International Handbook of Giftedness and Talent

2nd Edition

International Handbook of Giftedness and Talent

2nd Edition

Editors:

Kurt A. Heller

University of Munich, Germany

Franz J. Mönks

University of Nijmegen, The Netherlands

Robert J. Sternberg

Yale University, USA

and

Rena F. Subotnik

Hunter College, City University of New York

ELSEVIER

AMSTERDAM – LAUSANNE – NEW YORK – OXFORD – SHANNON – SINGAPORE – TOKYO

2000

ELSEVIER SCIENCE Ltd
The Boulevard, Langford Lane
Kidlington, Oxford OX5 1GB, UK

© 2000 Elsevier Science Ltd. All rights reserved.

This work is protected under copyright by Elsevier Science, and the following terms and conditions apply to its use:

Photocopying
Single photocopies of single chapters may be made for personal use as allowed by national copyright laws. Permission of the Publisher and payment of a fee is required for all other photocopying, including multiple or systematic copying, copying for advertising or promotional purposes, resale, and all forms of document delivery. Special rates are available for educational institutions that wish to make photocopies for non-profit educational classroom use.

Permissions may be sought directly from Elsevier Science Rights & Permissions Department, PO Box 800, Oxford OX5 1DX, UK; phone: (+44) 1865 843830, fax: (+44) 1865 853333, e-mail: permissions@elsevier.co.uk. You may also contact Rights & Permissions directly through Elsevier's home page (http://www.elsevier.nl), selecting first 'Customer Support', then 'General Information', then 'Permissions Query Form'.

In the USA, users may clear permissions and make payments through the Copyright Clearance Center, Inc., 222 Rosewood Drive, Danvers, MA 01923, USA; phone: (978) 7508400, fax: (978) 7504744, and in the UK through the Copyright Licensing Agency Rapid Clearance Service (CLARCS), 90 Tottenham Court Road, London W1P 0LP, UK; phone: (+44) 207 631 5555; fax: (+44) 207 631 5500. Other countries may have a local reprographic rights agency for payments.

Derivative Works
Tables of contents may be reproduced for internal circulation, but permission of Elsevier Science is required for external resale or distribution of such material.
Permission of the Publisher is required for all other derivative works, including compilations and translations.

Electronic Storage or Usage
Permission of the Publisher is required to store or use electronically any material contained in this work, including any chapter or part of a chapter.

Except as outlined above, no part of this work may be reproduced, stored in a retrieval system or transmitted in any form or by any means, electronic, mechanical, photocopying, recording or otherwise, without prior written permission of the Publisher.
Address permissions requests to: Elsevier Science Rights & Permissions Department, at the mail, fax and e-mail addresses noted above.

Notice
No responsibility is assumed by the Publisher for any injury and/or damage to persons or property as a matter of products liability, negligence or otherwise, or from any use or operation of any methods, products, instructions or ideas contained in the material herein. Because of rapid advances in the medical sciences, in particular, independent verification of diagnoses and drug dosages should be made.

Second edition 2000

British Library Cataloguing in Publication Data
A catalog record from the British Library has been applied for.

Library of Congress Cataloging in Publication Data
International handbook of giftedness and talent / edited by Kurt A. Heller . . . [et al.].--
2nd ed.
    p. cm.
  Rev. ed. of: International handbook of research and development of giftedness and
talent. 1st ed. 1993.
  ISBN 0-08-043796-6 (hardcover)
  1. Gifted children--Education--Handbooks, manuals, etc. 2. Gifted
children--Education--Research--Handbooks, manuals, etc. I. Heller, Kurt, A. 1931-II.
International handbook of research and development of giftedness and talent.

LC3993 .I596 2000
371.95--dc21   00-035438

ISBN: 0-08-043796-6 (HB)

♾ The paper used in this publication meets the requirements of ANSI/NISO Z39.48-1992 (Permanence of Paper).

Contents

CRM Library
JAN 16 2002
Acquisitions

CARRIE RICH MEMORIAL LIBRARY
CAMPBELL UNIVERSITY
BUIES CREEK, NC 27506

v

PART V   COUNSELING AND NURTURING GIFTEDNESS AND TALENT

Foreword

Franz E. Weinert

Max-Planck-Institute for Psychological Research, Munich, Germany

Most scientists do their work in seclusion, and only a small circle of experts is interested in their theoretical questions, methodological advances, and empirical findings. In contrast, like research on molecular genetics or communication technology, even small-scale scientific studies and local innovations leading to a better theoretical understanding, early identification, and specific promotion of gifted and talented individuals enjoy an international reception and discussion. This public interest has grown significantly in recent years and will probably continue to grow in the future. There are several reasons for this.

Talented individuals are nature's gift to society; this idea from Karl Marx reflects an intuitive belief shared by many persons across various cultures throughout history. In the past, persons with exceptional abilities and achievements were admired, honored, but also often feared and sometimes even persecuted. There have been hardly any changes in attitudes toward the phenomenon of giftedness right up to the present day. However, what has changed dramatically is the awareness of how important the gifted are for cultural progress, scientific innovation, and economic prosperity.

In an age of advancing globalization and continued international competition, the focus is no longer on the myth of individual genius, but on the identification and education of as many gifted children and adolescents as possible. The last few decades have seen a remarkable expansion of the arts, science, technology, business, and political administration throughout the world. This has been accompanied by continuing differentiation and specialization in job demands. Although the scientific production of new knowledge is advancing rapidly, this has not been accompanied by any decline in the amount and difficulty of problems to be solved. Demanding intellectual, personal, and social challenges can be found wherever one looks. There is a continuously growing need for gifted, creative, and talented persons to acquire specialized expertise and achieve high levels of performance and responsibility. This is why it is not surprising that research on giftedness receives so much public attention and is the focus of a variety of interests:

(1) International organizations (such as the United Nations, OECD) hope that the identification, psychological encouragement, and systematic training of the gifted will improve economic and social conditions in not only the industrialized, but, above all, the Third World and lead to a reduction in political tensions and conflicts.

(2) National, regional, and local administrations are initiating special programs for gifted children because they anticipate long-term advantages in terms of national and international competitiveness. There is an increasing awareness in many countries that human abilities and talents are one of the most important resources for future growth. Such administrations are seeking—often in desperation—a scientific orientation for their programs as well as professional evaluation.

(3) In the 1960s and 1970s, most educational institutions in the industrialized world—alongside their underlying philosophies and theories of education—went beyond their general tasks and focused on the problems of socially and intellectually disadvantaged children. Numerous programs were developed for them. Nowadays, there is a broad consensus that not only children with learning difficulties but also gifted children require special education lest they fail to live up to their promise. This has led to the emergence of numerous special schools, school classes, programs, and projects for gifted students in recent years. The practical experiences thus gained represent important sources for improving our understanding of gifted and talented students and designing more appropriate interventions.

(4) Scientists from many disciplines (e.g. differential psychology, cognitive psychology, developmental psychology, educational psychology, social psychology, human genetics, sociology, and educational science) have not only contributed to the current knowledge on giftedness but also pursue research in this field from different theoretical perspectives and with a lively critical interest. At the present time, despite a research tradition going back more than 100 years, we cannot assume a shared corpus of confirmed knowledge. Instead, there are various,

sometimes competing, theoretical, methodological, and educational approaches that each have to be judged with different sets of criteria.

(5) Parents who have, or believe they have, gifted children naturally exhibit a strong interest in those results of psychological research that possess practical relevance, in the instruments developed to identify gifted individuals, and the special education opportunities (or even needs!) of daughters and sons whose accelerated development often deviates from their peers. Such parents expect science to assist them in solving their problems. However, they also want to cooperate with scientists and often become committed and critical participants within the system of local or national programs for the gifted.

(6) Gifted children and adolescents often become aware at an early stage of development that they have other abilities, other ways of thinking, and other interests than their peers. Such an impression is reinforced when parents, teachers, or psychologists tell them they are gifted. At present, we know very little about how such a labeling process affects development in children with different degrees of giftedness. Nonetheless, empirical research has shown that many gifted children and adolescents develop an intensive personal interest in the available psychological research on this topic.

(7) Finally, the interests of many critics of research on giftedness and its consequences for education should not be neglected. These are not only scientists who question the theoretical, methodological, and empirical foundations of such research but also educational scientists, sociologists, and policymakers who fear a one-sided intellectual promotion of a small group of individuals and an instrumentalization of such interventions for purely economic purposes.

Although there can be no doubt that many sectors of society have a strong interest in the phenomenon of giftedness and its study, this is based on a variety of needs and reasons. Such external conditions would seem to make it impossible to follow the ideal sequence of basic and applied research, of developing and testing suitable instruments and programs, and finally, a broad implementation of scientific knowledge. Ever since the beginning of the 20th century, the field of giftedness has been characterized by a variety of extremely heterogeneous scientific and practice-related approaches that run concurrently. It is impossible to discern one general system in either the history of research or in practice. The outcome is a remarkably large number of psychological, biological, educational, and social findings that vary greatly in their reliability and validity. This makes it extremely difficult for both scientists and workers in the field, for both experts and laypersons, to find their way through this complex and complicated field of theoretical approaches, methodological procedures, empirical findings, practical experiences, and contradictory evaluations.

It can be seen that the number of special journals, monographs, edited books, and essays on giftedness research as well as on practical interventions with gifted children both inside and outside schools is now almost incalculable. Hundreds of new publications are appearing every year. All this information needs to be organized and assessed including the different scientific models and theories, and the practical projects and programs. What is the role, for example, of general intelligence (usually expressed in terms of intelligence quotients) in the definition of giftedness? Do highly intelligent individuals, in general, also possess high creative potential? How do intellectual abilities relate to special mathematical, verbal, artistic, or technical talents? Do gifted and highly talented children develop in different ways or only more quickly than their 'normal' peers? In what ways do special learning programs influence development in the gifted? How do genetic and environmental factors impact on cognitive abilities and performance? What is the contribution of non-cognitive motivational and personal traits? How can we minimize the risk of classifying children wrongly as gifted or non-gifted? Do gifted students require special teaching institutions, or can they be promoted sufficiently within mainstream schools? Why are some gifted children only moderately successful in their adult careers, whereas some exceptional scientists, technicians, physicians, or artists were only average achievers at school? We can see that each question can generate further questions at increasing levels of complexity.

This second edition of the International Handbook of Giftedness and Talent is not just a representative overview on the current state of the art in the major research approaches and on the application of their findings to identifying and promoting the gifted, but also offers competent answers to the main questions in theory and practice. This statement applies equally to the first edition published in 1993. Not only did reviews in scientific journals praise the work as the first comprehensive presentation of the theoretical principles, empirical findings, and practical application of research on giftedness, but the book also rapidly became an international bestseller exerting a strong influence on work about and with gifted children.

The present second edition represents an admirable continuation of this tradition. Because of the dynamic advances and successes in research on giftedness and talent during recent years, the editors Kurt A. Heller, Franz J. Mönks, Robert J. Sternberg, and Rena F. Subotnik have taken care to ensure that the book has been revised completely, that 80% of the information is new compared with the first edition, that 22 more chapters have been added, that the international and interdisciplinary approach has been strengthened, and that particularly important fields of research on giftedness are covered by several different chapters that each take a different theoretical and/

or practical perspective. Indeed, the list of authors reads like an international Who's Who of the top researchers in the field.

In his foreword to the first edition, Howard Gardner speculated on what the pioneers of research on giftedness might have had to say about this book and what would have surprised them the most. Considering the same question seven years later after reading the more than 60 chapters in the International Handbook of Giftedness and Talent, I believe that they would have been fascinated by the breadth of new theoretical and procedural knowledge and amazed by not only the continuities (e.g. the decisive role of IQ in defining giftedness) but also the discontinuities in the basic research approaches over a long period of time. Although some might have been rather disappointed by the fact that important questions (regarding, e.g. the effect of genetic and environmental factors or the prediction of career performance in the gifted on the basis of developmental indicators during childhood) are still unanswered, in general, they would be impressed strongly by the state of the art in international research, by the intensive programs for the gifted in many countries, and by a handbook that reports this in such a comprehensive, representative, critical, constructive, and brilliant way. I am confident that readers of this second edition of the International Handbook of Giftedness and Talent will reach a similarly positive conclusion.

May, 2000
Franz Emanuel Weinert

Preface of the 2nd edition

The first edition of this handbook was published in 1993 and received critical acclaim for its achievement in bringing together international perspectives on research and development in giftedness and talent. In the years since 1993, the scholarly field of giftedness and talent studies has expanded and developed, welcoming contributions from researchers in related disciplines. Several theoretical frameworks outlined in the first edition have now been empirically tested and a number of new trends have emerged.

The second edition, containing over 80% new material, brings scholars up-to-date with the latest research in the field. The new material includes:

- Substantially revised chapters taking into account recent developments in the field.
- Twenty-two completely new chapters.
- Significant contributions from scholars working in related fields.
- An increased focus on empirically supported scholarship.

The second edition of the *International Handbook of Giftedness and Talent* represents the most comprehensive, authoritative and up-to-date reference work on giftedness and talent. Bringing together leading scholars and teachers from around the world, this volume provides an invaluable research tool to academics, researchers and students interested in giftedness and talent.

For the better part of the 20th Century, and especially during the past two decades, the nature, nurture, problems and achievements of persons described as gifted or talented have been theorized about and researched. Hundreds of studies are done each year dealing with every conceivable aspect of giftedness. These studies include quantitative and qualitative designs, experiments, surveys, case studies, evaluations and simple descriptions of programs and practices. They range in significance of the problems studies as well as their quality.

The first edition of the *International Handbook* offered readers a synthesis and critical review of significant theory and research conducted through 1993 on all aspects of giftedness in order to provide a sound knowledge base on which to guide educational policy and practice, and help frame the next generation of research questions. We aimed to provide researchers, practitioners and policy makers with a comprehensive, critical review of theoretical and empirical research and descriptions of program and practice dealing with all aspects of the nature, nurture and realisation of giftedness and talent.

Prepared by over 100 researchers and program developers from 24 different countries, the chapters of the second edition of the *International Handbook of Giftedness and Talent* provide authentic, state-of-the-art international perspectives on all aspects of identification and development of giftedness and talent. We believe the chapters represent the best scholarly, theoretical and empirical knowledge available on the topic, reflecting the contributors' judgements of the important issues, programs and practices. The *Handbook* also highlights needed research and promising avenues of program development.

A. Harry Passow, the third editor of the first edition, passed away in 1996. Two new editors have been invited to participate as co-editors: Robert J. Sternberg (Yale University) and Rena F. Subotnik (Hunter College) – both well-known in the scientific community and in the field of gifted education.

In order to distinguish the new (2nd) edition from the original, three fundamental changes have been incorporated:

- Perspectives from scholars in related fields.
- New scholarship emerging in the late 1990's on talent development in various domains.
- More focus on empirically supported scholarship.

The second edition of the *International Handbook of Giftedness and Talent* is divided into seven parts with a total of 59 chapters. They are divided into seven sections (parts) as follows:

Part I: Changing conceptions of giftedness and talent.
Part II: Development of giftedness and talent.
Part III: Identification of giftedness and talent.
Part IV: Gifted education and programming.
Part V: Counseling and nurturing giftedness and talent.
Part VI: Examples of country efforts, policies, programs and issues.
Part VII: Present and future of research and education of the gifted and talented.

We have organized the *Handbook* to serve a broad audience of readers – students, teachers, researchers, decision-makers, administrators and others – who are concerned with nurturing talent potential. We think readers will find a meaningful balance of scholarship and practice which will provide a base for ideas and policies for the years ahead.

Finally, we would like to thank the contributors, most of whom have worked within a tight deadline. Without their efficient cooperation it would have been impossible to meet the publication goals of this second edition. Special thanks is owed to Franz E. Weinert for writing the Foreword of the second edition.

In addition, we would like to thank the editors of Pergamon Press/Elsevier Science—especially Gerhard Boomgaarden and Lesley Roberts and their colleagues in the production department—for their very professional handling of this publication.

Kurt A. Heller
Franz J. Mönks
Robert J. Sternberg
Rena F. Subotnik

Part I

Changing Conceptions of Giftedness and Talent

Conceptions of Giftedness from a Meta-Theoretical Perspective

Albert Ziegler and Kurt A. Heller

University of Munich, Germany

Introduction

In this chapter conceptions of giftedness will be presented from a meta-theoretical perspective. The intention here is not to present individual conceptions, contrast their inherent advantages and disadvantages with one another or identify those points they have or do not have in common. Rather, the objectives here are to deliniate meta-theoretical criteria which provide a sound basis for giftedness research and to examine the most important conditions which could influence the validity of conceptions of giftedness.

A brief survey of the present state of the theoretical development of conceptions of giftedness reveals the existence of three recurring points of criticism: (1) The empirical basis is often insufficient, (2) their ontological status is unclear, and (3) they often fall short of meta-theoretical standards set by the philosophy of science. In the following section, we want to explain these points of criticism in detail. The attempt to develop a constructive argument is the main purpose of this chapter. The goal is to formulate a conclusive response to them by the end of the chapter, which in and of itself enables a scientifically fertile coming to terms with the topic of giftedness research.

Empirical, Ontological and Meta-Theoretical Difficulties with Conceptions of Giftedness

The fact that there is no object one can simply point to which demonstrates the existence of a gift or a talent appears to be trivial for a scientific branch like psychology which is largely based on constructs. However, is there at least indirect evidence that would support the postulation of gifts? The most important denial comes from the field of expertise research. Howe, Davidson and Sloboda (1998) seriously question how realistic the assumption of the existence of gifts or talents is, or whether one is actually being taken in by a myth. Basically, there are at least three reasons for the empirical difficulties facing conceptions of giftedness. (1) Empirical evidence obtained with average gifted persons cannot easily be transferred to highly gifted persons. For example, several conceptions of giftedness incorporate genetic influences as a significant component of the basic meaning of talent. In fact, there is a large body of research that proves that genetic influences account for some inter-individual differences. Wagner (1999) indicates, and correctly so, that these genetic influences have only been proven by untrained persons. In the same vein, Ericsson (Ericsson & Crutcher, 1990; Ericsson, Krampe & Tesch-Römer, 1993; Ericsson & Pennington, 1993) arrives at the overwhelmingly convincing conclusion that the estimated performance barriers seen as genetically fixed upper boundaries can be overcome through suitable learning processes. (2) By and large, the second empirical difficulty can be attributed to the inadequate methods currently available for the identification of gifted persons. According to the predominant opinion, gifts are not automatically transformed into exceptional achievements which leads us to contend with the existence of quite talented underachievers (Butler-Por, 1993). On the other hand, it could very well be that we are speaking of persons who have attained eminent achievement; these could be either highly gifted or average gifted persons who have had successful learning careers. In sum, giftedness research can not make an absolutely clear distinction between a highly gifted person and a well-trained person or between an average gifted person and a highly gifted person not taking full advantage of his/her gift. (3) The last empirical problem is due to the rarity of talents. For example, a country like Germany would need to conduct several complete cohorts in order to find just one individual major chess master. The scope of the problem increases when one wants to ascertain specific components of giftedness such as genetic influence. For example, in order to assess these genetic influences among chess players one would need to implement twin and adoption studies within an already extremely

3

small population (cf. Thompson & Plomin in this handbook). Such samples are impossible to recruit.

From an ontological point of view, it is actually difficult to determine the precise ontological status of gifts. It seems to be clear that there is no direct correspondence between a gift and a natural entity, but rather that a construct is indicated. For example, Howe et al. (1998), in their devastating criticism of the talent construct, present a so-called list definition of talent, in other words talent as a composite of several necessary factors. Although some of the peer comments criticized of the individual points of the theory, none of them complained about the form of the definition as a list of criteria. A survey of the practical research reveals that talents seem to be handled as predictors indicated by variables such as intelligence or attributions of giftedness in a nomination procedure (see empirical publications in journals dedicated to questions involving talent and giftedness: *Creativity Research Journal, Exceptional Children, Gifted Child Quarterly, Gifted Child Today, Gifted Education International, High Ability Studies, Journal for the Education of the Gifted, Roeper Review*). On the other hand, it is difficult to accept talent as a proximal explanation for exceptional achievements. When an investigator attempts to explain why an exceptional achievement has occurred, he would need to analyze psychological processes, specific skills or physical structures (see Chi, Glaser & Farr, 1988; Ericsson & Smith, 1991; Hoffman, 1992). For example, when the basis or organization of the knowledge structures used by chess experts (Freyhof, Grub & Ziegler, 1992) or the capacity to mentally generate chess moves in advance (Holding, 1985) are investigated, an investigator would not be satisfied in using the expression 'giftedness' to explain such achievements. In certain ways, we are addressing the direct explanation of an exceptional achievement in terms of a methodological anti-gift-approach, since one would constantly attempt to break down gifts into psychological processes or entities.

From a meta-theoretical perspective, the consideration of current giftedness research as well as the existing theoretical basis of giftedness is striking in many respects. First, one must concede that it is difficult to justify the scientific necessity of gifts without becoming caught up in a vicious circle. Often, conceptions of gifts create their own legitimacy through empirical evidence of achievement eminence which are used to justify gifts themselves. Many arguments run along lines similar to this simplified example: If someone is a high achiever, it follows that he is gifted and vice versa; if someone is gifted, he will demonstrate exceptional achievements (as long as he is not restricted by unfavorable environmental conditions). Examples of this can particularly be found in the biographies of extraordinary persons (e.g., Ellis, 1927; Kretschmer, 1931). Therefore, conceptions of giftedness must also be capable of making a conceptional

differentiation between achievement eminence and gifts.

The second troublesome point concerning the construct of gifts from a meta-theoretical perspective is that there is a tendency to immunize them against potential falsification. This is of course not a problem if one is speaking of a theoretical term whose measurement more or less presupposes its existence (cf. Sneed, 1994; Sneed, Baber & Moulines, 1987), similarly to how a concept such as intelligence is handled. Intelligence, in the strictest sense of the word, cannot be falsified; at most it can be proven to be scientifically less fruitful. In the debate over the existence of talents and giftedness, the question as to who carries the burden of the proof of existence is posed often enough (cf. Howe, Davidson & Sloboda, 1998, as well as the open peer commentaries): Do talent researchers now need to come up with proof of the existence of gifts, or do their opponents need to offer proof of non-existence? In our opinion this question is poorly formulated and suffers under a petitio principii, i.e. the adoption of an unjustified tacit assumption. This exists within the universal assumption that gifts always—according to the proponents—or never—according to the opponents—are at the base of the behaviors leading to achievement eminence. In contrast, we believe that a conception of giftedness should allow for the possibility that a behavior leading to achievement eminence could, in fact, either be or not be based on the existence of a gift. A decision should be made in each case in collusion with an empirical clarification.

The third troublesome point from a meta-theoretical perspective is evidence of a significant decrease in progressiveness regarding the ability to move forward (Lakatos, 1978) seen in the last few years. Giftedness research is mainly a receptive research of psychology whereby methodological standards do suffer, in some respects, from deficits. In order to prove the first part of this claim one need only take a glimpse through the leading psychological journals. It becomes immediately obvious that practically all important scientific discoveries are not being obtained from subject pools with striking talents. Methodological deficits were evident in a meta-analysis of current empirical works appearing in peer-reviewed journals on giftedness by Ziegler and Raul (2000). Among other points, they confirmed that control groups were employed in less than one quarter of the studies! Some studies even neglected to indicate the number of subjects participating in their investigations.

The above depicted analyses of empirical, ontological and scientific aspects point to the necessity of a complete and thorough deliberation of the theoretical foundations of giftedness research. This does not necessarily entail the development and presentation of a new conception of giftedness, but rather a reflection on the basis upon which the forthcoming as well as current conceptions of giftedness can be evaluated.

In the next section of this chapter we will address the concept of giftedness, a term which has so far only been intuitively applied. In face of the abundance of various applications of the term currently in use, it is not possible to present an *all* encompassing concept of giftedness here nor to offer a complete overview of the various views of the construct. The only goal here is to provide an intuitive understanding for the following sections of this chapter; initially we will define the object, which giftedness research attempts to explain. Then a meta-conceptual model which we name the *critical state view of giftedness* will be presented, which should set the standards for the analysis and discussion of present conceptions of giftedness as well as for the development of future conceptions. Central components of such conceptions of giftedness will be addressed against this background, as will some virulent conceptual problems in the research field itself.

Conceptions of Giftedness and Their Central Object

Exceptional achievements have always held the interest of mankind, whether they be found in folklore, sagas, everyday encounters, theology, philosophy, art, or recently in empirical science. Two matters are of central concern; first, those individuals enjoying social privileges were always tied to certain demands apropos achievement. For example, the kings and lords in ancient Greece were often attributed with physical strength in addition to their leadership qualities; this strength turned them into an effective protective factor with respect to external enemies. This theme is illustrated by the renowned battle for Troy whereby every son of the Trojan King Priamos as well as every Greek leader was ascribed the status of a hero and, therefore, their actions mainly determined—besides the actions of the gods—the outcome of the battle. Second, in addition to this social legitimization function, there was always a vital interest in seeking out the source of exceptional achievement. Naturally, the explanations have varied to a great degree over the course of history. In hindsight, these constructs seem to have experienced a period of development which corresponds particularly well to the *Three Phase Model* proposed by the French founder of Positivism, Auguste Comte (1798–1857). In the first phase, the theological state, man interprets the worldly phenomenon in terms of supernatural beings, usually as gifts from the gods. In the second phase, the metaphysical or abstract state, the causes of all worldly phenomena can exist outside the physical world and are therefore secure from empirical encroachment. In the third and final phase, the scientific or positive state, a controlled empirical approach is incorporated into investigation.

In fact, initial encounters with exceptional achievements in the ancient world were explained through constructs borrowed from religion. In Greek mythology, divine descent (Sisyphus, Achilles) or divine mercy (Odysseus, Tiresias) were often believed to be the sources of heroism, intelligence or prophetic abilities. Plato in Greece and Confucius in China have already addressed the topic of 'heavenly' children. The Bible is explicit on the theme in Romans 12:6: "We have different gifts according to the grace that is given to us." The phase described as metaphysical is characterized by a gradual change in the understanding of gifts or talents which can now be more closely tied to individuality. Studies in speech etymology show that these facets in meaning had already started to differentiate by the 4th century, a change which first surfaced in middle and north European language groups in the 14th century. Talents were then understood more in terms of individual aptitudes (Kluge, 1967). The philosopher Paracelsus in 1537 already used the term 'talent' in the sense of a mental aptitude (Passow, Mönks & Heller, 1993). On the other hand, explanations of achievement eminence, although no longer referring to religious sources, were still not being investigated by means of empirical methods. During the middle ages, the belief was spread that exceptional achievements were the result of extra-sensory causes (Fels, 1999). The gifted were expected to die earlier as a sort of compensatorical justification (Stanley & Benbow, 1986). A further example is that of the genius cult in the age of Enlightenment and Romance, whereby genius was something spiritual, here represented by an entity in a state absolutely removed from that of normal comprehension. "Genius is another psycho-biological species, differing from man, in his mental and temperamental processes, as man differs from the ape" (Hirsch, 1931, p. 298). Along similar lines, Hollingworth recounts the opinion that: "The contemplation of genius thus came to be accompanied by a kind of superstitious awe, and the notion gained currency that people of genius constitute a separate species" (1929, p. 3). Metaphysically oriented explanations for giftedness have been common constructs in scientific theories, even in the 20th century, and can still be found in commonplace theories subscribed to today. A prominent example would be that of the 'blue blood' ascribed to the aristocracy in medieval class society which served to legitimize their social superiority and spiritual claim to leadership. Only with the dawn of psychology and the consequent development of methodological standards could the explanation of achievement eminence gradually enter the third phase, or the positive state. Here, unusually successful learning processes as well as talents or gifts were seen as the causes for exceptional achievements. Talents or gifts themselves became more assessable under scientific measurement than intelligence; they were seen as the interplay among several psychological components, a result of specific genetic dispositions or as the result of learning processes. From a historical angle, one can most probably say that Galton (1883) and, somewhat later, Binet (Binet & Simon, 1916) can be credited with leading giftedness research into the positive state. Their fundamental beliefs, that talent can be measured and that it differs from person to person in gradients rather than quality led to a revolution in the understanding of gifts.

Nowadays, a look through the relevant literature pertaining to giftedness research can be quite confusing due to the amazing variety of definitions for giftedness or gifted persons. A frequent definition, upon which many investigative studies are based, equates giftedness with high levels of intelligence. Often, an arbitrary point will be set beyond which one is considered to be gifted. Other definitions of giftedness have expanded on this limited definition and gone on to include exceptional achievement in various domains. For example, DeHaan and Havighurst (1957) named intellectual abilities, creative thinking, scientific abilities, social leadership qualities, mechanical abilities and artistic abilities in their definition. Another frequently quoted definition of gifted (children) was offered by Marland (1972, p. ix): "Gifted and talented children are those identified by professionally qualified persons who, by virtue of outstanding abilities, are capable of high performance." Similarly, Heller (1989) formulates giftedness as "the individual cognitive and motivational potential for—as well as social and cultural conditions of—achieving excellent performance in one or more areas such as mathematics, languages, or artistic areas with regard to difficult theoretical vs. practical tasks" (p. 141). Conspicuous in this definition is that it is based on achievement *potentials* which do not necessarily have to be realized; however, definitions based on *performance* can also be found. For instance, Götze (1916) wrote that talent can only be measured by achievement. Similarly, Tannenbaum (1986) sees talent as a product of a labeling process and the corresponding gifted persons as "outstanding contributors to the arts, sciences, letters and general well-being of fellow humans" (p. 33). Furthermore, he reserves *true* giftedness for adults, a talent which is distinguished by particular achievements, while children can only be accorded a *potential* giftedness. However, the general opinion is that the gifted do not necessarily need to demonstrate achievement eminence, but rather that they can attain this state more easily than other persons. Those who do not achieve to the levels predicted by their potential are said to be underachievers (cf. Butler-Por, 1993; see also Thompson & Plomin in this handbook).

Conceptions of Giftedness

Regardless of whether one is considering a psychometric conception of high ability in terms of the disposition for extraordinary achievements (in specific areas) or a cognitive conception regarding domain-specific competence vs. performance in the sense of achievement eminence, one finds that all new theories tend to favor *multi-dimensional* models of high ability (for example Gagné, 1985, 1993; Gardner, 1985; Heller & Hany, 1986; as well as Sternberg, 1985, 1988, 1990; Heller, 1989, 1990, 1991). Theoretically based diagnostic and promotional concepts need multi-dimensional formulations which cannot be adequately realized through (one-dimensional) IQ definitions which are limited by cut-off levels inherent in a model based on threshold values.

In early childhood, ability initially manifests itself as a relatively unspecific individual behavioral potential. Here, the *interaction* with the social learning environment is significant for highly gifted children in that a reciprocal influence between the child's behaviors and the parental breeding practices is characteristic. According to Scarr and McCartney (1983), inherited ability potentials—including inter-individual intelligence differences—become relevant for individual selection and engagement of information stimuli offered by or made available through the social environment (see Monks & Mason and Thompson & Plomin in this handbook). Modern intelligence and talent theories favor domain-specific conceptions, exemplified by the multiple intelligence model developed by Gardner or the Munich Dynamic Giftedness Model, both of which will be briefly described in the following text.

Gardner differentiates seven intelligences:

(1) *Linguistic* intelligence. This includes the sensitivity to the definitions of words as well as effective language based memory skills.

(2) *Logical-mathematical* intelligence. Here general logical and special mathematical thinking abilities are referred to.

(3) *Spatial* intelligence. This form of intelligence refers to the conception and perception of space as well as abilities involving spatial memory and thought processes.

(4) *Bodily-kinesthetic* intelligence. Psycho-motor abilities of this type are needed, for example in achievements in the fields of athletics or dance.

(5) *Musical* intelligence. This includes not only musical competencies in the narrowest of senses, but also includes mood and emotion. For a more detailed discussion see Perleth & Mönks, in this handbook.

(6) *Intrapersonal* intelligence. This refers to a sensibility regarding ones own sensory world.

(7) *Interpersonal* intelligence. This concept of social intelligence refers primarily to the ability to differentially perceive the needs of others.

Recently Gardner has added one further type of intelligence to these seven, and has suggested two further types as candidates for inclusion, namely:

(8) *Naturalistic* intelligence. Here the author is referring to the ability to discern patterns in the living world.

($8\frac{1}{2}$) *Existential* intelligence (in myth, art, science, philosophy) and *Spiritual* intelligence (whatever that may mean). Gardner labels the last two intelligences as intelligence candidates due to the lack (so far) of empirical validation.

Along the same line, the content of the Munich Model of Giftedness and Talent (see Fig. 1) makes distinctions among relatively independent forms of ability which themselves are relevant for specific achievement areas. Besides *intelligence* (linguistic, mathematical, technical-constructive and other dimensions), the following talent dimensions have been investigated:

(1) *Creativity* (originality, productivity, elaboration, flexibility, liquidity, etc.).

(2) *Social competence* (planning ability, leadership and the control of social interactions among others).

(3) *Musical-artistic* abilities (i.e. musicality).

(4) *Psychomotoric* (hand and body motor skills).

(5) *Practical intelligence* (i.e. the command over daily and or vocational challenges or problems).

These talent dimensions represent — as in Gardner's Theory — the fundamental, but by no means all possible forms of ability. In a variation of the model suggested by Ziegler and Perleth (1997), an attempt to make a connection between talent research and expertise research is made (see Fig. 2). Their model spans from the taking up of an activity to the achievement of expert status. In the model, antecedent and marginal conditions of exceptional performances are taken into consideration just as much as the use of talents in an active learning process.

Person's internal performance dispositions which set maximum performance levels are postulated as an antecedent condition of exceptional performances. Here, following Ackerman's theory (1987, 1992), cognitive, perceptual and motor talent factors are differentiated, whereby the importance of domain-specific foreknowledge is additionally included. However, only very roughly estimated talent factors are named, which, of course, would have to be subdivided more finely for single career fields. For example, cognitive abilities can be further subdivided into creative, analytical or logical abilities.

Talent factors require favorable marginal conditions for their use; without *active learning* which is supported through *favorable personality characteristics* and suitable *environmental features*, talents vanish unused. The resulting performance at a given point in time is, according to this, seen as a product of the

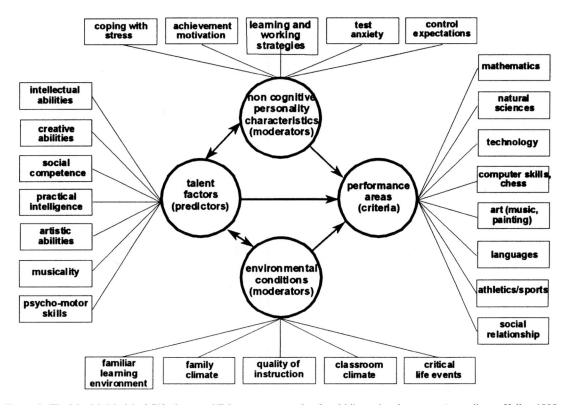

Figure 1. The Munich Model of Giftedness and Talent as an example of multidimensional concepts (according to Heller, 1990, 1991; Heller & Hany, 1986; Perleth & Heller, 1994).

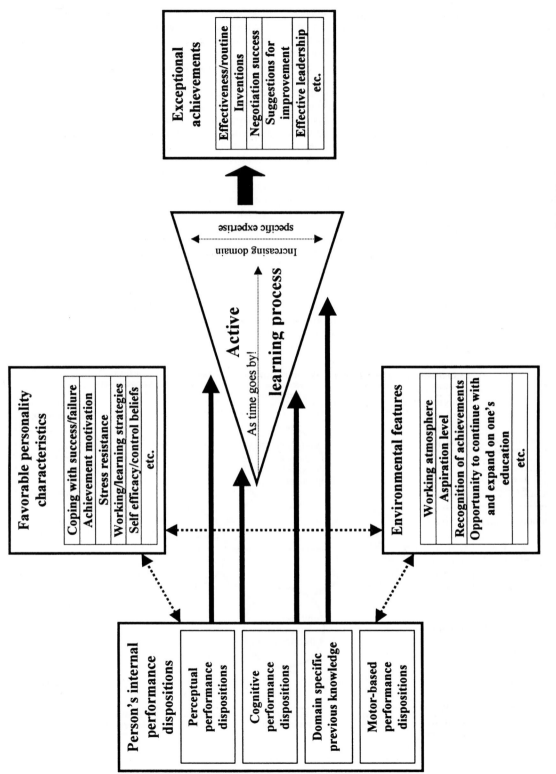

Figure 2. The variant of the Munich Dynamic Model of Giftedness by Ziegler & Perleth (1997).

interplay of the talent, motivational and environmental factors that are analytically differentiated in the model.

It should be clear that multiple interaction and compensation processes take place between these factors. The development of expertise is dependent upon the use of the opportunities for experience and learning offered in the environment, which, however, must not be seen as static factors. In contrast to that, the talented must deliberately look for them according to their growing abilities and match them to their increased performance level. Thus, a performance-oriented company climate can probably level out an unfavorable individual performance motivation; in the same vein non-optimal intellectual performance preconditions can be compensated for by further educational offers within the company. Therefore, not only a high domain-specificity concerning the task areas focused upon is to be expected, but also a highly individual expertise process.

A *psycho-social* conception of high ability was suggested by Tannenbaum (1983, 1991). Here the independence of every form of talent from social demands and validation contexts is emphasized. Furthermore, Tannenbaum points to the role *chance factors* can play in the transformation of individual talent potential into achievement behavior. Heller and Hany (1986) discuss *critical* life events, while Feldhusen (1986) sees *self-concept* as a central personality variable among the highly gifted. Such differentiated ability concepts are not only relevant for the identification of highly gifted adolescents, but also for the sponsorship of extremely talented members of specific domains.

Finally, a brief look should be taken at Renzulli's influential *Three Ring Model* (Renzulli 1978, 1986) of high ability, which has in the meantime been expanded upon by Mönks (1990) from the developmental psychological perspective of the social settings family, school and peer group. Despite some — justifiable — criticism of such implicit models, they often show a large affinity for the practical problems faced by educational psychologists (Sternberg, 1993), which may explain the attractiveness of the Renzulli Model: In this model giftedness s conceptualized as the lucky coincidence of above average (general) intelligence, creativity and task commitment; see also Renzulli & Reis in this handbook. In general, dynamic models as they are conceptualized in investigations based on cognitive approaches seem to be more effective for practical needs than psychometric models of ability which are preferred in the genetically oriented and neuroscientific basis research as well as in the developmental and differential branches of psychological and psychodiagnostic research and practice. Both research paradigms are indispensable, whereby at a glance the profit they bring in pedagogical applications pushes their supplementary functions into the foreground.

While the giftedness theories discussed thus far have been, more or less, psychometrically founded and, thereby, oriented on abilities and traits, recent research based on cognitive psychology has been gaining new significance. Included here are information theory models such as the cognitive component theory developed by Sternberg and his research group (Sternberg & Davidson, 1986).

In a further development of earlier research theories on analog thinking (Sternberg, 1977), Sternberg (1985) presents his *Triarchic Theory of Intelligence.* This consists of three subtheories designated as the context, two-facet and component theories.

The *context subtheory* refers to how intelligence is culture specific. Here, intelligence needs to be defined within a socio-cultural context, or in other words as the individual's goal-directed adaptation of a relevant living environment as well as its organization and selective integration. Aspects of social and practical intelligence are also addressed.

The *two-facet subtheory* attempts to bridge the (apparent) contradiction found between assumptions regarding information processing offered by thought psychologists and learning psychologists. Thought is only required for problem solution when the individual is confronted by an inadequate knowledge or experience base, in other words when one is dealing with a novel problem. According to Sternberg, human intelligence can be particularly well measured in situations where the application of existing information is necessary for, but not sufficient to, arrive at a solution for this new problem. In addition, available information bytes must be selectively encoded in that a decision must be made as to whether the information is relevant or irrelevant with respect to the solution of the problem. They must be suitably combined, and then these results must be reviewed and scrutinized. This process is, however, just one facet, the second facet refers to subroutines in the problem solving process or the automatization of information processing. The more extensive the repertoire of available automated (partial) processes, the less the burden on the actual thought which must be applied in the solution of the problem. A first grade student, who has not yet automated the operations associated with reading and writing readily available to older students and adults, would need much more time to manage writing tasks than, say, a seventh grade student. Similarly, a novice auto driver would progress at a much more cautious pace than a routine driver, so long as an insufficient number of automized driving elements are available.

Finally, in the *component subtheory*, Sternberg differentiates among (a) performance components, (b) meta-components and (c) knowledge acquisition components. *Performance* components refer to basis operations such as selection and routine organization. In addition, control processes are needed which are here called *meta*-components due to their presumed universal validity. Included here are operations such as problem recognition, selection of appropriate performance components and form of representation (verbal, numeric, figural, illustrative), strategy regarding the combination and re-ordering of performance components, as well as control over execution and solution. *Knowledge acquisition* components steer the learning process.

The *Triarchic Theory of Intelligence* considers: (1) internal (person related) process elements, i.e. meta-components of the control and evaluation of behavior; (2) performance components, which are responsible for the actual solution of the problem (through thinking and learning transfer which regulates behavior) and; (3) knowledge acquisition components, which refer to both declarative and procedural knowledge (i.e. factual knowledge vs. know-how). The object of Sternberg's (1985, 1986, 1988, 1991, 1997) analyses in the area of cognitive psychology is inductive thinking, whereby three insight skills, selective information processing, combination processes and comparative processes were experimentally investigated. According to a series of empirical studies, the highly gifted can particularly be differentiated from normally gifted persons in how these process components are engaged in the processing of information in open or complex and difficult logic problems.

Psychometric and cognitive approaches to giftedness research are often considered to be opposing and incompatible approaches. We are of another opinion. In the early stages of intelligence measurement, the psychometric approach and the experimental approach appeared to be completely irreconcilable, as observed in the memory experiments conducted by Ebbinghaus and Binet. It is only in recent years that signs of a cohesion have again become apparent; this change is only meaningful to the diagnostics of giftedness regarding the degree to which the psychometric and cognitive approaches can complement each other. While the psychometric paradigm for behavioral prognoses still forms an indispensable foundation (without bringing in 'psychological explanations'), important conclusions regarding the causes for and conditions surrounding human information processing and intellectual problem solving are expected from process analyses in the cognitive paradigm. In this manner, inter-individual cognitive ability differences are to be confirmed through a series of cognitive process analyses, i.e. those regarding language comprehension, logical thought patterns or spatial perception and understanding. Studies in the expert-novice paradigms appear to be particularly successful here. In such studies the cognitive processes which significantly differentiate beginners from advanced achievers in a certain area (language competence, mathematics, technology, chess, etc.) are specified.

Sternberg and his co-workers ascertained the following six components based on their component analyses of thought processes (Reasoning factor I = Induction), whereby highly gifted and normally gifted students were found to differentiate in the solution of difficult, complex problems: (1) decisions as to which problem needs to be solved, i.e. what the actual problem at hand is; (2) planning appropriate steps leading to a solution; (3) the choice of a suitable step; (4) choice of a level of representation (oral, symbolic, illustrative); (5) allocation of attention; (6) control over the range of problem solving activities. Evidently, the necessary planning and direction competencies in the sense of meta-components of cognitive control are responsible for each and every partial step (inference, mapping, application, comparison, justification, response).

Despite the striking diversity of concepts of giftedness, it is interesting to note that all conceptions agree that exceptional achievements can be explained by giftedness. Furthermore, concrete research on giftedness is concerned with a section of human behavior, one which can be measured against a standard of excellence — in the sense of being either better or worse (McClelland, Atkinson, Clark & Lovell, 1953). Usually, one can speak here of three types of standards of excellence: (1) achievements, which are assessed by applying a critical norm under the guidance of objective criteria; (2) inter-individual norms, which are used to contrast individuals on one assessment dimension; and (3) intra-individual norms, which offer the opportunity to compare the present achievements of a person with his earlier achievements. All of these measurement techniques have been used in giftedness research, whereby the first two have clearly been the dominant choices. For instance, unique artistic, scientific or athletic feats would be acceptable demonstrations of objective indicators of exceptional talents of the same caliber as age relevant exceptional academic achievement. Certainly, through intra-individual measurement, one could demonstrate a rapid growth in learning and accept this as a sign of exceptional talent (e.g. Feldman, 1980; Feldman & Goldsmith, 1986; Radford, 1990). To sum up, recent conceptions of giftedness are not united as to whether gifts are only potentials for eminent achievement or can only be indicated by eminent achievement. However, they all agree that gifts explain eminent behavior, which itself can be measured against a standard of excellence. Unfortunately, by accepting a standard of excellence in the field of giftedness research, four problems unique to this subject emerge which will be discussed in the following sections: (1) the application problem, (2) the focus problem, (3) the reference problem and (4) the significance problem. These four problems stand in a hierarchical relationship to one another whereby a decision must be finalized for one problem before the next one can be considered (see Fig. 3).

Application Problem

The application problem addresses the problem of how to determine which domains deal with differences in achievement levels, thereby permitting the application of a standard of excellence. Various researchers have indicated that these areas are also to be seen as valuable in another sense; when one thinks of achievement, one is more prone to think of academic and scientific areas, or artistic domains such as music, painting or literature. Idiosyncratic works of art, on the other hand, are not usually considered to be valid expressions of extraordinary talents (Tannenbaum, 1986). This does, however, reflect an unwarranted preference among researchers to react to changes in taste by seeing the blossoming of extraordinary talents tomorrow in an area which only yesterday was hardly worth mentioning. The concept of a standard of excellence thereby contains a feature of a relativistic nature which can be seen as a type of silent agreement. For example, Tannenbaum (1986) distinguishes among four types of talent: *Scarcity talents* lead to improvements considered to be socially valuable, *surplus talents* elevate people's sensitivities with splendid achievements in art or philosophy. *Quota talents* fulfill roles which are limited by the needs of the society. Tannenbaum's last category, *anomalous talents*, is interesting in that it concerns abilities which are of no use to society whatsoever, such as those depicted in the *The Guinness Book of World Records*. Included here are also anachronistic talents which may have been suitable to one of the other talent forms in a different era, but are worthless today. This type of list-forming makes it absolutely clear that the underlying classification is in no way founded on psychological considerations, but rather on extra-psychological criteria which are not further expounded upon by Tannenbaum, and which are probably based on some other social value, rarity or achievement component. The classification of talent in *Sternberg's pentagonal implicit theory of giftedness* is also dependent on the distribution of talent levels and social values (Sternberg, 1993). His five necessary and jointly sufficient criteria of excellence, rarity, productivity, demonstrability and value also circumvent psychological considerations by finding their roots in commonplace theories.

In fact, the starting point for most scientific constructs is rooted in common, everyday concepts (cf. Stegmüller, 1970); for example, color theory originated with sensual expressions which were accessible to all. However, the ultimate goal of a scientific branch is to be able to transform common, everyday concepts into scientific expressions such as the description of colors through the frequencies of light waves. In exercising self-criticism, the field of giftedness research must admit that it has not yet been able to attain the level of scientific advancement which allows for a common definition of its research object in favor of a psychologically based construct. We will, for the time being, set this point aside and address it once again later in the text.

Focus Problem

Binding standards of excellence are not readily available in all areas in which achievement is being investigated; this poses not only a serious problem for convergent achievements, but an even greater one for divergent achievements. Even when a consensus can be reached regarding whether a standard of excellence can be applied in a specific domain, one cannot be certain of which aspect to focus on. For example, one would assume that in order to evaluate a high jump, one would consider the height the jumper can attain. It goes without saying that specific types of jumps are ruled out by the regulations governing the sport (for example, today, the frequently employed flop technique in which an athlete jumps over the crossbar backwards is only permitted after a lengthy discussion). In the earlier phases of this sport discipline, the jump technique was assessed along with the height of the jump itself, similar to the manner in which ski jumps and figure skating are still assessed today. In subsequent domains, such as those in the academic field, complicated assessment techniques must be

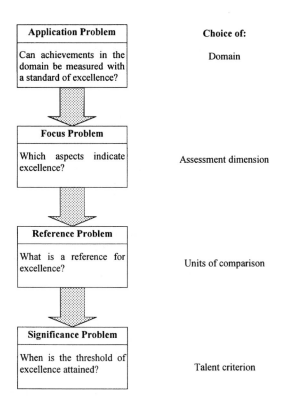

Figure 3. Hierarchical relationship among the four problems arising from the application of a standard of excellence.

devised or complex psychometric scales like IQ tests must be developed. It should be mentioned here that even by establishing which aspects of a domain are to be subjected to a standard of excellence, this cannot be based solely on objective criteria. Whether academic achievement is assessed with paper-and-pencil-tests, oral examinations or by the success in real life situations, is not an inevitable consequence of the choice of domain.

Reference Problem

Even when the dimension on which the achievement eminence in a domain can be determined is clear, it is still necessary to establish a norm against which achievement can be measured. Reference norms have already been introduced in this text: there are criteria-based, inter-individual and intra-individual norms. In using criteria-based norms, one highlights exceptional achievements that result from facets of a unique character or those which only very few people can reproduce. One can include discoveries and works of art among these types of achievement; these examples are founded on the assessment of products which are a result of actions undertaken. These actions can also be assessed on a criterial basis, for instance, the incredible feats performed by memory or arithmetic geniuses who can commit columns of numbers to memory or seem to have magical capacities for mental calculations at their disposal. Such achievements fall, in many cases, so far outside the range of normal abilities that the application of an inter-individual standard of excellence for these phenomena would only be a waste of time. Inter-individual achievement comparisons often make allowance for an age norm as well as for the rarity of the phenomenon (Sternberg, 1993). Thereby, an accomplishment which is sub-normal for adults would be unexpected for a younger person at an earlier developmental stage (e.g. child prodigies, early readers). In imposing an intra-individual norm, one would more than likely be looking for quick learning growth rates. The average age of subjects being evaluated using this type of reference norm should be relatively low, typically childhood or early adolescence is the ideal level. However, we want to stress the fact that there are no objective criteria available which allow us to prefer one type of reference norm over another.

Significance Problem

In the last stage, a classification or assessment, we are faced with the question of what qualifies as an achievement to be counted among the objects to be explained through giftedness research. Is it merely the top 10% or those who perform better than two standard deviations above the average who comprise the potential candidates for studies of giftedness? What sorts of learning growth would indicate talent? As long as no criteria regarding the actual understanding of gifted-

ness are at our disposal, one must be content to turn to ad hoc criteria such as percentages or international acknowledgments for the foreseeable future. The search for an end to the paralyzing and crippling discussion of percentages and optimal identification procedures will keep the community of giftedness researchers busy for quite some time as long as proven psychological criteria are not available to bring this discussion to a decisive end (cf. Rescher, 1995).

The Critical State View of Giftedness

In the following, we present the meta-conceptual framework for the *critical state view of giftedness*, a model which offers a meta-theoretical basis for an assessment regarding the content of present conceptions of giftedness. In the first step, four postulates will be introduced and substantiated which any conception of giftedness must be able to fulfill.

Postulate 1: Temporal Precedence

We will start with the assumption that gifts form a causal relationship with exceptional achievements; consequently, they must meet all of the theoretical and scientific criteria which are usually demanded in cases of causality (Achinstein, 1983; Bromberger, 1992). Of particular significance in this context is the criteria of temporal precedence, originally introduced by John Stuart Mill (1806–1873). Applied to the field of giftedness research, this criterion demands that a gift precedes the eminent behavior it is supposed to explain. The acceptance of this cause-and-effect postulate has decisive consequences for the formation of a conception of giftedness in that it precludes the possibility for a performance oriented definition. This becomes clear when one considers the prospects of seeing gifts as explanations for current actions; the negative consequences of this attempt are best demonstrated with an example of an explanation for an exceptional achievement. If one would want to explain an ingenious move made by the current strongest chess player in the world, Gary Kasparow, one would have to call attention to his outstanding specific knowledge of the game, his ability to conduct mental calculations or his evaluative abilities (Holding, 1985). It would now be awkward instead to want to explain this ingenious move through one particular gift or talent.

Important here is that the actions being undertaken can always be resolved through fundamental psychological constructs, without having to rely on explanations through gifts. This is also the fundamental reason for claiming that gifts precede the actions which lead to achievement; otherwise they would merely be unsophisticated, pointless constructs inferior to actual-psychological explanations. Therefore, Postulate 1 maintains that one must assume that the gifts which intend to explain exceptional achievement are temporally precedent.

Postulate 2: Fulfillment of the 'inus' Condition

Mackie (1975) suggested that causes need to fulfill an 'inus' condition when they intend to be granted some degree of explanatory value; his basic idea can also be applied to gifts. An *inus condition* for some effect *is an insufficient but non-redundant part of an unnecessary but sufficient condition*. Before trying to apply this complicated formulation to the field of giftedness, an example would best serve to clarify it. Assume that a burning cigarette has started a forest fire. The burning cigarette, by itself, is not sufficient (there are many forest fires not caused by burning cigarettes), but non-redundant (because in the circumstances hypothesized there was no other condition present which would have ignited the flammable materials). The burning cigarette is, however, a part of some constellation of conditions that are jointly sufficient for the forest fire. Moreover, given that this set of conditions occurred, rather than some other set sufficient for the forest fire, the burning cigarette was necessary: Without it, the fire would not have occurred. Usually, the causes of an event are complex, and we often single out one of those conditions because there is something unusual about that condition. The presence of oxygen may be just as necessary for the fire as the burning cigarette; but because that is a condition that we can usually take for granted, we would not mention it.

Gifts should, admittedly, be able to explain exceptional achievements, however, they are certainly not sufficient to do this in and of themselves. For instance, in addition to gifts one must take learning opportunities, a high level of motivation, and a supportive environment into consideration (e.g. Gagné, 1993). Let us further assume that this entire set of additional factors are realized, then the gift would be non-redundant within this set in that without this gift the exceptional achievement could not be accomplished. When one considers the entire constellation surrounding giftedness, gift inducing personality traits and a supportive environment, one concludes that they are sufficient for the prognosis of exceptional achievement, although not necessary. Similar exceptional achievements in this field could be based on completely different constellations of antecedent conditions. In the case of the forest fire described above, oxygen fulfills the inus condition just as well as the burning cigarette. We are, however, inclined to name the burning cigarette as the cause of the forest fire. In the same vein, the fulfillment of the inus condition is not sufficient to identify a gift, it only serves to single out potential candidates. The next two postulates offer assistance in recognizing which candidates are indeed actual gifts.

Postulate 3: Giftedness as a Personal Characteristic

Postulate 3 is more than likely to be acceptable to most giftedness researchers; gifts denote specific personal variables, and not environmental variables. Consequently, this excludes various further potential causes for achievement eminence which, although meeting the inus condition, do not meet that of Postulate 3. Let us assume that early behaviorists were correct in asserting that the environment is the ultimate cause of behavior. Thus, in a hypothetical case, which may be fully correct in the particular case of a specific achievement, the environmental circumstances alone would be sufficient in meeting the inus condition. Therfore, a particular gift would not have to exist in order to enable exceptional achievement.

Therefore, Postulate 3 disallows environmental factors as potential gifts, although it does not exclude the possibility that personal factors, which one would be reluctant to classify as gifts, could be distinguished as potential gifts. An extreme example of this, which adequately illuminates the problem here would be as follows: Each and every vital event in one's life (e.g. heartbeat), which could occur simultaneously with a gift is fully capable of fulfilling the first three postulates of temporal precedence, the inus condition and of being a personal variable. Nevertheless, one would be reluctant to accept a heartbeat or a functional digestive system as a cause for eminent achievement.

Postulate 4: Theoretical Significance

The postulate of theoretical significance gives expression to an established meta-theoretical criterion according to which a theoretically meaningful causal mechanism between antecedent (here: the gift) and explanandum (here: achievement eminence) must exist. In causal explanations, two or more states of affairs are theoretically tied to one another in such a way that one state of affairs brings about or produces the other state of affairs (Bunge, 1967; Stegmüller, 1970). In order for a gift to be a valid cause for achievement eminence, the achievement must be preceded by the gift (see Postulate 1). Furthermore, an invariant conjunction of the gift and the behavior leading to achievement eminence must be in evidence and an underlying mechanism or psychological structure must theoretically guarantee the necessity of the conjunction. One would not realistically expect to demand deterministic relations here, rather, one can give a new probabilistic interpretation to Postulate 4. However, the problem of when theoretical significance is manifest is now, as ever, unclear from a meta-theoretical viewpoint, and one can always resort to rules of thumb. In any case, it should be clear that gifts should have some effect on the behaviors leading to achievement eminence through processes which can be described by means of *psychological theory*. These theories could be based on a structure or configuration of attitudes, intelligence theories, cognitive theories etc. that facilitate or bring about the exceptional performance. On the other hand, no psychological theories take up the position that processes as vital for life as the heartbeat itself are of psychological significance for achievement eminence.

Often it is the empirical nature of a theoretically maintained mechanism which is difficult to command, particularly when the random samples are troublesome to recruit or the condition constellation of achievement eminence demonstrates unique characteristics. In this case, the empirical investigation of the theoretical significance should, at the very least, be substituted by verification that no third variable controls both, or mediates between, the gift and the behaviors leading to eminent achievement. This sort of makeshift operation does not ensure the identification of gifts, but it does preclude the identification of absurd internal factors as being gifts. It may be that these aforementioned vital processes preclude the behaviors leading to achievement eminence, that they fulfill the inus condition and are certainly personal variables, but they can in no way be established as mediators which arbitrate between an initial state and the behaviors leading to achievement eminence.

Another problem is presented by internal factors which promote the development of achievement eminence, but are traditionally not considered to be gifts; two examples can be differentiated according to the degree of their complexity. *Factors of a low level of complexity* find themselves in a *complementary relationship* with gift factors, in other words, talents and these other factors (i.e. variables which support gifts or favorable environmental conditions) are necessary for the development of achievement eminence. *Factors of a high level of complexity* are, in contrast, *inclusive* and encompass, in addition to further gift promoting factors, the gift itself.

An example of factors with low levels of complexity is offered by Gagné (1993; see also Sternberg in this handbook). He differentiated (to a large extent innate) gift variables (intellectual, creative, socio-affective, and sensori-motor aptitudes) from so-called (intra-personal and environmental) catalysts which are decisive for the translation of gifts into talent. Environmental catalysts have already been ruled out as gifts through Postulate 3. Problems are admittedly brought up by intra-personal catalysts such as motivation or personality. They do meet the requirements of Postulates 1, 2 and 3, but are incapable of demonstrating theoretical significance since no psychological mechanism can be cited which allows these catalysts to be converted into the very behavior which is considered to be eminent. For instance, if one were to decompose chess expertise as Holding (1985) did in his *SEEK Model* into the subskills *S*earch, *E*valuat*E* and *K*nowledge, one is left with motivational constructs on entities which are unknown to the theory, and which do not allow themselves to be converted into these three subskills within the language of the SEEK Model. On the other hand, the ability to perform complicated mental calculations could be a gift, since this ability

underlies one of the subskills (Search) of the SEEK Model.

An example of a factor of a high level of complexity is offered by Ericsson's theory of *deliberate practice* (e.g., Ericsson et al., 1993). In comparison with mere experience, deliberate practice (goal oriented and conscious training, which is maintained over a long time period) denotes an advanced form of experience. It is a behavioral style which encompasses personality factors such as motivation and cognitive skills as well. However, the decisive question here is whether highly inclusive constructs such as deliberate practice can be identified as gifts (for the sake of the discussion let us assume that their influence could also be empirically confirmed). Three facts speak against this. In the first place, they are of such a complex nature that they can encompass environmental factors and intra-individual catalysts as well as gifts themselves. Such a wide concept of giftedness seems also to have too much of an inflationary effect on the construct of giftedness. Second, this partially contradicts Postulate 3, according to which gifts can only be personal variables. One could take a more narrow definition of deliberate practice, exclude environmental factors and define all other internal factors as gifts; this, however, leads us to our third argument which was already addressed in the discussion of Gagnés intra-personal catalysts. For these type of intra-personal catalysts—such as Ericsson's suggestion of a high tolerance level for frustration which enables lengthy, strenuous learning processes— there exist no psychological mechanisms which lead to questionable behaviors which enable achievement eminence. Once again, we are confronted with various theoretical languages which refer to different psychological constructs.

Features of the Critical State

Behavior patterns which lead to achievement eminence are rooted in the interaction of several factors in which scientists are convinced that giftedness plays a crucial role. In the previous section criteria were named which must be fulfilled in order for a variable to be identified as a gift. The next point is concerned with placing this gift in a scientifically productive context.

Figure 4 reveals the outline for a meta-conceptual model for the field of giftedness research; from the point of view of giftedness research, giftedness is seen as the core of the field. From an *epistemological perspective*, however, this is an insufficient explanation of the genesis of achievement eminence. Further conditions must be met and fulfilled, a process which, in its entirety, will be denoted as a critical state.[1]

---

[1] The concept of a 'critical state' has already been employed in several branches of science and is referred to as a transitional phase. For instance, the term critical mass in nuclear physics refers to the state a mass is in during a chain reaction induced by nuclear fusion.

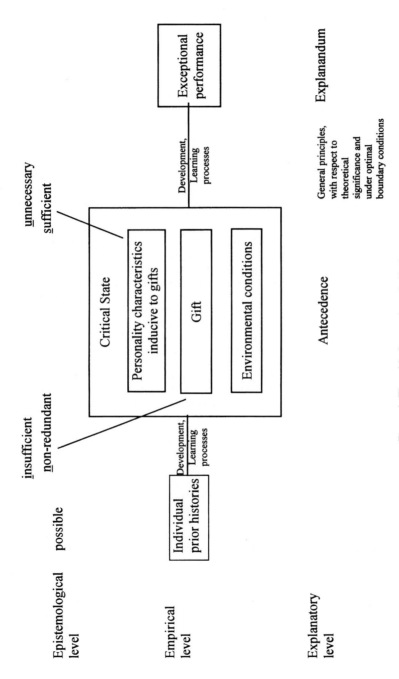

Figure 4. The critical state view of giftedness.

Giftedness, as a part of a critical state, is non-redundant, which legitimizes it as an integral field of research. The critical state, which in addition to giftedness, encompasses environmental and personality factors which promote the development of giftedness is, from an epistemological perspective and when the optimal boundary conditions exist, sufficient for the development of achievement eminence. However, this critical state is not a necessary condition in that achievement eminence can principally be attained via alternative avenues. In this respect, giftedness within the critical state fulfills the inus condition.

The meta-conceptual ordinal diagram illustrates a time span which covers the period preceding and following the critical state. The individual prior history is, from an epistemological perspective, a possible state in which it could very well be that the attainment of a specific manifestation of achievement eminence is already genetically fixed. In this case, it would be useless to consider an individual's prior history.

The eminent achievement can follow the critical state if optimal boundary conditions are present. Developmental and learning processes mediate between individual prior history and critical state as well as between critical state and achievement eminence. This last association must abide by the postulate of theoretical significance.

Let us now look at the model on the *explanatory level* within the framework of the model developed by Hempel and Oppenheim (Hempel & Oppenheim, 1953, cf. Fig. 4, Hempel, 1965). According to their model, an explanation bears three components: first, there must be some statement of a particular fact or facts (antecedence); second, it must incorporate one or more general principles or laws; and third, there must be a statement describing whatever it is that is being explained (explanandum). The explanation shows that the thing to be explained follows from the general principles, given that the particular facts also hold. In applying this to the ordinal diagram at hand, one sees that achievement eminence should be subject to explanation; the entire critical state (not just the gift) describes the particular facts. The general principles correspond to the psychological theory, so that achievement eminence can be theoretically derived from the critical state.

The preceding discourse clearly indicates that the critical state can only be *empirically* identified, and is distinguished for each domain. Thus, it may very well be the case that in one domain the critical state, on the average, can first be attained at the age of 12, while in another domain a critical state has already been reached as early as at the point of conception. In the first domain, all possible combinations of genetic, gene-environment interactions and pure environmental influences could be feasible conditions for the attainment of the critical state (Plomin, 1990; Plomin, DeFries & McClean, 1990), in the second domain,

giftedness was genetically determined. Decisive here is that the critical state view, in principle, offers equal validity to both possible scenarios. First, we must establish that ideological discussions without corresponding evidence in the form of data and without naming the domains in which the gifts are to be identified are more or less futile. Perhaps there is such a thing as a born violinist, but not a born author; conceptions of giftedness must allow for these possibilities.

The critical state also makes no concrete statements regarding what giftedness in a specific domain is; this is a question which must be empirically clarified by each separate domain in and of itself. Certainly, the critical state does not rule out the development of mistakes which could seriously endanger the progressiveness of the field of giftedness research. Let us here consider an example. It is well known that Terman (1925) established his longitudinal study on an intelligence-based operationalization of giftedness. Quite recently, increased theoretical efforts have been undertaken in the area of cognition research to better support cognitive super-constructs such as intelligence. They have been related to low-level biological measures (see Anderson, 1992; Gustafsson & Undheim, 1996, for reviews) such as inspection time (Deary & Stone, 1996), nerve conductance velocity (Vernon, 1987), and evoked potentials (Eysenck, 1988). In an another line of research, Kyllonen (Kyllonen & Christal, 1990; Kyllonen, 1996) has shown that there is enough good empirical evidence to accept the existence of a close to perfect relationship between reasoning ability (e.g., G_f) and working memory capacity. However indifferent the endeavors to make intelligence a theoretically more comprehensible entity may be, from the point of view of the critical state, this is possibly the wrong point from which to begin the process of identifying talents. The starting point should be the supported psychological analyses of the behaviors leading to eminent achievement and the developmental conditions conducive to these behaviors. Only then can a gift be identified which also fulfills the criterion of theoretical significance. If, in fact, it can be proven that academic achievements or the development of achievement eminence in the academic area is actually founded on intelligence, then it makes sense to identify the intelligence of a person as a gift. Then factors such as low-level biological measures, inspection time etc. could also be gainfully investigated as potential gifts.

Now, on the basis of the previous expositions, only a few recommendations can be proposed for inclusion into the terminology of giftedness research. *Gifts* should be denoted by those psychologically identifiable factors which: (1) precede behaviors leading to eminent achievement, (2) satisfy the inus condition, (3) describe personal factors and (4) are theoretically significant with respect to the behaviors leading to the eminent achievement as well as its acquisition. The term *talent* should be used to indicate persons who have reached the critical state. In contrast, an *underachiever* would be a person who has reached the critical state, but has not yet been able to evolve to achievement eminence. Finally, *experts* should refer to those people who have been able to exhibit achievement eminence.

Special Problems

Explanatory Relativisms

Most conceptions of giftedness lend themselves to the label of universal theories in that they are applicable to all domains; this also applies to the meta-conceptual viewpoint of the critical state, however not to the critical state's way of viewing giftedness. Here, gifts are always treated as being *relative* to specific forms of achievement eminence, thereby allowing for the express admittance of explanatory relativism regarding gifts. These are dependent on the determination of achievement eminence, or to put it another way, the solutions to the application problem, the focus problem, the reference problem and the significance problem. On their behalf, two aspects are to be emphasized. In the first place, it appears to be improbable that a general theory of giftedness could be established which would be entitled to universal domain validity. The demands made for such a claim by fields as diverse as sports, music and academics appear to be too great. In the second place, the limits of achievement can be altered, which brings about differing solutions for the significance problem, which in itself would lead to a variety of empirical consequences and theoretical implications. In this way, a lofty achievement from yesterday, which was only possible through fixed genetic provisions, may be easily learned tomorrow.

A further aspect of explanatory relativism ensues from the inus condition; a critical state, although sufficient for the attainment of achievement eminence, is not necessary; this implies that achievement eminence can also be attainable through alternative critical states. This seems to be thoroughly plausible and can also be conventionally defended in that in the identification of gifts it is not just one expression of the gift which is used to authorize recognition in domains such as academics, art or sports (Hany, 1993).

Ontological Status of Gifts

The critical state view proposes the framework for a conceptual model which, in principle, is an uninterpreted model which must be confirmed for every manifestation of achievement eminence. Gifts are empirically ascertainable psychological entities. Therefore, it can be that the emphasis is on one single trait, such as intelligence or a perceptual ability, or on an entire set of traits. At any rate, there is no guarantee that the conceptual model can be interpreted in specific cases, in other words, that a gift actually exists. In case there is a need to emphasize that a specific form of achievement eminence can be realized through externally controlled learning processes alone, then the domain in question is one in which giftedness plays no substantial role whatsoever.

Likewise, it is important to point out that gifts are not merely predictors, as for instance Heller and Hany (1986) or Ziegler and Perleth (1997) postulated in their prediction models of eminent behavior. The general problem with mere prediction models is their lack of an explanatory status; in order to further clarify this point, we look to another branch of science: astronomy. One can safely assume that a solar eclipse will take place when 99% of all astronomers agree on this prediction; this prognosis does not, however, satisfy the postulate of theoretical significance. By the same token, even a good predictor of achievement eminence, such as intelligence, cannot be automatically identified as a gift as long as the causal mechanism which leads to achievement eminence cannot be confirmed.

In summary, one can conclude that gifts are concerned with psychological personality characteristics or even configurations of such characteristics which must be empirically identified, satisfy the requirements of the four postulates discussed, and demonstrate an empirical correlation to reality.

Epistemological Perspective

Through the postulate of the inus condition, the critical state view holds various epistemological assumptions which require some clarification. Three aspects are of particular significance, the epistemological terms 'sufficient' and 'necessary', the question of a probabilistic interpretation of the critical state and finally the question surrounding the boundary conditions.

'Sufficient' and 'Necessary'

The critical state signifies the moment in the biography of a person at which, under specific conditions, achievement eminence will be attained with sufficient certainty. This, however, raises logical problems since there is no guarantee that a person who has reached the critical state will actually demonstrate achievement eminence. For this reason, the application of the term 'sufficient' seems to be too extreme from a strictly logical point of view. Actually, it should not be understood in a strictly logical sense as a description of actual empirical relationships, but rather as a subjective certainty in the estimation of the state by assessors (giftedness researchers, patrons, giftedness program administrators, etc.) of a person who finds him/herself in a phase of achievement development. This subjective certainty is not random, but rather relative to the available psychological knowledge and the available information regarding the ability to meet the conditions essential for fostering the development of achievement. Here, the assessments of the relevant experts will certainly deviate from one another, although the problem is not unknown. In certain respects, it is similar to the subjective certainty shown in the acceptance of a specific level of statistical error, whereby there is no compelling justification for one to deem a 5% or 1% error rate as being sufficient for the acceptance of a hypothesis. These considerations can effortlessly and logically be translated to the assessment of the term 'necessary'. The expressions 'sufficient' and 'necessary' refer to personal judgments which are based on subjective acceptance criteria which themselves have to be supported by current knowledge in the discipline.

Probability

The application of the terms 'sufficient' and 'necessary' suggests that the critical state view is concerned with a deterministic view of achievement development. At the very least, the discussions in the last text section should have made clear that this point of view is not intended, and that instead, probabilistic relationships are advocated.

Boundary Conditions

Scientific statements are only valid under certain conditions, which are referred to as the boundary conditions. In the same manner that a falling stone will be pulled towards earth as long as no obstacle blocks its path, a person who has reached the critical state will only be able to develop achievement eminence under certain boundary conditions. Each and every field of scientific research is faced with the challenge of determining the precise conditions under which their theories are valid; giftedness research is no exception to this rule. What is called for here is an *optimal process criterion*; in concrete terms, this means that we should place strict standards on the conditions of a critical state. The need to adopt an optimal process criterion is founded on the fact that achievement eminence concerns itself with a rare behavioral pattern which can only be mastered by a small minority. The higher the demands for quality placed on the *ceteris paribus* conditions are, the lower the level of achievement will be for a person who has been able to reach the critical state. This does open up the opportunity for theoretical advantages. Gifts are further removed temporally from achievement eminence, whereby more ambitious giftedness theories, as well as theories which secure theoretical significance, become essential. Furthermore, the optimal process criteria leads to an earlier indicator of talents.

What advantages are Offered by the Critical State View?

Forging a Link to Expertise Research

One point, which is also of the utmost significance for the further development of the field of giftedness research, is that the critical state view enables the forging of a frequently suggested link between two areas of research which are often unnaturally separated (Feldhusen, 1998; Sternberg, Gross in this handbook): Giftedness research and expertise research. While giftedness research has traditionally posed the question of where the gifted are heading towards and whether they will ever reach the point of eminent achievement, expertise researchers have always been interested in determining where experts come from. Figuratively speaking, from the perspective of the critical state view, the task of giftedness research is to establish this theoretical link between the talented (who have achieved the critical state) and experts (who have demonstrated exceptional performance).

Empirical, Ontological and Theoretical Criticisms of Expertise Research

The critical state view furnishes methodological references for the identification of gifts which eases empirical research of giftedness; since they are understood as constructs with an empirical correlate, their identification is, in principle, feasible. They could be referring to, for instance, specific motor characteristics, cognitive or perceptual abilities. Such qualities are already the focus of empirical investigation, and psychologists make a daily practice of placing them under examination.

Through such a consistent empirical point of view, various fruitless arguments such as the previously mentioned debate over the existence of talents or gifts become unnecessary. Whether giftedness is determined through genetics or learning processes (Sternberg & Grigorenko, 1997) becomes a subordinate question from the point of view of giftedness research; it only becomes important when one is investigating the conditions pertinent to the origination of giftedness. A more important and distinctly praiseworthy advantage of a critical state view is the compulsion it generates towards a theory guided style of empirical research.

From an ontological point of view, gifts are accredited with the same ontological status granted to the behaviors leading to eminent behavior. Here, we are referring to neither a composite of items from a list-based definition, nor to simple predictors (although they would provide a useful service), but rather to empirical factors capable of explaining the subsequent process of the development of eminent behavior.

Through these empirical and ontological interpretations of the traditional talent constructs, the above-mentioned meta-theoretical difficulties are avoided. The critical state view guarantees non-circularity, foremost on the grounds of the temporal displacement between the gifts and the behaviors pertinent to achievement eminence. Gifts are also not immune to falsification in that it has already been conceded that for a specific type of achievement eminence, no specific gift may exist. Through the explanatory relativity of gifts, it may very well be the case that a form of giftedness which is acceptable today may quickly become obsolete due to a redefinition of achievement eminence or advances in promotional techniques. Finally, the demand for theoretical progessiveness (Lakatos, 1978) is serenely met with a critical state view since a close-fitting link between gifts and achievement eminence is demanded, whereby the criterion of theoretical significance, which no longer extends mere predictive services, is easily met.

Summary

Exceptional performances have always fascinated mankind, but it was only when the theoretical concepts which resulted from empirical psychological investigation were available, that one could replace the theological and metaphysical explanations which have been hitherto pressed into service. It is on the meta-theoretical level that many current conceptions of giftedness need to confront criticism. With the critical state view presented in this chapter, a meta-conceptual model is being delineated which should serve to surmount these deficiencies. The critical state view, although it does not propose a substantive theory of giftedness, does show the manner in which one could be developed in the future on the basis of solid empirical research. Starting with an analysis of the behaviors which lead to achievement eminence, it is proposed that a critical state be established, based on disposable theoretical knowledge and the assumption of optimal conditions for achievement eminence. Within this critical state one can identify those possibly special gifts which meet the criteria developed in this chapter.

Acknowledgements

The authors would like to thank Hanna David, Letitia Hernandez and Thomas D. Raul for their assistance in the form of critical discussions and valuable comments to an earlier version of this chapter, and Alice Boetsch, Thomas D. Raul and Janet Townsend for their hard work in the translation of the text.

References

Achinstein, P. (1983). *The nature of explanation*. New York: Oxford University Press.

Ackerman, P. L. (1987). Individual differences in skill learning: An integration of psychometric and information processing perspectives. *Psychological Bulletin*, **102**, 3–27.

Ackerman, P. L. (1992). Predicting individual differences in complex skill acquisition: Dynamics of ability determinants. *Journal of Applied Psychology*, 5, 598–614.

Anderson, M. (1992). *Intelligence and Development*. Oxford, UK: Basil Blackwell.

Binet, A. & Simon, T. (1916). *The intelligence of the feeble-minded*. Baltimore: Williams & Williams.

Bromberger, S. (1992). *On what we know we don't know*. Chicago: University of Chicago Press.

Bunge, M. (1967). *Scientific research I: the search for system*. New York: Springer.

Butler-Por, N. (1993). Underachieving gifted students. In: K. A. Heller, F. J. Mönks & A. H. Passow (Eds), *International Handbook of Research and Development of Giftedness and Talent* (pp. 649–668). Oxford: Pergamon.

Chi, M. T. H., Glaser, R. & Farr, M. J. (Eds) (1988). *The nature of expertise*. Hillsdale, NJ: Erlbaum.

Deary, I. J. & Stone, C. (1996). Intelligence and inspection time: achievements, prospects, and problems. *American Psychologist, 51*, 599–608.

DeHaan, R. G. & Havighurst, R. J. (1957). *Educating the gifted*. Chicago: University of Chicago Press.

Ellis, H. (1927). *A study of British genius*. London: Constable.

Ericsson, K. A. & Crutcher, R. J. (1990). The nature of exceptional performance. In: P. B. Baltes, D. L. Featherman & R. M. Lerner (Eds), *Life-span Development and Behavior* (pp. 187–218). Hillsdale, NJ: Erlbaum.

Ericsson, K. A. & Smith, J. (Eds) (1991). *Toward a General Theory of Expertise. Prospects and Limits*. Cambridge: Cambridge University Press.

Ericsson, K. A. & Pennington, N. (1993). The structure of memory performance in experts: Implications for memory in everyday life. In: G. M. Davies & R. H. Logie (Eds), *Memory in Everyday Life* (pp. 241–272). Amsterdam: Elsevier.

Ericsson, K. A., Krampe, R. T. & Tesch-Römer, C. (1993). The role of deliberate practice in the acquisition of expert performance. *Psychological Review, 100*, 363–406.

Eysenck, H. J. (1988). The biological basis of intelligence. In: S. H. Irvine & J. W. Berry, (Eds), *Human Abilities in Cultural Context* (pp. 87–104). Cambridge, England: Cambridge University Press.

Feldhusen, J. F. (1998). A conception of talent and talent development. In: R. C. Friedman & K. B. Rogers (Eds), *Talent in context* (pp. 41–67). Washington, DC: APA.

Feldhusen, J. F. (1986). A conception of giftedness. In: K. A. Heller & J. F. Feldhusen (Eds), *Identifying and Nurturing the Gifted. An International Perspective* (pp. 33–38). Toronto: Huber.

Feldman, D. H. & Goldsmith, L. (1986). *Nature's gambit: child prodigies and the development of human potential*. New York: Basic Books/Teachers College Press.

Feldman, D. H. (1980). Beyond universals in cognitive development. In: R. J. Sternberg (Ed.), *The Nature of Creativity*. Cambridge: Cambridge University Press.

Fels, C. (1999). *Identifizierung und Förderung Hochbegabter in den Schulen der Bundesrepublik Deutschland* [Identifying and promoting gifted students in Germany]. Stuttgart: Haupt.

Freyhof, H., Gruber, H. & Ziegler, A. (1992). Expertise and hierarchical knowledge representation in chess. *Psychological Research*, **54**, 32–37.

Gagné, F.(1985). Giftedness and talent: re-examination of the definitions. *Gifted Child Quarterly, 29*, 103–112.

Gagné, F. (1993). Constructs and models pertaining to exceptional human abilities. In: K. A. Heller, F. J. Mönks & A. H. Passow (Eds), *International Handbook of Research and Development of Giftedness and Talent* (pp. 69–87). Oxford: Pergamon.

Galton, F. (1883). *Inquiry into human faculty and its development*. London: Macmillan Press.

Gardner, H. (1985). The role of crystallizing experiences. In: F. Horowitz & M. O'Brien (Eds), *Developmental Per-

spectives on the Education of the Gifted (pp. 74–102). Washington, DC: APA.

Götze, C. (1916). Schulbegabung und Lebensbegabung [Scholastic talent and talent]. In: P. Petersen (Ed.), *Der Aufstieg der Begabten. Vorfragen* (pp. 9–16). Berlin: Teubner.

Gustafsson, J.-E. & Undheim, J. O. (1996). Individual differences in cognitive functions. In: D. Berliner & R. Calfee (Eds), *Handbook of Educational Psychology* (pp. 186–248). New York: Macmillan.

Hany, E. A. (1993). Methodological problems and issues concerning identification. In: K. A. Heller, F. J. Mönks & A. H. Passow (Eds), *International Handbook of Research and Development of Giftedness and Talent* (pp. 209–232). Oxford: Pergamon.

Heller, K. A. (1989). Perspectives on the diagnosis of giftedness. *German Journal of Psychology*, **13**, 140–159.

Heller, K. A. (1990). Goals, methods and first results from the Munich Longitudinal Study of Giftedness in West Germany. In: C. W. Taylor (Ed.), *Expanding Awareness of Creative Potentials Worldwide* (pp. 538–543). New York: Trillium Press.

Heller, K. A. (1991). The nature and development of giftedness: a longitudinal study. *European Journal of High Ability*, **2**, 174–188.

Heller, K. A. (1993). International trends and issues of research on giftedness. In: W. T. Wu, C. C. Kuo & J. Steeves (Eds), *Growing Up Gifted and Talented. Proceedings of the Second Asian Conference on Giftedness* (pp. 93–110). Taipei, Taiwan: NTNU.

Heller, K. A. & Hany, E. A. (1986). Identification, development and achievement analysis of talented and gifted children in West Germany. In: K. A. Heller & J. F. Feldhusen (Eds), *Identifying and Nurturing the Gifted* (pp. 67–82). Toronto: Huber.

Hempel, C. G. & Oppenheim, P. (1953). The logic of explanation. In: H. Feigl and M. Brodbeck (Eds), *Readings in the Philosophy of Science* (pp. 319–352). New York: Appleton-Century-Crofts.

Hempel, C. G. (1965). *Aspects of scientific explanation.* New York: The Free Press.

Hirsch, N. D. M. (1931). *Genius and creative intelligence.* Cambridge: Sci-Art Publishers.

Hoffman, R. R. (Ed.). (1992). *The psychology of expertise: cognitive research and empirical AI.* New York: Springer.

Holding, D. H. (1985). *The psychology of chess skill.* Hillsdale, NJ: Erlbaum.

Hollingworth, L. S. (1929). *Gifted children: their nature and nurture.* New York: Macmillan.

Howe, M. J. A., Davidson, J. W. & Sloboda, J. A. (1998). Innate talents: reality or myth? *Behavioral and Brain Sciences*, **21**, 399–442.

Kluge, F. (1967). *Etymologisches Wörterbuch der deutschen Sprache* [Etymological handbook of German language]. Berlin: Walter de Gruyter.

Kretschmer, E. (1931). *Geniale Menschen* [Geniuses] (2nd ed.). Berlin: Springer.

Kyllonen, P. C. & Christal, R. E. (1990). Reasoning ability is (little more than) working-memory capacity?! *Intelligence*, **14**, 389–433.

Kyllonen, P. C. (1996). Is working memory capacity Spearman's g? In: I. Dennis & P. Tapsfield (Eds), *Human Abilities: Their Nature and Measurement* (pp. 77–96). Hillsdale, NJ: Erlbaum.

Lakatos, I. (1978). *The methodology of scientific research programs. Philosophical Papers, Vol. I.* Cambridge: Cambridge University Press.

Mackie, J. L. (1975). *The cement of universe: a study of causation.* Oxford: Oxford University Press.

Marland, S. P. (1972). *Education of the gifted and talented: Report to the Congress of the United States by the U. S. Commissioner of Education.* Washington: U. S. Government Printing Office.

McClelland, D. C., Atkinson, J. W., Clark, R. A. & Lowell, E. L. (1953). *The achievement motive.* New York: Appleton Century-Crofts.

Mönks, F. J. (1990). Hochbegabtenförderung als Aufgabe der Pädagogischen Psychologie [Promoting the gifted as a task for educational psychology]. *Psychologie in Erziehung und Unterricht*, **37**, 243–250.

Passow, A. H., Mönks, F. J. & Heller K. A. (1993). Research and education of the gifted in the year 2000 and beyond. In: K. A. Heller, F. J. Mönks & A. H. Passow (Eds), *International Handbook of Research and Development of Giftedness and Talent* (pp. 883–903). Oxford: Pergamon.

Perleth, Ch. & Heller, K. A. (1994). The Munich Longitudinal Study of Giftedness. In: R. F. Subotnik & K. D.Arnold (Eds), *Beyond Terman: Contemporary Longitudinal Studies of Giftedness and Talent* (pp. 77–114). Norwood, NJ: Ablex.

Plomin, R. (1990). *Nature and nurture: an introduction to human behavioral genetics.* Pacific Grove, CA: Brooks/ Cole.

Plomin, R., DeFries, J. C. & Mcclearn, G. E. (1990). *Behavioral genetics: a primer.* New York: Freeman.

Radford, J. (1990). Child prodigies and exceptional early achievers. *The Psychologist*, **7**, 359–360.

Renzulli, J. S. (1978). What makes giftedness? Reexamining a definition. *Phi Delta Kappan*, **60**, 180–184.

Renzulli, J. S. (1986). The three-ring conception of giftedness: a developmental model for creative productivity. In: R. J. Sternberg & J. E. Davidson (Eds), *Conceptions of Giftedness.* Cambridge: University Press.

Rescher, N. (1995). *Satisfying reason: studies in the theory of knowledge.* Dordrecht, NE: Kluwer.

Scarr, S. & McCartney, K. (1983). How people make their own environments: a theory of genotype-environent effects. *Child Development*, **54**, 424–435.

Sneed, J. (1994). Structural explanation. In: P. Humphreys (Ed.), *Patrick Suppes : Scientific Philosopher*, Vol. 2. *Philosophy of Physics. Theory Structure and Measurement Theory* (pp. 195–213). Dordrecht, NE: Kluwer.

Sneed, J., Balzer, W. & Moulines, C. U. (1987). *An architectonic for science: the structuralist approach.* Dordrecht, NE: Reidel.

Stanley, J. C. & Benbow, C. P. (1986). Youths who reason exceptionally well mathematically. In: R. J. Sternberg & J. E. Davidson (Eds), *Conceptions of Giftedness* (pp. 361–387). New York: Cambridge University Press.

Stegmüller, W. (1970). *Probleme und Resultate der Wissenschaftstheorie und Analytischen Philosophie (Bd. II. Theorie und Erfahrung: 1. Halbband. Begriffsformen, Wissenschaftssprache, empirische Signifikanz u. ihre theoretischen Begiffe)* [Problems in and results of scientific theory and analytical philosophy (Vol. II. Theory and experience: 1st Semi-volume terminological forms, scientific language, empirical significance and their theoretical terms)]. Berlin: Springer.

Sternberg, R. J. (1977). Intelligence, information processing and analogical reasoning. Hillsdale, NJ: Erlbaum.

Sternberg, R. J. (1985). *Beyond IQ: A triarchic theory of human intelligence.* Cambridge: University Press.

Sternberg, R. J. (1986). A triarchic theory of intellectual giftedness. In: R. J. Sternberg & J. E. Davidson (Eds), *Conceptions of Giftedness* (pp. 223–243). Cambridge, MA: Cambridge University Press.

Sternberg, R. J. (1988). *The nature of creativity. Contemporary Psychological Perspectives.* Cambridge: Cambridge University Press.

Sternberg, R. J. (1990). What constitutes a 'Good' definition of giftedness? *Journal for the Education of the Gifted*, **14**, 96–100.

Sternberg, R. J. (1991). The nature of creativity: Contemporary psychological perspectives. Cambridge, MA: Cambridge University Press.

Sternberg, R. J. (1993). Procedures for identifying intellectual potential in the gifted: A perspective on alternative 'Metaphors of Mind'. In: K. A. Heller, F. J. Mönks & A. H. Passow (Eds), *International Handbook of Research and Development of Giftedness and Talent* (pp. 185–207). Oxford: Pergamon.

Sternberg, R. J. & Davidson, J. E. (Eds) (1986). *Conceptions of giftedness.* Cambridge: Cambridge University Press.

Sternberg, R. J. & Grigorenko, E. L. (Eds) (1997). *Intelligence, heredity, and environment.* New York: Cambridge University Press.

Tannenbaum, A. J. (1983). *Gifted children: psychological and educational perspectives.* New York: MacMillan.

Tannenbaum, A. J. (1986). Giftedness: a psychosocial approach. In: R. J. Sternberg & J. E. Davidson (Eds), *Conceptions of Giftedness* (pp. 21–52). New York: Cambridge University Press.

Tannenbaum, A. J. (1991). The social psychology of giftedness. In: N. Colangelo & G. A. Davis (Eds), *Handbook of Gifted Education* (pp. 27–44). Boston: Allyn and Bacon.

Terman, L. M. (1925). *Genetic studies of genius. Mental and physical traits of a thousand gifted children* (Vol. 1). Stanford: University Press.

Vernon, P. A. (1987). *Speed of information-processing and intelligence.* Norwood, NJ: Ablex.

Wagner R. K. (1999). Searching for determinants of performance in complex domains. In: P. L. Ackerman, P. C. Kyllonen & R. D.Roberts (Eds), *Learning and Individual Differences* (pp. 371–388). Washington, DC: APA.

Ziegler, A. & Perleth, C. (1997). Schafft es Sisyphos, den Stein den Berg hinaufzurollen? Eine kritische Bestandsaufnahme der Diagnose- und Fördermöglichkeiten von Begabten in der beruflichen Erstaus- und Weiterbildung vor dem Hintergrund des Münchner Begabungsmodells [Will Sisyphus be able to roll the stone up the mountain? A critical examination of the status of diagnosis and promotion of gifteds in occupational education set against the Munich Talent Model]. *Psychologie in Erziehung und Unterricht*, **44**, 152–163.

Ziegler, A. & Raul, T. D. (2000). A review of empirical studies on giftedness. *High Ability Studies*, **10**, in press.

A History of Giftedness in School and Society*

Abraham J. Tannenbaum

Teachers College, Columbia University, New York, USA

Introduction

Does genius make history, or does history make the genius? A seemingly intriguing question for school children and scholars alike. But a deceptive one nonetheless, since the choice is not 'either-or'. Actually, neither individual geniuses nor historical forces predominate, the real relationship being interactive and interdependent. Great ideas by highly creative individuals often carry enough power to influence the course of history; conversely, the *Zeitgeist* (spirit of the times) exercises an enormous influence on great minds and on the domains of excellence in which their precious ideas are generated.

Western Perspectives on Domains of Excellence

Although the precise manner in which geniuses and their eras inter-relate will always be a mystery, one impression seems clear: the work of seminal thinkers throughout the ages and societies is so important that unless we learn to appreciate it we cannot hope to learn how the human family *makes* history. Indeed, there are historians whose theories are bound up with the nature and impact of creative accomplishments in every historical period.

Spengler (1918), who compared the development of a society to that of a human organism, each with its own life cycle and distinctive personality, believed that every stage of growth is *defined* by the style and substance of great creative works produced at that time.

Medieval Europe is characterized by the Gothic cathedral in architecture, the Gregorian Chant in music, and 'Everyman' in drama, all treasures of creative thinking and fitted perfectly to Church-State political leadership. In the Romantic Period, sumptuous government buildings and elegant homes for the bourgeoisie are the representative architecture of flourishing democracies; Beethoven's music and Shelley's poetry bespeak the idealization of the human collective spirit as it replaces the earlier authority of monarchy and aristocracy and the still earlier power of the Supernatural. It would therefore be anachronistic for a late twentieth-century composer to create music in the style of Mozart's Divertimenti or for an artist to produce a Gainsborough-type 'Blue Boy' in the 1990s. The voices of present-day genius are not only different from those of previous times—they also codify current history as both reflectors and shapers of the society in which *they* live, just as their predecessors did in their own idiomatic, but era-inspired, ways when Western society was younger.

In an essentially different approach to history, Toynbee (1967) emphasizes society's need to respond successful to periodic challenges as a condition of survival. Today, the most obvious obstacles facing the world include threats to the environment, huge regional pockets of overpopulation and hunger, the dread of nuclear warfare, urban decay and violence, inter-ethnic and inter-class tensions, and a host of diseases that resist cure thus far. Whatever progress is made in confronting these problems will be spear-headed by some of the most advanced thinkers of our times. Toynbee is explicit in estimating the importance of creativity in guaranteeing the survival of Western civilization when he writes:

> To give a fair chance to potential creativity is a matter of life and death for any society. This is all-important, because the outstanding creative ability of a fairly small percentage of the population is mankind's ultimate capital asset, the only one with which Man has been endowed (p. 24, italics in the original).

---

* Since the terms 'giftedness', 'talent', 'creativity', and 'genius' appear in this chapter, a brief note is in order concerning their intended meanings. 'Giftedness' and 'talent' are used synonymously to encompass publicly valued abilities possessed by no more than one to two percent of people at each developmental stage. 'Creativity' is regarded here as representing one of two aspects of 'giftedness' (or 'talent'), namely, innovation or invention that deserves critical acclaim, in contrast to the other aspect of 'giftedness' (or 'talent') which refers to highly developed proficiency in highly demanding tasks. 'Genius' is the most advanced extension of 'giftedness' (or 'talent') or 'creativity', denoting Olympian-level accomplishments by the rarest of adults.

In essence, then, there is not only a history *of* giftedness, but also history *and* giftedness. It makes little sense to recount the life of a people without taking special note of at least some of its best minds. These leading figures produce immortal artifacts that symbolize the distinctive nature of culture and civilization as they are preserved and changed in the course of time (according to Spengler). Viewed differently, the nature and degree of creative thinking are critical in determining whether a culture can survive and continue to grow or become truncated relics of an unrecoverable past (according to Toynbee).

Historical Drives

The human psyche seems to have a phenomenal potential for achievement. There are no known limits to the *kinds* of talents it can demonstrate and to the heights to which it can climb in any talent domain. But the mind is not motivated to achieve every possible form of excellence. The cultural milieu makes that decision in the broadest possible sense. Spengler suggested that the predominant characteristic of Western society is 'Faustian', a term based on the medieval legendary character, Faust, who is depicted in masterpieces by Marlowe, Goethe, Gounod, Boito, and Thomas Mann. In its reified form, this governing power is said to produce an insatiable urge in individuals to explore the unknown and even the unknowable, to reach the unreachable, to grasp at the fringes of eternity, as it were, no matter what sacrifices are necessary to solve the mysteries of the universe and to serve the cause of aesthetics. Spengler offers no clue as to why the West adopted Faust as its inspiration to thrust ever upward with the Gothic arch in the Middle Ages and into outer space and the firmament in our own time. But according to him, the high-intensity drive has always been there; penetration of the heavens with cathedral architecture in one period of history and with jet propulsion in another era represent similar Faustian impulses emanating from different world views. Both also represent accomplishments of some of the best minds of their respective generations. Thus, the history of a people comes to life and takes on meaning through feats of supreme intellect and artistry in every generation.

In the course of Western history, considerable consensus has evolved concerning domains of excellence that have come to receive highest valuation and emphasis. Phenix (1964) describes these domains from the perspective of a philosopher-educator, as follows:

(1) *Symbolics*, including basic forms of communication through ordinary language, mathematics, and such nondiscursive symbolic forms as gestures, rituals, and rhythmic patterns. These systems are structured according to socially accepted rules of formation and transformation and, as carriers of messages between human beings, they are the most basic of all realms of meanings since they have to be used to express ideas in each of the other realms.

(2) *Empirics*, comprising the sciences of the physical and living world. Their content includes factual descriptions, generalizations, and theoretical formulations based on objective evidence in a world of matter, life, mind, and society. Hypotheses introduced into these realms are tested according to specified rules of evidence and verification before acceptable truths can emerge.

(3) *Aesthetics*, including the various arts, such as music, painting, sculpting, theater, and literary creation. "Meanings in this realm are concerned with the contemplative perception of particular significant things as unique objectifications of ideated subjectivities" (pp. 6,7.).

(4) *Synnoetics*, derived from the Greek word *Synnoesis*, meaning 'meditative thought', or more specifically, a combination of *syn*, meaning 'with' or 'together', and *noesis*, meaning 'cognition'. Synnoetics therefore signifies insightful relationships between people or psychological understandings about people. It applies to other persons or to oneself in the sphere of *knowing*, just as sympathy relates to individuals in the sphere of *feeling*.

(5) *Ethics*, which emphasizes moral meanings that are concerned with *obligation* instead of fact, what ought to be rather than what was, is, or will be. "In contrast to the sciences, which are concerned with abstract cognitive understanding, to the arts, which express idealized aesthetic perceptions, and to personal knowledge which reflects intersubjective understanding, morality has to do with personal conduct that is based on free, responsible, deliberate decision" (p. 7).

(6) *Synoptics*, which embraces meanings that integrate history, religion, and philosophy comprehensively. The tools for building such meanings are empirical, aesthetic, and synnoetic, and the outcomes are new insights that amount to more than the sum of the parts from which they are derived.

Psychologists observing the trained and habituated skills in modern Western society classify human aptitude structures in fairly much the same way as Phenix does, albeit from a different vantage point. For example, DeHaan and Havighurst (1957) list the following domains of excellence:

(1) *Intellectual ability*, which is related most directly to success in school subjects, encompasses the verbal, number, spatial, memory, and reasoning factors of the primary mental abilities. Combinations of these aptitudes are regarded as basic to other talents, such as fine arts, social leadership, science, and mechanics.

(2) *Creative thinking*, which is revealed through some complex mental powers, such as the ability to recognize problems, to be flexible in thinking, to originate ideas or products, or to find new uses for old objects and materials.

(3) *Scientific ability*, including skills in the use of numbers and algebraic symbols, arithmetic reasoning, curiosity about the natural world, and facility with the scientific method.

(4) *Social leadership*, specifically the ability to help a group reach its goals and to improve human relationships within a group. Such skills are necessary for those who will eventually assume leadership positions in business and industry, labor unions, professional organizations, community groups, government, and international agencies.

(5) *Mechanical skills*, otherwise known as 'craft skills' and closely related to talents in the fine arts and in science and engineering. Success in this category depends on manipulative facility, spatial ability, and perception of visual patterns, details, similarities, and differences.

(6) *Talents in the fine arts*, which are required of artists, writers, musicians, actors, and dancers.

In a similar vein, Gardner (1983) lists seven human intelligences: (1) linguistic, (2) musical, (3) mathematical, (4) visual-spatial, (5) bodily kinesthetic, (6) social-interpersonal, and (7) intrapersonal. What is noteworthy about Gardner's theory is that it derives partly from his observations of individuals who had sustained injuries in different parts of the brain. This source of data is a far cry from the primarily cultural and historic corpus of material from which Phenix (1964) drew his observations. Yet, the overlap in their domain listings is extensive enough to give a clear picture of what is generally recognized as the major types of excellence treasured in modern Western civilization, in contrast to earlier times in the West and to present-day life in some Western subcultures and in parts of the world that remain relatively untouched by Western influence.

Among the talent domains that define the West's particular brands of Faustian strivings, there seems to be something of a prestige hierarchy which has remained fairly stable over the years. Highest in valuation are the *scarcity talents*, so called because they are always in short supply. Medieval society could never get its fill of leadership and inspiration from the clergy who created an orderly, protective environment and provided its constituents with keys to personal redemption from sin and from the threat of divine retribution. In our modern world there is also an insatiable need for people inventive enough to make life easier, safer, healthier, and more intelligible. But hopes for survival are no longer vested primarily in special talents possessed by leaders of the clergy. Instead, the creative scientist and social leader are seen as most indispensable, and therefore the demand for them cannot be satiated as long as life itself is vulnerable to extinction or dysfunction.

Although it takes only a single Jonas Salk to achieve the breakthrough in conquering polio, there can never be enough talent like his for the great leaps forward that still need to be made in medical science. The same can be said for an Abraham Lincoln in political leadership, a Martin Luther King Jr, in race relations, a Winston Churchill in defense of human freedom, and a Sigmund Freud in mental health. Society will always venerate such talents as they appear, while thirsting for more and more since the shortage can never be filled, principally because the public's motives are more self-preserving than self-serving. It makes sense, therefore, to consider these special abilities as symbols of excellence in greatest demand.

Ranking second are the *surplus talents*, so named because their cumulative accomplishments over the years are so abundant, rich, and varied that they exceed the capacity of individuals to sample and derive benefit from all of them. For example, it is said that multitudes acknowledge the greatness of Dante for his *Inferno*, but hardly anyone ever reads it even once in a lifetime. For the non readers, such a masterpiece is considered 'surplus' in the sense that it is underutilized as literary fare, although it could never be considered 'superfluous' inasmuch as some people, albeit a handful, do read and adore it.

Those who possess surplus talents have the rare ability to elevate people's sensibilities and sensitivities to new heights through the production of great art, literature, music, and philosophy. Few individuals can excel in this category, and some who do achieve celebrity status, which means that they are the most widely recognizable people in the eyes of the general public. But despite the fame and fortune of a Picasso and a Beethoven, they are treated as 'divine luxuries' capable of beautifying the world without guaranteeing its continued existence. Of course, a Michelangelo and a Bach are always welcome as cultural assets; still, the need for such talents represents a *craving* for ways in which to enhance the quality of life rather than a *demand* for finding means of preserving life itself. People are more likely to suppress their cravings than their demands, as evidenced by the vast treasures of art, literature, and music that are widely unappreciated.

The terms *scarcity talents* and *surplus talents* are not intended to express value judgments, as if one were superior to the other. They are simply different in the *kinds* of admiration they elicit from society and in the popular hierarchy of importance if a choice between them had to be made. Scarcity talents are treated as if they were vital human resources that will always be in short supply as long as utopia is yet to be attained. Their primary preoccupation is with fathoming the unknown and even the unknowable, and modern Western society has committed itself to investing all it can to further such an enterprise. The physical survival of individuals depends on the existence of scarcity talents, whereas the cultural survival of the civilization depends on surplus-type talents. Therefore, it is no surprise that many schools and their supporting communities are more eager to cultivate scarcity talents in order to keep body and soul together rather than to nurture surplus talents for the sake of keeping the human spirit alive.

Third in rank are the *quota talents*, which include specialized, high-level skills needed to provide goods and services for which the market is limited. The job to be done is fairly clear; there are no creative break-throughs expected and no way of knowing precisely how long the opportunities for such work will last. Job openings for the relatively few who qualify depend on supply and demand, which can be irregular and geographically bound. Thus, a person with aptitudes for local political leadership has a chance of becoming elected only on special days designated for voting in a democracy, provided that an appropriate vacancy in public office exists at that time. Physicians, teachers, engineers, lawyers, commercial artists, and business executives are but a few of the kinds of highly skilled people whose work is valuable. But they are sought after only in response to market demand and opportu-nity. Sometimes there are low supplies of such talents, as the case of physicians needed in poverty-stricken areas of the world; occasionally there are surpluses, such as liberal arts PhDs who are working at unskilled jobs because they cannot find professional employment for which they are trained, even though some positions are filled by less capable people hired ahead of them and protected by tenure policies.

Like scarcity and surplus talents, quota talents emerge in response to popular demand, but only up to the point where the public feels that its needs for such productivity are being met. For example, major symphony orchestras are kept alive by appreciative audiences that support first-rate performances by first-rate musicians. Sometimes there are vacancies to be filled in orchestral sections, and the search is on for candidates who qualify. But the number of such positions is necessarily limited by the number of orchestras the public is willing to sponsor. Hence, there is a quota system against which to measure shortage and surplus.

Schools have historically been most responsive to the public's needs for quota talents. These types of advanced skills are appreciated for the specialized services and goods they supply and for their market value. Schools can therefore be alerted to areas of expertise where there are many openings and the pay is good for those who are bright and trained enough to qualify. In many schools, the advanced training programs designed to fill quotas in various professions have traditionally constituted the total effort at differ-entiating education for the gifted.

Ranking last in the hierarchy are *anomalous talents*, including those which are either unappreciated or disdained. Yet, they reflect how far the powers of the human mind and body can be stretched and still not be recognized for excellence. Included among them are many prodigious feats, some having practical meaning, others being appreciated for the amusement they provide, and still others that strike fear and awe in people. Speed reading, mastery of mountains of trivia, gourmet cooking, trapeze artistry, performance of complex mathematical calculations faster than a com-puter, and even the numbers of sexual seductions boasted by a Doan Juan are just a few examples of such talents. In this category there are also 'extinct' abilities such as oratory and various types of manual craftsman-ship that belonged among the scarcity, surplus, or quota talents in another era, but can now be considered anomalous because they have become anachronisms. The condemned talents include the demagoguery and craftiness of a Hitler or a Stalin, which may require as much ingenuity as do extraordinary leadership skills for constructive purposes, except that they are threats rather than boons to humanity.

Schools have habitually emphasized the develop-ment of harmless anomalous talents, especially those that attract crowds and build morale, such as sports, glee clubs, and marching bands. The popularity of such activities among students and alumni, especially in the United States, is communicated to faculties who respond by mounting elaborate talent hunts and devoting considerable effort to sharpening these tal-ents.

Thus we see that scarcity, surplus, quota, and anomalous types of giftedness have always been valued differently by patrons of excellence. The four cate-gories may encompass all forms of giftedness, but the differential categorization helps describe, if not fully explain, their differential acceptance.

Historical Constraints

In his psychoeconomic approach to the study of creativity, Rubenson (1992) weighs the intrinsic and extrinsic costs as well as benefits of innovation in different historical periods. The intrinsic costs refer to the pressures on creative minds who, by virtue of their inventions and discoveries, render obsolete at least some cherished wisdom that had also been innovative at one time and had also upset established dogma before gaining acceptance. Indeed, iconoclasm and revisionist thinking is likely to meet resistance which can exercise restraint on the impulse to create, or even demoralize it. But the countervailing, if not over-powering, drive is toward newness, which is seen as progress in some domains of excellence and venture-someness in others. Among the sciences, changes in theory often meet the stiffest objections from those who have mastered and adopted older concepts, but eventually the change is accepted as progressive. For example, Galileo's proposition that the sun is immovable in the center of the universe and that the earth has a diurnal motion of rotation has long been seen as a major breakthrough in astronomy. Yet, Galileo languished in what amounted to house arrest for the last eight years of his life because his theories were considered heretical.

It is awesome to contemplate how much richer and more abundant the West's cultural treasures would be if countless potential geniuses had not elected to suppress or abort their creative impulses because they feared ostracism or even reprisal if they would dare revolutionize style and substance in the world of ideas.

Unlike intrinsic costs, which relate to the creative person's courage (or lack of it) to render received wisdom obsolete, extrinsic costs focus on societal influences that stimulate (or inhibit) creative activity. Obviously, freedom of expression encourages daring, avant-garde thought and productivity. Coupled with liberty is the impact of opportunity and access to audiences, clients, and customers. Rubenson (1992) cites evidence to show a relationship between the number of journals in an academic domain and research output by discoverers in that discipline. He also refers to patent data to measure how changes in demand can affect the frequency of invention. It is not just demand that makes a difference; patronage and sponsorship do also. And the effect is not only on quantity, but also on fashion and content of creative products. Simonton (1990a, b), for example, lists many instances where ingredients of musical and literary products relate directly to variations in external demand. How else to explain the special Russian thematic material—and indeed the very existence—of Beethoven's Rasumovsky Quartets without reference to their being subsidized by the person to whom these works are dedicated, and to his native origin?

The combination of personal freedom and encouragement would seem to create historical imperatives for the production of excellence. That is, times and places which provided these conditions should have been rewarded with a flowering of genius, whereas under oppressive and restrictive conditions the landscape of creativity would be expected to remain barren. However, here is an instance where logic and reality are not always compatible. Somehow, the human spirit that is strong enough to overcome internal restraints is sometimes able to survive and even create under brutal political regimes.

True, a Werner Von Braun could develop his considerable talents even in a police state under Hitler because his own Nazi convictions may have given him access to opportunities for cultivating and dedicating desperately needed talents in rocketry to help the German war effort. The same may apply to the multi-talented Albert Speer, whose superior abilities together with his deep loyalty to Hitler enabled him to design an enormously productive slave labor operation, as well as

a vision of a Third Reich capable of maintaining its hegemony for a thousand years. But how to explain the genius of an Osip Mandelstam, who wrote great poetry while declaring his enmity toward Stalin, which eventually led to his death by order of that tyrant? How did he, and his wife Nedezhda too, manage to achieve immortality for their literary works while suffering so much oppression and humiliation in their native country? Perhaps Amabile (1983) and Hennessey and Amabile (1988) are on target when they reveal the enormous power of intrinsic motivation in creative work. Indeed, it may even be strong enough in some cases to overcome the pain of extreme adversity.

The emphasis has to be on 'some cases', to point up the fact that wide generalizations cannot be drawn from them in any view of history. More typical are the consequences of changes in political leadership in late fourteenth- and early fifteenth-century China. As Mokyr (1990) points out, before the fourteenth century, Chinese technology was clearly superior to that of the West in textile production, ship building, the measurement of time, movable type printing, the invention of the wheelbarrow, and the development of chemicals for explosives, pharmaceuticals, and insecticides In fact, it would take the West several centuries to catch up with some of these technological feats. Artistic technique and imagination were similarly encouraged to flourish as China was approaching the fourteenth century. Grousset (1959) attributes this outpouring of creative productivity to the climate of cultural freedom, and probably public appreciation as well.

But as the Ming Dynasty came into power in the late fourteenth century, support by the ruling elite shifted away from technological and artistic creation to more immediate economic needs. Instead of emphasizing innovation, the regime urged imitation of the past. It also blocked the development of letter alphabets, preferring instead to stay with the old ideograms, which fostered artistic activity through calligraphy but stifled literary excellence for many years. Thus it appears that a relaxation of political policing of cultural life, together with a powerful popular thirst for excellence, helps account for periodic outbursts of greatness in different localities. These conditions were surely prominent in the early sixteenth-century Florence of Leonardo Da Vinci and Michelangelo, the late sixteenth and early seventeenth-century London of Shakespeare, Milton, Bacon, Jonson and Donne, the nineteenth-century Vienna of Beethoven, Schubert, and Mahler, the late nineteenth- and early twentieth-century Paris of Cezanne, Matisse, Monet, and Picasso, and the nineteen-twenties' Weimar Republic of Wedekind, Reinhardt, Thomas Mann, and the Bauhaus.

In a grotesque expression of political and public frenzy to generate progress, especially in science, nations at war can be 'credited' with 'inspiring' breakthroughs meant for human destruction but turned into major blessings for people at peace. Examples abound in the wake of World War II, but two obvious ones come to mind immediately. The first, of course, is the Manhatten Project, which brought together some of the world's greatest scientific minds to create an atomic bomb, and that in turn ushered in forever the real and potential peaceful benefits of nuclear energy. The other is experimentation with jet propulsion of bombs over Britain by Germany's scientists at Peenemünde, which paved the way to today's jet travel and space exploration. And who can gainsay the countless benefits to modern medicine of treatment drugs, devices, and methods developed originally for use on the wounded in battle? On the other hand, wars have destroyed, crippled, exiled, demoralized, and misdirected so many creative spirits that the discoveries and innovations gained in wartime, dramatic as they may be, cannot possibly make up for the real and potential talent lost in the upheavals of conflict.

Disastrous living conditions around the world have also brought scientific breakthroughs in recent decades. Witness, for example, the so-called 'green revolution', with its outcropping of agricultural abundance, thanks to new methods of selecting, planting, and fertilizing crops to produce enough surplus edibles to feed famine stricken areas of the world. But unfortunately, the magnitude and effects of famine clearly overwhelm the benefits of a green revolution in making enough of a difference worldwide. There are now some three billion people who have no easy access to fresh water, and millions of them live in arid climates, mostly in the southern hemisphere where the once fertile land is already, or is becoming, desert-like in its failure to yield any crops to sustain human life. Aside from the unspeakable misery that exists in that part of the world, there is the added tragedy of a scarcity of talent, brought on by the need to alleviate suffering which saps all energies, physical and mental.

Until the late eighteenth-century, starvation also threatened the lives of many settlers in the North American continent, and artistic life had to be compromised accordingly. But the settlers had brought with them from Europe a social legacy which eventually evolved to what Laski (1948) calls "the quintessence of a secularized puritanism" (p. 42). Its origins are in the familiar Protestant ethic (Weber, 1948), but is applied singularly to the North American condition. It extols effort and the belief that success is its inevitable consequence. In a pioneering society, it is praiseworthy to take risks, show courage, innovate and adapt, and even engage in 'rugged individualism' to build and maintain a modern society. It takes so much ingenuity and hard work to get the job done that there is hardly much time to cultivate the arts. Indeed, artistic life is a luxury that few can afford when so many shoulders have to be put to the wheel.

Only later, when the pioneering days in America were over and political, social, and economic institutions were established, could increasing numbers of people allow themselves to turn to the life of the mind. Great political theory and science flourished earliest in the post-pioneer years because they were rooted in the necessities of the pioneer period; great drama and music began to appear much later, also as symbols of hard work and self-perfection in conformance with the Protestant ethic. However, in too many parts of the southern hemisphere, where survival is constantly under threat, and living conditions are indescribably brutal, any confidence people may have had in their ability to overcome adversity has been buried beneath layers upon layers of tragedy accumulated over generations. If they ever inherited a belief in achieving excellence through hard work, their histories of abject misery *despite* hard work could only have had a demoralizing effect on them. And yet, faith in oneself and in the perfectibility of the world are prerequisite to creative activity that is of great value. Sadly, there are too many people today, especially in the southern hemisphere, whose life circumstances deprive them of such basis and deny them access to membership in a global circle of immortals.

Ancient Origins of Interest in the Gifted

Western society has generally looked to Ancient Greek (i.e. Athenian) and Judaeo-Christian traditions for sources of its own cultural identity. In following this practice, a reviewer of history of/and the gifted must beware not to view these forebears as child-like in their mental powers compared to the mature moderns simply because the age of the human species is older now and therefore presumably wiser. True, today's storehouse of music, art, literature, and scientific knowledge is much greater than ever before, a fact that makes contemporary Western society culturally richer than that of Ancient Athens, Judea, or Babylon. But for sheer intellectual power, and the ability to achieve immortality in creative production, the ancients could easily match the moderns in domains of excellence that were characteristic of their societies.

The Legacy of Athens

In the case of Athenian culture, the talent domains were fairly much the same as those which would eventually be valued in the West. They include intellectual ability, often expressed in philosophic speculation, moral excellence, political insight, literary, musical, oratorical, and artistic talents, as well as physical strength for beauty's sake. Hellenism also spread its influence to Ancient Rome and, indeed, to much of the Middle East long before it took hold in Western countries.

There was no state-sponsored education at any level in Athens, even though Plato advocated its establishment. Instead, private citizens opened schools for boys, ages 6 to 14, or to later ages for those who could afford it. (Girls studied at home where their mothers or nurses taught them how to weave, spin, embroider, sing, dance, and play an instrument.) The boys' course of study was divided into three parts: writing (including arithmetic and reading), music, and gymnastics. In Aristotle's time, drawing and painting were added. Everyone learned to play the lyre, and much of the instruction emphasized creating music and poetry. Although no time was spent on acquiring foreign languages, great care was taken in learning the correct usage of the mother tongue. Gymnastics were major features of the curriculum, especially wrestling, swimming, and the use of bow and sling. By age 16, the boys were well trained to run, leap, wrestle, hunt, drive chariots, and hurl the javelin, skills needed for military service. When they became soldier youths at age 18 they learned and practiced the skills of democratic governance and engaged in intensive studies of literature, music, geometry, and rhetoric before being sent off as 19-year-olds for a two-year assignment to a frontier garrison to protect the city.

For advanced study, Aristotle, who was recognized in his time as a philosopher, scientist, and statesman, established the Lyceum, a major learning center rivaling the Academy and the School of Isocrates. All three became severe competitors until they began to emphasize different courses of study. The School of Isocrates concentrated on rhetoric, the Lyceum on natural science, and the Academy on mathematics, metaphysics, and politics. At the Lyceum, Aristotle assigned his students to gather and coordinate knowledge in many fields: the customs of barbarians, the constitutions of the Greek cities, the chronology of victories in the Pithian Games and in the Athenian Dionysia, the organs and habits of animals, the character and distribution of plants, and the history of science and philosophy.

Athenian citizens, mainly the well-to-do aristocrats, could thus provide their sons with an education that came reasonably close to Plato's version of special enriched schooling for so-called Guardians, or men of silver, whose performance in advanced studies would determine who qualifies as a man of gold, or philosopher king. Plato believed that citizens in his republic should be trained to maximize their potentialities. He insisted that young men who possessed unusual mental ability, based on evidence derived from various tests, be separated from those of average intelligence and given a specialized type of education. The program would require mastery of science, philosophy, and metaphysics. Those who excelled in the program would form a pool out of which future leaders of the state could be drawn. Plato was convinced that Athenian democracy could sustain its greatness only as long as it provided the best educational opportunities for selected young people who would then become its future leaders.

The Classical idea of a ruling elite based on wealth and merit is anathema to modern Western democracies and has been effectively satirized by Young (1959) as a portent of social upheaval and possible disaster.

However, Athenian tradition highlights the need to nurture human excellence for its own sake and for the betterment of life in society, an ideal which should be made attainable without sacrifice of egalitarian principles. Classical society also calls attention to domains of excellence which came alive during the Renaissance period in Europe and which are so very much alive today in the entire Western world.

Judaic Influences

The Jewish people have often been called 'children of the book', with a tradition of studying, creating, interpreting, teaching, and disseminating ideas wherever they have lived in Western countries. This intense devotion to learning, which has spread its influence to the larger Western community, can be found in several biblical sources, of which the medieval Jewish philosopher, Maimonides, in Chapter 2 of *Laws of the Study of Torah (Mishna Torah)* singles out one: 'The *Torah* which Moses commanded us is a legacy for the congregation of Jacob (i.e. the Jewish people!' (Deuteronomy, 33:4). *Torah* encompasses a vast literature, including the Old Testament, Mishna and Talmud (i.e. codifications of centuries of Rabbinic exegeses of scriptural law, lore, and philosophy), along with the wisdom and scholarship of *Gaonim, Rishonim,* and *Acharonim,* leading exegetists of post-Talmudic times to the present day.

Maimonides' extolling the centrality of *Torah* learning in traditional Jewish life deserved some explication because it reflects the pronouncements of generations of scholars before him, and his influence has remained powerful, even in large segments of today's Jewish world. Here are just a few examples of his thoughts on Torah studies:

(1) There is no biblical positive commandment that outweighs the study of Torah.
(2) Torah should be studied for its own sake (i.e. self-betterment and enlightenment), not for the sake of material reward.
(3) Even if economic circumstances reduce persons to sustain themselves on bread and salt and on severely limited measures of water, and they are forced to sleep on the ground, they may not renounce immersion in Torah.

Religious Jews throughout their history have devotedly adhered to the sentiments expressed by Maimonides. To achieve the status of a *Talmid Chachum* (literally a student-scholar)—everybody a student, *including* the scholar—was an incomparable accomplishment in early Jewish history and remains so to this day. Not even material wealth could gain so much public veneration for its possessor. Indeed, the rich have often sought the brightest, most scholarly young bachelors for possible marriage to their daughters, and the promise of a substantial dowry could enable the groom to spend a lifetime in *Torah* study free from want, even while building a family. There is never any thought of using the money to enter the business or professional world, or even to support a luxurious lifestyle. Young women had no such educational opportunities until the early twentieth-century when seminaries were opened for them in various Western countries and have multiplied ever since, rapidly in recent years.

Usually, the male's advanced academic work is conducted at a *Yeshiva* (Torah Academy) where partners or small groups of three or four adolescents or adults study together for up to ten hours a day and attend regular lectures by leading student-scholars. Since there is no end to the breadth or depth of study, there is no completion of coursework and therefore no diplomas or any other material awards granted, or even sought, except for the few—not necessarily the brightest—who are ordained as Rabbis after some years of prescribed study, and they serve in pulpits, or in Jewish education, or in community leadership positions. This kind of intensive learning that begins soon after the cradle and extends to the grave has permeated large pockets of *Torah*-loyal Jewish life in every Western country where Jews have settled, since the destruction of the Temple in Jerusalem in AD 70.

When the male child enters the *Cheder* (i.e. a Jewish school containing one or more classrooms), with much joy and celebration, often as early as age 3, he quickly develops literacy in the Hebrew language and then spends most of the time, until the pre-adolescent years, mastering the scriptures and the accompanying commentaries. Thereafter, for the rest of his student years at Yeshiva, including the many informal learning periods outside of school hours and beyond the school years, most of the concentration, by far, is on the Talmud and its vast collection of related literature. His deep penetration into Judaic jurisprudence and codes of behavior requires a most sophisticated level of logical insight simply to understand the text, let alone to draw brilliant inferences from it. The highest honor bestowed by learned peers and even by the uneducated public is upon the rare student who can gain intimate familiarity with Talmudic thought in all its depth and breadth and can also create original interpretations that illuminate it as perhaps never before. This gifted individual thus qualifies as a student-scholar, the person for whom the Yeshiva is primarily meant to exist. In short, it is an educational system that fosters a kind of intellectual elitism in which the Talmudist *par excellence* reigns supreme.

Since Jews lived for many centuries as second class citizens in Western society, their Gentile neighbors were rarely inspired by the Jewish love for learning. In fact, some of the richest, most intensive scholarly activity took place in ghetto-like settings, small town (*Shtetl*) communities where religious oppression and separatism was greatest, and there was little desire or even opportunity for Gentile to emulate the often-hated Jew. It was not until the emancipation proclamations all across Europe and in the United States, mostly in the late eighteenth and early nineteenth centuries, that ghetto life began to crumble as Jews were given freedom to prosper in financial centers and to participate in Western cultural life. From that time on, a huge majority of 'children of *the* book' (i.e. *Torah*) became children of *all* books. The devotion with which Talmudic study was pursued shifted, for a vast majority of Jews, to secular learning, with far-reaching consequences for the Jewish *Shtetl* and for Western society in general.

The *Shtetl* lamented the hemorrhaging of religious commitment and Torah learning among its youth, while Western society gained a talent pool that enriched cultural life immeasurably and permanently in virtually every domain of advanced-level activity. Unreconstructed anti-semites have derided highly motivated, high achieving Jewish students as grindingly over-ambitious as they scramble and compete to get ahead. So conspicuous have these students been in their self-sacrifice for mastery, that the American novelist, Thomas Wolfe, whose university classes contained large Jewish enrollments, once described them as 'burning in the night' with a seemingly endless fire of enthusiasm for matters cerebral and secular.

For sheer volume of great Western achievements in the arts and sciences over the past two centuries, Jews have contributed far out of proportion to their numbers within the general population. Such immortals as Freud, Einstein, Kafka and von Neumann, among others, even succeeded in revolutionizing whole domains of productive activity far beyond their lifetimes, possibly for all time. Others, though lesser lights, have enriched cultural life in the West not only as creative contributors but also as patrons, mentors, and role models by enabling others to achieve renown while remaining virtually unknown themselves. The magnitude of Jewish constrictive involvement in Western arts and sciences can only be a matter of conjecture, the few hints coming out of facts concerning pre- and post-Holocaust Europe. Engelmann's (1984) powerful treatise on Germany without Jews reports on their critical role in German medicine, politics, higher education, artistic, literary, theatrical, and musical life, and even in that country's record in winning Nobel prizes. The precipitous drop in quality and abundance of German talent since the liquidation of almost all Jewry in that country illustrates how a life of the mind among ancient Jews, passed on from generation to generation, plays a vital role in the recent history of giftedness in Western society.

Christian Influences

To the extent that Christianity is rooted in Judaic sources, it has also extolled studiousness and achievement, concentrating in its early history on the scriptures, including the New Testament. When it was at its peak of power during the Middle Ages, it created an everlasting learning tradition without causing Europe to be "blissfully ignorant of the 'spell of the classics' and interested only in theological speculation" (Lamonte, 1949, p. 553). Great ideas in science, law, literature, philosophy, and art were, in fact, studied and propounded vigorously at that time. Yet, to the modern Westerner, Medieval Europe appears as a tradition-oriented society in which high-level talent was devoted primarily to the preservation, understanding, and enhancement of Church ideals.

Among the most significant developments in creative thinking by the end of the fifteenth-century, besides ideological treatises, were those associated with early technology and the renaissance. Advances in the chemistry of ink, skills in paper making, and metallurgy enabled Gutenberg to invent movable type sometime around the mid-fifteenth-century, and this new device almost immediately facilitated the wide dissemination of ideas, some of them highly critical of the Church. Among the most powerful polemics were Martin Luther's ninety-five theses which he nailed on the door of the Castle Church at Wittenberg, Germany, in 1517, a document that received wide circulation with the help of movable type. The theses bitterly attacked the Pope's practice of selling indulgences, whereby sinners were promised forgiveness if they sent substantial sums of money to the papal treasury. Luther was branded a heretic, but the authority of the Vatican was shaken, not only in his native Germany, but also in France and Switzerland, where John Calvin led the struggle for Church liberalization soon afterwards. These three countries were already leaning toward reformation, so they provided fertile ground for the sowing of new ideas by Luther and Calvin.

With the advent of the Protestant Reformation came the movement toward widespread growth of literacy. Protestants suggested that the masses can serve their religion directly without relying heavily on Church intermediaries. But in order to do so, everybody had to be able to read and understand the scriptures. True, it requires hard work, but the rewards are substantial, since human beings are considered perfectible through their own efforts, according to Protestant tradition.

The growth of the Protestant spirit and ethic over the past five centuries, and the conversion of the Western world from an agrarian to a highly commercial and industrial society have exerted deep influences upon present-day concerns about the development of talent. In the Protestant urban centers the individual quickly learned that the highest rewards in life could be attained through self-enlightenment and self-betterment in some culturally approved area of activity. This orientation to life's opportunities brought with it the seeds of universal education, scientific and technological development, and intense intellectual restlessness that conforms with the Faustian nature of Western society.

Reinforcing the spirit of reformation and humanism was the contemporaneous renaissance movement, which vitalized creative behavior through new freedom of style and substance. Although the Church and its sages retained their prominence in the art of Titian, Tintoretto, Michelangelo, and El Greco, among many others, these masterpieces reflected an inspiration to idealize the human form and to place the human being at center stage as divinely conceived and precious beyond measure. The powers of reason and the senses gained new respect as they brought back to life the Greek and Roman Classics. The scope of the new enthusiasm for learning widened rapidly, incorporating in it a need to advance the sciences for a better understanding of the laws of nature, of the structure of the planet, and the place of the planet in the wider universe. It was a break from the past in which intellectually gifted behavior was dominated by logicians trained in scholastic disputation and in speculating mostly about the human soul that was often shrouded in mysticism. The Renaissance replaced mysticism with humanism and its belief in the goodness and dignity of the human species, as well as its great powers of thought and imagination, as evidenced by the wealth of ideas inherited from the ancient Greeks and Romans.

The Modern Scene

The Reformation and the Renaissance eventually led to the industrial revolution which further reinforced belief in human potential for fashioning a new world with better-than-ever standards of living and qualities of life. Understandably, the public bestowed renown—sometimes fortune, too—upon those who excelled as conquerors of nature through science, producers of masterpieces, and masterful performance on the stage and in various professions. The names associated with these great achievements took on an importance of their own, sometimes exaggeratedly so, when the so-called 'Matthew Effect' drew critical accolades for inferior work simply because the high reputation of its creator had been earned through earlier success. Fame, or at least recognition among peers, became a powerful spur to self-fulfillment and self-advancement and remains to this day a prime incentive for potentially gifted people to fulfill their promise.

As popular belief in the powers of the individual and in opportunities for individualism grew over the past two centuries in Western countries, so did democracy as a preferred social system and form of government. Egalitarianism and excellence emerged as ideals to be preserved, even though they have always been counter-poised and resistant to reconciliation. Among the democracies there are constant changes and variations in emphases on people's rights to social, political, economic, and educational entitlements, especially those individuals who are poor in status and in finances. A democracy that leans far in the direction of egalitarianism seems to weaken its commitment to excellence and is therefore in danger of losing honor in the family of nations—a threat from without. On the other hand, a strong commitment to excellence can compromise equality of status and opportunity within a democracy and arouse serious civil unrest—a threat from within.

Examples of both kinds of threat seem to surface from time to time in modern Western history. Conscious efforts to foster excellence could be seen under the benevolent monarchy of late nineteenth-century Austria, which was determined to maintain its status as one of Europe's premier cultural centers. At that time, secondary education was of a kind that some of today's educators would consider elitist. The famous literary figure, Stefan Zweig, was then a student at a Viennese *Gymnasium*, along with others from bourgeois families, who could afford the tuition and who were bright enough to qualify for pre-university studies. In his autobiography (1943), Zweig described his *Gymnasium* as an eight-year program, following five years of elementary school, and requiring French, English, and Italian (the 'living' languages) along with Greek and Latin ('dead' languages) plus geometry and physics, among other subjects. In more egalitarian democracies, the Viennese program would perhaps qualify as differentiated education for the gifted, since the mainstream curriculum is geared to accommodate students who are closer to average in ability, many of whom have no plans to enter college.

In a fairly unusual situation where commitment to excellence is a national priority, one may consider the relatively short history of education for the gifted in Singapore. A city-state established in 1965 as an independent, Western-oriented democracy, it has adopted English as its official language and geared its educational system as a means of finding a place in the economic and cultural atmosphere of the much larger, more established Western nations. Law and order are strictly enforced, efficiency and proficiency are emphasized, and there are relatively few special educational provisions for handicapped learners. However, the academically gifted are placed in special programs which provide advanced-level studies in English language and literature, the maths and sciences, foreign languages, history, geography, social studies, moral education, and computer appreciation. Australia's commitment to the gifted, on the other hand, varies according to the social ideologies of its states. In Victoria, where there is a relatively strong emphasis on egalitarianism, political office holders tend to resist singling out the gifted for special enrichment experiences. They would rather 'cut down tall poppies' to equalize educational opportunity than adjust curricula to accommodate individual differences at the upper ability levels. As a result, proponents of special enrichment for the gifted have had to struggle hard, with only occasional success, in influencing public

policy. Not so in New South Wales, where egalitarianism seems to be a less sensitive issue and where there is more eagerness to single out the gifted for special studies.

It should be emphasized that modern Western democracies have always paid attention to the needs of the gifted, albeit with various degrees of intensity. From 1917 until Hitler came to power, Germany made some efforts on behalf of precocious children. Special schools and classes with enriched curricula were formed on the basis of psychological tests. France, Great Britain, Belgium, and Switzerland also have a modern tradition of identifying and training gifted children, or at least providing support for their continued advancement up the educational ladder. However, none of the democracies invested as heavily as did the dictatorships, which considered the gifted as vital human resources for furthering the power of the state. In its early period, the Soviet Union's overall curriculum emphasized heavy indoctrination in communism, but only incidental coverage of the physical sciences, mathematics, and languages. In later years, government leaders recognized that physics, chemistry, and mathematics are essential to national aspirations, culturally and militarily. Schools intensified requirements to the point where relatively few could manage to graduate from high school since requirements included five years of physics, biology, and foreign language, four years of chemistry, one year of astronomy, and as many as ten years of mathematics (*Soviet Commitment to Education*, 1959).

The United States has lived with the conflict between egalitarianism and excellence throughout its history, but it took on new meaning in 1918, when the Commission on Reorganization of Secondary Education issued its *Cardinal Principles of Secondary Education* (1918) which took careful note of human differences and characterized the function of the high school program as open to all young people but differentiated according to their abilities and aspirations. For some students, high school education remained preparatory to college studies, but for others it served as terminal schooling. Inasmuch as democracy is sweeping through the Western world and beyond, the American post-war history of balancing egalitarianism and excellence, and its effect on the gifted, is instructive to more and more societies in present times.

The American Experience: Pre-Sputnik

Since World War II, the greatest swings between devotion to excellence and to egalitarianism have occurred between the late nineteen-fifties and the early nineteen-seventies. Because of these changes, the five years following the launching of *Sputnik* in 1957 and the last half-decade of the 1970s may be viewed as twin peak periods of interest in gifted children. Separating the peaks was a deep valley of neglect in which the public fixed its attention more eagerly on the low functioning, poorly motivated, and socially handicapped at school. In the late 1960s, there was a revival of earlier sensitivities to the needs of the gifted. These fluctuations in national temperament seem to indicate that the country had not succeeded in paying equal attention *simultaneously* to its most and its least successful achievers at school.

Unlocking the secrets of the atom during World War II to produce the bomb represented a scientific as well as a military breakthrough that increased the dependency of armed power on the innovativeness of the scientist. Since the bomb was produced on American soil, its citizens had grown confident that America's leadership in science and technology was unchallengeable. The nation expected itself always to be the first in creating new gadgetry to make life and death easier, be it through sophisticated home appliances, computer systems, communications equipment, or explosives with the power of megatons of TNT. It is easy to imagine, therefore, the shock when this illusion was shattered with the orbiting of *Sputnik* by none other than America's arch enemy in the midst of a Cold War that any moment could turn hotter than any conflict in history. *Sputnik* was not just a demoralizing technological feat; it had potential military applications, too. Suddenly, the prestige and survival of a nation were jeopardized because some of the enemy's greatest minds of the day had taken the lead in achievement, and the Soviets capitalized on this coup by broadcasting to every nation on earth its success in reducing America to a second-class power at long last.

As might be expected, the targets of criticism for the national humiliation were elementary and secondary schools. But it was by no means the first time that American education had been put on the defensive in those years. Four years before *Sputnik*, a sensational indictment of public education had been published (Bestor, 1953), which accused the schools of practicing what the author considered their special brand of fraudulence on America's children. The main charge was that schools were not governed by learned educators but rather by know-nothing 'educationists', a term the author used in referrring to teachers, administrators, and those responsible for training them on college campuses. To his way of thinking, it was tragically ironic that 'educationists' should exert nearly total influence on the content of curricula while caring so little about the world of ideas. How could anyone presume to dictate what should be taught at school if he/she is not immersed personally in any scholarly discipline or artistic pursuit? Because of what he regarded as a misplacement of power in the hands of 'educationists', Bestor was convinced that schools provided meager intellectual nourishment or inspiration, especially for the gifted, who often marked time in their studies until graduation released them from boredom.

An even more prominent critic was Admiral Hyman Rickover, famous as the 'father' of the atomic submarine and long an advocate of programs that would identify and educate an intellectual elite for leadership in the United States. Rickover saw a deadly link between scientific advancement and military strength and warned that the Soviets were moving ahead menacingly on both fronts. Ennobling excellence was no longer just a means of improving the quality of life in a free society; it had also become a key to the survival of the free world.

Beyond the military advantages of producing knowledge and technology, there was also the matter of national prestige that Rickover saw clearly. He warned that the Soviets were in a do-or-die race with the democratic West to produce excellence in every arena that the world respected. Even the number of gold medals it accumulated at the quadrennial Olympics was counted as a badge of honour. Rickover warned that, in order to compete on an equal footing, America had to overcome its traditional guilt about singling out the gifted for special opportunities at school. Even after *Sputnik* was launched, he observed that "anti-intellectualism has long been our besetting sin. With us, hostility to superior intelligence masquerades as belief in the equality of man and puts forth the false claim that it is undemocratic to recognize and nurture superior intelligence" (Rickover, 1960, p. 30). In other words, America could not afford to indulge in a complacent sense of egalitarianism which granted compensatory education for those who needed it while denying enriched education for others who deserved it.

Since Rickover was not an educationist, his 'outsider' status prevented him from influencing school policy. However, the pre-*Sputnik* evidence that America was neglecting its gifted could hardly be ignored much longer. In a lengthy report prepared by the director of the Commission on Human Resources and Advanced Training (Wolfle, 1954), it was asserted that the United States failed to prepare enough men and women in the natural sciences, health fields, teaching, and engineering. Only six of the ten in the top five percent and only half of the top twenty-five percent of high school graduates went on to earn college diplomas. At the more advanced levels, a mere three percent of those capable of earning doctorates actually did so.

What made matters worse were expectations that the shortages would soon become even more acute in the late nineteen-fifties unless the schools succeeded in encouraging gifted students to continue on to advanced studies. These concerns were later echoed by the chairman of the U.S. Atomic Energy Commission when he warned the nation that its public schools were not maintaining educational standards, especially for gifted students, thereby causing dangerous shortages of scientists and engineers and other technically trained individuals (*New York Times*, November 27, 1995). An earlier *New York Times* report (May 1, 1955) estimated that, in 1954, American industry needed thirty thousand engineers but that colleges and universities had graduated only eighteen thousand. A mere two hundred physicists earned diplomas that year, and half chose not to enter the field of physics. Serious shortages existed also in industry, medicine, nursing, pharmacology, clinical psychology, and social work, among other important fields. The alarm spread to the National Education Association's Ninety-third Annual Convention in 1955. A committee report pointed out that each year two hundred thousand outstanding high school graduates did not enroll in a college before graduation. The report went on to warn that an annual loss of 400,000 highly trained men and women could force the United States to lose its superiority to the Soviet Union in the realm of technology.

And yet, pre-*Sputnik* America of the 1950s was not entirely unmindful of the nature and nurture of its gifted. In addition to conducting basic research that generated new hypotheses about intellectual functioning and preserving long-standing special school programs in a few scattered cities, behavioral scientists and educators were already demonstrating how university resources could reach out to schools and to school systems in order to further the cause of special education for the ablest. Pioneering such efforts on a nationwide scale was the Talented Youth Project under the direction of A. Harry Passow, at Teachers College, Columbia University. Initiated in 1954, three years before *Sputnik*, the project assisted school administrators and their staffs in different parts of the country to develop, implement, and evaluate their own programs for the gifted. This outreach service was in the tradition of the 1930s activities of Leta Hollingworth and her staff, also of Teachers College, who experimented with curriculum enrichment and conducted research on behalf of gifted children, albeit only in New York City's public schools rather than nationwide.

The Talented Youth Project existed for twelve years, during which time it provided technical assistance to many practitioners at their own sites and at various professional conferences concerned with the needs of the gifted. The Project staff also conducted some large-scale studies on ability grouping (Goldberg et al., 1966), underachievement (Raph et al., 1966), the comparative effectiveness of several special programs for the mathematically gifted (Goldberg et al., 1966), and the attitudes of high school students toward academic brilliance (Tannenbaum, 1962). At the outset of its service and research activities, Passow and his associates wrote a problems-and-issues monograph (Passow et al., 1955) that turned out to be not only time*ly* for its day but surprisingly time*less*, or at least as applicable nearly forty years after its publication as it was then.

The American Experience: Post-Sputnik

When the American educational community finally took action on behalf of the gifted, it did so with alacrity. Enormous public and private funds became available to assist in the pursuit of excellence, primarily in the fields of science and technology. Academic course work was telescoped and stiffened to test the brainpower of the gifted. Courses that had been offered only at the college level began to find their way into special enrichment programs in high school and eventually in elementary school.

Rickover's alarms concerning Soviet advancement in technology were finally taken seriously, especially since they were expressed by a man whose own career symbolized the marriage between science and the military. His criticisms of public schools were basically motivated by concerns about national security. This coupling of education and defense became public policy through a significantly titled piece of legislation, the National Defense Education Act of 1958, which revealed a new and far more critical role for the schools than they had ever played before. While remaining obliged to produce an enlightened people capable of living together happily, responsibly, and productively in a democratic system of government, schools are also in the business of protecting its citizens from being buried ideologically, and perhaps militarily too, by a fearsome foreign power. The Act provided funds to strengthen six components of American education, one of which was the identification of gifted children. In addition, it set aside money to help schools mount programs in science, mathematics, and foreign languages, which showed where the emphasis in high-level education was to be placed.

Another influential figure in promoting excellence in American schools was James B. Conant, a renowned chemist and public servant and a president of Harvard University. In his report, titled *The American High School Today* (1959), he addressed the concerns of the post-*Sputnik* 1950s by offering a broad twenty-one step plan for changing secondary education with special emphasis on core subjects that were challenging in content and required of all students regardless of their career plans. His proposal also took special note of the academically gifted (defined as the upper fifteen percent) and the highly gifted (defined as the upper three percent), and schools took serious note of his recommendations. Perhaps the combination of the report's timeliness and Conant's personal credibility in the public schools enabled his message to get through and retain its influence for a long time, while the earlier critics' ideas, which were fairly similar to his, were taken less seriously.

In addition to the outpouring of special enrichment activities initiated in the schools during the late nineteen-fifties and early nineteen-sixties, there was a good deal of research activity dealing with the characteristics and education of gifted children. Lewis M. Terman's studies of high-IQ children, which began in the early nineteen-twenties, had produced several landmark results that cleared the way for efforts on behalf of the gifted. One important outcome of his research was that precocious children are not mutants who possess some kinds of freakish powers bestowed upon them by biological accident. Instead, they differ from lesser abled peers in degree rather than in kind. Those who find themselves in the upper extreme of the ability continuum merely have more powerful versions of the same attributes possessed by those who are closer to average in ability.

A second enduring outcome of Terman's work was his finding that potential giftedness reveals itself even in childhood. 'Early ripe, early rot' is a once-popular platitude that he helped turn into a canard by his studies of high-IQ children growing up. Despite the many cases of aborted genius, his data provided some assurance that children with high potentialities and reasonably stable personalities stood a better-than-average chance to excel eventually in their careers, provided they were given the right opportunities at home and at school. Because of his finding that greatness does not materialize suddenly and unaccountably in adulthood, but instead has its roots in the early years of growth, professional education was convinced of its key position in helping bright children fulfill their promise. In other words, Terman confirmed the need for special educational programs for the gifted, an idea that would be irrelevant if there were no developmental connection between early promise and later fulfilment.

In claiming to reach beyond the IQ, Guilford's Presidential address at the American Psychological Association in 1950 introduced creativity as an unsung dimension of precocious development. The need to measure creativity encouraged psychometrists to abandon the assumption that tests of general intelligence, such as those developed in the early part of the century by Terman and his associates, could be used to locate the entire pool of children out of which virtually all the gifted would probably emerge. This led to a highly influential paper by Getzels and Jackson (1958) which reported a comparison of 'high-creative, low-IQ' and 'high-IQ, low-creative' students at the University of Chicago Campus High School. This study had a stunning influence on educational researchers because it announced a breakthrough in the use of so-called 'creativity' measures to identify a talent resource that was allegedly overlooked by IQ tests.

Other investigations in vogue in the immediate post-*Sputnik* period focused on the relative effectiveness of different administrative designs, such as ability grouping; enrichment in regular classes, and acceleration; the social status of the gifted at school and its effect on

their motivation to learn; the causes and treatment of scholastic underachievement among children with high potential; achievement motivation and other non-intellective factors in high-level learning; and the psychosocial correlates of divergent thinking processes. Professional journals in America were deluged with research reports and with exhortations to do something special for the gifted. So rapid was the build-up of literature in the field that one writer (French, 1959) claimed there were more articles published in the three-year period from 1956 to 1959 than in the previous thirty years.

Perhaps the most vivid recollection of the post-*Sputnik* years is that of the Great Talent Hunt. It was a time when every possible effort was exerted at federal, state, and local levels to identify gifted children and to educate them to the limits of their potential. So intense was the search for young brains, their nurture, and utilization that a parallel can be drawn between the way in which America dealt with high-level *human* resources in the 1950s and its approach to precious *natural* resources during the energy shortages of the late nineteen-seventies. Just as the nation grasped at new energy sources out of fear that it could not continue to function without them, so did the post-*Sputnik* leadership cast about frantically for signs of giftedness in the schools. And just as natural resources were dealt with in an objective, efficient manner, so did the talent hunt show signs of detachment and impersonality, as if gifted people's usefulness to society mattered more than their individualities and sensibilities as human beings.

High scholastic standards and standing, academic advancement, studiousness, and career mindedness were conspicuous themes in America's schools when the bandwagon for the gifted was rolling in reaction to the Soviet *Sputnik* threat. It became virtually unthinkable for a gifted child to bypass the more difficult courses in favor of the less demanding ones. It certainly was no time for young people to be free spirited or to enjoy the privilege of doing nothing. Instead they were brought up in a period of total talent mobilization, requiring the most able-minded to fulfill their potentials and to submit their developed abilities for service to the nation.

The American Experience: The 1960s Decade of Turmoil

The 1960s opened with John F. Kennedy's election to the Presidency amid promises and dreams of a modern utopia. There was excitement in the air as the nation prepared itself to sweep away the stodginess of the 1950s and to create a new age of excellence. Kennedy was particularly attractive to young people who saw in him (and his family) a refreshing blend of youthfulness, vitality, intelligence, idealism, and beauty. His earliest messages as President of the United States made it clear that brains and loyalty to the flag were among the nation's most precious assets. He announced boldly his intention to put a man on the moon by 1970, a clear sign that he was accepting the Soviet challenge for supremacy in space exploration and that the most brilliant scientists would be called upon to make such a feat feasible. This meant encouraging the largest possible number of able students to enroll in science programs that offered them the best possible specialized education. For who else but the gifted could yield forth from their ranks a team of scientists qualified to honour the President's commitment?

There were other hints of meritocracy in the air. Kennedy gathered around him some of the most precocious men (though few women) of his generation to advise him on governmental matters. Known then as the 'Whiz Kids', some had earned their reputations as scholars at leading universities and others as promising ideas men in industry. All of them projected an image of braininess with a zest for unravelling the Chief Executive's knottiest problems. They were gifted children grown up and enjoying the glamor of fame and power rather than living in relative obscurity as so many other gifted people have to do even in their most productive years. At last, able children had their own celebrity role models to emulate, much as budding athletes and entertainers have theirs. The nation's leaders were demonstrating by their own example that it pays to be smart at school if you want to get ahead in life. It certainly made good economic sense because the best paying jobs were going to the best educated.

It would, of course, be naïve to suggest that America had reached a time in history when brilliant students were taking their place alongside the sports stars as heroes on campus. Far from it. Research by Coleman (1962) and Tannenbaum (1962) demonstrated that acclaim among peers was achieved far more easily on the athletic field than on the honor roll. Still, the Kennedy years were making good on promises of social and economic rewards for those willing to cultivate their superior scholastic abilities despite the lack of enthusiastic cheering from schoolmates.

The bids were high for brains in the early 1960s, but there was a string attached. President Kennedy expressed it best in his immortal admonition to his countrymen: 'Ask not what your country can do for you—ask what you can do for your country'. It was a call for unselfish accomplishment, to dedicate the work of America's citizens to the greater glory of the nation. Those with higher abilities had more to contribute and were therefore under pressure not to bury their talents or even to indulge in creative productivity that was impractical. The feeling during the Cold War was that the scientist could better serve the nation than could the poet. Judging from the career plans of gifted children in the late nineteen-fifties and early nineteen-sixties, they evidently believed that the nation was worth serving. By far the largest number of students with high tested intelligence majored in the sciences, and many of them aspired to enter fields of technology that could somehow help the defense effort. Employment opportunities in these industries and professions were reinforced by the glamorization of science as humanity's most exciting modern frontier.

Yet the flurry of activity on behalf of the gifted left some unfinished business to haunt America ever since. Even the threat of *Sputnik* and the indulgence of excellence during the Kennedy era were not enough to guarantee that the needs of the gifted would be cared for perpetually at school. Instead, enrichment was considered a curricular ornament to be detached and discarded when the cost of upkeep became prohibitive. This is as true in the 1990s as it was in the 1960s, as evidenced by reports of cutting back on programs for the gifted as a result of budgetary crises and tax revolts in many school districts, where only programs for the handicapped learners are mandated by law to receive their usual share of special support (*New York Times*, November 29, 1992). Moreover, the fervor with which guidance counselors ushered gifted youths into sciences programs backfired to some degree as large numbers of these students changed their academic majors by the time they reached their sophomore years in college (Watley, 1968) and many who did stay on to pursue careers mapped out for them became victims of the shaky fortunes of the aerospace industry.

When the *Sputnik* scare began to wane, some special progams and curricula were retained, partly through the efforts of the newly formed advocacy groups on behalf of the gifted. But for the most part, the vast majority of educational innovations triggered by *Sputnik* and sustained in the Kennedy era proved trendy rather than long-lived despite their early promise. Perhaps the decline of interest in the gifted would have been inevitable, considering how conflicted the American public often feels about such children. Intimations of meritocracy can never fit easily into a democratic frame of reference. There will always be egalitarian-minded people who consider it necessary to withhold special opportunities that might aid the ablest to get far ahead of the pack. These critics often argue that bright children are advantaged and can fend for themselves, so why invest in them? This sentiment has circulated widely for a long time and is compatible with the popular notion of idealizing the norm, encouraging the deficient to reach as close to it as possible, and either ignoring or frowning on the efforts of the highly proficient to move far beyond it.

Nevertheless, it would be a mistake to assume that America merely grew tired of the gifted in the mid-1960s because its interest in them had been less than wholehearted all along. While attention might have declined, the fact is that there were pressures forcing the nation's preoccupation away from the gifted toward realities that seemed to be far more relevant to the events of those days. Among the most prominent were the Civil Rights Movement, school integration and compensatory education; Vietnam and the disenchantment of youth; and growing distrust of scientific discovery.

Focus on Underprivileged Minorities

The 1954 Supreme Court decision to desegregate public schools set off an inexorable movement toward updating the Constitution and the Bill of Rights. Once again education became the linchpin of a national priority, this time for social justice, as it had formerly been for the Great Talent Hunt. Separatism and equality were declared an impossible combination and therefore unconstitutional. In 1955, Martin Luther King Jr began his leadership in the struggle for racial integration in all community institutions, including employment, housing and transportation, as well as the schools, when he led his historic boycott of buses in Montgomery, Alabama, to protest at the treatment of black passengers, an event that led to similar action throughout the country. His efforts placed the classroom in perspective as one of many battlegrounds in America's all-out campaign to raise the status of its underclasses. Educators learned quickly that pressures were mounting everywhere—not just in the schools— to take decisive action to eliminate even the subtle forms of discrimination that had hardly been noticeable over the years. It was the wave of those times and it could not be ignored.

At the top of the educational agenda, far ahead of the needs of the gifted, was the cause of low-achieving, disadvantaged children. There was a new sense of urgency to avert internal unrest by using every possible means to close the gap between the 'haves' and the 'have-nots', and it was generally acknowledged that schools would figure prominently in the process. Attention was thus shifted away from the need of the nation's talent reservoir to be kept well filled for the sake of defense and world prestige. The feeling was that somehow these problems could take care of themselves while only lightly attended to, whereas failure at school among the disadvantaged could not. In short, America was more concerned about bolstering freedom and equality within its borders than in playing the lead on the world stage, despite the unabated pressures of cold warfare that brought confrontations between East and West in Europe, Southeast Asia, and the Middle East.

In addition to diverting interest away from the gifted the advocacy movement for the socially disadvantaged actually contested at least two features of special programs for able children: (1) the use of IQ tests and other conventional measures of mental functioning as means of determining who deserves to be called gifted, and (2) grouping children in special classes for the gifted on the basis of their performance on these kinds of assessments.

Since racial minorities, such as Hispanics, Blacks, Chicanos, and Native Americans, traditionally performed less well at school than did white majorities, it was logical to suspect ability grouping for the gifted as *de facto* racial segregation. Critics argued that schools were practicing blatant favoritism by creating special classes for children who were rated superior on conventional measures of intellect and also by offering the chosen few a kind of enrichment in their curriculum that was denied everyone else. Objections were not necessarily against special ability grouping *per se* for the gifted, or even the enriched educational experience reserved for them because of their ability. What created the furor was the practice of denying enough children from disadvantaged subpopulations their rightful access to these classes. There was an overwhelming sentiment favoring the idea that high potential is distributed equitably among all races, privileged or underprivileged, but that life's circumstances in some groups are oppressive enough to cast a shadow over their innate competencies. And since nobody had ever devised a way in which to locate and nurture giftedness that was thus hidden from view, it was impossible to integrate special classes for the gifted with balanced racial quotas.

American education could not reconcile its interest in the gifted with its concern for the disadvantaged, nor could it design a satisfactory methodology for locating and cultivating giftedness among minority groups. The dilemma was easy to resolve inasmuch as it reduced itself to a choice between battling for social justice to achieve egalitarianism as against pursuing excellence, and there was no doubt as to which of the two would better fit the mood of the post-Kennedy 1960s.

Vietnam and Dissenting Youth

Although Vietnam was by no means the first confrontation between West and East, it turned out to be disastrously different, despite the fact that Kennedy's successor, Lyndon B. Johnson, justified America's entanglement on the same grounds that his predecessor defended his risks of war in Berlin and Cuba. What started out as a limited police action that was supposed to last only a short time before the expected victory would be won and American soldiers returned home, degenerated into a nightmarish entanglement with staggering sacrifices of life and no end in sight. The leadership in Washington kept the public's hopes for a quick end to the war alive by issuing deceptive reports about success on the battlefield. Eventually, the nation grew tired of war, suspicious of politicians' promises of a quick victory, and increasingly convinced that America was meddling in affairs of other nations rather than serving as a judge and enforcer of what was normally right in the world.

Among the many casualties of the Vietnam conflict was America's perception of giftedness and political leadership. The Whiz Kids of the Kennedy years, many of whom had stayed on in the Johnson era to help formulate strategy for the war effort, eventually turned out to be *The Best and the Brightest* (Halberstam, 1972). while they were quick-minded, articulate, hard-working, and self-confident, Halberstam argued that they lacked wisdom and sensitivity to the feelings of the masses. Their cerebral artistry proved to be flashy rather than profound. They were rapidly losing their image as people who could become heroes in public life by virtue of their brainpower alone. In fact, their sad history seemed to prove that being super-smart scholastically was not a guarantee of super understanding of humanity's most serious problems and how to solve them. Gifted youths on campuses throughout the country learned to despise them for their role in the Vietnam debacle rather than revere them as graduated honors students distinguishing themselves as national leaders.

A serious by-product of Vietnam was growing unrest among students in the college. Many of them saw the war as an unprincipled adventure of the establishment in Washington and perhaps even of the senior generation (ages 30 and above) who either did not care or did not understand how their actions were affecting the conscience of idealistic young people.

Kenneth Keniston, who studied campus protestors in great detail, made it quite clear that a complex mix of personal attributes, familiar influences, peer associations, and school environments set them apart from their more conforming agemates (Keniston, 1971). However, it is noteworthy that a disproportionate number of disaffected youth on campus distinguished themselves in their studies at school and were frequently enrolled in some of the more enriched and prestigious programs. Their immediate targets were the colleges they were attending, which represented to them an establishment with archaic standards for success and unreasonable controls over their lives. Yet these same gadflies in centers of learning were themselves described in one study as possessing high degrees of intellectualism, defined as "concern with ideas—desire to realize intellectual activities—high valuation of intellectual creativities—appreciation of theory and knowledge—participation in intellectual activity (e.g. reading, studying, teaching, writing)—broad intellectual concerns" (Flacks, 1967, p. 70).

The unrest on campus underwent some dramatic changes over a relatively short time. As one observer remarked, "the key difference between the Berkeley [University] riots of 1964 and the Columbia [University] crisis of May 1968 is that in the pre-Columbian sense the major impetus for unrest stemmed from the perceived abuse or misuse of authority, whereas the later protest denied the legitimacy of authority . . ." (Bennis, 1970, p. 599). One might add that, when attention was called to the *misuse* of authority, it was an expression of protest, but when it evolved into doubts about the *legitimacy* of authority, it became a sign of insurrection.

The revolt was not only against institutions (educational or otherwise) and their leaders; it was also against a tradition of rationalism that sanctified ivory-tower scholarship. When Columbia University rioters willfully destroyed a professor's research files, the act may have carried a message that went beyond ordinary malicious mischief and vandalism. It seemed to imply that all the work invested in accumulating those files was a waste of the professor's talent, which ought to have been dedicated to building a better society rather than to dabbling in esoterica. And to make matters worse, the educational establishment expected its brightest students to follow in the footsteps of professors like him.

Many questions were raised among gifted college students as to whether they ought to funnel their psychic energies into a life of the mind. Many were attracted to the sensitivity-training movements, which told them that "talking is usually good for intellectual understanding of personal experience, but it is often not effective for helping a person to *experience*—to feel" (Shutz, 1967, p. 11). Accordingly, the human being was increasingly seen not as a thought machine but rather as a complex biological, psychological, and social organism that can fulfill itself through all these dimensions of being. Every part of the body had to be exercised to its fullest potential, which meant building up the strength and stamina of its muscles, its sensory awareness and aesthetic appreciation, its motor control, and the gamut of its emotional and social feelings. Inhibiting other aspects of self for the sake of the intellect was regarded as amounting to robbing life of its multi-dimensionality, so the task of individuals was to make something of *all* their capacities, even if in so doing they could not make the most of *any* of them.

Significantly, a new utopia emerged in the form of Consciousness III depicted by Charles A. Reich in his then best-seller, *The Greening of America* (1971). One of the postulates of this new world was described by Reich as follows:

Consciousness III rejects the whole concept of excellence and comparative merit . . . [it] refuses to evaluate people by general standards, it refuses to classify people, or analyze them. Each person has his own individuality, not to be compared to that of anyone else. Someone may be a brilliant thinker, but he is not 'better' at thinking than anyone else; he simply possesses his own excellence. A person who thinks very poorly is still excellent in his own way. Therefore people are in no hurry to find out another person's background, schools, achievements, as a means of knowing him; they regard all of that as secondary, preferring to know him unadorned. Because there are no governing standards, no one is rejected. Everyone is entitled to pride in himself, and no one should act in a way that is servile, or feel inferior, or allow himself to be treated as if he were inferior (p. 243).

Thus we see how life for campus dissidents becomes strangely paradoxical. Many of them espoused the habits of intellectualism generally associated with gifted students. At the same time they rejected excellence and its trappings as violations of democracy and too stultifying to the attainment of total job and liberation. Even those consenting to live the life of the mind learned an unforgettable lesson from the events in Vietnam. No longer could they be adjured to cultivate their talents for the sake of their country's prestige and need for survival. The war in Southeast Asia tarnished the nation's image enough to discourage such commitments among a large number of students who could potentially be counted among America's high-level human resources. Besides, some may have felt it faintly dehumanizing to be treated like natural resources; it simply did not fit well with the new spirit of selfhood and individuality.

The Devaluation of Science

Gifted youth in the age of *Sputnik* had been bombarded with the message that a lifetime devotion to achievement in science in particular was not only in the interests of the state but of humankind in general. Such pursuits had their own built-in ethic, that any efforts at pushing back the frontiers of theory and research deserve the highest commendation because they attest to humanity's divine-like power of mastering its environment and creating its own brand of miracles. Suddenly the nation was told that science is as fallible as the one who advances it. Among the most vocal critics were the environment-minded scientists who warned that, in America's enthusiasm for conquering nature, it may be destroying its people in the process unless it imposes restraints on such activity (Bereano, 1969).

Perhaps the best known writer of the 1960s to forecast doom if science were to continue on its conventional course was the biologist, Barry Commoner, whose book, *Science and Survival* (1966), enjoyed wide circulation and influence. Commoner took the ecological point of view that the elements of nature are integrated, but human knowledge of these elements is so limited that it is not yet possible to see their connectedness. Expressing deep concern about science's preoccupation with the elegance of its methods rather than the danger of its products, he directed much of his fire at the polluting effects of such symbols of technological giantism as nuclear testing and industrial waste. He acknowledged the need for brainpower to enrich scientific thinking, but he also warned that "no scientific principle can tell us how to make the choice, which may sometimes be forced upon us by the insecticide problem, between the shade of the elm tree and the song of the robin" (p. 104). With such

caveats, it became more difficult to convince gifted children that a life dedicated to science was the kind of high calling it had once been unless closer links were made between the intellect and the conscience.

Besides being tarnished because little account was taken of their human consequences, careers in science lost more of their glitter when the job market in various related fields began to tighten. The manpower crisis dramatized by *Sputnik* gradually calmed down when America began to overtake the Soviets in the technology race and achieved a victory of sorts by transporting the first man to the moon in 1969. Previous personnel shortages in the various fields of science were no longer critical, partly because the flood of graduates in the early 1960s had filled available jobs and also because the Cold War was not considered serious enough to create new jobs through lucrative defense contracts. In fact, by the late 1960s, many Americans were suspicious of the so-called 'military-industrial complex' for carving too much out of the tax dollar to support projects that they considered wasteful in times of peace. The primary need, as seen then, was to solve the problem of social unrest rather than to prop up defense technology. Many would-be scientists and engineers began to realize that these professions attracted neither the prestige nor the occupational rewards that would have been guaranteed only a few years earlier. However, the supply of scientific talent did not slow down in accordance with the reduced demand, and as a result of the imbalance, many highly trained personnel found themselves either unemployed or working at jobs outside their fields.

The American Experience: Renewed Interest in the Gifted in the 1970s

The decline of attention to the gifted in the 1960s is evident in the contrasting volume of professional publications on that subject at the beginning and end of the decade. The number of entries under 'Gifted children' in the 1970s volume of *The Education Index* was less than half the number in the 1960 volume. Nevertheless, by the outset of the 1970s, there were unmistakable signs of a revival of interest.

Probably the biggest boost came from a 1970 Congressional mandate that added 'Provisions Related to Gifted and Talented Children' to the Elementary and Secondary Educational Amendments of 1979. This document expressed a legislative decision to include gifted students among those receiving help from the Elementary and Secondary Educational Act and the Teacher Fellowship Provisions of the Higher Education Act of 1956. It also directed the Commissioner to: (1) determine the extent to which special education assistance programs are necessary or useful to meet the needs of gifted children; (2) show which federal assistance programs are being used to meet the needs of gifted children; (3) evaluate how existing federal educational assistance programs could be used more effectively to meet these needs; and (4) recommend new programs, if any, required to meet these needs. The target population was defined as the upper three to five percent of school-age children with outstanding promise in six categories of giftedness: general intellectual ability, specific academic aptitude, creative or productive thinking, leadership ability, visual and performing arts, and psychomotor ability.

In response to the mandate, the then-commissioner Sidney P. Marland, Jr issued a report of his findings and recommendations that set the stage for doing something significant about the deteriorated condition of programs for the gifted (Marland, 1961). He estimated that only a small percentage of the 1.5 to 2.5 million gifted school children were benefitting from special educational services and that such services had a low priority at virtually all levels of school administration. Furthermore, even in those localities where there were legal or administrative directives to provide special offerings, little was accomplished due to other funding priorities, more threatening crises, and the absence of adequately trained personnel. Clearly, Marland saw the gifted as a deprived group whose talents were in danger of serious impairment unless appropriate intervention strategies were planned. He therefore declared his intention to initiate a series of major activities at the federal level with the hope of inspiring and pressing for more commitment on behalf of the gifted throughout the nation's schools.

As a result of federal encouragement and some public and private initiatives, the gifted were exposed to an increasing number of special educational experiences in the 1970s. While as late as 1973 fewer than four percent of the nation's gifted were receiving satisfactory attention at school, and most of the fortunate ones were concentrated in ten states, the nationwide picture improved considerably within the decade. Zettel (1979) reports the following outcomes of a survey conducted in 1977:

(1) nearly 75% of the states already had statutory definitions of gifted children;
(2) thirty-three (or 66%) of the states reported an aggregate increase of nearly 25% over the previous year in the number of gifted children served;
(3) thirty-one (or 62%) of the states increased their appropriations for the gifted by 50%;
(4) forty-two states reported sponsoring some kind of in-service training for persons interested in serving the gifted, a 110% increase over the previous year.

There was talk about possible legislation that would change the Federal Bureau of the Handicapped to the Bureau of Exceptional Persons, thus including gifted individuals as eligible for sustained support of their education, along with the handicapped. If this kind of move had been made, it would have gone a long way toward erasing the image of gifted education as being only a periodic fad in the schools. It was admittedly a way of forcing attention on the ablest by tying their fortunes to those of the handicapped, for whom funding has rarely abated appreciably. The change in name never came to pass, possibly because the American public could never feel equally sympathetic to the needs of children at both ends of the ability continuum.

Despite the fact that the definition of giftedness had been broadened by the Marland report, little more than lip service was given to children who showed precocity in domains other than academics. Even less fortunate were the gifted among the underprivileged minority populations who remained largely neglected, except in the arts and sports, but not deliberately so. There is no doubt that many educators would gladly have initiated enrichment experiences for these children and that support was obtainable for such plans if they had stood a chance of success. However, the profession was stymied in its efforts to find a clear way of discerning high-level academic potential that was buried under a thick overlay of social and economic handicaps. In fact, it is hardly less difficult today than it was then to inspire the fulfillment of scholarly talent in the nation's underclasses.

In its desire to sustain interest in the gifted, the federal government funded projects designed to strengthen leadership in the field and to spread advocacy at the grass-roots level. The National/State Leadership Training Institute received federal funds to help state education departments develop viable plans for educating the gifted. In addition, Teachers College, Columbia University, was provided with support to coordinate efforts by seven universities in recruiting and training graduate students to become seminar figures in the field. It was seen as a long-range investment in the careers of men and women who had shown promise for making significant contributions in the 1980s and beyond. Besides these nationwide projects, the federal government, along with state, city, and private agencies, sponsored many regional and local programs for the gifted. The emphasis was mainly on enrichment practices, whereas research and experimentation received relatively little encouragement.

A review of the state of research for the years 1969 to 1974 reveals a fairly bleak picture (Spaulding, undated). These efforts continued to be limited throughout the 1970s, but there are several major exceptions worth noting. They include the 1971 initiation of Julian Stanley's (1976) continual studies of mathematical precocity, Halbert Robinson's (1979) investigations of the cognitive development of young able children, and Pauline Snedden Sears' (1979) and Robert Sears' (1977) assessment of the Terman population in their senior period of life.

What prompted the resurgence of activity in the education for gifted children after nearly a decade of quiescence? A full answer will probably never be known, but the explanation that seems most obvious is

America's backlash against what it saw as a youth turned excessively self-indulgent, indifferent to scholastic achievement, and hostile towards some sacred, scholarly traditions. Wagner (1976) published a scathing indictment of universities for compromising academic standards, inflating grades, and diluting degree requirements to fend off unrest among students. His sentiments, shared by many other educators at the time, were signs that the pendulum had swung away from extreme egalitarianism in the direction of excellence. It is hard to image the youth of the late 1970s accepting the Consciousness III notion that brilliant minds are not better at thinking than anyone else. However, the revival of interest was no more a sign of pure historical inevitability than was its decline a decade earlier. What accounted for the revival, at least in part, was evidence of initiatives taken by people who believed in differentiated education at every ability level and who participated in vigorous campaigns to save the schools.

Prescriptive Teaching for All Children

When Riessman published his highly influential book on the culturally deprived child in 1962, he reiterated a number of criticisms of the schools made some fifteen years earlier by Davis and Havighurst (1947). The charges were that the curriculum was excessively loaded with verbal content and therefore placed underprivileged children at a disadvantage; that the subject matter was irrelevant to the vital concerns of these children; that teachers espoused values and behavior codes that were oriented too narrowly toward middle-class living; and that schools were so preoccupied with teaching the disadvantaged how to become socially mobile that they were in effect trying to create a melting pot rather than striving to strengthen cultural pluralism. However, researchers did not take their lead from such charges. Instead of tampering with the old curriculum, they tried to create a learning environment that would enable the disadvantaged to meet the more conventional demands at school.

Among the most notable experiments that sustained their influence at the time were those conducted a decade earlier by Martin Deutsch (1964) and his associates. They attempted to forestall educational retardation by intervening early in children's lives and equipping them with the readiness skills that they could not derive from their social milieu. This required developing elaborate ways in which to diagnose individual learning profiles and to match instructional treatments to them. It paralleled developments in special education for the handicapped, which emphasized prescriptive teaching based on increasingly sophisticated methods of diagnosing intellective processes. This orientation led to nationally mandated requirements that every handicapped child have an individual diagnosis, prescription, and evaluation.

Attention to specific competencies among the handicapped dramatized the need for individualized education, with *all* children receiving a fair share of what is uniquely appropriate for them, regardless of how deficient or proficient they are in mastering curriculum content. Advocates for the gifted argued that these children should also receive special attention to accommodate their unique learning strengths and thereby demonstrate the educator's attention to human differences. These protagonists pointed out that the more sophisticated educators become in discerning human individuality, and the more inventive they are in providing for individual needs of the ablest, the more likely that America could achieve equality at school.

The Role of the Gifted in 'Rescuing' Public Education

It is no secret that educators in the 1970s searched desperately for ways in which to maintain order in thousands of classrooms. This was especially true in big-city schools where ten percent of the nation's pupil population was enrolled. The dismal picture was a familiar one: scholastic achievement levels were three, four, and even five years below norms; drugs, violence, vandalism, and truancy reached epidemic proportions; and costs climbed to such a height that there was always the danger of insufficient funds to pay the bills while maintaining an adequately staffed program. Many middle-class families fled the inner city in the 1970s or sought help from private schools in order to provide a meaningful educational experience for their children. This further aggravated the situation in urban centers.

School administrators became aware that one way in which to bring back the middle classes to inner-city schools was to initiate special programs for the gifted. They therefore opened so-called 'magnet schools' that offered enrichment activities in particular subject matter areas to attract sizeable numbers of children who would otherwise have been studying elsewhere. The presence of the ablest began to make a difference in the total school atmosphere, which demonstrated that these children were capable of enhancing all education if their learning capacities were properly respected. Again, special education for the gifted was initiated for the sake of solving social problems rather than solely for the sake of those who need, or could benefit from, it.

The American Experience: Peaks and Valleys in the 1980s

At the conclusion of his personal retrospective on three decades of education for the gifted in the United States, Passow (1980) wrote: "I was once again struck by the cyclical nature of our interest in and efforts on behalf of the gifted and talented" (p. xvi). Perhaps the most positive statement that can be made about the gifted in the 1980s is that they prevented George Orwell's 'Big Brother' era from arriving in 1984 as he had predicted.

In fact, if Orwellian forecasts ever come true, it will be tragic proof of how ineffectual educators have been in nurturing talent for the strengthening of selfhood in the human family. But even the failure of 'Big Brother' to materialize is no guarantee that America will succeed in finally breaking its vacillation between public enthusiasm and apathy toward gifted children in the foreseeable future. All that can be said about the 1980s is that there were both positive and negative developments in the school and society, and that it is too early to tell what the eventual effects of these developments will be.

New Sources of Talent

It was already apparent that women and low-status minorities were moving toward parity with middle-class white males in the extent and variety of their advanced education. Trends have indicated a sharply rising representation of women in every creative field over the ten-year span from 1975 to 1985, when there was only a 6% increase in first professional degrees for men, as compared to a huge 122% increase for women. During the same period, the number of earned doctorates among men inched up from slightly under 27,000 to about 28,000, or 4%, whereas for women the jump was from some 8000 to about 14,000, or about 75%.

Considering the changing status of women in society, it is difficult to imagine that talent among them will continue to be suppressed as in former generations. Parents of school-age girls do not tolerate such biases as readily as the girls' grandparents might have, especially if the mothers of these children are themselves members of the new generation of women with advanced training and are in mid-career. Furthermore, opportunities for employment at higher skill levels have increased dramatically for women in recent years, and will continue to do so in the foreseeable future. According to the U.S. Bureau of Labor Statistics, the number of men added to the labor force from 1979 to 1985 was 8.1 million, not even half the 16.5 million figure for women. By 1995, more than 60 of every 100 women of working age will be employed, an increase from 43 per 100 in 1970. They will then constitute over 45% of the prime-age work force. Some of the professional occupations filled mostly by males possessing marketable talents that require advanced training are now absorbing unprecedented numbers of women. These professions include engineering, law, medicine, dentistry, and the life sciences.

The educational and occupational opportunities for bright African-Americans has also improved over the past half century. In 1940, total black enrolment in post-secondary education was less than 50,000, and over 95% of that group was enrolled in traditionally Negro Colleges (Pifer, 1978). By 1976, the number of blacks in colleges and universities had risen dramatically to 1,062,000 and for the 1975–1976 academic year alone, more than 83,000 blacks earned baccalaureate, masters, medical, law, and PhD or EdD degrees (Pifer, 1978; National Center for Education Statistics, 1978).

There is reason to expect the upward trend to continue as more and more people from minority groups are accepted into the managerial, professional, and technical segments of the labor force. What women, blacks, and other minorities have found in the high-skill labor market in the late 1980s is an increase of about 29% over the mid-1970s in the number of professional, technical, and kindred occupations. What they also discovered, unfortunately, is that the total number of adults with advanced education increased more sharply, thus dimming the employment outlook for them. The openings for PhDs over the 1972–1985 period for growth and replacement was about 187,000, whereas the actual supply of new PhDs numbered as many as 580,000 in the second half of the 1980s. It stands to reason, therefore, that doctoral recipients from all subpopulations have found it difficult to locate work commensurate with their training. But the women and other minorities are most vulnerable on account of age-old prejudices that bar them from many positions of prestige.

New Trends in Diagnosing and Nurturing Excellence

Traditional tactics for identifying gifted who might qualify for the talent pool are under pressure to undergo change, some of it radical. There is no end in sight to the debate over the meaning of IQ, its measurement, and the nature-nurture issues that revolve about it, all of which arouse powerful emotions as well as scientific interest. In the 1970s, some behavioral scientists (Estes, 1976; Voss, 1976) foresaw a decline in the concept of intelligence as a useful description of higher-level cognitive powers. They expected it to be replaced by more diagnostic analyses of the patterns and processes of human functioning. This kind of orientation to the measurement of intellect conforms to the pioneering approach taken by Piaget (1952) in monitoring clinical development of children's problem-solving behavior.

Despite the criticisms of IQ for identifying gifted children, there has never been a complete let-up in such practice. In a recent review of all empirical studies published in the *Gifted Child Quarterly* over two years (1990 and 1991), Tannenbaum (1992) discovered that in the 22 published reports of research on the gifted, all of them listed IQ, or alternative tests that correlate highly with IQ, as the measure of choice for identifying experimental samples. This is not surprising in light of previous findings by Snyderman and Rothman (1988) which shows that psychologists and educators knowledgeable in areas related to intelligence testing generally agreed that IQ instruments are valid and useful in measuring some of the most vital aspects of intelligence. Obviously, test users have been paying little attention to the advice and efforts of academic psychologists to promote new ways of assessing high potential in children.

Among the changes strongly advised by theoreticians has been to examine specialized talents that demonstrate extraordinary rates of mastery and of creativity. Gardner's (1983) list of such aptitudes has been widely circulated, and includes linguistic, logical-mathematical, spatial, bodily-kinaesthetic, musical, interpersonal, and intrapersonal intelligences.

Another major trend in describing high potential in children is through the study of mental processes, exemplified by Sternberg's (1986) 'Triarchic Theory', so named because it contains three sub-theories. One of them is 'componential', and it consists of three kinds of components involved in the performance of separate mental operations: (1) metacomponents, or the executive processes needed for planning, monitoring, and decision-making in a problem-solving situation; (2) performance components, which include processes needed for executing a task; (3) knowledge acquisition components used in the selective encoding, selective combination, and selective comparison operations. Another sub-theory is called 'experiential', which incorporates the ability to deal with novelty and the ability to automatize or habituate information processing. The third sub-theory is called 'contextual', which refers to the organism's selecting, shaping, and adapting to its real-world environment.

Ramos-Ford and Gardner (1991) have experimented with ways of departing from the usual pencil-and-paper tests of ability to monitoring children carefully and systematically for their performance in learning environments that bear some resemblance to real working conditions. It remains to be seen whether such an approach can improve upon conventional testing methods, which critics consider antiquated and inefficient.

A sharply different testing method has been developed by Feuerstein (1979), who also opts for measuring the dynamics of human potential. This means determining the extent to which children's functioning levels can be modified through what he calls mediation, or the examiner's use of appropriate helping tactics and practice materials. The idea of mediating the child's entering behavior in a test situation is novel in that it revises the role of the examiner from that of an objective observer to a participant observer who orients the child to the underlying cognitive principles involved in the test experience. Feuerstein asserts that the organism is so modifiable that mediated learning affects not only the cognitive functioning of the individual but the structure of intellect as well. Such is the power of regulated encounters between the individual and environment.

Programs and Provisions

In 1954, Tannenbaum conducted an informal survey of American schools singled out in a 1941 published report as offering exemplary enrichment programs for gifted children. The purpose of the communication was to find out what had happened to those programs over the intervening 13 years and how schools in 1954 could benefit from the experiences, including the successes and failures, of the 1941 programs. Of the 100 schools contacted, nearly all replied, and in every case the original programs were no longer in operation. In fact, they were never meant to last a long time. What they had amounted to were imaginative projects initiated by talented teachers and supported by administrators who shared their concern about the plight of the gifted.

The survey revealed a fundamental difference between *programs* and *provisions* for the gifted. A program can be defined as a comprehensive offering, sequenced over a long period of time, usually designed as a requirement, and very much a major part of the total school curriculum. Thus, the school offers programs in mathematics, literature, art, social studies, and the like. A provision, on the other hand, is more fragmentary, an *ad hoc* offering, relatively brief in duration, often designed by an individual teacher with special abilities rather than by a curriculum committee, and supplemental to the major offerings, not integral with them. What the 1954 survey revealed is that the 1941 schools had offered provisions rather than programs. Indeed, wherever enrichment of any kind has been initiated into the school curriculum, in most cases it has amounted to add-on provisions that sooner or later disappeared because of lack of strong enough commitment or sufficient funds to retain what was generally seen as a curriculum luxury rather than necessity. In fact, the lesson learned in the 1954 study was confirmed more than 30 years later. The Richardson sponsored investigation (Cox et al., 1985) reports a survey of some 16,000 schools (of which only about 10% responded, an ominous sign in itself) that found once again only fragmentary enrichment provisions, not programs, in most schools that claimed to be servicing the needs of the gifted.

Despite schools' reluctance to invest in long-range programmatic development for the gifted, there were some encouraging signs in the 1980s that conceptual frameworks for curriculum development could at least be available to those interested in them. School officials were offered program paradigms that they could adapt or adopt for actual implementation. In Renzulli's (1986) *Systems and Models for Developing Programs for the Gifted and Talented* no fewer than fifteen such designs are described in detail by their creators. They are by no means the only ones available for implementation. Not included, for example, is the work of Stanley and the Johns Hopkins Study of Mathematically Precocious Youth (SMPY). Initiated in 1971, SMPY has spread to nearly every corner of the United States, with more and more school systems subscribing to Stanley's ideas about fast-paced instruction for junior high school-age children who are advanced in mathematics. By now, large numbers of young adolescents throughout America, and recently in Germany as well, are being tested in hopes of being placed in any of a number of enrichment settings, such as afternoon and summer classes as well as college courses that offer advanced study. If SMPY and other enrichment paradigms are adopted increasingly in the United States and in other Western countries, it will signal a movement away from *ad hoc* provisions to much longer range programs for the gifted.

Unquestionably, the largest-scale effort on behalf of the gifted in the last decade of the twentieth-century and possibly of all time, is the federally funded project conducted by the National Research Center on the Gifted and Talented. Initiated by Joseph S. Renzulli at the University of Connecticut, it involves three additional universities in joint leadership for the development of theory, research, and programs across the United States. More than 200 elementary and secondary schools throughout the country collaborate as experimental sites, and as many as eleven major so-called 'stakeholders' are targeted for dissemination and impact. 'Stakeholders' include lay and professional organizations, business, industry and labor, legislative bodies, and the media, among others.

In its own summary of objectives (Renzulli, Reid and Gubbins, undated), the Center is committed to designing and carrying out 'theory-driven quantitative and qualitative research that is problem-based, practice-relevant, and consumer-oriented' (p. 3). It has thus dedicated itself to providing intellectual leadership that will hopefully ensure continued public attention to the needs of the gifted for years to come into the twenty-first century.

It is much too early to assess the Center's realization of its lofty hopes. But it bears monitoring closely as a model that may deserve preservation and replication in Western countries because of its sheer scope, size, ambition, and organization, should it prove successful in the long run.

Final Thoughs About Present and Future Trends

Current prospects for recognizing the special needs of gifted children worldwide are still subject to the excellence-egalitarianism dilemma which Fetterman (1988) regards as universal. At the conclusion of his international survey of enrichment offerings for the gifted, Brickman (1979) observes: "the dogma that democracy is at the opposite pole from meritocracy based on individual talent, skill, aptitude, ambition, and ability is at least open to serious difference of opinion.... A democratic society can pursue an egalitarian policy if it provides the fullest possible education for each person without regard to background and status, social, economic, political, religious, racial, sexual, physical, and mental. Under such a policy, all individuals will receive their demo-

cratic due, including those who are gifted and talented' (p. 329).

Indeed, there are some signs that Brickman's optimism may be justified. The membership in the World Council on Gifted Children consists mainly of professionals and lay advocates from democratic nations, and its biennial meetings have drawn large numbers of participants from these and other countries. Similar lively participation is shown at conferences sponsored by national and local associations on behalf of the gifted in the United States. Educationally, European democracies have tended to maintain their traditional school structures which differentiates education for university-bound students. These countries have also exposed at least some of their precocious children to various kinds of enrichment experiences in and out of school. Some of this activity is especially noteworthy, as more and more Western and Western oriented democracies are making highly promising contributions to the field. For example, Heller's fifteen-year longitudinal study of the gifted in Germany (Heller, 1991/1996; 1992, 2000; Perleth & Heller, 1994; Perleth, 2000) is designed to clarify identification criteria that may be used in all special programs; Israel's Ministry of Education is sponsoring many adventurous enrichment experiences for the gifted at the elementary and secondary levels, and the newly established Israel Academy for the Sciences and Arts has initiated an extraordinarily imaginative program for the gifted that is attracting worldwide interest; the SMPY program for the mathematically gifted is spreading throughout the United States and beyond; and the enrichment curricula designed by a permanent committee of expert educators in Singapore has been operating with notable success in recent years.

Yet, ambivalent feelings toward the gifted persist even to this day. Aside from fears of elitism in a democracy, there are suspicions that only a thin line separates genius, or even giftedness, from insanity. Some argue that in the interest of cosmic fair play, nature somehow balances off mental superiority with emotional or physical handicap. Others are suspicious of the creative as potential iconoclasts who make life uncomfortable; they find it easier to live with the familiar than to be prodded into the unknown by unconventional ideas, be they political, social, artistic, literary, or scientific. Still another, more recent, tradition is the belief that super-rational powers, which are so popularly associated with so many kinds of giftedness, are not all that critical in affecting the human condition, either because irrational impulses also figure greatly in individual accomplishment (according to Freud), or because no amount of effort by any one person, however brilliant he/she may be, can cause more than a ripple in the inexorable tides of history (according to Marx).

Opponents of differentiated education for the gifted surface time and again in professional journals and forums. They believe that talent is irrepressible in some children and impossible to nurture in others. Why, then, invest in special programs for the gifted? Sometimes the question is raised cynically by those opposed to any kinds of special programs, except for the handicapped. Many more objectors are skeptical rather than cynical about the need for providing 'extras' to children who can allegedly excel without them. In the past, these periodic criticisms have placed advocacy for the gifted on the defensive despite anything anybody could say on its behalf.

The Changing Status of Gifted Achievement

Usually, an account of history of/and giftedness in Western society deals with outstanding individuals and their nurturance. There is rarely any doubt that gifted performance or production matters in the sense that it attracts critical admiration, even acclaim, temporarily or for all time. This seems to be changing. It is now necessary to take into account the prospects of noteworthy achievement per se by asking whether indeed it has a future.

Examples that come to mind include the classical symphony orchestra and its repertoire as well as the literary novel that is written by an author and bound in the usual print form. Of the symphony orchestra, the Arts and Leisure section of the *New York Times* (January 31, 1988) offers the following speculation:

> The date is January 31, 2038. At eight o'clock tonight, Carnegie Hall will be the scene of a special concert of rediscovered music—music that has not been played for three decades. There will, however, be no orchestra—not enough people play the violin, or the cello, or the oboe, anymore. All of the instruments will be played on a new computer, programmed for the occasion: the Bach 9000, which sounds more like an old-fashioned symphony orchestra than the real thing. For the last thirty years, Carnegie has specialized in Pop, Rock and Rage, the new fusion of New Age and Rock, but not tonight. The rediscovered works: Symphony #9 by Ludwig van Beethoven, Eine Kleine Nachtmusik by Wolfgang Amadeus Mozart, and Brandenburg Concerto #2 by Johann Sebastian Bach.

Such a scenario depicts a total break with the past rather than a creative accretion to it. Vivaldi and Schnittke do not survive in the company of their successors. Instead, the masterpieces of previous generations are banished to the archives, to be revived only on rare nostalgic occasions. Never before have artists and their art been declared obsolete, irrelevant, and unwelcome with such finality, as projected so seriously in the *New York Times* feature essay.

Should these speculations come true, they will constitute a major threat to the very concept of excellence as it is now known and accepted. No matter what differences exist in the way people define and evaluate giftedness, creativity, and genius, all agree that a high quality of human productivity or performance is a *sine qua non*. Some individuals who are celebrated for their work, even for many years, may eventually fall into disrepute. But at least the legacies of some *do* survive to maintain society's cultural treasures. By nullifying *all* of them at once, or even in time, raises doubts as to whether quality per se can survive as an essential ingredient of excellence. Surely *some* artists and their artistry contain enough brilliance to ensure their immortality. If they don't endure, then the criterion of quality has been replaced by something else. By what? Is it possible that mediocrity will some day be extolled for no other reason than its being new and different? How will music be critiqued, if not by its aesthetic value, however that is judged? Could Western society be entering an era when the beauty of musical statements counts for nothing, and all that matters is the arousal of people's deep impulses by *any* pounding, persistent beat with accompanying sound, however pedestrian it may be, even if it is programmed for 'performance' electronically rather than *interpreted* by an instrumental artist? If so, giftedness in music will take on a radically new meaning, if indeed it retains any real meaning at all.

With respect to the future of literature, the novelist, Robert Coover (*New York Times*, June 21, 1992) states:

> In the real world nowadays, that is to say, in the world of video transmissions, cellular phones, fax machines, computer networks, and in particular, out in the humming digitalized precinct of avant-garde computer hackers, cyber punks and hyperspace freaks, you will often hear it said that the print medium is a doomed and outdated technology, a mere curiosity of bygone days destined soon to be consigned forever to those dusty unattended museums we now call libraries. Indeed, the very proliferation of books and other print-based media, so prevalent in this forest-harvesting, paper-wasting age, is held to be a sign of its feverish moribundity, the last futile gasp of a once vital form before it finally passes away forever, dead as God.

Coover observes that the novel "is perceived by its would-be executioners as the virulent carrier of the patriarchal, colonial, canonical, proprietary, hierarchical and authoritarian values of a past that is no longer with us." In the novel, as it is traditionally constructed, the author is alleged to wield dictatorial power, not only over plot and character, but also over the format through which they are presented: on lines to be read from left to right (right to left in some languages), in sentences, paragraphs, pages and chapters. Freedom from this kind of literary tyranny is supposed to come from the so-called 'hypertext', in which the linear-sequential structure is eliminated with the help of computer programming. Unlike print text, hypertext

45

liberates readers from control by the novelist and, instead, allows them to become partners in the creative enterprise by involving them in the process of mapping and remapping textual content, "not all of which is provided by what used to be called the author" (in Coover's words).

As the novelist is relieved of the burden of unilateral creation, he/she is no longer the shaper of a complete narration, but instead becomes a collaborative arranger of text, together with erstwhile consumers of text. This is done by providing readers only with sketches of fictional events in no particular sequence and allowing them to fill in details independently in any way they choose to form webs of connection among the sketches. In other words, talent in writing novels becomes democratized, as everybody enjoys the right to participate in the process of producing plot and character on an equal footing with the gifted novelist. By thus being stripped of the task of composing stories in full detail from beginning to end *alone*, creatives in this domain lose their distinction and even their visibility as potential contributors to quality literature.

The mere speculation about such changes raises questions concerning gifted children with promising careers on the concert stage and superb young writers of narrative who may have the next great novel stored in their imaginations.

In another vein, consider Flynn's (1987) large-scale study of intergenerational gains in IQ in countries where such data were available. He found that present-generation 20-year-olds in Holland score about twenty points higher in IQ than did their counterparts some 30 years earlier. Both groups were compared on the same test using the same norms. An increase of such dramatic magnitude means that, in his sample at least, the number of persons with IQs of 150 and above has increased proportionately by a factor of almost 60 from the previous to the following generation. Yet, the number of patents granted has actually diminished, with the 1980s showing only sixty to sixty-five percent of the yearly rate for the 1960s. This may mean that IQ is no longer as relevant to the world of invention as it once was, or more probably, as scientific knowledge accumulates and inventions become more and more sophisticated, the threshold IQ has to rise in order to qualify a child as a potential producer of scientific ideas.

The Flynn (1987) results may be symptomatic of a trend toward fewer and fewer people capable of mastering more and more sophisticated knowledge, much of it sheltered from more popular consumption by convoluted neologisms. University professors in the 1960s were attacked by student activists who felt their would-be mentors were, in-effect, 'fiddling while Rome burned'. The students felt that the professors were elitist snobs, so tunnel-visioned that their own theories allowed no room for alternatives. Such criticisms may have led to the Consciousness III

declarations of exasperation and Reich's (1971) rejecting the concept of excellence and comparative merit.

The Reich suggestion that everybody is brilliant implies that brilliance has no distinctive meaning. It democratizes abilities and thus leads to the conviction that all products of the mind are created equal, free of criticism or comparative evaluation. This stance is entirely compatible with that of Paul de Man, the Belgian scholar who was instrumental in spreading the theory of deconstructionism in the liberal and fine arts. Supporters of the theory regard it as a reexamination of the humanist legacy, but opponents see it as an attack against the traditional canon.

According to deconstructionism, language in literature, art, and music, never means what it appears to mean. It discards the evaluational aspects of these creative products by declaring them neither good nor bad. Also discarded are attempts to analyze the ideas of writers, artists, and composers. What counts instead is the emotion that literature, art, and music generates in the reader, viewer, and listener, regardless of whether these feelings are embedded ion the creative products per se or in any way intended by the creators of these products.

The reactions to masterpieces are so personal and so differentiated according to who is reacting that the objects of these responses need not be masterpieces at all; anybody's work can qualify as a stimulator, which makes anybody as important a creator as everybody else. Sometimes the responses embody deeply felt political or social convictions, or even sexual meanings (McClary, 1987).

Aside from the philosophical consideration of deconstructionism, if the excellence of a creative product counts for nothing because there is no concern for standards or criticism or appreciation, what is the meaning of precocity and its cultivation? How can educators differentiate curriculums for the gifted when there are no human differences acknowledged in a society where *all* children are considered gifted, or not gifted? Can there be patronage of the arts which have no intrinsic value except as objects of highly personal projections? In other words, is the world of ideas witnessing the end of history of the gifted?

Similar questions may be raised in relation to a growing distortion of multicultural education. Traditionally, multiculturalism has advocated the incorporation of great ideas of all cultures and subcultures in the curriculum. It has also fostered the appreciation of the different histories, languages, lifestyles, and values of foreigners as a means of combating xenophobia and racism. However, these highly constructive and much needed additions to school curricula are occasionally ignored in favor of a radically different version of multiculturalism, exemplified in the Stanford University students' chant, "hey, hey, hey—ho, ho, ho, Western Civilization's got to go." 'Western Civilization', in this case, refers to the required course of reading great Western literature written by authors carricatured as dead white European males (DWEMs). Some of these great works, which have been treasured for centuries in Western society, had to be discarded from the requirements list and replaced by works selected primarily on the basis of their representing minority subcultures and achieving more of a balance of representativeness among the races and sexes.

Again, excellence is democratized by removing quality as the sole criterion for judging it and substituting in its stead an adherence to subcultural representation for its own sake. The gifted can continue making history and being part of history only if their products and performances are judged strictly by their worthiness, not as commonplace instruments for flushing out other people's emotions or *only* because they emanate from a minority group that seeks and deserves its place in the sun. It remains to be seen how long the element of quality in giftedness, talent, precocity, and genius will remain under attack in the years to come. The stakes are higher than ever in the world of the gifted, and indeed in the world at large.

The Study of Giftedness at the Beginning of the Twenty-First Century

Long before the first Christian millennium, the gifted were already subjects of special public attention. Indeed, people probably became interested in giftedness from the time they first recognized ability differences in each other and in their children. Then as now, general attitudes toward differentiating education for the ablest probably ranged from approval to apathy to ambivalence to antagonism. This lack of consensus is not about to change at the turn of a new century. Advocates for the gifted have enough commitment and influence on policy makers to keep many special enrichment services ongoing in the foreseeable future, while those who protest such services also enjoy sufficient influence to dampen full-scale support for the needs of highly creative and accelerated achievers at school. What lies ahead, then, is likely to be much more than minimal, and much less than maximal, opportunity for the most precocious schoolchildren to be challenged in full measure, educationally. 'Aye'-sayers to the desirability of exposing every qualified student to expanded and accelerated curricula, together with their 'nay'-saying opponents to such measures, constitute a small minority of those capable of influencing school policy. The vast majority either doesn't care or is conflicted about the issue, and will probably remain that way for years to come.

Relatively few school administrators take the initiative in mounting programs for the gifted. Instead of being pro-active, they tend to be reactive in response to bright students' parents who plead and pressure for more challenging educational fare to relieve their children's boredom in lock-step programs. Whatever

enrichment is then introduced tends to be provisional — easily discarded when school budgets are reduced or when the beneficiaries of temporary add-on learning exercises graduate, especially if there are no parent-advocates to clamor for the rights of a new wave of precocious students. Wherever special education for the gifted is treated as a curriculum elective rather than a requisite, a luxury instead of a necessity, the unique needs of most of these children will remain at the edge of school life, sometimes struggling to get in and sometimes in danger of falling out. The 'Aye'- and 'Nay'-sayers are locked in a seemingly endless struggle to capture the allegiance of the much greater numbers of educators whose attitudes are divided between indifference and indecisiveness. Both extremes alternate in winning battles, but neither has ever won the war decisively, and perhaps never will. At this historic change in eras, only the euphoric would dare anticipate universal special education for all children deemed gifted, by any means of identification. Some vital realities in school and society stubbornly resist change, and the treatment of unequals remains largely undifferentiated, except for handicapped learners.

Expansion of Advocacy and Service

Although widespread malaise in servicing the special needs of the gifted in public education still prevails at the turn of a new century and millennium, increasing numbers of professionals and lay people are active on behalf of this population, and the participation in these activities promises to grow in the course of time. Some two thousand educators and psychologists usually participate in the biennial conferences of the *World Council for the Gifted and Talented* (WCGT). Nearly that many attend the annual meetings of the *National Association for Gifted Children* (NAGC), a country-wide organization in the United States. In early December, 1999, the twenty-second annual conference of the *Texas Association for the Gifted and Talented* attracted more than 6,000 parents, teachers, psychologists, and school administrators to two days' attendance at some 400 seminars and several keynote addresses.

In other regions of the world, the *European Council for High Ability* (ECHA) and *Australia's Gifted Education Research, Resource and Information Centre* (GERRIC) bring together leading students and educators of the gifted periodically to share ideas with large numbers of their respective constituent colleagues. In addition to the efforts of worldwide, regional, and local advocacy organizations, many universities are providing sustained and intensive training to selected children, their parents, pre- and in-service teachers, supervisors, school administrators, and support personnel. In some instances, college faculty members teach qualified school-age children advanced topics in selected disciplines. Other courses may not necessarily be advanced, but are outside the scope of the regular school curriculum and fit into the range of a few children's interests as well as the instructors' areas of expertise.

Inasmuch as support services for precocious children already exist at many college campuses (too many to list here), it would be revealing to note some of the largest-scale efforts that promise to figure prominently in the years ahead. Thus far, the most duplicated, replicated and extensively researched program, based originally at Johns-Hopkins University, is Julian C. Stanley's *Study of Mathematically Precocious Youth* (SMPY). These services are still being adopted by a growing number of universities at various geographic locations. In the new century, SMPY-type programs show promise of becoming so widespread that nearly every mathematically advanced child may eventually have easy access to rapid-paced instruction in all countries where universities are receptive to the model. SMPY is noteworthy not only because of its proven success and popularity but also on account of its longevity. Too many other efforts at addressing the learning speed and capacity of the gifted through direct instruction have been short-lived. Hopefully, SMPY will serve as an object lesson on how and why to preserve effective services for the gifted in the next century, not only in mathematics but in all vital disciplines.

At the University of Connecticut, Joseph S. Renzulli continues to direct *The National Research Center on the Gifted and Talented* (NRCG/T), a consortium of four tertiary education institutions, including his own, Yale University, and the Universities of Georgia and Virginia. Besides building up a sizeable record of field service, research, and publication of position papers on various critical issues over the past decade, NRCG/T is anticipating its mission for the beginning of the next century by having issued a comprehensive needs assessment, based on reports of no fewer than 13,749 respondents, revealingly titled Setting an Agenda: Research Priorities for the Gifted and Talented Through the Year 2000 (Renzulli, Reid & Gubbins, 1992). Judging from the survey's scope and detail, and subsequent staff planning, NRCG/T — indeed the entire field of giftedness and its nurture — faces a huge agenda in the years ahead (see NRCG/T Newsletter, Fall 1999). The University of Connecticut also sponsors its yearly so-called 'Confratute' on the gifted, which is a huge attraction to educators seeking to learn from, and interact with, some of the best-known figures in the field.

The *Belin-Blank Center*, headed by Nicholas Colangelo at The University of Iowa, has also attracted worldwide attention to its biennial *Wallace Symposia* featuring lecturers on topics that are both directly and inferentially related to the gifted. The range of its study opportunities is so extensive that many targeted children and adults have been reached by them. For example, in his Comprehensive Report 1980–1999, Colangelo notes that in the last two decades over 20,000 school-age students have participated in the Center's talent searches, more than 5,000 students have attended its summer programs, and some 2,000 teachers have been enrolled in its courses and workshops. Considering the Center's past accomplishments and plans for the future, there is no doubt that *Belin-Blank* services will continue and probably expand, at least in the early part of the twenty-first century.

Still another example of a higher education institution that has long been offering wide varieties of special education to gifted children and to elementary and secondary school personnel is Purdue University in Indiana, where *The Gifted Education Resource Institute* (GERI), founded by John F. Feldhusen in 1978, is located. Here too, as in a growing number of colleges and universities, there is a rich array of advanced and unconventional courses for gifted children of all ages. The schedule of these learning experiences avoids conflict with school hours and the school calendar. This separation prevents power disputes between the 'home' schools and the enrichment centers concerning who is responsible for instructing gifted children in any content area.

As yet, this 'division of labour' is only a partial blessing for the gifted. On the positive side, it expands the children's exposure to domains and depths and breadths of knowledge they might never have encountered, at least at their ages. It challenges them closer to the limits of their abilities than anything they study in regular classrooms. Moreover, the direct college-based service to the gifted is at least somewhat of an accommodation of Martin's (1996) argument that we are living in an age of cultural superabundance which makes it impossible for conventional schools alone to fully educate tomorrow's children, including the gifted. Other institutions have to share the burden of public education. Furthermore, even school buildings may some day become fairly insufficient as locales of study if distance learning is eventually geared to reach and educate unprecedented numbers of students. In that case, a vast, complex, internet-based school system would become the major medium for confronting knowledge overload in the twenty-first century.

The limitation of dividing education for the gifted between school and college is that the two efforts are usually independent of each other rather than shared or coordinated. Elementary and secondary school rarely collaborate with colleges to offer an interrelated program to able children, a total package as it were. Instead, the colleges often provide supplementary learning experiences without much care about what is being supplemented. Worse still, the regular schools hardly ever consult the supplemental program content in designing curriculum enrichment or to gain insight into the special interests and abilities of their gifted students. Sometimes, compulsory education defers or defaults entirely to elective education to service the gifted, paying hardly any attention to what the gifted are experiencing in their after-school-hours studies. This failure of schools to fully assume its share of responsibility is a problem despite the impressive attendance at advocacy group conferences by more and more professionals interested in bright children. Perhaps these meetings amount to preaching to the converted, while the policy-making educationists and lay board members who need the orientation are not yet fully represented among the participants.

Expansion of Scholarly Activity

Among the encouraging signs of concern about the gifted is the mounting volume of theory and research that relates to them directly or by inference. This is true both for Europe and the United States (Heller, 1997). It is also clear from Heller's 1997 report that both areas of the world share similar scholarly concerns. Even at well-attended professional conventions where giftedness is not a first priority, there is often a sprinkling of papers delivered on aspects of childhood precocity, its meaning, origins, cultivation, and development. Needless to say, the many regional, national, and international meetings on the gifted are filled with such reports. Furthermore, there are at least three major journals on the gifted and one on the creative in the United States alone, which, along with similar periodicals in other countries, provide ample outlets for professional papers on these subjects. To illustrate the magnitude of scholarly work in the field, one educational psychologist, Kurt A. Heller, a co-editor of this Handbook, is credited or co-credited with no fewer than 91 publications, including books (written and edited), book chapters, journal articles, and scholarly papers published or delivered over a span of merely five years, 1995–1999. All of this material relates to the gifted, most of it directly, some indirectly. In addition, Heller has been readying nine reports for dissemination in the years 2000 and one in 2001. His total, so far, since 1995, and probably still growing: 101! Camilla P. Benbow and David Lubinski have likewise produced a large number of publications in recent years, reporting mostly on studies related to mathematical precocity, with present and former SMPY students as the subjects.

In the 1990s, and continuing into the next century, psycho-educational research and debate have concentrated heavily, though not exclusively, on long-standing, never-resolved issues. Still highly volatile is the familiar nature vs. nurture controversy relating to IQ, which has simmered for many years and was newly inflamed by the publication of *The Bell Curve*, by Herrnstein and Murray (1994). A major source of dissatisfaction among the book's critics is its claim that social success and failure depend heavily on individual differences in tested intelligence and that it

is impossible to achieve equity in education because some minority groups perform poorly on these measures (Fraser, 1995; Jacoby & Glauberman, 1995). Gould (1996) finds it preposterous to assert that a single metric can create a hierarchy of sorts among people and that the test score is genetically based and immutable. Some go so far as to denounce the book as a pseudoscientific attack against democratic ideals (Giroux & Searles, 1996).

Still, the barrage of criticism of *The Bell Curve* has not stifled arguments favoring nature over nurture and the importance of IQ in testing for giftedness in children. Despite Carroll's (1997) reasonably even-handed review of the Herrnstein–Murray thesis, in which he finds their data collection and analysis methods defensible but disagrees with the inferences they draw from the results, opinions on the issue have become mostly polarized. On the side of nature, Gottfredson (1998) states her view unequivocally, as follows: "We are born unequal in intellectual potential, and these differences portend social inequality in any reasonably free society. We may all be equal before the law and in the eyes of God, but we differ greatly in our abilities to perform well in school, work, and everyday life. Mother nature, it turns out, is not egalitarian. Gifted children are a stark reminder of this fact" (1998, p. 3).

One of the best-known advocates of the nature position is Judith Rich Harris, author of the much-discussed book, *The Nurture Assumption* (1998), which argues vigorously against the hitherto popular belief that caretakers' child-rearing strategies are critical in shaping children's personalities. Instead, the overwhelming influence at home is in the genes inherited from the parents. From an historical perspective, it doesn't matter that the study has been criticized by behavioral scientists (e.g. Williams, 1999; Plomin, 1999). Nor do too many people take notice of the work by Riksen and Walraven (1978) in Holland, Klein (1992) in Israel, and Moss (1992) in the United States on how effectively caretakers can enhance the cognitive development of infants and pre-schoolers through systematic mediation of the children's behavior. What matters is that the Harris thesis has received a plethora of media attention, much of it in the form of unrestrained endorsement. Perhaps the reason for the idea's current popularity is that it appeals to so many of today's parents who want to cast off the Freudian burden of responsibility for the kinds of people their offspring turn out to be, especially in cases where the children are considered 'bad seed'. These parents may prefer to feel complacent in the thought that 'molding' the genes they pass on to their young is impossible, rather than take heavy responsibility for 'molding' a healthy home environment to enrich their children's lives.

The role of media attention to the nature–nurture controversy is extremely powerful in influencing public opinion, far more persuasive than the technical scholarly reports from which the media elicit knowledge and information. How it is presented for public consumption, specifically with what bias, if any, is of critical importance. Sometimes, coverage of professional papers in the popular press carries with it an air of finality that was never intended. For example, a study comparing the sexes in performance on the Scholastic Aptitude Test showed that more male than female bright seventh graders scored high in mathematical reasoning (Benbow and Stanley, 1980). Five years later, Jacobs and Eccles (1985) noted that two of the most widely read news magazines interpreted these outcomes to mean that genetic or other biological factors accounted for the discrepancy in performances. Eleven years later, Freeman (1996) reported that British schoolgirls were functioning on a par with their male peers in mathematics. In light of these more recent data, what credence can be attached to the original media coverage? More important, what can a twenty-year history of scholarship on gender differences in mathematical aptitude reveal about the relative power of nature and nurture, if such differences are not universal, or if they change dramatically over time?

Is it plausible to assert that the genetic mix powering mathematical achievement is stronger in British than in American females? Or is there something in British schools and society that forecloses a gap in mathematical achievement between British schoolgirls and schoolboys, whereas such a preventative doesn't exist in the United States? Hardly, on both counts. It would therefore seem that extreme convictions in the nature–nurture debate are rooted more in dogma than in empiricism. Probably the only reasonable way to deal with the nature vs. nurture polarization is to revive from the history of science an interaction hypothesis suggesting that nature and nurture are not in conflict but rather combine to reinforce each other. It doesn't really matter which is stronger, as long as it is understood that each is powerless without the other.

Similar psycho-social forces may also be operating in research on monozygotic and dizygotic twins, some reared together, others reared apart (Bouchard, Jr. & Lykken, 1999; Bouchard Jr., Lykken, Tellegen & McGue, 1996). These studies have produced seemingly powerful arguments favoring heredity as the key determinant of gifted behavior. The data show that environment contributes little to the variance; it can help a budding historiographer decide whether to focus on French or Chinese history, but it contributes little to that person's competence in whatever choice he or she makes. But here too, the finding that genetic factors soak up so much of the variance may result, surprisingly, from similarities between the lifestyles of homes where the experimental populations are born and homes where they are raised. Stoolmiller (1999) reviewed several adoption studies relating to IQ and antisocial behavior and discovered a narrow range of differences between birthing and adoptive family environments. When corrections were made for range restrictions, the shared environment accounted for as much as 50% of the variance. Stoolmiller speculates that studies of adopted twins may also reveal a larger-than-expected portion of the variance explained by environments when range restrictions are corrected statistically. If evidence shows that home settings cannot be discounted, it may boost confidence in the role of education as a nurturing influence. Indeed, Ericsson and Charness (1994) have argued persuasively that skilled and imaginative training can stimulate expert performance effectively.

Again, a review of past and present scholarship on the nature–nurture controversy encourages even-handedness in the form of a revival of the long-neglected belief in the interdependence of both, to replace current orthodoxies about the supremacy of either.

Another seemingly perpetual debate that promises to continue well into the twenty-first century is between believers in general ability ('*g*') as the main source of vital mental functioning and those who point to separable aptitudes as the origins. Here again, sociopolitical differences, more than research evidence, may account for the rivalry. Those who emphasize the importance of *g* concentrate on human differences in the abilities that relate most strongly to *g* and are at the heart of every curriculum in sciences and letters. Whoever excels in these disciplines is deemed most likely to some day enlarge the world's knowledge bank and to preserve and advance cultural life on the planet. Discreditors of *g* focus mainly on diversity rather than just difference and prefer to show that more people can demonstrate excellence in at least one of a variety of aptitudes than in the restricted range of competencies subsumed under *g*. One side of the debate prides itself in being primarily selective in defining who qualifies as gifted, while the opposition seeks to be more inclusive and hence more egalitarian or expansive in formulating qualifications.

As would be expected, belief in the idea of multiple intelligences (Guilford, 1973; Gardner, 1983) is relatively popular, compared to favoring theories of general intelligence, since it would seem more equitable for the largest possible number of people to qualify as outstanding in any skill of more or less use to society. Sternberg (1997) calls attention to what he has labeled 'Successful Intelligence', or the ability to adapt to unfamiliar environments and their own practical challenges. His studies indicate that these abilities are not validly measured by conventional IQ tests, which are best suited for assessing *g*. Therefore, it is necessary to abandon *g*-centrism in identifying giftedness in the realm of successful intelligence, which is more closely related to practical, adaptive skills than to analytical or creative talents. However, some may wonder whether swift, ingenious adaptation to strange surroundings, often marked by 'street smarts', is an adequate sign of sophistication that denotes the familiar domains of excellence.

Those who appreciate the importance of *g* typically base their conviction on empirical data showing that *g* explains a high proportion of the variance in special aptitude tests (e.g., Thorndike, 1985). Some proponents of separable abilities also use mass data examination, particularly factor analysis, to bolster their theory (Thurstone & Thurstone, 1941; Guilford, 1967). Howard Gardner's approach is more ex-cathedra, although he uses specific criteria for including abilities in his list of intelligences. Possibly because his list of qualifiers is subjective, albeit rational, but not yet subjected to objective confirmation, he is regarded as more of a theorist than empiricist. Still, his theory has been enormously appealing to classroom teachers, especially those who work with exceptionally bright children. Commercial publishers have produced and sold many packets of instructional materials to stimulate growth of each intelligence he has posited thus far. These practical aids seem ready to retain their popularity well into the new century, probably because they are theory-driven, and their content and format seem engaging enough to capture children's attention. It remains to be seen whether learning is deepened or accelerated by education in Gardner's multiple intelligences.

One of the most enduring successes in expanding the concept of giftedness has been accomplished through the build-up of theory and research on creativity. Ever since J. P. Guilford introduced his sense of urgency about the topic at mid-twenty-first century in his presidential address to the American Psychological Association (Guilford, 1950), it has become the subject of intense scientific speculation, empirical research, and classroom attention. Some of it was initiated by Guilford himself, but he has been succeeded by a large number of scholars, some of whom are poised to carry on their work well into the twenty-first century. For example, Mark A. Runco, co-editor of the *Encyclopedia of Creativity* (Runco & Pritzker, 1999), has served as editor of the Creativity Research Journal since 1988 and is instrumental in disseminating some of the most important papers on the subject through this publication. Dean Keith Simonton (1999) has introduced a unique historiometric approach to the study of creativity and will likely continue this enlightening work in the years ahead. Jonathan A. Plucker (Plucker & Runco, 1998; Plucker & Renzulli, 1999) has been leading an initiative to restore confidence in divergent thinking as essential to the understanding and measurement of creativity. So insightful and engaging is the work of these specialists, along with the efforts of other scholars (too many to list here), that hardly any student of giftedness would exclude creativity from its realm.

In essence, then, scholarship on the gifted is alive and vigorous at the turn of a new century. Most of the subjects occupying the attention of theorists and researchers are not new, but are being addressed in innovative ways that generate new understandings for succeeding generations of scholars to accept, or build on, or dissent from, or replace with their own work. The twenty-first century promises to be the most exciting in history for future students of the gifted, thanks to the knowledge shared with them, and bequeathed to them, by their predecessors.

A Postscript on the Future

How daunting is it to forecast change initiated by the gifted for the next hundred years? Consider the hazards of making such an attempt in 1900 for the twentieth century. At that time, it was unthinkable to anticipate success in inventing incandescent bulbs to light homes, communities, and work places; formulating theories of relativity to revolutionize the physical sciences; harnessing atomic energy for awesome destructive and constructive potential; designing telecommunication devices, including telephone, television, audio and video recording, and computer technology to connect people with lives, ideas, events, materials, and places anywhere on the planet; achieving breakthroughs in medicine to prevent and cure hitherto uncontrollable diseases and to habilitate the organism's bodily, mental, and social functioning for a prolonged, healthier life; devising air travel, eventually jet-propelled, to enable people and cargo to reach distant places in relatively short time, and to use such unprecedented transport power for deep probes into the universe; and creating a cornucopia of artistic, musical, literary, theatrical, dance, and movie masterpieces to add meaning and pleasure to human life. This is merely a small sample of the countless gifts from the gifted to humanity, all given within a span of only one hundred years.

And yet, even the brightest of men and women at the outset of the twentieth century could not predict what miracles of the mind would materialize in the lifetimes of their children, grandchildren, and great-grandchildren. But they must have sensed that if anything so dramatic were to happen in their new century, precocious children, nurtured to fulfill their extraordinary promise and to serve rather than disserve society, would deserve the credit. We face the same mixture of mystery and expectation as our new century unfolds.

References

Amabile, T. (1983). *Social psychology of creativity*. New York: Springer.

Benbow, C. P. & Stanley, J. C. (1980). Sex differences in mathematical ability: fact or artifact? *Science*, **210**, 4475, 1262–1264.

Bereano, P. L. (1969). The scientific community and the crisis of belief. *American Scientist, 57*, 484–501.

Bestor, A. (1953). *Educational wastelands*. Urbana, IL: University of Illinois Press.

Bouchard, T. J., Jr. & Lykken, D. T. (1999). Life achievement in a sample of twins reared apart: estimating the role of genetic and environmental influences. In: N. Colangelo & S. G. Assouline (Eds), *Talent Development III* (pp. 81–97). Scottsdale, AZ.: Gifted Psychology Press.

Bouchard, T. J., Jr., Lykken, D. T., Tellegen, A. & McGue, M. (1996). In: C. P. Benbow & D. Lubinski (Eds), *Intellectual Talent* (pp. 5–43). Baltimore and London: Johns Hopkins University Press.

Brickman, W. W. (1979). Educational provisions for the gifted and talented in other countries. In: A. H. Passow (Ed.), *The Gifted and the Talented: Their Education and Development* (pp. 308–329). Chicago, Il: University Of Chicago Press.

Carroll, J. B. (1997). Psychometrics, intelligence, and public perception. *Intelligence*, **24** (1), 25–52.

Coleman, J. S. (1962). *The adolescent society.* New York: Free Press.

Commission on the Reorganization of Secondary Education, U. S. Department of Interior, Bureau of Education (1918). *Cardinal Principles of Secondary Education.* Washington, DC: Superintendent of Documents, Government Printing Office.

Commoner, B. (1966). *Science and survival.* New York: the Viking Press.

Conant, J. B. (1959). *The American high school today.* New York: McGraw-Hill.

Davis, W. A. & Havighurst, R. J. (1947). *Father of the man.* Boston: Houghton Mifflin.

DeHaan, R. G. & Havighurst, R. J. (1957). *Educating the Gifted.* Chicago: University of Chicago Press.

Deutsch, M. (1964). Facilitating development of the pre-school child: social and psychological perspectives. *Merrill-Palmer Quarterly*, **10**, 249–268.

Engelmann, B. (1984). *Germany without Jews.* New York: Bantam Books.

Ericsson, K. A. & Charness, N. (1994). Expert performance: Its structure and acquisition. *American Psychologist*, **49** (8), 725–747.

Estes, W. K. (1976). Intelligence and cognitive psychology. In: L. B. Resnick (Ed.), *The nature of intelligence.* (pp. 295-305). Hillsdale, NJ: Lawrence Erlbaum.

Fetterman, D. M. (1988). *Excellence and equality.* Albany, NY: State University of New York Press.

Feuerstein, R. (1979). *The dynamic assessment of retarded performers.* Baltimore, MD: University Park Press.

Flacks, R. (1967). The liberated generation: an exploration of the roots of student protest. *Journal of Social Issues*, **23**, 52–75.

Flynn, J. R. (1987). Massive IQ gains in 14 nations: what IQ tests really measure. *Psychological Bulletin*, **101**, 171–191.

Fraser, S. (Ed.). (1995). *The Bell Curve wars: race, intelligence, and the future of America.* New York: Basic Books.

Freeman, J. (1996). *Highly able girls and boys.* London: Department For Education and Employment.

French, J. L. (Ed.) (1959). *Educating the gifted.* New York: Henry Holt.

Gardner, H. (1983). *Frames of mind.* New York: Basic Books.

Getzels, J. W. & Jackson, P. W. (1958). The meaning of 'giftedness': an examination of an expanding concept. *Phi Delta Kappan*, **40**, 75–77.

Giroux, H. A. & Searles, S. (1996). The Bell Curve debate and the crisis of public intellectuals. In: J. L. Kincheloe, S. R. Steinberg & A. D.Gresson (Eds), *Measured lies: the Bell Curve examined.* New York: St. Martin's Press.

Goldberg, M. L., Passow, A. H., Camm, D. W. & Neill, R. D. (1966). *A comparison of mathematics programs for able junior high school students.* (Project No. S–0381. Washington, DC: U. S. Office of Education, Bureau of Research).

Goldberg, M. L., Passow, A. H., Justman, J. & Hage, G. (1966). *The effects of ability grouping.* New York: Bureau of Publications, Teachers College, Columbia University.

Gottfredson, L. S. (1998). *Intelligence and American ambivalence towards talent.* Paper presented at the fourth biennial Henry B. Wallace symposium, May 21–23, 1998, University of Iowa. Iowa City, Iowa.

Gould, S. J. (November 28, 1994). Curveball: Review of R. J. Herrnstein & C. Murray, The Bell Curve. *The New Yorker*, 139–149.

Grousset, R. (1959). *Chinese art and culture.* New York: The Orion Press.

Guilford, J. P. (1950). Creativity. *American Psychologist.* **5**, 444–454.

Guilford, J. P. (1967). *The nature of human intelligence.* New York: McGraw-Hill.

Guilford, J. P. (1973). Theories of intelligence. In: B. B. Wolman (Ed.), *Handbook of General Psychology* (pp. 630–643). Englewood Cliffs, N.J.: Prentice-Hall.

Halberstam, D. (1972). *The best and the brightest.* New York: Random House.

Harris, J. R. (1998). *The nurture assumption: why children turn out the way they do.* New York: Free Press.

Heller, K. A. (1991). The nature and development of giftedness: a longitudinal study. *European Journal for High Ability*, **2**, 174–188. Reprint in A. J. Cropley & D. Dehn (Eds), *Fostering the Growth of High Ability: European Perspectives* (pp. 31–56). Norwood, NJ: Ablex (1996).

Heller, K. A. (Ed.). (1992). *Hochbegabung im Kindes- und Jugendalter.* [High Ability in Children and Adolescence]. Göttingen: Hogrefe, 2nd ed. 2000.

Heller, K. A. (1997). *Gifted (children) education in the European community.* Paper presented at the International Congress on Gifted and Talented Children. Madrid, Spain, July 14–16, 1997.

Hennessey, B. A. & Amabile, T. M. (1988). The conditions of creativity. In: R. J. Sternberg (Ed.), *The Nature of Creativity* (pp. 11–38). Cambridge: Cambridge University Press.

Herrnstein, R. J. & Murray, C. (1994). *The bell curve: intelligence and class structure in American life.* New York: Free Press.

Jacobs, J. E. & Eccles, J. S. (1985). Gender differences in math ability: the impact of media reports on parents. *Educational Researcher, 13*, 20–24.

Jacoby, R. & Glauberman, N. (Eds) (1995). *The Bell Curve debate: history, documents, opinions.* New York: Times Books.

Keniston, K. (1971). *Youth and dissent: the role of a new opposition.* New York: Harcourt Brace Jovanovich.

Klein, P. S. (1992). Enriching the environments of gifted young children. In: P. S. Klein & A. J. Tannenbaum (Eds), *To Be Young and Gifted* (pp. 245–277). Norwood, NJ: Ablex.

Lamonte, J. L. (1949). *The world of the middle ages.* New York: Appleton-Century-Crofts.

Martin, J. R. (1996). There's too much to teach: Cultural wealth in an age of scarcity. *Educational Researcher*, **25**, 2, 4–10,16.

Moss, E. (1992). Early interactions and metacognitive development of gifted preschoolers. In: P. S. Klein & A. J. Tannenbaum (Eds), *To Be Young and Gifted* (pp. 278–318). Norwood, NJ: Ablex.

Perleth, Ch. (2000). Follow-up findings of the Munich Longitudinal Study of Giftedness. In: K. A. Heller (Ed.), *High Ability in Children and Adolescence* (2nd ed.) (pp. 357–446). Göttingen: Hogrefe.

Perleth, Ch. & Heller, K. A. (1994). The Munich Longitudinal Study of Giftedness. In: R. F. Subotnik & K. D. Arnold (Eds), *Beyond Terman: Contemporary Longitudinal Studies of Giftedness and Talent* (pp. 77–114). Norwood, NJ: Ablex, 2nd ed. 1998.

Plomin, R. (1999). Parents and personality. *Contemporary Psychology*, **44**, (4), 269–271.

Plucker, J. A. & Renzulli, J. S. (1999). Psychometric approaches to the study of human creativity. In: R. J. Sternberg (Ed.), *Handbook of Creativity* (pp. 35–61). New York: Cambridge University Press.

Plucker, J. A. & Runco, M. A. (1998). The death of creativity measurement has been greatly exaggerated: current issues, recent advances, and future directions in creativity assessment. *Roeper Review*, **21**, (1), 36–39.

Renzulli, J. S., Reid, B. D. & Gubbins, E. J. (1992). *Setting an agenda: Research priorities for the gifted and talented through the year 2000*. Storrs, CT: The National Research Center on the Gifted and Talented.

Riksen-Walraven, J. M. (1978). Effects of caregiver behavior on habituation rate and self-efficacy in humans. *International Journal of Behavioral Development*, **1**, 105–130.

Runco, M. A. & Pritzker, S. (Eds) (1999). *Encyclopedia of creativity*. San Diego, CA: Academic Press.

Simonton, D. K. (1999). Creativity from a historiometric perspective. In R. J. Sternberg (Ed.), *Handbook of Creativity* (pp.116–133). New York: Cambridge University Press.

Sternberg, R. J. (1997). Successful intelligence: a broader view of who is smart in school and in life. *International Schools Journal*, **17**, 19–31.

Sternberg, R. J. (1999). The theory of successful intelligence. *Review of General Psychology*, **3** (4), 1–25.

Stoolmiller, M. (1999). Implications of the restricted range of family environments for estimates of heritability and nonshared environment in behavior-genetic adoption studies. *Psychological Bulletin*, **125** (4), 392–409.

Thorndike, R. L. (1985). The central role of general ability in prediction. *Multivariate Behavioral Research*, **20**, 241–254.

Thurstone, L. L. & Thurstone, T. G. (1941). Factorial studies of intelligence. *Psychometric Monographs*, No. 2.

Williams, W. M. (1999). Peering into the nature-nurture debate. *Contemporary Psychology*, 44 (4), 267–269.

Giftedness as Developing Expertise

Robert J. Sternberg

Yale University, New Haven, Connecticut, USA

Introduction

Mary has an IQ of 140 on a standardized individual intelligence test and has been identified as 'gifted'. Ellen has an IQ of 120 on the same test and has not been identified as gifted. What do each of these scores, and the difference between them, mean? In this chapter, it is argued that the best available answer to this question is quite different from the one that is conventionally offered, which is that the scores and the difference between them reflect some largely inborn, relatively fixed 'ability' construct. Instead, it is argued that the difference in scores reflects a difference in one of many kinds of developing expertise (Sternberg, 1998), a kind that is especially important for school performance but less important for job performance later in life.

The expertise that all these assessments measure is referred to as 'developing' rather than as 'developed' because expertise is typically not at an endstate, but in a process of continual development. Gifted individuals need continually to be developing the kinds of expertise that render them gifted. If they do not, they stop being identified as gifted, or they become identified as gifted 'has-beens'. Indeed, part of the argument of this chapter is that the kinds of distinction that lead one to be identified as gifted differ at different points in the life span, which is why many people are gifted in childhood but not thereafter. It is not that the gifted children somehow later lose what they had; it's that they never developed the kind of expertise that would lead them to be identified as gifted adults (see Bamberger, 1986).

In a sense, the point of view articulated in this chapter represents no major departure from some modern points of view regarding abilities (e.g. Anastasi & Urbina, 1997). Abilities are broadly conceived, and are seen as important to various kinds of success. They are seen as modifiable in some degree, and as capable of being flexibly implemented, at the same time that they are viewed as having interactive genetic and environmental components. Of course, they are seen as important in giftedness, although only a part of it.

What is perhaps new here is the attempt to integrate three literatures—the literature on abilities, in general; the literature on giftedness, in particular; and the rather distinct literature on expertise. The abilities and expertise literatures, especially, may be talking, at some level, about the same thing, rather than about distinct constructs or even, as some believe, constructs in opposition (see Ericsson, 1996).

The Relation of Abilities to Expertise

Traditionally, abilities are typically seen either as (a) precursors to expertise (see essays in Chi, Glaser & Farr, 1988) or (b) as opposed to expertise (Fiedler & Link, 1994) as causes of behavior. Sometimes, abilities are held up (c) as causes of developing expertise in contrast to deliberate practice (see also Ericsson, Krampe & Tesch-Romer, 1993, who argue for the importance of the latter as opposed to the former). Here, abilities are seen as themselves a form of developing expertise. An important educational implication of this view is that abilities, like expertise, can be developed. It therefore follows that giftedness can be developed.

When we test for abilities in order to identify gifted individuals, we are as much testing a form of expertise as we are when we test for accomplishments of various kinds, whether academic achievement, skill in playing chess, skill in solving physics problems, or whatever. What differs is the kind of expertise we measure, and more importantly, our conceptualization of what we measure. The difference in conceptualization comes about in part because we happen to view one kind of accomplishment (ability-test scores) as predicting another kind of accomplishment (achievement test scores, grades in school, or other indices of accomplishment). But according to the present view, this conceptualization is one of practical convenience, not of psychological reality.

Consider, as an example, solving problems on a verbal-analogies test or a test of mathematical problem solving. Solving such problems requires expertise, just as does any other kind of problem solving. Moreover, the components of information processing on many of these kinds of tasks are highly overlapping (Sternberg, 1983, 1985; Sternberg & Gardner, 1983).

According to this view, although ability tests may have temporal priority relative to various criteria in their administration (i.e. ability tests are administered first, and later, criterion indices of performance, such as grades or achievement test scores, are collected), they have no psychological priority. All of the various kinds of assessments are of the same kind psychologically. What distinguishes ability tests from the other kinds of assessments is how the ability tests are used (usually, predictively), rather than what they measure. There is no qualitative distinction among the various kinds of assessments. When we believe that ability tests and achievement tests give us distinct insights into giftedness, we are wrong: Both kinds of tests measure largely the same construct, which is why ability and achievement tests correlate about as highly with each other as they do among themselves.

For example, verbal-analogies tests and mathematical problem-solving tests could be, and often are, used as predictors; but they could as well be predicted by other kinds of measures, such as school performance or other measures of achievement. Indeed, the murkiness of the distinction between abilities and achievement is shown by the fact that some of the types of items that appear as ability-test items (e.g. vocabulary) on one measure appear as achievement test items on another measure. For example, the *Kaufman Assessment Battery for Children* (Kaufman & Kaufman, 1983) labels as measuring achievement verbal items that the *Stanford-Binet Intelligence Scale* (Thorndike, Hagen & Sattler, 1986) labels as measuring abilities.

If we look at current theories of intelligence, we find they make a similar point. Conventional ability and achievement tests both measure largely analytical abilities and their outcomes according to Sternberg's (1985) theory and measure largely linguistic and logical-mathematical abilities and their outcomes according to Gardner's (1983) theory. Moreover, the kinds of outcomes they measure are limited by their paper-and-pencil format and by the narrow range of skills tested. Thus, these tests can identify only a narrow band of those who are gifted.

Although individual and group tests of intelligence are administered differently, they measure roughly the same skills and have underlying them the same theories of intelligence (Sternberg, 1990; Gustafsson & Undheim, 1996; Daniel, 1997). Thus, in this discussion, individual and group tests are considered jointly.

The literatures on abilities and expertise have grown up largely separately, with studies of ability testing dating back to work done by Binet and his colleagues (Binet & Simon, 1916) on children and studies of expertise dating back to work of DeGroot (1965) done on adults. The giftedness literature has grown up in tandem with the abilities literature, dating back at least

to the Terman studies (e.g. Terman, 1925). But the suggestion here is that the giftedness literature needs also to be aligned with the expertise literature, because in adulthood, expertise is what giftedness is really about. At any age, gifted individuals have always developed some kind of extraordinary expertise. In school, expertise in taking tests may be sufficient to label one as gifted. In adulthood, it almost never is. Little wonder, then, that there is only very partial overlap between who is identified as gifted in childhood versus adulthood.

A Model of Individuals' Abilities and Achievements

The model of abilities driving the present work is the triarchic theory of human intelligence and intellectual giftedness (Sternberg, 1984, 1985, 1988, 1996d). According to this theory, abilities take the form of various information processes operating upon mental representations at varying levels of experience in order to adapt to, shape, and select environments (see Sternberg, 1985, for more details). It is important to note, however, that one could accept the model of abilities as forms of developing expertise, in general, without accepting the triarchic theory, in particular. Where does the developing-expertise model lead us, both in terms of educational opportunities and in terms of societal outcomes for gifted individuals? One place it leads is to a view of abilities as flexible rather than fixed:

There is now substantial evidence that abilities are modifiable, at least in some degree (see Feuerstein, 1980; Nickerson, Perkins & Smith, 1985; Herrnstein, Nickerson, deSanchez & Swets, 1986; Nickerson, 1986; Sternberg, 1988, 1994a, 1996d; Ramey, 1994; Perkins, 1995; Sternberg & Spear-Swerling, 1996; Perkins & Grotzer, 1997). If they are, then we should probably hesitate to assign any individual to a fixed group, whether it be a 'cognitive elite' (Herrnstein & Murray, 1994) or any other. The best evidence, of course, is in favor of both genetic and environmental origins of intelligence, interacting in ways that are not, as yet, fully known (see Sternberg & Grigorenko, 1997). There is no one set of 'gifted individuals', on this view. People can become gifted by developing various kinds of expertise. But the kind of expertise they will need to be identified as gifted will change throughout their life span.

The Developing-Expertise Model of Abilities

There are views of abilities and their implications that diverge substantially from fixed-abilities views such as those advocated and reviewed by Herrnstein and Murray (1994). For example, Snow (1979, 1980, 1996; Snow & Lohman, 1984) presented a much more flexible view of human abilities, according to which abilities are not limited to the cognitive domain, and also overlap with aptitudes and achievements. Ceci

(Ceci, Nightingale & Baker, 1992; Ceci & Roazzi, 1994; Ceci, 1996) has proposed a bioecological model of abilities that shares some features with the view presented here, particularly with regard to the relevance of domains. Perkins (1995) and Renzulli (1986) have also proposed compatible views. The model presented here perhaps extends some of these views in its emphasis on abilities and hence gifted levels of abilities as representing developing forms of expertise.

Abilities as developing expertise. This alternative model sees scores on ability tests as measuring a form of developing expertise, much as would be represented by chess performance (Chase & Simon, 1973), physics performance (Chi, Glaser & Rees, 1982; Larkin, McDermott, Simon & Simon, 1980), radiology performance (Lesgold, 1984), teaching performance (Shulman, 1987; Livingston & Borko, 1990; Sabers, Cushing & Berliner, 1991; Sternberg & Horvath, 1995), or any of a number of other kinds of expertise (Bereiter & Scardamalia, 1993).

One comes to be an expert in the skills needed for success on ability tests in much the same ways one becomes an expert in doing anything else—through a combination of genetic endowment and experience. A gifted individual is thus someone who has developed and is continuing to develop a set of societally valued skills, using both the genetic and environmental resources available to him or her. Of course, people with more privileges and opportunities in their environment are at an advantage in developing expertise.

Expertise involves the acquisition, storage, and utilization of at least two kinds of knowledge: explicit knowledge of a domain and implicit or tacit knowledge of a field (see Sternberg et al., 1995), where *domain* refers to a knowledge base and *field* to the social organization of that knowledge base (Csikszentmihalyi, 1988, 1996). Explicit knowledge is the kind most frequently studied in the literature on expertise (see Chi, Glaser & Farr, 1988; Ericsson & Smith, 1991). It is knowledge of the facts, formulas, principles, and major ideas of a domain of inquiry. Implicit or tacit knowledge of a field is the knowledge one needs to know to attain success in a field that usually isn't talked about or even put into verbal form. For example, in psychology, Freud's theory of depression would constitute explicit knowledge, whereas how to get a grant would constitute informal or tacit knowledge. Giftedness in a domain (subject matter) may involve just explicit knowledge, but giftedness in a field (the social organization of subject matter) always involves tacit knowledge about the field as well (see Csikszentmihalyi, 1996). Children develop a variety of different kinds of expertise. Society places demands when it expects specialization, but individuals can and do make their own decisions. Virtually any kind of domain-related expertise can be incorporated into the purview of the school.

When abilities are measured, both explicit and implicit elements are involved. A verbal-analogies test, for example, measures explicit knowledge of vocabulary and reasoning with this knowledge, but the test also measures implicit knowledge of how to take a test. For example, one has to work within certain time constraints, choose the best of what often are all imprecise options, and so on. The connection between explicit and implicit knowledge can be fluid, as shown by the fact that courses are sometimes constructed to make implicit knowledge, explicit (see e.g. The Practical Intelligence for School Program of Williams et al., 1996). Gifted individuals may have tremendous domain knowledge but fail to utilize it effectively if they do not have the implicit knowledge of a field (which includes the workings of a school) that enables them best to exploit their domain-based knowledge.

Characteristics of expertise. The characteristics of experts as reflected in performance on ability tests are similar to the characteristics of experts of any kind (see Chi, Glaser & Farr, 1988; Sternberg, 1996a). Expertise is a prototypically rather than classically defined concept (Sternberg, 1994a). Operationally, by *expertise*, I refer, in a given domain, to a prototype of people's: (a) having large, rich schemas (organized networks of concepts) containing a great deal of declarative knowledge about a given domain, in the present case, the domains sampled by ability tests; (b) having well-organized, highly interconnected (mutually accessible) units of knowledge about test content stored in schemas; (c) spending proportionately more time determining how to represent test problems than they do in search for and in executing a problem strategy (Larkin, McDermott, Simon & Simon, 1980); (d) developing sophisticated representations of test problems, based on structural similarities among problems; (e) working forward from given information to implement strategies for finding unknowns in the test problems; (f) generally choosing a strategy based on elaborate schemas for problem strategies; (g) having schemas containing a great deal of procedural knowledge about problem strategies relevant in the test-taking domain; (h) having automatized many sequences of steps within problem strategies; (i) showing highly efficient problem solving; when time constraints are imposed, they solve problems more quickly than do novices; (j) accurately predicting the difficulty of solving particular test problems; (k) carefully monitoring their own problem-solving strategies and processes; and (l) showing high accuracy in reaching appropriate solutions to test problems. Rather than defining gifted individuals as simply high in some kind of abstract ability, the proposed notion defines them in terms of very high levels of these particular aspects of expertise.

Ability tests, achievement tests, school grades, and measures of job performance all reflect overlapping kinds of expertise in these kinds of skills. To do well in school or on the job requires a kind of expertise; but to do well on a test also requires a kind of expertise. Of course, part of this expertise is the kind of test-wiseness that has been studied by Millman, Bishop & Ebel (1965) and others (see Bond & Harman, 1994); but there is much more to test-taking expertise than test-wiseness.

Return, for a moment, to Mary and Ellen. Mary and Ellen test differently on an IQ test. This difference in test scores may reflect a number of factors: differential test wiseness, differential test anxiety, differential enculturation into a culture that values IQ tests, differential mood and alertness on the day of testing, differential readiness to take the test, and most importantly, differential developing expertise in the skills that the test measures. Only the last of these differences reflects a true difference in who properly should be identified as gifted.

People who are more expert in taking IQ-related tests have a set of skills that is valuable not only in taking these tests, but in other aspects of Western life as well. Taking a test, say, of verbal or figural analogies, or of mathematical problem solving, typically requires skills such as (a) puzzling out what someone else (here, a test constructor) wants, (b) command of English vocabulary, (c) reading comprehension, (d) allocation of limited time, (e) sustained concentration, (f) abstract reasoning, (g) quick thinking, (h) symbol manipulation, and (i) suppression of anxiety and other emotions that can interfere with test performance, among other things.

These skills are also part of what is required for successful performance in school and in many kinds of job performance. Thus, an expert test-taker is also likely to have skills that will be involved in other kinds of expertise as well, such as expertise in getting high grades in school. These kinds of expertise also matter in the work of adults, but perhaps less than in the schoolhouse. It is for this reason, again, that the child expert often does not become the adult expert.

It is, in my opinion, not correct to argue that traditional intelligence tests measure little or nothing of interest. Moreover, the tests do not all measure exactly the same constructs, although they measure related constructs. Clearly, these tests tap some range of cognitive abilities. At the same time, there are many important kinds of expertise that the tests do not measure (Gardner, 1983; Sternberg, 1985; Das, Naglieri & Kirby, 1994), for example, what Gardner (1983, 1993) would call musical, bodily-kinesthetic, interpersonal, and intrapersonal intelligences, and what I would call creative and practical intelligence (Sternberg, 1985, 1988, 1996d). These other kinds of expertise probably matter more in later life than in school. For example, an expert musician might not be identified as gifted in the school, but if he or she becomes an expert musician as an adult, will almost

certainly be identified as a gifted musician. The individual may be a wonderful dancer without the school's even knowing about it. Later in life, though, when this individual becomes a dancer, he or she will be identified as a gifted dancer.

Contrariwise, the individual who is an expert at solving given mathematics problems but who cannot recognize what problems are worth solving may be identified as gifted during youth, but is less likely to be identified as a gifted mathematician upon reaching adulthood. Similarly, the history student who can memorize all the facts in the middle-school history text may appear to be gifted at the middle-school level, but without accompanying analytical and creative skills, is unlikely to be identified as a gifted historian later on. The kinds of developing expertise required to be identified as gifted simply change. By using the single word 'gifted', we confuse the type (the word) with the token (the concept).

To the extent that the expertise required for one kind of performance overlaps with the expertise required for another kind of performance, there will be a correlation between performances. The construct measured by the ability tests is not a 'cause' of school or job expertise; it is itself an expertise that overlaps with school or job expertise. On the overlapping-expertise view, the traditional notion of test scores as somehow causal is based upon a confounding of correlation with causation. Differences in test scores, academic performance, and job performance are all effects—of differential levels of expertise.

Acquisition of expertise. The literature on the acquisition of expertise, in general, is reviewed in Ericsson (1996). How does this development relate to abilities, and to gifted levels of abilities, in particular?

Individuals gain the expertise to do well on ability tests in much the same way they gain any other kind of expertise—through the interaction of whatever genetic dispositions they bring to bear with experience via the environment. Tests measure *developing* expertise because the experiential processes are ongoing. In particular, individuals (a) receive direct instruction in how to solve test-like problems, usually through schooling; (b) engage in actual solving of such problems, usually in academic contexts; (c) engage in role modeling (watching others, such as teachers or other students, solve test-like problems), (d) think about such problems, sometimes mentally simulating what they might do when confronting such problems; and (e) receive rewards for successful solution of such problems, thereby reinforcing such behavior.

It is interesting to compare the acquisition of test-taking expertise with the acquisition of the kinds of expertise that will matter in adulthood, because the processes by which a person becomes gifted seem to be somewhat different.

First, once direct instruction in school is over (point (a) above), direct instruction in one's life is likely to diminish or vanish. What it takes to be a gifted expert artist, musician, scientist, or teacher as an adult goes well beyond the instruction one receives during the period of schooling. One needs to acquire a kind of productive expertise that goes beyond the reproductive expertise that may earn one identification as gifted in one's youth.

Second, the kinds of problem solving one does in adulthood often differs from the kinds of problem solving done in childhood (point (b) above). In particular, in adulthood the problems are not given to one in quite the same way as they are during childhood. In school, problems are presented in textbooks, on tests, in the classroom, and so on. In adulthood, the problems solved by teachers in the classroom, by physicists in the laboratory, by composers writing sonatas, or by entrepreneurs trying to start up a business are not handed to them directly. Often the hardest part of dealing with problems in adulthood is recognizing that they exist, and then, what their nature is. Adult giftedness requires sophisticated problem-recognition and problem-definition skills.

Third, although role modeling continues through adulthood, the time of life when perfect or near-perfect imitation of a role will lead to identification as gifted has ended (point (c) above). Indeed, a professional who does no more than perfectly imitate a mentor is likely to be viewed as nothing more than some kind of unimaginative clone, and certainly not as gifted.

Fourth, the mental simulations needed for success differ in school and in the world of work (point (d) above). In school, simulation often means reconstructing an algorithm one has learned from a teacher or a textbook (such as to solve a difficult mathematics problem or to write a term paper that basically follows guidelines a teacher has set out). In the world of work, simulation often means constructing one's own algorithms and heuristics and trying them out mentally before actually implementing them.

Fifth, the kind of feedback one typically receives in the world of work is quite different from that typically received in school (point (e) above). In school, most feedback is immediate and direct, often taking the form of a letter grade or other evaluation of a piece of work that has been turned in. In the world of work, feedback is much more sporadic, often indirect, and often extremely ambiguous. One needs much more sophisticated skills for monitoring and evaluating one's performance (Sternberg, 1985). Gifted individuals are able to take advantage of feedback to tune already exceedingly high levels of performance.

In sum, the processes that lead to successful development of high and indeed gifted levels of expertise differ between the worlds of school and of work. Little wonder that different people often end up being identified as gifted in the two different worlds.

Individual differences in expertise. Of course, there may be substantial differences in underlying capacities. The problem, as recognized by Vygotsky (1978), as well as many others, is that we do not know how directly to measure these capacities. Measures of the zone of proximal development (e.g. Brown & French, 1979; Feuerstein, 1979; Brown & Ferrara, 1985; Grigorenko & Sternberg, 1998) seem to assess something other than conventional psychometric g, but it has yet to be shown that what it is they do measure is the difference between developing ability and latent capacity.

Individual differences in expertise may stem from differences in rate of learning and ultimate asymptote, which are in turn likely to depend upon one's ability to learn from the way material is taught (see Sternberg, Ferrari, Clinkenbeard & Grigorenko, 1996; Sternberg, Torff & Grigorenko, 1998a, 1998b; Sternberg, Grigorenko, Ferrari & Clinkenbeard, 1999). But material is 'taught' in very different ways in the schools of one's youth versus the school of life. Our work on tacit knowledge finding little or no correlation between academic and practical intelligence (Sternberg, Wagner, Williams & Horvath, 1995) suggests that the people who learn well in school are not necessarily those who learn well in life. So again, who becomes gifted can depend a great deal on stage of life.

There is no compelling evidence that individual differences can be wiped out by the kind of 'deliberate practice' studied by Ericsson and his colleagues (e.g. Ericsson & Smith, 1991; Ericsson, Krampe & Tesch-Romer, 1993; Ericsson & Charness, 1994). Ericsson's work shows a correlation between deliberate practice and expertise; it does not show a causal relation, any more than the traditional work on abilities shows causal relations between measured abilities and expertise. A correlational demonstration is an important one; it is not the same as a causal one. Thus, the concept of giftedness will always be with us. No one has shown a way to wipe out individual differences.

The fact that experts have tended to show more deliberate practice than novices may itself reflect an ability difference (Sternberg, 1996b). Meeting with success, those with more ability may practice more; meeting with lesser success, those with lesser ability may give up. Or both deliberate practice and ability may themselves be reflective of some other factor, such as parental encouragement, which could lead both to the nurturing of an ability and to deliberate practice. Indeed, deliberate practice and expertise may interact bidirectionally, so that deliberate practice leads to expertise, and the satisfaction brought by expertise leads to more deliberate practice. The point is that a variety of mechanisms might underlie a correlational relationship. It seems unquestionable that deliberate practice plays a role in the development of gifted levels of expertise. But it also seems extremely likely that its role is as a necessary rather than sufficient condition.

Deliberate practice may play a somewhat lesser role in creative giftedness than in other kinds of giftedness (Sternberg, 1996b). We might argue over whether someone who practices memorization techniques can become a mnemonist. Probably, the individual can become a mnemonist at least within certain content domains (Ericsson, Chase & Faloon, 1980). Ericsson and his colleagues, for example, were able to work with a college student so that he attained truly impressive expertise in memorizing strings of digits, but his memorization of strings of letters was ordinary. The reason was that he could use the mnemonic of running times to memorize digits but not letters. He may have been an expert, but he was a limited expert and certainly not a gifted one.

Even limited practice effects do not seem to apply quite so well in other domains. It seems less plausible that someone who practices composing a lot will become a Mozart. Of course, one could always conveniently maintain that we have not proven that someone could not become a Mozart with sufficient deliberate practice. Null hypotheses do not lend themselves to proof. But in the real world, with many millions having practiced music very hard, the evidence to date appears discouraging.

Other factors seem far more important in the development of the kind of giftedness that is represented by creative expertise, in whatever field. These factors include pursuing paths of inquiry that others ignore or dread, taking intellectual risks, persevering in the face of obstacles, and so on (Sternberg & Lubart, 1995, 1996).

Relations Among Various Kinds of Expertise and Giftedness

There are various measures that correlate with IQ that do not, on their face, appear to be measures of achievement. But they are measures of forms of developing expertise. For example, the inspection-time task used by Nettelbeck (1987; Nettelbeck & Lally, 1976) to measure intelligence or the choice reaction-time task of Jensen (1982) both correlate with psychometric g. However, performances on both tasks reflect a form of developing expertise, in one case, of perceptual discriminations, in the other case, of quick responses to flashing lights or other stimuli. Of course, individuals may differ in the slopes and asymptotes of their acquisition functions.

An examination of the content of tests of intelligence and related abilities reveals that IQ-like tests measure achievement that individuals should have accomplished several years back. Tests such as vocabulary, reading comprehension, verbal analogies, arithmetic problem solving, and the like are all, in part, tests of achievement. Even abstract-reasoning tests measure achievement in dealing with geometric symbols, skills taught in Western schools (Laboratory of Comparative Human Cognition, 1982). One might as well use

academic performance to predict ability-test scores. The problem with regard to the traditional model is not in its statement of a correlation between ability tests and other forms of achievement, but in its proposal of a causal relation whereby the tests reflect a construct that is somehow causal of, rather than merely temporally antecedent to, later success. Thus, as stated earlier, ability and achievement tests do not provide anything approaching independent assessments of giftedness.

Even psychobiological measures (see, e.g. Vernon, 1990) are in no sense 'pure' ability measures, because we know that just as biological processes affect cognitive processes, so do cognitive processes affect biological ones. Learning, for example, leads to synaptic growth (Thompson, 1985; Kandel, 1991). Thus, biological changes may themselves reflect, in part, developing expertise. Thus, 'better biology' does not always lead to giftedness. Giftedness may lead to 'better biology'.

If we viewed tested abilities as forms of what is represented by the term *developing expertise*, then there would be no argument with the use of the term *abilities*. The problem is that this term is usually used in another way—to express a construct that is psychologically prior to other forms of expertise. Such abilities may well exist, but we can assess them only through tests that measure developing forms of expertise expressed in a cultural context. There is no a priori test of who is gifted, only a posteriori ones.

In sum, the present argument differs from the conventional one in rejecting the psychological priority of abilities or of giftedness. Even those who believe that abilities are developing may view them as somehow prior to achievement; on the present view, both abilities and achievement—and hence, giftedness—are forms of developing expertise. None is psychologically prior, although there may be temporal priority in a protocol of assessment.

The Specifics of the Developing-Expertise Model

The specifics of the developing-expertise model are shown in Fig. 1. At the heart of the model is the notion of *developing expertise*—that individuals are constantly in a process of developing expertise when they work within a given domain. They may and do, of course, differ in rate and asymptote of development. The main constraint in achieving expertise is not some fixed prior level of capacity, but purposeful engagement involving direct instruction, active participation, role modeling, and reward.

Elements of the Model

The model of developing expertise has five key elements (although certainly they do not constitute an exhaustive list of elements in the development of expertise): metacognitive skills, learning skills, thinking skills, knowledge, and motivation. All of these

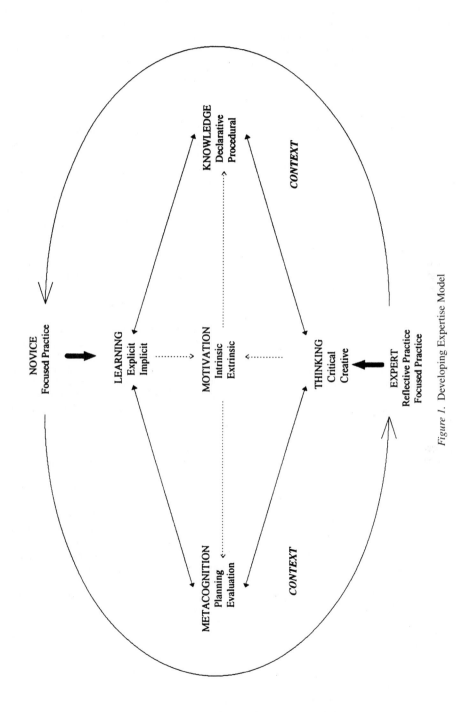

Figure 1. Developing Expertise Model

attributes have been associated in the past, individually or in various combinations, with giftedness (see Sternberg & Davidson, 1984). Although it is convenient to separate these five elements, they are fully interactive, as shown in the figure. They influence each other, both directly and indirectly. For example, learning leads to knowledge, but knowledge facilitates further learning.

1. Metacognitive skills. Metacognitive skills (or metacomponents—Sternberg, 1985) refer to people's understanding and control of their own cognition and are an important element of giftedness (Borkowski & Peck, 1986; Jackson & Butterfield, 1986). For example, such skills would encompass what an individual knows about writing papers or solving arithmetic word problems, both with regard to the steps that are involved and with regard to how these steps can be executed effectively. Seven metacognitive skills are particularly important: problem recognition, problem definition, problem representation, strategy formulation, resource allocation, monitoring of problem solving, and evaluation of problem solving (Sternberg, 1985, 1986). All of these skills are modifiable (Sternberg, 1986, 1988; Sternberg & Spear-Swerling, 1996).

2. Learning skills. Learning skills are also important elements of giftedness (Sternberg, 1984; Davidson, 1986; Feldhusen, 1986). Learning skills (knowledge-acquisition components) are essential to the model (Sternberg, 1985, 1986), although they are certainly not the only learning skills that individuals use. Learning skills are sometimes divided into explicit and implicit ones. Explicit learning is what occurs when we make an effort to learn; implicit learning is what occurs when we pick up information incidentally, without any systematic effort. Examples of learning skills are selective encoding, which involves distinguishing relevant from irrelevant information; selective combination, which involves putting together the relevant information; and selective comparison, which involves relating new information to information already stored in memory (Sternberg, 1985).

3. Thinking skills. Thinking skills are also essential to giftedness (Borkowski & Peck, 1986; Jackson & Butterfield, 1986; Stanley & Benbow, 1986; Sternberg, 1984). There are three main kinds of thinking skills (or performance components) that individuals need to master (Sternberg, 1985, 1986, 1994b). It is important to note that these are sets of, rather than individual, thinking skills. Critical (analytical) thinking skills include analyzing, critiquing, judging, evaluating, comparing and contrasting, and assessing. Creative thinking skills include creating, discovering, inventing, imagining, supposing, and hypothesizing. Practical thinking skills include applying, using, utilizing, and practicing (Sternberg, 1997). They are the first step in the translation of thought into real-world action.

4. Knowledge. Giftedness requires knowledge (Gruber, 1986). There are two main kinds of knowledge that are relevant in academic situations. Declarative knowledge is of facts, concepts, principles, laws, and the like. It is 'knowing that'. Procedural knowledge is of procedures and strategies. It is 'knowing how'. Of particular importance is procedural tacit knowledge, which involves knowing how the system functions in which one is operating (Sternberg, Wagner, Williams & Horvath, 1995).

5. Motivation.. Motivation is an important part of giftedness (Feldhusen, 1986; Haensly, Reynolds & Nash, 1986; Renzulli, 1986; Gardner, 1994). One can distinguish among several different kinds of motivation. A first kind of motivation is achievement motivation (McClelland, Atkinson, Clark & Lowell, 1976; McClelland, 1985). People who are high in achievement motivation seek moderate challenges and risks. They are attracted to tasks that are neither very easy nor very hard. They are strivers—constantly trying to better themselves and their accomplishments.

A second kind of motivation is competence (self-efficacy) motivation, which refers to persons' beliefs in their own ability to solve the problem at hand (Bandura, 1977, 1996). Experts need to develop a sense of their own efficacy to solve difficult tasks in their domain of expertise. This kind of self-efficacy can result both from intrinsic and extrinsic rewards (Amabile, 1996; Sternberg & Lubart, 1996). Of course, other kinds of motivation are important too. Indeed, motivation is perhaps the indispensable element needed for school success. Without it, the student never even tries to learn.

6. Context. Giftedness attains meaning from a context (Csikszentmihlayi & Robinson, 1986; Haensly, Reynolds & Nash, 1986; Tannenbaum, 1986). All of the elements discussed above are characteristics of the learner. Returning to the issues raised at the beginning of this document, a problem with conventional tests is that they assume that individuals operate in a more or less decontextualized environment. A test score is interpreted largely in terms of the individual's internal attributes. But a test measures much more, and the assumption of a fixed or uniform context across test-takers is not realistic. Contextual factors that can affect test performance include native language, emphasis of test on speedy performance, importance to the test taker of success on the test, and familiarity with the kinds of material on the test.

Interactions of Elements

The novice works toward expertise through deliberate practice. But this practice requires an interaction of all five of the key elements. At the center, driving the elements, is motivation. Without it, the elements remain inert. Eventually, one reaches a kind of expertise, at which one becomes a reflective practitioner of a certain set of skills. But expertise occurs at many levels. The expert first-year graduate or law student, for example, is still a far cry from the expert professional. People thus cycle through many times, on the way to successively higher levels of expertise. They do so through the elements in the figure.

Motivation drives metacognitive skills, which in turn activate learning and thinking skills, which then provide feedback to the metacognitive skills, enabling one's level of expertise to increase (see also Sternberg, 1985). The declarative and procedural knowledge acquired through the extension of the thinking and learning skills also results in these skills being used more effectively in the future.

All of these processes are affected by, and can in turn affect, the context in which they operate. For example, if a learning experience is in English but the learner has only limited English proficiency, his or her learning will be inferior to that of someone with more advanced English-language skills. Or if material is presented orally to someone who is a better visual learner, that individual's performance will be reduced.

Conclusion

The model proposed in this chapter is one of abilities, in general, and gifted levels of abilities, in particular, as forms of developing expertise. Individuals are viewed as novices capable of becoming experts in a variety of domains. A model of fixed individual differences, which essentially consigns some students to fixed levels of instruction based on supposedly largely fixed abilities, can be an obstacle to the acquisition of expertise. The key to developing expertise is purposeful and meaningful engagement in a set of tasks relevant to the development of expertise, something of which any individual is capable in some degree. For various reasons (including, perhaps, genetic as well as environmentally based differences), not all individuals will equally engage or engage equally effectively, and hence, individuals will not necessarily all reach the same ultimate level of expertise. But they should all be given the opportunity to reach new levels of competence and perhaps even giftedness well beyond what they, and in some cases, others may have thought were possible for them. The fact that Mary and Ellen have different IQs tells us something about differences in what they now do. It does not tell us anything fixed about what ultimately they will be able to do, and which, if either of them, will be identified as a gifted adult.

Author Notes

Preparation of this article was supported under the Javits Act Program (Grant No. R206R950001) as administered by the Office of Educational Research and Improvement, U.S. Department of Education. Grantees undertaking such projects are encouraged to express freely their professional judgment. This article, therefore, does not necessarily represent the position or policies of the Office of Educational Research and Improvement or the U. S. Department of Education, and no official endorsement should be inferred.

Requests for reprints should be sent to Robert J. Sternberg, Department of Psychology, Yale University, P. O. Box 208205, New Haven, CT 06520–8205

References

Amabile, T. M. (1996). *Creativity in context*. Boulder, CO: Westview.

Anastasi, A. & Urbina, S. (1997). *Psychological testing* (7th ed.). Upper Saddle River, NJ: Prentice-Hall.

Bamberger, J. (1986). Cognitive issues in the development of musically gifted children. In: R. J. Sternberg & J. E. Davidson (Eds), *Conceptions of Giftedness* (pp. 388–413). New York: Cambridge University Press.

Bandura, A. (1977). Self-efficacy: Toward a unifying theory of behavioral change. *Psychological Review*, **84**, 181–215.

Bandura, A. (1996). Self-efficacy: The exercise of control. New York: Freeman.

Bereiter, C. & Scardamalia, M. (1993). Surpassing ourselves: An inquiry into the nature and implications of expertise. Chicago: Open Court.

Binet, A. & Simon, T. (1916). The development of intelligence in children (E. S. Kite, trans.). Baltimore: Williams & Wilkins.

Bond, L. & Harman, A. E. (1994). Test-taking strategies. In: R. J. Sternberg (Ed.), *Encyclopedia of Human Intelligence* (Vol. 2, pp. 1073–1077). New York: Macmillan.

Borkowski, J. G. & Peck, V. A. (1986). Causes and consequences of metamemory in gifted children. In: R. J. Sternberg & J. E. Davidson (Eds), *Conceptions of Giftedness* (pp. 182–200). New York: Cambridge University Press.

Brown, A. L. & Ferrara, R. A. (1985). Diagnosing zones of proximal development. In: J. V. Wertsch (Ed.), *Culture, communication, and Cognition: Vygotskian Perspectives*. New York: Cambridge University Press.

Brown, A. L. & Frensch, L. A. (1979). The zone of potential development: Implications for intelligence testing in the year 2000. *Intelligence*, **3**, 255–277.

Ceci, S. J. (1996). *On intelligence: A bio-ecological treatise on intellectual development* (expanded ed.). Cambridge, MA: Harvard University Press.

Ceci, S. J., Nightingale, N. N. & Baker, J. G. (1992). The ecologies of intelligence: Challenges to traditional views. In: D. K. Detterman (Ed.), *Current Topics in Human Intelligence (Vol. 2). Is Mind Modular or Unitary?* (pp. 61–82). Norwood, NJ: Ablex.

Ceci, S. J. & Roazzi, A. (1994). The effects of context on cognition: Postcards from Brazil. In: R. J. Sternberg & R. K. Wagner (Eds), *Mind in Context: Interactionist Perspectives on Human Intelligence* (pp.74–101). New York: Cambridge University Press.

Chase, W. G. & Simon, H. A. (1973). The mind's eye in chess. In: W. G. Chase (Ed.), *Visual Information Processing* (pp. 215–281). New York: Academic Press.

Chi, M. T. H., Glaser, R. & Farr, M. (Eds) (1988). The nature of expertise. Hillsdale, NJ: Erlbaum.

Chi, M. T. H., Glaser, R. & Rees, E. (1982). Expertise in problem solving. In: R. J. Sternberg (Ed.), *Advances in the*

Psychology of Human Intelligence (Vol. 1, pp. 7–75). Hillsdale, NJ: Erlbaum.

Csikszentmihalyi, M. (1988). Society, culture, and person: A systems view of creativity. In: R. J. Sternberg (Ed.), *The Nature of Creativity* (pp. 325–339). New York: Cambridge University Press.

Csikszentmihalyi, M. (1996). *Creativity.* New York: Harper-Collins.

Csikszentmihalyi, M. & Robinson, R. E. (1986). Culture, time, and the development of talent. In: R. J. Sternberg & J. E. Davidson (Eds), *Conceptions of Giftedness* (pp. 264–284). New York: Cambridge University Press.

Daniel, M. H. (1997). Intelligence testing: Status and trends. *American Psychologist, 52,* 1038–1045.

Das, J. P., Naglieri, J. A. & Kirby, J. R. (1994). Assessment of cognitive processes. Needham Heights, MA: Allyn & Bacon.

Davidson, J. E. (1986). The role of insight in giftedness. In: R. J. Sternberg & J. E. Davidson (Eds), *Conceptions of Giftedness* (pp. 201–222). New York: Cambridge University Press.

Dawis, R. V. (1994). Occupations. In: R. J. Sternberg (Ed.), *Encyclopedia of Human Intelligence* (Vol. 2, pp. 781–785). New York: Macmillan.

DeGroot, A. D. (1965). *Thought and choice in chess.* The Hague: Mouton.

Ericsson, A. (Ed.). (1996). *The road to excellence.* Mahwah, NJ: Erlbaum.

Ericsson, K. A. & Charness, N. (1994). Expert performance: Its structure and acquisition. *American Psychologist, 49,* 725–747.

Ericsson, K. A., Chase, W. G. & Faloon, S. (1980). Acquisition of a memory skill. *Science, 208,* 1181–1182.

Ericsson, K. A., Krampe, R. T. & Tesch-Romer, C. (1993). The role of deliberate practice in the acquisition of expert performance. *Psychological Review, 100,* 363–406.

Ericsson, K. A. & Smith, J. (Eds) (1991). *Toward a general theory of expertise: Prospects and limits.* New York: Cambridge University Press.

Feldhusen, J. F. (1986). A conception of giftedness. In: R. J. Sternberg & J. E. Davidson (Eds), *Conceptions of Giftedness* (pp. 112–127). New York: Cambridge University Press.

Feuerstein, R. (1979). *The learning potential assessment device.* Baltimore, MD: University Park Press.

Feuerstein, R. (1980). *Instrumental enrichment: An intervention program for cognitive modifiability.* Baltimore: University Park Press.

Fiedler, F. E. & Link, T. G. (1994). Leader intelligence, interpersonal stress, and task performance. In: R. J. Sternberg & R. K. Wagner (Eds), *Mind in Context* (pp. 152–167). New York: Cambridge University Press.

Gardner, H. (1983). *Frames of mind.* New York: Free Press.

Gardner, H. (1993). *Multiple intelligences: The theory in practice.* New York: Basic Books.

Gardner, H. (1994). *Creating minds.* New York: Basic.

Gottfredson, L. S. (Ed.). (1986). The g factor in employment (special issue). *Journal of Vocational Behavior, 29,* 293–450.

Grigorenko, E. L. & Sternberg, R. J. (1998). Dynamic testing. *Psychological Bulletin, 124,* 75–111.

Gruber, H. E. (1986). The self-construction of the extraordinary. In: R. J. Sternberg & J. E. Davidson (Eds),

Conceptions of Giftedness (pp. 247–263). New York: Cambridge University Press.

Gustafsson, J. E. & Undheim, J. O. (1996). Individual differences in cognitive function. In: D. C. Berliner & R. C. Calfee (Eds), *Handbook of Educational Psychology* (pp. 186–242). New York: Macmillan.

Haensly, P., Reynolds, C. R. & Nash, W. R. (1986). Giftedness: Coalescence, context, conflict, and commitment. In: R. J. Sternberg & J. E. Davidson (Eds), *Conceptions of Giftedness* (pp. 128–148). New York: Cambridge University Press.

Herrnstein, R. J. & Murray, C. (1994). *The bell curve.* New York: Free Press.

Herrnstein, R. J., Nickerson, R. S., deSanchez, M. & Swets, J. A. (1986). Teaching thinking skills. *American Psychologist, 41,* 1279–1289.

Hunt, E. (1995). *Will we be smart enough? A cognitive analysis of the coming workforce.* New York: Russell Sage Foundation.

Hunter, J. E. (1986). Cognitive ability, cognitive aptitudes, job knowledge, and job performance. *Journal of Vocational Behavior, 29,* 340–362.

Jackson, N. E. & Butterfield, E. C. (1986). A conception of giftedness designed to promote research. In: R. J. Sternberg & J. E. Davidson (Eds), *Conceptions of Giftedness* (pp. 151–181). New York: Cambridge University Press.

Jensen, A. R. (1982). The chronometry of intelligence. In: R. J. Sternberg (Ed.), *Advances in the Psychology of Human Intelligence* (Vol. 1, pp. 255–310). Hillsdale, NJ: Erlbuam.

Kandel, E. (1991). Cellular mechanisms of learning and the biological basis of individuality. In: E. R. Kandel, J. H. Schwartz & T. M. Jessell (Eds), *Principles of Neural Science* (3rd ed.). New York: Elsevier.

Kaufman, A. S. & Kaufman, N. L. (1983). *Kaufman assessment battery for children: interpretive manual.* Circle Pines, MN: American Guidance Service.

Laboratory of Comparative Human Cognition. (1982). Culture and intelligence. In: R. J. Sternberg (Ed.), *Handbook of Human Intelligence* (pp. 642–719). New York: Cambridge University Press.

Larkin, J., McDermott, J., Simon, D. P. & Simon, H. A. (1980). Expert and novice performance in solving physics problems. *Science, 208,* 1335–1342.

Lesgold, A. M. (1984). Acquiring expertise. In: J. R. Anderson & S. M. Kosslyn (Eds), *Tutorials in Learning and Memory* (pp. 31–60). New York: Freeman.

Livingston, C. & Borko, H. (1990). High school mathematics review lessons: Expert-novice distinctions. *Journal of Research in Mathematics Education, 21,* 372–387.

McClelland, D. C. (1985). *Human motivation.* New York: Scott Foresman.

McClelland, D. C., Atkinson, J. W., Clark, R. A. & Lowell, E. L. (1976). *The achievement motive.* New York: Irvington.

Millman, J., Bishop, H. & Ebel, R. (1965). An analysis of test-wiseness. *Educational and Psychological Measurement, 25,* 707–726.

Nettelbeck, T. (1987). Inspection time and intelligence. In: P. A. Vernon (Ed.), *Speed of information processing and intelligence.* Norwood, NJ: Ablex.

Nettelbeck, T. & Lally, M. (1976). Inspection time and measured intelligence. *British Journal of Psychology, 67,* 17–22.

Nickerson, R. S. (1986). *Reflections on reasoning.* Hillsdale, NJ: Erlbaum.

Nickerson, R. S., Perkins, D. N. & Smith, E. E. (1985). *The teaching of thinking.* Hillsdale, NJ: Erlbaum.

Perkins, D. N. (1995). *Outsmarting IQ: The emerging science of learnable intelligence.* New York: Free Press.

Perkins, D. N. & Grotzer, T. A. (1997). Teaching intelligence and teaching for intelligence. *American Psychologist*, **52**, 1125–1133.

Ramey, C. T. (1994). Abecedarian project. In: R. J. Sternberg (Ed.), *Encyclopedia of Human Intelligence* (Vol. 1, pp. 1–3). New York: Macmillan.

Renzulli, J. S. (1986). The three ring conception of giftedness: A developmental model for creative productivity. In: R. J. Sternberg & J. E. Davidson (Eds), *Conceptions of Giftedness* (pp. 53–92). New York: Cambridge University Press.

Sabers, D. S., Cushing, K. S. & Berliner, D. C. (1991). Differences among teachers in a task characterized by simultaneity, multidimensionality, and immediacy. *American Educational Research Journal*, **28**, 63–88.

Shulman, L. S. (1987). Knowledge and teaching: Foundations of the new reform. *Harvard Educational Review*, **19**, 4–14.

Snow, R. E. (1979). Theory and method for research on aptitude processes. In: R. J. Sternberg & D. K. Detterman (Eds), *Human Intelligence: Perspectives on its Theory and Measurement* (pp. 105–137). Norwood, NJ: Ablex.

Snow, R. E. (1980). Aptitude processes. In: R. E. Snow, P.-A. Federico & W. E. Montague (Eds), *Aptitude, learning, and instruction: Cognitive process analyses of aptitude* (Vol. 1, pp. 27–63). Hillsdale, NJ: Erlbaum.

Snow, R. E. (1996). Abilities as aptitudes and achievements in learning situations. In: J. J. McArdle & R. W. Woodcock (Eds), *Human Cognitive Abilities in Theory and Practice.* Mahwah, NJ: Erlbaum. .

Snow, R. E. & Lohman, D. F. (1984). Toward a theory of cognitive aptitude for learning from instruction. *Journal of Educational Psychology*, **76**, 347–376.

Stanley, J. C. & Benbow, C. P. (1986). Youths who reason exceptionally well mathematically. In: R. J. Sternberg & J. E. Davidson (Eds), *Conceptions of Giftedness* (pp. 361–387). New York: Cambridge University Press.

Sternberg, R. J. (Ed.). (1982). *Handbook of human intelligence.* New York: Cambridge University Press.

Sternberg, R. J. (1983). Components of human intelligence. *Cognition*, **15**, 1–48.

Sternberg, R. J. (1984). Toward a triarchic theory of human intelligence. *Behavioral and Brain Sciences*, **7**, 269–287.

Sternberg, R. J. (1985). *Beyond IQ: A triarchic theory of human intelligence.* New York: Cambridge University Press.

Sternberg, R. J. (1986). *Intelligence applied.* Orlando, FL: Harcourt Brace College Publishers.

Sternberg, R. J. (1988). *The triarchic mind: A new theory of human intelligence.* New York: Viking-Penguin.

Sternberg, R. J. (1990). *Metaphors of mind: Conceptions of the nature of intelligence.* New York: Cambridge University Press.

Sternberg, R. J. (1994a). Cognitive conceptions of expertise. *International Journal of Expert Systems: Research and Application*, **7**, 1–12.

Sternberg, R. J. (1994b). Diversifying instruction and assessment. *The Educational Forum*, **59**, 47–53.

Sternberg, R. J. (1995). For whom the bell curve tolls: A review of The Bell Curve. *Psychological Science*, **6**, 257–261.

Sternberg, R. J. (1996a). *Cognitive psychology.* Orlando, FL: Harcourt Brace College Publishers.

Sternberg, R. J. (1996b). Costs of expertise. In: K. A. Ericsson (Ed.), *The Road to Excellence* (pp. 347–354). Mahwah, NJ: Erlbaum.

Sternberg, R. J. (1996c). Myths, countermyths, and truths about intelligence. *Educational Researcher*, **25**, 11–16.

Sternberg, R. J. (1996d). *Successful intelligence.* New York: Simon & Schuster.

Sternberg, R. J. (1996e). What should we ask about intelligence? *American Scholar*, **Spring**, 205–217.

Sternberg, R. J. (1997). *Thinking styles.* New York: Cambridge University Press.

Sternberg, R. J. (1998). Abilities are forms of developing expertise. *Educational Researcher*, **27**, 11–20.

Sternberg, R. J. & Davidson, J. E. (Eds) (1986). *Conceptions of giftedness.* New York: Cambridge University Press.

Sternberg, R. J., Ferrari, M., Clinkenbeard, P. & Grigorenko, E. L. (1996). Identification, instruction, and assessment of gifted children: A construct validation of a triarchic model. *Gifted Child Quarterly*, **40**, 129–137.

Sternberg, R. J. & Gardner, M. K. (1983). Unities in inductive reasoning. *Journal of Experimental Psychology: General*, **112**, 80–116.

Sternberg, R. J. & Grigorenko, E. L. (Eds) (1997). *Intelligence, heredity, and environment.* New York: Cambridge University Press.

Sternberg, R. J., Grigorenko, E. L., Ferrari, M. & Clinkenbeard, P. (1999). A triarchic analysis of an aptitude interaction. *European Journal of Psychological Assessment*, **15**, 1–11.

Sternberg, R. J. & Horvath, J. A. (1995). A prototype view of expert teaching. *Educational Researcher*, 24, 9–17.

Sternberg, R. J. & Lubart, T. I. (1995). *Defying the crowd: Cultivating creativity in a culture of conformity.* New York: Free Press.

Sternberg, R. J. & Lubart, T. I. (1996). Investing in creativity. *American Psychologist*, **51**, 677–688.

Sternberg, R. J. & Spear-Swerling, L. (1996). *Teaching for thinking.* Washington, DC: APA Books.

Sternberg, R. J., Torff, B. & Grigorenko, E. L. (1998a). Teaching for successful intelligence raises school achievement. *Phi Delta Kappan*, **79**, 667–669.

Sternberg, R. J., Torff, B. & Grigorenko, E. L. (1998b). Teaching triarchically improves school achievement. *Journal of Educational Psychology*, **90**, 374–384.

Sternberg, R. J., Wagner, R. K., Williams, W. M. & Horvath, J. (1995). Testing common sense. *American Psychologist*, **50**, 912–927.

Tannenbaum, A. J. (1986). Giftedness: A psychosocial approach. In: R. J. Sternberg & J. E. Davidson (Eds), *Conceptions of Giftedness* (pp. 53–92). New York: Cambridge University Press.

Terman, L. M. (1925). *Genetic studies of genius: Mental and physical traits of a thousand gifted children* (Vol. 1). Stanford, CA: Stanford University Press.

Thompson, R. F. (1985). *The brain: An introduction to neuroscience.* New York: Freeman.

Thorndike, R. L., Hagen, E. P. & Sattler, J. M. (1986). *Technical manual for the Stanford-Binet Intelligence Scale: Fourth edition.* Chicago: Riverside.

Vernon, P. A. (1990). The use of biological measures to estimate behavioral intelligence. *Educational Psychologist*, **25**, 293–304.

Vygotsky, L. S. (1978). *Mind in society: The development of higher psychological processes*. Cambridge, MA: Harvard University Press.

Wechsler, D. (1958). *The measurement and appraisal of adult intelligence* (5th ed.). Baltimore, MD: Williams & Wilkins.

Wigdor, A. K. & Garner, W. R. (1982). *Ability testing: Uses, consequences, and controversies: Part 1: Report of the Committee*. Washington, D.C.: National Academy Press.

Williams, W. M., Blythe, T., White, N., Li, J., Sternberg, R. J. &Gardner, H. I. (1996). *Practical intelligence for school: A handbook for teachers of grades 5–8*. New York: HarperCollins.

Understanding the Complex Choreography of Talent Development Through DMGT-Based Analysis

Françoys Gagné

Université du Québec à Montréal, Montreal, Canada

Introduction

In the first edition of this handbook (Gagné, 1993), I addressed two basic issues in the field of gifted education: (1) How should we define the key concepts of giftedness and talent? (2) How large is the population of gifted and talented individuals? As a response to the first question, I introduced my Differentiated Model of Giftedness and Talent (DMGT), whose six components (gifts, talents, intrapersonal catalysts, environmental catalysts, chance as well as learning and practising) cover all the variables relevant to the analysis of talent development. Concerning the prevalence problem, I proposed a generous threshold, namely the top 15% on any ability measure; to that minimum threshold was added a system of four progressively more selective levels, based on the first four standard deviations of the normal curve. Since the publication of the first edition of the *International Handbook*, the DMGT has undergone no major transformations. The only substantial change has involved the prevalence issue. Not only did I adopt a slightly more selective threshold (10%), but also I proposed a 5-level system of categories based on the metric system (Gagné, 1998). Recently, I tried to anchor more solidly the differentiated nature of gifts and talents, by explaining in more detail what was meant by the concepts of natural abilities (NAT) and systematically developed ones (SYSDEV). The operationalization of the NAT vs. SYSDEV dichotomy, as well as their relationship to the concepts of giftedness and talent took the form of a set of 22 logically interconnected statements, each accompanied by detailed comments (Gagné, 1999c). That text was discussed by five colleagues (Borland, 1999; Detterman & Ruthsatz, 1999; Feldman, 1999; Hany, 1999; Robinson, 1999); a rejoinder (Gagné, 1999a) completed that special issue of the *Journal for the Education of the Gifted*.

For this second edition of the *International Handbook*, I have chosen not to write a strict update of the 1993 chapter, but to discuss instead some practical uses for this model of talent development. My main purpose will be to describe the DMGT's usefulness as an analytical tool, what will be called *DMGT-based analysis*. It describes the way this model can serve to examine in a very systematic way various types of data related to the process of talent development: journal articles, research reports, lists of variables, biographical information, interview data, and so forth. It is my belief that the DMGT can be a valuable framework to classify information into appropriate causal categories. Thanks to that classification, it can help better understand the dynamic interplay between the five causal factors during that long period from the time individuals decide to systematically develop a set of skills in a particular field of human activity until they achieve some level of excellence within that field. I intend to remain at a molar level, that of the major events that mark the developmental process, and not address day-to-day interactions. But, before going any further, it might be useful to recall briefly, for those still unfamiliar with the DMGT, the basic structure of that developmental model.

Overview of the DMGT

The Differentiated Model of Giftedness and Talent proposes a clear-cut distinction between the concepts of giftedness and talent. The term 'giftedness' designates the possession and use of untrained and spontaneously expressed natural abilities (called aptitudes or gifts) in at least one ability domain, to a degree that places an individual among the top 10% of age peers. By contrast, the term 'talent' designates the superior mastery of systematically developed abilities (or skills) and knowledge in at least one field of human activity, to a degree that places an individual within the top 10% of age peers who are (or have been) active in that field.

Gifts (G)

The DMGT proposes four aptitude domains (see Fig. 1): intellectual, creative, socioaffective, and sensor-

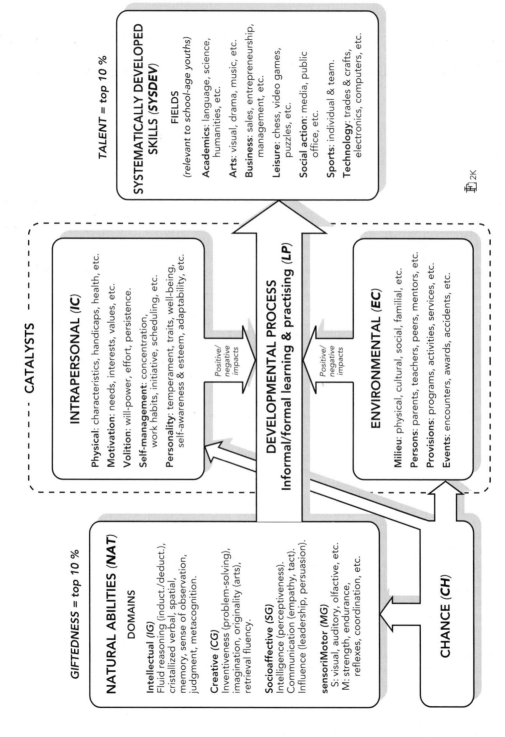

Figure 1. Gagné's differentiated model of giftedness and talent (DMGT.UK.2K)

imotor. These natural abilities, whose development and level of expression is partially controlled by the individual's genetic endowment, can be observed in every task children are confronted with in the course of their schooling: for instance, the intellectual abilities needed to learn to read, speak a foreign language, or understand new mathematical concepts, the creative abilities needed to solve different kinds of problems and produce original work in science, literature and art, the physical abilities involved in sport, music or woodwork, or the social abilities that children use in their daily interactions with classmates, teachers, and parents. High aptitudes or gifts can be observed more easily and directly in young children because environmental influences and systematic learning have exerted their moderating influence in a limited way only. However, they still show themselves in older children and even in adults through the facility and speed with which individuals acquire new skills in any given field of human activity. The easier or faster the learning process, the greater the natural abilities. It is these high natural abilities that some laypersons call 'talent' or, more appropriately, 'natural talent'.

Talents (T)

As defined in the DMGT, talents progressively emerge from the transformation of these high aptitudes into the well-trained and systematically developed skills characteristic of a particular field of human activity or performance. These fields can be extremely diverse. Figure 1 shows some of the many talent fields relevant to school-aged youths. A given natural ability can express itself in many different ways, depending on the field of activity adopted by the individual. For example, dexterity, as a natural physical ability, can be modeled into the specific manual skills of a pianist, a painter, or a video-game player. Similarly, intelligence as a natural ability can be modeled into the scientific reasoning of a chemist, the game analysis of a chess player, or the strategic planning of an athlete.

Talent development (LP)

In this model, natural abilities or aptitudes act as the 'raw materials' or constituent elements of talents. It follows from this relationship that talent necessarily implies the presence of well above average natural abilities; one cannot be talented without first being gifted. The reverse is not true, however. It is possible for well above average natural abilities to remain simply as gifts and not be translated into talents, as witnessed by the well-known phenomenon of academic underachievement among intellectually gifted children. The process of talent development manifests itself when the child or adolescent engages in systematic *learning and practising* (LP); that process can be either formal (e.g. within schools, conservatories, sports leagues or teams) or informal, that is self-taught. The

higher the level of talent sought, the more intensive and long-term these activities will be.

Catalysts (IC and EC)

This process is facilitated (or hindered) by the action of two types of catalysts; *intrapersonal* (IC) and *environmental* (EC). The intrapersonal catalysts are subdivided into physical and psychological factors, all of them under the partial influence of the genetic endowment. Among the psychological catalysts, motivation and volition play a crucial role in initiating the process of talent development, guiding it and sustaining it through obstacles, boredom, and occasional failure. Self-management gives structure and efficiency to the talent development process, and to other daily activities. Hereditary predispositions to behave in certain ways (temperament), as well as acquired styles of behaviour (e.g. personality traits and disorders), also contribute significantly to support and stimulate, or slow down and even block, talent development. The environment manifests its significant impact in many different ways. The *surroundings* exert their influence both at a macroscopic level (e.g. geographic, demographic, sociological) and in a more microscopic context (size of family, personality and parenting style of caregivers, socio-economic status, and so forth). Many different *persons*, not only parents and teachers but also siblings and peers, may exert a positive or negative influence on the process of talent development. Gifted education programs within or outside the schools belong to the *provisions* category; they are a more systematic form of intervention to foster or hinder the process of talent development. Finally, significant *events* (the death of a parent, winning a prize or award, suffering a major accident or illness) can influence the course of talent development.

Chance (CH)

Chance is spontaneously associated with the environment (e.g. the 'chance' of being born in a particular family; the 'chance' of the school in which the child is enrolled deciding to develop a program for gifted/talented students; the bad luck of suffering a major accident during athletic training). But, its influence also manifests itself in both the G and IC components of the model through the randomness inherent in the transmission of the genetic endowment.

Prevalence: threshold and levels

Any definition of normative concepts must specify how subjects differ from the norm and what it means in terms of the prevalence of the population subsumed under the label. In the DMGT, the threshold for both the giftedness and talent concepts is placed at the 90th percentile (approximately 1.3 standard deviations above the mean). In other words, those who belong to approximately the top 10% of the relevant reference group in terms of natural ability (for giftedness) or achievement (for talent) may receive the relevant label. It must be clearly noted, however, that this generous choice of threshold is counterbalanced by a recognition of levels or degrees of giftedness or talent. Within the top 10% of 'mildly' gifted or talented persons, the DMGT recognizes four progressively more selective subgroups. They are labelled 'moderately' (top 1%), 'highly' (top 1:1,000), 'exceptionally' (top 1:10,000), and 'extremely' (top 1:100,000). As in other fields of special education, the nature of the intervention program that a school develops for gifted or talented students should be influenced by the level of the student's gifts or talents, as well as the domains or fields to which they belong.

Two Practical Uses of the DMGT

As the preceding overview indicates, the dynamic interactions between the components of the DMGT in the course of talent development remain largely undeveloped. These interactions will be detailed by borrowing heavily from current developmental theories, since talent development is not qualitatively different, in most cases at least, from the acquisition of normal competencies. Until that enrichment is made, I hesitate to use the label 'theory', preferring the more modest one of 'model'. In the words of Keeves (1988), "the model, like the hypotheses which are contained within it, can be built from accumulated evidence, intuition by analogy, or derived from theory" (p. 559). Even in its present model state, the DMGT has a usefulness well beyond its primary goal of demonstrating that the terms giftedness and talent are both essential in our technical lexicon because they allow us to distinguish potential from achievement, natural abilities from systematically developed ones (Gagné, 1999a, 1999c). I will describe below two practical uses of the model, and will illustrate them by analyzing the talent development of a young Vietnamese musician.

A 'big picture' reminder

No one will deny that complex human behaviours have a multi-source aetiology, usually involving factors from each of the DMGT's causal components. Yet, that statement is too often given lip service, not only in daily life but in scientific research as well. We are all confronted in the course of our daily life with events that 'demand' an explanation. It can be our own unexpected behavior, that of a family member or a friend; it can also be some behavior observed in a public setting or presented by the media. These causal interpretations have been studied by social scientists under a variety of labels: 'implicit', 'personal', 'naive' or 'lay' theories, or expressions like 'folk psychology', preconceptions, beliefs, and so forth (Pajares, 1992; Goldman, 1993; Calderhead, 1996). Attribution theories (Weiner, 1984) also belong to that large field. These interpretations appear to result from a very spontaneous (inborn?) human propensity to give some

meaning to observed situations. Often called 'mind reading' (O'Hanlon & Hudson, 1995), they can mar human relations when lent wrongly to a friend or spouse's behaviour. What is so typical about most of these attributions and interpretations is their tendency to focus on one, and only one, explanatory factor, to reify that factor, and completely overlook other potential causes for the observed phenomenon. Media people do it when trying to understand the reason behind the latest mass killing; teachers do it when confronted with a student's misbehavior or under-achievement. In fact, we all do it in our personal and professional lives. The DMGT can help counterbalance that well-anchored human propensity to simplify causality, by reminding us that what appears to be the most evident cause of a behaviour is probably not the only significant one, and might even not be the most significant one.

Researchers also frequently resort to oversimple interpretations of human behaviour. Because of limited means, most social scientists are forced to observe or manipulate only one or two independent variables. But the pool of potentially influential factors is much larger. Just within our field, causal variables cover the whole spectrum suggested by the DMGT, including: (a) abilities (e.g. IQ, piagetian level, creativity); (b) specific learning processes or strategies (e.g. mathematical operations, problem solving strategies in specific learning situations, metacognitive activities); (c) personal characteristics (e.g. self-efficacy, intrinsic motivation, goal orientation, volition, self-regulation, self-concept); (d) specific pedagogical strategies (e.g. skinnerian reinforcement, individualised instruction, mastery learning, tutoring, co-operative learning); (e) diverse administrative practises (e.g. homogeneous grouping, accelerative enrichment, special schools); or (f) other forms of environmental influences (e.g. peer groups, parental supervision, teachers' characteristics, amount of television viewing, classroom climate). Such a list could be expanded almost without limits. Because they have invested considerable energy in the realisation of their study, researchers have a tendency when finding *statistically* significant results to over-estimate the *substantial* significance of these results, especially in the (usual) absence of effect size measures to temper their enthusiasm (Plucker, 1997). Again, if these scholars kept in mind the DMGT's message, namely the multi-source etiology of talent development, they would probably maintain a more relativistic (and modest) attitude toward the significance of their 'pet' variable within the more global explanatory picture.

Besides that natural human propensity to seek meaning, other motives may produce the same blinkered interpretation of talent development. I have especially in mind the tunnelling effect of strongly held theoretical beliefs about the pre-eminence of a particular explanatory variable. Ericsson's conviction that deliberate practise constitutes the most significant cause of talent emergence is a good example of such beliefs (see Ericsson & Charness, 1994). Even large-scale studies are not exempt from that narrowed explanatory perspective. For instance, Bloom (1985) supervised a series of interviews with twenty top American professionals in six distinct occupational fields (swimming & tennis, neurology & mathematics, music & sculpture). The summary chapter focuses quasi-exclusively on the LP process, and various environmental influences. Bloom's environmental leaning is well known and predates that particular study (e.g. Bloom, 1976). He clearly announced his theoretical position in the Preface of his 1985 book:

> The central thesis . . . is the potential equality of most human beings for school learning . . . it leads us to speculate that there must be an enormous potential pool of talent available in the United States. It is likely that some combinations of home, the teachers, the schools, and the society may in large part determine what portions of this potential pool of talent become developed. (1985, p. 5)

That environmental focus is unfortunate in view of the fact that many other causal influences must have been mentioned during the interviews. For instance, in a preliminary publication, Bloom (1982) acknowledged the existence of individual differences in natural abilities:

> In homes where other children were also interested in the talent area, the parents sometimes mentioned that one of the other children had even greater 'gifts' than the individual in the sample, but that the other child was not willing to put in the time and effort that the parents or the teacher expected and required. (pp. 512–513)

The potential significance of that causal source was not explored in depth, probably because it conflicted with Bloom's environmentalist tenets. One can only wonder how much information was lost for lack of an analytical framework open enough to encompass all potentially valuable factors of talent emergence. This comment leads us to the second practical use of the DMGT, namely as a classification tool.

An analytical tool

Researchers can adopt the DMGT's framework of categories and subcategories to classify data. That second practical application, which I have labelled *DMGT-based analysis*, finds usefulness in many different contexts. For example, one could survey the articles of a research journal (or several of them) to identify which types of independent variables appear more frequently in published empirical studies. Thus, longitudinal trends or short-term fads could be observed.

Alternatively, median effect sizes could be obtained within categories and subcategories, making it possible to assess their relative causal impact. Walberg and his colleagues did exactly that type of structured analysis in their ambitious attempt at synthesising the vast literature on school achievement. That literature is relevant to our interests in so far as talent development is but a specific case of the more general theme of competency development over the K–12 schooling process. Walberg and his team surveyed and synthesised close to 3000 empirical studies on the causal influences of student learning (Walberg, 1984). They identified nine significant factors, which they grouped under three headings: *Aptitude* (1. ability; 2. piagetian development; 3. motivation), *Instruction* (4. amount; 5. quality), and *Environment* (6. home; 7. classroom; 8. peers; 9. television). Walberg's model could be considered a coarse analogue of the DMGT. For instance, it confounds abilities and intrapersonal catalysts under the aptitude heading, separates instruction from other environmental inputs, and does not mention clearly the LP process (amount of instruction is dissociated from homework placed in Environment). Still, the goal is the same: bring structure to a large data set.

DMGT-based analysis can be applied to other types of information. Our research team tried it in two different contexts. In one case, we wanted to assess beliefs about the causes of talent emergence. The targets of that research program were educators and students in general education, music, visual arts, and sports. Not only did the DMGT guide the construction of the survey questionnaire, especially the choice of the most relevant causal factors, but it was used as the framework in the data analysis and the presentation of results (Gagné, Blanchard & Bégin, 1999a). DMGT-based analysis was also at the core of a labour-intensive research project recently completed. Forty-two multi-talented adolescents were first identified (Gagné, Neveu, St. Père & Simard, 1997); then, two in-depth interviews were conducted, one with the adolescents themselves and another with at least one parent. We examined the individual's whole life, beginning with the first signs of precocity in their natural abilities, then covering the major events in the development process of each of their talents. The 84 two-hour-long interviews yielded over 1200 pages of transcribed material. Each unit of information (a sentence) was then coded using a category system based on the DMGT (Gagné, 1999b). We found that all relevant information gathered from the interviewees could be codified with high inter-rater reliability, and that no significant information was left uncoded.

If the DMGT offers a useful framework for the study of talent development through interview material, it should apply equally well to biographical data. Because short biographies are easy to find, I decided to use that type of data to illustrate how DMGT-based analysis helps understand the complex dynamics of talent development. To demonstrate its applicability to any field of talent, I chose the talent development of a young Vietnamese musician.

DMGT-Based Analysis: An Illustrative Case Study

The descriptive information concerning Dat Nguyen's life story is borrowed from Bartholomew (1997). The story uses as much of her wording as possible, while reducing the length of her excellent article by about half.

Dat's story: Act I

Dat Nguyen was born blind in December 1970 in South Vietnam. Dat's father, an American service-man, went back to the United States in 1973. Dat's half-sister Yung was born in 1974. Her father, a Vietnamese, disappeared in 1975. When their Viet-namese mother died that same year, they were placed in an orphanage, but it closed after the Communists swept through. The two were taken in by an abusive woman who worked them like slaves. They ran away in 1977 and wandered across the countryside for two years before reaching Ho Chi Minh City (formerly Saigon). There, a man gave them lottery tickets to sell for a small commission. There was little left after they paid for food, however, so they slept on lawns or in alleys. After three years of that life of bare survival, Dat, aged 11, knew he was a triple outcast: blind, Amerasian, and beggar. Yet, even when treated harshly, he would pat his little sister's hand and say to her, "Don't worry, Yung, we will meet some kind people today who will help us".

Anyone reading without any further information this brief overview of Dat's first eleven years of life would find there a perfect scenario for disaster. How could anyone survive such an accumulation of unlucky intrapersonal (innate blindness) and environmental catastrophes (father's departure, second husband's disappearance, mother's death, closing of orphanage, abusive guardian). That series of disasters, succeeding each other within such a short period of time, would burst the top of any stress scale! Indeed, in most North-American school settings, just one of these events would be judged traumatic enough by itself to 'explain' a child's personal or social misadaptation. The fact that this 6-year old blind boy decided to run away from their abusive guardian, not alone but with his half-sister, demonstrates extremely precocious maturity and inner strength. The odds were so heavily against them, and yet he dared make that move. He was probably still too young to understand the negative impact of his mixed blood in the aftermath of the war, but no doubt

that it was pointed out to him regularly by their guardian, and by other people they met. The fact that both children survived two years of wandering plus three more of barest survival in Ho Chi Minh City implies above average resourcefulness, a form of practical intelligence (Sternberg & Wagner, 1986) that could fit in either the DMGT's cognitive or creative domains. During that period, the text mentions just one significant positive environmental input: being given lottery tickets to sell. Still, at that point in time, in fact at the midpoint of the period covered by this story, nothing could lead anyone to expect that an exceptional talent would ever emerge from such a terrible beginning. And yet, the miracle happened.

Dat's Story: Final Act

Some time in 1993, Professor David Grimes, head of the Fullerton classical-guitar program at Cal State University, auditioned all the newcomers. At five-foot-one and 95 pounds, 22-year-old Dat Nguyen looked like a child. He sat down to play, caressing his cheap guitar while coaxing extraordinary beauty from it. Grimes was astounded: Dat's technique was a bit raw, but his phrasing showed an intimate understanding of the material. What grabbed Grimes most was the power, the emotion. Grimes soon learned that he had to make only minimal accommodations for Dat's blindness, because he had a most extraordinary ear for music; he could play almost anything, note for note, after hearing it once. Dat practised up to eight hours a day, often getting up before dawn to play, muffling his guitar with a towel so as not to disturb the neighbours.

One day in October 1994, Grimes told his students he had some applications for the Southern California American String Teachers Association competition. He cautioned his students against setting their goals on winning: there would be strong competitors from other top music schools in California. Yet, Dat won easily and went on to win the state-wide competition. In Vietnam, music had given him the strength to survive. In America, it had brought him an acceptance he might never have known. He was, it seemed at that moment, a very lucky young man.

I skipped on purpose (for dramatic effect!) all intervening events to show immediately the endpoint of Dat's story: the confirmation of his exceptional talent as a classical guitarist. As unbelievable as it may seem, Dat went, in just eleven more years, from beggar and ticket peddler to undergraduate student in classical guitar at a U. S. university. I can imagine many readers itching to look immediately at the next framed text to see what happened in that time interval to bring about such a miracle. Please bear with me a little; this short finale deserves at least two comments. First, the DMGT's definition of talent and its system of prevalence levels are well illustrated. Recall that talent is defined strictly as high level performance, no more no less. Being accepted in a very selective university program no doubt places any music student well within the talent zone, probably within the top 1% of the appropriate reference group, namely all those who have attempted to learn to play the guitar, whether they kept at it or abandoned at some point (Gagné, 1993). Moreover, among all these university students in music, the odds of winning a regional competition would certainly not exceed 10%, easily placing such a winner one rung higher (1:1,000) on my metric-based talent ladder (Gagné, 1998). Finally, assuming that the state-level competition included at least ten participants, winning it would mean acceding to the next higher level. In other words, these achievements probably place Dat among exceptionally talented (1:10,000) guitarists. And that remarkable success was achieved in just eleven years.

Second, the text mentions one potential cause for that achievement, namely outstanding natural abilities: (a) the socio-affective ability to understand intimately the emotional meaning of a piece of music and express it with deep feelings, and (b) the cognitive ability to memorise almost any musical piece, note for note, after hearing it just once. Such a feat is beyond reach for the quasi-totality of professional musicians, yet extremely useful to a blind performer. Most people would probably conclude that this mnemonic ability was progressively developed with much deliberate practise because of Dat's blindness. Does not the need create the instrument? I will not deny that the advantage of such an ability in his case acted as an incentive to pursue the acquisition of that skill, and that much practise was involved. But, any professional musician knows how extremely difficult it is to develop such an extraordinary capacity, especially when one cannot see the musical score. It would be interesting to survey blind professional musicians and ask them to what extent they have mastered that instant mnemonic recording, a feat that compares, in its extreme rarity, to the better analysed phenomenon of eidetic memory (Haber & Haber, 1988). But, let us now look at the most significant events that bridge the first and final acts of Dat's story.

Dat's Story Act II: The Intervening Events

Dat's favourite place to sell tickets was the local barbershop. One of the things he liked best about the store was that its radio blared American songs. As he sang with the music, he pounded the back of a barber chair. One day, a local bandleader noticed him and said, "you like music?" Dat nodded: "It's my favourite thing." "You've got that drum riff down like a pro. How would you like to try a real set of drums?" The man led him to his house, handed Dat drumsticks and gave him a few instructions. Dat hammered away, amazed at the sounds booming through the room. Soon he was wildly drumming on cymbals, and the snare and bass drums. He played for hours before realising that he might have overstayed his welcome. But as he apologised, the man said: "Overstayed? You were just getting started. Come back tomorrow." So, he returned the following day, and almost every day after that. Within a few months, he was playing with the rock band.

One day when Dat was 12, another lottery customer suggested he meet Mr. Truong, one of Saigon's finest classical music teachers. "He loves to nurture young musicians," the customer explained, "and he is also blind." Truong listened to Dat play the drums. "You have talent," he said as Dat finished. "You will be my student." Truong explained that he never took money from a blind student. What's more, he would give Dat and his sister the money they needed to live. In the months that followed, he introduced Dat to the piano and several stringed instruments, and taught him to read Braille. As the instruments resonated under the boy's sensitive fingers, the old man beamed like a proud father.

One Sunday morning in 1988, Dat, now 17, tuned Truong's radio to the classical music hour, featuring a concert by the Spanish guitarist Segovia. Dat had never heard anything so beautiful and complex. In an instant he knew he had to learn to play the guitar like that. Dat bought a used guitar, and Truong found a music book in his Braille library. Dat played for hours at a time, the guitar freeing him to express himself as never before.

That same year, an Amerasian girl told Dat she was going to the United States under a new program that brought Amerasian children to America. "Why don't you apply?" she suggested. In January 1991, sponsored by a Vietnamese American, Dat and Yung arrived at their new home in Orange County, CA. Dat attended Anaheim High School for two years. He learned so quickly that his teachers encouraged him to enrol at Cal State Fullerton. And there he met David Grimes.

Talent Development: A Complex Choreography

As I have observed time and again when presenting that story, most people, professional educators and laypersons alike, tend to interpret the second half of Dat's life, the lifespan covered by Bartholomew's (1997) article, as the mirror image of the first half. To the same degree that the first eleven years saw an accumulation of bad luck, the second half was marked by an unending series of lucky environmental inputs. The series began with the chance encounter of the local bandleader; it continued one year later when another lottery customer directed Dat to Mr. Truong. The next major lucky event was the chance tune-in to Segovia's concert, soon followed by the chance meeting of an Amerasian girl who recommended to Dat that he apply for a special U. S. immigration program which targeted Amerasian Vietnamese children. Then, Dat was discovered by a Vietnamese American, who sponsored his (and his sister's) immigration to the U. S. Finally, his high school teachers, as well as Professor Grimes, paved the way for his admission and subsequent achievements in Cal State Fullerton's classical guitar program. So, as Dat himself reflects, is he just a lucky young man? A closer look at this short biography, aided by DMGT-based analysis, will reveal a much more complex picture of successive interactions between 'events' and personal characteristics that cover all five causal components of the DMGT.

Before examining the role played by each factor, the following comment must be made. The DMGT is a *talent* development model; it illustrates a process whose goal or endpoint is the achievement of talented performances. The choice of that particular goal was predetermined by this author's desire to better differentiate the concepts of giftedness and talent. And the best way, in my view, to operate that differentiation was to define them respectively as the beginning and endpoint of a developmental process through which high natural abilities (gifts) progressively give rise to high level systematically developed skills (talents) in a specific field of human activity. This comment introduces a *relevance rule*, which states that only those elements that have a direct, immediate, and significant impact—positive or negative—on the attainment of the sought goal, in this case musical talent, should be included in any causal component of the model. For example, I purposely avoided using the EC label for all the environmentally induced catastrophes suffered by Dat and his little sister during the first ten years of their life; similarly, I did not apply the IC label to extremely precocious indices of Dat's strength of character, and unfaltering optimism. Thus, retrospective information would be brought in only as supporting evidence for any element directly recognised as a causal factor in Dat's *musical* talent development. Let us now proceed to the separate examination of each causal component.

Natural abilities

Just as bringing an animal to the trough does not ensure its drinking, offering supportive environmental conditions does not guarantee that excellence will automatically ensue. The first question to ask is: "Why was Dat noticed by the bandleader, adopted by Mr. Truong, pushed toward Cal State by his high school teachers, and singled out by Professor Grimes? Are these environmental inputs pure chance events, the

result of proactive social gestures that just reflect human nature at its best? In fact, the text shows clearly that these individuals did react to behaviours they interpreted as signs of exceptional potential. The bandleader saw the 'drum riff' of a pro; Mr. Truong saw that he had 'talent', which meant without doubt 'natural' talent, or giftedness for music; the teachers also saw intellectual giftedness because of his rapid progress in spite of his visual handicap and past schooling history; Professor Grimes noticed Dat's exceptional emotional sensitivity and auditory memory. It is my conviction that *none* of these people's reactions and proposals would have ever happened if they had not observed at the outset exceptional natural abilities. In other words, each of these events was triggered by Dat's behaviour. I am not saying that there was no chance in any of them; indeed, there was chance on every occasion. But, that chance was activated by Dat's exceptional natural gifts. I will come back to the chance factor later.

And the giftedness observed at first sight by the bandleader, Mr. Truong, and Professor Grimes was subsequently confirmed through Dat's ease and speed of learning, the DMGT's best indicator of giftedness in the absence of aptitude testing. He learned so fast to play the drums, especially in spite of his handicap and the fact that this instrument is probably the most visually dependent of all musical instruments, that he was playing with the band within six months. Similarly, as a student of Mr. Truong, Dat learned in just a few months to play many instruments and read Braille; Dat's talent developed in fact so rapidly that Mr. Truong 'beamed like a proud father'. And again, it was his ease and speed of learning that brought him to the attention of his teachers at Anaheim High School. Note that Dat Nguyen received no formal schooling until he was 14 years-old (Dat Nguyen, personal communication, September 22, 1999). Even though the article does not mention it, we might surmise that learning Braille opened the door not only to written music but also to some academic knowledge. Even with that huge delay in formal schooling and a handicap that severely limits the educational accomplishments of most children affected (Blanchard, 1997), Dat obtained his high school diploma when he was just a few years older than the average American student. Finally, Dat only began learning the classical guitar when he was 17 years-old, attaining his high level of excellence with just five or six years of systematic LP, most of them self-taught (see Postscript).

Intrapersonal catalysts

The IC component may take different forms, of which only a few illustrative examples are shown in Fig. 1. Let us look first at the motivational aspects. They can be subdivided into two parts: a directional or goal component (e.g. drives, needs, interests) and a sustaining or volitional component (Corno, 1993) that works at overcoming any intervening obstacles (digressions, temptations, boredom, accidents) so that the chosen goal will be attained. The text mentions two 'directional' elements: (a) Dat's answer to the bandleader about music being his favourite thing, and (b) his 'love at first sight' (a double metaphor!) for the classical guitar as he listens to Segovia's concert. In this second instance, the term passion would be an appropriate label. The volitional component can be easily confounded with the LP process, since will power and persistence are commonly observed through the amount of work done, the intensity of the learning and practise. But volition implies effort in the face of difficulties; thus, amount of LP is not by itself a 'pure' indicator of volitional strength. For instance, in his first encounter with real drums, Dat played for hours; in that case it is just a sign of intense interest. Indeed, Bartholomew's (1997) article never mentions directly that volitional component. But it is always there, in filigree, through mentions of years upon years of bare survival, as well as long hours of music practise, day after day, week after week. This component brings to mind Sir Francis Galton's (1869/1962) often-cited comment:

> By natural ability, I mean those qualities of intellect and disposition, which urge and qualify a man to perform acts that lead to reputation. I do not mean capacity without zeal, nor zeal without capacity, nor even a combination of both of them, without an adequate power of doing a great deal of very laborious work. (p. 77)

A DMGT-based analysis of that quote will associate capacity with giftedness, disposition with temperament (IC), zeal with intrinsic motivation (interest, passion), and the power of laborious work with the volitional aspect of motivation. In Galton's terms, reputation (talent, eminence) will emerge from proper qualifications (high capacities, gifts), urges and zeal (needs, passions), as well as the power for laborious work (volition, perseverance). It is interesting that little importance is given to environmental influences.

The intrapersonal component of the DMGT includes many more 'ingredients' besides motivational constructs. Temperament and personality traits constitute a major subdivision, as well as personal beliefs (e.g. self-perceptions, implicit theories, attitudes, values). Bartholomew's (1997) short article does not explore that area in much detail. The few elements that stand out were mentioned earlier and predate Dat's musical talent development; so they cannot be included. But, to better illustrate the contents of the IC component, I could add resilience (O'Connell Higgins, 1994). Even after years of begging, he maintained an unflagging optimism, as witnessed by his comment to his little

sister when treated harshly: "Don't worry, Yung, we will meet some kind people today who will help us."

Environmental catalysts

Environmental catalysts are no doubt the most visible of all five causal factors. We are constantly surrounded by stimuli, and one of the major roles of our lower brain is to monitor that input and bring to consciousness only the most significant sensory information. That selection process needs to be mentioned because it points to a major difference between environmental *inputs* and environmental *catalysts*. Webster's dictionary proposes the following broad definition of a catalyst: "any agent that provokes significant change" (1991, p. 214). And there lies the difficulty: determining the degree of causal impact of any environmental stimulus. It is a well-known psychological fact that individuals do not react similarly, either cognitively or affectively, to any stimulation; indeed, studies in behavioural genetics have shown that, contrary to common-sense beliefs, familial environmental influences contribute much more to sibling *disparities* than to their similarities (Plomin, DeFries & McClearn, 1990). Moreover, according to the relevance rule stated earlier, these environmental inputs must affect the target phenomenon, here Dat's musical talent development. For instance, very good parents may have played a significant role in the development of their child's personality; yet, their role with regard to that child's talent development could have been much more unobtrusive (except maybe paying the bills!). With these caveats in mind, let us examine the text. In the case of Dat's first eleven years in this world, two opposite points of view could be defended. Some could argue that because the dramatic events preceded the beginning of Dat's musical talent development, they cannot be properly introduced as catalysts: catalysts play their role *during* the chemical reaction, don't they? Others might point out that if Dat had benefited from a more normal environment during his youth he would have encountered much earlier the occasions or favourable circumstances that often launch the systematic development of new skills; consequently, these events hindered the process by retarding its beginning. To be honest, I would feel comfortable with either of these two positions. Still, the first clearly relevant EC mentioned in Bartholomew's (1997) article is the bandleader inviting Dat to come and try his drums.

It is not surprising that all the major EC influences are significant persons: the bandleader, Mr. Truong, the Amerasian girl, the Vietnamese–American sponsor, a few Anaheim high school teachers, and Professor Grimes. No doubt that humans are more easily conceived as significant causal influences than inanimate objects. Some of these persons played their catalytic role over a long period of time (e.g. bandleader, Truong, Grimes), whereas others (e.g. the lottery customer who guided Dat to Mr. Truong, the Amerasian girl) just gave a nudge, albeit a very important one, in the right direction. But other EC categories appear in the text. For instance, even though it is not a direct musical provision, I would place the immigration program in the Provisions category. It is very relevant to Dat's talent development, because it allowed him to come to the U. S. and maximize his chances of finding a suitable environment to pursue his learning of the classical guitar. I would include in the Events category tuning in by chance to Segovia's concert; that event made Dat discover in himself the powerful addictive impact of the extremely refined and complex 'sound' of the classical guitar. That was one of those rare 'crystallising experiences' first described by Walters & Gardner (1986). Yet, we must ask ourselves what was more important for Dat's musical talent development: the guitar concert (EC) or Dat's special emotional sensitivity to that instrument or music (IC)? Thousands of persons probably listened to that particular concert on the radio, but only one among them was moved to the point of completely reorienting his life and career plans to include that musical instrument. I personally believe that such an impact says much more about Dat's emotional sensitivity than about the guitar's power of attraction. Granted that the event had to take place for that sensitivity to be aroused; but chances are that, because he was actively involved in music, Dat Nguyen would have encountered sooner or later that particular musical form.

Two additional comments. First, can the classical guitar program at Cal State Fullerton be considered a significant EC within the Provisions category? I am still debating that point. My present position leans toward a more selective interpretation of the relevance rule: a program should have a *unique* impact on the talent development of a person to receive the EC label, an impact that no other similar program could have had. In other words, because a college-level music program is a necessary constituent in the training of any professional musician, and so cannot serve to differentiate the more talented from the less talented ones, I would tend to include it instead within the LP component. I would argue similarly that any regular K–12 curriculum or school environment would not be considered an EC unless something special or unique existed in that program that contributed *directly and significantly* to a person's talent development. Second, many people believe in the 'formative' role of adversity, namely that difficult life situations during youth toughen individuals and prepare them to better confront the challenges of adult life. Adversity as a character builder is a very strange hypothesis in view of the overwhelming literature on the importance of an early supportive family environment to ensure normal development. I do not believe that adversities 'build' character; what they do is give those who already have some inborn strength of character, as I believe Dat

possesses, an excellent occasion to demonstrate that strength. Very few 6 year-old children, even with perfect eyesight, would have dared take Dat's decision to flee with his young sister; indeed, most would not even have thought of it.

The LP process

As a causal factor, the LP component plays a special role in the DMGT: it corresponds to the *process* through which high natural abilities (gifts) are transformed into the specific skills that characterise a particular field of talent. No one will deny that this component is crucial in talent development: no skills have yet been discovered that blossom overnight! One needs only to compare novices with experts to realise the huge amount of knowledge and skill generated by months and years of LP. From that macroscopic perspective, *mean* differences in performance will be evident between beginners and more advanced students (artists, athletes, etc.). On that point I totally agree with Ericsson and Charness's (1994) position: macroscopically speaking, practise does make perfect. But the real question is: "Does deliberate practise play the most important role in Dat's (or anyone's) success, as Ericsson and Charness would argue?" I strongly disagree. When we control the amount of LP (e.g. students in the same grade), we observe that yearly average improvements in performance are accompanied by large standard deviations; in other words, significant incremental differences in knowledge from one school grade to the next are accompanied by large *within-grade* differences in academic achievement (Biemiller, 1993; Schulz & Nicewander, 1997). These residual individual differences reflect, among other things (e.g. quality of instruction, motivation), disparities in *pace of learning*; indeed, some of the best students (performers, athletes) will not be practising more, sometimes even less, than more average peers. I observed that exact phenomenon in music in the results of a study by Sloboda & Howe (1991) with students in a special music school. The top-achieving half of their sample practised on average *a third less*; yet, their level of achievement was *twice as advanced* as that of students occupying the bottom half (Gagné, 1999d). Moreover, studies of the impact of homework on school achievement have shown only modest results (Walberg, 1984). In summary, while LP is no doubt an essential component of the talent development process, I believe that it accounts for only a modest percentage of the large individual differences in achievement observed among persons enrolled in a similar LP program.

Chance

Bartholomew (1997) states toward the end of her article that Dat Nguyen perceived himself to be "a very lucky young man." Is this whole story a poem to chance? I am not aware of any studies that have tried to assess individual differences in the role of chance over the course of people's lives. So, it is not possible to determine to what extent, normatively speaking, chance played a bigger role in Dat's life than it did for other individuals. One would also need to qualify the type of chance observed. Austin (1978) described four levels of chance events, differentiated by the degree of activity of the person, from passive 'blind luck' to the focused exploratory behaviour of the researcher. According to Austin, both the activity level and its focus increase the chances of fate showing its fickle finger. All these considerations make it difficult to circumscribe the exact role of chance in Dat's life.

The chance factor was borrowed from Tannenbaum's (1983) model, and first introduced in the DMGT to stress the randomness of many life events (being discovered by a mentor, accidents, etc.). In the first edition of this handbook (Gagné, 1993), chance was present as a fifth element among the environmental catalysts. But, it soon became clear that chance influences all the environmental catalysts (e.g. the socio-economic status of a child's family, the quality of the parenting, the existence of talent development programs in the neighbourhood school, and so forth). That is why it could not appear as one element within a list of ECs. Moreover, chance manifests itself in another major event, namely the transmission of hereditary characteristics; there are few human phenomena more dependent on chance than the specific mix of genes resulting from the random meeting of a particular ovum and one among billions of spermatozoids. In that respect, Tannenbaum cites Atkinson's (1978) belief that all human accomplishments can be ascribed to "two crucial rolls of the dice over which no individual exerts any personal control. These are the accidents of birth and background" (Tannenbaum, 1983, p. 221). Atkinson's 'accident of birth' stresses the role of chance outside of ECs, especially in the giftedness and IC components. If Dat is a 'lucky young man', it is first and foremost because of the exceptional gifts received from Nature. We could add to these natural abilities the strong temperament, again a gift of Nature, that allowed him to survive through an incredible series of traumatic events, and, finally, the lucky encounters that completely reoriented his life toward the development of an exceptional musical talent. In brief, as shown in Fig. 1, there is some degree of chance in all the causal components of the model, except maybe the LP process.

Summary

The above analysis of Dat Nguyen's musical talent development illustrates how his exceptional talent as a classical guitarist progressively emerged from complex interactions between all the causal factors that comprise the DMGT; and I would be hard-pressed to single out any of them as having played an overwhelming role. The analysis demonstrates the importance of Dat's high natural abilities (G), without which none of the chance (CH) events (EC) that launched his musical career would ever have materialised. At the same time, the significant individuals mentioned (EC) were essential to his talent development, since without their support Dat would probably have never discovered how musically gifted he was nor how strong was his attraction for that field. Moreover, without his passionate interest for music (IC), he would not have followed up on the bandleader's invitation to learn the drums, nor taken up Mr. Truong's invitation to become his music teacher, nor switched instantaneously to the classical guitar after listening to a Segovia concert. The hundreds of hours of practise (LP) were also essential to develop Dat's musical skills, but his giftedness allowed him to progress at a much faster pace than the vast majority of music students. Also, no doubt that a strong will power (IC) helped him stay on course during the difficult moments of his talent development process. In summary, it confirms that all the causal factors were *necessary* — in the statistical sense — to produce these exceptional achievements, and that none of them was by itself *sufficient* — again in the statistical sense — to bring about Dat's exceptional musical talent. This essential-but-not-sufficient character of each of the DMGT's components as contributors to Dat's exceptional talent, as well as their constant interplay over time, exemplifies my 'complex choreography' metaphor to describe the talent development process.

Conclusion

I have tried to describe in this text two practical uses of the Differentiated Model of Giftedness and Talent (DMGT). One of them is a cartographic representation of the major groups of determinants of talent development and, consequently, a constant reminder of the 'big picture', namely the rich diversity of potential causes of talent emergence. But, in my view, the DMGT should be most useful as an analytical tool, a system of categories and subcategories enabling professionals and scholars to classify developmental information gathered through interviews, biographies, surveys, and so forth. There is still much to discover about the dynamics of talent development, about the relative importance of various causal factors, or the most common causal direction when two factors influence each other over time in a bi-directional causal spiral, or the change in importance of these factors as individuals move from youthful precocity to mature talent. I am convinced that DMGT-based analysis could help researchers in the field bring better understanding to these still coarsely charted waters.

Postscript

As I was completing this manuscript in the fall of 1999, I decided to contact Dat Nguyen. We talked a few times on the phone. I sent him a tape of the manuscript, asking for his help to ascertain the correctness of the information, and the face validity of my analysis. He acknowledged that my outside analysis had given him new insights on his past. He confirmed two points about which I had lingering doubts. First, the Segovia concert was really a cristallising experience—as defined by Walters & Gardner, 1986—a falling in love with the classical guitar as sudden and intense as Bartholomew had described. Second, Dat stated that his instant memory for music and lyrics goes back as far as he can remember, even before he began studying music formally. That gift has improved over the years to a point where he can now easily memorise 8-note chords, as well as whole clusters played in rapid succession. He mentioned having tried to teach that ability to young musicians, so far without success. That failure strengthened his conviction that there was an inborn component to that ability. He also has perfect pitch; that ability goes back to his first music lessons, and is judged by him to be inborn to some degree. Finally, Dat pointed out that he began studying the classical guitar for a year with a professional teacher while still living in Ho Chi Minh City. But, during the next four years, as he moved from Vietnam to the U.S. and completed high school, he had no music teacher. Self-teaching alone brought his competence to a level high enough to be admitted to Fullerton. That makes his achievements even more remarkable.

Since the Bartholomew article, Dat Nguyen's career as a classical guitarist has progressed. In 1996, he was chosen to represent his state in a national competition of classical musicians called the Panasonic Young Soloist Award. The only guitarist among the 50 participants, he reached the finals (3 participants). Last spring, aged 28, Dat completed his bachelor's degree in guitar perform-ance at Fullerton. In October 1999, he played against 80 classical guitarists from seven countries in a world-level competition organised by the Guitar Foundation of America, and held in Charles-ton, SC. Unfortunately, he did not attain the finals (12 participants), but enjoyed tremendously that high-level experience. Dat has decided to take a sabbatical leave for a year or two to devote more time to performing and composing. Not only does he play the classical guitar repertoire, but he also loves jazz, flamenco, and Vietnamese music. To make ends meet, he performs regularly, either alone or with his own guitar quartet. For at least the last twelve years, he has been writing songs and composing instrumental music. He hopes to record some of his work in the near future. Dat plans to enroll within a year or two in a graduate music program.

References

Atkinson, J. W. (1978). Motivational determinants of intellec-tive performance and cumulative achievement. In: J. W. Atkinson & J. O. Raynor (Eds), *Personality, Motivation, and Achievement*, pp. 221–242. New York: Wiley.

Austin, J. H. (1978). *Chase, chance, and creativity.* New York: Columbia University Press.

Bartholomew, A. (1997). The gift of music was his passport. *Readers' Digest* (March), 149–154.

Biemiller, A. (1993). Lake Wobegon revisited: on diversity and education. *Educational Researcher*, **22** (9), 7–12.

Blanchard, P. (1997). *Quelques données concernant les personnes ayant une déficience visuelle: document de travail.* [Some data concerning individuals with a visual handicap; draft.] Drummondville, QC, Canada: Office des Personnes Handicapées du Québec.

Bloom, B. S. (1976). *Human characteristics and school learning.* New York: McGraw-Hill.

Bloom, B. S. (1982). The role of gifts and markers in the development of talent. *Exceptional Children*, **48**, 510–522.

Bloom, B. S. (1985). Developing talent in young people. New York: Ballantine Books.

Borland, J. (1999). The limits of consilience: a reaction to Françoys Gagné's "My convictions about the nature of abilities, gifts, and talents". *Journal for the Education of the Gifted*, **22**, 137–147.

Calderhead, J. (1996). Teachers: beliefs and knowledge. In: D. C. Berliner & R. C. Calfee (Eds), *Handbook of Educational Psychology* (pp. 709–725). New York: Mac-millan.

Corno, L. (1993). The best-laid plans: modern conceptions of volition and educational research. *Educational Researcher*, **22**, 14–22.

Detterman, D. & Ruthsatz, J. (1999). Toward a more comprehensive theory of exceptional abilities. *Journal for the Education of the Gifted*, 22, 148–158.

Ericsson, K. A. & Charness, N. (1994). Expert performance: its structure and acquisition. *American Psychologist*, **49**, 725–747.

Feldman, D. H. (1999). A developmental, evolutionary perspective on gifts and talents. *Journal for the Education of the Gifted*, **22**, 159–167.

Gagné, F. (1993). Constructs and models pertaining to exceptional human abilities. In: K. A. Heller, F. J. Mönks & A. H. Passow (Eds), *International Handbook of Research and Development of Giftedness and Talent* (pp. 69–87). Oxford: Pergamon Press.

Gagné, F. (1998). A proposal for subcategories within the gifted or talented populations. *Gifted Child Quarterly*, **42**, 87–95.

Gagné, F. (1999a). Is There Any Light at the End of the Tunnel? *Journal for the Education of the Gifted*, **22**, 191–234.

Gagné, F. (1999b). The multigifts of multitalented individ-uals. In: S. Cline & K. T. Hegeman (Eds), *Gifted Education in the Twenty-first Century: Issues and Concerns* (pp. 17–45). Delray Beach, FL: Winslow Press.

Gagné, F. (1999c). My convictions about the nature of human abilities, gifts and talents. *Journal for the Education of the Gifted*, **22**, 109–136.

Gagné, F. (1999d). Nature or nurture: a re-examination of Sloboda and Howe's (1991) Interview Study on Talent Development in Music. *Psychology of Music*, **27**, 38–51.

Gagné, F, Blanchard, D. & Bégin, J. (1999). Beliefs of American and Quebec educators and students concerning the major determinants of academic talent. In: F. A. Dixon & C. M. Adams, (Eds), *1999 Research Briefs*, pp. 1–16. Washington, DC: National Association for Gifted Children.

Gagné, F., Neveu, F., Simard, L. & St Père, F. (1996). How a search for multitalented individuals challenged the concept itself. *Gifted and Talented International*, **11**, 4–10.

Galton, F. (1869/1962). *Hereditary genius: an inquiry into its laws and consequences*. New York: Meridian Books.

Goldman, A. I. (1993). The psychology of folk psychology. *Behavioral and Brain Sciences*, **16**, 15–28.

Haber, R. N. & Haber, L. R. (1988). The characteristics of eidetic imagery. In: L. K. Obler & D. Fein (Eds), The Exceptional Brain: Neuropsychology of Talent and Special Abilities, pp. 218–241. New York: Guilford Press.

Hany, E. A. (1999). Do personal convictions promote scientific progress? Comment on Gagné's "My convictions about the nature of abilities, gifts, and talents." *Journal for the Education of the Gifted*, 22, 168–179.

Keeves, J. P. (1988). Models and model building. In: J. P. Keeves (Ed.), Educational Research, Methodology, and Measurement: an International Handbook, pp. 559–566. Oxford, England: Pergamon.

O'Connell Higgins, G. (1994). *Resilient adults: overcoming a cruel past*. San Francisco: Jossey-Bass.

O'Hanlon, B. & Hudson, P. (1995). *Love is a verb*. New York: W. W. Norton.

Pajares, M. F. (1992). Teachers' beliefs and educational research: cleaning up a messy construct. *Review of Educational Research*, **62**, 307–332.

Plomin, R., DeFries, J. C. & McClearn, G. E. (1990). *Behavioral genetics: a primer* (2nd ed.). New York: Freeman.

Plucker, J. A. (1997). Debunking the myth of the 'highly significant' result: effect sizes in gifted education research. *Roeper Review*, **20**, 122–126.

Robinson, N. (1999). Exchanging new hats for old: a response to Françoys Gagné's "My convictions about the nature of abilities, gifts, and talents." *Journal for the Education of the Gifted*, **22**, 180–190.

Schulz, E. M. & Nicewander, W. A. (1997). Grade equivalent and IRT representations of growth. *Journal of Educational Measurement*, **34**, 315–331.

Sloboda, J. A. & Howe, M. J. A. (1991). Biographical precursors of musical excellence: An interview study. *Psychology of Music*, **19**, 3–21.

Sternberg, R. J. & Wagner, R. K. (Eds) (1986). *Practical intelligence: nature and origins of competence in the eveyday world*. New York: Cambridge University Press.

Tannenbaum, A. J. (1983). *Gifted children: psychological and educational perspectives*. New York: Macmillan.

Walberg, H. J. (1984). Improving the productivity of America's schools. *Educational Leadership*, May, 19–27.

Walters, J. & Gardner, H. (1986). The crystallizing experience: discovering an intellectual gift. In: R. J. Sternberg & J. E. Davidson (Eds), *Conceptions of Giftedness* (pp. 306–331). New York: Cambridge University Press.

Webster's Ninth New Collegiate Dictionary (1991). Springfield, MA: Merriam-Webster.

Weiner, B. (1984). Principles for a theory of student motivation and their application within an attributional framework. In: R. Ames & C. Ames (Eds), *Research on Motivation in Education* (Vol. 1). Orlando, FL: Academic Press.

New Conceptions and Research Approaches to Creativity: Implications of a Systems Perspective for Creativity in Education

Mihaly Csikszentmihalyi and Rustin Wolfe

Claremont Graduate University and The University of Chicago, USA

Introduction

At the beginning of the third millennium, the importance of creativity becomes ever more critical. Age-old problems, such as coexistence on an increasingly interdependent planet, need new solutions for our species to survive. And the unintended results of the creativity of past centuries require even more creativity to be resolved, as we must learn to cope with the aftermath of previous successes, such as increasing population density and chemical pollution.

For several millions of years young people have learned how to adapt successfully by learning practical skills from their elders. But during the last few generations, they have become dependent on schools for acquiring the information necessary to cope with their environment. Thus we might expect that creativity, inasmuch as it can be taught, would be learned and practiced in schools. Yet — with notable exceptions — schools seem to be inimical to the development of creativity. For instance, Getzels and Jackson (1962) found that students who scored high on creativity tests were generally disliked by teachers, who preferred students who were highly intelligent but less creative.

In a recent study of 91 exceptionally creative writers, musicians, businessmen, and Nobel-prize winning scientists, these individuals almost never mentioned their elementary or secondary schools as having helped them to develop the interest and expertise that led to their later accomplishments. Almost every person could mention one or two very influential teachers, but classroom activities as such were generally remembered as boring and repressive (Csikszentmihalyi, 1996). Is this a necessary feature of institutionalized mass education? Or are there ways to make schools more friendly to the development of creativity? Before attempting to deal with such questions, it will be useful to present our perspective on what creativity consists of.

A Definition of Creativity

Creativity can be defined as an idea or product that is original, valued, and implemented. Traditionally creativity has been viewed as a mental process, as the insight of an individual genius. Psychologists have assumed that creativity consists of breaking down conceptual paradigms as they are solving problems. But where do paradigms come from? Where do problems come from? On second thought, it becomes obvious that creativity cannot exist in a vacuum; new is relative to old. Without norms there can be no variation; without standards there can be no excellence. Such obvious considerations should alert us to the fact that whatever individual mental process is involved in creativity, it must be one that takes place in a context of previous cultural and social achievements, and is inseparable from them.

While originality refers to any new idea or product, creativity is a subset of originality that is also valuable (Fig. 1). But how do we know whether or not an original solution is worth implementing? From where

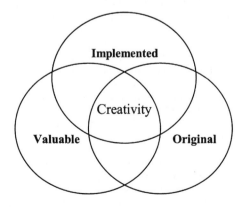

Figure 1. General Model of Creativity.

81

do we get our internal standards? Who is to judge what is valuable? These questions point at the importance of a supportive and evaluative context beyond the individual. Most definitions of creativity also stipulate that an idea must be implemented before its success can be evaluated. Implementation, in turn, requires inputs and resources that are usually beyond the individual's control.

While individual originality clearly plays a necessary role in the creative process, it is only one part. In this chapter, we will propose that an intrapsychic approach cannot do justice to the complex phenomenon of creativity, which is as much cultural and social as it is a psychological event. To develop this perspective, we will use a 'systems' model of the creative process that takes into account its essential features. Later, we shall consider what role educational institutions can play in fostering creativity according to the systems model.

The Systems Model of Creativity

Creativity research in recent years has been increasingly informed by a systems perspective. Starting with the observations of Morris Stein (Stein, 1953, 1963), and the extensive data presented by Dean Simonton showing the influence of economic, political, and social events on the rates of creative production (Simonton, 1988, 1990), it has become increasingly clear that variables external to the individual must be taken into account if one wishes to explain why, when, and where new ideas or products arise from and become established in a culture (Gruber, 1988; Harrington, 1990). Magyari-Beck (1988) has gone so far as to suggest that because of its complexity, creativity needs a new discipline of 'creatology' in order to be thoroughly understood.

The systems approach developed here has been described before, and applied to historical and anecdotal examples, as well as to data collected to answer a variety of different questions (Csikszentmihalyi, 1988b, 1990b, 1996, 1999; Csikszentmihalyi, Rathunde & Whalen, 1993; Feldman, Csikszentmihalyi & Gardner, 1994; Csikszentmihalyi & Sawyer, 1995).

Why is a Systems Approach Necessary?

When the senior author started studying creativity over 30 years ago, like most psychologists he was convinced that it consisted of a purely intrapsychic process. He assumed that one could understand creativity with reference to the thought processes, emotions, and motivations of individuals who produced novelty. But each year the task became more frustrating. In a longitudinal study of artists, for instance, it was observed that some of the potentially most creative persons stopped doing art and pursued ordinary occupations, while others who seemed to lack creative personal attributes persevered and eventually produced works of art that were hailed as important creative

achievements (Getzels & Csikszentmihalyi, 1976; Csikszentmihalyi & Getzels, 1988; Csikszentmihalyi, 1990b). To use just a single example, young women in art school showed as much, or more creative potential than their male colleagues. Yet twenty years later, not one of the cohort of women had achieved outstanding recognition, whereas several in the cohort of men did.

Psychologists have always realized that good new ideas do not automatically translate into accepted creative products. Confronted with this knowledge, one of two strategies can be adopted. The first was articulated by Abraham Maslow and involves denying the importance of public recognition (Maslow, 1963). In his opinion it is not the outcome of the process that counts, but the process itself. According to this perspective a person who re-invents Einstein's formula for relativity is as creative as Einstein was. A child who sees the world with fresh eyes is creative; it is the quality of the subjective experience that determines whether a person is creative, not the judgment of the world. While we believe that the quality of subjective experience is the most important dimension of personal life, we do not believe that creativity can be assessed with reference to it. In order to be studied by the interpersonally validated tools of science, creativity must refer to a process that results in an idea or product that is recognized and adopted by others. Originality, freshness of perceptions, divergent thinking ability are all well and good in their own right, as desirable personal traits. But without some form of public recognition they do not constitute creativity. In fact, one might argue that such traits are not even necessary for creative accomplishment.

In practice, creativity research has always recognized this fact. Creativity tests, for instance, ask children to respond to divergent thinking tasks, or to produce stories, or designs with colored tiles. The results are assessed by judges or raters who weigh the originality of the responses. The underlying assumption is that an objective quality called 'creativity' is revealed in the products, and that judges and raters can recognize it. But we know that expert judges do not possess an external, objective standard by which to evaluate 'creative' responses. Their judgments rely on past experience, training, cultural biases, current trends, personal values, idiosyncratic preferences. Thus whether an idea or product is creative or not does not depend on its own qualities, but on the effect it is able to produce in others who are exposed to it. Therefore it follows that what we call creativity is a phenomenon that is constructed through an interaction between producer and audience. Creativity is not produced by single individuals, but by social systems making judgments about individuals' products.

A second strategy that has been used to accommodate the fact that social judgments are so central to creativity is not to deny their importance, but to separate the process of *creativity* from that of *persuasion*, and then claim that both are necessary for a creative idea or product to be accepted (Simonton, 1988, 1991, 1994). However, this stratagem does not resolve the epistemological problem. For if you cannot persuade the world that you had a creative idea, how do we know that you actually had it? And if you do persuade others, then of course you will be recognized as creative. Therefore it is impossible to separate creativity from persuasion; the two stand or fall together. The impossibility is not only methodological, but epistemological as well, and probably ontological. In other words, if by creativity we mean *the ability to add something new to the culture*, then it is impossible to even think of it as separate from persuasion.

Of course, one might disagree with this definition of creativity. Some will prefer to define it as an intra-psychic process, as an ineffable experience, as a subjective event that need not leave any objective trace. But a definition of creativity that aspires to objectivity, and therefore requires an inter-subjective dimension, will have to recognize the fact that the audience is as important to its constitution as the individual to whom it is credited.

Thus, starting from a strictly individual perspective on creativity, we were forced to adopt a view that encompasses the environment in which the individual operates. This environment has two salient aspects: A cultural, or symbolic aspect which here is called the *domain*; and a social aspect called the *field*. Creativity is a process that can be observed only at the intersection where individuals, domains, and fields interact.

An Outline of the Systems Model

In the *Origin of Species*, Charles Darwin described the process by which nature 'invents.' To paraphrase:

> "Nature's mechanism of invention lies in the process of natural selection. Unpacked into its details, natural selection depends on three subprocesses: (1) genetic variation; (2) selection of adaptive results via the test of survival and reproduction; (3) inheritance of the adaptive results. According to the Darwinian perspective, this trio of subprocesses, over millennia, leads to the emergence of new species" (Perkins, 1988, p. 367).

Describing biological evolution may, at first, seem an odd way to present a model of creativity (Fig. 2), but the process of evolution at the level of species is analogous to the creativity at the level of cultural traits. Biological evolution occurs when an individual organism produces a genetic *variation* that is *selected* by the environment and *transmitted* to the next generation (see Campbell, 1976; Mayr, 1982; Csikszentmihalyi, 1993). In biological evolution, it makes no sense to say that a beneficial step was the result of a particular genetic mutation alone, without taking into account environmental conditions. For instance, a genetic

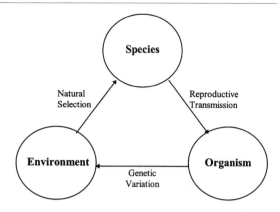

Figure 2. Model of Biological Evolution.

change that improved the size or taste of corn would be useless if at the same time it made the corn more vulnerable to drought, or to disease. Moreover, a genetic mutation that cannot be transmitted to the next generation is also useless from the point of view of evolution.

According to Sterman, this paradigm has now been widely accepted in the social sciences as a model of learning in general:

> "John Dewey ... recognized the feedback-loop character of learning around the turn of the century when he described learning as an iterative cycle of invention [variation], observation, reflection [selection], and action [transmission] (Schön, 1992). Explicit feedback accounts of behavior and learning have now permeated most of the social sciences. Learning as an explicit feedback process has even appeared in practical management tools such as Total Quality Management, where the so-called Shewhart-Deming PDCA cycle (Plan-Do-Check-Act) lies at the heart of the improvement process in TQM (Shewhart, 1939; Walton, 1986; Shiba et al., 1993)." (Sterman, 1994, p. 293).

Creativity occurs at the interface of three subsystems: An Individual who absorbs information from the culture and changes it in a way that will be selected by the relevant Field of gatekeepers for inclusion into the Domain, from whence the novelty will be accessible to the next generation (see Fig. 3).

The systems model of creativity is formally analogous to the model of evolution based on natural selection. The variation which occurs at the individual level of biological evolution corresponds to the contribution that the person makes to creativity; the selection is the contribution of the field, and the transmission is the contribution of the domain to the creative process (cf. Simonton, 1988; Martindale, 1989). Operating within a specific cultural framework, a person makes a variation on what is known, and if the

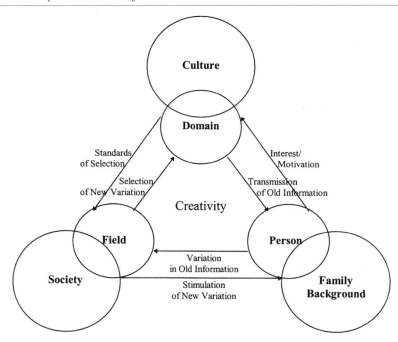

Figure 3. The Systems Model of Creativity.

change is judged to be valuable by the field, it will be incorporated into the domain, thus providing a new cultural framework for the next generation of persons (Csikszentmihalyi, 1988b). Thus creativity can be seen as a special case of evolution. Creativity is to cultural evolution as the mutation, selection, and transmission of genetic variation is to biological evolution. In creativity, it makes no sense to say that a beneficial step was the result of a particular person alone, without taking into account environmental conditions. To be creative, a variation has to be adapted to its social environment, and it has to be capable of being passed on through time.

What we call creativity always involves a change in a symbolic system—a change that, in turn, will affect the thoughts and feelings of other members of the culture. A change that does not affect the way others think, feel, or act will not be creative. Thus creativity presupposes a community of people who share ways of thinking and acting, who learn from each other and imitate each other's actions. Instead of 'genes', it is useful to think about creativity as involving a change in *memes*—the units of imitation that Dawkins (1976) suggested were the building-blocks of culture. Memes are similar to genes in that they carry instructions for action. The notes of a song tell us what to sing; the recipes for a cake tells us what ingredients to mix and how long to bake, the rules of mathematics tell us how to operate with numbers. But whereas genetic instructions are transmitted in the chemical codes we inherit on our chromosomes, the instructions contained in

memes are transmitted through learning. By and large we learn memes and reproduce them without change. The great majority of individuals are perfectly content to obey cultural instructions without dreaming of changing them. But occasionally some people develop the notion that they can write a new song, bake a better recipe, or develop a new equation—and then we may have creativity.

Creativity is the engine that drives cultural evolution. The notion of 'evolution' does not imply that cultural changes necessarily follow some single direction, or that cultures are getting any better as a result of the changes brought about by creativity. Following its use in biology, evolution in this context means increasing complexity over time. In turn, complexity is defined in terms of two complementary processes (Csikszentmihalyi, 1993, 1996). First, it means that cultures tend to become *differentiated* over time—they develop increasingly independent and autonomous domains. Second, the domains within a culture become increasingly *integrated*; that is, related to each other and mutually supportive of each others' goals—in analogy to the differentiated organs of the physical body that help each others' functioning.

The Place of Schools in the Systems Model

If we apply this model to educational institutions, schools might be seen as consisting of the same three components: a body of knowledge to be transmitted (Domain), teachers who controls the knowledge (Field), and finally a number of individuals, the students, whose task is to learn the knowledge and who are evaluated by teachers in terms of their learning.

This perspective immediately makes clear why schools and creativity are inimical. In a creative process, the point is to innovate on the content of the domain in such a way that the field will deem the innovation better than what existed before. But in schools, the point is for the students to replicate the content of the domain as closely as possible, without deviations. The teachers' task is to ensure conformity with prior knowledge, without even trying to evaluate whether the students' deviations might be 'better' than what is written in the textbooks. Thus the main task of schools is to transmit knowledge with as little change as possible—a necessary task which many might argue should not be tampered with.

On the other hand, good teachers everywhere have always been alert for signs of original thinking in their students. Even though it is very rare for a young student to improve on the content of an existing discipline, the very fact of trying to invent a new poetic expression, or a more efficient mathematical calculation, is taken by some teachers to show an involvement with learning that is extremely important to encourage and nurture. From such a perspective learning can be seen as a rehearsal and preparation for later creativity, when the student has mastered the content of the domain to the point that he or she can make a genuinely valuable innovation in it.

In terms of Education as an institution, typically the individual student, teacher, or administrator submits a novel idea to the teacher, administration, or school board, respectively. This field then selects which *good* ideas are to be, respectively, added to the curriculum, passed on to a higher level of management, or implemented as policy. The cumulative sum of these decisions becomes the domain of Education.

Figure 4 describes the specific manifestation of creativity in the classroom. When a student produces a variation in the curriculum of a subject, a variation that

the teachers feel is worthy of being preserved in some form, then we can observe an instance of creativity. Of course, the problem usually is that teachers are neither looking for innovations from their students, and even if they notice a promising one they have few mechanisms for incorporating it into the curriculum. It is for this reason that most instances of creativity in schools occur outside the classroom, such as in science fairs, artistic competitions, literary prizes, and so on.

The Individual's Contribution to Creativity

We have said that creativity occurs when a person makes a change in a domain, a change that will be transmitted through time. Some individuals are more likely to make such changes, either because of personal qualities, or because they have the good fortune to be well-positioned with respect to the domain—they have better access to it, or their social circumstances allow them more free time to experiment.

The systems model makes it possible to see the contributions of the person to the creative process in a theoretically coherent way. In the first place, it brings attention to the fact that before a person can introduce a creative variation, he or she must have access to a domain, and must want to learn to perform according to its rules. This implies that motivation is important— a topic already well understood by scholars in the field of creativity. But it also suggests a number of additional factors that are usually ignored; for instance, that cognitive and motivational factors interact with the state of the domain and the field. For instance, the domain of nuclear physics promised many interesting intellectual challenges during the first half of this century, and therefore it attracted many potentially creative young people; now the domain of molecular genetics has the same attraction.

Second, the system model reaffirms the importance of individual factors that contribute to the creative process. Persons who are likely to innovate tend to have personality traits that favor breaking rules, and early experiences that make them want to do so. Divergent thinking, problem finding, and all the other factors that psychologists have studied are relevant in this context.

Finally, the ability to convince the field about the virtue of the novelty one has produced is an important aspect of personal creativity. One must seize the opportunities to get access to the field and develop a network of contacts. The personality traits that make it possible for one to be taken seriously, the ability to express oneself in such a way as to be understood are also part of the individual traits that make it easier for someone to make a creative contribution.

Personal Qualities

Having the right background conditions is essential, but certainly not sufficient, for a person to make a

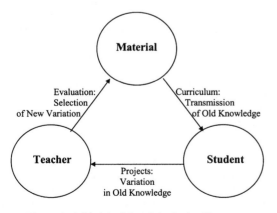

Figure 4. A Model of Creativity in the Classroom.

creative contribution. He or she must also have the ability and inclination to introduce novelty into the domain. These are the traits that psychologists have most often studied, and it is to these that we shall now turn. Because the individual traits of creative people have been so widely studied, we shall only touch on them briefly and without being able to do them justice.

Perhaps the most salient characteristic of creative individuals is a constant curiosity, an ever renewed interest in whatever happens around them. This enthusiasm for experience is often seen as part of the 'childishness' attributed to creative individuals (Gardner, 1993; Csikszentmihalyi, 1996). Without this interest, a person would be unlikely to become immersed deeply enough in a domain to be able to change it.

Besides this indispensable quality of being curious and interested, the picture becomes more complicated. One view we have developed on the basis of our studies is that creative persons are characterized not so much by single traits, but rather by their ability to operate through the entire spectrum of human characteristics. So they are not just introverted, but can be both extroverted and introverted depending on the phase of the process they happen to be involved in at the moment. When gathering ideas a creative scientist is gregarious and sociable; but as soon as he starts working, he might become a secluded hermit for weeks on end. Creative individuals are sensitive and cold, arrogant and humble, masculine and feminine, as the occasion demands (Csikszentmihalyi, 1996). What dictates their behavior is not a rigid inner structure, but the demands of the interaction between them and the domain in which they are working.

In order to want to introduce novelty into a domain, a person should first of all be dissatisfied with the status quo. It has been said that Einstein explained why he spent so much time on developing a new physics by saying that he could not understand the old physics. Greater sensitivity, naiveté, arrogance, impatience, and higher intellectual standards have all been adduced as reasons why some people are unable to accept the conventional wisdom in a domain, and feel the need to break out of it.

Values also play a role in developing a creative career. There are indications that if a person holds financial and social goals in high esteem, it is less likely that he or she will continue for long to brave the insecurities involved in the production of novelty, and will tend to settle instead for a more conventional career (Getzels & Csikszentmihalyi, 1976; Csikszentmihalyi, Getzels & Kahn, 1984). A person who is attracted to the solution of abstract problems (theoretical value) and to order and beauty (aesthetic value) is more likely to persevere.

Another way of describing this trait is that creative people are intrinsically motivated (Amabile, 1983).

They find their reward in the activity itself, without having to wait for external rewards or recognition. A recurring refrain among them goes something like this: "You could say that I worked every day of my life, or with equal justice you could say that I never did any work in my life." Such an attitude greatly helps a person to persevere during the long stretches of the creative process when no external recognition is forthcoming.

The importance of motivation for creativity has long been recognized. Cox advised that if one had to bet on who is more likely to achieve a creative breakthrough, a highly intelligent but not very motivated person, or one less intelligent but more motivated, one should always bet on the second (Cox, 1926). Because introducing novelty in a system is always a risky and usually an unrewarded affair, it takes a great deal of motivation to persevere in the effort. One recent formulation of the creative person's willingness to take risks is the 'economic' model of Sternberg and Lubart (Sternberg & Lubart, 1995).

Probably the most extensively studied attributes of the creative cognitive style are divergent thinking (Guilford, 1967) and discovery orientation (Getzels & Csikszentmihalyi, 1976). Divergent thinking—usually indexed by fluency, flexibility, and originality of mental operations—is routinely measured by psychological tests given to children, which show modest correlations with childish measures of creativity, such as the originality of stories told or pictures drawn (Runco, 1991). Whether these tests also relate to creativity in 'real' adult settings is not clear, although some claims to that effect have been made (Torrance, 1988; Milgram, 1990). Discovery orientation, or the tendency to find and formulate problems where others have not seen any, has also been measured in selected situations, with some encouraging results (Baer, 1993; Runco, 1995). As Einstein and many others have observed, the solution of problems is a much simpler affair than their formulation. Anyone who is technically proficient can solve a problem that is already formulated; but it takes true originality to formulate a problem in the first place (Einstein & Infeld, 1938).

Some scholars dispute the notion that problem finding and problem solving involve different thought processes; for example the Nobel-prize winning economist and psychologist Herbert Simon has claimed that all creative achievements are the result of normal problem-solving (Simon, 1985, 1988). However, the evidence he presents, based on computer simulation of scientific breakthroughs, is not relevant to the claim, since the computers are fed pre-selected data, pre-selected logical algorithms, and a routine for recognizing the correct solution—all of which are absent in real historical discoveries (Csikszentmihalyi, 1988a, c).

The personality of creative persons has also been exhaustively investigated (Barron, 1969, 1988).

Psychoanalytic theory has stressed the ability to regress into the unconscious while still maintaining conscious ego controls as one of the hallmarks of creativity (Kris, 1952). The widespread use of multi-factor personality inventories suggest that creative individuals tend to be strong on certain traits such as introversion and self-reliance, and low on others such as conformity and moral certainty (Csikszentmihalyi & Getzels, 1973; Getzels & Csikszentmihalyi, 1976; Russ, 1993).

How these patterns of cognition, personality, and motivation develop is still not clear. Some may be under heavy genetic control, while others develop under the conscious direction of the self-organizing person. In any case, the presence of such traits is likely to make a person more creative if the conjunction with the other elements of the system — the field and the domain — happen to be propitious.

Measurement Techniques

How can one appropriately measure individual creativity? By definition, the ability to develop useful products never before developed seems quite *un*predictable. Nevertheless, some attempts have been made. To expand on the categories of Davis (1983), these approaches are summarized by the following five methods: *Self-Assessment*, *Peer Nomination*, *Personality Correlates*, *Divergent Thinking Tests*, and *Historical Recurrence* (for greater detail see Davis, 1997; Wolfe, 1997).

One method is *Self-Assessment*. This approach elicits the subject's opinion of himself. A substantial problem with such tools is the desirability effect. People like to think of themselves of possessing a positive trait such as creativity. Other people are too modest to accurately report their own strengths. Further, it is extremely difficult to lay out a standard from which the subject can judge what is *creative*. Consequently, popular stereotypes shared in the culture conflate the findings.

A second method is *Peer Nomination*. This approach allows respondents to evaluate each other. The idea is that while creativity is difficult to operationalize, people will recognize it when they see it. As with self-assessment, this measure does not require an external framework. But unlike self-assessment, with other people evaluating the subject, the desirability effect is less intrusive. Amabile (1983) and Csikszentmihalyi (1996) are among those who have used this method by asking experts in specific domains to judge each other. This approach explicitly includes a component of social evaluation.

A third method is *Personality Correlates*. This approach uses personality traits to predict creativity. Dispositions believed to be associated with creativity include confidence, risk-taking, curiosity, and tolerance for ambiguity. Davis and Rimm (1982) developed an omnibus test called the *Group Inventory for Finding Interests* (GIFFI) I and II based on these assumptions. The problem with this approach is that in real life personality traits are dependent on context. What is important is whether these traits are present in a particular situation, within a particular domain. Furthermore, as previously argued the creative person is distinguished by the ability to alternate between usually fixed characteristics. For instance, he or she must be conformist enough to learn the knowledge available in the domain, and non-conformist enough to want to change it.

A fourth approach measures *Divergent Thinking*. Here creative ability is measured by the quality and quantity of responses to a series of hypothetical problems. The best known creativity tests are the Torrance Tests of Creative Thinking (TTCT) (Torrance, 1966; Davis, 1983, 1997). These pencil and paper tests show reasonable relationships to the preceding general creative personality traits. There is a question, however, as to how the hypothetical problems presented in divergent thinking tests translate into real life. Whether generating numerous fantastic uses for a box really predicts any sort of creative achievement is unclear. Further, divergent thinking as a general skill may not represent the reality of a domain specific world. Some support does exist for the generalizability of divergent thinking tests to creative behavior in later life as reported by Torrance (1988). An advantage of these tests is that they may pick up unrealized potential, if such a thing exists.

A fifth method is *Historical Recurrence*. This approach uses biographical data from previous creative involvement to predict future creative involvement. Simonton wrote "What distinguishes the [creative] genius is merely the cognitive and motivational capacity to spew forth a profusion of chance permutations pertaining to a particular problem" (1988b, p. 422). It follows that participation in a particular domain and public recognition of that participation can be measured and used as a predictive tool. Milgram (1990) designed a useful test for measuring creative activity and achievement applicable to ordinary school children. A criticism of this method is that it does not pick up latent divergent thinking ability. But is the detached latent ability of an individual relevant? The ability to merely think in original ways may not be an appropriate predictor of creative achievement. Csikszentmihalyi (1990a) has tried to measure the mechanism through which intrinsic motivation operates. In studying the creative *experience*, he coined the term 'flow' to describe the feeling people report when skills become so second nature that everything one does seems to come naturally, and when concentration is so intense that one loses track of time. Csikszentmihalyi argued that it is this optimal feeling of flow that fuels the intrinsic motivation engine which propels creativity (Schmidt & Wolfe, 1998).

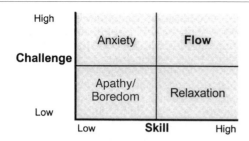

Figure 5. The Experience of Flow.

Flow

People report the most positive experiences and the greatest intrinsic motivation when they are operating in a situation of high opportunities for action (Challenges) and a high capacity to act (Skills); see Fig. 5.

Flow experiences also play a critical role in the development of complex patterns of thought and behavior and in the successful development of talent. This theoretical assumption has received empirical support in studies of adolescents (Csikszentmihalyi, Rathunde & Whalen, 1993; Adalai-Gail, 1994; Hektner, 1996; Heine, 1996).

Educational Implications at the Individual Level

In applying the Systems Model to education we shall begin on familiar ground, at the level of the person. After all, the great majority of psychological research assumes that creativity is an individual trait, to be understood by studying individuals. Considering which personal characteristics promote variation in thought and behavior suggests the following implications for educational practice.

Students' Curiosity and Interest are the Main Sources of Potential Creativity (Csikszentmihalyi, 1996)

To the extent that the curriculum and the methods of instruction will stimulate and sustain students' interests, the likelihood of them being motivated to ask new questions and explore divergent solutions will be enhanced. Unfortunately pedagogy usually either takes students' interests for granted, or ignores them altogether. One of the most important pedagogical steps would be for teachers to acquaint themselves with each student's particular inclination and interest, so that the curricular material could be connected with it.

Potential Creativity is Enhanced by Intrinsic Motivation, and Suppressed by Excessive Reliance on Extrinsic Rewards

If students learn to enjoy the acquisition of knowledge for its own sake, they will be more likely to engage in extended exploration and experimentation (Amabile, 1983). If teachers use mainly extrinsic rewards — grades, discipline, promises of conventional success — as inducements to study, it is less likely that

students will be stimulated to think new thoughts. Enjoyment does not imply relaxation or laziness; the most enjoyable activities are usually those that require great effort and skill.

Activities Need to be Designed With the Conditions Necessary for Flow in Mind

To experience flow, a challenging activity must meet the skills of the student. Therefore activities must be adapted, or at least adaptable, for each student's ability. Additionally, activities need to be designed such that goals are clear and relevant feedback is not delayed. Without clear goals, students are not certain where they should be headed; and without immediate feedback, they are not sure whether or not they are successfully headed toward that goal.

Learning to Formulate Problems Should be Part of the Curriculum

Educational practice currently relies almost exclusively on teaching students how to solve problems. The ability to formulate new problems (Getzels & Csikszentmihalyi, 1976) — or even to engage in divergent thinking — is seldom encouraged and even more rarely taught. Yet these are among the essential cognitive requirements for potentially creative thought.

Respecting Creative Personality Traits

Students who are potentially creative are almost by definition unusual in their attitudes, values, and demeanor. Therefore, they often come in conflict with teachers who consider their responsibility to enforce conformity and discipline. As a result, many young people who might contribute useful new ideas are intimidated into mediocrity. It is important for teachers to tolerate the idiosyncrasies of children who are otherwise curious and committed to learning.

Promoting the Internalization of Learning

A young person will be best prepared to introduce valuable novelty into a domain if he or she has identified himself with the rules and contents of a given discipline, and developed internal criteria of excellence in it. It is more important to nurture development of these internal standards than to make sure that students are able to perform according to standards set externally, as when they take tests and examinations.

The Contribution of the Domain

A new idea can be observed only against the background of already accepted ideas. These are grouped into domains that constitute the heritage of information we call a 'culture'. The purpose of education is to acquaint individuals with the contents of the most important domains. Howard Gardner (1983) has argued that there are at least seven main classes of such domains, each based on specific neurological potentialities. These include linguistic (e.g. poetry, literature, rhetoric, drama), logical-mathematical, musical, spatial (e.g. painting, sculpture, architecture), bodily-kinesthetic (e.g. dance, athletics), interpersonal (e.g. politics) and intrapersonal (e.g. philosophy, psychology) domains. Schools typically address only the content of the first two groups, and the emphasis is almost exclusively on the transmission of information, not on innovation.

As the system models suggests (cf. Fig. 3), in order for a creative process to begin, it is necessary that individuals become interested to assimilate the contents of a domain, and for the information contained in the domain to be transmitted to the person. These conditions suggest several issues for the enhancement of creativity in schools.

Educational Implications at the Level of the Domain

Among the issues to be considered for educational practice are the following questions.

How Attractive is the Information Presented to Students?

Regardless of the domain, if the information in it is not connected to students' interests and needs, few students will be motivated to learn beyond what is required to get good grades, and hence few will be in a position to know where the lacunae in knowledge are located, or will be moved to formulate new problems.

Given the nature of learning, it is inevitable that teachers should provide structure and goals to the curriculum, but unless students have some latitude in exploring and making decisions about the acquisition of their own knowledge, it is unlikely that they will feel enough ownership about the material to want to play with it for its own sake. The flow model also suggests that being able to match challenges with skills — in other words, to access information that is neither too difficult nor too easy — is essential for students to be attracted to learning.

How Accessible is the Information?

Often the creative process cannot start for the simple reason that the necessary information is either unavailable, or difficult to access. Textbooks and lectures are often unnecessarily abstract and mystifying, so that even motivated students often give up in frustration. It is important to encourage students to explore as many sources of information as possible, and to allow them some flexibility to do so at their own pace. Computers and the internet have a mixed record in supporting the acquisition of personalized knowledge so far, but these new information technologies have a great potential for making the contents of domains accessible.

How Integrated is the Information?

While it is important to delineate clearly the boundaries and limitations of each subject matter, it is also important for teachers to show how each subject relates to others — both differentiation and integration are essential for complex learning. Creative problems often arise at the interface of disciplines, and thus excessive compartmentalization stifles genuinely new ideas.

It is also important to help students integrate the knowledge they are acquiring — whether it is mathematics or history — to the issues students already know, and to what they care about. Few students care enough about purely abstract information to want to experiment with it. Courses that combine different disciplines (e.g. 'Physics for Poets') are only the first step in this direction; much more effort could be devoted to the planning of integrated curricula that while preserving the integrity of distinct domains, will attempt to show their mutual interaction.

Are there Opportunities for Mentorships and Apprenticeships?

In many domains, it is essential for a young person to be trained by experts as soon as possible, or the potential for creativity will not be fulfilled (Bloom, 1985). To study physics or music long enough to be able to innovate in it depends in part on whether there are laboratories or conservatories in which one can practice and learn state-of-the-art knowledge in the particular domain. Parents have to be able to afford tutors as well as the time and expense involved in driving the child back and forth to lessons and competitions. The careers of creative individuals are often determined by chance encounters with a mentor who will open doors for them, and such encounters are more likely in places where the field is more densely represented — certain university departments, laboratories, or centers of artistic activity.

Schools can contribute to matching potentially creative young people with tutors and enhancement programs through tests for identifying talent, and the organization of mentorships.

The Contribution of the Field

Novel ideas are not recognized or adopted unless they are sanctioned by some group entitled to make decisions as to what should or should not be included in the domain. These gatekeepers are what we call here the *field*. The term 'field' is often used to designate an entire discipline or kind of endeavor. In the present context, however, we want to define the term in a more narrow sense, and use it to refer only to the social organization of the domain — to the teachers, critics, journal editors, museum curators, textbook writers and foundation officers who decide what belongs to a domain and what does not. In physics, the opinion of a very small number of leading university professors was enough to certify that Einstein's ideas were creative. Hundreds of millions of people accepted the judgment of this tiny field, and marveled at Einstein's creativity without understanding what it was all about. It has been said that in the United States ten thousand people in Manhattan constitute the field in modern art. They decide which new paintings or sculptures deserve to be seen, bought, included in collections—and therefore added to the domain. A society can then be defined as the sum of its interrelated fields—from architects to zookeepers, from mothers to consumers of computer peripherals.

The recognition that culture and society are as involved in the constitution of creativity certainly does not answer all the questions. In fact, it brings a host of new questions to light. New ideas often arise in the process of artistic or scientific collaboration (Dunbar, 1993; Csikszentmihalyi & Sawyer, 1995), and peers play an important role in supporting the creativity of individuals (Mockros & Csikszentmihalyi, 2000).

Perhaps the major new question this perspective brings to light is: Who is entitled to decide what is creative? According to the individual-centered approach, this issue is not problematic. Since it assumes that creativity is located in the person and expressed in his or her works, all it takes is for some 'expert' to recognize its existence. So if some kindergarten teachers agree that a child's drawing is creative, or a group of Nobel Prize physicists judge a young scientist's theory creative, then the issue is closed, and all we need to find out is how the individual was able to produce the drawing or the theory.

But if it is true, as the systems model holds, that attribution is an integral part of the creative process, then we must ask: What does it take for a new meme to be accepted into the domain? Who has the right to decide whether a new meme is actually an improvement, or simply a mistake to be discarded? How are judgments of creativity influenced by the attributional process (Kasof, 1995)?

In any case, the point is that how much creativity there is at any given time is not determined just by how many original individuals are trying to change domains, but also by how receptive the fields are to innovation. It follows that if one wishes to increase the frequency of creativity, it may be more advantageous to work at the level of fields than at the level of individuals. For example, some large organizations such as Motorola, where new technological inventions are essential, spend a large quantity of resources in trying to make engineers think more creatively. This is a good strategy as far as it goes, but it will not result in any increase in creativity unless the field—in this case, management—is able to recognize which of the new ideas are good, and has ways for implementing them— i.e. including them in the domain. Whereas engineers and managers are the field who judge the creativity of new ideas within an organization such as Motorola, the entire market for electronics becomes the field that evaluates the organization's products once these have been implemented within the organization. Thus at one level of analysis the system comprises the organization with innovators, managers, and production engineers as its parts; but at a higher level of analysis the organization becomes just one element of a broader system that includes the entire industry.

Teachers constitute a field that judges the ideas and products of students. It is they who decide which test responses, essays, or portfolios are to be considered creative. So it is true that teachers can measure creativity—as long as it is recognized that what is meant by 'creativity' is not a real objective quality, but refers only to the acceptance by teachers. Such creativity, while part of the domain of Education, may have nothing to do with creativity in any other domain outside of it. At every level, from considering Nobel Prize nominations to considering the scribbles of four-year olds, fields are busy assessing new products and deciding whether or not they are creative—in other words, whether they are enough of an improvement to deserve inclusion in a particular domain. And as the biographies of creative individuals suggest, teachers are not particularly good at recognizing future creativity in their students.

Educational Implications at the Level of the Field

The Role of Funding

Other things being equal, a school that enjoys material resources is in a better position to help the creative process. A wealthier school is able to make information more readily available, allows for a greater rate of specialization and experimentation, and is better equipped to reward and implement new ideas. Subsistence schools have fewer opportunities to encourage and reward novelty, especially if it is expensive to produce. Only schools with ample material reserves can afford to build great gymnasiums, great auditoriums, great scientific laboratories

How Open are Teachers to New Ideas?

It is important that teachers enjoy students' explorations beyond the boundaries of textbooks and lesson plans, instead of feeling threatened by them. Teachers who allow deviation from the curriculum, who encourage students to ask questions, to explore alternative paths to solve problems, are more likely to see novelty produced by their students.

Do Teachers Stimulate Students' Curiosity and Interest?

Given the importance of problem formulation in the creative process, it seems important for teachers to stimulate students to find and frame problems of their own, problems that they care about. Every field sooner or later develops self-serving tendencies, so that the effort of its members goes towards making life easier for themselves instead of serving the social purposes for which they are paid.

For teachers, the danger is to teach with the least effort, relaying on familiar formulae and texts, without regard for the needs and interests of students. Teachers can stimulate creativity by keeping their lessons and outlines fresh, by exposing students to extracurricular opportunities to learn, by getting to know the interests and strengths of their students.

Can Teachers Distinguish Good New Ideas from Bad Ones?

As the evolutionary model makes clear, most variations are not an improvement on existing knowledge. Teachers who praise every novelty without discrimination do not help students develop the essential internalized criteria that will eventually allow them to make informed evaluations of their own ideas.

Like good parenting, good teaching requires both support and challenge, appreciation and evaluation, freedom and discipline (Csikszentmihalyi, Rathunde & Whalen, 1993). Here again extracurricular opportunities could help classroom activities: science fairs, writing contests, athletic tournaments expose students to accepted criteria of evaluation, helping them to internalize standards.

Are There Ways of Implementing Student Creativity in the School?

Recognizing a valuable novelty is the first step of the process, but bringing it to fruition is equally important. Schools can help through the production of plays, compositions, math competitions, science fairs. Similarly, it is important to pass the novel product on to others. Publication in a school paper or literary magazine, or a publicly viewed art exhibit, play, or science fair allow novelty to spread beyond the classroom.

Conclusion

It is perhaps unrealistic to expect schools to become a major force in the development of creativity. After all, the major function of formal education is to pass on knowledge to young people as accurately as possible, without losing much of the hard-earned knowledge of previous generations in the process. Yet, as we have argued, the future will require individuals who are able to formulate new problems, come up with new solutions, and adapt readily to the new ideas of others. Much of this training for a flexible, creative approach to information should be the responsibility of schools.

Traditionally, education has been focused on transmitting the knowledge of major socially sanctioned domains (i.e. Science, Mathematics, Literature), at the expense of encouraging the evolution of those domains which might lead to individual variation through challenging questions and original answers. The Systems Model suggests an important issue: To foster creativity, education needs to do more than transfer

information from teacher to student. So, without sacrificing the domain's information *transmission*, how can educators add to the field's value *selection* and the student's product *variation*?

Creativity in the past has been viewed as a mental process, as the product of individual genius. But new ideas come from existing domains of knowledge; problems arise and standards are internalized from them. And we know whether or not an original solution is worth implementing because of the evaluation of an expert field. It is certain that psychologists interested in the phenomenon of creativity will continue to focus on the individual and his or her thought processes. After all, the unique qualities of creative geniuses are so attractive that we cannot curb our curiosity about them.

What the present chapter seeks to accomplish, however, is to point out that creativity cannot be recognized except as it operates within a system of cultural rules, and it cannot bring forth anything new unless it can enlist the support of experts. If these conclusions are valid, then it follows that the occurrence of creativity in schools is not simply a function of how many gifted students there are, but also of how accessible is the information they need, and how responsive teachers are to novel ideas. Instead of focusing exclusively on students, it makes more sense to focus on educational institutions that may or may not nurture novelty. For in the last analysis creativity in schools is a joint result of well-presented knowledge, interested students, and stimulating teachers.

References

Adalai-Gail, W. S. (1994). *Exploring the Autotelic Personality*. Unpublished doctoral dissertation. The University of Chicago.

Amabile, T. M. (1983). *The Social Psychology of Creativity*. New York: Springer.

Baer, J. (1993). *Creativity and Divergent Thinking*. Hillsdale, NJ: Lawrence Erlbaum.

Barron, F. (1969). *Creative Person and Creative Process*. New York: Holt, Rinehart and Winston.

Barron, F. (1988). Putting creativity to work. In: R. J. Sternberg (Ed.), *The Nature of Creativity* (pp. 76–98). Cambridge, UK: Cambridge University Press.

Bloom, B. (1985). *Developing talent in young people*. New York: Ballantine Books.

Campbell, D. T. (1976). Evolutionary epistemology. In: D. A. Schlipp (Ed.), *The Library of Living Philosophers: Karl Popper*. La Salle, IL: Open Court.

Cox, C. (1926). *The early mental traits of three hundred geniuses*. Stanford, CA: Stanford University Press.

Csikszentmihalyi, M. (1975). *Beyond boredom and anxiety*. San Francisco: Jossey-Bass.

Csikszentmihalyi, M. (1988a). Motivation and creativity: Toward a synthesis of structural and energistic approaches to cognition. *New ideas in psychology*, **6** (2), 159–176.

Csikszentmihalyi, M. (1988b). Society, culture, person: a systems view of creativity. In: R. J. Sternberg (Ed.), *The Nature of Creativity* (pp. 325–339). New York: Cambridge University Press.

Csikszentmihalyi, M. (1988c). Solving a problem is not finding a new one: a reply to Simon. *New Ideas in Psychology*, **6** (2), 183–186.

Csikszentmihalyi, M. (1990a). *Flow: the psychology of optimal experience*. New York: Harper and Row.

Csikszentmihalyi, M. (1990b). The domain of creativity. In: M. A. Runco & R. S. Albert (Eds), *Theories of Creativity* (pp. 190–212). Newbury Park, CA: Sage.

Csikszentmihalyi, M. (1993). *The Evolving Self: a psychology for the third millennium*. New York: HarperCollins.

Csikszentmihalyi, M. (1996). *Creativity: flow and the psychology of discovery and invention*. New York: HarperCollins.

Csikszentmihalyi, M. (1999). Implications of a systems perspective for the study of creativity. In: R. J. Sternberg (Ed.), *The Handbook of Human Creativity* (pp. 313–338). New York: Cambridge University Press.

Csikszentmihalyi, M. & Getzels, J. W. (1973). The personality of young artists: An empirical and theoretical exploration. *British Journal of Psychology*, **64** (1), 91–104.

Csikszentmihalyi, M. & Getzels, J. W. (1988). Creativity and problem finding. In: F. G. Farley & N. R. W. (Eds), *The Foundations of Aesthetics, Art, and Art Education* (pp. 91–106). New York: Praeger.

Csikszentmihalyi, M., Getzels, J. W. & Kahn, S. P. (1984). *Talent and achievement: a longitudinal study of artists*. [A report to the Spencer Foundation]. Chicago: The University of Chicago.

Csikszentmihalyi, M., Rathunde, K. & Whalen, S. (1993). *Talented teenagers: the roots of success and failure*. New York: Cambridge University Press.

Csikszentmihalyi, M. & Sawyer, K. (1995). Shifting the focus from individual to organizational creativity. In: C. M. Ford & D. A. Gioia (Eds), *Creative Action in Organizations* (pp. 167–172). Thousand Oaks, CA: Sage Publications.

Davis, G. A. (1983). *Creativity is forever*. Kendall: Hunt Publishing Company.

Davis, G. A. (1997). Identifying Creative Students and Measuring Creativity. In: N. Colangelo & Davis (Eds), *Handbook of Gifted Education* (2nd ed., pp. 269–281). Boston: Allyn and Bacon.

Davis, G. A. & Rimm, S. (1982). Group inventory for finding interests (GIFFI) I and II: Instruments for identifying creative potential in the junior and senior high school. *Journal of Creative Behavior*, **16**, 50–57.

Dawkins, R. (1976). *The selfish gene*. Oxford, UK: Oxford University Press.

Dunbar, K. (1993). Scientific reasoning strategies for concept discovery in a complex domain. *Cognitive Science*, **17**, 397–434.

Einstein, A. & Infeld, L. (1938). *The evolution of physics*. New York: Simon & Schuster.

Feldman, D., Csikszentmihalyi, M. & Gardner, H. (1994). *Changing the world:* a framework for the study of creativity. Westport, CT: Praeger.

Gardner, H. (1983). *Frames of mind: the theory of multiple intelligences*. New York: Basic Books.

Gardner, H. (1988). Creative lives and creative works: a synthetic scientific approach. In: R. J. Sternberg (Ed.), *The Nature of Creativity* (pp. 298–321). New York: Cambridge University Press.

Gardner, H. (1993). *Creating minds*. New York: Basic Books.

Getzels, J. W. & Csikszentmihalyi, M. (1976). *The Creative Vision: a longitudinal study of problem finding in art*. New York: John Wiley and Sons.

Getzels, J. W. & Jackson, P. (1962). *Creativity and intelligence*. New York: J. Wiley & Sons.

Gruber, H. (1988). The evolving systems approach to creative work. *Creativity Research Journal*, **1** (1), 27–51.

Guilford, J. P. (1967). *The nature of human intelligence*. New York: McGraw-Hill.

Harrington, D. M. (1990). The ecology of human creativity: a psychological perspective. In: M. A. Runco & R. S. Albert (Eds), *Theories of Creativity* (pp. 143–169). Newbury Park, CA: Sage Publications.

Heine, C. (1996). *Flow and achievement in mathematics*. Unpub. Doctoral Dissertation. Chicago: The University of Chicago.

Hektner, J. (1996). *Exploring optimal personality development: a longitudinal study of adolescents*. Unpublished doctoral dissertation. The University of Chicago.

Kasof, J. (1995). Explaining creativity: the attributional perspective. *Creativity Research Journal*, **8** (4), 311–66.

Kris, E. (1952). *Psychoanalytic explorations in art*. New York: International Universities Press.

Magyari-Beck, I. (1988). New concepts about personal creativity. *Creativity and Innovation Yearbook, 1* (pp.121–26), Manchester, UK: Manchester Business School.

Martindale, C. (1989). Personality, situation, and creativity. In: R. R. J. Glover & C. R. Reynolds (Eds), *Handbook of Creativity* (pp. 211–232). New York: Plenum.

Maslow, A. H. (1963). The creative attitude. *The Structuralist*, **3**, 4–10.

Mayr, E. (1982). *The growth of biological thought*. Cambridge, MA: Belknap Press.

Milgram, R. M. (1990). Creativity: an idea whose time has come and gone? In: M. A. Runco & R. S. Albert (Eds), *Theories of Creativity* (pp. 215–233). Newbury Park, CA: Sage Publications.

Mockros, C. & Csikszentmihalyi, M. (2000). The social construction of creative lives. In: R. Purser & A. Montuori (Eds), *Social creativity*. Creskill, NY: Hampton Press, 175–216.

Perkins, D. N. (1988). The Possibility of Invention. In: R. J. Sternberg (Ed.), *The Nature of Creativity* (pp. 362–385). New York: Cambridge University Press.

Runco, M. A. (1991). *Divergent thinking*. Norwood, NJ: Ablex.

Runco, M. A. (Ed.). (1995). *Problem finding*. Norwood, NJ: Ablex.

Russ, S. W. (1993). *Affect and creativity*. Hillsdale, NJ: Lawrence Erlbaum.

Schmidt, J. A. & R. N. Wolfe. (1998) *Preparing for Careers in Technology: course-taking, time allocation, and daily experience of American adolescents*. Unpublished paper presented at the 6th Biennial Conference for the European Association for Research on Adolescence, June 1998. Budapest, Hungary.

Simon, H. A. (1985). *Psychology of scientific discovery*. Keynote presentation at the 93rd Annual Meeting of the American Psychological Association. Los Angeles, CA.

Simon, H. A. (1988). Creativity and motivation: A response to Csikszentmihalyi. *New Ideas in Psychology*, **6** (2), 177–181.

Simonton, D. K. (1988). *Scientific Genius*. Cambridge: Cambridge University Press.

Simonton, D. K. (1988b). Creativity, leadership, and chance. In: R. J. Sternberg (Ed.), *The Nature of Creativity* (pp. 386–426). New York: Cambridge University Press.

Simonton, D. K. (1990). Political pathology and societal creativity. *Creativity Research Journal*, **3** (2), 85–99.

Simonton, D. K. (1991). Personality correlates of exceptional personal influence. *Creativity Research Journal*, **4**, 67–68.

Simonton, D. K. (1994). *Greatness: who makes history and why*. New York: Guilford.

Stein, M. I. (1953). Creativity and culture. *Journal of Psychology*, **36**, 311–322.

Stein, M. I. (1963). A transactional approach to creativity. In: C. W. Taylor & F. Barron (Eds), *Scientific Creativity* (pp. 217–227). New York: John Wiley.

Sterman, J. D. (1994). Learning in and about complex systems. *System Dynamics Review*, **10** (2–3), 291–330.

Sternberg, R. J. & Lubart, T. I. (1995). *Defying the crowd: cultivating creativity in a culture of conformity*. New York: The Free Press.

Torrance, E. P. (1966). *Torrance Tests of Creative Thinking*. Bensenville, IL: Scholastic Testing Service.

Torrance, E. P. (1988). The nature of creativity as manifest in its testing. In: R. J. Sternberg (Ed.), *The Nature of Creativity* (pp. 43–75). Cambridge, UK: Cambridge University Press.

Wolfe, R. N. (1997). *Creative involvement, task motivation, and future orientation in adolescence*. Unpublished masters thesis. The University of Chicago.

Giftedness in Non-Academic Domains: The Case of the Visual Arts and Music

Ellen Winner[1] and Gail Martino[2]

[1] *Boston College and Harvard Project Zero, USA*
[2] *John B. Pierce Laboratory and Yale University School of Medicine, USA*

Introduction

It is common to distinguish between giftedness and talent. Children who are advanced in scholastic abilities or have a high IQ are labeled gifted, while those who show exceptional ability in an art form or an athletic area are called talented. In this chapter we argue against such a distinction, and refer to children with talent in an art form as gifted.

While there is no necessary link between a gift in art or music and a gift in terms of high IQ (Shuter-Dyson, 1986; Csikszentmihalyi, Rathunde & Whalen, 1993; Winner, 1996a; Miller, 1999), children with high ability in an art form are similar to academically gifted children in three respects (Winner, 1996a). First, they are precocious; they master the first steps in their domain at an earlier than average age and learn more rapidly in that domain. Second, they have a 'rage to master'—that is, they are intensely motivated to make sense of their domain and show an obsessive interest and ability to focus sharply in their area of high ability. In the visual arts, this means that they produce a large volume of work over a sustained period of time (Golomb, 1992; Pariser, 1997; Milbrath, 1998). In music, where giftedness usually emerges in performance rather than composition, this means that children develop a large repertoire of music that they can perform (Winner, 1996a). And third, they 'march to their own drummer', meaning that they do not just learn faster than ordinary children, they also learn differently. They learn virtually on their own, requiring minimum adult scaffolding, and often solve problems in their domain in novel, idiosyncratic ways.

Because these children solve problems in unusual ways, they are creative. But we distinguish sharply here between two levels of creativity: little-c and big-C creativity (Winner, 1997). Gifted children are creative in the little-c sense, meaning that they solve problems in novel ways and make discoveries about their domain on their own. Big-C creativity, or domain creativity, involves changing the domain. There is considerable evidence that creators do not make domain-altering changes until they have worked for at least ten years in their area (Gardner, 1993; Simonton, 1994). (Mozart and Picasso both created works as young children, but their domain-altering contributions came from their adult works.) Thus, children by definition cannot be domain creative.

In this chapter we consider three questions about giftedness in the visual arts and music. First, what are the characteristics typically displayed by children with such gifts? Second, what is the role of environmental factors in the development of these gifts? Third, what is the relationship between early prodigiousness in art and music and domain creativity in these areas in adulthood?

Characteristics of Children Gifted in Visual Arts

Children who may be labeled 'gifted' in drawing are not just more advanced than typical children in drawing milestones. Rather, they draw in a qualitatively different way. This has been demonstrated by Milbrath (1998) in a longitudinal and cross-sectional study of gifted young artists. Prior to the work of Milbrath, studies of artistically gifted children relied primarily on case studies. Milbrath made an important contribution to the study of artistic giftedness by following eight artistically gifted children over ten years, and also by comparing a group of artistically gifted children between ages 4–14 to a normal control group. Using the terminology of Piaget (Piaget & Inhelder, 1969), she argues that artistically gifted children are guided by 'figurative' rather than 'operational' processes (but see Pariser, 1995, for a critique of using a Piagetian framework to describe artistic milestones). According to Milbrath, these children actually *see* the world differently. To begin with, they encode visual information more accurately, and see the world less in terms of concepts and more in terms of

95

shapes and visual surface features. Second, they have superior visual memories (cf. Rosenblatt & Winner [1988] for corroborating evidence). And third, they attend more to the act of drawing itself, they can *see* when something looks wrong, and this leads to discoveries about how to represent the world on paper. Thus, in Milbrath's terms, these children are better at seeing, remembering, and doing.

Ability to Draw Realistically

Because artistically gifted children use figurative processes to represent (that is, they seem to be able to draw things as they appear, with all the distortions caused by point of view and perspective), their drawings typically appear highly realistic (Milbrath, 1998). This realism is a hallmark of gifted child art. The 'core' indicator of giftedness in drawing is the ability to draw recognizable shapes at least one year in advance of the normal time of emergence of this skill. While typical children begin to draw recognizable shapes representing objects in the world at around the age of 3 or 4 (Kellogg, 1969; Matthews, 1984; Golomb, 1992), gifted children have been noted to begin to draw representationally at the age of 2. Figure 1 shows a striking contrast between the way in which a typical and an artistically gifted 2-year-old drew

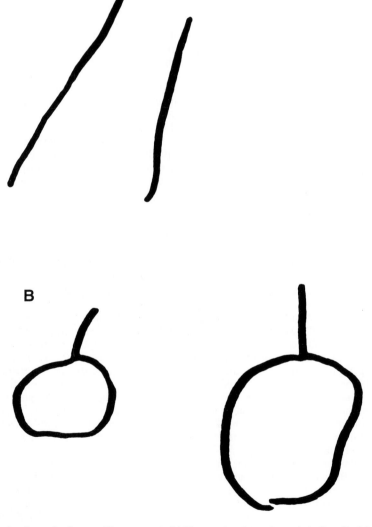

Figure 1. (a) Two apples drawn by 2-year-old on request; (b) Two apples drawn by artistically gifted 2-year-old on request. Reprinted with permission of Ryan Sullivan.

apples. The typical 2-year-old made a slash for each apple because he had not yet acquired the understanding that lines on the page stand for the edges of objects. For him, a line simply stood for 'thingness'. The gifted 2-year-old had grasped the concept of a line standing for an edge, and produced a fluid line describing the contour of each apple.

Milbrath (1998) also notes that a clear sign of artistic giftedness is the ability to use line to stand for edge, in contrast to typical children who use line to stand for thing. In Willats' (1981) terms, ordinary children use a denotation rule by which a one-dimensional picture primitive (i.e. a line) stands for a two-dimensional region or volume. Artistically gifted children bypass this rule. They also bypass another similar denotation rule by Willats (1981). While children ordinarily fill in planes to convey solidity (thereby using a 2-d primitive to stand for a 3-d volume), artistically gifted children emphasize the surface features of a plane by decorating its surface and retaining a line around its edge. In this way a plane is depicted correctly as a two-dimensional form.

Soon after gifted children begin to draw recognizable forms, they also begin to draw in a realistic manner. They are able to capture the precise shapes of objects, they add true-to-life details that most children would never add (e.g. gas tanks on cars), and they begin to represent the illusion of volume and depth. In place of the simple, schematic, flat, charming, child-like forms typically found in child art, one finds remarkable adult-like, differentiated, complex images that suggest an effort to understand and master how objects are structured. Gifted children draw realistic images quickly and with ease. They do not labor and erase. Instead, their lines are sure and confident (Gordon, 1987; Paine, 1987; Pariser, 1991, 92/93; Milbrath, 1998). The young Picasso, for example, could draw anything upon demand, and liked to start a figure from non-canonical places, for instance, by drawing a dog beginning with the ear (Richardson, 1991) A highly realistic pair of faces, copied by Millais at age 8 from an adult work is shown in Fig. 2.

The ability to draw realistically also means that gifted children's drawings capture the correct proportions of figures. Milbrath (1998) found that gifted children succeed in drawing human figures in proportion between the ages of four and ten. The non-gifted children that she studied were still unable to capture proportion by age 14 (which was the oldest age at which she observed their drawings).

Numerous examples of children with precocious ability to draw realistically have been reported (Kerchensteiner, 1905; Wilson & Wilson, 1976; Gardner, 1980; Hurwitz, 1983; Golomb, 1992; Winner, 1996a; Milbrath, 1998). One of the most striking examples of early realism is found in the work of Eytan, an Israeli child described by Golomb (1992). Eytan's family did not remember whether he scribbled, but the family does have drawings that he produced at 2, an age when most children are just beginning to scribble. At 2, Eytan drew recognizable shapes: people, tractors, fish, cars, etc. Normal children make their first tadpole-like representation of a human at about age 3, and do not differentiate the head from the trunk until several years later. In contrast, Eytan began to draw humans with a differentiated head and trunk at between 2 and 3.

Figure 2. Pencil copy of an adult work drawn by John Everett Millais at age 8.

One way Eytan achieved realism was through the meticulous depiction of details, such as exhaust pipes on his vehicles. Another way that realism was achieved was through the depiction of volume and depth. Typically children in Western culture do not begin to try to depict the third dimension until the middle elementary school years. By the age of $2\frac{1}{2}$, Eytan was not content with drawing vehicles from their canonical side view, and invented ways to depict their volume, showing their sides receding into depth. He first used an orthographic projection system to show more than the front or side of a vehicle. By the age of 3 he had abandoned this system and instead showed multiple sides of a vehicle by attaching the top and side faces to the front of a vehicle. After his third birthday, he used a mixture of three projection systems: horizontal and vertical oblique projection; isometric projection (in which the front view of a vehicle was its true rectangular shape, but the top and sides of his trucks were parallelograms); and divergent perspective, in which lines diverge outwards to show the front, top, and both sides of a vehicle. By the time he was 4 he showed an understanding of the perspectival rule that objects receding in the distance are reduced in size, and he was beginning to experiment with foreshortening. Figure 3 shows an attempt at perspective by Eytan at age $3\frac{3}{4}$.

According to Milbrath (1998), because artistically gifted children see the world in terms of its visible surface features, they are able to overcome the object-centered perspective that dominates typical children. Milbrath notes that artistically gifted children begin to make view-specific drawings long before ordinary children do so. This means that their drawings show figures in non-canonical positions (e.g. three-quarter views of faces by age 7, back views, profiles) as well as figures distorted and foreshortened by perspective. She observes, however, that while artistically gifted children use perspectival techniques at an early age, their drawings show mixed viewpoints (e.g. oblique projection mixed with linear perspective). These children do not appear to be able to make drawings with one single coordinated point of view until adolescence. According to Milbrath, the ability to coordinate a drawing through a single viewpoint must await Piagetian formal operations. However, whatever it is that constrains the development of the ability to coordinate a drawing through a unified viewpoint is not yet known, and research is needed to determine whether children could learn to draw with a single viewpoint at a pre-formal age with appropriate training. Given the fact that artistic savants such as Steven Wiltshire are able to use

Figure 3. Drawing of a truck by Eytan at age $3\frac{3}{4}$. From Claire Golomb, *The child's creation of a pictorial world*. Reprinted with permission of The Regents of the University of California, Copyright & Copy: 1992.

unified perspective despite being autistic and retarded, there are likely to be alternative routes to perspective besides operational understanding, a point on which Milbrath agrees.

The ability to draw realistically at an earlier than average age also marks the childhoods of those who go on to become established artists. Gordon (1987) studied the childhood works of thirty-one Israeli artists and found that all stood out for their early ability to draw realistically. The desire and ability to draw realistically at an early age also characterized the childhoods of those who go on to become sculptors: Sloane and Sosniak (1985) interviewed twenty sculptors about their childhoods, most of whom recalled drawing realistically at an early age. Numerous other well known artists' early drawings have been singled out for their advanced realism: e.g. Millais (Paine, 1987), Landseer (Goldsmith & Feldman, 1989), Seargent (Cox, 1992), and Picasso (Pariser, 1991).

Picasso provides a clear example of the ability to draw highly realistically at an early age. He claimed, perhaps apocryphally, that he bypassed the typical stage of early drawings in which children draw in a fanciful, playful, non-realistic manner. "I have never done children's drawings. Never" (Richardson, 1991, p. 29). However, since we have no records of his works before the age of 9, it is not clear whether this is true. What is clear is that Picasso wanted to see himself as a prodigy. When he went to see a show of child art, he noted, 'As a child I would never have been able to participate in a show of this kind: at age 12, I drew like Raphael' (Richardson, 1991, p. 29). And he recalled specific examples of this adult-like style: "Even when I was very small. I remember one of my first drawings.

I was perhaps six . . . In my father's house there was a statue of Hercules with his club in the corridor, and I drew Hercules. But it wasn't a child's drawing. It was a real drawing, representing Hercules with his club" (Richardson, 1991, p. 29). At 11, Picasso enrolled in his father's academic drawing class, in which students had to make detailed renderings of plaster casts. While most students considered this drudgery, Picasso loved it, and produced technically skilled and precise drawings.

Ability to Master Cultural Conventions

Realism as an early indicator of artistic giftedness may well be culturally determined. In the West, at least from the Renaissance until the twentieth century, artists have striven to capture the illusion of space, volume, and depth (Gombrich, 1960). While gifted children probably begin to draw realistically long before they have much if any exposure to examples of Western realistic art, they have certainly been exposed to realistic images on billboards, magazines, and picture books. The most well-known non-Western artistic prodigy is Wang Yani, a Chinese child who painted in the Chinese brush and ink style at an adult-like level in the preschool years (Zhensun & Low, 1991). As can be seen in Fig. 4, Wang Yani does not draw or paint in a realistic style, but rather in the style of classical Chinese painting. As young as four, Wang Yani had developed a sense of the adult art world, and could make the kind of art valued by the art 'field' in her culture—i.e. the art historians, the museum curators, etc. Wang Yani uses the classical Chinese wash technique and she paints in the loose spontaneous and abbreviated style of Chinese ink paintings. Thus, as

Figure 4. 'Pull Harder', painting by Wang Yani at age five. Reprinted by permission of Wang Shiqiang.

Goldsmith and Feldman (1989) point out, the technical sophistication of her work reveals itself along dimensions different from those of Western children.

Alexandra Nechita, a Romanian born artistic prodigy now in the United States, provides a similar example (Winner, 1997). She works in oil, on large canvases, some up to 5 feet by 9 feet, and she paints quickly and compulsively, often completing several large paintings in one week. Her paintings are clearly imbued in the Western modernist tradition — Cubism, Fauvism, Expressionism. One can see in them the styles not only of Picasso, but also of Gorky, Kandinsky, and Miro (Fig. 5).

The differences between Wang Yani and Alexandra Nechita are instructive. The domain — the body of works that make up the history of painting in one's culture — is shown here to exert as powerful an influence on child prodigies as on adult artists. It is unlikely that either could have painted as they did without the influence of their respective traditions.

The similarities between the two child artists are just as instructive as their differences. Both have an uncanny sense of the adult art world of their culture, and can paint the kinds of paintings that are prized by this art world. Both have an astonishing mimetic ability that allows them to do this. These two cases tell us not only about the power of the domain, but also about the strong role of the *field* — the gatekeepers, judges, curators and art critics who determine whether a work is considered creative (Csikszentmihalyi, 1988). If Alexandra Nechita had somehow been able to develop her style in China, her works would almost certainly have been seen as odd, as distorted, as ugly, as unskillful, and as something to be discouraged. They would have looked nothing like the art that the adult field values. Because she painted in the West and in the 20th century, where modernism and Picasso are revered, her art looks adult-like and has thus been deemed prodigious. Had she produced her paintings two hundred years ago in the West, her works would surely have attracted a negative reaction. A recent study by Pariser and Vandenberg (1997) found that views of what is considered aesthetic in child art in general (i.e. not specifically gifted child art) is also culturally determined, with Westerners valuing modernism, and Chinese-Americans valuing skill.

Further evidence that we place too high a value on early realism as a sign of artistic giftedness comes from Karpati (1994, 1997), who found that giftedness in design and construction did not predict a high level of ability to draw realistically. She concluded that different aspects of artistic talent are unrelated, and the ability to draw realistically is only one sign of such talent. There is in fact abundant evidence that artistically gifted children do not always draw realistically. Gifted children often draw in cartoon style, and cartoons are a non-realistic cultural convention (Wilson & Wilson, 1976). The childhood drawings of Toulouse

Lautrec were not realistic but were in the style of grotesque and expressive caricatures (Pariser, 1998). As a child, Picasso also often drew caricatures, as well as other playful non-realistic images (Pairser, 1998). Neither Picasso, Lautrec, nor Klee were advanced in the area of spatial rendering (Pariser, 1998). An analysis of Klee's 6-year-old drawings showed them to be at an adult level in realism (using the Goodenough Harris scale) but only at the 6-year-old level in terms of organization of pictorical space (Porath, 1992).

What unites all children with artistic gifts is thus not the ability or proclivity to draw realistically (though this is a common manifestation in the West), but rather the ability to master one or more of the culture's norms of artistry at a very early age. At the heart of artistic talent is the ability to master cultural conventions, whether the convention is realism in the case of Eytan or Millais, modernism's distortion in the case of Alexandra Nechita, grotesque caricature in the case of Lautrec, or allusionistic brush painting in the case of Wang Yani. It is a mistake to be blinded by our Western eyes and see realism as the prime sign of artistic talent, when realism is but one of many possible cultural conventions that artistically gifted children master so early and so independently.

Exploration of a Single Theme

Picasso viewed paintings as a logical sequence of explorations. "Paintings", he said, "are but research and experiment. I never do a painting as a work of art. All of them are researches. I search constantly and there is a logical sequence in all this research" (Liberman, 1960, p.33). Many artistically gifted children seem to exemplify this approach. In their drawings, a single theme is explored over and over gain. This repeated practice in drawing one kind of subject means that they are far more skilled in drawing their favored subject than in drawing other subjects. For Eytan, for instance, the theme was vehicles, and these were drawn far in advance of his human figures. Wang Yani painted only monkeys until the age of 7 (Goldsmith & Feldman, 1989; Goldsmith, 1992), and was far better at rendering monkeys than horses or humans, just as Lautrec rendered horses better than birds or humans (Pariser, 1997). Kerchensteiner (1905) described G. J. who drew only horses. Gardner (1980) described Gabriel who focused on portraits, and Stuart who focused on comic book style figures. Winner (1996a) described Peter who focused on women in flowing robes. As Pariser (1997, p.41) notes, the work of artistically gifted children is 'thematically specialized'.

The Invention of Imaginary Worlds and the Construction of Narratives

Particularly in middle childhood and adolescence, artistically gifted children create imaginary settings and fantasy characters in their drawings, and their drawings depict episodes in the lives of these invented characters. This is the age when gifted children begin to create superheroes and science fiction characters modeled after the images they see in comic books. Wilson and Wilson (1976) note that visual narrative need not be in the form of a series of frames, as in a comic strip. Each drawing functions as a shorthand for a complex plot. One episode may begin in one sketch book and then continue on disconnected pages. These fantasy worlds allow children an escape into a private world. According to one gifted child, "most people . . . just look at them and say 'that's a pretty picture'

Figure 5. 'Forgotten Values', Painting by 10-year-old Alexandra Nechita in a style reminiscent of Picasso. Reprinted by permission of International Art Publishers, Costa Mesa, CA.

101

without understanding what the people are really like and the story behind them" (Wilson & Wilson, 1976, p. 46). Gifted children are often much more interested in inventing imaginary worlds in their drawings than in experimenting with form and design. In the process, they produce countless drawings, and thus gain fluency and technical skill (Wilson & Wilson, 1976).

Advanced Compositional Strategies

The compositional strategies of artistically gifted children are advanced in comparison to those of typical children. Golomb (1992) studied the principles of composition in almost 1,500 drawings by typical children from 3–13 years of age. Younger children tended to align the parts of the drawing along either the horizontal or vertical axes. Older children moved on to symmetrical compositions, but only the most talented ones used asymmetrical balance. In contrast, Milbrath (1998) found that the drawings by even her youngest gifted children were constructed according to symmetry as well as complex symmetry and asymmetrical balance. Both complex symmetry and asymmetrical balance use different dimensions as counterbalances. Thus, large size may be counterbalanced by a heavy color. In Fig. 6, the large cat is balanced by the smaller ball of yarn which achieves weight because it is colored an intense yellow. Milbrath hypothesizes that the advanced compositional strategies of artistically gifted children are made possible by the fact that these children attend closely to the act of drawing itself, and thus can judge the visual weights of shapes, colors, empty spaces, and directional lines.

Characteristics of Children Gifted in Music

The core ability of the visually gifted child was described as the ability to capture one or more of the culture's graphic conventions, whether these be realistic depiction, modernism, caricature, or the allusionistic style of Chinese brush painting. The core ability of the musically gifted child is a sensitivity to the structure of music—tonality, key, harmony, and rhythm, and the ability to hear the expressive properties of music. Sensitivity to structure allows the child to remember music, to play it back with ease either vocally or with an instrument, and to transpose, improvise, and even invent. Just as there has been undue focus on realism as the core indicator of artistic giftedness, there has been undue focus on technical and analytic skill as the core indicator of musical giftedness. Sensitivity to expressive properties has been relatively ignored.

Musical giftedness reveals itself as young as 1 or 2, which is perhaps earlier than giftedness in any domain of skill (Scott & Moffett, 1977; Shuter-Dyson & Gabriel, 1981; Shuter-Dyson, 1986). For example, in a survey of forty-seven musicians, Scheinfeld (1956, cited in Shuter-Dyson & Gabriel, 1981) found that their ability had been detected on average at $4\frac{3}{4}$. Drake

Figure 6. Drawing by an 8-year-old gifted child showing asymmetrical balance. The large cat is balanced by the small ball of yarn because the cat is uncolored and the yarn is bright yellow. The color gives the smaller shape more weight. Reprinted by permission of Constance Milbrath and Cambridge University Press.

(1957, cited in Shuter-Dyson & Gabriel, 1981 found that 70% of the great violinists in Leahy's *Famous Violinists* were prodigies as young children. Mozart composed a concerto for the harpsichord at 4 (Water-house, 1988). Mendelssohn was even more of a prodigy, and the violinist Yehudi Menuhin performed with symphony orchestras at 7.

The strikingly early age at which musical giftedness often manifests itself may be a function of music's appeal and accessibility. However, musical talent may not always be recognized at an early age, as shown by Sloboda's (1985) finding that concert pianists are not always recognized as musically gifted in early child-hood.

Interest in Musical Sounds

Perhaps the earliest clue that a child is gifted in music is a strong interest and delight in musical sounds (Scott & Moffett, 1977; Sosniak, 1985; Radford, 1990). Stravinsky's first memories were of song (Gardner, 1992). And Mozart's ear was said to be so delicate that loud sounds made him physically ill (Schonberg, 1970). However, Sloboda (1985) points out that heightened attention to sounds per se is not in itself evidence of musical sensitivity: a response to a sound may simply be due to the infant's natural heightened attentiveness to novelty.

Musical children respond more to music than do average children, showing an intense interest in auditory information, both musical and environmental (Haroutounian, 1998, in preparation; Miller, 1989). Such children often have a strong sense of goodness of tone and timbre. For example, both Rubinstein and Menuhin broke toy violins because the tone of these toys was so poor (Radford, 1990).

Musical Memory

One of the earliest signs of musical giftedness is the ability to sing back heard songs with accuracy. This ability is made possible by exceptional musical mem-ory, a skill that has been said to be the ability most central to musical talent (Judd, 1988). While children ordinarily begin to sing and talk at about the same age (18 months) (Sloboda, 1985), musically gifted children may begin to sing at a younger age, and often before they can speak (Shuter-Dyson, 1986). E. N., the 7-year-old Hungarian musical prodigy studied by Revesz (1925) did not speak until the age of 3, but before the age of 1 he tried to sing back songs. Revesz reports also that Handel sang before he could speak.

In the normal course of development, children do not try to imitate heard songs until about 2–$2\frac{1}{2}$. Children are able to sing portions of these songs with accuracy at around 3, and can sing whole songs by about 4. However, intervals in these songs are only approx-imate, and children are not yet able to maintain the same tonality through a single song. It is not until about five that children can reproduce with accuracy the

familiar tunes of their culture (Gardner, Davidson & McKernon, 1981; Sloboda, 1985). Musically gifted children present a striking contrast: these children sing with great accuracy, demonstrating the ability to match pitches with precision by their second year (Revesz, 1925).

Musically gifted children can imitate a song after only one exposure, and familiar themes from TV are rapidly and effortlessly learned (Miller, 1989). Mozart began to pick out tunes on the piano at 3 (Schonberg, 1970). Pepito Areola, a child studied by Richet (1900) could play twenty pieces from memory by the age of $3\frac{1}{2}$. At 3, the pianist Arthur Rubinstein listened to his older sister playing the piano and surprised his family by faultlessly playing the pieces she had been practis-ing (Winn, 1979). At the beginning of his fourth year, a Hungarian prodigy, E. N. could reproduce with accuracy on the piano any tune that he overheard (Revesz, 1925); by seven he could play complex Beethoven sonatas from memory. Mozart at 14 was able to write down Alleferi's *Miserere*, a complex piece of music with nine parts, after listening to it only a few times (Henson, 1977).

A series of memory tests administered by Revesz showed the seven-year-old E. N. had a short-term musical memory almost equal to that of an adult musician tested. That is, E. N. performed as well as the musician when asked to listen to pieces of music, commit them to memory, and play them back. Moreover, E. N. revealed a long-term memory far superior to that of the adult musician: both were asked to reproduce music heard 24 hours earlier, but only E. N. succeeded, and he did so effortlessly and flaw-lessly.

E. N.'s memory gave evidence of a tacit under-standing of musical structure: he was better able to recall familiar structure, harmony, and rhythm than random harmonies, and had better recall for the music in the diatonic scale than for dissonant music built on the twelve tone chromatic scale. Thus, his memory was structure-preserving: it was somewhat dependent on familiar structure, and was thus not eidetic, mindless, or literal. Superior recall for familiar form indicates some representation (whether conscious or uncon-scious) of musical structure. Bamberger (1986) notes that the extraordinary ability of musically gifted children to play back what they hear is non-reflective and tacit. Such children often say that they cannot imitate a piece if they think about it.

Perfect Pitch

While one might predict that musically gifted children would show perfect pitch—the ability to name notes heard, and the ability to sing notes named—this is not the case. Certainly some prodigies have shown perfect pitch. E. N., for example, at the age of 3 could instantly locate on the piano notes that were sung to him. He could also recognize intervals and the notes in a chord and analyze chords. In fact, his capacity for resolving multiple chords has hardly ever been equaled (Revesz, 1925). Mozart also had perfect pitch: he could tell when violins were a quarter out of tune by the age of 4 (Schonberg, 1970).

However, perfect pitch is not consistently associated with musical giftedness (Walters, Krechevsky & Gardner, 1985). Rather, perfect pitch is related to the age at which musical instruction was begun, and is far more likely to be found in individuals who began musical instruction before the age of 4 than in those who began as late as 12 (Sergent and Roche, 1973). However, it is certainly possible that children who begin at an early age are those who are more gifted and also those who have perfect pitch.

Sight-Reading

As with the skill of perfect pitch, the ability to sight-read is also not consistently associated with giftedness in music (Walters, Krechevsky & Gardner, 1985). This ability is possessed by some but not all musical prodigies. Mozart possessed this skill. At seven, he could readily play a piece he had never seen before (Scott & Mofett, 1977). E. N. also had this ability at seven.

Musical Generativity: Ability to Transpose, Improvise, and Compose

There is a clear distinction between the act of performing existing music and the creation of new music. A further distinction exists between composing new music and two more constrained forms of creation: transposing a given piece to a new key, and improvising from a given musical theme. The transposer takes a given piece and shifts it to a new key. The improviser takes a given musical theme and improvises from this theme, without changing the essential style and structure of the already existing piece.

All children begin to produce their own spontaneous songs at around 18 months, and experiment with musical intervals. Their spontaneous songs lengthen and develop in internal organization between two and three. However, by five, spontaneous singing declines in frequency, as the child becomes concerned with making mistakes, and shows an interest in imitating heard songs with accuracy (Sloboda, 1985). Thus, most children in Western culture stop generating music by the end of the preschool years. This decline in playful experimentation with song has its parallel in a decline of flavorful, preconventional drawings of the pre-schooler, and a concern for literalness in drawing in the elementary school years (Gardner, 1980; Winner, 1982).

Once again, musically gifted children tell a different story. Most musically gifted children learn to play an instrument, and soon after they begin to play they show 'musical generativity' in the form of improvising, and in transposing tunes to new keys. E. N. could transpose pieces to new keys at seven, and by ten could transpose complex pieces into any key with ease. He could improvise by four and for the next three years he improvised more than he composed, both on his own themes as well as on those of others. Mozart improvised by four (Schonberg, 1970; Scott & Moffett, 1977). For other examples, see Richet (1900), and Walters, Krevchevsky & Gardner (1985).

The ability to compose in early childhood is far rarer than the ability to perform, and these are clearly two separate kinds of musical talent (Persson, 1997). Revesz (1925) argued that a gift for composition is rarely seen before late childhood. J. S. Bach, Handel, Beethoven, Mendelssohn, Brahms are examples of great musicians reported by Revesz who were performing virtuosi in early childhood but who did not compose until early adolescence or later. E. N. is a rare example of a child who began to compose as early as $3\frac{1}{2}$. Haydn, Mozart, Chopin, Mahler, Meyerbeer, Saint-Saens, and Strauss also produced their first compositions before 10 (Revesz, 1925; Radford, 1990). Mozart began composing at 4 and by 8 had already written six sonatas for piano and violin and three symphonies for small orchestra. However, the biographies of great composers show that the ability to compose at an early age is much rarer than the ability to interpret and perform music at an early age.

Multiple Representations of Musical Relations

Musically gifted children have an unusual capacity for representing musical relations in multiple ways (Bamberger, 1986). Bamberger demonstrated this by comparing musically gifted children to three other groups: musically untrained (presumably non-gifted) children, musically untrained adults, and musically trained adults. They were given a randomly ordered array of bells that formed the pitches of the C major scale along with two Cs, two Gs, and two Es. They were asked to construct a familiar tune (Twinkle Twinkle Little Star).

Children and untrained adults always added new bells to the bell path in their order of occurrence in the tune; they never moved backwards to hit the same note a second time. Thus they needed two different bells for the two Gs in the tune, because each was heard as different. These non-gifted and non-trained individuals used what Bamberger (1986) calls a 'figural' strategy, because they focused on the figure of the tune and heard each note within the context of the tune's shape. Doing this leads to the two Gs being heard as different because of their different functions in the tune.

The non-gifted but trained adults used a 'formal' strategy (since they had received musical training), building a C major scale and then playing the tune on the scale as if it were a keyboard. They focused on the formal structure of the tune. In contrast, the gifted children switched strategies. At first they began with a figural strategy, lining pitches up from left to right. But when the got to 'star', they switched to a formal strategy and moved backwards to hit the G already used for 'twinkle'. Thus they realized that one bell could be used for both. They felt a conflict between figural and formal strategies as they proceeded and made both figural and formal choices, showing that they represented the notes both in terms of their position on the C major scale and also in terms of their function within the tune. (Two notes can be identical yet serve a different function, and thus feel different.) Thus, Bamberger (1986) argued that musically gifted children have multiple internal representations for the same piece of music, and can move freely from one kind to another. While they are capable of formal strategies, they have also retained the capacity for a more intuitive figural approach. In contrast, non-gifted individuals, irrespective of age and musical training, use a single strategy and focus consistently on a limited set of musical dimensions.

A similar point has been made by Scripp and Davidson (1994), who showed that even musically gifted conservatory students face the challenge of developing and coordinating multiple representations of music. Scripp and Davidson found a lack of coordination between conservatory students' performance knowledge (their ability to play their instrument) and their understanding of musical notation, with the former often way ahead of the latter. For example, they found that conservatory students who have no trouble sightreading tunes on an instrument have considerable difficulty, and make many errors, if asked to sightsing. We should not, therefore, make the mistake of assessing musical development only by studying performance knowledge. Musical development is multi-dimensional, and musical giftedness does not develop at the same rate along all dimensions.

Expression

Just as researchers have, we believe, focused too narrowly on realism as an indicator of giftedness in the visual arts, so also have they focused too narrowly on sensitivity to analytical and notational aspects of music — structure, themes, transformation — as the indicator of musical giftedness (Kirnarskaya & Winner, 1997). Sensitivity to non-notational, expressive properties of music — register, timbre, loudness, articulation, and phrasing — has been overlooked. These are the features that carry the emotional and dramatic message of music. An individual with a heightened expressive ear for music might not be able to follow the details of musical structure, but can hear and respond to the emotional message of the music. Persson and his colleagues (Persson, 1996; Persson, Pratt & Robson, 1996) found that musicians judged pieces in terms of their emotional response, that positive emotional experiences with music were one of the most important factors prompting them to become musicians, and that

emotional aspects of music were often ignored in traditional conservatory training. Perhaps sensitivity to the emotional message of music is a better indicator of musical giftedness than is sensitivity to notational aspects.

The Seashore measures (Seashore, 1938), as well as most other musical aptitude tests (e.g. Bentley, 1966; Gordon, 1987; Stankov & Horn, 1980; Shuter-Dyson & Gabriel, 1981), are based on the assumption that individuals with musical talent have an excellent 'analytical ear' for music. The Seashore measures assess analytical skills such as the ability to make fine differentiations between tones and musical structures. Individuals are asked to listen to pairs of chords, intervals, rhythms, and brief melodies and to decide if they are the same or different. Cultures in which children are selected for musical training rely on these same kinds of measures: children are given brief tunes and patterns to recall and sing back. The more accurate their performance, the more musical they are considered to be. (This, for instance, has been the practice of music schools in Russia for decades.) The core of musical aptitude is thus assumed to be the ability to detect pitch, duration of pitch, and rhythm.

Some psychologists have argued that musical aptitude tests should assess not analytic ability but rather other qualities that would be more closely predictive of high creative achievement in music. Davies (1978), for example, suggests that aptitude tests should assess musical reasoning. He argues that the possession of a sharp ear for music may be no more predictive of musicality than possession of good eyesight is predictive of good reading ability. Similarly, Teplov (1966) argued that musical aptitude should not be equated with having a good musical memory and an ability to differentiate chords and melodies. Rather, he argued, the ability to respond emotionally to music is the core of musicality. Teplov reflects the traditional Russian musicological interest in expression and affect in music, and in non-notational aspects of music making (Asafiev, 1947; Medushevsky, 1983).

Kirnarskaya and Winner (1997) found that most people, even those with high levels of music training, respond to music analytically rather than expressively. When asked to group passages of music, both trained and untrained individuals grouped according to analytic structure rather than expressive properties. Even music educators with high levels of music training grouped analytically. In contrast, concert performers, who had no more formal training than the music educators, grouped according to expression. Kirnarskaya and Winner concluded that formal musical training does not foster an expressive ear for music. Sensitivity to expressive properties may, they argued, be a marker for inborn musical giftedness. This suggestion, which remains to be directly tested, follows from the fact that concert performers grouped expressively, while equally well-trained music educators (who are presumably less gifted since they did not become performers) grouped analytically.

Origins of Artistic and Musical Gifts

Practice

The origin of artistic and musical giftedness is a subject of much debate. The lay person's view is that these gifts are innate (Winner, 1996a), and music teachers often say that they can tell right away when a student has inborn ability: these are the students who learn quickly, self-correct, and have high self-confidence when they perform (Walters, Krechevsky & Gardner, 1985).

Not all music educators subscribe to this nativist view, however. Perhaps the most famous exception was Shinichi Suzuki, the founder of the Suzuki method of music teaching. "Every child is born with the capacity for becoming richly musical so long as he or she is brought up properly ... There is no inborn talent for music ability," wrote Suzuki (Herman, 1981, p. 36). Recently, some cognitive psychologists have developed this environmentalist position in the case of music, arguing that high achievement in music, like high achievement in any area, is due to hard work, perseverance, and what is termed 'deliberate practice' — goal-directed work on what is difficult (Ericsson & Faivre, 1988; Howe, Davidson & Sloboda, 1988; Howe, 1990; Ericsson et al., 1993).

The major problem with this environmental explanation is that there is no evidence that the hard work is causally related to high achievement (Torff & Winner, 1994; Winner, 1996a, b, 1998; Miller, 1999). It is just as likely that the intense motivation that leads prodigies (as well as savants) to work for hours at a time is due to the fact that they have high ability. Children are motivated to work hard at a domain in which they have special ability. But no typical child can be made to have a 'rage to master', and no typical child can be forced to work in the intense way that prodigies work. It is our position that hard work (or deliberate practice, in the case of domains in which one can reasonably talk about practice) is necessary for the development of any gift. But there is no evidence that hard work is sufficient, and thus no evidence to allow us to rule out an innate component to giftedness. Indeed, the strikingly early age of emergence of gifts in art and music, and the fact that high levels of skill make themselves known prior to formal training, are both strong pieces of indirect evidence for an innate component (Winner, 1996a, b).

Family and Teachers

Families of both artistically and musically gifted children tend to be supportive and encouraging, but families play a far more interventionist and active role in the case of the musically gifted (Csikszentmihalyi, Rathunde & Whalen, 1993). Without a supportive home environment, musically children often give up a musical instrument (Freeman, 1979). Almost all music prodigies come from musical families (Scheinfeld, 1956; Scott & Moffett, 1977; Judd, 1988; Radford, 1990). Similarly, artistically gifted children almost always have parents or close relatives who are artists or in fields related to the arts (Feldman & Goldsmith, 1986; Gordon, 1987; Goldsmith & Feldman, 1989). Of course, we have no idea how many artistically or musically gifted children have been born into non-supportive families and whose gifts have hence never developed (Persson, in press).

Music prodigies who continue to perform and compose as adults are nurtured and even pushed by their parents and teachers. The gift is never fully developed when first observed, and must be nourished through daily training. Those who continue with music as adults all report having had at least one parent or teacher who cared deeply about their talent, and who worked with them daily, sitting with them as they practiced and establishing a structure of discipline. Studies of prize winning musical performers show the universal presence of at least one parent who was 'fanatically' interested in music and in the child's musical development (Bastian, 1994). The violinist Isaac Stern remarked, "There *has* to be someone pushing, a parent or a teacher. Every one of the kids I've guided has someone like that in their lives, pushing them, sometimes gently, sometimes horribly, sometimes, unfortunately, to the point of driving the child away from music. It's the quality of parental pushing that helps determine the eventual outcome of the prodigy" (Winn, 1979, p. 40).

The importance of a first music teacher who is warm and supportive has been noted by many (e.g. Sosniak, 1985; Bastian, 1994; Howe & Sloboda, 1991). Most adult musical performers eventually attend a conservatory to get musical training in a department of music. While musically gifted children typically enter a regimen of formal training at a young age, and stress the necessity of hard work and practice for the development of their talent (Bastian, 1994), artistically gifted children often get little formal training in art. At least in the West, artistically gifted children are often suspicious of formal art education, believing such tutelage to be unnecessary and potentially destructive of their talent (Gardner, 1980). The typical art class in elementary and high school does not serve to stimulate these children's art. It is a sad commentary on the way that art is typically taught in school that none of the sculptors studied by Sloane and Sosniak had anything good to say about their elementary or high school art classes. Winner and Pariser (1985) also noted this: the artists they interviewed reported that what crystallized their identity as young artists was some professional artist who noted their ability. Contemporary Chinese artists show the same negative attitude towards their elementary school arts instructors (Winner, 1989). Thus, family and community appear more important than schools in the development of artistic ability. Not surprisingly, then, gifted children often make their best, most inventive work out of school (Hurwitz, 1983; Wilson & Wilson, 1976).

Relationship between Childhood Giftedness and Adult Eminence

Highly gifted children often face a crisis at adolescence. Bamberger (1982) points out that prodigies in music experience a midlife crises at adolescence, when they become increasingly critical of their playing, and this crisis often results in dropping out of music. The same situation may well be true of artistically gifted children. Adolescence is the time when prodigies must make the transition from technical perfection to innovation and big-C, domain creativity. Only those who can reinvent themselves will make the leap between childhood giftedness and adult creativity (Gardner, 1993). It is extremely difficult to predict those gifted children and prodigies who will make this transition, and those who will not (Simonton, 1994). We might predict that a six-year-old who can draw as realistically as a skilled adult will grow up to be the next Picasso. But again, if at twenty she is still just drawing with technical precision, and not doing anything innovative, she will begin to fade from public view. Take the case of Alexandra Nechita. She is famous now as a child for painting in the style of late Picasso. But will anyone take notice of her as an adult if she continues only to paint in the style of Picasso? Rostan et al. (1998) found that the childhood drawings of great artists (Picasso, Klee, Lautrec) were not distinguishable from drawings of contemporary gifted child artists. Yet surely few if any of this contemporary group will become great artists. Clearly, while high ability is necessary, it is not sufficient. Degree of skill in childhood cannot by itself predict later creative eminence; nor can early detection or the best and most rigorous course of training (Scripp & Davidson, 1994).

The situation is the same in music. A child who plays Mozart just like her teacher, or even just like a Heifetz recording, amazes us. But by twenty, if this prodigy does not play in a way that is new, with some deep understanding, and a new interpretation, serious musicians and critics will lose interest. Technical perfection will win a child adoration, but it will win the prodigy grown into adulthood little or nothing.

Almost all research on musical giftedness has limited itself to the study of children learning the Western classical tradition. We know little about the development of giftedness in the arena of Western popular or counter-cultural music, nor about the development of children in non-Western musical traditions. As pointed out by Persson (1995, 1997, in press), traditional Western conservatory training is highly competitive, stressful, inflexible, and places a strong value on conformity to tradition (see also Gelber, 1988; Kennedy, 1991). Is it not possible then that such training may constrain the emergence of domain-altering creativity? Given the far greater emphasis placed on rigorous formal training for young people in music than art, the musically talented child in our culture faces very different developmental hurdles from those faced by the artistically talented child.

Great artists, especially music performers, were often prodigies as children (Shuter-Dyson, 1986). However, the reverse is not the case: most children who are gifted in art or music do not become adult artists, musicians, or composers. When discussing artistically gifted children, the art historian Hartlaub commented that the promise of these "over-potential years of childhood is almost never fulfilled in adulthood" (Lark Horowitz et al., 1973, p. 190). Even among those who weather this crisis and do not drop out, most do not become known as creative geniuses. This is not surprising, as there is no direct route from precocity to inventiveness. But of course a few prodigies do go on to change their respective domains. These are the ones who earn the epithet 'creative' or 'creative genius'. These are the individuals who, at adolescence or early adulthood, take a new stance. They begin to take risks: they challenge the establishment (Gardner, 1992, 1993).

One reason why only a few artistically and musically gifted children and prodigies make the transition to become domain creators as adults is that the funnel is small: there is simply not enough room at the top for all prodigies to become creators; and so there is an inevitable weeding out. Any domain would be in chaos if there were as many creative adult innovators as there are child prodigies.

A second inevitable reason is that the skill of being a prodigy is not the same as the skill of being a big-C creator. A prodigy is someone who can easily and rapidly master a domain with expertise. A creator is someone who changes a domain. It is likely that personality factors play a major role in becoming a domain creator. Creators are restless, rebellious, and dissatisfied with the status quo (Simonton, 1994; Sulloway, 1996); and they have something new to 'say'.

In a study of seven creative geniuses, Gardner (1993) suggests that a certain degree of tension, or 'asynchrony' is required for a prodigy to grow into an adult artist or musician who would be classified as creative, or even as a genius. Gardner (1992) argues that creative geniuses differ from prodigies in how well the individual synchronizes with his or her domain as it currently operates within the society. The prodigy typically exhibits talents that fit well with a domain that is recognized by the society as important, and the skills of the prodigy are thus instantly recognized. In contrast, the creative genius often initially exhibits talents that do not fully fit within the domain in which the individual works, and which do not fit with the established tastes of the field (e.g. critics, gallery owners, conductors).

Of course, some individuals, such as Mozart, start out as prodigies and go on to become adults who transform their domains. As a prodigy, Mozart pleased the establishment. But it is only because of his later behavior, when he began to write music that we considered shocking, and which broke with established convention, that we now consider him to be a creative genius. The creative artist/musician takes risks, and breaks with conventions; the gifted child, or child prodigy, does not. As Hurwitz (1983) points out, gifted children have invested a great deal of energy in mastering a set of skills, and are often unwilling, or even unable, to experiment in the way that one must do in order to be creative.

Gardner's (1992) notion of asynchrony is compatible with Getzels and Csikszentmihalyi's (1976) notion of problem finding. In a study of art students, Getzels and Csikszentmihalyi found that the art students who went on to become recognized as creative artists did not differ from their art student peers in technical skill. Where they stood out was in their tendency and ability to find challenging problems. This problem-finding mentality is reminiscent of Picasso, who delighted in posing difficulties for himself which he could then go on to solve (Richardson, 1991). Even as a child, he fought against what came naturally, insisting on setting up difficult drawing challenges for himself such as beginning a drawing from an odd starting point, or drawing a profile facing right when the opposite orientation is more natural for a right-hander (Richardson, 1991). (For another example of a gifted child artist posing difficult challenges for himself, see Winner, 1996a, p.71).

Sheer hard work also plays a role in determining whether a prodigy becomes a creative adult artist or musician or composer. The personality characteristics associated with success in any field are drive, tenacity, and the willingness to overcome obstacles (Roe, 1953; Gardner, 1980; 1993; Simonton, 1994). "I believe in nothing but work," said Picasso, who had tremendous energy and drive (Richardson, 1991, p. 48).

Finally, historical and socio-cultural factors determine who becomes classified as an adult creator or genius. No individual or artistic work is inherently creative or not. Instead, creativity is an emergent property formed by an interaction among the individual's gift, the state of the domain at the time when the individual begins to exhibit talent, and the tastes and judgments of the field (e.g. critics, curators, publishers) (Gardner & Wolf, 1988; Csikszentmihalyi, 1988; Gardner, 1992, 1993; Pariser, 1992/93). There is a fair amount of serendipity involved in determining whether giftedness grows into creative genius. One needs to be born at the right time, at a time when the field is ready to recognize one's talents.

References

Asafiev, B. (1947). *Musical form as a process*. Leningrad: Musica.

Bamberger, J. (1982). Growing up prodigies: the midlife crisis. In: D. H. Feldman (Ed.), *Developmental Approaches to Giftedness and Creativity* (pp. 61–77). San Francisco, CA: Jossey-Bass, Inc.

Bamberger, J. (1986). Cognitive issues in the development of musically gifted children. In: R. Sternberg & J. Davidson (Eds), *Conceptions of Giftedness* (pp. 388–413). New York: Cambridge University Press.

Bastian, H. G. (1994). From the every-day world and the musical way of life of highly talented young instrumentalists. In: K. A. Heller & E. A. Hany (Eds), *Competence and Responsibility: The Third European Conference of the European Council for High Ability*, (Vol. 2), (pp. 153–163). Seattle: Hogrefe & Huber Publishers.

Bentley, A. (1966). *Musical ability in children and its measurement*. New York: October House.

Bloom, B. (1985). *Developing talent in young people*. New York: Ballantine Books.

Cox, M. (1992). *Children's drawings*. London: Penguin Books.

Csikszentmihalyi, M. (1988). Society, culture, and person: A systems view of creativity. In: R. Sternberg (Ed.), *The Nature of Creativity: Contemporary Psychological Perspectives*. New York: Cambridge University Press.

Cskikszentmihalyi, M, Rathunde, K. & Whalen, S. (1993). *Talented teenagers: the roots of success and failure*. New York: Cambridge University Press.

Davies, J. (1978) *The Psychology of Music*. London: Hutchinson.

Ericsson, K. A. & Faivre, I. A. (1988). What's exceptional about exceptional abilities? In: L. K. Obler & D. A. Fein (Eds), *The Exceptional Brain: Neuropsychology of Talent and Special Abilities* (pp. 436–473). New York: Guilford Press.

Ericsson, K. A., Krampe, R. T. & Tesch-Romer, C. (1993). The role of deliberate practice in the acquisition of expert performance. *Psychological Review*, **100** (3), 363–406.

Feldman, D. H. & Goldsmith, L. T. (1986). *Nature's gambit*. New York: BasicBooks.

Freeman, J. (1974). Talent in music and fine art. *Gifted Education International*, **2**, 107–110.

Freeman, J. (1979). *Gifted children: their identification and development in a social context*. Baltimore: University Park Press.

Gardner, H. (1980). *Artful scribbles: the significance of children's drawings*. New York: BasicBooks.

Gardner, H. (1992). *The 'giftedness matrix' from a multiple intelligences perspectives*. Paper presented at the Esther Katz Rosen Symposium on the development of Giftedness, University of Kansas, February.

Gardner, H. (1983). *Frames of mind: the theory of multiple intelligences*. New York: Basic Books.

Gardner, H. (1993). *Creating minds: an anatomy of creativity seen through the lives of Freud, Einstein, Picasso, Stravinsky, Eliot, Graham, and Gandhi*. New York: BasicBooks.

Gardner, H. & Wolf, C. (1988). The fruits of asynchrony: a psychological examination of creativity. *Adolescent Psychiatry*, **15**, 106–123.

Gardner, H., Davidson, L. & McKernon, P. (1981). The acquisition of song: a developmental approach. In: *Doc-*

umentary *Report of the Ann Arbor Symposium.* Music Educators National Conference. Reston, Virginia.

Gelber, G. S. (1988). Psychological development of the conservatory student. In: F. L. Roehmann & F. R. Wilson (Eds), *The Biology of Music Making. Proceedings of the 1984 Denver Conference.* (pp. 3–15). St. Louis, MO: MMB Music.

Goldsmith, L. (1992). Stylistic development of a Chinese painting prodigy. *Creativity Research Journal,* **5** (3), 281–293.

Goldsmith, L. & Feldman, D. (1989). Wang Yani: Gifts well given. In: W. C. Ho (Ed.), *Yani: The Brush of Innocence* (pp. 59–62). New York: Hudson Hills Press.

Golomb, C. (1992). *The child's creation of a pictorial world.* Berkeley, CA: University of California Press.

Gombrich, E. H. (1960). *Art and illusion.* London: Phaidon Press.

Gordon, A. (1987). Childhood works of artists. *The Israel Museum Journal,* **6,** 75–82.

Gordon, E. E. (1987). *The nature, description, measurement, and evaluation of music aptitudes.* Chicago, IL: GIA.

Haroutounian, J. *Musical talent—kindling the spark: recognizing and developing musical potential.* New York: Oxford University Press. (in preparation).

Haroutounian, J. (1998). Kindling a musical spark. *Communicator: California Association for the Gifted,* **29,** 2, 1, 24–17.

Henson, R. (1977). Neurological aspects of musical experience. In: M. Crichley & R. Henson (Eds), *Music and the Brain: Studies in the Neuropsychology of Music.* London: William Heinemann Medical Books Limited.

Herman, E. (1981). *Shinichi Suzuki: the man and his philosophy.* Athens, OH: Ability Associates.

Howe, M. J. A. (1990). *The origins of exceptional abilities.* Oxford: Blackwell.

Howe, M. J. A, Davidson, J. W. & Sloboda, J. A. (1998). Innate talents: reality or myth. *Behavioral and Brain Science,* **21** (3), 430–431.

Howe, M. J. A. & Sloboda, J. A. (1991). Young musicians' accounts of significant influences in their early lives. 2. Teachers, practising and performing. *British Journal of Music Education,* **8,** 53–63.

Hurwitz, A. (1983). *The gifted and talented in art: a guide to program planning.* Worcester, MA: Davis Publications.

Judd, T. (1988). The varieties of musical talent. In: L. Obler & D. Fein (Eds), *The Exceptional Brain: Neuropsychology of Talent and Special Abilities* (pp. 127–155). New York: Guilford Press.

Karpati, A. (1994). The Leonardo program. In: H. Kauppinen & M. Dicket (Eds), *Trends in Art Education in Diverse Cultures* (pp. 95–102). Reston, VA: National Art Education Association.

Karpati, A. (1997). Detection and development of visual talent. *Journal of Aesthetic Education,* 31, 4, 79–93.

Kellogg, R. (1969). *Analyzing children's art.* Palo Alto: National Press Books.

Kennedy, N. (1991). *Always playing.* London: Weidenfeld & Nicholson.

Kerschensteiner, G. (1905). *Die Entwicklung der zeichnerischen Begabung* (Development of drawing aptitude), Munich: Carl Gerber.

Kirnarskaya, D. & Winner, E. (1997). Musical ability in a new key: exploring the expressive ear for music. *Psychomusicology,* **16,** 2–16.

Lark-Horowitz, B., Lewis, H. & Luca, M. (1973). *Understanding children's art for better teaching* (2nd ed.). Columbus, OH: Charles E. Merrill.

Liberman, A. (1960). *The artist in his studio.* New York: Viking Press.

Matthews, J. (1984). Children drawing: are young children really scribbling? *Early Child Development and Care,* **18,** 1–39.

Medushevsky, V. (1983). *Intonation and plot in musical form.* Moscow: Musica.

Milbrath, C. (1998). *Patterns of artistic development in children: comparative studies of talent.* Cambridge, UK: Cambridge University Press.

Miller, L. K. (1989). *Musical savants: exceptional skill in the mentally retarded.* Hillsdale, N.J.: Lawrence Erlbaum Associates.

Miller, L. K. (1999). The savant syndrome: intellectual impairment and exceptional skill. *Psychological Bulletin,* **125** (1), 31–46.

Morgan, M. (1987). David Downes: Drawings from 4 to 10 years. In: S. Paine (Ed.), *Six Children Draw* (pp. 23–37). New York: Academic Press.

Morishima, A. & Brown, L. (1977). A case report on the artistic talent of an autistic idiot savant. *Mental Retardation,* **15,** 33–36.

Paine, S. (Ed.). (1987). *Six children draw.* New York: Academic Press.

Pariser, D. (1991). Normal and unusual aspects of juvenile artistic development in Klee, Lautrec, and Picasso. *Creativity Research Journal,* **4,** 457–472.

Pariser, D. (1992/93). The artistically precocious child in different cultural contexts: Wang Yani and Toulouse-Lautrec. *Journal of Multicultural and Cross-cultural Research in Art Education,* **10/11,** 49–72.

Pariser, D. (1995). Not under the lamppost: Piagetian and neo-Piagetian research in the arts. A review and critique. *Journal of Aesthetic Education,* **29** (3), 93–108.

Pariser, D. (1997). Conceptions of children's artistic giftedness from modern and postmodern perspectives. *Journal of Aesthetic Education,* **31** (4), 35–47.

Pariser, D. (1998). Looking for the muse in some of the right places: A review of Constance Milbrath's *Patterns of artistic development.*

Pariser, D. & Vandenberg, A. (1997). The mind of the beholder: Some provisional doubts about the U-curved aesthetic thesis. *Studies in Art Education,* **38** (9), 155–170.

Persson, R. S. (1995). Psychological stressors among student musicians: A naturalistic study of the teacher-student relationship. *International Journal of Arts Medicine,* **2,** 7–13.

Persson, R. S. (1996). Musical reality: Exploring the subjective world of performers. In: R. Monelle & C. T. Gray (Eds), *Song and Signification: Studies in Music Semiotics.* Edinburgh: University of Edinburgh Faculty of Music.

Persson, R. S. (1997). Annorlunda land: Sarbegavningens psykologi [In a different land: the psychology of high ability]. Stockholm: Almqvist & Wiksell. (translation of chapter, 'The artistic domain of giftedness: music and musical pursuits' provided by the author).

Persson, R. S. Survival of the fittest or the most talented? Deconstructing the myth of the musical maestro. *Journal of Secondary Gifted Education* (in press).

Persson, R. S., Partt, G. & Robson, C. (1996). Motivational and influential components of musical performance: A qualitative analysis. In: A. J. Cropley & D. Dehn (Eds), *Fostering the Growth of High Ability: European Perspectives*. Norwood, N.J.: Ablex.

Piaget, J. & Inhelder, B. (1969). *The psychology of the child*. New York: BasicBooks.

Porath, M. (1992). Stage and structure in the development of children with various types of 'giftedness'. In: R. Case (Ed.), *The Mind's Staircase: Exploring the Conceptual Underpinnings of Children's Thought And Knowledge* (pp. 303–318). Hillsdale, NJ: Lawrence Erlbaum Associates, Inc.

Radford, J. (1990). *Child prodigies and exceptional early achievers*. New York: The Free Press.

Revesz, G. (1925). *The psychology of a musical prodigy*. Freeport, NY: Books for Libraries Press. Reprinted in 1970.

Richardson, J. (1991). *A life of Picasso*. New York: Random House.

Richet, G. (1900). Note sur un cas remarquable de precocité musicale. IV Congrés Internationale de Psychologie. *Compte Rendu des Sciences*, 93–99.

Roe, A. (1953). *The making of a scientist*. New York: Dodd Mead.

Rosenblatt, E. & Winner, E. (1988). Is superior visual memory a component of superior drawing ability? In: L. Obler & D. Fein (Eds), *The Exceptional Brain: Neuropsychology of Talent and Superior Abilities* (pp. 341–363). New York: Guilford.

Rostan, S., Pariser, D. & Gruber, H. (1998). *What if Picasso, Lautrec and Klee were in my art class*? Paper presented at the American Educational Research Association, San Diego.

Scheinfield, A. (1956). *The new heredity and you*. London: Chatto & Windus.

Schonberg, H. (1970). *The lives of the great composers*. New York: W. W. Norton & Company, Inc.

Scott, D. & Moffett, A. (1977). The development of early musical talent in famous composers: a biographical review. In: M. Critchley & R. Henson (Eds), *Music and the Brain: Studies in the Neurology of Music* (pp. 174–201). London: William Heinemann Medical Books Limited.

Scripp, L. & Davidson, L. (1994). Giftedness and professional training. In: R. F. Subotnik & K. D. Arnold (Eds), *Beyond Terman: contemporary longitudinal studies of giftedness and talent* (pp. 186–211). Norwood, N.J.: Ablex.

Seashore, C. (1938). *The psychology of music*. New York: McGraw-Hill.

Selfe, L. (1977). *Nadia: A case of extraordinary drawing ability in an autistic child*. New York: Academic Press.

Sergent, D. & Roche, S. (1973). Perceptual shifts in the auditory information processing of young children. *Psychology of Music*, **1**, 39–48.

Shuter-Dyson, R. (1986). Musical giftedness. In: J. Freeman (Ed.), *The Psychology of Gifted Children* (pp. 159–183). Chichester: Wiley.

Shuter-Dyson, R. & Gabriel, C. (1981). *The psychology of musical ability* (2nd edition). London: Methuen.

Simonton, D. (1994). *Greatness: who makes history and why*. New York : Guilford Press.

Sloane, K. & Sosniak, L. (1985). The development of accomplished sculptors. In: B. Bloom (Ed.), *Developing Talent in Young People* (pp. 90–138). New York: Ballantine Books.

Sloboda, J. (1985). *The musical mind: the cognitive psychology of music*. Oxford: Clarendon Press.

Sosniak, L. (1985). One concert pianist. In: B. Bloom (Ed.), *Developing Talent in Young People* (pp. 68–89). New York: Ballantine Books.

Stankov, L. & Horn, J. (1980). Human abilities revealed through auditory tests. *Journal of Educational Psychology*, **72**, 19–42.

Subotnik, R. & Arnold, K. D.(Eds) (1994). *Beyond Terman: contemporary longitudinal studies of giftedness and talent*. Norwood, NJ: Ablex.

Sulloway, F. (1996). *Born to rebel: birth order, family dynamics, and creative lives*. New York: Pantheon.

Teplov, B. M. (1966). *Psychologie des aptitudes musicales*. Paris: Presses Universitaires de France.

Torff, B. & Winner, E. (1994). Don't throw out the baby with the bathwater: on the role of innate factors in musical accomplishment. (Commentary). *The Psychologist*, **7** (8), 361–362.

Walters, J., Krechevsky, M. & Gardner, H. (1985). *Development of musical, mathematical, and scientific talents in normal and gifted children*. (Technical Report No. 31). Project Zero, Harvard Graduate School of Education.

Waterhouse, L. (1988). Speculations on the neuroanatomical substrate of special talents. In: L. Obler & D. Fein (Eds), *The Exceptional Brain: Neuropsychology of Special Talent* (pp. 493–512). New York: Guilford.

Willats, J. (1981). What do the marks in the picture stand for? The child's acquisition of systems of transformation and denotation. *Review of Research in Visual Arts Education*, **13**, 18–33.

Wilson, B. & Wilson, M. (1976). Visual narrative and the artistically gifted. *The Gifted Child Quarterly*, **20**, 432–447.

Winn, M. (1979, December 23). The pleasures and perils of being a child prodigy. *New York Times Magazine*, **12–17**, 38–45.

Winner, E. (1982). *Invented worlds: the psychology of the arts*. Cambridge, MA: Harvard University Press.

Winner, E. (1989). How can Chinese children draw so well? *Journal of Aesthetic Education*, **23**, 41–63.

Winner, E. (1996a). *Gifted children: myths and realities*. New York: BasicBooks.

Winner, E. (1996b). The rage to master: the decisive case for talent in the visual arts. In: K. A. Ericsson (Ed.), *The Road to Excellence: the Acquisition of Expert Performance in the Arts and Sciences, Sports and Games* (pp. 271–301). Hillsdale, NJ: Erlbaum.

Winner, E. (1997). Giftedness vs. creativity in the visual arts. *Poetics*, **24** (6), 349–377.

Winner, E. (1998). Don't confuse necessity with sufficiency or science with policy. Commentary on Howe, M. J. A., Davidson, J. W. & Sloboda, J. A. Innate Talents: Reality or Myth. *Behavioral and Brain Science*, **21**, (3), 430–431.

Winner, E. & Pariser, D. (1985). Giftedness in visual arts. *Items*, **31** (4), 65–69.

Zhensun, A. & Low, A. (1991). *A young painter: the life and paintings of Wang Yani—China's extraordinary young artist*. New York: Scholastic, Inc.

Genius and Giftedness: Same or Different?

Dean Keith Simonton

Department of Psychology, University of California, Davis, USA

Introduction

Lewis M. Terman's monumental *Genetic Studies of Genius* is universally recognized as one of the classics in the research literature on giftedness. Each volume of this multi-volume work holds significant insights about the development of intellectual giftedness across the life span. Yet it is also essential to recognize why the set of six volumes must be styled 'studies' rather than as a single 'study'. The plural designation is required because Terman's magnum opus actually contains two rather different kinds of empirical inquiries. On the one hand, the bulk of *Genetic Studies* is allotted to Terman's impressive longitudinal study of gifted children. These results are treated in Volumes 1 and 3 through 6. Published over a 70-year period, these volumes cover almost the entire human life span (Terman, 1925; Burks, Jensen & Terman, 1930; Terman & Oden, 1947, 1959; Holahan & Sears 1995). Of these volumes, it is Volume 5 that is in many respects the most crucial (Terman & Oden, 1959; see also Oden, 1968). This volume, which was published posthumously, attempted to prove that those whom he had identified as talented children did in fact become highly successful adults. The gifts of childhood could even become the genius of adulthood (see also Subotnik & Arnold, 1994; Subotnik, Kassan, Summers & Wasser, 1993).

Volume 2 contrasts greatly with the others. Published in 1926, this is the only volume of the first five that Terman did not co-author. This 842-page tome was instead written by Catharine Cox, one of his graduate students. She chose a rather different approach to the study of giftedness across the life span. Instead of identifying a group of gifted children and then following them through adulthood to determine whether they attained eminence in some achievement domain, Cox opted to reverse the strategy: She identified a group of clearly famous adults and then looked to the biographies of their early childhood to discover whether they had shown any signs of giftedness. Hence, Terman's longitudinal investigation of children was complemented by Cox's retrospective investigation of adults. The explicit hope was that these two inquires would corroborate each other. Gifted children would develop into geniuses, and the geniuses would eventually prove themselves to have been gifted children. It was this hope that led Terman to include this otherwise misfit study among the set.

But was this hope actually realized? Does giftedness necessarily transform into genius? If not, why not? And, on the other side of the coin, does all genius display giftedness in youth? If not, again, why not? Significantly, this is a problem that deeply concerned Terman himself. Not every one of his gifted children realized their supposed potential, and so he made a big effort to explain away these failures. Cox was also cognizant of this problem. Many of the 301 geniuses in her sample would not have been qualified for membership among the elite Termites, as they affectionately came to be called. This discrepancy she tried to handle in a number of ways. Thus, the linkage between childhood and adulthood talent may be more complicated than the main theme of *Genetic Studies of Genius* would have us believe.

I will therefore devote this chapter to discussing some of the developmental complexities. Taking full advantage of subsequent research on both giftedness and genius (e.g. Albert, 1992, 1994; Subotnik & Arnold, 1994; Winner, 1996; Simonton, 1997b), I will survey the principal agreements and disagreements that have surfaced in longitudinal and retrospective studies of talent development. In particular, I concentrate below on three critical topics: intellect, disposition, and development—questions that were explicitly or implicitly introduced in *Genetic Studies of Genius*.

Intellect

Terman's children were specifically chosen according to their performance on the Stanford–Binet intelligence test, an instrument that Terman had himself developed just a few years previously. If a child earned an IQ score of 140 or better, he or she was considered sufficiently bright to be styled a 'genius'. In fact, the mean IQ score across the entire sample of more than

1,500 children was around 150, a rather impressive figure. IQ scores were also calculated for Cox's 301 geniuses, but in a necessarily different manner. Clearly the Stanford–Binet could not be administered to dead celebrities. Accordingly, Cox substituted a historiometric assessment for the psychometric. Because the intelligence quotient was then conceived as the ratio of mental age to chronological age (multiplied by 100), she and her collaborators—Terman among them—applied this definition to biographical data about the ages at which members of her distinguished sample demonstrated certain accomplishments. Actually, Cox was following a procedure originally developed by Terman (1917), who used this method to estimate the IQ of Francis Galton. In any event, her 301 geniuses also displayed a higher degree of intelligence, with IQ scores also averaging around 150 (prior to introducing the correction of data reliability).

Both Terman and Cox conceived of genius as a quantitative rather than qualitative characteristic. The more elevated an individual's IQ, the more impressive the talent, and hence the greater the magnitude of genius. Consequently, the IQ score should be strongly associated with a person's final accomplishments. It did not turn out this way. In the longitudinal study, not every intellectually gifted child grew to become an eminent adult. Even worse, differences in IQ could not discriminate between those who were successful from those who failed to realized their potential (Terman & Oden, 1959). The results were not much better in the retrospective study. Even though Cox found a small positive relationship between IQ and eminence, this correlation has been shown to be mostly artifactual (Simonton, 1976a). That is, the correlation shrinks to zero once the appropriate statistical controls are introduced. Later studies have arrived at similar conclusions for both psychometric and historiometric samples (e.g. McClelland, 1973; Simonton, 1984d; cf. Barrett & Depinet, 1991). Only a few studies have found that variation in intellectual ability can successfully predict the level of attained distinction (e.g. Simonton, 1986b, 1991a). So, why is it that adulthood genius is not always linked to childhood giftedness, as gauged by psychometric or historiometric IQ?

Thresholds and Triangular Scatterplots

Part of the answer comes from the fact that intelligence functions as a necessary but not sufficient basis for achievement. Below a certain IQ, the probability of adulthood success becomes minuscule. But beyond that threshold level, additional increases in IQ will not necessarily translate into proportional amounts of distinction (Guilford, 1967; Simonton, 1985a; Barron & Harrington, 1981). Admittedly, an exceptionally high intelligence *may* allow more accomplishments than a somewhat lesser intelligence (Benbow, 1992); it's just that there are no guarantees. In fact, the scatterplot describing the relationship between genius

and intelligence tends to be best described as triangular (Simonton, 1994). As intelligence increases, the highest possible level of attainment increases, but so does the cross-sectional variation. Hence, there can be extremely bright individuals who are no more successful than persons with IQs far lower.

Curvilinear Relations

Another phenomenon undermines the relationship even more: under special circumstances, an excessively high IQ can actually work to the *disadvantage* of a person. In the first place, unusual precocity may obstruct the development of the social maturity so essential to the emergence of an adult well-equipped for the rough-and-tumble world. Examples of intellectual prodigies who failed to actualize their potential for this particular reason are numerous. The classic illustration of this failure is William James Sidis (Montour, 1977). Furthermore, aside from social maturation, extremely bright persons often suffer many difficulties trying to convince others of the worth of their ideas. Too often the excessively brilliant will 'talk over the heads' of their audiences, and they thus can discover themselves dismissed by potential appreciators as unacceptably 'high brow', 'cerebral', 'theoretical', 'eccentric', 'radical', or 'avant-garde'. This liability is especially potent in those achievement domains in which success depends on the cultivation of a broad constituency. A mathematical physicist can afford to be understood by only a handful of experts; a politician, entrepreneur, commander, or religious leader cannot.

In fact, one mathematical model specifically predicts that for those areas of accomplishment where a person must appeal to the masses, the functional relation between IQ and effectiveness is curvilinear, with a maximum point around 119 (Simonton, 1985a). The predicted curve has been confirmed by an impressive body of psychometric and historiometric research (Simonton, 1994). Evidence for the model also appears in the Terman and Cox samples. Few Termites attained distinction in areas of leadership that required the ability to win popularity with the masses. And in the Cox 301, those who did attain fame in this fashion—such as the Presidents of the United States in her sample—displayed much lower IQs than did her other geniuses. Indeed, the lowest IQs were exhibited by the military leaders in the sample – individuals who must inspire confidence in the common soldier or sailor. Hence, it is possible to have too much of a good thing, so that a high IQ can be a bad thing.

Multiple Intelligences

In the early decades of the 20th century, psychologists were prone to view intelligence as a single, homogeneous construct. This coherence has even been given the name 'Spearman's *g*' to honor Spearman's (1927) advocacy of a unified, *general* latent variable underlying performance on all intelligence tests. Terman and Cox were not exceptions. Both implicitly believed in Samuel Johnson's (1781, p. 5) assertion that "the true Genius is a mind of large general powers, accidentally determined to some particular direction."

Nonetheless, research since Spearman, Terman, and Cox implies that intelligence may be a much more complicated construct than any single-factor theory can accommodate (Guilford, 1967; Sternberg, 1985). In Gardner's (1983) theory, for instance, at least seven distinct intelligences exist: verbal, logical-mathematical, spatial-visual, bodily-kinesthetic, musical, intrapersonal, and interpersonal (for more possibilities, see Gardner, 1998). As a consequence, there ought to be seven varieties of intellectual giftedness, as well as seven kinds of genius. In line with this inference, Gardner (1993) examined seven exemplars of each intelligence drawn from 20th-century celebrities: T. S. Eliot, Albert Einstein, Pablo Picasso, Martha Graham, Igor Stravinsky, Sigmund Freud, and Mahatma Gandhi. Even so, it is obvious that that Terman identified giftedness and genius using an IQ test that is heavily slanted toward the first two or three of these seven intelligences. It should not surprise us, therefore, that most of his children became professors, lawyers, doctors, and scientists rather than artists, choreographers, composers, psychoanalysts, or world leaders.

Naturally, this problem still plagues many modern definitions of giftedness and genius. Children will still be chosen for gifted programs according to their performance on narrowly defined psychometric instruments. In addition, there are still people who identify themselves as 'geniuses' simply because they score so many standard deviations above the mean on some equally restricted measure. Hence, an IQ of 132 allows someone to join Mensa, an IQ of 164 is the entrance criterion for the Four Sigma Society, and an IQ 228 puts someone in the *Guinness Book of Records* as the world's brightest person (McFarlan, 1989). These views of talent exhaust one specific type of intelligence and unjustly exclude the many equally valuable forms that intellect may take.

Are the foregoing criticisms inconsistent with the results of Cox's retrospective study? After all, didn't she discover that eminent geniuses had extremely high IQs? However, it is critical to note that Cox's operational definition of IQ was actually rather different from Terman's. In gathering evidence of childhood and adolescent precocity, Cox did not impose a homogeneous, unidimensional conception of intelligence. Rather, she allowed each one of her 301 geniuses to decide the particular intelligence on which they would be assessed. J. S. Mill had his IQ gauged according to his phenomenal analytical precocity, whereas Mozart was evaluated according to his attainments as a musical prodigy. Cox's judges did not penalize anyone for being mediocre or even retarded in some cognitive domain captured by the Standford–

Binet. Hence, Cox's IQ scores were implicitly based on the thesis that there exist multiple intelligences.

Skewed Distributions

Terman and Cox, following Galton (1869), thought that intelligence was distributed like so many other psychological and physical characteristics. That is, IQ was believed to exhibit a normal distribution in any large population—the classic bell-shaped curve. For the most part, moreover, that belief was justified, at least as an approximation. Typically, IQ will be distributed so that about two thirds of the population will have an IQ within one standard deviation from the mean, and virtually the entire human population will have an IQ score within four standard deviations from the mean. For example, only one person out of a million can be admitted to the Mega Society, which requires an IQ of 176.

If intelligence has such a close connection with accomplishment, then the distribution of achievements should also be roughly described by the same bell-shaped curve. Yet that is completely false. The marked discrepancy in the distributions is best seen by looking at an objective measure of accomplishment, such as income, influence, or productivity (Price, 1963; Walberg, Strykowski, Rovai & Hung, 1984; Simonton, 1988a). Creative output offers a case in point. No matter what is the domain of creative behavior, the distribution of lifetime productivity is highly skewed, with a small proportion of the contributors producing the overwhelming proportion of the total products (Dennis, 1954a, 1954b, 1955; Simon, 1955; Shockley, 1957; Albert, 1975). This skewed distribution is so firmly established empirically that it has already become the source of corresponding behavioral laws (Lotka, 1926; Price, 1963). For instance, the Price Law holds that if k designates the number of creators active in a particular achievement domain, then $\sqrt{k}$ provides the number of that select few who can be credited for *half* of everything contributed to that field (Price, 1963). A good illustration is found in classical music, where about 250 composers are responsible for at least one permanent contribution to the repertoire. So, the number of composers who should be responsible for half of that repertoire should be the square root of 250, or 15.8, which rounds off to 16. This is exactly the case (Simonton, 1984b). To indicate what this elitist disparity signifies more dramatically, assume that we translated this distribution into the same terms as IQ scores, labeling them *productivity coefficients* or PQ (Simonton, 1988c). Then the highest PQs would be almost 200 points higher than the highest recorded IQs! We often talk of geniuses as being giants in their fields. Well, imagine coming across a true giant whose height measures 21 standard deviations above the population average!

How can this conspicuous discrepancy between IQ and PQ be explained? There are many potential

113

explanations (Simonton, 1997a), but I want to consider just one long-standing explanation (Shockley, 1957; Eysenck, 1995). When we try to identify the predictors of some phenomena, behavioral scientists tend to think in terms of additive models. This means that each cause makes an independent contribution to the overall effect, the latter being simply the sum of the separate effects. Furthermore, should the diverse components be normally distributed in the population, any summation of those components will be similarly distributed. Yet outstanding talent could very well be a behavioral phenomenon in which the effects participate in a *multiplicative* fashion. All of the varied factors of exceptional attainment—intelligence, motivation, personality, developmental experiences and conditions, education, etc.—are multiplied together rather than merely added. Yet the multiplicative combination of normally distributed variables does not yield a normally distributed product but rather a composite variable with a highly skewed *lognormal* distribution (for demonstration and additional implications, see Simonton, 1999). This fits perfectly with what we see in distributions of lifetime accomplishments.

The same multiplicative model is compatible with the threshold and triangular distributions noted earlier. Persons who are very low on just one of the contributing factors will not manifest any gifts as adults. Zero times any number is zero. Accordingly, below the minimum intellectual requirement, we cannot expect genius to emerge. Yet additional increments in intelligence beyond the threshold requirement will not necessarily augment the odds for achievement. The contribution of the most exalted intelligence to the overall product can be negated by striking deficiencies in other components of the product. Indeed, this is precisely what occurred to those Termites who grew up to become adulthood underachievers. However impressive their IQs, some critical factor was missing from their personal makeup.

In comparison, other individuals with much lower IQs may compensate by having assets that enable them to achieve far more than the Termites. An example is William Shockley (Eysenck, 1995). As a child, Shockley was among the initial batch of children whom Terman tested for inclusion in the longitudinal sample. Yet his IQ was not high enough to certify him as a psychometrically established genius. So rather than become a gifted child, Shockley became a famous scientist instead, winning the Nobel Prize for Physics as co-inventor of the transistor. Not a single Termite received so high an honor. Obviously, Shockley had other virtues that helped him achieve despite his nominally 'sub-genius' IQ.

Disposition

Cox was cognizant of the existence of such tradeoffs. After assessing the personality traits of a subsample of 100 geniuses, Cox noted that drive and determination could more than compensate for a less than stellar IQ. Specifically, she confessed that "high but not the highest intelligence, combined with the greatest degree of persistence, will achieve greater eminence than the highest degree of intelligence with somewhat less persistence" (Cox, 1926, p. 187). This motivational facet of talent development is absolutely mandatory for success. High achievement demands an adult who can overcome the many trials and tribulations that dot the path to genius. Even after luminaries have established their reputations, their positions is never secure, and failures will follow successes throughout their careers (Simonton, 1977, 1985d, 1997a). Furthermore, to attain eminence in any field requires a childhood and adolescence packed with hard training and practice. Empirical studies have shown that potential talents must grapple with their domain several hours per day for a full decade before their latent capacity starts to become actualized (Bloom, 1985; Hayes, 1989; Simonton, 1991b; Csikszentmihalyi, Rathunde & Whalen, 1993; Ericsson, 1996). Such a massive commitment is not for the faint of heart. The members of the Cox sample who attained eminence notwithstanding mediocre intellects clearly had this mandatory quality in place. By the same token, those of the Termites who did not fulfill the original expectations often lacked this very requisite (Terman & Oden, 1959).

Dearth of enthusiasm and persistence is not the sole personality liability that may prevent a gifted child from transforming into an adult genius. The character profile necessary to attain greatness in maturity is very complex, requiring that a maturing talent be high on some traits and low on others (Cox, 1926; Cattell, 1963; Simonton, 1986b, 1991a; Eysenck, 1995). Yet this achievement profile is not what is always selected for whenever IQ tests provide the basis for identifying talent. The often-cited studies by Getzels and Jackson (1962) and Wallach & Kogan (1965) show this very well. Children chosen according to their high IQs tend to have personality profiles rather distinct from those who are selected according to their exceptional scores on tests that have a more direct claim to assess creativity. For example, the latter youths are prone to be more playful and humorous, to be less conventional in their life aspirations, and to be less conforming in their attitudes about their education and future careers.

But the most striking disparity concerns psychopathology. Terman (1925) collected data on his subjects' character traits in order to contradict the then-common opinion that genius was near to madness. Terman showed that his intellectually gifted children were certainly not abnormal. On the contrary, both psychologically and physically, the Termites tended to be well above the norms for the human population. Yet studies of eminent personalities reveal something rather different. These investigations have found support for Dryden's (1681, p. 6) famed dictum that "Great Wits are sure to Madness near ally'd,/ And thin Partitions do their Bounds divide."

It would require too much space to review all the pertinent literature on this point, but that has already been accomplished by others anyway (e.g. Richards, 1981; Prentky, 1989; Simonton, 1994; Eysenck, 1995). It should suffice to offer the following four points:

(1) Historiometric inquiries find that famous achievers displayed incidence rates for various mental disorders that exceed the rates observed in the general population (Ellis, 1926; Juda, 1949; Martindale, 1972; Goertzel, Goertzel & Goertzel, 1978; Post, 1994; Ludwig, 1995).

(2) Psychiatric investigations encounter comparably high percentages of mental and emotional illnesses among distinguished contemporaries (Andreasen & Canter, 1974; Andreasen, 1987; Jamison, 1989).

(3) Psychometric research on eminent personalities have found that they often obtain high scores on the clinical subscales of several standard personality measures, such as the EPQ and the MMPI (Barron, 1969; MacKinnon, 1978; Götz & Götz, 1979a, 1979b; Rushton, 1990).

(4) Genetic analyses of family pedigrees reveal that notable adults are more prone to emerge from lineages that exhibit high proportions of psychopathology (Myerson & Boyle, 1941; Juda, 1949; Karlson, 1970; Andreasen, 1987).

These four forms of evidence seem to corroborate the conclusion that genius-grade talent may reside at the delicate boundary between healthy and unhealthy personalities. Moreover, we have cause for thinking that this delicate placement is not incidental. Certain advantages can actually accrue to personalities that teeter-totter on the edge of sanity.

Such persons are less conforming, more unconventional, even iconoclastic (Eysenck, 1995). Such individuals may experience manic episodes replete with optimistic activity that results in a large body of outstanding work (Jamison, 1993; Weisberg, 1994). Such personalities may also entertain crazy thoughts, bizarre associations, or strange metaphors or analogies that later enable them to arrive at landmark insights (Woody & Claridge, 1977; Eysenck, 1995). Naturally, all of these proclivities can also go too far, giving the poor soul too much of a good thing; those who inherit or acquire an inclination to advance beyond the frontier into fantasy land may never see their gifts mature into genius (Rothenberg, 1990). Or, like Van Gogh or Schumann, these sad personalities may not permit their talents to progress as far as they would have in the absence of suicidal disorder. Nevertheless, it's just as hazardous to talent development for a gifted person never to break out of the shell of conventional complacency.

It is very likely that Terman's sampling procedures are to blame for the dearth of high-grade genius among his Termites. Rather than test the entire student population, Terman relied on teacher nominations to screen those students who their teachers thought had the most promise. How many kids were not so named because their teachers thought them more weird than bright? Furthermore, even if a few oddballs somehow got through this first filter, how many of them would have taken the Stanford–Binet with sufficient seriousness to provide answers indicative of their true intelligence? How many future geniuses would have had a diverting time offering humorous or Bohemian responses that would bring their scores down? Of course, we can never know, but is it possible that William Shockley was one of them?

Development

A false impression may have been stimulated by the previous discussion. It was noted that the borderline pathology that enhances the realization of intellectual talent may be inherited, because notable personalities frequently come from pathological family pedigrees. Thus, the familial lines of 'natural ability' described by Galton (1869) appear to roughly parallel familial lines of 'unnatural abilities'. When two such genetic lineages just so happen to intersect in exactly the correct proportions, giftedness turns into genius. Nonetheless, this inference would not be correct. Genius is not just born; it is also made—by the environmental circumstances in which the youth develops his or her talent. Genetic endowment solely provides the raw materials from which environmental events and conditions can configure talent growth. At this point as well, we can isolate some interesting contrasts between potential and actual talents. Below I concentrate on three categories of environmental factors: (a) birth order, (b) traumatic events, and (c) education and training; these have probably received the most attention in empirical research (Simonton, 1987, 1994).

Birth Order

Terman (1925) observed that first-borns were over-represented among his Termites. A like disproportion also appears to hold for child prodigies (Feldman & Goldsmith, 1986). Moreover, early investigations of adulthood genius suggested that primogeniture had the same advantage for them as well. The first such observation came from Galton's (1874) study of notable British scientists (see also Ellis, 1926; Albert, 1980). Nonetheless, later research indicated that birth-order's impact is more complicated. First-borns are more prone to achieve eminence in some domains, while other ordinal positions have the advantage in rather distinct domains. Hence, where first-borns become eminent scientific creators (Roe, 1952; Eiduson, 1962; Clark & Rice, 1982; Terry, 1989; Sulloway, 1996), later-borns become the artistic luminaries (Bliss, 1970; Clark & Rice, 1982). The main exceptions to this rule is that classical composers are more strongly aligned with the first-borns (Schubert, Wagner

& Schubert, 1977), whereas the scientific revolutionaries are more strongly aligned with the later-borns (Sulloway, 1996). A comparable pattern holds in leadership, where the first-borns are the source of status-quo politicians (Zweigenhaft, 1975; Wagner & Schubert, 1977), whereas the last-borns populate the revolutionaries (Stewart, 1977; Sulloway, 1996). Overall, a consistent pattern emerges from these data: First-borns tend to attain distinction in highly prestigious positions that are an integral part of the Establishment, whereas the later-borns are more prone to succeed as rebellious agents of a new order or even to serve as advocates of disorder.

We need not discuss the exact developmental foundation of this divergent outcome (but see Sulloway, 1996). The crucial point here is simply to note that we can now better understand why Terman's gifted children turned out so conventional. When first-borns predominate in a sample, we should predict a higher percentage of doctors, lawyers, professors, and other prestigious professions (Schachter, 1963), but a low percentage of artists, writers, revolutionaries, and others who are less willing to conform to societal definitions of success. Indeed, this developmental tendency may even explain why the first-borns were originally so prominent among the Termites. In the first place, first-borns may have been more inclined to seek the scholastic success that would have earned them a teacher nomination during the initial stages of the study. In addition, the first-borns may actually have been more enthusiastic about earning more conventional acclaim by performing so well during the IQ screening. Indeed, I wonder if the tendency for IQ to decline with ordinal position says more about attitudes than about aptitudes (cf. Zajonc & Mullally, 1997). The later-borns may have less respect for the authorities who unilaterally decide that these measures gauge something significant, and they may even prove too iconoclastic to accept the presumption that the test questions do in fact have a single correct response!

Whatever the upshot of the preceding speculation, one conclusion seems firm. Birth-order may not so much decide the magnitude of genius as the direction that genius takes (cf. Helmreich et al., 1980). To claim that first-borns are more successful because they enter prestigious occupations serves merely to perpetuate the first-born orientation toward talent development.

Traumatic Events

Empirical inquiries into the origins of famous achievers repeatedly discover that a significant percentage suffered less than happy childhoods (Goertzel, Goertzel & Goertzel, 1978). Perhaps the family experienced substantial ups-and-downs in economic and emotional well-being, or maybe the home was the locus of tragic events. Of the various ways that misfortunes can visit a talent's youth, the one that has earned the most attention has been orphanhood or parental loss (e.g.

Albert, 1971; Eisenstadt, 1978). For both leaders and creators, the proportion of geniuses who lost one or both parents before attaining majority is noticeably larger than what appears to hold in the population at large or in any other relevant comparison group (e.g. Martindale, 1972; Berrington, 1974; Silverman, 1974; Walberg, Rasher & Parkerson, 1980; Berry, 1981).

These statistics become all the more intriguing when we contrast them with the much more benign home circumstances that the Termites enjoyed (Terman, 1925; Holahan & Sears, 1995). His children were more likely to experience comfortable, stable, intact family environments. In addition, the same positive home settings tend to favor the emergence of child prodigies (Feldman & Goldsmith, 1986). What does this discrepancy tell us?

Perhaps 'trials and tribulations' in the early years have a beneficial impact on talent development; the developmental advantage may have three causes that may operate either individually or in some combination (cf. Simonton, 1987, 1994):

(1) Traumatic events may disrupt standard socialization to such a degree that the youth will find it less likely to conform to societal norms and expectations. Parents play a big role in inculcating societal normals and values, both as instructors and as models.

(2) The youth may experience a bereavement reaction that plunges development into a lasting emotional equilibrium that can only be alleviated by the attainment of distinction (Eisenstadt, 1978); fame and fortune serve as remedies for the underlying emotional scars.

(3) The experience of traumatic events can facilitate the acquisition of an emotional robustness that helps the person accommodate all the disappointments and frustrations that attend the quest for success (Simonton, 1994). Those talents that grow up in more benign circumstances may be totally ill-equipped for the hardships that await them in early adulthood.

Whatever the explanation, some qualifications are in order; for one thing, any advantage gained from an unhappy childhood or adolescence depends on the achievement domain. For instance, even though rates of parental loss are higher among famous scientists than among the general public, the rates among literary creators are higher still (Berry, 1981); artistic creativity may demand more life turmoil than does scientific creativity. Moreover, the impact of traumatic events must we gauged against the personal resources that the youth has at his or her disposal. Juvenile delinquents and suicidal depressives may also exhibit high incidence of parental loss (Eisenstadt, 1978). Thus, there probably exists an optimal level of developmental stress for each youth. What might not be enough challenge for one developing talent, might be just the right amount for a second, and yet far too much for a third. Hence, the numerous eminent individuals who attained distinction *without* having to endure orphanhood may be those for whom only less dramatic tests of character were required.

The intricacies be what they may, it is conceivable that most of the Termites were not adequately challenged during the course of their early development. They too frequently appear to illustrate Dylan Thomas' ironic comment that "There's only one thing that's worse than having an unhappy childhood, and that's having a too-happy childhood" (Ferris, 1977, p. 49).

Education and Training

Terman was proud of the academic successes of his gifted children; these intellectually bright youths tended to attain praiseworthy grades and to advance to higher degrees. Child prodigies also tend to make their first big splash in the news by their exceptional exhibitions of scholastic prowess. It is not rare to read about super-brains who entered high school at 10 and graduated at 11 with straight As—as well as full scholarships to Ivy League colleges.

Even so, when we turn our glance at those individuals who actually make a name for themselves in some achievement domain, the picture changes radically. In the first place, those who obtain excellent grades and scholastic honors are not necessarily likely to attain eminence in their chosen fields; the correlations are either zero or very weakly positive (Hudson, 1958; Hoyt, 1965; McClelland, 1973; Cohen, 1984). Consequently, examples abound of undoubted geniuses who proved themselves to be mediocre and even inferior students. Furthermore, the association between the magnitude of formal education and the realization of talent is not always unambiguous. This is quite evident from a reanalysis of the 301 geniuses in the Cox (1926) sample (Simonton, 1976a, 1983a). By plotting her eminence scores (from Cattell, 1903) as a function of formal education level attained, one gets a curious pair of functions. First, for leaders one obtains a strictly negative linear function, the most famous leaders tending to have the least amount of formal instruction. Second, for creators one gets an odd curvilinear function, an inverted-J curve, with a peak appearing in the last two years of undergraduate education. In neither case is achievement a positive linear function of the number of degrees acquired, and for both creativity and leadership talent development may actually undergo damage. Nor is this result peculiar to the Cox 301, for comparable results have been found in more contemporary samples of adulthood achievers (Simonton, 1984b, chap. 4).

Naturally, it is one thing to discover an interesting empirical relationship, and another to comprehend its actual meaning; but one obvious possibility should be considered: Formal education may not always make a positive contribution to the growth of talent, and in certain cases it may actually inhibit the development of talent. On the one hand, those who hope to become lawyers, doctors, professors, and other academically certified professionals certainly have little choice but to advance up the ladder of degrees; these were the attainments that predominated among the Termites. On the other hand, most artistic creators, revolutionary scientists, and other forms of unconventional achievement may have more to lose than to gain by going all the way to the highest available academic degree. Such creative activities may require just enough training to master certain basic knowledge and skills, but beyond that requisite, increased inculcation into more specialized disciplinary preoccupations may only interfere with more crucial endeavors. For example, success in many achievement domains is conspicuously linked with voracious and omnivorous reading, an undisciplined exploration of ideas that may suffer under intensified academic pressures (McCurdy, 1960; Simonton, 1984b). Furthermore, many achievement domains demand the gradual acquisition of rather specialized techniques that are not always taught—or taught well—in formal academic settings. Whatever the specifics, we must remember that it normally requires about 10 years of intense dedication to master the materials of a field. As a consequence, whenever formal schooling is not making a direct contribution to the needed mastery then it is necessarily retarding the acquisition of that expertise. Distaste for that interference inspires many talented youth adults to become college dropouts—to their gain and society's too.

If a growing talent must obtain an education beyond the educational system proper, one type of extracurricular training is particularly valuable: mentoring. This was not a matter that attracted the attention from either Terman or Cox. Yet research on talented youths demonstrates that this is a critical factor in the emergence of their special capacities (e.g. Bloom, 1985; Feldman & Goldsmith, 1986; Arnold & Subotnik, 1994). The talented youth must encounter an appropriate teacher who is well equipped to cultivate the youth's current capacity, and often the talent must change teachers as that capacity grows. Moreover, retrospective investigations into famous adults reveal the importance of this same developmental factor, but with some crucial contrasts that are usually ignored in the longitudinal literature (Simonton, 1983b, 1992b).

(1) Mentors can have a detrimental effect on talent development if they are motivated to clone themselves through their students. In part, it is for this cause that it is usually more advantageous to experience multiple mentors rather than lean heavily on just one (Simonton, 1984a, 1992c).

(2) The linkage between mentor characteristics and talent development is often complex, with interaction effects, curvilinear functions, and other causal complexities (Simonton, 1977, 1984a, 1992c). For instance, the most accomplished mentors are likely to be those who are at the peak of their own careers rather than those who are past their prime, and thus who may be less receptive to new ideas.

Lastly, it is also essential to note that a growing talent may receive appreciable benefits from rather more impersonal relationships with predecessors who are active in the same domain. Role models of exceptional achievement may be admired and emulated at a distance long after those paragons of excellence have died. This indirect role modeling can frequently be every bit as potent as personalized instruction (Simonton, 1975, 1984a, 1988b, 1992c). Einstein had the portraits of three deceased predecessors hanging in his home study—those of Newton, Faraday, and Maxwell. These three luminaries probably had much more impact on the emergence of Einstein's special gifts than did any of his teachers.

Conceivably, many of the Termites failed to grow up to become highly gifted adults simply because they failed to form the right linkages with those predecessors who embodied the best in their chosen domain of achievement. In the absence of an intense ambition to surpass these predecessors, even the most prodigious gifts will seldom convert into even the most mediocre genius.

Conclusion

In this brief space I could do little more than to provide an overview of what I consider a very profound puzzle. Many critical issues have been necessarily overlooked. I made no mention, for example, of the difficult question of how the adulthood realization of latent talents may differ for women and minorities (see, e.g. Vaillant & Vaillant, 1980; Helson, 1990; Tomlinson-Keasey & Little, 1990; Ochse, 1991; Simonton, 1992a, 1996, 1998; Arnold, Noble & Subotnik, 1996). Nor have I examined the matter of how the 'spirit of the times' (*Zeitgeist*) affects the growth and manifestation of adulthood achievement (e.g. Simonton, 1976b, 1976c, 1978, 1980; Martindale, 1990). And, finally, I have omitted discussion of the potential impact of crystallizing experiences, cultural and professional marginality, socioeconomic class, religious affiliation, and many other potentially crucial developmental factors (see, e.g. Lehman & Witty, 1931; Roe, 1952; Roe, 1952; Datta, 1967; Simonton, 1977, 1984c, 1986a; Walberg, Rasher & Parkerson, 1980; Berry, 1981; Walters & Gardner, 1986; Gardner, 1993). Nonetheless, those topics that I did cover should communicate the tremendous complexities in the process by which potential talent is converted into actual talent. We are a long way yet from comprehending all the factors that affect talent development. We are farther still from understanding how all of these factors intersect and interact in the emergence of the exceptional adult achiever. Further theoretical and empirical inquiries must attempt to consolidate all of these complicated forces and functions into a single, coherent, life-span developmental system. Besides encompassing the immense inventory of relevant developmental inputs, this system must accommodate all the interaction effects, curvilinear functions, and other causal relations that moderate the impact of these influences. Moreover, this systematic account must address what I view as two absolutely essential questions:

(1) Why do so many gifted children fail to realize their potential upon becoming adults? What are the places where the developmental trajectory is most likely to veer off target? What are the most common blind alleys? This is the problem of the 'nipped bud'.

(2) Why is it that many highly successful adults managed to display no clear signs of giftedness in their early years? Does the developmental trajectory for these unpromising youths differ in some qualitative manner from that which guides the precocious child to adulthood achievement? This is the problem of the 'late bloomer'.

If we could understand the developmental foundations for both the nipped bud and the late bloomer, we would have a much more firm idea about how best to intervene in the growth of talent—especially within our educational systems, where society's involvement is most direct and potent. Thus, we might learn how to prevent the promising youth from going astray, and we might grasp how to accelerate the flowering of a latent talent. Moreover, at a more theoretical level, we would comprehend why not all of Terman's children became geniuses, and why not all of Cox's geniuses would have qualified as gifted youth. A comprehensive theory of talent development must encompass both ends of this significant phenomenon.

Acknowledgments

This chapter is based on a keynote address delivered at the 1997 World Conference of the World Council for Gifted and Talented Children held in Seattle, Washington. I would like to thank Rena Subotnik and Robert J. Sternberg for their comments on an earlier draft of the chapter.

References

Albert, R. S. (1971). Cognitive development and parental loss among the gifted, the exceptionally gifted and the creative. *Psychological Reports*, **29**, 19–26.

Albert, R. S. (1975). Toward a behavioral definition of genius. *American Psychologist*, **30**, 140–151.

Albert, R. S. (1980). Family positions and the attainment of eminence: a study of special family positions and special family experiences. *Gifted Child Quarterly*, **24**, 87–95.

Albert, R. S. (1994). The achievement of eminence: A longitudinal study of exceptionally gifted boys and their families. In: R. F. Subotnik & K. D. Arnold (Eds), *Beyond Terman: Contemporary Longitudinal Studies of Giftedness and Talent* (pp. 282–315). Norwood, NJ: Ablex.

Andreasen, N. C. (1987). Creativity and mental illness: prevalence rates in writers and their first-degree relatives. *American Journal of Psychiatry*, **144**, 1288–1292.

Andreasen, N. C. & Canter, A. (1974). The creative writer: psychiatric symptoms and family history. *Comprehensive Psychiatry*, **15**, 123–131.

Arnold, K. D., Noble, K. D. & Subotnik, R. F. (Ed.). (1996). *Remarkable women: perspectives on female talent development*. Cresskill, NJ: Hampton Press.

Arnold, K. D. & Subotnik, R. F. (1994). Lessons from contemporary longitudinal studies. In: R. F. Subotnik & K. D. Arnold (Eds), *Beyond Terman: Contemporary longitudinal studies of giftedness and talent* (pp. 437–451). Norwood, NJ: Ablex.

Barron, F. X. (1969). *Creative person and creative process*. New York: Holt, Rinehart & Winston.

Barron, F. X. & Harrington, D. M. (1981). Creativity, intelligence, and personality. *Annual Review of Psychology*, **32**, 439–476.

Barrett, G. V. & Depinet, R. L. (1991). A reconsideration of testing for competence rather than for intelligence. *American Psychologist*, **46**, 1012–1024.

Benbow, C. P. (1992). Academic achievement in mathematics and science of students between ages 13 and 23: are there differences among students in the top one per cent of mathematical ability? *Journal of Educational Psychology*, **84**, 51–61.

Berrington, H. (1974). Review article: The Fiery Chariot: Prime ministers and the search for love. *British Journal of Political Science*, **4**, 345–369.

Berry, C. (1981). The Nobel scientists and the origins of scientific achievement. *British Journal of Sociology*, **32**, 381–391.

Bliss, W. D. (1970). Birth order of creative writers. *Journal of Individual Psychology*, **26**, 200–202.

Bloom, B. S. (Ed.). (1985). *Developing talent in young people*. New York: Ballantine Books.

Burks, B. S., Jensen, D. W. & Terman, L. M. (1930). *The promise of youth: follow-up studies of a thousand gifted children*. Stanford, CA: Stanford University Press.

Cattell, J. M. (1903). A statistical study of eminent men. *Popular Science Monthly*, **62**, 359–377.

Cattell, R. B. (1963). The personality and motivation of the researcher from measurements of contemporaries and from biography. In: C. W. Taylor & F. Barron (Eds), *Scientific Creativity: Its Recognition and Development* (pp. 119–131). New York: Wiley.

Clark, R. D. & Rice, G. A. (1982). Family constellations and eminence: The birth orders of Nobel prize winners. *Journal of Psychology*, **110**, 281–287.

Cohen, P. A. (1984). College grades and adult achievement: a research synthesis. *Research in Higher Education*, **20**, 281–293.

Cox, C. (1926). *The early mental traits of three hundred geniuses*. Stanford, CA: Stanford University Press.

Csikszentmihalyi, M., Rathunde, K. & Whalen, S. (1993). *Talented teenagers: the roots of success and failure*. Cambridge, England: Cambridge University Press.

Datta, L.-E. (1967). Family religious background and early scientific creativity. *American Sociological Review*, **32**, 626–635.

Dennis, W. (1954a). Bibliographies of eminent scientists. *Scientific Monthly*, **79**, 180–183.

Dennis, W. (1954b). Productivity among American psychologists. *American Psychologist*, **9**, 191–194.

Dennis, W. (1955). Variations in productivity among creative workers. *Scientific Monthly*, **80**, 277–278.

Dryden, J. (1681). *Absalom and Achitophel: a poem*. London: Davis.

Eiduson, B. T. (1962). *Scientists: their psychological world*. New York: Basic Books.

Eisenstadt, J. M. (1978). Parental loss. *American Psychologist*, **33**, 211–223.

Ellis, H. (1926). *A study of British* (rev. ed.). Boston: Houghton Mifflin.

Ericsson, K. A. (Ed.). (1996). *The road to expert performance: empirical evidence from the arts and sciences, sports, and games*. Mahwah, NJ: Erlbaum.

Eysenck, H. J. (1995). *Genius: the natural history of creativity*. Cambridge, England: Cambridge University Press.

Feldman, D. H. & Goldsmith, L. T. (1986). *Nature's gambit: child prodigies and the development of human potential*. New York: Basic Books.

Ferris, P. (1977). *Dylan Thomas*. London: Hodder & Stoughton.

Galton, F. (1869). *Hereditary: an inquiry into its laws and consequences*. London: Macmillan.

Galton, F. (1874). *English men of science: their nature and nurture*. London: Macmillan.

Gardner, H. (1983). *Frames of mind: a theory of multiple intelligences*. New York: Basic Books.

Gardner, H. (1993). *Creating minds: an anatomy of creativity seen through the lives of Freud, Einstein, Picasso, Stravinsky, Eliot, Graham, and Gandhi*. New York: Basic Books.

Gardner, H. (1998). Are there additional intelligences? The case for naturalist, spiritual, and existential intelligences. In: J. Kane (Ed.), *Education, Information, and Transformation* (pp. 111–131). Upper Saddle River, NJ: Merrill.

Getzels, J. & Jackson, P. W. (1962). *Creativity and intelligence: explorations with gifted students*. New York: Wiley.

Goertzel, M. G., Goertzel, V. & Goertzel, T. G. (1978). *300 eminent personalities: a psychosocial analysis of the famous*. San Francisco: Jossey-Bass.

Götz, K. O. & Götz, K. (1979a). Personality characteristics of professional artists. *Perceptual and Motor Skills*, **49**, 327–334.

Götz, K. O. & Götz, K. (1979b). Personality characteristics of successful artists. *Perceptual and Motor Skills*, **49**, 919–924.

Guilford, J. P. (1967). *The nature of human intelligence*. New York: McGraw-Hill.

Hayes, J. R. (1989). *The complete problem solver* (2nd ed.). Hillsdale, NJ: Erlbaum.

Helmreich, R. L., Spence, J. T., Beane, W. E., Lucker, G. W. & Matthews, K. A. (1980). Making it in academic psychology: demographic and personality correlates of attainment. *Journal of Personality and Social Psychology*, **39**, 896–908.

Helson, R. (1990). Creativity in women: outer and inner views over time. In: M. A. Runco & R. S. Albert (Eds), *Theories of Creativity* (pp. 46–58). Newbury Park, CA: Sage.

Holahan, C. K. & Sears, R. R. (1995). *The gifted group in later maturity*. Stanford, CA: Stanford University Press.

Hoyt, D. P. (1965). The relationship between college grades and adult achievement. *American College Testing Program*, Research Report No. 7, Iowa City, IA.

Hudson, L. (1958). Undergraduate academic record of Fellows of the Royal Society. *Nature*, **182**, 1326.

Jamison, K. R. (1989). Mood disorders and patterns of creativity in British writers and artists. *Psychiatry*, **52**, 125–134.

Jamison, K. R. (1993). *Touched with fire: Manic-depressive illness and the artistic temperament*. New York: Free Press.

Johnson, S. (1781). *The lives of the most eminent English poets* (Vol. 1). London: Bathurst et al.

Juda, A. (1949). The relationship between highest mental capacity and psychic abnormalities. *American Journal of Psychiatry*, **106**, 296–307.

Karlson, J. I. (1970). Genetic association of giftedness and creativity with schizophrenia. *Hereditas*, **66**, 177–182.

Lehman, H. C. & Witty, P. A. (1931). Scientific eminence and church membership. *Scientific Monthly*, **33**, 544–549.

Lotka, A. J. (1926). The frequency distribution of scientific productivity. *Journal of the Washington Academy of Sciences*, **16**, 317–323.

Ludwig, A. M. (1995). *The price of greatness: resolving the creativity and madness controversy*. New York: Guilford Press.

MacKinnon, D. W. (1978). *In search of human effectiveness*. Buffalo, NJ: Creative Education Foundation.

Martindale, C. (1972). Father absence, psychopathology, and poetic eminence. *Psychological Reports*, **31**, 843–847.

Martindale, C. (1990). *The clockwork muse: the predictability of artistic styles*. New York: Basic Books.

McClelland, D. C. (1973). Testing for competence rather than for 'intelligence'. *American Psychologist*, **28**, 1–14.

McCurdy, H. G. (1960). The childhood pattern of *Horizon*, **2**, 33–38.

McFarlan, D. (Ed.). (1989). *Guinness book of world records*. New York: Bantam.

Montour, K. (1977). William James Sidis, the broken twig. *American Psychologist*, **32**, 265–279.

Myerson, A. & Boyle, R. D. (1941). The incidence of manic-depression psychosis in certain socially important families: Preliminary report. *American Journal of Psychiatry*, **98**, 11–21.

Ochse, R. (1991). Why there were relatively few eminent women creators. *Journal of Creative Behavior*, **25**, 334–343.

Oden, M. H. (1968). The fulfillment of promise: forty-year follow-up of the Terman gifted group. *Genetic Psychology Monographs*, **77**, 3–93.

Post, F. (1994). Creativity and psychopathology: a study of 291 world-famous men. *British Journal of Psychiatry*, **165**, 22–34.

Prentky, R. A. (1989). Creativity and psychopathology: gamboling at the seat of madness. In: J. A. Glover, R. R. Ronning & C. R. Reynolds (Eds), *Handbook of Creativity* (pp. 243–269). New York: Plenum Press.

Price, D. (1963). *Little science, big science*. New York: Columbia University Press.

Richards, R. (1981). Relationships between creativity and psychopathology: An evaluation and interpretation of the evidence. *Genetic Psychology Monographs*, **103**, 261–324.

Roe, A. (1952). *The making of a scientist*. New York: Dodd, Mead.

Rothenberg, A. (1990). *Creativity and madness: new findings and old stereotypes*. Baltimore: Johns Hopkins University Press.

Rushton, J. P. (1990). Creativity, intelligence, and psychoticism. *Personality and Individual Differences*, **11**, 1291–1298.

Schachter, S. (1963). Birth order, eminence, and higher education. *American Sociological Review*, **28**, 757–768.

Schubert, D. S. P., Wagner, M. E. & Schubert, H. J. P. (1977). Family constellation and creativity: Firstborn predominance among classical music composers. *Journal of Psychology*, **95**, 147–149.

Shockley W. (1957). On the statistics of individual variations of productivity in research laboratories. *Proceedings of the Institute of Radio Engineers*, **45**, 279–290.

Silverman, S. M. (1974). Parental loss and scientists. *Science Studies*, **4**, 259–264.

Simon, H. A. (1955). On a class of skew distribution functions. *Biometrika*, **42**, 425–440.

Simonton, D. K. (1975). Sociocultural context of individual creativity: a transhistorical time-series analysis. *Journal of Personality and Social Psychology*, **32**, 1119–1133.

Simonton, D. K. (1976a). Biographical determinants of achieved eminence: a multivariate approach to the Cox data. *Journal of Personality and Social Psychology*, **33**, 218–226.

Simonton, D. K. (1976b). Philosophical eminence, beliefs, and zeitgeist: an individual-generational analysis. *Journal of Personality and Social Psychology*, **34**, 630–640.

Simonton, D. K. (1976c). The sociopolitical context of philosophical beliefs: a transhistorical causal analysis. *Social Forces*, **54**, 513–523.

Simonton, D. K. (1977a). Creative productivity, age, and stress: a biographical time-series analysis of 10 classical composers. *Journal of Personality and Social Psychology*, **35**, 791–804.

Simonton, D. K. (1977b). Eminence, creativity, and geographic marginality: a recursive structural equation model. *Journal of Personality and Social Psychology*, **35**, 805–816.

Simonton, D. K. (1978). The eminent genius in history: the critical role of creative development. *Gifted Child Quarterly*, **22**, 187–195.

Simonton, D. K. (1980). Thematic fame, melodic originality, and musical zeitgeist: a biographical and transhistorical content analysis. *Journal of Personality and Social Psychology*, **38**, 972–983.

Simonton, D. K. (1983a). Formal education, eminence, and dogmatism: the curvilinear relationship. *Journal of Creative Behavior*, **17**, 149–162.

Simonton, D. K. (1983b). Intergenerational transfer of individual differences in hereditary monarchs: Genes, role-modeling, cohort, or sociocultural effects? *Journal of Personality and Social Psychology*, **44**, 354–364.

Simonton, D. K. (1984a). Artistic creativity and interpersonal relationships across and within generations. *Journal of Personality and Social Psychology*, **46**, 1273–1286.

Simonton, D. K. (1984b). *Genius, creativity, and leadership: historiometric inquiries*. Cambridge, Mass.: Harvard University Press.

Simonton, D. K. (1984c). Is the marginality effect all that marginal? *Social Studies of Science*, **14**, 621–622.

Simonton, D. K. (1984d). Leaders as eponyms: Individual and situational determinants of monarchal eminence. *Journal of Personality*, **52**, 1–21.

Simonton, D. K. (1985a). Intelligence and personal influence in groups: Four nonlinear models. *Psychological Review*, **92**, 532–547.

Simonton, D. K. (1985b). Quality, quantity, and age: the careers of 10 distinguished psychologists. *International Journal of Aging and Human Development*, **21**, 241–254.

Simonton, D. K. (1986a). Biographical typicality, eminence, and achievement style. *Journal of Creative Behavior*, **20**, 14–22.

Simonton, D. K. (1986b). Presidential personality: biographical use of the Gough Adjective Check List. *Journal of Personality and Social Psychology*, **51**, 149–160.

Simonton, D. K. (1987). Developmental antecedents of achieved eminence. *Annals of Child Development*, **5**, 131–169.

Simonton, D. K. (1988a). Creativity, leadership, and chance. In: R. J. Sternberg (Ed.), *The Nature of Creativity: Contemporary Psychological Perspectives* (pp. 386–426). New York: Cambridge University Press.

Simonton, D. K. (1988b). Galtonian genius, Kroeberian configurations, and emulation: a generational time-series analysis of Chinese civilization. *Journal of Personality and Social Psychology*, **55**, 230–238.

Simonton, D. K. (1988c). *Scientific genius: a psychology of science*. Cambridge: Cambridge University Press.

Simonton, D. K. (1991a). Emergence and realization of: the lives and works of 120 classical composers. *Journal of Personality and Social Psychology*, **61**, 829–840.

Simonton, D. K. (1991b). Personality correlates of exceptional personal influence: a note on Thorndike's (1950) creators and leaders. *Creativity Research Journal*, **4**, 67–78.

Simonton, D. K. (1992a). Gender and genius in Japan: Feminine eminence in masculine culture. *Sex Roles*, **27**, 101–119.

Simonton, D. K. (1992b). Leaders of American psychology, 1879–1967: career development, creative output, and professional achievement. *Journal of Personality and Social Psychology*, **62**, 5–17.

Simonton, D. K. (1992c). The social context of career success and course for 2,026 scientists and inventors. *Personality and Social Psychology Bulletin*, **18**, 452–463.

Simonton, D. K. (1994). *Greatness: who makes history and why*. New York: Guilford Press.

Simonton, D. K. (1996). Presidents' wives and First Ladies: On achieving eminence within a traditional gender role. *Sex Roles*, **35**, 309–336.

Simonton, D. K. (1997a). Creative productivity: a predictive and explanatory model of career trajectories and landmarks. *Psychological Review*, **104**, 66–89.

Simonton, D. K. (1997b). *Genius and creativity: selected papers*. Greenwich, CT: Ablex.

Simonton, D. K. (1998). Achieved eminence in minority and majority cultures: vonvergence vs. divergence in the assessments of 294 African Americans. *Journal of Personality and Social Psychology*, **74**, 804–817.

Simonton, D. K. (1999). Talent and its development: an emergenic and epigenetic model. *Psychological Review*, **106**, 435–457.

Spearman, C. (1927). *The abilities of man: their nature and measurement*. New York: Macmillan.

Sternberg, R. J. (1985). *Beyond IQ: a triarchic theory of human intelligence*. New York: Cambridge University Press.

Stewart, L. H. (1977). Birth order and political leadership. In: M. G. Hermann (Ed.), *The Psychological Examination of Political Leaders* (pp. 205–236). New York: Free Press.

Subotnik, R. F. & Arnold, K. D. (Eds) (1994). *Beyond Terman: contemporary longitudinal studies of giftedness and talent*. Norwood, NJ: Ablex.

Subotnik, R. F., Kassan, L., Summers, E. & Wasser, A. (1993). *Genius revised: high IQ children grown up*. Norwood, NJ: Ablex.

Sulloway, F. J. (1996). *Born to rebel: birth order, family dynamics, and creative lives*. New York: Pantheon.

Terman, L. M. (1917). The intelligence quotient of Francis Galton in childhood. *American Journal of Psychology*, **28**, 209–215.

Terman, L. M. (1925). *Mental and physical traits of a thousand gifted children*. Stanford, CA: Stanford University Press.

Terman, L. M. & Oden, M. H. (1947). *The gifted child grows up*. Stanford, CA: Stanford University Press.

Terman, L. M. & Oden, M. H. (1959). *The gifted group at mid-life*. Stanford, CA: Stanford University Press.

Terry, W. S. (1989). Birth order and prominence in the history of psychology. *Psychological Record*, **39**, 333–337.

Tomlinson-Keasey, C. & Little, T. D. (1990). Predicting educational attainment, occupational achievement, intellectual skill, and personal adjustment among gifted men and women. *Journal of Educational Psychology*, **82**, 442–455.

Vaillant, G. E. & Vaillant, C. O. (1980). Determinants and consequences of creativity in a cohort of gifted women. *Psychology of Women Quarterly*, **14**, 607–616.

Wagner, M. E. & Schubert, H. J. P. (1977). Sibship variables and United States presidents. *Journal of Individual Psychology*, **33**, 78–85.

Walberg, H. J., Rasher, S. P. & Parkerson, J. (1980). Childhood and eminence. *Journal of Creative Behavior*, **13**, 225–231.

Walberg, H. J., Strykowski, B. F., Rovai, E. & Hung, S. S. (1984). Exceptional performance. *Review of Educational Research*, **54**, 87–112.

Wallach, M. A. & Kogan, N. (1965). Modes of thinking in young children. New York: Holt, Rinehart & Winston.

Walters, J. & Gardner, H. (1986). The crystallizing experience: discovering an intellectual gift. In: R. J. Sternberg & J. E. Davidson (Eds), *Conceptions of Giftedness* (pp. 306–331). New York: Cambridge University Press.

Weisberg, R. W. (1994). Genius and madness? A quasi-experimental test of the hypothesis that manic-depression increases creativity. *Psychological Science,* **5**, 361–367.

Winner, E. (1996). *Gifted children: myths and realities*. New York: Basic Books.

Woody, E. & Claridge, G. (1977). Psychoticism and thinking. *British Journal of Social and Clinical Psychology*, **16**, 241–248.

Zajonc, R. B. & Mullally, P. R. (1997). Birth order: reconciling conflicting effects. *American Psychologist*, **52**, 685–699.

Zweigenhaft, R. L. (1975). Birth order, approval-seeking, and membership in Congress. *Journal of Individual Psychology*, **31**, 205–210.

International Trends and Topics of Research on Giftedness and Talent

Kurt A. Heller[1] and Neville J. Schofield[2]

[1] *University of Munich, Germany and* [2] *University of Newcastle, Australia*

Introduction

During the last two decades a change has been taking place in the concepts of giftedness and talent as they are featured in research literature. Whereas until fifteen or twenty years ago the field was dominated by one dimensional giftedness concepts and corresponding IQ measurements, a large majority of more recent models are based on multidimensional or multifactorial psychometric concepts of intelligence—e.g. Gardner's (1985) theory of multiple intelligences—or on approaches from information theory and cognitive psychology—e.g. Sternberg's (1985) triarchic intelligence model. Other models still include elements from socialization theories, e.g. Mönks' (Mönks et al., 1986) extended Renzulli model. Furthermore, we agree with Sternberg's demand that (1990, p. 96): "We need to think in terms not only of multiple components of giftedness, but (also) of multiple kinds of giftedness". 'Giftedness' is thus defined as the individual cognitive and motivational potential for—as well as social and cultural conditions of—achieving excellent performances in one or more area/s such as in mathematics, languages, or artistic areas with regard to difficult theoretical vs. practical tasks (Heller, 1989, 1992). 'Talent' can be defined as a domain-specific gift or ability, e.g. 'scientific ability' as the competence for scientific expertise in the fields of psychology, medical sciences, or physics. However, the differentiation suggested by Gagné (1985) between 'giftedness' and 'talent' is infrequently maintained in the literature. In many languages—as in German—both concepts are used more or less synonymously. For this reason, no semantic differentiation was insisted upon in this handbook between 'giftedness' and 'talent'. When this makes sense in individual cases, the differentiation is explicated in that context. This also holds true for related terms, such as intelligence, creativity, or (high) ability, that are not independent of the theoretical basis in which they are found. In addition, the definition of giftedness, etc. is dependent on the intended use, for example, on the type and tasks of school programs, the aims of enrichment vs. acceleration programs, on empirical investigation goals and theory-based hypotheses, etc. Moreover, the term 'giftedness' or 'talent' is influenced by social norms and considerations (Tannenbaum, 1983). Last but not least, the definition of giftedness will be determined by the choice of measurement instruments, i.e. by the operationalization of the experimental variables examined.

A differentiation between descriptive and explanatory terms is also relevant when looking at research strategies. Whereas the *descriptive* term is linked to the psychometric paradigm, the *explanatory* term needs an experimental design in the cognitive science paradigm. For example, on the one hand, the psychometric intelligence structure theories enrich the ability phenomenology substantially, while on the other hand, the cognitive psychological (experimental) studies make it possible to explain the mechanism of cognitive processes and their individual sources. This also corresponds to the various identification strategies: status vs. process diagnosis (see Part III of this handbook). Both descriptive and explanatory terms are necessary for theoretically and practically efficient conceptualizations and measures.

Information Sources for the Data Analysis of Recent Research on Giftedness and Talent

The state of the art of research on giftedness and talent to be presented here was based on content analyses of the following *conference proceedings*:

(a) the last three published volumes of proceedings from the World Council for Gifted and Talented (WCGT) in 1991, 1995 and 1997; cf. Mönks and Peters (1992), Chan, Li & Spinks (1997), Leroux (1998);

(b) the until now published three volumes of proceedings from the European Council for High Ability (ECHA) between 1992 and 1996; cf. Heller and Hany (1994), Katzko and Mönks (1995), Spiel (1998);

(c) the previously published four volumes of proceedings from the Asia-Pacific Conferences (APC) between 1990 and 1996; cf. Roldan (1992), Wu, Kuv & Steeves (1993), Cho, Moon & Park (1995), Munandar and Semiawan (1997).

Proceedings for the first two ECHA Conferences in Zurich, 1988 and in Budapest, 1990, have not been published, nor have those for the 1993 WCGT Conference in Toronto. Those wishing to review the findings of the content analysis of the previously published nine volumes of proceedings from the WCGT Conferences held between 1975 and 1991 should refer to Heller (1993), Heller and Menacher (1992).

Furthermore, six major journals in the field (d–i) and two journals as a 'control group' (j–k) have been content analyzed over the last seven years (1992–1998):

(d) Gifted Child Quarterly (GCQ);
(e) Roeper Review (RR);
(f) Gifted Education International (GEI);
(g) Journal for the Education of the Gifted (JEG);
(h) High Ability Studies (HAS);
(i) Exceptionality Education Canada (EEC);
(j) Exceptional Children (EC);
(k) Journal of Educational Psychology (JEP).

The chapters and articles are classified according to seven categories:

• Learning and perception
• Identification
• Development
• Personal characteristics
• Physical/mental conditions
• Education and instruction
• Social issues.

Consequently, the various information sources can be evaluated with respect to corresponding vs. contradictory trends. We begin with an analysis of the conference proceedings (a–c). In addition, the WCGT Conference proceedings in the 1990s can be compared with those published in the volumes dating back to 1975 since the findings here corroborate those in the first edition of the Handbook (Heller, 1993). Furthermore, the structural concept of this handbook was included in the content analysis for comparative purposes. Supplementary to this, psychological subdisciplines as well as the differentiation between research vs. practice-related reports are used as categories.

Content Analysis—International Conference Proceedings

A total number of 163 manuscripts were published in the WCGT conference proceedings 1991–1997 of which approximately 38% were data based contributions; while a total of 95 manuscripts were published in the ECHA conference proceedings 1992–1995 with exactly 60% being data based contributions. Again, a total of 162 manuscripts were published in the APC proceedings 1990–1996, of which about 44% were data-based. Relatively speaking, the highest percentage of data based studies are to be found in the ECHA conference proceedings, and the lowest percentage among the WCGT conference proceedings. One must also remark that the percentage of data-based investigations in the WCGT conference proceedings in the past decade has risen by 13% with respect to the previous 15 years, namely from 25% (1979–1989) to 38% (1991–1997), a result which is pleasant indeed.

Significantly more modest differences are to be found for the three conference groups (WCGT, ECHA, APC) with respect to the age groups investigated (where middle age groups dominate in comparison with primary and pre-education groups as well as adults—the one exception being the European ECHA conferences). However, all three conference groups have common ground regarding the sample sizes of the data based proceedings in that a sample size of $n = 501$ or more is rather seldom found (see Table 1).

Further agreement is maintained regarding methodological aspects. With approximately 80%, the interview is clearly the preferred measurement technique whereas the use of research designs—with one or two exceptions—show no large differences among the three conference groups (Table 2). Gratifying is the rela-

Table 1. Age Groups and Sample Sizes in the Data Based Contributions to the WCGT (1991–1997), ECHA (1992–1996), and APC (1990–1996) Proceedings.

Age groups:	WCGT	ECHA	APC
preschool	9.3%	3.0%	6.5%
primary education	7.8%	10.6%	16.3%
elementary/secondary education (grades 4–8)	26.8%	27.3%	30.4%
later secondary education (grades 9–12)	18.7%	19.7%	22.8%
higher education	21.8%	15.2%	13.1%
adulthood	15.6%	24.2%	10.9%
Sample sizes: $n =$ under 100	47.3%	52.9%	37.1%
$n = 101–500$	35.2%	29.5%	33.3%
$n = 501$ and more	17.5%	17.6%	29.6%

Table 2. Measurement Techniques and Research Designs of the Data Based Contributions to the WCGT (1991–1997), ECHA (1992–1996), and APC (1990–1996) Proceedings.

Measurement techniques:	WCGT	ECHA	APC
interview	80.6%	85.5%	78.8%
observation	9.6%	5.5%	7.5%
(quasi) experiment	9.8%	9.0%	13.7%
Research designs: single-age group	34.4%	29.1%	10.9%
cross-sectional	24.3%	34.5%	51.6%
longitudinal	41.3%	36.4%	37.5%

tively large percentage of longitudinal studies which in the WCGT proceedings was, with 10%, significantly higher than during the earlier period (1975–1989). For a detailed comparison of individual changes in the WCGT proceedings articles within the past decade in contrast to the previous 15 years see Table 3 (age groups and sample sizes) and Table 4 (methodological aspects).

What sorts of trends develop regarding research topic or subject group? The most important results of our proceedings content analysis are illustrated in Figs 1 to 4, which are also presented as conference group comparisons.

It becomes apparent that the categories 'Educational/ Instructional Processes and Programming' in the WCGT conference proceedings 1991–1997 with a median of 43.5% (the corresponding figure for the period 1975–1989 was 35%) and 'Personal Character-istics' with a median of 30.5% (previously 25%) have

the most entries, relatively speaking (see Fig. 1a). One quickly notices that WCGT proceedings contributions concerning 'Development' (6%) and 'Identification' (3.5%) are only seldom occurrences, while the cate-gory 'Social Issues' is well represented with 11.5% of the contributions.

By contrast, in the European gifted conferences (ECHA), the individual categories are more balanced. Contributions in ECHA proceedings (1992–1996) most frequently concern the topic 'Personal characteristics' (37%), followed closely by 'Educational/Instructional processes and programming' (32.5%). The third most addressed topic here is 'Identification' (10.5%). Only slightly less contributions concern 'Physical/mental conditions' (8.5%), while 'Development' and 'Social Issues' are each covered in 5.5% of the contributions (see Fig. 1b).

The topic profile of the APC proceedings (Fig. 1c) proves to be largely similar to the WCGT conference

Table 3. Age Groups and Sample Sizes in the Data Based Contributions to the WCGT Conference Proceedings—Comparison Between the Period 1975–1989 and the Period 1991–1997.

Age groups:	(1975–1989)	(1991–1997)
preschool	3%	9%
primary education	13%	8%
elementary/secondary education (grades 4–8)	45%	27%
later secondary education (grades 9–12)	23%	12%
higher education	3%	22%
adulthood	13%	15%
Sample sizes: n = under 100	42%	47%
n = 101–500	42%	35%
n = 501 and more	16%	18%

Table 4. Measurement Techniques and Research Designs of the Data Based Contributions to the WCGT Conference Proceedings – Comparison Between the Period 1975–1989 and the Period 1991–1997.

Measurement techniques:	Period (1975–1989)	(1991–1997)
interview	71%	80%
observation	5%	10%
(quasi) experiment	24%	10%
Research designs: single-age group	23%	35%
cross-sectional	67%	24%
longitudinal	10%	41%

profile described above. With about 53%, the category 'Educational/Instructional processes and programming' is even more frequent. All in all, however, the structural agreement among all three profiles in Fig. 1 (Figs 1a, 1b, 1c) is larger than the individual differences depicted.

This picture does not change much if we redefine the categories somewhat. If one prefers to use the structural concept from this handbook, then we find the division as shown in Fig. 2—with comparisons of WCGT, ECHA and APC in Figs 2a, 2b, 2c.

The following analysis results are very informative regarding the psychological sub-disciplines which contributed to the three different conference proceedings (Fig. 3). There is a clear dominance of conference articles regarding Educational Psychology: 62.5% in the WCGT (Fig. 3a), 44% in the ECHA (Fig. 3b) and 62.5% in the APC (Fig. 3c). Although Personality

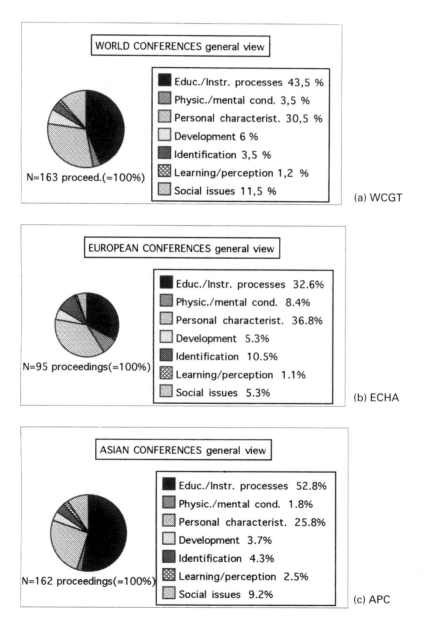

Figure 1. Content analysis of the WCGT conferences (1991–1997), the ECHA conferences (1992–1996) and the APC (1990–1996) proceedings: Percentages of the main topics.

Psychology makes up 25% of the proceedings in the WCGT and 26.5% in the APC, this topic is more frequently addressed in Europe (ECHA) with a share of 42%. The analysis of the WCGT proceedings in the time period between 1975–1989 resulted in a figure of approximately 70% regarding contributions which stem from Educational Psychology. On the other hand, topics relating to General Psychology were poorly represented by contributions (0.6% for both WCGT and APC proceedings and 1.1% in the ECHA proceed-

ings). Even when one takes into account that a stray basic research study could be hidden among the other categories (primarily in Personality Psychology), this finding can only be considered as disappointing from a research perspective.

This impression is confirmed in the following analysis results presented in Fig. 4. With theoretical contribution levels of 10% (Fig. 4a) to 20% (Fig. 4b)—with 14% the APC (Fig. 4c) lies in the middle—and only 0.6% (WCGT, APC),and 4.2% (ECHA) for basic

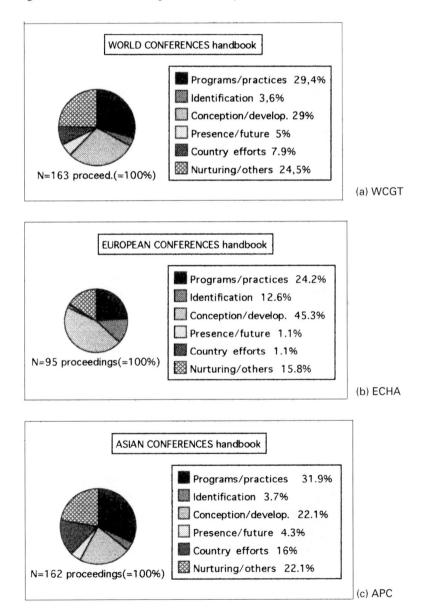

Figure 2. Percentages of the main topics of the WCGT conferences (1991–1997), the ECHA conferences (1992–1996) and the APC (1990–1996) proceedings according to the structure of the International Handbook.

(mainly experimental) research, these two areas are placed in direct contrast to data-based (empirical) studies, in the sense of applied research, shown to be 38% in Fig. 4a (WCGT), 45% in Fig. 4b (ECHA) and 36% in Fig. 4c (APC). This indicates a twofold increase in data-based research contributions for the WCGT proceedings for the last ten years in comparison to the preceding 15 year period (38% vs. 20%) whereby a simultaneous drop in the number of practical needs reports could be confirmed (18% vs.

40% previous). Real research contributions, i.e. those based on hypotheses made up approximately one quarter of all conference papers in the period 1975–1989. This level has made a gratifying increase in the past ten years in that about one third of all conference contributions now meet the usual scientific standards of applied research.

Further breakdowns regarding current research trends and topics can be expected in the content analysis of eight leading journals in the field. The

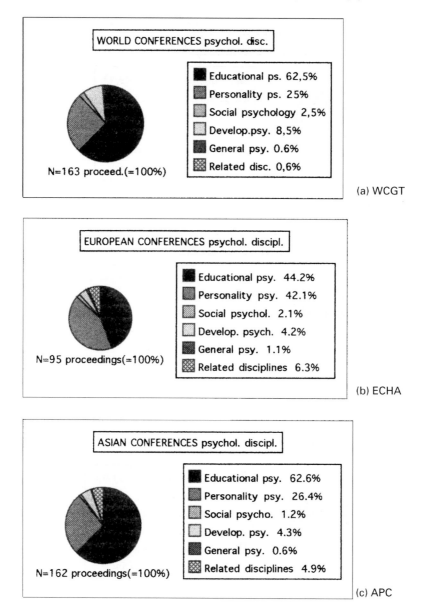

(a) WCGT

(b) ECHA

(c) APC

Figure 3. Classification of the papers published in the proceedings of the WCGT conferences (1991–1997), the ECHA conferences (1992–1996) and the APC (1990–1996) according to psychological subdisciplines.

results of this analysis will be presented in the following section.

Content Analysis—Major Journals

In the following section a content analysis of eight of the most important journals in this area of giftedness over the last seven years (1992–1998) is undertaken. The aim of such an analysis is to both consider the nature of the research currently being undertaken in terms of the general content headings of this handbook,

and to compare the results of such an analysis with those undertaken in the first edition of this handbook (Heller, 1993, pp. 51–56) some seven years ago. The eight journals analysed included the six used for the first edition: *Gifted Child Quarterly* (GCQ), *Roeper Review* (RR), *Gifted Education International* (GEI), *Journal for the Education of the Gifted* (JEG) as well as *Exceptional Children* (EC) and *Journal of Educational Psychology* (JEP) which were used as a 'control group', along with *High Ability Studies* (HAS)

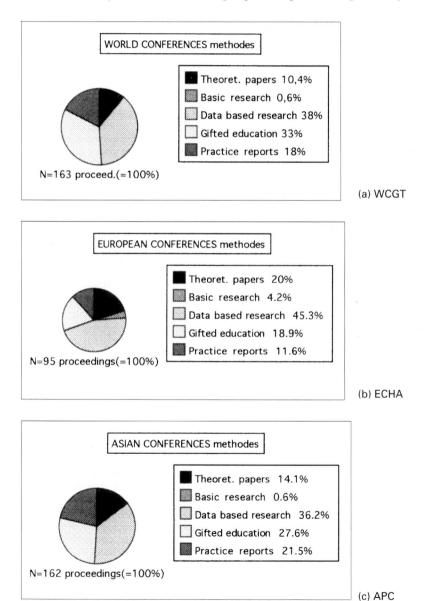

Figure 4. Classification of the papers published in the proceedings of the WCGT conferences (1991–1997), the ECHA conferences (1992–1996) and the APC (1990–1996) according to research vs practice reports.

[formerly *The European Council Journal for High Ability* (ECHA)] and *Exceptionality Education Canada* (EEC), also used as part of the control group. In particular, the analysis was concerned with:

(1) the nature of the topics most frequently addressed in those journals which deal with giftedness related research;

(2) relative differences between the five gifted journals in terms of their content and approach as well as the differences between the gifted journals and the control group in terms of the types of articles presented;

(3) whether, during the last seven years, there has been a shift in content, methodology or editorial approach, as reflected in the types of articles published.

In an effort to address these questions, the various journals were categorized along a number of dimensions, some of which overlap but each of which provides a theoretical framework which accords with a generally accepted view of either psychological or gifted research. In each series of analyses, all articles were categorized into one, and only one category, which inevitably resulted in relatively fine distinctions having to be drawn. In the first series of analyses undertaken on the five specified gifted journals (see Fig. 5), articles were categorized according to a generally discipline based formula, which revealed that there had been marked changes in the pattern of articles published in these journals since the previous analysis. Most notably, there was a decline in the number of articles devoted to 'Education and Instruction' so that, whereas previously up to 60% of articles fell into this category (in GEI), the highest percentage now found was only 41% (in RR). There was almost no change in the second most frequently reported category of article, namely 'Personal Characteristics', which meant that the decline in the first category resulted in a greater breadth in the nature of the articles published. Perhaps the greatest general spread of articles was to be found in the HAS, which was previously not included in the analyses. The category which was least represented was 'Physical/Mental' aspects of giftedness, mainly due to the very low representations in both the GCQ and the RR. Given that these are probably the two most prestigious journals in the North American group, one is forced to question why this category of research should be so scantily recognized. Another, somewhat related area, is that of 'Development', which was also poorly represented across the board. In particular, RR and JEG each had around 3% of their articles in this category, while the other three journals varied between 8% and 10%. It is impossible to tell from these analyses whether the low or changed figures given represent specific editorial policies or changes in general research interest. However, it could be assumed that the decline in representation across all five journals for articles related to 'Education and Instruction' does

represent a change in research interest over the period in question and the broader diversity which filled the void also suggests a more balanced approach to gifted research.

The second set of analyses, which is found in Fig. 6, corresponds to the general conceptual structure of this Handbook. This meant that, whereas in the First Edition 'Concepts and Development' was a single category, these two dimensions, which are conceptually discrete, are also separated in the analysis.

In all five journals the most frequently represented category was 'Programs and Practices', with percentages ranging from 26% (GEI) to 48% (JEG). This represents another shift in emphasis from the earlier analysis, where there had been a slight emphasis in favour of the area of 'Nurturing' (which largely involved Counseling of the gifted). This shift was particularly marked in JEG and, to a lesser extent, in the RR and GEI. The two categories of 'Concepts' and 'Development' were marked by a slight rise in overall percentages of articles with 'Concepts' receiving greater numbers in all but one (JEG) of the journals. The predominance of the 'Programs and Practices' category accords with the similar importance of the 'Education and Instruction' category in Fig. 5.

When the articles are classified according to psychological sub-disciplines (Fig. 7) there appears to be a dramatic shift from the earlier analysis which cannot easily be explained. In the previous analysis, the dominant category in all four journals was that of 'Personality Psychology', with figures ranging from 55% to over 80%. However, in the present analysis in those same four journals this category is hardly represented and instead the category of 'Educational Psychology' accounts for between 69% and 78% of all articles. While an initial reaction might be to decide that this is a clear case of faulty classification, the situation is actually made more confusing by the fact that the newest journal to be added to the group (HAS) reports some 61% of articles as coming from the area of 'Personality Psychology', which suggests that there may have actually been a major editorial shift in the four original journals over this period. Indeed, a relatively quick scan of these earlier journals suggests that, while there may have been some minor evidence of misclassification, the figures were generally correct, which only leaves a significant editorial shift as an explanation, particularly as it seems that such personality research is still being undertaken, given the number of articles published in HAS. One possible alternative explanation is that, since the HAS is largely focused on Europe and the other journals reflect more of an American and international focus, the change in emphasis reflects a cultural shift in research activity.

Overall then, given the size of the imbalance, it is not surprising that there are very few other sub-disciplines which are significantly represented in these analyses. Certainly, it could be argued that the very broad

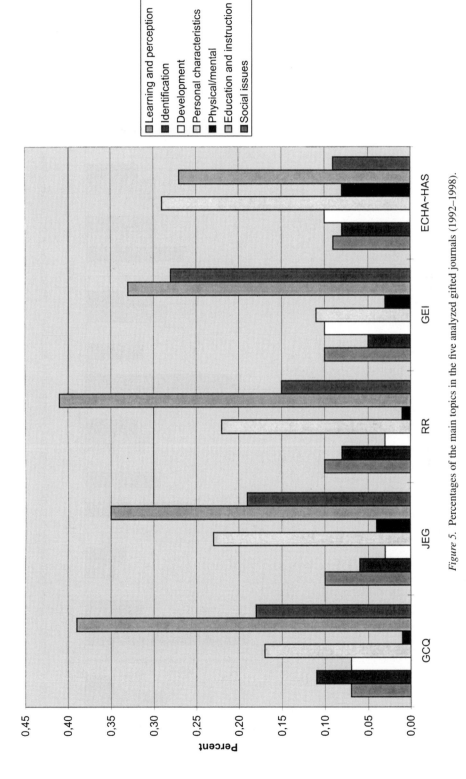

Figure 5. Percentages of the main topics in the five analyzed gifted journals (1992–1998).

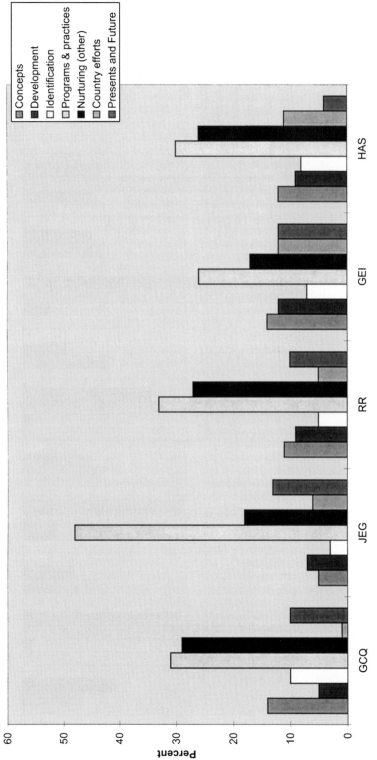

Figure 6. Percentages of the main topics in the five analyzed gifted journals according to the structure of this internatiobnal handbook (1992–1998).

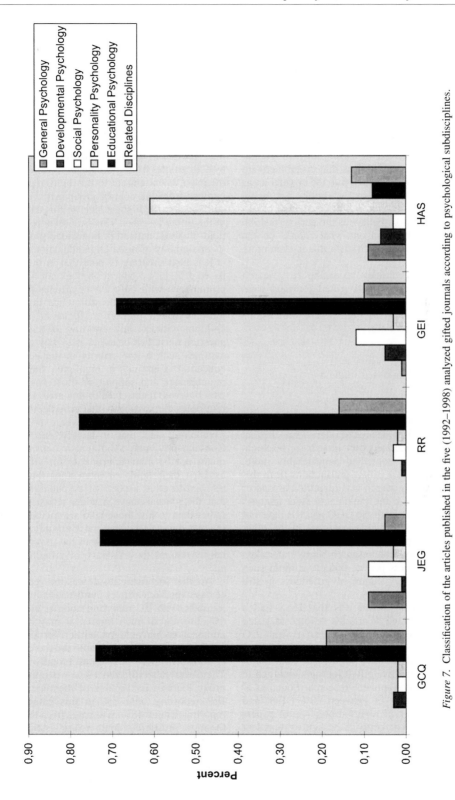

Figure 7. Classification of the articles published in the five (1992–1998) analyzed gifted journals according to psychological subdisciplines.

category of Educational Psychology is likely to be the province of most of the research on giftedness and this appears to have been reflected in all journals except for HAS. However the question remains as to whether there has been such a major shift in research emphasis in the non-European countries or whether there is some other factor at work here. If there has actually been such a shift in focus, then it perhaps should be a matter for some concern that researchers, both non-European and European, are not conducting research on gifted-ness in the broader areas of psychology in greater numbers. At the same time, if it is that researchers are actually undertaking the research into the broader areas of psychology but their work is simply not being published because of an editorial policy which has as its focus what the editors believe is the current fashion or perhaps even a belief about what *should* be the direction of giftedness research, then this is even more disquieting.

In an analysis of articles according to research methods and practice, the five gifted journals were compared with each other and with the three journals used as a control group (see Fig. 8). The dimensions which were considered were:

- theoretical papers
- basic research focused papers
- applied research (data-based studies)
- gifted education
- practical reports.

Amongst the five gifted journals there were definite variations in emphasis. One area of interest was the fact that GCQ and RR contained very little basic research, while the other three contained considerably more, with HAS reporting 28% of its contributions from this area. A lack of basic research was identified as one of the areas of concern in the previous content analysis and it is surprising that both the GCQ and RR have not reflected the changes that have emerged in the other three journals. This may also suggest that there is still a lack of good quality basic research being undertaken in the area of giftedness per se. Indeed, without such basic research, the very nature of giftedness is still open to question.

One other surprising result was that HAS had a relatively low percentage of articles devoted to gifted education (8%), especially when compared with GCQ (39%) and GEI (47%). Again, one must assume that this is a reflection of editorial policy. The final major difference between the five gifted journals emerged in the area of data-based (applied) research. Four out of the five reported figures of between 20% (JEG) and 37% (GCQ) whereas GEI reported only 4% of papers which fitted into this category. These figures represent 23% of all studies reported in these journals, which is a much lower proportion than that which was found in the earlier analysis (Heller, 1993, p. 53) where this category represented approximately 30%. It is

extremely disappointing that the area of gifted research is still so poorly served by both basic research and data-based research and that the warnings sounded so long ago in the Marland Report have not been heeded. Indeed, these figures suggest that the situation is actually deteriorating.

When a comparison is made between the gifted journals and the three control group journals, a number of other patterns emerge. In particular, the number of data-based studies is completely out of proportion to that reported in the gifted journals, with JEP reporting 89% of articles from this category, while EEC, which is the most recent entrant to this field, reports the lowest number from the control group with 37%, but this is still equal to the highest level of this category reported in the gifted journals. This is another reminder that the field of gifted education is decidedly out of step with the main body of research in educational psychology.

It is also sobering to note that in the more broadly based JEP, gifted education does not achieve any real prominence with only 2% of articles falling into that category. There is little difference in the other two journals which purport to focus on all exceptional children, with EC only reporting 3% and EEC 7%. The question must then be asked as to why gifted education assumes such a low priority in the general realm of education. Certainly it highlights the need for the maintenance and support of those specialist journals which devote themselves to this area. However, it also reinforces the possibility that gifted education has little of relevance to say to the rest of the world of psychology and that it largely exists in isolation. Consequently, one should also consider whether it might not be more appropriate for gifted journals to broaden their fields of interest so that they become relevant to other aspects of psychological research so that the journals have a wider appeal and relevance, rather than to just those who are focused on establishing giftedness as a discipline. Certainly, if these figures are any indication, the rest of the psychological world hardly notices the existence of giftedness research at all.

Another surprising result was the very low numbers of basic research articles published in the control group journals, with EC reporting none at all and JEP only 4%. In view of such figures, it may be that the low numbers commented on earlier for this category in GCQ were actually in line with the more general trends as shown in these other more broadly-based journals. There were also differences between the three control group journals in the area of theoretical papers, with JEP reporting only 5% in this category and EEC reporting a huge 48%. It appears from these figures that the more prestigious journals are less likely to publish theoretical papers and more likely to publish papers which are data based. However, given this trend, it is still surprising that more papers in the area of basic research are not published, which leads to the

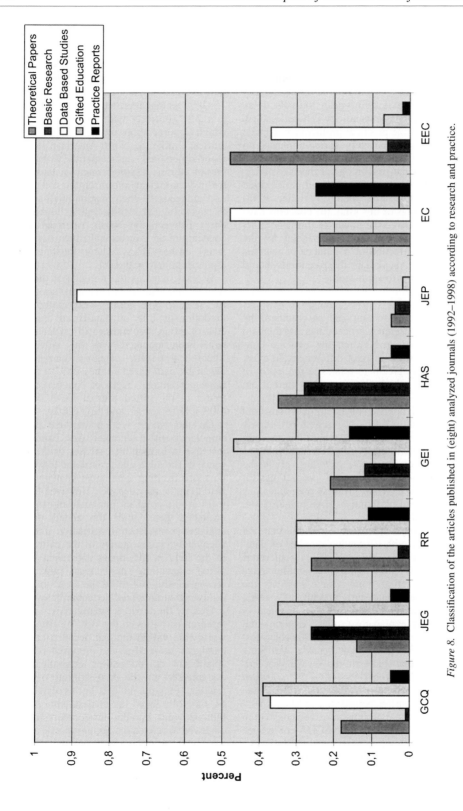

Figure 8. Classification of the articles published in (eight) analyzed journals (1992–1998) according to research and practice.

conclusion that there is very little basic research of sufficient quality for publication being undertaken.

In summary, these findings indicate that there has been relatively little change in most areas of gifted research in the last seven years, with the notable exception of a shift away from a focus on Personality Psychology within the non-European journals to an emphasis on Educational Psychology. There is still a general emphasis on the practical problems associated with gifted education and very little emphasis on research which is of a basic nature or which relies on an understanding of the psychological theories underpinning gifted performance. This was an issue which was highlighted in the earlier analysis (Heller, 1993) but, like most warnings of this kind, the concerns have fallen on deaf ears. Given the power of journal editors to shape research directions, as evidenced by the various changes in direction of a number of journals over the last seven years, perhaps these cautions should be specifically directed towards them.

Conclusion

When one compares the content analysis results of the two sections—the conference proceedings and the field journals—the similarities between the two are considerable, although some distinct differences do exist. The greatest area of agreement relates to the *topics of main emphasis*, of which 70% to 80% stem from Educational and Personality Psychology contributions. In these categories applied research questions and methods outweigh those of basic research (cf. Figs 1 and 3) by more than 90%, a fact which has recently been criticized by Persson (1999). Few contributions from the category of *General Psychology* are to be found in either source (conference proceedings or gifted journals), although the greatest preponderance from this category can be found in HAS and JEG (cf. Fig. 7) with nearly 10%.

Preferred *age groups* are school-aged children and youth (cf. Table 1), with a growing number of data-based contributions to the (WCGT) conference proceedings (Table 3) emphasizing early adulthood age groups (higher education). *Sub specie methods* the empirical studies dominate with around 80% using descriptive (interview) measurement techniques as compared with 10% explanatory (quasi) experimental studies (cf. Table 2). *Sample sizes* up to 500 occur most frequently (Table 3). There has been a gratifying increase in longitudinal studies in the WCGT proceedings during the period from 1991–1997 (41%) when compared with the period 1975–1989 (10%). When compared with this earlier period, the level of cross-sectional and longitudinal designs remained constant in the 1990s (from 35% to 36% for the ECHA conference proceedings). In the empirical papers of the APC, however, cross-sectional studies continue to outweigh longitudinal designs with 52% and 38% respectively (Table 2). This could be interpreted as being the result

of different economic and/or historical circumstances for longitudinal studies in East Asian vs. European and North American countries.

Gifted journals generally do not differ from one another greatly in their *topic profiles*. The one exception to this is in the area of 'social issues' which, with 15–20% being reported in North American gifted journals, contrasts with the European journal HAS which reports approximately only half this rate of entries. Unlike the North American journals, the HAS reports 'personal characteristics' as having the highest rate of entries, although many of these do not fit into the psychological sub-discipline of 'social psychology'. Indeed, the classification of all articles according to psychological sub-disciplines highlights the differences between the North American journals, which concentrate on Educational Psychology, and the European journal HAS, where Personality Psychology topics dominate with 60%.

If one compares the findings of the gifted journals with those of the so-called control group journals (JEP, EC, EEC), one notices—especially with JEP—the predominant role of data-based studies within the control group. Yet within EEC (which perhaps should have been included with the gifted journals), the 'theoretical papers' category dominates (48%), followed by data-based studies at 37% (cf. Fig. 8). This same percentage (37%) of data-based studies can be found in the gifted journal GCQ, followed by RR (30%), HAS (24%), and JEG (20%).

On the whole we can deduce that, aside from singular positive changes (for example the partial increase in longitudinal studies or the stronger observance of the adult age group), the 90s have contributed no more exciting qualitative changes to the research field than the past decades. However, this conclusion is valid at this point in time and only for the documents evaluated here, with the added proviso that the analyzed sources of information can be viewed as adequately representative of the entire research scene in the field of giftedness and talent with a focus on gifted education. There exists, however, no obvious reason for this not to be the case, so that perhaps the following summarized deduction may be allowed.

Despite the obvious quantitative increase of applied research activities in the field of giftedness and talent worldwide within the last decade, the topics of main emphasis, as well as the preferred research methods, apparently do not differ dramatically from those documented in the first edition of this handbook (Heller, 1993, pp. 49–60). In this respect, the 1993 (pp. 61–62) formulated list of desiderata *mutatis mutandis* remains valid. Parallel developments can, however, be observed in related disciplines (social sciences), so that we should not be too disappointed in this regard. Advances in knowledge can often only be achieved through small steps and extensive efforts in long-term research. To this end, an increase in the quality of research designs and measurement techniques, including data analysis, is necessary. But most importantly, basic research in the field of giftedness and talent must be improved, which requires the intensification of cooperation with researchers. This is particularly true within the areas of 'General and Personality Psychology' and 'Cognitive Science' (where basic experimental research traditionally holds a higher priority); for greater detail see Waldmann & Weinert (1990). In general, a stronger emphasis on interdisciplinary research—above and beyond the boundaries of the strongly pedagogical-psychological dominated field of research—is essential in order to discover more about the nature of giftedness and talent. Julian Stanley's assertion is as valid now as before, that in the meantime we know quite a bit about the 'whats', but very little about the 'whys' of high ability, etc. To change this should be the top goal of researchers within the field of giftedness and talent during the first decade of the new millennium.

Acknowledgments

The authors would like to thank Lea Salis and Jeffrey Reeves for their valuable assistance with data analysis.

References

Chan, J., Li, R. & Spinks, J. (Eds) (1997). *Maximizing potential: lengthening and strengthening our stride.* Proceedings of the 11th World Conference on Gifted and Talented Children (WCGT). Hong Kong: The University of Hong Kong, Social Science Research Centre.

Cho, S., Moon, J. H. & Park, J. O. (Eds) (1995). *Creativity for the 21st century.* Selected Proceedings of the 3rd Asia-Pacific Conference on Giftedness (APC). Seoul: The Korean Society for the Gifted.

Gagné, F. (1985). Giftedness and talent—reexamining a reexamination of the definitions. *Gifted Child Quarterly*, **29**, 103–112.

Gardner, H. (1985). *Frames of mind. The theory of multiple intelligences.* New York: Basic Books.

Heller, K. A. (1989). Perspectives on the diagnosis of giftedness. *The German Journal of Psychology*, **13**, 140–159.

Heller, K. A. (1992). Giftedness research and education of the gifted and talented in Germany. In: F. J. Mönks & W. A. M. Peters (Eds), *Talent for the Future: Social and Personality Development of Gifted Children* (pp. 149–154). Assen/Maastricht: Van Gorcum.

Heller, K. A. (1993). Structural tendencies and issues of research on giftedness and talent. In: K. A. Heller, F. J. Mönks & A. H. Passow (Eds), *International Handbook of Research and Development of Giftedness and Talent* (pp. 49–67). Oxford: Pergamon.

Heller, K. A. & Hany, E. A. (Eds) (1994). *Competence and responsibility*, Vol. 2. Proceedings of the 3rd Conference of the European Council for High Ability (ECHA). Seattle: Hogrefe & Huber Publ.

Heller, K. A. & Menacher, P. (1992). Research on giftedness and talent in the Proceedings of the WCGT Conferences 1975–1991. In: F. J. Mönks & W. A. M. Peters (Eds), *Talent for the Future: Social and Personality Development of Gifted Children* (pp. 138–148). Assen/Maastricht: Van Gorcum.

Katzko, M. W. & Mönks, F. J. (Eds) (1995). *Nurturing talent. individual and social ability.* Proceedings of the 4th Conference of the European Council for High Ability (ECHA). Assen/Maastricht: Van Gorcum.

Leroux, J. A. (Ed.) (1998). *Connecting the gifted community worldwide.* Selected Proceedings from the 12th World Conference of the World Council for Gifted and Talented Children (WCGT). Seattle: WCGT.

Mönks, F. J. & Peters, W. A. M. (Eds) (1992). *Talent for the future: social and personality development of gifted children.* Proceedings of the 9th World Conference on Gifted and Talented Children (WCGT). Assen/Maastricht: Van Gorcum.

Mönks, F. J., van Boxtel, H. W., Roelofs, J. J. W. & Sanders, M. P. M. (1986). The identification of gifted children in secondary education and a description of their situation in Holland. In: K. A. Heller & J. F. Feldhusen (Eds), *Identifying and Nurturing the Gifted* (pp. 39–65). Toronto: Huber.

Munandar, U. & Semiawan, C. (Eds) (1997). *Optimizing excellence in human resource development.* Proceedings of the 4th Asia-Pacific Conference on Giftedness (APC). Jakarta: University of Indonesia Press.

Persson, R. J. (1999). Editorial. *High Ability Studies*, **10**, 133–136.

Roldan, A. H. (Ed.) (1992). *Gifted children and youth today, gifted adults of the 21st century.* Selected Proceedings of the 1st Southeast Asian Regional Conference on Giftedness (APC). Manila, Philippines: Reading Dynamics Center, Inc.

Spiel, Ch. (Ed.) (1998). *Creativity and culture. talent development in the arts and sciences.* Selected Proceedings from the 5th Conference of the European Council for High Ability (ECHA). Abingdon/Oxford: Carfax. Special Issue of *High Ability Studies*, 9 (1), (pp. 3–124).

Sternberg, R. J. (1985). *Beyond IQ: a triarchic theory of human intelligence.* New York: Cambridge University Press.

Sternberg, R. J. (1990). What constitutes a 'good' definition of giftedness? *Journal for the Education of the Gifted*, **14**, 96–100.

Tannenbaum, A. J. (1983). *Gifted children: psychosocial and educational perspectives.* New York: MacMillan.

Waldmann, M. & Weinert, F. E. (1990). *Intelligenz und Denken. Perspektiven der Hochbegabungsforschung.* [Intelligence and Thinking Processes. Perspectives of the Research of Giftedness]. Göttingen: Hogrefe.

Wu, W.-T., Kuo, C.-C. & Steeves, J. (Eds) (1993). *Growing up gifted and talented.* Proceedings of the 2nd Asian Conference on Giftedness (APC). Taipei: National Taiwan Normal University, Department of Special Education.

Part II

Development of Giftedness and Talent

Developmental Psychology and Giftedness: Theories and Research

Franz J. Mönks[1] and Emanuel J. Mason[2]

[1]University of Nijmegen, The Netherlands
[2]Northeastern University, Boston, Massachusetts, USA

Introduction

Human development is generally regarded as an interaction between individual characteristics and environmental conditions. Historically, psychologists have debated whether development of an individual is determined more by organic or environmental factors. This nature–nurture issue is not only a concern for developmental psychology (Vernon, 1979). Education and socialization depend largely on theories and findings of developmental psychology. If proponents of the nature position predominate at a given time, human development is regarded as a process of maturation. If, however, the advocates of nurture are prevailing, the emphasis is on learning. Nowadays most developmental and educational psychologists hold a position somewhere between the two extremes.

The primary question in developmental research on the gifted is no longer whether nature or nurture is the most basic, but rather what is the kind of interaction that occurs between the two, and how this influences development. In other words, the results from the interaction of specific individual genetic attributes and experiences in a given social and cultural environment is the central concern.

Major developmental theories will be presented in this chapter. These theories will be related to conceptualizations and definitions of giftedness. The main intention is to elaborate on the contribution of developmental theories to our understanding of the gifted. Finally, teaching, instruction and educational reforms in gifted education will be discussed from a developmental perspective. In the present chapter, the authors treat the terms gifted, highly able, and talented synonymously.

Developmental Theories

The concept of development includes a complexity of processes and their organization. This complexity is constructed from conceptual and empirical elements. A theory of development depends on the accentuation of aspects of this complexity. Theories are most meaningful when they enable description, explanation and prediction of diverse phenomena (Mason & Bramble, 1997). It has been suggested that the usefulness of a theory of giftedness should be established in terms of what it implies about the nature of the gifted child, education and programs for the gifted, its structure and framework, and the criteria of good theory (e.g. logical consistency, parsimony) (Cohen, 1988). According to Marx (1963), a distinction is necessary between four different modes of theory construction. They are arranged from relatively more conceptual to relatively more empirical.

Deductive theory refers to any logically or deductively arranged cluster of concepts. The empirical data are explained from a conceptual structure. Such a formally organized theory can give direction to research but findings contribute little to produce a new or better theory.

Functional theory refers to the interaction of empirical findings and conceptualization. Empirical and conceptual activities are emphasized and have equal status in theory construction.

Inductive theory refers to the kind of theory that is essentially a summary of empirical data; it contains a minimum of deductive logic. Essentially it is the contrary of a deductive theory.

Model is a term for any conceptual analog that can be used for empirical research. Such an analog is often of a mathematical or physical nature. A model that directs the process of finding an answer or solution is called a heuristic. The result of such a process can be a hypothesis and as such contribute to a better conceptualization. Models often have a descriptive or explanatory function. Such a model accentuates the most important aspects. For example, the machine or deficit model has often been used to explain the human aging (i.e. the functioning of a machine decreases over time, parts of the machine getting old, which affects the functioning of the system). This increasingly poorly functioning model serves as an analogy for the human aging process. Thus, a model has value as a heuristic or tool. A model is not subject to the same kinds of rigorous demands for verification and falsification as a theory (Cook & Campbell, 1979).

Developmental theories can be grouped by their different perspectives. Divergent orientations will be presented to show the variety of explanations for human development. Sometimes theories cannot be easily classified into these groups because they came from multiple perspectives, e.g. Sternberg (2000) is working from a functional and inductive perspective, in his model.

Biologically Oriented Theories

In this context development is viewed as synonymous with evolution. Human development is mainly seen as growth and maturation of the organism, as unfolding of predispositions: i.e. heredity and temperament. In this view development is biologically determined. The environment plays a relatively unimportant role providing only the necessary ground for the growth of predispositions, comparable to a plant that needs favorable environmental conditions for its growth. Actually, development is a continuation of the genesis of the embryo.

Terman believed to his 'dying day' that intelligence is a genetically determined trait that is stable over the life of an individual (Minton, 1988, p. 199). However, by the time he was 77, his own empirical genetic studies, the longest developmental investigation in terms of duration ever attempted, convinced him that many of his 1500 subjects had never made use of their superior ability. He concluded that factors other than intelligence, such as personality and environment, determine in an essential way whether or not an individual reaches 'life success' (Terman, 1954). Nowadays, there are no serious proponents of this kind of theory. However, the relationship of genetics to behavior is currently an active issue among researchers as will be shown later in this chapter (e.g. Thompson and Plomin in this volume, Plomin, 1995).

Ecology-Oriented Theories

Learning and sociologically oriented theories belong to this group. The influence of the environment on the development of a person has a central position in these theories. Human development is seen as an ongoing social learning process in a complex ecological context (see, e.g. Bronfenbrenner, 1979).

Learning theories, although not identical, have a common feature that learning is viewed as a relatively stable change in the person's potential to behave; therefore, development means increase of potential to perform and to behave. Simple behavior like walking has to be learned once the maturational process makes walking possible. Similarly, social skills and thinking systematically have to be learned when the child is ready to do so. The potential to perform higher order activities is not the result of spontaneous organismic growth, but is the outcome of learning appropriate techniques. Therefore, the child learns to demonstrate milieu-specific behavior patterns in coordination with the developmental process.

It is important to search for the mechanisms that govern the acquisition and modification of behavior, but it is unknown whether this approach "actually looks for mechanisms of acquisition and modification or whether it merely applies the preconceived notion that the growth of all behavior is caused by conditioning and thereby overlooks the actual mechanisms governing acquisition and modification" (Langer, 1969, p. 85). Evidently much of our behavior is learned and its acquisition, such as with language learning, often depends on our social environment. But these theories neglect the inborn abilities and the diversity of human characteristics. A single environment with specific learning opportunities is not the same for every developing individual exposed to it. One child may profit optimally while another is not at all affected.

Psychodynamic Theories

Psychodynamic theories and learning theories both portray the environment as having a strong impact on human development. They differ in that the socio-affective component of personality and its development is considered to be fundamental in psychodynamic theories but is not central in theories of learning. The socio-affective component essentially determines the dynamics of the developmental processes.

Within the psychodynamic group, the most prominent theory is the psychoanalytic. According to this view the child is born with two fundamental forms of biological energy: libido and aggression. These two conflicting yet complementary classes of instincts are operative from birth. Libido or Eros is constructive, positive and life seeking; aggression or death instinct is destructive and life disturbing. The child is born with an id structure that is energized by libido and aggression. The id provides the child with the energy to satisfy his or her passions, but the environment inhibits this process. The id structure is transformed by its interactions with the environment into an ego structure. The superego emerges under the influence of the social environment, especially the parents, to control the behavior of the ego and the demands of the id.

Freud saw creative work as embedded in experience occurring early in one's life that is expressed in "a wish that finds fulfillment in the creative work" (1975, p. 133). John-Steiner (1987), in her provocative analysis of creative minds, emphasized the importance of visual imagery to the psychoanalytic approach to creativity. Visual images from wishes and fears in the unconscious are brought into conscious reality through a writer's (or artist's, poet's, scientist's) creativity with language and other forms of expression. From this kind of explanation, a creative person would be expected to be closer to his or her unconscious than would other people.

Psychodynamic theory is primarily a theory of socioaffective development. A problem with this theory is empirical validation of the id, ego and superego, and the stages of sexual development (which are not covered in this chapter). Findings are obtained by the clinical therapeutic method; the data are therefore confounded with the therapist's interpretation. "Thus, not only are the data not reliable, but it is also not always certain which theoretical assertions they are relevant to" (Langer, 1969, p. 49).

Erikson (1963) broadened the Freudian perspective; he introduced a relationship between psychological, educational, and cultural factors. Erikson took a lifespan perspective and developed a framework of eight distinct stages. Developing individuals pass through those stages at specific periods in their lives. Each stage represents a conflict that must be resolved successfully for the person to be psychologically healthy. This approach stimulated research, especially in the infancy and adolescent periods. However, questions remain about whether psychodynamic theory really can be considered as scientific theory (i.e. is it falsifiable, testable, and can it be revised?). The traditions of this approach looking at developmental conflicts through analysis to reveal the mind's working continues to some extent.

Interactionist Theory

The theories discussed so far are rather limited because each emphasizes a single dimension. A synthesis of the various aspects is necessary. The interactionist theory used by the great majority of Western psychologists and educators provides such a synthesis. The German psychologist William Stern (1871–1938) was the first to propose such a theory and called it the *theory of convergence*. In his view human development is a process in which personality and environmental factors converge (Stern, 1916). Yet, Stern never directly participated in the controversy concerning nature vs. nurture.

The former socialist countries favored the environmental theory. Human development was seen primarily as a mirror of the environment. According to Vygotsky, cognitive development is not a 'natural' process, but is determined by culture (see Van Parreren, 1983). Therefore, Vygotsky's position was that it is not necessary, as Piaget argued, to connect instruction in school with stages of development, but rather with the 'zone of proximal development', in other words, stimulate the child to do tasks that are just above his or her current ability level (Vygotsky, 1978).

Like Langer, some authors view Werner and Piaget as proponents of maturation. The human being is viewed as an active agent and development as merely a self-constructive process. Development occurs from within. Werner characterized development as an orthogenetic process that is "directed towards increasing differentiation, centralization, and hierarchic integration of the child's mental organization" (Langer, 1969, p. 9). On the other hand, Piaget (1967) characterized development as an equilibration process (i.e. development proceeds from relative disequilibrium to increasing equilibrium). The child will always function to achieve equilibrium; in doing so, the child changes and develops. Langer characterizes Werner and Piaget as *organic lamp* theorists. It is true that these theorists emphasize maturation of the organism as a central agent of development. However, development only then takes place when the child *interacts* with his environment.

Therefore, Piaget (1896–1980) can be regarded mainly as an interaction theorist; however, he emphasized only cognitive functioning and the related issue of moral development. According to Piaget, development is a continuation of embryogenesis. Development occurs in a sequence of stages which, when reached, permit the child to perform at a higher level of cognitive operations. The development of a higher stage depends on *maturation, experience*, and *social transmission*; education and language play roles in social transmission. The most central factor, however, is the spontaneous activity of the child, because this activity brings the child through interaction between maturation and social environment to new forms of *adaptation*. This means the child is increasingly able to react adequately to the demands of the reality.

Piaget called the process of adaptation of the organism *assimilation*. If the organism has to adapt to new elements of the environment, the process is called *accommodation*. This last form of adaptation requires flexibility in mental operations. As a process of establishing equilibrium, accommodation brings the child to a higher cognitive level and the child establishes a higher structure for thinking. Structure refers to the scheme developed by the individual to achieve equilibrium between the tendencies of assimilation and accommodation. The result is a new process of accommodation that is necessary to establish a new or higher kind of operation that will disturb the existing equilibrium. The process of actively breaking through the existing equilibrium to establish a higher structure of thinking is called equilibration by Piaget. This active form of achieving a new equilibrium is a kind of *self-regulation*.

Interaction refers to mutual or reciprocal action or influence between a person and other people, objects, processes, or other elements of the environment. This includes the notion that the acting and reacting individual shapes the environment (e.g. with family, friends, classmates, social class). On the other hand, the individual influences the environment through experiences. In short, the individual is both a product and a producer of the environment. The biological concept of *adaptation* introduced by Piaget has to be extended to emphasize the more active role of the individual. Sociologists use the term *emancipation*, to mean self-actualization, becoming an independent person, and detachment from inappropriate bondings.

It is evident that psychological development consists of more than cognitive development as emphasized by Piaget. Psychological development includes cognitive as well as social and personality aspects. Furthermore, it is a dynamic and life-long process; the interaction between the nature of the individual and the environment determines the motives that emerge and the kinds of behavior patterns that will become manifest. In short, psychological development is the result of interaction between the maturing individual and his or her environment. This view posits that development follows a universal pattern; a contrary view is that each individual develops differently (see Case, 1992).

As was emphasized earlier, conceptualizations of psychological development influence research directions and educational and psychological practice. All the theories briefly summarized here have influenced theory and concepts of giftedness and will continue to do so. Knowledge of developmental theories is necessary to understand what is 'behind' a definition.

Other Perspectives

It has been suggested that the traditional dependence on intelligence measures is misguided as a basis for identifying giftedness. One alternative is represented by the view that development in gifted children is an asynchronous process with unique cognitive and behavioral characteristics (Morelock, 1996). The assumption, is that the development of the child in the normative range of ability is synchronous.

Another type of asynchronous conceptualization of gifted development is provided by Feldman (2000). The approach here considers developmental activity to be on a continuum from universal (in all children) to non-universal (manifested relatively more in gifted children). The universal to non-universal dimension is based on the uniqueness of the domains of knowledge and experience across age, background, and culture. Therefore, Feldman claims that non-universal theory provides more appropriate framework for understanding gifted development and conducting research in the area.

Definitions of Giftedness

Defining giftedness is a task fraught with difficulty; a definition should give a formal and concise description of the meaning of a concept or a construct. Giftedness or the synonyms high ability and talent can assume different meanings. Frequently these meanings are tainted by an emotionalism that seems to engulf the concept of giftedness. For example, in German the

word for giftedness can be *Begabung* or *Hochbegabung*. The connotation of *Hochbegabung* can be value laden, associating giftedness with elitism. A similar situation exists in French (*doués* or *surdoués*). Such a connotation evokes emotional reactions and negative feelings that have hampered progress in programming for the gifted worldwide (Williams & Mitchell, 1989).

Further, a concise definition is almost impossible because the context in which the definition is made may refer to a process, key elements of giftedness, provisions for the gifted, or education of the gifted. In addition, it is not easy to separate theoretical and practical concepts because adherence to a theory of giftedness determines one's research and educational approaches. Finally, definitions seem more involved in practical concerns than in developmental theories.

Our definition is: *Giftedness is an individual potential for exceptional achievement in one or more domains.* On the other hand, according to Hany (1987) there are more than a hundred definitions of giftedness (and its synonyms). These definitions can be clustered in four distinctive groups. The first two of them refer to psychological constructs (i.e. genetically-based, and cognitively-based), a third focuses on achievement and accomplishment, and the fourth takes an environmental view. In the following section these four main groups of definitions of giftedness are presented.

Innate or Genetic-Oriented Definitions

The most prominent representative of the genetic-oriented approach is Lewis M. Terman (1877–1956) who popularized the concept of IQ and played a prominent role in the history of social science and management of scientific research. Terman believed that intelligence as revealed by intelligence tests is genetically determined and therefore stable over time. His belief in *biological determinism* was so strong that he only came to the conclusion in 1947 that "intellect and achievement are far from perfectly correlated" (Terman & Oden, 1947, p. 352). Evidence that he participated personally in that conclusion might be found in his own female students. In a carefully selected, highly talented group of thirty collaborators for his longitudinal research on gifted children, less than half of them were able to reach his standards for attaining the doctoral degree, and only a handful of those were able to reach prominence in the field (e.g. Florence Goodenough, Nancy Bailey) (see Rogers, 1999).

The new ideas that environmental and personality factors are significant determinants of "the extent to which a subject had made use of his superior ability" (Terman & Oden, 1947, p. 349) were most clearly spelled out in Terman's address at the University of California at Berkeley (Terman, 1954). Another central issue of Terman's work was the idea that he had a *mission* as a psychologist to contribute to the shaping of American society. He advocated a society that was a *meritocracy.* More precisely, individual differences in ability to perform at high standards should be reflected in the hierarchical structure of the society: the most responsible positions should be held by the most capable individuals (that is, those with the highest IQ scores). A meritocratic social structure, however, based on the results of mental tests that identify innate characteristics at school age is an unrealistic ideal, not only because high intelligence is not isomorphic with high achievement, but human beings develop in a dynamic way and through interaction with the environment. Terman's view of intelligence as a unitary inherited ability reappeared in modified form in Marland's well-known definition of giftedness proposed in 1972.

> Gifted and talented children are those identified by professionally qualified persons who by virtue of outstanding abilities are capable of high performance. These are children who require differentiated educational programs and services beyond those normally provided by a regular school program in order to realize their contribution to self and society. Children capable of high performance include those with demonstrated achievement and/or potential ability in any of the following areas:
>
> (1) General intellectual ability;
> (2) Specific academic aptitude;
> (3) Creative or productive thinking;
> (4) Leadership ability;
> (5) Visual and performing arts;
> (6) Psychomotor ability (Davis & Rimm, 1985, p. 10).

There were at least two new elements in this definition: (1) the definition goes beyond intelligence to other areas of high ability, and (2) abilities as well as achievement are criteria for identification. However, the definition excludes non-cognitive factors (e.g. motivation) as well as clear operationalization of the different forms of giftedness.

A committee convened by the U.S. government in 1993 generated the following definition:

> "Children and youth with outstanding talent perform or show the potential for performing at remarkably high levels of accomplishment when compared with others of their age, experience, or environment. These children and youth exhibit high performance capability in intellectual, creative, and/or artistic areas, possess an unusual leadership capacity, or excel in specific academic fields. They require services or activities not ordinarily provided by the schools. Outstanding talents are present in children from all cultural groups across all economic strata, and in all areas of human endeavor". (Ross, 1993, p.3)

Unfortunately, this definition was not an improvement but "reflects the tensions and shifts that have been occurring in the field" (Feldman, 2000). It serves more as a description of gifted children than as a definition of giftedness.

When Gardner (1983) proposed his theory of multiple intelligences, he argued "that individuals have a number of domains of potential intellectual competence which they are in the position to develop, if they are normal and if the appropriate stimulating factors are available" (p. 284). Furthermore, there are conditions and criteria that have to be taken into account to identify a specific kind of intelligence. Criteria of an intelligence may be, for example, potential isolation by brain damage, support from experimental psychological tasks, or support from psychometric findings. Gardner identified several intelligences related to a specific domain of potential (linguistic, musical, logical-mathematical, spatial, bodily-kinesthetic, intra- and interpersonal intelligence; recently he added naturalistic and existentialistic intelligence).

The description of multiple intelligences or traits is primarily based on qualitative findings and idiographic analyses rather than empirical results (see Gardner, 1993). The important extension beyond Terman's approach is that giftedness results from inborn abilities in interaction with an appropriately supportive environment. The other point is that this definition goes beyond the opinion that giftedness is high intelligence as such, but rather expresses itself in different domains.

The genetic-oriented approach has led to and enriched empirical research. It has enabled extension of knowledge concerning characteristics and conditions for the development of giftedness and has led to better understanding of the processes of achievement of gifted people (e.g. Holahan & Sears, 1995).

Cognitive Models

Cognitive definitions focus on thought process memory and related skills. For example, Piaget was less interested in the outcome of a test than the process of responding. Therefore, he emphasized clinical methods in which a single or small group of children were observed and interviewed while they were performing tasks rather than large-scale research in his approach. In his theory of knowledge, known as *genetic epistemology*, Piaget preferred to investigate how children attain knowledge and use it.

Proponents of the cognitive information processing approach have invested considerable effort in the direction suggested by Piaget's work. "The cognitive components approach is task analytic and attempts to directly identify the components of performance on tasks that have been generally used to assess mental abilities" (Pellegrino & Glaser, 1979 p. 188).

Sternberg is an important proponent of this approach (Sternberg, 1985; Sternberg & Davidson, 1986). A

145

central concept in Sternberg's experiential subtheory of intelligence is insight and response to novelty in task performance. Within this view a distinction is made between "three separate but related psychological processes" (Sternberg, 1985, p. 80): (1) *selective encoding*, i.e. sifting out relevant from irrelevant information; (2) *selective combination*, i.e. "combining what might originally seem to be isolated pieces of information into a unified whole that may or may not resemble its parts" (Sternberg, 1985, p. 80); (3) *selective comparison*, i.e. relating new information to that which was acquired in the past.

Insightful performance demonstrated as problem-solving skills or as knowledge-acquisition components are indicators of giftedness. The better these skills are, the more intellectually gifted a person appears to be. Moreover, according to the loci of information processing, Sternberg makes a distinction between three kinds of giftedness: analytic, synthetic, and practical abilities (Sternberg & Lubart, 1991). More recently he refers to analytic, creative and practical aspects of successful intelligence (Sternberg, 2000).

The constructive qualitative and empirical research approach of the cognitive models bodes well for the potential for progress in cognitive models. On the basis of current activity and interest in the field, it appears that as this approach matures, it will contribute to better understanding of the developmental processes underlying giftedness.

Achievement-oriented Models

Even Terman, the most rigidly genetic-oriented author, was convinced by his own empirical data that high intelligence was only a necessary but not a sufficient condition for highly able behavior. As a result he considered *achievement* as the observable output of giftedness. As early as 1916, the noted German psychologist William Stern considered high intelligence as a necessary but not sufficient condition for outstanding achievement. He considered personality traits like motivation and environmentally appropriate conditions important (Stern, 1916). However, his arguments were more supported by careful observation than by controlled empirical research.

The most influential author in the achievement orientation category is Renzulli. His article "What makes giftedness?" (Renzulli, 1978) has had a long lasting impact on the field. A thorough literature review revealed that there are at least three traits or factors involved in gifted achievement: (1) above average ability, (2) task commitment, and (3) creativity. These three clusters of variables are brought together in Renzulli's "three-ring conception" that charaterizes highly productive people.

The history of the groundbreaking 1978 article by Renzulli is more than interesting. Renzulli wrote in 1998: "November, 1998 was the twentieth anniversary of the publication of my article on the Three Ring Conception of Giftedness in *Phi Delta Kappan* magazine. This article, which was rejected for publication by the major gifted education journals at that time, is now the most widely cited publication in the field; and its influence is being manifested in the more flexible ways that schools go about identifying students for special services" (Renzulli, 1998–99, 1).

The research base of the three-ring conception has been attacked by Jarell & Borland (1990) who argued that the research they reviewed does not support this conception and moreover, the research is either irrelevant or contradictory to the triad.

The article by Jarell and Borland provided Renzulli (1990) with an opportunity to react in a constructive and convincing way. Most important, Jarell and Borland did not examine the most recent theory and research on the three-ring conception. Furthermore, the intention of Renzulli's conception is threefold: "(a) to call attention to the developmental nature of behaviors such as creativity and task commitment, (b) to highlight the dynamic interaction among behaviors that is necessary in order for gifted behaviors to emerge, and (c) to provide enough flexibility in selection procedures . . ." (Renzulli, 1990, p. 325). Giftedness has to be seen as a manifestation "of human potential that can be developed in certain people, at certain times, and under certain circumstances" (p. 324). Renzulli's overall intention in his approach is to be able to identify and to nurture giftedness appropriately. The multicomponent conceptualization of giftedness can be regarded as one of the better definitions.

However, a definition that strongly or exclusively emphasizes personality traits neglecting the interactive nature of human development does little justice to the dynamic interplay of the developmental processes. A multidimensional approach, including personality and social components as determining factors, seems to be an appropriate framework. The following modification was made by Mönks working from a developmental psychology perspective in his Triadic Interdependence Model of Giftedness (see Mönks, 1992a, p. 191), now called Multifactor Model (Mönks, 1998). This model consists of personality and environmental aspects. Task commitment was replaced by *motivation* which includes task commitment, risk taking, future time perspective, anticipation, planning and emotional factors. Emotional factors as aspects of ability are considered in the model (Golman, 1995).

Furthermore, the rather liberal above-average ability criterion was replaced by *outstanding abilities* in specific domains exceeding 5–10% of performance. Environmental factors include the main social contexts in which the child and adolescent mature: family, school and peer group. Emergence and development of gifted potential depend to a great extent on a supportive environment. Intellectual peers or developmental equals are significant people who are needed for healthy social and psychological development. All children need peers to interact with and from whom to learn, and this is true with the gifted.

Authors working with an achievement orientation make a distinction between potential and realized capacities. In serving the needs of underachievers it is important to know the potential of a person and how much of that potential has been realized. Knowledge of the discrepancy between potential and realized abilities provides opportunity for intervention. The advantage of achievement oriented models lies not only in the interconnection of identification and education, but also that attention is paid to the processes involved in achievement and the recognition that there are non-cognitive and environmental factors that influence the realization of innate human potential.

Systemic Models

As was indicated earlier, the social systems (family, school, and peers) have an impact on human development. However, it is evident that other systems also have an impact on the development of each individual. The *Zeitgeist* (or world view represented in the society at the time), the economic situation, the political orientation, and the culturally dominant values and beliefs all have influence on human development and therefore on the development of gifted youth. To a certain extent, it might be said that the systemic approach is the opposite of 'ontogenic stability'.

According to Tannenbaum (1983), who takes a systemic approach, outstanding achievements are determined equally by the following five factors: (1) general ability, (2) special ability, (3) non-intellective factors, (4) environmental factors, and (5) chance factors. Tannenbaum arranged these factors in the shape of a star, and thus his definition is called the star definition (see Tannenbaum, 1983, p. 87; Feldman, 1992). Society determines who is regarded as gifted. From the societal perspective, a distinction can be made between 'scarce talents', 'surplus talents', 'quota talents', and 'anomalous talents'. A society always has criteria for the attribution of what is talented and gifted in terms of outstanding achievement (see the first Tannenbaum chapter in this volume).

The systemic perspective includes interacting influences that affect a child's life and development. Beyond the family, they might include the schools, political system, economic environment, social agencies, cultural practices, and related factors. Development of giftedness may come from opportunities provided by different agendas within various units of the system.

Definitions of, and perspectives on, giftedness give direction to research and practice. The interconnection and interdependence of the individual and society affect both the gifted and the non-gifted. The detrimental effects of not serving the special needs of gifted individuals will affect society at large. Programs for the gifted are not special in the sense that they advocate giving to each individual what is appropriate for him or her.

Research on the Development of Gifted Children

A casual review of the literature suggests that definitions of giftedness are more influential on the research of gifted development than the theories of development. This may be the result of a practical and educationally oriented grounding of the definitions. For this reason, research presented here is organized more along definitional than theoretical lines.

Innate or Genetic-oriented Research

Although early interest in intelligence could be attributed to the work of Sir Francis Galton, Karl Pearson, Alfred Binet, and others, the beginning of formal scientific research in giftedness has frequently been credited to Terman for his development of a technically sound method of assessment of intelligence and his longitudinal studies of gifted individuals. In these studies, Terman postulated that individuals developed within the limits of their genetically preordained intellectual abilities (Grinder, 1990; Cravens, 1992). Terman's long developmental investigation started in the 1920s initially involved more than 1500 children and adolescents from 5 to 16 years of age, and is still ongoing. The group was selected based on an IQ score of 135 or higher as determined by the Stanford–Binet Test. This research has continued with latest results published in 1995 (Holahan & Sears, 1995).

Because of the influence of Terman's contributions, much of the research on giftedness has taken a genetic orientation emphasizing intelligence testing and other psychometric approaches to the identification of intelligence as a general static trait that determines gifted capacity (e.g. Macmann, Plasket, Barnet & Siler, 1991). However, other analyses have challenged the assumption that high IQ scores and general intelligence are (1) genetically determined, and (2) necessarily required for, or reflective of, gifted performance (O'Connor & Hermelin, 1988; Silver & Clampit, 1990).

The genetic-oriented view prevails in research looking for the multiple traits of the gifted child; in studies of the performance of gifted children, an IQ test is frequently used to identify the gifted sample. Such studies have investigated a wide range of traits of gifted populations in addition to performance and achievement. For example, the Shigaki and Wolf (1980) investigation of children's syllogistic reasoning; Carter's (1985) studies of Piagetian task performance; research by Derevensky and Coleman (1989) and Henderson, Gold and Clark (1984) on gifted children's fears and daydreaming, and various studies of personality and socialization (e.g. Altman, 1983; Olszewsky, Kulicke & Krasney, 1988; Luftig & Nichols, 1991; Keller, 1992).

In recent years, research that questions the validity of using IQ test scores for identifying present and future gifted performance in specific academic and skill areas has been increasing. Along with this drift away from the general trait conception of giftedness represented by the IQ score, interest has been directed to identification of giftedness in groups that had previously not been considered gifted such as handicapped, underprivileged, and ethnically divergent minority groups (Baldwin, 1987; Sekowski, 1992; Armour-Thomas & Gopaul McNicol, 1998). This new interest in giftedness among non-traditional populations is leading to a broadening of criteria for identification. For example, Schack and Starko (1990) reported that teachers emphasized creativity, learning speed and ease, curiosity, and initiative in seeking one's own learning experiences as essential for academic giftedness, but more experienced teachers also emphasized the IQ score. A trait model that emphasizes multiple intelligences like Gardner's is becoming more compatible with research evidence than the single trait models relying on IQ scores for identification of giftedness.

Another promising approach is that of human behavioral genetics. It is, for example, now possible to identify with greater precision of how the environment has an impact on cognitive abilities (see, e.g. Thompson & Plomin in this volume).

Cognitive Models

Much recent literature that comes under the influence of cognitive definitions seems to represent the trait of giftedness functionally rather than by intelligence test score. For example, numerous investigations of giftedness in mathematics emphasize mathematics performance as the criterion (e.g. Benbow & Arjmand, 1990; Benbow & Minor, 1990). Facaoaru and Bittner (1987) have advocated diagnostic procedures for identifying the gifted using techniques and concepts from cognitive research such as procedural thought processing, spatial abilities, and problem solving. Further, the analysis of thought processes determined by verbal comments recorded during problem solving has proven useful in identifying how gifted students learn (Shore et al., 1992). In a more extreme position, Mason (1992) advocated the identification of giftedness on the basis of analysis of task performance and cognitive skills. This approach has been successfully implemented by Claypool (1994) in a study of how young children learn to read. Children were identified as learning in accelerated or delayed rates using this method. The focus on functionality and mental processing is a reflection of the increased interest in the cognitive orientation in recent years.

Advances seem to be rapidly occurring as a result of cognitive science, spurred by the merging of numerous disciplines (e.g. psychology, computer science, engineering, mathematics, physiology, neuroscience) into a specialty that focuses on intelligence and ability to perform (Luger, 1994). From this position, Minsky (1986) argued that giftedness was in the management of learning and cognitions. Naglieri and Das (1997) have taken an approach to cognitive assessment that is very different from the more traditional IQ measures. It is founded in the neuropsychological theory of Luria (1980) and emphasizes the cognitive processes planning, attention, and simultaneous and successive processing (Naglieri, 1987; Naglieri, Das, Stevens & Ledbetter, 1991; Das, Carlson, Davidson & Lange, 1997). The impact of these newer approaches to cognitive ability on the identification of the gifted is still to be shown.

A factor leading to the increase of cognitive research in giftedness is the growth of the information sciences and computer technology. These advances in technology have been particularly influential on research in cognitive psychology (Thorndike, 1984; Beer, 1990). The new technology has greatly increased the ability to present complex stimulus and problem solving situations. It also renders the study of constructs like response time more plausible and accurate than was previously possible. In addition, computers have led to models of human information processing (e.g. Ellis & Hunt, 1989). Cognitive psychology has focused on the study of such subjects as the nature of expert thinking, the formation of a construct, and elements and structures of productive mental processing. This approach is reflected in studies showing that mathematically gifted students were able to express verbal statements of quantity and relationship mathematically more readily than their peers or college students taking mathematics courses (Dark & Benbow, 1990), and that verbally gifted students excel in different cognitive tasks than mathematically gifted students (Benbow & Minor, 1990). Further, by focusing on mental processing, Borland (1989) found divergent thinking was associated with a 'strict percept-strict concept' cognitive style. In addition, Carter (1986) reported that teaching students higher level thinking skills led to greater success among gifted students in learning the concepts and reasoning but not in leading the gifted students to reach higher developmental levels of thought. In addition, research emerging from a cognitive orientation is beginning to shed light on the complex relationship between the brain, high level performance and ability, and biological, psychological, and social status (Clark, 1986; Petersen, Crockett & Graber, 1990; Luger, 1994; Bownds, 1999).

Achievement-oriented Models

Achievement-oriented research on the gifted suggests rather consistently that children who are identified as gifted at a young age tend to continue to be identified as having high ability and accomplishment later in life (Milner & Elrod, 1986; Mönks, 1992b; Benbow, 1992). For example, accelerated readers seem to maintain an edge over other students, but the difference is less as they get older. Further, in Western cultures boys are more likely to sustain gifted performance and interest in science and mathematics than girls. In addition, experience with the contents of the educational curriculum prior to studying it (e.g. through involvement with preschool or after school programs or hobbies), family characteristics such as parents educational attainment level, and attitudes toward education, students' interests and attitudes towards learning, and access to experiences all seem to contribute to one's being identified as gifted (e.g. Hannah & Shore, 1995; Jones & Day, 1996).

The importance of special programming for the academic development of the gifted has been shown. For example, Brown and Rogan (1983) have addressed the effects of maintaining gifted children in rigid reading programs designed for a particular grade level. According to these authors, these children can become frustrated about independent reading because they already have skills above what they are being taught. This can lead to disillusionment and poor study habits and the paradox of poor levels of achievement by gifted students (Boyd, 1990).

Evaluation studies by Heller and his group (1998) demonstrate especially that the impact of peer interaction is of great and lasting value. From a developmental viewpoint it is extremely important that gifted individuals can interact with developmentally equals.

Systemic Models

Systemic models emphasize the effects of social systems on the development of the gifted. Research in this area has focused on the family and home environment of gifted children (e.g. Colangelo & Dettmann, 1983; Cornell & Grossberg, 1987; Prom, Johnson & Wallace, 1987; Green, Fine & Tolleson, 1988; Cornell, Callahan & Lloyd, 1991). This research suggests that the family and home environment play an important role in the development of the gifted. For example, the research suggests that the home environment affects emotional adjustment, achievement satisfaction, and academic success with a tendency for the most cohesive, child-centered, and functional family environments to produce the most successful students. On the other hand, giftedness in creative expression seemed to be greater from the less child-centered and tenser family situations. Similar findings for scholastic performance with low income minority families have been reported (Prom, Jackson, Johnson & Wallace, 1987). Other researchers (e.g. Klein & Cantor, 1976) have found lower self-esteem levels in gifted children in kindergarten to fourth grade. It has been suggested from this finding that the gifted child was more sensitive to the environment and had greater need for approval from family and friends than his or her less able peers. This social sensitivity was sup-

ported by a study of gifted and learning disabled children which reported the gifted were more able to identify and label prosocial behavior (Abelman, 1991).

Peer relations and cultural influences also seem to play a significant role in gifted development. For example, subtle cultural values may have been influential in producing the findings of Luftig and Nichols (1991) that gifted boys tended to be the most popular students while gifted girls least popular in a group of fourth through eighth graders. Young gifted students have also been found to show a tendency toward choosing older (Janos, Marwood & Robinson, 1985) and more popular (Schneider & Daniels, 1992) students and leaders to be their playmates and friends. In general, the social psychological literature seems to provide substantial support for the kind of model proposed by Mönks (1992a) which integrates Renzulli's three-part model with the family, peer, and school environments.

As was pointed out earlier in this chapter, cultural environment can determine whether or not a child is exposed to opportunities for the giftedness (Lowenstein, 1979; Merenheimo, 1991). Female students are often not selected to participate in gifted programs in societies in which male dominance is well established in the educational system (Ayles, 1992). In addition, research findings have suggested that children who come from different cultural backgrounds than the majority of their peers may experience reduced opportunity to become identified as gifted despite evidence that such children give a fairly good account of themselves when they are chosen to participate in gifted programs (Baldwin, 1987; Robinson, Bradley & Stanley, 1990; Cooley, Cornell & Lee, 1991; Smith, LeRose & Clasen, 1991).

General Trends in the Research Literature

The general trends in the research literature seem to be changing. Previously research in the field of development of giftedness tended toward descriptive and case study methodology rather than more complex designs and sophisticated statistical analysis (Carter & Swanson, 1990). As noted by Gallagher (1986), practical needs and realistic solutions seemed more influential in the contents of the research literature than high level theories of the sort proposed by Erikson (1963), Piaget (1967), or Bandura (1986). Theory-oriented research tends not to have immediate or widespread influence on practice.

More recent research seems to be directed toward the development of theories and models that would explain and provide methods for identifying and working with the gifted. For example, theories and approaches from cognitive psychology like Sternberg's (1985; Sternberg & Horvath, 1998) have been applied to performance studies of gifted (Zhang & Sternberg, 1998; Dai & Feldhusen, 1999). In addition, prior knowledge, matacognition (what is known about what one knows), cognitive flexibility, speed, and problem solving seem to be more prevalent in the recent literature (Mills, Ablard & Gustin, 1994; Hannah & Shore, 1995; Jones & Day, 1996; Dresl, Ziegler, Broome & Heller, 1998). In addition, advances in biology and genetics have begun to yield studies on specific genes that may be involved in the development of gifted performers (e.g. Skuder et al., 1995). However, this particular kind of effort still seems a long way from providing useful applications.

Finally, the newer research seems more focused on gifted performance in specific areas such as science, mathematics, and literature rather than general realms like total academic performance. In view of the themes in the recent literature, the reminder of Horowitz & O'Brien (1986), about the importance of the developmental perspective is useful. Better understanding of the processes of development to include learning, cognitive mechanisms, emotion and temperament, and social and environmental factors through the life span will lead to more effective identification and provision for the gifted.

Teaching and Instruction Based on Developmental Psychology

A considerable portion of the research literature deals with how to teach gifted students (e.g. Milgram, 1980; Wang & Walberg, 1983; Horowitz & O'Brien, 1986; Slavin, 1987; Reis & Renzulli, 1989; Whitlock & DuCette, 1989; Swiatek & Benbow, 1991; Vaughn, Feldhusen & Asher, 1991). As this literature would suggest, many forms of instructional practice exist to serve the special needs of gifted children. These approaches can include some form of ability grouping (between- or within-class), cooperative learning, or pull-out programs. A further distinction can be made between homogeneous and heterogeneous grouping. However, the content of the program rather than instructional practice is most important; certain instructional practices enable gifted children to learn at their own pace and level of ability. On the other hand, the content of the program enriches and motivates students who are highly able. Close examination of the research indicates that the various programs do tend to have positive influence on achievement, creativity or critical thinking (see Buchanan & Feldhusen, 1991). However, there is no clear indication of what is the most effective means of serving the academic needs of gifted students. To be able to identify the best practice requires comparison of all practices; this kind of research is both rare and difficult to do. Another conclusion that might be drawn from the literature is that academic arrangements designed to provide differentiated learning experiences for students of different ability levels are more effective than traditional undifferentiated approaches. It is also clear that the educational effectiveness of a particular instructional practice depends on the charateristics of both teacher and student, and on social and developmental factors. Certain methods are most beneficial in certain environments for particular students. Further, what is beneficial in grade 3 need not continue to be beneficial in later grades.

The most beneficial educational approach, however, is the approach that fits the developmental needs of the individual child. Vygotsky did not regard cognitive development as a process of nature (see Van Parreren, 1983), thus suggesting that education and instruction need not be fitted to a particular developmental level or stage, as Piaget argued. Vygotsky's position (1978) is that instruction creates development (to a certain extent), because learning and development take place within the zone of proximal development. Tasks within the zone of proximal development are too difficult for the child to do alone; these tasks become possible with guidance and assistance from adults or older children. As new technology comes into the classroom with its potential of making many aspects of education more experiential and meaningful to children, the challenge will be to use developmental theories to apply these powerful tools in effective ways to meet the needs of the gifted learner (Grabe & Grabe, 1998).

Montessori's and Petersen's Contribution to Gifted Education

Another developmental position has been defended and elaborated upon by Maria Montessori, a person who played a leading role in the school reform movement started in Europe in the early 1920s. This movement influenced schools to become institutions where children were accepted and treated as individuals. Child-centered education was felt to be most beneficial for the healthy development of children.

Maria Montessori (1870–1952) grew up as an only child in a family with a father who believed in traditional values and role patterns. She aspired to a technical career but a daughter in a 'male profession' was beyond her father's conservative value system, and he could not accept his daughter's choice of study. Maria Montessori was a mathematical prodigy, and at the age of 26 became the first woman physician in Italy's history. Although not a trained pediatrician, she became famous as an expert in children's illnesses.

A central component of the Montessori theory is the concept of *sensitive periods*, or genetically determined developmental periods during which the child is especially eager and able to master specific tasks, similar to critical periods. During these periods the child works with a high level of interest to improve these abilities. However, "if the child is prevented from enjoying these experiences at the very time when nature has planned for him to do so, the special sensitivity which draws him to them will vanish, with a disturbing effect on development . . ." (Montessori as cited in Crain, 1980, p. 56).

Other central concepts of Montessori education are *prepared learning environment* and *freedom of choice*. The proper environment will contain materials and means that correspond to the developmental needs of children; the role of parent and teacher can be described as 'facilitator'. To be successful in this role, parents must be aware of the specific developmental needs of the child, not only during early childhood but throughout the child's developmental period. Therefore, *ongoing careful observation* is necessary to give to the child needed experiences. Observation of the child enables the parent and teacher to make the right choices of supportive materials for the individual's development; freedom of choice is the opposite of teacher dictated learning.

The Montessori elementary school with its mixed age groups (normally more than one age group is found in a class) provides possibilities for independent as well as cooperative learning. Ability grouping is a normal instructional practice in the Montessori school. According to Maria Montessori, assigning children to grades on the basis of age is not a good practice (Holtstiege, 1991). A school must provide the possibility for an individual to progress at his or her own pace and level of learning; this principle is at the core of all gifted education.

The Montessori school encourages children to become independent learners and productive thinkers, and to love learning; a curriculum based on Montessori education principles provides for *qualitative differentiation*. That is, children are allowed to proceed at their own pace according to their own interests and needs. A differentiated curriculum is a prerequisite for appropriate and effective gifted education. Analysis of the Montessori system with regard to the elements beneficial for gifted education would be useful and helpful to the field. Crain (1980) accurately stated that, "Montessori demonstrated, as much or more than anyone else, how the developmental philosophies of Rousseau, Gesell, Piaget, and others can be put into effective practice. She showed how it is possible to follow children's spontaneous tendencies and to provide materials that will permit them to learn on their own" (p. 72).

Peter Petersen (1884–1952) was one of the prominent and influential leaders of the *School Reform Movement* or *Progressive Movement* (e.g. Dewey or Washburn). In 1923 he founded, as professor of education at the university of Jena (Germany), a laboratory school of which he was director until 1950, when the school was closed by the then socialist Government. This experimental school became the place for the realization of new educational concepts and an important institution for teacher training. Actually, it was a *School for the Gifted Learner*,

because all the necessary elements were included in his system. For example, he regarded the age graded class as 'unnatural' and realized an age heterogeneous grouping with three different age levels similar to that in a normal family. Actually, the roots for gifted education go back to the *School Reform Movement* and the Jena plan principles demonstrate that gifted education is possible in the regular school. The following principles are core concepts of the Jena plan:

ability grouping;
independent as well as group learning;
cooperative learning;
progress according to individual ability and pace;
social learning.

At the beginning of the new millenium we can conclude that the *School Reform Movement*, which has its roots in the beginning of the 20th century, established the road to the *Gifted Education Movement in Europe* a century later.

Concluding Remarks

Theories of development contribute to our understanding of the gifted. These theories provide different perspectives on the innate, systemic, psychological, and experiential background and tendencies affecting gifted performance. Developmentally oriented definitions of giftedness have broadened from the foundations laid by Terman and other early workers. Cognitive research and systemic views are becoming more influential. Research in the development of the gifted seems influenced by practical concerns but theoretical interests are becoming more evident. These efforts coupled with improvements in educational and instructional practice, the availability of technology, and public awareness of the developmental and learning needs of the gifted portend improved methods for development of the gifted (see Mönks, 1998).

References

Abelman, R. (1991). TV literacy: III. Gifted and learning disabled children: amplifying prosocial learning through curriculum intervention. *Journal of Research and Development in Education*, **24** (4), 51–60.

Altman, R. (1983). Social-emotional development of gifted children and adolescents: a research model. *Roeper Review*, **6** (2), 65–68.

Armour-Thomas, E. & Gopaul McNicol, S. (1998). *Assessing intelligence: applying a bio-cultural model*. Thousand Oaks, CA: Sage.

Ayles, R. (1992). Gifted girls: a case of wasted talent? In: F. J. Mönks, M. W. Katzko & H. W. van Boxtel (Eds),

Education of the Gifted in Europe: Theoretical and Research Issues (pp. 157–161). Amsterdam: Swets & Zeitlinger.

Baldwin, A. Y. (1987). Undiscovered diamonds: the minority gifted child. *Journal for the Education of the Gifted*, **10** (4), 271–285.

Bandura, A. (1986). *Social foundations of thought and action: a social cognitive theory*. Englewood Cliffs, NJ: Prentice Hall.

Beer, R. D. (1990). *Intelligence as adaptive behavior*. New York: Academic Press.

Benbow, C. P. (1992). Academic achievement in mathematics and science of students between ages 13 and 23: are there differences among students in the top one per cent of mathematical ability? *Journal of Educational Psychology*, **84**, 51–61.

Benbow, C. P. & Arjmand, O. (1990). Predictors of high academic achievement in mathematics and science by mathematically talented students: a longitudinal study. *Journal of Educational Psychology*, **82**, 430–441.

Benbow, C. P. & Minor, L. L. (1990). Cognitive profiles of verbally and mathematically precocious students: implications for identification of the gifted. *Gifted Child Quarterly*, **34** (1), 21–26.

Borland, J. H. (1989). Cognitive controls, cognitive styles, and divergent production in gifted preadolescents, *Journal for the Education of the Gifted*, **11** (4), 57–82.

Bownds, M. D. (1999). *The biology of the mind: origins of structures of mind, brain, and consciousness*. Bethesda, MD: Fitzgerald.

Boyd, R. (1990). Academically talented underachievers at the end of high school. *Gifted Education International*, **7** (1), 23–26.

Bronfenbrenner, U. (1979). *The ecology of human development: experiments by nature and design* Cambridge, MA: Harvard University Press.

Brown, W. & Rogan, J. (1983). Reading and young gifted children. *Roeper Review*, **5** (3), 6–9.

Buchanan, N. K. & Feldhusen, J. F. (Eds) (1991). *Conducting research and evaluation in gifted education*. New York: Teachers College Press.

Carter, K. R. (1985). Cognitive development of intellectually gifted: a Piagetian perspective. *Roeper Review*, **7** (3), 180–184.

Carter, K. R. (1986). A cognitive outcomes study to evaluate curriculum for the gifted. *Journal for the Education of the Gifted*, **10** (1), 41–55.

Carter, K. R. & Swanson, H. L. (1990). An analysis of the most frequently cited gifted journal articles since the Marland Report: implications for researchers. *Gifted Child Quarterly*, **34** (2), 116–123.

Case, R. (Ed.) (1992). *The mind's staircase: exploring the conceptual underpinnings of children's thought and knowledge*. New York: Erlbaum.

Clark, B. (1986). Early development of cognitive abilities and giftedness. *Journal of Children in Contemporary Society*, **18** (3–4), 5–15.

Claypool, A. M. (1994). *Elements of reading processing in beginning readers: a constructivist approach*. Doctoral dissertation, University of Kentucky, Lexington, KY.

Cohen, L. M. (1988). To get ahead, get a theory. *Roeper Review*, **11** (2), 95–100.

Colangelo, N. & Dettmann, D. F. (1983). A review of research on parents and families of gifted children. *Exceptional Children*, **50** (1), 20–27.

Cook, T. D. & Campbell, D. T. (1979). *Quasi-experimentation: design and analysis issues for field settings*. Chicago: Rand McNally.

Cooley, M. R., Cornell, D. G. & Lee, C. C. (1991). Peer acceptance and self-concept of Black students in a summer gifted program. *Journal for the Education of the Gifted*, **14**, 166–170.

Cornell, D. G., Callahan, C. M. & Loyd, B. H. (1991). Socioemotional adjustment of adolescent girls enrolled in a residential acceleration program. *Gifted Child Quarterly*, **35** (2), 58–66.

Cornell, D. G. & Grossberg, I. W. (1987). Family environment and personality adjustment in gifted program children. *Gifted Child Quarterly*, **31** (2), 59–64.

Crain, W. C. (1980). *Theories of development*. Englewood Cliffs, NJ: Prentice-Hall.

Cravens, H. (1992). A scientific project locked in time: the Terman Genetic Studies of Genius, 1920s–1950s. *American Psychologist*, **47**(2), 183–189.

Dai, D. Y. & Feldhusen, J. F. (1999). A validation of the Thinking Styles Inventory: implications for the gifted. *Roeper Review*, **21** (4), 302–307.

Dark, V. & Benbow, C. P. (1990). Enhanced problem translation and short-term memory: components of mathematical talent. *Journal of Educational Psychology*, **82**, 420–429.

Das, J. P., Carlson, J., Davidson, M. B. & Lange, K. (1997). *PREP: PASS remedial program*. Seattle, WA: Hogrefe.

Davis, G. A. & Rimm, S. B. (1985). *Education of the gifted and talented*. Englewood Cliffs, NJ: Prentice-Hall.

Derevensky, J. & Coleman, E. B. (1989). Gifted children's fears. *Gifted Child Quarterly*, **33** (2), 65–68.

Dresl, M., Ziegler, A., Broome, P. & Heller, K. A. (1998). (1998). Gender differences in science education: the double-edged role of prior knowledge in physics. *Roeper Review*, **21** (2) 101–106.

Ellis, H. C. & Hunt, R. R. (1989). *Fundamentals of human memory* (4th ed.). Dubuque, IA: William C. Brown.

Erikson, E. H. (1963). *Childhood and society*. New York: Norton.

Facaoaru, C. & Bittner, R. (1987). Kognitionspsychologische Ansiitze der Hochbegabungsdiagnostik. [Cognitive psychology approaches to the diagnosis of giftedness]. *Zeitschrift fur Differentielle und Diagnostische Psychologie*, **8** (3), 193–205.

Feldman, D.H. (2000). Developmental theory and the expression of gifts and talents. In: C. F. M. van Lieshout & P. G. Heymans (Eds), *Developing Talent Across the Life-Span: A Festschrift for Franz Mönks*. Hove, UK: Psychology Press.

Feldman, D. H. (1992). The theory of co-incidence: how giftedness develops in extreme and less extreme cases. In: F. J. Mönks & W. A. M. Peters (Eds), *Talent for the Future* (pp. 10–22). Assen/Maastricht, The Netherlands: Van Gorcum.

Freud, S. (1975). Creative writers and daydreaming. In: P. E. Vernon (Ed.), *Creativity*. Harmondsworth: Penguin.

Gallagher, J. J. (1986). A proposed federal role: education of gifted children. *Gifted Child Quarterly*, **30** (1), 43–46.

Gardner, H. (1983). *Frames of mind*. New York: Basic Books.

Gardner, H. (1993). *Creating minds*. New York: Doubleday.

Golman, D., (1995). *Emotional intelligence.* New York : Bantam Books.

Grabe, M. & Grabe, C. (1998). *Integrating technology for meaningful learning* (2nd ed.). New York: Houghton Mifflin.

Green, K., Fine, M. J. & Tollefson, N. (1988). Family systems characteristics and underachieving gifted adolescent males. *Gifted Child Quarterly, 32* (2), 267–272.

Grinder, R. E. (1990). Sources of gifted in nature and nurture. *Gifted Child Quarterly, 34* (2), 50–55.; Jones & Day, 1996;

Hannah, C. & Shore, B. M. (1995). Metacognition and high intellectual ability. *Gifted Child Quarterly, 39* (2), 95–109.

Hany, E. A. (1987). *Modelle und Strategien zur Identifikation hochbegabter Schüller.* [Models and strategies in the identification of gifted students]. Ph.D. Dissertation. University of Munich.

Henderson, B. B., Gold, S. R. & Clarke, K. (1984). Individual differences in IQ, daydreaming and moral reasoning in gifted and average adolescents. *International Journal of Behavioral Development, 7* (2), 215–230.

Holahan, C.K. & Sears, R.R. (1995). *The gifted group in later maturity.* The fifth volume in the Terman Study. Stanford, CA: Stanford University Press.

Holtstiege, H. (1991). *Modell Montessori-Grundsättze und aktuelle Geltung der Montessori-Pädagogik* [The Montessori Model: Principles and issues of the value of a Montessori education]. Freiburg/Basel: Herder.

Horowitz, F. D. & O'Brien, M. (1986). Gifted and talented children: state of knowledge and directions for research. *American Psychologist, 41* (10), 1147–1152.

Janos, P. M., Marwood, K. A. & Robinson, N. M. (1985). Friendship patterns in highly intelligent children. *Roeper Review, 8* (1), 46–49.

Jarrell, R. H. & Borland, J. H. (1990). The research base for Renzulli's three-ring conception of giftedness. *Journal for the Education of the Gifted, 13,* 288–308.

John-Steiner, V. (1987). *Notebooks of the mind: explorations in thinking.* New York: Harper Row.

Jones, K. & Day, J. D. (1996). Cognitive similarities between academically and socially gifted students. *Roeper Review, 18* (4), 270–273.

Keller, G. (1992). Schulpsychologische Hochbegabtenberatung: Ergebnisse einer Beratungsstudie [School psychological counseling of gifted children: results of a counseling study]. *Psychologie in Erziehung und Unterricht, 39* (2), 125–132,

Klein, P. S. & Cantor, L. (1976). Gifted children and their self-concept. *Creative Child and Adult Quarterly, 1* (2), 98–101.

Langer, J. (1969). *Theories of development.* New York: Holt, Rinehart and Winston.

Lowenstein, L. F. (1979). Discovering gifted children in a Third World nation. *School Psychology International,* l (l), 27–29.

Luftig, R. L. & Nichols, M. L. (1991). An assessment of the social status and perceived personality and school traits of gifted students by non-gifted peers. *Roeper Review, 13* (3), 148–53.

Luger, G. F. (1994). *Cognitive science: the science of intelligent systems.* New York: Academic Press.

Luria, R. A. (1980). *Higher cortical functions in man* (2nd ed.). New York: Basic Books.

Macmann, G. M., Plasket, C. M., Barnett, D. W. & Siler, R. F. (1991). Factor structure of the WISC-R for children of superior intelligence. *Journal of School Psychology, 29* (l), 19–36.

Marx, M. H. (1963). *Theories in contemporary psychology.* New York: Macmillan.

Mason, E. J. (1992). *Constructive approach to identification of the gifted.* Paper presented at the Second Asian Conference on the Gifted and Talented, Taipei, Taiwan, R.O.C., July 25, 1992.

Mason, E. J. & Bramble, W. J. (1997). *Research in education and the behavioral sciences: concepts and issues.* Madison, WI: Brown & Benchmark (McGraw-Hill).

Merenheimo, J. (1991). Cultural background and experience controlling the manifestation of giftedness. *Scandinavian Journal of Educational Research, 35* (2), 115–129.

Milgram, R. M. (1980). Gifted children in Israel: theory, practice, and research. *School Psychology International, 1* (3), 10–13.

Mills, C., Ablard, K. E. & Gustin, W. C. (1994). Academically talented students' achievement in a flexibly-paced mathematics curriculum. *Journal for Mathematics Education, 25,* 495–511.

Milner, J. O. & Elrod, M. M. (1986). Language reception in three modes. *Journal of Genetic Psychology, 147* (l), 123–133.

Minsky, M. (1986). *The society of the mind.* New York: Simon & Schuster.

Minton, H. L. (1988). *Lewis M. Terman: Pioneer in psychological testing.* New York: University Press.

Mönks, F. J. (1998). *Back to the roots of gifted education: a European perspective.* Paper presented at the Henry B. and Jocelyn Wallace National Research Symposium on Talent Development at The University of Iowa.

Mönks, F. J. (1992a). Development of gifted children: The issue of identification and programming. In: F. J. Mönks & W. A. M. Peters (Eds), *Talent for the Future* (pp. 191–202). Assen/Maastricht, The Netherlands: Van Gorcum.

Mönks, F. J. (1992). General introduction: from conception to realization. In: F. J. Mönks, M. W. Katzko & H. W. van Boxtel (Eds), *Education of the Gifted in Europe: Theoretical and Research Issues* (pp.13–21). Amsterdam: Swets & Zeitlinger.

Morelock, M. J. (1996). On the nature of giftedness and talent: imposing order on chaos. *Roeper Review, 19* (1), 4–12.

Naglieri, J. A. (1987). A cognitive processing theory for the measurement of intelligence. *Educational Psychologist, 24,* 185–206.

Naglieri, J. A. & Das, J. P. (1997) *Das-Naglieri Cognitive Assessment System.* Itasca, IL: Riverside.

Naglieri, J. A., Das, J. P., Stevens, J. J. & Ledbetter, M. F. (1991). Confirmatory factor analysis of planning, attention, simultaneous, and successive cognitive processing. *Journal of School Psychology, 29,* 1–18.

O'Connor, N. & Hermelin, B. (1988). Low intelligence and special abilities. *Journal of Child Psychology and Psychiatry and Allied Disciplines, 29,* 391–396.

Olszewski-Kubilius, P. M., Kulieke, M. J. & Krasney, N. (1988). Personality dimensions of gifted adolescents: a review of the empirical literature. *Gifted Child Quarterly, 32* (4), 347–352.

Pellegrino, J . W. & Glaser, R. (1979). Cognitive correlates and components in the analysis of individual differences. *Intelligence*, **3**, 187–214.

Petersen, A. C., Crockett, L. J. & Graber, J. (1990). Issues in the development of mathematical precocity. *Behavioral and Brain Sciences*, **13** (l), 192–193.

Piaget, J. (1967). *Biologie et connaissance* [Biology and understanding]. Paris: Gailimard.

Plomin, R. (1995). Nature, nurture, and intelligence. In: M. W. Katzko & F. J. Mönks (Eds), *Nurturing Talent: Individual Needs and Social Ability*. Assen, The Netherlands: van Gorcum.

Prom, J. S., Johnson, S. T. & Wallace, M. B. (1987). Home environment, talented minority youth, and school achievement. *Journal of Negro Education*, **56** (l), 111–121.

Reis, S. M. & Renzulli, J. S. (1989). Providing challenging programs for gifted readers. *Roeper Review*, **12** (2), 92–97.

Renzulli, J. S. (1978). What makes giftedness? Reexamining a definition. *Phi Delta Kappa*, **60**, 180–184, 261.

Renzulli, J. S. (1990). 'Torturing data until they confess': an analysis of the analysis of the three-ring conception of giftedness. *Journal for the Education of the Gifted*, **13** (4), 309–331.

Renzulli, J. S. (1998–99). From the desk of Joe Renzulli. *The Confratute Times—a Newsletter for Confratute Alumni*. Storrs: University of Connecticut.

Robinson, A., Bradley, R. H. & Stanley, T. D. (1990). Opportunity to achieve: identifying mathematically gifted black students. *Contemporary Educational Psychology*, **15** (l), 1–12.

Rogers, K. B. (1999). The lifelong productivity of the female talent researchers in Terman's Genetic Studies of genius longitudinal study. *Gifted Child Quarterly*, **43** (3),150–169.

Ross, P. O. (Ed.)(1993). *National excellence: a case for developing America's talent*. Washington, DC: U.S. Government Printing Office.

Schack, G. D. & Starko, A. J. (1990). Identification of gifted students: an analysis of criteria preferred by preservice teachers, classroom teachers, and teachers of the gifted. *Journal for the Education of the Gifted*, **13**, 346–363.

Schneider, B. H. & Daniels, T. (1992). Peer acceptance and social play of gifted kindergarten children. *Exceptionality: a Research Journal*, **3** (1), 17–29.

Sekowski, A. (1992). Problems of the education of the gifted in the countries of Middle East Europe. In: F. J. Mönks, M. W. Katzko & H. W. van Boxtel (Eds), *Education of the Gifted in Europe: Theoretical and Research Issues* (pp. 104–117). Amsterdam: Swets & Zeitlinger.

Shigaki, 1. S. & Wolf, W. (1980). Hierarchies of formal syllogistic reasoning of young gifted children. *Child Study Journal*, **10** (2), 87–106.

Shore, B. M., Coleman, E. B. & Moss, E. (1992). Cognitive psychology and the use of protocols in the understanding of giftedness and high level thinking. In: F. J. Mönks and W. Peters (Eds), *Talent for the Future*. Van Gorcum: Assen, The Netherlands.

Silver, S. J. & Clampit, M. K. (1990). WISC-R profiles of high ability children: interpretation of verbal-performance discrepancies. *Gifted Child Quarterly*, **34** (2), 76–78.

Skuder, P., Plomin, R., McClearn, G. E., Smith, D. L., Vigetti, S., Chorney, M. J., Chorney, K., Kasarda, S., Thompson, L.

A., Petrill, S. A., Daniels, J., Owen, M. J. & McGuffin, P. (1995). A polymorphismin mitocondrial DNA associated with IQ? *Intelligence*, 21, 1–11.

Slavin, R. E. (1987). Grouping for instruction in the elementary school. *Educational Psychologist*, 22(2), 109–127.

Smith, J., LeRose, B., & Clasen, R. E. (1991). Underrepresentation of minority students in gifted programs: Yes—It matters. *Gifted Child Quarterly*, 35 (2), 81–83.

Stern, W. (1916). Psychologische Begabungsforschung und Begabungsdiagnose [Psychological research on the gifted and diagnosis of giftedness]. In: P. Petersen (Ed.), *Der Aufstieg der Begabten* (pp. 105–120). Leipzig: Teubner.

Sternberg, R. J. (2000). Successful intelligence: a unified view of giftedness. In: C. F. M. van Lieshout & P. G. Heymans (Eds), *Developing Talent Across the Life-Span: A Festschrift for Franz Mönks*. Hove, UK: Psychology Press.

Sternberg, R. J. (1985). *Beyond IQ—a triarchic theory of human intelligence*. Cambridge: Cambridge University Press.

Sternberg, R. J. & Davidson, J. E. (Eds) (1986). *Conceptions of giftedness*. Cambridge: Cambridge University Press.

Sternberg, R. J. & Horvath, J. A., (1998). Cognitive conceptions of expertise and their relations to giftedness. In: R. C. Friedman & K. B. Rogers, (Eds), *Talent in Context: Historical and Social Perspectives on Giftedness* (pp. 177–191). Washington, DC: American Psychological Association.

Sternberg, R. J. & Lubart, T. 1. (1991). An investment theory of creativity and its development. *Human Development*, **34**, 1–31.

Swiatek, M. A. & Benbow, C. P. (1991). Ten-year longitudinal follow-up of ability-matched accelerated and unaccelerated gifted students. *Journal of Educational Psychology*, **83** (4), 528–38.

Tannenbaum, A. (1983). *Gifted children*. New York: Macmillan.

Terman, L. M. (1954). The discovery and encouragement of exceptional talent. *American Psychologist*, **9**, 221–230.

Terman, L. M. & Oden, M. H. (1947). The gifted child grows up: twenty-five years' follow-up of a superior group. In: *Genetic Studies of Genius*, Vol. 4. Stanford, CA: Stanford University Press.

Thorndike, R. L. (1984). *Intelligence as information processing*. Bloomington, IN: Phi Delta Kappa.

Van Parreren, C. F. (1983). *Leren door handelen* [Learning through experience]. Apeldoorn: Watraven.

Vaughn, V. L., Feldhusen, J. F. & Asher, W. J. (1991). Meta-analyses and review of research on pull-out programs in gifted education. *Gifted Child Quarterly*, **35** (2), 92–98.

Vernon, P. E. (1979). Intelligence testing and the nature/nurture debate, 1928–1978: what next? *British Journal of Educational Psychology*, **49**, 1–14.

Vygotsky, L. (1978). *Mind and society: the development of higher psychological processes*. Cambridge, MA: Harvard University Press.

Wang, M. C. & Walberg, H. J. (1983). Adaptive instruction and classroom time. *American Educational Research Journal*, **20** (4), 601–626.

Whitlock, M. S. & DuCette, J. P. (1989). Outstanding and average teachers of the gifted: a comparative study. *Gifted Child Quarterly*, **33** (l), 15–21.

Williams, W. G. & Mitchell, B. G. (1989). *From Afghanistan to Zimbabwe: gifted education in the world community.* New York: Peter Lang.

Zhang, L. & Sternberg, R. J. (1998). The pentagonal implicit theory of giftedness revisted: a cross-validation in Hong Kong. *Roeper Review,* **21** (2), 149–153.

Suggested Further Reading

Friedman, R. C. & Rogers, K. B. (Eds) (1998). *Talent in context: historical and social perspectives on giftedness.* Washington, DC: American Psychological Association.

Heller, K. A. (1992). Giftedness research and education of the gifted in Germany. In: F. J. Mönks, M. W. Katzko & H. W. van Boxtel (Eds), *Education of the Gifted in Europe: Theoretical and Research Issues* (pp. 71–85). Amsterdam: Swets & Zeitlinger.

Pulvino, C. J. & Lupton, P. E. (1978). Superior students: family size, birth order and intellectual ability. *Gifted Child Quarterly,* **22** (2), 212–216.

Scholnick, E. K., Nelson, K., Gelman, S. A. & Miller, P. (1999). *Conceptual development: Piaget's Legacy,* Mahwah, NJ: Erlbaum.

Genetic Tools for Exploring Individual Differences in Intelligence

Lee Anne Thompson[1] and Robert Plomin[2]

[1]Case Western Reserve University, USA
[2]Institute of Psychiatry, London, UK

Genetic Tools for Exploring Individual Differences in Intelligence

When the first edition of this handbook was published in 1993, general intelligence was the most widely studied behavior in the field of human behavioral genetics. A multitude of studies using a variety of research designs had clearly demonstrated that genetic influences on individual variation in intelligence are substantial. A survey of scientists found that most agree on this point (Snyderman & Rothman, 1987). The solidity of the finding led researchers in the field to conclude that no further quantitative genetic studies were required simply to demonstrate that genetic factors contribute to intelligence (Plomin et al., 1994, p. 107).

This statement should not be viewed as an endpoint but rather as a launching pad for the exciting cutting-edge research that has since ensued. Genetic research is now free to tackle more interesting issues surrounding the etiology of intelligence. For example, current molecular genetic research is uncovering specific genes that contribute to individual differences in cognitive function which will ultimately lead to a better understanding of the biochemical structure and regulation of cognitive processes. Advances in brain imaging have led to genetic studies of brain function during cognitive processing. New quantitative genetic techniques are merging with molecular genetic techniques to provide additional leverage on the genetic foundations of extreme groups, in this case, individuals with mental retardation and individuals who are intellectually gifted. Multivariate genetic analyses have revealed that the genetic variance influencing specific cognitive abilities is shared across abilities. In other words, genes are operating in a molar rather than a modular fashion. Perhaps most importantly, we can now tackle with greater precision issues of how the environment impacts on cognitive ability when genetic influences have been taken into account.

We hope to provide an overview of how this fascinating area is currently unfolding. Before we begin our update of current research, it is important to present a brief description of the methods used to study genetic influences on cognitive ability and also to highlight some common misconceptions.

Quantitative Genetics

The foundation for studying genetic influences on individual differences in intelligence and cognitive abilities is quantitative genetic methodology; primary to all quantitative genetic methods is the concept of variability or individual differences. Always bear in mind that quantitative geneticists do not try and explain the development of any one individual nor do they try and tackle species-wide developmental issues. Partitioning variance into either genetic or environmental categories simply explains how much of the observed differences across individuals can be explained by genetic or environmental factors. When you observe a classroom of first graders, you cannot help but wonder why some of the children are reading simple sentences effortlessly while others are still struggling with the identification of single letters and their sounds. To understand how genetic and environmental influences work together to create this striking pattern of variation in early reading skills, genetic and environmental influences must be separated.

The majority of research on the genetics of intelligence has involved the normal range of variation. Behavioral geneticists use a statistic called 'heritability' to describe the proportion of phenotypic variance that can be accounted for by genetics; to estimate the heritability of human behavior, samples of genetically informative individuals are studied. For example, adoptive parents and their adopted children share environments but not genes, while adopted children and their birth parents share genes but not environments. If adoptive parents resemble their adopted children, then environmental influences are operating; if adopted children resemble their birth parents, then genetic influences are operating. The comparison of identical and fraternal twins can also estimate heritability through the simple subtraction of correlations. Since identical twins are 100% genetically identical and fraternal twins are on average 50% genetically the same, subtracting the identical and fraternal twin correlation and doubling that difference, yields a rough univariate estimate of heritability or h^2. Currently, more sophisticated methods of estimating h^2 are typically used (McArdle & Prescott, 1997) and involve regression and/or structural equation models. These approaches are advantageous because they provide tests of significance through the simultaneous estimation of standard errors for the parameter estimates, allow for multivariate analyses, and in the case of regression analyses, are not as affected by non-normality in the distribution of the behavioral trait under study.

Traditionally, behavioral geneticists have broken environmental influences into two main categories, shared and non-shared. Shared family environmental influences (c^2) are those experiences that family members are all exposed to and that create similarities among family members. For example, they share the same home and neighborhood; the siblings may all attend the same school system and in some cases have the same teachers; parents may to some degree treat their children in a similar manner. In contrast, family members are also exposed to unique experiences; the oldest child may have more responsibilities than the youngest; one child may have a peer group that is dramatically different from another child; parents may also create unique experiences for each child. Experiences that create dissimilarity among family members are called non-shared environmental factors or e^2. Distinguishing the two types of environment is important because developmental psychologists have emphasized the importance of shared family environmental factors, while behavioral geneticists have consistently pointed out the relevance of non-shared factors (Scarr, 1996). Furthermore, many identified shared family environmental influences have been shown to be mediated by genetic factors (Plomin & Bergeman, 1991; Plomin & Petrill, 1997).

Although most behavioral genetic studies of intelligence tend to conceptualize environmental influences as experiential factors that are manifested in a psychological, social and/or cultural manner, it may be more accurate to portray environmental parameter estimates as 'non-genetic' instead of environmental (Jensen, 1997). Non-genetic biological factors would also be categorized as shared or non-shared environment. Jensen has further proposed that much of what is categorized as non-shared, excluding error variance, can be thought of as 'micro-environmental' influences. He hypothesizes that these are random small environ-

mental effects that accumulate to impact on individual variation.

To briefly summarize the vast literature on general intelligence across the normal range of ability, heritability accounts for roughly 50% of the phenotypic variation, shared environmental influences account for 10–20%, thus leaving 30–40% of the variation to non-shared environment and error (Chipeur, Rovine & Plomin, 1990; Plomin & Petrill, 1997). However, it is important to remember that these estimates are applicable only to the populations from which the samples were drawn and may vary across age; heritability represents what was happening in a given sample, at a specific time, on a particular trait as reflected by a specific measure. Change any of these conditions, and the parameter estimates may change as well. Although a great deal of research converges on these estimates of h^2, c^2, and e^2, the majority of the studies contributing to these estimates included a normally distributed group of relatively homogeneous individuals.

Recent Advances in Quantitative Genetic Research

As previously mentioned, estimates of heritability and environmentality are necessarily fluid; recent studies have begun to explore what factors can change the magnitude of these estimates. Some of the questions addressed include changes in heritability and environmentality across age, across levels of intelligence, and across environments.

Changes in heritability and environmentality across age. Developmental behavioral genetic studies have consistently suggested that as children mature from infancy through adolescence the magnitude of h^2 increases and c^2 decreases. Loehlin (1997) provides a nice overview of this literature. Twin studies show an overall pattern of high similarity for both Mz and Dz twin pairs early in life and a tendency for Mz twins to remain highly similar while the similarity of Dz twins gradually decreases across age. The increasing difference between Mz and Dz degree of similarity leads to higher heritability estimates with age; as the Dz pairs become less and less alike, the influence of shared family environment also drops. Adoption studies show a similar pattern in that adoptees have a moderate level of similarity with their siblings and parents with whom they share no genes during childhood; but once adolescence begins and especially after high school, the similarity drops to almost zero. In contrast, the resemblance between the biological parents and their adopted-away children increases throughout childhood and reaches a level similar to parents and children in non-adoptive families by adolescence (Plomin, Fulker, Chorley & DeFries, 1997).

An important Swedish study of twins reared apart and tested as elderly adults, called SATSA (Pederson, Plomin, Nessebroade & McClearn, 1992), indicates that the trend for increasing heritability continues throughout the lifespan and model-fitting results from this data set, yielding a heritability estimate of 0.80. Intelligence data collected in another study of twins reared apart based in Minnesota and tested during adulthood yielded similar results (Bouchard, Lykken, McGue, Segal & Tellegen, 1990). This trend towards higher heritability may not apply to very late in the life span. A study of Swedish twins over 80 years of age found a more modest heritability of 0.62, although this lower heritability might be due to lower reliability of psychometric tests with very old individuals (McClearn et al., 1997).

Changes in heritability and environmentality across levels of intelligence. Studies involving samples of selected individuals or individuals who score extremely high or low may provide different estimates of h^2, c^2, and e^2. Several recent studies have attempted to test for differential effects of genes and environments across the IQ range; two distinct regression approaches have been used that address different issues. The first approach involves an exploration of changes in individual difference h^2 or c^2 across the IQ continuum; for example, h^2 and c^2 are typically thought to be consistent across the normal range of IQ. These parameters can be estimated and tested for their significance by predicting one twin's IQ from their co-twin's IQ, a coefficient of relationship, R (R = 0.5 for Dz twins and R = 1 for Mz twins) and their product. The same approach can also test for a significant change in the amount of variation accounted for by h^2 and c^2 across the IQ continuum by adding an interaction term consisting of the product of the co-twin's IQ, the coefficient of relationship, and a diagnostic index in this example, the IQ score. This regression approach was developed in a series of papers by John C. DeFries and David W. Fulker (DeFries & Fulker, 1985, 1988; LaBuda, DeFries & Fulker, 1986) and is called DF analysis. This approach addresses a very interesting conceptual issue with practical implications. If heritability is significantly higher for one part of the continuum, then researchers could look for environmental factors that may account for the differences. Studies applying this methodology have been inconsistent to date; for example, two different papers have found evidence for higher heritability at the high end of the IQ continuum and higher common environmental influences at the low end (Bailey & Revelle, 1991; Thompson, Detterman & Plomin, 1993), while two other papers have found no differences in either h^2 or c^2 across the contiuum (Cherny, Cardon, Fulker & DeFries, 1992; Sundet et al., 1994). These inconsistencies may be due to several factors but three are most likely to be critical. First, sample sizes, while reasonably large for standard estimation of h^2 and c^2 , are inadequate to provide the necessary power to detect moderate-to-small changes in parameter estimates; much larger samples are

needed. Second, the majority of behavioral genetic studies have used samples that under-represent the low end of the IQ continuum. Subjects with IQs from the lower quartile are harder to recruit, harder to test, and harder to retain in studies. Finally, given that heritability increases and shared environment decreases across age, the age range of the subjects in the studies may have an impact on the findings. The studies included subjects ranging in age from infancy through old age; those that found significant differences included subjects who were predominantly between the ages of 5 and 18.

The second use of DF analysis is to estimate another type of heritability, group heritability or h_g^2. This parameter is not about individual variation but instead explains the etiology of mean differences for selected extreme groups. If a group of gifted individuals with a mean IQ of 150 is compared to a group of average IQ individuals with a mean IQ of 100, an obvious questions is "What factors create this 50-point mean group difference?" A significant estimate of h_g^2 would suggest that this difference is due in part to genetic differences across the groups. This is in contrast to the previous analysis which explains individual variation not mean differences between groups. Similarly, estimates of group shared environment, c_g^2, can also be obtained.

Group heritability was estimated for high and low IQ groups from the SATSA study conducted in Sweden and involving elderly twins (Saudino, Plomin, Pederson & McClearn, 1994), h_g^2 was high, hovering around 0.75, in both the high and low groups. In a sample of twins ages 5–13 years, Thompson, Tiu, Spinks & Detterman (1999) found similar results for a high IQ group (selected to be at least 1.25 standard deviation above the sample mean, $h_g^2 = 0.67 \pm 0.24$), but contrasting results for the low IQ groups (selected to be at least 1.25 standard deviations below the mean. For the low IQ group, group heritability was low and non-significant ($h_g^2 = 0.27 \pm 0.27$) while group common environment was appreciable ($c_g^2 = 0.63 \pm 0.23$). Once again, the discrepancies across the studies are most likely due to age and/or sampling differences across the studies.

Changes in heritability and environmentality across environments. Assuming that the evidence for the greater influence of common family environment at the lower levels of general cognitive ability can be shown to be a reliable effect, research should then address the issue of what causes the effect. Preliminary work from the Western Reserve Twin Project (Thompson et al., 1999) provides a small piece of evidence. The DF analyses that was previously conducted looking at differential heritability across the continuum for general cognitive ability was a univariate analysis in that the heritability of IQ was estimated across the continuum of IQ. These analyses can also be conducted in a bivariate manner where the heritability of IQ is estimated across the continuum of another variable, in this case fathers' occupation. The WRTP did not include direct assessments of the twins' environments; however, fathers' occupational status may be an indirect reflection of both the father's intellectual level and a global variable reflecting common environmental factors. Fathers' occupational status was measured on a 7 point scale, with low values representing more prestigious/higher paying occupations and high values representing relatively unskilled occupations. When the average twin pair differences for general cognitive ability for MZ and DZ twins was plotted against each of the 7 occupational categories, an interesting trend emerged. The average difference between MZ twins was between 0.4 and 0.5 standard deviations at the higher levels of father's occupation and increased slightly to about 0.55 for the lower levels of father's occupation. In contrast, the average difference between DZ twins was around 0.8 standard deviations for the higher occupational levels and dropped down to the same level as the MZ twins for the lower occupational levels. In other words, within pair similarity for the MZ twins stays relatively constant across levels of father's occupational status, but DZ twins become increasingly more similar (and approach the magnitude of the MZ resemblance) for general cognitive ability as father's occupational status goes down. Bivariate DF analyses supported the findings of this simple means analysis and suggested that heritability is significantly higher for general cognitive ability for higher levels of father's occupational status, and shared family environment becomes increasingly relevant for the lower levels of father's occupational status. Similar results showing increased heritability and decreased shared environment as a function of father's educational level have recently been reported in adolescence (Rowe, Jacobson & Van den Oord, in press). This study involved a much larger sample, a larger range for socioeconomic status, and in addition to twins, the study included full and half siblings as well.

How can we explain these preliminary findings? It is possible that heritability increases as environmental opportunities increase and heritability decreases when environmental opportunities are restricted. Individuals are not allowed a free range of choices through which to best express their own preferences. Rowe et al. (in press) suggest that below a certain level, some children are experiencing environments that are deleterious and the lower mean level of intelligence in the lower occupational groups may in part express this negative influence. Conversely, if families fall above this level, the environments are relatively homogeneous in terms of their impact on children's intellectual development and do not play a role in restructuring the causes of individual variation. However, the environments supplied by parent's from higher occupational levels may still have a positive mean effect on their children's IQ.

Clearly these hypotheses are just conjecture at this point and further research designed to measure specific aspects of the environment and/or opportunity is necessary before more definitive conclusions can be drawn.

General Intelligence and Separable Abilities. Thus far, this chapter has focused on genetic and environmental influences on general intelligence. A fascinating off-shoot from this topic is the exploration of how genes and environment impact on components of 'g' or specific cognitive abilities (Plomin & DeFries, 1998). Detterman and Daniel (1989) discovered a thought-provoking trend when they reanalyzed data collected in the standardization samples for several IQ tests. When the sample was divided into low and high ability groups based on general intelligence, the pattern of correlations among the subtests of each battery differed across low and high groups. Subtests are more highly correlated within low ability groups than they are within high ability groups. Although this study did not address genetic and environmental issues, genetically informative studies may be useful in explaining the origin of these group differences. This finding is especially interesting with respect to the high IQ because it suggests that the structure of general intelligence is fundamentally different among high ability individuals. What is needed are multivariate genetic analyses that investigate the genetic and environmental underpinnings of the structure of intelligence for high and low ability, but this has not as yet been done. This is a completely different issue from the topic described in the previous section concerning changes in heritability and environmentality across levels of intelligence. We return to the topic of multivariate genetic analysis later in this section.

Several studies have addressed the question of whether specific cognitive abilities are differentially heritable with respect to each other and to general intelligence. Specific abilities assessed through standard psychometric tests, for example verbal ability, spatial ability and memory appear to have heritabilities similar to general intelligence and to each other, although the heritability of memory may vary with the type of memory being assessed (Thapar, Petrill & Thompson, 1994). However, studies that have included tests of basic cognitive processing such as reaction times, have suggested differential patterns of heritability across tasks (Petrill, Thompson & Detterman, 1995; Neubauer et al., in press). One of the most interesting yet little known findings about cognitive abilities has emerged from multivariate genetic research, which examines the covariance among specific cognitive abilities rather than the variance of each cognitive ability considered separately: The same genetic factors largely influence different abilities (Petrill, 1997). That is, genetic correlations (the extent to which genetic factors that affect one ability also affect other abilities) among diverse cognitive abilities are very high, often near unity. These studies include twin analyses in childhood based on WISC-R subtests and specific cognitive ability factors and in adulthood using WAIS-R subtests and specific cognitive ability. Similar results have been reported in sibling and parent-offspring adoption analyses from the Colorado Adoption Project in childhood and in adulthood. The pattern of evidence suggests that genetic influences are responsible for linking together diverse areas of cognitive functioning, whereas environmental effects create differences between different domains.

In other words, the genetic basis of cognitive abilities is general (Petrill, 1997). What this finding means concretely is that if a specific gene were found that is associated with verbal ability, it would also be expected to be associated with spatial ability and other specific cognitive abilities. Conversely, *g* should be the best target for attempts to identify genes associated with cognitive abilities because genetic effects are general rather than specific. This finding is surprising because it goes against the tide of the popular modular theory of cognitive neuroscience, which assumes that cognitive processes are specific and independent and that genes work from the bottom up. That is, genes are assumed to be specific to elementary processes, with these modular effects then indirectly affecting more complex cognitive processes. However, multivariate genetic results are consistent with the opposite hypothesis of a top-down model in which genes have their primary influence on *g* and these genetic effects trickle down to affect other cognitive processes.

Insights Gained Through Advances in Molecular Genetic Technology

The field of molecular genetics has made remarkable advances in identifying genes that cause many diseases and physical anomalies; the vast majority of these successful identifications have been rare diseases determined by a single or major gene. The challenge today is to successfully identify genes that contribute to complex or polygenic traits where each gene only contributes to a small portion of the trait variation, also known as quantitative trait loci (QTLs; Plomin, Owen & McGuffin, 1994). Traits of interest to psychologists are likely to involve QTLs including general intelligence, personality, and many common psychiatric disorders. As molecular and statistical genetic methods for detecting QTLs are continually refined, studies searching for QTLs are on a scientific frontier.

There are many unknowns; thus, it is imperative that the trait or phenotype under study be well defined and accurately measured. General intelligence is a strong candidate for this pioneering research with strong social and functional importance as a predictor of academic success. Years of psychometric scrutiny have provided indices of general intelligence with high reliability, validity and stability; quantitative genetic studies have repeatedly found general intelligence to be heritable. Current advances in neuropsychology and cognitive neuroscience provide a strong biological and structural foundation upon which to bridge the gap between DNA codes and the resulting complex behaviors (Kosslyn & Plomin, in press).

As with many complex traits and diseases, there are several distinct challenges inherent in molecular genetic studies. First, measures of intelligence are continuous and normally distributed. Second, environmental factors account for a significant portion of the variance in intelligence and may make it more difficult to identify genetic effects. And finally as previously mentioned, because of the multiple genes involved, each gene will only have a small effect size thus requiring tremendous power to detect QTLs.

The likely effect size for QTLs important for general intelligence is around 1–2% of the variance. Traditional genetic methods that capitalize on the genetic similarities and differences among relatives like linkage analysis used for identifying single-gene effects are not powerful enough for such small effects (Risch & Merikangas, 1996). Even the newer QTL linkage methods which have been used to successfully identify and replicate linkage for reading disability on chromosome 6 (Cardon, et al., 1994; Grigorenko et al., 1997; Fisher et al., 1999; Gayan et al., 1999) must have an effect size of at least 10% for reliable detection.

Given the limitations of linkage studies, allelic association studies provide an attractive alternative. Unlike linkage studies, allelic association does not require related individuals; instead, it compares the differences in the frequencies of specific alleles between a target or affected group and an unrelated control group. One drawback to association studies is the need for DNA markers to be so close to the functional gene that the marker and gene are not separated by recombination. Therefore two options emerge for the successful identification of a relevant gene. Studies use either only candidate genes, known genes with a high probability of effect, or many, many markers in an effort to screen for relevant genes. To systematically scan the entire human genome for a relevant gene through association analysis, approximately 3500 DNA markers would be needed, a huge undertaking!

However, a line of ongoing research, called the IQ QTL Project, is attempting to do just that using a technique called DNA pooling (Fisher et al., 1999). The goal of the research is to locate genes that contribute to the highest end of the distribution for general intelligence. The strategy maximizes the chance for the identification of genes relevant for the entire distribution of intelligence because those individuals with high intelligence are most likely to have the highest proportion of alleles from the group of genes affecting intelligence, that lead to an increase in intelligence. In contrast, individuals from the low end of the distribution for intelligence may have a higher proportion of decreasing alleles, but may also be affected by idiosyncratic genetic and environmental factors that disrupt normal development and may obscure the effect of the QTLs relevant for normal variation. Analogous idiosyncratic effects that would impact on a group selected from the high end of the distribution seem less likely.

Because of the multiple comparisons required in an association study with 3500 markers, inflation of Type I error is an inherent problem. To compensate for this inflation, a replication design was used in the IQ QTL Project. An original high intelligence group (N = 51, mean IQ = 136, SD = 9.3) was compared with a control sample (N = 51, mean IQ = 103, SD = 5.6).

The IQ QTL Project attempted a preliminary search using a dense map of DNA markers associated with intelligence on the long arm of chromosome 6. For one marker, the frequency of one of its alleles was twice as high in two groups of children with high g as compared to two groups of children with average g (frequencies of about 30% vs. 15%, respectively). Both samples yielded a significant difference in the same direction and combining these results yielded a highly significant result ($\chi^2 = 12.41$, $p < 0.0004$). The DNA marker happened to be in the $3'$ untranslated region of the gene for insulin-like growth factor receptor-2 (IGF2R), which has recently been shown to be especially active in brain regions most involved in learning and memory (Wickelgren, 1998).

Pooling DNA from subjects within each group and comparing the pooled DNA across groups for a dense map of DNA markers offers a solution to the conundrum that linkage is systematic, but not powerful, whereas allelic association is powerful but not systematic. DNA pooling can be used to screen thousands of DNA markers for QTL associations by creating pools of DNA for cases and controls. For example, only 7,000 rather than 1.4 million genotypings would be needed in the previous example for screening 3,500 markers for two groups. An approach to DNA pooling has been developed in the IQ QTL Project that compares the allele image patterns (AIPs) from an automated DNA sequencer for two pools of DNA (Daniels et al., 1998). DNA pooling has been shown to be a reasonably accurate screening tool to detect the largest allelic frequency differences between two groups. A three-stage design in which pooled DNA is compared for an original sample and tested in a replication sample and then surviving markers are individually genotyped and tested using conventional statistics. The goal of this programme of research is to identify some of the oldest and largest QTLs, knowing that QTLs with complicated linkage disequilibrium histories and QTLs whose effect sizes are too small will be missed. DNA pooling is a screening device that greatly reduces the amount of genotyping needed to conduct a genome scan for allelic association using a dense marker map. DNA pooling results have been reported for 147 markers on chromosome 4 (Fisher et al., 1999) and for 66 markers on chromosome 22 (Hill et al., 1999). Three replicated associations on chromosome 4 were identified using DNA pooling and confirmed using individual genotyping. Encouraged by these first results of the application of DNA pooling for a systematic analysis of allelic association screening a dense map of markers, the IQ QTL Project is proceeding with a scan of 3,500 markers across the genome to find other QTLs for g. As specific genes are identified, their function can be investigated, not only at the biological level of cells, but also at the neuroscience level of the brain, as well as the psychological level of behavior.

Where do we go from here?

General intelligence has proven to be a valuable phenotype for both quantitative and molecular geneticists. Despite the fact that intelligence is a complex trait influenced by both genes and environment, quantitative geneticists have demonstrated that individual differences in intelligence are highly heritable, and molecular geneticists are beginning to identify genes associated with intelligence. The entire 'package' of studies that have over the years explored variation in intelligence serves as a model for researchers tackling other complex traits. The search for factors that influence individual differences in intelligence has been a successful journey, but the journey is far from complete. Recent technological, methodological and conceptual advances have opened the door for additional topics of study; we would like to suggest three areas that are ripe for further research on intelligence.

Neuroscience is making rapid advances in our understanding of the structure and function of the brain; as more and more studies begin to pinpoint how cognitive processes operate in general at a neurological level, the potential for extending these findings to the exploration of individual differences is enormous. As measures become more reliable, and as technology becomes more efficient and affordable, we should begin to concentrate on filling in the gap between the gene code at the level of DNA and behavior. For example, cognitive neuroscientists have used functional magnetic resonance imaging (fMRI), high resolution electroencephalogram (EEG) recordings, and positron emission tomography (PET) studies to characterize and localize neurologic processes involved in different types of memory. Quantitative genetic studies have for the most part lumped different types of memory measures into one generic category and molecular genetic studies of memory have yet to be tackled. Given the varying neurologic substrates of different types of memory, quantitative and molecular genetic studies should capitalize on this knowledge and begin to investigate neurologically defined measures of memory.

Although we have gained a considerable amount of knowledge about the nature of environmental factors that affect intelligence, we have not yet realized an understanding of how specific environmental factors, in the normal range, impact on individual variation in intelligence. Developmental studies and the recent finding by Thompson et al. (1999) and Rowe et al. (in press) that heritability decreased and shared environment increased with socioeconomic status suggests that shared environmental factors that impact on general intelligence may be stronger during childhood and in specific groups of families. Identifying systematic non-shared environmental influences that affect variation in intelligence may be quite difficult if Jensen's hypothesis is true and each small piece of the environment operates like one gene in a highly polygenic trait. Perhaps an extreme group association analysis strategy similar to the IQ QTL Project can be adapted using environmental markers in place of, or in addition to, genetic markers.

Psychologists continue to refine and improve indices of personality and emotion; a growing area of research today is in the understanding of the biology of personality and emotion. One of the most frequent criticisms of research on intelligence is that knowing someone's IQ seems to be only a partial predictor of their academic and/or career success. The mediation of intelligence through individual differences in personality and affect may partially address this weakness. Bivariate quantitative genetic analyses could be quite interesting in understanding how these areas are intertwined at a genetic and environmental level particularly when the phenotypes used in the analysis have a strong biological foundation. This approach might be especially fruitful when a child exhibits a large discrepancy between intelligence and global scholastic achievement.

These three suggestions for future research represent only a small fraction of potential research questions ripe for addressing given our current understanding of the genetics of intelligence.

References

Bailey, M. J. & Revelle, W. (1991). Increased heritability for lower IQ levels? *Behavior Genetics*, **21**, 397–404.

Bouchard, T. J., Lykken, D. T., McGue, M., Segal, N. L. & Tellegen, A (1990). Sources of human psychological difference: the Minnesota study of twins reared apart. *Science*, **250**, 223–228.

Cardon, L. R., Smith, S. D., Fulker, D. W., Kimberling, W. J., Pennington, B. R. & DeFries, J. C. (1994). Quantitative trait locus for reading disability on chromosome 6. *Science*, **266**, 276–279.

Cherny, S. S., Cardon, L. R., Fulker, D. W. & DeFries, J. C. (1992). Differential heritability across levels of cognitive ability. *Behavior Genetics*, **22**, 153–162.

Chipeur, H. M., Rovine, M. J. & Plomin, R. (1990). LISREL modeling: Genetic and environmental influences on IQ revisited. *Intelligence*, **14** (1), 11–29.

Chorney, M. J., Chorney, K., Seese, N., Owen, M. J., Daniels, J., McGuffin, P., Thompson, L. A., Detterman, D. K., Benbow, C., Lubinski, D., Eley, T. C. & Plomin, R. (1998). A quantitative trait locus (QTL) associate with cognitive ability in children. *Psychological Science*, **9** (3), 159–166.

Daniels, J., Holmans, P., Williams, N., Turic, D., McGuffin, P., Plomin, R. & Owen, M. J. (1998). A simple method for analyzing microsatellite allele image patterns generated from DNA pools and its application to allelic assocation studies. *American Journal of Human Genetics*, **62** (5), 1189–1197.

DeFries, J. C. & Fulker, D. W. (1985). Multiple regression analysis of twin data. *Behavior Genetics*, **15**, 467–473.

DeFries, J. C. & Fulker, D. W. (1988). Etiology of deviant scores versus individual differences. *Acta Genetica Medicae Gemellogic. Twin Research*, **37**, 205–216.

Detterman, D. K. & Daniel, M. H. (1989). Correlations of mental tests with each other and with cognitive variables are highest of low IQ groups. *Intelligence*, **13** (4), 349–359.

Fisher, S. E., Marlow, A. J., Lamb. J., Maestrini, E., Williams, D. F., Richardson, A. J., Weeks, D. E., Stein, J. F. & Monaco, A. P (1999). A quantitative-trait locus on chromosome 6p influences different aspects of developmental dyslexia. *American Journal of Human Genetics*, **64**, 146–56.

Gayan, J., Smith, S. D., Cherny, S. S., Cardon, L. R., Fulker, D. W., Brower, A. M., Olson, R. K, Pennington, B. F. & DeFries, J. C. (1999). Quantitative-trait locus for specific language and reading deficits on chromosome 6p. *American Journal of Human Genetics*, **64**, 157–164.

Grigorenko, E. L., Wood, F. B., Meyer, M. S., Hart, L. A., Speed, W. C., Schuster, A. & Pauls, D. L. (1997). Susceptibility loci for distinct components of dyslexia on chromosome 6 and 15. *American Journal of Human Genetics*, **60**, 27–39.

Hill, L., Asherson, P., Ball, D., Eley, T., Craig, I., Fisher, P. J., Turic, D., McGuffin, P., Owen, M. J., Chorney, K., Chorney, M. J., Benbow, C., Lubinski, D., Thompson, L. A. & Plomin, R. (1999). DNA pooling and dense marker maps: A systematic search for genes for cognitive ability. *NeuroReport*, **10** (4), 843–848.

Jensen, A. R. (1997). The puzzle of non-genetic variance. In: R. J. Sternberg & E. L. Grigorenko (Eds), *Intelligence, Heredity, and Environment*. New York: Cambridge University Press.

Kosslyn, S. & Plomin, R. Towards a neuro-cognitive genetics: goals and issues. In: D. Dougherty, S. L. Rauch, & J. F. Rosenbaum. *Psychiatric Neuroimaging Strategies: Research and Clinical Applications*. American Psychiatric Press, Washington DC, 1999. (in press).

LaBuda, M. C., DeFries, J. C. & Fulker, D. W. (1986). Multiple regression analysis of twin data obtained from selected samples. *Genetic Epidemiology*, **3**, 425–433.

Loehlin, J. C. (1997). Genes and environment. In: D. Magnusson (Ed.), *The Lifespan Development of Individuals: Behavioral, Neurobiological, and Psychosocial Perspectives: A Synthesis*. (38–51). New York: Cambridge University Press.

Luo, D., Petrill, S. & Thompson, L. A. (1994). Hierarchical factor analysis of genetic and environmental influences on specific cognitive abilities. *Intelligence*, **18**, 335–347.

McArdle, J. J. & Prescott, C. A. (1997). Contemporary models for the biometric genetic analysis of intellectual abilities. In: Dawn P. Flanagan and Judy L. Genshaft (Eds), *Contemporary Intellectual Assessment: Theories, Tests, and Issues* (pp. 403–436). New York, NY: Guildford Press.

McClearn, G. E., Johansson, B., Berg, S., Pedersen, N. L., Ahern, F., Petrill, S. A. & Plomin, R. (1997). Substantial genetic influence on cognitive abilities in twins 80+ years old. *Science*, **276**, 1560–1563.

Neubauer, A. C., Spinath, F. M., Riemann, R., Borkenau, P. & Angleitner, A. Genetic (and environmental) influence on two measures of speed of information processing and their relation to psychometric intelligence: evidence from the German Observational Study of Adult Twins. *Intelligence*. (in press).

Pedersen, N. L., Plomin, R., Nesselroade, J. R. & McClearn, G. E. (1992). A quantitative genetic analysis of cognitive abilities during the second half of the lifespan. *Psychological Science*, **3**, 346–353.

Petrill, S., Thompson, L. A. & Detterman, D. K. (1995). Genetic and environmental influences on elementary cognitive processes. *Behavior Genetics*, **25**, 199–209.

Petrill, S. A., Luo, D., Thompson, L. A. & Detterman, D. K. (1996). The independent phenotypic prediction of general intelligence by elementary cognitive tasks: genetic and common environmental influences. *Behavior Genetics*, **26** (2), 135–148.

Petrill, S. A., Plomin, R., McClearn, G. E., Smith, D. K., Vignetti, S., Chorney, M. J., Chorney, K., Thompson, L. A., Detterman, D. K., Benbow, C., Lubinski, D., Daniels, J., Owen, M. & McGuffin, P. (1996). DNA markers associated with general and specific cognitive abilities. *Intelligence*, **23**, 191–204.

Petrill, S. A. (1997). Molarity versus modularity of cognitive functioning? A behavioral genetic perspective. *Current Directions in Psychological Science*, **6** (4), 96–99.

Plomin, R. & Bergeman, C. S. (1991). The nature of nurture: genetic influence on 'environmental' measures. *Behavioral and Brain Sciences*, **14**, 373–427.

Plomin, R & DeFries, J. C. (1998). The genetics of cognitive abilities and disabilities. *Scientific American*, May, 62–69.

Plomin, R. & Petrill, S. A. (1997). Genetics and intelligence: What's new? *Intelligence*, **24** (1), 53–77.

Plomin, R., Owen, M. J. & McGuffin, P. (1994). The genetic basis of complex human behaviors. *Science*, **264**, 1733–1739.

Plomin, R., Fulker, D. W., Corley, R. & DeFries, J. C. (1997). Nature, nurture, and cognitive development from 1 to 16 years: a parent-offspring adoption study. *Psychological Science*, **8**, 442–447.

Risch, N. & Merikangas, K., (1996). The future of genetic studies of complex human diseases. *Science*, **273** (13), 1516–1517.

Rowe, D. C., Jacobson, K. C. & Van den Oord, E. J. C. G. Genetic and environmental influences on vocabulary IQ: parental education level as moderator. *Child Development*. (in press).

Saudino, K. J., Plomin, R., Pedersen, N. L. & McClearn, G. E. (1994). The etiology of low and high cognitive ability during the second half of the life span. *Intelligence*, **19**, 359–371.

Scarr, S. (1996). How people make their own environments: implications for parents and policy makers. *Psychology, Public Policy and Law*, **2** (2), 204–228.

Snyderman, M. & Rothman, S. (1987). Survey of expert opinion on intelligence and aptitude testing. *American Psychologist*, **42**, 137–144.

Sundet, J. M., Eilertsen, D. E., Tambs, K. & Magnus, P. (1994). No differential heritability of intelligence test scores across ability levels in Norway. *Behavior Genetics*, **24**, 337–340.

Thapar, A., Petrill, S. A. & Thompson, L. A. (1994). The heritability of memory in the Western Reserve Twin Project. *Behavior Genetics*, **24**, 155–160.

Thompon, L. A., Detterman, D. K. & Plomin, R. (1993). Differences in heritability across groups differing in ability, revisited. *Behavior Genetics*, **23**, 331–336.

Thompson, L. A., Tiu, R., Spinks, R. & Detterman, D. K. (1999). *Differential heritability for cognitive abilities across fathers' occupational levels*. Manuscript in preparation.

Wickelgren, I. (1998). Tracking insulin to the mind. *Science*, **280**, 517–519

Giftedness, Expertise, and (Exceptional) Performance: A Developmental Perspective

Wolfgang Schneider

University of Würzburg, Germany

Introduction

This chapter focuses on determinants of exceptional performance; in particular, the roles of intellectual abilities and domain-specific knowledge in predicting academic and professional success are carefully analyzed. Since the beginning of this century, educational researchers and psychologists have investigated long-term effects of early giftedness and a rich knowledge base to locate the sources of outstanding (academic) behavior and performance. A major purpose of this chapter is to give an overview of the findings of this research.

In a first section, developmental (longitudinal) research on giftedness and its impact on later performance is summarized. This paradigm—which has been used for a long time—is based on the psychometric approach; the next major section focuses on research on knowledge acquisition that has been conducted within the information processing framework. Theoretical models of skill acquisition are briefly described, followed by a review of recent empirical studies on the development of expertise and its relationship to (exceptional) cognitive performance. Finally, theoretical models that describe possible relationships between aptitude and the acquisition of expertise are briefly discussed.

The Relationship between Giftedness and Exceptional Performance

Although the question of whether early giftedness predicts outstanding academic achievement and subsequent professional success has been repeatedly examined in the literature, the number of longitudinal studies devoted to this issue is still rather small. Most information on the development of gifted children stems from prospective studies where participants are recruited at an early age and then followed through childhood and adolescence (in some rare cases even up to adulthood). Retrospective studies represent another interesting approach: here, eminent adults are selected for further study which consists of a careful analysis of their biography; the main goal is to identify early signs of subsequent exceptional performance. The findings of classic prospective and retrospective studies are summarized next.

Prospective Studies

There is little doubt that the well-known Terman Gifted Children Study (Terman, 1954) can be conceived as the most impressive attempt to explore the predictive power of high intellectual ability for subsequent academic performance and success in later life. In fact, the Terman study is the longest prospective study ever conducted; about 1500 young Californian children with an IQ of 135 and above (IQ range: 135–201; mean IQ: 151) were recruited in 1921 and followed until recently. The last questionnaires were sent to the participants in 1996 and answered by a total of 264 men and women (see Hastorf, 1997). Accordingly, this life-span longitudinal study created an enormous and invaluable body of information on developmental changes in gifted individuals.

One of Terman's main goals at the beginning of the study was to prove the assumption that the children in his sample were not only intellectually gifted but also above average in physical and social development. The findings supported this hypothesis and clearly pleased Terman, for he was motivated to disprove the popular belief of the time that high-IQ children are physically awkward and social misfits (see Rost, 1993, for a recent replication of these results). Although the theoretical focus of the study changed over the years, the body of data seems suited to evaluate the relevance of high aptitude for academic and professional performance. The vast majority of children (85%) were accelerated, and nearly half learned to read before entering school (Terman, 1954); as noted by Winner (1996a), early reading is a reliable sign of a high IQ. In accord with this, those 'Termites' with IQs above 170 were more than twice as likely to have read before the age of four than those with IQs below 170 (see

Hollingworth, 1942, for additional evidence regarding early reading skills in profoundly gifted children).

Terman and his colleagues found that participants' IQs remained high over the course of the study and that IQ differences were stable over time. They also reported that academic achievement of this special sample was clearly superior. Whereas in the general population of California at that time only 8% had graduated from college, about 70% of the male and 67% of the female Termites were college graduates (cf. Hastorf, 1997). Overall, they were also rather successful in later life. However, a closer look at the findings of the Terman study reveals that the expected collection of 'eggheads' and outstanding personalities was not found (cf. Sears, 1984). As noted by Howe (1982), the data collected by Terman and his colleagues provided little information that would have helped one to predict which of the children under study would be most successful in later life. When the small subgroup of children with IQs over 180 were compared to a small group chosen at random, no marked differences in accomplishment were found (Feldman, 1984). Although most Termites became respected professionals, not a single one grew up to become a creative genius. It seems ironic in this regard that two future Nobel laureates, William Schockley, who invented the transistor, and Luis Alvarez, who won the prize in physics, were actually rejected from the study because their IQs did not test high enough (cf. Winner, 1996a). Overall, the conclusion to be drawn from the Terman study is that even though most gifted children turn out to be academically successful, individual differences in giftedness do not sufficiently predict differences in educational achievement and subsequent professional success. A similar finding was reported by Subotnik, Kassan, Summers and Wasser 1993. Although several contemporary prospective studies on high IQ gifted children exist (e.g. Heller, 1991; Rost, 1993; for reports on these and other longitudinal studies, see Subotnik & Arnold, 1994), their findings confirm those outlined above and thus are in accord with our general conclusion.

Further research conducted with random samples of people indicated that the importance of the IQ predictor does not change much when aptitude is assessed considerably later, that is, during the college years (cf. Samson, Grane, Weinstein & Walberg, 1984). In this study, an average correlation of about 0.15 was found between college students' aptitude and their professional productivity assessed several years later, indicating that the subsamples representing 'schoolhouse giftedness' and 'production giftedness' do not have much in common (cf. Siegler & Kotovsky, 1986). Obviously, information about intellectual ability alone does not allow for reliable predictions of later academic and professional success. Given that one major incentive of research in giftedness was to illustrate the importance of early talent and potential for further

development, such an outcome may have contributed to what Weinert & Waldmann (1986) called a 'worldwide crisis' in this research program. Given that the correlations between early giftedness and later professional success obtained from prospective studies were only moderate, it seemed necessary to complement prospective studies with retrospective analyses, thereby exploring the determinants of outstanding professional success.

Retrospective Studies

Several reanalyses based on the data of the Terman longitudinal study explored the reasons for individual differences in academic and professional success among those intellectually gifted individuals. Oden (1968) assessed occupational success in a subgroup of 664 male Termites and compared 100 of the most successful (given an A rating) with 100 of the least successful (given a C rating). The two extreme groups were found to differ only by seven IQ points: the more successful averaged IQs of 157, and the less successful averaged IQs of 150. However, the A group was much more successful academically, with a high percentage (63%) graduating from college with honors. In comparison, only 11% of the C group graduated with honors. Where the two groups really differed was in their childhood ratings of motivation. The A group was described as more persevering, having greater self-confidence, and engaged in more extra-curricular activities.

Another secondary analysis of the Terman longitudinal study (Elder, Pavalko & Hastings, 1991) revealed that the picture may be more complex. In particular, Elder et al. (1991) explored how major historical events such as the Great Depression and World War II affected the life course of the male Termites. The wide range of birth years of these men placed them in two general birth cohorts relative to historical events: the older with birth dates of 1904 through 1910, and the younger with birth years mainly from 1911 through 1917. The reanalysis by Elder and colleagues illustrates that the two cohorts encountered the Great Depression and World War II at very different points in their life course. The older men were in their early 20s at the time of the economic collapse and thus experienced many problems when completing college and establishing careers. By comparison, the younger men largely missed the economic stagnation of the 30s and could complete their higher education before they were mobilized into the military service during World War II. Thus worklife disadvantages of the older cohort may be partly responsible for the fact that men in this cohort were more likely to end up in the low achievement group (the C group).

Another line of research focused on subjects with reliably superior performances, with the goal to reconstruct their cognitive and non-cognitive abilities. Most of that research was similarly motivated by the belief that exceptionally high levels of performance should reflect some basic cognitive ability such as general intelligence, atttention, or memory (e.g. Cox, 1926). Some researchers studied other stable individual characteristics, such as aspects of personality and motivation (Roe, 1952, 1953). In short, the results of these retrospective studies seem to confirm the outcomes of the prospective studies in that individual differences in intellectual abilities were not the crucial determinant of outstanding professional careers. For example, Roe's analysis of the careers of outstanding scientists showed that non-cognitive factors like endurance, concentration power, and committment to work were more important for professional success than the individuals' cognitive abilities, despite the fact that the latter were generally above average.

Roe's findings were confirmed in an interview study with outstanding scientists, sportsmen, and artists organized by Bloom (1985a). The data obtained from these subjects and their parents did not support the view that outstanding basic abilities were solely responsible for success in later life. Instead, the study provided strong evidence that no matter what the initial gifts or basic abilities of the individuals, extreme levels of capabilities in their fields of expertise were not attained unless there was a long and intensive process of encouragement, education, and training. Bloom concluded from these findings that his research raised serious questions about earlier views of special gifts and innate aptitudes as necessary prerequisites of talent development (1985, p.3).

Taken together, prospective and retrospective studies focusing on the impact of intelligence and other stable cognitive factors on academic and professional success have been largely unsuccessful in identifying strong and replicable relations (see Ericsson & Smith, 1991, for more evidence on this issue). Instead, most of these studies have shown that non-cognitive factors such as motivation, concentration, and endurance as well as parental and school support systems seem mainly responsible for exceptional performances in later life. However, please note that none of this evidence rules out the possible role of innate gifts.

The Expertise Approach

Studies with Adult Experts and Novices

Undoubtedly, the pioneering work on chess conducted by de Groot (1946/1978) and Chase & Simon (1973) has stimulated numerous studies on the nature of expertise. For most cognitive psychologists, an approach based on acquired characteristics seems much more suited to account for outstanding and superior performance than research on giftedness relying on stable inherited characteristics. The game of chess appears particularly attractive for researchers interested in the preconditions of outstanding performance because it is rather easy to produce and observe outstanding chess performance under standardized conditions. In addition it is possible to measure a subject's chess-playing ability from the results of matches against different opponents in different tournaments (cf. the index developed by Elo, 1978). Another related advantage is that chess players can be reliably differentiated by skill level. As chess skill can be measured with remarkable precision, the domain of chess seems ideal for the study of acquired skill, and models of chess skill have strongly influenced investigations of expertise in other domains such as physics, medical sciences, music, and sports.

One of the major outcomes of the chess studies was that exceptional performance was closely linked with exceptional memory for domain specific information. In order to capture skill differences in chess, de Groot (1946/1978) used a task that assessed memory for briefly presented chess positions. He found that when chess masters were shown a chess position consisting of 20–30 pieces for a very brief duration (e.g. 5 seconds), they were able to remember the position far better than less experienced chess experts. Chess masters were able to recall the positions of all pieces virtually perfectly, whereas the less experienced chess experts recalled between 50 to 70% of the positions. Chase & Simon (1973) followed up de Groot's finding by adding an important control—showing random arrangements of pieces; the experts' advantage in recall with structured positions disappeared.

In order to understand the chess masters' recall superiority for meaningful chess positions, Chase and Simon attempted to uncover the structure of their chess knowledge. They showed that superior recall depended on the master's ability to recognize familiar patterns or 'chunks'. That is, the master was able to recall pieces more effectively than the novice because groups of pieces, rather than single pieces, formed his chunks. According to this finding, quantitative differences in the memory performance of experts and novices could be largely explained by *qualitative differences* in memory behavior.

More recent, carefully designed studies of superior memory performance for chess positions have shown that experts store information about chess positions in long-term memory, not solely in short-term memory as Chase & Simon (1973) originally proposed (for a review, see Charness, 1991). These findings do not negate the basic assumption that there are qualitative differences in memory behavior of experts and novices. They indicate instead that Chase & Simon's (1973) original theoretical assumptions need to be replaced by more sophisticated views of skilled memory such as those by Chase & Ericsson (1982; see also Ericsson & Staszewski, 1989), stressing the importance of domain-specific, easily activated retrieval structures in recall performance.

Qualitative differences in the problem-solving and memory behavior of experts and novices have also been reported for other domains such as physics, medical diagnosis, reasoning, and sports (see Voss, Vesonder & Spilich, 1980; Chi, Glaser & Rees, 1981; Lesgold, 1984; Morris, Tweedy & Gruneberg, 1985; Anzai, 1991; Patel & Groen, 1991). Overall, a broad variety of studies based on the expert-novice approach have found evidence supporting a monotonic relation between recall of domain-related information and domain-specific knowledge. They have also supported the view that the main differences among experts and novices in a wide range of domains concern the speed of access to relevant knowledge as well as the sophistication of knowledge-based strategies.

The Acquisition Of Expertise

As emphasized by Ornstein & Naus (1985), an association between expert–novice status in a particular area and differential patterns of performance on tasks related to the area of expertise does not constitute an explanation of how such differences arise. Theoretical models describing the acquisition of expertise are helpful in clarifying the issue.

Several models of skill acquisition are described in the literature; the classic model developed by Fitts & Posner (1967) proposed three different acquisition stages: the 'cognitive stage' can be characterized by an effort to understand the task demands and to distinguish between important and unimportant aspects of the task. The focus is on the acquisition of declarative knowledge about the task. The 'associative stage' involves making the cognitive processes more efficient to allow rapid retrieval, thus transforming declarative knowledge into procedural forms. During the third and final phase, labeled the 'autonomous stage', performance is automatic, and conscious cognition and control is minimal (see Ackerman, 1987, 1988, and Anderson, 1982, for similar theoretical models).

According to these models, practice plays a crucial role in the acquisition of expertise; across a wide range of tasks, improvements in performance seem closely related to the amount of practice. Reviews of skills acquisition indicate that the relationship between performance is monotonic, and that a power function provides a very good fit for a variety of tasks and skills (Newell & Rosenbloom, 1981; Anderson, 1982).

Although these models of skill acquisition have been attractive for many researchers in the field, stimulating much important research, it remains unclear whether the learning mechanisms and developmental stages they propose generalize from adult learners to children. We know from numerous reports on the careers of chess experts, eminent musicians, or world-class tennis players that these individuals started their careers early, that is, between 6 and 10 years of age (e.g. Bloom, 1985a). We also know from several sources that it takes about 10 years between experts' first experiences with their domain of interest to attain international-level performance (Chase & Simon, 1973; Krogius, 1976;

Sosniak, 1985). This '10-year rule' first established by Simon and Chase (1973) for the area of chess, is supported by data from a wide range of domains, including sports, music, and science.

Given that the attainment of exceptional performance in real life usually takes place in childhood and adolescence, it seems important to identify the learning mechanisms, rules of practice, and support systems that enable this rapid development. Research conducted by Anders Ericsson and his colleagues (cf. Ericsson, Krampe & Tesch-Roemer, 1993; Ericsson & Charness, 1994; Ericsson, 1996, 1998) has led the authors to propose a theoretical framework for the acquisition of expert-level performance. The attractiveness of this model stems from the fact that hypotheses about the developmental history and practice intensity of expert-level performers have been systematically evaluated against empirical evidence on exceptional performances in various domains.

The Role of Deliberate Practice

The model presented by Ericsson and colleagues differs from the skill acquisition models presented above in that it explicitly considers developmental issues within a life-span perspective. Whereas skill acquisition has, for the most part, been studied with college students, most information relevant for Ericsson's theoretical framework stems from observations and retrospective reports dealing with performances in childhood and adolescence.

Ericsson and colleagues adopt and extend the basic characteristics of a framework first developed by Bloom (1985b). According to this framework, the preparation period for reaching exceptional performance can be conceived of as a sequence of states, each representing rather stable characteristics for a specific time period in the individual's life. The first stage corresponds to the playful introduction to the domain, the second to the start of systematic practice supervised by a coach or a teacher, and the third and most crucial stage to attaining exceptional levels of performance (cf. Ericsson et al., 1993).

This model suggests that the type and intensity of training may differ as a function of developmental stage. Whereas it is most important to keep children motivated and interested in the domain during the first stage, methods of instruction and the quality of teachers become more relevant with increasing levels of performance. An early start as well as parental interest and support seem particularly important for the earlier stages. With increasing skill, factors such as availability of excellent instruction, quality of practice equipment, and access to practice facilities become most relevant. As noted by Bloom (1985b), performers at an international level have nearly always been instructed by master teachers who themselves had once achieved that level.

Ericsson and colleagues provide multiple evidence from the domains of chess, sports, music, and arts that is in accord with the core assumptions of this model, and that show surprising parallels in developmental patterns observed across these domains. However, one apparent problem with their early conceptualization (Ericsson et al., 1993) is that it focused on the *extent* of practice, although individual differences in the *intensity or quality* of practice were also observed. Our everyday experiences show that not all people practising and working extensively in a specific domain end up as eminent experts in that area. Thus, there is little doubt that mere experience is insufficient for attainment of very high (expert) levels of performance. More recent descriptions of the theoretical model (e.g. Ericsson et al., 1993; Ericsson, 1996; Ericsson & Lehmann, 1996) addressed this problem by focusing on the role of *deliberate practice*. This term refers to practice activities that aim at maximizing improvement; deliberate practice is conceived of as a highly structured activity that requires effort and is not inherently enjoyable. According to Ericsson and colleagues, individuals are motivated to engage in deliberate practice only because practice improves performance, not because of monetary reward.

Other constraints inherent in the attainment of exceptional performance concern resources, effort, and motivation. In many cases, it has been shown that parental support is a major variable, and that extraordinary commitments by parents may be necessary to cope with the demands (cf. Bloom, 1985b). Further, as deliberate practice requires effort, fatigue is a frequent result; the success of deliberate practice seems to depend on a careful balance of intensive practice and recovery; disregard of recovery may result in maladaptation, injury, and even failure. Finally, as deliberate practice is not inherently enjoyable, motivation has to be given special attention; the loss of motivation can have different causes from problems with external support to temporary stagnation of performance quality. These issues are more pertinent to the initial stages of preparation and may lose their importance when individuals get more involved in a domain. As noted by Ericsson et al. (1993), at this point the motivation to practice becomes closely connected to the goal of becoming an expert performer and integrated into daily routines.

The importance of deliberate practice for attaining expert performance was first demonstrated by Ericsson et al. (1993), who used diaries and interview procedures to study how three groups of elite, adult violinists differing in levels of musical performance spent their daily lives. Whereas the top performance group played at an international level, the second best group was top-rated at the national level; the third group consisted of gifted violonists enrolled in a teacher education program. The musicians in the top performance group were found to spend more time in deliberate practice;

they had spent more practice hours per week than the violinists of the two other groups during early adolescence. From a retrospective estimate of practice, Ericsson et al. (1993) calculated the number of hours of deliberate practice that the different groups of musicians had accumulated until the age of 20. Whereas the best musicians had spent more than 10,000 hours of practice, the number of practice hours for the two less accomplished groups was about 7,500 and 5,000, respectively. The fact that the best violinists were also found to nap more in the afternoon than did the other groups was attributed to the effects of the greater intensity of practice. Since the early work of Ericsson and colleagues, several other studies have found a consistent relation between performance and amount and quality of deliberate practice (cf. Charness, Krampe & Mayr, 1996; Sloboda, 1996; Howe, Davidson & Sloboda, 1998).

One controversial issue emphasized in most of the more recent publications on effects of deliberate practice concerns the explanation of individual differences in expert performances. The core message forwarded by Ericsson and colleagues (as well as by Howe et al.) is that these differences should not be attributed to individual differences in natural, innate (i.e. mainly genetically-based) abilities. Instead, it is argued that expertise has to be conceived of as the result of extensive and intensive practice activities, and that individual differences in ultimate performance can be accounted for by differential amounts of past and current levels of practice. The claim is that once individuals have started deliberate practice, it is virtually impossible to distinguish the role of natural, innate ability from that of acquired skill in their current level of performance. According to Ericsson and colleagues, it is not the innate talent but rather the *perception* of talent that motivates parents to invest time and money to support deliberate practice.

The theoretical framework developed by Ericsson and colleagues seems to account for the causes of exceptional performance. However, the empirical evidence described above mostly consists of cross-sectional studies employing correlational data and are based on retrospective estimates of past behavior and interview data obtained from adults. Prospective studies carried out with child experts and novices may add substantially to our knowledge about the origins and determinants of exceptional performance, particularly as far as the role of domain knowledge and basic abilities is concerned. As a consequence, the empirical evidence on determinants of exceptional performance based on cross-sectional as well as longitudinal developmental studies with child experts and novices will be summarized next.

Studies with Child Experts and Novices

Most developmental studies using the expert/novice paradigm focused on the impact of domain-specific

169

knowledge on memory. In the field of memory development, numerous studies conducted during the past two decades have demonstrated the importance of the knowledge base for various aspects of memory performance (for reviews see Chi & Ceci, 1987; Schneider, 1993; Bjorklund & Schneider, 1996; Schneider & Pressley, 1997). According to many developmental researchers, the knowledge base seems to be one of the crucial sources of memory development in childhood and adolescence, probably outweighing other relevant factors such as capacity, strategies, or metamemory (cf. Bjorklund, 1990; Siegler, 1996). Although the number of developmental studies based on the expert/novice paradigm is still small, compared to the number of studies on expertise with adults, the findings have attracted much attention in the developmental literature. In the next section, developmental studies focusing on the role of knowledge will be presented first, followed by those studies that explored the importance of basic ability operating in concert with a knowledge base.

Developmental studies exploring the impact of domain knowledge on performance

From a developmental perspective, the major advantage of the expert/novice paradigm is that knowledge and chronological age are not necessarily confounded: it is not only possible to recruit adult chess novices but also to find young chess experts for experimental studies. The classic developmental study was conducted by Chi (1978) who recruited experienced and inexperienced chess players and gave them Chase and Simon's chessboard reconstruction task (see above). A most interesting result of this research was that subjects' knowledge correlated negatively with age: Chi found that the children's short-term memory for chess positions was superior to that of the adults. When dealing with a domain (i.e. digits) that adults were more familiar with, typical adult superiority in short-term memory capacity could be demonstrated for the memory span control task. Chi concluded from her results that short-term memory capacity was not inherently a function of the subjects' age, but rather of their knowledge.

From a methodological point of view, both the small sample size of Chi's study and the fact that only two of the four possible groups (i.e. child and adult experts and novices) were included, called for a replication and extension of Chi's work. Two subsequent developmental studies on chess expertise (Roth, 1983; Schneider, Gruber, Gold & Opwis, 1993) found supportive evidence. Roth (1983) did not assess memory performance but tested child and adult experts and novices on a chessboard comparison task. The magnitude of the knowledge effect was sufficient to eliminate any significant differences between child and adult experts. Further, the knowledge effect accounted for between-age group differences in that child experts

outperformed adult novices. Thus Roth's findings for the area of perceptual speed seem to validate Chi's results obtained for short-term memory processes.

Schneider et al. (1993) demonstrated that the more a memory task could be mediated by knowledge of chess, the greater the advantage of child and adult experts relative to novices. Groups of child and adult experts and novices (20 participants per group) were compared on various chessboard and control board reconstruction tasks which included both replications and extensions of Chi's original work. The major extension concerned a procedure that aimed at identifying possible sources of the experts' superior memory performance. Schneider et al. believed that several aspects, such as the experts' greater familiarity with the constellation of chess pieces on the board (i.e. meaning of constellations), and their greater familiarity with the characteristics of the chessboard (i.e. geometrical pattern, form and color of chess pieces), all contributed to superior performance. They expected all these factors to be effective in the meaningful chessboard reconstruction task. It was expected that the effects of expertise on performance would be considerably smaller (but still significant) in the random board reconstruction task because only familiarity with the basic characteristics of the chessboard was assumed to be greater for the experts, as compared to the novices. Finally, no performance differences between experts and novices were expected for a control task that required the reconstruction of wooden pieces on a board that had little in common with a chessboard.

The results of the study basically confirmed these assumptions; similar to the findings by Roth (1983), no performance differences between adult and child experts were found. Expert/novice differences on the chessboard reconstruction task were most pronounced for the meaningful chess positions, and considerably smaller but still significant for the random board positions. In accord with their hypothesis, Schneider et al. found that experts and novices did not differ in immediate reconstruction of items on the control board. They concluded from this finding that experts' performance on the chessboard reconstruction tasks is facilitated by the two context factors described above; probably due to these factors, experts are able to process information faster and in larger semantic units.

The results were inconsistent with those by Chi (1978) and also Chase and Simon (1973) in that no pronounced expert/novice differences in chunking were observed based on inter-response latency measures. The analysis of videotapes suggested qualitative differences in the reconstruction strategies used by the expert and novice groups. Although most experts seemed to start with the reconstruction of specific meaningful units, the novices focused on aspects such as color of pieces or specific positions on the board. From a developmental perspective, it seems particularly interesting that no qualitative differences in the strategies of the child and adult experts were detected. Regardless of age, however, qualitative differences between experts and novices were found for a chunking measure called the 'collective reconstruction index'. That is, most experts not only picked up chess pieces in a similar order when reconstructing the meaningful chess positions, but also created similar patterns ('chunks'); there were no similar effects for the novices. Thus, the chess studies provided evidence that rich domain knowledge enables a child expert to perform like an adult expert and better than an adult novice, showing the disappearance or even reversal of usual developmental trends.

The importance of practice was illustrated in a follow-up study of the Schneider et al. (1993) chess experiment (Gruber, Renkl & Schneider, 1994); in that study, children were presented with the same chessboard reconstruction tasks they had worked on three years earlier. The most interesting finding was that those children who had lost their expert status because of lack of interest and motivation reconstructed fewer chess positions from memory than those children who had shifted from novice to expert status.

Superior memory performance of child experts has not only been demonstrated in the domain of chess, but also of dinosaurs (Chi & Koeske, 1983), 'Star Wars' (Means & Voss, 1985), and sports such as baseball (Recht & Leslie, 1988) and soccer (Schneider, Körkel & Weinert, 1989, 1990). For instance, Schneider et al. (1989, 1990) proved that the reversal of the usual age effect could be demonstrated for text learning. In this study, about 500 third-, fifth- and seventh-graders were presented with a story about a soccer game, with the participants classifiable as soccer experts and novices. The expected differences between experts and novices were especially evident in the recall and comprehension of the soccer-related passage. Again, a reversal of developmental trends was demonstrated in that third-grade experts recalled significantly more text units than both fifth- and seventh-grade novices; moreover, a re-analysis of the data revealed qualitative differences in the way the soccer-related passage was recalled (Körkel & Schneider, 1992). Whereas experts of all ages recalled more important than unimportant aspects of the text, the soccer novices recalled as much important as unimportant text information, regardless of age. Taken together, the findings from the developmental studies on chess expertise corroborate those obtained from studies dealing with expert/novice differences in adults in that performance differences can be attributed to both quantitative and qualitative differences in information processing.

The developmental studies on expertise discussed above have all demonstrated the rapid development of domain-specific knowledge in child experts and its close relationship to performance in the domain of interest. With the exception of the soccer studies,

however, the variable of ability differences was not included in the design; as a matter of fact, only a small number of developmental studies considered the impact of both intelligence and domain knowledge on performance. These studies will be summarized next.

Developmental Studies Exploring the Impact of Aptitude and Knowledge on Performance

The assumption that domain-specific expertise can compensate for low overall ability on domain-related cognitive processing was first confirmed in studies that focused on adult populations. For example, Ceci & Liker (1986) demonstrated that adults with IQs in the 80s were capable of complex classification and reasoning processes when the stimuli were highly familiar. Walker (1987) compared high- and low-aptitude adults who were either baseball experts or novices; when presented with a baseball text passage, low-aptitude/high knowledge subjects recalled more than high-aptitude/low knowledge subjects.

Schneider et al. (1989, 1990) proved that this pattern of findings could be generalized to their child soccer experts and novices. When the samples of experts and novices were further subdivided into subgroups of high- and low-aptitude children, neither a single effect was found for psychometric intelligence, nor were there any interactions. This finding was stable over time: when the same children were retested one year later, neither main effects for intelligence nor any significant interactions were found. All in all, the findings of this study suggest that rich domain-specific knowledge can compensate for low overall aptitude on domain-related cognitive tasks. A similar conclusion was drawn by Ericsson et al. (1993) and Howe et al. (1998) from their research on adult expertise. Thus research on exceptional performance in adults and developmental studies on text processing in child experts and novices lead to similar insights, as far as the role of basic abilities is concerned.

Although the evidence seems impressive, findings from more recent studies indicate that some qualification is in order. For instance, aptitude effects on text recall (in addition to those of expertise) were found in studies on text processing when recall was delayed. This indicates that time of testing may be an important variable (Hall & Edmondson, 1992; Visé, 1997). Moreover, developmental studies by Schneider, Bjorklund and colleagues (Schneider & Bjorklund, 1992; Schneider, Bjorklund & Maier-Brückner, 1996) indicated that findings for text processing could not be easily generalized to other memory paradigms such as sort-recall tasks that explored effects of organizational strategies on memory performance. Schneider & Bjorklund (1992) adopted the basic design used by Schneider et al. (1989). However, instead of assessing text processing, they tested second- and fourth-grade soccer experts' and novices' performance on a sort-recall task dealing with soccer words. In accord with their expectations, Schneider & Bjorklund found significant effects of expertise on recall, thus confirming the results of the previous studies. However, soccer expertise did not modify a significant effect of IQ level, with high-IQ children recalling more than low-IQ children for all contrasts. The results thus demonstrate that domain knowledge played an important role in children's memory, but could not fully eliminate the effects of IQ on sort-recall tasks using domain-related materials. More precisely, although rich domain knowledge seemed to compensate for low aptitude, in that low-aptitude experts performed at the level of high-aptitude novices, its effects were not strong enough to eliminate performance differences between high- and low-aptitude soccer experts.

In a subsequent study, Schneider et al. (1996) confirmed this finding using a within-subject design; in two experiments, both text-recall and sort-recall measures related to the game of soccer were presented to high- and low-aptitude fourth-grade children who were either soccer experts or soccer novices. As a main result, effects of expertise but not of aptitude were found for text recall, whereas both expertise and aptitude predicted performance on the sort-recall task. The authors concluded from this that expertise does reduce but not eliminate the relationship of IQ to memory tasks involving deliberate strategies. Further support for this assumption stems from a study by Gaultney, Bjorklund & Goldstein (1996) who compared strategic memory in highly gifted and intellectually normal children. Gifted children were quicker to identify the advantages of memory strategies, suggesting that one advantage gifted children have on strategic memory tasks is in metamemory.

One problem related to studies with (child) experts is that usually we are not dealing with 'true' (in the sense of exceptional) experts but with knowledgeable individuals who instead may be classified as 'intermediate, semi-experts' or 'subexperts' according to recent classification attempts (cf. Patel & Groen, 1991). To my knowledge, only two developmental studies with 'true' child experts (Horgan & Morgan, 1990; Schneider, Bös & Rieder, 1993; Bös & Schneider, 1997) exist that allow for both a test of the 'deliberate practice' model and the significance of individual differences in basic abilities for subsequent performance. Both samples were exceptional in that they included elite subgroups. Most of the elite child chess players in Horgan & Morgan's study had skill ratings of 1300 and greater (the mean for all US tournament players of all ages is 1500 and the standard deviation is 200). The Bös & Schneider (1997) study referred to a secondary analysis of longitudinal data on the development of about 100 young (10 to 14-year-old) tennis talents that were collected in the late seventies and early eighties. The database included repeated assessments of basic motor abilities, skill-related tests, psychological tests concerning achievement motivation

and concentration skills, as well as interview data focusing on parental support and amount of practice. The careers of most of these tennis talents were very successful, with about 10% of the sample making it to the top 100 in the world (a few players belonged to the top ten players in the world, and two even gained the number one position).

Both studies provided additional evidence for the crucial importance of experience and motivation, thus providing impressive support for the 'deliberate practice' model developed by Anders Ericsson and colleagues. Horgan and Morgan showed that improvement in chess skill was significantly correlated with experience. Using age and pre-test chess ratings as covariates, the authors demonstrated a close relationship between expertise in terms of games played and post-test chess ratings. In sum, the experienced players played more and won more. Similarly, in the longitudinal study of young tennis talents (Schneider Bös & Rieder, 1993; Bös & Schneider, 1997), results of causal modeling procedures showed that parents' support, the amount and intensity of practice, as well as the level of achievement motivation significantly predicted children's tennis rankings several years later (see Schneider, 1997, for a more detailed account on these findings).

What about the impact of basic abilities in these two studies? The elite subsample in the Horgan and Morgan chess study was given two tasks that tapped general abilities (the Raven's Matrices test and a Piagetian task), and one test of domain-specific skill (the Knight's tour). When stepwise regression analyses on post-test scores were carried out for the elite subsample, pre-test chess skill accounted for about 65% of the variance in chess skill at the end of the study. When the Raven's test was added as a predictor, the amount of variance explained in the dependent variable increased to 77%. Another 10% of the variance were accounted for by the addition of numbers of games played. Horgan and Morgan concluded from this finding that both experience and non-verbal intelligence significantly contribute to improvements in chess skill. As the Piagetian task showed no significant correlation with chess skill in the young elite players, it appears that the type of reasoning assessed in general ability tests such as IQ makes an important difference in this regard.

One interesting aspect of the causal model estimated and tested by Schneider et al. (1993) was that although tennis-specific skills and the amount and intensity of practice accounted for most of the variance in children's tennis rankings several years later, the effects of basic motor abilities on tennis performance could not be ignored. That is, when the basic ability construct was omitted from the model, the model no longer fitted the data. Although individual differences in basic motor abilities were not large in this highly selected sample, they made a difference when it came to predicting individual tennis performance.

Taken together, the findings by Horgan & Morgan (1990) and Schneider et al. (1993) basically confirm the theoretical framework developed by Ericsson and colleagues. They all highlight the importance of deliberate practice in developing domain-specific expertise in children. The results provided by Schneider et al. (1993) additionally prove the significance of parental support systems for skill development. However, neither study supports the assumption that individual differences in basic ability can be completely neglected when it comes to predicting the development of expertise.

How to Reach Exceptional Performance: Concluding Remarks on Restrictions of the 'Deliberate Practice' Model and the Need for Alternative Theoretical Approaches

The evidence presented in this chapter clearly indicates that highly gifted children do not necessarily become famous and eminent adults. Although giftedness is usually seen as synonymous with high creativity and professional success, the available research does not support this causal link. In fact, case studies on gifted children, even prodigies, indicate that many of them burn out early, whereas others move on to other areas of interest (cf. Winner, 1996b). More recent research on the development of expertise has shown that exceptional performance is usually based on an extremely rich knowledge base, acquired through a very long lasting process of motivated learning. In order to reach this point, cognitive personality characteristics such as high intellectual ability seem less important than non-cognitive factors such as endurance, dedication, concentration, and motivation. The most important accomplishment of the skilled memory theory was to highlight and demonstrate the relevance of acquired skills in explaining exceptional performance. Later on, the development of the 'deliberate practice' model (cf. Ericsson, 1996, 1998; Howe et al., 1998) provided a framework suitable to describe and explain developmental changes in highly knowledgeable individuals. The developmental evidence clearly supports the assumptions made by Anders Ericsson, Michael Howe and their colleagues that individual differences in the amount of deliberate practice and motivation are key variables for predicting individual differences in the level of expertise in a given domain among high-ability individuals. By and large, my own developmental studies and others conducted in different areas such as soccer, tennis, and chess support the 'deliberate practice' model, thereby underlining the great merit and generalizability of the approach developed by Ericsson, Howe, and colleagues.

Although I can agree with basic assumptions of the deliberate practice model, its position regarding the negligible impact of basic ability differences seems too extreme. See Sternberg (1996), for a sophisticated elaboration on various biases and weaknesses of the expertise approach. One problem with most of the studies on adult expertise was that individual differences in basic intellectual abilities were not explicitly measured. Given the evidence from developmental studies on expertise that took those abilities into account, one is inclined to believe that the impact of individual differences in basic (intellectual) abilities cannot be completely ignored in theoretical models dealing with the acquisition of expertise. Although the evidence provided by Ericsson and colleagues clearly demonstrates the role of motivation, commitment, and hard work, it fails to rule out the possibility that innate talent plays a necessary role in high achievement (Sternberg, 1996; Winner, 1996b).

The impact of aptitude on cognitive performance most clearly shows up in the case of globally gifted children such as Michael Kearney, a child prodigy who has attracted considerable media attention recently because of his outstanding development (see Kearney & Kearney, 1995; Morelock, 1995). The development of a child who first spoke at the age of four months; began reading single words at the age of eight months; and proved the commutative, associative, and identity rules at the age of three years is difficult to explain by the core assumptions of the deliberate practice approach.

Given that prodigies such as Michael do exist and that their number is increasing, the tendency of promoters of the deliberate practice model to either ignore or doubt the existence of such early exceptional performance is not acceptable. In particular, the statement that objective data are not available in such cases (cf. Ericsson, 1998; Howe et al., 1998) can be easily rejected. For instance, Ericsson (1998) questioned the reports on Jonathan Estrada's precocious speaking and reading performance by noting that the data were provided by the parents without any independent testing by scientists. When I contacted Estrada's parents, I was told that family videos about the then one-year-old Jonathan exist that show him reading picture books, and that Jonathan was tested by a child psychologist at the age of two-and-a-half (Mary Estrada, personal communication, August 1, 1999). Although it may be true that many other prodigies have not been tested at the extremely young age at which they started to speak or read, there is simply no reason to doubt parents' retrospective accounts. As I noted in an earlier comment on the issue (Schneider, 1998), it is difficult to understand why such reports should be less reliable than the recollections of adult musicians concerning their early practice habits, information that is taken as valid by the promoters of the 'deliberate practice' approach.

Another point frequently raised by researchers questioning the impact of genetically-based influences on accelerated development is that rapid cognitive development in the early years is not 'innate' but mainly due to the impact of supportive environmental conditions. Although careful explorations of the role of family context in the case of profoundly gifted children show that family support is indeed important (see Morelock, 1995, for an impressive documentation), there is no reason to believe that early cognitive acceleration is mainly caused by parental stimulation. As noted by several researchers, one typical feature of highly gifted children is their obsessive desire to master a domain (Feldman, 1991; Morelock & Feldman, 1991). It is difficult to attribute their persistence, drive, and rage to learn and master solely to the specific conditions and supportive features of their environment. Extremely gifted children such as Michael Kearney or Jonathan Estrada can be characterized as stimulus seekers: if they are not sufficiently stimulated, they will produce stimulation for themselves with activity (Winner, 1996a).

Also, the fact that profoundly gifted children maintain their rapid development is well documented and can easily be proven (e.g. Kearney & Kearney, 1995). For instance, Michael Kearney is listed in the Guiness Book of World Records four times: (1) as the youngest person in history to receive a high school diploma (at age 6 years 5 months); (2) as the youngest person in history to enter college (at age 6 years 7 months); (3) as the youngest person in history to have grduated from college (at age 10 years 4 months), and (4) as the youngest person in history to receive a Master's degree (in biochemistry from Middle Tennessee Southern University at the age of 14 years in August, 1998). These impressive accomplishments and the fact that he is a top expert in several domains is difficult to reconcile with the 'ten-year rule' and the environmentalist position of the 'deliberate practice' approach. This is not to question the overall validity and utility of this approach, but just to emphasize the need to qualify and restrict its applicability.

Given that individual differences in basic ability cannot be completely ignored, I suggested a modification of the theoretical framework of expert performance (see Schneider, 1997). I proposed that two different models of exceptional performance explicitly consider the interplay between domain knowledge and basic abilities: a 'threshold' model and a 'partial compensation model'. The 'threshold' model can be described as follows: If the ability parameter of an individual person is close to or beyond a critical or 'threshold' value of ability (typically assumed to be slightly above average), then individual differences in non-cognitive variables such as commitment, endurance, concentration, or motivation determine peak performance. In other words, if the ability score of a given person exceeds a certain threshold value, it does not matter at all whether this individual is gifted or of only normal intelligence. Although this model appears intuitively plausible, one of its problems lies in the definition of critical or 'threshold' scores for different domains (cf. Weinert, 1992). The boundaries may be well above average for domains/tasks where complex problem-solving activities and strategy utilization are necessary components, and may be clearly below average for less complex domains or tasks that mainly rely on automatic processes (e.g. pattern recognition processes or text recall). Another problem with the 'threshold' model is that it cannot readily explain why basic abilities contributed to performance differences among the two elite subsamples described by Bös and Schneider (1997) and Horgan & Morgan (1990). In the light of these data, it appears that the 'partial compensation' model seems more appropriate, indicating that expertise reduces the contribution of general ability more and more as the amount of domain knowledge increases. Although the available developmental evidence supports such a view, clearly more research is needed to prove the validity of this theoretical approach.

Acknowledgments

I am grateful to Ellen Winner for valuable suggestions and to Martha Morelock for providing me with her impressive doctoral dissertation. My knowledge about profoundly gifted children was greatly enhanced through communications with Mary Estrada as well as Michael and Kevin Kearney. Last but not least, thanks are due to David Bjorklund for his helpful comments on a previous version of the chapter.

References

Ackerman, P. C. (1987). Individual differences in skill learning: an integration of psychometric and information processing perspectives. *Psychological Bulletin*, **102**, 3–27.

Ackerman, P. L. (1988). Determinants of individual differences during skill acquisition: Cognitive abilities and information processing. *Journal of Experimental Psychology: General*, **117**, 288–318.

Anderson, J. R. (1982). Acquisition of cognitive skill. *Psychological Review*, **89**, 369–406.

Anzai, Y. (1991). Learning and use of representations for physics expertise. In: K. A. Ericsson & J. Smith (Eds), *Toward a Theory of General Expertise – Prospects and Limits* (pp. 64–92). Cambridge: Cambridge University Press.

Bjorklund, D. F. (1990) (Ed.). *Children's strategies: contemporary views of cognitive development*. Hillsdale, NJ: Erlbaum.

Bjorklund, D. F. & Schneider, W. (1996). The interaction of knowledge, aptitude, and strategies in children's memory performance. In: H. Reese (Ed.), *Advances in Child Development and Behavior* (Vol. 26, pp. 59–89). New York: Academic Press.

Bloom, B. S. (1985a) (Ed.). *Developing talent in young people*. New York: Ballantine Books.

Bloom, B. S. (1985b). Generalizations about talent development. In: B. S. Bloom (Ed.), *Developing Talent in Young People* (pp. 507–549). New York: Ballantine Books.

Bös, K. & Schneider, W. (1997). *Talententwicklung im Tennis: Eine Reanalyse der Heidelberger Längsschnittstudie* [The development of tennis talents: a re-analysis of the Heidelberg longitudinal study]. Schorndorf: Hofmann.

Ceci, S. J. & Liker, J. (1986). A day at the races: the study of IQ, expertise, and cognitive complexity. *Journal of Experimental Psychology: General*, **115**, 225–266.

Charness, N. (1991). Expertise in chess: the balance between knowledge and search. In: K. A. Ericsson & J. Smith (Eds), *Toward a General Theory of Expertise – Prospects and Limits* (pp. 39–63). Cambridge: Cambridge University Press.

Charness, N., Krampe, R. T. & Mayr, U. (1996). The role of practice and coaching in entrepreneurial skill domains: an international comparison of life-span chess skill acquisition. In: K. A. Ericsson (Ed.), *The Road to Excellence: the Acquisition of Expert Performance in the Arts and Sciences, Sports and Games* (pp. 51–80). Mahwah, NJ: Lawrence Erlbaum Associates.

Chase, W. G. & Ericsson, K. A. (1982). Skill and working memory. In: G. H. Bower (Ed.), *The Psychology of Learning and Motivation* (Vol. 16, pp. 1–58). New York: Academic Press.

Chase, W. G. & Simon, H. A. (1973). The mind's eye in chess. In: W. G. Chase (Ed.), *Visual Information Processing* (pp. 215–281). New York: Academic Press.

Chi, M. T. H., Feltovich, P. J. & Glaser, R. (1981). Categorization and representation of physics problems by experts and novices. *Cognitive Science*, **5**, 121–152.

Chi, M. T. H. (1978). Knowledge structures and memory development. In: R. S. Siegler (Ed.), *Children's Thinking: What Develops?* (pp. 73–96). Hillsdale, NJ: Erlbaum.

Chi, M. T. H. & Ceci, S. J. (1987). Content knowledge: Its role, representation, and restructuring in memory development. In: H. W. Reese (Ed.), *Advances in Child Development and Behavior* (Vol. 20, pp. 91–142). Orlando: Academic Press.

Chi, M. T. H. & Koeske, R. D.(1983). Network representation of a child's dinosaur knowledge. *Developmental Psychology*, **19**, 29–39.

Cox, C. M. (1926). *Genetic studies of genius: the early mental traits of three hundred geniuses* (Vol. 2). Stanford: Stanford University Press.

de Groot, A. (1978). *Thought and choice in chess*. The Hague: Mouton. (Original work published in 1946).

Elder, G. H., Pavalko, E. K. & Hastings, T. J. (1991). Talent, history, and the fulfillment of promise. *Psychiatry*, **54**, 251–267.

Elo, A. E. (1978). *The rating of chess players, past and present*. New York: Arco.

Ericsson, K. A. (1996). The acquisition of expert performance: an introduction to some of the issues. In: K. A. Ericsson (Ed.), *The Road to Excellence—the Acquisition of Expert Performance in the Arts and Science, Sports and Games* (pp. 1–50). Mahwah, NJ: Lawrence Erlbaum Associates.

Ericsson, K. A. (1998). The scientific study of expert levels of performance: general implications for optimal learning and creativity. *High Ability Studies*, **9**, 75–100.

Ericsson, K. A. & Charness, N. (1994). Expert performance: its structure and acquisition. *American Psychologist*, **49**, 725–747.

Ericsson, K. A., Krampe, R. Th. & Tesch-Römer, C. (1993). The role of deliberate practice in the acquisition of expert performance. *Psychological Review*, **100**, 363–406.

Ericsson, K. A. & Lehmann, A. (1996). Expert and exceptional performance: evidence on maximal adaptations on task constraints. *Annual Review of Psychology*, **47**, 273–305.

Ericsson, K. A. & Smith, J. (1991). Prospects and limits of the empirical study of expertise: An introduction. In: K. A. Ericsson & J. Smith (Eds), *Toward a General Theory of Expertise: Prospects and Limits* (pp. 1–38). Cambridge: Cambridge University Press.

Ericsson, K. A. & Staszewski, J. J. (1989). Skilled memory and expertise: Mechanisms of exceptional performance. In: D. Klahr & K. Kotovsky (Eds), *Complex Information Processing: the Impact of Herbert A. Simon* (pp. 235–267). Hillsdale, NJ: Erlbaum.

Feldman, D. H. (1984). A follow-up of subjects scoring above 180 IQ in Terman's 'Genetic studies of genius'. *Exceptional Children*, **50**, 518–523.

Feldman, D. H. (with Goldsmith, L.T.) (1991). *Nature's gambit: child prodigies and the development of human potential*. New York: Teachers College Press.

Fitts, P. & Posner, M. I. (1967). *Human performance*. Belmont, CA: Brooks/Cole.

Gaultney, J. F., Bjorklund, D. F. & Goldstein, D. (1996). To be young, gifted, and strategic: Advantages for memory performance. *Journal of Experimental Child Psychology*, **61**, 43–66.

Gruber, H., Renkl, A. & Schneider, W. (1994). Expertise und Gedächtnisentwicklung: Längsschnittliche Befunde aus der Domäne Schach [expertise and memory development: longitudinal findings from the domain of chess]. *Zeitschrift für Entwicklungspsychologie und Pädagogische Psychologie*, **26**, 53–70.

Hall, V. C. & Edmondson, B. (1992). Relative importance of aptitude and prior domain knowledge on immediate and delayed post-tests. *Journal of Educational Psychology*, **84**, 219–223.

Hastorf, A. H. (1997). Lewis Terman's longitudinal study of the intellectually gifted: early research, recent investigations and the future. *Gifted and Talented International*, **12**, 3–7.

Heller, K. A. (1991). The nature and development of giftedness: a longitudinal study. *European Journal for High Ability*, **2**, 174–188.

Hollingworth, L. S. (1942). *Children above 180 IQ (Stanford–Binet): their origin and development*. Yonkers-on Hudson, NY: World Book.

Horgan, D. D. & Morgan, D. (1990). Chess expertise in children. *Applied Cognitive Psychology*, **4**, 109–128.

Howe, M. J. A. (1982). Biographical evidence and the development of outstanding individuals. *American Psychologist*, **37**, 1071–1082.

Howe, M. J. A., Davidson, J. W. & Sloboda, J. A. (1998). Innate talents: reality or myth? *Behavioral and Brain Sciences*, **21**, 399–407.

Kearney, K. & Kearney, C. (1995). *Accidental genius*. Murfreesboro, TN: Woodshed Press.

Körkel, J. & Schneider, W. (1992). Domain-specific versus meta-cognitive knowledge effects on text recall and comprehension. In: M. Carretero, M. Pope, R.-J. Simons & J. I. Pozo (Eds), *Learning and Instruction—European Research in an International Context* (Vol. 3, pp. 311–324). Oxford: Pergamon Press.

Krogius, N. (1976). *Psychology in chess*. New York: RHM Press.

Lesgold, A. M. (1984). Acquiring expertise. In: J. A. Anderson & S. M. Kosslyn (Eds), *Tutorials in Learning and Memory* (pp. 39–60). San Francisco, CA: Freeman.

Means, M. & Voss, J. (1985). Star wars: a developmental study of expert and novice knowledge structures. *Memory and Language*, **24**, 746–757.

Morelock, M. J. (1995). *The profoundly gifted child in family context*. Unpublished doctoral dissertation, Tufts University.

Morelock, M. J. & Feldman, D. H. (1991). Extreme precocity. In: N. Colangelo & G. A. Davis (Eds), *Handbook of Gifted Education* (pp. 347–364). Boston: Allyn and Bacon.

Morris, P. E., Tweedy, M. & Gruneberg, M. M. (1985). Interest, knowledge and the memorization of soccer scores. *British Journal of Psychology*, **76**, 415–425.

Newell, A. & Rosenbloom, P. S. (1981). Mechanisms of skill acquisition and the law of practice. In: J. R. Anderson (Ed.), *Cognitive Skills and Their Acquisition* (pp. 1–55). Hillsdale, NJ: Erlbaum.

Oden, M. H. (1968). The fulfilment of promise: forty-year follow-up of the Terman gifted groups. *Genetic Psychological Monographs*, **77**, 3–93.

Ornstein, P. A. & Naus, M. (1985). Effects of the knowledge base on children's memory strategies. In: H. W. Reese (Ed.), *Advances in Child Development and Behavior* (Vol. 19). New York: Academic Press.

Patel, V. L. & Groen, G. J. (1991). The general and specific nature of medical expertise: A critical look. In: K. A. Ericsson & J. Smith (Eds), *Toward a General Theory of Expertise—Prospects and Limits* (pp. 93–125). Cambridge: Cambridge University Press.

Recht, D. R. & Leslie, L. (1988). Effect of prior knowledge on good and poor readers'memory of text. *Journal of Educational Psychology*, **80**, 16–20.

Renzulli, J. S. (1986). The three-ring conception of giftedness: a developmental model for creative productivity. In: R. J. Sternberg & J. E. Davidson (Eds), *Conceptions of Giftedness* (pp. 53–92). Cambridge: Cambridge University Press.

Roe, A. (1952). *The making of a scientist*. New York: Dodd, Mead.

Roe, A. (1953). A psychological study of eminent psychologists and anthropologists, and a comparison with biological and physical scientists. *Psychological Monographs: General and Applied*, **67**, 1–55.

Rost, D. H. (1993) (Ed.). *Lebensumweltanalyse hochbegabter Kinder* [Analysis of environmental factors influencing gifted children]. Göttingen: Hogrefe.

Roth, C. (1983). Factors affecting developmental changes in the speed of processing. *Journal of Experimental Child Psychology*, **35**, 509–528.

Samson, G. E., Grane, M. E., Weinstein, T. & Walberg, H. J. (1984). Academic and occupational performance: a quantitative synthesis. *American Educational Research Journal*, **21**, 311–321.

Schneider, W. (1993). Domain-specific knowlege and memory performance in children. *Educational Psychology Review*, **5**, 257–273.

Schneider, W. (1997). The impact of expertise on performance: illustrations from developmental research on memory and sports. *High Ability Studies*, **8**, 7–18.

Schneider, W. (1998). Innate talent or deliberate practice as determinants of exceptional performance: Are we asking the right questions? *Behavioral and Brain Sciences*, **21**, 423–424.

Schneider, W. & Bjorklund, D. F. (1992). Expertise, aptitude, and strategic remembering. *Child Development*, **63**, 461–473.

Schneider, W., Bjorklund, D. F. & Maier-Brückner, W. (1996). The effects of expertise and IQ on children's memory: when knowledge is, and when it is not enough. *International Journal of Behavioral Development*, **19**, 73–96.

Schneider, W., Bös, K. & Rieder, H. (1993). Leistungsprognose bei jugendlichen Spitzensportlern [Performance prediction in adolescent top tennis players]. In: J. Beckmann, H. Strang & E. Hahn (Eds), *Aufmerksamkeit und Energetisierung*. Göttingen: Hogrefe.

Schneider, W., Gruber, H., Gold, A. & Opwis, K. (1993). Chess expertise and memory for chess positions in children and adults. *Journal of Experimental Child Psychology*, **56**, 328–349.

Schneider, W., Körkel, J. & Weinert, F. E. (1989). Domain-specific knowledge and memory performance: a comparison of high- and low-aptitude children. *Journal of Educational Psychology*, **81**, 306–312.

Schneider, W., Körkel, J. & Weinert, F. E. (1990). Expert knowledge, general abilities, and text processing. In: W. Schneider & F. E. Weinert (Eds), *Interactions Among Aptitudes, Strategies, and Knowledge in Cognitive Performance* (pp. 235–251). New York: Springer-Verlag.

Schneider, W. & Pressley, M. (1997). *Memory development between two and twenty*. Mahwah, NJ: Lawrence Erlbaum Associates.

Sears, R. R. (1984). The Terman Gifted Children Study. In: S. A. Mednick, M. Harway & K. M. Finello (Eds), *Handbook of Longitudinal Research* (Vol. 1). New York: Praeger.

Siegler, R. S. (1996). *Children's thinking (3rd ed.)*. Englewood Cliffs, NJ: Prentice-Hall.

Siegler, R. S. & Kotovsky, K. (1986). Two levels of giftedness: Shall ever the twain meet? In: R. J. Sternberg & J. E. Davidson (Eds), *Conceptions of Giftedness*. New York: Cambridge University.

Simon, H. A. & Chase, W. G. (1973). Skill in chess. *American Scientist*, **61**, 394–403.

Sloboda, J. A. (1996). The acquisition of musical performance expertise: Deconstructing the 'talent' account of individual differences in musical expressivity. In: K. A. Ericsson (Ed.), *The Road to Excellence—the Acquisition of Expert Performance in the Arts and Sciences, Sports and Games* (pp.107–126). Mahwah, NJ: Lawrence Erlbaum Associates.

Sosniak, L. A. (1985). Learning to be a concert pianist. In: B. S. Bloom (Ed.), *Developing Talent in Young People* (pp. 19–67). New York: Ballantine Books.

Sternberg, R. J. (1996). Costs of expertise. In: K. A. Ericsson (Ed.), *The Road to Excellence—the Acquisition of Expert Performance in the Arts and Sciences, Sports and Games*. Mahwah, NJ: Erlbaum Associates.

Subotnik, R. F. & Arnold, K. D.(1994). *Beyond Terman: contemporary longitudinal studies of giftedness and talent*. Norwood, NJ: Ablex.

Subotnik, R. F., Kassan, L., Summers, E. & Wasser, A. (1993). *Genius revisited. High IQ-children grown up*. Norwood, NJ: Ablex.

Terman, L. M. (1954). The discovery and encouragement of exceptional talent. *American Psychologist*, **9**, 221–230.

Visé, M. (1997). Metagedächtnis, Vorwissen und textbezo-genes Lernen: Zur Entwicklung der kurz- und langfristigen Gedächtnisleistung bei Kindern [metamemory, domain knowledge, and text learning: the development of short-term- and long-term memory in school children]. Lengerich, Berlin: Pabst Publishers.

Voss, J. F., Vesonder, G. T. & Spilich, G. J. (1980). Text generation and recall by high-knowledge and low-knowledge individuals. *Journal of Verbal Learning and Verbal Behavior*, **19**, 651–667.

Walker, C. H. (1987). Relative importance of domain knowledge and overall aptitude on acquisition of domain-related information. *Cognition and Instruction*, **4**, 25–42.

Weinert, F. E. (1992). Wird man zum Hochbegabten geboren, entwickelt man sich dahin oder wird man dazu gemacht [Are gifted people born to be gifted, do they develop giftedness, or are they taught to be gifted]. In: E. A. Hany & H. Nickel (Eds), *Begabung und Hochbegabung* (pp. 197–203). Bern: Huber.

Weinert, F. E. & Waldmann, M. R. (1986). How do the gifted think: Intellectual abilities and cognitive processes. In: A. J. Cropley, K. K. Urban, H. Wagner & W. Wieczerkowski (Eds), *Giftedness: a Continuing Worldwide Challenge* (pp.49–64). New York: Trillium Press.

Winner, E. (1996a). *Gifted children: myths and realities*. New York: BasicBooks.

Winner, E. (1996b). The rage to master: the decisive role of talent in the visual arts. In: K. A. Ericsson (Ed.), *The Road to Excellence—the Acquisition of Expert Performance in the Art and Sciences, Sports and Games* (pp. 271–301). Mahwah, NY: Erlbaum Associates.

Issues in the Cognitive Development of Exceptionally and Profoundly Gifted Individuals

Miraca U. M. Gross

The University of New South Wales, Sydney, Australia

Introduction

In the first edition of this handbook, Gross (1993b) reviewed a substantial body of research on three groups of extremely gifted individuals: (a) adults who made exceptional contributions to their fields, (b) historical studies of children whose remarkable academic achievements implied cognitive ability substantially beyond the norm, and (c) children who scored at or above IQ 160 on tests of cognitive ability.

This chapter will focus specifically on the third of these groups and will present the key research, particularly from the last decade, on the cognitive development of this population of extremely gifted children and adolescents. This chapter, therefore, should be viewed as an addendum to Gross's chapter in the first edition, building on the findings introduced within it.

Early Studies of Exceptionally and Profoundly Gifted Children

Many of the difficulties experienced in school by extremely gifted students arise from the lack of awareness, among teachers, of the enormous range of ability within the intellectually gifted population. Whereas teachers of impaired hearing or intellectually disabled students are trained to respond to different levels or degrees of the handicapping condition, teachers of the gifted are rarely given such training. Consequently, many educators assume that the intellectually gifted are a relatively homogeneous group—and, for students in the higher ranges of this group, this misconception frequently leads to misidentification, seriously inadequate curriculum provision, and inappropriate grade placement (Gross, 1993a).

Educators working with hearing impaired students recognise four levels of impairment—mild, moderate, severe and profound (Moores, 1987) while, similarly, the field of special education recognises at least three levels of intellectual disability. The level and type of intervention prescribed for hearing impaired or intellectually disabled students are dictated by the degree of severity of the condition (Payne & Patton, 1981). Few educators would expect a severely or profoundly deaf student to cope, in the regular classroom, with the relatively modest degree of intervention required by the child with a mild or moderate hearing loss. Yet exceptionally and profoundly gifted students are regularly placed in the heterogeneous classroom without access to other students who share their abilities and interests and with little or no curriculum differentiation.

Silverman (1989, p. 71) defines the highly gifted as "those whose advancement is significantly beyond the norm of the gifted." It is important to note, however, that by 'advancement' Silverman refers to aptitude or potential, rather than performance. Research on the school performance of the highly gifted suggests that the considerable majority of these children are required to work, in the regular classroom, at levels several years below their tested achievement (Hollingworth, 1926, 1942; Silverman, 1993; Gross, 1993a). Within the broader classification of 'highly gifted', however, are sub-categories of students with increasingly differentiated cognitive characteristics, and more specific terminologies have been developed to classify and describe these children.

Intellectually gifted children can be classified as mildly, moderately, highly, exceptionally, and profoundly gifted. Levels of intellectual giftedness, as defined by IQ ranges, and the level of prevalence of such children in the general population, appear as follows:

Level	IQ range	Prevalence
Mildly (or basically) gifted	115 – 129	1: – 1:40
Moderately gifted	130 – 144	1:40 – 1:1000
Highly gifted	145 – 159	1:1000 – 1:10,000
Exceptionally gifted	160 – 179	1:10,000 – 1:1 million
Profoundly gifted	180 +	Fewer than 1:1 million

As discussed in Gross (1993b), the literature on exceptional children over the last century contains a wealth of individual case studies of children whose academic achievements imply cognitive development far in advance of what might be expected for their age. Unfortunately, however, the majority of the earlier studies provide no specific information on the children's intellectual status.

Several larger-scale group studies which have compared children of IQ 160+ with moderately or highly gifted age-peers have focused on aspects of psychosocial development but have paid much less attention to cognitive or academic issues (see, for example, Gallagher, 1958; Selig, 1959; Sheldon, 1959; DeHaan & Havighurst, 1961; Barbe, 1964; Janos, 1983) These, and other studies have made extremely important contributions to our knowledge of the affective development of this population, and have been discussed in Gross (1993b) but will not be outlined in this review of cognitive studies.

The most rigorously conducted and influential study of profoundly gifted children was undertaken by Hollingworth (1942) who analysed current and previous conceptions of intellectual giftedness, described 19 children of IQ 180 and above reported by previous researchers, and described in great detail the intellectual, academic and social development of 12 New York children of IQ 180 and above whom she herself had been studying over 23 years.

Hollingworth found significant differences in both the cognitive and affective development of moderately and extremely gifted children. She defined the IQ range 125–155 as 'socially optimal intelligence' (Hollingworth, 1926) and noted that while children scoring within this range were self-confident, out-going individuals who won the confidence and friendship of classmates, children above IQ 160, were so different from their age-peers that, despite deliberate underachievement for peer acceptance, they frequently suffered from social isolation (Hollingworth, 1931) Hollingworth argued that to ensure the optimisation of their academic potential, as well as healthy social adjustment, extremely gifted children should be placed in full-time grouping with intellectual peers. "In the ordinary elementary school situation, children of IQ 140 waste half their time. Those above IQ 170 waste practically all their time" (Hollingworth, 1942, p. 299).

Silverman and Kearney (1989, 1992) have undertaken longitudinal studies of children in Denver and Maine who score above IQ 170 finding, as did Hollingworth, that these children have unusually advanced cognitive and affective development. Rogers and Silverman (in press) are engaged in possibly the largest-scale study of extremely gifted children yet undertaken—a comprehensive analysis of the cognitive and psychosocial development of 241 children of IQ 160+. Gross has been engaged since 1986 in a longitudinal study of Australian children scoring IQ 160+, which will continue at least until the children reach adulthood (Gross, 1986, 1992, 1993a, 1994, 1995, 1998a; Gross, in press (a); Gross & Start, 1990). Morelock is engaged in a longitudinal study of children of IQ 180 which includes six children of IQ 200 (Morelock, 1995); findings from all these studies are reported in this chapter.

Exceptionally and profoundly gifted students appear very rarely in the school population; this accounts, in part, for educators' lack of awareness of their needs and characteristics. A contributing cause, however, has been a serious neglect of these groups of children by the research community. Much of the empirical research on exceptionally and profoundly gifted children was undertaken in the years between the 1930s and the early 1960s, but the extremely egalitarian ethos of the 1960s and 1970s did not encourage research into the needs of the extremely gifted, and it is only in recent years that we have seen a revival of interest in this population.

Even this belated concern, however, is discouraged by writers such as Savon-Shepin who claims (incorrectly) that "a child with an IQ of 145 is, in fact, much more similar to a child with an IQ of 100, than is a child with a tested IQ of 55" (1994, p. 146), and Richert, who criticises the practice of "designating degrees of giftedness (which) creates implicit hierarchies (and) engenders elitism within programs" (1997, p. 76). Such criticism is unfortunate; there is an urgent need for further sustained observation of the academic, social and emotional development of children whose extraordinary intellectual abilities should qualify them to make significant contributions to the societies in which they live, provided that their youthful potential is permitted to flower into adult productivity.

The broadening of the concept of giftedness over the last 40 years, (see Gagné's discussion in this book) has led us to view giftedness as much more than intellectual precocity, and it would be simplistic to define intellectual giftedness solely in terms of IQ scores. Nonetheless, the intelligence quotient is a useful index of the relationship (and, in the case of the gifted child, the discrepancy) between mental age and chronological age. A moderately gifted 12-year-old with a mental age of 16 and thus an IQ of approximately 133 is 'out of synch' with her age-peers by a matter of four years before she has even passed through elementary school; however her exceptionally gifted age-mate with a mental age of 20 and an IQ of approximately 167 looks across a chasm of eight years from the age at which she is capable of reasoning to the grade level in which she is likely to be placed on the basis of her chronological age. The IQ can assist us in understanding fundamental differences in mental processing between moderately and highly gifted students.

Benbow & Lubinski (1993) note that the top one per

cent of students in almost any distribution of ability or achievement covers as broad a range as that encompassed by the 2nd to the 98th percentile. Goldstein, Stocking & Godfrey (1999) translate this to IQ scores, showing that the range of scores of children in the top 1% on IQ—from 135 to more than 200—is as broad as the range of scores from the 2nd percentile (IQ 64) to the 98th (IQ 132). Indeed, in terms of intellectual capacity alone, the profoundly gifted student of IQ 190 differs from moderately gifted classmates of IQ 130 to an even greater degree than the latter differ from intellectually disabled students of IQ 70. If they are to come anywhere near to maximising their remarkable intellectual and academic potential, extremely gifted students require an educational program which differs significantly in structure, pace and content from that which might be offered to the moderately gifted.

Exceptionally gifted children comprise a population characterised by their scarcity. The incidence of children scoring at or above IQ 160 on the *Stanford– Binet Intelligence Scale (L–M)*, as predicted by the statistical tables, lies somewhere between 1 in 10,000 and 1 in 30,000 (Marland, 1972), while children scoring above IQ 180 are fewer than one in one million. (It should be noted that the *Stanford–Binet Revision IV* is not regarded as appropriate for the measurement of very high levels of cognitive ability and its publishers, Riverside Press, have endorsed the continued use of the *L–M* for gifted assessment pending the imminent publication of the new *Revision V* (Wasserman, 1997). Over the last 70 years, researchers have repeatedly found that the number of children actually identified in the range 160+ far exceeds the theoretical expectations derived from the normal curve of distribution (Terman, 1925; Burt, 1968; Robinson, 1981; Silverman, 1989; Gross, 1993a); nevertheless, even the most generous over-prediction must acknowledge that these young people comprise an extremely small minority of the child population.

Differences in Cognitive Functioning

Comparative studies of the cognitive functioning of intellectually gifted and non-gifted children have identified significant differences in cognitive style, cognitive development and cognitive strategy selection between the two populations (Rogers, 1986).

Unfortunately very few large-scale comparative studies have been undertaken of differences between the cognitive functioning of moderately and extremely gifted children. A few such studies are reported here; however, as discussed earlier, exceptionally and profoundly gifted children appear rarely, and much of the evidence for significantly superior cognitive functioning in this group comes from single and (occasionally) multiple case studies. Examples of these are presented below and also in the later section on precocious early development in extremely gifted children.

Cognitive Style

In terms of cognitive style, defined by Rogers as "consistencies in the unique manner in which a learner acquires or processes information" (1986, p. 19) research consistently finds that intellectually gifted children prefer to study independently rather than in mixed-ability groups, function best within a modality which combines auditory and kinaesthetic learning (auditory input alone is often too slow because of their more rapid learning pace), are intrinsically rather than extrinsically motivated, and dislike being given responsibility for the learning achievements of classmates (Dunn, Dunn & Price, 1981; Ricca, 1984; Ristow and Edeburn, 1985).

In Australia Gross (1997), comparing the motivational orientation of academically gifted 7th grade students with an unselected population of age-peers, also found the gifted students to be significantly more task-oriented, focusing on the task and strategies to master it rather than on the ego-oriented desire for high grades or academic recognition. Similarly in Canada, Kanevsky (1994), comparing differences between the problem solving strategies used by young children of average ability (mean IQ 104) and those used by highly gifted age-peers (mean IQ 153) found ability-related differences in motivational orientation. Highly gifted children were more likely to display intrinsic motivation in enhancing their enjoyment of the problem-solving exercises by monitoring and maintaining the level of challenge available to them, whereas children of average ability appeared more extrinsically motivated by the researcher's interest in their progress. The Fullerton Study found that intellectually gifted children displayed stronger academic intrinsic motivation at age 7 and 8 than non-gifted age-peers, and showed a stronger orientation to test themselves against challenging and rigorous tasks (Gottfried, Gottfried, Bathurst & Guerin, 1994).

Case studies of exceptionally and profoundly gifted children often identify, as a dominant affective characteristic, a passionate desire to learn more, and improve, in the child's talent field. The father of one of Morelock's subjects of IQ 180+ described his son's hunger for intellectual stimulus as "a rage to learn" (Morelock, 1995). Sally Huang, a phenomenally gifted young mathematician in Gross's longitudinal study, planned her own program of radical acceleration through elementary and secondary school over a period of five years and, from the age of 8, personally negotiated each grade advancement with her teachers and school principals, explaining her unhappiness and frustration at being stalled in her learning process (Gross, 1993a, 1994, 1998a).

Terman's 'study within a study' which traced the development of those members of the gifted group who scored at or above IQ 170 (Burks, Jensen & Terman, 1930), found that 60% of the extremely gifted boys and

73% of the extremely gifted girls were reported by their teachers and parents as preferring to work or study alone rather than with other students. Terman believed strongly that this preference for working independently reflected a natural cognitive orientation.

This preference for independent study, combined with the sometimes startling differences in the cognitive strategies developed and applied by extremely gifted students which will be discussed below, and the findings of Schunk (1987) that children model on, and learn best from, students of similar ability to themselves, may explain why highly gifted students are often reluctant to act as tutors or assistants to children whose abilities are substantially inferior to their own. Many studies have found that the seeming social isolation and reluctance to assist classmates often displayed by the highly gifted disappear when they are placed in ability grouped or accelerated settings with intellectual peers (Hollingworth, 1926, 1942; Gross, 1993a, 1997, 1998b).

Gross's comparison study of the motivational orientation of academically gifted and unselected students also examined a third group; highly and exceptionally gifted students in a full-time ability grouped setting who were also telescoping the six years of secondary schooling into five years (Gross, 1997). These students were *very* significantly more task oriented than even the moderately gifted group, and, as the assessment of motivational orientation was made in the first few days of the program, it is probable that their unusual degree of task-orientation pre-dated their enrolment. Indeed, the opportunity to progress at a much faster pace than is usually permitted, within a class of children who are also highly gifted, may be more attractive to students who are intrinsically motivated and stimulated by intellectual challenge than to students who are extrinsically motivated and stimulated by external rewards.

As the program progressed, several of the teachers who worked with this highly gifted class commented on the 'cohort effect' of peer bonding, affectionate guidance and mutual encouragement that swiftly developed among this group of students who were similar in their abilities and interests, were task-oriented rather than ego-involved and had been presented with a common but intellectually challenging goal (Gross, 1998a). Yet many of these children stated that in elementary school, in the heterogeneous classroom, they had preferred to work independently and had actively disliked being required to act as tutors for less able classmates. Collaborative work became a delight, rather than a chore, when the students with whom they were now permitted to work were intellectual peers rather than simply age-mates.

Cognitive Development

A substantial amount of research support exists for the proposal that gifted learners differ from their age-peers of average ability at the age, and pace, at which they traverse the Piagetian stages of cognitive development: specifically, that while all children experience the stages of cognitive development in the same order, the gifted progress through the stages at significantly accelerated rates, thus reaching the formal operation stage at much earlier ages.

In a study of 25 exceptionally gifted children (IQ 160+) aged 6–11, Webb (1974) found that the entire group had mastered the most complex or advanced tasks at the concrete and (for the older children) formal operations stages significantly in advance of their age-peers. Keating (1975) studying gifted 11-year-olds, found a level of developmental precocity within the Piagetian framework which led him to suggest that it may be more important to think in terms of IQ, rather than age, in predicting children's developmental stages—thus echoing the advice of Hollingworth who advised that mental age, rather than chronological age, should serve as a predictor of children's success in cognitively mediated school subjects (Hollingworth, 1926, 1930).

Some researchers suggest that chronological age does set some limits on stage-to stage progression. Reviewing earlier research, Carter & Kontos (1981) suggested that at the pre-operational stage, gifted and non-gifted children were equal in task performance up to age 6, and that only in the middle years of elementary school does the relationship between IQ and developmental stage become more substantial. Kanevsky, however, found that as early as four years of age, intellectually gifted children were significantly superior to age-peers of average ability in acquiring and generalizing strategies for solving two different versions of the 'Tower of Hanoi' puzzle (Kanevsky, 1992).

Several studies (e.g. DeVries, 1974; Kemler, 1978) suggest that IQ, and mental age, are correlated to certain specific skills *within* each stage of development but not to others, and that this accounts for the differentiated levels of cognitive performance which can be noted in individual children across a range of tasks. Brown, for example, points out that mental age by itself cannot guarantee exceptional performance on those tasks which depend on pre-existing knowledge (Brown, 1978).

It is notable, however, that Holahan & Sears (1995), in the most recent volume reporting the results of Terman's longitudinal study, strongly endorse the validity of mental age as a determinant not only of academic achievement but also of vocational interests, recreational interests and affective development in childhood and adolescence.

"Through the school years and into adolescence these children's interests, attitudes and knowledge developed in correspondence with their mental age rather than with their chronological age. Their academic achievement as measured by tests, their interest and liking for various future occupational careers, their knowledge about and interest in games, their choice of recreational reading materials, and their moral judgments about hypothetical conduct were all characteristic of older non-gifted children whose mental age-range was approximated by this much younger and brighter group. Even the intellectual level of their collections was more mature than that of their chronological age-mates".

Holahan and Sears, 1995, p. 16.)

Cognitive Strategy Selection

A wealth of research is available on ways in which gifted individuals differ from non-gifted in the cognitive strategies they select and use both in structured problem-solving tasks and in their daily lives. Rogers (1986, p. 29) lists the higher-order (meta-componential) information processing strategies which are used more frequently and effectively by the gifted. These include: the swift and spontaneous generation of a series of steps towards the resolution of a problem, the setting of priorities, the systematic monitoring of progress and solutions, a longer period of thoughtful pre-analysis of the problem before beginning the attempt towards its solution, and the representation of information through structures more usually employed by an expert in the field.

Ian Baker, whose ratio IQ on the *Stanford–Binet L–M* is in excess of 200, was fascinated by cartography. By age nine he could identify and classify, in terms of his state's Department of Roads descriptors, any major or minor road in his home city of one million people. He drew maps to demonstrate his theories of how the road systems and traffic flow of various suburbs could be improved and synthesized the bus, train and streetcar timetables produced by the State Transport Authority to provide more effective service linkages (Gross, 1992).

Ian's fascination with structural analysis, and the strongly spatial orientation of his problem-solving strategies, were apparent in every area of his schoolwork and throughout his leisure pursuits. His parents and teachers were concerned by his reluctance to access or use narrative text. As his mother explained:

"The sort of things that excite him (are) factual books, books on computing or logic, or compendiums of math puzzles. He had a craze, at one stage, for 'Choose Your Own Adventure' stories, because he liked working out the different permutations of changes and endings. But even in writing, he doesn't go in for imaginative stories. When he was seven his teacher said to me that she would throw a party on the day he wrote an imaginative story because anything she asked him to do he would convert into a diagram, a maze, a flow-chart, a timetable, calendar—everything had to be set out and analyzed" (Gross, 1992, p. 123–124).

Sternberg (1981) has noted significant differences between gifted and non-gifted learners in tasks involving *analogical* thinking and in the skills of acquisition (learning new information), retention (retrieving information previously required and stored in long-term memory) and transfer (skills in applying various problem-solving heuristics across a range of problems.

Many of the cognitive traits which characterize moderately gifted children appear at even earlier ages, and in heightened or intensified forms, in the highly gifted. Ian Baker is only one of many highly gifted children who have developed, to an unusual degree, Sternberg's 'transfer components', the skills required for generalizing concepts from one context to another (Sternberg, 1981). Roedell describes a 4-year-old boy who had been learning about set theory in mathematics. Later, when someone asked him what he wanted to be when he grew up, he said, "Maybe I'll be doctor; no, I think I'll be a fireman". Then, describing, with his arms, an intersection set, he announced, "No—I'll be a paramedic!" (1989, p. 19). Tessa, aged 8, a highly gifted young musician and a member of Gross's longitudinal study of children of IQ 160+, when seeking to describe her new-found, but deeply important, friendship with two other highly gifted girls, found her metaphor in music "Each of us is a different note—we've each got our own voice and our own qualities—but put us together and it's like a D major chord! Something beautiful and better happens" (Gross, in press (b)).

A keen sense of humour in young children has often been noted as an indicator of intellectual giftedness (Torrance, 1977; Shade, 1991; Harrison, 1999) but the degree of sophistication of that humour increases with the level of ability. Specifically, the analogical reasoning noted by Sternberg (1981) and the capacity to transfer ideas between contexts at early ages and with unusual facility can help to explain the delight in puns and wordplay which seems to characterize extremely gifted children even in the early years.

Silverman (1989) describes the two-year-old who was playing beneath his mother's bed and when told she was trying to have a rest, spontaneously explained, "Does that mean I'm under arrest?" Gross (1995) describes four-year-old Steven whose pre-school teacher, cleaning up after morning recess, asked him to pass the plastic cup which had contained his fruit juice. Steven incurred her wrath by parading solemnly back and forth in front of the cup for several minutes and finally responding to her rebuke by assuring her that he was only doing what she had instructed—he had now passed the glass from several different directions.

A striking characteristic of exceptionally and profoundly gifted children is their capacity for 'dual focusing', the ability to process two sets of information simultaneously. Christopher Otway was assessed on the *Stanford–Binet (L–M)* at the age of 11 and passed virtually every item on the test, right up to Superior Adult Three. He scored at the ceiling of the test; however, a ratio calculation gave him an IQ of 200. The psychologist's assessment included some interesting analyses of Chris's styles of processing information.

"(Christopher) works hard at trying to put every piece of information or every problem which he has to solve into some sort of category. Perhaps at his level of intellectual activity this is the most efficient way of handling the multitude of information and ideas which he handles each day. I have also observed (as have his parents) that Christopher is one of the few people who truly seems to be able to handle information in parallel. For instance, when he was working on quite a difficult question in the assessment, and was obviously thinking and talking on that particular problem, he suddenly interrupted himself to produce the solution to a previous problem which he felt he could improve on."

(Gross, 1993, p. 15)

Chris's younger brother, Jonathon, who also ceilinged out on the *Stanford–Binet (L–M)* at the age of 8 years 4 months, obtaining a ratio IQ of 170, has a similar cognitive style, although, as the psychologist found, this often manifests itself differently through Jonathon's puckish sense of humor.

"Jonathon's verbal responses (were) of exceptionally high quality. He is a very fluent and articulate sort of child, who has highly developed abstract reasoning skills. It was also obvious that Jonathon has a well-developed sense of humour, too, and often he handled test items on two levels. Firstly he would answer the test question exactly as it was given at a very high level, but then he would give me a supplementary and much more humorous answer or interpretation of the item which he had just completed".

(Gross, 1993a, p. 17–18)

Lyndall Hendrickson, an Australian music teacher who has taught and mentored several extremely gifted young violinists, has noted this capacity for dual focusing in highly gifted musicians who also possess exceptional levels of cognitive ability. One of many illustrative examples is that of a nine-year-old girl, herself a child prodigy, whom Hendrickson took to hear a recital by another of her students. To Hendrickson's irritation, the child spent her time making detailed sketches of the soloist and other members of the orchestra on a drawing pad which she had brought with her. However, when questioned later on what she had learned from the recital, the young girl offered a reasoned and insightful critique of the performance, including a perceptive analysis of the soloist's phrasing (Hendrickson, 1985).

As can be seen, the cognitive functioning of exceptionally and profoundly gifted children differs in many ways from that of their moderately gifted counterparts. An overview of the early development of extremely gifted children can assist us to understand the origin of these differences.

Developmental Precocity in Extremely Gifted Children

As discussed earlier, exceptionally and profoundly gifted children appear rarely in the population, and research on extreme intellectual precocity has mainly comprised isolated case studies of individual children. Such group studies as do exist (Gallagher & Crowder, 1957; Barbe, 1964) are generally of short duration. Longitudinal studies which follow the subject group's development through adolescence into adulthood, such as Hollingworth's landmark study of children of IQ 180+ (Hollingworth, 1942), Terman's 'study within a study' of members of the gifted group who scored at or above IQ 170 (Burks, Jensen & Terman, 1930), or Gross's study of children of IQ 160+ (Gross, 1993a et seq.) are extremely rare. Furthermore, many reports of childhood precocity are retrospective, undertaken when the subjects have already attained adulthood, or even after the subject's death (Cox et al., 1926; Montour, 1977; Bergman, 1979).

For a fully accurate picture to be obtained of the cognitive or affective development of extremely gifted children, it is important that their development should be studied not retrospectively but *in current time*. In this way, events and situations which impact on the child's development can be observed as they occur, rather than being recalled by parents, or in adulthood by the subjects themselves, through the filter of an unintentionally biased and selective memory. In the case of exceptionally and profoundly gifted children, whose development may differ radically from that of age-peers, it is particularly important that the young child's perceptions should be recorded at the time when they are influencing his or her thoughts and actions, rather than related in later years.

The case study method is a sound approach for developing specific knowledge about exceptional giftedness; it is ideally suited to the investigation and description of events or people characterised by their rarity (Foster, 1986). It provides a holistic perspective and allows the researcher to develop and validate theories grounded in direct observation of individual students. Indeed, close observation of the student in natural settings, the analysis of subjective factors such as the subject's attitudes, desires and perceptions, and the use of a wide range of observation procedures, all of which are characteristic of good case study research, enable a more comprehensive observation of a subject or process than is possible with any other research methodology (Merriam, 1988).

Nonetheless, the retrospective nature of much of the case study research on the early years of gifted children has led researchers who support a wholly or largely environmental view of giftedness to suggest that records of very early speech, movement or reading may derive from flawed parental memory or inaccurate recording. However, the Fullerton Longitudinal Study of the early years of a group of gifted and non-gifted children has provided empirical evidence of the developmental advancement of intellectually gifted young children (Gottfried, Gottfried, Bathurst & Guerin, 1994).

The Fullerton Study traced the development of 107 children recruited through birth notifications of hospitals adjacent to California State University, Fullerton. The children were full term babies of normal birthweight who were free of visual and neurological abnormalities. The children, who were one-year-old at the commencement of the study, were given numerous developmental assessments through the first eight years of life. At the age of eight, they were assessed on the *Wechsler Intelligence Scale for Children—Revised (WISC–R)* and the 20 children who made a full-scale IQ score of 130 were designated the gifted group for comparison with the other 87 children. The IQ range in the gifted group was 130–145 with a mean of 137.6; the range in the non-gifted group was 84–128 with a mean of 110.9.

The Fullerton team thus possessed objective, systematically collected, data on the early development of a group of children who were *later* identified as gifted. This is not, therefore, a retrospective study, but a developmental study conducted in current time and the consistent superiority of the gifted group cannot be attributed to flawed memory or parental bias.

Indeed because the mean of the Fullerton comparison group (110.9) is significantly higher than the mean of the general population, the superiority of the gifted group would doubtless be even more striking if the comparison group had included a fuller representation of children of average ability. It is significant that the least able subject in the comparison group scored only slightly more than one standard deviation below the mean of the *WISC-R*.

The Fullerton Study found that differences in the level of intellectual performance between the gifted and non-gifted children appeared on psychometric testing as early as 1.5 years of age, and were sustained throughout the study. Interestingly, the earliest difference was found at age one, *on entrance to the study*, in receptive language. Given the evidence of extremely early responses to speech in young gifted children (e.g. Gross, 1993a) it is interesting to speculate how much earlier this difference might have been recorded if structured observation had been commenced in the first year of life. Significant differences in expressive language were consistently found from infancy onwards. Assessments of comprehension, gross and fine motor skill, memory, and personal-social development consistently found the gifted group superior. Indeed, the only academic skill on which the gifted children did not display significant superiority was on numeracy—and the researchers noted that this was due to a ceiling effect on the test for the gifted group! Indeed, the Fullerton team concluded: "Gifted IQ implies generalized high intelligence. Gifted children were superior across an array of cognitive tasks beginning as early as the pre-school period. Gifted children tended to be cognitively well rounded or adept. Globality rather than specificity in cognitive performance characterizes intellectual giftedness" (Gottfried, Gottfried, Bathurst & Guerin, 1994, p. 85).

Although, as might be predicted from the relatively small sample size, the Fullerton Study included no extremely gifted children—the highest IQ in the group was 145—its findings do lend credibility to retrospective assessments of unusual cognitive precocity in case studies of the intellectually gifted.

Early Development of Speech and Movement

Exceptionally and profoundly gifted children differ significantly from their age-peers of average ability both in their cognitive and in their socio-affective development and, as with the subjects of the Fullerton study, these differences generally become evident from their earliest years, with the precocious acquisition of speech and movement. Studies of the early movement of moderately gifted children report that these children learn to walk, on average, two to three months earlier than age-peers (for example Terman, 1925) but, in general, the extremely gifted show even more remarkable physical precocity. Silverman (1989) described a girl of 7 months who stood alone, climbed into chairs unassisted and went up and down stairs by herself. Gross (1993a) describes Rick, of IQ 162, who sat up by himself at four months, ran at 11 months, and rode a two-wheeled bicycle unaided at age three. Six subjects in Gross's study of children of IQ 160+ were able to sit up unsupported before the age of 5 months, and with only few exceptions the children in this study crawled, walked and ran at ages considerably younger than the population as a whole (Gross, in press (a)). One of the most remarkably precocious is Emma who began horse-riding lessons (at her own urgent insistence) at the age of 14 months and who at 18 months competed in a riding school gymkhana and won second prize in a competition against 12 other junior riders aged between three and seven (Gross, 1999).

Numerous researchers have noted the early development of speech which is characteristic of even moderately gifted children. Jersild (1960) studying the fluency of speech in young children, noted that at the age of 18 months, when children of average ability were uttering a mean number of 1.2 words, per 'remark', their gifted age-peers were uttering 3.7 words. By the age of four the difference was even more remarkable;

the mean number of words per 'remark' for average children was 4.6 whereas for the gifted it was 9.5.

Occasionally the speech of even extremely gifted children may be delayed. Probably the best known example of this is Einstein who did not talk until three years of age and who was suspected of being intellectually disabled (Goertzel and Goertzel, 1962). Similarly, the mother of two brothers in Gross's study who did not speak until 18 and 21 months respectively was warned by their pediatrician that they may be seriously developmentally delayed; the brothers later tested at IQ 170 and 200 (Gross, 1993a).

It is important, therefore, that delayed speech should not be taken as indicating that the child is not gifted. Research has shown, however, that very early speech, is a powerful indication of high levels of cognitive ability. A study of 241 children of IQ 160+ found that 91% were reported, by their parents as displaying unusually early language development (Rogers and Silverman, in press). The mean age at which the 58 IQ 160+ subjects of Gross's study uttered their first meaningful word (other than 'mamma-dadda' babble) was 8.7 months.

In general, exceptionally and profoundly gifted children display remarkably complex and advanced speech patterns. The case study literature on the extremely gifted is particularly rich in examples of this (Langenbeck, 1915; Terman & Fenton, 1921; Goldberg, 1934). Hollingworth (1926) reported on 'David' who was talking in sentences at the age of 11 months and who at the age of 8 months exclaimed, "Little boy!" when his shadow appeared on the wall. 'Ian' in Gross's study knew all the words of the song *My Grandfather's Clock* by the age of 23 months, and at 2 years 4 months announced to a family friend, "My father is a mathematician and my mother is a physiotherapist" (Gross, 1993a). Emma, whose unusual motor development was reported on earlier, is also linguistically precocious: by 13 months of age she had a vocabulary of more than 80 words.

The precocious development of movement permits extremely gifted children to move around and explore for themselves much earlier than their age-peers of average ability, while their very early speech enables them to express their ideas, seek information through questioning and interact verbally with their parents and other family members at an age when other children are only beginning to experiment with oral communication. Both early movement and early speech contribute significantly to these children's capacity to acquire and process information. Reading, a third and significant source of knowledge acquisition, also seem to develop at remarkably early ages in the extremely gifted.

Early Development of Reading

While some researchers question the relationship between early reading and intellectual giftedness (see Jackson & Klein, 1997 for a discussion of this) there is little doubt that the *extremely* early acquisition of reading is both one of the most powerful indicators of exceptional giftedness and a powerful predictor of later school success. Terman found that one of the few variables on which his IQ 170+ sub-group differed from the moderately and highly gifted subjects was the very early age at which they learned to read (Terman & Oden, 1947) while Hollingworth (1926) confirmed that it was very early reading which most clearly differentiated between moderately and extremely gifted children. All Hollingworth's subjects of IQ 180, read before school entry, while 80% of them read by age four (Hollingworth, 1942).

VanTassel-Baska (1983) studied 270 students aged 13 and 14 who had achieved within the 90th percentile on the Mathematics or Verbal subtests of the *Scholastic Aptitude Test*, and found that 80% of this group had read by age five and 55% by age four. More than 90% of Gross's subjects of IQ 160+ read by age five.

One of the most striking contrasts noted between the gifted and their age-peers of average ability is the age at which different books are read. Terman (1925) noted that books which were preferred by the average child of 11 or 12 were usually read with enjoyment by the moderately gifted child of 8 or 9.

Even more striking differences are noted in the reading interests of moderately and extremely gifted children. Gross (1993b) provided an overview of the literature since the early years of the century on the extremely advanced reading interests of exceptionally and profoundly gifted children. Current research suggests that extremely gifted children still prefer novels and non-fiction texts which are more usually selected by students 5–7 years their senior, and still tend to seek out books which address social and ethical issues, although what Halstead (1988) terms 'high fantasy'—adolescent or adult science fantasy novels, or series of novels, which trace a quest or a seeking for moral maturity by an individual or group—have replaced the classics which served a similar purpose for the highly gifted young people studied by Terman & Hollingworth. The literature on the highly gifted suggests that the majority of extremely gifted students deliberately moderate or conceal their exceptional abilities in the regular classroom in attempts to win social acceptance by age-peers (Hollingworth, 1926, 1942; Pringle, 1970; Silverman, 1993; Morelock, 1995). Gross found that 70% of the early readers in her study deliberately stopped reading, or significantly moderated their *in-class* reading, within the first few weeks to conform to peer expectations (Gross, 1993a). Significantly, however, their passion for reading, and the precocity of their reading abilities and interests was maintained at home.

This deliberate concealment of precocity for peer acceptance can easily be misinterpreted. Braggett (1983) proposed that many children who display unusually accelerated reading development in early childhood may not retain this capacity but may, rather, be 'developmental spurters' whose early promise is not fulfilled as the child progresses through elementary school. However, the persistence of exceptional reading accuracy and comprehension skill in Gross's Australian subjects of IQ 160+ indicate that these children are by no means 'developmental spurters'. In virtually every case the reading development of these children has followed the pattern reported in the studies of Burks, Jensen & Terman (1930), Hollingworth (1942), Durkin (1966) and VanTassel-Baska (1983), and in the numerous individual case studies of precocious readers (Terman and Fenton, 1921; Witty & Coomer, 1955; Feldman, 1986); that is, the precocity which was such a salient feature of the child's early development has persisted, and in many cases increased, through the children's elementary school years.

What has decreased, however, has been the opportunity for these children to display their reading precocity in the classroom The majority of these exceptionally gifted children are required to work lock-step through the curriculum at the same level and pace, and using the same school texts and materials, as their chronologically aged peers (Gross, 1998a). Thus, their continuing exceptionality in reading is displayed not in the classroom but at home, or in extra-curricular programs for gifted children organized by universities or advocacy groups, where their unusual reading abilities and reading interests are accepted and valued. In several cases the child has appeared, to his classroom teacher, to have developed a new, and apparently unrelated, gift or talent.

An important insight into the continuity, but transmutability, of precocity in reading is offered by Jackson (1992) who proposes that, since the challenge of learning to read extremely well may lose its excitement as the young gifted child progresses through the early years of school, she may seek other avenues for the expression of her precocious talent for decoding and encoding what is, in essence, a complex and sophisticated symbol system. We have discussed earlier, the unusual capacity of gifted children for generalizing concepts from one context to another. Some precocious readers may translate this facility into an enhanced capacity for learning mathematics or computer programming. In a peer culture which ridicules, rather than values, enhanced linguistic development, the child may deliberately choose to transfer her skills to another area in the hope that this new expression of talent may be accepted more readily by her teacher and classmates.

Rather than assuming that giftedness is transient and that developmental spurters are "possibly the largest single group of gifted children we may identify in the school" (Braggett, 1983, p. 14), we should seek to understand the continuity of giftedness through its diverse manifestations and transitions as the child matures.

Multiplicity of Talents in the Extremely Gifted

Models of intelligence which propose a number of specific, quasi-autonomous factors, abilities or aptitudes, for example Thurstone's (1938) seven 'primary mental abilities' or Gardner's (1983) theory of 'multiple intelligences' which bears some interesting parallels to Thurstone's model, require greater empirical support if they are to become the foundation for broad-based educational usage. More recent research has lent substantial support to Spearman's (1904) conception of a general mental ability factor *g*—"a highly general information-processing capacity that facilitates reasoning, problem solving, decision making and other higher order thinking skills" (Gottfredson, 1997, p. 81) and the placement of *g* at the apex of a pyramidal hierarchy of factors which comprises, in its lower layers, broader cognitive abilities which themselves comprise narrower, more specific abilities (Carroll, 1993). As discussed earlier, the Fullerton Study found powerful support for *g* in their study of pre-school children which noted the superiority of the gifted group across a whole range of cognitive tasks (Gottfried, Gottfried, Bathurst & Guerin, 1994).

The extraordinary superiority of extremely gifted children across a wide range of subject fields, and indeed domains gives powerful additional support to *g*. The case study literature over the last 70 years consistently documents children of IQ greater than 160 who have displayed astonishing multiplicity of talents (McElwee, 1934; Goldberg, 1934; Grost, 1970). A not untypical example is 'R', reported by Zorbaugh & Boardman (1936) who was reading omnivorously before school entry and by age eight had a large personal library of books on science, history and biography which he had catalogued himself on the Dewey decimal system. At age two he was modeling in clay and at age three began to design and make machines; he applied through his father to the United States patent office for two patents before he was eight years old; at the same age he was writing a book on electricity.

During the last 30 years reports of single case studies of extremely gifted children have only rarely appeared in journals of gifted education or psychology. One of the very few exceptions has been a report (Gross, 1986) of the academic and socio-affective development of Terence Tao, an Australian boy of IQ 220+ who taught himself to read before his second birthday through watching *Sesame Street*, scored 760 on the *Scholastic Aptitude Test—Mathematics (SAT–M)* at age 8 years 10 months, at nine was teaching one of his younger brothers chess, and the other piano, and at age 12 was amusing himself by translating *The Hitch-Hiker's Guide to the Galaxy* into Latin. Researchers' knowledge of the extremely gifted, and further research interest in them, would doubtless be enhanced if journals were willing to publish further rigorously conducted and comprehensive single-subject case studies of exceptionally or profoundly gifted children. It takes a researcher many years to locate and study large samples of this sparse population and the ongoing dissemination of research is needed!

The larger scale studies of Hollingworth and Cobb (1928) and Hollingworth (1926, 1942), however, also noted a consistent superiority of exceptionally gifted students over the moderately or highly gifted, over a wide range of subject areas. Hollingworth and Cobb's (1928) 'Public School 165' experiment, in which two classes of gifted children, one centering on IQ 146, the other centering on IQ 165, were given an identical curriculum, taught under identical circumstances, over a period of three years, showed that the IQ 165 group demonstrated superiority across 12 of the 14 areas tested, the sole exceptions being speed and quality of penmanship (handwriting) which are significantly moderated by sensorimotor ability.

Gross's subjects of IQ 160+ almost without exception display remarkable superiority across a range of academic fields and many also excel in music, computing and sport (Gross, 1993a) However both Gross (1992, 1993a, 1998a) and Rogers & Silverman (in press (a)) have found that their subjects of IQ 180+ have even a wider range of exceptionalities and a wider range of interests.

By the time Christopher Otway of IQ 200, was 12 years old he had been accelerated to 9th grade and was undertaking further subject acceleration with 11th grade students in physics, chemistry, maths, English and economics. Because of his unusual aptitude for music he commenced flute lessons with students four years older and while undertaking undergraduate study, played in a prestigious flute ensemble , the majority of whom were musicians of many more years experience. He plays competitive tennis, was until recently the organiser and captain of a mixed-sex netball team, enjoys contract bridge, served on the committee of his university's Science Fiction Club, plays piano, takes a keen interest in the Stock Market and reads voraciously.

Chris entered Grade 10 a few weeks after his 13th birthday but, rather than continuing his subject accelerations to Grade 12, he chose to 'repeat' Grade 11 in different curriculum areas, this time selecting English, legal studies, Australian history, accounting, and biology. The following year he entered Grade 12 and took, for university entrance, the five subjects he had taken in his 'first run' of Grade 11, and the year after that, he 'repeated' Grade 12 and took, for university entrance, his second set of five subjects.

It was Chris's own decision to take this somewhat unusual method of acceleration. He felt that he would not be ready, at age 13 or 14, to enter university and he was delighted with the opportunity to broaden his education by taking ten, rather than the usual five, subjects at Grade 12 level. Interestingly, in both of his Grade 12 years, he graduated as one of the top students in his state, majoring in mathematics (two subjects), physics. chemistry, economics, English, Australian history, legal studies, accounting and biology.,

Chris entered university at 16 and graduated with two degrees, a Bachelor of Economics and a First Class Honours degree in Computer Science and Pure Mathematics, before his 21st birthday. He was successful in winning a scholarship to a prestigious British university and now, aged 23 is in the final year of PhD study.

Radical Acceleration

"Someone has said that genius is necessarily solitary, since the population is so sparse at the highest levels of mental ability. However, adult genius is mobile and can seek out its own kind. It is in the case of extraordinarily high IQ that the social problem is most acute. If the IQ is 180, the intellectual level at six is almost on a par with the average eleven-year-old and at ten or eleven is not far from that of the average high school graduate... The inevitable result is that the child of IQ 180 has one of the most difficult problems of social adjustment that any human being is ever called upon to meet'

Burks, Jensen & Terman, 1930, p. 264).

Earlier in this chapter a brief review of the literature on the extremely gifted established the difficulties that arise when the differences between extremely gifted children and their age-peers so far outweigh the similarities as to hinder the formation of productive social relationships. Hollingworth identified an IQ of 160 as being the 'danger point' beyond which the gifted child is particularly at risk for social rejection by age-peers, and noted that the problems of social isolation seemed particularly acute between the ages of 4 and 9 (Hollingworth, 1931).

It cannot be sufficiently emphasized, however, that the problems of social isolation, peer rejection, loneliness and alienation which afflict many extremely gifted children arise *not* out of their exceptional intellectual abilities but as a result of society's response to them (Selig, 1959; Janos, 1983; Gross, 1993a). These problems arise when the school, the education system or the community refuses to create for the extremely gifted child a peer group based not on the accident of chronological age but on a commonality of abilities, interests and values.

The multiplicity of talents displayed by exceptionally and profoundly gifted children, coupled with the social and emotional maturity which characterizes these young people (Terman, 1925; Hollingworth, 1942; Janos, Robinson & Lunneborg, 1989; Gross, 1993a) makes them excellent candidates for radical acceleration, a series of grade-advancements which results in the student graduating from high school three or more years earlier than is customary.

It is now generally recognized (Hollingworth, 1942; Cronbach, 1996; Benbow, 1998) that for highly gifted children some form of acceleration is essential if they are to find significant numbers of students of their own mental age with whom they can form healthy and productive social relationships. The findings, since the early 1970s, of the Study of Mathematically Precocious Youth provide powerful arguments for the intellectual and social benefits of academic acceleration for highly gifted youth (Benbow et al., 1996).

However, Hollingworth (1942) and Terman & Oden (1947) in their follow-up research on the young adults in Terman's gifted group, argued forcefully that for extremely gifted children the more conservative accelerative procedures such as a single grade-skip were not sufficient; they strongly advised radical acceleration through several grade-skips spaced appropriately through the student's school career. Gross (1992, 1993a, 1998b) found that for children of IQ 160+ a token grade-skip of one year, even when supplemented with in-class enrichment or pull-out, has been no more effective, academically or socially, than retention in the heterogeneous classroom. In the considerable majority of cases, children who have not been radically accelerated display low levels of motivation and social self-esteem, are more likely to report social rejection by their classmates, and are required to perform in school at levels several years below their tested achievement.

In striking contrast, 16 of Gross's 58 subjects of IQ 160+ have been radically accelerated; nine have already entered university, at ages between 11 and 16 . All are experiencing high levels of academic success and have full social lives (Gross, 1998a). None regrets having taken such an accelerated pathway through school. As Roshni Singh, of IQ 162, comments; "I'm sorry it was necessary to do something that was so unusual at the time, but I certainly don't regret *doing* it. The alternative—staying with age-peers—would have been intolerable". Ian Baker of IQ 200 bleakly encapsulated his life in the heterogeneous classroom in a single word: "Hell" (Baker, 1991).

References

Baker, I. (1991). *Hell.* Unpublished presentation to graduate class in gifted education, University of Melbourne, Australia, July.

Barbe, W. B. (1964). *One in a thousand: a comparative study of highly and moderately gifted elementary school children.* Columbus, Ohio: F. J. Heer.

Benbow, C. P. (1998). Acceleration as a method for meeting the academic needs of intellectually talented children. In: J. VanTassel-Baska (Ed.), *Excellence in Educating Gifted and Talented Learners* (pp. 279–294). Denver: Love Publishing.

Benbow, C. P. & Lubinski, D. (1993). Psychological profiles of the mathematically talented: some sex differences and

evidence supporting their biological basis. In: G. R. Bock and K. Ackrill (Eds), *The Origin and Development of High Ability* (pp. 44–66). New York: John Wiley and Sons.

Benbow, C. P., Lubinski, D. & Sushy, B. (1996). The impact of SMPY's educational programs from the perspective of the participant. In: C. P. Benbow and D. Lubinski (Eds), *Intellectual Talent* (pp. 266–300). Baltimore: Johns Hopkins University Press.

Bergman, J. (1979). The tragic story of two highly gifted, genius-level boys. *Creative Child and Adult Quarterly*, **4**, 222–233.

Braggett, E. J. (1983). Curriculum for gifted and talented children: needs. In: Commonwealth Schools Commission (Eds), *Curriculum for Gifted and Talented Children* (pp. 9–30). Canberra, Australia: Commonwealth Schools Commission.

Brown, A. L. (1978). Conservation of number of continuous quantity in normal, bright and retarded children. *Child Development*, **44**, 376–379.

Burks, B. S., Jensen, D. W. and Terman, L. M. (1930). *The promise of youth.* Volume 3: *Genetic studies of genius.* Stanford, California: Stanford University Press.

Burt, C. (1968). Is intelligence normally distributed? *British Journal of Statistical Psychology*, **16**, 175–190.

Carroll, J. B. (1993). *Human cognitive abilities: a survey of factor-analytic studies.* New York: Cambridge University Press.

Carter, K. R. and Kontos, S. (1981). The application of developmental theories. *Roeper Review*, **4**, 17–20.

Cox, C. M. et al. (1926). *The early mental traits of 300 geniuses.* Vol. 2: *Genetic studies of genius.* Stanford, CA: Stanford University Press.

Cronbach, L. J. (1996). Acceleration among the Terman males: correlates in midlife and after. In: C. P. Benbow and D. Lubinski (Eds), *Intellectual Talent* (pp. 179–191). Baltimore: Johns Hopkins University press.

DeHaan, R. F. & Havighurst, R. J. (1961). *Educating gifted children* (revised edition). Chicago: University of Chicago Press.

DeVries, R. (1974). Relationships among Piagetian stages, IQ and achievement assessments. *Child Development*, **45**, 746–756.

Dunn, R., Dunn, K. & Price, G. E. (1981). Learning styles: research vs. opinion. *Phi Delta Kappen*, **62**, 645–646.

Durkin, D. (1966). *Children who read early.* New York: Teachers College Press, Columbia University.

Feldman, D. H. (1986). *Nature's gambit.* New York: Basic.

Foster, W. (1986). The application of single subject research methods to the study of exceptional ability and extraordinary achievement. *Gifted Child Quarterly*, **30** (1), 33–37.

Gallagher, J. J. (1958). Peer acceptance of highly gifted children in the elementary school. *Elementary School Journal*, **58**, 465–470.

Gallagher, J. J. & Crowder, T. (1957). The adjustment of gifted children in the regular classroom. *Exceptional Children*, **23**, 306–312, 317–319.

Gardner, H. (1983). *Frames of mind: the theory of multiple intelligences.* New York: Basic Books

Goertzel, V. & Goertzel, M. G. (1962). *Cradles of eminence.* Boston: Little, Brown & Co.

Goldberg, S. (1934). A clinical study of K., IQ 196. *Journal of Applied Psychology*, **18**, 550–560.

Goldstein, D., Stocking, V. B. & Godfrey, J. J. (1999). What we've learned from talent search research. In: N. Colangelo and S. G. Assouline (Eds), *Talent Development 111: Proceedings from the 1995 Henry B. and Jocelyn Wallace National Research Symposium on Talent Development.* Scottsdale, Arizona: Gifted Psychology Press.

Gottfredson, L. S. (1997). Why g matters: the complexity of everyday life. *Intelligence,* **24** (1), 79–132.

Gottfried, A. W., Gottfried, A. E., Bathurst, K. & Guerin, D. W. (1994). *Gifted IQ: early developmental aspects. the Fullerton longitudinal study.* Plenum Press: New York and London.

Gross, M. U. M. (1986). Radical acceleration in Australia: Terence Tao. *G/C/T,* **45**, 2–11.

Gross, M. U. M. (1992). The use of radical acceleration in cases of extreme intellectual precocity. *Gifted Child Quarterly,* **36** (2), 90–98.

Gross, M. U. M. (1993a) *Exceptionally Gifted Children,* London: Routledge.

Gross, M. U. M. (1993b). Nurturing the talents of exceptionally gifted individuals. In: K. A. Heller, F. J. Monks and A. H. Passow (Eds), *International Handbook of Research and Development of Giftedness and Talent* (pp. 473–490). Oxford: Pergamon Press.

Gross, M. U. M. (1992). The early development of three profoundly gifted children of IQ 200. In: P. S. Klein and A. J. Tannenbaum (Eds), *To Be Young and Gifted* (pp. 94–138). Norwood, NJ: Ablex.

Gross, M. U. M. (1994). Radical acceleration: responding to academic and social needs of extremely gifted adolescents. *Journal of Secondary Gifted Education,* **5** (4), 27–34.

Gross, M. U. M. (1995). Seeing the difference and making the difference for highly gifted students. *Tempo,* **15** (1), 1, 11–14

Gross, M. U. M. (1997). How ability grouping turns big fish into little fish—or does it? Of optical illusions and optimal environments. *Australasian Journal of Gifted Education,* **6** (2), 18–30.

Gross, M. U. M. (1998a). Fishing for the facts: a response to Marsh and Craven, 1998. *Australasian Journal of Gifted Education,* **7** (1), 16–28.

Gross, M. U. M. (1998b). Fishing for the facts: a response to Marsh and Craven, 1998. *Australasian Journal of Gifted Education,* **7** (1), 16–28.

Gross, M. U. M. (1999). Small poppies: highly gifted children in the early years. *Roeper Review,* **21** (3), 207–214.

Gross, M. U. M. "The road less travelled by": the different world of highly gifted children. In: J. F. Smutny (Ed.), *Underserved Gifted Populations.* Creskill, New Jersey: Hampton Press. (in press (a)).

Gross, M. U. M. *Ability grouping, self-esteem and the gifted: a study of optical illusions and optimal environments.* Keynote address: Proceedings of 4th Biennial Henry B. and Jocelyn Wallace National Research Symposium on Talent Development. Gifted Psychology Press, Inc: Scottsdale, Arizona (in press (b)).

Gross, M. U. M. & Start, K. B. (1989). Not waving, but drowning: the exceptionally gifted child in Australia. In: Bailey, S., Braggett, E. & Robinson, M. (Eds), *The Challenge of excellence: a vision splendid* (pp. 25–36). Proceedings of the Eighth World Conference on Gifted and Talented Children. Sydney, July. Wagga Wagga, Australia: Australian Association for the Education of the Gifted and Talented.

Grost, A. (1970). *Genius in Residence.* Englewood Cliffs, New Jersey: Prentice-Hall.

Halstead, J. W. (1988). *Guiding gifted readers from pre-school through high school.* Columbus, Ohio: Ohio Psychology Publishing Company.

Harrison, C. (1999). *Giftedness in early childhood.* Sydney: GERRIC.

Hendrickson, L. (1985). Personal communication.

Holahan, C. K. & Sears R. R. (1995). *The gifted group at later maturity.* Stanford University Press: Stanford, CA.

Hollingworth, L. S. (1926) *Gifted children: their nature and nurture.* New York: Macmillan.

Hollingworth, L. S. (1931). The child of very superior intelligence as a special problem in social adjustment. *Mental Hygiene,* **15** (1), 3–16.

Hollingworth, L. S. (1942) *Children above IQ 180: their origin and development.* New York: World Books.

Hollingworth, L. S. (1930). *The psychology of the adolescent.* New York: Staples Press.

Hollingworth, L. S. & Cobb, M. V. (1928). Children clustering at 165 IQ and children clustering at 146 IQ compared for three years in achievement. In: G. M. Whipple (Ed.), *Nature and Nurture: Their Influence Upon Achievement.* The Twenty-seventh Yearbook of the National Society for the Study of Education, Part 2 (pp. 3–33). Bloomington, Illinois: Public School Publishing Company.

Jackson, N. E. (1992). Precocious reading of English: sources, structure and predictive significance. In: P. N. Klein & A. J. Tannenbaum (1992) (Eds), *To Be Young and Gifted* (pp. 171–203). Norwood, NJ: Ablex.

Jackson, N. E. & Klein, E. J. (1997). Gifted performance in young children. In: N. Colangelo and G. A. Davis (Eds), *Handbook of Gifted Education* (2nd ed.). (460–474). Boston: Allyn and Bacon.

Janos, P. M. (1983). *The psychological vulnerabilities of children of very superior intellectual ability.* Unpublished doctoral dissertation. New York University.

Janos, P. M., Robinson, N. M. & Lunneborg, C. E. (1989). Markedly early entrance to college: a multi-year comparative study of academic performance and psychological adjustment. *Journal of Higher Education,* **60**, 496–518.

Jersild, A. T. (1960). *Child psychology.* London: Prentice-Hall.

Kanevsky, L. K. (1992). The learning game. In: P. S. Klein and A. J. Tannenbaum (Eds), *To Be Young and Gifted* (pp. 204–241). Norwood, NJ: Ablex.

Kanevsky, L. K. (1994). A comparative study of children's learning in the zone of proximal development. *European Journal of High Ability,* **5** (2), 163–175.

Keating, D. P. (1975). Precocious cognitive development at the level of formal operations. *Child Development,* **46**, 276–280.

Kemler, D. (1978). Patterns of hypothesis testing in children's discriminative learning: a study of the development of problem-solving strategies. *Developmental Psychology,* **14**, 653–673.

Langenbeck, M. (1915). A study of a five-year-old child. *Pedagogical Seminary,* **22**, 65–88.

Marland, S. P. (1972). *Education of the gifted and talented.* (2 vols.). Washington, DC: U.S. Government Printing Office.

McElwee, R. (1934). Seymour, a boy with 192 IQ. *Journal of Juvenile Research,* **18**, 28–35.

Merriam, S. B. (1988). *Case study research in education: a qualitative approach.* San Francisco, CA: Jossey Bass.

Montour, K. (1977). William James Sidis: the broken twig. *American Psychologist*, **32**, 265–279.

ores, D. F. (1987). *Educating the deaf: psychology, principles and practices* (3rd ed.), Boston: Houghton Mifflin.

Morelock, M. J. (1995). *The profoundly gifted child in family context.* Unpublished doctoral dissertation. Tufts University.

Payne, J. S. & Patton, J. R. (1981). *Mental retardation.* Columbus, Ohio: Merrill.

Pringle, M. L. K. (1970). *Able misfits.* London: Longman.

Ricca, J. (1984). Learning styles and preferred instructional strategies of gifted students. *Gifted Child Quarterly*, **28**, 121–126.

Richert, E. S. (1997). Excellence with equity in identification and programming. In: N. Colangelo and G. A. Davis (Eds), *Handbook of Gifted Education* (2nd ed.), (pp. 75–88). Boston: Allyn and Bacon.

Ristow, R. S. & Edeburn, C. E. (1985). Learning preferences: a comparison of gifted and above-average middle grades students in small schools. *Roeper Review*, **8**, 119–124.

Robinson, H. B. (1981). The uncommonly bright child. In: M. Lewis & L. A. Rosenblum (Eds), *The Uncommon Child* (pp. 57–81). New York: Plenum Press.

Rogers, K. B. (1986) Do the gifted think and learn differently? A review of recent research and its implications for instruction. *Journal for the Education of the Gifted*, **10** (1), 17–39.

Rogers, K. B. & Silverman, L. K. *Personal, social, medical and psychological factors in children of IQ 160 +.* Proceedings of the 4th Biennial Henry B. and Jocelyn Wallace National Research Symposium on Talent Development. Gifted Psychology Press: Scottsdale, Arizona (in press).

Savon-Shepin, M. (1994). *Playing favorites: gifted education and the disruption of community.* Albany, NY: State University of New York Press.

Schunk, D. H. (1987). Peer models and children's behavioral change. *Equity and Excellence*, **23**, 22–30.

Selig, K. (1959). *Personality structure as revealed by the Rorschach technique of a group of children who test above 170 IQ on the 1937 edition of the Stanford–Binet.* Unpublished doctoral dissertation, New York University.

Shade, R. (1991). Verbal humor in gifted students and students in the general population: a comparison of spontaneous mirth and comprehension. *Journal for the Education of the Gifted*, **14** (2), 134–150.

Sheldon, P. M. (1959). Isolation as a characteristic of highly gifted children. *The Journal of Educational Sociology*, January, 215–221.

Silverman, L. K. (1989). The highly gifted. In: J. F. Feldhusen, J. VanTassel-Baska & K. Seeley (Eds), *Excellence in Educating the Gifted* (pp. 71–83). Denver: Love.

Silverman, L. K. (1993). *Counseling the gifted and talented.* Denver: Love.

Silverman, L. K. & Kearney, K. (1989). Parents of the extraordinarily gifted. *Advanced Development*, **1**. 1–10.

Silverman, L. K. & Kearney, K. (1992). Don't throw away the old Binet. *Understanding Our Gifted*, **4** (4), 1, 8–10.

Spearman, C. (1904). General intelligence, objectively determined and measured. *American Journal of Psychology*, **15**, 201–193.

Sternberg, R. (1981). A componential theory of intellectual giftedness. *Gifted Child Quarterly*, **25**, 86–93.

Terman, L. M. (1925). *Genetic studies of genius* (Vol. 1). *Mental and physical traits of a thousand gifted children.* Stanford, CA: Stanford University Press.

Terman, L. M. & Fenton, J. C. (1921). Preliminary report on a gifted juvenile author. *Journal of Applied Psychology*, **5**, 163–178.

Terman, L. M. & Oden, M. H. (1947). *Genetic studies of genius* (Vol. 4), *The gifted child grows up.* Stanford, California: Stanford University Press.

Thurstone, L. L. (1938). *Primary mental abilities.* Chicago: University of Chicago Press.

Torrance, E. P. (1977). *Discovery and nurturance of giftedness in the culturally different.* Reston, VA: Council for Exceptional Children.

VanTassel-Baska, J. (1983). Profiles of precocity: the 1982 Midwest Talent Search Finalists. *Gifted Child Quarterly*, **27** (3), 139–144.

Wasserman, J. (1997). *Letter from John Wasserman, Director of Psychological Assessment, Riverside Press, to Dr L. K. Silverman*, December 1997.

Webb, R. A. (1974). Concrete and formal operations in very bright 6 to 11 year olds. *Human Development*, **17**, 292–300

Witty, P. & Coomer, A. (1955). A study of gifted twin boys. *Exceptional Children*, **22**, 104–108.

Zorbaugh, H. W. & Boardman, R. K. (1936). Salvaging our gifted children. *Journal of Educational Sociology*, **10**, 100–108.

Suggestions for further reading

Benbow, C. P. (1991). Mathematically talented children: can acceleration meet their educational needs? In: N. Colangelo and G. A. Davis (Eds), *Handbook of Gifted Education* (pp. 154–165). Boston: Allyn & Bacon.

Benbow, C. P. & Stanley, J. C. (1997). Inequity in equity: how 'equity' can lead to inequity for high potential students. *Psychology, Public Policy and Law*, **2** (2), 249–292.

Carroll, H. A. (1940). *Genius in the making.* New York: McGraw-Hill.

Dolbear, K. E. (1912). Precocious children. *Journal of Genetic Psychology*, **19**, 461–491.

Feldman, D. H. (1979). The mysterious case of extreme giftedness. In: A. H. Passow (Ed.), *The Gifted and Talented: Their Education and Development.* The 78th Yearbook of the National Society for the Study of Education (pp. 335–351). Chicago: University of Chicago Press.

Goertzel, V. & Goertzel, M. G. (1962). *Cradles of eminence.* Boston: Little, Brown and Co.

Hollingworth, L. S. (1936). The development of personality in highly intelligent children. *National Elementary Principal*, **15**, 272–281.

Hollingworth, L. S. (1936). The founding of Public School 500, Speyer School. *Teachers College Record*, **38**, 119–128.

Hollingworth, L. S., Garrison, G. G. & Burke, A. (1917). The psychology of a prodigious child. *Journal of Applied Psychology*, **1** (2), 101–110.

Hollingworth, L. S., Garrison, G. G. & Burke, A. (1922). Subsequent history of E.: five years after the initial report. *Journal of Applied Psychology*, **6** (6), 205–210.

Montour, K. (1977). William James Sidis the broken twig. *American Psychologist*, **32**, 265–279.

Morelock, M. J. and Feldman, D. H. (1997). High-IQ children, extreme precocity and savant sydrome. In: Colangelo and G. A. Davis (Eds), *Handbook of Gifted Education* (2nd ed.), (pp. 439–459). Boston: Allyn and Bacon.

Roe, A. (1951). A psychological study of eminent physical scientists. *Genetic Psychology Monographs*, **43**, 121–235.

Roe, A. (1951). A psychological study of eminent biologists. *Psychological Monographs*, **63** (14, Serial No. 31).

Roe, A. (1953). A psychological study of eminent psychologists and anthropologists. *Psychological Monographs*, **67** (2, Serial No. 352).

Silverman, L. K. (1998). The highly gifted. In: J. VanTassel-Baska (Ed.), *Excellence in Educating Gifted and Talented Learners* (pp. 115–128). Denver: Love Publishing.

Southern, W. T. & Jones, E. D.(1991). *The academic acceleration of gifted children*. New York: Teachers College Press.

Terman, L. M. (1905). A study in precocity and prematuration. *American Journal of Psychology*, **16**, 145–183.

Motivation and Cognition: Their Role in the Development of Giftedness

Willy Lens[1] and Per Rand[2]

[1]University of Leuven, Belgium
[2]University of Oslo, Norway

Introduction

When Thomas Edison said "Genius is 1% inspiration and 99% perspiration," 'genius' referred to an outstanding level of performance (in whatever type of achievement tasks) and Edison wanted to stress that such high achievements or excellent performances depend much more on individual differences in perspiration, transpiration, effort or motivation than on individual differences in inspiration, abilities, capacities. He made a distinction between ability and level of performance, and he certainly underestimated the relative importance of abilities and he overestimated the role of motivation as determinants of exceptional achievements.

Merriam Webster's Collegiate Dictionary (1993, 10th edition, p. 486) defines 'genius' as "extraordinary intellectual power especially as manifested in creative activity" and 'gifted' as "having great natural ability". For Marland (1971) gifted and talented children are capable of high performance, by virtue of outstanding abilities; children capable of high performance include those with demonstrated achievement and/or potential ability. Giftedness then refers to exceptionally high levels of general intellectual ability, or of specific abilities or aptitudes. Passow's (1985) brief review of the literature shows however quite clearly that there is no generally accepted common understanding of the nature of giftedness; it can refer to high abilities as well as to high achievement, or both.

> "Can giftedness be considered as potential or must it be made visible through actual performance? . . . While giftedness has long been associated with high intelligence and high academic achievement, the dominant conceptions of giftedness which have emerged in many cultures focus on high order of potential or achievement in a variety of areas other than academic alone (o.c., p. 2048).

Terman (1925, p. 19) limited giftedness to exceptionally high levels of ability when he defined it as:

> ". . . A degree of brightness that would rate them well within the top one per cent of the population",

Brightness refers then to very high (above 135 or 140) IQ scores, or levels of performance on an intelligence test. It was "Terman's hypothesis that early promise of intellectually gifted students is likely to culminate in relatively outstanding achievement during adulthood" (Passow, 1985, p. 2046).

Renzulli (1978) does not agree with Terman's unifactorial definition of giftedness and developed his own three components model. In addition to high levels of general or specific abilities and high levels of motivation or task commitment, Renzulli adds creativity as a third component. For him giftedness is constituted by the interaction of those three personality characteristics:

> "An interaction among three basic clusters of human traits—these clusters being above average general abilities, high levels of task commitment, and high levels of creativity. Gifted and talented children are those possessing or capable of developing this composite set of traits and applying them to any potentially valuable area of human performance" (Renzulli, 1978, p. 261).

Creativity refers to original and highly inventive ways of formulating and solving complex and difficult problems; creative people have high problem sensitivity, often concentrating their analyses on the novel aspects of the situation. They produce many and original ideas which they apply flexibly, using divergent rather than convergent thinking (Guilford, 1967).

It is interesting to notice already here (see also our next section) that Renzulli not only talks of 'possessing' but also of 'capable of developing' giftedness. For him, the three components are essential for giftedness and he refers to the common mistake made when identifying giftedness to exceptionally high intellectual abilities. That is because he also derives giftedness from creative, productive high achievements. For Mönks and his collaborators (Mönks & Span, 1984; Mönks & Knoers, 1994; Mönks & Ypenburg, 1996) these three components are not more than personality dispositions that must be stimulated and developed in a social context. The three most important social settings in which a child grows up and develops are the family, the school and the peers. The family can nurse and stimulate giftedness, but also suppress or hinder its development when it is not recognized as such. Schools that do not recognize the specific abilities and potentialities of gifted children de-motivate their development. Neglecting individual cognitive differences, focusing on the middle group and expecting an equal progress from all pupils has negative motivational and learning consequences, not only for the less able but also for the most intelligent pupils. Quite often, really gifted children are not accepted by their peers and this may also negatively affect their psychological development and their scholastic achievements.

It is clear that for Renzulli and for Mönks giftedness can refer to high abilities and/or to exceptionally high achievements; this conceptual confusion is very characteristic for the field. Renzulli's (1986) three-ring conceptualization and Mönks' triadic interdependency model of giftedness discuss mainly the determinants of high and creative achievements. But from the very beginning, an important part of the research on gifted children had to do with their underachievement or much too low school performances (Terman & Oden, 1947; Whitmore, 1980; Mooij, 1991; Butler-Por, 1993, 1995). When so-called 'gifted' children can be underachieving, 'giftedness' does only refer to high levels of intellectual abilities and potentialities; conceptually it is then clearly distinguished from high achievements. When we discuss the role of motivational processes in the development of giftedness, we do make a distinction between exceptionally high levels of abilities as potentialities and high intellectual (academic) achievements. It should become clear however that the two are mutually interdependent. Unique accomplishments require high levels of abilities (potentialities) and important achievements foster the further development of those abilities, as we will discuss.

Level of Performance as a Function of Motivation and Ability

As implied in Edison's dictum, a high achievement or level of performance depends not only on high ability but certainly also on motivational factors, be it probably much less than Edison argued. For Atkinson (1974) individual differences in intellectual abilities explain about 66% of the variance in academic achievement and motivation explains about 33% of the differences in school results. As expressed in Vroom's formula (1964, p. 203) and by many others before and after him, the level of performance in an achievement

task is indeed a multiplicative function of abilities and motivation: Level of Performance $= f$ (Ability $\times$ Motivation); but how can we know someone's level of ability unless we measure it?

To start with we will discuss the distinction between true abilities or potentialities (e.g. general intelligence), measured abilities or test performances (e.g. IQ scores) and cumulative achievement (e.g. a scholastic or a professional career). We will discuss the role of motivational and other conative variables as determinants of the development of individual differences in the three of them.

People do indeed more often things that they like to do than things that they do not like and by doing so, they become better at it. That is a first explanation for a developing positive correlation between motivation and ability. In the next paragraph we will discuss a second explanation for that developing correlation. Indeed people also like to do things that they are good at; people become more motivated for tasks that they can do well. In that section we will also discuss the different categories or types of motivation that are usually distinguished in motivational research in general and in educational motivational research in particular. We will discuss the circumstances in which (exceptionally) high levels of ability will have facilitating and debilitating effects on those different types of motivation that are most relevant in an educational context.

Test Performances and Cumulative Achievements

When analyzing the role of individual differences in ability and in motivation as determinants of the level of intellective performances Atkinson (1974; Atkinson, Lens & O'Malley, 1978) made an important distinction between test performances or the level of performance while at work (e.g. an exam, an intelligence test, studying maths) and cumulative achievements that are built up over time (e.g. grade point average in a given academic year; the level of educational achievement). Motivation has a different role in these two types of tasks.

Motivation and Intellective Test Performances: True Ability (the Ever Unknown) and Measured Ability (IQ Scores)

The level of performance that is reached at each moment in time when working at a cognitive task or test is a function of: (a) the true knowledge and intellectual capacities or abilities, and (b) the efficiency with which the individual makes use of those cognitive abilities. The strength of motivation affects the quality of cognitive functioning at each moment in time because motivation determines how efficiently abilities are applied. The relationship between motivation and efficiency of cognitive functioning is, however, not necessarily linear, as assumed when blindly applying linear statistics. It can be inverted U-shaped (Yerkes & Dodson, 1908; Atkinson, 1974, p. 198). Such a curvilinear relationship implies that the efficiency and the level of performance will increase when the motivation increases from low to medium or medium to high. But when the strength of motivation to perform well increases beyond an optimal level, the efficiency of cognitive functioning will decrease. The optimal level of motivation is that intensity of motivation at which the efficiency is 100% and the individual makes maximal use of his/her true abilities; lower as well as higher levels of motivation (lower or higher than the optimal level) cause inefficiency. The second part of the too often neglected Yerkes–Dodson Law holds that the optimal level of motivation depends on the difficulty of the task; the more difficult the task, the lower the optimal level, the higher the probability of being over-motivated.

"The more general guide provided by the old Yerkes–Dodson hypothesis is that the shape of the curve describing efficiency of performance in relation to strength of motivation will depend upon the nature of the task . . . A simple, overlearned task . . . may, perhaps, produce the monotonic increasing function we have traditionally assumed . . . A more complex activity . . . may produce the kind of curvilinear relationship . . .. Still other tasks, perhaps those which require a very cautious, deliberate or relaxed approach, might produce a decreasing function for most of the range of motivation . . ." (Atkinson, 1974, p. 199).

Individual differences in strength of the achievement motivation affect the quality of cognitive functioning and hence the level of performance in intelligence tests/intellective tasks. IQ scores or the level of performance in an intelligence test must be considered as the product of the individuals' 'true ability' and the "efficiency with which they make use of their true ability during the test performance," which may be curvilinearly related to the strength of motivation to perform well in the test (Atkinson, 1974; Nygard, 1977a, b; Lens & De Volder, 1980). Taking into account existing individual differences in achievement motive, test anxiety, perceived task difficulty, there is no reason to assume that a given standardized test situation arouses the achievement motivation to an optimal level for all subjects. Individuals who are more or less strongly motivated than the optimal level while taking the intelligence test, will have their true intelligence underestimated by their IQ scores; they are underachieving on the test. Not only low levels of motivation, but also a very high level of motivation to perform well on the test will interfere with efficient test behavior. For Atkinson (1974, p. 395):

"It is essential to emphasize that the mental test movement for many years has implicitly made the claim, without adequate justification and certainly in the absence of knowledge, that the level of motivation is either optimal for everyone being tested, or constant, or only negligibly different among all individuals at the time of performance. . . . Until proven otherwise, any measured difference in what has been called general intelligence, scholastic aptitude, verbal or mathematical ability, . . . which is always obtained from performance under achievement-oriented if not multi-incentive conditions, can be given a motivational interpretation with no less scientific justification than the traditional aptitudinal interpretation."

Interpreting individual differences in IQ scores as reflecting individual differences in intellectual ability as well as in motivation, implies that lower IQ scores do not always reflect lower intellectual ability. Highly gifted youngsters who are totally uninterested in their test performances or who are much too strongly motivated or aroused when taking the test will perform much below their true ability. They will not (immediately) be recognized as highly talented; it also implies that the true ability is the ever unknown.

Motivation and Cumulative Achievement

The level of cumulative achievement reached over time depends on the level of performance while at work and on the amount of time spent at the cumulative task (Atkinson, 1974); motivation affects both components. We discussed above the relationship between strength of motivation and the level (efficiency) of performance at each moment in time or while at work. In addition, people will spend more time on intellectual tasks the more they are motivated to excel in such tasks and the less numerous and strong are the competing behavioral tendencies. Atkinson and Lens (1980) distinguished two effects of spending more time in a particular endeavor; first, the cumulative achievement or the level of performance that is realized over shorter or longer time spans. The more years one spends in the school system, the higher will be the degree (e.g. high school degree, a college degree, a degree from graduate school); but as the proverb says, 'Practice makes perfect'. Spending more time (practicing more) will also have an effect on the individual; it results in a growth in knowledge, abilities, capacities. This explains why a positive correlation should develop between motivation and abilities: the more motivated for or interested in a particular domain (e.g. mathematics, a foreign language) the more time one will spend in that domain and the more one will develop those capacities, abilities, the better one becomes. Highly motivated students will study more and by

195

doing so they will not only obtain better school results but also become more able, more intelligent. Kagan and Moss (1962) concluded their developmental study of intelligence as follows:

> "For certain populations the IQ can serve as an index of achievement concerns ... when one is working with children whose IQ scores are average or above, level of intelligence and increases in test scores appear to be good indexes of the strength of overt achievement behavior during childhood, adolescence and adulthood, and a reflection of intensity of motivation to master intellectual tasks ' (o.c., pp. 151, 152).

Which intellectual abilities one prefers to develop and to what degree one wants to do so, depends on motivational variables; see for example Anastasi (1982, p. 352): "Even more important is the cumulative effect of personality characteristics on the direction and extent of the individual's intellectual development."

Behavior (B) does not only result from an interaction between personality characteristics (P) and perceived environmental variables (E), as implied by Lewin's famous formula $B = f$ (P, E). Quite often, doing something for a while affects the individual (for example, studying changes the content and the structure of the long term memory store) and it may have effects on the environment (e.g. operant behavior). There is a second process that can explain why a positive correlation between motivation and intellectual abilities will develop. In the foregoing we explained how individual differences in motivation or interest may affect the development of individual differences in (intellectual) abilities. A not too extremely high level of motivation for intellectual tasks and only very few competing side interests ensures a maximum free time to be devoted to intellectual development. (We do not want to say here that this is most optimal for the development of a rich personality). The causal influence can however also work in the opposite direction. Due to largely genetically determined individual differences in intelligence or other abilities, some children achieve more often and more important successes in tasks invoking those intellectual or other types of abilities. The intrinsic satisfaction of successfully applying one's competencies enhances the intrinsic motivation for such tasks; people are, or become, motivated to do things that they are good at. For Deci and Ryan (1985) the perception of competence (in circumstances of self-determination) creates intrinsic motivation; people are motivated to be competent and efficient in their interactions with the world. We refer here to White's concept of "competence motivation" (White, 1959) and Bandura's concept of 'self-efficacy' (Bandura, 1986, 1997).

A Motivational Explanation of Underachievement

Underachievement is a quite common problem among gifted children (Whitmore, 1980). Terman and Oden (1947) found in one of their follow-up studies that a rather high number of highly gifted subjects perform below what might be expected based on their intellectual potentialities. Butler-Por (1993, 1995) defines underachievement as a growing discrepancy between the high ability (as observed by teachers and parents or as expressed in measures of intelligence or creativity) and the much too low school results. Notice the important difference between underachievers and low achievers. Underachievers are performing in a criterion measure, such as grades in school, much lower than was predicted based on scores in a predictor measure such as a general intelligence test. This implies that highly gifted children who score in the middle or even the top of their class may be underachieving. They could do better, given their true ability. Taking into account that giftedness can be limited to a particular ability (e.g. mathematics, languages), pupils' relatively high scores in maths or languages can nevertheless be an underachievement, while their lower grades for other courses are not.

Whitmore (1980), Span (1988), Butler-Por (1993, 1995), Piirto (1994) and many other authors distinguish different types of underachieving gifted children and they refer to many explaining factors that can be situated in the children, in their home environment and at school. Several of these debilitating factors affect the level of performance and hence cause underachievement because they undermine the children's daily motivation for school work. Atkinson (1974) formulated the following motivational explanation for underachievement in general, but that can also explain underachievement among high ability pupils. At the moment that their abilities (e.g. general intelligence) were measured, they were optimally motivated and made maximal use of their true abilities. Their (very) high score on the test expresses their true high abilities or potentialities. However, for regular schoolwork they are less than optimally motivated and they perform way below their actual potentialities. Due to motivational problems, they perform lower than could be expected on the basis of their test scores and they do not develop their potentialities; their intellectual development levels off. They do not become 'perfect' because they do not 'practice' enough. Really bright young children end up as regular students (or even worse). Lack of motivation hinders both high achievement and becoming a real 'genius'. In the next section we will discuss how different types of motivation can be undermined at school and at home.

It is very easy and quite common to perform below one's abilities or to be an underachiever; it is of course impossible to be an overachiever if that means to perform better than one's abilities would allow. Overachievers are performing better than one would predict or expect on the basis of a predictor-measure, for example test scores. For Atkinson (1974) they are underachieving in the predictor measure; because they are not enough or too much motivated to do well on the test, (below or above the optimal level of motivation) they are not 100% efficient and their test scores underestimate their true abilities.

Motivational Effects of Individual Differences in Abilities

Different from the neo-behavioristic Hullian approach in psychology, we do not have any longer one global theory of motivation that is supposed to explain all aspects of motivated behavior. Basic and applied research has resulted in a number of more limited mini-theories, discussing and explaining some aspect(s) or component(s) of the total motivation instigating and/or sustaining behavior.

Theories of human motivation can be classified in two broad categories: content theories and process theories. Content theories reduce motivation to more or less stable, inborn or acquired instincts, drives, needs or motives (e.g. the motive to succeed or the need for achievement). Process theories consider motivation as a psychological process in which personality characteristics (e.g. motives, needs, abilities, expectancies) interact with perceived characteristics of the environment (e.g. content and difficulty of learning tasks, teachers, parents and peers). Lewin's conceptualization of behavior as resulting from the interaction between the individual and the perceived environment [B = f(P, E)] is extended to also cover motivational processes. For example, the strength of the achievement motivation is not only affected by the individual strength of the achievement motive, but also by the difficulty of the achievement task. Process theories imply that characteristics of both the individual and his or her behavioral situation should be taken into consideration when trying to understand, explain and influence motivation (Snow, 1989; Snow & Swanson, 1992).

Content theories attribute the motivational cause(s) of behavior (a movement) solely to the behaving individual (the moving object), and not to the environment in which the movement takes place (the behavioral situation). Process theories attribute the movement of an object to characteristics of that object and of the environment in which the movement takes place. The difference between Renzulli's and Mönks' definition of giftedness (see above) is very analogous to the difference between content theories and process theories.

In the following section we will discuss several process-theories of motivation that are relevant for understanding the role of motivation in the development of giftedness and in high levels of performance.

We will do this for intellectual giftedness and for academic performances; but it will become clear that the discussed models apply for other types of abilities and in other domains of achievement as well.

Intrinsic and Extrinsic Motivation

It holds for most of our behaviors that they are at the same time intrinsically and extrinsically motivated; actions are extrinsically motivated when they are done for the sake of rewards or other consequences that are not intrinsically related to the activity. The activity is instrumental and its motivation can be called 'instrumental motivation'; an activity is intrinsically motivated when it is done for its own sake, when it is a goal in itself. Although it is certainly true that learning and working can be both intrinsically and extrinsically motivated, it is quite striking to notice that research on work motivation traditionally concentrates on extrinsic motivation and that research on the role of motivation in education usually discusses different types of intrinsic motivation.

For many years it was assumed that student motivation, as well as work motivation, is the sum of intrinsic and extrinsic motivational components; each intrinsic and extrinsic goal can be conceived of as an additional source of motivation. At each moment in time, the total motivation can be increased by increasing either the intrinsic motivation or the extrinsic, or both; motivational problems at school are usually due to low levels of intrinsic motivation (Lens & Decruyenaere, 1991). Parents and teachers try to compensate insufficient (intrinsic) motivation by offering extrinsic rewards in order to increase the extrinsic motivation, and hence also the total motivation. As we will explain later, nothing is wrong with this practice, if the intrinsic motivation is missing or very low.

The additive model does however not hold when we look at dynamic interactions between intrinsic and extrinsic motivation; basic experimental research over the last twenty years shows that intrinsic and extrinsic motivation are not necessarily additive. Salient, promised extrinsic rewards that are exogenous to the nature of the task, and that are given for already intrinsically motivated activities, may undermine the intrinsic motivation (Deci, 1975; Lepper & Greene, 1978; Luyten & Lens, 1981; Deci & Ryan, 1985, 1992). They do so when they produce an over-justification effect; the individual sees too many reasons for doing the task: the already present intrinsic interest and the promised extrinsic reward. Due to the fact that rewards are usually more salient, they are progressively seen as the reason for doing the task and the intrinsic interest dies out. The rewards and other external controlling measures cause a shift in the locus of causality from internal to external. Intrinsically motivated individuals see their own interest in the subject matter or the task as their sole reason for doing it. When they then repeatedly receive extrinsic rewards, those rewards become the external reasons for learning and performing well. Not the intrinsic interest, but the extrinsic rewards are from then on controlling those activities; the intrinsic interest disappears. Not only announced rewards but also evaluation, surveillance, coercion, time pressure may cause such a change in the locus of causality from internal to external and undermine the intrinsic motivation.

The low level of intrinsic motivation among many high school pupils may be partly due to this undermining effect of the many extrinsic rewards they received in elementary and (junior) high school for doing their best at school and for high marks. Harter (1981) found "... a systematic, grade-related, shift from a predominantly intrinsic motivational orientation in third grade to a more extrinsic motivational orientation by ninth grade, the biggest shift occurred between the sixth grade elementary school students and the seventh grade junior high school students" (Harter & Jackson, 1992, pp. 223–224). This is even more so for gifted children who—at a young age—are usually very highly motivated to learn and develop their exceptional abilities (Gottfried, 1990; Gottfried et al., 1994). As we will explain in the next section, they are even more vulnerable to situational circumstances undermining their (different types of) intrinsic motivation.

More recent meta-analytic research shows however that "... detrimental effects of reward occur under highly restricted, easily avoidable conditions ..." (Eisenberger & Cameron, 1996, p. 1153). Extrinsic rewards do not have this negative effect on intrinsic motivation when they are given in such a way that their controlling aspect is much less salient than their informative aspect; they can be given in such a way that they tell students how good they are at the tasks for which the rewards are given. They then strengthen perceptions and feelings of competence, enhancing the intrinsic motivation (Deci & Ryan 1985). Extrinsic rewards "... can sometimes complement or increase intrinsic motivation ..." (Rigby, Deci, Patrick & Ryan, 1992, p. 168). The intrinsic motivation will not be undermined when people can stay "self determined even when offered extrinsic motivators" (o.c., p. 168).

Extrinsic rewards and other sources of extrinsic motivation may even instigate an intrinsic motivation. Activities such as studying, plumbing, jogging may originally be motivated only by extrinsic goals such as rewards, making a living, staying in good health; after a while the same activities may become intrinsically interesting for an individual. For example, an unmotivated pupil who hates maths tries to solve additional mathematical problems as homework because the teacher or parents promised a reward for doing it. If the problems are not too easy, nor too difficult, and when their content is related to the child's life (contextual or situated topics) that pupil may then find out that she is

good at it, that it is fun to find a solution for a challenging problem. Her feelings of competence will be strengthened and an intrinsic interest in mathematics may develop. Although this phenomenon has been well known in motivational psychology for many years, it is often neglected in the discussion on the interaction of intrinsic and extrinsic motivation. Allport (1961) calls it "the functional autonomy of motives." Actions that used to be instrumentally or extrinsically motivated become functionally autonomous and intrinsically motivated. Woodworth (1918) referred to this process as "mechanisms become drives."

Intrinsic motivation

Motivation in general and intrinsic motivation in particular, are important determinants of creativity, of high achievement and the development of high abilities. Renzulli, Mönks and many others consider a strong motivation, task-commitment and perseverance as basic components of giftedness. High abilities are necessary but not sufficient for outstanding achievement or for the development of genius. This implies that motivational problems can be an important cause of underachievement and less than optimal development of potentialities. We will now discuss several types of intrinsic motivation and why highly talented children may have problems with those different types of motivational orientation.

Curiosity

Intellectual or epistemic curiosity is probably the most typical type of intrinsic motivation for learning; the desire to know and to understand intellectual problems is aroused by moderately discrepant, complex and novel information. Familiar or simple information arouses only indifference, satiation and boredom, while information that is too complex or totally new may cause anxiety and/or withdrawal. This need for information and knowledge is very strong among young children, but seems to decrease and even disappear during the high school years; our schools do not seem to appeal to this intrinsic need (Bruner, 1966). The type of intellectual problems, information and knowledge that is offered in formal education in schools is for many children too much decontextualized to arouse their curiosity.

Developmentally, creativity presupposes on the motivational side in particular curiosity, often also a will to 'do it myself'. The favorable environment for both the development of creativity and curiosity in children is one where there is time, room and encouragement for the child's self-initiated exploratory behavior (Trudewind, 1975, p. 153–154).

Most high IQ-children with a typically high curiosity start to read, write and calculate at a much younger age than less gifted children do and they learn at a much faster rate; in intellectually heterogeneous classes, the program and its pace easily bore them. Some of them compensate their intellectual frustration in school by developing a special intellectual interest (e.g. computer programming, space exploration, and wars); but that will not greatly help their motivation at school.

Need for Competence and Efficacy

The need for mastery, competence and efficiency in solving challenging tasks is a second type of intrinsic motivation that is highly relevant for schoolwork in general and for very able pupils in particular. For Malone and Lepper (1987), curiosity is the need of humans as information processors and the need for mastery characterizes humans as problem solvers. Perceptions of competence and self-efficacy (e.g. "I am good at it; I can do it") are intrinsically motivating (Deci, 1975; Deci & Ryan, 1985). As mentioned earlier, people like to do things that they are good at and they also become good at things that they like to do; students are motivated and invest considerable effort when they can expect to master a challenging task. In addition Locke and Latham (1990) stress in their goal-setting theory of task motivation that people will be more strongly motivated and perform better when the tasks are difficult but attainable.

Perceptions of competence and efficacy require challenging tasks; tasks that are too easy or too difficult are not challenging, hence not motivating; in such tasks, one cannot expect to feel competent and efficient. Success in easy tasks is highly probable but it will not be attributed to abilities or competence, but to the low degree of task difficulty; it will not enhance the perception of competence and self-efficacy. Failure in an easy task is very informative about the (low) level of ability, but it is of course highly unlikely, certainly for gifted children. When the task is very difficult, success would give much information about high competence, but success in such tasks is highly unlikely. Success experiences stimulate academic self-concept and self-efficacy only when they can be internally attributed to abilities and/or effort.

We can expect that, in general, gifted children will score highly for perceived competence and academic self-efficacy (Wagner, Neber & Heller, 1995). Social comparison teaches them that they are much more gifted than their peers and that they have much less difficulties in understanding and solving school related problems; these are two important determinants of self-efficacy (Bandura, 1986).

However, we see several reasons why truly gifted children do not develop the motivating conceptions of high ability and high self-efficacy. First, the intellectual tasks they are confronted with in school are usually too easy and too simple and hence not challenging at all for them; in general, teaching is adapted to the middle slice of students. The learning and achievement tasks are then too easy for the able students and too difficult for the lowest third in the class to be motivating. Second,

for Mönks and Ypenburg (1995), perfectionism is a rather common trait among gifted children. Piirto (1994) distinguishes enabling and disabling perfectionism. Many gifted children strive for perfectionism; they set high standards of excellence and they are very critical for themselves; they are not easily satisfied with the quality of their work. When those high standards of excellence are highly motivating and facilitate high achievement, what they often do (Whitmore, 1980), it is an enabling perfectionism. However, perfectionism can also lead to unrealistic goals that cannot be achieved or realized, because they are too difficult or too complex. Perfectionism is then debilitating (disabling perfectionism), it creates anxiety, stress and psychosomatic symptoms; about 15 to 20% of gifted people will now and then suffer from their perfectionism. Studying perfectionism among gifted children, Parker (1997) found three types: the non-perfectionists (32.8%), the healthy-perfectionists (41.7%) and the dysfunctional perfectionists (25.5%). The latter group scores higher than the two others on perfectionism and neuroticism; they are also very competitive and perceive their parents as very demanding and very critical; this is a third reason why gifted children may not develop a motivating degree of self-efficacy. A stimulating and scaffolding social environment is an important prerequisite for giftedness and creativity (Mönks & Ypenburg, 1995), but when teachers and parents expect too much too soon, the children may develop lack of confidence, fear of failure, anxiety and stress; they will underachieve, certainly in terms of the unrealistically high expectations.

Achievement motivation

The need for mastery and efficacy is closely related to the achievement motive or the need for achievement. The strength of the resultant achievement motivation is the algebraic sum of two components: the positive tendency or motivation to strive for success and the negative tendency or motivation to avoid failure. The positive tendency is a multiplicative function of three factors: (a) the motive to succeed, (b) the subjective probability of success or the expected difficulty of the achievement task, and (c) the anticipated positive incentive value of success (the harder the task, the higher the incentive value of success). Analogously, the negative tendency to avoid failure is a multiplicative function of (a) the motive to avoid failure, (b) the subjective probability of failure, and (c) the anticipated negative incentive value of failure (the easier the task, the stronger the shame for failing) (Atkinson, 1964).

For success-oriented individuals, the resultant achievement motivation is a positive approach tendency and for failure-threatened or test-anxious individuals it is a negative, inhibitory tendency not to approach achievement tasks. Achievement tasks that are either too easy or too difficult do not arouse the achievement motivation; for the most gifted children in an intellectually heterogeneous class, the tasks will be too easy to be motivating and when competing with others they have a high probability of success; but an easy success has not much incentive value. Given that gifted children usually score low on test anxiety or fear of failure (Butler & Nissan, 1975; Milgram & Milgram, 1976; Gottfried et al., 1994) it can be expected that they will be more strongly motivated for success in homogeneous classes with more difficult tasks and more competition. Atkinson and O'Connor (1963) did indeed find that success-oriented pupils are more motivated in homogeneous classes.

Another important factor to be taken into account when determining the strength of a person's achievement motivation is future time perspective (Gjesme, 1996). For Atkinson and Raynor (1974, p. 5) future time perspective or future orientation is ". . . the impact on motivation for some present activity of perceiving its instrumental relationship, as a step in a longer path, to more distant future goals and threatening consequences" (Atkinson & Raynor, 1974, p. 5).

A person who has a long future time perspective will, compared to a person with a short future time perspective, 'see' further ahead, and include more distant future happenings in his/her plans. A person with a long time perspective will perceive a future goal closer than a person with a shorter time perspective does (Lens, 1986). The motivation for working towards a goal will be more strongly aroused the closer the person perceives the goal; chronological time distance is of course also an important factor influencing the perceived goal distance in time.

Gjesme found that ". . . the arousal of motives increases as the subjectively experienced goal distance in time decreases" (Gjesme, 1981, p. 124).

For Gjesme (1996) and Zaleski (1987) the influence of the future goal on the present motivation to work towards that goal depends partly on the importance of the final goal, the perceived instrumentality of present actions for reaching that goal, the distance in physical time and the individual future orientation.

Length or extension of future time perspective correlates positively with general intelligence (Nuttin et al., 1979). This means that highly intelligent children at a younger age can easily foresee the distant future and take it into account in the present. They perceive more easily the instrumental value or utility of their present actions and that will increase their motivation.

In summary, the three types of intrinsic motivation that we discussed above, are all very relevant in building cognitive structures and content, and play an important part in the development of giftedness. The creativity part (cf. Renzulli, 1978) is for its early development motivationally dependent on curiosity, and often also on a will to 'do it myself'; later in life intrinsic motivation may not play the same dominant part. Extrinsic motivation increases in importance, but must not be seen as the big bad wolf (Harter &

Jackson, 1992; Heyman & Dweck, 1992; Lens & Rand, 1997; Husman & Lens, 1999). One cannot assume that the moment a goal outside the ongoing activity enters the picture, all is ruined; one must accept performance goals. It is not possible only to pursue interesting things, and abstain from meeting the performance demands needed for entering or continuing studies, and thus spoiling the chances of reaching own long-term goals.

Dweck (1986) differentiates between three types of achievement goals as: (a) the wish to develop competence, (b) to reach competence, and (c) to demonstrate competence. According to Pintrich and Schunk (1996) Dweck's two first types of goals may be called learning or mastery goals (intrinsic ones), while the third is a performance (with extrinsic motivation).

An optimal level of motivation is usually connected with a high learning goal orientation, and low performance orientation. However, lately several authors report positive effects of performance goals on cognitive engagement, well adapted learning strategies and on academic performance (cf. Bouffard, Boisvert, Vezeau & Laroviche, 1995; Wolters, Yu & Pintrich, 1996; Skaalvik, 1997). To strive for performance goals through competition with others does not exclude working towards learning goals; simultaneous striving for both is possible, if there is a certain basis of learning goals. Wentzel (1991) actually found that pupils who strive towards both types of goals show a higher degree of self-regulation and higher performance than pupils who only work towards one type of goal. The authors who share this view often stress that the double goals are usually found in pupils/students on the higher steps of education (college and university students), who have chosen their courses themselves so that they are related to their future work career. At this level there may be a real need for competition, because further study in the wished-for direction may be restricted to the best part of the student group.

Conclusion

The close relationship between cognitive and motivational development might be explained in two ways. Differences in motivation may create differences in cognition, reflected in intelligence test scores and in cumulative intellectual achievements over time. Highly motivated individuals would always seek out a variety of challenging task situations; they work hard and they are persistent. As a consequence, they might accordingly develop higher ability to tackle new situations. But differences in cognitive ability/intelligence may also create differences in strength of motivation; a child with high abilities and a nurturing learning environment will have many opportunities to experience goal attainment, success and intellectual satisfaction. Those positive affects are the basis for the development of the several types of intrinsic and extrinsic (instrumental) motivation.

References

Allport G. W. (1961). *Pattern and growth in personality*. New York: Holt.

Anastasi (1982). *Psychological testing*. New York: Wiley.

Atkinson, J. W. (1964). *An introduction to motivation*. Princeton: Van Nostrand.

Atkinson, J. W. (1974). Motivational determinants of intellective performance and cumulative achievement. In: J. W. Atkinson & J. O. Raynor (Eds), *Motivation and Achievement* (pp. 389–410). Washington, DC: Winston & Sons.

Atkinson, J. W. & Lens W. (1980): Fähigkeit und Motivation als Determinanten momentaner und kumulativer Leistung. In: H. Heckhausen (Ed.), *Fähigkeit und Motivation in erwartungswidriger Schulleistung* (pp.129–192). Göttingen: Verlag für Psychologie, Dr. C. J. Hogrefe.

Atkinson, J. W., Lens, W. & O'Malley, P. M. (1978). Motivation and ability: interactive psychological determinants of intellective performance, educational achievement and each other. In: W. H. Sewell, R. M. Hauser & D. L. Featherman (Eds), *Schooling and Achievement in American Society* (pp. 29–66). New York: Academic Press.

Atkinson, J. W. & O'Connor, P. A. (1963). *Effects of ability grouping in schools related to individual differences in achievement-related motivation: final report*. Office of Education Cooperative Research Project 1238.

Atkinson, J. W. & Raynor, J. O. (1974). (Eds), *Motivation and achievement*. Washington, DC: Winston & Sons.

Bandura, A. (1986). *Social foundations of thought and action. a social cognitive theory*. Englewood Cliffs, NJ: Prentice-Hall.

Bandura, A. (1997). *Self-efficacy: the exercise of control*. New York: Freeman.

Bouffard, T., Boisvert, J., Vezeau, C. & Larouche, C. (1995). The impact of goal orientation on self-regulation and performance among college students. *British Journal of Educational Psychology*, **65**, 317–329.

Bruner, J. S. (1966). *Toward a theory of instruction*. Cambridge, Mass.: Harvard University Press.

Butler, R. & Nissan, M. (1975). Who is afraid of success? and why? *Journal of Youth and Adolescence*, **4**, 259–270.

Butler-Por, N. (1993). Underachieving gifted children. In: K. A. Heller, F. J. Mönks & A. H. Passow (Eds), *International Handbook of Research and Development of Giftedness and Talent* (pp. 649–668). Oxford: Pergamon.

Butler-Por, N. (1995). Gifted children: who is at risk for underachievement and why? In: M. W. Katzko & F. J. Mönks (Eds), *Nurturing talent: Individual Needs and Social Ability* (pp. 649–668). Oxford: Pergamon Press.

Deci, E. L. (1975). *Intrinsic motivation*. New York: Plenum.

Deci, E. L. & Ryan, R. M. (1985). *Intrinsic motivation and self determination in human behavior*. New York: Plenum Press.

Deci, E. L. & Ryan, R. M. (1992). The initiation and regulation of intrinsically motivated learning and achievement. In: A. K. Boggiano & T. S. Pittman, (Eds), *Achievement and Motivation: A Social-Developmental Perspective* (pp. 9–36). Cambridge: Cambridge University Press.

Dweck, C. S. (1986). Motivational processes affecting learning. *American Psychologist*, **41**, 1040–1048.

Eisenberger, R. & Cameron, J. (1996). Detrimental effects of reward: reality or myth? *American Psychologist*, **51**, 1153–1166.

Elliot, E. S. & Dweck, C. S. (1988). Goal: an approach to motivation and achievement. *Journal of Personality and Social Psychology*, **54**, 5–12.

Gjesme, T. (1981). Is there any future in achievement motivation? *Motivation and Emotion*, **5**, 115–138.

Gjesme, T. (1996). Future time orientation and motivation. In: T. Gjesme, & R. Nygård (Eds), *Advances in Motivation*. Oslo, Norway: Scandinavian University Press (pp. 210–222).

Gottfried, A. E. (1990). Academic intrinsic motivation in young elementary school children. *Journal of Educational Psychology*, **82**, 525–538.

Gottfried, A. W., Gottfried, A. E., Bathurst, K. & Guerin, D. W. (1994). *Gifted IQ: early developmental aspects. The Fullerton longitudinal study*. New York: Plenum Press.

Guilford, J. P. (1967) *The nature of human intelligence*. New York: McGraw-Hill.

Harter, S. (1981). A new self-report scale of intrinsic vs. extrinsic orientation in the classroom: motivational and informational components. *Developmental Psychology*, **17**, 300–312.

Harter, S., & Jackson, B. K. (1992). Trait vs. non-trait conceptualizations of intrinsic/extrinsic motivational orientations. *Motivation and Emotion*, **16**, 209–230.

Heyman, G. D. & Dweck, C. S. (1992).Achievement goals and intrinsic motivation: their relation and their role in adaptive motivation. *Motivation and Emotion*, **16**, 231–247.

Husman, J. & Lens, W. (1999). The role of the future in student motivation. *Educational Psychologist*, **34**, 113–125.

Kagan, J. & Moss, H. A. (1962). *Birth to maturity*. New York: Wiley.

Lens, W. (1986). Future time perspective: a cognitive-motivational concept. In: D. R. Brown & J. Veroff (Eds), *Frontiers of Motivational Psychology*. (pp. 173–190). New York: Springer-verlag.

Lens, W. & Decruyenaere, M. (1991). Motivation and demotivation in secondary education: student characteristics. *Learning and Instruction*, **1**, 145–159.

Lens, W. & De Volder, M. (1980). Achievement motivation and intelligence test scores: a test of the Yerkes–Dodson hypothesis. *Psychologica Belgica*, **20**, 49–59.

Lens, W. & Rand, P. (1997). Combining intrinsic goal orientations with professional instrumentality/utility in student motivation. *Polish Psychological Bulletin*, **28**, 103–123.

Lepper, M. R. & Greene, D. (1978). (Eds), *The hidden costs of reward*. Hillsdale, NJ: Erlbaum.

Locke, E. A. & Latham, G. P. (1990). *A theory of goal setting and task performance*. Englewood Cliffs, NJ: Prentice Hall.

Luyten, H. & Lens, W. (1981). The effect of earlier experience and reward contingencies on intrinsic motivation. *Motivation and Emotion*, **5**, 25–36.

Malone, Th. W. & Lepper, M. (1987). Making learning fun: a taxonomy of intrinsic motivations for learning. In: R. E. Snow & M. J. Farr (Eds), *Aptitude, Learning, and Instruction*. Vol. 3. *Conative and Affective Process Analyses* (pp. 223–253). Hillsdale, NJ: Erlbaum.

Marland, S. P., Jr. (1971). *Education of the gifted and talented.* Washington, DC: U.S. Government Printing Office.

Milgram, R. M. & Milgram, N. A. (1976). Creative thinking and creative performance in Israeli students. *Journal of Educational Psychology,* **68,** 255–259.

Mönks, F. J. & Knoers, A. M. P. (1994). *Ontwikkelings-psychologie [Developmental psychology].* Assen/ Maastricht: Van Gorcum.

Mönks, F. J. & Span, P. (1984). *Hoogbegaafden in de samenleving [Gifted people in society].* Nijmegen: Dekker & Van de Vegt.

Mönks, F. J. & Ypenburg, I. H. (1995). *Hoogbegaafde kinderen thuis en op school [Gifted children at home and in school].* Alphen aan den Rijn: Samson H. D.Tjeenk Willink.

Mooij, T. (1991). *Onderwijs aan hoogbegaafde kinderen [Teaching gifted children].* Muidenberg: Coutinho.

Nuttin, J., Lens, W., Van Calster, K. & Devolder, M. (1979). La perspective temporelle dans le comportement humain: Etude théorique et revue de recherches. In: P. Fraise et al. (Eds), *Du temps biologique ou temps psychologique* (pp. 307–363). Paris: Presses Universitaires de France.

Nygård, R. (1977a). *Personality, situation and persistence: a study with emphasis on achievement motivation.* Oslo, Norway: Universitetsforlaget.

Nygård, R. (1977b): IQ og intelligens. Noen betraktninger omkring individuelle forskjeller med utgangspunkt i en motivasjonsteori. (IQ and intelligence. Some thoughts regarding individual differences based on a theory of motivation.) In: T. Nordin & B. Sjövall (Eds), *Individualism Och Samhörighet. En Vänbok Till Wilhelm Sjöstrand.* Lund, Sweden: Bokförlaget Doxa (pp. 169–187).

Parker, W. D.(1997). An empirical typology of perfectionism in academically talented children. *American Educational Research Journal,* **34,** 545–562.

Passow, A. H. (1985). Gifted and talented, education of. In: T. Husen & T. Neville Postlehwaite (Eds), *The International Encyclopedia of Education: Research and Studies.* Vol. 4 (pp. 2045–2056). Oxford: Pergamon Press.

Piirto, J. (1994). *Talented children and adults: their development and education.* New York: Macmillan College Publishing Company.

Pintrich, P. R. & Schunk, D. H. (1996). *Motivation in education: theory, research, and applications.* Englewood Cliffs, NJ: Prentice Hall.

Raynor, J. O. (1981). Future orientation and achievement motivation: toward a theory of personality functioning and change. In: G. d'Ydewalle & W. Lens (Eds), *Cognition in Human Motivation and Learning* (pp. 199–231). Leuven & Hillsdale, NJ: Leuven University Press & Erlbaum.

Renzulli, J. S. (1978). What makes giftedness? Re-examining a definition. *Phi Delta Kappan,* **60,** 180–184 and 261.

Renzulli, J. S. (1986). The three-ring conception of giftedness: a developmental model for creative productivity. In: R. J. Sternberg & J. E. Davidson (Eds), *Conceptions of Giftedness* (pp. 53–92). Cambridge: Cambridge University Press.

Rigby, C. S., Deci, E. L., Patrick, B. C. & Ryan, R. M. (1992). Beyond the intrinsic-extrinsic dichotomy: self-determination in motivation and learning. *Motivation and Emotion,* **16,** 165–185.

Skaalvik, E. M. (1997). Self-enhancing and self-defeating ego-orientation: relations with task and avoidance orientation, achievement, self-perceptions, and anxiety. *Journal of Educational Psychology,* **89,** 71–81.

Snow, R. E. (1989). Toward assessment of cognitive and conative structures in learning. *Educational Researcher,* **18,** 8–14.

Snow, R. E. & Swanson, J. (1992). Instructional psychology: aptitude, adaptation, and assessment. *Annual Review of Psychology,* **43,** 583–626.

Span, P. (1988). Onderpresteren op school door hoogbegaafde leerlingen: Een 'geval' [Underachievement at school by gifted children: a case-study]. *Tijdschrift voor Orthopeda-gogiek, Kinderpsychiatrie en klinische Kinderpsychologie,* **13,** 121–129.

Terman, L. M. (1925). *Mental and physical traits of a thousand gifted children: genetic studies of genius* (Vol. 1). Stanford, CA: Stanford University Press.

Terman, L. M. & Oden, M. H. (1947). *The gifted child grows up—twenty-five years' follow-up of a superior group: genetic studies of genius* (Vol. 4). Stanford, CA: Stanford University Press.

Trudewind, C. (1975). *Häusliche Umwelt und Motive-ntwicklung.* Göttingen: Hogrefe.

Vroom, V. H. (1964). *Work and motivation.* New York: Wiley.

Wagner, H., Neber, H. & Heller, K. A. (1995).The BundesSchülerAkademie—a residential summer program for gifted adolescents in Germany. In: M. W. Katzko & F. J. Mönks (Eds), *Nurturing Talent: Individual Needs and Social Ability* (pp. 281–292). Assen: Van Gorcum.

Wentzel, K. R. (1991) Social and academic goals at school: motivation and achievement in context. In: M. Maehr & P. R. Pintrich (Eds), *Advances in Motivation and Achievement,* Vol. 7: *Goals and Self-Regulatory Processes* (pp. 185–212). Greenwich, CT: JAI.

White, R. W. (1959). Motivation reconsidered: the concept of competence. *Psychological Review,* **66,** 297–333.

Whitmore, J. R. (1980). *Giftedness, conflict and under-achievement.* Boston: Allyn & Bacon.

Wolters, C., Yu, S. & Pintrich, P. R. (1996). The relation between goal orientation and students' motivational beliefs and self-regulated learning. *Learning and Individual Differences,* **8,** 211–238.

Woodworth, R. S. (1918). *Dynamic psychology.* New York: Columbia University Press.

Yerkes, R. M. & Dodson, J. D.(1908). The relation of strength of stimulus to rapidity of habit formation. *Journal of Comparative and Neurological Psychology,* **18,** 459–482.

Zaleski, Z. (1987). Behavioral effects of self-set goals for different time ranges. *International Journal of Psychology,* **22,** 17–38.

Social-Emotional Development and the Personal Experience of Giftedness

Laurence J. Coleman[1] and Tracy L. Cross[2]

[1] *College of Education, University of Tennessee, USA*
[2] *Teachers College, Ball State University, USA*

Introduction

Social-emotional development is particularly important because it is clear that non-intellective factors are crucial to understanding the emergence of giftedness (Tannenbaum, 1983). The literature on social-emotional development of children who are gifted and talented is broad with much written on it, much expressed clinically about it, and scattered systematic study about it. Most of the literature is written from the perspective of detached scholars as well as staunch advocates for programs designed on behalf of the gifted. The result is a mass of interesting, sometimes contradictory, information and a fertile ground for all kinds of entrepreneurial activity as witnessed by the parent-help books and workshop training opportunities for teachers.

The purpose of this chapter is to provide a means for understanding the social-emotional development of gifted students. In this chapter we introduce a structure for understanding the topic that looks at giftedness and talent from the inside, attempt to clarify some of the issues and suggest how we might expand our knowledge base. We start with clarifying statements and assumptions about our topic, continue with some discussion of major questions that govern the topic of social-emotional development, and encourage two approaches to the study of experience as means of expanding our understanding of the topic. More specifically, issues such as nature/nurture concerns, universal and nonuniversal patterns of development, endogenous and exogenous characteristics of gifted students and culturally-based issues of giftedness are discussed. From all this, a means of considering the social-emotional development of gifted students is articulated that includes several components: social cognition, stigma management, and lived experience. The discussion uses experiences in school to illustrate meaningful interactions that affect the long term social-emotional development of gifted students.

Clarifying Statements and Assumptions

There are several important assumptions held by the authors that underpin the ideas proposed in this chapter. While many in the field of gifted education have focused on the social and emotional needs of gifted students, we assume more of a developmental approach. We prefer the term social-emotional development over the term emotional development because it makes it clear that emotional development occurs in a social matrix. Talking about development as if those influences do not exist makes little sense to us. We also contend that the separation of emotions from cognition is false. When we use the term social-emotional, we are always assuming the influence of thought. Therefore, gifted students are assumed to be active agents in their social-emotional development. For example, just as social forces influence development, the emotional content of symbols and actions as interpreted by the individual influence development. We rarely use the term personality in the discussion because it seems to be an even broader construct than social-emotional development. Lastly, our presentation wavers back and forth between normative issues that apply to all those who are gifted and unique personal issues that refer to individual development. In general our discussion begins with a normative discussion and moves toward the unique.

Terms Used in the Social-Emotional Realm: Needs, Characteristics and Issues

Researchers have claimed that the social-emotional needs of gifted students are a byproduct of one of two possibilities. The first possibility is that needs will exist as a function of specific individual characteristics (endogenous) the gifted student possesses. For example, excessive perfectionism is a personality characteristic that can influences a child's experience of the world in a certain way. Consequently, in this child's experience, this personality characteristic reflects needs he or she has. The second way social-emotional needs can emerge is as a function of the child interacting within a specific environment. This interaction of characteristics with the environment yields exogenous needs. For example, a child who is self-critical and who exists in a school environment that encourages competition might experience a greater sense of self-doubt or poor self-image due to the struggle that is associated with that personal characteristic as it interacts with that setting. In other settings, however, the characteristic may elicit no social-emotional need per se.

Issues are examples of large, more general concerns gifted students have in school, or that affect the context in which the child exists in school. For example, a common issue for gifted students is working as peers with other students who are not as passionate about their schooling as they are. This issue exists in many school settings, but the prevailing attitudes of teachers and administrators vary based on their beliefs and the values held about giftedness, the role of schooling etc. For example, many principals believe that all children are gifted, while many teachers believe that students should accommodate the curriculum rather than the other way around. Perhaps the most commonly held belief by these two groups is that the whole concept of giftedness is elitist, and therefore something to be discouraged. Consequently, even though issues always surround gifted students while they are in school, their experiences are lived with myriad other influences or factors that affect their social-emotional development.

Needs of All Children

It is generally assumed that all children have the same basic needs. Maslow's (1970) hierarchical theory provides a framework from which we can interpret the role of the needs. The theory asserts that people have several basic needs that must be satisfied before they can ascend to the higher tier needs. In the hierarchy, just after the first (physiological) and second needs (safety) are two needs relevant to the psychological and social domain – the need for belonging and love (level three) and esteem needs (level four). According to the theory, gifted children would have to have satisfied these two needs in the psychological and social realm before they would be able to move toward self-actualization (level five). The satisfying of needs consumes time and energy. In a very practical sense, the more time one spends trying to satisfy the lower level needs on Maslow's Hierarchy, the less time and energy can be spent operating at the higher levels that are generally more closely associated with being a successful student. An important conclusion from this theory applied to the development of the social-emotional needs of gifted students is that some of the influences on the development of gifted students are the same as those for nongifted students. While we

point this out, we do not conclude, however, that the influences are the same in either the experience of or effects on gifted and talented students.

Endogenous Characteristics of Gifted Students

Researchers have been exploring the efficacy of Dabrowski's (1967) theory of personality as a means for understanding gifted students (Silverman, 1993; Mendaglio, 1995; Cross, Cook & Dixon, 1996). Piechowski (1986, 1997) has been the leader in forwarding the basic tenets of the theory that has two components: overexcitabilities and levels of development. In his theory, Dabrowski posited that gifted individuals manifest super-sensitivity (translated into English as overexcitabilities) in several areas: psychomotor, intellectual, sensual, imaginational and emotional. Overexcitabilities are described as expanded awareness, intensified emotions, and increased levels of intellectual and/or physical activity. The research in this area shows early promise in greatly expanding the understanding we have about gifted students in the social-emotional realm. For example, it should not be surprising to see a young gifted child being very upset by social injustices around the world. The level of emotional intensity might appear more common to an adolescent than a child of elementary age. Understanding that these strong reactions are an aspect of their gifted personality rather than a behavioral or emotional disorder has implications for teachers, counselors and parents (Mendaglio, 1995).

A common topic appearing in the research lore that considers the endogenous social-emotional characteristics and needs of gifted students is that they experience uneven development; sometimes called asynchronous development (Delisle, 1992; Silverman, 1993). This can be seen in differences between the level of their general aptitude, or specific aptitude, and other aspects of their development such as their physical abilities, or social and emotional development. Many in the field believe that asynchronous development represents a need in and of itself, regardless of the student's environment.

A second often mentioned social-emotional need described in the literature emerges from some gifted children's tendency toward perfectionism (Webb, Meckstroth & Tolan, 1982). Perfectionism is being dissatisfied with the difference between one's ideal performance and one's perception of his or her actual performance. This characteristic is also described as having unreasonably high expectations for one's performance. Numerous manifestations of problems have been attributed to perfectionism, such as high levels of stress, uncompleted projects and an unwillingness to engage in healthy risk-taking behaviors (Baker, 1996).

Another frequently discussed endogenous need of gifted children results from their tendency for excessive self-criticism (Anderholt-Elliot, 1987). This need emerges from their pattern of being highly critical of themselves when they fall short of accomplishing an ideal performance. Since they may also have perfectionistic tendencies, their self-assessment will often be very disappointing, yielding excessive self-criticism.

Lastly, an often-discussed characteristic of gifted students is called multipotentiality (Silverman, 1993). Multipotentiality describes the way in which many gifted students show great promise and interest in numerous areas. Being successful in numerous areas is very difficult, and requires vast amounts of time and commitment to each area. According to some, multipotentiality often becomes problematic in the social-emotional lives of the gifted students because it can lead to higher levels of stress and emotional upset.

Exogenous Needs of Gifted Students

As noted previously, exogenous needs emerge from the characteristics of the person within the culture, norms and expectations of a specific environment; they are not extant characteristics of the individual per se. In this chapter, the discussion is limited to the social-emotional needs of gifted students in a school environment. Before discussing their need, one should note that all the previous endogenous characteristics and subsequent needs may exist within the school setting. Because each school has its own personality and distinct social milieu, it is difficult to accurately predict the extent to which a particular gifted student will thrive or struggle due to his or her social-emotional make-up (Cross, Coleman & Terhaar-Yonkers, 1991). It is, however, reasonable to illustrate commonalities to gifted students' experiences and how they evolve over time. Perhaps the most common example of a gifted child's characteristics leading to social-emotional needs emerges from their desire for academic engagement while interacting within a school environment that is not accepting of students who are very serious about learning (Cross, Coleman & Stewart, 1995). This interaction can yield any of the following needs in the social emotional realm: a need to feel accepted, a need to affiliate with other gifted students, and a need for recognition of accomplishments. In short, studies have shown that exogenous needs emerge from the characteristics the gifted child has in either their psychological or intellectual domains interacting in an environment that is perceived and/or experienced by the child as being at odds with their social-emotional nature (Cross, Coleman & Terhaar-Yonkers, 1991; Cross & Stewart, 1995; Cross, Coleman & Stewart, 1995). Therefore, the same qualities the individual gifted student has in a different environment may not manifest in social-emotional needs. To gain insight into their social-emotional development, one should consider larger issues of the relative influences of nature and nurture of gifted students.

Considering the Role of Nature and Nurture in Social-emotional Development

What governs social-emotional development? Is it nature or nurture? Is it universal or nonuniversal? Both questions seem to be foundational to the topic of social-emotional development. The first question looks at the biological-environmental bases of development; the second, at the everyperson-specialperson idea of development. Neither pole has unequivocal support; yet, the way in which the questions are answered by people influence interpretations about the topic of social-emotional development of the gifted.

Nature-Nurture

The question of nature and nurture is unanswerable, or only partially answerable, for many reasons. The most obvious is because the person we see is always a phenotype, never a genotype. Typical development is a consequence of multiple genes (polygenic), not a single gene, interacting in a changeable environment of some kind. Any person we meet is a product of interactions between genes expressed in the form of DNA messages and environments in the form of various social settings in the world. Thus, it may sound strange, yet it would be more accurate to use the adjective phenotypic before the word gifted or talented.

Acknowledging complexity does not mean that we cannot say something more definite about the relationship between nature and nurture. Research into the heritability of IQ indicates that about 50% or so of the score is attributable to genes and the rest to environment and to chance. It seems that, for IQ, nature may have the strongest influence among the three. However, two caveats are important to avoid an over interpretation of the statement's meaning. The first is that estimates of heritability refer to groups and not to individuals. The second caveat is that the statement refers specifically to general cognitive functioning and, most importantly for our topic, not directly to social-emotional development. There is no reason to assume that inherited factors are more or less important in social-emotional development than they are in cognitive development. In other words, the forces influencing development are nature and nurture, but how these forces play out for the individual is not knowable. This fact becomes most obvious when considering those persons who are the most gifted.

Commenting on the evidence on general intelligence and genetics, Plomin & Petrill (1997) offered a summary that applies to our discussion of social-emotional development. We recommend (recognizing the danger of this suggestion) that the reader substitute the term social-emotional development for the word intelligence in order to get a sense of the essential meaning of the nature-nurture discussion. It is important to emphasize what these findings do not imply. They do not imply that intelligence is predetermined.

The fact (sic) that intelligence is heritable does not mean that the genetic part of intelligence is non-malleable. It is also true that intelligence is often confused with a genetic predisposition to learn. Intelligence is a phenotype with about half of the variance of IQ scores having a nongenetic origin. Going further, because 50% heritability is an average estimate in the population, the importance of environmental factors may be greater for a particular individual's intelligence (p.73).

In recent years an idea – the niche-picking hypothesis – has emerged that speculates on the influence an individual's genetic make-up might have on his or her own development (Scarr, 1992). If the niche-picking hypothesis is valid, then persons may gravitate toward environments that fit their biological predisposition. This hypothesis is interesting because it suggests that unconscious forces have a role in a person's development by pushing a preference to be in settings that promote development. Thus, people are not simply passive beings waiting for their biological destiny to be played out, but active, yet oblivious seekers. While this idea is intriguing, our intent is not to endorse it but rather to underscore that nature-nurture interaction is dynamic. We are not suggesting that individual development is simply a matter of making choices among the social and natural forces that potentially influence development. One only has to imagine what it is like growing up in warring societies such as in the former Yugoslavia or in Rwanda to recognize that many forces are outside a person's control. However, the notion of finding oneself or placing oneself in the best environment for development reemerges later in our discussion of universal and unique development.

Universal-nonuniversal

The issue of universal-nonuniversal refers to the question of whether the social-emotional development of persons who are gifted and talented is the same as or different in some fundamental way from that of persons who are not gifted. This issue is related to the issue of whether gifted persons are qualitatively versus quantitatively different from the non-gifted. (Coleman & Cross, 2001).

In speaking of the development of giftedness, much is taken for granted about the topic. The conventional wisdom on the development of giftedness asserts that gifted children are children first and gifted second. Many in the field, including our own graduate students, often translate such assertions into the idea that gifted children develop like all children, an idea that might be inaccurate. We take the statement to be an announcement of value – that all children are valuable as persons first, and as gifted persons second – not as a statement of social-emotional development. We ask, is it possible that gifted children could develop in a manner that is different from that of non-gifted children? We know

that some persons accomplish or create in a way that seems to be unlike others. Does this mean that their developmental pattern is uniquely different from other children who are not gifted? Note that our questions do not ask whether the development of any individual is unique because we assume that always to be the case; no two individuals develop in precisely the same way. So, unique in this sense refers to the classes of persons who might be considered gifted in some manner.

Answers to the questions of universal/non-universal development fall within the field into three co-existing viewpoints about development: universal, universal with special characteristics, and non-universal. These views translate into these statements: the gifted are like all children (universal); the gifted are like all children and yet (some) have some special quality, too (universal with special characteristics); and the gifted are like persons who develop within a narrow domain of talent and few among them will be unique (non-universal). Here, we are using the term unique in a narrower sense than it is commonly used to convey the idea that some persons present an idea, model or performance that transforms a field.

The most common view, the universal, is that development of gifted children proceeds like that of all children. Typical development is an observable pattern common to all humans. In this category, whatever giftedness is, is generally accepted as development advanced from the expected pattern. Much of Terman's pioneering work can be seen as an attempt to show the universality of development of gifted children. A number of theories propose patterns of development that fit into the universal developmental view, e.g. Piaget, Erickson, Maslow, Kohlberg who speak of cognitive, identity, personality, and moral development respectively. Interestingly, these well-named theories are treated as independent from each other in most discussions of the gifted pertaining to their social-emotional development. Few acknowledge an association or interrelationship among them (Gowan, 1972; Coleman & Cross, 2001.) Although unevenness across developmental theories seems possible, it is their universality that is important.

Feldman (1980) identified four assumptions or criteria that are characteristic of universal developmental theories: universal achievement, spontaneous acquisition, invariant sequence and hierarchical integration toward transition. Note that the first two assumptions include all persons and are relatively independent of societal variations. It is this freedom that makes them universal and why they are applicable across a wide range of societal conditions. Regardless of the specific theory one accepts, buying into a universal theory means one accepts the assumptions underlying theories of that kind. Another smaller group which is growing in popularity in the field also speaks of universal patterns. This group sees gifted persons as possessing some quality or attribute more so than non-gifted persons (Silverman, 1993; Morelock, 1996). Gifted persons are believed to experience living more intensely and more deeply. Piechowski (1991) maintains that these differences mean the gifted are qualitatively different. Integral to this view of development is the notion that these qualities promote the emergence of discontinuity or asynchrony in the universal developmental patterns. Asynchronous development is thought to be fueled by increasing levels of cognitive complexity (IQ is the metric) and by universal internal psychological mechanisms that are more evident in the gifted (Dabrowski, 1967). The interplay of cognition and internal mechanisms is important. The idea that children with the highest IQs experience emotional difficulties reminiscent of 'older' persons at earlier ages has been observed for many years (Hollingworth, 1926, 1942). However, the corresponding idea of internal mechanisms driving development has roots in Freud, Maslow and other theorists, but here Dabrowski's Theory of Positive Disintegration is influential. In his theory, inner conflict builds tension that fuels further development. Heightened sensitivity to certain kinds of stimuli (overexcitability) yields tensions that propel development. In this process the individual influences his own development. Within the gifted group individuals can be further distinguished by increasing levels of cognitive complexity and sensitivity. While development proceeds along the same lines for all, the particular characteristics of the gifted (IQ and intensity) make the gifted group qualitatively different and hence their development is different. The proponents of this view refer most often to examples of highly gifted persons and maintain they are more concerned about social-emotional development than accomplishment (Morelock, 1996).

The third group, the smallest in the field, sees development as non-universal and links development to the emergence of advanced, specialized kinds of abilities or talents in relatively few persons. The non-universal perspective proposes the idea that development is not solely in the person (like the other positions) but is also governed by the structure of the domain in which the advanced development is evident. Persons in that field (e.g. music, mathematics) go through an invariant sequence with increasing levels of complexity and increasing time devoted to practice. Nonuniversal development does not happen spontaneously in the course of living. Rather a person must make a commitment (e.g. by devoting time and practice) to the field. Not all persons have the opportunity, nor take the opportunity, for such development. Because of this purposeful dimension, non-universal development is susceptible to social variation. This is in marked contrast to universal development that is resistant to social forces, hence its universal quality. The theoretical proponent behind non-universal development has been David Feldman (1980), although our interpretation of it as a means for understanding social-emotional development is not (Coleman, 1985; Coleman & Cross, 2001). The non-universal concept forwards the notion that commonalities will exist among persons in a field and reserves the notion of uniqueness to be applied to those few persons who alter the parameters of a field or create a new one. A significant feature of non-universal development is that rapid advances in development are regarded as normal rather than departures from normal. This view was developed based on the study of prodigies and the use of case studies (Feldman, 1991).

Moving From Influences to Theory

We have discussed needs, characteristics and issues in terms of exogenous, endogenous and their interaction with the environment and in terms of researchers' conceptions of developmental trends and influences. What do the three conceptions of development have to do with dealing with the social-emotional issues that some children experience? That is hard to answer. The notion that gifted children have special needs is present in many of the popular texts in the field (Webb, Meckstroth & Tolan, 1982; Silverman, 1992; Gallagher & Gallagher, 1994; Clark, 1997). (For purposes of clarity we are not discussing educational needs in this chapter.) Webb and colleagues make a distinction between endogenous needs originating from the individual and exogenous needs that are byproducts of specific characteristics being present in an environment. Their dichotomy is a useful way to think about some individuals in their particular lives, but we suspect that the distinction tends to reify endogenous characteristics in a way that leads to confusion about social-emotional development of persons who are gifted. From our interactionist perspective, personal characteristics have psychological and phenomenal meaning primarily in sociocultural contexts. For example, in conversations among advocates for the gifted it is not uncommon to hear, "I think Mary's passion for dinosaurs is an indicator of attention span, curiosity, and imagination, but others view her passion as obnoxious, obsessive and not gender appropriate." This illustrates that characteristics have primary meaning when linked to living in the world and it is debatable whether the needs are endogenous. That some children who are gifted and talented have social-emotional problems and need assistance in coming to terms with themselves is undeniable. As previously noted, the three characteristics that get the most attention (perfectionism, multipotentiality and developmental differences between cognitive and affective growth) are interpretable as either endogenous or exogenous. Helpful suggestions can be found for practitioners and parents for dealing with those problems. However, acceptance of the existence of these problems does not mean that the majority of gifted children have variants of those problems. To make such an inference distorts and dilutes the meaning of those problems. Furthermore, it is also unclear how the presence of those problems influence later development. Are our conventional assumptions about long term influence valid? Obviously, much more needs to be learned.

The Relationship Between Social-Emotional Development and Experience

What does this situation mean for our understanding of social-emotional development? Where do we go with these competing views of social-emotional development? How do they help us understand gifted persons? We endorse a postmodern view that the three views of social-emotional development tell us somewhat different stories about the phenomenon of social-emotional development. Obviously, universal developmental milestones are evident in gifted child. Also, we see some characteristics that seem exaggerated in some gifted children and we do not know why they are present. And, lastly, some of those considered gifted or talented seem to be best described by non-universal theory. We conclude that it would be premature to proclaim that there is or can be a unified theory of the social-emotional development of the gifted that can help us understand those persons and guide the implementation of appropriate educational and counseling programs. The following recommendations for learning more about social-emotional development will contribute to the creation of a new, more encompassing theory.

Moving Toward Personal Experience

In order to move toward greater understanding of the development of giftedness in general, and social emotional development in particular, we need to study development in ways that have not been typically done (Coleman, 1995, 1997.) More systematic inquiry is needed in all three developmental theories, but the latter two deserve more effort. In our view universal developmental theory is unlikely to yield significantly deeper understanding of giftedness than it already has. Our knowledge has been relatively static in that area for decades. We use the term static not in the sense that useful research is not going on, but rather that what is studied are finer and finer delineation of aspects of development that have yielded small dividends. One area that seems tied to the idea of universality is the study of the construct self-concept. Researchers continue to gather data on this elusive idea (Hoge & Renzulli, 1993).

More research needs to be focused on the latter two theoretical perspectives (universal with special characteristics and non-universal) to see what new insights they might provide. Research centered on the lives of gifted persons seems to be a potentially fruitful area. While the experience of giftedness has been studied over many years, we consider the personal experience of being gifted or talented, especially through child-hood, as a relatively unexplored area because the actual experience of the persons from the perspective of those persons has been missing. One exception would be autobiographies of persons who are gifted.

To understand social-emotional development, we need to understand more closely the personal experience of persons who are gifted. The pressures, joys, worries, conflicts and satisfactions of the experience of being a person who is gifted in various settings can become known as we gather evidence from empirical studies, biographies, clinical stories, life stories, etc. The experience of development contains much of the evidence of what social-emotional development is for this group and for subgroups. Our interest in this topic of experiences drives us toward two approaches to research described below.

Two Avenues of Research on the Experience and Giftedness

Experience of being gifted can actually be approached in two different ways. One approach is to try to explicate the experience of being gifted by understanding gifted students' understandings of their experiences. The other approach focuses on the lived experience of being gifted. 'Lived' experience is a term that phenomenologists use to illustrate the fact that people exist in the world in a primary way ahead of the establishment of second order meaning through symbols. Both approaches are similar in that they attempt to understand the meanings of the persons in a social setting. What distinguishes these approaches is when and where the researcher enters the life of the developing person. The experience of being gifted explores the meaning of the categories, symbols, and stories of one's life as people have reflected on them. On the other hand, lived experience explores the immediate experience of a person before meanings have been assigned to the experience (Van Manen, 1990; Holdstein & Gubrium, 1994). The former kind of research has a theoretical base or is moving toward one; the latter is atheoretical in the sense that experiences of people are their own. The two kinds of research are discussed below.

Research on the Experience of Being Gifted

The experience of being gifted has been pursued for many years by numerous researchers (e.g. Sanders, 1996; Bloom, 1985; Coleman and Cross, 1988; Cross, Coleman & Terharr-Yonkers, 1991; Csikszentmihalyi, Rathunde & Whalen, 1993). The approaches taken have included interviews, histories and biographies. Many important ideas and theories have emerged from these studies. In addition, the techniques used by researchers in this area have shed light on the relationship between the approach taken and what can be known as a consequence of an approach. For example, Csikszentmihalyi, Rathunde & Whalen, (1993) popularized the use of pagers as a means for collecting important data in a random but systematic fashion from a group of subjects, but without hampering the external validity of a study that comes from reducing the extent to which subjects are in their natural environment due to experimenter influence. In this study the researchers asked gifted teenagers to wear a pager and write down where they were and what they were doing several times a day when the pager was randomly signaled. Sanders (1996) conducted a study that attempted to tell the life histories of several very accomplished college students. Each person's individual story was portrayed with the researcher providing an analysis of the social historical context of their lives. Gardner has produced books containing histories of very prominent people. Their histories provide great detail of their experiences as the subjects made sense of them.

One of the best known studies on the experiences of gifted people was published by Bloom (1985). In this book, Bloom reported the interviews of eminent people in several professions. As in the previous examples, details about gifted persons' lives were revealed in a manner that has affected both what we currently believe about the highly successful gifted adult person and how we go about conducting research.

From earlier research on the experience of gifted students in school, we developed an Information Management Model (IMM; Coleman & Cross, 1988). The IMM was built on previous research the yielded a Stigma of Giftedness Paradigm (SGP; Coleman, 1985). The SGP underpins the IMM by providing insight in the social cognition of gifted students.

Stigma of Giftedness Paradigm

Coleman (1985) articulated a stigma of giftedness paradigm based on Goffman's stigma construct (1963), which asserted that being tainted (in this case, identified as gifted) makes apparent to other people a set of variables which influence the tainted person to alter the way he or she typically interacts with others. The SGP has three tenets: (1) gifted students desire normal social interactions; (2) they learn that others will treat them differently when they learn of their giftedness; and (3) they learn to manage information about themselves in order to maintain normal social interactions. Implicit in this theory is the existence of social cognition in gifted students.

There is another important idea underpinning this paradigm. That is, unlike certain stigmatizing qualities, i.e. visible differences one might have from a group of others, giftedness is only potentially stigmatizing; it can be masked or hidden. Consequently, researchers have tested the notion that gifted adolescents who feel threatened by the potentially stigmatizing association with giftedness attempt to control the information about themselves they make available to others (e.g. their score on a test) (Cross, Coleman & Stewart, 1993). Their findings supported the validity of tenets

two and three of the Stigma of Giftedness Paradigm. This controlling of information about oneself is considered a behavioral manifestation of social cognition (Cross, Coleman & Terharr-Yonkers, 1991). Some evidence does exist, however, that not all gifted adolescents control information others are allowed to have about them (Coleman & Cross, 1988; Cross, Coleman & Terharr-Yonkers, 1991; Cross, Coleman & Stewart, 1993). At this point we do not know how to account for these differences.

Social Cognition

Social cognition is a person's psychological mechanism for understanding social situations and the subsequent strategies created to reach desired outcomes (Shantz, 1977). According to Rice (1990), social cognition is "concerned with the processes by which children and adolescents conceptualize and learn to understand others: their thoughts, emotions, intentions, social behavior, and general point of view. Implied in the concept of social cognition is an ability to make inferences about other people's capabilities, attributes, expectations, and potential reactions" (p. 105). In short, social cognition refers to reasoning about social situations while it guides efforts to reach social goals.

The Information Management Model

From interviews with numerous gifted students about their experiences in school, an Information Management Model (see Fig. 1) was created. To follow the IMM one should read from left to right, first noticing a child approaching a specific setting. The IMM illustrates that in that student's mind are certain social expectations held for him/her. These expectations come from parents and teachers teaching them appropriate behavior for various settings (e.g. school, church). Upon entering school, the child creates an understanding of how to behave in accordance with expectations from the numerous cues. Whether a gifted student feels different from his or her peers will affect him or her. If the gifted child does not feel different (point A on the IMM), then he or she will have little need to develop social coping strategies. Studies have reported that some gifted students do not feel different from their nongifted peers (Coleman & Cross, 1988; Cross, Coleman & Stewart, 1995; Manor-Bullock, 1995).

Point (B) on the IMM reflects the fact that even though there are gifted students who do feel different, they do not develop social coping strategies per se. This point is debatable since many forms of coping strategies are quite subtle. In addition the strategies may originate as a strategy and later become a common part of the child's behavioral repertoire. Callahan, Sowa & May (1996) reported on this phenomenon by claiming that social coping strategies often later become more a part of the child's regular behavior and less of a specific coping strategy. Point C is where a

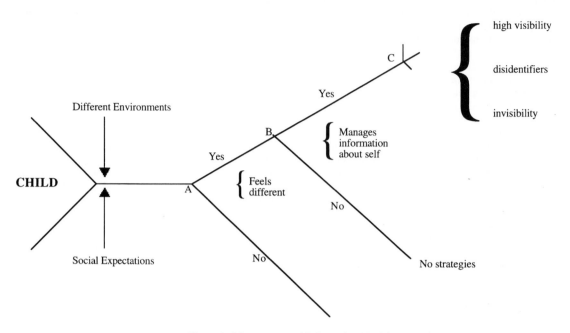

Figure 1. Management of Information Model.

gifted child feels different and engages in social coping strategies. The strategies can be characterized as falling on a Continuum of Visibility (see Fig. 2; Coleman & Cross, 1988: Cross, Coleman & Terhaar-Yonkers, 1991). The continuum was constructed to illustrate that, as gifted students act, they reveal social goals they have. The social goals can range from standing out further from other groups of students (high visibility) to becoming invisible (blending in with other groups). The third position on the continuum is called dis-identifiers. They are strategies that attempt to convince others, by association, that the gifted student is really more like a group of students stereotypically not thought to be gifted. For example, gifted students have told us that certain groups of students in their schools are believed to be quite distinct from gifted students (e.g., burners, doper, skateboarders, jocks) (Coleman & Cross, 1988; Cross, Coleman & Terhaar-Yonkers, 1991). Hence, some gifted students chose to use

prevailing stereotypes held in their school culture to disidentify from being thought of as gifted.

Consequently, gifted students' behaviors in school reflect their self-perceptions in terms of feeling different or the same, and how they choose to act in order to maintain as much social latitude as they desire. Their idiosyncratic plan for social latitude is defined as their social goals. Their self-perceptions and subsequent behavior patterns also reflect their social cognition and the social milieu of the school. The Stigma of Giftedness Paradigm in concert with the Information Management Model provide useful tools for understanding why gifted students make certain choices about how to cope in school. These concepts were outcomes of the meaning of experiences of gifted students as they reflect on their lives. The students offered windows into their lives that were constructions based on interpretations of events and behaviors as influenced by the historical times in which they lived. To get at pre-reflective descriptions of lived experience, a different approach is necessary.

Continuum of Visibility

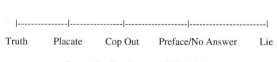

Figure 2. Continuum of Visibility.

Lived Experience

Because social-emotional experiences are part and parcel of development, our knowledge of social-emotional development of the gifted requires access to the lives of persons. The study of the lived experience of being gifted can be carried out through phenomenology, a form of scholarly inquiry (Giorgi, 1983). In phenomenology the connection between reality and the person is actively co-created such that there is no real distance between the two. A person's experience is what the world is to that person. Put succinctly, a person's subjectivity, not a denial of it, is the focus of study.

Phenomenology provides a means for entering parts of a person's life. By increasing our knowledge of the lived experience of being gifted, we will be advancing our understanding of giftedness itself. There are moments in person's lives when pathways change or diverge. In terms of the social-emotional development of giftedness, it would be useful to understand those moments. Several examples of such moments are presented below to convey the idea of what could be learned from this approach.

Moment 1. A person becomes aware that future development in an area or field requires a level of commitment that he or she does not want to invest.

Moment 2. A person who is gifted may have the ability to recognize something that outsiders do not, that is, he or she becomes cognizant that he or she does not have that special brilliance of another and must come to terms with that recognition. An example would be the moment in Amadeus when Soliari recognizes he cannot be a Mozart and must come to terms with that recognition.

Moment 3. Some persons are able to encounter the boundaries of a field and then transform that field. Is there an awareness of resistance to forces of conformity as a new way of approaching some field emerges? Is the person oblivious to outside influences in the pursuit of an idea or performance?

Moment 4. Feeling one's differentness has been reported by gifted persons. How is differentness experienced in circumstances where ability and interest is valued or devalued?

Moment 5. Moving toward excellence or originality is a part of some gifted persons lives. Is striving for excellence a nascent sensation that grows to some deeper awareness by the person during their life?

Moment 6. A person realizes that they are different from others who have common interests.

Moment 7. A person realizes an identity with another or others of similar interests and inclinations.

Each of these moments is fraught with personal significance. The apparent infrequency of these moments makes them appear mysterious, yet such experiences are part of being gifted for some persons. These are significant moments in development that the study of lived experience can open to scholarly inquiry.

Phenomenology can help us understand those moments better and deepen our appreciation of the social-emotional development of gifted persons (Cross, Coleman & Stewart, 1995).

Summary

This chapter attempted to introduce a structure for understanding the social-emotional development of gifted students. We began by reviewing terms and issues about social-emotional development. We outlined a postmodern view acknowledging that the three types of development (universal, universal with some differences, nonuniversal) tell us different stories about the social-emotional development of gifted students. We also illustrate the benefits to the understanding of social-emotional development of gifted students of exploring the personal experience of the individual. Two avenues of research on the experiences of gifted students were also noted. They included research on the experience of being gifted as presented from the accounts of the students. The second avenue attempts to describe the lived experience of gifted students prior to the application of language attempting to approximate the experiential qualities. The nature of our understanding of the development of gifted students in the social-emotional realm will be significantly forwarded as we combine research on the lived experience with the universal with differences and nonuniversal developmental theories.

References

Anderholt-Elliot, M. (1987). *Perfectionism: What's bad about being too good?* Minneapolis: Free Spirit Press.

Baker, J. (1996). Everyday stressors of academically gifted adolescents. *Journal of Secondary Gifted Education*, **7** (2), 356–368.

Bloom, B. (1985). *Developing talent in young people.* New York: Ballentine Books.

Csikszentmihalyi, M., Rathude, K. & Whalen, S. (1993). *Talented teenagers.* New York: Cambridge University Press.

Clark, B. (1997). *Growing Up Gifted* (5th ed.). Columbus. OH: Charles E. Merrill.

Colangelo, N. & Brower, P. (1987). Gifted youngsters and their siblings: Long term impact of labeling on their academic and personal self-concepts. *Roeper Review*, **10**(2), 101–103.

Coleman, L. (1985). *chooling the gifted.* Menlo Park, CA: Addison-Wesley.

Coleman, L.J. (1997). Studying ordinary events in a field devoted to the extraordinary. *Peabody Journal of Education*, **72**(3&4), 117–132.

Coleman, L. J. (1995). The power of specialized environments in the development of giftedness: The need for research on social context. *Gifted Child Quarterly*, **39**, 171–176.

Coleman, L. & Cross, T. (2001). *Being gifted in schools: Issues of development, guidance and teaching.* Prufrock Press.

Coleman, L. & Cross, T. (1988). Is being gifted a social handicap? *Journal for the Education of the Gifted*, **11**, 41–56.

Cross, T. & Stewart, R. (1995). A phenomenological investigation of gifted students in rural schools. *Journal of Secondary Gifted Education*, **6**(4), 273–280.

Cross, T., Coleman, L. & Stewart, R. (1993). The social cognition of gifted adolescents: An exploration of the stigma of giftedness paradigm. *Roeper Review*, **16**(1), 37–40.

Cross, T., Coleman, L. & Stewart, R. (1995). Psychosocial Diversity of gifted adolescents: An exploration of the stigma of giftedness paradigm. *Roeper Review*, **16**(1), 37–40.

Cross, T., Coleman, L. & Terhaar-Yonkers, M. (1991). The social cognition of gifted adolescents in schools: managing the stigma of giftedness. *Journal for the Education of the Gifted*, **15**, 44–55.

Cross, T., Cook, R. & Dixon, D. (1996). Psychological autopsies of three academically talented adolescent who committed suicide. *Journal of Secondary Gifted Education*, **7**(3), 403–409.

Dabrowski, K. (1967). *Personality shaping through positive disintegration*. Boston: Little Brown.

Delisle, J. (1992). *Guiding the social and emotional development of gifted youth: A practical guide for educators and counselors*. New York: Longman.

Giorgi, A. (1983). Concerning the possibility of phenomenological psychological research. *Journal of Phenomenological Psychology*, **14**(2), 129–169.

Feldman, D. H. (1980). *Beyond universals in cognitive development*. Norwood, NJ: Ablex.

Feldman, D. H. (with Goldstein, L.) (1986/1991). *Nature's gambit: Child prodigies and the development of human potential*. NY: Teachers College Press.

Gallagher, J.J. & Gallagher, S. (1994). *Teaching the gifted child* (4th ed.). Prentice Hall.

Goffman, E. (1963). *Stigma: Notes on the management of spoiled identity*. Englewood Cliffs, NJ: Prentice-Hall.

Gowan, J. C. (1972). *Development of the creative individual*. San Diego, CA: R.K. Knapp.

Hoge, R. D. & Renzulli, J. S. (1993). Exploring the link between giftedness and self concept. *Review of Educational Research*, **63**, 449–465.

Holdstein, J. A. & Gubrium, J.F. (1994). Phenomenology, ethnomethodology, and interpretive practice. In: N. K. Denzin, & Y. S. Lincoln (Eds), *Handbook of Qualitative Research* (pp. 262–272). Thousand Oaks, CA: Sage.

Hollingworth, L. S. (1926). *Gifted children: their nature and nuture*. NY: MacMillan.

Hollingworth, L. S. (1942). *Children above 180 IQ: Their origins and development*. Yonkers-on-Hudson, NY: World Book.

Howley, A., Howley, C. & Pendarvis, E. (1995). *Anti-intellectualism and public schools*. New York: Teachers College Press.

Kerr, B., Colangelo, N. & Gaeth, J. (1988). Gifted adolescents' attitudes toward their giftedness. *Gifted Child Quarterly*, **32**(2), 245–247.

Manor-Bullock, R. (1995). Is giftedness socially stigmatizing? The impact of high achievement on social interactions. *Journal for the Education of the Gifted*, **18**(3), 319–338.

Maslow, A. (1970). *Motivation and personality* (2nd ed.). New York: Harper and Row Publishers.

Mendaglio, S. (1995). Sensitivity among gifted persons: A multi-faceted perspective. *Roeper Review*, **17**(3), 169–172.

Morelock, M. (1996). On the nature of giftedness and talent: Imposing order on Chaos. *Reoper Review*, **19**(1), 4–12.

Piechowski, M. (1986). The concept of developmental potential. *Roeper Review*, **8**(3), 190–197.

Piechowski, M. (1991). Emotional development and emotional giftedness. In: N. Colangelo & G. A. Davis (Eds), *Handbook of Gifted Education* (pp. 285–336). Sydney: Allyn and Bacon.

Piechowski, M. (1997). Emotional giftedness: The measure of intrapersonal intelligence. In: N. Colangelo & G. A. Davis (Eds), *Handbook of gifted education* (pp. 366–381). Needham, MA: Allyn & Bacon.

Plomin. R. P. & Petrill, S. S. (1997). Genetics and Intelligence: What's New? *Intelligence*, **24**(1), 53–78.

Rice, P. (1990). *Adolescent psychology* (6th ed.). Needham, MA: Allyn and Bacon.

Sanders, M. (1996). Betty's story. *Journal of Secondary Gifted Education*, **8**(2), 87–95.

Scarr, S. (1992). Developmental theories for the 1990s: Development and individual differences. *Child Development*, **63**, 1–19.

Tomchin, E., Callahan, C., Sowa, C. & May, K. (1996). Coping and self concept. *Journal of Secondary Gifted Education*, **8**(1), 16–27.

Shantz, (1977). *The Development of social cognition*. New York: MacMillan.

Silverman, L. (1993). *Counseling the gifted and talented*. Denver: Love.

Tannenbaum, A. (1983). *Gifted children: Psychological and educational perspectives*. New York: MacMillan.

Van Manen, M. (1990). *Researching lived experience*. Albany: State University of New York.

Webb, J., Meckstroth, E. & Tolan, S. (1982). *Guiding the gifted child*. Columbus: Ohio Psychological Publishing.

A Life Span Approach to Talent Development

Ingrid Schoon

Department of Psychology, City University, London, UK

Introduction

We would expect gifted individuals to do well in life, to apply their abilities fruitfully to the area of their choosing, and to succeed in the world of work. Yet, many individuals who are identified as gifted and talented during childhood or adolescence do not fulfil their promise in later life. This holds true for academic achievements in the school environment, for the pursuit of a professional career, and occupational success (Gardner, 1983; Subotnik & Arnold, 1993b; Simonton, 1998). Only very few young people become committed to the cultivation and realisation of their talent, while most equally gifted teenagers lose interest and never develop their childhood skills (Solano, 1987; Csikszentmihalyi, Rathunde & Whalen, 1993). How is budding talent transformed into adult achievements? Why do not all gifted children succeed in the world of work? What factors promote or hinder the use and realisation of childhood gifts? These questions have occupied a number of researchers and led to the identification of key factors which stimulate or inhibit the development of childhood potential. The aim of this paper is not to formulate another componential theory of talent development, but to outline a framework for synthesising the key spheres of influence that shape the pathways of gifted individuals. The first step will be to define the key concepts.

Defining Giftedness

Over the last few decades the definition of giftedness has changed from being a one-dimensional conception linking giftedness to high intelligence to multi-dimensional conceptions acknowledging the existence of outstanding ability in different domains.[1] In opposition to the notion of one general intelligence factor (Spearman, 1927), researchers have identified a num-

ber of relatively independent groups and subgroups of abilities (Thurstone, 1938; Guilford, 1956; Cattell, 1971). Synthesising available knowledge from psychometrics, cognitive psychology and neuropsychology Gardner (1983) has formulated the theory of multiple intelligences, identifying seven distinct 'intelligences' or abilities: linguistic, logical-mathematical, spatial, musical, bodily-kinesthetic, inter- and intra-personal. Gardner argues that all human beings are capable of several forms of knowing, and that individuals differ from one another in strength and combination of these intelligences, for both genetic and cultural reasons. Both cultural and developmental determinants affect which of the intelligences is emphasised, with a biological component determining inclinations and susceptibility to environmental shaping. Gardner assumes that each of the intelligences corresponds to a particular type of giftedness, and is a system in its own right with its own form of memory, learning, and perception. Thus, his approach suggests that giftedness is largely domain specific, and the search for general processes across domains would be unsuccessful. However, there is evidence that intellectually gifted individuals excel in other areas as well (Janos & Robinson, 1985; Gagné, 1995) and that there are some common higher order processes that operate across domains. Critiques of Gardner's theory have furthermore focused on the use of the word intelligence to describe what would more accurately be labelled gifts or talents. Intellectual giftedness as such has been defined in terms of multiple loci by Sternberg (1985, 1991). According to the triarchic theory of human intelligence intellectually gifted individuals recognize and advance their strengths, and they recognize and either compensate for or remediate their weaknesses. According to this theory individuals may differ widely in how they are intelligent, but they find some way in which they excel and make the most of it.

Noting that the terms giftedness and talent are often used synonymously Gagné (1985, 1993) suggested a differentiation between the two concepts, defining giftedness as exceptional competence in one or more domains of ability, and talent as exceptional per-

---

[1] According to Csikszentmihalyi (1988, 1999) cultures are made-up of a variety of domains: mathematics, literature, dance, religion, music, etc. Each domain has its own set of rules, representations, or notations for instructing and assessing performance.

formance in one or more domains of human activity. Gagné specifies that genetically determined gifts form the infrastructure for talent development, while personal factors (such as motivation, interests, and personality traits), as well as environmental constituents (including parents, teachers, and the wider community), and systematic learning and training serve as catalysts for the expression of talent. Howe (1990, 1999) questioned the assumption of a genetic base to giftedness and suggested that outstanding abilities are not inborn but the product of a combination of personality, environment, and sheer hard work. He argues that gifted individuals are not fundamentally set apart from ordinary men and women, since the complexity and indirectness of genetic contributions to human activities and achievements rule out one-to-one relationships between genetic differences and ability differences. The debate about the role of nature versus nurture remains unresolved, yet there is a general consensus that multiple components must converge for outstanding achievement to occur.

Giftedness can therefore be defined as the potential for outstanding achievements, including cognitive, personal, biological, and social qualities of the individual. The development of exceptional abilities or talent in a particular domain can be conceptualised as the product of a combination of individual resources, a supportive environment, hard work, continuous training or practice. The processes by which individual potential is actualised into outstanding achievements are, however, not fully understood. Most theories of talent development do not relate directly to the major theories of development, and few describe the nature of environmental opportunities that nurture the realisation of potential (Horowitz & O'Brian, 1985; Mönks & Mason, 1993). Furthermore, most approaches investigating the realisation of potential only map the transition from childhood abilities to the formation of recognizable talents in particular domains, usually apparent from adolescence onwards and crystallising in a career choice (Feldman, 1992; Csikszentmihalyi et al., 1993; Gagné, 1993). Few researchers have investigated the experiences of young gifted people after their formal education has been completed, and still fewer have tried to describe and to follow the progress of gifted young people in the world of work. The current approach will address these issues, and outline a conceptual framework for analysing the influence of individual and contextual factors from a life-span developmental perspective.

Investigating the Realisation of Potential From a Life-span Perspective

Developmental processes can best be investigated by studying individuals over time. The approach will therefore be a developmental one, trying to understand the development of gifted young men and women

beyond their school and college years, and to trace how the gifts of youths are transformed into adult attainments. Reviewing three, rather distinct perspectives on the developmental linkages between childhood giftedness and outstanding achievements in adulthood, Simonton (1998) concluded that a comprehensive theory of talent development must capture the intricate and dynamic exchange between genetic constitution, contextual influences, and the individual's distinctive intellectual and motivational make-up together with their social maturation. Biological, sociological, and psychological aspects all have an explanatory part to play, and one cannot be considered in isolation from the others. To bring together the multitude of factors influencing the realisation of potential within a comprehensive framework is a major challenge. By adopting a 'life-span view of human development' (Baltes, Reese & Nesselroade, 1977; Baltes, Reese & Lipsitt, 1980; Featherman & Lerner, 1985; Baltes, 1987), we find a conceptual and methodological framework that allows for the study of individual and contractual variables as well as their dynamic interaction within a wider context.

Life-span developmental psychology is concerned with the description, explanation, and modification of constancy and change of behaviour throughout the life-course, underscoring the link between contextual change and individual development. Life-span psychology has been characterised by six theoretical propositions (Baltes, Reese & Lipsitt, 1980; Baltes, 1987). First, it emphasises that human development extends over the entire life-span, from conception into old age, and involves the mastery of successive life-span tasks in a series of contexts that have different importance and salience at different points in the life course. Second, development is considered to be multidimensional and multidirectional, since at any given time point, developmental outcomes can be both positive and negative in the sense of multifunctionality. Interactive functioning in earlier stages, for example, may generate protective and risk conditions for later phases of the life course. Third, development is not linear, incremental growth, but always consists of the simultaneous occurrence of gain and loss, of growth and decline. Any developmental progression involves at the same time new adaptive capacities as well as the loss of previously existing capacities. Forth, within-person variability (plasticity) of the developmental course can take many forms, depending on the life conditions and experiences of the individual. Fifth, developmental processes are historically embedded, which means they are influenced by the socio-cultural conditions that exist in a given historical period and the way in which these evolve over time. Sixth, declaring contextualism as a paradigm, individual development is understood as the outcome of the interactions among three systems of developmental influences: age-graded, history-graded, and non-normative conditions.

Critiques of the approach have pointed out that none of these propositions taken separately are new, and conclude that life-span work has little to offer (Kaplan, 1983). In a response to this criticism Baltes (1987) stresses that the significance of the life-span approach does not lie in the individual propositions, but in the whole complex of perspectives forming a metatheoretical framework for the study of development. The coordination of the different propositions form a coherent system, or 'family of perspectives', that together specify the life-span approach. Like other developmental specialities, such as child development, life-span developmental psychology is not a theory but an orientation, providing a framework for the theoretical and empirical study of behaviour development.

Perhaps the best studied domain of life-span developmental psychology is the area of cognitive functioning within the theoretical scenarios of child development or aging (Baltes & Staudinger, 1996; Pasupathi & Staudinger, this volume). The life-span view of human development has also been adopted for the study of career development, which is conceptualised as one feature of a person's development (Vondracek, Lerner & Schulenberg, 1986). The life-span approach stresses the mutual embeddedness of individual and context, conceptualising development as the dynamic interaction between a developing or changing individual in a changing context. The notion of dynamic interaction implies that individuals influence the contexts that influence them, that no one level of analysis in isolation can be considered the sole cause of change. The notion of embeddedness addresses the multiple levels of analysis, e.g. the biological, psychological, social, and historical context contributing to human functioning. The levels do not function in parallel, as independent domains, but there is a dynamic interaction between the levels. Each level may be both a product and a producer of the functioning and changes at all other levels. Different contextual conditions will lead to different developments when different individuals interact in them, and the same attributes in individuals will lead to different developments when they interact in different contexts.

In the following, the significance of the life-span perspective for the study of talent development will be illustrated by drawing on examples from the literature that describe the interaction between individual and contextual factors which shape the pathways of gifted individuals. The chapter will conclude with the formulation of a dynamic interactional model of talent development integrating the various spheres of influence.

Early Ripe, Early Rot?

Lewis Terman's pioneering study of gifted individuals is one of the few that followed individuals beyond their college years, and reports on the fulfilment of intellectual promise in mature adulthood (Terman, 1925; Terman & Oden, 1947, 1959). 1528 eleven year old school children with an IQ of 140 or higher were identified and followed from childhood in the 1920s to midlife and beyond. The twofold purpose of the study was to investigate whether child prodigies are psychotic or otherwise abnormal and whether they burn out quickly, or whether precocious children become exceptional adults.

The study shows that intellectually superior children become successful and well adjusted adults, who proved superior to the average person in most respects.[2] Despite the fact that the study was based on a single-cohort design, comprising overwhelmingly middle- and upper middle-class Anglo-Americans, it generated a reliance on the use of IQ scores for the early identification of giftedness The instrument used to select the superior children (the Stanford Binet Test) is, however, quite heavily influenced by socio-economic advantages, and it is difficult to say to what degree the obtained IQ of 140 or above may be in part a function of the excellent home background of these young people (Cattell and Butcher, 1968). Furthermore, the study did not operationalise contextual factors, but focused on individual differences in intellectual ability.

The accomplishments of the Terman sample were outstanding, but the study group did not produce a single truly prominent individual (Wallace, 1985).[3] Furthermore, the vocational accomplishments of the gifted women in the sample did not compare with those of men: they were in positions of lesser responsibility, opportunity, and renumeration then men (Terman & Oden, 1959; Feldman, 1984; Subotnik & Arnold, 1993b). Fewer than one-half were employed outside the home, and according to Terman & Oden (1959) opportunities for employment and for advancement were influenced by both the women's own attitudes towards work and the attitudes of society toward the role of women. They concluded that however efficient the tests may be in discovering exceptional ability, and whatever schools may do to foster the discovered individuals, it is the prevailing Zeitgeist that will decide, by the rewards it gives or withholds, what talents will come to flower. They recognised that adult achievement is influenced by many things other than the sum total of intellectual abilities, and stress the importance of social class, educational attainment and personality traits which reflect ambition, self-con-

---

[2] The Terman sample tended to be of slightly better physique, healthier, more popular, less neurotic, more dominant, and happier with their lives.
[3] Simonton (1998) reports that William Shockely, Nobel Prize laureat for Physics, was among those tested in 1921 for inclusion in Terman's sample, yet his score on the Stanford Binet was not high enough to be considered as gifted.

fidence and all-round mental and social adjustment.[4] Yet Terman did not address how these factors are related, what impact they had at different stages of the life course, and how development is influenced by the historical context encountered by the sample members.

Performance Potential in Context

Considering any monistic theory of talent development as inadequate, Ginzberg & Herma (1964) tried to delineate the principal factors that played an important role in shaping the careers of gifted individuals. Subjects of the study were those individuals who had been awarded graduate fellowships at Columbia University between 1944 to 1951. This group of gifted or talented men and women were re-contacted in 1961, when aged between 34 and 44 years, and were asked to complete a ten-page questionnaire. Like Terman's study, this project had to concentrate on male graduates, because women had responded furiously to the carefully drafted questionnaire that gave them no opportunity to talk about their homes and families, or to describe the impact these aspects had on their career development.[5]

Ginzberg & Herma (1964) could identify a number of factors that influenced the extent to which gifted individuals, after completing their education, performed to a high level of competence. Original endowment, or mental prowess, proved to be one of the crucial factors for the level of accomplishment that an individual eventually reached. A second factor is the quantity and quality of the education, training and practice, and other preparations taken before starting to work. Thirdly, the ease or difficulty experienced in resolving the question of occupational choice was an important issue. Participants in the study who did not have a clear career aim had great difficulties negotiating their way through the complex and varied opportunities they encountered. Other key factors include individual motivation, attitudes, and values: those who seek to achieve the most will, other things being equal, achieve more than their peers who are less inclined to invest in the pursuit of their careers. Furthermore in order to succeed, individuals have to 'build bridges between the present and the future' (p.203), to develop expectations, and to project oneself into the future, constantly monitoring and adjusting their ideas and ideals. As a sixth factor Ginzberg and Herma mention the support received from the home

environment, as provided by the wife or the family of origin. Both can be a major source of comfort, but also of stress and difficulties. Finally, man does not live by work alone, and there are many opportunities to gain satisfaction from activities outside the work place. To invest some time and energy into avocational interests and activities can be rewarding and constructive in relation to work, while preoccupation with non-work activities can lead to lessening of accomplishments at work, and ultimately to an unsuccessful career. Thus the response to opportunities in the non-work area is another important factor related to the differential performance of talented individuals.

Underlying these factors Ginzberg and Herma identified a general factor similar to Spearman's G-factor, the 'performance potential', that gives shape and direction to the careers and lives of the generally successful gifted individuals. However, superior performance potential does not guarantee high level performance. Other determinants, such as the social reality, and the way in which the encountered reality is interpreted by the individual, must also be taken into consideration to understand the process of occupational development. Social disadvantage at birth, late completion of the doctorate, military service, marital troubles, numerous job shifts, or a unresponsive, poorly structured job market are some of the social reality factors that can impede a successful career. However, such experiences can also act as a spur, bringing new challenges and opportunities to the individual. Situational factors can always be perceived as dualities: as opportunities or limitations, demands or pressures, stimulation or temptation, encouragement or discouragement. The significance of any situation depends on its objective aspects and the manner in which the individual perceives and responds to it. Ginzberg & Herma (1964) stress that the way individuals respond to different situations, how they interpret the reality, can vary widely, and has to be understood as part of their total personality. They go further and identify two general principles that influence career development. One is the principle of accumulative (dis-) advantage, or continuity-cumulating tendency: getting off to a good start enhances the likelihood of becoming successful later, while the experience of bad luck at the beginning lowers the odds for being successful later on. The other principle is the functional equivalence of subjective factors (such as motivation), and environmental factors (such as a supportive and encouraging context or family background), which while being discrete phenomena, act at times as rough equivalents in the structuring of career development. Some individuals overcome apparently unsurmountable obstacles by determination, drive, and hard work, while others with less drive will reach the top if they receive strong support and encouragement.

This complex multidimensional framework integrates individual and contextual aspects, it includes

---

[4] A comparison of the 150 most successful and the 150 least successful males among the gifted subjects brought out four personality traits on which these two groups differed most widely: persistence in the accomplishment of ends, integration toward goals, self-confidence, and freedom from inferiority feelings (Terman & Oden, 1959, p. 149).

[5] This led Ginzberg to design a questionnaire specifically for women and to undertake a separate investigation into 'The Life Styles of Educated Women' (Ginzberg & Herma, 1966).

explicit measures of the social context, and describes processes that link the individual and context, covering some of the propositions central to life-span psychology (multidirectionality, plasticity, historical embeddedness). In contrast to the life-span approach that extends over the whole life-span, the model concentrates on the transition from college to work. It assumes an ideal, straight pathway from outstanding achievement in college to outstanding achievements in the world of work, and does not differentiate between age-graded, history-graded, and nonnormative conditions. Furthermore it conceptualises individual and contextual factors as discrete phenomena that can act as functional equivalents, and does not account for their mutual embeddedness meaning that individuals can influence the contexts that influence them. It should also be remembered, that, the model is only based on the experiences of gifted men, as other studies of that time.[6] A comprehensive model of talent development has to account for the experiences of both men and women, and seek to describe how men and women respond to the demands and opportunities they face as they move through life.

Pathways of Gifted Women

The women in Terman's sample equalled or excelled men in school achievement, yet they ceased to compete with men in the world of work, due to lack of motivation and opportunities not a lack of ability (Subotnik & Arnold, 1993b). Women seeking a career outside the home at that time had to break through many more barriers and overcome many more obstacles than did men on the road to success.[7] Tomlinson-Keasey (1998) describes the careers of the Terman women as random, marked by improbable and serendipitous events. Their careers were buffeted by social and societal forces, with their husbands', children's, and even parents' needs often taking precedence over their own career plans. Some women gave up successful careers when the chance for a meaningful relationship arose, or when the demands of their family could not be combined with work commitments. The late 1970's saw the launch of new equal opportunity programmes with aims to help and assist diverse groups of women to fulfil their potentials,

especially targeted to identify and to overcome internal and external barriers to success. Yet women, and in particular gifted women, remain underrepresented in the higher ranks of the professions (Card, Steele & Abeles, 1980; Eccles, 1985; Kerr, 1985; Subotnik, Karp & Morgan, 1989; Arnold, 1993; Subotnik & Arnold, 1993b; Tomlinson-Keasey, 1998; Schoon, 1999). This worrisome fact indicates an underdevelopment or underuse of the intellectual talents of women who would otherwise be fully participating and contributing in a variety of settings, and has stimulated a number of researchers to investigate further the reasons for the incongruence that exists between women's abilities and their occupational attainment.

Is There a Measure of Successful Adult Attainments?

Defining success of adult achievement is generally a value-laden endeavour, involving a variety of criteria that reflect both objective and subjective evaluations: income, occupational status or rank, responsibility, status of the employing institution, personal productivity, or personal reputation. Sir Francis Galton (1869), for example, considered the social and professional life as a continuous examination, and success in proportion as the general estimate of aggregated merits. He defines reputation as 'the opinion of contemporaries, revised by posterity' (p. 37). Terman & Oden (1959) have stressed that 'greatness of achievement is relative both to prevailing patterns of culture and the individual's personal philosophy of life; there neither exists nor can be devised a universal yardstick for its measure' (p. 151).[8] Evaluating the meaning and consequences of sex differences in achievement is equally complex and value-laden. Too often a male standard of ideal achievement has been adopted when judging the value of achievements by women, asking 'why aren't women achieving at the same levels as the men?' (Eccles, 1985; Tomlinson-Keasey, 1998). Suggesting that the traditional definitions of achievement are stereotypically masculine, Eccles (1987) inspired a number of researchers to rethink definitions of achievement and success from a female perspective that is substantially different from men.

Generally women's career choice and commitment to work differs from that of men, and is distinctly influenced by the effects of life role expectations (Arnold, 1993b). Longitudinal studies of women's career development showed that women, unlike men

---

[6] For example Vaillant's (1977) study on the coping mechanisms of Harvard male graduates for decades after graduation. Vaillant could show that the way the cohort dealt with inevitable life difficulties is a key characteristic in explaining the profound differences in career achievement that separated gifted undergraduates from one another in later years. Yet, he cannot explain how specific adaptation or coping styles emerge, but points out that they are multidetermined, depending on a blend of conflict, inner strengths, and earlier outside help.

[7] Terman's study describes a cohort of women growing up in a time prior to the women's movement, the occurrence of dual career couples, and the single-parent family.

[8] Asking their respondents 'From your point of view, what constitutes success in life?' Terman & Oden (1959) identified a wide range of definitions. The five most frequently mentioned definitions of life success are: a. realisation of goals, vocational satisfaction, sense of achievement; b. a happy marriage and home life, bringing up a family satisfactorily; c. adequate income for comfortable living; d. contributing knowledge or welfare to mankind; e. peace of mind, well-adjusted personality (p. 152).

who progressively narrowed their career choice, pursued a 'contingency approach' with plans remaining open and shifting in the face of imagined constellation of future personal and professional roles (Almquist & Angrist, 1993). Rather than following an optimum career sequence, careers of women are characterised by several viable options that call for attention as the life course unfolds (Giele, 1982; Gilligan, 1982, 1991; Lubinski & Benbow, 1993; Tomlinson-Keasy, 1998). Findings from Hollinger & Fleming's (1992) study suggest that gifted women define achievement differently, placing equal value on personal and relational accomplishments as well as on career or educational achievements.

Life-role Expectations and Life-Style Choices

A number of studies suggest that intimacy is as central to women's lives as achievement is to men's lives (Gilligan, 1982; Harris, 1992; Hollinger & Fleming, 1992; Arnold, 1993a; Tomlinson-Keasey, 1998). It has been argued that women choose domains that are perceived as more person-oriented, affectionate and compassionate, involving interaction with people, while males prefer areas that have an image of being forceful, analytic, ambitious, individualistic and competitive, dealing with things rather than people (McClelland, 1975; Colley, 1995). In a longitudinal study of men and women who graduated from medical school in the 1980's Inglehart, Brown & Malanchuk (1993) showed that women entering medicine placed a higher emphasis on helping as the motivating factor for their occupational choice, while men stressed the reputation and status of the profession as well as the financial possibilities. In a sample of successful women, Gilligan (1982) found that women seldom mentioned their academic and professional distinctions, but rather described themselves as a mother, lover, or wife, focusing on the care they give to relationships rather then their achievements. In a follow-up study of 173 women who had been identified as gifted in their childhood (IQ greater than 132), and who finished college in the late 1960's, Tomlinson-Keasey & Blurton (1992) asked the same questions that the Terman women had answered at approximately the same age. This sample of women attached significantly more value to their careers than Terman's women. Although family life was rated lower in importance than in Terman's sample, the family was still regarded as their top priority, confirming the continuing importance of relationships, intimacy, and commitments among contemporary women. Arnold (1993b) shows that while the majority of young gifted women maintain a commitment to both relationships and careers, this dual priority can mean that each alternative is not pursued with the same dedication as a single goal. She stresses that values and life role expectations are the key to occupational attainment of gifted women, not ability, motivation, and academic

performance which although necessary are not sufficient to explain adult vocational achievement. Being able to see a potential self that combines high level career attainment with successful relationships allows gifted women to balance public and private spheres, work and family life. Arnold emphasises that aspirations[9] are crucial for the realisation of potential insofar as they enable or constrain self-images as aspiring career achievers.

These findings illustrate differential outcomes and adult achievements for gifted men and women. Early identification questions are not that crucial for capturing the pathways of gifted women. It is more the question of how giftedness develops across the life-span, and the kinds of achievement it leads to, that is of central importance. Gender role beliefs and stereotypes influence both expectations for success and the subjective evaluation of various life-style choices. Factors influencing the development of gifted individuals cannot be seen in isolation, but rather in relation to other spheres of life. The research findings indicate just how intertwined individual and contextual factors are, how their embeddedness in a wider socio-cultural context determines the pathways of gifted young men and women, and how different factors influence decisions and choices at different time points of the developmental process.

Towards a Model of Talent Development

Selecting key variables recognised as relevant for the development of budding talent, in both men and women, and bringing them together into a framework, the following model of talent development can be formulated (Fig. 1).

The model describes a setting for investigating the realisation of individual potential in a wider socio-cultural context. It adopts a life-span approach of development, as specified by Baltes (1987), Baltes, Reese & Lipsitt (1980), Vondracek, Lerner & Schulenberg (1986). The model differentiates between individual factors, conditions at birth, environmental factors, and the wider socio-historical and cultural context. Education, training, and practice take a special position, linking early and later stages in the process of talent development.

The Socio-Historical Context

The course of individual development is dependent on one's location in historical time, and the overarching cultural and economic context. Societal circumstances beyond the control of the individual contribute con-

---

[9] Aspirations or occupational choices are generally considered as an expression of a person's self concept, or more specifically self-perceptions (Super, 1980; Gottfredson, 1981).

siderably to the development of potential, and a major task confronting the gifted individual throughout the life-course is to cope effectively with the changing social reality. It has been stressed that we cannot understand the phenomenon of outstanding achievements by isolating individuals and their work from the socio-historical context in which their actions are carried out (Csikszentmihalyi, 1988; Simonton, 1987, 1997). The socio-historical context can spark ideas, nourish or suppress talent, and is crucial for the evaluation of ideas (Sternberg & Lubart, 1991). The prevaling Zeitgeist, or spirit of the times might cry out for the development of a particular ability, while at other times, or in other cultures, the same competence might be considered as of no particular value.

Achievements in Adulthood

Adult achievements refer to accomplishments at a stage in life and thus do not portray a life trajectory or pathway to particular achievements. In the model, the variable 'achievements' includes occupational attainments, but also takes into consideration other indicators, such as qualifications, status or income, a harmonious family or personal life, or general satisfaction with life. Such a broader conceptualisation of adult accomplishments accounts for the different definitions of achievements and success mentioned before, and takes into consideration the various domains of human activity in academic, artistic, or inter- and intrapersonal fields. High status, the realisation of educational and vocational goals, a happy family life, and a well adjusted personality are positive outcomes in themselves, but they are also intricately linked to each other. For example, good qualifications enable entry to prestigious occupations; the process of participating in further education itself can widen and deepen personal interests and might lead to a general contentment or satisfaction, while also opening up opportunities to meet potential partners for relationships or other support networks. On the other hand, good qualifications can coincide with unemployment, and might thus lead to discontentment and feelings of frustration.

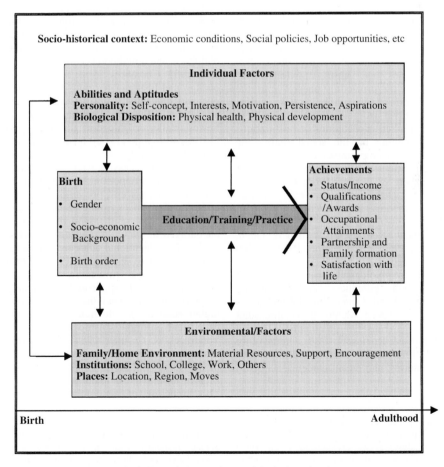

Figure 1. A dynamic-interactive model of talent-development.

Likewise the family of procreation can be a major source of life satisfaction and support in attaining one's occupational aims, or it can be the centre for difficulties and disturbances that drain one's energies (Ginzberg & Herma, 1964; Subotnik & Arnold, 1995). Thus outcomes at different life stages are linked with each other, they can always be perceived as dualities, and they can influence or become part of the environmental or individual factors influencing the ongoing process of development.

Individual Factors

Inter-individual differences in achievement are based on a mixture of aptitudes and abilities, personality characteristics, motivation and biological disposition, as well as the interaction of these factors with environmental factors and their embeddedness in a wider socio-cultural context. Specific aptitudes and abilities are a necessary but not a sufficient precondition for achievement in various domains. Determination and persistence in pursuing an ambition, or willingness to work hard for realising one's potential is another key ingredient (Terman & Oden, 1959; Ginzberg & Herma, 1964; Bloom, 1985; Renzulli, 1986; Heller, 1996; Heller & Vieck, 1999). Aspirations, in particular, play a crucial role in linking potential to fulfilment. Recognising and exercising one's own interests, competencies, and values, individuals formulate expectations by projecting oneself into the future. The formulation of such a life plan (Ginzberg et al., 1951) helps to direct and guide the transition from present to the future. Yet, expectations and aspirations might change depending on the social reality the individual encounters. Compromises might be necessary, adjusting aspirations that were either too high or too modest (Ginzberg & Herma, 1964; Gottfredson, 1981; Heckhausen, 1999).[10] Other personality characteristics such as autonomy, independence of thought, and self-confidence also play a key role in linking promise to fulfilment (Roe, 1953; Terman & Oden, 1959; MacKinnon, 1960, 1965; Gagné, 1993, Heller, 1996) and are included in this model. We also have to consider the role of biological dispositions as a underpinning of both giftedness and outstanding achievements in adulthood. General mental and physiological health have been identified as important factors facilitating the realisation of potential (Terman & Oden, 1959; Janos & Robinson, 1985). On the other hand, individual giftedness has been linked to psychopathology for centuries, and recent evidence seems to

support such a link (Eysenck, 1995; Prentky, 1989). Yet, Eysenck does stress that 'many other conditions must be fulfilled, many other traits added (e.g. ego strength), many abilities and behaviours added (e.g. IQ, persistence), and many socio-cultural variables present, before high creative achievement becomes probable' (Eysenck, 1995, p. 279).

Thus, those individuals who have the aptitudes, the disposition, the motivation, the belief in their own capacity, and who show personality characteristics appropriate to the demands of a special field[11] will try to make the most of their potential. Yet, the question also why so few individuals realise their potential cannot be answered by looking at individual factors alone, but depends as much on the social realities experienced by the individual.

Birth

Individuals are born as male or female, to more or less privileged parents, and into small or big families. All of these factors influence their consequent development. Gender differences in the development of talent are well documented and analysed, and some findings have been discussed earlier. Research on birth-order effects has shown consistent evidence that birth-order influences the emergence of exceptional ability in both childhood and adulthood (Galton, 1874; Terman, 1925; Roe, 1952; Chambers, 1964; Simonton, 1987). Social background is associated with educational aspirations, occupational status aspirations, and occupational status attainment (Blau & Duncan, 1967; Oden, 1968; Sewell, Haller & Ohlendorf, 1970; Zuckerman, 1977). Getting off to a good start, for example being born into a privileged family, can mean an increased likelihood of becoming successful later. A favourable objective situation creates opportunities that facilitate the realisation of ambitions and potential. The socio-economic and educational background of parents has shown to be a good indicator of the kind of intellectual interests encouraged in the child (Getzels & Jackson, 1961) as well as for educational achievement and occupational attainment (Trost & Sieglen, 1992; Tomlinson-Keasy, 1998). Individuals from more privileged homes have more educational opportunities, greater access to financial resources when they need them (i.e. to pay for higher education), role models, occupational knowledge, and informal/kinship networks (Schulenberg, Vondracek & Crouter, 1984). The same cumulative effect, in the opposite direction though, can occur for those who are not born so lucky and who consequently acquire an enhanced likelihood of risk, or bad luck. This principle of accumulative advantage or dis-

---

[10] Ginzberg & Herma (1964) emphasise the importance of recognizing when to adjust one's expectations: some individuals are more adept than others in profiting from their experiences and in adjusting their expectations when necessary, while others may waste much of their energy running after illusions, while still others might settle for too little.

---

[11] The term 'field' describes the social organisation of a domain. A field is made up of individuals who practice a given domain, who have the power to change it, or to act as 'gatekeepers' (Csikszentmihalyi, 1988, 1999).

advantage[12] has been described by Ginzberg & Herma (1964), and also by Merton (1968). What is not known, is how far the pathways between childhood circumstances and adult attainments are mediated through individual outcomes during the life course or through the continuous accumulation of (dis-) advantage which increases resilience or vulnerability of the individual to later problems. After all, some individuals from a disadvantaged family background break the vicious cycle (Elder, Pavalko & Hastings, 1991), while others from privileged backgrounds fail to succeed.

Environmental Factors

Much of the available information about the impact of external factors on the development of talent over the life course comes from Bloom's (1985) retrospective study of outstanding individuals in a variety of domains. Bloom illustrated the changing nature of the dynamic interaction between individual and contextual factors across different life stages. He differentiated between early, middle and later years of talent development to demarcate important signposts along a long and continuous process. The development of exceptional levels of talent requires certain types of environmental support, special experiences, excellent teaching, and appropriate motivational encouragement at each stage of development. During the early years of childhood, the individual is introduced to the domain, usually through parents or kin, with an emphasis on play and enjoyment. During the middle years of training, competition and work receive more emphasis. At this stage parents seek advise and support from teachers, coaches, or mentors and continue to provide emotional support. During the later years a definite commitment is required, the individual pursues training and practice on a full-time basis. The development of talent becomes a life-long career combining work and play. During this period the talented individual usually works with a teacher or coach who can also perform at an exceptional level in the relevant domain. Lack of economic and social support from parents, serious injury or disease, lack of teaching and encouragement, and other social and medical problems make full dedication difficult or impossible. Bloom's findings emphasise the crucial role of tutelage, nurturance, and support, and downplay the role of genetic endowment as prime cause of high-level achievement. Furthermore, a strong interest and emotional commitment, the desire to reach a high level of attainment, and willingness to work hard are crucial qualities present in all fields of accomplishment. According to Bloom these are socialised qualities, learned in the home, from teachers, and sometimes from peers and siblings. They can be acquired more easily if they are valued in the individual's immediate environment and should thus be encouraged and not undermined.

The school environment, for example, is powerful shaper or a deterrent to the development of individual potential (Mönks, Katzko, & Boxtel, 1992). School activities, both inside and outside the classroom, the interpersonal relations with teachers, students, and other staff, the various roles and role expectations, and the physical, structural, and material features, all render the school environment a most important context shaping the expectations and outlook of young people (Vondracek et al., 1986). In the school context the individual has its first encounter with a structured social arena within which to experience the 'sense of industry', the consequences of social and academic competence, competition, and power relationships (Erikson, 1959). The school setting also prepares the individual for the world of work, providing information, advise, and experience relevant to the impeding transition from school to work.

The experience of the world of work requires the developing person to become an active participant. Finding a job, changing jobs, losing jobs, or changing careers are major transitions in the life-course of every individual. The reason why some individuals are more likely than others to take action to achieve lies often in the nature of the chosen field, the necessary requirements for entry, and the structure of the organisations in which people work. Fields differ in the dynamics of their inner organisation, the stringency of their selective mechanisms, the sensitivity of the 'gatekeepers' who have wealth and power, or who are highly respected for their expertise (Csikszentmihalyi, 1988, 1999). Professional advancement structures, the funding climate for scientific research, and career constraints were identified as crucial factors influencing the career paths and achievements of talented individuals (Heller & Viek, 1999; Subotnik & Arnold, 1995). If there are not enough jobs, or opportunities, or social recognition to develop a domain related role, individual factors are insufficient to create viable careers.

Education, Training, Practice

It has been emphasised by Gagné (1993) that learning, training and practice illustrate best the longitudinal dimension of talent development. Gagné describes the unfolding of aptitudes and talent on the basis of four developmental processes: maturation, daily use of problem solving situations, informal training and practice, and formal training in a particular field. Without general and specialised forms of education and training, individuals will be excluded from a number of occupations or opportunities, regardless of their endowment. The quantity and quality of the training and practice and other preparations that an individual undertakes in order to pursue a particular

---

[12] This principle is sometimes referred to as the 'Matthew effect' due to its link to the Gospel passage that says 'For to every one who has will more be given, and he will have abundance; but from him who has not, even that he has will be taken away' (Matthew 25:29 in Simonton, 1998).

career or life-style, are clearly influencing differential outcomes, as well as the ability to learn rapidly and well (Bloom, 1985). Education, training and practice takes a central position in the model, forming a link between the present and the future, and as a key area for possible interventions (Mönks, Katzko, & Boxtel, 1992; Mönks & Mason, 1993).

Conclusion

The aim of the chapter was to develop a framework for investigating the development or realisation of child-hood gifts in adult achievements. By adopting a life-span developmental perspective, and drawing on examples from the literature, a dynamic interactive model of talent development has been formulated. Talent development has been conceptualised as one feature of person development, fuelled by the dynamic interaction between a changing individual and a changing context. Key aspects shaping the pathways of gifted individuals are conditions at birth, individual characteristics, environmental factors and the wider socio-historical context. Participation in education, training and practice plays a central role, bridging earlier and later stages of the developmental process. The model provides a framework for investigating how giftedness develops across the life-span, and the kinds of achievement it leads to. It accounts for the changing social contexts confronted by the maturing individual, such as, the changes in the number and kind of interacting partners (family, friends, peers, teachers, colleagues), and it illustrates how experiences in one sphere may affect those in others.

The model still requires an elaboration of the different spheres involved. There is need for further research along several lines. Firstly approaches for delineating and evaluating the individual factors and their dynamic interaction need to be explored further. The processes linking ability, personality, motivation, and biological disposition have to be more fully examined. There is a need to develop new method-ologies to investigate the reality of situations and the ways in which these are experienced and interpreted by the individual. Furthermore, the processes linking the different spheres have to be specified. Each sphere can have an impact on any of the others, and these relationships are bidirectional, which means that each sphere can both be product and producer of changes in other spheres. What we do not know is the relative influence of the different spheres on each other. There is also a need to define developmental markers, since one of the most important person characteristics is the location on the developmental path. As the individual grows older they become more able to transform, manipulate, or modify the environment with which they interact.

The model raises questions that have not yet been fully addressed and answered by research. There is clearly a need for comprehensive, longitudinal, multi-wave studies of the processes and variables that shape the pathways of gifted men and women. Unlike cross-sectional studies that can measure inter-individual differences at one point in time, or retrospective studies that have to rely on subjective reports that can be distorted by hindsight, prospective longitudinal studies allow us to explore the processes of change. Longitudi-nal designs allow us to define giftedness as a potential, and to follow the development of this potential across time (Trost, 1993). They provide causal explanations for intra-individual change and for inter-individual differences in intra-individual change, and they enable the researcher to describe the interactions of devel-opmental variables (Subotnik & Arnold, 1993a). By including all the individual and contextual variables that might have a significant longitudinal effect, the relative importance of various factors can be assessed in various contexts. Furthermore, by measuring all the relevant variables at several time points, the inter-relations among variables can be investigated.

Independently of the numerous clarifications that should be made to the proposed model, it is an important step to acknowledge the need for a devel-opmental perspective that captures the dynamic interaction between a changing individual and a changing context. Many questions raised by previous research on the topic could be answered if we knew more about the developmental course of gifted individ-uals and the nature of the forces that shape and stimulate the realisation of giftedness and talent.

References

Almquist, E. M. & Angrist, S. S. (1993). Families, careers, and contingencies. In: K. D. Hulbert & D. T. Schuster (Eds), *Women's Lives Through Time: Educated American Women of the 20th century.* San Fancisco: Jossey Bass.

Arnold, K. D.(1993). Undergraduate aspirations and career outcomes of academically talented women: a discriminant analysis. *Roeper Review,* **15,** 169–175.

Arnold, K. D.(1993b). The Illlinois Valedictorian Project.: Early adult careers of academically talented male high school students. In: R. F. Subotnik & K. D.Arnold (Eds), *Beyond Terman: Longitudinal Studies in Contemporary Gifted Education* (pp.24–51). Norwood, NJ: Ablex.

Baltes, P. B. (1987). Theoretical Propositions of Life-Span Developmental Psychology: On the dynamics between growth and decline. *Developmental Psychology,* **23,** 611–626.

Baltes, P. B., Reese, H. W. & Lipsitt, L. P. (1980). Life-Span Developmental Psychology. *Annual Review of Psychology,* **31,** 65–110.

Baltes, P. B., Reese, H. W. & Nesselroade, J. R. (1977). Life-span developmental psychology. Montery, CA: Brooks/Cole.

Baltes, P. B. & Staudinger, U. M. (1996). *Interactive Minds. Life-Span Perspectives on the Social Foundation of Cogni-tion.* Cambridge: Cambridge University Press.

Blau, P. M. & Duncan, O. D.(1967). *The American Occupa-tional Structure.* New York: John Wiley & Sons.

Bloom, B. S. (Ed.) (1985). *Developing talent in young people.* New York: Ballantine Books.

Card, J. J., Steele, L. & Abeles, R. (1980). Sex differences in realization of individual potential for achievement. *Journal of Vocational Behavior*, **17**, 1–21.

Cattell, R. B. (1971). *Abilities: Their structure, growth and action*. Boston: Houghton Mifflin.

Cattell, R. B. & Butcher, H. J. (1968). *The Prediction of Achievement and Creativity*. Indianapolis: The Bobbs-Merril Company.

Chambers, J. A. (1964). Relating personality and biographical factors to scientific creativity. *Psychological Monographs: General and Applied*, **78** (Whole No. 584), 1–20.

Colley, A. (1995). Psychology, Science and women. *Psychologist*, **8**, 346–352.

Csikszentmihalyi, M. (1988). Society, culture and person: a systems view of creativity. In: R. J. Sternberg (Ed.), *The Nature of Creativity* (pp. 325–339). Cambridge: Cambridge University Press.

Csikszentmihalyi, M. (1999). Implications of a systems perspective for the study of creativity. In: R. J. Sternberg (Ed.), *Handbook of creativity* (pp. 313–335). Cambridge: Cambridge University Press.

Csikszentmihalyi, M., Rathunde K. & Whalen S. (1993) (Eds), *Talented Teenagers. The Roots of Success and Failure*, Cambridge: Cambridge University Press.

Eccles, J. S. (1985). Why doesn't Jane run? Sex differences in educational and occupational patterns. In: F. D. Horowitz & M. O'Brien (Eds), *The Gifted and Talented: Developmental Perspectives*. (pp:251–295). Washington, DC: American Psychological Association.

Eccles, J. (1987). Gender roles and women's achievement-related decisions. *Psychology of Women Quarterly*, **11**, 135–172.

Elder, G. H., Pavalko, E. K. & Hastings, T. H. (1991). Talent, history and the fulfillment of promise. *Psychiatry*, **54**, 251–267.

Erikson, E. H. (1959). Identity and the life cycle. *Psychological Issues Monograph*, **1**. New York: International University Press.

Eysenck, H. J. (1995). *Genius. The natural history of creativity*. Cambridge: Cambridge University Press.

Featherman, D. L. & Lerner, R. M. (1985). Ontogenesis and sociogenesis. Problematics for theory about development across the life-span. *American Sociological Review*, **50**, 659–676.

Feldman, D. H. (1984). A follow-up of subjects scoring above 180 IQ in Terman's 'Genetic studies of genius'. *Exceptional Children*, **50**, 518–523.

Feldman, D. H. (1992). Intelligences, symbol systems, skills, domains and fields: A sketch of a developmental theory of intelligence. In: H. C. Roselli & G. A. MacLauchaln (Eds), *Proceedings from the Edyth Bush Symposium on Intelligence: Theory into Practice, Blue Printing for the Future* (pp. 37–43). Tampa: University of South Florida.

Gagné, F. (1985). Giftedness and Talent: Reexamining a Reexamination of the Definitions. *Gifted Child Quarterly*, **29**, 103–112.

Gagné, F. (1993). Constructs and models pertaining to exceptional human abilities. In: K. A. Heller, F. J. Mönks & A. H. Passow (Eds), *International Handbook of Research and Development of Giftedness and Talent* (pp.69–87). Oxford: Pergamon Press.

Gagné, F. (1995). Learning about the nature of gifts and talents through peer and teacher nominations. Piirto, J. (1995). In: M. W. Katzko & F. J. Mönks (Eds), *Nurturing Talent. Individual Needs and Social Ability* (pp. 20–30). Assen:Van Gorcum.

Galton, F. (1869). *Hereditary Genius*. London: Macmillan.

Galton, F. (1874). *English Men of Science*. London: Macmillan.

Gardner, H. (1983). *Frames of Mind. The theory of multiple intelligences*. New York: Basic Books.

Getzels, J. & Jackson, P. (1961). Family environment and cognitive style: A study of the sources of highly intelligent and of highly creative individuals. *American Sociological Review*, **26**, 351–359 .

Gilligan, C. (1982). *In a different voice: Psychological theory and women's development*. Cambridge, MA: Harvard University Press.

Ginzberg, E., Ginsburg, S. W., Axelrad, S. & Herma, J. L. (1951). *Occupational choice: An approach to a general theory*. New York: Columbia University Press.

Ginzberg, E. & Herma, J. L. (1964). *Talent and performance*. New York: Columbia University Press.

Ginzberg, E. & Herma, J. L. (1966). *Life styles of educated women*. New York: Columbia University Press.

Gottfredson, L. S. (1981). Circumscription and compromise: A developmental theory of occupational aspirations. *Journal of Counseling Psychology*, **28**, 545–579.

Guilford, J. P. (1956). The structure of intellect. *Psychological Bulletin*, **53**, 267–293. .

Harris, C. R. (1992). The fruits of early intervention: The Hollingworth group today. *Advanced Development*, **4**, 91–104.

Heckhausen, J. (1999). Developmental Regulation in Adulthood. Cambridge: Cambridge University Press.

Heller, K. A. (1996). The nature and development of giftedness: A longitudinal study. In: A. J. Cropley & D. Dehn (Eds), *Fostering the Growth of High Ability: European perspectives* (pp.41–56). Norwood, NJ:Ablex.

Heller, K. A. & Viek, P. (1999). Support for the gifted university students: Individual and social factors. In: C. F. M. van Lieshout & P. G. Heymans (Eds), *Talent, Resilience, and Wisdom Across the Life Span*. London: Psychology Press.

Hollinger, C. L. & Fleming, E. S. (1992). A longitudinal examination of life choices of gifted and talented young women. *Gifted Child Quarterly*, **36**, 207–212.

Horowitz, F. D. & O'Brian, M. (1985). Perspectives on research and development. In: F. D. Horowitz & M. O'Brien (Eds), *The Gifted and Talented: Developmental Perspectives* (pp. 437–454), Washington, DC: American Psychological Association.

Howe, M. J. A. (1990). *The origins of exceptional abilities*. Oxford: Blackwell.

Howe, M. J. A. (1999). *Genius explained*. Cambridge: Cambridge University Press.

Inglehart, M., Brown, D. R. & Malanchuk, O. (1993). University of Michigan medical graduates of the 1980s: The professional development of women physicians. In: K. D. Hulbert & D. T. Schuster (Eds), *Women's Lives Through Time: Educated American Women of the 20th Century* (pp. 374–392). San Fancisco: Jossey Bass.

Janos, P. M. & Robinson, N. M. (1985). Psychosocial development in intellectually gifted children. In: F. D Horowitz & M. O'Brien (Eds), *The Gifted and Talented: Developmental Perspectives* (pp. 149–195). Washington, DC: American Psychological Association.

Kaplan, B. (1983). A trio of trials. In: R. M. Lerner (Ed.), *Developmental Psychology: Historical and Philosophical Perspectives* (pp. 185–228). Hillsdale, NJ: Erlbaum.

Kerr, B. A. (1985). *Smart girls, gifted women.* Columbus, OH: Ohio Psychology.

Lerner, R. M. (1984). On the nature of human plasticity. New York: Cambridge University Press.

Lubinski, D. & Benbow, C. P. (1993). Reconeptualizing gender differences in achievement among the gifted. In: K. A. Heller, F. J. Mönks & A. H. Passow (Eds), *International Handbook of Research and Development of Giftedness and Talent* (pp. 693–707). Oxford:Pergamon Press.

MacKinnon, D. W. (1960). The highly effective individual. In: R. S. Albert (Ed.), *Genius and Eminence: The Social Psychology of Creataivtiy and Aexceptional Achievement* (pp. 114–127). New York: Oxford University Press.

MacKinnon, D. W. (1965). Personality and the realisation of creative potential. *American Psychologist,* **20,** 273–281.

McClelland, D. C. (1975). *Power: The inner experience.* New York: Wiley.

Merton, R. K. (1968). The Matthew Effect in Science. *Science,* **159,** 56–63.

Mönks, F. J. & Mason E. L. (1993). Developmental Theories of Giftedness. In: K. A. Heller, F. J. Mönks & A. H. Passow (Eds), *International Handbook of Research and Development of Giftedness and Talent* (pp. 89–102). Oxford: Pergamon Press.

Mönks, F. J., Katzko, M. W. & Boxtel, v. H. W. (Eds) (1992). *Education of the Gifted in Europe: Theoretical and Research Issues.* Amsterdam/Lisse: Swets & Zeitlinger.

Oden, M. (1968). The fulfillment of promise: 40-year follow-up of the Terman gifted group. *Genetic Psychology Monographs,* **77,** 3–93.

Perleth, C. H., Sierwald, W. & Heller, K. A. (1993). Selected results of the Munich Longitudinal Study of Giftedness: The multidimensional/typological giftedness model. *Roeper Review,* **15,** 149–155.

Prentky, R. A. (1989). Creativity and psychopathology: Gamboling at the seat of madness. In: J. A. Glover, R. R. Ronning & C. R. Reynolds (Eds), *Handbook of Creativity* (pp. 243–269). New York: Plenum Press.

Reis, S. M. (1995). Older Women's reflections on eminence: Obstacles and Opportunities. *Roeper Review,* **18,** 66–72.

Renzulli, J. S. (1986). The three-ring conception of giftedness: a developmental model for creative productivity. In: R. J. Sternberg & J. E. Davidson (Eds), *Conceptions of Giftedness* (pp. 53–92). Cambridge: Cambridge University Press.

Roe, A. (1952). *The Making of a Scientist.* New York: Dodd, Mead & Co.

Roe, A. (1953). A psychological study of eminent psychologists and anthropologists, and a cmparison with biological and physical scientists. *Psychological Monographs: General and Applied,* **67** (Whole No. 352).

Schoon, I. (1999). On the realisation of scientific talent. In: R. Silbereisen & J. Bynner (Eds), *Adversity and Challenge in Life in the New Germany and in England* (pp. 170–189). London: Macmillan.

Schulenberg, J., Vondracek, F. W. & Crouter, A. C. (1984). The influence of the family on voctional development. *Journal of Marriage and the Family,* **10,** 129–143.

Sewell, W. H., Haller, A. O. & Ohlendorf, G. W. (1970). The Educational and Early Occupational Status Attainment Process: Replication and Revision. *American Sociological Review,* **35,** 1014–1027.

Simonton, D. K. (1987). Developmental antecedents of achieved eminence. *Annals of Child Development,* **5,** 131–169.

Simonton, D. K. (1997). Creative productivity: A predictive and explanatory model of career trajectories and landmarks. *Psychological Review,* **104,** 66–89.

Simonton, D. K. (1998). Gifted child, genius adult: three life-span developmental persepctives. In: R. C. Friedman & K. B. Rogers (Eds), *Talent in Context: Historical and Social Perspectives on Giftedness* (pp. 151–175). Washington DC: American Psychological Association.

Solano, C. H. (1987). Stereotypes of social isolation and early burnout in the gifted: Do they still exist? *Journal of Youth and Adolescence,* **16,** 527–539.

Spearman, C. (1927). *The abilities of man.* London: MacMillan.

Sternberg, R. J. (1985). *Beyond IQ: A triachic theory of human intelligence.* Cambridge: Cambridge University Press.

Sternberg, R. J. (1991). Giftedness According to the triachic theory of human intelligence. In: N. Colangelo & G. A. Davis (Eds), *Handbook of gifted education* (pp. 45–54) Boston: Allyn & Bacon.

Sternberg, R. J. & Lubart, T. I. (1991). An Investment Theory of creativity and its development. *Human Development,* **34,** 1–31.

Subotnik, R. F. & Arnold, K. D. (1995). Passing through the gates: Career Establishment of Talented women scientists. *Roeper Review,* **18,** 55–61.

Subotnik, R. F. & Arnold, K. D. (1993a). Longitudinal Studies of Giftedness: Investigating the Fulfillment of Promise. In: K. A. Heller, F. J. Mönks & A. H. Passow (Eds), *International Handbook of Research and Development of Giftedness and Talent* (pp. 149–159). Oxford: Pergamon Press.

Subotnik, R. F. & Arnold, K. D. (1993b). *Beyond Terman: Longitudinal studies: Contemporary longitudinal studies of giftedness and talent.* Norwood, NJ: Ablex.

Subotnik, R., Kassan, L., Summers, E. & Wasser, A. (1993). *Genius revisited: High IQ children grown up.* Norwood, NJ: Ablex.

Subotnik, R. F. Karp, D. E. & Morgan, E. R. (1989). High IQ children at midlife: An investigation into the generalizability of Terman's genetic studies of genius. *Roeper Review,* **11,** 139–144.

Super, D. E. (1980). A life span, life space approach to career development. *Journal of Vocational Behavior,* **16,** 282–298.

Terman, L. (1925). *Genetic studies of genius: Vol. 1. Mental and physical traits of a thousand gifted children.* Stanford, CA: Stanford University Press.

Terman, L. M. & Oden, M. H. (1947). *Genetic studies of genius: Vol. 4. The gifted child grows up.* Stanford, CA: Stanford University Press.

Terman, L. M. & Oden, M. H. (1959). *Genetic studies of genius: Vol. 5. The gifted group at mid-life.* Stanford, CA: Stanford University Press.

Thurstone, L. L. (1938). *Primary mental abilities.* Psychometric Monograph, No.1.

Tomlinson-Keasey, C. (1998). Tracing the Lives of Gifted Women. In: R. C. Friedman & K. B. Rogers (Eds), *Talent in context: historical and social perspectives on giftedness,* (pp. 17–38). Washington DC: American Psychological

Association.

Tomlinson-Keasey, C. & Blurton, E. U. (1992). Gifted women's lives: Aspirations, achievements and persoanl adjustment. In: J. Carlson (Ed.), *Cognition and Educational Practice: An International Perspective* (pp. 151–176). Greenwich, Ct: JAI Press.

Trost, G. (1993). Prediction of Excellence in School, University and Work. In: K. A. Heller, F. J. Mönks & A. H. Passow (Eds), *International Handbook of Research and Development of Giftedness and Talent* (pp. 325–336). Oxford: Pergamon Press.

Trost G. & Sieglen, J. (1992). Biographische Frühindikatoren herausragender beruflicher Leistungen. In: E. A. Hany & H. Nickel (Eds), *Begabung und Hochbegabung* (pp. 95–104). Bern: Huber.

Vaillant, G. E. (1977). *Adaptation to Life*. Boston: Little Brown.

Vondraceck, F. W., Lerner, R. M. & Schulenberg, J. E. (1986). *Career development: A life-span developmental approach.* Hillsdale, NJ: Erlbaum.

Wallace, D. B. (1985). Giftedness and the construction of a creative life. In: F. D. Horowitz & M. O'Brian (Eds), *The Gifted and Talented: Developmental Perspectives* (pp. 361–385). Washington, DC: American Psychological Association.

Zuckerman, H. (1977). *Scientific Elite*. New York: Free Press.

Zuckerman, D. M. (1985). Confidence and aspirations: Self-esteem and self-concepts as predictors of students' life goals. *Journal of Personality*, **53**, 543–560.

Prodigies, Savants and Williams Syndrome: Windows Into Talent and Cognition

Martha J. Morelock[1] and David Henry Feldman[2]

[1]*Elmira College, Elmira, NY, USA*
[2]*Tufts University, Medford, Massachusetts, USA*

Introduction

Although extraordinary talent is always intriguing, it is perhaps most fascinating when found where least expected. This chapter deals with three groups of individuals whose capabilities are surprising in this sense. All have captured the imagination of those seeking to understand the origins and development of talent. Child prodigies display astounding adult-like mastery of a demanding domain of endeavor. Savants manifest islands of extreme capability showcased against a backdrop of overall severely deficient intellect. In recent years, people with Williams Syndrome, who show major deficits in general cognitive ability, have attracted interest because of their astonishing innate abilities in music and facile use of language.

Over the last two decades, the domain-specificity characterizing talents in these groups has provoked awareness that our concepts of intelligence, talent, and handicap need to be revised (Feldman, 1980, 1982; Gardner, 1983; O'Connor, 1989; Feldman & Goldsmith, 1991; Lenhoff, 1998). It has become clear that to understand giftedness and talent, we must seek more precise articulation of the relative roles of general cognitive ability and domain-specific intellective capacities as well as the interplay between them (Morelock & Feldman, 1993; Feldman, in press). Special groups such as these show promise of providing this understanding.

We begin this chapter with some general background about prodigies, savants and people with Williams Syndrome; the discussion then focuses on comparing their abilities in music—a shared talent domain. The chapter concludes by examining what we have discovered by juxtaposing these groups; possible directions for future research are also explored.

The Prodigy

A prodigy is a child who, before the age of 10, performs at the level of a highly trained adult in some cognitively demanding domain (Feldman with Goldsmith, 1991; Morelock & Feldman, 1999).

This precise definition of prodigiousness has only been in existence since 1979 (Feldman, 1979)—in spite of the fact that 'prodigy' was used loosely to refer to extraordinary youngsters for many years prior to that. Historically, the term was part of a prophetic tradition signaling impending change (Feldman with Goldsmith, 1991). It referred to an entire range of unnatural phenomena extending from the advent of notable uncanny or extraordinary happenings to the existence of humans or animals regarded as 'freak'.

Over time, the term began to be used more narrowly to refer to extreme human precocity (Morelock & Feldman, 1997). The 'sign' or 'portent' aspect of its meaning was dropped, while the essential connotation of 'unnatural' or 'inexplicable' remained. The term continued, however, to be used indefinitely to refer to a broad range of manifestations of precocity (Barlow, 1952).

With the advent of IQ and its widespread acceptance as the gauge of giftedness, the phenomenon of the prodigy became subsumed under the IQ umbrella (Feldman, 1979). Children who could compose sonata at the age of 6 were implicitly assumed to be high IQ children with penchants for given fields. Nevertheless, the four scientific studies of prodigies that have appeared in the literature[1] fail to support a straightfor-

---

[1] Although the literature contains only four systematic scientific studies of child prodigies, a number of biographical or psychohistorical accounts of the lives of prodigies have been published. See, for example, Kathleen Montour's William James Sidis: *The broken twig* (Montour, 1977), Norbert Wiener's 1953 autobiography, Ex-Prodigy: My childhood and Youth (Wiener, 1953); Amy Wallace's 1986 book (also about William James Sidis) The Prodigy (Wallace, 1986); Fed Waitzkin's 1984 book, Searching for Bobby Fischer: The World of Chess. Observed by the Father of a Child Prodigy (Waitzkin, 1984), and Claude Kenneson's

ward relationship between prodigious achievement and extraordinarily high IQ (Revesz, 1925, Baumgarten, 1930; Feldman, 1980, Morelock, 1995). Prodigies have been documented with IQs ranging from 120 (Baumgarten, 1930) to 200 + (Morelock, 1995). While IQ-associated verbal-conceptual reasoning alters the quality of performance across domains (Morelock & Feldman, 1993; Feldman, in press), the extent to which *large* endowments of general cognitive ability are necessary to talent development appears to vary according to the domain in question and the salience of IQ-independent components in performance. For example, the quality of a writing prodigy's work is heavily influenced by insights and perceptiveness arising out of abstract reasoning (see, for example, Morelock, 1995). However, no matter how great a child's abstract reasoning ability, musical talent cannot emerge without keen auditory perception and sensitivity. Indeed, as the talents of savants and many people with Williams Syndrome attest, impressive musical ability sometimes emerges in the absence of *average* general cognitive strengths, although certain skills of musicianship—such as reading music—appear to require IQ-associated competency (Miller, 1989; Lenhoff, 1998).

Feldman, as the result of his study of six child prodigies, became sensitized to the importance of such domain-specific requirements. He incorporated them into his theory of *Co-incidence*, which he constructed to explain prodigious talent (Feldman, 1980; Feldman with Goldsmith, 1991). Co-incidence, briefly defined, is the melding of many sets of forces interacting in the development and expression of all human potential. These extend from the level of the individual and his/ her family to that of the domain and its requirements and on to the macro level of differential cultural opportunities for the development and expression of various talents. Child prodigies result from a fortuitous concordance of the forces of co-incidence leading to the maximization of human potential. Thus, in most cases of prodigiousness, a child of extraordinary native ability is born into a family recognizing, valuing, and fostering that ability when the child's introduction to the culturally available domain reveals its presence. The child is generally exposed to master teachers who instruct the prodigy in a way most likely to engage the interest and sustain the commitment of the child. Invariably, as well, the child demonstrates a combination of inner-directedness and passionate commitment to the field of achievement.

Prodigious achievement only occurs in domains accessible to children, requiring little prerequisite

knowledge and using media and techniques adaptable for a child's use (e.g. a child-sized violin must be available for a 6-year-old prodigy violinist). Most child prodigies are found in chess and music performance. There have been, however, child prodigy visual artists (Pariser, 1987; Goldsmith & Feldman, 1989), infrequently, a child prodigy in mathematics (Bühler, 1981), and occasional writing prodigies (Radford, 1990; Feldman,1991; Morelock, 1995).

Having briefly touched on the literature pertaining to prodigious achievement, we turn now to consider the idiot savant.

The Idiot Savant

The emergence of exceptional skill in people with mental disability has been documented in the literature for over 200 years (Foerstl, 1989). However, the term 'idiot savant', did not appear in the literature until 1887 when Dr. J. Langdon Down (1887) used it to refer to severely mentally handicapped persons displaying advanced levels of learning in narrowly circumscribed areas. In Down's time, *idiot* referred to individuals operating at the lowest level of retarded functioning based on an evaluation of speech and language capabilities (Scheerenberger, 1983).

With the development of IQ tests, idiocy became translated as encompassing the lowest portion of the IQ scale—extending over an IQ range of 0 to 20 (Craft, 1979). In reality, however, the IQs of all known tested idiot savants have been above 20—and usually fall in the range of 40 to 70 (Treffert, 1989). Somewhat more appropriate, but still a misnomer, is the second part of the term, 'savant'—a straightforward adaptation from the French word meaning 'to know' or 'man of learning'.

Because of the failure of 'idiot savant' to capture the essence of the savant phenomena and because of the pejorative connotations of the first part of the term, a number of alternatives have been suggested (Rimland & Hill, 1984; Charness, Clifton & MacDonald, 1988; Treffert, 1989). In 1989, Treffert proposed a more precise classificatory terminology and suggested a theoretical explanatory framework. He also proposed an alternative term for the condition: *savant syndrome*—or, more simply, just *savant*.

Savant Syndrome Defined

As defined by Treffert (1989), Savant syndrome is a rare condition in which seriously mentally handicapped persons show spectacular islands of ability or brilliance standing in stark, markedly incongruous contrast to the handicap. In some, savant skills are remarkable simply in contrast to the handicap (talented savants, or savant I). In others, with a much rarer form of the condition, the ability or much rarer form of the condition, the ability or brilliance would be spectacular even if viewed in a normal person (prodigious savants or savant II).

---

[1] Continued
account of the lives of a number of musical prodigies, including Mozart, Paganini, and Clara Schumann, in his 1998 book, Musical Prodigies: Perilous Journeys, Remarkable Lives.

Savant syndrome can be either congenital or acquired by a normal person after injury or disease of the central nervous system. The skills can appear—and disappear—inexplicably and without warning (Selfe, 1977; Treffert, 1989).

Like prodigies, savants occur only within a limited number of areas (Treffert, 1989; Young, 1995). Documented savant skills include: calendar calculating (e.g. the ability to quickly calculate the answers to such questions as "On what day of the week will April 29 of the year 2245 A.D. fall?"; music (chiefly limited to the piano); lightning calculating (the ability to do extraordinary rapid mathematical calculations); art (painting, drawing, or sculpting); mechanical ability; prodigious memory (mnemonism); or, on rare occasion, unusual sensory discrimination (smell or touch) or extrasensory perception. Prodigious savants occur chiefly within the areas of music, mathematics (lightning and calendar calculating), and memory (Treffert, 1989).

Incidence of Savants

The literature reveals two major populations from which savants emerge: (1) those diagnosed as autistic, and (2) those diagnosed as mentally handicapped, but not autistic. Rimland (1978) estimates the percentage of idiot savants in the autistic population as 9.8%; while the prevalence of savants in the mentally handicapped population is estimated to be significantly less—0.06% (Hill, 1977). As the incidence of autism itself is only 0.04% of births, however, autistic individuals are far less numerous in the general population than are mentally handicapped people (O'Connor, 1989). Consequently, in absolute terms, idiot savants emerge from each source in approximately equal numbers. Savant skills occur six times as often in males as in females (Hill, 1977).

Features of Savant Functioning

A number of features are common to all savant functioning:

Impaired capacity for abstraction. Scheerer, Rothmann, and Goldstein (1945) first documented the "impairment of abstract attitude" typical of savant functioning. The researchers noted that, generally, savants display minimal abstract reasoning ability combined with almost exclusive reliance on concrete patterns of expression and thought. They wrote of one savant who memorized and sang operas in several languages, yet had no comprehension of the abstract conceptual and symbolic meaning of words.

More recent research suggests that the question of abstract reasoning in savants is more complex than originally thought. Studies show that savants have an immediate—seemingly intuitive—access to the underlying structural rules and regularities of their domain, be it music (Miller, 1989; Treffert, 1989), mathematical calculation (O'Connor & Hermelin, 1984; Hermelin &

O'Connor, 1986), or art (O'Connor & Hermelin, 1987). Intriguingly, these are the same as those applied by practitioners of normal or high reasoning ability who are skilled in the same area. Thus, although most savants can't reason conceptually, all can abstract to a degree—at least in circumscribed and domain-specific areas (O'Connor, 1989; Miller, 1999). Miller (1999) suggests that what may be missing in savants is a conceptual system that can reconstrue or relate domain-specific knowledge in a more general framework, leading to a decontextualized representation containing less perceptual detail but better adapted to varied application in cognition.

Lack of metacognition. Savants lack the ability to reflect upon their internal thinking processes (Scheerer et al., 1945)—what is now called 'metacognition'. When asked to account for how they can do whatever it is that they do, savants frequently respond with something strictly irrelevant. One calendar calculator, when asked how he managed his remarkably fast responses to date questions, said "I make all sorts of mathematical calculations, don't I?" In fact, he was usually unable to add or subtract without pencil and paper (O'Connor, 1989).

Extraordinary memory. All savants are notable for their extraordinary memories (Treffert, 1989). Indeed, the mnemonist savant's sole talent consists of impressive memory for miscellaneous or mundane happenings (e.g. some savants have been known to remember weather conditions for each day of most of their lives). In other savants, it is the norm for extraordinary memory to be limited to their domains of achievement.

Flattened affect. Savants exhibit a restricted range of emotion, or flattened affect (Treffert, 1989). The performance of musical savants, for example, frequently manifests this deficit by coming across as shallow, imitative expressiveness lacking subtlety or innuendo.

Music appears to be the only domain where there is some controversy about the 'flattened affect' observation (Howe, 1989; Miller, 1989; Treffert, 1989). There have been cases of musical savants demonstrating emotional connection with the music they were performing (Viscott, 1970; Miller, 1989). In one such case (Viscott, 1970), the savant possessed more expanded verbal abilities than is commonly the case in manifestations of savant talent. This may have allowed for an interpretive response to the music.

An additional consideration in the case of musical savants is the fact that emotional response to music may be, to some extent, the direct result of the physiological changes which it evokes (Winner, 1982). Music not only affects pulse, respiration, blood pressure, and the electrical resistance of the skin, but also delays the onset of fatigue (Mursell, 1937). These same types of changes occur during emotional experience. The question is raised whether the emotional response seen in musical savants may be more a straightforward reflection of specific physiological effect than is the case with musicians more conceptually and interpretively involved with the music.

Limited creativity. Savants appear to be incapable of producing totally original work. For example, while a musical savant might imitate, improvise, or embellish based on pre-established constraining musical rules, he or she is generally incapable of composing (Treffert, 1989). Sacks (1995a) distinguished between two different kinds of creativity, acknowledging as creative the individuality of savant ability based on perceptual talent while recognizing that even the prodigious savant does not achieve a higher order of creativity— the invention of new ideas and new ways of seeing things.[2]

Along this line of thought—there is evidence that musical savants with more highly developed language capacities may be more likely to be able to compose music. Miller (1989) documented the development of language in L. L., a musical savant. Over a period of months, L. L.'s language skills evolved from simple monosyllabic or echolalic responses to conversational generation of requests, comments and more sophisticated responses to questions. At the beginning of this period, L. L. remained musically confined to renditions of songs and melodies of others, with little inclination to improvise or compose. When he and Miller met for the last time, however, L. L. announced and played an original composition. This curious concordance of the development of expanded language skills and the onset of musical creativity led Miller to speculate that music and language are not mutually exclusive.

Cognitive profiles and family influences. In what is the largest series of studies of savants to date, Robyn Young (1995) investigated the talents and family backgrounds of 51 savants recruited throughout Australia and the United States. The selection of savants included varying degrees of talent, including prodigious and talented savants as well as cases of 'splinter skills'—levels of interest and competence only marginally above the level of general functioning. Young found that parents and siblings of the participants were an exceptionally able group, with above-average IQ and high frequency of high-level skills, though not necessarily the same skills as those displayed by the savants. In addition, there was a familial predisposition toward high achievement, possibly innate, which provided encouragement and reinforcement for savant skills. Young concluded that savants have an underlying biological predisposition towards high general ability that is tempered by neurological impairment. Furthermore, she found the level of precocity exhibited by a savant (i.e. prodigious or talented) to be positively correlated with level of general cognitive ability, as indexed by IQ.

In contrast to the generally held impression that savants manifest islands of extreme capability showcased against a backdrop of *overall severely deficient intellect*, Young found peaks and valleys in the WAIS profiles of her savant sample. Among her 51 savants, 16 had a subtest score at least one standard deviation above the population mean, and 60% had at least 1 subtest one standard deviation above the full-scale score. Block Design, Object Assembly, and Digit Span accrued highest scores; lowest scores were found on Comprehension, Coding and Vocabulary. Neither grouping is consistent with traditional verbal-performance classification of subtest scores, though the patterns are compatible with observed strengths and weaknesses of savant functioning documented in the literature (i.e. verbal/conceptual weaknesses and perceptual strengths).

Tasks requiring successive or sequential processing (digit span, coding, and arithmetic) distinguished prodigious from talented subgroups, though sequential processing ability did not differentially distinguish the type of skill (i.e. music, art, mathematics, etc.) manifested by the subject. Young concluded that although strengths in modes of processing may underlie *development* of a skill, they do not influence *type* of skill developed.

The Similarities subtest, which, in the normal population loads on the Verbal Comprehension factor, was aligned more clearly with the Perceptual Organization factor for Young's savants. Based on these findings, Young proposed that the subjects in her study approached the Similarities subtest using a different mode of information processing than would be expected among the normal population.

Like savants, people with Williams Syndrome display cognitive profiles with peaks and valleys of strengths and weaknesses and unusual modes of processing information. We turn now to explore the unique talents of this population.

Williams Syndrome

Williams Syndrome, a genetically based disorder manifesting in generalized mild-to-moderate mental

---

[2] In a discussion of prodigies and creativity, Morelock & Feldman (1999) introduce a classificatory system for levels of creativity: 'Low C Creativity' refers to "Everyday occurrences of creativity exemplified by original transformations in small products, thoughts or expressions. "Middle C Creativity" refers to "Creative products appreciated in terms of interpretive skill, mastery of technical forms, distinctive style, and success in achieving a technical, practical, commercial or academic goal". "High C Creativity/Genius" refers to "Unique reorganizations of knowledge resulting in substantial new contributions to bodies of knowledge". (Morelock & Feldman, 1999, p. 449). According to this system, most savant-generated creativity would be designated as 'Low C Creativity'.

retardation punctuated with corresponding peaks and valleys of specific abilities, is estimated to occur in 1 out of 20,000 births. It was first identified in 1961 by the New Zealand cardiologist, J. C. P. Williams. Williams had examined a number of young children with pixie-like facial features (e.g. a turned up nose and a small chin) and noted that all had similar heart problems and other medical symptoms as well as cognitive impairments. In a recent video,[3] the neurologist Oliver Sacks, observing that people with Williams Syndrome were "a highly musical species", commented that he chose to refer to them as "Williams People", adding that they had "an identity of their own, which is different". The term 'Williams people' has subsequently made its way into general parlance, even being adopted by the Board of the Williams Syndrome Foundation, a major advocacy group for people with the disorder (Lenhoff, 1998)

Because Williams people lack a group of specific genes from one of their chromosomes (a 'micro-deletion'), they share a range of similar physical and behavioral characteristics as well as cognitive impairments. In addition, they share a number of remarkable abilities (Lenhoff, 1998).

IQs of people with Williams Syndrome range from 40 to 100 (mean, ~ 60), accompanied by commensurate impairments in spatial, quantitative and reasoning abilities (Levitin & Bellugi, 1998). Most Williams people fail Piagetian tests (Piaget, 1963) for conservation of number, space, substance, weight, and quantity (Bellugi, Klima & Wang, 1996). In contrast, they exhibit better face processing and larger vocabularies than would be expected given their cognitive deficits. Typically talking fluidly and with feeling, they employ complex syntactic structures and a surprisingly large and unusual vocabulary (Bellugi, Wang & Jernigan, 1994). As a matter of fact, Williams adolescents show a *proclivity* for unusual words, typically matching correctly with a picture such words as 'canine', 'abrasive', and 'solemn'. In a task requiring subjects to name all the animals they could think of in a minute, adolescent and adult subjects included choices such as 'yak', 'Chihuahua', 'ibex', 'condor', 'vulture', 'unicorn', and 'saber-tooth tiger', far more often than controls matched for mental age (Bellugi et al., 1996). Based on such findings, researchers conclude that unusual word knowledge, processing and choice is characteristic of adolescent and adult Williams Syndrome subjects.

Williams people are characteristically highly sociable. They typically converse with anyone, are generally polite, and have learned a number of complex social

mores to the extent that they may be able to carry on a conversation for a long time without being suspected as mentally retarded (Levitin & Bellugi, 1998).

Williams people also exhibit a heightened auditory awareness. Levitin & Bellugi (1998) dubbed this condition 'soundscape sensitivity' (see Schafer, 1969) to characterize their ability to differentiate *quality* of sounds and classify them on the basis of timbre. Associated with this heightened sensitivity to sound is a strong attraction to and often a talent for music. They also commonly exhibit 'hyperacusis'—unusual sensitivity to noise with distress and discomfort or pain at levels of sound not causing discomfort in normal individuals (A. Don, personal communication, December 20, 1999).[4]

The above sections provided an introductory overview of what is known about prodigies, savants and Williams people. The following section examines more closely their comparative functioning in the domain of music.

Music

As was noted before, in addition to being a talent domain for many people with Williams Syndrome, music is the domain in which the largest number of both prodigies and savants are found. It is also the only domain in which there has actually been some detailed, though limited, systematic research comparing and contrasting prodigy and savant performance (Miller, 1989). We turn now to consider some of that research.

Case Study of A Musical Savant

Miller (1989) conducted a case study of Eddie, a musical savant pianist, who was 5 years old at the time of first contact. At the time Miller first saw the 5-year-old savant, the child had received no formal music lessons and there was no piano in the home. There was no history of a special musical talent in the family, and none of the other members of the family played an instrument. Miller's longitudinal study spanned a 4-year period during which Eddie, at the age of 6, began taking formal music lessons. This allowed Miller to observe the savant's progress during the period of the formal lessons as well as to devise research tasks to assess Eddie's natural acoustical and musical skills.

The researcher gained a more complete picture of Eddie's musical abilities by exploring the literature on musical savants and by selecting three groups of diverse musically talented living subjects with whom to compare Eddie's abilities. In addition, he compared Eddie's musical skills with those of the musical prodigy Erwin Nyiregyhazi, documented in Revesz's (1925) case study. Following is a synopsis of Miller's impressions and findings.

---

[3] The referenced video, made by the Dutch American subsidiary, EO Productions, Inc. (Mons, Wilmowski & Detweiler, 1996), is entitled *Williams Syndrome: A Highly Musical Species*. It has earned seven national film festival awards in the USA.

[4] Dr. Audrey Don is a Postdoctoral Fellow in pediatric neuropsychology with the Department of Developmental Pediatrics at the Children's Seashore House, Children's Hospital of Philadelphia.

Researcher meets savant: first impressions. Miller describes his first encounter with Eddie as unexpected and dramatic, admitting that he was skeptical about this severely handicapped 5-year-old child who was reported to play the piano surprisingly well. Eddie presented as "a very fragile child, bony thin and small for his age" whose motor delay was apparent in his hesitant, splay-footed walking" (Miller, 1989, p. 1). Eddie's speech was almost exclusively echolalic, except for a few conversational cliches such as "How are you?," "I'm fine," and "Good-bye."

Nevertheless, when Eddie's teacher mentioned the word 'piano', the child smiled excitedly and he turned to the room containing the piano, needing no prompting to exhibit his talent. At the piano, Eddie's hands found the keys easily and he started to play some melodious chords, "his head tilted back, staring through his thick glasses at the ceiling with an intent expression on his face" (Miller, 1989, p. 2).

Eddie's first recital for Miller consisted of a rendition of the Christmas carol, 'Silent Night'. The melody was well articulated, with an appropriate tempo, and a nice rolling broken chord figure in the bass. "Eddie's hands, which had difficulty holding a pencil, were clearly at home on the keyboard" (Miller, 1989, p.2).

On Miller's second visit, he tested the range of Eddie's musical sensitivity. Realizing that technical facility across all major and minor keys on the piano is generally achieved only with considerable instruction and practice, Miller questioned how well Eddie could follow a simple melody through a series of transpositions on the keyboard. Was the child's facility limited to a few common keys, or would the particular key of the piece prove irrelevant?

Miller engaged Eddie in a musical 'Game' in which the child was required to repeat a simple melody exactly as it had initially been played by the researcher. Through this little experiment, he discovered that Eddie's talent was not limited to a few, well-practiced patterns of movement on the keyboard. The boy had an impressive sensitivity to the tonal structure of a melody line, and he could follow that melody wherever it appeared in the pitch range represented by a piano keyboard. In addition, he was capable of improvisation—he could take a melodic line and produce variations consistent with the conventions of musical composition.

Such skill dramatically contrasts with musical ability of average 5-year-olds. Normally, a 5-year-old could be expected to have, at best, a slim grasp of interval relationships in even a simple melody (Bartlett & Dowling, 1980); and their spontaneous songs often wander from one tonal center to another, with little sense of an overall tonal structure (Hargreaves, 1986). Not only did Eddie demonstrate a much better grasp of the structure of music than would be expected for a child his age, but his understanding was manifested

naturally and concretely in his playing. Miller comments: "The piano seemed an extension of Eddie's body, and his fingers effortlessly explored its range of sounds as soon as he came in contact with its keyboard" (Miller, 1989, p.3).

Eddie's extraordinary musical ability led Miller to wonder what it was, exactly, that Eddie knew about music. Of what was this incredible musical intelligence—so disparate with the rest of Eddie's abilities—comprised? The results of his case study revealed some answers to these questions. Below we outline some of Miller's major findings; as they are reported, we will discuss their possible implications for our understanding of music prodigies, as well. This comparison and contrast will be followed by a short explication of talent in Williams people, outlined according to some of the same kinds of categorical topics as Miller explored with his study of savants.

Miller's Findings

Absolute pitch: definition and incidence. Absolute pitch is generally defined as 'the ability to name the note of any tone heard without either seeing it played or the benefit of a reference note' (Miller, 1989, p. 15). *Extended absolute pitch* means that the ability extends over the whole musical scale and is independent of the instrument used. Miller reported extended absolute pitch to be present in all well-documented cases of musical savants. A 100% incidence within this seems even more extraordinary when compared with the incidence in the general population, where it is estimated to be less than one-hundredth of 1% (Bachem, 1955).

For Eddie, absolute pitch was separate from knowledge of the verbal names of the notes: he was able to match tones to their equivalent piano notes before he had ever been taught the note names. Miller deduced that this would apply for other savants, as well, since their generally restricted language abilities made verbal association an unlikely means of learning. Once Eddie learned the names of the notes, however, he delighted in pointing out the 'names' of sounds. A passing police car's siren was F and G: while the bell in an elevator was identified as A#.

Exploring absolute pitch further. Miller tested Eddie and his comparison subjects on the identification of single tones and chord groups. Only the subjects who, like Eddie, possessed secure absolute pitch gave quick, accurate and confident judgments across the tasks presented—even when the chords contained dissonant notes.

Other subjects were able to use 'relative pitch' in identifying notes. That is, after a reference tone was sounded, they were able to recognize a second tone as identical, lower or higher, and perhaps estimate a proportionate distance by which the two presented notes differed. Even so, individuals with relative pitch characteristically identified notes more slowly, considering a number of options before settling on a 'guess'.

As Miller's absolute pitch subjects varied considerably in age, musical training, and level of general intelligence, he concluded that the consistency of their results argued for absolute pitch as a distinctive skill with important consequences for music perception.

Absolute pitch and musical syntax. Miller proposed that absolute pitch and the intuitive link it represents between chroma (note name) and tonal frequency suggests the faculty may provide a foundation for the development of higher order structures and a basis for higher order pattern extraction. The beginning musician must learn to map or represent musical notes in a reliable way before he can construct higher order groups in music. The savant, according to Miller, has a ready means of doing so by virtue of the 'internal standard' he possesses for each note of the chromatic scale, i.e. the faculty of absolute pitch.

Miller suggests that the concept of parallel distributed processing (PDP) (Rumelhart & McClelland, 1986) may prove helpful in explaining how a higher order musical structure or pattern emerges. PDP models characterize information processing as involving the activation of specific groups of units corresponding to aspects of information present in the stimulus array. In music performance, it might work like this: the presence of chroma information (e.g. hearing the note 'C') activates several candidate key signatures—keys in which the note 'C' naturally occurs, such as C, G, or F Major. At the same time, it inhibits orientation towards other keys in which 'C' does not appear—such as D Major. This restricted range of key signatures affects subsequent patterns of activation at the chroma level. Chroma values consistent with the suggested key are augmented; whereas, those inconsistent with the key are inhibited. Thus, by its frequency, a note not only specifies central categories (chroma), but it also suggests another series of relations among sounds in terms of candidate keys for the musical piece in question. The 'inevitability' of various frequency-chroma-scale links represents a pathway by which a young musician with a particularly good sense of chroma identification could start establishing a more complex system for extracting patterns in music—a hierarchical representation of the stimulus structure of music.

Eddie's musical performance, as well as that of other savants, does indeed reflect regularities and consistencies related to the structural rules embedded in musical composition. There is little evidence, however, that musical or other types of savants consciously apply a structured set of rules to their material of interest (Hermelin & O'Connor, 1986; Howe & Smith, 1988; Miller, 1989); and the speed of savant response seems to preclude the notion of some complex formal

rule structure. Miller concludes that, like the child whose language expression and comprehension reflects the rules of syntax, so the musical savant's performance shows 'musical syntax' rule use. In neither case is conscious knowledge of the system of rules necessary.

Absolute pitch and the prodigy. No one has completed a review of historically documented music prodigies to determine just what percentage has shown absolute pitch. Nevertheless, accounts of various prodigies' extraordinary faculties of absolute pitch do appear every now and then.

Revesz's prodigy, Erwin Nyiregyhazi, exhibited absolute pitch. Revesz noted the speed and confidence with which the prodigy identified the component notes of complex chords:

> Erwin's verdicts were given immediately without reflection and with perfect confidence. One characteristic of the boy's performance was that during these experiments he always smiled in a superior manner, the tasks put before him being so easy to him that he did not take them seriously (Revesz, 1925, p. 75).

An article appearing in the *New York Times Magazine* (Winn, 1979, December 23) included a fascinating account by pianist Lorin Hollander of how his father first discovered that Hollander was a prodigy . . .

> When I was $3\frac{1}{2}$, I went with my father to a rehearsal and heard them play a Haydn quartet. I was profoundly moved by the music. When I came home, I wanted somehow to put down what I had heard. I found some drawing paper and began to draw spirals. My father asked me what I was doing, and I began to sing him back the piece, which I remembered perfectly, and told him that I was trying to write it down. My father said, "No, you silly boy, we already have a way of writing music", and he brought out the score to show me. I fell into the music; that's the only way to describe it. Within four minutes I knew the notes, the clefs, everything. A car horn sounded outside and, just for fun, my father asked me what note it was. I immediately answered, 'F sharp'. He took a spoon and clinked a glass, 'B flat', I told him. Then he and my mother realized they had a prodigy on their hands and they started to run around to people to find out what to do' (Winn, 1979, December 23, p. 37).

Then, of course, there is Mozart. Of this legendary child prodigy, Marshall (1991) comments that his musical memory was perhaps the most formidable in history, going far beyond absolute pitch. It included the ability to hear and remember entire compositions—motets, concertos, even operas—and subsequently write them down. A letter from Mozart's father, Leopold, to his wife from Rome in April, 1770, when Mozart was 14 years old attests to this:

You have often heard of the famous Miserere in Rome, which is so greatly prized that the performers in the chapel are forbidden on pain of excommunication to take away a single part of it, to copy it or to give it to anyone. *But we have it already.* Wolfgang has written it down and we would have sent it to Salzburg in this letter, if it were not necessary for us to be there to perform it. But the manner of its performance contributes more to its effect than the composition itself. So we shall bring it home with us. Moreover, as it is one of the secrets of Rome, we do not wish to let it fall into other hands, *so that we shall not incur the censure of the Church now or later* (Marshall, 1991, p. 5).

It may well be that absolute pitch operates in prodigies as Miller suggests it does in savants—to provide a foundation for the structure and higher level abstraction of patterns in music. Given Mozart's extraordinary acoustical memory, could we expect him to recall equally well some extended set of random notes or sounds? While there are no specific data on Mozart addressing this question, Miller offers some findings that may be relevant.

Memory in musical savants. Miller (1989) presented a series of chord, melody, and rhythm tasks to Eddie and his comparison subjects to assess short-term memory capacities. The findings suggested that savants did extremely well when the task required retention of harmonic information. When tasks involved tonal material presented sequentially, or 'melody-like' information, they also did quite well, though their performance was not quite so exceptional.

Miller found savant musical memory was enhanced by increased structure or organization in the material to be remembered. The more the stimulus array was composed of 'just notes' (e.g. unconventional chords, random tones, or irregular intervals), the less remarkable savant performance was. Miller concludes that savant performance resembles the selective memory found among those with expert knowledge in a domain: ". . . the savant's memory excels most when the more meaningful or structured aspects of music are present. In each case, it seems most parsimonious to assume that the excellence of immediate memory reflects a complex and well-structured representation of the domain in long-term" (Miller, 1989, p. 112). Tasks requiring reproduction of portions of intact compositions suggested that this response to musical structure extended to a sensitivity to the implicit rules governing music composition in Western culture. For example, notes consistent with the underlying scale of a piece were more likely to be reproduced accurately.

Memory in the music prodigy. Revesz (1925) also assessed the memory of his young prodigy, establishing that Erwin easily memorized melodious pieces with simple harmony and had no difficulty remembering a large number of operatic arias, having learned them in a very short time. Revesz noted that as a rule, however, only the melodies without the harmonies were reproduced without error. This is interestingly to contrast to Eddie's superior performance in reproducing the harmonic dimensions of music as opposed to the melodic. In considering Revesz's findings, however, Miller (1989) states that in view of Erwin's proven ability to render complex chords with great precision, this conclusion about more extended musical excerpts may reflect an attentional bias or preference (Eddie loved operative arias) rather than a particular performance limitation.

Erwin, like Eddie, found unconventional musical excerpts more of a challenge. Revesz notes: "In the case of musical pieces of a strange character, such as melodies with complicated accompaniment and peculiar harmonies, his memory did not prove itself equal to the task" (Revesz, 1925, p. 90). Whether this would have proven to be the case as well with Mozart, one cannot tell for sure. But one might speculate that even Mozart's phenomenal musical memory may have been facilitated by the presence of conventional structure in whatever material he was memorizing at the moment.

Sight reading skills. Unlike Eddie, Erwin's extraordinary talent included a prodigious acquisition of sight reading capabilities. By the age of 6, Erwin already preferred optical exposure to the music rather than just hearing it; and he obviously benefited from seeing the written score while attempting to master a musical piece. Interestingly, while 'reading' a new score without benefit of hearing the music, Erwin would hum the melody to himself while moving his fingers as if he were playing the theme on the piano, thereby fixing the theme in his memory by motor means. Revesz noted that the child appeared to be trying to imprint the treble on his memory by singing, and the lower parts by the action of playing.

Language in the savant. Only two characteristics are possessed by *all* musical savants. The first is extended absolute pitch. The second is some significant degree of language disability (Miller, 1989). The language deficit appearing in musical savants has a specific form. Generally, savants show considerable facility in the phonetic (sounds of speech) and syntactic (rules for combining words into phrases and sentences) aspects of language, while manifesting severe deficits in semantics (the acquisition of words and the meanings associated with them) and pragmatics (using language to express one's intentions and for getting things done in the world). Echolalic speech, such as that manifested by Eddie, appears in the great majority of cases.

Miller argues that echolalia implies that the savant has considerable sensitivity to his or her surrounding language as a system of sounds. Additionally, there is some knowledge as to how these sounds are combined to produce extended sequences. What is missing is manifested awareness of the communicative function of language and its role in sharing meanings about environmental events and objects (Sigman & Mundy, 1987). The presence of this specific pattern of partial language ability tells us that development of extraordinary musical abilities in the savant does not require the *absence* of 'competing' language. In fact, Miller continues, the most gifted musical savants are *not* mute.

Miller (1989) provides a brief recapitulation of Eddie's language development, noting that at age $5\frac{1}{2}$, his language was monosyllabic and/or echolalic. Conversations were generally one-way, with Miller reminding Eddie to listen while a piece was played, informing him of the names of the pieces, and responding with verbal approval to Eddie's playing. Over time, Eddie started reliably repeating the names of requested tunes, although often not with the appropriate melody. Miller observed that the first notes of a song were more reliable cues for Eddie than was the song's title. With the advent of formal music lessons, Eddie gradually began to name notes and additional tunes; he also started commenting on pieces and including simple requests or instructions to the teacher during the lessons.

Language in Erwin, the prodigy. The semantic, pragmatic, and conceptual impoverishment of Eddie's savant mode of speech contrasts dramatically with the pragmatically astute, conceptually rich, and emotionally colored language of Erwin, the prodigy. Revesz observed that the child often asked if what he was about to say would get "into the book", for in this case, Erwin noted, "I want to express myself correctly, and you must pay great attention to me; for a single wrongly-chosen word may alter the meaning of the whole thing" (Revesz, 1925, p. 42).

Revesz also noted that Erwin, unlike most musicians or artists, grasped with absolute precision questions asked of him about his own experiences or processes of consciousness during creative activity or interpretation, and responded with incredible insight. For example, when Revesz asked him whether during the whole time he was composing a piece, he maintained the same state of feeling, Erwin replied that he did so as far as possible, adding "When composing, one must not always give way to one's *heart*, the head must also be consulted. Often it is necessary that the heart should be silenced, pushed into the background, otherwise the composition will become weak" (Revesz, 1925, p. 45).

A few final notes on the piano. Overwhelmingly, the piano proves to be the instrument of musical savants. Why? Miller (1989) points out that the piano keyboard maps its sound producing qualities onto the musical

culture in a direct fashion. It contains, in effect, the alphabet of the musical language laid out in a coherent spatial organization. Octaves and various harmonies appear in a recurring, spatial pattern, making it relatively easy to explore sound combinations in both direct and extensive ways. Piano keys release pleasing tones readily—without the application of subtle bowing or fingering techniques such as are needed for string or wind instruments. Finally, the piano is a popular instrument—one which is more commonly available to the young child.

The Musical Talents of Williams People

From music therapists, private music teachers, and parents has come mounting anecdotal evidence regarding the innate musical abilities of many people with Williams Syndrome (Lenhoff, 1998).[5] In addition, there is a small, but growing formal literature investigating the musical abilities of this population. What has been investigated so far allows us to compile some findings associated with the areas explored by Miller in his study comparing savant and prodigious musical performance.

Absolute pitch. Preliminary findings from research funded by the National Science Foundation at the University of California, Irvine, suggest that the incidence of absolute pitch in the Williams populations is higher than it is in the average population—perhaps as much as 5 times higher (H. M. Lenhoff, personal communication, July 9, 1999).[6]

Memory in Williams musicians. Some Williams musicians are able to retain complex music (some in a variety of languages), including both the words of many verses of long ballads and the melodies, for periods of years (Lenhoff, 1998). Those who learn to

---

[5] The reader is cautioned against presuming that all people with Williams Syndrome are musical. While unusual attraction to music is widespread Williams people and musical talent is common, the degree of talent across individuals varies widely. Furthermore, the Williams Syndrome Association (a membership organization representing nearly 4,000 families in the USA) often hears from parents who say their child is *not* musical. To date, there is no published study of the incidence and degree of musicality in persons with Williams Syndrome (S. E. Libera, personal communication, December 20, 1999). (Dr. Sharon E. Libera is Co-Founder and Coordinator of the Williams Syndrome Music and Arts Camp at Belvoir Terrace in Lenox, Massachusetts).

[6] Dr. Howard M. Lenhoff is Professor (Emeritus) in the Department of Developmental and Cell Biology, University of California, Irvine. He is co-founder of the Williams Syndrome Music and Arts Camp in Lenox, Massachusetts, and is currently Executive Vice-President of the Williams Syndrome Foundation. He is the principal investigator of a National Science Foundation grant to study music cognition in Williams Syndrome, and is father of the Williams musician, Gloria Lenhoff.

sing in foreign languages show near perfect accents. They have a sensitive ear and rapidly learn melody and lyrics simply by hearing a piece a number of times. Lenhoff (1998) notes that usually once they learn a piece, they rarely forget it.[7]

Sight reading. Most Williams people cannot read musical notation. Although some may be capable of doing so, and some can sight read, many feel more comfortable returning to learning by ear and playing without reading the notes (Lenhoff, 1998). Lenhoff observes that the cognitive processing of information involved in reading musical notes appears to interfere with their desire to produce music. On the other hand, some Williams musicians have been known to learn to sight read and at least one known Williams musician prefers sight reading to playing by ear (S. E. Libera, personal communication, December 20, 1999).

Language. The surprising facility with language that many Williams people have, given their general cognitive deficits, has already been mentioned. Most likely related to their sensitivity to nuances of sound, Williams vocalists are also generally good at mastering music in foreign languages. Lenhoff (1998) writes of his 43-year-old daughter, Gloria, who, with a trained voice has performed operatic and other kinds of music for a wide variety of audiences, is the most highly accomplished Williams musician known today [8]:

> Gloria, like many Williams people, has perfect pitch. She also has a lovely lyric soprano voice, great skill at playing the large piano accordion, and a repertoire

of over 2000 pieces in 25 languages. She does not read musical notation and only recently has been able to identify the white notes on the keyboard. (Lenhoff, 1998, p. 16).

Levitin and Bellugi (1998) wrote of one Williams musician who is a prolific creator of songs. When asked by an experimenter to write a song about the breakfast cereal, he spontaneously composed one on the piano, complete with verse, chorus, and rhyming lyrics!

Though fluidly creative with language in speech and lyrics in song, the linguistic products of Williams people typically have a naïve quality about them. Given their documented conceptual deficits, it is intriguing that many Williams people use metaphor and analogy in describing their experience (A. Don, personal communication, December 20, 1999). One Williams musician, 24-year-old pianist Christian Lawson, exuded "Music lights a fire in me and I feel it go right through my system! It's like I'm in paradise". (Scheiber, 1998, p. 1F). A second, Meghan Finn, when asked by her teacher what music was to her, described it as 'soup'—because you drank it down, it made you feel all warm inside, it was nourishing, and she had a really big spoon. (Mons, Wilmowski & Detweiler, 1996)

Rhythmicity and audiation. Levitin & Bellugi (1998) investigated the rhythmic abilities of Williams people. The researchers, noting that Piagetian theory stated that, across domains, conservation is required for activities involving temporal order, seriation, and rhythmic organization, deduced that rhythmic abilities ought to be impaired in children who have not yet reached the conservation stage. Indeed, in former research with normal children (Serafine, 1979) metric conservation in normal children was highly correlated with the standard (non-musical) Piagetian conservation tasks. In addition, Miller (1989) found no evidence for rhythmic abilities in musical savants and argued that their musical skills were focused in melodic and harmonic domains.

Using a graduated series of one- and two-measure rhythmic patterns clapped by the experimenter, the investigators engaged their subjects in an 'echo clapping' or 'rhythm repetitions task' (Levitin & Bellugi, 1998). The investigators noted that while not instructed to do so, all the subjects tended to look the experimenter in the eye (rather than watching the experimenter's hands) during the demonstration of the reference rhythm. In addition, in nearly every trial, the subjects clapped back the demonstrations immediately in perfect time, without missing a beat, as if their response formed part of the same rhythmic sequence. When Williams subjects failed to reproduce the presented rhythm perfectly, the rhythm they did clap bore a clear musical relationship to the referent—as

---

[7] Investigators at the University of Connecticut found some preliminary evidence that music can serve a memory and comprehension-enhancing function in Williams people attempting to master quantitative skills. (R. M. Schader, personal communication, June 18, 1999). (Dr. Robin M. Schader was Program Co-Director of the 1998 *Music and Minds* research initiative co-sponsored by the School of Education, the Music Department, and the NEAG Center of Gifted & Talented Education at the University of Connecticut).

[8] In 1988, an award-winning PBS documentary, *Bravo Gloria*, was produced describing Gloria Lenhoff's outstanding musical talents and telling about her life (Maas & Alda, 1988). In response to that documentary, Gloria's parents received a number of letters and phone calls suggesting that she had Williams Syndrome. Up until that point in time, they had never heard of the disorder (Lenhoff, 1998). The film also piqued the interest of a number of parents in training their Williams children in music. Lenhoff notes: "We often wondered if had we learned when Gloria was a child that she had WS, would we have been discouraged by counselors and teachers and not given her a good musical education?" (Lenhoff, 1998, p. 16.). As of December, 1999, Gloria Lenhoff sings in 26 languages, the most recently acquired being Arabic which, her father notes, "is full of quarter tones" (H. M. Lenhoff, personal communication, December 20, 1999).

though the subject were creating a musically logical completion to the rhythm provided. Furthermore, in contrast to the Piagetian theoretical prediction, all of the experimental subjects demonstrated *conservation of musical time*. If a subject clapped a greater or lesser number of musical notes, in most cases, the subject altered the length of the notes to take up the same amount of metrical time as the exemplar. The investigators concluded that subjects with Williams Syndrome show evidence for a quality that they called *rhythmicity*, or *rhythmic musicality*.

Williams musicians' highly developed, creative sense of rhythm contrasts with savant talent, which Miller found to be confined to melody and harmony. One could argue that Williams people's ability to transform rhythmic patterns while conserving musical time is reminiscent of the playful creativity of Mozart, who was given to making innumerable changes and transformations in speech, writing, and music, while skillfully conserving underlying patterns (Morelock & Feldman, 1999).

In another study, Don (1997) investigated audiation and rhythmic ability in Williams people, testing 19 individuals with Williams Syndrome using the tonal and rhythm subtests of *Gordon's Primary Measures of Music Audiation* (1980). Audiation, according to Gordon, "takes place when one hears music through recall or creativity, the sound not being physically present" (p. 107). Don compared her Williams Syndrome group with a comparison group of 19 normal children, equivalent in terms of receptive vocabulary age (8 yrs. 1 mo.) as measured by the Peabody Picture Vocabulary Test-Revised (PPVT-R). She found the level of audiation exhibited by her subjects to be commensurate with their preserved language skills rather than on a par with their levels of general cognitive ability (average receptive vocabulary score on the PPVT-R for the Williams group was 78; average full scale IQ score on the WISC-III was 53). Don concluded that, generally, musical skills among the population of Williams people are a *relative strength* rather than a 'savant skill', although she noted that some Williams people's musical abilities are more extreme and savant-like (A. Don, personal communication, December 20, 1999). Where the Williams children *did* stand out as different was in their *emotional response* to the music.

Affect. Given the 'flat effect' so often cited in the savant literature, the affective response of Williams people to music is of particular interest. Don (1997) used a *Child Music Interest Interview* and a *Parent Language and Music Questionnaire* to compare her groups in terms of their interest in music and their auditory characteristics. The groups differed neither in their musical background and environment nor in their history of creating music. However, emotional responsivity stood out in the Williams group. Of the Williams

group, 100% reported that music could make them feel happy, while 84% of the comparison group responded likewise. The 'negative' response of one Williams child had to be recoded as positive when he explained that music did not make him feel happy *because it made him feel **more** than happy*. Whereas 79% of the Williams Group reported that music could make them feel sad, only 47% of the comparison group made a comparable response.

Perhaps most striking are the spontaneous reports from the parents of the Williams children. Some noted that when their children were very young, they cried inconsolably when exposed to slow, sad music. One child screamed and refused to listen to a lullaby composed specifically for her (A. Don, personal communication, December 20, 1999).

Choice of instrument. Unlike savants, who overwhelmingly gravitate to the piano, Williams musicians choose a variety of instruments, musical genres, and styles of performance. These choices appear to be much more a matter of individual affinity (S. E. Libera, personal communication, July 1, 1999), though motor problems commonly associated with the disorder also play a role in determining which instruments remain viable options (H. M. Lenhoff, personal communication, December 20, 1999).[9]

Having explored what is known about the configurations of talent reflected by prodigy, savant and Williams populations, we are left with more questions than answers. This is to be expected, considering the fledgling state of research. Nevertheless, the following section considers what we have learned and where we might go next in juxtaposing the extremes.

Juxtaposing the Extremes

Accumulated research exploring savants, prodigies and Williams people appears promising. To date, no studies compare the abilities of Williams people with those of savants. Nevertheless, findings from independent investigations suggest that such a study would be worthwhile. While overall levels of general cognitive ability in these two populations are similar, their profiles of specific abilities show intriguing disparities and commonalities. Savants are deficient in language, while Williams people are particularly facile. While prosodic features of speech may be absent or disturbed in savants (O'Connell, 1974; Miller, 1989), Williams people use affective prosody far more frequently than even normal children (Bellugi et al., 1996).

A similarity between the two populations may be the incidence of absolute pitch;. it appears that the majority

---

[9] Howard Lenhoff cites voice, keyboard and drums as the most favored instruments among Williams musicians, noting that these are also the main instruments taught at the Williams Syndrome Music and Arts Camp at Belvoir Terrace in Lenox, Massachusetts. However, various Williams musicians have mastered trumpet, clarinet, violin, guitar, or accordion.

of savants (Judd, 1988; Miller, 1989) and, as mentioned previously, possibly a large proportion of Williams people have absolute pitch. A recent investigation (Schlaug, Jancke, Huang & Steinmetz, 1995) found individuals with absolute pitch to have a larger planum temporale in the left hemisphere. The publication of these results in the journal *Science* led neurologist Oliver Sacks (1995b) to suggest that the exaggerated leftward asymmetry of the planum temporale in musicians with perfect pitch may also underlie perfect pitch as a 'savant talent' in disabled persons. In response to Sack's speculations, Hickok, Bellugi & Jones (1995) sent a letter to the editor of the journal, reporting that they had used magnetic resonance images (MRI) to analyze the planum temporale in Williams Syndrome subjects. They found the planum temporale asymmetry for Williams subjects to be comparable to that of the group of musicians studied by the former investigators. Three of the four Williams subjects had greater asymmetry than that of the musicians, but less than that of musicians with perfect pitch. In addition, Williams subjects did not differ from normal subjects in planum temporale surface area despite the overall reduction of cerebral volume previously reported in subjects with Williams Syndrome (Jernigan, Bellugi, Sowell, Doherty & Hesselink, 1993).

The investigators cautioned, however, that since individuals with Williams Syndrome typically possess exceptional language abilities relative to other cognitive domains (and despite mental retardation), planum temporale asymmetry may be related to linguistic abilities rather than, or as well as, musical abilities.

While linguistic and musical abilities may be highly confounded in both Williams people and musical prodigies, they may be less so in musical savants. We might speculate that MRI research analyzing the planum temporale in musical savants may shed light on whether this focal area of the brain is specifically related to musical abilities rather than linguistic abilities. Or perhaps the question pertaining to the relationship between linguistic and musical abilities may prove more complex, as Morelock's (1995; Morelock & Feldman, in progress) studies of child writers seems to suggest.[10] Brain imaging techniques

may provide clues as to whether and how certain writing, such as poetry, with its emphasis on rhythmical cadence and the sound of words, may be linked in the brain to music production in a way that prose is not.

The connection between linguistic abilities and musical creativity is a related area that may also be explored through comparative studies of savants and Williams subjects. Miller's (1989) report of the savant whose enhanced language development coincided with an emerging ability to compose music is especially intriguing when viewed beside the fluidity of language and capacity for melodic and rhythmic creativity characterizing people with Williams Syndrome. What does this have in common, if anything, with the playful verbal creativity that Mozart exhibited alongside his extraordinarily creative musical achievements (Morelock & Feldman, 1999)? This is another question whose time has come.

Perhaps the purest essence of domain-specific talent is the ability to holistically intuit the syntactic core of rules and regularities lying at the heart of a domain of knowledge: the pattern of relationships between numbers, the pattern of tones in a musical scale, the pattern of images in the visual world, the pattern of words in a language (Morelock & Feldman, 1993). However, evidence has accrued that even in savants, general cognitive ability plays a role in degree of precocity (Young, 1995; Young & Nettelbeck, 1995; Nettelbeck & Young; 1996) as well as in the emergence of aesthetic qualities (O'Connor & Hermelin, 1987). Young's (1995) studies of the families of savants echoes Feldman's (Feldman with Goldsmith, 1991) and Morelock's (1995) findings in families of prodigies, where facilitative environments and supportive hereditary influences combine to encourage the flourishing of talent. A comparable exploration into the families of extraordinary Williams musicians would be of interest here. Might we find among the families of the more talented Williams musicians a suggestion of underlying biological predisposition toward high level ability and an overt valuing of achievement much like that which Young (1995) found in her families of savants? Longitudinal case studies tracing development over time and aiming for a comprehensive contextual understanding are needed (e.g. Feldman, 1980, Feldman with Goldsmith, 1991; Morelock, 1995, 2000).

Given what we have learned from the combination of case studies and empirical investigations, we are

---

[10] In two case studies of highly talented child writers, Morelock documented some intriguing parallel differences in terms of their creative processes as they wrote poetry and prose. Both children reported that poetry "came to them" suddenly, unbidden and fully-formed. One of the girls reported that when poems first started "coming to her", they were always accompanied by music. She would hear in her mind a voice singing the words of the poem. Eventually, the voice became her own, and over time, the music stopped accompanying the poetry. In contrast, for both girls, prose evolved out of play. Both children independently created a process in which they set up figures and/or dolls and proceeded to allow them to play out a scenario that the

[10] Continued
children narrated. The ensuing drama, upon its completion, got transformed into a written story. Morelock speculates that the creation of poetry requires different brain functioning, perhaps more akin to that required to create music and relying in a different way or to a different extent upon right brain processes.

beginning to see the wealth of knowledge that we can glean from comparison and contrast of extreme talent in its diverse forms exhibited by individuals with a variety of genetic and neurological substrates. We look forward to what investigators will find through continued explorations of the kind we have considered here.

Acknowledgements

The authors wish to express their appreciation to Professor Howard M. Lenhoff, Dr. Sharon E. Libera, Dr. Audrey Don and Dr. Robin M. Schader for freely sharing their knowledge and experience in the world of Williams people. To Professor Lenhoff and Dr. Libera go special thanks for reviewing the first draft of this paper and kindly offering invaluable comments and suggestions. Whatever shortcomings might be found in the final product are solely the responsibility of the authors.

References

Bachem, A. (1955). Absolute pitch. *The Journal of the Acoustical Society of America*, **27** (6), 1180–1185.

Barlow, F. (1952). *Mental prodigies*. New York: Philosophical Library.

Bartlett, J. & Dowling, W. (1980). The recognition of transposed melodies: a key-distance effect in developmental perspective. *Journal of Experimental Psychology: Human Perception and Performance*, **6**, 501–515.

Baumgarten, F. (1930). *Wunderkinder psychologische untersuchungen*. Leipzig: Johann Ambrosius Barth.

Bellugi, U., Klima, E. S. & Wang, P. P. (1996). Cognitive and neural development: clues from genetically based syndromes. In: D. Magnusson (Ed.), *The Life-Span Development of Individuals: A Synthesis of Biological and Psychological Perspectives*. (Proceedings of the Nobel Symposium, Stockholm, Sweden, June 19–22, 1994; pp. 223–243). New York: Cambridge University Press.

Bellugi, U., Wang, P. P. & Jernigan, T. L. (1994). Williams Syndrome: an unusual neuropsychological profile. In: S. Broman & J. Grafman (Eds), *Atypical Cognitive Deficits in Developmental Disorders: Implications for Brain Function* (pp. 23–56). Hillsdale, NJ: Lawrence Erlbaum Associates.

Bühler, W. K. (1981). *Gauss: a biographical study*. Berlin: Springer-Verlag.

Charness, N., Clifton, J. & MacDonald, L. (1988). A case study of a musical Mono-savant: a cognitive psychological focus. In: L. K. Obler & D. A. Fein (Eds), *The Exceptional Brain: Neuropsychology of Talent and Special Abilities* (pp. 277–293). New York: Guilford.

Craft, M. (Ed.) (1979). *Tredgold's mental retardation* (12th ed.). London: Bailliere Tindall.

Don, A. (1997). *Auditory pattern perception in children with Williams Syndrome (WMS)*. Unpublished doctoral dissertation, University of Windsor, Ontario, CA.

Down, J. L. (1887). *On some of the mental affections of childhood and youth*. London: Churchill.

Feldman, D. H. (1979). The mysterious case of extreme giftedness. In: A. H. Passow (Ed.), *The Gifted and the Talented: The 78th Yearbook of the National Society for the Study of Education* (pp. 335–351). Chicago: University of Chicago Press.

Feldman, D. H. (1980). *Beyond universals in cognitive development*. Norwood, NJ: Ablex Publishing Corporation.

Feldman, D. H. (1982). A developmental framework for research with gifted children. In: D. H. Feldman (Ed.), *Developmental Approaches to Giftedness and Creativity* (pp. 31–45). San Francisco, CA: Jossey-Bass.

Feldman, D. H. (1991). *The theory of Co-Incidence: how giftedness develops in extreme and less extreme cases*. Paper presented at the Ninth World Conference on Gifted and Talented Children, July 29–August 2, The Hague, Netherlands.

Feldman, D. H. (with Goldsmith, L. T.) (1991). *Nature's gambit: child prodigies and the development of human potential*. New York: Teachers College Press.

Feldman, D. H. (in press). A developmental, evolutionary perspective on giftedness. In: J. Borland & L. Wright (Eds), *Rethinking Gifted Education: Contemporary Approaches to Understanding Giftedness*. New York: Teachers College Press.

Flavell, J. H. (1968). *The development of role-taking and communication skills in children*. New York: Wiley.

Foerstl, J. (1989). Early interest in the idiot savant. *American Journal of Psychiatry*, **146**, 566.

Gardner, H. (1983). *Frames of mind: the theory of multiple intelligences*. New York: Basic Books.

Goldsmith, L. T. & Feldman, D. H. (1989). Wang Yani: gifts well given. In: W. C. Ho (Ed.), *Yani: The Brush of Innocence* (pp. 50–62). New York: Hudson Hills.

Gordon, E. E. (1986). *Primary measures of music audiation* (Book and sound recording). Chicago: G.I. A. Publications.

Hargreaves, D. (1986). *The developmental psychology of music*. Cambridge: Cambridge University Press.

Hermelin, B. & O'Connor, N. (1986). Idiot savant calendrical calculators: rules and regularities. *Psychological Medicine*, **16**, 1–9.

Hickok, G., Bellugi, U. & Jones, W. (1995). Asymmetrical ability. *Science*, **270** (5234), 219–220.

Hill, A. L. (1977). Idiots-savants: rate of incidence. *Perceptual and Motor Skills*, **44**, 161–162.

Howe, M. (1989). *Fragments of genius: the strange feats of idiots savants*. London: Routledge.

Howe, M. & Smith, J. (1988). Calendar calculating in 'idiots savants': How do they do it? *British Journal of Psychology*, **79**, 371–386.

Jernigan, T. L., Bellugi, U., Sowell, E., Doherty, S. & Hesselink, J. (1993). *Archives Of Neurology*, **50**, 186–191.

Judd, T. (1988). The varieties of musical talent. In: L. Obler & D. Fein (Eds), *The Exceptional Brain* (pp. 127–156). New York: Guilford Press.

Kenneson, C. (1998). *Musical prodigies: perilous journeys, remarkable lives*. Portland, OR: Amadeus Press.

Lenhoff, H. M. (1998). Insights into the musical potential of cognitively impaired people diagnosed with Williams Syndrome. *Music Therapy Perspectives*, **16** (1), 33–36.

Levitin, D. J. & Bellugi, U. (1998). Musical abilities in individuals with Williams Syndrome. *Music Perception*, **15** (4), 357–389.

Marshall, R. L. (1991). *Mozart speaks: views on music, musicians, and the world*. New York: Schirmer Books.

Maas, J. B. (Producer) & Alda, A. (Director) (1988). *Bravo Gloria* [Film]. (Available from the Williams Syndrome Association, P. O. Box 297, Clawson, MI 48017–0297).

Miller, L. K. (1989). *Musical savants: exceptional skill in the mentally retarded*. Hillsdale, NJ: Lawrence Erlbaum.

Miller, L. K. (1999). The Savant Syndrome: intellectual impairment and exceptional skill. *Psychological Bulletin*, **125** (1), 31–46.

Mons, A., Wilmowski, W. A. (Executive Producers) & Detweiler, C. (Director) (1996). *Williams Syndrome: A Highly Musical Species* [Videotape]. (Available from the Williams Syndrome Association, P.O. Box 297, Clawson, MI 48017–0297).

Montour, K. (1977). William James Sidis: the broken twig. *American Psychologist*, **32**, 267–279.

Morelock, M. J. (1995). *The profoundly gifted child in family context*. (University Microfilms No. 0234 TUFTS-D 9531439).

Morelock, M. J. (2000). A sociolinguistic perspective on exceptionally High-IQ children. In: R. C. Friedman & B. M. Shore (Eds), *Talents unfolding: Cognition and Development*. Washington, DC: American Psychological Association.

Morelock, M. J. & Feldman, D. H. Inner worlds and alternate dimensions: exploring the phenomenology of the child writer. In: L. V. Shavinina (Ed.), *Extracognitive Phenomena in High Ability*. Mahwah, N.J.: Erlbaum. (in progress).

Morelock, M. J. & Feldman, D. H. (1993). Prodigies and savants: what they have to tell us about giftedness and human cognition. In: K. A. Heller, F. J. Mönks & A. H. Passow (Eds), *International Handbook of Research and Development of Giftedness and Talent* (1st ed.). New York: Pergamon.

Morelock, M. J. & Feldman, D. H. (1997). High-IQ children, extreme precocity, and Savant Syndrome. In: N. Colangelo & G. Davis (Eds), *Handbook of Gifted Education* (2nd ed.) (pp. 439–459). Boston: Allyn & Bacon.

Morelock, M. J. & Feldman, D. H. (1999). Prodigies. In: M. A. Runco & S. R. Pritzker (Eds), *Encyclopedia of Creativity* (Vol. 2, pp. 449–456). Boston: Academic Press

Mursell, J. (1937). *The psychology of music*. New York: W. W. Norton.

Nettelbeck, T. & Young, R. (1996). Intelligence and Savant Syndrome: is the whole greater than the sum of the fragments? *Intelligence*, **22**, 49–68.

O'Connell, T. (1974). The musical life of an autistic boy. *Journal of Autism and Childhood Schizophrenia*, **3**, 223–229.

O'Connor, N. (1989). The performance of the 'idiot-savant': implicit and explicit. *British Journal of Disorders of Communication*, **24**, 1–20.

O'Connor, N. & Hermelin, B. (1984). Idiot savant calendrical calculators: maths or memory? *Psychological Medicine*, **14**, 801–806.

O'Connor, N., & Hermelin, B. (1987). Visual and graphic abilities of the idiot savant artist. *Psychological Medicine*, **17**, 79–90.

Pariser, D. (1987). The juvenilia of Klee. Toulouse-Lautrec and Picasso. *Visual Arts Research*, **13**, 53–67.

Piaget, J. (1963). *The origins of intelligence in children*. New York: Norton.

Radford, J. (1990). Child prodigies and exceptional early achievers. New York: Free Press.

Rest, J. (1974). *Manual for defining issue test: an objective test of moral judgment development*. Minneapolis: University of Minnesota.

Revesz, G. (1925). *The psychology of a music prodigy*. New York: Harcourt, Brace.

Rimland, B. (1978). Savant capabilities of autistic children and their cognitive implications. In: G. Servan (Ed.), *Cognitive Defects in the Development of Mental Illness*. New York: Brunner/Mazel.

Rimland, B. & Hill, A. L. (1984). Idiot savants. In: J. Wortis (Ed.), *Mental Retardation and Developmental Disabilities* (pp. 155–159). New York: Plenum.

Rumelhart, D. & McClelland, D. (1986). *Parallel distributed processing*. Cambridge, MA: MIT Press.

Sacks, O. (1995a). *An anthropologist on Mars*. New York: Alfred A. Knopf.

Sacks, O. (1995b, May 5). Musical ability: discussion and reply to the February 3, 1995 article. In vivo evidence of structural brain asymmetry in musicians. *Science*, **268**, 621–622.

Schafer, R. M. (1969). *The new soundscape*. New York: Associated Music Publishers.

Scheiber, D. (1998, September 6). Music lights a fire. *The St. Petersburg Times*, pp. 1F, 4F–8F.

Scheerenberger, R. C. (1983). *A history of mental retardation*. Baltimore: Brookes.

Scheerer, M., Rothmann, E. & Goldstein, K. (1945). A case of 'idiot savant': an experimental study of personality organization. *Psychology Monograph*, **58**, 1–62.

Schlaug, G., Jancke, L.,Huang, Y. & Steinmetz, H. (1995, February). In vivo evidence of structural brain asymmetry in musicians. *Science*, **267**, 699–701.

Selfe, L. (1977). *Nadia: a case of extraordinary drawing ability in an autistic child*. New York: Academic Press.

Serafine, M. L. (1979). A measure of meter conservation in music, based on Piaget's Theory. *Genetic Psychology Monographs*, **99**, 185–229.

Sigman, M. & Mundy, P. (1987). Symbolic processes in young autistic children. In: D. Cicchetti & M. Beeghly (Eds), *Symbolic Development in Atypical Children* (pp. 31–46). San Francisco: Jossey-Bass.

Smith, S. B. (1988). *The great mental calculators: the psychology, methods, and lives of calculating prodigies, past and present*. New York: Columbia University Press.

Treffert, D. A. (1989). *Extraordinary people: understanding 'idiot savants'*. New York: Harper & Row.

Viscott, D. S. (1970). A musical idiot savant: a psychodynamic study, and some speculations on the creative process. *Psychiatry*, **33**, 494–515.

Waitzkin, F. (1984). *Searching for Bobby Fischer: The world of chess, observed by the father of a child prodigy*. New York: Random House.

Wallace, A. (1986). *The prodigy*. New York: Dutton.

Wiener, N. (1953). *Ex-prodigy: my childhood and youth*. Cambridge, MA: MIT press.

Winn, M. (1979). The pleasures and perils of being a child prodigy. *New York Times Magazine*, December 23, 12–17, 38–45.

Winner, E. (1982). *Invented worlds*. Cambridge, MA: Harvard University Press.

Young, R. (1995). *Savant Syndrome: processes underlying extraordinary abilities*. Unpublished doctoral dissertation, University of Adelaide, South Australia.

Young, R. & Nettelbeck, T. (1995). The abilities of a musical savant and his family. *Journal of Autism and Developmental Disorders*, **25**, 229–245.

Addressing the Most Challenging Questions in Gifted Education and Psychology: A Role Best Suited to Longitudinal Research

Rena Subotnik[1] and Karen Arnold[2]

[1]Hunter College, City University of New York, USA
[2]Boston College, USA

Introduction

Fundamental challenges in the field of gifted education and psychology involve finding the right people and nurturing their gifts appropriately. Both aims require research that connects promise with attainment. Unique among research designs, longitudinal investigations, which collect information about the same individuals on multiple occasions over time, yield direct evidence about the conditions that lead to the fulfillment of talent. Repeated measures studies use a variety of quantitative and qualitative data, appear in a variety of social science disciplines, draw from a wide range of theoretical perspectives, and focus on both individual trajectories and group patterns.

The fields of gifted education and psychology have developed sufficiently over the decade to have elicited highly complex questions and concerns that require a comprehensive and long-term approach to problem solving and policy making. The continuing effects of all the variables we claim to be important to the study of gifted children and adolescents—programs, instructional strategies, mentoring, parenting styles, and innate qualities above and beyond IQ—are finally being addressed. As will be seen in the discussion that emerges from this chapter, the community of scholars that employ repeated measures methodology envision the need for more refined theoretical and design models to answer increasingly sophisticated questions about the development of giftedness and talent.

In the last edition of the *Handbook*, we provided readers with samples of classic longitudinal studies and a synthesis of the literature from the 1980s and early 1990s that were organized around issues of identification, sex differences, program effectiveness, definitions of success, and personality variables. In addition, the strengths and weaknesses of longitudinal research methodology were delineated. We urged scholars to conduct more research on young children, to use more sophisticated, multi-cohort methodologies, and to focus more on domain specific talent development.

Chapter Preview

Since 1993 a rich array of repeated measures studies have been conducted in countries around the world and published in English. We have organized the studies into categories and describe them briefly for readers. We then provide an analysis of the current literature in relation to our perspective of what is needed by the field. The final sections of the chapter provide a platform for presenting our views of the key issues in the field, and arguing that longitudinal data provide the most promising foundation for meaningful program design and policy making.

Recent Longitudinal Research

New single cohort longitudinal studies and several ongoing larger projects have appeared in the literature since the first edition of the International Handbook. Our review of classic and contemporary longitudinal studies in that volume was organized around the themes of gifted identification, educational intervention, and domain specific talent. Interestingly, the literature since 1993 only partly overlaps with these a priori conceptual categories. A heuristic grouping of recent studies follows, beginning with edited collections of repeated measures research and continuing in order of the prevalence of each topic within the longitudinal literature.

Collections of Longitudinal Studies

Collections of longitudinal studies provide relevant sources for assessing both longitudinal research findings and repeated measures methodology. Subotnik and Arnold edited a 1994 collection: *Beyond Terman:*

Contemporary Longitudinal Studies of Giftedness and Talent. The editors discuss the advantages of repeated measures methodology for addressing the central issues of gifted education. The 16 studies in the book investigate the determinants of later academic and career achievement for different populations identified on the basis of early demonstrated accomplishments, on intelligence test and achievement test scores, and on inclusion in educational programs for the gifted. The editors analyzed the body of findings to enable researchers, policy makers, and practitioners to compare the long-term effects of different identification procedures. Important patterns across the collected studies were: (1) the close relationship between individual outcomes and identification criteria or educational program emphasis; (2) the continuing salience of gender as a mediating variable in talent development; and (3) the general methodological weakness of most contemporary longitudinal studies in the field.

Subotnik and Arnold also edited a special longitudinal research issue in the gifted journal, *Roeper Review* (1993, Volume 15, Number 3). In addition to several studies that appeared in *Beyond Terman*, the issue included some longitudinal projects on academic acceleration, academic achievement, and IQ test stability.

Two other collected works contain studies about gifted populations as well as relevant analyses of methodological issues across longitudinal investigations. The earliest of these is a collection of research on educated American women from various Twentieth Century birth cohorts, *Women's Lives Through Time: Educated American Women of the Twentieth Century* (Hulbert & Schuster, 1993). The focus of the volume is on the interplay of changing societal forces and the life paths of college-educated women. The book's 15 studies explore changing definitions of success for women, relationships between personal values and levels and domains of accomplishment, and the impact of historical and social forces on women's talent development. Second, a special issue of the *Journal of Creativity Research* (1999, Volume 12, Number 2) edited by Runco, presents several studies specifically devoted to giftedness and features longitudinal studies across the related field of creativity.

Ongoing Major Studies

Two ongoing, major longitudinal studies of gifted students warrant special mention in connection with this chapter's topic. (See chapters by study directors in this volume for comprehensive discussions of the projects.) In the United States, the Study of Mathematically Precocious Youth (SMPY) is approximately halfway through a planned 50-year multiple cohort investigation (Benbow, 1992; Lubinski & Benbow, 1995) Participants were identified at age 13 as high scorers on the mathematics portion of the Scholastic

Aptitude Test (SAT-M) normally taken by American secondary students for the purposes of university entrance. Currently, 4000 students from four cohorts have participated in three or four waves of data collection. In a recent published study, vocational interests derived from the Strong–Campbell interest inventory at age 13 were found to predict adult career profiles at age 28 (Lubinski, Benbow & Ryan, 1995). Insights into the career and life choices of participants have richly rewarded the educational community.

The Study of Mathematically Precocious Youth was the model for a mathematics talent search and educational program at the University of Hamburg. This German program has also yielded some follow-up studies that indicate positive effects of identification via mathematics tests in early adolescence and for a challenging enrichment program (Wagner & Zimmerman, 1986; Wieczerkowski, Wagner & Birx, 1987).

A second large sample, multi-cohort longitudinal study is underway in Germany. The Munich Longitudinal Studies of Giftedness began in 1985 with a national sample of 26,000 children and adolescents in six cohorts (Perleth & Heller, 1994). Participants were identified based on a multi-dimensional definition of giftedness and followed through quantitative and qualitative measures of cognitive, personality, and achievement variables. The most comprehensive ongoing longitudinal study of giftedness in the world, the researchers publish regular follow-ups on various developmental issues and educational concerns.

IQ-Related Studies

One of the larger categories of new and on-going longitudinal studies found in the literature since 1993 comprises IQ-related studies. Several publications address the Terman data, and others report on the Fullerton Study, a 20-year follow-up of a cohort of Californian babies. These two studies have shaped the thinking about life-span studies in profound ways. In addition, a series of studies conducted in three different countries looks at the stability of IQ scores and the relationship of IQ to creativity and personal characteristics.

The Terman study, begun in the 1920s when the subjects were between nine and eleven years old, is the longest published investigation of human development. A series of books, *Genetic Studies of Genius*, (Terman, 1925; Terman & Oden, 1947, 1959, etc.) covered the childhood, early adulthood, and middle age of these high IQ men and women. Terman's protégés, and their respective protégés continue to collect information related to geriatric health and psychology. In addition, the publicly available data have been re-analyzed by countless scholars and graduate students. Holahan, Sears & Cronbach (1995) report on the development of the 'Termites' in their sixth and seventh decades. The focus is on the variables associated with successful aging through explorations of retirement and sources of life satisfaction. Cronbach (1996) conducted a re-analysis of the Terman data comparing males who completed high school at a normal rate with those who graduated at age 15 or 16 on variables associated with life satisfaction and accomplishment through late middle age. Elder (1987) studied the impact of the type and timing of wartime military service on the later lives of Terman study men. Subotnik, Kassan, Summers & Wasser (1993) compared the Terman group at mid-life with those of a cohort of high IQ adults who attended the highly selective Hunter College Elementary School in the 1940s and 1950s. The level drive and ambition in the Hunter group mirrored the small proportion of Terman study subjects who achieved eminence.

Gottfried, Gottfried, Bathurst & Guerin's (1994) contribution is methodologically unique. They began their study in 1979 by collecting data on the physical, cognitive, and social development of 130 one-year-olds who had all been born at the same community hospital within a specified time period. The subjects were tested for IQ at age eight and categorized as gifted or not-gifted, thereby providing a natural comparison group and avoiding validity issues associated with selection bias. In 1996, Gottfried and Gottfried reported that subjects categorized as gifted demonstrated significantly higher tested intrinsic motivation than unselected peers.

Other important longitudinal studies furthering the validity of IQ were conducted in Israel, Eastern Europe, and United States. Cahan and Gejman (1993) investigated the stability of IQ scores in 161 gifted Israeli children. A new repeated measures study was initiated by Belova (1996) to examine developmental characteristics of gifted East European children over time, with a special focus on the interaction between creativity, intelligence, and personality. The revised Wechsler-Scale for children was employed by Americans Spangler and Sabatino (1995) to test the reliability of test scores used to identify children admitted to special programs for the gifted over the course of six years.

No discussion of IQ can be complete without addressing the work of Flynn (1999), who brought global attention to the trend of rising IQ scores unaccompanied by increased indications of achievement in countries like the United States. The Flynn Effect serves to remind us that high IQ has limited explanatory power in predicting real world achievements.

Gender Differences Studies

Differences in achievement, life satisfaction, career choice, and other key psychological measures based on gender remain of great interest to researchers. *Women's Lives through Time* (Hulbert & Schuster, 1993) includes a 29-year follow-up study of career and life aspirations and accomplishments among 1961 women graduates of the University of California at Los Angeles (Schuster, Langland & Smith, 1993). A second chapter in Hulbert and Schuster re-analyzed the Terman data for female subjects (Tomlinson-Keasy, 1993). In an ongoing longitudinal study of American students ranked first in their high school classes, Arnold (1993a, 1993b, 1995) found that exceptional high school grades predicted post-secondary academic achievement and degree attainment. However, non-academic factors, such as gender, social class and ethnicity, overshadowed academic talent in determining career accomplishments by the former valedictorians. The most glaring differences in career and life satisfaction outcomes were between women and men. A later collaboration with Subotnik (1996), which included subjects from both the Valedictorian Project and Subotnik's Westinghouse study (Subotnik & Steiner, 1994) showed that women's conceptions of their role as parents continue to shape their career aspirations. Those who were on the 'fast-track' to high level science careers discussed their views of balancing family and work responsibilities, revealing a preference for balance over exclusive focus on work. The authors speculated as to whether their potential for future eminence would be jeopardized in the unforgiving career trajectory of research science.

In a related study, both girls and boys in a special program for mathematically gifted adolescents lost interest in mathematics during their two years in the program (Terwilliger & Titus, 1995). The girls' interests were less strong initially and dissipated much more dramatically than the boys. A Norwegian longitudinal study of school children between ages 10 and 16 found similar gender differences (Undheim, Nordvik, Gustaffson & Undheim, 1995). In that study, high-ability girls and boys were identified as the top 5% of scorers on a variety of cognitive ability tests taken by an unselected sample of 1000 10-year olds. By the end of middle school, at age 16, three to four times as many high-ability boys as girls earned top grades in mathematics. Furthermore, high-ability girls did not show the same superiority over gifted boys in English and Norwegian language study that characterized the larger sample of unselected students.

Kerr (1994) followed up on the women in her elementary school class of gifted students at the 10 and 20 year marks. Decisions made by the women in her group during their early years profoundly limited their later choices. Those who focused on marriage and family later in life were more likely to have met their aspirations. Some of Kerr's research participants found their giftedness a boon, while other women felt defensive about not using their high potential.

Runco (1999) reported on the latest data collected on a 20-year follow-up of two groups of gifted boys, one group with high IQs and a second with high scores on the SAT-M. Various predictive variables associated with creative productivity were explored, including mothers' expectations for their sons' independence as it relates to flexibility and divergent thinking ability in men's adulthood.

Although an interest in gender differences remained strong for researchers since the last edition of the Handbook appeared, a marked reduction of studies that included ethnic differences is evident. Garrison (1993) addressed the interaction of sex and ethnicity on identification, academic performance, and course selection with a diverse population of American students moving from the middle to the upper secondary school years. Surprisingly little longitudinal work has been conducted on gifted children with disabilities. Only two studies appeared in the English language literature since 1993. Vernon & LaFalce-Landers (1993) studied 57 American children with hearing impairments who were monitored over time on variables associated with their education, career, and mental health status. Over one-third had undergone therapy to address psychological problems including mental illness and less than half had acquired a baccalaureate level education by their early 20s, indicating a clear need for more research and intervention. A British study described the 16-year effects of treatments given to maladjusted able and highly able boys designed to help them succeed in school and in relationships (Lowenstein, 1996).

Education-related studies

Longitudinal research on the effects of educational experiences and schooling constitute another thread among prospective studies of giftedness and talent. Among this category are studies of the effects of educational interventions and the characteristics of gifted teachers.

Follow-up studies of participants in specific gifted educational programs are surprisingly rare. The most ambitious longitudinal study in progress in this arena comes out of the US National Research Center on the Gifted and Talented. The Learning Outcomes Study (Delcourt, Loyd, Cornell & Goldberg, 1994) began with a national sample of approximately 1000 elementary school students as they entered school programs for the gifted in grades 2 and 3; to date, only cross-sectional findings have been published. The purpose of the study was to compare the cognitive and affective outcomes of participants in the four common types of classroom arrangements for gifted education: within-class; pull-out; separate class; and special school.

Robinson and associates found positive effects of a constructivist classroom approach in a 2 year treatment/control study of early primary school students who displayed advanced mathematical skills (Robinson, Abbott, Berninger, Busse & Mukhopadhyay, 1997). A Canadian longitudinal study of gifted fifth graders demonstrated at least short-term positive effects in performance and attitudes of students grouped in heterogeneous as opposed to homogeneous ability classrooms (Shields, 1996). German and American follow-up studies, in contrast, have provided support for the practice of acceleration and grade skipping for gifted students (Swiatek, 1993; Burks, 1994; Prado & Schiebel, 1995).

In an unusual longitudinal project related to education, Sears, Marshall & Otis (1994) traced the professional development of five high-ability prospective public school teachers from their identification as high school seniors to their entrance into the teaching profession. Study subjects were indistinguishable from less academically gifted teachers in their professional attitudes and teaching performance. The authors concluded that education reform efforts that focus on recruitment of highly academically able teachers will not result in a better teaching force.

The predictive validity of school-based definitions of talent has been the basis for a varied group of longitudinal studies. Austrian researchers investigated the conditions that affected the stability of high level cognitive competence, school grades, and task commitment from early childhood to early adolescence (Speil & Sirsche, 1994). Israeli children from all segments of society were identified as talented in the arts or sciences by teacher ratings and portfolio assessment by professionals. Sixty children have been followed for seven years (Zorman, 1997). Katchadourian and Boli investigated the enduring effects of an elite college education in their 10 year follow-up study of highly able students who graduated from Stanford University (Katchadourian & Boli, 1994). In addition to assessing graduates' career and personal trajectories, researchers tested the predictive validity of a typology based on intellectualism and careerism which had characterized the participants as college students (Katchadourian & Boli, 1985). Katchadourian and Boli found that the educational elite move into prestigious professional ranks in the decade after graduation; the college typology that explained undergraduates' academic achievement and aspirations did not hold for professional attainment, however. Finally, Bok and Bowen (1998) studied ethnic minority students who had been admitted to Ivy League colleges with high school records and test scores below those of most white classmates. The study showed pronounced positive effects of elite undergraduate education on minority graduates' professional ranking and income.

Studies on Psycho-Social Variables

Freeman has been conducting a long-term investigation of British youngsters' social and emotional development, particularly in regard to the effects of both parenting and labeling (see this volume; 1991). Not only opportunity, but unforeseen problems can arise from being identified as gifted, especially when the services provided are not suitable to the child's academic needs. Swiatek (1994) compared the effects of acceleration on the self-esteem of gifted youngsters (1994) by following for five years, 340 students, some of whom were accelerated and some of whom were not.

A methodologically innovative study was conducted by Csikszentmihalyi, Rathunde & Whalen (1993) in which gifted high school students wore beepers and completed journals on their motivational, attention, and emotional state at whatever moment and location they were paged. The goal of the study was to address the factors that would lead some students to choose particular domains of interest and to sustain or diminish their involvement over time.

Hungarian researchers followed the top 10% of 1033 nine-year-old children who were tested on a variety of personality and ability measures (Herskovits & Gefferth, 1995). Retests two years later indicated that approximately a third of the high-ability children showed a significant decrease in their tested ability. Achievement motivation, academic self-concept, and family supportiveness differentiated children who remained high scorers from those whose intellectual potential had dissipated. The authors recommended repeated screening of children who exhibit early signs of giftedness in order to improve identification and support services.

Summary of Trends in Recent Longitudinal Research

In 1993, we outlined recommendations for future longitudinal studies of gifted populations (Subotnik & Arnold, 1993). More multiple cohort studies were needed, we argued, as well as more cross-cultural and cross-national research, and theory-driven designs. Finally, we saw the need for greater attention to follow-up studies of young children.

Given what we have learned about the development of intrinsic motivation in infancy and early childhood (Gottfried & Gottfried, 1996), and related findings on the central role of intrinsic motivation in talented teenagers (Csikszentmihalyi, Rathunde & Whalen, 1993), it appears that motivation is an especially fruitful avenue for identification and nurturing of highly able students. The juxtaposition of these two studies also points to promising possibilities for analyzing similar variables in populations across multiple studies.

Among longitudinal studies published in English since 1993, we find continued emphasis on IQ tests for identifying giftedness and for establishing longitudinal research populations. Stability of IQ over time is another prevalent theme in the recent literature. Gender continues as a focus for longitudinal study, along with interest in personality factors associated with the fulfillment of early promise in gifted populations.

Having considered the themes characterizing recent longitudinal literature, it is important to note those absent or poorly represented in the set of recently reported studies. As noted above, there was little cross-cultural research conducted even within countries or communities, a surprising finding given the large populations of immigrants and ethnic minorities in many nations that are home to established researchers. Similarly, cross national studies would inevitably shed light on new approaches to understanding and educating gifted students, yet we found none in the recent literature. A small and emerging category of studies that look longitudinally at gifted individuals with disabilities. Some insights into the factors that enhance or impede the academic and career development of these gifted individuals could be a catalyst for whole new interdisciplinary areas of study.

New program models are not proliferating, nor are studies that compare the efficacy of existing programs over time. We are sorely lacking in evidence-based decision making when it comes to establishing, maintaining, or closing gifted programs. Nor has the press for validating various identification schemes persisted over time: only IQ and SAT studies continued to appear regularly in the longitudinal literature. Comparing the effects of programming or identification using repeated methods is an important gap in our research literature. New multiple-cohort studies are not being reported in the journals, either, at least in the English language.

Fulfilling the Potential of Longitudinal Research

The central questions of gifted education and talent development continue to be those uniquely suited to longitudinal research designs; are educators identifying and serving the right people? Do high potential children, adolescents, and adults receive appropriate services? What factors can be positively influenced through intentional educational experiences? Only following people through time enables the establishment of causal connections between person, context, experiences, and achievement outcomes.

Despite the close match between longitudinal research methods and the fundamental issues of giftedness, repeated measures studies have fallen short of their potential contribution to education and policy. Recent longitudinal work seldom draws directly on either the emerging theoretical insights of the gifted field or the theoretical and methodological advances of sociology and developmental psychology. We suggest several directions to capitalize on the advantages of longitudinal methods.

Development in Context

Historical and cultural contexts play important roles in determining the forms of individual adaptation and development, and an explosion of theoretical and methodological work in the social sciences concerns contextual issues (Elder, 1974; Bronfenbrenner, 1979, 1993; Dannefer, 1984; Elder, Pavalko & Clipp, 1993; Lerner, 1996). Life course research has emerged over the past few decades, with a robust literature based in psychology and sociology (Giele & Elder, 1994). Different life paths, according to this model, result from the interaction of human agency (such as motivation, ability), one's historical and cultural location in time and place, the linked lives created by social relations, and the confluence of age, period, and the timing of life events (Giele & Elder, 1994). The importance of historical period and the actual sequence of life events are particularly important contributions of this literature. The life course model could speak directly to conceptualizing and specifying long-term effects of gifted identification, education, and talent development conditions.

The reciprocal interaction of persons and environments has been theorized and researched extensively outside the gifted field, but could be strengthened in the recent longitudinal work reviewed here and in future repeated measures designs. Some researchers of the gifted have incorporated Vygotskian theoretical understandings into cross-sectional or very short term follow-up studies of classroom instruction (see Chapter by Kanevsky). Theory viewing talent development within systems of individual, domain, and field also provides a promising framework for considering individuals within social and historical contexts (Gruber & Davis, 1988; Feldman, Csikszentmihalyi & Gardner, 1994).

In addition to capitalizing on advances in related social science disciplines, longitudinal research could benefit from a closer alignment with emerging insights about giftedness and talent within our own field, including conceptualizations about talent development versus schooling (Bloom & Sosniak, 1981; Subotnik & Coleman, 1996; Subotnik & Olszewski-Kubilius, 1997), attention to underachievers and at-risk gifted populations, and new schooling arrangements such as governor's schools and early entrance programs. None of these issues anchor recent longitudinal work, although the Learning Outcomes Study of comparative gifted program effects (Delcourt et al., 1994) might offer a particularly promising model of theoretical and practical significance for gifted education.

Longitudinal Methodology

More sophisticated theoretical models for longitudinal studies must be accompanied by stronger methodological designs in order for longitudinal research to reach its considerable potential in illuminating giftedness. Multiple cohort, cross-cultural, and cross-national designs are necessary to overcome threats to validity by cohort, period, and cultural effects in single-cohort longitudinal studies. Control groups also strengthen repeated measures studies. Many longitudinal studies use extremely small samples. Although small samples may be appropriate for intensive qualitative inquiries or exploratory studies, subject attrition and statistical power considerations argue for larger study groups wherever possible.

The Study of Mathematically Precocious Youth and the Munich Longitudinal Study of Giftedness are welcome examples of large-sample, multiple cohort longitudinal investigations. However, such studies involve enormous human and financial resources. Short of starting a series of similarly large research projects, several avenues remain open for improving the quality of longitudinal studies. Secondary analysis of existing longitudinal data sets is an especially promising direction for research; existing data may be mined in light of new questions, sub-populations, and theory-testing. The many re-analyses of the Terman data are good examples of this type of secondary analysis. Another extremely valuable form of secondary analysis that satisfies the need for large samples and multiple cohorts is re-analysis of gifted subgroups from nationally representative longitudinal study samples. In the United States, researchers have employed the NELS–88 follow-up of a nationally representative student cohort in order to ask specific questions about gifted populations (see for example Owings,1995; Russell & Meikamp, 1995; Sayler, 1996). Much of the NELS–88 work presented at academic meetings will appear in published form in the next few years.

Quantitative data from national longitudinal studies are readily available electronically; provision of data sets internationally would stimulate valuable comparative research. Qualitative longitudinal data are equally valuable for secondary analysis. The Murray Center for the Study of Lives, at Radcliffe College, provides an archive of raw qualitative and quantitative longitudinal study data from secondary analysis, replication, and follow-up. The promise of longitudinal inquiry requires the full utilization of existing data sets along with well-designed and theoretically-grounded new longitudinal studies.

Secondly, investigators can analyze findings across two or more existing longitudinal studies; cross-study analysis can provide information on variables of interest for different birth cohorts, age groups, and cultural or national populations. Meta-analysis of single-cohort longitudinal studies can reveal recurring patterns of findings about talent development. Researchers can replicate existing studies or collect a new wave of data on a previously followed study population. In order for more robust cross-study and cross-national investigations, the field needs better dissemination of longitudinal studies previously unpublished in English or unavailable internationally.

Third, retrospective data may be helpful in answering some research questions, especially when combined with cross-sectional or prospective information. The life course approach provides a theoretical framework for multiple methods in tracing individual trajectories. Questions about the timing of major life events, such as the effects on career attainment on the timing of women's marriage, childbirth, and labor force participation, lend themselves to retrospective designs. Researchers of the gifted need longitudinal and retrospective life course research designs that similarly investigate the differential effects of the timing of life events.

Proximal Distance

As noted above, the study of the fulfillment of talent has been conducted using two approaches. One involves the retrospective study of individuals who have met with notable success in achieving some desired outcome, whether the Nobel prize or admission to Stanford University. Participants of these studies are asked to reflect on the variables that led to reaching this goal. Another line of research identifies promising candidates in a cohort and monitors their progress toward attainment of one of these goals.

Retrospective studies suffer from selective memory, when subjects' reflections are colored by their current perspectives and psychological state. Long-term repeated measure studies tend to be inefficient; that is, very few members, if any, of the original cohort will achieve the desired outcome. We would argue that the best way to understand the trajectory of talent is to plan a series of longitudinal studies that work backwards from some valued end goal. An example follows.

Zuckerman (1977), provided a thorough account of the work and training of American Nobel laureates in science. She reported that 55% had attended the same five doctoral universities, and 52% had worked in the laboratory of a former laureate. Based on this work, it appears that (a) attendance at an elite university, and (b) mentorship by a laureate are good precursors for achieving eminence in science. The laboratory of a Nobel laureate is, therefore, an excellent place to start a longitudinal study of eminence in science; the lessons of the eminence literature could be brought to bear on this investigation. Researchers could administer IQ tests, (Roe, 1954), create personality profiles (MacKinnon, 1978), assess effects of marital and parental status (Kerr, 1994; Subotnik & Arnold, 1995), or map professional networks and tacit knowledge (Zuckerman, 1977; Wagner & Sternberg, 1986). We would then be able to get some insights into what distinguishes those who become and remain creatively productive over time from those who do not.

The next stage of the research would be to look at the applications of those who apply to work in the laureate labs. What distinguished the applications of those who were especially creative? What happened to those who were rejected from the lab who had similar characteristics? In this way, the researchers would work backwards in time, establishing the strongest possible levels of predictive validity along the way.

Conclusion

The essence of longitudinal research is predictive validity; this method of investigation is designed to answer questions like, how well does the Juilliard audition process select for solo violinists? How effective is the challenge provided by the Talent Search process in maintaining academically talented adolescents' interest in school? How does the imminence of the biological clock affect the decision making of female scientists? The answers to these sample questions are innately interesting, but more importantly, they provide road maps to interventions that may make talent development more efficient, and open the doors to greater inclusion in the process.

Scholars who investigate the development of giftedness and talent are in an excellent position to extend the sophistication and applied usefulness of repeated measures methodology. We repeat our 1993 call for a more complex approach to the study of predictive validity. The education public wants to know whether special programs or groupings meet the goals ascribed to by the program designers. The education community also wants to know if we are selecting the 'right' students. What is the effect of identifying and serving only the most talented? What happens when students who exhibit some potential in spite of incredibly difficult circumstances are served in gifted programs? At what point, if ever, is it too late for them to become 'competitive' with their advantaged peers? Finally, what components of the talent development process (and what domains) are most suitable to replication in schools? If we want to broaden the possibilities for children to discover and build on their potential talents, more of the talent development process will have to be accessible in schools. Longitudinal studies are the best way to address these questions, and we look forward to harvesting the results of those investigations.

References

Arnold, K. D.(1993a). Academically talented women in the 1980s: the Illinois Valedictorian Project. In: H. D.Hulbert & D. T. Schuster (Eds), *Women's Lives Through Time: Educated American Women of the Twentieth Century*. (pp. 393–414). San Francisco, CA: Jossey-Bass.

Arnold, K. D.(1995). *Lives of promise: what becomes of high school valedictorians*. San Francisco, CA: Jossey-Bass.

Arnold, K. D.(1993b). Undergraduate aspirations and career outcomes of academically talented women: a discriminant analysis. *Roeper Review*, **15**, 169–175.

Belova, E. (1996). Experimental study of intellectual and creative development of preschool-age children. *Journal of Russian and East European Psychology*, **34** (4), 39–47.

Benbow, C. P. (1992). Academic achievement in maths and science over a decade: are there differences among students in the top one percent of ability? *Journal of Educational Psychology*, **84**, 51–61.

Bloom, B. S. & Sosniak, L. A. (1981). Talent development vs. schooling. *Educational Leadership*, **39**, 86–94.

Bowen, W.. G. & Bok, D. (1998). *The shape of the river: long term consequences of considering race in college and university admissions*. Princeton, NJ: Princeton University Press.

Bronfenbrenner, U. (1993). The ecology of human development: research models and fugitive findings. In: R. H.

Wozniak & K. W. Fischer (Eds), *Development in Context: Acting and Thinking in Specific Environments* (pp. 2–44). Cresskill, NJ: Erlbaum.

Bronfenbrenner, U. (1979). *The ecology of human development*. Cambridge, MA: Harvard University Press.

Burks, L. C. (1994). Ability group level and achievement. *School-Community Journal*, **4**, 11–24.

Cahan, S. & Gejman, A. (1993). Constancy of IQ Scores among gifted children. *Roeper Review*, **15**, 140–143.

Cronbach, L. J. (1996). Acceleration among the Terman males: correlates in midlife and after. In: C. P. Benbow & D. J. Lubinski (Eds), *Intellectual Talent: Psychometric and Social Issues* (pp. 179–191). Baltimore, MD: Johns Hopkins University Press.

Csikszentmihalyi, M., Rathunde, K. & Whalen, S. (1993). *Talented teenagers: the roots of success and failure*. New York: Cambridge University Press.

Dannefer, D. (1984). Adult development and social theory: a paradigmatic reappraisal. *Sociological Review*, **49**, 847–850.

Delcourt, M. A., Loyd, B. H., Cornell, D. G. & Goldberg, M. D.(1994). *Evaluation of the effects of programming arrangements on student learning outcomes*. Research Monograph 94108. Charlottesville, VA: National Research Center on the Gifted and Talented.

Elder, G. H., Jr. (1974). *Children of the great depression: social change in life experience*. Chicago: University of Chicago Press.

Elder, G. H., Jr., Pavalko, E. K. & Clipp, E. C. (1993). *Working with archival data: studying lives*. Newbury Park, CA: Sage.

Elder, G. H., Jr. (1987). War mobilization and the life course: a cohort of World War II veterans. *Sociological Forum*, **2**, 449–472.

Feldman, D. H., Csikszentmihalyi, M. & Gardner, H. (1994). *Changing the world: a framework for the study of creativity*. Westport, CT: Praeger.

Flynn, J. R. (1999). Searching for justice: the discovery of IQ gains over time. *American Psychologist*, **54**, 5–20.

Freeman, J. (1991). *Gifted children growing up*. London: Cassell.

Garrison, L. (1993). Professionals of the future: will they be female? Will they be ethnically diverse? *Roeper Review*, **15**, 161–164.

Giele, J. A. & Elder, G. H., Jr. (1998). (Eds), *Methods of life course research*. Thousand Oaks, CA: Sage.

Gottfried, A. E. & Gottfried, A. W. (1996). A longitudinal study of academic intrinsic motivation in intellectually gifted children: childhood through early adolescence. *Gifted Child Quarterly*, **40**, 179–183.

Gottfried, A. W., Gottfried, A. E., Bathurst, K. & Guerin, D. W. (1994). *Gifted IQ: The Fullerton longitudinal study*. New York: Plenum.

Gruber, H. & Davis, S. N. (1988). Inching our way up Mount Olympus: the evolving systems approach to creative thinking. In: R. J. Sternberg (Ed.), *The Nature of Creativity* (pp. 243–270). New York: Cambridge University Press.

Herskovits, M. & Gefferth, E. (1995). Personality and motivational factors influencing the change of high intellectual potential. *Gifted Education International*, **10** (2), 71–75.

Holahan, C. K., Sears, R. R. & Cronbach, L. J. (1995). *The gifted group in later maturity*. Stanford, CA: Stanford University Press.

Hulbert, K. D. & Schuster, D. T. (Eds) (1993). *Women's lives through time: educated American women of the twentieth century*. San Francisco, CA: Jossey-Bass.

Katchadourian, H. & Boli, J. (1985). *Careerism and intellectualism among college students*. San Francisco, CA: Jossey-Bass.

Katchadourian, H. & Boli, J. (1994). *Cream of the crop: the impact of elite education in the decade after college*. New York: Basic Books.

Kerr, B. A. (1994). *Smart girls: a psychology of girls, women, and giftedness*. Dayton, Ohio. Psychological Press.

Lerner, R. M. (1996). Relative plasticity integration, temporality, and diversity in human development: a developmental contextual perspective about theory, process, and method. *Developmental Psychology*, **32** (4), 781–786.

Lowenstein, L. F. (1996). Diagnosing and treating the problems of able maladjusted children. In: V. P. Vara (Ed.), *The Inner Life of Children with Special Needs* (pp. 145–155). London, UK: Wuhrr.

Lubinski, D. & Benbow, C. P. (1995). Optimal development of talent: respond educationally to individual differences in personality. *Educational Forum*, **59** (4), 381–392.

Lubinski, D., Benbow, C. P. & Ryan, J. (1995). Stability of vocational interests among the intellectually gifted from adolescence to adulthood: a 15-year longitudinal study. *Journal of Applied Psychology*, **80**, 196–200.

MacKinnon, D. W. (1978). *In search of human effectiveness*. New York: Creative Education Foundation.

Perleth, C. & Heller, K. A. (1994). The Munich Longitudinal Study of Giftedness. In: R. F. Subotnik and K. D. Arnold (Eds), *Beyond Terman: Contemporary Longitudinal Studies of Giftedness and Talent*, (pp. 77–114). Norwood, NJ: Ablex.

Prado, T. M. & Schiebel, W. (1995). Grade skipping: some German experiences. *European Journal for High Ability*, **6**, 60–72.

Robinson, N. M., Abbott, R. D., Berninger, V. W., Busse, J. & Mukhopadhyay, S. (1997). Developmental changes in mathematically precocious young children: longitudinal and gender effects. *Gifted Child Quarterly*, **41** (4), 145–158.

Roe, A. (1953). *The making of a scientist*. New York: Dodd, Mead. (1999).

Runco, M. (1999). A longitudinal study of exceptional giftedness and creativity. *Creativity Research Journal*, **12** (2), 161–172.

Runco, M. (Ed.) (1999). Longitudinal studies of creativity. (Special issue). *Creativity Research Journal*, **12** (2).

Russell, S. & Meikamp, J. (1995). *Cultural diversity among gifted students and their teachers in rural West Virginia. Reaching to the Future*. Proceedings of the American Council on Rural Special Education. Las Vegas, NV.

Sayler, M. (1996). *Differences in the psychological adjustment of accelerated eighth grade students*. Paper presented at the Annual Meeting of the American Educational Research Association. New York, NY.

Schuster, D. T., Langland, L. & Smith, D. (1993). The UCLA gifted women, class of 1961: living up to potential. In: K. D. Hulbert & D. T. Schuster (Eds), *Women's Lives Through Time: Educated American Women of the Twentieth Century* (pp. 211–231). San Francisco, CA: Jossey-Bass.

Sears, J. T., Marshall, J. D. & Otis-Wilborn, A. K. (1994). *When best doesn't equal good: educational reform and teacher recruitment: a longitudinal study.* New York: Teachers College Press.

Shields, C. M. (1996). To group or not to group academically talented or gifted students? *Educational Administration Quarterly*, ??, 295–323.

Spangler, R. S. & Sabatino, D. A. (1995). Temporal stability of gifted children's intelligence. *Roeper Review*, **17**, 207–210.

Spiel, C. & Sirsche, U. (1994). Giftedness from early childhood to early adolescence: a pilot study. In: K. A. Heller and E. A. Hany (Eds), *Competence and Responsibility*, Vol. 2 (pp. 141–146). Goettingen, Germany: Hogrefe & Huber Publishers.

Stevens, R. J. & Slavin, R. E. (1995). The cooperative elementary school: effects on students' achievement, attitudes, and social relations. *American Educational Research Journal*, **32**, 321–351.

Subotnik, R. F. & Arnold, K. D. (Eds) (1993). Longitudinal studies in gifted education. (Special issue). *Roeper Review*, **15** (3).

Subotnik, R. F. & Arnold, K. D. (1996). Success and sacrifice: the costs of talent fulfillment for women in science. In: K. D. Arnold, K. D. Noble & R. F. Subotnik (Eds), *Remarkable Women: Perspectives on Female Talent Development* (pp. 263–280). Cresskill, NJ: Hampton.

Subotnik, R. F. & Coleman, L. J. (1996). Establishing the foundations for a talent development school: applying principles to creating an ideal. *Journal for the Education of the Gifted*, **20**, 175–189.

Subotnik, R. F., Kassan, L., Summers, E. & Washer, A. (1993). *Genius revisited: high IQ children grown up.* Greenwich, CT: Ablex.

Subotnik, R. F. & Olszewski-Kubilius, P. (1997). Distinctions between children's and adults' experiences of giftedness. *Peabody Journal*, **72**, (3/4), 101–116.

Subotnik, R. F. & Steiner, C. L. (1993). Adult manifestations of adolescent talent in science. *Roeper Review*, **15**, 164–169.

Subotnik, R. F., Steiner, C. L. & Chakraborty, B. (1999). Procrastination revisited: the constructive use of delayed response. *Creativity Research Journal*, **12** (2), 151–160.

Swiatek, M. A. (1994). Accelerated students' self-esteem and self-perceived personality characteristics. *Journal of Secondary Gifted Education*, **5**, 35–41.

Terman, L. M. (1925). *Genetic studies of genius.* Vol. 1: *Mental and physical traits of a thousand gifted children.* Stanford, CA: Stanford University Press.

Terman, L. M. & Oden, M. H. (1947). *Genetic studies of genius.* Vol. 4: *The gifted child grows up: 25 years' follow up of a superior group.* Stanford, CA: Stanford University Press

Terman, L. M. & Oden, M. H. (1959). *Genetic studies of genius*, Vol. 5: *The gifted group at mid-life.* Stanford, CA: Stanford University Press.

Terwilliger, J. S. & Titus, J. C. (1995). Gender differences and attitude changes among mathematically talented youth. *Gifted Child Quarterly*, **39**, 29–35.

Tomlinson-Keasey, C. & Keasey, C. B. (1993). Graduating from college in the 1930s: the Terman Genetic Studies of Genius. In: K. D. Hulbert & D. T. Schuster (Eds), *Women's Lives Through Time: Educated American Women of the Twentieth Century* (pp. 63–92). San Francisco, CA: Jossey-Bass.

Undheim, J. O., Nordvik, H., Gustafsson, K. & Undheim, A. M. (1995). Academic achievements of high-ability students in egalitarian education: a study of able 16-year-old students in Norway. *Scandinavian Journal of Education Research*, **39** (2), 157–167.

Vernon, M. & LaFalce-Landers, E. (1993). A longitudinal study of intellectually gifted deaf and hard of hearing people. *American Annals of the Deaf*, **138**, 427–434.

Wagner, R. K. & Sternberg, R. J. (1986). Tacit knowledge and intelligence in the everyday world. In: R. J. Sternberg & R. K. Wagner (Eds), *Practical Intelligence: Nature and Origins of Competence in the Everyday World* (pp. 51–83). New York: Cambridge University Press.

Wagner, H. & Zimmerman, B. (1986). Identification and fostering of mathematically gifted students. *Educational Studies in Mathematics*, **17**, 243–259.

Wieczerkowski, W., Wagner, H. & Birx, E. (1987). Die Erfassung mathematischer Begabun über Talentsuchen. *Zeitschrift für Differentielle und Diagnostische Psychologie*, **8** (3), 217–226.

Zhang, W. (1997). *Influences of internal and external frames of reference on math and verbal self-concepts for gifted and non-gifted tenth grade students.* Paper presented at the Annual Meeting of the American Educational Research Association. Chicago, IL.

Zorman, (1997). Eureka: the cross-cultural model for identifying hidden talent through enrichment. *Roeper Review*, **20** (1), 54–61.

Zuckerman, H. (1977). *Scientific elite: Nobel laureates in the United States.* New York: Free Press.

A 'Talent' for Knowledge and Judgment about Life: The Lifespan Development of Wisdom

M. Pasupathi* and U. M. Staudinger**

*Center for Lifespan Psychology,
Max Planck Institute for Human Development, Berlin, Germany*

Introduction

Most people would agree that wisdom is of great value to individuals and to societies. In the historical wisdom literature, it is often viewed as one of the four great virtues of paramount importance for human societies, and historically, even as a divine gift (Assmann, 1994; Kekes, 1995; Almond, 1997; Baltes, in press). Giftedness has similarly been characterized, and even lauded as the only human characteristic that could help us survive and evolve (Toynbee, 1967).

Wisdom as Divine Gift

Assmann (1994) reviews the historical transformation of wisdom into a divine quality during the Hellenistic period; thereafter, wisdom was a gift given by the gods. Within Christian traditions, wisdom became something achieved via revelation, prayer, faith, and vision. This divine gift was viewed as distinct from knowledge and as an antidote to human foolishness during the Middle Ages. During the Renaissance, the view of wisdom as a divine gift became questionable once more, as well as secularized. From current conceptions of giftedness and talent, the gift character of wisdom reappears, though in a different light.

Wisdom as Giftedness or Talent

Current ideas about giftedness often touch base with what we would think of as wisdom, when they emphasize talent for insightful psychological under-standings about the self or other, or the integration of history, religion, and philosophy to bring new insights about societies and individuals (DeHaan & Havighurst, 1957; Phenix, 1964; see also Gardner, 1993). Other conceptions of giftedness and talent have emphasized abilities like productive thinking, communicating, forecasting, decision-making, planning, implementing, human relations, and detecting opportunities (Taylor, 1986). Probably someone having a talent for all of these activities would be likely to be called wise as well. As we will discuss later in this chapter, parallels between conceptions of wisdom and giftedness are many, and multiple relationships between wisdom and giftedness can be fruitfully considered and have the potential to lead to interesting empirical work. Depending on the theoretical perspective taken on giftedness, some researchers would consider wisdom a kind of talent. Based on our conception of wisdom we would argue that wisdom may be better viewed as a *meta-talent*, comprised of knowledge and skills across many domains and the capacity to select and appropriately combine aspects of these domain-specific talents. We will return to this issue later in the chapter.

In this chapter, we concern ourselves with two general questions. First, what do we know from psychological research about the development of wisdom? Three general developmental predictions can be distinguished in the literature, and we present evidence bearing on these views. Second, how might wisdom and giftedness be related? In this part, we consider four ideas. First, can wisdom be viewed as a type of giftedness? Second, can giftedness itself help or hinder the development of wisdom? Third, is the life event of being identified as gifted one that facilitates the development of wisdom? We conclude with a discussion of the potential and peril in considering wisdom and giftedness together and of some of the common issues facing researchers interested in either of these concepts.

Developing Wisdom: Conceptions and Findings

Many people believe that age is the bringer of wisdom (Clayton & Birren, 1980; Sternberg, 1986; Sowarka,

---

* Now at University of Utah, Department of Psychology, Salt Lake City, USA.
** Now at Dresden University of Technology, Department of Psychology, Lifespan Development Area, 01062 Dresden, Germany.

1989; Orwoll & Perlmutter, 1990). But what is meant by wisdom? Wisdom has been variously conceived of as a quality of personhood, a feature of actions, a body of knowledge ('the wisdom of the bible'), or an expertise in difficult and fundamental aspects of life (Baltes, Smith & Staudinger, 1992; Oser, 1998). Wisdom is often seen as knowledge about the human condition at its boundaries, knowledge about the most difficult questions of the meaning and conduct of life, and knowledge about life's uncertainties. Commonalities in psychological definitions have emphasized the search for a moderate course between extremes, a dynamic between knowledge and doubt, sufficient detachment from the problem at hand, and a well-balanced coordination of emotion, motivation, and thought (see Staudinger & Baltes, 1994 for a review).

Psychological approaches to studying wisdom can be viewed as emphasizing either implicit views of wisdom, that is, the opinions and beliefs people hold about wisdom and wise people, or focusing on explicit theories of wisdom (Sternberg, 1990; Staudinger & Baltes, 1994; see Pasupathi & Baltes, 1999). Explicit theories typically define wisdom and then proceed to evaluate the degree to which expertise, knowledge, an action, or a person demonstrates wisdom as defined. Such theories sometimes point to the processes involved in producing wisdom, whether ontogenetically, or in terms of the particular response or task context. In the present chapter, we focus our review of empirical evidence primarily on explicit theories of wisdom, although we do review some of the findings on implicit theories in constructing different predictions about the development of wisdom.

Three different developmental courses for wisdom have been proposed in the literature. One suggests that age is associated with decreases in wisdom; a second implies that age should be associated with increases in wisdom, and a third proposes that complex qualities like wisdom are unlikely to show clear and consistent relationships with age, particularly in adulthood. Below, we review the theoretical frameworks leading to each of these three predictions in turn.

Aging and Loss of Wisdom

Walker Percy has argued that expertise can obscure our ability to really see what confronts us, hiding the thing observed behind a web of concepts and prior explanations. "The technician is never vague and never humble before the thing; he holds the thing disposed of by the principle, the formula, the textbook outline; and he thinks a great deal of equipment and jargon" (Percy, 1975, p. 61). Meacham (1990) makes a similar argument about wisdom. He proposes that the essence of wisdom is a view of knowledge as fallible, and a subsequent ability to strike a balance between doubt and certainty; this essence, he claims, is not developmental in that it is available to people of all ages. He goes on to suggest that a second dimension of wisdom

concerns the profoundness of the domain in which wisdom is being expressed, and that this dimension may vary systematically with age. Finally, he argues that children may represent the peak of wisdom, with development over the lifespan characterized by either maintenance or loss of wisdom. He argues, in fact, that it is easier to lose rather than gain wisdom as we mature, either by gaining knowledge and therefore inappropriate levels of certainty, or by becoming overwhelmed with contradictory information and therefore doubt. Meacham appears to exclude the idea that development not only brings more certainty or more contradiction, but might also lead to a balance between certainty and doubt, nor does he provide empirical findings directly testing his interesting predictions. This is a view presented by other conceptions of wisdom, and the evidence reviewed below thus has implications for Meacham's view as well. Further, increasing personality rigidity and decreasing openness to experience with aging, along with losses in cognitive ability (Costa & McCrae, 1994; Schaie, 1995; Baltes, Lindenberger & Staudinger, 1998) suggest that some of the ingredients necessary for wisdom may in fact be lost with increasing age (Staudinger, 1999).

Gaining Wisdom with Age: Implicit Theories, Personality and Neo-Piagetian/Post-Formalist Approaches

Among the most commonly shared, or even stereotypical, assumptions about wisdom is that older adults are more likely to possess it (Clayton & Birren, 1980; Sternberg, 1985; Sowarka, 1989; Orwoll & Perlmutter, 1990). It must be noted, though, that age is not typically the most central characteristic in people's images of a wise person. Further, the older the person being asked, the less likely it is that age and wisdom are viewed as connected (Clayton & Birren, 1980).

Stage-like developmental frameworks underly both personality approaches to wisdom (e.g. Erikson, Erikson & Kivnick, 1986) and post-formalist or neo-Piagetian approaches (e.g. Alexander & Langer, 1990; Kitchener & Brenner, 1990; Kramer, 1990). Typically, these approaches argue for a sequential, stage-like emergence of the personality characteristics or cognitive ability considered central to wisdom; such approaches do not imply that all people eventually attain wisdom. Rather, there are personality stages (or resolved psychological crises) and/or cognitive abilities that serve as important and necessary prerequisites for wisdom, and that the eventual attainment of wisdom occurs relatively later in adulthood. This in turn implies that wisdom should be positively correlated with age.

According to the Eriksonian theory of personality development, personality develops via a sequence of age-related crises (Erikson, Erikson & Kivnick, 1986; Whitbourne, Zuschlag, Elliot & Waterman, 1992). The crisis of late life involves coming to terms with one's life-as-lived, including both the successes of that life and the failures and unresolved problems. Mastery of this crisis leads to ego-integrity, or wisdom, according to many theorists (Erikson et al., 1986). Because earlier crises and their resolutions are viewed as contributing to later ones, the crisis of middle-age, which concerns whether and how to be generative (e.g. either by bearing and raising children or via professional contributions), may also be an important contributer to wisdom. When ego-integrity and generativity are successfully resolved, the result is someone who contributes to the world and who has a sense of integrity about themselves and their life. Both of these qualities figure centrally in implicit views of wisdom (e.g. Orwoll & Perlmutter, 1990). Other personality conceptions, such as the notion of developmental changes in psychological maturity (e.g. Vaillant, 1995), also imply increases in wisdom with increasing age; the empirical evidence employing personality approaches to wisdom is limited. Those nominated as wise do score higher on measures of ego-integrity (Orwoll & Perlmutter, 1990), confirming the validity of this approach to studying wisdom. Older adults do show higher ego-integrity than younger adults, although not all older adults attain ego-integrity (Ryff & Heincke, 1983; Whitbourne et al., 1992). Vaillant (1995) has provided substantial evidence for increasing psychological maturity in his longitudinal studies, but these studies focus on a relatively elite group of individuals.

Post-formalist or neo-Piagetian approaches to wisdom concentrate on features of thinking or reasoning, such as the structure with which people reason about problems, the stance people take on knowledge, or the degree to which people integrate cognitive and affective information in their thinking (e.g. Kramer, 1990; Labouvie-Vief, 1980). A common thread in many of these approaches is the notion of uncertainty or fallibility of knowledge, consistent with Meacham's propositions; relativism, and the ability to make sense of conflicting elements in a dialectic or synthesized whole, are also emphasized. Here again, though specific theories vary, the usual proposition is a series of increasingly advanced, mature, or wise stages in thinking through which people progress in a linear fashion. Although not all individuals are expected to show increases, and not all individuals are expected to attain the top levels of performance, the general expectation is one of linear increases with age. However, at which age people are able to attain the 'peak' level of functioning varies with the particular conception of post-formal development examined.

For example, reflective judgment, which involves a person's capacity to understand the fallibility of knowledge and still make conclusions despite this awareness, seems positively correlated with age. Samples examined with this measure have been relatively young, however (Kitchener & Brenner, 1990; Kitchener, Lynch, Fischer & Wood, 1993). Other

approaches, such as that taken by Labouvie-Vief and her colleagues (e.g. Labouvie-Vief, 1980; Labouvie-Vief, DeVoe & Bulka, 1989; see also Kramer, 1990 for similar theoretical views), suggest the importance of integrating cognition and affect in reasoning for developing wisdom. Their work shows improvements in integrative thinking into middle-age, but small to moderate declines in later life (see, e.g. Labouvie-Vief et al., 1989). Thus, the development of cognitive abilities viewed as indicators of wisdom suggests curvilinear development with age, where evidence on the full adult lifespan is available.

Age is not Sufficient for Becoming Wise: The Berlin Wisdom Paradigm

Our own approach attempts to integrate some of the elements of the theories reviewed so far with additional influences from expertise approaches to development (e.g. Ericsson & Smith, 1991) and lifespan psychology (Baltes, 1987). We have defined wisdom as "an expert knowledge system in the fundamental pragmatics of life permitting exceptional insight, judgment, and advice involving complex and uncertain matters of the human condition" (Baltes & Smith, 1990, p. 95). Wisdom-related knowledge and judgment apply to difficult problems in managing, planning, and making sense of life. Such knowledge is characterized more specifically by a family of five criteria (see Table 1).

Two of the five criteria (rich factual and rich procedural knowledge) are drawn from general conceptions of expertise (e.g. Chi, Glaser & Farr, 1991; Ericsson & Smith, 1991). Factual and procedural knowledge about the conduct, interpretation, and meaning of life are *basic* criteria in that they are necessary but not sufficient for defining wisdom-related knowledge and judgment. The remaining three criteria (lifespan contextualism, value relativism, recognition and management of uncertainty) are *meta*-criteria, and are viewed as specific to the fundamental pragmatics of life. They are grounded in the cultural and historical literature on wisdom (Assmann, 1994; Baltes, in press), neo-Piagetian research as reviewed above, and propositions of lifespan developmental psychology (e.g. Baltes, Lindenberger & Staudinger, 1998). Assessment of an individual's wisdom-related knowledge and judgment follows from the definition and employs these five criteria. Study participants are presented with difficult and ill-defined life dilemmas faced by hypothetical people, and are asked to think aloud about what the person facing the situation might do or consider. Following a standardized procedure (Staudinger, Smith & Baltes, 1994), a carefully selected, extensively trained, and well-calibrated rater panel evaluates how well responses reflect the five criteria outlined above. Note that this expertise-related approach resonates with the literature on giftedness; some researchers argue for reconceptualizing giftedness as expertise in a particular domain

Table 1. A Family of Five Criteria Used to Evaluate Wisdom-Related Performances.

Basic criteria	High performances demonstrate . . .
Rich Factual Knowledge About Life	consideration of general (human condition) and specific (e.g. life events, institutions) features of life matters as well as scope and depth in coverage of issues.
Rich Procedural Knowledge About Life	consideration of decision strategies, goal selection, choosing means to achieve goals, people to consult with, as well as strategies of advice-giving.

Meta criteria	High performances demonstrate . . .
Lifespan Contextualism	consideration of past, current, and possible future life contexts and the circumstances in which a life is embedded.
Value Relativism	consideration of variations in values and life priorities and the importance of viewing each person within an individual framework, but also the importance of a small set of universal values oriented towards the good of others and oneself.
Awareness & Management of Uncertainty	consideration of the inherent uncertainty of life (in terms of interpreting the past and predicting the future) and effective strategies for dealing with uncertainty.

(Adapted from Baltes et al., 1992)

(Gruber & Mandl, 1992). However, expertise approaches also imply the routinization, and resulting lack of flexibility, of knowledge use. The meta-criteria concerning the awareness and management of uncertainty is meant to require that wisdom involve transcending the limitations of 'typical' expertise, and that those who are wise retain flexibility 'despite' expertise.

Thus far, we have addressed how wisdom is conceptualized and assessed in this model, but not the expectations about the ontogeny of wisdom derived from this model. Our developmental framework is shown in Fig. 1. As depicted, general person characteristics like intellectual capacity, personality, social skills, or creativity are related to whether individuals develop wisdom or not. The model also proposes

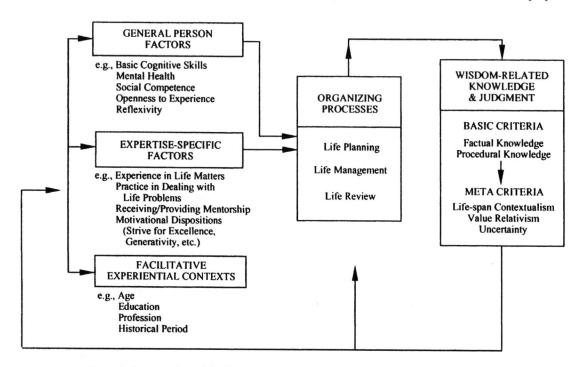

Figure 1. Ontogenetic model of the development of wisdom-related knowledge and judgment.

expertise-specific factors in the development of wisdom, which include access to relevant experiences, extensive practice, mentorship for making use of such experiences, and the motivation to excel at knowledge and judgment about life. Individual differences in motivation and access to relevant experience are expected to be critical in terms of who becomes wise and who does not. A final category of factors, termed facilitative experiential contexts, highlights the way in which age or profession provide differential access to experiences relevant for the development of wisdom. Such contextual variables also, as shown, may be related to general person qualities; as when specific personality characteristics are more prevalent among some occupational groups than in others or particular aspects of intellectual ability improve or decline over adulthood (see, e.g. Staudinger, Maciel, Smith & Baltes, 1998).

All of these factors are 'activated' by a set of organizing processes—those of life planning, management, and review—which provide an instance for the activation, transformation, and expression of wisdom-related knowledge and judgment. Such processes are considered critical for the acquisition of wisdom-related knowledge and judgment within our model, but are only beginning to be considered (see Smith, 1996; Staudinger, 2000; Staudinger, 1999). These processes form the core of our own procedure for accessing an individual's wisdom-related knowledge.

As is probably clear, this framework does not imply any obvious linear relationship between age and wisdom. Rather, it suggests that a complex interplay between experience and individual can allow for the emergence of wisdom, or at least for high levels of wisdom-related knowledge and judgment, at any adult age. Age may allow for time within which experience can be acquired, but may also produce changes that are less supportive of wisdom, as we discuss in more detail below (see also Staudinger, 1999). Not only is the role of age potentially both facilitative or debilitative, leading to no clear age-wisdom expectations, but there are many roads to wisdom in Fig. 1, and not all intersect with age.

What about the evidence? Our own findings have been thoroughly summarized elsewhere (Staudinger, 1999), and the story about age-relationships with general wisdom-related performance is relatively simple. Across several studies with heterogeneous samples of adults (ages 25–80 years), we have found no systematic relationships between our measure of wisdom-related performance and age. In a more recent study of adolescents and young adults, a much stronger age relationship emerged (r = 0.46; Pasupathi, Staudinger & Baltes, 2000). Figure 2 shows the relationship between age in adulthood and wisdom-related performance across several studies. As can also be seen in Fig. 2, a slightly more negative relationship emerges for participants over age 80 (see Baltes et al., 1995; Staudinger, 1999, for discussion).

In sum, as can be seen, age plays a much smaller role in wisdom than might be expected from stereotype or common sense views. Generally, findings support the expertise-contextual model in that there is no clear relationship with age for wisdom-related performance.

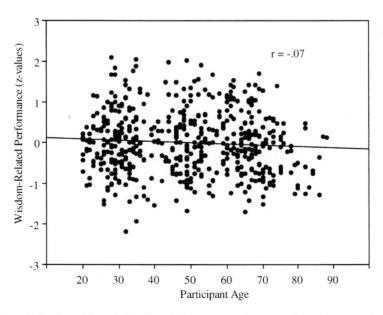

Figure 2. During adulthood (25–75 yrs.), it is not enough to grow older to become wiser.

At some stages of life, there is a normative age relationship—specifically, during adolescence, almost all data suggest growth. Similarly, during very old age, enough people may show declining performance, although more data are needed for this later part of the lifespan. In between, probably some individuals do become wiser, or even wise, over time; while others may remain stable, and others actually show decline. Which people show what developmental pattern may be predicted by features of the ontogenetic model described above, that is, by individual differences in personality, intelligence, and experiences.

Below, we shall see that when the correlates of wisdom-related knowledge and judgment in our own work are examined, potential explanations for age stability emerge. Two of these explanations are (1) the complexity of typical developmental changes in factors which facilitate or support wisdom-related performance and those which are detrimental to that performance, and (2) the relatively unexplored territory of individual differences in developmental trajectories for these same factors. An additional relatively unexamined issue concerns within-person patterns of wisdom-relevant characteristics. Below, we turn to the more complex picture emerging from examining wisdom-relevant characteristics; in doing so, we focus on the antecedents identified in our own ontogenetic model.

Person Characteristics and Their Contribution to the Development of Wisdom

Individual differences in the antecedents for the development of wisdom are presumed to relate to who becomes wiser and who does not. Such differences could take at least three (potentially inter-related) forms. First, stable mean-level differences in factors which support the acquisition of wisdom may predict which individuals become wise in adulthood. Those individuals who are creative and reflective may simply be advantaged in the attainment of wisdom. Second, differences in individuals' *development* of these supportive factors may influence which individuals attain greater life insight or maintain such insights for a longer time. For example, a person who remains open to experience throughout their adulthood may continue to acquire the kind of knowledge and judgment associated with wisdom; another person who becomes increasingly rigid from early adulthood to old age may eventually lose the ability to respond reflectively and sagely to a difficult life problem. Third, individuals may differ in the profile of characteristics and experiences they have, with some patterns of characterstics facilitating wisdom and others not. A person who has many difficult life experiences may gain insight only in combination with other qualities, such as a structured and reflective way of thinking about those experiences or a motivation to gain insight, or both. Below, we take the ontogenetic model as a framework and review what

is known about the typical developmental trajectory of characteristics associated with wisdom-related knowledge and judgment.

Intelligence. Our conception views wisdom as a prototype of the pragmatics of the mind (see Baltes, Lindenberger & Staudinger, 1998; Staudinger, 1999), that is, the aspect of intelligence characterized by content-rich, knowledge-driven processing. This implies that indicators of cognitive pragmatics, such as vocabulary or practical knowledge, will be more strongly related to wisdom-related performance than indicators of cognitive mechanics, such as fluid intelligence. This has in fact been the case in both adolescent and adult lifespan samples (Staudinger, 1999; Staudinger & Pasupathi, 2000). Intelligence has not been a unique predictor of wisdom-related performance in adult samples (see Staudinger, 1999). In relatively elderly populations and in adolescent populations, however, where intellectual functioning may drop below a critical threshold required for performance, intelligence appears to play a stronger predictive role than across the remainder of adulthood (Baltes, Staudinger, Maercker & Smith, 1995; Staudinger & Pasupathi, 2000; Staudinger, 1999). Some minimum level of intellectual ability is required for accessing and integrating knowledge in formulating a response to wisdom-related dilemmas, whether in our laboratory conditions, or in the actual life contexts in which people reason about difficult life matters.

In addition to normative change in intelligence, such as the increases in performance occurring over adolescence, and the decreases identified in later life, there are inter-individual differences in the developmental trajectory of intellectual functioning (e.g., Schaie, 1994; Arbuckle, Maag, Pushkar & Chaikelson, 1998; Baltes et al., 1998). Such differences may be due to differences in mechanisms thought to account for general age-related changes in cognitive mechanics (e.g. working memory capacity or processing speed). Alternatively, different trajectories of cognitive aging may also be due to other factors that appear to moderate individual differences in intellectual change, such as personality traits like flexibility or exposure to environments that are complex and intellectually stimulating (Schaie, 1994). The implication for the development of wisdom-related knowledge and judgment is that individual variability in the development of intellectual capacities across the lifespan may mean that individuals differ in the age at which they do not have the minimum intellectual capacity needed to support wisdom-related performances, whether during childhood and adolescence, or during late life. This in turn, would mean that the age-trajectory of wisdom-related performance would vary across these individuals.

Finally, particular domains of knowledge within the broader category of pragmatics of the mind may be of special relevance for developing wisdom-related knowledge. Consider the case of knowledge about human psychological functioning—sometimes referred to as theory-of-mind research (see also Staudinger & Pasupathi, 2000). Theory-of-mind has predominantly been examined in young children (infancy through middle-childhood), and results here show increasing sophistication in the way that children and adolescents understand concepts like beliefs, thoughts, and desires, the way that they differentiate between different types of mental activities, and the way they use concepts like that of belief to explain actions (Fabricius, Schwanen-flugel, Kyllonen, Barclay & Denton, 1989; Perner, 1991; Flavell, Green & Flavell, 1995). In one study, improvements were demonstrated across the adult lifespan, with older adults actually outperforming other groups in terms of the complexity of their belief-based reasoning (Happé, Winner & Brownell, 1998). As another special case, consider knowledge about typical adult biographies. Here, too, the evidence points to increasing knowledge about both typical and idiosyn-cratic biographies over childhood and adulthood (see, e.g. Greene, Wheatley & Aldava, 1992; Strube, Gehringer, Ernst & Knill, 1985; Heckhausen, 1999).

Personality. Among the personality characteristics uniquely associated with wisdom-related knowledge and judgment are openness to experience and an orientation towards personal growth (Clayton & Bir-ren, 1980; Staudinger, Lopez & Baltes, 1997). An additional performance advantage accrues to those individuals who are balanced between being intro-verted and extraverted. Characteristics like these tend to show small declines with increasing age in adult-hood, particularly after middle-age (Costa & McCrae, 1994; Ryff & Keyes, 1995). Normative personality changes may in fact hinder the development and expression of insight about life matters over adulthood (Staudinger, 1999). Of course, here again, there may be wide variability in individual patterns of stability and change over adulthood, and relatively little empirical work addresses the possibility of such patterns (but see Schaie, 1995). Some types of people appear to be 'changers' while others remain stable, as identified by Block (1971), and combinations of personality, intelli-gence, and environmental factors may interact to determine developmental trajectories (see, e.g. Schaie, 1995).

Interface of personality and intelligence. Qualities like creativity, social intelligence, and cognitive styles are important predictors of wisdom, demonstrating the largest unique relationships with wisdom-related per-formance in our own past work (Staudinger, Lopez & Baltes, 1997). Cognitive styles, defined as character-istic preferences for using cognitive abilities in particular ways, represent a prototypical interface between intelligence and personality. People perform-

ing well on our measure of wisdom-related knowledge and judgment display a judicial style—that is, they are more concerned with understanding the reasons for and implications of someone's thoughts and actions than with judging the thought or action as good or bad (Sternberg, 1990, p. 51). Higher performances are also given by those who are progressive in thinking rather than conservative, and those who are more creative (Staudinger et al., 1997, 1998). Little empirical evidence speaks to developmental changes on these characteristics; during adolescence, people may improve in social intelligence and related capacities (e.g. Gurucharri & Selman, 1982; Keller & Wood, 1989). Creativity, when assessed by standardized tests, may follow a curvilinear pattern of development over adolescence, decreasing from early into middle adoles-cence, then increasing again (Ross, 1976; Smith & Carlsson, 1985). When actual products are employed in assessing creativity, this appears to peak in early or middle adulthood, depending on the field examined, and then to decline (Simonton, 1990). Further, over adulthood and aging rigidity may increase (Stevens & Truss, 1985; Costa & McCrae, 1994). Even less evidence is available on individual differences in developmental trajectories of creativity or cognitive styles; to the extent that these are viewed as trait-like, non-changing attributes of the individual, change is expected to be minimal. However, Sternberg and Grigorenko (1997) argue that in fact, cognitive styles probably do change over time and across situations, largely dependent on what is rewarded in a particular context at a particular time. Similar arguments have been made concerning creativity and giftedness, also at times viewed like traits (Jackson & Butterfield, 1986).

Expertise-specific antecedents: life experiences and motivation. Thus far, we have concentrated on general characteristics of people, normative developmental trajectories in these characteristics, and where possible, individual differences in the way that these character-istics change. We now focus on the role of life experiences in acquiring wisdom-related knowledge and judgment, and briefly address motivational issues, as little empirical work has directly addressed these aspects of wisdom-related knowledge and judgment.

The role of specific life experiences in contributing to wisdom has a large role in implicit views and philosophical approaches (e.g. Jaspers, 1932; Ass-mann, 1994). Further, different contexts can offer varying opportunities for wisdom-relevant experiences. For example, some types of professional training offer extensive practice and experience in difficult matters of life management, planning, and interpretation. In our own work, clinical psychologists, who receive exten-sive training and practice in dealing with difficult life matters, outperform other highly educated profession-als with less exposure to knowledge of life pragmatics (Staudinger, Smith & Baltes, 1992; Smith, Staudinger

& Baltes, 1994). In one recently completed study we investigated participants subjective conceptions about the development of wisdom and their wisdom-related performance. First results suggest that mention of events with deeply existential qualities (such as death, guilt) were especially related to higher levels of wisdom-related performance (Staudinger & Reimer, 1999). This finding fits well with Jaspers' notions of existential confrontations and their contribution to deepening insight into human nature (see also Maercker, Böhmig-Krumhaar & Staudinger, 1998).

Both the experience of events and reflecting upon or integrating such experiences appear necessary for extracting wisdom-related knowledge and judgment (Staudinger & Dittmann-Kohli, 1994; Staudinger, 2000). These processes of extracting meaning, in the case of traumatic events, may have implications for later well-being as well (Davis, Nolen-Hoeksema & Larson, 1998). In fact, extracting benefits from a loss, rather than simply making sense of the loss in terms of what the person already knows, seems most important for adaptation over the longer-term (Davis et al., 1998). Identifying and understanding the mechanisms by which people construct meaning and knowledge from their life experiences are an important direction for future work; some existing findings suggest that these mechanisms may vary as a function of age and other person characteristics. For example, older adults report more frequently using the past in preparation for death, and also in teaching or informing others (Webster, 1997). Both of these uses of the past might produce more wisdom-related insight than other functions of remembering, such as using the past to reduce boredom; however, this speculation has not yet been addressed empirically.

How people reflect on their experiences may also be a function of personality, cognitive style, intellectual ability, and motivation, as well as a function of the social contexts in which they perform such reflections. For example, those high in openness to experience tend to reminisce differently than those low on this personality dimension, considering more philosophically weighty issues in their thinking (Webster, 1994). People highly open to new experience also engaged in reminiscence more frequently (Webster, 1994). Such differences suggest that personality influences the way people think about and make sense of their past experiences; such 'processing' differences may in turn have consequences for the amount and quality of knowledge and insight individuals extract. Some preliminary results support this with our own measure of wisdom-related knowledge and judgment. In one study, moral reasoning interacted with age in predicting wisdom-related performance (Pasupathi & Staudinger, in press); this interaction, though based on cross-sectional data, suggested that individuals with high-level moral reasoning ability did gain in wisdom with age. We interpreted this finding, admittedly

speculatively, in terms of experience (assessed indirectly by age) and ways of extracting meaning (principled moral reasoning abilities). Moral reasoning at complex and sophisticated levels may endow people with a rich way of extracting meaning from their experiences. As experiences accumulate with increasing age, the benefits of higher moral reasoning ability for wisdom-related knowledge and judgment emerge. This account is quite preliminary, but suggests one interesting path to wisdom.

Motivations. Motivational factors have been identified or mentioned as having great importance in research on talent and giftedness (Renzulli, 1986; Sternberg & Davidson, 1986; Csikszentmihalyi, Rathunde & Whalen, 1993; Gagné, 1993), research on expertise (Bloom, 1985; Ericsson & Smith, 1991; Winner, 1996), and in our own work on wisdom-related knowledge and judgment (Staudinger, 1999). Unfortunately, specific conceptions of a motivation for excellent life insight are not, to our knowledge, available. Perhaps the sorts of biographical factors proposed to lead to generative lives, such as an early sense of purpose and a feeling that one has a duty to society, may also be connected to the motivation to become wiser (see McAdams, Diamond, de St. Aubin & Mansfield, 1997).

Obviously, existing findings on the expertise-specific antecedents of wisdom specified in our own model are sparse—very little work has been done examining mentoring, and an analysis of the role of specific life experiences, and ways of coping with those experiences, is in its infancy. This remains a very promising arena for future research.

Contextual factors as facilitators of wisdom. Development, whether of athletic skill or life insight, does not take place in a vacuum of intrapsychic processes. As giftedness researchers note, cultures define what abilities constitute important talents, and talents included in a culture's definition will be supported and encouraged via resources and attention (see, e.g. Sternberg & Davidson, 1986; Csikszentmihalyi et al., 1993; Tannenbaum, 1993). Although cultures tend to show relatively good cross-cultural consensus about the components of wisdom (see Assmann, 1994; Baltes, in preparation), contextual factors may provide more or less support for an individual's development of wisdom. Here, we address the role of contextual factors in the acquisition and expression of wisdom-related knowledge and judgment, with a particular focus on age and cohort.

Although age is not related to wisdom-related performance per se, age may play a role in many ways; it does provide individuals with time within which they can accumulate experience. Further, due to the biological constraints and the societal institutionalization of the life course (Havighurst, 1972), age is sometimes necessary for certain experiences. These two propositions do imply that a person's age may sometimes matter in responding to wisdom-related dilemmas, particularly when the content of those dilemmas concerns a particular age period.

Findings from two studies suggest that participants sometimes do show performance advantages for problems relevant to their own age group (Staudinger et al., 1992; Smith et al., 1994). This effect, which we call the 'age-match' effect, is more straightforward for life-review tasks than for life-planning tasks. For the former task type, older adults do better than younger adults on older adult problems, younger adults outperform older adults on younger adult problems. For the latter task type, younger adults tend to outperform older adults on younger adult problems; whether older adults show a similar advantage depends on the normativeness of the life problem and the older adults' degree of expertise (see Staudinger, 1999, for more details).

Cohort can also limit people's access to particular kinds of experiences; for example, a sample of individuals nominated by the community as wise had biographies characterized by resistance and/or persecution by the Hitler regime (cf. Baltes et al., 1995). Such experiences are necessarily limited by the historical time of a person's birth. Similar statements can be made of many other variables, including nationality, ethnicity, and gender. Such categories permit or deny some experiences to the individuals who fit into them. The ramifications of major historically-determined experiences, such as combat experience, can extend to the timing of the entire lifecourse (Elder, 1998). Presumably, differences in lifecourse timing can have implications for the development of life insight, both supportive and detrimental; these differences have not been thoroughly examined with respect to wisdom-related knowledge and judgment. These findings do underscore the complexity of developmental approaches to wisdom, reminding us that our knowledge and judgment may be inextricably bound up with our own position in life.

Thus far, we have concerned ourselves primarily with developmental and individual differences in personality, intellectual capacity, interface qualities, and life experiences that have developmental implications for wisdom. We have argued that individual differences in stable personal characteristics, or in access to particular experiences may predict who becomes wise, and who does not. We have also argued that individual differences in the developmental trajectory of these qualities, though relatively under-investigated, also have importance for the development of wisdom. Of course, we want to highlight the fact that complex interactions among these factors may provide many roads to wisdom. One such possibility was mentioned above when we discussed the potential for age, personality and other person characteristics to influence the way individuals extract knowledge and insight from events they encounter. Another such possibility is raised by the findings mentioned above on moral reasoning, age, and wisdom-related performance. Still a third possibility concerns cross-sectional and developmental profiles of characteristics within individuals, which we know very little about. Such a wholistic picture seems important for understanding a variety of person qualities as well as for understanding the acquisition, maintenance, and expression of wisdom.

Wisdom and Giftedness

Having now spent some time on the complicated evidence about the development of wisdom, we wish to consider how wisdom intersects with the theme of this Handbook. We believe there are at least three ways in which that intersection can be considered. First and perhaps most straightforwardly, wisdom can be viewed as a talent for a particular domain: the domain of fundamental life pragmatics; we prefer, however, to think about it as a meta-talent, and say more about this below. Second, we may consider how giftedness as a characteristic might help or hinder the development of wisdom; we will refer to these as primary effects of giftedness on wisdom. Third, we consider how the experience of being a gifted child may relate to the development of wisdom, or what we will call secondary effects of giftedness on wisdom.

Wisdom as a Meta-Talent: A Gift for Life Insight

Whether one looks at conceptual, methodological, or intervention aspects of the literatures, wisdom and giftedness or talent appear to overlap. Our conception of wisdom-related knowledge and judgment, as well as the other views mentioned above, is explicitly not a trait-like approach. In this sense, views of giftedness as a stable, enduring, trait-like characteristic would provide a contrast with wisdom research (but see Mönks & Mason, 1993). However, more recent conceptions of giftedness seem more analogous to our own views about wisdom, emphasizing the interaction and integration of various personal characteristics and socio-cultural factors in the development of giftedness or talent, regardless of which domain. For example, Gagné (1993) conceives of giftedness as potential, and talent as specific ability, and attempts to understand the way that giftedness gets translated (developed) into talent. He regards both individual characteristics, such as persistence, and environmental catalysts, such as encounters with mentors or chance exposure to activities, as critical. Similarly (for our purposes), Renzulli (1986) argues for redefining giftedness in terms of initial above-average ability, motivation (task commitment), and creativity. Finally, as noted earlier, proposals to view giftedness as expertise are well in line with our own views of wisdom (Gruber & Mandl, 1992; Winner, 1996). In this way, considering wisdom as a kind of talent, in the domain of fundamental life pragmatics, seems appropriate. The very nature of the domain, however, implies that conceiving of wisdom as a meta-talent means that wisdom cannot be understood as a single ability or skill, but rather as the ability to orchestrate multiple talents to fit the demands of the occasion.

Taking these conceptions above as a starting point is illustrative. Like other talents, wisdom involves *exceptional* performance in the domain to which it is applied (life planning, life management and life review). Like other talents, those who attain high levels of wisdom often embody a profile of person characteristics and experiences that support their expertise. These clear analogies between giftedness and wisdom suggest the fruitfulness of using approaches taken in one field to investigate the other, and there is some methodological overlap. For example, nomination of wise or gifted people followed by careful study of these individuals is an approach taken in both areas with rich results (Csikszentmihalyi et al., 1993; Baltes et al., 1995). Other kinds of methodological borrowing might be interesting for researchers in both contexts. Importantly, the roles of mentoring and motivation in talent development have been, arguably, more investigated than in the case of wisdom, at present (see, e.g. Bloom, 1985; Subotnik & Arnold, 1993).

Additional similarities and differences: looking at interventions. As gifts with high relevance for societies, interventions to enhance the realization of gifted children's potential and interventions to improve individuals' wisdom-related knowledge and judgment have been of considerable interest. Interventions for gifted children can be loosely divided into acceleration, in which children are permitted faster movement through the traditional educational system, and enrichment, which involves additional educational experiences aimed at providing gifted children with a more challenging and elaborated environment (Southern, Jones & Stanley, 1993; Moon & Feldhusen, 1995). The latter often involves specific training (e.g. scientific method, library skills, etc), and a focus on additional and more elaborative exposure than the typical classroom environment. This is analogous to the two interventions we have employed to enhance wisdom-related performance in our own work.

In line with the idea of wisdom as a meta-talent, however, our interventions have focused on changes in the performance context more than on changes in the specific contents participants engaged with. Specifically, in one study, imagined or actual discussion with a trusted partner prior to responding to a wisdom dilemma enhanced wisdom-related performance substantially. This enhancement was presumably due to the more elaborative and comprehensive 'search' of the

person's existing knowledge, aided by the other person's actual or imagined dialogue and the increased perspective-taking provided by considering another person's viewpoint (Staudinger & Baltes, 1996). In another study, a specific criterion, value relativism, was the focus (Böhmig-Krumhaar, Staudinger & Baltes, in press). A mnemonic strategy was adapted for use in cueing consideration of cultural variability while thinking about a wisdom-related dilemma, and participants trained with this strategy not only received higher scores on value relativism, but also higher scores on rich factual knowledge and lifespan contextualism as well. This latter finding is in line with the idea of providing gifted students with specific skills in research in order to enhance their ability to learn independently (Southern et al., 1993). Participants provided with a specific method of accessing knowledge about other cultures were able to apply this method to different dilemmas.

Despite the similarity of giftedness research and wisdom research at the conceptual, basic research method, and intervention level, at this point some fundamental differences between these two bodies of research must be noted. In our conceptualization, wisdom is conceived of as time-transcendent in nature and pertaining to life, rather than specific domains of performance. Examinations of the cultural and historical literatures on wisdom suggest that cultures display much consensus about wisdom (Assmann, 1994; Baltes, in preparation). Giftedness, by comparison, is often explicitly held up as a cultural construction (see, e.g. Sternberg & Davidson, 1986; Tannenbaum, 1986; Csikszentmihalyi et al., 1993). Further, ideas about giftedness often center around a specific ability in a structured and well-defined domain, although empirical investigations often focus on individuals with talents in multiple such domains or individuals with very high general intelligence (e.g. Csikszentmihalyi et al., 1993; Alexander, Carr & Schwanenflugel, 1995; Robinson & Clinkenbeard, 1998). The domain of wisdom is by contrast broad, ill-defined and ill-structured (Baltes et al., 1992). While gifted intervention research seeks to identify the most talented people in a domain and to ensure the fruition of their ability, in our own research we have sought to enhance the potential of normal individuals who were not identified because of specific talents. Perhaps most critically, wisdom is conceived of as the integration of knowledge from various domains (Baltes & Staudinger, 2000). In sum, wisdom cannot be purely treated as a kind of gift for knowledge about life; such an equation might lose the wholistic, integrative aspect of wisdom. From our view, it is better to think of wisdom as a meta-talent. Wisdom is the kind of expertise that allows individuals to maximize their own gifts or to give insightful advice to others about how to do so. That optimization process will draw not only on gifts within a specific domain, say, a particular talent, but also on knowledge and abilities in many other domains.

Giftedness as Superior Ability Influencing the Development of Wisdom: Primary Effects

Does being gifted or talented in some specific domain, such as mathematics or science, contribute to wisdom-related knowledge and judgment? Answering this question requires direct empirical evidence that doesn't exist. However three competing predictions can be made based on existing literatures, and taking high IQ performance as the indicator of giftedness. We do not mean to suggest that high IQ is the only type of giftedness there is, but it may be the best-studied form of giftedness at present.

The first two hypotheses are simply competing predictions. Notions of wisdom as a balanced integration of intellectual and personality resources imply that an imbalance towards intellectual superiority (intellectual giftedness) might actually make wisdom more difficult to achieve. On the other hand, the idea that 'good things go together' might suggest that high intellectual ability would be a facilitator of wisdom-related performance. In fact, some of the very strengths of gifted children have been argued to come with specific vulnerabilities, related both to possessing high ability and to the experience of being labelled gifted (see, e.g. Webb, 1993). Such vulnerabilities might be taken as evidence for the idea that wisdom and intellectual giftedness are somewhat at odds with one another. The general picture of gifted adolescents, however, suggests that they are normal to above-average on most personality and self-concept measure that have been used (Perleth & Heller, 1995; Robinson & Clinkenbeard, 1998). What about good things going together? In a study we conducted, an array of positive intellectual, personality, and interface characteristics (those in between personality and intelligence, like creativity and cognitive style) predicted better moral reasoning performance and better wisdom-related performance, supporting the 'good things go together' idea at least within the domain of intraperson factors (Pasupathi & Staudinger, in press).

Of course, it might also be more complicated than simple facilitative or detrimental effects. The ontogenetic model implies that interactions among several different positive qualities are needed to produce peak levels of wisdom-related knowledge and judgment. Thus, high intelligence paired with the motivation to find out about life might be a powerful enhancer of wisdom-related performance. High intelligence without the necessary personality or motivational qualities might be irrelevant to wisdom-related performance. This may be why high intelligence does not seem to unequivocally provide unique benefits for wisdom-related performance, whether in our own work (see, e.g. Staudinger et al., 1997; Staudinger, 1999) or indeed, in work employing other conceptions of

wisdom (e.g. Labouvie-Vief et al., 1989; Kitchener & Brenner, 1990). Lastly, our own prior work does support a 'threshold' model of the relationship between fluid IQ and wisdom-related performance (see Staudinger 1999), that is, the relationship between wisdom-related performance and fluid IQ is neutral above a threshold value. Below that threshold, the two are positively related. A similarly discontinuous relationship might be evident for extremely high levels of intelligence, that is, at very high levels of intelligence, a relationship between intelligence and wisdom may emerge that is not like the relationship we observe in samples of normal intellectual ability.

The above discussion related primarily to the idea of intellectual giftedness. In other work, we have been able to show relationships between creativity and wisdom (Staudinger et al., 1997) and between moral reasoning and wisdom (Pasupathi & Staudinger, in press). As mentioned in the opening of this chapter, some conceptions of giftedness provide explicit domains of talent that can be seen as overlapping with wisdom; clearly, for those interested in peak human potential of all kinds, here is a rather open research agenda.

Giftedness as a Life Experience that can Result in Wisdom: Secondary Effects

Considerations of specific life experiences in the development of wisdom often highlight crisis-like, existential situations. But the experience of being labelled as gifted can be a very profound and far-reaching event for a child. Such an experience places the child apart, separate from others, and gives the child special status, which may be viewed positively or negatively by the surrounding society. As an event with such profound possibilities, being labelled gifted is an experience which may be 'mastered' or failed. In fact, there is some very limited evidence that being labelled gifted can create its own set of problems (Webb, 1993). Gifted adolescents in one study did react more negatively to failure, with more irrational beliefs, negative effect, and physiological stress, than did high achievers who were not labeled gifted and a randomly selected group of same-aged students (Roberts & Lovett, 1994). But the time between being labelled and this kind of assessment of psychological functioning may be critical; as a difficult life event, being labelled as gifted very likely requires some time for children to adapt to their status.

The experience of being labelled a gifted child may provide the opportunity for insight about relations between individuals and groups, experiences of separateness, even in some cases prejudice and stereotyping. Such labelling could also lead to a sense of being privileged and of owing a debt to society, as illustrated in the narratives of highly generative adults studied by McAdams and his colleagues (McAdams et al., 1997). Whether a child gains such insight from the experience is likely to depend on many other factors, including the responses of caregivers and mentors, the child's own proclivities, and whether being labelled gifted has noticeable consequences at all in that child's particular context. But the examination of more diffuse and long-lasting experiences in considering pathways to profound life insight might prove very interesting.

Conclusions and Outlook

We have suggested considering wisdom as a meta-talent, which acknowledges both similarities and differences between our conception of wisdom and existing conceptions of giftedness and talent. Wisdom-related knowledge and judgment, and by extension, wisdom itself, show non-linear, idiosyncratic paths of development over the lifespan. Whether a particular individual increases in wisdom-related knowledge and judgment depends on a constellation of factors, including everything from their own genetically consti-tuted temperament to chance experiences and supportive contexts that help them gain insight about themselves and their worlds. There is little evidence for linear upward progressions with increasing age after adolescence, and little evidence for any decreases in performance after adolescence as well.

Giftedness researchers and those investigating wis-dom and wisdom-related performances face similar difficulties in some ways. For example, identifying individuals who are qualitatively different than average based on largely quantitative indices remains a problem (for a discussion in relation to giftedness, see Gagné, 1993). Although normative (standard deviation based) approaches are often employed (e.g. we select the top 15 to 20% of individuals in our own work to examine what we refer to as wise performance), such approaches are only approximations of the qualitative distinctions we are often theorizing about. Another is trying to avoid a trait-like approach. Although our model focuses on wisdom-related knowledge and judgment, rather than on the identification of wise people per se, that assessment is necessarily made at the level of individuals. Similarly, although giftedness researchers would like to focus on gifted performances, the literature, for historical and pragmatic reasons, often focuses on gifted individuals (Jackson & Butter-field, 1986). In addition to these common methodological hurdles, juxtaposing giftedness and wisdom may suggest interesting and fruitful new directions for empirical inquiry. From a societal viewpoint, wisdom, like other important societal resources, is certainly a gift worth developing in all individuals, to the extent possible. How we encourage the development of wisdom is a question we psycholo-gists have only begun to ask.

References

Alexander, J. M., Carr, M. & Schwanenflugel, P. J. (1995). Development of metacognition in gifted children: direc-tions for future research. *Developmental Review*, **15**, 1–37.

Alexander, C. & Langer, E. J. (Eds) (1990). *Beyond formal operations: alternative endpoints to human development.* New York: Oxford University Press.

Almond, B. (1997). Seeking wisdom. *Philosophy*, **72**, 417–433.

Arbuckle, T. Y., Maag, U., Pushkar, D. & Chaikelson, J. S. (1998). Individual differences in trajectory of intellectual development over 45 years of adulthood. *Psychology and Aging*, **13**, 663–675.

Assmann, A. (1994). Wholesome knowledge: concepts of wisdom in a historical and cross-cultural perspective. In: D. L. Featherman, R. M. Lerner & M. Perlmutter (Eds), *Life-Span Development and Behavior* (Vol. 12, pp. 187–224). Hillsdale, NJ: Erlbaum.

Baltes, P. B. (1987). Theoretical propositions of lifespan psychology: on the dynamics between growth and decline. *Developmental psychology*, **23**, 611–626.

Baltes, P. B., Lindenberger, U. & Staudinger, U. M. (1998). Life-span theory in developmental psychology. In: R. M. Lerner (Ed.), *Handbook of Child Psychology*, Vol. 1: *Theoretical Models of Human Development*, (5th ed., pp. 1029–1143). New York: Wiley

Baltes, P. B., Smith, J. & Staudinger, U. M. (1992). Wisdom and successful aging. In: T. B. Sonderegger (Ed.), *Nebraska Symposium on Motivation* (Vol. 39, pp. 123–167). Lincoln, Nebraska: University of Nebraska Press.

Baltes, P. B. & Smith, J. (1990). Toward a psychology of wisdom and its ontogenesis. In: R. J. Sternberg (Ed.), *Wisdom: Its Nature, Origins, and Development* (pp. 87–120). New York: Cambridge University Press.

Baltes, P. B. & Staudinger, U. M. (2000). Wisdom: a meta-heuristic (pragmatic) to orchestrate mind and virtue towards excellence. *American Psychologist*, **55**, 122–136.

Baltes, P. B., Staudinger, U. M., Maercker, A. & Smith, J. (1995). People nominated as wise: a comparative study of wisdom-related knowledge. *Psychology and Aging*, **10**, 155–166.

Baltes, P. B. (in press) *Wisdom: Orchestrating mind and virtue.* Boston: Blackwell.

Block, J. (1971). *Lives through time.* Berkeley, CA: Bancroft Books.

Böhmig-Krumhaar, S. A., Staudinger, U. M. & Baltes, P. B. (in press). *Tolerant but Not: Ahtivisung West-relativier-enden Wissens und Urtailens. Feitschrift für Entswichungspsychologic und Pädagogivolcc Psychologic* (in press).

Caspi, A. (1990). Why maladaptive behaviors persist: sources of continuity and change across the life course. In: D. C. Funder, R. D. Parke, C. Tomlinson-Keasey & K. Widaman (Eds), *Studying Lives Through Time: Personality and Development* (pp. 343–376).Washington, D.C.: American Psychological Association.

Chi, M. T. H., Glaser, R. & Farr, M. J. (1991). *Toward a general theory of expertise.* Hillsdale, NJ: Erlbaum.

Clayton, V. P. & Birren, J. E. (1980). The development of wisdom across the life span: a re-examination of an ancient topic. In: P. B. Baltes & O. G. Brim (Eds), *Life-Span Development and Behavior* (Vol. 3, pp. 103–135). New York: Academic Press.

Costa, P. T. & McCrae, R. R. (1994). Set like plaster? Evidence for the stability of adult personality. In: T. F. Heatherton & J. L. Weinberger (Eds), *Can Personality Change?* (pp. 21–40). Washington, D.C.: APA.

Csikszentmihalyi, M., Rathunde, K. & Whalen, S. (1993). *Talented teenagers: the roots of success and failure.* Cambridge: Cambridge University Press.

Davis, C. G., Nolen-Hoeksema, S. & Larson, J. (1998). Making sense of loss and benefiting from the experience: two construals of meaning. *Journal of Personality and Social Psychology*, **75**, 561–574.

DeHaan, R. G. & Havighurst, R. J. (1957). *Educating the gifted.* Chicago: University of Chicago Press.

Elder, G. H. (1998). The life course and human development. In: R. M. Lerner (Ed.), *Handbook of Child Psychology*, Volume 1: *Theoretical Models of Human Development* (5th ed., pp. 939–991).

Ericsson, K. A. & Smith, J. (1991). *Toward a general theory of expertise: prospects and limits.* Cambridge, MA: Cambridge University Press.

Erikson, E. H., Erikson, J. M. & Kivnick, H. Q. (1986). *Vital involvment in old age: the experience of old age in our time.* New York: Norton.

Fabricius, W. V., Schwanenflugel, P. J., Kyllonen, P. C., Barclay, C. R. & Denton, S. M. (1989). Developing theories of the mind: children's and adult's concepts of mental activities. *Child Development*, **60**, 1278–1290.

Fischer, K. W., Bullock, D. H., Rogenberg, E. J. & Raya, P. (1993). The dynamics of competence: how context contributes directly to skill. In: R. H. Wozniak & K. W. Fischer (Eds), *Development in Context: Acting and Thinking in Specific Environments.* (pp. 93–120). Hillsdale, NJ: Erlbaum.

Flavell, J. H., Green, F. L. & Flavell, E. R. (1995). Young children's knowledge about thinking. *Monographs of the Society for Research in Child Development*, **60**, 1–96.

Gagné, F. (1993). Constructs and models pertaining to exceptional human abilities. In: K. A. Heller, F. J. Mönks & A. H. Passow (Eds), *International Handbook of Research and Development of Giftedness and talent* (pp. 69–88). Oxford: Pergamon.

Gardner, H. (1993). *Multiple intelligences: the theory in practice.* New York: Basic Books.

Greene, A. L., Wheatley, S. M. & Aldava, J. F. (1992). Stages on life's way: adolescents' implicit theories of the life coures. *Journal of Adolescent Research*, **7**, 364–381.

Gruber, H. & Mandl, H. (1992). Begabung und Expertise [Ability and Expertise]. In: E. A. Hany & H. Nickel (Eds), *Begabung und Hochbegabung* (pp. 59–73). Bern: Huber.

Gurucharri, C. & Selman, R. L. (1982). The development of interpersonal understanding during childhood, pre-adolescence, and adolescence: a longitudinal follow-up study. *Child Development*, **53**, 924–927.

Happé, F. G. E., Winner, E. & Brownell, H. (1998). The getting of wisdom: theory of mind in old age. *Developmental Psychology*, **34**, 358–362.

Havighurst, (1972). *Developmental tasks and education* (3rd. ed.). New York: McKay.

Heckhausen, J. (1998). *Developmental regulation in adulthood: age-normative and sociostructural constraints as adaptive challenges.* Cambridge, Cambridge University Press.

Jackson, N. E. & Butterfield, E. C. (1986). A conception of giftedness designed to promote research. In: R. J. Sternberg & J. E. Davidson (Eds), *Conceptions of Giftedness* (pp.151–181). Cambridge: Cambridge University Press.

Jaspers, K. (1932). *Philosophie II: Existenzerhellung.* Berlin: Springer.

Kekes, J. (1995). *Moral wisdom and good lives.* Ithaca, NY: Cornell University Press.

Keller, M. & Wood, P. (1989). Development of friendship reasoning: a study of interindividual differences in intra-individual change. *Developmental Psychology*, **25**, 820–826.

Kitchener, K. S., Lynch, C. L., Fischer, K. W. & Wood, P. K. (1993). Developmental range of reflective judgment: the effect of contextual support and practice on developmental stage. *Developmental Psychology*, **29**, 893–906.

Kitchener, K. S. & Brenner, H. G. (1990). Wisdom and reflective judgment: knowing in the face of uncertainty. In: R. J. Sternberg (Ed.), *Wisdom: Its Nature, Origins, and Development* (pp. 212–229). Cambridge: Cambridge University Press.

Kramer, D. (1990). Conceptualizing wisdom: the primacy of affect-cognition relations. In: R. J. Sternberg (Ed.), *Wisdom: Its Nature, Origins, and Development* (pp. 279–316). Cambridge: Cambridge University Press.

Labouvie-Vief, G. (1980). Beyond formal operations: uses and limits of pure logic in life-span development. *Human Development*, **23**, 141–161.

Labouvie-Vief, G., DeVoe, M. & Bulka, D. (1989). Speaking about feelings: conceptions of emotion across the life span. *Psychology and Aging*, **4**, 425–437.

Lubinski, D. & Benbow, C. P. (1995). The study of mathematically precocious youth: the first three decades of a planned 50-year study of intellectual talent. In: R. F. Subotnik & K. D. Arnold (Eds), *Beyond Terman: Contemporary Longitudinal Studies of Giftedness and Talent* (pp. 255–281). Norwood, NJ: Ablex.

Maercker, A., Böhmig-Krumhaar, S. A. & Staudinger, U. M. (1998). Existentielle Konfrontation als Zugang zu weisheitsbezogenem Wissen und Urteilen: Eine Untersuchung von Weisheitsnominierten. *Zeitschrift für Entwicklungspsychologie und Pädagogische Psychologie*, **30**, 2–12.

McAdams, D. P., Diamond, A., de St. Aubin, E. & Mansfield, E. (1997). Stories of committment: the psychosocial construction of generative lives. *Journal of Personality and Social Psychology*, **72**, 678–694.

Meacham, J. (1990). The loss of wisdom. In: R. J. Sternberg (Ed.), *Wisdom: Its Nature, Origins, and Development* (pp. 181–211). Cambridge, MA: Cambridge University Press.

Mönks, F. J. & Mason, E. J. (1993). Developmental theories and giftedness. In: K. A. Heller, F. J. Mönks & A. H. Passow (Eds), *International Handbook of Research and Development of Giftedness and Talent* (pp. 89–102). Oxford: Pergamon.

Moon, S. M. & Feldhusen, J. F. (1995). The program for academic and creative enrichment (PACE): a follow-up study ten years later. In: R. F. Subotnik & K. D. Arnold (Eds), *Beyond Terman: Contemporary Longitudinal Studies of Giftedness and Talent* (pp. 375–400). Norwood, NJ: Ablex.

Orwoll, L. & Perlmutter, M. (1990). The study of wise persons: integrating a personality perspective. In: R. J. Sternberg (Ed.), *Wisdom: Its Nature, Origins, and Development* (pp. 160–177). New York: Cambridge University Press.

Oser, F. (1998, July). *Wisdom and religious development in Hungary and Switzerland: criteria of wisdom.* Paper presented at the annual meetings of the International Society for the Study of Behavioral Development, Bern, Switzerland.

Pasupathi, M. & Baltes, P. B. (1999). Wisdom. In: A. E. Kazdin (Ed.), *Encyclopedia of Psychology.* New York: Oxford University Press.

Pasupathi, M. & Staudinger, U. M. (in press). The link between two educational ideals: do advanced moral reasoners also show wisdom? *International Journal of Behavioral Development.*

Pasupathi, M., Staudinger, U. M. & Baltes, P. B. (2000). *Seeds of wisdom: adolescents' knowledge and judgment about difficult life matters.* Max Planck Institute for Human Development, Berlin, Germany. Manuscript submitted for publication.

Percy, W. (1975). *The message in the bottle.* New York: Farrar, Straus & Giroux.

Perleth, C. & Heller, K. A. (1995). The Munich longitudinal study of giftedness. In: R. F. Subotnik & K. D. Arnold (Eds), *Beyond Terman: Contemporary Longitudinal Studies of Giftedness and Talent* (pp. 77–114). Norwood, NJ: Ablex.

Perner, J. (1991). *Understanding the representational mind.* Cambridge, MA: MIT Press.

Phenix, P. H. (1964). *Realms of meaning.* New York: McGraw-Hill.

Renzulli, J. S. (1986). The three-ring conception of giftedness: a developmental model for creative productivity. In: R. J. Sternberg & J. E. Davidson (Eds), *Conceptions of Giftedness* (pp. 53–92). Cambridge: Cambridge University Press.

Roberts, S. M. & Lovett, S. B. (1994). Examining the 'F' in gifted: academically gifted adolescents' physiological and affective responses to scholastic failure. *Journal for the Education of the Gifted, 17,* 241–259.

Robinson, A. & Clinkenbeard, P. R. (1998). Giftedness: an exceptionality examined. *Annual Review of Psychology, 49,* 117–139.

Ross, R. J. (1976). The development of formal thinking and creativity in adolescence. *Adolescence, XI,* 609–617.

Ryff, C. D. & Keyes, C. L. M. (1995). The structure of psychological well-being revisited. *Journal of Personality and Social Psychology, 69,* 719–727.

Ryff, C. D. & Heincke, S. G. (1983). Subjective organization of personality in adulthood and aging. *Journal of Personality & Social Psychology, 44,* 807–816.

Schaie, W. K. (1994). The course of adult intellectual development. *American Psychologist, 49,* 304–313.

Schaie, W. K. (1995). *Intellectual development in adulthood: the Seattle longitudinal study.* New York: Cambridge University Press.

Simonton, D. K. (1990). Creativity in the later years: optimistic prospects for achievement. *Gerontologist, 30,* 626–631.

Smith, G. & Carlsson, I. (1985). Creativity in middle and late school years. *International Journal of Behavioral Development, 8,* 329–343.

Smith, J., Staudinger, U. M. & Baltes, P. B. (1994). Occupational settings facilitative of wisdom-related knowledge: the sample case of clinical psychologists. *Journal of Consulting and Clinical Psychology, 62,* 989–1000.

Smith, J. (1996). Planning about life: toward a social-interactive perspective. In: P. B. Baltes & U. M. Staudinger (Eds), *Interactive Minds: Life-Span Perspectives on the Social Foundation of Cognition* (pp. 242–275). Melbourne, Australia: Cambridge University Press.

Southern, W. T., Jones, E. D. & Stanley, J. C. (1993). Acceleration and enrichment: the context and development of program options. In: K. A. Heller, F. J. Mönks & A. H. Passow (Eds), *International Handbook of Research and Development of Giftedness and Talent* (pp. 387–409). Oxford: Pergamon.

Sowarka, D. (1989). Weisheit und weise Personen: Common-Sense-Konzepte älterer Menschen. *Zeitschrift für Entwicklungspsychologie und Pädagogischer Psychologie, 21,* 87–109.

Staudinger, U. M. (2000). *Life Review or Life Reflection: Epistemic and Emancipatory Functions.* Dresden: Dresden University of Technology. Manuscript submitted for publication.

Staudinger, U. M. (1999). Older and wiser? Integrating results on the relationship between age and wisdom-related performance. *International Journal of Behavioral Development, 23,* 641–664.

Staudinger, U. M. & Pasupathi, M. (2000). *Predicting wisdom-related performance in adolescence and adulthood.* Max Planck Institute for Human Development, Berlin, Germany. Manuscript submitted for publication.

Staudinger, U. M. & Pasupathi, M. (2000). Lifespan perspectives on self, personality, and social cognition. In: F. I. M. Craik & T. Salthouse (Eds), *Handbook of Cognition and Aging.,* pp. 633–688.

Staudinger, U. M. & Baltes, P. B. (1996). Interactive minds: a facilitative setting for wisdom-related performance? *Journal of Personality and Social Psychology, 71,* 746–762.

Staudinger, U. M., Smith, J. & Baltes, P. B. (1992). Wisdom-related knowledge in a life-review task: age differences and the role of professional specialization. *Psychology and Aging, 7,* 271–281.

Staudinger, U. M. & Baltes, P. B. (1994). The psychology of wisdom. In: R. J. Sternberg (Ed.), *Encyclopedia of Intelligence* (pp. 1143–1152). New York: Macmillan.

Staudinger, U. M., Smith, J. & Baltes, P. B. (1994). *Manual for the assessment of wisdom-related knowledge and judgment* (Technical report No. 46). Berlin: Max Planck Institute for Human Development.

Staudinger, U. M., Maciel, A., Smith, J. & Baltes, P. B. (1998). What predicts wisdom-related knowledge? A first look at personality, intelligence, and facilitative experiential contexts. *European Journal of Personality, 12,* 1–17.

Staudinger, U. M., Lopez, D. F. & Baltes, P. B. (1997). The psychometric location of wisdom-related performance. *Personality and Social Psychology Bulletin, 23,* 1200–1214.

Staudinger, U. M. & Reimer, M. (1999). *What helps us to become wise? Subjective conceptions about the ontogenesis of wisdom.* Berlin: Max Planck Institute for Human Development. Manuscript in preparation.

Staudinger, U. M. & Dittmann-Kohli, F. (1994). Lebenserfahrung und Lebenssinn. In: P. B. Baltes, J. Mittelstraß & U. M. Staudinger (Eds), *Alter und Altern: Ein interdisziplinärer Studientext zur Gerontologie* (pp. 408–436). Berlin: de Gruyter.

Sternberg, R. J. (1985). Implicit theories of intelligence, creativity, and wisdom. *Journal of Personality and Social Psychology*, **49**, 607–627.

Sternberg, R. J. (1990). Wisdom and its relations to intelligence and creativity. In: R. J. Sternberg (Ed.), *Wisdom: Its Nature, Origins, and Development* (pp. 142–149). Cambridge, MA: Cambridge University Press.

Sternberg, R. J. & Grigorenko, E. (1997). Are cognitive styles still in style? *American Psychologist*, **52**, 700–712.

Sternberg, R. J. & Davidson, J. E. (1986). Conceptions of giftedness: a map of the terrain. In: R. J. Sternberg & J. E. Davidson (Eds.), *Conceptions of Giftedness* (pp. 3–20). Cambridge: Cambridge University Press.

Stevens, D. P. & Truss, C. V. (1985). Stability and change in adult personality over 12 and 20 years. *Developmental Psychology*, **21**, 568–584.

Strube, G., Gehringer, M., Ernst, I. & Knill, K. (1985). *Knowing what's going to happen in life II: biographical knowledge in developmental perspective*. Unpublished manuscript. Munich: Max Planck Institute for Psychological Research.

Subotnik, R. F. & Arnold, K. D. (1993). Longitudinal studies of giftedness: Investigating the fulfillment of promise. In: K. A. Heller, F. J. Mönks & A. H. Passow (Eds.), *International Handbook of Research and Development of Giftedness and Talent* (pp. 149–160). Oxford: Pergamon.

Tannenbaum, A. J. (1986). Giftedness: a psychosocial approach. In: R. J. Sternberg & J. E. Davidson (Eds.), *Conceptions of Giftedness*. Cambridge: Cambridge University Press.

Taylor, C. W. (1986). Cultivating simultaneous student growth in both multiple creative talents and knowledge. In: J. S. Renzulli (Ed.), *Systems and Models for Developing Programs for the Gifted and Talented* (pp. 306–351). Mansfield Center, CT: Creative Learning Press.

Toynbee, A. (1967). Is America neglecting her creative talents? In: C. W. Taylor (Ed.), *Creativity Across Education* (pp. 23–29). Salt Lake City, University of Utah Press.

Vaillant, G. (1995). *The wisdom of the ego*. Cambridge, MA: Harvard University Press.

Vygotsky, L. S. (1978). *Mind in society: the development of higher psychological processes*. Cambridge, MA: Harvard University Press.

Webb, J. T. (1993). Nurturing social-emotional development of gifted children. In: K. A. Heller, F. J. Mönks & A. H. Passow (Eds.), *International Handbook of Research and Development of Giftedness and Talent* (pp. 525–538). Oxford: Pergamon.

Webster, J. D. (1997). The reminiscence functions scale: a replication. *International Journal of Aging and Human Development*, **44**, 137–148.

Webster, J. D. (1994). Predictors of reminiscence: a lifespan perspective. *Canadian Journal on Aging*, **13**, 66–78.

Whitbourne, S. K., Zuschlag, M. K., Elliot, L. B. & Waterman, A. S. (1992). Psychosocial development in adulthood: a 22-year sequential study. *Journal of Personality and Social Psychology*, **63**, 260–271.

Winner, E. (1996). The rage to master: the decisive role of talent in the visual arts. In: K. A. Ericsson (Ed.), *The Road to Excellence: The Acquisition of Expert Performance in the Arts and Sciences, Sports, and Games* (pp. 271–301). Mahwah, NJ: Erlbaum.

Part III

Identification of Giftedness and Talent

Identification of Gifted and Talented Youth for Educational Programs

John F. Feldhusen[1] and Fathi A. Jarwan[2]

[1] *Purdue University, USA*
[2] *Noor-Hussein Foundation, Jordan*

Introduction

Gifted and talented youth are major national resources. With supportive and nurturing parents and high level and challenging educational services they can become the professionals, artists, care givers, and leaders of our nation and the world. Appropriate parenting and education are also needed to help them develop all of their human potential and lead rich and satisfying lives.

Meeting the needs of gifted and talented youth in the family and school begins with their identification as especially able individuals and includes assessment of their special aptitudes, talents, and interests. Educational programs and curricula that are general in nature and offer enrichment experiences to all identified youth are far less effective than programs that address specific talents and interests. The needs of mathematically precocious youth are far different from the needs of artistically or verbally talented youth. Appropriate curriculum and instruction recognize both the nature and level of gifted students' talents and aptitudes.

As a prelude to identification and assessment of gifted and talented youth it is essential that parents and educators have clear conceptions of the nature and manifestations of giftedness and talent. This means definition of terms and the relationships among them; giftedness and talent are not simply scores on tests and/ or rating scales. They are descriptors of complex abilities as interactive components of human behavior that develop throughout the lifetime of gifted individuals; the major growth periods, however, are childhood and adolescence. We will address the conception of abilities, gifts, and talents at length in this chapter.

Once conceptions and definitions of giftedness, aptitude, and talent are delineated, the next task is to devise methods and procedures for implementing them in work with precocious youth. This means defining the goals of the identification program, the target population. Will it focus on a few particular talents or a broad range of abilities? What tests, rating scales, behavioral observations, or product evaluations shall we use? How will the data we gather be synthesized or summarized to arrive at selection judgments? How will we assess specific talents and interests? How do we effect the transition from data or profiles to actual classroom experiences and family support? These are the critical questions we will address in this chapter with a view to paving the way to educational services and family support that help gifted and talented youth realize their full potential and achieve the highest levels of expertise, artistry, or professional contribution to society.

We will begin with a review of conceptions of giftedness and talent.

Conceptions of Giftedness and Talent

General intelligence has served as the major representation of intellectual ability during most of the twentieth century. Beginning with the work of Binet (1902) in France, Spearman (1927) in England, and Terman (1916) in the United States, the metaphor of intelligence as the nexus of mental abilities grew to be the salient psychological construct representing human cognition. While the factor analyses of Thurstone (1938) and Guilford (1967) began to identify components or factors of intelligence, the concept of general intelligence represented by the IQ continued and still continues to hold sway in much of psychology and education as well as the practical worlds of business and industry

The course of development in most scientific fields is from broad to ever finer and more detailed analyses. After decades of medical research we now delineate many specific forms of cancer and in clinical psychological research many specific types of mental illness. We can better understand, control, and minister to phenomena by addressing components, as for example blood cells in the cancer condition called leukemia or specific areas of the brain in mental illness.

Beginning with the extensive work of Thurstone (1938), Cattell (1971), Guilford (1967), and others in factor analyzing intelligence tests, a new conception of human abilities began to emerge, identifying specific factors of intelligence. Methods of factor analysis changed over time so that while Thurstone's analyses yielded a parsimonious set of six or seven major factors of intelligence, Guilford's analyses seemed to reveal over a hundred and possibly several hundred factors. Both Thurstone and Guilford also brought creativity factors into the realm of intelligence: Thurstone with 'fluency' and Guilford with an extensive set of divergent thinking factors.

The history of gifted education has witnessed extensive efforts in both theoretical and empirical areas to define the construct *giftedness*. Yet, there is little agreement among researchers and educators on a precise definition and measurement of giftedness (Horowitz & O'Brien, 1985; Janos & Robinson, 1985). The widespread disagreement is a result of varying and conflicting conceptions about the relationships among and definitions of giftedness, intelligence, and talent (Gagné, 1985; Feldhusen & Hoover, 1986). Hallahan and Kauffman (1982), however, argued that the reasons for disagreement are mainly due to differences regarding four issues: the range of skills and behaviors to which the term giftedness should be applied, the measurement of giftedness, the cutoff point above which a child is considered gifted, and the nature of the comparison group. In an insightful analysis of the term and the conception of giftedness Gallagher (1991) concluded that it is time to change our terminology because the term 'gifted' connotes unearned privilege and creates problems for students who are so designated. Recent research and theory development by Carroll, Sternberg, Gardner, Gagné, and others show the way to new and better terms and conceptions of superior ability.

Carroll, Sternberg, Gardner, and Gagné

During the last two decades of the twentieth century the work of four psychologists dominated the new analytical approach to human mental ability, intelligence, or cognition—Carroll, Sternberg, Gagné, and Gardner. These four and a host of other researchers sought to map out the terrain of human intelligence. Although their maps differ a great deal, their insights about human cognitive functioning have given us a better understanding of the intellectual processes underlying the general mental operation called 'intelligence'.

Carroll's Three Stratum Theory

The factor analytic tradition in psychology that sought to identify the components of human intelligence or ability reached its peak in the large factor analyses conducted by John B. Carroll on 461 data sets. Based on the empirical data and the factor analyses Carroll proposed (1996) a three-stratum theory of intelligence in which *g* or general intelligence supersedes all

intellectual functioning. Stratum II includes eight broad areas of ability: fluid intelligence (2F), crystallized intelligence (2C), general memory and learning (2Y), broad visual perceptions (2V), broad auditory perception (2U), broad retrieval ability (2R), broad cognitive speediness (2S), and processing speed (2T). Based on his factor analysis of 461 data bases, he goes on to specify 70 subfactors under these eight Stratum II abilities. They included, for example, five reasoning abilities under 2F; sixteen knowledge acquisition abilities under 2C; six memory factors under 2Y; eleven visual and imagery factors under 2V; fifteen auditory factors under 2U; nine creativity and fluency factors under 2R; four cognitive speed factors under 2S; and four processing speed factors under 2T. Carroll goes on to suggest that the abilities represented in these factors "refer to variations in individuals' capabilities to respond successfully to a class of tasks that differ in difficulty . . ." (p. 14). Among the 70 subfactors the reasoning, imagery, creativity, and fluency factors are especially relevant to our efforts to identify specific aspects of giftedness and talent.

Sternberg's Triarchic Theory

Sternberg (1985) proposed and elaborated a triarchic theory of intelligence that has become a major new theory in the worlds of education and psychology; the model is fundamentally an information-processing approach to human intellectual functioning. The three major parts of the model are metacomponents, performance components, and knowledge-acquisition components.

The metacomponents are essentially metacognition processes including: (1) recognizing problems, (2) clarifying problems, (3) planning, (4) creating strategies to solve problems, (5) mental representation of problems, (6) pulling together the cognitive resources needed to solve problems, (7) surveillance of problem solving, and (8) judging the adequacy or quality of solutions.

Knowledge-acquisition components are forms of intelligence in which new information is dealt with and committed to long-term memory. Selective encoding is sorting among all the information we encounter and deciding which pieces are relevant and useful in our intellectual operations. Selective combination is uniting pieces of information into integrated and more useful wholes. In essence it is "putting two and two together". Selective comparison is seeing relationships among pieces of information in long-term memory and new information in working or short-term memory.

Performance components are lower order or less complex forms of intelligence that serve to carry the metacomponential processes. They are often fairly specific pieces of knowledge or skills that are related to a problem being addressed. Again, we might see them as the particular mental skills needed to execute moves in chess, solve water jar problems, write poetry, or solve algebraic problems. They constitute the working abilities we need to function well in a special domain of activity.

While we await good measures of all the components, it is clear that all of the metacomponents are specific abilities that can be assessed and nurtured by schools as the higher level thinking skills. The knowledge acquisition components deal with the learning and retention of information and the development of knowledge bases. The performance components represent specific behavioral skills that students need to function well in their particular domains of talent. The Sternberg abilities represent much more practical and applicable aspects of giftedness and talent than the Carroll factors; they can more readily be assessed and they point the way to specific curricular and instructional activities (Sternberg, 1997).

Gagné's Differentiated Model of Giftedness and Talent

The most well articulated theory of giftedness and talent development was first presented by Gagné in 1985. In the years following, Gagné has carried on a substantial program of research based on and growing out of the theory, and he has continued to refine the overall theoretical model of talent development. This model recognizes general or basic gifts but goes on to delineate how more specific talents grow out of environmental influences and interactions. The 'gifts' are the genetic endowments while talents are the product of the synergistic interaction of genetic predispositions with home, school, and the physical and social environments surrounding a child. In an extensive study of 2343 students in 88 classrooms Gagné (1993), using 42 talent descriptions and teacher and peer nominations, found substantial sex differences in the incidence of talents in the areas of creativity, cognitive abilities, socio-affective activity, physical prowess, academic talent, technical skills, artistic talent, and interpersonal functioning.

The theory proposes that there is a basic set of gifts that evolve into specific talents through the cognitive interactions that the child experiences with persons, events, environments, and chance factors. An emerging set of interpersonal factors in the realms of personality and motivation are also manifested and influence the course of talent development. Much of the influence on talent development derives specifically from learning, training, and practice. Gagné's research has focused a great deal of attention on delineation of fields and categories of talent. Since the theory is presented elsewhere in this volume, no further elucidation of it will be presented here. However, we wish to make clear that the theory is a major basis for current research, theory, and school practice in talent development (Gagné, 1997). The recent publication by Gagné (1999) of rating scales for self, peer, and teacher ratings of talents and the profile methodology developed by Kay (1999) make the model now a practical procedure for identification in school settings.

Gardner's Multiple Intelligences Model

Garner has revived and reconceptualized factors of human ability. Gardner's model of multiple intelligences (1993) is now recognized as the most popular and widely applied model of human abilities. The broad categories of (1) linguistic, (2) logical-mathematical, (3) spatial, (4) musical, (5) bodily-kinesthetic, (6) interpersonal, and (7) intrapersonal abilities or 'intelligences' as they are called are being used extensively to structure general school programs, gifted programs, and 'key' schools that serve as model programs. However, there is little evidence to show that they are being used to identify specific youth talents or to individualize programming for gifted and talented youth. Schools and teachers have embraced the model avidly as a guide to curriculum and instruction, yet there are few specific tests or assessment guidelines to identify precocity, giftedness, or talent in the seven domains. Nevertheless the model and the intelligences, preferably called 'talents' as Gardner, Walter & Hatch (1992) suggested, enhance both our conception of giftedness and identification of its component abilities.

The work of Carroll, Sternberg, Gagné, and Gardner has been influential in promulgating the concepts of multiple aptitudes, talents and abilities. While the field of gifted education often clings to a unitary conception of giftedness, the new work of these researchers is broadening our views of giftedness and should lead to totally new approaches to identification and assessment in programs for gifted and talented youth.

Definitions of Giftedness and Talent

An explicit definition of giftedness is considered by many authors to be a keystone for the development of programs for the gifted. It is important because of the close link that must exist between the definition and the identification system (Ward, 1983; Feldhusen, Asher & Hoover, 1984; Hoge, 1988). It is also important because of its relationship with program goals and curriculum offerings (Feldhusen, 1982). Finally, the definition adopted or developed by a school will determine in general terms who will be selected and who will be excluded.

Technically a 'gifted' child is one who scores high on an intelligence test or an academic achievement test and who has partially or totally inherited his or her ability. However, a 1993 policy report from the U.S. Office of Education, *National Excellence: Developing America's Talent* proposed that the term 'gifted' be used to denote mature achievement, not developing ability; that report also spells out all the types of abilities as talents. However, we argue that giftedness is basically genetic endowment that paves the way to the development of specific abilities, aptitudes, and talents.

Talent is a specific ability within a domain of human activity such as art, music, mathematics, political science, drama, or literature. It may also be physical talent as in tennis, golf, or bowling. Some talents are broad as, for example, 'verbal' talent while others are narrow or circumscribed such as 'gun repair'. Individuals may have one or a number of superior talents; talents vary in level or proficiency. Most youth have some special talents but a relatively small number have superior talents.

The Identification Process

Identification of youth talents often begins with a general measure of mental ability, intelligence, or achievement to determine a child's general level of precocity. The steps leading up to such testing may include teacher and/or parent observations of such behaviors as learning to read before entering school, early facility with numbers and arithmetic operations, oral-verbal fluency and extended vocabulary, ability to use logic in reasoning, or strong interests in science topics. Generally the child may show capacity to function well at age levels two or more years beyond his or her chronological age.

The initial assessment may also come about because the child demonstrates personal or social problems in addition to the precocity. Peer relations may not be going well, regular school activities may be rejected by the child, achievement in the form of classroom tests and teacher grades may be far under expectations, the child may be inattentive in school, and/or misbehaviors may even be exhibited. Assessment as a result of such problems may lead to a need to find alternative curricula and instructional methods to better serve the child.

Ideally the label 'gifted' is not ascribed to the child at this point nor at any time in the identification process. While schools try to avoid labeling children in either positive or negative ways, there is a special need to avoid the 'gifted' label because of its high genetic pretence, because it mistakenly communicates to the majority of children that they have no special gifts or abilities, because it may evoke negative peer reactions, and finally because it may communicate to the labeled child that he or she has superior ability and hence should not have to work hard in school.

Having determined that a child has superior ability or is precocious in school achievements, the next step is to determine a child's specific talents, areas of precocious achievement, aptitudes, or abilities. Children who are designated as 'gifted' are not superior in all forms and areas of ability; each has unique patterns of high achievement, aptitude or talent (Achter, Lubinski & Benbow, 1996). Efforts to meet their educational needs must be directed to their specific talent strengths, not to giftedness in general.

Using Multiple Criteria

In almost every program and service for gifted and talented youth there is a limited number of openings and resources; the identification criteria are general conditions regarding eligibility for consideration or nomination. They function as a means of controlling the number of nominees or applications within a reasonable range. The use of multiple procedures for identification has been emphasized as a response to theories of human abilities which stress multiple factors (Gardner, 1991). It is important, however, to recognize that this approach does not necessarily guarantee making valid decisions. The quality and relevance of measures place limits on the reliability and validity of such decisions. The question to be raised, therefore, is not how many measures are used in the identification process, but rather what contribution each piece of information has to making valid decision or to serving specific objectives (Piirto, 1994). It is a waste of money, time, and effort to collect data that are not going to be used or are not contributing to more valid and reliable decisions.

A variety of data sources are suggested in the literature for the identification of academically gifted and talented children for special services (Feldhusen, Jarwan & Holt, 1993). The list includes standardized tests, school grades, rating scales, references, essay writing (Feldhusen & Baska, 1989), past accomplishments (Coleman, 1985), interviews, creativity tests (Torrance, 1984), and creativity inventories (Rimm, 1984). Feldhusen, Jarwan & Holt (1993) present comprehensive descriptions and evaluations of tests and scales they recommend for identification of generally gifted and specifically talented youth.

Identifying Giftedness and Talent Among Special Populations

Identifying gifted students from special populations and identifying their specific talents has posed a challenging problem for professionals and educators in the field of gifted education (Feldhusen, Asher & Hoover, 1984; Bragget, 1990; U.S. Office of Education, 1993). Research on special populations in the past focused more on their deficits rather than on their strengths (Baldwin, 1985; Baum & Owen, 1988); however, an identification system should guarantee that no one who is qualified is overlooked. Frasier (1994) has carried out pioneering work on methods and procedures for the identification of general giftedness and specific talents among minority populations.

The National Association for Gifted Children's Committee on Special Populations (Jennings-Friedman, Richert & Feldhusen, 1991, pp. vi–viii), adopted a position statement relating to the definition and identification of special populations. The term is defined to include "groups who differ from those who have been traditionally well represented in school programs for the gifted" and it "can be applied to children and young adults who are Black, Hispanic, Native American, Asian Pacific, rural, economically disadvantaged, handicapped, and female, as well as students whose gifts are in domains not traditionally recognized in school settings." The statement also indicates that typical instruments and procedures used to identify gifted students for special programs are often inadequate and insensitive to the unique qualities and characteristics of special populations. Ignoring the needs and special problems associated with identifying gifted/talented students from special populations also leaves the field vulnerable to charges of elitism and racism (VanTassel-Baska, 1989).

It is imperative, as we argued earlier, that identification of giftedness and talent among special populations focus both on the possible presence of superior general abilities, *g*, or general intelligence but also on emerging talents or capabilities. Feldhusen (1995) has proposed that those talents may be academic or intellectual in nature, artistic, in business and technical fields, and/or personal-social in nature. Superior intelligence should never be the sole or pre-requisite criterion for identification and eligibility for programs.

Handicapped Gifted

The term 'gifted handicapped' refers to children who have two sets of characteristics: giftedness or talent and disability (Clark, 1992). They are impaired by one or more specific conditions that include: learning disability, hearing impairment, visual difficulty, neurological disorders, emotional problems, and motor disabilities (Whitmore & Maker, 1985; Yewchuk, 1985). Obstacles to identifying disabled children as mentally gifted or talented include: stereo-typical expectations, developmental delays, incomplete information about the child, lack of challenge, and lack of appropriate tests or rating scales. It is also a problem in many schools that non-handicapped children qualify quickly and easily for all the available program openings, especially when the program is limited to generally 'gifted' youth, and thus no effort is made to search for giftedness or talent among youth whose handicaps or minority status hide their gifts or talents.

Gifted Underachievers

'Gifted underachiever' is another category of gifted special populations. Whitmore (1980) defined 'underachievement' as "performance judged either by grades or achievement test scores, or both, that are significantly below the student's measured or demonstrated potential for academic achievement" (p. 168). Although there are many different definitions (Seeley, 1989), the underlying concept is that there is a discrepancy between potential and actual performance (Mooij, 1992). The problem of gifted underachievers is simply that they are often not identified for any special services because they do not meet the criteria for selection which require high achievement or perform-

ance (Boyd, 1990). If the popular conception that many outstanding women and men were poor achievers or indifferent scholars as children is correct (Reynolds & Birch, 1977), and if the magnitude of the problem is huge as has been estimated (Whitmore, 1980), then identification of gifted underachievers should be one of the important concerns reflected in systems for identifying gifted students. Rimm (1995) has been a leader in efforts to identify and help gifted students who are underachieving in school; she offers comprehensive guidelines for assessment of the underlying achievement problems and for corrective educational therapy.

Gifted Females

Gifted girls and women are considered a 'minority' group or special population because of their under-representation in higher levels of schooling, professions, and achievement in mathematics and science (Gallagher, 1988; Callahan & Reis, 1996). Sex differences on the mathematics portion of the Scholastic Aptitude Test (SAT-M), were found in the first talent search of Johns Hopkins University (Stanley & Benbow, 1983). Fewer girls than boys scored at high levels of mathematical reasoning ability. At the high school level, the authors found sex differences favoring males mathematics course enrollment, performance on the SAT-M, and taking of, and performance on, mathematics achievement and Advanced Placement Program Examinations. Also, in the Study of Mathematically Precocious Youth (SMPY), males performed better than females on achievement tests measuring knowledge and understanding of biology, chemistry, and physics.

Kerr (1997), a leading scholar in the study of gifted girls concluded that the problems of gifted girls in the realm of gifted education are in both the identification process and in educational programming. She offers insights for increasing equity and opportunities for gifted girls in the classroom and practical guidelines for enhancing achievement behavior, social self-esteem, and exploratory behavior of gifted girls.

Minority and Disadvantaged Student

Frasier (1994) developed a 'culture-specific' assessment system that evaluates "the intelligence of each person in relation to others who come from similar socioeconomic backgrounds and who have had the same opportunity to acquire the knowledge and skills needed to answer questions on an intelligence test designed for an Anglo-American society." She also recommends using standardized tests that allow for culturally different manifestations and interpretations of intellectual ability. Frasier cited many references regarding the inappropriateness of traditional intelligence tests for black students.

VanTassel-Baska (1998) argued that minority and disadvantaged student are the most neglected of all the school subpopulations and especially African-American students. She suggests that the identification process should focus on special attributes of minority subcultures, use non-traditional measures, and search for creative and psychomotor talents; and programs should address issues of motivation and related non-cognitive skills. She concludes by delineating a number of effective intervention tactics especially focused on curricular adaptations.

From the review of literature on identification of gifted students from special populations (Frasier, Garcia & Passow, 1995) we conclude that the problems associated with identifying and serving these gifted students are major concerns for both educators and policy makers. A defensible program for the gifted must deal with the diverse talents and abilities that characterize different ethnic and cultural groups (Frasier & Passow, 1994). A variety of objective and subjective assessment data should be used to ensure the discovery of talents existing across and within populations and sub-populations of children.

Phases of Identification

A sound identification system typically is carried out through a series of steps. The order and sequence of steps, clarity of objectives, purposefulness of each component, and the modifiability of the system are important foundations for a defensible identification system. The number of steps and the purpose of each step is dependent upon the nature of the program for the gifted and the talent areas it strives to serve. Is the program restricted to a school building? Is it a program serving a school district or statewide population of students? Does it address academic, artistic, vocational-technical, and personal-social talents?

Application

Many programs for gifted and talented youth begin with an announcement of the program, descriptions of what will be offered, and detailed criteria for admission or acceptance. Youth and their parents may then decide to submit an application. The identification criteria often include test scores, letters of evaluation, and rating scales to be completed. Often the youth-candidates are asked to write a letter setting forth why they want to be in the program and why they believe themselves to be qualified; an admissions committee then reviews applications, and using the criteria as guides, selects youth for the program. Often such programs and identification systems make little pretence as to the levels of giftedness nor to the specific talents of the youth who are selected.

Screening and /or Preliminary Assessment In School Program

Screening or preliminary assessment is often the second step in the identification process. Many activities are carried out during this process such as: getting information from school records, collecting and categorizing information from nomination forms and referrals, testing, synthesizing information, and selecting students for further testing. The ultimate function of screening activities is to find youth who have superior talent potential. The following guidelines are suggested to achieve this goal: (1) use multiple criteria, (2) train staff on the identification procedures, and (3) use reliable and valid screening tests and rating scales. The screening process should and probably will produce more students than will ultimately be selected for the program.

In addition to existing school records and group test scores, nominations from teachers, counselors, peers, parents, and the students themselves can be used. Setting cutoff points on some screening measures should not lead to ignoring strong evidence from other sources. In school practice it is common to have 10–20% of the school population in the initial screening pool, especially if a broad definition of giftedness is used, including academic and artistic talent. Inclusion in the initial screening pool, not exclusion, is recommended (e.g. Feldhusen, 1989; Clark, 1992). Borland and Wright (1994) suggested two practices to serve this purpose: (1) set low cutoff points on screening measures, and (2) include every student who meets the cutoff score on any one screening measure. It is extremely important to follow Borland's suggestions if one is searching for nominees among special populations.

Effectiveness and subsequent efficiency of the screening process can be substantially improved by providing adequate training for all staff who participate in the screening process. Hoge and Cudmore (1986) reviewed the literature on teacher accuracy in identifying gifted students and concluded that the validity of teacher judgments or ratings can be improved substantially through appropriate training. Such training should include clarification of the processes of screening and identification, communication of the overall goals of the program, and tryouts of all the forms and procedures. Finally, the tests and rating scales should be of the highest quality obtainable. Evaluation information about tests is quite readily available in the *Mental Measurement Yearbooks*. Nomination forms and rating scales, however, are often locally produced with little or no attention to their validity or reliability; they should be used therefore with extreme caution.

Data Synthesis

An enormous number of research studies and writings have argued strongly and persuasively in support of using multiple selection criteria (Richert, Alvino & McDonnel, 1982; Feldhusen, 1989; McLeod & Cropley, 1989). However, very few studies have discussed the emerging problems of: (1) how to reduce and combine data in a defensible way that facilitates selection decisions, and (2) what practical procedures need to be used in validating those decisions.

It is important to recognize that the use of multiple selection criteria does not necessarily guarantee making valid decisions. The quality of the identification measures and the manner in which the data are synthesized and interpreted is critical in making valid selection decisions. Therefore, as stated earlier, the question to be raised is what contribution each measure makes to the validity and efficiency of the system. Three methods will be discussed: (1) standard score method; (2) multiple-cutoff method; (3) multiple regression method.

Standard Score Method

If the goal of identification is to find the 'all-purpose gifted child', the most appropriate metric of psychological measurement is the standard score system (Lauer & Asher, 1988). The use of the basic standard score scale (z-score) or any of its derivatives (e.g. t-scores) achieves comparability of means, dispersions, and the form of distribution (Guilford & Fruchter, 1973). Equality of units is an important characteristic of standard-score scales.

The standard score metric can also be used to get a composite score for several identification measures. For example, while it is indefensible to combine measures from mathematics, verbal ability, and artistic talent to select students for a program stressing science and technology, the standard score method can be used after selecting appropriate measures such as science achievement test scores, ratings by teachers of students' technological aptitude, and quantitative aptitude from a cognitive skills index. Here the measures may all have theoretical relevance to the program goals in science and technology; however, the matrix method fails completely to identify youths' specific talents.

Multiple-Cutoff Method

According to this method, a minimum score is set for each measure in the identification system; students who have scores equal to or in excess of all the minimums are selected for the program. Any student who fails to meet the standard on any one measure is not selected. The rationale underlying this method is that high aptitude or ability in one area does not counterbalance low aptitude or ability in another (Hills, 1971). The major problem with this method is that the cutoff points are often arbitrarily set without adequate evidence of the validity of the measures or without any reference to the criterion measure of success in the program. Also, as the measures become less reliable and highly correlated the method becomes less and less defensible for selection (Lord, 1962). In actual practice, the cutoff points are often established on the basis of external determinants, such as the number of applicants, the number to be selected, and the distribution of scores on one measure.

Multiple Regression Method

Multiple regression is a correlational method that makes it possible to take several identification scores and find a single composite correlation with measures of student achievement later in or at the end of a program. It serves to test the predictive power of the identification scores in relation to student outcomes or achievement in the program. The multiple regression method is based on the assumption that synthesis of the identification data should lead to relatively accurate prediction of student success in the program. The question of how effective and efficient the system is, should be carefully tested and validated against stated criteria of success in the program. The underlying conception behind the use of measures in educational selection is that they have predictive validity (Cronbach, 1970; Hoge, 1988; Feldhusen & Baska, 1989), that is that they select students who will be able to meet the goals of the program and exclude students who would fail to achieve the goals. For such an assumption to stand, "data must be collected which indicate that the instruments used to identify students do indeed predict success in the gifted program" (Feldhusen, Asher & Hoover, 1984, p. 151). Correlational and multiple regression analyses are appropriate means for dealing with the problems of synthesizing data and validating identification systems. The major advantages of this method are: ·

(1) The use of multiple regression implies the need for establishing solid relationships among three major components of any well-structured program for gifted and talented youth: (a) selection measures (predictors), (b) the instructional program, and (c) measures of outcomes (criteria).

(2) Multiple regression yields the most accurate predictions, and is never improved upon by using additional methods.

(3) Multiple regression provides an unbiased selection index that is a best weighted linear combination of identification criteria with minimal error of prediction.

(4) Regression equations have the advantage of the compensation principle over the multiple-cutoff method. The simultaneous processing of all measures in the regression equation allows a high score on one measure to compensate for a low score on another. This principle is very important for the inclusion of some students who score very high on one measure but who fail to meet the cutoff on another (Jarwan & Asher, 1994).

(5) The relative importance of each selection measure in the regression equation can be determined using beta coefficients when all measures are stated in standard score form. The measures with beta

coefficients near zero can be dropped from the selection system, and the cost of the identification process can be reduced.

(6) Multiple regression can be run using available computer statistical packages.

Identifying Specific Talents

The next major task in the identification process is to identify the specific talents, aptitudes, or abilities of prospective students so that the programs and curriculum can be tailored to students' specific needs. Feldhusen (1999) proposed that talents should be assessed in the areas of academics, arts, vocational-technical skills, and interpersonal-social activities. The vocational-technical area has also been incorporated into the talents domain by Bals (1999) and the arts by Baum, Owen & Oreck (1996).

A number of excellent diagnostic instruments for identifying giftedness and talent are described in detail by Feldhusen, Jarwan & Holt (1993). They especially focus on cognitive tests of intelligence, aptitude and school achievement that are useful in academically oriented programs.

Several sets of diagnostic rating scales are also useful such as *Scales for Rating The Behavioral Characteristics of Superior Students* by Renzulli et al (1997), and the *Academic Talents Rating Scales* and the *Vocational-Technical Rating Scales* by Feldhusen, Hoover & Sayler (1997). The ten Renzulli scales assess strengths or talents in art, music, drama, learning, leadership, motivation, expressiveness and precision in communication, creativity, and planning. The *Academic Rating Scales* are used to assess specific talent in mathematics, science, social studies, English, and foreign languages. Finally the *Vocational-Technical Rating Scales* focus on talent in agricultural studies, business, shop-mechanical, and social-interpersonal activities.

Gagné (1999) has also published new rating scales to identify multiple talents through ratings by peers, teachers, and self assessment for cognitive abilities, academic talents, social skills, physical-sports abilities, and technological and artistic talent. All of these rating scales have been carefully developed and have good technical qualities including evidence of reliability and validity. However, the problems of identifying talents in special populations should be addressed specifically. Plucker, Callahan & Tornchin (1996) did just that using Gardner's multiple intelligence framework (Gardner, 1993) and Udall & Passe's (1993) *Multiple Intelligence Assessment Technique*. Observations, performance-based activities, and teacher rating measures were adapted for the project. They found some good evidence of reliability in the assessments and limited evidence of convergent and discriminate validity of the scales.

Identification of talents in the arts has been addressed by several researchers, notably Piirto (1994),

Haroutounian (1993), and Clark & Zimmerman (1994). Programs for the gifted and talented should and can identify youth talents in the arts and provide individually appropriate services to them.

Selection-Placement

In many programs for talent development there is a fixed number of openings and limited resources; therefore, the ultimate goal of this phase is to select students who show the greatest talent potential and need for the service. Further testing may be required to make more valid decisions and especially to make sure that students from special populations have equal access to the programs. Individual tests, group tests, essays, auditions, and interviews are possible sources of additional information that might be relevant to program services.

The final phase of the identification process is placement of students in the program or service. Ideally there should be more than enough openings so that students who may be borderline cases or from special populations can try out in the program for a time to determine if they can perform well and profit from participating. The ultimate final stage of the identification process comes later when empirical tests of performance in the program or service are carried out to determine if those who were picked perform up to expectations and profit from the program services (Jenkins-Friedman, Richert & Feldhusen, 1991). The program services should, of course, be tailored to address students' specific talent strengths and interests. Kay (1999) and Feldhusen (1999) have both developed profile methods for delineating the specific talents of students as a prelude to selecting appropriate services, activities, resources, and experiences that will minister most effectively to the specific talents of individual students.

Summary

A special program for gifted or talented students should provide more advanced, rigorous curriculum experiences to satisfy intellectual needs, which are not addressed in regular classes. Thus, selection strategies must be focused on finding those youths who need and can profit from the advanced learning experiences and excluding those who would not benefit from it or who would fail in the program. An efficient identification system can play a role in meeting the requirements for making selection decisions not only on the basis of 'who is best' but also 'who is qualified'. It is important for administrators of programs to be as clear as possible in adopting a selection strategy that assures that those who are selected meet minimum standards for success in the program. Decisions regarding minimum standards are influenced by the selection strategy and the orientation of the program. Empirical evidence and/or professional judgment can be used to make a sound decision.

Over a period of years we have reviewed, analyzed, and critiqued identification processes in gifted education (Feldhusen, Baska & Womble, 1981; Feldhusen, Asher & Hoover, 1984; Feldhusen, 1991, 1992). Hoge (1988, 1989) also critiqued practices and the literature on identification of the gifted (1989). He concluded that there is a need to be explicit in defining the giftedness constructs and component traits, talents, and aptitudes. Definitions should be derived from theory concerning human abilities in general and superior ability in particular. Then the specific identification or selection procedures should be derived directly from the definition and supporting theory. Finally, there should be substantial efforts to verify or validate the identification system empirically.

Our recommendations then are as follows:

(1) Identification processes in gifted education should be based on the best current conceptions and theories of human aptitude, talent, and abilities.

(2) Test instruments and rating scales with established reliability and validity should be selected for use in the identification process.

(3) Identification should be viewed as an ongoing process. One should not conclude that assessment at one point in time, even with multiple tests, finally and unequivocally identifies the gifted child. Giftedness and talent are emerging abilities calling for repeated evaluation as youth mature.

(4) Labeling children as 'gifted' should be avoided; it is preferable to regard the process as selecting children for programs or services. Implicit labeling of children who are not selected as 'ungifted' is also a serious problem, especially when the labeling process openly labels others as 'gifted'. Ideally a good program should help all youth to identify, understand, and develop their talents, whatever the initial level, to the highest level possible.

(5) Identification should always be diagnostic in nature, identifying strengths, aptitudes, and talents as well as problems, weaknesses, and needs.

The concepts of 'general giftedness', 'gifted child', and 'gifted education' are no longer tenable in light of emerging research and theory on human abilities, psychometric shortcomings, and social offensiveness. Decades of research on factors of human intelligence as well as more recent research on human talents lead to a broader conception of human abilities as embracing not only academic-intellectual ability, as has been the focus of the 'gifted movement', but also talents in the arts, personal and social capabilities, and vocational aptitudes. The work of a number of researchers, notably Ericcson (1996), also lead to a much greater conception of plasticity in the development of human abilities. While Plomin (1990), Bouchard (1994), Wachs (1992) and others delineate the genetic potentials and limits in human abilities, it is also clear that emerging talents, aptitudes, and abilities are to a great extent products of learning experiences. Thus, the field of gifted education must heed the warning of a report from the U.S. Office of Education (1993) that the term 'gifted' no longer characterizes well the children who are subjects of our interest and that we should shift our view and effort to a broader range of talents in children.

Thus, the task of identification shifts from a search for the gifted few to assessment of the talent strengths and aptitudes of all students, and to identification of high level talent potential among those who are especially precocious or advanced in their talent development. None of what has been presented in this chapter implies that all children are 'gifted' in the traditional sense of that term, but it is becoming clear that relatively large numbers of youth demonstrate one or more potential talent strengths and a smaller but significant number demonstrate high talent potential which if identified and nurtured may lead to high level creative achievement in adulthood.

References

Achter, J. A., Lubinski, D. & Benbow, C. P. (1996). Multipotentiality among the intellectually gifted: It was never there and already its vanishing. *Journal of Counseling Psychology*, **43** (1), 65–76

Baldwin, A. Y. (1985). Programs for the gifted and talented: issues concerning minority populations. In: F. D. Horowitz & M. O'Brien (Eds), *The gifted and Talented: Developmental Perspectives* (pp. 223–250). Washington, DC: American Psychological Association.

Balogh, L. & Nagv, K. (1990). Developing talented children: problems and experiences. *European Journal for High Ability*, **1**, 179–186.

Bals, T. (1999). Fostering talents in vocational training: current strategies in Europe. *High Ability Studies*, **10** (1), 97–105.

Baum, S. & Owen, S. V. (1988). High ability/learning disabled students: how are they different? *Gifted Child Quarterly*, **U32** (3), 321–326.

Baum, S. M., Owen, S. V. & Oreck, B. A. (1996). Talent beyond words: identification of potential talent in dance and music. *Gifted Child Quarterly*, **40** (2), 93–101.

Binet, A. (1902). *The experimental study of intelligence*. Paris: Schleicher.

Birely, M. (1995). Identifying high ability/high achievement giftedness. In: J. L. Genshaft, M. Birely & C. L. Hollinger (Eds), *Serving Gifted and Talented Students* (pp. 49–66). Austin, TX: Pro-Ed.

Bloom, B. S. (1985). *Developing talent in young people*. New York: Ballantine Books.

Borland, J. H. (1989). *Planning and implementing programs for the gifted*. New York: Teachers College Press.

Borland, J. H. & Wright, L. (1994). Identifying young, potentially gifted, economically disadvantaged students. *Gifted Child Quarterly*, **38**, 164–171,

Bouchard, T. J. (1994). Genes, environment, and personality. *Science*, **264**, 1700–1701.

Boyd, R. (1990). Academically talented underachievers. *Gifted Education International*, **7**, 23–26.

Braggett, E. J. (1990). A wider concept of giftedness: providing for special populations. *Gifted International*, **6** (1), 71–80.

Callahan, C. M. & Reis, S. M. (1996). Gifted girls, remarkable women. In: K. Arnold, K. D. Noble & R. F. Subotnik (Eds), *Remarkable Women: Perspectives on Female Talent Development* (pp. 171–192). Cresskill, NJ: Hampton Press.

Carroll, J. B. (1996). A three stratum theory of intelligence: Spearman's contribution. In: I. Dennis & P. Tapsfield (Eds), *Human Abilities, Their Nature and Measurement* (pp. 1–17). Mahwah, NJ: Lawrence Erlbaum.

Cattell, R. B. (1971). *Abilities: their structure, growth and action*. Boston: Houghton-Mifflin.

Clark, B. (1992). *Growing up gifted: developing the potential of children at home and at school* (4th ed.). Columbus, OH: Macmillan Publishing Co.

Clark, G. A. & Zimmerman, E. D. (1994). *Programming opportunities for students gifted and talented in the visual arts*. Storrs, CT: The National Research Center on The Gifted and Talented.

Colangelo, N. & Kerr, B. (1990). Extreme academic talent: profiles of perfect scorers. *Journal of Educational Psychology*, **82** (3), 404–449.

Coleman, L. J. (1985). *Schooling the gifted*. Menlo Park, CA: Addison-Wesley Publishing.

Coleman, M. R. & Gallagher, J. J. (1995). Gifted education: historical perspectives and current concepts. In: J. L. Genshaft, M. Birely & C. L. Holinger (Eds), *Serving Gifted and Talented Students* (pp. 3–16). Austin, TX: Pro-Ed.

Cronbach, L. J. (1970). *Essentials of psychological testing*. New York: Harper & Row.

Csikszentmihalyi, M., Rathunde, K. & Whalen, S. (1993). *Talented teenagers: the roots of success and failure*. New York: Cambridge University Press.

Davis, G. A. & Rimm, S. B. (1985). *Education of the gifted and talented*. Englewood Cliffs, NJ: Prentice-Hall.

DeHaan, R. G. & Havighurst, R. J. (1957). *Educating gifted children*. Chicago, IL: University of Chicago Press.

DeHaan, R. G. & Kough, J. (1956). *Identifying students with special needs*. Chicago, IL: Science Research Associates.

Ericsson, A. (1996), *The road to excellence*. Mahwah, NJ: Erlbaum.

Feldhusen, J. F. (1982). Meeting the needs of gifted students through differentiated programming. *Gifted Child Quarterly*, **26** (1), 37–41.

Feldhusen, J. F. (1986a). A conception of giftedness. In: R. J. Sternberg & J. E. Davidson (Eds), *Conceptions of Giftedness* (pp. 112–127). New York: Cambridge University Press.

Feldhusen, J. F. (1986b). A new conception of giftedness and programming for the gifted. *Illinois Council for the Gifted Journal*, **5**, 2–6.

Feldhusen, J. F. (1989). Synthesis of research on gifted youth. *Educational Leadership*, **46** (6), 6–11.

Feldhusen, J. F. (1991). Identification of gifted and talented youth. In: M. C. Wang, M. C. Reynolds & H. J. Walberg (Eds), *Handbook of Special Education* (Vol. 2) (pp. 7–22). New York: Pergamon Press.

Feldhusen, J. F. (1995). *Talent identification and development in education (TIDE)*. Sarasota, FL: Center for Creative Learning.

Feldhusen, J. F. (1995). Talent as an alternative conception of giftedness. *Gifted Education International*, **11** (3), 4–7.

Feldhusen, J. F. (1998). Programs for the gifted few or talent development for the many. *Phi Delta Kappan*, **79** (10), 735–738.

Feldhusen, J. F. (1999). Talent identification and development in education: the basic tenets. In: S. Kline & K. T. Hegeman (Eds), *Gifted Education in the Twenty-First Century* (pp. 89–100). New York: Winslow Press.

Feldhusen, J. F. & Baska, L. K. (1989). Identification and assessment of the gifted. In: J. F. Feldhusen, J. VanTassel-Baska & K. Seeley (Eds), *Excellence in Educating the Gifted* (pp. 85–101). Denver, CO: Love Publishing.

Feldhusen, J. F. & Hoover, S. M. (1986). A conception of giftedness: intelligence, self-concept and motivation. *Roeper Review*, **8** (3), 140–143.

Feldhusen, J. F., Asher, J. W. & Hoover, S. M. (1984). Problems in identification of giftedness, talent, or ability. *Gifted Child Quarterly*, **28** (4), 149–151.

Feldhusen, J. F., Baska, L. K. & Womble, S. R. (1981). Using standard scores to synthesize data in identifying the gifted. *Journal for the Education of the Gifted*, **4**, 177–185.

Feldhusen, J. F., Hoover, S. M. & Sayler, M. F. (1997). *Identifying and educating gifted students at the secondary level*. Unionville, NY: Royal Fireworks Press.

Feldhusen, J. F., Jarwan, F. & Holt, D. (1993). Assessment tools for counselors. In: L. K. Silverman (Ed.), *Counseling the Gifted and Talented* (pp. 239–259). Denver: Love Publishing.

Frasier, (1994). *A manual for implementing the Frasier Talent Assessment profile*. Athens, GA: Georgia Southern Press.

Frasier, M. M. & Passow, A. H. (1994). *Toward a new paradign for identifying talent potential*. Storrs, CT: National Research Center/Gifted and Talented, Rm 94112.

Frasier, M. M., Garcia, J. H. & Passow, A. H. (1995). *A review of assessment issues in gifted education and their implications for identifying gifted minority students*. Storrs, CT: National Research Center/Gifted and Talented, No. Rm 95204.

Gagné, F. (1985). Giftedness and talent: re-examining a re-examination of the definitions. *Gifted Child Quarterly*, **29** (3), 103–112.

Gagné, F. (1993). Sex differences in the aptitudes and talents of children as judged by their peers and teachers. *Gifted Child Quarterly*, **37** (2), 69–77.

Gagné, F. (1995). From giftedness to talent: a developmental model and its impact on the language of the field. *Roeper Review*, **18** (2), 103–111.

Gagné, F. (1997). Critique of Morelock's definition of giftedness and talent. *Roeper Review*, **20** (2), 76–85.

Gagné, F. (1999). *Tracking talents: examiner's manual*. Waco, TX: Prufrock Press.

Gallagher, J. (1975). *Teaching the gifted child* (2nd ed.). Boston, MA: Allyn & Bacon.

Gallagher, J. J. (1988). National agenda for educating gifted students: statement of priorities. *Exceptional Children*, **55** (2), 107–114.

Gallagher, J. J. (1991). The gifted: a term with surplus meaning. *Journal for the Education of The Gifted*, **14** (4), 353–365.

Gallagher, J. J., Coleman, M. R. & Nelson, S. (1995). Perceptions of educational reform by educators representing middle schools, cooperative learning, and gifted education. *Gifted Child Quarterly*, **39** (2), 66–76.

Galton, F. (1869). *Hereditary genius*. London: Macmillan.

Gardner, H. (1991). *The unschooled mind*. New York: Basic Books.

Gardner, H. (1993). *Multiple intelligences: the theory into practice*. New York: Basic Books.

Gardner, H. (1993). *Multiple intelligences* (2nd ed.). New York: Basic Books.

Gardner, H., Walter, J. & Hatch, T. (1992). If teaching had looked beyond the classroom: The development and education of intelligence. *Innotech Journal*, **16** (1), 18–35.

Gold, M. J. (1980). Secondary level programs for the gifted and talented. In: H. J. Morgan, C. G. Tennant & J. Gold (Eds), *Elementary and Secondary Level Programs for the Gifted and Talented* (pp. 32–65). New York: Teachers College, Columbia University.

Guilford, J. P. (1967). *The nature of human intelligence*. New York: McGraw-Hill.

Guilford, J. P. & Fruchter, B. (1973). *Fundamental statistics in psychology and education* (5th ed.). Tokoyo, Japan: McGraw-Hill Kogakusha.

Hallahan, D. P. & Kauffman, J. M. (1982). *Exceptional children* (2nd ed.). Englewood Cliffs, NJ: Prentice-Hall.

Haroutounian, J. (1993). Identifying talent in the performing arts. *Spotlight*, **3** (2), 8–12.

Hills, J. R. (1971). Use of measurement in selection and placement. In: R. L. Thorndike (Ed.), *Educational Measurement* (2nd ed.) (pp. 680–732). Washington, DC: American Council on Education.

Hoge, R. D. (1988). Issues in the definition and measurement of the giftedness construct. *Educational Research*, **14** (1), 12–17.

Hoge, R. D. (1989). An examination of the giftedness construct. *Canadian Journal of Education*, **14** (1), 6–17.

Hoge, R. D. & Cudmore, L. (1986). The use of teacher-judgment measures in the identification of gifted pupils. *Teaching & Teachers Education*, **2** (2), 181–196.

Hollingworth, L. (1929). *Gifted children: their nature and nurture*. New York: Macmillan.

Horowitz, F. D. & O'Brien, M. (Eds) (1985). *The gifted and talented: developmental perspectives*. Washington, DC: The American Psychological Association.

Howe, M. J. A. & Sloboda, J. A. (1991). Early signs of talent and special interests in the lives of young musicians. *European Journal for High Ability*, **2**, 102–111.

Janos, P. M. & Robinson, N. M. (1985). Psychosocial development in intellectually gifted children. In: F. D. Horowitz & M. O'Brien (Eds), *The Gifted and Talented: Developmental Perspectives* (pp. 149–196). Hyattsville, MD: American Psychological Association.

Jarwan, F. A. & Asher, J. W. (1994). Evaluating selection systems in gifted education. In: J. B. Hansen & S. M. Hoover (Eds), *Talent Development: Theories and Practice* (pp. 47–65). Dubuque, IA: Kendall/Hunt.

Jenkins-Friedman, R., Richert, E. S. & Feldhusen, J. F. (Eds) (1991). *Special populations of gifted children*. New York: Trillium Press.

Kay, S. I. (1999). The talent profile as a curricular tool for academics, the arts, and athletics. In: S. Kline & K. T. Hegeman (Eds), *Gifted Education in the Twenty First Century* (pp. 47–59). New York: Winslow Press.

Kerr, B. (1997). Developing talents in girls and young women. In: N. Colangelo & G. A. Davis (Eds), *Handbook of Gifted Education* (2nd ed.) (pp. 483–497). Boston: Allyn and Bacon.

Kerr, B. A. & Colangelo, N. (1988). The college plans of academically talented students. *Journal of Counseling and Development*, **67**, 42–48.

Kirk, S. & Gallagher, J. (1983). *Educating exceptional children* (4th ed.). Boston, MA: Houghton Mifflin.

Lauer, J. M. & Asher, J. W. (1988). *Composition research: empirical design*. New York: Oxford University Press.

Lord, F. M. (1962). Cutting scores and errors of measurement. *Psychometricka*, **27**, 19–30.

Maker, C. J. (1989). Program for gifted minority students: a synthesis of perspectives. In: C. J. Maker & S. W. Schiever (Eds), *Critical Issues in Gifted Education* (Vol. II) (pp. 293–309). Austin, TX: Pro-Ed.

Maker, C. J. (1996). Identification of gifted minority students: a national problem, needed changes, and promising solutions. *Gifted Child Quarterly*, **40**, 41–50.

Marland, S. P. (1971). *Education of the gifted and talented*. Report to the Congress of the United States by the Commissioner of Education. Washington, DC: U.S. Government Printing Office.

McLeod, J. & Cropley, A. (1989). *Fostering academic success*. Oxford, England: Pergamon Press.

Mooij, T. (1992). Predicting (under)-achievement of gifted children. *European Journal for High Ability*, **3**, 59–74.

Passow, A. H. (1997). International perspective on gifted education. In: N. Colangelo & G. A. Davis (Eds), *Handbook of Gifted Education* (2nd ed.) (pp. 528–535). Boston: Allyn & Bacon.

Patton, J. M., Prillaman, D. & VanTassel-Baska, J. (1990). The nature and extent of programs for the disadvantaged gifted in the United States and territories. *Gifted Child Quarterly*, **34** (3), 94–96.

Piirto, J., 1994. *Talented children and adults*. New York: Merrill.

Plomin, R. (1990). *Nature and nurturance: an introduction to human behavioral genetics*. Pacific Grove, CA: Brooks/Cole.

Plomin, R. (1994). *Genetics and experience: the interplay between nature and nurture*. Oaks, CA: Sage Publications.

Plucker, J. A., Callahan, C. M. & Tomchin, E. M. (1996). Wherefore art thou, multiple intelligences? Alternative assessments for identifying talent in ethnically diverse and low income students. *Gifted Child Quarterly*, **40** (2), 81–92.

Renzulli, J. S. (1978). What makes giftedness? Re-examining a definition. *Phi Delta Kappan*, **60**, 180–184.

Renzulli, J. S. (1984). The triad/revolving door system: a research-based approach to identification and programming for the gifted and talented. *Gifted Child Quarterly*, **28** (4), 163–171.

Renzulli, J. S. (1986). A three-ring conception of giftedness: a developmental model for creative productivity. In: J. S. Renzulli & S. M. Reis (Eds), *The Triad Reader* (pp. 2–19). Mansfield Center, CT: Creative Learning Press.

Renzulli, J. S. (1998). A rising tide lifts all ships. *Phi Delta Kappan*, **80** (2), 104–111.

Renzulli, J. S., Smith, L. H., White, A. S., Callahan, C. M. & Hartman, R. K. (1997). *Scales for rating the behavioral characteristics of superior students*. Mansfield Center, CT: Creative Learning Press.

Reynolds, M. C. & Birch, J. W. (1977). *Teaching exceptional children in all America's schools*. Reston, VA: The Council for Exceptional Children.

Richert, E. S., Alvino, J. & McDonnel, R. (1982). *The national report on identification of gifted and talented youth*. Assessment and recommendations for comprehensive identification of gifted and talented youth. Sewell, NJ: Educational Improvement Center South.

Rimm, S. (1984). The characteristics approach: identification and beyond. *Gifted Child Quarterly*, **28** (4), 181–187.

Rimm, S. (1995). Impact of family patterns upon the development of giftedness. In: C. L. Hollinger (Eds), *Serving Gifted and Talented Students* (pp. 243–256). Austin, TX: Pro-Ed.

Seeley, K. R. (1989). Under-achieving and handicapped gifted. In: J. Feldhusen, J. VanTassel-Baska & Seeley, K. (Eds), *Excellence in Educating the Gifted* (pp. 29–37). Denver,CO: Love Publishing.

Spearman, C. (1927). *The abilities of man: their nature and measurement*. New York: Macmillan.

Stanley, J. C. (1979). Identifying and nurturing the intellectually gifted. In: W. C. George, S. J. Cohn & J. C. Stanley (Eds), *Educating the Gifted: Acceleration and Enrichment* (pp. 172–180). The Johns Hopkins University Press.

Stanley, J. C. & Benbow, C. P. (1983). SMPY's first decade: ten years of posing problems and solving them. *The Journal of Special Education*, **17** (1), 11–25.

Sternberg, R. J. (1985). *Intelligence applied*. New York: Harcourt Brace Jovanovich.

Sternberg, R. J. (1997). The concept of intelligence and its role in lifelong learning and success. *American Psychologist*, **52** (10), 1030–1037

Sternberg, R. J. & Davidson, J. E. (Eds) (1986). *Conceptions of giftedness*. New York: Cambridge University Press.

Tannenbaum, A. (1986). *The gifted movement forward or on a treadmill*. Indianapolis, IN: Indiana Department of Education, Office of Gifted & Talented Education.

Terman, L. M. (1916). *Measurement of intelligence: an explanation of and a complete guide for the use of the Stanford revision and extension of the Binet-Simon intelligence scale*. Boston: Houghton-Mifflin.

Terman, L. M. (1925). *Genetic studies of genius* (Vol. 1), *Mental and physical traits of a thousand gifted children*. Stanford, CA: Stanford University Press.

Terman, L. M. & Oden, M. H. (1959). *Genetic studies of genius* (Vol. V), *The gifted group at mid-life: thirty-five years' follow-up of the superior child*. Stanford, CA: Stanford University Press.

Thurstone, C. L. (1938). *The primary mental abilities*. Chicago, IL: University of Chicago Press.

Torrance, E. P. (1984). The role of creativity in identification of the gifted and talented. *Gifted Child Quarterly*, **28** (4), 153–156.

U.S. Office of Education (1993). *National excellence: a case for developing America's talent*. Washington, DC: U.S. Government Printing Office.

Udall, A. J. & Passe, M. (1993). Gardner-based performance-based assessment notebook. Charlotte, NC: Charlotte-Mecklenburg Schools.

VanTassel-Baska, J. (1989). The disadvantaged gifted. In: J. Feldhusen, J. VanTassel-Baska & K. Seeley (Eds), *Excellence in Educating the Gifted* (pp. 53–70). Denver, CO: Love Publishing.

VanTassel-Baska, J. (1998). Disadvantaged learners with talent. In: J. VanTassel-Baska (Ed.), *Gifted and Talented Learners* (pp. 95–114). Denver: Love Publishing.

vonArdenne, M. (1990). Facilitating the development of talents. *European Journal for High Ability*, **1**, 127–135.

Wachs, T. D. (1992). *Nature and nurturance*. Newbury Park, CA: Sage Publications.

Ward, V. S. (1983). *Gifted education: exploratory studies or theory and practice*. Monassah, VA: The Reading Tutorium.

Whitmore, J. R. (1980). *Giftedness, conflict, and under-achievement*. Boston, MA: Allyn & Bacon.

Whitmore, J. R. & Maker, C. J. (1985). *Intellectual giftedness in disabled persons*. Rockville, MD: Aspen Publishers.

Yewchuk, C. R. (1985). Gifted/learning disabled children. *Gifted Education International*, **3**, 122–126.

Young, C. (1988). Concerns and issues relating to the education of talented girls. *Gifted Education International*, **5** (3), 186–191.

Dynamic Assessment of Gifted Students

Lannie Kanevsky

Faculty of Education, Simon Fraser University, Burnaby, British Columbia, Canada

Introduction

Dynamic assessment is an interactive methodology designed to evaluate latent learning potential, i.e. a learner's ability to benefit from instruction (Sternberg, 1986). The dynamic aspects are evident in its format (pretest—teach/learn—post-test) and its commitment to nurturing and measuring change. It has been used extensively in work with students who are young, culturally different, disadvantaged, or learning disabled (Lidz, 1987, 1991; Haywood & Tzuriel, 1992; Hamers, Sijtsma & Ruijssenaars, 1993; Swanson, 1994), yet only recently entered into identification procedures and research in gifted education.

Traditional, 'static' intelligence tests have been found to underestimate the intellectual potential of culturally, linguistically, and socio-economically different children (Skuy, Kaniel & Tzuriel, 1988; Tellegen & Laros, 1993; Frasier & Passow, 1994). The individuals' test scores were reduced by gaps in knowledge rather than ability because they had not had equivalent opportunities to learn information derived from mainstream culture represented in the tests' items. This bias has contributed to the disproportionate representation of minority learner groups in educational programs requiring cut-offs on test scores: programs for developmentally delayed students and programs for gifted students. This situation stimulated a search for alternatives that more accurately assessed the dynamic *processes* that contribute to intellectual development rather than products based on experience.

Conceptions of giftedness or intelligence emphasizing potential (e.g. Tannenbaum, 1983) also create the need for "techniques which assess not only current manifest ability, but ascertain what the children concerned might be capable of" (Skuy et al., 1988, p. 91). The influences of socio-cultural theories of development bring with them a focus on the role of social interaction in the development of higher intellectual functions. Keeping in mind that the best predictor of any criterion is a sample of that performance (Anastasi & Urbina, 1997), it becomes essential to assess processes, like learning, that contribute to talent development.

Bolig and Day (1993) have summarized the ways in which dynamic assessments address concerns related to traditional intelligence tests:

(1) Dynamic assessment allows for the fact that children with identical competencies on static tests may profit differentially from instruction.

(2) Dynamic assessment provides information that could be used in the creation of intervention programs to facilitate the child's development.

(3) Dynamic assessment techniques were developed to overcome biases against minorities induced by traditional intelligence tests.

(4) Dynamic assessments focus on what children can learn (rather than what they do not know) and can be tailored to a child's unique personality and/or preferred learning styles.

(5) Dynamic assessments are domain specific indicators of learning ease, not general measures of ability (e.g. IQ tests) (p. 111–112).

The majority of dynamic assessment research involving high ability children has investigated its potential utility in identification of giftedness; other work has explored ability-related differences in the nature of learning. Following a brief description of dynamic assessment and its roots, these two lines of research will be examined. The chapter closes with a discussion of issues, trends, and recommendations.

Static and Dynamic Assessments

The broad view of psychological assessment is of a conceptual, flexible, problem-solving process for "understanding individuals for defined and useful purposes" (Tallent, 1992, p. ix). Tests can be part of the process, however they provide a restricted view of an individual's potential. Both static and dynamic measures are necessary when generating a diagnostic profile for a student (Vygotsky, 1978; Day, Englhardt, Maxwell & Bolig, 1997) and both can make valuable contributions to identification and education.

Traditional measures of intelligence are characterized as static, normative, and standardized (Haywood, Brown & Wingenfeld, 1990). They are considered static because they are designed "to assess

283

performance at some specific moment, with no attempt to change that performance" (p. 411); normative because a child's score is compared to that expected to be earned by an 'average' individual in the norm group; and standardized because standard procedures used to administer the tests and interpret the scores have been followed. Traditional intelligence tests can answer questions related to a child's relative strengths and weaknesses when compared to age or grade-level norms; a score reflects what an individual knows as a result of past experience.

In contrast, dynamic measures of learning potential involve supporting the child's efforts to perform the 'test' task. They are most "concerned with the different ways in which individuals who earned the same [static] score achieved that score" (Palinscar et al., 1991, p. 76). The assessor leaves the session with information regarding the amount and nature of improvement that took place, and the assistance needed for the child to perform the task independently (Brown & Ferrara, 1986). The many versions of dynamic assessment share a commitment to assessing learning-in-process by activating the complex relationship between teaching, learning, and assessment. Considering all three in unison provides a "prospective" view of children's potentials while they are learning from others, and that information can play a key role in multidimensional identification processes and educational planning.

Foundations of Dynamic Assessment

The modifiability of intelligence has been a recurring theme in psychology. Binet (1909), Dearborn (1921), and Henmon (1921) were a few of the early researchers who argued that intelligence was modifiable and that learning capacity ought to be considered a prime index of intelligence. Binet even developed activities he called 'mental orthopedics' to improve learning skills and test performance (Snow, 1990). This was followed by decades of attempts to explain and measure intelligence as a fixed or static, genetically-determined characteristic of an individual. Assessment technologies focused on the knowledge an individual had accumulated and could recall in response to the items on an intelligence test. Vygotsky (1978) was particularly frustrated by this orientation.

"Suppose I investigate two children upon entrance into school, both of whom are ten years old chronologically and eight years old in terms of mental development. Can I say that they are the same age mentally? Of course. What does this mean? It means that they can independently deal with tasks up to the degree of difficulty that has been standardized for the eight-year-old level. If I stop at this point, people would imagine that the subsequent course of mental development and of school learning for these children will be the same, because it depends on their intellect ... Now imagine that I do not

terminate my study at this point, but only begin it. These children seem to be capable of handling problems up to an eight-year-old's level, but not beyond that. Suppose that I show them various ways of dealing with the problem. Different experimenters might employ different modes of demonstration in different cases; some might run through an entire demonstration and ask the children to repeat it, others might initiate the solution and ask the child to finish it, or offer leading questions. In short, in some way or another I propose that the children solve the problem with my assistance. Under these circumstances it turns out that the first child can deal with problems up to a 12-year-old's level, the second up to a nine-year-old's. Now, are these children mentally the same?" (p. 85–86).

Most forms of dynamic assessment claim a connection to Vygotsky's work. Unfortunately, the Soviet political climate and Western psychometric orientation limited attention to his work until the 1970s. He proposed a construct, the zone of proximal development (ZPD; Vygotsky, 1978) to characterize the relationship between learning and development. A "ZPD is created by the interaction and is a function of the interaction" (Lidz, 1995, p. 148) in a teaching/learning context. It appears in the gap between the most difficult task a learner can complete independently (the actual level of development; ALD) and the most difficult task a learner can *learn* to perform independently with support (the level of proximal development). The broader the ZPD, the greater the learning potential.

The dynamism of learning in the ZPD is apparent in the nature of the social interaction between the learner and the tutor; learning is characterized by the child's 'progressive internalization' of the support offered by the tutor.

The process of internalization is gradual; first the adult or knowledgeable peer controls and guides the child's activity, but gradually the adult and the child come to share the problem-solving functions, with the child taking the initiative and the adult correcting and guiding when she falters. Finally, the adult cedes control to the child and functions primarily as a supportive and sympathetic audience (Brown & Ferrara, 1986, p. 281–282).

Throughout the intervening years, others insisted that any ecologically valid theory of individual differences in ability must reflect the fact that all learning occurs within the context of experience. Information-processing theories of intelligence began to distinguish more and less able individuals according to differences in their 'adaptive, goal-directed behavior' (e.g. Sternberg, 1985). Both of these pressures have brought us back to the orientations of the early 20th century with an emphasis on the role of adaptive interactions in context. Extensive descriptions of the history of efforts assess learning ability can be found in Grigorenko & Sternberg (1998) and Guthke & Wingenfeld (1992).

Research Employing Dynamic Assessment Methods

Dynamic assessment (DA) researchers have selected tasks and designed protocols based on the goals, theoretical orientation, and practical demands of their work (Bransford, Delclos, Vye, Burns & Hasselbring, 1987; Hamers & Sijtsma, 1993). Many have modified the administration of tasks drawn from intelligence tests like the Ravens Standard Progressive Matrices and the WISC, and recent work has expanded this repertoire to include curriculum-based activities (e.g. Zorman, 1997). The nature of the support offered to students has ranged widely from providing standardized concrete hints (Kanevsky, 1990, 1992, 1994a, 1994b), examples (Stanley, Siegel, Cooper & Marshall, 1995), or graduated prompts (Brown & Ferrara, 1986), to unstandardized mediation (Feuerstein, Rand & Hoffman, 1979) involving "familiarization of materials, instruction of rules and problem solving strategies, and extensive feedback" (Hamers & Sijtsma, 1993, p. 369).

The next three sections describe studies employing a variety of DAs according to their purpose: identification processes using DA, improving test performance with mediation, and assessing ability-related differences in the zone of proximal development. This summary is limited to studies involving high ability students, however extensive summaries of the work involving other groups abound (e.g. Missiuna & Samuels, 1988; Campione, 1989; Haywood et al., 1990; Grigorenko & Sternberg, 1998). The DA work on giftedness is extremely young and diverse; as a result, this chapter will focus on methods rather than findings.

Identification Processes Using Dynamic Assessment

Both projects outlined here employ a multitude of instruments and procedures to locate the 'hidden talents' of students who are currently under-represented in programs for gifted students. In Project Synergy, Borland & Wright (1994) embedded a DA task in a comprehensive, three phase, identification process. Participants were from a low achieving, inner city school where the student population is 75% African-American and 25% Hispanic; and economically disadvantaged. Rather than investigating the validity of any one element of the procedure, they wholistically examined the validity of the entire year-long process.

The goal of Phase I was to develop a candidate pool of 35 to 40 from the Kindergarten classes totaling approximately 100 students. Classroom observations, multicultural curriculum-based enrichment activities, standardized assessment, portfolio assessment, and teacher nominations were considered. An academic profile of each candidate was developed in Phase II; the DA task was administered along with a literature-based activity, standardized assessments of mathematics, reading and vocabulary, and an interview with the child.

For the DA task, Borland & Wright (1994) adapted matrix tasks like those in the Ravens Standard Progressive Matrices (RSPM; Raven, 1947) into a hands-on, interactive format for young children. One cell of each 2×2 matrix was empty so the child was to identify the correct block to complete the pattern.

> "Children who understand the task, apply an effective strategy, and solve many or most of the items correctly are allowed to complete the test without interruption. Children who do not solve most of the items correctly are questioned and given instruction to correct errors in strategy conception or execution. They then repeat the items missed. This continues until they experience success or it becomes clear that they are becoming frustrated and success is not forthcoming ... We record the number of correct responses, the number of spontaneous corrections, the number correct following instruction, the child's strategy, and any other behavior displayed" (p. 167).

In Phase III, all of the information was considered and each case categorized as: (a) no special needs yet detected; (b) equivocal evidence, reassess in the future; or (c) clear signs of potential giftedness. Students in the first two categories were recommended for placements in regular classrooms with continued monitoring. Students in the third category were recommended for participation in a summer transition program intended to prepare them for placement in a school for gifted students. Five students (5% of the original Kindergarten intake) were ultimately admitted to the special school.

Preliminary efforts to examine the validity of this process were undertaken with follow-up testing during Grades 1 and 2; the results are promising. The students moved from the bottom quarter to the top third of the population on standardized tests of reading and maths by the end of first grade. By the end of Grade 2, their Stanford–Binet scores had gone from the 1991 range of 68 to 109 to a range of 104 to 139; a second cohort was identified in 1991–2 and efforts to track all of these students are currently underway.

The Project Synergy identification process has many strengths including its multi-dimensionality and rich information base for educational planning. Its disadvantages include the time and expense of broad-based testing and analyzing the information collected for each case study; still, Project Synergy demonstrates these costs may be worth the investment.

The Eureka Project is a long-term approach to identification through enrichment. Data are collected before, during, and after classroom intervention; this test-teach-test design is consistent with the principles of DA. Other long-term procedures have been developed, however they lack baseline measures, distinguishing them as more performance-based than dynamic (e.g. Baldwin, 1994; Kay & Subotnik, 1994).

Eureka's two-phase process has spread from two schools in Tel-Aviv to 56 schools across Israel, serving students from a range of socio-economic and cultural backgrounds. The first phase (Exposure) involved DA in the visual arts and sciences, professional evaluation of portfolios (end of Grade 2) and task performance (end of Grade 2). The DAs of art and science potential employed a teacher rating tool for "specific aptitudes, interests and persistence in these talent areas" (p. 55). At the beginning of Grade 1 and the end of Grade 2, teachers used this instrument to evaluate the products and processes of students' work. It was the assess-learn-assess design that was considered dynamic, not the rating process. Once these data were collected at the end of Grade 2, each student's profile was examined for strengths and weaknesses. If a student was high in two of the three indicators in science or art, the student was encouraged to pursue special opportunities to develop that talent area in Phase II: Immersion. Non-identified students continued to participate in Exposure activities and assessments continued in order to find 'late bloomers'. In Immersion, the types of enrichment opportunities available varied depending upon school resources and students' needs.

Zorman (1997) provides preliminary and encouraging evidence of the reliability and validities (content, concurrent, and predictive) of the science and artistic potential instruments based on the performance of 34 science and 26 art students identified in the first two Tel Aviv schools. The project has also had positive effects on the overall school environment (e.g. art exhibits, science and art learning centers) and on the curriculum.

"Some of the teachers began to utilize items for the science and artistic potential instruments for observing students' behavior in their classroom in various subjects. For instance, some teachers observe and record students' process of developing hypotheses in the language arts, while other teachers observe student's motivation to cope with tasks and employ them in history and geography" (p. 60).

Both Project Synergy (described in Borland & Wright in this volume) and Eureka involve staff development to support the use of the new methods, raise teachers' sensitivity to indicators of latent potential, and encourage efforts to differentiate curriculum. These projects have operationalized the five elements in the identification paradigm proposed by Frasier & Passow (1994): new constructs of giftedness, absolute attributes and specific behaviors, cultural and con-

textual variability, more varied and authentic assessment and identification through learning opportunities. The preliminary indications of their validity, as well as these results, suggests a bright future for the contributions DA tasks, tools, and procedures may make to identification processes. In order to implement these approaches, schools will need to relinquish the common practice of one-shot assessment for a commitment to identification as a continuous process.

Improving Test Performance with Mediation

This group of studies focuses on change in unassisted test scores before and after instruction. The extent of the change was interpreted as the index of learning potential.

The first study to involve high IQ children was part of a series implementing three versions of the Learning Potential Tests (variants of the RSPM) to distinguish 'educationally retarded' children from developmentally delayed children who were more or less trainable (Badad & Budoff, 1974). All tests were administered in group settings; students were taught a pattern recognition strategy in the second session. Surprisingly, the 'subnormal' (mean IQ = 68) and 'average' (mean IQ = 85) groups made larger gains than the bright group (mean IQ 113); although the authors discounted the possibility of a ceiling effect, this possibility lingers.

Stanley et al. (1995) administered unmediated and mediated versions of the Peabody Picture Vocabulary Test (PPVT) to 39 students (19 gifted program participants from grades 2 to 9 and 20 regular Grade 4 students) to investigate the feasibility of their use in the identification of gifted students in rural settings. The PPVT assesses receptive vocabulary by asking the child to select one of four pictures that best illustrates each word's meaning. Two weeks after completing the PPVT without mediation, students were offered mediation with the words beyond their first session's top performance. This time the examiner repeated the word and used it in a sentence before the child selected a picture. No feedback or other instructional support was provided, making this the least instructive intervention of those offered in any of these studies; it could be argued that the limited nature of the mediation and the lack of a post-test mitigates its claims to being a DA study.

Not surprisingly, group means rose with the examples provided in the mediation; the gains reflected the same trends and concerns that were evident in Badad and Budoff's findings, i.e. the non-gifted group made greater gains. A ceiling effect was undeniable in this case as eight gifted and six non-gifted students achieved ceiling scores. The lack of a control group that had not received mediation on the second administration leaves potential practice effects unaddressed. The authors also used unmediated performance norms for the purposes of determining giftedness, e.g. "With mediation, 55% score as gifted" (p. 87); this is an untenable practice as the mediation invalidates the norms (Embretson, 1987).

The next group of investigations employ tasks from the most comprehensive and fully developed DA measures (Grigorenko & Sternberg, 1998), the Learning Potential Assessment Device (LPAD; Feuerstein, Rand, Haywood, Hoffman & Jensen, 1986). The LPAD operationalizes Feuerstein's theory of cognitive modifiability in a set of instruments and procedures designed to "(a) to assess potential rather than manifest ability, and (b) to decrease the gap between functioning and potential" (Skuy et al., 1988). They involve static pretests and post-tests with mediated learning experiences between the testing sessions; the mediation, or instructional support, has cognitive and metacognitive elements.

The major difference between Feuerstein's work and other DAs is that the instruction is not standardized in any way; students are offered direct, personalized instruction in principles and strategies involved in task performance. This feature and minimal evidence of validity have attracted the most criticism (see Frisby & Braden, 1992; Büchel & Scharnhorst, 1993). Guidelines for the individually administered version are much more extensive than those for group administration (Rand & Kaniel, 1987). In both formats, eliciting a learner's 'peak performance' is the goal of the assessment process.

Feuerstein, Rand, Jensen, Kaniel & Turiel (1987) state, "the only group of individuals who are not viewed as legitimate targets for DA are those, who by virtue of their high and efficient levels of functioning, do not require modification" (p. 43). Therefore the LPAD and its variants (see for example, Wallace & Adams, 1988) have been recommended and applied in efforts to locate potentially gifted students in groups from disadvantaged, low SES contexts (e.g. Rand & Kaniel, 1987; Skuy et al., 1988; Hickson & Skuy, 1990; Sibaya, Hlongwane & Makunga, 1996). Only the group version of LPAD has been used thus far in efforts to locate gifted students, and consequently, only quantitative performance scores have been analyzed. Without the qualitative analysis of examiner–learner interactions from individual administrations, this work cannot extend the validity of Feuerstein's theory of structural cognitive modifiability to include high functioning students.

The three tasks implemented in these studies were selected from the LPAD battery because they involve "abstract thinking and representational behavior" and "possess a relatively high degree of complexity." They are the Organizer, Set Variations (I & II) and the Verbal Analogies Test. Like the tasks in the two preceding studies, they are based on items common on static intelligence tests; the items in Set Variations I & II are elaborations of the items on the RSPM (see Fig. 1). The student chooses the correct answer from eight alternatives; the mediation involves problem-definition, focusing, rules for matrix problems, and sequencing. The Organizer asks the student to determine the possible location of objects based on incomplete information (Tzuriel, 1992; see Fig. 2); students need to analyze relationships, plan, and test hypotheses. This instrument is considered to have "a higher ceiling than other subtests" (Skuy et al., 1988, p. 96). In the Verbal Analogies Test (VAT), the examinee chooses one of six alternatives to complete standard verbal analogies ($A:B = C:?$).

LPAD studies have focused on the relationships between gain scores and traditional measures of cognitive ability, school performance, and temperament. Skuy has been the lead author on all three LPAD studies with high ability students from low SES and immigrant backgrounds and the LPAD. The first and largest (total $N = 1041$; 165 superior students; 867 classmates) was undertaken in Israel with 9–11 year-olds (Skuy et al., 1988).

Intact classes of students completed the RSPM, the MILTA (Ortar, 1966; an Israeli test of intellectual ability), and the three LPAD instruments.

"In this study, mediation was applied to the planning, learning and execution of particular strategies required for dealing with the tasks/tests presented. The 'tester-as-mediator' adopted a teaching stance and promoted a learning set in her students. She attempted to communicate to the students the value and significance of the tasks, and led a discussion on the principles underlying the task, and an exploration of their application beyond the immediate situation, to a broader range of tasks and situations. In addition, by being given encouragement and specific and realistically positive feedback regarding their performance, the subjects' sense of competence was addressed and fostered" (Skuy et al., 1988, p. 92).

Comparisons of pre- and post-LPAD scores indicate superior students made relatively greater average gains only on the Organizer, not the RSPM. Group means did not change on the VAT. Thus it appears that only the mediation for the Organiser was more effective for the superior students.

Two South African studies reported by Skuy and his colleagues (Skuy, Gaydon, Hoffenberg & Fridjhon, 1990a; Skuy, Hoffenberg, Visser & Fridjhon, 1990b) included a control group (no mediation). In Skuy, et al. (1990a), numerous measures of school performance, cognitive ability (traditional and LPAD), and temperament were assessed as potential predictors of the criterion, performance in the Soweto Gifted Child Program (SGCP), a weekly five-hour enrichment program for superior students. In the second study, they limited their investigation to the relationship of LPAD gain scores and cognitive ability to teacher-rated temperament scores (Skuy et al., 1990b). Both reports drew on the same sample of more than 90, 13 to 18

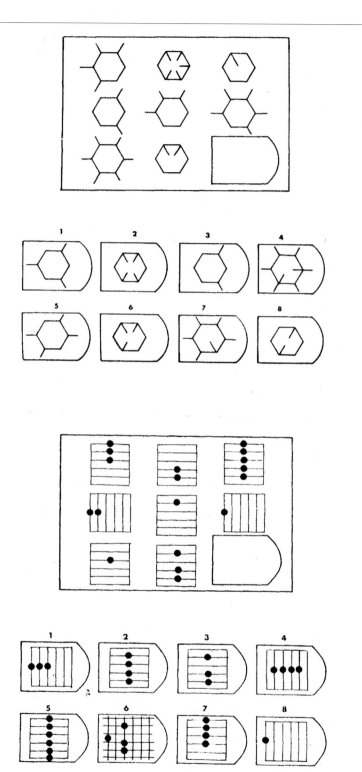

Figure 1. Example of Set Variations item from the LPAD. (Reprinted with permission)

Place the five children in their appropriate places.
A. In the three places to the left are Don, Mike, and Tammy (not necessarily in that order).
B. Mike and Allan are in the two outside places.
C. John is on the right of Don.

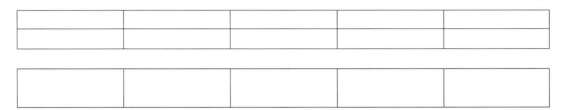

Figure 2. Sample item from The Organizer (Skuy, Kaniel & Tzuriel, 1988).

year-old black students from 'impoverished black ghettos' participating in the SGCP.

The four variables accounting for 50% of the variance in SGCP performance were the VAT learning task (31%), school performance (a further 10%), the Organizer post-test (6%), and the Similarities post-test (3%). All of these measures, even for a group considered to be disadvantaged, reflect the type of verbal skills which consistently contribute to the academic success of superior students.

It is interesting that no mediated/non-mediated group differences were found on the LPAD tasks. The authors suggest this may have been due to the inexperience of the mediators, however this finding raises other questions as well. Considering the lack of ability-related differences on the VAT reported in the first study, the specter of ceiling effects looms, as do questions about the appropriateness of the mediation. It may be that mediation based on a deficit-oriented theory of cognitive modifiability needs to be revised to promote the growth of high functioning disadvantaged students.

The results of the study of temperament (Skuy et al., 1990b) indicated students judged to be high on Task Orientation (persistence) were higher academic achievers and high scorers on the LPAD learning tasks and post-tests. Those higher on Personal-Social Flexibility (more flexible and adaptable) performed better on the Organizer and Set Variations I and II, and the Ravens post-test. There were no group differences for Reactivity (frustration tolerance). These findings suggest personality variables need to be considered as factors affecting students' learning potential.

Overall, the LPAD studies indicate the group administration of the Organizer has potential to screen 'disadvantaged' students for enriched learning opportunities. Perhaps one-to-one administrations in the future will enlighten efforts to revise the mediation offered in group administrations to enhance effectiveness when screening for potential giftedness. This work will also bring work with gifted students in line with the original intent of the LPAD; it "seeks to determine the type and intensity of interventions that have to be offered to the examinee to produce a realization of that potential for change that may become revealed with the LPAD" (Jensen & Feuerstein, 1987, p. 395).

The consistent appearance of ceiling effects in all of these studies is evidence that even the 'experts' underestimate the learning potential of bright children when designing their research. Future research must attend to this and should give serious consideration to the controversies surrounding the use of gain scores (see Cronbach & Furby, 1970; Embretson, 1987; and Glutting & McDermott, 1990).

Assessing Ability-Related Differences in the Zone of Proximal Development

Like the LPAD, the post-tests in the next group of studies require demonstrations of transfer. Students continue to receive assistance if needed. The focus here is on the amount and nature of the assistance students need to achieve mastery (independent performance on the learning and transfer tasks). This distinguishes it from the work in the preceding sections, which has focused on the amount of improvement achieved from pretest to post-test (Brown & Ferrara, 1986). In addition, the samples in these studies were from 'majority', middle class, English-speaking backgrounds. Although the majority of Brown and her colleagues' work has involved low functioning and disadvantaged students, only the work with high IQ children will be included here.

The theoretical orientation of Brown, Campione and their colleagues is explicitly Vygotskian and was stimulated by Brown's first visit to the Institute of Defectology (Moscow) in 1978 (Brown & Ferrara, 1985). Brown and her colleagues interpret the ability to use learning from the first task to reduce the need for assistance (number of hints) on transfer tasks as an index of the breadth of the ZPD. In a study involving children having a broad range of normal and high IQs (88–150), Ferrara, Brown & Campione (1986) reported evidence of the concurrent and predictive validity of graduated prompting procedures. In a graduated prompting procedure, the tutor provides the learner with a series of standardized supports. Examples of the tasks and hint procedures described below are from the Letter Series Completion task used in the validation study:

Original learning task: N G O H P I Q J _ _ _ _
Far Transfer task: U C T D S E R F _ _ _ _

". . . hints proceed from quite general or abstract hints to extremely explicit and concrete ones. The two initial prompts were general ones that redefined the task. The next five were more specific and pointed to the periodicity and relations among the letters. The following four hints were more concrete in that they involved colorful transparencies that made the relations and periodicity even more salient . . . The last four hints gave the answer to the child one letter at a time" (Ferrara, Brown & Campione, 1986, p. 1090–1091).

Concurrent validity was established by the significant relationship found among the amount of assistance needed (number of hints), IQ, and age. The amount of assistance required decreased with increasing IQ and age. These relationships were not perfect, indicating that although intelligence and this measure of learning potential were related, the measures are not redundant. Predictive validity was evident in the significant relationship between gain scores and IQ.

In other studies using standardized prompts, Brown and her colleagues found consistent IQ related differences in children's transfer propensity (potential to generalize their learning) (e.g. Campione, Brown, Ferrara, Jones & Steinberg, 1985). This relationship increases with greater transfer distance, i.e. children with higher IQs needed less assistance as the extent of differences between the learning and transfer tasks increased. Based on theirs and related work, they concluded that bright children have broader zones of proximal development, i.e. they learn more quickly and transfer more broadly. They explain that this is

". . . because they know more about learning in general and *supply for themselves* the information that is not afforded. They apportion effort appropriately, continually monitor progress, know when and how to seek advice, and so on . . . More capable students also prepare for transfer and engage in sophisticated reasoning aimed at accessing and using current knowledge. They prepare for transfer, for example, by regarding 'new' problems, not as isolated ones, but as instances of a general class (e.g. Scribner & Cole, 1973); they expect that what they learn may be relevant elsewhere and entertain hypotheses about where and when. Simply knowing that transfer is desirable from prior situations to the current one, or from the current one to future ones, is

itself part of the battle. Good learners perform thought experiments, seek appropriate analogies, and understand some of the principles involved in learning and reasoning from incomplete knowledge" (Campione & Brown, 1984, p. 286).

Kanevsky extended this work and its theoretical implications. She maintained the test-train-test-near transfer-far transfer procedure, yet differences were evident in the sampling strategy, the task, the hints and the addition of a qualitative analysis of the children's behavior. Her analyses explored differences in young (ages 4–8) children's problem solving related to chronological age, mental age, and IQ using an extremely high IQ comparison group (Kanevsky, 1990, 1992, 1994a). The mean IQs for the average ability students was 104 and 153 for the high. The high IQ preschoolers had been matched for mental age with the average ability Grade 2s.

Two versions of the Tower of Hanoi puzzle (hands-on and computer-based; see Fig. 3) were used because, according to Piaget (1976), young children would not be able to complete them independently. The goal of the 'game' was to move the three layers from one outside peg to the other outside peg, one layer at a time, in seven moves. The hints offered were concrete (direct instruction consisting of the best next move toward the goal) compared to Brown & Ferrara's (1986) more strategic support.

Like Brown & Ferrara (1986), analyses of the total number of hints used indicated that the high IQ children had broader ZPDs, as they learned more quickly and generalized their learning to a greater extent (Kanevsky, 1990). The high IQ and older children were also found to be more accurate in the moves they made, they were more independent, understood their mistakes better, and learned from them. 'Floor' and ceiling effects were apparent. The 'floor' was too high for 11 average IQ pre-schoolers who found the computer-based puzzle too difficult. A ceiling effect arose among the high IQ Grade 2s. Their erratic performance and comments indicated the task was too easy (Kanevsky, 1994). Neitze & Rohr-Sendlemeier (1992) also found that levels of performance and effort deteriorated when gifted adolescents were given an unchallenging, but age appropriate version of the Catell Culture Fair Test.

Kanevsky's (1992) qualitiative analysis documented ability-related differences in the interplay of children's goals, motivation, and metacognition. Some of the high-IQ children were intrinsically motivated to enhance their fun by monitoring and maintaining their own challenge level. They spontaneously elaborated on the basic task or connected the game with personal experiences. The average-IQ children appeared more extrinsically motivated by the researcher's interest in their success. Scruggs (1986) also observed this pursuit of complexity in his examination of the learning

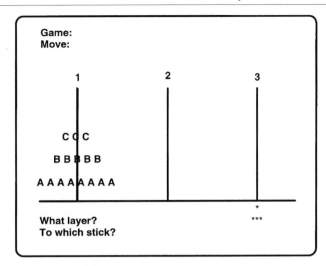

Figure 3. Screen display for the computer-based Tower of Hanoi (Kanevsky, 1990).

strategies employed by average and high ability seventh- and eighth-grade students. He reported: "The results were remarkable. These gifted students had transformed what appeared to be a rote learning task into a problem solving activity, in which the problem was: 'How can I learn these nonsense words most effectively?'" (p. 294).

Further evidence of their concern for efficiency was apparent when the high-IQ children spontaneously decided to pursue a quick, independent solution in the least number of moves (Kanevsky, 1992). A meta-cognitive interpretation of this group difference would be that while the OA child was asking herself, "What is any move I can make?" the high IQ child would be asking, "What is the *best* next move I can make?"

Ferrara et al. (1986) and Kanevsky (1994c) both found significant, but far from perfect correlations between IQ and hint totals, indicating static measures of general intellectual ability are related to the breadth of the ZPD, but are not perfect predictors. Thus, the ZPD and IQ provide related, but different views of learning. Additionally, the ZPD appears to be domain specific (Tissinck, Hamers & van Luit, 1993; Day et al., 1997) while most intelligence tests target more general cognitive abilities.

Issues, Trends and Recommendations

Psychometric Concerns

The desire for levels of standardization and objectivity expected of psychological tests (Hamers & Sijtsma, 1993; Anastasi & Urbina, 1997) are vigorously challenged by those, like Feuerstein, who argue for flexibility. Certain individually administered domain- or task-specific DAs using standardized prompts (e.g. Brown) have come closer to achieving these goals than group versions that rely on flexible interaction procedures (e.g. the group LPAD).

DA techniques have evolved to a point where researchers and advocates of each approach can no longer ignore calls for evidence of their reliability and validity (Embretson, 1992; Grigorenko & Sternberg, 1998). In clinical applications, it may be more appropriate to seek 'credibility' (as in qualitative research) rather than traditional forms of validity. Embretson (1987) and Sijtsma (1993a, 1993b) suggest DA research should move away from Classical Test Theory to Item Response Theory and latent trait modelling, because these techniques will more accurately test and reflect the complexity of interactive learning environments and the multidimensional nature of learning.

It seems every feature of DA has been criticized by psychometricians and often with good reason (e.g. Cronbach & Furby, 1970; Embretson, 1987, 1992; Sijtsma, 1993b; Guthke, Beckmann & Dobat, 1997; Grigorenko & Sternberg, 1998). Practitioners and researchers interested in measuring potential giftedness using this methodology would be wise to consult these sources to avoid the pitfalls of the research and development efforts that have preceded them.

Methodological concerns

Samples. Passow & Frasier (1996) pointed out, "A paradigm or model for identifying talent potential should have applicability to all students, not just the economically disadvantaged or the advantaged" (p. 200). All of the DA techniques here need to be tested with a broader spectrum of students. Eureka-style programs and the LPAD need to be applied to samples of 'advantaged' children, as well as ZPD studies of high functioning disadvantaged students.

Differential effects of interventions/mediation. Comparisons of the various interventions (e.g. Brown's graduated prompts vs. Feuerstein's mediated learning) with non-gifted students indicate that they differ in their effectiveness (Bransford et al., 1987; Jitendra & Kameenui, 1993). These studies should be extended to include gifted students so as to investigate potential interactions between the nature of the assistance (i.e. abstractness and complexity, feedback, metacognitive content, verbalization) and non-intellective variables (i.e. personality, creativity) (e.g. Carlson & Wiedl, 1992).

Task difficulty. To avoid the ceiling effects found in many of these studies, future research must raise or, if possible, remove the ceiling on task difficulty so the full breadth of the ZPD can be activated and explored.

Scoring and coding. Limiting analyses to pre-post changes in test scores ignores the potential of DAs to provide rich data regarding interactions among many variables: changes in the nature of children's knowledge and skill, their goals, interest, motivation, personality, etc. Reliable and valid coding systems can be developed to track these changes as well as those in the tutor/learner interaction. Clinicians and researchers are encouraged to consult Smagorinsky's (1995) discussion of the methodological challenges in assessing the ZPD, include subjectivity and purity of data, and identifying an appropriate unit of analysis.

Ecological validity is the extent to which the ability being assessed is authentically contextualized in 'actual working conditions' (Gardner, 1992). One approach to establishing the ecological validity of DA for school-based learning potential has been to assess learning potential and the differential influences of classroom instructional strategies (e.g. Campione & Brown, 1987; Palinscar et al., 1991; Kanevsky, 1994c; Jitendra & Kameenui, 1996).

Individual and group assessments. The test format must be appropriate to the purpose to be served by the results. In individual assessments, "A diagnostician has to concentrate on assessment using some qualitative criteria of the developmental stages of different functions, their interactive relationships, and individual profiles of processing capabilities" (Gajdamaschko, 1999, p. 90). This information can contribute to educational planning in ways that group test scores and gain scores cannot. In contrast, group dynamic testing can be useful in preliminary screening for enrichment (Rand & Kaniel, 1987).

Theoretical concerns

Vygotsky was "concerned about the development of processes that generalize across domains, processes

also referred to as meta-cognitive or executive, that express unique human characteristics of self-consciousness and permit self-regulation" (Lidz, 1995, p. 149). This concern for the shift from other- to self-regulation has not always been evident in the goals of instruction/mediation, data collected or its analysis. For example, gain scores may reflect change but show no concern for the interactions so essential to learning in the ZPD (Minick, 1987; Lidz, 1995) or the nature of the changes in learning or understanding.

Feuerstein has a theoretical and methodological commitment to overcoming cognitive deficits resulting from a lack of appropriate mediation. He has stated, "Children at a low functioning level in school can benefit most from mediated learning experience" (p. 206). It was never his intention to apply his theory of the LPAD with advantaged, high functioning, successful students. Inconsistent results found with the LPAD tasks raise doubts regarding the feasibility of extending his work beyond disadvantaged students. This suggests that DAs driven by Vygotsky's work, or other more inclusive, developmental theories may be more appropriate for work with gifted students.

Practical concerns

First and foremost, advocates must remember that DA is a methodology, not a complete identification procedure; it can act as one dimension of multi-dimensional identification procedure, as it does in Project Synergy and Eureka.

DAs have some practical obstacles to overcome. Individually administered tasks (pretest/baseline, teaching/learning, and posttest/transfer) are costly in terms of the time required to train examiners as well as the time required for administration and interpretation (Stanley, 1993; Borland & Wright, 1994). The range of tasks and materials available is limited and those that are available may have ceilings so low that they are ineffective with high functioning students. Developing a reliable, valid, standardized series of tasks, prompts, scoring and interpretation procedures is a monumental challenge.

On the other hand, the time, effort, and money may be the key to ensuring that the potentials of all students are fairly assessed. DAs can be designed to provide static *and* dynamic results, thereby reducing the need for separate static tests of domain knowledge. This is unlikely to happen, however, unless the demand increases for finding students with potential to become gifted in the future, in addition to those who are already outstanding.

Informal DA and instruction can be designed by teachers for particular skills, such as vocabulary building, summarizing (Paris & Jacombs, 1987), solving mathematical problems (Jitendra & Kameenui, 1996), and to suit the needs of particular communities. Bolig & Day (1993) suggest teachers can use it to "determine what a child has already learned (i.e. pretest performance), how easily the child learns (i.e. the number of hints needed, the number of explanations required, or the amount learned from an instructional session), and how readily the child transfers newly acquired knowledge or skills following complete instruction" (p. 112).

In addition to these benefits, Tzuriel (1992) points out that DAs can reduce the 'communication gap' that often exists between educators and psychologists when discussing the results of a student's assessment.

"Instead of talking with teachers about remote concepts that mainly concern psychologists (e.g. discrepancy between verbal and performance scales, the psychological meaning of figure drawings), I can talk about learning processes, behavior problems that might affect learning, mediational styles, strategies for effective change, and the educational philosophy that I believe should be adopted in dealing with learning problems" (p. 320).

Conclusion

Learning is complex and so is the problem of assessing it well; DA has only begun to contribute to understanding, identifying, and responding to extraordinary learning potential. Future research should pay closer attention to the basic methodological and psychometric lessons learned by earlier researchers with non-gifted samples. We also need to take advantage of more sophisticated technology and statistical procedures when appropriate, and to analyze the rich process data available in DAs; this is happening outside of the gifted literature. One example of the DA research benefiting from the power of computer technology is apparent in the work of Guthke, Beckman & Dobat (1997). They have developed a computer-administered, individualized, standardized, adaptive battery of learning tests. In terms of the potential for improved statistical techniques, one can refer to the work of Embretson (1987). Among others, she has recommended and applied Item Response Theory and latent trait analyses to examine the data derived from her research implementing DA methods.

The flexibility of the test – learn – test paradigm offers teachers, psychologists, and researchers enormous opportunities to address their shared concerns for fair assessment, a better understanding of the learning process, and its role in talent development. With this tool, we can strengthen the theoretical and practical foundations of gifted education.

References

Anastasi, A. & Urbina, S. (1997). *Psychological testing* (7th ed.). Upper Saddle River, NJ: Prentice Hall.

Babad, E. Y. & Budoff, M. (1974). Sensitivity and validity of learning-potential measurement in three levels of ability. *Journal of Educational Psychology*, **66** (3), 439–447.

Baldwin, A. Y. (1994). The Seven Plus story: developing hidden talent among students in socio-economically disadvantaged environments. *Gifted Child Quarterly*, **38** (2), 80–84.

Binet, A. (1909). *Les idées moderes sur les enfants*. Paris: Flammarion.

Bolig, E. E. & Day, J. D. (1993). Dynamic assessment and giftedness: the promise of assessing training responsiveness. *Roeper Review*, **16** (2), 110–113.

Borland, J. H. & Wright, L. (1994). Identifying young, potentially gifted, economically disadvantaged students. *Gifted Child Quarterly*, **38** (4), 164–171.

Bransford, J. D., Delclos, V. R., Vye, J. I., Burns, M. S. & Hasselbring, T. S. (1987). State of the art and future directions. In: C. S. Lidz (Ed.), *Dynamic Assessment: An Interactional Approach to Evaluating Learning Potential* (pp. 479–496). New York: Guilford Press.

Brown, A. L. & Ferrara, R. A. (1985). Diagnosing zones of proximal development. In: J. V. Wertsch (Ed.), *Culture Communication and Cognition* (pp. 273–305). New York: Cambridge University Press.

Büchel, F. P., Scharnhorst, U. (1993). The learning potential assessment device (LPAD): discussion of theoretical and methodological problems. In: J. H. M. Hamers, K. Sijtsma & A. J. J. M. Ruijssenaars (Eds), *Learning Potential Assessment: Theoretical, Methodological and Practical Issues* (pp. 83–116). Berwyn, PA: Swets & Zeitlinger.

Campione, J. C. (1989). Assisted assessment: a taxonomy of approaches and an outline of strengths and weaknesses. *Journal of Learning Disabilities*, **22** (3), 151–165.

Campione, J. C. & Brown, A. L. (1987). Linking dynamic assessment with school achievement. In: C. S. Lidz (Ed.), *Dynamic Assessment: An Interactional Approach to Evaluating Learning Potential* (pp. 82–115). New York: Guilford Press.

Campione, J. C. & Brown, A. L. (1984). Learning ability and transfer propensity as sources of individual difference in intelligence. In: P. H. Brooks, R. Sperber & C. McCauley (Eds), *Learning and Cognition in the Mentally Retarded* (pp. 265–293). Hillsdale, NJ: Erlbaum.

Campione, J. C., Brown, A. L., Ferrara, R. A., Jones, R. S. & Steinberg, E. (1985). Breakdowns in flexible use of information: intelligence-related differences in transfer following equivalent learning performance. *Intelligence*, **9**, 297–315.

Carlson, J. S. & Wiedl, K. H. (1992). Principles of dynamic assessment: the application of a specific model. *Learning and Individual Differences*, **4** (2), 153–166.

Cronbach, L. J. & Furby, L. (1970). How we should measure 'change'—or should we? *Psychological Bulletin*, **74** (1), 68–80.

Day, J. D., Englhardt, J. L., Maxwell, S. E. & Bolig, E. E. (1997). Comparison of static and dynamic assessment procedures and their relation to independent performance. *Journal of Educational Psychology*, **89** (2), 358–368.

Dearborn, W. G. (1921). Intelligence and its measurement: a symposium. *Journal of Educational Psychology*, **12**, 210–212.

Embretson, S. E. (1987). Toward development of a psychometric approach. In: C. S. Lidz (Ed.), *Dynamic Assessment:*

An Interactional Approach to Evaluating Learning Potential (pp. 141–170). New York: Guilford Press.

Embretson, S. E. (1992). Measuring and validating cognitive modifiability is an ability: a study in the spatial domain. *Journal of Educational Measurement*, **29**, 25–50.

Ferrara, R. A., Brown, A. L. & Campione, J. C. (1986). Children's learning and transfer of inductive reasoning rules: studies of proximal development. *Child Development*, **57**, 1087–1099.

Feuerstein, R., Rand, Y. & Hoffman, M. B. (1979). *The dynamic assessment of retarded performers: the Learning Potential Assessment Device: theory, instruments and techniques*. Baltimore: University Park Press.

Feuerstein, R., Rand, Y., Haywood, C., Hoffman, M. & Jensen, M. R. (1986). *Learning potential assessment device, Manual* (Jerusalem: Hadassah WIZO-Canada Research Institute.

Feuerstein, R., Rand, Y., Jensen, M. R., Kaniel, S. & Tzuriel, D. (1987). Prerequisites for assessment of learning potential: the LPAD model. In: C. S. Lidz (Ed.), *Dynamic Assessment: An Interactional Approach to Evaluating Learning Potential* (pp. 35–51). New York: Guilford Press.

Feuerstein, R., Rand, Y., Hoffman, M. B. & Miller, R. (1980). *Instrumental enrichment*. Baltimore, MD: University Park Press.

Frasier, M. M. & Passow, A. H. (1994). *Toward a new paradigm for identifying talent potential* (Research Monograph 94112). Storrs, CT: National Research Center on the Gifted and Talented.

Frisby, C. L. & Braden, J. P. (1992). Feuerstein's dynamic assessment approach: a semantic, logical, and empirical critique. *Journal of Special Education*, **26** (3), 281–301.

Gajdamaschko, N. (1999). Totalitarian societies: Ukraine. In: A. Y. Baldwin & W. Vialle (Eds), *The Many Faces of Giftedness: Lifting the Masks* (pp. 85–100). Belmont, CA: Wadsworth.

Gardner, H. (1992). Assessment in context: the alternative to standardized testing. in B. R. Gifford & M. C. O'Connor (Eds), *Alternative Views of Aptitude, Achievement, and Instruction*. Boston: Lummer.

Glutting, J. J. & McDermott, P. A. (1990). Principles and problems in learning potential. In: C. R. Reynolds & R. W. Kamphause (Eds), *Handbook of Psychological and Educational Assessment of Children* (pp. 296–347). New York: Guilford Press.

Grigorenko, E. L. & Sternberg, R. J. (1998). Dynamic testing. *Psychological Bulletin*, **124**, 75–111.

Guthke, J. & Wingenfeld, S. (1992). The learning test concept: origins, state of the art and trends. In: H. C. Haywood & D. Tzuriel (Eds), *Interactive Assessment* (pp. 64–93). New York: Springer.

Guthke, J., Beckmann, J. G. & Dobat, H. (1997). Dynamic testing—problems, uses, trends and evidence of validity. *Educational and Child Psychology*, **14** (4), 17–32.

Hamers, J. H. M. & Sijtsma, K. (1993). Learning potential assessment epilogue. In: J. H. M. Hamers, K. Sijtsma & A. J. J. M. Ruijssenaars (Eds), *Learning Potential Assessment: Theoretical, Methodological and Practical Issues* (pp. 365–376). Berwyn, PA: Swets & Zeitlinger.

Hamers, J. H. M., Sijtsma, K. & Ruijssenaars, A. J. J. M. (Eds) (1993). *Learning potential assessment: theoretical, methodological and practical issues*. Berwyn, PA: Swets & Zeitlinger.

Haywood, H. C., Brown, A. L. & Wingenfeld, S. (1990). Dynamic approaches to psycho-educational assessment. *School Psychology Review*, **19** (4), 411–422.

Haywood, H. C. & Tzuriel, D. (Eds) (1992). *Interactive assessment*. New York: Springer.

Henmon, V. A. C. (1921). Intelligence and its measurement: a symposium. *Journal of Educational Psychology*, **12**, 195–217.

Hickson, J. & Skuy, M. (1990). Creativity and cognitive modifiability of gifted disadvantaged pupils. *School Psychology International*, **11**, 295–301.

Jensen, M. R. & Feuerstein, R. (1987). The Learning Potential Assessment Device: from philosophy to practice. In: C. S. Lidz (Ed.), *Dynamic Assessment: An Interactional Approach to Evaluating Learning Potential* (pp. 379–402). New York: Guilford Press.

Jitendra, A. K. & Kameenui, E. J. (1993). Dynamic assessment as a compensatory assessment approach: A description and analysis. *Remedial and Special Education*, **14** (5), 6–18.

Jitendra, A., K. & Kameenui, E. J. (1996). Experts' and novices' error patterns in solving part–whole mathematical word problems. *Journal of Educational Research*, **90** (1), 42–51.

Kanevsky, L. S. (1990). Pursuing qualitative differences in the flexible use of a problem solving strategy by young children. *Journal for the Education of the Gifted*, **13**, 115–140.

Kanevsky, L. S. (1992). The learning game. In: P. Klein & A. J. Tannenbaum, *To be Young and Gifted* (pp. 204–241). Norwood, NJ: Ablex.

Kanevsky, L. S. (1994a). A comparative study of children's learning in the zone of proximal development. *European Journal of High Ability*, **5** (2), 163–175.

Kanevsky, L. S. (1994b). Exploring the implications of dynamic and static assessments for gifted education. *Exceptional Education Canada*, **4** (2), 77–98.

Kanevsky, L. S. (1994c). *Exploring ability-related differences in children's acquisition and application of pattern recognition strategies in text and numbers*. Paper presented at the Annual Meeting of the American Educational Research Association, New Orleans, LA.

Kanevsky, L. S. & Rapagna, S. O. (1990). Dynamic analysis of problem-solving by average and high ability children. *Canadian Journal of Special Education*, **6** (1), 15–30.

Kay, S. I & Subotnik, R. F. (1994). Talent beyond words: unveiling spatial, expressive, kinesthetic and musical talent in young children. *Gifted Child Quarterly*, **38** (2), 70–79.

Lidz, C. S. (Ed.) (1987). *Dynamic assessment: an interactional approach to evaluating learning potential*. New York: Guilford.

Lidz, C. S. (1991). *Practitioner's guide to dynamic assessment*. New York: Guilford Press.

Lidz, C. S. (1995). Dynamic assessment and the legacy of L. S. Vygotsky. *School Psychology International*, **16**, 143–153.

Minick, N. (1987). Implications of Vygotsky's theories for dynamic assessment. In: C. S. Lidz (Ed.), *Dynamic Assessment: An Interactional Approach to Evaluating Learning Potential* (pp. 116–140). New York: Guilford Press.

Missiuna, C. & Samuels, M. (1988). Dynamic assessment: review and critique. *Special Services in the Schools*, **5** (1/2), 1–22.

Neitzke, C. & Röhr-Sendlmeier, U. M. (1992). Achievement motivation of intellectually gifted students when confronted with challenging and unchallenging tasks. *European Journal for High Ability*, **3**, 197–205.

Ortar, G. R. (1966). *MILTA Intelligence Test*. Jerusalem: Hebrew University School of Education.

Palinscar, A. S., Brown, A. L. & Campione, J. C. (1991). In: H. L. Swanson (Ed.), *Handbook on the Assessment of Learning Disabilities: Theory, Research and Practice* (pp. 75–94). Austin, TX: Pro-Ed.

Paris, S. G., Jacombs, J. E. & Cross, D. R. (1987). Toward an individualistic psychology of exceptional children. In: J. D. Day & J. G. Borkowski (Eds), *Intelligence and Exceptionality: New Directions for Theory, Assessment and Instructional Practices* (pp. 215–248). Norwood, NJ: Ablex.

Passow, A. H. & Frasier, M. M. (1996). Toward improving identification of talent potential among minority and disadvantaged students. *Roeper Review*, **18** (3), 198–202.

Piaget, J. (1976). *The grasp of consciousness*. Cambridge, MA: Harvard University Press.

Rand, Y. & Kaniel, S. (1987). Group administration of the LPAD. In: C. S. Lidz (Ed.), *Dynamic Assessment: An Interactional Approach to Evaluating Learning Potential* (pp. 196–214). New York: Guilford Press.

Raven, J. C. (1947). *Raven Standard Progressive Matrices*. London: H. K. Lewis.

Sibaya, P. T., Hlongwane, M. & Makunga, N. (1996). Giftedness and intelligence assessment in a third world country: constraints and alternatives. *Gifted Education International*, **11**, 107–113.

Sijtsma, K. (1993a). Classical and modern test theory with an eye toward learning potential testing. In: J. H. M. Hamers, K. Sijtsma & A. J. J. M. Ruijssenaars (Eds), *Learning Potential Assessment: Theoretical, Methodological and Practical Issues* (pp. 117–133). Berwyn, PA: Swets & Zeitlinger.

Sijtsma, K. (1993b). Psychometric issues in learning potential assessment. In: J. H. M. Hamers, K. Sijtsma & A. J. J. M. Ruijssenaars (Eds), *Learning Potential Assessment: Theoretical, Methodological and Practical Issues* (p. 175). Berwyn, PA: Swets & Zeitlinger.

Skuy, M., Gaydon, V., Hoffenberg, S. & Fridjhon (1990a). Predictors of performance of disadvantaged adolescents in a gifted program. *Gifted Child Quarterly*, **34** (3), 97–100.

Skuy, M., Hoffenberg, S., Visser, L. & Fridjhon, P. (1990b). Temperament and the cognitive modifiability of academically superior black adolescents in South Africa. *International Journal of Disability, Development and Education*, **37** (1), 29–43.

Skuy, M., Kaniel, S. & Tzuriel, D. (1988). Dynamic assessment of intellectually superior Israeli children in a low socio-economic status community. *Gifted Education International*, **5**, 90–96.

Smagorinsky, P. (1995). The social construction of data: methodological problems of investigating learning in the zone of proximal development. *Review of Educational Research*, **65** (3), 191–212.

Snow, R. E. (1990). Progress and propaganda in learning assessment. *Contemporary Psychology*, **35**, 1134–1136.

Speece, D. L., Cooper, D. H. & Kibler, J. M. (1990). Dynamic assessment, individual differences and academic achievement. *Learning and Individual Differences*, **2** (1), 113–127.

Stanley, N. (1993). Gifted and the 'zone of proximal development'. *Gifted Education International*, **9**, 78–81.

Stanley, N., Siegel, J., Cooper, L. & Marshall, K. (1995). Identification of gifted with the Dynamic Assessment Procedure (DAP). *Gifted Education International*, **10**, 85–87.

Sternberg, R. J. (1986). The future of intelligence testing. *Educational Measurement, Issues and Practices*, **5** (5), 19–22.

Swanson, H. L. (1994). The role of working memory and dynamic assessment in the classification of children with learning disabilities. *Learning Disabilities Research & Practice*, **9** (4), 190–202.

Tannenbaum, A. J. (1983). *Gifted children*. New York: McMillan.

Tellegen, P. J. & Laros, J. A. (1993). The Snijders-Oomen non-verbal intelligence tests: general intelligence tests or tests for learning potential? In: J. H. M. Hamers, K. Sijtsma & A. J. J. M. Ruijssenaars, (Eds), *Learning Potential Assessment: Theoretical, Methodological and Practical Issues* (pp. 267–283). Berwyn, PA: Swets & Zeitlinger.

Tissink, J., Hamers, J. H. M. & van Luit, J. E. H. (1993). Learning potential tests with domain-general and domain-specific tasks. In: J. H. M. Hamers, K. Sijtsma & A. J. J. M. Ruijssenaars, (Eds) *Learning Potential Assessment: Theoretical, Methodological and Practical Issues* (pp. 243–266). Berwyn, PA: Swets & Zeitlinger.

Tzuriel, D. (1992). The dynamic assessment approach: a reply to Frisby and Braden. *Journal of Special Education*, **26** (3), 302–324.

Vygotsky, L. S. (1978). *Mind in society: the development of higher psychological processes*. Cambridge, MA: Harvard University Press.

Wallace, B. & Adams, H. B. (1988). Assessment and development of potential of high school pupils in the third world context of Kwa Zulu/Natal. *Gifted Education International*, **5**, 72–78.

Zorman, R. (1997). Eureka: the cross-cultural model for identifying hidden talent through enrichment. *Roeper Review*, **20** (1), 54–61.

Early Identification of High Ability

Christoph Perleth, Tanja Schatz and Franz J. Mönks

University of Rostock, Germany

Introduction

Approaches to Identifying Early Indicators of Giftedness

One of the first complex study designed to determine indicators of intellectual giftedness was carried out by Terman (1925) and his colleagues. The longitudinal investigation beginning in 1920 included 1528 school children having an IQ of 135 or above. Although one may criticize the Terman study for its lack of a control group, the selection procedure and other reasons (e.g. Rost, 1993), the researchers did determine—retrospectively—several differences between their more gifted and less gifted children. The more gifted children were able to walk about one month earlier and their language development began about 3.5 months earlier than the less gifted children. In addition, approximately 50% of the children studied could read before entering school. Parental interviews suggest that these children can be characterized by rapid comprehension, insatiable curiosity, familiarity with things, excellent memories, large vocabularies and an unusual interest in numerical relationships (Terman & Oden, 1947).

Following in the footsteps of Terman, giftedness researchers attempted to identify indicators which predict excellent performance in school or even in later life. In considering the promise of development, researchers have primarily worked on the following areas: sleep, habituation, memory, concentration or attention, information processing and accelerated development in individual areas, etc. Most of the research was done in a retrospective way, i.e. questionnaires with possible indicators were given to the parents of gifted children and youth asking about interesting aspects of the (early) development. On the basis of these, behavioral checklists (e.g. Stapf & Stapf, 1994) were then constructed for early identification of gifted or promising children.

When faced with the problem of identifying and fostering infant or early development of high ability today, it is apparent that the traditional approach of identification has become increasingly questionable.

Tannenbaum (1992), for example, compared different studies of child prodigies. He demonstrated that the hope placed in such children by researchers, teachers and/or parents was frequently misplaced.

This contribution will primarily emphasize a developmental or prospective perspective. It will to a considerably lower extent take a retrospective approach about the developmental relevancy of personality and environmental factors of infant prodigies as expertise researchers do (Perleth, 1997). Crook & Eliot (1980) showed that predictions of this sort are often faulty. A more fruitful approach is to prospectively examine indicators which can be used to predict the developmental course of gifted individuals.

When considering early identification of children with intellectual gifts and talents, one question should always be asked: Is it necessary to identify such children before school age, or as some research (e.g. habituation and sleep studies) indicates as early as infancy? Obviously, during the preschool years, the primary goal should be the guarantee of optimal child development. Decisions about the fostering of giftedness should be based on adequate diagnostic information about the status and prediction of personality development.

Models of High Ability

In this chapter, our understanding of high ability or giftedness are those capacities and competencies found in the infant and child which are relevant for learning processes. We, therefore, do not subsume constructs such as musical or psychomotor giftedness under the term high ability, but view this, as Campione, Brown & Ferrara (1982) expressed, as: "the ability to perform well in school-like and test-like situations" (p. 392). In the following, we will therefore only deal with a segment of that which makes up modern conceptions of giftedness (e.g. Gardner, 1983, 1995; Tannenbaum, 1986; Perleth & Heller, 1994; Perleth, 1997, 2000).

Traditional Psychometric Approaches

Traditional approaches to intelligence and giftedness continue to play the most important role in the research

297

about and fostering of gifted children. These include psychometric measures, especially intelligence tests, which are the most often employed instruments for identifying gifted children in research and everyday practice. The most widespread tests are, with very few exceptions, e.g. the German Rasch-scaled test for 'Adaptive Intelligence Diagnosis' by Kubinger and Wurst (2000), based on formulas of classical test theory (e.g. Lord & Novick, 1974).

Information Processing Approaches

In the framework of psychometric intelligence theories, primarily the relationship of various dimensions of intelligence as well as the concurrent and predictive validity of the tests is important. On the other hand, information processing or cognitive approaches aim at identifying and analyzing the components and processes which interact when cognitive tasks are solved (Waldmann & Weinert, 1990).

Frequently cited and reliable cognitive or information processing models of intelligence are those of Sternberg (e.g. 1985, 1993) and Campione & Brown (1978; see also Borkowski & Peck, 1986). Whereas Sternberg's model certainly initiated fruitful research in the area of giftedness, the Campione and Brown model seems useful for classifying some often cited early indicators of giftedness, despite the fact that this model was originally derived from research with retarded children.

In the Campione & Brown model (1978; see also Borkowski & Peck, 1986) the 'architectural' level, i.e. the 'hardware' of the cognitive apparatus, comprise a three-storage space memory model (sensory register, short-term memory STM, long-term memory LTM; for summary see Wessells, 1984). The characteristics of these entities, i.e. their capacity (number of entities that can be stored in the STM or LTM), duration, and efficiency, do not underlay developmental processes. Therefore, they are neither changeable nor trainable.

The speed of information processing and retrieval represents the operative efficiency of the system. While capacity and duration are—according to the authors—not related to intelligence, the efficiency is regarded by Campione et al. (1982) as a determinant of intelligent behavior. Other authors (e.g. Jensen, 1969; Neubauer & Knorr, 1998) put this speed of information processing in the center of their theoretical conceptions of intelligence. These and similar conceptions of intelligence refer directly to the unchangeable hardware properties of the cognitive apparatus.

The higher 'executive' system in Campione & Brown (1978) is made up of the following components: (a) The knowledge base in which the whole world knowledge of the child is organized and represented, whereby the knowledge can be regarded both as a symptom and as a determinant of extraordinary achievement. Further components represent (b) rules and strategies, and (c) metacognition/metamemory

(knowledge about strategies, knowledge about the task, knowledge about characteristics of one's own cognitive apparatus) and executive metacognitive control processes. The latter are used as metacognitive components in the regulation in memory tasks (see also Borkowski & Peck, 1986), processes of comprehension, or in problem solving. These components of the executive level which are considered, for example, to strongly influence memory performance, underlay 'dramatic development' processes (Campione & Brown, 1978, p. 284), and can also be improved by training measures.

Achievement Oriented Approaches

A third approach for investigating gifted children is represented by the expert-novice approach (Ericsson, 1996; Ackerman, 1992; see also Schneider, 1993, or Perleth, 1997, who summarize theories and research of acquisition of expertise). In this research paradigm, the special abilities or skills of young experts, prodigies, or precocious children are investigated. Fields of interest for research on the gifted are early reading/writing, mathematics, music and arts, and so on (see e.g. Burns, Collins & Paulsell, 1991; Lamb & Feldhusen, 1992; Winner & Martino, 1993; Davidson & Scripp, 1994; Baum, Owen & Oreck, 1996; Robinson, Abbott, Berninger & Busse, 1996; Snowden & Conway, 1996; Stainthorp & Hughes, 1998).

Methodologically, research using this approach compares young experts in a specific domain with average children who do not possess the skills under investigation, or to a lesser extent. One research question is to analyze what precocious children do when solving tasks, so that aspects of the cognitive component and the cognitive correlates approach are touched upon. The other question is whether intellectually precocious children will maintain their advantage in later school years so that these extraordinary skills can be used as early indicators of high ability (see Perleth, 2000). Because of the limited space of this chapter, however, we have to refer to other chapters in this volume which cover areas of infant and child expertise or precocity.

Identifying Young Gifted Using Psychometric Methods

Psychometric instruments for the assessment of high ability or rather intelligence are broadly used in research and practical attempts at identifying and nurturing gifted children. Nevertheless the psychometric approach in identifying the young gifted is crucial: We know from research with 'normal' samples that we cannot assume either high reliability of intelligence tests nor stability of measured traits in preschool children (see Sattler, 1988, for a comprehensive review). The following short descriptions of different tests focus on test properties which are most important for identification of gifted children: above all reliability, norms, and predictive validity. Especially with regard to the latter, we have to face the fact that nearly no longitudinal studies have been conducted which followed preschool and early elementary school children for a minimum of several years to analyze possible indicators and determinants of giftedness and achievement. The volume by Subotnik and Arnold (1994) on newer longitudinal studies of giftedness, for example, lists only three projects which investigated the development of giftedness in young children (younger than 8 or 9 years); one of these is limited to the musical domain, a second to the evaluation of a gifted program, and only the third one covered a broad area of giftedness factors and achievement areas (Perleth & Heller, 1994; see also Perleth, 1997, 2000).

Tests of 'General' Intelligence

Although newer conceptions of giftedness or intelligence more frequently make use of multidimensional models, the tests generally used in the identification of gifted children represent measures of general intelligence subsuming verbal, mathematical, figural, memory, and other tasks in one or few global scores. While such a procedure can be criticized when applied to youth and adolescents, it can be considered less problematic in young children because factor analytic research seems to show that the structure of intelligence become more differentiated with increasing age. Therefore, multidimensional tests such as the Cognitive Abilities Test series (Thorndike & Hagen, 1987) propose global intelligence scores for young children. In the following we provide an overview of the intelligence tests most frequently used with young gifted children including information available on their reliability and predictive validity in this population. See Sattler (1988) for a comprehensive critical overview of intelligence tests available in English-speaking countries.

Stanford-Binet Intelligence Scale

The Stanford-Binet Intelligence Scale: Fourth Edition (SB:FE) by Thorndike et al. (1986) is the current version of the Stanford-Binet intelligence test originally developed by Terman on the basis of Binet and Simon's scale. The SB:FE is the successor of the 1960 Standford-Binet: Form L-M (SB:L-M) for which new norms were published in 1973 by Thorndike. These 1973 norms were used for much of the research reported in this chapter. According to the very informative manual by Thorndike et al. (1986), the new SB:FE provides the examiner with an overall score for general intelligence which is composed of three dimensions measuring crystallized abilities, fluid abilities, and short-term memory. The crystallized abilities contain two scales for verbal and quantitative reasoning, while fluid abilities are made up of items of

abstract/visual reasoning. The test can be used with children from the age of 2 years.

Since Terman (1925) used the Stanford-Binet (SB) in his classical giftedness study, the SB is still very popular in the field of giftedness-research and practice, although the modern version has not too much in common with the SB Terman used. Many authors stress that the SB differentiates better in the extremely high range of intelligence. This additional advantage could be concluded from the fact that the norm tables provide values up to IQ 170 (e.g. Freeman, 1979). In our view, this is too optimistic for the following reasons. First, the standard deviation (s) of the SB is 16 so that in comparison with the 'normal' IQ-scale (mean: M = 100, s = 15) the SB provides slightly higher values. A SB-IQ of 130, for example, is equivalent to an IQ of 128 measured by a Wechsler test. Second, the standardization samples of both the SB:L-M and the SB:FE are much too small to calculate IQ scores above 130 (see below).

To judge the predictive validity of the SB for gifted children, the classical study by Terman & Oden (1959) is often cited. These authors discovered a good concordance between childhood and adult IQ scores. Interpreting this, however, you must take into account that Terman (1925) did not begin his study solely with young children but with 4–14 year olds (median between 9 and 10). Kangas & Bradway (1971) report for the preschoolers of the 1937 standardization sample of the SB correlations of r = 0.59 and r = 0.41 with SB-scores measured 25 (N = 109) and 38 years (N = 48) later.

Perleth, Lehwald & Browder (1993) report a number of studies in normal samples which showed that the prognostic validity of the SB between early childhood or preschool age at the one side and primary school age at the other is quite low (not higher than about r = 0.35). For samples of gifted children Robinson (1987) reported a retest correlation of r = 0.75 for preschoolers assessed at age 2 and 6 (N = 16), r = 0.59 between children of age 3 and 6 (N = 117), r = 0.61 between age 4 and 6 (N = 74), and r = 0.71 between age 5 and 6 (N = 25). Although Robinson (1987) judges these results as 'relatively low' (p. 162), they show in our opinion that intelligence as measured by the SB is a relatively stable trait even in the preschool age. Laurent, Swerdlik & Ryburn (1992) also give a positive judgement about the usefulness of the SB:F-E for diagnostic in gifted children.

Shapiro, Palmer, Antell, Bilker, Ross & Capute (1989) tried to predict WISC-R IQs measured at age 7.5 (a sample of 200 children containing 36 gifted) with developmental indicators assessed at 7–12 months and SB:L-M scores evaluated at 3 years. While the correlation between the SB-scores and the WISC-R were medium at least for the WISC-R full-scale, it was not possible to predict giftedness at age of 7.5 with the SB in a discriminant analysis. The results were not better for the other indicators in the study. The authors conclude that "the expectation for precocious infants to become precocious children, while appealing, is not supportable" (Shapiro et al., 1989, p. 209).

Sometimes short-form versions of the SB are used (e.g. McCallum & Karnes, 1990, for the SB:F-E). In some studies these forms turned out to perhaps be appropriate for screening purposes (see Perleth et al., 1993; McCallum & Karnes, 1990, found—on average—slightly higher results with the full form). In any case we would completely agree with Robinson (1992) who argues that the SB:L-M should not be used any longer in the identification of gifted children.

Wechsler Intelligence Scale

The Wechsler Preschool and Primary Scale of Intelligence—Revised (WPPSI-R) (Wechsler, 1989; the WPPSI was published in 1967) and the Wechsler Intelligence Scale for Children—Third Edition (WISC-III) (Wechsler, 1991) which suceeded the WISC-R (Wechsler, 1974) are the second most widely used intelligence tests in gifted children. The tests measure 'the aggregate or global capacity of the individual to act purposefully, to think rationally and to deal effectively with his environment' (Wechsler, 1958, p. 7). In consequence, the most frequently used indicators derived from the tests are the total score and the global scores for the verbal and performance scale. Although there have been some studies of the factor structure of the test (see Sattler, 1988, for a comprehensive overview; also Brown, Hwang, Baron & Yakimowski, 1991; Wilkinson, 1993; Masten, Morse & Wenglar, 1995), alternative scores or the profile are seldomly used for scientific or practical purposes. As in the Stanford-Binet, the Wechsler scales have been shown to be sufficiently reliable and valid for the assessment of general intelligence in gifted children (Kaufman, 1992; Kaplan, 1992; Bracken & McCallum, 1993; Spangler & Sabatino, 1995; Sparrow & Gurland, 1998).

A major problem in using the Wechsler test for studying gifted young children occurs when longitudinal research is planned. The WPPSI-R covers an age range from about 3 to 7 years while the WISC-III is constructed for 6 to 16;6 year-olds. As the WPPSI-R does not contain all subtests of the WISC-III and the two tests overlap only for the 12 month period between 6 and 7 years, it is problematic to switch between the two tests. Sattler (1988) questions the general interchangeability of both scales (referring to the WISC-R of course, the argument, however, can be extended to the WISC-III).

From their factor analytical findings, Schneider & Gervais (1991) conclude that the verbal and non-verbal part of the WPPSI-R should be considered separately (see also Wilkinson, 1993). According to Mark, Beal & Dumont (1998) a short form of the WISC-III can be used as a screening method for identifying gifted

children. Linville, Rust & Kim (1999) showed that even a single subscale of the WISC-III (picture completion) could be applied as such a screening tool.

Tests of Specific Abilities

Kaufman Assessment Battery for Children

The Kaufman Assessment Battery for Children (K-ABC) (Kaufman & Kaufman, 1983) can be used with children from 2;6 to 12;6. The four scales available give information on the sequential and simultaneous information processing, the child's factual knowledge and skills (so-called Achievement Scale), and non-verbal reasoning abilities (score composed of subtests from the sequential and simultaneous processing scales). The K-ABC was normed with 200 to 300 children for each age group. The reliability of the test is as sufficient as those for the SB or WPPSI/WISC-R, the validity with regard to the underlaying information processing model of intelligence seems unclear (see Sattler, 1988, for a critical review of the test).

Swanson, Brandenburg-Ayres & Wallace (1989) investigated the construct validity of the K-ABC in children from gifted classes (N = 169). They found a factor structure of the test which differs from the one reported for normal children in the manual. In the sample of Swanson et al. (1989) a hierarchical model was established by exploratory factor analysis. The model subsumized a verbal memory, non-verbal memory and non-verbal reasoning factor under a (weak) factor of general intelligence. Therefore, the usual K-ABC factor structure supporting the model of simultaneous and sequential processing was not confirmed for gifted children. From the methodological point of view, however, it has to be stated that the intercorrelations between the K-ABC subtests were very low (< 0.25). Analyzing the K-ABC subtests, Cameron, Ittenbach, McGrew, Harrison, Taylor, Hwang (1997) found support for Cattell's or Horn's distinction between fluid and crystallized ability.

With respect to the fairness of the K-ABC, Nolan, Watlington & Willson (1989) could not find indications of a systematic bias in the K-ABC items against gender and race in gifted and non-gifted children (using the standardization sample of the test). This confirms the results of McCallum, Karnes & Edwards (1984) who found hints that the K-ABC is more suited for the identification of minority children than the WISC-R or the SB. Meanwhile, however, a verification of the norms with respect to gifted children seems to be necessary.

Tests of Nonverbal Reasoning Abilities

The Progressive Matrices (Raven, Court & Raven, 1983, 1986) measure non-verbal reasoning abilities (inductive reasoning) without verbal, quantitative, or memory aspects. Therefore they are sometimes classified as tests for general intelligence in the sense of Spearman (Heller & Perleth, 2000). The Colored and

Standard Progressive Matrices are available for the purpose of assessing intelligence in gifted young children. They cover an age range from 5 to 11 and 6 to 17 years, respectively. The fact that there are no verbal items makes the tests attractive for the assessment of children from minority groups or risk groups (e.g. foreign children, children from underprivileged families and so on).

Peabody Picture Vocabulary Test

The Peabody Picture Vocabulary Test—Revised (Dunn & Dunn, 1981) or the British Picture Vocabulary Test (Dunn, Dunn, Wetton & Burley, 1997) is—in spite of its exclusively verbal character—sometimes used as a screening test for the selection of gifted children (see Hayes & Martin, 1986). Norms are available from 3 to 16 years. Sattler (1988) judges the reliability and validity as sufficient, warns, however, against the use of the PPVT-R as a "screening device for measuring intellectual level of functioning" (p. 350). Bracken, Prasse & McCallum (1984) give an overview of research available on the PPVT-R. The use of the test as a (screening) instrument for identifying gifted children, however, can be criticized from methodological point of view (e.g. Hayes & Martin, 1986; Tarnowski & Kelly, 1987) as well as because of the exclusively verbal character of the test.

Developmental Tests

As the intelligence scales described above are not available for very young infants, developmental scales such as the Bayley Scales of Infant Development (BSID-II, Bayley, 1993; original version published 1969) are sometimes used for the estimation of the cognitive level of gifted children. The Bayley Scales, from which an index for mental development can be derived, for example, can be applied from 1 months to $3\frac{1}{2}$ years of age. In this age, however, the course of development is inter- and intraindividually very unstable, and thus the use of these scales is questionable for the detection of early signs of giftedness.

Results of the prospective studies using developmental tests indicated, all in all, that developmental indicators of early infancy are not appropriate for prognosis of later intelligence or ability in gifted children (Perleth et al., 1993). The overview by McCall (1979) for normal children shows that higher correlations could be obtained with children older than 18 months because in the first month the developmental tests assess sensorimotor more than cognitive functioning (Sattler, 1988; Shapiro et al., 1989).

Comparison of Different Measures and Problems Related to the Psychometric Approach

Nearly all studies in gifted young children employ tests of cognitive functioning. The results of these tests are, on the one hand used as indicator of intelligence, high abilities, or giftedness itself. On the other hand, if an alternative definition of giftedness is used, intelligence or abilities tests are used as reference variables, e.g. to make the samples of different studies comparable. There are several problems to be regarded if the psychometric approach is used in giftedness research.

As mentioned above, many practitioners and researchers look for tests which provide them with differentiated norms in the upper extreme. Concerning the SB, the SB L-M is therefore sometimes preferred to the newer SB:FE because of better discrimination in gifted children (Kitano & DeLeon, 1988; Silverman & Kearney, 1992). A similar argument was, for example, expressed against the K-ABC by Roberson (1988, cited by Storfer, 1990). In our opinion, this seems to be an unrealistic expectation. The 1973 standardization of the SB was done on the basis of about 2,100 testees, the one of the SB:FE on the basis of about 5,000. This means that, on the average, the norms for each age group were computed on the basis of only 100 or 300 persons. In samples of that size, you find on the average 2 or 6 persons with an IQ higher than 2 standard deviations (s) from the mean (M), and you probably find no person with an IQ higher than M + 3s (i.e. SB-IQ > 148). To be sure that a sample contains 10 gifted persons with an IQ over M + 2s (SB-IQ > 132) you have to collect a representative sample of N = 438. In order to find a single person with an IQ higher than M + 3s (SB-IQ > 148), respectively M + 4s (SB-IQ > 164) on the basis of the deviation IQ you need a sample of 741 and 31,546 persons respectively. These examples show that it is not at all realistic to gain valid IQ-scores that are able to finely differentiate between persons with an IQ higher than M + 2s (SB-IQ > 132, Wechsler-IQ > 130). Thus, norm tables that provide you with such extreme values are constructed on the basis of random extrapolation and smoothing but not on the basis of empirical data of representative samples.

As a consequence, profile analysis with gifted children is in most cases very difficult or even impossible as these children may score beyond the ceiling of the subtests. Reynolds & Clark (1986) propose a procedure with the help of which the subtest scores can be restandardized intraindividually using the norms of older children or those from higher grades and thus making profile analysis possible. Prerequisite for this is that age or grade norms of the test are available and the reliabilities and the structure of the subtests across age or grade are the same.

There is a great deal of evidence that there has been a shift in the mean IQs of children and adults (Flynn, 1987; see also Storfer, 1990). There also was a shift in the IQs from the SB L-M of about 10 points from the 1960 to the 1973 norms (see e.g. Roedell et al., 1989). As can be read in the SB:FE manual (Thorndike et al., 1986), a sample of gifted individuals which was administered the SB L-M and the SB:FE scored 13.5 points higher on the 1973 SB L-M than on the 1986

SB:FE (similar results are reported by Robinson, Dale & Landesman, 1990; Kluever & Green, 1990; McCall et al., 1989). With respect to the other tests, the SB:FE manual contains information that children classified as gifted by their schools reached a mean composite IQ of 123.2. In comparison with the WISC-R full scale score, the SB composite score turned out to be slightly lower (1.4 points), while children scored even lower in the K-ABC composite score than in the SB:FE (4.7 points). As can be seen from Thorndike et al. (1986), the differences are smaller for samples of individuals with average ability.

Findings on mean differences between tests was confirmed for gifted by McCallum et al. (1984) who report that gifted children score lower on the K-ABC than on the WISC-R or the SB L-M. With respect to the PPVT, Knoff & Blednick (1986) found a difference of more than 10 points between the older PPVT and the newer PPVT-R, while in a study by Bondy et al. (1984) gifted children scored 8–20 IQ points higher in the Slosson test than in the McCarthy test.

Results of such studies are of major importance for giftedness practice and research as severe consequences for recruited samples of gifted children are related to the question of which test and which norms were used. If the IQ shift between the SB L-M and the SB:FE is 13 points in the upper extreme, a gifted sample gathered using IQ > 132 using the old SB L-M in 1985 does not contain the top 2% of the population but the best 10%.

Apart from the problem of the test norms, comparing samples recruited by different measures of intelligence requires 'comparable' instruments. The question of concurrent construct validity, however, is difficult to solve for gifted children. For average, heterogeneous samples, Thorndike et al. (1986) report high correlations between the SB:FE and the WISC-R (r = 0.83), the WPPSI (r = 0.80), as well as the K-ABC (r = 0.89) which is even higher than the correlation between the SB:FE and the SB L-M which is r = 0.81. Such correlations are necessarily lower with gifted samples because of the reduced variance in such samples (Perleth & Sierwald, 2000). McCallum et al. (1984), for example, report a correlation of r = 0.5 between the WISC-R and the K-ABC for gifted samples. For a sample of 82 gifted primary school students, Thorndike et al. (1986) found a correlation of only r = 0.26 between the SB L-M and the SB:FE which has to be explained by reduced variances and invalid IQ scores in the extreme upper range of the SB L-M. Comparing tests for identifying gifted children should also include a comparison which children are identified as gifted by the respective tests and which not. The results of Beal (1995) show that for example the WISC-III and the Otis-Lennon assign children to similar giftedness groups.

Modern approaches in constructing measures of cognitive functioning—apart from the further develop-

ment of traditional, well-accepted tests—can be described by at least three important trends. First, the results of the information processing approaches should be used in a stronger way to establish measures for components of intelligence. The K-ABC may be given as a first attempt for of this, other examples of genuine information processing character, however, have still to be developed (see Pyryt, 1996).

The second trend refers to the placing of training and transfer in the center of theories of intelligence. Using a pretest-treatment-posttest design, Guthke (1974, 1992) began in the sixties to develop so-called learning tests which assess the 'learning potential' of the child in the sense of Wygotsky's theory of zone of proximal development. Later, a similar test-teach-test approach was developed independently in the Anglo-American countries under labels such as dynamic assessment or learning potential assessment device (Feuerstein, 1980; see also Campione et al., 1982; Bolig & Day, 1993; Borland & Wright, 1994; Kirschenbaum, 1998). The ideas common to both the German and the American tradition is the assessment of the level a child can achieve given ideal teaching or the advancements that can be obtained through training. But up till the present time, no real usable tests of this kind are available (see Pyryt, 1996).

A third trend is the development of adaptive or tailored tests. If tests of this kind are given to children, the children work only on these items that are best suited to measuring their ability. This means that gifted children only complete rather difficult items. This normally necessitates computer-aided testing. With the help of probabilistic test theory, ability parameters for each child are available and comparable, even if completely different subsets of items are administered to every child (e.g. Embretson, 1985; Embretson & Hershberger, 1999). For German-speaking countries, Kubinger & Wurst (2000; see also Kubinger, 1998) presented an paper-pencil-test for adaptive intelligence diagnosis. Following a concept similar to the WISC-R, this AID II enables the measurement of intelligence in gifted primary school children with good precision.

With regard to the question of the extent to which later (superior) performance can be predicted on the basis of tests administered during preschool and early school years, we have to state that no precise answer can be given based on the presently available (or rather lack of) empirical evidence. There are far too few prospective studies or at least combined longitudinal-cross sectional studies which could provide practitioners and researchers with respective data.

In general, the abilities measured by intelligence tests are quite unstable in preschoolers. While Sattler (1988) found a correlation of r = 0.5 from 7 to 8 years of age with youth and adult intelligence and achievements, the same author states: "The older the child is when first tested and the shorter the interval is between tests, the greater the constancy of the IQ" (p. 73). Thus,

IQ scores measured prior to 5 years of age must be interpreted cautiously. Fluctuations of as much as 20 IQ points are possible, even if the oscillation of the IQ for the majority of children is lower after age 5 (Sattler, 1988; Cahan & Gejman, 1993, report quite stable IQ-scores for primary school children; similar Perleth & Sierwald, 2000). The same holds true for the relationship between intelligence and achievement (which can be moderated, for example, by external factors).

In view of this state of the art, further evaluation of relatively well-known tests in samples of gifted children are preferable to the construction of new instruments for identifying young gifted children. On the other hand it should be stated that the situation is totally different for older students. Perleth (1997, 2000) for example found for the German CAT high stabilities of intelligence scores over 2 years in samples of over average and gifted students. The intelligence measures also showed satisfactory prognostic validity with school completion grades over up to 8 years.

Nevertheless, practitioners and researchers should be sceptical of too much optimism about the possibility of predicting high ability and high achievement from early age. According to Howe's (1990; see also Ericsson, 1996) critical summary prognoses must be made with extreme caution. This holds even more true as most of the research was done with older children or youth. Also considering the results from the Terman study, Howe (1990) concludes that "such tests are especially ineffective at making predictions that concern the achievements of individuals who are highly able" (p. 202).

Information Processing of the Young Gifted

The subsequent section follows the outlined information processing model of intelligence presented above. Since parameters of information processing in newborn and infants are measured primarily in habituation studies, we have included a subsection on this. We have also included a section on sleeping behavior under the topic architectural level as this is frequently reported as an important early indicator of giftedness, especially in German-speaking countries. Possible links of sleep parameters to giftedness have to be on this 'hardware' level. With concern to the higher order components, we summarize knowledge base and strategies as declarative and procedural knowledge on the one hand and strategy use, metacognition, and executive control on the other hand.

Architectural Level

Attention and Habituation
As infant intelligent tests have little predictive validity, researchers have turned to other areas promising better results. Indeed it would seem that cognitive functioning makes great developmental leaps during the first two years of life. In habituation studies, a (generally visual) stimulus is repeatedly presented until the subject ceases to attend to it. Typically, infants placed in otherwise homogenous environments will orient and attend to a novel stimulus. This attention will diminish if the stimulus is presented continuously or repeatedly. Bornstein (1988, 1989) explains habituation using a two-component process: The infant develops a mental image of the stimulus and continually compares the mental image to the stimulus presented. A representational match will not hold the baby's attention, but mismatches maintain it. Abroms (1982) reported that high newborn cry counts, rapidity of visual habituation, and other parameters of early attention and information processing might precede advanced cognitive development.

From our point of view, it is important that habituation studies have linked intelligence or cognitive functioning to early habituation results. Lewis & Brooks-Gunn (1981) view habituation to redundant information and recovery when stimulus is changed as perceptual-cognitive ability or information processing. These are abilities which can be examined even in very young infants. The developmental theory upon which their research is based assumes that different skills develop at different ages and 'those central to a specific age group are most likely to be predictive of the next major skill, even though the next skill might be quite different from the preceding one' (Lewis & Brooks-Gunn, 1981, p. 132).

To put it briefly, cognitive ability is a transformation of skills from one age level to another. The research of Lewis & Brooks-Gunn (1981) did, in fact, provide a better prediction of intellectual functioning at 24 months (Bayley scores) from 3-month habituation/recovery than 3-month (Bayley scales) global intelligence or object permanence scores. Their research results are also supported by Bornstein & Sigman (1986), who showed that attention focussing at six months may be used as a predictor of subject's IQs between two and eight years of age, and Rose & Wallace (1985), Fagan & McGrath (1981), and Fagan and Singer (1983) also discovered a relationship between preference for novel stimuli and mental abilities. Bornstein & Sigman (1986) explain the early habituation and the later intelligence as both reflecting effectiveness in encoding information. Thus, more intelligent infants encode everything of interest or perhaps they more quickly match it to their mental representation. Lécuyer (1989), however, judges these correlations as less substantial and argues that—amongst other methodological problems—the '0.05 syndrome' (p. 149) might have suppressed the publication of lower correlations or studies in which no relationships between habituation and later cognitive indicators were found.

Of course, as Tannenbaum (1992), points out, neither habituation nor response to novelty actually requires reasoning or logic, but rather are viewed as being measures of efficiency in information processing. That is, they are a means of predicting later intellectual functioning without explaining the relationship between habituation and IQ. But all in all the amount data is rather small with respect to young gifted children.

Memory Capacity and Durability

Although it has often been shown that gifted children's memory performance is better than that of average children (Abroms, 1982), these results are generally not interpreted as meaning higher memory capacity or memory durability in gifted children. Memory capacity here means the number of 'slots' of the working and long-term memory rather than measures of the memory span where the number of recalled words or numbers can be increased, for example, by using appropriate strategies. On the contrary, there is much evidence that there are hardly differences in the capacity and durability of the short-term or working memory as well as the long-term memory of children and adults of different level of giftedness and of different ages (Howe, 1990).

All differences in memory performance reported in the literature have to be attributed to differences in speed of information processing (memory or cognitive efficiency) or in higher order components as knowledge, metamemory, and executive control which lead to a more efficient use of the limited capacities of the short-term memory (see e.g. the surveys of Campione et al., 1982; Jackson & Butterfield, 1986; Borkowski & Peck, 1986; Brewer, 1987; Torgesen, Kistner & Morgan, 1987). In addition, Schneider & Pressley (1997) argue that intraindividual development changes in memory performance cannot be linked either to changes in capacity or to speed of information processing.

Memory Efficiency

Although Schneider & Pressley (1997) deny a causal relationship between intraindividual development of memory performance and speed of information processing, the efficiency of the memory system is considered to be the main cause on the architectural level of interindividual differences in the achievement of gifted, average, and retarded children (see literature cited in the last paragraph). Memory or cognitive efficiency refers primarily to the speed of information processing. This includes properties of the sensory system and the short-term memory and, in consequence, the speed of registering, identifying, and analyzing incoming information, the speed of storing new information in long-term memory as well as the speed of retrieving information from memory, the speed with which information in the working memory is processed etc. All in all, cognitive efficiency enables one to make better use of the limited capacities of the

working memory. Memory efficiency increases as cognitive processes become more and more automatic: Automation frees capacity of the working memory and at the same time attention for more complex problems. Thus, the superiority of gifted children may be attributed to higher cognitive efficiency, i.e. to a higher basic speed of information processing and a higher level of automation.

While aspects of attention, memory, and cognitive efficiency are regularly included in checklists for the early identification of gifted children, there is not much empirical evidence for the concurrent and predictive validity of these indicators in young children. In our opinion this is a consequence of the methods employed. Information processing in infants up to one year is measured using the habituation paradigm (see above; for a methodological discussion see Daehler & Greco, 1985) while recognition tasks, reaction time tasks and so on have normally been applied in children older than nine or ten years. Thus, there are few studies with children under eight or nine years of age investigating cognitive efficiency in gifted children. On the other hand, there are many more studies dealing with retarded or learning disabled children. Possible relations between cognitive efficiency and later achievements were demonstrated, for example, by Jackson & Myers (1982) who could show for 37- to 66-month-old preschoolers that rapid letter naming and backward digit span was a predictor of reading skills six months later while no relationship could be found between measures of IQ (e.g. Stanford-Binet, WPPSI-subscores).

There is some evidence that memory efficiency concerning retrieval processes cannot be associated uniquely with differences in the basic speed of information processing (Brewer, 1987). The superiority of the gifted in cognitive efficiency may be also caused by enhanced attention processes, a superior organization of the knowledge base, more effective strategies, a better motivational structure, longer and more intensive practice, or the complex interaction of all these and other components.

Sleep

Occasionally, descriptions of young gifted children include the idea that the gifted child sleeps less than other children and/or has sleep problems (see Freeman, 1979; also Louis & Lewis, 1992). Frequently, behavioral checklists, especially ones for the hand of parents and teachers, include an item such as the following from Geuss & Urban (1982): Needs comparatively little sleep and this irregularly (p. 94, checklist for early identification of giftedness). This continues to be reported by parents, practitioners, and is reflected to a certain extent in the literature. As a consequence of this reduced need of sleep and irregular sleeping times of gifted newborns and infants—according to respective literature—the parents of the gifted may be under considerable strain (e.g. Webb, Meckstroth & Tolan, 1985; Stapf & Stapf, 1988; Heinbokel, 1996).

The empirical evidence for these indicators is rather poor. Despart (1949, cited along with Busby & Pivik, 1983), for example, reported shorter sleep periods of the gifted but did not present any statistical or polygraphical evidence for this statement. On the contrary, Terman (1925) stated that his sample of gifted children (age 7 to 14) slept even longer than normal children. In accordance with this result, Freeman (1979) reports that in her study no differences were found concerning sleep behavior and sleep problems between gifted controls and non-gifted control children. Only the parents of the children of the so-called 'target group' which consisted of gifted children whose parents were members of the English National Association for Gifted Children reported a lower amount of sleep and more sleeping problems for their children. In a similar way, the sample of Stapf & Stapf (1988), who also report a low sleep need for young gifted children, was collected in a counseling center. Browder (1993), on the other hand, could not find a difference in the sleep length between gifted and average children, using reports of the parents who did not know that their children were gifted.

Freeman (1983) suggests that sleep problems tend to be more an indication of parental attitudes: The parents of the gifted children tend to be middle class, and at the same time expect their children to sleep more than working class parents. Thus they put their children to bed earlier. "Quantity of sleep depends on what parents expect and on the children's psychological adjustment" (Freeman, 1983, p. 30) and, therefore, in her opinion sleep cannot be regarded to be an indicator of giftedness.

This view is confirmed by a look at the general sleeping behavior of infants and toddlers. As Wolke (1993) points out, the variance of sleeping behavior is intra- and interindividually, as well as interculturally, extremely high. Twenty to 38% of all parents, for example, consider night-waking a mild or serious problem for their families' life; about 6–10% of all toddlers wake more than twice per night.

A major problem in the research on the sleeping behavior of gifted infants is the retrospective way in which the indicators were collected. To our knowledge, there are no prospective studies investigating the relationship between sleeping behavior of newborn or young infants which turned out to be gifted in later childhood or in primary school. On the other hand, there are some longitudinal studies on representative samples or on children at risk which can provide some information about the correlation between sleep behavior and intelligence and other indicators of cognitive capacity in school time. Pollock (1992), for example, reports that the British Birth Survey (17,196 children) "has failed to show any association" (p. 165) between sleeping behavior at early infancy and intellectual

abilities at age ten, only a slight superiority of the children with sleeping problems in a vocabulary test at age five and a reading test at age ten was found.

Researchers who compared not sleeping behavior but sleep patterns and sleep variables of mentally retarded and normal children were a little more successful. From such research it seems to be obvious that the REM latencies are longer, the REM sleep is shorter, and the eye movement density during REM sleep is less in the mentally retarded (Busby & Pivik, 1983; Grubar, 1985). Studying normal children alone, however, Borrow, Adam, Chapman, Idzekowski & Oswald (1980) could not find any association between these parameters and intellectual ability. In general, however, the reliability and validity of such research is critical as the recording of physiological functions is stressful and often unacceptable in infants and young children so that their ecological validity has to be questioned (Wolke, 1993). In consequence, sleep studies with gifted children under the age of eight years are, to our knowledge, not available.

All in all, the evidence from the sleep studies of Busby & Pivik (1983) and Grubar (1985) is small, contradictory and drawn from samples of older children. Considerably more efforts have to be undertaken to clarify the sleep characteristics of gifted infants or children. At the present state of research, sleep variables cannot be taken as early indicators of giftedness, even if Grubar (1985) hopes that the measurement of sleep variables may enable a new way of assessment of intellectual potential. In consequence, corresponding items in checklists reflect myths or more or less subjective impressions of the staff in counseling centers rather than empirical findings.

Higher Order Components
Knowledge Base and Strategies

The knowledge base is frequently regarded as an important component of giftedness (e.g. Chi, 1984). Muir-Broaddus & Bjorklund (1990) see differences between gifted and average children not so much in the use of strategies or executive processes but in non-strategic aspects, above all the knowledge base (also Harnishfeger & Bjorklund, 1990). The authors report that their research results show that 'typicalness' evaluation of concepts with regard to their categories of more intelligent 10 to 14-year-old children are similar to those of adults. In comparison with average children, this adult-like knowledge base can be observed primarily in the reproduction time of words of different categories, while no differences between giftedness groups could be found concerning words of the same category. On the other hand, with regard to clustering behavior, Muir-Broaddus & Bjorklund (1990) found no significant differences between the groups, whereby a trend in favor of the average students had to be reported. Hasselhorn (1996) concludes on the basis of a series of well designed studies that during primary school time there is a substantial change from non-strategic, knowledge base driven 'clustering' to intentional strategic behavior. This might indicate that cognitively advanced children use more strategies but respective studies are rare, last but not least because studies investigating strategies, knowledge and metacognition (see next section) in young children are very critical from the methodological point of view (Schneider & Sodian, 1988). Meanwhile Bjorklund and coworkers also reported a strategic superiority—at least partly—of gifted children (e.g. Gaultney, Bjorklund & Goldstein, 1996).

Bjorklund & Schneider (1996) gave an overview of the research investigating the connections between intellectual ability, knowledge base, strategic behavior and memory achievement. The authors stress that measures of intelligence include aspects of metacognition and processing speed, both of which also exert an influence on memory and learning. So a large, elaborated and well structured knowledge base can be considered as a core function of all (intellectual) achievements even if one does not follow the extreme position of Ericsson (1996; see above). Concerning aspects of the knowledge base in (young) gifted children, still too few studies are available. McFarland & Wiebe (1987) already stated that "there is a certain irony here: the complexity and methodological sophistication used to study mentally retarded children clearly surpasses that used to study cognitively superior children" (p. 109).

Strategy Use, Metacognition and Executive Control

In the tradition of Flavell & Wellman (Flavell, 1971; Flavell & Wellman, 1977; Flavell, 1978, 1984), we use the term metamemory or metacognition, on the one hand, to refer to the knowledge about the capacity/ efficiency and about the function of one's memory or the whole cognitive set-up. Seen from an alternative theoretical point of view (e.g. Brown, 1978, 1984), metacognition means the cognitive processes which— referring to the respective demands—plan cognitive processes, which choose adequate cognitive strategies, which execute and control them in reference to their efficiency.

As demonstrated above, metacognitive knowledge and metacognitive control processes play an eminent role in newer theories of intelligence and giftedness (Campione & Brown, 1978; Sternberg, 1985, 1991; Ferretti & Butterfield, 1992). Quite surprisingly, however, there are only a handful of studies on metamemory or metacognition in younger gifted children. Studies with gifted pupils have been carried out mainly with primary school children or adolescents older than 8 years (for a summary see Perleth et al., 1993). One of the reasons for this might be the fact that research in metacognition—especially if one focuses on knowledge aspects—calls for a certain reflection

ability which emerges only gradually during the course of childhood development. This would indicate that it should be even easier with gifted children whose language might be more elaborate.

Some research, however, has been conducted in young children investigating metacognitive control processes. Here the way children cope with a problem, whether they adopt a trial-and-error strategy or whether they switch to systematically checking and comparing different possibilities, or whether they reflect on the problem-solving processes are aspects of metacognitive control with direct relations to success in the respective task. Such control activities are acquired in interaction with parents or other persons while the child is brought up (Karnes, Shwedel & Steinberg, 1982; Kontos, 1983; Browder, 1993).

In order to increase our understanding of how the antecedents of metacognition are structured, we must deal closely with the caregiver-child interaction, in which metacognitive directions are provided as verbal or non-verbal aids. They help the child wake up to his/ her own storage capacities. Gifted children eagerly seize on such metacognitive directions provided by a caretaker (information about task and strategy characteristics, and about the child's personality characteristics that interfere with the problem-solving process). Without subjecting them to much experimentation, gifted children use directives to expand their repertoires of verification procedures (Lehwald, 1992).

Moss (1990) and Moss & Strayer (1990) investigated the problem-solving behavior of three to four-year-old gifted and average nursery school children of a (upper) middle class area in Montreal. They examined their play with blocks when the problem was solved in the presence and with the help of the mothers. As a result, Moss & Strayer (1990) determined that the mothers of the gifted focussed the attention of their children on important relations between problem aspects while the mothers of the average gave more hints about concrete solutions. All in all, the mothers of the gifted provided their children with a more favorable environment for the formation of metacognitive competencies. The gifted children used metacognitive strategies after the modelling of their mothers, but also more and more spontaneously during the task (see also Browder, 1993).

With respect to primary school children Perleth (1994) conducted a series of studies to investigate differences in strategy use and metamemory (related to a sort-recall-task) between groups of different levels of giftedness and to analyze whether training and transfer effects depend on the level of giftedness. As main results Perleth (1994) had to state that the differences in strategy use between gifted and normal children were smaller than expected, especially less apparent among second-graders (about 8 years old) but relatively larger in more distant transfer tasks. Intelligence correlated better with memory performance than did metamemory.

As a result of his compact survey, on a very general level one can state (e.g. Heller, 2000), that gifted can be distinguished from the average by their better information-processing competencies. They make use of relevant information for problem solving, they perform comparison processes more quickly, and spend, however, more time for the encoding phase (more careful problem analysis). Gifted use more and better strategies for problem solving in different areas, they substitute more favorable strategies for unsuitable ones more quickly, and their cognitive monitoring is better (for summary see Waldmann & Weinert, 1990; Robinson, 1993; Shore & Kanevsky, 1993; Sternberg, 1993).

Some authors, however, could not find superiority of gifted children in metacognitive variables in general. Swanson, Christie & Rubadeau (1993), for example, report good strategic behavior of gifted children or youth which, however, was independent of metamemory. Swanson (1992) attributes the superiority of gifted children to their superior central processing system. Carr, Alexander & Schwanenflugel (1996) summarize the research on metacognition in gifted children by conceding better declarative metacognitive knowledge and strategy transfer but they do not outperform average children in strategy use and monitoring abilities in general. The metacognitive superiority of gifted children is above all obvious in high achievement in specific domains. Coyle, Read, Gaultney & Bjorklund (1998) could show that cognitive stability and low variability in strategy use was the prominent characteristics of gifted children which lead to higher achievement in memory tasks.

Up till now there is a body of evidence worth mentioning which shows that gifted children profit from strategy use and metacognitive abilities especially in more complex and more demanding tasks. So efforts for improving especially strategy use and metamemory of gifted children (see Manning, Glasner & Smith, 1996, or Van Der Westhuizen & Rautenbach, 1997) seem to be promising.

Motivational Characteristics

While motivational aspects are regarded as core presumption of excellence in general from all theoretical positions—see for example the controversy between Ericsson & Charnes (1994) and Gardner (1995)—motivational aspects play a smaller role in investigations in preschool or young children (also Porath, 1996). More information is available for primary school and older children (e.g. Clinkenbeard, 1996). In his representative and methodologically well controlled study in primary school children, Rost (1993) found that gifted children can be positively distinguished from average controls with respect to achievement motivation and causal attribution. Moreover, their strategies of working through their failure are more favorable. Concerning other aspects of personality, only a few differences were found, but when, then to the advantage of the gifted children.

As motivational characteristics develop to a great extend during primary school time, most studies in motivational variables concentrate on older children and youth. At the end of primary school gifted children show higher intrinsic motivation (Gottfried & Gottfried, 1996).

An important motivational aspect important for development of high ability can be seen in the curiosity and interest of even the young infant, i.e. the attention and preferences which are given to objects in the environment (Howe, 1990; Johnson & Beer, 1992). These motivational characteristics manifest themselves in a child's behavior. Because of their curiosity, gifted children already attract attention in early stages of development (Schneider, 1987). Berg & Sternberg (1985) view curiosity as an integral part of giftedness. In a meaningful and profound manner, the gifted children typically integrate the information acquired into their knowledge base. On the basis of their knowledge and a critical analysis of the consequences of their knowledge, they make decisions on courses of action geared to their original intention (acquisition of knowledge). Even at an early age, the behavior of gifted children is marked by a clear goal orientation. That orientation and its development is facilitated by these children's enhanced concentration power (Freeman, 1990).

During childhood, curiosity manifests itself in exploratory behavior. Therefore, the latter may be used as an early indicator of intellectual functioning. Exploratory acts are forms of active learning typical of young or preschool children. We are dealing with these when children expand and differentiate cognitive structures or when they incorporate these into a wider system (Keller, Gauda, Miranda & Schölmerich, 1985). In the course of mental development, the forms of exploratory behavior undergo change. These forms range from simple experimentation (mouthing, beating, shaking things) through functional/relational manipulations (assembling and integrating objects) to the asking of questions, a language-based information-seeking process. For differential diagnostic purposes, exploratory behavior may be used in a particularly impressive way, as a 'response to novelty'. In such situations gifted children focus their attention on relevant pieces of information. It may be that this has to do with the exceptional ability of gifted children to identify problems (Renzulli & Delisle, 1982).

Empirical work (Lehwald, 1990) has shown that gifted, curious children make impressive use of their exploratory skills in puzzles. They relate single objects to complex units significantly more frequently than do less curious children. Thus, in a largely unstructured situation (at play, for example) they generate information themselves, and in doing so are engaged in an intensive information gathering process about the properties of objects, how objects are interrelated, what functions they have, and what functional relationships can be established. In the long run, such active learning is conducive to the development of cognitive abilities. Follow-up studies using an intelligence test showed curious children to be clearly superior to less curious children. Thus, the exploratory actions which gifted, curious children engage in are of high 'cognitive relevance'. If environmental conditions are fortunate, they perform a developmental function. If a child's social environment provides an abundance of information, exploratory actions will build up a rich knowledge base, which is characteristics of gifted children (Siegler & Kotovsky, 1986).

Social Environment of the Young Highly Able Child

As Tannenbaum (1992) pointed out, many children showing signs of giftedness in toddlerhood or in the preschool age, do not achieve an outstanding level at school or later achievement in life. According to Lewis & Michalson (1985), one explanation for this discrepancy between promise and fulfillment can be the family background and educational-career opportunities. Families select and produce opportunities and experiences for the development of their children, and thus play an essential part in the growing of giftedness. Consequently, the development of giftedness is a function of individual characteristics, environmental experiences, and the interaction between both factors (also Bloom, 1985; Perleth, 1997, 2000)—apart from the role of mentors and models for the development of gifted children (Pleiss & Feldhusen, 1995).

Analyzing the socio-economic background of the families of gifted children and adults, a number of typical factors were identified. The majority of the students identified and traced by the classical Terman study turned out to stem from a wealthy and intellectual milieu. These findings of above-average education and socio-economically well placed families of the gifted was replicated regularly in giftedness studies (see Lewis & Michalson, 1985; Birx, 1988, for mathematically talented).

Howe (1990) points out that among extremely successful scientists (e.g. winners of the Nobel prize) religion, size of the home city, etc. distinguish them from the population in general. Considering these findings that so many identified gifted children come from the middle and upper socio-economic classes, Roedell et al. (1989) address the problem of identification of gifted from other social and educational classes, a topic on which more research was done during the last decade (Ford & Harris, 1990; Rhodes, 1992; Scott, Deuel, Stoyko & Urbano, 1996; Passow & Frasier,

1996; Tomlinson, Callahan & Lelli, 1997).

According to Howe (1990), individuals who later became scientists in particular come from intact families, enjoyed their childhood, and their career was straight and not interrupted by (family caused) critical life events. The parents of the gifted children from Berger's (1984) sample reported that their children were planned, and that pregnancy and birth were free from worries and problems. Most children had attended kindergarten.

The more sociological family characteristics described, however, cannot explain why they favor the development of highly able children. To obtain more insight into the shaping of giftedness, factors such as educational style, family climate, or attitude about learning and schooling have to be analyzed. According to Lewis & Michalson (1985), for example, an optimal amount and balance of freedom and pressure most favorably influences a child's motivation to learn and to explore the environment. Sometimes, however, gifted stem from families where parents stress discipline from the early childhood on (Berger, 1984). Gruber, Weber & Ziegler (1996) report that many members of A-class orchestras as the Munich symphonic orchestra were forced to exercise during their youth crisis by their parents.

Beginning with a representative sample totaling more than 7000 eight-year-old pupils recruited all over Germany (all of whom were tested individually), Rost (1993) compared 151 gifted elementary school children with 137 average control children which were matched by social class, age, school, grade, and sex. In contrary to other findings comparable family structures and family relationships were found in both the gifted and the control group. Moreover, the fathers and mothers of both groups had the same educational goals, and no differences were found with respect to patterns of parental behavior and parental beliefs.

Based on an example of Jewish families descending from Europe, Howe (1990) describes mechanisms of how giftedness can be fostered by the family environment and background factors such as educational aims, attitude towards achievement, religion, and so on (see also Storfer, 1990). The Jewish families are mostly intact and stable, with two parents at home. Their living circumstances in urban or suburban environments provide good cultural opportunities. As demanded by the Talmud, the fathers are the first to teach their children and this takes place at an early age. The parents encourage activities that lead to success at school, while little emphasis is placed on sports. The whole lifestyle is one where scholastic activities are enjoyed and respected, the families witness the successful outcomes of sustained efforts to learn new skills. Most interestingly, studying is allowed on Sabbath but other activities are forbidden.

Roedell et al. (1989) draw the conclusion from research on the family environment of the gifted that parents should spend a great deal of time with their children, read frequently to them, answer their children's questions in a proper way, support their children's own reading attempts and interests, and all in all, demonstrate a positive basic attitude towards intellectual learning. According to Howe (1990), however, girls are often confronted with traditional role models and encounter severe opposition to careers from their families. Encouraging and helping every child to acquire knowledge and skills should be focus of parental educational efforts. On the other hand, Howe (1990) warns that some parents are too anxious and too ambitious about the development of their children (see also Perleth & Sierwald, 2000). In any case, families of gifted children have to be seen as to be at risk (Robinson, 1998)

Practical and Research Desiderata

Early identification of young gifted children necessitates methods which are able to discover those children who promise high achievement in later school or professional careers. With respect to psychometric tests and as well to other early indicators of giftedness described in this chapter or in (behavioral) checklists, this necessitates first of all high reliability, fairness, and high predictive validity. To prove that a test has sufficient reliability for purposes of identifying promising children, it is not enough to determine its parallel test or consistency reliability. Instead one has to show that the retest reliability is high since the assumption is that the measured trait or indicator is stable over the course of time.

For identifying young gifted children, proving prognostic validity of the test and the giftedness indicators used plays a central role. This seems to be a main problem as the predictive power of a method can only be demonstrated in longitudinal studies. In the case of identifying gifted children, such studies would require very large samples and the tracing of the sample over many years. Moreover, all tests and questionnaires should be completed under the supervision of trained researchers, as for example Rost (1993) did in his study. To check the prognostic validity of an instrument, it is namely not enough to watch a sample of gifted and checking whether they indeed achieve outstanding but it is necessary to do such research with appropriate design including different control groups (if not representative samples). If identification methods are used for selecting children for special programs, for example, at the very least, the levels of achievement which selected children are able to achieve with and without the program need to be examined, as well as the progress made by the non-selected with and without the program.

Therefore longitudinal studies with representative samples are extremely crucial for the evaluation of methods suited for the early identification of gifted

children. Unfortunately, such research is difficult to organize, expensive, and requires a great deal of manpower. A possible solution therefore could be to reanalyze data of big representative longitudinal surveys to obtain information on the usefulness of the identification methods (e.g. the British Birth Survey cited earlier). Such studies collect numerous variables on the motor and cognitive development as well as on the academic achievement of the children. Their size enables the investigation of groups of gifted children recruited without dubious screening by parents or teachers as has to be done in most giftedness studies for practical reasons.

Information obtained by checklists, however, have to be used carefully. Especially for young children, the competence of teachers to identify gifted children is often questioned (e.g. Fatouros, 1986) or nearly denied (e.g. Rost, 1993). Rost (1993) also judges peer and self nomination as totally useless for the identification of gifted (primary school) children (also Fatouros, 1986; Gagné, 1989). Although some authors argue that the best information on gifted preschool children is available from their parents (e.g. Hagen, 1989), according to the results of Johnson & Lewman (1990), parental perception of giftedness indicators in three- to four-year-old boys and girls has to be doubted, as the answers of parents showed drastic role stereotypes: While, in comparison with girls, boys are nominated considerably more frequently in the categories 'remarkable abstract thinking', "extraordinary curiosity', and 'problem solving', while girls are perceived as possessing a 'large vocabulary' (30% more nominations).

If indicators of giftedness—for example in the form of (behavioral) checklists (Robinson, 1993; Stapf & Stapf, 1994)—are used, effective and practical statistical methods for the combination and weighting of the single information have to be used (see e.g. Hany, 1993). One possibility could be Bayes' rule which combines given probabilities of the occurrence of indicators in gifted and non-gifted children to evaluate the probability that a single child exhibiting some indicators and not exhibiting others is gifted. Modern statistics has provided more methods for combining probabilities. The mechanisms of these (e.g. the modern Shafer-Dempster theory) should be cautiously examined by practitioners and researchers.

At any rate, such combination of probabilities demands knowledge about the frequency of the indicator in gifted and unselected or non-gifted population (or in every group which is diagnostically relevant) and therefore necessitates respective research with representative samples. It should be noticed, that especially with indicators used for checklists, sometimes myths arise and are spread (e.g. Tannenbaum, 1992, cites a table from Lewis & Louis, 1991, who report that Freeman, 1985, found that gifted children are characterized by their sense of humor, although

Freeman, 1985, states the opposite; or see the section on sleep above).

As a quintessence, identification of young gifted children is problematic. Psychometric measures as well as diverse indicators of giftedness have up till now not proven to be suitable to identify these children which promise exceptional achievements later in school or in professional career. As early as 1896, the German founder of the experimental psychology, Wilhelm Wundt (1914) wrote: "The experimental method is almost without application for early childhood, and the results of experiments which have nevertheless been undertaken should be more or less considered purely coincidental because of the unbelievable weighting of error sources" (p. 364). Even if, nevertheless, much research with high standards has been undertaken, psychometric measures as well as diverse indicators of giftedness have, to date, not proven to be suitable for identifying those children who promise exceptional achievements later in school or in professional life.

Aside from possible principal obstacles to early identification, this is due to a considerable lack of appropiate research: There are too few prospective longitudinal studies and too few studies with representative samples or at least with adequate control groups (see Subotnik & Arnold, 1994). Giftedness research in young children too often fall back on to samples of counseling centers with their highly preselected clientele, thus finding and generalizing results which are not representative for the population of gifted children (see for example, the different results which Freeman, 1979, found for her gifted target and her gifted control group). In addition, too little effort in giftedness research is made in minority groups, in underpriviledged children, in the handicapped, and in other risk groups. A possible way out of this dilemma could be the reanalysis of data from large surveys and other representative studies at least to generate hypotheses which can be tested in following giftedness studies.

Finally we have again to ask the question of why and for what purpose gifted children in infancy, preschool age or in the early elementary school years are to be identified. Usually answers refer to the danger that children who are not identified early are not adequately stimulated so that their gifts will not develop (e.g. Karnes & Johnson, 1990). Concerning infants and toddlers, however, Robinson (1987, 1993) is skeptical about the usefulness of early training to force the development of giftedness. Nevertheless the author draws the conclusion 'that successful parents are flexible, in tune with their children's progress, and ready to introduce a new idea when the child is ready, but that even those who are most planful also work with the children's own skills' (Robinson, 1987, p. 164). This means gifted children need stimulation, and they may require a variety of material so their intellectual needs can be fully met.

References

Abroms, K. I. (1982). The gifted infant tendalizing behaviors and provocative correlates. *Journal of the Division for Early Childhood*, **5**, 3–18.

Ackerman, P. L. (1992). Predicting individual differences in complex skill acquisition: dynamics of ability determinants. *Journal of Applied Psychology*, **5**, 598–614.

Baum, S. M., Owen, S. V. & Oreck, B. A. (1996). Talent beyond words: Identification of potential talent in dance and music in elementary students. *Gifted Child Quarterly*, **40**, 93–101.

Bayley, N. (1993). *Bayley Scales of Infant Development* (2nd ed.). San Antonio, TX: The Psychological Cooperation.

Beal, A. L. (1995). A comparison of WISC-III and OLSAT–6 for the identification of gifted students. *Canadian Journal of School Psychology*, **11**, 120–129.

Berg, C. A. & Sternberg, R. J. (1985). Response to novelty: continuity versus discontinuity in the developmental course of intelligence. In: H. W. Reese (Ed.), *Advances in Child Development and Behavior* (pp. 1–47). New York: Academic Press.

Berger, M. (1984). Klassenbeste—eine Untersuchung bei 10jährigen Schülern [The best of class—a study in 10-year-old students]. In: G. Nissen (Ed.), *Psychiatrie des Schulalters* (pp. 101–118). Bern: Huber.

Birx, E. (1988). *Mathematik und Begabung* [Mathematics and giftedness. Evaluation of a fostering program for mathematically gifted high school students]. Hamburg: Krämer.

Bjorklund, D. F. & Schneider, W. (1996). The interaction of knowledge, aptitude, and strategies in children's memory performance. *Advances in Child Development and Behavior*, **26**, 59–89.

Bloom, B. S. (1985). *Developing talent in young people*. New York: Ballantine.

Bolig, E. E. & Day, J. D. (1993). Dynamic assessment and giftedness: The promise of assessing training responsiveness. *Roeper-Review*, **16**, 110–113.

Bondy, A. S., Constantino, R., Norcross, J. C. & Sheslow, D. (1984). Comparison of Slosson and McCarthy Scales for exceptional preschool children. *Perceptual and Motor Skills*, **59**, 657–658.

Borkowski, J. G. & Peck, V. A. (1986). Causes and consequences of metamemory in gifted children. In: R. J. Sternberg & J. E. Davidson (Eds), *Conceptions of giftedness* (pp. 182–200). Cambridge, UK: Cambridge University Press.

Borland, J. H. & Wright, L. (1994). Identifying young, potentially gifted, economically disadvantaged students. *Gifted Child Quarterly*, **38**, 164–171.

Bornstein, M. (1988). Perceptual development across the life cycle. In: M. H. Bornstein & M. E. Lamb (Eds), *Developmental psychology: An advanced textbook*. Hillsdale, NJ: Erlbaum.

Bornstein, M. H. (1989). Information processing (habituation) in infancy and stability in cognitive development. *Human Development*, **32**, 129–136.

Bornstein, M. H. (1989). Stability in early mental development: from attention and information processing in infancy to language and cognition in childhood. In: M. H. Bornstein & N. A. Krasnegor (Eds), *Stability and Continuity in Mental Development: Behavioral and Biological Perspectives* (pp. 147–170). Hillsdale, NJ: Erlbaum.

Bornstein, M. H. & Sigman, M. D. (1986). Continuity in mental development from infancy. *Child Development*, **57**,

251–274.

Borrow, S. J., Adam, K., Chapman, K., Idzekowski, C. J. & Oswald, I. (1980). Adolescent growth and intellectual ability in relation to sleep. *Sleep Research*, **9**, 98.

Bracken, B. A. & McCallum, R. S. (Eds) (1993). *Wechsler Intelligence Scale for Children* (3rd ed.). Brandon, VT: Clinical Psychology Publishing.

Bracken, B. A., Prasse, D. P. & McCallum, R. S. (1984). Peabody Picture Vocabulary Test-Revised: An appraisal and review. *School Psychology Review*, **13**, 49–60.

Brewer, N. (1987). Processing speed, efficiency, and intelligence. In: J. D. Borkowski & J. D. Day (Eds), *Cognition in Special Children: Comparative Approaches to Retardation, Learning Disabilities, and Giftedness* (pp. 15–48). Norwood, NJ: Ablex.

Browder, C. S. (1993). Aspekte der Metakognitionsentwicklung im Vorschulalter [Aspekts of the development of metacognition in preschool age]. In: K. A. Heller (Ed.), *Entwicklungsaspekte und Entwicklungsdeterminanten der Metakognition*. Munich: University of Munich.

Brown, A. L. (1978). Knowing when, where, and how to remember: a problem of metakognition. In: R. Glaser (Ed.), *Advances in Instructional Psychology* (Vol. 1, pp. 77–165). Hillsdale, NJ: Erlbaum.

Brown, A. L. (1984). Metakognition, Handlungskontrolle, Selbststeuerung und andere, noch geheimnisvollere Mechanismen [Metacognition, action control, self-direction and other even more secret mechanisms]. In: F. E. Weinert & R. H. Kluwe (Eds), *Metakognition, Motivation und Lernen* (pp. 60–109). Stuttgart: Kohlhammer.

Brown, S. W., Hwang, M. T., Baron, M. & Yakimowski, M. E. (1991). Factor analysis of responses to the WISC-R for gifted children. *Psychological Reports*, **69**, 99–107.

Burns, J. M., Collins, M. D. & Paulsell, J. C. (1991). A comparison of intellectually superior preschool accelerated readers and nonreaders: Four years later. *Gifted Child Quarterly*, **35**, 118–124.

Busby, K. A. & Pivik, R. T. (1983). Sleep patterns in children of superior intelligence. *Journal of Child Psychology and Psychiatry and Allied Disciplines*, **24**, 587–600.

Cahan, S. & Gejman, A. (1993). Constancy of IQ scores among gifted children. *Roeper-Review*, **15**, 140–143.

Cameron, L. C., Ittenbach, R. F., McGrew, K. S., Harrison, P. L., Taylor, L. R. & Hwang, Y. R. (1997). Confirmatory factor analysis of the K-ABC with gifted referrals. *Educational and Psychological Measurement*, **57**, 823–840.

Campione, J. C. & Brown, A. L. (1978). Toward a theory of intelligence: contributions from research with retarded children. *Intelligence*, **2**, 279–304.

Campione, J. C., Brown, A. L. & Ferrara, R. A. (1982). Mental retardation and intelligence. In: R. J. Sternberg (Ed.), *Handbook of Human Intelligence* (pp. 392–490). Cambridge, MA: Cambridge University Press.

Carr, M., Alexander, J. & Schwanenflugel, P. (1996). Where gifted children do and do not excell on metacognitive tasks. *Roeper Review*, **18**, 212–217.

Chi, Michelene T. H. (1984). Bereichsspezifisches Wissen und Metakognition [Domain-specific knowledge and metacognition]. In: F. E. Weinert & R. H. Kluge (Eds), *Metakognition, Motivation und Lernen* (pp. 211–229). Stuttgart: Kohlhammer.

Clinkenbeard, P. R. (1996). Research on motivation and the gifted: implications for identification, programming and evaluation. *Gifted Child Quarterly*, **40**, 220–221.

Coyle, T. R., Read, L. E., Gaultney, J. F. & Bjorklund, D. F. (1998). Giftedness and variability in strategic processing on a multitrial memory task: evidence for stability in gifted cognition. *Learning and Individual Differences*, **10**, 273–290.

Crook, T. & Eliot, J. (1980). Parental death during childhood and adult depression: a critical review of the literature. *Psychological Bulletin*, **87**, 252–259.

Daehler, M. W. & Greco, C. (1985). Memory in very young children. In: M. Pressley & Ch. J. Brainerd (Eds), *Cognitive Learning and Memory in Children. Progress in Cognitive Development Research* (pp. 49–79). New York: Springer.

Davidson, L. & Scripp, L. (1994). Conditions of giftedness: musical development in the preschool and early elementary years. In: R. F. Subotnik & K. D. Arnold (Eds), *Beyond Terman: Contemporary Longitudinal Studies of Giftedness and Talent* (pp. 155–185). Norwood, NJ: Ablex.

Despart, J. L. (1949). Sleep in pre-school children: a preliminary study. *Nerveous Child*, **8**, 8–27.

Dover, A. & Shore, B. M. (1991). Giftedness and flexibility on a mathematical set-breaking task. *Gifted Child Quarterly*, **35**, 99–105.

Dunn, L., Dunn, L., Wetton, C. & Burley, J. (1997). *The British Picture Vocabulary Scale (BPVS II)* (2nd ed.). Circle Pines, MN: American Guidance Service.

Dunn, L. M. & Dunn, L. M. (1981). *Peabody Picture Vocabulary Test—Revised*. Circle Pines, MN: American Guidance Service.

Embretson, S. E. (ed.). (1985). *Test design. Developments in psychology and psychometrics*. Orlando, FL: Academic Press.

Embretson, S. E. & Hershberger, S. L. (eds). (1999). *The new rules of measurement: what every psychologist and educator should know*. Mahwah, NJ: Lawrence Erlbaum Associates.

Ericsson, K. A. (1996). The aquisition of expert performance. In: K. A. Ericsson, (Ed.), *The Road to Excellence: the Aquisition of Expert Performance in the Arts and Science, Sports and Games* (pp. 1–50). Mahwah, NJ: Erlbaum.

Ericsson, K. A. & Charness, N. (1994). Expert performance: Its structure and acquisition. *American Psychologist*, **49**, 725–747.

Fagan III, J. F. & Krahe McGrath, S. (1981). Infant recognition memory and later intelligence. *Intelligence*, **5**, 121–130.

Fagan III, S. F. & Singer, L. T. (1983). Infant recognition memory as a measure of intelligence. In: L. P. Lipsitt (Ed.), *Advances in Infancy Research* (Vol. 2, pp. 31–72). Norwood, NJ: Ablex.

Fatouros, C. (1986). Early identification of gifted children is crucial, but how should we go about it? *Gifted Education International*, **4**, 24–28.

Ferretti, R. P. & Butterfield, E. C. (1992). Intelligence-related differences in the learning, maintenance, and transfer of problem-solving strategies. *Intelligence*, **16**, 207–223.

Feuerstein, R. (1980). *Instrumental enrichment. An intervention program for cognitive modifiability*. Baltimore: University Park Press.

Flavell, J. H. (1971). First discussant's comments: What is memory development the development of? *Human Development*, **14**, 272–278.

Flavell, J. H. (1978). Metacognitive development. In: J. M. Scandura & C. J. Brainerd (Eds), *Structural Process Theories of Complex Human Behavior*. Alpen a. d. Rijn, Netherlands: Sijtoff and Noordhoff.

Flavell, J. H. (1984). Annahmen zum Begriff Metakognition sowie zur Entwicklung von Metakognitionen [Assumptions about the concept of metacognition and the development of metacognition]. In: F. E. Weinert & R. H. Kluwe (Eds), *Metakognition, Motivation und Lernen* (pp. 23–31). Stuttgart: Kohlhammer.

Flavell, J. H. & Wellman, H. M. (1977). Metamemory. In: R. V. Kail, Jr. & J. W. Hagen (Eds), *Perspectives on the Development of Memory and Cognition* (pp. 3–33). Hillsdale, NJ: Erlbaum Associates.

Flynn, J. R. (1987). Massive IQ gains in 14 nations: what IQ tests really measure. *Psychological Bulletin*, **101**, 171–191.

Ford, D. Y. & Harris, J. J. (1990). On discovering the hidden treasure of gifted and talented Black children. *Roeper Review*, **13**(1) 27–32.

Freeman, J. (1979). *Gifted children*. Lancaster, UK: MTP.

Freeman, J. (1983). Identifying the able child. In: T. Kerry (Ed.), *Finding and helping the able child* (pp. 19–39). London: Croom Helm.

Freeman, J. (1985). The early years: preparation for creative thinking. *Gifted Education International*, **3**, 100–104.

Freeman, J. (1990). The early development and education of highly able young children. *European Journal for High Ability*, **1**, 165–171.

Gagné, F. (1989). Peer nominations as a psychometric instrument: many questions asked but few answered. *Gifted Child Quarterly*, **33**, 53–58.

Gardner, H. (1983). *Frames of mind. The theory of multiple intelligences*. New York: Basic Books.

Gardner, H. (1995). Expert performance: Its structure and acquisition: comment. *American Psychologist*, **50**, 802–803.

Gaultney, J. F., Bjorklund, D. F. & Goldstein, D. (1996). To be young, gifted, and strategic: Advantages for memory performance. *Journal of Experimental Child Psychology*, **61**, 43–66.

Geuss, H. & Urban, K. K. (1982). Hochbegabte Kinder (Gifted children). In: W. Wieczerkowski & H. zur Oeveste (Eds), *Lehrbuch der Entwicklungspsychologie* (Vol. 3, pp. 85–110). Düsseldorf: Schwann.

Gottfried, A. E. & Gottfried, A. W. (1996). A longitudinal study of academic intrinsic motivation in intellectually gifted children: childhood through early adolescence. *Gifted-Child-Quarterly. Special Issue: Motivation and giftedness.*, **0**, 179–183.

Grubar, J.-C. (1985). Sleep and mental efficiency. In: J. Freeman (Ed.), *The Psychology of Gifted Children*. Chichester: Wiley & Sons.

Gruber, H., Weber, A. & Ziegler, A. (1996). Einsatzmöglichkeiten retrospektiver Befragungen bei der Untersuchung des Expertiseerwerbs [Possibilities of using retrospective interviews in studies of acquisition of expertise]. In: H. Gruber & A. Ziegler (Eds), *Expertiseforschung. Theoretische und methodische Grundlagen* (pp. 150–168). Opladen: Westdeutscher Verlag.

Guthke, J. (1974). *Zur Diagnostik der intellektuellen Lernfähigkeit* [Diagnostic of the intellectual learning potential] (2nd ed.). Berlin: Deutscher Verlag der Wissenschaften.

Guthke, J. (1992). Lerntests auch für Hochbegabte [Learning tests for the gifted, too?]. In: E. A. Hany & H. Nickel (Eds), *Begabung und Hochbegabung. Theoretische Konzepte, Empirische Befunde, Praktische Konsequenzen* (pp. 125–141). Bern: Huber.

Hagen, E. (1989). *Die Identifizierung Hochbegabter* [German translation of 'Gifted Young Children', 1980, New York: Techers College Press]. Heidelberg: Asanger.

Hany, E. A. (1993). Methodological Problems and Issues Concerning Identification. In: K. A. Heller, F. J. Mönks & H. A. Passow (Eds), *International Handbook of Research and Development of Giftedness and Talent* (pp. 209–232). Oxford: Pergamon.

Harnishfeger, K. K. & Bjorklund, D. F. (1990). Strategic and nonstrategic factors in gifted children's free recall. *Contemporary Educational Psychology*, **15**, 346–363.

Hasselhorn, M. (1996). *Kategoriales Organisieren bei Kindern. Zur Entwicklung einer Gedaechtnisstrategie* [Categorial organization in children. The development of memory strategy]. Göttingen: Hogrefe.

Hayes, F. B. & Martin, R. P. (1986). Effectiveness of the PPVT-R in the screening of young gifted children. *Journal of Psychoeducational Assessment*, **4**, 27–33.

Heinbokel, A. (1996). *Hochbegabte. Erkennen, Probleme, Lösungswege*. Münster: Lit.

Heller, K. A. (Ed.) (2000). Begabungsdiagnostische Anwendungsfelder. In: K. A. Heller (Ed.), *Begabungsdiagnostik in der Schul-und Erziehungsberatung* (2nd ed.) (pp. 217–258). Bern: Huber.

Heller, K. A. & Perleth, Ch. (2000). Informationsquellen und Meßinstrumente [Information sources and measurement methods]. In: K. A. Heller (Ed.), *Begabungsdiagnostik in der Schul- und Erziehungsberatung* (2nd ed.) (pp. 96–216). Bern: Huber.

Howe, M. J. A. (1990). *The origin of exceptional abilities*. Cambridge, MA: Blackwell.

Jackson, N. E. & Butterfield, E. C. (1986). A conception of giftedness designed to promote research. In: R. J. Sternberg & J. E. Davidson (Eds), *Conceptions of Giftedness* (pp. 151–181). Cambridge: Cambridge University Press.

Jackson, N. E. & Myers, M. G. (1982). Letter naming time, digit span, and precocious reading achievement. *Intelligence*, **6**, 311–329.

Jensen, A. R. (1969). How much can we boost IQ and scholastic achievement? In: H. Skowronek (Ed.), *Umwelt und Begabung* (pp. 1–123). Stuttgart: Klett.

Johnson, L. & Beer, J. (1992). Specific and diversive curiosity in gifted elementary students. *Perceptual and Motor Skills*, **75**, 463–466.

Johnson, L. J. & Lewman, B. S. (1990). Parent perceptions of the talents of young gifted boys and girls. *Journal for the Education of the Gifted*, **13**, 176–188.

Kangas, J. & Bradway, K. (1971). Intelligence at middle age: A 38-year follow-up. *Developmental Psychology*, **5**, 333–337.

Kaplan, C. (1992). Ceiling effects in assessing high-IQ children with the WPPSI-R. *Journal of Clinical Child Psychology*, **21**, 403–406.

Karnes, M. B. & Johnson, L. J. (1990). A plea: serving young gifted children. *Early Child Development and Care*, **63**, 131–138.

Karnes, M. B., Shwedel, A. M. & Steinberg, D. (1982). *Styles of parenting among parents of young gifted children*. Urbana: Univ. of Illinois.

Kaufman, A. S. (1992). Evaluation of the WISC-III and WPPSI-R for gifted children. *Roeper Review*, **14**, 154–158.

Kaufman, A. S. & Kaufman, N. L. (1983). *K-ABC: Kaufman Assessment Battery for Children*. Circle Pines, MN: American Guidance Service.

Keller, H., Gauda, G., Miranda, D. & Schölmerich, A. (1985). Die Entwicklung des Blickkontakts im ersten Lebensjahr [The development of eye contact during the first year of life]. *Zeitschrift für Entwicklungspsychologie und Pädagogische Psychologie*, **17**, 258–269.

Kirschenbaum, R. J. (1998). Dynamic assessment and its use with underserved gifted and talented populations. *Gifted Child Quarterly*, **42**, 140–147.

Kitano, M. K. & de Leon, J. (1988). Use of the Stanford Binet Fourth Edition in identifying young gifted children. *Roeper Review*, **10**, 156–159.

Kluever, R. C. & Green, K. E. (1990). Identification of gifted children: a comparison of the scores on Stanford-Binet 4th Edition and Form LM. *Roeper Review*, **13**, 16–20.

Knoff, H. M. & Blednick, M. L. (1986). A comparison of the PPVT and the PPVT-R with gifted elementary school children. *Educational and Psychological Research*, **6**, 173–180.

Kontos, S. (1983). Adult-child interaciton and the origins of metacognition. *Journal of Educational Research,*, **77**, 43–54.

Kubinger, K. D. (1998). Psychological assessment of high ability: Worldwide-used Wechsler's Intelligence Scales and their psychometric shortcomings. *High Ability Studies*, **9**, 237–251.

Kubinger, K. D. & Wurst, E. (2000). *Adaptives Intelligenz Diagnostikum 2 (AID 2)*. Göttingen: Hogrefe.

Lamb, P. & Feldhusen, J. F. (1992). Recognizing and adapting instruction for early readers. *Roeper Review*, **15**, 108–109.

Laurent, J., Swerdlik, M. & Ryburn, M. (1992). Review of validity research on the Stanford-Binet Intelligence Scale (4th ed.). *Psychological-Assessment*, **4**, 102–112.

Lécuyer, R. (1989). Habituation and attention, novelty and cognition: where is the continuity? *Human Development*, **32**, 148–157.

Lehwald, G. (1990). Curiosity and exploratory behaviour in ability development. *European Journal for High Ability*, **1**, 204–210.

Lehwald, G. (1992). Mikroanalyse eines Konstruktionsspiels – Erfassung von Prüfprozeduren im Vorschulalter unter dem Aspekt der Begabungsentwicklung [Analysis of a construction game – assessment of control procedures in preschool age with respect to development of giftedness.] In: K. K. Urban (Ed.), *Begabungen Entwickeln, Erkennen und Fördern* (pp. 134–139). Hannover: Univ. of Hannover.

Lewis, M. & Brooks-Gunn, J. (1981). Visual attention at three months as a predictor of cognitive functioning at two years of age. *Intelligence*, **5**, 131–140.

Lewis, M. & Louis, B. (1991). Young gifted children. In: N. Colangelo & G. A. Davis (Eds), *Handbook of gifted education* (pp. 365–381). Boston: Allyn & Bacon.

Lewis, M. & Michalson, L. (1985). The gifted infant. In: J. Freeman (Ed.), *The Psychology of Gifted Children. Perspectives on Development and Education* (pp. 35–57). Chichester, UK: Wiley & Sons.

Linville, J. N., Rust, J. O. & Kim J. K. (1999). The information and picture completion dyad of the WISC-III as a screening test for gifted referrals. *Journal of Instructional Psychology*, **26**, 98–104.

Lord, F. M. & Novick, M. P. (1974). *Statistical theories of mental test scores* (2nd ed.). Reading, MA: Addison-Wesley.

Louis, B. & Lewis, M. (1992). Parental beliefs about giftedness in young children and their relation to actual ability levels. *Gifted Child Quarterly*, **36**, 27–31.

Manning, B. H., Glasner, S. E. & Smith, E. R. (1996). The self-regulated learning aspect of metacognition: a component of gifted education. *Roeper Review*, **18**, 217–223.

Mark, R., Beal, A. L. & Dumont, R. (1998). Validation of a WISC-III Short-Form for the identification of Canadian gifted students. *Canadian Journal of School Psychology*, **14**, 1–10.

Masten, W. G., Morse, D. T. & Wenglar, K. E. (1995). Factor structure of the WISC-R for Mexican-American students referred for intellectually gifted assessment. *Roeper Review*, **18**, 130–131.

McCall, R. B. (1979). The development of intellectual functioning in infancy and the prediction of later I. Q. In: J. D. Osofsky (Ed.), *Handbook of Infant Development* (pp. 707–741). New York: Wiley.

McCall, V. W., Yates, B., Hendricks, S. & Turner, K. (1989). *Contemporary-Educational-Psychology*, **14**, 93–96.

McCallum, R. S. & Karnes, F. A. (1990). Use of a brief form of the Stanford-Binet Intelligence Scale (Fourth) for gifted children. *Journal of School Psychology*, **28**, 279–283.

McCallum, R. S., Karnes, F. A. & Edwards, R. P. (1984). The test of choice for assessment of gifted children: a comparison of the K-ABC, WISC-R, and Stanford-Binet. *Journal of Psychoeducational Assessment*, **2**, 57–63.

McFarland, C. E. & Wiebe, D. (1987). Structure and utilization of knowledge among Special Children. In: J. D. Borkowski & J. D. Day (Eds), *Cognition in special children: Comparative Approaches to Retardation, Learning Disabilities, and Giftedness* (pp. 87–121). Norwood, NJ: Ablex.

Moss, E. (1990). Social interaction and metacognitive development in gifted preschoolers. *Gifted Child Quarterly*, **34**, 16–20.

Moss, E. & Strayer, F. F. (1990). Interactive problem-solving of gifted and non-gifted preschoolers with their mothers. *International Journal of Behavioral Development*, **13**, 177–197.

Muir-Broaddus, J. E. & Bjorklund, D. F. (1990). Developmental and individual differences in children's memory strategies: The role of knowledge. In: W. Schneider & F. E. Weinert (Eds), *Interactions Among Aptitudes, Strategies, And Knowledge in Cognitive Performance* (pp. 99–116). New York: Springer.

Neubauer, A. C. & Knorr, E. (1998). Three paper-and-pencil tests for speed of information processing: psychometric properties and correlations with intelligence. *Intelligence*, **26**, 123–151.

Nolan, R. F., Watlington, D. K. & Willson, V. L. (1989). Gifted and non-gifted race and gender effects on item functioning on the Kaufman Assessment Battery for Children. *Journal of Clinical Psychology*, **45**, 645–650.

Passow, A. H. & Frasier, M. M. (1996). Toward improving identification of talent potential among minority and disadvantaged students. *Roeper Review*, **18**, 198–202.

Perleth, Ch. (1994). Strategy use and metamemory in gifted and average primary school children. In: K. A. Heller & E.

A. Hany (Eds), *Competence and Responsibility. The Third European Conference of the European Council for High Ability* (Vol. 2, pp. 46–52). Göttingen: Hogrefe.

Perleth, Ch. (1997). *Zur Rolle von Begabung und Erfahrung bei der Leistungsgenese. Ein Brückenschlag zwischen Begabungs- und Expertiseforschung* [The role of giftedness and experience in the genesis of achievement. A bridge over the gap between giftedness and expertise research]. (Habilitationsschrift). München: LMU.

Perleth, Ch. (2000). Neue Tendenzen und Ergebnisse in der Begabungs- und Intelligenzdiagnostik [New trends and results in giftedness and intelligence diagnostics]. In: H. Joswig (Ed.), *Begabungen erkennen – Begabte fördern* (pp. 35–64). Rostock: Univ. Rostock.

Perleth, Ch. & Heller, K. A. (1994). The Munich Longitudinal Study of Giftedness. In: R. Subotnik & K. Arnold (Eds), *Beyond Terman: Longitudinal Studies in Contemporary Gifted Education* (pp. 77–114). Norwood, NJ: Ablex.

Perleth, Ch., Lehwald, G. & Browder, C. S. (1993). Indicators of high ability in young children. In: K. A. Heller, F. J. Mönks & H. A. Passow (Eds), *International Handbook ffor Research on Giftedness and Talent* (pp. 283–310). Oxford: Pergamon Press.

Perleth, Ch. & Sierwald, W. (2000). Entwicklungs- und Leistungsanalysen zur Hochbegabung [Analyses of development and achievement of the gifted]. In: K. A. Heller (Ed.), *Hochbegabung im Kindes- und Jugendalter* (2nd ed.) (pp. 172–357). Göttingen: Hogrefe.

Pleiss, M. K. & Feldhusen, J. F. (1995). Mentors, role models, and heroes in the lives of gifted children. *Educational Psychologist*, **30**, 159–169.

Pollock, J. I. (1992). Predictors and long-term association of reported sleeping difficulties in infancy. *Journal of Preproductive and Infant Psychology*, **10**, 151–168.

Porath, M. (1996). Affective and motivational considerations in the assessment of gifted learners. *Roeper Review*, **19**, 13–17.

Pyryt, M. C. (1996). IQ: Easy to bash, hard to replace. *Roeper Review*, **18**, 255–258.

Raven, J. C., Court, J. H. & Raven, J. (1983). *Manual for Raven's Progressive Matrices and Vocabulary Scales (Section 3)—Standard Progressive Matrices (1983 ed.)*. London: Lewis.

Raven, J. C., Court, J. H. & Raven, J. (1986). *Manual for Raven's Progressive Matrices and Vocabulary Scales (Section 2) – Coloured Progressive Matrices (1986 edition)*. London: Lewis.

Raven, J. C., Court, J. H. & Raven, J. (1998). *Standard Progessive Matrices (SPM)*. London: Lewis.

Renzulli, J. S. & Delisle, J. R. (1982). Gifted person. In: H. E. Mitzel (Ed.), *Encyclopedia of educational research* (5th ed.) (pp. 723–730). New York: Free Press.

Reynolds, C. R. & Clark, J. H. (1986). Profile analysis of standardized intelligence test performance of very high IQ children. *Psychology in the Schools*, **23**, 5–12.

Rhodes, L. (1992). Focusing attention on the individual in identification of gifted Black students. *Roeper Review*, **14**, 108–110.

Robinson, N. M. (1987). The early development of precocity. *Gifted Child Quarterly*, **31**, 161–164.

Robinson, N. M. (1992). Which Stanford-Binet for the brightest? Stanford-Binet IV, of course! Time marches on. *Roeper Review*, **15**, 32–34.

Robinson, N. M. (1993). Identifying and nurturing gifted, very young children. In: K. A. Heller, F. J. Mönks & A. H. Passow (Eds), *International handbook of research and development of giftedness and talent* (pp. 507–524). Oxford: Pergamon.

Robinson, N. M. (1998). Synergies in the families of gifted children. In: M. Lewis & C. Feiring (Eds), *Families, risk, and competence* (pp. 309–32). Mahwah, NJ: Erlbaum.

Robinson, N. M., Abbott, R. D., Berninger, V. W. & Busse, J. (1996). Structure of abilities in math-precocious young children: gender similarities and differences. *Journal of Educational Psychology*, **88**, 341–352.

Robinson, N. M., Dale, P. S. & Landesman, S. (1990). Validity of Stanford-Binet IV with linguistically precocious toddlers. *Intelligence*, **14**, 173–186.

Roedell, W. C., Jackson, N. E. & Robinson, H. B. (1989). *Hochbegabung in der Kindheit: besonders begabte Kinder im Vor- und Grundschulalter* (German translation of 'Gifted young children'). Heidelberg: Asanger.

Rose, S. A. & Wallace, J. F. (1985). Visual recognition memory: a predictor of later cognitive functioning in preterms. *Child Development*, **56**, 843–852.

Rost, D. H. (1993). *Lebensumweltanalyse hochbegabter Kinder* [Analysis of living circumstances of gifted children]. Göttingen: Hogrefe.

Sattler, J. M. (1988). *Assessment of children*. San Diego, CA: Sattler.

Schneider, B. H. & Gervais, M. D. (1991). Identifying gifted kindergarten students with brief screening measures and the WPPSI-R. Special Issue: Wechsler Preschool and Primary Scale of Intelligence (WPPSI-R). *Journal of Psychoeducational Assessment*, **9**, 201–208.

Schneider, K. (1987). Subjective uncertainty and exploratory behavior in preschool children. In: D. Görlitz & J. F. Wohlwill (Eds), *Curiosity, imagination, and play* (pp. 127–150). Hillsdale, NJ: Erlbaum & Associates.

Schneider, W. (1993). Acquiring expertise: determinants of exceptional performance. In: K. A. Heller, F. J. Mönks & A. H. Passow (Eds), *International handbook of research and development of giftedness and talent* (pp. 311–324). Oxford, UK: Pergamon Press.

Schneider, W. & Pressley, M. (1997). *Memory development between two and twenty* (2nd ed.). Mahwah, NJ: Lawrence Erlbaum Associates.

Schneider, W. & Sodian, B. (1988). Metamemory-memory behavior relationships in young children: evidence from a memory-for-location task. *Journal of Experimental Child Psychology*, **45**, 209–233.

Scott, M. S., Deuel, L. L. S., Jean Francois, B. & Urbano, R. C. (1996). Identifying cognitively gifted ethnic minority children. *Gifted Child Quarterly*, **40**, 147–153.

Shapiro, B. K., Palmer, F. B., Antell, S. E., Bilker, S., Ross, A. & Capute, A. J. (1989). Giftedness: can it be predicted in infancy? *Clinical Pediatrics*, **28**, 205–209.

Shore, B. M. & Kanevsky, L. S. (1993). Thinking processes: being and becoming gifted. In: K. A. Heller, F. J. Mönks & A. H. Passow (Eds), *International handbook of research and development of giftedness and talent* (pp. 133–147). Oxford, UK: Pergamon.

Siegler, R. S. & Kotovsky, K. (1986). Two levels of giftedness: shall ever the twain meet? In: R. J. Sternberg & J. E. Davidson (Eds), *Conceptions of giftedness* (pp. 417–435). Cambridge: Cambridge University Press.

Silverman, L. K., & Kearney, K. (1992). Which Stanford-Binet for the brightest? The case for the Stanford-Binet L-M as a supplemental test. *Roeper Review*, **15**, 34–37.

Snowden, P. L., & Conway, K. D. (1996). A comparison of self-reported parenting behaviors and attitudes of parents of academically precocious and nonprecocious preschool children. *Roeper Review*, **19**, 97–101.

Spangler, R. S., & Sabatino, D. A. (1995). Temporal stability of gifted children's intelligence. *Roeper Review*, **17**, 207–210.

Sparrow, S. S., & Gurland, S. T. (1998). Assessment of gifted children with the WISC-III. In: A. Prifitera, D. H. Saklofske et al. (Eds), *WISC-III clinical use and interpretation: scientist-practitioner perspectives* (pp. 59–72). San Diego, CA: Academic Press.

Stainthorp, R., & Hughes, D. (1998). Phonological sensitivity and reading: evidence from precocious readers. *Journal of Research in Reading*, **21**, 53–68.

Stapf, A., & Stapf, K. H. (1988). Kindliche Hochbegabung in entwicklungspsychologischer Sicht [Childhood giftedness from a developmental psychological point of view]. *Psychologie in Erziehung und Unterricht*, **35**, 1–17.

Stapf, A., & Stapf, K. H. (1994). Identifikation hochbegabter Vorschulkinder [Identifying gifted preschool age children]. In: D. Bartussek & M. Amelang (Eds), *Fortschritte der Differentiellen Psychologie und Psychologischen Diagnostik* (pp. 77–90). Göttingen: Hogrefe.

Sternberg, R. J. (1985). *Beyond IQ: A triarchic theory of human intelligence*. Cambridge, MA: University Press.

Sternberg, R. J. (1991). Giftedness according to the triarchic theory. In: N. Colangelo & G. A. Davis (Eds), *Handbook of gifted education* (pp. 45–54). Boston: Allyn and Bacon.

Sternberg, R. J. (1993). Procedures for identifying intellectual potential in the gifted: A perspective on alternative 'metaphors of mind'. In: K. A. Heller, F. J. Mönks, & H. A. Passow (Eds), *International handbook for research on giftedness and talent* (pp. 185–207). Oxford: Pergamon Press.

Storfer, M. D. (1990). Intelligence and giftedness. In: *The Contributions of Heredity and Early Environment*. San Francisco: Jossey-Bass.

Subotnik, R. F., & Arnold, K. D. (1994). Longitudinal study of giftedness and talent. In: R. F. Subotnik & K. D. Arnold (Eds), *Beyond Terman: Contemporary longitudinal studies of giftedness and talent* (pp. 1–23). Norwood, NJ: Ablex.

Swanson, H. L. (1992). The relationship between metacognition and problem solving in gifted children. *Roeper Review*, **15**, 43–48.

Swanson, H. L., Brandenburg Ayres, S., & Wallace, S. (1989). Construct validity of the K-ABC with gifted children. *Journal of Special Education*, **23**, 342–352.

Swanson, H. L., Christie, L., & Rubadeau, R. J. (1993). The relationship between metacognition and analogical reasoning in mentally retarded, learning disabled, average, and gifted children. *Learning Disabilities Research and Practice*, **8**, 70–81.

Tannenbaum, A. (1992). Early signs of giftedness: Research and commentary. *Journal for the Education of the Gifted*, **15**, 104–133.

Tannenbaum, A. J. (1986). Reflection and refraction of light on the gifted. *Roeper-Review*, **8**, 212–218.

Tarnowski, K. J., & Kelly, P. A. (1987). Utility of the PPVT-R for pediatric intellectual screening. *Journal of Pediatric Psychology*, **12**, 611–614.

Terman, L. M. (1925). *Genetic studies of genius: Mental and physical traits of 1000 gifted children*. Stanford, CA: Stanford University Press.

Terman, L. M., & Oden, M. H. (1947). *The gifted child grows up*. Stanford, CA: Stanford University Press.

Terman, L. M. & Oden, M. H. (1959). *The gifted group of mid-life*. Stanford, CA: Stanford Univ. Press.

Thorndike, H. L., & Hagen, E. (1987). *Cognitive Abilities Test*. Boston: Houghton-Mifflin.

Thorndike, R. L., Hagen, E. P. & Sattler, J. M. (1986). *Stanford-Binet Intelligence Scale Fourth Edition. Technical manual*. Chicago, IL: The Riverside Publishing Company.

Tomlinson, C. A., Callahan, C. M., & Lelli, K. M. (1997). Challenging expectations: case studies of high potential, culturally diverse young children. *Gifted Child Quarterly*, **41**, 5–17.

Torgesen, J. K., Kistner, J. A., & Morgan, S. (1987). Component processes in working memory. In: J. D. Borkowski & J. D. Day (Eds), *Cognition in special children: comparative approaches to retardation, learning disabilities, and giftedness* (pp. 49–85). Norwood, NJ: Ablex.

Van Der Westhuizen, C. P., & Rautenbach, E. M. (1997). The teaching of higher-order thinking skills to gifted pupils at the elementary level. *Early Child Development and Care*, **130**, 1–12.

Waldmann, M., & Weinert, F. E. (1990). *Intelligenz und Denken. Perspektiven der Hochbegabungsforschung* [Intelligence and thinking. Perspectives of the research in giftedness]. Göttingen: Hogrefe.

Webb, J. T., Meckstroth, E. A., & Tolan, S. S. (1985). *Hochbegabte Kinder, ihre Eltern, ihre Lehrer. Ein Ratgeber* [German translation of 'Guiding the gifted child', 1985, Columbus, OH: Ohio Psychology Publishing Company] Bern: Huber.

Wechsler, D. (1958). *The measurement and appraisal of adult intelligence* (4th ed.). Baltimore, MD: Williams & Wilkins.

Wechsler, D. (1967). *Wechsler Preschool and Primary Scale of Intelligence WPPSI*. New York: Psychological Corporation.

Wechsler, D. (1974). *Manual for the Wechsler Intelligence Scale for Children – Revised*. New York: Psychological Corporation.

Wechsler, D. (1989). *Manual for the Wechsler Preschool and Primary Scale of Intelligence-Revised*. San Antonio, TX: Psychological Corporation.

Wechsler, D. (1991). *Wechsler Intelligence scale for Children* (3rd ed.) (WISC-III). San Antonio, TX: Psychological Corporation.

Wessells, M. G. (1984). *Kognitive Psychologie* [German translation of 'Cognitive psychology']. New York: Harper & Row (UTB).

Wilkinson, S. C. (1993). WISC-R profiles of children with superior intellectual ability. *Gifted Child Quarterly*, **37**, 84–91.

Winner, E., & Martino, G. (1993). Giftedness in the visual arts and music. In: K. A. Heller, F. J. Mönks, & H. A. Passow (Eds), *International handbook for research on giftedness and talent* (pp. 253–281). Oxford: Pergamon Press.

Wolke, D. (1993). Feeding and sleeping across the lifespan. In: M. L. Rutter & D. F. Hay (Eds), *Developmental principles and clinical issues in psychology and psychiatry.* Oxford: Blackwell Scientific Publications.

Wundt, W. (1914). *Grundriß der Psychologie* [Outline of psychology] (12th ed.). Leipzig: Engelmann.

Prediction of Excellence in School, Higher Education, and Work

Günter Trost

Institute for Test Development and Talent Research Ltd., Bonn, Germany

Introduction

How predictable is exceptional performance in school, higher education, and work? What is the predictive value of a variety of information gathered in a variety of ways with respect to excellence in these three areas? In attempting to provide answers to these questions by reviewing the literature, this contribution will focus on person-related predictors (abilities, motivation, further personality variables), while environmental factors will also be taken into account.

Before the empirical data can be reviewed, a brief discussion of the criterion referred to as 'excellence' seems appropriate.

The Criterion of Excellence

'Excellence' is not a scientific term, and a clear-cut, unanimously accepted definition of it does not exist. In none of the standard textbooks on giftedness except one (Sternberg & Davidson, 1986) does the key-word 'excellence' appear in the subject index. Nevertheless, the term is frequently used in literature and mostly in the sense of outstanding achievement, brilliant performance, or 'eminence' (Hunt, 1983; National Commission on Excellence in Education, 1983; Feldhusen, 1984; Tannenbaum, 1986). Ochse (1990) uses the term 'excellence' in the title of her book as a synonym of creativity: "creative people excel—they go beyond what others have done" and "produce something of cultural value" (p. 3).

The borderline between 'excellence' and 'above-average achievement' has been drawn at very different points of the achievement continuum, depending on the author. Some set it extremely high, admitting only the epoch-making achievement of a genius brought forth once in a century. Others use listing in *Who's Who* as a criterion for that person's excellence, and still others rely on more or less exclusive awards or on peer nomination. Another approach is to define excellence statistically, e.g. as achievement that can be measured on a discrete scale and exceeds a certain value, or as a characterization of persons who, when rank-ordered according to their respective accomplishments, reach positions beyond a certain percentile rank.

The small common denominator of all definitions is achievement far above average. Consequently, excellence can be observed in all domains of human performance. The scope of this chapter is restricted to the predictability of excellence in school, in higher education, and in work. (For a discussion about the methodological problems faced by empirical research into the determinants of excellence, see Subotnik and Arnold in this handbook.)

Prediction of Excellence in School

Excellence in school, defined as outstanding overall achievement, can be measured by grade point average, by rank in class, or by teacher ratings. Excellent performance in particular subjects is reflected in top grades, teacher ratings, or achievement test scores. The predictors that have gained the most attention in this context are measures of intelligence, scholastic aptitude, creativity, interests, motivation, and other personality traits as well as parent and teacher ratings.

Lewis Terman (1925) started his famous longitudinal study in 1922 on 1,528 children who had scored at least 140 on an intelligence test before the age of 12; he and his co-researchers followed the persons in this sample over their entire life span. On an average, the highly intelligent children performed very well in school, but not exceedingly so (Terman, 1965).

In the context of the Munich Study of Giftedness (Heller & Hany, 1986; Perleth & Heller, 1994) the predictive validity of a battery of cognitive ability tests and creativity measures was determined on three samples of 11, 13, and 15 year old secondary school students. The criterion was the average of school grades in German, mathematics, and English three years after the assessment of the predictor data. The validity coefficients for the combined test score were 0.48, 0.45, and 0.32.

317

In the well-known Study of Mathematically Precocious Youth (SMPY) initiated by Julian Stanley and
carried on under the directorship of Camilla Benbow,
the predictive value of the quantitative section of the
Scholastic Aptitude Test (SAT-M) with respect to high
school achievement could be examined. The SAT-M
proved to be a good predictor of excellent performance
in mathematics and science, even when applied to
12-year-old students (Benbow & Minor, 1986).

Teacher ratings on achievement in a special mathematics course offered to gifted tenth-graders were the
criteria in the Hamburg study on mathematically
precocious youth carried out by Birx (1988). Among
the predictors were the score in a German version of
the quantitative section of the Scholastic Aptitude Test
(GSAT-M) and the total score on an intelligence test.
For two cohorts and a prediction period of two and
three years, validity coefficients of 0.43 and 0.17 were
found for the scholastic aptitude test score, and of 0.37
and 0.17 for the intelligence test score.

From the many studies covering the whole range of
general cognitive abilities it can be concluded that
intelligence and related ability test scores are satisfactory predictors of success in school with
correlations around 0.40 to 0.50 (cf. Cattell & Butcher,
1968; Bloom, 1976; Parkerson et al., 1984; Kuusinen
& Leskinen, 1988). The findings indicate, however,
that even though high intelligence is a necessary
prerequisite for top achievement in school, it is by far
not sufficient. Other, non-cognitive factors are needed
in addition (cf. Helmke, 1992; Schiefele et. al., 1992).

Not surprisingly, teacher ratings turned out to be
fairly good predictors of later achievement in school. In
the Munich Study of Giftedness, a combined teacher
rating of students' cognitive and creative abilities
proved better than the combined results of a battery of
ability and creativity tests as predictors of participants'
grades in German, mathematics and natural sciences,
assessed in secondary school after one-year and two-
year intervals. In primary school the tests were superior
to teacher judgments (Perleth & Heller, 1994). Denton
(1986) reports good agreement between teacher ratings
of excellent students and their classroom achievement
two years later.

In a meta-analysis, Schiefele et al. (1992) examined
the results of longitudinal studies from 18 countries
that addressed the predictive validity of interest scales
with respect to achievement in school, as measured by
grades or achievement test scores. As this review
includes a great number of studies initiated by the
International Association for the Evaluation of Educational Achievement (IEA) using achievement tests with
a fairly high ceiling as criteria, the authors' conclusions
deserve to be mentioned here, even though the studies
were not specifically focused on outstanding achievement. The mean value of 121 correlation coefficients
was 0.31, after correction for attenuation it amounted
to 0.40.

Basing their findings on the analysis of 40 studies,
Ugurogulu & Walberg (1979) reported an average
coefficient of 0.34 for the correlation between measures of motivation and self-concept on the one hand
and achievement in school on the other. Hansford &
Hattie (1982), in their meta-analysis of data from 128
studies on the predictive validity of self-concept
measures, found an average value of 0.21. In Bloom's
study (1976), "self-concept of ability" was the strongest predictor of success in school among three types of
self-concept. For 'affective characteristics' as predictors of school achievement, Fraser et al. (1987)
found in their meta-analysis of 335 studies a mean
validity coefficient of 0.12.

In sum, the findings suggest that teacher ratings,
cognitive tests, and measures of non-cognitive features
such as interests, motivation, and self-concept can be
used for the prediction of outstanding achievement in
school and that they should be used in combination.
What the optimal combination is cannot be derived
from the available data; however, cognitive abilities far
above average seem to be indispensable for excellence
in school.

There is only indirect evidence as to the contribution
parent ratings can make to the prediction of outstanding achievement in school. Jacobs (1971) and
Ciha et al. (1974) report findings indicating that parents
are reasonably successful in identifying gifted children.
Other studies raise doubts about the predictive value of
parent judgments (e.g. Ferdinand, 1961; Miles, 1965).
In general, parents tend to overestimate their children's
giftedness (Ferdinand, 1961), while highly-educated
parents tend toward underestimation (Martinson,
1975). In all, parent ratings do not seem to be very
valid predictors of achievement in school. However,
parents are apparently in a position to identify, at an
early stage of their children's development, high
potential in music or in the arts (Sloane & Sosniak,
1985; Sosniak, 1985a).

Prediction of Excellence in Higher Education

Excellence in higher education can be operationalized
by outstanding grade point averages or marks in
intermediary or final examinations as well as by awards
and honors degrees. It was possible to follow up on the
participants in the above-mentioned Study of Mathematically Precocious Youth (SMPY) for another five
years after graduation from high school. They had been
selected at age 12, primarily on the basis of above-
average performance on the quantitative section of the
Scholastic Aptitude Test that had been designed for a
much older age group (Stanley & Benbow, 1986). As
college graduates, almost half ranked among the top
10% of their class, 11% reported awards or honors in
mathematics, 10% in science (Benbow & Arjmand,
1990; Lubinski & Benbow, 1994). The canonical
correlation for the SAT-M—when administered at high
school age—as a predictor of university achievement

was 0.30. Other important predictors were attitude toward mathematics and science, encouragement to pursue academic and career goals, and paternal educational level (Benbow & Arjmand, 1990).

In a four-year follow-up study of 1,200 German students who had ranked among the top 10% in the final class of upper secondary school, low but highly significant correlations were found between grades in the 12th school year and grades on the first university examination (0.25), and also between the total score in a scholastic aptitude test and the same criterion (0.16). Forty per cent of those whose test scores were in the top quartile within the pre-selected group subsequently earned top grades at university (Trost, 1986).

Chauncey and Hilton (1965) examined validity studies on samples of highly able students. They concluded that scholastic aptitude tests can discriminate reliably even among very gifted students and predict their academic performance.

Willingham (1985) summarizes his review of empirical data on the predictability of success in college as follows: "The two traditional academic predictors, high school rank (HSR) and admissions test score (SAT) were by far the best at forecasting the scholastic types of achievement. In a comparison of the two, HSR was a somewhat better predictor of college honors (based on cumulative grade average), while the SAT was a somewhat better predictor of departmental honors. The latter were based on independent scholarship, arguably more characteristic of pre-professional work in the discipline than is grade point average" (p. 179). Willingham also presents data demonstrating that both high school records and scores on the Scholastic Aptitude Test have their highest predictive validities within student sub-samples above the 90th percentile (p. 29). In a more recent survey Lubinski & Dawis (1992) came to similar conclusions.

There is also some evidence of the relationship between superior intelligence and outstanding achievement in higher education. Hollingworth (1942) studied the educational development of 12 children up to their early twenties who had scored 180 or above on the Stanford–Binet intelligence test before the age of 12. They did exceedingly well in college and won a long list of prizes and honors.

Feldman (1984) identified those 26 persons in Terman's group of highly intelligent children with IQs above 180 and compared their educational careers with those of 26 subjects selected at random from Terman's original group of 1,500. On the whole, both groups were highly successful throughout their college years, with a markedly larger percentage of persons winning honors and receiving advanced degrees in the above–180 IQ group. For his total sample of highly intelligent persons Terman (1965) reports that "close to 90% entered college and 70% graduated. Of those graduating, 30% were awarded honors and about two-thirds remained for graduate work" (p. 12).

The relative importance of non-cognitive factors for achievement in higher education has been demonstrated in various studies (see, e.g. the reviews by Lavin, 1965; Cattell & Butcher, 1968; Khan, 1969; Mabe & West, 1982; Steinkamp & Maehr, 1983; Schiefele, Krapp & Winteler, 1992).

Nichols & Holland (1963) and Nichols (1966) attained considerable improvement in the prediction of college grades of a highly selective sample of finalists and scholars of the National Merit Scholarship program when they included attitude, interest, and personality scales in the set of predictors: "For predicting college grades, high school grades were the best predictor (average validity 0.33), followed by the non-intellective scales (average validity 0.27), and finally by the aptitude test (average validity 0.12)" (Nichols, 1966, p. 911).

The overall conclusions which may be drawn from the findings on the predictability of excellence in higher education are: achievements in secondary school and performance on scholastic aptitude tests are the best predictors; high scores on intelligence tests also have satisfactory predictive validity. Other factors, particularly interest, motivation, and self-concept, have, on their own, a lower predictive power. However, they do add to the overall prediction of academic success, and among highly intelligent students, these factors seem to differentiate between the very good and the excellent.

Prediction of Excellence in Work

Authors operationalize excellence in work in a variety of different ways including: recognition as geniuses who have revolutionized their fields in some way, distinguished awards persons have won for their work, outstanding ratings by experts in the field, high number of publications, patents, or exhibitions, etc.

One of the ways to uncover the determinants of excellence in work is analyzing biographies of eminent persons. The first study of this type was Sir Francis Galton's work on 'hereditary genius' (1869). He found three common elements: capacity, zeal, and the power of hard work. His study on eminent scientists (1874) led to the conclusion that "these people were endowed with superior intellectual ability, tremendous energy, good physical health, a sense of independence and purposefulness, and exceptional dedication to their fields of productivity", as Tannenbaum (1986, p. 27) summarizes.

As part of Lewis Terman's genetic studies of genius, Catherine Cox (1926) reported on the early development of 300 famous persons from the past 450 years who had made outstanding contributions to their cultures. The sample included Byron, Cromwell, Darwin, Kant, Luther, Michelangelo, Mozart, Newton, and Robespierre. From the information given in the biographies, estimates were made as to the persons' IQs and more than sixty other personal traits. Within her sample, Cox compared a subgroup of the most creative subjects with the total group. The intelligence ratings assigned to the persons in the total sample were high: for the subgroup of eminent philosophers the average IQ estimate in childhood was 173, for the scientists 164, for the statesmen 159, and for the soldiers 133. However, the estimated IQ did not differentiate between high and exceptionally high achievement. Cox concluded from her data that given high intelligence, persistence, motivation, and effort influence whether the highest level of accomplishment will be achieved or not. Other features that she found particularly characteristic for the 100 leading geniuses in her sample were confidence in their abilities, and 'strength of character' (p. 50).

Twenty-five years after the Cox study, Anne Roe (1952a, 1952b, 1953) selected, on the basis of nomination by panels of experts in each field, 64 of the most eminent living American scientists: 20 biologists, 22 physicists, and 22 social scientists (psychologists and anthropologists) and examined them comprehensively by interviews and tests. Although there were marked group differences between the natural scientists and the social scientists, and between the biologists and the physicists, certain common patterns did appear in the group as a whole.

The scientists typically came from middle-class and upper middle-class families. Of the individuals surveyed, 53% were the sons of professionals, another 19% the sons of businessmen. Learning for its own sake was highly valued in their families. They developed early independence, read a lot, and enjoyed school and university. The intelligence level of the eminent scientists—as measured at the time of the study—was very high, their average scores in verbal and quantitative tests corresponding to an IQ of approximately 160. Furthermore, the interviews revealed that one of the features all 64 eminent scientists had in common was the "driving absorption in their work" (Roe, 1952a, p. 25).

MacKinnon (1960, 1978) conducted a series of both retrospective and cross-sectional studies on creative architects, engineers, industrial researchers, mathematicians, physical scientists, and writers nominated by experts in the fields. Apart from features that were characteristic to each of the respective groups, he found the following traits common among the highly effective persons in all of these fields: openness to experience, independence in goal-setting, enthusiasm, and high tolerance for frustration in the course of solving problems.

Goertzel & Goertzel (1962) and Goertzel et al. (1978) examined the biographies of 314 eminent personalities of the twentieth century, stressing environmental rather than individual factors. Their results confirmed many of the previously mentioned findings. In contrast to other authors, however, they found that 85% of the eminent persons came from disturbed

homes. Nevertheless, parents—as well as other mentors—seemed to play a significant role in evoking the children's and adolescents' motivation to achieve.

Walberg et al. (1981) asked biographers working for the Encyclopedia Britannica to rate the presence or absence of traits in the childhood of those persons from Cox's sample whose biographies the authors had written. According to the ratings, the most distinctive trait common to 97% of the 221 eminent men was intelligence; they also had superior communicative skills. Eighty-two per cent were permitted by their parents to explore environments on their own. Eighty per cent were very successful in school.

Simonton (1984, 1987) re-analyzed the Cox and the Goertzel family data. According to his findings, the eminent persons came from intellectually and culturally stimulating homes; they acquired numerous demanding hobbies and were omnivorous readers. In their later educational and professional careers they displayed immense productivity. Simonton also gathered evidence that "intelligence is the single best personological predictor of leadership in general" (1988, p. 399). For all subgroups of eminent persons except for "celebrities" (including athletes, businessmen, editors, and performers) he found an inverted U-shaped curve for the relation between attained educational level and eminence.

A series of retrospective studies on 120 living persons who, before age 40, had attained distinction as concert pianists, sculptors, swimmers, tennis-players, research mathematicians, and research neurologists was carried out under the directorship of Benjamin Bloom (1985). Interviews with the individuals and their parents revealed a number of communalities over the groups under study. The majority of the parents placed high value on achievement, success, and persistence at work. They encouraged and supported the interests their children pursued and were willing to devote time, resources, and energy to providing the best conditions for the development of their children's talents. They viewed their children as gifted and expected hard work and high attainments from them. In terms of parental interests and activities the climate was consistently favorable: the parents of the swimmers and tennis-players were interested in athletics (Kalinowski, 1985; Monsaas, 1985); in the homes of the concert pianists music played an important part (Sosniak, 1985a); there was a certain emphasis on the arts in the sculptor's homes (Sloane & Sosniak, 1985); the parents of the mathematicians and neurologists had themselves attained high levels of education and offered a wide range of intellectual stimulation to their children (Gustin, 1985; Sosniak, 1985b).

The children can be characterized as rather self-guided and independent in their interests and activities; they had soon become highly self-confident with respect to their abilities. In their adolescence they were strongly motivated to learn, to practice, and improve upon their accomplishments. The academic records of the pianists, sculptors and athletes were inconspicuous; those of the research neurologists were very good but not necessarily brilliant; most of the research mathematicians had attained excellent results both in secondary and higher education.

Harriet Zuckerman (1977) examined the biographies of 92 Nobel laureates, partly by means of interviews, and concluded that their socioe-conomic backgrounds were considerably higher than those of 'non-eminent' scientists, that they were significantly influenced by role models ('elite masters') and had a particularly high level of self-confidence.

Several retrospective studies comparing exceptional managers with average managers yielded fairly consistent results as to the predictors of outstanding managerial achievement: superior cognitive abilities, high interpersonal skills, vigorous desire for achievement, and strong self-confidence (Klemp & McClelland, 1986; Cascio, 1987; Northouse, 1997).

While the studies mentioned so far were designed as retrospective analyses, other studies started with more or less selected samples of children or adolescents who were followed up until life achievement could be measured.

The most famous longitudinal study of this kind, is the one by Lewis Terman begun in 1922 with a sample of 1,528 six- to twelve-year-old children with IQs of at least 140 (Terman, 1925). The 800 males in his sample (only a minority of the women had pursued professional careers at that time) developed impressive records of adult life achievement: "By 1950,... they had published 67 books,... more than 1,400 scientific, technical, and professional articles; over 200 short stories, novelettes, and plays. ... They had also authored more than 150 patents. ... Of the scientists, 47 are listed in the 1949 edition of American Men of Science. Nearly all of these numbers are from 10 to 20 or 30 times as large as would be found for 800 men of corresponding age picked at random in the general population" (Terman, 1965, p. 12). According to Terman, these figures prove that tests of general intelligence, given at school age, "tell a great deal about the ability to achieve either presently or 30 years hence" (1965, p. 13). Notably, the 150 most and the 150 least successful men in the sample did not differ in their average measured intelligence. They did, however, differ in personality traits such as "persistence in the accomplishment of ends, integration toward goals, self-confidence, and freedom from inferiority feelings, all-round emotional and social adjustment, and ... drive to achieve" (Terman & Oden, 1959, p. 148).

By comparing the professional careers of the 26 persons from Terman's sample—persons who, before age 12, had scored above 180 in the intelligence test—with the careers of a control group of 26 persons drawn at random from the same sample, Feldman (1984) found only "some margin of benefit from the extra IQ points" (p. 520) in terms of professional achievement.

Tomlinson-Keasey & Little (1990) factor-analyzed data gathered by Terman—parent and teacher trait ratings from the year 1922, family of orgin characteristics described retrospectively by the subjects, and variables of adult accomplishment—and represented the relationships in a path model. Of all the 'early' predictors, the factor 'parental education' showed the highest correlation to the criterion factors 'educational attainment' (0.26) and 'occupational achievement' (0.13).

In another re-analysis of the Terman data, Walberg et al. (1994) differentiated between relatively fixed and relatively alterable predictor variables. They found that alterable variables (e.g. hours of instruction, health, leisure activities) contributed little to the prediction of educational and occupational outcome beyond that already afforded by the fixed variables (including abilities and socio-economic status).

Two studies carried out recently at the Institute for Test Development and Talent Research in Bonn, Germany deserve mention in this context. Heilmann (1999) investigated the educational and professional careers of all national winners of the German Federal Mathematics Competition for grades 11–13 since 1971, the year the competition was introduced. Every year, some 10 national winners emerge from a total of 1,600 participants. In her retrospective analyses Heilmann included several control groups: One was a sample from the most selective German scholarship program for highly gifted university students, matched to the 'winners' group in terms of age, gender, and choice of courses in higher education. Another comparison group consisted of a representative sample of 2,220 persons—matched to the 'winners' group with respect to gender—who had graduated from upper secondary school in 1973 and had been followed up since that year in a longitudinal study (Trost, 1987).

The winners' parents offered their children significantly more support than the parents of the students in the representative group, both in terms of assistance in developing their abilities and pursuing their interests, and in terms of emotional warmth. As to the parents' academic backgrounds, the proportion of parents who held university degrees was nearly three times as high for the mothers of the winners and nearly twice as high for the fathers of the winners than for the mothers and fathers of the persons in the representative group.

Throughout school age the winners were highly committed to working on mathematical problems and earned top grades in mathematics. It should be pointed out that their performance in other subjects was also exceptional: Their average grade in the school-leaving certificate ranged more than two standard deviations above the average grade of the representative group. Of the winners, 1 in 6 had skipped one school year, as

321

compared to 1 in 12 National Merit scholarship recipients and 1 in 63 members of the representative group. With respect to extra-curricular interests during the school years, the 'winners' differed from the 'scholars' in that the latter were much more interested in the political/social field (comparable data for the representative group was not available).

A comparison of the career-related motives and values of the groups under study yielded marked discrepancies. The career goals of the representative group were more 'extrinsic' in nature (earning money, job security), and associated with social values (working for changes in society, working on a team). The winners clearly favored 'intrinsic' aims (tackling challenging tasks, pursuing personal interests, contributing to progress in personal area of specialization).

The Mathematics Competition winners' post-secondary careers are characterized by outstanding achievement: they earned top grades in university, 81% completed their doctoral dissertations (representative group: 12%) and they were, on average, two years younger than the persons in the representative sample upon receipt of their doctoral degrees. The 'winners' group was able to list about three times as many indicators of success in science and technology (e.g. number of publications, participation in inventions, awards) as the representative control group.

In another retrospective study, Sieglen (1998) identified 121 adults who have been exceptionally successful as scientists (41), engineers (40), and businessmen (40). Here the control group consisted of a nationally representative sample of about 3,600 Germans who had graduated from secondary school in 1973—persons who had been included in the same long-term follow-up study that provided control data for Heilmann's 1999 investigation.

The outstanding scientists, engineers, and businessmen differed from the representative group with regard to a variety of features characterizing their behavior and motives at school age, during the period of higher education, and at the time of their entry into professional life, as well as their home environments. The patterns were very similar for outstanding scientists and engineers while the outstanding businessmen differed largely in other respects from the unselected control group.

At school age, both the outstanding scientists and engineers developed scientific curiosity, perseverance, concentration, and a desire to seek intellectual challenge to a much greater extent than the control group; they also had a wider range of interests. Their academic achievements both in school and in higher education were far beyond those of the representative group, and their career motives were much more achievement-oriented and 'intrinsic'. The outstanding managers also differed from the control group in terms of the desire to seek intellectual challenge at school age; their academic achievements, however, were not distinctly

superior. The aspects most significantly distinguishing this top group from the representative group at school age were the striving to influence others and the ability to take initiative. With respect to career motives, the outstanding businessmen were—like the scientists and engineers—achievement-oriented and 'intrinsically' motivated; at the same time they differed from the control group to an even greater extent in their appreciation of the 'materialistic' rewards of their work and in their general professional ambitions. In terms of home environment and parental support, the three top groups differed from the representative group much less than they did in terms of the aspects mentioned above.

To sum up, the evidence gathered from these two recent studies emphasizes the relevance of individual predictors such as cognitive abilities, interests, and motives as well as academic achievement for exceptional performance in the professions. The results also support the notion of 'differential predictability': The sets of information that prove to contribute best to the prediction of outstanding success in differing career paths are to some extent themselves different, i.e. whereas a certain set of abilities, interests, or motives is best suited for prediction of excellence in one domain, a partially or wholly different set of traits may be the best predictors in another, etc.

Torrance (1988) also conducted longitudinal studies on unselected groups. He operationalized 'creative adult achievement' as "quantity of publicly recognized and acknowledged creative achievements" and "quality of creative achievements" (p. 58) according to three judges' quality ratings of what the subjects had identified as their most creative achievements. For a sample of 254 high school seniors who had taken creativity, intelligence and school-based achievement tests in 1959 and were followed up until 1979, Torrance (1988) obtained the following correlations with the quantitative and the qualitative criteria of adult creative achievement respectively: 0.32 and 0.36 for the total score in the creativity test battery, 0.21 and 0.38 for the total intelligence score, and 0.27 and 0.47 for the total achievement test score. For another sample of 211 subjects tested at elementary school level and followed up for 22 years, Torrance found validity coefficients of 0.46 for the total creativity score with respect to the quantitative criterion and 0.58 with respect to the qualitative criterion of achievement.

Empirical findings as to the predictability of job success in general (i.e. not only in view of excellence) complete the picture. The results of a meta-analyses indicate that overall cognitive ability is the best single predictor with an average correlation coefficient of 0.45 (Hunter & Hunter, 1984). The correlation between college grade-point average and job success is considerably lower, the average correlation coefficient being 0.30 (Roth, BeVier, Switzer & Schippmann, 1996).

Among non-cognitive variables, biographical data on past attainments in particular areas tend to be the best predictors of similar attainments in adult life, the mean validity coefficient being 0.37 (Taylor & Ellison, 1967; Hunter & Hunter, 1984). The predictive validity of interests as measured by questionnaires is lower, the respective values ranging around 0.20 or below (Hunter & Hunter, 1984). The relation between general personality traits as they are assessed by personality inventories and measures of job success seems to be rather weak: the average correlation coefficient amounts to 0.15 (Hunter & Hunter, 1984; Klitgaard, 1985).

Summary and Conclusions

What, then, are the characteristics which can be assessed at earlier stages of a person's life that contribute to the prediction of excellence at later stages? In the first place, the results of all pertinent research clearly show that there is no such thing as one exclusive predictor of outstanding achievement. Instead, excellent performance is the product of a highly complex intra-individual interaction of a variety of traits (cognitive and non-cognitive abilities, motivational and emotional attributes, additional personality variables), as well as of an interaction between these individual traits and environmental factors (influences of family, peers, school, university, extra-curricular experiences, the media, etc.). The prevailing conceptions of giftedness as they are proposed, for instance, by Feldhusen (1986), Gagné (1991), Heller (1989) and Tannenbaum (1986) emphasize these interactions and thus are in line with the findings reported in this chapter (see also Gagné; Hany & Weinert; Ziegler & Heller in this handbook).

Second, there is hardly any single predictor that accounts for more than 30% of the variance in any criterion of achievement if predictors and criteria are measured in longitudinal studies. In cross-validation studies, even optimal combinations of several predictors rarely explain more than 50% of the variance in later achievement. These figures reflect the degree of predictability of achievement in unselected populations where the full range of individual achievements, from very low to very high, can be observed. In cases of highly selected groups where we aim at predicting extraordinary performance, our expectations concerning the degree of predictability must be placed even lower. One of the reasons for this is the restriction of variance with regard to both the predictors and the criteria, a circumstance that tends to diminish the correlations between the variables under study. It is therefore safe to say that, even by using the best predictors available (both individual and environmental) and combining them in the most appropriate way, less than half of 'what makes excellence' can be accounted for (see also Subotnik & Arnold in this handbook).

Within these limits, though, certain variables have fairly consistently proved to be more predictive than others. For a large number of areas of excellence, intelligence and other cognitive abilities are the most important single predictors, particularly in terms of outstanding performance in school, in higher education, in vocational training, in the professions, in business, and in all fields of scientific research. "It appears that individuals who end up known in history as highly productive achievers in those fields requiring extensive formal schooling are likely to have an IQ of at least 145" (Albert & Runco, 1986, p. 349). Other abilities, e.g. psychomotor, perceptual and social abilities, hold the highest rank positions as predictors of exceptional performance in sports, in the fine arts and the performing arts, in music, and in some areas of leadership. Abilities assessed by tests are better predictors than abilities rated by parents or teachers, at least in the cognitive domain. Whenever the accomplishment of something novel is the criterion, creativity is an important additional predictor. However, a fairly high, though not exceptional level of intelligence is also necessary for high degrees of creative achievement (Roe, 1952b; Cattell, 1963; Barron, 1969).

Although the predictive value of specific abilities can be different, depending on the particular domain of achievement, some motivational, affective, and environmental characteristics are obviously relevant predictors across domains. Aside from ability variables, a high and task-oriented motivation is probably the most powerful predictor of excellence. Its importance has been confirmed in practically all studies searching for the determinants of outstanding achievement. Aspects of it are the willingness to work hard and persistently on things that are of particular interest to the individual, perseverance in the face of obstacles, a high level of aspiration, competitiveness, and ambition. High motivation without high abilities will not bring about extraordinary accomplishments; inversely, even persons endowed with maximum abilities but who lack 'task commitment' (Renzulli, 1986) will never excel.

The connecting link between ability and motivation seems to be the individual's self-concept, another relevant predictor of excellence. It is a set of perceptions and evaluations of one's own traits. Persons characterized by outstanding accomplishments were, as a rule, quite aware of their extraordinary capabilities at the time of their childhood and adolescence. As a consequence, their self-confidence was boosted which encouraged them to set their stakes higher and improve their achievements.

There are some further personality traits in which persons who later excel, be it in their educational records, their extra-curricular achievements, or their vocational accomplishments, already differ from their peers in childhood and adolescence. One of them is independence, both emotionally and intellectually. They are more self-directed in setting their goals and in

323

choosing the objects of their activities and the problems they are going to tackle; they are more willing to work alone and to accept responsibility for their products. A tendency toward non-conformity, unconventionality, even radicality of thinking goes along with this independence. However, the predictive validity of these personality traits, as they are assessed by interviews or questionnaires, is not very high.

Interests as measured by inventories can make a useful contribution to the prediction of outstanding achievement. They are obviously domain-specific predictors; in general, the predictive validity of interests is considerably lower than the validity of abilities.

Lastly, there are some aspects of the home environment that can serve as predictors of excellent achievement, not as isolated factors but rather as 'catalysts' (Gagné, 1991), aiding in the gradual manifestation of potential and development of abilities. One relevant aspect is the parents' value system: Positive attitudes toward learning, practice, and achievement in general shape and foster children's achievement motivation. A second aspect is exposure to a variety of experiences—e.g. frequent discussions, shared hobbies and other leisure time activities—serving the children as incentives in the discovery and development of their own interests and abilities. A third aspect is the relative freedom with which the children are allowed to pursue their interests. The fourth relevant contribution is the parents' support for the development of their children's abilities. In the course of adolescence and thereafter, the importance of the home environment diminishes as the influence of role models outside the home increases; it has been pointed out earlier that virtually all of the research data leading to these conclusions were obtained retrospectively. The degree to which information on the home environment can contribute to the prediction of excellence in longitudinal studies is presumably very modest, for two reasons: first, the home environment is a moderator rather than a genuine predictor variable; second, it is difficult to assess reliable indices of the situational factors mentioned above.

A further group of predictors might be called 'second-order predictors', as they are in a sense both predictors and (early) criteria of achievement: performance in school, in higher education, and extracurricular accomplishments during all stages of education. Quite naturally, past achievement is the best predictor of similar future achievement. This is why teacher ratings of classroom performance are good predictors of school grades, school grades are good predictors of college grades, early accomplishments in sports, music or the arts are good predictors of later accomplishments in the same areas, etc., especially in the upper part of the achievement continuum. Both society and researchers, however, have a keen interest in identifying the potential of (future) outstanding performance at a point in time when high accomplishment in the respective (or closely corresponding) area cannot yet be observed. Where this is the case, there is no choice but to try and assess the individual traits (abilities, motivation, interests, self-concept) and the environmental predictors discussed above.

An Outlook

Much has been done to uncover the predictors of excellence since Galton set out to study geniuses more than a century ago. Several interesting investigations have been carried out since the first edition of this handbook appeared in 1993; yet much remains to be done. Most of the knowledge available on this subject has been gathered by means of retrospective studies; throughout the history of research into giftedness, longitudinal studies have been scarce. It seems, however, that within the past decade or so efforts to conduct longitudinal research have been increasing (see Subotnik & Arnold and Ziegler & Heller in this handbook). Still there is a need for more long-term longitudinal studies based on large unselected samples and assessing a broad spectrum of predictor variables. In cases where the samples have already been highly selected, unselected control groups ought to be included. In the latter respect, progress has also been made since the handbook was first issued.

Better assessment instruments are needed as well: instruments such as complex tests of information processing and problem solving, with good discriminative power in the upper range of the performance continuum. Computer-based adaptive ability tests and complex problem scenarios we already have at our disposal should be further developed and applied to investigations of the predictability of exceptional performance. In addition, we require more reliable instruments for assessing the motivational, affective, and environmental variables that have proved essential for outstanding performance.

Finally, more use should be made of methods for modeling the complex interactions of predictors and their relationships to achievement criteria (see, e.g. Jöreskog, 1979). To date, few researchers have applied such structural models to the analysis of longitudinal data on the predictability of extraordinary achievement.

With the help of longitudinal studies, better instruments of assessment, and the application of complex structural models to longitudinal data, we can further enhance our understanding of the sources of outstanding achievement and thus create a more solid basis for the identification and support of individuals with extremely high potential.

References

Albert, R. S. & Runco, M. A. (1986). The achievement of eminence: a model based on a longitudinal study of exceptionally gifted boys and their families. In: R. J. Sternberg & J. E. Davidson (Eds), *Conceptions of Gifted-*

ness (pp. 332–357). Cambridge: Cambridge University Press.

Barron, F. (1969). *Creative person and creative process.* New York: Holt, Rinehart & Winston.

Benbow, C. P. & Arjmand, O. (1990). Predictors of high academic achievement in mathematics and science by mathematically talented students: a longitudinal study. *Journal of Educational Psychology*, **82**, 430–441.

Benbow, C. P. & Minor, L. L. (1986). Mathematically talented males and females and achievement in the high school sciences. *American Educational Research Journal*, **23**, 425–436.

Birx, E. (1988). *Mathematik und Begabung (Mathematics and giftedness).* Hamburg: R. Krämer.

Bloom, B. S. (1976). *Human characteristics and school learning.* New York: McGraw-Hill.

Bloom, B. S. (Ed.) (1985). *Developing talent in young people.* New York: Ballantine.

Cascio, W. F. (1987). *Applied psychology in personnel management* (3rd ed.). Englewood Cliffs, NJ: Prentice-Hall.

Cattell, R. B. (1963). The personality and motivation of the researcher from measurements of contemporaries and from biography. In: C. W. Taylor & F. Barron (Eds), *Scientific Creativity* (pp. 119–131). New York: Wiley.

Cattell, R. B. & Butcher, H. J. (1968). *The prediction of achievement and creativity.* Indianapolis/New York: Bobbs-Merrill.

Chauncey, H. & Hilton, T. L. (1965). Are aptitude tests valid for the highly able? *Science*, **148**, 1297–1304.

Ciha, T. E., Harris, R., Hoffman, S. & Potter, M. W. (1974). Parents as identifiers of giftedness, ignored but accurate. *The Gifted Child Quarterly*, **18**, 191–195.

Cox, C. M. (1926). *The early mental traits of three hundred geniuses. Genetic studies of genius*, Vol 2. Stanford, CA: Stanford University Press.

Denton, S. C. J. (1986). Identifikation durch Lehrer (Identification by teachers). In: W. Wieczerkowski, H. Wagner, K. K. Urban & A. Cropley (Eds), *Hochbegabung—Gesellschaft—Schule (High giftedness—society—school)* (pp. 172–184). Bad Honnef: Bock.

Feldhusen, J. F. (1984). The pursuit of excellence in gifted education. In: J. F. Feldhusen (Ed.), *Toward Excellence in Gifted Education* (pp. 1–16). Denver, Col.: Love.

Feldhusen, J. F. (1986). A conception of giftedness. In: R. J. Sternberg & J. E. Davidson (Eds), *Conceptions of Giftedness* (pp. 112–127). Cambridge: Cambridge University Press.

Feldman, D. H. (1984). A follow-up of subjects scoring above 180 IQ in Terman's 'Genetic studies of genius'. *Exceptional Children*, **50**, 518–523.

Ferdinand, W. (1961). Wir beurteilen Eltern die Intelligenz ihrer Kinder (How do parents judge their children's intelligence)? *Schule und Psychologie*, **8**, 239–246.

Fraser, B. J., Walberg, H. J., Welch, W. W. & Hattie, J. A. (1987). Syntheses of educational productivity research. *International Journal of Educational Research*, **11**, 145–252.

Gagné, F. (1991). Toward a differentiated model of giftedness and talent. In: N. Colangelo & G. A. Davis (Eds), *Handbook of Gifted Education* (pp. 65–80). Boston: Allyn and Bacon.

Galton, F. (1869). *Hereditary genius.* New York: Macmillan.

Galton, F. (1874). *English men of science, their nature and nurture.* New York: Macmillan.

Goertzel, M. G., Goertzel, V. & Goertzel, T. G. (1978). *Three hundred eminent personalities.* San Francisco, CA: Jossey-Bass.

Goertzel, V. & Goertzel, M. G. (1962). *Cradles of eminence.* London: Constable.

Gustin, W. C. (1985). The development of exceptional research mathematicians. In: B. S. Bloom (Ed.), *Developing Talent in Young People* (pp. 270–331). New York: Ballantine.

Hansford, B. C. & Hattie, J. A. (1982). The relationship between self and achievement/performance measures. *Review of Educational Research*, **52**, 123–142.

Heilmann, K. (1999). *Begabung—Leistung—Karriere (Giftedness—achievement—career).* Göttingen: Hogrefe.

Heller, K. A. (1989). Perspectives of the diagnosis of giftedness. *German Journal of Psychology*, **13**, 140–159.

Heller, K. A. & Hany, E. A. (1986). Identification, development and analysis of talented and gifted children in West Germany. In: K. A. Heller & J. F. Feldhusen (Eds), *Identifying and Nurturing the Gifted. An International Perspective* (pp. 67–82). Toronto: Huber.

Helmke, A. (1992). *Selbstvertrauen und schulische Leistungen (Self-confidence and achievements in school).* Göttingen: Hogrefe.

Holahan, C. K. & Sears, R. R. (1995). *The gifted group in later maturity.* Stanford, CA: Stanford University Press.

Hollingworth, L. S. (1942). *Children above 180 IQ Stanford–Binet: Origin and development.* New York: World Book.

Hunt, J. (1983). *Action for excellence.* Denver, Col.: Education Commission of the States, Task Force on Education for Economic Growth.

Hunter, J. E. & Hunter, R. F. (1984). Validity and utility of alternative predictors of job performance. *Psychological Bulletin*, **96**, 72–98.

Jacobs, J. C. (1971). Effectiveness of teacher and parent identification of gifted children as a function of school level. *Psychology in the Schools*, **8**, 140–142.

Jöreskog, K. G. (1979). Statistical estimation of structural models in longitudinal-developmental investigations. In: J. R. Nesselroade & P. B. Baltes (Eds), *Longitudinal Research in the Behavioral Sciences: Design and Analysis* (pp. 303–351). New York: Academic Press.

Kalinowski, A. G. (1985). The development of Olympic swimmers. In: B. S. Bloom (Ed.), *Developing Talent in Young People* (pp. 139–192). New York: Ballantine.

Khan, S. B. (1969). Affective correlates of academic achievement. *Journal of Educational Psychology*, **60**, 216–221.

Klemp, G. O. & McClelland, D. C. (1986). What characterizes intelligent functioning among senior managers? In: R. J. Sternberg & R. K. Wagner (Eds), *Practical Intelligence. Nature and Origins of Competence in the Everyday World* (pp. 31–50). Cambridge: Cambridge University Press.

Klitgaard, R. (1985). *Choosing elites.* New York: Basic Books.

Kuusinen, J. & Leskinen, E. (1988). Latent structure analysis of longitudinal data on relations between intellectual abilities and school achievement. *Multivariate Behavioral Research*, **8**, 103–118.

Lavin, D. E. (1965). *The prediction of academic performance: a theoretical analysis and review of research.* New York: Russell Sage Foundation.

Lubinski, D. & Benbow, C. P. (1994). The study of mathematically precocious youth: the first three decades of a planned 50-year study of intellectual talent. In: R. F. Subotnik & K. D. Arnold (Eds), *Beyond Terman: Contemporary longitudinal studies of giftedness and talent* (pp. 255–281). Norwood, NJ: Ablex.

Lubinski, D. & Dawis, R. V. (1992). Aptitude, skills and proficiency. In: M. D. Dunnette & L. M. Hough (Eds), *The Handbook of Industrial/Organizational Psychology*, 2nd ed., Vol. 3 (pp. 3–59). Palo Alto, CA: Consulting Psychologists Press.

Mabe III, P. A. & West, S. G. (1982). Validity of self-evaluation of ability: a review and meta-analysis. *Journal of Applied Psychology*, **67**, 280–296.

MacKinnon, D. W. (1960). The highly effective individual. In: R. S. Albert (Ed.), *Genius and Eminence: The Social Psychology of Creativity and Exceptional Achievement* (pp. 114–127). New York: Oxford University Press.

MacKinnon, D. W. (1978). *In search of human effectiveness*. Buffalo: Creative Education Foundation.

Martinson, R. A. (1975). *The identification of the gifted and talented*. Reston, VA: Council for Exceptional Children.

Miles, C. C. (1965). Gifted children. In: L. Carmichael (Ed.), *Manual of Child Psychology* (pp. 984–1063). New York: Wiley.

Monsaas, J. A. (1985). Learning to be a world-class tennis player. In: B. S. Bloom (Ed.), *Developing Talent in Young People* (pp. 211–269). New York: Ballantine.

National Commission on Excellence in Education. (1983). *A nation at risk: the imperative for educational reform* (A report to the Nation and the Secretary of Education). Washington, D.C.: U.S. Government Printing Office.

Nichols, R. C. (1966). Non-intellective predictors of achievement in college. *Educational and Psychological Measurement*, **26**, 899–915.

Nichols, R. C. & Holland, J. L. (1963). Prediction of the first year college performance of high aptitude students. *Psychological Monographs: General and Applied*, **77**, Whole No 570, 1–29.

Northouse, P. G. (1997). *Leadership. theory and practice*. Thousand Oaks, CA: Sage.

Ochse, R. (1990). *Before the gates of excellence. The determinants of creative genius*. Cambridge: Cambridge University Press.

Parkerson, J. A., Lomax, R. G., Schiller, D. P. & Walberg, H. J. (1984). Exploring causal models of educational achievement. *Journal of Educational Psychology*, **76**, 638–646.

Perleth, C. & Heller, K. A. (1994). The Munich Longitudinal Study of Giftedness. In: R. F. Subotnik & K. D. Arnold (Eds), *Beyond Terman: Contemporary Longitudinal Studies of Giftedness and Talent* (pp. 77–114). Norwood, NJ: Ablex.

Renzulli, J. S. (1986). The three-ring conception of giftedness: a developmental model for creative productivity. In: R. J. Sternberg & J. E. Davidson (Eds), *Conceptions of Giftedness* (pp. 53–92). Cambridge: Cambridge University Press.

Roe, A. (1952a). A psychologist examines 64 eminent scientists. *Scientific American*, **187**, 21–25.

Roe, A. (1952b). *The making of a scientist*. New York: Dodd, Mead.

Roe, A. (1953). A psychological study of eminent psychologists and anthropologists, and a comparison with biological and physical scientists. *Psychological Monographs: General and Applied*, **67**, Whole No 352.

Roth, P. L., BeVier, C. A., Switzer, F. S. & Schippmann, J. S. (1996). Meta-analyzing the relationship between grades and job performance. *Journal of Applied Psychology*, **81**, 548–556.

Schiefele, U., Krapp, A. & Winteler, A. (1992). Interest as a predictor of academic achievement: a meta-analysis of research. In: K. A. Renninger, S. Hidi & A. Krapp (Eds), *The Role of Interest in Learning and Development* (pp. 183–212). Hillsdale, NJ: Erlbaum.

Sieglen, J. (1998). *Erklärung und Vorhersage außergewöhnlicher beruflicher Leistungen (Elucidation and prediction of outstanding occupational achievements)*. Frankfurt: Peter Lang.

Simonton, D. K. (1984). *Genius, creativity, and leadership: historiometric inquiries*. Cambridge, MA: Harvard University Press.

Simonton, D. K. (1987). Developmental antecedents of achieved eminence. *Annals of Child Development*, **5**, 131–169.

Simonton, D. K. (1988). Creativity, leadership, and chance. In: R. J. Sternberg (Ed.), *The Nature of Creativity. Contemporary Psychological Perspectives* (pp. 386–426). Cambridge: Cambridge University Press.

Sloane, K. D. & Sosniak, L. A. (1985). The development of accomplished sculptors. In: B. S. Bloom (Ed.), *Developing Talent in Young People* (pp. 68–89). New York: Ballantine.

Sosniak, L. A. (1985a). Learning to be a concert pianist. In: B. S. Bloom (Ed.), *Developing Talent in Young People* (pp. 19–67). New York: Ballantine.

Sosniak, L. A. (1985b). Becoming an outstanding research neurologist. In: B. S. Bloom (Ed.), *Developing Talent in Young People* (pp. 348–408). New York: Ballantine.

Stanley, J. C. & Benbow, C. P. (1986). Youths who reason exceptionally well mathematically. In: R. J. Sternberg & J. E. Davidson (Eds), *Conceptions of Giftedness* (pp. 361–387). Cambridge: Cambridge University Press.

Steinkamp, M. W. & Maehr, M. L. (1983). Affect, ability, and science achievement: a quantitative synthesis of correlational research. *Review of Educational Research*, **53**, 369–396.

Sternberg, R. J. & Davidson, J. E. (Eds) (1986). *Conceptions of giftedness*. Cambridge: Cambridge University Press.

Tannenbaum, A. J. (1986). *Giftedness: a psychosocial approach*. In: R. J. Sternberg & J. E. Davidson (Eds), *Conceptions of Giftedness* (pp. 21–52). Cambridge: Cambridge University Press.

Taylor, C. W. & Ellison, R. L. (1967). Biographical predictors of scientific performance. *Science*, **155**, 1075–1080.

Terman, L. M. (1925). *Genetic studies of genius*: Vol 1. *Mental and physical traits of a thousand gifted children*. Stanford, CA: Stanford University Press.

Terman, L. M. (1965). The discovery and encouragement of exceptional talent. In: W. B. Barbe (Ed.), *Psychology and Education of the Gifted: Selected Readings* (pp. 8–23). New York: Appleton-Century-Crofts. (Reprinted from *American Psychologist*, **9**, 1954, 221–130.)

Terman, L. M. & Oden, M. H. (1959). *Genetic studies of genius*: Vol 5. *The gifted group at mid-life: thirty-five years' follow-up of the superior child*. Stanford, CA : Stanford University Press.

Tomlinson-Keasey, C. & Little, T. D.(1990). Predicting educational attainment, occupational achievement, intellectual skill, and personal adjustment among gifted men and women. *Journal of Educational Psychology, 82*, 442–455.

Torrance, E. P. (1988). The nature of creativity as manifest in its testing. In: R. J. Sternberg (Ed.), *The Nature of Creativity. Contemporary Psychological Perspectives* (pp. 43–75). Cambridge: Cambridge University Press.

Trost, G. (1986). Identification of highly gifted adolescents: methods and experiences. In: K. A. Heller & J. F. Feldhusen (Eds), *Identifying and Nurturing the Gifted: An International Perspective* (pp. 83–91). Toronto: Huber.

Trost, G. (1987). Hochbegabte und eine Repräsentativgruppe deutscher Abiturienten in elfjähriger Längsschnittbeobachtung: Vergleich der Studien- und Berufswege. Ein Zwischenbericht (Highly gifted and a representative group of German 'Abiturienten' followed up over 11 years: comparison of educational and professional careers. An intermediary report). *Empirische Pädagogik, 1*, 6–26.

Uguroglu, M. E. & Walberg, H. J. (1979). Motivation and achievement: a quantitative synthesis. *American Educational Research Journal, 16*, 375–389.

Walberg, H. J. (1988). Creativity and talent as learning. In: R. J. Sternberg (Ed.), *The Nature of Creativity: Contemporary Psychological Perspectives* (pp. 340–361). Cambridge: Cambridge University Press.

Walberg, H. J., Tsai, S.-L., Weinstein, T., Gabriel, C. L., Rasher, S. P., Rosecrans, E. R., Ide, J., Trujillo, M. & Vukosavich, P. (1981). Childhood traits and environmental conditions of highly eminent adults. *The Gifted Child Quarterly, 25*, 103–107.

Walberg, H. J., Zhang, G., Haller, E. P., Sares, T. A., Stariha, W. E., Wallace, T. & Zeiser, S. F. (1994). Early educative influences on later outcomes: the Terman data revisited. In: K. A. Heller & E. A. Hany (Eds), *Competence and Responsibility*, Vol. 2 (pp. 164–177). Toronto: Hogrefe & Huber.

Willingham, W. W. (1985). *Success in college: the role of personal qualities and academic ability*. New York: College Entrance Examination Board.

Zuckerman, H. (1977). *Scientific elite: Nobel laureates in the United States*. New York: Free Press.

Part IV

Gifted Education and Programming

Conceptual Foundations and Theoretical Lenses for the Diversity of Giftedness and Talent

LeoNora M. Cohen[1], Don Ambrose[2] and William N. Powell[3]

[1] *Oregon State University, Corvallis, Oregon, USA*
[2] *Rider University, Lawrenceville, NJ, USA*
[3] *Oregon State University, Corvallis, Oregon, USA*

Conceptual foundations include definitions and conceptions of giftedness; philosophical bases and ethical issues; theories and models; historical, social, political, and economic considerations; influences from outside the field; and trends, issues, and future directions for the field. Other chapters in this book deal with some of these aspects, particularly chapters by Tannenbaum, Heller and Ziegler, Simonton, Gagnè, and Monks and Mason. This chapter will therefore focus largely on philosophical and theoretical considerations.

Philosophical frameworks and theoretical lenses provide guidance for coordinating meaningful research and for building coherent practices in gifted education. Without a solid conceptual base and theoretical awareness, researchers and practitioners tend to develop conceptual blind spots and ignore important aspects of giftedness and talent. Worse still, they can perpetuate current socio-political power structures and give no voice to the gifted in under-represented groups.

These blind spots arise from tacit entrapment within dominant philosophical frameworks or favored theoretical perspectives. For instance, mechanistic philosophical beliefs (reality as machine-like) encourage assumptions that intelligence is objectively measurable and culture-transcendent. Such assumptions obscure alternative conceptions of intelligence and perpetuate long-established sorting practices that ignore gifts and talents valued by minority populations. At their worst, these practices have reinforced the power of dominant classes, while promoting exploitation, racism, and even eugenics policies (Powell, 1999). The prominence of these assumptions and practices in the historical development of gifted education eventually led to the quagmire in which the field currently finds itself, namely, under-inclusion of children from racial and ethnic minorities and impoverished groups (Passow & Frasier, 1996; Rudnitski & Kearney, 1996).

Gifted education is still based on dominant-culture conceptions of giftedness. What continues to be ignored are ways to understand and define giftedness and talents of non-mainstream children outside of the dominant hierarchical social order. Their gifts and talents may be overlooked, according to Passow & Frasier (1996), due to overemphasis on standardized tests, narrow definitions of giftedness, failure to consider attributes and specific behaviors in cultural context, deficit orientations, and lack of dynamic assessment through learning opportunities. This is in spite of major focus in the field in the 1960s and 1970s and efforts by Frasier, Garcia, and Passow (1995), Frasier et al. (1995), Ford (1996), Ford & Harris (1999), Maker (1996), Maker and Schiever (1989), Peterson (1999) and others to conceptualize giftedness in diverse groups and to identify and serve diverse children.

Although there has been some progress in developing conceptual underpinnings for the field of gifted education, the issue of diversity has not yet been sufficiently addressed. Several researchers and practitioners have focused on addressing under-represented groups, particularly the identification of children from these groups, but there has been little attention to the related theoretical or philosophical dimensions of the field that shape exclusionary, possibly Eurocentric definitions of giftedness and talent.

Theorists, researchers, and practitioners need to critique their own assumptions in efforts to ensure that they are not ensnared in insular, ethnocentric thinking about giftedness and talent. One way to carry out such a critique is to explore the philosophical and theoretical roots of thinking in the field. Another is to look beyond the borders of the field to discover research findings, theoretical frameworks, and philosophical perspectives that can reveal new ways of thinking about optimal development of creativity, intelligence, and other aspects of children's potential. This chapter is a broad-based exploration of conceptual foundations and theoretical lenses for the diversity of giftedness.

Current Fragmentation and Incoherence of Approaches to Education of the Gifted and Talented

Reflection about the core assumptions and the evolution of the field has been emerging (see Ambrose, 1998a, 1998b; Ambrose, Cohen & Coleman, 1999; Borland, 1990, 1996; Callahan, 1996; Cohen, 1996; Coleman, Sanders & Cross, 1997; Gallagher 1996; Pendarvis & Howley, 1996). Much of this deliberation has to do with equity issues, perceived lack of purpose, and qualitative differentiation concerns in quick-fix programming and instruction, as well as the viability of gifted education per se. Attacks from outside the field (e.g. Oakes, 1985; Sapon-Shevin, 1994; Margolin, 1996) have catalyzed some of this reflection.

In spite of the development of several excellent conceptual models (e.g. Benbow, 1986; Betts, 1985; Clark, 1992; Feldhusen, 1998; Gagné, 1993; Jellen and Verduin, 1986; Kaplan, 1986; Milgram, 1989; Piirto, 1999a; Renzulli, 1986, 1994; Renzulli & Reis, 1985; Tannenbaum, 1983, 1986; Taylor, 1986; Treffinger & Sortore, 1994; VanTassel-Baska, 1992; Ward, 1980), simplistic approaches to programming and instruction are too often implemented with the claim that they are specifically designed for the gifted. Yet these 'easy' approaches pay little attention to the nuances of, or rationale for, these models. Practices disconnected from strong, conceptual underpinnings open gifted education to criticism. Even though important meta-analyses have clarified research-practice connections (e.g. Shore, Cornell, Robinson & Ward, 1991; Kulik & Kulik, 1992; Rogers, 1992), justification of qualitatively different programming and practices for gifted children is built on shifting sands due to a lack of coherent theory and philosophical awareness. Moreover, the needs of children from diverse cultures and socio-economic backgrounds remain obscured.

Limitations of Research

Research paradigms partially determine what will be studied in a field (Ambrose, 1998a; Borland, 1990; Coleman, Sanders & Cross, 1997; Lincoln & Guba, 1985). For instance, the positivistic paradigm biases research toward analytic investigation of decontextualized variables while the post-positivist paradigm embraces the complexities of context. The contexts for gifted education include the larger school system and the socio-economic, political, and cultural aspects of society. If most of the research in a field is positivistic, that field may ignore important contextual influences.

Renzulli (1991) points out that the dominance of traditional research designs and instruments limit what can be studied in gifted education, and that this obscures visibility of the needs of minority and economically-disadvantaged groups. Cross (1994) notes that gifted education lags behind general education in the employment of alternative research methods (e.g. constructivism, critical theory, or varied qualitative methodologies). The dominance of the traditional research paradigm, he claims, protects the research base from unconventional ideas, data, and theories. In addition, research in the field has been largely atheoretical, dealing with small issues often in a piecemeal approach that misses the whole picture. Without theoretic guidance, the 'so what' of research does not become integrated into practice (Cohen & Ambrose, 1993).

Philosophical Underpinnings of Gifted Education

One reason for fragmentation and insularity of theory, research, and practice in the field is that opposing world views tacitly influence the thinking of scholars and practitioners at the philosophical level. World views are broad, meta-theoretical conceptual lenses based on root-metaphorical filters through which individuals perceive reality (Gillespie, 1992; Overton, 1984; Pepper, 1942). These world views, which include mechanism, organicism, contextualism, and formism, implicitly shape basic assumptions about theory, research, and practice.

Tacit entrapment within the conceptual framework of one world view can cause scholars and practitioners to misunderstand or devalue the work of others whose world views differ from their own. The broad scope of each world view can mislead a scholar or practitioner into thinking that his or her perspective provides a sufficient view of the whole, but each world view highlights some aspects of phenomena while obscuring others. For example, the mechanistic view, based on the root metaphor of a machine, encourages perceptions of reality as stable and fixed, predisposing researchers to reductive analyses and the search for the simplest cause-effect explanations. It promotes reductive conceptions of mind, such as behaviorist theory or strictly inside-the-cranium computer metaphors of mind, while denying the validity of holistic or contextual accounts.

Actually, each world view has sufficient breadth of scope to provide useful alternative explanations, and complex phenomena require multiple investigations based on more than one world-view (Ambrose, 1996, 1998a; Gillespie, 1992; Overton, 1984; Pepper, 1942). Table 1 provides an overview of the essential characteristics of the world views, their connections with well-known philosophical paradigms, and some examples of their influences on conceptual foundations.

Paradigm Shifts in Gifted Education

An investigative paradigm is a collection of implicit assumptions that influences scientific research and shapes the formation of theories and conceptual models (Kuhn, 1970). Treffinger & Sortore (1994) claim that

Table 1. Root-Metaphorical World Views: Their Tenets, Limitations, and Influences on Conceptions of Giftedness © 1999 Don Ambrose.

World View	Organicism	Contextualism	Formism	Mechanism
Root metaphor	– Organism developing through stages toward a particular end	– Ongoing event within its context	– Similarity	– Machine
Connections with philosophical traditions	– Absolute or Objective Idealism, Existentialism (Hegel, Husserl)	– Pragmatism (Peirce, James, Dewey)	– Platonic Idealism and some Realism (Plato, Aristotle)	– Materialism, Realism, Naturalism (Descartes, Locke, Hobbes, Hume)
What the world view highlights	– Coherence and totality of systems (the whole transcending its parts) – Integrative connections – Long-term development	– Contextual influences – Unpredictable emergence of novelty	– Patterns of similarity in diverse phenomena	– Reduction of the whole to its component parts – Precision, detail – Linear causality – Objectivity
Weaknesses of the perspective	– Limited applicability beyond the system under study – Misses detail of the moment	– Imprecision	– Imprecision	– Obscures context and systemic interconnections
Preferred mode of inquiry	**Postpositivist:** – Seeks big-picture, qualitative essence patterns in multiple interpretations (constructed realities) of complex, holistic phenomena. – Assumes that elements and processes in these phenomena are inextricably intertwined, mutually shaping, and inescapably influenced by context – Assumes inseparability of researcher and the object of study. Clarifies values and biases of the researcher on assumption that research is not value-free			**Positivist:** – Seeks prediction and control of linear cause-effect relationships between isolated variables – Uses objective, value-free experimental, quantitative analyses
Examples of research projects primarily influenced by the world view	– In a case study of a creative individual, a researcher seeks ways in which intrasystemic, mutually shaping interactions among cognitive, affective, and conative subsystems promote long-range purpose	– Qualitative researcher seeking effects of socioeconomic influences on talented minority children who show resilience in dealing with unpredictable environments	– Complexity theorists discovering patterns of similarity in the dynamics of human brains and the US economic system – Philosophical analysis of metaphors that underpin research in gifted education	– Experimental, quantitative analysis of effects of instructional strategy on students' achievement scores
Perspectives on intelligence and giftedness (derived from Fischer et al., 1996)	**Social Construction Paradigm:** Intelligence is a socially constructed and changeable consequence of political choices. It is (a) a complex collection of interactive and context-dependent elements, (b) plastic and developing, (c) amenable only to approximate assessment. Cross-cultural similarities in children's reactions to deprivation (e.g. anxiety, resignation) suppress the development of intelligence. 'Giftedness' encompasses the skills, knowledge, and dispositions that are valued or needed in a given society in a given era. Finding diverse talents in diverse settings is preferable to 'sorting' children for giftedness on the basis of a few narrow academic measures.			**Natural Inequality Paradigm:** Intelligence is innate and largely immutable. It can be objectively and precisely measured. The 'gifted' can be sorted out based on test scores.

paradigms in gifted education shape the attitudes and beliefs that dominate the field. Undergoing paradigm changes in gifted education is necessary and natural; the field is part of a larger system of education and an aspect of a much larger system of global evolution. Currently, fundamental changes in values and beliefs are influencing the evolution of societies around the globe (Inglehart, 1997). These changes are fueling a major paradigm shift that is altering educators' values and assumptions; shifts such as this are abrupt and disturb the status quo, causing periods of instability and unrest.

There have been several paradigm shifts in the gifted child movement (Cohen, 1998). The traditional paradigm in gifted education was based on assumptions of clearly defined, measurable, culture-transcendent intelligence and the selection and labeling of the gifted (usually through IQ tests) for their inherent abilities.

The second paradigm was derived from special-education emphases on individual educational plans and least restrictive environments based on assessments of students' individual needs. This paradigm ran counter to the one-size-fits-all programming emphasis of the traditional paradigm and was more sensitive to the nuances of individual development, but it was detrimental wherever it over-emphasized students' weaknesses.

Aspects of the as yet ill-defined third paradigm shift seem to include emphases on multidimensional talents (Feldman, 1992; Piirto, 1999; Treffinger & Feldhusen, 1996), multidimensional and context-sensitive conceptions of intelligence (Gardner, 1983, 1993, 1999; Perkins, 1995; Purcell, 1996; Sternberg, 1990, 1993, 1997, 1999b), and awareness of diversity and societal context (Ford, 1996; Ford & Harris, 1999; Frasier, 1995a, 1995b, 1995c; Frasier et al., 1995; Maker, 1996; Peterson, 1999; Piirto, 1999a). If educators of the gifted come to understand the nature of paradigm shifts in the field, they will be able to appreciate the ways in which their work fits into broader educational and societal contexts. In addition, they are more likely to recognize the limitations of earlier paradigms for identifying and serving diverse learners.

What Is Theory and Why Is It Important?

Research appropriately provides much of the direction in any academic field. But by its very nature, most empirical research emphasizes specific pieces of phenomena and cannot adequately address big-picture frameworks. This is especially the case in complex fields. Research in gifted education has not portrayed the whole picture because it tends to address important but small-scale issues in a scattershot approach while phenomena in the field pertain to the most complex system in the universe: the human mind.

Theory can provide big-picture guidance for researchers and practitioners by transcending and connecting the important, but fragmented empirical findings upon which researchers necessarily focus. Theory is also needed to: (a) account for extant research findings and organize these into a cogent whole, (b) provide research heuristics and suggest new directions for research by highlighting gaps in the knowledge base, (c) provide explanatory frameworks that can help educators discern the special nature and needs that do or do not manifest in gifted and talented children, and (d) clarify the scope and scale of phenomena deemed important to research and practice.

Theories of narrow scope tend to have clarity of detail and strong predictive capacity; theories of broad-scope tend to have strong descriptive and explanatory potential and context-sensitivity. It seems important to embrace both narrow- and broad-scope theoretical perspectives when studying complex phenomena such as the human mind.

The scale of a theory refers to the level of analysis at which it operates; theorists can focus on different levels ranging from macrolevel philosophical frameworks and panoramic, overarching theories, to levels dealing with thought processes and other factors influencing mind development, to practical instructional frameworks and specific learning processes. In order to fully understand the comprehensiveness of conceptual foundations, scholars must appreciate the levels in which their theories fit, and ensure that theorizing in the field addresses all levels (see Cohen & Ambrose, 1993 for more detail about theoretic scope and scale).

Competing Views About Methods for Theory Development

Unfortunately, strengthening conceptual foundations through theoretic awareness is not so simple. While there are varied ways of making philosophical sense of a field, there are also diverse, often conflicting perspectives on theoretic work. Some scholars believe that formal theory usurps too much attention in educational inquiry, and has detrimental effects on practice. For instance, Thomas (1997) claims that theory can be seductive, trapping investigators in preconceived idea frameworks and inhibiting creative solution of educational problems. In a similar vein, Grant and Piechowski (1999) claim that attending to theory development in gifted education may not do much for gifted children, or may even be counter-productive. They claim that formal social-science theory does little good unless that theory is rooted in student-centered, case-based naturalistic inquiry. Without this rooting, much of the theorizing in the field tends to promote morally problematic outside-the-child visions of achievement and productivity as opposed to the inner life and emotional well being of the child.

Others see positive roles for theory in educational investigation. For instance, Ambrose (1996, 1998a) claims that it is necessary to expand and clarify the conceptual foundations that underpin the field in order to overcome the insularity of our own assumptions about complex phenomena such as creativity and giftedness. Expansion can come from broad searches for relevant formal and implicit theories both within and beyond the field. Clarification can come from careful consideration of the specific contributions each theoretical perspective can make to our understanding of a phenomenon as a whole.

Based on similar assumptions, Sternberg (1990, 1993) develops metaphors of mind that reveal diverse perspectives from which theorists can view intelligence. Sternberg claims that many intelligence theorists mistakenly overgeneralize their theories to the entire phenomenon of intelligence when, in reality, each theory applies to a part of the whole. The metaphorical representations of intelligence make explicit the diverse perspectival differences while collectively enabling more comprehensive visions of mind.

There are proposals to integrate theory in the field; for instance, Cohen (1988, 1992) advocates non-competitive interdisciplinary dialogue and comparisons of diverse theories of giftedness and creativity. Cohen and Ambrose (1993) map out influential theories of intelligence, creativity, and giftedness, categorizing them into theory families according to the tenets of the mechanistic and organismic world views, and highlighting some integrative connections among the diverse theories.

Others point out that complex phenomena of mind require investigation from multiple levels of analysis because theorists, researchers, and practitioners tend to lock into one level while assuming that they have adequate perception of the whole (Ambrose, 1998a; Midgley, 1995, 1998; Wahlsten & Gottlieb, 1997). For instance, Wahlsten and Gottlieb (1997) claim that the intricate systemic interconnections among genetic and environmental influences on intelligence can become visible only if we consider research at multiple levels of analysis including the cultural, societal, anatomical, hormonal, cellular, and genetic, among others.

There are additional reasons for large-scale mapping of theoretic perspectives. For example, Newell (1990) claims that while much impressive 'local' cognitive theory currently provides frameworks for interpretation of small bodies of data in cognitive science, global, integrative, broad-scope theorizing is needed to bring together dissonances and contradictions. It is contradiction that promotes problem-solving and insight in a field.

Sternberg (1999a) uses the dialectical process, advocated by philosopher Georg Hegel, to expose and capitalize on contradictions among diverse philosophical and theoretical camps in cognitive psychology. In the dialectical process, a dominant perspective in a field (the thesis) brings forth an opposing reaction (the antithesis). The dynamic interplay between thesis and antithesis can bring about a productive synthesis of the two perspectives. From this vantage point, conflicting conceptions of giftedness and talent (e.g. general intelligence vs. multiple intelligences) represent golden opportunities for progress in the field.

Unfortunately, theoretic aspects of education for the gifted and talented are too often ignored by researchers and practitioners. In spite of valid points made by those who caution against the hypnotic effects of formal theory in education (e.g. Grant & Piechowski, 1999; Thomas, 1997), research and practice without theory tends to be banal, superficial, fragmented, and insular. Acknowledging and integrating the necessary and reciprocal relationships of theory, research, and practice can give the field a stronger foundation (Cohen & Ambrose, 1993).

We advocate an eclectic approach to clarification and expansion of theoretical perspectives in gifted education because such an approach is consistent with emerging meta-theoretical insights in other fields and because only through diverse perspectives can we discover the multiple realities of giftedness among diverse groups. These insights imply that large-scale theoretic mapping is necessary because the entirety of any complex phenomenon is simply not visible from a single perspective or a single level of analysis. For instance, in the field of neuroscience, Rose (1998) argues for a more expansive research agenda that would incorporate but go well beyond currently dominant reductive studies of electrochemical processes within individual crania to include socio-cultural shaping influences on mind. At the same time, eclectic does not mean stirring together random bits and pieces, lest we fall into the same traps of fragmented practices. Instead, it is the careful consideration of these various theoretical perspectives and the mapping of the luminous elements within their area(s) of explanation/vision onto a large frame that differentiates what we advocate from sloppy thinking.

In order to gain a comprehensive grasp of a complex phenomenon, it seems necessary to map as many as possible of the elements of that phenomenon in order to provide big-picture guidance to those who prefer to incisively analyze small subsets of its elements. Interdisciplinary conceptual navigation throughout multiple levels of analysis can promote big-picture appreciation of the intricacies of, and contradictions in, complex phenomena such as intelligence, creativity, and giftedness while preventing scholarly entrenchment and insularity. Expanding our view of a complex phenomenon makes it less likely that theorists and researchers will overgeneralize their own local theories to the whole phenomenon, and less likely that educators will be mislead by such overgeneralizations.

Influential and Promising Theories Pertaining to Giftedness and Talent

Gifted education largely rests on theories of intelligence, creativity, and giftedness. In the first edition of

335

this book, we outlined many of the diverse theories that were influential at that time in gifted education, or that had the potential to influence the field. Due to their number and complexity, these theories are not described again in detail here (see Cohen & Ambrose, 1993 for an extensive overview). Instead, the following outlines some representative recent developments in theories of intelligence, creativity, and giftedness, as well as some potentially informative theories from beyond the field.

Developments in intelligence theory. The debate over IQ-based definitions of intelligence continues to rage unabated. The publication of *The Bell Curve* (Herrnstein & Murray, 1994) set off yet another round of altercations between those defending the credibility of the general intelligence factor (e.g. Gottfredson, 1999) and those highlighting the limitations of IQ-based definitions while portraying intelligence as much more multidimensional and context-situated (e.g. Gardner, 1999; Perkins, 1995; Purcell, 1996; Sternberg, 1999b). In the midst of this debate, other related controversies swirl; for instance, recent developments in genetic research are prompting new rounds of nature-nurture debates. Proponents of behavior-genetic theories of intelligence emphasize the role of genetics, and proponents of socialization theories emphasize the importance of socio-cultural influences (see Sternberg & Grigorenko, 1997 for an overview of these theories).

Yet another debate rages among cognitive scientists who argue over the credibility of two artificial-intelligence-based models of cognition (Baumgartner & Payr, 1995). Proponents of the symbolist view of mind (e.g. Newell, 1990; Simon, 1979) portray cognition as the result of linear, primarily logical, symbolic information processing in the brain. Proponents of the connectionist view (e.g. Churchland & Sejnowski, 1992) highlight nonlinear thought by portraying cognition as arising from parallel distributed processing within the brain's intricate neural networks. Both of these viewpoints are based on computer metaphors of mind.

Still other cognitive scientists believe that the computer metaphors ignore strong contextual effects on human thought. For instance, Cicourel (1995) claims that cognition is embedded in, and strongly influenced by, the subtle nuances of interpersonal interaction and cultural belief systems. Lakoff (1993, 1995) demonstrates ways in which metaphorical frameworks from our shared language systems exert subtle yet strong contextual shaping influences on cognition.

There are some other notable developments in intelligence theory. For instance, Gardner (1999) has expanded his theory of multiple intelligences by adding the naturalist (ability to recognize and categorize natural objects) to his seven original intelligences while proposing the existential (recognition of deep, fundamental questions) as a potential candidate for yet another intelligence.

In recognition of the abstract, somewhat school-bound, decontextualized nature of most intelligence theories, Sternberg (1997) posits practical intelligence as a necessary theoretical perspective. Practical intelligence is the dimension of mind that enables one to artfully navigate the problem-solving requirements of the real world.

Developments in creativity theory. Some scholars claim that early research on creativity erroneously portrayed the creative process as dependent on domain-transcending traits, skills, or dispositions and that recent research corrects this misconception. Instead, creativity should be considered domain-specific (e.g. Baer, 1993, 1998). Others (e.g. Cramond, 1994; Plucker, 1998) argue that claims about the domain-specificity of creativity are premature.

Some recent theory blurs the boundaries between creativity, intelligence, and giftedness; for instance, Heller (1995) suggests that creativity and intelligence are complementary components of mind, which in tandem support complex problem solving. Along similar lines, various scholars explore the ways in which critical, convergent, thought processes support divergent, creative thinking (see Runco, 1998).

Much recent theory portrays creativity as emergent from the complex, systemic intermingling of diverse elements. For instance, Feldhusen & Goh (1995) claim that an understanding of creative development requires an integrative view of cognitive processes (e.g. critical thinking, decision making, metacognition), interests, motivation, attitudes, the nature of creative products and performances, and the shaping influences of environment. In a similar argument, Amabile (1995) and Urban (in press) advocate for systemic views of creativity, which encompass the characteristics of the individual and the nature of the environment instead of narrow conceptions of one or the other.

Others highlight the diversity-creativity nexus. For instance, Arnold, Noble & Subotnik (1996) incorporate a wide range of perspectives that reveal the effects of race, class, and other aspects of social/historical context on the manifestation of women's creative potential. Esquivel & Houtz (1998) provide a similar forum for explorations of the ways in which creativity emerges in culturally and linguistically diverse populations.

Developments in theories of giftedness and talent. The major recent theoretical shift in the field of gifted education is the growing emphasis on talent development, which highlights mutliple talents at multiple levels of development. For instance, Treffinger & Feldhusen (1996) describe "a strong shift away from the limited academic-intellectual orientation of gifted education toward a recognition of the nature and importance of talents in the arts, vocational domains, and social-interpersonal areas of human activities" (p. 182).

Gagné (1985, 1993) helped catalyze the shift to talent development with a theoretical model portraying talent as emergent from genetically determined gifts that, under the influence of intrapersonal and environmental impacts, develop into more and more specific talents. Feldhusen (1998) uses Gagne's construct, among others, in his model of talent development. In Feldhusen's model, the interaction of genetically determined abilities with environmental stimulation produces emerging aptitudes, abilities, and intelligences, which integrate to support the pursuit of career goals.

Piirto (1999a) presents yet another talent development model, which incorporates genetic foundations, emotional-personality elements, a minimum IQ threshold, and environmental influences (home, school, community, culture, chance, and gender). Given these constraints and influences, the individual's domain-specific talents are selected and developed according to a calling or vocation.

Rea (2000) borrows from motivation theory to create a different theory of talent development. According to Rea, children can become engaged in counterproductive cycling between anxious overexcitement and apathetic boredom, or highly productive cycling between exciting exploration and calm, serious reflection. The latter cycling emerges from interactions among optimal challenge, undivided interest, and optimal arousal.

As in creativity and intelligence theory, most theorists are recognizing that giftedness and talent emerge from the complex interaction of diverse elements; consequently, they are using broad-scope perspectives to incorporate the expansiveness and intricate complexities of mind-related phenomena. For instance, Simonton (1998) uses three disciplinary vantage points (biology, sociology, psychology) to explain differing developmental processes leading from childhood promise to adult achievement. Simonton claims that biological-genetic factors, sociocultural and economic influences, and specialized expertise and motivation all intertwine to enhance or suppress the development of specific talents.

Some Promising Theories from Outside the Field of Gifted Education

As Piaget (1981) noted, reading around a field mitigates against parochialism and promotes creativity in that field. Consideration of the established theoretical terrain pertaining to giftedness and talent helps clarify conceptual foundations. But a truly eclectic, epistemologically diverse treatment of theoretical perspectives would push back the edges of the map to explore potentially fruitful theories from disciplines normally thought of as beyond the field. This section includes some examples of outside-the-field theories and constructs that could influence thinking about giftedness and talent; these examples are by no means exhaustive of potentially influential interdisciplinary connections.

Complexity theory. The rapidly growing interdisciplinary science of complexity is one body of knowledge with potential implications for conceptions of giftedness and talent. Complexity theory includes broad-based, interdisciplinary searches for patterns of similarity in the structure and dynamics of complex adaptive systems. These systems evolve unpredictably through states of orderly stability and chaotic turbulence, sometimes finding new patterns of order at higher levels of complexity (Axelrod, 1997; Jervis, 1997; Kauffman, 1995). Kelso (1995) and Sterling (1992) promote theories of the brain as a nonlinear dynamic system in which new thought patterns emerge from self-organization. These theories highlight the importance of environmental influence, ambiguity, and unpredictability in creativity.

Cognitive science. Some scholars are continuing the recent trend of borrowing insights from cognitive science to expand conceptions of giftedness and talent. For instance, Pelletier & Shore (in press) use comparisons of novices and experts to illuminate the nature of giftedness. They use research findings on flexibility, metacognition, and knowledge organization to clarify processes that promote development from novice levels to expert levels in a domain. Sternberg & Hovarth (1998) also explore the expertise-giftedness nexus, delineating eight different ways in which conceptions of expertise correspond with conceptions of giftedness. These include differential degrees of knowledge accumulation, knowledge organization, automaticity of skills, metacognitive capacity, creative capacity, and practical savvy among others.

Quantum physics. Theories of mind based on quantum physics have been operating at the fringes of mind-related fields (Eccles, 1996; Goswami, 1988, 1990, 1995, 1996; Penrose, 1994). These theories detail ways in which the strange paradoxes of the submicroscopic quantum world (e.g. non-local causality) can operate within microstructures of the brain, thereby contradicting traditional eliminative-materialist assumptions that the mind is little more than an epiphenomenon of electrochemical actions within individual crania. If on target, quantum theories of mind eventually could undermine the dominant mechanistic theories of cognitive science. They raise the possibility that underlying, holistic interconnections influence those processes beyond the scope of sensate perception and material causality.

Table 2. Some Recent Developments in Theoretical Perspectives in Gifted Education and some Foreign Theories: Potential Luminous Elements and Potential Problems. © 1999 Don Ambrose.

Theoretical Perspective	Source Discipline(s) and World-View Derivation (The latter is in italics)	Current or Potential Luminous Elements for Understanding Giftedness and Talent and Some Potential Problems with the Perspective
Talent-Development Theories and Models (Feldhusen, 1998; Gagne, 1985, 1993; Piirto, 1999b; Rea, 2000)	Primarily psychology, gifted education *organicism, contextualism, and some mechanism*	– Reveal dynamics conducive to development of diverse talents. – Could 'democratize' gifted education by supporting talent development for all. – Could over-emphasize precocity.
Multidimensional, Systemic, Context-Situated Theories of Intelligence (Gardner, 1999; Sternberg, 1999b), **Creativity** (Amabile, 1995; Feldhusen & Goh, 1995; Heller, 1995), and **Giftedness** (Simonton, 1998)	Primarily psychology *organicism, contextualism*	– Raise awareness that gifts and talents can be diverse and mutually shaping. – Highlight influences of socioeconomic, political, and cultural environment. – Undermine mechanistic-reductionist assumptions.
Behavioral-Genetic Theories: Specific genes are the basis of cognitive abilities. (Plomin, 1997; Scarr, 1997)	Molecular biology *primarily mechanism*	– May specify heritability factors that underlie variance in some cognitive abilities. – Could obscure influence of context on intelligence.
Critical and Socialization Theories of Intelligence: Societal context shapes the development of intelligence (Fischer et. al., 1996; Wahlsten & Gottlieb, 1997)	Psychology, sociology *contextualism, organicism*	– Could keep genetic determinists honest at a time when new technology is highlighting genetic discovery. – Could aid in considering attributes and behaviors of giftedness in cultural context.
Artificial-Intelligence, Computer-Based Models of Cognition – **Symbolist:** Cognition emerges from linear, primarily logical, symbolic information processing in the brain (Newell, 1990; Simon, 1979) – **Connectionist:** nonlinear emergence of cognition from parallel distributed processing of neural networks (Churchland & Sejnowski, 1992)	Cognitive science (an interdisciplinary field) *mechanism, formism* (symbolist) *contextualism, formism* (connectionist)	– Symbolists refine our knowledge of logical cognitive processes. – Connectionists emphasize the importance of unpredictable connection making in creative thought processes. – Both symbolists and connectionists promote the belief that cognition derives from inside-the-head computation.
Context-Embedded Models of Cognition from Cognitive Science: Culture and language strongly shape and partially structure cognitive processes (Cicourel, 1995; Gillespie, 1992; Lakoff, 1993, 1995)	Sociology, linguistics, and psychology *strong contextualism, some formism*	Could prevent entrapment within the computer metaphor by showing that cognition is more than inside-the-head computing. Highlight sociocultural influences on giftedness and talent.
Economic Theories of Creativity: Supply and demand processes influence creative work (Rubenson, in press; Rubenson & Runco, 1992; Sternberg & Lubart, 1993)	Economics, psychology *contextualism, some formism*	Reveal motivational patterns in creativity.

Table 2. Continued.

Theoretical Perspective	Source Discipline(s) and World-View Derivation (The latter is in italics)	Current or Potential Luminous Elements for Understanding Giftedness and Talent and Some Potential Problems with the Perspective
Creativity Through the Lenses of Gender and Cultural-Linguistic Diversity (Arnold, Noble, & Subotnik, 1996; Esquivel & Houtz, 1998)	*contextualism*	– Strengthen awareness of environmental opportunity and shaping influences on manifestation of creativity.
Postmodern Theory: rejects mechanistic assumptions such as objectivity and reductionism; Highlights sociocultural and political influences such as effects of power and privilege on 'identification' of the gifted (Piirto, 1999a; Cahoone, 1996)	Interdisciplinary, but primary influence is from philosophy *primarily contextualism*	– Challenges basic assumptions (e.g. the giftedness construct, the 'gifted' as a national resource). – Highlights 'gifts' of collaboration and altruism while putting competitive, self-interested individual achievement in better perspective. – Could mitigate greed, conflict, and social stratification in society. – Challenges dominance of positivistic inquiry.
Complexity Theory: Minds, children, classrooms are complex, self-organizing, context-sensitive, unpredictable, chaotic-orderly, dynamic systems (Kelso, 1995; Sterling, 1992)	Originally physics and chemistry, now applied in diverse fields such as biology, economics, and political science *primarily contextualism, formism*	– Highlights context-sensitivity and spontaneous cognitive transformations – Undermines prediction and control.
Quantum Theories of Mind: Consciousness is a fundamental aspect of mind with causal influence, not simply an epiphenomenon of electrochemical, cranial processes (Eccles, 1996; Goswami, 1988, 1990, 1995, 1996; Penrose, 1994)	Theoretical physics and neuroscience *formism, organicism, contextualism*	– Emphasize intuitive processes of mind. – Raise possibility that cognition has very deep, untapped levels, with holistic, transcendent effects beyond the scope of mechanistic tools and constructs. – Could transcend world views. – Could undermine mechanistic, materialist theories.

Economic theories. Economic concepts have been influencing theories of creativity. For instance, two emerging economic perspectives highlight the motivational aspects of creative activity. The psycho-economic model (Rubenson, in press; Rubenson & Runco, 1992) portrays creative activity as emergent from supply and demand interactions between the individual, the field (which determines market demand for creative activity), and a particular domain (the market itself). According to another economic perspective, the investment theory of creativity (Sternberg & Lubart, 1993), successful creators tend to recognize ideas that are undervalued and invest themselves in these ideas, using aspects of their intelligence, intellectual style, knowledge, personality, motivation, and environmental context to produce creative ideas.

Philosophical developments. The often ignored field of philosophy can contribute important perspectives on giftedness, creativity, and intelligence. For instance, postmodern theory is challenging modernist (primarily mechanistic) assumptions in most of the social and behavioral sciences, and the field of gifted education is not immune. Postmodern theorists regard most of the mechanistic tenets of modern scholarship as obsolete, illegitimate, or at least inadequate bases for inquiry (Cahoone, 1996). For instance, They reject assumptions that investigators can achieve objectivity, simplicity, completeness, and certainty, and that the study of human phenomena can be based on or reduced to the methods of the physical sciences. They point out that socio-cultural and political contexts strongly shape the assumptions of scholars, as well as the nature of the phenomena they study.

Piirto (1999a) details some overarching themes from postmodern scholarship, and uses them as critical lenses for analysis of education of the gifted and talented. For instance, the theme of constitutive otherness highlights the ways in which commonly accepted constructs such as giftedness are maintained through exclusion of those labelled nongifted. Exclusion obscures the 'gifts' of women, minorities and others while highlighting the abilities of those whose gifts more closely match modernist (i.e. mechanistic) values.

Critical theory. While not purporting a theory per se, Fischer et al. (1996) report compelling evidence from sociological theory and research that encourages second thoughts about traditional theories of intelligence and giftedness. They show how systems of socio-economic stratification around the world depress the opportunities and initiative of underprivileged racial and ethnic groups. Deprivation, segregation, and stigmatization of lower-caste groups in many nations produce consistent patterns of anxiety, fatalism, and resignation in underprivileged children. These patterns, combined with inequality of educational opportunity,

undermine intelligence test scores and academic achievement. Of most pertinence to conceptions of giftedness, patterns of low intelligence and achievement scores persist in populations that were initially captured or conquered by ancestors of the dominant culture because these populations face long-term stigmatization. In contrast, low intelligence and achievement scores rise to levels comparable with the dominant populations within a few generations in immigrant groups for whom socio-economic deprivation is temporary. Fischer et al. (1996) claim that race or genetics cannot explain the dramatic intergenerational rebound in intelligence among the immigrant groups, but dramatic changes in socio-economic status can explain it. These patterns highlight the importance of societal power-control structures in showcasing the abilities of some children while suppressing those of others.

In general, these theories and perspectives from beyond the field raise some new possibilities for conceptions of intelligence, creativity, and giftedness; they also raise some issues about research methods, philosophical assumptions, and political issues in the field.

Clarifying and Expanding Conceptual Foundations Through Luminous Elements of Theory

It is important to scrutinize new theoretical developments in the field and interesting theories from beyond the field for their philosophical bases and biases, and for their potential impact on gifted education. In terms of philosophical bias, if we analyze new theoretical developments for their consistency with the tenets of the four root-metaphorical world views and discover that most or all of them are rooted in one world view, we can surmise that new theory suffers from entrapment within a single perspective, or that it is compensating for a prior world-view imbalance. If, on the other hand, some new theories are consistent with one world view, while others are consistent with another, we can assume that new thinking in and outside of the field makes room for diverse perspectives. If so, there is more hope for comprehensiveness and structural corroboration in our emerging understanding of giftedness and talent and more opportunity to embrace both diverse conceptions of giftedness and diverse gifted and/or talented learners.

In terms of potential impact on the field, wide-ranging considerations of diverse theories can tease out luminous elements that stretch our thinking about intelligence, creativity, or giftedness. Cohen (1992) calls the strengths of a given theory its 'luminous elements', as they have an aesthetic rightness and light-shedding quality that resonates with knowledgeable theorists, researchers, or practitioners. In recognition that no single theory captures all important aspects of mind (Ambrose, 1998a; Newell, 1990; Rose, 1998;

Sternberg, 1990, 1993, 1999a; Wahlsten & Gottlieb, 1997) it can be helpful to carry out an active search for luminous elements of theory from diverse inter-disciplinary sources with relevance to intelligence, creativity, and giftedness: a search such as the rudimentary example in the previous section.

The beauty, truthfulness, and relevance of these luminous elements enables them to reveal the depths, nuances, and the importance of specific phenomena. Such revelations can provide important keys to understanding the entirety of a complex phenomenon such as optimal mind development. They can help reveal gaps in the knowledge base and establish connections among diverse theoretical perspectives while keeping important aspects of mind development at the forefront of our attention.

Table 2 is an embryonic example of a search for luminous elements in recent theory, and in theories beyond the field. The overview highlights some emerging conceptual conflicts and possibilities for syntheses. It also details the current or potential impact of each perspective on conceptions of giftedness and talent and possible problems from these perspectives.

Theorists, researchers, or practitioners exposed to diverse theoretical luminous elements such as those outlined in Table 2 have the opportunity to expand their conceptions of giftedness and talent while preventing implicit entrapment within any single perspective. Consistent with advice to employ more than one world-view perspective when analyzing complex phenomena (Ambrose, 1996, 1998a; Gillespie, 1992; Overton, 1984; Pepper, 1942), Table 2 enables considerations of giftedness and talent from all four world-view perspectives. Also, consistent with advice to consider complex phenomena from multiple levels of analysis (Ambrose, 1998a; Midgley, 1995, 1998; Wahlsten & Gottlieb, 1997), Table 2 enables conceptions of giftedness and talent from the microlevels of molecular biology and neuroscience to the macrolevels of sociology, economics, and political science. It is the macroperspectives that reveal the subtle influences of socio-economic and political contexts, thereby revealing the conceptual blind spots that obscure the gifts and talents of minority populations. In addition, conflicting viewpoints in the table (e.g. behavioral-genetic vs. socialization theories of intelligence) create opportunities for attempts at dialectical syntheses such as those advocated by Sternberg (1999a).

We advocate for a largely philosophical meta-discourse in and around the field: a dialogue with the purpose of discerning emerging new big-picture patterns, and how these augment, extend, or work against the old. It should be a search for new connections and new possibilities.

We agree with the critics of theory who warn against blind acceptance of ideologically saturated social-science theories as tools for prediction and control of human phenomena (e.g. Thomas, 1997; Grant &

Piechowski, 1999). Instead, diverse theories should be used collectively as potentially useful clues that can guide our investigations of the many facets of human potential. A consideration of a wide range of diverse theories and philosophical perspectives can provide new perceptions of varied dimensions of giftedness and talent in diverse populations.

References

Amabile, T. M. (1995). Attributions of creativity: What are the consequences? *Creativity Research Journal*, **8**, 423–426.

Ambrose, D. (1996). Unifying theories of creativity: Metaphorical thought and the unification process. *New Ideas in Psychology*, **14**, 257–267.

Ambrose, D. (1998a). A model for clarification and expansion of conceptual foundations. *Gifted Child Quarterly*, **42**, 77–86.

Ambrose, D. (1998b). Comprehensiveness of conceptual foundations for gifted education: A world-view analysis. *Journal for the Education of the Gifted*, **21**, 452–470.

Ambrose, D., Cohen, L. M., & Coleman, L. J. (Eds.). (1999). Exploring theoretical foundations for gifted education [Special issue]. *Journal for the Education of the Gifted*, **22**(4).

Arnold, K., Noble, K. D., & Subotnik, R. F. (1996). *Remarkable women: Perspectives on female talent development*. Cresskill, NJ: Hampton Press.

Axelrod, R. (1997). *The complexity of cooperation: Agent-based models of competition and collaboration*. Princeton, NJ: Princeton University Press.

Baer, J. (1993). *Divergent thinking and creativity: A domain-specific approach*. Hillsdale, NJ: Lawrence Erlbaum Associates.

Baer, J. (1998). The case for domain specificity of creativity. *Creativity Research Journal*, **11**, 173–177.

Baumgartner, P., & Payr, S. (Eds.). (1995). *Speaking minds: Interviews with twenty eminent cognitive scientists*. Princeton, NJ: Princeton University Press.

Benbow, C. P. (1986). SMPY's model for teaching mathematically precocious students. In J. S. Renzulli (Ed.), *Systems and models for developing programs for the gifted and talented* (pp. 1–26). Mansfield Center, CT: Creative Learning Press.

Betts, G. (1985). *The autonomous learner model*. Greeley, CO: Autonomous Learning Publication Specialists.

Borland, J. H. (1990). Postpositivist inquiry: Implications of the 'new philosophy of science' for the field of education of the gifted. *Gifted Child Quarterly*, **34**, 161–167.

Borland, J. H. (1996). Gifted education and the threat of irrelevance. *Journal for the Education of the Gifted*, **19**, 129–147.

Brodsky, R. (1994). From the attic. *Roeper Review*, **17**, 70.

Cahoone, L. E. (Ed.). (1996). *From modernism to postmodernism: An anthology*. Oxford, England: Blackwell.

Callahan, C. M. (1996). A critical self-study of gifted education: Healthy practice, necessary evil, or sedition? *Journal for the Education of the Gifted*, **19**, 148–163.

Churchland, P. S., & Sejnowski, T. (1992). *The computational brain*. Cambridge, MA: MIT Press.

Cicourel, A. V. (1995). Cognition and cultural belief. In P. Baumgartner & S. Payr (Eds.), *Speaking minds: Interviews with twenty eminent cognitive scientists* (pp. 33–46). Princeton, NJ: Princeton University Press.

Clark, B. (1992). *Growing Up Gifted*. (4th ed.). Columbus, OH: Charles Merrill.

Cohen, L. M. (1988). To get ahead, get a theory: Criteria for evaluating theories of giftedness and creativity applied to education. *Roeper Review*, **11**, 95–100.

Cohen, L. M. (1992). From ownership to 'allship': Building a conceptual framework for educating the gifted and creative. In: N. Colangelo, S. G. Assouline & D. L. Ambroson (Eds.), *Talent development: Proceedings from the 1991 Henry B. and Jocelyn Wallace National Research Symposium on Talent Development* (pp. 204–222). Unionville, NY: Trillium.

Cohen, L. M. (1996). Mapping the domains of ignorance and knowledge in gifted education. *Roeper Review*, **18**, 183–189.

Cohen, L. M. (1998, Fall). Paradigm change in gifted education: Developing the talent-Is this the optimal set of possibilities?. *Conceptual Foundations Newsletter*, **6**, 3–5.

Cohen, L. M., & Ambrose, D. (1993). Theories and practices for differentiated education for the gifted and talented. In K. A. Heller, F. J. Mönks & A. H. Passow (Eds.), *International handbook of research and development of giftedness and talent* (pp. 339–363). Oxford, England: Pergamon.

Coleman, L. J., Sanders, M. D., & Cross, T. L. (1997). Perennial debates and tacit assumptions in the education of gifted children. *Gifted Child Quarterly*, **41**, 105–111.

Cramond, B. (1994). We can trust creativity tests. *Educational Leadership*, **52**, 70–71.

Cross, T. (1994). Alternative inquiry and its potential contributions to gifted education: A commentary. *Roeper Review*, **16**, 284–285.

Eccles, J. C. (1996). Evolution of complexity of the brain with the emergence of consciousness. In B. Pullman (Ed.), *The emergence of complexity in mathematics, physics, chemistry, and biology* (pp. 369–391). Vatican City: Pontifical Academy of Sciences.

Esquivel, G. B., & Houtz, J. C. (1998). *Creativity and giftedness in culturally diverse students*. Cresskill, NJ: Hampton Press.

Feldhusen, J. F. (1998). A conception of talent and talent development. In R. C. Friedman & K. B. Rogers (Eds.), *Talent in context: Historical and social perspectives on giftedness* (pp. 193–209). Washington, DC: American Psychological Association.

Feldhusen, J. F., & Goh, B. E. (1995). Assessing and accessing creativity: An integrative review of theory, research, and development. *Creativity Research Journal*, **8**, 231–247.

Feldman, D. H. (1992). Has there been a paradigm shift in gifted education? In N. Colangelo, S. G. Assouline, and D. L. Ambroson (Eds.), *Talent development: Proceedings from the 1991 Henry B. and Jocelyn Wallace National Research Symposium on Talent Development* (pp. 89–94). Unionville, NY: Trillium Press.

Fischer, C. S., Hout, M., Jankowski, M. S., Lucas, S. R., Swidler, A., & Voss, K. (1996) *Inequality by design: Cracking the bell curve myth*. Princeton, NJ: Princeton University Press.

Ford, D. Y. (1996). *Reversing underachievement among gifted black students: Promising practices and programs*. New York: Teachers College Press.

Ford, D. Y., & Harris, J. J. III (1999). *Multicultural gifted education*. New York: Teachers College Press.

Frasier, M. M., Garcia, J. H., & Passow, A. H.(1995). A review of assessment issues in gifted education and their implications for identifying gifted minority students. *Research Monograph 95204*. Storrs, CT: National Research Center on the Gifted and Talented.

Frasier, M. M., Martin, D., Garcia, J., Finley, V. S., Frank, E., Krisel, S., & King, L. L. (1995). *A new window for looking at gifted children* (Guidebook). ERIC Clearinghouse Number EC305218. Storrs, CT: National Research Center on the Gifted and Talented.

Gagné, F. (1985). Giftedness and talent: Reexamining a reexamination of the definition. *Gifted Child Quarterly*, **29**, 103–112.

Gagné, F. (1993). Constructs and models pertaining to exceptional human abilities. In K. A. Heller, F. J. Mönks & A. H. Passow (Eds.), *International handbook of research and development of giftedness and talent* (pp. 69–87). Oxford, England: Pergamon.

Gallagher, J. J. (1996). A critique of critiques of gifted education. *Journal for the Education of the Gifted*, **19**, 234–249.

Gardner, H. (1983). *Frames of mind*. New York: Basic Books.

Gardner, H. (1993). *Multiple intelligences: The theory in practice*. New York: Basic Books.

Gardner, H. (1999). A multiplicity of intelligences. *Scientific American*, **9** (4), 19–23.

Gillespie, D. (1992). *The mind's we: Contextualism in cognitive psychology*. Carbondale, IL: Southern Illinois University Press.

Goswami, A. (1988). Creativity and the quantum theory. *Journal of Creative Behavior*, **22**, 9–31.

Goswami, A. (1990). Consciousness in quantum physics and the mind-body problem. *The Journal of Mind and Behavior*, **11**, 75–96.

Goswami, A. (1995). Monistic idealism may provide better ontology for cognitive science: A reply to Dyer. *The Journal of Mind and Behavior*, **16**, 135–150.

Goswami, A. (1996). Creativity and the quantum: A unified theory of creativity. *Creativity Research Journal*, **9**, 47–61.

Gottfredson, L. S. (1999). The general intelligence factor. *Scientific American*, **9** (4), 24–29.

Grant, B. A., & Piechowski, M. M. (1999). Theories and the good: Toward child-centered gifted education. *Gifted Child Quarterly*, **43**, 4–12.

Heller, K. A. (1995). The role of creativity in explaining giftedness and exceptional achievement. *European Journal for High Ability*, **6** (1), 7–26.

Herrnstein, R. J., & Murray, C. (1994). *The bell curve: Intelligence and class structure in American life*. New York: The Free Press.

Inglehart, R. (1997). *Modernization and postmodernization: Cultural, economic, and political change in 43 societies*. Princeton, NJ: Princeton University Press.

Jellen, H., & Verduin, J. R. (1986). *Handbook for differential education of the gifted: A taxonomy of 32 key concepts*. Carbondale, IL: Southern Illinois University Press.

Jervis, R. (1997). *System effects: Complexity in political and social life*. Princeton, NJ: Princeton University Press.

Kaplan, S. N. (1986). The grid: A model to construct differentiated curriculum for the gifted. In J. S. Renzulli (Ed.), *Systems and models for developing programs for the gifted and talented* (pp. 180–193). Mansfield Center, CT: Creative Learning Press.

Kauffman, S. (1995). *At home in the universe: The search for laws of self-organization and complexity.* New York: Oxford University Press.

Kelso, J. A. S. (1995). *Dynamic patterns: The self-organization of brain and behavior.* Cambridge, MA: MIT Press.

Kulik, J. A., & Kulik, C. C. (1992). Meta-analytic findings on grouping programs. *Gifted Child Quarterly, 36,* 73–77.

Kuhn, T. S. (1970). *The structure of scientific revolutions* (2nd ed.). Chicago, IL: Chicago University Press.

Lakoff, G. (1993). The contemporary theory of metaphor. In A. Ortony (Ed.), *Metaphor and thought* (2nd ed.) (pp. 202–251). New York: Cambridge University Press.

Lakoff, G. (1995). Embodied minds and meanings. In P. Baumgartner & S. Payr (Eds.), *Speaking minds* (pp. 115–129). Princeton, NJ: Princeton University Press.

Lincoln, Y. S., & Guba, E. G. (1985). *Naturalistic inquiry.* Beverly Hills, CA: Sage.

Maker, C. J. (1996). Identification of gifted minority students: A national problem, needed changes and a promising solution. *Gifted Child Quarterly, 40,* 41–50.

Maker, C. J., & Schiever, S. W. (Eds.). (1989). *Critical issues in gifted education: Defensible programs for cultural and ethnic minorities.* Austin, TX: Pro-Ed.

Margolin, L. (1996). A pedagogy of privilege. *Journal for the Education of the Gifted, 19*(2), 164–180.

Midgley, M. (1995). Reductive megalomania. In J. Cornwell (Ed.), *Nature's imagination: The frontiers of scientific vision* (pp. 133–147). Oxford, England: Oxford University Press.

Midgley, M. (1998). One world, but a big one. In S. Rose (Ed.), *From brains to consciousness: Essays on the new sciences of the mind* (pp. 246–270). Princeton, NJ: Princeton University Press.

Milgram, R. M. (Ed.). (1989). *Teaching gifted and talented learners in regular classrooms.* Springfield, IL: Charles C. Thomas.

Newell, A. (1990). *Unified theories of cognition.* Cambridge, MA: Harvard University Press.

Oakes, J. (1985). *Keeping track: How schools structure inequality.* New Haven, CT: Yale University Press.

Overton, W. F. (1984). World views and their influence on psychological thoughts and research: Khun-Lakatos-Laudan. In H. W. Reese (Ed.), *Advances in child development and behavior* (Vol. 18, pp. 91–226). New York: Academic.

Passow, A. H. & Frasier, M. M. (1996). Towards improving identification of talent potential among minority and disadvantaged students. *Roeper Review, 18* (3), 198–202.

Pelletier, S., & Shore, B. M. (in press). The gifted learner, the novice, and the expert: Sharpening emerging views of giftedness. In D. Ambrose, L. M. Cohen & A. J. Tannenbaum (Eds.), *Creative intelligence: Toward theoretic integration.* Cresskill, NJ: Hampton Press.

Pendarvis, E. D., & Howley, A. (1996). Playing fair: The possibilities of gifted education. *Journal for the Education of the Gifted, 19* (2), 215–233.

Penrose, R. (1994). *Shadows of the mind: A search for the missing science of consciousness.* Oxford, England: Oxford University Press.

Pepper, S. C. (1942). *World hypotheses.* Berkeley, CA: University of California Press.

Perkins, D. (1995). *Outsmarting IQ: The emerging science of learnable intelligence.* Old Tappan, NJ: The Free Press.

Peterson, J. S. (1999). Gifted-through whose cultural lens? An application of the postpositivistic mode of inquiry. *Journal for the Education of the Gifted, 22,* 354–383.

Piaget, J. (1981). Creativity: Moving force of society. Appendix to J. M. Gallagher & D. K. Reid, *The learning theory of Piaget and Inhelder.* Monterrey, CA: Brooks/Cole.

Piirto, J. (1999a). *Talented children and adults: Their development and education* (2nd ed.). Columbus, OH: Prentice Hall/Merrill.

Piirto, J. (1999b). Implications of postmodern curriculum theory for the education of the talented. *Journal for the Education of the Gifted, 22,* 324–353.

Plucker, J. A. (1998). Beware of simple conclusions: The case for content generality of creativity. *Creativity Research Journal, 11,* 179–182.

Powell, W. N. (1999). *The structural oppression of African Americans in higher education.* Doctoral Dissertation, Oregon State University.

Purcell, J. H. (1996). Preparing for fall-out: A perspective on The Bell Curve. *Roeper Review, 18,* 248–252.

Rea, D. (2000). Optimal motivation for talent development. *Journal for the Education of the Gifted, 23,* 187–216.

Renzulli, J. S. (1986). The three-ring conception of giftedness: A developmental model for creative productivity. In R. J. Sternberg & J. E. Davidson (Eds.), *Conceptions of giftedness* (pp. 53–92). New York: Cambridge University Press.

Renzulli, J. S. (1991). The National Research Center on the Gifted and Talented: The dream, the design, and the destination. *Gifted Child Quarterly, 35,* 73–80.

Renzulli, J. S. (1994). *Schools for talent development: A practical plan for total school improvement.* Mansfield Center, CT: Creative Learning Press.

Renzulli, J. S., & Reis, S. M. (1985). *The schoolwide enrichment model: A comprehensive plan for educational excellence.* Mansfield Center, CT: Creative Learning Press.

Rogers, K. B. (1992). A best-evidence synthesis of the research on acceleration options for gifted learners. In N. Colangelo, S. G. Assouline & D. L. Ambroson (Eds.), *Talent development: Proceedings from the 1991 Henry B. and Jocelyn Wallace National Research Symposium on Talent Development* (pp. 406–409). Unionville, NY: Trillium.

Rose, S. (Ed.). (1998). *From brains to consciousness: Essays on the new sciences of the mind.* Princeton, NJ: Princeton University Press.

Rubenson, D. L. (in press). Art and science, ancient and modern: A psycho-economic perspective on domain differences in creativity. In D. Ambrose, L. M. Cohen & A. J. Tannenbaum (Eds.), *Creative intelligence: Toward theoretic integration.* Cresskill, NJ: Hampton Press.

Rubenson, D. L., & Runco, M. A. (1992). The psychoeconomic approach to creativity. *New Ideas in Psychology, 10,* 131–148.

Rudnitski, R. A., & Kearney, K. (1996, November). *A walk on the 'other side'.* Paper presented at the annual convention of the National Association for Gifted Children, Indianapolis, IN.

Runco, M. A. (Ed.). (1998). *Critical Creative Processes.* Cresskill, NJ: Hampton Press.

Sapon-Shevin, M. (1994). *Playing favorites: Gifted education and the disruption of community.* Albany: State University of New York Press.

Shore, B. M., Cornell, D., Robinson, A., & Ward, V. (1991). *Recommended practices in gifted education.* New York: Teachers College Press.

Simon, H. A. (1979). *Models of thought.* New Haven, CT: Yale University Press.

Simonton, D. K. (1998). Gifted child, genius adult: Three life-span developmental perspectives. In R. C. Friedman & K. B. Rogers (Eds.), *Talent in context: Historical and social perspectives on giftedness* (pp. 151–175). Washington, DC: American Psychological Association.

Sterling, A. (1992). *Human creativity as a function of chaotic dynamics: Implications for research and practice in education* (Doctoral dissertation, University of Oregon, 1992). *Dissertation Abstracts International, 53,* 2749A.

Sternberg, R. J. (1990). *Metaphors of mind: Conceptions of the nature of intelligence.* New York: Cambridge University Press.

Sternberg, R. J. (1993). Procedures for identifying intellectual potential in the gifted: A perspective on alternative 'metaphors of mind'. In K. A. Heller, F. J. Mönks & A. H. Passow (Eds.), *International handbook of research and development of giftedness and talent* (pp. 185–207). Oxford, England: Pergamon.

Sternberg, R. J. (1997). *Successful intelligence: How practical and creative intelligence determine success in life.* New York: Plume.

Sternberg, R. J. (1999a). A dialectical basis for understanding the study of cognition. In R. J. Sternberg (Ed.), *The nature of cognition* (pp 51–78). Cambridge, MA: MIT Press.

Sternberg, R. J. (1999b). How intelligent is intelligence testing? *Scientific American, 9* (4), 12–17.

Sternberg, R. J., & Grigorenko, E. L. (Eds.). (1997). *Intelligence, heredity, and environment.* Cambridge, England: Cambridge University Press.

Sternberg, R. J., & Hovarth, J. A. (1998). Cognitive conceptions of expertise and their relations to giftedness. In R. C. Friedman & K. B. Rogers (Eds.), *Talent in context: Historical and social perspectives on giftedness* (pp. 177–191). Washington, DC: American Psychological Association.

Sternberg, R. J., & Lubart, T. I. (1993). Creative giftedness: A multivariate investment approach. *Gifted Child Quarterly, 37,* 7–15.

Tannenbaum, A. J. (1983). *Gifted children: Psychological and educational perspectives.* New York: MacMillan.

Tannenbaum, A. J. (1986). The enrichment matrix model. In J. S. Renzulli (Ed.), *Systems and models for developing programs for the gifted and talented* (pp. 391–428). Mansfield Center, CT: Creative Learning Press Inc.

Taylor, C. W. (1986). Cultivating simultaneous student growth in both multiple creative talents and knowledge. In J. S. Renzulli (Ed.), *Systems and models for developing programs for the gifted and talented* (pp. 306–350). Mansfield Center, CT: Creative Learning Press.

Thomas, G. (1997). What's the use of theory? *Harvard Educational Review, 67,* 75–104.

Treffinger, D. F., & Feldhusen, J. F. (1996). Talent recognition and development: Successor to gifted education. *Journal for the Education of the gifted, 19,* 181–193.

Treffinger, D. J., & Sortore, M. R. (1994). *Programming for giftedness-A contemporary view* (Volume 1). Melbourne: Hawker-Brownlow.

Urban, K. (in press). Towards a componential model of creativity. In D. Ambrose, L. M. Cohen & A. J. Tannenbaum (Eds.), *Creative intelligence: Toward theoretic integration.* Cresskill, NJ: Hampton Press.

VanTassel-Baska, J. (1992). *Planning effective curriculum for gifted learners.* Denver, CO: Love Publishing.

Wahlsten, D., & Gottlieb, G. (1997). The invalid separation of effects of nature and nurture: Lessons from animal experimentation. In R. J. Sternberg & E. L. Grigorenko (Eds.), *Intelligence, heredity, and environment* (pp. 163–192). Cambridge, England: Cambridge University Press.

Ward, V. S. (1980). *Differential education for the gifted.* Ventura, CA: Ventura County Superintendent of Schools.

Theory and Research on Curriculum Development for the Gifted

Joyce VanTassel-Baska

College of William and Mary, Williamsburg, Virginia, USA

Introduction

How can educators help a gifted student to excel? The answer to this question is a complicated one because much of our research on what impacts the lives of gifted individuals relates more to the role of parents (Feldman, 1985; Bloom, 1985), the role of internal factors such as motivation (VanTassel-Baska & Olszewski-Kubilius, 1989; Csikszentmihalyi, Rathunde & Whalen, 1993), the role of crystallizing experiences (Gardner, 1985), the role of conative factors such as will and passion (Snow, 1994), or the role of chance (Tannenbaum, 1983).

Yet what happens to a child in school should have a significant positive effect on the processes of learning. Gifted and talented students, like all students, have the right to a continuity of educational experience that meets their present and future academic needs. When an organized, thoughtful curriculum plan is in place and when that curriculum is supported by an articulate, informed educational leadership, the probability of capturing the interest and energy of our ablest young thinkers is markedly enhanced. Certainly an organized and appropriate curriculum is a key ingredient in this complex blending of circumstance so central to the transformation of a gifted learner's initial capacity for intellectual activity into a mature competence for academic and professional accomplishment.

Key beliefs and assumptions have guided the thinking of most curriculum theory in gifted education (Passow, 1982; Gallagher, 1985; Maker & Nielson, 1996; VanTassel-Baska, 1998). These beliefs may be stated succinctly as follows:

(1) All learners should be provided curriculum opportunities that allow them to attain optimum levels of learning.
(2) Gifted learners have different learning needs compared with typical learners. Therefore, curriculum must be adapted or designed to accommodate these needs.
(3) The needs of gifted learners cut across cognitive, affective, social, and aesthetic areas of curriculum experiences.
(4) Gifted learners are best served by a confluent approach that allows for accelerated and advanced learning, and enriched and extended experiences.
(5) Curriculum experiences for gifted learners need to be carefully planned, written down, and implemented in order to maximize potential effect.
(6) Curriculum development for gifted learners is an ongoing process that uses evaluation as a central tool for future planning and revision of curriculum documents.

Over twenty years ago, national reports in the United States ushered in a new era for educational and curricular change, predominantly in science and mathematics. Today, educators are still faced with a barrage of reports that describe deficiencies in the current instruction in mathematics and science and in other content disciplines as well. *A Nation at Risk* (National Commission on Excellence in Education, 1983) reported on the abysmal failure of public education in exposing students to full secondary programs in science and mathematics. The Carnegie Report (1986) further documented the need for more advanced course taking in these subjects by larger numbers of the secondary school population. The College Board's *Project Equality* (1983) outlined maximum competency skills in academic areas that require mastery in today's technologically advanced world. The most stringent recommendations on curriculum were reported by the National Science Commission (1983) which prescribed four full years of science and mathematics for the majority of students in American schools.

In the early 1990s, the American reform movement had taken on global significance; all countries focused on the importance of education. All countries see their future economic hopes linked to an educated citizenry, skilled in the world technologies. Moreover, the demographic make-up of many developed countries is pluralistic, thus instantly globalizing the issues. The results of the Third International Math and Science Study (National Center for Education Statistics, 1997) attest to the sense of importance attached to student performance at elementary and secondary levels worldwide.

Based on the proliferation of reports on problems and remedies, it is clear that education has and is experiencing significant pressure for reform and curricular change. In particular, there is a strong interest in focusing efforts on raising the level of performance for all learners and a belief that the successful approaches to the achievements of the gifted can also enhance the educational enterprise for those who are less able.

Although many local school efforts have not been responsive to the perceived needs of a modern technological society, curriculum for the gifted and talented provides a starting point to upgrade these efforts, particularly in areas that reports have cited as most deficient: mathematics, science, technology, and foreign language. Yet practitioners of theoretical ideas about curriculum for the gifted must be sensitive to the organizational structure of the schools, contemporary K-12 curriculum needs, and the recommendations for change being advocated by these major studies.

The Forces That Drive Curriculum

Based on the calls for reform at steady rates over the last decade, one would expect a commensurate interest in curriculum development projects. Yet very few large-scale curriculum projects have been funded since the splurge of the 1960s. However, curriculum development in math and science is now in the forefront of educational reform. Examples include the Amoco Foundation's $50 million grant to the University of Chicago to change the shape of American mathematics education at the elementary and secondary levels, new NSF-funded projects in science and mathematics with a heavy focus on technological application, and AAAS science projects that capitalize on new science concepts. Within gifted education, major curriculum development projects have been funded by the United States Department of Education under the Javits Gifted and Talented Act. These projects presage a renewed interest in serious curriculum work for gifted learners.

What has caused this resurgence of interest in curriculum? One of the social forces at work is our concern as a nation for meeting future workforce needs. Wirsup (1986) reported on the dismal status of America's students in math and science when compared to their Russian, Japanese, and West German counterparts. Numerous reports over the last few years continue to document similar deficiencies in performance (Darling-Hammond, 1990; Stevenson & Stigler, 1992). At the national level there has been a pronounced shift in focus from issues like discipline and community involvement to hard questions about the content and sequence of curriculum. The egalitarian philosophy that dominated the last twenty years of educational policy altered curriculum standards, reduced requirements, and created an elective system that spawned low test scores and gaps in traditional knowledge. A concomitant focus on the education of the disabled sparked an examination of our educational priorities. The billions of dollars allocated to tailoring educational programs to the special needs of disabled children as a result of the passage of PL 94–142 raised consciousness about the cost of responding to individual needs of learners at appropriate levels. The current concerns about changing demographics, work force, competency issues, and negative international education comparisons further exacerbate the need for reform.

Juxtaposed with these social, political, and economic forces within educational systems is new research that affects thinking about the nature of curriculum change desired. New studies about intelligence (Gardner, 1983; Sternberg, 1985) and how children learn are available to shape the curriculum process.

While limited research has been conducted on curriculum for the gifted per se, current research in teaching and learning appears important to our conceptual framework for understanding appropriate curriculum for the gifted. For example, curriculum planners for the gifted have long advocated the optimal match between learner capacity and level of experiences provided; new evidence for this principle has emerged from studies of human development where it was found that when both personal skill level and challenge level are correspondingly high, adolescents experience a state of 'flow' which allows for optimal learning (Csikszentmihalyi, 1990).

Current learning research is also deeply rooted in the basic disciplines of reading, writing, mathematics, and science. Much on-going research is attempting to explain how children master complex knowledge structures and procedures (Brown & Campione, 1986). In both reading and mathematics, current research has supported a meaning-based approach that provides appropriate drill and practice in key activities (Resnick, 1984; Anderson, Herbert, Scott & Wilkinson, 1985).

Studies of thinking also contribute to understanding curriculum directions for the gifted. Expert-novice comparisons in various fields (Sommers, 1980; Berliner, 1985) have yielded differences favoring experts in metacognitive acts like planning and revising. A collection of research on expertise has revealed that the successful utilization of these skills may be content-specific. Rabinowitz & Glaser (1985) found that expert performance entailed a large knowledge base of domain-specific patterns, rapid recognition of situations in which these patterns apply, and the use of forward reasoning based on pattern manipulation to reach solutions. Ericsson & Lehman (1996) in studies of athletes and chess masters assert that domain specific expert behavior emerges out of a triad of experience, instruction, and practice.

Further support for such domain-specific research comes out of studies which use general content-independent cognitive strategies and which find no clear benefits outside the specific domains in which they are taught (Pressley, Snyder & Carigha-Bull, 1987). Thus, research on transfer suggests that "thinking at its most effective [level] depends on specific context-bound skills and units of knowledge that have little application to other domains" (Perkins & Saloman, 1989, p. 119).

Curriculum is also being affected by larger social and political contexts. Computer technology has found its way into the curriculum as a 'basic' subject rather than as a peripheral. Global interdependence has become a major organizational theme of special programs in all content areas, not just social studies. On the other side of the ledger, moral majority advocates have brought about the dissolution of values education, and other educational foci that encouraged free and open inquiry by students.

A number of years ago, Goodlad (1979) posited that curriculum decision-making is done at two levels, each in isolation from the other. School boards effect curriculum policy, and teachers implement classroom curriculum. Little curriculum leadership is provided at a middle level by building principals or central office staff. Consequently, curriculum implementation as a standardized process does not occur in most public school settings. Even skeptical parents are not likely to challenge teachers in an area heavily loaded with issues of expertise and academic freedom.

But curriculum is still mostly driven by the inertia of the status quo, a system of skill-based areas of inquiry that proceeds on a continuum from first grade to twelfth grade, buttressed by basal texts and little examination of the 'why' of a curriculum offering at a particular point in the sequence. For example, algebra was not in the school curriculum sixty years ago, and now the debate rages as to its appropriateness at the ninth-grade level where it was initiated and has tended to stay. Reading continues to follow a similar illogical path of development based on a curriculum model that ignores individual readiness issues.

Since curriculum is at a point of potential change, the opportunity for educators of the gifted to take a strong role in defining what it should be for the most able, the process by which it is formulated, and the diversity of products or outcomes to be anticipated is at hand. It is through appropriate curriculum design and delivery for the top five per cent of the population that the whole of curriculum can be upgraded and enhanced. The curricular work for the gifted can spearhead higher standards and more rigorous methodologies in addressing the needs of the rest of the student body.

A Curriculum Philosophy for the Gifted

Eisner & Vallance (1974) presented five conceptions of curriculum that have shaped the thinking of many educators, and represent strong philosophical orientations for what a view of curriculum for the gifted might be. Moreover, educators of the gifted have influenced curriculum philosophy through both the venue of new conceptions of intelligence (Sternberg & Davidson, 1986; Gardner, 1991) but also through new ways of thinking about nurturing our best learners in schools (Gagne, 1995; Piirto, 1999).

1. Curriculum as the development of cognitive process. This orientation in the education of the gifted has focused on process skill development and has led to the adoption of curriculum materials organized around higher level thinking skills. Having its roots in cognitive psychology, it has fostered an information-processing model of curriculum that uses cognitive and meta-cognitive skills as the centerpiece of all learning activities. Implicit in this view is the assumption that learning cognitive skills will translate across, apply to, and enhance any field of inquiry a student may encounter. Many programs for the gifted, which reflect this orientation, have emphasized critical thinking, creative thinking, and problem solving as the substance of their curricula, treating these process skills as content dimensions in their own right. Research would support this orientation if there are also ample opportunities for applying cognitive skills directly to content (Perkins & Saloman, 1989; Sternberg, Torff & Grigorenko, 1998a).

2. Curriculum as technology. This approach to curriculum is also process-oriented, but focuses on the organization of curriculum into student inputs and outputs. This view of curriculum relies heavily on stated behavioral or performance objectives with measurable outcomes that can be tested in order to determine educational progress or achievement. Learner outcomes developed in individual states and by several national groups attest to the current centrality of this curriculum orientation. It assumes that curriculum standards must be explicit, taught to, and tested for. This view of curriculum sees curricular effectiveness and efficiency realizable if a learning system is adopted by schools rather than piecemeal changes (Spady & Marshall, 1991; O'Day & Smith, 1993). Clearly this view of curriculum dominates the work of the reform movement calling for systemic changes at all levels of existing educational systems (Fuhrman, 1993).

3. Curriculum as personal relevance. This orientation promotes a child-centered model that values curriculum experiences which are tailored to individual student needs. The interest of students in specific areas guides the curriculum. The goal of such curriculum is to be personally engaging and to offer consummatory experiences that will provide growth at each student's level of understanding. Several curriculum models in gifted education employ this orientation. Renzulli & Reis (1994), Moon & Feldhusen (1994), and Betts (1991), favor this orientation because of its emphasis on self-directed learning. Gifted students become responsible for their own curriculum through contracts with a facilitator who assesses interest and ability. The interaction of student and facilitator in mutually agreed upon work form the central core of curriculum experiences.

4. Curriculum as social reconstruction. This view of curriculum holds that the purpose of educational institutions is to be an agent for social change and that the content of curriculum should be viewed within the larger social and cultural realm. Banks (1999) has identified four levels of a curriculum that moves toward social action. At the first level, students encounter specific material related to diverse cultures; at a second level they encounter an understanding of the contributions of various cultures; at a third level they transform their understanding based on exposure to multiple perspectives and viewpoints of diverse cultures. At this level, key concepts like discrimination, tolerance and social justice become a central focus. At the fourth level, social action occurs. Engaging students in social action such as drafting a piece of legislation, taking a poll of neighborhood opinions regarding nuclear energy, or organizing a school anti-pollution campaign typify the curricular experience as part of social reform. Most multicultural trends in curriculum have their philosophic roots in this orientation (Hernandez, 1989; Ford-Harris, 1996)).

5. Curriculum as academic rationalism. This curriculum orientation has its roots in the Western tradition of rational humanism. Specifically, it adheres to an ideal of education as a way of providing students with an understanding of great ideas and an ability to analyze and synthesize past achievements. It recognizes a core of work as central to our evolution as a culture (Hirsch, 1989). It further espouses a belief in the structure of knowledge as embodied in the organization of academic and artistic fields of inquiry, and seeks to instruct students within those content disciplines. Most of the 'durable' curriculum that is used in gifted programs flows from this general orientation. Both Advanced Placement (AP) and International Baccalaureate (IB) curriculum focus on this view. This philosophy is heavily oriented toward a discipline- or content-based approach to learning and organizes experiences accordingly. In many respects the multiple intelligences view of curriculum is also grounded in this philosophical orientation (Gardner, 1995).

Although educators are free to choose among these curriculum philosophies, the most effective curricula incorporate all of them to some extent. Yet the academic rationalist's view most closely accommodates the current curricular organization of schools, and has guided most long-term curriculum efforts. The major challenge to the traditional view in gifted child education has come from those models favoring individual student-centered approaches to curriculum (e.g. the School-wide Enrichment Model, and the Autonomous Learner Model). This viewpoint has impacted greatly the thinking of gifted child education worldwide.

Research on Curriculum Models

The history of curriculum development for the gifted has been fraught with problems just as the general history of curriculum development in this country has been. The curriculum enterprise in general has suffered from neglect since the Sputnik craze in the 1960s. Only with the new national standards movement have we seen a renewed interest in the issue of curriculum. Such contemporary interest, however, has also spawned additional concerns about differentiating for gifted learners rather than raising the standards for all learners. Negotiating between the need to respond to advanced learners as a group and the need to provide high level equitable access to all learners creates an interesting challenge for gifted educators.

The most successful curriculum models for gifted learners have been developed based on acceleration principles for advanced secondary students (VanTassel-Baska, 1998). The International Baccalaureate program and the College Board Advanced Placement Program are perceived by many American school districts to represent the highest levels of academic attainment possible for secondary students and are thought to provide important stepping stones to successful college work. Thus one approach to curriculum development for the gifted may be seen as a 'design down' model where all curriculum at K-12 is organized to promote readiness for college and the process is both speeded up and shortened along the way for the most apt.

Alternatives to this viewpoint abound, however, and tend to focus on learning beyond or in lieu of traditional academics. Most of the curriculum models cited in this chapter ascribe to an enriched view of curriculum development for the gifted, one that addresses a broader conception of giftedness, taking into account principles of creativity, motivation, and independence as crucial constructs to the development of high ability (Renzulli, 1986; Maker & Nielson, 1995). These enrichment views also tend to see process skills such as critical thinking and creative problem solving as central to the learning enterprise, with content choices being more incidental. Evidence of student work through high quality products and performances is also typically highly valued in these models.

Most of the enrichment-oriented approaches to curriculum development for the gifted emanated from the early work of Leta Hollingworth, and her curriculum template for New York City self-contained classes. Strongly influenced by Deweyan progressivism, she organized curriculum units that allowed students to discover connections about how the world worked, to discover the role of creative people in societal progress by having students study biography, and promoting the role of group learning through discussion and conversation about ideas (Hollingworth, 1926). In some respects, contemporary curriculum development efforts have not surpassed her early work in scope, purpose, and delivery.

Accelerative approaches to learning owe much to the work of Terman & Oden (1947), Pressey (1949), and early developers of rapid learning classes which enabled bright students to progress at their own rate. Early educational examples of auto-didacticism and tutorials also encouraged a view of learning that promoted independent interest and a self-modulated pace (VanTassel-Baska, 1995). Thus current curriculum models are grounded in a history of research, development, and implementation of both accelerative and enrichment approaches, typically implemented in self-contained classes since the level of content instruction could be modified based on the group. Chief differentiation approaches early in the history of this field then lay in attention to differences between gifted and non-gifted populations. One might argue that today's views of differentiation tend to center far more on individual differences among the gifted in respect to aptitudes, predispositions, styles, and experiences (Gardner, 1995; Benbow & Stanley 1996; Lubinski, 1996; Snow, 1989) than on the group difference paradigm, for both curriculum employed in and out of school.

Analysis of curriculum models

As curriculum has become more a centerpiece of program activity for the gifted, the field has deepened its connections to key criteria that constitute a viable curriculum model. Curriculum models have to provide a system for developing and designing appropriate curriculum for a target population. As such they have to identify elements of design and show how they interact in a curriculum product; a model has to be utilitarian in that it can be easily applied to all major areas of school-based learning. A model also has to be flexible in respect to age groups to which it would apply; the central elements need to work for kindergarten age gifted children as well as high school students. A curriculum model must also have relevance in multiple locations and learning settings; it would need to work in tutorials as well as large classes. Finally, curriculum models for the gifted have to differentiate the particular needs of this population for curriculum and instruction.

Each of the models discussed in the following section meet these criteria. The two most researched models and best known are described first, the talent search model and the School-wide Enrichment Model (SEM), because both have defined the major curriculum efforts of the gifted education field since the middle 1970s and both also represent well the persistent programmatic division in the field between accelerative and enrichment approaches. Moreover, each of these models has over a decade of research, development, and implementation behind it; none of the other models described have enjoyed such longevity, widespread use, or research attention.

The Talent Search Model of Talent Identification and Development

The overall purpose of the talent search model is to educate for individual development over the lifespan (Benbow & Stanley, 1983; Benbow, 1986; Stanley, 1991). Major principles of the model include: (1) use of a secure and difficult testing instrument that taps into high level verbal and mathematical reasoning to identify students, (2) a diagnostic testing – prescriptive instructional approach (DT-PI) in teaching gifted students through special classes allowing for appropriate level challenge in instruction, (3) use of subject matter acceleration and fast-paced classes in core academic areas, as well as advocacy for various other forms of acceleration, and (4) curriculum flexibility in all schooling (Daurio, 1978; Stanley & Benbow, 1983). The model has been developed at key university sites across the country with some adoptions by local school districts who have established fast-paced classes.

The Study of Mathematically Precocious Youth (SMPY) officially started in September of 1971 at Johns Hopkins University (JHU) and is now being continued, since 1986, at Iowa State University. From 1972 through 1979, SMPY pioneered the concept of searching for youth who reason exceptionally well mathematically (i.e. a talent search) (George, 1976; Stanley, 1976, 1977, 1978). In 1980, the talent search was extended to verbally gifted youth by others at JHU. For the students identified by the talent searchers, SMPY provided educational facilitation by utilizing acceleration or curricular flexibility and by developing fast-paced academic programs. Gifted students in 7th and 8th grade can participate in these talent searches by taking the College Board's Scholastic Aptitude Test (SAT) or the ACT; almost 150,000 gifted students do so every year. Residential and commuter academic programs in several disciplines are also offered by these centers and other universities and organizations to qualified students.

The research work of SMPY has been strong over the past 27 years, with more than 300 published articles, chapters, and books about the model. Findings of these studies have consistently focused on the benefits of acceleration for continued advanced work in an area by precocious students (Stanley, Keating & Fox, 1974; Kolitch & Brody, 1992), a clear rationale for the use of acceleration in intellectual development (Keating, 1976), and the long-term positive repeated impacts of accelerative opportunities (Benbow & Arjmand, 1990; Hendricks, 1997). Case study research has also been undertaken to demonstrate how these processes affect individual students (Brody & Stanley, 1991; Benbow & Lubinski, 1994). Other studies have focused more specifically on student gains from fast-paced classes (VanTassel-Baska, 1982; Lynch, 1992). The use of the model has been extensive across all of the United States and in selected foreign countries. Curriculum materials have been developed by talent search staff at various sites and by individual teachers in the summer and academic year programs. Especially noteworthy are the curriculum guides for teaching Advanced Placement courses developed at the TIP program at Duke University. Strong use of articulated course materials are employed on the way to Advanced Placement coursework and testing in mathematics, science, and the verbal areas including foreign language. These materials have been reviewed by practicing professionals and content specialists.

Over the entire 27 years of operation, the model has been very well received by parents and students who constitute the major client groups; schools have been less receptive based on their conservative attitude toward accelerative practices and the emphasis on highly gifted students in subject areas (Lynch, 1990; Benbow & Lubinski, 1996; Benbow & Stanley, 1996).

The model does not have a formal training component, although selection of teachers is a rigorous process carried out carefully in each university and school setting. Content expertise and work with highly gifted secondary students are primary considerations for selection; the model is easy to understand but difficult to implement in schools based on prevailing philosophies. The application of the model that has been most successful is in after school and summer settings in which students complete the equivalent of high school honors classes in three weeks (Benbow & Stanley, 1996).

The SMPY model has proven to be highly sustainable, exhibiting strong replication capacity. Even where countries do not conduct talent searches, students from those countries routinely attend summer programs at talent search universities.

Because the model is content-based, it aligns well with national standards although some of the enrichment emphasis of the standards would be overlooked in implementation. SMPY represents core curriculum on an accelerated and streamlined level. The model is not totally comprehensive in that it addresses students in grades 3–12 who reason exceptionally well mathematically and verbally (Lupkowski & Assouline, 1993; Stanley, 1993). Some studies on spatially gifted students at those levels have also been conducted; curriculum areas are comprehensive, including all of the 33 Advanced Placement course strands. Scope and

sequence work has been articulated for grades 7–12 in some areas of learning. Northwestern University has developed a guide for educational options for grades 5–12.

Longitudinal data, collected over the past 20 years on 300 highly gifted students, have demonstrated the viability of the Stanley model in respect to the benefits of accelerative study, early identification of a strong talent area and the need for assistance in educational decision-making (Swiatek & Benbow, 1991a; 1991b; Swiatek, 1993; Lubinski & Benbow, 1994). A fifty year follow-up study (1972–2022) is in progress at Iowa State University with 6000 students in the sample (Lubinski & Benbow, 1994). This study already rivals Terman's longitudinal study in respect to its longevity and exceeds it in regard to understanding the talent development process at work.

The Schoolwide Enrichment Model (SEM)

The Schoolwide Enrichment Model (SEM) evolved after 15 years of research and field testing by both educators and researchers (Renzulli, 1988). It combined the previously developed Enrichment Triad Model (Renzulli, 1977) with a more flexible approach to identifying high-potential students called the Revolving Door Identification Model (Renzulli, Reis & Smith, 1981). This combination of services was initially field tested in 11 school districts of various types (rural, suburban, and urban) and sizes. The field tests resulted in the development of the SEM (Renzulli & Reis, 1985), which has been widely adopted.

In the SEM, a talent pool of 15%–20% of above-average ability/high-potential students is identified through a variety of measures, including achievement tests, teacher nominations, assessment of potential for creativity and task commitment, as well as alternative pathways of entrance (self-nomination, parent nomination, etc.). High achievement test and IQ scores automatically include a student in the talent pool, enabling those students who are underachieving in their academic school work to be included.

Once students are identified for the talent pool, they are eligible for several kinds of services. First, interest and learning styles assessments are used with talent pool students; second, curriculum compacting is provided to all eligible students; that is, the regular curriculum is modified by eliminating portions of previously mastered content and alternative work substituted; third, the Enrichment Triad Model offers three types of enrichment experiences. Types I, II, and III Enrichment are usually more appropriate for students with higher levels of ability, interest, and task commitment.

Type I Enrichment consists of general exploratory experiences such as guest speakers, field trips, demonstrations, interest centers, and the use of audiovisual materials designed to expose students to new and exciting topics, ideas, and fields of knowledge not ordinarily covered in the regular curriculum. Type II Enrichment includes instructional methods and materials purposefully designed to promote the development of thinking, feeling, research, communication, and methodological processes. Type III Enrichment, the most advanced level of the model, is defined as investigative activities and artistic productions in which the learner assumes the role of a first-hand inquirer: thinking, feeling, and acting like a practicing professional, with involvement pursued at as advanced a professional level as possible, given the student's level of development and age.

One comparative study (Heal, 1989) was completed comparing the effects of SEM to other enrichment models or strategies. Other studies report results using within-model comparisons (Delisle, 1981; Reis, 1981) or the SEM program as compared to no intervention (Karafelis, 1986; Starko, 1986). Because control or comparison groups of students participating in alternate or comparison models were not used, it is difficult to attribute various results to participation in the SEM.

Evaluation studies have been conducted in 29 school districts on the perceptions of the model with parents, teachers, and administrators (Reis, 1981; Cooper, 1983; Olenchak & Renzulli, 1989). Positive change in teacher attitudes toward the work as documented.

Delcourt (1988) investigated characteristics related to creative/productive behavior in 18 high school students who consistently engaged in first-hand research on self-selected topics within or outside school. Burns (1988) and Starko (1986) also examined the effects of the Schoolwide Enrichment Model on student creative productivity. Results indicated that students who became involved in independent study projects in the SEM more often initiated their own creative products both *in and outside school* than did students in the comparison group and that multiple creative products were linked to self-efficacy (Schack, Starko & Burns, 1991; Baum, Renzulli & Hebert, 1995).

Several studies have examined the use of the model with underserved populations. Emerick (1988) investigated underachievement of high-potential students. Baum (1985, 1988) and Olenchak (1991) examined highly able students with learning disabilities, identifying both characteristics and programmatic needs. Findings suggest positive effects of the model with these populations.

Compacting studies have sought to document the fact that gifted students are capable of rapidly progressing through regular school curriculum in order to spend time on Type III project work. Results demonstrate knowledge scores as high or higher on in-grade standardized tests than non-compacted peers (Reis & Purcell, 1993).

Two SEM longitudinal studies have been conducted with 18 and nine students respectively. These studies showed that students in the sample maintained similar or identical career goals from their plans in high school, remained in major fields of study in colleges, and were satisfied in current project work. Moreover, the Type III process appeared to serve as important training for later productivity (Delcourt, 1993, 1994; Hebert, 1993).

The SEM is widely used in schools nationally and internationally in some form; summer training on the model is available at the University of Connecticut, reportedly training 600+ educators annually. The model is perceived by the developer to be closely linked to core curriculum, offers a scope and sequence within Type II activities, and has the potential to be aligned with national standards (Renzulli & Reis, 1994). Teachers are especially enthusiastic about the model as are selected students.

The Autonomous Learner Model

The autonomous learner model for the gifted and talented was developed to meet the diverse cognitive, emotional and social needs of gifted and talented students in grades K-12 (Betts & Knapp, 1980). As the needs of gifted and talented students are met, gifted students will develop into autonomous learners responsible for the development, implementation and evaluation of their own learning. The model is divided into five major dimensions: (1) Orientation, (2) Individual Development, (3) Enrichment Activities, (4) Seminars and (5) In-Depth Study.

One of the criteria used for assessing the appropriateness of a curriculum model is the evidence of research to support its use with gifted and talented learners. To date, no research evidence of effectiveness has been shown with regard to this model's student learning impact, or longitudinal effectiveness with gifted learners. However, six curriculum units and curriculum guides have been produced as a result of dissemination of its ideas. One article reviewed and described the model by presenting guidelines for developing a process-based scope and sequence as well as independent study programs for gifted learners (Betts & Neihart, 1986).

Regardless of the paucity of data on this model, it is one of the most widely recognized and used in the United States (Betts, 1986); teachers have commented positively on its implementation; the model has also been employed at selected sites in other countries. Formal teacher training occurs in three- and five-day segments annually; in its design, a three-year timeline is suggested for model implementation. It does contain a degree of comprehensiveness in that the model applies broadly to all curriculum domains and ages of learners; however, it does not incorporate any features of accelerated learning, thereby limiting one aspect of its comprehensiveness.

The Multiple Intelligences Model

Multiple intelligences (MI) as a curriculum approach was built on a multidimensional concept of intelligence (Gardner, 1983). Seven areas of intelligence were defined in the original published work in 1983, with an eighth intelligence added by Gardner in 1995. They are (1) Verbal/linguistic, (2) Logical/mathematical, (3) Visual/spatial, (4) Musical/rhythmic (5) Bodily/kinesthetic, (6) Interpersonal, (7) Intrapersonal, and (8) Naturalistic.

Evidence of research based on multiple intelligences translated into practice has recently been documented (Rosnow, Skleder, Jaeger & Rind, 1994; Strahan, Summey & Banks, 1996; Latham, 1997). Most of the research, however, lacks control groups, and therefore generalizations about the model are difficult to infer (Latham, 1997). Longitudinal evidence of effectiveness with gifted students over at least three years has not been documented, although some research has been conducted on incorporating multiple intelligences with other forms of curriculum models (Maker, Nielson & Rogers, 1994).

The Multiple Intelligences Model has been used in the formation of new schools, to identify individual differences, for curriculum planning and development, and as a way to assess instructional strategies (Gardner & Hatch, 1990; Fasko, 1992). A plethora of curriculum materials have been produced and marketed based upon Multiple Intelligences (MI). It holds widespread appeal for many educators because it can be adapted for any learner, subject domain or grade level. The model is not easy to implement and does require teacher training, financial resources and time. Best known project sites for the model are the Key School in Indianapolis, Indiana and the Atlas Project in New York City. While the model has been readily adapted to curriculum, it remains primarily a conception of intelligence applied broadly to school settings as a way to promote talent development for all learners.

Developer concerns about application fidelity of the ideas and variability in implementation quality are strong, leading to a new project specifically designed to monitor implementation of MI in classrooms where positive impacts have been reported.

The Purdue Three-Stage Enrichment Model for Elementary Gifted Learners (PACE) and The Purdue Secondary Model for Gifted and Talented Youth

The concept of a three-stage model initiated by Feldhusen and his graduate students was first introduced as a course design for university students in 1973; it evolved into The Three-Stage Model by 1979 (Feldhusen & Kolloff, 1979). The model is primarily an ordered enrichment model that moves students from simple thinking experiences to complex independent activities (Feldhusen and Kolloff, 1986; Feldhusen, Kolloff, Cole & Moon, 1988). Stage I focuses on the development of divergent and convergent thinking skills; Stage II provides development in creative problem solving, and Stage III allows students to apply research skills in the development of independent study skills. The Purdue Secondary Model is a comprehensive structure for programming services at the secondary level. It has eleven components supporting enrichment and acceleration options with each component designed to act as a guide for organizing opportunities for secondary gifted students. They are: (1) counseling services, (2) seminar, (3) advanced placement courses, (4) honors classes, (5) math-science acceleration, (6) foreign languages, (7) arts, (8) cultural experiences, (9) career education, (10) vocational programs, and (11) extra-school instruction (Feldhusen & Robinson-Wyman, 1986).

Research has documented gains with regard to enhancement of creative thinking and self-concept using the Three-Stage Enrichment model for elementary gifted students (Kolloff & Feldhusen, 1984), and one study was conducted documenting limited long-term gains of the elementary program PACE (Moon & Feldhusen, 1994; Moon, Feldhusen & Dillon, 1994).

The application and implementation of either the elementary or secondary models are not conclusive yet appear to be sustainable (Moon, Feldhusen, Powley & Nidiffer, 1993; Moon & Feldhusen, 1994). Teacher training has accompanied the site implementation of both the elementary and secondary models; however, it is difficult to ascertain the degree of widespread application beyond the state of Indiana. Neither model utilizes a scope and sequence and may not be viewed as a comprehensive model in terms of applying broadly to all areas of the curriculum, all types of gifted learners or to all stages of development.

The Grid

The Grid was a model designed to facilitate the curriculum developer's task of what constitutes differentiated curriculum and how one can construct such a curriculum. The model uses the components of process, content and product organized around a theme. Content is defined as "the relationship between economic, social, personal and environmental displays of power and the needs and the interests of individuals, groups, and societies (interdisciplinary)" (Kaplan, 1986). The process component utilizes productive thinking, research skills and basic skills; the product component culminates the learning into a mode of communication.

Research has not been conducted to support the effectiveness of this model with a target population. The quality of the curriculum products that have been produced based upon this model has not been reported in the literature; however, there has been extensive implementation of the approach both at state and local levels.

Teacher training has been conducted throughout the United States initially through the National/State

Leadership Training Institute and now independently by the developer so that practitioners can learn how to implement it; thousands of teachers have developed their own curriculum based upon the model. The Grid is intended as a developmental framework for curriculum planning for gifted learners, but it does not contain a scope and sequence; additionally, within the model itself, no provisions are explicitly made for accelerated learning.

The Matrix

The Matrix model was developed to categorize content, process, environmental, and product dimensions of an appropriate curriculum for the gifted; it represents a set of descriptive criteria that may be used to develop classroom-based curriculum (Maker, 1982; Maker & Nielson, 1996). Recent work on the model primarily represents an enhancement of the problem solving component of it. The Discover project is a process for assessing problem solving in multiple intelligences (Maker, 1993); the problem-solving matrix incorporates a continuum of five problem types for use within each of the intelligences; Types I and II require convergent thinking. Type III problems are structured but allow for a range of methods to solve them and have a range of acceptable answers. Type IV problems are defined but the learner selects a method for solving and establishing evaluation criteria for the solution. Type V problems are ill structured and the learner must define the problem, discover the method for solving and establish criteria for creating a solution (Maker, Nielson & Rogers, 1994). The project is typically used by teachers for curriculum planning and assessing learner problem-solving abilities.

Research is currently underway involving 12 classrooms in a variety of settings; however, to date the results have not been published. A pilot study has shown that use of the matrix enhances the process of problem solving (Maker, Rogers, Nielson & Bauerle, 1996); studies to evaluate the long-term validity of the process are in progress.

School systems in several areas have applied the matrix as a framework for organizing and developing classroom level curriculum; there is evidence of individual teacher-developed curriculum, and teachers have been receptive to its use; some training exists for its application. The sustainability of the matrix for at least three years is not known; it is not comprehensive in nature, yet it does have a strong emphasis in its relationship to core subject domains.

The Structure of Intellect Model (SOI)

The Structure of Intellect Model (SOI) for gifted education was based upon a theory of human intelligence called the Structure of Intellect (SI) developed by J. P. Guilford (1967); the SI model of human intelligence describes ninety kinds of cognitive functions organized into content, operation and product abilities. The SOI system applies Guilford's theory into the areas of assessment and training. The model is definable as a system and applies broadly to all types of gifted learners at varying developmental stages but due to its comprehensiveness and emphasis on cognition, only a few sites have actually implemented the model (Meeker, 1985). Those sites have used it for identifying students or for training teachers to view intelligence as a non-fixed entity.

Studies of the model do not include effectiveness data (Meeker, 1976); rather they primarily focus on findings for use as identification criteria or as a means for organizing information about a gifted child or for overall program design. SOI has been successfully used in selected sites for identification of culturally diverse students (Hengen, 1983) and preschool screening for multi-ethnic disadvantaged gifted students (Bonne, 1985).

Although now somewhat dated, SOI offered a means of understanding students by delineating profiles of their intellectual abilities. It contained a teacher training component that used teacher modules that were designed to train one SOI ability at a time. Training materials included mini lesson plans for group teaching and self-help modules for individualized instruction with selected students (Meeker, 1969).

The Models for Talents Unlimited, Inc. and Talents Unlimited to the Secondary Power (TU²)

Talents Unlimited (Schlichter, 1986b) was also based upon Guilford's (1967) research on the nature of intelligence. Taylor and colleagues (Taylor, Ghiselin, Wolfer, Loy & Bourne,1964), also influenced by Guilford, authored The Multiple Talent Theory, which precipitated the development of a model to be employed in helping teachers identify and nurture students' multiple talents. Talents Unlimited features four major components: (1) a description of specific skill abilities or talents, in addition to academic ability, that include productive thinking, communication, forecasting, decision making, and planning; (2) model instructional materials; (3) an inservice training program for teachers; and (4) an evaluation system for assessing students' thinking skills development (Schlichter, 1986b). Talents Unlimited Inc. is the K-6 model and Talents Unlimited to the Secondary Power is a model for grades 7–12 (Crump, Schlichter & Palk, 1988; Schlichter, Hobbs & Crump, 1988).

Research has documented gains using the model in developing students' creative and critical thinking (Schlichter & Palmer, 1993). Additionally, there is evidence that the use of the model enhances academic skill development on standardized achievement tests (McLean & Chisson, 1980); however, no longitudinal studies have been conducted.

Staff development and teacher training constitute a strong component of the model (Schlichter, 1986a;

Schlichter et al, 1997); teachers may become 'certified' as Talents Unlimited trainers. Due to the strong emphasis on teacher training, Talents Unlimited has widespread applicable student use across the United States and worldwide. Part of its implementation success came as a result of funding and membership in the United States Office of Education, National Diffusion Network.

The model has been used most effectively as a classroom-based approach with all learners (Schlichter, 1988), thus rendering it less differential for the gifted in practice than some of the other models.

The Triarchic Componential Model

The triarchic componential model of curriculum is based upon an information processing theory of intelligence (Sternberg, 1981). In the metacomponent area, three components must be present in mental processes used in thinking. The executive process component is used in planning, decision making and monitoring performance. The performance component processes are used in executing the executive problem-solving strategies within domains. The knowledge-acquisition component is used in acquiring, retaining, and transferring new information. The interaction and feedback between the individual and his/her environment within any given context allows cognitive development to occur.

An initial study has shown the effectiveness of the triarchic model with students learning psychology in a summer program (Sternberg & Clinkenbeard, 1995); more recent work has been conducted in studies using psychology as the curriculum base with larger samples of students. Students continue to show growth patterns when assessment protocols are linked to measuring ability profiles (Sternberg, Ferrari, Clinkenbeard & Grigorenko, 1996). Primary to these studies is the validation of the STAT (Sternberg Triarchic Abilities Test) and its utility for finding students strong on specific triarchic components; other recent studies (Sternberg, Torff, and Grigonerko, 1998a, 1998b) focus on the use of triarchic instructional processes in classrooms at the elementary and middle school levels. Results suggest slightly stronger effects for triarchic instruction over traditional and critical thinking approaches. Descriptions of teacher-created curriculum and instructional instrumentation processes were limited but are clearly organized along discipline-specific lines of inquiry; sustainability of the curriculum model beyond summer program implementation and pilot settings is not known.

There is not a packaged teacher training or staff development component, partially because the model is based upon a theory of intelligence rather than a deliberate curriculum framework; it is a systemic but not a comprehensive model with applications made in selected classrooms.

The William and Mary Integrated Curriculum Model (ICM)

The Integrated Curriculum Model (ICM) (Van Tassel-Baska, 1986) was specifically developed for high ability learners and has three dimensions: (1) advanced content, (2) high level process and product work, and (3) intra- and interdisciplinary concept development and understanding. VanTassel-Baska, with funding from the Jacob Javits Program, developed specific curriculum frameworks and underlying units in language arts, science and social studies, using the ICM.

Research has been conducted to support the effectiveness of these curriculum units with gifted populations within a variety of educational settings. Specifically, significant growth gains in literary analysis and interpretation, persuasive writing, and linguistic competency in language arts have been demonstrated for experimental gifted classes using the developed curriculum units in comparison to gifted groups not using them (Van Tassel-Baska, Johnson, Hughes & Boyce, 1996; Van Tassel-Baska, Zuo, Avery and Little, in press). Other studies have shown that using the problem-based science units embedded in an exemplary science curriculum significantly enhances the capacity for integrating higher order process skills in science regardless of the grouping approach employed (Gallagher, Stepien, Sher & Workman, 1995; Boyce, VanTassel-Baska, Burruss, Sher & Johnson, 1997; Van Tassel-Baska, Bass, Ries, Poland & Avery, 1998). Further, research has documented positive change in teacher attitude, student motivational response, and school and district change (Van Tassel-Baska, Avery, Little & Hughes, 2000) as a result of using the William and Mary curriculum over three years.

Teacher training is an integral component of the ICM; training workshops have been conducted in 30 states, and The College of William and Mary offers training annually. There is a strong relationship to core subject domains as well as national standards alignment; the curriculum based on the model was developed using the national standards work as a template. Alignment charts have been completed for national and state standards work in both language arts and science.

The William and Mary units are moderately comprehensive in that they span grades 2–10 in language arts and 2–8 in science. New language arts units developed in 1997–98 now offer K–11 coverage in language arts; the ICM has been used for specific district curriculum development and planning.

There is evidence of broad-based application but some question remains as to the ease of implementation of actual teaching units and to the fidelity of implementation by teachers (Burruss, 1997); some districts use the units as models for developing their own curriculum. The developer reported that 100 school districts are part of a National Curriculum Network using both the science and language arts units; data have been collected from over 100 classrooms nationally on student impact.

Studies of effectiveness are on-going in classrooms nationally. and the curriculum is reported to be used in 45 states. Internationally, the model is being used in 15 countries with systematic unit development occurring in two states in Australia.

Findings

Seven models showed evidence of research being conducted on them; of those, six of the models employed comparison groups where treatment might be attributed to the curriculum approach employed. The Stanley, Renzulli, Feldhusen, Sternberg, VanTassel-Baska, and Schlichter models all have some evidence of effectiveness with gifted populations in comparison to other treatments. However, only Stanley has amassed a comprehensive body of literature to support his model. While the Talents Unlimited Model has some evidence of effectiveness, much of it is on non-gifted populations.

Evidence for the translation of these curriculum models into effective practice varies considerably; seven models have training packages that provide staff development for implementation; only four models explicitly consider scope and sequence issues. The Autonomous Learner Model (ALM) and SEM consider scope and sequence within their model. For the ALM, it is in the movement from one stage to another; for SEM, it occurs within Type II activities. Both talent search and ICM have developed scope and sequence models linked to Advanced Placement work; ICM has also developed alignment models to the national standards projects and 15 state frameworks as well.

Data on curriculum and instructional practices with the gifted clearly favor accelerative approaches in the core subject areas of language, arts, science, and mathematics, although the approach to content acceleration may vary. While both the talent search and ICM models have elements of acceleration within them, only the talent search model has empirically demonstrated the strong impact of accelerative study on learning.

Curriculum organized around higher order processes and independent study have yielded few studies of student impacts, nor are the findings across studies consistent; even longitudinal studies, such as those on the PACE and SEM models, have produced limited evidence of outcomes relevant to clear student gains. Limited sample size and other confounding variables such as lack of comparison groups also render these studies less credible.

Conclusions

A strong body of research evidence exists supporting the use of advanced curriculum in core areas of learning at an accelerated rate for high ability learners; some evidence also exists that more enrichment-oriented models are effective; this conclusion has not changed much in the past 20 years (Daurio, 1979). Moreover, recent meta-analytic studies continue to confirm the superior learning effects of acceleration over enrichment in tandem with grouping the gifted (Kulik & Kulik, 1992). In comparison to strategies such as independent study, various modes of grouping, and problem-solving, acceleration also shows superior effect sizes (Walberg, 1991). Despite the lack of convincing research to support their use, several of the enrichment models enjoy widespread popularity and are used extensively in schools.

Implications

Several implications might be drawn from these findings, related to both research and practice in gifted education. Research-based practice is critical to defensible gifted programs; therefore, practitioners must proceed carefully in deciding on curriculum for use in these programs. The evidence strongly suggests that content-based accelerative approaches should be employed in any curriculum used in school-based programs for the gifted and that schools need to apply curriculum models faithfully and thoroughly enough to realize their potential impacts over time.

In the area of research, it is clear that there is a limited base of coherent studies that can make claims about the efficacy of enriched approaches to curriculum for the gifted. Thus an important direction for future research would be to conduct curriculum intervention studies, testing the extant models as well as replicating existing studies to build a base of deeper understanding about what works well with gifted students in school programs. More research on differential student learning outcomes in gifted programs, using discrete curricular approaches clearly needs to be undertaken. The field of gifted education has a long way to go before being able to say "what intervention works best with what type of gifted learner at what stage of development?" Future research efforts need to define at a more discrete level the impacts of curriculum interventions on the prototypes of gifted learners that inhabit our schools.

The relationship of curriculum for the gifted to general school reform initiatives

The standards-based educational reform movement in the United States and abroad has been instrumental in underscoring the need for curriculum development work (Cohen & Spillane, 1993; O'Day & Smith, 1993). This movement advocates the articulation of challenging content standards which become the basis for the alignment of policies, practices, and resources directed toward student proficiency in meeting or exceeding the standards (McLaughlin & Shepard, 1995). At national and state governance levels, these standards serve as the foundation for establishing policies and distributing resources across districts and schools. At the district level, the standards facilitate the design of curriculum frameworks to guide the curriculum and staff development initiatives. At the classroom level, the content standards are translated into specific curriculum and instructional units.

After a decade of work on analysis, design and development of curriculum for the gifted learners that is consonant with state and national curriculum standards in the United States and other countries it appears that there is goodness of fit between the standards for all and the components of a desirable curriculum for the gifted.

The similarities between curriculum development efforts in general education, and the principles of gifted education curriculum development are very complementary. While the translation of these principles into practice still require greater flexibility and latitude when dealing with the range of high ability learners, it is important to note the commonalities of general approaches to curriculum reform with those principles of good gifted education. Both approaches value learner outcomes that emphasize higher level thinking and conceptual understanding, authentic instruction and assessment, deep involvement in inquiry, use of multiple resources and technology applications, and helping students develop metacognitive tools. The standards also reflect an attempt to view the curriculum experience as one that promotes the habits of mind of a practicing professional, whether it be a scientist, writer or mathematician; all of these components have been staples of gifted curriculum philosophy for the past 20 years. Because of the complementarity of discipline-specific reform efforts and gifted education tenets, educators of the gifted should align their efforts in curriculum with the work currently going on in all the content disciplines. As a field, gifted education has much to contribute to the debate on national and international standards in all of the core domains of inquiry.

While there is considerable overlap in the proposed exemplary content-based curriculum for all learners and curriculum differentiation issues for the gifted, there still remain two issues that must be accounted for in working with the gifted. The differentiation for these learners in such a model must still emanate from a clear understanding of the capacity of such learners at a given grade level to engage in a faster pace of learning at an advanced level. Moreover, high ability learners require access to more sophisticated curriculum treatment at earlier stages of development. Consequently, curriculum expectations for these students need to reflect such adaptations, at advanced and even world

class levels. Curriculum grounded in intra- and interdisciplinary concepts, however, provides enormous opportunities to enhance more advanced and sophisticated learning for gifted students.

Based on the thorough review of existing subject matter materials, it appears appropriate to underscore the extent to which cost-effective exemplary curriculum materials are readily available for use in classrooms. One problem uncovered, however, was the very limited use those materials were receiving, even in schools and districts that have purchased them (Johnson, Boyce & VanTassel-Baska, 1995). Some of the best materials may be characterized as unleveled in respect to grade, interdisciplinary in orientation, and comprised of multiple modes of learning, usually including video or computer technology as a key feature. It is paradoxical that the very curricular components valued for their appropriateness with high ability learners are overlooked when they are 'packaged' into ready-made curriculum materials. The lesson to be learned may be that there already are excellent curricula for high ability and other learning groups; the problem rests with: (a) continuing the development process through extending and refining that which is already available using existing frameworks, and (b) removing barriers (such as lack of experimental materials and/or equipment and lack of human resource assistance in implementing classroom procedures) to getting the new curriculum institutionalized in classroom practice.

Many basal text materials are inadequate for the task of curriculum reform, especially for high ability learners. For example, in the 1995 study cited, no basal text reached the level of being recommended for use with high ability learners with the exception of the BSCS biology program originally developed in the 1960s. There is a clear need for schools to select materials carefully that respond to the more powerful current curricular models in general and gifted education in particular.

Developmental and ability levels of students appear to impact on the use of new curriculum materials but not to the degree anticipated by many educators. The William and Mary curriculum units, for example, were pilot tested in various classroom settings: gifted self-contained, resource rooms, high ability classes, and heterogeneous classrooms. Teachers who worked with gifted students daily reported greater success with the curriculum than did those who saw students only once or twice a week. Based on teacher log data, it was found that high ability learners were more receptive to the curriculum than other learners; however, some students *not* identified as gifted displayed aptitude and interest through the use of the materials, and teachers felt that most learners benefitted more from the approaches embedded in this curriculum than from a traditional text model (VanTassel-Baska, Bass, Reis, Poland & Avery, 1998). This finding tends to support the premise that more high-powered curriculum in regular classrooms would enhance the learning for all.

Clearly the major thrust in curriculum reform in all areas for high ability learners must be in the arena of teacher training; the need for specific subject matter training is great, given the need to attend to discipline-specific reform and rigorous curriculum for the gifted. In science, for example, all teachers are teachers of the high ability learner, except in special schools or self-contained classes; thus the need to engage with general science educators in their staff development efforts to reform science education for all learners may be a crucial part of our role as educators of the gifted.

Teacher training for gifted learners also needs to target specialized concerns. In respect to curriculum in general, preservice and inservice work needs to focus on how to implement discipline-specific models of curriculum and instruction that are responsive to the underlying needs of gifted learners, how to engage learners as investigators, providing the tools and processes used by real world problem solvers, and how to raise standards and expectations for gifted learners in regular classrooms.

Curriculum Issues for Special Populations of Gifted Learners

Whether we are talking about low income, minority, or disabled gifted students, one factor remains common to each group; they reside outside the mainstream networks that provide access to educational advantage. This knowledge is crucial to converting high aspirations into creative productive achievement at various stages of development; thus the role of special programs is critical to this conversion process.

At their best, in-school programs have provided rigorous coursework comparable to what advantaged learners in the best school settings would receive. At the same time, other school programs have focused on remediating skill deficits or offering programs in non-academic areas, such as the performing arts. A survey of existing programs for disadvantaged gifted students at the local level identified over 100 districts thought to be providing service (VanTassel-Baska, Patton & Prillaman, 1991). The majority of these programs were not differentiating service delivery for disadvantaged gifted students, even though they were careful to include them in programs for gifted students.

Yet there is evidence from the general literature on disadvantaged populations of the importance of key differential interventions with these learners based on the variables that separate them from their more advantaged peers in the first place. These needed interventions include early education, classroom environment, curriculum, and counseling.

Historically, the Upward Bound program, which assists high school students in preparing for college, emphasized language-based skills such as reading, composition, ethnic literature, and creative writing

(Koe, 1980). Yet recent curriculum concerns have centered on the paucity of minority students pursuing advanced programming in math and science. Anick, Carpenter & Smith (1981) noted that serious inequities exist in math education of Black and Hispanic students and that their achievement levels were not only well below the national average, but that differences from the larger population increased for each consecutive age group. Their study showed though, that while Blacks appear to take less math than other groups, they reported positive feelings about the subject. The authors concluded that motivation may not be a major problem and that general approaches used for all students would be appropriate for minorities.

In a review of 24 studies of participation and performance of minorities in math done since 1975, Mathews (1984) found that parents desire but often do not know how to help their children, that minority role models appear to have a positive effect on enrollment in math courses, and that math may be seen as lacking utility by lower SES children.

Several researchers have focused on group rather than individual models of learning as more facilitative for minority group students. Slavin & Oickle (1981) found a greater increase in black students' academic performance when cooperative learning groups were used; Hale-Benson (1986) advocated peer tutoring, while Holliday (1985) emphasized enhanced teacher-student interactions.

The literature has suggested several differentiated approaches for working with gifted learning disabled children, including separate class grouping (Daniels, 1983), counseling and adaptive behavior programs (Wolf & Gygi, 1981), the use of technological aids (Tobin & Schiffman, 1983), after-school structured timetables (Sah & Borland, 1989), and the teaching of compensation strategies (Suter & Wolf, 1987). Moreover, most writers also urge the use of strategies appropriate for all gifted learners. A list of adaptations for use at school and home to enhance learning for gifted learning disabled students include: use visuals and hands-on experiences; provide a quiet place for work; use a sight approach to reading rather than phonics; use a word processor with a spell correct program; practice visualization as a memory aid; tape record lectures instead of taking notes; and concentrate on the child's strengths, especially in order to compensate for weaknesses (Hansford et al., 1987; Suter & Wolf, 1987; Silverman, 1989).

While the research base on the under-representation of low-income and culturally diverse gifted learners was fairly substantial, there were fewer studies that reported on educational practices addressing their needs. VanTassel-Baska et al. (1991) synthesized the generic features of interventions that work well with disadvantaged and culturally different gifted students: (1) early and systematic attention to their needs, (2) parental and family involvement in their educational program, (3) use of effective schools' strategies, (4) experiential and 'hands-on' learning approaches, (5) activities that allow for self-expression, (6) mentors and role models, (7) counseling that addresses cultural values and facilitates talent development, (8) building on the strengths and differential learning styles of at-risk learners. Maker and Schiever (1989) presaged many of these same elements in their earlier synthesis of the literature on programs and curricula for cultural and ethnic minorities. Their summary included the following: (1) plan the curriculum based on students' strengths, (2) provide for the development of basic skills and other abilities that the student may lack, (3) consider differences as positives, (4) arrange for mentors, and (5) create and maintain a classroom with a multicultural emphasis.

Frasier (1993) cited several examples of U.S. programs that had success in working with dis-advantaged and minority gifted populations, including the Skills Re-enforcement Project (SRP) and the Program of Assessment, Diagnosis, and Instruction (PADI). Tomlinson, Callahan & Lelli (1997) found that multicultural emphases, language immersion, use of manipulatives, participation in mentorships, and family outreach were essential for the success of low-income and/or minority primary-aged gifted students in Project START (Support to Affirm Rising Talent).

Other researchers have focused on the larger cultural context for understanding the needs of specific minority groups. Clasen (1992) and Ogbu (1994) have both commented on the alienation experienced by involuntary minorities struggling to juggle the expectations of conflicting worlds. For instance, African-American gifted students, who demonstrate academic aptitude, can be rejected by their black peers for 'acting White'; as a result, these students must develop coping mechanisms in order to straddle the value systems of competing allegiances (Patton & Baytops, 1995). Such demands create additional psychological stressors in minority gifted populations that need psycho-social support (Ford-Harris, Schuerger & Harris, 1991).

In studying the needs of at-risk gifted adolescents, Olszewski-Kubilius, Grant & Seibert (1994) noted that programs that address only one aspect of the child's life, such as the provision of an appropriate academic program, have "little hope of having long-term impact" (p. 23). This underscores the need for parental involvement in the child's education. Parent involvement has been found to have a positive effect for students by providing appropriate modeling, reenforcement, and even direct instruction within a holistic context of family, school, and community (Epstein, 1995; Hoover-Dempsey & Sandler, 1995). Epstein (1995) found that developing school, family, and community partnerships improved school programs and school climate and provided a basis for connecting families to services in the community. Such refrains are

also echoed in the literature on resilience (Werner & Smith, 1992), which advocated for multifaceted, systemic interventions in the home, school, and community.

Several curricular interventions also appear promising:

(1) Separate instructional opportunities for students with the same developmental profile. Data across special populations suggest the importance for within-group instructional time that allows for interaction based on similar conditions whether it be gender, social background, or handicapping conditions.

(2) The use of technology, especially microcomputers, to aid in the transmission of learning for many special population learners. While it has been used most predominantly with disabled gifted learners, it holds promise for targeted use with other learners who evidence discrepant learning patterns and can profit from compensatory intervention.

(3) The use of small group and individual counseling, mentorships, and internships for special population learners appears promising since these interventions all constitute individual attention to affective as well as cognitive issues of development.

(4) A focus on the arts as a therapeutic intervention as well as a creative and expressive outlet appears important to consider for all of these special populations. Through the arts, the dissynchronies of one's experience can be reduced and absorbed into a higher pattern of integration. Thus it serves as an enhancement to higher level functioning for such individuals.

(5) Use of materials rich in ideas and imagination coupled with a focus on higher level skills appears to be an important intervention approach for special populations. Both self-concept and motivation are in jeopardy if prolonged use of compensatory strategies and basic level materials are used in the educational process of these learners. Challenging content with a focus on ideas and creative opportunities are essential to combat further discrepant performance.

(6) An emphasis on one-to-one instruction through tutorial approaches appears to be very helpful in working with gifted special populations.

Thus research on the learning needs of many of these students, particularly from African-American and Hispanic populations, has provided some guidance about program and curriculum interventions that have worked. Key features of successful programs included early identification and sustained intervention, experiential and hands-on learning, and use of curricula with multicultural emphases that allow for student choice. In addition, an awareness of the importance of parental involvement or support by a mentor who encourages academic achievement, permeated this segment of the literature.

Conclusion: The Challenge for the Future

Where is curriculum and instruction for the gifted headed over the next several years? It is clear that the field of gifted education is changing: our conceptions of intelligence and therefore of giftedness have changed, our conceptions of the delivery context for serving the gifted have changed, and our population focus has also changed. This shift in focus is both a dilemma and a challenge that provides us with new opportunities to grow and develop as a field, hopefully more responsive to the individual needs of children than to preordained labels; to the social context of schools and the networks that hold them together than to the categorical approach to gifted education as a separate enterprise; and more responsive to change in general that requires us to compromise hard positions and join forces with all educators who care about students with special needs.

Curriculum planners for the gifted need to be cognizant of the importance of maintaining a balanced perspective toward key issues if gifted education is to be meaningful for the students it wants to serve. The theme for approaching and dealing with these issues is that of balance—a balance that must be effected between alliances with general and special education models without diffusing efforts to maintain a distinguishable set of curriculum principles that are appropriate *only* for gifted learners. One of the dangers of stretching to reach out to the more entrenched curriculum models of general education or the specialized administrative models of special education is a loss of identity in what gifted education itself represents. If it is shown by current research efforts that the degree of exceptionality is not sufficiently great enough to warrant a special administrative structure and special settings for gifted learners, then our claims as a field to separate program considerations becomes weakened. If at the same time, it is sufficiently demonstrated that exemplary approaches to curriculum in general education are in fact both necessary and sufficient for gifted learners, then our claims to a qualitatively different set of educational experiences for the gifted are weakened. While we as a field may have made too much of our distinctiveness and specialness, by the same token we must guard against too quickly abandoning the very principles on which the field has been grounded for the last 80 years—the basic principles of the gifted student's unique needs that call for acceleration, grouping, and enrichment in school settings in order to receive an appropriate education.

Balance is also important in considering the needs of learners who are gifted in all cognitive areas in comparison to those gifted only in one; how do we provide appropriate curricular experiences for specialized talents as well as provide comprehensive services to more broad-based ones? This issue is particularly worthy of our reflection at the level of developing a curriculum scope and sequence. Should the outcome expectations of secondary school for the science-prone, for example, differ from the expectations for the intellectually gifted student whose interests and aptitudes are more broad-ranging? If they should, how might these differential expectations be articulated K-12? Or should specialized talent development even be a function of the public school arena? Certainly Bloom's work on talent development (1985) would support the contention that it has not been traditionally a part of what public schools have taken on as their responsibility. Perhaps it is in the specialized areas of talent—art, music, mathematics, chess—where the school's major role may be that of broker and facilitator of talent development for students who show early promise. It is for these learners that tutorials, mentorships, and internships in the larger community are reserved since their aptitudes and interests are more finely attuned to the need for individualized adult expert instruction early.

Balance is also a theme in our consideration of the domains of study to be valued in a comprehensive curriculum for gifted learners. The aesthetic, and social domains of study deserve as much attention as the cognitive in the overall development of the gifted learner (VanTassel-Baska, 1998). This balanced perspective on curriculum development is needed lest we limit the recognition of the integrated needs of the gifted learner and narrow the educational options available to her. Inclusion of the arts, for example, in a curriculum for the intellectually gifted is significant because it provides a vehicle for the development of aesthetic appreciation and an expressive outlet that enhances the creative impulse. Scientists foreshadow discoveries in metaphors and visual symbols; mathematicians strive for elegance in form; philosophers value the symmetry of an argument. In most professional fields at high levels of creative work, the aesthetic and artistic aspects of the work come strongly into focus. Thus to ensure that curriculum for gifted learners is heavily infused with such an emphasis throughout their schooling years seems vital.

Honoring the affective development of the gifted is also an important aspect of a comprehensive balanced curriculum view. These students need to understand their own exceptionality, their intensity and sensitivity of feelings, their need for coping strategies to help them deal with their own perfectionism and vulnerability. These needs require a strong affective orientation to the curriculum to be delivered by teachers sensitive to the nature of gifted students. Such needs also demand a set of counseling services that can respond to psychosocial, academic planning, and career planning needs at requisite periods during schooling.

Another facet to a balanced view of curriculum for the gifted is in the area of social development, undertaken with the long view toward adult leadership. While much of the work in leadership curriculum for the gifted has focused on political leadership (e.g. Karnes & Chauvin, 2000), there is a need to expand our thinking in this area to embrace a concept of leadership that recognizes the other forms of leadership that gifted individuals in a society provide including intellectual leadership in various areas and for many gifted women, social service leadership. The skills of understanding group dynamics, the organization of complex tasks, and how to motivate others, however, are fundamental to all forms of leadership and thus must underlie a curriculum in this area.

Another issue related to a balanced perspective in curriculum planning for the gifted rests with a need to view our purposes in constructing specialized curriculum for gifted learners. We have often argued that differentiating curriculum for the gifted was important to meet individual needs, yet we also view the potential contribution of the gifted to society as an equally important purpose. The metaphor of the gifted as national resource has been exploited more than once in our history as a field; in the policy arena, at least, it seems important to be able to keep these purposes in a healthy tension that allows for both views to be made explicit. For, at a fundamental level, the gifted develop as individuals in a reciprocal relationship with their society; thus their creative work carries meaning beyond themselves whether it is fully intended to or not. By the same token, a society is enriched by having individuals actively engaging in self-chosen creative endeavors.

The translation of this paradox of individual and societal needs at the classroom level can be seen in the issue of cooperative learning and the gifted. To what extent does the use of the gifted learner as a tutor/teacher/model to others in group settings become exploitation and costly to their own individual development? To what extent does prolonged independent or homogeneous group work carried out in isolation contribute to a rejection by the gifted of their natural connection to other learners in the classroom? Again the healthy balance must be struck between independent and group opportunities in order to ensure the full development of the gifted learner in a social context. Can we tolerate individual excellence within a social framework that honors the integrity of everyone and is hospitable to all learners? This it seems is the fundamental question in school classrooms today.

As curriculum planners reflect on these somewhat traditional issues, they must not reject their importance in favor of the more 'trendy questions' that may be asked. For if curriculum planning is to have merit, then the need for a balanced perspective in the areas of general and specialized talent development, equal valuing of cognitive, affective, aesthetic, and social development of the gifted, and a concern for both individual and social contributions must be satisfied.

For groups of typical gifted learners as well as individual-need gifted learners, such as those from special populations, attention to these issues is crucial. Curriculum for the gifted, its goals and purposes, as well as its delivery systems speaks loudly as to how talent and its development is honored and nurtured in a society.

References

Academic Preparation for College (1983). *Project equality*, NY: College Board.

Anderson, R., Herbert, E., Scott, J. & Wilkinson, I. (1985). *Becoming a nation of readers*. The report of the commission on reading. Washington, DC: National Institute of Education.

Anick, C. M., Carpenter, T. P. & Smith, C. (1981). Minorities and mathematics. *Mathematics Teacher*, **74** (7), 560–566.

Banks, J. A. (1999). *Teaching strategies for the social studies: Decision-making and citizen action* (5th ed.). New York: Longman.

Baum, S. (1985). *Learning disabled students with superior cognitive abilities: A validation study of descriptive behaviors*. Unpublished doctoral dissertation, The University of Connecticut, Storrs, CT.

Baum, S. (1988). Enrichment program for the gifted learning disabled students. *Gifted Child Quarterly*, **32**, 226–230.

Baum, S., Renzulli, J. & Hebert. T. P. (1995). Reversing under-achievement: Creative productivity as a systematic intervention, *Gifted Child Quarterly*, **39**, 224–235.

Benbow, C. P. (1986). SMPY's model for teaching mathematically precocious students. In: J. S. Renzulli (Ed.), *Systems and Models for Developing Programs for the Gifted and Talented* (pp. 1–25). Mansfield Center, CT: Creative Learning Press.

Benbow, C. P. & Arjmand, O. (1990). Predictors of high academic achievement in mathematics and science by mathematically talented students: A longitudinal study. *Journal of Educational Psychology*, **82**, 430–431.

Benbow, C. P. & Lubinski, D. (1994). Individual differences amongst the mathematically gifted: Their educational and vocational implications. In: N. Colangelo, S. G. Assouline & D. L. Ambroson (Eds.), *Talent Development* (Vol. 2, pp. 83–100). Dayton, OH: Ohio Psychology Press.

Benbow, C. P. & Lubinski, D. (1996). *Intellectual talent: Psychometric and social issues*. Baltimore: Johns Hopkins University Press.

Benbow, C. P. & Stanley, J. C. (1983). *Academic precocity*. Baltimore, MD: Johns Hopkins University Press.

Benbow, C. P. & Stanley, J. C. (1996). Inequity in equity: How 'equity' can lead to inequity for high-potential students. *Psychology Public Policy, and Law*, **2**, 249–292.

Berliner, D. (1985). *Presidential address to the American Educational Research Association*. San Francisco, CA.

Betts, G. T. & Knapp, J. (1980). Autonomous learning and the gifted: A secondary model. In: A. Arnold (Ed.), *Secondary Programs for the Gifted* (pp. 29–36). Ventura, CA: Ventura Superintendent of Schools Office.

Betts, G. T.(1986). The autonomous learner model for the gifted and talented. In: J. S. Renzulli (Ed.), *Systems and Models for Developing Programs for the Gifted and Talented* (pp. 27–56). Mansfield Center, CT: Creative Learning Press.

Betts, G. T. & Neihart, M. (1986). Implementing self-directed learning models for the gifted and talented. *Gifted Child Quarterly*, **30**, 174–77.

Betts, G. (1991). The autonomous learner model for the gifted and talented. In: N. Colangelo and G. A. Davis (Eds), *Handbook of Gifted Education* (pp.142–153). Boston, MA: Allyn & Bacon.

Bloom, B. (1985). *Developing talent in young people*. NY: Ballantine.

Bonne, R. (1985). *Identifying multi-ethnic disadvantaged gifted*. Brooklyn, NY: Community School District #19.

Boyce, L. N, VanTassel-Baska, J., Burruss, J. D, Sher, B. T. & Johnson, D. T. (1997). A problem-based curriculum: Parallel learning opportunities for students and teachers. *Journal for the Education of the Gifted*, **20**, 363–379.

Brody, L. E. & Stanley, J. C. (1991). Young college students: Assessing factors that contribute to success. In: W. T. Southern & E. D. Jones (Eds), *Academic Acceleration of Gifted Children*. New York: Teachers College Press.

Brown, A. & Campione, J. (1986). Psychological theory and the study of learning disabilities. *American Psychologist*, **14** (10), 1059–1068.

Burns, D. (1988). The effects of group training activities on students' creative productivity. In J. S. Renzulli (Ed.), *Technical Report of Research Studies Related to the Revolving Door Identification Model* (2nd ed), (pp. 147–174). Storrs, CT: Research Report Series, School of Education, University of Connecticut.

Burruss, J. D. (1997, April). *Walking the talk: Implementation decisions made by teachers*. Presentation at the American Educational Research Association (AERA), Chicago, IL.

California Department of Education (1990). *Science framework for California schools K-12*. Sacramento, CA: California Department of Education.

Carnegie Forum on Education and the Economy, Task Force on Teaching as a Profession (1986). *A nation prepared: Teachers for the 21st century*. NY: Author.

Clasen, D. R. Changing peer stereotypes of high-achieving adolescents. *Nassp Bulletin*, **76**, 95–102.

Cohen, D. K. & Spillane, J. P. (1993). Policy and practice: The relationship between governance and instruction. In: S. H. Fuhrman (Ed.), *Designing Coherent Education Policy* (pp.35–95). San Francisco, CA: Jossey-Bass.

Cooper, C. (1983). *Administrators' attitudes toward gifted programs based on the enrichment triad/revolving door identification model: Case studies in decision making*. Unpublished doctoral dissertation, The University of Connecticut, Storrs, CT.

Csikszentmihalyi, M. (1990). *Flow: The psychology of optimal experience*. New York: Harper and Row.

Csikszentmihalyi, M., Rathunde, K. & Whalen, S. (1993). *Talented teenagers: The roots of success and failure*. Cambridge: Cambridge University Press.

Crump, W. D., Schlichter, C. L. & Palk, B. E. (1988). Teaching HOTS in the middle and high school: A district-level initiative in developing higher order thinking skills. *Roeper Review*, **10**, 205–211.

Daniels, P. R. (1983). *Teaching the gifted/learning disabled child*. Rockville, MD: Aspen.

Darling-Hammond, L. (1990). Achieving our goals: Superficial or structural reforms. *Phi Delta Kappa*, **72**, 286–295.

Daurio, S. (1978). Educational enrichment and acceleration. In: J. C. Stanley, W. C. George & C. H. Solano (Eds), *Educational Programs and Intellectual Prodigies* (pp. 90–120). Baltimore, MD: Johns Hopkins University.

Daurio, S. P. (1979). Education enrichment versus acceleration: A review of the literature. In: W. C. George, S. J. Cohn & J. C. Stanley (Eds), *Educating the Gifted: Acceleration and Enrichment* (pp. 13–63). Baltimore: Johns Hopkins University Press.

Delcourt, M. A. B. (1988). *Characteristics related to high levels of creative/productive behavior in secondary school students: A multi-case study*. Unpublished doctoral dissertation, The University of Connecticut, Storrs, CT.

Delcourt, M. A. B. (1993). Creative productivity among secondary school students: Combining energy, interest, and imagination. *Gifted Child Quarterly*, **37**, 23–31.

Delcourt, M. (1994). Characteristics of high-level creative productivity: A longitudinal study of students identified by Renzulli's three ring conception of giftedness. In: R. Subotnik & K. D. Arnold (Eds), *Beyond Terman: Contemporary Longitudinal Studies of Giftedness and Talent* (pp. 375–400). Norwood, NJ: Ablex.

Delisle, J. R. (1981). *The revolving door identification model: Correlates of creative production*. Unpublished doctoral dissertation, The University of Connecticut, Storrs, CT.

Eisner, E. W. & Vallance, E. (Eds) (1974). *Conflicting conceptions of curriculum*. Berkeley, CA: McCutchen.

Emerick, L. (1988). *Academic underachievement among the gifted: Students' perceptions of factors relating to the reversal of the academic underachievement pattern*. Unpublished doctoral dissertation, The University of Connecticut, Storrs, CT.

Epstein, J. (1995). School, family, community partnerships. *Phi Delta Kappan*, **76**, 701–712.

Ericsson, K. A. & Lehmann, A. C. (1996). Expert and exceptional performance: Evidence of maximal adaptation to task constraints. *Annual Review of Psychology*, **47**, 273–305.

Fasko, D., Jr. (1992). *Individual differences and multiple intelligences*. Paper presented at the annual meeting of the Mid-South Education Research Association, Knoxville, TN.

Feldhusen, J. & Kolloff, M. (1978). A three stage model for gifted education. *Gifted Child Today*, **1**, 53–58.

Feldhusen, J. F. & Kolloff, M. B. (1979). A rationale for career education activities in the Purdue Three-Stage model. *Roeper Review*, **2**, 13–17.

Feldhusen, J. F. & Kolloff, M. B. (1986). The Purdue three-stage model for gifted education. In: J. S. Renzulli (Ed.), *Systems and Models for Developing Programs for the Gifted and Talented* (pp. 126–152). Mansfield Center, CT: Creative Learning Press.

Feldhusen, J. F., Kolloff, M. B., Cole, S. & Moon, S. (1988). A three-stage model for gifted education. *Gifted Child Today*, **11**, 14–20.

Feldhusen, J. F. & Robinson-Wyman, A. (1986). The Purdue secondary model for gifted education. In: J. S. Renzulli (Ed.), *Models for Developing Programs for the Gifted and Talented* (pp. 153–179). Mansfield Center, CT: Creative Learning Press.

Feldman, D. (1985). *Nature's gambit*. NY: Basic Books

Ford, D. Y. (1996). *Reversing underachievement among gifted black students: Promising programs and practices*. New York: Teachers College Press.

Ford-Harris, D. Y., Schuerger, J. M. & Harris, J. J. (1991). Meeting the psychological needs of gifted Black students:

A cultural perspective. *Journal of Counseling and Development*, **69**, 577–579.

Frasier, M. M. (1993). Issues, problems and programs in nurturing the disadvantaged and culturally different talented. In: K. A. Heller, F. J. Mönks & A. H. Passow (Eds), *Research and Development of Giftedness and Talent* (pp. 685–692), NY: Pergamon.

Fuhrman, S. (Ed.) (1993). *Designing coherent education policy*. San Francisco: Jossey-Bass.

Gagné, F. (1995). From giftedness to talent: A developmental model and its impact on the language of the field. *Roeper Review*, **18**, 103–111.

Gallagher, J., et al. (1984). *Leadership unit*. NY: Trillium Press.

Gallagher, J. & Gallagher, S. (1995). *Teaching the gifted child*. Boston: Allyn & Bacon.

Gallagher, S. A., Stepien, W. J., Sher, B. T. & Workman, D. (1995). Implementing problem-based learning in science classrooms. *School Science and Mathematics*, **95**, 136–146.

Gardner, H. (1983). *Frames of mind*. NY: Basic Books.

Gardner, H. (1991). *Creating minds*. New York: Basic Books.

Gardner, H. (1995). Reflections on multiple intelligences: Myths and messages. *Phi Delta Kappan*, **77**, 200–203, 206–209.

Gardner, H. & Hatch, T. (1990). *Multiple intelligences go to school: Educational implications of the theory of multiple intelligences*. Technical Report No. 4. NY: Center for Technology in Education.

George, W. C. (1976). Accelerating mathematics instruction for the mathematically talented. *Gifted Child Quarterly*, **20**, 246–261.

Goodlad, J. I. (1979). *Curriculum inquiry: The study of curriculum practice*. NY: McGraw-Hill

Guilford, J. P. (1967). *The nature of human intelligence*. New York: McGraw-Hill.

Hale-Benson, J. E. (1986). *Black children: Their roots, culture and learning styles* (2nd ed.). Baltimore, MD: Johns Hopkins University Press.

Hansford, S. J., Whitmore, J. R., Kraynak, A. R. & Wingenbach, N. G. (1987). *Intellectually gifted learning disabled students: A special study*. Reston, VA: ERIC Clearinghouse on handicapped and gifted children.

Heal, M. M. (1989). *Student perceptions of labeling the gifted: A comparative case study analysis*. Unpublished doctoral dissertation, The University of Connecticut, Storrs, CT.

Hebert, T. P. (1993). Reflections at graduation: The long-term impact of elementary school experiences in creative productivity. *Roeper Review*, **16**, 22–28.

Hendricks, M. (1997). Yesterday's whiz kids: Where are they today? *Johns Hopkins Magazine*, **49** (3 June), 31–36.

Hengen, T. (1983). *Identification and enhancement of giftedness in Canadian Indians*. Paper presented at the annual meeting of the National Association of Gifted Children, New Orleans, LA.

Hernandez, S. (1989). *Multicultural education*. Columbus, OH: Merrill Publishing.

Hirsch, E. D. (1989). *Cultural literacy*. Boston: Houghton Mifflin.

Hodgkinson, H. (1993). American education: The good, the bad, and the task. *Phi Delta Kappan*, **74**, 619–623.

Holliday, B. G. (1985). Towards a model of teacher-child transactional processes affecting Black children's academic achievement. In: M. B. Spencer, G. K. Brookins & W R. Allen (Eds), *Beginnings: The Social and Affective Development of Black Children* (pp. 117–131). Hillsdale, NJ: Erlbaum.

Hollingworth, L. (1926). *Gifted children*. New York: World Book.

Hoover-Dempsey, K. V. & Sandler, H. M. (1995). Parental involvement in children's education: Why does it make a difference? *Teachers College Record*, **97**, 227–239.

Johnson, D. T., Boyce, L. N. & VanTassel-Baska, J. (1995). Science curriculum review: Evaluating materials for high-ability learners. *Gifted Child Quarterly*, **39**, 36–43.

Kaplan, S. (1986). The Kaplan grid. In: J. S. Renzulli (Ed.), *Systems and Models for Developing Programs for the Gifted and Talented* (pp. 56–68) Mansfield Center, CT: Creative Learning Press.

Karafelis, P. (1986). *The effects of the tri-art drama curriculum on the reading comprehension of students with varying levels of cognitive ability*. Unpublished doctoral dissertation, The University of Connecticut, Storrs, CT.

Karnes, F. A. & Chauvin, J. C. (1998). *Leadership development program*. Scottsdale, AZ: Gifted Psychology Press.

Keating, D. P. (Ed.) (1976). *Intellectual talent: Research and development*. Baltimore: Johns Hopkins University Press.

Keating, D. (1976). *Intellectual talent*. Baltimore: Johns Hopkins University Press.

Koe, F. T. (1980). Supplementing the language instruction of the culturally different learner: Upward Bound program. *English Journal*, **69**, 19–20.

Kolitch, E. R. & Brody, L. E. (1992). Mathematics acceleration of highly talented students: An evaluation. *Gifted Child Quarterly*, **36**, 78–86.

Kolloff, M. B. & Feldhusen, J. F. (1981). PACE (Program for Academic and Creative Enrichment) An application of the Three-Stage Model. *Gifted Child Today*, **18**, 47–50.

Kolloff, M. B. & Feldhusen, J. F. (1984). The effects of enrichment on self-concept and creative thinking. *Gifted Child Quarterly*, **28**, 53–57.

Kulik, J. & Kulik, C. (1992). Meta analytic findings on grouping programs. *Gifted Child Quarterly*, **36**, 73–77.

Latham, A. S. (1997). Quantifying MI's gains. *Educational Leadership*, **55** (1), 84–85.

Lubinski, D. (1996). Applied individual differences research and its quantitative methods. *Psychology, Public Policy, and Law*, **2**, 187–203.

Lubinski, D. & Benbow, C. P. (1994) The study of mathematically precocious youth: The first three decades of a planned 50-year study of intellectual talent. In R. Subotnik & K. D. Arnold (Eds) *Beyond Terman: Contemporary longitudinal studies of giftedness and talent* (pp. 375–400). Norwood, NJ: Ablex.

Lupkowski, A. E. & Assouline, S. G. (1993). Identifying mathematically talented elementary students: Using the lower level of the SAT. *Gifted Child Quarterly*, **37**, 118–123.

Lynch, S. J. (1990). Credit and placement issues for the academically talented following summer studies in science and mathematics. *Gifted Child Quarterly*, **34**, 27–30.

Lynch, S. J. (1992). Fast-paced high school science for the academically talented: A six-year perspective. *Gifted Child Quarterly*, **36**, 147–154.

Maker, C. J. (1982). *Curriculum development for the gifted.* Rockville, MD: Aspen.

Maker, C. J. (1993). Creativity, intelligence, and problem solving: A definition and design for cross-cultural research and measurement related to giftedness. *Gifted Education International, 9*, 68–77.

Maker, C. J. (1996). Identification of gifted minority students: A national problem, needed changes and a promising solution. *Gifted Child Quarterly, 40*, 41–50.

Maker, C. J. & Nielson, A. B. (1995). *Teaching models in education of the gifted* (2nd ed.). Austin, TX: Pro-Ed.

Maker, C. J. & Nielson, A. G. (1996). *Curriculum development and teaching strategies for gifted learners* (2nd ed.). Austin, TX: Pro-Ed.

Maker, C. J. & Schiever, S. W. (1989). Defensible programs for cultural and ethnic minorities. *Critical issues in gifted education*, Vol. II. Austin, TX: Pro-Ed.

Maker, C. J., Nielson, A. B. & Rogers, J. A. (1994). Multiple intelligences: Giftedness, diversity, and problem-solving. *Teaching Exceptional Children, 27* (1), 4–19.

Maker, C. J., Rogers, J. A., Nielson, A. B. & Bauerle, P. R. (1996). Multiple intelligences, problem solving, and diversity in the general classroom. *Journal for the Education of the Gifted, 19*, 437–460.

Mathews. W. (1984). Influences on the learning and participation of minorities in math. *Journal for Research in Math Education, 15* (2), 84–95.

McLaughlin, M. W. & Shepard, L. A. (1995). *Improving education through standards-based reform.* Stanford, CA: The National Academy of Education.

McLean, J. E. & Chisson, B. S. (1980). *Talented Unlimited program: Summary of research findings for 1979–80.* Mobile, AL: Mobile County Public Schools.

Meeker, M. (1969). *The structure of intellect: Its interpretation and uses.* Columbus, OH: Charles E. Merrill.

.Meeker, M. (1976). *A paradigm for special education diagnostics: The cognitive area.* (ERIC Document Reproduction Service No. ED 121 010)

Meeker, M. (1985). *A partial compendium of SOI patterns on sub-groups of gifted people.* Paper presented at the annual convention of the Council for Exceptional Children, Anaheim, CA.

Moon, S. & Feldhusen, J. F. (1994). The program for academic and creative enrichment (PACE): A follow-up study ten years later. In: R. Subotnik & K. D. Arnold (Eds), *Beyond Terman: Contemporary Longitudinal Studies of Giftedness and Talent* (pp. 375–400). Norwood, NJ: Ablex.

Moon, S. M., Feldhusen, J. F. & Dillon, D. R. (1994). Long-term effects of an enrichment program based on the Purdue Three-Stage Model. *Gifted Child Quarterly, 38*, 38–48.

Moon, S. M., Feldhusen, J. F., Powley, S. & Nidiffer, L. (1993). Secondary applications of the Purdue Three-Stage Model. *Gifted Child Today, 16* (3), 2–9.

National Center for Education Statistics. (1997). *Pursuing excellence: Initial findings from the Third International Mathematics and Science Study (TIMSS): Synthesis report.* Washington, DC: United States Department of Education.

National Commission on Excellence in Education (1983). *A nation at risk.* Washington, DC: U.S. Department of Education.

National Science Board Commision on Precollege Education in Mathematics, Science and Technology (1983). *Educat-*

ing Americans for the 21st century. Washington, DC: National Science Foundation.

O'Day, J. A. & Smith, M. 5. (1993). Systemic reform and educational opportunity. In: S. H. Fuhrman (Ed.), *Designing Coherent Education Policy* (pp. 250–312). San Francisco, CA: Jossey-Bass.

Ogbu, J. U. (1994). Understanding cultural diversity and learning. Reprinted in *Journal for the Education of the Gifted, 16*, 355–383.

Olenchak, F. R. (1991). Assessing program effects for gifted/learning disabled students. In: R. Swassing & A. Robinson (Eds). *NAGC 1991 Research Briefs.* Washington, D.C.: National Association for Gifted Children.

Olenchak, F. R. & Renzulli, J. S. (1989). The effectiveness of the Schoolwide Enrichment Model on selected aspects of elementary school change. *Gifted Child Quarterly, 33*, 36–46.

Olszewski-Kubilius, P., Grant, B. & Seibert, C. (1994). Social support systems and the disadvantaged gifted: A framework for developing programs and services. *Roeper Review, 17*, 20–25.

Passow, A. H. (1982). Differential curricula for the gifted/talented. Committee Report to the National/State Leadership Training Institute on the Gifted and Talented. Ventura County, CA: Office of the Superintendent of Schools.

Patton, J. M. & Baytops, J. L. (1995). Identifying and transforming the potential of young, gifted African-Americans: A clarion call for action. In: B. A. Ford, F. E. Obiakor & J. M. Patton (Eds), *Effective Education of African-American Exceptional Learners* (pp. 27–66). Austin, TX: Pro-Ed, Inc.

Perkins, D. & Saloman, G. (1989). Are cognitive skills context bound? *Educational Researcher, 18* (1), 16–25.

Piirto, J. (1999). *Talented children and adults: Their development and education* (2nd ed.). Upper Saddle River, NJ: Merrill.

Pressey, S. L. (1949). *Educational acceleration: Appraisal and basic problems.* Bureau of Educational Research Monographs (31). Columbus, OH: The Ohio State University Press.

Pressley, M., Snyder, B. & Carigha-Bull, T. (1987). How can good strategy use be taught to children? Evaluation of six alternative approaches. In: S. M. Corner & J. D. Hagman (Eds), *Transfer of Learning* (pp. 81–120). NY: Academic

Rabinowitz, M. & Glaser, R. (1985). Cognitive structure and processes on highly competent performance. In: E. D. Horowitz & M. O'Brien (Eds), *The Gifted and Talented: Developmental Perspectives* (pp. 75–98). Washington. DC: American Psychological Association.

Reis, S. M. (1981). *An analysis of the productivity of gifted students participating in programs using the Revolving Door Identification Model.* Unpublished doctoral dissertation, The University of Connecticut, Storrs, CT.

Reis, S. M. & Purcell, J. H. (1993). An analysis of content elimination and strategies used by elementary classroom teachers in the curriculum compacting process. *Journal for the Education of the Gifted, 16*, 147–170.

Renzulli, J. S. (1977). *The enrichment triad model: A guide for developing defensible programs for the gifted and talented.* Mansfield Center, CT: Creative Learning Press.

Renzulli, J. S. (Ed.). (1988). *Technical report of research studies related to the revolving door identification model.*

Storrs, CT: Bureau of Educational Research, The University of Connecticut.

Renzulli, J. S. & Reis, S. M. (1985). *The schoolwide enrichment model: A comprehensive plan for educational excellence*. Mansfield Center, CT: Creative Learning Press.

Renzulli, J. S. & Reis, S. M. (1994). Research related to the school wide enrichment triad model. *Gifted Child Quarterly*, **38**, 7–20.

Renzulli, J. S., Reis, S. M. & Smith, L. (1981). The revolving-door model: A new way of identifying the gifted. *Phi Delta Kappan*, **62**, 648–649.

Renzulli, J. S. (1986). *Systems and models for developing programs for the gifted and talented*. Mansfield Center, CT: Creative Learning Press.

Resnick, R. (1984). Beyond error analysis: The role of understanding elementary school arithmetic. In H. N. Check (Ed.), *Diagnostic and prescriptive mathematics: Issues, ideas & insight*. Kent, OH: Research Council for Diagnostic & Prescriptive Mathematics.

Rosnow, R. L., Skleder, A. A., Jaeger, M. E. & Rind, B. (1994). Intelligence and the epistemics of interpersonal acumen: Testing some implications of Gardner's theory. *Intelligence*, **19**, 93–116.

Sah, A. & Borland, J. H. (1989). The effects of a structured home plan on the home and school behaviors of gifted learning-disabled students with deficits in organizational skills. *Roeper Review*, **12** (1), 54–57.

Sarason, S. B. (1997). *How schools might be governed and why*. New York: Teachers College Press.

Schack, G. D., Starko, A. J. & Burns, D. E. (1991). Self-efficacy and creative productivity: Three studies of above average ability children. *Journal of Research in Education*, **1**, 44–52.

Schlichter, C. (1986a). Talents unlimited: An inservice education model for teaching thinking skills. *Gifted Child Quarterly*, **30**, 199–123.

Schlichter, C. (1986b). Talents unlimited: Applying the multiple talent approach in mainstream and gifted programs. In: J. S. Renzulli (Ed.), *Systems and Models for Developing Programs for the Gifted and Talented* (pp. 352–390). Mansfield Center, CT: Creative Learning Press.

Schlichter, C. L. (1988). Thinking skills for all classrooms. *Gifted Child Today*, **11** (2), 24–29.

Schlichter, C. L., Hobbs, D. & Crump, W. (1988). Extending Talents Unlimited to secondary schools. *Educational Leadership*, **45** (7), 36–40.

Schlichter, C. L., Larkin, M. J., Casareno, A. B., Ellis, E. S., Gregg, M., Mayfield, P. & Rountree, B. (1997). Partners in enrichment: Preparing teachers for multiple ability classrooms. *Teaching Exceptional Children*, **29** (4), 4–9.

Schlichter, C. L. & Palmer, W. R. (Eds) (1993). *Thinking smart: A premiere of the Talents Unlimited model*. Mansfield Center, CT: Creative Learning Press.

Silverman, L. K. (1989). Invisible gifts, invisible handicaps. *Roeper Review*, **12**, 103–108.

Slavin, R. E. & Oickle, E. (1981). Effects of cooperative learning teams on student achievement and race relations: Treatment by race interactions. *Sociology of Education*, **54**, 174–180.

Snow, R. E. (1989). Aptitude-treatment interaction as a framework for research on individual differences in learning. In: P. L. Ackerman, R. J. Sternberg & R. Glaser (Eds), *Learning and Individual Differences* (pp. 13–59). New York: W. H. Freeman.

Snow, R. E. (1994). Aptitude development and talent achievement. In: N. Colangelo, S. G. Assouline & D. L. Ambroson (Eds), *Talent Development* (pp. 101–120). Dayton, OH: Ohio Psychology Press.

Sommers, N. (1980). Revision strategies of student writers and experienced writers. *College Composition and Communications*, **31**, 378–387.

Spady, W. J. & Marshall, K. J. (1991). Beyond traditional outcome-based education. *Educational Leadership*, **49** (2), 67–72.

Stanley, J. C. (1976). Youths who reason extremely well mathematically: SMPY's accelerative approach. *Gifted Child Quarterly*, **20**, 237–238.

Stanley, J. C. (1977). Rationale of the Study of Mathematically Precocious Youth (SMPY) during its first five years of promoting educational acceleration. In: J. C. Stanley, W. C. George & C. H. Solano (Eds), *The Gifted and the Creative: A Fifty Year Perspective* (pp. 73–112). Baltimore: Johns Hopkins University Press.

Stanley, J. C. (1978). SMPY's DT-PI mentor model: Diagnostic testing followed by prescriptive instruction. *ITYB*, **4** (10), 7–8.

Stanley, J. C. (1991). An academic model for educating the mathematically talented. *Gifted Child Quarterly*, **35**, 36–42.

Stanley, J. C. (1993). Boys and girls who reason well mathematically. In: G. Bock & K. Ackrill (Eds), *The Origins and Development of High Ability* (pp. 119–138). New York: Wiley.

Stanley, J. C. & Benbow, C. P. (1983). Intellectually talented students: The key is curricular flexibility. In: S. P. Harris, G. Olson & H. Stevenson (Eds), *Learning and Motivation in the Classroom* (pp. 259–258). Hillsdale, NJ: Erlbaum.

Stanley, J. C., Keating, D. & Fox, L. (1974). *Mathematical talent*. Baltimore, MD: Johns Hopkins University Press.

Starko, A. J. (1986). *The effects of the revolving door identification model on creative productivity and self-efficacy*. Unpublished doctoral dissertation, The University of Connecticut, Storrs, CT.

Sternberg, R. (1981). A componential theory of intellectual giftedness. *Gifted Child Quarterly*, **25**, 86–93.

Sternberg, R. & Clinkenbeard, P. R. (1995). The triarchic model applied to identify, teach, and assess gifted children. *Roeper Review*, **17**, 255–260.

Sternberg, R. J. & Davidson, J. E. (Eds) (1986). *Conceptions of giftedness*. Cambridge: Cambridge University Press.

Sternberg, R. J., Ferrari, M., Clinkenbeard, P. & Grigorenko, E. L. (1996). Identification, instruction, and assessment of gifted children: A construct validation of the triarchic model. *Gifted Child Quarterly*, **40**, 129–137.

Sternberg, R. J., Torff, B. & Grigorenko, E. L. (1998a). Teaching for successful intelligence raises school achievement. *Phi Delta Kappan*, **79**, 667–699.

Sternberg, R. J., Torff, B. & Grigorenko, E. L. (1998b). Teaching triarchically improves school achievement. *Journal of Educational Psychology*, **90**, 374–384.

Sternberg, R. J. (1985). *Beyond IQ*. NY: Basic Books.

Stevenson, H. W. & Stigler. J. W. (1992). *The learning gap: Why our schools are failing and what we can learn from Japanese and Chinese education*. NY: Summit Books.

Strahan, D., Summey, H. & Banks, N. (1996). Teaching to diversity through multiple intelligences: Student and teacher responses to instructional improvement. *Research in Middle Level Education Quarterly*, **19**, (2), 43–65.

Subotnik, R. F. & Arnold, K. D. (Eds). (1994). *Beyond Terman: Contemporary longitudinal studies of giftedizess and talent*. Norwood, NJ: Ablex.

Suter, D. P. & Wolf, J. 5. (1987). Issues in the identification and programming of the gifted/learning disabled child. *Journal for the Education of the Gifted*. **10** (3), 227–238.

Swiatek, M. A. (1993). A decade of longitudinal research on academic acceleration through the study of mathematically precocious youth. *Roeper Review*, **15**, 120–124.

Swiatek, M. A. & Benbow, C. P. (1991a). A 10-year longitudinal follow-up of participants in a fast-paced mathematics course. *Journal for Research in Mathematics Education*, **22**, 138–150.

Swiatek, M. A. & Benbow, C. P. (1991b). Ten-year longitudinal follow-up of ability-matched accelerated and unaccelerated gifted students. *Journal of Educational Psychology*, **83**, 528–538.

Tannenbaum, A. (1983). *Gifted children*. New York: Mac-Millan.

Taylor, C. W., Ghiselin, B., Wolfer, J., Loy, L. & Bourne, L. E. Jr. (1964). *Development of a theory of education from psychology and other basic research findings*. Final Report, USOE Cooperative Research Project, No. 621, Salt Lake City, UT: University of Utah.

Terman, L. M. & Oden, M. H. (1947). *The gifted child grows up*. Stanford, CA: Stanford University Press.

Tobin, D. & Schiffman, G. B. (1983). Computer technology for learning-disabled gifted students. In: L. H. Fox, L. Brody & D. Tobin (Eds), *Learning-Disabled Gifted Children: Identification and Programming* (pp. 195–206). Baltimore, MD: University Park Press.

Tomlinson, C. A., Callahan, C. M. & Lelli, K. M. (1997). Challenging expectations: Case studies of high potential, culturally diverse young children. *Gifted Child Quarterly*, **41**, 5–17.

United States Department of Education, Office of Educational Research and improvement (1993). *National excellence: A case for developing America's talent*. Washington, DC: Author.

VanTassel-Baska, J. (1982). Results of a Latin-based experimental study of the verbally precocious. *Roeper Review*, **4** (4), 35–37.

VanTassel-Baska, J. (1986). Efffective curriculum and institutional models for talented students. *Gifted Child Quarterly*, **30**, 164–169.

VanTassel-Baska, J. (1992). *Planning effective curriculum for gifted learners*. Denver, CO: Love Publishing.

VanTassel-Baska, J. (1993). *Comprehensive curriculum for gifted learners*. Boston, MA: Allyn & Bacon.

VanTassel-Baska J. & Olszewski-Kubilius, P. (1989). *Patterns of influence: The home, the self, and the school*. NY: Teachers College Press.

VanTassel-Baska, J., Patton, J. & Prillaman, D. (1991). *Gifted youth at risk*. Reston, VA: Council for Exceptional Children.

VanTassel-Baska, J., Avery, L. D., Little, C. A., and Hughes, C. E. (2000). Where the rubber meets the road: An evaluation of the implementation of curriculum innovation: the impact of the William and Mary units on schools, *28*, 244–272.

VanTassel-Baska, J., Bass, G. M., Ries, R. R., Poland, D. L. & Avery, L. D. (1998). A national pilot study of science curriculum effectiveness for high-ability students. *Gifted Child Quarterly*, **42**, 200–211.

VanTassel-Baska, J., Johnson, D. T., Hughes, C. E. & Boyce, L. N. (1996). A study of the language arts curriculum effectiveness with gifted learners. *Journal for the Education of the Gifted*, **19**, 46.

VanTassel-Baska, J. (1982). Results of a Latin-based experimental study of the verbally precocious. *Roeper Review*, **4** (4), 35–37.

VanTassel-Baska, J. (1998). *Excellence in educating the gifted* (3rd ed.). Denver, CO: Love.

VanTassel-Baska, J. (1995). A study of life themes in Charlotte Bronte and Virginia Woolf. *Roeper Review*, **18**, 14–19.

Walberg, H. (1991). Productive teaching and instruction: Assessing the knowledge base. In: H. C. Waxman & H. J. Walberg (Eds), *Effective Teaching: Current Research* (pp. 33–62). Berkeley, CA: McCutchan.

Walters, J. & Gardner, H. (1986). The crystallizing experience: Discovering an intellectual gift. In: R. J. Sternberg & J. E. Davidson (Eds), *Conceptions of giftedness* (pp. 306–331). New York: Cambridge University Press.

Werner, E. E. & Smith, R. S. (1992). *Overcoming the odds: High risk children from birth to adulthood*. Ithaca, NY: Cornell University.

Wirsup, I. (1986). The current crises in mathematics and science education: A climate for change. In: J. VanTassel-Baska (Ed.), *Proceedings from the 9th Annual Research Symposium*. Evanston, IL: Phi Delta Kappa.

Wolf, J. & Gygi, J. (1981). Learning disabled and gifted: Success or failure? *Journal for the Education of the Gifted*, **4**, 199–206.

The Schoolwide Enrichment Model[1]

Joseph S. Renzulli and Sally M. Reis

University of Connecticut, Storrs, Connecticut, USA

Introduction

Enrichment programs for gifted and talented students have been the true laboratories of the world's schools because they have presented ideal opportunities for testing new ideas and experimenting with potential solutions to long-standing educational problems. Programs for high potential students have been an especially fertile place for experimentation because such programs are not usually encumbered by pre-scribed curriculum guides or traditional methods of instruction. It was within the context of these programs that the thinking skills movement first took hold in American education, and the pioneering work of notable theorists such as Benjamin Bloom, Howard Gardner, and Robert Sternberg first gained the attention of the education community. Other developments that had their origins in special programs are currently being examined for general practice. These developments include: a focus on concept rather than skill learning, the use of interdisciplinary curriculum and theme-based studies, student portfolios, performance assessment, cross-grade grouping, alternative scheduling patterns, and perhaps most important, opportunities for students to exchange traditional roles as lesson-learners and doers-of-exercises for more challenging and demanding roles that require hands-on learning, first-hand investigations, and the *application* of knowledge and thinking skills to complex problems.

The Schoolwide Enrichment Model (SEM) is a detailed blueprint for total school improvement that allows each school the flexibility to allow each school to develop its own unique programs based on local resources, student demographics, and school dynamics

as well as faculty strengths and creativity. Although this research-based model is based on highly successful practices that originated in special programs for the gifted and talented students, its major goal is to promote both challenging and enjoyable high-end learning across a wide range of school types, levels and demographic differences. The idea is to create a repertoire of services that can be integrated in such a way to create "a rising tide lifts all ships" approach. This approach allows schools to develop a collaborative school culture that takes advantage of resources and appropriate decision-making opportunities to create meaningful, high-level and potentially creative opportunities for students to develop their talents. SEM suggests that educators should examine ways to make schools more inviting, friendly, and enjoyable places that encourage the full development of the learner instead of seeing students as a repository for information that will be assessed with the next round of standardized tests. Not only has this model been successful in addressing the problem of students who have been under-challenged but it also provides additional important learning paths for students who find success in more traditional learning environments.

The present reform initiatives in general education have created a more receptive atmosphere for enrichment approaches that challenge all students, and accordingly, the Enrichment Triad Model has evolved over the last 20 years based on the previous experiences and current changes in general education. The evolution of the Enrichment Triad Model will be described in this chapter as well as the newest adaptation of the Schoolwide Enrichment Model including a description of the school structures upon which the model is targeted and the three service delivery components.

The original Enrichment Triad Model (Renzulli, 1976) was developed in the mid–1970s and initially implemented by school districts primarily in Connecticut in the United States. The model, which was originally field tested in several districts, proved to be quite popular and requests from all over the United

[1] Research for this chapter was supported under the Javits Act Program (Grant No. R206R00001) as administered by the Office of Educational Research and Improvement, U.S. Department of Education. Grantees undertaking such projects are encouraged to express freely their professional judgment. This report, therefore, does not necessarily represent positions or policies of the Government, and no official endorsement should be inferred.

States for visitations to schools using the model and for information about how to implement the model increased. A book about the Enrichment Triad Model (Renzulli, 1977) was published, and more and more districts began asking for help in implementing this approach. It was at this point that a clear need was established for research about the effectiveness of the model and for practical procedures that could provide technical assistance for interested educators to help develop programs in their schools. We had become fascinated by the various kinds of programs being developed by different types of teachers. In some programs, for example, teachers consistently elicited high levels of creative productivity in students while others had *few* students who engaged in this type of work. In some districts, many enrichment opportunities were regularly offered to students not formally identified for the program, while in other districts only identified 'gifted' students had access to enrichment experiences. We wondered how we could replicate the success of one teacher or one district in implementing the model. For example, if one teacher consistently produced high levels of creative productivity in students, how could we capture that technology and replicate it in other teachers? And if certain resources proved to be consequential in promoting desirable results, how could we make these resources available to larger numbers of teachers and students?

In the more than two decades since the Enrichment Triad Model has been used as the basis for many educational programs for gifted and talented students, an unusually large number of examples of creative productivity have occurred on the parts of young people whose educational experiences have been guided by this programming approach. Perhaps, like others involved in the development of theories and generalizations, we did not fully understand at the onset of our work the full implications of the model for encouraging and developing creative productivity in young people. These implications relate most directly to teacher training, resource procurement and management, product evaluation, and other theoretical concerns (e.g. motivation, task commitment, self-efficacy) that probably would have gone unexamined, undeveloped, and unrefined without the favorable results that were reported to us by early implementers of the model. We became increasingly interested in how and why the model was working and how we could further expand the theoretical rationale underlying our work, and the population to which services could be provided. Thus, several years of conceptual analysis, practical experience, and an examination of the work of other theorists, has brought us to the point of tying together the material in this chapter, which represents approximately twenty years of field testing, research, evolution and dissemination.

In this chapter, an overview of the conception of giftedness upon which this model is based is presented, and a description of the original Enrichment Triad Model is provided as is a chronology of how the model has expanded and changed. Research about the model is presented as is a brief summary of research dealing with selected studies about student creative productivity. In the final section, new directions for the model are presented along with suggestions for future directions for research on creative productivity.

A Broadened Conception of Giftedness

The field of gifted education, like any other specialized area of study, represents a spectrum of ideologies that exists along a continuum ranging from conservative to liberal points of view. *Conservative* and *liberal* are not used here in their political connotations, but rather according to the degree of restrictiveness that is used in determining who is eligible for special programs and services.

Restrictiveness can be expressed in two ways; first, a definition can limit the number of specific performance areas that are considered in determining eligibility for special services. A conservative definition, for example, might limit eligibility to academic performance only, and exclude other areas such as music, art, drama, leadership, public speaking, social service, creative writing or skills in interpersonal relations. Second, a definition can limit the degree or level of excellence that one must attain by establishing extremely high cutoff points.

Although liberal definitions have the obvious advantage of expanding the conception of giftedness, they also open up two theoretical concerns by introducing: (1) a values issue (How do we operationally define broader conceptions of giftedness?) and (2) the age-old problem of subjectivity in measurement. In recent years the values issue has been largely resolved. Very few educators cling tenaciously to a 'straight IQ' or purely academic definition of giftedness. 'Multiple talent' and 'multiple criteria' are almost the bywords of the present-day gifted education movement, and most people have little difficulty in accepting a definition that includes most areas of human activity which are manifested in socially useful forms of expression.

The problem of subjectivity in measurement is not as easily resolved. As the definition of giftedness is extended beyond those abilities that are clearly reflected in tests of intelligence, achievement, and academic aptitude, it becomes necessary to put less emphasis on precise estimates of performance and potential and more emphasis on the opinions of qualified persons in making decisions about admission to special programs. The crux of the issue boils down to a simple and yet very important question: How much of a trade-off are we willing to make on the objective to subjective continuum in order to allow recognition of a broader spectrum of human abilities? If some degree of subjectivity cannot be tolerated, then our definitions of giftedness and the resulting programs will logically be limited to abilities that can be measured only by objective tests.

Two Kinds of Giftedness

It is generally accepted that intelligence is not a unitary concept, but rather there are many kinds of intelligence and therefore single definitions cannot be used to explain this multifaceted phenomenon (Neisser, 1979). The confusion and inconclusiveness about present theories of intelligence has led Sternberg (1984) and others to develop new models for explaining this complicated concept. Sternberg's 'triarchic' theory of human intelligence consists of three subtheories: a contextual subtheory, which relates intelligence to the external world of the individual; a two-facet experiential subtheory, which relates intelligence to both the external and internal worlds of the individual; and a componential subtheory, which relates intelligence to the internal world of the individual. Gardner (1983) proposed seven distinctive types of intelligent behavior which he called linguistic, logical-mathmematical, spatial, bodily-kinesthetic, musical, interpersonal, intrapersonal, and the recently added naturalist intelligence.

In view of these recent works and numerous earlier cautions about the dangers of trying to describe intelligence through the use of single scores, it seems safe to conclude that this practice has been and always will be questionable. At the very least, attributes of intelligent behavior must be considered within the context of cultural and situational factors. Indeed, some of the most recent examinations have concluded that "[t]he concept of intelligence *cannot* be explicitly defined, not only because of the nature of intelligence but also because of the nature of concepts" (Neisser, 1979, p. 179).

There is no ideal way to measure intelligence and therefore we must avoid the typical practice of believing that if we know a person's IQ score, we also know his or her intelligence. Even Terman warned against total reliance on tests: "We must guard against defining intelligence solely in terms of ability to pass the tests of a given intelligence scale" (as cited in Thorndike, 1921, p. 131). E. L. Thorndike echoed Terman's concern by stating "to assume that we have measured some general power which resides in [the person being tested] and determines his ability in every variety of intellectual task in its entirety is to fly directly in the face of all that is known about the organization of the intellect" (Thorndike, 1921, p. 126).

The reason we have cited these concerns about the historical difficulty of defining and measuring intelligence is to highlight the even larger problem of isolating a unitary definition of giftedness. At the very least, we will always have several conceptions (and therefore definitions) of giftedness. To help in this analysis, we will begin by examining two broad categories of giftedness that have been dealt with in the research literature: 'schoolhouse giftedness' and 'creative-productive giftedness'. Before describing each type, we want to emphasize that:

(1) Both types are important.
(2) There is usually an interaction between the two types.
(3) Special programs should make appropriate provisions for encouraging both types of giftedness as well as the numerous occasions when the two types interact with each other.

Schoolhouse Giftedness

Schoolhouse giftedness might also be called test-taking or lesson-learning giftedness. It is the kind most easily measured by IQ or other cognitive ability tests, and for this reason it is also the type most often used for selecting students for entrance into special programs. The abilities people display on IQ and aptitude tests are exactly the kinds of abilities most valued in traditional school learning situations. In other words, the tasks required in ability tests are similar in nature to tasks that teachers require in most lesson-learning situations. A large body of research tells us that students who score high on IQ tests are also likely to get high grades in school, and that these test-taking and lesson-learning abilities generally remain stable over time. The results of this research should lead us to some very obvious conclusions about schoolhouse giftedness: it exists in varying degrees, it can be identified through standardized assessment techniques, and we should therefore do everything in our power to make appropriate modifications for students who have the ability to cover regular curricular material at advanced rates and levels of understanding. Curriculum compacting (Renzulli, Smith & Reis, 1982; Reis, Burns & Renzulli, 1992) is a procedure used for modifying standard curricular content to accommodate advanced learners. Other acceleration techniques should represent essential parts of every school program that strives to respect the individual differences that are clearly evident from classroom performance and/or scores yielded by cognitive ability tests.

Creative-Productive Giftedness

If scores on IQ tests and other measures of cognitive ability only account for a limited proportion of the common variance with school grades, we can be equally certain that these measures do not tell the whole story when it comes to making predictions about creative-productive giftedness. Before defending this assertion with some research findings, we briefly review what is meant by this second type of giftedness, the important role that it should play in programming, and, therefore, the reasons we should attempt to assess it in our identification procedures—even if such assessment causes us to look below the top 3 to 5% on the normal curve of IQ scores.

Creative-productive giftedness describes those aspects of human activity and involvement in which a premium is placed on the development of original material and products that are purposefully designed to have an impact on one or more target audiences. Learning situations that are designed to promote creative-productive giftedness emphasize the use and application of information (content) and thinking skills (process) in an integrated, inductive, and real-problem-oriented manner. The role of the student is transformed from that of a learner of prescribed lessons to one in which she or he uses the *modus operandi* of a firsthand inquirer. This approach is quite different from the development of lesson-learning giftedness, which tends to emphasize deductive learning, structured training in the development of thinking processes, and the acquisition, storage, and retrieval of information. In other words, creative-productive giftedness is simply putting one's abilities to work on problems and areas of study that have personal relevance to the student and that can be escalated to appropriately challenging levels of investigative activity. The roles that both students and teachers should play in the pursuit of these problems have been described elsewhere (Renzulli, 1977, 1982), and have been embraced in general education under a variety of concepts such as constructivist theory, authentic learning, discovery learning, problem based learning, and performance assessment.

"Why is creative-productive giftedness important enough for us to question the 'tidy' and relatively easy approach that has traditionally been used to select students on the basis of test scores? Why do some people want to rock the boat by challenging a conception of giftedness that can be numerically defined by simply giving a test? The answers to these questions are simple and yet very compelling. A review of the research literature (Renzulli, 1986) tells us that there is much more to identifying human potential than the abilities revealed on traditional tests of intelligence, aptitude, and achievement. Furthermore, history tells us it has been the creative and productive people of the world, the producers rather than consumers of knowledge, the reconstructionists of thought in all areas of human endeavor, who have become recognized as 'truly gifted' individuals. History does not remember persons who merely scored well on IQ tests or those who learned their lessons well. The definition of giftedness (See Fig. 1) which characterizes creative productive giftedness and serves as part of the

rationale for the Enrichment Triad Model is the three-ring conception of giftedness (Renzulli, 1978, 1986), in which giftedness: ... consists of an interaction among three basic clusters being above average general ability, high levels of creativity. Gifted and talented capable of developing this composite set of potentially valuable area of human performance or capable of developing an interaction among these require a variety of educational opportunities and services those not normally through regular instructional programming. (1978, p. 6)

We have advocated that gifted behaviors can be developed through systematic enrichment opportunities described in the Enrichment Triad Model (Renzulli, 1977, 1978, 1988b).

An Overview of the Enrichment Triad Model

The Enrichment Triad Model was designed to encourage creative productivity on the part of young people by exposing them to various topics, areas of interest, and fields of study, and to further train them to *apply* advanced content, process-training skills, and methodology training to self-selected areas of interest. Accordingly, three types of enrichment are included in the Triad Model (see Fig. 2).

Type I enrichment is designed to expose students to a wide variety of disciplines, topics, occupations, hobbies, persons, places, and events that would not ordinarily be covered in the regular curriculum. In schools that use this model, an enrichment team consisting of parents, teachers, and students often organizes and plans Type I experiences by contacting speakers, arranging minicourses, demonstrations, or performances, or by ordering and distributing films, slides, videotapes, or other print or non-print media.

Type II enrichment consists of materials and methods designed to promote the development of thinking and feeling processes. Some Type II training is general, and is usually carried out both in classrooms and in enrichment programs. Training activities include the development of: (1) creative thinking and problem solving, critical thinking, and affective processes; (2) a wide variety of specific learning how-to-learn skills; (3) skills in the appropriate use of advanced-level reference materials; and (4) written, oral, and visual communication skills. Other Type II enrichment is specific, as it cannot be planned in advance and usually involves advanced methodological instruction in an interest area selected by the student. For example, students who become interested in botany after a Type I experience might pursue additional training in this area by doing advanced reading in botany; compiling, planning and carrying out plant experiments; and seeking more advanced methods training if they want to go further.

Type III enrichment involves students who become interested in pursuing a self-selected area and are willing to commit the time necessary for advanced content acquisition and process training in which they assume the role of a first-hand inquirer. The goals of Type III enrichment include:

- providing opportunities for applying interests, knowledge, creative ideas and task commitment to a self-selected problem or area of study,
- acquiring advanced level understanding of the knowledge (content) and methodology (process) that are used within particular disciplines, artistic areas of expression and interdisciplinary studies,
- developing authentic products that are primarily directed toward bringing about a desired impact upon a specified audience,
- developing self-directed learning skills in the areas of planning, organization, resource utilization, time management, decision making and self-evaluation,
- developing task commitment, self-confidence, and feelings of creative accomplishment.

The Revolving Door Identification Model

As our experience with Triad Programs grew, our concern about who was being identified to participate in these programs also grew. We became increasingly concerned about students who were not able to participate in enrichment programs because they did not score in the top 1–3% of the population in achievement or intelligence tests.

Research conducted by Torrance (1962, 1974) had demonstrated that students who were rated highly on creativity measures do well in school and on achievement tests but are often not selected for gifted programs because their scores are often below the cutoff for admission. Some of our own research (Reis, 1981) indicated that when a broader population of students (15–20% of the general population called the 'talent pool') were able to participate in Types I and II enrichment experiences, they produced equally good Type III products as the traditional 'gifted' students (the top 3–5%). This research produced the rationale for the Revolving Door Identification Model (RDIM) (Renzulli, Reis & Smith, 1981) in which a talent pool of students receives regular enrichment experiences and the opportunity to 'revolve into' Type III creative productive experiences. In RDIM, we recommend that students be selected for participation in the talent pool on the basis of multiple criteria that include indices of creativity, because we believe that one of the major purposes of gifted education is to develop creative

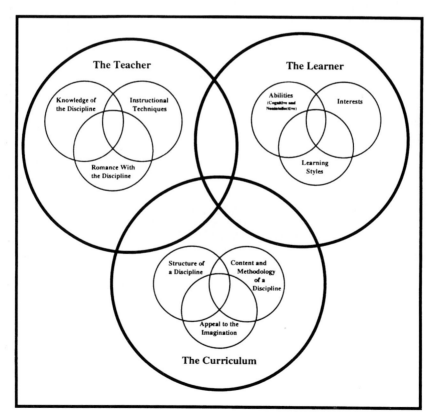

Figure 1. The three-ring conception of giftedness. (Reprinted with permission from Creative Learning Press).

thinking and creative productivity in students. Once identified and placed in the talent pool through the use of test scores, teacher, parent, or self-nomination, and examples of creative potential or productivity, students are observed in classrooms and enrichment experiences for signs of advanced interests, creativity, or task commitment. We have called this part of the process 'action information' and have found it to be an instrumental part of the identification process in assessing students' interest and motivation to become involved in Type III creative productivity. Further support for expanding identification procedures through the use of these approaches has recently been offered by Kirschenbaum (1983) and Kirschenbaum and Siegle (1993) who demonstrated that students who are rated or test high on measures of creativity tend to do well in school and on measures of achievement. The development of the RDIM led to the need for a guide dealing with how all of the components of the previous

Triad and the new RDIM could be implemented and the resulting work was entitled *The Schoolwide Enrichment Model* (SEM) (Renzulli & Reis, 1985, 1997).

The Schoolwide Enrichment Model (SEM)

In the SEM, a talent pool of 15–20% of above average ability/high potential students is identified through a variety of measures including: achievement tests, teacher nominations, assessment of potential for creativity and task commitment, as well as alternative pathways of entrance (self-nomination, parent nomination, etc.). High achievement test and IQ test scores automatically include a student in the talent pool, enabling those students who are underachieving in their academic school work to be included.

Once students are identified for the talent pool, they are eligible for several kinds of services; first, interest and learning styles assessments are used with talent

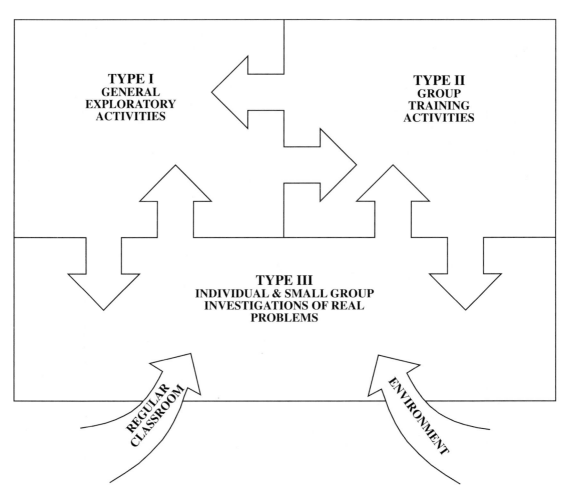

Figure 2. The enrichment triad model.

pool students. Informal and formal methods are used to create or identify students' interests and to encourage students to further develop and pursue these interests in various ways. Learning style preferences which are assessed include: projects, independent study, teaching games, simulations, peer teaching, programmed instruction, lecture, drill and recitation, and discussion. Second, curriculum compacting is provided to all eligible students for whom the regular curriculum is modified by eliminating portions of previously mastered content. This elimination or streamlining of curriculum enables above average students to avoid repetition of previously mastered work and guarantees mastery while simultaneously finding time for more appropriately challenging activities (Reis, Burns & Renzulli, 1992; Renzulli, Smith & Reis, 1982). A form, entitled The Compactor (Renzulli & Smith, 1978), is used to document which content areas have been compacted and what alternative work has been substituted. Third, the Enrichment Triad Model, offers three types of enrichment experiences. Type I, II, and III Enrichment are offered to all students; however, Type III enrichment is usually more appropriate for students with higher levels of ability, interest, and task commitment.

Separate studies on the SEM demonstrated its effectiveness in schools with widely differing socio-economic levels and program organization patterns (Olenchak, 1988; Olenchak & Renzulli, 1989). The SEM has been implemented in several hundred school districts across the country (Burns, 1998) and interest in this approach continues to grow.

Newest Directions for the Schoolwide Enrichment Model

The present reform initiatives in general education have created a more receptive atmosphere for more flexible approaches that challenge all students, and accordingly, the Schoolwide Enrichment Model (SEM) has been expanded to address three major goals that we believe will accommodate the needs of gifted students, and at the same time, provide challenging learning experiences for all students. These goals are:

To maintain and expand a continuum of special services that will challenge students with demonstrated superior performance or the potential for superior performance in any and all aspects of the school and extracurricular program.

To infuse into the general education program a broad range of activities for high-end learning that will: (a) challenge all students to perform at advanced levels, and (b) that will allow teachers to determine which students should be given extended opportunities, resources, and encouragement in particular areas where superior interest and performance are demonstrated.

To preserve and protect the positions of gifted education specialists and any other specialized personnel necessary for carrying out the first two goals.

A graphic representation of the newest adaptation of the model is presented in Fig. 3.

School Structures

The Regular Curriculum

The regular curriculum consists of everything that is a part of the predetermined goals, schedules, learning outcomes, and delivery systems of the school. The regular curriculum might be traditional, innovative, or in the process of transition, but its predominant feature is that authoritative forces (i.e. policy makers, school councils, textbook adoption committees, state regulators) have determined that the regular curriculum should be the 'centerpiece' of student learning. Application of the SEM influences the regular curriculum in three ways. First, the challenge level of required material is differentiated through processes such as curriculum compacting and textbook content modification procedures. Second, systematic content intensification procedures should be used to replace eliminated content with selected, in-depth learning experiences. Third, types of enrichment recommended in the Enrichment Triad Model (Renzulli, 1977) are integrated selectively into regular curriculum activities. Although our goal in the SEM is to influence rather than replace the regular curriculum, application of certain SEM components and related staff development activities has resulted in substantial changes in both the content and instructional processes of the entire regular curriculum.

The Enrichment Clusters

The enrichment clusters, one component of the Schoolwide Enrichment Model, are non-graded groups of students who share common interests, and who come together during specially designated time blocks during school to work with an adult who shares their interests and who has some degree of advanced knowledge and expertise in the area. The enrichment clusters usually meet for a block of time weekly during a semester. All students complete an interest inventory developed to assess their interests, and an enrichment team of parents and teachers tally all of the major families of interests. Adults from the faculty, staff, parents, and community are recruited to facilitate enrichment clusters based on these interests, such as creative writing, drawing, sculpting, archeology and other areas. Training is provided to the facilitators who agree to offer the clusters, and a brochure is developed and sent to all parents and students that discusses student interests and select choices of enrichment clusters. A title and description that appeared in a brochure of clusters in a school using the SEM follows:

Invention Convention

Are you an inventive thinker? Would you like to be? Brainstorm a problem, try to identify many solutions, and design an invention to solve the problem, as an inventor might give birth to a real invention. Create your invention individually or with a partner under the guidance of Bob Erikson and his students, who work at the Connecticut Science Fair. You may share your final product at the Young Inventors' Fair on March 25th, a statewide daylong celebration of creativity.

Students select their top three choices for the clusters and scheduling is completed to place all children into their first, or in some cases, second choice. Like extra-curricular activities and programs such as 4-H and Junior Achievement, the main rationale for participa-

tion in one or more clusters is that *students and teachers want to be there.* All teachers (including music, art, physical education, etc.) are involved in teaching the clusters; and their involvement in any particular cluster is based on the same type of interest assessment that is used for students in selecting clusters of choice.

The model for learning used with enrichment clusters is based on an inductive approach to solving real-world problems through the development of authentic products and services. Unlike traditional, didactic modes of teaching, this approach, known as enrichment learning and teaching (described fully in a later section), uses the Enrichment Triad Model to create a learning situation that involves the use of methodology, develops higher order thinking skills,

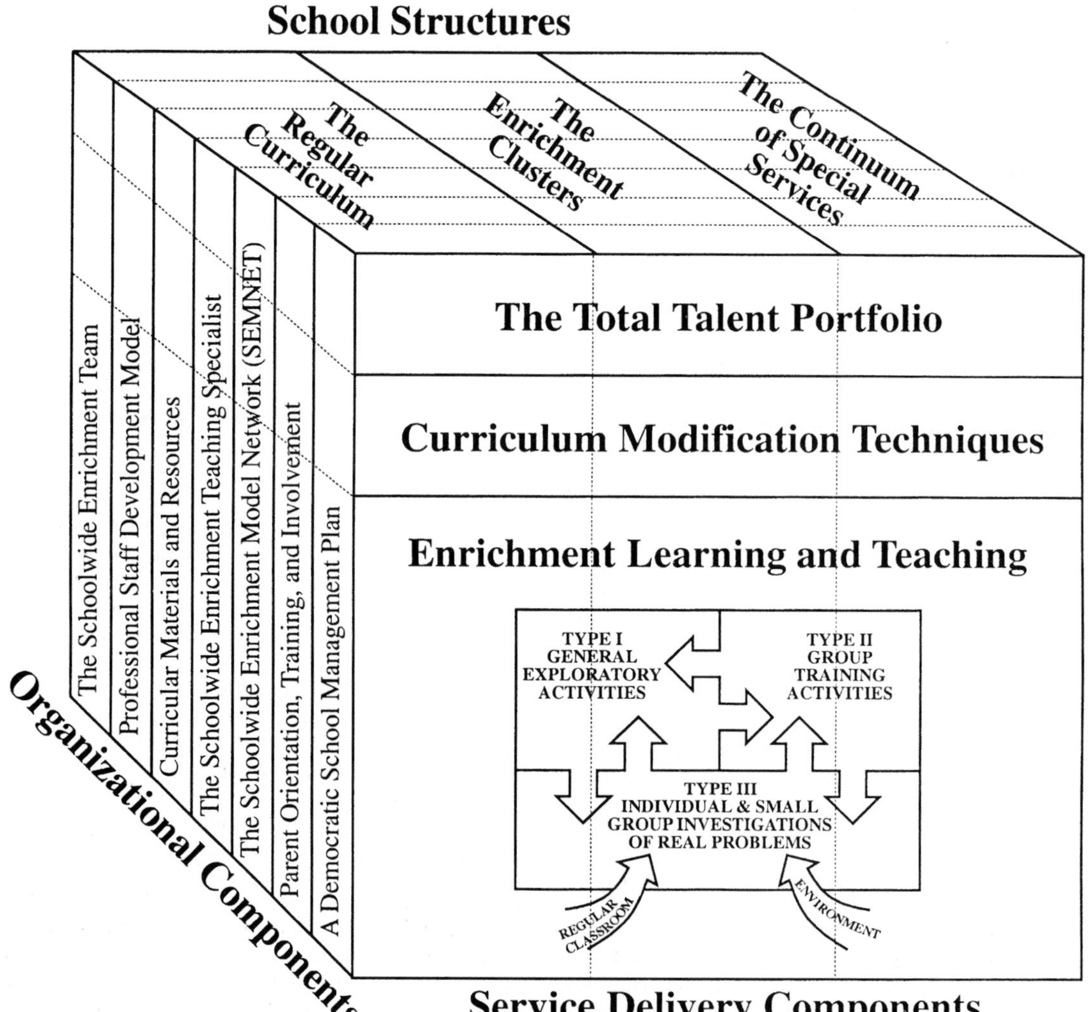

Figure 3. The schoolwide enrichment model.

and authentically applies these skills in creative and productive situations. Enrichment clusters promote cooperativeness within the context of real-world problem solving, and they also provide superlative opportunities for promoting self-concept. "A major assumption underlying the use of enrichment clusters is that *every child is special if we create conditions in which that child can be a specialist within a specialty group*" (Renzulli, 1994, p. 70).

Enrichment clusters are organized around various characteristics of differentiated programming for gifted students on which the Enrichment Triad Model (Renzulli, 1977) was originally based, including the use of major disciplines, interdisciplinary themes, or cross-disciplinary topics (e.g. a theatrical/television production group that includes actors, writers, technical specialists, costume designers). The clusters are modeled after the ways in which knowledge utilization, thinking skills, and interpersonal relations take place in the real world. Thus, all work is directed toward the production of a product or service. No lesson plans or unit plans are created in advance by the cluster facilitator; rather, direction is provided by three key questions addressed in the cluster by the facilitator and the students:

(1) What do people with an interest in this area (e.g. film making) do?
(2) What knowledge, materials, and other resources do they need to do it in an excellent and authentic way?
(3) In what ways can the product or service be used to have an impact on an intended audience?

Enrichment clusters incorporate the use of advanced content, providing students with information about particular fields of knowledge, such as the structure of a field as well as the basic principles and the functional concepts in a field (Ward, 1960). Ward defined functional concepts as the intellectual instruments or tools with which a subject specialist works, such as the vocabulary of a field and the vehicles by which persons within the field communicate with one another. The methodology used within a field is also considered advanced content by Renzulli (1988a), involving the use of knowledge of the structures and tools of fields, as well as knowledge about the methodology of particular fields. This knowledge about the methodologies of fields exists both for the sake of increased knowledge acquisition, and also for the utility of that know-how as applied to the development of products, even when such products are considered advanced in a relative sense (i.e. age, grade, and background considerations).

The enrichment clusters are not intended to be the total program for talent development in a school, or to replace existing programs for talented youth. Rather, they are one vehicle for stimulating interests and developing talent potentials across the entire school population. They are also vehicles for staff development in that they provide teachers an opportunity to participate in enrichment teaching, and subsequently to analyze and compare this type of teaching with traditional methods of instruction. In this regard the model promotes a spill-over effect by encouraging teachers to become better talent scouts and talent developers, and to apply enrichment techniques to regular classroom situations.

The Continuum of Special Services

A broad range of special services is the third school structure targeted by the model; a diagram representing these services is presented in Fig. 4. Although the enrichment clusters and the SEM-based modifications of the regular curriculum provide a broad range of services to meet individual needs, a program for total talent development still requires supplementary services that challenge young people who are capable of working at the highest levels of their special interest and ability areas. These services, which cannot ordinarily be provided in enrichment clusters or the regular curriculum, typically include: individual or small group counseling, direct assistance in facilitating advanced level work, arranging for mentorships with faculty members or community persons, and making other types of connections between students, their families, and out-of-school persons, resources, and agencies.

Direct assistance also involves setting up and promoting student, faculty and parental involvement in special programs such as Future Problem Solving, Odyssey of the Mind, the Model United Nations program, and state and national essay, mathematics, art, and history contests. Another type of direct assistance consists of arranging out-of-school involvement for individual students in summer programs, on-campus courses, special schools, theatrical groups, scientific expeditions, and apprenticeships at places where advanced level learning opportunities are available. Provision of these services is one of the responsibilities of the schoolwide enrichment teaching specialist or an enrichment team of teachers and parents who work together to provide options for advanced learning. A schoolwide enrichment teaching specialist in Barrington, Rhode Island, estimates she spends two days a week in a resource capacity to the faculties of two schools, and three days providing direct services to students.

Service Delivery Components
The Total Talent Portfolio
The Schoolwide Enrichment Model targets specific learning characteristics that can serve as a basis for talent development. Our approach to targeting learning characteristics uses both traditional and performance-based assessment to compile information about three dimensions of the learner—abilities, interests, and

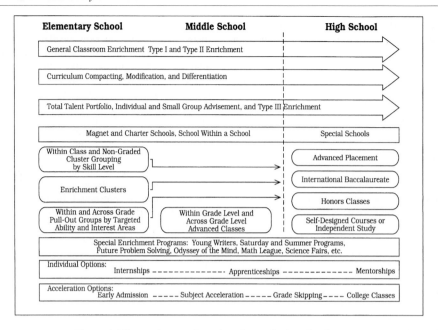

Figure 4. The continuum of services for total talent development.

learning styles. This information, which focuses on strengths rather than deficits, is compiled in a management form called the 'Total Talent Portfolio' (see Fig. 5) which is used to make decisions about talent development opportunities in regular classes, enrichment clusters, and in the continuum of special services. The major purposes of the Total Talent Portfolio are:

(1) To *collect* several different types of information that portray a student's strength areas, and to regularly update this information.

(2) To *classify* this information into the general categories of abilities, interests, and learning styles and related markers of successful learning such as organizational skills, content area preferences, personal and social skills, preferences for creative productivity, and learning-how-to-learn skills.

(3) To periodically *review and analyze* the information in order to make purposeful decisions about providing opportunities for enrichment experiences in the regular classroom, the enrichment clusters, and the continuum of special services.

(4) To *negotiate* various acceleration and enrichment learning options and opportunities between teacher and student through participation in a shared decision making process.

(5) To *use the information* as a vehicle for educational, personal, and career counseling and for communicating with parents about the school's talent development opportunities and their child's involvement in them.

This expanded approach to identifying talent potentials is essential if we are to make genuine efforts to include more under-represented students in a plan for *total* talent development. This approach is also consistent with the more flexible conception of *developing* gifts and talents that has been a cornerstone of our work and our concerns for promoting more equity in special programs.

Curriculum Modification Techniques

The second service delivery component of the SEM is a series of curriculum modification techniques designed to: (1) adjust levels of required learning so that all students are challenged, (2) increase the number of in-depth learning experiences, and (3) introduce various types of enrichment into regular curricular experiences. The procedures that are used to carry out curriculum modification are curriculum compacting, textbook analysis and surgical removal of repetitious material from textbooks, and a planned approach for introducing greater depth into regular curricular material. Due to space restrictions, curriculum compacting is described in depth here and other modification techniques are described in detail in other publications (see, for example, Renzulli, 1994; Reis et al., 1993).

How to Use the Compacting Process

Defining goals and outcomes. The first of three phases of the compacting process consists of defining the goals and outcomes of a given unit or segment of instruction. This information is readily available in most subjects because specific goals and outcomes can usually be found in teachers' manuals, curriculum guides, scope-and-sequence charts, and some of the new curricular frameworks that are emerging in connection with outcome based education models. Teachers should examine these objectives to determine which represent the acquisition of new content or thinking skills as opposed to reviews or practice of material that has previously been taught. The scope and sequence charts prepared by publishers, or a simple comparison of the table of contents of a basal series will provide a quick overview of new vs. repeated material. A major goal of this phase of the compacting process is to help teachers make individual programming decisions; a larger professional development goal is to help teachers be better analysts of the material they are teaching and better consumers of textbooks and prescribed curricular material.

Identifying students for compacting. The second phase of curriculum compacting is identifying students who have already mastered the objectives or outcomes of a unit or segment of instruction that is about to be taught. This first step of this phase consists of estimating which students have the potential to master new material at a faster than normal pace; knowing one's students is, of course, the best way to begin the assessment process. Scores on previous tests, completed assignments, and classroom participation are the best ways of identifying highly likely candidates for compacting. Standardized achievement tests can serve as a good general screen for this step because they allow us to list the names of all students who are scoring one or more years above grade level in particular subject areas.

Being a candidate for compacting does not necessarily mean that a student knows the material under consideration. Therefore, the second step of identifying candidates consists of finding or developing appropriate tests or other assessment techniques that can be used to evaluate specific learning outcomes. Unit pretests, or end-of-unit tests that can be administered as pretests are readymade for this task, especially when it comes to the assessment of basic skills. An analysis of pretest results enables the teacher to document proficiency in specific skills, and to select instructional activities or practice material necessary to bring the student up to a high level on any skill that may need some additional reinforcement.

Joseph S. Renzulli

Abilities	**Interests**	**Style Preferences**			
Maximum Performance Indicators	Interest Areas	Instructional Styles Preferences	Learning Environment Preferences	Thinking Styles Preferences	Expression Style Preferences
Tests	Fine Arts	Recitation & Drill		Analytic	Written
•Standardized	Crafts	Peer Tutoring	***Inter/Intra***	(School Smart)	
•Teacher-Made	Literary	Lecture	***Personal***		Oral
Course Grades	Historical	Lecture/Discussion	•Self-Oriented	Synthetic/	
Teacher Ratings	Mathematical/Logical	Discussion	•Peer-Oriented	Creative	Manipulative
Product Evaluation	Physical Sciences	Guided Independent	•Adult-Oriented	(Creative, Inventive)	
•Written	Life Sciences	Study *	•Combined		Discussion
•Oral	Political/Judicial	Learning /Interest Center		Practical/	
•Visual	Athletic/Recreation	Simulation, Role Playing,	***Physical***	Contextual	Display
•Musical	Marketing/Business	Dramatization, Guided	•Sound	(Street Smart)	
•Constructed	Drama/Dance	Fantasy	•Heat		Dramatization
(Note differences between assigned and self-selected products)	Musical Performance	Learning Games	•Light	Legislative	Artistic
	Musical Composition	Replicative Reports or Projects*	•Design		
Level of Participation in Learning Activities	Managerial/Business	Investigative Reports or Projects*	•Mobility	Executive	Graphic
	Photography	Unguided Independent	•Time of Day		Commercial
Degree of Interaction With Others	Film/Video	Study*	•Food Intake	Judicial	
	Computers	Internship*	•Seating		Service
	Other (Specify)	Apprenticeship*		Ref: Sternberg, 1984, 1988, 1990	
Ref: General Tests and Measurements Literature		*With or without a mentor	Ref: Amabile, 1983; Dunn, Dunn, & Price, 1977; Gardner, 1983		Ref: Kettle, Renzulli, & Rizza, 1998; Renzulli & Reis, 1985
	Ref: Renzulli, 1997	Ref: Renzulli & Smith, 1978			

Figure 5. The total talent portfolio.

The process is slightly modified for compacting content areas that are not as easily assessed as basic skills, and for students who have not mastered the material, but are judged to be candidates for more rapid coverage. First, students should have a thorough understanding of the goals and procedures of compacting, including the nature of the replacement process. A given segment of material should be discussed with the student (e.g. a unit that includes a series of chapters in a social studies text), and the procedures for verifying mastery at a high level should be specified. These procedures might consist of answering questions based on the chapters, writing an essay, or taking the standard end-of-unit test. The amount of time for completion of the unit should be specified, and procedures such as periodic progress reports or log entries for teacher review should be agreed upon. Of course, an examination of potential acceleration and/or enrichment replacement activities should be a part of this discussion.

Another alternative is to assess or pretest all students in a class when a new unit or topic is introduced; although this may seem like more work for the teacher, it provides the opportunity for all students to demonstrate their strengths or previous mastery in a given area. Using a matrix of learning objectives, teachers can fill in test results and establish small, flexible, and temporary groups for skill instruction and replacement activities.

Providing acceleration and enrichment options. The final phase of the compacting process can be one of the most exciting aspects of teaching because it is based on cooperative decision making and creativity on the parts of both teachers and students. Efforts can be made to gather enrichment materials from classroom teachers, librarians, media specialists, and content area or gifted education specialists. These materials may include self-directed learning activities, instructional materials that focus on particular thinking skills, and a variety of individual and group project oriented activities that are designed to promote hands-on research and investigative skills. The time made available through compacting provides opportunities for exciting learning experiences such as small group, special topic seminars that might be directed by students or community resource persons, community based apprenticeships or opportunities to work with a mentor, peer tutoring situations, involvement in community service activities, and opportunities to rotate through a series of self-selected mini-courses. The time saved through curriculum compacting can be used by the teacher to provide a variety of enrichment or acceleration opportunities for the student.

Enrichment strategies might include a variety of Type I, II, or III or a number of options included on the continuum of services. Acceleration might include the use of material from the next unit or chapter, the use of

the next chronological grade level textbook or the completion of even more advanced work. Alternative activities should reflect an appropriate level of challenge and rigor that is commensurate with the student's abilities and interests.

Decisions about which replacement activities to use are always guided by factors such as time, space, and the availability of resource persons and materials. Although practical concerns must be considered, the ultimate criteria for replacement activities should be the degree to which they increase academic challenge and the extent to which they meet individual needs. Great care should be taken to select activities and experiences that represent individual strengths and interests rather than the assignment of more-of-the-same worksheets or randomly selected kits, games, and puzzles! This aspect of the compacting process should also be viewed as a creative opportunity for an entire faculty to work cooperatively to organize and institute a broad array of enrichment experiences. A favorite mini-course that a faculty member has always wanted to teach, or serving as a mentor to one or two students who are extremely invested in a teacher's beloved topic are just a few of the ways that replacement activities can add excitement to the teachers' part in this process as well as the obvious benefits for students. We have also observed another interesting occurrence that has resulted from the availability of curriculum compacting. When some previously bright but underachieving students realized that they could both economize on regularly assigned material and 'earn time' to pursue self-selected interests, their motivation to complete regular assignments increased; as one student put it, "Everyone understands a good deal!"

The best way to get an overview of the curriculum compacting process is to examine an actual example of how the management form that guides this process is used. This form, 'The Compactor', presented in Fig. 6, serves as both an organizational and record keeping tool. Teachers should fill out one form per student, or one form for a group of students with similar curricular strengths. Completed Compactors should be kept in students' academic files, and updated on a regular basis. The form can also be used for small groups of students who are working at approximately the same level (e.g. a reading or maths group). The Compactor is divided into three sections:

- The first column should include information on learning objectives and student strengths in those areas. Teachers should list the objectives for a particular unit of study, followed by data on students' proficiency in those objectives, including test scores, behavioral profiles and past academic records.
- In the second column, teachers should detail the pretest vehicles they select, along with test results. The pretest instruments can be formal measures, such as pencil and paper tests, or informal measures,

such as performance assessments based on observations of class participation and written assignments.

Specificity is extremely important; recording an overall score of 85% on ten objectives, for example, sheds little light on what portion of the material can be compacted, since students might show limited mastery of some objectives and high levels of mastery on others.

• Column three is used to record information about acceleration or enrichment options; in determining these options, teachers must be fully aware of students' individual interests and learning styles. We should never replace compacted regular curriculum work with harder, more advanced material that is solely determined by the teacher; instead, students interests should be taken into account. If for example, a student loves working on science fair projects, that option may be used to replace material that has been compacted from the regular curriculum. We should also be careful to help monitor the challenge level of the material that is being substituted. We want students to understand the nature of effort and challenge and we should ensure that students are not simply replacing the compacted material with basic reading or work that is not advanced.

Rosa: A Case Study in Curriculum Compacting

Rosa is a fifth grader in a self-contained heterogeneous classroom; her school is located in a lower socio-economic urban school district. While Rosa's reading and language scores range between four or five years above grade level, most of her 29 classmates are reading one to two years below grade level. This presented Rosa's teacher with a common problem: what was the best way to instruct Rosa? He agreed to compact her curriculum. Taking the easiest approach possible, he administered all of the appropriate unit tests for the grade level in the Basal Language Arts program, and excused Rosa from completing the activities and worksheets in the units where she showed proficiency (80% and above). When Rosa missed one or two questions, the teacher checked for trends in those items and provided instruction and practice materials to ensure concept mastery.

INDIVIDUAL EDUCATIONAL PROGRAMMING GUIDE
The Compactor

Prepared by Joseph S. Renzulli
Linda M. Smith

NAME_____ AGE_____ TEACHER(S)_____

Individual Conference Dates And Persons
Participating in Planning Of IEP

SCHOOL _____ GRADE_____ PARENT(S) _____ _____ _____ _____ _____

CURRICULUM AREAS TO BE CONSIDERED FOR COMPACTING Provide a brief description of basic material to be covered during this marking period and the assessment information or evidence that suggests the need for compacting.	PROCEDURES FOR COMPACTING BASIC MATERIAL Describe activities that will be used to guarantee proficiency in basic curricular areas.	ACCELERATION AND/OR ENRICHMENT ACTIVITIES Describe activities that will be used to provide advanced level learning experiences in each area of the regular curriculum.

☐ Check here if additional information is recorded on the reverse side.

Copyright © 1978 by Creative Learning Press, Inc. P.O. Box 320 Mansfield Center, CT 06250. All rights reserved.

Figure 6. The compactor.

Rosa usually took part in language arts lessons one or two days a week; the balance of the time she spent with alternative projects, some of which she selected. This strategy spared Rosa up to six or eight hours a week with language arts skills that were simply beneath her level. She joined the class instruction only when her pretests indicated she had not fully acquired the skills or to take part in a discussion that her teacher thought she would enjoy. In the time saved through compacting, Rosa engaged in a number of enrichment activities. First, she spent as many as five hours a week in a resource room for high ability students. This time was usually scheduled during her language arts class, benefiting both Rosa and her teacher, since he didn't have to search for all of the enrichment options himself. The best part of the process for Rosa was she didn't have make-up regular classroom assignments because she was not missing essential work.

Rosa also visited a regional science center with other students who had expressed a high interest and aptitude for science. Science was a second strength area for Rosa, and based on the results of her *Interest-A-Lyzer,* a decision was made for Rosa to proceed with a science fair project on growing plants under various conditions. Rosa's Compactor, which covered an entire semester, was updated in January. Her teacher remarked that compacting her curriculum had actually saved him time—time he would have spent correcting papers needlessly assigned! The value of compacting for Rosa convinced him that he should continue the process. The Compactor was also used as a vehicle for explaining to Rosa's parents how specific modifications were being made to accommodate her advanced language arts achievement level and her interest in science. A copy of The Compactor was also passed on to Rosa's sixth grade teacher, and a conference between the fifth and sixth grade teachers and the resource teacher helped to ensure continuity in dealing with Rosa's special needs.

The many changes that are taking place in our schools require all educators to examine a broad range of techniques for providing equitably for *all* students. Curriculum compacting is one such process. It is not tied to a specific content area or grade level, nor is it aligned with a particular approach to school or curricular reform. Rather, the process is adaptable to any school configuration or curricular framework, and it is flexible enough to be used within the context of rapidly changing approaches to general education. The research study described above, and practical experience gained through several years of field testing and refining the compacting process have demonstrated that many positive benefits can result from this process for both students and teachers.

Enrichment Learning and Teaching

The third service delivery component of the SEM, which is based on the Enrichment Triad Model, is enrichment learning and teaching which has roots in the ideas of a small but influential number of philosophers, theorists, and researchers such as Jean Piaget (1975), Jerome Bruner (1960, 1966), and John Dewey (1913, 1916). The work of these theorists coupled with our own research and program development activities, has given rise to the concept we call enrichment learning and teaching. The best way to define this concept is in terms of the following four principles:

(1) Each learner is unique, and therefore, all learning experiences must be examined in ways that take into account the abilities, interests, and learning styles of the individual.

(2) Learning is more effective when students enjoy what they are doing, and therefore, learning experiences should be constructed and assessed with as much concern for enjoyment as for other goals.

(3) Learning is more meaningful and enjoyable when content (i.e. knowledge) and process (i.e. thinking skills, methods of inquiry) are learned within the context of a real and present problem; and therefore, attention should be given to opportunities to personalize student choice in problem selection, the relevance of the problem for individual students at the time the problem is being addressed, and authentic strategies for addressing the problem.

(4) Some formal instruction may be used in enrichment learning and teaching, but a major goal of this approach to learning is to enhance knowledge and thinking skill acquisition that is gained through formal instruction with applications of knowledge and skills that result from students' own construction of meaning (Renzulli, 1994, p. 204).

The ultimate goal of learning that is guided by these principles is to replace dependent and passive learning with independence and engaged learning. Although all but the most conservative educators will agree with these principles, much controversy exists about how these (or similar) principles might be applied in everyday school situations. A danger also exists that these principles might be viewed as yet another idealized list of glittering generalities that cannot be manifested easily in schools that are entrenched in the deductive model of learning; developing a school program based on these principles is not an easy task. Over the years, however, we have achieved success by gaining faculty, administrative, and parental consensus on a small number of easy-to-understand concepts and related services, and by providing resources and training related to each concept and service delivery procedure. Numerous research studies and field tests in schools with widely varying demographics have been carried out (Renzulli & Reis, 1994). These studies and field tests provided opportunities for the development of large amounts of practical know-how that are readily available for schools that would like to implement the SEM. They also have shown that the SEM can be implemented in a wide variety of settings and used with various populations of students including high ability students with learning disabilities and high ability students who underachieve in school.

References

Amabile, T. (1983). *The social psychology of creativity.* New York: Springer-Verlag.

Bruner, J. S. (1960). *The process of education.* Cambridge, MA: Harvard University Press.

Bruner, J. S. (1966). *Toward a theory of instruction.* Cambridge, MA: Harvard University Press.

Burns, D. E. (1998). *SEM network directory.* Storrs, CT: University of Connecticut, Neag Center for Gifted Education and Talent Development.

Dewey, J. (1913). *Interest and effort in education.* New York: Houghton Mifflin.

Dewey, J. (1916). *Democracy and education.* New York: Macmillan.

Dunn, R., Dunn, K. & Price, G. E. (1977). Diagnosing learning styles: avoiding malpractice suits against school systems. *Phi Delta Kappan,* 58(5), 418–420.

Gardner, H. (1983). *Frames of mind.* New York: Basic Books.

James, W. (1885). On the functions of cognition. *Mind, 10,* 27–44.

Kirschenbaum, R. J. (1983). Let's cut out the cut-off score in the identification of the gifted. *Roeper Review: A Journal on Gifted Education, 5,* 6–10.

Kirschenbaum, R. J. & Siegle, D. (1993, April). *Predicting creative performance in an enrichment program.* Paper presented at the Association for the Education of Gifted Underachieving Students 6th Annual Conference, Portland, OR.

Neisser, U. (1979). The concept of intelligence. In R. J. Sternberg & D. K. Detterman (Eds.), *Human Intelligence* (pp. 179–189). Norwood, NJ: Ablex.

Olenchak, F. R. (1988). The schoolwide enrichment model in the elementary schools: a study of implementation stages and effects on educational excellence. In: J. S. Renzulli (Ed.), *Technical Report on Research Studies Relating to the Revolving Door Identification Model* (2nd ed., pp. 201–247). Storrs, CT: University of Connecticut, Bureau of Educational Research.

Olenchak, F. R. & Renzulli, J. S. (1989). The effectiveness of the schoolwide enrichment model on selected aspects of elementary school change. *Gifted Child Quarterly, 32,* 44–57.

Piaget, J. (1975). *The development of thought: equilibration of cognitive structures.* New York: Viking.

Reis, S. M. (1981). *An analysis of the productivity of gifted students participating in programs using the revolving door identification model.* Unpublished doctoral dissertation, University of Connecticut, Storrs.

Reis, S. M., Burns, D. E. & Renzulli, J. S. (1992). *Curriculum compacting: the complete guide to modifying the regular curriculum for high ability students.* Mansfield Center, CT: Creative Learning Press.

Reis, S. M., Westberg, K. L., Kulikowich, J., Caillard, F., Hébert, T. P., Plucker, J. A., Purcell, J. H., Rogers, J. & Smist, J. (1993). Why not let high ability students start school in January? the curriculum compacting study (Research Monograph 93106). Storrs, CT: University of Connecticut, The National Research Center on the Gifted and Talented.

Renzulli, J. S. (1976). The enrichment triad model: a guide for developing defensible programs for the gifted and talented. *Gifted Child Quarterly,* 20, 303–326.

Renzulli, J. S. (1977). *The enrichment triad model: a guide for developing defensible programs for the gifted and talented.* Mansfield Center, CT: Creative Learning Press.

Renzulli, J. S. (1978). What makes giftedness? Re-examining a definition. *Phi Delta Kappan, 60,* 180–184, 261.

Renzulli, J. S. (1982).What makes a problem real: stalking the illusive meaning of qualitative differences in gifted education. *Gifted Child Quarterly, 26,* 147–156.

Renzulli, J. S. (1986). The three ring conception of giftedness: A developmental model for creative productivity. In R. J. Sternberg & J. E. Davidson (Eds.), *Conceptions of giftedness* (pp. 53–92). New York: Cambridge University Press.

Renzulli, J. S. (1988a). The multiple menu model for developing differentiated curriculum for the gifted and talented. *Gifted Child Quarterly, 32,* 298–309.

Renzulli, J. S. (Ed.). (1988b). *Technical report of research studies related to the enrichment triad/revolving door model* (3rd ed.). Storrs, CT: University of Connecticut, Teaching The Talented Program.

Renzulli, J. S. (1994). *Schools for talent development: a practical plan for total school improvement.* Mansfield Center, CT: Creative Learning Press.

Renzulli, J. S. & Reis, S. M. (1985). *The schoolwide enrichment model: A comprehensive plan for educational excellence.* Mansfield Center, CT: Creative Learning Press.

Renzulli, J. S. & Reis, S. M. (1994). Research related to the Schoolwide Enrichment Model. *Gifted Child Quarterly, 38,* 2–14.

Renzulli, J. S. & Reis, S. M. (1997). *The schoolwide enrichment model: a how-to guide for educational excellence.* Mansfield Center, CT: Creative Learning Press.

Renzulli, J. S., Reis, S. M. & Smith, L. H. (1981). *The revolving door identification model.* Mansfield Center, CT: Creative Learning Press.

Renzulli, J. S. & Smith, L. H. (1978). *The compactor.* Mansfield Center, CT: Creative Learning Press.

Renzulli, J. S., Smith, L. H. & Reis, S. M. (1982). Curriculum compacting: an essential strategy for working with gifted students. *The Elementary School Journal, 82,* 185–194.

Sternberg, R. J. (1984). Toward a triarchic theory of human intelligence. *Behavioral and Brain Sciences, 7,* 269–287.

Sternberg, R. J. (1988). Three facet model of creativity. In R. J. Sternberg (Ed.), *The Nature of Creativity* (pp. 125–147). Boston: Cambridge University Press.

Sternberg, R. J. (1990). Thinking styles: keys to understanding student performance. *Phi Delta Kappan,* 71(5), 366–371.

Thorndike, E. L. (1921). Intelligence and its measurement. *Journal of Educational Psychology, 12,* 124–127.

Torrance, E. P. (1962). *Guiding creative talent.* Englewood Cliffs, NJ: Prentice-Hall.

Torrance, E. P. (1974). *Norms-Technical manual: torrance tests of creative thinking*. Bensenville, IL: Scholastic Testing Service.

Ward, V. S. (1960). Systematic intensification and extensification of the school curriculum. *Exceptional Children*, **28**, 67–71, 77.

Instructional Psychology and the Gifted

Hans Gruber[1] and Heinz Mandl[2]

[1]University of Regensburg, Germany
[2]University of Munich, Germany

1. Fostering Excellence: The Role of Dispositions and Practice

Instructional psychology aims at fostering learning or even the growth of 'excellence'—a term we are going to use synonymously with the term 'high-level performance'. There are two bodies of research dealing with this topic that are only loosely connected: research on 'giftedness'—we are going to use this term synonymously with the term 'high ability'—(Sternberg & Davidson, 1986; Heller, Mönks & Passow, 1993), and research on 'expertise' (Ericsson & Smith, 1991; Ericsson, 1996; Gruber & Ziegler, 1996). Both are taking different theoretical perspectives on the same educational processes, and they frequently argue that the respective other research is doing the wrong thing. If the narrow viewpoints are left aside it can be recognized that both directions contribute to the same phenomena, and that both are dependent on each other, because the complex goal of fostering the development of excellence requires both favourable individual dispositions and intensive deliberate practice (Ericsson, Krampe & Tesch-Römer, 1993) over a long period. Analyses of expert information processing and of processes of the learning of the gifted are necessary pre-conditions of instructional fostering of the development of excellence, if instruction is aimed to go beyond the pure placement of subjects in different pre-existing learning environments. The notion of situated learning gives opportunity to adequately foster any learners in demanding learning environments by making use both of the evidence from research on expertise and on giftedness. Of course, the idea of integrating research on giftedness and research on expertise is not entirely new, but has only rarely been discussed. Some approaches exist in the U.S. as well as in Europe (Sternberg, 1990b; Gruber & Mandl, 1992; Waldmann, 1996; Perleth, 1997), which is reflected in this book's contributions, and parts of the discussion can be found in the nurture-or-nature controversy which re-inflamed after the publication of Herrnstein and Murray's (1994) theses on differences in intelligence and their instruc-tional consequences (Neisser et al., 1996; Devlin, Fienberg, Resnick & Roeder, 1997). Resnick (1996) convincingly argued that nature and nurture factors have to be integrated, and that within situated learning theories, promising instructional approaches were developed for fostering the acquisition of excellence. These approaches basically view learning as tuning of prepared structures and, therefore, include both dis-positional factors and practice factors.

This chapter consists of six parts. Sections 2 and 3 provide an overview of research on conditions of the development of high-level performance. The main outcomes from traditional research on giftedness (section 2) and from traditional research on expertise (section 3) are reported; reasons for the empirical lack of substantial correlations between both are then discussed (section 4). Their interaction during the acquisition of excellence despite low correlations is then described (section 5). Theories of the acquisition of expertise and high abilities are discussed in order to explain and model changes in the relation between giftedness and instructional support; at the core, it is argued that dispositions influence information process-ing. Local instructional efforts try to foster singular individual capabilities for reaching better performance. On the other hand, individual learning processes are embedded in complex social contexts. Approaches for complex learning based on situated cognition models integrate these perspectives and provide guidelines for the design of learning environments that are helpful for acquiring excellence, including adequate fostering of the gifted. In these approaches, authenticity and complexity of learning environments are considered crucial (section 6).

2. Traditional Research on Giftedness: Focus on Dispositions

The assumption that some people are more intellec-tually gifted than others is an attractive one for instructional psychology: The task of fostering excel-lence is much facilitated if high-level performance can be reliably predicted by a set of abilities that are stable over time and that can be assessed by (e.g.) IQ tests. Identifying the gifted then is a major task of instructional psychology, but not an easy one, because unanimously agreed upon definitions do not exist.

This handbook shows that a number of different conceptions of giftedness have been elaborated in various research programs. Part I of the handbook deals with changing conceptions on giftedness and talent and thus should prevent argumentative oversimplifications. Traditional research on giftedness focused on innate dispositions. Conceptions that consider high ability as an innate disposition stress the 'nature' component of human development and view giftedness as rather stable property of (some) individuals. The most important and most widely discussed dispositional factor of this kind is 'general intelligence' ('g'; Jensen, 1998), and much effort in assessing giftedness and in identifying gifted persons is closely tight to research on 'g'. Of course, nobody would deny that environmental factors also play an important role in the emergence of high-level performance, but the consequences of the focus on dispositions for instructional psychology are substantial. Giftedness conceived as a relatively stable property predicts the potential of development and limits the effects of what can be achieved by instructional efforts. In terms of the equation 'Nature + Nurture = Performance', traditional approaches to research on giftedness tend to neglect the nurture part. In section 3, we will discuss research that prefers the opposite model: in research on expertise some have argued that dispositional factors play a negligible role in the acquisition of high-level performance (e.g. Ericsson & Charness, 1994; Howe, Davidson & Sloboda, 1998). Mixed models that conceive giftedness via (high) performance resulting from the convergence of positive dispositions and positive environmental factors put their focus on the interaction of both components (Holling & Kanning, 1999). They have to struggle with the argument that environmental variables can frequently clearly be operationalized and experimentally varied whereas dispositions cannot.

Of course, 'g' is not the only feature characteristic of the gifted (Van Tassel-Baska, 1998). However, many of the observable correlates of intellectual giftedness are related to constructs measured by IQ tests: excellence in logical thinking; quick comprehension of abstract thoughts; correct inductive reasoning; understanding of complex relations; quick and correct learning; flexible use of an elaborated vocabulary; outstanding memory, etc. (Heller & Hany, 1996). The ascribed importance of 'g' is to a substantial degree a result of the research method used. Ceci and Ruiz (1992) argued that a psychometric approach, which aims at identifying the most important components of mental performance by computing a Principal Component Analysis, more or less automatically results in 'g' as the factor explaining the largest portion of variance. It has been argued that

factorial theories are theories about the structure of correlation matrices of abilities tests, but not theories of the human mind. Approaches using a research paradigm different from factor analysis come to different conclusions. For example, models using the analysis of cognitive processes stress that differences in cognitive performance result from differences in (the dispositions of) information processing speed (Kail & Salthouse, 1994; Schweizer, 1998) or in working memory capacity (Kyllonen & Christal, 1990).

Non-intellectual abilities have frequently have been included in models of giftedness, but have not received as much attention, because they do not explain as much variance as 'g'. Their role for high-level performance cannot as clearly be identified as with working memory or information processing speed. One notable exception is the concept of emotional intelligence (Goleman, 1995, 1998; Salovey & Mayer, 1997), which recently received wide public attention. Descriptive analyses of successful people show that they are not just good at their jobs, but they also tend to be smart, resilient and optimistic. To be successful at work, the ability is needed to restrain negative feelings (e.g. self-doubt) and to focus on the positive (e.g. confidence). From an instructional point of view, such kinds of emotional intelligence are attractive, because they can be built and learned, whereas IQ is relatively fixed; however, little empirical research in this direction exists.

Correlational studies revealed relations between intellectual components of giftedness and achievement motivation (Dai, Moon & Feldhusen, 1998): gifted students have strong motivation, they show higher academic self-efficacy than others, they surpass others in prediction accuracy and in precision of estimation of their own ability. Consequently, multifactorial theoretical models of giftedness have been developed that include non-intellectual components (cf. Fels, 1999). Many of these models are described in other chapters of this handbook. It is important to stress the theoretical argument that giftedness includes not only innate intellectual abilities. Be it Vygotsky's 'Dynamic Theory of Giftedness' (cf. Babaeva, 1999) with its focus on the social determination of development and defining gifted performance as overcoming emerging barriers; or be it Renzulli's (1986) 'Three-Ring Conception' including task commitment and creativity as parts of giftedness, or be it Mönks' (1992) 'Triadic Interdependence Model': all stress the dispositional nature of giftedness, but hypothesize the necessity of intensive instructional efforts in order to foster excellence. IQ in these models reflects only a particular type of cognition (namely academic-verbal performance) rather than the general aptitude for complex thinking. Sternberg (1990a) argued that metaphors of mind determine the nature of theories of intelligence, and the biological 'look inward' metaphor of theories of intelligence stressing 'g' is one kind of description, but not the only one. (For an outline of his preferred model of intelligence and instructional implications see section 5 of this chapter.) Simonton (1999) convergently argued that complex models of innate giftedness and talent are necessary. He described talent "as a multidimensional and multiplicative developmental process. This point is elaborated in the form of a 2-part emergenic-epigenetic model" (p. 435). Both the analysis of individual differences in dispositional traits that faciliate the manifestation of expert performance and the development of innate components during life have to be considered.

In different multi-dimensional theories of giftedness, the relationship between person-internal and environmental factors is conceived quite differently. Gallagher and Courtright (1986) therefore classified theories as either 'psychological' (e.g. Renzulli, 1986) or as 'educational' (e.g. Tannenbaum, 1986). This dualism does not imply that instructional psychology is considered relevant only in the latter group, because special needs of the gifted have to be met even if the relative importance of environmental factors is conceptualized as small. Many chapters of Part IV of this handbook address instructional tasks of education of the gifted, as the needs for a challenging education, for 'true peers', for adult empathy, for responsive parenting or—in our context most important—for special instruction. Heller (1999a, b) described education of the gifted as the fit between individual cognitive and motivational pre-conditions of the learning process and the instructional situation (cf. Feger & Prado, 1998). Such education can follow the strategies of grouping (forming groups homogeneous in achievement), of acceleration of instruction (changing the speed of instruction; cf. Southern, Jones & Stanley, this volume), or of enrichment (changing the quality of contents of instruction; cf. Renzulli & Reis, this volume). In terms of school achievement, research provided more support for acceleration programs than for enrichment programs, but the particular outcomes of enrichment programs perhaps are not in the scope of school achievement measures. New developments in instructional psychology (see section 6 of this chapter) led into the design of learning environments that seek to avoid the problem of inert knowledge and that facilitate the acquisition of complex, applicable knowledge and skills. Such efforts resemble enrichment programs much more than acceleration programs.

3. Traditional Research on Expertise: Focus on Practice

The second research stream that has to be dealt with when discussing instructional efforts for fostering excellence is research on expertise. Some agents in this stream strongly argue that giftedness or talent are not at all important and that high-level performance is predominantly acquired rather than inherited (Ericsson & Charness, 1994). This implies that instruction in whatever manifestation is believed to impose certain

effects on acquisition of expertise. "The necessity for innate talents has been questioned and recently collected evidence shows that superior performance reflects primarily acquired skills and other attributes attained as the result of extended training and practice." (Ericsson, 1998, p. 75) Undoubtedly, no excellent person in any complex skill can be found that did not practice within this domain for a long period. As a consequence, giftedness (if it exists at all) and practice inevitably are confounded and can hardly be analyzed separately. (Simonton, 1999, p. 435, referred to a quotation that is ascribed to the famous violin virtuoso Sarasate when called a genius: "A genius! For thirty-seven years I've practiced fourteen hours a day, and now they call me a genius!)" Effortful—and often not enjoyable—commitment in training activities over a long period of time that solely has the purpose of improving the performance is an important characteristic of the process of acquisition of excellence; Ericsson et al. (1993) described this kind of work as 'deliberate practice'. However, some components of the acquisition of excellence can preferably be interpreted in terms of giftedness, whereas others clearly underlie mechanisms of extended practice. Ericsson (1998) admitted limits of the deliberate practice approach: "However, the motivational factors that sustain the expert performers' commitment toward gradual effortful improvement for extended periods of time still remain mostly unexplored." (p. 96)

Empirical studies from research on expertise are most frequently based on the contrastive approach (Voss, Fincher-Kiefer, Greene & Post, 1986). By cross-sectionally comparing experts with novices, the 'nature of expertise' (Chi, Glaser & Farr, 1988) can comprehensively be revealed. The primary aim of expert–novice studies is to identify contrasting characteristics, both qualitative and quantitative, of subjects with various levels of knowledge and skills in a certain domain, and thus to establish theories by incorporating the variables so isolated to account for the observed differences in their performance in that domain. The practical concern is to draw some instructional implications from these studies for training novices into experts (Law, 1995). One of the descriptive findings is that experts in any complex domain have been active within this domain for many years so that the argument is supported that extensive practice is the most important explaining variable for reaching high-level performance. Most researchers on expertise (more or less implicitly) assume that extensive practice is not only a necessary, but a sufficient condition for the acquisition of expertise. As a consequence, individual differences in dispositions are regarded as unimportant, and findings of zero-correlations between, for example, level of expertise and intelligence seem to support this interpretation. (Section 4 is devoted to arguments that show that this conclusion is not necessarily valid.) The instructional consequence is that experts in an earlier stage of their career did not differ from novices at that particular stage, so that the cross-sectional comparison between both allows longitudinal interpretation. The finding that experts possess much more domain knowledge than novices then leads to the interpretation that fostering excellence is simply adding knowledge. In view of the fact that experts organize knowledge and approach problem-solving differently from novices, the goal of instruction from a cognitive perspective, then, seems to be to replicate the knowledge structure and cognitive processes of the expert in the mind of the learner (Glaser, 1989). We will return to that argument later, but will first review further basic findings of research on expertise.

Among the most interesting results of research on expertise is the evidence for experts' excellent memory for domain-specific material. A chess master is able to correctly remember a chess position (containing more than 20 pieces) after being presented with it for only a few seconds (De Groot, 1965). In contrast, novices remember no more than about seven pieces (effect size in contrastive studies often has scores $d > 2$!). Such dramatic differences in memory performance cannot be explained by differences in memory dispositions as could be suspected: in control tasks (e.g. digit-span), no differences between experts and novices can be traced (Schneider, Gruber, Gold & Opwis, 1993). This implies that it is domain-specific practice that contributes to differences in memory performance. The concept of 'pattern recognition' (Chase & Simon, 1973; Gobet & Simon, 1996) was developed to explain (and simulate) the contrastive differences; it is plainly based on accumulation of knowledge units (chunks) through practice. Experts' ability to analyze newly presented domain-specific information very quickly and to recognize semantically relevant patterns is based on a large knowledge base they already possess. It was shown that the integration of perception and knowledge in memory performance can be explained by (1) chunking processes for semantical association of information units (De Groot & Gobet, 1996), and by (2) building up a highly organized memory structure for fast storing and recalling of domain knowledge (Ericsson, 1985).

The related cognitive processes do not depend on specific dispositions so that it has been argued that everyone could become expert in any domain, given only extended practice within that domain. Ericsson and Crutcher (1990) speak of about ten years needed for the acquisition of expertise in any complex domain. Evidence exists across many domains that experts have extensive knowledge at their disposal, and that they intensively practiced over many years. Additionally, given the fact that experts per definition excel in domain-specific performance, the conclusion can be drawn that the construction of a large knowledge base is sufficient for the acquisition of expertise. However, the relationship between high-level performance on the one hand and memory skill and knowledge structure on the other is correlative in nature so that causal interpretations remain speculative.

Rather, there exists evidence that the availability of a large knowledge base is not necessarily connected with high-level performance, at least as far as declarative knowledge is concerned. The problem of 'inert knowledge' has emerged as one of the most urgent problems for instructional psychology in the last decades (Bransford, Goldman & Vye, 1991; Renkl, Mandl & Gruber, 1996). Besides knowledge accumulation a careful design of learning environments is important that gives opportunity to make 'right' experiences and to apply the knowledge-to-be-learned in relevant situations (Prerau, Adler & Gunderson, 1992).

The problem of inert knowledge has not yet received much attention within research on expertise, despite the fact that some authors have illuminated 'costs of expertise' (Arkes & Freedman, 1984). One of the reasons is that many studies have been performed in domains that can be described as well-defined (e.g., programming), in which the problem is not as urgent as in others. In such domains, the problems usually to be solved are clearly defined; there exist optimal solutions, the veridicality of knowledge is rarely doubted. Within well-defined domains, the epistemological conclusion seems to be obvious that knowledge can be described as isolated objective entities existing independently from individuals and their experiences. Only then the idea of reaching excellence by accumulation of objectively relevant knowledge units can be expressed. This is not trivially transferable from well-defined domains to ill-defined domains like medical diagnosis, writing lyrics, etc.

The study of ill-defined domains thus is one of the most urgent desiderata in research on expertise; some evidence exists that results obtained from the study of well-defined domains cannot be directly transferred (Voss, 1990). Ford and Adams-Webber (1992) argue that a constructivistic epistemology might be more appropriate in such cases, in which (for example) the truth of knowledge is doubted. Of course, knowledge is of immense importance in ill-defined domains as well, but the nature of relevant knowledge might be different: declarative knowledge is less important, practical knowledge is more important. A helpful differentiated analysis of types of knowledge was provided by De Jong and Ferguson-Hessler (1996). The problems to be solved are more complex; the problem-solver has to show more flexibility in the use of solutions strategies (Krems, 1996). A conclusion from situated-cognition approaches is that in complex domains the situativity of knowledge and problems has to be taken into account, and that successful learning heavily depends on experience dealing with the uncertainty of domain-specific information and with the irrgularity of cases to be met. It has repeatedly been doubted that systematic presentation of information and systematic accumulation of knowledge is adequate for teaching complex skills. The constructive learner activity during learning and the kind of approach to problems and creatively solving them then is of increasing importance. This, however, suggests that individual differences in dispositions that underlie information processing might play an important role. Additionally, problem solving in relevant situations within complex domains suggests that the social context of learning processes is important; individual differences in the ability to deal with the social context are also related with the outcomes of learning. Martin and Double (1998) argued that processes of peer observation and collaborative reflection are important factors in the development of complex skills; in section 6, this argument will be addressed in more detail.

Whereas the descriptive results of contrastive studies cannot be neglected, the basic lack of research on expertise obviously concerns longitudinal studies of the acquisition of high-level performance in complex domains. First studies (e.g. Gruber, Renkl & Schneider, 1994) indicate that intensive practice within a domain may not be sufficient for the acquisition of expertise. Other conditions also play a role, that are not necessarily of a cognitive nature; reasons have to be identified why some individuals are motivated to work and practice for many years, whereas others are not.

The amount of exposure to relevant information during practice then is not the only relevant factor during learning. Many individuals were exposed to much practice and did not reach expert level, because they lacked the ability to integrate facts to derive complex insights. The interaction between dispositions and practice seems to be important even if a substantial correlation between them can not be observed in experts.

4. Do Giftedness and Expertise Meet? The Lack of Substantial Correlations is No Counter-Evidence!

The relation between dispositions and practice can most clearly be analyzed by studying the role of giftedness for expert behavior. As Schneider (this volume) shows, in complex domains intelligence is not a very good predictor of expert achievement. Rather, low correlations between intelligence and level of expertise are usually found; this may lead to the assumption that dispositional factors do not influence expertise and its acquisition. There are three reasons why this assumption may not be accurate. Since the potential relation between dispositional factors and practice factors has a major impact on instructional efforts, these arguments have to be considered carefully.

(1) *"Limited variance" argument.* The lack of a substantial correlation between intelligence and level of expertise may be an artifact because the variance of intelligence is limited to what can be observed in studies on expertise. Schneider (this volume) argued that within many domains, intelligence has to be above a certain threshold value for the successful acquisition of expertise; as a consequence, expert samples of contrastive studies usually have limited variance in intelligence. Thus, the argument that intelligence does not play a substantial role, cannot be generalized. Ackerman and Rolfhus (1999) found that for middle-aged adults, intelligence significantly predicts knowledge if a lower level of expertise is assumed or if knowledge across a variety of domains is analysed. The notion of the development and maintenance of 'intelligence-as-knowledge' as correlates of task performance of adults implies that the scope of what is analysed as 'intelligence' dramatically influences the correlation between dispositional factors and practice. (In section 5, the concept of practical intelligence instead of 'g' is discussed as a solution for this problem.) In developmental psychology, arguments have been collected that the adequate use of the terms 'intelligence' or 'excellence' is different for different age groups (Kliegl & Mayr, 1997).

(2) *"Drop-outs make it difficult!" argument.* The interpretation of low correlations between intelligence and level of expertise may be speculative because almost no data are available about drop-out rates and specific characteristics of the drop-outs during the acquisition of expertise. Only very few persons reach excellence—the factors responsible for this phenomenon of drop-outs have not yet been analysed sufficiently, and there is a lack of adequate longitudinal studies.

(3) *"Different roles in different phases" argument.* In early phases of the acquisition of expertise, dispositional factors may play a larger role than in later phases, in which domain-specific knowledge becomes increasingly important. Thus, contrastive studies contain another artifact, because the sample of experts already reached late phases in development, whereas the novice sample did not even start with gaining excellence. The role of intelligence during the acquisition of expertise might be more significant in other phases than those usually considered (this argument was extended in Ackerman's comprehensive theory of the acquisition of high-level performance which is addressed in section 5).

Doubts therefore may be expressed; even convincing evidence that intensive deliberate practice is necessary for reaching high-level performance does not exclude the impact of dispositional factors. Deliberate practice over a very long period of time requires the existence of some enduring individual characteristics that support strong motivation and commitment. "Hard work and innate ability are very likely confounded. Those children who have the most ability may also be those who are most interested in a particular activity, who begin to work at that activity at an early age, and who work the hardest at it. One is likely to want to work hard at something when one is able to advance quickly with relatively little effort, but not when every step is a painful struggle. Thus, Ericsson's research (. . .) demonstrates the importance of hard work but in no way allows us to rule out the role of innate ability" (Winner, 1996, p. 273). It is hardly possible to isolate ability from practice.

So, on the other hand, even an assumed strong role of innate talent does not rule out the importance of practice and hard work—even the most gifted develop their performance through intense work. However, the gifted may differ from ordinary people in respect of their learning speed, their intrinsic motivation to acquire domain-specific skills, and so on; research on expertise has not yet sufficiently dealt with such analyses. As will be shown, attempts to model the acquisition of complex expertise resulted in a number of assumptions which (at least implicitly) include components of the integration of approaches about giftedness and expertise.

5. Interaction of Dispositions and Practice in the Acquisition of Excellence

Among the arguments expressed in the previous section, the third one, the "different roles in different phases" argument, has been elaborated in the most explicit way. For different kinds of human skills, theories have been developed that describe distinctive phases during learning, in which dispositions and practice interact in different ways.

In his ACT* theory (and some derivatives), Anderson (1982) described three phases of skill acquisition: declarative phase, compilation phase, and tuning phase. The basic idea is that learners first require much declarative knowledge, which can be later proceduralized and recognized as patterns with associated action sequences. They can then automatize and tune skills through repeated practice. Anderson assumes innate cognitive structures for the acquisition of knowledge in the declarative phase, which he did not elaborate as much as the practice-based mechanisms of compilation (composition and proceduralization) and tuning.

With growing skills, more and more parts of the knowledge base become proceduralized, that is, practice helps to change the nature of information processes from controlled and effortful to automatized and compiled processes. Automatized processing is quick, needs few cognitive resources, and cannot easily be controlled. Its development is based upon extensive practice within consistent problem-solving conditions, that is, preferably within well-defined domains. Information processing remains in the declarative phase, if task consistency is not present; in this case, effortful controlled processing remains necessary.

In his theory of *ability determinants of skilled performance*, Ackerman (1986, 1987, 1992) discussed the change from controlled processing to automatized processing in terms of dispositions vs. practice (cf. Mack, 1996). He proposed an hierarchical three-phase model similar to ACT*, in which a cognitive phase, an associative phase, and an autonomous phase are distinguished. The relationship between intellectual abilities and practice is moderated by task characteristics (consistency, complexity).

The cognitive phase makes high demands on the subject. S/he has to understand task instructions, comprehend relevant goals, express strategies, memorize knowledge, etc. General, dispositional ability regarding giftedness plays an important role in this phase, which is only decreased if consistent task characteristics allow the emergence of proceduralized knowledge. In the case of inconsistent tasks, the correlation between general dispositional measures and performance is much higher than estimated within research on expertise.

In the associative phase strategies are being proceduralized; performance is increasingly bound to perception, and the compilation of knowledge leads to an increased speed of information processing.

Skills are being automatized during the autonomous phase; conscious attention for domain-specific actions is no longer necessary; in ill-defined, inconsistent domains, however, the autonomous phase is only rarely reached.

Obviously, the size of correlations between dispositional abilities and performance depends on the nature of the task or the domain. Given inconsistent demands, performance is well predicted by general abilities. If demands within a domain are consistent, more and influential processes of compilation are happening, the importance of practice increasing, the correlation between general abilities and performance is decreased. The gifteds' intellectual advantages are thus more important in domains with less consistent demands. Consistency of tasks is thus related to skill specificity in learning (Ackerman, 1990): the more skilled a subject is, the more specific components of information processing are relevant, so that the correlation between dispositions and performance decreases. Characteristic of many complex vocational domains (Ackerman, 1992, worked on air-traffic control), however, is inconsistency of demands; in such domains, general abilities do not lose their importance for high-level performance.

Thus, there is some evidence that dispositional factors like giftedness or intelligence influence the nature of human information processing, e.g., the way in which individuals notice, accumulate, process, and apply the stimuli presented in their environment. The use of learning strategies, the degree of activity during learning as well as the degree of self-regulation in learning, the skill of knowledge management or the degree of cooperative learning activities, are examples of the information processing than might be influenced by dispositional factors (cf. Weinert & Schrader, 1997). As a consequence, dispositions possess some relevance for the acquisition of excellence. It has been argued (e.g. Renzulli, 1986) that learning environments with high demands optimally foster the development of the gifted because complex learning is supported. The basic ideas of situated cognition (see section 6) include some similar thoughts.

Of course, it is not only intellectual abilities that influence information processing. Pekrun and Schiefele (1996) stressed the role of emotions for performance, e.g., through the allocation of cognitive resources, the selection of information processing strategies, the representation and recall of knowledge, or the amount of intrinsic motivation.

A number of instructional means have been developed that attempt to directly foster processes in which the gifted transfer their superior intellectual (and other) abilities in order to make progress in the quality of their information processing. General didactical advice was administered that aimed at promoting subjects' general abilities; examples are strategy training, metacognitive training, fostering of cooperative learning and social exchange, imparting values and norms, etc. (George, 1993). Teo and Quah (1999) stressed that the analysis of non-achieving behaviour of the gifted gives hints for instructional efforts. Such problems can be attributed to a lack of knowledge, volition and action of the gifted. Consequently, gifted education has to care about knowledge of the self, knowledge about volition, consultation, time management, stress management, and so on. Teachers' perceptions of the problems of the gifted play a crucial role in such instruction (Chyriwsky & Kennard, 1997).

Gifted instruction traditionally focused on the principles of developmental differentiation (Montgomery, 1996) and enrichment of the curriculum for the gifted. A couple of programs have been developed that systematically investigate possibilities of identifying and fostering high ability subjects (Heller & Hany, 1996; Mönks, 1999), e.g., 'The Study of Mathematically Precocious Youth' (Benbow, 1986), 'Purdue Three-Stage Enrichment Model' (Feldhusen & Kolloff, 1986), 'Enrichment Triad/Revolving Door Model' (Renzulli & Reis, 1986); see also the chapters on acceleration of instruction (Southern, Jones & Stanley, this volume) and on instructional enrichment (Renzulli & Reis, this volume).

Montgomery (1998) stressed the complex relationship between high ability and performance and concluded that the mechanisms of just testing and identifying the gifted do not suffice, but cognitive processes during learning have to be taken into account. Analysis of gifted thinking and problem-solving yields a more valid basis for instructional support of the gifted (Waldmann & Weinert, 1990; Waldmann, 1996). Future development of research on high ability should thus lead to research about the nature of cognitive processes that make the gifted excel, that is, investigations about individual differences in cognitive structures and processes. Obviously, this again argues in favour of reciprocal influences of research on giftedness and research on expertise.

The implications of this proposal are clear: on the one hand, individual cognitive processes have to be analysed, and reasons for individual differences have to be investigated. For this purpose the assumptions of situated learning with its stress on active constructive processes are important. On the other hand, experts' activities are bound to specific domains and thus are part of a large social system. Social and application contexts therefore influence information processing as well. This implies that more complex conceptions of information processing than just 'g' have to be used in theories of the development of excellence (Sternberg, 1985, 1996, 1997). Sternberg and Wagner's (1989, 1993) notion of practical intelligence and practical knowledge seems to be useful for this purpose, and its instructional implications are eminent (Sternberg, 1998).

Based on his triarchic theory of human intelligence, Sternberg developed a model of intelligence in which the perspective of information processing is reflected, and which proved satisfactory in prediction of professional success. *Practical intelligence* describes how people successfully interact with their environment; it includes components of human ability of adaptation in the environment, shaping of one's own environment, and the selection of adequate environmental contexts. Learning then comprises three basic processes of selection, namely selective encoding, selective combination, and selective comparison.

The operationalization of practical intelligence differs substantially from the operationalization of 'g'. Whereas 'g' is measured via (IQ) tests that include tasks which are well-defined, lacking complex embedding, and which are presented completely, practical intelligence measures assess the skills of high-performing people (Sternberg & Caruso, 1985). Their ability is focused to apply their knowledge as a consequence of their professional experience (Gruber, 1999). The problems concerned are usually ill-defined, always embedded in relevant situational and/or cultural contexts, and they rarely appear in completely worked formats.

In some respects, the difference between 'g' and practical knowledge reflects the relation between theory and practice. As Kessels and Korthagen (1996) noticed, this relation was quite imbalanced in 20th-century research: abstract knowledge in most theories is much more appreciated than practical abilities or "tacit knowledge of good performance." After all, at the end of the century the situated cognition movement provided ample evidence that it is a very plausible assumption that knowledge is context-bound in principle (see section 6). Accordingly, Sternberg and Wagner (1993) chose the provocative title 'The *g*-ocentric view of intelligence and job performance is wrong' to express the opinion that research on the description of excellence as well as instructional efforts to foster high-level performance should focus on the contextualization of knowledge and skills (cf. Mandl, Gruber & Renkl, 1993; Nake, 1998). Thus, they implicitly argue that research on dispositions cannot be separated from research on expertise through practice and from research on the social and cultural contextualization of human activity.

Recent models on the acquisition of expertise argued similarly, even if they did not explicitly include the giftedness argument nor the contextualization argument. However, the same topics are involved when ideas about the development of complex skills are expressed.

Boshuizen and Schmidt (1992) investigated the development of expertise in medicine. They proposed a three-phase model in which the relations between (abstract) biomedical knowledge and practical experience are changing, and are leading into an integration of theoretical and experiential knowledge in some kind of 'encapsulated' knowledge. Through professional activity, the medical doctors' knowledge undergoes qualitative changes. Declarative biomedical knowledge is proceduralized as result of experience with real cases. The resulting knowledge structures ('illness scripts') are generalized across cases, but nevertheless based on episodic experience and thus closely related to application contexts. The use of illness scripts leads to quick diagnosing without the need to effortfully activate declarative knowledge (compare with Anderson's ACT* theory). In the first phase of development, declarative biomedical knowledge about diseases has to be gathered and learned; during this phase, individual differences in general abilities lead to differences in learning. Then, the declarative knowledge is developed into 'illness scripts' as a result of real diagnoses with patients. It is important to note, however, that the declarative knowledge remains available if necessary. But it is no longer necessary in most cases, because the knowledge encapsulated in clinical experience with cases is sufficient.

The subjectively perceived relevance of experienced episodes and the conscious reflection of these episodes plays an important role for learning. In her model of dynamic memory, Kolodner (1983) explained how episodes are represented in memory, and how people apply episodic experiential knowledge. Representing knowledge through 'episodic definitions' that include the subjective perception and assessment of episodes as well as knowledge about applicability and application errors, are key features of this model. Learning through

experience with cases alters general knowledge structures. Instructional consequences are evident: the acquisition of excellence can instructionally be fostered by fostering reflective application of knowledge through the presentation of complex learning environments in which real application situations occur and which teach the relevance of the to-be-learned. Case-based learning is a preferable mode of learning (Kolodner, 1997) in which many components are included that contribute to high-level performance. Thus, this kind of learning is suited to make best use of the advantageous dispositions of high ability learners, but it also provides ample learning opportunities for the less gifted. Learning by this means—taking individual differences in dispositions as well into account as the amount of practice and the social and cultural contextualization—is exactly what the theories of situated cognition and situated learning focus on.

6. Situated Cognition: Environments for Complex Learning

It has been argued that understanding the development of excellence cannot be constrained either to dispositional factors or to practice factors. A focus on dispositions (or even biological prepared structures) does not mean neglecting social processes in which learning is embedded. "Prepared structures do not substitute for learning but rather make learning possible by constraining and guiding attention." (Resnick, 1996, p. 342) The notions that mental activity involves social coordination, and that knowledge is acquired in and attuned to specific social and cultural situations, on the other hand, do not necessarily have to disappear. Even if the social nature of cognitive activity is stressed, individual differences in information processing substantially influence the learning outcome. Resnick (1996) proposed a combination of both views in the perspective of situated rationalism, which can "provide an account of how individuals learn both the universal concepts for which they appear to be biologically prepared and the much greater variety of culturally specific knowledge and ways of acting that characterize mature people. The issue addressed here is how to understand the relations between the prepared structures and the cultural domains; it is assumed that there are cultural elaborations of conceptions initially founded on the biologically prepared structures." (p. 344) Learning can then be described as tuning of prepared structures.

The resulting learning environments can be described as 'constructivistic'. They are based on two assumptions: (1) individual mental constructive (rather than receptive) activity; (2) social embeddedness of learning and, thus, perspective on the acquisition of excellence as increasing participation in expert communities of practice. Instructional psychology has to consider both by giving the opportunity for constructive activity of learners and by preparing complex, authentic learning environments.

Constructive Activity of Learners

A fundamental assumption of all situated cognition theories is that the reality is constructed by a learner based upon his/her own perceptions, and that learners do so by actively interpreting perceptual experiences in terms of prior knowledge, current mental structures and existing beliefs. Instructional psychology has to investigate the nature of and possibilities for implementation of learning environments that encourage such generative processes.

Learning, from a constructivist perspective, does not occur by passively receiving information but by actively interpreting it. Effective learning thus depends not only on the quality of instruction and of the material presented, but also on the learner's intentions, meta-cognitive skills (e.g. self-monitoring), elaboration activities, and intrinsic motivation. Despite the subjective character of learning, the learning environment needs to be highly adaptive in order to foster the possibilites resulting from the idea of learning as active, self-regulating, and reflective process.

As an instructional strategy, situated cognition has been seen as a means for relating subject matter to the needs and concerns of learners (Stein, 1998). Learning as creating meaning from the real everyday activities leads to practical intelligence. By embedding subject matter in the ongoing experiences of the learners and by relating the learning environment to the real world, knowledge is acquired in an applicable way, so that it does not remain inert and can be transferred outside the learning environment.

From the situated-learning perspective, four basic assumptions about activities during learning can be derived (Wilson, 1993): (1) learning is grounded in the actions of everyday situations; (2) knowledge is acquired situationally; (3) learning is the result of a social process encompassing ways of thinking, perceiving, problem solving, and interacting in addition to declarative and procedural knowledge; (4) learning is not separated from the world of action but exists in robust, complex, social environments made up of actors, actions, and situations. Conclusions about instructional practices can be drawn from these assumptions: theories from a situated perspective on learning propose an increased use of cooperative and participative teaching methods in order to create possibilities to negotiate knowledge through the interactions of the learner with other learners, with teachers and/or experts, and with the environment, its tools and materials.

Obviously the 'situation' plays a central role in approaches of 'situated' learning. The notion of learning as active, constructive process instead of carriage of invariable mental entities lays stress upon the situation in which learning occurs. It is important to note that 'situation' does not only characterize material aspects, but also includes the social environment; participation in social processes plays a central role in situated learning approaches.

Social Contextualization of Learning

Participation denotes the process by which learners are working together and with experts in a social organization in order to solve problems related to everyday life circumstances (Lave, 1988; Brown, Collins & Duguid, 1989). Learning becomes a social process dependent upon interactions with others placed within a social context that should—for learning to be successful—resemble as closely as possible the practice environment.

Lave and Wenger (1991) proposed a theoretical framework in which learning is conceived as situated activity which has its central defining characteristic in a process called *legitimate peripheral participation* by which learners or newcomers become *enculturated* into a *community of practice*. Both concepts, legitimate peripheral participation and community of practice, though not precisely defined by Lave's work, refer to the notion of using out-of-school learning processes as models for school learning.

The essential parts of the arrangements in a community of practice that influence learning are the relations between newcomers and old-timers, the relations among newcomers, the typical activities in the community, and the artifacts of the domain. The process by which a newcomer becomes a 'full participant' or an 'expert' is fundamentally social; newcomers as apprentices learn from the old-timers and also from the other newcomers. Even learning with physical or symbolic tools (e.g. books) is fundamentally social, because the tools as artifacts carry a substantial proportion of content knowledge that has historically grown in the respective communities of practice. Finally, learning is viewed as enculturation, not only as acquisition of knowledge. Thus, learning concerns many social aspects such as ways of speaking, belief systems, social customs, etc.

Acquiring excellence is thus not confined to the acquisition of declarative knowledge or skills but a social process of enculturation. It means to become a full participant in a community of practice that can cope with the problems typical for the respective domain in a flexible manner.

Rogoff's (1990) theoretical approach shares some similarity with that of Lave, but puts more emphasis on cognitive development in childhood. Rogoff takes up the Vygotskian notion of the *zone of proximal development* and uses the term *guided participation* to describe the process by which children learn in the course of interaction with expert partners (e.g. parents or teachers). Rogoff (1990) underlines the importance of expert modelling, active observation, guidance by more able partners, and joint participation for the development of expertise.

Both approaches ascribe a novel role to learners who are regarded as apprentices. The learner is, right from the beginning, an active participant in authentic practices; learning and acquiring expertise are essentially viewed as processes of enculturation (Gruber, Law, Mandl & Renkl, 1995).

The conceptions of learning described above have serious consequences for the design of learning environments. The call for maximal similarity between a learning situation and application situation, which is based on the argument that knowledge in principle is context-bound, dramatically changes the nature of learning environments as well as the nature of teaching and learning processes. The consequences are as follows: (1) By using complex initial problems learners get interested, they get a notion of the relevance of the to-be-learned. Active, constructive learning processes are fostered by presentation of motivating problems in which learners perceive relevance for daily life. (2) Authenticity and situativity of learning environment enable learners to learning in near-to-application situations, and to make experiences in complex episodes of learning. (3) Using multiple perspectives on the same subject matter helps to avoid oversimplifications and enhances transferability of the to-be-learned. The learners' skill is enhanced to flexibly transfer knowledge onto a variety of problem situations. Experiencing common characteristics of episodes helps to induce general knowledge structures. (4) The methods of articulation and reflection help learners to transform concrete experience into abstract knowledge including the learner's subjective perspective and experiences.

These principles of situated learning have been realized in a couple of instructional models for complex learning; most convincingly, this has been done in the models of cognitive apprenticeship and of cognitive flexibility.

Complex Learning Through Cognitive Apprenticeship

As already described, the authors from the situated-cognition camp favor apprenticeship arrangements for learning; the apprenticeship metaphor is taken from craft domains, such as tailors or midwives. Collins, Brown and Newman (1989) have proposed an instructional approach for more cognitive domains. In the Cognitive Apprenticeship model, it is intended to introduce the learner into an expert culture by authentic activities and social interaction, just as in craft apprenticeship.

The core of the Cognitive Apprenticeship model is a special instructional sequence and the employment of authentic learning tasks; cognitive processes are externalized by experts within authentic application situations. Learning then leads the student to acquire knowledge that is applicable to a certain class of situations; further learning takes place in sequenced learning environments of increasing complexity and diversity. At all these learning stages of the apprenticeship approach, the expert is assigned an important role as a *model* and as a *coach* providing *scaffolding*. However, the learner has to increasingly take over an active role, as the expert is gradually *fading out*. In this course, *articulation* and *reflection* are promoted by the expert, i.e. the normally internal mental problem solving processes are externalized. Thus, one's own strategies can be compared with strategies of experts and are then open to feedback. In addition, one's own cognitive strategies should be compared with those of other learners. As a result of this instructional sequence, the learner increasingly works on his own (*exploration*) and may take over the role initially assumed by the expert. This sequence resembles the development from legitimate peripheral participation to full participation described by Lave and Wenger (1991).

Ideally, the following process takes place: the learner starts out from the very beginning with authentic tasks, as far as he or she can accomplish with his or her present knowledge state, which should be corrected and enlarged in the further learning process. The teacher or expert supports the learner by modelling, coaching, and scaffolding. The expert's scaffolding helps the student to successfully cope with problems that are somewhat beyond the scope of the learner if he or she works alone. The social-communicative exchange between expert and learner as well as among different learners is ascribed a central role. By this way, the cognitive concepts and processes are articulated and thereby explicated. Thus, they can be an object of reflection which fosters the induction of more general and abstract concepts or schemata. In addition, the communicative exchange provides the opportunity for the learner to get to know the concepts, strategies, and beliefs of the expert and also of other learners that are in some respect more advanced. From this point of view, learning is a process of enculturation into an expert community; with growing skills the learner can work more and more independently; the support by the expert is gradually withdrawn (fading). The setting, however, keeps its cooperative character; the fading of the support formerly provided by the expert ends up with the fostering of self-guided exploration. This means that the learner attacks novel problems and works primarily on his or her own.

A critical point of all instructional models that focus on the applicability of the to-be-learned is how to make the acquired knowledge not remain bound to the very context of acquisition. In the Cognitive Apprenticeship approach, the model should not only show how to solve problems, but also explicate the rationale behind his strategies. Thus, the concrete model behavior is connected with more general principles of the respective domain. Furthermore, students should articulate and reflect upon their problem solving strategies and compare them with others; this means should also 'free' the acquired knowledge from the very context of learning.

Complex Learning by Acquiring Cognitive Flexibility

To make knowledge applicable outside the learning situation requires the acquisition of knowledge that can be applied in many different situations. One instructional means to reach this goal is to confront the learner with a variety of situations in which the respective knowledge occurs.

Spiro and his colleagues (e.g. Spiro, Feltovich, Jacobson & Coulson, 1991) propose to employ *multiple perspectives* to make knowledge more transferable. A learner should deal with a concept at different times, in different contexts, with different purposes, and in different roles (e.g. as tutee and as tutor); thus, oversimplification and too narrow ties to a specific context are avoided.

Cognitive flexibility theory stresses the importance of providing multiple perspectives in which the knowledge to be acquired is embedded (Spiro et al., 1991; Spiro, Vispoel, Schmitz, Samarapungavan & Boerger, 1987). Cognitive flexibility theory mainly deals with advanced knowledge acquisition in ill-structured domains (e.g. diagnosis of heart diseases, literary interpretation). These domains can be described by two basic characteristics, complexity of concepts and cases, and irregularity of cases with large variability of relevant features across different cases. Instruction following the theory of cognitive flexibility aims to induce multiple and, as a consequence, flexible representations of the knowledge which can be applied for problem solving in a great many contexts. An instructional means to induce flexible multiple representations is to elucidate the same concept at different times, in different contexts, with different problem-solving goals, and from different perspectives. Only this allows the learner to create a rich collection of aspects of the same concept, which helps him or her to apply the knowledge in many different situations. Furthermore, this kind of instruction renders it possible to identify multiple relations to other concepts as well as common misconceptions and oversimplifications. Transferability of knowledge increases through multiple perspectives on the problem rather than through abstract context-free learning.

Concluding Remarks

To sum up: "Instructional psychology and the gifted" has gone beyond its own scope. Its aim of fostering the growth of excellence and high-level performance needs research on specific instructional efforts for high-ability people, but adequate fostering needs knowledge about the way in which these people process information, in which they acquire expertise, in which they make use of the affordances and constraints of the environment, and in which they are getting members of communities of practice. Research, thus, cannot only deal with identification and fostering of intellectual abilities, but has to investigate the interaction between dispositional abilities and practice as well as the cognitive structures of expert knowledge and the social processes which help to integrate individuals in real-life application situations. In this chapter, we attempted to report evidence in favour of the argumentation, that the traditional research lines dealing with high ability on the one side, and with expertise on the other, have to be combined. Extending central concepts (like intelligence) is a necessary pre-condition for this. Instructional approaches using the concept of situated learning (in Resnick's, 1996, words: approaches that take the position of 'situated rationalism') seem to offer good starting points for such a kind of research.

References

Ackerman, P. L. (1986). Individual differences in information processing: An investigation of intellectual abilities and task performance during practice. *Intelligence*, **10**, 101–139.

Ackerman, P. L. (1987). Individual differences in skill learning: An integration of psychometric and information processing perspectives. *Psychological Bulletin*, **102**, 3–27.

Ackerman, P. L. (1990). A correlational analysis of skill specificity: learning, abilities, and individual differences. *Journal of Experimental Psychology: Learning Memory, and Cognition*, **16**, 883–901.

Ackerman, P. L. (1992). Predicting individual differences in complex skill acquisition: dynamics of ability determinants. *Journal of Applied Psychology*, **77**, 598–614.

Ackerman, P. L. & Rolfhus, E. L. (1999). The locus of adult intelligence: Knowledge, abilities, and non-ability traits. *Psychology and Aging*, **14**, 314–330.

Anderson, J. R. (1982). Acquisition of cognitive skill. *Psychological Review*, **89**, 369–406.

Arkes, H. R. & Freedman, M. R. (1984). A demonstration of the costs and benefits of expertise. *Memory & Cognition*, **12**, 84–89.

Babaeva, J. D. (1999). A dynamic approach to giftedness: theory and practice. *High Ability Studies*, **10**, 51–68.

Benbow, C. P. (1986). SMPY's model for teaching mathematically precocious students. In: J. S. Renzulli (Ed.), *Systems and Models for Developing Programs for the Gifted and Talented* (pp. 1–26). Mansfield: Creative Learning.

Boshuizen, H. P. A. & Schmidt, H. G. (1992). On the role of biomedical knowledge in clinical reasoning by experts, intermediates and novices. *Cognitive Science*, **16**, 153–184.

Bransford, J. D., Goldman, S. R. & Vye, N. J. (1991). Making a difference in people's ability to think: reflections on a decade of work and some hopes for the future. In: R. J. Sternberg & L. Okagaki (Eds.), *Influences on Children* (pp. 147–180). Hillsdale: Erlbaum.

Brown, J. S., Collins, A. & Duguid, P. (1989). Situated cognition and the culture of learning. *Educational Researcher*, **18** (1), 32–41.

Ceci, S. J. & Ruiz, A. (1992). The role of general ability in cognitive complexity: a case study of expertise. In: R. R.

Hoffman (Ed.), *The Psychology of Expertise. Cognitive Research and Empirical AI* (pp. 218–230). New York: Springer.

Chase, W. G. & Simon, H. A. (1973). The mind's eye in chess. In: W. G. Chase (Ed.), *Visual Information Processing* (pp. 215–281). New York: Academic Press.

Chi, M. T. H., Glaser, R. & Farr, M. J. (Eds.). (1988). *The Nature of Expertise*. Hillsdale: Erlbaum.

Chyriwsky, M. & Kennard, R. (1997). Attitudes to able children: a survey of mathematics teachers in English secondary schools. *High Ability Studies*, **8**, 47–59.

Collins, A., Brown, J. S. & Newman, S. E. (1989). Cognitive apprenticeship: teaching the craft of reading, writing and mathematics. In: L. B. Resnick (Ed.), *Knowing, Learning and Instruction: Essays in Honour of Robert Glaser* (pp. 453–494). Hillsdale: Erlbaum.

Dai, D. Y., Moon, S. M. & Feldhusen, J. F. (1998). Achievement motivation and gifted students: a social cognitive perspective. *Educational Psychologist*, **33**, 45–63.

De Groot, A. D. (1965). *Thought and choice and chess*. The Hague: Mouton.

De Groot, A. D. & Gobet, F. (1996). *Perception and memory in chess: studies in the heuristics of the professional eye*. Assen: Van Gorcum.

De Jong, T. & Ferguson-Hessler, M. G. M. (1996). Types and qualities of knowledge. *Educational Psychologist*, **31**, 105–113.

Devlin, B., Fienberg, S. E., Resnick, D. P. & Roeder, K. (Eds.). (1997). *Intelligence, genes, and success: scientists respond to 'The bell curve'*. New York: Springer.

Ericsson, K. A. (1985). Memory skill. *Canadian Journal of Psychology*, **39**, 188–231.

Ericsson, K. A. (Ed.). (1996). *The road to excellence. The acquisition of expert performance in the arts and sciences, sports and games*. Mahwah: Erlbaum.

Ericsson, K. A. (1998). The scientific study of expert levels of performance: general implications for optimal learning and creativity. *High Ability Studies*, **9**, 75–100.

Ericsson, K. A. & Charness, N. (1994). Expert performance: its structure and acquisition. *American Psychologist*, **49**, 725–747.

Ericsson, K. A. & Crutcher, R. J. (1990). The nature of exceptional performance. In: P. B. Baltes, D. L. Featherman & R. M. Lerner (Eds.), *Life-Span Development and Behavior* (Vol. 10, pp. 187–217). Hillsdale: Erlbaum.

Ericsson, K. A., Krampe, R. T. & Tesch-Römer, C. (1993). The role of deliberate practice in the acquisition of expert performance. *Psychological Review*, **100**, 363–406.

Ericsson, K. A. & Smith, J. (Eds.). (1991). *Toward a general theory of expertise: prospects and limits*. Cambridge: Cambridge University Press.

Feger, B. & Prado, T. M. (1998). *Hochbegabung. Die normalste Sache der Welt*. Darmstadt: Primus.

Feldhusen, J. F. & Kolloff, M. B. (1986). The Purdue three-stage enrichment model of gifted education at the elementary level. In: J. S. Renzulli (Ed.), *Systems and Models for Developing Programs for the Gifted and Talented* (pp. 126–152). Mansfield: Creative Learning.

Fels, C. (1999). *Identifizierung und Förderung Hochbegabter in den Schulen der Bundesrepublik Deutschland*. Bern: Haupt.

Ford, K. M. & Adams-Webber, J. R. (1992). Knowledge acquisition and constructivist epistemology. In: R. R.

Hoffman (Ed.), *The Psychology of Expertise. Cognitive Research and Empirical AI* (pp. 121–136). New York: Springer.

Gallagher, J. J. & Courtright, R. D. (1986). The educational definition of giftedness and its policy implications. In: R. J. Sternberg & J. E. Davidson (Eds.), *Conceptions of Giftedness* (pp. 93–111). Cambridge: Cambridge University Press.

George, D. R. (1993). Instructional strategies and models for gifted education. In: K. A. Heller, F. J. Mönks & H. A. Passow (Eds.), *International Handbook of Research and Development of Giftedness and Talent* (pp. 411–425). Oxford: Pergamon.

Glaser, R. (1989). Expertise and learning: how do we think about instructional processes now that we have discovered knowledge structures? In: D. Klahr & K. Kotovsky (Eds.), *Complex Information Processing: The Impact of Herbert A. Simon* (pp. 269–282). Hillsdale: Erlbaum.

Gobet, F. & Simon, H. A. (1996). Templates in chess memory: a mechanism for recalling several boards. *Cognitive Psychology*, **31**, 1–40.

Goleman, D. (1995). *Emotional intelligence: why it can matter more than IQ*. New York: Bantam Books.

Goleman, D. (1998). *Working with emotional intelligence*. New York: Bantam Books.

Gruber, H. (1999). *Erfahrung als Grundlage kompetenten Handelns*. Bern: Huber.

Gruber, H., Law, L.-C., Mandl, H. & Renkl, A. (1995). Situated learning and transfer. In: P. Reimann & H. Spada (Eds.), *Learning in Humans and Machines: Towards an Interdisciplinary Learning Science* (pp. 168–188). Oxford: Pergamon.

Gruber, H. & Mandl, H. (1992). Begabung und Expertise. In: E. A. Hany & H. Nickel (Eds.), *Begabung und Hochbegabung: Theoretische Konzepte—Empirische Befunde—Praktische Konsequenzen* (pp. 59–73). Bern: Huber.

Gruber, H., Renkl, A. & Schneider, W. (1994). Expertise und Gedächtnisentwicklung. Längsschnittliche Befunde aus der Domäne Schach. *Zeitschrift für Entwicklungspsychologie und Pädagogische Psychologie*, **26**, 53–70.

Gruber, H. & Ziegler, A. (Eds.). (1996). *Expertiseforschung. Theoretische und methodische Grundlagen*. Opladen: Westdeutscher Verlag.

Heller, K. A. (1999a). Hochbegabtenförderung: Individuelle und soziale Bedingungsfaktoren akademischer Leistungsexzellenz im Jugend- und frühen Erwachsenenalter. In: W. Hacker & M. Rinck (Eds.), *Zukunft gestalten* (pp. 288–302). Lengerich: Pabst.

Heller, K. A. (1999b). Individual (learning and motivational) needs vs. instructional conditions of gifted education. *High Ability Studies*, **10**, 9–21.

Heller, K. A. & Hany, E. A. (1996). Psychologische Modelle der Hochbegabtenförderung. In: F. E. Weinert (Ed.), *Psychologie des Lernens und der Instruktion. Enzyklopädie der Psychologie, D/I/2* (pp. 477–513). Göttingen: Hogrefe.

Heller, K. A., Mönks, F. J. & Passow, H. A. (Eds.). (1993). *International handbook of research and development of giftedness and talent*. Oxford: Pergamon.

Herrnstein, R. J. & Murray, C. (1994). *The bell curve: intelligence and class structure in American life*. New York: Free Press.

Holling, H. & Kanning, U. P. (unter Mitarbeit von A. J. Wittmann & F. Preckel). (1999). *Hochbegabung. For-*

schungsergebnisse und Fördermöglichkeiten. Göttingen: Hogrefe.

Howe, M. J. A., Davidson, J. W. & Sloboda, J. A. (1998). Innate talents: reality or myth? *Behavioral and Brain Sciences*, **21**, 399–442.

Jensen, A. R. (1998). *The g factor.* New York: Praeger.

Kail, R. & Salthouse, T. A. (1994). Processing speed as a mental capacity. *Acta Psychologica*, **86**, 199–225.

Kessels, J. P. A. M. & Korthagen, A. J. (1996). The relationship between theory and practice: back to the classics. *Educational Researcher*, **25**, 17–22.

Kliegl, R. & Mayr, U. (1997). Kognitive Leistung und Lernpotential im höheren Erwachsenenalter. In: F. E. Weinert & H. Mandl (Eds.), *Psychologie der Erwachsenenbildung. Enzyklopädie der Psychologie, D/I/4* (pp. 87–114). Göttingen: Hogrefe.

Kolodner, J. L. (1983). Towards an understanding of the role of experience in the evolution from novice to expert. *International Journal of Man-Machine Studies*, **19**, 497–518.

Kolodner, J. L. (1997). Educational implications of analogy: a view from case-based reasoning. *American Psychologist*, **52**, 57–66.

Krems, J. (1996). Expertise und Flexibilität. In: H. Gruber & A. Ziegler (Eds.), *Expertiseforschung: Theoretische und Methodische Grundlagen* (pp. 80–91). Opladen: Westdeutscher Verlag.

Kyllonen, P. C. & Christal, R. E. (1990). Reasoning ability is (little more than) working-memory capacity?! *Intelligence*, **14**, 389–433.

Lave, J. (1988). *Cognition in practice: mind, mathematics, and culture in everyday life.* Cambridge: Cambridge University Press.

Lave, J. & Wenger, E. (1991). *Situated learning: legitimate peripheral participation.* Cambridge: Cambridge University Press.

Law, L.-C. (1995). *Constructivist instructional theories and acquisition on expertise* (Research report No. 48). München: Ludwig-Maximilians-Universität, Lehrstuhl für Empirische Pädagogik und Pädagogische Psychologie.

Mack, W. (1996). Expertise und Intelligenz. In: H. Gruber & A. Ziegler (Eds.), *Expertiseforschung. Theoretische und methodische Grundlagen* (pp. 92–114). Opladen: Westdeutscher Verlag.

Mandl, H., Gruber, H. & Renkl, A. (1993). Kontextualisierung von Expertise. In: H. Mandl, M. Dreher & H.-J. Kornadt (Eds.), *Entwicklung und Denken im kulturellen Kontext* (pp. 203–227). Göttingen: Hogrefe.

Martin, G. A. & Double, J. M. (1998). Developing higher education teaching skills through peer observation and collaborative reflection. *Innovations in Education and Training International*, **35**, 161–170.

Mönks, F. J. (1992). Ein interaktionales Modell der Hochbegabung. In: E. A. Hany & H. Nickel (Eds.), *Begabung und Hochbegabung: Theoretische Konzepte—empirische Befunde—praktische Konsequenzen* (pp. 17–22). Bern: Huber.

Mönks, F. J. (1999). Begabte Schüler erkennen und fördern. In: C. Perleth & A. Ziegler (Eds.), *Pädagogische Psychologie. Grundlagen und Anwendungsfelder* (pp. 94–102). Bern: Huber.

Montgomery, D. (1996). Differentiation of the curriculum for the highly able. *High Ability Studies*, **7**, 25–37.

Montgomery, D. (1998). Gifted education: Education of the highly able. In: D. Shorrocks-Taylor et al. (Eds.), *Directions in Educational Psychology* (pp. 244–264). London: Whurr.

Nake, F. (1998). Schwierigkeiten beim semiotischen Blick auf die Informationsgesellschaft. In: H. Zimmermann (Ed.), *Knowledge Management und Kommunikationssysteme* (pp. 455–468). Konstanz: Universitäts-Verlag.

Neisser, U., Boodoo, G., Bouchard, T. J., Boykin, A. W., Brody, N., Ceci S. J., Halpern, D. F., Loehlin, J. C., Perloff, R., Sternberg, R. J. & Urbina, S. (1996). Intelligence: knowns and unknowns. *American Psychologist*, **51**, 77–101.

Pekrun, R. & Schiefele, U. (1996). Emotions- und motivationspsychologische Bedingungen der Lernleistung. In: F. E. Weinert (Ed.), *Psychologie des Lernens und der Instruktion. Enzyklopädie der Psychologie, D/I/2* (pp. 153–180). Göttingen: Hogrefe.

Perleth, C. (1997). *Zur Rolle von Begabung und Erfahrung bei der Leistungsgenese. Ein Brückenschlag zwischen Begabungs- und Expertiseforschung.* Unveröff. Habilitationsschrift, Ludwig-Maximilians-Universität München.

Prerau, D. S., Adler, M. R. & Gunderson, A. S. (1992). Eliciting and using experiential knowledge and general expertise. In: R. R. Hoffman (Ed.), *The Psychology of Expertise. Cognitive Research and Empirical AI* (pp. 137–148). New York: Springer.

Renkl, A., Mandl, H. & Gruber, H. (1996). Inert knowledge: analyses and remedies. *Educational Psychologist*, **31**, 115–121.

Renzulli, J. S. (1986). The three-ring conception of giftedness: a developmental model for creative productivity. In: R. J. Sternberg & J. E. Davidson (Eds.), *Conceptions of Giftedness* (pp. 53–92). Cambridge: Cambridge University Press.

Renzulli, J. S. & Reis, S. M. (1986). The enrichment triad/revolving door model. In: J. S. Renzulli (Ed.), *Systems and Models for Developing Programs for the Gifted and Talented* (pp. 216–266). Mansfield: Creative Learning.

Resnick, L. B. (1996). Situated learning. In: E. De Corte & F. E. Weinert (Eds.), *International Encyclopedia of Developmental and Instructional Psychology* (pp. 341–347). Oxford: Elsevier.

Rogoff, B. (1990). *Apprenticeship in thinking: cognitive development in social context.* New York: Oxford University Press.

Salovey, P. & Mayer, J. (1997). *Emotional development and emotional intelligence.* New York: Basic Books.

Schneider, W., Gruber, H., Gold, A. & Opwis, K. (1993). Chess expertise and memory for chess positions in children and adults. *Journal of Experimental Child Psychology*, **56**, 328–349.

Schweizer, K. (1998). Complexity of information processing and the speed-ability relationship. *The Journal of General Psychology*, **125**, 89–102.

Simonton, D. K. (1999). Talent and its development: an emergenic and epigenetic model. *Psychological Review*, **106**, 435–457.

Spiro, R. J., Feltovich, P. J., Jacobson, M. J., & Coulson, R. L. (1991). Cognitive flexibility, constructivism, and hypertext: random access instruction for advanced knowledge acquisition in ill-structured domains. *Educational Technology*, **31** (5), 24–33.

Spiro, R. J., Vispoel, W. P., Schmitz, J. G., Samarapungavan, A. & Boerger, A. E. (1987). Knowledge acquisition for application. In: B. K. Britton & S. M. Glynn (Eds.), *Executive Control Processes in Reading* (pp. 177–199). Hillsdale: Erlbaum.

Stein, D. (1998). *Situated learning in adult education.* Columbus: ERIC Clearinghouse on Adult, Career, & Vocational Education.

Sternberg, R. J. (1985). *Beyond IQ: a triarchic theory of human intelligence.* Cambridge: Cambridge University Press.

Sternberg, R. J. (1990a). *Metaphors of mind. Conceptions of the nature of intelligence.* Cambridge: Cambridge University Press.

Sternberg, R. J. (1990b). Prototypes of competence and incompetence. In: R. J. Sternberg & J. Kolligian (Eds.), *Competence Considered* (pp. 117–145). New Haven: Yale University Press.

Sternberg, R. J. (1996). Myths, countermyths, and truths about intelligence. *Educational Researcher, 25* (2), 11–16.

Sternberg, R. J. (1997). The concept of intelligence and its role in lifelong learning and success. *American Psychologist, 52*, 1030–1037.

Sternberg, R. J. (1998). Principles of teaching for successful intelligence. *Educational Psychologist, 33*, 65–72.

Sternberg, R. J. & Caruso, D. (1985). Practical modes of knowing. In: E. Eisner (Ed.), *Learning the Ways of Knowing* (pp. 133–158). Chicago, IL: Chicago University Press.

Sternberg, R. J., & Davidson, J. E. (Eds.). (1986). *Conceptions of giftedness.* Cambridge: Cambridge University Press.

Sternberg, R. J. & Wagner, R. K. (1989). Individual differences in practical knowledge and its acquisition. In: P. L. Ackerman, R. J. Sternberg & R. Glaser (Eds.), *Learning and Individual Differences: Advances in Theory and Research* (pp. 255–278). New York: Freeman.

Sternberg, R. J. & Wagner, R. K. (1993). The g-ocentric view of intelligence and job performance is wrong. *Current Directions in Psychological Science, 2* (1), 1–4.

Tannenbaum, A. J. (1986). Giftedness: a psychosocial approach. In: R. J. Sternberg & J. E. Davidson (Eds.), *Conceptions of giftedness* (pp. 21–52). Cambridge: Cambridge University Press.

Teo, C. T. & Quah, M. L. (1999). The knowledge, volition and action programme in Singapore: the effects of an experimental intervention programme on high ability achievement. *High Ability Studies, 10*, 23–35.

Van Tassel-Baska, J. (Ed.). (1998). *Excellence in educating gifted and talented learners* (3rd ed.). Denver: Love.

Voss, J. F. (1990). Das Lösen schlecht strukturierter Probleme—ein Überblick. *Unterrichtswissenschaft, 18*, 313–337.

Voss, J. F., Fincher-Kiefer, R. H., Green, T. R. & Post, T. A. (1986). Individual differences in performance: the contrastive approach to knowledge. In: R. J. Sternberg (Ed.), *Advances in the Psychology of Human Intelligence* (Vol. 3, pp. 297–334). Hillsdale: Erlbaum.

Waldmann, M. R. (1996). Kognitionspsychologische Theorien von Begabung und Expertise. In: F. E. Weinert (Ed.), *Psychologie des Lernens und der Instruktion. Enzyklopädie der Psychologie, D/I/2* (pp. 445–476). Göttingen: Hogrefe.

Waldmann, M. R. & Weinert, F. E. (1990). *Intelligenz und Denken. Perspektiven der Hochbegabungsforschung.* Göttingen: Hogrefe.

Weinert, F. E. & Schrader, F.-W. (1997). Lernen lernen als psychologisches Problem. In: F. E. Weinert & H. Mandl (Eds.), *Psychologie der Erwachsenenbildung. Enzyklopädie der Psychologie, D/I/4* (pp. 295–335). Göttingen: Hogrefe.

Wilson, A. (1993). The promise of situated cognition. In: S. B. Merriam (Ed.), *An Update on Adult Learning Theory* (pp. 71–79). San Francisco: Jossey-Bass.

Winner, E. (1996). The rage to master: the decisive role of talent in the visual arts. In: K. A. Ericsson (Ed.), *The Road to Excellence. The Acquisition of Expert Performance in the Arts and Sciences, Sports and Games* (pp. 271–301). Mahwah: Erlbaum.

The Education and Development of Verbally Talented Students

Paula Olszewski-Kubilius[1] and Samuel P. Whalen[2]

[1]*Center for Talent Development, Northwestern University, Evanston, IL, USA*
[2]*Chapin Hall Center for Children at the University of Chicago, Chicago, IL, USA*

Introduction

Among the domains of human excellence there is none more fundamental than the capacity for language. Indeed, language and communication are so intrinsic to human experience that their absence may preclude fully human development. Past and recent studies indicate that 'wild' children deprived of early inter-active speech suffer linguistic, emotional, and social deficits that permanently limit their cognitive potential (Itard, 1801/1982; Frith, 1989). And while researchers differ over the degree to which language is 'hard-wired', much about language is clearly special, both as a cognitive capacity and a medium of socialization and cultural evolution.

Yet if language distinguishes humans as a species, it also divides us; language is among the most powerful factors defining membership within ethnic and national populations. While translation is among the highest arts, nuances in accent, inflection, grammar and idiom remain elusive to non-native speakers, and act as surface markers of sub-group membership. Even within monolingual populations, subgroups defined by age, class, occupation and geographical region actively cultivate specific vocabularies and speech patterns that reinforce group identity and in-group cohesion. To the extent that such linguistic subgroups map also to distinctions between social and economic class, facility with language further implies access to economic and social opportunity.

Given the intimate links between linguistic compe-tence, identity, and opportunity, it is not surprising that efforts to identify individual differences in verbal talent generate resistance and controversy. Disputants across a range of communities correctly perceive that the stakes involved in controlling how verbal ability is defined and measured are high (Winch, 1990). For the community devoted to the development of verbal talent, the dual challenge has been to establish the validity of individual differences in verbal ability, while convincing educators and policy makers of their stake in the future of verbal excellence. It is a challenge complicated both by the accelerated pace of recent research into language, and by the acrid climate of controversy surrounding the contemporary 'language wars'.

This chapter first surveys five major areas of controversy surrounding language development and literacy. These debates exercise considerable influence over how linguistic excellence is understood, as well as who is understood to possess it, and how the commu-nity of practitioners most concerned with verbal talent defines itself. We then review major conceptions of verbal and linguistic ability, and go on to summarize the range of proposals to identify and educate excep-tional verbal competence. Finally we suggest some core lessons learned in recent research into the education of verbal excellence, and propose some priorities for research into verbal excellence in the next decade.

Critical Debates About Language and Literacy

We want to emphasize here debates that really impact on how the community of researchers and practitioners into verbal talent development are able to work:

First, there are issues related to the nature of verbal ability and individual differences, including:

> Is language acquistion innate?
> Is language critical to rationality?
> Is language a separate intelligence?
> Is language ability heritable?
> Is verbal ability independent of specific language or linguistic experience?

Second, issues of what should be taught?

> Bilingual education and who will be included among the verbally able?
> The cultural corpus: what books are appropriate to age groups?

What is the future of the written word? Does cyberspace heighten or reduce the importance of the traditional literacies?

Third, issues of how literacies ought to be taught:

Questions about ability grouping and early reading Technique: whole language vs. phonics

Survey any community at the dawn of the 21st century and you are likely to uncover at least one contentious issue related to language and literacy. Ubiquitous to these conflicts is an historical tension between literacy and eliticism. Throughout most of history societies have cultivated elites, both religious and administrative, to exploit the powerful tools of literacy and restrict the dissemination of ideas more broadly through the society. That is, policies regarding literacy have been closely tied to political and religious philosophies and considerations, affecting both access to and applications of literacy. In the West, Medieval European theocracies tended to restrict access. Reformation theocracies challenged these restrictions, but regulated what could be expressed about religious and political matters. It is only more recently that notions such as universal literacy have been embraced. Yet modern history offers many variations on who has access to literacy, and how literacy is employed—either to reinforce old ideas, or to cultivate the development of new ideas.

In many respects what distinguishes modern democracies is the unprecedented scope they grant both in terms of access and useage of literacy, and the consistency of debate about issues of literacy. From the Modern Language Association to the local school board to the Amazonian tribe fighting to preserve its mother tongue, communities are asked to situate their specific concerns within a broader context of unprecedented, dynamic linguistic change. Discourse within the community concerned with verbal talent is influenced by a range of contemporary debates and ideas, from questions about the origins and nature of language, to questions about whether certain forms of expression and pedagogy ought to occupy a privileged position within Western culture. In this section we briefly survey five critical debates that form the broader context for thinking about the nature and nurture of verbal talent.

How much of language is nature or nurture?

In the arena of language acquisition strong differences of opinion remain about both the timing and weight of biological and social factors. These debates shape the general climate of opinion about the relative mutability of verbal ability, and the amenability of talent to environmental influence. The strongest assertion of linguistic innateness holds that linguistic ability emerges too early and too powerfully in human childhood to be explained by social influences. In

particular, purely inductive models of learning can not account for how young children surmise the syntactical and grammatical conventions in their mother tongues, with little guidance or exposure to examplars (Wexler & Culicover, 1980; Pinker, 1989). Denying the 'learnability' of language, Chomsky has hypothosized the existence of a universal grammar whereby children instinctively orient to the fundamental patterns of spoken language (Chomsky, 1986). Other linguistic researchers, while not arguing as exclusively for innate capacity, emphasize the early operation of adaptive constraints in shaping the attention of children to patterns and regularities in human speech (Bloom, 1990; Kelly, 1992; Gardner, 1993).

Drawing particularly on the theories of the Soviet psychologist Lev Vygotsky (Vygotsky, 1962), social interactionist researchers argue that it is a mistake to ignore the essentially social nature of early linguistic exchange. Both the vocal tone and facial expressions of the primary caregiver selectively orient infants to the particulars of their primary language, from the simple phonetic level to the elaboration of word meanings and expected styles and conventions of conversation (Nelson, 1989, 1991). Cross-cultural evidence, for example, indicates that significant parameters of speech acquisition (e.g. the ratio of verbs to nouns employed) correlate closely to the emphases of maternal speech—what Nelson (1989) calls 'motherese' (Choi & Gropnik, 1995). Further, the role of psychosocial processes becomes increasingly prominent as language development moves from primary acquisition to the elaboration of more sophisticated abilities and sensibilities (Feldman, 1980; Hoff-Ginsberg, 1990; Huttenlocher, Haight, Bryk, Seltzer & Lyons, 1991). Jerome Bruner has argued for the operation of a 'Language Acquisition Support System' working in tandem with maturational processes to catalyze language development toward advanced, culturally specific modes of expression (Bruner, 1983).

How heritable is linguistic ability?

Just as brain research has fueled the biological debates surrounding language acquisition, so the explosion in genetic research has spurred controversy about the heritability of verbal ability. First, serious disagreement remains over the importance and interpretation of ethnic and racial differences in intelligence, best illustrated by the furore caused by the publication of Herrnstein & Murray's *The Bell Curve* in 1994. Proponents of these differences focus less on explaining their origins than on validating their authenticity, primarily on grounds that IQ measures are methodologically sound and largely free of cultural bias. While noting that members of all groups can be found at all points of the bell curve, they insist that group differences in innate intelligence contribute to class differences and social problems, and should be acknowledged in shaping social policies (Herrnstein & Murray, 1994; Gottfredson, 1997).

The most general criticism of this stance points out that within-group differences are much more profound than between-group differences in predicting phenotypic outcomes, and that group differences are confounded with historical and socioeconomic factors (Cole & Cole, 1996; Sternberg, 1996). Other critics focus on the risks of cultural and educational bias posed by heavily verbal test formats (Miller-Jones, 1989). Claude Steele has argued that the conditions of standardized testing negatively impact the confidence and motivation of minority students, leading to cognitive interference and underperformance in evaluative situations (Steele, 1991).

A second sphere of controversy involves the significance of early environmental risks for long-term outcomes in adulthood. There is general agreement that environmental stressors such as poverty, family conflict and malnutrition all suppress the intellectual performance of children in the short run. Researchers differ sharply, however, over their long-term impacts. Critics of environmental effects on intelligence point to evidence that while the correlation of early risk to intellectual performance decreases with age, the concordance of intelligence to genetic affinity (e.g. identical twins vs. fraternal twins) actually increases (Fischbein, 1981). They interpret this to indicate that genetic factors tend to override environmental disadvantage over time. Proponents of environmental effects argue that cumulative advantages building within lives and across generations account for the relative intransigence of class and economic differences. Such conditions are likely to suppress or impair the expression of otherwise high genetic potential (Bronfenbrenner & Ceci, 1994).

Are some languages better than others?

Debates about language primacy or plurality are now encountered in almost all industrialized countries that have opened their borders and economies (Crawford, 1992). These debates, both interlinguistic and intralinguistic, are likely to become more prominent in the 21st century as traditionally monolingual nations are challenged to consider multicultural and multiethnic national identities. At both linguistic levels three issues are engaged. First, is one language 'better' than another in ways that warrant privileging its speech? Second, do the costs of elevating one language over others outweigh the benefits? Third, should the power of the state be brought to bear in enforcing (or undermining) language hegemony?

In the United States, for example, a vocal 'English Only' movement has emerged from regional roots to significantly influence language and education policy discussions. Organizations such as U.S. English and English First urge government action to enforce the use of standard American English in public places, and

particularly in schools. Rationales include the economic advantages posed by the globalization of English, the centrality of English to American political and cultural institutions, and the need to stem the tide of ethnic fragmentation through one common language (Arias & Casanova, 1993). Opponents of these arguments cite examples of successful multi-lingual societies and warn against the social and educational costs of monolingualism. These include the exclusion of large numbers of citizens from democratic participation, the isolation of America from the world community, and intellectual deprivation of children with no exposure to a second language (Resnick, 1991; Secada & Lightfoot, 1993).

The recent uproar over the decision of the Oakland (California) school board to acknowledge 'Ebonics' or Black English as the 'primary language' of local African American children highlights many of the characteristics of intralinguistic conflict (Ogbu, 1999). Proponents of Ebonics vary in their claims about the degree of distance between Black English and standard American forms. But they agree that urban African American children encounter significant difficulty in making the transition from their home dialect to the standard English required for success in school (Perry & Delpit, 1998; Baugh, 2000). In their view the Oakland decision aimed only to institutionalize existing curricula that approached African American children as a bilingual population at risk for school failure (Smitherman & Wayne State University, Center for Black Studies, 1981; Smitherman, 2000).

Opponents of the Oakland decision reflected the full range of opinion and anxiety about racial distinctions as public policy: many white-identified critics saw the Ebonics agenda as divisively political rather than educational. African American critics feared further stigmatization of Black students and warned that the debate would distract attention from systemic and cultural sources of Black underachievement (United States. Congress. Senate. Committee on Appropriations. Subcommittee on Departments of Labor Health and Human Services Education and Related Agencies., 1997). The emotionality of the debate suggests how language can become a lightning rod for more fundamental questions of social justice, racial identity, and educational opportunity, including the chance to develop excellence in the idiom of one's early and most formative experience.

Are some books better than others?

Another contentious debate between conservative and progressive voices in pluralistic societies involves the content and legitimacy of the literary canon. In a number of countries this debate pits the supposed 'Great Books' of the mainstream tradition against a range of challengers, old and new, embodying voices and opinions at odds with the cultural elite. On the one hand advocates for conservation of the canon argue for both the cultural and educational importance of a restricted range of classic texts and ideas. These texts represent a time-honored source of 'cultural literacy' for the young, a focus of cultural cohesion for civic society, and a standard of excellence toward which the most talented members of each generation may aim. While the strongest arguments for a restricted canon align closely with political conservatism (Hirsch, 1987), it should be noted that attention to the canon as an educational resource is common to a number of reform proposals (Adler, 1982; Sizer, 1984; Gardner, 1999).

In the United States the agenda of cultural literacy collides most directly with the emphases and commitments of multicultural education (Sleeter, 1995). Two proposals are common to most multicultural approaches. First, the challenges of tolerance facing a pluralistic society demand an education that acquaints future citizens with a diversity of cultures and ideas. Stringent adherence to one cultural canon thus incurs prohibitive intellectual as well as civic costs. Second, for literacy to thrive, children must be able to identify with the themes and characters in the literature they encounter. Failure to provide culturally accessible materials to immigrant and minority children in particular can cause disengagement from full verbal development, leading to inequitable educational outcomes. Many multiculturalists view early experiences of cultural incompatibility as the key to later shortfalls in literacy among historically disenfranchised minority children (Tharp, 1989; Ogbu, 1991).

Finally in many parts of the world state censorship continues to significantly restrict the range of ideas available to stimulate literary development (Lunsford, Moglen, Slevin & Modern Language Association of America, 1990). The overall impact of censorship on intellectual freedom has receded dramatically since the end of the Cold War, while in the West battles over overt censorship tend to focus on isolated texts (Edwards, 1998). Nonetheless to the extent that verbal excellence thrives in an atmosphere of intellectual plurality, censorship remains among the fundamental international obstacles to literary development.

Are some forms of instruction better than others?

Several controversies involve how best to instruct and cultivate literacy and verbal excellence. At the inter-linguistic level arguments about the aims and techniques of bilingual education continue to impact directly the quality of instruction available to students of minority language households. In the United States debate about the techniques of Spanish bilingual education reflects fundamental differences in understandings of American pluralism. The strongest multicultural advocates combine support for sustained Spanish language instruction with a broader agenda of language diversification. Opponents argue that most ESL students adapt to English quickly, and require only limited bilingual structure to transition effectively to full English immersion. Recently the latter argument has significantly altered the commitment to bilingual instruction in states such as California and Texas (Arias & Casanova, 1993; Brizuela & Garcia-Sellers, 1999).

The most protracted debate regarding the instruction of literacy involves the contrast between phonetic and whole language approaches to early reading and writing (Nelson & Clafee, 1998). These approaches rely on contrasting models of verbal development, models that often do not adequately encompass the needs of precocious verbal learners. In Chall's view of phonetic development, for example, novice readers lack the decoding skills necessary to bridge from symbol to sound; the process of reading alters qualitatively from the early labor of decoding to the mature pleasures of interpretive reading. Reading proficiency is accelerated to the extent that decoding strategies are taught and encouraged; failure to teach these skills particularly impacts the educational prospects of poor and minority children (Chall, Jacobs & Baldwin, 1990).

The 'whole language' view gives higher prominence to experiences of meaning, enjoyment and activity early in literacy development, with special emphasis on the needs of language minority learners (Goodman & Goodman, 1990). This reflects a view of language development that sees children as active language makers, and formal literacy as a further extension of early language play. Emphasis on the conventions of literacy (e.g. 'correct' spelling) is replaced with activities that integrate reading, writing and listening as media of meaningful learning. More recent whole language approaches embed phonetic instruction within highly interactive contexts of literacy development (Adams, 1990; Brown, Campione, Reeve, Ferrara & Palincsar, 1992). However, neither phonetic nor whole language curricula narrowly applied are well matched to the often autonomous and highly self-motivated learning styles of verbally precocious children (Winner, 1996).

To conclude, this review can only suggest the broad matrix of critical questions about language and literacy in which more specific debates about exceptional verbal talent are located. On the near horizon, for example, are profound questions about technology and the future of communication. Increasingly children are engaged in a diverse range of written and verbal activities in cyberspace that challenge the conventions of formal schooling and family socialization (Kerr, 1996). How the internet will shape the literacy of the next century and the media of verbal excellence remains to be seen, but it will undoubtedly contribute to shifts in our contemporary map of verbal potential. In the next sections we review how verbal ability currently is conceptualized, as well as the present state of the art in identifying and nurturing verbal talent.

Psychometric Definitions

Verbal ability or verbal talent can be and is often defined by performance on standardized tests, such as IQ and achievement tests. Most IQ tests or broad scale assessments of intellectual ability consist of subscales, including ones that measure constructs called 'verbal ability', 'verbal concepts', or 'verbal comprehension'. Some tests give a separate score for a composite of the verbal subtests; the WISC III for example, yields a verbal IQ score, a performance IQ score, and a full scale score. The Cognitive Abilities Test gives verbal, quantitative, and non-verbal composite scores. In educational practice, the verbal subtest scores are often used as a measure of verbal ability and high scores are considered indicative of exceptional verbal ability.

The types of items included within a verbal subtest or verbal subscore vary greatly. They are usually a mixture of items that directly assess information taught in school and items that require a child to draw on information acquired in school and/or informally in other settings. The arithmetic and vocabulary subtests of the verbal portion of the WISC are illustrative of the former type and the similarities and comprehension subtests of the WISC are representative of the latter type (Flanagan, Andrews & Genshaft, 1997). Although most intelligence tests do have a verbal subtest(s), the extent to which academic achievement-like items (the first type described above) are included varies greatly; for example, 50% of the items of the Test Composite of the Stanford Binet IV and the WISC Full Scale IQ are of this type compared to only 14% of the items of the Woodcock-Johnson Revised Tests of Cognitive Ability (Flanagan, Andrews & Genshaft, 1997).

Because of the mix of types of items on most verbal tests, there is some discussion within the literature as to whether they are measures of fluid or crystallized intelligence.

> However, because the knowledge that is necessary to respond correctly to verbal items on intelligence tests is dependent on accumulated knowledge and experience, that derives from living in mainstream American culture (or other highly industrialized societies), in addition to formal education, the verbal scales of intelligence tests may be interpreted more appropriately as measures of crystalized intelligence (Flanagan, Andrews & Genshaft, 1997, pp. 461).

The mix of items within a verbal intelligence scale affects the interpretation of its predictive validity and its usefulness for deciding upon educational interventions. Scores from different tests may predict children's future performances equally well but tests that are comprised of tasks of information processing may be more meaningful in terms of deciding upon educational interventions than scores on tests that are composed of achievement-like tasks. In practice, scores on verbally laden achievement-like tasks are more readily available to educators and therefore, more typically used for educational placement or selection into special programs.

Studies involving children with a wide range of abilities indicate that the relationship between verbal IQ and general IQ is moderate and varies with the age of the subject. For younger children (early elementary school aged children), scores on different subtests are more highly inter-correlated than they are for older children (pre-adolescence). A young child's relative standing in one ability, e.g. verbal, is highly predictive of his/her standing in others, e.g. quantitative. Not so for older children whose patterns become much more variable. For an older child, a profile showing the relative standing on each subtest is more informative and valuable than a composite IQ score. These trends with age may or may not be true of gifted children and there is some evidence to suggest that gifted children exhibit variance in subtest performance earlier than non-gifted children (Winner, 1996). There is also evidence that children who exhibit strength in the quantitative area have more varied cognitive profiles than children who exhibit strength in verbal areas (see later sections for a fuller discussion of this issue).

Verbal intelligence is maintained into old age and shows a sharp decline just before death (Hunt, 1978). Scores on verbal intelligence tests are not predictive of precocity in specific verbal skills such as early reading but precocity in oral language is an indicator of later high verbal intelligence in children (Jackson & Kearney, 1993; Jackson & Klein, 1997).

Achievement tests also include verbal and quantitative subtests. Typically, verbal subtests include tests of reading comprehension, vocabulary, decoding or word attack skills, spelling, and language mechanics.

Prior research indicated that girls scored higher on aspects of verbal ability, as assessed by standardized achievement tests, compared to boys, particularly in the elementary grades (Macoby & Jacklin, 1974). A more recent meta-analysis conducted by Hyde and Linn (1988) on the magnitude of gender differences in verbal ability concluded that most observed gender difference on verbal tests are so small as to be considered negligible. Specifically, gender differences on subtests such as vocabulary, reading, analogies, essay writing are small to negligible. The single area in which females substantially outperformed males was the quality of speech production, $d = +0.33$; However, the meaning of this finding is not clear. Males performance on the Scholastic Aptitude Test is slightly better than females, but the effect size is small ($d = -.11$).

Stanley, Benbow, Brody, Dauber and Lupkowski (1992) conducted an analysis of 86 nationally standardized tests for gender differences and found that males almost always outperformed females. They found small effect sizes favoring females for the Test of Standard Written English (TSWE) of the Scholastic Aptitude Test (SAT) and the American College Test–English Usage test (ACT–E), a slight advantage for males on the SAT–Verbal and PSAT–Verbal (females had historically outscored males on the SAT–V until 1972.), no differences between males and females on the verbal portions of the Graduate Record Exam (GRE) or the Law School Admissions Test (LSAT), and a small effect size (0.19) favoring females on the verbal subtest of the Graduate Management Admissions Test (GMAT).

Stanley et al. found small (0.08 to 0.09) effect sizes favoring females for College Board Achievement Tests in French and English Composition but moderate effect sizes favoring males for tests in Biology, American History, and European History, which presumably rely on strong verbal skills such as vocabulary and reading comprehension. On Advanced Placement (AP) exams, there were small effect sizes favoring females on German Language and French Literature and small to moderate effect sizes favoring males for subjects using verbal skills such as Biology, American History, and European History.

Stanley and his associates note that while most researchers believe that gender differences on standardized tests aren't large and are getting smaller, even small differences can have a significant impact, particularly on whether females will qualify for high status programs of study. They report the largest effect favoring females for the spelling subtest of the Differential Aptitude Test (DAT). Differences also favored females on the language usage and clerical speed and accuracy subtests of the DAT for students in grade 8–12. Lohman (1994) concurs that females' advantage over males is greatest for spelling tests, intermediate for tests of grammar and style, and non-existent on general measures of verbal comprehension.

Since the early 1980s, the SAT and ACT have been used to identify mathematical and verbal talent among 7th and 8th graders who are already scoring well on standardized in-grade achievement tests. Among the middle school students who take either the ACT or SAT as part of a talent search program, mean differences favor females for the ACT English and Reading but are small and probably of negligible effect size (Center for Talent Development, 1998).

What is not clear is the meaning of high scores on verbal subtests of IQ tests or standardized achievement tests. IQ and achievement test scores are predictive of general school achievement. However, the relationship between verbal ability as assessed by standardized tests and achievement in specific performance areas is less clear and may be dependent upon the nature of the subject and the way it is taught. For example, Gustin and Corazzo (1994) found that SAT–Verbal was more predictive of performance by gifted middle school

students in a summer, fast-paced biology course than SAT–Math while SAT–Math was predictive of performance in quantitatively oriented science courses such as physics. An important question is how does verbal intelligence measured in childhood or adolescence relate to achievement or choice of career in adulthood. Benbow (1992) demonstrated that scores on the SAT–M obtained in the 7th or 8th grade was related to the pursuit of careers in science and mathematics ten years later. Similar evidence regarding the predictive validity of SAT–V or other verbal measures has not been presented.

Gardner and the Multiple Intelligences Approach to Verbal Talent

Gardner postulates the existence of a linguistic intelligence among his list of eight intelligences. According to Gardner (1983), there is substantial evidence across many criteria that supports the autonomy of human competencies in the linguistic area. Gardner's criteria (1983) for the existence of a separate intelligence include the following: that the area of the brain primarily responsible for those functions can be isolated by brain damage; the existence of idiot savants, prodigies and other exceptional individuals with the intelligence; an identifiable core operation or set of operations; a distinct developmental history of the intelligence along with a definable set of end state performances; an evolutionary history for the intelligence; support from experimental psychological tests for the intelligence; susceptibility to encoding as a symbol system; and support from psychometric findings.

Gardner states that individuals who are aphasic can perform very well on cognitive tasks that are not related to language. For example, individuals who are severely aphasic may not be able to write or be authors but they will retain their abilities to be musicians or artists. This supports the existence of a specific area of the brain, the left hemisphere, as the primary locus for language functions.

There are three core functions of language, phonological discrimination and production, the pragmatic uses of language, and the semantic and syntactic uses of language (Gardner, 1983). Further, Gardner says that there are four aspects of language that are very important to human society: the rhetorical function of language or the ability to use language to convince others to take a course of action, the mnemonic function of language or the use of language to remember information, the role of language in explanation and teaching, and the metalinguistic function of language or the capacity for language to explain itself.

The ontogeny of language in humans is well documented from the first babblings of infants to the sophisticated use of language by poets, writers, and orators. Individuals with highly developed levels of linguistic intelligence can be easily identified and found in writers, politicians or evangelists with unusual rhetorical powers, story tellers, poets, novelists. The one criteria which Gardner (1983) postulates for which there does not seem to be a lot of evidence is the existence of idiot savants or prodigies. In fact, Feldman (1986) says that child prodigies in writing are very rare because the field has few organized supports or strategies for instruction and because children normally lack the kind of experience, insight, and understanding needed to convey complex thoughts in language. Piirto (1992) disagrees and believes that writing prodigies occur more frequently than previously thought. According to Gardner (1983), while oral and written forms of language draw on the similar capacities, written language, in addition, requires the author to supply the context that is often apparent from non-linguistic cues.

We have already reviewed the evidence regarding psychometric findings in support of verbal talent above, another of Gardner's criteria. In the next section, we review the findings on experimental and verbal information processing types of tasks. However, for both areas of research, there is support for the existence of individual differences in verbal ability and skills. There is also support for a relationship between verbal psychometric measures and performance in related, verbally laden, school achievement tasks. What is less well established is the relationship between individual differences on psychometric or information processing tasks and gifted adult performances and between information processing type tasks and achievement in school subjects (see Lohman's results below as an example). These seem to be important evidence that is needed to support the existence of a linguistic intelligence.

Language is a very sophisticated symbol system. It is interesting to speculate about the relationship between facility in one symbol system such as language and others such as those involved in mathematics, computer languages, musical notation, and the alphabet. Jackson (1988) has investigated this issue with early readers and found that children who speak early do not necessarily read early and children who read early do not necessarily have high verbal intelligence as measured by standardized tests. Early code breaking as is involved in precocious reading may be related to a very specific facility with decoding symbol systems that later takes the form of musical or mathematical talent. Further research in this area is also needed.

Gardner's theory of multiple intelligences, including his assertions regarding the existence of linguistic intelligence, are still considered largely speculative. His theory offers a useful rubric to think about cognitive abilities as they relate to performance in various school subjects and skill areas (e.g. mathe-matics, language, arts) and to achievement in domains of adult activity (e.g. scientific research, writing).

Other Definitions of Verbal Talent

Benbow and Minor (1990) studied the cognitive profiles of verbally vs. mathematically talented students. They identified students who were mathematically gifted (SAT–M above 700 before age 13), students who were verbally gifted (SAT–V above 630 before age 13), and students who were both mathematically and verbally gifted (met both score criteria). They gave students a variety of subtests drawn from well known standardized tests to assess speed of processing, memory, spatial visualization, non-verbal reasoning, vocabulary, knowledge of English expression, and mechanical comprehension. The mean score of the students on each test was approximately equal to students who were 4 to 5 years older. After a factor analysis of all the tests used, analyses revealed that the mathematically talented students outperformed the verbally talented students on the spatial/speed and non-verbal reasoning factors which included the spatial visualization test, the clerical speed and accuracy test, the mechanical comprehension test, and the Ravens Progressive Matrices test. The verbally talented students did better than the other groups on the verbal factor which included the assessments of vocabulary and knowledge of written English. The authors suggest that their results indicate that enhanced speed and memory are more strongly associated with mathematical than verbal talent. Benbow's and Minor's findings established that verbal and mathematical precocity are distinct forms of intellectual giftedness with unique intellectual profiles.

One interesting finding was that the presence of exceptionally high verbal ability increased the likelihood of the presence of exceptional mathematical ability. Only one of the verbally exceptional students had an SAT–M score of less than 500, while the reverse was not true. Benbow and Minor (1990) suggest that verbally talented students may be more even in their cognitive profiles than mathematically talented students. This finding is reiterated by Winner (1996); who asserts that it is far rarer to find verbally precocious children who do poorly in maths than the opposite pattern because these students can use verbal strategies to solve mathematical problems. According to Winner, children who are mathematically precocious are less balanced in their skills and more likely to achieve lower overall IQ scores than children who are verbally precocious.

Dark and Benbow (1991) studied the relationship between intellectual precocity in mathematical vs. verbal areas and a variety of working memory measures using different types of stimuli. They were interested in basic memory processes such as the accuracy with which information is maintained in working memory, the accuracy with which information in working memory can be manipulated by associating it with other information, and the speed with which information is activated from long term memory into working memory. Subject groups were defined by differential performance on SAT–V and SAT–M as above. They found that mathematical talent was associated with better memory for digit and spatial location stimuli while verbal ability was associated with better memory of word, but not letter stimuli. The authors suggested a 'differential compactness' theory to account for their results. Verbally talented individuals have more compact word representations and mathematically talented individuals have more compact representations of digits and locations. Their results also showed that quantitative ability was associated with slower loss of information from working memory. A correlate of verbal ability was the speed of activating a word's representation from long term memory into working memory; verbally talented individuals have quicker access to the word like stimuli that are stored in long term memory. The authors concluded that enhanced working memory functions are associated with mathematical talent while exceptional speed of encoding is more strongly associated with verbal talent.

Hunt, Lunnenborg & Lewis (1975) undertook a study to determine if there was a relationship between psychometrically defined verbal intelligence and information processing tasks. They identified college students who were considered verbally talented by virtue of their performance on the Washington Pre-College Test (WPCT). The verbal composite on the WPCT was a weighted sum of performance on the spelling, reading comprehension, vocabulary, and English usage subtests. Hunt et al. found that one of the abilities of the high verbals was being able to make a rapid conversion from a physical representation to a conceptual meaning—that is to recognize a particular visual pattern as a word or letter. Another ability of the verbally talented students was facility with retaining information about the order of stimulus presentation within short term memory. Lohman (1994) asserts that this latter aspect of verbal ability underlies phonological fluency, a component of exceptional and precocious reading. Hunt and his associates concluded that it is possible to distinguish low and high verbal university students who were identified via standardized psychometric tests by their performance on information processing types of tasks.

Lohman (1994), whose interests include the high spatial individual as defined by performance on visual spatial tasks, asserts that there are gender differences favoring females in sequential processing of letter or phonemes or linear order codes. These differences account for females slight advantages, compared to males, on spelling tests and tests of grammar and linguistic style. According to Lohman, phonological awareness which includes knowledge of phonetic

coding or spelling is among the best predictors of reading performance and in other forms, of foreign language aptitude.

Components of Verbal Ability

Another way to think about verbal ability is to break it down into its component parts. There are two perspectives from which to do this—that of adult performances and products and that of the skills or subjects that children study and acquire.

We can identify many areas of adult productive performance that rely on verbal skills and performances; these include all forms of creative writing such as poetry, short stories, and novels, and writing of a more informative kind such as non-fiction books, journal articles, or newspaper, or magazine writing. Verbal talent underlies exceptional oratorical performances such as is evident in acting, speech-making, or debating. Verbal ability would also presumably be involved in facility in foreign languages such as is found in interpreters or individuals who easily acquire a foreign language or read, write, and speak many languages with ease. There are many other adult professions that could require a high level of verbal ability such as law but do not readily yield critically acclaimed, observable verbal products. Exceptional adult performances and/or products presume a high level of ability but not necessarily childhood precocity in the domain; also, it is not clear that higher levels of verbal ability lead to more exceptional performances or products, beyond a certain, albeit high, minimum level.

From the perspective of skill acquisition, components of verbal ability could include early speech, an advanced receptive or productive vocabulary, early reading, early writing, or early facility with foreign language acquisition.

What is the evidence regarding precocity in any aspect of verbal ability and later talent? There is very little research on these issues with the exception of early reading.

Precocity in the production and comprehension of oral language in infancy or early childhood is a predictor of later verbal intelligence at least as measured by standardized tests (Jackson & Klein, 1997). The age of production of first words by a child is predictive of level of verbal intelligence. However, it is also reported in case studies that many highly gifted adults began speech production later than most children but, once begun, it proceeded very rapidly (Jackson and Klein).

Case studies highlight the variety of patterns of exceptional verbal skills found in children. According to Winner (1996), Michael Kearney, a very gifted boy who finished college by the age of 10, uttered his first words at 4 months of age and began reading off of a television screen at age 8 months. Michael was also very precocious in mathematics.

Similarly, David had an excellent receptive vocabulary and also began to speak at the age of 8 months, about four months earlier than most children (Winner, 1996). By age 5, David showed interest in language as a system—he wanted to learn other languages and made up his own. He read phonetically at age 3 and was able to read words he did not understand. By the time he entered kindergarten, he was reading at a 6th grade level. He was also advanced in writing, producing non-fiction pieces and stories at age 5. Michael and David were two examples of children who showed precocity in both the verbal and mathematical areas, which Winner admits is more the exception than the rule.

Raphaela (see Winner, 1996) spoke her first words at age 9 months and spoke in long, complex sentences by the age of 2 years; she was reading at age 3 and read chapter books by age 5. At the same age her writing was advanced; she could read cursive writing. She spelt correctly from the start and not phonetically; she was somewhat advanced in mathematics but not remarkably so. Her drawings and physical development were also age appropriate.

These examples of verbally precocious children raise several issues; one is the relationship between precocity in one area of the verbal domain and precocity in another, e.g., early reading and early writing. A second is the relationship between precocity in two very different domains, mathematics and verbal. According to Winner (1996), despite the examples of Michael Kearney and David, unevenness is typically the pattern across disparate domains. Similarly, according to the research conducted by Jackson and her associates, young children who produce or understand language at unusual levels do not necessarily read early (Jackson & Klein, 1997).

The evidence regarding precocity in writing is also equivocal. Feldman (1986) asserts that writing is not an area in which prodigious achievement typically occurs; he also notes that writing prodigies rarely become writers in adulthood. However, Feldman does report on a child, Randy, who was exceptional as a child at least in the amount he wrote and his use of language. Randy's father was a writer and thus could provide an unusual amount of support for his writing activities; his father was his first teacher. Randy showed an early interest in words and their tonal qualities; he began to read without instruction at age two and a half. He wrote constantly about everything he read and studied. According to Feldman, Randy's strength as a writer was in his evocative use of language to set tone and create a style but not in his ability to tell a really good story. Only occasionally did Randy express powerful emotions or feelings in his writing; his spelling was also exceptional.

Randy had many other interests including music and acting; he eventually pursued these more vigorously than his writing although he continued with his writing to some extent. Feldman (1986) notes that typically, when talent emerges very early, parents serve as the first teachers. Eventually, another adult takes over the instructional process; but in writing, there are few mentors available to children to serve as teachers or role models. Also, writing is a lonely craft and for Randy, the draw of performing in front of an audience, made it and other endeavors more attractive.

Piirto (1992) claims that the reported incidence of writing prodigies may be inaccurately low due to inadequate documentation. She lists 16 qualities of advanced writing of children including the use of paradox, parallel structure, rhythm, visual imagery, unusual figures of speech, reverse structure, unusual adjectives or adverbs, unusual melodic combinations, a feeling of movement, uncanny wisdom or humor, sophisticated syntax, prose lyricism, an 'ear' for the rhythm and sounds of language, a philosophical or moral bent in writings and a playfulness with words. Characteristics of outstanding prose writing include giving a refreshing twist to old ideas, keeping ideas within a story organized, and choosing descriptive words that show perception and precision. Piirto asserts that the characteristics of children with creative writing talent include early and voracious reading and attention to words and expressions of words. Piirto agrees that precocity in writing is not necessary for adult achievement and says that incipient writers are characterized by high emotionality and strong imaginations.

According to Bailey (1996), writing development has its roots in drawing, an interesting hypothesis that has not been studied to any great extent. Bailey asserts that most 3 year olds would not be able to tell a true story in response to a picture; what they would produce would be more like a description of the picture. A *verbally gifted* 3 year old can tell a logical and creative story. By age 5, dialogue would be used creatively and the story could be highly imaginative and include expressively vivid and complex language.

By far, the most well researched area of early precocity is that of reading; most of this work has been done by Nancy Jackson and her associates. Jackson (1988) notes that many eminent individuals are purported to have been early and voracious readers; she raises the interesting question of the meaning and significance of early reading. After all, advancement in reading does not last; eventually other children who start at the normal time catch up. Does early reading have any predictive value or long lasting effects? Jackson (1988) argues that even if we cannot answer that question, it is clear that early reading has *immediate* profound effects because it alters the way teachers and parents respond to and interact with a child.

As stated earlier, there is no relationship between early oral language fluency and precocious reading (Jackson & Klein, 1997). Early reading is not necessarily a start to an excellent career in school and precocious readers may or may not have high verbal IQ's (Jackson & Klein); they may or may not be exceptional or early writers. As a group, early readers tend to be somewhat above average in IQ and most tend to remain at least above average in reading (Jackson, 1992, 1988).

Precocious readers differ in their specific subskill patterns. Some precocious readers rely on phonics and can decode virtually any word. Others rely heavily on context to decipher new words (Jackson, Donaldson & Cleland, 1988). The most critical factor is a child's ability to use relevant knowledge or reading strategies effectively, appropriately, and flexibly (Jackson, Donaldson & Cleland, 1988). Thus, there are individual differences among precocious readers in what and why they read as well as how they do it. The most striking feature of precocious readers is their ability to read text very rapidly (Jackson & Klein, 1997) although not more precisely than a comparative group (Jackson, 1988). Precocious reading is associated with the ability to name letters rapidly, which indicates a more general ability to quickly retrieve information from long term memory.

Jackson proposes that precocious reading has a heterotypic pattern of continuity, which means that it is part of a trait that gets expressed in different ways with age. Precocious reading has diverse roots and diverse sequalae (Jackson & Klein, 1997). Early reading may be indicative of later interest and remarkable performance or achievement in another symbol system such as music, computer languages, or mathematics. Efficient processing of auditory-sequential information may underpin exceptional representation and retrieval of phonological information and abstraction of oral-graphemic rules' leading to early reading and, somewhat later, early exceptionality in music (Jackson & Klein). Alternatively, efficient processing of visual-spatial information may also lead to early reading and somewhat later, exceptional achievement in mathematics (Jackson & Klein).

There may be more of a contribution of specific teaching to early reading than has been thought. Burns, Collins & Paulsell (1991) studied four year olds who had a Stanford-Binet IQ of 120 or higher; some were readers and some were not. At age 4 there were no significant differences between the readers and non-readers on listening comprehension, understanding of concepts about print, ability to recite the alphabet, or ability to verbalize the names of written letters. Accelerated readers did perform better on tasks which asked them to read specific words in print, use invented spelling, or verbally produce vowel and consonant sounds when shown corresponding letters. It was found that the majority of mothers of readers (66%) had used reading kits or programs at home with their children and the remaining readers had received formal reading instruction in their preschools. At ages 8 and 9, the readers did significantly better than the non-readers in

using phonetic analysis to identify nonsense words or to spell dictated words; there were no differences on word identification or comprehension, key aspects of reading. However, the authors suggest that more differences might have existed at ages 8 and 9 had the early readers continued to be exposed to an accelerated or advanced language arts curriculum during the early elementary grades.

Research Findings on the Development of Verbally Gifted Adults

Retrospective studies of talented adults reveal a complex picture of the talent development process including the following factors—personality characteristics of the individual, environmental circumstances and supports, access to mentors, and childhood experiences. The group of individuals who have been studied and written about most extensively are writers.

VanTassel-Baska (1996a, 1996b) has studied the development of female writers including Virginia Wolfe and Charlotte Bronte. She discovered eight themes that were characteristic of these women: adversity typically involving the deaths of close family members and/or poverty; autodidactism or self-learning sometimes resulting from a lack of access to formal education and consisting of informal instruction from family members or literary family friends; practice of the craft which often included daily journal or diary writing; need for emotional support (which came from others and also from their own writing) because they lacked confidence in their writing; vulnerability to criticism and high strung personalities; a defined philosophy of being which involved believing that one was subject to the whims of impersonal 'fate' but could also rise above difficult circumstances to create something of beauty; the influence of place which showed in the use of familiar locations and childhood environments as settings for stories; loneliness which was evident in the lack of friends and the erratic nature of friendships due in part to lifestyle and location; and the search for a mother figure and understanding of a mother's role which was often a theme within their writing.

VanTassel-Baska (1996a, 1996b) also identified four stages of development of the talented female writers. The first stage was a family that valued the literary and intellectual life and spoke freely about the world of ideas; this period was also characterized by opportunities for the child to spend time alone indicating a more isolated and atypical childhood. The second stage consisted of an informal early development of the craft of writing; during this stage, the child engaged in imaginative play, played with words in writing, and created skits and plays. An important element of this early experimentation was an audience, usually consisting of family members who provided constructive feedback. The third stage was an active experimentation with the various forms and genres of writing. The final stage was the development of a mature form in successive works.

Simonton's (1986) research suggests that writers tend to be from cities, have small, non-religious families with non-supportive fathers and generally unhappy home environments. Many experienced severe childhood trauma such as the loss of a parent, alcoholic parents, or serious illness, their own or their parents.

As children, writers were often very responsive to the emotional climate and stresses of their family household. They were often compelled to retreat away from these situations into reading or daydreaming, which often facilitated the development of their talent. Writers, as children, had intense imaginational and intellectual reactions to the written word (Piirto, 1992). They tended not to be joiners, preferring to be alone, and did not care for physical activities. Many writers reported hating school and school curricula (Piirto).

Writers' personalities tend to include the characteristics of independence and unconventionality (Piirto, 1992). On the Meyers Briggs Type Indicator, writers are found to be introverted, intuitive, feeling, and perceptive, a profile that is similar to visual artists (Piirto). Many writers are also artistic and/or have great interest in the visual arts (VanTassel-Baska 1996b); distinguished writers are frequently schizoid, depressive, hysterical, or psychopathic. Many were self abusive and self destructive. Writers may write because of deep seated pathologies and their writing is often an outlet for childhood trauma (Piirto).

Writers are risk takers; they must submit manuscripts over and over again risking rejection and criticism; they are characterized as resilient, stubborn, persistent, and good at self promotion (Piirto, 1992).

According to Piirto (1992), writers value productivity; the number of pieces a writer produces is related to his or her success. More successful writers produce more written pieces overall. Simonton's (as cited in Piirto, 1992) research shows that poets reach their peak of productivity at age 39 on the average and fiction and non-fiction writers at age 43.

An important environmental component of a writer's development is a group of connected friends—particularly other writers who can provide support and constructive criticism. Often this means living in areas of cities where writers are known to live (Piirto, 1992). "The 'loft culture' of artists . . . also exists in the writing world. Writers keep in touch with one another and often seek to establish themselves through public readings, which unfortunately, are frequently attended only by other writers." (p. 148, Piirto, 1992). Friends can help get a writer's work published; for many writers, the first works were published by small presses or by one friend for another. While writers need one another they often feel threatened by other writers.

Another critical component of a writer's environment is the literary agent (Piirto).

Educational Programs for the Development of Verbal Talent

Educational programs for children with verbal talent vary widely. These include grouping arrangements that allow children who possess advanced skills to proceed at a faster pace or do accelerated work (e.g. reading groups), early foreign language study, or comprehensive, integrated language arts programs for high ability learners. Most programs in early elementary school focus on the area of reading since this is such a crucial and fundamental skill area. Few programs for elementary school aged children single students out for special instruction on the basis of advanced writing ability, exceptional creative writing ability, exceptional spelling ability, or facility with foreign languages. In most cases, school personnel rely on in-grade achievement tests to identify children who are performing above grade level in reading or language arts and to place them in special, advanced programs.

According to VanTassel-Baska (1996b), characteristics of verbally gifted learners upon which a program should be built include: reads well and fluently, is interested in words and word relationships, uses an advanced vocabulary, processes key ideas about what is read, enjoys talking about literature, writes descriptively and communicates a story, enjoys verbal puzzles and games, reads often and outside of class, plays with language in its oral and written forms, and exhibits understanding of the structure of language in speaking and writing. Bailey (1996) adds, fluid and descriptive oral language, advanced ability to use a linguistic symbol system, ability to express a complex thought, and playful doing of a skill coupled with a seriousness of purpose.

Programs at the junior high or middle school level may include strong literature programs with literary analysis by genre or theme as a major focus. Writing may be incorporated into the literature class or be a separate strand, particularly a focus on the development of strong non-fiction writing skills. Foreign language study typically begins in high school but many schools now begin instruction in middle school or even in the elementary grades.

High school programs for verbally talented youths include the International Baccalaureate program which helps to prepare students for facility with another language. It also emphasizes writing in the formal exams that students take in order to obtain the prestigious IB diploma. A key component of the program is a 4000 word research report.

The Advanced Placement program(AP) of The College Board has many courses that are appropriate for verbally talented students including AP English Literature and Composition, AP Language and Composition, and AP courses in several foreign languages and the social sciences. AP courses give high school students the opportunity to study college level material; students can, by examination, earn college credits for these courses.

Other options for secondary students include dual enrollment programs which currently exist by legislation in 19 U.S. states. These programs allow students to be simultaneously enrolled in high school and college. Students can take college courses on college campuses, and usually earn both college and high school credit for them. With the increasing use and capabilities of the internet to reach remote audiences, distance education programs can allow verbally gifted youths to take advanced courses in many language arts areas. These courses may be high school or college level courses.

Other opportunities for verbally gifted youths include summer programs, study abroad options, and contests and competitions. Summer programs abound in the U.S. and many of these have courses for verbally gifted youth in writing, literature, foreign language, debate, philosophy and the social sciences. Many of these are connected to talent search programs and rely on SAT and ACT scores for entrance. Study abroad programs offer a unique opportunity for students to learn about another culture and acquire facility in a second language at a high level. Contests and competitions can give students an outlet for their writing, an opportunity to have their work evaluated by a professional writer, chances for publication, and potentially cash prizes or scholarship money.

An important question is what should be the components of a program for verbally gifted youth. These might include foreign language study, reading or literature study, writing, oral communication, or language and grammar study. Reading/literature and writing are most typically included in programs for verbally gifted youths. Thompson (1996) recommends, however, that language/grammar study is also an essential component of the education of verbally talented youth; the study of language includes grammar, vocabulary, etymology, and poetics. Language study offers gifted students content that is complex and abstract; it is inherently interdisciplinary according to Thompson. It "is an enabling curriculum that will strengthen students' abilities in all other curricula and invigorate their powers of articulation for all purposes" (p. 152). Thompson goes on to say that "because grammar is so often studied as a thing in itself, an intellectual amputation severed from its context of living ideas in literature, poetry, and other forms of language, it is easy for us to forget what a decisive analytical thinking technique grammar can be in the interpretation of literature and poetry" (p. 153, Thompson, 1996).

Thompson and Thompson (1996) suggest that foreign language study begins early in the elementary school years; they stress that foreign language study can develop verbal ability in a way that the study of one's native language cannot. The advantages of studying a foreign language include a deeper understanding of language, accelerated vocabulary development, new understanding of grammar through comparison between the native and foreign language, training of the poetic ear, ability to read literature in another language, mental flexibility gained through knowledge of language elements that are non-existent in the native language, and a multicultural perspective. According to these authors, studying a foreign language forces one to become more language conscious in general. Further, the study of foreign language is interdisciplinary because the student does not just study the language but also the culture, history, literature, geography, and customs.

Speaking and listening activities of a higher level are frequently not a component of the school curriculum; these could include forensics, debate, or rhetoric. According to Chaney (1996), oral communication should be conceptualized as 'thinking in action' and involves listening, non-verbal communication, information gathering, synthesis and analysis of arguments, comparison of alternative choices, identification of values, and giving and responding to feedback. Students who can read and write at high levels of proficiency may not be able to communicate orally at the same level. All students, but particularly those who are verbally talented, need and can benefit from experiences that can systematically develop speaking and listening competencies.

Very little in terms of special language arts curricula for gifted learners exists; most programs rely on using materials designed for older learners to increase complexity and abstractness of the content. Consequently, there are few evaluations of the effects of specialized curricula designed for gifted learners (VanTassel-Baska, Johnson, Hughes & Boyce 1996). These authors studied the impact of a 40 hour language arts curriculum designed for gifted learners in 4th though 6th grades. The curriculum was integrated and used selected literature, writing exercises, and a self-study grammar packet and was employed with seven experimental groups. Performances of the experimental students on a reading assessment, a performance-based persuasive writing task, and a grammar test were compared to three control classes. Results showed large effect sizes favoring the experimental group on the grammar and writing assessments and small effect sizes for the reading test. The authors suggest that their data support the use of more powerful language arts curricula for high-ability learners.

Conclusions

What can we conclude about the development of verbal talent and the education of verbally talented youths? At this point we can easily and quite reliably identify children with high scores on certain types of tests that we believe measure meaningful aspects of verbal ability and that predict performance in verbal subjects or school tasks. Most researchers would agree that verbal ability is multi-faceted, consisting of skills, components, or subparts, even though they may not agree on what they are nor their importance relative to one another or to expert-adult performances. There are only a few studies about the more basic cognitive processes such as memory or encoding processes that underlie exceptional verbal abilities; more research is needed in this area.

We are also unclear about the emergence of certain components of verbal ability and the significance of precocious emergence in children with the exception of early reading. The connection between drawing and literacy skills in young children is worthy of investigation and the work of Jackson and her associates on the relationship between early reading and other domains offers hope for a more comprehensive, in-depth understanding of the development of symbol use.

As is the case in many areas of gifted education, curricula for verbally talented children have developed despite a lack of clear consensus on the construct of verbal ability. Well developed programs exist particularly at the secondary level. In elementary school, the heavy emphasis on reading has precluded the systematic development of other verbal skills; this is an area where change is vitally needed. Also required are more studies of the VanTassel-Baska et al (1996) variety in which special curricula for gifted learners are implemented and their effects studied.

References

Adams, M. J. (1990). *Learning to read: thinking and learning about print*. Cambridge, MA: MIT Press.

Adler, M. J. (1982). *The paideia proposal*. New York: Macmillan Publishing Co.

Arias, M. B. & Casanova, U. (1993). *Bilingual education: politics, practice, and research*. (Vol. 92 (2)). Chicago: National Society for the Study of Education.

Bailey, J. M. (1996). Literacy development in verbally talented children. In: J. VanTassel-Baska, D. T. Johnson & L. N. Boyce (Eds.), *Developing Verbal Talent. Ideas and Strategies for Teachers of Elementary and Middle School Students* (pp. 97–114). Needham Hts., MA: Allyn & Bacon.

Baugh, J. (2000). *Beyond ebonics : the linguistic legacy of American slavery*. New York: Oxford University Press.

Benbow, C. P. (1992) Academic achievement in mathematics and science of students between ages 12 and 23: are there differences among students in the top one percent of mathematical ability? *Journal of Educational Psychology*, **84**, 57–61.

Benbow, C. P. & Minor, L. L. (1990). Cognitive profiles of verbally and mathematically precocious students: implications for identification of the gifted. *Gifted Child Quarterly*, **34** (1) 21–26.

Bloom, P. (1990). Syntactic distinctions in child language. *Journal of Child Language*, **17**, 343–355.

Brizuela, B. M. & Garcia-Sellers, M. J. (1999). School adaptation: a triangular process. *American Educational Research Journal*, **36** (2), 345–370.

Bronfenbrenner, U. & Ceci, S. J. (1994). Nature-nurture reconceptualized in developmental perspective: a bioecological perspective. *Psychological Review*, **101**, 568–586.

Brown, A. L., Campione, J. C., Reeve, R. A., Ferrara, R. A. & Palincsar, A. S. (1992). Interactive learning and individual understanding: the case of reading and mathematics. In: L. T. Landsman (Ed.), *Culture, Schooling, and Psychological Development*. Hillsdale, NJ: Erlbaum.

Bruner, J. S. (1983). *Child's talk: learning to use language*. New York: W. W. Norton.

Burns, J. M. Collins, M. D. & Paulsell, C. J. (1991). A comparison of intellectually superior preschool accelerated readers and nonreaders: four years later. *Gifted Child Quarterly*, **35** (3), 118–124.

Center for Talent Development (1998). *1998 Midwest Talent Search Statistical Summary*. Northwestern University, Evanston, IL.

Chall, J., Jacobs, V. A. & Baldwin, L. E. (1990). *The reading crisis: Why poor children fall behind*. Cambridge, MA: Harvard University Press.

Chaney, A. L. (1996). Oral communication: thinking in action. In: J. VanTassel-Baska, D. T. Johnson & L. Neal Boyce (Eds.), *Developing Verbal Talent. Ideas and Strategies for Teachers of Elementary and Secondary Students* (pp. 115–132). Needham Hts., MA: Allyn & Bacon.

Choi, S. & Gropnik, A. (1995). Early acquisition of verbs in Korea: a cross-linguistic study. *Journal of Child Language*, **22**, 497–529.

Chomsky, N. (1986). *Knowledge of language: Its nature, origins, and use*. New York: Praeger.

Cole, M. & Cole, S. R. (1996). *The development of children*. New York: W. H. Freeman.

Crawford, J. (1992). *Hold your tongue: bilingualism and the politics of English only*. Reading, MA: Addison-Wesley.

Dark, V. J. & Benbow, C. P. (1991). Differential enhancement of working memory with mathematical vs. verbal precocity. *Journal of Educational Psychology*, **83** (1), 48–60.

Edwards, J. (1998). *Opposing censorship in the public schools: religion, morality, and literature*. Mahwah, N.J.: L. Erlbaum Associates.

Feldman, D. H. (1980). *Beyond universals in cognitive development*. Norwood, NJ: Ablex.

Feldman, D. H. (1986). *Nature's gambit: child prodigies and the development of human potential*. New York: Basic Books.

Fischbein, S. (1981). Heredity-environment influences on growth and development during adolescence. In: L. Gedda, P. Parisi & W. E. Nance (Eds.), *Twin research 3: Pt. B. Program in Clinical and Biological Research*. New York: Liss.

Flanagan, D. P., Andrews, T. J. & Genshaft, J. (1997). The functional utility of intelligence tests with special education population. In: D. P. Flanagan, J. L. Harrison (Eds.), *Contemporary Intellectual Assessment. Theories, Tests and Issues*, (pp. 457–483). New York: The Guilford Press.

Frith, U. (1989). *Autism*. Oxford: Oxford University Press.

Gardner, H. (1983). *Frames of mind: the theory of multiple intelligences*. New York: Basic Books.

Gardner, H. (1993). *The unschooled mind*. New York: Basic Books.

Gardner, H. (1999). *The disciplined mind*. New York: Basic Books.

Goodman, Y. E. & Goodman, K. S. (1990). Vygotsky and the whole language perspective. In: L. C. Moll (Ed.), *Vygotsky* and Education: Instructional Implications and Applications of Sociohistorical Psychology. New York: Cambridge University Press.

Gottfredson, L. S. (Ed.). (1997). *Intelligence and social policy*. (Vol. 24). Greenwich, CT: Ablex Publishing Corporation.

Gustin, W. & Corazzo, L. (1994). Mathematical and verbal reasoning as predictors of science achievement. *Roeper Review*, **16** (3), 160–162.

Herrnstein, R. J. & Murray, C. (1994). *The bell curve: intelligence and class structure in American life*. New York: Free Press.

Hirsch, E. D. (1987). *Cultural literacy*. Boston: Houghton Mifflin.

Hoff-Ginsberg, E. (1990). Maternal speech and the child's development of syntax: a further look. *Journal of Child Language*, **17**, 85–99.

Hunt, E. (1978). Mechanics of verbal ability. *Psychological Review*, **85** (2), 109–130.

Hunt, E., Lunnenborg, C., & Lewis, T. (1975). What does it mean to be high verbal? *Cognitive Psychology*, **7**, 194–227.

Huttenlocher, J., Haight, W., Bryk, A., Seltzer, M. & Lyons, T. (1991). Early vocabulary growth: relation to language and gender. *Developmental Psychology*, **27**, 236–248.

Hyde, J. S. & Linn, M. C. (1988). Gender differences in verbal ability: a meta-analysis. *Psychological Bulletin*, Vol. **104** (1), 53–69.

Itard, J. M. G. (1801/1982). *The wild boy of Aveyron* (Humphrey, G. Humphrey, M., Trans.). New York: Appleton-Century-Crofts.

Jackson, N. E. (1992). Understanding giftedness in young children: Lessons from the study of precocious readers. In: N. Colangelo, S. G. Assouline & D. L. Ambroson (Eds.). *Talent Development: Proceeding from the 1991 Henry B. and Jocelyn Wallace National Research Symposium on Talent Development*, (pp. 163–179). Unionville, NY: Trillium Press.

Jackson, N. E. (1988). Precocious reading ability: what does it mean? *Gifted Child Quarterly*, **32** (1), 200–204.

Jackson, N. E., Donaldson, G. W. & Cleland, L. N. (1988). The structure of precocious reading ability. *Journal of Educational Psychology*, **80** (2), 234–243.

Jackson, N. E. & Kearney, J. M. (1993). *Achievement of precocious readers in middle childhood and young adulthood*. Paper presented at the 1993 Henry B. and Jocelyn Wallace National Research Symposium on Talent Development, University of Iowa, Iowa City, IA.

Jackson, N. E. & Klein, E. J. (1997). Gifted performance in young children. In: N. Colangelo & G. A. Davis (Eds.), *Handbook of Gifted Education* (2nd ed.) (pp. 460–474). Boston, MA: Allyn & Bacon.

Kelly, M. H. (1992). Using sound to solve syntactic problems: the role of phonology in grammatical category assignments. *Psychological Review*, **99**, 349–364.

Kerr, S. T. (1996). *Technology and the future of schooling*. (Vol. 96 (2)). Chicago: National Society for the Study of Education.

Lohman, D. F. (1994). Spatially gifted, verbally inconvenienced. In: N. Colangelo, S. G. Assouline & D. L. Ambroson (Eds.), *Talent Development: Proceedings from the 1993 Henry B. and Jocelyn Wallace National Research Symposium on Talent Development* (pp. 251–264). Dayton, OH: Ohio Psychology Press.

Lunsford, A. A., Moglen, H., Slevin, J. F. & Modern Language Association of America. (1990). *The Right to literacy*. New York: Modern Language Association of America.

Maccaby, E. E. & Jacklin, C. N. (1974). *The psychology of sex differences*. Stanford, CA: Stanford University Press.

Miller-Jones, D. (1989). Culture and testing. *American Psychologist*, **44**, 360–366.

Nelson, K. (1989). Strategies for first language teaching. In: M. L. Rice & R. L. Schiefelbusch (Eds.), *The Teachability of Language*. Baltimore: Paul H. Brooks.

Nelson, K. (1991). Concepts and meaning in language development. In: N. A. Krasnegor, R. L. Rumbaugh, R. L. Schiefelbusch & M. Studdert-Kennedy (Eds.), *Biological and Behavioral Determinants of Language Development*. Hillsdale, NJ: Erlbaum.

Nelson, N. & Clafee, R. C. (1998). *The reading-writing connection*. (Vol. 97 (2)). Chicago: National Society for the Study of Education.

Ogbu, J. U. (1991). Minority status and literacy. In: S. R. Graubard (Ed.), *Literacy: An Overview by 14 Experts*. New York: Hill and Wang.

Ogbu, J. U. (1999). Beyond language: ebonics, proper English, and identity in a Black-American speech community. *American Educational Research Journal*, **36** (2), 147–184.

Perry, T. & Delpit, L. D. (1998). *The real ebonics debate: power, language, and the education of African-American children*. Boston: Beacon Press.

Pinker, S. (1989). *Learnability and cognition*. Cambridge, MA: MIT Press.

Piirto, J. (1992). *Understanding those who create*. Dayton, OH: Ohio Psychology Press.

Resnick, D. P. (1991). Historical perspectives on literacy and schooling. In: S. R. Graubard (Ed.), *Literacy: An Overview by 14 Experts*. New York: Hill and Wang.

Secada, W. G. & Lightfoot, T. (1993). Symbols and the political context of bilingual education in the United States. In: M. B. Arias & U. Casanova (Eds.), *Bilingual Education: Politics, Practice, and Research* (Vol. 92 (2)). Chicago: National Society for the Study of Education.

Simonton, D. K. (1986). Biographical, typicality, eminence and achievement styles, *Journal of Creative Behavior*, **20** (1) 17–18.

Sizer, T. R. (1984). *Horace's compromise: the dilemma of the American high school*. Boston: Houghton Mifflin.

Sleeter, C. E. (1995). Curriculum controversies in multicultural education. In: E. Flaxman & A. H. Passow (Eds.), *Changing Populations/Changing Schools* (Vol. 94 (2)). Chicago: National Society for the Study of Education.

Smitherman, G. (2000). *Black Talk: Words and Phrases from the Hood to the Amen Corner*. (Rev. ed.). Boston: Houghton Mifflin.

Smitherman, G. & Wayne State University. Center for Black Studies. (1981). *Black English and the education of Black children and youth: proceedings of the National Invitational Symposium on the King Decision*. Detroit, Mich.: Center for Black Studies Wayne State University.

Stanley, J. C., Benbow, C. P., Brody, L. E., Dauber, S. & Lupkowski, A. (1992). Gender differences on eighty-six nationally standardized achievement and aptitude tests. In: N. Colangelo, S. G. Assouline & D. L. Ambrosen (Eds.), *Talent Development: Proceedings from the 1991 Henry B.*

and Jocelyn Wallace National Research Symposium (pp. 42–61). New York: Trillium Press.

Steele, C. (1991). Race and the schooling of Black Americans. *Atlantic Monthly,* **269** (4), 68–78.

Sternberg, R. J. (1996). Myths, countermyths, and truths about intelligence. *Educational Researcher,* **25** (2), 11–16.

Tharp, R. G. (1989). psychocultural variables and constants: effects on teaching and learning in schools. *American Psychologist,* **44**, 349–359.

Thompson, M. C. (1996). Formal language study for gifted students. In: J. VanTassel-Baska, D. T. Johnson & L. Neal Boyce (Eds.), *Developing Verbal Talent. Ideas and Strategies for Teachers of Elementary and Middle School Students* (pp. 149–173). Needham Hts., MA: Allyn & Bacon.

Thompson, M. C. & Thompson, M. D. (1996). Reflections on foreign language study for highly able learners. In: J. VanTassel-Baska, D. T. Johnson & L. Neal Boyce (Eds.), *Developing Verbal Talent. Ideas and Strategies for Teachers of Elementary and Middle School Students* (pp. 174–188). Needham Hts., MA: Allyn & Bacon.

United States. Congress. Senate. Committee on Appropriations. Subcommittee on Departments of Labor Health and Human Services Education and Related Agencies. (1997). *Ebonics : hearing before a subcommittee of the Committee on Appropriations, United States Senate, One Hundred Fifth Congress, first session, special hearing.* Washington: U.S. G.P.O.: For sale by the U.S. G.P.O. Supt. of Docs. Congressional Sales Office.

VanTassel-Baska, J. (1996a). The talent development process in women writers: a study of Charlotte Bronte and Virgina Woolf. In: K. Arnold, R. D. Noble & R. F. Subotnik (Eds.), *Remarkable Women. Perspectives on Female Talent Development* (pp. 295–316). Cresskill, NJ: Hampton Press, Inc.

VanTassel-Baska, J. (1996b). The process of talent development. In: J. VanTassel-Baska, D. T. Johnson & L. Neal Boyce (Eds.), *Developing Verbal Talent. Ideas and Strategies for Teachers of Elementary and Middle School Students* (pp. 3–22). Needham Hts., MA: Allyn & Bacon.

VanTassel-Baska, J., Johnson, D. T., Hughes, C. & Boyce, L. N. (1996). A study of language arts curriculum effectiveness with gifted learner. *Journal for the Education of the Gifted,* **19** (4), 461–480.

Vygotsky, L. (1962). *Thought and language* (Hanfmann, E. Vakar, G., Trans.). Cambridge, MA: MIT Press.

Wexler, K. & Culicover, P. (1980). *Formal principles of language acquisition.* Cambridge, MA: MIT Press.

Winch, C. (1990). *Language, ability, and educational achievement.* New York: Routledge.

Winner, E. (1996). *Gifted children. Myths and realities.* New York: Basic Books.

Nurturing Talents/Gifts in Mathematics

Wilhelm Wieczerkowski, Arthur J. Cropley and Tania M. Prado

University of Hamburg, Germany

Introduction

Reliable diagnostic strategies and error-free identification of any psychological characteristic are difficult without a satisfactory operational definition derived from an unequivocal theory. Thus, the first step in considering strategies for nurturing giftedness in mathematics is to make a clear statement of what is actually meant by the construct. This definition determines how highly gifted pupils are to be identified (selected), and what measures are to be included in special provision aimed at nurturing their gifts.

The variety of conceptions of mathematics leads not only to varying perceptions of what mathematical giftedness is, but also apparently affects the contents of instruction and the way information is imparted by instructors (Wagner & Zimmermann, 1986; Zimmermann, 1992). These aspects have not been explicitly discussed in scientific debate to date.

Aspects of mathematical giftedness are, not least, an expression of subjective experience and expectations of the individual person. Statements on mathematical giftedness and its structure exhibit commonalities and uniformity as well as specificity supposedly stemming from different philosophies of mathematics (Steen, 1979, 1981) and the rich variety of aspects within mathematics (David & Hersh, 1981).

Decisive predictors of giftedness are not restricted to special skills or the degree of development of certain abilities or special aptitudes at a particular time. Of equal importance are the interactions of potential with personal characteristics such as motivation and task commitment, as well as with environmental factors including level of support or challenge at home and at school in a particular area of knowledge. Excellence can, in this sense, be regarded as the optimal goal for the development of the gifted, not as a fixed state. According to this view, the unfolding of talent is a continual reorganization of the internal structure of knowledge and the metacognitive competencies of an individual, according to the person's stage of development.

Mathematical Core Variables in Research on Intelligence

The parameters of mathematical ability have occupied the interest of researchers for more than fifty years. Two central questions have recurred over and over again:

1. Is mathematical giftedness an expression of specific cognitive characteristics, or is it simply the result, at least to a considerable degree, of high general intellectual ability?
2. Is mathematical giftedness a uniform construct, or are there many different profiles of exceptional mathematical ability?

Questions such as these are not simply of academic interest; depending on the answers, quite different strategies of special provision would be implemented.

As a rule, research on intelligence from the Thirties to the Sixties concentrated on general factors of intelligence, and did not look into explicit parameters of mathematical giftedness. Specific factors of intelligence such as spatial relations, visualization and orientation, numerical facility, reasoning, induction, deduction, and flexibility (see the overview in Pawlik, 1968) were first introduced in studies involving unusual proficiency in solving mathematical problems (Siegvald, 1944; Terman & Tylor, 1954; Maccoby & Jacklin, 1974; Lloyd & Archer, 1976; Merz, 1979; Halpern, 1986). Since early research on the structure of intelligence (e.g. Thorndike, Thurstone Guilford) was basically concerned with attributing complex cognitive processes to general operations (primary factors), the relative lack of attention given to specific abilities, such as those related to mathematical giftedness, is understandable.

Areas of achievement strength in different individuals or within homogeneous groups were ascertained by means of profiles on scales of general ability. This procedure is still common in current test diagnosis, and is also regularly applied when describing components of mathematical giftedness. In this context, more general cognitive operations such as ability in abstracting concrete problems, the ability to generalize, flexibility, reversibility of operations, fluency of thought, or strategic decision-making have been regarded as core variables for mathematical giftedness.

The main objection to the use of general ability parameters for defining mathematical giftedness lies in their lack of specificity. In order to facilitate understanding of a special gift (or special measures to nurture it), it seems reasonable to assume that the primary cognitive operators mentioned above are not interchangeable across specific academic domains such as mathematics, biology, physics or even the social sciences. In the case of mathematics, concepts of general academic giftedness should, at the very least, be augmented by identifying potentially relevant specific characteristics, which should then be analyzed to ascertain their importance for mathematical talent (Sternberg, 1981; Dummer, 1983; Heid, 1983; Gardner, 1983).

Structure of Mathematical Abilities

The Russian psychologist Krutetskii made a significant contribution to understanding the nature and structure of specifically mathematical abilities. He showed that there are three components: reception; processing; and retaining of mathematical information (see Table 1). These are closely related and influence one another, and constitute a complete integral system or distinctive syndrome of mathematical talent: the mathematical cast of mind (Krutetskii, 1976, p. 350). According to this view, mathematically gifted schoolchildren are mainly distinguished from the less talented by internalized qualitative differences in cognitive processes. This

discipline-related analysis of talent has been accepted by other researchers (e.g. Bright, 1977; Marjoram & Nelson, 1985), but is still relatively loosely defined.

According to Krutetskii (1976, p. 351), characteristics such as speed of mental processing, computational ability, memory for symbols, numbers and formulae, ability in spatial concepts, and ability to visualized abstract mathematical relationships and dependencies are not absolutely vital for high mathematical aptitude. However, it cannot be denied that in maths lessons some students master tasks rapidly and effectively with the help of such abilities; apparently they enable the students to apply internalized cognitive processing strategies with great success. More recently, Kiesswetter (1985, 1988, 1999) has argued that the core of purposeful mathematical thinking is the systematic organizing of insights and findings into higher order structures. He identified six 'mathematical activities' which he regarded as central to this process (see Table 2). The most striking feature of these activities is their operative mode or the 'action' definition entailed in them. In this system, mathematics is understood to be an active process of devising theories, in the course of which four steps can be identified: (1) ascertaining constellations (questions) of interest; (2) focusing on the mathematical question under consideration and specifying the steps involved in its solution; (3) creatively and with the help of heuristic procedures arriving at new terms, mathematical formulations, proofs and broadly applied lines of attack; (4) placing the established interconnections within a network (Kiesswetter, 1992, p. 11).

According to this approach, mathematical giftedness manifests itself in the form of complex thinking

---

Table 1. Structure of mathematical abilities (Krutetskii, 1976, p. 350).

Obtaining mathematical information

- The ability for formalized perception of mathematical material, for grasping the formal structure of a problem

Processing mathematical information

- The ability for logical thought in the sphere of quantitative and spatial relationships, number and letter symbols; the ability to think in mathematical symbols
- The ability for rapid and broad generalization of mathematical objects, relations, and operations
- The ability to curtail the process of mathematical reasoning and the system of corresponding operations; the ability to think in curtailed structures
- Flexibility of mental processes in mathematical activity
- Striving for clarity, simplicity, economy, and rationality of solutions
- The ability for rapid and free reconstruction of the direction of a mental process, switching to a reverse train of thought (reversibility of the mental process in mathematical reasoning)

Retaining mathematical information

- Mathematical memory (generalized memory for mathematical relationships, type characteristics, schemata for arguments and proofs, methods of problem-solving, and principles of approach)

Table 2. System of complex mathematical activities (Kiesswetter, 1985).

(1) Organizing materials

(2) Recognizing patterns or rules

(3) Changing the representation of the problem and recognizing patterns and rules in this new area

(4) Comprehending and working with highly complex structures

(5) Reversing and inverting processes

(6) Finding (constructing) related problems

processes. These can be identified even in young people by using a relatively open approach such as that of the *Hamburg Test for Mathematical Giftedness (HTMB—Hamburger Test für Mathematische Begabung)*, which was developed along the lines of Kiesswetter's variables. It recognizes in its evaluation not only correct answers, but also the sensible application of these six activities (Wagner, Zimmermann & Stüven, 1986). High scores in the test indicate probable success in creative work within mathematical domains and/or related areas (Wagner & Zimmermann, 1986).

Essentially, this approach regards mathematical giftedness as involving special ways of looking at and attempting to solve mathematical problems, what Zimmermann (1998) called 'active structuring'. It involves higher order thinking, which has the following characteristics: (a) it is non-algorithmic (i.e. the pathway to the required solution is not specified in advance); (b) it is complex; (c) it often yields multiple solutions; (d) it requires 'nuanced judgment' from the learner (i.e. there are choice points where the learners must decide between lines of attack on the basis of experience, intuition and the like); (e) it involves multiple criteria; (f) it involves uncertainty; (g) it requires self-regulation; (h) it requires that the learner impose meaning on apparent disorder, rather than discover a pre-existing meaning. These characteristics can be contrasted with those of thinking aimed at acquisition of fixed knowledge that is then reapplied, in the case of talented individuals with great speed and accuracy (Resnick & Resnick, 1992).

Resnick and Resnick also emphasized the 'executive processes' necessary for higher order thinking; these encompass what are referred to later in this chapter as 'metacognitive' aspects of learning. They include: (a) keeping track of one's own understanding of the issue under consideration; (b) organizing attention; (c) organizing available resources; (d) reviewing one's own progress. To these can be added (Frederiksen & Collins, 1996) (e) effectively representing and solving problems; (f) choosing more promising approaches when existing ones fail to yield a solution; (g) understanding how systems work; (h) applying this understanding. The ability of students to articulate their own metacognitions is also of considerable importance. Articulation permits conscious self-reflection, highly specific feedback (correction) by teachers, and discussion with other learners of methods, precise differences between approaches, and similar topics.

Mathematical Giftedness from the Perspective of Gifted Youth

Theoretically derived systems for describing talented activities do not, however, necessarily accord with the experiences of mathematically gifted students actually dealing with mathematical problems. Former participants in the Hamburg Talent Searches aged between 16 and 20 (N = 234; male = 174, female = 60), of whom 71 took part in the *Hamburg Tutorial Program in Mathematics* for up to six years, responded to a questionnaire containing 63 items. The factor analytic approach yielded six dimensions, four of them cognitive (general traits; memory for symbols, numbers, formulae and principles; mathematical structures and patterns; visualization of problems and relations), one task oriented, and one creative (see Table 3). Thus, there is quite a strong resemblance to Renzulli's (1986) three-dimensional model of giftedness, according to which talent is a combination of high intelligence, creativity, and goal-directed motivation. This approach has been supported by other authors too (Wieczerkowski & Wagner, 1985; Mönks, 1992; Mönks & Mason, 1993).

In the view of these highly achieving young students, as Fig. 1 shows, cognitive flexibility (factor V) is the most important dimension, followed by perception of structures and patterns (factor IV), the ability to visualize abstract problems and relations (factor VI), and sensitivity to the aesthetic value and elegance inherent in a solution. In these aspects, differences between persons who participarted in the tutorial program and those who did not were not significant, but they were highly significant in task commitment (factor II) and memory for symbols, numbers and principles (factor III) ($p < 0.01$). Tenacity in problem-solving, ability to concentrate, ambition, goal orientation, i.e. facilitative working habits, and memory for formulae, etc. were given less importance for excelling in mathematical activities by those

Table 3. Six aspects of mathematical talent from the perspective of gifted youth.

I. General Trait	Understanding and empathy	0.679
	Emotional stability	0.612
	Originality of formulation	0.605
	Sensitivity	0.604
	Originality in connecting ideas and information	0.585
	Unusual suggestions	0.572
	Fantasy	0.566
II. Task Commitment	Tenacity in problem-solving	0.763
	Task commitment	0.727
	Goal orientation	0.719
	Ambition	0.702
	Constancy in mastering tasks	0.696
	Permanent readiness to learn	0.605
	Ability to concentrate	0.537
III. Memory for Symbols, Numbers, Principles	Memory for formulae	0.730
	Memory for numbers and symbols	0.676
	Memory for relations	0.637
	Memory for methods and principles	0.604
	Swift and precise calculations	0.603
	Memory for mathematical proofs	0.549
	Reconstructing learning process	0.480
	Searching out most obvious solutions	0.431
IV. Mathematical Structures and Patterns	Striving towards elegance in solutions	0.636
	Sensitivity for the beauty of a solution	0.574
	Perception of structure	0.534
	Abstracting concrete problems	0.515
	Interest in complex systems	0.494
	Recognizing formal structures	0.484
V. Flexibility in Mathematical Abilities	Flexibility of thought	0.734
	Inversion of thought processes	0.508
	Shifting representational level	0.437
	Flexible application of solution principles	0.384
	Generalizing a problem in terms of a problem area	0.346
	Trying various approaches to a problem	0.324
VI. Visualization of Problems and Relations	Ability to visualize problems	0.776
	Imagining spatial relations	0.774
	Ability to imagine visually	0.768
	Visualizing abstract relations	0.738

included in the program, apparently an effect of the special tutoring they had received.

Defining mathematical giftedness as successful cognitive problem solving in various areas emphasizes the importance of discovering the inherent structure of a problem and finding adequate operations for solving it. As a rule, this may well be a nonlinear process, for which appropriate knowledge and thinking strategies or, in the sense of Bauersfeld (1988), ease of interaction among areas of experience and a high level of goal directedness and achievement motivation, may be prerequisites. Experimenting by trying out different

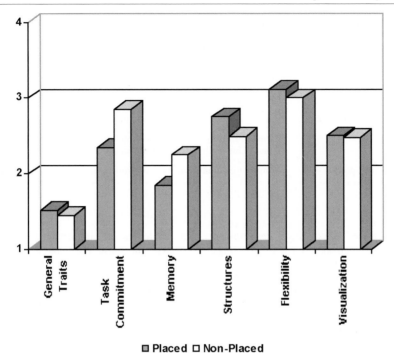

Figure 1. Aspects of mathematical talent

lines of attack on a problem then becomes a very important part of the complex system of mathematical behavior exhibited by talented young mathematicians.

Mathematical Excellence as a Developing State of Mind

The idea that giftedness is 'in process' and that the development of special ability involves changes in the internalized structure of a discipline achieved by an individual has often emerged in scientific research (cf., Geuss, 1981). According to this point of view, giftedness unfolds hand in hand with ongoing work in a given field. Abilities are then extended within a dialectical relationship between subject and (learning) object, that is to say, between the learner and the subject material. This conception, which sees changes in cognitive structure as the result of constant interaction of existing structures with accumulated and new experience, has been put forward primarily by Piaget (1970).

Such an interactionistic-constructivistic perspective has been emphasized in most recent discussions of mathematical giftedness by, among others, Bauersfeld (1988, 1987). Two fundamental qualities of processes are mentioned: (1) being able to shift easily from one subjective reality to another, and (2) being able easily to form new subjective realities. According to Bauersfeld (1988), there are six steps within these constructivistic processes that correspond to meta-

cognitive competencies worked out by Sternberg (1981, 1985) (see Table 4).

An analysis such as this probably comes closer to the problem-solving process than do ability-oriented definitions of mathematical giftedness. It must be added, however, that mathematical activities of young people will not always follow this ideal algorithm of thinking linearly and without interruptions to the course of progress (Zimmermann, 1992).

Quantitative vs. Qualitative Approaches to Defining Mathematical Giftedness

A crucial conceptual issue in this context is the distinction between the development of mathematical giftedness as a *quantitative* phenomenon, according to which development would be understood as accumulation of greater quantities of conventional, standard knowledge and skills (i.e. acquiring, ever larger quantities of the same), and as a *qualitative* phenomenon. In the latter case, development is seen as a series of cognitive advances involving acquisition and perfection of new kinds of strategies and systems for dealing with mathematical material, rather than as increasing the extent of existing knowledge and skills. Sheer quantity of mathematical knowledge at an early age involves one form of giftedness, to be sure, but this is different from the giftedness resulting from the development of higher order cognitive and metacognitive skills. Adopting a Piagetian position, Case (1979)

Table 4. Metacognitive analysis of progress in mathematical activities (Bauersfeld, 1988).

Recognizing the problem	Activating relevant subjective realities (constructions)
Planning strategies of problem-solving	Finding an appropriate initial approach
Selecting steps of action	Choosing from among a wider range of alternatives because of realities created by the learner
Mental representation of the problem	Finding a concise, condensed and generalized form of representation
Distributing attention	Frequent shifting of perspective and looking at wide overview of connected topics (This facilitates complex decision making)
Monitoring solution related process	Monitoring the informational network at each phase of the process

identified a fifth phase of cognitive development beyond the stage of formal operations. In this stage, second-order relations are recognized. Sternberg & Dowing (1982) extended this to third-order relations (analogies between analogies). Commons, Richards & Kuhn (1982) also argued for a fifth stage, the stage of 'Systematic Operations', at which operations are carried out on classes to build systems, as well as for a sixth stage of 'Metasystematic Operations' involving operations on systems.

The discussion of qualitative and quantitative approaches to mathematical giftedness can be linked to the general distinction between thinking aimed at finding the one only correct answer to a problem (referred to as 'convergent thinking' in the tradition of Guilford, 1950) and thinking aimed at producing novelty (to follow Guilford, 'divergent thinking'). It is possible to be very successful in school via the application of convergent thinking. However, there is evidence that at university (e.g. Cropley & Field, 1969) or in practical settings (e.g. Facaoaru, 1985), not only in Arts but also in Science and Technology, a combination of knowledge of the facts, logical thinking, speed and accuracy (i.e. convergent thinking) with branching out, seeing unexpected possibilities and finding novel solutions (divergent thinking) is necessary for gifted performance. Cropley (1994) argued that this combination defines 'true' giftedness.

This line of argument suggests that defining mathematical giftedness as simply mastering conventional knowledge at an early age (the quantitative approach) would lead to emphasis on convergent thinking in programs and strategies for fostering it, whereas the qualitative approach would emphasize divergent thinking. However, Cropley (e.g. 1992) warned against 'going overboard' for divergent thinking. While essential for true gifteness, divergent thinking is not sufficient; mastery of basic facts, speed, accuracy, rapid recall of material from memory and similar factors are also part of mathematical giftedness.

Fundamental cognitive processes such as retrieving, associating, synthesizing, transforming and constructing analogies are important for the production of novelty, but these must be accompanied by interpreting, inferring, shifting contexts, hypothesis testing, and searching for limitations (for more detailed discussions see Finke Ward & Smith, 1992). However, the production of mathematical novelty is not simply a matter of diverging from the traditional in an unregulated, more or less random process, in the hope that effective novelty will be produced by 'brute force' (Simon, 1989). What is needed are, on the one hand, control processes that make it possible, for instance, to distinguish in advance between promising lines of attack and dead ends, and on the other evaluative strategies and skills that make it possible for the individual to reject or modify inappropriate solutions, recognize promising aspects of rejected solutions, and use these in new attacks on the problem. The metacognitive aspects of effective mathematical activities listed in Table 4 thus take on renewed importance.

Non-cognitive Factors in Mathematical Giftedness

The metacognitive components of giftedness such as frequent shifting of perspective (see Table 4) require not only knowledge and skills, but also personal characteristics such as flexibility, openness (for the new), or tolerance for ambiguity, as well as confidence in oneself in the form of positive self-image. Also of considerable importance are motivational factors like curiosity, willingness to take risks, and task commitment. In research on the question of why some schoolchildren are willing to invest a great amount of time and effort in striving for mastery of a discipline such as mathematics—i.e. why they are motivated to study it intensively—Wieczerkowski (1998) identified two subjective factors: on the one, hand children's assumptions about the difficulty of mathematics, especially in relation to their own perceived ability to master this degree of difficulty, on the other, their assessment of the value and importance of mathematics, including its interestingness, its ability to help them satisfy personal needs (for success, social standing, and a feeling of self-worth), and its usefulness in achieving life goals (academic success, a good job, and the like).

Thus, although there is little doubt that attitudes to mathematics, mathematics-related self-concept and estimates of the utility of mathematics are closely linked to objective factors such as level of skill in the discipline and past success in the area, they are also affected by children's self-image and their stereotypes about mathematics and people who engage in it. Although he was writing about creativity, Csiksy-zentmihalyi (1996) emphasized the role of the social environment in fostering such subjective aspects of giftedness by stressing the necessity of a 'congenial' environment. This is characterized by tolerance of differences, openness for the new, positive attitudes to novelty, and willingness to reward clever failures, to give some examples.

Considerations such as these permit a broader understanding of Krutetskii's concept of a mathematical cast of mind and how to foster it. His approach was essentially cognitive and couched in terms of 'abilities', although elements such as 'flexibility' or 'striving for clarity' touch on personality or motivational aspects. However, it is now apparent that a special cast of mind would be characterized not only by abilities but also by non-cognitive components such as willingness to expend great effort on mathematical issues (motivation), placing a high value on mathematics (attitudes and values) or seeing oneself as capable of being successful in the mathematical field (self-image). A strategy for fostering mathematical ability would thus have as its goal provision of a mathematically 'congenial' environment that promoted both cognitive and non-cognitive aspects.

Gender Differences in Mathematics Achievement

Although the evidence for gender differences in mathematics achievement is not unequivocal across the full range of ability, differences in achievement between gifted boys and girls have repeatedly been reported in both North America and Europe (for detailed discussions, see LeMaistre & Kanevsky, 1997; Wieczerkowski & Prado, 1990). Among gifted children, boys are regularly observed to do better in mathematics and to show greater interest in the discipline; these differences are seen not only in school performances such as grades or choice of mathematics as subject specialization, but also in out-of-school activities such as participation in maths-oriented summer programs or in mathematics competitions.

Typical explanations of the causes of gender-related differences in mathematics (see LeMaistre & Kanevsky, 1997) have emphasized cognitive differences, either global (such as greater speed of certain functions of the central nervous system or superior right hemisphere performance in boys), or more specific (such as superior spatial relations or pattern formation in boys). It seems that there may well also be cognitive differences of the kind referred to here as 'qualitative'. Linn & Hyde (1989), for instance, showed that on the SAT-M girls typically (although naturally not exclusively) preferred to solve test items by reapplying standard algorithms in a meticulous but time consuming way. Boys, by contrast, often produced intuitive and fast solutions that gave them more time to attempt more items.

Some explanations emphasize particularly strongly that differences between boys and girls are acquired during the interactions of individual males and females with the conventions, beliefs, habits and values of the culture in which they grow up (see Wieczerkowski & Prado, 1990, 1992). The position adopted in this chapter (intellectual talent is a dynamic phenomenon that develops as a result of an interaction between an individual's potentials and a particular set of environmental conditions) suggests that the latter approach is more fruitful.

According to Wieczerkowski and Prado's analysis, the culture makes certain assumptions about sex roles that may be seen as stereotypes of what is typically 'male', and what is 'female'; these are maintained and transmitted in the typical family, in the form of attitudes and goals. The child develops a self-image and goals with regard to certain areas, for instance mathematics, while these areas acquire a subjective value for the child. Finally, the child develops expectations of success or, of course, of failure.

On the basis of a study of 436 12-year-old participants in a mathematics talent search (292 boys and 144 girls), Wieczerkowski (1998) identified two basic 'orientations' in the children's academic interests: on the one hand, an orientation towards musical-artistic pursuits, on the other towards scientific-technological activities. Independent of level of ability, these orientations encapsulate the kinds of activity that are seen by individual young people as capable of satisfying their needs. They define the immediate goals pursued by the individual, but do not necessarily develop into long term interests (i.e. a scientific-technological orientation in a young person promotes interest in learning mathematics, but may or may not lead to a career in mathematics).

Two findings concerning subject orientations in girls are of great interest here; even mathematically talented girls showed a significantly lower level of interest in science and technology than boys. In girls, the strength of the scientific-technological orientation increased with increasing level of achievement in relevant subjects, but this was not the case in boys. Wieczerkowski (1998) concluded that this was the result of sex-role stereotypes: boys regard themselves as talented in science and technology regardless of achievement (as of right, as it were), whereas girls need to convince themselves by obtaining high grades, since sex-role stereotypes indicate that girls are not good in these areas. Mathematically-talented boys judged their own ability more favourably, chose independently to enter a special program for the mathematically able, and expected to be successful. Girls, by contrast, were more modest in their self-estimates, needed encouragement from their teachers and parents to take part in the program, and estimated their likelihood of success less favourably than boys.

According to analyses of this kind, problems for girls in developing mathematical talent include (see also Feldhusen, VanTassel-Baska & Seeley, 1989): more rigid stereotypes than for boys; greater fear of failure in an 'unknown', atypical subject area; less favorable self-image with regard to mathematics; lower ability to recognize their own strengths; and lack of conviction of the worthwhileness of studying mathematics. This means that measures for fostering mathematical talent in girls need, to a degree greater than for boys, to go beyond the cognitive aspects of mathematics achievement, paying more attention to aspects such as communicating high expectations to girls and avoiding overprotection, encouraging them to take on difficult tasks, even if this risks failure, encouraging them to trust in their own ability, supporting mathematical interests outside school, and encouraging friendships with children with similar interests.

Strategies for Promoting Mathematical Talent

As has already been pointed out, the above discussions are not simply academic in nature, but are of great practical importance for the design of programs for fostering mathematical giftedness; practical consequences can be demonstrated with the help of a simple example from teaching practice. The authoritative *Third International Mathematic and Science Study* of the *International Association for the Evaluation of Educational Achievement* (IEA) evaluated videotapes of 8th grade mathematics instruction in over 200 American, German, and Japanese classrooms. German and American teachers concentrated on imparting standard skills; teachers demonstrated standard solutions to problems, then gave the students further problems of the given type, requiring them to apply the solution just demonstrated in a more cookbook manner. By contrast, Japanese teachers required students to work out their own solutions to problems and then discussed the wider application of these solutions in class. Japanese children were the third best achievers out of 41 countries in the project, whereas the Germans reached place 23 and the Americans place 28.

Educational programs for gifted students can be classified within a two-dimensional system, with one dimension involving instructional settings (in-school vs. out-of-school), the other the special approach to provision (acceleration and enrichment). This two-fold formal structure is made more complex by the additional aspect of grouping according to either ability

or interest. Although both of these criteria are, in practice, applicable to the same program in most cases, ability or interest groupings are of significant importance for placement and selection when considered separately. Programs in advanced mathematics for the mathematically highly able and interested can be divided into several types using the dimensions just outlined: whether they are offered in or out of school and according to the dominant didactic ideas underlying them (acceleration vs. enrichment). A two-dimensional matrix cannot, of course, account for the wide range of programs for the gifted; the sheer number of programs for the highly gifted at regional, national and international level thwarts any effort to ascertain their structure (see Fig. 2).

Acceleration and Enrichment

Traditionally, a distinction has been made between acceleration (children cover conventional material in less than the usual time, for instance by grade skipping or by enroling in special classes that work at a faster rate than usual) and enrichment (the children are exposed to material from outside the traditional curriculum, for instance in resource rooms or through the visits of resource teachers). However, more recent discussions (e.g. Stanley,1986) have concluded that the two approaches are merely two sides of the same coin. In the most obvious variant of this arrangement, children work through the conventional material faster than foreseen in the curriculum plan, in order to free up time for additional activities such as resource room or resource teacher, visits from knowledgeable members of the public, or excursions. Another variant involves giving the children material from higher classes as enrichment; the two could also be combined.

However, the argument that acceleration and enrichment more or less inevitably go hand in hand fails to distinguish between the quantitative and qualitative approaches outlined above. It is undeniable that acceleration (learning the usual material faster) is essentially the same as enrichment if the latter consists of no more than doing more difficult or more complex examples of the usual material. However, when enrichment is understood qualitatively (i.e. exposing children to material of a different kind and not just to more difficult or more complex examples of the usual), it becomes apparent that acceleration and enrichment are not simply different organizational forms of the same thing. In this sense it is possible to imagine acceleration without enrichment, as well as enrichment without acceleration; despite this, it may turn out that, in practice, a combination of the two is most effective.

Exclusive Grouping

Exclusive grouping requires satisfying a prerequisite for participation, and is based on three types of preselection: selection with the use of objective ability tests, placement on the basis of previous extraordinary

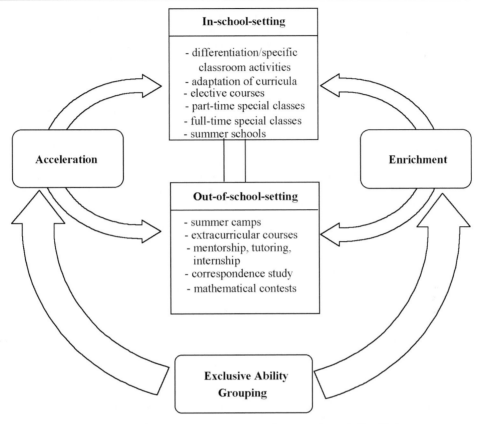

Figure 2. Strategies for special provision for the mathematically gifted

achievement in regular class instruction, or strong interest in mathematics. These three criteria are not mutually exclusive, and often come into play in combination. On the one hand, interest in mathematical problems is almost always tied in with a higher level of achievement and conception of oneself as a bright achiever. On the other hand, the readiness to demonstrate one's own skills in a talent search and to take part

in a program is, as a rule, coupled with exceptional interest in mathematics. Generally, grouping procedures follow a four-step strategy (Fig. 3):

Individually Paced Sequences vs. Open Syllabus

Two different tutorial models, applied by the *Center for Talented Youth* (IAAY at the Johns Hopkins University) and the *William Stern Society for Research on Gifted-*

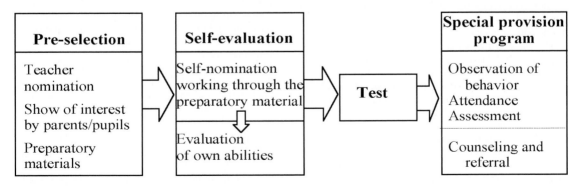

Figure 3. Identification by pre-selection, self-evaluation, testing, and special provision in advanced courses

ness (University of Hamburg) respectively, can be regarded as representing contrasting basic types of provision, and serve to demonstrate the variety of programs around the world.

Talent searches are conducted by the *Center for Talented Youth* (CTY) using the *College Board Scholastic Aptitude Test* (SAT), a standardized test for 17 to 18-year-olds. The idea underlying the search is that "12 to 13-year-olds who score highly on the SAT-M have enhanced problem transiation ability and are superior in their ability to represent and manipulate information in short term memory" (Benbow, 1990, p. 96). The Center offers fast-paced mathematics classes during summers in intensive three-week residential courses for students who scored at or above a cutoff score on the SAT-M. Participants registered in, for example, the Precalculus Mathematics Sequence are then given an Algebra Diagnostic Test in order to place them at an appropriate instructional starting point. In accordance with the principle of diagnostic testing followed by prescribed instruction, the students' approach is tailored to their individual needs (for details of the DT→PI model see Stanley, 1978, 1991; Lupkowski et al., 1990). Progress in course work is paced according to the learners' unique intellectual talents and motivation. The rationale of the approach is to support young mathematically gifted pupils in the swift and improved mastery of concepts within the conventional maths curricula in a manner that would not otherwise be possible in most public or private school instruction. CTY students use their academic program coursework for credit or placement at their local school (Barnett & Corazza, 1993, p. 56, see also internet sites of IAAY). In this pragmatic approach, mathematical giftedness is above all defined by an extraordinary level of speed in processing and retaining basic mathematical information and in successfully applying this to solving new examples of conventional tasks. Thus, the CTY approach is essentially quantitative in nature: it equates mathematical giftedness with possession of exceptionally large amounts of mathematical knowledge and outstanding success in obtaining correct solutions to conventional problems. Yet, speed components and memory for symbols, numbers and formulae are not considered by mathematicians to be essential for mathematical talent.

The underlying philosophy of mathematics of the *Hamburg Model* (Kiesswetter, 1992, 1988) is basically different from the rationale of the CTY. As Wagner and Zimmermann (1986, p. 275) pointed out, the emphasis of the Hamburg Program is on informal mathematics and mathematical ideas rather than on abstract structures. In this way, 'good mathematics' is defined by the quality of problem-solving strategies; in this context, mathematics is seen as an open process of thought rather than a universe of fixed products. Therefore, the main educational goal is exploring mathematics by micro-research processes, with as little guidance as possible; finding and creating problems is, in this view of mathematical provision, of greater or at least equal importance to solving them.

The different basic positions of these two approaches are obvious: while the CTY approach intends to speed up learning, a rather radical form of fast-pacing learning of prescribed contents, aided by skilled mentors, the Hamburg approach is guided by the central thought of improving mathematical abilities through working with (for the students in question) new kinds of relatively complex problems.

Four prototypical strategies more or less cover the full range of approaches to fostering mathematical talent: the two outlined above plus *Mathematics Olympics* and *student clubs*. This section will end by presenting a brief overview of the ways in which these strategies differ from each other.

(1) Acceleration/Self-Pacing

- Course contents are clearly structured and oriented to the regular syllabus. They are hierarchically organized.
- Participation is highly selective. Admission is by means of tests; a high score on a standardized abilities test is required. In addition to a diagnostic test for selecting a course with an appropriate level of difficulty, achievement tests are used to decide how much credit is to be given.
- The central motives for participating are exposing oneself to a challenge, saving time, and avoiding periods of stagnation in which nothing new is learned.
- Successful implementation of this strategy is dependent upon a readiness on the part of the society to give due recognition to individual effort.

(2) Enrichment/Open Syllabus

- Contents are usually taken from areas that are not covered in conventional classroom instruction. They are broad and open, e.g. 'Applied Algebra', 'Mathematics and Music', or 'Probability and Statistics', and are intended to awaken students' curiosity.
- Participation is selective to highly selective, and is dependent upon passing an entry exam. Further tests have no point. The duration of participation is determined by the opportunities available and the students' needs.
- Motivation arises principally from interest in the discipline, the expectation of being confronted by challenging material, and the chance to work with people with similar interests.
- Successful implementation of this strategy is dependent upon an instrinsic interest in the subject.

(3) Mathematics Olympics

- Courses with the specific goal of preparing students to participate in these international competitions are, naturally, particularly clearly oriented towards the goal of doing as well as possible in comparison with competitors from other countries. Contents are usually based on areas and topics that have appeared in previous competitions. In other words, the contents are determined by the contest.

- Participation is extremely selective and is usually decided by success in preliminary competitions, for instance in regional elimination contests.
- The reasons why participants expose themselves to the risks of such competitions are undoubtedly complex: in addition to the motivation provided by prizes and other rewards for the winners, they probably include the desire to prove oneself and to obtain prestige. In all probability, motivation is rather extrinsic.
- The degree to which special efforts are made to encourage broad participation in national contests depends upon the political climate in each particular country.

(4) Mathematics Student Clubs

- The contents that seize the interest of the participants and hold it over a certain timespan are usually unstructured, as are the groups themselves, that form to pursue a common activity.
- Participation is determined by interest, and depends in the first instance on whether the expectations that led initially to joining up are satisfied. The decisive characteristic of participants is, almost without exception, an interest in the subject and, conceivably, a 'personal disposition'.

Concluding Remarks

Participation in a special program whether on the basis of high test scores in a talent search, exceptional achievement in the classroom, or by virtue of expressing a strong interest in mathematical subjects and thought processes has unmistakable consequences for the individual's further development. As Eccles and her colleagues have shown in their General Model of Achievement Choice (Eccles, 1985; Eccles & Jacobs, 1986), dynamic processes set off by participation in challenging activities within a subject can have a significant bearing on how such activity is experienced subjectively and the way ensuing decisions concerning career paths are made (see the earlier discussion of gender differences in mathematical achievement).

Taking part in a special program for the mathematically gifted and experiencing the challenge that is inherent in such participation causes change not only in the cognitive structure of knowledge and thought of the young person, i.e. heightened mathematical competence, but also induces change in non-cognitive structure. Up to the present, only modest empirical contributions on these dynamics can be found in studies concerning the effects of such changes. Con-

cepts of the characteristics and components of mathematical giftedness mark the beginning and remain central to any effort to identify and nurture the mathematically highly able. Not only the selection process, but also concepts dealing with the form and content of what optimally should be included in a program are directly affected by assumptions made about the structure of mathematical giftedness. Assumptions which are implicitly presented to schoolchildren assist them in forming their 'perception of mathematics', their subjective realities, which presumably later influence their attitude toward the subject. Special provision for highly able students of mathematics may implicity induce, as knowledge and mathematical competence increase, a continuous change toward a specific mathematical cast of mind (Krutetskii, 1976). In most programs, this aspect is not explicitly considered.

The variety of approaches that can be used to nurture talent is enormous. The multiplicity of organisational principles, course contents, formal as well as informal settings, regional and national set-ups within the gamut of special provision concepts makes clear that a large number of program forms exist. When selecting or constructing a program from such a large variety of possibilities, the main issue is not that of finding the 'right' one, but of finding the one that is most stimulating for particular participants. All strategies aimed at nurturing mathematical giftedness have their own specific goals and contents, and, as Gallagher (1985) pointed out, they all have their own intrinsic value.

References

Barnett, L. B. & Corazza, L. (1993). Identification of mathematical talent and programmatic efforts to facilitate development of talent. *European Journal for High Ability*, **4**, 48–61.

Bauersfeld, H. (1988). Exploration aus Mikroanalysen mathematischer Lehr-Lern-Prozesse zur möglichen Förderung sogenannter Hochbegabter. In: K. Kiesswetter (Ed.), *Das Hamburger Modell zur Identifizierung und Förderung von mathematisch besonders befähigten Schülern. Berichte aus der Forschung*. Heft 2 (pp. 69–89). Hamburg: Fachbereich Erziehungswissenschaft, Universität Hamburg.

Bauersfeld, H. (1987). Interaction, construction, and knowledge. Alternative perspectives for mathematics education. In: T. Cooney & D. Grouws (Eds.), *Effective mathematics teaching*. Reston, VA: National Council of Teachers of Mathematics.

Benbow, C. P. (1990). Mathematical talent and females: from a biological perspective. In: W. Wieczerkowski & T. M. Prado (Eds.), *Hochbegabte Mädchen* (pp. 95–113). Bad Honnef: K. H. Bock.

Bright, G. S. (1977). Critique, and analysis of the psychology of mathematical abilities in schoolchildren. *Investigations in Mathematics Education*, **10**, 43–47.

Case, R. (1979). Intellectual development from birth to adulthood: a neo-Piagetian interpretation. In: R. S. Siegler (Ed.), *Children's thinking: What develops?* (pp. 37–71). Hillsdale, N.J.: Erlbaum.

Commons, M. L., Richards, F. A. & Kuhn, D. (1982). Systematic and metasystematic reasoning: a case for levels of reasoning beyond Piaget's stage of formal operations. *Child Development*, **53**, 1058–1069.

Cropley, A. J. (1992). *Fostering creativity in the classroom*. Norwood, NJ: Ablex.

Cropley, A. J. (1994). Creative intelligence: a concept of 'true' giftedness. *European Journal for High Ability*, **5**, 6–23.

Cropley, A. J. & Field, T. W. (1969). Achievement in science and intellectual style. *Journal of Applied Psychology*, **53**, 132–135.

Csikszentmihalyi, M. (1996). *Creativity: Flow and the psychology of discovery and invention*. New York: Harper Collins.

David, P. J. & Hersh, R. (1981). *The mathematical experience*. Basel: Birkhäuser.

Dummer, L. (1983). Zur mathematisch-technischen Begabungsstruktur. *Psychologie in Erziehung und Unterricht*, **30**, 192–199.

Eccles, J. (1985). Model of students' mathematics enrollment decisions. *Educational Studies in Mathematics*, **16**, 311–314.

Eccles, J. & Jacobs, J. E. (1986). Social forces shape math attitudes and performance. *Signs*, **11**, 367–389.

Facaoaru, C. (1985). *Kreativität in Wissenschaft und Technik*. Bern: Huber.

Feldusen, J., VanTassel-Baska, J. & Seeley, K. (1989). *Excellence in educating the gifted*. Denver, CO: Love.

Finke, R. A., Ward, T. B. & Smith, S. M. (1992). *Creative cognition*. Boston, MA: MIT Press.

Frederiksen, J. R. & Collins, A. (1996). Designing an assessment system for the future workplace. In: L. B. Resnick & J. G. Wirth (Eds.), *Linking school and work* (pp. 193–221). San Francisco: Jossey Bass.

Gallagher, J. J. (1985). *Teaching the gifted child* (3rd ed.). Boston: Allyn & Bacon.

Gardner, H. (1983). *Frames of the mind: The theory of multiple intelligences*. New York: Basic Books.

Geuss, H. (1981). Zur Problematik der Identification von Hochbegabung. In: W. Wieczerkowski & H. Wagner (Eds.), *Das hochbegabte Kind* (pp. 52–67). Düsseldorf: Schwann.

Guilford, J. P. (1950). Creativity. *American Psychologist*, **5**, 444–454.

Halpern, D. F. (1986). *Sex differences in cognitive abilities*. Hillsdale, NJ: Lawrence Erlbaum.

Heid, M. K. (1983). Characteristics and special needs of the gifted student in mathematics. *Mathematics Teacher*, **76**, 221–226.

Kiesswetter, K. (1985). Die Förderung von mathematisch besonders begabten und interessierten Schülern—ein bislang vernachlässigtes sonderpädagogisches Problem. *Der Mathematische und naturwissenschaftliche Unterricht*, **38**, 300–306.

Kiesswetter, K. (1988). Das Hamburger Fördermodell und sein mathematik-didaktisches Umfeld. In: K. Kiesswetter (Ed.), *Das Hamburger Modell zur Identifizierung und Förderung von Mathematisch besonders Befähigten Schülern. Berichte aus der Forschung*. Heft 2 (pp. 6–34). Hamburg: Fachbereich Erziehungswissenschaft, Universität Hamburg.

Kiesswetter, K. (1992). 'Mathematische Begabung'. Über die Komplexität der Phänomene und die Unzulänglichkeiten von Punktbewertungen. In: K. Kiesswetter (Ed.), *Mathematische Begabungen. Der Mathematikunterricht. Beiträge zu seiner Fachinhaltlichen und fachdidaktischen Gestaltung*, **38**, 5–18.

Krutetskii, V. A. (1976). *The psychology of mathematical abilities in schoolchildren*. Chicago: University of Chicago Press.

LeMaistre, C. & Kanevsky, L. (1997). Factor influencing the realization of exceptional mathematical ability in girls: an analysis of the research. *High Ability Studies*, **8**, 31–46.

Lloyd, B. & Archer, J. (Eds.). (1976). *Exploring sex differences*. London: Academic Press.

Lupkowski, A. E., Assouline, S. G. & Stanley, J. C. (1990). Applying a mentor model for young mathematically talented students. *Gifted Child Today*, **13**, 15–19.

Maccoby, E. E. & Jacklin, C. N. (1974). *The psychology of sex differences*. Stanford: Stanford University Press.

Marjoram, D. T. E. & Nelson, R. D.(1985). Mathematical gifts. In: J. Freeman (Ed.), *The psychology of gifted children. perspectives on development and education* (pp. 185–200). Chichester, New York: John Wiley & Sons.

Merz, F. (1979). *Geschlechtsunterschiede und ihre Entwicklung. Ergebnisse und Theorien der Psychologie*. Göttingen: Hogrefe.

Mönks, F. J. (1992). Ein interaktionales Modell der Hochbegabung. In: E. A. Hany & H. Nickel (Eds.), *Begabung und Hochbegabung. Theoretische Konzepte, empirische Befunde und praktische Konsequenzen* (pp. 17–22). Bern: Huber.

Mönks, F. J. & Mason, E. J. (1993). Developmental theories on giftedness. In: K. A. Heller, F. J. Mönks & A. H. Passow (Eds.), *International handbook of research and development of giftedness and talent* (pp. 89–101). Oxford: Pergamon.

Pawlik, K. (1968). *Dimensionen des Verhaltens. Eine Einführung in Methoden und Ergebnisse faktorenanalytischer psychologischer Forschung*. Bern: Huber.

Piaget, J. (1970). Piaget's theory. In: P. H. Mussen (Ed.), *Carmichael's manual of child psychology* (3rd ed.) (pp. 703–732). New York: John Wiley & Sons.

Renzulli, J. S. (1986). The three-ring conception of giftedness: a developmental model for creativity. In: R. S. Sternberg & J. E. Davidson (Eds.), *Conceptions of giftedness* (pp. 53–92). Cambridge: Cambridge University Press.

Resnick, L. B. & Resnick, D. P. (1992). Assessing the thinking curriculum: new tools for educational reform. In: B. R. Gifford & M. C. O'Connor (Eds.), *Changing assessments: alternative views of aptitude, achievement, and instruction* (pp. 37–75). Boston: Kluwer.

Siegvald, H. (1944). *Experimentella undersökningar rörande intellektuella könsdifferenser*. Lund: Ohlsons Boktryckeri.

Simon, H. A. (1989). The scientist as a problem solver. In: D. Klahr & K. Katovsky (Eds.), *Complex information processing* (pp. 375–398). Hillsdale, N.J.: Erlbaum.

Stanley, J. C. (1978). SMPY's DT→PI mentor model: diagnostic testing followed by prescriptive instruction. *Intellectually Talented Youth Bulletin*, **4**, 7–8.

Stanley, J. C. (1986). Fostering use of mathematical talent in the USA: SMPY rationale. In: A. J. Cropley, K. K. Urban, H. Wagner & W. Wieczerkowski (Eds.), *Giftedness: A continuing worldwide challenge* (pp. 227–243). New York: Trillium.

Stanley, J. C. (1991). An academic model for educating the mathematically talented. *Gifted Child Quarterly*, **35**, 36–42.

Steen, L. A. (1979). *Mathematics today*. New York: Springer.

Steen, L. A. (1981). *Mathematics tomorrow*. New York: Springer.

Sternberg, R. J. (1981). A componential theory of intellectual giftedness. *Gifted Child Quarterly*, **25**, 86–93.

Sternberg, R. J. (1985). *Beyond IQ: A triarchic theory of human intelligence*. Cambridge: Cambridge University.

Sternberg, R. J. & Dowing, D. C. (1982). The development of higher order reasoning in adolescence. *Child Development*, **53**, 209–221.

Terman, L. M. & Tylor, L. E. (1954). Psychological sex differences. In: L. Carmichael (Ed.), *Manual of child psychology* (2nd ed.) (pp. 1064–1114). New York: John Wiley & Sons.

Wagner, H. & Zimmermann, B. (1986). Identification and fostering of mathematically gifted students. In: A. J. Cropley, K. K. Urban, H. Wagner & W. Wieczerkowski (Eds.), *Giftedness: A continuing worldwide challenge* (pp. 273–287). New York: Trillium.

Wagner, H., Zimmermann, B. & Stüven, N. (1986). Identifizierung und Förderung mathematisch besonders befähigter Schüler. Bericht über einen Modellversuch. In: W. Wieczerkowski, H. Wagner, K. K. Urban & A. J. Cropley (Eds.), *Hochbegabung-Gesellschaft-Schule* (pp. 239- 251). Bad Honnef: K. H. Bock.

Wieczerkowski, W. (1998). *Mathematisch besonders befähigter Schüler. Einstellungen und Selbstkonzepte in einer 12jährigen Talentgruppe*. Hamburg: William-Stern-Gesellschaft.

Wieczerkowski, W. & Prado, T. M. (1990). *Hochbegabte Mädchen*. Bad Honnef: K. H. Bock.

Wieczerkowski, W. & Prado, T. M. (1992). Begabung und Geschlecht. In: E. A. Hany & H. Nickel (Eds.), *Begabung und Hochbegabung. Theoretische Konzepte, empirische Befunde, praktische Konsequenzen* (pp. 39–57). Bern: Huber.

Wieczerkowski, W. & Wagner, H. (1985). Diagnostik von Hochbegabung. In: R. S. Jäger, R. Horn & K. Ingenkamp (Eds.), *Tests und Trends 4. Jahrbuch der Pädagogischen Diagnostik* (pp. 109–134). Weinheim: Beltz.

Zimmermann, A. (1998). Verändertes Denken, Sprechen, Wahrnehmen und Verhalten bei Schülerinnen und Schülern. *Labyrinth*, **58**, 3–5.

Zimmermann, B. (1992). Profile mathematischer Begabung. Fallstudien aus dem Hamburger Projekt sowie aus der Geschichte der Mathematik. In: K. Kiesswetter (Ed.), *Mathematische Begabungen. Der Mathematikunterricht. Beiträge zu seiner fachinhaltlichen und fachdidaktischen Gestaltung*, **38**, 19–41.

Talent Development in Science and Technology

Michael C. Pyryt

University of Calgary, Centre for Gifted Education, Calgary, Alberta, Canada

Overview

The purpose of this chapter is to discuss effective strategies and programs for developing talent in science and technology. It is organized in five broad sections. The first deals with the development of scientific talent over the lifespan; the second section describes several approaches for discovering talent in science; the third highlights a variety of curricular approaches for developing talent in science; the fourth discusses continual challenges impacting the development of scientific talent. Finally, the chapter provides directions for the future.

Scientific Development: A Life-Span Approach

The basic tenet underlying this chapter is that the process of talent development in science mirrors the process of career development of scientists; by understanding how individuals become successful scientists, we gain insight into the individual and environmental dynamics that facilitate talent development in science. Piirto (1999) views talent development as a multi-faceted phenomenon in which the genetic attributes, personality traits, cognitive capacities, influenced by the home, school and community coalesce into a vocation. Albert (1980) proposed that two transformations are necessary to achieve eminence. The first involves channeling intellectual giftedness into creative giftedness and the second involves channeling creativeness into the configuration of talent, drive, and values that it takes to succeed. These transformations are viewed as occurring as a result of the dynamic interaction of early talent recognition, family socialization experiences and career development experiences. This interaction is most likely to occur when the particular talent is of special interest to the family.

The Development of Talent Research Project at The University of Chicago (Bloom, 1985) provides insights into the socialization factors that promote talent development. Sosniak (1985) described the developmental precursors of commitment to science for a sample of outstanding research neurologists. Their parents who provided intellectual stimulation and high expectations actively nurtured the initial curiosity of these potential scientists; they often purchased science kits or toy microscopes, which were used by these future scientists to conduct experiments at home. As they grew older, their experiments grew in complexity; their commitment to research as a career was crystallized by their introduction to formal research in prestigious universities and medical schools.

They chose neurology as an area of study because of its intellectual challenge, complexity, and importance. Sosniak (1999) views the main ingredients of talent development to be time commitment, engagement in authentic tasks, and involvement with communities of like-minded committed individuals.

As one pursues a career there are 'Matthew Effects' (Merton, 1968) or cumulative advantages that accrue from any initial advantage that an individual might have; potential scientists who matriculate at elite undergraduate institutions often have the opportunity to pursue post-baccalaureate study at elite graduate institutions. Five universities (Columbia, Harvard, Johns Hopkins, Princeton, and the University of California at Berkeley) produced over half of the American Nobel Laureates in science (Zuckerman, 1977). After finishing graduate school, laureates were most likely to begin employment or pursue post-doctoral training at prestigious institutions; as part of their training, laureates were likely to have had at least one Nobel Laureate as supervisor or senior collaborator. Potential laureates were socialized to attempt important problems, to appreciate elegant solutions, to maintain high standards of performance, and to work hard to achieve these standards. This work pattern initiated early publication of significant research and subsequent recognition among peers and academic promotions.

The research of MacKinnon and associates at The University of California at Berkeley (MacKinnon, 1962, 1965, 1975; 1978; Barron, 1963, 1969; Helson & Crutchfield, 1970) is the basis for our understanding of the personality characteristics of eminent individuals in a variety of domains, including mathematics and science. Eminent individuals possess the unique combination of theoretical and aesthetic values because they are motivated to find elegant solutions to discovering the truth; they possess ego-strength and are capable of tolerating ambiguity and disharmony to a greater extent than most people. They are curious and prefer novelty and complexity; typical self-descriptive adjectives of eminent individuals include individualistic, self-reliant, spontaneous, flexible, assertive, ambitious, competitive, and self-confident. Research by Mac-Kinnon (1962) indicates that a certain level of intelligence, typically one standard deviation above the mean, is necessary for creative achievement; once this threshold is reached, intelligence and creativity are uncorrelated. In addition to this threshold effect, the distribution of productivity in domains is skewed (Simonton, 1997); eminent individuals are highly productive individuals, whose output dramatically surpasses the average contributor in a domain.

Heller's (1993) review of the literature on scientific ability makes accessible some important studies from Germany. The five highest effect sizes in a 17 year longitudinal comparison of over 3500 high and average achievements in science and technology were motivation and ability to solve problems (0.71), desire to influence, initiative, and leadership success (0.62), search for knowledge (0.43), early upbringing focusing on independence (0.42), and self-evaluation of school performance in the last three years at school (0.35).

Discovering Talent in Science

This section highlights a variety of approaches for discovering talent in science and technology: cognitive and affective approaches, profile approaches, and invitational approaches; one of the challenges in developing any identification procedure is to differentiate potential and performance. Students in elementary schools have limited potential to explore scientific content; measures of science knowledge and competencies would be inappropriate. Predictors of science achievement such as mathematics ability would be useful for identifying potential; once the opportunity for learning science content and process is provided measures of science achievement would be more direct measures of developed science ability than indirect measures such as mathematical ability.

The pioneering work of Julian Stanley (1976, 1996; Stanley, Keating & Fox, 1974) through the founding of the Study of Mathematically Precocious Youth (SMPY), originally known as the Study of Mathematically and Scientifically Precocious Youth in 1971, has greatly influenced our thinking about the discovery of mathematical and scientific talent. SMPY uses a talent search approach (Cohn, 1991; Stanley, 1976; Assouline & Lupkowski-Shoplik, 1997; Olszewski-Kubilius, 1998) to identify superior mathematical reasoners. Seventh graders who score at the 97th percentile (national norms) on a standardized achievement test

are invited to take a more difficult test (the Scholastic Aptitude Test). Seventh grade students scoring higher than the average university-bound high school senior on the SATs are given opportunities to participate in a wide variety of educational experiences. Currently regional talent searches for junior high school students using either the SAT or ACT are conducted throughout the United States via the Institute for the Academic Advancement of Youth (IAAY) at The Johns Hopkins University, the Talent Identification Program (TIP) at Duke University, the Center for Talent Development (CTD) at Northwestern University or the Rocky Mountain Talent Search at the University of Denver. Through its international talent searches, The Johns Hopkins University provides the opportunity for students throughout the world to determine their developed verbal and mathematical ability. A new development is the administration of talent searches at the elementary level. The Belin Elementary School Talent Search (BESTS) conducted by the Belin-Blank Center at The University of Iowa administers a test called EXPLORE, a standardized test for eight graders to fourth, fifth, and sixth graders. The EXPLORE test has a science reasoning subtest which requires the test taker to evaluate scientific information and design experiments. The BESTS approach has been successfully imported to Australia and Canada (Assouline, Colangelo, Gross & Pyryt, 1999); talent searches at the elementary school level are also conducted by IAAY, CTD, and TIP.

In addition to mathematical ability, it might also be useful to assess spatial visualization ability. Humphreys & Lubinski (1996) reanalyzed Project Talent (Flanagan et al., 1962) data using canonical correlation and showed that spatial ability in addition to mathematics ability is useful in predicting graduate majors in science and engineering. Spatial-visualization ability is one of the broad factors identified by Carroll (1993) in his monumental factor analytic survey of 476 datasets dealing with human cognitive abilities.

In addition to assessing cognitive components, it is important to address affective dimensions, particularly motivation and interests; among the various conceptions of giftedness (Sternberg & Davidson, 1986), motivation is a common ingredient. In Tannenbaum's (1986) psychosocial model of giftedness, motivation to achieve is one of the non-intellective factors; task commitment is a major component of Renzulli's (1986) three-ring conception of giftedness. Feldhusen (1986) also includes motivation in his conception of giftedness; Haensly, Reynolds & Nash (1986) incorporate motivation in their focus on commitment; Stanley & Benbow (1986) include motivation in their recommendations for talent development in mathematics. Despite its importance in conceptions of giftedness, domain specific measures of motivation are lacking; interviews and observations seem to be the best way to assess motivation for specific areas like science and technology. Holland's (1973) theory of vocational choice provides a mechanism for assessing interests related to science and science activities; this theory suggests that occupations can be classified by the personality types involved in the occupations. Holland's system classifies occupations as a combination of three of six ideal personality types (realistic, investigative, artistic, social, enterprising, and conventional). Investigative types who prefer occupations that permit searching for the truth dominate science. A variety of career interest inventories such as the *Vocational Preference Inventory* (Holland, 1978), the *Self-Directed Search* (Holland, 1974) or *Strong Interest Inventory* (Hansen & Campbell, 1985) can be used to determine the investigative interests of adolescents.

Rather than using scores on cognitive and affective measures as criteria for selection into specialized programs for talent development in science and technology, it is possible to evaluate potential in science through a profile analysis; Renzulli & Reis (1997) use the Total Talent Portfolio in their School-wide Enrichment Model. In addition to standardized and teacher-made tests, the portfolio includes grades, teacher ratings, products, level of participation, and interaction with others as indicators of maximum performance. The Total Talent Portfolio includes interests in Physical Science, Life Science, Mathematical/Logical and Computers as science and technology related interest clusters. The Talent Portfolio also includes a wide variety of preferences (learning styles, thinking styles, instructional styles, and expression styles) to gain a wholistic picture of a child's needs. Treffinger's (1986) Individualized Programming Planning Model (IPPM) also uses profile analysis in determining needs.

The use of competitions, such as science contests and olympiads provide the opportunity for scientifically talented students to demonstrate their ability in science and technology; these invitational practices permit the opportunity for self-selection since students' participation is voluntary. One of the most prestigious scientific competitions in the United States is the Westinghouse Science Talent Search (Berger, 1994); this competition, now sponsored by Intel, has been in operation since 1942. Each year high school students submit 1000 word research summaries reporting results of an original research investigation; from these submitted reports, 300 are selected as honors recipients and forty participants are designated as semi-finalists and interviewed to compete for 10 positions as Westinghouse finalists. Winners in the talent search have gone on to win Nobel prizes, become MacArthur fellows, and earn election in the National Academy of Science. Subotnik (1986, 1988a, 1988b, Subotnik & Steiner, 1994) is conducting a longitudinal study of a sample of 146 combined honors, semi-finalists and finalists in the 1983 Westinghouse Talent Search. She reported that many of the participants (61%) were

assisted in problem selection by laboratory supervisors and professors. Much of the work was carried out in laboratories in hospitals and universities with practicing scientists serving a mentoring function; subjects tended to attribute curiosity as the major motivating reason for conducting research. Olympiad programs also capitalize on self-selection since individuals typically try out for olympiad teams.

Curricular Approaches to Talent Development in Science

This section highlights curricular approaches to talent development in science and technology. In addition to three main approaches to gifted education curriculum (content-based, process/product research based, and epistemological concept) identified by VanTassel-Baska (1994), this section also includes a description of community-based approaches and highlights the power of the internet for stimulating scientific activity. Since there are numerous content-based approaches that have been proven effective, content-based approaches will predominate; exemplary models such as specialized schools will combine several approaches.

Content-based approaches focus on the importance on content acquisition as a precursor to scientific productivity; as exemplified by the Study of Mathematically Precocious Youth, the goal is to provide educational experiences that enable talented and motivated youth to master the content of various science disciplines. Over the past quarter century SMPY has pioneered a variety of content-based approaches including DT–PI, accelerated courses, and opportunities for university coursework; it has also supported specialized classes and schools that provide a content-rich experience.

Diagnostic Testing–Prescriptive Instruction (DT–PI) enables students to master content rapidly by concentrating on those skills that students still need to acquire (Stanley, 1978, 1998); this instructional approach involves performing an error analysis of items missed on a given standardized test to determine instructional needs. An instructional program is designed and implemented to address these needs; students are retested on a parallel form of the initial test to determine mastery; if the course content is mastered, students proceed to the next content level using the same approach (Benbow, 1986). Stanley (1998) suggests that computer programs can be used to facilitate the diagnostic testing-prescriptive instruction process. Followers of Renzulli implement a variant of the DT–PI approach when they use curriculum compacting (Renzulli, Smith & Reis, 1982; Starko, 1986; Reis, Burns & Renzulli, 1992).

SMPY has also pioneered the use of fast-paced classes in science (Mezynski, Stanley & McCoart, 1983; Stanley & Stanley, 1986; Lynch, 1990) and mathematics (George & Denham, 1976; Bartkovich &

George, 1980). In these classes, students learn content far more rapidly than in traditionally-paced approaches; Stanley & Stanley (1986) described the use of the fast-paced class approach in science instruction implemented in 1982. During an intense three-week summer institute, students ages 11–15, who scored at least 500 on the mathematics section of the Scholastic Aptitude Test (SAT) and at least 930 on the combined mathematics and verbal sections of the SAT before age 13, learned the equivalent of a year of high school biology or a year of high school chemistry; four students studied both subjects in six weeks. The biology class met approximately 5.5 hours a day including laboratory instruction for 15 days. Pretesting of students, *who had not taken a course called biology*, on the biology achievement test developed by the College Entrance Examination Board (CEEB) indicated that the 25 students in the class earned scores ranging from 420 to 690. The median score of 560 placed the sample at the 52nd percentile. At the end of the three-week course, which was taught by a well-qualified and enthusiastic instructor, knowledgeable about biology content at the high school and college levels, scores on an alternate form of the CEEB Biology Achievement Test ranged from 590 to 800 (the maximum possible score). The median score of 727 placed the group at the 95th percentile on National norms. The 13 students enrolled in the chemistry course earned a median score of 743 (95th percentile) on the CEEB Chemistry Achievement Test; as a result of this initial success, a fast-paced physics course was also developed. Lynch (1990) provided results from fast-paced science classes conducted between 1982 and 1987. Mean post-test scores on CEEB achievement tests were 627 for 353 students in biology, 630 for 339 students in chemistry, and 644 for 213 students in physics; these mean scores represent the 73rd, 67th, and 70th percentiles in biology, chemistry, and physics respectively.

Earning credit by examination through the Advanced Placement Program (Advanced Placement Program, 1994; Hanson, 1980) is a viable way to accelerate one's progress in science and technology; students can earn college credit by receiving a specified score on an Advanced Placement examination. In the area of science, there are examinations in general biology, general chemistry, magnetism, physics, physics/mechanics, and physics/electricity; there are also two computer science examinations. Approximately 1400 colleges and universities award sophomore standing to students who earn satisfactory examination scores on enough (typically 3) AP examinations. Since tuition fees at elite universities in the United States continues to escalate, the ability to pass several AP examinations will result in significant financial benefits for the student.

The Advanced Placement Program distributes course descriptions of the objectives that will be assessed on the AP examinations; approximately 11,000 high schools offer Advanced Placement courses that address content assessed on the AP examinations. Some universities offer AP Summer Teaching Institutes to prepare secondary school teachers to instruct specific AP courses; fast-paced classes can be geared to AP examinations (Mezynski, Stanley & McCoart, 1983). SMPY implemented courses in physics and chemistry that were taught by college professors to students ages 12 to 17. Seven of the ten students, who completed the physics earned a grade of 3 or higher on both the mechanics and electricity and magnetism sections of the AP Physics: C examination; three students earned a grade of 2 on both sections of the AP Physics:C examination. Eighteen students completed the chemistry course. Twelve of the 14 students who took the AP Chemistry examination earned a grade of '3' or higher; homework performance, in-class test scores, and AP practice test scores were predictive of Advanced Placement Examination scores. Longitudinal studies have indicated that AP students are more likely than non-AP students to select an academic or scientific career, graduate early, and apply to selective colleges (Advanced Placement Program, 1994). Brody, Assouline & Stanley (1990) found that the number of Advanced Placement credits was the only statistically significant predictor of first semester GPA, cumulative GPA, percentage of semesters on the Dean's List, and honors at graduation in their study of early entrants at Johns Hopkins.

SMPY has also pioneered the notion of content acquisition through early university coursework either on a part-time or full-time basis. Solano & George (1976) examined the university achievement of 131 adolescents identified by SMPY; overall grade point average on a 4-point scale after taking 277 college courses was 3.59. The majority of these courses were in the areas of mathematics and the natural sciences. Early admission to college (two years earlier than normal) is a possible option for some highly able and motivated students. SMPY's first radical accelerant entered The Johns Hopkins University at age 13 and completed the requirements for a B.A. degree in quantitative studies and an M.S. in Engineering specializing in Computer Science at age seventeen years and ten months (Stanley, 1974). He went on to earn a Ph.D. in computer science from Cornell University and is currently a professor at Carnegie Mellon University (Hendricks, 1997). Stanley & McGill (1986) correlated demographic variables (age, gender, SMPY affiliation, credits at college entrance, attendance at private high schools, Oriental parentage) and indices of college performance (age at graduation, number of credits earned, simultaneously earning Bachelor's and Master's degrees, percentage of time on the Dean's List, cumulative GPA, Honors at graduation) for 25 students who entered The Johns Hopkins University two-to-five-years earlier than usual. They reported two significant canonical correlations of 0.87 and 0.78 between composites of demographic variables and outcomes. Further analysis indicated that SMPY affiliation, credits at college entrance and attendance at private schools were most related to Honors at graduation, cumulative Grade Point Average, age at graduation, and number of credits earned. Brody, Assouline & Stanley (1990) expanded Stanley & McGill's (1986) study to include 65 students, who entered Johns Hopkins between the ages of 13 years 8 months and 17 years 7 months. Accelerants were more likely than non-accelerants to simultaneously earn bachelor's and master's degrees, win general honors and departmental honors at graduation, and be elected to honor societies such as Phi Beta Kappa or Tau Beta Pi, the national engineering honor society. Hendricks (1997) describes a twenty-year follow-up of some of SMPY's initial early entrance group; for the most part, the early entrants have had successful careers and have benefited greatly by their acceleration experience. Brody & Benbow (1987) examined the effectiveness of the smorgasbord of educationally accelerative opportunities model. Students who made use of accelerative options attended more selective colleges, had higher college GPAs, won more honors, and had higher career aspirations than students who decided against making use of these accelerative options.

The SMPY model has been replicated throughout the United States. Other Universities operating projects based on the SMPY model include: The University of Washington, Northwestern University, Duke University, Arizona State University, University of Denver, Iowa State University, the University of North Texas, Purdue University, Sacramento State University, and the University of Wisconsin in Eau Claire (Stanley, 1991a). The SMPY model has also been successfully implemented in China (Stanley, Huang & Zhu, 1986).

There are various models of specialized schools for students who show promise for achievements in science and technology. Stephens (1998/1999) described the 11 state-supported residential mathematics and science high schools in the United States with a total enrollment of 3,366 students. Models differ primarily in the initial age at entry, length of experience, degree of acceleration permitted, and the amount of university-level experiences provided. Entry to selective residential programs is typically based on performance on examinations or through participation in regional or national science olympiads; the majority of the faculty hold advanced degrees. Students graduating from these residential high schools receive scholarship offers from prestigious universities.

Stanley (1987) advocated that three-year state residential high schools for science and mathematics be established. for all states having at least 300 National Merit semi-finalists each year. He recommended identification in terms of established minimum scores on the Scholastic Aptitude Test, performance on measures of non-verbal reasoning ability, mechanical comprehension, spatial visualization, and knowledge of science and mathematics, demonstrated interest through participation in science fairs and contests, and recommendations by science and mathematics teacher. Faculty qualifications would include at least a master's degree in the subject area taught and successful experience as Advanced Placement teachers. The goal of the curriculum would be to facilitate successful performance on the Advanced Placement examinations in biology, chemistry, physics, computer science, and calculus; proximity to a college campus, would enable students to take college level courses; participation in prestigious competitions such as the Westinghouse Science Talent Search would be strongly encouraged. Aspects of Stanley's (1987) vision has been realized with the establishment of the Texas Academy of Mathematics and Science (TAMS), which is located on the campus of the University of North Texas in Denton, Texas (Stanley, 1991b). Scores of at least 550 on the mathematics section of the Scholastic Aptitude Test and combined scores of at least 1000 on the mathematics and verbal sections of the SAT are minimum entrance requirements for entering eleventh grade students. Students are required to complete at least 57 semester hours of university courses consisting of two semesters each of biology, chemistry, physics, and calculus; 24 semester hours of English, humanities, and social science; and additional electives to earn their high school diploma. Students who complete TAMS can matriculate as juniors at institutions of higher education in Texas or throughout the United States. The TAMS model is cost-effective because the use of college professors and university facilities saves the typical capital expenses of school buildings with science laboratories and dormitories as well as personnel expenses. The residential aspect of TAMS also promotes social interaction. Another model for state-wide residential high schools is the North Carolina School for Science and Mathematics (NCSSM), which was established in 1980 and located on a 27-acre campus in Durham, Carolina (Eilber, 1987; Eilber & Warshaw, 1988). The NCSSM also enrolls eleventh and twelfth graders; admission is determined through a two-step process. The first step involves rating a selection portfolio consisting of scores on the mathematics and verbal sections of the SAT taken in tenth grade, scores on a non-verbal test of critical thinking, grades in maths and science in grades 9 and 10, ratings on a teacher checklist, student essays, and recommendations. The second step involves selecting students based on interviews of students with promising selection portfolios. There are 20 possible courses in mathematics and computer science, 16 courses in biology, 8 courses in chemistry, and 8 courses in physics at NCSSM. Student requirements include: at least one course in biology, chemistry and physics; two years of English courses which emphasize writing;

choice of Spanish, French, German, Russian, Latin, or Chinese as Foreign Language; and American History. Courses in social science, music, visual arts, and interdisciplinary courses are taken as electives. Although the content is advanced, the courses are not designed to ensure success on Advanced Placement examinations. Students are given opportunities to conduct research at NCSSM facilities or participate in yearlong mentorships with researchers and professionals in the Durham-Raleigh-Chapel Hill area. Students are also required to perform three hours of work service each week during their stay at NCSSM and 60 hours of community service work in their home communities during the summer following their junior year. The NCSSM offers workshops each summer for secondary teachers in science and mathematics and coordinates summer research and laboratory-oriented courses held for eleventh and twelfth graders throughout the state of North Carolina. About two thirds of the graduates enter universities in North Carolina and about a third enter selective universities elsewhere; a follow-up study of the graduating class of 1986 indicated that most (80%) were pursuing a career in science or mathematics.

Specialized schools for those talented in science and technology have been described by Pyryt, Masharov & Feng (1993). The development and establishment of an exciting residential school in Israel has been described by Amram (1999); the Israeli Arts and Sciences Academy brings together students with talents in the arts and sciences from throughout Israel. In addition to project-oriented content in the sciences and humanities, students participate in a variety of community service activities. The Israeli Arts and Sciences Academy also runs a Discovery Program to facilitate the educational development of economically disadvantaged students.

Non-residential specialized high schools for the scientifically gifted can be successfully implemented in large urban centers. For over 50 years, the Bronx High School of Science has been developing the scientific talents of students in New York City (Taffel, 1987; Kopelman, Galasso & Schmuckler, 1988). Performance on an entrance examination, consisting of language aptitude and mathematics aptitude and reasoning, is used to select 1000 students from a pool of 4000 applicants. (The school has recently instituted a special program to admit minority and disadvantaged students based on examination performance, feeder school nomination, and completion of an intensive summer program in English and mathematics). The core curricular requirements include: four years of English, four years of social studies, four years of science including biology, chemistry, and physics, three years of a foreign language, three years of mathematics, one year of mechanical drawing, one-half year of shop experience. Two advanced electives from among courses in science, mathematics, computer

science, and advanced scientific laboratory techniques are required; courses in computer literacy, music, art, health education and hygiene are also required. A unique aspect of the science curriculum is the use of block scheduling, whereby students have two consecutive science periods each day permitting more intensive exposure to scientific content and integration of classroom discussions and laboratory experiences. Students are encouraged to do independent research in mathematics and science; they are mentored by the teaching staff at Bronx High School of Science and volunteer scientists from universities, laboratories, hospitals, museums, zoos, and botanical gardens in New York City. Students are expected to communicate the results of their research by writing research reports and submitting them to various competitions such as the New York City and New York State Science Fairs, and the Westinghouse Science Talent Search. The school also publishes annual journals highlighting the best research in mathematics, biology, and physical sciences.

Data reported by Berger (1994) indicates that the number of finalists in the Westinghouse Talent Search from the Bronx High School of Science (118), as of 1990, was more than double every other high school in the United States, with one exception, Stuyvesant High School, another specialized school in New York City, which had 70 winners. Over a 50-year period, about 65% of the graduates of the Bronx High School of Science have become scientists.

Successful programs can also be offered in non-specialized schools; the pioneering work of Brandwein (1955, 1962, 1981, 1986 1988, 1992) at Forest Hills High School in New York City provides insights into how schools can organize science programs to challenge scientifically gifted students. In contrast to the previous programs described, no tests are given; students are given the opportunity to conduct independent research. Brandwein suggested that three clusters of traits called genetic, predisposing, and activating are necessary for developing scientific talent. Genetic factors are the mathematical and verbal aptitudes that a student brings to the situation; these abilities contribute to the acquisition of scientific knowledge and the communication of the results of scientific investigations. Predisposing factors are motivational traits and include the student's persistence and questioning attitude; activating factors relate to the school climate and environment variables that facilitate scientific development. Some of the components of the specialized curriculum in science pioneered by Brandwein include: conducting original research, learning laboratory techniques and the use of laboratory equipment; engaging in library research; taking adequate preparation in mathematics, preparing research reports and exhibits, participating in seminars and conferences, entering the Westinghouse Science Talent Search, and taking college-level courses. The model developed at

Forest Hills High School has been successful in developing scientific talent as evidenced by the success of its students in the Westinghouse Talent Search. Forest Hills ranks third among high schools in the United States in producing the number of finalists (42) in this prestigious competition (Berger, 1994).

The process product approach focuses on the incorporation of the scientific method into projects aimed to produce knowledge; the research component of the specialized high schools and the products submitted to the Science Talent Search are exemplars of this approach. In gifted education, Renzulli's original enrichment triad model (Renzulli, 1977) and current schoolwide enrichment model (Renzulli & Reis, 1997) provided the opportunities to apply the research method to the individual and small group investigations that comprise Type III enrichment. Renzulli & Reis (1997) describe a Type III science project, entitled 'Bobby Bones', which is a life-sized model of the human skeletal structure.

The National Curriculum Science Project at the Center for Gifted Education at the College of William & Mary has produced a problem-based science curriculum that uses real problems to integrate science concepts, process, and systems (Center for Gifted Education, 1997). The curriculum includes units on topics such as pollution, nuclear waste, electricity, and acid spills. Evaluation data has supported the effectiveness of the William & Mary units for developing science process skills.

Thematic units are another way to integrate science content and processes into the curriculum. VanTassel-Baska (1994) classifies this approach as the epistemological concept model, since it focuses on how we come to understand knowledge and uses Hayes-Jacobs and Borland's (1986) interdisciplinary concept model as an exemplar for this approach. The exploration of concepts from an interdisciplinary perspective permits the student talented in science and technology to solve science-related problems for a theme. For example, using the theme, 'flying', a student with an interest in science might examine the physics of flight.

There are a variety of worthwhile opportunities for students interested in learning more about science; Passow (1988a) highlighted some programs available for high-ability pre-college students. These included programs offered by prestigious universities such as Johns Hopkins and Columbia; conducted by national laboratories such as the Argonne National Laboratory (Illinois), the Fermi National Accelerator Laboratory (Illinois), the Lawrence Livermore National Laboratory (California), and the Los Alamos National Laboratory (New Mexico); and provided by museums such as the Chicago Museum of Science and Industry. These programs provide opportunities for students to take courses, engage in research, or combine coursework and research; similar opportunities are provided at science centers (Sitkoff, 1988) such as the Talcott

Mountain Science Center in Connecticut (LaSalle, 1979).

The internet has become an invaluable tool for expanding science knowledge. A visit to the National Science Teachers Association website (www.nsta.org) will yield five pages of links covering archeology, astronomy, biology, chemistry, earth and space science, environmental science, general science, geology, mathematics, and physics. Featured articles from science magazines such as *Scientific American* are also available online. The December 1999 featured article by Sir John Maddox (www.sciam.com) suggests that the discoveries of the next 50 years will begin with our cataloguing of our current ignorance; the article has numerous links related to the history of science. Government agencies such as the National Aeronautical and Space Administration have development a wide variety of science-related resources for educators, students, and the community (http://education.nasa-.gov). The NSTA museum link has connections to general and specialized science museums in the United States, Canada, Italy, Sweden, and Singapore. The Study of Exceptional Talent at The Johns Hopkins University (www.jhu.edu/ ~ gifted/set) has an extensive set of links to scientific competitions such as the Science Talent Search (www.sciserv.org/sts).

Continual Challenges in Developing Science Talent

There are several continual challenges that affect the talent development process in science. The first is the continual differential performance of males and females and differential persistence in science careers; the next is the need for science education to address the ethical dimensions of science; the third continual challenge is the development of teacher/mentors who can appropriately challenge students talented in science and technology.

Since the initiation of talent searches, gender differences in mathematics performance on the Scholastic Aptitude tests have been rampant (Stanley, Keating & Fox, 1974). Stanley, Benbow, Brody, Dauber & Lupkowski, 1992) found dramatic gender differences on a wide-variety of high-level cognitive tests. These differences are correlated with values and career interests (Fox, Pasternack & Peiser, 1976; Fox, Brody & Tobin, 1980; Lubinski, Benbow & Sanders, 1993). Longitudinal studies (Subotnik & Arnold, 1994, 1996) highlight the dilemma that gifted professionals face as they try to balance career and family issues. Several models have been proposed to understand the nature of differential scientific achievement paths of males and females (Eccles & Harold, 1992; Benbow & Lubinski, 1993a, 1993b; Noble, Subotnik & Arnold, 1996; Reis, 1996). These models have much in common and focus on how the combination of individual cognitive and personality traits interact with socialization factors and in producing career paths consistent with one's interests and value patterns; they highlight the importance of mentors and role models. Mentorship experiences give students the opportunity to learn the nature of the discipline by personal interaction with practicing professionals. Through such experiences, individuals are socialized into the cognitive processes scientists use as well as their work habits, attitudes, and values. Exposure to appropriate role models seems especially critical for scientifically gifted females (Tobin & Fox, 1980).

There is also a need for the science curriculum to address the ethical dilemmas that scientists face (Passow, 1957, 1988b; Pyryt, 1979; Tannenbaum, 1979; Frazer & Kornhauser, 1986). This need has been stated most eloquently by Tannenbaum (1979), who quotes Commoner's (1966) dictum that "no scientific principle can tell us how to make the choice, which may sometimes be forced upon us by the insecticide problem between the shade of the elm tree and the song of the robin" (p. 104). Computer espionage and sabotage through viruses provide another example of the need for gifted individuals to use technology as a productive rather than destructive force.

All of the successful programs for nurturing gifts/talents in science and technology acknowledge the importance of the teacher/mentor. Passow (1957) identified the following characteristics as exemplifying a quality science teacher: he\she is inspired and inspiring; knows science and its techniques; understands the meanings of science and its relationship to the world, encourages individual excellence; guides the student to locate resources; adapts teaching methods to stimulate problem solving; attempts to provide flexible programming to meet the unique needs of rapid learners.

Directions for Future Research

This chapter summarized important conceptions and research related to the development of science and technology; still, much remains to be done. Various multidimensional models have been proposed to account for development in science and technology and differential achievement patterns of males and females; these models tend to propose numerous interacting variables over a long time span. The models appear to be heuristic and at this stage represent implicit theories (Sternberg & Davidson, 1986) rather than explicit ones. Many of the variables such as self-concept of ability, self-efficacy, and attributions are likely to be highly correlated; models that include measures of all of these constructs may be unnecessarily complex. There is a need for large sample, longitudinal studies using structural equation modeling techniques to determine the most parsimonious models. There is also a need for longitudinal studies that relate the characteristics of young children and adolescents to those of eminent scientists; most studies of eminence in science examine the characteristics of eminent adults after they have achieved acclaim; we need to know more about their cognitive and affective traits as children. There is also the issue of domain-specificity; more research is needed to determine whether or not the models hold across all science disciplines. If all of the curricular approaches described are beneficial, research is needed on the amount of time that should be dedicated to each approach to maximize science achievement. It is likely that there will be an interaction between a person's cognitive and affective profile and the variety of curricular options needed.

References

Advanced Placement Program (1994). *College and university guide to the Advanced Placement Program* New York: College Entrance Examination Board.

Albert, R. S. (1980). Family positions and the attainment of eminence. *Gifted Child Quarterly, 24*, 87–95.

Amram, R. (1999). Israeli Arts and science Academy: Interim Report, December, 1994. (pp. 219–240). In: N. Colangelo & S. M. Assouline (Eds.), *Talent development III*. Scottsdale, AZ: Gifted Psychology Press.

Assouline, S. G., Colangelo, N., Gross, M. U. M. & Pyryt, M. C. (1999, November). *International talent search results: comparisons with TIMMS*. Paper presented at the meeting of the National Association for Gifted Children, Albuquerque.

Assouline, S. G. & Lupkowski-Shoplik, A. (1997). Talent searches: a model for the discovery and development of academic talent. In: N. Colangelo & G. A. Davis (Eds.), *Handbook of Gifted Education* (2nd ed.) (pp. 170–179). Needham Heights, MA: Allyn and Bacon.

Barron, F. X. (1963). *Creativity and psychological health.* New York: D. Van Nostrand.

Barron, F. X. (1969). *Creative person and creative process.* New York: Holt, Rinehart & Winston.

Bartkovich, K. G. & George, W. C. (1980). *Teaching the gifted in the mathematics classroom.* Washington, DC: National Educational Association.

Benbow, C. P. (1986). SMPY's model for teaching mathematically precocious youth. In: J. S. Renzulli (Ed.), *Systems and Models for Developing Programs for the Gifted and Talented* (pp. 2–25). Mansfield Center, CT: Creative Learning Press.

Berger, J. (1994). *The young scientists: America's future and the winning of the Westinghouse.* Reading, MA: Addison-Wesley.

Benbow, C. P. & Lubinski, D. (1993a). Psychological profiles of the mathematically talented: Some sex differences and evidence supporting their biological basis. In: G. R. Bock & K. Ackrill (Eds), *The origins and development of high ability: Proceedings of a symposium on the origins and development of high ability held at the CIBA Foundation, London, January 25, 1993* (pp. 44–66). Chichester, UK: Wiley.

Benbow, C. P. & Lubinski, D. (1993b). Consequences of gender differences in mathematics reasoning ability: Some biological linkages. In: M. Haug, R. E. Whalen, C. Aron & K. L. Olsen (Eds), *The development of sex differences and similarities in behaviour* (pp. 87–109). The Hague: Kluwer.

Bloom, B. S. (Ed.). (1985). *Developing talent in young people.* New York: Ballantine.

Brandwein, P. F. (1955). *The gifted student as future scientist: The high school student and his commitment to science.* New York: Harcourt Brace.

Brandwein, P. F. (1962). Beginnings in the art of investigation. In: P. F. Brandwein, J. Metzner, E. Morholt, A. Roe & W. Rosen (Eds.), *Teaching High School Biology: A Guide to Working with Potential Biologists* (pp. 43–60). Washington, DC: American Institute of Biological Sciences.

Brandwein, P. F. (1981). *Memorandum: on renewing schooling and education.* New York: Harcourt Brace Jovanovich.

Brandwein, P. F. (1986). A portrait of gifted young with science talent. *Roeper Review*, **8**, 235–243.

Brandwein, P. F. (1988). Science talent: in an ecology of achievement. In: P. F. Brandwein & A. H. Passow (Eds.), *Gifted Young in Science: Potential Through Performance* (pp. 73–103). Washington, DC: National Science Teachers Association.

Brandwein, P. F. (1992). Science talent: the play of paradigm in the science education of science-prone young. *Science Education*, **76**, 121–139.

Brody, L. E., Assouline, S. G. & Stanley, J. C. (1990). Five years of early entrants: predicting achievement in college. *Gifted Child Quarterly*, **34**, 138–142.

Brody, L. E. & Benbow, C. P. (1987). Accelerative practices: how effective are they for the gifted? *Gifted Child Quarterly*, **31**, 105–110.

Carroll, J. B. (1993). *Human cognitive abilities: a survey of factor analytic studies.* New York: Cambridge University Press.

Center for Gifted Education, College of William and Mary. (1997). *Guide to teaching a problem-based science curriculum.* Dubuque, IA: Kendall-Hunt.

Cohn, S. J. (1991) Talent searches. In: N. Colangelo & G. A. Davis (Eds.), *Handbook of Gifted Education* (1st ed.), (pp. 166–177). Needham Heights, MA: Allyn and Bacon.

Commoner, B. (1966). *Science and survival.* New York: Viking.

Eccles, J. S. & Harold, R. D. (1992). Gender differences in educational and occupational patterns among the gifted. In: N. Colangelo, S. G. Assouline & D. L. Ambroson (Eds.), *Talent Development* (pp. 2–30). Unionville, NY: Trillium.

Eilber, C. R. (1987). The North Carolina School of Science and Mathematics. *Phi Delta Kappan*, **68**, 773–777.

Eilber, C. R. & Warshaw, S. J. (1988). North Carolina School of Science and Mathematics: the special environment within a statewide science high school. In: P. F. Brandwein, & A. H. Passow (Eds.), *Gifted Young in Science: Potential Through Performance*. Washington, DC: National Science Teachers Association.

Feldhusen, J. F. (1986). A conception of giftedness. In: R. J. Sternberg & J. E. Davidson (Eds.), *Conceptions of Giftedness* (pp. 112–127). New York: Cambridge University Press.

Flanagan, J. C., Dailey, J. T., Shaycroft, M. F., Gorham, W. A., Orr, D. B. & Goldberg, I. (1962). *Design for a study of American youth.* Boston-Houghton-Mifflin.

Fox, L. H., Brody, L. & Tobin, D. (Eds.), (1980). *Women and the mathematical mystique.* Baltimore: The Johns Hopkins University Press.

Fox, L. H., Pasternack, S. R. & Peiser, N. L. (1976). Career-related interests of adolescent boys and girls. In: D. P. Keating (Ed.), *Intellectual Talent: Research and Development* (pp. 242–261). Baltimore: The Johns Hopkins University Press.

Frazer, M. J. & Kornhauser, A. (Eds.). (1986). *Ethics and social responsibility in science education.* Elmford, NY: Pergamon.

George, W. C. & Denham, S. A. (1976). Curriculum experimentation for the mathematically talented. In: D. P. Keating (Ed.), *Intellectual Talent: Research and Development* (pp. 103–131). Baltimore: The Johns Hopkins University Press.

Haensly, P., Reynolds, C. R. & Nash, W. R. (1986). Giftedness: coalescence, context, conflict, and commitment. In: R. J. Sternberg & J. E. Davidson (Eds.), *Conceptions of Giftedness* (pp. 128–148). New York: Cambridge University Press.

Hansen, J. C. & Campbell, D. P. (1985). *Manual for the Strong Interest Inventory* (4th ed.). Stanford, CA: Stanford University Press.

Hanson, H. P. (1980). Twenty-five years of the Advanced Placement Program. Encouraging able students. *College Board Review*, **115**, 8–12, 35.

Hayes-Jacobs, H. & Borland, J. H. (1986). The interdisciplinary concept model: Theory and practice. *Gifted Child Quarterly*, **30**, 159–163.

Heller, K. A. (1993). Scientifc ability. In: G. R. Bock & K. Ackrill (Eds.), *Origins and Development of High Ability* (pp. 139–150). London: Wiley.

Helson, R. & Crutchfield, R. S . (1970). Mathematicians: The creative researcher and the average Ph.D. *Journal of Consulting and Clinical Psychology*, **34**, 250–257.

Hendricks, M. (1997, June). Yesterday's whiz kids: where are they today? *Johns Hopkins Magazine*, pp. 30–36.

Holland, J. L. (1973). *Making vocational choices: a theory of careers.* Englewood Cliffs, N. J.: Prentice-Hall.

Holland, J. L. (1974). *The Self-Directed Search: a guide to educational and vocational planning.* Palo Alto: Consulting Psychologists Press.

Holland, J. L. (1978). *Vocational Preference Inventory manual.* Palo Alto: Consulting Psychologists Press.

Humphreys, L. G. & Lubinski, D. (1996). Assessing spatial visualization: an underappreciated ability for many school and work settings: In: C. P. Benbow & D. Lubinski (Eds.), *Intellectual Talent: Psychometric and Social Issues* (pp. 116–140). Baltimore: The Johns Hopkins University Press.

Koppelman, M., Galasso, V. G. & Schmuckler, M. (1988). A program for stimulating creativity in a citywide high school: the Bronx High School of Science. In: P. F. Brandwein & A. H. Passow (Eds.), *Gifted Young in Science: Potential through Performance* (pp. 209–216). Washington, DC: National Science Teachers Association.

LaSalle, D. (1979). On Talcott Mountain. *Science and Children*, **16** (6), 27–29.

Lubinski, D., Benbow, C. P. & Sanders, C. E. (1993). Reconceptualizing gender differences in achievement among the gifted: an outcome of contrasting attributes for personal fulfillment in the world of work. In: K. A. Heller, F. J. Mönks & A. H. Passow (Eds.), *International Handbook for Research on Giftedness and Talent* (pp. 693–708). Oxford: Pergamon.

Lynch, S. J. (1990). Fast-paced science for the academically talented: Issues of age and competence. *Science Education*, **74**, 585–596.

MacKinnon, D. W. (1962). The nature and nurture of creative talent. *American Psychologist*, **17**, 484–495.

MacKinnon, D. W. (1965). Personality and the realization of creative potential. *American Psychologist*, **20**, 273–281.

MacKinnon, D. W. (1975). IPAR's contribution to the conceptualization and study of creativity. In: I. A. Taylor & J. W. Getzels (Eds.), *Perspectives in Creativity* (pp. 60–89). Chicago: Aldine.

MacKinnon, D. W. (1978). *In search of human effectiveness: Identifying and developing creativity.* Buffalo: Creative Education Foundation.

Merton, R. K. (1968). The Matthew effect in science. *Science*, **159**, 56–63.

Mezynski, K., Stanley, J. C. & McCoart, R. F. (1983). Helping youths score well on AP examinations in physics, chemistry, and calculus. In: C. P. Benbow & J. C. Stanley (Eds.), *Academic Precocity: Aspects of its Development* (pp. 86–112). Baltimore: The Johns Hopkins University Press.

Noble, K. D., Subotnik, R. F. & Arnold, K. D. (1996). A new model for adult female talent development: a synthesis of perspectives from 'Remarkable Women'. In: K. D. Arnold, K. D. Noble & R. F. Subotnik (Eds.), *Remarkable Women: Perspectives on Female Talent Development* (pp. 1427–439). Cresskill, NJ: Hampton Press.

Olszewski-Kubilius, P. (1998). Research evidence regarding the validity and effects of talent search education programs. *Journal of Secondary Gifted Education*, **9**, 134–138.

Passow, A. H. (1957). Developing a science program for rapid learners. *Science Education*, **41**, 104–112.

Passow, A. H. (1988a). School, university, and museum cooperation in identifying and nurturing potential scientists. In: P. F. Brandwein & A. H. Passow (Eds.), *Gifted Young in Science: Potential Through Performance* (pp. 245–253). Washington, DC: National Science Teachers Association.

Passow, A. H. (1988b). The educating and schooling of the community of artisans in science. In: P. F. Brandwein & A. H. Passow (Eds.), *Gifted Young in Science: Potential Through Performance* (pp. 27–38). Washington, DC: National Science Teachers Association.

Piirto, J. (1999). *Talented children and adults: Their development and education* (2nd ed.). Columbus, OH: Prentice-Hall/Macmillan/Merrill

Pyryt, M. C. (1979). Helping scientifically gifted children. *Science and children*, **16** (6), 16–17.

Pyryt, M. C., Masharov, Y. P. & Feng, C. (1993). Programs and strategies for nurturing gifts/talents in science and technology. In: K. A. Heller, F. J. Mönks & A. H. Passow (Eds.), *International Handbook for Research and Development of Giftedness and Talent* (pp. 453–471). Oxford: Pergamon.

Reis, S. M. (1996). Older women's reflections on eminence: obstacles and opportunities. In: K. D. Arnold, K. D. Noble & R. F. Subotnik (Eds), *Remarkable women: Perspectives on female talent development* (pp. 149–168). Cresskill, NJ: Hampton Press.

Reis, S. M., Burns, D. & Renzulli, J. S. (1992). *Curriculum compacting: the complete guide to modifying the regular curriculum for high ability learners.* Mansfield Center, CT: Creative Learning Press.

Renzulli, J. S. (1977). *The enrichment triad model: a guide for developing defensible programs for the gifted and talented.* Mansfield Center, CT: Creative Learning Press.

Renzulli, J. S. (1986). The three-ring conception of giftedness: a developmental model for creative productivity. In: R. J. Sternberg & J. E. Davidson (Eds.), *Conceptions of Giftedness* (pp. 53–92). New York: Cambridge University Press.

Renzulli, J. S. & Reis, S. M., (1997). The Schoolwide Enrichment Model: New directions for developing high-end learning. In: N. Colangelo & G. A. Davis (Eds.), *Handbook of Gifted Education* (2nd ed.). (pp. 136–154). Needham Heights, MA: Allyn and Bacon.

Renzulli, J. S., Smith, L., H. & Reis, S. M. (1982). Curriculum compacting: an essential strategy for working with gifted students. *Elementary School Journal*, **82**, 185–194.

Simonton, D. K. (1997). When giftedness becomes genius: how does talent achieve eminence? In: N. Colangelo & G. A. Davis (Eds.), *Handbook of Gifted Education* (2nd ed.). (pp. 335–349). Needham Heights, MA: Allyn and Bacon.

Sitkoff, S. (1988). Science centers—an essential support system for the teaching of science. In: P. F. Brandwein & A. H. Passow (Eds.), *Gifted Young in Science: Potential Through Performance* (pp. 189–187). Washington, DC: National Science Teachers Association.

Solano, C. H. & George, W. C. (1976). College courses for the gifted. *Gifted Child Quarterly*, **20**, 274–285.

Sosniak, L. (1985). Becoming an outstanding research neurologist. In: B. S. Bloom (Ed.), *Developing Talent in Young Children* (pp. 348–408). New York: Ballantine.

Sosniak, L. (1999). An everyday curriculum for the development of talent. *Journal of Secondary Gifted Education*, **10**, 166–172.

Stanley, J. C. (1974). Intellectual precocity. In: J. C. Stanley, D. P. Keating, & L. H. Fox (Eds.), *Mathematical Talent: Discovery, Description, and Development* (pp. 1–22). Baltimore: The Johns Hopkins University Press.

Stanley, J. C. (1976). Identifying and nurturing the intellectually gifted. *Phi Delta Kappan*, **58**, 234–237.

Stanley, J. C. (1978). SMPY's DT-PI model: Diagnostic testing followed by prescriptive instruction. *Intellectually Talented Youth Bulletin*, **4** (10), 7–8.

Stanley, J. C. (1987). State residential schools for mathematically talented youth. *Phi Delta Kappan*, **68**, 770–773

Stanley, J. C . (1991a). An academic model for educating the mathematically talented. *Gifted Child Quarterly*, **35**, 36–42.

Stanley, J. C. (1991b). A better model for residential high schools for talented youths. *Phi Delta Kappan*, *72*, 119–122, 471–473.

Stanley, J. C. (1996). In the beginning: the Study of Mathematically Precocious Youth. In: C. P. Benbow & D. Lubinski (Eds.), *Intellectual Talent: Psychometric and Social Issues* (pp. 225–235). Baltimore: The Johns Hopkins University Press.

Stanley, J. C. (1998, May). *Helping students learn only what they don't already know.* Paper presented at Fourth Biennial Henry B. and Jocelyn Wallace National Research Symposium on Talent Development, Iowa City.

Stanley, J. C. & Benbow, C. P. (1986). Youths who reason extremely well mathematically. In: R. J. Sternberg & J. E. Davidson (Eds.), *Conceptions of Giftedness* (pp. 361–387). New York: Cambridge University Press.

Stanley, J. C., Benbow, C. P., Brody, L. E., Dauber, S. & Lupkowski, A. E. (1992). Gender differences on eigty-six nationally standardized achievement tests. In: N. Colangelo, S. G. Assouline, and D. L. Ambroson (Eds.), *Talent Development*. (pp. 42–65). Unionville, NY: Trillium.

Stanley, J. C., Huang, J. F. & Zhu, X. M. (1986). SAT-M scores of highly selected students in Shanghai tested when less than 13 years old. *College Board Review*, **140**, 10–13, 28–29.

Stanley, J. C., Keating, D. P. & Fox, L. H. (Eds.). (1974). *Mathematical talent: discovery, description, and development*. Baltimore: The Johns Hopkins University Press.

Stanley, J. C. & McGill, A. M. (1986). More about 'Young entrants to colleges: How did they fare?' *Gifted Child Quarterly*, **30**, 70–73.

Stanley, J. C. & Stanley, B. S. K. (1986). High-school biology, chemistry, or physics learned well in three weeks. *Journal of Research in Science Teaching*, **23**, 237–250.

Starko, A. (1986). *It's about time: inservice strategies for curriculum compacting*. Mansfield Center, CT: Creative Learning Press.

Stephens, K. R. (1998/1999). Residential math and science high schools: a closer look. *Journal of Secondary Gifted Education*, **10**, 85–92.

Sternberg, R. J. & Davidson, J. E. (Eds.). (1986). *Conceptions of giftedness*. New York: Cambridge University Press.

Sternberg, R. J. & Davidson, J. E. (1986). Conceptions of giftedness: A map of the terrain. In: R. J. Sternberg & J. E. Davidson (Eds.) *Conceptions of Giftedness* (pp. 3–18). New York: Cambridge University Press.

Subotnik, R. F. (1986). Scientific creativity: Westinghouse Talent Search winners' problem finding behavior. In: A. J. Cropley, K. K. Urban, H. Wagner & W. Wieczerkowski (Eds.), *Giftedness: A Continuing Worldwide Challenge* (pp. 147–156). New York: Trillium.

Subotnik, R. F. (1988a). The motivation to experiment: a study of gifted adolescents' attitudes toward scientific research. *Journal for the Education of the Gifted*, **11** (3), 19–35.

Subotnik, R. F. (1988b). Factors from the Structure-of-Intellect model associated with gifted adolescents' problem finding in science: research with Westinghouse Science Talent Search winners. *Journal of Creative Behavior*, **22**, 42–54.

Subotnik, R. F. & Steiner, C. L. (1994). Adult manifestations of adolescent talent in science: A longitudinal study of 1983 Westinghouse Talent Search winners. In: R. F. Subotnik & K. D. Arnold (Eds.), *Beyond Terman: Contemporary Longitudinal Studies of Giftedness and Talent* (pp. 52–76). Norwood, NJ: Ablex.

Subotnik, R. F. & K. D. Arnold (Eds.). (1994). *Beyond Terman: contemporary longitudinal studies of giftedness and talent*. Norwood, NJ: Ablex.

Subotnik, R. F. & Arnold, K. D. (1996). Success and sacrifice: the costs of talent fulfillment for women in science. In: K. D. Arnold, K. D. Noble & R. F. Subotnik (Eds.), *Remarkable Women: Perspectives on Female Talent Development* (pp. 263–280). Cresskill, NJ: Hampton Press.

Taffel, A. (1987). Fifty years of developing the gifted in science and mathematics. *Roeper Review*, **10**, 11–24.

Tannenbaum, A. J. (1979). Pre-Sputnik to post-Watergate concern about the gifted. In: A. H. Passow (Ed.), *The Gifted and Talented: Their Education and Development (Seventy-Eighth Yearbook of the National Society for the Study of Education*, Part I.) (pp. 5–27). Chicago: University of Chicago.

Tannenbaum, A. J. (1986). Giftedness: a psychosocial approach. In: R. J. Sternberg & J. E. Davidson (Eds.), *Conceptions of Giftedness* (pp. 21–52). New York: Cambridge University Press.

Tobin, D. & Fox, L. H. (1980). Career interests and career education: a key to change. In: L. H. Fox, L. Brody & D. Tobin (Eds.), *Women and the Mathematical Mystique* (pp. 171–191). Baltimore: The Johns Hopkins University Press.

Treffinger, D. J. (1986). Fostering effective independent learning through individualized programming. In: J. S. Renzulli (Ed.), *Systems and Models for Developing Effective Programs for the Gifted and Talented* (pp. 429–460.). Mansfield Center, CT: Creative Learning Press.

VanTassel-Baska, J. (1994). The National Curriculum Development Projects for high ability learners: key issues and findings. In: N. Colangelo, S. G. Assouline & D. L. Ambroson (Eds.), *Talent Development:* Volume II (pp. 19–38). Dayton, OH: Ohio Psychology Press.

Zuckerman, H. (1977). *Scientific elite: Nobel laureates in the United States*. New York: Free Press.

Promotion of the Gifted in Vocational Training

Rudolf Manstetten

University of Osnabrück, Germany

Introduction

Giftedness is a central research field of psychology and it is also of basic importance for other sciences, especially for educational science which is not only in need of the results of psychological giftedness research, but also has to examine adequate measures in order to promote the gifted. However, in psychology, as well as in educational science *vocational giftedness* has been a research desideratum.

In the following study the promotion of vocationally gifted young people in the fields of business and commerce, crafts and trades and others will be introduced and discussed. The study deals with those young people who have passed their initial vocational training in the German dual system. Academic qualifications will be excluded. The *Promotion of the Gifted in Vocational Training* which started in Germany at the beginning of the nineties, is quite a new phenomenon, contrary to the old dual system of vocational training. The following ideas try to discuss the theoretical models and practical measures of this newly designed promotion program for gifted young people in vocational education.

The young people participating in the program as grant recipients receive 9,000 German marks for a period of three years. The grant is seen as a support for further vocational training. A prerequisite to participate in the program are excellent results in the final examination of initial vocational training. Since 1991 about 3,000 young people have been enrolled in the program yearly. In the meantime nearly 10,000 young people have benefited from this program which is financed by the German Government with 25 million German marks per year.

The program has been scientifically tested since 1991. Three questions were closely studied:

- Which special personal characteristics are shown by the vocationally gifted young people?
- Which training measures did they choose?
- Which effects did the promotion program have on vocational careers?

These research results will be depicted and discussed here. The study is partly related to the research of entire age-groups, and it also includes the analysis of representative samples based upon sociometric tests and interviews. The following findings refer to the most important research results. The complete results are stated in a special report which also includes the applied research methods and statistical analysis (Manstetten, 1996).

Current Importance of the Research Topic

The program *Promotion of the Gifted in Vocational Training* emphasizes a rather neglected area of giftedness promotion. In Germany and many other countries multiple promotion activities exist in various educational fields such as kindergartens, schools (special classes, etc.), as well as in academical institutes, universities and others. A promotion of giftedness for about 1.5 million young people who spent a non-academic practical vocational training in the dual system of school and company has not yet happened.

This fact is rather surprising because the dual system of vocational training is typical for Germany and is passed by most of the young people between the age of 16 and 19. Furthermore, there are no studies in psychology that deal with the specially gifted in this field; the following sections, therefore, present concepts and preliminary results on this topic. We hope that interest in psychological research of giftedness will be stimulated to undertake further efforts in this research area.

Historical Importance of the Research Topic

The necessity for the study of *vocational* giftedness and its promotion was already seen at the beginning of the last century. Contributions to the promotion of giftedness of young people in technical, industrial and trade vocations already appeared in a report of Petersen, entitled *The Rise of the Gifted* (Der Aufstieg der Begabten, 1916). The main idea of this report was astonishingly similar to the intention of the program of the German Government 75 years later:

(1) "It is economically, socially and ethically necessary to find ways to identify, to evaluate and to promote giftedness better; giftedness means practical giftedness related to the sense of duty and strength of mind.

(2) The promotion of the gifted has to be carried out in an organized way.

(3) Promotion of the gifted should not lead to an increase in academic professions; on the contrary, the danger of economic and social over-estimation of the academic professions should be opposed as much as possible and should attempt to reach a more suitable appraisal and appreciation of the practical vocations" (Petersen, 1916, p. 205; translation from German).

Stern (1916, p. 106) asks the German Science in his contribution to this report to prepare for the understanding of intelligence as a national treasure and to utilize this for educational and vocational abilities: Modern psychology should deal with research and diagnosis of giftedness.

Furthermore, Stern also complains that we know very little about the assumed demands of giftedness in commercial, technical and industrial vocations. Therefore, he already urged schools to introduce measures such as lessons in crafts and trades for example, because hidden technical and manual talents would then have the opportunity to come to the surface (Stern, 1916, p. 115).

Until now, these demands for research and promotion of vocational giftedness have mostly remained unfulfilled, although giftedness had been a major point of German pedagogical psychology in the sixties. Research results of that time are reported in the book *Giftedness and Learning* by Roth (Begabung und Lernen, 1969) for example, which influenced sciences and politics of education greatly at that time. With regard to important publications of educational science for the last 20 years, it seems, however, that this topic has nearly disappeared from pedagogical discussion although psychological giftedness research has intensified at the same time. The dispute of this topic is equally missing in vocational educational science as well as in the practice of vocational training. Nevertheless, there was already an approach to promote vocational giftedness in Germany in 1954, but this approach was confined to young craftsmen only who received a prize for their excellent examination results (Schubert, 1958).

To the Relevance of Models of Giftedness

In order to emphasize specifics of vocational giftedness, the knowledge in the psychological field of giftedness research should be referred to. Because there are numerous definitions, Roth (1969) proposed that each researcher should define his own term of 'giftedness'. Furthermore, totally different terms such as 'talent', 'high talent', 'special giftedness' and others are used in a partly synonymous and partly different way.

Without extending the terms, we shall preliminarily define 'vocational giftedness' as special dispositions which are shown in special achievements of (non-academic) vocational learning and action. In this way, the term 'gifted in vocational training' shall be understood.

Another problem must be seen here if 'giftedness' is explained by the term 'achievement' which also has to be defined. We will not discuss 'achievement' here, but according to Schiefele/Krapp (1975) the terms 'giftedness' and 'achievement' should not be used in the same way. The term 'giftedness' shall be used as a theoretical construct for the explanation of special phenomenona such as special achievement, but not for the description of these phenomenona. Stern already stressed that "giftedness is only a possibility respectively an imperative prerequisite of achievement, but it does not signify achievement itself" (Stern, 1916, p. 110). Therefore we understand that 'vocational giftedness' should be defined as disposition of abilities that explain oberservable (vocational) achievements.

The terms 'giftedness', as well as 'achievement' must also be seen in a sociological aspect; this aspect signifies that achievements on their part are determined and evaluated by societal norms (Heid, 1969). Whether a person is gifted or not shall be determined by the way this person shows excellent achievements in relation to a comparative group, whose achievements are evaluated positively by society. The reason that vocational giftedness has not yet been researched and promoted can also be seen as an indicator that vocational achievements have not been evaluated favorably by society.

Giftedness must also be seen in an anthropological aspect. This aspect signifies the question whether giftedness is genetically or environmentally determined. The question whether giftedness is either a matter of innate abilities or social and cultural influences, is not only as old as the research of giftedness itself, but there have not been clear empirical results to answer this question. Psychologists seem to have a more pragmatic understanding which states that both inheritance *and* environment have an interactive effect on the development of giftedness. Since giftedness is no longer seen as a static phenomenon, but a dynamic developmental process—in the interaction of inheritance and environment—the dynamic-interaction approach is consequently preferred.

It seems to be undoubtedly certain that these aspects of giftedness can be regarded as decisive factors for vocational giftedness; much more of a problem is the identification of factors, criteria and components that constitute vocational giftedness. Psychology with its models of giftedness, can probably help to find basics for this.

Without describing the various models of giftedness in detail, it can be said that giftedness is very often identified with intelligence in pedagogical-psychological references. In contrast, Stern (1916, p. 111) already emphasized "that not intellectual giftedness determines selection, but also the strength of interest and the excellence of will."

There are various complex models in the psychological research of giftedness which describe the factors and components of giftedness in different ways. These can mainly be reduced to the following aspects:

- Which cognitive (e.g. intelligence) and/or non-cognitive factors of personality (e.g. motivation) are essential?
- Are environmental factors included?
- How far are areas—besides sports, arts or sciences—such as trades, commerce, communication, etc. also involved?

As a further category, models should be taken into account that define high-giftedness as achievement and which partly overlap with the already mentioned aspects. According to Sternberg (1993) a person is highly gifted if evident achievements are produced that are—in relation to a comparative group—excellent, rare, productive and valuable.

For further clarification the models of Renzulli (1978, 1986), Gagné (1985, 1993) and the new variant of the Munich model of (high-)giftedness (Heller et al., 1994) shall be introduced briefly, examining how far these models can offer a basis for the explanation of vocational giftedness.

In Renzulli's three-ring conception "giftedness consists of an interaction among three basic clusters of human traits—being above average general abilities, high levels of task commitment and high levels of creativity" (1979, p. 23).

This often cited model is also criticized, however, because Renzulli does not draw a line between *giftedness* and *achievement*; but this differentiation is especially important for the educational field because achievement and not giftedness is measured here. It seems to be possible to draw the conclusion that special achievement indicates special giftedness. Contrary to that it is not possible, however, to infer from low achievement a low giftedness. There are pupils who achieve bad results although they show excellent abilities according to psychological tests; these pupils would not be regarded as gifted in the model of Renzulli. Furthermore, it should be criticized that this model depicts creativity as a constitutive factor for giftedness. Contrary to that, there is the example of a sportsman who is highly gifted, but seldom especially creative (Holling et al., 1996). These examples show that the model of Renzulli is hardly adequate to explain

giftedness sufficiently; therefore it can hardly be used for the description of vocational giftedness.

The *differentiated model of giftedness and talent* is introduced by Gagné (1993) who distinguishes between *giftedness* and *talent:* Genetically determined and not yet developed abilities (giftedness), on the one hand, and systematically developed abilities or expertise in special fields of action (talent), on the other hand, are separated from each other. The development of a special talent is supported by intrapersonal catalysts such as motivation and personality and environmental catalysts as well as learning, training and exercise.

Without returning to this model and the differentiation made between giftedness and talent, which is also controversially discussed in the psychological literature, the following can be stated: On the one hand, there are no exclusively creative or intellectual abilities being used as a basis, as in other models of giftedness, but 'socioaffective' and 'sensorimotor' aptitude domains and others are also named here. Therefore, vocational abilities can also be included. On the other hand, talent is not only related to arts, athletics, sciences and technology, as well as education, but is also related to vocational fields such as business and commerce, crafts and trades, health services, transportation and communication. Concerning vocational giftedness, it is also essential that *learning, training* and *practice* in a special field are emphasized in its significance for the development of talent. It has to be pointed out, however, that this model does not differentiate between *giftedness* and *achievement*.

The Munich giftedness model of Heller et al. (1994) does not differentiate between giftedness and talent, as in the Gagné model, but it distinguishes between *giftedness* and *achievement*. The differentiated structure of this concept is quite similar to the Gagné model. Heller et al. point out intellectual and creative, as well as social and sensorimotor factors of giftedness, on the one hand, and technical and social achievements besides sports, mathematics and others, on the other. Therefore, both models can be seen as a basis for giftedness research in non-academic vocations in the field of technics and commerce, crafts and trades, as well as in social vocations. Nevertheless, both models do not sufficiently explain the specific factors of vocational giftedness itself.

According to Mönks (1991) it should also be mentioned that social competences, should be emphasized more as important internal catalysts, because they are particularly significant for the occurrence of excellent achievements. It also has to be mentioned that social competences gain importance in various vocational fields without being especially nurtured in schools.

All in all it has to be criticized that some models are too inadequate to offer a basis for a concept of vocational giftedness; they can hardly explain giftedness at all. This is not only true for one-sided models that are focused on intellectual abilities, but also for those that do not differentiate between giftedness and achievement or which start out from creativity as a constitutive factor (e.g. Renzulli, 1986).

Similar to Gagné, the Munich model of giftedness (Heller et al., 1994) also focuses on a differentiated understanding of giftedness which seems to be suitable for explaining factors of vocational giftedness. Furthermore, *learning, training* and *practice* which are stressed by Gagné (1993, p. 72) also seem to be very important for vocational giftedness. He emphasizes abilities, skills and knowledge which were developed at a certain point of time and which are the reason for particularly successful practice of (vocational) activities.

It becomes clear so far that a differentiation between general and vocational giftedness is hardly meaningful because there is no general giftedness as Trost (1991, p. 2) stated. This would only be true if giftedness is seen as intelligence (as a general ability to learn and solve problems). If this is rejected, however, as described at the beginning, giftedness will always be a special giftedness, i.e. "giftedness for special achievements" (Trost, 1991, p. 2). With this it can be stressed that giftedness is not related to a narrowly limited ability (e.g. adding numbers), but always to more complex achievement areas (e.g. commercial giftedness).

If we are not to speak of general giftedness, but of giftedness for special achievements then the question arises how those factors that were confirmed by giftedness research can also be confirmed by vocational giftedness research. In order to preliminarily clarify that question the following results from the scientific research of the promotion program are described and discussed (Manstetten, 1996).

Evaluation of Current Strategies in Germany

Personal Characteristics

The empirical results of vocational giftedness research are based upon interviews and sociometrical tests of young employed persons who were selected as grant recipients by the responsible Chambers of Commerce, Trade and others.

Summarizing the research results some considerable differences to previous findings of giftedness research can be depicted. There are, for instance, differences regarding constitutional environmental characteristics in the family and school area (Bals, 1996, p. 324). While previous giftedness research has identified first born and single children as highly gifted this could not be verified by our random sample of grant recipients tested here. It also cannot be confirmed that higher education and social status of parents determine vocational giftedness; the grant recipients mostly come from lower status families. According to the findings, most of these grant recipients see a chance of a vocational career in their vocational training. That can also be regarded as a reason why these young people show a different profile in their school careers, compared to previous results of giftedness research. There are excellent school achievements in our sample, but more typical are discontinuous curricula vitae showing grave problems (Bals, 1996, p. 324).

Psychometric tests with grant recipients (Holling et al., 1996, p. 109) also show considerable deviations related to factors such as intelligence and creativity which are regarded as basic giftedness factors (e.g. Renzulli). In this respect grant recipients only showed average results. Therefore, these factors, which are controversially discussed, are inadequate for vocational giftedness and cannot explain excellent vocational achievements.

A remarkable consensus about motivational factors is shown by the findings. Compared to test persons of non-grant recipients of the same age group, the grant recipients analyzed here showed stronger work-related interests, more distinct engagement in their occupation and a higher general achievement motivation. A further indicator for high motivation is seen in the strong interest in further education, which is documented in the more intensified use of vocational and non-vocational training measures.

All in all these results indicate that vocational giftedness shows specific characteristics which are partly different from current giftedness research results. A reason for this could be found in the present practice of selecting grant recipients by the Chambers of Commerce, Trade and others.

Grant recipients are selected primarily according to their results in the final examination of initial vocational training; this selection process is not going to be described here. It should be mentioned, however, that this program does not concern promoting young people during their training; examination results are the criteria for their selection, but the examinations only refer to special vocational knowledge and experience; other skills that might be important for a vocational career are not considered.

Promotional Measures

Contrary to the selection process, which uses functional examination achievements as a criterion, promotion is not only limited to vocational qualifications. Apart from vocational education, general education is supported as well, which can refer to different topics. Grant recipients are offered a broad spectrum of educational possibilities so that they can choose among a wide range from public and private suppliers; young employees have many possibilities which they can use for their individual vocational career chances. The program's objective, therefore, tries to enable young people to see attractive vocational careers as an alternative to studying at the university.

The attraction of vocational education, however, cannot only be improved by financing pretentious measures of further education. The motives for going into further education are manifold, resulting from economic and technological developments, the competition between genders for occupational positions, the increasing internationalization of labor markets etc.

The evaluation of the 3,000 grant recipients enrolled yearly since 1991 draws a reliable and complete picture of further educational interests. About 80% of the grant recipients' choices of courses concentrate on the six categories of the following ranking list:

(1) technical skills
(2) foreign languages (mostly English)
(3) economic knowledge
(4) information technology (computer)
(5) management tasks
(6) communication.

This can be divided into two groups, *specific* (number 1 and 3) and *non-specific* (number 2, 4, 5, and 6) vocational measures.

Apart from foreign languages which were primarily chosen in the first promotion years, the profile of the following promotion years has remained relatively stable; but the career possibilities that are connected with these measures are different. In recent years technical and economic courses have had the highest priority in order to achieve higher vocational levels (e.g. examination for the title of a *master craftsman*), which are less attainable with courses for computing, management and communication. The reason for this is that technical and economic qualifications are directed towards special occupations; the other topics are *non-specific*, i.e. they are related to various vocations. Therefore, the chosen courses indicate different preferences for careers; while some serve vocational advancement directly, others enable a higher vocational qualification that is important for various vocations.

It is interesting that the decision for one of the two groups is related to gender. Female grant recipients mostly chose foreign languages followed by economic courses; technical and information technological courses range significantly lower. Male grant recipients mostly selected technical and information technological courses. This shows that there are specific career plans for young gifted employees according to gender and generally this is typical for the vocational selection process of young people.

Significant for the interests of further education is also the school level already achieved; 30% of all the high school graduates (A-level) chose foreign languages and 20% economic topics, so that 50% of the grant recipients concentrate on only two categories. Contrary to that, nearly 50% of the non-high school graduates (lower than A-level) chose technical and information technological topics.

Also the statistical correlation of analysis showed significant coherence between the variable *topic of further education,* on the one hand, and the variables *gender* and *school grade,* on the other; i.e. foreign languages are mostly chosen by women and high school graduates while men and non-high school graduates prefer technical courses which make it possible to achieve a higher vocational level. Career planning strongly depends on gender and school grade; female grant recipients are obviously less interested in a vocational career than men. High school graduates dislike a career oriented further vocational training more than non-high school graduates.

Career Promotion

How far can the program *Promotion of the Gifted in Vocational Training* effectively nurture the career of former grant recipients? This question is of foremost interest because the results are also a control for the success and the efficiency of this program.

The first analysis of efficiency was already completed in 1994 (Manstetten, 1996, p. 354; p. 378); it referred to those grant recipients who were enrolled in the promotion program in 1991 and 1992. Positive short-term effects on vocational developments could already be found here.

The second analysis of efficiency, which was carried out in autumn 1997 by Fauser/Schreiber, was aimed at the research of longer term effects of the promotion program (Fauser/Schreiber, 1998). This analysis covers the following two groups of grant recipients annually admitted in various years:

• First there were 1,400 grant recipients admitted in 1991/92. Those grant recipients had already taken part in the research study of 1994.
• Second there were 4,300 grant recipients admitted in 1994.

The questionnaires were answered by 3,093 grant recipients (63%). The benefits of the promotion program for the vocational career of the grant recipients were more positively evaluated in the study from 1997 than in the study from 1994; the reason for this increase can be found in the different use of the promotion program by the grant recipients. As shown in the previous section, *specific* and *non-specific* vocational promotion measures can be distinguished. With the increase of *specific* vocational measures, which enable higher vocational degrees, a promotion in the vocational career could be realized more often. Higher responsibility, higher positions and better payments were the indicators of such a promotion of vocational career in this questionnaire. Although the period since participating in the program for both test groups was quite different, it is surprising that the positive effect was similarly evaluated.

Furthermore, those who chose the *non-specific* vocational measures, evaluated the promotion program quite positively, even though, it was less important for their vocational career. More essential for the grant recipients was obviously their personal benefit.

Another important variable for the analysis of the promotion conditions was the size of the companies employing grant recipients. Particularly grant recipients of smaller firms could benefit more from their promotion of careers than grant recipients of bigger companies. The cause can be seen in the context that higher vocational degrees (e.g. master craftsman), mostly in the technical area, are demanded by those grant recipients who did not pass high school. These are young employees who mostly come from small craft and trade companies.

The conditions in mostly bigger sized commercial companies are just the opposite. For A-level grant recipients who more often chose commercial vocations and mostly took part in non-specific vocational training courses instead of courses that lead to higher vocational levels, a promotion of career is less often possible in their companies. Another disadvantage for the careers of young employees of bigger sized companies can also be seen in the fact that leading positions are mostly occupied by academic personnel.

Another study of 300 representatively selected top managers, however, showed different results (Manstetten, 1996, p. 63). Here non-specific vocational qualifications, such as problem solving, leadership, teamwork etc. were evaluated as being very important for the promotion of gifted young employees. But this is not a contradiction insofar as specific and non-specific vocational qualifications should be regarded as complementary, but not as alternative; i.e. non-specific vocational qualifications must obviously be regarded as very important, but not sufficiently so for successful attainment of higher positions in a company.

Therefore, it is a positive aspect that the program also supports—apart from specific vocational qualifications—non-specific vocational qualifications. Those were not only chosen quite often, but they were also evaluated positively by the former grant recipients. Particularly valuable were foreign language courses combined with stays in foreign countries, measures for the promotion of communicative abilities and personal abilities. Grant recipients who passed these measures felt more competent and self-confident in various areas of their personal and vocational lives.

All in all more than 20% of the questioned persons have improved considerably since their promotion by the program; nearly 50% have reached a higher position in their companies. Grant recipients from the first test group had attained more attractive positions and responsibilities than their peers; three-fifths work as trainers in their companies whereas this share is normally only 15%; 30% occupy leadership positions compared to 18% of the same age group (Fauser/ Schreiber, 1998, p. 6). In this regard a positive career development can be observed shortly after the partici-

pation in the promotion program. Along with the goal that this program should primarily promote attractive careers as an alternative to university studies, the research results showed how far the positve effects could be stated. The question is very interesting because 50% of the grant recipients have the prerequisite to study at a university.

A total of 24% of these grant recipients decided to study at academic institutions like universities; this seems to be rather low compared to a ratio of 40% of the same age-group. The propensity to study at universities of the second test group decreases to 19%. At the same time—as described above—both groups showed that a decision for higher specific vocational degrees had increased. Therefore, it can be summarized that the promotion program contributes to a higher attractiveness of vocational careers because it offers an alternative to academic studies (Fauser/Schreiber, 1998, p. 8).

Résumé and Concluding Remarks

Vocational education has been regarded as equal to general education in Germany since the beginning of the 20th century. Today, 100 years later, vocational giftedness seems to have a similar fate: Vocational giftedness has long been ignored as a research field in pedagogy as well as in psychology. This deficit was already criticized at the beginning of this century. New impulses for the research field were set by the program *Promotion of the Gifted in Vocational Training* in Germany as late as the beginning of the nineties.

A first research step has been taken by asking how far psychological gifted models can be used to explain and describe giftedness in the non-academic vocational field. The preliminary analysis of these models shows some positive results. This is particularly true for the models of Gagné and Heller et al. Both models can be seen as a basis for giftedness research in non-academic vocations in the field of technics and commerce, crafts and trades, as well as in social vocations. Nevertheless, both models do not sufficiently explain the specific factors of vocational giftedness itself.

The empirical research of the German Government's promotion program discloses personal and social factors of the gifted in vocational training. The grant recipients are not so much characterized by intelligence and creativity, but more so by the above average achievement motivation in work and learning behavior. On the other hand, this study serves as an evaluation of the grant recipients' preferred courses of further vocational training, as well as the consequences for their vocational career. In this respect former grant recipients evaluated the non-specific vocational courses quite positively even a few years after they finished their program. However, specific vocational courses that lead to higher vocational degrees were particularly useful for a vocational career. Specific vocational courses were mostly chosen by non-high school grant recipients who primarily qualified in technical areas. Grant recipients with high school degrees—although to a lower extent—see better career opportunities in academic study.

The promotion program seems to be especially career oriented for those grant recipients who have special gifts and achievements in the technical area. This is an area, however, which does not occur in curricula of general, non-vocational schools; therefore, it is obvious that the questioned grant recipients regard their vocational training as a new chance and a highlight.

It has to be criticized that the promotion program of the German Government is restricted to promote gifted young people after their graduation from initial vocational training. There are hardly any concrete measures during the initial vocational training. The few examples that exist in vocational schools for the promotion of specially gifted young people are mostly related to the extension of general teaching contents (e.g. additional lessons), or they are based upon higher degrees which were acquired at former general schools (e.g. establishing special classes for A-level trainees in vocational schools). Therefore, they are primarily aimed at the promotion of general education and not at the promotion of vocational qualifications (Manstetten, 1996, p. 24; Kusch, 1995, p. 57).

Promotion by companies during the initial vocational training of young gifted employees is mainly limited to the performance of additional high-level tasks or the participation in vocational achievement contests (Pütz, 1998, p. 32). These measures are—contrary to the school examples named—related to the extension of vocational qualifications, but they lack continuity and systematization which is typical for learning processes in schools.

For all these reasons a systematic vocational promotion of gifted young people is still in its early stages; the deficits which were criticized at the start of this century, still exist. This is not only related to the introduction of concrete vocational promotion measures, but also for the development of adequate procedures and instruments to identify vocational giftedness. The solution of these problems will be an important task for the future and is equally demanded by psychology, as well as by pedagogy.

References

Bals, T. (1996). Ausbildungserfolg und Berufsbildungsbiographie. (Training success and biographies in vocational education.) In: R. Manstetten (Ed.), *Begabtenförderung in der beruflichen Bildung*. (Promotion of the gifted in vocational training.) (pp. 252–338). Göttingen/Bern/Toronto/Seattle:Hogrefe.

Fauser, R. & Schreiber, N. (1998). *Wirkung und Nutzen der Begabtenförderung berufliche Bildung*. (Effects and bene-fits of the promotion of the gifted in vocational training.) Konstanz (unpublished).

Gagné, F. (1985). Giftedness and talent: reexamining a reexamination of the definitions. *Gifted Child Quarterly*, **19**, 103–112.

Gagné, F. (1993). Constructs and models pertaining to exceptional human abilities. In: K. A. Heller, F. J. Mönks & A. H. Passow (Eds.), *International handbook of research and development of giftedness and talent*. (pp. 69–87) Oxford: Pergamon.

Heid, H. (1969). Sozialkulturelle Bedingtheit der 'Begabung' in pädagogischer Betrachtung. (Sociocultural condition of 'giftedness' in pedagogical perspective.) *Die Deutsche Berufs- und Fachschule*, **8**, 561–579.

Heller, K. A., Mönks, F. J. & Passow, A. H. (Eds.). (1993). *International handbook of research and development of giftedness and talent*. Oxford: Pergamon.

Heller, K. A., Perleth, Ch. & Hany, E. A. (1994). Hochbegabung—eine lange Zeit vernachlässigtes Forschungsthema. (Giftedness—a longtime neglected research topic.) *Einsichten—Forschung an der Ludwig-Maximilians-Universität München*, **1**, 18–22.

Holling, H., Wübbelmann, K. & Geldschläger, H. (1996). Kriterien und Instrumente zur Auswahl von Begabten in der beruflichen Bildung. (Criteria and instruments for the selection of the gifted in vocational training.) In: R. Manstetten (Ed.), *Begabtenförderung in der Beruflichen Bildung*. (Promotion of the gifted in vocational training.) (pp. 85–174). Göttingen/Bern/Toronto/Seattle: Hogrefe.

Kusch, W. (Ed.). (1995). *Begabtenförderung in der beruflichen Erstaus- und Weiterbildung*. (Promotion of the gifted in initial and further vocational training.) Neusaess: Kieser.

Manstetten, R. (Ed.). (1996). *Begabtenförderung in der beruflichen Bildung*. (Promotion of the gifted in vocational training.) Göttingen/Bern/Toronto/Seattle: Hogrefe.

Mönks, F. J. (1991). Kann wissenschaftliche Argumentation auf Aktualität verzichten? (Are scientific arguments dispensable in the discussion on identification of the gifted?) *Zeitschrift für Entwicklungspsychologie und Pädagogische Psychologie*, **23**, 232–240.

Petersen, P. (Ed.). (1916). *Der Aufstieg der Begabten*. (The rise of the gifted.) Leipzig/Berlin: Teubner.

Pütz, H. (1998). Bericht zum Forschungsbericht des BIBB. (Report on the research report of the BIBB.) In: M. Selzer, M. Weinkamp & C. Heese (Eds.), *Leistungsstarke Auszubildende nachhaltig fördern*. (Promotion of Excellent Achievements of Vocational Trainees.) Dettelbach: Röll.

Renzulli, J. S. (1978). What makes Giftedness? Reexamining a definition. *Phi Delta Koppa*, **60**, 180–184.

Renzulli, J. S. (1979). What makes giftedness: A reexamination of the definition of the gifted and talented. Ventura, CA.

Renzulli, J. S. (1986). The three-ring conception of giftedness: a developmental model for creative productivity. In: R. J. Sternberg & J. E. Davidson (Eds.), *Conceptions of Giftedness*. pp. 53–92. New York: Cambridge University Press.

Roth, H. (1969). *Begabung und Lernen*. (Giftedness and learning.) Stuttgart: Klett.

Schiefele, H., & Krapp, A. (1975). *Studienheft zur Erziehungswissenschaft. Teil I: Grundzüge einer empirisch-pädagogischen Begabungslehre*. (Studies on educational science. Part I: Principles of an empirical-pedagogical giftedness instruction.) (2nd ed.), München: Oldenbourg.

Schubert, H. (1958). Die Begabtenförderung im Handwerk. (Promotion of gifted craftsmen.) *Berufserziehung im Handwerk*. Issue No 14. Köln: Universität Köln.

Stern, W. (1916). Psychologische Begabungsforschung und Begabungsdiagnose. (Psychological research and diagnosis of giftedness.) In: P. Petersen (Ed.), *Der Aufstieg der Begabten*. (The rise of the gifted.) (pp. 150–120). Leipzig/Berlin: Teubner.

Sternberg, R. J. (1993). Procedures for identifying intellectual potential in the gifted: a perspective on alternative 'metaphors of mind'. In: K. A. Heller, F. J. Mönks & A. H. Passow (Eds.), *International handbook of research and development of giftedness and talent*. (pp. 185–207). Oxford: Pergamon.

Trost, G. (1991). Begabung und Bildung. (Giftedness and education.) In: C. Krekelau & J. Siegers (Eds.), *Handbuch der Aus- und Weiterbildung*. (2330, pp. 1–6). Köln: Deutscher Wirtschaftsdienst.

Giftedness: The Ultimate Instrument for Good and Evil

Abraham J. Tannenbaum

Teachers College, Columbia University, New York, USA

Introduction

Probably with a mixture of pride and relief, the renowned psychologist, Edward L. Thorndike, once observed that gifted individuals tend to be friends, rather than enemies, of the people. Applied to outstanding adults, this truism would seem self-evident, because their giftedness is virtually defined by their notable service to society. For after all, they are the ones who design ingenious ways to prevent and heal sickness in body and soul; who enhance the quality of life by creating aesthetic treasures; who make invaluable discoveries ranging from elemental matter to phenomena in the broad universe; who contribute incomparably to the world's knowledge bank; and who demonstrate wide or deep expertise in existing knowledge. Indeed, the extraordinary abilities of these men and women *are* their most prominent virtues, to the extent that the human family benefits from them.

Missing from this euphoric definition of mature giftedness is its ugly reverse side. The selfsame creative and cognitive strengths that serve society with distinction are sometimes turned against it with tragic effect. For example, the so-called 'Angel of Death', Dr. Joseph Mengele, used his medical research talents to conduct some of the most outrageous experiments on innocent people whose living bodies he regarded as disposable slabs of meat, bones, and sinew. In the world of art, Leni Riefenstahl's riveting cinematography is on display in the documentary, 'Triumph of Will', which depicts the revolting pageantry of a pre-war Nazi rally in Nürnberg. The setting is an ornate facade of a building and a huge plaza that faces it, where torches and floodlights pierce a black night, revealing long streamers, emblazoned with swastikas, that seem to hang from the top of the building to the ground of the plaza. A phalanx of uniformed, banner-bearing troops marches into the plaza, row by row in perfect formation. Automaton-like, they tramp to the sound of a martial drumbeat that goes on and on until all the marchers have taken their places at attention.

Adolph Hitler then appears on a tall balcony of the building, his face beaming against the backdrop of night, and he proceeds to harangue his huge audience of uniformed and civilian adorers, whipping them into a state of ecstasy. What a vivid foreshadowing of the bloodbath soon to spread over Europe and much of the rest of the world, captured in a masterpiece of filmmaking! How priceless its propaganda value must have been!

Mengele and Riefenstahl and other highly gifted scoundrels are understandably absent from any list of notable achievers, but they do belong in a rogue's gallery of brilliant villains. Of course, such a galaxy of sinister movers and shakers consists only of adults. In children, however, giftedness is generally viewed in value-neutral terms. Rather than defining and identifying them by what they can contribute to society today or someday, they qualify as gifted only if they think faster or deeper or more creatively than most of their age peers. The school years are often considered too early in a person's life to worry about right and wrong applications of faster, deeper, and more creative thought.

Such complacency is unfortunate because so much is at stake in guiding gifted children to dedicate their special abilities eventually to pro-social, rather than anti-social, causes. Since there is a proven link, imperfect as it may be, between early promise and mature performance and productivity (Oden, 1968), it is essential for the gifted to learn that great character has to serve as the mediator of great accomplishments; otherwise, the brilliant mind can become the most destructive force in the world. The purpose of this chapter is, therefore, to help psychologists and educators: (1) see a clearer picture of moral principles and their relationship to brainpower; (2) appreciate more fully how giftedness carries with it enormous potential for evil as well as good; and (3) explore the possibilities of interweaving 'duties of the heart' with brilliance of the mind.

Issues in Defining Moral Codes

Morality is recognizable through pro-social values, including empathy, humanism, justice, and the like, along with appropriate derivative traits. It seems unnecessary to define morality, a term that is well known to be associated with "what one ought to be, to do, or to have," in contrast to "what one is, was, or may become." The operative referent, as Havighurst & Taba (1949) point out, is *character*, with its subsumed attributes that are judged on a scale of right or wrong, in contrast to *personality*, which includes only those descriptors that delineate a person's individuality in non-evaluative terms. Thus, character calls attention to love, ethics, charitableness, and trustworthiness, among other qualities one is obliged to have. Personality, on the other hand, is reflected in people's tastes (e.g. music, art, literature, etc.) and interests (e.g. sports, recreation, travel, etc.), or in anything that is viewed with a live-and-let-live attitude, even by those who do not necessarily share another's tastes and interests. Character also incorporates immorality, when it involves publicly resented traits, such as misanthropy, misogyny, bigotry, and brutality.

For a formal psychosocial definition of morality, perhaps none is more serviceable than Martin L. Hoffman's (1979): "[M]orality is the part of personality that pinpoints the individual's very link to society, and moral development epitomizes the existential problem of how humans come to manage the inevitable conflict between personal needs and social obligations" (p. 958).

Subjectivity in Defining Morality

Beneath the surface rendering of the concept, there are complications, the first of which is its parameters. Does it require not only moral *judgment* and a feeling of moral *responsibility*, but also *acting* in accordance with this judgment and responsibility? Secondly, there is the matter of conflicting applications. In the name of morality, people have argued pro and con regarding abortion rights, genetic engineering, mercy killing, legalizing drugs, and recognizing homosexual marriages. This suggests that while there may be general consensus on the *need* for moral codes to guide human belief and action, there can also be considerable discord on how, where, and when to employ the codes. A third issue relates to the question of "whose ox is being gored." One side in an armed conflict condemns the enemy guerrillas as terrorists, whereas the other side idolizes these partisans as freedom fighters. Are both attitudes valid, morally, depending on who espouses either of them? Fourth, there are questions of internal consistency and generality among those who subscribe to particular moral principles. Is a person who is honest in family life necessarily honest in reporting financial data for income tax purposes? If a President of the United States is proven guilty of marital infidelity while in office, does it necessarily cast doubt on his (or her) sincerity in promoting family values as public policy?

Behavioral scientists are especially concerned about a fifth issue pertaining to the psychological structure of morality. Is it analogous to a cognitive 'g' factor, defined by the religiously oriented as belief and involvement in the *sanctity* of life, or by secularists as the active *celebration* of life? Or, as Gruber (1993) argues, there are various forms of morality, including "Justice Morality (Kohlberg, Piaget); Caring Morality (Gilligan); Truth Morality (Asch); Freedom Morality (Fromm, 1941); The Work Ethic (Veblen, 1914); Planetary Morality (Ehrlich & Ehrlich, 1991); Religious Morality" (pp. 8, 9). All of these are subsumed under a general life morality which Gruber defines as "the superordinate combination of caring and planetary morality" (1993, p. 9). Shades of theories of intelligence proposed by Spearman (1927) and Vernon (1960) which make room for overarching general abilities and related specific aptitudes.

Finally, there are various orientations concerning the origins of moral codes in humans. From a theological point of view, a Jewish scholar (Hutner, undated) quotes the Biblical passage in *Genesis* (II, 7) ". . . and He breathed into [Adam's] nostrils the soul of life, and Adam became a living being," and comments that the 'soul' of life carried with it a nobility of character which Adam shared with Eve and which both bequeathed to all subsequent generations. Specifically, the all-virtuous Creator transmitted part of Himself, as it were, to the human race by breathing virtue, along with life, into Adam.

From a completely different orientation, the zoologist (and editor of *The Economist*), Matt Ridley (1996) offers an evolutionary explanation of morality's origins by tracing cooperative behaviors in humans to similar traits in other living creatures, including ants, fish, naked mole rats, and baboons. Ridley believes that people tend to work together constructively when they are prepared to trust and trade with each other.

Still another perspective is suggested by the classical scholar, Moses Hadas (1967) who locates the roots of modern society's humanism in ancient cultures that populated the Tigris-Euphrates valley. It was then reinforced by the multitudes who were inspired by the Old Testament's vision of people caring and taking responsibility for each other. But nowhere did it flower more richly than in the ancient Greece of Homer, Socrates, Plato, Aristotle, and in the accompanying classical art and literature. This confluence of Hellenistic genius spread its influence to other parts of the world, and it still inspires humanistic leadership in modern society. However, Greek sophists took humanism to a dangerous extreme by encouraging individuals to place themselves at the center of the universe, with little concern for the needs and plights of others. Such a belief is perhaps best expressed by Shakespeare's foolish schemer, Polonius, in his oft-quoted advice to

Laertes: "This above all—to thine own self be true. . . ," not to some higher principle of morality.

What creates social harmony, then, in a world of Ayn Rand-type radical egotists is the social contract, as in Thomas Hobbes' *Leviathan* (1996), which recognizes no intrinsic principles of right and wrong. Instead, human beings adopt a mutual survival pact, not unlike the United States–Soviet Union mutual deterrence of mass destruction, based on the fear that each possessed the means to annihilate the other in relatively short order. And there was enough hatred between them to render their 'peace' into a more realistic 'cold war'.

People usually subscribe to principles of morality and can even agree on what these values are; but they interpret and invoke them in different ways that often lead to dispute or even conflict. The sheer complexity of morality as a construct may help explain why it is difficult to penetrate below the surface of platitudes that overlay the phenomenon so often in everyday conversation. Educators are also stymied by the puzzle and may assume that it is futile to teach morality in school until the fog of mixed meanings is lifted. Besides, many teachers are convinced that such instruction rightly belongs in the home and places of worship.

Perhaps most discouraging to scientists and educators is that, to them, morality seems approachable either pragmatically or dogmatically, neither of which is appealing to the rational mind. From a pragmatic point of view, there are no eternal values, only those which fit transitory needs. Schwartz (1990) suggests that values are contextually determined and supports his contention with evidence on how they can be created or destroyed in laboratory experiments. They therefore do not lend themselves to scientific generalization about their origins, how they change over time, and how they influence behavior. Instead, according to Schwartz, they are subject to the specifics of times, places, social norms, and the institutions that exert leadership. Consequently, "[A]ttempts to extract what is timeless and universal about the formation of human values from the particulars that are important at any given time or place are likely to lead to distortion. This distortion can be especially serious if historical contingencies are mistakenly identified as natural laws" (p. 15).

No wonder that scientists who see the systematization of moral principles and their origins as an impossibility often ignore the subject in their studies; they are more committed to generalizing than to particularizing; and without some rules about the nature of morality, educators may lack, or think they lack, the guidelines for nurturing it. If a sizable number of scientists and educators consider dogmatism as the only alternative to Schwartz's brand of pragmatism, they could find themselves in the precarious position of promoting eternal verities in a laboratory or a schoolroom where proselytizing is unacceptable, even in a non-sectarian format. For similar reasons, warning against evil is not a popular practice in psychological counseling or classroom instruction.

Some Ideational Visions of Morality

Clearly, 'ought's' and 'ought not's' are elusive by nature, even among those who take a strict-construction view of morality. Loving-kindness is an unquestionably noble trait under ordinary circumstances, but hazardous foolishness when practiced by innocent victims toward their assailants bent on hurting them. Equally, self-defense is occasionally an acceptable excuse for pre-emptive strikes against an imminent attack. But even though there are times and places for violating good or practicing evil, ideationally, good and evil are timeless—yes, even dogmatic—constructs. Benevolence is virtuous and aggression is vile despite the fact that they can be misapplied and often are.

Behavioral and social scientists and educators seem reluctant to posit ideational descriptors of morality as they do for cognitive, creative, motivational, and social portrayals of people. Perhaps they consider the nature and nurture of the utopian good life self-evident, and words are not adequate to describe it without sounding preachy. Thus, instead of approaching the phenomenon as a universal concept, contemporary theory and research concentrate mainly on how morality develops, how its development can be measured, how it can be clarified subjectively by those in search of personal values to live by, and what its mental and emotional correlates are, with only casual attention to the true nature of the profound 'it' in all its glory. Hesitation among students of human nature to commit themselves to a vision of morality, even in a chimerical state bordering on fantasy, probably helps inhibit teachers and counselors from daring to promote virtue and to discourage harmful inclinations in children's belief systems. For the gifted, this reluctance can have devastating consequences since superior brain power, harnessed to unprincipled motives, poses threats to the human family that are far out of proportion to the incidence of such couplings in society. In simple terms, a brilliant villain or a brilliant dupe serving villainous causes, though mercifully rare in public life, is the most dangerous of living species, just as the high-minded, highly able handful is the world's most precious possession.

The Need to Concretize the Visions

For many centuries, the Ten Commandments, the Seven Deadly Sins, and The Confucian Analects have individually or collectively addressed the conscience of huge segments of the world's population. The purpose of this widespread dissemination has been simply to guide people to embrace righteousness and to reject wrongdoing. Yet, there are people who express respect for these keys to morality but are guilty of causing death, hunger, and bondage among countless humans. Is it just a tiny minority, consisting of those who give only lip service to morality, guilty of spreading havoc, whereas the vast majority abide by the ancients' tenets about the good life? Or is it possible that traces of cruelty lie dormant in most people and can be brought to life by authority figures, as in Milgram's (1974) experiment with normally law-abiding citizens who followed orders to administer what they thought were near-lethal electric shocks to strangers? If so, the popular, age-old precepts and scriptures serve merely as a thin veil to cover people's baser instincts that can be aroused to turn masses into willing executioners of innocents (Goldhagen, 1996).

It is conceivable that the printed word and the vocal plea for universal morality, such as peace on earth and goodwill toward mankind are only ideational visions with limited persuasive power. Possibly, even the language of Beethoven's music, combined with Schiller's 'Ode to Joy' are only powerful enough to arouse deep aesthetic sensitivity, but not to advance the cause of the brotherhood and sisterhood of all humanity. The only alternative, then, is to concretize these lofty ideals into behaviors of individuals who qualify as role models. Instead of drawing the big picture of morality, the concept may best be approachable through its constituent details as exemplified by single specific behaviors or habits of the famous, not so famous, and even unknowns. What follows, then, is a sample of some defining morality attributes and the names of real individuals who have been known to possess them, and at least a few of whose lives deserve to become familiar to young students.

Morality is the *passion for freedom* that characterized Dietrich Bonhöffer, Osip Mandelstam, and Arturo Toscanini, whose self sacrifice in their battles against tyranny is legendary. Bonhöffer died at the hands of the Nazi regime; Mandelstam was tortured and finally put to death in a Soviet Gulag; and Toscanini lived in self-imposed exile from the Fascist domination of his beloved Italy.

Morality is the *dedication to world peace* displayed by Mildred Norman, the 'Peace Pilgrim', who hiked well over 25,000 miles to campaign for peace on earth. An earlier heroic figure of her kind was the great French writer Romain Rolland who passionately rallied the intelligentsia of Europe to use their prestige and influence to avert World War I, albeit without success.

Morality is the *dedication to racial equality*, as personified by the likes of W. E. B. DuBois, Martin Luther King, Jr., and Arthur Schomburg, who contributed so much to overcome resistance to black integration in American society. Even today, long after

their death, their influence remains alive and powerful against bigotry, separatism, and ignorance.

Morality is belief in the *sanctity or celebration of human life*, as perfected by Eleanor Roosevelt through self-discovery, self-acceptance, and self-deliverance from emotional pain and from feelings of inadequacy, to become the conscience of the fledgling United Nations and the beloved caretaker of the downtrodden throughout the world. In their study of her values and behaviors, Piechowski & Tysk (1982) conclude that she was a truly self-actualized 'Doer' in the sense that Maslow (1970) defines the term.

Morality is the *leap from expressing sympathy to feeling empathy* for fellow humans, especially the broken spirits, that Mother Teresa demonstrated in the squalor of Calcutta, India. Her values contrasted sharply from those who loudly profess a love for humanity and for identifiable segments thereof, but fail tragically in one-to-one relationships, be it in marriage, family life, the workplace, or in informal social groups.

Morality is *modesty and honesty* that characterized the psychometrist and researcher, Robert L. Thorndike, who spent about five of the last years of his highly productive life preparing a revision of the Stanford-Binet Test. Soon after its completion, he remarked to this author, "Abe, my job is finished, but I'm not sure that the new instrument is an improvement over the previous one." How many productive behavioral scientists would be willing to confess doubts about their success after completing an exhausting labor of love?

Morality is *personal integrity*, as practiced by behavioral scientists, Irving Lorge and Miriam L. Goldberg, who would not agree to be listed as co-authors of their respective students' or colleagues' publishable research without actively participating in the conduct of the studies and in the reports of outcomes. Lorge and Goldberg resisted the temptation to lengthen their lists of publications, and thus enhance their professional reputations, even when they played vital roles in advising on the study designs, the accurate presentation of results, and honesty in interpretation.

Morality is just plain *human decency and thoughtfulness*, as exhibited by this author's four-year-old grandson who would accept a cookie from his mother only if she also gave one to his playmate. This habit was practiced without ulterior motives to curry favor from his mother or out of fear of punishment if he were to act selfishly. Sharing and caring behavior as a matter of principle among mere four-year-olds is an oddity that does not seem compatible with age- and stage-related theories of moral development.

Obviously, morality embraces a much greater array of human attributes than the ones listed above. Furthermore, to those familiar with the personalities of the real people who are named as exemplifying these aspects of morality, it is equally self-evident that the descriptive behaviors are not context bound or restricted to the single traits attributed to these individuals. The campaigners for peace felt that way about warlike situations in general; so did the individual exponents of empathy, honesty, and decency generalize their defining characteristics in large varieties of situations involving these principles. But while they were consistent in demonstrating the values that made them notable, the question is to what extent their moral superiority crossed over to other domains of prosocial behavior. For example, did those described as possessing uncommon personal integrity also distinguish themselves in fostering social equality? Again, the question reduces itself to the issue of whether morality manifests itself in discrete ways, or whether there is at least a partial common denominator among them. If there were a kind of 'g' factor combining aspects of all forms of morality, it would probably be defined, as Gruber (1993) suggests, an extraordinary regard for the human race, its sub-populations, and its individual members.

The most promising advantage of illustrating specific moral traits through the behaviors of real people is that the concept thus becomes more teacher friendly. It is easier to teach earthbound, kindly habits than to deal with morality as a vague, Utopian abstraction and trying to make it a governing influence on students' lifestyles. Easier, but not easy. If the instructors are virtuous role models and able to show how heroic figures and unknowns, even four-year-olds, behave laudably, there is a chance that students will try to adopt at least some of these habits and absorb at least some of the underlying convictions. In the last analysis, pedagogic methods have to be tested and confirmed as effective and applied to instill morality in children at school. For to neglect the humane development of young personalities,—either out of fear of failure or out of conviction that such matters belong outside of school—is clearly risky; riskier when it involves the gifted. The reason is that there is no way of knowing precisely where the talents of unprincipled able students will be directed—towards good or towards evil—when early promise is fulfilled in the adult years.

Conflict and Consensus on How to Examine Morality

Occasional Conflict

There seems to be a fair amount of contrast in scholarly approaches to morality and immorality. Hutner's (undated) theory of God instilling virtue in human beings is countered by belief in original sin (Hoffman, 1970) which emphasizes the need for proper upbringing and other supportive experiences to counteract people's immoral inclinations. Behavior management specialists move nurturance into the realm of specifics by itemizing virtues to be reinforced and by elaborating on proper reinforcement tactics. No rationale for reward or punishment is necessarily communicated to the person whose behavior is being modified.

A much different dynamic is suggested by Freud (1955) who, unlike reward and punishment change agents, was most interested in the antecedents and causes of moral behavior and proposed elaborate methods of helping clients to engage in intensive introspection for better self-understanding. Freud believed in deep analysis to expunge guilt feelings which can surface if moral principles do not suppress antisocial impulses from operating at the conscious level.

Guilt has no place, however, in Maslow's (1954) humanitarian orientation, with its focus on self-perfection through self-fulfillment, which can be accomplished by human beings nurturing their potential for dignity, autonomy, personal integration, and by satisfying their needs for social attachment and altruism. According to Schneider (1998), Maslow's protagonism for personal worth and perfectibility continues to influence the work of social scientists who study personology, industrial organizational psychology, and educational psychology. Schneider concludes: "Thanks to the influence of Maslow and other existential-humanistic psychologists (e.g. Rogers), there have been significant increases in the trends toward worker participation in management, meaning-based jobs, and human relations training. . . . There has also been an increased recognition of the roles played by empathy, emotions, and creativity within the educational setting. . . . Arguably, these factors are integral to the . . . social responsibility movement in our culture and to a resurgent quest for meaning . . ." (p. 282). These views are in sharp contrast to Elliot's (1997) observation that psychologists today often perceive Maslow's ideas as quaint, romantic anachronisms in the worlds of social and behavioral sciences. Friedman (1992) goes so far as to hold Maslow partly responsible for the 'me-generation's' narcissism in the 1970s.

In essence, then, the aggregate of theories of morality are basically in a point-counterpoint, thrust-and-parry relationship with each other rather than in a complementary, mutually reinforcing arrangement. To make matters even more complicated, the theories have to deal with change in American value priorities. For example, Rokeach & Ball-Rokeach (1989) report an encouraging increase, from 1968 to 1971, and then a disturbing decrease, from 1971 to 1974 to 1981, in America's valuation of *egalitarianism*. The authors note that these findings contrast with outcomes of another survey which shows impressive increases in positive attitudes toward *integration* between 1942 and 1983. Also noted are the generally lower levels of support for *equality* as reflected in attitudes toward implementing racial integration through legislation, government aid, and the like. Rokeach and Ball-Rokeach suspect that the differences in findings resulted from variations in questionnaire formats in these surveys.

There is reason to believe that values do change over time, regardless of how they are tapped by surveyors. Note, for example, the more recent study by Wolfe (1998) which shows that Americans have more respect for *diversity* than they have had in the past, clearly another sign that values are changeable. This kind of instability may help explain why some researchers prefer to study how people mature in their understanding of why they embrace particular moral beliefs rather than just studying the nature of these beliefs per se. It may also be a reason for the delayed popularity of Piaget's book, *The Moral Judgment of the Child* (1932) which was fairly neglected for decades until psychologists began to view morality from a developmental cognitive perspective. Piaget's monitoring of moral maturation in children has served as a strong basis for Kohlberg's contributions to the field.

Occasional Consensus

No other body of thought about morality has attracted as much testing and commentary (pro and con) as Lawrence Kohlberg's theory of moral development (Puka, 1994a, 1994b, 1994c, 1994d, 1994e, 1994f, 1994g). It is redundant to repeat much of what has already been written, except to add comments and comparisons that are not often made. One probable reason for its popularity is that it has the distinction of dealing with morality and yet does not promote a package of virtues. Moral relativists and pragmatists can relate to it easily. Even dogmatists can identify with insights into their own maturation in embracing what they consider eternal values.

Kohlberg (1963, 1964, 1966) acknowledges Piaget's influence on his thinking, but he also argues for the need to discredit the earlier work of Hartshorne & May (1928–1930) who defined a package of virtues consisting of *honesty* (i.e. avoidance of cheating, lying, and stealing); *service* (i.e. sacrificing personal possessions for others' welfare); and *self control* (i.e. task persistence). The basic method for assessing these virtues was to note the frequency of occurrence in situations where children's behavior was not disciplined or monitored by authority figures. The outcomes of these investigations convinced the researchers that honesty depends on the situation, not on an internalized, consistent set of values.

Kohlberg (1964) disputes this conclusion, offering alternative ways of interpreting the results. More important, he expresses disappointment in the Hartshorne and May belief that moral principles are determined in early childhood by the home environment and that character education and religious education had no real impact on children's honesty and service, as measured by the Hartshorne and May tests (Kohlberg, 1966). These outcomes seem to help account for Kohlberg's avoidance of positing a virtue

package and for moving him closer to Piaget's (1932) developmental theory. They may also account for the lukewarm commitment (at best) of schools toward mounting serious character and citizenship education programs.

In his book on the unity of knowledge, Wilson (1998) uses the term 'concilience' to describe the sense of accordance of two or more lines of induction drawn from different sets of phenomena. Kohlberg's model which is primarily developmental and cognitive, along with Dabrowski's (1964) paradigm on positive disintegration, which is also developmental, but non-intellective, combine with each other and with Perry's (1970) framework of epistemological development to form a concilient relationship that sheds combined light on moral maturity, albeit from different conceptual sources. Their parallelisms and convergences can best be illustrated by placing them side-by-side, as shown in Table 1.

A simple inspection of the three models reveals a fairly invariant stage progression from rigidity, self-absorption, and dependence on authority to more sophistication, flexibility, and independence as the person matures. The number of stages is roughly the same, and there is either a conceptual or empirical relationship between the models at various stages. Yet, there are differences in interpretation of what *causes* movement from one stage to the next. As a cognitive psychologist, Kohlberg (1966) saw role taking and guided personal reflection as powerful facilitators of moral development. This was demonstrated in Turiel's (1966) study of three sixth grade groups, matched for IQ, which were engaged in role-play and discussion sessions that centered on hypothetical conflict situations similar to the ones that appear on Kohlberg's tests of moral development. Each group used moral judgments at one of three levels, either at its own, or one above its own, or one below its own. Only in the case where the children engaged in one above their levels did they show meaningful absorption of the older group leader's own moral judgments. Another experiment involving classroom discussion produced similarly encouraging results (Blatt & Kohlberg, 1975). Kohlberg et al. (1972) also used the role taking and discussion methods to help prison cottage populations to become justice-oriented communities, with moderate success.

The process of moving to higher developmental stages was seen by the psychiatrist, Dabrowski (1964) as an active effort by the organism to transform itself from within rather than rely passively on maturation and on cognitive stimulation from without. He calls the mechanism for change 'positive disintegration', marked by a deep inner struggle to reject one's present, familiar value motives in order to reach a higher level of belief and understanding. In other words, less mature psychological structures are broken down by profound, disturbing restlessness and distress and

Table 1. Three Developmental Theories and Their Parallelisms..

Stage	Kohlberg (1969) (Cognitive development in moral reasoning)	Dabrowski (1964) (Stages in positive disintegration)	Perry (1970) (Epistemological development)
1	Avoidance of punishment and the superior power of authorities.		Relevant experiences are judged as absolutely right or wrong, true or false, good or bad, and authorities are believed to have the right answers to all questions.
2	To serve one's own needs or interests in a world where you have to recognize that other people have their interests too.	Primary integration, marked by egocentrism. Lack of sympathy or self-examination, personal ambition without a sense of personal responsibility.	
3	The need to be a good person in your own eyes and in those of others. Belief in the golden rule. Desire to maintain rules and authority which support stereotypical good behavior.	Uni-level disintegration: moral relativism, conformity to mainstream values, and indecisiveness in choosing between competing values.	Alternative judgments are possible and equally valid, but there is no standard of preference of one over the other.
4	To preserve the social system and one's own conscience. Worry that the system may break down if individuals deviate from it. The violator's conscience may thus be threatened, too.	Spontaneous multi-level disintegration, in which the person develops an hierarchical sense of values. A dissatisfaction with what one is because of awareness of what one ought to be. The struggle between the 'is' and the 'ought to be' can produce anxiety, self-doubt, and a restless need for personal change.	Recognition of relativism only in academic tasks and exercised only when allowed by authorities.
5	A sense of obligation to law because of one's social contract to make and abide by laws for the welfare of all and for the protection of all people's rights. The greatest good for the greatest number.	Organize multi-level disintegration; the individual is finding a way to reach his or her personal ideals and thereby achieve a new sense of autonomy of thought and action, self-awareness, and acceptance of others. This degree of maturation resembles and is comparable to Maslow's advanced progress toward self-actualization.	Relativism begins to permeate all thought. Knowledge itself requires relativistic reasoning in the sense that an interpretation is right only in terms of a particular context or frame of reference. This means that a variety of perspectives have to be considered.
6	The belief, as a rational person, in the validity of universal moral principles and a sense of personal commitment to them.	Secondary integration of values and ideals on the one hand and everyday living on the other. The person's social space makes room for compassion toward others and a sense that every aspect of experience is guided by principles, not by personal motives or social dictates.	The possibility of commitment within the relativistic universe is recognized. That commitment evolves over time, as contexts change.

replaced by greater moral responsibility, empathy, sensitivity, and autonomy. As in the Kohlberg and Perry models, few people ever reach the highest stage. Those who do are the rare creative souls who seem capable of experiencing a commitment to what Gowan (1979) calls 'agape love', or an all-embracing, total identification with humanity. 'Agape love' is the peaceful culmination of a turbulent development from narcissism, on to oedipal attachments to parents, and love partnerships in the years when such feelings can be aroused. These particularized expressions of love form the basis for an all-embracing 'agape love', which are closely associated with profound creative impulses.

Powering the inner transformations from one stage to the next are five overexcitabilities that can be expressed in any of the following forms: psychomotor, sensual, intellectual, imaginational, and emotional. According to Piechowski (1979), these overexcitabilities combine with "original endowment [to determine] what level of development a person may reach under optimal conditions" (p. 28). In a study of graduate students, Lysy & Piechowski (1983) found that the emotional and intellectual excitabilities were most closely associated with higher development, as defined by Dabrowski. Within an adolescent population, Piechowski & Colangelo (1984) detected two different types of exceptionally bright children, (1) the *rational altruistic*, who possess short-term goals and engage in little introspection; and (2) the *introspective-emotional*, who demonstrate more concern about understanding life's existential meanings. Small wonder that the Dabrowski model, with its emphasis on self-regeneration and its hyper-motivational drives, is of such growing interest to scholars concerned about understanding and stimulating gifted behavior (Maxwell & Silverman, 1995; Nelson, 1995; Morrissey, 1996; Piechowski, 1997).

Besides showing some resemblances to the Kohlberg and Dabrowski models in the form of change from early stages of rigidity and conformity, to the higher levels of freedom and flexibility, Perry's theory of epistemological development seems to add a dynamic dimension to understanding Kohlberg's model. In a study by Clinchy, Lief & Young (1977), a high correlation (0.7) was discovered between Perry's and Kohlberg's systems among high school senior girls. This is important, in light of speculation by Gruber (1993) and Runco (1993) that morals may be immutable principles and therefore orthogonal in their relationship to the spontaneity and venturesome of creativity. One would expect Perry's developmental stages leading toward relativistic moral thinking to describe the unfolding of creative impulses that veer away from what seems to be the uncompromising, conservative nature of moral beliefs. Yet, the Clinchy, Lief & Young results reveal the opposite—that the relationship is strong, despite other empirical evidence to the contrary (Andreani & Pagnin, 1993a). The latter study uses a categorical analysis and measures creativity through a divergent thinking test, the type of instrument that has been criticized as questionable in validity (Baer, 1993, 1993/1994). Besides, if morality and creativity relied on opposite cognitive styles, shouldn't the correlation hover around −1 rather than 0?

Perry's model and its subsequent evaluation suggests that it may be simplistic to consider moral values as hard-and-fast rules applied predictably in every moral dilemma. Kohlberg's stage 6 and Dabrowski's stage 5-type people are not superficial idealogues at peace with their values. Instead, they are cognitively flexible enough to weigh alternatives before judging how, where, and when to apply them, by Kohlberg's standards, and emotionally mature enough to sense the nuances of right and wrong, case-by-case, according to Dabrowski's standards. Inasmuch as the Clinchy, Lief & Young study is only a single investigation of a female high school sample, it should be replicated on more representative populations. If the first results are confirmed, moral development would take on new clarity. Further, the more recent investigation of culture and conformity (Bond & Smith, 1996), which discovered a decline in conforming behavior over the past four decades, especially in 'individualist', as opposed to 'collectivist', countries, may also signal a general rise in epistemological development and, by extension, moral maturity.

Giftedness and Morality: Are They Compatible?

As a social construct, giftedness can be defined at will, unlike objective phenomena, such as height and weight. Even when children are viewed strictly in their early and school-age years without concern about their ability to sustain excellence in adulthood, arbitrary standards are used, such as an IQ level or signs of asynchronous development (Silverman, 1997), in which intellect and creativity are observed as outracing social, emotional, and physical development, at some unspecified speed. The same kind of subjectivity accounts for the tendency to cast specific talents in a morally upright mold. For example, it is assumed that Gardner's (1983) intelligences are meant as pro-social potentialities, with no thought that they can and might be used for evil purposes. Similar positive applications of gifts and talents are implied in Gagne's (1991) model of differentiated forms of excellence.

Some Basic Issues About the Relationship

Talents are sometimes turned into destructive forces, even if the association is too rarely noted in the scientific literature. Moreover, when individuals are guilty of anti-social behavior, they are usually placed near the low end of moral maturity, which is to be expected. For example, Kohlberg (1958) describes the delinquents he was attempting to reform as considerably less mature in moral judgment than those in the comparison sample. Nelson (1995) likewise places one notorious General Secord, who promoted bloody wars in Iran and in Nicaragua out of lust for money, at the lowest primary integration level in Dabrowski's hierarchy. Ignored is the likes of an Adolph Hitler, a genius (or more appropriately an evil genius) who used his talent for demagoguery, and whose charisma and great skills in manipulating masses captivated his countrymen more effectively than any other political leader in his nation's history. He surely climbed to the top of the heap as a political power through rare interpersonal ingenuity, combined with intimidation. Without ever forgetting his immoral *behavior*, one has to admit that he climbed the ladder of immoral *maturity* in a way that parallels the *process* by which exemplary figures move from one *moral* stage to the next. For him, disintegration of earlier beliefs was surely negative in effect, but it helped him escape his personal demons that held him captive in his early years. Later, through some kind of epiphany, which he recorded in his book, *Mein Kampf* (My Struggle) while in jail, he reached a state of idealism, twisted to be sure, that enabled him to gather the inner strength of a visionary fanatic and to rally a powerful following that would encourage him to actualize a dream of fashioning a master race to rule the world.

The point is that gifted villains can reach Kohlberg's and Dabrowski's highest developmental stages and use their combination of brains and hate-filled over-excitabilities to threaten the quality, and even the existence, of life on our planet. Schwebel (1993) describes how creative artists and writers can be forces for the common good through the exemplary works they produce. Conversely, in an equally searching analysis, McClaren (1993) brings to light the destructive potential of arts, sciences, and technology. Whether intellectual and creative gifts will be used for positive or negative purposes depends upon the values of those who possess them. No wonder that Piechowski (1997) pleads for more attention to the moral needs of able children.

A Classification of Talents from a Moral Perspective

In addition to focusing on childhood precocity, one may also consider the connection between early promise and its later fulfillment. Does the child show early signs of social leadership, or scientific reasoning, or legal acumen, or a flair for literary or musical expression, or any other developed talent that is appreciated in the broad cultural world? Of course, the public celebrates superior brain power that is directed to a common good, which makes it morally defensible. Viewed from this perspective, talents can be categorized as follows:

(1) *Scarcity talents*, that are rare and universally appreciated because they heal, preserve, and prolong life. The world is always in need of people inventive enough to make it easier, safer, healthier, more intelligible, and more obstacle-free. Although it takes only a single Jonas Salk to achieve the breakthrough in conquering polio, there can never be enough talent like his for the great leaps forward that still need to be made in medical science. The same can be said for extraordinary leadership in politics, race relations, mental health, and in all matters that are critical to well being. Society will always venerate such talents as they appear, while thirsting for more and more because the shortage has never been filled.

(2) *Surplus talents*, that are also rare and universally appreciated, not for their making survival possible, but because they make life meaningful. Included are the arts, music, literature, theater, and philosophy, among others, that elevate people's sensibilities and sensitivities. Without them, life would reduce itself to a hollow existence. They are labelled 'surplus' to suggest that our cultural treasures are super-abundant and life is too short for an individual's possible exposure to all that exists and all that is being added constantly. But nothing in that treasure should be considered superfluous so long as its contents can have deep meaning for people who savor them.

(3) *Quota talents*, which include specialized high-level skills needed to provide goods and services for which the market is limited. The jobs to be done are fairly clear; there are no creative breakthroughs expected and no way of knowing precisely how long the opportunities for such work will last. Job openings for the relatively few who qualify depend on supply and demand, which can be irregular and limited geographically. Schools are probably most responsive to the public's needs for quota talents, and advanced training programs designed to fill top level positions in various occupations constitute the major effort at differentiating education for the gifted.

(4) *Anomalous talents* are different from the ones already mentioned, not in their nature but in their applications. Some include feats that are intellectually and creatively sophisticated but are not often judged to be signs of excellence. Examples include speed reading, mastery of mountains of trivia, gourmet cooking, trapeze artistry, performance of complex mathematical calculations faster than a computer, and even the numbers of sexual seductions boasted by Don Juan.

Those who possess anomalous talents also include people who possess scarcity, surplus, and quota talents but use them for anti-social purposes. It takes sophisticated talent to develop biological and chemical weaponry. If the results of such efforts are placed by the researchers in the hands of an unscrupulous political power, the results could be the annihilation of life rather than its preservation. Likewise, cultural activity and high level quota productivity can serve a tyrannical state either by helping build it or simply as 'window dressing'. It is obvious, then, that giftedness has its moral and immoral applications, and it would be a serious mistake for its nurturers to regard it as invariably pro-social or even value-free.

What Is (and Isn't) Clear about the Relationship

Whether or not giftedness and moral behavior belong together depends on how the relationship is examined. One source of evidence is historical, which takes the long, impressionistic view, and the other is empirical, which relies on the examination of relatively small sample populations, closely and methodically. Nobody can doubt that great men and women have played important roles in making history, for better or worse, but mostly better. The liberal arts and sciences have always served society brilliantly and continue to do so, even if a few of their most gifted exponents work against the common good or have chosen these professions primarily to gain prestige or material security. This may be 'only' a historical perception, but it is hard to escape the feeling that those who possess scarcity, surplus, and quota talents deserve to be proud of their tradition of virtuous leadership in human affairs. The mean-spirited among them have never succeeded in destroying that tradition, even if they have weakened it from time to time.

As for the empirical evidence, there are problems in interpreting it, due to restrictive methods of gathering data on both independent and dependent variables. In most studies, giftedness is defined exclusively as a high score on an IQ test. Ignored are personality and social indicators as well as special aptitudes that are not measured by IQ. Besides the oversimplicity of equating precocity with high IQ, there may be implicit bias in relating IQ scores with performance on pencil-and-paper tests or interviews on moral reasoning, which are used so popularly today, since they are all measures of cognition. Instruments for assessing the latter essentially reveal how maturely people rationalize the values they espouse, regardless of what these values are. The instruments do not pretend to clarify whether a person is a do-gooder or even a believer in doing good; to further complicate matters, the relationship between moral reasoning and moral behavior is not established. Thus, even though it is likely that having a high IQ gives its possessors an advantage in moral reasoning, it does not necessarily guarantee their putting those morals into practice.

Methodologically, there are two approaches to studying giftedness and morality. One is *categorical*, in which high-functioning subjects are compared with those of lesser ability; the other is *correlational*, involving samples that range widely in ability. Of the two kinds of studies, the categorical yields more consistently encouraging results. Probably the earliest categorical study on the subject was conducted by Terman (1925) on more than 600 elementary school children with an average age between 9 and 10 and with IQs above 140. Taking into account the fact that the instruments used for measuring moral status were

not as valid as the ones assessing moral reasoning today, the children apparently showed a healthy set of virtues, including unwillingness to claim undeserved credit for work accomplished, choosing socially constructive activities relatively often, rather than those that were just personally gratifying. When the Terman high-IQ sample reached its senior year in high school and freshman year in college, these students again responded to a pencil-and-paper test of trustworthiness. Results showed that their scores were comparable to those of other well-educated late adolescents (Burks et al., 1930).

The outcomes of Terman's longitudinal study seem to have been reinforced by Hollingworth's (1942) finding that children with IQs of 180 and above are particularly tortured by universal problems of good and evil, justice and injustice, honesty and dishonesty, and other such ethical issues. Hollingworth (1942) concludes, "The higher the IQ, the earlier does the pressing need for an explanation of the universe occur, [and] the sooner the demand for a concept of the origin and destiny of the self appears" (p. 281).

In later years, Boehm (1962) studied the moral reasoning of 237 children between the ages of 6 and 9, among them a subgroup identified as 'gifted' (with IQs of 110 and higher). The children were tested on Piaget's three levels of morality: (1) automatic obedience to rules without reasoning or judgment; (2) internalization of rules without evaluating them; and (3) evaluation of intentions rather than deeds or outcomes alone. Results show that above-average IQ children matured earlier in their moral judgments concerning distinctions between intention and outcome of an action than children of average intelligence. Moreover, the difference was greater among the upper middle class children than among those coming from the working class.

Less encouraging outcomes were revealed in research by Hoffman (1977) involving children ages 7–8 and 11–12 divided into subgroups of average IQ (91–109) and superior IQ (124–156). The criterion measure was also a test based on Piaget's stages of moral development. Results show that age was a more important predictor than IQ, as the older children with close to average IQs scored higher than did younger children with superior tested intelligence. Karnes & Brown (1981) likewise produced strong support for a relationship between age, along with high IQ, and advanced moral reasoning. Their sample consisted of 233 children, ages 9–15 with a mean IQ of 126.5. The data reveal the expected steady increase in appropriate Level 3 responses from ages 11 to 15. There is also a positive correlation between intellectual functioning and the ability to make more mature moral judgments. The evidence suggests that high-IQ children may reach Level 3 moral reasoning in their high school years, even though most people never reach this level at any age. In fact, the estimated 10–15% of the general population that succeeds in reaching it usually does so in adulthood.

In a study using Kohlberg's Moral Judgment Interview, Form A, Bear (1983) compared 14 intellectually gifted 6th graders with 46 of their non-gifted peers. In this case, giftedness was defined as a score above the 95th percentile on the Vocabulary scale of the Stanford Achievement Test. Bear found that the high achievers scored approximately one-third of a stage higher than their lower achieving peers on the Kohlberg instrument.

More than half a century after Hollingworth's report, Gross (1993) also assessed a small sample of children with extremely high IQs and of late elementary and early junior high school age. This Australian group took Rest's (1986) Defining Issues Test (DIT) which is influenced by Kohlberg's theory of mental development although, as Rest, Thoma & Edwards (1997) acknowledge, "DIT researchers have taken some turns [in the design of the instrument] that Kohlberg would not have endorsed himself" (p. 6). Of the eight children whose IQ scores ranged from 160–175+, five had z-scores of at least +1.00, compared to the norms obtained from a somewhat older American junior high school population, and two of the children exceeded the senior high school average by a z-score of more than 1.00. The other four children also exceeded the junior high school norm, which further indicates a positive relationship between high tested intelligence and moral reasoning.

In contrast to the categorical studies, correlational research provides little confirmation of links between giftedness and morality or moral reasoning. In her review of the evidence, Gross cites several studies that "have found significant correlations between scores on individual group tests of the intelligence and scores on measures of moral development" (p. 253). On the other hand, Janos & Robinson (1985) appear less impressed with the outcomes of several studies cited by Gross, despite the encouraging results of their own investigation. From their review of empirical evidence, they conclude as follows: "In early research on the character of gifted children and in more recent work on moral judgment within a social-cognitive framework, significant relations with IQ have been found. These studies have not, however, yielded satisfactory predictors of moral behavior" (p. 152). Hoffman (1970) also reviewed several investigations and concluded that "The relation between IQ and the moral attributes formulated by Piaget are consistently positive" (p. 271). A close inspection of the various correlational studies confirms a fairly high consistency in positive results but it does not dispel the conclusion that IQ explains only a small portion of the variance.

Other correlational studies confirm the fact that IQ figures in moral reasoning, as it does with other forms of logical analysis, without serving as a powerful

factor. A study by Durkin (1959) sampled children from grades 2, 5, and 8 whose scores ranged widely on a group intelligence test. The objective was to investigate the children's concept of justice, as described by Piaget, and its relationship to age and IQ; results confirmed Piaget's contention of a relationship between chronological age and feelings of equity. However, no such clear result was obtained in relating IQ to an understanding of justice. In another study involving a moral judgment measure based on Piaget's work, Johnson (1962) tested 807 subjects in grades 5, 7, 9, and 11, all approximating the United States norms in parental occupation and IQ. In this case, IQ and chronological age were significantly related to scores on most of the subtests.

In sum, how can one characterize the relationship between giftedness and moral development? The only sizable body of literature on the subject confines itself to high-IQ subjects to represent the entire spectrum of gifted children, an approach that is obviously inadequate. What the categorical studies reveal about children with high IQs is that their ability gives them at least some moderate advantage in moral reasoning. This is to be expected if moral development is boosted by the kinds of cognitive skills that are measured by IQ tests. But, as Winner (1996) points out, "While the fascination with ethical issues may come with the territory of a high IQ, the *content* of one's moral code seems far more likely to be determined by the values of one's family" (p. 221). Her reasoning is in line with Kohlberg's (1969) speculation that the moderate predictive strength of IQ may be represented in the connection between more rapid cognitive and social development. The enriched social interaction opportunities within families of high-IQ children and adolescents may account for some advancement in their moral reasoning.

In Rothman's (1992) assessment of research on the subject, "Age accounts for most of the variance in moral reasoning . . . with variables such as IQ and socioeconomic status playing more moderate roles" (p. 329). However, the correlation between moral maturity and IQ increases as individuals grow older, perhaps on account of an accumulation of educational experiences which are enhanced in high-IQ individuals (Colby et al., 1983).

All in all, there appears to be some compatibility between giftedness and moral maturity, judging from impressions of the history of great ideas and from evidence on high-IQ populations who seem to be advanced in moral reasoning.

Conclusions about the Compatibility

Reflecting on both the systematic-empirical and the impressionistic-historical perspectives on giftedness and morality leads to several moral dilemmas and reflections; some have already been noted, but are worth repeating because they persist. One nagging question is whether moral development, which is currently measured by interviews and pencil-and-paper tests of a cognitive variety concerning moral dilemmas, favor test takers who may not necessarily act morally out of lofty conviction but who possess the brainpower to be labeled gifted and to see the wisdom of subscribing *intellectually* to more principled moral codes.

Conversely, is the instrument 'biased' against those who lack the reasoning skills to *express* the higher moral principles that are reflected in their actual *behavior*? Also, what if more serious attention were paid to partialling out, or controlling for, such variables as socioeconomic status, risk-taking behavior, home environment, school achievement, and whatever else correlates with measures of giftedness? Would it change the relationship between giftedness and moral development appreciably? Are other superior intelligences or special aptitudes, which correlate poorly with IQ, also associated with moral advancement? Why is the correlation between IQ and moral reasoning only 0.13 in one study (Andreani & Pagnin, 1993a) and range from only 0.20 to 0.50 in another (Rest, 1984)? Does IQ really explain so little of the variance, even without partialling out related factors? Finally, and perhaps most important, how does one account for the rather poor connection between moral reasoning and moral behavior, even at the highest levels, as described by Rothman (1992), and between moral reasoning and moral responsibility, as discussed by Gruber (1985)?

Perhaps one way of escaping some of these difficulties is to stop thinking about relationships between giftedness and morality and to consider, instead, the possibility that morality is a *form* of giftedness. Colby & Damon (1992) have already studied adults whose only claim to prominence was their legendary kindness. But that does not diminish the ethical imperative of researching other forms of giftedness and its relation to moral behavior.

Extra Cautions in Interpreting Relevant Evidence

Empirical studies usually come in two varieties: (1) mass data analysis and (2) single-subject clinical diagnosis. Both require strict objectivity in the exploratory phase of the research. After the *facts* are gathered and analyzed, there is a changeover to the search for *truth* through interpreting the facts and drawing inferences from the interpretation. In the quest for truth, there is always the danger of personal bias or just plain misjudgment. For example, producers and consumers of research sometimes stretch their comprehension of study outcomes beyond reasonable meaning, as in the case of overgeneralizing central tendencies in mass data analysis and in fitting clinical diagnosis outcomes into private predilections. These

are especially sensitive matters when they pertain to moral values and practices of the gifted.

The Invited Tyranny of Central Tendency

In the analysis of mass data, scientists look for statistical central tendencies from which to draw generalizations. Reporters and readers of research acknowledge exceptions to a generality and yet often accept it so dogmatically that the exceptions hardly seem to count. The consequences can be harmful, as in the case of the bold, but not perfect, correlation between IQ and scholastic achievement. In much of the literature on the gifted who are not excelling in their studies, it is assumed that if a child scores high on an IQ test, he or she should perform at a comparably high level in school work. Whoever fails to measure up to expectation is dubbed an 'underachiever', a failure, when in reality whoever labels the child that way may be guilty of neglecting to prove that the failure is *not* due to the *imperfect* relationship between IQ and achievement, which can be explained by test error and which would occasionally account for the discrepancy. The unfortunate consequence is stigmatizing some children with an unfair label and force-feeding them with unnecessary 'intervention' which can cause embarrassment to them and to the interveners, all of whom are laboring under unrealistic expectations.

Overlooking exceptions to a rule that is relevant to 'underachievement' can be a serious matter. But trivializing exceptions to the rule of strong ties between giftedness and morality can result in far more monstrous threats to society. In his long essay, *When Learned Men Murder*, Patterson (1996) reminds readers that the notorious Wannsee conference, organized on January 20, 1942 by the Nazi leadership to facilitate the 'final Solution', took only two hours to work out the ways and means of murdering all Jewish people in lands under current and future Nazi control and influence. Of the small group of fourteen conferees, eight held Ph.Ds from prestigious universities, and included among them, ironically, was the Minister of Justice. One can only speculate as to how many highly educated individuals played important roles in 'ethnic cleansing' more recently in the Balkans. Of course, there is room for quibbling over whether earning a Ph.D is a sign of giftedness, an argument that this author can appreciate since he, too, owns that degree. But at the very least, people who have successfully completed advanced schooling must have been exposed to great ideas, as taught by instructors with impeccable credentials in scholarship and who must, or should, have taught something about the greatness of the human mind and soul. What could have been lacking in the Wannsee Ph.Ds' education?

Sometimes, gifted people who are probably not mean-spirited can become the instruments of others' evil intentions, either out of naiveté, indifference, or greed. For example, it wasn't outlaw science that has posed what may become a permanent insult to the planet's biosphere. In his collection of essays on mortality and morality, the philosopher Hans Jonas (1996) attacks members of the scientific community for failing to reconcile nature and humanity, following or leading to the belief that both the universe and life on earth have no intrinsic meaning. No wonder that the work of relatively few superior rational minds has facilitated fouling the environment without malice aforethought, but also without concern that organic life may face extinction as a consequence. Fortunately and ironically, though, Jonas sees hope albeit only in the kinds of rare gifted intellects that created the problem of human survival in the first place. Lesser brainpower would not be sophisticated enough to discover remedies for our environmental ills. Thus, some creative individuals in some branches of science deserve to be condemned for bringing about the impending tragedy. Yet, science has to be advanced along with proper nurture of the consciences of its budding practitioners so that they can dedicate their research to undoing what a few of their predecessors have wrought.

In sum, a *sine qua non* of studying an aggregate of gifted children and providing adequate education for them is to take seriously the minority among them who may not turn out to be pillars of society. These are not just negligible, non-conforming minorities; their superior abilities may someday be used for harmful purposes, so harmful in fact that they can threaten the good accomplishments of the overwhelming majority of their gifted peers. It is not just another case of a rotten apple spoiling the healthy ones in a barrel; this kind of rotten apple has the contagion power to contaminate a whole orchard.

Clinical Understanding vs. Moral Judgment

There is also a lesson to be learned by scientists who study individuals in clinical detail. Hoffman (1992) reports that during World War II, behavioral scientists working for the American government produced a number of innovative studies on the nature of Nazism, Adolph Hitler's personality, the German national character, and Germans' reactions to the war. One of the committees in this effort consisted of a group of psychologists working on "Hitler's Mentality and Personality," directed by none other than Lewis M. Terman whose famous *Genetic Studies of Genius* is still the largest scale, most ambitious longitudinal investigation of high-IQ children.

The original purpose of the project was to undermine Nazism by waging psychological warfare against Hitler and other German leaders. Although some of these studies amounted to breakthroughs in clinical research, the methodology and purposes have evolved into occasional blurring of the boundaries between deep understanding and justifying anti-social behavior. For example, the revered psychoanalyst Erich Fromm seems to have allowed his clinical insights to over-

power strict accountability for the crime of genocide, as reported in his 1973 book, *The Anatomy of Human Destructiveness*. His subject was Adolph Hitler whom Fromm regarded as a victim of necrophilia, a love of death and dead bodies. Unlike popular notions that Hitler suffered abuse from a cruel and aggressive father, Fromm's thesis focuses on the mother, Klara, as guilty of a 'malignant incestuousness' with her son. According to Fromm, Germany became the central symbol for mother, and his hatred for the Jews whom he saw as threatening Germany, actually concealed a deeper, long-repressed desire to destroy his mother. Thus, Hitler's deepest hatred wasn't Jews—it was Germans. This kind of analysis can be used to justify Hitler's spearheading genocide as the product of an understandably deranged, and therefore blameless, mind.

A similar sentiment was expressed by a Harvard Medical School Psychologist (Westen, 1998) who suspects Ted Kaczinski (the convicted Unabomber) of being a victim of paranoid schizophrenia and therefore possibly treatable. Westen asks, "Is Kaczinski any more morally responsible for his acts than a person who becomes impulsive or dangerous after a damaging blow to the head?" (p. 16). It causes one to wonder whether the clinical and behavioral sciences are reaching a point where enemies of the people, brilliant or not, can be understood and treated without penalty, thus reducing the legal system to punishing only violators of the law who are somehow confidently declared sane or socially adjusted at the moment of committing a crime.

Teaching Moral Values to the Gifted (and to the Non-Gifted, too!)

Experimental programs in moral, or character, education are not often evaluated. Those that report somewhat encouraging results feature mostly discussions of moral dilemmas and how to solve them more maturely (Rest & Thoma, 1986). In such cases, the criterion measures assess moral reasoning, not moral values or behaviors; in the rare instances where programs sought to build pro-social habits, the impact has been minimal (Andreani & Pagnin, 1993b). Why? Is it because schools are basically weak in affecting students' habits of honesty, decency, and compassion? Or are they not trying hard enough or with much pedagogic ingenuity?

If laxity is the cause of failure, it is well for educators of the gifted to memorize, or at least reflect on, the sentiments of a now-deceased popular psychologist who was a World War II Holocaust survivor.

> My eyes saw what no person should witness. Gas chambers built by learned engineers. Children poisoned by educated physicians. Infants killed by trained nurses. Women and babies shot and killed by high school and college graduates. So I'm suspicious

of education. My request is: help your students to be human. Your efforts must never produce learned monsters, skilled psychopaths, or educated Eichmanns. Reading and writing and spelling and history and arithmetic are important only if they serve to make our students human. (Ginott, 1972, p. 317)

In Tannenbaum's book, *Gifted Children: Psychological and Educational Perspectives* (1983), he suggests a curriculum framework for enriching the education of the gifted. One of its elements refers to the social and affective consequences of becoming a high-level producer or performer. In introducing this feature, Tannenbaum warns: "Perhaps the worst possible outcome of an enriched program is that it will produce a cadre of technocrats who are brilliant in the work they do but have no conscience or commitment to a set of values, and are willing to sell their talents to the highest bidder" (p. 438). It is no surprise that the warning has gone unheeded.

Character education has not had a notable history in America's schools, possibly because Hartshorne and May have shown how futile it is to instill moral values in the classroom, or perhaps because the American public is just plain worried about exposing children to hot issues that they see as belonging only in family and religious environments. A *New York Times* (July 8, 1995) report on efforts to introduce such a program in the Mount Lebanon, PA school system describes how sensitive the topics of study have been. For example, 'Respect for Life' was discarded because of suspicions that it might have led to disputes over abortion and euthanasia. 'Respect for the Environment' was also never introduced because ecology activists and industrialists could disagree on its meaning; and, of course, the topic of 'Race' was avoided because of the extreme emotions it would arouse. It is no surprise that the warning has gone unheeded by psychologists and educators who seem to attend only to cognition and creativity in children with high potential.

The Lebanon effort is fairly unique among schools across the United States, and this lack of widespread commitment is also evident in educational efforts on behalf of the gifted. For example, the National Research Center on the Gifted and Talented has produced a publication entitled *Setting an Agenda: Research Priorities for the Gifted and Talented Through the Year 2000* (Renzulli, Reid & Gubbins, undated), which reports a needs assessment study involving 13,749 respondents to a questionnaire that canvassed their priorities in the field. In the Personal and Social Development section of the questionnaire, items included social adjustment, emotional adjustment, guidance and counseling, peer relations, family relations, and underachievement. No mention is made of moral education which is so critical to the gifted.

What follows, then, are some suggested exercises in moral education that may arouse or restore interest in

alerting the gifted to the centrality of moral principles in their lives. It is by no means comprehensive, but its fragmentary nature suggests further development possibilities wherever desirable or feasible.

A. "Know Thyself"—the Issue of Self-Knowledge

"Who am I?" (the development of a time-unlimited portfolio into which entries are made whenever something important can be added in the following four categories)

(1) *Pride in Specific Accomplishment.* Describe or enclose anything you have achieved that gives you unusual satisfaction. It may be academic documents that you have produced, acts of kindness, creative works, etc.

(2) *Personal Identify.* Describe how you would distinguish yourself in a crowd. It could be through your deeply absorbed values, beliefs, and aspirations; perceived personal strengths, weaknesses, physical features, etc.

(3) *Choice of Heroes, If Any.* If you have a hero, or more than one hero, such persons may be of any age group and not necessarily well known to anybody else. Write something about these heroes that supports your choice.

(4) *Deepest Commitments.* Indicate what values or beliefs you are willing to embrace, even if it means suffering discomfort to embrace them. Are there any that are so precious to you that you are willing to make real sacrifices for their sake? If so, record your feelings.

This "Who Am I" portfolio contains each student's private documents, and the privacy has to be respected by staff and administration. However, staff should meet with students periodically, perhaps bimonthly or once every semester, to discuss whatever the student wishes to share with the staff member. Needless to say, the importance of building such a portfolio may have to be communicated periodically to the student body. Under no circumstances should students feel that this is a formal 'assignment'; instead, it is a format for helping them to serve their own needs to clarify their own personae.

B. Learning that Life can be a Challenge

Conflict Resolution. Staff members familiar with the work of Morton Deutsch and Herbert Kellman, who have written extensively about conflict resolution, may then use the derivative methodology for dealing with strained personal relations. The Internet can retrieve the strategies tested and successful in reaching this goal, or at least approaching it more closely.

Surviving and Benefiting from Frustration. Since gifted students experience frustration in school work relatively rarely, it should be pointed out to them that creative writers sometimes suffer writers' block, scientists' experiments don't always unfold as planned, musicians don't always hit the right notes in concerts, and artists sometimes 'climb the walls' while trying to express an aesthetic message. But these creative minds persevere and even push themselves to greater heights, rather than become discouraged and give up.

Experiencing and Overcoming Temporary Failures. Artists, writers, and scientists are not only occasionally frustrated in the process of creating, but sometimes their work turns out to be unsatisfactory to them. Instead of having a demoralizing effect, the failure encourages them to continue or to renew their efforts. Alexander Fleming's early failure in his search for penicillin and Thomas Edison's repeated failures to produce the light bulb, followed by success in both cases, are excellent examples of overcoming temporary failures, and worth studying.

Delay of Gratification. Many students demonstrate their precocity by giving quick, accurate answers to teachers' questions and solving problems at high speed. Some of these students may have learned that impatience is a virtue and either refuse, or are unable to wait for results to come in due course. Biologists always experience delay of gratification because plants and insects and animals have to grow to the point where success or failure of an experiment can be determined. This habit of patience should be emphasized in the course of teaching in all disciplines.

Risk Taking. Some students prefer guaranteeing success for themselves by concentrating on what they know they can accomplish, thus sustaining their positive self-image. But it is important for them to be encouraged to enter into unknown realms which increase the possibilities of frustration or even failure, so that they can reach higher levels of achievement.

Teachers may use various methodologies for emphasizing the principle of professional life's challenges. One way is to introduce students to the productive experiences of artists, writers, and scientists, with special attention to their resolution of conflicts, frustrations, temporary failures, delays of gratification, and occasional willingness to take necessary risks. Teachers may even use their own experiences to illustrate these principles.

C. Alienation and Changes in Identity

Dehumanization. Reading Franz Kafka's *The Trial* will illustrate to students the meaning of having no name and about being victimized by legal accusations and processes that are not understood by the accused. In Kafka's *Metamorphosis*, the central character is not viewed as a human being, but rather as an insect. Students can also learn that racism and genocide have strong elements of dehumanization directed at the victims. There is a subtle but profound difference between lower status in social life and being regarded as a non-person and thus disqualified from membership in the human community.

Misogyny and Liberation. Henrik Ibsen's *A Doll's House* illustrates marital relations gone sour because of the diminutive role of the wife; it would be interesting for the gifted to speculate on what happens to Nora after the end of the play. August Strindberg's *Miss Julie* can also help students see how women's identity has been so marginalized in literature and society. It is important for the gifted to see how females' status has become far more honorific at the end of the twentieth century than at its beginning. Finally, a study can be done on Betty Friedan's vision of women's status in *Feminine Mystique* and the changes that have occurred in her later book, *Beyond Gender: Individualism vs. the Voice of the People*. Sometimes, personal identity can be so strong that it is forced to battle against consensus. All agree that the majority should rule, but the majority can be wrong while the individual who thinks differently is right. A good example of that is Ibsen's *Enemy of the People*, which should be read and discussed.

In the sciences and arts, too, there are notable examples of individuals who contested conventional thinking and the *status quo* and were even unpopular on account of their courage. But eventually, their individualism proved to be productive and creative. Teachers in the sciences and arts should make students aware of the professional histories of prominent people in their fields who have become immortalized, despite their swimming upstream.

D. Language, Knowledge, Creativity, and Values

As underscored in other parts of this chapter, scholars and creative thinkers are mostly moral benefactors as well as moral role models in society. But it is necessary for schools to work toward the ideal of enabling all gifted young people to become that way, because the few who do not may someday use their superior brainpower to cause incredible harm in the life of humanity.

An Introduction to General Semantics. S. I. Hayakawa has written the book, *Language in Thought and Action*. This work includes instructions and exercises to help the reader distinguish between fact and opinion and how words are used to manipulate the reader's or the listener's emotional reactions. It is a valuable guide for students, who are already advanced in language comprehension, to learn how to read newspaper reports that use words for the sake of persuasion rather than enlightenment. Hayakawa's approach to general semantics can also be useful in reading or listening to political pronouncements, analyzing advertisements, and generally strengthening the relationship between communicating knowledge in any field and the degree of subjectivity and value coloration it contains.

Medical Ethics. Issues surrounding euthanasia and assisted suicide have swept through the medical profession in recent years. But they are not the only ethical issues that people in the health services face every day. In every region of the country, there are people in the health professions who are becoming more and more aware of the importance of Bio-ethics, and children who may someday enter these sciences should become aware of this developing field and of the growing concerns it addresses.

Scientific Truth and Empirical Fact. The case of Dr. David Baltimore, a Nobel Prize winner and former president of Rockefeller University in New York City, reads like Greek drama and the rise and fall of an assortment of tragic heroes. One of several major issues raised in that episode in American science relates to the risk that researchers take in seeking out truths in their empirical data that may deviate from the hard facts. Another issue deals with the freedom of scientists to experiment and to explore in their fields without governmental controls that are intended to avert possible harmful effects of research. A full report on the Baltimore case by Daniel J. Kevles (1998) deserves to be read and debated in great detail among students in the sciences, especially in biology.

Genetic Engineering and Its Possible Consequences. Although this is a widely addressed topic in newspapers and journals, gifted students should review the experimentation with sperm and eggs from high-IQ people in order to produce an intellectually able population. Also, the 'creation' of Dolly in Great Britain has stirred a good deal of commentary. Students ought to discuss the possible connection between the eugenics of creating a generation of high-IQ individuals and the cloning of animals, on the one hand, and the production of a master race on the other.

E. A Rogues' Gallery of Great Minds.

It is important for students to have concrete examples of people who have achieved greatness while living evil lives. Even though they constitute only a minority of geniuses, the power of their depravity, combined with their creativity, had a negative and often lethal effect on countless individuals. Gifted students should be introduced to at least some of these historic figures and remember them in infamy for the rest of their lives:

(1) Wilhelm Furtwaengler is the major subject of a powerful play titled *Taking Sides*, which deals with a conflict between the great orchestral conductor's devotion to recreating immortal music while serving Hitler as an unwitting or guilty emissary of Nazism.

(2) Ezra Pound and T. S. Eliot, two of the leading literary figures of the twentieth century, were both anti-Semites, although Pound was also a major spokesman for Mussolini's Fascism.

(3) Joseph Stalin, Adolph Hitler and Mao Zedong, highly gifted leaders who could manipulate millions of subjects through their political intrigue, demagoguery, and social skills, and yet guilty of wholesale murder at home and abroad. Though tiny in number, but notorious in tyranny, these despots deserve far more than their proporionate share of blame for the massacre of some 170 million civilians and the war-related deaths of roughly 30 million soldiers in all of the twentieth century (Conquest, 2000), a total approximate the entire population of the United States today.

(4) Leni Riefenstahl, actress and highly gifted filmmaker, whose Nazi-era masterpieces include the films *Triumph of Will* and the *1936 Olympics in Berlin*, both used as propaganda instruments at a crucial time in Nazi history.

(5) Joseph Mengele, whose brutal experimentation with human beings may have produced meaningful results. Should these outcomes be added to our storehouse of scientific knowledge? The same can be asked about psychological studies by Nazi behavioral scientists, and the circulation of the '*Pernkopf Anatomy*', a classic anatomy atlas, produced by the Nazi doctor Eduard Pernkopf, onetime dean of the medical faculty at the University of Vienna.

(6) Werner Heisenberg, the Nazi scientist who nearly completed the development of an atomic bomb for Hitler's Germany ahead of the American scientists. Heisenberg's position in this rogues' gallery is particularly strange and interesting. In 1967, the New Americana Library initiated a series of studies under the general heading 'Perspectives in Humanism', with a Board of Editors consisting of distinguished scholars, among them Werner Heisenberg. This is the same man who had visited the United States to participate in a high-level conference on science in the 1930s, and was urged by other participants at the meetings to remain in the West and enjoy its freedom, but he refused. Cassidy (1996) suggests two possible reasons for Heisenberg's loyalty to his homeland and its outlaw government. One is that he craved personal advantage, prestige, and high status in his field, which he felt only Germany could provide for him. The second is that he was never aware of the need to share with fellow Nobel prize winners the responsibility of battle against injustice and oppression. In a strange way, this may help explain his identification with humanism, for as the eminent social

psychologist, Brewster Smith (1991), points out, humanism serves as an umbrella for individualism and sometimes even for narcissism.

(7) Werner Von Braun, one of Nazi Germany's leading rocket scientists who helped rain rocket-propelled bombs on London late in the war and who was brought to the United States after the war to contest the Soviet Union's domination of deep space exploration. Did the United States solve this moral dilemma?

(8) 'The Monster' is a brief biographical study of a famous composer by the music critic, Deems Taylor. Should his music be appreciated even though he was a monstrous megalomaniac, liar, and cheat?

(9) Albert Speer, whose autobiography should be 'must' reading for the gifted, because of its revelation of the author's genius combined with unspeakable evil.

(10) Pablo Picasso, one of the twentieth century's greatest artists, whose mistreatment of women was unforgivable, despite his ability to depict women with so much insight in his artistic works.

A Final Thought

This chapter is but a brief outline of some prominent ideas that have been propagated by theorists and researchers on the concept of morality. The summary was intended to lead in the direction of a sincere plea to persist with dedication and imagination in making moral education an integral part of enrichment for the gifted in the hope that it will enhance their learning experiences and encourage them to serve society with guidance from its highest ideals. The plea for unrelenting efforts is best captured in the final paragraph of Patterson's (1996) essay:

> The event of loving embrace that distinguishes teaching is a consecration of life through a testimony and pursuit of the sacred, for the sake of all that is sacred. However, simply asserting this is not enough. It is needful but not sufficient. From here we must return once more to begin again and ever again. Though the task has been met a million times, it remains forever yet to be done; for the debt increases in the measure that it is paid. And so, having said this, let us return to our students for the encounter that lends life meaning (p. 162).

References

Andreani, O. D. & Pagnin, A. (1993a). Moral judgment in creative and talented adolescents. *Creativity Research Journal*, **6** (142), 45–63.

Andreani, O. D. & Pagnin, A. (1993b). Nurturing the moral development of the gifted. In: K. A. Heller, F. J. Mönks & A. H. Passow (Eds.), *International Handbook of Research and Development of Giftedness and Talent* (pp. 539–553). New York: Pergamon.

Baer, J. (1993). *Creativity and divergent thinking.* Hillsdale, NJ: Erlbaum.

Baer, J. (1993/1994). Why you shouldn't trust creativity tests. *Educational Leadership*, **53** (1), 80–83.

Bear, G. G. (1983). Moral reasoning, classroom behavior and the intellectually gifted. *Journal for the Education of the Gifted*, **6**, 111–119.

Blatt, M. M. & Kohlberg, L. (1975). The effects of classroom moral discussion upon children's level of moral judgment. *Journal of Moral Education*, **4**, 129–161.

Boehm, L. (1962). The development of conscience: A comparison of American children at different mental and socioeconomic levels. *Child Development*, **33**, 575–590.

Bond, R. & Smith, P. B. (1996). Culture and conformity. *Psychological Bulletin*, **119** (1), 111–137.

Burks, B. S., Jensen, D. W. & Terman, L. M. (1930). *The promise of youth: Follow-up studies of a thousand gifted children.* Stanford, CA: Stanford University Press.

Cassidy, D. (1984). German scientists and the Nazi atomic bomb. *Dimensions*, **10** (2), 15–22.

Clinchy, B., Lief, J. & Young, P. (1977). Epistemological and moral development in girls from a traditional and a progressive high school. *Journal of Educational Psychology*, 69 (4), 337–343.

Colby, A. & Damon, W. (1992). *Some do care: contemporary lives of moral commitment.* Unpublished manuscript.

Colby, A., Kohlberg, L., Gibbs, J. & Lieberman, M. (1983). A longitudinal study of moral judgment. *SRCD Monographs*, **48** (1–2).

Conquest, R. (2000). *Reflections on a ravaged century.* New York: W. W. Norton & Co.

Dabrowski, K. (1964). *Positive disintegration.* London: Little Brown.

Durkin, D. (1959). Children's concepts of justice: a comparison with the Piaget data. *Child Development*, **30**, 59–67.

Ehrlich, P. R. & Ehrlich, A. H. (1991). *The population explosion.* New York: Simon and Schuster.

Elliot, R. (1997). The persistence of being. *Contemporary Psychology*, **42** (7), 579–580.

Freud, S. (1955). *Civilization and its discontents.* London: Hogarth Press (originally published in 1930).

Friedman, M. (1992). *Dialogue and the human image: Beyond humanistic psychology.* Newbury Park, CA: Sage.

Fromm, E. (1941). *Escape from Freedom.* New York: Rinehart.

Fromm, E. (1973). *The anatomy of human destructiveness.* New York: Holt, Rinehart and Winston.

Gagne, F. (1991). Toward a differentiated model of giftedness and talent. In: N. Colangelo & G. Davis (Eds.), *Handbook of Gifted Education* (pp. 65–80). Boston: Allyn & Bacon.

Gardner, H. (1983). *Frames of mind: the theory of multiple intelligences.* New York: Basic Books.

Ginott, H. (1972). *Teacher and child: a handbook for parents and teachers.* New York: Macmillan.

Goldhagen, D. J. (1996). *Hitler's willing executioners.* New York: Knopf.

Gowan, J. C. (1979). The development of the creative individual. In: J. C. Gowan, J. Khatena & E. P. Torrance (Eds.), *Educating the Ablest* (pp. 58–79). Itasca, IL: Peacock.

Gross, M. U. M. (1993). *Exceptionally gifted children.* London and New York: Routledge.

Gruber, H. E. (1985). Giftedness and moral responsibility: Creative thinking and human survival. In: F. D. Horowitz &

M. O'Brien (Eds.), *The Gifted and Talented: Developmental Perspectives* (pp. 301–330). Washington, DC: American Psychological Association.

Gruber, H. E. (1993). Creativity in the moral domain: OUGHT implies CAN implies CREATE. *Creativity Research Journal*, **6** (1&2), 3–15.

Hadas, M. (1967). *The living tradition*. New York: New American Library.

Hartshorne, H. & May, M. A. (1928–1930). *Studies in the nature of character* (3 vols.). New York: Macmillan.

Havighurst, R. J. & Taba, H. (1949). *Adolescent character and personality*. New York: Wiley.

Hobbes, T. (1996). *Leviathan*. New York: Oxford University Press (Republication, Edited by J. C. A. Gaskin)

Hoffman, L. E. (1992). American psychologists and wartime research on Germany, 1941–1945. *American Psychologist*, **47** (2), 264–273.

Hoffman, M. L. (1970). Moral development. In: P. H. Mussen (Ed.), *Carmichael's Manual of Child Psychology* (3rd ed.), pp. 261–359. New York: Wiley.

Hoffman, M. L. (1979). Development of moral thought, feeling, and behavior. *American Psychologist*, **34** (10), 958–966.

Hoffman, S. (1977). Intelligence and the development of moral judgement in children. *Journal of Genetic Psychology*, **130**, 27–34.

Hollingworth, L. S. (1942). *Children above 180 IQ Stanford-Binet: Origin and development*. Yonkers, NY: World Book Co.

Hutner, I. (n.d.). Heard at several public, unpublished lectures at the Gur Aryeh Institute for Advanced Jewish Scholarship.

Janos, P. M. & Robinson, N. M. (1985). Psychosocial development in intellectually gifted children. In: F. D. Horowitz & M. O'Brian (Eds.), *The Gifted and Talented: Developmental Perspectives* (pp. 149–195). Washington, DC: American Psychological Association.

Johnson, R. C. (1962). A study of children's moral judgements. *Child Development*, **33**, 327–354.

Jonas, H. (1996). *Mortality and morality: a search for the good after Auschwitz*. Evanston, IL: Northwestern University Press.

Karnes, F. A. & Brown, K. E. (1981). Moral development and the gifted: an initial investigation. *Roeper Review*, **3**, 6–13.

Kevles, D. J. (1998). *The Baltimore Case*. New York: W. W. Norton & Co.

Kohlberg, L. (1958). *The development of modes of moral thinking and choice in the years ten to sixteen*. Unpublished doctoral dissertation, University of Chicago.

Kohlberg, L. (1963). Moral development and identification. In: H. Stevenson (Ed.), *Child Psychology*. Chicago: University of Chicago Press.

Kohlberg, L. (1964). The development of moral character and ideology. In: M. Hoffman & L. W. Hoffman (Eds.), *Review of Child Development Research*. New York: Russell Sage Foundation.

Kohlberg, L. (1966). Moral education in the schools: a developmental view. *School Review*, **74** (1), 1–30.

Kohlberg, L. (1969). Stage and sequence: The cognitive developmental approach to socialization. In: D. A. Goslin (Ed.), *Handbook of Socialization Theory and Research* (pp. 347–480). Chicago: Rand McNally.

Kohlberg, L., Hickey, J. & Scharf, P. (1972). The justice structure of the prison: a theory and intervention. *Prison Journal*, **51**, 3–14.

Lysy, K. Z. & Piechowski, M. M. (1983). Personal growth: an empirical study using Jungian and Dabrowskian measures. *Genetic Psychology Monographs*, **108**, 267–320.

Maslow, A. H. (1954). *Motivation and personality*. New York: Harper and Row.

Maxwell, E. & Silverman, L. K. (1995). Inner conflict as a path to higher development. *Advanced Development* (Special Edition), 57–64.

McClaren, R. B. (1993). The dark side of creativity. *Creativity Research Journal*, 6 (1&2), 137–144.

Milgram, S. (1974). *Obedience to authority*. New York: Harper and Row.

Morrissey, A.-M. (1996). Intellect as prelude: The potential for higher level development in the gifted. *Advanced Development*, **7**, 101–116.

Nelson, K. C. (1995). Dabrowski's theory of positive disintegration. *Advanced Development* (Special Education), 43–56.

Oden, M. H. (1968). The fulfillment of promise: 40-year follow-up of the Terman gifted group. *Genetic Psychology Monographs*, **77**, 3–93.

Patterson, D. (1996). *When learned men murder*. Bloomington, In: Phi Delta Kappa Educational Foundation.

Perry, W. G. (1970). *Forms of intellectual and ethical development in the college years*. New York: Holt, Rinehart and Winston.

Piaget, J. (1932). *The moral judgment of the child* (M. Gabain, trans.). London: Kegan Paul, Trench, Trubner.

Piechowski, M. M. (1979). Developmental potential. In: N. Colangelo & R. T. Zaffran (Eds.), *New Voices in Counseling the Gifted* (pp. 25–57). Dubuque, IA: Kendall/Hunt.

Piechowski, M. M. (1997). Emotional giftedness: The measure of intrapersonal intelligence. In: N. Colangelo & G. A. Davis (Eds.), *Handbook of Gifted Education* (pp. 366–381). Boston: Allyn and Bacon.

Piechowski, M. M. & Colangelo, N. (1984). Developmental potential of the gifted. *Gifted Child Quarterly*, **28**, 80–88.

Piechowski, M. M. & Tyska, C. (1982). Self-actualization profile of Eleanor Roosevelt, a presumed non-transcender. *Genetic Psychology Monographs*, **105**, 95–153.

Puka, B. (Ed.). (1994a). *Kohlberg's original study of moral development*. New York: Garland.

Puka, B. (Ed.). (1994b). *The great justice debate: Kohlberg criticism*. New York: Garland.

Puka, B. (Ed.). (1994c). *New research in moral development*. New York: Garland.

Puka, B. (Ed.). (1994d). *Fundamental research in moral development*. New York: Garland.

Puka, B. (Ed.). (1994e). *Reaching out: Caring, altruism, and prosocial behavior*. New York: Garland.

Puka, B. (Ed.). (1994f). *Defining perspectives in moral development*. New York: Garland.

Puka, B. (Ed.). (1994g). *Caring voices and women's moral frames: Gilligan's view*. New York: Garland.

Renzulli, J. S., Reid, B. D. & Gubbins, E. J. (n.d.). *Setting an agenda: Research priorities for the gifted and talented through the year 2000*. Storrs, CT: The National Research Center on the Gifted and Talented.

Rest, J. (1986). *Moral development: advances in research and theory*. New York: Praeger.

Rest, J. (1984). The major components of morality. In: W. Kurtines & J. Gewirtz (Eds.), *Morality, Moral Behavior, and Moral Development* (pp. 24–40). New York: Wiley.

Rest, J. R. & Thoma, S. J. (1986). Educational programs and interventions. In: J. R. Rest (Ed.), *Moral Development: Advances in Research and Theory* (pp. 59–88). New York: Praeger.

Rest, J., Thoma, S. & Edwards, L. (1997). Designing and validating a measure of moral judgment: Stage preference and stage consistency approaches. *Journal of Educational Psychology*, **89** (1), 5–28.

Ridley, M. (1996). *The origin of virtue: Human instincts and the evolution of cooperation*. New York: Viking.

Rokeach, M. & Ball-Rokeach. (1989). Stability and change in American value priorities, 1968–1981. *American Psychologist*, **44** (5), 775–784.

Rothman, G. R. (1992). Moral reasoning, moral behavior, and moral giftedness: A developmental perspective. In: P. S. Klein & A. J. Tannenbaum (Eds.), *To Be Young and Gifted* (pp. 321–347). Norwood, NJ: Ablex.

Runco, M. A. (1993). Creative morality: International and unconventional. *Creativity Research Journal*, **6** (1 & 2), 17–28.

Schneider, K. J. (1998). Toward a science of the heart. *American Psychologist*, **53** (3), 277–289.

Schwartz, B. (1990). The creation and destruction of value. *American Psychologist*, **45** (1), 7–15.

Schwebel, M. (1993). Moral creativity as artistic transformation. *Creativity Research Journal*, **6** (1 & 2), 65–81.

Silverman, L. K. (1997). The construct of asynchronous development. *Peabody Journal of Education*, **72** (3 & 4), 36–58.

Smith, M. B. (1991). *Values, self, and society: toward a humanist social psychology*. New Brunswick, NJ: Transaction.

Spearman, C. E. (1927). *Abilities of man: their natures and measurement*. New York: Macmillan.

Tannenbaum, A. J. (1983). *Gifted children: Psychological and educational perspectives*. New York: Macmillan.

Terman, L. M. (1925). *Mental and physical traits of a thousand gifted children*. Stanford, CA: Stanford University Press.

Turiel, E. (1966). An experimental test of the sequentiality of developmental stages in the child's moral judgments. *Journal of Personality and Social Psychology*, **3**, 611–618.

Veblen, T. (1914). *The instinct of workmanship*. New York: Macmillan.

Vernon, P. E. (1960). *The structure of human abilities*. London: Methuen.

Westen, D. (1998). Should we have second thoughts about Kaczinski? *APA Monitor*, **29** (3), 16.

Wilson, E. O. (1998). *Concilience: The unity of knowledge*. New York: Knopf.

Winner, E. (1996). *Gifted children*. New York: Basic Books.

Wolfe, A. (1998). *One nation after all: What middle-class Americans really think about God, country, family, racism, welfare, immigration, homosexuality, work, the right, the left, and each other*. New York: Viking.

New Trends in Research on Moral Development in the Gifted

Adriano Pagnin and Ornella Andreani

Istituto di Psicologia, Universita di Pavia, Italy

Introduction

Morality is generally conceivable as a set of basic guidelines for determining how decisions about action and solution of conflict between different interests/points of view are to be settled and a consequent behavior is to be accomplished.

As morality has to do with judgements about rightness of behavior, it is based on strictly cognitive aspects on the one hand (analysis of behaviors and their consequences, discussion of normative assumptions), and on motivational and affective aspects (motives for following assumptions in practice, and capacity to do so) on the other.

So, we believe that we need two sets of reflections on the development of morality:

- moral behavior is based on specific cognitive ability and specific education towards rational analysis and discussion of actions concerning rights, duties, consequences (about life, affects, well being, etc.) of self and others;
- moral behavior is based on affective roots and emotional education (in terms of empathy, commitment to others, care for others).

Much research has been devoted to the study of development of moral judgement in general, starting from the classical studies of Piaget (1932) and Kohlberg (1969); but a few were devoted to connection of moral judgement with moral behavior, and to interventions aiming to enhance them, and very few to analyzing those specific aspects in the gifted.

But we can also study characteristics of the gifted by considering the highest intelligence subjects in studies aiming to other objectives, where data for those subjects are reported. So we will emphasize the interest of research results for the gifted and for gifted education.

We shall consider moral judgement as related to intelligence, special abilities or academic success: not only moral judgement in the gifted, as only few researches have been made specifically on the gifted in this topic, as the Psychinfo database can show, except for some retrospective biographical study.

In the meanwhile, social development of the gifted was studied aiming mostly to analyze their adjustment to others, popularity, leadership, or problems in interacting with friends. Only a few studies were devoted to altruistic or pro-social behaviors and to moral development.

Definition of the problem

We have assumed as gifted subjects those subjects with a high IQ (5–10% superior of the population), rather than those with an extraordinary IQ (2% superior or less), so we have considered a relatively wide range of people. This way we examine high intelligence subjects from a point of view that intersects basic qualities (those also determined in relationship with their genetic background) with the opportunities for action and the cultural and environmental chances that enable them to 'cultivate' the genetic endowments in due course. Therefore our attention is laid more on the cultivation processes, being more interesting and more promising in the research fields, rather than on the selected ones.

Moreover, we consider giftedness as a high general ability rather than a specific skill: we do not examine here peculiar skills or abilities – music, painting, mathematics . . . but only the development of generally gifted subjects, seen from the viewpoint of moral thinking and moral behavior. This way we feel it important to draw our attention to the moral development of the gifted, rather than starting from the theory of an existing specific giftedness in the moral, a theory that we see as rather doubtful. So, our attention is driven to the moral development of the generally gifted subjects, rather than to the strict selection of the morally gifted ones.

Then, we shall consider the relationship between some concepts, frequently used in similar contexts: they need a few specifications and they may elicit a few problems, too. We are talking about the concepts of moral judgement, moral behavior, and morality.

In the concept of moral judgement, the importance of the evaluation process is stressed, rather than the decision-making one (it is to judge if an action is right or wrong, and not to decide if making it or not), and the focus is settled on the cognitive and developmental aspects, on which a large part of the psychological research has concentrated its efforts and to these aspects we will also pay a great deal of attention.

The concept of moral behavior is, on the other hand, particularly complex, because it covers different themes and problems, and only some of these can be treated and studied by psychology:

- social behavior aspects, among which are different social abilities. We have to remember that not all abilities concerning social success are involved, but a major part is played here by the empathic role-play, rather than self-presentation and manipulation skills, and the back up ability is considered more important than persuasion and influence capacities;
- structural individual features, as the so-called 'psychological maturity', defined differently by the authors; we could recall here the 'classical' definition by Freud, as the "ability to love and work";
- personality features in the social field, such as identifications and basic social relationships;
- altruism and prosocial behavior, expressed in several forms, depending on which society or culture we are investigating; nevertheless, we can presume the presence of a general common (super-cultural) basis, which seems to send us back to biological grounding;
- in the concept of moral behavior there is a reference to subjects (which actions are moral?) that eventually send us to philosophy or religion; to avoid the intervention of philosophy, some psychologists have tried to study this aspect on the subjective side. This way they have tried to analyze what people think when they morally value or label a fact or an action: what do people mean by morality and moral judgement in their common language?

Basically, most difficulties are due to the superimposition of three different approaches: two psychological and an extra-psychological one:

(1) Moral judgement can be seen as a problem connected to society (and to the human species as a social species). It consists of leading to patterns of behavior which fit social survival (of manhood), seen both as physical survival and as the chance to nourish the quality of cultural relationships and achievements which found the specific heritage of the species;

(2) Otherwise, moral judgement can be seen as an expression of the individual qualities of a person. Those qualities enhance his whole performance, when not measured just as thinking abilities in the traditional meaning, or even as social abilities totally rule-oriented, but they also include environmental adaptability in the sense of the best balance and wellness possible. So they include empathy, comfort ability and the skill of finding patterns of actions meant to minimize pain and to satisfy the most important needs to oneself and to one's fellow creatures, both on the psychological and the cultural side;

(3) Moreover, the extra-psychological approach identifies the word 'morality' as a concept including a range of behaviors and rules defined by a particular philosophy or religion, or common basis to many of them, considered as lore which shall be pedagogically transmitted. We do not share the same ground, but this approach has to be taken into account when thinking about the problem, because its presence is widespread in the shared representations and expectations. This way those representations can be the objects of our studies: what do people mean when they talk about morality? Which contents do they put into this concept? Which conditions subdue to a morally considered act or problem and what is the difference between morality and legality, opportunity or social ability? Are these conditions the same in different social classes, cultures or societies? This is a typical ground for psychosocial studies.

Aware of the complexity of the problem, we will try to show some guidelines and to give a few remarks on what we consider the most interesting aspects that researches providing useful data have investigated.

Moral development

The wide range of researches on moral judgement analyze either the relationship between cognitive development or academic success and the stages of moral judgement, or the essential conditions suitable to developing the skills of moral judgement.

On that approach, several books have been recently published, addressed both to a specific or a generic audience (that of educators or parents). And the titles are really catchy ones, as "100 ways to enhance values and morality in schools and youth," "365 ways to develop your child's values" or the more recent, "The moral intelligence of children: how to raise a moral child" (Coles, 1997).

Many books about related topics, as values or character education, have been issued in recent years.

The varied meanings of the idea of moral judgement used in the researches cover angles and perspectives different from time to time: moral rationality and decision-making, the development of the sense of fairness and justice, and of pro-social dispositions, moral self and moral identity.

Although these concepts are strictly linked together, we must underline that there is a clear distinction between:

- the problem of the nature of values, concerning the planning of the action and representing the ideal domain of social psychology, as well as anthropology and sociology and that of the nature and the development of character, inherant to personality psychology, and

- the domain of moral judgement, more specific and connected to its own tradition in the research, formerly in the philosophical field and more recently also within the sphere of psychology.

Some questions of emerging importance are posed:

(1) the researches on cognitive and social-cognitive components of moral reasoning: many studies, both psychometric (even conducted with fine statistical techniques, as LISREL) and experimental, have considered the different component of understanding problems and decision making in moral matters, both in cognitive psychology perspective and in the perspective of social psychology.
(2) the relationship between strictly logical, computational abilities (traditionally emphasized by cognitive stage theories, as well as traditional philosophical approaches) and social-affective components of thinking in moral judgement, which characterize human reasoning: is moral giftedness only a matter of a good computational machine?
(3) the discourse analysis on moral judgement and the social representation of moral judgement. The place of moral judgement in everyday thinking and the role of social conventions and pragmatic aims in conversations have been the object of a certain number of works: is moral giftedness only a matter of dialectical ability in sustaining one own rights or interests, making them coherent and acceptable to others?
(4) the researches on moral reasoning in special professional fields (education, economy, and medicine . . .): is moral reasoning part of the so-called 'social intelligence' and of good professional performance?
(5) the problem of moral giftedness as a special ability: is there moral giftedness at all?

Psychologists have studied this problem for some decades and the traditional perspective distinction is divided into cognitive, behaviorist and psycho-dynamic approaches. Nowadays, the most recent approach is based on new patterns, taking new alternatives into account:

- the choice between the perspective of the subject (decision-making process) and the perspective of the observer (what an observer sees as the object of the moral judgement from the outside);
- the choice between global approaches (where the problem is to value if a judgement is fully developed or not) and component approaches (mainly cognitive: the role of information, of the de-codification, of the euristhics);

- the alternative between individual level (which studies individual performance) and processes of interactive construction (how judgement is formed through language and speech);
- the alternative between the pre-eminence of the self (and so of the processes of identification of the defense mechanisms) and the supremacy of the social self (so the pre-eminence of the social expectations and representations which determine it).

The classical cognitive-developmental approach

Cognitive developmental studies about moral development have stated the existence of a succession of stages in judgement about the nature of rules (both in play and in interpersonal behavior), rightness of actions, distributive and retributive justice.

Piaget (1932) named such stages as egocentric, realistic-heteronomous and autonomous, where reciprocity, consideration of intentions of agents and reference to the functional aims of rules are the discriminatory issues for autonomous moral behaviour.

Kohlberg (1969) searched for a more detailed succession of stages and attributed a central role to the concept of social convention and social rule, differentiating the six stages he found in three groups:

- two pre-conventional, where the rule is a way to avoid punishment or harm and to satisfy one's needs (in the second stage, even reciprocally);
- two conventional stages, where the rule is a way to feel good and to meet the expectations of the social group (stage 3), or expresses the priority of a general social point of view (stage 4);
- and two post-conventional stages, where the rule expresses a more abstract point of view, referring to meta-rules to solve conflicts between specific different norms (stage 5), or to abstract general, absolute principles (stage 6).

In this approach, the sequence of stages is structured in the same developmental sequence as intelligence operations: each new stage employs more differentiated, reversible and equilibrated operations and has a higher degree of generality and abstraction.

The cognitive-developmental approach to moral judgement has sustained the existence of a series of stages in the judgement. They are related to the nature of social rules, the agreement or the liability to punishment of deeds, the modality of the retributive justice (concerning nature and measure of reward and punishment) and the distributive one. Piaget identified three main stages in this development (egocentric, realistic-heteronomous and autonomous), stressing the importance of the very origin of the idea of social rule as a peculiar moment in the general cognitive development of the child.

Kohlberg gave a wider meaning to the existence of stages in the moral judgement and he ordered the levels on the basis of the concept of social convention-rule (two pre-conventional, two conventional and two post-conventional stages). His effort compelled the researchers to overcome the context of social cognition, that is the construction analysis, the understanding and the mastering of social reality, to stretch out towards the idea of a cognitive genesis in the moral individual orientations and behaviors.

We shall remember here that Kohlberg and his students had devoted themselves to the study of moral judgement for more than two decades, using the 'dilemma' method, in which short problematic episodes are shown to the subjects. These episodes are based on several principles, usually known as morally relevant ones, which appear as opposite and incompatible in that specific situation. So the subject is asked to elaborate answers or to choose between different courses of action, and to justify his/her choice answering a series of questions and remarks.

Kohlberg thought morality concerned the managing of the general idea of justice, and he aimed to study the performance of his subjects in the thinking process, which centers on the social justification of action (right or wrong). From this point of view it should be intended as an intellectual performance, though not measurable through a traditional problem-solving process. As a matter of fact, it is not concerned either in the manipulation of univocal premises into defined logical systems, or can it be reduced to a conditional reasoning where logical connections between premises and consequences are univocal, too (e.g.: if you want x, you have to do y). So, Kohlberg underlines that in moral judgement the gagged ability is firmly connected to the understanding of social rules that are the basis of the building up of relationships between people.

The rationalist tradition, to which Kohlberg seems tightly linked (starting from his direct cooperation with Rawls, a clear representative of contractualistic moral philosophy), tends to regard moral judgement as an intellectual production that has to be analyzed mainly on a logical consistency and formal legitimacy level.

For this reason, too, and getting over Piaget's legacy, Kohlberg underlines the idea of a stage evolution that focuses on the changing of the formal legitimacy of judgement during the development process. The basic idea here is that all the different perspectives the subjects show could meet in a common ground, where the keystone is represented by the general idea of justice, which can be understood and discussed following different patterns. These methods will be closely related to the stage the subject has reached in his/her moral development.

In this way, Kohlberg stresses the topic of the validation of the judgement, while he deliberately overlooks the problem of the de-codification of real positions (transformations and distortions made when we understand situations in which a decision on reality is needed), because he makes clear that moral judgement only concerns what is inside the frame of aware experience and of personal interpretation of situations.

Those studies affirmed a central relation between cognitive development and moral development, and stated the importance of a higher intellectual level to reach the higher moral stages: and, if no specific study was conducted on the gifted, nevertheless they are supposed to have a privileged position with respect to the theory.

In this approach moral behavior is considered as largely dependent on moral judgement: moral judgement, in fact, is viewed both as a necessary condition (you can't behave fairly if you don't know what is fair), and as a motivating condition (if you really know what is good, this assumes a positive value for your action). Moral education assumes the same possibilities and limits of intellectual education: you can't develop by simply memorizing norms or by repeating prescribed and positively reinforced actions, but is necessary to develop a broader comprehension of nature of rules, difference of perspectives, relations between different aspects, both through intellectual and social stimuli: this was done in the 'just community' approach by Kohlberg and other researchers.

In the meanwhile, other theorists (especially social learning theorists, starting with Bandura & McDonald, 1963) focused on moral behavior as influenced by reinforcement and modeling procedures, and analyzed conditions for the efficacy of such procedures (for instance, characteristics of models and of their behaviors, efficacy of preaching vs. modeling).

Those theorists considered moral behavior mainly in its concrete and social effects, not only as an extension of judgement (as coherence with judgement) as cognitivists do. So, many kinds of 'pro-social' behavior have been considered: such as sharing goods, helping others in distress, acting altruistically by giving time, money and effort for altruistic and social purposes.

Developments in discussion on moral development

Piaget did not suggest a reductionist position. His analysis was better aimed to demonstrate how, even in the moral judgement area, those stadial phenomena show themselves, phenomena that explain the evolution of deep mental structures during the growth. He considered and studied moral thinking because here the occurrence was evident.

On the other hand, Kohlberg reaches a more ontologically cognitive viewpoint as he considers moral thinking as the core of the morality and virtue debate, giving it an explicit value connotation. To him, following Socrates and Plato, understanding is a transformation in the way of living, rather than a mere ability.

To balance this 'hard' position, other supplementary components (and not only the cognitive one) have eventually appeared in further research, as in Rest's contribution to the discussion.

Rest distinguished four major components of moral behavior: interpreting the situation in terms of how people's welfare is affected by possible actions of the subject; figuring out what the ideally moral course of action would be; selecting among possible outcomes in deciding what is actually to be done; executing and implementing a plan of action (see Rest, 1983, 1986).

Rest's theory on moral action

FOUR COMPONENTS

---

1 *Understanding the situation*

2 *Deciding what should, morally, be the right thing to do*

3 *Choosing what to do, among different possibilities and motivations*

4 *Executing and carrying out the action*

Cognitive elaboration of moral judgement

The de-codification of situations and the awareness of transformations or distortions in the processes that lay between perception and judgement represent a central problem in the social-cognitive perspective. Several contemporary researches have shown the importance of context, cultural condition, choice in the verbs used, availability of distortion mechanisms (as the 'moral disengagement' ones, studied by Bandura) in judgement.

So, moral judgement becomes a complex thematic area, which covers various aspects. The main ones are: understanding and de-codifying stimulus situations, knowing and representing socially learnt rules, elaborating the norms deriving from actual experiences and conflicts, realizing the pertinence of the rules to the situation, applying the right regulations. Again, anticipating the material and/or psychological consequences of one's choices on oneself and on the other people implied, valuing the consequences on the self image and the self-esteem related to personal values and identifications, anticipating the blame, using strategies that protect from blame and from damage of self image (e.g. through 'moral disengagement' mechanisms), developing and using verbal arguments.

Recognizing this complexity does not invalidate the central role of the cognitive angle, widely recognized: moral reasoning is a complex form of human cognition that challenges theoretical models of cognitive science (May, Friedman & Clark, 1996)

Nevertheless, facing this complexity, the simple classical analysis of moral judgement, the one traditionally carried out on Kohlbergian dilemma, seems incomplete and reductive. Rest's model, too, underestimates the complexity in the processes and does not take into account verbal expressions and their influence on moral judgement.

Many different aspects of cognitive elaboration may be considered: decisions in the moral judgement field are deeply influenced by the kind, quantity and ways of approaching information related to the object (event, situation) we have to value.

For instance, the presence of more information items obliges the subjects to reflect more deeply on the nature of factors that suggest either support for or making an exception to the rule in the considered situation. Even when we apply a well-known moral rule, judgement is influenced both by the rule involved and by the contradicting factors suggesting that an exception may be made (Langford, 1992b). In another research by Wainryb (1991), 80% of the moral evaluations changed in response to informational changes and in all subjects significant relationships were found between the evaluations and the informational assumptions. Cognitive context factors represented by characteristics of moral dilemmas and issues account for substantial variability (for instance, transpersonal dilemmas account for higher stage scores than do personal dilemmas: Teo, Becker & Edelstein, 1995).

Access to specified information and knowledge produces relevant influence on judgement: two crucial aspects are the relationship between actions and omissions and the role given to negligence. When substantial a priori negligence is explicitly provided or can be inferred implicitly from contemporaneous information about the actor, there is a change in moral evaluation, especially in relation to a posteriori outcome information (Enzle & Hawkins, 1992).

Information about the size of the 'job' and intent of offenders is relevant for moral judgement even for convicted offenders (Wolf et al., 1995).

Information is relevant also when judging between intentions and outcomes: the use of the 'conjunction rule' (punishment is related to bad intention and bad outcome) is understood even by young subjects (since 4 years old: Zelazo, Helwig & Lau, 1996); moreover, when outcomes are foreseeable, more mature subjects pay more attention to them (Sanvitale, Saltzstein & Fish, 1989).

Information processing rules and heuristics are also important: judgment for commissions is harsher than for omissions ('omission bias', Spranca, Minsk & Baron, 1991). So, an important effect on cognitive elaboration of moral judgement is provided by the difference between commissions and omissions.

Andreani and Pagnin (1992, 1993, 1994), have underlined that expressing moral judgement involves different cognitive processes: valuing the situation (specifically, roles and needs of the actors) and the immediate or long-term consequences of one's deeds; understanding the rules, which control expectations and define rights and their enforcement field; and affective-emotional processes such as the affective involvement of needs and consequences committed in the action (particularly in terms of empathy); and the tendency to look after those needs and consequences.

How to survey moral judgement

Many controversies lay in the way of analysis and measurement of what we define as moral judgement. The main tools in this field have been the Standard Interview (SI), or Moral Judgement Interview (MJI) by Kohlberg, to analyze through the scoring procedure defined by Colby & Kohlberg (1987) and the Defining Issues Test (DIT) by Rest. Those instruments, particularly the SI, so complex and time-consuming, have often been applied in a revised short form, fitted in form and contents to different situations.

Nevertheless, other instruments have been used, such as the Ethic of Care Interview by Skoe and Marcia, the Ethics Position Questionnaire by Forsyth, the Sociomoral Reflection Measure by Gibbs, and many others. In different cases, alternative projects have studied the scoring method used in the analysis of the classical dilemmas, as in the method proposed by Langford (1992a).

On the methodological level, then, researchers have tried to verify the unity of the stadial meaning. For instance, principal axis factor analysis and LISREL were used to test the hypothesis that moral stages form structured wholes (Cortese, 1989): the results supported the idea of moral stages as unitary wholes: a single underlying factor accounted for between issue correlation in moral stage scores: there is a unitary factor across the different context of various dilemmas. Bush, Krebs & Carpendale (1993) also showed that moral judgement was structurally consistent across three sets of dilemmas.

Controversies about gender and culture bias of moral judgment measures

A classical controversy in this field deals with the relationship between contents classified within different stages and their cultural and sexual definition. Sexual specification has been a crucial point raised by one of Kohlberg's students, Carol Gilligan (1982). She revealed the presence of two main moral orientation, 'care' and 'justice', which appeared in different percentages in the answers of men and women.

Gilligan thought that Kohlberg's traditional scoring clearly favors male orientation to 'justice' rather than female orientation to 'care'. Hence, several studies proved controversial: first Walker then Krebs (Krebs et al., 1991) showed there were no striking differences between male and female subjects, while Baumrind ratifies and makes a thorough study of Gilligan's findings. Again, some researches on adolescent subjects revealed the presence of a more cognitively evolved moral judgement in women.

Perry & McIntyre (1995) point out this phenomenon through the distinction between three ways to make moral decisions: a care mode (others should not suffer), a justice mode (decisions made according to the golden rule), and a narrowly concerned or selfish mode. As the authors say: "All three modes were used by males and females; however, males were more likely to choose the narrowly concerned mode than were females, who chose the justice and care modes more often." Garmon et al. (1996), too, showed that "in moral judgement stage, females were more advanced than males during early adolescence. Care-related and ethically ideal expressions were more prevalent in females' moral judgement. Results reject Gilligan's claim of stage bias, but support was found for gender-related moral orientation differences."

Even more clearly than the disputed sexual difference, cultural tradition has been stated as playing a major role in the definition of moral orientation and in the various aspects considered in its valuation. Even though Kohlberg had found correspondence in the results of the researches led with his method in different countries (Western, Eastern cultures, Northern and Southern cultures of the world), a clear advantage for North-western countries was found, and it aroused several doubts on the fairness of his method.

More recent studies show the nature of cultural influence on moral judgement. For instance, in the Mille & Luthar's (1989) research on Indian and American subjects it is stated that "Indians tended to categorize role-related interpersonal responsibilities as moral issues, Americans tended to regard them in personal terms." Hence, the idea that moral reasoning may be based on role-based interpersonal responsibilities and not merely on justice considerations. Haidt et al. (1993), too, reveal that "cultural norms and culturally shaped emotions have a substantial impact on the domain of morality and the process of moral judgment." Again, Miller & Bersoff (1994) underline that "interpersonal reciprocity is invested with a deontological moral status rather than viewed in purely utilitarian terms in cultures emphasizing interdependent, as contrasted with independent, views of the self."

The role of situation in moral judgement: abstract judgment and real situation reasoning

An important difference arises between testing and thinking in a real situation. Different researches corroborate this remark: Foster & Sprinthall (1992) find that, when having to decide about abortion in real life, there were no major differences between adolescent and adult women on the level of reasoning that directly assessed the specific decision concerning abortion, while in general test of moral reasoning there were clear developmental differences between the adolescent group and the older groups.

In a quite different life domain, decision making in business, Weber (1996) shows that the type of harm embodied in a moral dilemma and the magnitude of its consequences significantly influence the moral rationales used in managerial moral decision making.

In decisions relating to real behavior the moral situation is interpreted from the self's perspective prior to a behavioral decision, whereas in the case of evaluation it is construed from the perspective of an observer judging the actor's decision after the event.

This is clearly shown in a social-psychological study from Denton & Krebs (1990), where subjects responding hypothetically attributed to themselves moral integrity, while in a real situation analogous to that of the test, when they were really induced to an illegal behavior, they behaved in a different way.

Other studies show that moral judgments are situation-specific. For instance, Keltikangas (1989) found that in many fields of life, moral cognition of aggressive subjects did not differ from those of their non-aggressive peers: the behavioral choices differ only when specific conflicts arise.

Even studies on incarcerated subjects show that they are not significantly differentiated from controls in moral judgement, when principal social variables (status, education, race, and gender) are controlled.

A crucial issue: moral judgement and action

In Rest's componential model of moral development a separate place is given to executing and implementing a plan of action (component 4), that affects the relationship between belief and action. This component involves 'ego strength' and self-regulation skills; to this aspect are referred the incongruities between moral judgement and behavior observed by many researchers (see Blasi, 1980). For instance, in an often quoted research, Damon (1977) asked young children how 10 candies ought to be distributed as rewards: when these same children actually were given the 10 candy bars to distribute, they deviated from their espoused schemes of fair distribution. And Sobesky (1983) showed that when information about different types of consequences is added even to hypothetical moral dilemmas, as the severity of personal consequences increases, people favor self-interest over principled reasoning.

The radical critics see moral judgement as representative only of fancy talk and argument, of ability in verbal fluency or in elaborating excuses, not of social action and behavior.

In the face of such criticisms, even cognitive theorists recognize that verbal moral judgement does not explain the whole moral behavior. In fact, many studies have been carried out about relation between moral judgement and behavior, using various kinds of measures for behavior: both laboratory measures (like as Prisoner Dilemma Game, cheating in the solution of difficult problems, sharing rewards, etc.) and naturalistic measures (such as systematic ratings in school, clinical ratings, reports of anti-social behavior, delinquency, performance in caring activities by doctors, or

conscientious objectors, etc.). As Rest (1986) remarks, "in general, the finding from these studies is that moral judgement is consistently statistically related to behavior measures, but the strength of the relation is only moderate (approximately a correlation in the 0.3 range)."

To understand the relationship between moral judgement and action, some researchers referred to Ajzen's theory on reasoned action. For instance, Kramer & Hofmann (1990) showed that, fitting moral judgements, behavioral intentions, expected personal consequences, and expected social consequences in the analysis model, the level of moral judgment moderates the prediction of behavioral intentions: so, moral judgement is a moderating factor, but only a partial determinant of behavioral intentions.

Using structural equation techniques, specifically Lisrel path analysis, Lombardo & Pagnin (in work) show that a modified model of reasoned action has to be used, because not only personal moral judgement level but also moral disengagement mechanisms (see Bandura, 1991) result as main moderators upon behavioral intentions. In different types of dilemmas, concerning situations near to everyday life (loyalty to friends, love relationships, bullying and reporting a physical assault to the authority), main components of decision process were investigated: expected outcomes of the intended action, evaluation of such outcomes as positive or negative, representation of reference groups (parents, best friends, and schoolmates) norms about the problem, subjective importance of conforming to those reference groups expectations, personal principles about the problem, moral disengagement mechanisms; behavioral intention and moral stage assessed by classical DIT dilemma were considered. More than 400 students (16–17 year old) were tested.

The model resulting from the use of structural equations as best fitting with data collected from a research on 400 subjects is shown in Fig. 1.

In conclusion, we think it is necessary to maintain a certain distance between judgement and action:

- as a perspective: judgement as a third person evaluation, outside or after the act, action as a first person choice, before the act;
- as a process: while in behavior motivational and affective aspects play their role, in judgement this role is basically given to skills in social reasoning;
- the difference between the two processes is symbolized by two characters, which express the peculiar qualities of each level at the highest degree. The first is the pro-social altruist (that could be the 'saint' or the 'hero'), the second is the 'wise man', able to judge for himself and for the others, more than being only a man of learning or the guardian of law, and he can act in different ways, following various needs and roles. Only a few outstanding people embody both figures.

MODIFIED MODEL OF MORAL ACTION
(Lombardo & Pagnin)

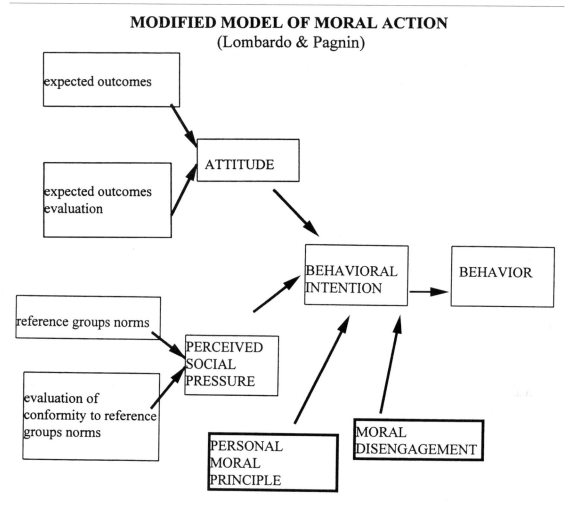

Figure 1.

Moral judgement and action: the role of motivation and values

A principal aspect of moral development concerns motives for moral action. In fact, whether a subject is able to apply his or her moral competence to a real-life context seems to be a problem of affectively dealing with personal needs and self-interest in a situation.

Moral judgement is based not only on logic: moral judgement enters into a descriptive account of our emotions, and our emotional responses to situations and to each other necessarily inform the moral judgments. Emotional responses to situations and to others inform the moral judgement.

In this perspective, also, the role of defense mechanisms on moral judgement was considered, embedding moral judgement research within the broader sphere of personality: adolescents with mature profiles of defen-

ses reasoned at higher stages of moral judgment (Hart & Chmiel, 1992). On the other side, moral problems that are overwhelming reflect problems in primary relationships, calling to mind developmentally primitive moral strategies (Blakeney & Blakeney, 1992).

As Bandura (1991) notes, "a person's level of moral judgement may indicate the types of reasons likely to be most persuasive to that person, but it does not ensure a particular kind of conduct ... different people can arrive at different judgements from the same principle of justness, depending on what factors they consider relevant and how they weight them." From such a point of view, a broader conception of morality requires more than skill in abstract reasoning: affective and social factors play a vital regulative role in moral conduct.

The problem of moral motivation sees the competition of three kinds of theories: emotion centered theories, rationality centered theories, and social (and self) centered theories.

A. Emotion centered theories. Guilt feeling is the first and more traditional reference in psychodynamic theories; but other psychologists also consider it as the basis for moral behavior. Even behaviorists utilized guilt in the same direction, though giving a different interpretation of its origins:

- in psychoanalysis guilt has a wide meaning, from normal remorse to absurd self-rebukes in severe depression. It is an affective state following an action that the subject considers bad; but, as the critical and punitive agent (the super-ego) is differentiated from the conscious self since childhood (in the Oedipal stage), guilt feelings, though tied to the internalization of demands and prohibitions of parents, have a largely unconscious origin and not-rational outcomes (Freud S., 1923); for behaviorists, on the other hand, guilt feeling can be interpreted as anxiety anticipating punishment, or fear of punishment: conditioned negative affect motivates morality (Aronfreed, 1968; Eysenck, 1976);
- a somewhat different emotional state, near to guilt, which has been considered as source for morality, is empathy: Hoffman (1977) considers empathy, and empathy-based guilt as the basis for altruistic motivation. Empathy is defined as "a vicarious affective response that does not necessarily match another's affective state, but is more appropriate to the other's situation than to one's own" (Hoffman, 1984, p. 285): this appropriateness depends on the knowledge about others and self, and definitely on one's cognitive level. So it is possible to identify some different developmental levels of the empathic distress: Hoffman identifies four levels: global empathy, 'egocentric' empathy, empathy for another's feelings, empathy for another's life condition (Hoffman, 1991).

B. Rationality centered theories. The general nature of moral obligation is seen in the rational necessity of putting oneself beyond the particular:

- in the more abstract and philosophical expression, this is made by the Kant's categorical imperative, that expresses the general nature of obligation, besides specific, conditional imperatives (like those studied by deontic logic: "if you want x, you must do y").
- in the cognitive developmental theory of Piaget, obligation comes out from social understanding of how cooperation functions and from one's own stake in making it work (Piaget, 1932)
- in a similar way, in Kohlberg's work the origin of moral motivation is seen in the experience of living in just and caring communities: this can lead to understanding how cooperative communities are possible and to moral commitment (Kohlberg, 1984; the philosophical roots of this conception are exposed by Rawls, 1971)
- impartial cognitive role taking is postulated by cognitive developmental theories as the source of principled reasoning. So rationality dictates morality: it is not possible to do right if you don't know what is right; and when you know what is right, the need for cognitive equilibrium and the knowledge of general consequence of evil urges you to do right.

C. Social and self theories. From classical social learning, according to which people just respond to reinforcement and/or modeling opportunities and learn social behavior (Bandura, 1977), to social cognitive theory, where the role of self and self-regulation mechanisms are included.

- According to Bandura (1991) in social cognitive theory moral conduct is regulated by two major sources of sanctions: social sanctions and internalized self-sanctions. So, people's belief in their efficacy to exercise control over their own motivation, thought patterns and actions, plays an important role.

  But the self is not seen as disembodied from social reality, as social influences affect the operation of the self system in three major ways: contributing significantly to the development of self-regulatory competence, providing collective support for adherence to moral standards, and facilitating selective activation and disengagement of moral self-regulation.

  In this perspective, even moral thought is not solely an intrapsychic affair: "impartial role reversibility is imaginable in the abstract, but social experiences create too many human biases for impartiality of view and universalization of interest to be achievable in reality" (Bandura, 1991, p. 48).
- Other researchers consider the role of the self central in moral motivation: concern for self integrity and one's identity is the main moral agent for Blasi (1985); identification with something great and highly valued as part of the construction of the self has the same function for Erikson (1958).

  We can note that social influence affects the operation of the self system in four major ways: contributes to the development of self-regulatory competence, provide collective support for adherence to moral standards, facilitate selective activation or disengagement of moral self-regulation, states the areas and situations affected by moral meanings.

  So, in a social cognitive perspective moral judgement is regulated by two major sources: social sanctions and internal processes referring to the self-concept. Moreover, people's knowledge about their values and feelings and belief in their efficacy of exercising control over thought patterns and actions plays an important role.

- In a social perspective centered on the self also values and life philosophy have a substantial impact on moral behavior (also more than in moral judgement).

A research shows, for instance, that in adolescents, nominated by community leaders for having demonstrated commitments to care for others or the community, and interviewed on issues of self-understanding, moral judgement, and implicit personality theories, personal beliefs and philosophies are crucial: care exemplars were more likely to describe themselves in terms of moral personality traits and goals[1] (Hart & Fegley, 1995).

Also the acquisition of optimistic values seems to favor moral judgement development: a strong positive relationship between meaning in life and moral judgement levels was found for males and females regardless of education or religiosity, and for criminals and noncriminals (Addad & Leslau, 1990).

Discourse and social representations in moral judgement

Moral judgements are apparent in discourse about most forms of human interaction: what is their content, how are they constructed by language and interaction? Parents provide moral training of their children not only through punishment or approval, but also, primarily, by discussing situations and behavior to be punished or approved. For instance, in the case of aggressive behavior, parents take the lead in promoting their younger son's narrative and logical understanding of his offensive action. The family's court is an important natural moral training ground for the child's acquisition of reasoning, narrative understanding of aggression, critical thinking, and the arguments used in proving a case (see Beck & Wood, 1993).

Discourse can also determine the extent in which individuals construct the situation as moral or nonmoral (Smetana, 1994): a business matter, a political matter, or even a friendship matter may become a moral problem and require reasoning and decision, or merely be considered from a 'matter of fact' aspect. Personal language and, moreover, shared language in conversations strongly influences the moral status of a problem: most intelligent children are more sensible to the language expressions, and rapidly identify their implicit consequences. This is also the reason for the importance of media presentations of social problems, as they create a shared language about them.

For many years verbal expressions have been considered crucial in moral judgement research. Kohl-

berg had already shown—even with a pure 'diagnostic' aim in answering classification—the importance of verbal expressions. He observed (Colby & Kohlberg, 1987) how moral domain is characterized by the ways of moral language, and how they express the actions useful to the individual to face the situations of moral conflict. According to Kohlberg, they are: "obeying, approving or blaming, punishing or proving one's innocence, having rights and duties."

In pre-school children, having suitable linguistic abilities is a major condition for being able to discern between morality and behaving (the observance of conventional behavior), (see Smetana & Braeges, 1990), and later, mainly during adolescence, for learning more complex levels in moral judgement. The essential role of linguistic knowledge is confirmed by research in hearing impaired adolescents, that are unable to fully handle reciprocity and equality in a contractual relationship (Sam & Wright, 1988).

Other researchers have given great importance to verbal expressions used by the subjects to understand the application field and the extension of moral judgement in real life. Some of them have proposed an autobiographical collection of real dilemma situations and their subsequent content analysis (Walker, De Vries & Trevethan, 1987; Wark & Krebs, 1996); situations found in these cases are very different in their dilemma intensity and in their creative richness. Others have devoted to verbal and speech characterization of the moral judgement levels, which have been hypothesized by the classical cognitive-developmental theory, when asking, for instance, to describe and typify characters that give morally high judgements. Wygant & Williams (1995) found that subjects describe people using high and moderate levels of postconventional reasoning, positively in terms of rationality and intelligence but negatively in interpersonal terms (e.g. unfriendly, insensitive, selfish, indifferent, phony, inconsiderate, inhumane), compared to people using low levels of post-conventional reasoning.

Finally, to us a crucial point is the attribution of moral value to problems and the identification of the core of meaning requested by this attribution: on the semantic level, which content presents the moral connotation of a situation, according to people with different life conditions? To answer this question we have used procedures such as lexical analysis to the answers to dilemmas (Pagnin & Zanetti, 1997; Pagnin & Bajoni, 1997), narrative analysis and conversational analysis.

Social and professional impact of moral judgment

It could be stated that the link between social relationship and moral judgement is double: on one hand, positive social experiences favor the development of an evolved moral judgement, as Kohlberg hypothesized (he thought only the experience of a

---

[1] The differences between subjects and control groups vanished in measures of developmental stages of moral judgement.

supporting community and of the peers gives way to an evolution in moral judgement in young people) and as it has been ratified by specific researches. For instance, adolescent moral judgement is consistently related to reports of positive intra-familiar relationships (Speicher, 1992); and children's moral judgements are related to positive social experiences associated with peer acceptance (Buzzelli, 1992).

On the opposite side, the level of morality influences social acceptance: moral characterization of a subject or situation is a powerful element in social categorization, with a strength even superior to traditionally important features as high ability (Martijn et al., 1992).

This awareness led not only researchers working with public and health institutions to carry out surveys on moral judgement, but even company personnel dealing with directors training and marketing (McIntyre et al., 1995).

Moral judgement and the attribution of moral features theme spreads out and involves several fields: from the classical criminology (Przygotski & Mullet, 1993; Gregg, Gibbs & Basinger, 1994), to food behavior (Stein & Nemeroff, 1995), from marketing and company management (Weber, 1996), to medicine (Testa & Simonson, 1996; Reiter & Hiddemann, 1997; Crichton, 1997). Moral judgement can influence many people's behavior: not only law, caring and health workers, but also consumers. That has been clearly shown by the reaction spread out from the accusations made against some sports corporations to exploit young workers in the third world. Or the 'Nestlé affair', related to an evaluation on the negative effects of the dried milk diffusion in some countries of the third world. With this growth of the consumer awareness, company management also have to become involved in this side of company and products image.

Moral dimension becomes an important part in social image of people and even of institutions: we have to consider not only the developmental side (moral judgement seen as a way in cognitive and emotional growth), but also its relevant social impact.

Even in scientific literature, the double soul of this subject—developmental and social—is assessed by the fact that some of the most interesting researches have been published on the one hand in *Child Development* and, on the other, in *Journal of Personality and Social Psychology*, which are two fundamental keystones in their area of study.

Specific relationships between moral judgment and high ability

High cognitive ability and high education are the main contributors to high level of moral judgment: most researches find strongest relations between intelligence (or general cognitive ability) or educational achievement and measures of moral judgement.

Many data were found supporting those assumptions. For instance, years in college are the strongest predictor of moral judgement (Finger, Borduin & Baumstark, 1992); intellectual perspective taking in academic settings accounts for more of the moral judgement variance than does any other factor (Mason & Gibbs, 1993); stages of logical and socio-moral judgement are strongly related to each other (Gibson, 1990). At least, above-average cognitive ability is necessary for higher scores in moral judgement, as higher cognitive achievement ability appears to provide a foundation for higher scores in moral judgment, even if it is not the only element needed (not every high achiever obtains a high score on moral judgement) (Narvaez, 1993); creative gifted give more original solutions to the dilemmas (Andreani & Pagnin, 1993).

Also, researches on personality traits (e.g. referred to the 'big five' model) assess that the element connected to intellectual performance is tightly linked to the level in moral judgement: principled moral reasoning relates to markers of intellectual-academic ability and to the big-five factor of openness to experience: "openness to experience is the big-five factor that best predicts moral reasoning" (Dollinger & LaMartina, 1998: moral reasoning was measured by the DIT; nevertheless, in our research [not published], good correlation was also found with consciousness and sociability).

Intellectually gifted children appear to reach a relatively high stage of moral reasoning earlier than their chronological peers (Karnes & Brown, 1981; Tan-Willman & Gutteridge, 1981). Some may be able to use principled reasoning during mid-teens, while it is normally reached only in adulthood by a small segment of the population. Using the DIT, Janos & Robinson (1985) also found significantly advanced moral judgement (compared with standards) in older gifted students (up to 18 years old).

Other researches underline as reaching a high level in thinking, talking about intellectual stages, is a fundamental pre-requirement for reaching the highest stages in moral judgement in the Kohlberghian sense (see Walker & Richards, 1979). As Walker (1991) states, "moral reasoning is based on, and constrained by, cognitive development: adequate solutions to difficult moral problems require systematic thought and logical analyses." So, advancements in cognitive development place individuals in a state of readiness for moral growth, as they may more easily understand higher moral reasoning and recognize deficiencies in common moral thinking.

Examining the available studies, we see that children and adolescents intellectually gifted generally have better results than their fellow-mates in 'paper and pencil' tests on moral thinking (see Rest's resourceful review, 1986).

Then, we can stress that some personality features in the gifted, shown by Andreani (1975), or by Janos & Robinson (1985), are potentially linked to some components of moral behavior, as Ego-strength and the ability to implement the correct course of action (see component four in the Rest's model).

Andreani (1975), examining personality of gifted adolescents through projective tests such as Rorschach, found that the ones that combined high intelligence with creativity were characterized by apparently conflicting traits: empathy, emotional reactivity, strong drives for aggression and sex (even if usually well controlled), low conformity, high need for achievement.

We also notice that features such as aggressiveness, competition and a great ambition for individual success (see Freeman, 1991), which could give way to anti-social behavior, may be bent to socially positive directions; for instance, towards creative aims, or, at least, trying to excel in one's social and professional duties. We shall remember that, from the 'morality of responsibility' point of view, being suitable to do one's social duty (so, one's professional fulfillment) is one of the basic aspects in the moral behavior of a rational type (aimed at enhancing common wellness). Such a statement is validated also on the empirical and factual side, where we notice a positive correlation between high scores in moral judgement and the existence of success orientation in one's job, in civic duties, career fulfillment, educational orientation, civic political awareness (Rest, Deemer, et al., 1986).

Moreover, even if the gifted tend to face to adults and to socially superimposed rules, they do not act in an anti-social way, as they typically conform to reasoned expectations and engage in cooperative relationships.

On the other hand, we note that findings regarding favorable social adjustment come from studies of moderate rather than extremely gifted children: the most talented are more vulnerable, as they are 'out of synchrony' with others (Janos & Robinson, 1985); as Freeman (1985, 1991) notes, highly gifted children are particularly sensitive and reactive to social stimuli they meet, and so are exposed both to most positive, highly intellectually and socially developed experiences, both to negative ones; and their development is inhibited—at any level—without adequate material and psychological conditions. Such susceptibility to environmental conditions show the importance of sustaining interventions, both in the intellectual and in the personality domain; as Heller notes from the experience of his very large Munich Longitudinal Study on gifted students, the "prejudice that the gifted do not need any special support or counseling belongs to those assumptions which have been empirically proven incorrect" (Heller, 1992).

Andreani & Pagnin (1992, 1996), in works on large samples of students, which used Kohlberg's and Rest's concepts and utilized various kinds of tests, showed that gifted, compared to other students, give higher approval of abstract and general principles (post-conventional in the sense of Kohlberg) and with respect to law and contracts and higher coherence of reasoning; and give less importance to other people's opinion and agreement, and also to sentimental-humanitarian expressions, which constituted the basis for a more intuitive morality in the lower ability groups.

On the basis of these results, we proposed a two-level method of moral judgement: a morality of sentiments (based on common sense and sympathetic feelings) and a rational morality (centered on rational principles and the attempt to weigh the consequences of actions): the first one more typical of average and low intelligence subjects, the second one of the gifted. While the first adheres to common standard, the second requires a calculation of benefit of different actors, a forecast of the outcome of actions, a balance of the different aspects of rights, an examination of different possible roles to be assumed (Andreani & Pagnin, 1992). Besides this general characteristic, in the gifted two different patterns of moral orientations can be identified, where there are important differences in the contents and in the values involved in judgements (Andreani & Pagnin, 1996). In fact, focusing on logical coherence and on personal needs (for instance need for achievement), some subjects tend to neglect the immediate feelings of empathy and the common moral immediate references.

The Moral Giftedness problem

The idea of moral giftedness involves several levels, which could invalidate the nature of giftedness. In fact, this has been traditionally valued on the basis of the shifting aside from the mean in tests on abstract reasoning or a group of tests including verbal, numerical aspects, deductive abilities (as matrices), and tests on creativity, mainly regarding verbal performance, and of more uncertain validity.

We have not normally considered social ability as an independent variable, for which good measurement exist, and the emotional one, stressed but not defined in a univocal way or by those positions that have recently enhanced the so-called 'emotional intelligence' (a somewhat contended definition). Goleman (1995) cites narrative cases of exceptional ability in resolving social conflicts and potentially dangerous interpersonal or public situations, among children and adults.

There is a common recognition of the existence of such kind of people: in many cultural traditions they are pointed out as models, at least if their actions are congruent with values and discourses of that tradition. Of course here we do not think about mere intellectual ability (the intelligent killer is a well-known figure in fiction literature, but sometimes exists in reality), nor about the kind of social ability we see in the successful politician or salesman, or even in the able cheater: here social ability is really partial and limited, and sometimes is accompanied by quite bad personal and social adjustment. Emotional ability implies a more profound interest in other people feelings, in their happiness or physical and psychological suffering. The affective side of moral judgement and behavior is crucial here. But also crucial is the ability to communicate and participate in the reasons of choices and decisions: moral judgement requires a high level of (at least, potential) exchange of reasons and motives.

Enhancing moral judgment in the gifted

The development of morality needs a positive context to enhance cognitive, social and emotional aspects of morality. Both Berkowitz (1985) and Keller & Reuss (1985) underline the importance of communication in moral development. To them, the moral judgement ability is linked to experiencing speeches and discussions about decisions: "The child must acquire the ability to express his or her own needs, interests, feelings and convictions, and at the same time to consider the claims of others. How adequately the child is able to do this depends on two factors: first, on the latitude of unconstrained discussion in factual communication and life practice, as well as in the context of institutionalized learning processes; second, on the child's level of development." (Keller & Reuss, 1985, p. 121).

To be at liberty to form an opinion, to justify it, and to come to terms with possible objections, is something the child learns only when given a fair chance, as a member of a relaxed discourse community, where the child can experience directly what it means to be involved in the tension of an ongoing communication process based on real life experiences. The moral discourse involves the goal of coming to a justified agreement, that is, an agreement shared by those concerned, beyond the 'prima facie duties'.

In fact, cognitive-developmental oriented researchers used communication, discussion and cooperation to enhance moral development: Kohlberg himself conducted interventions based on the 'just community' approach to moral education (see Kohlberg, 1984), where such principles were applied. This theory emphasizes the role of a good social context for moral development: but this does not mean a mere mechanical transmission: even an apparently deprived or antisocial social context may allow the main experiences that enhance significant social exchange about values, life experiences, responsibilities and decisions. But an external intervention will emphasize more direct ways to do it.

The efficacy of interventions in enhancing levels of moral reasoning is pointed out by many researches (for instance Erikson et al., 1976; Whiteley, 1982; Willging & Dunn, 1982): a good review of them (comprehensive of unpublished dissertations) is in Rest & Thoma, 1986, that conclude the meta-analysis stating that "moral education programs emphasizing dilemma discussion and those emphasizing personality development both produce modest but definite effects." (Rest

& Thoma, 1986, p. 85). More recently, positive results of intervention have also been found by Keen (1990).

As Rest states, to obtain measurable results interventions must be long enough (at least three weeks); and these results are probably linked to cognitive pre-requirements and role-taking skills owned by the subjects, like the ones shown by Walker (1980) (see Rest & Thoma, 1986, p. 86).

The exclusive over-emphasis put by cognitivist authors on the main role of cognitive conflict as a stimulus to the development of moral thinking has been discussed by researchers who also investigated other aspects of social interaction, which can boost the development of moral judgement. For instance, Walker has studied the influence of parents on moral development of their children, using a sophisticated analysis of the relationship of the family taken as a whole (thanks to micro-analytical methods applied to interactions). He has revealed that "children who evidenced the greatest development had parents who provided the stimulation of a relatively high level of moral reasoning as well who engaged in behaviors such as eliciting the child's opinion, asking clarifying questions, paraphrasing, and checking for understanding" (Walker, 1991). Those are typically cognitive interventions, but Walker notes that parenting behavior predicting the greatest development also entails supportive interactions, while the least moral development involves affectively conflictual interactions (Walker & Taylor, 1991).

Many authors have expressed doubts on the efficacy on interventions based on rational aspects only, and particularly on the discussion of dilemmas (hypothetical or real-life). We note, for instance that the usual cognitive interventions succeed much more in theoretical moral judgement than in moral discussions of real-life arguments (Villenave-Cremer & Eckensberger, 1985).

Critics remark that the constructivist educational intervention is based on the function of cognitive conflict in development. The strategy in order to induce cognitive conflict is discussion, involving comparison and contrast: but it is not clear whether the discussion strategy will suffice for moral growth, as it works for cognitive growth. Nevertheless, it seems the best way of intervention where it is not possible to act on the primary socialization quality and on the presence of strongly positive models in the community.

The ways of intervention may favor development at least in the aspect concerning skills implied in moral judgement:

- understanding the complexity of working of social rules (e.g. reciprocity, agreement, balance);
- understanding the domain of attribution of moral quality to a decision or an action (and of attribution of responsibility or guilt) in the social interaction;
- foreseeing the application to oneself and to the others and its danger level;

- understanding and using argumentative rules useful to comprehend other's point of view and to compare them to one's own (e.g. not being contradictory, accepting deductions, recognizing the link cause and effect);
- anticipating the consequences of the moral attribution on the self-image (on its wholeness and articulation) and the effects on the self even at an emotional and implicit level.

The attention on the ability aspect seems particularly profitable in the gifted and in the age of the maximum development in cognitive abilities: adolescence.

An educational program for social and moral abilities enhancement in selected groups of gifted adolescents was carried out by Pagnin and Zanetti (1997): it was based on exercises of dilemmas discussion, role-taking, social inferences, free expression of personal values, social behavior strategies discussion and dramatized simulation. The outcome of such intervention, analyzed by classic stage scores analysis and by an analysis of verbal expressions and meanings, showed the reaching of higher moral reasoning level.

The aim of the intervention was to enhance four main dimensions:

- general social-cognitive abilities: understanding other people's intentions, feelings and expectations;
- values understanding and selection in social context;
- identification of specific norms for different social domains;
- strategies for pursuing goals.

A set of exercises was used to enhance those abilities:

- discussion of hypothetical dilemmas;
- analysis of intentions, personal values, personality traits of the actors who play different roles in dilemmas, in comparison with one's own values and personality;
- role-taking concerning the different characters;
- identification and description of different aspects and components of real life dilemmas and of life events in one own life, and discussion on such dilemmas;
- expression of personal values, life goals, events which elicit happiness or sufferance, and which produce self-fulfillment or self-blame feelings in personal life;
- social behavior strategies and moral disengagement strategies discussion and dramatized simulation.

We point out also the possibility of using new means to foster moral development: a first experience in the use of computer simulation has been performed by Sherer (1998).

Conclusion

Summarizing our considerations, we look at moral development as a multi-dimensional construct that involves some principal social-cognitive abilities, concerning:

- comprehension and evaluation of the situation or problem in its cognitive-social aspects: in particular, the ability to understand other person's intentions, feelings and expectations;
- experiencing empathy with other person's (or living being's) state, and positive feelings toward basic social relationships;
- understanding norms and rules, and the conditions for their selection and use in social context and in specific areas;
- identifying a specific course of action that optimizes the outcomes in terms of social, cognitive and affective requirements;
- eliciting strategies for pursuing and sustaining the selected course of action notwithstanding obstacles.

From such a point of view, moral judgement requires more than skill in abstract reasoning: a specific social experience and a social construction of moral expectations, values and meanings is needed.

In the face of those problems, the classic Kohlberghian approach focuses on judgement legitimization in terms of just-unjust: his rationalist point of view, rooted in a Platonic (even more than Kantian) conception and mediated by the philosophical contractualism of Rawls (opposed, for instance, to the utilitarianism of Hare), consider moral judgement as a form of thinking to be analyzed at the level of logical coherence and formal legitimization. Kohlberg's approach neglects the problem of situation decoding: he explicitly states that moral judgement concerns only what is circumscribed by conscious experience and personal interpretation of the situation.

On the contrary, a social cognitive approach notes that 'a person's level of moral judgement may indicate the types of reasons likely to be most persuasive to that person, but it does not ensure a particular kind of conduct...different people can arrive at different judgements from the same principle of justness, depending on what factors they consider relevant and how they weight them' (Bandura, 1991): but it does not give account for the evidence of a development in moral judgement with age and experience, and for the effect of such development on behavior.

On the basis of those considerations, we think that two problems have to be faced in the study of moral judgement:

- on the one hand, moral judgement has to be analyzed not only by a stage-driven codifying system, but also at a more 'ecologically social' level, by analyzing semantic aspects of reasoning about problems
- on the other hand, moral judgement has to be studied as an ability which has some roots in the quality of basic social relationship and trust, and is supported and enhanced by social discussion.

Regarding this second aspect, we think that the working group is a context that contributes to the aim of enhancing moral reasoning and expression. We mean a context where people are at liberty to form an opinion, to justify it, and to come to terms with possible objections; it is something the young person (and especially a young gifted) learns as a member of a relaxed discourse community, where the young can experience directly what it means to be involved in the ongoing communication process based on real life experiences.

In the working group, the moral discourse involves the goal of coming to a justified agreement, that is, an agreement shared by those concerned, beyond the 'prima facie[2] duties'. Group discussion focuses rational justification of values. During the discussion of moral dilemmas, persons are asked to put into discussion their choices: those are not simply accepted, but must be justified: behind the tolerance for different ways of reasoning, there is a clear understanding that moral criteria are not equally sustainable in the discussion, both on a intellectual basis and on affective-emotional basis.

Intellectually gifted children and adolescents are mainly open to this kind of intervention, as they can better recognize the value of a good reasoning context. Nevertheless, social and emotional aspects also have to be considered: developing good basic relationships, identifying with positive adult models, being exposed to language, discourses and values giving meaning to life.

A specific giftedness in social relationship management could and should be fostered: this should include moral judgement ability and general moral development. Special attention to this aspect should give a broader education to the gifted and favor a more open and positive social representation and social appreciation of the gifted.

References

Addad, M. & Leslau, A. (1990). Immoral judgement, extraversion, neuroticism, and criminal behaviour. *International Journal of Offender Therapy and Comparative Criminology*, **34** (1), 1–13.

Andreani Dentici, O. (1975). *Le radici psicologiche del talento*. Bologna: Il Mulino.

Andreani Dentici O. & Pagnin A. (1992), Moral reasoning in gifted adolescents: cognitive level and social values, *European Journal for High Ability*, **3** (1), 105–114.

Andreani Dentici, O. & Pagnin, A. (1993). Moral judgement in creative and talented adolescents. Special Issue: creativity in the moral domain. *Creativity Research Journal*, **6** (1–2), 45–63.

Andreani Dentici, O. & Pagnin A. (1993b). Nurturing moral development for gifted. In: K. A. Heller, F. J. Monks, & A. H. Passow (Eds.), *International Handbook of Research and Development of Giftedness and Talent* (556–605). Oxford: Pergamon Press.

Andreani Dentici, O. & Pagnin A. (1994). Due modalità di giudizio morale nel'adolescenza. *Psicologia e Società*, **23** (44/3), 23–49

Andreani Dentici, O. & Pagnin, A. (1996) Moral reasoning in gifted adolescents. In: A. J. Cropley, D. Dehn (Eds.), *Fostering the Growth of High Ability: European Perspectives*. Norwood, N.J.: Ablex Publishing Company.

Andreani Dentici, O., Pagnin, A. & Zanetti, A. (1995). Advanced reasoning in gifted adolescents: stages and strategies. In: F. Monks & M. Katzko (Eds.), *Nurturing Talent*. Assen: Van Gorcum.

Aronfreed, J. (1968). *Conduct and conscience*. New York: Academic Press.

Bandura, A. (1977). *Social learning theory*. Englewood Cliffs, NJ: Prentice-Hall.

Bandura, A. (1991). Social cognitive theory of moral thought and action. In: W. Kurtines & J. Gewirtz (Eds.), *Handbook of Moral Behavior and Development*, Vol. I (pp. 46–103). Hillsdale, N.J.: L. Erlbaum.

Bandura, A. & McDonald, F. (1963). Influence of social reinforcement and the behavior of models in shaping children's moral judgement. *Journal of Abnormal and Social Psychology*, 67.

Basinger, K. S., Gibbs, J. C., Fuller, D. (1995). Context and the measurement of moral judgment. *International Journal of Behavioral Development*, **18** (3), 537–556.

Baumrind, D. (1986). Sex differences in moral reasoning: response to Walker's conclusion that there are none. *Child Development*, **57**, 511–521.

Beck, R. J. & Wood, D. (1993). The dialogic socialization of aggression in a family's court of reason and inquiry. *Discourse Processes*, **16** (3), 341–362.

Berkowitz, M. W. (1985). The role of discussion in moral education. In: M. W. Berkowitz & F. Oser (Eds.), *Moral Education: Theory and Application* (pp. 197–218). Hillsdale (NJ): Erlbaum.

Blakeney, R. A. & Blakeney, C. D.(1992). Growing pains: a theory of stress and moral conflict. *Counseling and Values*, **36** (3), 162–175.

Blasi, A. (1980). Bridging moral cognition and moral action: a critical review of the literature. *Psychological Bulletin*, **88**, 1–45.

Blasi, A. (1985). The moral personality: Reflections for social science and education. In: M. . Berkowitz & F. Oser (Eds.), *Moral Education: Theory and Application* (pp. 433–443). Hillsdale (NJ): Erlbaum.

Bush, A. J., Krebs, D. L., Carpendale, J. I. (1993). The structural consistency of moral judgments about AIDS. *Journal of Genetic Psychology*, **154** (2), 167–175.

Buzzelli, C. A. (1992). Popular and rejected children's social reasoning: Linking social status and social knowledge. *Journal of Genetic Psychology*, **153** (3), 331–342.

Carpendale, J. I., Krebs, D. L. (1995) Variations in level of moral judgement as a function of type of dilemma and moral choice. *Journal of Personality*, **63** (2), 289–313.

Colby A. & Kohlberg L. (1987). *The measurement of moral judgement*, Vol. 1. New York: Cambridge University Press.

Coles, R. (1997). *The moral intelligence of children*. New York: Random House.

---

[2] Literally: 'at first glance'; the philosopher Hare uses this expression to underline the presence of immediate forms of judgement, based on personal and social experience, prior to more complex processes of moral evaluation.

Cortese, A. J. (1989). Structural consistency in moral judgement. *British Journal of Social Psychology*, **28** (3), 279–281.

Crichton, J. (1997). The response of nursing staff to psychiatric inpatient misdemeanour. *Journal of Forensic Psychiatry*, **8** (1), 36–61.

Damon W. (1977). *The social world of the child*. San Francisco: Jossey-Bass.

Denton, K. & Krebs, D. (1990). From the scene to the crime: the effect of alcohol and social context on moral judgement. *Journal of Personality and Social Psychology*, **59** (2), 242–248.

Dollinger, S. J. & LaMartina, A. K. (1998). A note on moral reasoning and the five-factor model. *Journal of Social Behavior & Personality*. **13**, 349–358.

Enzle, M. E. & Hawkins, W. L. (1992). A priori actor negligence mediates a posteriori outcome effects on moral judgement. *Journal of Experimental Social Psychology*, **28** (2), 169–185.

Erickson, B., Colby, S., Libbey, P., Lohmann, G. (1976). The young adolescent: a curriculum to promote psychological growth. In: G. D.Miller (Ed.), *Developmental Education*. St. Paul, MN: Minnesota University.

Erikson, E. (1958). *Young man Luther*. New York: Norton.

Eysenck, H. J. (1976). The biology of morality. In: T. Lickona (Ed.), *Moral Development and Behavior* (pp. 108–123). New York: Holt, Rinehart & Winston.

Finger, W., Borduin, C. M. & Baumstark, K. E. (1992). Correlates of moral judgement development in college students. *Journal of Genetic Psychology*, **153** (2), 221–223.

Foster, V. & Sprinthall, N. A. (1992). Developmental profiles of adolescents and young adults choosing abortion: stage sequence, decalage, and implications for policy. *Adolescence*, **27** (107), 655–673.

Freeman, J. (1985). Emotional aspects of giftedness. In: J. Freeman (Ed.), *The Psychology of Gifted Children*. New York: Wiley.

Freeman, J. (1991). *Gifted children growing up*. Portsmouth, NH: Heinemann.

Freud, S. (1923). Das Ich und das Es. *Gesammelte Werke*, Vol. 13.

Garmon, L. C., Basinger, K. S., Gregg, V. R. & Gibbs, J. C. (1996). Gender differences in stage and expression of moral judgment. *Merrill-Palmer Quarterly*, **42** (3), 418–437.

Gibson, D. R. (1990). Personality correlates of logical and sociomoral judgement. *Journal of Personality and Social Psychology*, **59** (6), 1296–1300.

Gilligan C. (1982). *In a different voice: psychological theory and women's development*. Cambridge, MA.: Harvard University Press.

Gilligan C., Ward J. V. & Mclean Taylor J. (1988). *Mapping the moral domain*. Cambridge, MA.: Harvard University Press.

Goleman, D. (1995). *Emotional intelligence*.

Gregg, V., Gibbs, J. C. & Basinger, K. S. (1994). Patterns of developmental delay in moral judgment by male and female delinquents. *Merrill-Palmer Quarterly*, **40** (4) 538–553.

Hague, W. J. (1998). Is there moral giftedness? *Gifted Education International*, **12**, 170–174.

Haidt, J., Koller, S. H. & Dias, M. G. (1993). Affect, culture, and morality, or is it wrong to eat your dog? *Journal of Personality and Social Psychology*, **65** (4), 613–628.

Hart, D. & Chmiel, S. (1992) Influence of defense mechanisms on moral judgement development: a longitudinal study. *Developmental Psychology*, **28** (4), 722–730.

Hart, D. & Fegley, S. (1995). Prosocial behavior and caring in adolescence: relations to self-understanding and social judgement. *Child Development*, **66** (5), 1346–1359.

Heller, K. A. (1992). Goals, methods and results of the Munich longitudinal study of giftedness. *European Journal for High Ability*, **3** (1).

Hoffman, M. L. (1977). Moral internalization. In: L. Berkowitz (Ed.), *Advances in Experimental Social Psychology*: Vol. 10. New York: Academic Press.

Hoffman, M. L. (1984). Empathy, its limitations, and its role in a comprehensive moral theory. In: W. M. Kurtines & J. L. Gewirtz, (Eds.), *Morality, Moral Behavior and Moral Development* (pp. 283–302). New York: Wiley & Sons.

Hoffman, M. L. (1991). Empathy, social cognition, and moral action. In: W. M. Kurtines & J. L. Gewirtz, (Eds.), *Handbook of Moral Behavior and Development*, Vol. 1 (pp. 275–301). Hillsdale, NJ: Erlbaum.

Janos, P. M. & Robinson, N. M. (1985). Psychosocial development in intellectually gifted children. In: F. D.Horowitz & M. O'Brien (Eds.), *The Gifted and Talented: Developmental Perspectives*. Washington, DC: American Psychological Association.

Karnes, F. & Brown K. E. (1981). Moral development and the gifted: an initial investigation. *Roeper Review*, **3**, 8–10.

Keen, C. H. (1990). Effect of a public issues program on adolescent's moral and intellectual development. In: J. C. Kendall (Ed.), *Combining Service and Learning: A Resource Book for Community and Public Service*, Vol. 1 (pp.393–404). Washington, DC: American Psychological Association.

Keller, M. & Reuss, S. (1985). Moral decision making and discourse. In: M. W. Berkowitz & F. Oser (Eds.), *Moral Education: Theory and Application* (pp. 109–123). Hillsdale (NJ): Erlbaum.

Keltikangas Jarvinen, L. (1989). Moral judgements of aggressive and non-aggressive children. *Journal of Social Psychology*, **129** (6), 733–739.

Kohlberg L. (1969). Stage and sequence: the cognitive developmental approach to socialization. In: D. A. Goslin (Ed.), *Handbook of Socialization: Theory and Research*. Chicago: Rand Mc Nally.

Kohlberg L. (1984). *The psychology of moral development*. Vol. 2: *Essays on moral development*. San Francisco: Harper & Row.

Kramer, M. & Hofmann, J. M. (1990). Die Bereitschaft zur Teilnahme an der Volkszahlung 1987: Erwartungs-werttheoretische Analysen unter Einbeziehung von Niveaus des moralischen Urteils. *Zeitschrift fur Sozialpsychologie*, **21** (1), 27–39.

Krebs, D. L., Denton, K. L., Vermeulen, S. C. & Carpendale, J. I. (1991). Structured flexibility of moral judgment. *Journal of Personality and Social Psychology*, **61** (6), 1012–1023.

Langford, P. E. (1992a). Refining a non-Kohlbergian decision-making approach to the production of justifications for moral judgements. *Psychological Reports*, **71** (3), 883–895.

Langford, P. E. (1992b). Depth of processing during moral judgement interviews. *Genetic, Social, and General Psychology Monographs*, **118** (3), 221–247.

Martijn, C., Spears, R., Van der Pligt, J., Jakobs, E. (1992). Negativity and positivity effects in person perception and inference: ability versus morality. Special Issue: Positive-negative asymmetry in affect and evaluations: Part I. *European Journal of Social Psychology*, **22** (5), 453–463.

Mason, M. G. & Gibbs, J. C. (1993). Social perspective taking and moral judgement among college students. *Journal of Adolescent Research*, **8** (1), 109–123.

May, L., Friedman, M. & Clark, A. (Eds.). (1996) *Mind and morals: essays on cognitive science and ethics*. Cambridge, MA: MIT Press.

McIntyre, R. P., Capen, M. & Minton, A. P. (1995). Exploring the psychological foundations of ethical positions in marketing. *Psychology and Marketing*, **12** (6), 569–583.

Miller, J. G. & Bersoff, D. M. (1992). Culture and moral judgment: how are conflicts between justice and interpersonal responsibilities resolved? *Journal of Personality and Social Psychology*, 62 (4), 541–554.

Miller, J. G. & Bersoff, D. M. (1994). Cultural influences on the moral status of reciprocity and the discounting of endogenous motivation. *Personality and Social Psychology Bulletin*, **20** (5), 592–602.

Miller, J. G., Luthar, S. (1989). Issues of interpersonal responsibility and accountability: a comparison of Indians' and Americans' moral judgements. *Social-Cognition*, **7** (3), 237–261.

Narvaez, D. (1993). High achieving students and moral judgement. *Journal for the Education of the Gifted*, **16** (3), 268–279.

Pagnin, A. & Bajoni, A. (1997). Le parole della morale: aspetti lessicali della rappresentazione della colpa e del dovere in giovani con difficoltà sociofamiliari. In: A. Scopesi & M. Zanobini (Eds.), *Processi Comunicativi e Linguistici Nei Bambini e Negli Adulti* (pp. 291–309). Milano: Angeli.

Pagnin, A. & Zanetti, M. A. (1997). *Moral development: an educational program in the PLUS project*. ECHA International Conference, Wien.

Perry, C. M. & McIntire, W. G. (1995). Modes of moral judgement among early adolescents. *Adolescence*, **30** (119), 707–715.

Piaget J. (1932). *Le jugement moral chez l'enfant*. Paris: Alcan.

Przygotski, N. & Mullet, E. (1993). Relationships between punishment, damage, and intent to harm in the incarcerated: an information integration approach. *Social Behavior and Personality*, 21 (2), 93–102.

Rawls, J. (1971). *A theory of justice*. Cambridge, MA: Harvard University Press.

Reiter, T. S, & Hiddemann, W. (1997). The 'patient's forum medical ethics'. *Medizinische klinik*, **92** (9), 552–557.

Rest J. (1974). Judging the important issues in moral dilemmas: an objective measure of development, *Developmental Psychology*, **10** (4), 491–501.

Rest J. (1983). Moral development. In: P. Mussen (Ed.), *Handbook of Child Psychology*, vol. 3, New York: Wiley.

Rest J. (1984). The major components of morality. In: W. Kurtines & J. Gewirtz (Eds.), *Morality and Moral Development*. New York: Wiley.

Rest, J. R. (1986). *Moral development: advances in research and theory*. New York: Preager.

Rest, J., Deemer, D., Barnett, R., Spickelmier, J. & Volker, J. (1986). Life experiences and developmental pathways. In:

J. R. Rest (Ed.), *Moral Development: Advances in Research and Theory* (pp. 28–58). New York: Preager.

Rest, J. & Thoma, S. J. (1986). Educational programs and interventions. In: J. R. Rest (Ed.), *Moral Development: Advances in Research and Theory* (pp. 59–88). New York: Preager.

Sam, A. & Wright, I. (1988). The structure of moral reasoning in hearing-impaired students. *American Annals of the Deaf*, **133** (4), 264–269.

Sanvitale, D., Saltzstein, H. D. & Fish, M. C. (1989). Moral judgements by normal and conduct-disordered preadolescent and adolescent boys. *Merrill-Palmer Quarterly*, **35** (4), 463–481.

Sherer, M. (1998) The effect of computerized simulation games on the moral development of junior and senior high-school students. *Computers in Human Behavior*, **14**, 375–386.

Smetana, J. G. (1994). The relation between moral judgement and behavior: a social-cognitive and decision-making analysis. Commentary. *Human Development*, **37** (5), 313–318.

Smetana, J. G. & Braeges, J. L. (1990). The development of toddler's moral and conventional judgements. *Merrill-Palmer Quarterly*, **36** (3), 329–346.

Sobesky, W. E. (1983). The effects of situational factors on moral judgements. *Child Development*, **54**, 575–584.

Speicher, B. (1992). Adolescent moral judgement and perceptions of family interaction. *Journal of Family Psychology*, **6** (2), 128–138.

Spranca, M., Minsk, E. & Baron, J. (1991). Omission and commission in judgement and choice. *Journal of Experimental Social Psychology*, **27** (1), 76–105.

Stein, R. I. & Nemeroff, C. J. (1995). Moral overtones of food: judgements of others based on what they eat. *Personality and Social Psychology Bulletin*, **21** (5), 480–490.

Tan-Willman, C. & Gutteridge, D. (1981). Creative thinking and moral reasoning on academically gifted secondary school adolescents. *Gifted Child Quarterly*, **25**, 149–153.

Teo, T., Becker, G., Edelstein, W. (1995). Variability in structured wholeness: context factors in L. Kohlberg's data on the development of moral judgement. *Merrill-Palmer Quarterly*, **41** (3), 381–393.

Testa, M. A. & Simonson, D. C. (1996). 'Assessment of quality of life': Reply. *New England Journal of Medicine*, **335** (7), 521–522.

Trevethan, S. & Walker, L, J. (1989). Hypothetical versus real-life moral reasoning among psychopathic and delinquent youth, *Development and Psychopathology*, **1**, 91–103.

Villenave-Cremer, S. & Eckensberger L. H. (1985). The role of affective process in moral judgement performance. In: M. W. Berkowitz & F. Oser (Eds.), *Moral Education: Theory and Application* (pp. 175–194). Hillsdale (NJ): Erlbaum.

Wainryb, C. (1991). Understanding differences in moral judgements: the role of informational assumptions. *Child Development*, **62** (4), 840–851.

Wainryb, C. (1993). The application of moral judgements to other cultures: relativism and universality. *Child Development*, **64** (3), 924–933.

Walker, L. J. (1980). Cognitive and perspective-taking prerequisites for moral development, *Child Development*, **51**, 131–140.

Walker L. J. (1984). Sex differences in the development of moral reasoning: a critical review of the literature, *Child Development*, **55**, 677–692.

Walker, L. J. (1991). Moral reasoning: cognitive sources and cosnstraints. In: O. Andreani (Chair), *Logical and Moral Reasoning in Gifted Adolescents and Young People*. Symposium at the IX World conference on gifted and talented children, The Hague, The Netherlands.

Walker L. J., De Vries B. & Treventhan S. D. (1987). Moral stages and moral orientations in real life and hypothetical dilemmas, *Child Development*, **58**, 842–858.

Walker, L. J. & Richards, B. S. (1979). Stimulating transitions in moral reasoning as a function of stage of cognitive development. *Developmental Psychology*, **15**, 95–103.

Walker, L. J. & Taylor, J. H. (1991). Family interactions and the development of moral reasoning. *Child Development*, **62**, 264–283.

Wark, G. R. & Krebs, D. L. (1996). Gender and dilemma differences in real-life moral judgement. *Developmental Psychology*, **32** (2), 220–230.

Weber, J. (1996). Influences upon managerial moral decision making: nature of the harm and magnitude of consequences. *Human Relations*, **49** (1), 1–22.

Whiteley, J. (1982). *Character development in college students*. Schenectady, NY: Character Education Press.

Willging, T. E. & Dunn, T. G. (1982). The moral development of law students. *Journal of Legal Education*, **31**, 306–358.

Wolf, Y., Friedlander, M., Addad, M. & Silfen, P. (1995). Moral judgement among incarcerated offenders from a psychotherapeutic background. *International Journal of Offender Therapy and Comparative Criminology*, **39** (3), 242–257.

Wygant, S. A. & Williams, R. N. (1995). Perceptions of a principled personality: an interpretative examination of the Defining Issues Test. *Journal of Social Behavior and Personality*, **10** (1), 53–66.

Zelazo, P. D., Helwig, C. & Lau, A. (1996). Intention, act, and outcome in behavioral prediction and moral judgement. *Child Development*, **67** (5), 2478–2492.

Programs and Strategies for Nurturing Creativity

Arthur J. Cropley[1] and Klaus K. Urban[2]

[1]*University of Hamburg, Germany*
[2]*University of Hanover, Germany*

Creativity and Giftedness

Almost from the beginning, modern research on creativity, intelligence, and achievement showed that although, as a group, students with high IQs obtained good grades both at school and university, they were consistently outstripped by those with not only a high IQ but also high creativity (e.g. Cropley, 1967a, 1967b). In Sierwald's later (1989) longitudinal study, students with high creativity surpassed those merely high on intelligence at all levels of school. Hudson (1968) showed that students admitted to Cambridge University on the basis of a creativity test graduated with grades equal to those of students selected on the basis of extraordinarily good high school marks. Gibson & Light (1967) and Bayer & Folger (1966) found that many gifted scientists had IQs below 130. More recently, Facaoaru (1985) showed that gifted engineers displayed not only high ability in knowing, recognizing, recalling and reapplying, but also in seeing possibilities, discovering problems, branching out, or inventing. Taken together, these findings indicate that a combination of intelligence and creativity defines giftedness. This is already the case by Grade 7, and increases through school, university and later career.

In accordance with this conclusion, creativity and intelligence will be regarded here as integral elements of giftedness. Referring to research in the former Soviet Union, Matyushkin (1990) supported this approach. Writing in a Western European context, Cropley (1995) regarded creativity as indispensable for 'true' giftedness, and in the United States Sternberg & Lubart (1995) concluded that 'contrarianism' (a combination of cognition, motivation and personality) is a characteristic of all gifted individuals. Hassenstein (1988) argued that a new term is needed to refer to intellectual giftedness, since 'intelligence' is too narrow, and suggested *Klugheit* (cleverness), arguing that this incorporates both intelligence (e.g. factual knowledge, accurate observation, good memory, logical thinking, and speed of information processing) and creativity (e.g. inventiveness, unusual associations, fantasy, and flexibility).

Ward, Saunders & Dodds (1999) identified two major approaches to conceptualizing the relationship between giftedness and creativity: According to Renzulli's 'three ring' approach (e.g. 1986), creativity and intelligence – together with motivation – are separate *sub-components* of giftedness. By contrast, according to the *overlapping skills* model gifted achievement and creativity require some of the same cognitive skills such as problem definition, selective encoding, shifting context, or transcending limitations (Finke, Ward & Smith, 1992; Sternberg & Lubart, 1995). Cropley (1999a) adopted a somewhat different approach, arguing that *production of novelty* (the central element of creativity) is one possible 'style' for applying intellectual ability, *production of orthodoxy* (at the core of intelligence) another. These two styles are possible at all levels of ability, so that the difference is qualitative rather than quantitative. Production of novelty leads to gifted achievement when the novelty is 'effective'. Such achievement has a quantitative aspect, since high levels of specific and general knowledge, a strongly developed connection to reality, well-grounded self-evaluation, a superior grasp of what the surrounding environment can tolerate, and a high level of command of a medium of expression and communication are necessary for effectiveness.

The Process of Creativity

Despite what has just been said, a definition that places less emphasis on products is particularly fruitful for discussions of creativity in children. They do not possess the years of experience that are almost always necessary for acclaimed products, even in the case of extraordinary precocious geniuses like Mozart (Howe, 1990), and, in fact, most of them will never produce acclaimed works. Calls for the fostering of creativity in the classroom should not be based on the desire to force an élite group of extraordinary children to exceptional achievements, but on the humanistic goal of fostering the fullest possible development of all children in all aspects of their personality. An approach based on the *process* of creativity rather that its products is most appropriate for this.

Producing Novelty

The only constant factor in all definitions of creativity is novelty (Morgan, 1953). This was later defined in a more psychological way by Bruner (1962) as the achieving of 'surprise' in the beholder. However, surprisingness alone is not sufficient. Genuine creativity requires two further elements: *relevance* and *effectiveness* (Bruner, 1962). Thus, creativity is nowadays widely defined as the production of relevant and effective novel ideas (Engle, Mah & Sadri, 1997; Cropley, 1999a). In addition, as Grudin (1990), among others pointed out, the purpose of fostering creativity is not self-aggrandisement or exploitation of other people, but promotion of the common good, i.e. it has an ethical element.

Solving Problems

An important aspect of problem solving is the distinction between 'solving' by eliminating a difficulty or removing an impediment and 'solving' in the sense of envisaging, posing or formulating questions that need to be raised in order to deal more effectively or elegantly with an existing situation. The latter is referred to as 'problem finding', and is proactive and constructive rather than reactive and destructive, since it involves bringing into existence a new way of looking at the issue in question. Tardiff & Sternberg (1988) stressed the importance in creativity of *sensitivity to problems*, especially finding 'good' problems. This is more closely related to creativity (see above) than 'merely' solving them (Jay & Perkins, 1997). A striking example (Fromm, 1998) is Einstein's recognition that existing theories of electrodynamics were inadequate, which led to the theories of relativity. A further aspect of creative problem solving involves the ability to *recognize a solution* (e.g. Ghiselin, 1955), even if it falls outside traditional boundaries.

Teachers are accustomed to specifying the problems on which students are to work, laying down the procedures to be used in solving the problems, and defining the criteria for deciding on the value of solutions. However, creative students need to take responsibility for at least some of these aspects. One attempt to promote creativity through problem solving is Creative Problem Solving (CPS) which has a long tradition in the United States (Feldhusen (1993), and has widely and successfully been applied since Parnes (1967). It involves the following steps:

(1) Mess finding
(2) Data finding
(3) Problem finding
(4) Idea finding

(5) Solution finding
(6) Acceptance finding.

What Must be Fostered?

Appropriate Thinking Skills and Strategies

The initial approach to describing creative thinking was based on Guilford's (1950) distinction between convergent thinking (finding the single best answer) and divergent thinking (generating alternative possibilities). Subsequently, the process of branching out was described in terms of remote associations to stimuli (Mednick, 1962), or linking domains of meaning (e.g. 'bisociation'; Koestler, 1964). In the present chapter, thinking is regarded as a process that uses existing information to produce further information. In the case of creativity, this further information contains effective novelty. This involves *analyzing* the particular form of the problem, *selecting* from among the masses of information available at any moment, *relating* new information to what is already known, *combining* elements of new and old information, *evaluating* newly emerging combinations, *selectively retaining* successful combinations, and *communicating* the results to others.

Although some authors argue that novel combinations result from random associations (e.g. Simonton, 1988), Resnick (1987) emphasized that thinking must be guided by 'executive' processes. Otherwise, creativity would become blind trial and error. A related approach focuses on 'heuristics'. These consist, on the one hand, of rules or techniques for recognizing from the start blind alleys or their opposite, particularly promising lines of attack, and, on the other, of evaluation skills for determing the progress that has been made and how the present approach should be altered (if this proves necessary).

Executive processes and heuristics are part of what is often referred to as 'metacognition' (Sternberg, 1988), that allows people to keep track of their own thinking. It includes review of knowledge, organization of attention, and marshalling of resources. Further metacognitive processes include defining the problem, selecting an appropriate set of processes for solving it, and combining these into a workable strategy. To these can be added evaluation of one's own progress, effective changing of course should the evaluation make this necessary, and identifying of one or more promising alternatives.

Martinson (1995) identified two 'strategic dispositions' in thinking: Some people consistently seek to deal with the new by reapplying existing knowledge and solution strategies, whereas others recognize the need for new ways of dealing with new situations. The nature of this disposition can be clarified by borrowing from Piaget and emphasizing *assimilation* and *accommodation*. Assimilation involves fitting new information in with existing cognitive structures, accommodation is based on recognizing that current structures are not adequate. Intuitively, production of novelty (creativity) is related to accommodating, sticking to the known (intelligence) to assimilating.

General and Specific Knowledge

Broad general experience leads to *knowledge*, often obtained outside school and possibly without conscious awareness. This serves as a source of ideas, and is thus favorable to the production of novelty. Thus, linking learning outside the classroom with school learning enhances the chances of creativity. However, thinking alone will not lead to creative excellence, since creativity does not occur in a vacuum but in a particular field: Guilford himself pointed out that divergent thinking seems not to be a general trait, but changes with different contents and specific tasks. Brown (1989) emphasized that area-relevant knowledge and skills are fundamental to creativity. Walberg & Stariha (1992) also emphasized the central role in creativity of relevant knowledge, accompanied by sensitivity to gaps in this knowledge. Henle (1974) regarded the urge to fill such gaps constructively or elegantly as the primary motivation for creativity. In keeping with this view, increasing attention is being given nowadays to domain-specific knowledge—what Feldhusen (1995) called the 'knowledge base'—as a prerequisite for generating creative ideas and products.

These findings indicate that fostering creativity in schoolchildren would require promotion of:

- rich and varied experience in many different settings
- a fund of general knowledge
- specialized knowledge
- an active imagination
- analyzing and synthesizing skills
- skill at seeing connections, overlaps, similarities and logical implications (convergent thinking)
- skill at making remote associations, linking apparently separate fields (bisociating), and forming new gestalts (divergent thinking)
- preference for accommodating rather than assimilating
- ability to recognize and define problems
- ability to plan one's own learning and evaluate progress (executive or metacognitive abilities).

Creativity Facilitating Personality Factors

Reviews of the relevant research (e.g. Eysenck, 1997) typically list autonomy, non-conformity, openness to stimuli, flexibility, tolerance of ambiguity, inner directedness, and ego strength, among others, as favorable for creativity. However, Helson (1996) concluded that there is no unitary personality profile that is both typical of highly creative people as a group and also distinguishes them from the less creative. According to an early study (McMullan, 1978), creativity requires possession of a 'paradoxical' personality. This is characterized by 'polarities' such as openness com-

bined with drive to close incomplete gestalts or acceptance of fantasy combined with maintenance of a strong sense of reality. More recently Csikszentmihalyi (1996) emphasized the importance of a 'complex' personality, combining, among others, sensitivity with toughness, or high intelligence with naivité. Striking is that the personality characteristics regarded as important for creativity are often contradictory: for instance, the creative personality is simultaneously stereotypically 'masculine' (autonomous, self-confident, tough) and yet stereotypically 'feminine' (sensitive, intuitive, responsible). These findings imply that both rigid maintenance of strict gender roles as well as insistence on a well-balanced or harmonious personality would inhibit creativity. An 'integration of opposites' (Urban, 1995a, 1997) seems necessary.

Fostering creativity thus requires promotion in children of:

- openness to new ideas and experiences
- adventurousness
- autonomy
- ego strength
- positive self-evaluation and high self-esteem
- acceptance of all (even contradictory) aspects of one's own self
- preference for complexity
- tolerance for ambiguity.

Motivation for Creativity

It is intuitively obvious that the acquisition of comprehensive and detailed area-specific knowledge and skills (see earlier discussions of the knowledge base) requires disciplined task commitment and a high level of persistence. The problem in question and the connecting thematic field have to be maintained as the focus of attention over a long period of time and with varying intensity (Hayes, 1989). Concentration and selectivity are necessary for collecting, analysing, evaluating, and elaborating information and data. In fact, studies of highly creative people have demonstrated the importance of dedication almost to the point of obsession (e.g. Biermann, 1985; Csikszentmihalyi, 1988). At a more everyday level, Baldwin (1985) argued that intense motivation for activity in a particular area may be the best indicator of creativity in members of disadvantaged groups.

The creation of novelty requires readiness to diverge, defy conventional opinion, or expose oneself to the possibility of being wrong: in other words, taking risks (e.g. Williams, 1976). Basadur & Hausdorf (1996) emphasized the importance of placing a high value on new ideas. Early research in aesthetics as well as Gestalt psychology showed the importance of preference for complexity in creative people, and this was confirmed by Shaughnessy & Manz (1991).

A widely accepted position is that creativity is based on intrinsic motivation (Amabile, 1996), the wish to carry out an activity for the sake of the activity itself. This can be contrasted with working for external rewards, such as praise, prizes, even avoidance of punishment (extrinsic motivation). More recently, however, the possibility of fostering creativity in the classroom by the application of external rewards has been demonstrated by Eisenberger & Armeli (1997). They showed that extrinsic reward led to enduring improvements even in a creative area such as music, when children were rewarded for specific 'creative' behaviors such as incorporating unexpected elements or producing alternative possibilities. Thus, children need a clearly-defined concept of creativity.

Cropley & Cropley (2000) extended this by showing that engineering students who received a concrete definition of what was meant by 'creative' in a particular class, and were counselled individually on the basic of a personal profile of their own specific strengths and weaknesses, were more original on creativity tests, and built more creative models in a laboratory exercise, despite the fact that they were working for grades.

The findings just presented suggest that teachers should seek to foster in students

- a concept of creativity and a positive attitude to it
- curiosity
- willingness to risk being wrong
- drive to experiment
- task commitment, persistence and determination
- willingness to try difficult tasks
- desire for novelty
- freedom from domination by external rewards (intrinsic motivation)
- readiness to accept a challenge
- readiness for risktaking.

A Supportive Environment

A product must be communicated to other people and at least tolerated by them ('sociocultural validation') if it is to be acclaimed as creative. What Csikszentmihalyi (1996) called a 'congenial' environment is vital. In schools, this means that the atmosphere or climate of the classroom is of major importance. Where the teacher and classmates reject differentness or non-standard solutions, the environment will inhibit creativity.

The result is that creativity requires on the part of the creator:
- independence and nonconformity
- knowledge of the social rules
- courage
- ability to communicate.

On the part of the social environment, creativity requires:

- acceptance of differentness

- openness and tolerance of variability
- renunciation of rigid sanctions against (harmless) mistakes
- provision of a 'creativogenic' climate.

Creativity Fostering Teacher Behavior

Early in the modern era, Feldhusen & Treffinger (1975) reported that 96% of teachers believed that creativity should be fostered in the classroom. However, even in Grade 2, children who scored highest on tests of creativity were rated by their classmates as the ones most often in trouble with their teachers (Stone, 1980). In fact, studies both in the United States and elsewhere have shown that many teachers dislike the characteristics and behaviors associated with creativity (e.g. Howieson, 1984; Obuche, 1986), despite their theoretical support of it. Nonetheless, 'creativity fostering' teachers are particularly good at promoting students' creativity (Cropley, 1992). They provide a model of creative behavior, reinforce such behavior when pupils display it, protect creative pupils from conformity pressure, and establish a classroom climate that permits alternative solutions, tolerates constructive errors, encourages effective surprise, and does not isolate nonconformers.

Clark's (1996) research on teachers who had been rated as particularly successful with gifted children made a direct link between giftedness and creativity: These teachers, among other things, emphasized 'creative production', showed 'flexibility', accepted 'alternative suggestions', encouraged 'expression of ideas', and tolerated 'humor'. They were themselves creative, and had stronger personal contacts with their students.

Creativity fostering teachers are those who:

- encourage students to learn independently
- have a cooperative, socially integrative style of teaching
- do not neglect mastery of factual knowledge
- delay judgment of students' ideas
- encourage flexible thinking
- tolerate 'sensible' errors
- promote self-evaluation
- take questions seriously
- offer opportunities to work with varied materials under different conditions
- help students learn to cope with frustration and failure
- reward courage as much as being right.

Instructional Resources for Fostering Creativity

Treffinger, Sortore & Cross (1993; first edition of this handbook) reported in excess of 250 published materials that can be regarded as instructional resources for fostering creativity. Huczynski's (1983) encyclopedia of methods listed dozens that could be applied to nurturing creativity in schoolchildren, including 'buzz groups', 'flexastudy', 'lateral thinking', and 'mathetics'.

Some consist of simple, specific games, such as 'bridge building', 'idea production', or 'creative connections' (Cropley, 1992). Others involve mental techniques that can be learned quickly and then applied in a wide variety of settings as general ways of getting ideas, such as the *SCAMPER* procedure, originally developed by Osborn. This approach assumes that production of novelty simply involves changing what already exists, and includes seven change techniques: substituting, combining, adapting, magnifying, putting to a different use, eliminating and rearranging/reversing.

Other procedures are more formal, but still consist of specific procedures that can be learned and then applied in many different situations, usually in order to get ideas (e.g. *Synectics, Brainstorming, Morphological Methods, Bionics, Imagery Training, Mind Maps*, the *KJ Method*, or the *NM Method*). Most of these are described by Torrance (1992) or Michalko (1998). Although they are suitable for use with schoolchildren, they are often applied in business, for instance in product development, or in advertising.

Probably the best known of all these is *Brainstorming* (Osborn, 1953), which has become the prototype for a number of related techniques. 'Classical' *Brainstorming* is a group activity in which each member is encouraged to put forward ideas without any constraints, no matter how implausible the idea. Criticism is not permitted, because of its inhibitory effect. Quantity of ideas is important, rather than quality, and 'hitchhiking' by attaching one's ideas to those of others is encouraged. There are various procedures for selecting, recording, testing and otherwise ultimately relating ideas to reality. In the *KJ Method*, individual members of the group write on cards their ideas for defining the core of the problem at hand (one idea per card). The cards are then sorted into 'sets', i.e. groups of cards containing similar statements defining the nature of the problem, and the different sets are given labels which summarize the essence of the problem. Sets of solutions are then constructed in a similar way.

Some procedures retain the idea of unhindered production, but go beyond simple 'blind' generating of ideas. In *Mindmaps*, for instance, the central theme is written down and then a 'spray' of associations recorded, each association functioning as the beginning of a new spray of further associations. Solutions are found by identifying patterns or threads found in the masses of associations. The *Hierarchical Method* (e.g. Butler & Kline, 1998) involves an even stronger element of organization and structure. Although the idea of generating large numbers of possible solutions is retained, this approach is based on the idea that a hierarchical organization of ideas (rather than simple masses of ideas or associational chains) produces

solutions of better quality. Suggested solutions are sorted into classes on the basis of common content. Subsequently, hierarchies can be formed by combining lower level classes into superordinate classes, or by contrast, by breaking down higher order classes into lower level categories.

Many of the instructional resources now available involve *programs*—often based on a model of creativity, and sometimes with substantial special materials—that are used systematically over a period of at least several weeks (for instance, a school term or year) with the intention of inculcating a general disposition to be creative. (Such programs often include training in various techniques.) The United States Patent and Trademark Office (1990) listed about 25 such packages, and Treffinger, Sortore and Cross briefly described a number of them. A number of examples of programs of this kind are summarized in Table 1.

Popular and Commercial Programs

In addition to more scientific works on fostering creativity, there is a substantial number of semi-scientific or popular publications with essentially commercial goals aimed at organizations (business/commerce, the armed forces, government) and individuals (adults interested in self-help, teachers, parents). Many of these were developed by practitioners, not necessarily researchers or even traditional educators. Probably the best known are deBono's publications, in which he has elaborated the concept of 'lateral thinking' (e.g. deBono, 1970). Originally a medical practitioner, he has developed not only a graphic and picturesque terminology (e.g. 'water' and 'rock' logic), but has also published the *CoRT Thinking Program* (deBono, 1978), a set of strategies for creative thinking that has been widely applied in business and education. Michalko (e.g. 1996, 1998), a former officer in the U.S. Army, has recently become prominent in the USA, with programs such as *Thinkertoys* (aimed at nurturing business creativity), or *Cracking Creativity* (self-training).

Such books are often based on scholarly findings, even if the connection is sometimes loose. They are frequently technically well-produced, extremely readable, easy to understand, and plausible. In addition, they often contain sensible and humane advice with which very few people would disagree, and many of them are undoubtedly capable of bringing benefits.

However, there are problems with much of this popular literature, and these were summarized by Hruby (1999)—he was reviewing a specific book, but his comments are very pertinent and can be applied here in a more general way. He complained that enthusiasm for educational reform can 'run away with itself' (1999, p. 326). Among other weaknesses, he identified: presenting speculations, conjectures and hypotheses as established facts; confusing correlations

Table 1. Main characteristics of well-known creativity programs.

Program	Level	Materials	Aimed at Promoting
Imagi/Craft	Elementary School	Dramatized recordings of great moments in the lives of famous inventors and discoverers	• The feeling that their own ideas are important • Widened horizons • Career aspirations of a creative kind
Purdue Creative Thinking Program	Fourth Grade	Audiotapes and accompanying printed exercises	• Verbal and figural fluency, flexibility, originality, and elaboration
Productive Thinking Program	Fifth and Sixth Grades	Booklets containing cartoons. Uses principles of programmed instruction	• Problem-solving abilities • Attitudes to problem solving
Myers-Torrance Workbooks	Elementary School	Workbooks containing exercises	• Perceptual and cognitive abilities needed for creativity
Creative Problem Solving	All Levels	No special materials. Makes great use of Brainstorming	• Finding problems • Collecting data • Finding ideas • Finding solutions • Implementing solutions
Talents Unlimited	All Levels	Workbooks based on idea of 'inventive thinking', aimed at problem solving Emphasis on Brainstorming	• Thinking productively • Communicating • Planning • Making decisions • Forecasting
Khatena Training Method	Adults and Children	No special materials—Simple teacher-made aids	• Breaking away from the obvious • Transposing ideas • Seeing analogies • Restructing information • Synthesizing ideas
Osborne-Parnes Program	High School and College Level	No special materials Primary emphasis on Brainstorming,	• Getting many ideas • Separating idea generation and idea evaluation
Clapham-Schuster Program	College Level	No special materials Relaxation exercises Definition of creativity as involving combining ideas Brainstorming, Synectics, etc	• Getting ideas • Understanding creativity • Using metacognitive techniques (setting goals, expecting success, coping with failure)

with causal relationships; making unjustified sweeping generalizations that are either not unequivocally supported by research or are even contradicted by some findings; drawing unwarranted conclusions about the implications of research findings for practice; failing to understand the factors that inhibit conversion of admirable recommendations into practice. Some popular books proclaim incompletely digested research findings as containing a 'revolutionary' panacea that can be applied in a set way in any and all situations, without taking account of the individuals involved, the special characteristics of the situation, or the personal or structural factors facilitating or impeding imple-

mentation of good practice. We recommend moderation, flexibility and sensitivity in their use.

The Need for a Holistic Approach to Fostering Creativity

From almost the beginning, doubts have been expressed about whether procedures for fostering creativity really achieve what they set out to do (e.g. Mansfield, Busse & Krepelka, 1978). Wallach (1985) showed that effects are very specific. Treffinger, Sortore and Cross came to the conclusion that it has not been shown that there are clearly-definable effects of creativity training on specific cognitive or personal characteristics, for instance that particular programs foster specific aspects of children's psychological development, or that children with one particular psychological profile benefit from a specific program, whereas other children need a different one.

Although later programs include knowledge, problem solving and decision making (Treffinger, Sortore & Cross, 1993), Cropley (1997a) argued that they still concentrate overwhelmingly on the cognitive aspects of creativity, even if factors such as self-concept or positive attitudes to problem solving are sometimes considered (see Table 1). He criticized the narrowness in the conceptualization of creativity inherent in the programs, and called for an integrative, holistic approach, as also did Urban (e.g. 1997).

Treffinger, Sortore & Cross also stressed the importance of what they called the "full 'ecological system' of creativity" (1993, p. 560). This involves recognition of creativity's interaction with other psychological properties of the individual, aspects of the creative process, effects of the situation, characteristics of the task itself, and the nature of the desired product. They concluded that it is possible to foster creativity in this 'ecological' or 'interactionist' sense, but that the factors just mentioned must be specified.

Cropley (1999b) called for 'differential diagnosis' of creativity, and suggested that the different kinds of creativity tests that are now emerging could provide the tools for this. Table 2 shows the theoretically possible combinations of knowledge, thinking, motivation and personal properties. A plus sign indicates a favorable state for creativity, a minus sign an unfavorable one.

Column 1 depicts a child in whom all four elements are favorably developed, and represents 'fully realized' creativity, Column 2 describes a child in whom the personal properties are unfavorable ('stifled' creativity), Column 3 a child in whom motivation is missing ('abandoned' creativity), and Column 4 a child without the necessary thinking skills ('frustrated' creativity). Children with different combinations of psychological prerequisites would require different emphases in procedures to nurture their creativity: For example, where only motivation is lacking (Column 3), a different approach would be needed in comparison with a child who was highly motivated but lacking in openness, flexibility and self-confidence (Column 2).

In order to base programs on the full ecological system of creativity, it will be necessary to specify: (a) the factors that are involved in the development of children's capacity to be creative (for instance, abilities, motivation, personal properties, and positive social conditions); (b) the nature of the interactions among these factors; (c) the nature of the creative process. The analysis of the process needs to be capable of integrating research findings showing the simultaneous importance of conflicting factors such as divergent and convergent thinking, intrinsic and extrinsic motivation, or apparently contradictory personality characteristics. An appropriate model is presented below.

A Comprehensive Theoretical Framework for Fostering Creativity

The Componential Model of Creativity

Urban's (1990) components model specifies the relationships among characteristics of the learner and the setting. It is based on six components, each with a set of subcomponents that work together for and in the creative process, within a framework of environmental conditions (see Fig. 1). The first three components, which are cognitive in nature, are:

(1) Divergent thinking and acting
(2) General knowledge and a thinking base
(3) A specific knowledge base and area specific skills.

The other three components, representing personality, are:

(4) Focusing and task commitment
(5) Motivation and motives
(6) Openness and tolerance of ambiguity.

The model (for more detail see Urban, 1990, 1994, 1995a, 1997) emphasizes that the elements of creativity form an interacting, mutually dependent system. A simple example is that divergent, associational thinking is linked with deep domain-specific knowledge, broad, open perception, and networking in the processing and storing of information. Other related subcomponents are the resistance to group pressure that is necessary for non-conformist behavior and autonomy of thinking, at least at certain times and in certain settings (such as the classroom). Readiness to take risks permits remote

Table 2. Possible combinations of psychological prerequisites for creativity..

| | Possible Combinations | | | | | | | | | | | | | | | |
	1	2	3	4	5	6	7	8	9	10	11	12	13	14	15	16
Knowledge	+	+	+	+	−	−	−	−	+	+	+	+	−	−	−	−
Thinking Skills	+	+	+	−	+	+	−	−	−	−	−	+	+	+	−	−
Motivation	+	+	−	+	+	−	+	−	−	+	−	−	+	−	+	−
Personal Properties	+	−	+	+	+	+	+	+	−	−	+	−	−	−	−	−

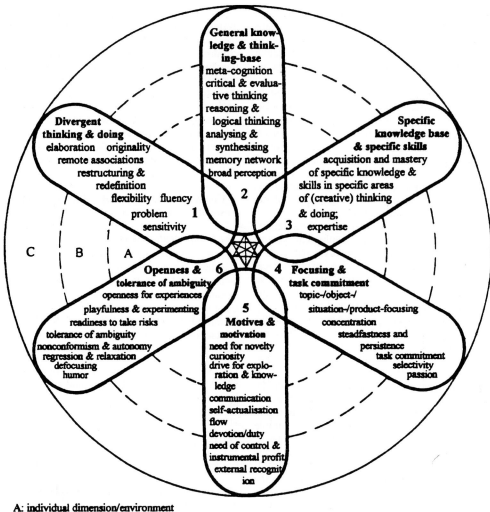

A: individual dimension/environment
B: group- or local dimension/environment
C: societal, historical, global dimension/environment

Figure 1. The componential model of creativity.

associations, playfulness and willingness to experiment go with fluency and flexibility, and tolerance of ambiguity is supported by passion.

No single component alone is sufficient or responsible for the whole creative process leading to a creative product. The (sub)components are used for, participate in, or determine the creative process to differing degrees, and work with differing subcomponents or combinations of subcomponents. Each (sub)component plays its interdependent, functionally adequate role at a certain stage or phase of the creative process, a certain level, or in a certain situation. Each component is a prerequisite for and at the same time a result of others.

The dynamics and mechanics of the componential functional system are dependent on the discouraging/inhibiting versus nurturing/stimulating/inspiring/cultivating influences of the various environmental systems in which creative individuals become active. These may be classified in a threefold way:

(1) The individual, subjective dimension, with the direct, situational, material, and social environment.
(2) The group or local dimension with family, peer group, school, local educational system (the microenvironment).

(3) The societal, historical, global dimension with the cultural, political, and scientific conditions (the macro- and meta-environment).

The Stage Model of Creativity

Cropley (1997a) focused attention on the process of creativity, emphasizing especially its 'paradoxical' nature (Cropley, 1997b). Taking Wallas's (1926) phase model as a starting point, he expanded it by adding to Wallas's phases ('Information', 'Incubation', 'Illumination', 'Verification') further stages of 'Preparation', 'Communication' and 'Validation' (see Table 3). Preparation makes the stage of problem finding more explicit. Communication and Validation are necessary because without them novelty may be produced, but cannot receive 'sociocultural validation'.

In each stage (see left hand column), psychological processes (second column) produce a psychological 'configuration' (Simonton, 1988) shown in the third column, that forms the material for the next stage. The psychological processes are made possible or at least facilitated by motivational states (fourth column) and personality characteristics (fifth column). Table 3 depicts a process culminating in a socially-validated product. The process can, however, be broken off earlier, for instance when executive or metacognitive processes indicate that the current configuration is doomed to failure. The creative process can also start part way through, for instance when a person who has in the meantime learned more returns to a configuration previously abandoned, thus restarting the process.

Dividing the emergence of effective novelty into stages, as in Table 3, aids understanding of paradoxical aspects of creativity. For instance, in the stage of information, convergent thinking, naiveté, and intrinsic motivation might be of paramount importance, whereas in the stage of illumination, divergent thinking, general knowledge and openness might predominate, or in that of verification, toughness, courage, extrinsic motivation, specific knowledge and convergent thinking. Rather than pursuing a vague, global goal of 'fostering creativity', teachers need to be aware of which aspects of creativity they wish to promote, and which particular activity is likely to do this, while students need to understand in a more specific and concrete way the precise purpose of what they are learning. The extended phase model offers a framework for doing this.

Fostering Creativity in the Classroom

Teachers need to review their own practices in order to evaluate how far their teaching is suited to fostering

Table 3. The emergence of a creative product.

Stage	Process	Result	Motivation	Personality
Preparation	identifying problem setting goals convergent thinking	initial activity general knowledge special knowledge	problem-solving drive (intrinsic) hope of gain (extrinsic)	critical attitude optimism
Information	perceiving learning remembering convergent thinking	focused special knowledge rich supply of cognitive elements	curiosity preference for complexity willingness to work hard hope of gain	knowledgeability willingness to judge and select
Incubation	divergent thinking making associations bisociating building networks	configurations	freedom from constraints tolerance for ambiguity	relaxedness acceptance of fantasy nonconformity adventurousness
Illumination	recognizing a promising new configuration	novel configuration	intuition reduction of tension	sensitivity openness flexibility
Verification	checking relevance and effectiveness of novel configuration	appropriate solution displaying relevance and effectiveness	desire for closure desire to achieve quality	hardnosed sense of reality self-criticism
Communication	achieving closure gaining feedback	workable product capable of being made known to others	desire for recognition (intrinsic) desire for acclaim or reward (extrinsic)	self-confidence autonomy courage of one's convictions
Validation	judging relevance and effectiveness	product acclaimed by relevant judges (e.g. teacher)	desire for acclaim mastery drive	toughness flexibility

development of children's creative thinking, learning, and acting. In this section we provide guidelines they can refer to in order to become 'creativity fostering' teachers.

A Framework for Stocktaking

Creativity is not simply a matter of helping children get better at having as many ideas as possible in the shortest possible time. On the contrary, it involves both the whole person and all aspects of personal development as well as all phases of the creative process. The questions below are based on the components model, and provide a framework for teachers to evaluate their own classroom practices. They refer to classroom instruction at all levels.

Component 1: Divergent thinking

- Is asking questions allowed and appreciated?
- Is the teacher open and sensitive to problems raised by students?
- Does the teacher try to make children aware of open questions, sensitive to their environment, and willing to use all their senses?
- Are problems simply presented, or (to the maximum degree possible) discovered? Are preexisting answers simply presented?
- Do time and organisation allow more than one attempt at finding a solution?
- Are objects and topics considered from different aspects?
- Are phases or ways and/or goals/products kept open or shaped openly?
- Are students encouraged not always to be satisfied with the first correct solution?
- Is a 'deviant' method or solution—originality—expected and appreciated?
- In general, does anything happen (in school) that could be called 'divergent thinking'?

Or is learning nothing more than regurgitation of accumulated knowledge that has been obtained from textbooks or teachers?

Component 2: General knowledge and thinking base

- Do learning tasks require and promote broad and differentiated perception, or do they restrict focus?
- Does learning use different sensory channels and varying methods, so that experiences and knowledge may be anchored and accessible in memory storage in various ways?
- Is the structure of learning objects/subjects analysed?
- Is there a focus on the learning process, not simply on the result?
- Are solution methods questioned or optimized?
- Are 'why?' questions asked and answered, so that cause-effect relations can be studied?

- Is there instruction on systematic analysing and synthesising of problems, topics, facts, situations etc.?
- Are there challenges requiring both inductive and deductive reasoning?
- Is evaluation asked for and desired?
- Is the learning process made explicit and reflected upon with students, so that metacognitive thinking is initiated and furthered?

Component 3: Specific knowledge base and specific skills

- Is the development of special interests encouraged? For example, by additive or extracurricular provision, mentor systems, competitions, etc.?
- Are individual interests brought into or built into school work?
- Are there opportunities/possibilities for students to obtain experience via in-depth studies?
- Is both experts' and children's expertise appreciated?

Component 4: Focusing and task commitment

- Is sustained occupation with a special activity allowed or supported (for example, research work on a project carried on for the entire school year)?
- Do the timetable and school organisation support such activities?
- Is task commitment rewarded?
- Is there an expectation that tasks have to be fulfilled and brought to an end?
- Are children supported in recognizing and avoiding distractions?
- What is the role of self-evaluation and external reward?

Component 5: Motives and motivation

- Are children's questions accepted and expanded upon?
- Is the curiosity of the children stimulated and supported?
- Are there opportunities for self-directed learning and discovery learning, in order to support and promote intrinsic motivation?
- Are individual interests appreciated and supported?
- Is unnecessary repetition avoided?
- Can children identify with their work?

Component 6: Openness and tolerance of ambiguity

- Is school not only a place for traditional instruction, but a place of living, of fun, of (mental) adventure?
- Does instruction bring the real world into school, does instruction reach out into reality?
- Is school a place for fantasy and imagination?
- Is school a place for eu-stress and relaxation?
- Is there a place for laughter (not at the expense of others) and appreciation of humor?

- Is the teacher able to accept an open result for an instructional unit?
- Are there opportunities to explore and investigate objects in a playful and experimental way?
- Are errors allowed, or are quick and correct results demanded?
- Is the individuality and uniqueness of each person appreciated, or is conformist behavior demanded?

Introducing 'Open Learning'

The pedagogical concept of *open teaching and learning* seems to provide essential conditions for fostering creativity and giftedness (Urban, 1995b, 1996). When adopted by highly competent teachers, open learning and instruction mean:

- offering meaningful enrichment of the children's perceptual horizons;
- enabling self-directed work, allowing a high degree of initiative, spontaneity, and experimentation without fear of sanctions against incorrect solutions, errors, or mistakes;
- encouraging and accepting non-conformist behavior and the adaptation of original ideas;
- providing for challenging and stimulating learning materials;
- creating organisational and structural conditions that allow open and reversible distribution of roles, themes, and problems, as well as sharing of activities;
- providing support and positive feedback for questioning and exploring behavior and problem finding, and not just problem solving;
- fostering identification of the child with school (learning) activities by allowing self-determination and joint responsibility;
- supporting development of positive self-assessment and a favourable self-concept;
- increasing autonomy in/of learning by recognition and self-evaluation of progress;
- making it possible for children to experience social creativity and the 'creative plus' during group interactions and through joint projects with self-selected partners;
- reducing stress on achievement and avoiding negative stress by introducing playful activities;
- fostering intense concentration and task commitment through high motivation and interest in self-selected topics;
- creating an atmosphere free from anxiety and time pressure;
- establishing psych(olog)ical security, openness, and freedom;
- nurturing sensibility, flexibility, and divergent thinking.

This kind of concept implies a changed and enriched role of the educator or teacher, who is no longer just instructor, evaluator, censor, and authority, but stimulator, elicitor, moderator, stabiliser, helper, mediator, counsellor, friend, participating observer, initiator, partner, instructor, organiser, expert, mentor, and model (Urban, 1996).

Recommendations for Stimulating and Nurturing Creativity in School

These recommendations, though formulated for teachers in school, are in principle also true for other educational institutions, as well as settings such as the workplace, where there is a felt need for creative productivity or innovation.

(1) Stimulate and maintain a creative group atmosphere, which allows learners to speak, think, and work free of stress and anxiety and without fear of sanctions.
(2) Avoid group pressure and factors such as envy associated with competition, but allow and support a cooperative climate.
(3) Try to avoid and prevent negative reactions or sanctions by classmates.
(4) Provide for adequate alternation of periods of activity and relaxation that foster musing.
(5) Demonstrate and appreciate humor.
(6) Stimulate and support free play and manipulation of objects and ideas (e.g. 'What if . . .?').
(7) Support self-initiated questioning and learning.
(8) Provoke and provide for situations challenging, stimulating, requiring creative behavior.
(9) Be careful with/hold back (excessively) rapid feedback promoting (rigid) patterns of behavior or solutions.
(10) Act as a model for and support questioning of rules or seemingly indispensable facts or patterns.
(11) Try to avoid 'suggestive' questions or questions that require a simple 'yes/no' answer, as much as possible.
(12) Instead of questions try to formulate statements that may stimulate or provoke questions by the students.
(13) Do not provide strategies for finding solutions too quickly, but give hints step-by-step in order to stimulate independent thinking.
(14) Allow errors and mistakes (as long as they are not physically or psychologically harmful to the child or to others).
(15) Interpret errors as signs of individual and constructive effort towards a self-detected solution.
(16) Try to discover the 'other' or deviant or poor or incorrect strategy that led to an error (qualitative error analysis).
(17) Try to make students sensitive to stimuli from different aspects of the environment (material, symbolic, social).
(18) Support interest in and acquisition of knowledge in a broad variety of different areas.

(19) Give stimulation and examples for systematic investigating, redefining, altering of ideas, stories, statements, presentations, etc.

(20) Demonstrate tolerance and appreciation of unusual thoughts, original ideas, or creative products.

(21) Teach students, to accept, acknowledge, and appreciate their own creative thinking, behavior and production as well as that of others.

(22) Provide for manifold and stimulating material for the elaboration of ideas.

(23) Support and attach importance to the full elaboration or realisation (of all implications) of creative ideas.

(24) Develop and demonstrate constructive criticism, not just criticism.

(25) Make students sensitive to possible implications and consequences of solutions.

Some idea of what these processes would mean in everyday practice can be gained from the following examples. Information could be drawn from students' experiences outside school, for instance during camping trips, out-of-school projects, hobby activities, or even shopping (Introducing Open Learning, first point: "Offering meaningful enrichment of the child's perceptual horizon"). The teacher could also go beyond setting tests on which answers can be scored either 'correct' or 'incorrect', and include at least some open items, or even items that are insoluble. Students could be required to describe the thinking that led to the best answer they could find to such questions, and grades could be based on the nature of this reasoning, regardless of formal correctness (or not) of the actual answer (Framework for Stocktaking, Component 2, fourth point: "Is there a focus on the learning process and not simply the result?"). In a history lesson, for instance, instead of asking for a list of the causes of the American War of Independence a teacher could ask students to describe what the modern world would be like if the British had granted the North American colonies representation in the House of Commons (Recommendations for Stimulating and Nurturing Creativity, Number 6: "Stimulate and support free play and manipulation of objects and ideas").

Fostering creativity is an integral part of education, and should be a guiding principle for teaching *all* children. In the case of the gifted, however, it takes on special importance, because it permits 'true' giftedness. However, fostering creativity should not be reduced to a collection of set exercises carried out at fixed times as part of a 'creativity program'. The desire to foster it is at the heart of a philosophy or principle that should underlie *all* teaching and learning, in all subject areas and at all times.

References

Amabile, T. M. (1996). *Creativity in context*. Westview Press, Boulder, CO.

Baldwin, A. Y. (1985). Programs for the gifted and talented: Issues concerning minority populations. In: F. D. Horowitz & M. O'Brien (Eds.), *The gifted and talented: Developmental perspectives* (pp. 223–250). Washington, D.C.: American Psychological Association.

Basadur, M. & Hausdorf, P. A. (1996). Measuring divergent thinking attitudes related to creative problem solving and innovation management. *Creativity Research Journal*, **9**, 21–32.

Bayer, A. E. & Folger, J. (1966). Some correlates of a citation measure of productivity in science. *Sociology of Education*, **39**, 381–390.

Biermann, K.-R. (1985). Über Stigmata der Kreativität bei Mathematikern des 17. bis 19. Jahrhunderts [On indicators of creativity in mathematicians of the seventeenth to nineteenth centuries]. *Rostocker Mathematik Kolloquium* [Rostock Mathematics Colloquium], **27**, 5–22.

Brown, R. T. (1989). Creativity: What are we to measure? In: J. A. Glover, R. R. Ronning & C. R. Reynolds (Eds.), *Handbook of creativity* (pp. 3–32). New York: Plenum.

Bruner, J. S. (1962). The conditions of creativity. In: H. Gruber, G. Terrell & M. Wertheimer (Eds.), *Contemporary approaches to creative thinking* (pp. 1–30). New York: Atherton.

Butler, D. L. & Kline, M. A. (1998). Good versus creative solutions: a comparison of brainstorming, hierarchical, and perspective-changing heuristics. *Creativity Research Journal*, **11**, 325–331.

Clark, C. (1996). Working with able learners in regular classrooms. *Gifted and Talented International*, **11**, 34–38.

Cropley, A. J. (1967a). Creativity, intelligence and achievement. *Alberta Journal of Educational Research*, **13**, 51–58.

Cropley, A. J. (1967b). Divergent thinking and science specialists. *Nature*, **215**, 671–672.

Cropley, A. J. (1992). *More ways than one: fostering creativity in the classroom*. Norwood, NJ: Ablex.

Cropley, A. J. (1995). Creative intelligence: a concept of true giftedness. In: J. Freeman, P. Span & H. Wagner, H. (Eds.), *Actualizing talent: A lifelong challenge* (pp. 99–114). London: Cassell.

Cropley, A. J. (1997a). Fostering creativity in the classroom: general principles. In: M. Runco, (Ed.), *Handbook of creativity* (pp. 81–112). Cresskill, NJ.: Hampton Press.

Cropley, A. J. (1997b). Creativity: A bundle of paradoxes. *Gifted and Talented International*, **12**, 8–14.

Cropley, A. J. (1999a). Creativity and cognition: producing effective novelty. *Roeper Review*, **21**, 253–260.

Cropley, A. J. (1999b). Education. In: M. A. Runco & S. Pritzker (Eds.), *Encyclopedia of creativity* (pp. 629–642). San Diego: Academic Press.

Cropley, D. H. & Cropley, A. J. (in press). Fostering creativity in engineering undergraduates. *High Ability Studies*.

Csikszentmihalyi, M. (1988). Motivation and creativity: towards a synthesis of structural and energetic approaches. *New Ideas in Psychology*, **6**, 159–176.

Csikszentmihalyi, M. (1996). *Creativity: Flow and the psychology of discovery and invention*. New York: Harper Collins.

deBono, E. (1970). *Lateral thinking*. London: Ward Lock Education.

deBono, E. (1978). *Teaching thinking*. London: Pelican.

Eisenberger, R. & Armeli, S. (1997). Can salient reward increase creative performance without reducing intrinsic creative interest? *Journal of Personality and Social Psychology,* **72,** 652–663.

Engle, D. E., Mah, J. J. & Sadri, G. (1997). An empirical comparison of entrepreneurs and employees: Implications for innovation. *Creativity Research Journal,* **10,** 45–49.

Eysenck, H. J. (1997). Creativity and personality. In: M. A. Runco (Ed.), *The creativity research handbook,* Vol. 2 (pp. 41–66). Cresskill, NJ: Hampton Press.

Facaoaru, C. (1985). *Kreativität in Wissenschaft und Technik* [Creativity in science and technology]. Bern: Huber

Feldhusen, J. F. (1993). A conception of creative thinking and creativity training. In: S. G. Isaksen, M. C. Murdock, R. L. Firestien & D. J. Treffinger (Eds.), *Nurturing and developing creativity: The emergence of a discipline* (pp. 31–50). Norwood, NJ: Ablex.

Feldhusen, J. F. (1995). Creativity: a knowledge base, metacognitive skills, and personality factors. *Journal of Creative Behavior,* **29,** 255–268.

Feldhusen, J. F. & Treffinger, D. J. (1975). Teachers' attitudes and practices in teaching creativity and problem solving to economically disadvantaged and minority children. *Psychological Reports,* **37,** 1161–1162.

Finke, R. A., Ward, T. B. & Smith, S. M. (1992). *Creative cognition.* Boston, MA: MIT.

Fromm, E. (1998). Lost and found half a century later: letters by Freud and Einstein. *American Psychologist,* **53,** 1195–1198.

Ghiselin, B. (1955). *The creative process.* New York: Mentor.

Gibson, J. & Light, P. (1967). Intelligence among university scientists. *Nature,* **213,** 441–443.

Grudin, R. (1990). *The grace of great things: Creativity and innovation.* New York: Ticknor and Fields.

Guilford, J. P. (1950). Creativity. *American Psychologist,* **5,** 444–454.

Hassenstein, M. (1988). *Bausteine zu einer Naturgeschichte der Intelligenz* [Building blocks for a natural history of creativity]. Stuttgart: Deutsche Verlags-Anstalt.

Hayes, J. R. (1989). Cognitive processes in creativity. In: J. A. Glover, R. R. Ronning & C. R. Reynolds (Eds.), *Handbook of creativity* (pp. 135–146). New York: Plenum.

Helson, R. (1996). In search of the creative personality. *Creativity Research Journal,* **9,** 295–306.

Henle, M. (1974). The cognitive approach: the snail beneath the shell. In: S. Rosner & L. E. Aber (Eds.), *Essays in creativity* (S. 23–44). Croton on Hudson, NY: North River Press.

Howe, M. J. A. (1990). *The origins of exceptional abilities.* Oxford: Blackwell.

Howieson, N. (1984, August). *Is Western Australia neglecting the creative potential of its youth?* Paper presented at the 1984 Annual Conference of the Australian Psychological Society, Perth, August 12–17.

Hruby, G. G. (1999). Review of Jensen, E. (1998). Teaching with the brain in mind. *Roeper Review,* **21,** 326–327.

Huczynski, A. (1983). *Encyclopedia of management development methods.* Aldershot: Gower.

Hudson, L. (1968). *Contrary imaginations.* London: Methuen.

Jay, E. S. & Perkins, D. N. (1997). Problem finding: the search for mechanisms. In: M. A. Runco (Ed.), *The creativity research handbook,* Vol. 1 (pp. 257–294). Cresskill, NJ: Hampton Press.

Koestler, A. (1964). *The act of creation.* London: Hutchinson.

Lehwald, G. (1985). *Zur Diagnostik des Erkenntnisstrebens bei Schülern* [Identifying thirst for knowledge in schoolchildren]. Berlin: Volk und Wissen.

Mansfield, R. S., Busse, T. V. & Krepelka, E. J. (1978). The effectiveness of creativity training. *Review of Educational Research,* **48,** 517–536.

Martinson, O. (1995). Cognitive styles and experience in solving insight problems: replication and extension. *Creativity Research Journal,* **8,** 291–298.

Matyushkin, A. (1990). Gifted and talented children: the nature of giftedness, screening and development. *European Journal for High Ability,* **1,** 72–75.

McMullan, W. E. (1978). Creative individuals: paradoxical personages. *Journal of Creative Behavior,* **10,** 265–275.

Mednick, S. A. (1962). The associative basis of creativity. *Psychological Review,* **69,** 220–232.

Michalko, M. (1998). *Cracking creativity.* Berkeley, CA: Ten Speed Press.

Morgan, D. N. (1953). Creativity today. *Journal of Aesthetics,* **12,** 1–24.

Obuche, N. M. (1986). The ideal pupil as perceived by Nigerian (Igbo) teachers and Torrance's creative personality. *International Review of Education,* **32,** 191–196.

Osborn, A. F. (1953). *Applied imagination.* New York: Scribner.

Parnes, S. J. (1967). *Creative behavior guidebook.* New York: Scribner.

Renzulli, J. S. (1986). The three-ring conception of giftedness: a developmental model for creative productivity. In: R. J. Sternberg & J. E. Davidson (Eds.), *Conceptions of giftedness.* Cambridge: Cambridge University Press.

Resnick, L. B. (1987). (Ed.). *Education and learning to think.* Washington, DC: National Academy Press.

Shaughnessy, M. F. & Manz, A. F. (1991). Personological research on creativity in the performing and fine arts. *European Journal for High Ability,* **2,** 91–101.

Sierwald, W. (1989, September). *Kreative Hochbegabung— Identifikation, Entwicklung und Förderung kreativ Hochbegabter* [Creative giftedness—identifying, developing and fostering the creatively gifted]. Referat auf der 2. Jahrestagung der Arbeitsgruppe Pädagogische Psychologie der Deutschen Gesellschaft für Psychologie [Paper presented at the second annual meeting of the working group on Educational Psychology], Munich.

Simonton, D. K. (1988). *Scientific genius: a psychology of science.* Cambridge: Cambridge University Press.

Sternberg, R. J. (1988). *The nature of creativity.* New York: Cambridge University Press.

Sternberg, R. J. & Lubart, T. I. (1995). *Defying the crowd: cultivating creativity in a culture of conformity.* New York: Free Press.

Stone, B. G. (1980). Relationship between creativity and classroom behavior. *Psychology in the Schools,* **17,** 106–108.

Tardif, T. Z. & Sternberg, R. J. (1988). What do we know about creativity? In: R. J. Sternberg (Ed.), *The nature of creativity* (pp. 429–440). New York: Cambridge University Press.

Torrance, E. P. (1992, January/February). A national climate for creativity and invention. *Gifted Child Today*, pp. 10–14.

Treffinger, D. J., Sortore, M. R. & Cross, J. A. (1993). Programs and strategies for nurturing creativity. In: K. A. Heller, F. J. Mönks & A. H. Passow (Eds.), *International handbook for research on giftedness and talent* (pp. 555–567). Oxford: Pergamon.

United States Patent and Trademark Office. (1990). *The Inventive Thinking Curriculum Project*. U.S. Patent and Trademark Office, Washington, DC.

Urban, K. K. (1990). Recent trends in creativity research and theory in Western Europe. *European Journal for High Ability*, **1**, 99–113.

Urban, K. K. (1994). Recent trends in creativity research and theory. In: K. A. Heller & E. A. Hany (Eds), *Competence and responsibility*, Vol. 2 (pp. 56–67). Seattle: Hogrefe and Huber.

Urban, K. K. (1996). Encouraging and nurturing creativity in school and workplace. In: U. Munandar & C. Semiawan (Eds), *Optimizing excellence in human resource development* (pp. 78–97). Jakarta, Indonesia: University of Indonesia Press.

Urban, K. K. (1995a). Different models in describing, exploring, explaining and nurturing creativity in society. *European Journal for High Ability*, **6**, 143–159.

Urban, K. K. (1995b). Openness: a 'magic formula' for an adequate development and promotion of giftedness and talents?! *Gifted and Talented International*, **10**, 15–19.

Urban, K. K. (1997). Modelling creativity: the convergence of divergence or the art of balancing. In: J. Chan, R. Li & J. Spinks (Eds.), *Maximizing potential: lengthening and strengthening our stride* (pp. 39–50). Hong Kong: The University of Hong Kong, Social Sciences Research Centre.

Walberg, H. J. & Stariha, W. E. (1992). Productive human capital: learning, creativity and eminence. *Creativity Research Journal*, **5**, 323–341.

Wallas, G. (1926). *The art of thought*. New York: Harcourt Brace.

Wallach, M. A. (1985). Creativity testing and giftedness. In: F. D. Horowitz & M. O'Brien (Eds.), *The gifted and the talented: Developmental perspectives* (pp. 99–123). Washington, DC: American Psychological Association.

Ward, T. B., Saunders, K. N. & Dodds, R. A. (1999). Creative cognition in gifted adolescents. *Roeper Review*, **21**, 260–266.

Williams, F. E. (1976). Intellectual creativity and the teacher. In: W. R. Lett (Ed.), *Creativity and education* (pp. 17–31). Melbourne: Australian International Press and Publications.

Developing Gifted Programs

Sidney M. Moon[1] and Hilda C. Rosselli[2]

[1] *Purdue University, West Lafayette, Indiana, USA*
[2] *University of South Florida, Tampa, Florida, USA*

Introduction

The word 'program' has been used in many ways in the field of gifted and talented education. At a *macro level*, a national or regional ministry of education might specify parameters for gifted education for an entire country and call that a gifted program. For example, Israel's ministry of education established a Department of Gifted Children and Science Oriented Youth to be responsible for the gifted education program in Israel (Burg, 1992) and the gifted education program in Singapore was initiated, planned, and implemented by the Singapore ministry of education (Goh, 1994). Similarly, Siberia developed a large-scale regional project to develop science talent that involved selecting talented high school seniors for accelerated university education, engagement in research, and postgraduate work at research institutes (Masharov, 1993).

At the *local level*, there are numerous examples of local school districts developing gifted programs to fit a specific local context (see for example Powley & Moon, 1993; Whitman & Moon, 1993; Nidiffer & Moon, 1994). In between these extremes are programs developed to serve an entire city such as CEDET, a comprehensive, individualized, enrichment program for Brazilian students in grades 1–8 (Guenther, 1995). What all of these efforts have in common is an articulated set of services for an identified subpopulation of gifted and talented students in a specific location or region. These services include identification procedures and differentiated educational experiences in a specified delivery format and are designed to develop the talents of high ability youth.

Theoretical models for gifted programs also range from the general to the specific. At the general level, a model such as the Purdue Secondary Model (Feldhusen & Robinson, 1986) provides a generic framework for comprehensive programming for gifted and talented students at the secondary level. Other general models provide templates for the development of specific program components in specific contexts, but are not really programs themselves. The Purdue Three-Stage Model (Feldhusen & Kolloff, 1986; Moon, 1993; Moon, Feldhusen, Powley, Nidiffer & Whitman, 1993) and the Kaplan grid model (Kaplan, 1986) are examples. Both of these models provide frameworks for program and curriculum design that can be applied in a wide variety of contexts. At the specific level, a model such as the Program for Academic and Creative Enrichment (PACE) (Kolloff & Feldhusen, 1981) specifies the identification procedures, format, and curriculum for a two-hour/week pullout enrichment program for children aged 9–11. In between, models such as the Schoolwide Enrichment (Renzulli & Reis, 1985) and the Autonomous Learner (Betts, 1985) specify in great detail the design parameters of enrichment programs with integrated, embedded program components. Theoretical program models provide guidance for the development of gifted and talented programs but are not themselves programs unless they are implemented in a specific local context.

This chapter focuses on the *process* of developing programs for gifted and talented students, rather than on specific program models. As used here, a *program* is an educational experience that is planned and implemented in a specific location or region for the purpose of enhancing the development of identified gifted and talented students. The chapter provides guidance for persons charged with developing programs for gifted and talented students by: (a) discussing theoretical, cultural, and political issues that influence the program development process; (b) outlining strategies that are helpful in planning and designing gifted programs. Throughout, the emphasis is on *situated program development*, i.e. program development that is designed to fit a specific local context.

Contextual Issues

Theoretical

Before one develops a program for high ability students, it is helpful to spend time clarifying the theoretical basis of program development efforts.

499

Program developers should be aware of the conceptual foundations of the field, competing theories of giftedness, and differing viewpoints on key issues in gifted education. Ambrose (1998) has proposed a hierarchical model of the conceptual foundations of gifted education that includes world views (e.g. mechanism, contextualism, organicism, and formism); disciplinary perspectives (e.g. the 'hard' vs. the 'soft' sciences), and levels of operation (e.g. theory, research, and. practice). This model can be used by program developers to organize the various theoretical perspectives in the literature and prevent the polarization that can result when different individuals hold different world views or come from different disciplinary specializations. Using Ambrose's (1998) framework either/or thinking can be replaced by a broader more divergent consideration of many ideas and potential integrative connections. Ideally, this integrative process will occur when stakeholders work together to develop a shared philosophy of gifted education at the beginning of program development efforts.

Conceptions of Giftedness

One of the most important conceptual foundations of a gifted program is the theory of giftedness that undergirds the program. Theories of giftedness influence all aspects of program development including program philosophy and goals, identification procedures, program delivery format, and instructional strategies. On a less tangible level, conceptions of giftedness influence perceptions of the need for specialized programming, the cast of stakeholders who will play a pivotal role in the development of the program, and the level and type of advocacy necessary to support program efforts. Numerous conceptions of giftedness have been proposed by scholars in the fields of psychology and education (Sternberg & Davidson, 1986). Although some believe the field of gifted education needs a unifying conception of giftedness (Gagne, 1999), others feel a plethora of competing conceptions is both necessary and valuable (Borland, 1999).

Existing conceptions of giftedness have been categorized in different ways. For example, Sternberg (1986), has categorized conceptions of giftedness into implicit vs. explicit theories. *Implicit theories* are definitions that lie within the heads of the theorists whether those 'theorists' are experts or lay persons. Such theories cannot be empirically tested. It is important for program developers to be aware of the implicit theories of giftedness held by various program stakeholders, particularly if these implicit theories differ from the conception of giftedness that the program developers are using as a foundation for program development efforts. *Explicit theories* are testable theories that assume specific definitions and seek to relate those definitions to other constructs through empirical research. Often the assumptions underlying the definitions of giftedness used in research studies have not

been critically examined by the researchers. Program developers also need to be discerning about the assumptions about giftedness underlying much of the empirical research literature in order to interpret that literature effectively in a specific context.

Conceptions of giftedness are influenced by definitions of the constructs that underlie them as well as by the hypothesized relationships between those constructs. At the close of the 20th Century, there is little consensus among scholars in the fields of psychology and education about such constructs as *intelligence* (Gardner, 1983; Sternberg, 1985, 1986, 1996; Neisser et al., 1996), *creativity* (Glover, Ronning & Reynolds, 1989; Runco & Albert, 1990; Sternberg, 1999), *motivation* (Pintrich & Schunk, 1996; Clinkenbeard, 1997), *expertise* (Ericsson, Krampe & Tesch-Romer, 1993; Ericsson, 1996; Sternberg & Horvath, 1998), *levels of ability* (Gagne, 1998), and *gifts and talents* (Feldhusen, 1998; Gagne, 1999). There is also little consensus about the relationships among these constructs in the development of giftedness (Renzulli, 1986b; Stanley, 1997; Feldhusen, 1998).

A recent, striking example of the controversy surrounding these core constructs was stimulated by Gagne's (1999) treatise on his beliefs about abilities, gifts, and talents. Gagne distinguished between natural abilities (giftedness) and abilities that have been systematically developed through a structured program of learning, development, and practice (talents). Gagne's essay garnered an interesting array of responses that ranged from viewing exceptional human ability as a regression equation consisting of general intelligence, domain-specific skills, and practice (Detterman & Ruthsatz, 1999) to a reaffirmation of the distinction between gifts as general, system-wide capabilities and talents as specific, within-domain capabilities (Feldman, 1999). Given this diversity of viewpoints, it is helpful if some members of a program development team can familiarize themselves with the literature on conceptions of giftedness prior to beginning program development efforts. Ideally, program developers should receive training in the field of gifted education and/or talent development psychology. If extended training and/or independent study is not possible, consultants can be hired to help develop a coherent theoretical foundation for program development efforts.

Critical appraisals of gifted education

Even if the debate regarding conceptions of giftedness were to be resolved, there would still be a need for ongoing critical reflection about the fundamental premises and practices of the field of gifted education. Gifted education has been shaped through advocacy, but advocacy without self-examination can border on fanaticism (Borland, 1996). Thus, this chapter would be incomplete without mentioning some of the critiques of gifted education. Seldom has there been as cogent a collection of critical appraisals of the field as the one compiled by Lawrence Coleman in the Winter 1996 issue of the *Journal for the Education of the Gifted*. This issue provided a powerful array of essays from both proponents and opponents of the field. Readers were roused to question the field's reluctance to ask of ourselves the questions asked by critics of gifted education (Borland, 1996), to recognize impressive accomplishments of the field as well as areas still worthy of scrutiny (Callahan, 1996), and to consider talent development as a new conceptual framework that extends and redefines the nature of giftedness, identification, and programming (Treffinger & Feldhusen, 1996). Margolin (1996) argued that gifted education is really a strategy to develop a class of people who lead and direct others, and, thus, a pedagogy of the oppressed. In a similar vein, Sapon-Shevin (1996) argued that gifted education is a form of 'educational triage' in that programs are created for those for whom educational failure would be unacceptable. The result is a continued focus on improving education for the privileged rather than considering a comprehensive overhaul of the entire educational system. Sapon-Shevin also reminded us that when we define "what gifted students need," we are using a blanket approach that may fail to recognize the unique educational needs of particular gifted students. Gallagher (1996) noted that many of the criticisms raised in the special issue were really questions of ethics and philosophy.

This collection of essays, along with other critical appraisals of the field of gifted education, can help program developers clarify their values and viewpoints. Program development teams would benefit from reading such critiques in a reflective mode, using their context as the backdrop for spirited discussion of these critical appraisals of gifted education and their relevance to local program development efforts.

Cultural

Cultural influences on gifted and talented programs are often quite marked (Robinson, 1992b). These influences stem from beliefs and values. Many cultures have deeply ingrained beliefs about concepts such as the nature of giftedness and the purpose of education. These beliefs can have a strong influence on educational policies for gifted and talented students (Freeman, 1992), as can cultural values (Braggert, 1993; Taylor, 1993; Stevenson, 1998).

Beliefs

Socio-cultural influences often shape the implicit conceptions of giftedness that evolve in particular settings. Historically, many cultures believed that human talents were an endowment of the gods (Hunsaker, 1995). For example, in the ancient greco-Roman culture special intellectual and artistic abilities were believed to come from the Muses. In modern times, belief in divine dispensation is less prevalent. Instead, modern cultures tend to believe that unusual abilities are the result of heredity, environment, individual effort, or some combination of these. Which of the three receives the greatest emphasis in a particular culture can have a dramatic impact on gifted education.

In the United States and Canada, a prevailing cultural belief is that individual differences in abilities are largely the result of natural endowments. For example, the province of Saskatchewan in Canada defines giftedness as "superior natural ability or exceptional talent" (Goguen, 1993). This belief in natural gifts leads to an educational focus on measuring individual differences and providing educational programming that is an appropriate match for an individual's measured abilities (Tannenbaum, 1986; VanTassel-Baska, 1998b). In most Asian countries, on the other hand, the prevailing cultural belief is that individual differences in abilities are largely the result of effort (Stevenson, 1994, 1998). Hence the emphasis in Asian education is on teacher skill and pupil diligence.

Some cultures foster a unified belief system about the nature of giftedness. Others encourage a variety of competing beliefs in an open marketplace of ideas. Where a single belief system holds sway it is very difficult to implement gifted and talented programming that flows from another conception of giftedness. For example, Nowicka (1995) cited denial of the existence of genetic differences during the communist period as a historical barrier to the development of gifted education in Poland.

The United States (Gallagher, 1993), Canada (Goguen, 1993), and Western Europe (Urban & Sekowski, 1993) are examples of cultures which foster competing conceptions of giftedness. In these cultures, the prevailing conception of giftedness in a given locality tends to be determined by political processes rather than by cultural ones. Hence many types of gifted programming are found in these countries and beliefs about the nature of giftedness tend to be seen as values held by certain groups of people rather than as shared beliefs about the 'Truth'.

The Purpose of Education. Cultures also differ dramatically in their beliefs about the purpose of education, especially for talented individuals. Some cultures emphasize education as a means to individual development while others believe education is a means of achieving collective or national goals. Often cultural beliefs about the purpose of education will change over time. For example, traditional African societies viewed the purpose of education to be establishing a favorable environment for the development of special abilities; children who demonstrated special abilities were viewed as needing specialized education to prepare them for their adult roles as priests, herbalists, etc.

(Hunsaker, 1995). Taylor (1993), however, suggests that modern African societies believe that the purpose of education is to enhance togetherness and communal responsibility rather than to promote individual development; as a result, African nations today tend to place greater priority on educating the majority and disadvantaged students than on educating students with special talents.

Israel is an example of a modern culture that believes the purpose of education is multi-faceted: encouraging the pursuit of individual excellence, as well as enhancing the ability of young people to contribute to society (Burg, 1992; Passow, 1994). Perhaps as a result, Israel has a well-developed national policy of gifted education that encourages a wide variety of types of gifted and talented programming including special schools, special classes, and enrichment schools (Burg, 1992).

Both China and Korea have been heavily influenced by Confucianism (Robinson, 1992b, Oh-Hwang, 1993). Confucianism holds that success is equivalent to wealth and prestige and is attained primarily through education. Hence cultures influenced by Confucianism believe that education is important for success in life and have a long tradition of promoting achievement and talent on the basis of examinations. Since higher education is a scarce resource in these countries, much of the focus of pre-college education is on achieving a high enough score on national college entrance examinations for selective college entrance (Robinson, 1992b; Oh-Hwang, 1993). This narrow focus on academic achievement as measured by competitive examinations makes it very difficult to develop gifted and talented programs for any other purpose than improving examination scores (Hsueh, 1998).

Under communist leadership, Eastern European countries, the USSR, and China, banned the study and testing of individual differences but promoted the development of individuals with unusual potential in sports, science, and the arts because such individuals could enhance national honor by winning international competitions (Urban & Sekowski, 1993; Stevenson, 1998). Hence beliefs about talent development in communist countries were bifurcated: one set of beliefs governed normal education for most students and another governed the education of extremely talented individuals in domains where excellent performance could bring national prestige. These bifurcated beliefs appear to have been largely political in nature, rather than truly cultural. In most of these countries, these beliefs are being replaced by beliefs that are more consistent with underlying cultural traditions i.e. eastern Europe is aligning itself with the beliefs of democratic countries (Urban & Sekowski, 1993) and mainland China is aligning itself with the traditional beliefs of Confucianism (Robinson, 1992b).

Some cultures believe that the primary purpose of education, especially in the pre-high school/college

years, is the reduction of individual differences, e.g. Japan (Stevenson, 1998), while others believe that education should help even very young children differentiate, e.g. England, Germany, and Holland (Urban & Sekowski, 1993). When beliefs are deeply rooted, shared by most individuals in a nation or region they can have a strong influence on gifted education . For example, most people in the Scandinavian countries hold egalitarian beliefs about the purpose of education; as a result these countries tend to be opposed to special provisions for gifted students (Freeman, 1992; Urban & Sekowski, 1993; Persson, 1998).

Values

Family values. Differences in family values can affect program development efforts. In cultures where filial piety is a strongly held value, and parents exercise considerable control over their children's lives, parental pressures may heavily influence gifted and talented programming. For example, in Taiwan parents value good grades and high scores on exams to the exclusion of other aspects of talent development (Hsueh, 1998). As a result it is very difficult to get parental support for programs to develop humanistic or artistic talents in Taiwan. Similarly, in Korea parents are the absolute authority and value conformity so it is difficult to develop programs to nurture creativity or flexible, creative learning environments (Oh-Hwang, 1993). In some subcultures in the United States, such as the African American, families may view gifted programs as threatening to their family and cultural values and so may not be supportive of their children's participation in such programs (Exum, 1983).

Conformity vs. independence. One of the ways the values of cultures differ is with respect to the conformity-independence continuum (Sisk, 1990). Cultures like the American and Western European that value individualism and independent thinking tend to be supportive of many different types of gifted and talented programming, while cultures that value conformity tend to be supportive of a narrower range of programs. For example, programs that focus on the development of creative talents are common in the United States (see for example, Kolloff & Feldhusen, 1981; Renzulli & Reis, 1985) and Brazil (see for example, CDET, Guenther, 1995), two countries that value independent thinking, but rare in Japan (Stevenson, 1998) and Korea (Oh-Hwang, 1993), countries that value conformity and obedience.

Cultures also differ in the amount of conformity that is expected with respect to curriculum and pedagogy. In countries where educational policy and curriculum are established at the national level, local efforts to develop gifted and talented programming are not likely to be successful unless they occur in the private sector (Urban & Sekowski, 1993; Wu & Cho, 1993). If broadly-based gifted education is to occur in these countries, a mandate for it must become integrated into national policy. In countries with decentralized educational systems, on the other hand, regional and/or local program development may be strongly encouraged (Gallagher, 1994; Passow & Rudnitski, 1994; Robinson, 1999).

Differential Weighting of Talent domains. Cultural values can also influence levels of support for talent development in specific domains. In some regions such as Western Europe (Freeman, 1992; Tirri & Uusikyla, 1994), Taiwan (Hsueh, 1998), and Korea (Oh-Hwang, 1993), a traditional emphasis in the educational system on academic subjects makes it difficult to develop programs to nurture creativity or non-traditional talents. Exactly the opposite pattern can prevail in egalitarian countries such as Finland (Tirri & Uusikyla, 1994), where special classes may be supported for children gifted in music and sports but not for the intellectually gifted.

In Africa, cultural values include community and togetherness and the importance of affective and social development. As a result, the African culture values social giftedness more than academic or technological giftedness (Taylor, 1993). African nations are likely to be more supportive of gifted education if an emphasis is placed on the social/emotional domain in addition to academics or if programming focuses on developing social/emotional talent. Another country that emphasizes social goals for gifted education is Singapore (Goh, 1993) where gifted education is viewed "as benefiting society as a whole, not just the individual" (Goh, 1994, p. 52). Similarly, Israel's residential high school for the arts and sciences was motivated by the belief that Israel must "encourage her youth to achieve excellence, not only in their areas of talent potential, but excellence as human beings by nurturing deep moral, social, and civic commitment" (Passow, 1994, p. 54. A desired outcome of gifted education in both countries is talented adults who have a strong commitment to their society.

National goals can also influence levels of support for different talent domains. In Eastern Europe under the communists, special schools were established to develop the most talented pupils for international competitions in sports, art, music, and science, but no individualization or differentiation was provided in academic subjects at regular schools or for individuals with more moderate levels of talent in sports, art, music, and science (Urban & Sekowski, 1993). China has supported gifted education in part because it has been seen as promoting the need of their society for modernization; similarly, one of the reasons Taiwan supports gifted education is the belief that an island economy with scarce national resources needs to develop its human resources (Stevenson, 1994). The talent domains supported by national welfare rationales are usually science and technology.

Philosophies of education. Perhaps the most important cultural influences on gifted education are those related to educational philosophies (Freeman, 1992; Wu & Cho, 1993; Stevenson, 1998). The *egalitarian* philosophy holds that the primary purpose of education is to create similar outcomes for all students (Freeman, 1992; Robinson, 1992a; Persson, 1998). Thus an important educational goal in an egalitarian culture is the reduction of individual differences. In contrast, an *equal opportunity* culture values equality of opportunity more than equality of outcomes and recognizes that providing equal opportunities may actually increase the differences between individuals (Gallagher, 1993; Urban & Sekowski, 1993). A core educational value in an equal opportunity culture is adapting instruction to meet individual needs. In an egalitarian culture, achieving excellence beyond age-group norms is discouraged. In an equal opportunity culture, achieving excellence beyond age-group norms is encouraged to the extent that resources are available.

Both types of cultures emphasize educational equity but they do so in different ways. In the egalitarian culture, equity is achieved by making sure that all students experience exactly the same educational experiences regardless of their individual differences. A common educational experience is provided and similar outcomes are expected for all students. For example, in the Sweden (Persson, 1998), Poland during the communist regime (Ekiert-Grabowska, 1994) , and Japan (Stevenson, 1994; Stevenson, 1998), one rationale for providing a uniform curriculum to all children in the elementary grades has been equity—all children are perceived as being given equal chances to learn because they all experience the same education. In the equal opportunity culture, on the other hand, educational opportunities are adapted to meet the needs of students with different interests and abilities. Equity is perceived to be achieved by ensuring that students who vary by race, gender, ethnicity, and socio-economic background have equal access to opportunities to develop their abilities. For example, in the United States achieving equity has been a major goal of the Jacob Javits legislation (Berger, 1992). This legislation funded a variety of projects that designed better ways to identify (Borland & Wright, 1994; O'Tuel, 1994; Maker, 1996) and serve (Baldwin, 1994; Hiatt, 1994; Tomlinson, Callahan & Lelli, 1997) students from minority and/or low SES backgrounds in gifted and talented programs.

In general, egalitarian cultures are either hostile towards gifted education or supportive of gifted education only in inclusive settings. Where egalitarian ideologies or politics are dominant in a culture, the conception of giftedness espoused by program developers can make a big difference in the success of program development efforts. Egalitarians tend to reject gifted education when it is based on narrow conceptions of giftedness as innate, fixed, measurable intellectual superiority and to be open to gifted education when it is based on broader conceptions of giftedness that focus on multiple talents that are malleable and can be developed through appropriate educational experiences in inclusive settings. This trend can be seen in Australia and New Zealand (Braggert, 1993), Italy (Pagnin, 1995), Scandanavia (Urban & Sekowski, 1993), and many Asian countries (Wu & Cho, 1993).

Equal opportunity cultures, on the other hand, usually encourage the development of a broad smorgasbord of talent development opportunities (Feldhusen & Moon, 1995; Robinson, 1999). Hence programming options tend to proliferate in these cultures if resources are ample. However, when resources are scarce in a culture with an equal opportunity philosophy, the needs of the gifted are usually a lower priority than the needs of disadvantaged and disabled students. In South America and Africa, for example, the primary barrier to the development of programs for gifted children is not educational philosophy but resources (Alencar, 1993; Taylor, 1993; Guenther, 1995; Kolo, 1996). Much of the population in these countries is poor, the quality of the general education system is also poor, and there is little money available for infrastructure or staff training. Even if there is a belief that differential opportunities should be provided to students with talents to enable them to fulfill their potential, the human and material resources are not available to do so. In addition, given the immensity of the educational problems in these countries, the needs of gifted and talented students are usually seen as a lower priority than improvements to general education and/or special provisions for disadvantaged students (Taylor, 1993). Thus, in practice, it is usually the wealthier nations with an equal opportunity philosophy that provide the most support for gifted education.

Politics

Educational Policies

An educational policy is a plan which provides written guidelines for action. The role of policy in gifted education varies greatly in different countries and is heavily influenced by political processes (Passow, 1993). In some countries education is highly centralized and one educational philosophy dominates (Burg, 1992; Goh, 1994; Stevenson, 1998). Other countries are characterized by locally determined educational philosophies with strong value conflicts among different subgroups (Braggert, 1993; Gallagher, 1993; Goguen, 1993; Purcell, 1995; Robinson, 1999). In countries with centralized educational systems, national legislation and/or policy can have a tremendous influence on the development of gifted and talented programming.

In countries with decentralized educational systems, the climate for program development may vary considerably in different regions and/or in different historical time periods. In Canada, for example, gifted and talented programming varies by province (Goguen, 1993) and, in the United States, it varies by state and school district (Purcell, 1995; Landrum, Katsiyannis & DeWaard, 1998; Robinson, 1999). In Australia, gifted and talented programming tends to be influenced by the views of the political party that is in power, and thus varies by time as well as by region. Australian political parties with social democratic traditions favor policies aimed at equalizing social outcomes and don't believe that the absence of special programming handicaps gifted students; conservative political parties geared to a free market economy favor wider choice and a diversity of school provisions for gifted and talented students (Braggert, 1993). Countries that have traditionally had uniform egalitarian educational philosophies can sometimes be influenced by advocacy to consider modifying their uniform stance. For example, Finland, a country which has deeply held egalitarian values, has become more receptive to gifted education because of pressures from industry for a greater investment in excellence (Tirri & Uusikyla, 1994).

The Interface Between General and Gifted Education

When gifted students spend all or part of their time in general education classrooms, program developers must pay attention to the interface between gifted and general education. Research on what happens in general education classrooms for gifted and talented students in the United States has been discouraging and provides only limited guidance for persons wanting to develop differentiated, inclusive programming for gifted and talented students. For example, a survey of more than 7,000 third and fourth grade classroom teachers on their current differentiation practices revealed that few teachers were modifying the curriculum for gifted and talented learners (Archambault et al., 1993). When observations were conducted in 46 of the classrooms, the same research team found that 84% of the activities in the regular classrooms observed provided no differentiation for gifted and talented students and a majority of the teachers observed reported that they had no professional training in gifted education (Westberg, Archambault, Dobyns & Salvin, 1993).

A multi-site qualitative follow-up study was somewhat more encouraging (Westberg & Archambault, 1997). The study investigated ten schools with a reputation for successful differentiation of instruction for high ability students in regular classrooms. The teachers in these schools who were effective in differentiating appeared to be life-long learners who were interested in continuous improvement of their skills, willing to embrace changes in their practices, engaged in some form of voluntary collaboration, and able to view their students as individuals rather than a mass. In some sites there was strong leadership support for the teachers' efforts at the school or district level. This study thus provides some guidance for the development of differentiated, inclusive education for gifted and talented learners.

Friedman & Lee (1996) studied three popular models that could be used to help general classroom teachers serve high-achieving/gifted students: the Enrichment Triad Model, the Multiple Talent Model, and the Cognitive-Affective Interaction Model. Only the Cognitive-Affective Interaction Model showed substantial gains in the cognitive complexity of teacher queries and student responses. An analysis by Johnson & Ryser, 1996 of over 675 articles appearing in gifted education journals and databases yielded only a small number of recommended practices that currently have research support for enhancing the learning of gifted students in inclusive programs. Their conclusions supported the use of problem finding, problem solving, and transfer strategies for the development of problem solving skills; competitions and special programs for improving thinking skills; and independent learning and interest centers for developing positive attitudes toward learning and creative productivity. Direct instruction was found useful for some groups of students and acceleration was considered useful for varying the rate of instruction. The authors expressed concern about the dearth of studies examining the effects of these practices on other students in the general classroom. They also recommended that future studies identify critical attributes of the strategies and methods that determine whether recommended practices are actually implemented in the classroom. Clearly more research is needed to guide the development of inclusive education programs that seek to adapt instruction for gifted and talented learners in general education classes.

Program developers also need to pay attention to the interface between the gifted and general education when specialized gifted programs are housed in general education settings, especially when gifted students spend only part of their school day in special programming. In such situations, increasing numbers of gifted program teachers consult and collaborate with general educators. Many gifted program administrators are also assuming new roles as collaborators with their general education colleagues, helping to guide the instruction of gifted learners in the regular classroom. Interviews have been conducted with respected individuals in gifted education and general education to explore ways in which the two fields might more effectively interface (Tomlinson, Coleman, Allan, Udall & Landrum, 1996). Collaboration between gifted education and general education was viewed by those interviewed as a means of balancing concerns about equity and excellence, reinforcing the reality that both groups share common goals, and maximizing the strengths of both generalists and specialists to the benefit of the total school community. However, those interviewed also felt that gifted education must maintain a sufficiently separate identity to facilitate advocacy goals. Barriers to collaboration identified in this study included scarce resources, isolationism, and negative attitudes between the two groups.

Tomlinson (1996) has also argued that as a field, gifted educators "have not conveyed effectively how we do what we do when we do it well." To address this concern, Shore & Delcourt (1997) identified recommended practices in gifted education that have research support as distinctive to gifted education, practices needing further research to ascertain their uniqueness to gifted education, practices effective for gifted students but applicable to all students, and finally, practices for which there is no evidence for their uniqueness for gifted students. Five strategies considered uniquely appropriate to gifted education received strong empirical support: acceleration; career education, especially for girls; program arrangements influencing academic and affective outcomes; ability grouping; and high-level curriculum materials. Strategies that received moderate support as uniquely appropriate for gifted students included paying attention to cultural and social differences, learning styles, and affective development; individualized reading; investigation of real problems; supervised independent study; and rapid pacing. The authors categorized an additional 13 strategies as effective with gifted students but applicable to all students. They also identified thirteen strategies where there was insufficient evidence to make a case for their uniqueness for the gifted. This research can be utilized by program developers to make an empirically grounded case for the value of specialized programming for gifted and talented students, especially when that programming emphasizes strategies that have been documented to be uniquely appropriate for such students.

In summary, program developers need to be aware of issues surrounding the interface between general education and gifted education and strive to develop a collaborative relationship with general educators. The issues that must be addressed to achieve a cooperative relationship between gifted and general educators vary by culture, context, and type of programming being implemented. Issues related to the interface are particularly important when programs for gifted students will be housed in general education settings, when gifted students will be spending only part of their time in special programming and the rest in a general education settings, and when general educators are opposed to special programming for gifted and talented students.

Attitudes of Stakeholders Towards Gifted Education

It is important for program administrators to monitor the attitudes of stakeholders and the general public toward gifted education. Unfortunately, a review of the research on attitudes toward gifted education revealed no consistent predictors of stakeholder attitudes (Begin & Gagne, 1994). Therefore, it is essential for program developers to monitor stakeholder attitudes empirically. In the United States, a recent Gallup Organization national survey suggested that the general public as well as parents of school age children were more supportive of using public school funds to provide services for students with learning problems than for students who were gifted and talented when both types of programs were perceived as competing for the same funds (Larsen, Griffin & Larsen, 1994). However, in a situation where funding for gifted children would not diminish what was offered to average and slow learners, nearly 85% of the general public was supportive of special funding for gifted and talented programs. This kind of information can be very helpful to advocacy and program development efforts. When information about public opinion is not available through large, national surveys, program administrators may want to administer a local needs assessment to assess stakeholder attitudes toward gifted and talented programming.

Principles of Educational Change

Those responsible for program development also need to be knowledgeable about educational change theory. Much is known about the educational change process and those who are most effective in facilitating change (Moon & Swift, 1989; Maier, 1993). Both bottom-up and top down efforts are necessary to bring about lasting change (Fullan, 1993). Goals that are effective in influencing change do not have a single solution but recognize a variety of alternatives and are accompanied by the resources needed for implementation (Sarason, 1996). Although building-level administrators are key to change in schools, teachers, curriculum coordinators, and others are also an integral ingredient in the change process for education and must be viewed as such and prepared as leaders (Hord, Rutherford, Huling-Austin & Hall, 1987; Tietel, 1996). Boles & Troen (1996) have defined five areas of leadership development critical for encouraging teachers' growth: pedagogical innovation, pre-service teacher education, curriculum development, research, and governance. When program developers are aware that their efforts will require substantial changes in an educational system, they would be wise to spend some time reading the educational change literature prior to beginning their program development efforts.

Legal Rights of Gifted Students

Although relatively few cases involving the rights of gifted students are heard in judicial systems around the world, program developers need to be aware of the laws governing student rights in their jurisdiction (Ford, Russo & Harris, 1995). For example, under-representation of ethnic minority groups in gifted programs poses potential legal challenges to identification systems that under-identify ethnic minorities in the United States (Brown, 1997; Ford, 1995). The Office of Civil Rights (OCR) in the Department of Education in the United States is responsible for helping to resolve issues of discrimination with respect to gifted students. The primary purpose of the OCR is to investigate the compliance of school districts with federal legislation (Marquandt & Karnes, 1994). The OCR has investigated cases involving protected groups such as ethnic minorities and disabled students in four areas of gifted education: admission to gifted programs, identification procedures, placement in gifted programs, and procedures involving notification, communication, and/or testing of gifted students (Karnes, Troxclair & Marquandt, 1997). Program developers need to be aware of the laws governing the rights of special populations of gifted students in their area so they can ensure that the programs they develop protect those rights.

The Development Process

Introduction

The contextual issues discussed in the first part of this chapter influence all aspects of gifted program planning and implementation. Because theoretical, cultural, and political issues pervade the design process, program design is most effective when it is contextualized. General principles can be derived from theory and practice, but they must be modified to fit specific situations. Hence the focus of the remainder of the chapter is on *situated program development*, defined as program development that occurs in a specific local context and addresses that context throughout the development process.

The development of a program for gifted and talented students is a complex endeavor that involves the mobilization of human and material resources and is often controversial. Some aspects of the development process are inherent in the nature of the task. For example, a well-designed program must specify identification procedures, program goals, and a program format (Borland, 1989; VanTassel-Baska, 1998a). Other aspects of the program development process are more strategic. They are designed to facilitate the change process in a specific context. For example, including a wide variety of stakeholders on the development team is a strategy that can increase support for a new gifted program (Moon & Swift, 1989; VanTassel-Baska, 1998a). Program developers need skill in change facilitation, planning, and program design strategies. Strong change facilitation strategies lead to broad-based support for gifted and talented programs and program longevity; strong planning and design skills lead to coherent, theoretically sound programs.

Change Facilitation Strategies

Advocacy

In an environment where prevailing attitudes are opposed to any form of special education for gifted and talented students the first stage of program development may be a prolonged period of advocacy. An adovocate has been defined as "one who supports, defends, maintains, and convinces with knowledgeable arguments in favor of a cause" (Gifted, 1998, p. 8). The role of advocacy is to draw attention to a need (Maier, 1993). Advocacy is a political process that can have an impact on the creation of policies and legislation favorable to gifted education as well as on local program development efforts (Dettmer, 1991; Riley & Karnes, 1991; Maier, 1993; Purcell, 1995). Where cultural values or educational policies are unfavorable to gifted education, a period of advocacy may be necessary prior to beginning program development efforts (DeLeon & VandenBox, 1985). It has been the experience of many nations around that world that advocacy must precede program development because program development simply does not occur when the prevailing educational philosophy is opposed to any form of special educational services for students with high abilities (Braggert, 1993; Stevenson, 1994). An effective advocacy effort can pave the way for vigorous program development. Even when educational philosophies and policies are favorable to gifted education, ongoing advocacy and attention to public relations can help enhance the viability and effectiveness of gifted and talented programming (Dettmer, 1991; Karnes & Riley, 1991; Renzulli & Reis, 1991).

Advocacy, like program development, is a problem solving process. Maier (Maier, 1993) has identified the steps in advocacy problem solving as follows:

(1) A problem emerges
(2) People gather to discuss the problem
(3) Advocates present the issues to others to raise awareness
(4) A multiplication of concern builds and creates power forces
(5) Strategic intervention ends in action.

The goal of advocacy efforts on behalf of gifted and talented students is usually to bring about educational change (Maier, 1993). Therefore, persons attempting to develop programs for gifted and talented students should be familiar with the principles of educational change (Moon & Swift, 1989). More specific guidance on advocacy procedures is beyond the scope of this chapter. The interested reader is referred to Moon & Swift, 1989; Dettmer, 1991; Karnes & Riley, 1991; Riley & Karnes, 1991; Troxclair & Karnes, 1997; California Association for the Gifted, 1998 for more concrete suggestions and information on how to advocate effectively for gifted and talented students.

Leadership

Gifted programs can be conceptualized as educational innovations (Goh, 1993). The planning and implementation of a gifted program requires changing existing educational systems, beliefs, and structures. Scholars in both business and education have found that strong leadership is a key factor in successful efforts to implement innovations in institutional settings (Peters & Waterman, 1982; Tuttle & Becker, 1983b; Peters & Austin, 1985; Moon & Swift, 1989).

Two types of leadership have been recommended in the institutional change literature: (a) 'champions' who are committed to creating change and given sufficient leeway by the relevant institutional structures that they can do so (Peters & Austin, 1985; Moon & Swift, 1989), and (b) broad-based advisory groups with representation from various groups of stakeholders that can steer program development efforts that flow from policy changes (VanTassel-Baska, 1998a). The role of a *champion* is to take responsibility for initiating and overseeing the change process. When there is a policy mandate for change in place, champions may be appointed by the policy makers. When there is not, champions often arise from the ranks of gifted education advocates. However, it is difficult for a champion to provide leadership for program development efforts unless they have some official role or position within the institution they desire to change, i.e. have been elected to a public office or are employed by a ministry of education or school system. If a school district has a coordinator or director of gifted education, that person is in an ideal position to be the champion for the development of new gifted program components (see for example Moon & Swift, 1989). Similarly, university professors with positions in gifted education can serve as champions for the development of university-based gifted programs (Stanley, 1997; Wood & Feldhusen, 1996) and members of ministries of education can serve as champions for national efforts to develop gifted programs (Burg, 1992; Goh, 1994). Teachers (Powley & Moon, 1993; Whitman & Moon, 1993) and members of state or national associations for the gifted (George, 1992) can also champion program development efforts.

The role of a *broad-based advisory group* is to address key issues that affect the program development effort and participate in all aspects of the planning process (Juntune, 1982; Tuttle & Becker, 1983b; Moon & Swift, 1989; VanTassel-Baska, 1998a). For district-level program development, VanTassel-Baska (1998a) recommends that the advisory committee include representation from administrators, teachers, parents, gifted students, pupil personnel services (counselor, social worker, psychologist), and community members (businesss, arts, and professional). Additional relevant stakeholders for regional or national program development efforts would include representatives from regional departments of education, government officials, and university professors. The purpose of the broad-based advisory group is to provide diversified input into the program planning process and increase ownership in the new program.

Planning Strategies

Needs Assessment
Situated program development requires a thorough needs assessment (Borland, 1989). The purpose of the needs assessment is to gather information on the program development context so that program development efforts can be tailored to that context (Boyd, 1992). Elements of the program development context that should be assessed include: (a) regional or national policies on gifted education or the lack thereof; (b) attitudes of stakeholders toward gifted education; (c) the incidence of giftedness types and levels; (d) existing educational practices; (e) material and financial resources and constraints; (f) human resources and constraints. Ideally, all of these contextual elements should be assessed by program developers prior to beginning the design phase of program development.

Methods of assessment include document analysis, reviews of the literature, surveys, interviews, observations, and analysis of student records. Document analysis is particularly appropriate for the examination of relevant gifted education policies. Such policies should be analyzed to determine whether they are mandatory or advisory in nature, and how they will facilitate or inhibit program development efforts. Curriculum materials can be examined to determine how effective the existing curriculum in specific subjects is in challenging the most able students in that domain. In some parts of the world, document analysis can be used to assess material and human resources because statistics on these resources are collected and analyzed on a regular basis. Where documents are not available, surveys, interviews, and/or observations can be utilized for the same purpose. However, these methods are more time and labor intensive so decisions will need to be made about which areas are the most important to assess in order to complete the needs assessment in a timely manner. Reviews of the literature can provide information on the status of programs for gifted students in other states (Purcell, 1995) or countries (Part VI, this volume); alternate conceptualizations of giftedness (Gardner, 1983; Sternberg & Davidson, 1986; Benbow & Lubinski, 1996; Neisser et al., 1996); different program models (Renzulli, 1986a; Maker & Nielson, 1995); and the steps involved in program design (Borland, 1989; Goh, 1993; VanTassel-Baska, 1998a).

Surveys are especially helpful in assessing attitudes of stakeholders toward gifted education. Surveys require careful construction if they are to provide reliable and valid data (Fink & Koscecoff, 1985). For example, it is important that items be easily understood by the respondents (Borland, 1989) and constructed in a way that will facilitate analysis (Fink & Koscecoff, 1985). If program developers are not trained in survey design, they should consult methodological texts and/ or collaborate with a researcher in developing their needs assessment questionnaires and analyzing and interpreting the results.

An analysis of student records, particularly standardized testing results, can provide a rough guide to the numbers of students who need special services in the academic areas. Existing standardized test results are usually less useful in providing information on the highly gifted population. To estimate numbers of students with high levels of giftedness, tests with a high ceiling and/or off-level tests must be used (Benbow & Lubinski, 1997; Silverman, 1998). In addition, standardized tests are also not good guides to many important talent domains such as leadership, creativity, and the visual arts (Clark & Zimmerman, 1984, 1987; Sternberg, 1993). Estimating the number of students who are talented in these domains is far more difficult than estimating the number intellectually talented students. Surveying parents and/or teachers can yield a very rough estimate; however, surveys will probably underestimate the true talent pool because many children with talents in these domains are not given sufficient encouragement to develop their abilities to the point where they would be evident to parents and/or teachers. Hence, estimates obtained by surveying parents and teachers on the incidence of talent in areas such as music, art, creative writing, leadership, and creativity should be considered conservative.

Development of a Shared Philosophy
In countries, such as the United States (Purcell, 1995; Robinson, 1999), Australia (Robinson, 1992a; Braggert, 1993), and Canada (Goguen, 1993), where there is no national mandate for gifted education and considerable latitude is given to individual school districts to develop programs for gifted students that fit the local context, a key early phase task in local program development efforts is the creation of a shared philosophy of gifted education (VanTassel-Baska, 1998a). The development of a philosophy of gifted education can occur concurrently with, before, or after the needs assessment, but should precede the creation of action plans for the development of specific program components. The process of creating a formal philosophy statement involves discussion of the conceptual, political, and cultural issues discussed earlier in this chapter, as well as issues more specific to programming like the relative value of acceleration and enrichment in developing talent. The goal is to create consensus

around a shared philosophy of gifted education. Ideally, this process will be undertaken by a broad-based committee of stakeholders so that diverse viewpoints will be represented. The process of shaping a shared philosophy can clarify areas of agreement and disagreement among stakeholders and help build ownership in gifted programming within the specific context where services will be provided (Moon & Swift, 1989). The end product should be a formal philosophy statement that includes a working definition of giftedness and summarizes the educational philosophy that will guide the development and implementation of specific program components in that context (VanTassel-Baska, 1998a).

In countries where a particular philosophy of gifted education is mandated by state or national policy documents, as in Korea and Japan (Wu & Cho, 1993; Stevenson, 1994; Stevenson, 1998), a different approach is needed. Instead of creating local philosophies of gifted education, program developers must either translate the national philosophy into effective programming in specific school contexts and/or advocate for more effective national policies prior to beginning program development efforts.

Action Plan

Once the needs assessment has been completed and a philosophy of gifted education developed or adopted, the program developers need to create an action plan. The action plan is a blueprint for program development in a specific context over a specific time period. An action plan should include the following information:

(1) The formal philosophy statement.
(2) Goals of the overall program development effort
(3) A brief description of the major tasks to be accomplished in achieving the goals with the persons(s) responsible for each tasks
(4) Timelines for each aspect of the overall project
(5) Projected budget
(6) Evaluation procedures for each major task/component of the plan
(7) Process for periodic revisions of the action plan after implementation begins.

Once the overall action plan has been written and approved by the relevant governing bodies the design and implementation of specific program components can begin.

Design Strategies

Using the strategic planning strategies suggested above can help galvanize broad-based support, elicit planning priorities from various stakeholder groups, and provide a contextualized structure for the design of program components. The component design and implementation process frequently involves many practical decisions such as who will be in charge of the program,

how the program will be delivered, how it will be funded, how students will be identified and served at various developmental levels, what will be taught, and who will teach it. At this stage of program development, it is essential that the contextual issues be integrated into a design for a specific program component that considers local, state, and/or national policies as well as the results of local needs assessments.

To a great extent, the success of the implementation process is linked to the gifted specialist or program administrator who will be directly responsible for program implementation in a specific context. Changes in educational reform have transformed the role of the gifted specialist in many regions (Hertzog, 1998), giving these individuals more responsibility as change agents. From very small communities, where there is only one gifted specialist who is also responsible for teaching, to large metropolitan programs that include a range of specialists in charge of different delivery systems, the competencies and skills needed by gifted specialists share some common features. Each serves as an advocate for gifted students and as a matchmaker seeking to match students' identified strengths and talents with program options that meet their needs. The gifted specialist may be expected to provide direct instruction, co-teach or identify resources for other program teachers. In larger programs, the gifted specialist may also have responsibilities for managing the program budget, overseeing both formative and summative evaluation of the program, providing professional development opportunities for staff, parents, general education personnel, families and the community. If at all possible, the gifted specialists who will be responsible for overseeing the implementation of a new gifted program component should be involved in all stages of the design of that component.

The array of program options available in gifted education can be overwhelming (Renzulli, 1986a; Maker & Nielson, 1995). Though seemingly convenient, a packaged approach to the design of program components can ignore important contextual needs identified during the planning phase and may result in a gifted program that is viewed as out of sync with the community's larger array of educational programs and services. In the situated approach to program development program developers are charged with fashioning program components that are tailored to local situations. Situated program development also requires a systems approach to the selection of program formats to prevent the proliferation of fragmented and marginalized services that characterized much of the early development of gifted programs in the United States (Cox, Daniel & Boston, 1985; Borland, 1989). The situated approach ensures that gifted program components can be integrated into the larger educational system (Borland, 1989; Moon & Swift, 1989). For an example of the use of the situated approach to the development of a multi-faceted middle school program in a single school district in the United States see Moon & Swift, 1989.

Funding issues

Program development must balance vision with pragmatism. Funding is one of the most important factors on the pragmatic side of the program development equation. For successful implementation, funding must be considered during the design stage. Generally, funding for gifted and talented programming comes from one of four sources: national or regional legislation; ministries of education; local allocations from a general education budget; or special, experimental projects.

Currently there are several countries that have broad-based, legislated, national funding for special education, but few that have broad-based, national, funding for gifted education. In the United States, for example, programs for special education students have high levels of national funding, but gifted education programs have been developed without federal funding. In most cases, gifted program costs in the United States are supported by a combination of state and district funds, with the greatest percentage of the funds used for personnel (Gallagher, Weiss, Oglesby & Thomas, 1983; VanTassel-Baska, 1998a). A similar situation exists in Canada (Goguen, 1993) and Australia (Braggert, 1993). In these countries program development most often occurs at the local level and it is imperative that the budget consequences of the components designed be carefully considered. In general, program design proposals must include realistic budgets in order to be approved by local school boards. In addition, advocacy to increase both regional and local funding availability may be required.

In other countries such as Singapore and Korea, categorical funding is available for gifted education through national ministries of education. The most successful program development efforts in these countries occur at the national level through the ministry of education and there is less support for local program development efforts in state supported schools (Wu & Cho, 1993; Goh, 1994). Occasionally, both national and local funding are available for gifted education. In Israel, for example, some programs, such as special schools for mathematically, scientifically, and artistically talented students, are funded entirely by the national government and others are partially funded by local school districts with the encouragement of national policy (Burg, 1992).

When legislation or ministry of education policies provide regional funding for gifted education, funding formulas can vary. Sometimes a set amount of dollars is allocated to gifted programming, which may necessitate a cap on the number of students served. In other cases, a weighted model is used based on a formula that includes such variables as the type of exception-

ality and the hours of services provided. A new model that was recently developed in the United States uses the services needed by the student and the intensity of the student's need as the key variables in determining program costs. In at least one state where this approach has been used, the model has helped create a more student-centered approach to programming. Program developers must pay attention both to what funds are available and to how those funds are allocated.

A final source of funding in many countries is special project funds. Such funds have supported demonstration projects for serving disadvantaged gifted students in the United States under the Jacob Javits Act (Berger, 1992; Gallagher, 1994); a longitudinal study of experimental, individual and group programming options in China (Zha, 1993a, 1993b, 1997); and a large-scale project to identify and develop science talent in Siberia (Masharov, 1993). Program developers need to find out whether such funds are available in their area. If they are, developers should consider whether there is a match between the goals of the special project and local needs. Where a match exists, it may be worthwhile to apply for special project funds to support program development efforts. However, such funds are usually limited in duration. Therefore, a plan also needs to be created for financing the new program when the special project funds terminate. A more ambitious approach to special project funding involves attempting to convince funding agencies and/or legislatures to develop a new, funded special project to support the type of programming envisioned by the developers.

Unfortunately, in far too many countries, scarce financial resources for education in general, and gifted education in particular, are a major barrier to program development (Alencar, 1993; Taylor, 1993; Ekiert-Grabowska, 1994; Kolo, 1996). In these countries it is particularly important for program developers to pay attention to the cost-effectiveness of gifted programs and/or seek a source of special project funds.

Identification Procedures

Although needs assessments, advocacy efforts, and stakeholder input can help establish a common understanding of the target population that a gifted program is intended to serve, the determination of identification procedures can still be one of the most controversial aspects of program development. By definition, an identification procedure is an operational definition of giftedness and therefore subject to all of the controversy surrounding the construct of giftedness discussed earlier in this chapter. The difference between an identification procedure and a definition of giftedness is that an identification procedure is an operational definition of giftedness for the purpose of identifying students who would benefit from a particular gifted program. Prior to designing an identification procedure for a particular program component, program designers should have defined the domains and levels of giftedness that will be served in the program.

One of the most important criteria for evaluating identification procedures is the degree of 'fit' between the procedures and the program component. In other words, an identification procedure should identify students who need and would benefit from the program. In addition, identification procedures should include at least two stages and multiple methods of data collection (Tuttle & Becker, 1983a; Gallagher & Gallagher, 1994; VanTassel-Baska, 1998b). The first stage is usually an inclusive screening process to find all students who might possibly benefit from the program that will be offered. In the second stage, additional data may be collected and the final selection decisions are made. A well-designed identification procedure also has formal appeal and exit procedures and is revised periodically (Moon, Feldhusen & Kelly, 1991).

The use of multiple identification criteria is strongly recommended (Feldhusen & Jarwan, 1993). As of 1992 in the United States, 34 states were using multiple criteria for ascertaining a student's eligibility for the gifted program (Coleman & Gallagher, 1992a). A position paper developed by the National Association for Gifted Children stated:

> Given the limitations of all tests, no single measure should be used to make identification and placement decisions. That is, no single test or instrument should be used to include a child in or exclude a child from gifted education services . . . Best practices indicate that multiple measures and valid indicators from multiple sources must be used to assess and serve gifted students'. (NAGC, 1997)

Both formal and informal sources of data can be used to provide identification information (Spicker, 1987). *Formal sources* include standardized achievement tests, personality measures, normative behavioral checklists, and group or individual intelligence tests. *Informal sources* include portfolios of student work, authentic assessments, interviews, criterion-referenced rating scales, and parent/teacher/peer/self nominations. It is also a good idea to use the information gathered during the identification process to inform instructional planning. When used to plan and deliver instruction, knowledge of students' abilities can have a positive impact on student performance (Sternberg, Ferrari, Clinkenbeard & Grigorenko, 1996).

Issues in Identification. Issues in identification include: (a) equitable identification of students of different genders, ethnicities, and socio-economic background; (b) measurement concerns; (c) data aggregation and decision making concerns. Identification decisions are 'high stakes' decisions because they impact the lives of individuals. Therefore, each step in the procedures must be carefully reviewed to insure

that they are equitable for different subgroups (Frasier, 1991; Baldwin, 1994; Borland & Wright, 1994; O'Tuel, 1994; Plucker, 1996). For example, teacher nomination has consistently contributed to the under-inclusion of economically disadvantaged and minority students in U.S. gifted programs due to low teacher expectations and the type of impoverished schools that such students are often attending (Frasier & Passow, 1994; Frasier et al., 1995). Those responsible for overseeing the identification process must insure that teachers and staff become knowledgeable about the diverse ways in which gifted characteristics, behaviors, and indicators may be exhibited. The process must include a variety of individuals from various contexts who are invited to refer or nominate students and provide educational settings that can stimulate early signs of giftedness through students performances that can be observed in classrooms.

The are a number of measurement issues that can affect the validity of an evaluation procedure. The most important is validity with respect to program goals and services (Feldhusen, 1991; Feldhusen & Jarwan, 1993). Other measurement concerns frequently cited in the literature include *reliability*, especially for locally constructed and nonstandardized assessment techniques; and the *ceiling effects* on many standardized tests that make it difficult to distinguish levels of giftedness among the highly gifted.(Feldhusen, 1991; Feldhusen & Jarwan, 1993). *Developmental appropriateness* is also a measurement issue (Zorman, 1998). For example, Kolo (1999) studied instruments suitable for nominating potentially gifted preschoolers in Nigeria found that instruments designed specifically for the age group being targeted that had been modified for use by making more relevant item descriptors were more effective than instruments that had been locally developed for older students. For assistance in the challenging process of selecting standardized instruments appropriate for identification of gifted students, readers are encouraged to use Callahan, Hunsaker, Adams, Moore & Bland's (1995) careful review of identification instruments and Callahan, Tomlinson & Pizzat's (1995) discussion of innovative approaches to identification.

Data aggregation techniques and methods of making selection decisions are also controversial. For example, the use of matrices where points are assigned to diagnostic data in order to categorize them or produce totals have been criticized because such aggregation systems can distort the underlying raw scores (Feldhusen, Baska & Womble, 1981; Feldhusen & Jarwan, 1993). A more reliable way to synthesize data from different instruments is to convert the raw scores to standard scores prior to aggregation (Feldhusen et al., 1981; Feldhusen & Jarwan, 1993). The strengths and weaknesses of professional judgement methods of decision making have also been debated in the literature. When using the professional judgement decision making method with multiple selection criteria, it is important to make the weighting systems used by members of the selection committee explicit and uniform (Moore & Betts, 1987). In sum, the development of an identification procedure is a controversial, technical, and vitally important aspect of program development. If the program planning team does not included an expert in measurement and the principles of identifying talent, a consultant should be hired to assist with the development of the identification procedures for each program component that will be developed by the team.

Program Format and Curriculum

Format. One of the most important tasks in designing gifted program components is the selection of a delivery format and a curriculum that fit together and will achieve program goals for a targeted group of gifted students. The *format* of a gifted program is the administrative delivery system utilized. Examples of program formats include special schools (Burg, 1992), early college entrance (Robinson, 1992b; Robinson, 1997), pullout enrichment (Kolloff & Feldhusen, 1981), regular classroom with differentiation (Tomlinson, 1995), and after-school, Saturday, and summer programs (Goldstein & Wagner, 1993; Wood & Feldhusen, 1996). The format tells whether, how, and when students will be grouped for instruction but says little about what kind of instruction students will receive. Selection of a program format requires careful consideration of a number of factors including the program talent domain, the level of giftedness of the target population of students, cultural and family values, and resources such as funding, space, and personnel.

There are different cost differentials associated with the staffing demands of various program models. Hence, decisions about program format require particularly close attention to personnel resources. The flexible use of human resources has been suggested as a means of increasing the cost effectiveness of gifted programs. Planned use of community volunteers, differentiated staffing, and extended school day and year are all strategies that have been suggested as ways to make gifted programming more cost effective (VanTassel-Baska, 1998a). Selecting a program format that facilitates use of these cost-effective personnel strategies may make it possible to develop gifted programs in contexts where lack of funding is a major barrier to gifted education.

Curriculum. Curriculum describes the type of learning experiences students will have irregardless of the delivery format. Curriculum development can be one of the most demanding aspects of the development of a gifted program component. Often there is no existing curriculum that will provide sufficiently challenging learning experiences for the target population of high ability students so curriculum must be written by the program developers, perhaps with the guidance of outside consultants, a time and labor intensive task. Full consideration of the complexities of developing articulated and differentiated curriculum for a specific gifted program is beyond the scope of this chapter. The interested reader is referred to the following references for guidance on this crucial program development task: (VanTassel-Baska, 1992, 1994; Maker & Nielson, 1996).

Developmental Issues. Those responsible for planning programs for gifted students must carefully consider the developmental needs of the age group of students for whom a program is intended, e.g. young gifted children vs. gifted adolescents. Although there is strong evidence supporting early recognition of giftedness (Kingore, 1998), early intervention (Diamond, 1988; Clark, 1998), and special programming for talented preschoolers (Karnes, 1983; Borland & Wright, 1994), the young gifted child is still frequently overlooked in the continuum of gifted programming (Smutny, 1998). For example, many educators and researchers are reluctant to recommend young children for psychometric testing and/or to trust the results of such testing. Those providing services to young gifted children will need to plan for children who may already know how to read, have advanced understandings of mathematical concepts and operations, and/or have a natural curiosity that requires opportunities for individualized investigations (Vydra & Leimbach, 1998). Responding to a child's readiness to learn is pivotal to the philosophy characterizing the learning environments considered best suited to working with developmentally advanced young children (Meininger, 1998).

The middle grades pose another series of developmental challenges that interface with a student's giftedness. Although there are many areas of agreement between gifted education and middle grades education (Chance, 1998), the current emphasis on heterogeneous grouping favored by middle schools contributes to the lack of challenge that many gifted students report when compared to elementary and high school (Coleman & Gallagher, 1992b; Tomlinson, 1994). Although this issue seemed to create a chasm between middle school educators and gifted educators in the early 1990s in the United States, recent reviews of the literature suggested that the debates have served as a forum for both fields to move beyond the rhetoric of differences towards a healthier focus on programs and practices (Rosselli, 1997; Tomlinson, 1997). For example, the 'touchstone' approach permits the testing of practices that may or may not be under the nomenclature of gifted education to insure that gifted middle schoolers' needs are met (Rosselli, 1997). This approach involves asking questions such as: Will the program services support excellence over mediocrity? Do the program offerings eliminate an artificial ceiling for learning? Do the program offerings support students' varying learning needs, e.g. pace and style? Will the program offerings help students see in themselves a strength, passion or capability that can become a highly developed talent? The dialogue between middle school and gifted education in the United States has provided gifted program administrators with more information on the unique needs of this age group and creative new ways to meet the needs of gifted and talented middle schoolers.

Staffing

Teacher characteristics. Although much has been written about desirable attributes of teachers for gifted programs, there is little empirical evidence supporting agreement on a definitive profile of an effective teacher of gifted students (Borland, 1989). Traits and characteristics such as hard working, high energy level, emotionally mature, self-confident, knowledgeable in the content area, highly intelligent, flexible, and creative are generally suggested with disclaimers that recognize the problems that such lists invoke (Feldhusen, 1997). In an attempt to move beyond this type of list mentality, which has limited usefulness for administrators charged with selecting personnel to teach gifted students, Olenchak (1990) has recommended that those hiring teachers for gifted programs include interview questions that create simulations in which candidates can demonstrate their use of reflection. Another suggestion for interview protocols can be drawn from the research of Armenta (1997) who found that the motivation for teachers to work with gifted students was fueled by strong feelings of identification with gifted children and memories of inadequate services during their own school histories. Thus, interview protocols inquiring about candidates' own backgrounds and motivations for seeking employment in gifted education may prove useful in the selection process.

The increasing use of consultation models as primary or supporting delivery system for gifted services, suggests that attention be paid to the qualities found in those who are able to successfully implement consultation and collaboration models. Critical attributes/behaviors needed for collaboration include: the ability to establish an easy rapport, the ability to communicate effectively, expertise in the area of gifted education, a view of the consultative relationship as mutually beneficial, resourcefulness, and empathy (Purcell & Leppien, 1998; Kirschenbaum, Armstrong & Landrum, 1999).

All too often staffing is limited to only those individuals who serve as teachers in a particular program. Feldhusen & Moon (1995) encourage the use of a systems-ecological perspective to involve families and communities, as well as school personnel, in programs for gifted students. In addition, guidance counselors, social workers, and other school support personnel can assume important responsibilities relative to gifted programs such as: (a) matching student needs with appropriate services, (b) facilitating grade acceleration, and (c) serving as a catalyst for developing services that are none existent.

Staff development. An important responsibility of any program administrator is the design, facilitation, and evaluation of professional development activities. Effective professional development increases job retention, helps individuals prepare for role changes, enhances personal growth, and provides inspiration. No longer viewed as simply an exhaustive list of mini-workshops offered on a standardized inservice day, today's models of professional development are results-driven, systems oriented and influenced by constructivist approaches (Sparks & Hirsh, 1997). A full continuum of approaches to professional development must consider learning that takes place formally and informally, as well as within and outside school settings. In best case scenarios, teachers have opportunities to prioritize their own professional development needs while simultaneously supporting school agendas.

Although professional development has been recognized as one of the seven key directives for gifted education (Ross, 1993) and there is empirical evidence that teachers who receive training are more effective with gifted students than those who have not received training (Hansen & Feldhusen, 1994), professional development opportunities that address the needs of capable learners are still sorely lacking. Westberg and colleagues (Westberg et al., 1998) examined survey responses from over 1,200 school districts and found that:

- A very small proportion of school districts' total professional development dollars is spent on gifted education topics;
- The majority of districts do not evaluate the impact of their professional development practices in gifted education;
- Peer coaching between classroom teachers and gifted education teachers is seldom or never used to provide professional development; and
- Although more professional development experiences were found in districts with state mandates to identify and serve gifted students, there were no differences in terms of differentiated levels of professional development being offered for beginning, intermediate, and advanced levels of educators.

Similarly, the United States Council of State Directors of Programs for the Gifted has reported only 17 states with mandated training leading to teacher endorsement in gifted education (1994).

Ideally, candidates hired to teach in gifted programs should participate in formal professional coursework designed to help teachers develop proficiency in gifted education. Towards this direction, NAGC has provided guidance through the publication of professional standards for graduate programs in gifted education (Parker, 1996). Program format has an influence on the type of formal training needed by teachers who will be working with gifted and talented youth. In countries where responsibility for meeting the needs of gifted students rests with general education teachers teaching in general education classrooms, it is desirable that those teachers receive coursework on gifted education during their *preservice* teacher education programs. When gifted education is delivered to adolescents in special schools, the teachers who will be teaching in such schools should have intensive *graduate* coursework in both gifted education pedagogy and their disciplinary specialization prior to and/or concurrent with their teaching assignment.

When such formal training is lacking, local staff development must be planned and implemented as a part of program development efforts. Dettmer & Landrum (1998) have distinguished between inservice and staff development in gifted education. *Inservice* tends to be a single event offered by an individual with expertise in gifted education. Staff development is a multi-year process that is targeted at school goals. *Staff development* involves careful planning based on assessment processes and is usually focused on goals that include involvement, commitment, and renewal. District personnel who oversee gifted programs embedded within general education settings have an especially complex mission in creating staff development programs that can be responsive to three different groups of stakeholders: veteran teachers in gifted programs, novice teachers in gifted programs, and general education and support personnel who by virtue of their interaction with gifted students need knowledge and skills relative to gifted education. For an excellent guide to planning and conducting local staff development see Dettmer & Landrum, 1998.

Building Ownership

It is critical for administrators to develop ownership for gifted programs in ways that go beyond simply training the educational personnel directly involved in delivering services. The support of general education teachers, administrators, the participating students and their families are all integral to a situated approach to program planning. For example, use of instruments such as the Parent Experience Scale (Keirouz, 1992) can assist administrators in better understanding parental concerns, allowing for program revisions as appropriate. Similar processes involving other stakeholder groups are necessary as part of the climatization process which Goh (1993) describes as the development of trust and effective communication patterns within the organization in order to gain participation and support: "Climatization should be an ongoing

activity with different levels of intensity at different stages of program development and implementation, and aimed internally at the whole school environment as well as externally to the community outside of the school" (p. 576). Without this important step, a gifted program may become isolated from the rest of the educational system and be vulnerable to elimination.

In order to be effective in building ownership, gifted program administrators must be knowledgeable about change and innovation in educational systems (Moon & Swift, 1989; Goh, 1993; Maier, 1993). After all, new gifted programs are an innovation that need support from members of the school community to grow and develop (Goh, 1993). Use of the Concerns Based Adoption Model (CBAM), which views change as a process, can help administrators assess teachers' concerns about a new program and examine the relationship between the teachers' concerns and their actual practices in the classroom which can then be compared to the original design of the program innovation (Burns & Reid, 1990). This approach is helpful in examining the progress of a pilot program or when the program development spans a complex multi-year plan of action. It can help program administrators monitor multiple aspects of the program once it is implemented in order to resolve any problems that were not detectable at the design stage.

District personnel who attempt to change programs and services run the minefield of miscommunication, misidentification, and misapprehension due to the varying perceptions of stakeholders regarding the purpose and intent of gifted programs McGonagill (1997). Some of this confusion can be defused when district personnel pay adequate attention to the interaction of services across levels in ways that allow all stakeholders to recognize how each service at each level serves as an important precursor for future program endeavors and an integral step towards the program's goals (McGonagill, 1997). Often overlooked at the implementation stage are the students who will participate in the program. Orientation sessions for students and their parents can help clarify the goals and expected outcomes of the program, address fears and concerns, strengthen ownership for the program, and even serve as an ideal setting for collecting data that may be useful in a pre- and post-program assessment model.

Along with building ownership in the program, the program administrator, advisory committee, parents, teachers, and students can all serve as advocates for the program (Karnes, Lewis & Stephens, 1999; Kiger, 1998). Publicizing the program and its offerings and accomplishments helps others recognize the merit of special services for gifted students. A strong public relations approach can also facilitate a quick and effective response to legislative and policy initiatives that may impact the program (Riley & Karnes, 1991; Troxclair & Karnes, 1997). Holliday (1996) suggests two types of public relations that are needed: a political approach that addresses needs of the program and seeks resources to support those needs and a more relational approach which effects the way the school personnel and community members work together to provide students with quality services. Again, it is clear that advocacy and program development go hand in hand.

Accountability

Gifted programs are not exempt from the increased focus of the public and legislatures on accountability. In fact the opposite is true, because measures of student outcomes are increasingly being linked to resources. Gallagher (1998) suggests that accountability should be thought of in the spirit of "Trust, but verify." He also recommends that two levels of objectives be considered when measuring accountability: management objectives that include specific actions that the district intends to take to improve the program and program objectives that articulate expected changes as a result of the program, e.g changes in student knowledge, skills, attitudes, and motivation. Both types of objectives are important, so Gallagher cautions that meeting management objectives means little if the program has fallen short in meeting its program objectives.

A well-designed formative evaluation can document that a gifted program is fulfilling its intention and provide information that can be utilized for program improvement (Callahan & Caldwell, 1984; Carter, 1991; Fetterman, 1993). Although many experts in the field believe that program designs should always include an accompanying evaluation design (Renzulli, 1975; Tomlinson & Callahan, 1993; Callahan & Caldwell, 1995), in practice program evaluation is among the most neglected aspects of program development (Hunsaker & Callahan, 1993). Many reasons have been suggested for the neglect of program evaluation including program vagueness and variability (Callahan, 1993), problems related to the use of standardized tests (Archambault, 1984; Reis, 1984; Robinson, 1991; Callahan & Caldwell, 1993), the complexity of gifted program outcomes (Carter, 1991; Callahan, 1993), and lack of time, resources, or technical assistance (Moon, 1996).

Although it can be difficult to evaluate gifted programs, it is essential to do so in order to ensure program excellence and viability. A full discussion of the principles of gifted program evaluation is beyond the scope of this chapter. For guidelines for planning effective evaluations of gifted programs see (Renzulli, 1975; Fetterman, 1993; Tomlinson & Callahan, 1993; Callahan & Caldwell, 1995; Seeley, 1998). For guidance on developing locally constructed instruments for evaluation purposes see (Nielsen & Buchanan, 1991). For good discussions of some of the complex issues that must be addressed in planning evaluations of

gifted programs see (Callahan, 1983, 1993; Carter, 1986, 1991).

Conclusion

Situated program development is a complex task. The foundational stage of situated program development is a careful examination of both the conceptual foundations of the field of gifted education and the socio-cultural environment in which the program will be implemented. The second stage of situated program development involves strategic planning that results in a long-term action plan for the development of gifted and talented programming in a particular context. Finally, program components are custom-designed to develop talent in specific subpopulations of gifted and talented students in a particular context. When high levels of expertise in each aspect of program design are combined with a strong conceptual foundation and wise strategic planning, the result is exciting and effective educational programs for gifted and talented students.

References

Alencar, E. M. L. S. (1993). Programs and practices for identifying and nurturing giftedness and talent in Central and South America. In: K. A. Heller, F. J. Monks & A. H. Passow (Eds.), *International Handbook of Giftedness and Talent* (pp. 849–864). New York: Pergamon.

Ambrose, D. (1998). A model for clarification and expansion of conceptual foundations. *Gifted Child Quarterly*, **42** (2), 77–86.

Archambault, F. X. (1984). Measurement and evaluation concerns in evaluating programs for the gifted. *Journal for the Education of the Gifted*, **7** (1), 12–25.

Archambault, F. X., Westberg, K. L., Brown, S. W., Hallmark, B. W., Emmons, C. L. & Zhang, W. (1993). *Regular classroom practices with gifted students: Results of a national survey of classroom teachers*. Storrs, CT: National Research Center on the Gifted and Talented.

Armenta, C. (1997). Understanding our passion for the gifted. *Research Briefs*, **11**, 100–111.

Baldwin, A. Y. (1994). The seven plus story: developing hidden talent among students in socio-economically disadvantaged environments. *Gifted Child Quarterly*, **38** (2), 80–84.

Begin, J. & Gagne, F. (1994). Predictors of attitudes toward gifted education: a review of the literature and a blueprint for future research. *Journal for the Education of the Gifted*, **17** (2), 161–179.

Benbow, C. P. & Lubinski, D. (Eds.). (1996). *Intellectual talent: psychometric and social issues*. Baltimore: Johns Hopkins University Press.

Benbow, C. P. & Lubinski, D. (1997). Talent searches: a model for the discovery and development of academic talent. In: N. Colangelo & G. A. Davis (Eds.), *Handbook of Gifted Education*. Boston: Allyn & Bacon.

Berger, S. L. (Ed.). (1992). *Programs and practices in gifted education: projects funded by the Jacob K. Javits Gifted and Talented Students Education Act of 1988*. Reston, VA: The Council for Exceptional Children.

Betts, G. T. (1985). *Autonomous learner model for the gifted and talented.* Greely, CO: ALPS.

Boles, K. & Troen, V. (1996). Teacher leaders and power: Achieving school reform from the classroom. In: G. Moller & M. Katzenmeyer (Eds.), *Every Teacher as a Leader: Realizing the Potential of Teacher Leadership* (pp. 141–162). San Francisco: Jossey-Bass.

Borland, J. H. (1989). *Planning and implementing programs for the gifted and talented.* New York: Teachers College Press.

Borland, J. H. (1996). Gifted education and the threat of irrelevance. *Journal for the Education of the Gifted*, **19** (2), 129–147.

Borland, J. H. (1999). The limits of consilience: a reaction to Francoys Gagne's "My convictions about the nature of abilities, gifts, and talents." *Journal for the Education of the Gifted*, **22** (2), 137–147.

Borland, J. H. & Wright, L. (1994). Identifying young, potentially gifted, economically disadvantaged students. *Gifted Child Quarterly*, **38** (4), 164–171.

Boyd, L. N. (1992). The needs assessment-who needs it? *Roeper Review*, **15** (2), 64–66.

Braggert, E. J. (1993). Programs and practices for identifying and nurturing giftedness and talent in Australia and New Zealand. In: K. A. Heller, F. J. Monks & A. H. Passow (Eds.), *International Handbook of Research and Development of Giftednes and Talent* (pp. 815–832). New York: Pergamon Press.

Brown, C. N. (1997). Gifted identification as a constitutional issue. *Roeper Review*, **19** (3), 157–160.

Burg, B. (1992). Gifted Education in Israel. *Roeper Review*, **14** (4), 217–221.

Burns, D. E. & Reid, B. D. (1990). CBAM: Three methodological techniques for research and evaluation in gifted education. *Research Briefs*, **5**.

California Association for the Gifted (1998). *Advocacy in action: an advocacy handbook for gifted and talented education.* Mountain View, CA: California Association for the Gifted.

Callahan, C. & Caldwell, M. (1984). Using evaluation results to improve programs for the gifted and talented. *Journal for the Education of the Gifted*, **7** (1), 60–75.

Callahan, C. M. (1993). Evaluation programs and procedures for gifted education: International problems and solutions. In: K. A. Heller, F. J. Monks & A. H. Passow (Eds.), *International Handbook of Research and Development of Giftedness and Talent* (pp. 605–618). Oxford, England: Pergamon.

Callahan, C. M. (1996). A critical self-study of gifted education: healthy practice, necessary evil, or sedition? *Journal for the Education of the Gifted*, **19** (2), 148–163.

Callahan, C. M. & Caldwell, M. S. (1993). Establishment of a national data bank on identification and evaluation instruments. *Journal for the Education of the Gifted*, **16** (2), 201–219.

Callahan, C. M. & Caldwell, M. S. (1995). A practitioner's guide to evaluating programs for the gifted. Washington, D. C.: *National Association for Gifted Education*.

Callahan, C. M., Tomlinson, C. A. & Pizzat, P. M. (1995). *Contexts for promise: Noteworthy practices and innovations in the identification of gifted students.* Storrs, CT: The National Research Center on the Gifted and Talented.

Callahan, C. M. (1983). Issues in evaluating programs for the gifted. *Gifted Child Quarterly*, **27** (1), 3–7.

Carter, K. R. (1986). Evaluating design: issues confronting evaluators of gifted programs. *Gifted Child Quarterly* (30), 2.

Carter, K. R. (1991). Evaluation of gifted programs. In: N. K. Buchanan (Ed.), *Conducting Research and Evaluation in Gifted Education: A Handbook of Methods and Applications* (pp. 245–273). New York: Teachers College Press.

Chance, P. L. (1998). Meeting in the middle: gifted education and middle schools working together. *Roeper Review*, **21** (2), 133–138.

Clark, G. A. & Zimmerman, E. D. (1984). *Educating artistically talented students.* Syracuse, NY: Syracuse University Press.

Clark, G. A. & Zimmerman, E. D. (1987). *Resources for educating artistically talented students.* Syracuse, NY: Syracuse University Press.

Clinkenbeard, P. R. (1997). Research on motivation and the gifted: implications for identification, programming, and evaluation. *Gifted Child Quarterly*, **40** (4), 220–221.

Coleman, M. R. & Gallagher, J. J. (1992a). *Report on state policies realted to the identification of gifted students.* Chapel Hill, NC: University of North Carolina at Chapel Hill.

Coleman, M. R. & Gallagher, J. J. (1992b). *Report on state policies related to the identification of gifted students.* Chapel Hill, NC: University of North Carolina at Chapel Hill.

Cox, J., Daniel, N. & Boston, B. O. (1985). *Educating able learners: programs and promising practices.* Austin: University of Texas.

DeLeon, P. H. & VandenBox, G. R. (1985). Public policy and advocacy on behalf of the gifted and talented. In: F. D. Horwitz & M. O'Brien (Eds.), *the Gifted and Talented: Developmental Perspectives* (pp. 409–435). Washington, D.C.: American Psychological Association.

Detterman, D. K. & Ruthsatz. (1999). Toward a more comprehensive theory of exceptional abilities. *Journal for the Education of the Gifted*, **22** (2), 148–158.

Dettmer, P. (1991). Gifted program advocacy: overhauling bandwagons to build support. *Gifted Child Quarterly*, **35** (4), 165–172.

Dettmer, P. & Landrum, M. (Eds.). (1998). *Staff Development: The Key to Effective Gifted Education Programs.* Washington, D.C.: National Association for Gifted Children.

Diamond, M. (1998). *Enriching heredity: The impact of the environment on the anatomy of the brain.* New York: The Free Press.

Ekiert-Grabowska, D. (1994). Creativity and gifted education in the context of current political changes in Poland. *Gifted and Talented International*, **9** (2), 36–46.

Ericsson, K. A. (1996). *The road to excellence*: Lawrence Erlbaum.

Ericsson, K. A., Krampe, R. T. & Tesch-Romer, C. (1993). The role of deliberate practice in the acquisition of expert performance. *Psychological Review*, **100** (3), 363–406.

Exum, H. A. (1983). Key issues in family counseling with gifted and talented black students. *Roeper Review*, **5** (3), 28–31.

Feldhusen, J. F. (1991). Identification of gifted and talented youth. In: M. C. Wang, M. C. Reynolds & H. J. Walberg (Eds.), *Handbook of Special Education: Research and Practice*. New York: Pergamon.

Feldhusen, J. F. (1997). Educating teachers for work with talented youth. In: N. Colangelo & G. A. Davis (Eds.), *Handbook of Gifted Education* (pp. 547–5552). Boston: Allyn & Bacon.

Feldhusen, J. F. (1998). A conception of talent and talent development. In: R. C. Friedman & K. R. Rogers (Eds.), *Talent in Context: Historical and Social Perspectives* (pp. 193–209). Washington, D.C.: American Psychological Association.

Feldhusen, J. F., Baska, L. K. & Womble, S. R. (1981). Using standard scores to synthesize data in identifying the gifted. *Journal for the Education of the Gifted*, **4**, 177–185.

Feldhusen, J. F. & Jarwan, F. A. (1993). Identification of gifted and talented youth for educational programs (pp. 233–252). Oxford, England: Pergamon.

Feldhusen, J. F. & Kolloff, P. B. (1986). The Purdue Three-Stage Enrichment Model at the Elementary Level. In: J. S. Renzulli (Ed.), *Systems and Models for Developing Programs for the Gifted and Talented* (pp. 153–179). Mansfield Center: Creative Learning Press.

Feldhusen, J. F. & Moon, S. M. (1995). The educational continuum and delivery of services. In: J. L. Genshaft, M. Birely & C. L. Hollinger (Eds.), *Serving Gifted and Talented Students: A Resource for School Personnel* (pp. 103–121). Austin, TX: Pro Ed.

Feldhusen, J. F. & Robinson, A. (1986). The Purdue Secondary Model for Gifted and Talented Education. In: J. S. Renzulli (Ed.), *Systems and Models for Developing Programs for the Gifted and Talented* (pp. 153–179). Mansfield Center, CT: Creative Learning Press.

Feldman, D. H. (1999). A developmental, evolutionary perspective on gifts and talents. *Journal for the Education of the Gifted*, **22** (2), 159–167.

Fetterman, D. M. (1993). *Evaluate yourself*. Storrs, CT: The National Research Center on the Gifted and Talented.

Fink, A. & Koscecoff, J. B. (1985). *How to conduct surveys: a step by step guide*. Newbury Park, CA: Sage.

Ford, D. Y. (1995). Desegregating gifted education: a need unmet. *Journal of Negro Education*, **64** (1), 52–62.

Ford, D. Y., Russo, C. J. & Harris, J. J. (1995). Meeting the educational needs of the gifted: a legal imperative. *Roeper Review*, **17** (4), 224–228.

Frasier, M. M. (1991). Disadvantaged and culturally diverse gifted students. *Journal for the Education of the Gifted*, **14** (3), 234–245.

Frasier, M. M., Hunsaker, S. L., Lee, J., Finley, V. S., Frank, E., Farcia, J. H. & Martin, D. (1995). *Educator's perceptions of barriers to the identification of gifted children from economically disadvantaged and limited English proficient backgrounds (Research Mongograph 95216)*. Storrs, CT: The National Research Center on the Gifted and Talented.

Frasier, M. M. & Passow, A. H. (1994). *Toward a paradigm for identifying talent potential*. Storrs, CT: The National Research Center on the Gifted and Talented.

Freeman, J. (1992). Education for gifted in a changing Europe. *Roeper Review*, **14**(4), 198–201.

Friedman, R. C. & Lee, S. W. (1996). Differentiating instruction for high achieving/gifted children in regular classrooms: a field test of three gifted education models. *Journal for the Education of the Gifted*, **19**(4), 405–436.

Fullan, M. (1993). *Change forces*. New York: Falmer Press.

Gagne, F. (1998). A proposal for subcategories within gifted or talented populations. *Gifted Child Quarterly*, **42**, 87–95.

Gagne, F. (1999). My convictions about the nature of abilities, gifts, and talents. *Journal for the Education of the Gifted*, **22** (2), 109–136.

Gallagher, J., Weiss, P., Oglesby, K. & Thomas, T. (1983). *The status of gifted/talented education: United States surveys of needs, practices, and policies*. Ventura County, CA: Ventura County Superintendent of Schools Office.

Gallagher, J. J. (1993). Current status of gifted education in the United States. In: K. A. Heller, F. J. Monks & A. H. Passow (Eds.), *International Handbook of Research and Development of Giftedness and Talent* (pp. 755–770). Oxford: Pergamon Press.

Gallagher, J. J. (1994). A retrospective view: the Javits program. *Gifted Child Quarterly*, **38** (2), 95–96.

Gallagher, J. J. (1996). A critique of the critiques of gifted education. *Journal for the Education of the Gifted*, **19** (2), 234–249.

Gallagher, J. J. & Gallagher, S. G. (1994). *Teaching the gifted child*. Boston: Allyn & Bacon.

Gardner, H. (1983). *Frames of mind: the theory of multiple intelligences*. New York: Basic Books.

George, D. (1992). Gifted education in England. *Roeper Review*, **14** (4), 201–204.

Glover, J. A., Ronning, R. R. & Reynolds, C. R. (Eds.). (1989). *Handbook of creativity*. New York: Plenum.

Goguen, L. J. (1993). Right to Education for the Gifted in Canada. In: K. A. Heller, J. F. Monks & A. H. Passow (Eds.), *International Handbook of Research and Development of Giftedness and Talent* (pp. 771–777). Oxford, England: Pergamon Press.

Goh, B. (1994). Reflections on gifted education in Singapore and the USA. *Gifted and Talented International*, **9** (2), 52–53.

Goh, B. E. (1993). Administrative issues in organizing programs for the gifted. In: K. A. Heller, F. J. Monks & A. H. Passow (Eds.), *International Handbook of Research and Development of Giftedness and Talent* (pp. 569–583). New York: Pergamon Press.

Goldstein, D. & Wagner, H. (1993). After school programs, competitions, school olympics, and summer programs. In: K. A. Heller, F. J. Monks & A. H. Passow (Eds.), *International Handbook of Research and Development of Giftedness and Talent* (pp. 593–604). Oxford, England: Pergamon.

Guenther, Z. C. (1995). A center for talent development in Brazil. *Gifted and Talented International*, **10** (1), 26–30.

Hansen, J. B. & Feldhusen, J. F. (1994). Comparison of trained and untrained teachers of gifted students. *Gifted Child Quarterly*, **38** (3), 115–121.

Hertzog, N. B. (1998). The changing role of the gifted education specialist. *Teaching Exceptional Children*, 30, 39–43.

Hiatt, E. L. (1994). Promises to keep: the story of project promise. *Gifted Child Quarterly*, **38** (2), 85–88.

Holliday, A. E. (1996). Ninety nine ways to increase/improve school-community relations. *The Journal of Educational Relations*, **17** (3), 2–6.

Hord, S. M., Rutherford, W. L., Huling-Austin, L. & Hall, G. (1987). *Taking charge of change*. Alexandria, VA: Association for Supervision and Curriculum Development.

Hsueh, W. & Moon, S. (1998). Families of gifted children in Taiwan: a comparative review of the literature. *Gifted and Talented International*, **13**, 5–13.

Hunsaker, S. L. (1995). The gifted metaphor from the perspective of traditional civilizations. *Journal for the Education of the Gifted*, **18** (3), 255–268.

Hunsaker, S. L. & Callahan, C. M. (1993). Evaluation of gifted programs: current practices. *Journal for the Education of the Gifted*, **16** (2), 190–200.

Johnson, S. K. & Ryser, G. R. (1996). An overview of effective practices with gifted students in general education settings. *Journal for the Education of the Gifted*, **19** (4), 379–404.

Juntune, J. E. (1982). Program development. St. Paul, MN: National Association for Gifted Children.

Kaplan, S. N. (1986). The grid: a model to construct differentiated curriculum for the gifted. In: J. S. Renzulli (Ed.), *Systems and Models for Developing Programs for the Gifted and Talented* (pp. 180–193). Mansfield Center, CT: Creative Learning Press.

Karnes, F. A., Lewis, J. D. & Stephens, K. R. (1999). Parents and teachers working together for advocacy through public relations. *Gifted Child Today*, **22** (1), 14–18.

Karnes, F. A. & Riley, T. (1991). Public relations strategies for gifted education. *Gifted Child Today*, **14** (6), 35–37.

Karnes, F. A., Troxclair, D. A. & Marquandt, R. G. (1997). The Office of Civil Rights and the gifted: An update. *Roeper Review*, **19** (3), 162–165.

Keirouz, K. (1992). Assessing the concerns of gifted parents: the parent experience scale. *Research Briefs*, **6**, 162–165.

Kiger, L. (1998). Public relations for gifted education. *Gifted Child Today*, **21** (5), 42–44.

Kingore, B. (1998). Seeking advanced potentials: Developmentally appropriate procedures for identification. In J. F. Smutny (Ed.) *The young gifted child: Potential and promise, an anthology (31–51)*. Cresskill, NJ: Hampton Press.

Kirschenbaum, R. J., Armstrong, D. C. & Landrum, M. S. (1999). Resource consultation model in gifted education to support talent development in today's inclusive schools. *Gifted Child Quarterly*, **43** (1), 39–47.

Kolloff, M. B. & Feldhusen, J. F. (1981, May/June). PACE (Program for Academic and Creative Enrichment): an application of the three-stage model. *Gifted Child Today*, 47–50.

Kolo, I. A. (1996). Reflections on the development of gifted education in Nigeria. *Roeper Review*, **19**(2), 79–81.

Kolo, I. A. (1999). The effectiveness of Nigerian vs. United States teacher checklists and inventories for nominating potentially gifted Nigerian preschoolers. *Roeper Review*, **21**(3), 179–183.

Landrum, M. S., Katsiyannis, A. & DeWaard, J. (1998). A national survey of current legislative and policy trends in gifted education: life after the *National Excellence* report. *Journal for the Education of the Gifted*, **21** (3), 352–371.

Larsen, M. D., Griffin, N. S. & Larsen, L. (1994). Public opinion regarding support for special programs for gifted children. *Journal for the Education of the Gifted*, **17**(2), 131–142.

Maier, N. (1993). Advocacy as a force in the education of the gifted and talented. *Gifted International*, **8**(1), 20–26.

Maker, C. J. (1996). Identification of gifted minority students: a national problem, needed changes, and a promising solution. *Gifted Child Quarterly*, **40** (1), 41–50.

Maker, C. J. & Nielson, A. B. (1995). *Teaching models in education of the gifted*. (2nd ed.). Austin, TX: Pro Ed.

Maker, C. J. & Nielson, A. B. (1996). *Curriculum development and teaching strategies for gifted learners*. (2nd ed.). Austin, TX: Pro Ed.

Margolin, L. (1996). A pedagogy of privilege. *Journal for the Education of the Gifted*, **19** (2), 164–180.

Marquandt, R. G. & Karnes, F. A. (1994). Gifted education and discrimination: The role of the Office of Civil Rights. *Journal for the Education of the Gifted*, **18** (1), 87–94.

Masharov, Y. P. (1993). A 30-year global experiment with gifted children in the USSR. *Gifted International*, **7** (2), 1–6.

McGonagill, B. (1997). Gifted education and long-range planning: Using time wisely with TQM. *Roeper Review*, **19**, 200–203.

Meininger, L. (1998). Curriculum for the young gifted children. In: J. F. Smutny (Ed.), *The Young Gifted Child: Potential and Promise, An Anthology* (pp. 492–500). Cresskill, NJ: Hampton Press.

Moon, S. M. (1993). Using the Purdue Three-Stage Model: developing talent at the secondary level. *The Journal of Secondary Gifted Education*, **5** (2), 31–35.

Moon, S. M. (1996). Using the Purdue Three-Stage Model to facilitate program evaluations. *Gifted Child Quarterly*, **40**, 121–128.

Moon, S. M., Feldhusen, J. F. & Kelly, K. W. (1991). Identification procedures: Bridging theory and practice. *Gifted Child Today*, **14** (1), 30–38.

Moon, S. M., Feldhusen, J. F., Powley, S., Nidiffer, L. & Whitman, M. (1993). Secondary applications of the Purdue Three-Stage Model. *Gifted Child Today*, **16** (3), 2–9.

Moon, S. M. & Swift, M. (1989). Leadership in program development. *Gifted Child Today*, **12** (4), 16–21.

Moore, A. D. & Betts, G. T. (1987). Using judgment analysis in the identification of gifted and talented children. *Gifted Child Quarterly*, **31** (1), 30–33.

NAGC (1991). Position pgsu: Using tests to identify gifted children. Washington, DC: National Association for Gifted Chidren.

Neisser, U., Boodoo, G., Bouchard, R. J., Boykin, A. W., Brody, N., Ceci, S. J., Halpern, D. F., Loehlin, J. C., Perloff, R., Sternberg, R. J. & Urbina, S. (1996). Intelligence: knowns and unknowns. *American Psychologist*, **51** (2), 77–101.

Nidiffer, L. G. & Moon, S. M. (1994). Middle school seminars. *Gifted Child Today*, **17** (2), 24–27,39–41.

Nielsen, M. & Buchanan, N. K. (1991). Evaluating gifted programs with locally constructed instruments. In: N. K. Buchana & J. F. Feldhusen (Eds.), *Conducting Research and Evaluation in Gifted Education* (pp. 275–310). New York: Teachers College Press.

Nowicka, R. (1995). Supporting gifted and talented children within the Polish educational system. *Gifted and Talented International*, 37–39.

Oh-Hwang, Y. (1993). Linkage between home environments, child psychosocial maturity, and child academic achievement. *Gifted International*, **8** (1), 32–38.

Olenchak, R. F. (1990). Successful teachers of the gifted and reflective practices. *Research Briefs*, **4**.

O'Tuel, F. S. (1994). APOGEE: equity in the identification of gifted and talented students. *Gifted Child Quarterly*, **38** (2), 75–79.

Pagnin, A. (1995). Excellence and equality in education: conflicting values in a democratic society. *European Journal for High Ability*, **6**, 128–136.

Parker, J. P. (1996). NAGC Standards for personnel preparation in gifted education: A brief history. *Gifted Child Quarterly*, **40** (3), 158–164.

Passow, A. H. (1993). National/state policies regarding education of the gifted. In: K. A. Heller, F. J. Monks & A. H. Passow (Eds.), *International Handbook of Research and Development of Giftedness and Talent* (pp. 29–46). Oxford, England: Pergamon.

Passow, A. H. (1994). Israel's residential high school for gifted in the arts and science. *Gifted and Talented International*, **9** (2), 54–57.

Passow, A. H. & Rudnitski, R. A. (1994). Transforming policy to enhance educational services for the gifted. *Roeper Review*, **16** (4), 271–275.

Persson, R. S. (1998). Paragons of virtue: Teacher's conceptual understanding of high ability in an egalitarian school system. *High Ability Studies*, **9** (2), 181–196.

Peters, T. & Austin, N. (1985). *A passion for excellence: the leadership difference*. New York: Warner Books.

Peters, T. J. & Waterman, R. H. (1982). *In search of excellence: lessons from America's best run companies*. New York: Warner Books.

Pintrich, P. R. & Schunk, D. H. (1996). *Motivation in education: theory, research, and applications*. Englewood Cliffs, NJ: Prentice Hall.

Plucker, J. A. (1996). Gifted Asian-American students: identification, curricular, and counseling concerns. *Journal for the Education of the Gifted*, **19** (3), 314–343.

Powley, S. A. & Moon, S. M. (1993). Secondary English theme units: a pragmatic approach. *Gifted Child Today*, **16** (4), 52–61.

Purcell, J. H. (1995). Gifted education at a crossroads: the program status study. *Gifted Child Quarterly*, **39** (2), 57–65.

Purcell, J. H. & Leppien, J. H. (1998). Building bridges between general practitioners and educators of the gifted: a study of collaboration. *Gifted Child Quarterly*, **42** (3), 172–181.

Reis, S. M. (1984). Avoiding the testing trap: using alternative assessment to evaluate programs for the gifted. *Journal for the Education of the Gifted*, **7** (1), 45–59.

Renzulli, J. S. (1975). *A guidebook for evaluating programs for the gifted and talented*. Ventura, CA: Office of the Ventura County Superintendent of Schools.

Renzulli, J. S. (1986a). *Systems and models for developing programs for the gifted and talented*. Mansfield Center, CT: Creative Learning Press.

Renzulli, J. S. (1986b). The three-ring conception of giftedness: a developmental model for creative productivity. In: R. J. Sternberg & J. E. Davidson (Eds.), *Conceptions of Giftedness* (pp. 53–92). Cambridge, England: Cambridge University Press.

Renzulli, J. S. & Reis, S. M. (1985). *The schoolwide enrichment model: a comprehensive plan for educational excellence*. Mansfield Center, CT: Creative Learning Press.

Renzulli, J. S. & Reis, S. M. (1991). Building advocacy through program design, student productivity, and public relations. *Gifted Child Quarterly*, **35** (4), 182–187.

Riley, T. L. & Karnes, F. A. (1991). The tools for success for concerned citizens: Shaping public policy in gifted education. *Gifted Child Today*, **16** (2), 23–25.

Robinson, A. (1991). Tests in perspective: the role and selection of standardized instruments in the evaluation of programs for the gifted. In: N. K. Buchanan & J. F. Feldhusen (Eds.), *Conducting Research and Evaluation in Gifted Education* (pp. 311–335). New York: Teachers College Press.

Robinson, M. (1992a). A vision splendid: gifted education in Australia. *Roeper Review*, **14** (4), 206–208.

Robinson, N. M. (1992b). Radical acceleration in the People's Republic of China: early entrance to university. *Roeper Review*, **14** (4), 189–192.

Robinson, N. M. (1997). Acceleration as an option for the highly gifted adolescent. In: C. P. Benbow & D. Lubinski (Eds.), *Intellectual Talent: Psychometric and Social Issues* (pp. 169–178). Baltimore: Johns Hopkins University Press.

Robinson, N. M. (1999). Necessity is the mother of invention: The roots of our 'system' for providing educational alternatives for gifted students. *Journal of Secondary Gifted Education*, **10** (3), 120–128.

Ross, P. O. (1993). *National excellence: a case for developing America's talent*. Washington, DC: United States Department of Education.

Rosselli, H. C. (1997). Differing perspectives, common ground: the middle school and gifted education relationships. In: J. L. Irvin (Ed.), *What Current Research Says to the Middle Level Practitioner* (pp. 11–20). Columbus, OH: National Middle School Association.

Runco, M. A. & Albert, R. S. (1990). *Theories of creativity*. Newbury Park: Sage.

Sapon-Shevin, M. (1996). Beyond gifted education: building a shared agenda for school reform. *Journal for the Education of the Gifted*, **19** (2), 194–214.

Sarason, S. B. (1996). *Revisiting the culture of the school and the problem of change*. New York: Teachers College Press.

Seeley, K. (1998). Evaluating programs for the gifted. In: J. V. Tassel-Baska (Ed.), *Excellence in Educating Gifted and Talented Learners* (pp. 295–308). Denver: Love.

Shore, B. M. & Delcourt, M. A. (1997). Effective curricular and program practices in gifted education and the interface with general education. *Journal for the Education of the Gifted*, **20** (2), 138–154.

Silverman, L. K. (1998). The highly gifted. In: J. Van Tassel-Baska (Ed.), *Excellence in Educating Gifted and Talented Learners* (pp. 115–128). Denver: Love.

Sisk, D. A. (1990). Expanding worldwide awareness of gifted and talented children and youth. *Gifted Child Today*, **13** (5), 19–25.

Smutny, J. F. (Ed.). (1998). *The young gifted child: potential and promise*. Hampton Press: Cresskill, NJ.

Sparks, D. & Hirsh, S. (1997). *A new vision for staff development*. Alexandria, VA: Association for Supervision and Curriculum Development.

Spicker, H. H. (1987). *The Indiana Guide for the Identification of Gifted and Talented Students*. Indianapolis, IN: Indiana Department of Education.

Stanley, J. C. (1997). In the Beginning: the study of mathematically precocious youth. In: C. P. Benbow & D. Lubinski (Eds.), *Intellectual Talent: Psychometric and Social Issues* (pp. 225–235). Baltimore: Johns Hopkins.

Sternberg, R. J. (1985). *Beyond IQ: a triarchic theory of human intelligence*. Cambridge, England: Cambridge University Press.

Sternberg, R. J. (1986). Identifying the gifted through IQ: why a little bit of knowledge is a dangerous thing. *Roeper Review*, **8** (3), 143–147.

Sternberg, R. J. (1993). Procedures for identifying intellectual potential in the gifted: A perspective on alternative 'metaphors of the mind'. In: K. A. Heller, F. J. Monks & A. H. Passow (Eds.), *International Handbook of Research and Development of Giftedness and Talent* (pp. 185–207). Oxford, England: Pergamon.

Sternberg, R. J. (1996). *Successful Intelligence*. New York: Simon & Schuster.

Sternberg, R. J. (1999). *Handbook of creativity*. Cambridge, England: Cambridge University Press.

Sternberg, R. J. & Davidson, J. E. (Eds.). (1986). *Conceptions of Giftedness*. Cambridge, England: Cambridge University Press.

Sternberg, R. J., Ferrari, M., Clinkenbeard, P. & Grigorenko, E. (1996). Identification, instruction, and assessment of gifted children: a construct validation of a triarchic model. *Gifted Child Quarterly*, **40** (3), 129–137.

Sternberg, R. J. & Horvath, J. A. (1998). Cognitive conceptions of expertise and their relations to giftedness. In: R. C. Friedman & K. R. Rogers (Eds.), *Talent in Context: Historical and Social Perspectives* (pp. 177–191). Washington, D.C.: American Psychological Association.

Stevenson, H. W. (1994). Education of gifted and talented students in mainland China, Taiwan, and Japan. *Journal for the Education of the Gifted*, **17** (2), 104–130.

Stevenson, H. W. (1998). Cultural interpretations of giftedness: The case of East Asia. In: R. C. Friedman & K. B. Rogers (Eds.), *Talent in Context: Historical and Social Perspectives on Giftedness* (pp. 61–77). Washington, D.C.: American Psychological Association.

Tannenbaum, A. J. (1986). Giftedness: a psychosocial approach. In: R. J. Sternberg & J. E. Edwards (Eds.), *Conceptions of Giftedness* (pp. 21–52). Cambridge, England: Cambridge University Press.

Taylor, C. A. (1993). Programs and practices for identifying and nurturing giftedness and talented in Africa. In: K. A. Heller, F. J. Monks & A. J. Passow (Eds.), *International Handbook of Research and Development of Giftedness and Talent* (pp. 833–848). New York: Pergamon.

Tietel, L. (1996). Finding common ground: teacher leaders and principals. In: G. Moller & M. Katzenmeyer (Eds.), *Every Teacher as a Leader: Realizing the Potential of Teacher Leadership* (pp. 139–154). Alexandria, VA: Association for Supervision and Curriculum Development.

Tirri, K. & Uusikyla, K. (1994). How teachers perceive differentiation of education among the gifted and talented. *Gifted and Talented International*, **9** (2), 69–73.

Tomlinson, C. (1995). *How to differentiate instruction in mixed ability classrooms*. Alexandria, VA: Association for Supervision and Curriculum Development.

Tomlinson, C., Coleman, M. R., Allan, S., Udall, A. & Landrum, M. (1996). Interface between gifted education and general education: toward communication, cooperation, and collaboration. *Gifted Child Quarterly*, **40** (3), 165–171.

Tomlinson, C. A. (1994). Gifted learners: the boomerang kids of middle school? *Roeper Review*, **16** (3), 177–182.

Tomlinson, C. A. (1996). Good teaching for one and all: does gifted education have an instructional identity? *Journal for the Education of the Gifted*, **20** (2), 155–174.

Tomlinson, C. A. (1997). Curriculum and Instruction for gifted learners in the middle grades: what would it take? In: J. L. Irvin (Ed.), *What current research says to the middle level practioner* (pp. 21–34). Columbus, OH: National Middle School Association.

Tomlinson, C. A. & Callahan, C. M. (1993). Planning effective evaluations for programs for the gifted. *Roeper Review*, **17** (1), 46–51.

Tomlinson, C. A., Callahan, C. M. & Lelli, K. M. (1997). Challenging expectations: case studies of high-potential, culturally diverse young children. *Gifted Child Quarterly*, **41** (2), 5–17.

Treffinger, D. J. & Feldhusen, J. F. (1996). Talent recognition and development: Successor to gifted education. Journal for the Education of the Gifted, 19(2), 181–193.

Troxclair, D. & Karnes, D. (1997). Public relations: Advocating for gifted students. *Gifted Child Today*, **20** (3), 38–41, 50.

Tuttle, F. B. & Becker, L. A. (1983a). *Characteristics and identification of gifted and talented students*. Washington, DC: National Education Association.

Tuttle, F. B. & Becker, L. A. (1983b). *Program design and development for gifted and talented students*. (2nd ed.). Washington, D.C.: NEA Professional Library.

Urban, K. K. & Sekowski, A. (1993). Programs and practices for identifying and nurturing giftedness and talent in Europe. In: K. A. Heller, F. J. Monks & A. Passow (Eds.), *International Handbook of Research and Development of Giftedness and Talent* (pp. 779–795). Oxford, England: Pergamon Press.

VanTassel-Baska, J. (1992). *Planning effective curriculum for gifted learners*. Denver: Love.

VanTassel-Baska, J. (1994). *Comprehensive Curriculum for Gifted Learners*. (2nd ed.). Boston: Allyn and Bacon.

VanTassel-Baska, J. (1998a). A comprehensive model of program development. In: J. VanTassel-Baska (Ed.), *Excellence in Educating Gifted and Talented Learners* (pp. 309–334). Denver: Love.

VanTassel-Baska, J. (1998b). *Excellence in educating gifted and talented learners*. Denver: Love.

Vydra, J. & Leimbach, J. (1998). Planning curriculum for young gifted children. In: J. F. Smutny (Ed.), *The Young Gifted Child: Potential and Promise, an Anthology* (pp. 462–475). Cresskill, NJ: Hampton Press.

Westberg, K. L. & Archambault, F. X. (1997). A multi-site case study of successful classroom practices for high ability students. *Gifted Child Quarterly*, **41** (1), 42–51.

Westberg, K. L., Archambault, F. X., Dobyns, S. M. & Salvin, T. J. (1993). *An observational study of instructional and curricular practices used with gifted and talented students in regular classrooms*. Storrs, CT: National Research Center on the Gifted and Talented.

Westberg, K. L., Burns, D. E., Gubbins, E. J., Reis, S. M., Park, S. & Maxfield, L. R. (1998, Winter). Professional development practices in gifted education: the results of a national survey. *NRC/GT Newsletter*.

Whitman, M. W. & Moon, S. M. (1993). Bridge Building: conducting scientific research redefines the roles of teacher and student. *Gifted Child Today*, **16** (5), 47–50.

Wood, B. & Feldhusen, J. F. (1996). Creating special interest programs for gifted youth: Purdue's Super Saturday serves as a successful model. *Gifted Child Today*, **19** (4), 22–25, 28–29, 40–42.

Wu, W. T. & Cho, S. (1993). Programs and practices for identifying and nurturing giftedness and talented in Asia (Outside of mainland China). In: K. A. Heller, F. J. Monks

& A. H. Passow (Eds.), *International Handbook of Research and Development of Giftedness and Talent* (pp. 797–807). Oxford, England: Pergamon.

Zha, Z. (1993a). Programs and practices for identifying and nurturing giftedness and talent in the People's Republic of China. In: K. A. Heller, F. J. Monks & A. H. Passow (Eds.), *International Handbook of Research and Development of Giftedness and Talent* (pp. 809–814). New York: Pergamon Press.

Zha, Z. (1993b). Twelve-year study of the mental development of gifted children in China. *Gifted International*, **7** (2), 7–17.

Zha, Z. (1997). Mental development of gifted and non-gifted children in China. *Gifted and Talented International*, **12** (1), 31–35.

Zorman, R. (1998). A model for adolescent giftedness identification via challenges (MAGIC). *Gifted and Talented International*, **13**, 65–72.

Academic Competitions and Programs Designed to Challenge the Exceptionally Talented

James Reed Campbell,[1] Harald Wagner[2] and Herbert J. Walberg[3]

[1]*St. John's University, Jamaica, New York, USA*
[2]*Institute Bildung und Begabung, Bonn, Germany*
[3]*University of Illinois at Chicago, USA*

Introduction

Many chapters of this *International Handbook* concern in-school programs or conceptual frameworks designed for schools with gifted programs. The intent of both of these advances involves the development of talent. This chapter deals with a variety of out-of-school programs that are designed to challenge the exceptionally talented. We examine after school programs, competitions, including national academic Olympiads, and summer programs that have the same objective—the development of talent.

Bloom (1985) conducted a series of studies about how extraordinary talent is developed for concert pianists, sculptors, research mathematicians, research neurologists, Olympic swimmers, and tennis champions. His research teams examined the roles that teachers, parents, and out-of-school personnel played in the developmental process. One of the findings of these studies was that once parents became aware of their child's exceptional talent, they took a more active role in developing that talent. In many cases parents used out-of-school resources to develop their child's talent. They secured coaches, specialized teachers, or programs.

In this chapter we will continue this research focus by examining the ways teachers, parents, and other individuals (mentors) contribute to the development of academic talent.

A Framework for the Development of Talent

A useful framework for the development and fostering of talent was proposed by Weinert (Weinert & Wagner, 1987). It may serve as a theoretical underpinning for programs for the talented. He concluded that effective measures to support the development of potential in young people should contain the following features:

(1) Incitements: Curiosity, quest for knowledge and the interest in learning has to be incited by a multitude of attractive sources of information within easy access.

(2) Options: A variety of options has to be available to engage in learning activities such as workshops, courses, summer programs or competitions.

(3) Challenges: The difficulty and the level of the activities should match the level of ability so that very able pupils feel sufficiently challenged and have to exert considerable effort to reach the goal.

(4) Incentives: The activities should be exciting and attractive and should provide the experience of success, rewards, and personal recognition.

(5) Counseling: The young people, their parents and teachers should be able to obtain qualified information on the specific aspects of the students' potential and on available support programs.

(6) Cooperation: Very able young people should be brought up and educated in a community of peers to experience a variety of social contacts to acquire social responsibility and to facilitate a harmonious development of their personality.

According to this framework, at least in the domain of intellectual abilities, it seems to be quite unrealistic to strive for a comprehensive, valid and reliable system of early assessment of potentials followed by a closed system of support programs. Instead, every effort should be made to provide a variety of measures to meet the needs of those who are eager to achieve and show a high degree of motivation. They should be able to be implemented pragmatically, to be easily accessible, differentiated and as open as possible.

In the ideal case such measures would be free of charge, the admission entirely voluntary and based on self selection and the treatment effective both for talent development and for the identification of the most able. Quite often, however, the specific properties of a support program and/or the large number of applicants demand a selection procedure.

523

There are essentially two ways to accomplish this task. One can create an arena where individuals are allowed to perform some task or set of tasks with those being selected as eligible whose level of performance is judged superior, by whatever definition or criterion. Alternatively, one can use a psychometric approach, relying on standardized tests that are, or at least should be, valid predictors of talent or high ability. The first approach is best exemplified by academic competitions; the second by the talent search.

In this chapter we examine the various facets of out-of-class programs and services, including the identification of high ability students through talent searches and academic competitions and special programs held after school, on weekends, or during summer holidays. While the chapter attempts to be inclusive in its coverage of the numerous out-of-class efforts currently in existence, detailed attention is paid to a small number of representative efforts in order to demonstrate in specific ways how these programs work and what they have accomplished.

After school and Saturday Programs

Parent Initiated Programs

Parents are generally the first adults in a child's life to become aware of the child's talent. When the child enters school, it may become especially necessary for parents to provide supplementary activities by introducing the child to exciting and fascinating subjects. For many parents this task is rather intimidating. When they seek professional help and advice from pediatricians, teachers, school psychologists or educational counselors they are sometimes confronted with ignorance and prejudice about the talented child and imputations that they are 'pushy' parents.

Faced with the predicament of having to solve their problems more or less on their own, the parents of highly able children in many countries have established self-help groups in the form of associations such as the Gifted Child Society in the United States, the British National Association for Gifted Children (NAGC), the Deutsche Gesellschaft für das hochbegabte Kind in Germany, 'Pharos' in The Netherlands, 'Bekina' in Belgium, Association nationale pour les enfants intellectuellement precoces (ANPEIP) in France, or Elternverein für hochbegabte Kinder (EHK), Schweiz, in Switzerland.

Their joint aims are to:

(1) give help, advice and information to parents of gifted children.
(2) increase community awareness and understanding of the need to develop links with and information for local professionals such as teachers, social workers and medical practitioners.
(3) provide an opportunity for gifted and talented children to meet and to pursue their interests in company.

(4) facilitate contact with interesting and informed adults, offering children intellectual stimuli and an introduction to a wide range of interests.

Most of the associations have formed regional branches in order to better serve the needs of their members. Joint activities or enrichment programs for the children are usually run by adult volunteers, often a parent of one of the children or someone who is generally interested in the children's progress. They determine to a large extent the selection of activities available.

Long-term Courses

The array of courses offered by parents' associations is dependent on diverse, often chance, influences such as the number of children of a certain age group interested and willing to participate, the availability of course instructors, or special rooms, materials and equipment. A considerably more intensive form of provision are intellectually demanding long-term courses which take place in the afternoons, on weekends, or during holidays and which allow for a more systematic approach to a specific area.

As an example of this type of program, the 'Hamburg model' to find and foster mathematically able pupils will be described in more detail. In 1983, inspired by the work of Stanley and his group at Johns Hopkins University (Benbow & Stanley, 1983), a group of psychologists and mathematicians at the University of Hamburg developed an annual regional search for mathematically able pupils at the end of grade 6 (12-year-olds) (Wagner & Zimmermann, 1986). Selection criteria were: (1) German versions of the mathematical parts of the Scholastic Aptitude Test (SAT), and (2) a test of mathematical problem solving consisting of seven items both of which were taken during an examination of three hours' duration.

Pupils interested in the talent search received a preparation booklet in advance containing a complete version of the mathematical parts of the SAT to be worked through and attempted at home. About 40 students, that is 20 to 25% of the participants in the talent search, are annually admitted to the program that takes place on Saturday mornings at Hamburg University. The pupils work in small groups on challenging mathematical problems, with topics that vary from week to week. Expert secondary school maths teachers, mathematics students and mathematicians serve as instructors.

Rather than cover future curriculum material, the mathematical areas selected are predominantly those which pupils would find interesting and appealing and at the same time are important for the application of modern mathematics (e.g. graph theory, combinatorics, representation of numbers in connection with measuring, number theory, geometry and game theory). The problems are always chosen in such a way that they can be extended to allow the development of a small mathematical theory and put pupils in an elementary research situation. New problem areas are introduced by a short paper including a few initial questions which help motivate the pupils. In addition to developing and practicing strategies for problem solving, special importance is attached to recognizing, formulating and perhaps solving subsequent problems.

Despite the considerable length of the course (participation is possible for up to six consecutive years) and the very challenging course work, the extremely low dropout rate together with the high rate of attendance and the very positive opinions that the pupils have of the course are all indications that this type of program successfully meets such pupils' needs. The program's success is due, in part, to the stimulus provided by the assignments and to the informal manner of working in small groups, in pairs, or even alone, which is quite unlike that at school. There is, on the other hand, an important social motive for taking part: in this group, pupils meet age-mates of a similarly high intellectual level and with mutual interests, without encountering incomprehension or even rejection. This type of separate provision for the highly able does not (as is sometimes implied) lead to social isolation but actually causes participants to feel less like outsiders. Most of them have for the first time been faced with a challenge commensurate with their capability and aptitude.

Funds from the German Federal Government initially helped to get the program started. After three years the program was self-supporting through contributions from the parents. Offshoots of the Hamburg project show that even when confronted with the typical transport and distance problems of a rural area the appeal of the program prevails despite the long journeys involved.

Residential Programs

The difficulties of commuter programs are overcome by residential programs which typically last from one to several weeks. This setting allows total involvement in a certain subject with intensive tutoring and a multitude of social contacts. Particularly in the United States, such programs have long been a fixed element of out-of-school provisions for highly able students (Olszewski-Kubilius, 1997). One of the most sound and consistent approaches was developed in 1979 at the Johns Hopkins University's Center for Talented Youth (CTY). It has been emulated by several institutions in the USA including Duke University, Northwestern University, the University of Denver, Arizona State University and California State University at Sacramento (Benbow & Lubinski, 1997).

By means of regional, national and international talent searches several thousand highly able students are identified annually. They are eligible for three-week residential summer programs which in 1999 served about 4,000 participants at the CTY sites alone.

The German Schülerakademien

Inspired by the American approach to providing summer programs for highly able young people, in 1988 Bildung und Begabung, a non-profit German association, started residential summer programs for 16–19-year-old secondary school pupils, thus filling a critical gap between the last school years and higher education. Within a few years these 'Schülerakademien' (pupils' academies) have developed into an outstanding opportunity for academically highly talented and motivated adolescents which seems to be unique in continental Europe.

The main objectives of the academies are: (1) to offer several fields for scientific endeavor in order to develop and improve methods and abilities of knowledge acquisition, interdisciplinary thinking, research techniques and autonomous learning; (2) to challenge intellectual potentials to their limits; (3) to provide role models through encounters with highly creative, able, motivated and inspiring teachers and scientists; and (4) to experience a community of equally able and motivated peers, to develop lasting friendships and thus to accept one's own personality as valuable and 'normal'.

The 17-day academy typically embraces 90 boys and girls, each participating in one of six courses covering a broad range of diverse academic disciplines, e.g. mathematics, physics, foreign languages, creative writing, music, biology, chemistry, computer science, philosophy, history, economics, psychology, rhetoric and visual arts. The amount of time spent on course work within the 17 days is about 45 hours. The level of work is mostly comparable to advanced university seminars. Two teachers (scholars, expert school teachers or free-lancers) plan and conduct each of the courses with a minimum daily duration of 4–5 hours. The rest of the day is filled with additional optional activities such as sports, music, excursions, discussions and drama.

Between 1988 and 1998, 42 academies with over 3,600 participants were held in boarding schools which have proven to be ideal locations for these programs in Germany. Within a few days, each of the academies develops a unique and special atmosphere, filled with enthusiasm and motivation of both participants and instructors, characterized by intensive and open personal relations and discussions until late at night.

The participants are expected to pay a fee that covers board and lodging, the rest of the expenses being subsidized by the Government, by foundations and private donations. Financial assistance is available to needy families. Pupils are invited to apply for a place after successful participation in one of the intellectually demanding competitions in Germany or being recommended by headmasters, teachers, educational consultants, or psychologists. In 1998, 1,015 (86%) of the 1,178 boys and girls who were invited applied for the 540 available places in six academies.

Extensive evaluations of the academies (Wagner, Neber & Heller 1995, Neber & Heller, 1997) have shown their long-lasting positive effects on the participants, especially with regard to their motivation, self-efficacy, self-assertion, self-reliance, cooperativeness and communication skills. Similar effects are reported from residential summer programs in the United States (Olszewski-Kubilius, 1997).

The major benefit of these programs seems to be that they provide opportunities for interaction with equally able and motivated peers. Pupils feel accepted often for the first time in their lives and many of them are astounded to discover how easy it is to communicate with and to make friends within this group. The results are frequently long-lasting relationships and communication networks.

Encounters with excellent instructors provide valuable role models for an academic orientation. They can be helpful in career counseling and might open perspectives into yet unconsidered professional areas. The intense atmosphere of residential programs is capable of activating and stimulating dormant potentials. Many of these pupils relate with amazement what they were able to achieve in a short time.

In short, these programs have a tremendously beneficial impact on young lives. It would be highly desirable to increase the number of such programs, as the current demand far exceeds the existing supply of places.

Academic Competitions

Competitions are increasing by being made available to talented students in Europe, Asia, and the United States. In the United States 275 competitions (Karnes & Riley, 1996) are currently being used. These competitions have been developed in every academic area and in many non-academic areas. Some of these competitions are targeted at elementary school children, others concern middle school children, and others are reserved for advanced high school students. Campbell (1998) found that American teachers use these competitions to challenge their gifted students.

Potential Benefits and Liabilities of Competitions

Competitions are funded by governments, foundations, and companies to develop extraordinary talent. Maths, science, and engineering contests are conducted with the expectation of developing talent needed to supply the technical workforce (S & E work force). The S & E workforce is essential for a nation's economic health

and development. In the United States several of the high school competitions were initially developed after the Russians launched Sputnik. One of President Eisenhower's science advisors was Edwin Teller who urged the president to start academic contests that would get young people involved in the technical areas at early ages. This stimulus resulted in the initiation of several of the competitions that are still being used in America.

The chief benefit of these competitions for schools is their low cost. Competitions involving nationally administered tests can be done at very low costs per pupil. The supporters of competitions note that most societies are competitive. Certainly, businesses must, of necessity, be competitive, and the global economy has accelerated this process. Governments are also competitive not only in terms of their businesses but in many other areas. Competition exists even in academia where authors compete for publications and grants. Sports are competitive by definition; therefore, with all these levels of competition, it follows that competitions would emerge as a mechanism to uncover exceptional talent.

Competitions in Europe, Russia, U.S., and Asia

The Russians were the first to realize the potential of academic competitions and initiated the academic Olympics. The first academic Olympic program involved mathematics and was started in Leningrad in 1934 (Kukushkin, 1996). This Mathematics Olympic competition was extended to city programs in Moscow and Kiev in 1935. These Olympic programs eventually spread to the entire USSR and beyond. The Russians used these competitions to funnel talent into areas where they were needed. A student scoring exceptionally high on one of the academic Olympic exams was given automatic admission to some of the best universities. This admission placed the exceptional student in the Soviet S & E pipeline. In socialized countries national testing programs were conducted that assured the identification of a steady stream of gifted individuals. Once identified, these talents could be funneled into areas where development was needed.

European Competitions

In Europe, the Federal Republic of Germany probably has the most elaborate system of competitions for school children at all levels. Competitions are considered to be important and valuable additional instruments in the educational process.

They are relatively easy to administer and to organize, they can be made accessible to a broad number of participants and they can be differentiated to suit any level of ability. Competitions are an excellent tool to elicit, stimulate and challenge talents in many different fields. They are supposed to activate and strengthen the inclination for the subject matter and thus to improve knowledge and ability. Struggling with the tasks of the competition enhances the abilities of working autonomously while researching, experimenting, problem solving, learning and practicing release energies and enhance perseverance.

By taking the challenge of a competition, the participants gain insight into their abilities and their position in comparison with peers beyond the confinement of their classroom and school. Coming together with other participants, they have the opportunity to meet similarly interested and able peers who are usually not so easily found. Attractive prizes like scholarships, summer programs, or money are additional incentives.

In Germany, there are more than twenty federal (nationwide) competitions and dozens of smaller competitions at the state or regional level. On the federal level well over 100,000 students participate annually either individually or in groups in disciplines such as mathematics, science (biology, chemistry, physics, technology, computer science, environmental studies), foreign languages, social studies, history, creative writing, music, composing, drama, film and video production. Most of these competitions are subsidized by the Federal Government, with a total allocation of c. 4 million Euro in 1999. In addition, a considerable part of the cost is covered by sponsoring foundations and industry. While most of the academic competitions are aimed at upper secondary school students (16+ years of age), there is, however, in most cases no lower limit for the age of participation thus granting admission to all kinds of accelerated talents.

Without doubt, one of the most remarkable competitions is the 'Bundeswettbewerb Fremdsprachen' (Federal Languages Contest), as it is a unique comprehensive approach to support acquisition and application of foreign languages among secondary school students. The contest was initiated in 1979 by the Stifterverband für die Deutsche Wissenschaft (Donors' Association for the Promotion of Science in Germany) as a means to encourage students to learn foreign languages and to become interested in other countries and cultures at an early age. It has been developed and administered by independent experts from universities, schools and industry. Since 1985, the Federal Languages Contest has been sponsored mainly by the Federal Ministry of Education and Research. Bildung und Begabung e.V., a non-profit-making private association, and is responsible for the organization and coordination of the contest.

The contest comprises four levels:

(1) A group contest for students in grades 7–10 (13–16 years, in their third to sixth year of foreign language learning). The group contest encourages project work to produce a presentation (audio or video tape and additional written material) on a self-assigned subject (cf. Blüm, Hertel & Schröder, 1992).

(2) An individual junior contest for students in their fifth or sixth year of foreign language learning (15–16 years of age). It consists of an oral section (listening comprehension and oral production) and a written section (a cloze test, i.e. a text in which missing parts of words have to be filled in) and a creative writing task. The best participants in English usually demonstrate a higher proficiency than first year university students in English studies.

(3) An individual senior contest for students in grades 11–13 (17–19 years) in which at least two foreign languages must be presented. This contest consists of four rounds over a period of twelve months. It begins with an oral production in two languages (e.g. explaining the situation depicted in a cartoon, reading a text and answering questions on the text). The second round is a written examination with elements of translating, writing and summarizing. The task of the third round is writing a 3000-word essay on a given subject within a six-week period. The final round consists of a one-hour multilingual debating session in groups of four together with language experts and of individual oral examinations (cf. Hertel, Joppich, Schröder & Stütz 1991). Placement in all rounds depends upon achievement only. The participants do not compete against each other as in a sports contest.

Successful participants can expect a variety of prizes. Winners of a first prize in the final round ('federal winners') are granted a scholarship for university studies from the most prestigious scholarship foundation in Germany (Studienstiftung des deutschen Volkes). Second and third prizes consist of cash. Several prizes (e.g. travel grants, books, records) are awarded by foreign embassies for special languages. The Federal Minister of Education and Research annually awards a five-week stay in a summer studies program at a university in the United States to three participants who wrote outstanding essays on U.S. related subjects.

(4) A group contest for apprentices and for students at vocational schools. Here, again, a presentation on audio or videotape is required which has to relate to their working sphere. Many of the entries are multilingual.

More than 20,000 students participate in these four contests each year, the main languages being English, Latin, French, Spanish, Italian and Russian. Additionally, special contests are offered to pupils who study Japanese or Chinese.

Some competitions are held at an international European level. To promote the idea of European integration the 'European Competition' has been held since 1954. Each year students at all age levels in 19

European countries receive identical assignments to produce a pictorial or written treatment of European perspectives in social, economic, political or cultural affairs. In Germany alone over 100,000 students participate.

Most European countries run competitions for young researchers in the sciences. In 1990 the most famous science competition in Germany ('Jugend forscht') was sponsored by 'Deutsche Bank' to initiate a European competition for environmental studies. Up to three entrants from (1998) 39 nations may participate in the 'Young Europeans' Environmental Research (YEER)'.

Another recent development was initiated by Romania in 1993: the Central European Olympiad in Informatics (CEOI) with (1998) Croatia, Poland, Slovak Republic, Czech Republic, Slovenia and Hungary as participating countries. Other countries are expected to join in the following years.

Types of Competitions in the U.S.

In the United States three types of competitions are currently employed. The first type uses teams of gifted students; the second type involves encouraging gifted students to do long-term independent research projects (preferably with scientists or scholars); and the third type utilizes a series of tests to identify the exceptionally talented.

The two most widely used American team competitions are Future Problem Solving and Odyssey of the Mind (Campbell, 1998). The Future Problem Solving Program has three levels of competition (junior, intermediate, senior) (Grades 4–12). The teams are given problems that require creativity and imagination to solve. Successful teams learn to problem solve together. The problems frequently deal with futuristic scenarios. This program has local, state (state bowls), and international competitions.

The Odyssey of the Mind also emphasizes solving problems and creativity. Five problems are presented each year which require unique solutions. The problems range from engineering problems to literature analyses. The age range extends from K-12 and is organized into four divisions.

The next type of competition involves individual students doing independent research projects. Local Science and Engineering Fairs are very common in the U.S. At the high school level the projects become more advanced with many students working directly with scientists, mathematicians, and scholars (see Campbell, 1985; 1988). This direct involvement with the 'producers' of technical knowledge has been accelerated by the Science Training Programs that are offered for talented students each summer throughout the United States. These programs are designed for advanced high school students to join research labs and participate in up-to-date research projects. These students become members of graduate research teams and serve as apprentices. The same process is used year-round for

high schools located near universities or research labs. These projects are written up by the high school students and entered in the different competitions.

There are three national project competitions in the U.S. of which the most prestigious is the Intel (Westinghouse) Talent Search (started in 1941). Each year this competition accepts applications from approximately 1,500 high school seniors. These applications must include descriptions of original research projects in mathematics, biology, physics, chemistry, engineering, or the social sciences (psychology, anthropology, sociology). The research papers follow standard scientific methods and scholarly reporting procedures.

The 300 best papers are selected by the Science Service as semifinalists. From this pool the top 40 (finalists) are then invited for a series of interviews in Washington, D.C. A final ranking is determined on the basis of the interviews, and $330,000 (U.S.) in scholarships are awarded to the top finalists. Colleges and universities in the United States compete for the Intel winners (finalists and semifinalists). Their research skills are especially applicable at institutions that are committed to original research studies.

Over the 58-year history of this competition, 17,400 semifinalists and 2,320 finalists have been selected. The Science Service did a follow-up survey of the Intel finalists and found that they won five Nobel prizes, two Field Medals, and eight MacArthur Fellowships. However, the finalists comprise less than 13% of the Intel winners. There has been no comprehensive follow-up study to ascertain the number of the Intel winners in the United States S & E labor force.

Two other national research paper competitions are the Junior Science and Humanities Symposium (JSHS) and the International Science and Engineering Fair. The JSHS competitions are subdivided into 48 regionals, which are located in 50 states and Puerto Rico. The finalists from each regional attend a national meeting and compete for scholarships. Each year this competition involves more than 3,000 high school students (Grades 9–12). The national conference has 240 finalists and awards $343,000 (U.S.) in scholarships. Many of these finalists are also Intel winners.

The International Science and Engineering Fair is the largest research paper competition. In 1995 this competition reached 1,021,936 high school students (Grades 9–12). This competition is organized with local school fairs, regional, and state fairs and one national fair. Those selected for the national fair number 1,200 students. Again, many students enter other competitions and have the opportunity to win other contests.

The other types of national competitions involve testing of select groups of high school students. One of the largest is the National Merit Exam which tested 1,200,000 students in 1998. The top 50,000 students were contacted, and a sifting was performed where

34,000 received commendations and 16,000 are designated semifinalists. A further sifting narrowed down to 15,000 finalists who received $28,000,000 (U.S.) in scholarships.

Another national program (Study of Mathematically Precocious Youth-SMPY) tests 7th-grade students with the SAT-M exam (Scholastic Aptitude Test Maths). This program invites schools to test their top maths students. These talent search programs identify the most talented maths students and provide year-round activities and summer programs to help in developing this talent. These programs exist in every state and serve over 140,000 mathematically precocious participants (Goldstein & Wagner, 1993).

The other national testing programs are the Olympiad Competitions (maths, physics, chemistry). These competitions utilize multiple levels of tests to isolate very small sets of finalists. In maths, three levels of tests are used to isolate the highest scoring eight students (6 finalists and 2 alternates), and in physics and chemistry the same process is used to isolate talent pools of 20 students from which the international finalists are selected (5 for physics; 6 for chemistry).

A total of 2,226,436 high school students participated in the competitions listed above (although many high ability students participated in multiple contests). The total U.S. school age population in Grades 9–12 was 12,214,000, which indicates that a substantial percentage of talented students were involved in these competitions (Statistical Abstract of the United States, 1997).

Rationale

All competitions operate under a series of assumptions that constitute a distinctive rationale:

(1) Children with talent need to be identified early.
(2) Competitions are needed because most schools do not have the differentiated curriculum or the resources that are needed to develop the talents of extraordinary students.
(3) Contests will attract participants with extraordinary talent.
(4) Contests will motivate the early development of talent.
(5) Once developed, this talent is expected to contribute to society.

Every expert since Lewis Terman (1922) has called for the early identification of talent. Terman used IQ tests to identify the intellectually talented. He believed that with these tools schools could identify the gifted and then develop their talent accordingly. Unfortunately, Terman's expectations were never realized due to limited administration of the early IQ tests or to the failure of the schools to initiate programs that would develop the talents of those children that were identified.

The second assumption gets at the heart of the problem. Few would argue that schools have developed the differentiated curriculum or obtained the resources that are needed to develop the talents of the full range of extraordinary students. Perhaps this failing rests with the extensive range of talents (both academic and non-academic) that gifted students possess. Schools simply do not have the resources to accomplish this worthy goal.

The third assumption deals with the expectation that the talented will find out about the contests dealing with their special talent and this will stimulate their development (4th assumption). Both of these assumptions depend on getting the needed information to the students with the talent.

The last assumption—once developed, this talent is expected to contribute to society—is an open research question that is a vital topic to investigate. It must also be emphasized that in the United States millions of gifted students participate in academic competitions each year. Because of the shear numbers that participate, it is crucial to see what the competitions achieve. The answer to this question can only come by conducting long-term follow-up studies that track down the winners of important competitions and determine the contribution they made to society.

Unfortunately, American schools have a poor record in evaluating gifted programs (Callahan & Caldwell, 1995). Campbell (1998) found that only 7% of the schools with gifted programs that he studied conducted rigorous evaluations. This reluctance to evaluate extends to the competitions. Many of the organizations sponsoring them operate on very limited funds and do not have the resources or the manpower to carry out follow-up studies. Furthermore the funding sources (governments, foundations, companies) might not want to conduct such studies when they realize the possibility that their investment might not be justified. It would be difficult to explain negative findings to government officials or to boards of directors.

Academic Olympiad Studies

A definitive answer to this question can only come when each of the different competitions undergoes long-term follow-up studies of their adult participants by outside evaluators. But we will provide a partial answer to this question by presenting information about three retrospective academic Olympiad studies.

Campbell, Feng & Verna (1999) tracked down 15–27 years of winners of the American Maths, Physics and Chemistry Olympiad programs. These long-term retrospective follow-up studies asked the following research questions:

Research Questions

Do the Olympiad competitions serve the national purpose? Do the academic Olympians make important contributions? Do they fulfill their high potential? The specific questions we asked within this framework included: What careers do the Olympians select? Do they do well in their careers? Do the Olympians remain in the field originally identified? How many doctoral degrees were earned by the Olympians? How productive were the Olympians? How many publications and patents did they produce? Finally, we evaluated the effects of the Olympiad programs by asking the following questions: What effect did participation in the Olympiad program have on these talented individuals? Did it widen their horizons? Did it open doors for them? Were there negative side-effects?

To answer these questions we followed 229 Olympians through their college years to graduation (ages 15–22), into their graduate training (early careers) (ages 23–30), and finally onto their professional careers (career) (ages 30–46). They received information from substantial percentages of the national finalists (94% Math Olympians; 70% Physics Olympians, 68% Chemistry Olympians) (229 Olympians). Within the three age brackets there was much variation among the subject areas because of different starting dates for the programs. The Math Olympiad program started in 1972 and therefore contains the largest number of Olympians in the mature career bracket. The Chemistry Olympiad started in 1984, and the Physics Olympiad program started in 1986. These late starting points put more Olympians in the younger brackets. In the Physics study 49% of the Olympians are in the youngest age bracket, which means that fewer have had the time to establish publication records or to get advanced degrees.

One measure of success involves enrollment in the most selective colleges and the completion of college/universities degrees. The Olympians were successful in enrolling in the most prestigious colleges/universities in the United States (see Table 1). The institutions listed in this table constitute the most elite in the nation. The top five (Harvard, Princeton, MIT, U. C. Berkeley, University of Chicago) absorbed most of the Olympians and provided them with sound foundations for their careers. With their high GPA's and exceptional SAT scores, it is no surprise to find the Olympians at such institutions. However, a few of the Olympians had trouble completing their undergraduate degrees and some dropped out of college and took many years to finish. The majority finished their degrees within a four year period and enrolled in advanced degree programs.

The extent of the Olympians' graduate training is evident from the graduate institutions listed in the table. The same selective colleges are listed at the graduate level. One hundred and sixteen Olympians completed, or are in the process of completing, doctoral degrees (MD; Ph.D.; JD). The average time the Olympians take in getting their doctorate degree is approximately 8 years from their high school graduation year. The shortest time any Olympian earned a doctorate degree was 6 years; the longest was 13 years. Overall, 51% of the Olympians have received, or will receive, doctorate degrees (Math 57%; Chemistry 49%; Physics 41% (see Table 2). Among the doctorate degrees there are five law degrees. The percentage for the Math Olympians is more illuminating because of the ages of these Olympians. The other subject areas

Table 1. Colleges and Universities Attended by Olympians.

Colleges/Universities	Number enrolled Undergraduate	Number enrolled Graduate	Total enrolled
Harvard	46	37	83
MIT	17	21	38
Princeton	22	12	34
Stanford	8	16	24
U.C. Berkley	8	14	22
Cal. Tech.	10	7	17
U. Chicago	5	11	16
Cambridge (UK)	4	6	10
U. Illinois	3	7	10
Duke	7	3	10
Rice	6	2	8
Carnegie Mellon	4	2	6
U. Michigan	4	2	6
Yale	3	3	6
Cornell	4	2	6
Northwestern	3	2	5
UCLA	1	3	4
Oxford (UK)	4		4
Johns Hopkins	1	2	3
Columbia	2	1	3

Table 2. Doctoral Degrees Attained by Olympians.

Advanced Degrees	Mathematics	Physics	Chemistry
Ph.D.	48	18	35
M.D.		1	9
J.D.	2	2	1
Total	50	21	45
Number of Olympians in Subject Areas	87	51	91
Percent with Doctorate Degrees	57%	41%	49%

contain many more college-age Olympians who will probably enroll in doctoral programs. Terman (1954), in his monumental longitudinal study, found that 26.3% of 800 gifted males had their doctorate or law degrees. The Olympians far exceed this percentage.

Most of the Olympians select careers in academia—teaching at colleges or universities or doing research. These Olympians finish their doctorate degrees between 26 to 28 years of age and many go on to post doctorate experiences that take another two years.

Consequently, most of these Olympians do not formally start their academic careers before the age of 30.

How successful are these Olympians? One measure of post-secondary faculty and staff productivity involves tabulating the number of publications produced. Table 4 contains the total publication data for the 229 Olympians. The Olympians have produced a total of 2,921 publications. Most of these publications are written by the Olympians employed in colleges and

Table 3. Olympians' Occupations (not in Colleges and Universities).

Number	Occupation/Job Title
Computer Occupations	
4	Computer Programmer/Analyst
2	Computer Music Companies
2	Software Developer
2	Software Engineer
2	Founded Software Companies
1	Software Company Exec.
1	Founder Internet Co.
1	Director Product Design (Software)
1	Microsoft Program Manager
1	Computer Programmer/Algorithm Designer
Scientific Occupations	
18	Scientists/Engineers (including 1 Principal Engineer with 9 patents, 1 at Los Alamos Nat. Lab, 2 at Bell labs (ATT) 1 at IBM 1 at DuPont)
1	Consultant - Scientific Programmer
1	President & CEO Technology Corp.
1	System Integrator
1	Product Line Manager
Other Occupations	
8	Wall Street (including 3 financial analysts, 1 bond trader)
5	Lawyer
4	Teacher (2 Authored Text Books)
2	Talmud Scholar
1	Executive Director of Non-profit Corp.
1	Correspondent (Scientific Magazine)
1	Independent film Maker

Table 4. Total Publications.

Age Cohorts	Olympiad		
	Mathematics	Physics	Chemistry
Ages 15–22 PreCollege/College	10 (1.4/person) N=7	113 (4.5/person) N=25	107 (3.5/person) N=31
Ages 23–29 Early Career	231 (7.7/person) N=30	141 (6.1/person) N=23	401 (9.8/person) N=41
Ages 30–46 Mature Career	1,622 (32/person) N=50	14 (4.7/person) N=3	280 (14.7/person) N=19
Total Publications in Subject Areas	1,863 N=87	268 N=51	788 N=91

universities, and most are in refereed journals. The Math Olympians published 1,865 items, the Chemistry Olympians produced 788 items, and the Physics Olympians produced 268. The bulk of these publications were written by Olympians in their thirties or forties.

The National Center for Educational Statistics has a national study underway of 11,000 higher education faculty in 480 institutions (National Survey of Post-secondary Faculty—NSOFF) (Kirshstein, Matheson & Jing, 1997). The NSOFF data for 1992 showed the average number of publications for all college faculty was 4.6 per year. However, the faculty publication rate was much higher at research institutions (7.35/year for public colleges/universities; 7.95/year for private ones).

Some Olympians have higher publication rates than the NSOFF faculty. Four of the Olympians have over 100 publications, and eight Olympians in their 30s have produced between 50 and 99 publications. These academic 'stars' are in positions of leadership. For example, one is director of Whitehead/MIT Center for Genome Research at 42 years of age and has already made contributions to cancer research. He has published 229 articles, research papers, technical reports, and two books, and serves on 12 editorial boards. Another 44 year old Olympian served as the editor for two journals, published one book, has 6 chapters in books, 51 articles in refereed journals, and 37 research papers. He is active in research dealing with electrical and computer engineering projects and in 1994 served as a member of the Defense Science Board studying Cruise Missile defense.

By contrast, some of the Olympians may be underachievers. Thirteen of the mature career Math Olympians have produced less than 10 publications. Some of these Olympians are in fields where publications are irrelevant to performance. Still, some Olympians reported psychological problems or drug problems, which have undermined their productivity.

The Olympians' publication activities fit the pattern that Terman found in his longitudinal studies. Terman (1954) recorded the publications of 67 books and 1,400 articles and research papers for 800 gifted males. The average number of publications was 1.9 publications per person; for the Olympians the rate is greater at 12.8 publications per person. It must be emphasized that 69% of the Olympians are younger than 30 years old and can be expected to publish many more articles, books, papers, and secure more patents. The oldest cohort (ages 30–46), which has already produced 1,916 publications (26.6/person) can also be expected to continue to publish actively.

One factor involved in this high level of productivity is the mentoring done during the Olympians' undergraduate and graduate years. The disparity between Olympians who have been mentored and those who were not mentored is startling (see Table 5). The majority of publications was done by those who were mentored.

Table 5. Total Publications in Terms of Mentoring.

	Mentored %	Non-mentored %
Math Olympians	84	16
Chemistry Olympians	64	36
Physics Olympians	72	28

A substantial number of Olympians have careers outside academia. Some gravitate to science and engineering careers, a good number are employed in computer areas, and still others are employed in the business sector (see Table 3). How successful are the Olympians in the non-college/universities occupations? There is no way to determine the contribution made by the Olympians in the non-academic community, but the job titles indicate a number of responsible positions. The most successful might include the eight Olympians employed by financial institutions on Wall Street. One is an executive at the prestigious Salomon Brothers; one is a bond trader; one is an associate with Goldman, Sachs; and two are financial analysts with major banks. Two of these individuals are in charge of the research on derivatives. One of the lawyers is the council for the mayor's office in one of the largest cities in the U.S.

There are several Olympians employed in the computer industry. Three Olympians founded software companies. Two are currently the CEO of their companies, and another remains an executive with his company. Another Olympian is the executive director of a non-profit corporation.

A number of Olympians are scientists or engineers. One is a principal engineer with nine patents; another is a scientist at Los Alamos National lab; two are researchers at the Bell Labs (AT&T); two others are senior scientists at IBM; and one is a scientist with DuPont.

Two of the Olympians are Talmud scholars. Four of the Olympians are teachers, two of these teachers co-authored two textbooks. Another Olympian founded a journal that is in its 12th year, and another is a correspondent with a science magazine. One Olympian performed with a musical ensemble at Carnegie Hall; another is an independent film maker.

Would the Olympians have turned out as well without the Olympiad programs? This is a fundamental question to ask the adult Olympians and their parents. It is also a question that should be asked by independent evaluators who have no connection to these programs.

Both the Olympians (76%) and their parents (70%) expressed the view that they would not have accomplished as much without the programs. When asked if the programs helped or hindered their acceptance of their talents, 76% of the Olympians and 74% of their parents concluded that the program helped. Only 4% of the Olympians and none of the parents thought it hindered the development of their talent in any way. Most Olympians (76%) and their parents (83%) reported that the program helped to increase their awareness of educational opportunities.

Delayed Recognition

The Olympiad programs had some profound effects on the participants. When asked to comment about what the Olympiad experience meant to them, many responded with lengthy statements. Most of the Olympians had supportive families that nurtured confidence in their abilities, but to score in the top places in a national exam was a more important milestone for their confidence. They described their reactions to this achievement in these ways: "confirmation of my abilities," "realization I had potential," "confidence booster," "discovering I had the right to believe in my own abilities," "a chance to be recognized," "made me aware, for the first time, that my talent was really unusual," "validating," "confirmed my merit," "a more objective indication of my talent," "It helped me gauge my talent," and "First indication I had of how good I really was."

This theme is entitled 'delayed recognition' because so many of the Olympians did not realize the extent of their talent. Some of them had undervalued their capabilities and had set more modest goals for themselves. Their high scores on the Olympiad exams supplied them with much more confidence in their abilities. It also helped them to evaluate their potential more realistically and to set higher goals for themselves. The program also had several other benefits. After announcing the results of the exams, the Olympians were invited to an intensive summer training program. This training brought the Olympians in contact with other bright students and exposed them to stimulating presentations by well-known scientists and mathematicians. The effects of being exposed to equally bright peers had beneficial effects. One of the side effects of the national training program was to alert the Olympians to a select number of colleges and universities where their talents could be optimally developed. It is our contention that this experience was somewhat responsible for so many of the Olympians enrolling in Harvard, Princeton, MIT and U.C. Berkeley.

Rewarding Accomplishment

The Olympiad studies underscore the need to identify and develop those with most talent. But in America these needs clash with equity issues (Tannenbaum, 1997). Consequently, gifted and accomplished adolescents often go unrecognized and unrewarded for their efforts. Most of the federal supplemental funding of schools, for example, supports programs for disabled, limited-English speaking, and poor children. Within the past decade, new privately funded programs have arisen to support students of higher abilities and reward them for their effort. The National Alliance for Excellence, for example, gives strictly merit-based university scholarships for near perfect scores on matriculation examinations, the completion of university work in secondary school, and related criteria.

Some psychologists and other experts believe that even more immediate monetary rewards would have bigger effects in encouraging adolescents to put forth greater effort on advanced academic study. Walberg

(1998) recently evaluated apparently the largest program of its kind—the Dallas, Texas-based O'Donnell Foundation's Incentive Program.

The Foundation agreed to pay teachers $2,500 to take a course on how to teach Advanced Placement (AP) university-level courses and $100 for each of their students who passed. The students also received $100 for each AP exam they passed in English, calculus, statistics, computer science, biology, chemistry, and physics, plus a reimbursement for the cost of taking the exam.

In the nine participating Dallas schools, sharply increasing numbers of boys and girls of all major ethnic groups took and passed the AP exams. The number rose more than twelve-fold from 41 the year before the program began to 521 when it ended in 1994–95. After terminating, the program continued to have carry-over effects: in the 1996–97 school year, two years after the program ended, 442 students passed, about eleven times more than the number in the year before the program began.

Though these numbers speak for themselves, interviews with students, teachers, and college admission officers revealed high regard for the Incentive Program. They felt that even students who failed AP exams learned better study habits and the importance of hard work to meet high standards.

In addition, the program had other benefits: students could take more advanced courses in college. Those that passed a sufficient number of AP courses could graduate from college early, which saves their families tuition and tax payers subsidies. Those who passed AP courses also had a better chance for merit scholarships and entry into selective colleges.

The Incentive Program suggests that, at least in the U.S., incentivized standards work in schools as they do in many spheres of life. The lack of incentives in school seems an important reason why American students find academics so boring and sports so exciting. It may also account for the poor showing of typical U.S. students on international comparisons of achievement.

Conclusions

The data presented above supplies answers to the questions we asked earlier in this chapter: Do the Olympiad competitions serve the national purpose? Do the academic Olympians make important contributions? Do they fulfill their high potential? When the contributions are summed, including the number of doctorate degrees earned, the number of Olympians working as professors (many in technically needed areas), the number of scientists (some in sensitive and needed areas), the 2,921 publications produced, the number working in the computer industry, including several who have founded or managed software companies, and the Olympians working on Wall Street, we must conclude that the Olympians serve the national interest. They do make important contributions and a number of them fulfill their high potential. Overall, the quality of their contributions outweighs their small numerical numbers. Many of the Olympians are working in leadership positions that magnify their influence.

It must also be remembered that many of these contributions listed above are limited to the oldest Olympiad cohort (72 individuals between the ages of 30–42). These Olympians are in the prime of their careers and can be expected to make many more contributions over the next 20 or 30 years. Furthermore, the younger cohorts can also be expected to assemble a long list of their own contributions.

Having evaluated three competitions, what inferences can be made about the other American competitions? Do they serve the national interest? It is reasonable to infer that the Intel Talent Searches, the JSHS competitions, the SMPY programs, the Science Fairs, and the National Merit Exams all funnel talented students into the United States' science and engineering pipeline. Perhaps this is one of the secrets of America's uncanny ways of developing talent. Campbell (1985, 1992) studied the impact of the Intel Talent Searches on the participants and found that in order to succeed in this competition the students needed to develop the following skills, attitudes, and orientations: learn to manage time; develop library skills needed to conduct technical searches; learn how to read scientific and other advanced material; develop the organization skills to manage a research project; and finally develop the discipline needed to conduct scholarly research studies or to learn how to study for challenging examinations. These enhanced skills not only help the student do well in the contests but can also be applied in future schooling or later in their careers. Even if participants do not win the contest, these newly developed skills will prove very useful. In this sense there may be no 'losers' in a competition where the participants learn things that they can use to enhance their development.

There are some international implications from these analyses. The cost of most of the American competitions is surprisingly low. For example, participation in the Math Olympiad program costs the school only $15.00 (U.S.) and 75 cents per pupil. The costs for the science fairs, the Intel Talent Search, the JSHS regionals and national, and the National Merit Exams are paid by companies, foundations, or by the government. For the most part students competing in these contests use resources outside the schools. Campbell (1985) found that individual teachers in exemplary schools negotiated lab space for their gifted students in universities or research labs nearby. There was no need to improve or upgrade facilities or computers at the schools.

Therefore, many of these competitions are cost-effective, inexpensive ways to develop talent. Any extra expenses, including transportation costs, are willingly met by the parents. Consequently, we believe that competitions should be much more widely used internationally. Third world developing countries with limited financial resources for education should develop a wide range of competitions to nurture the indigenous talent that exists in these countries.

References

Benbow, C. P. & Lubinski, D. (1997). Intellectually talented children: How can we best meet their needs? In: N. Colangelo & G. Davis (Eds), *Handbook of Gifted Education* (2nd ed.), (pp. 155–169). Boston, MA: Allyn and Bacon.

Benbow, C. P. & Stanley, J. C. (Eds) (1983). *Academic precocity. Aspects of its development*. Baltimore, MD: The Johns Hopkins University Press.

Bloom, B. S. (1985). *Developing talent in young people*. New York: Ballantine.

Blüm, W., Hertel, E. & Schröder, K. (Eds) (1992). *Bundeswettbewerb Fremdsprachen. Leseproben. Projekte aus dem Gruppenwettbewerb 1985 bis 1990*. Berlin, Germany: Cornelsen.

Callahan, C. & Caldwell, M. (1995). *A practitioner's guide to evaluating programs for the gifted*. Washington, DC: National Association for Gifted Education.

Campbell, J. R. (1985). The phantom class. *Roeper Review: A Journal on Gifted Education*, **7** (4) 228–231

Campbell, J. R. (1988). Secrets of award winning programs for gifted in mathematics. *Gifted Child Quarterly*, **32** (4) 362–365.

Campbell, J. R. (1992). *Study of Westinghouse Talent Search winners*. Paper presented to the National Science Foundation, Committee on Equal Opportunities in Science and Engineering. Washington, DC.

Campbell, J. R. (1998). *Messages from the field*. Paper presented at the Annual Meeting of the American Educational Research Association.

Campbell, J. R., Feng, A. & Verna, M. (1999). *United States Olympiad studies: Math, Physics, Chemistry*. Paper presented at the 13th Biennial World Conference of the World Council for Gifted and Talented Children.

Goldstein, D. & Wagner, H. (1993). After school programs, competitions, school Olympics and summer programs. In: K. Heller, F. Mönks, A. H. Passow (Eds), *International Handbook of Research and Development of Giftedness and Talent*. Oxford: Pergamon.

Hertel, E., Joppich, K.-H., Schröder, K. & Stütz, W. (Eds) (1991). *Der Bundeswettbewerb Fremdsprachen. Zweite Dokumentation: 1987–1990. Aufgaben, Lösungen, Handreichungen*. Berlin, Germany: Cornelsen.

Karnes, F. & Riley, T. (1996). *Competitions: Maximizing your abilities*. Texas: Prufrock Press.

Kirshstein, R., Matheson, N. & Jing, Z. (1997). *Instructional faculty and staff in higher education institutions: Fall 1987 and Fall 1992*. Washington, DC: Office of Educational Research and Improvement (NCES 97–470).

Kukushkin, B. (1996). The Olympiad movement in Russia. *International Journal of Educational Research*, **25** (6) 553–562.

Neber, H. & Heller, K. A. (1997). *Deutsche SchülerAkademie. Ergebnisse der wissenschaftlichen Begleitforschung*. Bonn, Germany: Bundesministerium für Bildung, Wissenschaft, Forschung und Technologie; (Research report).

Olszewski-Kubilius, P. (1997). Special summer and Saturday programs for gifted students. In: N. Colangelo & G. Davis (Eds), *Handbook of Gifted Education* (2nd ed.), (pp. 180–188). Boston, MA: Allyn and Bacon.

Statistical Abstract of the United States (1997). Washington, DC: US Department of Commerce.

Tannenbaum, A. (1997). The meaning and making of giftedness. In: N. Colangelo & G. Davis (Eds), *Handbook of Gifted Education* (2nd ed.). Boston, MA: Allyn and Bacon.

Terman, L. (1922). New approach to the study of genius. *Psychological Review*, **29** (4) 310–318.

Terman, L. (1954). Scientists and non-scientists in a group of 800 gifted men. *Psychological Monographs*, **68** (7), 1–44.

Wagner, H. & Zimmermann, B. (1986). Identification and fostering of mathematically gifted students. *Educational Studies in Mathematics*, **17**, 243–259.

Wagner, H., Neber, H. & Heller, K. A. (1995). The BundesSchülerAkademie: a residential summer program for gifted adolescents in Germany. In: M. W. Katzko & F. J. Mönks (Eds), *Nurturing Talent. Individual Needs and Social Ability. Proceedings of the Fourth Conference of the European Council for High Ability* (pp. 281–291). Assen, The Netherlands: Van Gorcum.

Walberg, H. (November 4, 1998). Incentivized school standards work. *Education Week*, **18** (10), 48.

Weinert, F. & Wagner, H.(Eds) (1987). Die Förderung Hochbegabter in der Bundesrepublik Deutschland: Probleme, Positionen, Perspektiven. Bad Honnef, Germany: Bock.

Evaluation as a Critical Component of Program Development and Implementation

Carolyn M. Callahan

University of Virginia, Charlottesville, Virginia, USA

Introduction

The ways in which gifted and talented students are educated continues to be criticized at the local, state and national levels. On the one hand, parents of these students and some educators raise concerns about the lack of services and/or the quality of services that are offered. On the other hand, critical educators question the degree to which such services are really a means for parents of certain students to create a private school education within the public school or a way to create 'exclusively defined' sub-populations, or even whether gifted programs are created for political rather than educational reasons (e.g. Borland, 1997; Sapon-Shevin, 1987, p. 40). Underlying these criticisms lie claims that there is insufficient evidence that the offerings under the umbrella of gifted education really benefit the students to whom they are offered. The second basis of criticism is the claim that educators have not demonstrated that other students in the schools would not have benefited equally well from the offerings. Finally, critics assert that the program offerings are not based on documented needs of the identified populations (Sapon-Shevin, 1987, 1994).

One reason why the criticisms persist is that school personnel have failed to conduct evaluations that provide the evidence that counters those arguments. It is rare for a school division to evaluate and it is even rarer to find evaluations that document the processes or outcomes of their services to gifted students in ways that confirm that the needs of gifted students are being met through provisions not possible within the framework of the general education program (Hunsaker & Callahan, 1993). There is little documentation that the curriculum is sufficiently challenging and provides a depth and complexity of learning that could only be realized by those students identified as gifted. Finally, there is little evidence that students who are in the program are benefiting from it. Unfortunately, the program evaluation processes that could provide this data or other valuable data for maximizing the educational value of services offered by gifted programs is too often an afterthought—if even given any thought at all. Or, as Southern suggests, evaluations that are conducted tend to "focus on the wrong questions, oversimplify results or are so tightly constrained that the real goals and objectives are overlooked" (1992, p. 103).

While the need to document program outcomes is one important reason why a school division might engage in program evaluation, the usefulness of evaluation when appropriately executed extends well beyond documentation of outcomes to many other domains that may serve to improve services to gifted student. Among other purposes served by program evaluation are documenting the need for a program, justifying a particular program approach, documenting feasibility of selected program approaches, documenting implementation, and generating information about program strengths and weaknesses that can be used for program revision decisions (Callahan & Caldwell, 1995). These purposes are either well served or neglected depending on the role the evaluator assumes and the orientation of program personnel toward the process.

The Role of the Evaluator and the Evaluation Process in Light of Evolving Conceptions of Program and Service Delivery Models in Gifted Education

In many school districts there has traditionally been one model for the program for gifted students. In this paradigm, a service delivery model (e.g. pull-out, special school, full-time classes for the gifted) and/or a curriculum model (Kaplan's Matrix) are selected by the school division and then the students who 'fit' the model are assigned to receive instruction within the limits of those models. In these school divisions, the evaluator needs to consider at least two fundamental questions. First, is there a match between the models selected and the students selected for the program?

That is, is the model meeting the students' educational needs and are the goals of the model appropriate for the population selected? A second set of evaluation questions revolve around the degree to which one service delivery option or curricular approach is appropriate for *all* gifted students. Are there gifted students who are *not* identified and/or served appropriately by the given model? For example, do the identification procedures limit the selection of children to a narrow band of high IQ/high achieving children? Or is a child with extraordinary achievement and/or potential for mathematics achievement being well served in a program which once a week gives him opportunities for enrichment in social studies topics?

This second question suggests a more eclectic approach—one that focuses on evaluating services rather than 'a' program. It also reflects a growing exhortation among educators of all special populations, that services for exceptional children be matched to the learner, rather than finding learners who fit the programs (e.g. Tomlinson, 1995). At this point it is critical that the evaluator and the client are in agreement that the evaluation may go beyond judging the current program model and make judgements about the program relative to the state of the art in gifted education. Sharing of standards and criteria to be used for judging 'state of the art' is critical for ensuring that the program and general school personnel value the same criteria as the evaluator. To collect data according to standards not acceptable to the stakeholders will be a waste of time and energy (see later discussion of Evaluation Utility for further information on sources of such standards).

The Program Evaluation Standards

Standards for the quality of gifted programs provide important benchmarks for consideration in the process of collecting information relative to the efficiency and effectiveness of programming efforts. Equally important in the evaluation process is adherence to the evaluation standards of the Joint Committee on Standards for Educational Evaluation (1994). These standards are organized into four categories representing the four important attributes of quality evaluation (utility, feasibility, accuracy and propriety). The particular standards provide guidelines useful in the design, implementation and assessment of evaluations of gifted programs that will be fair, valid, useful and ethical.

Evaluation Utilization

A well-conceived and well-implemented evaluation process can provide critical information that can be utilized by two sets of clientele. The first and foremost is the group of stakeholders who are in the position to make decisions about the program under examination. A second audience for evaluations is the group of educators outside the program who will benefit in the design and implementation of other gifted programs from the data collected. However, neither of these audiences is well served if the process and report (or reports) do not have those characteristics that lead to both attention to and appropriate response to the information and recommendations presented.

Whatever the reasons for undertaking an evaluation, the persons who initiate and carry out the process do so with some expectation that the findings will actually be used. However, the application of the evaluation findings and recommendations in making commendable decisions and bringing about improvement in the services offered to gifted students has been documented to be dependent on many factors (Tomlinson, Bland & Moon, 1993). Some of these factors are outside of the control of the evaluator; other factors can at least be somewhat under the control of the evaluator. Whether the factors are those that can be controlled or not, consideration of their impact will provide cautions and guidance in improving the effectiveness of the process and sometimes even prevent the expenditure of precious resources in a fruitless endeavor (Shadish, Cook & Leviton, 1991).

Researchers in the field of evaluation in general and from the field of gifted education have identified many factors in the evaluation context which are out of the evaluator's control (e.g. Weiss, 1983). For example, economic factors within the school or school division influence the likelihood of the implementation of the recommendations of the evaluation (Patton, 1988). If the evaluator recommends fundamental changes in the program that are clearly outside the financial capabilities of the institution, the report is liable to be shelved with little consideration of the findings. Or decision-makers may focus on the less costly, but probably ineffectual, recommendations which have little probability of having a significant impact on children's learning but will giving the appearance of having 'done something'.

Of course, there are times when the fiscal decisions rest on political values and concerns (Patton, 1988; Shadish, Cook & Leviton, 1991). If decision-makers are not committed to a program or to improving services to gifted students, the prospect of a major infusion of funds to bring about change is very unlikely, even if the school division financially capable of appropriating monies for suggested change. The evaluator should also be aware of a school division's basic philosophies about general education, giftedness and/or gifted services before undertaking an evaluation. To make recommendations for a full-time school for the gifted in a school division that has just taken an emphatic public stance supporting the inclusion of children with handicapping conditions will probably make all other recommendations suspect. Or to recommend that a gifted program be extended to include children with talents in the arts in a school division with no art teachers is folly.

The Utility Standards

The Utility Standards of the Joint Committee were designed to guide evaluations so they would be 'informative, timely and influential'—the critical variables determined by the Committee to influence utility (p. 8). The Joint Committee (1994) and Tomlinson, Bland & Moon (1993) have provided a summary of the research supporting the eight specific standards: Stakeholder Identification, Evaluator Credibility, Information Scope and Sequence, Values Identification, Report Clarity, Report Timeliness and Dissemination, and Evaluation Impact.

Stakeholder Identification

To meet this standard, the evaluator would identify all persons involved in or affected by the gifted program, so that their informational needs can be addressed and so that no critical information is either missed or ignored. Reineke (1991) concludes that evaluation experts discussing evaluation utility concur that involving stakeholders early, continuously, actively, and within a clearly focused structure leads to the most efficient and effective identification of concerns. To be sure all stakeholder are involved in an evaluation of gifted services, an evaluator should consider, for example, the stakeholder defined as the parent of a child not identified and served as part of the gifted program services. Further, an evaluator should always make special efforts to ascertain whether there are less powerful groups or individuals who may not be included in initial lists of informants (for example, representatives of the full range of socio-economic groups; racial, cultural, or language minority groups). In the sensitive case of gifted services these steps are of particular concern due to the charges of elitism that are already likely aimed at services. Unfortunately, a study of evaluation reports on gifted programs revealed that the majority failed to address this standard adequately. The questions, data collection and recommendations were directed primarily toward administrator concerns (Hunsaker & Callahan, 1993). One systematic procedure for gathering stakeholder input was prescribed by Renzulli (1975). In this process of 'Front End Analysis', key informants are asked to identify their greatest concerns through an open-ended survey, interviews, and focus groups. Data from these procedures are subject to content analysis. A more statistical approach is offered by Miller, Klein & Troutt (1985) and involves prior specification of goals and sub-goals, which are then submitted to focus groups for weighting.

A critical second step in appropriately addressing the stakeholder concerns is to inform stakeholders that not all interests can be equally addressed and then to choose the issues which reflect important and answerable questions. In a gifted program one might find that an individual parent may raise concerns unique to his/her child, but not relevant to program issues.

Evaluator Credibility

The second standard, Evaluator Credibility, calls for evaluators to be appropriately trained in technical and substantive knowledge and to exhibit trustworthiness and integrity as well as public relations skills. The Committee suggests that the wide range of skills and knowledge called for are often not present in one individual necessitating the creation of a team of evaluators. In gifted education, with the range of loyalties to definitions, philosophies, models and practices within the field, it is critical that the evaluator be well-versed in these before attempting an evaluation. Multiple perspectives from a team allows for the data to be interpreted across a variety of perspectives and provides balance to interpretation.

Information Scope and Selection

The third standard flows naturally from the first and requires the evaluator to collect data relevant to the issues that have been identified by stakeholders (within realistic expectations and the budget for evaluation). But it requires that in the evaluation process, evaluators must collect information from multiple sources and across "important variables (e.g. effectiveness, harmful side effects, costs, responses to learner needs, meaningfulness of assumptions and values underlying the program) whether or not the stakeholders ask for such information" (p. 39). It is this standard where most evaluations of gifted programs are lacking (Hunsaker & Callahan, 1993). Reviewing the literature in the field of evaluation of gifted programs reveals evaluation studies that fail to address little more than participant (parent and/or student) perceptions of services received. Accountability, in the form of examination of classroom instruction or outcome variables is still lacking and the literature continues to call for greater accountability in these domains (Southern, 1992; Gallagher, 1998). Often the standard is not addressed fully because the evaluators rely on the simplest strategy for gathering data, the survey, (Hunsaker & Callahan, 1993) which will provide only limited information about programs.

Values Identification

Values Identification is a standard that has obviously grown out of the increased recognition that judgements are made relative to some "pertinent and defensible idea of what has merit and what does not" (p. 43). Two useful, and somewhat parallel, guides offering criteria potential criteria for gifted program evaluation are the Key Features components identified by experts in the field and reported and described by Renzulli (1973) and the *Gifted Education Programming Criteria* (National Association for Gifted Children (1998). The Key Features include philosophy and definition of giftedness, identification, staff selection and training, curriculum, program organization and operation of the program. The *Gifted Education Programming Criteria* provide statements describing both requisite and exemplary attributes across the domains of curriculum and instruction, program administration and management, program design, program evaluation, socio-emotional guidance and counseling, professional development, and student identification. Examples from the standards are provided in Table 1.

Report Clarity/Report Timeliness and Dissemination

As one might expect, the format of an evaluation report (regardless of whether it is an oral report, series of written memos, or a lengthy document) and its timeliness are key in leading to understanding and implementation of recommendations. The report(s) should be characterized by full descriptions of the purposes, the context, the process, the conclusions and recommendations. Making the report(s) as brief, direct and simple as possible without sacrificing necessary detail and precision will serve the clients more effectively than complex and technical documentation. An executive summary helps direct the consumer to the most salient and important conclusions and recommendations. Having the client and select representatives of the intended audiences for the report read and comment on a draft prior to final distribution is a useful strategy for ensuring clarity to various audiences.

Evaluation Impact

Finally, the standards urge evaluators to assume responsibility for helping stakeholders use the evaluation findings, but to avoid taking on the role of the client. The urge to create (or re-create) the ideal gifted program for a school district must be avoided. Not only do evaluators not have the power or authority to direct program reconstruction, if they assume a direct role in that process, the client and stakeholders are deprived of the respect they deserve and need to maintain in the institution.

Effects of Adhering to the Utility Standards

Tomlinson, Bland, Moon & Callahan (1994) examined the utilization standards relative to the impact that adhering to the standards had on producing quality evaluation reports and the ultimate use of evaluation results to change programs. Hunsaker & Callahan (1993) provided a conceptual framework for the study by describing the current state of practice in evaluating programs for the gifted and identifying factors associated with 'strong' and 'weak' evaluation designs and practices in gifted programs. Hunsaker and Callahan described as weaker those reports which:

(1) were disseminated solely to district administrators as opposed to broader stakeholder audiences,
(2) failed to include recommendations for action; and
(3) lacked apparent mechanisms for translating findings into action.

Reports categorized as stronger were disseminated more broadly, included recommendations for action, and outlined mechanisms for translating findings into positive program change. Tomlinson, et al. then interviewed the stakeholders of programs, which had received the 'stronger' and 'weaker' reports to determine the degree to which reports from stronger and weaker districts were utilized for positive program change. For purposes of this study change was defined as use of formative and/or summative evaluation information that affect a program for gifted learners in at least one of three ways: (1) altering ways in which program participants, evaluation audiences and/or decision-makers thought about the program; (2) changing the decision-making process and/or decisions made by stakeholders in the program; or (3) invoking some action regarding implementation of the program. One unexpected, but very important finding, was that districts using *any* evaluation process at all used the information gathered through the process to bring abut some level of change. The clear goals of the evaluation process in the stronger districts led to more specific,

Table 1. Sample Gifted Education Programming Criteria.

Guiding Principle	Minimum Standard	Exemplary Standard
Learning opportunities for gifted learners must consist of a continuum of differentiated curricular options, instructional approaches, and resource materials.	Diverse and appropriate learning experiences must consist of a variety of curricular options, instructional strategies, and materials. Flexible instructional arrangements (e.g. special classes, seminars, resource rooms, mentorships, independent study, and research projects (1) must exist.	Appropriate service options for each student to work at assessed level(s) and advanced rates of learning should exist. Differentiated educational program curricula for students pre-K–12 should be modified to provide learning experiences matched to students' interests, readiness, and learning style.
Gifted education must be adequately funded.	Gifted education funding should be equitable compared to the funding of other local programming.	Gifted education programming must receive funding consistent with the program goals and sufficient to adequately meet them.

Table 2. The Nature of Changes in Districts Using Weak and Strong Evaluation Practices.

Weak Evaluation Practices	Strong Evaluation Practices
Evaluation goals not stated, therefore changes not tied to goals, 'random'	Goals are focused on specific program elements, 'systematic'
Nature of services was changed to better meet the needs of students	Nature of services was changed to better meet the needs of students
Additional program resources secured staff development; provided to clarify misconceptions	Additional staff development provided to assist with meeting the needs of students and the parameters of the new program initiatives
Schedules and other program elements were changed to assist in general instruction in the school	Additional resources provided by the school board to enact those changes
Information on the program provided to parents	Staff development implemented to prepare for change in the services provided

Note: From 'Case Studies of Evaluation Utilization in Gifted Education', by Carol Tomlinson, Lori Bland, Tonya Moon & Carolyn Callahan, 1994, Evaluation Practice, 15, p. 160.

targeted recommendations and subsequent program changes. Table 2 outlines the commonalities and distinctions between the nature of changes resulting from the two categories of reports.

Two key factors correlated with use of evaluation findings in districts studied—will and skill. It appears that the will to evaluate on the part of some key personnel in a district, supplemented with systematic procedures and resources for doing so, results in generation of evaluation findings and translation of those findings into program change. This will to evaluate existed in both the weaker and stronger districts studied. The second factor, skill in evaluation and related processes, appeared to be the demarcation between the two categories of districts and affects the robustness of program change stemming from evaluation findings. Utilization appeared more likely and changes from the findings more potent and systemic in direct relationship to the following conditions:

(1) Evaluation of programs for the gifted was a part of a district-wide policy requiring routine evaluation for all program areas.
(2) Systematic written plans were in place delineating steps and procedures for ensuring implementation of findings.
(3) Multiple stakeholders were consistently involved in planning, monitoring, and reviewing the evaluation process and its findings.
(4) Stakeholders played an active role in planning for and advocating before policy makers for program change based on evaluation findings.
(5) Key program personnel were knowledgeable about gifted education, evaluation, the political processes in their districts and the interconnectedness of the three. In instances where program administrators with expertise in both gifted education and evaluation were not available, leaders invoked volunteer

steering committee members with such expertise. (Tomlinson et al., 1994, p. 165.)

Callahan, Tomlinson, Hunsaker, Bland & Moon (1995) used the results of the reviews of the literature and these utility studies to create a set of fundamental guidelines for the evaluation of gifted programs (see Table 3) and these guidelines have been given further explication by Tomlinson & Callahan (1993, 1994).

Feasibility Standards

One delicate balance that is often difficult to achieve in evaluating gifted programs is the one between the ideal plan and the affordable plan. While in theory the evaluator would like to conduct comprehensive and in-depth evaluations across a myriad of questions identified by stakeholders, gifted programs are not likely to have unlimited, excess, and uncommitted funds to expand on evaluation. The feasibility standards were designed to help the program staff and evaluators design evaluations that are "realistic, prudent, diplomatic and frugal" (p. 63).

Practical Procedures

Maximizing practicality and minimizing disruption are the core of this first feasibility standard. The standard cautions evaluators to attend to the steps in implementation that include choice of data sources; instruments; administration procedures; data and information collection, storage and retrieval. In particular, it would suggest that evaluators of gifted programs should ensure that appropriate instruments are available or can be developed to assess the evaluation questions. Cautions abound in the literature on gifted program evaluation regarding the validity of using traditional standardized assessments as outcome measures (e.g. Renzulli, 1975; Callahan, 1983; Gallagher, 1985; Callahan & Caldwell, 1986). While performance and product rating scales (e.g. Schack, 1994), guides

Table 3. Principles Derived from Evaluation Utilization Study

- Make evaluation part of planning from the earliest stages of program development or a part of planning when program changes are proposed.
  * A program which anticipates and builds in systematic processes and timelines is more likely to yield data which are useful to varied stakeholders and is more likely to be aimed at positive, focused program change.
  * A commitment to evaluation by the gifted education staff is essential, but needs to be accompanied by a clear division-wide expectation that all program areas will be evaluated regularly and appropriately. Without a commitment that evaluation should result in program change on the part of the people in positions of power and influence, little attention is likely to be given to evaluation findings.
- Develop clear program descriptions and goals.
  * These should provide a roadmap for evaluation as you seek to determine whether the program is meeting specific goals and is functioning as described. Be sure that goals are specific, focused and clear, and that descriptions are accurate.
- Provided adequate funding for evaluations and time for evaluation procedures to be executed fully,
  * It is unlikely that a broadly useful evaluation will be conducted in the absence of funding for preparation of evaluation materials, support personnel, data processing, etc. A well-planned evaluation will require ample time in order to involve key stakeholders and to assess varied aspects of program function.
- Prepare staff for conducting and analyzing the results of the evaluation.
  * In evaluating programs for the gifted, it is important that persons knowledgeable of both evaluation and gifted education play lead roles throughout the evaluation. It is likely that in many school divisions that key personnel will need meaningful training in one or both areas.
- Clearly identify all audiences who have an interest in or need for evaluation results and involve them in the full evaluation process. Involvement of multiple stakeholders throughout the process gives more people a sense of ownership of both the program and its outcomes, and yields more advocates for positive program change stemming from evaluation findings. Be sure to include relevant policy makers in the group of stakeholders.
- Ask questions which are well focused to provide information about the goals, structures and activities of the program being evaluated – questions which will aid in making significant program improvements
- Use multiple data sources in order to understand the values and perspectives of various groups of stakeholders.
  * Members of school boards, building and central office administrators, identified students, regular classroom teachers, g/t program staff, counselors, and many others will be able to give interesting insights into program functioning.
- Develop evaluation designs that address complex issues of measurement in programs for the gifted.
  * Assess both process and product outcomes.
  * Quantitative designs may be more effective in looking at product outcomes and qualitative designs mat be more effective in looking at process outcomes, but the most important criteria in selecting an approach is to match the evaluation question with the most appropriate data collection strategy.
  * Avoid reliance on traditional standardized measures that offer little promise of reflecting academic growth in learners (consider instead options such as authentic performance and product assessments).
- Use a variety of data gathering methods designed to reflect the unique structure and goals of programs for gifted learners (e.g. out of level testing, portfolio assessment, product rating with common criteria and demonstrated inter-rater reliability, qualitative studies which describe unique settings, interviews, surveys, observation checklists, etc.)
- In evaluation reports describe fully procedures for data collection and interpretation so that audiences understand processes which were followed and conclusions which were drawn
- Disseminate to all appropriate audiences reports that are timely and designed to encourage follow-through in translating findings into action. Develop a specific plan for turning findings into positive program growth as an essential part of each evaluation, including roles which various program personnel, evaluators and stakeholders play in that plan.

for exemplary high level rubrics (Wiggins, 1996), and non-traditional assessments have been recommended and developed (e.g. Treffinger, 1994; Callahan, Covert, Aylesworth & Vanco, 1976), the expense and reliability and validity issues surrounding those assessment tools should be examined to ensure that there are sufficient resources and adequately trained personnel to develop, validate and score such tools (Baker, O'Neil, & Linn (1994). In evaluating programs for gifted children in schools with high mobility stemming from poverty or other factors, the evaluator who seeks to track children longitudinally must take care that an adequate sample size is selected to ensure data analysis will be meaningful given attrition. And whenever possible, assessments should be piloted to ensure clarity and

reasonable assessment time requirements. This includes testing and survey instruments. Because the use of non-traditional instruments often requires special testing or assessment procedures, there is always potential for disruption and the intrusion on limited instructional time. In gifted programs where students are served in special pullout arrangements such assessment is particularly disruptive. All efforts should be made to minimize lost instructional time and minimize disruption of normal routine.

Political Viability

If the guidelines for including all critical stakeholders suggested by the utility standards have been followed, then the first step has been taken to ensure that this standard has been adhered to. However, there are always potential political pitfalls. In conducting an evaluation of gifted programs, the evaluator should be aware of the many potential political pressure groups that may be using the evaluation process to advance an agenda. An evaluation may be a veiled attempt to do away with a particular program model, or to change the funding patterns in the program, or even to change staffing. It is critical that all stakeholders be given the opportunity to voice any potential political issues and that during the process of evaluation to give a complete and balanced opportunity for all groups to have input into the data collection process. It is also critical that agreements be made at the beginning of the process regarding the conditions surrounding data collection—particularly assuring access to all needed data and assurances of appropriate control over editing and dissemination of the report. During the process of data collection evaluators should take every possible step to ensure that there is neither appearance of nor actual bias in giving opportunities to one group over another in providing data. In addition to careful selection of samples for surveys, interviews, observations, etc., one practice to avoid such bias is the scheduling of at least one open forum that is announced publicly and open to any interested parties.

Cost Effectiveness

This standard is seemingly self-explanatory; however, the most important concerns relative to gifted programs is an assurance that there is a proper balance between the human and financial costs in terms of student and staff time, financial costs and the potential benefits to the client. Appropriate attention to this standard requires careful budgeting and planning, seeking the most cost efficient means of data collection, and ensuring that funds are in place to carry out the full evaluation before the process is begun. Not all products must be assessed, not all parents must be surveyed, and not all children must be assessed on all instruments.

Propriety Standards

The propriety standards ensure that the legal and ethical standards of evaluations are met and that the welfare of those involved in the evaluation is safeguarded. These standards serve the rights of the client and the various stakeholders and other sources of information.

Service Orientation

This standard reflects the broader interests of evaluators in ensuring that the program examined addresses educational goals that are important, that learner development is addressed, promised services are delivered, and ineffective and harmful programs are removed. The standard urges evaluators to design the evaluations that promote excellence. The question "Is this gifted program really better than no program at all?" is often raised in program evaluation. This standard would suggest that the question, "Is this an excellent program?" would be a better focus of the evaluation. Further, it mandates that evaluations look at features most likely to positively or negatively affect participants. Hence, examining after-school program options while giving only cursory attention to the core school day program for gifted students illustrates inappropriate application of the standard. The NAGC program standards clearly call for a program that is integrated with the school day. After-school programs are not as likely to affect the students in positive ways. Attention to after-school programs is warranted if there is a sense that undue resources committed to those programs may actually be detracting from a core program of the school.

Formal Agreements

The recommendations for formal agreements include statements of purposes, identification of stakeholders and evaluation questions, deliverables, data collection procedures, analysis procedures, management plan, reporting plans, commitments of services, materials, personnel, timeline, budget and payment schedule (if external), provision for review and modification of the agreement.

Rights of Human Subjects and Human Interactions

Any evaluation of children and programs with limited enrollment and a small faculty such as gifted programs are subject to very special problems with privacy protection. Evaluators not only have to ensure that everyone is aware of the process and has full and complete understanding of the process, they must also take steps to ensure that rights of participants are protected and confidentiality is guaranteed. When anonymity is promised, every effort should be made to preserve that promise. Descriptions of classrooms or reports of classroom activities in gifted special classes will often breach that anonymity.

Complete and Fair Assessment, Conflict of Interest and Disclosure of Findings

When engaged in gifted program evaluation as an educator who supports gifted services, it is easy to allow oneself to become attached to a person or persons in the school division who share beliefs, philosophy or even just commitment to the population to be served. When this occurs, it is difficult, but critical that the evaluator take precautions to report on both strengths and weaknesses as revealed by the data and not commit the error of "manipulating the reporting of strengths and weaknesses to please partisan individuals or interest groups or allowing deletion from the report of weaknesses that might prove embarrassing or to further or protect the evaluator's personal interests or biases" (p. 106). The outside evaluator who ascribes to a particular model (or worse, is the developer of a curricular or program model of the school) is particularly susceptible to such issues and should take the extra step to have data reviewed by those with differing perspectives to screen for bias in interpretation.

Full disclosure requires the open and candid sharing of reports and information, except of course, when the disclosure of particulars would in some way violate assurances of anonymity, confidentiality or any other breach of ethics or would embarrass or violate human rights considerations. The credibility of the evaluation report rests on confidence that the conclusions drawn are warranted. Any potential biases that influence decisions or equivocal conclusions should be clearly noted. Evaluators with any financial interest in the success of the program or the reporting of findings (positive reports may lead to positive recommendations for further contracts; positive evaluations of models proposed by the evaluator may lead to further consultation) need to disclose those interests and publicly explicate the procedures that will be used to bring more independent judgements to the data analysis and interpretation. Full disclosure of procedures, data and reports will also increase credibility.

Accuracy Standards

Most of the accuracy standards parallel those one finds guiding sound research studies so will not be described in full in this text. They include program documentation, context analysis, described purposes and procedures, defensible information sources, valid information, reliable information, systematic information, appropriate analysis of qualitative information, appropriate analysis of quantitative information, justified conclusions, and impartial reporting.

Current Evaluation Practices

The reporting of evaluation practice in the literature is very limited. This is likely due to three factors. First, evaluation is not research and not subject to the same constraints to ensure generalizability and/or attribution of cause. Second, in many cases, the evaluation report is the property of the school division and the officials of school divisions are not apt to feel comfortable with publication of results which may point to serious flaws in the implementation of their gifted programs. Finally, the evaluation report that meets all of the technical requirements that have specified by the standards is likely to be too lengthy for the typical journal publication.

Measurement of Student Outcomes

Experts in gifted education and assessment continue to call for the measurement of student outcomes in gifted program evaluation. Gallagher (1998) outlines the domains of mastery of a body of knowledge, mastery of new skills and competencies such as designing and executing a scientific experiment, attitudes, motivation, products, process, problem finding and problem solving as worthy of the expenditure of time and effort in program evaluation. Treffinger (1994) has created a taxonomy of levels of creative learning and production and identified assessment or evaluation approaches to match each level (Table 4).

The limited literature that is available documenting program evaluation efforts in gifted education reflects continued reliance almost entirely on formative and process data with little attention to the measurement of student outcomes except student or parent satisfaction with the program and/or teacher report of accomplishment through surveys, post hoc interviews, or incidental observation of group discussions (e.g. Dor-

Table 4. Assessment and Evaluation of the Creative Learning Model.

Assessment or Evaluation Approach	Level 1: Basic Tools	Level 2: Learn/Practice Process	Level 3 Real Problems
Tests	Useful to assess level of proficiency or growth in basic areas (e.g. creative or critical thinking).	Expansion to multiple choice or written responses to assess process skills may be useful.	Not recommended.
Performance Tasks	Tasks of brief scope and duration can yield information relating to skill or proficiency in basic tools.	Wide variety of tasks can be used to provide realistic assessment of performance (e.g. cases, scenarios, practice problems)	Extended tasks or group projects can contribute to assessing and documenting proficiency.
Portfolio	Might include documentation or applications of specific tools or strategies in particular contexts.	Might include documentation of involvement in competitions, contests, or other structured programs.	Includes a variety of ways to document success and experience in dealing with real problems.

Note: From 'Productive Thinking: Toward Authentic Instruction and Assessment', by Donald J. Treffinger, 1994, *Journal of Secondary Gifted Education*, **6**, 30–37.

544

sal & Wages, 1993; Forster, 1994; Taplin, 1996; Davalos & Haensly, 1997; Frasier, Lee & Winstead, 1997).

Some exceptions have included measurement of changes in self-concept using the Self- Description Questionnaire (SDQIII) (e.g. Clark & Dixon, 1997) and achievement using the ETS Cooperative Mathematics Test in Calculus (McBride & Lewis, 1993). But these studies measured pre- and post-test score differences with no control or comparison groups or even comparison to norms of the tests. Even if significant differences were found across time, change could not be attributed to the program offered.

Although not carried out as an evaluation study of a particular district's gifted program, the curricular evaluation done by Sternberg, Ferrari, Clinkenbeard & Grigorenko (1996) provides a model of using an outcome measure structured to match the curricular goals of a program and also designing an evaluation where outcomes can be clearly attributed to the intervention. This intervention, offered to a particular, specifically defined group of gifted students was evaluated only by outcome variables. By structuring the program so that all students received services, but they receive clearly delineated curricular interventions, the authors were able to document those curricular modifications most effective with particular students.

Affective outcomes relating to peer social competence relations were examined by comparing sociometric assessments, evaluations of friendship relationships, and peer nominations as aggressors and as victims of aggression in an evaluation of a pull-out program by Cohen, Duncan & Cohen (1994). In this case, the measures with program students were compared with students not served by the program.

Case study data was used to supplement questionnaire data collected by Moon, Feldhusen & Dillon (1994). While this approach provided stronger perceptual data due to the in-depth data collection process, the retrospective and perceptual nature of the reflections makes attribution of outcomes less justifiable than would be achieved by measuring student change more directly.

Looking at incidental, non-intended outcomes, has been the focus of Marsh's evaluations of the effects being placed in gifted classrooms on the self-concept of gifted students (e.g. Marsh, Chessor, Craven & Roche, 1995). While Marsh et al., like Sternberg et al. (1996), have presented research results, their studies suggest measures and assessment strategies that might be adopted for evaluation paradigms. These paradigms, however, require planning for data collection and the assignment of students in ways that are not normally considered in program development, bringing to the forefront once again the notion that gifted program evaluation will be most effective if planned in conjunction with program planning or revision.

Inhibitors to Quality Program Evaluation

Given the general standards of program evaluation and the specific guidance offered by so many, why do we still fail to see extensive quality program evaluation? Moon's survey of program administrators (1996) provides us some insights. Not surprisingly, lack of time, lack of knowledge of qualitative analysis, lack of knowledge of program evaluation, lack of knowledge of statistics, and lack of knowledge of survey design were the biggest inhibitors to internal evaluation efforts. Surprisingly, lack of funds was rated quite low, raising questions about the lack of evidence in the literature of use of external evaluators.

Conclusions

The last twenty years has brought about the development of a professional field of evaluation with clearly established guidelines for educational program evaluation. Parallel translation of the guidelines and studies of evaluation utility in the field of gifted education have provided educators with a sufficient number of strategies, recommendations for evaluation procedures, models, and exhortations to evaluate more systematically and comprehensively. Yet, the literature suggests that these evaluations are still not occurring. The identification of reasons for the lack of internal evaluation gives us some insight into the lack of such models, but we still have no reasons to explain the lack of involvement of external evaluators. We might speculate on the reasons why. Obviously, there are no mandates for evaluations of gifted programs so the legal requirements will not spur the kind of evaluation that accompanies Title I legislation or drop-out programs, etc. So there is a reliance on the judgement of local school administrators that program evaluation will be worth the time and effort and financial commitment that will be required. The cost of external evaluation may be prohibitive to school divisions with minimal allocation of funds to gifted programs. Program administrators may be threatened by the prospect of evaluations, feeling that their personal competence as administrators may be judged. Or there may be some well-founded fear that the programs are not representative of excellence, fail to challenge the high-end learner or to produce the desired outcomes. Perhaps, evaluation is avoided because it will reveal that the goals of the program are not clearly delineated and the staff feels lacking in an ability to articulate the goals. Or perhaps, more simply, administrators simply have no understanding of the importance of the evaluation process in helping to identify program strengths and weaknesses, program improvement, or in documenting program effects and the importance of examining ways to maximize those effects. We owe it to gifted students to address these issues and provide the data that will enhance the educational opportunities afforded to them. Program evaluation provides the local schools or state systems that opportunity.

References

Baker, E. L., O'Neil, H. F. & Linn, R. L. (1994). Policy and validity prospects for performance assessment. *Journal for the Education of the Gifted*, **17**, 332–353.

Borland, J. H. (1997). The construct of giftedness. *Peabody Journal of Education*, **72**, 6–20.

Callahan, C. M. (1983). Issues in evaluating programs for the gifted. *Gifted Child Quarterly*, **27**, 3–7.

Callahan, C. M. & Caldwell, M. S. (1995). *A practitioner's guide to evaluating programs for the gifted*. Washington, DC: National Association for Gifted Children.

Callahan, C. M. & Caldwell, M. S. (1986). Defensible evaluations of programs for the gifted. In: C. J. Maker (Ed.), *Critical Issues in Gifted Education: Defensible Programs for the Gifted and Talented*. Rockville, MD: Aspen.

Callahan, C. M., Covert, R., Aylesworth, M. S. & Vanco, P. (1976). *SEA Test*. Charlottesville, VA: University of Virginia, Bureau of Educational Research.

Callahan, C. M., Tomlinson, C. A., Hunsaker, S. L., Bland, L. C. & Moon, T. R. (1995). *Instruments and evaluation designs used in gifted programs* (Research Monograph No 95132). National Research Center on the Gifted and Talented.

Clark, J. J. & Dixon, D. N. (1997). The impact of social skills training on the self-concepts of gifted high school students. *Journal for Secondary Gifted Education*, **8**, 179–188.

Cohen, R., Duncan, M. & Cohen, S. (1994). Classroom peer relations of children participating in a pull-out enrichment program. *Gifted Child Quarterly*, **38**, 33–37.

Davolos, R. A. & Haensly, P. A. (1997). After the dust has settled: youth reflect on their high school mentored research experience. *Roeper Review*, **19**, 204–207.

Dorsal, T. N. & Wages, C. (1993). Gifted, residential education: outcomes are favorable, but there are some cautions. *Roeper Review*, **15**, 239–242.

Forster, J. (1994). Mentor links program. *Gifted Education International*, **10**, 24–30.

Frasier, M. M., Lee, J. & Winstead, S. (1997). Is the Future Problem Solving Program accomplishing its goals? *Journal of Secondary Gifted Education*, **8**, 157–163.

Gallagher, J. J. (1985, September). Educational strategies for gifted students in secondary schools. *Nassp Bulletin*, **69**, 17–24.

Gallagher, J. J. (1998). Accountability for gifted students. *Phi Delta Kappan*, **79**, 739–742.

Hunsaker, S. & Callahan, C. M. (1993). Evaluation of gifted programs: current practice. *Journal for the Education of the Gifted*, **16**, 190–200.

Joint Committee on Standards for Educational Evaluation (1994). *The program evaluation standards* (2nd ed): *How to assess evaluations of educational programs*. Thousand Oaks, CA: Sage.

Marsh, H. W., Chessor, D., Craven, R. & Roche, L. (1995). The effects of gifted and talented programs on academic self-concept: the big fish strikes again. *American Educational Research Journal*, **32**, 285–319.

McBride, R. O. & Lewis, G. (1993). Sharing the resources: Electronic outreach programs. *Journal for the Education of the Gifted*, **16**, 372–386.

Miller, A., Klein, J. & Troutt, G. (1985). *Gifted and talented program evaluation: a multiattribute utility approach*. Frankfort, KY: Kentucky State Department of Education. (ERIC Document Reproduction Service No. ED 283 854 (1).

Moon, S. M., Feldhusen, J. & Dillon, D. (1994). Long-term effects of an enrichment program based on the Purdue Three-Stage Model. *Gifted Child Quarterly*, **3**, 38–48.

Moon, S. M. (1996). Using the Purdue three-stage model to facilitate local program evaluations. *Gifted Child Quarterly*, **40**, 121–128.

National Association for Gifted Children (1998). *Gifted education programming criteria*. Washington, DC: National Association for Gifted Children.

Patton, M. Q. (1988). Six honest serving men for evaluation. *Studies in Educational Evaluation*, **14**, 301–330.

Reineke, R. A. (1991). Stakeholder involvement in evaluation: Suggestions for practice. *Evaluation Practice*, **12**, 39–44.

Renzulli, J. S. (1975). *A guidebook for evaluating programs for the gifted and talented*. Ventura Co., CA: Office of the Ventura County Public Schools.

Sapon-Shevin, M. (1987). Giftedness as social construct. *Teachers College Record*, **89**, 39–53.

Schack, G. D. (1994). Authentic assessment procedures for secondary students' original research. *Journal of Secondary Gifted Education*, **6**, 38–43.

Shadish, W. R., Cook, T. D. & Leviton, L. C. (1991). *Foundations of program evaluation: Theories of practice*. Newbury Park, CA: Sage.

Southern, W. T. (1992). Lead us not into temptation: issues in evaluating the effectiveness of gifted programs. In: Ohio Department of Education, *Challenges in gifted education: Developing potential and investing in knowledge for the 21st century* (pp. 103–108). Columbus, OH: Ohio Department of Education.

Sternberg, R. J., Ferrari, M., Clinkenbeard, P. & Grigorenko, E. L. (1996). Identification, instruction, and assessment of gifted children: A construct validation of a triarchic model. *Gifted Child Quarterly*, **40**, 129–137.

Taplin, M. (1996). Student teachers providing programmes for gifted and talented children: A cooperative venture between universities and schools. *Gifted Child International*, **11**, 95–99.

Tomlinson, C. A. (1995). *How to differentiate instruction in mixed ability classrooms*. Washington, DC: Association for Supervision and Curriculum Development.

Tomlinson, C. A. & Callahan, C. M. (1994). Planning effective evaluations for programs for the gifted. *Roeper Review*, **17**, 46–51.

Tomlinson, C. A., Bland, L. & Moon T. R. (1993). Evaluation utilization: a review of the literature with implications for gifted education. *Journal for the Education of the Gifted*, **16**, 171–189.

Tomlinson, C., Bland, L., Moon, T. & Callahan, C. (1994). Case studies of evaluation utilization. *Evaluation Practice*, **15**, 153–168.

Tomlinson, C. A. & Callahan, C. M. (1993). A planning guide for evaluating programs for the gifted. *Quest*, **4** (2), 1–4.

Tomlinson, C. A. & Callahan, C. M. (1994). Planning effective evaluations for programs for the gifted. *Roeper Review*, **17**, 46–51.

Treffinger, D. J. (1994). Productive thinking: Toward authentic instruction and assessment. *Journal of Secondary Gifted Education*, **6**, 30–37.

Weiss, C. H. (1983). Ideology, interest, and information: The basis of policy decisions. In: D. Callahan & B. Jennings (Eds), *Ethics, the social sciences, and policy analysis* (pp. 213–245). New York: Plenum.

Cross-Cultural Studies in Gifted Education

Edna Leticia Hernández de Hahn

University of Munich, Germany
Iboamerican and National University, San Diego, California, USA

Introduction

Although giftedness and talent development are topics that have fascinated humans since ancient times, cross-cultural studies in gifted education are a relatively recent endeavor. The factors that have fostered the emergence of cross-cultural studies in gifted education include the theoretical and methodological developments in cross-cultural psychology, the creation of international competitions in various academic areas, and the serious concern that important differences in academic achievement exist across cultures and that these differences have an impact on other areas of performance.

This chapter examines historical, theoretical and methodological issues related to the development of cross-cultural research in gifted education. The first section explores the meaning of culture and the ways in which it affects giftedness. The second section deals with the methods and research strategies that are used in the field. Also included is a brief history of the methodological approaches used in research on cultural differences. The third section analyzes studies in three major areas of cross-cultural research, namely, cognitive processes, affective issues and academic performance. The final section provides guidelines for future studies in this domain.

Giftedness and Culture

Since giftedness is a socio-cultural phenomenon and not a quality that can be directly observed and measured (Feldhusen & Heller, 1986), its nature has been the object of much debate and it has been defined in many different ways (e.g. Sternberg, 1986). Although the 'gifted construct' may be similar across cultures (Frasier & Passow, 1994), the way in which abilities and talents are manifested and the procedures that are required to identify gifted individuals in the various cultural groups are different (e.g. Brush, 1971; Baldwin, 1991). Culture also has a direct influence on the type of gifted behaviors that are valued and fostered (e.g. Frasier, Garcia & Passow, 1995). Thus, time and space factors are determinants of the gifts and talents

that any given society nurtures and the way in which it chooses to identify individuals who possess or who are able to develop these qualities. The way giftedness is interpreted depends on the values and world views of each culture.

This emphasis on culture in the field of giftedness has an important implication. Namely, that human abilities are not immutable and that perceived differences in talent and capacity among groups of people (sometimes labeled 'races') are not entirely biologically determined (e.g. Nisbett, 1995). In fact, the term 'human race' has lost its meaning due to the enormous genetic diversity and has simply become a social construct (Cavalli-Sforza, Menozzi & Piazza, 1994).

Throughout history, culture has been the basis for identifying groups of people who differ in some behavioral aspects from other groups due to their ethnicity, national origin, place of residence, or other related factors. Like giftedness, culture has many definitions. In the past, emphasis was placed upon the notion that culture is "a shared way of life of a group of socially interacting people" (Segall, Lonner & Berry, 1998, p. 1104) and that it is transmitted from one generation to the next. More recently, emphasis has been placed upon the fact that culture is not simply an external reality that affects human behavior, but that it is actively created by each person throughout daily interaction with their surroundings (Segall et al., 1988; Shweder & Sullivan, 1993).

As the 19th century drew to a close, a new interest in 'culture' emerged and the empiricist conception of the person, which assumes humans are natural beings that exist materially in the space time continuum, declined (Kashima, 2000). The empiricist conception of the person had its origins in the 18th century Enlightenment Period, when psychology and education attempted to emulate Newtonian physics in the area of research methodology. The successful physical scientist viewed experimentation and causal explanation as fundamental to the process of finding universal truths. As psychologists were compelled to follow the tracks of positivism, culture was regarded as a material process, external to the person, and therefore, not an object of study for psychology. Psychology developed to utilize causal laws to explain human behavior. Kashima argues that the decline of the empirical perspective in the 1970s and 1980s was the logical consequence of the political, economical, historical and technological changes that took place after World War II. In the following years, theorists proposed an interpretive conception of culture. This perspective saw culture as an integral part of a person and stressed human intentions. It also suggested that the socio-cultural context must be examined in order to interpret human behavior. This is the assumption on which all cross-cultural research is based.

Cross-cultural research investigates the differences in behavior among cultures and attempts to interpret these differences. Since ancient times, travelers, missionaries and philosophers have recorded and attempted the interpretation of the differences they observed between cultures. However, it was not until the 19th century that cultural diversity was studied systematically (Klineberg, 1980). Systematic cross-cultural research in gifted education is a recent phenomenon and has focused on studying issues related to cognitive performance, affective factors and academic achievement. The following section discusses topics related to the methods and paradigms utilized in cross-cultural research.

Methodological Issues in Cross-cultural Research

Research Strategies in Cross-cultural Studies

Because education is a field of study in which many other sciences converge, educational researchers have traditionally used methods of inquiry that are used in other fields, in particular, psychology, anthropology, sociology and history (e.g. Borg & Gall, 1989; Gay, 1996). These methods may be grouped into two paradigms, the scientific model and the humanistic model (Husen, 1999). The first method models the natural sciences, emphasizing empirical, quantifiable observations and attempts to find causal relationships. These relationships are usually guided by a hypothesis that is drawn from a theoretical framework. The second method is derived from the humanities and focuses on holistic, qualitative information and interpretive approaches. This type of approach is commonly used in exploratory studies. Since the early 1990s, researchers have acknowledged that neither paradigm can answer all the questions posed and that the methods are not mutually exclusive, but rather complement each other (Husen, 1999; Landsheere, 1999).

Not surprisingly, the cross-cultural studies in gifted education have used research methodologies and theoretical approaches that are typically used in cross-cultural psychology and in comparative education. Cross-cultural psychology has not only provided the field of education with useful knowledge about cultures, but has also helped to develop theoretical perspectives and frameworks that have been useful in cross-cultural research in education (e.g. Harkness & Keefer, 2000). Likewise, comparative education has investigated topics (e.g. international comparisons in academic achievement) and used methodological tools that have attracted the interest of cross-cultural researchers. Given these connections between disciplines, several historical, theoretical, and methodological issues related to cross-cultural psychology and comparative education will be discussed.

Cross-cultural psychology seeks to determine the effects of culture on behavior and psychological development through the use of various types of comparative research (Segall, Lonner & Berry, 1998). The field of cross-cultural psychology emerged shortly after World War II, developed rapidly during the Cold War years, and was institutionalized in the 1960s (Johda & Krewer, 1977). During the early stages of cross-cultural psychology, researchers, like those in other disciplines (e.g. biology, linguistics, sociology and anthropology), focused on the discovery of universal ideas. To achieve this, two tasks had to be completed. First, the current psychological knowledge had to be tested in other cultures. Second, new aspects of various psychological phenomena had to be explored or discovered (Berry & Dasen, 1974). These early stages were characterized by methodological problems that originated in the tendency of the researchers to use Euro-American theoretical frameworks. One of the consequences of this approach was that the instruments developed and validated in one culture were used in another culture. The assumption was that the instrument would be measuring the same constructs. When the flaws of this approach became evident, researchers argued that the existence of psychological universals could only be supported if the psychological phenomena was first explored within each culture (emic research) and then across other cultures (etic research) (Segall et al., 1998).

Berry, Poortinga, Segall & Dasen (1992) identified three theoretical orientations in cross-cultural research: *absolutism*, *relativism* and *universalism*. The *absolutist* orientation takes for granted that all humans exhibit the same basic psychological processes and that culture has little, if any, effect upon their manifestations (etic research). Therefore, instruments validated in one culture may be used indiscriminately in other cultures and evaluative comparisons may be made. The results are then interpreted from an ethnocentric perspective and all views are excluded except those pertaining to the culture in which the researcher is immersed. The second orientation is *cultural relativism*, which neglects the relevance of similarities among different cultural groups and avoids making comparisons, particularly those of an evaluative nature. The last orientation is *universalism*, which most cross-cultural researchers adhere to. It is also called the integrationist approach (Kim, Park & Park, 2000). Followers of this approach argue that culture produces differences among groups, as well as among individuals within groups. They also believe that processes may only be considered universal after their existence in all cultures has been empirically proved. Although all humans share certain characteristics, their manifestations vary due to cultural differences. In the context of assessment, this implies that only instruments that take these differences into account can accurately measure the underlying processes and that, when interpreting the results, perspectives from the various cultural groups must be considered.

Most of the cross-cultural research conducted in the past concentrated on international work that involved exploring other cultures (Berry & Annis, 1988). These cultures were compared and, after analyzing the results, some dichotomies were created that would aid in the classification of cultures. These dichotomies included individualist vs. collectivist models and Western vs. non-Western societies. Despite clear evidence that the world society is becoming more interconnected, Hermans & Kempen (1998) found that many researchers still use these dichotomies and assume that culture is geographically localized, internally homogenous and externally distinctive. Some researchers continue to disregard the fact that cultures are increasingly more complex and less stable, coherent and independent. With new technologies and improved means of transportation, the process of globalization is fostering the interaction between people of all cultural backgrounds. The connections between societies exist in all areas: ecological, demographical, economical and political (Wolf, 1994). As Hermans et al. indicate, examples that render this phenomenon evident include the huge number of multi-national corporations and global institutions, the growing number of migrations throughout the world and the creation of new geographical groups such as the European Union.

Since the traditional approach of cultural dichotomies is not effective in studying today's world, researchers are looking for alternative perspectives. Hermans et al. (1998) suggest focusing on the contact zones of cultures rather than on their center because it is in the periphery that cultures meet. Thus, instead of comparing countries or regions, researchers should study the cultural changes that occur in the meanings and practices of people as they interact with individuals of other cultural groups. Contact with members of other cultures may occur within one region, as is the case of multi-cultural societies. Some of the issues that could be studied include the way in which communication and misunderstandings in cross-cultural interactions produce cultural changes, and changes in beliefs regarding how a culture is perceived by members of other cultures.

Berry & Annis (1988) indicate that the powerful process of globalization and immigration that have taken place during recent decades are leading researchers to dedicate more attention to issues of diversity and acculturation within multi-cultural societies. These researchers argue that immigrants, native people, ethnic groups, refugees and sojourners are no longer merely considered 'minorities' but 'cultures'. Even when people migrate to other nations, many aspects of their cultural background prevail and even shape the acculturation process. Given the worldwide impact of international migration, cross-cultural researchers in education must avail themselves to what cross-cultural psychology offers (Harkness et al., 2000). This includes the knowledge and understanding related to the beliefs and practices that people bring to their cross-cultural encounters.

Comparative education, another discipline that has contributed to the development of cross-cultural research, investigates educational systems in different societies, including aspects related to educational modernization and reform (Fischer, 1970; Altbach, Arnove & Kelly, 1982). Like cross-cultural psychology, it developed quickly during the Cold War, when the 'superpowers' were trying to compete in every sphere. Knowing that education is a factor that influences scientific and economic development, these powerful countries kept an eye on each other's educational practices and concluded that the enemy was training their youth to believe in and to perpetuate an unjust economic and political system (Ryba, 1997; Matthews, 1982; Gutmann, 1999). The fast development of comparative education after the end of World War II was triggered by this interest in knowing about the educational systems of other countries. To understand the differences that exist between systems, comparative researchers analyze how a number of contextual variables (e.g, economic, political and social) interact with educational issues. Although cross-cultural researchers in gifted education have investigated topics that are commonly addressed in comparative education (e.g. international comparisons in academic performance), they have not focused so much on the relationship between educational phenomena and the economic and political context, but rather on the relationship between school/home environment and the cognitive, affective and social development of the person.

Comparative education has adopted methodological tools of other disciplines such as sociology, anthropology, political science, and economics. One of the methods that has been widely used in this discipline and that can be very helpful in cross-cultural studies in gifted education (e.g. in studying the beliefs and attitudes of groups of people) is content analysis. This tool is the systematic and analytical study of information that reflects people's minds as opposed to behavior (Krippendorff, 1980). It involves counting frequencies of words in written or verbal productions in order to identify categories or themes that the researcher can then analyze from either a quantitative or a qualitative approach. This method can be used with a variety of research designs (e.g. statistical, descriptive, explanatory); and, although it used to be time consuming, the currently available computerized techniques make it very fast and convenient.

Cross-cultural research in education has taken knowledge and methodological tools from the previously mentioned disciplines. The first educational issues that were investigated cross-culturally were the universality of cognitive development (e.g. international studies on Piaget's stages of development) and the contexts for learning provided in different cultures (Harkness et al., 2000). With regard to the second, some aspects that were explored include the variability in learning styles and the differences in rearing patterns in collectivist vs. individualistic cultures. As cross-cultural research in education evolves, it is influenced by the same forces that have shaped the development of research strategies in cross-cultural psychology and in comparative education.

Cross-cultural Research Types

Van de Vijver & Leung (2000) developed a taxonomy of cross-cultural studies that is useful in identifying the strengths and weaknesses of the research carried out in the field of gifted education. It also provides some useful information to future researchers as they choose a research design and attempt to avoid methodological flaws. This taxonomy classifies cross-cultural studies into four categories: generalizability studies, theory driven studies, psychological differences studies and external validation studies.

In *generalizability studies*, a theoretical framework is developed and research hypotheses are developed. Usually, quantitative approaches are used to determine the universality of a particular structure (e.g. intelligence) without taking contextual variables into consideration.

Theory driven studies, like generalizability studies, have a strong theoretical background and a priori hypothesis that must be tested. This type of design differs from the previous one in that researchers gather contextual information and acknowledge the relationship between behavioral and cultural factors. The drawback, however, is that alternative interpretations are not considered when interpreting the results. Chen and Stevenson's (1995) study on the motivation and mathematical achievement of Asian-American, Caucasian-American, and East Asian students is such an example. Assuming that culture, through the social contexts of family, school and peers, has an impact on the academic achievement of students, the correlation between mathematical achievement and several characteristics of their cultural context was studied. It was

found that there is a relationship between achievement and several aspects associated with the lives of the students, including diligence and beliefs regarding the importance of effort.

Psychological differences studies focus on either exploring the stability of Western structures across cultures or on comparing cultures with regards to their scores on certain processes. Usually, instruments that were validated in one culture were used with other groups without consideration of the contextual factors. The open-mindedness regarding cross-cultural differences is the major advantage of using them, particularly when it comes to studying unexplored domains. The problem, though, is that once differences among cultures have been defined, the interpretation becomes ambiguous due to the lack of criteria to identify, among a large number of possible interpretations, a reliable way of explaining the results. The research of McIntosh, Nohda, Reys & Reys (1995) provides an example. The purpose of their study was to explore performance on several mental computational tasks utilizing a visual and oral presentation format. The correlations between levels of performance and contextual factors were not examined, but the differences in computational performance among American, Australian and Japanese students was analyzed.

External validation studies, like psychological differences studies, are not driven by hypotheses, but focus on exploration. They differ, however, in that the external validation studies consider contextual factors and are more successful in interpreting cross-cultural differences. The reason for this is that researchers examine the correlations between the indicators (i.e. possible explanatory variables) in order to discover a set of predictors or the general underlying factor that best explains each cross-cultural difference.

Bereday (1964) proposed an interesting way of classifying comparative studies based on whether explicit comparisons are made and on the level of their sophistication. Thus, studies are categorized according to the approach they follow in their comparisons. The *descriptive approach* is the simplest of all. Data is gathered on some aspect of education in one country and then it is described. In fact, this approach does not suggest any comparisons. In the second approach, called *juxtaposition and comparison*, data is gathered in more than one country and patterns are identified and compared. The third one is called *problems approach*. A problem or an issue is identified, data is collected in two or more countries, and the results are analyzed, usually in terms of implications and consequences. Finally, the last approach is *total analysis*. The ultimate objective of this approach is to develop theories or laws that can explain certain phenomena that are related to education. All aspects that affect, or that are affected by education, are considered and analyzed. Most of the cross-cultural studies that have been conducted in gifted education have followed one of the first three approaches. The following section analyzes some of these studies.

Cross-cultural Studies in Gifted Education

Due to the fact that giftedness is not objectively observed and measured and that there is no one single definition upon which all theorists agree, there are large variations among the studies with respect to their operational definition of giftedness. In some of the following cross-cultural studies, the authors explicitly indicate the type of giftedness that is being studied. In other cases, the researchers simply use the term 'high achievers' and do not delve into the subject of whether or not their subjects have any type of gift or outstanding talent. In still other studies, researchers only examine the factors that contribute to differential levels of achievement or the differences among groups on some variable associated with achievement, such as intelligence.

As mentioned above, cultural studies in gifted education differ based on whether data was collected from one or from at least two cultures. When only one culture is examined, the findings are sometimes compared with those of previous studies. However, the problem with monocultural research is that, although two studies may claim to examine the same process or construct, their operational definitions may be so different that no sound comparisons are able to be made. This section presents studies that are both representative of cross-cultural research in gifted education and which have focused on making explicit comparisons between cultures. For purposes of analysis, they were divided into three categories:

(1) academic performance,
(2) cognitive and affective issues
(3) diversity in multi-cultural societies.

Some of the studies, however, deal with topics from several categories.

Academic Performance

One of the main interests of cross-cultural researchers in education is to determine how groups differ with respect to academic performance and what may be the cause of these differences. As far as research in gifted education is concerned, mathematics, science and technology are the fields in which cross-cultural differences have been widely investigated. In this part of the chapter, an analysis of the influence of gender on mathematical performance is presented, as well as the results of international efforts to compare the mathematical performance of several cultures.

Studies in many places of the world have consistently found differences in academic performance between males and females. Much attention has been paid to differences in the verbal ability of females who perform better than males during the school years (Epstein, Elwood & Hey, 1998) and to the differences in mathematics particularly. Research studies indicate that although females do well in computational tasks, males outperform females in spatial ability and complex problem solving skills (e.g. Armstrong, 1985; Dossey, Mullis, Lindquist & Chambers, 1988; Becker & Forsyth, 1990; Gallagher, 1992; Low & Over, 1993; Benbow, Casey, Nuttal & Perzaris, 1995; Friedman, 1995). Even though the mathematical achievement of females in general has improved, a significant gender gap continues to exist in the gifted population (Kerr, 1994; Gallagher, 1996). These differences have been considered to be one of the factors that account for the under-representation of females in the fields of mathematics and science (Adams, 1996, Reis, 1998). While gender differences in academic performance have been widely investigated, only some of these studies have addressed giftedness issues from a cross-cultural perspective. The following is a sample of the topics that have been commonly investigated in cross-cultural research in gifted education, especially in mathematics; some of these studies focus on issues that arise in multicultural settings.

Chen & Stevenson (1995) studied the mathematical achievement of Asian-American, Caucasian American and East Asian high school students and found that the achievement scores of Asian-American students were higher than those of Caucasian-Americans, but lower than those of Chinese and Japanese students. The cultural factors found were associated with the Asian-American and East Asian students having had parents and peers with high academic standards, their belief in the importance of effort, a positive attitudes regarding mathematics, studying diligently and having less interference from jobs and informal peer interactions. It is possible that these differences in achievement may be correlated with how students allocate their time to various activities. For example, Fuligni & Stevenson (1995) examined the daily lives of American, Chinese and Japanese high school students to determine the amount of time devoted to a wide variety of activities. The interviews revealed that Chinese students spent more time than the American students in academic endeavors. Although no differences were found between Japanese and American students with respect to time spent studying or attending after school classes, the findings indicate that Japanese students spent more time attending school, whereas their American counterparts spent more time working and socializing with friends. Another study that involved Asian students indicated that, in the 8th grade, the mathematical performance of Hispanic students was lower than that of Asian students, with Asian females performing slightly higher than Asian males. It also showed that attitudes toward mathematics were good predictors of math achievement across cultures (Simich-Dudgeon, 1996).

Campbell & Wu (1994) used quantitative and qualitative research methods to study the factors that influence mathematical achievement among gifted and non-gifted 5th and 6th grade students from Taipei and Taiwan. Their findings indicated that boys received more pressure, support and help in intellectual pursuits and that, in the case of non-gifted boys, this additional pressure had a dysfunctional effect on their achievement. Non-gifted girls, on the other hand, were more neglected, as far as academics was concerned, but this did not undermine their overall achievement. In the case of gifted girls, more parental help was related to lower achievement in mathematics. These girls reported having more intellectual resources and, over-all, experienced a near optimal mix of family processes that fostered their academic development. Similar studies (Campbell, 1994; Campbell & Uto, 1994; Pitiyanuwat & Campbell, 1994) found that certain family processes, such as support and intellectual resources, positively affected mathematical achievement, but that excessive pressure and parental help had negative effects among Greek American, Caucasian American, Latino, Asian American, Japanese and Taiwanese students.

Success in mathematical achievement has also been related to students' estimation and mental computational skills. Research studies among Australian, Japanese and American students (Reys, Reys, Nohda, Ishida, Yoshikawa & Shimizu, 1991; McIntosh, Nohda, Reys & Reys, 1995) found that there is a correlation between students' confidence in their ability to estimate and their performance on actual estimation tasks. It was also found that, whereas American students outperformed their Japanese counterparts on orally presented items, the opposite is true when the items are presented visually. To explain these results, the authors hypothesized that high scores on visual tasks may be due to a greater reliance on the use of the standard written algorithms, whereas a higher performance on the oral items may suggest a tendency to use invented mental algorithms. This is an area that requires further research. The performance of Japanese students was higher at the early grades but, by grade 8, it decreased when compared to the American sample and disappeared when compared to the Australian sample. It appears that Japanese students tend to apply learned computational procedures mentally, instead of estimating.

Among the first well-known systematic comparisons are the studies connected with the Olympiad competitions. Some issues that have been studied include the differences in mathematical performance between different countries and the way in which the competition impacts the subsequent development of the participants.

Although the International Mathematical Olympiad was first held in 1959, it was not until recently that American and Chinese scholars decided to conduct joint research on whether the competition reached its stated goals (Campbell, 1996b). Studies (Campbell, 1996a) that analyzed various aspects of the Math Olympiad found that psychological support and parental help are the key to success in all cultures. Also, Olympians reported similar views across cultures regarding the attribution of ability and effort. American Olympians had a higher self-concept and published more research papers than their Chinese and Taiwanese counterparts, but also reported more hostility and claims of elitism. Although other International Olympiads exist, for example in physics and chemistry (Pyryt, Masharov & Feng, 1993), there are few cross-cultural studies on the characteristics of their participants and on the impact of these competitions.

Another important cross-cultural study in mathematical achievement is the Third International Mathematics & Science Study (TIMSS). It is the largest international study on mathematics and science ever undertaken and is conducted under the auspices of the International Association for the Evaluation of Education Achievement (IEA). This study focuses on making cross-national comparisons in educational attainment (Schmidt & McKnight, 1995). Three categories of characteristics, curriculum, instruction and student achievement, were assessed in more than 40 nations, among which Japan, the United States and Germany were the most widely studied. Some of TIMSS findings regarding curriculum and instruction (Beaton, Mullis, Martin, Gonzalez, Kelly & Smith, 1996) were as follows. Content taught in 8th grade maths classrooms in the United States was at a 7th grade level in comparison with other countries. Topic coverage in eight mathematics classrooms in the United States was not as focused as it was in Germany and in Japan. American 8th graders spend more hours per year in mathematics and science classes than German and Japanese students. In regards to instruction, some of the findings indicate that in the United States and in Germany, the goal of the lessons is that the students acquire principal skills, while in Japan it is to develop mathematical thinking.

The findings of these types of studies are useful in determining what educational practices promote high achievement throughout a country and they provide invaluable insight as to what changes in curricular content and teaching strategies may be appropriate in different cultures.

Cognitive and Affective Factors

This section presents research studies that have explored cognitive and affective issues in which researchers have found are correlated with either high achievement or giftedness. The topics that will be analyzed include intelligence, creativity, learning styles, attributional style, self-efficacy, anxiety and attitudes.

Several questions have emerged in the field of cross-cultural research regarding *intelligence*. Researchers have inquired into whether the structure of intelligence is the same across cultures and what relationships exist among the different intelligence tests and between these tests and other aspects such as personality and environmental variables (Bleichrodt, Hoksbergen & Khire, 1999). Bleichrodt et al. worked on the development of an intelligence test that would be useful in testing school-aged children in both India and the Netherlands. They developed the ICIT (Indian Child Intelligence Test), which is an adaptation of the RAKIT (Revisie Amsterdam Kinder Intelligentie Test). The test scores of Indian children were lower than those of children in the Netherlands in several areas. The researchers believe this could be due to the fact that children in the Netherlands start school earlier and that some children in India leave school earlier in order to work. In India, it was discovered that the scores for girls in three subtests (closure, verbal meaning and mazes) were significantly lower than those of boys. This may be due to the higher level of encouragement that boys receive to do well in school. Based on the overall results, the researchers concluded that a correspondence exists between the factor structure of both tests. This supports their psychometric equivalence. Research similar to this one has been done with various intelligence tests (e.g. WISC) as they are adapted to other cultures. Another topic that has been explored is the usefulness of different intelligence tests in identifying gifted children from diverse cultural backgrounds. Saccuzzo, Johnson & Guertin (1994a, 1994b), for instance, studied the effectiveness of the Raven Progressive Matrices Test (RPM) in identifying gifted children from cultural groups that are traditionally under-represented in gifted programs in the United States (eg., Latinos and African-Americans). They found that the RPM, as compared to the WISC-R, is a more equitable test for identifying students from ethnically diverse groups and for ensuring more gender equity. An aspect that has to be studied in more depth is the role of the environment, the culture and, in particular, of specific types of nurturing strategies in the development of intellectual abilities.

In the area of *creativity*, Lubart & Sternberg (1998) argue that this construct is time and place dependent and that it originates in the interaction between a person and his culture. Based on an analysis of previous research, it was concluded that the Eastern perspective of creativity does not emphasize innovative ideas, but that it focuses on emotional, personal and *intrapsychic* aspects of the creative process. In contrast, Western cultures have a problem-solving orientation and assume that creativity is linked to the creation of an observable solution that is novel and appropriate. The researchers also indicated that the level of creativity allowed and the degree to which it is fostered varies between cultures. In a study of technical creativity among Chinese and German students, Heller & Hany

(1997) found that the German students scored higher in the production tasks and in the practical verbal test of creativity. Chinese students, on the other hand, scored higher in logical thinking with geometrical figures and in the non-verbal part of the test, which involved constructing geometrical analogies. It would be a very interesting study to analyze, from a qualitative perspective, the mechanisms through which different cultures, and in particular these two, promote different levels of skills among their students. After more than two decades of studying creativity, Csikszentmihalyi (1988) concluded that it is not possible to study this construct by isolating individuals and their works from their social and historical environment. For this reason, the study of creativity is both fascinating and very complex.

With respect to *learning styles*, Milgram, Dunn & Price (1993) stated: "We are becoming increasingly aware of the unique impact of culture on intellectual and personal-social development, in general, and on giftedness and learning style, in particular." (p. xi). Because there are differences in the way individuals receive, store and retrieve information (i.e. learning style), it is imperative to provide educational experiences that respond to those differences (Dunn & Milgram, 1993). In a cross-cultural study of learning styles among students from Brazil, Canada, Egypt, Greece, Guatemala, Israel, Korea, the Philippines and the United States, Price & Milgram (1993) found that numerous differences exist among students from these cultures and between gifted and non-gifted students. One of the findings indicated that gifted students prefer learning alone rather than in groups. Even in the face of difficulty, they prefer to receive direction from an authoritative adult rather than work cooperatively with other students. This finding challenges the suggestion made by several researchers (e.g. Johnson & Johnson, 1985, 1989) regarding the benefits of using cooperative learning in heterogeneous ability groups. Other researchers (e.g. Anderson, 1988; Dunn, 1993; Ewing & Yong, 1993) have analyzed differences in learning styles among students of various ethnic groups in multicultural societies, finding differences between genders, between gifted and non-gifted students, and among ethnic/cultural groups.

Attributional style is related to the causes to which people attribute their successes and failures. Birenbaum & Kraemer (1995) studied the causal attributions for success and failure in mathematics and language examinations of Jewish and Arab 9th graders. Large gender differences were noticed in the mathematical abilities of Jewish students, with boys attributing success more to their ability in maths and girls attributing failure due to their lack of ability. Jewish girls displayed adaptive attributional patterns only in language. In another study, Heller & Ziegler (1997) examined gender differences in attributional styles in Germany, Israel, China and Korea and successfully trained the female subjects to attribute their successes to ability and their failures to lack of effort and to certain external factors.

Self-efficacy is a person's beliefs regarding their ability to perform at certain levels in particular tasks (Bandura, 1994). One of the mechanisms that may increase self-efficacy is social persuasion which, like other forms of social interaction, is shaped by culture. Many studies have been conducted in this field in various countries and particular attention has been paid to gender differences in self-efficacy in mathematics (e.g. Junge & Dretzke, 1995), with the result that females have lower self-efficacy than males. However, there is a lack of studies that analyze this phenomenon from a cross-cultural perspective.

Anxiety is another factor that is strongly correlated with achievement. Satake & Amato (1995) found a negative correlation between math achievement and maths anxiety. According to their results, Japanese students experience high levels of anxiety when they have to perform calculations or solve problems. With regards to testing, it was reported that 5th and 6th grade female Japanese students experienced significantly higher levels of test anxiety in maths than their male counterparts, regardless of achievement level. It was also found that elementary teachers are more likely to call upon high achievers in order to give them more opportunities to demonstrate success in classroom performance, which is one of the criteria that determines whether a student will be admitted into a prestigious middle school.

Another area in which the negative effects of anxiety have been reported is computers. Due to technological advances and the need to incorporate computers into our everyday lives, it has become imperative to develop educational programs that guarantee computer literacy. However, affective factors such as anxiety have been found to affect one's success in learning to use computers (Marcoulides, 1988). It has been argued that these programs will be successful only if the presence of computer anxiety is accurately measured (Marcoulides, 1991). However, construct invariance, in this case computer anxiety, is a sine qua non in the measurement of psychological variables and must be taken into account when making comparisons across cultures. Having identified this need, Marcoulides (1991), tested the invariance of a two-factor computer anxiety model with college students in two different cultures. He found that his model was invariant, which means that his Anxiety Scale is useful in identifying individuals who experience computer anxiety. Rosen & Weil (1994) conducted a similar study, but obtained different results. Using factor analysis procedures, it was demonstrated that the meaning of the construct of computer anxiety differs across cultures. It was found that each country had a unique culture-dependent

model for computer anxiety. The results also indicated that computer anxiety for university students in the United States and in Australia meant students were anxious regarding learning to use computer technology, including encountering and dealing with problems. To other students, it meant visiting a computer center or sitting in front of a home computer. For American and Australian students, computer problems were a part of the process of learning to use the computer, but these problems caused anxiety to students from Germany, Japan and Israel.

Attitudes have also been investigated in the field of computers. In a study of Canadian and Chinese adolescents, Collis & Williams (1987) found that Chinese students had a more positive attitude regarding the impact of computers on society, that they showed a greater tendency to label computer users as smart and less to label them as unsociable and that they were less confident in their computer abilities than Canadian students. In this study, girls expressed the belief that women and men were equally capable in scientific and technological endeavors. Markrakis (1992) studied attitudes towards computers among Japanese and Swedish students. He hypothesized that gender differences in one's attitude towards computers would reflect socio-cultural structures and the efforts of each country in reducing gender inequality. His findings indicated that Japanese female students were more interested in learning about computers than Swedish female students based upon a more positive perception regarding the need to master computer skills. The findings also showed that Japanese students of both genders exhibited a greater tendency to stereotype the area of computers as a male domain. Markrakis believed that these differences were related to the cultural characteristics of each country.

Regarding attitudes toward gifted students, Feather (1988) investigated differences in attitudes toward high achievers in Australia, Canada and the United States. Because the cultures in these three countries emphasize individual values, the researcher expected that all students would be in favor of rewarding high achievers, rather than rewarding their defeat. Indeed, this is what his findings confirmed. On the other hand, previous research (Feather & McKee, 1993) had indicated that in collectivist cultures, people showed a tendency to want to see high achievers fail. Further research is necessary that investigates how people's attitudes toward high achievers influence the motivation of gifted and talented students to perform at high levels in different cultures.

Issues of Diversity in Multi-cultural Societies

The process of globalization and international immigration have produced deep changes in today's society. Some of these changes are related to issues of diversity and acculturation in multicultural settings. In the field of gifted education, the problems that researchers have addressed include the identification of culturally diverse students, the creation of effective services and intervention strategies that adequately address their needs and the retention of these students in gifted programs. Some of the factors that have been studied include the adequacy of the instruments used for identification, differences in learning styles among cultural groups as previously discussed, the impact of non-intellectual barriers to achievement, and the classroom climate (Ford, 1994).

Most studies have been conducted in the area of identification of diversity. In discussions regarding identification, the psychometric, test-driven approach has been widely criticized due to its limited success in the identification of culturally diverse students. Consequently, efforts have been made to explore alternative ways of identification that are culturally impartial without compromising levels of excellence. Researchers at the Szold Institute for Research in the Behavioral Sciences in Israel (Zorman, 1997), developed a model to identify hidden potential in the visual arts and sciences through enrichment of students of various cultural backgrounds, including Arab, Jewish, Bedouin and Druze children. The model proved to be successful, but needs to be validated in other settings. Callahan, Tomlinson, Moon, Tomchin & Plucker (1995) used the Multiple Intelligence Model to identify and develop talent among minority and at-risk students. Some of their results indicated that student attitudes regarding self improvement and how their parents saw them were more successful. In another study, O'Tuel (1994) found that the Academic Program for Gifted with Excellence and Equity (APGEE) followed identification procedures that assured a more adequate representation of minorities, the disadvantaged, under achievers and persons with limited English skills into the program. Most of the systematic research in this area has been conducted in the United States (see Borland & Wright, in this book, Part V, chapter 3)). To find patterns across cultures more research needs to be conducted in other countries.

Future Directions in Cross-cultural Studies in Gifted Education

This section presents several suggestions regarding theoretical, methodological and statistical aspects that should be considered in future cross-cultural studies. Although some of these recommendations were originally proposed in the field of cross-cultural psychology, they equally apply to educational research, including cross-cultural studies in gifted education.

Some of the following guidelines (guidelines 1 through 6) concerning theoretical, methodological and statistical issues derive from suggestions proposed by van de Vijver & Leung (2000). In various cases, perspectives from other theorists are added to the suggestions.

(1) Effort should be made to eliminate the various types of bias that affect cross-cultural research. To begin with, not only target constructs, but also presumed biasing contextual factors should be measured. This would allow researchers to verify or falsify particular interpretations of the differences found across cultures. Second, bias due to measurement artifacts may be dealt with by using at least three different methods when gathering data. Third, sampling procedures must be sound enough to avoid confounding cross-cultural differences with differences due to biased sampling. Borg & Gall (1989) indicate that sampling bias may exist when volunteers have been used, when subjects have been lost and when the subjects selected differ regarding important aspects. This would make them non-equivalent samples and the subjects are, to a large extent, not representative of the population. The fourth type of bias is very difficult, and in some cases impossible, to avoid. However, researchers must be aware of it. The values, attitudes and beliefs of the researcher, as well as the research paradigm being used, affect many aspects of the study. They determine what questions are asked and how they are answered and prod the researcher to ignore other methodological approaches.

(2) Instruments must adequately cover the constructs under investigation. If only one part of the construct is measured, the results cannot be validly compared to those obtained from studies that included other aspects of the same construct.

(3) When reporting results, effect size estimates should be used. They provide a clearer picture of the magnitude of the difference between groups, thus making them easier to compare. Significant levels may be misleading because they are a combination of cultural differences and sample size.

(4) Item response theory should be used in developing instruments for cross-cultural research. This modern theory of measurement provides useful guidelines in the construction and equation of tests that are intended to measure traits such as aptitudes and cognitive abilities (Hambleton, Swaminathan & Rogers, 1991; Stocking, 1999). Item response theory assists in adapting the instrument to the cultures in which it will be used. It also provides a useful framework for comparing scales that measure the same construct but that include non-identical items.

(5) The use of multiple latent variable models which include factor analysis (exploratory and confirmatory), path analysis and structural equation modeling, is recommended when dealing with complex, real-life phenomena (Loehlin, 1998) such as that found in cross-cultural research. Confirmatory factor analysis, termed a 'measurement model' in structural equation modeling (Byrne, 1998), is useful in comparing factor models of different groups. As van de Vijver and Leung indicate, structural equation modeling is useful in eliminating bias affecting observed scores by compar-

ing factors for which equivalence has been established.

(6) Van de Vijver and Leung indicate that multi-level modeling may be very useful in analyzing differences in the score levels among individuals of the same cultural group, as well as across cultural groups. It may also help determine whether a particular construct has the same meaning across aggregation levels.

(7) The ethnocentric approach, in which only Western instruments and perspectives are considered, should be avoided (Harkness & Keefer, 2000).

(8) Constructs must not be oversimplified (e.g. individualism vs. collectivism) (Harkness et al., 2000).

(9) As Keller & Greenfield (2000) suggest, methods that study behavior in context (e.g. naturalistic observation) should be included in the repertoire of methodological tools. Until now, most of the research has focused on variables that are verbally reported.

(10) Not only quantitative, but also qualitative methods are necessary in cross-cultural research. Researchers should avail themselves of the rich heritage of methods and theories that anthropology and psychology have to offer. In particular, qualitative methods may be extremely useful in gaining a deeper understanding of the nature of the cross-cultural differences and of the factors that generate those differences.

A comment is in order regarding the dissemination of cross-cultural and multicultural studies. The results of many investigations that cover a wide variety of educational topics, including issues of diversity in some nations, appear in publications that are not always accessible to English-speaking persons or persons from the Western world. When traveling to other countries, it is not uncommon to discover that researchers in different parts of the world are working on similar, or even identical, issues unaware that others are conducting the same research. Therefore, it is imperative to develop more effective means of making ideas and research findings accessible to wider audiences.

Finally, given that culture plays such an important role in human performance, it makes sense to emphasize the development of policies geared toward eliminating the disadvantages suffered by some groups in the field of talent development. In addition, researchers must be aware of how the political system in which educational practices are embedded influences the types of issues that are investigated and the methodologies that are chosen.

References

Adams, C. M. (1996). Gifted girls and science: revisiting the issues. *The Journal of Secondary Gifted Education*, **7** (4), 447–458.

Altbach, P. G., Arnove, R. F. & Kelly, G. P. (1982). *Comparative Education*. New York: Mcmillan.

Anderson, J. A. (1988). Cognitive styles and multicultural populations. *Journal of Teacher Education*, **39** (1), 2–9.

Armstrong, J. M. (1985). A national assessment of participation and achievement of women in mathematics. In: S. F. Chipman, L. R. Brush & D. M. Wilson (Eds.), *Women and Mathematics: Balancing the Equation* (pp. 59–94). Hillsdale, NJ: Lawrence Erlbaum.

Baldwin, A. Y. (1991). Ethnic and cultural issues: handbook of gifted education. Needham Heights, MA: Allyn and Bacon.

Bandura, A. (1994). Self Efficacy. In: V. S. Ramachandran (Ed.), *The Encyclopedia of Human Behavior*, (Vol. 4, pp. 71–81). San Diego, CA: Academic Press.

Beaton, A. E., Mullis, I. V. S., Martin, M. O., Gonzalez, E. J., Kelly, D. L., Smith, T. A. (1996). *Mathematics achievement in the middle school years: IEA's third international mathematics and science study (TIMSS)*. Chestnut Hills, MA: CSTEEP, Boston College.

Becker, D. & Forsyth, R. A. (1990, April). *Gender differences in academic achievement in grades 3 through 12: a longitudinal analysis*. Paper presented at the annual meeting of the American Educational Research Association, Boston, MA.

Benbow, C. P., Casey, M. B., Nuttal, R. & Perzaris, E. (1995). The influence of spatial ability on gender differences in mathematics college entrance test scores diverse samples. *Developmental Psychology*, **31** (4), 697–705.

Bereday, G. Z. F. (1964). Comparative method in education. New York: Holt, Rinehart & Winston.

Berry, J. W. & Annis, R. C. (Eds.). (1988). *Ethnic psychology: research and practice with immigrants, refugees, native peoples, ethnic groups and sojourners*. Lisse, the Netherlands: Swets & Zeitlinger.

Berry, J. W. & Dasen, P. R. (1974). Introduction. In: J. W. Berry & P. R. Dasen (Eds.), *Culture and Cognition* (pp. 1–20). London: Methuen.

Berry, J. W., Poortinga, Y. H., Segall, M. H. & Dasen, P. R. (1992). *Cross-cultural psychology: Research and applications*. New York: Cambridge Unversity Press.

Birenbaum, M. & Kraemer, R. (1995). Gender and ethnic-group differences in causal attributions for success and failure in mathematics and language examinations. *Journal of Cross-Cultural Psychology*, **26** (3). 342–359.

Bleichrodt, N., Hoksbergen, R. A. C. & Khire, U. (1999). Cross-cultural testing of intelligence. *Cross-Cultural Research* **33** (1), 3–25.

Borg, W. R. & Gall, M. D. (1989). Educational research: an introduction (5th ed.). New York: Longman.

Brush, C. (1971). Modification of procedures for identification of the disadvantaged gifted. *Gifted Child Quarterly*, **15**, 267–272.

Byrne, B. M. (1998). *Structural equation modeling with LISREL, PRELIS, and SIMPLIS: Basic concepts, applications and programming*. New Jersey: Lawrence Erlbaum.

Callahan, C. M., Tomlinson, C. A., Moon, T., Tomchin, E. M. & Plucker, J. A. (1995). *Project START: Using a Multiple Intelligences Model in Identifying and Promoting Talent in High-Risk Students* (Research Monograph 95136). Storrs, CT: The National Research Center on the Gifted and Talented, University of Connecticut.

Campbell, J. R. (1994). Ethnic enclaves–cul-de-sacs or conduit: sifferential aspirations in Greek American, Caucasian American, Latino, and Asian American

Neighborhoods in New York City. *International Journal of Educational Research*, **21** (7), 723–747.

Campbell, J. R. (1996a). Developing cross-national instruments: using cross-national methods and procedures. *International Journal of Educational Research*, **25** (6), 485–496.

Campbell, J. R. (1996b). Implications of the Olympiad studies for the development of mathematical talent in schools. *International Journal of Educational Research*, **25** (6), 473–582.

Campbell, J. R. & Uto, Y. (1994). Educated fathers and mothers have differential effects on oversears Japanese boys' and girls' maths achievement. *International Journal of Educational Research*, **21** (7), 697–711.

Campbell, J. R. & Wu, R. (1994). Gifted Chinese girls get the best mix of family processes to bolster their maths achievement. *International Journal of Educational Research*, **21** (7), 686–695.

Cavalli-Sforza, L., Menozzi, P. & Piazza, A. (1994). *History and geography of human genes*. Princeton, NJ: Princeton University Press.

Chen, C. & Stevenson, H. W. (1995). Motivation and mathematics achievement: a comparative study of Asian-American, Caucasian-American, and East Asian high school students. *Child Development*, **66**, 1215–1234.

Collis, B. A. & Williams, R. L. (1987). Cross-cultural comparison of gender differences in adolescents' attitudes toward computers and selected school subjects. *Journal of Educational Research*, **81** (1), 17–27.

Csikszentmihalyi, M. (1988) Society, culture, and person: A systems view of creativity. In: R. J. Sternberg (Ed.), *The Nature of Creativity: Contemporary Psychological Perspectives* (pp. 325–339). New York: Cambridge University Press.

Dossey, J. A., Mullis, J. V. S., Lindquist, M. M. & Chambers, D. L. (1988). *The mathematics report card: are we measuring up? Trends and achievement based on the 1986 national assessment*. Princeton, NJ: The Nation's Report Card, NAEP, Educational Testing Service.

Dunn, R. (1993). Learning styles of the multiculturally diverse. *Emergency Librarian*, **20** (4), 24–32.

Dunn, R. M. & Milgram, R. M. (1993). Learning styles of gifted students in diverse cultures. In: R. M. Milgram, R. Dunn & G. E. Price (Eds.), *Teaching and Counseling Gifted and Talented Adolescents: An International Learning Style Perspective* (pp. 2–24). Westport, CT: Praeger.

Epstein, D., Elwood, J. & Hey, V. (Eds.). (1998). *Failing boys? Issues in gender and achievement*. Philadelphia: Open University Press.

Ewing, N. J. & Yong, F. L. (1993). Learning style preferences of gifted minority students. *Gifted Education International*, **9** (1), 40–44.

Feather, N. T. & McKee, I. R. (1993). Global self-esteem and attitudes toward the high achiever for Australian and Japanese students. *Social Psychology Quarterly*, **56**, 65–76.

Feather, N. T. (1998). Attitudes toward high achievers, self-esteem, and value priorities for Australian, American, and Canadian students. *Journal of Cross-Cultural Psychology*, **29** (6), 746–759.

Feldhusen, J. F. & Heller, K. A. (1986). Introduction. In K. A. Heller & J. F. Feldhusen (Eds.), *Identifying and Nurturing the Gifted: An International Perspective* (pp. 19–32). Toronto: Huber Publ.

Fischer, J. (1970). *The social sciences and the comparative study of educational systems*. Scranton, Pennsylvania: International Textbook Company.

Ford, D. Y. (1994). *The recruitment and retention of African-American students in gifted education programs: implications and recommendations* (RBDM 9406). Storrs, CT: The National Research Center on the Gifted and Talented, University of Connecticut

Frasier, M. M. & Passow. A. H. (1994). *Toward a new paradigm for identifying talent potential* (Research Monograph 94112). Storrs, CT: The National Research Center on the Gifted and Talented, University of Connecticut.

Frasier, M. M., Garca, J. H. & Passow, A. H. (1995). *A review of assessment issues in gifted education and their implications for identifying gifted minority students* (RM95204). Storrs, CT: The National Research Center on the Gifted and Talented, University of Connecticut.

Friedman, L. (1995). The space factor in mathematics: gender differences. *Review of Educational Research*, **65** (1), 22–50.

Fuligni, A. J. & Stevenson, H. W. (1995). Time use and mathematics achievement among American, Chinese, and Japanese high school students. *Child Development*, **66**, 830–842.

Gallagher, S. A. (1996). A new look (again) at gifted girls and mathematics achievement. *The Journal of Secondary Gifted Education*, **7** (4), 456–475.

Gallagher, A. M. (1992). *Sex differences in problem-solving strategies used by high-scoring examinees on the SAT-M*. New York: College Board Publications. (ERIC Document Reproduction Service No. ED 352 420)

Gay, L. R. (1996). *Educational research: Competencies for analysis and applications* (5th ed.). New Jersey: Prentice Hall.

Gutmann, A. (1999). *Democratic education*. Princeton, N.J.: Princeton University Press.

Hambleton, R. K., Swaminathan, H. & Rogers, H. J. (1991). *Fundamentals of item response theory*. California: Sage Publications.

Harkness, S. & Keefer, C. H. (2000). Contributions of cross-cultural psychology to research and interventions in education and health. *Journal of Cross-Cultural Psychology*, **31** (1), 92–109.

Heller, K. & Hany, E. A. (1997). German-Chinese study on technical creativity: Cross-cultural perspectives. In: J. Chan, R. Li & J. Spinks (Eds.), *Maximizing Potential: Lengthening and Strengthening our Stride* (pp. 237–241). Hong Kong: Social Sciences Research Centre, The University of Hong Kong.

Heller, K. A. & Ziegler, A. (1997). Gifted females: a cross-cultural survey. In: J. Chan, R. Li & J. Spinks (Eds.), *Maximizing Potential: Lengthening and Strengthening our Stride* (pp. 242–246). Hong Kong: Social Sciences Research Centre, The University of Hong Kong.

Hermans, H. J. M. & Kempen, H. J. G. (1998). Moving cultures: the perilous problems of cultural dichotomies in a globalizing society. *American Psychologist*, **53** (10), 1111–1120.

Husen, T. (1999). Research paradigms in education. In: J. P. Keeves & G. Lakomski (Eds.), *Issues in Educational Research* (pp. 31–39). The Netherlands: Elsevier Science.

Johda, G. & Krewer, B. (1997). History of cross-cultural and cultural psychology. In: J. W. Berry, Y. H. Poortinga & J.

Pandey (Eds.), *Handbook of Cross-cultural Psychology: Theory and Method*. Vol. 1 (pp. 1–42). Boston: Allyn & Bacon.

Johnson, D. W. & Johnson, R. T. (1985). The internal dynamics of cooperative learning groups. In: R. Slavin, S. Sharan, S. Kagan, R. Hertz-Lazarowitz, C. Webb & R. Schmuck (Eds.), *Learning to Cooperate, Cooperating to Learn* (pp. 103–124). New York: Plenum Press.

Johnson, D. W. & Johnson, R. T. (1989). Cooperative learning in mathematics education. In: P. R. Trafon (Ed.), *New Directions for Elementary School Mathematics* (pp. 234–245). Reston, VA: NCTM.

Junge, M. E. & Dretzke, B. J. (1995). Mathematical self-efficacy gender differences in gifted/talented adolescents. *Gifted Child Quarterly*, **39** (1), 22–28.

Kashima, Y. (2000). Conceptions of culture and person for psychology. *Journal of Cross-Cultural Psycology*, **31** (1), 14–32.

Keller, H. & Greenfield, P. M. (2000). History and future of development in cross-cultural psychology. *Journal of Cross-Cultural Psychology*, **31** (1), 52–62.

Kerr, B. A. (1994). *Smart girls: a new psychology of girls, women and giftedness*. Dayton, OH: Ohio Psychology Press.

Kim, U., Park, Y. & Park, D. (2000). The challenge of cross-cultural psychology: The role of the indigenous psychologies. *Journal of Cross-Cultural Psychology*, **31** (1) 63–75.

Klineberg, O. (1980). Historical perspectives: Cross-cultural psychology before 1960. In: H. C. Triandis & W. W. Lambert (Eds.), *Handbook of Cross-Cultural Psychology*: Vol. 1. *Perspectives* (pp. 31–68). Boston: Allyn & Bacon.

Krippendorff, K. (1980). *Content Analysis: an introduction to its methodology*. Newbury Park, CA: Sage Publications.

Landsheere, G. (1999). History of educational research. In: J. P. Keeves & G. Lakomski (Eds.), *Issues in Educational Research* (pp. 15–30). The Netherlands: Elsevier Science.

Loehlin, J. C. (1998). *Latent variable models: An introduction to factor, path, and structural analysis* (3rd ed.). New Jersey: Lawrence Erlbaum.

Low, R. & Over, R. (1993). Gender differences in solution of algebraic word problems containing irrelevant information. *Journal of Educational Psychology*, **85** (2), 331–339.

Lubart, T. I. & Sternberg, R. (1998). Creativity across time and place: life span and cross-cultural perspectives. *High Ability Studies*, **9** (1), 59–74.

Marcoulides, G. A. (1988). The relationship between computer anxiety and computer achievement. *Journal of Educational Computing Research, 4* , 151–158.

Marcoulides, G. A. (1991). An examination of cross-cultural differences toward computers. *Computers in Human Behavior*, **7**, 281–289.

Markrakis, V. (1992). Cross-cultural comparison of gender differences in attitude towards computers in Japan and Sweden. *Scandinavian Journal of Educational Research*, **36** (4), 275–287.

Matthews, M. (1982). *Education in the Soviet Union: policies and institutions since Stalin*. Boston: Allen & Unwin.

McIntosh, A., Nohda, N., Reys, B. & Reys, R. (1995). Mental computation perforance in Australia, Japan and the United States. *Educational Studies in Mathematics*, **29** (3), 237–258.

Milgram, R. M; Dunn, R. & Price, G. E. (Eds.). (1993). *Teaching and Counseling gifted and talented adolescents: An international learning style perspective*. Westport, CT: Praeger.

Nisbett, R. (1995). Race, IQ, and Scientism. In: S, Fraser (Ed.), *The Bell Curve Wars: Race, Intelligence, and the Future of America* (pp. 36–57). New York: Harper Collins.

O'Tuel, F. S. (1994). APOGEE: equity in the identification of gifted and talented students. *Gifted Child Quarterly*, **38** (2), 75–79.

Pitiyanuwat, S. & Campbell, J. R. (1994). Socio-economic status has major effect on math achievement, educational aspirations and future job expectations of elementary school children in Thailand. *International Journal of Educational Research*, **21** (7), 713–721.

Price, G. E. & Milgram, R. M. (1993). The learning styles of gifted adolescents around the world: differences and similarities. In: R. M. Milgram, R. Dunn & G. E. Price (Eds.), *Teaching and Counseling Gifted and Talented Adolescents: An International Learning Style Perspective* (pp. 229–248). Westport, CT: Praeger.

Pyryt, M. C., Masharov, Y. P. & Feng, C. D.(1993). Programs and strategies for nurturing talents/gifts in science and technology. In: K. A. Heller, V. J. Mönks & A. H. Passow (Eds.), *International Handbook of Research and Development of Giftedness and Talent* (pp. 453–471). Oxford: Pergamon

Reis, S. M. (1998). *Work left undone: choices and compromises of talented females*. Connecticut: Creative Learning Press.

Reys R, E., Reys B. J., Nohda N., Ishida J. & Yoshikawa, K. (1991). Computational estimation performance and strategies used by fifth- and eighth-grade Japanese students. *Journal for Research in Mathematics Education*, **22** (1), 39–58.

Rosen, L. D. & Weil, M. M. (1994). Computer anxiety: a cross-cultural comparison of university students in ten countries. *Computers in Human Behavior*, **11** (1), 45–64.

Ryba, R. (Ed.). (1997). *Education, democracy and development: an international perspective*. Dordrecht, the Netherlands: Kluwer Academic Publishers

Saccuzzo, D. P., Johnson, N. E. & Guertin, T. L. (1994a). *Identifying underrepresented disadvantaged gifted and talented children: a multifaceted approach*. Volume 1. (Available from D. P. Saccuzzo, Ph.D.; San Diego State University; 6363 Alvarado Court, Suite 103; San Diego, CA 92120–4913).

Saccuzzo, D. P., Johnson, N. E. & Guertin, T. L. (1994b). *Use of the Raven Progressive Matrices Test in an ethnically diverse gifted population*. San Diego, CA.: San Diego State University. (ERIC Document Reproduction Service No. ED 368 096).

Satake, E. & Amato, P. (1995). Mathematics anxiety and achievement among Japanese elementary school students. *Educational and Psychological Measurement*, **55** (6), 1000–1007.

Schmidt, W. H. & McKnight, C. (1995). Surveying educational opportunity in mathematics and science: An international perspective. *Educational Evaluation and Policy Analysis*, **17** (3), 337–353.

Segall, M. H., Lonner, W. J. & Berry, J. W. (1998). Cross-cultural psychology as a scholarly discipline: on the flowering of culture in behavioral research. *American Psychologist*, **53** (10), 1101–1110.

Shweder, R. A. & Sullivan, M. A. (1993). Cultural psychology: who needs it? *Annual Review of Psychology*, **44**, 497–527.

Simich-Dudgeon, C. (1996, April). *Ethnicity, gender, attitudes and mathematics achievement: The 1992 NAEP trial state assessment*. Paper presented at the Annual Meeting of the American Educational Research Association, New York, NY.

Sternberg, J. E. & Davidson, J. E. (Eds.). (1986). *Conceptions of giftedness*. New York: Cambridge University Press.

Stocking, M. L. (1999). Item response theory. In: G. N. Masters & J. P. Keeves (Eds.), *Advances in Measurement in Educational Research and Assessment* (pp. 55–63). The Netherlands: Elsevier Science.

van de Vijver, F. J. R. & Leung, K. (2000). Methodological issues in psychological research on culture. *Jorunal of Cross-Cultural Psycology*, **31** (1), 33–51.

Wolf, E. R. (1994). Perilous ideas: Race, culture, people. *Current Anthropology*, **35**, 1–12.

Zorman, R. (1997). Eureka: The cross-cultural model for identification of hidden talent through enrichment. *Roeper Review*, **20** (1), 54–61.

Part V

Counseling and Nurturing Giftedness and Talent

Global Professionalism and Perceptions of Teachers of the Gifted

Alexinia Y. Baldwin,[1] Wilma Vialle[2] and Catherine Clarke[3]

[1]University of Connecticut, USA
[2]University of Wollongong, Australia
[3]Newcastle University, UK

Introduction

The Terman studies set into motion an interest in the education of gifted students; however, one element of this educational package—the teacher—has gone without the intense research that other aspects of programming for the gifted have received. There has been little research which involved the direct observations of teachers in order to clarify those characteristics that are attributable to the teacher of the gifted rather than a global set of characteristics for all teachers. There has been a plethora of research reports on the interactions between teachers of the gifted and their students. Many of the studies that exist have focused on students' perceptions of various personality traits, intellectual acumen, and creativity of teachers of the gifted. From these studies, much has been extrapolated about the desired characteristics of the teachers of the gifted. The fact that these characteristics are good for all teachers makes it difficult for one to distinguish between those characteristics necessary for teachers of the gifted and the ones necessary for those who are not teachers of the gifted.

A series of questions were posed by Baldwin (1993) as the ones most frequently asked. They are:

(1) Should the teacher of the gifted be highly gifted; if so what should the IQ score be?
(2) How extensive should the knowledge of the teacher of the gifted be?
(3) Should the basic characteristics required to teach gifted elementary grade students be the same for gifted students at all levels?
(4) What type of educational background should the teacher of the gifted have?
(5) What is the difference between a teacher of the gifted and a good teacher of all the other students?
(6) What specialized training should teachers of the gifted have? (p. 621)

The question of the high intellectual ability needed for teaching gifted students is addressed tangentially by Skipper (1970) in his research with female pre-service teachers who scored at the 90 percentile or more on the American College Test and maintained a 3.5 average as university students. The premise of his study was that attitudes toward teaching as measured by several different scales would vary between intellectually gifted teachers and the unsampled set of pre-service teachers. The questions asked were: ". . . what are some of the personal attributes students may adopt from intellectually gifted teachers? Will gifted teachers' attitude toward students be conducive to the process of identification?" (p. 3). The findings of this study showed that the main difference in the two research groups was that intellectually gifted teachers like to discover new facts and have strong interest in skills required for science, and engineers. As teachers of the gifted it appears that the high intellectual teacher is more prepared personality wise, to help students process information and explore new ideas. This research showed, however, that the high intellectual teachers were much lower than the control group teachers in their interest in artistic affairs. Information processing and discovery of new facts are areas that have been listed as important for gifted students. Although this research might show that a teacher of the gifted who is of superior intelligence can address the areas considered important for gifted students of high *academic* ability what about those students who are highly creative—will they suffer? The answer to the question of how gifted must the teacher of the gifted be does not have an easy answer.

Much work has been done in the last ten years to develop standards for educational programs for teachers of the gifted. Knowledge of the domain—its constructs and the processes necessary to meet the needs of the gifted—have been the foundation for these standards as listed below. The literature which documents the efforts of researchers to answer the questions above has been an invaluable resource for the various committees' work on these standards.

The early research of Bishop (1968) which is referred to most often, determined that the teachers of the gifted in his sample were mature and experienced teachers of superior intellect. He also determined that they were creative, had high personal achievement needs and were student-oriented. Story's (1985) review of the literature revealed what she felt were important attributes of teachers of the gifted. They provide a supportive environment, have high verbal interactions, allow flexible scheduling, and give individualized attention. Whitlack & DuCette (1989) as shown in Table 1 also compared and ranked competencies for outstanding and average teachers.

Maker (1982) & Baldwin (1993) indicated that there are three important aspects of the educational development of the teacher of the gifted. These are: *philosophical awareness* of the constructs of education of the gifted which extends into a depth of understanding of human nature; *professional preparedness*; and *personal qualities* which are usually innate but can be enhanced through the proper training. These studies reveal the angst that researchers have felt in attempting to determine what is professionally appropriate for teachers of the gifted. They also provide the challenges that will face researchers in the future.

Since many of the questions listed earlier are still unanswered definitively, there remains a need to focus future research in these areas. Medley & Mitzel's (1963) statement over three decades ago that, "the development of a science of effective teacher behavior is almost certainly the most urgent research program that faces the profession today," is relevant for theoreticians and researchers as the agendas for

education of the gifted are set during the next millennium (p. 81)

Professional Development

Students for Teacher Training

Karnes & Parker (1983) reviewed the criteria used in various institutions. Out of this review came a recommendation that state certification should be based on "the prevailing philosophy that teachers for gifted program[s] should be practitioners of excellence in scholarly endeavours as well as in teaching performance" (p. 19). This earlier work has led to the development of Standards for Graduate Programs in Gifted Education as proposed by the National Association for Gifted Children (1996).

These standards for the post-bachelor's training programs for teachers of the gifted included four categories considered important in setting standards. The categories were:

(1) A *conceptual framework* which included the philosophy goals, and knowledge base of the curriculum. In summary, the proficiency expected in this area included a list of indicators of knowledge and understanding, the ability to interpret and apply this knowledge to identification, design of a program, the development of curricula, integrated instruction in a wide range of disciplines, and field experiences that are well sequenced and related to the conceptual framework.

(2) *Candidates for graduate programs in gifted education* which set a standard for candidates who had potential for professional success. Under these guidelines, recruitment and admission would be designed to attract a high quality of student including those from diverse backgrounds. The candidate should also have a

Table 1. Rank Order of the Ten Highest Rated Competences By the Outstanding and Average Teachers..

Item	Rank Order	
	Outstanding	Average
Likes gifted children	1	1
Ability to respond flexibly to the spontaneous needs of children	2	17
An advocate for gifted children	3	16
Emphasizes and looks for strengths in children	4	6
Ability to develop a gifted program appropriate to the needs of a particular community	5	36
Friendly, warm and accepting	6	24
Willingness to experiment with the unknown	7	20
Ability to admit error	8	5
Appreciates the uniqueness of individual gifted children	9	3
Encourages children to develop and present their own ideas	10	2
Ability to adapt materials (creatively and imaginatively) for the individual child	15	7
Ability to accept students' sense of humour	21	9
Fair (just)	23	4
Possesses and models joy in learning	26	8
Likes him/herself	33	10

Note: From Outstanding and Average Teachers by Whitlack, S. and DuCette, J., 1989, *Gifted Child Quarterly, 33* (p. 19)

record of successful teaching and academic ability as shown by various methods of assessment. There should also be an ongoing assessment of their progress throughout the program to the completion of their studies.

(3) The *professional education faculty* included several indicators but stressed the requirement that the faculty would be trained in the field of education of the gifted and able to conduct scholarly research in this area. It was also indicated that the faculty in charge of training students in graduate programs of education of the gifted should have a doctorate degree. There should also be evidence of their collaboration with colleagues and practitioners in research, teaching, and placement of graduates of the program.

(4) *Necessary resources* included the need for faculty to be actively involved and provided the resources with which to work. This includes an adequate library, and other technological and media resources as well as appropriate and flexible load assignments.

The extensive detail of each of the categories represents a thorough self-analysis of the fundamental requirements for professionalism in this field.

As the field has grown, these criteria have been necessary for all levels of teaching in education of the gifted. Many of the training activities, however, are done as inservice with all teachers. Gross' (1997) research noted below focused on the effects of inservice and training on the change of teachers' attitudes toward planning and programming for the gifted.

Research

It is quite evident that the primary focus of research on the teacher of the gifted has been the professional preparation of these teachers as shown by the many studies that have appeared in the literature. Berliner (1984) in his review of research on teaching cautioned that, "Teaching is a highly cognitive activity that requires an extraordinary level of competence for making decisions in complex and dynamic environments" (p. 52). This is important to understand as we attempt to make a science out of the field of education of the gifted. We can reflect on Berliner's summary of factors under a teacher's control as we consider the professionalism of teachers. The factors that can affect student attitude, achievement, and classroom behavior are: engaged time, time management, success rate, academic learning time, monitoring, structuring and questioning. He has strongly recommended that professional education for teachers should include a study of these factors.

In Gross' (1997) study of the effects of training and inservice on the attitudes and knowledge of teachers of the gifted, she indicated that the term *training* is more appropriately used for those students who are primarily enrolled in specialized degree programs at the graduate level while the term *inservice* is more appropriately used for short term courses for teachers. She compared the shifts in attitude toward gifted students, of teachers enrolled in single day inservice and those enrolled in intensive training programs. The principal research questions were:

(1) Do teachers in single-day inservice display significant positive attitudinal changes towards the gifted over the course of the inservice?

(2) Do teachers in specialist gifted education training display significant positive attitudinal changes toward the gifted over the course of their training?

(3) Do teachers in specialist gifted education training experience more powerful attitudinal changes than teachers in single-day inservice?

(4) Do teachers who choose to enter an intensive training program in gifted education display significantly more positive attitudes towards gifted students than professional colleagues who do not choose to enter training?

(5) Are there any aspects of the intensive training program, or any events or 'crystallizing experiences' associated with the program, which participants believe contributed significantly to shifts in their attitudes towards gifted students? (p. 12)

The findings of Gross' study indicated an expected difference in the level of change between the two groups in the area of knowledge gained and the confidence participants had in working with other teachers. Those who were in certificate programs were more prepared; however, on the two factors that traditionally have produced roadblocks for gifted programs—*needs of gifted and support for services* and *objectives based on ideology and priorities*—change as a result of both inservice and training experiences was evident. Gross concluded that planned professional training was certainly the important need for programs of the gifted, but inservice also plays an important role in changing the attitudes of teachers and administrators toward the value of addressing the needs of gifted students.

Studies by Hansen & Feldhusen (1994) focused on the observation of teachers who were trained in the education of gifted students vs. those who were not trained. Fifty-four trained and 28 untrained teachers in the field of education of the gifted were included in this study. Trained teachers were defined as those that completed three to five graduate courses and were teaching gifted students as part of their training. The 28 teachers included in the study were those who had been assigned to teach the gifted but had not completed course work in this area. The findings of this study gave evidence that trained teachers had greater teaching skills and were able to develop more positive class climates than untrained teachers.

In Australia, Whitton's (1997) study of the practices of 606 primary school teachers in New South Wales found that these teachers demonstrated a lack of knowledge about gifted children and made only minor modifications to their curriculum. This situation is attributed, in part, to the paucity of formal training in education of the gifted at both the preservice and inservice levels. Wellisch (1997) found that the younger the gifted child, the less likely their needs would be recognized and met by classroom teachers. Wellisch emphasized that teacher attitudes improve where they have some training in education of the gifted.

Curriculum modification. Reis & Westberg (1994) took another approach to looking at the effect of training on the development of good teachers of the gifted. This research focused on the ability of the teacher to modify curriculum for gifted students. The suggested type of modification was called curriculum compacting. The research questions that they wanted to answer were:

(1) In what areas and to what degree do teachers modify instructional practices and regular curricular materials to meet the needs of gifted and talented students in regular classroom settings?
(2) Is there a significant difference among treatment groups and teachers' decisions about whether they will compact curriculum in the future?
(3) Is there a significant difference among treatment groups with regard to the quality of the compactor forms completed by teachers? (p. 130)

It was found that teachers modified mathematics and language most often. The results showed that there was a significant difference in those who were trained in curriculum modification following the curriculum compacting formula, and the groups that did not have the specialized training. In answer to the next research question, some of the teachers indicated that they would definitely use compacting in the future, however; statistical analyses showed that there was a lack of relationship between those in the various treatment groups. In response to the third question, the researchers found that the quality of the compactor forms increased as the training became more intensified.

Holistic Professional Development for Teachers of Gifted Students

In the United Kingdom, a very different approach to professional development has been taken by one researcher. It has been developed for the purpose of helping teachers to make appraisals of their teaching in an environment with other teachers. In this environment, teachers share their intellectual skills and help each other to grow in creative thinking, problem-solving and managing and organizing classrooms. Although this system is not without its problems,

narratives such as that which exist in the popular portfolios, is nevertheless a valuable way of researching the complexities of life in classrooms and schools. By focusing the process on the achievements of teachers as well as their concerns, efforts made by teachers to meet the needs of their gifted students are acknowledged and explicitly valued during the process. When this is done, ideas, techniques and approaches can be considered and accepted with modification or rejection.

Gifted students around the globe need to be nurtured if they are to achieve at the level of which they are capable (Matthews, 1997). Teachers play an important role in this nurturing and as Her Majesty Inspectorate in the U.K. reported, "The judicious intervention of the teacher to urge pupils to a higher level of knowledge, skill, understanding and thinking was crucial" (1992 p. viii). In order for teachers to function at their best and facilitate the learning of gifted students appropriately, they themselves need, what Brandis & Ginnis (1990) describe as 'nurturing' attention. Brandis and Ginnis see this as an integral aspect of holistic staff development, an approach to staff development which has as its aim student centered education. An holistic approach is described as being based on participatory management, close interpersonal communication, a strong school-wide commitment to minimum ground rules, self and negotiated appraisal, pre and inservice training which emphasizes positive human interaction, and a creative and open curriculum (p. 160).

Clark (1992, 1996, 1997) has explored ways in which professional development can be holistic and incorporate many of the characteristics as listed above. In order to be holistic it should be participatory, utilizing close interpersonal communication with a minimum of ground rules, giving the opportunity for self and negotiated appraisal, and emphasizing positive human interaction and creative and open curriculum. This research of teachers should start out by first celebrating their work-effort and helping them to know that what they did and were attempting to do every day in their classroom is valued. In this model, teachers are encouraged even at this early stage in the program to conduct research in their classrooms.

The hypothesis underlying this model is that it is more likely that teachers who have taken part in holistic professional development programs will be able to offer holistic educational experiences to their gifted pupils and this will in turn enhance their intellectual progress but also their emotional and social development. This model is based on the theory that teachers given a chance to talk generally about their school and their classroom experiences of teaching and learning and to examine through their personal research the areas they need to change or enhance, will become better teachers. As Schon (1987) suggests, they can begin to explain what is usually left unexplained and thus understand more clearly what they are doing and why they are doing it. A holistic development approach can be done through several different activities; (a) through the use of teacher narrative, (b) through unstructured classroom observation, and (c) through action research.

Teacher narrative procedure. Eight primary school teachers all of whom were concerned to meet the challenges of individual differences in a mixed ability classroom, became participants in this study. Teachers were asked to keep a diary and prepare to deliver a short presentation about how they were currently managing and organizing learning in their classrooms and the concerns and issues arising which they wished to work on during the experimental session. The session agenda was agreed upon by the participants and this immediately put them at ease. First, they had to identify an area of their practice which they wished to change, after which they had to decide how they intended to implement the change, evaluate the outcomes, and plan for their future practice in the light of their findings. The group acted as a research community where each member had a chance to tell their story and present the data they had collected through reading and their classroom analysis. Responses from teachers were expressed in terms of how they were able to analyze their own teaching styles, their personal concerns about understanding the levels of abilities in their class, and modeling of this process with their students.

Unstructured classroom observation. This helps teachers tell more of the story about what is happening in their classes. These data in transcript form are used to facilitate a debate between the teacher in whose classroom the observation has been conducted and ideally two other colleagues who have participated in the observation provides the triangulation necessary for the analysis of data to be more systematic and rigorous. Observation which is unstructured seems to be particularly helpful because it can tell more of the whole story, that is, data collected can paint a full picture of what is happening. The ground rules for this discussion are exactly the same as those used for the discussion about diaries. A great deal of self-appraisal goes on during this time. The analysis of data provides a useful opportunity for story telling and the sharing of anecdotes which serve the purpose of making the exercise far less threatening and more meaningful.

Action research. This is the process of having teachers conduct research in their classes and implementing the changes that this research was able to show as needed. Clark (1997) explains that in this project teachers were taught how to do action research on the education of gifted children in their own classrooms and also on the education of gifted children across the school as a whole. After identifying an area which they wanted to change, they had to decide how they intended to change it, implement the change, evaluate the outcomes and plan for their future practice in light of their findings. The group acted as a research community where they discussed their data and their analysis through engagement in dialectical dialogues which are diametrically opposed to the one being put forward. What this appeared to do was as one teacher said "open up new vistas" and it also encouraged the teachers to link the data with their experiences as teachers and learners. Some of the conversations focused on the wider issues of current educational, political, economic and social context which broadened the entire scope of the professional development project.

Holistic professional development does not fit the usual mold for developing effective teachers of the gifted; however, teachers who participated in these holistic professional development programs were prepared to take risks, consider alternatives, tolerate ambiguities, and encourage task commitment. They were able to give learners more time to study in-depth and were flexible in finding ways within themselves to model those competencies they wished to develop in their students.

Perceptions of Teachers of the Gifted

Although much of the research presently available on the teacher of the gifted relates to teacher attitudes toward gifted students, assumptions are often made by researchers as to the desirable qualities of teachers of gifted students; however, there is comparatively little research that explores the attitudes of gifted students to their teachers. In an exploratory study, Vialle (1998) questioned primary school students (year 5 and 6) enrolled in a gifted program. In semi-structured interviews, the students were asked to describe the qualities that make a good teacher. The findings from these interviews clearly demonstrated that personal qualities are as highly regarded as academic qualities, a finding that is reminiscent of the study conducted by Abel & Karnes (1994). The students in Vialle's study rated understanding and helpfulness as the key qualities in their ideal teacher. Although their teachers needed to be smart according to 15% of the students, the ability to facilitate their learning through setting challenging tasks was described as a key factor by a large majority of the sample. A sense of humor, creativity, and curiosity were also qualities in their teachers that were highly valued by the students. Finally, the students required their teachers to make the work interesting and to be well organized.

Perceptions of the Characteristics of Teachers of the Gifted

In a study by Ferrell, Kress & Croft (1988), "it appeared that there were characteristics of a teacher of the gifted which were different from those of teachers who were commonly recognized as 'good' teachers" (p. 136). Efforts were made by these researchers to find characteristics of the gifted teacher by using the Teacher Perceiver Interview (TPI) Selection Research, Incorporated (1977). The themes of the TPI were seen by the researchers to be consistent with the qualities desired in a teacher of the gifted. These themes as described by SRI and shown in Table 2 are: mission, empathy, rapport drive, individual perception, listening, investment, input drive, activation, innovation, gestalt, objectivity, and focus.

In this study it was found that there were six themes that differentiated the two groups of teachers. They were focus, Gestalt, innovation, mission, rapport drive, and investment. The researchers found that three of these themes—Gestalt, innovation, and rapport drive were also characteristics frequently found in the literature on teachers of the gifted. Among these three, Gestalt was found to be the one important distinction. Other themes from TPI did not differentiate between teachers and non-teachers of the gifted. The researchers concluded that 'further study is needed to pinpoint the qualities of teachers who work with children which differentiate them from teachers in other capacities" (p. 137)

The list of desired characteristics for the teacher of the gifted and the levels of training they must have appears to be endless.

Summary

Professionalism of teachers of the gifted is a global concern. The paradigm for developing this professionalism is becoming more formalized around the world. Efforts to develop this paradigm have been more advanced in the USA but there are strong signs of a growing global acceptance of the value of teacher training in some systematic way. In each country, there will be political, cultural, and attitudinal factors that will require the basic paradigm to be shifted. Baldwin & Vialle (1999) have highlighted the importance of including in the paradigm for change a need to understand that giftedness can exist in many guises. They have encouraged that professionals in the field of education of the gifted, metaphorically 'lift the masks' and look beneath because there are many faces of giftedness. Tsui (1997) discussed the need for scrutiny of the principles underlying the policies that determine the programs to be offered. In a society whose educational system is academically oriented and where flexibility of teaching processes to accommodate different aptitudes and learning styles are not the rule,

Table 2. Description of SRI Teacher Perceiver Inventory Themes..

Theme	Description
Mission	Sees education as the foundation for all that comes later in a young person's life. This teacher wants to be a part of helping children to grow and maintain or improve society.
Empathy	Perceives the emotion of the moment and responds directly to the emotion. This teacher understands and accepts students' emotions on a cognitive level without trying to solve the problem for the student.
Rapport Drive	Sees him or herself as a warm friendly person who students like. This teacher works purposefully to build a positive working relationship with the students, which the teacher perceived as beneficial for the students.
Individualized Perception	Gets to know the individual needs and interests of each student and builds or adapts the educational program based on these need[s] and interests. Different activities are provided so that students can express their individuality through their work.
Listening	Spontaneously listens to others and facilitates the speaker by accepting what is said. This teacher perceives that the answer to the problem lies within the speaker and that talking will benefit the speaker.
Investment	Wants students to learn and sees any lack of student success as his or her concern. This teacher's satisfaction in teaching derives from student learning rather than his or her own performance.
Input Drive	Is excited about own learning and uses the new things learned to help others. This teacher is always seeking out new knowledge, learning from everything surrounding, including the students.
Activation	Sees success in learning as a key variable for helping students to learn. This teacher builds a wide repertoire of techniques to motivate learning and gets students involved in wanting to learn.
Innovation	Is looking for and trying new or different ways to approach learning in the classroom. This teacher focuses his or her creativity on helping students develop creativity and to become actively involved in learning.
Gestalt	Is well organized with a drive toward completing tasks even at a perfectionist level. This teacher transfers the need for closure to students but does so by working from where the student is.
Objectivity	Responds to the total situation, getting facts first before reaching a conclusion.
Focus	Has personal role models and goals which help him or her to move in a purposeful direction professionally. A major part of the goal involves teaching and this teacher sees teaching as a life-long career.

Note: From Teachers of Gifted Children by B. Farrell, M. Kress & J. Croft (1988). *Roeper Review*, **10**, (p. 137)

the process for change requires an approach which fits the needs of the culture and the policies that exist.

A recognition of the need for this professionalism can be seen in the increased number of international students in the USA enrolled in graduate programs designed to provide training in education of the gifted. A three-summers program to obtain an MA degree in education of the gifted and a two-week Confratute (conference and institute) which is held at the University of Connecticut, Storrs, Connecticut, have provided during its 23 year existence, thousands of teachers, and administrators with inservice knowledge about processes to use in developing the abilities of gifted students.

Where funding is lacking for involvement in this training for international personnel, Baldwin (1986) has suggested that modules be transported and used for each level of training with each level becoming more comprehensive and inclusive. *Level one* module would include—awareness training, definitions, characteristics. *Level two* module would include—more indepth awareness, definitions, psychology of needs, identification, teaching strategies. *Level three* would include—philosophy, definitions, psychology of needs, identification, curriculum development, teaching strategies. *Level four* would include—historical perspectives, rationale for defense of programs, administrative strategies, psychology of needs, identification, analysis of assessment protocols, curriculum development, teaching strategies, models of evaluation, advocacy strategies.

The University of Nijmegen (The Netherlands) have developed a postgraduate training course for teachers (elementary and secondary levels) to meet the needs of teachers of the gifted. This course consists of 14 modules, each 40 hours, for theoretical and practical training in gifted education. After fulfilment of all requirements the teachers receive a diploma with the qualification 'Gifted Education specialist'. This course is offered in cooperation with the European Council for High Ability (ECHA); therefore, the diploma is called ECHA-Diploma. To-date, 200 teachers, mainly from Hungary, Austria, Switzerland, Germany, and The Netherlands have received this diploma. Currently almost 300 teachers participate in the training program.

Without exception however, there is a need for training of teachers globally which in turn will prepare them to recognize and meet the needs of children from all cultures who exhibit gifted attributes.

References

Abel, T. & Karnes, F. A. (1994). Teacher preferences among the lower socioeconomic rural and suburban advantaged gifted students. *Roper Review*, **17**, 52–57.

Baldwin, A. Y. (1986). Teacher training in developing countries. *Giftedness: a continuing worldwide challenge.* New York: Trillium Press, 434–439.

Baldwin, A. Y. (1993). Teachers of the gifted. In: K. Heller, F. Monks & H. Passow, *International Handbook of Research and Development of Giftedness and Talent* (pp. 621–629).

Baldwin, A. Y. & Vialle, W. (1999). *The many faces of giftedness: lifting the masks.* Belmont, CA: Wadsworth Publishing Co.

Berliner, D. (1984). The half-full glass: a review of research on teaching. In: P. Hosford (Ed.), *Using What We Know About Teaching*, (pp. 51–77). Alexandria, VA: Association of Supervision and Curriculum Development.

Bishop, W. (1968). Successful teaching of the gifted. *Exceptional Children*, **34**, 317–325.

Brandis, D. & Ginnis, P. (1990). *The student-centered school.* London: Blackwell.

Clark, C. (1992). *Teacher-centered development: a way of helping able and talented students to achieve.* Proceedings of the International Conference of the National Association for Able Children in Education, Middlesex University Publications **80**, 84.

Clark, C. (1996). Working with able learners in regular classrooms in the United Kingdom. *Gifted and Talented International*, **11**, 34–38.

Clark, C. (1997). Using action research to foster a creative response to teaching more able pupils. *High Ability Studies* **8** (1), 95–113.

Ferrell, B., Kress, M. & Croft, J. (1988). Characteristics of teachers in a full day gifted program. *Roeper Review*, **10**, 136–139.

Gross, M. (1997). Changing teacher attitudes toward gifted children: an early and essential step. In: J. Chann, R. Li & J. Spinks (Eds.), *Maximizing Potential: Lengthening and Strengthening Our Stride.* Proceedings of the 11th World Conference on Gifted and Talented Children (pp. 3–22). Hong Kong: University of Hong Kong Social Services Center.

Hansen, J. & Feldhusen, J. (1994). Comparison of trained and untrained teachers of gifted students. *Gifted Child Quarterly*, **38**, 115–123.

Her Majesty's Inspectorate (1992). *Education observed: the education of very able children in maintained schools.* London: Her Majesty's Stationary Office.

Karnes, F. & Parker, J. (1983). Teacher certification in gifted education: the state of the art and considerations for the future. *Roeper Review*, **6**, 18–21.

Maker, C. J. (1982). *Curriculum development for the gifted.* Rockville, MD: Aspen Systems Corporation.

Matthews, D. J. (1997). Diversity in domains of development: research findings and their implications for gifted education and programming. *Roper Review*, **19**, 172–177.

Medley, D. & Mitzel, H. (1963). The scientific study of teacher behavior. In: A. Ballach (Ed.), *Theory and Research in Teaching* (p. 81). New York: Bureau of publications, Teachers College Columbia University.

National Association for Gifted and Talented (1996). NAGC Standards for graduate programs in gifted education. *Gifted Child Quarterly*, **4**, 162–164.

Reis, A. & Westburg, K. (1994). The impact of staff development on teachers' ability to modify curriculum for gifted and talented students. *Gifted Student Quarterly*, **38**, 127–135.

Selection Research, Inc. (1997). *SRI Perceiver Academies Teacher Themes.* Lincoln, NB: Selection Research, Inc.

Schon, D. (1987). *Educating the reflective practitioner.* San Francisco: Josey-Bass.

Skipper, C. (1970). *Personal attributes of intellectually gifted teacher candidates and their implication for student identification.* (ERIC Document Reproduction Service no. ED 079–245).

Story, C. (1985). Facilitator of learning: a micro-ethnographic study of teachers of the gifted. *Gifted Child Quarterly,* **9**, 155–159.

Tsui, H. (1997). Toward the development of potential in all children: policy comprehensiveness and teacher quality. In: J. Chan, R. Li & J. Spinks (Eds.), *Maximizing Potential: Lengthening and Strengthening Our Stride.* Proceedings of the 11th World Conference on Gifted and Talented Children

(pp. 598–600). Hong Kong: University of Hong Kong Social Services Center.

Vialle, W. (1998). [Perceptions of teachers of the gifted]. Unpublished raw data.

Wellisch, M. (1997). A pilot study: teachers' views on the concept of giftedness in the early childhood setting. *Australian Journal of Early Childhood,* **22**(2), 22–28.

Whitlack, M. & DuCette, J. (1989). Outstanding and average teachers of the gifted: a comparative study. *Gifted Child Quarterly,* **33**, 15–21.

Whitton, D. (1997). Regular classroom practices with gifted students in grades 3 and 4 in New South Wales, Australia. *Gifted Education International,* **12**(1), 34–38.

Families: the Essential Context for Gifts and Talents

Joan Freeman

School of Lifelong Learning and Education, Middlesex University, London, UK

Introduction

There is no lack of evidence to show that children's development, outlooks and achievements are influenced by the life-style of the families in which they grow up, and that from the beginning, the urge to learn is tempered by opportunity. Simonton (1998), though, in his investigations of world-class achievers has shown that there is no ideal family for producing giftedness: his subjects came from very varied backgrounds.

Indeed, families vary greatly in composition—from isolated one-parent units in big cities, to large families which are well integrated within a local community; from African families where children are cared for by several 'mothers', to large polygamous families where the father is shared, as well as residential homes for children without parents. It is not an easy matter to separate the effects of interactions between children and their parents from those with the wider culture, because each family provides its own unique mini-culture, 'translated' and adapted from that of the greater society. This special context not only provides a guide for the children's development, but also largely defines the opportunities in which all the family members can exercise their abilities. As far as we know, human parenting is not driven by instincts; every individual mother and father decides what to do, based on their own culture, experience and hopes.

The Early Promotion of Gifts

Children's aptitudes, in whatever area they show promise, can only develop into exceptionally high achievement in circumstances which are rich in the appropriate material and psychological learning opportunities. All long-term studies on the development of talent have shown the cumulative effects of family attitudes on high level achievement (e.g. Bloom, 1985; Freeman, 1991; Perleth & Heller, 1994). In general, as children get older, there is a widening gap in average intelligence scores between those from differently supportive homes (Mascie-Taylor, 1989).

Gifted achievement, though, cannot be predicted from early experiences alone: self-esteem, genetic, constitutional and social trajectories impose powerful limits. Using children's precocity as the prime identifying feature of giftedness is probably partly responsible for its later apparent loss, often called 'burn out', which is usually due to the others catching up. Giftedness may also take many different forms; it may appear in quite unexpected situations and at different points during a lifetime (Subotnik, Kassan, Summers & Wasser, 1993). Trost (1993) calculated that less than half of "what makes excellence" can be accounted for by measurements and observations in childhood. The key to success, he said, lies in the individual's dedication, but given a high level of aptitude, intelligence and other cognitive factors are the most reliable indicators.

In fact, very high intelligence, as measured by IQ tests, is by far the most popular criterion for defining children as very able or gifted. Just one problem is that IQ testing is strongly influenced by belief systems, learned in the family, which include social and moral values. An example is in the Stanford-Binet Intelligence Scale in the question "What's the thing to do if another boy/girl hits you without meaning to do it?" The correct response must involve forgiveness. Consequently, children who come from families who are part of that belief system are likely to be advantaged on these tests. The vocabulary aspect too is dependent on having heard those words.

A very close positive relationship was found when children's (Stanford-Binet) IQ scores were compared with their home backgrounds (Freeman, 1991). The higher the children's IQ scores, especially over IQ 130, the better the quality of their educational support, measured in terms of reported verbal interactions and activities with parents, number of books and musical instruments in the home, etc. In a detailed review of influences on the development of children's IQ, Slater (1995) concluded that the best predictor of all is parents' IQ, education and socio-economic status.

The family culture

Due to its mediating role in a culture, the family 'belief system', or what is taken as 'common sense' in one home, may bear little relevance to what is taken equally for granted by a neighbour. In his studies of creative people, Perkins (1981) found that they were able to produce great works, not solely as a result of their talent, but as a function of their values and beliefs, which were demonstrated individually in terms of originality, knowing, and independence. After all, as Csikszentmihalyi (1998) wrote, genius cannot exist independently of the culture: one has to be a genius in something. Lubart & Sternberg (1998) showed that culture influences the definition and expression of creativity, channelling it into certain task domains and social groups. "The quantity of creative activity can be further affected by cultural factors such as the value placed on conformity" (p. 59)

Cultural and family attitudes have a considerable effect on high-level achievement. For example, Berry (1990) found highly significant geographical and religious differences between Nobel prize-winners. In proportion to their numbers, Jews were heavily over-represented; in certain subject areas 50 times more. Zuckerman (1977) suggested that as 75% of Jewish Laureates came from lower socio-economic back-grounds, it could not have been social advantage which produced that excellence, but rather—in line with other research—the cultural influence of the family's drive for success. Indeed, in their late adulthood, the most successful of the Terman sample were neither distinguishable by IQ nor by earlier school achievement but by family background, notably the aim for success (Holahan & Sears, 1995). In many Pacific Rim countries, as well as Russia, measured intelligence is largely ignored and success is attributed to sheer effort, hence the growth of out-of-school crammers. Both Flynn (1991) and Stevenson (1998) have concluded that the culture of hard work is probably responsible for so many Asian youngsters' greater school and work success than their higher IQ class-mates. In fact, Hess & Azuma's (1991) in-depth research showed that American children needed much more help and praise than Japanese children in their motivation to learn.

Home outlook and style of upbringing provides a large part of the bridge between home and school. In Poland, Niebrzydowski (1997) compared mothers' styles of upbringing; mothers of high attaining kinder-garten children showed a greater capacity to control the child. Being themselves more sensitive to the child's concerns and competent with educational problems allowed the child greater autonomy. When parents and teachers are in agreement, the path to the child's achievement is smoother, in ways which are not always obvious.

Positive cooperation may be seen, for example, in the amount and quality of homework that a child does, a well recognised factor in school success. In a comprehensive review of research on homework, Hallam & Cowan (1997) conclude that the family is essential for seeing that it is done by young children.

American teachers, pupils and parents appear to be more negative than Europeans. For highly achieving Canadian inner-city children the combination of pos-itive parental attitudes, parent-school links, and homework were the three key supports for high level achievement (Zeigler, Hardwick & McCreath, 1989). In an overview of international research on education of the gifted, it was quite clear that without family support, schools would not be able to help a potentially gifted child to achieve (Freeman, 1998).

Cultural values may inhibit the achievements of bright children. These too can be subtle, such as the effect of expectations: if children do not fit the cultural stereotypes they are less likely to be recognised as potentially highly able. Currently, the common Western stereotype of a gifted child is of a weedy lad: he (for he is usually male) is bespectacled, lonely, and much given to solitary reading. He is, in fact, a juvenile 'egg-head', at times referred to by his schoolmates and maybe his teachers as 'the little professor'.

Very able children who do not speak the language of the test-makers or who think in different ways are also less likely to be recognised as having high potential. In an overview of 20 research-based international papers on the gifted disadvantaged across five continents, Wallace & Adams (1993) concluded that it is not only culture which can cut such children out of recognition and special provision, but poverty. There is, they wrote starkly, "the equation, in reality, of wealth with giftedness, special educational provision and gifted-ness." (p. 446).

Parents who have been brought up in culturally impoverished circumstances may lack familiarity with easy verbal communication, which affects their child-ren's intellectual growth. Cultural disadvantage usually brings psychological handicaps in the areas of percep-tion and attention, verbal and intellectual abilities, and motivation. Those parents who, for example, give orders more frequently than explanations are less likely to discuss daily events with their children. Where the children's questions are ignored or rejected, and play-material and psychological 'permission' to play is scarce, their development will be accordingly nar-rowed, and bright children may have to develop complex strategies to get any verbal interaction from their parents. The intellectual poverty of children from unstimulating homes is noticeable by the age of five years. Perceptual deficiency in children who are not talked with is shown when they recognise fewer objects and situations, and their interests are limited by their inability to describe them.

The use of language

The single most effective help parents can give towards future giftedness is the early encouragement and enrichment of language. Vygotsky (in Wertsch, 1990) suggested that with specific provision and mediation (adult guidance, especially through language) children can learn at a far greater speed than otherwise.

Based on 20 years of experimental research, Fowler (1990) showed how enriched language enabled children to shoot ahead of others with equal measured ability. From the earliest days, the key for parents is to take turns with the baby at initiating and responding to communication; the parent is not teaching but enabling. Early fluency in using language involving stimulation and practice from adults, such as being read to and talked with from the time of birth, enables children to deal more effectively with later complexities. His follow-up of 14 children with enriched early language showed them to have become "outstanding students in school" in all subject areas including the sciences and mathematics. Looking at the early lives of recognised gifted adults, he found that they had enjoyed an enormous amount of verbal stimulation, both spoken and written. Radford, too, in his survey of exceptional early achievers, found that although some appeared to come from homes of low socio-economic status, these homes were all lively, stimulating, and usually highly verbal (Radford, 1990).

Advanced language is probably the first thing to look for in assessing a potentially high intellectual level, and the advantage usually lasts; infants are able to manipulate language correctly, both in its comprehension and its production, earlier than had previously been thought. In intellectually gifted children, this is followed by the ability to reflect upon and control language using metalinguistic abilities—a reflective attitude to the comprehension and production of oral and written language—which is different from ordinary verbal communication (Gombert, 1992). However, children who are advanced in verbal ability are not, on average, more advanced in motor skills (Robinson, 1996).

In poor countries, literacy is often the key to the promotion of giftedness; having a literate family both improves a child's chances of going to school, and encourages familiarity with the written word. But it is unfortunate that education is so often identified with status, self-esteem, and empowerment, because not all members of the family are seen as having the same needs or rights. For example, where women's' lives are restricted to the home, they may be denied literacy; all communication with the wider (male) society being filtered through to them by their male relatives. Literacy for women has a proven value: in an area of high illiteracy, where one group of mothers were taught to read and a control group was not, it was found that those with even a little literacy produced healthier and cognitively brighter children (Hundeide, 1991).

Even within a strongly literate cultural tradition, one cannot make the assumption that parent-child relationships have a similar nature; adult development is as important as child development. Some mothers are aged 16 and some are 45; for this and other reasons,

their mental and educational development may be quite different. The interaction between parents and children is not just between them as individuals, but also between their cognitive capacities and needs, which change with age. For example, physical contact is most important in the first year of life, conversation and responsiveness in the second, responsiveness to the child's talk in the third, and from then on, more variety of contacts with a range of other adults. From the age of five, maternal responsivity is less important, but parental encouragement and the availability of a range of play materials and learning experiences remains salient. For example, a London study found that as children were learning to read, those who read out loud to their parents at home had markedly higher reading attainments than those who did not; this could not be explained by any factor other than their reading aloud (Tizard, 1985). Gottfried, Gottfried, Bathurst & Guerin (1994) found that "Ongoing reading to the child in the early years is consistently associated with gifted intelligence (130 IQ) at 8 years." (p. 161)

Can parents make a child gifted?

Studies of successful people brought Howe (1990) to the conclusion that "in the right circumstances almost anyone can . . . acquire exceptional skills" (p. 62). He argues that self direction, self confidence, a sense of commitment and persistence, can effectively produce gifted performance. But Freeman (1998) has responded that in all history "no one has ever taken a number of children at random and obliged them to practice to a world-class level of talent in any area." (p. 415)

In fact, attempts to analyse and teach the specific skills of expertise to adults have been carried out in laboratory studies for some years (Ericsson & Lehman, 1996). But even though motivation and practice made a vast difference to results in those strictly controlled conditions, the trainees differed in the level of expertise they could reach. The researchers concluded that the most important variable in gaining expertise is sufficient ability to gain a foothold in the learning process, and then to put in thousands of hours of learning and practice. Although Ericsson (1998) concluded that "expert performance can be attained without unique and innate capacities (talent)," he states that the mystery lies in the motivation for anyone to practice sufficiently to get there.

Children's interests may provide a clue. These offer parents a lead in selecting provision (Gottfried, Gottfried, Bathurst & Guerin, 1994; Renzulli, 1995; Hany, 1996). Able youngsters' interests and leisure activities have been found to be a reliable predictor of future high achievement in that area. Although such choice is largely self-directed, showing task commitment, intellectual abilities, persistence and other personal attributes, it also depends on provision and culture. Eighteen years after secondary school, 48 of the original 159 subjects of a high school in Tel Aviv,

Israel, were surveyed for their occupational accomplishments and outstanding career achievements. A third of the sample had continued to work seriously in their childhood leisure areas with relatively higher attainment than their school-fellows whose careers were unrelated to their interests (Milgram & Hong, 1997) It was concluded that serious adolescent leisure activities were highly indicative of future successful careers and that this form of self-identification should be encouraged and provided for.

Parents And Children Together

Things that parents do together with their children have a far-reaching effect on the child's understanding: games, chatter, stories, even arguments can be a stimulating means of fostering the child's intellectual growth. The cognitive functions most closely linked to family social relationships are the executive regulators—the way we plan, monitor, and check the outcome of problem-solving; the system works because adults have learned it and share the same cultural assumptions. However, close friends of children, who spend more time with them than other children do, are also cognitive mediators, in that they help each other to understand the world.

The problem for research is how to establish what results in what. A highly verbal and demanding child, for example, can affect parents' behaviour by stimulating them to have more conversation and read more stories aloud. On the other hand, parents who talk to children a lot are themselves verbal people.

By adaptation from the study of animals (e.g. by Konrad Lorenz, 1965), it has been proposed that there are specific times in development when a child is sensitive to certain influences. Danger points in physical development were revealed at the time of the thalidomide tragedy—if the mother took the drug at a specific stage in the development of the foetus, the baby could be born with deficiencies related to that time. But the general existence of critical periods for cognitive development in human beings is less sure, although foreign language learning does seem to be affected in this way. Since attempts to acquire another tongue after 15 years of age are very much less successful than earlier learning, it is important to start language teaching as early as possible. In general, however, the benefits of good learning experiences in the early years can be lost if subsequent experiences are bad, and conversely, there can be substantial recovery if early bad experiences are followed by good ones in middle childhood.

Maria Montessori designed a system of early childhood education using the similar idea of 'prime developmental times' (Montessori, 1964). She wrote that should those special times be used well, then good learning will happen, but if not, the moment may pass and the child may not have the chance again. Intellectual progress is 'at risk' between 7 and 36 months, because that is a period which is particularly sensitive to lack of good stimuli. White (1985) concluded that probably not more than one in ten children get sufficient educational input at that time for the fulfilment of their potential. Shavinina (1997), suggested that prodigiousness is itself a consequence of accelerated development during sensitive periods, expressed in exceptional perceptions of the world.

Imitation

The ability to imitate is extremely important in learning, and without it, the gifted would not reach their full potential. So fundamental and universal is this human ability that its absence in newborns is a sign of retardation. Imitation is not only a means of learning; it is also an emotional bonding process which begins from the first day of life, with the two-way imitative 'conversations', which mothers and babies enjoy. Mothers introduce their babies into their culture, such as one would do for a verbally helpless foreigner, by establishing a 'dialogue'; to do this, she is sensitive to what her baby initiates, as well as suggesting and demanding certain behaviours from him. She encourages the activities of which she approves and discourages those she considers inappropriate, trying to extend the baby's grasp of what is appropriate by being sensitive to signs, which she can reinforce, that he is understanding what is wanted of him. It is not just physical behaviour that she is moulding, but a conceptual learning system. From the earliest days, "Sensitive parents may not only be maintaining infant interest in the events during social interaction, but also maintaining infant state at an optimal level for processing information" (Messer, 1994, p. 27).

Babies initiate as well as imitate, making their own mark on their world. For example, those babies who are demanding may receive special family attention and resources, and if these demands are of an appropriate nature, they can stimulate the infant's intellectual development. But this option is not open to all babies—interaction is the key; it is only in families where the parents are good communicators that the baby's demands are likely to be beneficially effective. This implies a specifically active role for the baby, but one which also positively involves the parents. It is open to question, though, whether demanding babies are always those with the potential for high ability, and whether parents should stimulate passive babies into demanding more, on the grounds that this will encourage intellectual development.

The mother's emotions influence the interactions, which can significantly affect the intellectual growth of the baby; even infants of ten weeks can recognise the difference between happiness, sadness, or anger in the mother. Her happiness encourages them to explore, joy in one producing joy in the other, whereas her distress causes them to withdraw, her sadness producing sadness or anger. The implications are profound. A negative emotional atmosphere inhibits good learning, but positive emotions have an encouraging effect; any condition that causes stress to infants increases their need for their mothers, and decreases their urge to explore. What is more, when toddlers experience a series of anxiety-arousing experiences, the effect is cumulative. Sensitive parents are aware of times when the baby's attention begins to diminish, and change their behaviour to keep its interest, such as a change of voice or holding the toy in a different light. Infants cared for in this way are more likely to persist with their own explorations later on, especially as the tasks become more complex.

The Promotion of Motivation

Children's feelings about what they are able to achieve start early; young children do not understand ability in the same way as they will at about age 11. They start by expecting effort to lead to results (Heyman & Dweck, 1996). Differences in motivation to learn in young children may also be more connected to their ideas of goodness and badness than to specific ideas of intellectual competence. Increasing motivation to learn, then, implies taking the blame away from personal deficiencies, such as perceived low ability over which children have no control, and putting it on lack of effort or appropriate learning strategies over which they do have control.

Lehwald (1990) concluded that the major base of future problem-solving behaviour at a gifted level is an infant's curiosity coupled with confidence to explore the environment, which each one acquires as the result of favourable social processes. There is evidence that four year-olds who have high self-concepts are not only more intelligent and socially responsible, but better able to plan ahead, which is a vital part of creative thinking (Mischel, Shoda, Flavell & Rodriguez, 1989). However, these studies involve difficulties in measurement, for instance in accounting for the effects of influences such as gender, education, and socio-economic-status. For example, Power et al. (1998) in Britain, investigated young men who had been identified while at school as 'academically able', and found that their perceptions of a masculine identity could either foster or jeopardise their academic achievement.

Empowering children by giving them a feeling of competence and a goal to aim for (even examinations) generally increases both their motivation to study and the accompanying rise in level of work (Freeman, 1992). On the other hand, too much adult control implies constant dependence on someone else's decisions, removing their 'locus of control'—the place from which power comes (Rotter, 1966). If children see control of their learning as outside themselves, resting with the teacher or some other authority figure, then they will tend to be less involved and motivated to work. The urge to learn may also be improved when poorly motivated youngsters are empowered to help others, as when unsuccessful adolescents take on the role of tutors to younger children.

Improving motivation through feedback

Knowing how well one is doing allows aims to be set at an appropriate level, avoiding both certain failure and too-easy success; both success and failure tend to perpetuate themselves. A parent or teacher can modify feedback to give a child the feeling of success by raising the standard of the task so that when the child succeeds, her outlook on learning is encouraged to be one of success and optimism. Motivational factors are as important to high-level human accomplishment as intellectual ones. The existing body of research on intrinsic (deep and meaningful) motivation, as distinct from superficially trying to please, is particularly relevant for high levels of performance. Deci & Ryan (1985) analyzed over 200 studies on motivation, from which they formulated a theory of human motivation, which included personality factors. They found that when children feel competent, it motivates them to exercise and elaborate their abilities.

Yet the situation is not entirely controllable by parents or other adults; children can interpret feedback in different ways, depending both on the psychological context and on the child's personality. Telling one child he is doing badly may be interpreted as an excuse to stop work because it does not seem worth the effort, while for another, the response may be an increase in motivation to prove 'them' wrong. Paradoxically, too much praise, particularly in a system of close super-vision, may tell a child that he is doing the bidding of the teacher, rather than developing his own compe-tence. It then becomes psychologically impossible for the child to feel in control of his own progress in learning.

All children, whatever their ability, want to feel effective and engaged by challenge, which must include a risk of failure; the gifted need challenge at least as much as any others. If children are given a superficial reward, such as money or sweets, they are far more likely to choose the easiest ways of succeed-ing, whereas if they are enjoying the activity for itself, they choose harder tasks, usually just above the level of previous success. When children are interested in what they are doing, they seem to have a natural tendency to take on challenges that exercise and expand their limits of competence.

Positive feedback, particularly a positive attitude on the part of adults, can be very effective; there is always something specific to praise, some form of recognis-able success, and the possibility of offering a reward. Sloboda, (1993) found that the best music students had received more praise than the others, and their parents had made them feel 'special'. Negative feedback, such as sarcasm, punishment, or detention, are much less effective: for emotional reasons the child may have been seeking extra attention, and such punishment may simply fulfil what was wanted.

Social cognition

Social cognition is the way an individual perceives other people and comes to understand their thoughts, emotions, intentions, and viewpoints, first described by Flavell (1977); parents are cognitive mediators with a special relationship. Children's experiences in the family are used to develop a system of inferences which they use to make predictions about others, especially in relation to themselves, and consequently how they think and behave. Although social cognition is related to intelligence, actual social behaviour comes from children's involvement in a variety of social situations, and benefits from adult guidance. Socially positive attitudes, such as being sensitive to the feelings of other people, are more often shown by confident young children, especially if they are highly intelligent. They are also better at making use of adults as resources and tend to play more imaginatively.

To explore their awareness of other people's feelings, 3–6 year-old children were asked to predict what someone else would like as a birthday present, rather than what they themselves would like to receive (Flavell, Botkin, Fry, Wright & Jarvis, 1968). Each child was presented with an array of objects, and asked to select a birthday present for each of his or her parents, siblings, and teachers. Choices were judged as role-appropriate on the basis of age and gender. The 3 year-olds disregarded both the age and gender of the intended recipient, while 4 and 5 year-olds' choices represented a type of transitional level, and all the 6 year-olds made appropriate role responses. Age seemed to improve social cognition, which was more advanced for the highest IQ children in each age-group. However, the available research does not reveal a recognisable relationship between social cognition and actual behaviour towards others, whether intellectual or emotional; nor does this seem to be the case for moral reasoning.

It is strange that highly intelligent children are often thought of as having poor social cognition and therefore few friends. In fact, as research has shown (Freeman, 1997), they tend to have sympathy, adaptability and compassion in abundance, and do not usually choose to be without friends. Using one-to-one interviews in Germany, Rost and Czeschlik (1994), compared the responses of 50 high-IQ with 50 average-IQ primary school children, and concluded that the former were the better adjusted. Later, working with mixed-ability primary school children, they found that those with high-IQs were the most popular (Czeschlik & Rost, 1995).

Follow-ups

Detailed studies of gifted children as they grow up at home are rare. In America, Feldman (with Goldsmith 1986) spent ten years following-up just six young boys, described as prodigies; he used a term from biology, 'trace elements', to describe unrecognised events which are vital for gifted development. In a historical case-study of outstanding individuals such as Darwin and Piaget, Howard Gruber (1981) saw a similar combination, and referred to such creative achievers as people in "networks of enterprise," i.e. they have many things going on at the same time. In a four-year research project, Benjamin Bloom and his team (1985) looked back at the lives of 120 young men and women who had reached world-class levels of accomplishment. The subjects told them that no matter what their initial gifts, those high levels of achievement were due to a long and intensive process of encouragement and teaching, usually combined with long hours of practice under parents who drove them hard. Although several crucial factors which appeared to help the potentially gifted to achieve highly have emerged from such studies, we do not know what the effect of similar parenting behaviour would have been on other children, as there were neither comparison groups of families, nor any more intimate view of their lives—in fact, most of the Bloom interviews seem to have been done by telephone.

In a review of 14 American and German follow-up studies of varying design and loss of subjects over time, Arnold & Subotnik (1994) suggested an "inextricable link" between the identification of potential and timing due to age-related stages of development: accuracy in predicting achievement increases with the age of the sample studied. Accordingly, for the greatest reliability, information should be collected at different points in an individual's life, most reliably within specific subject areas in which the child shows promise and interest.

Reports from a 15-year Chinese study of 115 extremely high-IQ children (Zha, 1995), showed the strong influence of family provision, both in achievement and emotional development. The children were first identified by parents (two boys to every girl) and then validated as gifted by a psychologist; every year parents were given a questionnaire and interviewed several times. The parents-to-be had taken their future responsibilities very seriously by studying parenthood. As the toddlers were learning to speak, the parents often taught them to read, and some children even mastered writing at the same time. By the age of three many children could recognise 2000 Chinese characters, and at four many could not only read well, but also wrote compositions and poems. However, these 'hot-housed' children were found to be lacking in easy social relationships, and the parents had to be given some more lessons in how to help their children to some social life.

Measurements of certain aspects of learning in the first three years of life provide reliable indicators of life-long attributes, such as advanced physical control, which can predict gymnastic talent (Lewis & Louis, 1991). The strongest early indicator, which can be traced from the age of three months, is verbal ability, but spatial and non-verbal signs are also valuable indications for future talents. These researchers found that the greatest overall intellectual stability was at the extremes of the IQ range—both gifted and low—and suggest that this intellectual development is qualitatively different from that of individuals with more average scores. Indeed, the parents of the exceptionally high IQ children in the follow-up study by Freeman (1991), compared with those of more average IQ children, reported very early signs of exceptional concentration, memory, and talking. Clearly, early infancy is the time when family sensitivities and influences are the most vital means of developing potential giftedness.

A unique study in California began with 130 one-year-olds of unknown potential, the only criterion being that they were healthy (Gottfried, Gottfried, Bathurst & Guerin, 1994). Various measures of intellectual, physical and social development were made regularly until they were 9 years old. Those with an IQ of 130 or more on the Wechsler Intelligence test were designated gifted and compared with the others. The researchers concluded that giftedness is a developmental phenomenon, which can rise—and fall—over time: late bloomers' do exist and can be missed in a single testing. In a detailed examination of the family environments, they found a rich continuous educational environment to be essential in developing intrinsic motivation for curiosity and love of learning; children from higher SES families tended to have higher IQs. According to the researchers, this was neither due to the parents' occupations or intelligence, nor to the amount of parent-child contact, but rather to the parents' educational accomplishments. "The families of gifted children provided more stimulating activities than did the families of non-gifted children. Moreover, the parents were more involved and apparently more invested in providing their children with a cognitively advantageous home environment" (p. 156). These differences, which were clear at three years-old and remained throughout the early elementary years, were notably of an academic and cultural nature, such as use of library or musical instruments. The gifted IQ children also influenced their environments, demanding more learning activities compared with the non-gifted children.

Individual Differences Within Families

Most studies of the effects of the social environment on children's development examine factors that are supposedly similar for all the siblings in the family, such as social class, marital conflict, or pressure to perform. But a child is neither a passive nor an unbiased recipient; there are indications that the most influential environmental factors may be those which are different for siblings in the same family (Dunn, 1984). Thus, there may be social and biological mechanisms which increase the differences between experiences which siblings have in the same family. These are termed non-shared environmental effects, and might, for example, include variations in how each child is treated by the same parent, peer relationships, school interactions, and when they are older, differences in their marital and occupational experiences. Discovering exactly how different kinds of influences are received by different kinds of children is extremely difficult; parental divorce, for example, might either cause a temporary halt to a child's development or have life-long effects.

In order to study family interaction effects on different siblings in a family, it would be necessary to define the individual difference between the siblings (in families of at least two siblings) and the relationship of these differences to simple family structural variables. Only then would it be possible to distinguish the environmental variables which are likely to be important developmental differences. These could be relationships with the parents, as in the study which showed considerable consistency in parent's differential treatment of their children (Abramovitch, Pepler & Corter, 1982). There are also the differences in the way siblings see themselves as being treated by the family, and peer group relationships can also be different for children in the same family.

To some extent, these differences are attributable to recognised variables such as birth order, age spacing, and gender. Gottfried, Gottfried, Bathurst & Guerin (1994) found, as have many others, that birth order was important; firstborns and only children do better. They strive harder to please their parents because they identify more strongly with them, and in addition to having higher IQ scores, they usually achieve more than their siblings throughout life. Even their leisure-time pursuits often have an educational aspect. First-born and only children are more likely to be more concerned with the effect they have on adults, and to be more responsible; the second-born is more easy-going and has more friends; the third-born is often more difficult to live with; while the fourth is often babied and so learns to be more dependent.

Speed of reaction may also be an innate ability which shows itself in many facets of behaviour that can affect relationships, etc., and which are regarded as important if not vital aspects of intelligence (Eysenck, 1998). There has also been considerable evidence of even young children's ability to shape interactions with their families; indeed Scarr & McCartney (1983) have suggested that to some extent, children make their own environments. Long-term research (eg. Reiss, Plomin & Hetherington, 1991)) has shown that children may identify with one parent and strive to follow the path of that example, differentiating themselves from the other siblings, and so accentuating different parent-child relationships.

Studies in various parts of the world have concluded that better nutrition leads to an improvement in children's IQ scores, correlated with increases in their head size and height (Lynn, 1989). Clearly, the better-nourished child will function more effectively at a biological level, and this can be expected to support a higher level of mental functioning; it could make the difference as to whether or not giftedness will develop in bad circumstances. This effect is recognised for instance in Brazil and some areas of the USA, where feeding very poor children is an important part of school life; indeed, it is some children's reason for coming to school.

Gifted Girls and Boys

Many studies have shown that in most cultures, families encourage boys more than girls to be independent, self-reliant, and able to assume responsibility, and that this alters their approach to both school and work. In Germany, Rost & Hanses (1994) found "dramatic gender effects" in the toys gifted children were given. There is a strangely stable ratio of two boys to every girl when parents identify their children as gifted; this was the proportion in an American study by Johnson & Lewman (1990) of parent's selection of four to six year-olds as gifted. In China, in a 15 year follow up study, in which parents made the first judgement of giftedness, which was then confirmed by the teachers, 69.5% were boys and 30.5% were girls (Zha, 1995). Given the supposed differences in the Chinese attitudes, in which girls are seen as inferior, remarkably similar proportions appeared in Freeman's U.K. study (1991) where parents made the first recommendation—64.3% boys and 35.7% girls. The reason appeared to be that the boys had more behaviour problems as well as being more demanding in general; this also fitted better with the stereotyped image parents often had of the gifted child.

The effects of being a boy or girl are different for the gifted than for those of more average ability (Freeman, 1996); many studies have shown gender to be the strongest single influence on high level achievement. Intellectually gifted girls appear to be cognitively more like gifted boys than girls of average ability (Stapf, 1990). Emotionally, though, in America they have been found to be more depressed than equally able boys, often underestimating their abilities because of conflicts between of success and 'femininity' (Luthar, Zigler & Goldstein, 1992). Golombok & Fivush (1994) wrote that: "Careful statistical analyses across hundreds of studies have demonstrated that gender differences in ability in maths and language are so small as to be virtually non-existent for all practical purposes" (p. 177). They concluded that the measurable sex differences in aptitude are due to "a complex interaction between small biological differences and larger gender differences in socialisation experiences" (p. 176).

However, schoolgirls in Britain are currently achieving higher national examination grades than boys in all subjects at 16 and in everything except physics at 18 (Arnot, Gray, James, Rudduck with Duveen, 1998). Several other countries are moving in this direction, notably Australia. Investigating mathematically precocious American youth, Benbow & Lubinski (1993) although recognising the effects of cultural influences, concluded that there is a genetic mathematical bias in favour of boys. The British results, though, refute this. Taking a long-term look at giftedness in mathematics in the USA, Jacobs & Weisz (1994) found that parents held somewhat fixed and conventional gender expectations; this influenced the girls' self-esteem more than their actual performances, and inhibited their ambitions. Power et al. (1998) in Britain, investigated young men who had been identified at school as 'academically able', and found that their perceptions of a masculine identity could either foster or jeopardise their academic achievement.

An international review of research on gender differences in the highly able in mathematics and natural sciences, failed to find any reliable evidence that girls are inherently less able than boys in these subjects (Heller & Zeigler, 1996/7). So, because they have similar abilities, girls and boys can act as experimental controls for each other to gauge the power of social effects, probably best seen in career outcomes. Heller pointed out that, for example, even on present tests of spatial abilities at which boys do better, we could expect only twice as many male engineering graduates as females, whereas there are 30 times as many. This effect was found to be more pronounced among the gifted. Clearly, girls are being more influenced by social pressures than boys, e.g. by the 'unfemininity' of subjects such as physics, as well as much less practice and fewer role-models. Most importantly, the often-noted 'learned helplessness' of girls (a feeling that events and outcomes are beyond their control) was considered to be the result of 'wrong' attributions, so that girls often think their success is due to luck rather than their own ability. Thus, Heller states, believing that they are not good at maths, simply lucky to have done well that time, girls adjust their behaviour to fit their belief (attribution), and 'confirm' it by doing less well as time goes by.

Biological Differences

There is a limit to the extent that family influences can affect children's achievements because of biological differences. The IQ scores from studies of more than 400 sets of identical and non-identical twins separated at birth were investigated in later life (Plomin, 1998). This work discovered about 70% genetic influence on IQ, the strongest correlation found for any psychological characteristic; in isolating the genetic input, such studies have highlighted environmental influences, notably that the younger the child, the more potent the environment. However, no specific gene for giftedness has yet been discovered.

Lykken (1998) points out that identical twins are affected by uterine environmental influences, causing differences, e.g. in size and handedness, in quite enough ways for parents to tell them apart. It is the configural or 'emergenic' aspects of inheritance, he writes, which mark the truly gifted from the merely assiduous. He demolishes the idea that it is only practice which makes perfect, pointing out that perfect pitch or the aptitude to become a Olympic gold medallist are not the birthright of every child.

The perceptual responses of even tiny babies to shapes and noises can be related to the type of care they receive, which in turn reflects the care which their parents themselves experienced. Harlow's (1958) observations of monkeys were the basis for work which showed how both animal and human behaviour patterns are learned and transmitted over generations; but of course, the baby's individual responses are important. For example, girl babies seem to have more sensitive skins than boy babies, responding more positively to stroking, which reinforces the parent's pleasure in doing this, so that baby girls may receive more soothing attention of this kind; similarly, heavy babies often respond less quickly than thin ones, which must affect parental responses to them, and they seem to continue in this way as children.

Freeman (1983) concluded that genetic and environmental influences on IQ are unlikely to be in the same proportion for all children. She found that when their environmental support was poor, children, who scored in the top 1% on the (relatively culture-free) Raven's Matrices test of intelligence, sometimes scored at a much lower level on the Stanford-Binet test (contaminated by learning). However, the brightest appear to be relatively more able to extract benefit from whatever environment they are in.

Emotional Influences

Although gifted children are possibly more sensitive than others to emotional nuances in the family, there is no evidence that they are emotionally less stable than other children—even though it is sometimes argued that they are. On the contrary, an American meta-analysis pointed to low intelligence and attention problems as being associated with delinquency (Maguin & Loeber, 1996). Investigators who describe the gifted as having emotional problems have usually taken their data from clinical settings and case-studies, where the population is self-selecting and no comparisons are made with other equally able children (e.g. Silverman, 1993; Gross, 1993). In fact, the gifted appear to be emotionally stronger than other children, with lower levels of anxiety, higher productivity, and higher motivation. Perhaps those who are to be high

achievers need to be stronger than most because their exceptionality makes them more likely to come up against some special problems.

Research, unique in its in-depth approach, was carried out in Britain over 14 years (Freeman, 1991). A target group of 70 children, identified (but untested) by their parents as gifted, were compared with a second group of 70 who were unlabelled—but of equal measured ability—and a third group of 70 randomly selected children. In the target group 82% of parents either reported emotional problems or were expecting them. Typically, the child showed over-activity, clumsiness, tantrums, excessive demands, poor sleep and had few friends of any age. However, the comparison children in the study—of identical high ability—who did not exhibit problem behaviour, were much less likely to be seen as stereotypically gifted, simply outstanding at what they did. Freeman also found that about 10% of the children presented by parents as gifted were only of average ability on IQ tests, and had achieved accordingly at school; this perceived 'failure' was then sometimes blamed by parents on the school, or as teacher discrimination against the child. Ten years later, the parent identified youngsters had often remained the least happy (as measured by rating scales), for which their gifts were sometimes blamed. Labelling appeared to have the effect of putting pressure on children to live up to it in high achievements, notably those who had been wrongly labelled and could not fulfil their parents' ambitions. Whatever problems already exist in the family, these can be intensified when there is an unusual child present.

Emotions help or hamper learning at all levels. German research on gifted young children has found that fear can inhibit the development of curiosity, an important motivator in learning, thinking and creative endeavour (Lehwald, 1990). Boekaerts' (1991) overview of international research on the learning of gifted young children found that those who achieve most highly are not only very curious but have a hunger to learn, often along with a strong urge to control. Canadian research with young children has also found an extra quality of playfulness in the learning of highly able little children (Kanevsky, 1994). Investigating the current work of creative scientists in California and later that of living 'classical' composers, although some of this work was retrospective, Simonton (1994) could demonstrate that above a certain high level, personal characteristics such as independence contributed more than intellect to reaching the highest levels because of the great demands of effort and time needed. Perhaps for that reason, a four-year follow-up investigation of talented American teenagers, Csikszentmihalyi et al. (1993) found that in learning to tackle difficult tasks, the stronger the social support the more developed the youngster's skills, though schools were found to be much less effective in this than parents.

Vygotsky's (in Wertsch, 1990) Dynamic Theory of Giftedness suggests that either giftedness or defectiveness are possible outcomes when a child is faced with emotional barriers to development. Failure to overcome such barriers can lead to a child hiding behind the weakness, which then becomes reinforced. In a six-year experimental study in Moscow (Babaeva, 1999) investigated how to overcome such barriers in 31 children aged 6–7, identified as non-gifted by teachers and conventional tests. Following a specially devised therapeutic educational programme of 6 years, measures of the experimental group's abilities were equal to those of the identified gifted children, and considerably surpassed those of the non-gifted control children.

Even often-referenced studies may have tiny samples which are possibly unrepresentative. In Australia, Gross (1993) used the contentious IQ of 200 to select just three 'profoundly gifted' young children. They were described as exhibiting the 'typical' gifted symptoms of emotional disturbance, such as school-refusal and friendlessness, because for them, Gross wrote, being with normal children was the same as interacting "solely with children who are profoundly intellectually handicapped" (p. 475). But are the described heavy emotional problems a result of subtle messages from home that the child is 'too clever' and thus too sensitive to fit in socially? No comparisons with other children were made.

In fact, some studies of the gifted have found them to be emotionally stronger than others, with higher productivity, higher motivation and drive, and lower levels of anxiety. An Israeli study (Kener, 1993), found that gifted junior-school boys and girls showed significantly higher self-esteem when compared with those of average ability from similar backgrounds. In Italy, a sample of 300 high school pupils were given tests and open-ended questionnaires, although the follow-up only managed to trace 63 of them eight years later (Boncori, 1996). There were three sub-samples, 'highly gifted' (the top 10% of the general population), 'less gifted' and 'average'. The 'highly gifted' not only had far greater academic success than the other two groups, but also right through university enjoyed better social integration, wider interests, less materialism—and more satisfaction.

High achieving learners and labelled 'gifted' children are sometimes susceptible to extra pressure from parents to be continually successful, possibly at the expense of more challenging intellectual, artistic and emotionally satisfying activities (Freeman, 1997). What is more, no individual can perform at a high level all the time, not least because these children's abilities may develop at different and extreme rates, which can bring difficulties of coordination (Terassier, 1985; Silverman, 1993). Additionally, the highly able may suffer from false stereotyping and its expectations—along a spectrum which varies from expecting them to be emotionally handicapped to perfect in every respect.

Fear of failure and feelings of failure and of disappointing others' expectations are likely to develop, with possibly negative emotional consequences for life.

The particular pressures which the very able may experience, usually stem from others' reactions and expectations of them. For example, although the gifted may be expected to be too clever to enjoy normal relationships with ordinary people, in most findings, higher IQ youngsters have better all-round social relationships (e.g. van Leishout, 1995; Boncori, 1996). Other researchers have pointed to the tendency to perfectionism in the gifted (Stedtnitz, 1995; Robinson, 1996). Nevertheless, we cannot be sure about the causes, or whether this kind of obsessionality is found more among the gifted than other children; certainly the gifted can suffer from adults who mistake the abilities for the child.

Conclusions

All babies are born with potential, but it is clear that only some develop this to its full, and fewer still to a recognisable level of excellence. What is it that makes the crucial difference in later behaviour between people who start out in life with much the same potential ability? That vital provision starts in the family; parents have to be both willing and able to make the effort if their children are to take advantage of the opportunities that exist around them. However, there is no single type of parent-child interaction which is critical to the development of high level abilities in children; the process is complex because parents and children each have their respective intellectual capacities as well as their own personalities, but genuine and regular interaction between parents and children is decidedly effective.

Good parenting for nurturing and enhancing children's gifts involves the following:

- Interaction between parent and children from birth, which is positive and supportive, providing a structure in which a child can grow with security.
- Meaningful stimulation, which provides opportunities for children's learning, including other people outside the family, especially as the child develops interests which may need specialist help.
- A variety of experiences, which can be followed up by the child if wished.
- Provision of both materials and tuition with which to reach advanced heights of learning and creative production; this includes good relations with the child's school.
- Gifted children need the emotional freedom and materials to play and experiment, both for their mental health and for creative thinking. Would-be artists need far more than a few scraps of paper and a pencil stub, a mathematician needs a teacher, a linguist has to hear the language, and a budding violinist needs the instrument.

- Teaching skills are needed by parents to develop general and specific areas of their children's potentials. This starts with the basic teaching of language, and through it the family culture.
- Sensitivity of parents to their children's potential talents from a very early age is different from attempting to mould them into the image that the adults may prefer. Knowing when to take action and when not to is a matter of sensitivity. Parents also have to be aware of their own feelings, notably to avoid labels and categories such as gender, in bringing up children who can demonstrate their gifts.
- Children need to be taught specific skills and be given the opportunities to practise them.
- Real emotional support is not quite the same as love: parenting in the name of love can be directive and so inhibit the growth of children's gifts where they are not acceptable. Pride and pleasure in children's accomplishments (or efforts), along with suggestions and encouragement to practice, provide excellent feedback for improving performance.

Like other children, the potentially gifted with emotional problems generally achieve less well than those of the same ability who enjoy peace of mind. The best results in human terms are found when children are treated with respect, allowing them enough responsibility to make many of their own discoveries and decisions. There are some, though, especially in the arts, who seem to have an inbuilt impetus—a spark which can light up the world, bringing them great inspiration and success.

References

Abranovitch, R., Pepler, D. & Corter, C. (1982). Patterns of sibling interaction among pre-school children. In: M. E. Lamb & B. Sutton-Smith (Eds). *Sibling Relationships: Their Nature and Significance Across the Life Span*. Hillsdale, NJ: Lawrence Erlbaum Associates.

Arnold, K. D. & Subotnik, R. F. (1994). Lessons from contemporary longitudinal studies. In: R. F. Subotnik & K. D. Arnold, (Eds.) *Beyond Terman: Contemporary Longitudinal Studies of Giftedness and Talent* (pp. 437–451). Norwood, NJ: Ablex.

Arnot, M., Gray, J., Rudduck, J. with Duveen, G. (1998). *Recent research on gender and educational performance*. London: The Stationery Office.

Babaeva, J. D.(1999). The dynamic theory of giftedness: conception and practice, *High Ability Studies*, **10**, 51–68.

Benbow, C. P. & Lubinski, D. (1993). Psychological profiles of the mathematically talented: some sex differences and evidence supporting their biological basis. In: Bock, G. R. & Ackrill, K. A. (Eds), *The Origins and Development of High Ability* (Ciba Foundation Symposium). (pp. 44–59). Chichester; Wiley.

Berry, C. (1990). On the origins of exceptional intellectual and cultural achievement. In: Michael J. A. Howe (Ed.), *Encouraging the Development of Exceptional Skills and Talents*. (pp. 49–70). Leicester: British Psychological Society.

Bloom, B. S. (1985). *Developing talent in young people*. New York: Ballantine.

Boekaerts, M. (1991). The affective learning process and giftedness. *European Journal for High Ability*, **2**, 146–160.

Boncori, L. (1996), *A longitudinal study on academic success and satisfaction*. Paper given at the 5th conference of the European Council for High Ability, Vienna.

Csikszentmihalyi, M., (1998). Creativity and genius. In: A. Steptoe, (Ed.), *Genius and the Mind: Studies of Creativity and Temperament*. pp. 39–64, OUP: Oxford.

Csikszentmihalyi, M., Rathunde, K. & Whalen, S. (1993). *Talented teenagers. the roots of success and failure*. Cambridge: Cambridge University Press.

Czeschlik, T. & Rost, D. H. (1985). Sociometic types and children's intelligence. *British Journal of Development Psychology*, **13**, 177–189.

Deci, E. L & Ryan, R. M. (1985). *Intrinsic motivation and self determination in human behaviour*. New York: Plenum.

Dunn, J. (1984). *Sisters and brothers*. London: Fontana.

Ericsson, K. A. & Lehman, A. C. (1996). Expert and exceptional performance: evidence of maximal adaptation to task constraints. *Annual Review of Psychology*, **47**, 273–305.

Ericsson, K. A. (1998), The scientific study of expert levels of performance: general implications for optimal learning and creativity [1]. *High Ability Studies*, **9**, 75–100.

Eysenck, H. J. (1998). *A new look at intelligence*. London: Transaction Publishers.

Feldman, D. H. with Goldsmith L. T. (1986) *Nature's gambit: child prodigies and the development of human potential*. New York: Basic Books.

Flavell, J. (1977). *Cognitive development*. Prentice-Hall, Englewood Cliffs, N.J.

Flavell, J., Botkin, P., Fry, C., Wright, J. & Jarvis, P. (1968). *The development of role-taking and communication skills in young children*. New York: John Wiley.

Flynn, J. R. (1991). *Asian Americans: Achievement beyond IQ*. London: Erlbaum.

Fowler, W. (1990). *Talking from Infancy: How to Nurture and Cultivate Early Language Development*. Cambridge, MA: Brookline Books.

Freeman, J. (1983). Environment and high IQ: a consideration of fluid and crystallised intelligence. *Personality and Individual Differences*, **4**, 307–313.

Freeman, J. (1991). *Gifted children growing up*. London: Cassell.

Freeman, J. (1992). *Quality education: the development of competence*. Geneva: UNESCO.

Freeman, J. (1996). *Highly able girls and boys*. London: Department of Education and Employment.

Freeman, J. (1997). The emotional development of the highly able. *European Journal of Psychology in Education*. **12**, 479–493.

Freeman, J. (1998a). *Educating the very able: Current international research*. London: The Stationery Office.

Freeman, J. (1998b). Inborn talent exists. *Behavioral and Brain Sciences*, **21** (3), 415.

Golombok, S. & Fivush, R. (1994). *Gender development*. Cambridge: Cambridge University Press.

Gombert, J. E. (1992). *Metalinguistic development*. Hemel Hempstead: Harvester Wheatsheaf.

Gottfried, A. W., Gottfried, A. E., Bathurst, K. & Guerin, D. W. (1994). *Gifted IQ: early developmental aspects*. New York: Plenum.

Gross, M. U. M. (1993). Nurturing the talents of exceptionally gifted individuals. In: K. A. Heller, F. J. Monks & A. H. Passow, (Eds.), *International Handbook of Research and Development of Giftedness and Talent.* (pp. 473–490). Oxford: Pergamon Press.

Gruber, H. E. (1981). *Darwin on Man: a Psychological Study of Scientific Creativity.* Chicago: University of Chicago Press.

Hallam, S. & Cowan, R. (1997). *What do we know about homework: a literature review.* Occasional Paper, London: Institute of Education.

Hany, E. A. (1996). How leisure activities correspond to the development of creative achievement: insights from a study of highly intelligent individuals, *High Ability Studies, 7,* 65–82.

Harlow, H. F. (1958). The nature of love, *American Psychologist, 13,* 673–685.

Heller, K. A. & Ziegler, A. (1996/7). Gender differences in mathematics and natural sciences; can attributional retraining improve the low performance of gifted females? *Gifted Child Quarterly, 41,* 200–210.

Hess, R. D. & Azuma, H. (1991). Cultural support for schooling: Contrasts between Japan and the United States. *Educational Researcher, 20,* 2–9.

Heyman, G. D. & Dweck, C. S. (1996). Development of Motivation. In: E. de Corte & F. E. Weinert (Eds.), *International Encyclopedia of Developmental and Instructional Psychology.* (pp. 209–213), Oxford: Pergamon.

Holahan, C. K. & Sears, R. R. (1995). *The Gifted Group in Later Maturity.* Stanford, CA: Stanford University Press.

Howe, M. J. A. (1990). *The Origins of Exceptional Abilities.* Oxford: Blackwell.

Hundeide, K. (1991). Helping *Disadvantaged Children.* London: Jessica Kingsley; Norway: Sigma Forlag.

Jacobs, J. E. & Weisz, V. (1994). Gender stereotypes: implications for gifted education. *Roeper Review, 16,* 152–155.

Johnson, L. J. & Lewman, B. S. (1990). Parents perceptions of the talents of young gifted boys and girls. *Journal for the Education of the Gifted, 13,* 176–188.

Kanevsky, L. S. (1994). A comparative study of children's learning in the zone of proximal development. *European Journal for High Ability, 5,* 163–175.

Kener, Y. (1993). *Realistic and ideal self-concept of gifted children.* Unpublished MA thesis, Tel Aviv University (in Hebrew).

Lehwald, G. (1990). Curiosity and exploratory behaviour in ability development. *European Journal for High Ability, 1,* 204–210.

Lewis, M. & Louis, B. (1991). Young gifted children. In: N. Colangelo & G. A. Davis (Eds.), *Handbook of Gifted Education.* (pp. 365–381), Boston: Allyn and Bacon.

Lorenz, K. Z. (1965). *Evolution and the modification of behaviour.* Chicago: University of Chicago Press.

Lubart, T., & Sternberg, R. J. (1998), Creativity across time and place: life-span and cross-cultural perspectives, *High Ability Studies, 9,* 59–74.

Luthar, S. S., Zigler, E. & Goldstein, D. (1992), Psychosocial adjustment among intellectually gifted adolescents: the role of cognitive-developmental and experiential factors. *Journal of Child Psychology and Psychiatry, 33,* 361–373.

Lykken, D. T. (1998). The genetics of genius. In: A. Steptoe. (Ed.) *Genius and the Mind: Studies of Creativity and Temperament.* (pp. 15–37). OUP: Oxford.

Lynn, R. (1989). A nutrition theory of the secular increases in intelligence: positive correlations between height, head size and IQ. *British Journal of Educational Psychology, 59,* 372–377.

Maguin, E. & Loeber, R. (1996). Academic performance and delinquency. In: M. Tonry & N. Morris (Eds.), *Crime and Justice,* Vol 20 (pp. 145–264) Chicago: Chicago University Press.

Marsh, H. W., Chessor, D., Craven, R. & Roche, L. (1995). The effect of gifted and talented programs on academic self-concept: the big fish strikes again. *American Educational Research Journal, 32,* 285–319.

Mascie-Taylor, C. G. N. (1989). Biological and social aspects of development. In: N. Entwistle (Ed.), *Handbook of Educational Ideas and Practices.* (pp. 992–997). London: Routledge.

Messer, D. J. (1994). *The development of communication: from social interaction to language.* Chichester: Wiley.

Milgram, R. M. & Hong, E. (1997). Leisure activities and career development in intellectually gifted Israeli adolescents. In: B. Bain, H. Janzen, J. Paterson, L. Stewin & A. Yu (Eds.), *Psychology and Education in the 21st Century.* (pp. 223–227). Edmonton: ICP Press.

Mischel, W., Shoda, Y. & Rodriquez, M. (1989). Delay of gratification in children. *Science, 244,* 933–938.

Montessori, M. (1964). *The Montessori method.* New York: Schocken.

Niebrzydowski, L. (1997) Influences which promote high-level attainment in children of pre-school age. *High Ability Studies, 8,* 179–188.

Perkins, D. N. (1981). *The mind's best work: a new psychology of creative thinking.* Harvard: Harvard University Press.

Perleth, C. & Heller, K. A. (1994). The Munich longitudinal study of giftedness. In: R. F. Subotnik & K. D. Arnold (Eds.) *Beyond Terman: Contemporary Longitudinal Studies of Giftedness and Talent* (pp. 77–114). Norwood, NJ: Ablex Publishing.

Plomin, R., (1998). *The genetic inheritance debate today.* Address at ECHA/NACE conference, Oxford.

Power, S., Whitty, G., Edwards, T. & Wigfall, V. (1998). Schoolboys and schoolwork: gender identification and academic achievement. *International Journal of Inclusive Education, 2,* 135–153.

Radford, J. (1990). *Child prodigies and exceptional early achievers.* London: Harvester Wheatsheaf.

Reiss, D., Plomin, R. & Hetherington, E. M. (1991). Genetics and psychiatry: an unheralded window on the environment. *American Journal of Psychiatry, 143,* 283–291.

Renzulli, J. S. (1995). New directions for the schoolwide enrichment model. In: M. W. Katzko & F. J. Monks (Eds.), *Nurturing Talent: Individual Needs and Social Ability.* (pp. 162–167). Assen, NL: Van Gorcum.

Robinson, N. (1996). Counselling agendas for gifted young people: a commentary. *Journal for the Education of the Gifted, 20,* 128–137.

Rost, D. H. & Czeschlik, T. (1994). The psycho-social adjustment of gifted children in middle-childhood. *European Journal of Psychology of Education, 9,* 15–25.

Rost, D. H. & Hanses, P. (1994). The possession and use of toys in elementary school boys and girls: does giftedness make a difference? *Educational Psychology, 14,* 181–194.

Rotter, J. B. (1966). Generalised expectancies for internal vs. external control of reinforcement. *Psychological Monographs* (whole no. 609).

Scarr, S. & McCartney, K. (1983). How people make their own environments: a theory of genotype → environment effects. *Child Development*, **54**, 424–435.

Shavinina, L. (1997), Extremely early high abilities, sensitive periods, and the development of giftedness: a conceptual proposition. *High Ability Studies*, 8, 247–258.

Silverman, L. K. (1993). The gifted individual. In: L. K. Silverman (Ed.), *Counselling the Gifted and Talented*. (pp. 3–23), Denver: Love.

Simonton, D. K. (1994). *Greatness: who makes history and why*. New York: The Guildford Press.

Simonton, D. K. (1998). Gifted child, genius adult: three life-span developmental perspectives. In: R. Freidman & K. B. Rogers (Eds.) (1998). *Talent in Context: Historical and Social Perspectives on Giftedness*. (pp. 151–175). Washington: American Psychological Association.

Slater, A. (1995). Individual differences in infancy and later IQ. *Journal of Child Psychology and Psychiatry*, 36, 69–112.

Sloboda, J. (1993), Musical ability. In: G. R. Bock. & K. A. Ackrill (Eds.), *The Origins and Development of High Ability* (Ciba Foundation Symposium) Chichester: Wiley.

Stapf, A. (1990). Hochbegabte Madchen: Entwicklung, Identifikation und Beratung, insbesondere im Vorschualter (Highly able girls: development, identification and counselling, especially at pre-school age). In: Hochbegabte Madchen, W. Wieczerkowski & T. M. Prado (Eds.). (pp. 45–58). Bad Honnef: K. H. Bock.

Stedtnitz, U. (1995). Psychosocial dimensions of high ability: a review of major issues and neglected topics. In: J. Freeman, P. Span & H. Wagner (Eds.), *Actualizing Talent: A Lifelong Challenge*. (pp. 42–55). London: Cassell.

Sternberg, R. J. & Lubart, T. I. (1998). Creativity across time and space: life span and cross-cultural perspectives. *High Ability Studies*, **9**, 59–74.

Stevenson, H.W. (1998). Cultural interpretations of giftedness: the case of East Asia. In: R. Friedman & K. B. Rogers (Eds). *Talent in Context: Historical and Social Perspectives on Giftedness*. (pp. 61–77). Washington: American Psychological Association.

Subotnik, R., Kassan, L., Summers, E. & Wasser, A. (1993). *Genius revisited: high IQ children grown up*. Norwood, NJ: Ablex.

Terassier, J. C. (1985). Dysynchrony: uneven development. In: J. Freeman (Ed.), *The Psychology of Gifted Children*. (pp. 265–274). Chichester: John Wiley.

Tizard, B. (1985). Social relationships between adults and young children, and their impact on intellectual functioning. In: R. A. Hinde, A-H. Perret-Clermont and J. Stevenson-Hinde (Eds) *Social Relationship and Cognitive Development*. Oxford, Clarendon.

Tizard, B. & Hughes, M. (1984). *Young Children Learning: Talking and Thinking at Home and School*. London: Fontana.

Trost, G. (1993). Prediction of excellence in school, university and work. In: K. A. Heller, F. J. Monks & A. H. Passow, *International Handbook of Research and Development of Giftedness and Talent*. (pp. 325–336). Oxford: Pergamon Press.

van Leishout, C. F. M. (1995). Development of social giftedness and gifted personality in context. In: M. W. Katzko & F. J. Monks (Eds.), *Nurturing Talent: Individual Needs and Social Ability*. (pp. 31–42). Assen, NL: Van Gorcum.

Wallace, B. & Adams, H. B. (Eds.), (1993). *Worldwide Perspectives on the Gifted Disadvantaged*. Bicester: AB Academic Publishers.

Wertsch, J. D. (1990). *Voices of the mind: a sociocultural approach to mediated action*. London: Harvester Wheatsheaf.

White, B. (1985). Competence and giftedness. In: J. Freeman (Ed.), *The Psychology of Gifted Children*. (pp. 59–73). New York: John Wiley.

Zeigler, S., Hardwick, N. & McCreath, G. (1989). *Academically successful inner city children: What can they tell us about effective education?*. Toronto: Toronto Board of Education.

Zha, Z. (1995), *The influence of family education on gifted children*. Paper presented at World Conference on Gifted and Talented Children, Hong Kong.

Zuckerman, H. (1977). *Scientific elite: Nobel laureates in the United States*. New York: Free Press.

Identifying and Educating Poor and Under-represented Gifted Students

James H. Borland and Lisa Wright

Teachers College, Columbia University, USA

The Extent of the Problem

Historical Indicators of the Under-representation of Economically Disadvantaged and Minority Children

It has been a commonplace observation, usually accompanied by sincere but ineffectual expressions of concern, that certain children have been and continue to be chronically and systematically, if unintentionally, under-represented in programs for gifted students. In the United States, under-representation has been primarily associated with economic disadvantage and racial and ethnic minority status. This is the situation that we will address in this chapter. Our knowledge of gifted education in other countries is insufficiently comprehensive to permit us to generalize globally, although we would be surprised if the forces that have led to inequities in the identification and education of gifted children in the U.S. were absent or, some particulars aside, radically different in many other countries.

From the very beginning of the field, individuals labeled as gifted, either for educational or research purposes, have deviated significantly upward from population-wide demographic patterns. For example, in *Hereditary Genius* (1869), Sir Francis Galton concluded that eminence in 'mental work' is 400 times as likely to be found among children of upper-class parents than among the children of laborers. Somewhat later, in *Mental and Physical Traits of a Thousand Gifted Children* (1925), the first volume of Lewis M. Terman's *Genetic Studies of Genius*, the author revealed that, whereas 4 to 5% of the adult general population was engaged in occupations denoted as 'professional', 50% of the fathers of his high-IQ subjects were so-classified. Moreover, children of Italian, Portuguese, Spanish, and Mexican descent were statistically under-represented, and the nearly total absence of African-American children was so much in line with expectations that it was not deemed worthy of mention.

In 1960, Horace Mann Bond, the noted African-American educational researcher, studied the relationship between socio-economic status and the awarding of National Merit Scholarships. His findings revealed a pronounced skewing of awards toward higher SES students, prompting him to ask whether we have "developed a class system that is almost as fixed and immutable as that long established in Western European social hierarchies" (1960, p. 117). In the same anthology on gifted education in which Bond's paper appeared, Martin D. Jenkins, another prominent African-American educator, felt compelled to point out that mean differences in the IQs of Whites and Blacks did not imply that no 'superior cases' would be found among the latter group, nor did it mean that African-Americans were lacking in "the ability to participate in the culture at the highest level" (1960, p. 111; see Kearney & LeBlanc, 1993, for more about the work of Bond, Jenkins, and other 'forgotten pioneers' in the study of gifted African-American children).

Contemporary Indicators of the Under-representation of Economically Disadvantaged and Minority Children

Current data suggest that the under-representation of economically disadvantaged and minority students in gifted programs has not disappeared. For example, the National Educational Longitudinal Study conducted by the U.S. Department of Education (1991) revealed that eighth grade students whose families' socio-economic status placed them in the top quartile of the population were about five times more likely to be in programs for gifted students than were students from families in the bottom quartile. Moreover, almost half of the eighth grade students identified as gifted and placed in gifted programs were from families in the top SES quartile, whereas about 9% were from the bottom quartile.

Ford & Harris (1999) used data from 1978 through 1992 to compute indices of under-representation and over-representation of certain groups by comparing

587

their representation in the general population with their representation in gifted programs. Their data show that Hispanic Americans were under-represented by 24% in 1978 (accounting for 6.8% of the school population but only 5.15% of students in gifted programs) and by 42% in 1992. American Indians were under-represented by 62% in 1978 and by 50% in 1992, and the indices for African Americans were 33% and 41% respectively.

The serious and destructive consequences of this state of affairs can be illustrated in the form of a syllogism that we think is valid. Take the two following premises:

• Students typically derive at least some benefits from being placed in gifted programs, benefits that are realized in school and later in life
• Gifted programs disproportionately serve white middle- and upper-middle-class students

If these premises are true, and we believe they clearly are, the following conclusion is a logical necessity:

• Therefore, gifted programs are serving to widen the gap between society's 'have's' and 'have-not's' and between White and minority families.

The existence and the consequences of under-representation are not in doubt. What is less certain is why the problem exists, a question to which we will now turn.

Possible Causes of the Problem of Under-representation

It is useful to distinguish between those causes of under-representation over which we have an appreciable degree of control and those over which we do not. Among the latter, we will identify conditions in the larger society and, among the former, practices in the field of gifted education. This is a bit of a simplification if one views education, including gifted education, as an instrument for social change, but for purposes of discussion, we will maintain this dichotomy. Let us first examine factors outside the field of gifted education.

Social and Cultural Factors

Poverty, racism, class bias—inequity in all of its ugly forms—are malignant and insidious forces that can damage people, and children are especially vulnerable. Thus, a child who is born into poverty and experiences the consequences of racism for the first five years of his or her life is likely, whatever his or her innate capacity for academic achievement, to enter kindergarten at a disadvantage educationally. In attempting to understand the underachievement and corresponding under-representation in gifted programs of children from certain groups, we sometimes lose sight of the simple and undeniable fact that such things as poverty hurt all but the most resilient children in ways that can

deny them their basic rights in our schools and our society.

How this translates into academic under-achievement and under-representation in gifted programs is a difficult question. Descriptive data are plentiful. For example, Natriello, McDill & Pallas (1990) list five "key indicators associated with the educationally disadvantaged ... [that are] correlated with poor performance in school" (p. 16). These are: (a) being Black or Latino, (b) living in poverty, (c) living in a single-parent family, (d) having a poorly educated mother, and (e) having limited English proficiency. Useful as this might be, these data are correlational rather than explanatory, so we have to turn elsewhere for possible insights into how what Natriello et al. refer to as 'educational disadvantage' comes about.

The work of Ogbu and Fordham. John Ogbu (e.g. 1978, 1985, 1992) and Signithia Fordham (e.g. 1988, 1991; Fordham & Ogbu, 1986) have provided a useful theoretical framework for investigating the causes and mechanisms of educational disadvantage. Briefly (see Borland, Schnur, & Wright (2000), for a more detailed synopsis), Ogbu's explanation rests on a distinction between 'voluntary minorities', those whose minority status results from voluntary immigration in search of a better life, and 'involuntary minorities', such as African-Americans in the U.S., who were originally brought to this country against their will, denied assimilation into the mainstream, and relegated largely to menial occupations. It is the latter group who most acutely and persistently experience educational disadvantage and, as a result, under-representation in gifted programs.

Although voluntary-minority children may initially experience school difficulties, they do not typically fail generation after generation as many involuntary-minority children do. According to Ogbu, this is because, whereas both voluntary and involuntary minorities experience *primary cultural differences*—differences in language, religious practice, dress, child rearing—that existed before they came to the United States—involuntary minorities also experience what Ogbu calls *secondary cultural differences*, which arise in reaction to negative contacts with the dominant culture and serve as "coping mechanisms under 'oppressive conditions' " (Ogbu, 1992, p. 10). Whereas voluntary minorities see primary cultural differences as barriers to assimilation that must be overcome, involuntary minorities use secondary cultural differences as protectors of their very identity and "have no strong incentives to give up these differences as long as they believe they are still oppressed" (Ogbu, 1992, p. 10).

One possible form secondary cultural differences can take is *cultural inversion*, "the tendency ... to regard certain forms of behavior, events, symbols, and meanings as inappropriate ... because these are characteristic of White Americans" (Ogbu, 1992, p. 8).

In other words, denied opportunities to assimilate into the mainstream culture, involuntary minorities develop a subgroup identity based on values, attitudes, and behaviors that are directly oppositional to those of the White culture. Socializing children thus involves teaching behaviors and values discrepant from those of the mainstream culture, and sanctions are often applied to those who appear to embrace the values and behaviors perceived as being typical of White America, such as employing standard English or striving for academic achievement. Clearly, cultural inversion would militate against involuntary-minority parents desiring placement in gifted programs for their children and could be a cause of the under-representation under examination here.

This creates a dilemma for potentially gifted involuntary-minority students, which Fordham (1988, 1991); Fordham & Ogbu, 1986; refers to as the "burden of acting white."

> Learning to follow the standard academic practices of the school is often equated by the minorities with . . . "acting white" while simultaneously giving up acting like a minority person. School learning is therefore consciously or unconsciously perceived *as a subtractive process:* a minority person who learns successfully in school or who follows the standard practices of the school is perceived as becoming acculturated into the white American frame of reference at the expense of the minorities' cultural frame of reference and collective welfare (Fordham & Ogbu, 1986, pp. 182–183).

The quandary faced by gifted students from involuntary-minority groups can be a painful one: either adopt attitudes and behaviors that, although facilitative of school success, serve to alienate one from friends and culture, or maintain loyalty to friends and culture by sacrificing one's prospects for academic and vocational success.

Research by Ford (1992, 1993, 1996) suggests that this is indeed a significant problem for some bright involuntary-minority students. In her sample of 148 African-American fifth and sixth graders identified as either gifted, above-average, or average in academic ability, 97 "reported exerting low levels of effort in school" (1992, p. 134). This included 38 of the 48 gifted students, despite their endorsement of what Ford calls the "American achievement ideology" (p. 11).

The work of these researchers suggests that there is a powerful array of forces that work to lower the academic achievement of involuntary-minority children. Fordham & Ogbu (1986), referring to African-American children, summarize these as follows:

> The low school performance of black children stems from the following factors: first, white people provide them with inferior schooling and treat them

differently in school; second, by imposing a job ceiling, white people fail to reward them adequately for their educational accomplishments in adult life; and third, black Americans develop coping devices which further limit their striving for academic success. (p. 179)

Clearly, the under-representation of economically disadvantaged children, especially those from racial and ethnic minority groups, in programs for gifted students is a problem that, in Ford's words, is "complex and perplexing . . . requiring movement away from traditional theories and paradigms, including those which hold that under-achievement results only from a lack of motivation to achieve" (1992, p. 134). Moreover, it is part of a larger problem, the failure of our educational system to educate economically disadvantaged and minority students, that is the product of persistent structural inequities in our society.

Factors Within the Field of Gifted Education
Although the under-representation of economically disadvantaged and minority children in gifted programs is in part a function of inequities in our society, we also believe that beliefs and practices within the field of gifted education have contributed to the problem. Among the factors within the field that contribute to the problem are the following.

Conceptions of giftedness. Giftedness is context-specific and socially constructed (see, for example, Sapon-Shevin, 1994; Borland, 1996). It is not a fact of nature but rather a concept that was created by human beings because it was thought to be necessary. As a construct, giftedness is inevitably tied to notions of excellence and potential, and these ideas of excellence reflect the society in which individuals live. In fact, some writers, such as Tannenbaum (1983, 1986) in his "psycho-social conception of giftedness," argue that the environment, the social context, is a component of giftedness. In multicultural societies, conceptions of excellence and giftedness are likely to be shaped by the values of the dominant culture or subculture. In the U.S., for example, intellectual and academic giftedness, as it has traditionally been understood and operationalized, has largely been White middle- and upper-middle-class giftedness.

The point is that giftedness as a concept, as a label in the schools, and ultimately as a descriptor of certain adults is likely to reflect the values and strengths of the dominant culture and to slight those of other cultures, especially those of involuntary minorities who employ such secondary cultural differences as cultural inversion as a means to define and protect their identities. Thus, we would argue that *giftedness*, the very notion that gave rise to this book, has embedded in it the basis for the under-representation of certain groups outside the mainstream of any culture in which the concept is employed.

One need not view this as reflecting malign intent, although some do. According to social or cultural reproduction theory (see, for example, Katz, 1975; Apple, 1982; Spring, 1989), society's inequities, among them racism and wide disparities in wealth, work to the benefit of a wealthy and powerful elite. Society is structured to maintain the dominance of those in power and to perpetuate the subordinate status of those in the underclass, and social institutions, such as the educational system, are designed to perpetuate inequities that benefit the elite by reproducing, in the educational system, the hierarchical stratification found in the larger society.

One way the schools serve to maintain the status quo and the current power structure, according to social reproduction theory, is by denying an adequate education to the poor and the non-White. Gifted education is seen by some as an instrument of social reproduction and one of the means whereby schools perpetuate racism and economic injustice. Sapon-Shevin (1994) writes, "Whether or not the intention of gifted programs is to reproduce existing economic and racial hierarchies or to produce cultural capital held by an elite group of students, these are in fact the consequences of such a system" (p. 192).

Although we do not believe that gifted education is the result of a conscious intention to perpetuate inequities in society, there remains the nagging question of whether the very concept of giftedness necessarily leads to or reinforces racial and economic inequities, whether it might be impossible to conceptualize and operationalize the distinctions at the heart of the concept independent of such factors as race, ethnicity, and SES. The most pessimistic answers to that question hold some troubling implications for the field of gifted education.

Identification practices. That White middle-class children are identified as gifted in proportions that exceed their proportion in the general school population is a fact of educational life in the U.S. In part, this is a consequence of the ways we have traditionally identified students as gifted, which are themselves rooted in the values of the white middle class. For example, IQ tests have traditionally played a major role in identifying gifted students. Although no-one in the field of gifted education of whom we are aware advocates using these tests as Terman (1925) and Hollingworth (1942) used them, such tests and other measures that correlate substantially with IQ are still widely used in the schools to identify gifted students.

Standardized tests can play an important role in the equitable identification of gifted students (see, for example, Borland, 1986; Pendarvis & Howley, 1996). However, unless we also use non-traditional methods for identification (Borland & Wright, 1994), inequities will be inevitable. Furthermore, our traditional conception of identification as a method whereby we separate

the gifted students from the rest of the student population has, despite some challenges (e.g. Renzulli, Reis & Smith, 1981), continued to dominate our thinking. As long as this is the case, we may be faced with the problem we address in this chapter.

Some Thoughts About How to Address the Problem of Under-representation

Without pretending to have the answer to the question of how to remedy the problem of under-representation, we will present some of what we learned through our work in Project Synergy at Teachers College, Columbia University. To begin our discussion, let us take the two topics we identified above as being endogenous to the field of gifted education.

Conceptions of giftedness. We need to rethink giftedness as a concept and to do so radically, to go to the root of the concept and examine what it means, what it connotes and implies, and what value it actually brings to our field. At the very least, we need to examine our conceptions of giftedness in order to identify whether and how they might lead to the inequities we discuss above. Take as an example Renzulli's three-ring conception of giftedness (e.g. 1978, 1986), probably the most influential conception of giftedness in recent times. Renzulli challenged some well-entrenched, fundamental assumptions about giftedness, including the primacy of high levels of general ability, a legacy of Terman, Hollingworth, et al. This alone makes the definition a significant contribution to our literature. Yet, even this definition, in which giftedness is conceived of as an interaction among above-average ability, creativity, and task commitment, can, contrary to its author's intention, be operationalized in a manner that reinforces social inequities.

Creativity and task commitment are necessarily assessed subjectively, that is, without the use of standardized tests, since valid standardized measures of these constructs do not exist. This is not necessarily a liability; in fact, we strongly advocate the use of subjective measures in gifted education (see, for example, Wright & Borland, 1993; Borland & Wright, 1994). But problems can occur when any conception is applied in the practical sphere. For example, the New York City Public Schools serve 1.1 million students in a system in which the teachers are predominantly White and middle class and the students are not. It is not difficult to conceive of how conceptions of task commitment might be quite discrepant in the cultures in which, on the one hand, the majority of teachers and, on the other, the majority of students live. Teachers might, without any malign intent, conceive of this construct in a manner that predisposes them to see it in children culturally like themselves and not to see it in students unlike themselves.

If this can happen with a conception of giftedness that breaks with a prevailing psychometric tradition that favors White middle-class students, few if any conceptions are immune to this problem. This seems to leave us with two options. The first is to attempt to develop conceptions of giftedness that are either culture-fair or equitably multicultural. This may prove to be as difficult as the attempt to develop culture-fair tests has been.

A second approach led one of us a few years back to "think the unthinkable: that there might be effective gifted education without gifted programs" (Borland, 1996, p. 144). Perhaps it is time to ask an even more radical question: Can there be effective gifted education without gifted children? By this, we mean to ask whether we can accomplish the goals that gave rise to the field of gifted education without identifying children as gifted or even having recourse to the construct of giftedness at all. This latter course of action would constitute nothing short of a revolution in the field of gifted education. It would, no doubt, be strongly resisted by many of our colleagues, but as a thought experiment it could be a productive exercise. We suggest that it is once again necessary to think the unthinkable.

Identification practices. We would like to propose two possibilities for dealing with problems of inequity deriving from identification practices. The first of these is to work within the traditional conception of identification as a sorting process and to make the process more equitable and sensitive to diverse expressions of giftedness. Since we are most familiar with our own work in Project Synergy, we will use that as an example (see Borland, 1994; Borland & Wright, 1994). In this project, we learned that certain features of an identification process can make it more effective for identifying economically disadvantaged students. They include:

- a post-positivistic approach to assessment (see Borland, 1990), including the use of observation and other forms of the 'human instrument' (Lincoln & Guba, 1985);
- a focus on 'best performance' (Roedell, Jackson & Robinson, 1980) instead of averages of scores and ratings;
- curriculum-based assessment and other forms of 'authentic assessment' instead of, or in conjunction with, standardized measures;
- portfolio assessment (Wright & Borland, 1993);
- dynamic assessment, based on the work of Vygotsky (e.g. 1978) and Feuerstein (e.g. 1980), in which assessment is carried out in Vygotsky's "zone of proximal development";
- open-ended teacher referrals instead of checklists;
- a case-study approach to identification that relies on human judgment instead of a mechanical approach such as combining scores, which is characteristic of a matrix;

- conceiving of identification as a process, not an event; that is, making the identification process a long-term one, extending at least over a period of months.

We strongly believe that modifying identification procedures as we did in Project Synergy and has been done in other Javits Grant projects (e.g. Baldwin, 1996; Coleman, 1994; O'Tuel, 1996; Feiring, Louis, Ukeje & Lewis, 1997) can improve our field's performance with respect to equity. However, there is a second possible direction for the field, and this is the course of action we suggested above: the possibility of gifted education without gifted students, or the concept of 'the gifted student'.

It is often said that, in an ideal educational world, special education, including gifted education, would not be necessary because curricula would be sufficiently responsive to individual differences to make separating children into exceptionality categories unnecessary. We have worked with school districts to move in this direction by helping them plan and implement programs that combine school-wide enrichment; flexible grouping across grade levels in major subjects; and, for a very few truly exceptional students, individual educational plans. The result is a form of gifted education that does not look like traditional gifted education and that requires little in the form of traditional identification, save for those few students who require individual plans (whose identification involves a process that begins with pre-kindergarten screening and continues for two or three years).

In many ways, identification is at the crux of the problem of under-representation, for this is the process whereby more students from some groups and fewer children from other groups are designated as gifted. It seems to us that a major decision has to be made if we do not want to live with the inequities that have plagued the field since its inception. Either we have to make our practice equitable by modifying the way we do the things we have always done, or we have to give these things up while still hewing closely to our core values. In other words, we need to determine whether we can have gifted education, that is, its fundamental goals, without not only gifted programs as we have traditionally known them but without gifted children, labeled as such, as well.

If we give up the processes of conceiving of giftedness as a trait, or even state, possessed by some and not others and also forego the process of sorting children into 'gifted' and 'not gifted' groups and instead attempt to achieve the goals inherent in the practice of gifted education through curriculum reform and more creative administrative arrangements such as flexible grouping, large-scale equity problems in education will not disappear. However, the problem of under-representation that we are analyzing here would become a moot point, for program placement, the activity that gives rise to under-representation, would no longer be a concern. Discrepancies in educational achievement would and should, of course, continue to be a concern. However, addressing these as issues of educational achievement instead of gifted or non-gifted status strikes us as a slightly, but significantly, more tractable matter for educators.

Curriculum. We will briefly address two issues related to curriculum for gifted students that are germane to the problem of under-representation. The first is the role multicultural education can play in gifted education. Ford & Harris (1999) advance the perhaps controversial idea that gifted education and multicultural education are complementary and point to some practical steps educators can take to effect this synthesis. To the extent that such educational streams as gifted education and multicultural education are seen as having a potential confluence, the goal of remedying the under-representation of economically disadvantaged and minority children in gifted programs will seem less remote.

The second approach derives from our work in Project Synergy. Working with kindergarten children in a severely under-resourced school in Central Harlem, we quickly became aware of two things. The first was that there were potentially gifted students in this school just as there are in any other. The second was that the students were not ready academically for placement in gifted programs. Our approach was to implement what we called 'transitional services', curriculum designed to help young students identified as potentially gifted develop their potential so that subsequent placement in gifted programs would be successful and appropriate. Such a curriculum need not be terribly elaborate. In Project Synergy, the emphasis was on traditional skills of reading, writing, and mathematics. We employed a diagnostic-prescriptive model, along with some cultural enrichment, work on thinking skills, and help developing academic 'meta-skills', behaviors and attitudes that seem to be part of the tacit knowledge of successful students. Parent education was another important emphasis.

We think the concept of transitional services has potential in the field of gifted education for students who have not had the nurturance given to students from more economically favored circumstances. In cases where the only alternatives seem to be benign neglect or placement in a demanding sink-or-swim environment, the effort involved in developing transitional services curricula may be amply repaid. This does not mean that the gap between potentially high achieving poor and minority children and their high achieving age peers would necessarily be eliminated, for we are not advocating that the latter mark time while the former catch up. 'Catching up' is not our concern; the development of potential that is too often frustrated by inequities in our society and our schools is.

Some Final Thoughts

In this chapter, we have tried to describe the extent of the problem of the under-representation of economically disadvantaged and minority children in gifted programs, to discuss some of the forces contributing to the problem, and to suggest some measures that might be palliative, if not curative. It is our hope that the problem can be addressed and substantial progress can be made. This should be a major priority for the field of gifted education, both as a matter of educational effectiveness and a moral imperative. However, we also need to confront the troubling possibility that a complete resolution of the problem may not be possible.

The philosopher Isaiah Berlin, in an essay entitled 'The Pursuit of the Ideal' (1990; see also, Gray, 1996), advances his notion of 'value pluralism', which, we believe, has relevance here. This is the idea that we might not be able to attain a perfect state in which all goods, all desirable outcomes, are realizable. Some goods, Berlin argues, may be incompatible or incommensurable. That is, A may be a good, a desirable, even necessary thing; so, too, might B, which is equal in importance to A. But it may be impossible for both A and B to co-exist, for them both to be realized.

Berlin writes, "Values may easily clash within the breast of a single individual; it does not follow that, if they do, some must be true and others false" (p. 12). That is, contrary to what many philosophers, at least since the time of Plato, have argued, there may be no perfect system, no ideal world in which the competing claims of various desirable but incompatible outcomes can be realized. As Berlin argues, "The notion of the perfect whole, the ultimate solution, in which all good things coexist, seems to me to be not merely unattainable—that is a truism—but conceptually incoherent" (1990, p. 13).

It occurs to us to ask whether striving for a world in which the goals of both gifted education and perfect equity are pursued is, in Berlin's sense, a striving for that which is conceptually incoherent and, therefore, impossible. Might it be the case that, in any multicultural society in which there are discrepancies in socioeconomic status, the concept of giftedness and the practice of gifted education inevitably lead to the under-representation of certain groups of individuals and obviate the very possibility of equity?

This is a troubling thought. However, since we have been urging our readers to think the unthinkable, we feel obligated to suggest thinking what may be the most unthinkable thing of all within our field. And this is the possibility that two essential, core values—pursuing the goals inherent in the practice of gifted education and striving for racial, ethnic, and socioeconomic equity—may be incompatible. We may be able to realize one or the other, but not both.

This is, in essence, the question Gardner (1961) confronted in his book *Excellence: Can We Be Equal and Excellent Too?* Gardner raised the issue and expressed optimism over the possibility of a resolution, but he did not show how it could be effected. His concluding line, "But who ever supposed it would be easy?" (p. 161) is certainly more optimistic than the response Berlin's idea of value pluralism suggests: "It is not only far from easy, it is impossible."

Perhaps Berlin was wrong, or, if he was not, this may not be one of those situations in which seemingly competing goods are truly incommensurable. And perhaps, until it can be convincingly demonstrated that excellence and equity are, in some ways relevant to the practice of gifted education, mutually antagonistic, we need to proceed as if they were not. That is, we should not give up on either good, we should strive both for excellence and for equity. But we need to consider the disturbing possibility of their incompatibility and, if all evidence suggests that, in this world at least, incompatible they are, we need to make some extremely difficult choices.

References

Apple, M. W. (1982). *Education and power.* Boston: Routledge and Kegan Paul.

Baldwin, A. Y. (1996). The seven plus story: developing hidden talent among students in socioeconomically disadvantaged environments. *Gifted Child Quarterly,* **38**, 80–84.

Berlin, I. (1990). *The crooked timber of humanity Chapters in the history of ideas.* Princeton, NJ: Princeton University Press.

Borland, J. H. (1986). IQ tests: Throwing out the bath water, saving the baby. *Roeper Review,* **8**, 163–167.

Borland, J. H. (1990). Post-positivist inquiry: implications of the 'new philosophy of science' for the field of the education of the gifted. *Gifted Child Quarterly,* **34**, 161–167.

Borland, J. H. (1994). Identifying and educating young economically disadvantaged urban children: the lessons of Project Synergy. In: N. Colangelo, S. G. Assouline & D. L. Ambroson (Eds), *Talent Development: Proceedings of the Second Biennial Wallace Conference on Talent Development* (pp. 151–172). Dayton, OH: Ohio Psychology Press.

Borland, J. H. (1996). Gifted education and the threat of irrelevance. *Journal for the Education of the Gifted,* **19**, 129–147.

Borland, J. H., Schnur, R. & Wright, L. (2000). Economically disadvantaged students in a school for the academically gifted: a post-positivist inquiry into individual and family adjustment. *Gifted Child Quarterly,* **44**, 13-32.

Borland, J. H. & Wright, L. (1994). Identifying young, potentially gifted, economically disadvantaged students. *Gifted Child Quarterly,* **38**, 164–171.

Bond, H. M. (1960). The productivity of national merit scholars by occupational class. In: J. L. French (Ed.), *Educating the Gifted: a Book of Readings* (pp. 115–118). New York: Henry Holt and Company.

Coleman, L. J. (1994). Portfolio assessment: a key to identifying hidden talents and empowering teachers of young children. *Gifted Child Quarterly,* **38**, 65–69.

Feiring, C., Louis, B., Ukeje, I. & Lewis, M. (1997). Early identification of gifted minority kindergarten students in Newark, NJ. *Gifted Child Quarterly,* **41**, 15–21.

Feuerstein, R. (1980). *Instrumental enrichment: an intervention program for cognitive modifiability.* Baltimore: University Park Press.

Ford, D. Y. (1992). Determinants of under-achievement as perceived by gifted, above-average and average Black students. *Roeper Review,* **14**, 130–136.

Ford, D. Y. (1993). An investigation of the paradox of underachievement among gifted Black students. *Roeper Review,* **16**, 78–84.

Ford, D. Y. (1996). *Reversing underachievement among gifted Black students.* New York: Teachers College Press.

Ford, D. Y. & Harris J. J. III. (1999). *Multicultural gifted education.* New York: Teachers College Press.

Fordham, S. (1988). Racelessness as a strategy in Black students' school success: Pragmatic strategy or Pyrrhic victory? *Harvard Educational Review,* **58** (1), 54–84.

Fordham, S. (1991). Peer proofing academic competition among Black adolescents: 'Acting White: Black American style . In: C. E. Sleeter (Eds.), *Empowerment Through Multicultural Education* (pp. 69–93). Albany, NY: State University of New York Press.

Fordham, S. & Ogbu, J. U. (1986). Black students' school success: coping with the burden of 'acting white'. *The Urban Review,* **18**, 176–206.

French, J. L. (Ed.). (1960). *Educating the gifted: a book of readings* (pp. 115–118). New York: Henry Holt and Company.

Galton, F. (1869). *Hereditary genius.* London: Macmillan.

Gardner, J. W. (1961). *Excellence: can we be equal and excellent too?* New York: Harper & Brothers. (pp. x–xiv; 3–45; 65–75; 109–167).

Gray, J. (1996). *Isaiah Berlin.* Princeton, NJ: Princeton University Press.

Hollingworth, L. S. (1942). *Children above 180 IQ: Stanford-Binet.* New York: World Book Company.

Jenkins, M. D. (1960). The upper limit of ability among American Negroes. In: J. L. French (Ed.), *Educating the Gifted: a Book of Readings* (pp. 110–115). New York: Henry Holt and Company.

Katz, M. B. (1975). *Class, bureaucracy, and schools* (expanded edition). New York: Praeger.

Kearney, K. & LeBlanc, J. (1993). Forgotten pioneers in the study of gifted African-Americans. *Roeper Review,* **15**, 192–199.

Lincoln, Y. S. & Guba, E. G. (1985). *Naturalistic inquiry.* Beverly Hills, CA: Sage Publications.

Natriello, G., McDill Edward L. & Pallas, A. M. (1990). *Schooling disadvantaged children: racing against catastrophe.* New York: Teachers College Press.

Ogbu, J. U. (1978). *Minority education and caste: The American system in cross-cultural perspective.* New York: Academic Press.

Ogbu, J. U. (1985). Minority education and caste. In N. R. Yetman (Ed.), *Majority and Minority* (4th ed.), pp. 370–383. Boston: Allyn & Bacon.

Ogbu, J. U. (1992). Understanding cultural diversity and learning. *Educational Researcher,* **21** (8), 5–14.

O'Tuel, F. S. (1996). APOGEE: equity in the identification of gifted and talented students. *Gifted Child Quarterly*, **40**, 75–79.

Pendarvis, E. D. & Howley, A. (1996). Playing fair: the possibilities of gifted education. *Journal for the Education of the Gifted*, **19**, 215–233.

Renzulli, J. S. (1978). What makes giftedness? *Phi Delta Kappan*, **60**, 180–184, 261.

Renzulli, J. S. (1986). The three-ring conception of giftedness: a developmental model for creative productivity. In: R. J. Sternberg & J. E. Davidson (Eds), *Conceptions of Giftedness* (pp. 53–92). New York: Cambridge University Press.

Renzulli, J. S., Reis, S. M. & Smith L. H. (1981). *The revolving door identification model*. Mansfield Center, CT: Creative Learning Press.

Roedell, W. C., Jackson, N. E. & Robinson, H. B. (1980). *Gifted young children*. Perspectives on Gifted and Talented Education. New York: Teachers College Press.

Sapon-Shevin, M. (1994). *Playing favorites: gifted education and the disruption of community*. Albany, NY: State University of New York Press.

Spring, J. (1989). *The sorting machine revisited: national educational policy since 1945*. New York: Longman.

Tannenbaum, A. J. (1983). *Gifted children: psychological and educational perspectives*. New York: Macmillan.

Tannenbaum, A. J. (1986). The enrichment matrix model. In: J. R. Renzulli (Ed.), *Systems and Models for Developing Programs for the Gifted and Talented* (pp. 391–428). Mansfield Center, CT: Creative Learning Press.

Terman, L. M. (1925). *Genetic studies of genius: Vol. 1. Mental and physical traits of a thousand gifted children*. Stanford, CA: Stanford University Press.

United States Department of Education. (1991). *National educational longitudinal study 88. Final report: Gifted and talented education programs for eighth grade public school students*. Washington: United States Department of Education, Office of Planning, Budget, and Evaluation.

Vygotsky, L. (1978). *Mind in society*. Cambridge, MA: Harvard University Press.

Wright, L. & Borland, J. H. (1993). Using Early Childhood Developmental Portfolios in the Identification and Education of Young, Economically Disadvantaged, Potentially Gifted Students. *Roeper Review*, **15**, 205–210.

Counseling Gifted Students[1]

Nicholas Colangelo and Susan G. Assouline

The Connie Belin & Jacqueline N. Blank International Center for Gifted Education and Talent Development
University of Iowa, Iowa City, USA

Introduction

Educating gifted students has focused mainly on meeting their learning needs. Counseling needs, while long recognized, are a relatively recent emphasis. Over the years there have been two main (and conflicting) views regarding psychological well being of gifted students (Neihart, 1999). One view is that gifted children are generally very well adjusted; at least as well adjusted as the general student population. In light of this view, there is little need for specialized school counseling for gifted students. Essentially, what gifted students need most is the typical counseling that is available in schools and their needs for counseling are not dependent on their 'giftedness' but on whatever aspects of their personalities may need attention.

The other view is that giftedness brings with it an array of intrapersonal and interpersonal issues that are unique to their 'giftedness'. Gifted students by their very advanced cognitive abilities and intensity of feelings deal with issues about self and others in ways that are unique from the general population and therefore require specialized understanding. Interpersonally, gifted students are handed the task of adjusting to a peer culture that is often ambiguous if not downright hostile to those with intellectual talent. In this second view, counseling for gifted is seen as a specialty. Counselors need to be aware of those unique needs of gifted students as they try to navigate the challenges of their development and the challenges of an environment of confusing and 'mixed' messages. The assumption in this view is that while the majority of gifted students will and do make satisfactory psychological adjustment, there is a sizeable minority that are psychologically 'at risk' and need counseling that is focused on their needs.

Our contention is that the latter view is more helpful and accurate. From our experience and research, gifted students do have recurring and significant counseling needs based on their 'giftedness'. The focus of this chapter is on counseling needs of the gifted student and the role of the school counselor in addressing those needs. We recognize that counseling gifted students can take place in private practice and community mental health centers; however, our focus will be on the counseling that can be done in a school setting.

Historical Overview

A brief historical overview of counseling with gifted students will help set the present-day context. The gifted-child movement in the United States can be traced back to Lewis M. Terman, whose pioneering longitudinal study of 1,528 gifted children formed the project titled *Genetic Studies of Genius* (Terman, 1925; Burks, Jensen & Terman, 1930; Terman & Oden, 1947, 1959). The Terman studies grounded the study of giftedness in an empirical and psychometric tradition. Also, the work dispelled negative myths and traditions regarding the gifted. For example, Terman and his colleagues showed that gifted children were physically superior and psychologically and socially more stable than their intellectually average peers. The studies indicated that giftedness was a 'positive' and initially distracted professionals from issues of a psychological nature.

Because Terman's studies seemed to provide evidence that concern for gifted students' social/psychological needs was not necessary, any initial focus on counseling for gifted students was essentially derailed. However, since the sample from Terman's seminal studies is no longer considered representative of the broader gifted population, it is no longer valid to assume that there is a general absence of concern for the social-emotional well-being of the gifted student.

Terman's sample was identified by use of the Stanford-Binet intelligence test, and his sample was nearly exclusively white and middle-class youngsters (Holahan & Sears, 1995). The original group recommended for the Stanford-Binet testing was picked by teachers, and so some teacher biases probably entered

[1] Parts of this chapter are taken from Colangelo, N. (1997). Counseling gifted students: issues and practices. In: N. Colangelo & G. A. Davis (Eds.), *Handbook of Gifted Education* (2nd ed.). Needham Heights, MA: Ally and Bacon.

into the selection process even before the standardized testing. Further, although Terman erased a number of myths, he created others, most notably the myth that gifted children are uniformly well adjusted and therefore do not need counseling services. Thus, counselors and those in related professions were not an integral part of gifted education during its early development (Webb, Meckstroth, & Tolan, 1982; Kerr, 1986).

Leta Hollingworth (1926, 1942) was the first to contribute evidence indicating that gifted children do have social and emotional needs meriting attention. Hollingworth also emphasized strongly that the regular school environment did not meet the educational needs of the gifted. Rather, she wrote that the school environment was more likely to lead to apathy with these youngsters. She anticipated some of the emotional difficulties and peer problems that receive attention today. Especially, noting that there is often a gap between a gifted student's intellectual and emotional development, she stated, "To have the intellect of an adult and the emotions of a child combined in a childish body is to encounter certain difficulties" (Hollingworth, 1942, p. 282).

The 1950s witnessed some major attention to counseling gifted students and the establishment of research and guidance programs. John Rothney, a counselor educator, founded the Wisconsin Guidance Laboratory for Superior Students (University of Wisconsin-Madison), which was headed by Rothney and later by Marshall Sanborn. The Guidance Institute for Talented Students (GIFTS) was headed by Charles Pulvino, followed by Nicholas Colangelo and then by Philip Perrone (Colangelo & Zaffrann, 1979).

John Curtis Gowan was a major force from the 1950s to 1970s in promoting counseling services for the gifted. A. Harry Passow and his students Abe Tannenbaum and Miriam Goldberg founded the Talented Youth Project in 1954 which had a strong counseling component. The 1960s and 1970s also witnessed increased sensitivity to issues dealing with gifted women, minorities, and disadvantaged students, and to the counseling needs of the gifted.

The 1980s saw the establishment of the Supporting the Emotional Needs of Gifted (SENG) program by James T. Webb at Wright State University after the suicide of Dallas Egbert, a highly gifted 17-year-old. SENG has continued its focus on addressing the counseling and psychological needs of gifted students. The issues of depression and suicide among the gifted have continued to expand with the work of James Delisle at Kent State University (e.g. Delisle, 1992).

In 1982 Barbara Kerr established the Guidance Laboratory for Gifted and Talented at the University of Nebraska-Lincoln, to extend the work of both GIFTS and SENG (Myers & Pace, 1986). Linda Silverman (1993), a psychologist, established the Gifted Child Development Center at Denver, Colorado. In 1988, The University of Iowa established the comprehensive

Connie Belin National Center for Gifted Education (renamed The Connie Belin & Jacqueline N. Blank International Center for Gifted Education and Talent Development in 1995) with Nicholas Colangelo as director. The Belin-Blank Center has a strong focus on personal counseling, career guidance, family counseling, and psychological assessment. The clinical programs at the Belin-Blank Center are headed by Susan Assouline, associate director and school psychologist.

In a historical overview of counseling gifted students, Karen St. Clair (1989) divided counseling into several areas which we find useful.

(1) Early 1900s—recognition of the counseling needs of gifted students focusing on the work of Terman and Hollingworth.
(2) The 1950s—a non-directive approach to counseling the gifted student which acknowledged the influence of Carl Rogers (Rogers, 1951) to the entire counseling profession.
(3) The 1960s—the beginning of counseling the gifted in schools where the role of the school counselor was emphasized in the development of all students with some special attention to the gifted.
(4) The 1970s—program development for counseling gifted students emphasized a full fledged program of counseling in schools focusing not only on counseling sessions, but counseling programs, evaluations, and research related school counseling.
(5) The 1980s—diversity in counseling the gifted indicated a decade of special issues in counseling including focus on underachievement, females, minority students, and stress. This period was also characterized by diversity in terms of models and approaches to counseling.

To St. Clair's review we add the following:

The 1990s—counseling gifted-special-needs students provided a strong emphasis on gifted students as special-needs learners. There was a focus on gifted students who were double labeled, e.g. gifted/learning disabled. There was also a focus on providing programs (counseling and curriculum) that matched the dual exceptionalities of the students, (see for example Cash, 1999). A focus on families and sexual identity issues were also important trends in this decade.

The year 2000 and beyond—in the next decade we anticipate a sharper focus on ethics and moral issues as well as the continued focus on the 'emotional intelligence' of students. In addition there will be an expanding focus on rural issues and on international issues as the vision of giftedness will include a global perspective.

Self-Concept

The interest in self-concept, which by no means was initiated in the 1990s, has seen a very powerful revival during that decade. Almost everything 'good' in school life seems related to a positive self-concept and almost all that is 'at risk' has at least an aspect of negative self-concept associated with it. Robyn Dawes (1998) indicated that pop psychology associates positive mental health with self-esteem (i.e. self-concept). His brief review indicates that there are a number of destructive behaviors that are done by adolescents and adults who seem to have quite positive evaluations of themselves. His insightful comments at least give cause to consider that simply having high self-esteem/self-concept does not assure prosocial behavior and that we must consider that students with high (positive) self-concepts may also perform actions with negative consequences.

The self-concept construct has deep historical roots in psychology and education. The self-concept can be viewed as a "powerful system of cognitive structures that is quite likely to mediate interpretation of and response to events and behaviors directed at or involving the individual" (Nurius, 1986, p. 435). The definition of self-concept has evolved from a "collection of self-views" (e.g. Snygg & Combs, 1949; Rogers, 1951) to general good and bad feelings about oneself (Shavelson, Hubner & Stanton, 1976; McGuire, 1984) to recent theory and research on operationally defining the structures and contents of the self-concept (Nurius, 1986; Marsh, 1990; Colangelo & Assouline, 1995). Neihart (1999) states that self-concept is the collection of ideas that one has about oneself, an essential component of what is usually called personality.

Self-concept of gifted youngsters has received considerable attention in the past two decades. Neihart (1999) indicates that a number of studies have concluded that there are no differences between gifted and non-gifted students; however, a number of studies have concluded that there are differences in favor of gifted students particularly when measuring assessment of one's academic abilities. These studies typically have investigated: (1) how gifted and average children's self-concepts compare (Karnes & Wherry, 1981; Kelly & Colangelo, 1984; Loeb & Jay 1987; Hoge & Renzulli, 1993); (2) whether self-concept is a developmental construct (Karnes & Wherry, 1981; Harter, 1982; Hoge & McSheffrey, 1991; Marsh, 1992, 1993; Hoge & Renzulli, 1993); and (3) how programming affects a child's self-concept (Maddux, Scheiber & Bass, 1982; Kelly & Colangelo, 1984; Loeb & Jay, 1987).

Self-concept and giftedness represent complex constructs, and the study of each is made more difficult by theoretical controversies within each field. For example, the developmental nature and processes of self-concept have been debated (Ketcham & Snyder, 1977; Karnes & Wherry, 1981; Harter, 1982). Additionally, there are concerns about the reliability and validity of measures of self-concept (Wylie, 1989;

Marsh, 1990, 1993, 1994). In the area of gifted education, the question of uni-dimensionality versus multi-dimensionality has also permeated almost every aspect of the field.

Our research lends credibility to the multi-dimensional nature of self-concept. In a research study (Colangelo & Assouline, 1995) investigating the self-concept of 563 gifted students spanning grades 3–11, we found support for the general notion that the overall self-concept of gifted students is positive. However, there were peaks and valleys across the grade levels and the various domains as measured by the Piers-Harris Children's Self-Concept Scale. Most importantly for school counselors were the following findings:

(1) General self-concept scores were high for elementary, middle, and high school students; however, high school students had the lowest scores. High school girls in particular had the most significant drop in self-concept scores.
(2) As gifted students progress in school they become more anxious and feel more isolated.
(3) The lowest scores of the 563 students in the study were found in the domains of interpersonal skills and self-satisfaction.
(4) The highest scores were in the domains of intellectual and school status.

Closely related to self-concept is the attitude that gifted students have toward their own giftedness. Three books—*On Being Gifted* (American Association for Gifted Children, 1978), *Gifted Children Speak Out* (Delisle, 1984), and *Gifted Kids Speak Out* (Delisle, 1987)—present testimonials from gifted children describing the impact of giftedness on their lives.

One conclusion that can be drawn from these testimonials is that these children have mixed feelings about their giftedness. Research has provided some confirmation of this ambivalence. Colangelo & Kelly (1983) found that while gifted youngsters were positive about their being labeled gifted, they perceived non-gifted peers and teachers as having negative views of them. A study by Kerr, Colangelo & Gaeth (1988) indicated that the attitude of gifted adolescents toward their own giftedness was multifaceted. Adolescents reported that being gifted was a positive in terms of their own personal growth and in terms of academics. In terms of social peer relations, however, they reported it to be a negative. In a partial replication of the Kerr et al. study, Monaster, Chan, Walt & Wiehe (1994) supported the finding that attitudes toward giftedness are multifaceted. In addition, Monaster and colleagues found that those who knew the gifted child well had positive attitudes toward the child, and that attitudes became more negative toward 'giftedness' as respondents were removed from personal knowledge of a gifted youngster.

597

The Kerr et al. and Monaster et al. findings are very relevant for school counselors because the issues focus on human interaction. In individual counseling sessions, counselors can discuss issues such as: What does it mean to be gifted? What do I like about being gifted? What do I not like about being gifted? If I were not gifted, what would be better for me? If I were not gifted, what would be worse for me?

Career Counseling with Gifted

When gifted students are about to graduate high school and begin to plan for a college and career, parents and educators often get involved to ensure that the student 'does not waste the gift.' From our experience with this phenomenon, not wasting the gift translates into 'making a decision(s) that is reasonable to the adult.' Without articulating specifics, it seems there are a number of adults who believe certain careers are 'worthy' of a gifted student, and that others are not. Medical doctor, lawyer, engineer and physicist typically fall into the category of worthy, while elementary/secondary school teacher, social worker, school counselor, and nurse typically fall into a less worthy category.

Career planning for high ability students has not always been smooth (Kaufmann, 1981; Kerr, 1985, 1991, 1998). Gifted students do not always know what they want to do for the "rest of their lives" and while they may have the academic credentials to succeed in classes, this does not mean that they have the information to 'plan' for a career. Ability and ambition do not always translate into planned or purposeful action.

Multipotentiality

The most written about aspect of the unique career needs of gifted students is 'multipotentiality'. As the term implies, it refers to individuals who have diverse talents (and interests also) and who could 'succeed' at a high level in a number of different fields. The problem is how to make a decision, how to choose a path, from so many realistic possibilities. While this may seem a problem one would gladly 'suffer' it is a significant problem for gifted students. "Multi-potentialed young people may anguish over an abundance of choices available to them during career planning unless appropriate interventions are available" (Rysiew, Shore & Leeb, 1999, p. 423). The most useful definition of multipotential comes from Frederickson & Rothney (1972), "the ability to select and develop any number of competencies to a high level" (p. vii). Without the stipulation of developing competencies *at a very high level* the concept of multipotentiality loses any sense of meaningfulness. Most educators in the field of gifted education adhere to the belief of multipotentiality. While there has been some discussion that the term should be reserved for abilities and not interests (see Rysiew, Shore & Carson, 1994), there has been little

disagreement as to the existence and importance of this concept in understanding giftedness.

Where there has been an absence of empirical data supporting the notion of multipotentiality, there have been considerable anecdotal and clinical reports regarding the concept (Rysiew, Shore & Leeb, 1999). The only serious challenge to the usefulness and existence of multipotentiality has come from Achter, Lubinski & Benbow (1996) and Achter, Benbow & Lubinski (1997). These authors "have challenged the utility of the entire notion of multi-potentiality based on their observation of widely varying patterns of specific abilities and interests in a large sample of gifted adolescents, thereby challenging the ubiquity of low differentiation or high flat interest profiles" (Rysiew, et al., p. 424).

Rysiew et al. (1999) outline some of the main problems or concerns in dealing with multipotentiality, especially as it deals with career choices:

(1) Students find it hard to 'narrow' to a career since they have so many equally viable options.
(2) Multipotential students also suffer from perfectionism, thus look for the perfect or ideal career.
(3) Students feel 'coerced' from parents and others to make decisions based on status and high earning potential.
(4) Students must make commitments which may have long term schooling (graduate, professional) and a delay of independence in terms of earning a salary as well as starting families. These long term 'training' investments are also difficult to change once a student has embarked for several years towards a particular career, even if there are serious doubts about the chosen career path.

Rysiew, et al. (1999) review a number of writings regarding what counselors can do to help multipotential gifted students with career decisions. Among the recommendations are:

(a) Career is explored as a way of life, a lifestyle rather than a particular job/position.
(b) One does not have to limit to one career but that there can be career changes as well.
(c) Use leisure activities as a way to continually develop areas of abilities and interests apart from one's career.
(d) Use career counseling as a value-based activity, exploring broad categories of life satisfaction.
(e) Emphasize peer discussions and group work with other multipotential youth so that one can see that he/she is not alone with concerns.

Since 1988, the students selected for the Belin-Blank Center programs have participated in a Counseling Lab for Career Development. This career development program incorporates the recommendations listed by Rysiew, et al. (1999). In particular, the values-based component of the Counseling Lab for Career Development has proven highly successful with secondary students.

Group Counseling

Gifted students are considerably smarter about course work than about themselves. They have the ability to be insightful about themselves, but seldom the opportunity to articulate and share their insights.

Counselors can offer no more powerful tool for the social and emotional growth of gifted students than group counseling. Group counseling is a rich arena that affords students a rare opportunity to share with one another their struggles and questions about growing up and what it means to be 'gifted'. But simply sitting around talking about feelings and values is not enough. Group counseling is a structured situation with a trained leader (e.g. a school counselor) who has knowledge of both gifted youngsters and group dynamics.

Why Group Counseling for Gifted Students?

All students grow by having opportunities to discuss feelings and perceptions in an atmosphere of trust and understanding. Also, students need to share with peers. To think of *peers* as one's age-mates trivializes the concept. A peer is more a "soul-mate than an age-mate," someone who understands what you mean, has experienced what you are talking about, and can respond to you. Gifted students seldom have the opportunity to talk to one another about what it means to be gifted or how it feels to understand things that many age-mates cannot seem to grasp. These are subjects that educators do not encourage for discussion, and gifted students are bright enough to know it's best to keep such things to oneself.

Grouping gifted students for the sole purpose of helping them discuss, in a safe and open atmosphere, issues of a more personal and social nature gives them an opportunity to enjoy and grow from their peers. Most of the time gifted students 'hide' who they are (Colangelo, 1991). Group counseling is a situation in which they are encouraged to share themselves with others who understand and accept. We would guess that if gifted students were given a chance to meet as a small group for the purpose of self-discovery, for most of them this would be their first opportunity to share with true 'peers'. If a rationale is needed for group counseling with gifted students, it is that in the course of school life such a situation will not arise naturally.

Topics for Group Counseling

A counselor may wonder what topics are useful or of interest to gifted students meeting for group counseling sessions. These students will not find it difficult to generate discussion. In our experience with groups, the challenge is in ending the discussions rather than in starting them.

A counselor needs to set the atmosphere for a group. He or she must be clear on the ethics, purpose, rules, and norms. The overall purpose is for gifted students to be able to talk about themselves and learn about one another in an atmosphere of safety and respect. The following are some stems that a counselor may use in generating discussions:

(1) What does it mean to be gifted? We have found exciting and varied discussions generated by such a question. Students will see it in different ways. Questions that help elaborate this topic are:
    (1a) What do your parents think it means to be gifted?
    (1b) What do your teachers think it means to be gifted?
    (1c) What do other kids in school think it means?
(2) How is being gifted an advantage for you? How is it a disadvantage?
(3) Have you ever deliberately hidden your giftedness? If so, how?

Colangelo (1991) reported on group discussion with gifted students in which they talked about 'deliberate underachievement'—purposely getting lower grades so that their friends would be more accepting of them. Many gifted students will be able to articulate how they make decisions to avoid demonstrating their giftedness.

(4) How is your participation in this group different from your regular school day?

Colangelo (1991) also reported that students in groups talked about how, "Finally, I can be myself" or "I can say what's on my mind without someone making fun of me or saying I'm a snob."

In studies reported by Colangelo & Kerr (1990) and Kerr & Colangelo (1988), it is obvious that gender and ethnicity are important variables related to giftedness. A variation of questions we have found useful are:

(5) Would you rather be a gifted boy? Gifted girl? What does it mean to be gifted and Latino? Students will find it stimulating to discuss such issues. Also, they will achieve much better insight into gender and ethnic issues.
(6) Is there a time in school (elementary, middle, high school) when it is easiest to be gifted? Most difficult? Why? The foregoing questions are by no means exhaustive and they will lead to other related questions and directions.

Dynamics and Techniques

The essence of group counseling is to transform students from *spectators* to *participants*. Although there is evidence of the positive effects of being a spectator in a group, its value pales compared to the value of being a participant (Yalom, 1985). To be a spectator means to observe and listen, but to be only tangentially associated with the topic of discussion. A group is not effective when the primary role of its members is that of spectator.

A counselor can transform spectators into participants by taking opportunities to make any topic of discussion a connector to each group member. Following is a specific example using the concepts of *vertical* and *horizontal* self-disclosures.

Let's say a student is talking about her feelings about having been labeled gifted. The counselor could ask her questions to help her elaborate on these feelings: "How long have you felt this way?" "Is it changing at all for you?" "Who knows that you felt this way?" All of these are good questions that help the student talk more about her feelings. These questions lead to what can be called *vertical* self-disclosure (Yalom, 1985) because they help 'build' more information on how the student feels about labeling. As we build this mound of information, the rest of the students in the group are listening (perhaps nodding in agreement), being empathic, and so on. Their role is primarily that of spectator (albeit sympathetic and interested ones) in that they are observing this interaction between the one student and the counselor.

Using the same incident, the counselor could transform the group members from spectators to participants by moving from vertical to *horizontal* self-disclosure. Instead of asking for more information on the feelings about labeling, the counselor asks the student, "Who in this group do you think feels the same way you do?" or "Who in this group do you think feels most different from you about labeling?" These types of questions are *horizontal* in that they connect students to one another (Yalom, 1985). The students in the group are no longer simply spectators, listening to one girl talk about labeling. Instead, they are actively involved in their own feelings and perceptions about labeling. In every group there will be countless opportunities to take what a student says and make *horizontal* connections. Every *horizontal* connection makes better use of group dynamics and generates more energy and participation.

The second technique we want to share is not so much focused on transforming spectators to participants as it is on helping students to pay better attention to the processes in their group. At the end of every group session, the counselor can ask one student to "process for the group." What this means is to take the last three to five minutes of the session to articulate to everyone what he or she thought happened in the group. This group process time is an opportunity to share how the group went about its task for the session. This simple technique accomplishes several important tasks. First, over time, it gives each student a chance to share what he or she 'saw' happening in the group. It also offers other students a chance to hear the perspective of one member on what happened during a session. To paraphrase T. S. Elliot, you can have the experience but miss the meaning. This technique minimizes the possibility of missing the meaning. Second, ending every session with group process time is a good way to summarize the session. Third, the group process time can often be an excellent stem for the start of the next group session. For instance, it is not uncommon in groups we have led to have a student start a session with, "When Bob did group process, he said some things that I saw very differently. I want to talk about how I saw them. . . ." The group session is off and running.

Group counseling is an effective means of helping gifted students in their social and emotional growth. It is rare that gifted students ever have the opportunities for grouping when the primary purpose is personal growth rather than academics. Group counseling is most vibrant when members are *transformed* from spectators to participants. For a more extensive treatment of group counseling with the gifted, see Colangelo & Peterson (1993).

Counseling with Families

The family has been recognized as a primary and critical component in the development of talent and the success of children in school. Bloom's (Bloom, 1985; Bloom & Sosniak, 1981) seminal work on talent development made a compelling case for the demands on, as well as the influences of, the family on the development of talent. Although research and writings on families of gifted students have increased in the last two decades (see reviews by Colangelo & Assouline, 1993; Moon & Hall, 1998), counseling with families is still an area of exceptional need and challenge.

In the special anniversary issue of *Roeper Review*, it was emphasized that one of the most significant trends in gifted education over the next ten years would be a focus on families (Colangelo, 1988). Although there has been an increase in counseling families, counselors and therapists who work with families of gifted children rarely have expertise in the area of the gifted (Wendorf & Frey, 1985; Moon & Hall, 1998). Their expertise is in family counseling.

A major review of family issues was done by Colangelo & Dettmann (1983). Recently, the major review on family counseling and family therapy has been done by Moon & Hall (1998). A summary of the findings by Moon & Hall (1998) includes:

(a) Parents of gifted have unique stressors and concerns brought about by the unique cognitive and personality characteristics of gifted children.
(b) Parenting styles tend to be child-centered, with high expectations for education and achievement, and a value of cultural and intellectual activities.
(c) While families of gifted children have been found to have general close relationships, with flexibility and bonding, others have been found to experience

stress, disorganization and dysfunctional inter-actions.

(d) Moon and Hall discuss that family therapists, while they are experts in family dynamics, do not have the expertise regarding the unique cognitive and affective characteristics of gifted children. With some parents seeking guidance in family issues, family therapists (and school counselors) will need to complement their clinical expertise with knowledge of giftedness so that they can be effective helpers for these parents.

Sibling Relationships and the Label 'Gifted'

School counselors should anticipate difficulties in families when a child is first labeled *gifted*. It is at this time that the family needs assistance. First, school counselors need to be certain that parents clearly understand why their child has been identified as gifted. Many counselors hold parent discussion groups to clarify this issue. Second, counselors should help families anticipate changes as they attempt to adjust to the label. For siblings, the *gifted* label throws into question their role and their importance in the family.

Cornell and Grossberg (1986) found that in families with labeled gifted children, the non-labeled children are more prone to personality adjustment problems. Grenier (1985) reported increased competition and diminished cooperation by non-labeled siblings (see review by Jenkins-Friedman, 1992; Moon & Hall, 1998).

The good news is that the family will become accustomed to the label and positive adjustments are likely over time. Colangelo & Brower (1987) reported that, after a while, the negative effects of labeling disappear. Counselors can effectively ease the initial strain and disruption by helping the family communicate openly about the gifted label. Also, families simply alerted to likely changes seem better able to take some strain and disruption in stride and thus appear to adjust even more quickly.

Giftedness as a Family Organizer

In working with families of gifted children, it is fair to ask, "To what extent is any issue simply what all families must confront, and to what extent is this issue unique because of the presence of a gifted child?" Giftedness in many families becomes an 'organizer'— that is, a rationale for understanding behavior and actions (see Jenkins-Friedman, 1992).

In some families, behaviors are tolerated because the parents perceive that "this is how it is with a gifted child," or not tolerated because, "such behavior should not come from a gifted child." The giftedness of a child can structure how parents relate to him or her as well as siblings (Moon & Hall, 1998). Many families feel they must put greater energy and resources into the development of a gifted child's talents. Negatives from such organizers can occur when a family loses

'balance' with regard to the needs of other children. As in any case of exceptionality (e.g. a child with a disability), the 'exceptionality' can organize the energy and resources of a family, at times to the detriment of other aspects of the family.

A Family Counseling Program

At The Connie Belin & Jacqueline N. Blank International Center for Gifted Education and Talent Development (Belin-Blank Center), we have established a family counseling program to respond to the needs of families with a gifted child. The brief counseling approach lasts a maximum of five to six sessions per family. The focus is on helping the family develop its own strengths in the resolution of issues. Families receive services at no cost, and in return for these services they participate in research related to family counseling.

The majority of families who participated in the Belin-Blank Center Clinic sought services for their gifted child's perceived underachievement. The perception is an important concept in the work that we do with families. In some cases, there was significant underachievement. In others, however, the notion of underachievement was the 'symptom' that initiated the contact with the Belin-Blank Center's Clinic. It was not so much a case of the student underachieving as an issue of expectations.

We have also found that although a child's 'giftedness' may be the stated reason for seeking counseling, there are often other issues within these families that have been subsumed under giftedness (e.g. marital discord, alcoholism, delinquency). When this is the case, the families are referred to a family counselor who can provide longer-term therapy.

Parent-School Interactions

One of the most important issues confronting school counselors is the parent-school relationship (Dettmann & Colangelo, 1980; Colangelo & Dettmann, 1983, 1985; Moon & Hall, 1998). The underlying issue regarding this relationship is the role the school should take in providing special educational opportunities for gifted students. Colangelo & Dettmann (1982) developed a counseling model conceptualizing four types of parent-school interactions involving gifted students (Fig. 1).

Type I (cooperation) is an interaction based on the attitude by both parents and schools that the school should be active in gifted education. The tendency here is for open sharing of information about the child and cooperation between parents and schools. Typically, the gifted are identified and given special educational opportunities commensurate with their needs. The underlying assumption by both parents and schools is that the most effective way to develop exceptional ability is through overt special educational considerations based upon objective information concerning the student's learning needs (e.g. honors classes, advanced classes, resource rooms, independent projects, ability groupings, and grade skipping).

Type II (conflict) is an interaction based on conflicting attitudes by (active) parents and a (passive) school regarding the role of the school. Parents believe that their gifted child needs special programming by the school in order to develop his or her abilities. However, the school believes that the typical school curriculum is adequate to meet the needs of all youngsters, including the gifted. Also, it is typical for the school to believe that special programs should be a priority for students with disabilities. The school in this situation feels that

parents are pushy and demand unnecessary attention for gifted youngsters. The parents feel they must be aggressive, or the school will ignore the needs of their child.

Type II interactions are often the most difficult for parents and school. These schools tend to view gifted education as an albatross. Parents tend not to support the school and often blame the school for problems their child may have with boredom or lack of motivation and achievement. Parents sometimes encourage the child not to accept the school's evaluations and requirements (e.g. report card grades, class work) as accurate assessments of his or her abilities.

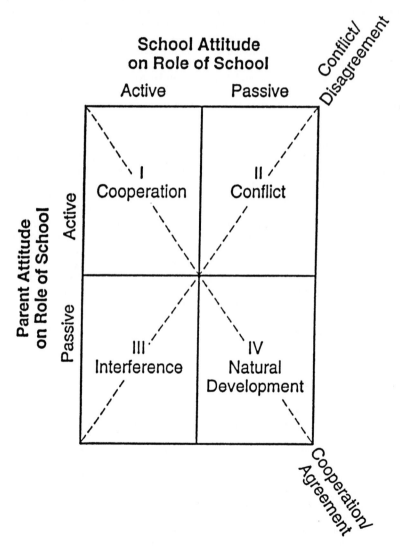

Figure 1. A Conceptual Model of Four Types of Parent-School Interactions

Source: Reprinted by permission of the authors and publisher from N. Colangelo and D. F. Dettman (1982), "A Conceptual Model of Four Types of Parent-School Interactions," *Journal for the Education of the Gifted*, Vol. 5, pp. 120–126

We have found that parents usually take one of three approaches in this Type II conflict. One is that they continually fight the school. They may either demand meetings for further discussion or join forces with other parents to assert their position. In the second approach, parents take it upon themselves to provide the special programs needed by a child. These may include summer enrichment activities, museum trips, college courses, tutors, mentors, and sometimes even private schools. Obviously, this approach is limited by educational background and financial resources of the parents. The third approach occurs when parents feel hopeless. They believe that they can have no real effect and that all they can do is complain. For many parents, the end result is a withdrawal from direct communication with the school.

Type III (interference) interactions are also based on conflict, but with a reversal of the dynamics found in Type II. In Type III the school actively wants to provide for the gifted child but the parents do not agree. Parents are unsure if special programs for the gifted are helpful or necessary. They are concerned about what effect identification and labeling may have on their (gifted) child as well as on siblings who may not be identified. Parents may be concerned that special recognition will damage their child's peer relationships. Parents may also view identification and special programs as an interference in the normal educational development of their child. Meanwhile, the school believes that the child *does* need special consideration and is willing to provide it. Of course, the school is often frustrated by the parents' refusal to let their child participate in the school's special program.

Type IV (natural development) interactions are based on agreement by both parents and schools that the role of the school should be passive. This belief is founded on the premise that high ability will take care of itself ("cream rises to the top") and that very little can be done meaningfully to nourish extraordinary ability. Essentially, both parents and schools view the typical school curriculum and extra-curricular activities as providing enough challenge and variety to stimulate the development of high potential and ability. In Type IV interactions, parents and schools recognize and support the youngster's efforts but believe that the natural development of talent will take its course, if the talent is truly there.

Implications of Parent-School Interactions

The model in Fig. 1 accounts for both *process* and *outcome*. The process relates to the nature of the interactions—that is, cooperative or conflictual. The outcome relates to the four possible types of content and results of the interactions when parents and school communicate about the school's role in gifted education.

The model can be used as a diagnostic instrument for helping both parents and school staff understand their interactions. The model also provides counselors with a framework for understanding their interactions with parents and other school staff—thus gaining insight into *how* they will deal with issues regarding programming for gifted children. Counselors can use this model not only to determine the type of interaction that *exists* between the school and parents, but also to assess what type of interaction would be *preferred*.

Underachievement

Perhaps the most intense counseling focus has been on the underachieving gifted student. In the Family Counseling program at The Connie Belin & Jacqueline N. Blank International Center for Gifted Education and Talent Development, underachievement has been the number one presenting problem. The issue of underachievement is confusing because of disagreement about its definition and the inconsistency of results from interventions (Whitmore, 1980; Dowdall & Colangelo, 1982; Delisle, 1992; Peterson & Colangelo, 1996; Reis, 1998).

Underachievement is seen as a discrepancy between assessed potential and actual performance. The discrepancy may be between two standardized measures (e.g. IQ and achievement tests), or between a standardized measure and classroom performance (e.g. teacher expectation and performance on daily assignments). The label 'gifted underachiever' implies a learner with a high level of potential (Reis, 1998). There are some measures, usually a standardized test, where a student meets the criteria for giftedness, while actual school performance is well below the assessed potential.

There have been a number of attempts to categorize underachievers. Reis (1998) distinguished between chronic and temporary (situational) underachievement. Temporary underachievement is often in response to a situational stress or event (e.g. divorce, loss of a friend, problems with a teacher). A chronic underachiever is one who has a 'history' and pattern of underachievement which appear to cut across a particular incident or circumstance.

Whitmore (1980) proposed three types of underachievers: aggressive, withdrawn, and combination. Aggressive students demonstrate disruptive and rebellious behaviors; withdrawn underachievers are bored and uninvolved. The third type is a combination of aggressive and withdrawn and the underachiever vacillates between aggressive and withdrawn behaviors.

Delisle (1992) proposes the categories of underachiever and a non-producer. Delisle makes an extensive comparison between the two categories. For counselors, however, the most important distinction revolves around the counseling needs of the student. The non-producer has minimal counseling needs and is the type of student whose non-productive behaviors can be reversed with minimal intervention. Underachieving behaviors require a strong counseling program that may include family counseling. Most significantly, underachievement, according to Delisle is a problem that demands a long-term solution.

To a school counselor, technical definitions and categories are not as critical as the interpersonal dynamics involved in underachievement. Rather than looking at it as a psychometric event, we see it as a relationship between the gifted student and teachers, parent(s), and sometimes peers. For some gifted students underachievement is a way to express either a need for attention or a need for control over a situation. Underachievement brings considerable attention from both teachers and parents, in extreme cases almost doting behavior. Adults are so concerned that the gifted youngster will not make good use of his or her gifts that they give a great deal of energy and time to the student.

Counselors can often break the attention-getting cycle by having parents and teaches avoid responding too strongly to the underachieving behavior or even ignoring it. They can give attention when the child achieves well and minimize attention when the child is not achieving. The equation is simple. If the child wants attention, he or she will soon learn that the attention is forthcoming only when certain achieving behaviors (and attitudes) are present. The child will want to do more of these kinds of behaviors because the reward is the attention.

A gifted youngster who uses underachievement as a means to gain control of a situation offers a more difficult challenge. For such youngsters, poor achievement is a way to show teachers and parents that they (the students) can do what they want. A typical reaction by teachers and parents to this kind of defiance is to attempt to force the student to do the task and do it at levels comparable to expectation. This situation can lead to a vicious and non-useful cycle of 'power struggle'. The counselor can work with teachers and parents to help them quit the fight. It is likely the student will diminish the fight relationship if there is no one to fight with.

Minimizing the power struggle will allow more opportunity for the student to perform because he or she is more free to do so. Again, we propose that group counseling can help gifted students better understand their behaviors and motives and learn new patterns of interactions. It is in the rich atmosphere of a group of peers with a trained leader (school counselor) that a gifted youngster can explore motives and consequences of underachieving behavior.

Finally, it is important for the school counselor to use school records as a source of information in understanding gifted underachievers, especially at the secondary level. In a comprehensive study of 153 gifted underachievers, grades 7–12, Peterson and

Colangelo (1996) found data on attendance, tardiness, course selection and course grades, by gender and by age, that provided differential patterns that distinguished gifted students who achieved from those who underachieved. Peterson and Colangelo reported that patterns of underachievement established in junior high school, though not impossible to alter in high school, do tend to persist through high school. The school records are ubiquitous in schools and are a good resource for counselors.

While the issues surrounding underachievement are complex and research findings inconclusive and even contradictory, Reis (1998) provides a good summary of the current research on underachievement in the following eight points:

First, it appears that the beginnings of underachievement in many young people occur in elementary school.

Second, underachievement appears to be periodic and episodic, occurring some years and not others and in some classes, but not others.

Third, a direct relationship seems to exist between inappropriate or too-easy content in elementary school and underachievement in middle or high school.

Fourth, parental issues interact with the behaviors of some underachievers, yet no clear pattern exists about the types of parental behaviors that cause underachievement.

Fifth, peers can play a major role in keeping underachievement from occurring in their closest friends, making peer groups an important part of preventing and reversing underachievement.

Sixth, busier adolescents who are involved in clubs, extracurricular activities, sports and religious activities are less likely to underachieve in school.

Seventh, many similar behavioral characteristics are exhibited by bright students who achieve and underachieve in school.

Eight, there are some students who may underachieve as a direct result of an inappropriate and unmotivating curriculum.

Dual Exceptionalities

Much of the literature on underachievement either states or implies psychological undercurrents (e.g. intrapersonal, interpersonal, and family dynamics). While the psychological issues have clearly been shown to play a role in underachievement, it is critical to note that not all underachievement behaviors have a psychological root. The presence of learning and developmental disabilities have been shown to be associated with both giftedness and underachievement.

The later 1980s as well as the 1990s brought a new awareness to the field of gifted education: gifted students who also have disabilities, especially learning, developmental, and social-emotional disabilities. Dual exceptionalities may include: autistic savant syndrome; developmental delays in speech, language and motor coordination; disruptive behavior (including conduct and oppositional-defiant disorders); anxieties, and eating disorders (Moon & Hall, 1998). Gifted children may also have specific learning disorders (LD), and attention deficit/hyperactivity disorder (AD/HD) (Moon & Hall, 1998).

The most common behavior disorder in gifted children is AD/HD (Moon & Hall, 1998) which can interfere with academic and social functioning. For gifted with LD or AD/HD, individualized testing will reflect patterns of inconsistency across talent areas (Moon & Hall, 1998). Multiple testing methods are typically needed to pinpoint areas of giftedness and disability (Moon & Dillon, 1995).

Dual-exceptionality students are at risk for under-achievement because they will have barriers to achieving at their level of giftedness. Such students can become easily frustrated (and frustrating) since their inability to perform or 'behave' can bring about questions regarding their motivation and commitment. From observation, it seems dual exceptionalities are more common than most educators may think.

We strongly recommend a battery of individualized tests to determine exceptionalities in cases where gifted students are underachieving in academics and unable to function effectively in the classroom. Dual exceptionalities require a 'team' approach. School psychologists are in the best position to test and diagnose exceptionalities while the school counselor (and at times a school social worker) has the expertise for counseling the student and family regarding the dual exceptionalities.

School Counseling Programs for Gifted Students

There are two ways to envision a school counseling program for gifted students: as *remedial* or as *developmental*. In the remedial approach, the emphasis is on problem solving and crisis intervention. In this approach, the counselor is primarily a 'therapy expert' who intervenes in problem situations either to help solve the problem or to minimize the difficulty. The counselor is involved in staffing, referrals, and one-on-one counseling. Where there is group counseling, the students are selected because they share a common problem (e.g. underachievement, behavior problems), and the purpose is to correct the problem.

In the developmental approach, the counselor does use his or her expertise to serve a therapeutic function and is available for problem solving, but therapy and problem solving are not their primary purpose. The real work of the developmentally oriented counselor is to establish an environment in school that is conducive to the educational growth of gifted students. Such an approach is predicated on knowledge of both affective and cognitive needs of gifted youngsters. The focus of individual counseling is to get to know students and help them better understand their own strengths and weaknesses as decision makers and formulators of their lives.

Group counseling focuses on sharing perceptions and learning more effective interpersonal skills. Group members do not necessarily have a common problem to resolve. Work with families is based not on a problem with their child, but on the recognition that gifted children pose a unique challenge to parents. Family work is based more on discussion groups with parents in which the parents share information and connect with other families.

We strongly advocate a developmental approach to counseling with gifted students; giftedness is not a problem to be solved but a unique challenge to be nourished. In a therapy model, evidence of a problem would be necessary to justify having a counselor with expertise in working with the gifted. However, a developmental approach does not depend on research evidence that gifted youngsters are 'at risk'.

A developmental counseling program requires the following components:

(1) An articulated and coherent rationale.
(2) A program of activities based on the affective and cognitive needs of youngsters.
(3) Trained counselors who are well grounded not only in counseling but also in giftedness.
(4) A minimum of attention to rehabilitative (therapy) services, but a strong component of individual, family, and teacher consultations.
(5) Input and participation from teachers, administrators, parents, and the youngsters who are served.
(6) A component for the continued professional development of the counselor so that he or she may keep pace with the latest research and practices on the counseling needs of gifted youngsters.

Summary

Although concern for the counseling needs of gifted students can be traced back to Leta Hollingworth's work of nearly seventy years ago, the emergence of counseling as a major force in the education of the gifted and talented is a phenomenon of the last two decades. Individual, group, and family counseling are predicated on the assumption and evidence that youngsters with exceptional ability and talents also have unique social and emotional needs.

These unique needs exist and interact in the successful or unsuccessful development of talent. Counseling is a necessary component in the successful development of talent. For counselors to be successful, they need knowledge and expertise both in counseling and in giftedness. A developmental counseling program in a school will foster both the cognitive and the affective growth of gifted youngsters.

References

Achter, J. A., Benbow, C. P. & Lubinski, D. (1997). Rethinking multipotentiality among the intellectually gifted: A critical review and recommendations. *Gifted Child Quarterly*, **41**, 5–15.

Achter, J. A., Lubinski, D. & Benbow, C. P. (1996). Multipotentiality among the intellectually gifted: It was never there and already it's vanishing. *Journal of Counseling Psychology*, **43**, 65–76.

American Association for Gifted Children (1978). *On being gifted*. New York: Walker & Company.

Bloom, B. S. (Ed.). (1985). *Developing talent in young people*. New York: Ballantine Books.

Bloom, B. S., & Sosniak, L. A. (1981). Talent development vs. schooling. *Educational Leadership*, **39**, 86–94.

Burks, B. S., Jensen, D. W. & Terman, L. M. (1930). *Genetic studies of genius: Vol. 3. The promise of youth*. Stanford, CA: Stanford University Press.

Cash, A. B. (1999). The profile of gifted individuals with autism: The twice-exceptional learners. *Roeper Review*, **22**, 22–27.

Colangelo, N. (1988). Families of gifted children: The next ten years. *Roeper Review*, **11**, 16–18.

Colangelo, N. (1997). Counseling gifted students: Issues and practices. In: N. Colangelo & G. A. Davis (Eds.), *Handbook of gifted education* (2nd ed.) (pp. 353–365). Needham Heights, MA: Allyn and Bacon.

Colangelo, N. (1991). Counseling gifted students. In: N. Colangelo & G. A. Davis (Eds.), *Handbook of gifted education* (pp. 273–284). Boston: Allyn and Bacon.

Colangelo, N. & Assouline, S. G. (1993). Families of gifted children: A research agenda. *Quest*, **4**, 1–4.

Colangelo, N., & Assouline, S. G. (1995). Self-concept of gifted students: Patterns by self-concept, domain, grade level, and gender. In: F. Monks (Ed.), *Proceedings from the 1994 European Council on High Ability Conference* (pp. 66–74). New York: Wiley.

Colangelo, N., & Brower, P. (1987). Labeling gifted youngsters: Long-term impact on families. *Gifted Child Quarterly*, **31**, 75–78.

Colangelo, N. & Davis, G. A. (Eds.) (1997). *Handbook of gifted education 2nd ed.* Boston: Allyn and Bacon.

Colangelo, N. & Dettmann, D. F. (1982). A conceptual model of four types of parent-school interactions. *Journal for the Education of the Gifted*, **5**, 120–126.

Colangelo, N. & Dettmann, D. F. (1983). A review of research on parents and families of gifted children. *Exceptional Children*, **50**, 20–27.

Colangelo, N. & Dettmann, D. F. (1985). Families of gifted children. In: S. Ehly, J. Conoly & D. M. Rosenthal (Eds.), *Working with Parents of Exceptional Children* (pp. 233–255). St. Louis: C. V. Mosby.

Colangelo, N. & Kelly, K. R. (1983). A study of student, parent, and teacher attitude towards gifted programs and gifted students. *Gifted Child Quarterly*, **27**, 107–110.

Colangelo, N. & Kerr, B. (1990). Extreme academic talent: profiles of perfect scorers. *Journal of Educational Psychology*, **82**, 404–409.

Colangelo, N. & Peterson, J. S. (1993). Group counseling with gifted students. In: L. S. Silverman (Ed.), *Counseling the Gifted and Talented* (pp. 111–129). Denver: Love.

Colangelo, N. & Zaffrann, R. T. (Eds.). (1979). *New voices in counseling the gifted*. Dubuque, IA: Kendall Hunt.

Cornell, D. G. & Grossberg, I. W. (1986). Siblings of children in gifted programs. *Journal for the Education of the Gifted*, **9**, 252–264.

Dawes, R. M. (1998). The social usefulness of self-esteem: A skeptical review. *The Harvard Mental Health Letter*, **15**(4), 4–5.

Delisle, J. R. (1984). *Gifted children speak out*. New York: Walker.

Delisle, J. R. (1987). *Gifted kids speak out*. Minneapolis: Free Spirit.

Delisle, J. R. (1992). *Guiding the social and emotional development of gifted youth*. New York: Longman.

Dettmann, D. F. & Colangelo, N. (1980). A functional model for counseling parents of gifted students. *Gifted Child Quarterly*, **24**, 139–147.

Dowdall, C. B. & Colangelo, N. (1982). Underachieving gifted students: Review and implications. *Gifted Child Quarterly*, **26**, 179–184.

Frederickson, R. H. & Rothney, J. W. M. (Eds.) (1972). *Recognizing and assisting multipotential youth*. Columbus, OH: Merrill.

Grenier, M. E. (1985). Gifted children and other siblings. *Gifted Child Quarterly*, **29**, 164–167.

Harter, S. (1982). The perceived competence scale for children. *Child Development*, **53**, 87–97.

Hoge, R. D. & McSheffrey, R. (1991, December-January). An investigation of self-concept in gifted children. *Exceptional Children*, pp. 238–245.

Hoge, R. D. & Renzulli, J. S. (1993). Exploring the link between giftedness and self-concept. *Review of Educational Research*, **63**, 449–465.

Holahan, C. K. & Sears, R. S. (1995). *The gifted group in later maturity*. Stanford, CA: Stanford University Press.

Hollingworth, L. S. (1926). *Gifted children: Their nature and nurture*. New York: Macmillan.

Hollingworth, L. S. (1942). *Children above 180 IQ*. New York: World Book.

Jenkins-Friedman, R. (1992). Families of gifted children and youth. In: M. J. Fine & C. Carlson (Eds), *The Handbook of Family School Interventions: a Systems Perspective* (pp. 175–187). Boston: Allyn and Bacon.

Karnes, F. A. & Wherry, J. N. (1981). Self-concepts of gifted students as measured by the Piers-Harris children's self-concept scale. *Psychological Reports*, **49**, 903–906.

Kaufmann, F. (1981). The 1964–1968 Presidential Scholars: a follow-up study. *Exceptional Children*, **48**, 164–169.

Kelly, K. R. & Colangelo, N. (1984). Academic and social self-concepts of gifted, general, and special students. *Exceptional Children*, **50**, 551–554.

Kerr, B. A. (1985). *Smart girls; gifted women*. Columbus, OH: Ohio Psychology Publications.

Kerr, B. A. (1986). Career counseling for the gifted: assessments and interventions. *Journal of Counseling and Development*, **64**, 602–604.

Kerr, B. A. (1991). *Handbook for counseling the gifted and talented*. Alexandria: VA: AACD Press.

Kerr, B. A. (Summer/Fall 1998). Career planning for gifted and talented youth. *Iowa Talented and Gifted Newsletter.*

Kerr, B. & Colangelo, N. (1988). The college plans of academically talented students. *Journal of Counseling and Development,* **67,** 42–48.

Kerr, B., Colangelo, N. & Gaeth, J. (1988). Gifted adolescents' attitudes toward their giftedness. *Gifted Child Quarterly,* **32,** 245–247.

Ketcham, B. & Snyder, R. T. (1977). Self-attitudes of the intellectually and socially advantaged student: Normative study of the Piers-Harris children's self-concept scale. *Psychological Reports,* **40,** 111–116.

Loeb, R. C. & Jay, G. (1987). Self concept in gifted children: Differential impact in boys and girls. *Gifted Child Quarterly,* **1,** 9–14.

Maddux, C. D., Scheiber, L. M. & Bass, J. E. (1982). Self-concept and social distance in gifted children. *Gifted Child Quarterly,* **26,** 77–81.

Marsh, H. W. (1990). A multidimensional, hierarchical model of self-concept: Theoretical and empirical justification. *Educational Psychology Review,* **2,** 77–172.

Marsh, H. W. (1992). Content specificity of relations between academic achievement and academic self-concept. *Journal of Educational Psychology,* **84,** 35–42.

Marsh, H. W. (1993). The multidimensional structure of academic self-concept: Invariance over gender and age. *American Educational Research Journal,* **30,** 841–860.

Marsh, H. W. (1994). Using the national longitudinal study of 1988 to evaluate theoretical models of self-concept: The self-description questionnaire. *Journal of Educational Psychology,* **86,** 439–456.

McGuire, W. J. (1984). Search for self: Going beyond self-esteem and reactive self. In: R. A. Zucher, J. Arnoff & A. I Rubin (Eds.), *Personality and the Prediction of Behavior* (pp. 73–120). New York, Academic Press.

McKernan, J. R. (Chair). (1994). *The national education GOALS report.* Washington, DC: U.S. Government Printing Office.

Monaster, G. J., Chan, J. C., Walt, C. & Wiehe, J. (1994). Gifted adolescents' attitudes toward their giftedness: A partial replication. *Gifted Child Quarterly,* **38,** 176–178.

Moon, S. M. & Hall, A. S. (1998). Family therapy with intellectually and creatively gifted children. *Journal of Marital and Family Therapy,* **24,** 59–80.

Moon, S. M. & Dillon, D. R. (1995). Multiple exceptionalities: A case study. *Journal of the Education of the Gifted.* **18,** 111–130.

Myers, R. S. & Pace, T. M. (1986). Counseling gifted and talented students: Historical perspectives and contemporary issues. *Journal of Counseling and Development,* **64,** 548–551.

Neihart, M. (1999). The import of giftedness and psychological well-being: What does the empirical literature say? *Roeper Review,* **22,** 10–17.

Nurius, P. S. (1986). Reappraisal of the self-concept and implications for counseling. *Journal of Counseling Psychology,* **33,** 429–438.

Peterson, J. S. & Colangelo, N. (1996). Gifted achievers and underachievers: A comparison of patterns found in school files. *Journal of Counseling and Development,* **74,** 399–407.

Reis, S. (Winter 1998). Underachieving for some: Dropping out with dignity for others. *Communicator,* **29** (1), Newsletter of the California Association for the Gifted.

Rogers, C. (1951). *Client-centered therapy: its current practice, implications, and theory.* Boston: Houghton Mifflin.

Rysiew, K. J., Shore, B. M. & Leeb, R. T. (1999) Multipotentiality, giftedness and career choices: A review. *Journal of Counseling & Development,* **77,** 423–430.

Rysiew, K. J., Shore, B. M. & Carson, A. D. (1994). Multipotentiality and overchoice syndrome: Clarifying common usage. *Gifted and Talent International,* **9**(2), 41–46.

Shavelson, R. J., Hubner, J. J. & Stanton, G. C. (1976). Validation of construct interpretations. *Review of Educational Research,* **46,** 407–441.

Silverman, L. K. (Ed.). (1993). *Counseling the gifted & talented.* Denver: Love.

Snygg, D. & Combs, A. W. (1949). *Individual behaviors: A perceptual approach to behavior* (rev. ed.). New York: Harper.

St. Clair, K. L., (1989). Counseling gifted students: A historical review. *Roeper Review,* **12,** 98–102.

Terman, L. M. (1925). *Genetic studies of genius* (Vol. 1). *Mental and physical traits of a thousand gifted children.* Stanford, CA: Stanford University Press.

Terman, L. M. & Oden, M. H. (1947). *Genetic studies of genius.* (Vol. 4). *The gifted child grows up.* Stanford, CA: Stanford University Press.

Terman, L. M. & Oden, M. H. (1959). *Genetic studies of genius.* (Vol. 5). *The gifted group at mid-life.* Stanford, CA: Stanford University Press.

Webb, J. T., Meckstroth, E. A. & Tolan, S. S. (1982). *Guiding the gifted child.* Columbus: Ohio Psychology Press.

Wendorf, D. J. & Frey, J. (1985). Family therapy with intellectually gifted. *American Journal of Family Therapy,* **13,** 31–37.

Whitmore, J. (1980). *Giftedness, conflict, and underachievement.* Boston: Allyn and Bacon.

Wylie, R. C. (1989). *Measures of self-concept.* Lincoln: University of Nebraska Press.

Yalom, I. D. (1985). *The theory and practice of group psychotherapy* (3rd ed.). New York: Basic Books.

Underachievement in Gifted Children and Adolescents: Theory and Practice

Willy A. M. Peters, Helga Grager-Loidl and Patricia Supplee

Center for the Study of Giftedness, University of Nijmegen, Netherlands

Introduction

One of the risks that gifted students face is underachievement. According to Richert (1991) there is reason to assume that "at least 50% of students identified through IQ have been designated as academic underachievers" (p. 140). This figure does not include students who were identified as gifted on a basis other than an IQ-test, so the problem seems widespread among the population of gifted students.

The most basic definition of underachievement is a discrepancy between actual achievement and intelligence. In the famous study by Terman, it appeared that gifted individuals did not achieve as well as could be expected on the basis of their intelligence scores (Terman & Oden, 1947). Durr (1964) defined underachievement as a difference between IQ-score and actual school achievement, measured in grades or achievement tests. However, the measurement of ability or the potential to achieve is problematic according to Raph, Goldberg & Passow (1966). For that reason, many attempts have been made to operationalize underachievement in ways that minimize the three problematic measurement issues: ability, performance and the discrepancy between them. Despite the difficulty, according to Tannenbaum (1991) one should try to define underachievement because there are few teachers who would deny the existence of students who exhibit this phenomenon. He cited Thorndike (1963, in Tannenbaum, 1991) who warned researchers to be careful and keep psychometric theory in mind while operationalizing underachievement.

There have been many descriptions of ability domains. Tannenbaum (1993) gives several examples, with the Marland report being of historical interest for its influence on provisions for gifted students in the USA. Supplee (1990) cites the Education Consolidation and Improvement Act (PL 97–35) which defines gifted children as those "who give evidence of high performance capability in areas such as intellectual, creative, artistic, leadership capacity, or specific aca-demic fields, and who require services or activities not ordinarily provided by the school in order to fully develop such capabilities" (Sec. 582). This text implicitly suggests that some children will not develop their potential if special support is not given, thus becoming underachievers. Gardner (1983) is currently influential in enumerating domains of ability.

The achievement-oriented and socio-cultural/psychosocial oriented models of giftedness (Mönks & Mason, 1993) include other variables in addition to general intelligence that must be present to allow gifted potential to develop and lead to high level achievement (e.g. Renzulli, 1978; Tannenbaum, 1983; Heller 1992). By default, this model of giftedness implicitly recognizes the fact that ability does not automatically imply achievement of the same level. Intervening factors can lead to lower achievement.

The lack of a widely accepted model of giftedness or consensus about the nature of intelligence implies that every theory about underachievement must be evaluated within the framework of a specifically defined theory of intelligence. This chapter deals with underachievers in the realm of logical-mathematical and verbal intelligence as Gardner (1983) would describe it.

Among the factors that contribute to underachievement, motivation can be regarded as one of the most important. Loss of motivation accompanies a decrease in achievement (Terman & Oden, 1947; Rimm, 1986; Butler-Por, 1993). Kaufmann (1999) has a different approach, seeing underachievement as a result of discouragement. Kaufmann's position might lead to a different view on interventions, but also recognizes the role of the environment in bringing about underachievement.

In this chapter, first the identification of underachievement is discussed. Assessing underachievement is viewed in two strands. The first type of assessment is through the practice of education and counseling. It is a task for teachers and counselors to recognize underachievement when it happens. Researchers carry out the second strand. They assess underachievement in order to be able to study the phenomenon and develop strategies to overcome it. Groups at risk are discussed before factors that induce underachievement are presented. These factors include family and school factors, the influence of peers, and personality characteristics of the individual. To conclude, programs and intervention strategies are presented.

Identification of Underachievers

In Research

Due to the lack of consensus regarding the nature of the discrepancy, it appears nearly impossible to create standards. The empirical literature reveals a number of different approaches to the problem of distinguishing between achievers and underachievers, each using criteria that are to some extent arbitrary (Ziegler, Dresel & Schober, 2000). An early attempt to set a standard was carried out by Shaw (1964). It was proposed that in those cases where the IQ-score belonged to the top quartile while achievement scores were below average, one might truly speak of underachievement. However, as Span (1988) stated, achievement scores can be on or above an average level and still the difference between achievement and ability can be so great that it is appropriate to speak about underachievement. Hanses & Rost (1998) believed that a relative criterion alone would not be sufficient. A student with an IQ score of 160, for example, and school results at the 95th percentile could be underachieving. Of course, one could argue that the reliability of the measurement of IQ scores at that level is so very low that the argument does not hold in practice

Ziegler, Dresel & Schober (2000) proposed an assessment procedure in four phases. It is the first phase that is of interest here. The discrepancy between actual and expected achievement has to be determined. According to these authors, there are so many ways to measure actual achievement in the school as well as in other domains, that this part would not be problematic. The measurement of expected achievement is another matter. The diagnosis of what can be expected from a student has to be determined from several variables that predict achievement. The decision of which variables to include depends on the framework of the specifically defined theory of intelligence in which the concept of underachievement is couched, the theoretical perspective. When sound criteria in the form of standardized tests are not available to measure ability, so-called Delphi-criteria may be used. These are estimations of experts in the field, e.g. a sports trainer, who can estimate the possible level that a pupil might attain. However, this type of assessment yields great problems in the case of academic underachievers. Prejudice may arise in the minds of raters due to long

lasting underachievement, and an intelligence test seems to be essential in order to counteract it.

It must be clear that intelligence is not the only variable that would predict achievement. Ziegler et al. (2000) pointed to the criterion proposed by Hanses & Rost (1998) who formulated the significant discrepancy as the difference between ability at the top 5% and achievement below 50%. A similar criterion was formulated by Colangelo, Kerr, Christensen & Maxey (1993). Unfortunately, using these criteria, students who attain school results on or a little above average are not considered to be underachievers. As Ziegler et al. (2000) noticed, this criterion as well as the use of one standard deviation are both arbitrary; they suggest that everyone should establish criterion of their own.

Thorndike (1963, in Tannenbaum, 1991) warned of methodological problems in the determination of underachievers. He suggested the following questions as guidelines:

(1) Have I an appropriate procedure for determining expected achievement?
   (a) Have I taken account of statistical regression?
   (b) Have I used the best team of predictors to establish expected achievement? Have I included aptitude? Initial achievement? Other appropriate factors?
(2) Do I have a criterion measure of achievement that has the same meaning for all cases?
   (a) Have I procedures to check for criterion heterogeneity?
   (b) Have I a plan to deal with heterogeneity if it is found?
(3) Am I aware of the effect of errors of measurement on my study
   (a) In reducing sensitivity?
   (b) In producing bias? (p. 65).

Thorndike's questions remain a solid basis on which to develop criteria that have greater authority, if only because of the psychometric standards that are set. Similar to these guidelines, Van Boxtel, Mönks, Roelofs & Sanders (1986) developed a methodologically sound procedure to identify underachievers. This procedure is based on psychometric theory and takes into account the psychometric properties of the measurement procedures that are used. Basically, their approach focuses on the discrepancy between obtained test scores for intelligence and school results that are reflected in grades. The first step is to transform both test results and school grades to standardized scores $(\overline{X} = 100, s = 15)$. In assessing the intelligence score, one has to deal with the regression effect. This means that extreme scores usually reflect a true score that lies closer to the mean. So, the intelligence score has to be corrected for this regression to the mean. The school grades consist of repeated measures, since the grades should be obtained not from one test only, but preferably by taking the average results over a longer period of time. The next step would be to determine the regression equation for the 'prediction' of school results on the basis of the intelligence score. This regression equation is needed to determine the reliability of the difference between the 'predicted' and the actual school results. With the reliability coefficient, it can be determined whether a difference between actual and 'predicted' school results is significant (p. 171–176). This procedure was used in later empirical research (Van Boxtel & Mönks, 1992, p. 175–176).

Another procedure was proposed by Lupart & Pyryt (1996). In their approach, the first step was to determine the correlation between the IQ and school achievement, as expressed in the last report form from the school. Next, the expected achievement was determined in different school subjects on the basis of the IQ-score. The standard error of estimate for predicting grades in each school subject was determined and the actual achievement score was subtracted from the predicted achievement scores. Finally, individuals with a discrepancy beyond one standard error of estimate for the grades were nominated as underachievers. The rationale for this approach can be found in Thorndike (1963, in Tannenbaum, 1991).

In Practice

As in research, the assessment of underachievement in practical settings such as education and counseling does not have fixed standards. The procedures described above are hard to apply in practical settings such as schools.

A completely different approach was used by Baum, Renzulli & Hébert (1995). In their investigation, underachievers were assessed by asking the teachers to determine who was underachieving. These assessments were made by the classroom teachers and the teachers of special programs for gifted students.

Hany (1991) compared intricate scientific procedures with teachers' judgement. Although the standardized procedures yielded results, Hany suggested that teachers' judgements can be improved by informing them about aspects of giftedness and underachievement. The level of reliability of their judgement could then come close to the quality of standardized procedures.

Butler-Por (1993) also emphasized the importance of training teachers. She proposed a procedure for use in schools that is applicable when teachers possess a minimal understanding about underachievement. This procedure has five steps:

(1) Identification of discrepancies between cognitive abilities expressed in formulating questions and hypotheses and normal school performance in the accomplishment of assignments, homework, and tests.
(2) Identification of great differences between general and expert knowledge derived from extensive reading at home, yet failure to complete reading assignments at school.
(3) Comparison between a student's wide interests outside the school with minimal effort invested in school projects.
(4) Combined student and teacher evaluation of academic strengths and weaknesses, academic personal choices and effort invested in the different subjects.
(5) Consulting parents, previous teachers and professional personnel at school on student's learning habits and social behavior. A consistent drop in scholastic performance of approximately two years indicates that the student is underachieving. (p. 651).

In comparison to the meticulous pyschometric way of dealing with the identification problem in research, this practical approach gives criteria for teachers to use, teachers whose task is to work with children and improve their situation, not merely study them.

Other approaches to identifying underachievers in school settings have been reported in the literature. Peterson & Colangelo (1996) suggested that data from school files could be used to determine which students were underachieving. Variables that could be used were: attendance, tardiness, and course selection. Redding (1989) argued that (verbally gifted) underachievers lack task commitment and appreciation for detail. In the assessment procedure, the educator would be wise to focus on the possibility of partially high test scores. This means that full-scale scores such as IQ are not the only, maybe even not the most important, variable to consider. Attention should be paid to the pattern of subtests across domains to identify the areas in which strengths of the individual are to be found.

Underachievement in Testing Situations

A phenomenon that has attracted little explicit attention so far, is underachievement in testing situations. Of course, test anxiety is a known phenomenon, but it seems that investigators seldom take the implications into account. In addition to test anxiety, other factors may play a negative role during testing: high expectations of others, specific learning problems that are related to the testing procedure (e.g. multiple choice exams) and fear of failure due to unsuccessful experiences with tests (Kerr, 1991). Research of error patterns in test responses, shows that 'illogical' mistakes may point at certain characteristics of students that: (a) evoke underachievement behavior and (b) result in lower test scores than would have been appropriate (Peters & Van Boxtel, 1999). Investigators should keep in mind what Kaufman (1994) wrote about this:

When an examiner is able to relate observations of the child's behaviors in the testing situation to the profile of obtained scores (e.g. by noting that the child's anxiety disrupted test performance on all timed tasks), two things occur: (a) The examiner learns important information about the child that can be translated to practical educational suggestions, thereby enhancing the value of the intelligence test; and (b) the actual IQs earned by the child may become gross underestimates of his or her real intellectual abilities. In general, the actual IQs are valuable because they provide evidence of a child's mental functioning under a known set of conditions and permit comparison with youngsters of a comparable age. The value of the scores increases when the examiner functions as a true experimenter and tries to determine why the child earned the particular profile revealed on the record form; the IQs become harmful when they are unquestioningly interpreted as valid indicators of intellectual functioning and are misconstrued as evidence of the child's maximum or even typical performance. (p. 9).

Groups at Risk

There is ample evidence that certain groups of individuals are more prone to underachievement than others. When dealing with these groups, educators and counselors should be more open for signals that could indicate underachievement. A number of groups can be found in the literature to be at risk for underachievement. Feger & Prado (1998) and Butler-Por (1993) described a number of groups that can be distinguished:

(1) Geographic—ecological factors: Living in areas that offer few challenges due to geographic or ecological reasons.
(2) Ethnic factors: Being member of a nation that is discriminated against on the basis of ideological or religious reasons.
(3) Economic factors: Living in poverty or lacking the means to develop abilities.
(4) Gender factors: In many cases girls are in disadvantaged positions.
(5) Educational deprivation: Often due to the factors mentioned above, but also due to other reasons, such as the school providing too few opportunities.
(6) (Sub)-Cultural factors: Growing up in a sub-culture that is deviant from the dominating culture.
(7) Physical or psychological problems: Physical or psychological illness will have a negative effect on achievement.
(8) Family factors: Disturbed relations between parents and their children, e.g. when a child is unwanted or rejected, or when family stressors such as divorce or separation are present.
(9) Active disrespect for societal norms: Taking part in delinquent activities.

(10) Being highly creative: Children in this category may be pressed to become more conforming.

Gifted Girls

Gender is a returning theme in the search for factors that contribute to underachievement. Just as in giftedness in general, researchers have tried to learn from successful women how their development was shaped (Arnold, Noble & Subotnik, 1996). An important issue to be dealt with is whether girls themselves take an underachieving position due to certain personality or other factors, or whether the environment in which they grow up puts them in a vulnerable position.

There is evidence that personality characteristics play a role in turning girls into underachievers. Non-assertiveness, fear of success, perceived low social competence, and perceived negative self-concept could be identified as such (Hollinger & Fleming, 1984). Highly able girls are more at risk to develop psychosomatic illnesses such as anorexia nervosa, in comparison to girls with an average ability (Detzner & Schmidt, 1985). Girls show less ambition than do boys (Freeman, 1993) and hide their abilities (Kerr, 1991). In programs for science and maths, girls tend to be underrepresented (Wieczerkowski & Prado, 1992; Feldhusen & Jarwan, 1993), which might be due to a different value-system in girls which does not include pursuing academic achievement. The differences between girls and boys become more visible at the onset of adolescence, when the priority changes to social approval instead of academic achievement (McCormick & Wolf, 1993). Case studies have shown that gifted girls need an accepting and stimulating environment which supports their academic activities (Reis & Diaz, 1999).

Of course, these characteristics of girls do not exist in a social vacuum. The social environment influences the genesis of these characteristics to a large extent. One could argue that most, if not all, characteristics mentioned above are induced through environmental influence. Probably because of this, some authors have shifted their attention more explicitly to environmental influence on the (under)achievement of girls. Often the academic ability of girls remains unnoticed (Heinbokel, 1996). Parents, together with their daughters, tend to choose a lower form of higher education for girls than they do for boys (Freeman, 1993). Also participation in gifted programs is rejected more frequently for girls than for boys (Butler-Por, 1995). Academic success can lead to negative responses because it is not part of the set of characteristics expected of girls (Gallagher & Gallagher, 1994). It is the environment that urges girls to give up aspirations in the fields of science and maths (McCormick & Wolf, 1993). The phenomenon, which encourages girls not to accelerate, is called 'fear of success': the negative effects outweigh the positive. A stimulating environment for girls should offer them support to achieve and follow their own aspirations (Reis & Diaz, 1999).

Cultural Minorities

Another group that is prone to underachievement consists of children from cultural minorities. It is widely reported that these groups are under-represented in programs for gifted students (Butler-Por, 1993; Ford & Webb, 1994; Butler-Por, 1995; Ford & Thomas, 1997). One of the factors that may cause children from cultural minorities to appear to underachieve would be the fact that curriculum activities do not match their cultural competencies (Hébert, 1998). (Sub)cultural differences in values and beliefs influence achievement. If a (sub)culture does not acknowledge success at school as important, children from this background have to deal with different standards and expectations in the school and non-school worlds in which they live (Kitano, 1991; Ford, 1992, Ford & Harris, 1992). Another important factor that contributes to underachievement is the lack of early appropriate academic experiences (Diaz, 1998), yet different cultures hold widely different beliefs about the importance of formal preschool. These differences may affect the daily activities of children such as reading books and time usage.

Many children live the first years of their life in their own (sub)culture then enter school, an entirely different culture. An example of this is Turkish children in Berlin, Germany (Feger & Prado, 1998). The differences between cultures will yield differences in personality structures. The value conflict may affect their sense of self-worth (Ford & Thomas, 1997).

Children in Critical Situations

Environmental disadvantages that may lead to underachievement are connected with critical events that might take place within the family or within the direct living environment of the child. Such critical events might be: marriage problems between the parents or divorce, unstructured family relations, early separation of the child from the parents, especially the mother, birth of siblings, illness and death of family members, having handicapped siblings, and violence and/or sexual harassment within the family. No-one will wonder that these experiences will have a negative effect on the achievement potential of a child (Friedrich, 1998). Typical behaviors that follow such trauma could be a drop in achievement, concentration problems, memory gaps, and perceptual difficulties (p. 91). Other events may also have an effect that could be underestimated. Webb, Meckstroth, & Tolan (1982) noticed that gifted children are more sensitive than their peers. Because of this, they may experience more of an impact from stressful events. Typically results include avoiding contact and even more, being unable to concentrate simply because one's mind is some-

where else. Children might even unconsciously ask for help by dropping achievement. "The gifted student, aware of his or her reputation as an excellent scholar, may be counting on the counselor to notice the change in his or her grades, to comment upon them, and to offer help and support" (Kerr, 1991; p.62). Butler-Por (1993; 1995) asked for attention towards children in a divorce situation.

Etiology of Underachievement

Research on etiological factors of underachievement has made clear that it is unlikely that only one factor will be the cause. Usually, several factors come together to contribute to sudden drops in achievement or in a slow decline in achievement scores. In determining what factors would be most important, Baker, Bridger & Evans (1998) distinguished three etiological models: individual, family and school. In their report, all three models turned out to predict significantly whether or not an individual student would develop into an underachiever. Yet, the combined model gave the best goodness-of-fit. This means that underachievement is best predicted when all three models are taken into account.

Mönks' triarchic model of giftedness (Mönks & Mason, 1993) included peers as a separate area of influence. Since this achievement-oriented model was also concerned with how ability can be realized, it seems logical to combine the factors from these two models. Therefore, the factors that evoke underachievement behavior can be ordered as follows: family, school, personality, peers.

Family Factors

The relationship between children and their parents is of the utmost importance. Butler-Por (1993) described the situation of these children: "Rejected children who are not receiving appropriate nurturing, reinforcement, and support are unable to understand what is happening to them and what is expected of them. They are unable to acquire coping skills, to gain confidence and build a realistic self-concept" (p. 653). Children from divorced parents are at risk as well, as described before. Nevertheless, Lee-Corbin & Evans (1996) described that parents may diminish the negative influence of the divorce situation by investing time and effort in their children and by avoiding involvement of the children in the conflict between the partners. Another factor of influence is the expectations that parents hold; high expectations seem to support achievement. Richert (1991) also stressed parental influence and described that the difficult task for parents would be to model the behavior that they wish to stimulate in the child. It may be hard for parents to tune their expectations to the level that is appropriate for the child. In many cases, parents expect too little from the child (Stapf, 1998), e.g. when parents try to hold back the young child from reading because he may get bored later in school. The result may be that pleasure in reading, arithmetic, thinking will be gone.

But expectations can also be too high. In many cases the child is being pushed "to be continually successful in examinations, possibly at the expense of more challenging intellectual, artistic and emotionally satisfying activities" (Freeman, 1998; p. 7). In some cases, these parents see a second chance for themselves in their children. They wish to compensate for their own unfulfilled wishes. The children's achievements and successes become more important than the abilities and needs of the children themselves (Webb, Meckstroth & Tolan, 1982; Mönks & Ypenburg, 1998). Children will hesitate to show school results to their parents if they do not meet the high standards of the parents (Perleth & Sierwald, 1992; Zielinski, 1998). This will occur even more so if the affective relationship between parents and child depends on the achievement of the child. When parents overvalue achievement, gifted children who are already at risk of becoming perfectionists will get an even greater push in that direction (Freeman, 1997; Mönks & Ypenburg, 1998).

The best parents can do is demonstrate the behavior that they want the child to display. The consistent and thorough style of working that is necessary for success in the academic realm, especially, can best be learned from models within the family (Winner, 1996). When children grow up in an environment where it is normal to read books, go to museums or experience other ways of exploring the world, they regard it as normal to adopt these behavioral patterns. Not only the activity per se, but also the pleasure in exploring can be handed down to the children by their parents. One has to start showing the joy in exploration while the children are as young as possible (Freeman, 1992). The parents not only function as models, but also as partners that can help to get access to resources.

As a background variable, the achievement goals that parents hold for their children may influence achievement behavior. Achieving children tend to have parents whose achievement goals are more in learning rather than in performing (Ablard & Parker, 1997). When parents and child join in this type of behavior on a basis of mutual interest, an important basis for understanding adequate achievement will be formed. This may be easier said than done, since the exploration need that is displayed by some children will get on the parents' nerves. Children need supportive parents and teachers, but must also have qualities of their own, such as concentration and presentation skills, task commitment, a positive self-concept and social abilities. Achievement is negatively influenced when various combinations of these factors are missing (Lee-Corbin & Denicolo, 1998).

The parenting style that is used should be neither authoritarian nor too permissive (Zielinski, 1998). A good optimum between these two extremes offers the best possibilities for children to develop explorative behavior in a safe environment. When parents hold the right amount of control over their children, the urge to discover new things will be maintained in the child (Butler-Por, 1993). However, with too few guidelines, there is a risk that children will grow up with too little sense of responsibility, or 'caring' (Webb, 1995).

School Factors

School is the place where most underachievement behavior becomes visible. But as research indicates, it cannot be the only place where underachievement is overcome, since the etiological factors can also be found outside of the classroom (Baker, Bridger & Evans, 1998). In many cases, a latent underachievement pattern may become visible when the child enters school; an example could be creative thinking. When a child notices that parents have some problems with 'creative initiatives' that are taken by the child, the child may conclude that it is better to try as much as possible to adapt to the standards that are set. This will lead to a loss of creative potential. Problems may also arise for the child in trying to adjust: "The inability of highly creative children to satisfy the demands of parents and school may lead them to choose to psychologically 'opt-out' and adopt underachievement behaviors" (Butler-Por, 1995; p. 253).

According to Heller (1992) the organization of teaching and the personality of the teacher were the two main factors that influenced the achievement of children in the classroom. Butler-Por (1993) added to this the attitude that the pupil has towards school; this may be displayed in less care for their schoolwork, e.g. with a sloppy handwriting (Lee-Corbin & Evans, 1996). Underachieving students tend to have peers with more negative school-attitudes (Ziv, 1977). This effect is strong, because peers among each other influence their mutual attitudes; when the students are not actively involved in their work, it will be impossible to recognize abilities (Drewelow, 1992). Inactivity and boredom not only hinders the teacher in observing capacities in students, it also induces underachievement (Freeman, 1993). In the classroom, the student needs to find impulses that strengthen his motivation; in order to respond to student needs, the learning situation should, as much as possible, allow students to delve into areas of their own interest. In so doing, motivation increases and the students actually work and develop their learning skills. This development of learning skills, especially self-regulating skills, is an important factor in preventing or overcoming underachievement (Redding, 1990; Baum, Renzulli & Hébert, 1995; Lee-Corbin & Evans, 1996). Effective goal setting for academic achievement and appropriate instruction and curriculum are interventions that can reverse underachievement (Emerick, 1992).

On the other hand, teachers' lack of awareness of aspects of giftedness and underachievement may evoke underachievement in students (Gross, 1999). Teachers' low expectations for children can encourage underachievement in three ways: (1) the mechanism of self-fulfilling prophecy will make students behave according to the expectations of the teacher; (2) perceptual bias will give the teacher wrong ideas about the abilities of students; (3) incompatability of teaching and learning styles of teacher and student may also mislead the teacher about students' capabilities.

Grading practices, e.g. when teachers give lower grades as a punishment for rule-breaking classroom behavior, also encourage underachievement because students may feel rejected by the teacher (Kolb & Jussim, 1994). When teachers' conceptions are changed, it alters the negative impact on the students. There is evidence that preconceptions can be altered which in turn will positively affect the achievement (Ribich, Barone & Agostino, 1998).

Teacher characteristics may reverse underachievement. One teacher characteristic that has a very positive influence on underachieving students is what Renzulli (1992) calls "romance with the profession." Being actively and emotionally involved with their own discipline, teachers function as powerful role models. Feldhusen (1986) listed characteristics that are useful if not necessary for teachers of gifted students: (1) good organization of their teaching; (2) self confidence; (3) flexibility; (4) capable of enthusing students; (5) positive attitude towards excellence; and (6) extensive general knowledge. Next to these more or less formal characteristics, good teachers of the gifted need the knowledge to be able to generate questions. They need to feel free to raise questions, and they need the courage to question the answers (Webb, 1995). These characteristics make teachers supportive or cooperative (Lee-Corbin & Denicolo, 1998).

Of course, it cannot be expected that teachers will understand (gifted) underachievers without any help; a support system, may be in the form of in-service training, is needed to teach them how to deal with underachievers (Freeman, 1997). It is known that teachers have a limited capability to recognize gifted potential without any training, yet this ability can be improved (Hany, 1991; 1997; Rost & Hanses, 1997). Teachers also need to know what characteristics describe underachievers. Because of the hidden character of underachievement, it may be hard for teachers to recognize underachievement when it is taking place. Information about students that comes from other sources may help them; an example would be the school files that are gathered during the years that students are at school (Peterson & Colangelo, 1996). Information that may be found could include school attendance and tardiness, course selection, and onset and duration of underachievement.

Another aspect of teacher behavior is praising. Kaufmann (1999) considered underachievement to be a matter of discouragement, claiming that praise has especially negative results on discouraged students. Praise may strengthen the notion that one is valued only for the achievement that has been reached. It will "foster the dependency, conformity and external motivation at the heart of the underachievement phenomenon" (p. 9). On the other hand praise can be regarded as advantageous when it is used properly. Winner (1996) underlines that it is necessary to praise when work of substance has been done; the repeated acknowledgment of good work and effort should help to overcome underachievement behavior (Freeman, 1998).

Personality Factors

When gifted children experience extreme boredom, when they cannot develop and train their thinking skills, and when they do not develop satisfying social relations, their self-concept will deteriorate (Gallagher, 1991; Heller, 1991; Van Boxtel & Mönks, 1992; Gallagher & Gallagher, 1994; Freeman, 1998; Hanses & Rost, 1998; Lee-Corbin & Denicolo, 1998). The nature of the relationship between achievement and self-concept is under debate. Does achievement develop a positive self-concept? Or can one achieve better when the self-concept is positive? Both seem to be true, although there seems to be some evidence that achievement should have priority over the self-concept (Helmke & Van Aken, 1995). This would mean that leading students to greater achievement changes their self-concept more than vice versa.

Closely related to self-concept is the notion of control. Individuals who possess a positive self-concept tend to believe that they, themselves, are in control of what happens to them (Laffoon, Jenkins-Friedman & Tollefson, 1989). Individuals with a more positive self-concept are more motivated and believe that they are responsible for their success, e.g. in maths (Vlahovic-Stetic, Vidovic & Arambasic, 1999). However, this relationship between locus of control and achievement is not clear. It seems that gifted children in general tend to have a more internal locus of control. There seems to be no clear relationship between underachievement and locus of control (McClelland, Yewchuk & Mulcahy, 1991; Peters & Van Boxtel, 1999). Yet, gifted students who undergo so-called attributional retraining do gain in achievement (Heller, 1999). Could it be that an internal locus of control can increase achievement, but does not have the impact to overcome underachievement?

As can be expected, motivation is a part of the underachievement problem. It is obvious that underachievers possess less motivation then their more successful peers (Baum, Renzulli & Hébert, 1995). The discouragement notion of Kaufmann (1999) implies this notion. Underachievers are reported to have lower expectations of themselves, but also of what their teachers and peers could offer them (Colangelo, Kerr, Christensen & Maxey, 1993). A training program which includes volition as one of the targets proved to be successful in improving achievement in a non-academic setting (Teo & Quah, 1999).

Behavioral problems, overt or more concealed, were reported by many authors. Stapf (1998) describes signs of protest behavior in children in kindergarten, such as school refusal, disturbing play and classes, motoric restlessness, emotional disturbances, aggressive behavior, psychosomatic complaints and daydreaming. Behavioral problems will not always be displayed in school; on the contrary, parents have to deal with this problem most of the time at home (Freeman, 1994).

Among other variables, self-regulation and inter-action with an appropriate peer-group may have a positive effect on underachievers (Baum, Renzulli & Hébert, 1995). One factor that influences behavior is the extent to which the individual is resilient (Bland, Sowa & Callahan, 1994); resilience enhances achievement (Ford, 1994).

One reason for problems in the realm of personality development or behavior, could be the lack of meta-cognitive and strategic skills; for example, underachievers are less capable of transferring skills from one situation to another (Muir-Broaddus, 1995). It seems, that underachievers can do well on holistic and divergent tasks, where no strategy has to be selected, in comparison to analytical and convergent tasks (Redding, 1990). The selection of strategies turns out to be a difficult issue for this group.

This lack of metacognitive ability in underachievers may have a cause that can be traced. It is commonly assumed that the process of learning must be learned, or trained, as well as the content of a curriculum. For this reason, the curriculum needs to offer instruction in how to learn as well as enough challenge on the level of difficulty of the content. Learning skills may not develop when the content of the curriculum does not match the level of cognitive functioning of the child (Perleth & Sierwald, 1992; Ulbricht, 1998).

Peer Influence

The influence of peers on gifted children gets special attention, due to the fact that it might be difficult to actually find peers for this group. Problems arise when the gifted child tries to adapt to the behavior of the peer group when this behavior does not match the interests and needs of the gifted child himself. One reason for underachieving has been known for a long time already: simply lower the results so the peer group will not let one down (Colangelo & Dettmann, 1983; Perleth & Sierwald, 1992; Baum, Renzulli & Hébert, 1995). In some cases, not doing homework can become a condition of being accepted in the peer group. Winner (1996) also recognizes this phenomenon. Finding the balance between receiving social acceptance and

excelling in school is a major task for gifted students; this problem is especially present for girls. Luftig & Nichols (1991) discovered that there seemed to be a huge difference in the way peers perceive gifted girls and boys. Gifted boys were more popular in comparison with boys of normal ability. For girls, this phenomenon was just the opposite; this could be a good reason for some individuals to adopt under-achieving behavior—to find oneself accepted again. Winner (1996) argued that the typical image of the gifted student was more in line with an acceptable image for boys. For girls a role conflict arose between the pursuit of excellence and the demonstration of feminine behavior to adapt to the standards of the peer group and gain social acceptance.

Furtherance and Interventions

Underachievement is a persistent phenomenon that is not easily overcome. Several approaches have been developed and tested, all of them based in different theoretical and practical backgrounds. This makes comparison difficult; nevertheless one can learn from the work done by others.

As a start, it has to be said that intervention programs for underachievers still have to prove their effectiveness (Baum, Renzulli & Hébert, 1995). In the last decade, more and more programs have been presented. In these interventions there is a tendency to address not just one element, but to regard under-achievement as a complex problem that needs to be worked on at several levels (Emerick, 1992).

As a prerequisite, parents need to give their consent for their child to participate in a program to overcome underachievement. It is better to include the parents in the program and show them ways in which they can help their child become a more effective learner (Colangelo & Dettmann, 1983; Rimm, 1991; Emerick, 1992). An important role for parents is to enhance the self-esteem of the child. Another is to become aware of stereotypical patterns of interaction that hamper achievement behavior.

An approach to reversing underachievement is to distract the attention of student, parents and educators from all that is not functioning well and to emphasize and elaborate on the strengths that are present in the individual (Willings, 1998). This enables the personal growth that is necessary to give the individual the strength to direct his own behavior again. Redding (1989) stressed the importance of paying attention to self-initiated successes gained by the children themselves. Furthermore, one could avoid continuously looking at school records to evaluate the development of the child. In the 'prism-metaphor', underachievement behavior is seen as an intertwined set of problematic factors that need to be understood, and separately addressed within the context of an intervention program (Baum, Renzulli & Hébert, 1995). This focus on broader programs is shared by other authors (e.g. Redding, 1989; Emerick, 1992). Such an approach will be more effective than focusing on just one aspect of the behavior.

General psychological well-being, brought about through guided discussion in groups, can be targeted as a goal for underachievement programs (Peterson & Espeland, 1995). This program offers ready-made hand-outs and other materials to encourage discussion among peers. The goals that can be reached with this method are a better understanding of themselves with more self-awareness and self-esteem, a feeling of being more in control of their lives and having more confidence in the future.

A school program that involves parents and offers a broad variety of activities was developed by Supplee (1990). It focused on activities that can be programmed in school in different subject areas. Underlying the program for pupils in kindergarten through grade 8 was a focus on working and study skills. The training was made more attractive by transferring the assignments as much as possible to real-life situations and inviting the students to think about different solutions themselves. This program offered a holistic approach, yet was organized within the context of school; a similar type of program can be found in Kerr (1991). In some cases, the help of a counselor is included in the program (Fehrenbach, 1993).

The opposite can also be found; sometimes emotional problems reach a severity that requires psychological counseling. Focusing on these problems could turn out to be symptom-curing while allowing the underlying problem to continue. A behavioral approach can be better, giving insight through cognitive therapy (Golden, 1993) or family therapy using a narrative approach (Thomas, 1999). Another entry on a more psychological level would be attributional retraining (Heller, 1999). A program was developed to help students take responsibility for their own behavior based on attributional and achievement motivation theories. The program was designed for use in a school setting. One important aspect of underachievement behavior that can be changed in this way would be helplessness.

Aspects of the underachievement syndrome can be addressed with good results. A program that gave writing process instruction to gifted, learning- disabled and low achieving 2nd grade pupils proved to be successful in improving their attitudes towards writing, but also in the achievement that was realized in this area (Zaragoza & Vaughn, 1992).

Another example of focusing on an aspect of the underachievement syndrome is the training of meta-cognitive skills in early childhood (Manning, Glasner & Smith, 1996). This approach was successful in enabling young gifted pupils to develop their meta-cognitive skills and, in so doing, prevent underachievement; this type of training is also valuable for older pupils (Redding, 1989).

For secondary school pupils, a possible approach to reducing underachievement would be to individualize the goals that are set for educational provisions (Fehrenbach, 1993). This might enhance motivation and it supports the students in those areas where they need it. Another specific way of trying to overcome or prevent underachievement is grade skipping (Rimm & Lovance, 1992). Parents reported that the decision to skip a grade was successful, and in many cases, they even regretted not having taken this measure earlier. Early entrance however, does not seem fruitful in preventing underachievement (Sweeney, 1995). A comparison between gifted students who did and did not enter school before the regular date did not show meaningful differences in achievement between these two groups. The small difference that was found, though, was in favor of the early-entrance group.

If underachievement is mainly due to lack of motivation, a program from Singapore may be helpful (Teo & Quah, 1999). This 'Knowledge/Volition/ Action'-program tries to foster the will to achieve in students. The result that achievement in the non-academic area seemed to benefit most from this program was striking.

The APOGEE-program brought students from different backgrounds together who were identified as gifted, but belonged to underprivileged groups such as handicapped or underachieving students (O'Tuel, 1994). In the program group work, projects and self-regulation were encouraged; results showed increases in critical thinking ability, self-esteem, and school attendance. Behavioral problems decreased and the students reported more positive attitudes towards themselves as learners.

A specific group that needs attention are gifted girls. For them, maths and sciences programs have been created, without boys present, to let girls develop skills in these areas where they tend to be underachieving (Lupart & Wilgosh, 1998). The content of the program is designed, among other things, to bridge the gap between school maths and science and post-secondary settings, such as college or business. Other programs focus on this group at another point in time. Early intervention and strengthening the ability of girls in the realm of maths and science is necessary to prevent the loss of ability and motivation in these subject areas (McCormick & Wolf, 1993).

Within a group of underachievers, one can distinguish subcategories that might need different types of programs (Richert, 1991; Schneider, 1998). Four categories of underachievers are the conformist, the rebel, the withdrawn, and the transcender (Richert, 1991). Each of them needs support in six areas: (1) strengthening self-concept; (2) learning to cope with failure and success;(3) learning to unleash creative potential; (4) learning how to plan; (5) developing ways to evaluate results; and (6) providing role models.

The way this is done differs for every subcategory. A similar system is provided by Schneider (1998). Contrary to Richert (1991), the system of Schneider (1998) does not seem to be based on personality characteristics, but on behavior patterns.

In Conclusion

Underachievement among the gifted appears to be a widespread phenomenon. Identification of these children has been attempted both psychometrically and informally, with many issues remaining in this area. Certain groups appear to be at greater risk, with risk factors cited including geographic, ethnic and gender, economic, educational deprivation, sub-cultural, physical, psychological and sociological factors. A number of interventions have been described that attempted to reverse underachievement with the most successful programs involving parents and addressing students' individual affective and cognitive needs in a manner appropriate for their age and the circumstances of their life.

References

Ablard, K. E. & Parker, W. D.(1997). Parents' achievement goals and perfectionism in their academically talented children. *Journal of Youth and Adolescence*, **26** (6), 651–667.

Arnold, K. D., Noble, K. D. & Subotnik, R. F. (1996). *Remarkable women: Perspectives on female talent development*. Cresskill, NJ: Hampton Press.

Baker, J. A., Bridger, R. & Evans, K. (1998). Models of underachievement among gifted preadolescents: the role of personal, family, and school factors. *Gifted Child Quarterly*, **42** (1), 5–15.

Baum, S. M., Renzulli, J. S. & Hébert, T. P. (1995). Reversing underachievement: creative productivity as a systematic intervention. *Gifted Child Quarterly*, **39** (4), 224–235.

Bland, L. C., Sowa, C. J. & Callahan, C. M. (1994). An overview of resilience in gifted children. *Roeper-Review*, **17** (2), 77–80.

Butler-Por, N. (1993). Underachieving Gifted Students. In: K. A. Heller, F. J. Mönks & A. H. Passow (Eds), *International Handbook of Research and Development of Giftedness and Talent* (pp. 649–668). Oxford: Pergamon Press.

Butler-Por, N. (1995). Who is at risk for underachievement and why? In: M. W. Katzko & F. J. Mönks (Eds), *Nurturing Talent: Individual Needs and Social Ability* (pp. 252–261). Assen: Van Gorcum.

Colangelo, N. & Dettmann, D. F. (1983). A review of research on parents and families of gifted children. *Exceptional-Children*, **50** (1), 20–27.

Colangelo, N., Kerr, B., Christensen, P. & Maxey, J. (1993). A comparison of gifted underachievers and gifted high achievers. *Gifted Child Quarterly*, **37** (4), 155–160.

Detzner, M. & Schmidt, M. H. (1986). Are highly gifted children and adolescents especially susceptible to anorexia nervosa? In: K. A. Heller & J. F. Feldhusen (Eds), *Identifying and Nurturing the Gifted* (pp. 149–162). Toronto-Bern: Huber.

Diaz, E. I. (1998). Perceived factors influencing the academic underachievement of talented students of Puerto Rican descent. *Gifted Child Quarterly*, **42** (2), 105–122.

Drewelow, H. (1992). Begabungsförderung in der Schule. In: E. A. Hany & H. Nickel (Eds) *Begabung und Hochbegabung: theoretische Konzepte—empirische Befunde—praktische Konsequenzen* (pp. 171–194). Göttingen-Toronto-Seattle: Huber.

Durr, W. H. (1964). *The Gifted Student*. New York: Oxford University Press.

Emerick, L. J. (1992). Academic underachievement among the gifted: students' perceptions of factors that reverse the pattern. *Gifted Child Quarterly*, **36** (3), 140–146.

Feger, B. & Prado, T. M. (1998). *Hochbegabung: die normalste Sache der Welt*. Darmstadt: Wissenschaftliche Buchgesellschaft.

Fehrenbach, C. R. (1993). Underachieving gifted students: intervention programs that work. *Roeper Review*, **16** (2), 88–90.

Feldhusen, J. F. (1986). Lehrer für Hochbegabte: Eigenschaften und Ausbildung. In: W. Wieczerkowski (Ed.), *Hochbegabung—Gesellschaft—Schule* (selected papers from the 6th World Conference on Gifted and Talented Children; pp. 194–209). Bad Honnef : Bock.

Feldhusen, J. F. & Jarwan, F. A. (1993). Identification of gifted and talented youth for educational programs. In: K. A. Heller, F. J. Mönks & A. H. Passow (Eds), *International Handbook of Research and Development of Giftedness and Talent* (pp. 233–251). Oxford: Pergamon Press.

Ford, D. Y. (1992). Self-perceptions of underachievement and support for the achievement ideology among early adolescent African-Americans. *Journal of Early Adolescence*, **12** (3), 228–252.

Ford, D. Y. (1994). Nurturing resilience in gifted Black youth. *Roeper Review*, **17** (2), 80–85.

Ford, D. Y., & Harris, J. J. (1992). The American achievement ideology and achievement differentials among preadolescent gifted and nongifted African American males and females. *Journal of Negro Education*, **61** (1), 45–64.

Ford, D. Y. & Harris, J. J. (1997). A study of the racial identity and achievement of Black males and females. *Roeper Review*, **20** (2), 105–110.

Ford, D. Y. & Thomas, A. (1997). *Underachievement Among Gifted Minority Students: Problems and Promises. Underachievement among Gifted Minority Students: Problems and Promises*. (ERIC Digest E544). Reston, VA.: ERIC Clearinghouse on Disabilities and Gifted Education.

Ford, D. Y. & Webb, K. S. (1994). Desegregation of gifted educational programs: the impact of Brown on underachieving children of color. *Journal of Negro Education*, **63** (3), 358–375.

Freeman, J. (1992). The development of gifted infants. In: F. J. Mönks & W. A. M. Peters (Eds), *Talent for the Future* (pp. 23–36). Assen: Van Gorcum.

Freeman, J. (1993). Boredom, high ability and achievement. In: V. P. Varma (Ed.), *How and Why Children Fail* (pp. 29–40). London: Jessica Kingsley Publishers.

Freeman, J. (1994). Some emotional aspects of being gifted. *Journal for the Education of the Gifted*, **17** (2), 180–197.

Freeman, J. (1997). The emotional development of the highly able. *European Journal of Psychology of Education*, **12** (4), 479–493.

Freeman, J. (1998). *Educating the very able: current international research*. (Ofsted reviews of research series). London: Stationary Office.

Friedrich, M. H. (1998). *Tatort Kinderseele: Sexueller Missbrauch und die Folgen*. Wien: Überreuter.

Gallagher, J. J. (1991). Personal patterns of underachievement. *Journal for the Education of the Gifted*, **14** (3), 221–233.

Gallagher, J. J. & Gallagher, S. A. (1994). *Teaching the gifted child* (4th ed.). Boston: Allyn and Bacon.

Gardner, H. (1983). *Frames of Mind*. New York: Basic Books.

Golden, L. B. (1993). The boy who trashed his final. In: L. B. Golden, & M. L. Norwood (Eds), *Case Studies in Child Counseling* (pp. 27–38). New York, NY: Merrill/Macmillan.

Gross, M. U. (1999). Small poppies: highly gifted children in the early years. *Roeper Review*, **21** (3), 207–214.

Hanses, P. & Rost, D. H. (1998). Das 'Drama' der hochbegabten Underachiever: 'Gewöhnliche' oder 'aussergewöhnliche' Underachiever? *Zeitschrift für Pädagogische Psychologie*, **12** (1), 53–71.

Hany, E. A. (1991). Sind Lehrkräfte bei der Identifikation hochbegabter Schüler doch besser als Tests? *Psychologie in Erziehung und Unterricht*, **38** (1), 37–50.

Hany, E. A. (1997). Modeling teachers' judgment of giftedness: a methodological inquiry of biased judgment. *High Ability Studies*, **8** (2), 159–178.

Hébert, T. P. (1998). Gifted Black males in an urban high school: factors that influence achievement and underachievement. *Journal for the Education of the Gifted*, **21** (4), 385–414.

Heinbokel, A. (1996). *Hochbegabte: Erkennen, Probleme, Lösungswege*. Münster: Lit.

Heller, K. A. (1991). Schuleignungsprognostik. In: K. A. Heller (Ed.), *Begabungsdiagnostik in der Schul- und Erziehungsberatung* (pp. 213–235) Bern-Stuttgart-Toronto: Huber.

Heller, K. A. (Ed.). (1992). *Hochbegabung im Kindes- und Jugendalter*. Göttingen: Hogrefe.

Heller, K. A. (1999). Individual (learning and motivational) needs versus instructional conditions of gifted education. *High Ability Studies*, **10** (1), 9–21.

Helmke, A. & Van Aken, M. A. G. (1995). The causal ordering of academic achievement and self-concept of ability during elementary school: a longitudinal study. *Journal of Educational Psychology*, **87** (4), 624–637.

Hollinger, C. L. & Fleming, E. S. (1984). Internal barriers to the realization of potential: correlates and interrelationships among gifted and talented female adolescents. *Gifted-Child-Quarterly*, **28** (3), 135–139

Kaufman, A. S. (1994). *Intelligent Testing with the WISC-III*. New York: Wiley.

Kaufmann, F. (1999). The courage to succeed: another look at underachievement. In: S. Cline & K. Hegeman (Eds.), *Gifted Education in the 21st Century: Issues and Concerns*. New York: Winslow Press.

Kerr, B. (1991). *A handbook for counseling the gifted and talented*. Alexandria, VA.: American Association for Counseling and Development.

Kitano, M. K. (1991). A multicultural educational perspective on serving the culturally diverse gifted. *Journal for the Education of the Gifted*, **15** (1), 4–19.

Kolb, K. J. & Jussim, L. (1994). Teacher expectations and underachieving gifted children. *Roeper Review*, **17** (1), 26–30.

Laffoon, K. S., Jenkins-Friedman, R. & Tollefson, N. (1989). Causal attributions of underachieving gifted, achieving gifted, and non-gifted students. *Journal for the Education of the Gifted*, **13** (1), 4–21.

Lee-Corbin, H. & Denicolo, P. (1998). Portraits of the able child: highlights of case study research. *High Ability Studies*, **9** (2), 207–218.

Lee-Corbin, H. & Evans, R. (1996). Factors influencing success or underachievement of the able child. *Early Child Development and Care*, **117**, 133–144.

Luftig, R. L. & Nichols, M. L. (1991). An assessment of the social status and perceived personality and school traits of gifted students by non-gifted peers. *Roeper Review*, **13** (3), 148–153.

Lupart, J. L. & Pyryt, M. C. (1996). 'Hidden gifted' students: underachiever prevalence and profile. *Journal for the Education of the Gifted*, **20** (1), 36–53.

Lupart, J. L. & Wilgosh, L. (1998). Undoing underachievement and promoting societal advancement of women and girls. *Gifted Education International*, **12** (3), 159–169.

Manning, B. H., Glasner, S. E. & Smith, E. R. (1996). The self-regulated learning aspect of metacognition: a component of gifted education. *Roeper Review*, **18** (3), 217–223.

McClelland, R., Yewchuk, C. & Mulcahy, R. (1991). Locus of control in underachieving and achieving gifted students. *Journal for the Education of the Gifted*, **14** (4), 380–392.

McCormick, M.E. & Wolf, J. S. (1993). Intervention programs for gifted girls. *Roeper Review*, **16** (2), 85–88.

Mönks, F. J. & Ypenburg, I. H. (1998). *Unser Kind ist hochbegabt: ein Leitfaden für Eltern und Lehrer*. München-Basel: E. Reinhardt.

Mönks, F. J. & Mason, E. J. (1993). Developmental theories and giftedness. In: K. A. Heller, F. J. Mönks & A. H. Passow (Eds), *International Handbook of Research and Development of Giftedness and Talent* (pp. 89–101). Oxford: Pergamon Press.

Muir-Broaddus, J. E. (1995). Gifted underachievers: insights from the characteristics of strategic functioning associated with giftedness and achievement. *Learning and Individual Differences*, **7** (3), 189–206.

O'Tuel, F. S. (1994). APOGEE: Equity in the identification of gifted and talented students. *Gifted Child Quarterly*, **38** (2), 75–79.

Perleth, C. & Sierwald, W. (1992). Entwicklungs- und Leistungsanalysen zur Hochbegabung. In: K. Heller (Ed.), *Hochbegabung im Kindes- und Jugendalter* (pp. 166–350). Göttingen-Toronto-Zürich: Huber.

Peters, W. A. M. & Van Boxtel, H. W. (1999). Irregular error patterns in Raven's Standard Progressive Matrices: A sign of underachievement in testing situations? *High Ability Studies*, **10** (2), 213–232.

Peterson, J. S. & Colangelo, N. (1996). Gifted achievers and underachievers: a comparison of patterns found in school files. *Journal-of-Counseling-and-Development*, **74** (4), 399–407.

Peterson, J. S. & Espeland, P. (Eds). (1995). *Talk with teens about feelings, family, relationships, and the future: 50 guided discussions for school and counseling groups*. Minneapolis, MN: Free Spirit Publishing.

Raph, J. B., Goldberg, M. L. & Passow, A. H. (1966). *Bright Underachievers*. New York: Columbia University Teachers College Bureau of Publications.

Redding, R. E. (1989). Underachievement in the verbally gifted: implications for pedagogy. *Psychology in the Schools*, **26** (3), 275–291.

Redding, R. E. (1990). Learning preferences and skill patterns among underachieving gifted adolescents. *Gifted Child Quarterly*, **34** (2), 72–75.

Reis, S. M. & Diaz, E. (1999). Economically disadvantaged urban female students who achieve in schools. *Urban Review*, **31** (1), 31–54.

Renzulli, J. S. (1978). What makes giftedness? Reexamining a definition. *Phi Delta Kappa*, **60**, 180–184.

Renzulli, J. S. (1992). A general theory for the development of creative productivity in young people. In: F. J. Mönks & W. A. M. Peters (Eds), *Talent for the Future* (pp. 51–72). Assen: Van Gorcum.

Ribich, F., Barone, W. & Agostino, R. (1998). Semantically different: preservice teachers' reactions to the gifted student concept. *Journal of Educational Research*, **91** (5), 308–312.

Richert, E. S. (1991). Patterns of underachievement among gifted students. In: M. Bireley & J. Genshaft (Eds), *Understanding the Gifted Adolescent: Educational, Developmental and Multicultural Issues* (pp. 139–162). New York: Teachers College Press.

Rimm, S. B. (1986). *Underachievement Syndrome: Causes and Cures*. Watertown, WI: Apple.

Rimm, S. B. (1991). Parenting the gifted adolescent: special problems, special joys. In: M. Bireley & J. Genschaft (Eds), *Understanding the Gifted Adolescent: Educational, Developmental and Multicultural Issues* (pp. 18–32). New York, NY: Teachers College Press.

Rimm, S. B. & Lovance. K. J. (1992). The use of subject and grade skipping for the prevention and reversal of underachievement. *Gifted Child Quarterly*, **36** (2), 100–105.

Rost, D. H. & Hanses, P. (1997). Wer nichts leistet, ist nicht begabt? Zur identifizierung hochbegabter Underachiever durch Lehrkräfte. *Zeitschrift für Entwicklungspsychologie und Pädagogische Psychologie*, **29** (2), 167–177.

Schneider, S. (1998). *Understanding the Complex Needs of the Underachiever*. Norristown, PA: PAGE. (Published at the website of PAGE: http://www.penngifted.org/bulletins/b2.html)

Shaw, M. C. (1964). Definition and identification of academic underachievers. In: L. French (Ed.), *Educating the Gifted* (pp. 139–155). New York: Holt, Rinehart and Winston.

Span, P. (1988). Onderpresteren op school door hoogbegaafde leerlingen. *Tijdschrift voor Orthopedagogiek, Kinderpsychiatrie en Klinische Kinderpsychologie*, **13** (3/4), 121–129.

Stapf, A. (1998). Hochbegabung: Was ist das? In: C. Engemann & M. Franz (Eds), *Begabungen fördern: hoch begabte Kinder in der Grundschule* (pp. 12–26). Stuttgart: Ministerium für Kultus, Jugend und Sport.

Supplee, P. L. (1990). *Reaching the gifted underachiever: program strategy and design*. New York, NY, USA: Teachers College Press.

Sweeney, N. S. (1995). The age position effect: school entrance age, giftedness, and underachievement. *Journal for the Education of the Gifted*, **18** (2), 171–188.

Tannenbaum, A. J. (1983). *Gifted Children*. New York: MacMillan.

Tannenbaum, A. J. (1991). Unmasking and unmaking underachievement among the gifted. In: R. Feuerstein & P. S. Klein, (Eds), *Mediated Learning Experience (MLE): Theoretical, Psychosocial And Learning Implications* (pp. 315–346). London: Freund Publishing House.

Tannenbaum, A. J. (1993). History of Giftedness and 'Gifted Education' in World Perspective. In: K. A. Heller, F. J. Mönks & A. H. Passow (Eds), *International Handbook of Research and Development of Giftedness and Talent* (pp. 3–27). Oxford: Pergamon Press.

Teo, C. T. & Quah, M. L. (1999). The knowledge, volition and action programme in Singapore: the effects of an experimental intervention programme on high ability achievement. *High-Ability-Studies*, **10** (1), 23–35.

Terman, L. M. & Oden, M. H. (1947). *Genetic Studies of Genius II*. California: Stanford University Press.

Thomas, V. (1999). David and the family bane: Therapy with a gifted child and his family. *Journal of Family Psychotherapy*, **10** (1), 15–24.

Ulbricht, H. (1998). *Hochbegabung: Ein Thema für die Schulberatung?* Munich: Website of the Bavarian School Advice Center (http://www.schulberatung.bayern.de/llhob.htm).

Van Boxtel, H. W. & Mönks, F. J. (1992). General, social, and academic self-concepts of gifted adolescents. *Journal of Youth and Adolescence*, **21** (2), 169–186.

Van Boxtel, H. W., Mönks, F. J., Roelofs, J. J. W. & Sanders, M. P. M. (1986). *De Identificatie van Begaafde Leerlingen in het Voortgezet Onderwijs en een Beschrijving van hun Situatie: Onderzoeksresultaten, konklusies en aanbevelingen*. Nijmegen: Hoogveld Instituut/Vakgroep Ontwikkelingspsychologie KUN.

Vlahovic-Stetic, V., Vidovic, V. V. & Arambasic, L. (1999). Motivational characteristics in mathematical achievement: a study of gifted high-achieving, gifted underachieving and non-gifted pupils. *High Ability Studies*, **10** (1), 37–49.

Webb, J. T. (1995). Cultivating courage, creativity and caring. In: Katzko, M. W. & F. J. Mönks (Eds), *Nurturing Talent: Individual Needs and Social Ability* (pp. 129–138). Assen: Van Gorcum.

Webb, J. T., Meckstroth, E. A. & Tolan, S. S. (1982). *Guiding the gifted child: a practical source for parents and teachers*. Columbus, OH.: Ohio Psychology Publishing Corporation.

Wieczerkowski, W. & Prado, T. (1992). Begabung und Geslecht. In: E. A. Hany & H. Nickel (Eds), *Begabung und Hochbegabung: Theoretische Konzepte, Empirische Befunde, Praktische Konsequenzen* (pp. 39–57). Bern-Göttingen-Toronto: Huber.

Willings, D. (1998). A radical approach to discovering the real self. *Roeper Review*, **20** (3), 227–230.

Winner, E. (1996). *Gifted children: myths and realities*. New York: Basic Books.

Zaragoza, N. & Vaughn, S. (1992). The effects of process writing instruction on three 2nd-grade students with different achievement profiles. *Learning Disabilities Research and Practice*, **7** (4), 184–193.

Ziegler, A., Dresel, M. & Schober, B. (2000). Underachievementdiagnose: Ein Modell zur Diagnose partieller Lernbeeinträchtigungen. In: K. A. Heller (Ed.) *Begabungsdiagnostik in der Schul- und Erziehungsberatung* (2nd ed.). Bern: Huber.

Zielinski, W. (1998). *Lernschwierigkeiten: Ursachen, Diagnostik, Intervention*. (3rd ed.). Suttgart-Berlin-Köln: Kohlhammer.

Ziv, A. (1977). Parental perceptions and self-concept of gifted and average ability underachievers. *Perceptual and Motor Skills*, **44** (2), 563–568.

Attention-Deficit/Hyperactivity Disorder in Gifted Students

Felice A. Kaufmann[1] and F. Xavier Castellanos[2]

[1]6520 Lone Oak Court, Bethesda, Maryland, USA
[2]National Institute of Mental Health, Bethesda, Maryland, USA

Introduction

The issue of Attention-Deficit/Hyperactivity Disorder (ADHD) among gifted students poses challenging questions for researchers and practitioners. The most fundamental is the question of validity. Some authors (Lind, 1993; Cramond, 1995; Baum, Olenchak & Owen, 1998; Rimm, 1999) have questioned whether ADHD in high ability students is just a misinterpretation of gifted, creative or 'overexcitable' behaviors or a mismatch between school curriculum and child. Others (Kohn, 1989; Reid, Maag & Vasa, 1993; Armstrong, 1995; Freed & Parsons, 1997; Breggin, 1998; Diller, 1998) have argued that the concept is more reflective of society's ills than an actual medical condition.

In this chapter, we will present information about the co-incidence of giftedness and ADHD with the assumption that the combination is real. We must acknowledge at the outset that much of the following material is based on our experiences as an educator and pediatrician/child psychiatrist, respectively, because to date there are no controlled and peer-reviewed studies on ADHD in gifted students. The bulk of the scientific information, therefore, will focus on what is known about ADHD in the general population but will be augmented by our speculations concerning the application of the material to gifted students.

What is ADHD?

Attention-Deficit/Hyperactivity Disorder is the most common neuropsychiatric disorder of childhood (American Psychiatric Association, 1994). It is not a single disease, but a 'syndrome', i.e. a grouping of symptoms that typically occur together. The core symptoms of ADHD are impulsivity, inattention, and hyperactivity. These symptoms and related problems can be mild, moderate or severe, and may manifest in different combinations within familial, academic and social contexts.

Estimates of the prevalence of ADHD among school age children vary from 0% to 16% (Lahey et al., 1999), a range that reflects differences in research methodology as well as the heterogeneity and complexity of the condition. The median estimate across all definitions of ADHD and all types of studies is 2% in boys and girls combined (Lahey et al., 1999). The symptoms typically emerge in early childhood and frequently continue into adulthood, although the manifestations of the condition usually change over time (Biederman, 1998).

What Causes ADHD?

A comprehensive review of the literature on the causes of ADHD is well beyond the scope of this chapter; a more extensive discussion of the empirical research on the topic is presented in another version of this chapter (Kaufmann, Kalbfleisch & Castellanos, 2000).

The question 'nature or nurture?' which underlies so much discussion about giftedness, also applies to ADHD. On the 'nature' side, family studies have confirmed that the chances that an individual will have ADHD is at least five times higher if he or she is closely related (sibling, parent, or child) to someone who also has ADHD (Faraone & Biederman, 1998). Moreover, recent research (Barkley, 1997) has revealed that a child of a parent with ADHD has up to a 50% chance of having the condition. Adoption studies also found greater similarities between children with ADHD and their biological parents than between those children and their adoptive parents (Castellanos & Rapoport, 1992). Furthermore, studies comparing the degree of similarity (concordance) between identical twins and fraternal twins have consistently converged on estimates of the heritability of ADHD ranging from 75% to 90% (Faraone & Biederman, 1998). Taken together, these investigations confirm that genetic factors strongly influence the development of ADHD.

Environment also contributes to the etiology of ADHD. Such factors as premature birth (Lou, 1996), head injury (Max et al., 1998), fetal alcohol syndrome (Streissguth et al., 1994), pre-natal cocaine (Levitt et al., 1997), pre-natal smoking (Milberger et al., 1996), and high levels of psychosocial stress (Mayes et al., 1992; Richardson & Day, 1994) have all been linked to ADHD. Although diet has been implicated in popular literature, placebo-controlled studies of refined sugar have failed to reveal an association (Wolraich, Wilson & White, 1995). However, there continues to be interest in the possibility that dietary causes may be etiologically important in some fraction of cases (Breakey, 1997; Arnold, 1999; Baumgaertel, 1999; Jacobson & Schardt, 1999).

To summarize, there is no one cause of ADHD, any more than there is one 'cause' of giftedness. Both genetics and environment contribute to the condition as they interact with a child's growth and development.

What is the Role of Development in ADHD?

Children with ADHD trail about 2–3 years behind age-peers in social development (Dykens et al., 1990) and in cognitive tests of prefrontal brain functions (Amin et al., 1993; Chelune et al., 1986). While children with ADHD and children without ADHD progress at the same rate, the developmental lag between them remains relatively constant. This gap is more evident in childhood when an individual is less able to exert control over his or her circumstances than in later life (Mannuzza et al., 1998).

Other social and neurodevelopmental changes occur as a child matures. Locomotor hyperactivity, which is the most visible characteristic of ADHD in young children, eventually decreases whether or not the condition is treated (Frick et al., 1994). Symptoms of inattention, by contrast, remain relatively constant (Hart et al., 1995) and in time become increasingly identifiable. Thus, many cases of Predominantly Inattentive Type ADHD (see Table 1) are not identified until the middle grades, or later.

Changes in brain anatomy and chemistry also are evident over time. Studies of brain chemistry have suggested that changes in the brain chemical dopamine may contribute to the physiology of ADHD (Castellanos, 1997). A recent study (Ernst et al., 1998) found evidence of decreased dopamine and/or norepinephrine neurons in the frontal lobes of the brain of adults who have ADHD. Researchers have also found that portions of the frontal lobes are smaller in children who have ADHD (Castellanos et al., 1996; Filipek et al., 1997). These neurochemical and neuroanatomic findings are consistent with the theory that the underlying cognitive deficits in ADHD are impairments in *executive functioning* (Denckla, 1989; Barkley, 1996; Denckla, 1996) which includes such processes as task analysis, strategy control and strategy monitoring. Impairments in these operations affect an individuals' ability to inhibit and delay responses, initiate and sustain activity, set priorities, and organize, which are among the most salient traits of ADHD (Barkley, 1997).

While researchers have not yet definitively shown "what ADHD is," they have learned "what it is not." This distinction is crucial to the diagnostic process. Among the many psychiatric and medical conditions that may co-exist with ADHD or be confused with it are oppositional defiant disorder and conduct disorder (Quay, 1999), substance abuse and dependence (Biederman et al., 1997), learning disorders (Pliszka, 1998), tic disorders (Freeman, 1997), mood or anxiety disorders (Angold, Costello & Erkanli, 1999), post traumatic stress disorder (Famularo et al., 1996) and sleep disorders (Bowen, Fenton & Rappaport, 1991; Stein et al., 1996).

That such a broad array of conditions can mimic or accompany ADHD makes the assessment and diagnosis of the disorder problematic. In the next section we will present some of the best known assessment and identification instruments used for ADHD.

How is ADHD Assessed and Diagnosed?

The current criteria for ADHD, taken from the fourth edition of the Diagnostic and Statistical Manual of Mental Disorders (DSM-IV), the diagnostic 'bible' of the American Psychiatric Association (1994), are presented in Table 1. That these behavioral descriptions are inevitably subjective means that, even under research conditions, the repeated application of the criteria does not result in the same diagnosis 100% of the time. It is important to note that these criteria, like all those included in DSM-IV, are provisional and like any single diagnostic assessment, have an appreciable chance (at least 20–25%) of being incorrect (Lahey et al., 1994).

While this level of inaccuracy is undesirable, uncertainty has and always will accompany medical or psychological diagnoses. Errors in diagnosis, however, are bi-directional. Thus while some children have been misdiagnosed and treated for ADHD that was *not* present (false positives), many others have ADHD or specific learning disorders that have not been diagnosed (false negatives). For example, in a county-wide Tennessee sample, less than a third of children who were diagnosable with ADHD by teacher ratings had been so identified, and less than one quarter had been treated for the condition (Wolraich et al., 1998).

Gender also appears to affect identification. Epidemiological studies have confirmed that while most children with ADHD are male, a substantial fraction (25–30%) is female (Lahey et al., 1999). Yet the proportion of children who are referred for evaluation and treatment has remained 70–90% male (Gaub & Carlson, 1997).

We believe that the diagnosis of ADHD is also affected by giftedness. Silverman (1998) noted that some professionals erroneously assume that a child who demonstrates sustained attention, such as a gifted child who is occupied with an activity in a high-interest area, cannot have ADHD. The state of rapt attention,

Table 1. Diagnostic Criteria for Attention-Deficit/ Hyperactivity Disorder..

A. Either (1) or (2):

(1) six (or more) of the following symptoms of inattention have persisted for at least 6 months to a degree that is maladaptive and inconsistent with developmental level:

Inattention

 (a) often fails to give close attention to details or makes careless mistakes in schoolwork, work, or other activities
 (b) often has difficulty sustaining attention in tasks or play activities
 (c) often does not seem to listen when spoken to directly
 (d) often does not follow through on instructions and fails to finish schoolwork, chores, duties in the workplace (not due to oppositional behavior or failure to understand instructions)
 (e) often has difficulty organizing tasks and activities
 (f) often avoids, dislikes or is reluctant to engage in tasks that require sustained mental effort (such as schoolwork or homework)
 (g) often loses things necessary for tasks or activities (e.g. toys, school assignments, pencils, books or tools)
 (h) is often easily distracted by external stimuli
 (i) is often forgetful in daily activities

(2) six (or more) of the following symptoms of hyperactivity-impulsivity have persisted for at least 6 months to a degree that is maladaptive and inconsistent with developmental level:

Hyperactivity

 (a) often fidgets with hands or feet or squirms in seat
 (b) often leaves seat in classroom or in other situations in which remaining seated is expected
 (c) often runs about or climbs excessively in situations in which it is inappropriate (in adolescents or adults, may be limited to subjective feelings of restlessness)
 (d) often has difficulty playing or engaging in leisure activities quietly
 (e) is often 'on the go' or often acts as if 'driven by a motor'
 (f) often talks excessively

Impulsivity

 (g) often blurts out answers before questions have been completed
 (h) often has difficulty awaiting turn
 (i) often interrupts or intrudes on others (e.g. butts into conversations or games)

B. Some hyperactive-impulsive or inattentive symptoms that caused impairment were present before age 7 years

C. Some impairment from the symptoms is present in two or more settings (e.g. at school and at home).

D. There must be clear evidence of clinically significant impairment in social, academic or occupational functioning.

E. The symptoms do not occur exclusively during the course of a Pervasive Developmental Disorder, Schizophrenia, or other Psychotic Disorder and are not better accounted for by another mental disorder (e.g. Mood Disorder, Anxiety Disorder, Dissociative Disorder, or a Personality Disorder).

Code based on type:

314.01 Attention-Deficit/Hyperactivity Disorder, Combined Type-. if both Criteria Al and A2 are met for the past 6 months

314.00 Attention-Deficit/Hyperactivity Disorder, Predominantly Inattentive Type- if Criterion Al is met but Criterion A2 is not met for the past 6 months

314.01 Attention-Deficit/Hyperactivity Disorder, Predominantly Hyperactive-impulsive Type: if Criterion A2 is met but Criterion Al is not met for the past 6 months

---

sometimes referred to as 'flow' (Csikszentmihalyi, 1990), may also be described as 'hyperfocus', which individuals with ADHD frequently experience (Hallowell & Ratey, 1994a; Kaufmann, Kalbfleisch & Castellanos, 2000).

Activities that are continuously reinforcing, and 'automatic', such as video or computer games or reading for pleasure, do not distinguish children who have ADHD from controls, whereas effortful tasks do (Borcherding et al., 1988; Douglas & Parry, 1994;

Wigal et al., 1998a). By the nature of their giftedness, the range of tasks that are perceived as 'effortless' is broader for gifted children. However, ADHD is not characterized by an *inability* to sustain attention, but rather, by the inability to appropriately regulate the application of attention to tasks that are not intrinsically rewarding and/or that require effort. Such tasks are characteristic of much of the work that is required in school.

Types of ADHD

Four subtypes of Attention-Deficit/Hyperactivity Disorder are recognized in the DSM-IV: Predominantly Hyperactive/Impulsive, Predominantly Inattentive, Combined, and Not Otherwise Specified (American Psychiatric Association, 1994). The criteria for each of these subtypes are presented in Table 1. In order to meet the criteria for one of the specific subtypes, at least six of the nine symptoms of hyperactivity/impulsivity, or at least six criteria from the nine symptoms of inattention must be present. (Combined type means both sets of criteria are met.) The symptoms must occur *in more than one setting*, must persist for *at least six months*, and must affect the individual "to a degree that is *maladaptive and inconsistent with developmental level* (p. 83).

We have italicized parts of the previous sentence to emphasize that attention deficit disorders cannot and should not be diagnosed on the basis of a few fleeting observations. That a child occasionally shows symptoms of hyperactivity at home or inattention in the classroom is insufficient to warrant a formal diagnosis. The diagnostic label ADHD should only be applied when many factors are considered over time in multiple settings and then, only with deliberate consideration.

Impairment and Age-of-Onset

The diagnostic criteria for ADHD emphasize that "there must be clear evidence of *clinically significant impairment* in social, academic, or occupational functioning" (p. 84). Moreover, some impairing symptoms must be present before the age of seven. Several researchers (Applegate et al., 1997; Barkley & Biederman, 1997, 1998) have criticized the age criterion as being too limiting. Until this issue is resolved, however, the age criterion remains a requirement for the diagnosis.

Diagnosis by Team

While the DSM-IV criteria can be used by anyone as a simple checklist, a diagnosis reached in this way has uncertain validity. In optimal circumstances a team, *including a qualified clinician*, such as a pediatrician, family physician, psychiatrist, neurologist or psychologist, should make the diagnosis because only specialists can assess the aforementioned physical and psychological problems that mimic ADHD. Informa-

tion about all these conditions is rarely available to school personnel, no matter how observant, experienced or well trained they may be.

Clinicians cannot function in a vacuum and therefore need assistance from parents and school personnel. A recent study (Barbaresi & Olsen, 1998) revealed, however, that teachers receive only minimal information about ADHD in their undergraduate education. Therefore, until pre-service education programs offer more comprehensive training, school systems must assume responsibility for providing the relevant information. Opportunities to learn about such crucial issues as identification, assessment, legal rights, and educational interventions should be made available to school personnel, parents, and the community at large to ensure the effectiveness and efficiency of assessment and diagnostic procedures.

The Teacher's Role in Assessment and Identification

Although most children with ADHD display their symptoms prior to reaching elementary school, the majority can be identified only when their behavior is observed and compared to other children over a sustained period of time. The classroom teacher, therefore, is professionally best suited to this task. When the child in question is gifted, an individual who specializes in giftedness should also be included in the process so the child's behavior can be compared to children of comparable abilities (Silverman, 1998). In all settings, however, appropriate identification instruments such as well-researched behavioral rating scales must be employed.

There are two types of rating scales for ADHD (Dykman, Ackerman & Raney, 1993). One type, which includes such instruments as the Child Behavior Checklist (for parents) and the Teacher Report Form (Achenbach & Edelbrock, 1983), is designed to assess a wide range of behaviors and symptoms. The strengths of these instruments are that they have large normalization samples, and require open-ended observations about the child's strengths and the adult's areas of greatest concern. Their weakness is that they are not constructed with reference to any particular diagnostic system.

The other category of rating scale focuses on a narrower range of behaviors or symptoms. The earliest of these, devised by Conners (Goyette, Conners & Ulrich, 1978), has been widely used in research and clinical settings for over two decades. The most recent revisions have been re-normed and are now compatible with DSM-IV diagnostic criteria for ADHD for children, adolescents, and adults (Conners, 1997). Other rating scales that are widely used to diagnose ADHD and to track treatment progress include the Attention Deficit Disorder Evaluation Scale (ADDES) (Bussing *et al.*, 1998), the SKAMP (Wigal *et al.*, 1998b), the Behavior Assessment System for Children

(BASC) (Vaughn *et al.*, 1997), and the Adolescent Behavior Checklist (Adams, Kelly & McCarthy, 1997).

All rating scales include separate age-related norms for males and females because the population means differ for boys and girls (Gaub & Carlson, 1997). Also, within the Conners normalization sample, teacher ratings of African Americans are higher than for comparison subjects (Epstein et al., 1998). Unfortunately, no normalization samples among other sub-populations, including the gifted, exist. Although rating scales can identify ADHD, they are inherently subjective and minor differences in rating scales can lead to different results. Trained personnel, therefore, remain the crucial component in the evaluation process.

New neuroimaging tools such as positron emission tomography (PET) (Zametkin et al., 1990; Ernst et al., 1998), single photon emission computed tomography (SPECT) (Lou et al., 1998), and magnetic resonance imaging (MRI) (Castellanos et al., 1996; Filipek et al., 1997; Vaidya et al., 1998) are currently being used in research studies and may eventually generate new means of diagnosing ADHD. But even these sophisticated techniques are insufficient to address the key issue of ADHD in relation to giftedness that is the focus of this chapter.

ADHD or Gifted?

In recent years, several authors (Lind, 1993; Webb & Latimer, 1993; Cramond, 1995; Freed & Parsons, 1997; Tucker & Hafenstein, 1997; Baum, Olenchak & Owen, 1998) have expressed concern that giftedness is often misconstrued as ADHD. In the absence of relevant data, we accept the possibility of occasional over-diagnosis among gifted children. However, it is worth noting that there is no evidence of substantial over-diagnosis of ADHD among the general population (Goldman et al., 1998).

While a misdiagnosis of ADHD is clearly undesirable, another diagnostic error may be even more prevalent among gifted students. This difficulty occurs when a student's over-reliance on strengths inadvertently obscures the disability. While this strategy may highlight a student's gifts, it does not eliminate the reality of the impairment, which is likely to reveal itself at some point in the student's development. On the other hand, if a student is allowed to acknowledge and experience the disability, he or she may learn appropriate compensatory or coping skills. Accepting that a child can be both gifted and ADHD and exploring the ways in which these conditions interact in each individual would seem to be a more productive way of looking at the problem than agonizing about a false dichotomy.

Sternberg's (1986) componential theory of intelligence, though not intended for this purpose, provides one way of describing the interaction between gifted-

ness and ADHD. This model suggests three components related to mental processes: knowledge-acquisition components (processes used in learning new material), metacomponents (higher-order processes used in planning, monitoring and decision making), and performance components (processes used in executing a task.)

For the purposes of this discussion, we have adapted this triarchy into the three stages of *input, processing*, and *output*. In this model, the *input stage* refers to the processes required for taking information in—listening, reading, kinesthetic learning, etc.; this stage corresponds to knowledge-acquisition. Learning disabilities, such as reading disorder (often called dyslexia), presumably have their greatest effects at this stage.

Processing refers to what happens 'in the head' of the thinker and would be roughly analogous to some metacomponents. While definitions of intelligence are controversial, most theories acknowledge that gifted individuals have an exceptionally rich set of mental links within which to embed new knowledge. It is at this stage, then, that giftedness has its greatest impact.

While ADHD can influence the input and processing stages, the most pronounced effect of the symptoms typically occur in the *output* or performance stage (Sergeant, Oosterlaan & Van der Meere, 1999). Until this stage, gifted/ADHD students may appear similar to other gifted students in terms of the amount of information they take in and process. Unlike other gifted students, however, they cannot summon their resources effectively and consistently at the output stage. This causes problems for the student who tries to produce written work because he or she is unable to process linearly the large amount of disparate information that were previously acquired. Oral communication, on the other hand, enables students with ADHD to reveal the extent of their knowledge through multiple channels such as tone of voice, facial expression, body and hand gestures, eye contact and intensity.

The contention that ADHD is merely misdiagnosed giftedness is likely derived from prematurely assessing the gifted student during the input and processing stages. Therefore, when evaluating ADHD in a student who is gifted, teachers should observe the quality and effectiveness of *all* stages of a student's learning.

Given the realities of the co-existence of giftedness and ADHD, 'ADHD or gifted?' is a less critical question than 'how impaired is a student by ADHD?' Some children are able to compensate in most situations for their susceptibility to ADHD; others are seriously handicapped. The former would not be diagnosed with ADHD as per the DSM-IV if they did not manifest impairment. Therefore, the single most relevant element that must be considered in evaluating ADHD is the degree of *impairment* a child experiences as a result of his or her behaviors.

A child who is far enough on the continuum of ADHD-like behaviors to be impaired academically, interpersonally, or in the development of sense of self, should be examined from a clinical/medical perspective to exclude treatable conditions and to distinguish ADHD from more benign 'overexcitabilities' (Silverman, 1993; Piechowski, 1997) and other temperamental or psychological traits. However, this does not mean that every child who may be somewhat impaired needs medical evaluation. As many authors (Hartmann, 1993; Lerner, Lowenthal & Lerner, 1995; Diller, 1998; Flick, 1998) have noted, nonmedical interventions can be used within the school and home and should be tried before more intrusive interventions are employed.

What is the Treatment for ADHD?

A comprehensive treatment plan for children with ADHD includes counseling, behavior management, educational modifications and, in cases where these do not suffice, medication. For the purposes of this chapter, however, we will limit our discussion to those issues that are most relevant to education and to gifted students in particular.

Educational Interventions

Once again, we must acknowledge the lack of data pertinent to gifted children. We also must limit our review of general educational accommodations. However, several resources (Hartmann, 1993; Hallowell & Ratey, 1994b; Lerner, Lowenthal & Lerner, 1995; Diller, 1998; Flick, 1998; Wiggins, 1998) provide more in-depth information about classroom organization, curriculum modification, behavior management, listening and memory techniques, social skills training and time management.

Generally speaking, the best educational programs for students with ADHD are based on structure, stimulation, and individualization (Lerner, Lowenthal & Lerner, 1995; Flick, 1998). While these are similar to qualities found in programs for the gifted (VanTassel Baska, 1997), this does not mean that a student's placement in a gifted program precludes further accommodations. In a program that stresses gifts, talents, and creativity (Renzulli & Reis, 1997), the student's need for ancillary services may be inadvertently camouflaged. An optimal program, therefore, should provide *complexity* and *challenge* to nurture a student's gifts and *support* and *structure* to accommodate the ADHD.

This duality presents immense challenge to educators, especially in light of the dearth of well-researched models designed specifically for this purpose. Of the models currently available in general education, we believe that those emphasizing diverse types of learning and production (Gardner, 1991; Renzulli, 1994; Kaplan & Gould, 1995; Sternberg et al., 1996) are the most promising for gifted students with ADHD

because they acknowledge and support many ways in which students can be productive and successful.

The information in the following chart demonstrates how common instructional practices from the lexicon of gifted child education might be modified for ADHD (Kaufmann, Kalbfleisch & Castellanos, 2000). The strategies listed in column one are representative of those frequently recommended for students with ADHD; column two specifies techniques and activities commonly used in gifted child education. The third column suggests ways in which the two might be combined to effectively teach gifted children with ADHD. While these suggestions cannot be construed as a curriculum or program, they do provide a springboard for application and research.

Although classroom modifications are important, the most significant school-based adjustment must be in the attitudes of educators. Teachers and students alike must learn to cope with giftedness (Galbraith & Delisle, 1996; Colangelo, 1997) and ADHD (Stern & Ben-Ami, 1998) and learn how each condition can enhance or inhibit the other. Educators should also be willing to substitute multi-modal assessment tasks for traditional evaluation techniques to more accurately identify a child's true range of abilities and interests (Renzulli, 1994; Wiggins, 1998). Finally, educators must change their definitions of success to reflect process and diversity in addition to conventional indications of achievement (Tomlinson, Callahan & Lelli, 1997; Flick, 1998).

Even in the best educational environment, however, with the most informed and flexible teachers, most students who have ADHD, including gifted students, require additional help. While non-medical interventions have their strong proponents (Lerner, Lowenthal & Lerner, 1995; Flick, 1998), medication remains the most well-researched and commonly recommended mode of treatment for ADHD in the United States.

Medical Interventions

The issue of medications and attention deficit disorders is too complex and contentious to be adequately addressed in a chapter, especially in light of the present emphasis on giftedness. However, certain information about stimulant medications, their possible benefits, and side effects should be mentioned.

Extensive research has repeatedly shown that psychostimulants such as methylphenidate (Ritalin) and the amphetamines (Dexedrine and Adderall) (Swanson et al., 1993) are remarkably safe and effective treatments for ADHD in the short-term. These drugs, which act by increasing the amount of the neurotransmitters dopamine and norepinephrine, have significant short-term benefits in about 70% to 80% of children who have ADHD (Spencer et al., 1996) with a slightly lower positive response rate in children who have Predominantly Inattentive Type ADHD. The benefits of these

Standard Modification for Students with ADHD	Standard Instructional Strategy from Gifted Child Education	Modified Instructional Strategy for Gifted Students with ADHD
To increase sustained attention, break complicated tasks into smaller parts to be completed at different times.	Synectics (Gordon, 1960; Gordon, 1974; Gordon & Poze, 1972)	Present Synectics stages in isolation rather than teach the entire process at one time.
To improve listening ability, use visual aids.	Creative/Future Problem Solving (Eberle & Stanish, 1985; Isaksen & Treffinger, 1985; Torrance & Sisk, 1997)	Write the rules and vocabulary of CPS/FPS on a poster or cue cards and refer to them often rather than rely solely on verbal instructions.
To minimize distractions, announce transitions in advance of their occurrence.	Creative/Future Problem Solving, Synectics	Announce each stage of the process before moving to the next.
To promote performance, use a buddy system in which students assist each other in concluding the day's work and reviewing the requirements for the next day.	Enrichment Clusters (Renzulli, 1994; Renzulli & Reis, 1997)	Assign buddies within each enrichment cluster, as well as in the student's regular classroom.
To cultivate organizational skills, provide a schedule so that the student knows exactly what to do for each class period.	Curriculum Compacting (Reis, Burns & Renzulli, 1993; Renzulli, 1994)	Create and identify daily compacting procedures in addition to or instead of longer-term goals.
To encourage performance, promote the use of tape recorders, computers, word processor and other technological advances.	Mentorships (Clasen & Clasen, 1997; Noller & Frey, 1994)	Employ alternative types of mentorships, e.g. on-line, correspondence, video, etc., rather than rely exclusively on in-person relationships.
To improve listening ability, eliminate extraneous noise and visual stimulation whenever possible.	Independent study (Betts, 1991; Kaplan & Gould, 1995; Schlichter, 1997)	Create a 'quiet area' for student-teacher conferences rather than hold meetings at the teacher's desk or in other high- traffic area.
To promote socialization, teach students effective communication skills that will generalize to a variety of situations.	Type III activities (Reis, Burns & Renzulli, 1993; Renzulli, 1994)	Encourage students to present their work to a variety of audiences rather than limit themselves to one type of audience.
To develop pro-social behavior, create a list of behaviors to be ignored as well as alternative behaviors.	Bibliotherapy (Frasier & McCannon, 1999; Schlichter, 1997)	Present biographies of eminent persons and fictitious gifted characters focusing on learning and problem solving instead of emphasizing success, e.g. process vs. product.
To encourage persistence, help students identify environmental distracters.	Guided fantasy (Eberle, 1996; Torrance & Safter, 1999)	Guide students through a Perfect Day Fantasy, allowing them to identify those factors that interfere with their goals.
To help students understand the consequences of their behavior, use appropriate reinforcers.	Interest inventories (Renzulli, 1977)	Allow students to select challenging, high-interest rewards such as reading or puzzles as well as standard reinforcers such as food or stickers.

medicines include a reduction of the core symptoms of inattention, impulsivity and hyperactivity, as well as improvement in motor, social and emotional functioning.

When these symptoms are reduced or eliminated, other improvements in classroom learning and productivity (Douglas et al., 1988; Balthazor, Wagner & Pelham, Jr., 1991), short term memory (Swanson et al.,

627

1978), interactions with parents, teachers and peers (Barkley et al., 1984; Pelham et al., 1985), and perceptual efficiency (Rapport et al., 1986), can also occur. At the same time, the most robust effects are on behavioral symptom ratings (Swanson et al., 1993). Although stimulants produce mild to moderate side effects, such as appetite suppression, headaches, irritability and trouble falling asleep, these usually subside when the prescribing physician changes the timing, dosage or formulation of the drug (Miller & Castellanos, 1998). For most children, however, the benefits of improved functioning in school, at home and with peers outweigh the temporary discomfort of side effects.

The recent increase in the prescription of stimulant medications, particularly in the U.S., has caused alarm and incited headlines worldwide. Studies of trends in prescriptions indicate that this pattern is not due to unscrupulous prescribing or illegal diversion but to increased treatment of previously neglected groups such as girls and children with Predominantly Inattentive ADHD (Goldman et al., 1998). Other explanatory factors for the increase in prescriptions are that treatment with medications is now being extended longer into adolescence and young adulthood and is more likely to be administered daily and year round, instead of just during school hours (Safer & Krager, 1994).

The long-term effects of stimulants appear to be relatively benign, although one longitudinal study raised the possibility that childhood use of stimulant medications may be associated with a later increased risk of smoking and stimulant abuse beyond that expected from ADHD alone (Lambert & Hartsough, 1998) although other investigators found that stimulant medications decrease the later risk of substance abuse (Biederman et al., 1999; Paternite et al., 1999). Since stimulant medications do not 'cure' ADHD and are not absolutely risk-free, their use should be reserved for those individuals who are significantly impaired and for whom psychosocial and behavioral programs and significant academic accommodations have not provided adequate benefit (Overmeyer & Taylor, 1999). Based on the most extensive randomized controlled trial of treatment modalities in ADHD (Jensen et al., 1999), Taylor argued that even in a low-medication culture, such as in most European countries, "children with suboptimal responses to behavioral approaches should be offered medication as well" (p. 1097, Taylor, 1999).

Conclusion

Clearly, this chapter must conclude with a plea for empirical research on giftedness and attention deficit disorders as no such data currently exist. A simple but profoundly important question such as the incidence of DSM-IV subtypes of ADHD among the gifted must be investigated. If research were to show that current DSM-IV criteria identify significantly different proportions of gifted students compared to the general population, subsequent studies would be able to explore the sources of such discrepancies. The existence of data would in turn facilitate and encourage the development of strategies for appropriate identification and curriculum development.

Although we have focused on the negative aspects of ADHD in this chapter, we do not believe that ADHD is a defect that must be 'cured'. In fact, we have often observed that ADHD can enhance as well as inhibit the realization of gifts and talents.

Educators of gifted students with ADHD face a formidable task in that they must provide opportunities for students to apply their strengths while ameliorating their deficits. Although the same might be said of any sound educational program, this is more daunting for gifted students with ADHD because of the disparity these conditions can create. Only through consistent attention, immeasurable creativity and patient understanding by educators, parents and students, coupled with substantive research will these challenges be adequately addressed.

References

Achenbach, T. & Edelbrock, C. (1983). *Manual for the Child Behavior Checklist and Revised Child Behavior Profile.* University of Vermont, Department of Psychiatry: Burlington, VT.

Adams, C. D., Kelly, M. L. & McCarthy, M. (1997). The Adolescent Behavior Checklist: development and initial psychometric properties of a self-report measure for adolescents with ADHD. *Journal of Clinical Child Psychology*, **26**, 77–86.

American Psychiatric Association (1994). *Diagnostic and Statistical Manual of Mental Disorders.* (4th ed.). Washington, D.C.: American Psychiatric Association.

Amin, K., Douglas, V. I., Mendelson, M. J. & Dufresne, J. (1993). Separable/integral classification by hyperactive and normal children. *Development and Psychopathology*, **5**, 415–431.

Angold, A., Costello, E. J. & Erkanli, A. (1999). Comorbidity. *Journal of Child Psychology and Psychiatry and Allied Disciplines*, **40**, 57–87.

Applegate, B., Lahey, B. B., Hart, E. L., Biederman, J., Hynd, G. W., Barkley, R. A., Ollendick, T., Frick, P. J., Greenhill, L., McBurnett, K., Newcorn, J. H., Kerdyk, L., Garfinkel, B., Waldman, I. & Shaffer, D. (1997). Validity of the age-of-onset criterion for ADHD: a report from the DSM- IV field trials. *Journal of the American Academy of Child and Adolescent Psychiatry*, **36**, 1211–1221.

Armstrong, T. (1995). *The myth of the A.D.D. child.* New York: Dutton.

Arnold, L. E. (1999). Treatment alternatives for attention-deficit/hyperactivity disorder (ADHD). *Journal of Attention Disorders*, **3**, 30–48.

Balthazor, M. J., Wagner, R. K. & Pelham, W. E., Jr. (1991). The specificity of the effects of stimulant medication on classroom learning-related measures of cognitive processing for attention deficit disorder children. *Journal of Abnormal Child Psychology*, **19**, 35–52.

Barbaresi, W. J. & Olsen, R. D. (1998). An ADHD educational intervention for elementary schoolteachers: a pilot study. *Journal of Developmental and Behavioral Pediatrics*, **19**, 94–100.

Barkley, R. A. (1997). Behavioral inhibition, sustained attention, and executive functions: constructing a unifying theory of ADHD. *Psychological Bulletin*, **121**, 65–94.

Barkley, R. A. (1997). *ADHD and the nature of self control.* New York: Guilford Press.

Barkley, R. A. & Biederman, J. (1997). Toward a broader definition of the age-of-onset criterion for attention-deficit hyperactivity disorder. *Journal of the American Academy of Child and Adolescent Psychiatry*, **36**, 1204–1210.

Barkley, R. A. & Biederman, J. (1998). Age of onset for ADHD [letter]. *Journal of the American Academy of Child and Adolescent Psychiatry*, **37**, 569–570.

Barkley, R. A., Karlsson, J., Strzelecki, E. & Murphy, J. (1984). Effects of age and Ritalin dosage on the mother-child interactions of hyperactive children. *Journal of Consulting and Clinical Psychology*, **52**, 750–758.

Baum, S. M., Olenchak, F. R. & Owen, S. V. (1998). Gifted students with attention deficits: fact and/or fiction? Or, can we see the forest for the trees? *Gifted Child Quarterly*, **42**, 96–104.

Baumgaertel, A. (1999). Alternative and controversial treatments for attention-deficit/hyperactivity disorder. *Pediatric Clinics of North America*, **46**, 977–992.

Betts, G. (1991). The autonomous learner model for the gifted and talented. In: N. Colangelo & G. Davis (Eds.), *Handbook of Gifted Education.* (1st ed.), pp. 142–153. Boston: Allyn and Bacon.

Biederman, J. (1998). Attention-deficit/hyperactivity disorder: a life-span perspective. *Journal of Clinical Psychiatry*, **59**, 4–16.

Biederman, J., Wilens, T., Mick, E., Faraone, S. V., Weber, W., Curtis, S., Thornell, A., Pfister, K., Jetton, J. G. & Soriano, J. (1997). Is ADHD a risk factor for psychoactive substance use disorders? Findings from a four-year prospective follow-up study. *Journal of the American Academy of Child and Adolescent Psychiatry*, **36**, 21–29.

Biederman, J., Wilens, T., Mick, E., Spencer, T. & Faraone, S. V. (1999). Pharmacotherapy of attention-deficit/hyperactivity disorder reduces risk for substance use disorder. *Pediatrics*, **104**, E201-E205.

Borcherding, B., Thompson, K., Kruesi, M. J. P., Bartko, J., Rapoport, J. L. & Weingartner, H. (1988). Automatic and effortful processing in attention deficit/hyperactivity disorder. *Journal of Abnormal Child Psychology*, **16**, 333–345.

Bowen, J., Fenton, T. & Rappaport, L. (1991). Stimulant medication and attention-deficit hyperactivity disorder. *American Journal of Diseases of Children*, **145**, 291–295.

Breakey, J. (1997). The role of diet and behaviour in childhood. *Journal of Paediatrics and Child Health*, **33**, 190–194.

Breggin, P. R. (1998). *Talking back to Ritalin: what doctors aren't telling you about stimulants for children.* Monroe, ME: Common Courage Press.

Bussing, R., Schuhmann, E., Belin, T. R., Widawski, M. & Perwien, A. R. (1998). Diagnostic utility of two commonly used ADHD screening measures among special education students. *Journal of the American Academy of Child and Adolescent Psychiatry*, **37**, 74–82.

Castellanos, F. X. (1997). Toward a pathophysiology of attention-deficit/hyperactivity disorder. *Clinical Pediatrics*, **36**, 381–393.

Castellanos, F. X., Giedd, J. N., Marsh, W. L., Hamburger, S. D., Vaituzis, A. C., Dickstein, D. P., Sarfatti, S. E., Vauss, Y. C., Snell, J. W., Lange, N., Kaysen, D., Krain, A. L., Ritchie, G. F., Rajapakse, J. C. & Rapoport, J. L. (1996). Quantitative brain magnetic resonance imaging in attention-deficit/hyperactivity disorder. *Archives of General Psychiatry*, **53**, 607–616.

Castellanos, F. X. & Rapoport, J. L. (1992). Etiology of attention-deficit hyperactivity disorder. *Child and Adolescent Psychiatric Clinics of North America*, **1**, 373–384.

Chelune, G. J., Ferguson, W., Koon, R. & Dickey, T. O. (1986). Frontal lobe disinhibition in attention deficit disorder. *Child Psychiatry and Human Development*, **16**, 221–234.

Clasen, D. & Clasen, R. (1997). Mentoring: a time-honored option for education of the gifted and talented. In N. Colangelo & G. Davis (Eds.), *Handbook of Gifted Education* (2nd ed.), pp. 218–229. Needham Heights, MA: Allyn & Bacon.

Colangelo, N. (1997). Counseling gifted students: issues and practices. In: N. Colangelo & G. Davis (Eds.), *Handbook of Gifted Education* (2nd ed.), pp. 353–365. Needham Heights, MA: Allyn & Bacon.

Conners, C. K. (1997). *Conners' Rating Scales-Revised User's Manual.* North Tonawanda, NY: Multi-Health Systems, Inc.

Cramond, B. (1995). *The coincidence of attention deficit hyperactivity disorder and creativity.* Storrs, CT: The National Research Center on the Gifted and Talented.

Csikszentmihalyi, M. (1990). *Flow: the psychology of optimal experience.* New York: Harper & Row.

Denckla, M. B. (1989). Executive function, the overlap zone between attention deficit hyperactivity disorder and learning disabilities. *International Pediatrics*, **4**, 155–160.

Denckla, M. B. (1996). A theory and model of executive function: a neuropsychological perspective. In: G. R. Lyon & N. A. Krasnegor (Eds.), *Attention, Memory, and Executive Function* (pp. 263–278). Baltimore, MD: Paul H. Brookes Publishing Co.

Diller, L. H. (1998). *Running on Ritalin: a physician reflects on children, society and performance in a pill.* New York: Bantam Books.

Douglas, V. I., Barr, R. G., Amin, K., O'Neill, M. E. & Britton, B. G. (1988). Dosage effects and individual responsivity to methylphenidate in attention deficit disorder. *Journal of Child Psychology and Psychiatry and Allied Disciplines*, **29**, 453–475.

Douglas, V. I. & Parry, P. A. (1994). Effects of reward and non-reward on frustration and attention in attention deficit disorder. *Journal of Abnormal Child Psychology*, **22**, 281–302.

Dykens, E., Leckman, J. F., Riddle, M., Hardin, M., Schwartz, S. & Cohen, D. (1990). Intellectual, academic, and adaptive functioning of Tourette Syndrome children with and without Attention Deficit Disorder. *Journal of Abnormal Child Psychology*, **18**, 607–615.

Dykman, R. A., Ackerman, P. T. & Raney, T. J. (1993). Research synthesis on assessment and characteristics of children with attention deficit disorder. In: Chesapeake Institute (Ed.), *Executive Summaries of Research Syntheses and Promising Practices on the Education of Children with*

Attention Deficit Disorder (pp. 4–21). Washington, D.C.: Chesapeake Institute.

Eberle, R. (1996). *SCAMPER: Games for imagination development*. Waco,TX: Prufrock Press.

Eberle, R. & Stanish, B. (1985). *CPS for kids*. Carthage,IL: Good Apple.

Epstein, J. N., March, J. S., Conners, C. K. & Jackson, D. L. (1998). Racial differences on the Conners Teacher Rating Scale. *Journal of Abnormal Child Psychology*, **26**, 109–118.

Ernst, M., Zametkin, A. J., Matochik, J. A., Jons, P. H. & Cohen, R. M. (1998). DOPA decarboxylase activity in attention deficit hyperactivity disorder adults, a [fluorine–18]fluorodopa positron emission tomographic study. *Journal of Neuroscience*, **18**, 5901–5907.

Famularo, R., Fenton, T., Kinscherff, R. & Augustyn, M. (1996). Psychiatric comorbidity in childhood post traumatic stress disorder. *Child Abuse and Neglect*, **20**, 953–961.

Faraone, S. V. & Biederman, J. (1998). Neurobiology of attention-deficit hyperactivity disorder. *Biological Psychiatry*, **44**, 951–958.

Filipek, P. A., Semrud-Clikeman, M., Steingard, R. J., Renshaw, P. F., Kennedy, D. N. & Biederman, J. (1997). Volumetric MRI analysis comparing attention-deficit hyperactivity disorder and normal controls. *Neurology*, **48**, 589–601.

Flick, G. L. (1998). *ADD/ADHD behavior-change resource kit*. New York: Simon & Schuster.

Frasier, M. & McCannon, C. (1999). Using bibliotherapy with gifted children. *Gifted Child Quarterly*, **25**, 81–85.

Freed, J. & Parsons, L. (1997). *Right-brained children in a left-brained world: unlocking the potential of your ADD child*. New York: Simon & Schuster.

Freeman, R. D. (1997). Attention deficit hyperactivity disorder in the presence of Tourette syndrome. *Neurologic Clinics*, **15**, 411–420.

Frick, P. J., Lahey, B. B., Applegate, B., Kerdyck, L., Ollendick, T., Hynd, G. W., Garfinkel, B., Greenhill, L., Biederman, J., Barkley, R. A., McBurnett, K., Newcorn, J. & Waldman, I. (1994). DSM-IV field trials for the disruptive behavior disorders: symptom utility estimates. *Journal of the American Academy of Child and Adolescent Psychiatry*, **33**, 529–539.

Galbraith, J. & Delisle, J. (1996). *The gifted kids' survival guide*. Minneapolis, MN: Free Spirit Press.

Gardner, H. (1991). *The unschooled mind: how children think & how schools should teach*. New York: Basic Books.

Gaub, M. & Carlson, C. L. (1997). Gender differences in ADHD: a meta-analysis and critical review. *Journal of the American Academy of Child and Adolescent Psychiatry*, **36**, 1036–1045.

Goldman, L. S., Genel, M., Bezman, R. J. & Slanetz, P. J. (1998). Diagnosis and treatment of attention-deficit/hyperactivity disorder in children and adolescents. Council on Scientific Affairs, American Medical Association. *Journal of the American Medical Association*, **279**, 1100–1107.

Gordon, W. J. (1960). *Synectics*. New York: Harper & Row.

Gordon, W. J. (1974). *Making it strange*. New York: Harper & Row.

Gordon, W. J. & Poze, T. (1972). *Teaching is listening*. Cambridge, MA: SES Associates.

Goyette, C. H., Conners, C. K. & Ulrich, R. F. (1978). Normative data on revised Conners Parent and Teacher Rating Scales. *Journal of Abnormal Child Psychology*, **6**, 221–236.

Hallowell, E. M. & Ratey, J. J. (1994a). *Answers to distraction*. New York: Pantheon Books.

Hallowell, E. M. & Ratey, J. J. (1994b). *Driven to distraction*. New York: Pantheon Books.

Hart, E. L., Lahey, B. B., Loeber, R., Appelgate, B. & Frick, P. J. (1995). Developmental change in attention-deficit/hyperactive disorder in boys: a four year longitudinal study. *Journal of Abnormal Child Psychology*, **23**, 729–749.

Hartmann, T. (1993). *Attention deficit disorder: a different perception*. Novato, CA: Underwood-Miller.

Isaksen, S. G. & Treffinger, D. J. (1985). *Creative problem solving: the basic course*. Buffalo, NY: Bearly.

Jacobson, M. F. & Schardt, D. (1999). *Diet, ADHD & behavior: a quarter-century review*. Washington, D.C.: Center for Science in the Public Interest.

Jensen, P. S., Arnold, L. E., Richters, J. E., Severe, J. B., Vereen, D., Vitiello, B., Schiller, E., Hinshaw, S. P., Elliott, G. R., Conners, C. K., Wells, K. C., March, J., Swanson, J., Wigal, T., Cantwell, D. P., Abikoff, H. B., Hechtman, L., Greenhill, L. L., Newcorn, J. H., Pelham, W. E., Hoza, B. & Kraemer, H. C. (1999). A 14-month randomized clinical trial of treatment strategies for attention-deficit/hyperactivity disorder. *Archives of General Psychiatry*, **56**, 1073–1086.

Kaplan, S. & Gould, B. (1995). *Frames: Differentiating the core curriculum*. Calabasas, CA: Educator to Educator.

Kaufmann, F. A., Kalbfleisch, M. L. & Castellanos, F. X. (2000). *Understanding and helping the gifted child with attention deficit disorders*. Storrs, CT: The National Research Center on the Gifted and Talented.

Kohn, A. (1989, October). Suffer the restless children. *The Atlantic Monthly*, 90–100.

Lahey, B. B., Applegate, B., McBurnett, K., Biederman, J., Greenhill, L., Hynd, G. W., Barkley, R. A., Newcorn, J., Jensen, P. & Richters, J. (1994). DSM-IV field trials for attention deficit hyperactivity disorder in children and adolescents. *American Journal of Psychiatry*, **151**, 1673–1685.

Lahey, B. B., Miller, T. L., Gordon, R. A. & Riley, A. W. (1999). Developmental epidemiology of the disruptive behavior disorders. In: H. C. Quay & A. E. Hogan (Eds.), *Handbook of Disruptive Behavior Disorders* (pp. 23–48). New York: Plenum Press.

Lambert, N. M. & Hartsough, C. S. (1998). Prospective study of tobacco smoking and substance dependencies among samples of ADHD and non-ADHD participants. *Journal of Learning Disabilities*, **31**, 533–544.

Lerner, J. W., Lowenthal, B. & Lerner, S. R. (1995). *Attention deficit disorders: assessment and teaching*. Pacific Grove, CA: Brooks/Cole Publishing.

Levitt, P., Harvey, J. A., Friedman, E., Simansky, K. & Murphy, E. H. (1997). New evidence for neurotransmitter influences on brain development. *Trends in Neuroscience*, **20**, 269–274.

Lind, S. (1993). Something to consider before referring for ADD/ADHD. *Counseling & Guidance*, **4**, 1–3.

Lou, H. C. (1996). Etiology and pathogenesis of attention-deficit hyperactivity disorder (ADHD): significance of prematurity and perinatal hypoxic-haemodynamic encephalopathy. *Acta Paediatrica*, **85**, 1266–1271.

Lou, H. C., Andresen, J., Steinberg, B., McLaughlin, T. & Friberg, L. (1998). The striatum in a putative cerebral network activated by verbal awareness in normals and in ADHD children. *European Journal of Neurology*, **5**, 67–74.

Mannuzza, S., Klein, R. G., Bessler, A., Malloy, P. & LaPadula, M. (1998). Adult psychiatric status of hyperactive boys grown up. *American Journal of Psychiatry*, **155**, 493–498.

Max, J. E., Arndt, S., Castillo, C. S., Bokura, H., Robin, D. A., Lindgren, S. D., Smith, W. L. J., Sato, Y. & Mattheis, P. J. (1998). Attention-deficit hyperactivity symptomatology after traumatic brain injury: a prospective study. *Journal of the American Academy of Child and Adolescent Psychiatry*, **37**.

Mayes, L. C., Granger, R. H., Bornstein, M. H. & Zuckerman, B. (1992). The problem of prenatal cocaine exposure. a rush to judgment. *Journal of the American Medical Association*, **267**, 406–408.

Milberger, S., Biederman, J., Faraone, S. V., Chen, L. & Jones, J. (1996). Is maternal smoking during pregnancy a risk factor for attention deficit hyperactivity disorder in children? *American Journal of Psychiatry*, **153**, 1138–1142.

Miller, K. J. & Castellanos, F. X. (1998). Management of attention-deficit/hyperactivity disorders. *Pediatrics in Review*, **19**, 373–384.

Noller, R. & Frey, R. (1994). *Mentoring: Annotated bibliography*. Sarasota, FL: Center for Creative Learning.

Overmeyer, S. & Taylor, E. (1999). Annotation: principles of treatment for hyperkinetic disorder: practice approaches for the UK. *Journal of Child Psychology and Psychiatry and Allied Disciplines*, **40**, 1147–1157.

Paternite, C. E., Loney, J., Salisbury, H. & Whaley, M. A. (1999). Childhood inattention-overactivity, aggression, and stimulant medication history as predictors of young adult outcomes. *Journal of Child and Adolescent Psychopharmacology*, **9**, 169–184.

Pelham, W. E., Bender, M. E., Caddell, J., Booth, S. & Morrer, S. H. (1985). Methylphenidate and children with attention deficit disorder: dose effects on classroom academic and social behavior. *Archives of General Psychiatry*, **42**, 948–952.

Piechowski, M. M. (1997). Emotional giftedness: The measure of intrapersonal intelligence. In: N. Colangelo & G. Davis (Eds.), *Handbook of gifted education* (2nd ed.), pp. 366–381. Needham Heights, MA: Allyn & Bacon.

Pliszka, S. R. (1998). Comorbidity of attention-deficit/ hyperactivity disorder with psychiatric disorder: an overview. *Journal of Clinical Psychiatry*, **59**, 50–58.

Quay, H. C. (1999). Classification of the disruptive behavior disorders. In: H. C. Quay & A. E. Hogan (Eds.), *Handbook of Disruptive Behavior Disorders* (pp. 3–21). New York: Plenum Press.

Rapport, M. D., DuPaul, G. J., Stoner, G. & Jones, T. J. (1986). Comparing classroom and clinic measures of attention deficit disorder: differential, idiosyncratic, and dose-response effects of methylphenidate. *Journal of Consulting and Clinical Psychology*, **54**, 334–341.

Reid, R., Maag, J. W. & Vasa, S. F. (1993). Attention deficit hyperactivity disorder as a disability category: a critique. *Exceptional Children*, **60**, 198–214.

Reis, S. M., Burns, D. & Renzulli, J. S. (1993). *Curriculum compacting: the complete guide for modifying the regular curriculum for high ability students*. Mansfield Center, CT: Creative Learning Press.

Renzulli, J. S. (1977). *The interest-a-lyzer*. Mansfield Center, CT: Creative Learning Press.

Renzulli, J. S. (1994). *Schools for talent development: a practical plan for total school improvement*. Mansfield Center, CT: Creative Learning Press.

Renzulli, J. S. & Reis, S. M. (1997). The school-wide enrichment model: new directions for developing high end learning. In: N. Colangelo & G. Davis (Eds.), *Handbook of Gifted Education* (2nd ed.), pp. 136–153. Needham Heights, MA: Allyn & Bacon.

Richardson, G. A. & Day, N. L. (1994). Detrimental effects of prenatal cocaine exposure: illusion or reality? *Journal of the American Academy of Child and Adolescent Psychiatry*, **33**, 28–34.

Rimm, S. (1999). Attention deficit disorder: a difficult diagnosis. *Parenting for High Potential* **12**–13–28.

Safer, D. J. & Krager, J. M. (1994). The increased rate of stimulant treatment for hyperactive/inattentive students in secondary schools. *Pediatrics*, **94**, 462–464.

Schlichter, C. (1997). Talents unlimited model in programs for gifted students. In: N. Colangelo & G. Davis (Eds.), *Handbook of Gifted Education* (2nd ed.), pp. 318–328. Needham Heights, MA: Allyn & Bacon.

Sergeant, J., Oosterlaan, J. & Van der Meere, J. (1999). Information processing and energetic factors in attention-deficit/hyperactivity disorder. In: H. C. Quay & A. E. Hogan (Eds.), *Handbook of Disruptive Behavior Disorders* (pp. 75–104). New York: Plenum Press.

Silverman, L. (1993). The gifted individual. In: L. Silverman (Ed.), *Counseling the Gifted and Talented* (1st ed.), pp. 3–28. Denver, CO: Love Publishing.

Silverman, L. (1998). Through the lens of giftedness. *Roeper Review*, **20**, 204–210.

Spencer, T., Biederman, J., Wilens, T. E., Harding, M., O'Donnell, D. & Griffin, S. (1996). Pharmacotherapy of attention-deficit hyperactivity disorder across the life cycle. *Journal of the American Academy of Child and Adolescent Psychiatry*, **35**, 409–432.

Stein, M. A., Blondis, T. A., Schnitzler, E. R., O'Brien, T., Fishkin, J., Blackwell, B., Szumowski, E. & Roizen, N. J. (1996). Methylphenidate dosing: twice daily vs. three times daily. *Pediatrics*, **98**, 748–756.

Stern, J. and Ben-Ami, U. (1998). Talking to children about their attention deficit disorder. *Attention! The Magazine of Children and Adults With Attentional Disorders*, **15**, 25–28.

Sternberg, R. (1986). A triarchal theory of intellectual giftedness. In: R. Sternberg & J. E. Davidson (Eds.), *Conceptions of Giftedness* (pp. 223–243). New York: Cambridge University Press.

Sternberg, R., Ferrari, M., Clinkenbeard, P. & Grigorenko, E. (1996). Identification, instruction and assessment of gifted children: a construct validation of a triarchic model. *Gifted Child Quarterly*, **40**, 129–137.

Streissguth, A. P., Barr, H. M., Sampson, P. D. & Bookstein, F. L. (1994). Prenatal alcohol and offspring development: the first fourteen years. *Drug and Alcohol Dependence*, **36**, 89–99.

Swanson, J., Kinsbourne, M., Roberts, W. & Zucker, K. (1978). Time-response analysis of the effect of stimulant medication on the learning ability of children referred for hyperactivity. *Pediatrics*, **61**, 21–29.

Swanson, J. M., McBurnett, K., Wigal, T., Pfiffner, L., Lerner, M. A., Williams, L., Christian, D. L., Tamm, L., Willcutt,

E., Crowley, K., Clevenger, W., Khouzam, N., Woo, C., Crinella, F. M. & Fisher, T. D. (1993). Effect of stimulant medication on children with attention deficit disorder: a 'review of reviews'. Special Issue: Issues in the education of children with attentional deficit disorder. *Exceptional Children*, **60**, 154–161.

Taylor, E. (1999). Development of clinical services for attention-deficit/hyperactivity disorder. *Archives of General Psychiatry*, **56**, 1097–1099.

Tomlinson, C. A., Callahan, C. M. & Lelli, K. M. (1997). Challenging expectations: case studies of high-potential, culturally diverse young children. *Gifted Child Quarterly*, **41**, 5–17.

Torrance, E. P. & Safter, T. (1999). *Making the creative leap beyond* . . . Buffalo, NY: Creative Education Foundation Press.

Torrance, E. P. & Sisk, D. S. (1997). *Gifted and talented children in the regular classroom*. Buffalo, NY: Bearly.

Tucker, B. & Hafenstein, N. L. (1997). Psychological intensities in young gifted children. *Gifted Child Quarterly*, **41**, 66–75.

Vaidya, C. J., Austin, G., Kirkorian, G., Ridlehuber, H. W., Desmond, J. E., Glover, G. H. & Gabrieli, J. D. (1998). Selective effects of methylphenidate in attention deficit hyperactivity disorder: a functional magnetic resonance imaging study. *Proceedings of the National Academy of Sciences of the United States of America*, **95**, 14494–14499.

VanTassel Baska, J. (1997). What matters in curriculum for gifted learners: Reflections on theory, research and practice. In: N. Colangelo & G. Davis (Eds.), *Handbook of Gifted Education* (2nd ed.), pp. 126–135. Needham Heights, MA: Allyn and Bacon.

Vaughn, M. L., Riccio, C. A., Hynd, G. W. & Hall, J. (1997). Diagnosing ADHD (predominantly inattentive and combined type subtypes): discriminant validity of the Behavior Assessment System for Children and the Achenbach Parent and Teacher Rating Scales. *Journal of Clinical Child Psychology*, **26**, 349–357.

Webb, J. T. & Latimer, D. (1993). ADHD and children who are gifted. *ERIC Digest, E522.*

Wigal, S. B., Gupta, S., Guinta, D. & Swanson, J. M. (1998b). Reliability and validity of the SKAMP rating scale in a laboratory school setting. *Psychopharmacology Bulletin*, **34**, 47–53.

Wigal, T., Swanson, J. M., Douglas, V. I., Wigal, S. B., Wippler, C. M. & Cavoto, K. F. (1998a). Effect of reinforcement on facial responsivity and persistence in children with attention-deficit hyperactivity disorder. *Behavior Modification*, **22**, 143–166.

Wiggins, G. (1998). *Educative assessment*. San Francisco: Josssey-Bass Publishers.

Wolraich, M. L., Hannah, J. N., Baumgaertel, A. & Feurer, I. D. (1998). Examination of DSM-IV criteria for attention deficit/hyperactivity disorder in a county-wide sample. *Journal of Developmental and Behavioral Pediatrics*, **19**, 162–168.

Wolraich, M. L., Wilson, D. B. & White, J. W. (1995). The effect of sugar on behavior or cognition in children. A meta-analysis. *Journal of the American Medical Association*, **274**, 1617–1621.

Zametkin, A. J., Nordahl, T. E., Gross, M., King, A. C., Semple, W. E., Rumsey, J., Hamburger, S. D. & Cohen, R. M. (1990). Cerebral glucose metabolism in adults with hyperactivity of childhood onset. *The New England Journal of Medicine*, **323**, 1361–1366.

Gender Differences in Engineering and the Physical Sciences Among the Gifted: An Inorganic-Organic Distinction

David Lubinski, Camilla P. Benbow and Martha J. Morelock

Vanderbilt University, USA

Introduction

Beginning in 1968 and essentially complete by 1972, there was in the U.S. a legal revolution in women's education and employment rights (Rossiter, 1995); it promised in the U.S. broad ramifications for women's careers across a wide range of professions. Over the ensuing three decades, many of the unenlightened barriers preventing women from achieving educational credentials and occupational status commensurate with their abilities were removed. In many educational programs, gender representation began to approach parity. Just as the protagonists urging the removal of the aforementioned barriers had predicted would occur, women entering the field of Law, for example, exhibited exceptional performances on bar exams and achieved high grades and honors in their classes. In 1995, 29.5% of the doctorate degrees earned in Law and legal studies in the U.S. went to women, up from less than 1% of doctorate degrees awarded to women in 1971 (U.S. Bureau of the Census, 1998).

The health and social sciences also saw striking gains in the U.S. Of the doctorate degrees awarded in health sciences in 1995, 58.1% went to women—up from 16.5% in 1971. Of the doctorate degrees awarded in social sciences in 1995, 37.7% went to women; whereas only 13.9% went to women in 1971. In psychology, women accounted for 62.6% of the doctorates awarded in 1995, up from the 24% of awarded doctorates credited to them in 1971.

This trend served to reinforce further the well-grounded arguments for removing gender-discriminating educational barriers. Arguments originally stemming primarily from political-ideological concerns now became buttressed by economic and psychological justification: not only were women performing admirably in these areas, the disciplines themselves were benefiting from a more able student population. The optimism spawned by these changes is reflected in a 1988 text: "A transformation is underway . . . fueled by feminist concerns and by the entry of increasing numbers of women into the scientific professions" (Lips, 1988).

When one looks at inorganic scientific fields, however, a marked winnowing of the male/female ratio is not observed. Despite gains, the participation of women in the physical sciences, mathematics, and engineering reflects a persistent gender disparity (National Science Foundation, 1999). For example, 1 in 6, or 17%, of engineering *bachelor's* degrees were awarded to women in 1995 (still, an increase from the less than 1% of the total in 1966). And women were awarded 35% of the *bachelor's* degrees in mathematics and computer science in 1995—only a slight increase over 1966.

At the graduate level, 23.5% of awarded Doctorates in physical sciences and science technologies went to women in 1995, up from 5.6% in 1971. In mathematics, women accounted for 22.1% of the awarded Doctorates in 1995, having been credited with 7.6% in 1971. The smallest proportion of women doctorate recipients in any broad field was in engineering. While men earned 5,313 engineering doctoral degrees in 1995, women earned 694 engineering degrees—just 12% of the total engineering doctorates. Even so, this represented a notable increase over the 7% of engineering doctorates awarded to women in 1985 (National Science Foundation, 1999) and the 0.6% of doctorates in engineering and engineering technology awarded to women in 1971 (U.S. Bureau of the Census, 1998).

Why has such gender disparity persisted in engineering and the physical sciences? Have we completely removed from these disciplines the barriers that previously prevented women from entering other fields, such as law and medicine? Are there factors unique to engineering and the physical sciences that discourage women from entering and excelling within

633

them? These questions, among many others, are being investigated through our research. Here we focus specifically on factors related to educational/vocational choice, exceptional educational/vocational achievement, and gender differences in educational and vocational outcomes within the gifted population. Our research, however, is also aimed at experimentation with and refinement of well-known educational interventions. That is, in working with intellectually talented students, individually and in groups, we attempt to find and provide environments wherein their talents can best blossom and come to their full fruition. Understanding what constitutes those environments and learning how to create them are two of the more central goals of our applied research (Lubinski & Benbow, 2000); we shall draw upon that work as well.

Our work with mathematically and verbally precocious youth is particularly relevant to exploring the critical determinants of gender differences in advanced achievement. Noteworthy professional achievements in the sciences tend to be within the exclusive purview of the highly able—people located within the top few percentage points of the distribution of intelligence. Thus, our Study of Mathematically Precocious Youth (SMPY) provides a data bank especially well suited to speak to male/female differences in educational achievement and vocational choice, inasmuch as it contains large proportions of individuals, of both genders, who possess the intellectual potential for achieving excellence in engineering, mathematics and the physical sciences, as well as for a variety of other intellectually demanding careers.

Our empirical studies have indeed revealed unique factors operating to preserve gender-disparities in inorganic vs. organic disciplines. Instead of stemming solely from external, culturally imposed barriers to vocational and educational opportunities, however, these factors appear to be more related to personal choice. Our empirical findings lead us to propose here that gender differences in achievement are a reflection of such choices. Furthermore, these choices naturally emerge from a number of longitudinally-stable, gender-differentiating attributes critical for a commitment to, and excellence in, contrasting careers.

It is the thesis of this chapter that the theoretical model guiding our research on the optimal development of intellectual talent (which we will explicate) has implications for analyzing and better understanding gender differences in various careers. Our model addresses why some intellectually demanding disciplines and occupations are over-represented by women, while others are over-represented by men. We suggest that it might be profitable to reconceptualize the professional and the public view of gender differences in maths/science achievement, namely, as consequences of the different perspectives and personal qualities those males and females bring to situations. It is our view that too much negativity has been attached

to the under-representation of women in the physical sciences, as if women possessed a deficit of some kind because, naturally, more females should be interested in such career possibilities. It is our position that young adults (particularly intellectually gifted young adults) are in a better position to make informed decisions on their personal development than some theorists give them credit for. To be sure, educators and policy makers should ensure opportunities for all students to develop as fully as their abilities and motivations take them. But if this results in some disciplines being over-represented by men, while others are over-represented by women, we are not as concerned, especially when the overall proportion of advanced educational degrees are comparable for men and women (Benbow et al., 2000; Lubinski et al., in press).

To illustrate how this might be accomplished, we shall draw on findings from SMPY to document gender differences in key antecedents to educational and vocational choice. We shall first describe the design of our study and its theoretical framework; this is followed by a discussion of gender differences in particular kinds of achievement among the mathematically talented. Some empirical findings involving gender differences on familiar as well as neglected variables critical for choosing contrasting educational and vocational paths are reviewed. Finally, we close with a brief discussion of the implications of our current state of knowledge and how these implications might be used to both guide and organize the direction of future research on the intellectually gifted.

Study of Mathematically Precocious Youth (SMPY)

SMPY was founded by Julian C. Stanley in September 1971 at Johns Hopkins University and predicated on the philosophy of conducting research through service to intellectually talented students. SMPY was interested in first identifying adolescents who possess exceptional intellectual abilities and, then, to ascertain factors that contribute to their optimal educational and vocational development. Yet, special attention has always been devoted to maths/science disciplines. One intervention, implemented from the start, was to provide these students, through acceleration and special classes, with better opportunities to develop their already exceptional quantitative skills, which we have now referred to as *appropriate developmental placement* (Lubinski & Benbow, 2000). To facilitate the uncovering of other beneficial interventions and to answer basic research questions about intellectual giftedness more generally, SMPY established in 1972 a planned 50-year longitudinal study, now being conducted at Vanderbilt University. Through this study, which currently includes over 5000 talented individuals identified over approximately a 20-year period, SMPY is beginning to bring into focus the factors contributing to gifted students' educational, intellectual, personal, and vocational development (Lubinski & Benbow,

1994, 2000; Benbow, Lubinski & Suchy, 1996; Stanley, 1996).

Participants in SMPY were identified through a talent search, a concept developed by Stanley and initially limited to mathematical talent (Keating & Stanley, 1972; Stanley, 1973; Stanley, Keating & Fox, 1974; cf. Cohn, 1991). The concept of a talent search has been refined over the past three decades and extended from 450 students in 1972 to well over 200,000 on an annual basis and from a focus on mathematics only to include verbal and overall intellectual abilities. Yet the basic premise of the talent search has remained the same: students in 7th or 8th grade (12- to 13-year-olds) who are already known to have scored in the top 3% on national norms on standardized achievement tests (e.g. the Iowa Test of Basic Skills) administered routinely by American schools are invited to take the College Board Scholastic Aptitude Test (SAT) [now the Scholastic Assessment Test] or, in some places, the ACT at regular administrations. The SAT measures mathematical reasoning (SAT-M) and verbal reasoning (SAT-V) ability and is designed for 11th and 12th graders who plan to attend college. This form of assessment is known as above-level testing (Stanley, 1990; Benbow & Stanley, 1996), inasmuch as the SAT was designed for students 4 to 5 years older than SMPY participants. Nonetheless, the score distributions manifested by these gifted 7th or 8th graders are similar to those observed in random samples of high school students (Keating & Stanley, 1972; Benbow, 1988). It is through this mechanism—the talent search—that the SMPY subject pool for the longitudinal study was formed. All 5000+ subjects, except for one group, were selected for high SAT scores placing them in at least the top 1% in intellectual

ability. Although several 'types' of gifted students are being studied, a dominant emphasis has remained on the maths/science disciplines.

Four SMPY cohorts of gifted students, initially identified at age 13, are being tracked longitudinally, as well as a fifth cohort comprised of graduate students in this nation's top math/science departments (see Table 1). Each cohort is separated by a few years. Collectively, the five cohorts span 25 years. Because the students in the first four cohorts were identified over a 25-year period, using the same criteria, our design allows us to assess historical influences to a degree (cf. Grinder, 1985). This is a great advantage; lack of historical control is a problem associated with most longitudinal studies.

Thus, over 5000 students are currently participating in the SMPY longitudinal study; all of the students in the five cohorts are being surveyed at critical junctures throughout their youth and adult lives. Moreover, each cohort will be surveyed at the same age to ensure developmental comparability of our cross-cohort findings. This serves as a rough sketch of the SMPY database and how it was constructed. Let us conclude this section by saying that, alas, SMPY is becoming more of a misnomer with time, inasmuch as many of our participants are now approaching age 40 and, since the early 1980s, just as much emphasis has been placed on identifying verbally talented youth as mathematically talented youth. Time is demanding that we do something about our initially appropriate but no longer descriptively apt name of SMPY.

Theoretical Structure Guiding SMPY Research

The conceptual framework for our research is explicated in (Lubinski & Benbow, 2000); it draws heavily

Table 1. The SMPY Longitudinal Study..

Cohort	N	When Identified	Age when Identified	SAT criteria	Ability level %
1	2188	1972–1974	12–13	Verb $\geq$ 370 or Math $\geq$ 390	1
2	778	1976–1979	12	Top 1/3 of Talent Search Participants	0.5
3	423	1980–1983	< 13	Math $\geq$ 700 Verb. $\geq$ 630	0.01
		1983	12	SAT-M + SAT-V $\leq$ 540	5
Comparison Groups					
		1982	12	500–590 SAT-M 600–690 SAT-M	0.5
4	$\approx$ 1500	1987	12	Math $\geq$ 500 or Verb. $\geq$ 430	0.5

Note. A fifth cohort, Cohort 5 includes 750 students enrolled in top-ranked graduate departments in the U.S. in various math-science disciplines; they were surveyed at age 23–25 in 1992 (Lubinski et al., under review).

from findings on individual differences, which cut across educational, counseling, and industrial psychological contexts. Primarily, our work is based upon a well-known model of vocational adjustment (Fig. 1), the Theory of Work Adjustment (TWA), a model that has been developed by Rene V. Dawis and (the late) Lloyd H. Lofquist (Lofquist & Dawis, 1969, 1991; Dawis & Lofquist, 1984). An especially attractive feature of TWA is that it extends to critical antecedents of vocational adjustment (e.g. choosing a college major).

According to TWA, to assess optimal learning and work environments it is useful to parse an individual's work personality and the environment into two broad, but complementary, subdomains. An individual's work personality is primarily defined by two components: (1) repertoire of specific skills or abilities and (2) personal preferences for content found in contrasting educational/vocational environments. Similarly, different environmental contexts (educational curricula and occupations) are defined by: (1) their ability requirements and (2) the nature of their reinforcement capabilities. Optimal learning and work environments are then viewed as requiring two levels of correspondence, *satisfactoriness* and *satisfaction*.

Satisfactoriness denotes correspondence between abilities and the ability requirements of a particular environment (viz., occupation or educational curriculum), whereas satisfaction denotes correspondence between the preferences and the types of reinforcers provided by an occupation or educational track. Collectively, satisfactoriness (how the environment

will respond to the individual) and satisfaction (how the individual is likely to respond to the environment) are useful for predicting the length of time individuals remain in various educational or career tracks. They are continuous as opposed to discrete concepts and one's psychological adjustment to any given environment at any point in time is, to a large degree, a joint function of these two broad correspondence dimensions (see Fig. 1). One implication of the model is that assessing the environment (for its requirements and reward capabilities) is just as important as assessing the individual's learning and work personality (i.e. abilities and preferences). TWA also stresses the importance of assessing *both* abilities and preferences *concurrently* to ascertain the readiness of a given individual for a particular educational or career track (Lubinski, 1996, 2000). Next we turn to the particulars of the individual-differences constructs relevant to this model (see Fig. 1).

Personality Structure: Critical Dispositions for Learning Readiness and Efficient Work

Abilities

How are intellectual abilities best conceptualized? There is actually a remarkable consensus that intellectual abilities are nicely outlined by Guttman's (1954) early formulation of the Radex (Humphreys, 1979; Snow et al., 1984, 1996; cf. Ackerman, 1987; Lubinski & Dawis, 1992; Carroll, 1993); a Radex representation of intellectual abilities, taken from Snow's work, is provided in Fig. 1 (upper left). In this organization, cognitive abilities are differentiated along two dimen-

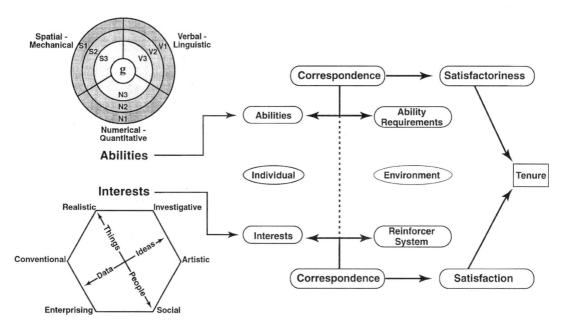

Figure 1. Theory of Work Adjustment

sions, *complexity* (viz., sophistication of the intellectual repertoire, general intelligence, or *g*) and *content* (viz., lower-order factors composed of three relatively distinct symbolic systems: verbal/linguistic, numerical/quantitative and spatial/pictorial). Both level and pattern are important to assess. In our work with the gifted, for example, we have found it useful to assess the complexity dimension to determine the extent to which educational acceleration is warranted (to provide a more correspondent learning environment), plus lower-order factors to ascertain the precise nature of the *appropriate developmental placement* required (thus providing a more individualized and optimal learning environment, responsive to students' unique strengths). Different 'types' of gifted students, for example, verbally vs. mathematically precocious, assimilate certain course work at different rates and more learning occurs when curricula are responsive to such individual differences (Benbow & Stanley, 1996; Lubinski & Benbow, 2000).

Preferences

In our research (and as part of our summer programs), the assessment of personal preferences is teamed with ability assessment to paint a more comprehensive picture of the unique aspects of each student; and counseling is based on how these distinct personality dimensions might form constellations, which factor into educational and career decision-making. Often students find this information useful in considering educational and career possibilities with counselors, teachers, and parents. Probably the most useful model for analyzing educational/vocational preferences is Holland's (1985) hexagonal structure, consisting of **R**ealistic, **I**nvestigative, **A**rtistic, **S**ocial, **E**nterprising, and **C**onventional interests (see Fig. 1, lower left). RIASEC is certainly the most widely used model in educational-vocational practice and research (Savickas & Spokane, 1999), and its cross-cultural generality has recently received empirical support (Day & Rounds, 1998).

We assess these normative attributes for identifying optimal learning environments (those likely to be most enjoyable and rewarding) for gifted students of comparable abilities, but who differ in non-intellectual attributes ultimately related to career choice. Our use of preference assessments is supported by empirical investigations, showing that preferences are sufficiently crystallized in the gifted by early adolescence to carry some applied utility. Lubinski, Benbow & Ryan (1995) provided evidence for the longitudinal stability of the Strong Interest Inventory (Hansen & Campbell, 1985) over a 15-year interval (ages 13–28); and, using an independent sample, Lubinski, Schmidt & Benbow (1996) documented the longitudinal stability of Allport, Vernon & Lindzey's (1970) Study of Values (SOV) over a 20-year interval (ages 13–33). Schmidt, Lubinski & Benbow (1998) added to this literature by

documenting the construct validity of the Strong for intellectually talented young adolescents. A wide range of individual differences is displayed by gifted young adolescents on the Strong (Harmon et al., 1994), which incorporates Holland's hexagon (Achter, Lubinski & Benbow, 1996). This suggests that these instruments—like the SAT used to sort out the wide range of abilities represented within the upper 1% of mathematical talent among 13-year-olds—might be useful for sorting out individual differences in motivational attributes among this special population.

Finally, additional empirical support for preference assessment with this special population was provided through a discriminant function analysis of educational outcomes (Achter, Lubinski, Benbow & Sanjani, 1999). A sample of 432 SMPY participants, assessed with both the SAT and the SOV during the 1970s, at or before age 13, were followed up 10 years later and asked about the areas in which they had earned their 4-year degree. These majors were then categorized into three groups: 'humanities', 'maths-science' and 'other'. Two discriminant functions significantly discriminated these three groups, with both the SAT and the SOV adding incremental validity relative to each other (Fig. 2). These two discriminant functions accounted for 23% of the variation between the three groups, which is amazing given the amount of within group heterogeneity. When abilities were initially entered, they accounted for 11% of group membership variance; when the SOV measures were added, an additional 12% of the variance was accounted for. Moreover, the functions clearly reveal support for the psychological reality of C. P. Snow's (1967) 'two cultures', the humanists (high-verbal abilities, high-aesthetic preferences) and the scientists (high-mathematical abilities, high-theoretical, low-social, low-religious); the authors discuss these functions in some detail. The point here is that abilities and preferences can be coordinated to better tailor learning opportunities (or select more correspondent learning niches) for each student based on the salient features of their (intellectual and motivational) individuality.

Environment Structure: Assessing Critical Features of Environmental Ecologies for Learning and Work

Up to this point we have talked about the personality structure of the individual (abilities and preferences); school and work environments can also be analyzed using analogous dimensions. Educational/vocational environments may be construed as molecular ecologies defined by: (1) their capability to reinforce certain preferences, and (2) the response requirements (or the abilities) that they demand of individuals. In engineering and the physical sciences, the response requirements particularly involve high mathematical and spatial/mechanical reasoning abilities, while investigative interests and theoretical values are among the most salient personal preferences for gravitating toward scientific environments, finding the content of these disciplines reinforcing (for developing one's intellectual talent) and maintaining a commitment toward such disciplines (Roe, 1953; MacKinnon, 1962; Southern & Plant, 1968; Dawis & Lofquist, 1984; Holland, 1985; Lubinski & Benbow, 1992). These environments require intense abilities and preferences for manipulating and working with sophisticated things and gadgets for lengthy periods of time. Individuals with pronounced or relatively higher social values (or stronger need for people contact), in contrast, are not as readily reinforced in such environments.

The above is what many have found to be the person-environment correspondence structure for engineering and the physical sciences (Roe, 1953; Dawis & Lofquist, 1984; Holland, 1985; Dawis, 1991; Lubinski & Benbow, 1992; Lubinski et al., under review). Although students are not formally selected for advanced scientific training based on their theoretical values, their investigative interests, or their spatial and mechanical reasoning abilities (but they are on mathematical reasoning ability), they appear to self-select scientific careers based on all of these attributes, whether they are explicitly aware of their abilities and preferences or not (Humphreys, Lubinski & Yao,

1993). Moreover, an individual will remain in the sciences to the extent that congruence is established between: (1) his/her abilities and preferences, and (2) the skill requirements and reinforcers provided by the scientific environment, respectively. Satisfaction (need-reinforcer correspondence) *and* satisfactoriness (ability-ability requirement correspondence) are essential for optimal intellectual development; helping individuals achieve both is the central goal of SMPY's programmatic work with gifted youth.

Optimal Educational Correspondence for the Extremely Gifted

A proper response to this topic requires, first of all, a full appreciation of the range of interventions that need to be considered when creating optimal learning environments for the exceptionally gifted (Benbow & Stanley, 1996; Lubinski, Webb, Morelock & Benbow, in press). That is, if giftedness is arbitrarily defined as being in the top 1%, individual differences in IQs among the gifted range from approximately 135 to over 200 (roughly one-third of the entire IQ range). Paralleling this vast ability range is an equally wide spectrum of ideal learning environments. Because learning environments can range from discorrespon-

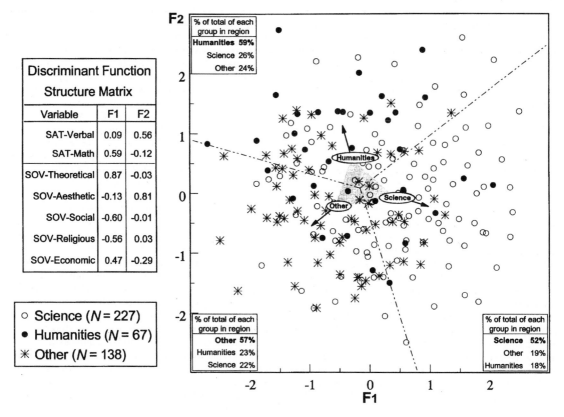

Figure 2. Discriminant Function Analysis

dent to optimally correspondent, a key component of our research is designed to uncover unique ways to enhance the learning experiences and intellectual development of the *exceptionally* able-to make it as optimally correspondent as possible. We suggest that Harriet Zuckerman's (1977) work provides clues for how to enhance educational correspondence among the exceptionally able, and this corresponds highly with what earlier writers have suggested (Seashore, 1922; Hollingworth, 1926, 1942). For this part of our thinking, we blend Zuckerman's hypothesis on the accumulation of advantage with Tannenbaum's (1983, 1986) work on the critical elements for world-class achievement. Considering exceptional achievement is important for purposes here, because it is this population that provides the intellectual leadership and role models for subsequent generations.

Zuckerman (1977) studied the career paths of Nobel Laureates and occupants of the 'forty-first chair' (scientists generally acknowledged to have done research of Nobel prize quality, but not awarded the prize). These individuals almost universally show promise extremely early in their careers and this evidenced precocity appears not only to respond to but also to create greater opportunities for intellectual development. For example, most Laureates receive an advantage in graduate work by attending the most distinguished universities (10 universities produced 55% of the laureates) and by studying with the best minds of the day-other Nobel Laureates or occupants of the 41st chair-thereby begetting a pattern of eminence's creating eminence. Zuckerman claims that the development of scientific taste, standards and self-confidence are the most beneficial results of the Laureate's apprenticeships (Stanley, 1992).

Moreover, future Nobel Laureates obtain degrees and start publishing earlier and more copiously than other scientists. Soon, by the quality of their scientific contributions, they become distinguished from their age-equivalent peers; this opens up further opportunities for their development. Zuckerman suggested that the descriptions of Nobel Laureates' careers fits well with the model of "the accumulation of advantage: the spiraling of augmented achievements and rewards for individuals and a system of stratification that is sharply graded" (p. 249). Moreover, almost all future Nobel Laureates were 'active' in creating this beneficial environment (Scarr & McCartney, 1983; Scarr, 1996; Bouchard, 1997).

Thus, among the gifted, it would seem that those who have the personal potentialities for manifesting exceptional achievement require special encounters with the appropriate environment to facilitate the emergence of world-class accomplishments (Lubinski et al., under review). Consistent with this view, Bloom (1985) noted from interviews of talented performers in a variety of disciplines that special experiences, sometimes interventions, are important for the develop-

ment of talent. Moreover, Tannenbaum (1983, 1986) postulated that great performance or productivity results from a rare blend of superior general intellect, distinctive special aptitudes, the right combination of non-intellectual traits, a challenging environment and the smile of good fortune at crucial periods of life. (The first three components seem to parallel the abilities and preferences discussed in the Theory of Work Adjustment and the latter two the work of Zuckerman.) According to Tannenbaum, success depends upon a combination of facilitators, whereas failure may result from even a single deficit. By virtue of its 'veto' power, then, every one of the five qualifiers is a necessary requisite of high achievement and none of them has sufficient strength to overcome inadequacies in the others.

The above discussion presents the scaffolding for our work on the dispositional determinants of contrasting educational/career paths of the gifted and, thus, leads to the conclusion that individuals who are ideally suited for careers in the physical sciences are gifted individuals with highly developed mathematical and spatial/mechanical reasoning abilities and intense investigative/theoretical preferences. It is these individuals who will *choose* careers in the physical sciences and engineering and remain committed to them. Gifted individuals with other ability and preference profiles will choose careers in other areas. Given this line of reasoning, to the extent that the sexes differ on specific abilities and preferences relevant to educational and career choice, disparate males/female ratios in certain academic and vocational domains will result. This will not only occur in math/science disciplines, but other disciplines as well; males would be expected to remain over-represented in some areas, whereas females would be anticipated to remain over-represented in others. Moreover, these differences should intensify at the higher educational levels; empirical evidence supporting these expectations is presented next.

Gender Differences in Abilities/Preferences: Their Implications According to TWA

Abilities

Over the past two decades reports seem to indicate that certain gender differences in cognitive abilities are steadily diminishing in normative samples (Feingold, 1988; Hyde, Fennema & Lamon, 1990). That is, males and females appear to be converging toward a common mean on a variety of intellectual abilities. These trends, however, have not been noted among the most able (Stumpf & Stanley, 1998). Among the gifted, there are sizable gender differences at age 13, favoring males, in mathematical reasoning and in spatial and mechanical reasoning abilities (abilities required for engineering and the physical sciences). Moreover, at the end of high school and college, these differences remain and accompany gender differences favoring males in maths/science achievement test scores (as well as other test scores), whereas females tend to do slightly better than males on a number of verbally oriented achievement tests (Stanley et al., 1992; Hedges & Nowell, 1995; Stumpf & Stanley, 1998). Before profiling these differences in some detail, we will first address the question: how can normative male/female means be converging while gender differences among the gifted remain pronounced? There are at least two possible explanations (and probably both operate to a degree): test construction practices and gender differences in ability dispersion.

First, Stanley et al. (1992) point out that it is difficult to assess group changes in performance on cognitive tests over the last few decades, inasmuch as a number of test publishers have routinely culled from their instruments items that characteristically generate the most conspicuous gender differences. This procedure is referred to by some as correcting for 'gender bias' or 'equity in testing'. Thus, it is possible that the apparent convergence of male/female group means is due to test construction practices as much as, or perhaps even more than, a genuine change in the cognitive attributes assessed by these measures.

Second, if meta-analytic reviews are indeed detecting a degree of genuine gender-convergence, consumers of meta-analytic reviews must keep in mind that this methodology provides information only on group differences in *overall level* of the attribute under analysis. Meta-analytic reviews do not provide information on group differences in other statistics such as those indexing ability dispersion. There are other parameters on which the genders can differ and a critically important one is *variability* (cf. Benbow, 1988).

Many lines of evidence suggest that males are more widely dispersed than females on a variety of intellectual variables. This phenomenon has been observed over several decades in normative samples (Lubinski & Humphreys, 1990a, 1990b; cf. Feingold, 1992; Lubinski & Benbow, 1992; Lubinski & Dawis, 1992; Hedges & Nowell, 1995; Halpern, 1997). Moreover, this phenomenon appears to hold even for variables on which females have superior means; an example of how this works might be helpful. Stanley et al. (1992) noted that the largest gender difference favoring females on the Differential Aptitude Test (DAT) is observed in DAT-Spelling. Grade 12 females score approximately 0.5 standard deviations above the males on this measure. Alternatively, one may state that only 30% of males score above the female mean; yet, because of greater male variability, male/female proportions are relatively uniform among students within the top 1% in 'spelling talent'. This finding and the general phenomenon of gender differences in ability dispersion has important implications for understanding male/female differences at exceptional levels of

achievement (Feingold, 1995). When assessing gender differences in achievement among the gifted, it is the upper tail of the ability distribution that is being examined; and this upper tail contains an inordinate number of males. Moreover, gender differences in dispersion and level often operate in concert to produce especially disparate male/female ratios at the extremes, as we will illustrate next by returning to SMPY's work with the mathematically talented.

In nationwide talent searches in the U.S., discussed previously, gifted students taking the College Board Scholastic Aptitude Test (SAT) have consistently generated the following pattern of scores. Gender differences in SAT-V are typically small. Yet, on SAT-M the difference between means approximates 0.4 standard deviations, favoring males, and males are more variable than females. Together, these differences in level and dispersion produce the following male/female ratios among 12- to 13-year-olds: SAT-M–500 (average score of college-bound 12th-grade males), 2:1, SAT-M—600 (83rd percentile of college-bound 12th-grade males), 4:1, and SAT-M—700 (95th percentile of college-bound 12th-grade males), 13:1 (Benbow & Stanley, 1983). Comparable ratios have been replicated across the U.S. in a number of talent searches across several years (Benbow & Stanley, 1996), as well as in other cultures. Score ranges beginning at SAT-M—500 are important for a 12-year-old to consider. They reflect important individual differences in quantitative sophistication (Benbow, 1992) and mark the level at which successful graduate work in engineering and the physical sciences at the very best universities becomes probable (Lubinski et al., under review).

The above gender difference in mathematical reasoning ability does not operate in isolation, however, to produce the profound gender disparities in educational attainment and pursuits along the maths/science pipeline. Gender differences in other abilities required by quantitatively demanding inorganic disciplines, especially spatial and mechanical reasoning, amplify the disparities. These abilities are frequently overlooked by investigators trying to come to grips with the underrepresentation of women in engineering and the physical sciences. Table 2 contains data that bear on this issue. They were collected on Cohort 4 by SMPY over a 6-year period (1992–1997). In addition to the SAT, students in Cohort 4 were administered a variety of non-verbal tests including Raven's Advanced Progressive Matrices, three-dimensional spatial visualization and mechanical reasoning. (A number of personal preference questionnaires were also administered, see below.) Gifted students at or above the cutting score for the top 1% in overall mathematical reasoning ability display trivial gender differences in not only SAT-V but also in Advanced Raven scores; yet significant gender differences were revealed for spatial ability and mechanical reasoning.

Table 2 also parallels the findings of Stanley et al. (1992). These investigators analyzed gender differences on the Differential Aptitude Test (DAT) in effect-size units, taken from a national sample of over 61,000 students. The most pronounced gender difference in this battery was observed in Grade 12 on the Mechanical Reasoning measure, the male-female effect-size difference was almost a full standard deviation (.89) favoring males. These gender differences in spatial and mechanical reasoning ability (Halpern, 1997; cf. Jensen, 1998), combined with the well-known gender differences in mathematical reasoning ability (Benbow, 1988), help explain why disparate male/female proportions are observed in inorganic scientific disciplines. Jensen (1998) has pointed out that in spite of these types of differences in specific abilities, there is a near-zero sex difference in overall general cognitive ability (g). This recalls Tannenbaum's assertion, discussed earlier, that success depends upon a combination of every one of his five qualifiers, two of which are general and specific abilities-and none of them has sufficient strength to overcome inadequacies in the others.

We conclude that because of sex differences in the configuration of specific abilities, the satisfactoriness criterion for engineering and physical science is less frequently met by gifted females compared to gifted males. This is only part of the picture, however. There are gender differences in *non*-ability personal attributes (vocational interests and values), in addition to life style preferences, that exacerbate disparities stemming from gender differences in satisfactoriness for the physical sciences. We turn to these next.

Preferences

As noted earlier, physical scientists are characterized primarily by their high theoretical/investigative preferences (Humphreys et al., 1993; Humphreys & Lubinski, 1996; Achter et al., 1999) coupled with a *relatively* low need for people contact. Table 4 contains

some typical findings from talent search participants collected by SMPY during the 1990s. Both mathematically gifted males and females have, relative to their own sex norms, strong theoretical values and investigative interests. Yet, there are prominent gender differences in critical preferences for maintaining a commitment to careers in the math/science pipeline that mirror the aforementioned spatial/mechanical abilities among the gifted at age 13. Mathematically talented males are more theoretically oriented on the SOV (see Table 3). Further, their primary interests lie in the investigative and (secondarily) the realistic sectors of Holland's Hexagon (Achter et al., 1996; Schmidt et al., 1998). In contrast, mathematically talented females are more socially and aesthetically oriented and have interests that are more *evenly divided* among investigative, social and artistic pursuits (Achter et al., 1996; Schmidt et al., 1998). Females are more balanced and less narrowly focused in terms of their interests and values. (One could also say this about their abilities.) Consequently, the TWA satisfaction criterion is less often achieved for females than males when considering the physical sciences.

Thus, at age 13 more males than females possess ability and preference profiles that are congruent with choices to pursue highly focused careers necessary for distinction in the physical sciences. Due to their more evenly distributed preferences and abilities, the career choices of mathematically gifted females and the amount of time they devote to scientific careers will be less marked than their male counterparts. Males will be more exclusively committed to the sciences, while females will have competing interests and will tend to develop their talents in relatively equal proportions across artistic, social, and investigative educational/vocational domains (Achter et al., 1996). That is exactly what is found in our educational programs designed for adolescents in the top 1% in ability. Females enroll in courses in maths/science and English/foreign language in essentially equal proportions,

Table 2. Ability Profiles of Mathematically Gifted Students (Top 1%) Attending a Summer Academic Program (1992–1997) by Gender..

	Males			Females		
	N	$\bar{X}$	SD	N	$\bar{X}$	SD
Age-Adjusted SAT-M	238	519.5	82.9	141	517.0	72.6
Age-Adjusted SAT-V	226	434.7	90.0	137	445.3	82.8
Advanced Raven's	229	25.2	4.6	133	24.4	4.7
Mental Rotation Test	229	30.5	8.0	133	24.0	9.2
Mechanical Reasoning	229	50.9	6.9	133	44.6	6.3

Note: All SAT Scores are reported on the original scale. Any scores from the recentered scale have been converted back to the original scale using tables provided by the College Board. Scores from testers greater than the age of 160 months (13 years, 4 months) at the time of testing have been adjusted down by a factor of 5.4 points on the SAT-M and 4.6 points on the SAT-V per month for every month of age beyond 160.

Table 3. Interest and Values Profiles of Mathematically Gifted Students (Top 1%). Attending a Summer Academic Program Across Six-Years (1992–1997) by Gender..

	Males			Females		
	N	$\bar{X}$	SD	N	$\bar{X}$	SD
Holland's RIASEC						
Themes						
Realistic	215	48.9	8.8	129	44.1	7.9
Investigative	215	54.1	7.8	129	54.9	8.2
Artistic	215	44.5	10.1	129	54.4	9.5
Social	215	39.6	9.4	129	50.7	10.4
Enterprising	215	44.1	9.0	129	46.5	10.5
Conventional	215	47.1	9.4	129	49.2	10.2
Study of Values						
SOV-Theoretical	227	47.7	7.2	139	42.5	8.4
SOV-Economic	227	42.9	7.5	139	36.6	7.2
SOV-Aesthetic	227	38.7	7.9	139	44.5	8.0
SOV-Social	227	35.2	6.9	139	41.4	8.4
SOV-Political	227	43.0	6.6	139	39.5	6.8
SOV-Religious	227	32.5	11.2	139	35.6	10.8

whereas males were approximately six times more likely to enroll in maths/science areas than in English/foreign languages. TWA would predict that the same pattern will reveal itself when career choices, made at a later age, are examined. Indeed, this is the case.

This can be seen in the secured educational credentials that mathematically gifted students in Cohort 1 achieved (or were intending to achieve) 10 years following their identification at age 13 (Lubinski & Benbow, 1992): Less than 1% of the females in the top 1% of mathematical ability are pursuing doctorates in mathematics, engineering, or physical sciences (Lubinski & Benbow, 1992); eight times as many males are doing so. Benbow & Lubinski (1992) presented similar data just collected for SMPY's Cohorts 2 and 3. Finally, in our 20-year follow up of Cohorts 1 and 2 (Benbow et al. 2000), both males and females achieved uniformly high and commensurate numbers of advanced degrees. However, they did so in contrasting disciplines: males were more likely to choose engineering and the physical sciences, while females were more likely to choose the humanities, law, social science, and life science.

An alternative way to capture the essence of these gender-differentiating outcomes takes us back to Thorndike (1911) and one of the most celebrated dimensions of individual differences, "people vs. things." In normative samples, females tend to gravitate towards the former, while males gravitate towards the latter (cf., Lubinski & Humphreys, 1990a) and this parameter of individual differences operates among the gifted as well (Achter et al., 1996; Schmidt et al., 1998). Given the male-female comparability within medicine and the biological sciences, however, com-

pared to the physical sciences, perhaps it would be more precise to state that gender differences in vocational preferences and outcomes are structured around 'organic' vs. 'inorganic' content domains (Benbow et al., 2000; Lubinski et al., under review). It is not science, per se, that turns off many females but, rather, its inorganic nature (coupled with competing interests for other areas).

Life-style choices. Before leaving the domain of preferences, there is one critical gender difference in lifestyle preference that is essential to document (and one that is typically not assessed on standardized interest or values questionnaires). This gender difference is likely to exert a huge effect on gender differences even in disciplines in which male/female ratios in achieved educational credentials are comparable: commitment to full-time work as young adults. In our first three cohorts, for example, about 95% of mathematically talented males vs. less than 60% of such females plan to work full-time until retirement. This latter statistic would indicate that females, as a group, tend to devote less time to their vocational development relative to males. They tend to prefer a more balanced life. Females prefer to devote more time to family and avocational pursuits, relative to males. Further, in most research in this area, questions to respondents are typically framed in terms of full-time vs. various part-time options, not in terms of how much they are willing to work. Thus, we are currently assessing how the gifted feel about 50- to 70-hour work weeks, schedules more in line with people at the cutting edge of their discipline; this reveals further gender disparities. Males are much more likely than females to be willing to work more than a 40-hour work week (Lubinski & Benbow, 2000, Figure 2, p. 143), whatever the reasons and their validity.

In sum, therefore, mathematically gifted females, in addition to having a more multifaceted interest profile *and* a more complex mixture of value orientations for evaluating their experiences and structuring their lifestyle, prefer to devote less time to vocational pursuits. They have more to balance, or more competing needs at comparable intensities. Mathematically gifted males, however, are more focused on a theoretical/investigative style of life with fewer competing pulls, and they prefer to devote a greater amount of time to vocational pursuits. Their lives are less balanced.

Contemporary Research Trends: Viewed From the Context of TWA

We have illustrated above how the personal attributes of females compared to males will lead them to *choose* inorganic scientific careers less frequently, as a group, and to distribute their educational development across artistic, investigative, and social areas more evenly. Of course, conventionally purported barriers (Kerr, 1985; Silverman, 1986; Noble, 1989; Reis & Callahan, 1989; Eccles & Harold, 1992) might still remain. Our work does not address that issue. We suggest, however, that these and other purported barriers be evaluated from a broader context using TWA and its key components, satisfaction and satisfactoriness, to establish expectations on the degree to which comparable gender representation might be anticipated. According to TWA, because of their differing ability and preference profiles, highly able males and females achieve, as a group, satisfaction and satisfactoriness through different means. Consequently, they respond to the environment differently, as does the environment to them. Gender differences as a reflection of choice need to be factored into existing models and perceptions, and taken into consideration when thinking about how best to meet educational needs (Benbow & Lubinski, 1997). Failure to do so can result in inaccurate assumptions about 'multipotentiality' in the intellectually gifted (Achter et al., 1996), with less than cautious educational and vocational decisions leading to dissatisfaction and loss of productivity for males or females. Seeking equity in educational provisions by ignoring gender-associated patterns of choice will, paradoxically, result in *in*equity of educational opportunity (Benbow & Stanley, 1996). In contrast, considering each individual's unique constellation of talents and preferences (Lubinski, 1996, 2000) and the way these may interact to structure and direct adult intellectual development (Ackerman, 1996; Ackerman & Heggestad, 1997) bodes well for the possibility of excellence in achievement (Lubinski & Benbow, 2000).

Satisfactoriness and satisfaction baselines might also be useful for appraising theoretical explanations of gender differences in achievement more generally. For example, Eccles et al. (1983) introduced the expectancy-value model of motivation, which they proposed as a framework for understanding the relationship between values/personality attributes and academic achievement, as well as gender differences therein. This popular model describes two primary factors affecting achievement behavior: (1) expectations for success and failure, and (2) subjective task value. Moreover, it conceptualizes gender differences in achievement, just as we do, from a *choice* perspective rather than a *deficit* perspective. It also views choices as being made from a variety of options presented within a complex social reality, wherein gender roles and stereotypes operate (see Eccles & Harold, 1992, for a discussion of this model as it pertains to the gifted). Yet to what extent do expectations and subjective task value reflect realistic personal estimates of the degree to which TWA's correspondence dimensions, satisfactoriness and satisfaction, respectively, are achievable in contrasting educational and work environments? Is self-confidence and self-efficacy, for example, a reflection of the extent to which one is in a correspondent environmental ecology in the TWA sense?

Inadequate maths/science preparation is another factor often mentioned as curtailing women's career options. Sells (1980), for example, perceived mathematics in high school as a 'critical filter', screening out females from engineering and science majors. Indeed, the number of mathematics and science courses taken in high school is found to relate to choice of college major as well as career (Berryman, 1985; Ethington & Wolfe, 1986); gifted females, even mathematically gifted ones, do take somewhat less mathematics (and science) in high school compared to such males (Benbow & Stanley, 1982; Benbow & Minor, 1986). Consequently, it has been suggested that more females would enter and remain in the maths/science pipeline if they were required to take more mathematics and science courses in high school. But to what extent is course-taking among mathematically gifted females a reflection of their preferences and abilities? Preference and ability profiles are in place long before high school. Can they be changed appreciably as a function of course-taking? Would *requiring* mathematically gifted females with intense preferences for social and artistic content to take more mathematics, chemistry, physics, and computer science in high school increase their representation in the maths/science pipeline? Would *requiring* mathematically and spatially gifted boys with intense preferences for building and manipulating physical materials to take more high school courses in English increase their representation in the humanities? We do not have answers to these questions. To be clear, however, we are not arguing that such course-taking is not beneficial in and of itself; we are certain that it would be. We simply do not know whether (or how much) it would change the direction of a student's development (e.g., see Holden, 2000; Kleinfeld, 1998–1999).

Some of the other factors thought to attenuate the professional development of women include those that women 'do to themselves'. These are, among others, the Queen Bee Syndrome (Staines, Tavis & Jayaratne, 1974), the Great Impostor Phenomenon (Machlowitz, 1982; Clance, 1985; Warschaw, 1985), the Cinderella Complex (Kerr, 1985) and the Perfection Complex (Reis, 1987). The Queen Bee and Perfection Complex are similar in that females feel that they have to be perfect in every way and in how they handle the multiple roles of professional, mother, and wife. The Great Impostor Phenomenon captures how many successful women feel they achieved their success-not through their hard work and ability but rather through luck: and they are waiting to be found out. To avoid being 'found out' they get caught in a circle of working even harder, achieving greater success and developing greater fear of being detected as the impostor they truly believe they are (Kerr, 1985, 1991). To what extent is this depiction characteristic of a gifted female with several competing interests at comparable intensities? These questions and others like them will be pursued in our future research. In all of our research, however, detailed assessments of well-known personal attributes critical for satisfaction and satisfactoriness in specialized careers and advanced educational tracks are conducted, not only to establish expectations for gender representation in the maths/science pipeline, but also the degree to which the self-perceptions of our students are reality based. Investigators in other areas of educational/vocational development, as well as theorists interested in indexing the magnitude of social psychological influences, might find this strategy profitable too.

Conclusions

In this chapter, using TWA, we have organized data collected at SMPY with data of other investigators on key gender-differentiating attributes that channel the nature and degree of educational/vocational achievement among the gifted. We feel that this model is useful for conceptualizing and better understanding many different kinds of gender differences surrounding the manifestations of intellectual talent. We conclude with three points: one intended for researchers, another for theoreticians, and finally one for educators and applied psychologists. Although the expressed thoughts shared by these three categories possess appreciable overlap, they also reflect a unique emphasis.

First, for the researcher, if one thing is apparent from the last 30 years of research on the gifted and gender differences therein, it is the need to conduct multi-attribute assessments of key characteristics relevant to criterion behaviors of interest. Our particular area of interest involves the determinants of educational and career excellence in engineering and the physical sciences. It behooves us, therefore, to incorporate measures of spatial and mechanical reasoning into our correlational and experimental designs, in addition to assessing critical vocational interests and values and life-style preferences. We simply cannot restrict investigations solely to abilities, preferences, *or* attitudes (or any 'favorite' class of personal attributes) and expect findings to generalize with fidelity. There are simply too many gender differences observed in key variables relevant to multiple educational/vocational paths to make one-shot, one-variable designs unquestionably defensible.

Second, theoretical formulations must at least attempt to genuinely embrace all available evidence before casting highly integrative frameworks for interpreting research findings. Theorists certainly should not ignore relevant auxiliary data that speak to the tenability of certain conclusions. In another context, we have suggested that researchers employ the Total Evidence Rule for evaluating the verisimilitude of competing theoretical formulations. This rule of induction was formulated by Rudolph Carnap (1950). It maintains that consideration of all relevant information is essential when evaluating a proposed scientific assertion. There are multiple examples in the gifted literature for the relevance of this important rule, but the following two involving gender differences will suffice to illustrate its significance. First, if social influences are operating in isolation to attenuate the development of exceptional levels of mathematical reasoning abilities in females (as some have suggested), theorists must address why it is that females are superior to males in arithmetic computation and also tend to get better grades than males in high school math courses (cf. Benbow, 1988; Kimball, 1989). A second example involves sex-role identification. The masculine identification hypothesis has been used to explain the relative superiority of males compared to females in mathematical reasoning ability. This formulation must come to grips with the fact that regardless of how giftedness is defined (e.g. by selecting subjects based on exceptional levels of verbal, spatial, or mathematical ability), gifted adolescents of all 'types' are less gender stereotyped than their average-ability peers in a variety of interests (Lubinski & Humphreys, 1990a). Moreover, Lytton & Romney's (1991) *meta*-analytic review, covering the literature on parents' differential socialization practices as a function of their child's gender, uncovered many *in*significant effect sizes for a number of abilities and social behaviors.

Finally, we, like most vocational psychologists working with young adults, feel it is important that gifted adolescents are provided with the opportunity to develop in ways commensurate with their unique abilities and personal preferences (Lubinski & Benbow, 2000). If this means that more gifted females *choose* to become biologists, lawyers, and physicians, relative to physical scientists, electrical engineers, or computer scientists, *as long as they are aware of their full potential* we are not concerned. We view gifted students as individuals *first*, and try to be as responsive to their individual differences and uniqueness as possible. One can never be all that one has the potential to become, because life is too short and developing expertise requires much time. But people do possess wide variation for how readily expertise development is likely to take. As the great counseling psychologist, Leona Tyler (1992) noted: The important life decision is not what you can be as much as it is choosing what you would like to become from an array of possibilities. We only have one life to develop, and we don't have time to actualize all of our possibilities.

To paraphrase Maslow's, one must be responsive to one's true nature, a theme that cuts across many fulfillment theories and formulations aimed at construing optimal forms of human development and positive psychological states, including those of Gordon Allport, Carl Rogers & Carl Jung. It might be advisable for counselors and educators to keep such wisdom in mind when working with clients and students searching for direction in their educational and vocational development, and, perhaps also, to remind clients of Jane Loevinger's (1976) observation (contained in her treatment of ego development) that "personality develops by acquiring successive freedoms." All of this is actually encompassed by various models of educational and vocational development stemming from individual differences research (Dawis, 1992; Tyler, 1992; Williamson, 1965; Lubinski, 1996) and, in particular, TWA. TWA is an empirically based model of personal fulfillment within the world of work (Lofquist & Dawis, 1969, 1991; Dawis & Lofquist, 1984).

Acknowledgment

This work was supported by a grant from an anonymous funding agency and the Kennedy Center at the College of Education and Human Development, Vanderbilt University.

References

Achter, J. A., Lubinski, D., Benbow, C. P. & Sanjani, H. (1999). Assessing vocational preferences among gifted adolescents adds incremental validity to abilities: a discriminant analysis of educational outcomes over a 10-year interval. *Journal of Educational Psychology*, **91**, 777–786.

Achter, J. A., Lubinski, D. & Benbow, C. P. (1996). Multipotentiality among the intellectually gifted: it was never there and already it's vanishing. *Journal of Counseling Psychology*, **43**, 65–76.

Ackerman, P. L. (1987). Individual differences in skill learning: an integration of psychometric and information processing perspectives. *Psychological Bulletin*, **102**, 3–27.

Ackerman, P. L. (1996). A theory of adult intellectual development: process, personality, interests, and knowledge. *Intelligence, 22*, 227–257.

Ackerman, P. L. & Heggestad. E. D. (1997). Intelligence, personality, and interests: evidence for overlapping traits. *Psychological Bulletin*, **121**, 219–245.

Allport, G. W., Vernon, P. E. & Lindzey, G. (1970). *Manual for the study of values*. Boston: Houghton-Mifflin.

Benbow, C. P. (1988). Sex differences in mathematical reasoning ability among the intellectually talented: their characterization, consequences and possible explanations. *Behavioral and Brain Sciences*, **11**, 169–232.

Benbow, C. P. (1992). Academic achievement in mathematics and science between ages 13 and 23: are there differences among students in the top one percent of mathematical ability? *Journal of Educational Psychology, 84*, 51–61.

Benbow, C. P. & Lubinski, D. (1992). Gender differences among intellectually-gifted adolescents: implications for the maths/science pipeline. Invited address at the annual convention of the American Psychological Society, San Diego.

Benbow, C. P. & Lubinski, D. (1997). Intellectually talented children: how can we best meet their needs? In: N. Colangelo & G. Davis (Eds.), *Handbook of Gifted Education* (2nd ed.), Boston: Allyn and Bacon.

Benbow, C. P., Lubinski, D., Shea, D. L. & Sanjani, H. E. (2000), Sex differences in mathematical reasoning ability: their status 20 years later. *Psychological Science*, **11**, 474–480.

Benbow, C. P., Lubinski, D. & Suchy, B. (1996). The impact of SMPY's educational programs from the perspective of the participant. In: C. P. Benbow & D. Lubinski (Eds.), *Intellectual Talent: Psychometric and Social Issues* (pp. 266–300). Baltimore, MD: The Johns Hopkins University Press.

Benbow, C. P. & Minor, L. L. (1986). Mathematically talented males and females and achievement in high school sciences. *American Educational Research Journal*, **23**, 425–436.

Benbow, C. P. & Stanley, J. C. (1980). Sex differences in mathematical ability: fact or artifact. *Science, 210*, 1262–1264.

Benbow, C. P. & Stanley, J. C. (1982). Consequences in high school and college of sex differences in mathematical reasoning ability: a longitudinal perspective. *American Educational Research Journal, 19*, 598–622.

Benbow, C. P. & Stanley, J. C. (1983). Sex differences in mathematical reasoning ability: more facts. *Science, 222*, 1029–1031.

Benbow, C. P. & Stanley, J. C. (1996). Inequity in equity: how 'equity' can lead to inequity for high-potential students. *Psychology, Public Policy, and Law, 2*, 249–292.

Berryman, S. E. (1985). *Minorities and women in mathematics and science: who chooses these fields and why?* Paper presented at the annual meeting of the American Association for the Advancement of Science, Los Angeles.

Bloom, B. S. (1985). *Developing talent in young people*. New York: Ballentine.

Carnap, R. (1950). *Logical foundations of probability*. Chicago: University of Chicago Press.

Carroll, J. B. (1993). Exploratory factor analysis: a tutorial. In: D. K. Detterman (Ed.), *Current Topics in Human Intelligence:* Vol. 1, *Research Methodology* (pp. 25–58). Norwood, NJ: Ablex.

Clance, P. R. (1985). The impostor phenomenon. *New Woman*, **15**, 40–43.

Cohn, S. J. (1991). Talent searches. In N. Colangelo & G. A. Davis (Eds.), *Handbook of Gifted Education* (pp. 166–177). Boston: Allyn & Bacon.

Dawis, R. V. (1991). Vocational interests, values and preferences. In: M. Dunnette & L. Hough (Eds.), *Handbook of Industrial and Organizational Psychology*, (2nd ed.), Vol. 2 (pp. 833–871). Palo Alto: Consulting Psychologist Press.

Dawis, R. V. (1992). The individual differences tradition in counseling psychology. *Journal of Counseling Psychology*, **39**, 7–19.

Dawis, R. V. & Lofquist, L. H. (1984). *A psychological theory of work adjustment: an individual differences model and its applications*. Minneapolis: University of Minnesota Press.

Day, S. X. & Rounds, J. (1998). The universality of vocational interest structure among racial/ethnic minorities. *American Psychologist*, **53**, 728–736.

Dick, T. P. & Rallis, S. F. (1991). Factors and influences on high school student career choices. *Journal for Research in Mathematics Education*, **22**, 281–292.

Eccles (Parsons), J., Adler, T. F., Futterman, R., Goff, S. B., Kaczala, C. M., Meece, J. L. & Midgley, C. (1983). Expectations, values and academic behaviors. In: J. T. Spence (Ed.), *Perspective on Achievement and Achievement Motivation*. San Francisco: W. H. Freeman.

Eccles, J. & Harold, R. D. (1992). Gender differences in educational and occupational patterns among the gifted. In: N. Colangelo, S. G. Assouline & D. L. Ambroson (Eds.), *Talent Development. Proceedings from the 1991 H. B. & J. Wallace National Research Symposium on Talent Development* (pp. 2–30). Unionville, NY: Trillium Press.

Ethington, C. A. & Wolfe, L. M. (1986). A structural model of mathematics achievement for men and women. *American Educational Research Journal*, **23**, 65–75.

Feingold, A. (1988). Cognitive gender differences are disappearing. *American Psychologist*, **43**, 95–103.

Feingold, A. (1992). Sex differences in variability in intellectual abilities: a new look at an old controversy. *Review of Educational Research*, **62**, 61–84.

Feingold, A. (1995). The additive effects of differences in central tendency and variability are important in comparisons between groups. *American Psychologist*, **50**, 5–13.

Flanagan, J. C., Dailey, J. T., Shaycoft, M. F., Gorham, W. A., Orr, D. B. & Goldberg, I. (1962). *Design for a study for American youth*. Boston: Houghton Mifflin.

Fox, L. H., Pasternak, S. R. & Peiser, N. L. (1976). Career-related interests of adolescent boys and girls. In: D. P. Keating (Ed.). *Intellectual Talent: Research and Development* (pp. 242–261). Baltimore: Johns Hopkins University Press.

Grinder, R. E. (1985). The gifted in our midst: by their divine deeds, neuroses and mental test scores we have known them. In: F. D. Horowitz & M. O'Brien (Eds.), *The Gifted and Talented: Developmental Perspectives* (pp. 5–36). Washington, DC: American Psychological Association.

Guttman, L. (1954). A new approach to factor analysis: The radex. In: P. Lazarsfeld (Ed), *Mathematical thinking in the social sciences* (pp. 258–348). Glencoe, Il: Free Press.

Halpern, D. F. (1997). Public policy implications of sex differences in cognitive abilities. *American Psychologist*, **52**, 561–574.

Hansen, J. C. & Campbell, D. P. (1985). *Manual for the SCII* (4th ed.) Palo Alto, CA: Stanford University Press.

Harmon, L. W., Hansen, J. C., Borgen, F. H. & Hammer, A. L. (1994). *Applications and technical guide for the Strong Interest Inventory*. Palo Alto: Consulting Psychologists.

Hedges, L. V. & Nowell, A. (1995). Sex differences in mental test scores, variability, and numbers of high-scoring individuals. *Science*, **269**, 41–45.

Holden, C. (2000). Parity as a goal sparks bitter battle. *Science*, **289**, 380.

Holland, J. C. (1985). *Making vocational choices: a theory of vocational personalities and work environments* (2nd ed.). Englewood, Cliffs, NJ: Prentice-Hall.

Hollingworth, L. S. (1926). *Gifted children*. New York: Macmillan.

Hollingworth, L. S. (1942). *Children above 180 IQ*. New York: World Book.

Humphreys, L. G. (1979). The construct of general intelligence. *Intelligence*, **3**, 105–120.

Humphreys, L. G., Lubinski, D. & Yao, G. (1993). Utility of predicting group membership: exemplified by the role of spatial visualization in becoming an engineer, physical scientist, or artist. *Journal of Applied Psychology*, **78**, 250–261.

Humphreys, L. G. & Lubinski, D. (1996). Brief history and psychological significance of assessing spatial visualization. In: C. P. Benbow & D. Lubinski (Eds.), *Intellectual talent: Psychometric and Social Issues* (pp. 116–140). Baltimore: Johns Hopkins University Press.

Hyde, J. S., Fennema, E. & Lamon, S. J. (1990). Gender differences in mathematics performance: a *meta*-analysis. *Psychological Bulletin*, **107**, 139–155.

Jensen, A. R. (1998). *The g factor: The science of mental ability*. Westport, CT: Praeger

Keating, D. P. & Stanley, J. C. (1972). Extreme measures for the mathematically gifted in mathematics and science. *Educational Researcher*, **1**, 3–7.

Kerr, B. A. (1985). *Smart girls, gifted women*. Dayton, OH: Ohio Psychology Publishing Co.

Kerr, B. A. (1991). Educating gifted girls. In: N. Colangelo & G. Davis (Eds.), *Handbook of Gifted Education* (pp. 402–415). Boston: Allyn & Bacon.

Kimball, M. M. (1989). A new perspective on women's maths achievement. *Psychological Bulletin*, **105**, 198–214.

Kleinfeld, J. (1998–1999). The Morella Bill, my daughter Rachel, and the advancement of women in science. *Academic Quarterly, Winter*, 79–86.

Lipps, H. M. (1988). *Sex & gender: an introduction*. Mountain View, CA: Mayfield.

Loevinger, J. (1976). *Ego development: conceptions and theories*. San Francisco: Jossey-Bass.

Lofquist, L. H. & Dawis, R. V. (1969). *Adjustment to work*. New York: Appleton-Century-Crofts.

Lofquist, L. H. & Dawis, R. V. (1991). *Essentials of person environment correspondence counseling*. Minneapolis: University of Minnesota Press.

Lubinski, D. (1996). Applied individual differences research and its quantitative methods. *Psychology, Public Policy, and Law*, **2**, 187–203.

Lubinski, D. (2000). Scientific and social significance of assessing individual differences: "Sinking shafts at a few critical points." *Annual Review of Psychology*, **51**, 405–444.

Lubinski, D. & Benbow, C. P. (1992). Gender differences in abilities and preferences among the gifted: implications for the maths/science pipeline. *Current Directions in Psychological Science*, **1**, 61–66.

Lubinski, D. & Benbow, C. P. (1994). The Study of Mathematically Precocious Youth: the first three decades of a planned 50-year study of intellectual talent. In R. F. Subotnik & K. D. Arnold (Eds.), *Beyond Terman: Contemporary Longitudinal Studies of Giftedness and Talent* (pp. 255–281). Norwood, NJ: Ablex.

Lubinski, D. & Benbow, C. P. (2000). States of excellence. *American Psychologist*, **55**, 137-150.

Lubinski, D., Benbow, C. P. & Ryan, J. (1995). Stability of vocational interests among the intellectually gifted from adolescence to adulthood: a 15-year longitudinal study. *Journal of Applied Psychology*, **80**, 196–200.

Lubinski, D., Benbow, C. P., Shea, D. L., Sanjani, H. & Halvorson, M. B. J. Men and woman at promise for scientific excellence: they are not as different as you might think. (under review).

Lubinski, D. & Dawis, R. V. (1992). Aptitudes, skills and proficiency. In: M. D. Dunnette & L. M. Hough (Eds.), *The Handbook of Industrial/Organizational Psychology*, (2nd ed.), Vol. 3 (pp. 3–59). Palo Alto, CA: Consulting Psychologists Press.

Lubinski, D. & Humphreys, L. G. (1990a). A broadly based analysis of mathematical giftedness. *Intelligence*, **14**, 327–355.

Lubinski, D. & Humphreys, L. G. (1990b). Assessing spurious 'moderator effects': Illustrated substantively with the hypothesized ('synergistic') relation between spatial visualization and mathematical ability. *Psychological Bulletin*, **107**, 327–355.

Lubinski, D., Schmidt, D. B. & Benbow, C. P. (1996). A 20-year stability analysis of the Study of Values for intellectually gifted individuals from adolescence to adulthood. *Journal of Applied Psychology*, **81**, 443–451.

Lubinski, D. & Thompson, T. (1986). Functional units of human behavior and their integration: a dispositional analysis. In: T. Thompson & M. Zeiler (Eds.), *Analysis and Integration of Behavioral Units* (pp. 275–314). Hillsdale, NJ: Erlbaum.

Lubinski, D., Webb, R. M., Morelock, M. J. & Benbow, C. P. Top 1 in 10,000: a 10-year follow up of the profoundly gifted. *Journal of Applied Psychology*, (in press).

Lytton, H. & Romney, D. M. (1991). Parents' differential socialization of boys and girls: a *meta*-analysis. *Psychological Bulletin*, **109**, 267–296.

MacKinnon, D. W. (1962). The nature and nurture of creative talent. *American Psychologist*, **17**, 484–495.

Machlowitz, M. (1982). The great impostors. *Working Women*, **7**, 97–98.

Maple, S. A. & Stage, F. K. (1991). Influences on the choice of maths/science majors by gender and ethnicity. *American Educational Research Journal*, **28**, 37–60.

National Science Foundation (1999). *Women, minorities, and persons with disabilities in science and engineering: 1998*. Arlington, VA. (NSF 99–338).

Noble, K. (1989). Counseling gifted women: becoming heroes of our own stories. *Journal for the Education of the Gifted*, **12**, 131–141.

Reis, S. M. (1987). We can't change what we don't recognize: understanding the special needs of gifted families. *Gifted Child Quarterly*, **31**, 83–89.

Reis, S. & Callahan, C. (1989). Gifted females: they've come a long way-or have they? *Journal for the Education of the Gifted*, **12**, 99–117.

Roe, A. (1953). *The making of a scientist*. New York: Dodd, Mead.

Roe, A. (1956). *The psychology of occupations*. New York: Wiley.

Rosenthal, R. & Rubin, D. B. (1982). Further meta-analytic procedures for assessing cognitive gender differences. *Journal of Educational Psychology*, **74**, 708–712.

Rossiter, M. (1995). *Women scientists in America: struggles and strategies to 1940*. Baltimore, MD: Johns Hopkins University Press.

Savickas, M. L. & Spokane, A. R. (1999). *Vocational interests: Their meaning, measurement, and use in counseling*. Palo Alto, CA: Davies–Black.

Scarr, S. (1996). How people make their own environments: implications for parents and policy makers. *Psychology, Public Policy, and Law*, **2**, 204–228.

Scarr, S. & McCartney, K. (1983). How people make their own environments: a theory of genotype→environment effects. *Child Development*, **54**, 424–435.

Schmidt, F. L. & Hunter, J. E. (1998). Development of causal model of processes determining job performance. *Current Directions in Psychological Science*, **1**, 89–92.

Schmidt, D. B., Lubinski, D. & Benbow, C. P. (1998). Validity of assessing educational-vocational preference dimensions among intellectually talented 13-year-olds. *Journal of Counseling Psychology*, **45**, 436–453.

Seashore, C. E. (1922). The gifted student and research. *Science*, **56**, 641–648.

Sells, L. W. (1980). The mathematics filter and the education of women and minorities. In: L. H. Fox, L. Brody & D. Tobin (Eds.), *Women and the Mathematical Mystique*. Baltimore: Johns Hopkins University Press.

Silverman, L. K. (1986). What happens in the gifted girl? In: C. J. Maker (Ed.), *Critical Issues in Gifted Education: Defensible Programs for the Gifted* (pp. 43–89). Rockville, MD: Aspen.

Snow, C. P. (1967). *The two cultures*. Cambridge: Cambridge University Press.

Snow, R. E., Corno, L. & Jackson III, D. (1996). Individual differences in affective and conative functions. In: D. C. Berliner & R. C. Calfee (Eds.) *Handbook of Educational Psychology* (pp. 243–310). New York: MacMillan.

Snow, R. E., Kyllonen, P. C. & Marshalek, B. (1984). The topography of ability and learning correlations. In: R. J. Sternberg (Ed.), *Advances in the Psychology of Human Intelligence*: Vol. 2 (pp. 47–104). Hillsdale, NJ: Lawrence Erlbaum Associates.

Southern, M. L. & Plant, W. T. (1968). Personality characteristics of very bright adults. *Journal of Social Psychology*, **75**, 119–126.

Stains, G., Tavris, C. & Jayaratne, C. (1974). The queen bee syndrome. *Psychology Today*, **7**, 55–60.

Stanley, J. C. (1973). Accelerating the educational progress of intellectually gifted youths. *Educational Psychologist*, **10**, 133–146.

Stanley, J. C. (1990). Leta Hollingworth's contributions to above-level testing of the gifted. *Roeper Review*, **12**, 166–161.

Stanley, J. C. (1992). A slice of advice. *Educational Researcher,* **21**, 25–26.

Stanley, J. C. (1996). In the beginning: the Study of Mathematically Precocious Youth. In: C. P. Benbow & D. Lubinski (Eds.), *Intellectual Talent: Psychometric and Social Issues* (pp. 225–235). Baltimore, MD: The Johns Hopkins University Press.

Stanley, J. C., Benbow, C. P., Brody, L. E., Dauber, S. & Lupkowski, A. E. (1992). Gender differences on eighty-six nationally standardized aptitude and achievement tests. In: N. Colangelo, S. G. Assouline & D. L. Ambroson (Eds.), *Talent Development* (pp. 42–65). Unionville, NY: Trillium Press.

Stanley, J. C., Feny, J. & Zhu, X. (1989). Chinese youths who reason extremely well mathematically: threat or bonanza? *Network News and Views,* **8**, 33–39.

Stanley, J. C., Keating, D. P. & Fox, L. H. (Eds.) (1974). *Mathematical talent: discovery, description and development.* Baltimore: Johns Hopkins University Press.

Stumpf, H. & Stanley, J. C. (1998). Stability and change in gender-related differences on the college board advanced placement and achievement tests. *Current Directions in Psychological Science,* **7**, 192–196.

Tannenbaum, A. (1983). *Gifted children: psychological and educational perspectives.* New York: Macmillan.

Tannenbaum, A. (1986). The enrichment matrix model. In: J. S. Renzulli (Ed.). *Systems and Models for Developing Programs for the Gifted and Talented* (pp. 391–428). Mansfeld Center, CT: Creative Learning Press.

Tyler, L. E. (1992). Counseling psychology-why? *Professional Psychology: Research and Practice,* **23**, 342–344.

Thorndike, E. L. (1911). *Individuality.* Cambridge, MA: Riverside Press.

U.S. Bureau of the Census (1998). *Statistical abstract of the United States: 1998* (118th ed.). Washington, DC: Bernan Press.

Warschaw, T. (1985). The "I-don't-deserve-it" syndrome. *New Woman,* **15**, 134–137.

Williamson, E. G. (1965). *Vocational counseling: some historical, philosophical, and theoretical perspectives.* New York: McGraw-Hill.

Willson, E. O. (1998). *Consilience: the unity of knowledge.* New York: Knopf.

Zuckerman, H. (1977). *Scientific elite: Nobel laureates in the United States.* New York: Free Press.

Guiding Gifted Girls and Young Women

Barbara Kerr

Arizona State University, USA

Introduction

One of the most profound transformations in human society has taken place in the last three decades as women's roles have changed throughout the world. In the United States, girls have pulled even with boys in many ways. Eighth grade girls have caught up in maths achievement, belying hypotheses from a mere ten years ago that biological differences would preclude girls from the highest attainments in mathematics. Bright girls enroll in challenging biology, chemistry, and physics classes in almost the same numbers as bright boys. Strong efforts to help girls to raise their career aspirations, to attempt course work of greater rigor, and to claim leadership positions have been strikingly successful. As many young gifted women as gifted men now plan careers in medicine, law, and many other fields once dominated by males (Campbell & Clewell, 1999). About 80% of high school leadership positions are now held by girls, and girls' and women's athletics have captured the nation's imagination. Similar trends have been noted in England and Australia, as well as other developed nations.

Changes in Girls' and Women's Roles

In industrialized countries, optimism about the gains that have been made by bright girls and women must be tempered by the fact that new problems have emerged. As girls and women become more assertive and enter leadership positions, they often take on the problems that have traditionally been the province of males: substance abuse, violence, and self-destructiveness (Phillips, 1998). In addition to these newly acquired difficulties, achieving girls and women are oppressed more that ever by societal images of the 'perfect' woman. Eating disorders are rampant as women try to achieve impossible ideals of physical beauty. Ninety per cent of people with eating disorders are women, and eating disorders have the highest mortality rate of any mental illness (National Institute of Mental Health, 1993). Finally, many of the gains that have been made in female achievement have been at the middle and high school level.

Gifted women in college and in young adulthood apparently still face both internal and external barriers to the attainment of their goals (Le Roux, 1994.) The gap in mathematics achievement test scores, particularly at the top range, have remained intractable, excluding gifted women from colleges and academic opportunities (Campbell & Clewell, 1999). College women encounter a virulent 'culture of romance' that forces them into competition for relationships with high prestige males (Holland & Eisenhart, 1990). Once in the workplace, bright women often face subtle forms of discrimination that prevent them from moving ahead. Young professional women face barriers not only in the workplace, but in their own homes, where the men they marry often do not support their ambitions or goals. As a result, gifted women continue to subvert their own dreams, compromising their goals and aspirations in an attempt to compose a lifestyle that will work for all the members of their families (Tomlinson-Keasey, 1999). Many of the conditions that make gifted women vulnerable to pressures to underachieve as college students and adults begin to take effect in early childhood (Eccles, 1987).

In developing countries, there have also been striking changes in the condition of women that have directly affected the lives of gifted girls. In many countries where girls once received little or no education, the benefits of educating girls are becoming apparent; societies that educate their girls find that they marry later, have fewer children, contribute to the economic well being of their communities more than uneducated women. New efforts are being made to identify and nurture the talents of girls. However, girls' education still lags behind boys' education in much of the world, and worldwide, the economic and social status of women remains inferior to that of men. Bright women in many cultures still face forced marriage, prohibition from owning property, and legal and social support for emotional and physical abuse (Kitano & Perkins, 1996).

Therefore, the radical changes in women's roles in both the developed and developing countries have brought about some dramatic improvements in the education and guidance of gifted girls in the last three decades; but much remains to be done to help bright females overcome the internal and external barriers to the achievement of their goals.

Changes in the Construct of Intelligence

In addition to changes in the role of women, there have also been extraordinary changes in the ways in which psychologists, teachers, and counselors view the construct of intelligence (Morelock, 1996). Twenty years ago, the construct of general intelligence reigned supreme; it was an unquestioned premise of psychology that intelligence was a unitary phenomenon. Intelligence was considered so indivisible that school psychologists were cautioned to avoid at all costs the interpretation of separate scale scores for the WISC-R; so that verbal and spatial scores were always combined to create one intelligence score. There was indeed considerable data to support the notion of *g* or general intelligence: factor analyses of ability tests have inevitably shown an overall tendency for most of the major talents to cluster together (Anastasi, 1998). An advantage of this way of construing intelligence is that the tests devised to measure this set of general intellectual abilities have been good predictors of academic achievement. That is, intelligence tests have done a good job of identifying children who can benefit from increased academic challenge. Another advantage of this construction of intelligence is that the tests based on *g* were constructed to identify as many girls as boys and continue to identify girls equitably.

The major disadvantages of this construction of intelligence are the consistent failure of intelligence tests to identify children from cultures with world views that diverge from that of the test developers. Therefore, girls from non-competitive cultures as well as girls with limited English ability have not been able to display their superior reasoning abilities as well as white or Asian middle class children who have been brought up to value test-taking and academic achievement. Another disadvantage of this construction of intelligence is that children with specific extraordinary abilities in music and art—and even maths and linguistic areas are less likely to be labeled gifted. At the highest levels of performance, the concept of *g* breaks down: few child prodigies are gifted across domains of talent, and adolescents at the highest levels of achievement in specific talent areas are unlikely to be more than above average in other talent areas (Morelock & Feldman, 1993; Colangelo & Kerr, 1991). Therefore, it is conceivable that brilliant girl artists, musicians, mathematicians, and writers will be left out of gifted programming because they do not score brilliantly across the board.

Finally, although intelligence tests show asynchronous development fairly clearly, they are not reliable predictors of academic achievement until children are at least nine years old. However, precocious intellectual behavior may be manifested in girls earlier than boys. If girls are not tested until nine because that is when the tests become useful for prediction of achievement, then many gifted girls whose cognitive complexity outstrips their social development may be missed (Silverman, 1995).

Gardner's (1983) theory of intelligence, which has led to many investigations of specific abilities and which has been enthusiastically embraced by many educators of the gifted, would seem to address many of the criticisms of the construct of general intelligence. His theory of seven intelligences does indeed account for the existence of both child prodigies in specific talent domains as well as for the evidence that specific abilities can exist in isolation in damaged brains. This theory is also useful in that it is much more inclusive; it brings many more young people into the 'gifted fold' who previously would have been left out. Because the theory is largely tested by the observation of achievement in talent domains rather than by paper and pencil or interview based testing, it can be argued that it provides a more practical and direct means of predicting future eminence in a talent domain. Proponents of this view of intelligence point out that eminent individuals are nearly always people with specific extraordinary talents, whereas many eminent people have only above average scores on tests of general intelligence (Gardner, 1993).

Silverman's perspective on this issue is that the newer theories of specific intelligences have clear gender biases. She says, "Current thinking in the field . . . from a masculine perspective—rejects IQ tests because the tests fail to predict who will win acclaim in specific domains in adult life. However, the tests do manage to locate approximately equal numbers of gifted girls and boys in early childhood . . . In fact, 47% (31) of the 66 children we have found above 180 I.Q. are female compared to less than 2% of the eminent! It is ironic that the very instrument that proved females to be equal or superior to males in intelligence is falling into disrepute. It has been replaced by a more vigorous emphasis on performance, achievement, and accomplishment in the new National Excellence report . . . the potential for eminence in another disguise—and educators are being warned not to 'label preschool and primary students as gifted and talented' despite the fact that gifted girls tend to go underground by the middle grades."

These changes, taken together, mean that our very definition of the gifted girl is in flux, as well as the attitudes of societies around the world toward the development of talent in women. Are gifted girls those who are asynchronous in their development, those whose overall intellect and capacity for perceiving the world seem to be developing out of pace with their age peers, or are gifted girls those whose talents combine with personality traits in such as way as to promote them toward eminence? Despite the suggested 'rapprochement' of the two models by Morelock (1996), research and theory on the education and guidance of girls has not reflected an integrative approach. The model of female talent development proposed by Noble, Subotnik & Arnold (1997) may hold hope for more synthetic understanding of giftedness in girls. This model, developed to provide an understanding of giftedness in women, takes into account intelligence, achievement, and distance from the center of power within the domains of human activites. In addition, it assumes that achievement and self-actualization are possible on many levels, ranging from personal to societal. In applying this model to girls, it may be possible to construct a means of identification of giftedness that assesses girls' innate abilities, their motivation and record of achievement, and the characteristics that put them closer or farther from the center of power in the dominant culture. In this model, a Navajo girl living on an isolated reservation who converses in both Navajo and English, who can read at the average level for urban white children, and who can perform at an average level on achievement tests normed on people with a world view entirely at odds with her own is gifted. The white, upper class suburban girl who scores in the 90th percentile on achievement tests and gets a B average may be less gifted than the tests say she is.

With regard to societal attitudes, we are in a time of ambivalence, when gifted girls are being urged to actualize their talents, particularly in maths and science, but discouraged at the same time from inconveniencing their families, communities, and society as a whole. The work of Kitano & Perkins (1996), Kitano (1998), Napier (1995), and Martinez-Thorne (1995) with international women, women of color, and indigenous women are illustrative of gifted females' struggle with societal ambivalence toward their giftedness. Kitano & Perkins (1996) found that the extraordinary achievement required extraordinary determination for international women. In many cases, women had initial support of their families for education only to learn that they are still expected to marry a man of their parents' choosing and to subjugate their goals to that of their husband. One of the women in Kitano's study told of escaping into education because her family wished to marry her to an old man she hated. Napier tells of Native American women leaders who struggled to maintain their cultural identities while participating in educational systems that could not recognize or understand their world view. Martinez-Thorne explains the pressure upon Hispanic American women scholars to remain loyal to traditional roles.

The research reviewed here reflects a diversity of perspectives on giftedness in girls, and suggests ways of providing guidance to girls and young women based on that diversity.

Gifted pre-school girls

Gifted pre-school girls go unidentified for a number of reasons; one of the most common reasons is that parents are diffident about bringing in girls for testing. Research has shown for later grades that parents are less likely to enroll girls in special gifted programming than parents of boys, perhaps because they are more reluctant to challenge them (Silverman, 1986.) Generally, parents of girls tend to 'overhelp' them, protecting girls from the rigors of difficult problem solving. There is reason to believe that this phenomenon is at work in parents' resistance to testing gifted girls (Kerr, 1997). Second, many psychologists are unwilling to test pre-school girls, because of the unreliability of intelligence tests for predicting later achievement; there is also the possibility that they are less willing to challenge girls than to challenge boys. Third, there is considerable confusion among psychologists and educators about the meaning of precocious reading (Jackson & Kearney, 1999). Because it is well known among educators that precocious reading does not necessarily predict giftedness, many discount parent diagnoses of giftedness based on precocious reading. This, however, is a misunderstanding of the nature of the relationship of female giftedness to reading. Most gifted girls learn to read earlier than gifted boys, and are more advanced in their reading skills than gifted boys throughout school. Although not all precocious readers become intellectually gifted students, nearly all gifted students—particularly gifted female students—were precocious readers. Therefore, precocious reading in a girl should not be discounted as a developmental fluke, but should be investigated as a possible sign of giftedness.

Although sex role behavior is learned as early as three years old, gifted girls tend to be less rigid in their sex role identification than average girls (Terman & Oden, 1935; Kerr, 1997). They are likely to be more open to playing with both girls and boys, and are likely to enjoy adventurous, active play that is usually preferred by boys. They may play with toys in a more complex way, inventing new games with even the most passive feminine toys (doing surgery upon a Barbie or marrying her off to Lego robot). Pre-school gifted girls have vivid fantasy lives, and are more likely than average girls to have invisible playmates or imagined characters.

Jane Piirto's advice for the guidance of children with specific creative talents is relevant to gifted girls (1998), as are counseling strategies recommended by Kerr (1997) for girls with specific extraordinary abilities. Gifted girls of three and four can benefit from exposure to a second language. They are likely to learn both languages in a bilingual family very quickly. Fears about linguistic confusion, leading parents to speak in only one language, are probably unfounded. Second languages learned at this age tend to be learned with near perfect accents, particularly by gifted girls, who seem to excel in language acquisition. Musical instruction should also begin at this age; recent studies show that musical instruction must begin by age 6 if a child is to have a 'natural' talent. Pitch, tonal memory, and rhythm memory may all be better learned at this very early age, since music is one of the earliest developing talents.

Mathematical precocity may appear in girls just before kindergarten as well, and because it is, like music, an early maturing ability, needs immediate challenge and guidance. Gifted girls tend to love counting games and early computational games, and computer programs that offer 'jump starts' are often very enjoyable to pre-school gifted girls. Social mathematics, like counting games, seem particularly appropriate for girls, who will throughout school prefer maths instruction that is linked to real life and to sociable activities. One of the most neglected areas of pre-school stimulation for girls is spatial-visual activities other than art. Because girls receive so little opportunity to play with Legos, construction toys, and other toys requiring mechanical and spatial manipulation, they may fall behind boys in spatial-visual skills. Therefore, spatial-visual challenge is particularly important, because later these skills will be needed for mathematics and effective use of technology.

Gifted girls who come to the attention of counselors and psychologists in the pre-school years are usually brought to professionals for testing when parents observe their unusual precocity and become concerned. Among upper middle class families who have not yet encountered the school system, there is often the belief that proper identification of their girl's giftedness will lead to better educational opportunities. This belief is often rapidly challenged by the unwillingness of educators to provide those opportunities.

One of the most frequent questions asked of guidance providers is whether to enroll gifted girls in school early. In most societies, early admission to schooling or early grade skipping were the tools of choice for accommodating gifted children's special abilities. In the early twentieth century, when Terman & Oden (1935) set out to identify gifted children, they found that an overwhelming number of the children identified by their teachers as gifted were the youngest or second youngest in the class. In contemporary United States and Australia, however, where a sort of radical egalitarianism holds sway, it is considered wrong to give bright children the special 'privilege' of early admission or grade skipping. In addition, in these societies, social adjustment is considered more important than intellectual challenge, and parents are discouraged from making a decision for early schooling. As a result, many parents are confused, and consult guidance providers about this decision.

Although of course every gifted girl is unique in her needs, and decisions must be made based on other variables besides early reading or maths ability, there is both clinical and research evidence that early admission to schooling for gifted girls is a simple and effective way of providing for intellectual challenge (Silverman, 1986, 1993). Gifted girls usually read earlier than gifted boys, are less physically active, and better adjusted socially, so they are a better bet for early admission than gifted boys. If girls are moderately gifted, have good social skills and have already mastered reading, then early admission may be indicated. Parents of highly gifted girls need to be warned that early admission alone will probably not address their child's needs; highly gifted girls are likely to still be so asynchronous in their development that entry by just one year is not enough, and two or more years places them at risk for being bullied by much larger children. Small, ungraded classes emphasizing self-paced learning may be the best option for these girls.

Primary age gifted girls

Across cultures, the early primary grades mark the time when the intellectual gifts of girls are most evident (Kerr, 1997). Most nations have compulsory schooling until at least fourth grade, so all over the world, girls at this age are afforded the opportunity to display their gifts. In addition, girls of this age have not yet internalized beliefs about female inferiority. As a result, most gifted girls are eager to show their superior reasoning and memory and happy to be asked to recite, draw, sing, play an instrument, or dance. They do their best because they have not yet learned the costs of being different from the other girls or superior to boys; they continue to behave like first class citizens. Gifted girls in primary grades outperform boys in all areas of academics, receiving higher grades and higher achievement test scores. In terms of psychological adjustment, primary age gifted girls are also superior to gifted boys and average girls and boys (Janos & Robinson, 1985) Even for highly gifted girls, ages five through nine are likely to be less troubling than later years, as long as they can find sufficient challenge for their abilities. Gifted girls at this age are filled with the excitement of learning, and usually reading, learning, and practicing skills take precedence over the pursuit of popularity.

Research confirms that gifted girls have higher grades than gifted boys throughout the school years. However, a disturbing pattern begins to emerge in fourth and fifth grade when gifted boys begin to receive higher achievement test scores in maths and science than gifted girls. It is the beginning of a gap between the achievement scores of the most highly gifted girls and boys that will continue throughout their lives, reducing the choices of gifted girls and women while opening doors for gifted boys and men. Sadker & Sadker (1994) have shown persuasively how achievement tests are biased against girls. Items on achievement tests reflect boys' experiences more than that of girls; items about sports, machinery, and wagering are of little interest to girls. In addition, studies have shown that girls do less well on tests of speed; timed tests of maths are nearly always biased against the more reflective style of problem-solving that is characteristic of girls. All of the major achievement tests are not just tests of knowledge or reasoning ability; they are tests of speed and brashness, characteristics which may predict little about a girl's true capacity for learning. It should be noted that girls excel at the language sections of achievement tests. However, boys' inferiority in reading and language skills is seldom held up as a cause for major concern the way girl's lesser performance is in mathematics. Girls are assumed to be deficient in the area of maths and science, and the difference in scores at the highest level, although attributable to many causes, is often held up as proof of gifted girls' deficiencies.

Although girls in the late primary grades begin to fall somewhat behind the boys in achievement tests, they continue to outshine boys not only in grades but in overall adjustment and self-esteem. Gifted girls before age 11 are strikingly confident. They assert themselves in groups, and will argue for their opinions. They have high self-efficacy, believing they are good at many things, particularly school work. At both five years old and eight years old, they have strong self-concepts; they have high opinions of their physical self, their academic selves, and their social selves (AAUW, 1991; Brown & Gilligan, 1992)

Finally gifted girls have high career aspirations. Gifted girls' career aspirations since the time of Terman have been higher than those of average girls. In the last twenty years, gifted girls' aspirations have continued to climb; at this point their career goals are just as high as those of gifted boys (Gassen, Kelley & Feldhusen, 1993). The major difference between the aspirations of gifted girls and gifted boys are the stronger altruistic and social motivations behind the goals. Gifted girls nearly always want careers that make people's lives better, or that make the world more safe and more beautiful for its beings. Gifted girls are idealistic and optimistic about their potential to do good.

When gifted girls come to the attention of counselors and psychologists, it is seldom for conduct disorders, underachievement, or adjustment disorders. Gifted girls' good mental health and frequently observed resilience usually mitigates against the need for in-depth treatment (Czeschlik & Rost, 1994). It is more likely to be some extraordinary situational disturbance that brings gifted girls into therapy: the death of a parent, a very difficult divorce, or exposure to abuse are some of the few situations that gifted girls may not be able to adjust to without professional help. In addition, therapists who counsel gifted girls who have some other risk factor such as inherited depression, autism, or personality disorders may find these conditions complicated by giftedness. Some have even called

gifted children with this combination 'dual diagnosis' clients because of the complex ways in which gifted-ness interact with other disorders. Therefore, it is important that guidance providers recognize that when a bright girl is referred for counseling, her situation and condition may be very bad indeed.

In addition to gifted at-risk girls, another category of bright schoolgirls who may need professional help are the highly gifted girls. Leta Hollingworth noted the severe burdens that are placed upon girls of great genius to be 'normal', and showed several girls' valiant efforts to do so. However, gifted girls of over 150 IQ or in the 99 + percentile on measures of achievement may simply be too different to camouflage their true abilities. Upon showing these abilities, many gifted girls will be cruelly rejected by other girls and will find themselves isolated. Kaufmann (1981) found that many of the highly gifted Presidential Scholars in her study had been unrecognized as high achievers and labeled as loners as children. Therefore, guidance providers have a special responsibility for highly gifted girls. Highly gifted girls need a caring, listening adult who will not only help them to get the academic stimulation they crave, but who will understand their loneliness and isolation. These girls often need assurance that they will some day find peers with whom they can talk, and the counselor's help in making that possible. Referral to conferences and camps for highly gifted, as well as support groups may be one of the most powerful interventions. Hollingworth (1926) and Silverman (1993) have both noted that if highly gifted girls can find just a few friends of similar intellectual ability, they can have quite normal lives. This is perhaps one of the great beauties of the highly specialized chat rooms on the Internet; many of these allow highly gifted children from all over the world to converse with one another about their interests, both esoteric and common. Counselors who familiarize themselves with chat rooms and websites frequented by gifted children can do a great service by connecting their young clients with this great source of friendship and fun.

Gifted adolescent girls

Once a topic spurned by feminists and non-feminists alike, the plight of the adolescent girl now is featured in the media everyday. The facts about girls' self-esteem plunge between 11 and 17; girls' loss of confidence in their own voices; and the high rates of eating disorders, substance abuse, and sexually transmitted diseases among teenage girls are fairly well known. However, many people believe that gifted girls are somehow protected by their intelligence. The vast majority of gifted girls continue to receive high grades and to have very high levels of involvement in extracurricular activities. However, there is evidence that they are also vulnerable to loss of self-esteem and to risky behaviors that can jeopardize their goals and dreams (Kerr & Kurpius, 1998).

653

Studies of the self-concept of gifted girls show a similar decline to that of average girls. Terman's girls actually declined in their performance on intelligence tests; administrators even speculated that they were no longer trying as hard. Groth's (1969) cross-sectional studies of gifted girls and women showed a sharp difference between the wishes of ten year olds and fourteen year olds, with ten year olds valuing the pursuit of achievements and the enhancement of their self esteem and fourteen year olds focusing almost entirely on desires for love and belonging. Groth commented that the fourteen year olds seemed to believe that achievement and love were mutually exclusive. Contemporary studies show the same transformation, as gifted girls "go into hiding." Gifted girls' concept of themselves slides in all dimensions—physical, academic, and social (Czeschlik & Rost, 1994).

How does the rapid change of fortunes in the psychological lives of gifted girls come about? The role of family, societal, and school expectations, achievement tests and grades, and girls' attitudes toward themselves have all been examined in an effort to understand what happens to adolescent gifted girls.

Gifted girls, particularly in traditional families and cultures, are expected to do an 'about-face' in adolescence (Reis & Callahan, 1996; Kerr, 1997); there is strong evidence that women who become eminent or achieving in Hispanic and Asian cultures are those who receive family encouragement that is out of the ordinary (Kitano, 1998). Up until puberty, intelligence in a girl is considered a positive characteristic, and little girls are encouraged in their school work and precocious behavior. However, with adolescence comes the expectation that the gifted girl will turn her attention to becoming an attractive potential mate. Few cultures perceive intelligence as an attractive characteristic in a woman; men tend to marry their equals or inferiors in ability (Kerr, 1997). As a result, most bright girls adjust to their culture's expectations of them. Girls all over the world tune in carefully to the media portrayals of women, and seek to emulate their television and musical stars in their makeup and dress. Gifted girls may focus their intelligence and creativity on diet schemes, shopping, and grooming rituals. In addition, gifted girls may become social experts, working their peer group in such a way as to increase their status and popularity with Machiavellian skill.

Portrayals of girls and women in academic materials are little improvement on media portrayals. Sadker & Sadker (1994) analyzed the content of commonly used maths, language, arts, and history books and found that girls and women were greatly underrepresented, with two to four times as many males depicted, and only 11 women's names mentioned in a popular 631 page history textbook. The items on tests and achievement tests, particularly in science and maths, feature problems that are more interesting to boys than to girls; items about machines, wagering (If you had a poker hand that had two aces . . .), and sports tend to be of less interest to girls. Girls do less well on these items, but perform better on items with the same level of difficulty that pertain to issues of interest to them: nature and animals, arts and crafts, and people.

Adolescent gifted girls may also be at a disadvantage in the classroom because of teacher attitudes. Siegel & Reis (1995) found that teachers perceive their gifted girls as working harder and producing higher quality work than gifted boys, but still assign higher grades to the boys. Girls then seem to accept their teachers' judgments, and evaluate themselves as less able than the boys in mathematics and science. Cooley, Chauvin & Karnes (1984) found similar stereotyping, with teachers of gifted perceiving gifted boys as having superior critical thinking skills and problem solving abilities, and perceiving gifted girls as having superior creative writing abilities. It is interesting that although most teachers are opposed to sex role stereotyping, and while most make an effort to avoid stereotyping in general, they tend to see gifted boys as liking maths and being better at it than girls (Fennema, 1990).

According to Sadker & Sadker (1994), achievement test scores may be the biggest culprit in gifted girls' sudden slide in self esteem. Because the gap in maths and science achievement is largest at the highest levels of achievement, gifted girls are particularly aware of the differences in their scores from those of gifted boys. Despite the evidence they have from their high grades that they can have outstanding performance in maths and science, they seem to give achievement test scores more credence. As a result, many gifted girls lower their estimate of their abilities as well as lowering their self-esteem.

Talented at risk girls are particularly vulnerable to this process. Because most achievement tests do not provide accurate predictions of the academic abilities of Native American, African American, and Hispanic girls, these girls are often greatly dismayed by achievement test scores. These girls may have had consistently high grades, but low achievement test scores come as a blow; many very bright girls will insist that they are not gifted after receiving their scores (Kerr & Kurpius, 1999.)

Adolescent gifted girls seek counseling and are referred for counseling for a wide variety of reasons, although again, it must be stressed that the incidence of severe behavioral problems is much lower in gifted girls than in average or low ability girls (Janos & Robinson, 1985). At risk behaviors include bulimia and anorexia; drug and alcohol abuse; unsafe sex and unwanted pregnancy. In gifted girls, these behaviors take on different meanings than with the general population of girls (Kerr & Kurpius, 1999). Eating disorders are often an extension of adolescent gifted girls' high needs for achievement. When society demands a thin, attractive body as opposed to an educated mind, these girls may attempt to become the thinnest girls in the school. Drug and alcohol abuse are compounded by gifted girls' ability to hide their problem behaviors, to create cover stories, and to distract adults with academic achievement. Even alcohol abuse can be a sort of achievement for the gifted girl who wants to prove her ability to binge with the boys. On the other hand, unsafe sex and unwanted pregnancies are sometimes the result of gifted girls wanting to prove their femininity; early sexual activity may mean acceptance into the social group by a girl who is otherwise an outsider.

The problems of being multipotential can also bring gifted girls into counseling. Multipotentiality of gifted students, first identified as a major problem of gifted students at the Wisconsin Guidance Laboratory for Superior Students (Sanborn, 1979) is the ability to select and develop any interest. These students have a wide variety of extracurricular activities, 'high flat' interest profiles showing them to be interested in almost every occupational category, and high grades across the board. For gifted girls, being multipotential often translates into excessive involvement in out of class activities and difficulty making decisions about colleges and career directions. Counselors may see girls who are physically exhausted from their rigorous schedule, and who have sudden long absences as a result of stress-related illnesses. In addition, gifted girls may agonize over college choices because of their inability to define a career interest.

The tendency of gifted young women to camouflage their abilities and to deny their giftedness is itself well hidden; that is, bright young women continue to receive very high grades and to perform well in the classroom while telling their friends that they are just lucky, or using other strategies to diminish their own accomplishments (Reis & Callahan, 1996). The slide in self-esteem is seldom evident to counselors. Therefore, only those counselors who carefully question girls about their abilities will be able to discern the inner barriers to achievement and actualization that are well developed by adolescence.

A great number of career development and counseling interventions are now available for adolescent gifted girls. A wide variety of National Science Foundation funded projects to encourage girls and young women in maths and science are now available for replication (NSF, 1999). Interventions specifically for gifted girls that have been developed include a counseling workshop to raise aspirations and overcome multipotentiality (Kerr & Erb, 1991); a workshop for raising self esteem and self-efficacy in maths and science as well as overcoming at-risk behaviors (Kerr & Kurpius, 1999); a method of attributional retraining to help gifted girls re-attribute difficulties with maths scores (Heller & Zeigler, 1996); and a diagnostic-prescriptive workshop to overcome internal and external barriers (Hollinger & Fleming, 1992).

Over 100 National Science Foundation experimental and model projects are aimed at increasing girls' and women's participation in maths and sciences. Projects range from in-school changes to Girl Scout projects. Although not specifically targeted for gifted girls, many of the projects created guidance interventions that are appropriate for gifted girls. The Girl Scout project, for example, links girls with mentors who are scientists in a wide variety of fields and allows them to engage in experiments that will eventually be presented or published. Another project fills classrooms with posters of women mathematicians and scientists, and shows how they attained their goals. Another coaches girls and young women on how to improve scores on maths and science portions of achievement tests. Therefore, many of the projects, by encouraging career development through mentoring, modeling, and coaching, are excellent models for the development of maths and science talent in gifted girls.

Kerr & Erb (1991) developed a counseling procedure that is effective in overcoming multipotentiality as well as developing a sense of identity and purpose. This counseling procedure involved individual assessment on vocational and personality tests; group counseling in which students visualized the future and set goals; and individual test interpretation and goal-setting. Students who experienced these workshops were more likely than controls to set higher goals, to change interests to those in keeping with their values, to increase their understanding of their personal identity, and to make career plans for future. Kerr & Robinson-Kurpius (1999) redesigned the counseling intervention for talented at risk girls, adding a group counseling intervention for overcoming at risk behaviors. They found that girls in the experimental group, the majority of whom were poor Native American, Hispanic, and African American girls, had increased self-esteem, increased maths-science efficacy, increased hope for the future, and decreased risky behaviors.

Heller & Ziegler (1996) used nine sessions of re-training, modeling, and feedback to teach gifted young women to attribute their successes in statistics to ability and effort and their failures to lack of effort or to the consensus that the problems were difficult for everybody. They were successful in retraining attributions to a great degree; the control group got worse, and the tendency to attribute failure to an internal, stable trait ("I'm stupid in maths") completely disappeared in the treatment group.

In Hollinger & Fleming's (1992) Project CHOICE (Creating Her Options in Career Education), counselors diagnosed barriers that stood in the way of gifted girls' achievement, and then prescribed strategies for overcoming those barriers. Gifted girls' self-esteem, achievement motivation, and attitudes toward success were assessed, as well as the support they received from family, peers, and schools. For each girls, a set of barriers were identified, and a means of overcoming those barriers through mentoring programs, career education, counseling, and discussions with parents were developed. Follow-ups of students from five to fifteen years after the program showed that participants had benefitted greatly from the program. The majority had gone on to professional and other high level careers in their chosen areas, and had successfully combined marriage and family with rewarding work.

Conclusion

There is reason for both optimism and concern about the condition of gifted girls and young women, and the guidance available to them. Internationally, the achievement of gifted girls is increasing, and the participation of gifted women in leadership roles in their societies is expanding. New methods of identifying and providing for the education of gifted girls are proliferating. Nevertheless, problems in identifying the talents of girls in societies where male talent development is the norm remain. Both the timing and the nature of the assessments of female giftedness need to be examined, so that early developing intelligences are nurtured. Efforts to operationalize the model of female talent development suggested by Noble, Subotnik, and Arnold need to be considered.

In addition, guidance remains necessary to help girls to survive pressures to subvert or camouflage their talents, to overcome at risk behaviors, and to learn ways of developing their career dreams and goals. Many promising methods of encouragement and guidance of gifted girls are being tested and implemented; these methods need to be disseminated and shaped to fit the cultures of girls throughout the world.

References

American Association of University Women (1991). *Short-changing girls, shortchanging America*. Washington, D. C.: AAUW.

Anastasi, A. (1998). *Psychological testing*. Upper Saddle River, NJ: Prentice-Hall.

Arnold, K. D. (1993). Academically talented women in the 1980's: the Illinois Valedictorian Project. In: K. D. Hulbert & D. L. Schuster (Eds.), *Women's Lives Through Time: Educated American Women of the Twentieth Century* (pp. 393–414). San Francisco: Jossey-Bass.

Arnold, K., Noble, K. D. & Subotnik, R. F.(1997). *Remarkable women: perspectives in female talent development*. Cresskill, NJ: Hampton Press.

Brown, L. & Gilligan, C. (1992). *At the crossroads*. Cambridge, MA: Harvard University Press.

Callahan, C. M. (1986). The special needs of gifted girls. *Journal of Children in Contemporary Society*, **18** (3–4), 105–117.

Campbell, P. & Clewell, B. C. (1999). Science, maths, and girls: still a long way to go. *Education Week*, 9/15/99, 50–51.

Colangelo, N. & Kerr, B. A. (1991). Extreme academic talent: Profiles of Perfect Scorers. *Journal of Educational Psychology*, **82**, 404–410.

Cooley, D., Chauvin, J. C. & Karnes, F. A. (1984). Gifted females: A comparison by male and female teachers. *Roeper Review*, **6**, 3, 164–167.

Czeschlik, T. & Rost, D. H. (1994). Socio-emotional adjustment in elementary school boys and school girls: Does giftedness make a difference? *Roeper Review*, **16** (4), 294–297.

Eccles, J. S. (1987). Gender roles and women's achievement related decisions. *Psychology of Women Quarterly*, **11**, 135–172.

Fennema, E. (1990). Teachers' beliefs and gender differences in mathematics. In: E. Fennema & G. Leder (Eds.), *Mathematics and Gender* (pp. 1–9). New York: Teachers College Press.

Gardner, H. (1983). *Frames of Mind. The theory of multiple intelligences*. New York, NY: Basic Books.

Gassin, E. A., Kelly, K. R. & Feldhusen, J. F. (1993). Sex differences in the career development of gifted youth. *School Counselor*, **41** (2), 91–95.

Groth, N. (1969). Vocational development for gifted girls. ERIC Document ED941737. Reston, VA: ERIC.

Heller, K. & Ziegler, A. (1996). Gender differences in mathematics and sciences: can attributional retraining improve the performance of gifted females? *Gifted Child Quarterly*, **40** (4), 200–210.

Holland, D. C. & Eisenhart, M. A. (1990). *Educated in romance: Women, achievement, and college culture*. Chicago, IL: University of Chicago.

Hollinger, C. L. & Fleming, E. S. (1992). A longitudinal examination of life choices of gifted and talented young women. *Gifted Child Quarterly*, **36**, 207–212.

Hollingworth, L. S. (1926). *Gifted children: Their nature and nurture*. New York: Macmillan.

Jackson, N. E. & Kearney, J. N. (1999). Precocious reading and the gifted child. In: N. Colangelo & S. G. Assouline (Eds.), *Talent Development* (pp. 230–236.) Scottsdale, AZ: Gifted Psychology Press.

Janos, P. M. & Robinson, N. M. (1985). Psychosocial development in intellectually gifted children. In: F. D. Horowitz & M. O'Brien, (Eds.), *The Gifted and Talented: Developmental Perspectives* (pp. 186–207). Washington, D.C.: American Psychological Association.

Kaufmann, F. (1981). The 1964–1968 Presidential Scholars: a follow-up study. *Exceptional Children*, **48**, 2–10.

Kerr, B. A. (1991) *Handbook for counseling the gifted*. Reston, Va: American Counseling Association.

Kerr, B. A. (1997) *Smart girls: a new psychology of girls, women, and giftedness*. Scottsdale, AZ: Gifted Psychology Press.

Kerr, B. A. & Erb, C. (1991). Career counseling with academically talented students: effects of a value-based intervention. *Journal of Counseling Psychology*, **38**, 309–314.

Kerr, B. A. & Kurpius, S. R. (1999). Brynhilde's Fire: talent, risk, and betrayal in the lives of gifted girls. In: J. Leroux, (Ed.) *Connecting the Gifted Community Worldwide* (261–271). Ottawa: World Council on Gifted and Talented,.

Kitano, M. K. & Perkins, C. O. (1996). International gifted women: developing a critical resource. *Roeper Review*, **19** (1), 34–40.

Kitano, M. K. (1997). Gifted Asian American women. *Journal for the Education of the Gifted.* **21** (1) , 3–37.

Kitano, M. K. (1998). Gifted Latina women. *Journal for the Education of the Gifted*, **21** (2) 131–159.

Leroux, J. A. (1994). A tapestry of values: gifted women speak out. *Gifted Education International*, **9** (3) 167–171.

Martinez-Thorne, Y. (1995). Achievement motivation in high achieving Latina women. *Roeper Review*, **18** (1) 44–49.

Morelock, M. & Feldman, D. (1993). Prodigies and savants: What they have to tell us about giftedness and human cognition. K. A. Heller & F. J. Mönks (Eds.). *International Handbook of Research and Development of Giftedness and Talent*.

Napier, L. A. (1995). Educational profiles of nine gifted American Indian women and their own stories about wanting to lead. *Roeper Review*, **18** (1) 38–43.

National Institute of Mental Health (1993). *Eating disorders.* NIH Publication No. 93–3477/ Washington, D.C.: U.S. Department of Health and Human Services.

National Science Foundation (1999). *Model and experimental projects for women and girls*. Arlington, VA: NSF.

Noble, K. D., Subotnik, R. F. & Arnold, K. D. (1997). A new model of adult female talent development. In: K. D. Arnold, K. D. Nobel & R. F. Subotnik (Eds.), *Remarkable Women*. (pp. 427–429). Cresskill, NJ: Hampton Press.

Piirto, J. (1998). *Understanding those who create*. Scottsdale, AZ: Gifted Psychology.

Phillips, L.(1998) *The girls report*. New York: National Council for Research on Women.

Reis, S. & Callahan, C. (1996). My boyfriend, my girlfriend, or me: the dilemma of talented teenage girls. *Journal of Secondary Education*, **3**, 434–445.

Sadker, M. & Sadker, D. (1994). *Failing at fairness: how America's schools cheat girls*. New York: Charles Scribner's Sons.

Sanborn, M. (1979). Problems of gifted and talented students. In: N. Colangelo & R. Zaffran (Eds.) *New Voices in Counseling the Gifted* (pp.186–190). Dubuque, IA: Kendall- Hunt. Siegel, D. & Reis, S. M. (1995). Gender differences in teacher and student perceptions of student ability and effort. *The Journal of Secondary Gifted Education*, **6** (2), 86–92.

Silverman, L. K. (1986). What happens to the gifted girl? In: C. J. Maker (Ed.), *Critical Issues in Gifted Education: Defensible Programs for the Gifted* (pp. 43–49). Rockville, MD: Aspen.

Silverman, L. K. (1995). Why are there so few eminent women? *Roeper Review*, **18** (1), 5–13.

Terman, L. M. & Oden, M. (1935). The promise of youth. Genetic Studies of Genius. Vol 3. Palo Alto, CA: Stanford University Press.

Tomlinson-Keasey, C.(1999). Gifted women's lives. In: N. Colangelo & S. G. Assouline (Eds.), *Talent development* (271–291). Scottsdale, AZ: Gifted Psychology Press.

657

Inclusive Education for Gifted Students with Disabilities

Carolyn Yewchuk[1] and Judy Lupart[2]

[1]University of Alberta, Canada
[2]University of Calgary, Canada

Introduction

In our initial chapter (Yewchuk & Lupart, 1993), we presented a broad overview of many areas of study and practice associated with giftedness and disability. In the present chapter, we report on ensuing changes in the field reflected most predominantly in current educational settings throughout the world. The first change we have made is in our terminology. The term *gifted handicapped* has been changed to *gifted students with disabilities* to be consistent with contemporary usage which differentiates the qualities of the person from his or her disability. The initial chapter sections entitled *Definition*, *Incidence*, and *Identification* have been revised under one heading, *Gifted Students With Disabilities*, in the present chapter. This represents a general trend away from labeling and diagnosis to providing information that will be relevant and helpful to general classroom teachers who are the individuals most likely to bear responsibility for the learning and talent development of gifted students with disabilities.

Two previous sections, *Emotionally Disturbed Gifted* and *Preschool Handicapped Gifted*, have been deleted in the present chapter since there has been no relevant new information in these two areas, and two new topics, *Gifted Students with Attention Deficit/Hyperactivity Disorders* and *Gifted Students with Visual Impairment* have been added. The remaining topics have been revised and updated with particular attention to the move towards inclusive schooling. Finally, in light of recent general and special education reforms throughout the world, we have emphasized inclusive educational programming in our presentation of *Primary Subgroups of Gifted Students with Disabilities*.

Gifted Students with Disabilities: Still a Desultory Duality

The growing momentum of the inclusive education movement in the last two decades has increased concern with providing appropriate education for all children in the mainstream classroom, including those with exceptional learning needs (Lupart, McKeough & Yewchuk, 1996; Booth & Ainscow, 1998; Friend, Bursuck & Hutchinson, 1998). During this same time period, there have also been tremendous gains in the relatively late-developing area of gifted education (Heller, Monks & Passow, 1993; Yewchuk, 1996). Unfortunately, the educational needs of certain subgroups of this population of children, gifted students with disabilities, have been slow to receive recognition (Lupart, 1992; Johnson, Karnes & Carr, 1997).

Interest in individuals with high potential and disability is not just a contemporary phenomenon. There are many historical examples of gifted men and women with handicapping conditions who have made significant contributions to society, for example, Thomas Edison, Helen Keller, and Franklin Roosevelt (Goertzel & Goertzel, 1962). Other notable persons, such Albert Einstein, Woodrow Wilson, and Auguste Rodin had learning difficulties in reading, writing, and spelling (Thompson, 1971). Despite the widespread recognition of a few such individuals, we have no way of knowing how many more individuals with disabilities failed to develop areas of potential giftedness because of lack of recognition and support or inappropriate schooling. In the past, gifted children with disabilities were generally underserved. Where they received special educational services, it was in the area of disability without provision for their gifts and talents. Only those few individuals who had the support of informed, concerned families and/or visionary, innovative educators were able to develop their potential giftedness (Johnsen & Corn, 1989).

Since the 1970s there has been increased professional awareness of gifted students with disabilities as an underserved subpopulation of students (Whitmore, 1986; Gallagher, 1988). In the United States, the Association for the Gifted, a division of the Council for Exceptional Children, established a subcommittee of educators of gifted children with handicaps. The first national conference on gifted and talented students with disabilities was held in 1976 and in 1977 the term 'gifted handicapped' was added to the Educational Resources Information Center indices (Porter, 1982). By the mid 1970s in the United States, at least eight special programs for gifted children with disabilities had been developed (Maker, 1977), and special interest groups advocating on behalf of these children had been created (Johnsen & Corn, 1989).

One notable example is Very Special Arts, an organization founded in 1974 to enrich the lives of children, youth, and adults with disabilities (Johnson, Karnes & Carr, 1997). This affiliate of the John F. Kennedy Center for the Performing Arts sponsors non-competitive programs and festivals in drama, dance, music, literature, and the performing arts. It has since expanded to include international affiliates in over 83 countries around the world (see the VSA website at http://www.vsarts.org).

By the early 1980s, education of gifted children with disabilities was being hailed as a 'new frontier' (Whitmore, 1981), and educators were being challenged to develop procedures for identifying creative potential in these children (Ford & Ford, 1981), and to make appropriate use of new technology in the classroom (Higgins, 1981), while attending to areas of deficit (Karnes, Schwedel & Linnemeyer, 1982). Despite this early flurry of professional interest in gifted students with disabilities, leading American advocates noted a general neglect of the actual special educational needs of these students during the 1980s (Whitmore, 1989) and continuing on into the 1990s.

Barriers to the Appropriate Education of Gifted Students with Disabilities

Over the past two decades general education, special education, and gifted education have undergone tremendous reform (Fullan, 1991; Lupart, McKeough & Yewchuk, 1996; Yewchuk, 1996). Unfortunately, these reforms tend to be separately channeled through the dual systems of regular and special education (Lupart & Webber, 1996; Skrtic, 1996; Lupart, 1998). Paradoxically, reform efforts associated with special education have been mainly focused on equity issues, and reform efforts associated with general and gifted education have addressed excellence issues (Skrtic, 1996; Lupart, 1998). As a result, continued separation of regular and special education in contemporary schools may lead to a single outcome, either excellence or equity, not both (Skrtic, 1995).

Critiques and discussions by leading American advocates for gifted students with disabilities reflect the inconsistencies that arise out of dual systems of education (Whitmore, 1989). In one of Whitmore's interviews, Karnes noted that teachers of the gifted are usually unaware of handicap services, while teachers of children with handicaps are not trained to recognize

potential gifts or talents. In some instances, state consultants for gifted children may not even know their fellow consultants for children with disabilities (Whitmore, 1989).

From Gallagher's perspective, the neglect may be attributed to both administrative, logistical, and psychological barriers (Whitmore, 1989). The problem lies in allocating limited resources for special program development to the very small number of students who are both gifted and disabled, while psychologically, people who work with one group of students may not be able to respond appropriately to the other group. "Children who are gifted almost seem to be disliked . . . for their potential, or disregarded at the very least" by professionals trained to work with the handicapped, while educators of the gifted "can be made uncomfortable even by the presence of handicapped children in the same program" (Whitmore, 1989, p. 8–9).

To Hanninen, the emphasis within special education programs on the handicapping condition rather than on serving the whole child has contributed to neglect of potential giftedness (Whitmore, 1989). When the handicapping condition is very severe, teachers consider the development of basic skills so important that other considerations, including encouragement of gifts and talents, are relegated to a position of secondary importance.

Johnson, Karnes & Carr (1997) identify the following barriers hindering the identification and programming for gifted students with disabilities: (1) inappropriate identification procedures; (2) stereotypic attitudes; (3) lack of information about the nature and impact of developmental delays; (4) inadequate training of professionals; (5) lack of program models, research, and dissemination strategies; (6) lack of supportive technology; (7) lack of appropriate career counseling; and (8) inadequate funding.

In spite of the perceived neglect in educational provisions for gifted students with disabilities during the 1980s and 1990s, professional concern for this subpopulation of students has remained strong. Many reform leaders are now promoting a merged or unified system of educational provision for all students, in the belief that all children, particularly those with exceptional learning needs stand to reap significant, positive benefit (Goodlad & Lovitt, 1993; Skrtic, 1995, 1996; Lupart & Webber, 1996; Lupart, 1998).

Future Promise in Inclusive Education

Although educators are, in general, positive about the notion, there are wide variations in the ways inclusion is defined and practised in the schools (Bunch, Lupart & Brown, 1997; Booth & Ainscow, 1998). According to Andrews & Lupart (1999), inclusive education means that all children have the right to be educated in their community schools, and that general classroom teachers have the ultimate authority and responsibility for educating them. Emphasizing professional collaboration that merges the best of regular and special education practice (Idol, 1996; Wong, 1996), and a belief in the simultaneous attainment of excellence and equity (Skrtic, 1996; Richert, 1997; Lupart, 1998), three enabling conditions for inclusive education are: (1) professional training and development; (2) pooling of material and professional resources; and (3) administrative leadership and support (Andrews & Lupart, 1999).

Moving toward truly inclusive education systems will not happen easily or overnight; however, the potential benefits for gifted students with disabilities are immediately obvious. First, an emphasis on the continuous progress of all students means that teachers are concerned about discovering and nurturing personal talents and learning abilities, rather than what category a child belongs to. Second, by eliminating a costly, time-consuming, and possibly elitist special education identification process, limited resources can be effectively deployed to support teachers in developing and implementing individually appropriate classroom programming adaptations. Third, expertise can be shared and extended for specialists and classroom teachers through collaborative consultation. Fourth, shared responsibility for all students fosters innovation and teaming in educator relationships. Fifth, a commitment to achieving both excellence and equity provides the challenge necessary for creating a true learning community.

Although inclusive education placements for children with multiple disabilities is widely supported (Fuchs & Fuchs, 1994), parents and professionals working with gifted children who learn best with specially trained teachers in segregated class settings are actively opposed to the inclusion movement. They are concerned that bright and talented children who flourish in special classes with their intellectual peers may again find themselves unchallenged in classes geared toward students of average ability (Yewchuk, 1996). There is strong support in many quarters for maintaining educational placements outside the inclusive classroom for those students who need it (Fuchs & Fuchs, 1994). The (American) National Association for Gifted Children (1992, back page) is on record as supporting grouping of students because it "allows for more appropriate, rapid, and advanced instruction, which matches the rapidly developing skills and capabilities of gifted students." With these possibilities in mind, we present a general overview of the contemporary field of gifted students with disabilities, followed by specific information relevant to general classroom teachers for each primary subgroup of gifted students with disabilities.

Gifted Students With Disabilities

The incidence of gifted students with disabilities is low compared to other segments of the school population. Estimates range from a conservative 2% of all students

with disabilities in the United States, or between 120,000 and 180,000 (Schnur & Stefanich, 1979) to a more liberal 5% or between 300,000 and 540,000 (Whitmore & Maker, 1985). Data from studies of specific subpopulations of gifted students with disabilities have varied even more. Mauser (1980) found 2.3% of students with learning disabilities to be gifted. Karnes and Johnson (1986) reported that 9.2% of preschool children with disabilities met their criteria of giftedness. Among students with hearing impairment, the reported rates are 4.2% (Gamble, 1985) and 6.1% (Yewchuk & Bibby, 1989a). Approximately 2 to 5% of school-aged children with visual impairment are considered gifted (Ferrell, 1994). Neither the estimates nor the empirically derived percentages can be considered definitive because of the range in criteria for giftedness and the nature, severity, and effect of disabilities.

Gifted students with disabilities require special education services for one or more areas of potential giftedness, and one or more types of disability. These students form an extremely heterogeneous group, with great variability in profiles of strengths and weaknesses.

Students with disabilities include those who require special education services for mental retardation, hearing impairment, speech impairment, visual impairment, serious emotional disturbance, specific learning disability, or orthopedic or other health impairment, either singly or in combination (Individuals with Disabilities Education Act, 1997). Special education services are indicated if the disability prevents children from performing appropriately in regular school programs.

Definitions of giftedness based on multiple criteria of high potential are more amenable to the identification of gifts and talents in children with disability than the more stringent traditional definitions based only on extremely high intelligence. The definition proposed by Marland (1972) and subsequent amendments by the U.S. Congress (1978, 1988) that included not only high intellectual ability but also high performance capability in specific academic areas, the arts, leadership, and creativity have influenced broadening the concept of giftedness to include children with disabilities. A student with disabilities, like any other student, can meet the criteria for giftedness by showing high potential and/or performance in at least one of the specified areas, irrespective of average or even deficient performance in other areas.

The characteristics of giftedness which students with disabilities exhibit (Whitmore, 1981; Pledgie, 1982; Udall, 1985; Whitmore & Maker, 1985; Yewchuk & Bibby, 1989a) are similar to those reported for nondisabled students (Davis & Rimm, 1998), such as:

- Superior memory and general knowledge
- Superior analytical and creative problem solving skills

- Notable drive to know, or master
- Superior use of language, oral or written
- Exceptional comprehension
- Keen sense of humor
- Persistence in pursuit of academic or intellectual tasks
- Awareness and/or ability to capitalize on personal strengths.

Furthermore, successful gifted students with disabilities have been observed to have an intense drive to succeed in reaching their goals and the capability of devising creative coping strategies for goal attainment. These have been shown to include strategies for overcoming personal limitations (Whitmore & Maker, 1985), and alternate solutions to attainment of a goal (Robertson, 1985). Gifted individuals with disabilities, in general, have a positive vision of their potential, accurate self-knowledge of their strengths, and a high degree of energy in trying to reach their goals (Whitmore & Maker, 1985; Wingenbach, 1985).

Some of the positive qualities of gifted students with disabilities, however, may not appear praiseworthy to adults around them (Friedrichs, 1990). For instance, these students might aspire to negative goals, such as identifying and criticizing inconsistent school policies (Rosner & Seymour, 1983). They may also exhibit negative characteristics associated with having a disability (Meisgeier, Meisgeier & Werblo, 1978; Whitmore & Maker, 1985; Nielsen & Mortorff-Albert, 1989; Vespi & Yewchuk, 1992):

- Struggles with self-acceptance
- Fragile self-concept
- Feelings of social discomfort, embarrassment, shame
- Intense frustration and anger
- A need to release or vent pent-up energies
- Interpersonal difficulties with peers, teachers, and family
- Academic difficulties in selected skill areas.

For some gifted students with disabilities, the interaction between positive and negative characteristics may develop into emotional/behavioral difficulties (Schiff, Kaufman & Kaufman, 1981), social isolation through withdrawn or aggressive behaviors (Meisgeier, Meisgeier & Werblo, 1978), suicidal tendencies (Yewchuk & Jobagy, 1992), avoidance of academic and social involvement because of a powerful fear of failure or rejection (Vespi & Yewchuk, 1992), psychologically painful school experiences (Reis, Neu & McGuire, 1997), external locus of control, field dependence, poor achievement motivation, and learned helplessness (Bireley, 1991). Where gifted students with disabilities are treated as handicapped to the neglect of their intellectual ability, a 'handicapped' or dependent pattern of behavior is likely to emerge. However, a supportive, facilitative environment can foster the emergence of a 'gifted' pattern geared toward success in academic endeavors and social interactions with peers (Bireley, 1991). Special educational interventions in supportive settings are crucial if gifted students with disabilities are to come to terms with the discrepancy between expectations based on self-perception of high abilities and low achievement resulting from the disabilities (Vespi & Yewchuk, 1992).

Because disabilities can mask intellectual ability, talent, and creativity (Maker & Grossi, 1985), gifted students with disabilities are not as likely as non-disabled gifted students to be identified as gifted for special school programming (Davis & Rimm, 1998). Disabilities can disguise a child's true potential and abilities, and impede the expression of characteristics revealing giftedness (Maker, 1976, Gerken, 1979). Identifying the true ability of a child with handicaps who cannot speak or hold a pencil, for example, presents a unique challenge to educators (Minner, Prater, Bloodworth & Walker, 1987; Minner, 1990).

The key to recognition of giftedness in students with disabilities lies in adequately trained special educators, gifted educators, and mainstream educators (Johnson, Karnes & Carr, 1997). Classroom teachers require special training to identify giftedness in students with learning disabilities (Minner, 1990). Gifted educators require familiarization with disabling conditions and their effects on learning. Until teachers received inservicing on the characteristics and educational needs of gifted students with disabilities, Eisenberg & Epstein (1981) did not receive a single nomination for their gifted program from teachers of 60,000 students with handicaps in New York City. In Minnesota, concerted state efforts to ensure that all student groups were represented in gifted programs yielded positive results: 77% of special education program coordinators and 81% of gifted education coordinators reported that gifted students with disabilities were being served in gifted programs (Grimm, 1998).

The following practices are conducive to identification of gifts and talents in students with disabilities:

- Be familiar with the characteristics of giftedness and talent, and how they can be manifested by students with handicapping conditions. Create situations where students with handicaps have the opportunity to display gifted and talented behavior.
- Ideally, an examiner who is similarly disabled should be involved in the testing process (Stefanich & Schnur, 1979).
- The norm group for a student with disabilities should include a subgroup of peers with similar disabilities who have experienced a similar degree of developmental delay in language development and intellectual functioning through lack of access to information, opportunity, and resources (Maker, 1977).

- Standardized tests of intelligence and achievement developed specifically for subpopulations of students with handicaps, such as the Hiskey Nebraska Test of Learning Aptitude (Hiskey, 1966) for deaf children, or the Perkins-Binet for blind children (Warren, 1984) should be used. Where such instruments are not available, checklists and tests should be examined and assessed for appropriateness of use, bearing in mind the unique characteristics of the particular subgroup (Corn, 1986; Johnson, 1987). Another suggestion is to consider a cut-off of 120 or 125 on any one of the Verbal, Performance, or Full Scales of the Wechsler instead of the more conventional 130+ for identifying gifted students with learning disabilities (Schiff, Kaufman & Kaufman, 1981; Fox, 1983; Udall & Maker, 1983; Yewchuk, 1986).
- Tests should be modified only if the examiner is thoroughly familiar with the limitations imposed by specific types of disability and the special concessions appropriate for that type of disability (Pendarvis & Grossi, 1980). Ways in which students compensate for a disabling condition, and characteristics instrumental in successful adaptation should be given special emphasis. If normal channels of expression are inaccessible, tasks requiring problem solving, memory, critical thinking, and creativity might be appropriate (Whitmore, 1981; LaFrance, 1995).
- Multiple sources of information, including standardized tests (achievement, ability, aptitude), teacher and parent referral, and student observation, maximize the likelihood of identification and facilitate a balanced, holistic view of the child's abilities (Lupart, 1990; Grimm, 1998).
- Special educators should have course work in gifted education, gifted educators should have course work addressing disability issues, and classroom teachers need familiarity with both fields to recognize the needs of gifted students with disabilities in inclusionary settings (Karnes & Johnson, 1991; Johnson, Karnes & Carr, 1997). Provision of appropriate educational programming for gifted students with disabilities is facilitated when teachers, psychologists, counselors, parents, and others can work together to provide services for children with special needs in the inclusive classroom.

Primary Subgroups of Gifted Students with Disabilities

Gifted Students with Learning Disabilities

Unlike other groups of gifted students with special needs, who can be identified by some type of discrete loss such as visual impairment, children with learning disabilities do not constitute an easily identifiable group (Brody & Mills, 1997). Learning disabilities may take many forms and involve some or all of the abilities inherent in using spoken or written language

and mathematics. Disorders in basic psychological processes underlying oral expression, listening comprehension, written expression, basic reading skills, reading comprehension, mathematics calculation, and mathematics reasoning are presumed to arise from central nervous system dysfunction (Individuals with Disabilities Education Act, 1997).

Many gifted students with learning disabilities appear intelligent and excel in one or more areas, but they have major difficulties in other areas. There may even be great variability in performance within a subject area such as reading (McGuire & Yewchuk, 1995, 1996). These students are often identified incidentally as a result of assessment for other purposes (Fox, 1983; Brody & Mills, 1997). Utilizing advanced abilities to compensate for the learning difficulties (Weill, 1987), they may function at or near grade level, and the teacher may not be aware of their gifted potential (Gunderson, Maesch & Rees, 1987). Some are initially referred for assessment of learning difficulties, and found to have IQs in the gifted range. Still others are referred for psychological assessment because of personal and social problems and subsequently found to be gifted (Schiff, Kaufman & Kaufman, 1981).

Surveys of special education and gifted programs in Texas have shown that gifted students with learning disabilities often fall into the gap between the two types of programs (Boodoo, Bradley, Frontera, Pitts & Wright, 1989; Tallent-Runnels & Sigler, 1995). Students receiving special education services for a learning disability may not have the opportunity to exhibit superior abilities, because of the remedial emphasis of such programs. Teachers who have training in special education, however, are more likely to identify gifted students with learning disabilities than regular classroom teachers without such training (Waldron, Saphire & Rosenbaum, 1987). Screening checklists can alert regular classroom teachers to the characteristics of these students (Dix & Schafer, 1996).

Many parents of children with learning disabilities in special class placements are apprehensive about the merging of regular education and special education. It took 30 years of lobbying to get recognition of, and instructional provision for, their children's learning needs in special classes (Learning Disability Association of Canada, 1993), and they are concerned about potential loss of these gains. Indiscriminate full-time inclusive placement of all children with learning disabilities would not meet the needs of those children who require intensive and continual instruction from specialists trained in learning disabilities.

Given the multiplicity of possible combinations of areas of giftedness and learning disability, comprehensive assessment aimed at developing an individual program plan should follow initial screening. The assessment should include both a summary profile of the student's intelligence, achievement, creativity, self-concept, teacher evaluation, and family support. This information can be derived from interviews with teachers, parents, and counselors; the student's cumulative record, and additional testing as required; and a structured individual interview focusing on the student's self-perception as a learner, approach to academic tasks, organization of work, and work habits (Lupart, 1990).

The individual program plan derived from the assessment should include strategies for enrichment of gifts and talents, strategies for remediation of and compensation for deficits, and strategies for enhancing personal development (Yewchuk, 1992). Individualized programs developed in accordance with Kaplan's (1986) Differentiated Curriculum Model (Hishinuma, 1991; Clements, Lundell & Hishinuma, 1994) and Renzulli's (1977) Enrichment Triad Model (Baum, 1984, 1988, 1994; Baum & Kirschenbaum, 1984; Baum & Owen, 1988; Baum, Emerick, Herman & Nixon, 1989; Olenchak, 1995) extend, challenge, and stimulate creative productivity in areas of strength, encourage development and use of alternate modes of thinking and communicating, and foster critical thinking and research skills in independent project activities. Remedial activities directed at areas of deficiency are addressed in the context of the enrichment activities, and compensatory techniques for bypassing areas of difficulty are encouraged. Involvement of parents in monitoring and reinforcing homework and afterschool activities can result in improved academic performance and classroom behaviors (Sah & Borland, 1989). In addition to differentiated and/or individual programming in the regular classroom, gifted students with learning disabilities may require individual or group counseling of social and emotional needs, such as a powerful fear of failure resulting from the conflict of high expectations and low achievement in academic subjects (Vespi & Yewchuk, 1992); feelings of frustration, resentment and anger directed at themselves, their parents, their peers and their teachers (Mendaglio, 1993); low self-concept (Hishinuma, 1993; Olenchak, 1994); and willful repression of negative school experiences (Reis, Neu & McGuire, 1997).

Gifted Students with Attention-Deficit/Hyperactivity Disorders

Attention-deficit/hyperactivity disorders (AD/HD) are characterized by symptoms of inattention, hyperactivity, and/or impulsivity that are developmentally inappropriate and not the result of other conditions (Turnbull, et al., 1999). These disorders fall into three subtypes.

The inattentive type is characterized by day-dreaming, distractibility, forgetfulness, apathy, underachievement, social withdrawal and/or difficulty paying attention in class. In contrast, the hyperactive-impulsive type includes students who are restless, talkative, fidgety, rebellious and/or impulsive. In the third, combined type, students manifest characteristics of both inattention and hyperactivity-impulsivity (Turnbull, et al., 1999; Kaufmann & Castellanos, Chapter 6, Part V, of this Handbook).

Many gifted students are mistakenly diagnosed as having AD/HD, while others are not appropriately identified (Delisle, 1995; Silverman, 1998). Since many of the behaviors associated with AD/HD may be exhibited by high-energy, high-intensity gifted students and highly creative students without actually having the disorder, distinguishing between the two conditions is not easy. Close examination of the environmental, curricular and contextual factors associated with the problematic behaviors is required (Webb & Latimer, 1993; Lind & Silverman, 1994; Delisle, 1995; Reid & McGuire, 1995). It is important to distinguish between the two conditions because the educational treatment is different (Lind & Silverman, 1994).

Children with AD/HD exhibit the behaviors in all settings, to a greater or lesser degree, while for gifted children problem behaviors are situation specific, e.g. lack of challenge. With the possible exception of television and computer games, children with AD/HD have short attention spans, in contrast to gifted students who can focus on tasks of interest for long periods of time. In general, children with AD/HD are inconsistent in the quality of their performance, unlike gifted students who, providing they are intellectually challenged, maintain consistent efforts and high standards.

Gifted students with AD/HD are characterized by asynchrony between advanced intellectual/academic abilities and immature social skills or emotional reactions, which may be poorly tolerated, even by gifted peers. They may have increased intensity and emotional reactivity to environmental stimuli, and heightened intellectual and imaginative excitation (Lovecky, 1994). Strengths of gifted students with AD/HD include ability to work quickly and produce work of significant quality, a spontaneous and joyful approach to life, and a sweet temperament and trust of people (Lovecky, 1994).

Successful educational interventions for gifted students with AD/HD address both conditions on an individualized basis (Wolfle & French, 1990; Hartley, 1993; Lind & Silverman, 1994; Reid & McGuire, 1995; Ramirez-Smith, 1997). Suggestions for changing disruptive classroom behaviors include use of behavior management techniques, social modeling and self-monitoring techniques, and providing a structured environment. The curriculum must be differentiated to challenge and stimulate. Instructional strategies modified to accommodate gifted students with AD/HD are detailed in Kaufmann & Castellanos, Chapter 6, Part V, of this Handbook.

A controversial recommendation for treatment of AD/HD concerns the prescription of stimulant drugs such as Ritalin, which, in children, can produce a calming effect and a focusing of attention. Between 70% and 80% of children with AD/HD respond positively to Ritalin (Pancheri & Prater, 1999). But it also has numerous possible side effect such as loss of appetite, insomnia, tics, headaches, and stomachaches (Pancheri & Prater, 1999). Medication should be used as a last resort, only after behavior management and instructional interventions have proved ineffective (Howell, Evans & Gardiner, 1997).

Gifted Students with Hearing Impairment

The historical pattern for educating students with hearing impairment has involved placement in special programs based on disability rather than giftedness. In segregated settings such as schools for the deaf or special classes for hearing impairment, emphasis has been placed on development of language and speech, and opportunities for exploring areas of creative and intellectual potential have been minimal. Students with hearing impairment have been less likely to be identified as gifted than their hearing counterparts (Yewchuk & Bibby, 1989a, b; Vialle & Paterson, 1996). Nevertheless, many in the deaf community and some professionals working with deaf students believe that deafness has its own culture and language that can only be taught effectively in segregated classes and schools for the deaf (Commission on the Education of the Deaf, 1988; Fuchs & Fuchs, 1994).

The basic referral, assessment, and selection procedures used with gifted children, may be applied to hearing-impaired populations (Whitmore & Maker, 1985), in segregated or inclusive settings, with appropriate concessions to handicapping effects of hearing impairment (Pendarvis & Grossi, 1980), and the pervasive influence of deafness as a cultural difference (Vialle & Paterson, 1996). Verbal test scores should be given less prominence than non-verbal and performance scores (Rittenhouse & Blough, 1995). Intelligence tests should be individually administered and non-verbal in nature (Sattler, 1992). Functioning at or somewhat above grade level on standardized achievement tests may be indicative of giftedness (Yewchuk, Bibby & Fraser, 1989). Referrals by both teachers and parents should be part of the identification process (Yewchuk & Bibby, 1989a).

Suggestions for designing and implementing programming to meet the learning needs of gifted students with hearing impairment include the following (Maker, 1981; Pollard & Howze, 1981; MacDonald & Yewchuk, 1994; Rittenhouse & Blough, 1995):

- Programs should be flexible in both design and use to allow latitude in investigation of complex issues.
- Programs should emphasize the use of advanced reasoning and analytical skills over memorization.
- Programs should be individualized to match student interests, learning styles, and exceptional skills.

- Programs should include thematic units with alternatives for stretching and extending exceptional gifts and talents of students.
- Programming should include special education services for areas in need of remediation.

A school-based model consistent with these general guidelines was developed at the Texas School for the Deaf (Pollard & Howze, 1981). At the elementary level, two gifted resource teachers worked with the regular classroom teacher to enrich the curriculum. In the middle school, the gifted students were placed together for instruction in core subjects but integrated with other students for elective classes. Teachers of the core subjects were provided with inservice regarding gifted education, and had access to the services of a gifted education specialist. In high school, gifted students attended regular classes, as well as a special class for gifted students where they worked individually with a gifted education specialist.

Gifted Students with Visual Impairments

Like students with hearing impairments, students with visual impairments have been educated historically in residential schools with other similarly affected students. Accompanying the trend towards placement of students into regular classrooms is an increasing awareness of the unique needs of those students who also have special gifts and talents (Ferrell, 1994).

Gifted students with visual impairment meet the criteria of giftedness and visual impairment. Visual impairment includes low vision (ability to read large print, with or without magnification), functional blindness (sufficient vision to move through environment, but braille required for reading and writing), and total blindness (Turnbull et al., 1999). Approximately one of every thousand children of school age have visual impairment, and of these 2 to 3% are gifted (Ferrell, 1994).

Giftedness is not as readily apparent in students with visual impairment as in the normal population because of the barriers to assessing true potential (Corn, 1986, 1992; Hackney, 1986). A teacher of students with visual impairment makes referrals for in-depth intellectual assessment upon evidence of only three of the characteristics usually associated with giftedness (Johnson, 1987).

Special problems arise when a student with visual impairment is placed with sighted students. Paskewicz (1986) found the major stumbling block to be the lack of adequate brailled materials and the waiting time for brailling of additional materials, which severely limits the depth and spontaneity of exploration of subject matter. Instruction in braille usage, orientation and mobility, socialization skills, and independent living must continue as part of the individual program plan

(Corn, 1986, 1992; Hackney, 1986). Successful placement in inclusive classrooms involves collaboration between regular classroom teachers, special educators, specialists in visual impairment, professional support personnel, parents, and the students themselves (Ingraham, Daugherty & Gorrafa, 1995; Lichtenstein, 1997).

Gifted Students with Intellectual Disabilities

This must be the most paradoxical of all dually labeled children. How can an individual be unable to manage independent living, while simultaneously being capable of remarkable mental feats in other areas of endeavour? Such is the puzzle of the individuals referred to as 'savants'. Savants constitute an estimated 0.06% of all institutionalized retarded individuals (Hill, 1977) and 9.8% of institutionalized patients with early infantile autism (Rimland, 1978). Their areas of brilliance are judged not against others with similar disability, but against those of the normal population. Some savants, such as Yoshihiko Yamamoto, the "Van Gogh of Japan," have become famous for their creative productions (Morishima, 1974).

The extraordinary abilities of idiots savants are manifested in a number of discrete ways categorized by Hill (1974) and Rimland (1978). Best known categories include calendar calculating, artistic ability, musical ability, memorization of obscure facts, mathematical abilities, mechanical ability, and pseudo-verbal ability. Savants may excel in more than one area.

In most documented cases, the specialized skills of savants have developed in unsupportive environments without specific training (Yewchuk, 1999). In some instances, systematic interventions combining opportunities for developing specific areas of talent with counseling and individualized programming to develop social and life skills have produced dramatic results (Donnelly & Altman, 1994). Morishima & Brown (1977) document how, under the tutelage of special education teachers, a student with severe mental retardation developed sufficient observational, graphic, and artistic skills to become a renowned Japanese illustrator of insects. Individualized programs that address areas of deficit and islands of excellence hold promise for meeting the exceptional educational needs of savants. Their special talents can be fostered and developed within inclusive classrooms that emphasize continuous progress and development of all students, irrespective of general intellectual ability.

Conclusion

Important changes have been taking place over the past decade in regular education, gifted education, and special education that will eventually have a significant positive effect on the education and full development of the learning potential of gifted students with disabilities. The adoption of a simultaneous commitment toward excellence and equity in our schools holds promise for all participants within the learning community. Inclusive education offers the context for this to happen in general classrooms throughout the world, and eventually should figure strongly in helping to eliminate many of the limitations and barriers created out of separate, dual systems of regular and general education.

General guidelines for successful inclusion of gifted students with disabilities into regular classrooms, drawn from Cline and Schwartz (1999), Federico, Herrold & Venn (1999), and Turnbull, et al. (1999) include the following:

- The entire school, from the principal to the school custodian, needs to be committed to inclusive education. Teachers cannot do it alone.
- Collaboration among everyone involved in the educational process (students, families, teachers, paraprofessionals, special service providers, school staff, administrators, agencies, community members) is vital.
- Psychological and counselling services to students with and without disabilities, their parents, and teachers is important in establishing comfort and commitment to the inclusive education process.
- Staff development and training, material resources, physical resources, and human resources to support disabling conditions should be readily available.
- The appropriateness of inclusion for gifted students with disability must be decided on a case-by-case basis. Some children might be better served in segregated settings.

Even though much of our current knowledge base and classroom practice in educating gifted students with disabilities is still best depicted as a 'desultory duality', the future is decidedly brighter with a growing confluence of interests, practices, and visions in the education of all students from regular and special education. Though the review of the literature reveals apprehension about inclusive education among some parents and professionals working with children with special needs, and a somewhat disconnected and unmethodical knowledge base, progress in understanding the challenges and benefits associated with the blending of programs and services to best meet the unique needs of those identified is becoming more apparent. Certainly there have been impressive gains in both research and educational practice; unfortunately there are still only small pockets of this exemplary work being carried out.

The ultimate merging of general and special education into a unified educational system will hopefully generate schools that can provide an appropriate education for all students, including gifted students with disabilities. Indeed, successful efforts in this area might contribute significantly to the general reform, if not transformation of education in the future.

References

Andrews, J. & Lupart, J. (1999). *The inclusive classroom: educating exceptional children* (2nd ed.). Scarborough, ON: Nelson.

Baum, S. (1984). Meeting the needs of learning disabled gifted students. *Roeper Review, 7* (1), 16–19.

Baum, S. (1988). An enrichment program for gifted learning disabled students. *Gifted Child Quarterly, 32*(1), 226–230.

Baum, S. (1994). Meeting the needs of gifted/learning disabled students. *The Journal of Secondary Gifted Education, 5* (3), 6–16.

Baum, S., Emerick, L. J., Herman, G. N. & Nixon, J. (1989). Identification, programs and enrichment strategies for gifted learning disabled youth. *Roeper Review, 12* (1), 48–53.

Baum, S. & Kirschenbaum, R. (1984). Recognizing special talents in learning disabled students. *Teaching Exceptional Children, Winter*, 92–98.

Baum, S. & Owen, S. V. (1988). High ability/learning disabled students: how are they different? *Gifted Child Quarterly, 32*(3), 321–326.

Bireley, M. (1991). The paradoxical needs of the disabled gifted. In M. Bireley & J. Genshaft (Eds.), *Understanding the Gifted Adolescent* (pp. 163–175). New York: Teachers College Press.

Boodoo, G. M., Bradley, C. L., Frontera, R. L., Pitts, R. & Wright, L. B. (1989). A survey of procedures used for identifying gifted learning disabled children. *Gifted Child Quarterly, 33*(3), 110–114.

Booth, T. & Ainscow, M. (Eds.). (1998). *From them to us: an international study of inclusive education*. London: Routledge.

Brody, L. & Mills, C. (1997). Gifted children with learning disabilities: a review of the issues. *Journal of Learning Disabilities, 30* (3), 282–296.

Bunch, G., Lupart, J. & Brown, M. (1997). *Resistance and acceptance: Educator attitudes to inclusion of students with disabilities*. Research report submitted to the Social Science and Humanities Research Council of Canada, Ottawa, ON.

Clements, C., Lundell, F. & Hishinuma, E. (1994). Serving the gifted dyslexic and gifted at risk. *Gifted Child Today, 17* (4), 12–14, 16–17, 36–37.

Cline, S. & Schwartz, D. (1999). *Diverse populations of gifted children*. Upper Saddle River, NJ: Prentice Hall.

Commission on the Education of the Deaf (1988). *Toward equality: education of the deaf*. Washington, DC: U.S. Government Printing Office. (ERIC Document Reproduction Service No. ED 303 932).

Corn, A. (1986). Gifted students who have a visual handicap: can we meet their educational needs? *Education of the Visually Handicapped, 18* (2), 71–84.

Corn, A. (1992). Education of children with visual handicaps who are also gifted. *Division for the Visually Handicapped, Council for Exceptional Children, Quarterly, 38* (1), 19–22.

Davis, G. A. & Rimm, S. B. (1998). *Education of the gifted and talented*. (4th ed.). Boston: Allyn and Bacon.

Delisle, J. (1995). ADD gifted: how many labels can one child take? *Gifted Child Today Magazine, 18* (2), 42–43.

Dix, J. & Schafer, S. (1996). From paradox to performance: practical strategies for identifying and teaching GT/LD students. *Gifted Child Today, 19* (1), 22–25, 28–31.

Donnelly, J. A. & Altman, R. (1994). The autistic savant: recognizing and serving the gifted student with autism. *Roeper Review, 16* (4), 252–256.

Eisenberg, D. & Epstein, E. (1981). *The discovery and development of giftedness in handicapped children*. Paper presented at the CEC-TAG National Topics Conference on the Gifted and Talented Child, Orlando, FL.

Federico, M. A., Herrold, W. G. & Venn, J. (1999). Helpful tips for successful inclusion. *Teaching Exceptional Children, 32* (1), 76–82.

Ferrell, K. (1994, April). *Twice exceptional: gifted and visually impaired*. Paper presented at the TAG Symposium of the Annual Meeting of the Council of Exceptional Children, Denver.

Ford, B. G. & Ford, R. D. (1981). Identifying creative potential in handicapped children. *Exceptional Children, 48* (2), 115–122.

Fox, L. H. (1983). Gifted students with reading problems: an empirical study. In: L. Fox, L. Brody & D. Tobin (Eds.), *Learning-Disabled/Gifted Children: Identification and Programming* (pp. 117–140). Baltimore, MD: University Park Press.

Friedrichs, T. P. (1990). Gifted handicapped students: the way forward. Richmond, Virginia: State Department of Education (ERIC Document ED 332 460).

Friend, M., Bursuck, W. & Hutchinson, N. (1998). *Including exceptional students: a practical guide for classroom teachers*. (Canadian ed.). Scarborough, ON: Allyn and Bacon Canada.

Fuchs, D. & Fuchs, L. S. (1994). Inclusive schools movement and the radicalization of special education reform. *Exceptional Children 60* (4), 294–309.

Fullan, M. (1991). *The new meaning of educational change*. New York: Teachers College Press.

Gallagher, J. J. (1988). National agenda for educating gifted students: Statement of priorities. *Exceptional Children, 55* (2), 107–114.

Gamble, H. W. (1985). A national survey of programs for intellectually and academically gifted hearing-impaired students. *American Annals of the Deaf, December*, 508–518.

Gerken, K. C. (1979). An unseen minority: handicapped individuals who are gifted and talented. In: N. Colangelo & R. T. Zaffrann (Eds.), *New Voices in Counseling the Gifted* (pp. 321–325). Dubuque, IA: Kendall/Hunt.

Goertzel, V. & Goertzel, M. G. (1962). *Cradles of eminence*. Boston, MA: Little, Brown.

Goodlad, J. I. & Lovitt, T. C. (Eds.). (1993). *Integrating general and special education*. New York: Merrill.

Grimm, J. (1998). The participation of gifted students with disabilities in gifted programs. *Roeper Review, 20* (4), 285–286.

Gunderson, C. W., Maesch, C. & Rees, J. W. (1987). The gifted/learning disabled student. *Gifted Child Quarterly, 31* (4), 158–160.

Hackney, P. W. (1986). Education of the visually handicapped gifted: a program description. *Education of the Visually Handicapped, 18* (2), 85–95.

Hartley, D. (1993). John Adam Hartley: an ADD story. *Gifted Child Today, 16* (2), 34–37.

Heller, K. A., Monks, F. & Passow, A. H. (Eds.) (1993). *International handbook of research and development of giftedness and talent*. Oxford: Pergamon.

Higgins, S. (1981). Reaching for that golden ring: some thoughts on educating gifted/talented handicapped students. *American Annals of the Deaf, September*, 572–577.

Hill, A. L. (1974). Idiot savants: a categorization of abilities. *Mental Retardation*, **12** (6), 12–13.

Hill, A. L. (1977). Idiot-savants: rate of incidence. *Perceptual and Motor Skills*, **44**, 161–162.

Hishinuma, E. S. (1991). Assets school: serving the needs of the gifted/learning disabled. *Gifted Child Today, Sept/Oct*, 36–38.

Hishinuma, E. S. (1993). Counseling gifted/at risk and gifted/dyslexic youngsters. *Gifted Child Today*, **16** (1), 30–33.

Hiskey, M. S. (1966). *Hiskey-Nebraska test of learning aptitude*. Lincoln, NA: Union College Press.

Howell, K., Evans, D. & Gardiner, J. (1997). Medications in the classroom: A hard pill to swallow? *Teaching Exceptional Children*, **29** (6), 58–61.

Idol, L. (1996). Collaborative consultation and collaboration in schools. In: J. Lupart, A. McKeough & C. Yewchuk (Eds.), *Schools in Transition: Rethinking Regular and Special Education* (pp. 220–241). Scarborough, ON: Nelson.

Individuals with Disabilities Education Act, 20. Washington: U.S. Congress. 1400 *et seq.* (1997).

Ingraham, C., Daugherty, K. & Gorrafa, S. (1995). The success of three gifted deaf-blind students in inclusive educational programs. *Journal of Visual Impairment & Blindness*, **89** (3), 257–261.

Johnsen, S. K. & Corn, A. L. (1989). The past, present, and future of education for gifted children with sensory and/or physical disabilities. *Roeper Review*, **12** (1), 13–28.

Johnson, L. (1987). Teaching the visually impaired gifted youngster. *Journal of Visual Impairment and Blindness*, **81** (2), 51–52.

Johnson, L., Karnes, M. & Carr, V. (1997). Providing services to children with gifts and disabilities: a critical need. In: N. Colangelo & G. Davis (Eds.), *Handbook of Gifted Education* (2nd ed.). (pp. 516–527). Boston: Allyn & Bacon.

Kaplan, S. N. (1986). The grid: a model to construct differentiated curriculum for the gifted. In: J. S. Renzulli (Ed.), *Systems and Models for Developing Programs for the Gifted and Talented* (pp. 180–193). Mansfield Center, CT: Creative Learning Press.

Karnes, M. B. & Johnson, L. J. (1986). Identification and assessment of gifted/talented handicapped and non-handicapped children in early childhood. *Journal of Children in Contemporary Society*, **18** (3–4), 35–54.

Karnes, M. B. & Johnson, L. J. (1991). Gifted handicapped. In: N. Colangelo & G. A. Davis (Eds.), *Handbook of Gifted Education* (pp. 428–437). Boston: Allyn & Bacon.

Karnes, M. B., Schwedel, A. M. & Linnemeyer, S. A. (1982). The young gifted/talented child: programs at the University of Illinois. *The Elementary School Journal*, **82** (3), 195–213.

Kaufmann, F. M. & Castellanos, F. X. (2000). Attention-deficit/hyperactivity disorder in gifted students. In: K. A. Heller, F. J. Mönks & R. J. Sternberg. *International Handbook of Giftedness and Talent* (2nd ed.). (pp. 615–626) Elsevier Science.

LaFrance, E. B. (1995). Creative thinking differences in three groups of exceptional children as expressed through completion of figural forms. *Roeper Review*, **17** (4), 248–252.

Learning Disabilities Association of Canada. (1993). *Making the most of the law: education and the child with learning disabilities*. Ottawa: LDAC.

Lichtenstein, J. (1997). The essence of empowerment: Richard's story. *Teaching exceptional children*, **30** (2), 16–19.

Lind, S. & Silverman, L. K. (1994). ADHD or gifted? *Understanding Our Gifted*, **6** (5), 13–16,

Lovecky, D. (1994). Gifted children with attention deficit disorder. *Understanding Our Gifted*, **6** (5), 1, 7–10.

Lupart, J. L. (1990). An in-depth assessment model for gifted/learning disabled students. *Canadian Journal of Special Education*, **6** (1), 1–14.

Lupart, J. L. (1992). The hidden gifted: Current state of knowledge and future research directions. In: F. J. Monks & W. A. M. Peters (Eds.), *Talent for the Future: Social and Personality Development of Gifted Children*. (pp. 177–190). Netherlands: Van Gorcum.

Lupart, J. L. (1998). Setting right the delusion of inclusion: implications for Canadian schools. *Canadian Journal of Education*, **23** (3), 251–264.

Lupart, J. L., McKeough, A. & Yewchuk, C. (Eds.) (1996). *Schools in transition: rethinking regular and special education*. Scarborough, ON: Nelson.

Lupart, J. L. & Webber, C. (1996). Schools in transition: issues and prospects. In: J. Lupart, A. McKeough & C. Yewchuk (Eds.), *Schools in Transition: Rethinking Regular and Special Education* (pp. 3–39). Scarborough, ON: Nelson.

MacDonald, P. & Yewchuk, C. (1994). Differentiating curriculum for gifted and talented deaf students in whole language classrooms. *The Association of Canadian Educators of the Hearing Impaired Journal*, **20** (3), 96–106.

Maker, C. J. (1976). Searching for giftedness and talent in children with handicaps. *The School Psychology Digest*, **5**, 24–36.

Maker, C. J. (1977). *Providing programs for the gifted handicapped*. Reston, VA: CEC.

Maker, C. J. (1981). The gifted hearing-impaired student. *American Annals of the Deaf*, **126** (6), 631–645.

Maker, C. J. & Grossi, J. (1985). *The gifted and talented handicapped*. (ERIC Document ED 262 522).

Marland, S. P. (1972). *Education of the gifted and talented*. Report to the Congress of the United States by the U.S. Commissioner of Education. Washington, DC: Government Printing Office.

Mauser, A. (1980). Learning disability in children. *Association for Children with Learning Disabilities Newsbriefs*, **130** (2).

McGuire, K. & Yewchuk, C. (1995). Gifted learning disabled students' knowledge of metacognitive reading strategies. In M. Katzko & F. Monks (Eds.), *Nurturing Talent: Individual Needs and Social Ability* (pp. 239–251). The Netherlands: Van Gorcum, Assen.

McGuire, K. & Yewchuk, C. (1996). Use of metacognitive reading strategies by gifted learning disabled students: an exploratory study. *Journal for the Education of the Gifted*, **19** (3), 293–314.

Meisgeier, C., Meisgeier, C. & Werblo, D. (1978). Factors compounding the handicapping of some gifted children. *Gifted Child Quarterly*, **22** (3), 325–331.

Mendaglio, S. (1993). Counseling gifted learning disabled: individual and group counseling techniques. In: L. K.

Silverman (Ed.), *Counseling the Gifted and Talented* (pp. 131–149). Denver: Love.

Minner, S. (1990). Teacher evaluations of case descriptions of LD gifted children. *Gifted Child Quarterly*, **34** (1), 37–39.

Minner, S., Prater, G., Bloodworth, H. & Walker, S. (1987). Referral and placement recommendations of teachers toward gifted handicapped children. *Roeper Review*, **9** (4), 247–249.

Morishima, A. (1974). Another Van Gogh of Japan: the superior artwork of a retarded boy. *Exceptional Children*, **41**, 92–96.

Morishima, A. & Brown, L. F. (1977). A case report on the artistic talent of an autistic idiot savant. *Mental Retardation, April*, 33–36.

National Association for Gifted Children. (1992). Policy statement on ability grouping. *Gifted Child Quarterly*, **36** (2), back page.

Nielsen, M. E. & Mortorff-Albert, S. (1989). The effects of special education service on the self-concept and school attitude of learning disabled/gifted students. *Roeper Review*, **12** (1), 29–36.

Olenchak, F. R. (1994). Talent development. *The Journal of Secondary Gifted Education*, **5** (3), 40–52.

Olenchak, F. R. (1995). Effects of enrichment on gifted/learning-disabled students. *Journal for the Education of the Gifted*, **18** (4), 385–399.

Pancheri, C. & Prater, M. (1999). What teachers and parents should know about Ritalin. *Teaching Exceptional Children*, **31** (4), 20–26.

Paskewicz, M. (1986). Mainstreaming the gifted visually handicapped child. *Journal of Visual Impairment and Blindness*, **80** (9), 937–938.

Pendarvis, E. D. & Grossi, J. A. (1980). Designing and operating programs for the gifted and talented handicapped. In: J. B. Jordan & J. A. Grossi (Eds.), *An Administrator's Handbook on Designing Programs for the Gifted and Talented* (pp. 66–88). Reston, VA: Council for Exceptional Children.

Pledgie, T. K. (1982). Giftedness among handicapped children: identification and programming development. *Journal of Special Education*, **16** (2), 221–227.

Pollard, G. & Howze, J. (1981). School-wide talented and gifted program for the deaf. *American Annals of the Deaf, September*, 600–606.

Porter, R. M. (1982). The gifted handicapped: a status report. *Roeper Review*, **4** (3), 24–25.

Ramirez-Smith, C. (1997). Mistaken identity: gifted and ADHD. (ERIC Document Reproduction Service No. ED 413 690).

Reid, B. & McGuire, M. (1995). *Square pegs in round holes—these kids don't fit: High ability students with behavioral problem*. Storrs, CT: National Research Center on the Gifted and Talented.

Reis, S., Neu, T. & McGuire, J. (1997). Case studies of high-ability students with learning disabilities who have achieved. *Exceptional Children*, **63** (4), 463–479.

Renzulli, J. S. (1977). *The enrichment triad model: a guide for developing defensible programs for the gifted and talented*. Mansfield Centre, CT: Creative Learning Press.

Richert, E. S. (1997). Excellence with equity in identification and programming. In: N. Colangelo & G. Davis (Eds.), *Handbook of Gifted Education* (2nd ed.). (pp. 75–88). Boston: Allyn & Bacon.

Rimland, B. (1978). Inside the mind of the autistic savant. *Psychology Today*, **12** (3), 69–80.

Rittenhouse, R. & Blough, L. (1995). Gifted students with hearing impairments: suggestions for teachers. *Teaching Exceptional Children*, **27** (4), 51–53.

Robertson, J. (1985). Gifted adults incurring severe disabilities. In: J. R. Whitmore & C. J. Maker (Eds.), *Intellectual Giftedness in Disabled Persons* (pp. 135–169). Rockville, MD: Aspen.

Rosner, S. L. & Seymour, J. (1983). The gifted child with a learning disability: clinical evidence. In: L. H. Fox, L. Brody & D. Tobin (Eds.), *Learning-Disabled/Gifted Children* (pp. 77–97). Baltimore, MD: University Park Press.

Sah, A. & Borland, J. H. (1989). The effects of a structured home plan on the home and school behaviors of gifted learning-disabled students with deficits in organizational skills. *Roeper Review*, **12** (1), 54–57.

Sattler, J. M. (1992). *Assessment of children*. (Rev. and updated 3rd ed.). San Diego: J. M. Sattler Publisher.

Schiff, M., Kaufman, A. & Kaufman, N. (1981). Scatter analysis of WISC-R profiles for learning disabled children with superior intelligence. *Journal of Learning Disabilities*, **14**, 400–404.

Schnur, J. O. & Stefanich, G. P. (1979). Science for the handicapped gifted child. *Roeper Review*, **2** (2), 26–28.

Silverman, L. K. (1998). Through the lens of giftedness. *Roeper Review*, **20** (3), 204–210.

Skrtic, T. (1995). The organizational context of special education and school reform. In: E. L. Meyen & T. M. Skrtic (Eds.), *Special Education and Student Disability* (pp. 731–791). Denver, CO: Love.

Skrtic, T. (1996). School organization, inclusive education, and democracy. In: J. Lupart, A. McKeough & C. Yewchuk (Eds.), *Schools in Transition: Rethinking Regular and Special Education* (pp. 81–118). Scarborough, ON: Nelson.

Stefanich, F. & Schnur, J. O. (1979). Identifying the handicapped gifted. *Science and Children, November/December*, 18–19.

Tallent-Runnels, M. & Sigler, E. (1995). The status of the selection of gifted students with learning disabilities for gifted programs. *Roeper Review*, **17** (4), 246–248.

Thompson, L. J. (1971). Language disabilities in men of eminence. *Journal of Learning Disabilities*, **4** (1), 34–45.

Turnbull, A., Turnbull, R., Shank, M. & Leal, D. (1999). *Exceptional lives: special education in today's schools* (2nd ed.). Upper Saddle River, NJ: Merrill.

U.S. Congress (1978). *Gifted and talented children's act of 1978* (P. L. 95–561). Washington, DC: Government Printing Office.

U.S. Congress (1988). *Jacob K. Javits gifted and talented students education act of 1988* (Title IV-H. R. 5). Washington, DC: Government Printing Office.

Udall, A. (1985). Chapter reaction (to Intellectually gifted persons with specific LD). In: J. R. Whitmore & C. J. Maker (Eds.), *Intellectual Giftedness in Disabled Persons* (pp. 207–209). Rockville, MD: Aspen.

Udall, A. & Maker, C. (1983). A pilot program for elementary-age learning disabled/gifted children. In: L. H. Fox, L. Brody & L. Tobin (Eds.). *Learning-Disabled/Gifted Children* (pp. 223–242). Baltimore, MD: University Park Press.

Vespi, L. & Yewchuk, C. (1992). A phenomenological study of the social/emotional characteristics of gifted learning disabled children. *Journal for the Education of the Gifted,* **16** (1), 55–72.

Vialle, W. & Paterson, J. (1996). *Constructing a culturally sensitive education for gifted deaf students.* (ERIC Document Reproduction Service No. ED 419 336).

Waldron, K. A., Saphire, D. G. & Rosenbaum, S. A. (1987). Learning disabilities and giftedness: identification based on self-concept, behavior, and academic patterns. *Journal of Learning Disabilities,* **20** (7), 422–427.

Warren, D. (1984). *Blindness and early child development.* New York: American Foundation for the Blind.

Webb, J. & Latimer, D. (1993). ADHD and the children who are gifted. *Exceptional Children,* **60** (2), 183–184.

Weill, M. P. (1987). Gifted/learning disabled students. *The Clearing House,* **60**, 341–343.

Whitmore, J. R. (1981). Gifted children with handicapping conditions: a new frontier. *Exceptional Children,* **48** (2), 106–113.

Whitmore, J. R. (1986). Conceptualizing the issue of underserved populations of gifted students. *Journal for the Education of the Gifted,* **10** (3), 141–153.

Whitmore, J. R. (1989). Four leading advocates for gifted students with disabilities. *Roeper Review,* **12** (1), 5–13.

Whitmore, J. R. & Maker, C. J. (1985). *Intellectual giftedness in disabled persons.* Rockville, MD: Aspen.

Wingenbach, N. (1985). Chapter reaction (to Intellectually gifted persons with specific LD). In: J. R. Whitmore & C. J. Maker (Eds.), *Intellectual Giftedness in Disabled Persons* (pp. 210–211). Rockville, MD: Aspen.

Wolfle, J. & French, M. (1990, October). *Surviving gifted attention deficit disorder children in the classroom.* Paper presented at the annual conference of the National Association for Gifted Children. Little Rock. (ERIC Document Reproduction Service No. ED 374 630).

Wong, B. (1996) The TEAM model: a potential model for merging special education with regular (general) education. In: J. Lupart, A. McKeough & C. Yewchuk (Eds.), *Schools in Transition: Rethinking Regular and Special Education* (pp. 194–219). Scarborough, ON: Nelson.

Yewchuk, C. R. (1986). Gifted/learning disabled children: problems of assessment. In: A. J. Cropley, K. K. Urban, J. Wagner & W. Wieczerkowski (Eds.), *Giftedness : A Continuing Worldwide Challenge* (pp. 40–48). New York: Trillium Press.

Yewchuk, C. (1992). Educational strategies for gifted learning disabled children. In: F. Monks & W. Peters (Eds.), *Talent for the Future: Social and Personality Development of Gifted Children* (pp. 285–295). Assen/Maastricht, Netherlands: Van Gorcum.

Yewchuk, C. (1996). Gifted education and school reform. In: J. Lupart, A. McKeough & C. Yewchuk (Eds.), *Schools in Transition: Rethinking Regular and Special Education* (pp. 164–193). Scarborough, ON: Nelson.

Yewchuk, C. (1999). Savant syndrome: intuitive excellence amidst general deficit. *Developmental Disabilities Bulletin,* **27** (1), 58–76.

Yewchuk, C. R. & Bibby, M. A. (1989a). Identification of giftedness in severely and profoundly hearing impaired students. *Roeper Review,* **12** (1), 42–48.

Yewchuk, C. R. & Bibby, M. A. (1989b). The handicapped gifted child: problems of identification and programming. *Canadian Journal of Education,* **14** (1), 102–108.

Yewchuk, C., Bibby, M. A. & Fraser, B. (1989). Identifying giftedness in the hearing impaired: the effectiveness of four nomination forms. *Gifted Education International,* **6** (2), 87–97.

Yewchuk, C. & Jobagy, S. (1992). Gifted adolescents: At risk for suicide. *European Journal for High Ability,* **2** (1), 73–85.

Yewchuk, C. & Lupart, J. (1993). Gifted handicapped: a desultory duality. In: K. A. Heller, F. Monks & A. H. Passow (Eds.), *International Handbook of Research and Development of Giftedness and Talent* (pp. 709–725). Oxford: Pergamon.

Part VI

Examples of Country Efforts, Policies, Programs and Issues

National/Provincial Gifted Education Policies: Present State, Future Possibilities

Rose A. Rudnitski

State University of New York at New Paltz, USA

Introduction

This is a sequel to the chapter on policy in the first edition of the *Handbook of Research on Giftedness and Talent*, 'National/State Policies Regarding the Education of the Gifted', written by A. Harry Passow, to whose memory this study is dedicated. That chapter focused on the policies of developed countries primarily situated in the Northern Hemisphere. Though this focus made sense because the policies and public educational systems of these countries are mature, this update takes a different perspective by presenting a critical analysis of gifted educational policy, comparing the gifted education policies of nations at different stages of development, delineating issues involved in designing national policies, and making recommendations. My intention is to be more inclusive and to highlight and critique the dominance of the conceptions and models used in developed countries as well as to raise questions about the assumptions upon which gifted educational policies are founded and their appropriateness, in their current construct, for all countries.

Educational Policy

All educational policy decisions are political acts. They are made primarily to resolve tensions created by competing interests in any society. These tensions generally emanate from the desire for a high standard of living, making education a potentially high-stakes policy area, for we know that educational attainment correlates highly with development and material success (OECD, 1997). Restricting access to high levels of educational attainment has the effect of restricting access to economic success, and there are some groups in every society who believe that policies should reinforce these restrictions as they maintain the social order.

Other points of view on education that may create tensions that policies must attempt to resolve are the view of some that education is a human right, while others view it primarily as an investment in economic development. There is friction between the view of education as having a general/academic purpose and those who view it as training in specific areas and skills. How important are the arts to a society? Are they important enough to merit the allocation of significant resources for the development of talented individuals, resources significant enough to limit those allocated for academics? These are the conflicts that are created when society tries to define what a general education entails.

There are major tensions created between the view that public education should support basic literacy and numeracy for all citizens and restrict access to post-basic education and training only to those who manifest potential spontaneously at the appropriate stage in life, and the view that advanced education for many enhances economic and social development for all (Hallak, 1990). No educational policy totally resolves these tensions. Some argue that gifted education policies sometimes exacerbate conflict and competition, not only within the borders of one nation, but also between nations. This is done through the basic assumptions on which gifted education policies are based, its 'fundamental canons', and on the assumptions inherent in defining giftedness as it is expressed in virtually every governmental policy that mentions it.

Passow (1993) defined policy as a plan that provides guidelines for action. He states, "A fundamental canon of a policy in support of gifted education is that there are children who, because they have manifested potential for outstanding achievement in a socially valuable area, require differentiated educational experiences adequate and appropriate to their special needs" (p. 29). The basic principle behind this canon is a sound one because gifted children do require educational experiences appropriate to their special needs, but the same argument can be made for all children. The fundamental canon of gifted education that makes so much sense when one is considering only the needs of the gifted, loses its cogency when the needs of all children are taken into consideration. Educational policy makers must consider the needs of all children, and resource allocations in education are inadequate to ensure an adequate education for every child. Unless an educational policy ensures that the special educational needs of every child can be met through some sort of personalization or individualization, then a policy that ensures that for only some children appears to be exclusionary to all the others. This is a common problem in many countries that have gifted educational policies (Passow, 1993).

Another problem with the logic of the fundamental canon is that many of the other children vying for the same resources, given the adequate or enriched educational experiences that those resources can provide, might manifest the potential for outstanding achievement. The goal of a gifted education policy could be broadened to expand exponentially as the policy succeeds in nurturing heretofore hidden gifts in some children. Most current policies aim to nourish the development only of those who manifest their gifts spontaneously with little nurturance and support. Can educational policy dare to expand the possibility for the development of talent in broader segments of the population? The purpose of the policy for the education of gifted students is a key factor in determining its effect on the students and on the society. Is success for gifted students enough in our global society?

Conceptions of what is gifted are also problematic. Gifted education was born on the cusp of the nineteenth and twentieth centuries, when the mental measurement movement dominated the conceptual and research paradigms in education and the social and behavioral sciences (Tannenbaum, 1983). Policy for gifted and talented students did not begin to develop to any extent until after the Marland Report (1971) was released in the United States and that country enacted legislation to encourage the development of state policies for the education of the gifted (Passow & Rudnitski, 1993). Some countries in Western Europe quickly followed suit (Passow, 1993). Now, on the cusp of the twenty-first century, conceptions of giftedness have broadened and are no longer very easily measured as the IQ was when the field was in its youth. This complicates the policy development process and the nature of policy at its core. What is socially valuable, the aspect that determines the meaning of giftedness, at one time in a society may not, in another age or under another political system, be as highly valued. What is socially valued varies from culture to culture, so even if it were possible to have homogeneous societies, the definitions of giftedness would have to be fluid to change over time. Who determines what is valued in a multicultural society? Should this determination always be made by a dominant culture in a Darwinian context of competition and domination and survival of the mightiest? Should the intent of gifted education

policy in an increasingly interconnected global culture be to mitigate the vicissitudes of the constant struggle for dominance by fostering cooperation and compromise through the integration of many conceptions of what might be socially valuable in determining definitions of giftedness? Perhaps it is time to take a critical view of our current national and state policies in the light of the needs of our fast-changing global society, keeping what is appropriate and changing for the future.

Research Method

This study builds on the chapter in the first edition of this work (Passow, 1993), and on the author and her colleague's previous policy analyses (Passow & Rudnitski, 1993, 1994). It is based on an extensive review of the literature on educational policy, specifically targeting policies on the gifted, and on a survey of the gifted policies of several countries, developed and developing, Western and Non-Western, Northern and Southern. In the fall of 1998, faxes were sent to the ministries of education of 40 nations. Fifteen ministries responded to the initial inquiry by sending either letters explaining their policies or lack of them, or by sending the policy, itself. Additional policy information was gathered through Internet databases such as *Eurydice*. Though extensive data were gathered from this survey, general themes and trends will be summarized for this chapter, which focuses not so much on what each country does, but on the fact that the notions of what services are needed for gifted children and how they should be educated have not changed much in the latter part of the twentieth century. Recommendations for changes and the development of policies that are more likely to be congruent with the needs of a global society are presented at the end of the chapter.

Findings/Trends

Though most countries reported having no policy to specifically deal with gifted or highly able students, the countries that did (N = 8) had several things in common.

- Their policies, even when they stated that they wanted to avoid fixed definitions of giftedness and talent, defined the gifted population in terms of intelligence and/or performance in formalized school settings. Performance almost invariably was assumed to be performance on tests, national, regional, or school-based. When appropriate to the discipline (e.g. art or music) performance was more traditionally defined as performance within the specific discipline.

- The services and accommodations for the gifted were ones that are normally provided locally, such as acceleration to tertiary education, summer programs, academic competitions and Olympiads, special classes within schools, and special schools. The most predominant services such as acceleration and pull out enrichment have been characterized as more popular with educators because they are low cost and less threatening than separate services, which are expensive and construed as taking away resources from other children (Freeman, 1992).

- The policies of European countries and their former colonies had striking similarities because the educational systems of the former colonies were still based on the colonizing country's model. These first three bullets were characteristics of the Traditional model, which reflects the traditions of Western civilization in terms of its definition of education and its definition of giftedness.

- The policies of former colonies that diverge from the Traditional model, though the difference is slight, have educational systems that are built on their own distinct national culture. This is true of the United States, Australia and New Zealand, which have some of the most mature policies regarding the education of gifted students. The policies of these countries also have a focus on providing opportunities for a diversity of students to partake of services for the gifted. This is an aspect that is unique to these countries, but is one that is espoused in general education policies in developing countries that exhibit a commitment to equalizing educational opportunity across groups. In this chapter, these are called 'Talent Development' model policies. These policy models, though in need of more development, demonstrate the most promise for fulfilling the need to integrate multiple conceptions of socially valuable talents and abilities. Their intent is to be inclusive rather than to filter and narrow the field, though they are constrained by formidable remnants of strongly held conceptual foundations in the field and by the overwhelmingly widespread low priority given to the education of all children in every country. Every country, no matter what its education policy, allocates a relatively small amount of resources for education in comparison to resources allocated for military and other governmental functions (OECD, 1997).

Discussion of Policy Content and Trends

Present State: Identification and Filtering Processes

The policy of Hungary is an example of the prevalent Traditional model of gifted educational policy. Students move through a system in which primary and early secondary education are compulsory, then they must qualify for further free education through performance on tests or in auditions and exhibitions, when appropriate. Some students thus identified early are placed in special schools that are connected to universities, which 'collect' them and place them on an accelerated track for tertiary education. Others are encouraged to participate in competitions and attend special classes. This model has worked for a long time

and is effective. However, a drawback that will emerge in the coming century as the world becomes a more global society economically, politically and socially, is that this model is most effective in more culturally homogeneous societies.

With a global marketplace, people are not only interacting more electronically, they are travelling more and farther than ever before in history, crossing borders not only for commerce, but to live. Almost all member countries of UNESCO acknowledged at its recent World Conference on Higher Education that providing higher education for a more diverse student population within their borders is a growing concern for the 21st century (Miller, 1999). This, coupled with a trend toward more global mobility in general, will pose many of the same issues that countries such as the U.S., Australia, and New Zealand face today in formulating educational policy—providing services that do not reflect cultural biases against indigenous and minority cultures and in favor of the dominant culture in resource allocation and human resource development. Traditional model countries would be well served if they looked to the policies of these three, which are currently paving the way toward more variability in options and definitions to prepare more citizens for citizenship and work in the knowledge-based global economy as well as to identify and serve the gifted.

Future Possibility: Traditional Program Options with New Funding Sources

None of the policies that were analyzed for this study diverged very much from the normal services that are offered to gifted and talented students, e.g. acceleration, special schools, etc. The United Kingdom outlined a new initiative for what the minister of education called *specialist schools*. Schools that apply for status as specialist schools receive funding to provide 'master classes' in specific areas in maths, science, technology, languages, sports and the performing arts. The ministry has assembled a national group of expert advisors to provide the philosophical foundations for the program, including definitions and identification procedures, and technical assistance to the schools. The most extraordinary aspect of this program is that it is privately funded. The government has collected more than 30 million pounds for the project from private sources so far. This raises the question of governmental funding for programs for the gifted, a core function of policy.

Hallak (1990) points out that governments are entrusted with the role of equalizer, simply because they distribute the public good. He contends that to fulfill the role of equalizer, "the State is required to finance education and training services for those unable to purchase them on the private market" (1990, p.78). Education is 'quasi public' because it can be provided either publicly or privately, at least by those who can afford it. It is the responsibility of governmental policy to not only provide access to education for those who cannot afford it at all, but also to provide funding for those who cannot pay for the total cost of their instruction. This would require governments to fund all types of education, both formal and informal, at all levels, which is admittedly impossible. With limited resources, all governments must set priorities in their educational policies, and these are always reflected in the financial aspects of the policy. The new initiative in the UK is a first step in a new direction because it represents governmental use of private funds for education of a specific population, and the funds are not provided by the parents of the students to educate their own. These are private funds distributed through a governmental program to benefit the public. This epitomizes a new trend in educational policy that should be noted and followed, where appropriate.

Examples of the Traditional model of education policy being adopted by former colonies can be found in Asia, Africa and Latin America (Passow, 1993). The system of formal schooling with high stakes examinations determining the future path of the student's education is prevalent on all continents—a vestige of the lingering influence of colonization that possibly creates inappropriate models for the very students the policies are attempting to serve. Some countries have taken steps to formulate their own unique models.

Present State: Some Problems with the Traditional Model

A Latin American country where the traditional model has not helped to adequately serve the needs of the gifted or to equalize educational opportunity enough to have a positive, widespread impact on economic and social development is Brazil, where many of the common pitfalls of the traditional model are evidenced. Yet it also has examples of good program and policy elements that can be replicated elsewhere. An example of an equalizing program is the summer enrichment program for disadvantaged gifted students in Minas Gerais. This program is like a summer camp, where children live on a farm and do projects and hands-on problem solving activities that stimulate their interests and abilities. The small group attention and the setting make this an expensive endeavor, so the program is in financial trouble (Alencar, 1994). This is typical of many special programs for the gifted in countries where there are Traditional models of gifted education policy and generally traditional models of schooling for all children. It also typifies countries where the national economy cannot sustain adequate educational services for all children and where education is not the highest political priority.

The pitfalls of the policy manifested in Brazil are summarized in the following list and are characteristic of the pitfalls of the traditional model, especially for developing countries, which are usually former colonies with few economic resources and reserves, and multicultural populations with indigenous populations with special needs caused by a history of oppression.

- Adoption of the Marland Report (1971) definition of giftedness or a variation on that definition with the accompanying assumption that only a small percentage of students, the upper end of the Bell Curve, will meet the criteria:

Gifted and talented children are those capable of high performance and/or high potential ability in any of the following areas, singly or in combination:

(1) General intellectual ability
(2) Specific academic aptitude
(3) Creative or productive thinking
(4) Leadership ability
(5) Visual and performing arts
(6) Psychomotor ability.

It can be assumed that utilization of these criteria for identification of the gifted and talented will encompass a minimum of 3 to 5% of the school population (p. IX).

- Over-reliance on American or other experts from developed countries with predominantly Western cultures as consultants in the development of the national policy for gifted education.
- Inadequate allocation of resources for education in general, with even less for gifted students.
- Tension between goals of equity and excellence manifested in attitudes toward the gifted such as expectations of perfection, over-identification of already privileged students from upper and middle classes, assumptions that giftedness is rare and that the gifted are a homogeneous population with many common traits (Alencar, 1994).

The adoption of the definition published in the Marland Report across the United States and much of the world in the 1970s and 80s can now be viewed from a historical perspective. It was a major step forward for the field. The leadership of the United States in "pushing the envelope" throughout the twentieth century cannot be denied in terms of policy, definitions, curriculum, and programming. The Marland Report provided a reasonably broad and very official definition that governments and legislative bodies could use with the confidence that it had credibility. It was a catalyst that started a chain reaction of policy development. That was a giant step forward. In the intervening years, the field has opened to include more theories of giftedness than the IQ (e.g. Gardner, 1983; Sternberg, 1988; Gagne, 1995). Program models have been replicated across the globe and a few new ones have been developed, though U.S. models continue to dominate. Clearly, the culture and economic system of the United States dominate the rest of the globe. It is time now to ask whether this domination is necessary or appropriate in the area of educational policy, especially for the gifted. The adoption of a definition of giftedness from another culture communicates what is socially valuable in that culture. Though the adopting culture may share some of that value, surely every culture has its own socially valuable talents and skills that must be included in its definition of giftedness in order for its policy to be culturally appropriate. If this is not considered when adopting a definition, the adoption becomes an imposition.

One of the effects of calling in the most prominent experts in the field is the perpetuation of the dominance of developed countries. Developed countries produce the most experts, and developing countries look to them for guidance. This guidance usually takes the form of transmission of the ideas and values of the culture from which the expert hails. The similarities between the policies of most of the countries is probably due to this transmission. Now that some policies are in place and others are beginning to be developed, we must ask if this is one of the effects that we desired as a global field. Do we want the policy of every country to be similar? What purpose does this serve?

Most educational policies will continue to be ineffective until educators around the world unite and act as advocates for the children of the world. Is this not one of the commitments of educators of the gifted? When education is one of the highest priorities of every nation and it receives resources that are consistent with that high priority, there will be enough money to provide adequate services to meet the special education needs of gifted students and all students.

Gifted education policies with the goal of equalizing educational opportunity can be designed. Equalizing policies are more appropriate for developing countries where there are high rates of illiteracy and many children do not have the opportunity to attend school or access to a free education.

Future Possibility: Expanding Program Models and Definitions

An example of a country that has attempted to formulate its own unique model is Nigeria, where, in the 1980s, a magnet school approach was designed to accommodate the needs of talented students (Kolo, 1996). In this model, students exhibiting a propensity, talent, or disposition for a subject or area of human endeavor, choose a school based on that area and learn all subjects through themes that are related to the area of strength and focus. This is more in keeping with the talent development model adopted in the United States after the *National Excellence* report (Callahan & Hiatt, 1998). This model takes into account the fact that giftedness is not fixed and that talent enables students to provide the focused attention necessary to persevere and practice enough to develop talents, propensities and dispositions into gifts. Much of the policy in the

U.S., Australia and New Zealand that is focused at groups that are underrepresented in gifted programs uses the talent development model rather than the gifted programming model that prevails in more Traditional type frameworks, which were reflected in the policies of these three countries until very recently. The Javits legislation and the funding that accompanied it to develop models for identifying and serving diverse populations of gifted children helped to spur research and development and to redirect the field. This is a good example for developing countries to follow when development of educational policy for the gifted is initiated. A relatively small amount of funding to a large national pool of researchers to develop processes and models for specific regional, ethnic, economic and racial populations can make a big difference in the direction that policy takes.

Future Possibilities

An aspect of the Talent Development policies for gifted education is that they acknowledge that heretofore prevailing constructs of giftedness and what Miller (1999) calls educational merit have been strongly affected by economic and social privilege. Because of this, groups have been disenfranchised from access to identification as being gifted and therefore to programs and services. If one takes either the view that equalizing educational opportunity is necessary for economic development or what has traditionally been the opposing view that education is a human right, the obligation to equalize access to appropriate services for all students, including the disadvantaged, is central to the mission of governmental policy. For this reason, national and state policies for gifted education that neglect the obligation to equalize access to and opportunity for appropriate services are inappropriate for the 21st century. The talent development model should be the major push in the policy area in this field in every nation. Traditional models, unless they are designed with the purpose of exponentially expanding the population of gifted students through providing educational contexts and opportunities that elicit high levels of performance, simply serve to re-privilege the already advantaged students in a society. Policies should be designed to newly-privilege the marginalized.

In a recent international study using educational researchers from nine nations in four geopolitical regions, using Delphi techniques and trend extrapolations, Parker, Ninomiya & Cogan (1999) found that the most significant challenges that the world is thought to face in this century include:

• The widening economic gap between the wealthy and the poor within countries;
• The inequalities between those who have access to information technologies and those who do not and the increasing disparity between them;

- Increasing conflicts of interest between developing and developed nations (Parker, Ninomiya & Cogan, 1999).

The authors suggest that, to meet these challenges, students must have educational experiences that develop their:

- Ability to look at and approach problems as a member of a global society.
- Ability to work with others in a cooperative way and to take responsibility for one's roles/duties within society.
- Ability to understand, accept, appreciate, and tolerate cultural differences.
- Capacity to think in a critical and systematic way.
- Willingness to resolve conflict in a non-violent manner.
- Willingness and ability to participate in politics at local, national, and international levels.
- Willingness to change one's lifestyle and consumption habits to protect the environment.
- Ability to be sensitive toward and to defend human rights (e.g. rights of women, ethnic minorities) (p. 125).

Can the field of gifted education meet these challenges with its current policies? Will our students, as a result of the education that we provide them, be prepared to take the leadership positions that we assume they will take in order to help the world meet these global challenges? Or will our education simply prepare them to get good jobs and make more money? Do we want to complacently design policies that maintain the ever-growing global inequalities that result in an ever-increasing waste of human potential? Or do we want to solve the problem of the widening wealth and opportunity gap? Policy is a political plan of action. It is a societal commitment to move in a direction. It is time for new policy directions in gifted education, locally, nationally, and internationally that reflect our commitment to a peaceful, cooperative, global society.

It is moral and wise for developed countries to begin the process of viewing policy as a means of equalizing educational opportunity internationally. Though there is no world government, there is a worldwide network of educators and researchers in gifted education. There are also many global, international corporations that are willing to fund initiatives that promote world peace and prosperity. A statement from the gifted field on equalizing educational opportunity and access to gifted services and talent development opportunities would be a major innovation and contribution to the future. It has historically been the place of this field to be the first field of experimentation in pedagogic and curricular practices. Policy innovations should also be our purview. Using private funds to formulate a statement and an experimental program that is less rooted in Western constructs and that acknowledges cultural

differences such as those outlined by Stevenson (1998) and Sternberg (1997) as well as disparities in privilege would be in keeping with current trends and meet global needs for the future.

Conclusion

Policies on educating gifted students worldwide are generally traditional in their definitions of giftedness and models of providing accommodations for those students in school settings. These settings are defined in formal, traditional ways in those policies, thus cementing the foundations of these policies in the early 20th century constructs of intelligence and schooling. New models that reflect the needs of a global, information society and economy are needed. Talent development models and international models are the first step toward meeting the needs of the 21st century.

References

Alencar, E. M. L. S. (1994). *Brazilian policies and the education of the gifted*. Unpublished paper.

Callahan, C. & Hiatt, E. (1998). Assessing and nurturing talent in a diverse culture: what do we do, what should we do, what can we do? In: R. Friedman & K. Rogers (Eds.), *Talent in Context: Historical and Social Perspectives on Giftedness* (pp. 3–17). Washington, DC: APA.

Freeman, J. (1992). Recent developments for the highly able in Britain. In: F. Monks, M. Ktazko & H. W. van Boxtel (Eds.), *Education of the Gifted in Europe: Theoretical and Research Issues* (pp.58–70). Amsterdam: Swets & Zeitlinger.

Gagne, F. (1995). From giftedness to talent: a developmental model and its impact on the language of the field. *Roeper Review*, **18**, 103–111.

Gardner, H. (1983). *Frames of mind: the theory of multiple intelligences*. New York: Basic Books.

Hallak, J. (1990). *Investing in the future: setting educational priorities in the developing world*. (UNESCO Institute for Educational Planning). Oxford: Pergamon Press.

Kolo, I. A. (1996). Reflections on the development of gifted education in Nigeria, *Roeper Review*, **19** (2), 79–81.

Marland, S. P. (1971). *Education of the Gifted and Talented* (Report to the Congress of the United States by the U.S. Commissioner of Education). Washington, DC: U.S. Printing Office.

Miller, M. A. (1999). Access in a global context, *Change*, **31** (1), 4.

Organisation for Economic Co-Operation and Development (OECD). (1997). *Education at a glance: OECD indicators*. Paris, France: OECD.

Parker, W. C., Ninomiya, A. & Cogan, J. (1999). Educating world citizens: toward multinational curriculum development. *American Educational Research Journal*, **36** (2), 117–147.

Passow, A. H. & Rudnitski, R. A. (1993). *State policies regarding the education of the gifted as reflected in legislation and regulation*. Storrs, CT: NRCGT.

Passow, A. H. & Rudnitski, R. A. (1994). *Transforming policy for the education of the gifted*. Paper presented at the annual meeting of the American Educational Research Association.

Passow, A. H. (1993). National/State Policies on the Gifted and Talented. In: K. A. Heller, F. Mönks & A. H. Passow

(Eds.), *Handbook of Research on Giftedness and Talent* (pp. 29–46). Oxford: Pergamon Press.

Sternberg, R. J. (1988). *The Triarchic mind: A new theory of human intelligence*. New York: Viking.

Sternberg, R. J. (1997). *Successful intelligence: how practical and creative intelligence determine success in life*. New York: Plume.

Stevenson, H. W. (1998). Cultural interpretations of giftedness: the case of East Asia. In: R. Friedman & K. Rogers (Eds.), *Talent in Context: Historical and Social Perspectives on Giftedness* (pp. 61–79). Washington, DC: APA.

Tannenbaum, A. J. (1983). *Gifted children: psychological and educational perspectives*. New York: Macmillan.

Changing Paradigms for Gifted Education in the United States

James J. Gallagher

The University of North Carolina at Chapel Hill, The Frank Porter Graham Child Development Center, USA

Introduction

The end of one century and the beginning of another is an ideal time to reflect, and look forward, to consider where the United States is going in this field of education of gifted children. The new millennium provides us a chance to ask old questions and to see if we have some new answers bolstered by experience and research. Some of the questions concern gifted children and youth themselves. How are they different from the average child? How can one find them? What should we be doing to enhance their capabilities?

Then there is the cultural context in which the gifted child is growing up. Is the child growing up in a one-parent home in poverty able to show his/her capabilities as well as the child of two professionally educated parents who can provide many advantages to aid the development of their child?

What about the educational context? What themes and theories are driving the educational enterprise and what effect is that having on the stimulation of gifted children? We are aware of a continuing struggle between *equity* and *excellence*, two important American values, for the scarce resources available to educational programs. The beginning of the twenty-first century is a good time to review all of these broad issues and chart a course for a rapidly changing future.

We have become accustomed to using a variety of paradigms or models as a way of organizing this complex field. We have had one paradigm for *intelligence*, another for our *public education system*, and still another for how we should educate *students high in intelligence*. All of these models or paradigms have been under challenge in recent times with many persons demanding change. If we are going to move forward into the twenty-first century we need to reexamine these guiding paradigms to see how they fit our current knowledge.

The Paradigm of Intelligence

One of the major changes that have taken place in the past few decades has been our changing view of the concept of intelligence. While intelligence had previously been thought to be predominantly hereditary in nature, we have now come to believe that there is a complex interaction between heredity and environment that produces the product that we call intelligence in the child of five or ten or fifteen (Plomin, 1997).

We have also expanded the scope of the concept of intelligence beyond a measure on an IQ test. Sternberg (1986) has produced the *triarchic model* of intelligence that features the executive and control functions of intelligence, the decision making function not well addressed in the past. Gardner (Ramos-Ford & Gardner, 1997) has stressed multiple intelligences including linguistic, logical-mathematical, spatial, bodily kinesthetic, musical, interpersonal, and intrapersonal. It is difficult to provide a functional definition of high intelligence or giftedness for the schools without first coming to terms with the construct itself.

Perkins (1995) has presented three competing paradigms or models that have all purported to represent intelligence in the past.

- *Neural Intelligence*: A kind of neural efficiency composed of the speed and precision of information processing in the neural system.
- *Experiential Intelligence*: The knowledge we gain through extended experience in academic areas like physics, or non-academic areas such as raising a family,
- *Reflective Intelligence:* The presence of thinking strategies, a positive attitude towards investing oneself in good thinking and metacognitive awareness, and management of one's own mind.

According to Perkins, all of these paradigms are partially correct so now we have the task of combining them to create a new and more adequate paradigm or model of intelligence. We can also note that the presence of *experiential intelligence* and *reflective intelligence* both mean that experience and education can play a meaningful role in the final intellectual development and functioning. While we have previously believed that there was a set proportion of children who would fall into the 'gifted' category (the neural intelligence model) we now see that the limits of high intelligence have yet to be discovered, so we can create experiences and design environments in order to enhance this valuable characteristic.

Gagné (1999) has proposed a breakdown of human abilities based on native and learned experiences that closely resembles the models of Perkins and Sternberg who also stress the interaction of native ability and experiences as resulting in the outstanding performances that we call gifted.

One of the most dramatic pieces of evidence for the influence of environment on the development of intelligence has been provided by Flynn (1999). He examined the retesting of students and adults over time on intelligence tests and found that the IQ scores tend to go up in the retesting over large spans of time. The increases in performance are so great that test constructors have been forced to renorm their intelligence tests to prevent a skewing to the positive end of the test, raising the issue whether we, as a society, are becoming more intelligent or just more proficient test takers.

One of the general understandings that have been accepted regarding intelligence is that it distributes itself roughly along a *normal curve*. But this is surely *not correct* at the ends of the distribution. At the low end, children with mental retardation do not dip lower than two standard deviations below the mean, unless there is some pathological condition present (Burack, Hodapp & Zigler, 1998). However, at the top end of the distribution there are documented cases of students performing as much as six or seven standard deviations above the mean on IQ tests (Morelock & Feldman, 1997)! As in the case of our calling our planet Earth 'round' when in fact it is flat at both poles, intelligence is not really normally distributed at the extremes. There is increasing evidence that the proportions of students at the higher end of the IQ distribution are also much greater than would be predicted by a normal curve of distribution (Silverman, 1997).

There is considerable evidence to suggest that genetics does play a significant role in the development of various intelligences. Studies of twins and adoptive children clearly indicate that some children are born with more potential for learning rapidly than others. These differences apply within various racial and ethnic groups, not necessarily between them (Plomin, 1997); but that is only part of the picture. The rest of the story is that environment and sequential experiences play a significant role in the crystallization of native abilities. If a particular environment allows a

child to have more experiences and to obtain more encouragement from adults and peers whom he or she considers important, then the child's abilities will flourish. Thus boys who are encouraged to work with mathematics and are told (implicitly or explicitly) that excelling in maths is a masculine trait that will develop their native mathematical abilities beyond those of girls who are told that they are not supposed to be good in this subject and that maths ability is gender-specific to males (Reis & Callahan, 1989).

Just as the concept of intelligence had been believed to be one of maturational unfolding within the individual, the concept or model of *creativity* was one in which some special characteristics of the 'creative' child (fluency, flexibility, risk taking, etc.) would be activated given the proper educational settings and conditions. Even as the development of intelligence is now being viewed as an interactive process, so creativity is beginning to be seen as a process that is environmentally interactive as well.

Csikszentmihalyi (1996) views creativity as an interaction among persons, products and environments. This change from focusing intense attention on the 'creative individual' to focusing on the interaction between individual and environment helps us to focus more on how to create a fruitful educational environment. By teaching children how to behave independently and how to search for new ideas we can help many students become more creative, not just those with extraordinary intelligence.

Definition

With these changing models or paradigms of intelligence and creativity, what has this done to our definition of gifted children? The definition most widely accepted appeared in the report on *National Excellence*.

> Children and youth with outstanding talent perform or show the potential for performing at remarkably high levels of accomplishment when compared with others of their age, experience, or environment. These children and youth exhibit high performance capability in intellectual, creative, and/or artistic areas, possess an unusual leadership capacity, or excel in specific academic fields. They require services or activities not ordinarily provided by the schools. Outstanding talents are present in children and youth from all cultural groups, across all economic strata, and in all areas of human endeavor (Ross, 1993).

Note that there is a broader scope to what is giftedness in this definition that was true of past definitions plus a recognition that outstanding talents can and should be found in all ethnic groups. Finally, there is a recognition that special educational services will be *required* if we expect these students to reach their expected level of educational attainment.

Characteristics

Social. The social relationships of gifted students continued to be a matter of concern despite the continuing evidence (Mayseless, 1993) that they are at least as popular as other students their age. The negative social reaction to students who appear to be outstanding can be judged by the number of unfavorable terms assigned to them. Few children relish being called 'brain' or 'geek' or 'nerd'. Consequently one of the most favorite of strategies is for the gifted students to deny their own giftedness, with the most gifted students being most likely to protest their giftedness (Swiatek, 1995). Many minority students who are gifted feel under additional social pressure to conform to general student norms. It is only those gifted Black students who were less concerned with peer pressure who felt comfortable with their high ability (Ford, 1993).

The self concepts of gifted students have been reported as higher than average. However, this high self image includes 'academic self concept' and it would be strange indeed if students who can easily perceive themselves to be years in advance of their peers do not think of themselves as superior in that domain (Robinson & Clinkenbeard, 1998). When non-academic areas (social or physical self image) are reviewed the gifted students appear only slightly superior to other students in their self image.

Emotional. There has been a trend to rethink the role of emotional development in the gifted child. Instead of seeing emotions as separate characteristics to be correlated with intellectual development, the trend has been to view emotions as an integral part of the makeup of the creative and gifted children. Two of Gardner's multiple intelligences represent what has been traditionally viewed as emotional behavior: interpersonal *intelligence*, the ability to understand other individuals; and *intrapersonal intelligence* a person's understanding of one's own cognitive strengths, feelings, and range of emotions.

There has been a revisiting of Dambrowski's concept of *overexcitabilities*, meaning a surfeit of emotional reactions, an intense personal reaction to an experience (Dabrowski, 1967). This passionate and intense response to the world is not seen as a negative, but one, which can lead to extraordinary achievement. Kurcinka (1991) refers in a similar fashion to the 'spirited' child meaning a child with more intense, sensitive, perceptive, persistent, and energetic characteristics. Of course, the more sensitive the child, the more vulnerable to psychic pain. Silverman (1994) reports a common observation that gifted children are more aware than their age peers of the disjunction between our moral pretensions and our actual behavior.

> Dozens of cases on record of gifted children fighting injustice, befriending and protecting handicapped children, conserving resources, responding to others' emotional needs, becoming terribly upset if a classmate is humiliated, becoming vegetarians in a meat eating family, crying at the violence in a cartoon (p. 111).

The intensity of feelings, drive, and passion about one's interests reminds one of Csikszentmihalyi's (1990) concept of *Flow*, a period of intense and single-minded attention to a particular problem or project that is currently under consideration by those who create. This is not to say that all gifted students have such drive and passion and sensitivity, some appear to be no more sensitive than a rock, but the blending of the intellectual and emotional sides is a fascinating and potentially productive area for further investigation.

The creative child, or the child who creates, seems to reveal a constellation of traits and abilities necessary for the innovative mental productivity desired. Davis (1997) assembled some of these traits as independence, risk taking, sense of humor, a fascination with complexity, tolerance for ambiguity, curiosity, etc. Such traits seem important if one is to turn one's back on the traditional lessons and seek other answers to those classroom responses traditionally given.

Terman and Hollingworth early noted that there seemed to be a greater prevalence of first-born children who are gifted. Solloway (1996) studied the lives of social rebels and concluded with the interesting observation that many of them are *not* first born, that first born children tend to be traditional and conservative following their parents' values and wishes. Later born children, in order to seek a niche for themselves in the family, tend to be less traditional and more willing to explore other ways, other answers. We have long been aware of the important role that families play in the lives of gifted individuals, but such findings as the birth order lead us to pursue further the family dynamics for clues as to the nurturing of creative and gifted performance.

In a search for the roots of success and failure for talented teenagers, Csikszentmihalyi, Rathunde & Whalen (1993) introduced a new device for collecting useful information, the Experience Sampling Method (ESM). By using a beeper (an electronic signal) to trigger a student's response at various times of the day we can determine who were his companions, and what he was thinking or feeling, and where he was. It is possible in this manner to gain a portrait of the intellectual and social life of these students.

A study of 394 teacher-nominated, secondary school students yielded such a portrait. Aside from confirming previous findings of the importance of a supportive family and sensitive teachers the study yielded the following about the life space of talented teenagers.

> Talented students spent less time just socializing or hanging out with friends. Instead they shared more active and challenging pursuits with friends, for example hobbies and studying. They learned to modulate attention: more concentration in school and less when socializing, doing chores and watching TV. They also spent a greater amount of time alone, which is essential for anyone building future skills. More solitude and more productive activities probably accounted for more somber weekly moods than average teenagers (p. 244).

In short, these teenagers were creating a productive learning environment for themselves, inside and outside of school, by avoiding or reducing some of the non-functional aspects of teenage society in the United States.

Special Populations

During the last decade in the United States there has been increasing interest in a variety of special populations within the broad general area of gifted education. Among these populations are women, gifted individuals with disabilities, gifted underachieving, and culturally different gifted students.

Women. One of the continuing puzzles in this field is why women, making up half of the population and clearly showing academic and intellectual equality in the early grades to males, do not have a stronger track record of adult production or eminence (Feldman, Csikszentmihalyi & Gardner, 1994). Western culture, with its bias in favor of white males, has been considered a major barrier to the further development of women and have stimulated a series of special programs that provide opportunities for the talent development of women (Kerr, 1997; Noble & Smyth, 1995).

A recent review of the topic of gifted women (Noble, Subotnik & Arnold, 1999) identified three major barriers to their progress and productivity that result from this relatively unfriendly culture. First, is the importance of *high self-esteem* necessary for setting important goals, taking risks, and confronting challenges. The authors feel that such high self-esteem is admired when it appears in men, but discouraged as immodest in women.

Second, women are automatically treated as minorities or token members of high-level male-dominated achievement settings. The lack of role models and the 'glass ceiling' which limits promotion to top positions contribute to problems in women reaching potential. Finally, there is the balancing act that women are faced with in juggling family and career. Some adaptation of organizational structures and expectations to take into account this conflict between career and home might be

helpful. The clear advance of gifted women in many different fields will provide role models and success paths that can be followed by the next generation of gifted girls.

Disability. We have long been aware of the outstanding accomplishments of gifted individuals who have had a particular physical handicap. Franklin D. Roosevelt, Ludwig Von Beethoven, Helen Keller, etc. are examples of twice exceptional individuals that are easily recognized. But recently, another area of disability has come to the attention of investigators and educators. These are twice exceptional children who are *gifted with a learning disability.* These would be youngsters who may have a variety of perceptual problems, such as dyslexia, that interfere with their learning and sometimes in their even being identified as gifted.

Reis, Neu & McGuire (1995) conducted case studies of twelve college students with learning disabilities who had attained high IQ scores in their youth but who had never been placed in a program for gifted students. These students reported a variety of negative school experiences including (1) their talents not being recognized, (2) an assumption that learning disabilities meant below average ability, and (3) frustration with some teachers' expectations. They also reported that other teachers provided them with support with special lessons and challenging the students at their level of performance. These students revealed high motivation and determination and were aided by a special college program for students with learning disabilities in which they learned various coping strategies, time management schemes, etc.

Coleman (1992) compared 21 matched pairs of middle grade students, one member of the pair being gifted-learning disability and the other average ability learning disability, on their academic coping skills. She found that the gifted LD students had been able to develop on their own a series of positive coping skills that enabled them to perform adequately in school in contrast to the average LD students, who manifested a type of learned helplessness and pessimism in academic situations. She recommended that the development of positive coping skills be part of the curriculum for both gifted and average LD students.

Concern has been felt for what happens to these 'twice exceptional' children when they become adults. Holliday, Koller & Thomas (1999) followed 80 adult rehabilitation clients who were high ability–learning disability subjects. They found that their adult performance was more characteristic of the learning disability dimension than the high ability side of their intelligence, calling for more attention to this combination of characteristics.

Another twice exceptional set of individuals has received attention recently because of the revived interest in autism. A special version of autism appears to be the 'Asperger Syndrome' where the child has high abilities concomitant with the more traditional symptoms of autism (social distance and isolation, special linguistic patterns, etc.) (Schopler, Mesibov & Kunce, 1998).

Underachievers. Ever since Terman called attention to the gifted underachiever (students performing much more poorly than their capabilities would indicate) in his monumental longitudinal study (Terman & Oden, 1947), there have been periodic concerns about finding such youngsters and remediating them. The original findings that such students lacked motivation, had a low self concept, and blamed others for their troubles, seems to be borne out in subsequent studies (see Colangelo, Kerr, Christensen & Maxey 1993).

Rimm (1997) presents a systematic way of approaching such children including individual assessment, family communication, identification of appropriate role models, correcting academic skill deficiencies, etc. Rimm reports widespread success using this model. It should not be imagined however that modification of the coping styles of such students is either quick or easy (see Butler-Por, 1987). After all, it took nine or ten years to form these dysfunctional habits and reversing them or replacing them requires an intensity of effort and individualization of care that few school systems have available to them. Gallagher & Gallagher (1994) described the dance of the underachiever as consisting of "two steps forward, one step back, one step to the side, and pause." The biggest disappointments appear to occur whenever we underestimate the amount of time and effort needed to achieve our goals.

Cultural Difference. One of the topics receiving the most attention during the last two decades are differences in ability and achievement between various students from different racial, ethnic, and parental income backgrounds. The finding that there are strong differences in prevalence of giftedness from various racial groups with African-American and Hispanic underrepresented; Asians overrepresented (Robinson & Clinkenbeard, 1998) has been taken as clear evidence of unfairness in the educational system or the culture itself. Dornbush, Glasgow & Lin (1996) in a review of the social structure of schooling point out that:

> In a system of mass education, group differences in achievement are seen as a glaring problem. The ideology underpinning mass education implies that equality in educational opportunities leads to equality in educational outcomes, but this expectation has not been realized (p. 404).

Various methods other than traditional intelligence tests have been used in an attempt to find 'hidden gifted' students from minority populations. These usually take the form of using multiple indices. Frasier & Garcia (1995) pointed out that using multiple measures is not sufficient unless one has a defensible way of combining the results from these measures. Another approach has been to use observation in an enriched classroom along with portfolio assessment that can create a pool of students for further consideration (Borland & Wright, 1994). Others use tests like the Raven Progressive Matrices test as a preferred 'culturally neutral' test and report promising results (Mills & Tissot, 1995). There will likely be many more attempts to provide enrichment for minority gifted students in the near future since it has become a priority of state and federal agencies as well as individual teachers.

Changing Paradigm of Public Education of Gifted Students

How gifted students are educated in the United States depends in large measure of how we view our public education enterprise, an unwieldy collection of about 15,000 school districts that is overseen by 50 separate states while the Federal government merely supports some research and development activities and provides some financial support for the education of special populations of economically disadvantaged children and children with disabilities.

The portrait of total chaos that many foreign observers imagine as a result of these many people influencing educational decision making from 15,000 separate school districts and 50 states, is overdrawn. While theoretically they could all go off in their own directions, educators often follow the lead of other states or districts so that trends like the Internet in multiple intelligences, or the use of portfolios, quickly become widespread across the country through successive modeling and example setting.

A report released by the U.S. Department of Education, *National Excellence* (Ross, 1993) has had a powerful impact on many educators and school systems. The report indicates many shortcomings of American Education in their dealing with talented and gifted students. Among the shortcomings of elementary school programs were:

• The regular school curriculum does not challenge gifted and talented.
• Most academically talented students have already mastered up to one-half of the required curriculum offered to them in elementary school.
• Classroom teachers do little to accommodate the different learning needs of gifted students.
• Most specialized programs are available for only a few hours a week.
• Students talented in the arts are offered few challenging opportunities.

Some of the shortcomings of the secondary school programs were noted as:

- Appropriate opportunities in middle schools are scattered and uncoordinated.
- High school schedules do not meet the needs of talent students
- The college preparatory curriculum in the U.S. generally does not require hard work from able students.
- Small town and rural schools often have limited resources and are unable to offer advanced classes and special learning opportunities.
- Specialized schools, magnets, and intensive summer programs serve only a fraction of the secondary students who might benefit from them.

According to the *National Excellence Report* all of this leads to a 'quiet crisis' in the words of Secretary of Education Richard Riley (p. iii) and leads to such undesirable consequences as the following:

> Compared with top students in other industrialized countries, American students perform poorly on international tests, are offered a less rigorous curriculum, read fewer demanding books, do less homework, and enter the work force or post-secondary education less well prepared (p. 1).

The report urged American educators to pay attention to student excellence in addition to their well-documented emphasis on student equity. Other reports appear to support the National Excellence findings.

The TIMSS report (Third International Mathematics and Science Study, 1997) stressed the low performance of American students compared with students from other countries. This was particularly true at the twelfth grade level. Even gifted students in the United States enrolled in advanced calculus and physics classes were only able to perform at the level of average students from other countries in these subject areas.

One of the common reactions of gifted students in the U.S. to public school is *boredom*. An inquiry of 871 gifted students in nine separate school systems (Gallagher, Harradine & Coleman, 1997) documented the reports of over half of these students that the standard academic subjects lacked challenge. Mathematics and the special enhancement program for gifted students were the only areas in these districts where the students felt challenged.

This group of students was saying, "Give me more work." Not just more of the same curriculum that has already been too easy for them, of course, but more conceptually challenging materials so that they can use these special abilities that they have. They want to flex their academic muscles. They are as bored as would be a student who has aspirations to be a world class sprinter and has been told he has been entered in a race with a bunch of fourth graders. Some of the comments that these gifted students made were:

- "Sometimes social studies doesn't challenge me because we mostly just copy things down and go slow."
- "No it is not challenging, because all we do is take notes, memorize, then regurgitate information for a test."
- "We are not allowed to be challenged—everything is explained for you with no room for personal views. Sometimes it is not hard enough."
- "The stories I read are simple and so are the questions. We just read and summarize and answer questions."

Equity and Excellence. Many observers have noted the mixed feelings expressed towards gifted students on the part of the general public, and of a subset of professionals. On one hand, we are proud of their accomplishments and honor them through scholarships and various prizes, but on the other hand our envy of their ease of performance communicates itself to these students who wonder what it is they have to do to obtain acceptance. Also, if we see our society as one fueled by competition then helping gifted students means giving them additional advantages over our own non-gifted children.

Two contradictory values have been competing for predominance in American education: *equity versus excellence*. Those who stress equity focus on the vastly different opportunities that exist from one subculture to another in the U.S. They focus on bringing the economically disadvantaged students up to a higher performance level, a level indicated by their potential. There is also a subset of the academic community that sees evil designs in the attempt to provide special help for gifted students. They see this as part of a class struggle. Margolin (1996) suggests that we are providing aid and comfort to the 'oppressors' of our society by establishing special programs for gifted students.

Those supporting *equity* (see Oakes, 1985; Margolin, 1996; Sapon-Shevin, 1996) are particularly concerned that many minority students have not had the chance to show what they can do and may be kept out of special services for gifted students because of their limited scores on aptitude tests. In this way, they observe, the majority of high income parents will continue to see to it that their children dominate the special programs.

One of the most influential of trends over the past decade has been the move towards *inclusion*. This is a term from special education describing the proposed integration of children with disabilities with other students in the same classroom. This inclusion philosophy is on the way to replacing the resource room as the primary model for educating children with disabilities (Kirk, Gallagher & Anastasiow, 2000).

Part of the reason for this inclusion movement has stemmed from the overrepresentation of minority children in pull-out programs for children with disabilities leading to suggestions that they were being discriminated against and given an inferior education. Inclusion would at least put such children in the same environment as the mainstream children (Stainback & Stainback, 1996).

There is a similar push for inclusion of gifted students because of under-representation of minorities in separate educational settings for gifted children, again leading to the suspicion that minority students were being kept out of desirable educational experiences (Sapon-Shevin, 1996). Regardless, there seems to be a trend towards educating gifted students in the regular classroom with help from a consultant teacher, or by organizing *cluster groups* (6 to 10 gifted students forming a subgroup in the regular classroom) (Gentry & Owen, 1999).

The general dissatisfaction of parents with the status quo of public education has led to the development of several alternative environments. *Charter schools* (schools that are free from the bureaucratic regulations of the regular school but with its same responsibilities) have been one way in which parents of gifted students have tried to gain more decision making control over the school program.

Another device is *magnet schools*, so-called because they present a visible program in certain educational areas such as advanced mathematics, or art, or creative writing, and thus draw students interested in their special program. Though we are currently short of evaluation of such programs, the informal messages from magnet school students has been largely positive.

A final change of setting has been *home schooling* whereby the parents agree to help the student learn necessary facts and master skills in exchange for being allowed to keep their child at home. The growing prevalence of computers in American homes has helped this Home School movement, which began as a move by some parents to give their children a religious orientation and background that they could not get in the public schools. In the case of parents of gifted students, home schooling has been used to allow the child to go forward on his/her own and not be tied to an inappropriate curriculum or educational setting.

Oakes (1985) complained that ability groupings for gifted students have failed to show any academic superiority and wishes to have all students educated together. At least in this fashion all would be getting the same education and no special opportunities would be given to upper middle class, white students. On the other hand, Kulik & Kulik (1991) have analyzed many grouping studies and have come to the conclusion that when grouping is accompanied by advanced conceptual curriculum, the ability grouped programs show a clear advantage over the heterogeneous classroom.

During the Cold War with the Soviet Union, programs for gifted students profited from the fears and anxieties of the public who felt we were falling behind in our educational programs, particularly those in mathematics and the sciences. Given a competition for national survival, all necessary steps to improve our performance were acceptable, particularly for those gifted students who had the potential to make a difference in scientific discoveries and engineering prowess. With the Cold War over, there is less of a press to challenge our brightest students although some efforts have been made to substitute Asian countries, such as Japan, as an economic competitor in the information age.

The discovery that there was an under-representation of African Americans, Hispanics, and Native Americans in advanced programs fueled the suspicions of observers who felt that these advanced programs and services were being reserved for those children of families that possessed political power and could influence the decision making as to who will receive special services. This perception of a love-hate relationship with the general public has caused some gifted students to reject special programs and flee to the anonymity and social safety of the general education program. Other gifted students complain, however, that they are not being challenged in their classrooms and have found it too easy to attain high grades with minimal effort. While we honor the athletes who give '110% effort' and whose exertion lead them to outstanding performance we do not often demand the same level of effort from the intellectually gifted. The result is similar to that of a six-cylinder car running on four cylinders, adequate for some purposes but far from its potential.

The Paradigm of Educating Gifted Students

Our changing view of intelligence, and what should be a good public school education, has inevitably influenced how we provide special services for gifted students in the schools. These changes occur in *where* the student is educated, *what* the student is taught, and the type of *skills* they are expected to master.

Where. There have been a wide variety of efforts designed to counteract the lack of challenge provided to gifted students in the typical educational setting. One of these involves a drastic change in the educational environment itself. A number of states have established special residential schools designed to provide stimulation for highly talented students at the secondary level (Koloff, 1997).

These schools have elaborate procedures for selecting the students involved, and they bring together a faculty with special expertise in the curricular areas emphasized by the school, often science and mathematics and art that seem to be the central focus of many of these programs. These schools provide an advanced curriculum of college level content and difficulty to these students who, often for the first time, find themselves among other students with similar abilities,

687

interests, and aspirations. The results have reported great student and faculty enthusiasm, a laboratory for instructional strategies, (Stepien, Gallagher & Workman, 1993) and a reputation for excellence. Eleven states now have created similar schools for the purpose of challenging the top students in their community or state.

Another approach using existing institutions was developed by Julian Stanley, called the Study of Mathematically Precocious Youth (SMPY). The program was initiated at Johns Hopkins University and now includes four other universities. Its purpose is to identify youth with extraordinary talent in mathematics through administering tests while the youngsters are in their early teens. While originally viewed as a talent search, the SMPY became a base for student acceleration and, through special summer programs, allowed talented students to earn credit for advanced mathematics courses.

Benbow & Lubinski (1996) have reported the beginnings of a fifty-year longitudinal study to determine the fate of SMPY students identified in the talent search. Some preliminary findings indicated substantial later academic success and student satisfaction with the program. The talent search portion of SMPY was also responsible for the discovery of great gender differences in mathematics between girls and boys and has been one of the leading forces to build special math and science programs for girls in this country (Lubinski & Benbow, 1994).

Ability Grouping

Several major attempts have been made to determine if placement, by itself, seemed to be of significance in academic achievement. The Learning Outcomes Study involved over 1,000 students. The teachers worked in a variety of settings providing special services for gifted students from fourteen school districts in grades 2 and 3. These students were placed in four separate settings: *Special School*, *Special Class*, *Pull-Out*, and *Within-Class* settings. The students were tested at the end of the year with the Iowa Test of Basic Skills and a variety of attitude and self-concept measures (Delcourt, Loyd, Cornell & Goldberg, 1994).

The results did indicate major achievement differences between the four groups with the advantage accruing to the special schools and special class programs. There also were differences in self concept with the highest measures obtained by the gifted students in the heterogeneous classrooms. This is a phenomenon noted before. Your social reference comes from the peer group in which you are assigned. If you are surrounded by peers of relatively equal ability to yourself your self image is likely to be lower than if you have peers who are manifestly lower in performance than yourself. There were no group differences obtained on social acceptance, however. Although the gifted youngsters in this study were quite young there did seem to be an advantage in grouping them together, allowing the teacher to press on to more challenging and complex materials and topics with these students.

Table 1 provides a breakdown of desirable practices in gifted and general education that seem to be supported by solid research (Shore & Delcourt, 1996). Many educators have pointed out that various educational strategies that have been recommended for gifted students could be profitably used for all students. Examples of such approaches are enrichment, inquiry, discovery, problem solving, problem finding, etc. All students profit from the challenge of doing their own thinking instead of memorizing predigested content.

For gifted students the content level involved in the discovery and problem solving could be at a higher abstract level than possible for the average student. The high level curriculum noted in Table 1 as uniquely appropriate for gifted would be an example of raising the conceptual level of the curriculum, such as studying various forms of government through the ages rather than just mastering the current workings of government in their own country. Also Shore and Delcourt note that *ability grouping*, *acceleration*, and *differential programming* are particularly useful for gifted students, mainly because they have already mastered the standard curriculum provided in general education.

Table 1. Desirable Practices In Gifted And General Education..

Uniquely Appropriate for Gifted	Effective with Gifted and General Education
Acceleration	Enrichment
Career education (girls)	Inquiry, discovery, problem solving, and creativity
Ability grouping	Professional end products as standards
High level curriculum	Microcomputers
Differential programming	

Adapted from Shore, B. & Delcourt, M. (1996). Effective curricular and program practices in gifted education and the interface with general education. *Journal for the Education of the Gifted*, **20** (2), 138–154.

More and more educators seem to be convinced that differentiating the standard curriculum is the key to effective education of gifted students but examples of such differentiation are few and far between. Gallagher & Gallagher (1994) have detailed four different ways in which the standard curriculum might be modified for gifted students. Such modified content can represent acceleration, enrichment, sophistication or novelty.

(1) *Acceleration.* The material presented to the gifted student may be drawn from the established curricula of a grade or more in advance of the students' current status (e.g. algebra in the seventh grade).
(2) *Enrichment.* The same curriculum goals are used as for the regular class members but the material is extended and more in depth (e.g. studying the diaries of the Lewis and Clark expedition as the class discusses westward movement).
(3) *Sophistication.* The material presented to gifted students is at a higher level of complexity, representing systems of knowledge, than that given to the regular student (e.g. studying the laws of Physics and their applications).
(4) *Novelty.* Material that is unique to the regular curriculum but which has some interest to gifted students (e.g. the study of the stock market and its operations).

The proliferation of high academic standards recently published by professional groups in mathematics, history, science, etc. have proved another anchor point for differentiated curriculum for gifted students.

Productive Thinking

One of the continuing arguments about productive thinking is whether we can instruct students in the general heuristics of problem solving or problem finding so that such mastery can then be transferred to whatever subject matter the student has to be dealing with at the moment (deBono, 1986). Much of gifted education of recent origin has held that assumption. Teach for creative thinking and the student will be creative in whatever topic area he will operate in (Torrance, 1964). An alternative position is that the student should be taught heuristics only within a particular field and that such complex strategies will be useful to him/her only within that field, with the transfer of these skills to other fields to be mainly limited or non-existent.

The field of artificial intelligence seems to provide some useful insight to the problem. There was an earlier attempt to develop a 'General Problem Solver' designed to use general principles to address a wide variety of problems in mathematics, chess playing, etc. (Newell, 1990). Basically, the 'General Problem Solver' became less useful in an area such as chess playing than were programs that had deliberately been written for only chess playing.

A series of studies contrasting the strategies of experts versus novices in physics, medical diagnoses, chess players, etc., tended to indicate that it was the knowledge base of the experts that allowed them to respond more effectively in problem situations. Perkins & Soloman (1989) summarize the contending parties as follows:

> General heuristics that fail to make contact with a rich domain-specific knowledge base are *weak*. But when a domain specific knowledge base operates without general heuristics, it is brittle—it serves mostly in handling formulaic problems (p. 23).

They conclude by arguing for an approach that calls for the intimate intermingling of generality and context-specificity in instruction. The message for us in gifted education would seem to be that if we wish to teach the student problem solving skills or creative thinking strategies we should do it within the context of a strong content base.

The desire to blend together the processes of productive thinking and sophisticated content in an integrated curriculum model is presented by VanTassel Baska (1997) in three dimensions: (1) emphasizing advanced content knowledge that frames disciplines of study; (2) providing higher order thinking and processing; and (3) focusing learning experiences around major issues, themes, and ideas that define both real world applications and theoretical modeling within and across areas of study (p. 128).

Examples of such models may be found in the problem based learning model and the enrichment triad model that follow.

One of the increasingly popular instructional strategies being used in American education is *problem-based learning* (PBL). This approach is a distinct departure from the didactic lectures and reading often used in our schools and universities. There are three critical features to the PBL approach (Stepien, Gallagher & Workman, 1993):

- *Learning is initiated with an ill-structured problem.* (This is one in which the solution to the problem is *not* embedded in the statement of the problem itself as would be true in an in arithmetic reasoning problem)
- *The student is made a stakeholder in the situation* (may be asked to play the role of a legislator or scientist forced to make a decision about the situation)
- *The instructor plays the role of metacognitive coach* (helps guide the student in their search for important knowledge by helping with the organization of information).

This PBL approach appears to heighten student interest and motivation without losing content mastery for the subject matter (Gallagher & Stepien, 1996). Since students of varying ability levels can respond to the problems at various intellectual levels this PBL approach allows for challenge for gifted students without losing the interest of other students.

The Renzulli Enrichment Triad is another instructional device designed to help students become more productive thinkers. The three stage approach is to: (1) introduce students to major topics, (2) provide students with methods and skills for finding answers, and (3) take a real problem and conduct an independent investigation using skills learned in step 2. Table 2 gives an example of this approach.

Baum, Renzulli & Hebert (1995) report positive gains in attitude, achievement tests for a group of seventeen underachievers (grades 3–9) who were educated through the Enrichment Triad approach. But how will we know whether our differentiated environments, content, or strategies have achieved their goals?

Accountability

One of the most persistent reform movements in education in the U.S. has been that of accountability. A central question in this endeavor is, "Do the schools achieve the instructional goals that they set for themselves?" Since there is strong suspicion in the minds of many that the schools do not achieve instructional goals for gifted, a complex system of testing is often mandated to determine the achievement of students in various content fields (mathematics, history, etc.). Aside from the unwarranted assumption that student performance is the exclusive responsibility of the school, instead of the psycho-social-cultural and economic worlds in which they exist (Gallagher, 1998; Evans, 1999) such broad scale attempts at evaluation must also assume common goals across schools and districts. Once one goes beyond simple skills such as reading and arithmetic, that assumption of common instructional goals and experiences also suffers.

Does this general education accountability movement aid educators of gifted students in their own attempt to determine if their special services or programs are having a positive effect on the students? Not really! There are problems in trying to apply general goals to gifted education which, after all, is supposed to have been differentiated from the average instruction. Gallagher (1998) notes several problems in evaluation:

- *Ceiling Effects.* Standard measures for average students will find the gifted student performing at the top of the test and we will only know that the gifted student has mastered the material on that test, we will not be testing their depth or breadth of knowledge.
- *Content Emphasis.* Part of differentiated content for gifted means that they may be studying Ancient History of Egypt or Space Exploration. If these topics are not on the standard examination, how will we know how the student has performed?
- *Content Complexity.* Most of the standard tests focus on factual knowledge or simple association and will not test the student on elaboration of thinking or depth of understanding of the subject again underestimating the gifted student's mastery of the topic.

One key to the proper assessment of programs for gifted students is to clearly state the specific instructional goals and a description of the educational procedures by which these goals are to be met (Callahan & Caldwell, 1995; Borland, 1997). There has been an attempt to employ *authentic assessment* (using measures that link to the instructional goals such as writing an essay for a measure of writing skills) and *performance assessment* (if the student produces a product such as a scientific experiment as part of his assignment then that product is the proper basis for careful evaluation). Such efforts then become qualitative (the use of human judgment in evaluation) in

Table 2. The Renzulli Enrichment Triad: How Did Our City or Town Begin?.

Step	Teacher Activity	Student Activity
I	Exploratory activities that introduce students to a major topic. Field trips, special speakers, etc., help to stir students' interest	Students are asked to consider why their town started and developed here. They may read old newspapers and documents to stir their curiosity.
II	Students are introduced to methods by which they can find answer to these questions.	Students learn how to find historical documents, how to use school and community libraries, how to deal with conflicting information.
III	Students take a real problem and conduct an independent investigation using some of the skills they learned in Step II.	They can use diaries and reports to study the role played by the initial settlers in establishing the community. They can study the role played by trade via the roads and rivers that shape community growth.

SOURCE: Renzulli, J. (Ed.). (1986). *Systems and models for developing programs for the gifted and talented.* Mansfield Center, CN: Creative Learning Press.

form but the qualitative methods approach is becoming increasingly well accepted (Wiggins, 1989; Nielson & Buchanan, 1991).

While well crafted evaluations for programs for gifted students are rare at the present time, they are not non-existent. Evaluations of new curricula in science and language arts for gifted students have shown meaningful gains in cognitive growth through a mix of quantitative and qualitative measures used (Hughes, Van Tassel-Baska, Boyce & Quek, 1994). Evaluation is a growth industry in American Education and will be much in evidence during the next decade.

2000 and Beyond

What lies in the immediate future for gifted education in the U.S.? Prediction is always a dangerous business since there are often *wild cards* that appear (events that cannot be predicted in advance that change the landscape) but some trends seem evident.

Intelligence. We have had two decades of exciting work on delineating what we mean by high intelligence and we would seem to be only in the midst of that work now. We should count on more interesting findings about the link of emotions and intelligence or what controls the *executive function* by which we make decisions, etc. and above all what we can do as educators to enhance its development.

Young Gifted. Most of the educational efforts over the past few decades for gifted students have started in the age range of 8–12, after the child has fairly well established patterns. Our realization of the flexibility of intellectual growth enhances the need to look at the development of these children earlier. Education is also in a slow and painful, but inevitable, process of extending its influence and responsibility to four-year-olds and perhaps to go to three year olds as well. They will be responsible now for young gifted students and will have to learn new approaches appropriate to that age level.

Culturally Different. We have spent a decade of attention on how to find the 'hidden' gifted students from culturally different environments but relatively little time in trying to enhance the intellectual development of these bright students once we have found them. This trend should be reversed soon. A much greater effort should be made in documenting attempts to upgrade the abilities of culturally different gifted, one of the major untapped resources of our society.

Differentiated Curriculum. There has been a realization that moving bright students from one environment to another is a relatively useless endeavor unless, at the same time, we modify the basic curriculum that they receive. Much effort has already been started on blending sophisticated content with instructional strate-

gies designed to help the students master complex ideas and systems. We should see a blossoming forth of a wide sample of model curricula in many content areas that will be of substantial aid to the teacher of gifted students.

Gifted Women. Ever since there has been a significant effort to attend to the special needs of gifted girls we have seen an upturn in their performance. Since this slice of the population turns out to be slightly more than 50% of the entire population, there would seem to be much to be gained socially as well as individually to continue our efforts to help girls "be the best that they can be" in the educational setting and later in the workplace and family.

Support Services. Just as gifted education has been influenced by more general trends in education so should they be influenced by a coming change in the organization of special education in the schools. There is a strong trend to bring a wide variety of auxiliary services into the schools (social work, mental health, special education, health, nutrition, etc.). It seems likely that the support services (including the psychologists, counselors and special teachers serving gifted students) will probably be brought under one department of special services within the educational complex of the school district. Whether this will be a favorable move for gifted students remains to be seen.

Public Policy and Excellence. As noted in this report, the United States has been wavering back and forth between two important educational goals, *equity* and *excellence*. The last two decades has seen the pendulum swing strongly in the direction of *equity* as we have become aware of the many problems facing young children growing up in poverty and social disorganization and most of our initiatives have been designed to use the educational system to counterbalance some of the negative social forces. The new millennium is likely to see a swing of that pendulum back to more emphasis on *excellence* as we become more and more embedded in the information age. It becomes more and more important for bright students to be using their abilities to stimulate this new era with economic and political productivity. But this will not happen if the current 'laissez faire' approach to gifted students continues into the next decade.

References

Baum, S. Renzulli, J. & Herbert, T. (1995). Reversing underachievement: Creative productivity as a systematic intervention. *Roeper Review*, **39**, 224–235.

Benbow, C. & Lubinski, D. (Eds.). (1996). *Intellectual talent: psychometric and social issues*. Baltimore, MD: Johns Hopkins University Press.

Borland, J. (1997). Evaluating gifted programs. In: N. Colangelo & G. Davis (Eds.). *Handbook of Gifted Education* (2nd ed.). (pp. 253–266). Boston: Allyn & Bacon.

Borland, J. & Wright, L. (1994). Identifying young, potentially gifted economically disadvantaged students. *Gifted Child Quarterly,* **38,** 164–171.

Burack, J., Hodapp, R. & Zigler, E. (Eds.). (1998). *Handbook of mental retardation and development.* Cambridge, England: Cambridge University Press.

Butler-Por (1987). *Underachievers in school: issues and Intervention.* New York: Wiley.

Callahan, C. & Caldwell, M. (1995). *A practitioner's guide to evaluating programs for the gifted.* Washington, DC: National Association for Gifted Children.

Colangelo, N., Kerr, B., Christensen, D. & Maxey, J. (1993). A comparison of gifted underachievers and gifted high achievers. *Gifted Child Quarterly,* **37,** 155–160.

Colangelo, N. & Davis, G. (Eds.). (1991, 1997). *Handbook of Gifted Education.* Boston: Allyn & Bacon.

Coleman, M. (1992). A comparison of how gifted LD and average LD boys cope with school frustration. *Journal for the Education of the Gifted,* **15,** 239–265.

Csikszentmihaley, M., Rathunde, K., Whalen, S. (1993). *Talented teenagers: the roots of success and failure.* Cambridge, UK: Cambridge Univ. Press.

Csikszentmihalyi, M. (1996). *Creativity.* New York, Harper Collins.

Csikszentmihalyi, M. & Getzels, J. W. (1990). *Flow: the psychology of optimal experience.* New York: Harper Perennial.

Dabrowski, K. (1967). *Personality-shaping through positive disintegration.* Boston: Little Brown

Davis, G. (1997). Identifying creative students and measuring creativity. In: N. Colangelo & G. Davis, *Handbook of Gifted Education* (2nd ed.) (pp. 269–281). Boston: Allyn & Bacon.

deBono, E. (1986). *Six Thinking Hats.* New York: Viking.

Delcourt, M., Loyd, B., Cornell, D. & Goldberg, M. (1994). *Evaluation of the Effects of Programming Arrangements on Student Learning Outcomes.* Charlottesville, VA: University of Virginia, The National Research Center on the Gifted and Talented.

Dornbush, S., Glasgow, K. & Lin, I. (1996). The social structure of schooling. *Annual Review of Psychology,* **47,** 401–429.

Feldman, D., Csikszentmihalyi, M. & Gardner, H. (Eds.). (1994). *Changing the world: a framework for the study of creativity.* Westport, CT: Praeger.

Evans, R. (1999). The great accountability fallacy: commentary: *Education Week,* February 3, 1999.

Flynn, J. (1999) Searching for justice: the discovery of IQ gains over time. *American Psychologist,* **54** (1), 5–20.

Ford. D. (1993). An investigation of the paradox of underachievement among gifted Black students. *Roeper Review,* **16,** 78–84.

Frasier, M. & Garcia, J. (1995). *Education and their implications for identifying gifted minority students.* Storrs, CT: The National Research Center on the Gifted and Talented.

Gagné, F. (1999). My convictions about the nature of abilities, gifts and talents. *Journal for the Education of the Gifted,* **22** (2), 109–136.

Gallagher, J. (1998a). Education, alone, is a week treatment. *Education Week,* July 8, 42–43.

Gallagher, J. (1998b). Accountability for gifted students. *Phi. Delta Kappan,* 739–742.

Gallagher, J. (2000). Unthinkable thoughts. *Gifted Child Quarterly,* **4** (1), 5–12.

Gallagher, J. & Gallagher, S. (1994). *Teaching the gifted child* (4th ed.). Boston: Allyn and Bacon.

Gallagher, J., Harradine, C. & Coleman, M. (1997). Challenge or boredom: gifted students. *Roeper Review,* **19** (3), 132–136.

Gallagher, S. & Stepien, W. (1996). Content acquisition in problem-based learning: depth versus breadth in American studies. *Journal for the Education of the Gifted,* **19** (3), 257–275.

Gentry, M. & Owen, S. (1999). An investigation of the effects of total school flexible cluster grouping on identification achievement and classroom practices. *Gifted Child Quarterly,* **43** (4), 224–243.

Holliday, G., Koller, J. & Thomas, C. (1999). Post-high school outcomes of high IQ adults with learning disabilities. *Journal for the Education of the Gifted,* **22** (3), 266–281.

Hughes, C., Van Tassel-Baska, J., Boyce, L. & Quek, C. (1994). *The William & Mary pilot of change and the search for meaning: A national language arts unit for high ability students in grades 4–6.* Williamsburg, VA: Center for Gifted Education, College of William and Mary.

Kerr, B. (1997). Developing talents in girls and young women. In: N. Colangelo & G. Davis (Eds.). *handbook of Gifted Education.* (pp. 483–497). Needham Height, MA: Allyn & Bacon.

Kirk, S., Gallagher, J. & Anastasiow, N. (2000). *Educating Exceptional Children* (9th ed.). Boston: Houghton Mifflin.

Kirschenbaum, R., Armstrong, D. & Landrum, M. (1999). Resource consultation model in gifted education to support talent development in today's inclusive schools. *Gifted Child Quarterly,* **43** (1), 39–47.

Koloff, P. (1997). Special residential high schools. In: N. Colangelo & G. Davis (Eds.), *Handbook of Gifted Education* (2nd ed.) (pp. 198–206). Boston: Allyn & Bacon.

Kulik, J. & Kulik, C. (1991). Ability grouping and gifted students. In: N. Colangelo and G. Davis (Eds.), *Handbook of Gifted Education.* (pp. 178–196). Boston: Allyn & Bacon.

Kurcinka, M. (1991). *Raising your spirited child: a guide for parents whose child is more intense, sensitive, perceptive, persistent, energetic.* New York Harper Collins.

Lubinski, D. & Benbow, C. (1994). The study of mathematical precocious youth (SMPY): the first three decades of a planned fifty-year longitudinal study of intellectual talent. In: R. Subotnik & K. Arnold (Eds.), *Beyond Terman: Longitudinal Studies in Contemporary Gifted Education* (pp. 255–281). Norwood, NJ: Ablex

Margolin, L. (1996). A pedagogy of privilege. *Journal for the Education of the Gifted,* **19** (2), 164–180.

Mayseless, O. (1993). Gifted adolescents and intimacy in close same-sex relationships. *Journal of Youth and Adolescence,* **22,** 135–146.

Mills, C. & Tissot, S. (1995). Identifying academic potential in student from underrepresented populations: is using the Raven Progressive Matrices a good idea? *Gifted Child Quarterly,* **32,** 347–352.

Morelock, M. & Feldman, D. (1997). High IQ children, extreme precocity and savant syndrome. In: N. Colangelo & G. Davis (Eds.), *Handbook of gifted education.* (2nd ed.) (pp. 382–397). Boston: Allyn & Bacon.

Newell, A. (1990). *Theories of cognition.* Cambridge, MA: Harvard University Press.

Nielson, E. & Buchanan, N. (1991). Evaluating gifted programs with locally constructed instruments. In: N. Buchanan & J. Feldhusen (Eds.), *Conducting Research and Evaluation in Gifted Education* (pp. 275–310) New York: Teachers College Press.

Noble, K. & Smyth, R. (1995). Keeping their talents alive: young women's assessment of radical acceleration. *Roeper Review*, **18**, 49–55.

Noble, K., Subotnik, R. & Arnold, K. (1999). To thine own self be true: a new model of female talent development. *Gifted Child Quarterly*, **43** (3), 140–149.

Oakes, J. (1985). *Keeping track.* New Haven, CT: Yale University Press.

Perkins, D. & Solomon, G. (1989) Are cognitive skills context-bound? *Educational Researcher*, **18**, 14–25.

Perkins, D. (1995). *Outsmarting IQ: The Emerging Science of Learnable Intelligence.* New York: The Free Press.

Plomin, R. (1997). Genetics and intelligence. In: N. Colangelo & G. Davis (Eds.), *Handbook of Gifted Education* (pp. 67–74). Boston: Allyn & Bacon.

Ramos-Ford, V. & Gardner, H. (1997). Giftedness from a multiple intelligences perspective. In: N. Colangelo & G. Davis (Eds.), *Handbook of Gifted Education* (2nd ed.) (pp. 54–74). Boston: Allyn and Bacon.

Reis, S. & Callahan, C. (1989). Gifted females: they've come a long way—or have they? *Journal for the Education of the Gifted*, **12**, 99–117.

Reis, S., Neu, T. & McGuire, J. (1995). *Talents in two places: case studies of high ability students with learning disabilities who have achieved.* Storrs, CT: The National Research Center on the Gifted and Talented.

Renzulli, J. (Ed.). (1986). *Systems and models for developing programs for the gifted and talented.* Mansfield Center, CN: Creative Learning Press.

Rimm, S. (1997). Underachievement syndrome: a national epidemic. In: N. Colangelo & G. Davis (Eds.), *Handbook of Gifted Education* (2nd ed.) (pp. 416–434). Boston: Allyn & Bacon.

Robinson, A. & Clinkenbeard, P. (1998). Giftedness: an exceptionality examined. *Annual Review of Psychology*, **49**, 117–139.

Ross P. (Ed.). (1993). *Natural Excellence.* Washington DC: U.S. Department of Education.

Sapon-Shevin, M. (1996). Beyond gifted Education: building a shared agenda for school reform. *Journal for the Education of the Gifted* **19**, 194–214.

Schopler, E., Mesibov, G. & Kunce, L. (Eds.). (1998). *Asperger Syndrome or high functioning autism.* New York: Plenum Press.

Shore, B. & Delcourt, M. (1996). Effective curricular and program practices in gifted education and the interface with general education. *Journal for the Education of the Gifted*, **20**, 138–54.

Silverman, L. (1994). The moral sensitivity of gifted children and the evolution of society. *Roeper Review*, **17**, 110–116.

Silverman, L. (1997). Family counseling with the gifted. In: N. Colangelo & G. Davis (Eds.), *Handbook of Gifted Education* (2nd ed.) (pp. 382–397).. Boston: Allyn & Bacon.

Solloway, F. (1996). *Born to rebel.* New York: Pantheon Books.

Stainback, S. & Stainback, W. (1996). *Inclusion: a guide for educators.* Baltimore, MD: Paul H. Brookes.

Stepien, W., Gallagher, S. A. & Workman, D. (1993). Problem-based learning for traditional and interdisciplinary classrooms. *Journal for the Education of the Gifted*, **16** (4), 5–17.

Sternberg, R. (1986). A triarchic theory of intellectual giftedness. In: Sternberg, R. & Davidson, J. (Eds.). *Conceptions of Giftedness* (pp. 223–243). New York: Cambridge University Press.

Swiatek, M. (1995). An empirical investigation of the social coping strategies used by gifted adolescents. *Gifted Child Quarterly*, **39**, 154–160.

Terman, L. & Oden, M. H. (1947). *The gifted child grows up: twenty-five years follow-up of a superior group* (Vol. 4). Stanford, CA: Stanford University Press.

The Third International Mathematics and Science Study (TIMSS). (1997). Washington, DC: U.S. Department of Education.

Torrance, E. (1964). *Rewarding creative behavior.* Englewood Cliffs, NJ: Prentice Hall.

VanTassel-Baska, J. (1997). Contributions to gifted education of the Talent Search concept. In: C. Benbow & D. Lubinski (Eds.), *Psychometric and Social Issues Concerning Intellect and Talent* (pp. 236–245). Baltimore, MD: Johns Hopkins Univ. Press.

VanTassel-Baska, J. (1997). What matters in curriculum for gifted learners: reflections on theory, research, and practice. In: N. Colangelo & G. Davis (Eds.), *Handbook of Gifted Education* (2nd ed.) (pp. 126–135). Boston: Allyn & Bacon.

Wiggins, G. (1989). A true test: toward more authentic and equitable assessment. *Phi Delta Kappan*, **70**, 703–713.

A Study of Education for High Ability Students in Canada: Policy, Programs and Student Needs

Janice A. Leroux

University of Ottawa, Canada

Introduction

Elementary and secondary education in Canada is currently in a state of major change. Since education in Canada is the direct responsibility of each province and territory, the changes are a reflection of the broader state of the economy and governments' emphasis on economic restraint. Ten years ago there were numerous provincially supported programs for gifted students across all grade levels. The promotion of excellence was a public goal and a wide range of services for these students, along with other exceptional students with special needs, was the prevailing pattern.

With the election of a number of more conservative provincial governments across the country, support for education (and concurrently, health care) began to wane. Economic and technological advancement became the current goals espoused by educational reformers in the provinces (Government of Canada, 1991a, b). A national trend towards inclusion and 'least restrictive environments' became the philosophical argument driving educational dollars.

Providing a range of services, although still on the books in many provincial regulations, was less in evidence as high ability students spent more time in regular classrooms. Educational innovations questioned the value of pull-out programs and stressed the notion of inclusion for all (Lipsky & Gartner, 1989; Pearpoint & Forest, 1992).

While student abilities in the classroom were showing greater variability, teacher competence and commitment to such diversity was declining (Lovitt, 1993). Yet at the same time, within faculties of education, teachers who were being exposed to the needs of special education students, received few, if any, training modules focusing on gifted and talented students. Teacher education and the need for advanced qualifications in education of gifted students became less popular in the faculties of education; this trend appeared all across the country.

It should be stated that education is mandatory for all children up to the age of 16, with exceptions made with parental consent at the age of 14. All schooling is free up to the age of 18. Only at post-secondary levels does the federal government in Ottawa provide financial support to subsidize education. Thus, each province is free to plan policy, implement change and provide support services for its student population. The results are quite varied from region to region in this land that is geographically the largest country in the world.

In order to determine the current provisions for gifted students, in 1998 a survey was carried out across Canada asking school boards, provincial Ministries of Education and Faculties of Education. Because of the vast numbers of school boards in each province, a purposive sample reaching a cross-section of geographic areas was surveyed. Seventy-eight responses were received from nine provinces and the North West Territories. Fifteen responses came from faculties of education in eight provinces. Ministries of Education from the North West Territories and three provinces were also received. The total of survey returns represents a 42% response rate. The following chapter reports on the conclusions of the survey.

Ministries of Education

All the provinces and territories stated that there were provincial mandates to provide equal educational opportunities for all students. Policy statements ranged from Individual Education Plans (IEP) required for all identified exceptional students (New Brunswick, Yukon, and Ontario) to program policies developed as required at the local board level (Manitoba). There appeared to be consensus about the right of all students to an appropriate educational program, however, the form for establishing and conducting such programs was not legislated uniformly across the country.

Across Canada, 'Gifted' for the purposes of legislation, is usually defined as intellectually ability. Hence, there is little attempt to accommodate special abilities such as creativity, kinesthetic or psycho-social talents. Any legislated services are based on demonstrated

695

intellectual aptitudes generally identified at the local school board level by a variety of assessment measures such as the Canadian Cognitive Abilities Tests, the Revised Wechsler Intelligence Scales, teacher, and in some cases, parent nominations.

As a result of varying educational policies, program offerings for high ability students differed from province to province. Some Ministries reported no separate legislation for programs for these students beyond what was available in the regular classrooms (New Brunswick, Yukon, North West Territories). Another Ministry, similar to Alberta and Ontario, reported legislation under special education services that allowed for mandatory education plans, yearly reviews of programs and services, or district supervisors responsible for enrichment services (New Brunswick). In general, it appeared that while equity in education is publicly legislated policy across Canada, programs and services for gifted children most frequently are subsumed in the regular classroom because there is no consistent legal mandate or support for a wide range of other services.

When asked what research was available to determine the effectiveness of such policies, all the respondents reported there were no provincial research or evaluation programs in place. Manitoba and the North West Territories, similar to Ontario, indicated that local educational districts provided various school-based measures such as parent conferencing, or curriculum review studies. Thus, if local school boards have advocates for high ability students within the educational and parental community, then indications are that some educational provisions for a range of services and accountability might occur. This issue is developed further in the survey results from individual school boards.

Funding for establishing and conducting programs for gifted students is generally not allocated from provincial Ministries of Education. All four provinces and territories reported that block grants were provided to school districts which in turn were responsible for education of all students. Any transportation, supervision, special programs or personnel for services for identified gifted students have to be budgeted by the local education authorities in each school district. All respondents reported that such funding was optional for high ability students in their areas.

When asked about pre-service education requirements and professional development training available for teachers of gifted students, all respondents said there was no specific training mandatory for teachers in their provinces or territories. Courses were optional, general special education upgrading qualifications were encouraged, and district level professional in-service was available. In all reports, however, nothing was mandated regarding qualifications for teachers responsible for gifted and talented students in the provinces. School systems were under no obligation to hire teachers with special educational certification for teaching gifted students.

When asked to outline future plans for educational provisions for gifted and talented students in their province or territories, respondents described: (1) the development of curriculum documents (Manitoba); (2) the development of teacher training modules, with an emphasis on Renzulli's Enrichment Triad Model (New Brunswick, Yukon); (3) the organization of in-service workshops and professional development for teachers (North West Territories). The latter are also current initiatives underway in Alberta and Ontario.

In summary, while Ministries of Education are the ultimate authority responsible for education of high ability students, much of the actual planning and implementation is the responsibility of local educational authorities. Ministries do not set down qualifications for teachers of the gifted, nor mandate levels of training. Little specific funding is set aside for projects or transportation related to gifted students, teacher in-service development is optional, and curriculum documents are left to the discretion of local school boards. In addition, research and evaluation relating to gifted and talented students is rare at the provincial level.

Local School Boards

Nine provinces and one Territory making a total of 78 districts, responded to the survey. Questions ranged from identification and placement criteria, types of programs offered for gifted students, criteria for teacher selection, to community collaboration. The following provides a synopsis of the data both from demographic and open-ended responses received.

The majority of the school boards which responded indicated that there were special provisions made for gifted and talented students in their jurisdiction. About 80% of the school districts reported providing various types of school programs at various times during the school day. These programs included services such as:

- enrichment classrooms, full or part-time
- independent study programs
- advanced placement (for secondary schools)
- subject acceleration
- pull-out programs
- mentorships with community and university personnel
- regular classroom with enrichment
- different programs within regular classroom

Grade acceleration of high ability students was available in over 70% of the school districts, although a number of respondents wrote that this was only offered 'occasionally' or 'rarely'.

Community activities such as Science fairs, Music festivals and mini-course enrichment programs at a local university were considered in some provinces as part of the school program and hence, reported as types of programs offered. Ontario, Alberta, British Columbia, and Saskatchewan indicated that for advanced secondary school students who were motivated, the International Baccalaureate Program was also provided as a means to accelerate gifted students. This allowed them to gain academic credits for university while still in their secondary school environment.

It appeared that most school boards supported the concept that opportunities for enriched learning should be available to children who demonstrated intellectual ability and motivation to learn. The form that programs took was extremely varied, with most activities taking place at the school level in a home classroom among groups of normative ability children.

It should also be noted that prior to 1993 in larger provinces such as Ontario, Saskatchewan, Alberta and to some extent British Columbia, homogeneous classes of gifted and talented children were funded in many urban centres. Sometimes these classes were designated 'pilot classes', but they continued to operate for over 15 years because parents and teachers supported this placement option.

Over the last seven years, however, the rapid growth of special needs, at-risk students, and increased societal demands for fiscal accountability across all sectors of society in Canada, has led to extensive restructuring of school programs. Educational, health and welfare resources were reduced at all levels, both provincially and federally. In the midst of such changes, the wide range of program services for high ability children began to shrink. Successful congregated classes for these students were among the first programs to be cancelled. It remains for a coalition of new advocates among parents and teachers to ensure access to congregated ability classes for our current and future gifted students.

Part of the reason there seems to be no consistent policy for gifted and talented children across each province is that individual school boards have autonomy to plan and implement school programs according to perceived local needs. When asked if the local school authority had a written policy for the education of its high ability students, over 75% of the school districts reported no such policy was in place. Ontario, the province with the highest number of districts with school provisions for gifted students (90%), reported the highest percentage of districts with specific policies in place (67%). Considering that Ontario has had legislation since 1980 recognizing the legal rights of education once defined as 'Exceptional-Gifted', it is somewhat surprising that a third of individual school boards report having no policies to accommodate gifted students.

Jurisdiction of programs for gifted students appeared to be divided between special education and curriculum departments of the local school authorities. Responses indicated that 63% of school boards assigned responsibility for programs to the special education department, while 36% reported giving jurisdiction to the curriculum department. There seemed to be no relationship between whether there was a policy in place for education of gifted students and the assignment of program jurisdiction.

A variety of other administrative patterns were also listed under the category, 'Other'. These included assigning administration of programs to such sections as individual school staff and support services, and student services. Once again such data highlight the autonomy of the majority of local school boards across the country.

When asked to rank the importance of identification procedures used in the individual school boards, the three most important measures were: (1) teacher selection, (2) individual psychological tests, and (3) group academic tests. Since most of the school boards currently use a variety of procedures for screening and identification of gifted students, it is not surprising that parent nominations and peer nominations also ranked closely with group academic tests in the majority of school boards. However, it should be noted that the latter two measures, when used in local school systems, do not carry the same weight or ranking strength as either individual or group psychological assessments.

Once identified, programs for high ability students begin in late primary grades (ages 9–10) across the country. In very rare cases, such as the Halton Board of Education, and the former Ottawa School Board in Ontario, younger students may have access to congregated enrichment classes. Generally, regular classroom teachers are expected the know the needs of their students and provide enrichment to complement the regular curricula.

Only Ministries of Education (Special Education branches) in Alberta and Ontario have issued curriculum Guidelines with special resources materials to help teachers work with gifted students in these provinces. The majority of school boards reported that they had developed their own support documents and resource materials for these students. It can be assumed that in the 22% of school districts that did not report having their own curriculum materials for gifted students, that the teachers carried a great deal of responsibility for locating and implementing special programs.

Before the new wave of economic utility hit Canadian educational systems, there were often district wide consultants available to offer resources support for teachers in the classroom. These were teachers trained in special educational needs of high ability students and available to a family of schools for help with enrichment materials, teaching strategies, reading resources, etc. At the current time, these consultants are generally teaching in regular classes once again, or have been reassigned to work with teachers who have special education students with disabilities and limited learning needs. Only 20% of the school boards reported still staffing a consultant responsible for programs and teacher support for gifted students.

On the other hand, over 60% of the school boards reported using a special assignment teacher in their schools as the personal responsible for the programs and teaching of identified gifted students. This person might be a school librarian, a principal (head teacher) who taught part-time, a special education teacher, or other classroom teachers designated responsible for gifted students part of the week. The program delivery and personnel assigned to serve gifted students in extremely varied across the provinces.

Likewise, transportation, a major concern in school districts that are as large as some European countries, is a concern and source of restriction for accessing special programs for gifted students. Less than 40% of the reporting school boards provided transportation to any special classes for these students. Several of the large urban districts (less than 5%) reported issuing bus passes for students in special programs.

If a school was noted for its special programs, but was too far away, then generally the onus was on parents to provide transportation. That assumes that an open boundary policy allowed this choice to parents and their children. Not all provinces or districts allow cross boundary school placements without a fee, and there have been cases of litigation where parents of gifted children have sued (and won), the right to have a child placed in another jurisdiction at no cost and with transportation provided (Leroux, 1990).

The result of transportation restrictions means that if a local school does not provide special programs for gifted children or adolescents (and this often applies to middle and secondary school students), then the students cannot access a wide range of services and must accept the limited programs available in their community school. Because transportation costs are a large portion of school board budgets, individual schools are expected to serve a growing range of special education needs. More and more we see gifted students integrated into regular classrooms in their local schools, served by hard-working teachers, but with educational provisions that are often sporadic and underfunded.

The issue of funding for programs and services for gifted students is difficult to determine. Not all school boards reported information as to costs per pupil or for program development. Because responsibility for these students comes under a variety of categories such as special education, transportation, curriculum departments and staffing, to name a few, a clear picture does not emerge across the provinces. Where congregated classes are reported for gifted learners, class size ranges between 18 to 25 pupils. In general, it appears that school districts are extremely creative in attempting to access resources, modify curricula, fund field studies to extend the curriculum, promote cooperative programs, and use community mentors and volunteer experts, in efforts to provide unique educational experiences at reduced costs for their high ability students. It remains for future research to assess the results of these endeavours.

All of the school boards reported providing in-service workshops for teachers on issues relating to education of gifted students. In addition, over 90% indicated that they provided opportunities for teachers to go to conferences and workshops to up-grade their knowledge of the field. Several districts also noted that workshops and in-service activities were organized when teachers requested such support. No information was gathered, however, as to the frequency of these training provisions or to the number of teachers who actually attended. If teachers are primarily responsible for adapting and providing programs for individual students, then training assistance is a key component for success. Once again there is great variability in the degree of expertise available for and utilized by, educators responsible for serving high ability students in Canada.

It was interesting to note that when asked to rank criteria important in the selection of teachers for gifted and talented students, the following ranking represents the collective response:

- commitment   1
- creativity   2
- flexibility   3
- personality/human relations   4
- intellectual ability   5
- academic qualifications   6

Although the above ranking reports the average of responses, it should be noted that many school boards ranked many of the traits of similar importance. It was evident that many of the districts wanted personnel with a combination of the listed qualities. Since the survey was completed by one person in a district, however, rankings might have been arbitrarily assigned. Caution should be taken when interpreting this item.

When comparing this ranking with that of a similar survey done by the Canadian Educational Association in 1980 (Borthwick, Dow, Levesque & Banks, 1980), the item 'flexibility' was then ranked number one, and 'intellectual ability' was ranked number 4. This may indicate a small shift in importance over the years, but generally the criteria have remained quite constant in the expectations of educators responsible for the selection of teachers for high ability students.

The last item on the survey asked how the school boards evaluated programs for gifted students in their systems. The following processes and frequency of responses were indicated:

- system review by the school board   50%
- informal evaluation   50%

- teacher assessments   40%
- products produced by students   35%
- student achievement   40%
- parent assessment   10%
- no evaluation reported   50%

Figures total more than 100% because most respondents described a variety of evaluation processes at work. In addition to the above items, one school board in New Brunswick indicated that guidance personnel were also part of their evaluation process.

Where boards did not have a system-wide process for program evaluation, individual schools and teachers were responsible for evaluation procedures. This 'informal evaluation' was for the purpose of adjusting programs and rationalizing services at the school level. This seems to indicate that many school systems still leave the responsibility to individual teachers to meet the needs of high ability students.

Also, the fact that school boards in seven provinces reported having no evaluation procedures for their gifted programs raises a number of questions. Where is the accountability? Who is ultimately responsible for program quality, review and revision? Why are there no consistent policies and procedures from the central school administrations and provincial Ministries of Education?.

Provincial Special Education departments in Ontario and Alberta require that yearly reviews of individual pupil placements and educational programs be conducted and reported by school boards for students identified as gifted. These proceedings, involving parents along with school personnel, are costly and time-consuming. Could these be reasons why more provinces have not mandated formal evaluation for services for gifted students?

It should be noted that currently Alberta is opening educational options to allow school boards to establish charter schools. In 1998 in Calgary, parents supported the opening of three charter schools to serve gifted children in the city. This was a direct result of a public review of the city's board of education. Evaluation results indicated that special needs programming for gifted students was insufficient and ineffective in the regular school system. Armed with such information, parents took the opportunity to hold administrators accountable.

Educational administrators have an important role to play in ensuring the quality of education for all students, but without systematic program evaluation, the onus falls back to the classroom teacher again to provide assessment and evaluation to justify continuation of services for high ability students. It is evident there is a great need for consistent program evaluation across the country and accountability to parents may be the powerful force needed for renewal.

In summary, school boards in the provinces have the major responsibility for educational policies, programs and services for gifted learners in their jurisdictions. There is great diversity in educational provisions across Canada. Local budgets drive the availability of services and resources: the increase of inclusive, least-restrictive environments for education fuels the placement for gifted students. Regular classroom teachers are most likely to be the primary educators responsible for program development and implementation. Educational qualifications for teaching gifted learners is the decision of individual school boards.

Though a wide range of educational programs and services are available in most school boards, only Ontario has legislation which mandates such services for gifted students. School boards are creative and diverse in their development of programs, utilization of community resources and provision of services. The percentage of gifted students served varies from 1 to 10% across the country, with urban centres reporting the largest numbers of students.

Program evaluation and yearly reviews are, for the most part, sporadic, and dependent on the policies of local school authorities. In some urban centres, notably Ottawa, Calgary, and Toronto, parents have been valuable advocates for enhanced program services to meet the needs of gifted children. The current movement towards economic utility has spilled over to education and school boards are reorganizing and amalgamating many services for these students. There is a need for strong advocacy for gifted students lest they be lost in the turmoil of current educational reforms in Canada. As well, research is needed to show the complex links among teacher effectiveness, programs and groupings, and special populations of students in order to inform any proposed educational changes.

Faculties of Education

The responsibility for teacher preparation lies with faculties of education in the ten provinces of Canada. In general, knowledge and training in the area of high ability learning is incorporated into the broad field of special education for new teachers. This section will summarize responses to the survey which were received from 15 faculties in eight provinces.

The questionnaire asked if programs in teacher education were offered at the faculty of education. Responses indicated that 86% of the institutions did not have specific courses available for the beginning teachers. The fact that some faculties provide a minor focus on gifted and talented students is laudable, but this situation is not extensive. Universities in British Columbia, Alberta, Ontario and Quebec described some credit courses available, but these are elective courses which means that not all undergraduate teachers would receive this training.

Descriptions of program offerings ranged from one module in special education studies, to an optional three-credit course concentrating on the gifted learner.

When studying about special needs students, the beginning teachers would be encouraged to explore the range of abilities of various populations of exceptional children or complete a case study of a special child during the practicum weeks. However, because this remains an option, there is little reason to suggest that all beginning teachers learn about gifted students. Such options are a prevailing pattern in undergraduate programs at the faculties of education.

When asked if a graduate program in special education was offered, 60% of the faculties responded 'Yes'. However, majoring in education of gifted learners is rarely available because no institution reported a wide range of graduate courses focusing on this concentration. Of the total responses to the survey, 54% indicated there were no actual credit courses available in this field. Individual faculties, such as those in McGill University, Bishops University, and Universities of British Columbia, Alberta, Brandon, Ottawa, and Toronto, offer a graduate course in education of gifted and talented students. Since one or two courses do not constitute a total program, it appears that at the graduate level in Canada there is little opportunity to specialize in the education of high ability learners.

On the other hand, many faculties of education reported providing seminars and professional development training for teachers in programs for gifted learners or who want to upgrade additional qualifications in this area. Over 66% of institutions indicated that they offered activities such as conferences, summer institutes, invited speakers, seminars or credit qualifications for teaching certification in this specialty. Again, these programs were generally subsumed under special education diplomas and often reflect the direction of provincial policies in education. (It should be noted here that many of the provinces tie teacher salary levels to the number of advanced qualifications completed by a teacher, and special education is one of the general categories for this training opportunity.)

In summary, there is little education offered to prepare undergraduate teachers in the developmental and educational needs of high ability learners in Canada. What courses are available are optional, not required courses. This phenomenon seems to reflect society's reduced commitment to the needs of gifted learners and the pervasive philosophy of inclusive education for all. Some faculties of education offer excellent courses at the graduate level for educators interested in the field, however, no institution provides a major specialty.

Many institutions, as a response to demonstrated need from the educational community, provide advanced qualifications in education of gifted and talented learners. If a community of educators requests such professional upgrading, or the faculty of education provides leadership in developing such programs, then it appears educators avail themselves of the opportunities. However, since no numbers of actual teachers enrolled in such advanced programs were solicited, it remains for further research to determine the interest and viability of professional development courses across the country.

It should be noted that two programs provide outstanding examples of professional development for teachers in Canada. McGill University in Montreal continues to offer its summer credit program for teachers of the gifted. A variety of teaching models are explored and applied with classes of gifted children for a number of weeks, exemplary role models teach and supervise instruction, and graduate credits are provided for teacher participants.

At the University of Calgary, along with teacher in-service sessions, a school outreach program is in place which teams master teachers with local classroom teachers in an on-site learning experience. Here university personnel go into the local schools when requested to train teachers, inform parents, and help administrators upgrade their skills in supporting the high ability learners in their communities.

It is evident from both these examples that universities can provide leading roles in the education of teachers of gifted and talented students. It remains for other universities to consider undertaking similar systematic programs based on the examples of these institutions.

Conclusions

Education of gifted and talented children in Canada has seen major changes in the last ten years, Systemic reforms based on economic utility have led to cutbacks in personnel, and the number of students served in withdrawal or homogeneous classes for high ability students.

Provincial and Territorial Ministries of Education have individual approaches to serving the needs of gifted students. There is no clear evidence that indicates support for this group of students other than the mandates designed for special education policies. With the exception of Alberta, Ontario and New Brunswick, no provinces reported specific legislation beyond that of equal education opportunities for all students. When funding is available to local school boards, it comes under the aegis of special education and hence, allocation is left to the decisions of local authorities. Transportation of students, funding for programs, identification procedures, teacher certification, and program evaluation are the responsibilities of school boards which in turn receive little if any, specific funding from the Ministries of Education for gifted students. Ministries of Education need to evaluate their policies regarding education of gifted students and consider assuming a higher priority in this area.

Within the school boards on the other hand, school administrators are being asked to ensure that enrichment programs are available to a wider student population. Regular classroom teachers are being required to provide more enrichment strategies within heterogeneous groups of students. There is little indication that vast numbers of school administrators or their teachers are receiving systematic professional development for the special needs of students identified as gifted learners. Hence, one questions that educational interventions are being consistently provided for these learners.

Although many school boards report providing funding for field studies, community mentorship programs and enrichment activities outside of the school building, limited numbers of gifted students are reported in homogeneous groupings, in withdrawal programs, and working with a resource teacher in middle and secondary schools. Because more and more classroom teachers are being asked to provide enrichment activities in the regular classroom, the onus is on the teacher to be flexible, creative and committed to serving the needs of the high ability students in her/his care. Opportunities for advanced placement and acceleration are reported available in many jurisdictions, however, these strategies are used with only a small number of students, particularly in the higher grades.

A number of school boards reported developing curricula and program guidelines for their teachers. Other jurisdictions reported supplying resource personnel with varying expertise to help classroom teachers with the needs of gifted students. Other areas reported excellent cooperation among teachers, parents and community members in providing transportation, expertise, and collaboration in enrichment activities for their gifted students.

Here is where the true creativity of our teachers stands out. There are islands of exciting programs being developed and implemented through the efforts of outstanding teachers across the country. Whether it is working with seniors to develop historical narratives, organizing community relief drives, communicating with international peers using computer interface systems, or planning experiments for use in our space programs, high ability students are being challenged by teachers who are committed to excellence for their students.

These are the same educators who take personal time to attend seminars and take additional qualifications courses to upgrade their teaching abilities. Because they care about gifted learners, they continue to learn how better to provide educational opportunities for them. Likewise school administrators, intent on ensuring the best learning for all, provide resources and support for their school faculty so that gifted students receive equal education just as do other exceptional students. Where gifted education thrives in Canada, we see a harmonious orchestration among administrators, teachers and parents. Greater sharing of these educational innovations should occur and celebration of exemplary school programs needs greater attention across the country.

There is another section in this orchestra and that is the faculties of education. Clearly there is a need for a systematic appraisal of provisions to address the needs of gifted learners in both undergraduate and graduate programs. Universities could provide more required courses in the developmental and educational needs of high ability children so that all teachers would be introduced to this important population early in their careers. They could take leadership in research studies to evaluate policies and programs across the country. Studies such as those from the Ontario Institute for Studies in Education at the University of Toronto provide good examples of relevant research which can inform classroom practice. If faculties of education wish to remain players in the educational composition, they need to provide trained teachers for our gifted learners.

The results of this survey, though limited in numbers, represent a cross-section of Canada's educational communities. The very fact that so many educators took time to complete the questionnaires is a testament to their commitment to gifted education. During this period of change in educational circles, there is also an opportunity for renewal. Concerned educators and parents can take advantage of such reformations to advocate for educational commitment to gifted learners. There is expertise in Canada: it is imperative that we capitalize on this and make the educational welfare of our gifted students once again a high priority everywhere.

Summary

The changing face of education in Canada has an impact on education of high ability students. In order to ascertain the current state of policies and programs for gifted students, a survey of provincial Ministries of Education, Faculties of Education and selected school boards across the country was undertaken. Results indicate that policies of inclusion are popular, diversity of program services is the norm, and regular classroom teachers, with some support from local school resource teams, carry the major responsibility for these students. Also, there is no consistent undergraduate or graduate credit training for teachers at faculties of education in the provinces. Advocacy by concerned educators and parents is an on-going need.

Acknowledgments

Grateful appreciation is acknowledged for research support from the University of Ottawa and in particular, Maria Cuffaro, M. A., for her invaluable research assistance with the data collection and analysis. Lastly, my heartfelt thank you to all the educators at all levels across the country who took time to complete the questionnaires.

References

Borthwick, B., Dow, I., Levesque, D. & Banks, R. (1980). *The gifted and talented students in Canada: results of a CEA survey*. Toronto: Canadian Educational Association.

Government of Canada. (1991a). *Learning well . . . Living well*. Ottawa: Minister of Supply and Services.

Government of Canada. (1991b). *Prosperity through competitiveness*. Ottawa: Minister of Supply and Services.

Leroux, Janice A. (1990). Are the rights of young gifted children really protected under the law? *Canadian Journal of Education*. **6** (1), 72–78.

Lipsky, D. K. & Gartner, A. (Eds.). (1989). *Beyond separate education: quality education for all*. Baltimore: Paul H. Brookes Publishing Co.

Lovitt, T. C. (1993). Recurring issues in special and general education. In: J. I. Goodlad & T. C. Lovitt (Eds.), *Integrating General and Special Education* (pp. 49–71). New York: Merrill.

Pearpoint, J. & Forest, M. (1992). Foreword. In: S. Stainback & W. Stainback (Eds.), *Curriculum Considerations in Inclusive Classrooms: Facilitating Learning for all Students* (pp. xv-xviii). Baltimore: Paul H. Brookes Publishing Co.

Gifted Education in Europe: Programs, Practices, and Current Research

Roland S. Persson,[1] Helga Joswig[2] and Laszlo Balogh[3]

[1]*Jönköping University, Jönköping, Sweden*
[2]*Rostock University, Rostock, Germany*
[3]*Kossuth Lajos University, Debrecen, Hungary*

Introduction

The fact that some individuals are capable of more than most others has been recognized in Europe for a considerable period of time. The philosophers of Ancient Greece, for example, bringing into the world the foundations of Science and Democracy, were generally respected, if not revered, by their disciples and the contemporary society (Grinder, 1985). They believed they were divinely inspired by *daemons*—tutelary spirits guiding and teaching them. Later, in the Roman Empire, the same notion was taken over, and such divine inspiration then became known as *genius* (or in Moslem mythology: a *jinni*); a word more familiar to modern proponents of Gifted Education.

There have been many illustrious Europeans following in the footsteps of, for example, Plato and Aristotle in terms of impacting with their brilliance, creativity and audacity—for good and for worse—the way Western history has unfolded, or at the very least, they have in their own unique way changed our understanding of history and society. Isaac Newton, Galileo Galilei, Vasco da Gama, Marco Polo, Martin Luther, Leonardo da Vinci, Karl Marx, Raol Wallenberg, Carl Friedrich Gauss, Wolfgang Amadeus Mozart, François Champollion, Carl von Linné, Sigmund Freud, Albert Einstein, Niccolò Macchiavelli, Marie Curie, Pablo Picasso, Lev Vygotsky, Niels Bohr, Ingmar Bergman and Winston Churchill are only a few from all over Europe, whose skills and insights have inspired—and occasionally threatened—the society of their time.

The fact that high ability potentially may pose a threat is to some extent a European dilemma too, which needs to be considered in outlining and understanding the status of Gifted Education and related research and educational policies in Europe. While there are numerous exceptionally gifted and talented individuals in European history, most of them did not experience the reverence and respect awarded many a philosopher and thinker of Ancient Greece. Talent used for the well-being of a nation is a tremendous asset, but talent as a potential foe may well be a formidable threat, as European history shows well (cf. Persson, 1999).

The gifted European has been treated somewhat ambivalently over the years. There is in much of Europe a continuous, and mainly political, struggle between the ideals of elitism and egalitarianism, that has resolved very differently in the various nations of Europe. While differences between individuals in cognitive ability was regarded as something natural to the citizens of ancient Athens (Durazzo, 1997), such differences have become increasingly more contentious, and politically sensitive, since the time of Enlightenment in 18th century Europe. Above all, the legacy of Communist and Socialist tenets—as they pertain to education and individual differences—largely eliminated the significance of innate and genetically determined factors. In the former USSR, for example, and in countries then under Soviet influence, psychological tests were forbidden. They were regarded as instruments of class discrimination (Mönks, Katzko & van Boxtel, 1992; Urban & Sekowski, 1993 Heller & Hany, 1994).

Dorothée Wilms (1986), for example, Minister of Education and Science in the former Federal Republic of Germany, pointed out that, "detecting talent is not a selection process in the sense of social selection . . . Support of talent is an educational process and no social mechanism. Excellence is in principle independent of social rank" (p. 19). It is obvious that Wilms is endeavoring to negotiate a balance between opposing values in order to make Gifted Education politically possible. The ambivalence towards Gifted Education still looms large in Post-Communist Europe. On the one side, it seems, stand critics who equal talent

703

selection to creating a socially privileged societal stratum potentially beyond democratic principles. On the other side stand proponents arguing the democratic rights of all children to develop to their full potential. While both factions appeal to the importance of upholding democracy and the equal rights of citizens secured by it, they nevertheless base their arguments on very different aspects and understandings of the notion of equality. One faction argues the right to be *different* for the common good, in which case special provision for talent as well as for the learning disabled is seen as a necessity. The other faction, however, rather argues the right to be *similar*—also for the common good. But the result is that special provision for the highly able becomes controversial, since such children are often regarded as privileged by their ability. Hence, by a flawed conclusion—as is obvious by the research on genetic influence on cognitive ability presented elsewhere in this Handbook—they are often not regarded as in need of any special support. The aim for a proponent of similarity must therefore be to bring children of low ability up to a higher level, thereby offering them their democratic right to become 'more similar' (cf. Husén, 1979).

The Purpose and Structure of this Chapter

For the sake of convenience, but also to some extent based on European nations' understanding and implementation of Gifted Education, Europe may be divided largely into three areas: Northern Europe (including Scandinavia, The British Isles, The Baltic States, and Russia), Middle, Western and Southern Europe, and Eastern Europe (including The Balkans and The Ukraine). The outline of Gifted Education in 25 of the larger European nations follows this tripartite division, the purpose of which is to convey an overview of the status of Gifted Education in Europe in terms of existing policies, provision, relevant practices and specific research. The chapter is concluded with a summary, which also endeavors to answer the question whether there exists a typically European approach to high ability and its education and research.

The authors aimed at covering all European countries and not restrict the survey to the 15 nations of the European Union. Geographical Europe consists of some 40 nations inhabited by approximately 700 million people. For this purpose a standardized questionnaire was devised, which asked questions concerning the political recognition of high ability in the national school system and legislation, the history of Gifted Education in each country, the nature of specific provision offered for the highly able, and questions on the existence of special training for teachers. Also, in the event that a particular country has no legislation or any special provision, national representatives were asked to explain why this is not the case, to elaborate on their understanding of Gifted Education, and speculate whether it might eventually

develop. Furthermore, each respondent was specifically asked to name indigenous research on high ability and Gifted Education, if available, since the existence of such in any nation is a fair indicator of status and will be invaluable in focusing cultural differences in educational practice and policy.

The questionnaire was sent to Embassies, Ministries of Education and Science or bodies and agencies sorting under these, and to national experts known by the authors. Considering the often contentious nature of Gifted Education in Europe we wished to provide national authorities with an opportunity to respond and outline their reasons for acting in favor of the highly able in their school systems or, as in some cases, the reason behind their lack of action and interest. In particular, the national correspondents of the European Council for High Ability were reliable sources of current information—scientific when available, and their own personal experience and observations when required. The contribution of personal experiences is a particular concern to the outline of Gifted Education in Eastern Europe, The Balkans, and The Ukraine, since the amount of published material so far is limited—and more so in some countries than in others.

Information was received pertaining to 25 European countries, thus excluding 15. The reason for exclusion was generally due to lack of response from authorities and/or individuals contacted. However, the number of respondents is more than sufficient, and representative, in order to convey the status and nature of Gifted Education and relevant research in Europe reliably.

Eastern Europe and the Balkans

Bulgaria, Croatia, Hungary, Poland, Romania, Slovakia, Slovenia, and the Ukraine generally recognize high ability through legislation—most commonly through the national Act of Education—which regulates how the issue of high ability is dealt with. The manner in which Gifted Education is managed, however, is broad. Some prescribe provision for talents as obligatory for state organizations (e.g. ministries, public schools and so on). Others only mention it for calling the issue to attention. Note that such legislation has mainly developed in the 1990s, reflecting directly the programs of political change of the Post-Communist Era. However, the fact that educational efforts now are made, and even thrive, can be traced back to the Communist period in each individual country. In spite of the imposed egalitarian dogma, most of these countries already had a tradition of nurturing high ability in special classes, workshops and courses, predating Communism. These efforts were often tolerated and endorsed by the authorities, but on the condition that talents were made 'ambassadors' to promote the ideals of the Communist State internationally. Such provision, however, was not always pursued with the welfare of the talented individuals in mind, which has been very painfully revealed, particularly in the former German

Democratic Republic, where researchers have now been given access to previously classified archives (e.g. Berendonck, 1993). The pursuits focused during this era were traditionally Sports, the Arts, and the Sciences. The knowledge and experience acquired regarding the nurture of talent, albeit under dubious political circumstances, were influential far beyond Eastern Europe. Particularly models pertaining to talent detection and development in Sports (Régnier, Salmela & Russell, 1993), Musical Performance (Neuhaus, 1969), and Music Education (Kabalevsky, 1988) became internationally recognized and often adopted or adapted elsewhere.

With a new political agenda, founded on democracy, this long-standing experience of nurturing talent facilitates the further development of Gifted Education in this area of Europe. Significant developments have already been made during the Post Communist Era. Also, with the continued development of specialized educational practices, indigenous research has followed and improved, since research and findings are now communicated freely across national borders. For example, researchers and educators in several Eastern European countries have joined the European Council for High Ability (ECHA) as well as the World Council for Gifted and Talented Children (WCGTC). They participate actively for the exchange of experience and the dissemination of research findings.

However, the current political agenda is recent and the aftermath of the previous era are still obvious. One of the greatest obstacles for further improvement and development is limited financial means, which is reflected in, for example, the current lack of systematic special training for teachers in Gifted Education, as well as the lack of scope in these efforts. In spite of difficulties progress has been quite remarkable in a relatively short period of time. Given that this trend is maintained, it is only a matter of time before the current differences in research quality, effectiveness and educational provision for the highly able between Eastern and Western Europe are leveled out.

Bulgaria

Article no. 43 of the Bulgarian Code of Education states the responsibility of the Ministry of Education and Science to identify high ability and provide for its subsequent educational provision. However, during the 1990s significant changes have taken place, and the State is no longer sole provider. There have emerged several foundations, non-state organizations and a number of new programs, all of which have been organized to cater to the highly able. The St. Cyril and St. Methodius International Foundation, for example, plays a significant and active role in educating young talented individuals by means of vocational training and career planning. The *Reference Book of Non-Governmental Organizations (1997)*, published by the Bulgarian Foundations and Associations Union, lists more than 20 non-governmental organizations, that have the nurturing of talent as well as specific teacher and parental training as their expressed aim.

Of particular interest are the Bulgarian special schools devoted to the Arts, Mathematics, the Sciences and Languages. Some of these were already founded in the 1960s, but with a changed political climate, they have increased in numbers. Such schools tend to provide a greater number of study hours and a greater variety in the subject on which such a school specializes. Regular schools also make provision for gifted students. They offer special classes in Mathematics, Informatics, the Sciences and Languages. In addition, after the seventh school year, children also have a choice of certain optional subjects extending and enriching the general curriculum, thus matching a child's specific interests more effectively. Bulgarian educational expertise is aware of the need to provide a rich and stimulating learning environment for optimal development, which is indeed reflected in a number of recent studies (Jakova, 1993; Stoycheva, 1994, 1996; Trifonova, 1994; Stoyanova, 1995; Kaftandjieva, 1996; Milanova-Kamburova, 1996).

Competitions are regularly held for able children on local, regional, national, and international levels. Winning such competitions generally entails gaining admission to universities or to prestigious Arts or Sports Academies. Award winners of international competitions, on the other hand, receive more public attention and are often recognized by the media. In addition to available competitions for students there is the St. Cyril and St. Methodius International Foundation Awards for teachers of Mathematics, Chemistry, and Biology, in recognition of their outstanding contribution to the identification and encouragement of young talents.

In the wake of Post-Communist societal changes regular schools, as a whole, are now more alert to talented students, and the development towards even greater awareness seems to continue. There are several programs worked out by individual teachers, or teams of teachers, who often establish educational centers with a specialized focus. This is done to some extent in response to a series of international seminars organized by the Ministry of Education and Science between 1979 and 1989, on modern trends in Education—with special focus on giftedness and creativity. This effort alone has stimulated more than 30 schools to launch special programs for educating gifted students. Furthermore, between 1982 and 1987 Edward De Bono's methods for teaching thinking skills were adapted in many schools under the auspices of the Ministry of Education and Science.

In addition, there are currently a variety of extracurricular programs for highly able children available, such as clubs, summer camps, summer schools, festivals, shows, and exhibitions. There is no official mentorship program for teachers focusing on the highly able, but teachers tend to cooperate in matters of Gifted Education. Basic teacher training, as yet, does not include a systematic preparation for the nurturing of special talent, though student teachers are given some relevant, albeit basic, information. Note, however, that there exist graduate programs at universities focusing on high ability (cf. Jakova, 1996).

Croatia

High ability is also recognized by the Croatian Government, but action for special provision is taken mainly at preschool and primary school levels. A national preschool program with such a focus is endorsed. Gifted Education at primary level is regulated by the Code of Practice for Gifted Students from 1991, and addresses issues like different domains of giftedness, identification methods, programs for enhancing and nurturing giftedness, as well as evaluation models (Koren, 1994).

The current state of Gifted Education in Croatia has, to some extent, roots in former Yugoslavia, at which time most of the activities were coordinated and supervised by the Ministry of Employment and its agencies (i.e. State Employment Offices and Vocational Services). The most important fields of study and learning in which development of Gifted Educational practice is currently taking place are the Fine Arts, Mathematics, the Sciences, and Sports (Arambasic, 1996; Vizek-Vidovic, 1996). Able students in Croatia attend extracurricular classes—within the regular school setting—that are specially organized in these fields of interest. This type of provision exists in several different varieties (Sekulic-Majurec, 1993, 1996; Vizek & Vlahovic, 1993; Vlahovic-Stetic, 1993; Cvetkovic, George, Sekulic-Majavec et al., 1996; Kolesaric & Koren, 1996).

There are several special summer schools and courses for talented students in Mathematics, the Fine Arts, Literature, and Astronomy, lasting from one to two weeks at a time. Also, a mentorship system exists at secondary school level, in which some teachers from the general school staff are specially appointed as 'mentors' to especially prepare able students for national and international competitions. Competitions, as a means of Gifted Education, are highly valued particularly in primary schools. They are organized in all subjects and are highly respected, since a victory will mean receiving scholarships for grammar schools or universities. There is no special program in Croatia for training teachers specifically in Gifted Education, however, but the topic is sometimes addressed by further training programs for teachers.

While high ability is indeed recognized by the Croatian Government, there is currently a lack of funding, administrative support, and adequately specialized teacher training. There are some private initiatives promoting Gifted Education such as, for example, Smarties—a parental association organizing special preschool activities for fostering children's creativity and ability. For talented individuals in the Performing Arts there exist drama centers for youth. And in 1998 the Croatian Psychological Association uniquely established a special division within its framework dedicated to the promotion of giftedness.

Hungary

Hungary also recognizes the necessity of nurturing talent and emphasizes its significance for the future wellbeing of the nation by establishing a legislation to govern the educational provision regarding the highly able. The Public Education Act of 1993, The Higher Education Act of 1995, and Regulations for the Development of Public Education of 1996, are all examples of current—and recent—legislation securing the continued development of Gifted Education in Hungary. Consequently, with such legislative support, Gifted Education is making significant strides forward in the new political climate.

To cater to, and provide for, talents, however, is not new in Hungarian educational history. To some extent, this continued development under new circumstances is based on already existing traditions. Interest in nurturing talent specifically was evident already in the early years of the twentieth century. Teachers, as well as researchers, have paid particular attention to the development of giftedness—although not always explicitly—since the time of World War II.

In addition to the Hungarian system of public schools, private schools and schools maintained by churches and foundations, have also participated in developing practices.

The current frameworks for nurturing talent were established already prior to 1980, and entail special groups, workshops and special classes. These three are common in schools at both primary and secondary levels. The most successful special fields include the Arts, Mathematics, the Sciences, and Sports (Laczó, 1993; Majoros, 1993; Harsányi, 1996; Kárpáti, 1996; Süle, 1996; Pásku, Kerekes & Fekete, 1997). Since the late 1980s, however, so-called complex programs have been implemented. These aim not only to develop skills and abilities, but also take into account the personal background of the individual student (Balogh & Nagy, 1991, 1995; Czeizel, 1995; Oppelt, 1995; Balla, Hanoi & Molnárné, 1996; Balogh, Dávid, Nagy & Tóth, 1997). Basic Art schools (teaching Fine Arts, Music, Dance and so on) traditionally hold a special position in Hungarian Gifted Education. Talent in Sports is provided for by special classes in primary schools and in region-based Sports Schools. High ability is also advanced by the existence of Special Colleges.

The tutorial system is increasingly becoming an established form of supporting gifted students. Professors and outstanding researchers allow secondary students to participate in research work. This type of activity is organized by the larger universities.

Competitions are also a means for promoting talent in Hungary. The school system has promoted local, regional and national competitions for a long period of time. One of the most significant is the National Academic Competition of Secondary Schools, where winners are awarded admission to the universities. The number of competitions for primary schools is increasing.

Higher education is currently experiencing a return to Faculty Colleges, which are tertiary institutions gathering the most able among students in certain academic fields; providing them with special programs to facilitate their continued development and training (Pásku & Imre, 1993).

The dynamic development of Gifted Education in Hungary in the last decade is reflected in indigenous research work too. Specific research is increasingly being published all over the country at universities, colleges and research institutions and is being disseminated at international conferences. Such publications on Gifted Education, specific to Hungary, are helpful points of reference for a continued effective advancement (Gefferth & Herskovits, 1991; Herskovits & Gyarmathy, 1995; Bóta, 1996; Dávid, Pásku & Vitális, 1996).

The success so far has been accompanied by an increasing focus on high ability in in-service training for teachers, the culmination of which prompted the Kossuth Lajos University at Debrecen to launch a Teacher of Gifted Education Program in 1997/1998. This program is a four-semester, graduate, in-service training, comprising more than 600 hours worth of study. It is based on the syllabus required by the University of Nijmegen, The Netherlands, to gain The European Advanced Diploma in Education the Gifted (often termed the ECHA Diploma). Note that special training of parents is also becoming increasingly common in Hungary (cf. Györik, 1993; Herskovits, 1994; Varga & Gyarmathy, 1996; Dávid & Balogh, 1997).

In addition to the public and general system of education, other public institutions also take part in providing for talent students (i.e. centers for culture, community centers and so on). There are organizations that endorse the promotion of talent, fully, or as part of their agenda. A few of the more important ones are The Hungarian Association for High Ability, The Corporation for Public Academic Activities, The Bolyai Association, MENSA, The Hungarian Association for Professional Training, and so on. The number of foundations fostering the development of giftedness is increasing and the establishing of regional Giftedness Centers is in progress. These are intended to facilitate

identification procedures and host special educational programs. The first center has already opened in Budapest.

Poland

The first move towards legislating Gifted Education in Poland took place in 1991. That is not to say, however, that Gifted Education was non-existent prior to this. Some educational provision was available, but it was neither comprehensive nor particularly well organized. Presently, enforced by the new legislation, Gifted Education is recognized by the Polish authorities, and all three educational levels are considered: primary, secondary, and tertiary.

In programs aimed at developing appropriate educational practices, talent in Music, Mathematics, and Visual Talent are given priority (Kepinska-Welbel, 1991; Limont, 1993a, b; Klimas-Kuchtowa, 1996; Manturzewska, 1996). In these fields, specific provision begins already in primary school. Children have, for example, special Ballet and Sports classes. In secondary education Music, Ballet, the Fine Arts, the Social Sciences, and Mathematics become focus. Highly able students tend to have special classes after school, but The Polish Children Fund (PCF) also organizes special summer schools and courses. However, these usually focus on the Arts. PCF additionally provides special meetings and workshops on Modern Languages, History, Astronomy, Physics, and so on, in which talented students are given the opportunity to meet with adult experts in their fields of interest. PCF is also in charge of organizing mentorship programs.

The current system is appealing to children, and is effective. Students in primary schools may exchange one or two classes, whereas students in secondary schools, simultaneously with their studies in school, may also attend university courses.

Competitions are numerous and varied in Poland. For example, there are 24 competitions available in the Arts, Astronomy, Biology, Chemistry, Philosophy, Physics, Geography, History, Information Technology, Modern Languages (e.g. English, Beylo Russian, French, Latin, German, Russian, and Polish), Mathematics, Ecology, Economy, Technology, Polish Studies, Universal History, Law, Agriculture, and Nursing. Some of these contests are held both for primary and secondary school children. Others are organized for secondary schools only. The winners of primary school competitions will gain free admission to secondary schools, and the winners of secondary school competitions obtain several priorities when applying to study at university.

There is no special training of Polish teachers in Gifted Education, however, but high ability is often discussed as part of Further Education Programs. There are programs for parents, some of which aim at shaping parents' attitudes to better be able to provide a creativity-inducing environment (Ledzinska, 1993,

1996; Mendecka, 1996a; Niebrzydowski & Poraj, 1996; Swietochowski & Poraj, 1996). Note that research in the field of giftedness and Gifted Education is considered important in Poland, and creativity appears to be a field of study of particular interest (Strelau, 1992; Limont, 1995; Sekowski, 1995; Mendecka, 1996b; Necka, 1996; Niebrzydowski & Poraj, 1996).

Romania

Romania follows the legislative trend of the rest of former Communist Europe. The latest Act of Education was passed in 1995, and endorses the recognition of gifted education at primary, secondary, and university level. It includes aspects such as educational acceleration, creating special classes, identification criteria, provision requirements, the special conditions for admission to universities, and special resources needed for Gifted Education. Note that the Romanian authorities are still at the early stages of implementing this new legislation. One problem currently posing an obstacle to making it effective is organizational in nature; there is lacking a department within the Ministry of Education that could specifically coordinate and organize all matters pertaining to Gifted Education.

Similar to Hungary, the traditions of nurturing talent predate Communism. Educational legislation, from as early as 1904 and 1939, recognizes giftedness as a special and separate issue. Following World War II, however, the sole provision for highly able children was made in placing them in special classes.

Current strategy gives priority to special provision in The Arts (Music and Folklore), Sports, Informatics, Mathematics, Physics, and Biology. New areas for provision are Communication Skills, Leadership, and Creativity. There are special schools for the Arts and Sports in most larger cities, and there exists an abundance of secondary schools with special provision in Informatics, Modern Languages, Mathematics, Physics, and the Sciences. Regular schools do not often consider differentiation; a common problem is the difficulty for teachers to actually apply educational theory in practice. Note that training programs in Pedagogy and Psychology were banned at universities from 1970 to 1990.

Summer courses are common in Romania; not only as staged by the Ministry of Education, but also by private organizations. One of these organizations: RO-Talent, has a leading position; but there is also the Henry Coanda Foundation and others. Competitions regularly take place for pupils from their fifth school year and on, in their local school, at regional, and national levels. Particularly able children also participate in international contests. The awards are attractive: winners are awarded with foreign travel and admission to universities. Unfortunately, these competitions often lack an appropriate pedagogical basis, but the need to carry out such activities on a sound basis is increasingly understood and considered (Cretu, 1992, 1993, 1996; Lazar, 1993).

Student teachers currently obtain some introductory courses in Psychology and Pedagogy relevant to high ability provision. Iasi University, for example, offers a course in Gifted Education, which is obligatory for student teachers. But whether Gifted Education is part of teachers' further education training or not, depends on the policies of each of the Local Education Authorities, which are mainly organized by the 'Casa Corpului Didactic'.

In sum, while high ability is certainly a focus of Romanian educational policy, its implementation is often missing. The main reasons for this are lack of professional knowledge and information, no priority in funding, a shortage of expertise in Gifted Education, and the need for specific administration of these matters at ministry level. There are some new developments in Romania in spite of difficulties, however, which bode well for the future. There is indigenous research in progress (e.g. at the Institute of Educational Sciences at Bucharest and its centers throughout Romania), and an additional program for teachers in Gifted Education at Iasi University is being launched. Also, there have been several doctoral dissertations produced focusing different aspects of Gifted Education from the universities at Iasi, Bucharest, and Cluj-Napoca.

Slovakia

Legislation relevant to Gifted Education in Slovakia is derived from the legislation of former Czechoslovakia. Beyond general guidelines, however, suggestions as how to operationalize these guidelines are presently absent. Provision for talented children is available but mainly at primary and secondary school levels.

Preceding contemporary Gifted Education in Slovakia were so-called People's Art Schools, which were established following World War II. During the 1960s a system of special classes with enrichment in a few particular subjects—still in operation—was conceived, and implemented. However, after 1989, and the break with Communism, the system has also been implemented in private schools. Special teaching in Music, Dance, Visual Art, Literature, and Drama is available in so-called Basic Art Schools, which are spread throughout the country; about 10% of all children attend these schools. In addition, there are several Music Conservatoires and Industrial Art Schools at secondary level available. Children with special abilities in Sports attend Sports Schools (Dockal, 1996; Kovac, 1996). Children highly able in Mathematics may attend special Mathematics classes from their fifth school year, or may proceed to study at independent secondary schools specializing in Mathematics (Laznibatova, 1993). Earlier, special classes in Foreign Languages were available from the fourth school year, but with the changed political climate, every school now teaches Foreign Languages. Particularly able children may therefore start learning new languages as early as from their first year of school (Farkasova, 1993).

Since 1989 a system of eight-year grammar schools has been established (succeeding the fourth year of primary school) for highly able children, where teachers provide advanced training aiming at high-level proficiency in every taught subject (Dockal, Laznibatova & Kovac, 1992; Dockal & Kovac, 1993; Farkasova, 1993; Kovac & Matejik, 1993; Lazibatova, 1993; Ostatnikova & Dohnanyiova, 1996). There are no special programs for gifted children in regular schools, however, but grade skipping is practiced promoting particularly able children ahead of normal grade placement, or allowing promotion in particular subjects only.

Several competitions are organized for able pupils on regional, national, and international levels in the Arts and Sports. Teachers have the opportunity to attend further education with a focus on Gifted Education, but there is currently no special teacher training available.

In addition to schools, different professional associations take a special interest in able children. One of the most active is the Slovak Association of Mathematicians and Physicists, which organizes competitions and summer camps; such camps are also similarly organized by the different Arts Associations (i.e. Fine Arts and Music). The Czecho-Slovakian Association for Gifted Children was founded in 1991, and its members are actively involved in specific research and/ or education. The Association arranges conferences, seminars for parents and teachers, and summer camps focussing on creativity involving both the able children and their parents.

Slovenia

The needs of gifted children in Slovenia attract much less attention than do the needs of children with learning disabilities. State institutions are less active in Gifted Education than they are in traditional Special Education, which tend to emphasize various disabilities. The result of current priorities is that financial means to pursue Gifted Education are relatively scarce; however, private initiatives have increased substantially. Private resources are available and private institutions make available scholarships, talent education, and schools for the highly able.

Interest in safeguarding the continued development of gifted individuals, however—just as in most other Eastern European and Balkan nations—has a long-standing tradition. Special provision for talent has been given attention for almost two centuries. However, to better and more effectively operationalize and implement legislation relevant to Gifted Education, systematic efforts are now being made to establish a Ministry of School and Sports which, when fully functioning, will also coordinate provision for the highly able in Slovenia.

Gifted Education in Slovenia emphasizes the need for differentiated curricula and training programs in the different domains of talent: Sports, Music, Arts, Drama, and so on (Ferbezer, 1993, 1996; Makarovic, 1993, 1996; David, 1997).

Post-Communist Slovenia is developing towards educational pluralism, which entails the possibility of choice at each educational level, and in each direction, as well as emphasizing the autonomy of the individual students. Schools are being made more independent from government authorities; also, international comparisons with other educational systems are made, and competitions are held; furthermore, it is now possible to study abroad, and the funding of scholarships for gifted children has increased. Teacher training has become more focused on Gifted Education; while teachers tend to learn the theory, however, they often fail to apply theory in practice.

In spite of some success in developing Gifted Education, full recognition is still wanting. To some extent, this may be explained by prejudices (in terms of the legacy of previous political ideologies), financial difficulties, lack of theoretical knowledge and expertise, insufficient teacher training, lack of scholarships, insufficient recognition of initiatives, and the fact that there is currently no national organization with an expressed interest in the promotion and education of highly able children. However, in the past ten years there have been several conferences addressing Gifted Education and related issues, for example, Gifted Children in the Educational Process at Maribor in 1987, Extra-Curricular Activities in Primary Schools, also at Maribor in 1988, and Gifted Children: Their Situation, Problems and Possibilities of Development at Novo Mesto in 1994.

A need for developing Gifted Education more comprehensively has been brought to the attention of the Slovenian authorities several times. It is important for future and continued development, however, that it be sensitive to Slovenian culture and traditions.

The Ukraine

Provision for the highly able in the Ukraine has been an issue in Education since the 1930s; it largely failed to develop due to the Communist egalitarian ideology. Specific research into the field began in the 1950s, but governmental recognition of such research did not arrive until the 1980s. Research in the field is currently being pursued at, for example, L'viv State University, where a project has been launched focusing on the development of intellectual and social talent in non-traditional educational programs, as well as on the impact of family education on high ability. Of interest

to this research project are also methods of identification (Partyko, 1996).

The change in policy and attitude to Gifted Education in Post-Communist Romania is largely due to a
political desire to make the Ukraine comparable with
most other nations in the world. It is now 'fashionable'
to address issues of Gifted Education, and recognizing
young talents is believed to improve the Ukraine's
standing in the global community.

The Ukrainian Government's actions officially demonstrate that Gifted Education is indeed recognized in
primary education and in secondary education; Gifted
Education pertaining to higher education, however, is
currently not similarly recognized. Priority is given to
Sports, Music, Visual Arts, Dance, the Sciences and
Verbal Skills (i.e. talented poets and writers). There is
some attention given to provision for talented individuals in Business and Management, which is a field of
talent gaining increasingly more interest.

Educational provision is mainly focussing the development of cognitive abilities (Kholodnaja, 1993;
Borodchuk, 1996; Partyko, 1996; Shavinina, 1996a),
but the need for addressing creativity is also recognized
and promoted by some researchers (Shavinina,
1996b).

In the Ukraine there are special schools and studios
for Music, Painting, and Dance; children talented in the
Sciences are provided for in grammar schools. Able
students in the mixed-ability environment of regular
schools are occasionally given individual assignments.
This type of provision is fickle, however, and always
dependent on teachers' sole initiatives, and is therefore
not common. There exists an experimental program
called The Development of Creative Giftedness and
summer schools organized by the so-called Minor
Academy of the Sciences (Kokotko, 1996). Other
available programs involve particularly gifted youth
from the rural areas of the Ukraine; competitions are
held in each of the prioritized subjects at school level,
regional level, and national level; the national level
competition is usually followed by an International
Olympiad. Note that Ukrainian teachers generally are
trained on how best to prepare able children and
adolescents to take part in the competitions on offer;
one means of preparation is to gather candidates in
special classes.

In addition to provision within the national school
system, there are several specially appointed Counselors in the Ukraine, acting as moral support to the
gifted and the talented, are available for consultations;
such consultations are always free of charge.

Western, Middle and Southern Europe

State ordinances and laws guiding education in Austria,
Belgium, France, Germany, Italy, Portugal, Switzerland, Spain, and The Netherlands tend to be *inclusive*.
That is, ideally all education should be integrated
within the regular school system (cf. Daunt, 1995;

Mitchell, 1995), as recommended by the UNESCO
World Conference on Special Needs Education: Access
and Quality, at Salamanca, Spain, in 1994. Legislation,
therefore, often contains general formulations on the
rights of all children to receive education and states
that such education should adequately support, and
meet, their abilities and interests; such formulations
also imply the possibility of making provision for
highly able students. In some legislation there is also
emphasis on accelerated and enrichment programs,
which could be interpreted as recognizing Gifted
Education. However, the acceleration possibilities
formulated in these legislative frameworks refer mainly
to early admission to schools, grade skipping or
moving through grades at a faster rate than normal.
Acceleration activities such as these are not accepted
practice in all Western, Middle, and Southern European
nations; prejudice and bureaucracy often complicate
their implementation.

With regard to enrichment as a means of providing
for highly able students, European school documentation contains, and suggests, different forms of
expanding and deepening knowledge and skills, which
is also relevant to Gifted Education, and therefore
supportive of gifted children. Such suggestions are
based on various forms of 'inner' and 'outer' differentiation.

Inner differentiation is carried out by conveying
different and additional subject matter to the existing
curriculum, as well as employing special teaching
methods—especially project-oriented and multi-sub-
ject based learning. Allowing students to develop at
their own pace, and making use of their own unique
knowledge and experience, obtained prior to entering a
certain school year, are important aspects of this
strategy (Hany, 1995). However, taking such individual
components into consideration in groups, where students have been matched with regard to their level of
achievement, has proven to be somewhat problematic.
There is no single specific method available for
teaching the highly able. The countries discussed here
are all working at different levels of intensity in
establishing curricula for specifically supporting and
promoting gifted students (Pagnin, 1994; Hany, 1995;
Heller, 1995, 1996; Cardoso, Coutinho & Fernandes,
1997; Martins, 1997; Joswig, 1998; Touron, Iriarte,
Reparaz & Peralta, 1998).

The possibilities of *outer differentiation* are also
discussed in European educational documentation.
General guidelines do exist, which may be operationalized and allow further development; these refer
to differentiation in school systems and to special
courses in different types of schools and institutions.

Austria

The Austrian school system is supportive of the needs
of the gifted in that it differentiates between general
and professional education, between electives, and

optional and elective subjects. It also allows flexibility in core and extension subjects, and accepts autonomy by means of, for example, allowing schools to choose a certain profile and become a 'special school'. Paragraph no. 17 of the Austrian 'Schulunterrichtsgesetzt' (Code of School Teaching) requires that every pupil be instructed according to his or her natural ability as far as this is possible; in this legislation there are defined possibilities for acceleration and enrichment.

The Austrian school system commences with four years of primary education ('Grundschule'). It then divides into two tracks, namely the main track school ('Hauptschule', which has four levels), followed either by polytechnical training (leading to a vocation) or by attending a so-called 'extension school'. The General Upper School (which has eight school levels) follows primary education and concludes with the 'Matura' diploma.

One of the main tasks of Austrian school policy during the last twenty years or so, has been to create a system, which was flexible—vertically as well as horizontally. It is therefore now possible to enroll a child earlier in the first grade, if parents wish it and if the principal agrees that this is a feasible strategy. It is also possible to switch between the two school tracks (Bundeskanzleramt, 1994). Paragraph no. 26 of the 'Schulunterrichtsgesetz' allows for skipping grades once in the 'Grundschule' (pupils 6 to 10 years of age), again between the Grundschule and the eighth grade (pupils 10 to 14 years of age), and also after the eighth grade (pupils 14 to 18 or 19 years of age). It is also possible to sit for the 'Matura' at age 15.

In addition to these options, the Austrian legislation differentiates between achievement groups, and there exist numerous forms of outer differentiation relevant to gifted education. Partial learning at higher-grade levels, for example, is possible. Furthermore, there are the so-called Plus Courses in Salzburg, in Oberpullendorf, and in Tirol.

Some of the main track schools and the general secondary schools host special forms, which emphasize Music, Sports, or Modern Languages. In Vienna, for example, there is an experimental primary school ('Die bilinguale Volksschule'), where German and English are used as the languages of instruction. Similar schools exist in Graz and Linz. There is also The Vienna International School, where children are taught from age five and on to the International Baccalaureate (cf. Bundeskanzleramt, 1994). It should also be noted that Austria has six Colleges of the Arts. The first school specially designated to the highly able—the Sir Karl Popper School—was launched in 1998, with two classes at secondary level, based at the Wiedner Gymnasium in Vienna. There are plans to expand this school progressively and also include primary education. It is the explicit aim of this school to support particularly gifted individuals in different

intellectual and social domains; the curriculum has been developed by the Popper Club, and one of the characteristics of the school is the use of a coaching system (cf. Witzmann, 1998).

Yet another method of outer differentiation in Austria is the possibility to attend university courses for particularly talented individuals. The 'Landschulräte' (the state school boards) of Salzburg and Tirol, as well as the 'Stadtschulrat' (municipal school board) of Vienna, have several agreements of cooperation with the Universities of Salzburg and Innsbruck, the 'Mozarteum' Conservatory of music, and the Technical University of Vienna (cf. http://www.bmuvie.gv.at/pbegabung/). In addition, so-called home schooling is allowed in Austria as long as it is pursued under state control.

In regard to inner differentiation, the 'Schulunterrichtsgesetz' provides for differentiation of course content and teaching methods for pupils of different achievement levels, who are being taught together. There are currently experimental pilot schools, and in five of the federal states—at a higher-education level— there are also pilot courses relating to the curricular coursework, as offered by the European Council for High Ability (ECHA) in conjunction with the University of Nijmegen in the Netherlands. A three-part basic teacher training course, leading toward the European Advanced Diploma in Educating the Gifted, is available for teachers interested in gifted education.

Pupils at all school levels may put their talent to the test in annual competitions in Modern Languages and in the Social Sciences, such as 'Europa macht Schule' (i.e. Europe goes to school) or 'Jugend Innovativ' (i.e. The innovative young). They may also compete in Sports (in tournaments and championships), the Arts (e.g. Prima La Musica), as well as in the Olympics for Mathematics, Physics, Chemistry, and Computer Sciences. The Federal Ministry for Teaching and Culture is currently planning an evaluative study to examine the long-term effects of such contests on the personality development of students who participate in these events. A special effort to support gifted education are the annual summer academies offered in some states and the initiatives of a parent group (i.e. Austrian Club for highly talented children), which was founded in 1994 and now has chapters in six of the Austrian states.

In conclusion, it is clear from all the current initiatives and activities in Austria, that supporting the gifted and talented is increasingly becoming more and more important both from the perspective of Austrian authorities but also from the perspective of society as a whole.

Belgium

Belgium is a federal state with three communities (the Flemish, the French, and the German community), and two regions: Flanders and Wallonia. Both regions are autonomous and have separate educational legislation. In neither region, however, is giftedness recognized; at least not by the same token as special provision for the physically handicapped children or for children with severe learning difficulties is. In Flanders and Wallonia there are well developed, but separate, systems of special education also, divided into eight domains; however, neither of these special educational systems include a domain targeting gifted children.

While highly able children are not recognized as a specific target group, gifted children may nevertheless benefit from the more general measures taken toward this end on kindergarten and primary education levels made possible by a recent policy focusing 'extended care'. This policy aims at enhancing the abilities of schools and teachers to deal with differentiation in a more efficient way. Gifted children can certainly benefit from this novel educational approach in spite of the fact that its main target group are children other than the highly able. This special program was launched in 1993, as it became clear that too many children were not appropriately benefiting from the general way of teaching in mainstream primary schools.

However, there are at present no specific efforts made by the Ministries of Education to provide for gifted children. On the other hand, private schools, five secondary Arts Schools and three secondary Sports Schools, have been established in Flanders to cater to the highly able. But for all other gifted students, special provisions are supplied only in the regular classroom. The measures usually taken to aid highly able children in the regular school involve grade skipping, early school admittance, part-time attendance in a higher class, special support provided by a peripatetic teacher, mixed-age classes (especially in small schools), projects for the gifted, informal differentiation, autonomous study, and homogeneous classes (streaming). During holidays, private organizers provide courses in Modern Languages, Sports, Creative Writing, and Computing for gifted and motivated students aged 12 and older. There are also annual Belgian Olympics in Mathematics, Physics, Chemistry, Biology, and Modern Languages for students in their final year of the secondary school.

There is currently no special teacher training targeting the education of talented children and adolescents, but there are two-day seminars available to teachers on "Differentiated curriculum in primary and secondary education," which has been on offer since 1995 (Kieboom, 1994). Also, the Belgian Association for Gifted Children and Adolescents (Begaafde Kinderen en Adolescenten—BEKINA), founded in 1986, takes a leading role in providing information and raising the general awareness in Belgium of the necessity and significance of providing suitable education also for gifted students.

France

The notion of high ability/giftedness has so far been somewhat inconsistently recognized in France. While recognized by the government as an issue in primary and secondary education, there has as yet been no special policy implemented. The French school system is organized around the 'Lycées', which are schools focusing on the Social and Natural Sciences, and Economy, followed by a two-year preparatory period, which may lead to admission to elite schools—the so-called 'Grande Ecoles'. These different school systems are usually seen by the authorities as sufficient in also meeting the special needs of gifted students.

However, special efforts to promote gifted children do exist; for example, early school admittance is possible. There is no longer a standard minimum age for when to enroll in the school system, nor is special approval needed from the Local Education Authority; approval for admission is given by the school in which the child is to be enrolled. So-called home schooling under state control is also possible, and grade skipping is an option. A student may skip one grade when in primary school, and in the 'collège' (which students enter at age 12) there is in addition the possibility of shortening the four-year program to three years. This means that, given special permission, the examination concluding secondary school may be obtained before the age of 17.

There are also a number of private schools in France, accepting students mainly on the basis of their achievement. Such schools, additionally, often consider parental financial status when deciding whether or not a student should be admitted; in other words, tuition is expensive and such schools are therefore open only to the socially privileged. There is only one amongst the private schools—the Lycée Michalet at Nice—hosting approximately 150 students, that is entirely devoted to intellectually talented students (from ages eight to 16). But there are 13 of the colleges that provide special courses for intellectually talented students between the ages of 11 to 15. The first such special course was launched in 1990 at Collège du Cèdre, in Le Vèsinet, near Paris, which is a state school. Since the 1970s, however, there have existed special schools in every region of France for talents in Music and Sports; the most famous of these is Ecole de L'Opera at Paris.

A number of competitions are organized regularly in France, including sports tournaments and competitions in chess and music. Most such competitions are broadcast on TV or Radio. In addition, a variety of French associations organize scientific or mathematical games such as 'Les Olympiades de Chimie et de Physique', or Mathematics competitions like 'Kangourou' and 'Logic Flip'. One Parisian university (Jussieu) regularly organizes courses and meetings to specifically challenge teenagers from different fields of pursuit. Once a year they gather young scientists from all over France to the Mathematics and Jeans Congress. The 'Ministère de l'Education Nationale' also organizes competitions in subjects such as French, Philosophy, Mathematics, English, German, and Physics for the most outstanding students in the 'Terminales' (i.e. the examinations concluding secondary education) at the end of the school year (Monnier, 1998).

A very active organization in France, aiming at promoting giftedness and talent, is the 'Association Française pour les Enfants Précoces (AFPE)'. It aims ultimately at changing the French school system in a way beneficial to gifted children, but also to continue to provide special training for teachers, advising parents of gifted children, as well as organizing meetings and conferences where scientists, teachers, and parents meet and discuss the different aspects of supporting and nurturing gifted and talented individuals (Côte, 1996; Côte, Adda, & Capron, 1997; Côte, Adda & Cancill, 1998 ; Côte, Bouchard & Delcros, 1998).

Germany

Germany is a federal republic with control of education resting with the individual states; legislation stipulates that each young person is to be provided with an education regardless of his or her heritage or economic situation. Furthermore, education must reflect the child's talents, interests, and inclinations; it is the responsibility of schools to make provision as stipulated by legislation.

Early education in Germany tends to be very similar all over the country; but with regard to secondary education, however, several German states tend toward a division into three types of schools (cf. Bals, 1999). School legislation does provide for the possibility of specially supporting the gifted. Such provision includes inner differentiation, flexible enrollment in the first grade, grade skipping, the use inclination courses, electives and free-choice requirement courses, as they are included in the curriculum. In the 'new' federal states there is also school legislation taken over from the former German Democratic Republic (GDR), which largely still follows the previous system of support for talented individuals. This legislative legacy allows for some schools to support the particularly gifted by following a special curriculum as well as offering a diverse array of extra-curricular activities (Sprengel, 1999a). There are currently 26 special schools in the new federal states of Eastern Germany promoting gifted children, all of which are part of the GDR legacy.

Following the German Unification in 1990, however, many of these schools were taken over by new sponsors (other than the state). Nine of them are devoted to Mathematics and the Natural Sciences, eleven specialize in the Arts and in Music, and six focus on Modern Languages. In addition, three schools support and specially promote intellectually gifted students, namely the Landesschule Pforta, The Free School at Rostock, and Torgelow—which is a private secondary school (a so-called 'gymnasium'). However, there are also special classes: one at the Jugendorf-Christophorus school in Braunschweig and one at the Christophorus school in Rostock, that cater to talented children from the 9th grade. Since 1985, in the state of Baden-Württemberg state-wide enrichment courses at secondary school level were established (Hany & Heller, 1988) and in a large-scale investigation evaluated (Hany & Heller, 1992; Heller & Hany, 1993). Furthermore, statewide acceleration programs for highly gifted students from the German Gymnasium have been implemented in Baden-Württemberg (Heller, Neber & Wystrychowski, 1993; Heller, Osterrieder & Wystrychowski, 1995; Heller & Reimann, 1999) and in Rhineland-Palatinate (Kaiser, 1997). For an overview of the concerned program evaluation studies see Heller (1995b). In the state of Bavaria, the Ministry of Culture is planning to launch three special support classes for students commencing school during the 1999/2000 school year in Munich, Nürnberg, and Regensburg (Sprengel, 1999b). Two years ago, a combined acceleration-enrichment program was established at the Maria Theresia Gymnasium in Munich. In addition, there are special classes, particularly for Music and Sports, at a number of German gymnasia. Considering former GDR's considerable prowess in Sports, it is not surprising that, as part of the East German legacy, 20 gymnasia devoted to Sports still remain; this should be compared to only nine similar gymnasia in the rest of Germany ('Kleine Sportasse', 1998).

One particularly significant German initiative in Gifted Education was taken by 'Jugenddorf Hannover' in 1995 to make provision for highly able children already in kindergarten and in primary schools. When leaving kindergarten, children enter a primary school, which has developed a program much along the lines of the proceeding kindergarten. In this environment children learn in mixed-ability groups, but the special needs of the gifted children are taken into account and are carefully monitored and supported (Hartmann, 1998). The Jugenddorf Hannover also offers advisory services for parents and highly talented children regarding identifying giftedness and discovering means of support. Such advisory channels are also provided by the Jugenddorf-Christophorus schools at Braunschweig and Rostock. More counseling and advice are available through the institutes of psychology at the universities of Hamburg, Munich, and Tübingen. The first German Counseling Center for the Gifted was founded in Hamburg in 1984/85 (Feger & Prado, 1986), another one in Munich 1987 (Heller & Geisler, 1989; Heller, 1992a, b, 1993). The main emphasis is on individual counseling for parents, teachers, and gifted pupils as well as in giving advice to schools on how to recognize and further giftedness; meanwhile, further counseling centers were established, e.g. with the support of the municipal government in Hamburg (Quittmann & Manke, 1998).

Extracurricular support in Germany is apparent in regional and state contests, conducting work groups, correspondence networks, and specialist camps or art studios, along with summer schools and camps, which are offered through the 'Deutsche SchülerAkademie' (Pupils Academy) and others. There are competitions for talented and motivated pupils, such as 'Jugend forscht/Schüler experimentieren' (Young people's research/Students experiment), which is a Natural Sciences contest. There are also selection rounds for the International School Olympiads in Mathematics, Physics, Chemistry (see Engel, Gronau, Langmann & Sewerin, 1999; Heller & Lengfelder, 1999, 2000), Biology, and more uniquely: to a federal German environmental competition too. Able students may also show their prowess in different Language competitions, Political Education, German and Contemporary History contests, as well as in the Pan-European contest 'Europe in School'. In the domains of Music and Culture there are further competitions in Rhetoric, Creative Writing, Singing, Drama, Film and Video-making, and in musical composition: Young People Making Music, which is a federal contest (Bildung und Begabung e. V., 1997).

The 'Deutsche SchülerAkademie' was started as a special form of supporting talented and interested young individuals in out-of-school fields of pursuit. It was initiated by 'Bildung and Begabung e.V'. at Bonn in conjunction with the Federal Ministry of Education and the Sciences, and evaluated by Neber and Heller (1997). Since 1988 it has provided holiday programs for able students. In 1993, however, the German Parliament—and in 1994 by a unanimous vote at the Ministry for Culture's Conference—a permanent federal budget was set to form a starting point for supporting gifted and talented individuals. Since 1988 over 3000 highly able students have participated in the holiday courses offered (Bildung und Begabung e. V., 1998). For greater detail see Peters, et al. in this handbook.

In higher education, a dozen (and more) gifted supporting programs exist in Germany. Ten of these were evaluated in recent years (Heller et al., 1997; Heller & Viek, 2000).

Some teacher training in Gifted Education is on offer in Germany, and specific programs have been developed (Heller, 1992a, b, 1995a, b, 1996, 1997a; Neber, 1995; Heller & Ziegler, 1996; Ziegler & Heller, 1998, 2000). The international MA study program 'Psychology Excellence' at the University of Munich is one pioneering initiative in gifted education and research. This pilot program conveys, to educators and psychologists, the issues relating to recognizing and supporting giftedness. It runs as a four-semester continuing education program (cf. http://www.paed.uni-muenchen.de/excellence/).

Germany also hosts a number of organizations and associations with a wide range of activities pertaining to talent and giftedness. There is the 'Hochbegabtenförderung e. V', established by parents. It offers a total of 63 courses for 470 children in 13 German cities. The organization also offers individual assessment and counseling to gifted children and their parents. Furthermore, the 'Deutsche Gesellschaft für das hochbegabte Kind e.V.'—founded in 1978—has 3000 members in 15 regional groups and also organizes advanced courses for children, as well as arranging special days of study at the universities. It provides advice to parents, does a wide range of publicity work, and arranges activities for entire families with gifted children. 'Müsteraner Zentrum für Begabtenförderung' is yet another German association focusing on giftedness and contributing to special provision. In addition, 'Bildung und Begabung e.V'. organizes competitions, the courses of the 'Deutsche SchülerAkademie', and is of particular interest to the European perspective, since the organization has strong links with the 'European Council for High Ability (ECHA). Furthermore, 'Arbeitskreis Begabungsforschung und Begabungsförderung e.V. (ABB)' in Rostock, is an association of researchers, educational policy-makers, and teachers, supporting giftedness research, and aims at integrating research findings into actual teaching (cf. Urban & Joswig, 1998).

Not all of the numerous German initiatives started over the past few years can be presented in detail here for lack of space. Yet the initiatives mentioned do signify that a considerable effort is being made to bring gifted education more into the foreground of education as well as providing a solid base for it (Heller, 1995c, 1997a, 1999; Heller & Hany, 1996).

Italy

Supporting the highly gifted is not a recognized issue in the educational policies in Italy. Although an interest in higher ability and talent is clearly emerging in Italian society as a whole, the notion of suspected elitism, the fear that non-liberal and undemocratic education could be rekindled and, because of this, that efforts towards gifted education therefore could be misunderstood, present a problem in the current Italian debate. As a result suggestions of establishing, for example, special schools or specially designed curricula, are indeed met with interest but are not put into action. The Italian experience regarding educational strategies for highly able children is therefore, by and large, limited.

However, private pre-schools for gifted, and generally for upper class children, have been organized, but these have so far had only limited success. There are also a few private schools, usually supported by the Roman Catholic Church, as well as a few universities, which previously selected students on the basis of financial as well as intellectual ability, thereby potentially creating a mainly social elite. These schools are akin to the place and status of the famous boarding schools in the English educational tradition. However, Italian authorities now prohibit this type of selection for education, and as a result educational initiatives and research lean toward the general rather than toward the particular. Authorities seek to support ability, avoid any obstacle for development, and to seek out and promote possibilities for developing excellence. Research programs at the Universities of Genoa, Pavia, and Rome, for example, are currently studying the development of social and moral learning and motivation, the way gifted individuals live and behave, and identification by means of adequate testing—without the need of a separate educational environment for the gifted student. Research results have been presented at international conferences, and one workshop on creative potential has been held at Pavia in 1994 in cooperation with the ECHA.

In Italy, as well as in many other European countries, there are competitions; however, these tend to be staged by private sponsors, who arrange competitions in Mathematics and in the Sciences as well as in the Arts (Painting, Writing, and Film Making) (cf. Pagnin, 1994).

Portugal

Educational provision for high ability in Portugal is not handled in a manner similar to traditional special education; that is, to regard special education as mainly including a variety of learning difficulties, physical disabilities and social-emotional disorders. There is in Portugal a concern for educational differentiation, which took legal form during the 1990s in ratifying and publishing the General Law for the New Reform, in which the rights of students' 'different learning rhythms' are made a specific issue. This legislation, indirectly, also paves the way for accepting the special needs of gifted children. For example, the Portuguese Department for Basic Education (DEB) published and distributed a brochure to all primary schools entitled *Gifted Students,* and by legislation the Department made possible for gifted students to begin their compulsory education at age five instead of at the mainstream age of six. In 1996 DEB launched and implemented a project to specifically support intellectual precocity: 'Projecto de Apoio ao Desenvolvimento Precoce (PADP)'. It provided extracurricular enrichment for students in primary and intermediate level schools.

There are also special courses for teachers available in Portugal, and conferences are held aiming at informing and promoting creativity in schools, as well as making teachers sensitive to the special needs of the highly able. In 1997 two such conferences were held in Lisbon and in Palmela (Martins, 1997).

Special endeavors to promote giftedness consist of available summer programs. For example, the Portuguese Center for Creativity, Innovation and Leadership (CPCIL) has provided summer programs for talented students since 1989. The Center cooperates with DEB and summer program participants are invited to take part also in the PADP. These programs are aimed at general enrichment, such as divergent thinking, communication, and leadership skills. In July of 1998 the DEB organized a similar summer program for 150 participants to which highly able students from grades 3 to 9 were invited. This particular event should be considered the first *official* summer program for highly able students ever staged in Portugal.

There are three private non-profit associations in Portugal devoted in various ways to giftedness; in 1986 the Association in Portugal for Gifted Children (APGC) was created; it organizes conferences and has also made available relevant publications. In 1989 the Portuguese Center for Creativity, Innovation and Leadership (CPCIL) was founded by parents and teachers in order to disseminate knowledge of identification and provide counseling, enrichment sessions, teacher training, conferences and summer programs for Portuguese and foreign students, making interchange and partnership with other similar associations abroad possible. Furthermore, in 1995 The Portuguese Association for the Study of the Problems of Intelligence, Creativity, and Talent (APEPICTA) was launched and staged a conference (cf. Martins, 1997). All three associations have been instrumental in changing how giftedness is perceived in Portugal and have been of considerable value in providing significant assistance in a large number of cases, where children have been identified as gifted.

Spain

There has been a growing awareness in Spain, since the 1970s, that there exists a need to cater to diversity in education and to provide personal attention to students. However, not until important changes were made in the educational legislation (particularly the 'Ley de Ordenación General del Sistema Educativo—LOGSE, 1/1990, 3 October'), did a more systematic development towards gifted education become possible. The new legislation has many implications for the education of gifted children. High intellectual ability is indeed represented in the legislation as a bona fide category of special educational needs. As a result, the Ministry of Education has issued various legal measures to cater to diversity. The 'Real Decreto 696/1995', Article 3.2, however, stipulates that gifted students must be educated in regular teaching and programs but that there is also a possibility for such students to attend specialized centers of education. Furthermore, other legal stipulations (e.g. The Order of 24 April 1996) state that compulsory schooling should be made more flexible for students who are academically gifted;

715

and the most recent legal development (The Resolution of 29 April 1996) actually outlines procedures to be followed to help educators and schools to implement the educational needs associated with high ability. This Resolution establishes the following available provision: early entrance to the school system, grade skipping, an appropriate form of psychopedagogical assessment, the use of special curricular measures, and ways of guiding the highly able in accordance with their educational response.

Thus, acceleration in the form of early entrance or grade skipping is now possible. School enrollment may be reduced by two years, but this may be done at only one grade level. Enrichment in the form of special measures like grouping or restructuring schedules and locations, however, still need to be put more into practice to gain enough experience for effective procedures to be found. Researchers and teachers are increasingly becoming aware of the need to make the teaching-learning process more flexible, and to adjust teaching to the pace and needs of the individual.

Support programs have been developed, which aim at supporting gifted children individually or in groups (cf. Martin Bravo, 1997, Prieto Sánchez, 1997; Aceveda & Sastre, 1998; Touron, Iriate, Reparaz & Peralta, 1998). In order to prompt the development of such programs into appropriate and consistent practice, teacher training programs have also been developed; such further training opportunities for teachers are to be launched at the University of Madrid. These will target two main issues, namely the development of specific diagnostics and identification instruments and the planning and development of suitable programs of action. In addition to teacher training there are also summer schools aiming at supporting the families of gifted children; international exchange programs have been developed. In 1998 university staff, teachers and researchers, with an interest in the study and promotion of high ability, established an organization: 'Sociedad Espanola para el Estudio de la Superdotación' (cf. *http://www.ucm.es/info/sees*), which publishes *FAISCA (Revista de Altas Capacidades)*—a national scholarly journal devoted to the study of high ability.

Switzerland

In Switzerland the Kantons (i.e. Switzerland's administrative regions) have authority regarding matters of education, and the need for gifted education is only slowly finding its way into the educational policy agendas of individual Kantons. At universities, for example the University of Zürich, work relevant to the highly gifted is anchored in the realm of special education. But universities do not have a direct influence on educational planning or its implementation. Since the end of the 1980s high ability has increasingly become a publicly discussed issue in the German and French speaking Kantons, but it is still largely ignored in the Italian speaking Kantons. There

has been some coverage in the national media since 1997, brought on by pressure from the press and public interest in this field. The state ministries, however, are not yet active in this area on their own accord; but first attempts at special provision for the talented and gifted can nevertheless be discerned. In Zürich there is an experimental and special school "for artistically and athletically talented young individuals." In 1998, also in Zürich, 'Talenta' opened, which is a private primary school for gifted children. Nineteen children have been selected as students so far by means of psychological tests and interviews with the children and their parents. The program for which they have been selected is a two-year experimental program. There are private schools also at Basel ('Minerva') and Solothurn, offering special training for highly able secondary pupils. Talented athletes may attend a private gymnasium at Graubünden, and young and promising Swiss scientists may participate in 'Jugend forscht' (i.e. Young people research). In addition, 'Schweizerische Studienstiftung' (a foundation) offers talented young students the chance to participate in diverse international programs thereby gaining international experience (Schweizerische Studienstiftung, 1998).

State policies, however, are aimed at keeping highly able children in the mainstream education and there are relatively few acceleration or enrichment measures offered. In the Kanton Zürich, skipping a grade as a means of providing for able children was made possible by legislation (i.e. 'Promotionsreglement'), which allows for skipping one grade at primary level. On 27 January 1998 the Local Education Authority at Kanton Zürich, however, passed a resolution, which extended the use of grade skipping. It is now possible to skip grades at all levels of school and also, under certain circumstances, to skip more than one grade (Bähr, 1998b). The Zürich LEA based this decision on specific research, pursued between 1995 to 1997, which showed that grade skipping most certainly may be seen as one of the ways in which to reduce the often insufficient demands of achievement placed upon gifted students (Bähr, 1998a).

In the city of Zürich the first ideas and funds for an enrichment teacher (a special teacher for gifted education) are available. Individualization in the classroom is recommended, and work is under way creating new teaching and support materials for teachers. One of the first nation-wide in-service teacher seminars on supporting giftedness in schools was held in 1998 at the Pestalozzianum, in Zürich; more courses concluding with appropriate certification are planned.

The Netherlands

High ability/giftedness is recognized by the Dutch government as an issue in primary and secondary education. The Dutch Ministry of Education stimulated and supported specific research between 1980–1987 at the University of Nijmegen, focusing on elementary schools, and at the University of Utrecht focusing on secondary schools; and in 1988 the Center for the Study of Giftedness (CSG) was founded at the University of Nijmegen, together with a Chair given the designation "The growth and development of the gifted child." This Chair, unique in European academia, has been held by Franz J. Mönks since its inauguration in 1988. The Center has, since it was launched, been instrumental in facilitating the development of Gifted Education and the understanding for high ability in much of Europe (cf. Mönks, 1994).

From 1988 and on, more specific attention was given to the gifted students in the Netherlands. The Secretary of Parliament recognized the importance of the subject and promoted research and study. In 1993 the Platform Gifted Education was founded on request by the government, which aims at better educational provision for gifted students and to stimulate new developments benefiting them. However, during 1998 the Platform activities decreased due to lack of funding, reflecting the increasing dominance of inclusive policies. The most celebrated policy at the moment endorses the motto "Together in school again," which signals that fewer children should attend special schools, and that regular schools should rather feature increased differentiation. Gifted children are thought to benefit more from this. However, this is rather difficult to operationalize. There is also another school form in the Netherlands, in addition to the 'regular' primary schools, namely the so-called New Schools. These alternative schools (run as Jena-plan schools, or in accordance with the ideas and philosophies of Montessori or Dalton), can more easily offer special provision for gifted students, since children tend to work individually to a greater extent than in the regular schools. There are also special schools for pupils talented in music, dance, or sports, however, and children can attend these schools from about 10 years of age.

Like in most other European countries there are various competitions (or Olympics) available in the Netherlands; these are organized by the Specialists in Curriculum Development (SLO), the Ministry of Education and/or universities in fields like Mathematics, Physics, Chemistry, and Information Technology. The participating students study either at secondary schools or at university. The aim of these Olympics is simply to promote the practice of the different Sciences; winners may continue to take part in the international equivalents or obtain a prize (up to 5000 NFG).

Other Dutch activities aimed at supporting gifted individuals include summer courses for 14 to 17-year old Europeans, which have been staged at several universities (i.e. Rotterdam, Delft and Twente at Enschede) since 1996 (Pluymakers, 1997). In addition, the Talent Support Foundation organizes summer courses in Mathematics, Arts and Culture, Economy,

History, and Sports. FACTA, another foundation, similarly organizes summer courses focusing on Computer Science (for further aspects of Gifted Education in the Netherlands cf. Mönks, 1992; Mönks, van Boxtel, Roelofs & Sanders, 1996; Span, 1992; Dijk, Kok & Poorthuis, 1996; Mooij, 1996; Peters, 1998).

'Pharos' is the Dutch parent organization, founded in 1987, and like other European sister-associations, it offers provision for gifted children and hosts weekend camps (Nawroth, 1997). The goal of the Dutch Talent Support Foundation is to offer special support; furthermore, HINT, yet another organization, promotes gifted children in terms of offering information to schools and education authorities, as well as organizing lectures, courses, and activities for gifted children.

The Faculty of Social Sciences of the University of Nijmegen, in cooperation with The Center for the Study of Giftedness (CSG) and the European Council for High Ability (ECHA), uniquely offers a European Advanced Diploma in Educating the Gifted. This postgraduate course is designed to serve teachers or others involved in education wishing to specialize in Gifted Education. The certification has been available to European teachers since 1994 (Kayser, 1994). The CSG organizes workshops for primary school teachers about once a month. In addition, there are also one-day workshops offered for secondary school teachers. Teachers receive general information in these workshops about the identification of giftedness and how one can meet the special learning needs of gifted students in the classroom.

There are some teacher training colleges that specifically offer one or two modules (one module equals 40 hours of study) for primary teachers in their third or fourth year of study. For secondary teachers special training is being planned. The first specialized course, however, will be offered during 1999 by the University of Nijmegen. More generally, there are a number of School Advisory Officers in The Netherlands who offer information about gifted education to teachers.

Although high ability/giftedness is increasingly accepted as an issue needing attention, it is still common to think that high ability does not qualify as bona fide special educational need; but due to the continued dissemination of knowledge it is most probable that high ability/giftedness will become an even more significant and accepted field of special practice and knowledge. One reason for this is likely to be the increasingly more assertive stance taken by the parents of gifted children.

Northern Europe, The British Isles, The Baltic States, and Russia

Scandinavia

While egalitarianism is a problem for gifted individuals in much of Europe, in spite of considerable progress in developing policies and special provision for the highly able, Scandinavia stands out from other European nations as exceptional in this respect. No European nation, and few in a global perspective, are likely to display and enact egalitarian convictions and policies as do the Scandinavian countries of Denmark, Norway, Sweden, and also to a lesser extent, Finland. However, the notion of equality and social collectivism in Scandinavia, at all levels of society, is best understood as an inherent cultural characteristic, in which certain political ideals have merged with indigenous traditions and sentiments, which draw on historical facts and events dating from early medieval times and the Viking Era (Sawyer & Sawyer, 1993; Persson, 1998a).

In modern times, as separate nations have emerged from a culturally and often politically common ancestry, political scientists and historians tend to speak of all the Scandinavian countries as politically similar. Together they embody 'The Nordic Model' (Petersson, 1994). The similarities between the Scandinavian countries also in terms of social dynamics were observed in Hofstede's (1982) monumental research on international differences in work-related values. Hofstede developed, for example, the Masculinity Index (MAS) by which he compared 39 different nations worldwide. High MAS indicates, for example, an independence ideal, an achievement ideal and a propensity for embracing and promoting individual excellence. Low MAS, on the other hand, much signifies the opposite: an inter-dependence ideal, a service ideal and a reluctance to reward or promote policies or actions that would cause some individuals to excel more than others. All Scandinavian countries—except Finland—are rated as low MAS: Sweden (MAS 6), Norway (MAS 10) and Denmark (MAS 22), which should be compared to, for example, Japan (MAS 87), Austria (MAS 75) and the United States (MAS 62). Finland receives a much higher rating than other Scandinavian countries (MAS 51), which has some significance in relation to Scandinavian Gifted Education and practice.

Due to the close cultural and social relationship between the Nordic nations, one should expect that attitudes toward Gifted Education, high ability and its research are more or less shared also. Particularly in Denmark, Norway and Sweden, the basic ethos by which individual excellence is commonly considered is known as 'The Law of Jante'; an expression coined by Danish novelist Aksel Sandemose in 1933. The expression signifies the impropriety of pride of self. Therefore, no-one must believe they are 'special'. A similar expression with much the same paradoxical meaning is The Tall Poppy Syndrome in Australia and New Zealand (see Mitchell, 1991; Thompson, 1994). The social reality of this often-debated issue in Scandinavia has resulted in, as Swedish journalist Göran Skytte (1997) puts it, "a begrudging and nationally endorsed attitude of envy."

Sweden

It is somewhat paradoxical that a nation hosting the internationally acclaimed Nobel Prize Ceremony, where highly accomplished individuals from all over the world come to collect their prestigious awards in recognition of their work, does not itself recognize politically that talent is an issue deserving particular attention in its educational system. While concern for the rights and welfare of every individual student in the regular classroom has been safeguarded in every national school curriculum since 1920, special needs have only been identified in reference to children with learning disabilities or a variety of physical or psychological disorders (cf. Rosenquist & Sandling, 1995). High ability has officially never been singled out as a separate issue in education, and amongst school teachers it is occasionally even considered unethical to argue that high-achieving children are in need of special provision (Persson, 1997a).

There exist special music schools in virtually all Swedish towns and cities available to anyone interested in music from age 6 to age 18 (Kommunförbundet, 1976). In addition, there are special secondary schools devoted to a variety of Sports and Music. It is difficult, however, to regard these as an intentional strategy to nurture talent specifically. While such special training does occasionally produce very able athletes and musicians, selection is mainly based on special interest rather than on special ability, although there are formal criteria as well as proficiency examinations in order for applicants to be accepted. However, a limited number of educational experiments have recently been launched, usually at a secondary level and in Science or Mathematics, which could be regarded as more akin to traditional Gifted Education. High-achieving students have been offered the possibility of taking more advanced courses than is typically offered at their level of education. These efforts, however, are local and limited to a handful of schools. Also, a recent action taken by the Stockholm Local Education Authority involves the creation of six special classes at primary and lower secondary levels. This particular effort is made possible by the fact that local education authorities have a certain degree of autonomy obliged mainly to make possible the targets and follow the guidelines stipulated by the National Curriculum. How these targets are to be reached falls within the jurisdiction of local education authorities. The special classes in the Stockholm school system will be in operation in the fall of 1999, and are carried out, it would seem, contrary to the wishes of the Ministry of Education. It is feasible to assume that there are political motives at the heart of these experiments, rather than a sudden understanding of the special needs of gifted children. The Stockholm City Council currently has a conservative majority, and it is possibly tempting for local politicians to act out against the Social Democratic government, rather than to consider the actual needs of gifted children in the school system. Interestingly, and somewhat alarmingly, special teacher training has not been considered, nor have strategies by which to evaluate this type of special school or program been devised (Melander, 1995; Nyman, 1998).

Swedish educational research over the years has indeed focused ability differentiation in the regular classroom (Husén, 1948; Gustafsson & Härnqvist, 1977; Dunér & Törestad, 1980), but it has been difficult to reconcile discovered variety and different levels of ability with dominating political ideals and cultural traditions forming the basis of national curricula (cf. Husén, 1979). Above all, education "plays a crucial role in supporting active citizenship and makes it possible for individuals to employ citizens' rights and meet necessary civic obligations" (Ministry of Education and Science, 1993, p. 125).

In Sweden formal groups and organizations tend to be strong and influential in contrast with individuals, who are generally considered weak and are often ignored; a tradition much influenced by dominant political ideals. Daun (1994) argues the considerable influence of the Swedish Social Democratic party, which has been in power with few interruptions since 1932. Due to the fact that individuals are largely legitimate only if representing a group, Daun concludes, that

> Swedes are ambivalent about their 'stars' … whether in sports, show business, or culture. Successes may be admired, but their exclusiveness and out-of-the-ordinary achievements often give rise to envy and therefore to malicious pleasure when the stars 'fall'. The high value awarded to *sameness* makes all personal success problematic (p. 107).

The notion of sameness also applies to Swedish education. Edfelt (1992), for example, points out that in Sweden "it is considered undemocratic not only to be mentally gifted, but also to be gifted and demand special treatment because of this fact" (p. 47).

While high ability and individual success may not readily be acknowledged in individuals, it is certainly recognized if occurring group-wise. One curious example of this—qualifying *both* as group-orientation and elite-orientation—is the so-called 'Gnosjö spirit'. Gnosjö is a small community in South Sweden in which entrepreneurial talent and prowess in the realm of small and medium-sized businesses is flourishing quite independently of political guidelines and policies decreed in Stockholm, making the area not only financially very affluent, but it also knows virtually no unemployment (Karlsson & Larsson, 1993; Gummesson, 1997). This phenomenon has been subject to much study and praise by politicians and researchers alike and, interestingly, more or less regardless of their political creed.

In spite of the cultural legitimacy of group-achievement and the collectivist protectionism of educational policies, however, one must juxtapose education with general professional practice encouraged in Swedish society as a whole. There exists a paradoxical discrepancy between stated and argued traditional values and politically encouraged behavior to support the market economy by professional expertise and talent. While education is 'protected' from what is argued to be 'elitism', elitism is indeed practiced, recognized and widely supported in professional life (Persson, 1997b). There is understandably, therefore, often a considerable disagreement between industry and governmental education policy (Nicolin, 1996). Conflicts between unique and very able individuals and the Swedish societal system has occasionally led to accusations of anti-intellectualism (Segerstedt, 1979), as well as to a certain 'brain drain', the most spectacular of which is likely to be film director Ingmar Bergman's decision in 1976 to leave Sweden after a series of accusations of tax evasion (Bergman, 1987).

Some change is under way, however, and interestingly it originates in individual initiatives rather than in governmental policies or group-efforts. Individual teachers, who have trained abroad, bring back knowledge and practices of Gifted Education with them, and share this information with others (e.g. Wahlström, 1995). Implementation and effort, however, is always local and receives neither official recognition nor special funding. The most significant change, and with the greatest potential of affecting the compulsory school system in a direction commensurate with the recommendations of the European Council on education for the highly able (cf. Council of Europe, 1994), is an effort made by Jönköping University, in which all students in the comprehensive teacher training programs are provided with rudimentary knowledge of high ability and the special needs of the highly able. A special course is also available, but applicants are few (Persson, 1997c, 1998c), in spite of the fact that indigenous research has shown that Swedish teachers themselves recognize both the special needs of highly able children and their own lack of information on how to support them (Persson, 1997a).

Denmark

In Denmark too, the ideals of the collectivist Welfare State, have prevented high ability from growing into a particular focus of attention in education. Inclusion, as well individualization, are basic principles of the Danish compulsory school system, as they are also in the rest of Scandinavia. All children's varied educational needs, according to Danish legislation, should be met by differentiation within the regular classroom (Tetler, 1995; Lau & Pagaard, 1996; Robenhagen, 1996). The Danish comprehensive school, as functioning under the latest Reform Act of 1993, shall "familiarize the pupils with Danish culture and contribute to their understanding of other cultures and of man's interaction with nature. The school shall prepare the pupils for active participation, joint responsibility, rights and duties in a society based on freedom and democracy. The teaching of the school and its daily life must therefore build on intellectual freedom, equality and democracy" (Ministry of Education, 1996, p. 2).

While differentiation is a basic prerequisite to cater also for particularly talented pupils, however, there is still the problem of teachers' common sense understanding of high ability in the inclusive classroom. Their basis for dealing with talent in the Danish school is to count on such children as always being resilient; that is, they will somehow manage whatever the circumstance (Jansen, 1996).

While the philosophical foundations of educational systems in Denmark, Sweden, and Norway are virtually identical, the Danish Ministry of Education—unlike educational authorities in Norway and Sweden—has "shown some interest" in the work of a research team of educators and psychologists established in 1995 in the Danish National Institute for Educational Research at Copenhagen, whose objectives are to "investigate potential problems and their incidence in relation to talented children" (Rabøl-Hansen & Robenhagen, 1996, p. 5).

Finland

Finland, although endorsing 'The Nordic Model' also (Petersson, 1994), differs to some extent from other Scandinavian countries in educational objectives and relationship to high ability. Note that Finland stands apart substantially from the rest of Scandinavia in terms of work-related values as estimated by Hofstede (1982).

While attitudes towards specific teaching for the highly able traditionally has been negative and rejecting, this is changing due to "increasing communication to educators and administrators of research findings, indicating the advantages of nurturing the highly able and the techniques to do this" (Ojanen & Freeman, 1994, p. 7). This development towards a greater flexibility in the Finnish understanding of equality, is largely due to a governmental decision to decentralize decision-making in the school system and, in fact, abandoning the concept of a national curriculum. Individuality and freedom of choice are emphasized more strongly in the Finnish school system than in any other Scandinavian country. As a result, schools have been encouraged to draft more individual curricula, which in turn allows flexible decisions for appropriate acceleration for the highly able (Tirri, 1997). This new trend of individual consideration and choice allows flexible decision-making. Parents may decide that their child is ready to start school at age six (earlier all children started at age seven), and there is a movement

towards allowing parents to choose which school to send their children to. In addition, students in secondary schools may have their study schedule more or less 'customized' due to the fact most upper secondary schools operate on an ungraded basis (Laukkanen, 1995). Also, opportunities for able children to attend extracurricular enrichment on a voluntary basis have arisen in recent years. Some primary schools, for example, arrange groups where students may advance those skills and interests in which they show talent. Such groups have so far focused on Thinking Skills, Mathematics, Computers, and the Arts within a project-oriented framework. Mathematically gifted secondary school students regularly meet at the University of Tampere and also take part in summer courses where they gain credits in Linear Algebra and Physics for later studies at university. This project is sponsored both by the Ministry of Education and Finnish Industry (cf. Nieminen & Piche, 1995).

A new strategic plan for the Finnish school system, ratified by Parliament in 1993, outlines the main objectives of education and science policy to maintain a high and varied level of training, to further spiritual growth, to encourage individual initiative and entrepreneurship, to improve education and research quality, to widen the basis for industry and strengthen innovation, to combine work, training and changing life situations, and develop further professional skills and facilitate employment (National Board of Education, 1997). This plan for the Finnish school system is unlike other Scandinavian strategic guidelines for schools and education, and does not only reflect recent political developments in Finland but also, at a more fundamental level, cultural differences. Note that there is also a growing base of original Finnish research with regard to high ability, competence, talent and its training (Merenheimo, 1991; Välijärvi, 1992; Tirri & Uusikylä, 1994; Uusikylä, 1994, 1996; Engeström, Engeström & Kärkkäinen, 1997; Räty & Snellman, 1997).

Norway

In 1997 the Norwegian Ministry of Church, Education and Science implemented an educational reform resulting in a new national curriculum reinforcing the Nordic notion of communality. It states, as do similarly other Scandinavian educational policies, that "the school system is based on the principle of inclusion; on equality and the individual adaption of the teaching of a unifying curriculum in an integrated school system" (Ministry of Church, Education and Science, 1997, p. 1). While the new curriculum clearly states that the Norwegian school system is structured so as to satisfy both the individual student's needs as well as society's need for competence, there is little to suggest that high ability would be a particular concern. On the contrary, it appears that the egalitarian ethos is reinforced to an even higher degree in the new reform, and to an even greater extent, than is the case in recent Danish and Swedish school reforms. It may well be, that in Scandinavia, the egalitarian ethos is strongest in Norway (Williams & Mitchell, 1989; Undheim & Nordvik, 1992).

While authorities expect that high ability as well as low ability should have their needs satisfied in the integrated and inclusive classroom, they also argue—somewhat contentiously in the light of Gifted Education research—that "all pupils aspire to achieve the same goals, and the demands of differentiation and individualization inside the class are a central concern of the teaching staff" (Arne Gundersen, personal communication, 29 September, 1998).

However, the Ministry of Church, Education and Science also points out that while there are no special schools available, and no summer schools are held for the special benefit of highly able children, schools may well take the initiative to invite experts in different fields to inspire not only students but also their teachers. As in most other European (and Scandinavian) nations there are competitions in Mathematics, Computing and Physics also in Norway attracting the talented.

THE FUTURE OF GIFTED EDUCATION IN SCANDINAVIA

It is not likely that the Scandinavian countries will conceptualize high ability in a way similar to, for example, Germany, Austria, The Netherlands, Canada or much of the United States. Nor is it likely that they will adopt current, and predominantly American, models by which to develop Gifted Education. That is not to say, however, that high ability will always remain of no or little interest, or that some precaution to secure the democratic rights of talented children to obtain training commensurate with their unique ability, will not be taken.

One interesting observation is that all the recent Scandinavian national curricula are implicitly approaching the notion of Multiple Intelligences (Gardner, 1983). In addition, MI-theory is increasingly seen by researchers as a way forward in which to cater to highly able children in the inclusive classroom also (Baltzer, 1996; Tirri, 1997; Persson, 1998), since—in a sense—a classroom based on the notion of multi-faceted competences much bypasses the egalitarian dilemma. The social and ideological sensitivity to whether an individual is of high or low ability would become lessened by a focus on competence differentiation rather than on achievement level differentiation in a few IQ-related skills. It is likely that with indigenous values and tradition as a basis, the Scandinavian countries may well develop their own culture-specific approach to provide also for the gifted and the talented.

Russia and the Baltic States

Russia

One easily associates contemporary Russia, as well as the former Soviet Union, with a passion for talent and a national pride for its high-achievers, considering the number of internationally known and prominent Russian artists, athletes, and scientists. Indeed, in fields such as Painting, Ballet and Music talented children from all over Russia have been sent to Moscow and Saint Petersburg to schools, rich in tradition, for training since before the Russian Revolution in 1917. Composer Peter Ilyich Tchaikovsky, for example, argued in his time, with reference to training in music, that "schools must be started in our capital cities, and also in our regional centers and towns . . . The purpose of these schools would be to train young people for the conservatoire" (Kabalevsky, 1988, p. 139). However, the assumption that Russia also has a long-standing tradition of Gifted Education in, for example, the Sciences and in Mathematics is false. Firsov (1993) declares the early development of special educational networks to further gifted mathematicians and scientists to be a myth; and as such a Western product of the now defunct Cold War. The first special school on a secondary level, with a special focus on advanced mathematical education, was created by Semyon Schwarzburd: a Mathematics teacher in Moscow School No. 444 in 1959.

High ability is recognized politically by the Russian Government, but there are no stated priorities regarding which subjects or fields of pursuit in which particular provision should be developed. Note that in providing training for gifted and talented individuals in Russia, the term 'gifted' is usually avoided. For example, in Moscow, where there are approximately 1250 federal and about 250 private schools, half of these host enrichment programs (or in Russian terms 'deepened programs') rather than 'programs for the gifted'.

There are both special schools and special classes available ranging in focus from Mathematics, Natural Science and Technology (cf. chapter 6, part V, in this Handbook) to Verbal Skills (including Foreign Languages), Music, the Arts, Sports as well as vocational and practical skills. A special program for Leadership was launched in 1991 and programs in Business and Management are currently under development. There are special boarding schools for mathematically gifted children from the remote and rural areas of Russia. In addition, such children may also participate in a special correspondence course hosted by Moscow State University. Interestingly, mentorship programs exist, but they have not been planned in order to reinforce educational provision; they have emerged spontaneously. Some schools use tutoring in which an expert works with a small group of students for a number of years; these experts, as a rule, are always former students of that particular school. The intention is to transfer the best of intellectual and cultural traditions of that school to the next generation of gifted individuals, challenge them in a particular subject, and facilitate their transition from school and to university.

An extensive network of extracurricular activities—often in cooperation with universities—where highly able children may find additional stimulation for their particular interests also exists. These involve lectures, workshops, projects, fieldwork, and cooperative learning endeavors in traditional school subjects and in other more specialized subjects such as the study of Animal Behavior, Astronomy, Archeology, Cosmology, Paleontology, Folklore, Ikebana (i.e. Japanese flower arrangement), Esoterics, and so on. Special summer schools and programs are numerous. Perhaps the most spectacular example of such provision is the Summer School of Cosmonautics in the Siberian city of Krasnoyarsk.

Special schools, which are relatively few, are generally intended for the exceptionally gifted children. Training entails radical acceleration, individually tailored instruction, psychological support, creativity training and communication training (Babaeva, 1999).

General guidelines for the Russian school system do not focus talent in a mixed-ability setting. They rather emphasize the necessity for differentiation and individualization of instruction. Whether or not these guidelines are adhered to, however, is dependent on the individual schoolteachers; number of students in the classroom, teachers' workload, individual interest and enthusiasm. There is a tendency amongst schoolteachers to devote more time to children with learning disabilities. Special training for teachers regarding the nature and special needs of highly able children does exist but takes place irregularly and usually as in-service training on the initiative of the Local Education Authorities. Such training typically includes the psychology of high ability, identification, strategies and models of Gifted Education, curriculum development, and the principles of creativity training.

Gifted Education in Russia, although already extensive more or less by tradition, has to some extent lacked specific and centralized guidelines. This is changing, however, indigenous research in the field is growing stronger (cf. Leites, 1996), and a group of specialists have been working on such guidelines for some time. There is currently in press an official document that includes a general conceptualization of the giftedness construct, its assessment, types of giftedness, and what manner of provision is suitable and recommended for the stated types of giftedness. The document has recently been approved by the Ministry of General and Professional Education of the Russian Federation. This further development is linked to the current Post-Communist turmoil, in which far-reaching reforms are creating transitional difficulties. During this transition, however, a particular concern has been expressed that gifted individuals must not be wasted or overlooked in the course of societal change. Rather, they represent a necessary national investment, which eventually may help to solve the crisis. One example of this concern is the latest federal program Gifted Children, launched in 1996 and constituting an important part of the Presidential program Children of Russia.

Latvia

To nurture talent is essential also to the Republic of Latvia; one of the Baltic nations, and largely for the same reasons high ability is becoming increasingly important for Russia and in the rest of former Communist Europe. Inara Akmene (1994), of the Latvian Ministry of Education and Science, declares that "the education of highly able school children is essential to Latvia. We work together with universities and public organizations to bring up a generation of talented young people, who in due time may constitute the intellectual basis of this nation" (p. 8).

High ability is thus endorsed politically in Latvia, and has been the focus of particular interest for many years. The Ministry of Education and Science at Riga, for example, hosts the Educational Advancement Institute; a body specifically assigned to promote competitions (usually termed Olympics), programs and activities for gifted and talented children and adolescents. Such provision rests mainly on all-year mentorships, seasonal enrichment programs (such as summer camps), and an abundance of competitive opportunities in several fields and disciplines. Highly able children are likely to be assigned to expertise from the universities; be it either in Mathematics, Physics, Chemistry, Biology, The Visual Arts, or in Modern Languages. There are incentives for university staff to participate in these schemes. A particularly successful mentor, in recognition of his or her success, may be eligible for the Atis Kronvald's Prize. No specialized training is provided to prepare these mentors for their role nor is such training available for school teachers.

The success of programs, courses, and studies, is always tried in a variety of Olympics on different levels, from subject competitions in single school units to nationwide and international competition, where number and type of prizes are important to local as well as national self-esteem. As in Russia, competitions and provision for mathematically prodigious children appear to be regarded as particularly important, as well as particularly prestigious (cf. Andzans, undated).

The British Isles

England and Wales

The status of Gifted Education in England and Wales is somewhat paradoxical; the issue exists as such in education. It is frequently the focus of debate in a complex social setting, where stratification is relatively distinct (cf. Giddens, 1989). Class consciousness exists alongside a tradition of very prestigious schools for the social elite, the political and egalitarian ideals of the working class, influential charities, and parent organizations of the middle class. In addition, there is a strong academic tradition of research on the various aspects of ability. The current international knowledge base of high ability owes a great deal to well known scholars such as Sir Francis Galton, Charles Spearman, Philip E. Vernon and more recently Hans-Jürgen Eysenck, Richard Dawkins, John Sloboda, John Radford, Alan Baddeley, and many more. Indigenous research specifically focusing on Gifted Education, however, is still scarce (Freeman, 1998), whereas specific literature for parents of highly able children, and for teachers interested in Gifted Education, is readily available (Denton & Postlewaithe; 1985; Leyden, 1985; Freeman, 1991; George, 1992; Young & Tyre, 1992; Faludi & Faludi, 1996; Montgomery, 1996; Eyre, 1997).

Recognizing and nurturing high ability has, in a sense, been an integral part of English society for a long time. Interest in high ability, however, has been largely class-bound, and has become a part of the sometimes conflicting interests of the higher and lower strata of English society. This conflict has occasionally also been voiced in research. Howe (1990), for example, argues in over-viewing the traditional nature/nurture problem, that

> it may be comforting for recipients of a privileged upbringing to have chosen to believe that Nature has ordained some people to be born quick-witted and others dull, some to lead and the remainder to follow. But the findings of empirical research contradict this conclusion (p. 57).

It needs to be pointed out, therefore, that while elite training in English boarding schools has a long-standing tradition—often hailed and commended for its excellence—it has, in fact, little to do with the growing recognition of the need to establish Gifted Education as based in the national school system. The famed tradition of English boarding schools is above all a matter of *social* positioning in society, where high ability certainly is an expressed target, but where tradition and a certain social fostering are likely to constitute a more powerful *raison d'être* than is differentiation and concern for ability profiles of individual students. Such schools may, contrary to belief, not necessarily facilitate the development of high ability. It is known by research that this type of institution may well have a long-term negative impact on the emotional lives of their pupils. They tend to foster in some children a particular style of coping whereby distress is actively suppressed from consciousness rather than confided in someone willing to listen (Boyd, 1985; Fisher, Frazer & Murray, 1987; Harris, 1989).

Due to the dominance of politically egalitarian convictions, as in the Scandinavian countries and in former Communist Europe, resistance to focus Gifted Education as a separate issue in the English school system—irrespective of the existence of traditional elite schools—has been formidable (cf. Young & Tyre, 1992). The process of recognizing the notion of special needs in education as inclusive of provision for the highly able also, has been a long one and, interestingly, largely separate from government decisions and legislation. High ability is not recognized, for example, under the Special Needs Legislation of 1981 and 1993, which also conveys the principle of inclusion: special needs should be provided for in the regular school (O'Hanlon, 1995). The provision for gifted and talented children in schools has nevertheless been the specific focus of officially commissioned reports (DES, 1977; HMI, 1992; Eyre, 1995; Freeman, 1998), or mentioned by these as an issue in need of serious consideration (DES, 1979; Askew & Wiliam, 1995).

As early as 1973—preceding the Warnock Committee Report on Special Education (DES, 1978), which to some extent accelerated the interest in providing for highly able children too—The Department of Education and Science in London offered a first course for teachers on the special education of gifted children. In-service training of teachers has continued, and some research on how best to implement such training is being pursued (Clark, 1996, 1997; Montgomery, 1997).

Note that teachers and parents organizations have been of paramount importance in prompting a development towards special provision for gifted and talented children in England and Wales (cf. Freeman, 1995). The National Association for Gifted Children (NAGC) was founded in 1966 by parents to promote knowledge of high ability, and in 1982 the National Association for Curriculum Enrichment and Extension (NACE) was founded by, and for, teachers to support teachers nationally in matters pertaining to the education of gifted and talented children. More recently NACE has also established a research center at Westminster College, Oxford: The Centre for Able Pupils.

Implementation of Gifted Education, always subject to egalitarian legislation—and influenced by parents and teachers organizations—has been mainly the concern of Local Education Authorities (LEAs). For example, in 1992 about 35 LEAs (out of a total of 108) were employing at least one individual with official responsibility for the gifted (Freeman, 1992), and five LEAs had one person employed with highly able children as their *sole* responsibility (Raffan & Short, 1992). Development towards national guidelines for Gifted Education, however, is slow (DES, 1989), and Freeman (1998) expresses some doubts as to a central and immediate political solution to the problem. The 1995 revision of the new National Curriculum has to some extent opened up to high ability provision through the so-called Access Statement, which declares that "for the small number of pupils who may need provision, material may be selected from earlier or later key stages where this is necessary to enable individual pupils to progress and demonstrate achievement" (cf. Freeman, 1998, p. 53). The level description for each Attainment Target in the National Curriculum also addresses 'exceptional performance' and does mention 'very able pupils'. However, it would appear that, at least for the time being, the further development and advancement of Gifted Education in England and Wales, rests mainly with individual schools and the local policy adopted on how to make provision for the highly able child (Eyre, 1997; Freeman, 1997, 1998). The number of schools expressing an interest in such policies is steadily on the increase. For example, there are presently ten experimental classes set up all over England geared towards special provision. In addition, a group of advisors has been set up to guide the British Government in the further development of Gifted Education, and a group of Members of Parliament has very recently launched a special investigation into the education of the most able (Joan Freeman, personal communication, 5 January, 1999). Freeman (1998) points out that this "accelerating development is likely to be the result of some government guidance, official and government-supported conferences and free publications focusing high ability, school standards in education inspections, parents and teachers organizations, as well as due to the recent large-scale NACE/DFE-project entitled Supporting the Education of Able Pupils in Maintained Schools' (cf. Eyre, 1995), which involved some 20,000 teachers in 37 LEAs.

Is There a Specific European Approach to Gifted Education?

Europe is a continent with a great deal of cultural, ideological, and economical variety. This is clearly reflected in the way Gifted Education is approached and valued. European ideals may be *ideologically* and *culturally* divided between policies striving for differentiation and policies promoting similarity, which largely divide the Continent in two halves: one Northern part and one Southern/Eastern/Middle/Western part. While special provision for the highly able is an expressed education-political agenda, albeit not always uncontroversial and legislated, in Southern, Eastern, Middle and Western Europe, Northern Europe (i.e. Scandinavia) largely resists any attempt to single out any individual in educational contexts for any reason, since generally the group is the culturally decided unit rather than the individual. It is often more important to be similar rather than different.

In spite of the demise of the 'Iron Curtain' between Communist and Non-Communist Europe, however, the continent is also divided in an Eastern and a Western part depending largely on current differences in national economies. This divide creates an interesting discrepancy between East and West as far as Gifted Education is concerned.

On the assumption that high ability is essential in promoting the development of a nation's Industry, Science, and Economy, all of former Communist Europe has embraced Gifted Education with some fervor and ingenuity; which in part is reviving a rich cultural tradition, that was largely dormant and suppressed during the time of Soviet influence. This part of Europe, however, currently lacks the financial means, and in some cases also efficient administration and organization, to implement their intentions, and bring to life again their interest in providing for talents. There is also little controversy in the East parts of Europe regarding Gifted Education.

In Western parts of Europe (including Scandinavia), however, national economies are relatively strong; there is generally no lack of funding for national education; but while high ability is recognized as instrumental in professional life and in competing with other world economies—professionally, developmentally and scientifically, Gifted Education is paradoxically a controversial issue, although more so in some countries than in others. This resistance tends to be ideological in nature, and is perhaps based on the fear that promoting an elite, which potentially could supersede democratic principles, could also proceed from being an intellectual/professional elite to becoming a social and exclusively privileged and potentially secluded elite. However, such fear is largely unwarranted. Most sociologists agree that no democracy can, in fact, exist without the support of an elite (Giddens, 1989).

The sensitivity of the issue in most of Western Europe has prompted national school systems to opt for Inclusive Education as recommended by the so-called Salamanca Statement, on the assumption that all children's educational needs can be satisfied, more or less, within the regular classroom in a mixed-ability setting.

The nations of the Western part of Europe, therefore—to the extent that national education authorities recognize the need of special provision for highly able children—enact Gifted Education mainly in an inclusive setting (see Table 1). For such endeavors to be successful, specific teacher training, means of instruction, research, and school system flexibility, are of the utmost importance. Significant to this development is the fact that the European Council—a body for intergovernmental cooperation between 25 European states—issued a recommendation for all of its member states in 1994 regarding, specifically, the education of gifted children (Council of Europe, 1994). This document recommends all member states

• to legislate for the special educational needs of gifted children to be recognized;

- to promote research on identification, the nature of success, and reasons for school failure;
- to provide information on gifted children and in-service training for all teachers;
- to make special provision for gifted children *within* the ordinary school system (i. e. Inclusive education);
- to take measures to avoid the negative consequences of labeling someone as gifted and talented;
- and to promote debate and research amongst psychologist, sociologists, and educators, on the
- vague and relatively undefined giftedness construct.

This document carefully addresses the sensitivity of the issue by emphasizing, that "special educational provision should . . . in no way privilege one group of children to the detriment of the others" (p. 1).

Is there then a typical European approach to Gifted Education? Clearly, the conditions for developing provision for the highly able are unique in the sense that the complexity of the issue demands European-based research to find ways of implementation, and to develop strategies commensurate with the psychological nature of highly able individuals, compatible with the cultural legacies of Europe, and agreeable to current political ideologies. The variety of problems encountered in developing Gifted Education, however, is not unique to Europe. Suspicion towards high-achievers, irrespective of their field of pursuit, is a problem in Scandinavia (Daun, 1994) as well as in Australia and New Zealand (Mitchell, 1991; Thompson, 1994), and to some extent also in the so-called Third World (Raina, 1996); and allegations of school systems nurturing anti-intellectualism have been made

Table 1. An Overview of Different Aspects of European Provision for the Gifted and Talented.

Countries	Legislation	Type of provision				
		Schools	Classes	Extracurricular	Training	Other
Bulgaria	•	•	•	•	•	-
Croatia	•	-	-	•	•	-
Hungary	•	•	•	•	•	-
Poland	•	-	•	•	•	-
Romania	•	•	•	•	•	-
Slovakia	•	•	-	•	•	-
Slovenia	•	•	-	•	•	-
The Ukraine	•	•	•	•	-	-
Austria	•	•	-	•	•	•
Belgium	-	•	-	•	•	•
France	-	•	•	•	•	•
Germany	•[a]	•	•	•	•	•
Italy	-	•	-	•	-	•
Portugal	-	-	-	•	•	•
Switzerland	-	•	-	•	•	•
Spain	-	-	-	•	•	•
The Netherlands	-	•	-	•	•	•
Sweden	-	-	•[b]	-	•	•
Denmark	-	-	-	-	•	•
Finland	-	-	-	•	-	•
Norway	-	-	-	-	-	•
Russia	•	•	•	•	•	-
Latvia	•	-	-	•	-	-
England/Wales	-	•	•[c]	-	•	•

Legend: Note that legislation refers to legislation specific to making provision for the highly able. Similarly, schools and classes refer to specially designated learning environments (also specially designated higher education)—private and/or state-controlled. Extracurricular pertains to all manner of provision or specially designated activities, which are not part of a school system. By training is meant all types of teacher training, either by in-service training, specially offered courses, or unique teacher training programs. Other includes means of provision typical of inclusive strategies such as grade skipping, within-class provision and/or a variety of enrichment strategies.

[a]*There is legislation in a few federal states, especially in the 'new states' of former GDR.*
[b]*Note that these are six experimental classes, launched in 1999 in Stockholm by initiative of the Stockholm LEA.*
[c]*Note that these are experimental classes.*

in the United States (Howley, Howley & Pendarvis, 1995) as well as in Sweden (Segerstedt, 1979).

To be different than most others has probably always been a dilemma in any culture and in any historical era; and being exceptionally able is only one possible way in which an individual may be different from others (Persson, 1999). Berenson's (1959) definition of 'genius' in the world of Visual Arts as "the capacity for productive reaction against one's training" (p. 201), for example, speaks of the potential and *social* impact of creating something new. Hence, by implication, to be 'deviant' from what is considered the general norm, is also to be made suspicious by peers and contemporaries holding on to that norm. There is safety in recognition and in that, which is generally accepted. Common to all nations, presumably, are abilities, which deviate from accepted norms by level or nature. Many of the problems encountered by implementing Gifted Education worldwide are likely to be the same rather than unique, or at least related, on social-psychological grounds.

It is likely, however, that in time Gifted Education will be established in a way unique to Europe, the reason being that such provision will need to follow not only psychological characteristics, and specifically European needs, but also the culture of which the gifted psyche is an inevitable part.

Acknowledgements

The authors would like to extend their gratitude to the multitude of staff at European Embassies and Ministries of Education and Science, who have willingly and expertly assisted us in providing current information relevant to high ability and Gifted Education. We are also particularly indebted to the following individuals, who graciously and exhaustively contributed their considerable professional experience in their respective countries as well as material and relevant information, which was not readily available by any other means than by colleague-to-colleague contact: Inara Akmene, Juan A. Alonso, Lidija Arambasic, Konstatin Bähr, Kirsten Baltzer, Dominique Barthélemy, Edward Chitham, Carmen Cretu, Carl D'hondt, Vladimir Dockal, Ivan Ferbezer, Joan Freeman, Margarida Goveia Fernandes, Arne Gundersen, Jarkko Hautamäki, Annette Heinbokel, Kurt A. Heller, Liane Hoogeveen, Thomas Köhler, Ole Kyed, Wieslawa Limont, Theo Mardulier, Sylviane Monnier, Franz J. Mönks, Tetyana B. Partyko, Willy A. M. Peters, Ludmila Popova, Vagn Rabøl-Hansen, Katya Stoycheva, Kirsi Tirri, Javier Touron, Kari Uusikylä, Vlasta Vizek-Vidovic, Vesna Vlahovic-Stetic, and Levcho Zdravchev.

References

Aceveda, A. & Sastre, S. (1998). *La superdotación* [Gifted Education]. Madrid: Sintesis.

Akmene, I. (1994). *Development of high ability pupils in Latvia.* Paper presented at The Fourth Conference of The European Council for High Ability in Nijmegen, The Netherlands.

Andzans, A. (undated). *Elementary mathematics and advanced teaching of it in Latvia.* Unpublished manuscript, University of Latvia at Riga.

Arambasic, L. (1996). Mathematics, anxiety and social support in mathematically gifted and non-gifted children. Paper presented at The Fifth Conference of The European Council for High Ability in Vienna, Austria.

Arrte ministeriel (1997). *Le système éducatif de la Belgique-Communaute française* [Educational system of the French community in Belgium]. Brussels, Belgium: Enseigement de la Communaute francaise.

Askew, M. & Wiliam, D. (1995). *Recent research in mathematics education* (OFSTED reviews of research). London: HMSO.

Babaeva, J. D. A. (1999). A dynamic approach to giftedness: theory and practice. *High Ability Studies,* **10** (1), 51–68.

Bähr, K. (1998a). *Bericht der verwaltungsinternen Arbeitsgruppe zum Thema 'Hochbegabte'* [Report by the self-contained working group on high ability]. Zürich, Switzerland: Erziehungsdirektion des Kantons Zürich, Pädagogische Abteilung. Available http://www blacklotus. ch/EHK/Recht/ERB98.html.

Bähr, K. (1998b). *Überspringen einer Klasse im Kanton Zürich. Ergebnisse einer Untersuchung der Jahre 1995–1997* [Skipping a grade in the Zürich Kanton: Results of a study from 1995 to 1997]. Zürich, Switzerland: Erziehungsdirektion des Kantons Zürich, Pädagogische Abteilung. Available http://www.blacklotus.ch/EHK/Recht/ UEB97.html.

Balla, L., Hanol, J. & Molnárné-Duschek, E. (1996). *Grammar school—different school systems.* Paper presented at The Fifth Conference of The European Council for High Ability in Vienna, Austria.

Balogh, L. & Nagy, K. (1991). The development of personality, abilities and social relations in a special class. *European Journal for High Ability,* **2** (2), 134–138.

Balogh, L. & Nagy, K. (1995). A follow-up study of pupils having taken part in a complex talent development program. In: M. W. Katzko & F. J. Mönks (Eds.), *Nurturing Talent: Individual Needs and Social Ability* (pp. 210–216). Assen, The Netherlands: Van Gorcum.

Balogh, L. & Nagy, K. (1996). Developing talented children: problems and experiences. In: A. J. Cropley & D. Dehn (Eds.*), Fostering the Growth of High Ability: European Perspectives* (pp. 65–74). Norwood, NJ: Ablex.

Balogh, L., Dávid, I., Nagy, K. & Tóth, L. (1997). Learning techniques and self-knowledge with talented school children. *Acta Psychologica Debrecina,* **20,** 173–182.

Bals, T. (1999). Fostering talents in vocational training: current strategies in Germany. *High Ability Studies,* **10** (1), 97–106.

Baltzer, K. (1996). Talentfulde børn [Talented children]. In: V. Rabøl-Hansen & O. Robenhagen (Eds.), *På det jævne og i det himmelblå. Talenter i skolen* (pp. 99–109). Copenhagen, Denmark: The Danish National Institute for Educational Research.

Berendonck, B. (1993). *DDR doping: Medaljer, ära, fördärv* (DDR doping: medals, glory, destruction) (A. Bredberg, Transl.). Kungsängen, Sweden: Musclemedi Publishing and Powerproducts AB.

Berenson, B. (1959). *The Italian painters of the Renaissance.* London: Phaidon Press.

Bergman, I. (1987). *Laterna magica.* Stockholm: Norstedts.

Bildung und Begabung e.V. (1997). *Tätigkeitsbericht 1996/97* [Annual Report for 1996/97]. Bonn, Germany: Bildung und Begabung e.V.

Bildung und Begabung e.V. (1998). *Deutsche Schüler-Akademie. Program 1998* [German Pupils' Academy. Program 1998]. Bonn, Germany: Bildung und Begabung e.V.

Borodchuk, I. (1996). *The Role of the Small Academy of Sciences in the formation of abilities of village pupils.* Paper presented at The Fifth Conference of The European Council for High Ability in Vienna, Austria.

Bota, M. (1996). *The family environment and the self-concept of gifted children in Hungarian primary school children.* Paper presented at The Fifth Conference of The European Council for High Ability in Vienna, Austria.

Boyd, W. (1985). *School ties.* London: Hamish Hamilton.

Bundeskanzleramt (1994). *Das sterreichische Bildungswesen* [The Austrian Education System]. Vienna, Austria: Bundespressedienst.

Bundesministerium für Unterricht und Kunst (1994). *Begabungsförderung: Eine Herausforderung für Schule und Gesellschaft* [Supporting the gifted: a challenge for school and society]. Vienna, Austria: Bundesministerium für Unterricht und Kunst.

Cardoso, M. L. S., Coutinho, A. M. & Fernandes, P. B. (1997). New perspectives, new directions in the discovery and development of gifted and talented children in Portugal. In: J. Chan, R. Li & J. Spinks (Eds.), *Maximizing Potential: Lengthening and Strengthening our Stride* (pp. 76–79). Hong Kong: The University of Hong Kong.

Clark, C. (1996). *More able and talented pupils: developing practice in Cleveland primary and secondary schools.* Cleveland, UK: Cleveland Local Education Authority.

Clark, C. (1997). Using action research to foster a creative response to teaching more able pupils. *High Ability Studies,* **8** (1), 95–111.

Côte, S. (Ed.). (1996). *Pédagogie pour enfants intellectuellement précoces* [Pedagogy for intellectually gifted children]. Paris: ACP Editions.

Côte, S., Adda, A. & Capron, C. (1997). *Précocité intellectuelle: de la mythologie à la génétique* [Precocious intelligence: from myth to genetics]. Paris: ACP Editions.

Côte, S., Adda, A. & Cancill, G. (1998). *Les Enfants Précoces* [The highly able children]. Paris: ACP Editions.

Côte, S., Bouchard, P. & Delcros, X. (1998). *Le paradoxe de l'enfant précoce* [The paradox of the highly able child]. Paris: ACP Editions.

Council of Europe (1994). *Recommendation no. 1248 on education for gifted children.* Strasbourg, France: Council of Europe.

Cretu, C. M. (1992). The educational system of gifted and talented people in Romania. In: F. J. Mönks & H. W. van Boxtel (Eds.), *Education of the Gifted in Europe: Theoretical and Research Issues* (pp. 171–176). Amsterdam: Swets & Zeitlinger.

Cretu, C. M. (1993). *Global success in learning: how to improve it?* In: E. A. Hany & K. A. Heller (Eds.), *Competence and Responsibility,* Vol. 1 (pp. 27–28). Seattle: Hogrefe & Huber Publ.

Cretu, C. M. (1996). *What makes the highly creative musician?* Paper presented at The Fifth Conference of The European Council for High Ability in Vienna, Austria.

Cvetkovic, L. J., George, D., Sekulic-Majavec, A., Glogovac, V. & Stritik, B. (1996). *Gifted pre-school children in Croatia.* Paper presented at The Fifth Conference of The European Council for High Ability in Vienna, Austria.

Czeizel, A. (1995). Heredity and giftedness: from eugenics to euphenics. In: M. W. Katzko & F. J. Mönks (Eds.), *Nurturing Talent: Individual Needs and Social Ability* (pp 102–112). Assen, The Netherlands: Van Gorcum.

Daun, Å. (1994). *Swedish mentality* [Jan Teeland, Trans. Original work published in 1989]. University Park, PA: The Pennsylvania State University Press.

Daunt, P. (1995). Introduction: integration practice and policy for children with special needs in Europe. In: C. O'Hanlon (Ed.), *Inclusive Education in Europe* (pp. 1–8). London: David Fulton Publishers.

David, G. (1997). *The gifted child as a challenge.* Ljubljana, Slovenia: Zavod Republike Slovenije za solstvo.

Dávid, I. & Balogh, L. (1997). Teachers' Opinion about the Nature of Giftedness. *Acta Psychologica Debrecina,* Vol. 20 (pp. 189–196). Debrecen, Hungary: Kossuth University Press.

Dávid, I., Pásku, J. & Vitális, E. (1996). *Correlations between IQ, Creativity and SES (Socio-Economic Status).* Paper presented at The Fifth Conference of The European Council for High Ability in Vienna, Austria.

Denton, C. & Postlewaithe, K. (1985). *Able children: identifying them in the classroom.* Staines, England: NFER Nelson.

Department of Education and Science (1977). *Gifted children in middle and comprehensive schools.* London: HMSO.

Department of Education and Science (1978). *Special educational needs.* London: HMSO.

Department of Education and Science (1979). *Aspects of secondary education.* London: HMSO.

Department of Education and Science (1989). *Standards in education 1988–1989.* London: HMSO.

Dijk van, W., Kok, W. A. M. & Poorthuis, G. T. M. (1996). Educating gifted pupils in regular schools. In: A. J. Cropley & D. Dehn (Eds.), *Fostering the Growth of High Ability: European Perspectives* (pp. 447–458). Norwood, NJ: Ablex.

Dockal, V. (1996). *Social conditions of sports and dance talent development.* Paper presented at The Fifth Conference of The European Council for High Ability in Vienna, Austria.

Dockal, V. & Kovac, T. (1993). On talent development. *Studia Psychologica,* **3–4,** 193–194.

Dockal, V., Laznibatova, J. & Kovac, T. (1992). The research on talent in Slovakia. In: F. J. Mönks, M. W. Katzko & H. W. van Boxtel (Eds.), *Education of the Gifted in Europe: Theoretical and Research Issues* (pp. 177–179). Amsterdam: Swets & Zeitlinger.

Dunér, A. & Törestad, B. (1980). *Toppbegåvningar i svensk skola* [Highly gifted in the Swedish school system] (Reports from the Department of Psychology, No. 34). Stockholm: Stockholm University.

Durazzo, F. M. (1997). Les représentations mythiques de l'intelligence dans le débat sur l'enfant précoce [Mythical representations of intelligence in the debate of gifted children]. In: J. C. Grubar, M. Duyme & S. Cte (Eds.), *La Précocité Intellectuelle de la Mythologie à la Génétique* (pp. 17–25), Sprimont, Belgium: Mardaga.

Edfelt, Å. W. (1992). Can early reading lead to academic prowess? In: F. J. Mönks, M. W. Katzko & H. W. van

Boxtel (Eds.), *Education of the Gifted in Europe: Theoretical and Research Issues* (pp. 47–57). Amsterdam: Swets & Zeitlinger.

Engel, W., Gronau, H.-D., Langmann, H.-H. & Sewerin, H. (1999). *The German Teams at the International Mathematical Olympiads 1959–1998.* Bad Honnef: Bock.

Engeström, Y., Engeström, R. & Kärkkäinen, M. (1997). The emerging horizontal dimension of practical intelligence: polycontextuality and boundary crossing in complex work activities. In: R. J. Sternberg & E. Grigorenko (Eds.), *Intelligence, Heredity, and Environment* (pp. 440–462). Cambridge, UK: Cambridge University Press.

Eyre, D. (1995). *School governors and more able children.* London: HMSO.

Eyre, D. (1997). *Able children in ordinary schools.* London: David Fulton Publishers.

Faludi, T. & Faludi, A. (1996). *A little edge of darkness: a boy's triumph over Dyslexia.* London: Jessica Kingsley.

Farkasova, E. (1993). *Special abilities in learning foreign language by young pupils.* In: E. A. Hany & K. A. Heller (Eds.), *Competence and Responsibility*, Vol. 1 (p. 41). Seattle: Hogrefe & Huber Publ.

Feger, B. & Prado, T. (1986). The first information and counseling center for the gifted in West Germany. In: K. A. Heller & J. F. Feldhusen (Eds.), *Identifying and Nurturing the Gifted* (pp. 139–148). Toronto: Huber Publ.

Ferbezer, I. (1993). *Teacher's observation by scales for rating the behavioral characteristics of superior pupils (Renzulli) in Slovenia.* In: E. A. Hany & K. A. Heller (Eds.), *Competence and Responsibility*, Vol.1 (p. 42). Seattle: Hogrefe & Huber Publ.

Ferbezer, I. (1996). *Teachers' standpoints to programs for culturally deprived gifted children.* Paper presented at The Fifth Conference of The European Council for High Ability in Vienna, Austria.

Firsov, V. (1993). Schools for gifted children. *Nämnaren, 2* (20), 40–43.

Fisher, S., Frazer, N. & Murray, K. (1987). Homesickness and health in boarding school children. *Journal of Environmental Psychology, 6,* 35–47.

Freeman, J. (1991). *Bright as a button: how to encourage your children's talents 0–5 years.* London: Macdonald Optima.

Freeman, J. (1992). Recent developments for the highly able in Britain. In: F. J. Mönks, M. W. Katzko & H. W. van Boxtel (Eds.), *Education of the Gifted in Europe: Theoretical and Research Issues* (pp. 58–70). Amsterdam: Swets & Zeitlinger.

Freeman, J. (1995). Towards a policy for actualizing talent. In: J. Freeman, P. Span & H. Wagner (Eds.), *Actualizing Talent. A Lifelong Challenge* (pp. 174–190). London: Cassell.

Freeman, J. (1998). *Educating the very able. Current international research* (OFSTED reviews of research). London: The Stationary Office.

Gardner, H. (1983). *Frames of mind: the Theory of Multiple Intelligences.* New York: Basic Books.

Gefferth, E. & Herskovits, M. (1991). Leisure activities as predictors of giftedness. *European Journal for High Ability, 2* (1), 43–51.

George, D. (1992). *The challenge of the able child.* London: David Fulton Publishers.

Giddens, A. (1989). *Sociology.* Oxford, UK: Polity Press.

Gobierno de Navarra: Departamento de Educación y Cultura (1995). *La Atención a la Diversidad* [Catering to Diversity]. Pamplona, Spain: Gobierno de Navarra. Departamento de Educación y Cultura.

Grinder, R. E. (1985). The gifted in our midst: by their divine deeds, neuroses, and mental test scores we have known them. In: F. D. Horowitz & M. O'Brien (Eds.), *The gifted an talented: developmental perspectives* (pp. 5–36). Washington, DC: American Psychological Association.

Gummesson, O. (1997). *Därför lyckas Gnosjö. Bygden som har blivit ett begrepp* [That is why Gnosjö succeeds. The community that set an example]. Stockholm: Ekerlids förlag.

Gustafsson, J. E. & Härnqvist, K. (1977). *Begåvningstyper och undervisningsmetoder* [Types of ability and teaching methods]. Stockholm: Liber läromedel/Skolöverstyrelsen.

Györik, F. (1993). *The experiences from consultations with talented children's parents.* In: E. A. Hany & K. A. Heller (Eds.), *Competence and Responsibility*, Vol. 1 (pp. 49–51). Seattle: Hogrefe & Huber Publ.

Hany, E. (1995). Eines schickt sich nicht für alle: Eine Führung durch das Methodenarsenal der Begabtenförderung [One is not necessarily suitable for all: a guide to the arsenal of methodology in support of gifted education]. In: H. Wagner (Ed.), *Begabung und Leistung in der Schule* (pp. 52–75). Bad Honnef, Germany: Bock.

Hany, E. A. & Heller, K. A. (1988). *Enrichment Program for Highly Gifted Students in Baden-Württemberg: A Project of Applied Developmental Psychology.* Paper presented at the Third European Conference on Developmental Psychology in Budapest (Hungary), June 15–19, 1988.

Hany, E. A. & Heller, K. A. (1992). *Förderung besonders befähigter Schüler in Baden-Württemberg: Ergebnisse der Wissenschaftlichen Begleitforschung.* [Educating the Gifted Students in Baden-Württemberg: Results of a program evaluation study]. Heft 15 der Reihe 'Förderung besonders befähigter Schüler', Ed. Ministry of Culture, Education and Sports Baden-Württemberg. Stuttgart: MKS.

Harris, P. L. (1989). *Children and emotion: the development of psychological understanding.* Oxford, UK: Blackwell.

Harsányi, L. (1996). Ability for athletics: Identification and improvement of talent. In: A. J. Cropley & D. Dehn (Eds.), *Fostering the Growth of High Ability: European Perspectives* (pp. 343–352). Norwood, NJ: Ablex.

Hartmann, Ch. (1998). *The 'Jugenddorf Hannover': a concept including kindergarten, primary school and extracurricular activities.* Paper presented at the Sixth Conference of The European Council for High Ability in Oxford, UK.

Heinbokel, A. (1996). *Überspringen von Klassen* [Grade skipping]. Münster, Germany: LIT Verlag.

Heller, K. A. (1992a). Aims and methodological problems of an intervention study in gifted and talented girls. In: F. J. Mönks & W. A. M. Peters (Eds.), *Talent for the Future: Social and Personality Development of Gifted Children* (pp. 149–154). Assen: Van Gorcum.

Heller, K. A. (1992b). Giftedness research and education of the gifted and talented in Germany. In: F. J. Mönks, M. W. Katzko & H. W. Boxtel (Eds.), *Education of the Gifted in Europe: Theoretical and Research Issues* (pp. 71–85). Amsterdam: Swets & Zeitlinger.

Heller, K. A. (1993). Identifying and counselling the gifted students. In: E. G. Demetropoulos et al. (Eds.), *Europe 2000—Tendencies and Perspectives in Counselling and Guidance. International Conference Proceedings* (pp.

48–62). Athens: Hellenic Society of Counselling and Guidance (HE.S.CO.G.).

Heller, K. A. (1995a). Begabungsdefinition, Begabungserkennung und Begabungsförderung im Schulalter [Defining, recognizing and supporting giftedness in school-aged children]. In: H. Wagner (Ed.), *Begabung und Leistung in der Schule* (pp. 6–36). Bad Honnef, Germany: Bock.

Heller, K. A. (1995b). Evaluation of programs for the gifted. In: M. Katzko & F. J. Mönks (Eds.), *Nurturing Talent: Individual Needs and Social Ability* (pp. 264–268). Assen/Maastricht: Van Gorcum.

Heller, K. A. (1996). Erkennen und Fördern hochbegabter Kinder und Jugendlicher [Recognizing and supporting highly gifted children and youths]. In: H. Kretz (Ed.), *Lebendige Psychohygiene* (pp. 207–249). München: Eberhard.

Heller, K. A. (1997a). *Gifted (children) education in the European community.* Paper presented at the International Congress on Gifted and Talented Children in Madrid, Spain, July 14–16, 1997.

Heller, K. A. (1997b). Individuelle Bedingungsfaktoren der Schulleistung: Literaturüberblick [A literature review of individual prerequisites for school achievement]. In: F. E. Weinert & A. Helmke (Eds.), *Entwicklung im Grundschulalter* (pp. 181–201). Weinheim, Germany: Beltz/PVU.

Heller, K. A. (1998). Gender differences in performance and in attributional styles among the gifted. In: R. Zorman & N. Krongold (Eds.), *Nurturing Gifted Girls in the Natural Sciences* (Englisch: pp. 9–37/Hebrew: pp. 9–24). Jerusalem: The Henrietta Szold Institute/The National Institute for Research in the Behavioral Sciences.

Heller, K. A. (1999). Individual (learning and motivational) needs versus instructional conditions of gifted education. *High Abilitiy Studies,* **9**, 9–21.

Heller, K. A. & Geisler, H.-J. (1989). *The Munich Counseling Center of Technical Creativity.* Paper presented at the Tenth Biennial Meetings of ISSBD in Jyväskylä (Finland), July 9–13, 1989.

Heller, K. A. & Hany, E. A. (1993). *Statewide Enrichment Program for Highly Gifted Students in Baden-Württemberg: A Longitudinal Follow-up Study (1985–1990).* Paper presented at the 10th World Congress on Gifted and Talented Education in Toronto (Canada), August 8–13, 1993.

Heller, K. A. & Hany, E. A. (Eds.). (1994). *Competence and Responsibility,* Vol. 2. Seattle: Hogrefe & Huber Publ.

Heller, K. A. & Hany, E. A. (1996). Psychologische Modelle der Hochbegabtenförderung [Psychological Models of Gifted Education]. In: F. E. Weinert (Ed.), *Psychologie des Lernens und der Instruktion,* Vol. 2 der Pädagogischen Psychologie (Enzyklopädie der Psychologie) (pp. 477–513). Göttingen: Hogrefe.

Heller, K. A. & Lengfelder, A. (1999). *Wissenschaftliche Evaluation der Internationalen Schülerolympiaden in Mathematik, Physik und Chemie (1977–1997)* [Evaluation Longitudinal Study on the International Olympiads in Maths, Physics and Chemistry (1977–1997)]. Final Report to the Federal Ministry of Education, Science and Technology in Bonn. München: LMU.

Heller, K. A. & Lengfelder, A. (2000). *German Olympiad Studies: Math, Physics and Chemistry.* Paper presented at the 2000 AERA Annual Meeting in New Orleans (USA), April 24–28, 2000.

Heller, K. A. & Reimann, R. (1999). *Achter Bericht über die wissenschaftliche Evaluation des baden-württembergischen Schulmodellversuchs 'Gymnasium mit achtjährigem Bildungsgang'.* Methoden und Ergebnisse der ersten acht Untersuchungswellen (1992–1999) an achtjährigen Gymnasien unter Einschluß dreier Erhebungswellen (1997–1999) an neunjährigen Regelgymnasien [Eighth Report on the Evaluation of the Acceleration Gifted Program at the German Gymnasium in Baden-Württemberg]. München: LMU/Stuttgart: MKS.

Heller, K. A. & Viek, P. (2000). Support for the gifted university students: individual and social factors. In: C. F. M. van Lieshout & P. G. Heymans (Eds.), *Talent, Resilience, and Wisdom Across the Life Span* (pp. 299–321). London: Psychology Press.

Heller, K. A. & Ziegler, A. (1996). Gender differences in mathematics and the natural sciences: can attributional retraining improve the performance of gifted females? *Gifted Child Quarterly,* **40**, 200–210.

Heller, K. A., Neber, H. & Wystrychowski, W. (1993). *Statewide Acceleration Program for Highly Gifted Students from the German Gymnasium: A Longitudinal Follow-up Evaluation Study (1991–2000).* Paper presented at the 10th World Congress on Gifted and Talented Education in Toronto (Canada), August 8–13, 1993.

Heller, K. A., Osterrieder, K. & Wystrychowski, W. (1995). A longitudinal follow-up evaluation study of a statewide acceleration program for highly gifted students at the german gymnasium. In: M. Katzko & F. J. Mönks (Eds.), *Nurturing Talent: Individual Needs and Social Ability* (pp. 269–274). Assen/Maastricht: Van Gorcum.

Heller, K. A. Viek, P., Becker, U. & Schober, B. (1997). *Explorationsstudie zur Begabtenförderung im Tertiärbereich* [Gifted Program Evaluation Study in Higher Education]. Final Report to the Federal Ministry of Education, Science and Technology in Bonn. München: LMU.

Herskovits, M. (1994). *Parental strategies for developing their highly able children.* Paper presented at The Fourth Conference of The European Council for High Ability in Nijmegen, Netherlands.

Herskovits, M. & Gyarmathy, E. (1995). Gifted children's early years by parental interviews. In: M. W. Katzko & F. J. Mönks (Eds.), *Nurturing Talent: Individual Needs and Social Ability* (pp. 58–63). Assen, The Netherlands: Van Gorcum.

HMI (Her Majesty's Inspectors of Schools). (1992). *Education observed: the education of very able children in maintained schools.* London: HMSO.

Hofstede, G. (1982). *Culture's consequences: international differences in work-related values.* London: Sage.

Howe, M. J. A. (1990). *The origins of exceptional abilities.* Oxford, UK: Blackwell.

Howley, C. B., Howley, A. & Pendarvis, E. D. (1995). *Out of our minds: anti-intellectualism and talent development in American Schooling.* New York: Teachers College Press.

Husén, T. (1948). *Begåvning och miljö* [Ability and environment]. Stockholm: Hugo Gebers förlag.

Husén, T. (1979). *The school in question: a comparative study of the school and its future in Western society.* Oxford, UK: Oxford University Press.

Jakova, M. (1993). *Creativity of the child and development of individual giftedness.* In: E. A. Hany & K. A. Heller (Eds.),

Competence and Responsibility, Vol. 1 (pp. 64–65). Seattle: Hogrefe & Huber Publ.

Jakova, M. (1996). *Social dimensions in children's creativity.* Paper presented at The Fifth Conference of The European Council for High Ability in Vienna, Austria.

Jansen, M. (1996). De klarer sig nok de tidlige læsere [Early readers will always be alright]. In: V. Rabøl-Hansen & O. Robenhagen (Eds.), *På det jævne og i det himmelblå— Talenter i skolen* (pp. 31–42). Copenhagen: The Danish National Institute for Educational Research.

Joswig, H. (1998). Innere Differenzierung und Begabungsentwicklung. [Inner differentiation and development of giftedness]. In: K. K. Urban & H. Joswig (Eds.), *Begabungsförderung in der Schule* (pp. 51–59). Rodenberg, Germany: Klausur-Verlag.

Kabalevsky, D. B. (1988). *Music and education: a composer writes about musical education.* London: Jessica Kingsley/ UNESCO.

Kaftandjieva, F. (1996). *Creativity measurement: Item Response Theory Approach.* Paper presented at The Fifth Conference of The European Council for High Ability in Vienna, Austria.

Kaiser, A. (Ed.). (1997). *Entwicklung und Erprobung von Modellen der Begabtenförderung am Gymnasium mit Verkürzung der Schulzeit* [Development and Evaluation of an Acceleration Gifted Program at the German Gymnasium]. Mainz: Hase & Koehler.

Karlsson, C. & Larsson, J. (1993). A macroview of the Gnosjö entrepreneurial spirit. In: C. Karlsson, B. Johannisson & D. Storey (Eds.*), Small Business Dynamics. International, National and Regional Perspectives* (pp. 175–202). London: Routledge.

Kárpáti, A. (1996). *Identifying visual talent: the Project-Portfolio Method.* Paper presented at The Fifth Conference of The European Council for High Ability in Vienna, Austria.

Kayser, R. E. (1994). European Advanced Diploma in Educating the Gifted. *ECHA News*, **8** (3), 11–13.

Kepinska-Welbel, J. (1991). Psychological counselling in music schools in Poland. *European Journal for High Ability*, **2** (1), 86–90.

Kepinska-Welbel, J. (1996). Psychological counseling in music schools in Poland. In: A. J. Cropley & D. Dehn (Eds.), *Fostering the Growth of High Ability: European Perspectives* (pp. 263–270). Norwood, NJ: Ablex.

Kholodnaja, M. (1993). *The cognitive mechanisms of intellectual giftedness.* In: E. A. Hany & K. A. Heller (Eds.), *Competence and Responsibility*, Vol. 1 (pp. 73–74). Seattle: Hogrefe & Huber Publ.

Kieboom, T. (1994). Where we want to go: Antwerp, Belgium. *ECHA NEWS*, **8** (3), 9.

Kleine Sportasse werden in M–V besonders gefördert [Little sports marvels receive special support in M–V]. (1998, 21/22 March). *Ostseezeitung*, p. 3.

Klimas-Kuchtowa, E. (1996). Creative thinking as a predictor of achievement in music. In: A. J. Cropley & D. Dehn (Eds.), *Fostering the Growth of High Ability: European Perspectives* (pp. 429–436). Norwood, NJ: Ablex.

Kokotko, N. (1996). *An educational summer program for gifted children in The Ukraine.* Paper presented at The Fifth Conference of The European Council for High Ability in Vienna, Austria.

Kolesaric, V. & Koren, I. (1996). The effect of identification and differential treatment of gifted elementary school pupils. In: A. J. Cropley & D. Dehn (Eds.), *Fostering the Growth of High Ability: European Perspectives* (pp. 501–512). Norwood, NJ: Ablex.

Kommunförbundet. (1976). *Den kommunala musikskolan* [The community music schools]. Stockholm: Kommunförbundet.

Koren, I. (1994). *Identification of the gifted.* In: K. A. Heller & E. A. Hany (Eds.), *Competence and Responsibility*, Vol. 2 (pp. 253–269). Seattle: Hogrefe & Huber Publ.

Kovac, T. (1996). Is creativity independent of heredity? *Studia Psychologica, 1–2*, 63–66.

Kovac, T. & Matejik, M. (1993). *Creativity, intelligence and anxiety in Middle European youth.* In: E. A. Hany & K. A. Heller (Eds.), *Competence and Responsibility*, Vol. 1 (pp. 78–79). Seattle: Hogrefe & Huber Publ.

Laczó, Z. (1993). *Cognitive processes in music listening.* In: E. A. Hany & K. A. Heller (Eds.), *Competence and Responsibility*, Vol. 1 (pp. 81). Seattle: Hogrefe & Huber Publ.

Lau, J. & Pagaard, P. E. (1996). De velfungerende elever. En dansk undersøgelse [The well-functioning pupils: a Danish study]. In: V. Rabøl-Hansen & O. Robenhagen (Eds.), *På det jævne og i det himmelblå—Talenter i skolen* (pp. 46–57). Copenhagen: The Danish National Institute for Educational Research.

Laukkanen, R. (1995). The formation of evaluation policies in education in Finland. In: Y. Yrjönsuuri (Ed.), *Evaluating Education in Finland.* Helsinki: National Board of Education.

Lazar, A. (1993). *Competence, achievement motivation and responsibility.* In: E. A. Hany & K. A. Heller (Eds.), *Competence and Responsibility*, Vol. 1 (pp. 84). Seattle: Hogrefe & Huber Publ.

Laznibatova, J. (1993). *The personality structure of the mathematically gifted.* In: E. A. Hany & K. A. Heller (Eds.), *Competence and Responsibility*, Vol. 1 (pp. 85). Seattle: Hogrefe & Huber Publ.

Ledzinska, M. (1993). *Interaction between abilities, information processing and school achievement in pupils.* In: E. A. Hany & K. A. Heller (Eds.), *Competence and Responsibility*, Vol. 1 (pp. 86–87). Seattle: Hogrefe & Huber Publ.

Ledzinska, M. (1996). *Teacher as a creator of professional role conception.* Paper presented at The Fifth Conference of The European Council for High Ability in Vienna, Austria.

Leites, N. S. (Ed.). (1996). *Psikhologiya odarennosti detei i podrostkov* [The psychology of giftedness in children and adolescents]. Moscow: Academia.

Leyden, S. (1985). *Helping the child of exceptional ability.* London: Routledge.

Limont, W. (1993a). *Model of the structure of visual art abilities.* In: E. A. Hany & K. A. Heller (Eds.), *Competence and Responsibility*, Vol.1 (pp. 88–90). Seattle: Hogrefe & Huber Publ.

Limont, W. (1993b). *The effectiveness of creativity training by means of controlled visual expression.* In: E. A. Hany & K. A. Heller (Eds.), *Competence and Responsibility*, Vol. 1 (pp. 90–91). Seattle: Hogrefe & Huber Publ.

Limont, W. (1995). The figurative and visual metaphor: a means or basis of creative thinking? In: M. W. Katzko & F. J. Mönks (Eds.), *Nurturing Talent: Individual Needs and*

Social Ability (pp. 125–128). Assen, The Netherlands: Van Gorcum.

Majoros, M. (1993). *Experiences of a course aimed at addressing mathematically gifted children held by Lajos Posa.* In: E. A. Hany & K. A. Heller (Eds.), *Competence and Responsibility*, Vol. 1 (pp. 93–95). Seattle: Hogrefe & Huber Publ.

Makarovic, J. (1993). *The system of talent identification in Slovenia.* In: E. A. Hany & K. A. Heller (Eds.), *Competence and Responsibility*, Vol. 1 (pp. 95–96). Seattle: Hogrefe & Huber Publ.

Makarovic, J. (1996). *Identifying talent in Slovenia—30 years of Experience.* Paper presented at The Fifth Conference of The European Council for High Ability in Vienna, Austria.

Manturzewska, M. (1996). Identification and promotion of musical talent. In: A. J. Cropley & D. Dehn (Eds.), *Fostering the Growth of High Ability: European Perspectives* (pp. 271–286). Norwood, NJ: Ablex.

Martin Bravo, C. (Ed.). (1997). *Superdotados. Problemática e intervención* [Gifted children. Problems and intervention]. Valladolid, Spain: Servicio de Apoyo a la Ensenanza, Universidad de Valladolid.

Martins, M. (1997). Correspondent's Report from Portugal. *ECHA News, 11*(2), 7.

Melander, Å. (1995). '*Duktiga elever klarar sig alltid— eller?' Om specialbegåvade elever i svensk grundskola* ["Clever students always manage—or do they?" On highly able students in the Swedish compulsory school system]. Unpublished Master thesis, Department of Political Science, Lund University, Lund, Sweden.

Mendecka, G. (1996a). Attitude of parents and development of creativity. In: A. J. Cropley & D. Dehn (Eds.), *Fostering the Growth of High Ability: European Perspectives* (pp. 563–570). Norwood, NJ: Ablex.

Mendecka, G. (1996b). Development of creativity through Performing Arts. *High Ability Studies, 7*(2),151–156.

Merenheimo, J. (1991). Cultural background and experience: controlling the manifestation of giftedness. *Scandinavian Journal of Educational Research, 35* (2), 115–129.

Milanova-Kamburova, I. (1996). *For encouragement of the talent and for development of creativity in the children by learning foreign languages.* Paper presented at The Fifth Conference of The European Council for High Ability in Vienna, Austria.

Ministerie van de Vlaamse Gemeenshap, Department Onderwijs (1997). *Education in Flanders.* Brussels: Afdeling Informatic en Documentatie.

Ministry of Church, Education and Science (1997). *Læreplanverket for den 10-årige grunnskolen: prinsipp og retningslinjer for opplæringa i grunnskolen* [National Curriculum for the 10-year comprehensive school system: Principles and guidelines for teaching]. Available http://skolenettet.nls.no/dok/sn/

Ministry of Education (1996). *The Folkeskole* (Factsheet no. 2). Copenhagen: Ministry of Education.

Ministry of Education and Science. (1993*). The Swedish way towards a learning society.* Stockholm: Ministry of Education and Science/Allmänna Förlaget AB.

Ministry of Education and Science. (1994). *Information om 1994 års Läroplan för det obligatoriska skolväsendet: Lpo 94* [Information on the 1994 National Curriculum of the compulsory school system: Lpo 94]. Stockholm: Ministry of Education and Science.

Misgeld, K., Molin, K. & Åmark, K. (Eds.). (1988). *Socialdemokratins samhälle. SAP och Sverige under 100 år* [The Social Democrat society. The 100 years of SAP and Sweden]. Stockholm: Tiden.

Mitchell, D. (1995). Best practices criteria in Inclusive Education: a basis for teacher education. In: P. Mittler & P. Daunt (Eds.), *Teacher Education for Special Needs in Europe* (pp. 26–36). London: Cassell.

Mitchell, S. (1991). *Tall poppies too.* Ringwood, Australia: Penguine.

Mönks, F. J. (1992). From conception to realization. In: F. J. Mönks, M. W. Katzko & H. W. van Boxtel (Eds.), *Education of the Gifted in Europe: Theoretical and Research Issues* (pp. 13–21). Amsterdam / Lisse: Swets & Zeitlinger.

Mönks, F. J. (1994). Begabungsförderung—eine Europäische Perspektive [A European perspective on supporting talent]. In: H. Drewelow & K. K. Urban (Eds.), *Begabungsförderung—eine Europäische Perspektive* (pp. 17–20). Rostock, Germany: Universität Rostock.

Mönks, F. J., van Boxtel, H. W., Roelofs, J. W. J. & Sanders, M. P. M. (1986). The identification of gifted children in secondary education and a description of their situation in Holland. In: K. A. Heller & J. F. Feldhusen (Eds.), *Identifying and Nurturing the Gifted* (pp. 39–65). Toronto: Huber Publ.

Mönks, F. J., Katzko, M. W. & Boxtel, H. W. van (Eds.). (1992). *Education of the Gifted in Europe: Theoretical and Research Issues.* Amsterdeam: Swets & Zeitlinger.

Monnier, S. A. (1998). What's the situation of talent development like in France? *ECHA News, 12* (2), 5–7.

Montgomery, D. (1996). *Educating the able.* London: Cassell.

Montgomery, D. (1997). Teaching teachers for creativity. *High Ability Studies, 8* (1), 79–93.

Mooij, T. (1996). Predicting (under)achievement of gifted children. In: A. J. Cropley & D. Dehn (Eds.), *Fostering the Growth of High Ability: European Perspectives* (pp. 459–477). Norwood, NJ: Ablex.

National Board of Education (1997). *Finlands utbildningssystem* [The Finnish Educational System]. Available http://www.edu.fi/info/system/reform.

Nawroth, E. (1997). Niederländischer Verein 'Pharos' feierte Zehnjähriges [The Netherlands' 'Pharos' Association celebrates its ten years]. *DGhK, Labyrinth, 53*, 9.

Neber, H. (1995). Explanations in problem-oriented, co-operative learning. In: R. Olechowski & G. Khan – Svik (Eds.), *Experimental Research on Teaching and Learning* (pp. 158–167). Frankfurt/M.: Lang.

Neber, H. & Heller, K. A. (1997). *Deutsche Schülerakademie. Ergebnisse der wissenschaftlichen Begleitforschung* [German Pupils' Academy. Results of the program evaluation]. Bonn, Germany: BMBF.

Necka, E. (1996). Levels of mind: a multilevel model of intellect and its implications for identification of the gifted. In: A. J. Cropley & D. Dehn (Eds.), *Fostering the Growth of High Ability: European Perspectives* (pp. 95–102). Norwood, NJ: Ablex.

Neuhaus, S. (1969). *Die Kunst des Klavierspiels* [The art of playing the piano] (L. Fahlbusch, Transl.). Leipzig, Germany: VEB Deutscher Verlag für Musik.

Nicolin, C. (1996). *Ny strategi för Sverige* [A new strategy for Sweden]. Stockholm: Ekerlids förlag.

Niebrzydowski, L. & Poraj, G. (1996). School adjustment of high ability students. In: A. J. Cropley & D. Dehn (Eds.), *Fostering the Growth of High Ability: European Perspectives* (pp. 479–488). Norwood, NJ: Ablex.

Nieminen, K. & Piche, R. (1995). The 1994 Finnish Summer Math Camp and the Edutech Mathematics and Physics Enrichment Program for gifted high-schoolers 1993–1995. In E. Pehkonen (Ed.), *Proceedings of the Nordic Conference on Mathematics Teaching (NORMA 1994)* (Research Report No. 141, Department of Teacher Education) (pp. 143–147). Helsinki: Helsinki University.

Nyman, S. (1998). *Satsar den svenska skolan på begåvningar?* [Is the Swedish school system interested in talents?] Unpublished undergraduate dissertation, Teachers College, Lund University, Sweden, Department of Instruction and Subject Theory.

O'Hanlon, C. (1995). Integration practice and policy in the UK for pupils with special educational needs. In: C. O'Hanlon (Ed.), *Inclusive Education in Europe* (pp. 122–132). London: David Fulton Publ.

Ojanen, S. & Freeman, J. (1994). *The attitudes and experiences of headteachers, class-teachers, and highly-able pupils towards the education of the highly able in Finland and Britain* (University of Joensuu Research Reports of the Faculty of Education No. 54). Joensuu, Finland: University of Joensuu.

Oppelt, K. (1995). Identification of high ability and special enrichment programmes for Gypsy children. In: M. W. Katzko & F. J. Mönks (Eds.), *Nurturing Talent: Individual Needs and Social Ability* (pp. 206–209). Assen, The Netherlands: Van Gorcum.

Ostatnikova, D., Dohnanyiova, M. & Laznibatova, J. (1996). *Testosterone influence on spatial cognition in gifted prepubertal boys and girls.* Paper presented at The Fifth Conference of The European Council for High Ability in Vienna, Austria.

Pagnin, A. (1994). Die Situation der Hochbegabtenforschung in Italien [The situation of giftedness research in Italy]. In: H. Drewelow & K. K. Urban (Eds.), *Begabungsförderung—eine Europäische Perspektive* (pp. 71–73). Rostock, Germany: Universität Rostock.

Partyko, T. (1996). *The influence of the traditional primary education in the Ukraine on intelligence and the mnemonic abilities of children.* Paper presented at The Fifth Conference of The European Council for High Ability, Vienna in Austria.

Pásku, J. & Imre, D. (1993). *Empathy and communication skills: Developing training for teachers.* In: E. A. Hany & K. A. Heller (Eds.), *Competence and Responsibility*, Vol. 1 (pp. 113–114). Seattle: Hogrefe & Huber Publ.

Pásku, J., Kerekes, I. & Fekete, F. (1997). Non-specific effects of musical education in childhood. *Acta Psychologica Debrecina*, **20**, 183–188.

Paszkowska-Rogacz, A. (1996). Non-verbal aspects of creative thinking: studies of deaf children. In: A. J. Cropley & D. Dehn (Eds.), *Fostering the Growth of High Ability: European Perspectives* (pp. 383–388). Norwood, NJ: Ablex.

Pérez Sanchez, L. (1993). *10 palabras claves en superdotados* [Ten key words for Gifted Children]. Estella, Navarra, Spain: Verbo Divino.

Persson, R. S. (1997a). *High ability in egalitarian contexts: able children and commonsense teacher roles in the Swedish school system* (Insikt 1997:3). Jönköping, Sweden: School of Education and Communication, Jönköping University.

Persson, R. S. (1997b). *Annorlunda land: särbegåvningens psykologi* [In a different land: the psychology of high ability]. Stockholm: Almqvist & Wiksell.

Persson, R. S. (1997c). Correspondent's report: Sweden. *ECHA News*, **11** (1), 12–13.

Persson, R. S. (1998a). Competence beyond IQ: on domain specificity and the need for a differentiated and culture-sensitive taxonomy of gifted behaviours. *Educating Able Children*, **2**, 20–26.

Persson, R. S. (1998b). Paragons of virtue: teachers' conceptual understanding of high ability in an egalitarian school system. *High Ability Studies*, **9** (2), 181–196.

Persson, R. S. (1998c). Correspondent's report: Sweden. *ECHA News*. **12** (1), 5–6.

Persson, R. S. (1999). High ability, society and its future: the broader curriculum. *Australasian Journal of Gifted Education*, **8** (1), 5–14.

Peters, W. A. M. (1998). *The self-concept of able young adolescents in China and The Netherlands: a comparative study.* Doctoral dissertation, University of Nijmegen, The Netherlands.

Petersson, O. (1994). *The government and politics of the Nordic Countries* (F. G. Perry, Trans.). Stockholm: Fritzes.

Pluymakers, M. (1997). Opportunities for highly able Students. *ECHA News*, **11** (2), 5–6.

Prieto Sánchez, M. D. (Ed.). (1997). *Identificación, evaluación y atención a la diversidad del superdotado* [Identification, evaluation and attention to the diversity of the gifted]. Málaga, Spain: Algibe.

Quittmann, H. & Manke, W. (1998). Die Hamburger Beratungsstelle besondere Begabungen [The Hamburg helpdesk for the especially gifted]. In: K. K. Urban & H. Joswig (Eds.), *Begabungsförderung in der Schule* (pp. 1145–1146). Rodenberg, Germany: Klausur-Verlag.

Rabøl-Hansen, V. & Robenhagen, O. (Eds.). (1996). *På det jævne og i det himmelblå—Talenter i skolen* [To stay low or to soar: talents in school]. Copenhagen: The Danish National Institute for Educational Research.

Raffan, J. M. & Short, M. (1992). A new era in education: England and Wales in the 1990s. In: F. J. Mönks, M. W. Katzko & H. W. van Boxtel (Eds.), *Education of the Gifted in Europe: Theoretical and Research Issues* (pp. 198–202). Amsterdam: Swets & Zeitlinger.

Raina, M. K. (1996). *Talent search in the Third World: the phenomenon of calculated ambiguity.* New Dehli, India: Vikas Publishing House.

Räty, H. & Snellman, L. (1997). Children's images of an intelligent person. *Journal of Social Behavior and Personality*, **13**, 773–784.

Régnier, G., Salmela, J. & Russell, S. J. (1993). Talent detection and development in sport. In: R. N. Singer, M. Murphy & L. K. Tennant (Eds.), *Handbook of Research on Sport Psychology*. New York: Macmillan.

Richardson, G. (1994). *Svensk utbildningshistoria* [The history of Swedish education]. Lund, Sweden: Studentlitteratur.

Robenhagen, O. (1996). Gør skolen noget for højdespringerne—og de andre talenter? [Does the school provide for high-achievers and other types of talents?] In: V. Rabøl-

Hansen & O. Robenhagen (Eds.), *På det jævne og i det himmelblå—Talenter i skolen* (pp. 78–98). Copenhagen: The Danish National Institute for Educational Research.

Rosenquist, J. & Sandling, I. (1995). The training of special educators in Sweden. In: P. Mittler & P. Daunt (Eds.), *Teacher Education for Special Needs in Europe* (pp. 160–167). London: Cassell.

Rychlicka, A. (1996). Intellectual abilities and the use of metaphors in solving problems. In: A. J. Cropley & D. Dehn (Eds.), *Fostering the Growth of High Ability: European Perspectives* (pp. 167–174). Norwood, NJ: Ablex.

Sawyer, B. & Sawyer, P. (1993). *Medieval Scandinavia. From Conversion to Reformation, circa 800–1500.* London: University of Minnesota Press.

Schweizerische Studienstiftung (1998). *Fonds für begabte junge Menschen* [Funds for gifted young individuals]. Available   http://www.acess.ch/studienstiftung/Was_will.html.

Segerstedt, T. (1979). *Antiintellektualism i Sverige* [Anti-intellectualism in Sweden]. Stockholm: Ratio.

Sekowski, A. (1995). Metacognition and achievements of gifted students. In: M. W. Katzko & F. J. Mönks (Eds.), *Nurturing Talent: Individual Needs and Social Ability* (pp. 114–119). Assen, The Netherlands: Van Gorcum.

Sekulic-Majurec, A. (1993). *New chances (and old barriers) for the development of the gifted and talented in Croatia.* In: E. A. Hany & K. A. Heller (Eds.), *Competence and Responsibility*, Vol. 1 (pp. 149–150). Seattle: Hogrefe & Huber Publ.

Sekulic-Majurec, A. (1996). *Program for developing the productive giftedness of potentially gifted students.* Paper presented at The Fifth Conference of The European Council for High Ability in Vienna, Austria.

Shavinina, L. V. (1996a). Specific intellectual intentions and creative giftedness. In: A. J. Cropley & D. Dehn (Eds.), *Fostering the Growth of High Ability: European Perspectives* (pp. 373–382). Norwood, NJ: Ablex.

Shavinina, L. V. (1996b). *The cognitive experience as a psychological basis of giftedness and creative talent.* Paper presented at The Fifth Conference of The European Council for High Ability in Vienna, Austria.

Skytte, G. (1997). *Självbekännelser och andra texter* [Confessions and other texts]. Stockholm: Sellin.

Span, P. (1986). Concepts of giftedness, and research into the education of gifted children in the Netherlands. In: F. J. Mönks, M. W. Katzko & H. W. van Boxtel (Eds.), *Education of the Gifted in Europe: Theoretical and Research Issues* (pp. 118–134). Amsterdam / Lisse: Swets & Zeitlinger.

Sprengel, H. J. (1999a). Aus Sachsen-Anhalt: Massnahmen des Kulturministeriums zur unterrichtlichen und ausserunterrichtlichen Begabungsförderung [From Sachsen-Anhalt: Measures of the Ministry of Education for curricular and extra-curricular giftedness provision]. *ABB e. V. Information*, **27**, 16–17.

Sprengel, H. J. (1999b). In Bayern 1999/2000: Drei Förderklassen am Gymnasium [In Bavaria: Three special support classes in upper secondary education]. *ABB e. V. Information*, **28**, 22–23.

Stoyanova, F. (1995). Intelligence, gender and self-esteem. In: M. W. Katzko & F. J. Mönks (Eds.), *Nurturing Talent:*

Individual Needs and Social Ability (pp. 75–84). Assen, The Netherlands: Van Gorcum.

Stoycheva, K. (1994). *Intelligence-creativity relationship: are creative motivation and need for achievement influencing it?* In: K. A. Heller & E. A. Hany (Eds.), *Competence and Responsibility*, Vol. 2 (pp. 40–45). Seattle: Hogrefe & Huber Publ.

Stoycheva, K. (1996). *The school: a place for children's creativity?* Paper presented at The Fifth Conference of The European Council for High Ability in Vienna, Austria.

Strelau, J. (1992). Temperament and giftedness in children and adolescents. In: F. J. Mönks & W. A. M. Peters (Eds.), *Talent for the Future* (pp. 73–86). Assen/Maastricht, The Netherlands: Van Gorcum.

Süle, F. (1996). Imaginative psychotherapy in the psychological care of top athletes. In: A. J. Cropley & D. Dehn (Eds.), *Fostering the Growth of High Ability: European Perspectives* (pp. 367–370). Norwood, NJ: Ablex.

Swietochowski, W. & Poraj, G. (1996). Parental attitudes and Type-A behavior patterns in high and low creative adolescents. In: A. J. Cropley & D. Dehn (Eds.), *Fostering the Growth of High Ability: European Perspectives* (pp. 555–562). Norwood, NJ: Ablex.

Tetler, S. (1995). The Danish efforts in integration. In: C. O'Hanlon (Ed.), *Inclusive Education in Europe* (pp. 9–23). London: David Fulton Publ.

Thompson, E. (1994). *Fair enough: Egaliarianism in Australia.* Sydney: University of New South Wales Press.

Tirri, K. (1997). How Finland meets the needs of gifted and talented pupils]. *High Ability Studies*, **8** (2), 213–222.

Tirri, K. & Uusikylä, K. (1994). How teachers perceive differentiation of education among the gifted and talented. *Gifted and Talented International*, **9** (2), 69–73.

Tourón, J., Peralta, F. & Reparaz, Ch. (1998). *La superdotación intelectual: Modelos, identificación y estrategias educativas* [The intelectually gifted: models, identification and educational strategies]. Pamplona, Spain: EUNSA.

Tourón, J., Iriarte, C., Reparaz, Ch. & Peralta, F. (1998). Diversity and school curriculum: the response of the Spanish education system to the needs of academically highly able pupils. *High Ability Studies*, **9** (2), 165–180.

Trifonova, M. P. (1994). *Subjects' semantic orientation and creative thinking.* In: K. A. Heller & E. A. Hany (Eds.), *Competence and Responsibility*, Vol. 2 (pp. 94–100). Seattle: Hogrefe & Huber Publ.

Undheim, J. O. & Nordvik, H. (1992). Socio-economic factors and sex differences in an egalitarian educational system: academic achievement in 16-year-old Norwegian students. *Scandinavian Journal of Educational Research*, **36** (2), 87–98.

Urban, K. K. & Joswig, H. (Eds.). (1998). *Begabungsförderung in der Schule* [Support for talent in school.] Rodenberg, Germany: Klausur-Verlag.

Urban, K. K. & Sekowski, A. (1993). Programs and practices for identifying and nurturing giftedness and talent in Europe. In: K. A. Heller, F. J. Mönks & A. H. Passow (Eds.), *International Handbook of Research and Development of Giftedness and Talent* (pp. 779–795). Oxford, UK: Pergamon Press.

Uusikylä, K. (1994). *Gifted Education.* Helsinki: WSOY.

Uusikylä, K. (1996). *The development of creative talent.* Paper presented at the Fifth Conference of the European Council for High Ability in Vienna, Austria.

Välijärvi, J. (1992). Teaching gifted children and adolescents and related research in Finland. In: F. J. Mönks, M. W. Katzko & H. W. van Boxtel (Eds.), *Education of the Gifted in Europe: Theoretical and Research Issues* (pp. 217–220). Amsterdam: Swets & Zeitlinger.

Varga, B. & Gyarmathy, E. (1996). *High ability. Is it a problem? The second Year of the Counselling Centre for the Gifted.* Paper presented at the Fifth Conference of the European Council for High Ability in Vienna, Austria.

Vizek-Vidovic, V. & Vlahovic-Stetic, V. (1993). *Vocational planning and salience of life roles of gifted and non-gifted secondary school students.* In: E. A. Hany & K. A. Heller (Eds.), *Competence and Responsibility*, Vol. 1 (pp. 180–181). Seattle: Hogrefe & Huber Publ.

Vizek-Vidovic, V. (1996). *Intrinsic motivation and situational interest of mathematically gifted students in elementary school.* Paper presented at the Fifth Conference of the European Council for High Ability in Vienna, Austria.

Vlahovic-Stetic, V. (1993). *Work values and perceived self-competence of gifted and non-gifted secondary school students.* In: E. A. Hany & K. A. Heller (Eds.), *Competence and Responsibility*, Vol. 1 (pp. 182–183). Seattle: Hogrefe & Huber Publ.

Wahlström, G. (1995). *Begåvade barn i skolan: Duglighetens dilemma?* [Gifted children in school. The problem of doing too well in school?] Stockholm: Liber.

Williams, W. G. & Mitchell, B. M. (1989). *From Afghanistan to Zimbabwe: gifted education in the world community.* New York: Lang.

Wilms, D. (1986). Patron's opening address. In: A. J. Cropley, K. K. Urban, H. Wagner & W. Wieczerkowski (Eds.), *Giftedness: A Continuing Worldwide Challenge* (pp. 16–20). New York: Trillium Press.

Witzmann, E. (1998, 21 April). Namenspatron Popper und 48 Fünfzehnjährige [The patron Popper and 48 fifteen-year-olds]. *Die Presse, 7.*

Young, P. & Tyre, C. (1992). *Gifted or able? Realizing children's potential.* Buckingham, England: Open University Press.

Ziegler, A. & Heller, K. A. (1998) An attribution retraining for self-related cognitions among women. *Gifted and Talented International*, **12**, 36–41.

Ziegler, A. & Heller, K. A. (2000). Conditions for self-confidence among boys and girls achieving highly in chemistry. *Journal of Secondary Education of the Gifted*, *10*, 192–199.

Russian Gifted Education in Technical Disciplines: Tradition and Transformation

Elena L. Grigorenko

Department of Psychology, Yale University, New Haven, Connecticut, USA.

Introduction

Russia's program of education for the gifted in maths and science has undergone tremendous change since the late 1980s. Once a centralized program that carefully selected, trained, and harnessed young talent, it can now best be described as a mosaic of traditional and innovative forms—an uneasy combination embedded in a context of pedagogical, financial, social, and political challenges.

All Russian children are familiar with a specific type of mathematical problem, in which Train 1 leaves Station A bound for Station B, while Train 2 departs from Station B and travels toward Station A. Although there are parallel tracks for two-way traffic, both trains must, at a certain point, pass through the same switch in railway track. If the trains arrive at the switch in track simultaneously, they will collide. The problem specifies the distance between Stations A and B, the distance from both stations to the switching point, and the time constraints of the train schedules. The students' task is to calculate the speed at which each train must travel to avoid a collision.

Metaphorically, this simple maths problem evokes the present dilemma confronting the Russian system of gifted education. Train 1 represents the inertia of the traditional centralized and controlled educational system, while Train 2 symbolizes the momentum established by recent developments beginning in the late 1980s. The trains departed from different places, but at some point they must pass through the same switch. The choices are that they can collide, pass each other without rendering an explosion, or, unlike it goes in the maths problem, get assembled in a single train. Somehow, Russia must find a way to integrate these two systems.

Unfortunately, the task before Russia is more complicated than the schoolchildren's train problem. We are not certain how far apart—how truly distinct—the two educational strands are, and we cannot be sure when each much be reconciled with the other. Never-theless, the 'trains' have left their respective stations, and decisions about the future of gifted education must be made. We need to understand, first, the defining features of Train 1 (the 'old' way) and Train 2 (the 'new' way); and, most importantly, we must determine how these different ways of schooling can be brought into productive harmony within the Russian educational system. How, in other words, can we avoid an educational 'train wreck'?

Train 1: Hallmarks of the Old Way

In Russia's traditional regular classes, all students received virtually identical training; they used the same textbooks and took the same exams. The Ministry of Education and local educational authorities established the programs to be carried out in regular classrooms. No schools could do less; but they could do more.

In general, the old system of gifted instruction pursued the following goals, in descending order of importance: (1) education for the good of the whole society, (2) education to promote progress, and (3) education for the personal growth of the individual. Society's needs came first, and technological and societal progress took second priority; personal development for the sake of the individual was the least important of the three major goals.

The system of education for the gifted was designed accordingly. To capitalize on the nation's intellectual resources and further the reputation of Soviet society, the designers of the system established a network of competitions. These contests identified gifted students, whose talents were then developed through extracurricular support and specialized schooling. The Russian system of intellectual competition has been evolving for over 50 years and includes competitions of multiple types and levels (school, district, town, region, and so on). Particular emphasis has been placed on the preparation and support of students engaged in international competitions. The most widespread types of intellectual competitions are olympiadas, tournaments, long-term extramural courses/competitions by correspondence, and pupils' conferences. These competitions present competitors with different sorts of tasks and feature a variety of structures and time constraints. Their major function, however, has been consistent: to identify talent (so that it could be developed to society's advantage) and to demonstrate Soviet/Russian achievement.

The second traditional goal of gifted education—assuring 'progress'—was accomplished by engaging talented youth in solving 'real problems'. Competitions and fairs exposed gifted children to the most advanced ideas. The problems and topics addressed at these events were those of concern to professionals working at the cutting-edge of their fields. In addition, most leading specialized schools for the gifted were run by Soviet academics. For example, Math-Physics school #18 was founded as an offshoot of Moscow State University's Department of Math and Mechanics by the famous Russian mathematician Alexei Kolmogorov. The majority of the teachers in this school were university professors, and many of the students conducted scientific research in the professors' labs. The gifted were channeled through a system—consisting of identification, different levels of education, and then work in appropriate jobs—carefully designed to develop and then harness their talents for 'progress'.

The achievement of the third goal—the optimal development of the individual person—was the least crucial in the old system. In fact, little organized support existed to further this aim. For one thing, specialized education emphasized learning in certain domains of giftedness (e.g. maths and science) and paid little attention to other subject areas (such as the humanities and the arts). (In fact, this was characteristic of Soviet education in general. In regular schools great attention was paid to the teaching of maths, physics, and other general sciences. However, instruction in the humanities was shaped, to a large degree, by ideology, and schools largely ignored the arts.) Second, students received little social and emotional support; up until very recently, no gifted programs utilized professional psychologists or social workers. Third, gifted education programs minimized the role of parents, who were rarely consulted. Moreover, only a few cities had day schools for the gifted, so in many cases gifted adolescents were placed in boarding schools far away from home.

Nevertheless, gifted education rewarded individuals for natural gifts. Compared with their less-talented counterparts, gifted children attended better schools (and, in the case of boarding schools, the government paid for tuition, room, and board), had better teachers (often teachers working with gifted children also taught at universities), gained access to more esteemed universities (participation in intellectual competitions and diplomas from certain schools were 'tickets' to the best universities), and received more desirable jobs

(special governmental committees assigned jobs such that higher-achieving students had better choices than their less-accomplished peers).

Traditionally, gifted education focused on the modification and enrichment of content in specific subject areas. This approach assumed that talent in specific subjects could be identified. Students were to be identified early and either placed in special schools for the gifted or enrolled in special programs. Nowhere was this more evident than in gifted education focused on maths and science. Thanks to the technical orientation of the educational system in general, gifted education in maths and science exemplified the best of specialized education within the Soviet system. Russia established numerous schools for gifted mathematicians; some of the leading ones are well-known both nationally and internationally. Among these are Moscow School No. 57, Saint Petersburg School No. 239, Moscow Boarding School No. 18 (now called the Specialized Education-Research Center of Moscow State University), and the Novosibirsk School for Gifted Children in mathematics (now called the Specialized Education-Research Center of Novosibirsk State University).

These four schools have much in common. Selection for admission is based on results from zonal or regional olympiads, summer/winter break maths schools, intellectual competitions by correspondence, entrance exams, and special competitions organized by school staff. Each of these four schools has its own independent curriculum, hires its own staff, ensures compliance of content with national standards, and adopts an individualized approach to students' education as necessary. Each of the schools has established links to top higher-educational institutions, and each offers courses aimed at preparing students for entrance exams, as well as activities that involve young mathematicians in research. Yet, each of these institutions has its own individual profile of strengths, weaknesses, and priorities. For example, graduates of Moscow School No. 57 and Saint-Petersburg School No. 239 have excellent track records in international competitions, whereas the other two schools (the university schools) are known for developing outstanding research skills in graduates. Graduates of these and other specialized schools have traditionally been channeled into the maths and science departments of quality higher-educational institutions and could later expect to receive job assignments appropriate for their talents. For example, among the graduates of Novosibirsk School for Gifted Children there are 12 members of the Russian Academy of Sciences (the highest academic rank in Russia), 120 Professors in leading universities, and 700 Ph.D.s.

In sum, the framework for traditional gifted education was a natural, high-end extension of the Soviet educational system in general. It was subject-oriented, based on ideas of acceleration and enrichment, subordinated to societal goals, financially supported by the state, attendant to both identification and training, designed to accommodate different levels of education, and underpinned by a labor market dependent on its products.

Train 2: Recent Developments

More recent developments in the education of the gifted and talented can also best be understood in the context of the larger educational system. Russian education started changing dramatically in the late 1980s and early 1990s. The first main characteristic of this 'brave new world' of education is democratization, which has produced an explosion of different programs and approaches. There are now many different types of schools (such as lyceums and gymnasias) and innovative educational programs. Essentially, the old homogeneous system has broken up into a constellation of different approaches. Today, of the 67,200 schools in Russia, 9,126 (or 13%) are of a new type; 540 (0.8%) are private. This differentiation distinguishes between children of different abilities and of different socio-economic backgrounds. The new system also increasingly assumes that the educational process should be individualized. A. Tikhonov, the Minister of Education of the Russian Federation, has described this trend as "a transition from unified education to varied education." This increasing differentiation, however, has been countered somewhat by federal declarations calling for equal educational opportunity for all.

The second major trend in regular education today is increased interest in education in the humanities, arts, and social sciences and, simultaneously, decreased interest in maths and science education. Under the old system, every student was expected to pay his or her dues studying integrals, Newton's Laws, and so on, but now a significant number of programs minimize, or even abandon, rigorous study of these topics. Under the old system, maths was taught according to a particular system named after Kiselev. Now, however, innovation in maths education is overwhelmingly varied and difficult to describe. But the general tendency has been aptly summarized by Russian mathematician Vladimir Arnold, who warned of the danger of "a decrease of hours of maths education in favor of horse-breeding and macramé." In addition to this departure from the tradition of polytechnic education, the modern Russian system has introduced new fields of study that supplement—and sometimes supplant—teaching the logic of a given subject (such as maths). Instead, students learn the logic of a broader subject area (such as the sciences or the humanities) through interdisciplinary study; such programs are aimed at developing particular thinking skills.

The third distinct characteristic of schooling in Russia today is the lack of financial support given the educational structure by the federal government. For example, as of December 31, 1997, only 76.1% of the budget allotted by the government for educational expenses for the year was actually distributed to the institutions and programs. The subordinate structures of the Ministry of Education (i.e. schools, higher-educational institutions, educational services, etc.) lack sufficient money for supplies, equipment, activities, renovations, meals, and so on.

Finally, the role of parents has changed. In the past, parents were involved primarily in discussions of disciplinary problems. The system was so stable that school environments did not change much from generation to generation. Parents knew that their children were experiencing very much what the parents themselves had gone through when they were school-children. Parents so familiar with the system did not feel that their own involvement was necessary. Today, however, the school environment has changed radically, and so parents have felt a need to become increasingly involved. At the same time, schools struggling in the face of inadequate federal support have encouraged the active participation of parents who can provide essential goods and services. Increased parental involvement has, however, brought complications—namely, disagreement between parents and teachers about what and how teachers should teach.

All of these general characteristics of Russia's modern educational system have impacted education for the gifted and talented. First, the democratization of schooling has gradually reshaped gifted education. In the middle of the 1980s, the Soviet government began financing specialized educational centers for the gifted. However, a 1990 document, 'The State Program of Identification, Education, and Upbringing of Gifted Children and Youth with Creative Giftedness', objected to the closed nature of gifted education and suggested an alternative in which programs could be made available to all educational institutions across the country. This pronouncement called for the development of both specialized schools and gifted programs for use in regular schools.

The budget reflected this overall shift in emphasis from specialized schools to more inclusive, broad-based gifted instruction. Initially, support was gradually withdrawn from the existing system of specialized schools (which focused on the highly gifted) and invested in new programs designed for the gifted and able. However, due to a severe nationwide budget deficit beginning in the early 1990s, the federal government began withdrawing virtually all financial support from specialized programs. The participation of parents and universities in specialized education has increased, but donations, tuition, and university support cannot begin to make up for the loss created by federal cuts in funding. Budget cuts have impacted both old and new forms of gifted education. However, the old system has been more severely affected, because it had no time to develop alternative financing, whereas proponents of the new system had sought out creative ways to raise necessary funds from the beginning.

Today, federal support of gifted education is carried out under a federal program called 'Gifted Children'. The program's three-year budget is 20,000,000 rubles (or about 3,500,000 USD). In 1997, a total of 21,400,000 students attended Russian schools. Assuming that 1% of these students are gifted (and this is surely an underestimate), the budget provides the equivalent of no more than 5.45 USD per gifted student per year.

The changing role of parents in education has also affected the system of gifted education. In essence, the 'educational niche' of gifted children in Russia is undergoing change. Schematically, this niche includes four components: the child, the family (including parents and children), the school, and the society at large. The modus operandi of the old system was from top to bottom; the societal component dominated the school component, the family component, and, to a large degree, the individual (child) component. The family's role was primarily to motivate and prepare the child, the child's role was to excel, and the rest of the educational program was accomplished by a merging of the school and the society. In contrast, the new system operates from the bottom up; the family, focused on the child, now serves as both initiator and promoter of gifted education. Now, the state's responsibility is all but gone, while the family component of the educational niche grows in importance. The school component remains in the middle, but the school is essentially being 'sold' by the state to the parents; a transition of power has gone hand-in-hand with this reshaping of the educational niche.

Educational goals for the gifted and talented also have been redefined. Before, the system cultivated special talents because it benefited from them; now, however, the system simply is not able to use these talents, so the traditional motivation for developing them is eroding. The second original aim of gifted education—assuring progress—is also in jeopardy. The federal government is no longer funding technological development. Any innovations that are being made are carried out in the private sector. Most of the old connections between federal scientific and industrial centers have been destroyed and nascent networks in the private sector are not yet fully established. Only the third goal—education for the sake of personal growth—has emerged unscathed; in fact, it has grown in importance; attention at last is being paid to children's overall individual development.

Accordingly, Russia is pursuing two new approaches to gifted education, in addition to continuing the traditional one (focused on the modification and enrichment of the standard curriculum in specific subject areas). These approaches are: (1) the accelera-

tion of education; and (2) the redefinition and restructuring of general goals and specific content.

In the acceleration approach, children with a high level of ability are taught (or teach themselves) the regular school program, but they progress at their own pace. These children often skip classes and graduate from high school much earlier than their peers. Only a few schools in the country have accelerated programs. One such school is Moscow Lyceum No. 1524. The experiences of one student there, Daniil, are typical. At age 9, Daniil began his first year at the lyceum in a regular classroom. However, he was way ahead of his classmates, so he decided to study independently, consulting with teachers when necessary. In his first year at the lyceum, Daniel zoomed through three regular grades. After three years, Daniil graduated from the lyceum at age 12 and was accepted at Moscow State University.

The second new approach to gifted education consists of a redefinition of the goals and content of gifted education. This framework assumes that gifted students do not merely know a lot about a particular subject area; rather, they think and act differently. And so, the theory goes, they need an education that not only fills them with knowledge but also helps them develop, both intellectually and emotionally, into balanced individuals.

Some schools have responded accordingly. Moscow School No. 1624, for example, implemented an interdisciplinary program called Constellation that prioritizes emotional and intellectual growth over content-specific knowledge. This program seeks to supplement the imparting of knowledge with programs that help children master higher-order thinking and bring together different areas of studies. The program first enrolled students in 1988 based on IQ scores. Since then, teachers and psychologists have monitored the subject-specific achievements of these students, who were classified into three groups depending on their IQ scores. The jury is still out on the ultimate success of the Constellation program. Notably, however, those in the top IQ tier upon entry have maintained a high level of subject-specific and general achievement. (This is a good sign since, typically, the achievement level of gifted students actually drops upon entry into a specialized school.)

Sizing up the Current System

How can we assess how well the system is performing at this point? We have no hard data that allow us to compare gifted education in Russia with that in other countries. However, we can evaluate the success of Russian education for the gifted based on the results of various competitions. For example, we can, to some degree, estimate the effectiveness of Russia's gifted education in maths and science by analyzing the success of Russian teams in competitions from 1995 to 1997. The most prestigious contests for young mathematicians and computer scientists are the international subject olympiadas. International competitions are held in maths, physics, biology, ecology, geography, chemistry, and computer science. On average, 70–80 teams of high school students from all over the world attend these competitions.

Twenty-seven Russian teenagers participated in the 1995 competitions. They won 25 medals: 10 gold, 7 silver, and 8 bronze. Russian students won 6 medals in maths and 5 medals in computer science. In 1996, Russia again sent 27 students to the international competitions. Again, the students returned with 25 medals: 11 gold, 7 silver, and 7 bronze. Six were in maths and 4 were in computer science. The following year, 31 Russian students competed in the competitions. This time around, 29 of them earned medals: 9 gold, 12 silver, and 8 bronze. Of these, 6 were in maths and 4 were in computer science. These successes are not specific to the last few years. In fact, this trend of achievement began in the 1960s and has been fairly stable since then.

However, the function of intellectual competitions is changing, and so is their value as indicators of intellectual attainment. In the 'old' system, winners had to rise to the top from the bottom. Individuals had to move systematically up the ladder of competitions from those at the school level to those at the top rung of intellectual achievement. Some exceptions existed; students could enter at different points (e.g. students from specialized schools might join the competition at later stages because their schools could have more than one eligible candidate). In general, however, students progressed from the bottom up, and anyone could start the climb.

In the 'new' system, students use alternative modes of entrance into the system more frequently. For example, of the six Russian winners of the international maths competition held in Toronto in 1995, five were from one St. Petersburg School: School No. 239, for children gifted in maths. This school has an impressive track record of producing winners of international maths and computer science competitions. School No. 239 has developed a special training program with carefully selected teachers to groom students for these competitions. In fact, schools featuring competition-oriented training are on the rise. No longer are the competitions themselves primarily ways to identify talented individuals so that they can then receive appropriate schooling. Now, the young people competing are already receiving specialized schooling. For these individuals, the competitions represent a prize to be achieved 'for the record'. In most cases, having a strong record guarantees acceptance to the better higher-educational institutions.

Some Russian experts have decried this motivational shift, suggesting that teachers be renamed 'trainers' and students be called 'intellectual sportsmen'. In fact, intellectual competition at any but the lowest levels is turning into a closed system. Children are selected for abilities very specific to these competitions-and then groomed and selected further. At the same time, the olympiada tasks increasingly have a distinctive style; consequently, students can receive focused, competition—specific training. More and more, gaining the skills necessary to solve specific types of olympiada problems is taking precedence over acquiring broad knowledge.

Educators, parents, and experts have noticed these trends. Some educators have responded by developing different ways to identify talent. These avenues are open to children whose 'competitive' skills have not been carefully honed to meet the requirements and time constraints of the olympiadas. One of the most popular of these alternatives is the 'intellectual marathon', which involves competitors in three age groups and three subject domains (maths, human sciences, and natural sciences). It is assumed that these alternative competitions allow for the identification of a wider circle of talented children. Clearly, then, even though success in competitions is impressive, the identification role that these competitions traditionally played has diminished, and the intellectual achievement that these triumphs once indicated is under question.

We also can assess the health of gifted education by observing what happens to talented students after their school years are over. Consider, first, the following general trends in Russian higher education. As of 1997, Russian had 555 federal and 250 non-federal higher-educational institutions (including colleges, universities, technological institutions, and so on.) Collectively, the federal institutions enrolled more than 3,000,000 students, while the non-federal schools served an additional population of 160,000 students. In 1997, there were 220 students per 10,000 people; 174 of these attended federal institutions, and 46 attended nonfederal schools. Russian higher education experienced a dramatic drop in enrollment in 1991–1992. Since 1993, however, the situation has been stabilizing, with an incremental growth in enrollment of 5% between 1995 and 1996, and a 77% growth rate between 1996 and 1997. (Interestingly enough, increased enrollment has occurred primarily in non-federal institutions.) Yet, the enrollment rates of 1997 have still not reached those of 1989.

It is also important to understand that Russian higher education is subject-specific. When students enter a university, they choose a specific subject of study and apply to the appropriate department by entrance exam. Applicants must apply in person. With the exception of a few highly competitive schools (such as Moscow State University), each applicant can typically apply to only one institution per year. (At Moscow State University, the entrance exam is held one month before the exams at the other institutions, so applicants who are not accepted have the opportunity to apply to a different institution that same year.)

How, then, have gifted students fared in this broader picture of higher education? Most graduates of gifted programs in maths apply to the best departments in maths, computer science, and economics. Preferred institutions include Moscow State University, Moscow Physics and Technology University, and Novosibirsk University. These institutions have special programs—and sometimes special departments—to prepare gifted children for entrance examinations. Such school-university partnerships serve both types of institutions: schools and programs for gifted children establish links with institutions of higher education in order to ensure acceptance of graduates, and higher educational institutions forge bonds with schools in order to ensure that the best students will eventually apply and enroll.

For example, statistics for School No. 18 (a specialized boarding school for gifted children in mathematics, established as a part of Moscow State University's Department of Math and Mechanics) graduates are supportive of these practices. This school enrolls 250–300 students from all over the country every year. The typical program lasts three years, but some students join for only a year or two. In 1997, 100% of School No. 18 graduates were accepted by highly prestigious higher-educational institutions. In 1998, the figure was 98%.

Here—at the moment of enrollment in higher-educational institutions—our formal data about gifted graduates ends. Observations from professors tell us little; gifted students are initially ahead of their peers, but this discrepancy, in most cases, is overcome by the second or third year of higher education.

The Track Ahead: Challenges for the Future

Still, we know enough to realize that the challenges confronting Russia's program of gifted education are many and various. Three major issues that deserve special mention here are the funding of gifted education, the reeducation of teachers, the establishment of theory-based instruction, and the harnessing of talents.

First, as federal support for gifted education has diminished, the need for alternative sources of funding has become pressing. Yet the list of potential donors is small. Tax law does not stimulate non-profit sponsorship, and so the funding of schools and programs is left first to parents, then to the potential 'consumers' of 'brainpower' (universities, banks, and high-tech corporations), and finally to alumni. But none of these potential supporters will fund Russian gifted education for the sake of its original primary goal: the benefit of the country. The current financial situation, then, requires a restructuring of the goals of this system of education. Now, gifted education must be aimed, first, at the good of the child (which can motivate parental support), then at the promotion of technological progress (which should draw the support of the 'consumers' of talent), and, lastly, at the well-being of

the country (which should stimulate some federal support-however small it may be).

Second, the training of teachers for the gifted must be refashioned to suit the changing needs and desires of the student population. Traditionally, gifted students have been educated by 'subject professionals': researchers or professors who were experts in particular subjects, but not necessarily in child and adolescent psychology and pedagogy. Moreover, the overwhelming majority of these instructors had no special training focused on the education of the gifted. An emphasis on content knowledge so dominated gifted education that these deficiencies did not matter much. But, in a system that stresses the balanced development of the talented, knowledge of psychology and teaching is crucial. The new system can survive only if it reeducates its teachers. What they know already about teaching their specific subjects is useful and should be retained, but additional teaching and mentoring skills must be developed as well.

One telling 1997 study of educators and gifted children found that gifted children want their teachers to be creative and to allow students to be creative as well. Teachers, on the other hand, did not prioritize creativity when they described either ideal teachers or ideal students. If the expectations of children and adults cannot be merged, the new system of gifted education, targeted primarily at meeting the needs of students, will not thrive.

Third, greater effort should be made to ground gifted education on a solid theoretical basis. Traditionally, Russian gifted education was essentially atheoretical, even though Soviet and Russian psychologists have developed theories covering a wide range of relevant topics—from the role of intuition in giftedness, to the nonlinear nature of the development of giftedness. In general, theoretical work has concluded that giftedness involves cognitive motivation, creative inquisitiveness, an ability to arrive at original solutions, an ability to anticipate and make prognoses, and an ability to create standards of performance meeting high aesthetic, moral, and intellectual criteria.

Along with these general concepts of giftedness, additional theories more specifically address the concept of the gifted child. For example, Nikolai Leites argues that the variability of giftedness must be taken into account. He suggests three different categories of gifted children: (1) children with accelerated intellectual development-those characterized by amazing intellectual activity and insatiable cognitive motivation; (2) children with early mental specialization-those who may have an average level of intelligence and even confront difficulty in some subject areas but who have a predisposition to high achievement in a specific domain; and (3) children who perform exceptionally well in a number of domains.

Clearly, the spectrum of possible theoretical approaches to giftedness is extensive. However, few ways of thinking about giftedness have been verified empirically in school settings. Psychologists penetrated school systems in the late 1980s and early 1990s and, in the process, established some experimental programs in gifted education. However, programs have not been evaluated formally so that they can be either recommended or ruled out.

The latest programmatic documents of the Russian federal government and the Ministry of Education consistently reveal a new federal push for the theory-based identification and education of the gifted. While this call for theory has some merit, we must be wary of too hastily seizing and promoting one dominant theoretical approach. Right now, there are three possible developments: (1) the new system could adopt multiple theoretical approaches and, at the same time, develop a system to compare and verify their effectiveness; (2) the system could adopt a single theoretical paradigm and test it empirically; or (3) the system could remain essentially atheoretical. The second choice would likely lead to a confrontation between the federal government and the extant variety of approaches to giftedness. And the third option would weaken federal authority in the increasingly theoretical field of gifted education. The first option, it seems, is the best; this path would allow the federal government to replace its unified but atheoretical program with a theory-based program that allows verification of different approaches.

Finally, Russia needs to find ways to harness the developed brainpower that emerges from gifted education programs. In the old system, the Soviet government ensured not only the nurturing but also the consumption of natural gifts. Presently, however, the government cannot pay those it already employs; hiring new talent is out of the question. Thus, one of the most urgent problems facing gifted education today is not education so much as it is productive use of talents once they are developed.

This problem is closely linked to current conditions in the Russian scientific community. Prior to about 1989, approximately 80% of the graduates of the old system became academic scientists in Russia. The situation today suggests the extent of recent change. For instance, about 10% of the 300 1992 graduates of Moscow School No. 18 are working and studying abroad, whereas less than 5% are pursuing academic careers in Russia. A significant portion of the class of 1992 entered the private sector of Russia's developing economy; other graduates simply left no record of their pursuits. For better or worse, graduates of specialized schools and programs for gifted children are entering a much-changed world of work.

What should be done in light of this fundamental shift? Presently, the system produces many gifted young people whose talents are not utilized by today's Russian society. The old system could ignore students' social and emotional development in part because it

protected them when they entered the working world. To be fair to its students, the new system should equip those growing up today with survival skills. There are now fewer guarantees in the adult world than there used to be.

In sum, Russian experts have proposed three immediate actions: (1) the development of diverse models of gifted education including expert validation prior to implementation, (2) the promotion of investment in gifted education, with careful oversight, and (3) the development of a theoretical model of gifted education that allows for a diversity of approaches but incorporates hard-won, traditional knowledge.

In gifted education in Russia today, old traditions and new developments coexist in the dynamic context of a society undergoing profound transformation. Still, the system functions. In fact, at the superficial level of success in international competition and higher education admission, it functions no less well than in the past. The residual stability of the traditional system (train 1) and the acceleration of the new (train 2) coexist and keep gifted education rolling along. But soon the old system will not be effective at all; already its vital signs are dwindling. In a best-case scenario, the new system will inherit the best of the old ways and move on, while the old system will willingly allow some of its components to be altered to fit the new context. All of us concerned—educators, parents, policy-makers, and social scientists—must work to ensure that this inevitable integration will be as harmonious and productive as possible.

References

Arnold, V. (1998). *Matematicheskaia bezgramotnost' khuzhe kostrov inkvizitsii* [Math illiteracy is worse than the Inquisition bonfires]. Izvestia, January 16.

Druzhinin, V. N. (1995). *Psikhologia obshchikh sposobnostei* [The psychology of general abilities]. Moscow: Logos.

Leites, N. S. (1984). *Sposobnosti i odarennost' v detskie gody* [Abilities and giftedness in childhood]. Moscow: Pedagogika.

Matiushkin, A. M. (1993). *Zagadki odarennosti* [Puzzles of giftedness]. Moscow: Pedagogika.

Paramonov, A. I., Bykov, V. V., Zavarzin, A. K., Pavlov, I. S., Orlov, V. A., Vinogradov, L. I., Kucher, N. I., Iniakin, Yu. S., Petrova, L. P., Shtykalo, F. E., Salakhetdinova, V. A., Kozlov, N. V., Lazareva V. I., Zakharchenko, O. V., Smirnova, L. A. & Gorskikh, V. A. (1997). *Odarennye deti* [Gifted children]. Moscow: Russian Ministry of Education.

Ponomarev, Ya. A. (1988). *Psikhologia tvorchestva* [The psychology of creativity]. Moscow: Nauka.

Popova, L. V. (1997). Podgotovka uchitelia dlia raboty s odarennymi [Teacher training for teaching gifted children]. In: V. P. Lebedeva & V. I. Panov (Eds.), *Utchiteliu of Odarennukh Detiakh* (pp. 49–73). Moscow: Molodaia Gvardia.

Rubinstein, S. L. (1981). Problema sposobnostei i voprosy psukhologicheskoi teorii [Abilities and psychological theory]. In: A. Zhdan (Ed.), *Khrestomatia po Vozrastnoi i Pedagogicheskoi Psikhologii* (pp. 44–55). Moscow: MGU.

Shumakova, N. B. (1997). Obuchenie i razvitie odarennykh detei v shkole [The education and development of gifted children in school]. In: V. P. Lebedeva & V. I. Panov (Eds.), *Utchiteliu of odarennukh detiakh* (pp. 203–233). Moscow: Molodaia Gvardia.

Teplov, B. M. (1985). *Sposobnosti i odarennost'* [Abilities and giftedness]. Moscow: Pedagogika.

The Committee of the USSR Ministry of Education (1989). *O pervoocherednykh merakh po vyiavleniui i vospitaniu osobo odarennukh uchatsikhsia* [Toward urgent actions regarding the identification and upbringing of highly gifted pupils] (No. 11/1). Moscow: Gosudarstvennyi Komitet SSSR po Narodnomu Obrazovaniu.

The Committee of the USSR Ministry of Education (1990). *O tselevoi kompleksnoi program 'Tvorcheskaia odarennost'* [On the targeted program Creative giftedness] (No. 2/3). Moscow: Gosudarstvennyi Komitet SSSR po Narodnomu Obrazovaniu.

The Committee of the USSR Ministry of Education (1991). *O razvitii programmy 'Tvorcheskaia odarennost'* [On the development of the targeted program 'Creative giftedness'] (No. 3/1). Moscow: Gosudarstvennyi Komitet SSSR po Narodnomu Obrazovaniu.

The Federation Committee of the Federal Assembly of Russian Federation (1998). *O sostoianii i perspectivakh razvitia sistemy vysshego professional'noogo obrazovania* [On the state and perspectives of the system of higher education] (No. 214-SF). Moscow: Russian Government Printing Office.

The Russian Government (1997). *Programma social'nykh reform v Rossiiskoi Federatsii* [The Program of Social Reforms in the Russian Federation (1996–2000)] (No. 222). Moscow: Russian Government Printing Office.

The USSR Cabinet of Ministers (1988). *Ob organizatsii specializirovannych uchebno-nauchnykh tsentrov Moskovskogo i Novosibirskogo gosudarstvennykh universitetov* [On the organization of the specialized education-research centers for gifted children of Moscow and Novosibirsk universities]. Moscow: the USSR Government Printing Office.

Middle East Region: Efforts, Policies, Programs and Issues

Taisir Subhi[1] and Netta Maoz[2]

[1]Al al-Bayt University in Amman, Jordan
[2]Weizmann Institute of Science in Rehovot, Israel

Introduction

The purpose of this chapter is to provide an explanation of the provisions for gifted and talented children in the Middle East including the Arabic countries and Israel. Because we are dealing with issues that have such important consequences for resource allocation and for the future of children in the region, it is important to look critically at the present situation and future trends in the region. This chapter concerns itself with practices, and current thinking on a number of major issues in the area of identification and the development of giftedness and creativity.

The Arabic Countries

In the Middle East, like other developing regions, gifted children are important to the modernization of society. About 50% of the population is under fifteen, every third person is a student, and the region's governments spend about 8% of its annual budget on education. Skills are among the region's chief exports.

School is organized around three cycles: elementary (6–12 year olds), preparatory (13–15 year olds), and secondary (16–19 year olds). The first two cycles are compulsory for all boys and girls. All schools follow the curriculum laid down by the Ministry of Education, and Arabic is the medium of instruction. In elementary school children learn Arabic, religion, mathematics, geography, science, drawing (for boys), embroidery (for girls), music, drama, and physical education. Starting from the fifth grade, all children learn English as their second language.

The preparatory cycle was added in the 1960s, providing children with an education designed to prepare them for secondary education or the labor market. This cycle is seen as enabling students to develop scientific thinking; to form positive notions about life and society; to have respect for truth, discipline, and work; and to recognize their rights and responsibilities. Those students who pursue the secon-dary cycle take the General Secondary Examination (Tawjihi) at the end of the cycle. Arabic is the medium of instruction and English is a compulsory subject.

All teacher training in the Arabic countries is conducted at the post-secondary level in teachers' colleges that offer special diplomas and have demonstration schools attached to them. As of 1998, 74.9% of academic and vocational secondary school teachers were untrained, but an increasing number of teachers are attending two-year part-time postgraduate diploma courses in education offered by universities. The universities now also offer courses for a B.Ed. degree.

Although many educational bodies in the Arabic countries are responsible for minor aspects of education, the Ministry of Education in every Arabic country maintains centralized control of all education other than in the universities. The Ministry recruits all teachers to state schools through the Civil Service Commission, administers the General Secondary Examination (Tawjihi), and provides all educational resources including textbooks, prepared centrally, which are given out free of charge to children in the compulsory cycle and at cost to students in the secondary cycle. In recent years, however, the Ministry of Education in each country has taken a number of steps to decentralize control. For example, it now delegates responsibility for implementing Ministry decisions with regard to staffing, scholarships, and building.

The Educational Process: Aims and Philosophy

The aims of the educational process in the Arabic countries were formally set out in the 1960s and were derived from a variety of sources. These sources reflect the diverse strands in the region's historical development including their Arabic Islamic heritage, British and French influences, and aspirations towards international standards of education and modernization. Prior to the 1960s, education was based on the Arabic

Islamic heritage and a view of knowledge inherited from the British and the French. This philosophy emphasized cognitive development. Its purpose was to develop the mental ability of children, but it did not take into account the development of the whole person or the needs of the society. The old aims of education concentrated on inculcating knowledge, facts, and information. Students learned by heart the subject matter, which often did not link with their daily lives. This means that there has been a shift from knowledge-centered aims to child and society-centered aims.

A new philosophy and new aims for education were introduced in the 1960s. They reflect the influence of international developments in education and broader aims for the education systems in the region. The problem has become whether the new philosophy and its associated aims of education can be realized in practice by societies that possess traditional attitudes towards education.

Article 4 of the 1964 Jordanian Education Act, for example, sets out a detailed set of curriculum aims [translated from Arabic Text]:

(1) To prepare the righteous citizen who believes in the following:
    (a) The principles of educational philosophy in Jordan; while drawing on the basic ingredients of Arab Islamic heritage a certain amount of emphasis is placed upon the possibility of modernization.
    (b) The rights and responsibilities of citizenship.
    (c) The practical realization of ethical ideals whether collectively or by individuals.
    (d) Initiative in work and in behaviour, fruitful cooperation with others and the application of democratic principles in human relations.
(2) Understanding the environment including its natural, social, and cultural forms, beginning in the family home to school, village, city, district, or country (Jordan), Arab home, and human society, provided that it is accompanied by the following:
    (a) An analytical understanding of all the features, varied problems, and current and future needs of the environment.
    (b) It should be achieved in such a way that it develops positive feelings in the individual concerning his/her duties for participation in the development of the environment, in accordance with his/ her aptitude and his/her ability.
(3) To develop basic skills such as:
    (a) Calculation and communication such as speaking, hearing, reading and writing standard Arabic, and enjoying reading and increasing knowledge.
    (b) To pursue the scientific method in research, thinking, inference, and to make distinctions between right and wrong.

    (c) To adjust, achieve, change, develop and progress and to minimize boredom, confusion, and frustration.
(4) To provide students with an educational environment that will provide the greatest possible development of their abilities.
(5) To promote collective and individual health by disseminating health information and the development of healthy habits.
(6) To promote collective and individual recreation by developing habits of healthy recreation and varied features of Arab and Jordanian Folk Art.
(7) To promote collective and individual economic advancement, and to increase the national income, by providing educational opportunities for all, by the diversification of educational programs which meet the interests and desires of individuals on the one hand, and on the other hand, satisfy the future and present needs of Jordan in all fields within a comprehensive economic blueprint of the State (Ministry of Planning, 1990).

The aims are general and vague, and not sufficiently defined to permit easy translation into curriculum objectives or instructional materials, making it difficult to institutionalize them and realize them adequately in practice. In brief, the aims do not show where and how they could fit into the general philosophy of education for these countries. Neither does it show how they can be used to develop specific curriculum measures.

The Character of the Educational Process

The Arabic countries face a number of problems and challenges in relation to education in general and gifted education in particular. Problems vary in complexity and magnitude from state to state. The First Conference for Education Development (1987) which took place in Jordan summarized the weaknesses of the Arabic educational process as follows:

(1) The region suffered from educational neglect during many centuries of foreign domination. During the earlier years of this century, efforts were directed primarily toward expansion of available resources and little attention was paid to quality.
(2) The region is still far from providing sufficient facilities for all school-age males and females.
(3) Among the most serious problems which reduce the efficiency and increase the real cost of education are excessively high dropout and repetition rates in all education cycles.
(4) Teachers making suitable provisions for gifted and talented students are not always appreciated.
(5) Lack of ability and interest in creating a supportive environment essential for nurturing gifts and talents.

(6) Lack of opportunities for participation by students in the discussion of educational and social issues of concern to them.

(7) Lack of interest on the part of males in joining the teaching profession, coupled with a high turnover rate due to a variety of moral, material, professional, and social causes.

(8) Shortage of qualified teachers in academic and vocational secondary schools.

Change and innovation have always been a vital part of human existence, yet only in the recent past has the process of change been transformed into a worldwide revolution. This revolution originated in Western Europe, but the process of modernization has become an increasingly universal experience. In one Arabic country after another, the transformation of traditional society and culture has taken place, though at varying speeds and in different ways (Subhi, 1997). Schools are viewed as instruments of change, and maxims about this are frequently encountered in the speeches of Arab officials (Szyliowics, 1973; Al-Tal, 1979).

Before the fourteenth century, the Middle East enjoyed a civilization which endured for more than five hundred years, and witnessed intellectual, artistic, scientific, and cultural achievements that influenced world culture (Huxley, 1963; Sa'ab, 1980). Yet, in the end this rich culture withered, and the high achievements of the Arabs in science, literature, medicine, and fine arts became dim memories (Al-Tal, 1979). One of the reasons for this decline was the failure of the education process to respond to changing demands, including production of gifted and talented scholars, statesmen, and administrators.

Practically every country is seeking to achieve a rapid rate of economic growth. Underlying the huge investment being made in education is the belief that schooling is a major variable determining the level of economic development. In general, researchers have concluded that positive relationships do exist between the formation of human capital – in which education is a major component – and economic growth. Experts have calculated that much of the rise in income in the U.S.A. between 1900 and 1956 was due to improvements in workers' educational qualifications. The (former) U.S.S.R. and Japan are often cited as further evidence of this relationship. All three countries possessed highly developed educational processes, and a significant proportion of their population was literate before the economy began to undergo rapid development (Szyliowics, 1973; Sa'ab, 1980).

Provisions for Gifted Children in the Arabic Countries

Changing philosophies and goals, economic priorities, and what we know about gifted children suggest a number of aims for gifted education in the Arabic countries including: developing an efficient and comprehensive procedure for identifying gifted and talented students in school as early as possible; providing gifted and talented students with an educational environment that enhances their abilities; developing problem solving abilities and creative thinking skills, research skills, individual interests, independent study skills, communication skills in the humanities (visual, oral, and written), and intellectual learning activities. Problem formulation abilities are also very valuable in all endeavors.

An appropriate curriculum is crucial to gifted education, and some instructional strategies may be more efficient than others in delivering the appropriate content to gifted students (Fox, 1981). Renzulli (1980) noticed that gifted programs are too often patchwork collections of random practices and activities; he suggested that differentiated programs for the gifted must include modification of the ways in which advanced materials are presented. Because we are dealing with an issue that has such important consequences for resource allocation and for the future of children, it is important to look critically at the nature of the process involved in identifying gifted and talented children and provide them with special provision and programs to meet their special needs.

The Multiple Criteria Identification Processes

According to Hallahan and Kauffman (1981):

> People who are gifted, or at least have the potential for giftedness, can go through life almost totally unrecognized for their talents. Sometimes the gifted go undiscovered because their families and intimates simply place no particular value on their special abilities. Sometimes they are not recognized because they are not given the opportunities or training necessary to show what they can do. Especially in the case of children who are poor or members of minority groups, the gifted may be deprived of chances to demonstrate and develop their potential. How many more outstanding artists and scientists would we have if every child had the opportunity and the training necessary to develop his or her talents to the fullest possible extent? There is no way of knowing, but it is safe to say we would have more (p. 434).

Gifted children are identified in this region as those who have demonstrated high ability (including high intelligence), high creativity, and high task commitment. In addition, three Arabic countries including Jordan, Bahrain, and Egypt have added achievement (e.g. in mathematics) as the fourth criterion. In the adopted definition, standardized intelligence tests, creativity tests, and achievement tests measure abilities. Task commitment is measured by tests of achievement, rating scales, and judgment of teachers and parents.

The multiple criteria identification procedure adopted by the Arabic countries, is based on a number of principles (or rationales), including:

(1) gifted and talented children should be identified as early as possible in their educational careers;
(2) the focus of identification is not to label students, but to recognize and respond to gifted and talented students' educational needs;
(3) the identification of gifted and talented students requires the utilization of formal and informal measures obtained from many sources in a wide variety of settings; and
(4) identification instruments and procedures must match with the program provided to gifted and talented children.

The major purpose of a multiple criteria identification process is to determine which children have a need for special educational provision, whether as a supplement or as an alternative to regular mainstream instruction, and to pinpoint or diagnose their special needs (Subhi, 1992). The multiple criteria identification process should be flexible and inclusive rather than exclusive (Feldhusen & Wyman, 1980).

Alternative Models of Provision

Included in the very broad spectrum of forms of special provision for the gifted and talented are acceleration and enrichment, and it is increasingly being recognized that they are best seen as complementary. A number of acceleration models are in place such as grade skipping in Bahrain, Iraq, Jordan, Qatar, and Kuwait; and grade or advancement placement in single subjects in Egypt, Morocco, and Lebanon. Other special provisions include grouping within the ordinary class, special schools and special classes, provision of resource rooms, extra courses, and similar measures. Provision outside the traditional school has also been reported, such as through competition, summer camps, and mentoring programs (Urban, 1993). Private groups, such as the National Association for Gifted Children, support family emotional needs, offer summer schools, and promote the children's interests to the public. New enrichment materials have been produced, and a number of workshops were conducted in the region.

Survey studies conducted in the region (Subhi, 1997) indicated that the most common form of provision for gifted children at the primary level is to leave their normal classes for a resource room or computer lab with a specially trained teacher. This is followed by self-contained classes. At the secondary level, grade skipping, special classes, and independent studies were applied most often. In addition, mathematically gifted students profit by participating in accelerated mathematics programs.

Enrichment

Gifted children need greater pace, breadth, and depth than most other children. This implies a need to provide all kinds of provisions which enrich the normal academic curriculum (Urban, 1993). It is clear that enrichment should give opportunity for creative production and expression of ideas and training of general strategies or techniques of study, which can then be applied to intellectual work in general.

In Arabic countries, three enrichment programs are provided for children from grade three up to grade twelve. These programs are conducted on a part time withdrawal basis one morning or afternoon per week. The Enrichment Triad Model (Renzulli, 1977) has been implemented in a large number of private schools in Jordan, the West Bank, and Bahrain. Resource rooms, as a special provision for gifted and talented children, are used in several Arabic countries. In special room(s) within the school building students work independently or are guided by a special resource teacher on freely chosen or assigned projects. These rooms include books and other publications; electronic, audiovisual equipment, and computer hardware; computer software; CAL packages; word processing, spread sheets, and data bases; instruments and apparatus for work in the sciences, materials and requisites for art and music, etc. (Urban, 1993). We must however take into consideration that the effective and efficient use of the resource room(s) in other Arabic countries depends on the availability of the trained and experienced resource teacher.

Problem Solving

In our rapidly changing world, the need for critical and creative problem solving is crucial. The question arises as to whether or not we can teach children to think creatively. The task, however, is to find realistic ways to implement programs which develop thinking skills in the classroom (McCluskey & Walker, 1991). Problem solving sessions, activities, and programs are available in a large number of schools in the Arabic countries. Both public and private schools provide educational experiences that use a set of problem solving strategies, such as looking for a pattern, making a list, guessing and testing; searching randomly, setting up a question, and working backward.

In Lebanon, Dr. Iman Osta and her colleagues have established a new agenda for teaching mathematics as an active process of discovery and inquiry. Talented maths students are provided with curricular opportunities, provisions, and classroom practices to experience the delights of mathematical communication, reasoning, creative thinking, and creative problem solving.

In the West Bank, for the last forty years, the Palestinian educational system continues in the traditional form, where the schools' staff has never had the chance to be exposed to new approaches and has never received training. As a result, no provisions are available to meet the special needs of gifted and talented students. The majority of children do not even have the chance to practice thinking skills. During the next decade, the main focus should be on using different approaches to provide students with opportunities to explore and experience logical, critical, analytical, and creative thinking derived from their own social environment.

Individualized Educational Programs (IEPs)

The IEPs can range from independent study activities planned to supplement, extend, or substitute classroom work for gifted and talented students to the formalized long term planning IEPs involving adaptation of the content, the process, the product, and the learning environment. The individualized instruction is diagnostic and prescriptive. The prescription is cooperatively developed by both the teacher and the gifted student, and can include information from different sources. Self-direction and self-selection of topics are key aspects in an individualized program. Up to now there are no IEPs being implemented in the Arabic countries. Further research needs to focus on this type of special provision and investigate how we could employ such provision effectively and efficiently.

Grade Skipping

It is now becoming possible for gifted and talented students in Bahrain, Egypt, Iraq, Jordan, Kuwait, Qatar, Lebanon and Morocco to 'skip grades'. After decades of neglect, giftedness and creativity are receiving more attention in Kuwait. It is for this reason that little attention has been paid to grade skipping there. Very limited numbers of schools include creative activities as an instructional strategy for reaching all children.

In Morocco the Ministry of Education has established a National Committee for Gifted and Talented. Scholars and interested people are planning to form a law to enforce consideration of gifted children in education. In addition, a national association for the gifted will be formed. However, little attention has been paid to grade skipping yet in Morocco.

Friday and Summer Programs

In Jordan, Bahrain, United Arab Emirates, and Egypt, special Friday courses constitute one of the main services provided for gifted children. Many different topics are offered for pupils in grades 6–8 (e.g. computer science, journalism, archeology, space and astronomy, philosophy). Privately organized Friday morning or after-school classes for special tuition are common in a number of Arabic countries, including those designed to foster cultural traditions and languages.

In both Syria and Lebanon there are still no official definitions of either giftedness or creativity nor public policy for educating gifted and talented children.

Currently, there are a few special programs for gifted students offered in individual schools, in clusters of schools, or run as private enterprises mainly after-school or on Friday or Sunday. These centers offer students opportunities to interact with and be stimulated by other gifted and talented students. From time to time (not on a regular basis) there is a special workshop or field trip organized by private schools.

Competition

Freeman (1990) pointed out that competition can be a strategic way of finding and defining children's capabilities, whether compared to others or to his/ her own best performance. She added: "Many highly able children used [competition] quite consciously to improve their skills, because of the reward it offered them. But they knew that in order to be effective, the comparison had to be meaningful, as well as part of the process of getting to the top, which is not the same as the simple thrill of winning" (pp. 93–94). During the last decades, competitions have become very popular in many countries in the region; the number of participants in international competitions or educational Olympiads has greatly increased. International, national, and regional competitions may be valuable assessments of and incentives for achievement. Further, competitions may provide feedback as to how the student compares with others who are interested in the same area. Regional and national competitions can be found in Arabic countries in most fields, including maths, science, computer programming, writing, engineering, geography, environmental, art, music, and dance.

Special Schools

The Jubilee School Project was first announced in 1977 during Jordan's celebrations of the late King Hussein's accession to the throne. The School is a tribute to His Majesty's development efforts, especially in the field of education. In 1984, Queen Noor accepted a request by the Prime Minister to assume responsibility for the project, and in 1985, when the Noor Al Hussein Foundation was established, the Jubilee School became one of its projects.

After years of research, planning, and teacher training, the Jubilee School was founded as an independent coeducational secondary school for outstanding scholarship students. In the Fall of 1993, 87 Jordanian ninth graders, chosen for their exceptional individual and academic potential embarked on a pioneering educational experience. The School expanded the following year to include 197 ninth and tenth graders. A rigorous multiple-criteria system is used for selecting Jubilee School students that includes school achievement over the last five semesters, ratings of behavioral characteristics, general mental ability, specific mathematical ability, and creativity level.

On May 2, 1995, on the 42nd anniversary of his assumption of the throne, the late King Hussein laid the foundation stone for the first phase of the construction of the Jubilee School campus near Amman. In addition to boarding facilities, which enables the School to welcome a larger number of students from remote areas of the kingdom and to open its doors to students from the rest of the Arab world, the campus also includes a comprehensive library providing access to databases worldwide, modern computer and language laboratories, vocational and teacher training centers, a music and drama center, and athletic facilities.

The Jubilee School reflects a Noor Al-Hussein Foundation's philosophy that is sensitive to traditional values and responsive to the needs, talents, and aspirations of the people of Jordan. As with other Foundation projects, the School's innovative approach to education encourages initiative and democratic participation, while contributing to national education standards.

The Jubilee School provides educational opportunities for gifted and talented students, with a special emphasis on students from less developed areas of the country. Convinced that gifted and talented students represent a national wealth that should be carefully nurtured, the School seeks to develop future leaders committed to the service of their country and capable of addressing the constantly changing challenges of our region and the world.

Beside the basic requirements of the Jordanian Ministry of Education, Jubilee School students are required to take courses especially designed to develop their critical thinking, problem solving, investigative, creative and decision-making abilities. The School is the only educational institution in Jordan presently linked to the Internet, facilitating interaction with schools, institutes, and databases worldwide. In addition to rigorous training in mathematics, science, and the humanities, the Jubilee School students are also required to choose from subjects such as advanced calculus, advanced physics, astronomy, computer graphics, debate, drama, economics, human genetics, journalism, literary criticism, and world history.

The Jubilee School is committed not only to equip its students with a strong academic base, but also to build character and a sense of social responsibility through two programs. The Leadership Guest Speakers Program introduces students to successful leaders in various fields, and fosters open discussion and debate designed to help students develop their own leadership qualities and self-esteem. The second, the Community Service Program, requires all students to participate in community service projects.

The Jubilee School also sponsors the Center for Excellence in Education, established in 1999 to develop and disseminate knowledge of innovative approaches and advances in mathematics, science and the humanities. The Center has become a resource for

secondary school teachers in Jordan, where curriculum modules which successfully integrate these disciplines are currently being developed. Deeply committed to a democratic learning environment, the School encourages freedom of thought and expression. Further, as a center for excellence in education, one of the School's primary functions is to provide a variety of educational services to public and private institutions through workshops and training programs for staff and faculty. The Counseling and Career Center was established to provide personal and career guidance to students and to address their emotional and social needs. Counseling programs are also held for the benefit of teachers and counselors from across Jordan and other countries. The Jubilee School students will also be able to sit for external examinations, including the SAT, TOEFL and GRE. A special advanced placement program is being studied whereby students can earn university credits for advanced courses in science, mathematics, computer science, and literature. The School also plans to develop an Educational Testing Service (ETS)-like organization in Jordan. Instruments similar to the SAT are currently being developed to be used as admission tests to the Jubilee School and local universities.

In Egypt, the first school for high achievers was established in 1955. Eleven years later, more programs designed and special classes were founded. These programs were established in recognition of the special educational needs of gifted and talented children. Egypt is a country with a long tradition of respect for education and high standards at all levels. Special classes are comprised of intellectually gifted children, although on the whole, the formation of special classes is not a policy used extensively in the Arabic countries, especially at primary school level. The argument used against special schools or special classes are that they promote elitism, prevent gifted children from learning to interact with their age peers, and prevent other children from benefiting from their presence.

In Saudi Arabia, research was conducted to describe the most effective approach for identifying gifted and talented children. In addition, the Ministry of Education has established a new foundation to support projects designed to meet the needs of gifted and talented children and serve the country's population of gifted and talented students. The Foundation will establish high schools for gifted youth, enrichment programs as well as other projects of merit.

Mentorship Programs

Mentor Connection is a new, three-week, residential summer program held at the Jubilee School for national and international young people entering the last two years of their high school experience. The program provides opportunities to participate in creative projects and investigations under the supervision of university mentors. Each year, accomplished university professors and graduate students work side-by-side with students on research projects, productions, and other works-in-progress in shared areas of interest. Students and mentors become a community of scholars of all ages working together on important problems that are on the cutting edge in the arts and sciences.

Mentor Connection students have the opportunity to participate in a variety of other experiences in addition to their preselected mentorship. Young people attend workshops designed to teach them about computer technology, and state-of-the-art electronic data retrieval systems. Program participants enter the real world of research; engage in hands-on, high-level learning; and emerge from the program with new visions of who they might become. This program allows students to achieve to their highest potential by participating in experiential research projects that provide direct, apprentice-based involvement with faculty members who are conducting research in their respective disciplines.

Computerized Provision for Gifted Children

Pelgrum & Plomp (1991) argued that many countries throughout the world are facing serious questions about the role of computers in education: what is the place and role of computers in the schools? How can the computer be used effectively in existing subjects? What will be the effect of computers on students' learning, on teachers' behaviour, on the school and classroom organization? Hawkridge et al. (1990) reported that in developed countries, computers were used for four main purposes:

(1) To become aware of the uses and limitations of computers.
(2) To learn computer programming.
(3) To learn the correct uses of application programs, which are sometimes called productivity tools because they have the potential to increase productivity.
(4) To learn selected topics from school subjects (p. 15).

Children in developed countries easily master use of keyboards, and understand texts and pictures on a computer screen more readily than students in developing countries. Blease & Cohen (1990) pointed out that "a familiarity with the potential of the new technology leads us to newer, quicker, and more efficient ways of doing things and, in some cases, to a realization that we are now able to accomplish what previously was totally beyond our grasp. In the classroom context this is particularly true of such things as simulation, word processing, desktop publishing and data bases" (p. 1). Many reasons have been presented for introducing computers in education. Hawkridge et al. (1990) summarize these reasons in terms of six rationales. First, a social rationale: to equip all students for a future in which technological awareness and basic computer skills will be necessary. This implies that

individuals should follow courses on computer awareness. Second, a vocational rationale: to build a resource-base of people skilled in information technology. Computer education should be related to future jobs, and individuals should be prepared to function adequately as professional workers in a technological society. Third, a pedagogical rationale: to use new technology to enrich the existing curriculum and improve instructional processes and learning outcomes. Fourth, a catalytic rationale: to promote changes in education by moving towards a more relevant curriculum and by bringing educational opportunities to a larger number of people. Fifth, an information technology rationale: to stimulate the national computer industry by governmental expenditure on large numbers of nationally produced or nationally assembled computers in the schools. Finally a cost effectiveness rationale which argues that computers can reduce the overall cost of education. In the context of Jordan and other Arabic countries, one might distinguish another rationale, namely, the opportunistic rationale: the expectation that the use of computers in private schools may contribute to attracting more students to those schools. However, if there is no explicit policy, computers are used in an uncoordinated fashion. Teachers are not trained, software is scarce, and hardware is incompatible, and spares, repairs, and maintenance hardly exist (Hawkridge et al., 1990).

A mixed picture emerges from a survey conducted in this region (Subhi, 1997). While computers are quite widely used in schools, they are thinly distributed and few teachers have training in their use. There are problems with availability of software and the most frequent educational use of computers is for drill and practice rather than for developing cognitive ability through problem solving and open-ended computer programs. This implies that the most worthwhile use of computers in schools lies with more innovative software. When we start to consider cognitive development to be of more central interest, and place children in the most appropriate educational settings, then we can see impressive achievements through the use of innovative software (e.g. open-ended simulation, Logo, problem solving, spread sheets, data bases, productivity software, etc.). If the Arabic countries are to achieve the potential of the computer which led Papert (1980) to anticipate an educational revolution, then they need to optimize the use of computers in the Arabic schools and to overcome the obstacles mentioned previously. In other words, real innovation can only take place when good quality software products are available in both Arabic and English languages, and teachers are well acquainted with these products by being trained in using them and integrating them into their instructional approaches.

If computerized problem solving is to be the focus of the mathematics curriculum, then it must also be given a place in teacher training programs. In other words, we must make effective and efficient use of what we know about how gifted children become problem solvers to design training programs for teachers. In addition, this implies requiring a course in computerized problem solving for all mathematics teachers. Teachers working with computer programming should be aware of the ideas gifted and talented children are forming and assist them in improving their performance and developing their mathematical skills. Yet, there are still many debates on how and how much the computerized programming environment can enhance schooling outcomes, and how this computer environment can provide special provision for gifted and talented children. There are no recent Arabic or cross-cultural large scale studies on the impact of computerized programming environment on children's achievement and creativity (Subhi, 1999).

Some obstacles exist to greater and better computer utilization. Computers must be purchased, software must be selected, facilities must be prepared, and then a curriculum has to be written for the inclusion of computers. Once these steps have been taken, staff development must proceed and, finally, teachers must change the way they teach. We must not expect effective use of computers to be developed in a year or even two. But with careful long-range planning, a computer-enhanced learning environment can be established in order to improve the teaching/ learning process.

The need to keep accurate records of the abilities that children display has been clearly demonstrated. In the absence of these records, teachers' memory of specific abilities seems to fade, so judgments based on memory alone are likely to be based on overall and unreliable impressions. In addition, the effective record keeping we have recommended (Subhi, 1997) should be computerized and used continuously to permit teachers to monitor each student's progress. The computer software we have developed and designed (Subhi, 1997) could play a major role in proposed computerized record keeping. Despite the problems and obstacles, clearly there are benefits to increasing the effective and efficient use of computers in teaching mathematics and other subjects.

The Arab Council

In 1996, Prof. Joan Freeman, Dr. Taisir Subhi, Dr. Abdul Aziz Kamal, and other Arabic scholars founded the Arab Council for the Gifted and Talented, in Amman, Jordan. The ACGT now represents 13 Arabic countries, including: Bahrain, Egypt, Jordan, Kuwait, Lebanon, Libya, Morocco, Qatar, Saudi Arabia, Syria, Tunisia, United Arab Emirates and the West Bank.

The ACGT aims at providing a network for the exchange of ideas and research findings and results related to teacher training of gifted and talented students among individuals and institutions in the Arabic countries; promoting public awareness of the exceptional abilities of gifted and talented children; conducting research and providing database and technical facilities to meet the special needs of gifted and talented children.

Recommendations

In sum, Arabic countries seem to be developing too few special curricular materials for classes and programs and special provision for gifted and talented children. The classroom teacher is expected to design or adapt existing materials despite the fact that gifted education for teachers is not widely available, compared to other areas of special education.

Third World problems in educating gifted and talented children arise from unique political and economic issues. The issues frequently concern the perceived needs of the country, the availability of jobs in the present market, and demographic surveys which reflect the present rather than the future status of the nation's economy, including health problems and population figures. These issues rarely center on the children themselves, on their needs, or on their potential to contribute to a global as well as domestic society (Harris, 1986; Subhi, 1997). In the Arabic countries, the picture of gifted education is far from rosy particularly in the case of a small developing countries like Jordan and Lebanon, which are currently undergoing political, economic, and social upheaval that leaves little time for matters such as providing special provision for gifted and talented children.

In Arabic countries we should not be content to wait for improvement and development to occur spontaneously in teaching gifted and talented children. If we really want to improve our education systems and to meet the special needs of gifted and talented children in our society, it will be necessary for us to take some very direct and deliberate actions. Earlier studies on giftedness did not make use of computers or related forms of educational technology. One of the key considerations in the early stages of our chapter was to determine whether, and how, educational technology could be used to benefit gifted children. More recently, the range of possibilities for using computers and multimedia in education has increased significantly.

One of our beliefs in choosing to carry out research with the gifted was that innovations developed and tested with gifted children might benefit mainstream education. We have anecdotal evidence that this may be the case. It would be good to have the opportunity to test this belief more rigorously, through inclusion of children from mainstream schooling in comparative experiments (using Logo and CAL).

It is important for gifted and talented programs implemented in any developing country to gain notice and recognition, not only within their own borders, but in interchange with others. We suggest establishment of a network that provides a forum of exchange, provides information, support, encouragement, examples and ideas, to strengthen opportunities for both the gifted and their countries. In addition, the network could branch off into research areas, provide an arena for follow up studies, stimulate planning efforts, provide a way of sharing concerns, serve to illustrate what giftedness means to emerging nations, and promote international awareness.

The Israeli Experience in Gifted Education

Israel's well-developed educational system was established at the beginning of the century, before the British mandate, and continued with the establishment of the Jewish State in 1948. The school system, like that in the Arabic region, is based on the structure of 6:3:3. Education in the kindergarten through 9th grade (5–15 years) is compulsory, and studies from ages 5 to 18 are free of charge. In areas that absorb many new immigrants, free education starts even earlier at the age of 3. Education is 10% of the annual national budget.

The provision for the gifted by the state began in 1973. It grew out of the 1971 Knesset (Parliament) educational policy and budget, presented by the Minister of Education and Culture. He stated that each child had the right to develop his abilities and that it was the task of the Ministry to provide proper frameworks and content, which would enable such development (Burg, 1988).

Starting from its creation in 1973, the Department for the Gifted began to establish special classes and afternoon workshops. Most of the larger cities and smaller towns have such enrichment programs. At the time, the Department rejected special schools for sociopolitical reasons and opted instead for expanding the after-school enrichment centers. By 1981, more than 5,000 students—an estimated 30–40% of the potentially gifted population—was being served by the centers which were funded on a shared cost basis by parents' tuition, the Ministry of Education, and the local sponsoring agency. These centers focus on mathematics and science including computer-based and laboratory experiences, plus offerings in art, music, literature, history, philosophy, creative writing, and journalism.

The Israeli Ministry of Education carries several delivery systems for its gifted and talented children:

(1) Dual University enrollment—gifted high school youngsters start their higher education while still in high school.
(2) Pullout classes in the big cities where every child identified as gifted is served once a week.
(3) Enrichment programs for gifted school pupils in the universities, mainly in science and mathematics.

In 1996 the Ministry of Education, Culture and Sport decided to adopt a new policy of identification and treatment of gifted children by broadening the definition of giftedness, identifying the gifted and nurturing

them (Rachmel, 1997). According to the new policy, the schools will be responsible for initial identification of their gifted children, and teachers themselves will propose special programs to teach these pupils at the schools. Gifted education in Israel is now in a transition state; identification and treatment are still conducted mainly by the old methods, while the new approach is in the process of being implemented. At the beginning of the academic year 2000/2001 the following changes will be implemented: (a) the identification process will be versified; (b) the high school students in the special classes for gifted education will have an option to get a weekly one-day university education in special centers; (c) special multi-regional centers for weekly enrichment day will be intensified.

Neglected Resources—The Professionals

Since youth programs in universities and research institutes are relatively rare, these resources are the 'neglected resources' in the education of the gifted and talented.

Science and art museums are most active in extracurricular and informal education. Almost every museum has an education department. These departments offer instruction to two populations: first; to the general public, so that scientific research and the arts become familiar to youngsters who, in the future, may become the decision and policy makers, and second; to gifted and talented children in their areas of interest. Thus, youth develop contacts with professionals and are exposed to resources not otherwise readily available. While art museums do have the appropriate professionals to cater to gifted children in the art domain, the high level personnel suitable for working with gifted children in science are found in the universities and research institutions.

Extracurricular and Informal Science Education in Israel

Israel offers its young gifted and talented science enthusiasts (4th–12th graders) a nationwide network of science activities based in the universities and research institutions to enhance what is offered by the schools. These activities include science clubs, summer camps, mathematics and science Olympiads, programs in science museums, etc. Most activities are in the life sciences, medicine, exact sciences, computers, mathematics and technology. About 16% of the students who participate take humanities and social science courses. Most programs are offered to students, who enroll on an individual basis, during the afternoons and holidays.

The programs in the universities are offered to two categories of youngsters: (a) Children who were identified as gifted and (b) science-motivated children. One of the most important aspects of the programs for science-motivated children is the 'self selection' approach. The students choose to come to the academic center, and thus have a very high commitment to participate. These children give up their after-school time, or sometimes their holidays, because they want to join the extracurricular framework. Their parents must pay, at least partially, for the activities and in many cases they have to transport them to the center. The Ministry of Education subsidizes the activities by 20%.

The courses for 7th–12th graders are not necessarily offered to children labeled as 'gifted', but to those who are challenged by high level courses; thus, the children are not labeled, but the courses are. The topics are either an enrichment to school curriculum or completely new. Participation in such a course enables the highly intelligent youngster to meet with other children with similar interests; this interaction is of great importance to the children. Some highly intelligent children have few friends in their own neighborhood, while others are not motivated to learn, since they acquire knowledge very easily. When they meet other children like themselves they are able to feel validated and better understand their abilities.

Science Projects

School students in Israel are encouraged to work on a special independent project, as a substitute for taking a final examination in one of their school subjects. Science projects for credit in physics, chemistry, biology, mathematics, and computers are done at the universities or research institutes. The student works with a mentor in his laboratory on a science project. The work done in this framework is usually related to a real research project being conducted by the scientist. Upon completion, the students summarize and report on their work to the school. Learning from a scientist engaged in high-level research offers an unparalleled opportunity for a youngster to gain real and valuable insights into science.

Annual Science Clubs

All Israeli universities and research institutions offer afternoon science clubs in the afternoons to students ages 10–18. Some even start at age 7. The programs vary from one institute to another, with the differences related to the nature of the institute. A university can offer subjects in the life sciences, medicine, exact sciences, social sciences, and humanities, while a technical institute focuses on topics such as aerodynamics and computer engineering. A research institute offers courses mainly in its own special fields such as agricultural research, marine biology, environment and so on. Usually learning is stimulated by discussions, films, presentations made by students, and, last but not least, the planning and execution of experiments and reporting of the results.

Summer Science Programs

Summer courses in universities and museums are similar to those run in science clubs throughout the academic year; the students participate daily, for two weeks, in courses offered by the university. These enables children who do not live in big cities or close to the facility to participate in courses offered by the universities and museums.

Five universities and research institutes in Israel provide on-campus residential programs; these programs enable the participants to get involved in real research laboratories and experience mentorship; they are encouraged to present their extracurricular projects, listen to lectures given by top professors of the hosting institute and engage in social activities. Mentorship programs are offered to 16–17 year old school students; participants in these programs are involved in actual research projects and work in small groups with mentors who are scientists.

Special Residential Summer Programs at the Weizmann Institute

INTERNATIONAL SUMMER SCIENCE INSTITUTE

This program provides some 75 outstanding 12th grade science students from Europe, Asia, the Americas, and Israel with an opportunity to work alongside top Weizmann Institute researchers, as well as to learn something about life in Israel today. Many students selected for this program are chosen when they excel in national science fairs or competitions; their teachers refer others. Upon completing an extensive application form, selected candidates are invited to an interview-after which a committee composed of scientists and professional staff from the Weizmann Institute office interviews the students in their home countries.

The intensive 30 days program is conducted in English and the participants are matched with mentors in groups of 2 or 3, and work in the research labs on current research topics such as: structural differences in normal and tumor cells, applications of lasers and the use of computers in modeling and simulations. Students work with sophisticated scientific instruments including the electron microscope, lasers and computers. The mentors are drawn from among the Institute's researchers and graduate students. Laboratory work is supplemented with lectures given by senior Institute scientists; each participant can choose a subject in accordance with his or her interests. At the conclusion of three weeks of laboratory work, the students are required to present a seminar and submit a report, and the reports are eventually published as scientific articles in the program's book. The group then shifts to an altogether different scientific focal point—a field school in the desert located in the southern part of the country. By observing the life systems, geology, and climatology in the field, students are able to formulate questions that can be explored in the laboratory.

SCIENCE, MUSIC AND ART PROGRAM

This special two-week program, run in cooperation with the Society for Excellence through Education, is aimed at sixty 14-year-old students who show potential to excel either in science, music, or art; the purpose of this program is to broaden the scope of youngsters by establishing connections among the disciplines (Maoz, 1990). The Israel Art and Science Academy (which is discussed below) was established several years later, after this experience proved to be successful.

The science, music, and art students go through a selection process that focuses on their ability in their field of interest; the science candidates receive a questionnaire with some problems in science and maths designed to examine their scientific thinking abilities; those who succeed are interviewed at the Weizmann Institute. The most meaningful criteria for the music and art candidates is their creative abilities (composing, improvising, drawing, and sculpting) based on the merits of their portfolio or audition.

In the mornings the participants study in groups based on their interests; in the afternoons they participate in interdisciplinary workshops, working with youngsters drawn from the three domains; evenings are devoted to either lectures by top scientists raising special issues in science, or meeting with professional actors and musicians. The students also have the opportunity for social and sport activities during the lunch break. At the end of the camp, the students organize a farewell party, during which they have a chance to showcase their talents and knowledge gained from the course, including original music performances by the music students, an exhibition of sculptures made by the art students, and demonstration of science concepts. Bringing together three seemingly disparate groups of science, music, and art enthusiasts provides a unique opportunity to enrich and advance students in their own field of interest, and open new horizons in other fields of interest.

NATIONAL SUMMER SCIENCE WORKSHOP

This program provides some 30–40 outstanding 11th grade Israeli students with the opportunity to work alongside researchers in a research institute. Senior staff members interview the candidates for this program and decide who will be accepted; they stay at the Weizmann Institute for 13 days, working mainly in small groups of two or three with a mentor in the research laboratories. The evenings are devoted to students presentations, lectures by top scientists, and some social activities. At the end of the program, participants are requested to write a scientific article for the program book.

IMPORTANCE OF RESIDENTIAL PROGRAM

Residential programs have special qualities for gifted children: they enable children to meet peers and make friends with other children whom they are not able to meet in any other way. Many gifted children do not socialize easily since they do not find peers who understand them. In some cases they feel like the 'ugly duckling' in their regular environment, while in the camps they find that they are 'swans' in a group composed of similar individuals. On the other hand, many gifted children do not bother to work at school; they acquire knowledge very easily or are not sufficiently challenged. At the residential programs they find out that there are many more students like them and they must make serious efforts if they want to succeed in their fields of interest.

The international program has these qualities as well, but also provides an international flavor and opportunity to meet people like themselves from different cultures. The participants might be the leaders in scientific fields in their own countries in the future. Getting to know potential leaders from other countries may advance understanding among nations, with consequential benefits.

The essence of these programs and the key to their success is 'mentorship'; the student meets his or her mentor in an everyday situation and learns about the mentor's career and way of life through personal example. Historically, mentor-student relationships are the oldest method of educating the gifted and talented (Milgram & Goldring, 1991); research has shown that this approach is very promising (Cox, Daniel & Boston, 1985). This approach is only limited by the difficulty in matching a student with a suitable mentor, as mentors are not easily available. The qualities possessed by the mentor are also crucial: a mentor must be able to anticipate the child's needs in addition to being a high-level professional in his or her field. Similarly, the student should have more qualities than simply being gifted—he or she should be very devoted and persistent; a creative, critical thinker and willing to sacrifice short term satisfactions for the sake of long term accomplishment (Tannenbaum, 1983; Passow, 1991).

MATHEMATICS PROJECTS

Tel-Aviv and Bar-Ilan Universities and the Technics accept mathematically gifted high school students into university courses based on passing a special examination; they get university credit for the courses and can even complete university mathematics while still in high school.

Special enrichment program for gifted children in mathematics, Math–by–Mail, is offered by the Weizmann Institute, to gifted children, 3rd–10th grades, all around the country. Mathematicians and mathematics educators prepare the educational materials. The problems, which emphasize the development of mathematical thinking, are written for each of four grade levels: Level 1 (3rd–4th grades), Level 2 (5th–6th grades), Level 3 (7th–8th grades), and Level 4 (9th–10th grades).

At the beginning of the school year, youth magazines and newspapers advertise the commencement of the year's Maths-by-Mail program with a thought-provoking, though easily solvable problem. Students interested in learning to solve such problems are asked to send in their name, address, and grade level. Those students receive worksheets addressing subject matter and new approaches that differ from that studied at school. For example, problems may deal with graph theory, number theory, statistics, topology, or set theory. Solutions are corrected, graded, and returned to the students with a printed solution and another worksheet. Five such rounds occur during the year. At the end of the year the best students are invited to the Weizmann Institute to participate in a hands-on mathematics experience. They are given a worksheet containing mathematical problems that are clues to a treasure hunt and compete in groups to solve the puzzle.

Experience indicates that all over the country, teachers use these work sheets for enhanced lessons for gifted children and many times an entire family will work together to solve the problems. Some highly gifted students are identified in the Maths-by-Mail program and are subsequently invited to participate in the National Mathematics Olympiad for high school students while still in junior high school. Every few years the material is collected and published; this material is a useful tool for teachers who have gifted children in their regular classes, or those who teach gifted children either in special schools or enrichment programs. It is also interesting to note that the program 'Science-by-Mail' run by the Science Museum of Boston originated from the 'Maths-by-Mail' program in Israel.

COMPETITIONS AND OLYMPIADS

Mathematics

The Weizmann Institute of Science runs two nation-wide olympiads, one for high school and one for junior high school students. There are no prerequisites for participation in the national Mathematics Olympiad for high school students. Those who apply receive a sample questionnaire used in previous olympiads, which gives them the basis to decide for themselves if they are on an appropriate level to participate. The Mathematics Olympiad for junior high school students is run in two stages: the first questionnaire is distributed to 7th–9th graders at their schools. The questionnaires are checked at the Weizmann Institute and the best students are invited for the second stage held at the Institute; other universities in Israel, such as Tel Aviv University and the Technion hold maths

competitions as well. The best students from all these competitions participate in the International Math Olympiad.

Physics

The Weizmann Institute also operates a physics tournament, which is a team competition for high school students. The task for the teams, each with five high-school students per group, is to design a lock for a safe using principals of physics. Each team is scored according to three categories: (i) the skill and creativity utilized in the building of the lock mechanism; (ii) the level of comprehension of the other teams' designs; and (iii) the level of success achieved in unlocking the respective teams' safes. In addition, the Technion runs physics Olympiad and Tel Aviv University sponsors a Space Competition. The Ministry of Education supports all of the above projects.

Israel Art and Science Academy

In 1990 the Society for Excellence through Education established the Israel Art and Science Academy which is a special boarding high school which combines formal and informal education and where the students have the opportunity to meet and work with professionals in art, science, and music. It hosts gifted and able youngsters from all parts of the Israeli society who study science, music, and plastic arts.

The Society for Excellence through Education was founded in 1987 in order to nurture excellence, creativity, and educational leadership among Israeli youngsters gifted in music, art and science. The Society developed and implements a three-year Discovery Program for Junior High School pupils throughout the country. (The name of the program was recently changed to 'Excellence 2000'.) The aim of this program is to nurture excellence among these students, concentrating mainly on developing analytic mathematical thinking, inquiry skills, tools for scientific thinking, broadening of their horizons, and strengthening their self-confidence. The programs are four hours a week for three years. The arts program consists of two hours of sketching and drawing and two hours of photography. The music program deals with composing, improvising, and music appreciation; and the science program works on scientific and mathematical thinking. The children accepted for the programs have to be very good musicians or demonstrate their achievements in drawing. These programs are based on the experience gained in the Science, Music, and Art Summer Program. The Society through Excellence also operates national and international seminars and summer camps for able children in science, music and art, some with the Weizmann Institute of Science as mentioned above.

THE ADMISSIONS PROCESS

The first screen looks for youngsters who are highly motivated to excel; the second stage involves an interview and participating in a workshop, carried out under boarding conditions. The accepted students have high learning ability and special interest in either science, visual art, or music and they are highly motivated to put a lot of effort in their studies.

THE EDUCATIONAL PROGRAM

The educational program is unconventional and reflects the conviction that science education must abandon the attitude of narrow specialization. The School believes that an integrative and interdisciplinary approach is essential to deepening students' understanding in the areas that they will choose as their main occupation. For example, science students get expertise in one scientific field, but within this framework they also study the history, philosophy, and sociology of this field and the interrelations of this field with other scientific fields. The students also dedicate 3 hours a week during their time at the school to work in the community.

Summary

At the end of the millenium Israel has a developed gifted education system within the formal education system. Gifted children are still identified centrally by special identification methods developed many years ago. However, new thinking about identification and provision are broadening conceptions of giftedness. Identification of children with higher potential will be carried out by school teachers who will also guide the programs at the primary schools. At the beginning of Junior High School, the gifted children will be provided with special programs at the universities and research institutions.

Special resources such as universities, research institutions, museums, and other professional organizations are still neglected resources in educating gifted and talented children. These bodies have the knowledge, the personnel, and the equipment that can cater to highly intelligent students and give them insight into exciting and challenging areas and methods of study. These settings can also provide gifted individuals with mentors. Globally, there appears to be only sporadic efforts to use these resources. Israel provides a good example of a national network of extracurricular science education in all its universities and some research centers, but still more can be done in science, music, and the arts.

Science, natural history, and art museums are now active in the field of education, while music institutions are less so. A promising sector is science-based industry with research and development departments. These industries can also adopt youngsters into their research and development departments and enable them to work with their professionals; implementing such programs in most universities and other institutions is neither complicated nor expensive. The most important factor—the personnel—is already in place, together with the necessary knowledge and equipment. However, commitment is needed to implement unique education programs, shaped by the mission of the individual institute.

Conclusion

There are increasing number of research papers in many Arabic countries in the Middle East, focusing on both the conception of giftedness and the conception of creativity and education of the gifted and talented. In addition, teacher training programmes, professional development courses and research projects are carried out at some Arabic universities concerning developmental, motivational, social, emotional, and cognitive aspects of gifted children and adolescents. Since 1980, the number of gifted and talented children in special provisions or programs has increased significantly, however teacher education is not keeping pace. In Israel, considerable emphasis has been placed on gifted and talented children, and extensive resources are allocated to their identification and the development of programs and special provisions to meet their special needs. If we are truly concerned about optimizing the region's educational systems and processes, then we must continue to develop special provisions to meet the needs of gifted children, nurturing the national resources that our gifted and talented students represent.

References

Al-Tal, A. (1979). *Education in Jordan (1921–1977)*. Pakistan: National Book.

Blease, D. & Cohen, L. (1990). *Coping with Computers: an Ethnographic Study in Primary Classroom*. London: Paul Chapman.

Burg, B. (1988). Programs for Gifted Children in Israel. *Gifted Education International*, **5** (2), 110–113.

Cox, J., Daniel, N. & Boston, B. O. (1985). *Educating able learners: programs and Promising practices*. Austin, TX: University of Texas Press.

Feldhusen, J. F. & Wyman, A. R. (1980). Super Saturday: design and implementation of Purdue's special program for gifted children. *Gifted Child Quarterly*, **24**, 15–21.

Fox, L. H. (1981). Identification and the Academically Gifted. *American Psychologist*, **36** (10), 1103–1111.

Freeman, J. (1990). The Intellectually Gifted Adolescent. In: M. J. A. Howe (Ed.), *Encouraging the Development of Exceptional Skills and Talents* (pp. 89–108). London: The British Psychological Society.

Hallahan, D. & Kauffman, J. (1981). *Exceptional Children: Introduction to Special Education*. Englewood Cliffs, NJ: Prentice-Hall.

Harris, C. R. (1986). Third World Networking: Problems, Issues and Practical Solutions. In: A. J. Cropley, et al.

(Eds.), *Giftedness: A Continuing Worldwide Challenge* (pp. 343–350). New York: Trillium Press.

Hawkridge, D., Jaworski, J. & McMahon, H. (1990). *Computers In Third-World Schools: Examples, Experience, And Issues.* London: Macmillan.

Huxley, J. (1963). The Future of Man. In: G. Walstenholme (Ed.), *Man and His Future* (pp. 1–24). Boston: Brown.

Maoz, N. (1990). A special program for gifted children in science and music. In: S. Bailey et al. (Eds.), *The Challenge of Excellence: A Vision Splendid* (pp. 377–379). Wagga Wagga, Australia: The Australian Association for the Education of Gifted and Talented.

McCluskey, K. W. & Walker, K. D. (1991). *The Doubtful Gift: Strategies for Educating Gifted Children in the Regular Classroom.* Toronto: Ronald P. Frye.

Milgram, R. M. & Goldring, E. B. (1991). Special education options for gifted and talented learners. In: R. Milgram (Ed.), *Counseling Gifted and Talented Children: a Guide for Teachers, Counselors and Parents* (pp. 23–36). Norwood, NJ: Ablex.

Ministry of Planning (1990). *Five-Year Plan for Economic and Social Development (1986–1990)* [In Arabic]. Amman: National Press.

Papert, S. (1980). *Mindstorm: Children, Computers, and Powerful Ideas.* Sussex: The Harvester Press.

Passow, A. H. (1991). Nurturing the affective aspects of giftedness: a neglected component of talent development. In: F. Mönks & W. Peters (Eds.) , *Talent and the Future* (pp. 222–226). Assen/ Maastricht: Van Gorkum.

Pelgrum, W. J. & Plomp, T. (1991). *The Use of Computers in Education Worldwide: Results from the IEA Computers in Education Survey in 19 Education Systems.* Oxford: Pergamon Press.

Rachmel, S. (1997). *Gifted Education in Israel: a Search for New Directions.* Paper presented at the 12th World Conference of the World Council for Gifted and Talented Children in Seattle, Washington (USA).

Renzulli, J. S. (1977). *The Enrichment Triad Model: a Guide for Developing Defensible Programs for the Gifted and Talented.* Wethersfield, CT: Creative Learning Press.

Renzulli, J. S. (1980). Will the gifted child movement be alive and well in 1990? *Gifted Child Quarterly,* **24** (1), 3–9.

Sa'ab, H. (1980). *Studies on the Cultural Revolution Necessary for the Arab Progress in the Modern Age.* Beirut: Dar al-Elm Lilmalayeen.

Subhi, T. (1997). Who is gifted? A computerized identification procedure. *High Ability Studies,* **8** (2), 189–211.

Subhi, T. (1999). The impact of LOGO on gifted children's achievement and creativity. *Journal of Computer Assisted Learning,* **15** (1), 1–11.

Subhi, T. (1992). *Giftedness and Creativity: The Computerized Comprehensive Identification Procedure.* Amman, Jordan: Scientific Enlightenment Publishing House.

Szyliowics, J. (1973). *Education and Modernization in the Middle East: A Comparative Analytical Study of Education Development, and Modernization in three Countries in the Middle East: Turkey, Iran, and Egypt (including Some of other Arab Countries).* Ithaca: Cornell University Press.

Tannenbaum, A. J. (1983). *Gifted Children: Psychological and Educational Perspective.* New York: MacMillan.

Urban, K. K. (1993). Fostering Giftedness. *International Journal of Educational Research,* **19** (1), 31–49.

Psychological Research on and Education of Gifted and Talented Children in China

Jiannong Shi and Zixiu Zha

Institute of Psychology, Chinese Academy of Sciences, Beijing, China

Introduction

In ancient China, there was a folk custom called 'shi er' (child prediction). According to this custom, when a child was one year old, he or she would be tested by exposing stationery objects, such as writing brushes and paper, sewing items, such as threads and needles, foods and cosmetics before him/her. People thought that the first object the child tried to grasp could tell whether he or she would be avaricious or disinterested, intelligent or not (Yang, 1994). The official selection and education of gifted and talented children, called 'child prodigies', dates back to the 18th century. An examination system for selecting gifted children known as 'Tong Zi Ke' (the Child Examination) existed in the feudal dynasties since the Western Han Dynasty (206 BC.). But a relatively strict and formal law procedure for selecting gifted and talented children was established in the Tang Dynasty. The law of the Tang Dynasty prescribed that a child under 10 years old who was able to read and understand either 'shi jing' (the Book of Songs) or 'lun yu' (the Analects of Confucius) and say over ten articles would be instated as placeman, while one who was able to read and understand the Book of Songs or the Analects of Confucius and say over seven articles would be dubbed a certificate. The policy of the Child Examination lasted until the end of the Qing Dynasty.

However, it is only since 1978 that widespread, systematic and scientific research on and education of gifted children has been undertaken in the mainland of China. The year 1978 marked an abrupt turn in Chinese history. The country energetically encouraged modernization in the areas of agriculture, industry, defense and science and technology. Since then, large numbers of talented scientists, engineers and other experts have been urgently needed. In response to this need, a Cooperative Research Group of Supernormal Children of China (CRGSCC) was set up across the country under the leadership of Professor Zha et al. and a special class for intellectually gifted adolescents was set up in the University of Science and Technology of China (USTC) in 1978. These were two milestones in the history of research on and education of gifted and talented children in China since 1949 (Shi & Xu, 1999). Since then, a new research project on identifying, studying and educating gifted children has been undertaken (Zha, 1985, 1993).

The purposes of the research are: (1) to identify and distinguish extraordinary children who are gifted intellectually and to educate them in order to promote and accelerate the proper development of their potential; (2) to explore the factors which accelerate the development of intelligence in such children and to analyze the process of formation in order to improve the education of all children and thus raise the level of mental development of future generations; and (3) on the basis of the above results, to accumulate material for exploring theoretical problems concerning children's development, such as the relationship between intelligence and personality, the function of nature and nurture in the growth of children and so on.

Under the leadership and influence of the CRGSCC much has already been achieved, and hundreds of gifted children and adolescents have been identified, investigated and followed up; a series of comparative studies on mental abilities and personality traits between gifted and normal children have been carried out; a battery of cognitive ability tests and personality trait questionnaires have been compiled; and various kinds of gifted education programs have been established and developed rapidly.

In Hong Kong, the gifted education movement started relatively later. Even though a non-profit organization devoted to the provision of gifted education in Hong Kong named Gifted Education Council (GEC) was formed in 1988, the governmental policies of the provision for gifted education or a strange structure were not included in the Education Commission Report until 1990 (Wu & Cho, 1993; Tsui, 1995).

Since then, several enrichment programs for the gifted have been created and researchers from the Gifted Education Council, the Hong Kong Institute of Education, the University of Hong Kong, and the Hong Kong Polytechnic University have been involved in several psychological and educational projects that study gifted and talented children. In addition, the G. T School (School for gifted and talented children) was established in 1996 under the control of the Gifted Education Council.

Conception and Identification

Conception

The term 'supernormal children' was created and employed by psychologists in mainland China since 1978 when the CRGSCC was set up. There are two reasons for Chinese psychologists to create the term of supernormal children: (1) 'gifted' in Chinese 'tian cai' means the God's bestowal upon man; and Chinese psychologists do not think that high ability is totally inborn. (2) 'Supernormal' means some children are relatively superior to most normal children. Hence, 'supernormal' is a term with statistical meaning (Liu, 1983). In general, the performances of an unselected age group follow the rule of normal distribution and can be mathematically expressed as

$$f(x) = \frac{1}{\sigma\sqrt{2\pi}} e^{-\frac{(x-\mu)^2}{2\sigma^2}}$$

where, x represents the real performance of an individual; μ represents the expected performance or mean performance of the whole; and σ represents the standard deviation. If $x \geq \mu + 2\sigma$, then the individual can be treated as a supernormal child (Shi & Xu, 1998).

In Hong Kong the definition of giftedness in Marland's (1971) report to the United States Congress was employed. According to Marland's definition of giftedness, an individual with the following features will be identified as the gifted. These features are: (1) high IQ or high level of conventional intelligence; (2) special academic aptitude; (3) creative thinking; (4) superior talents in the visual and performance arts; (5) high leadership ability; (6) psychomotor ability (Zha, 1993, p. 8; Tsui, 1995, p. 35). But an increasing number of psychologists and educators are influenced by Gardner's theory of multiple intelligences. Then, the definition of giftedness must be defined in a broader sense.

Identification

How can gifted and talented children be identified? What are the criteria and methods to be used? These problems are closely related to the concept of giftedness. In our opinion, gifted children are not only highly developed in intelligence or ability but also possess greater creative potential and other positive personality traits. All of these factors interact with each other to form the mental structure of the gifted. On the basis of this view of giftedness, the principles and procedures for identifying the gifted were explored and formed progressively (Zha, 1983, 1986a, 1990b; Shi & Xu, 1997).

Principles for Identifying the Gifted

In light of foreign experience (Roedell et al., 1980; Khatena, 1982; Tannenbaum, 1983; Freeman, 1985) and on the basis of our own practice and exploration in identifying the gifted, the following principles for identifying gifted children have been formulated (Zha, 1986, 1993):

(1) Identification in a dynamic comparative investigation. Since the intelligence of gifted children is developing rather than fixed, and because that development is influenced by cultural, environmental and educational factors, identification of the gifted ought to be carried out in a dynamic comparison with normal children of the same age under similar societal conditions.

(2) Identification with multi-criteria and multi-methods. Since the manifestations of giftedness are different, multiple criteria and different methods should be employed.

(3) Investigation of personality traits as well as intelligence. Excellent achievement depends not only on superior intelligence but also on certain personality traits. Moreover, the intelligence potential itself is influenced by the personality traits, as a result, both intelligence and non-intelligence factors are equally important for the identification of gifted children.

(4) Quantitative and qualitative responses recorded and analyzed. In viewing the development of intelligence as a dialectic unity of quantitative and qualitative changes, children should be identified on the basis of the results, speed of their responses, and the processes, forms and strategies of the responses.

(5) Identification with special education. Identification as a means to serve the education of gifted children and education can not only raise the level of giftedness but also serves to continue the identification in a practical setting. Giftedness is shaped by the environment and education to which the children have been exposed. Therefore it is necessary to continue monitoring the gifted during the educational process as a continuation of the identification process.

Criteria and Methods for Identifying the Gifted

On the basis of the above-mentioned principles, the following criteria and methods for identifying the gifted showed in Table 1 were adopted (Zha, 1993).

The Identification Procedure

In general, both individual identification and collective identification or mass screening have been used to select the gifted and talented children in the past twenty years. The individual identification was mostly used in the initial stage of the research of CRGSCC though it is still used now. There are four steps for identifying a gifted individual: (1) A child is nominated by his/her parents or teachers or reported in newspapers, or on television and broadcast; (2) the child is sent to institutions and introduced to the professional researchers; (3) the child is tested with the standardized intelligence test or cognitive ability test and the parents of the child are asked to obtain the information about some personality traits of the child; (4) the child is continually observed and identified dynamically. The individual identification seems efficient but not sufficient as it is too time-consuming.

For the collective identification or mass screening mainly the following steps are followed (Zhou & Zha, 1986; Zha, 1993; Shi & Xu, 1998):

Step 1, Application. Individuals who want to be enrolled in a special class for gifted children, are asked to fill in the application forms and to present information about their developmental history, facts of gifted expression, family education, family background etc.. In the case of young children, their parents or recommenders are asked to fill in the application forms.

Step 2, Primary screening test. The general or conventional intelligence of the children is measured with intelligence tests such as Stanford-Binet Intelligence Test (revised) and the Wechsler Preschool and Primary Scale of Intelligence (revised). In addition, the knowledge and ability of children concerning the major subjects are measured by experts.

Step 3, Retest. The children who pass the primary tests will be tested with 'Test for Identifying the Cognitive Ability of Supernormal Children (TICASC)' developed by the CRGSCC. The child who can meet one of the following three criteria will be expected to enter the special class for the gifted. The three criteria are: (a) a score which is two or more standard deviations above the mean score of the same aged children; (b) a score which is above the mean score of the children two years older; and (c) a score which is over the 95th percentile of the same aged children. For the children with special talents, their school works such as composition, painting, machine models, etc., should be appraised by experts.

Step 4, Further confirmation. To gather more information about the personality traits and physical conditions of the children who are expected to enter the special class, the children need to take some physical tests, and their parents or former teachers need to be interviewed or complete some questionnaires.

Step 5, Identifying through practice. In order to determine whether a child who is identified as gifted should stay in the regular classroom or should participate in a special program, the child will be placed in a special class for several weeks. Here, further identification through practice (student's learning process) is emphasized. The major practical activity of children is learning, i.e. being educated. Hence, to educate them in equal conditions and environment and investigate their potential and actual performance levels is a continuation of the identification procedure.

In the mainland of China, the instruments and methods that could be used in the identification of the gifted are far from satisfactory. Our research implied that as there are different kinds of gifted children, they also differ from normal children in different ways. Therefore, various criteria should be determined for the design of effective tests and appropriate methods for identifying different kinds of gifted children. This problem involves not only the need for better instruments but also requires a better comprehension of the concept of giftedness. Consequently, the solution of the improved instrument problem should be based on theoretical research.

Table 1. Criteria and Methods of the Study and Identification.

	Dynamic comparative research	
	Criteria	Methods
Cognition	thinking observation memory	cognitive experiment intellectual test
Creativity	creative thinking creative imagination ability to solve problems creatively	creative thinking test analysis of the process of creative activities etc.
Learning ability	speed style of mastery depth of knowledge firmness	test concerning learning ability and achievement, observation and analysis of learning process
Special talent	math foreign language leadership drawing, calligraphy music	test concerning special talent, assessment and observation of product (or home work)
Personality traits	interest, motivation intellectual curiosity confidence persistence independence	questionnaire observation, educational experiment, interview

In Hong Kong, a battery of tests in addition to self/peer nominations was used in identifying and selecting gifted students for the limited gifted programs in the initial stage (Wu & Cho, 1993). Recently, with the impact of the Gardner's multiple intelligences theory, different aspects of children's intelligence were considered. A set of multiple intelligences tests was developed by the Gifted Education Council and used to identify gifted children (Li & Chan, 1996).

Psychological Research

Development of cognition

The Memory and Metamemory of Gifted Children
According to common findings of the previous studies, the ability of excellent memorization is one of the obvious characteristics of intellectually gifted children (Huang, 1990; Zha, 1993). However, finding the phenomena is one thing, knowing its cause is another one. In order to detect why gifted children have, in general, stronger memory ability than normal children, the abilities of memory monitoring and memory organization of gifted children were tested and the relationship between memory performance and metamemory of gifted and normal children was analyzed (Shi, 1990a, 1990b). The results show that (1) gifted children were superior to normal children not only in the amount of recall, but also in the speed of remembering and in some aspects of metamemory, such as memory monitoring and memory organization; (2) there were close relationships between the memory performance and the organization of memory, especially between the speed of remembering and memory organization; (3) the relationship between memory performance and memory monitoring was complicated, but the speed of remembering, as one important aspect of memory performance, significantly correlated with memory monitoring; (4) there was a close correlation between the two components of metamemory, memory monitoring and the organization of memory. The results of these studies indicated that it was better to use both, the amount of recall and the speed of remembering, as an index of memory performance.

Thinking and Reasoning Ability of Gifted Children

In the last twenty years, Chinese researchers have found that the ability of analogy or analogical reasoning is one of the main aspects where there are significant differences between gifted and normal children. A set of analogical reasoning tests, including geometrical or figural analogy, numerical analogy, and verbal or semantic analogy was developed (Zha, 1984). With this set of analogical reasoning tests, the researchers can not only record the scores of the performance, but also analyze the level of analogical reasoning of the children. Zha and her colleagues found that gifted children were not only able to get higher scores than

normal children, but have a higher level of analogical reasoning as well (Zha, 1984, 1990; Wang, 1990).

The Development Oof Creativity in Gifted Children

Because many psychologists have suggested that creativity is one of the most important manifestations of giftedness, the creative thinking of gifted children is the main aspect that Chinese researchers and educators have focused on. A creativity test was developed and included, as a sub-test, in the Cognitive Ability Test for Identifying Supernormal Children (CATISC) (Zha, 1986c). Several comparative studies have been conducted on creative thinking between intellectually gifted and normal children in the last twenty years. Furthermore, psychologists from the Institute of Psychology, Chinese Academy of Sciences, joined the collaborative cross-cultural study on technical creativity of gifted and normal children between China and Germany. This study was supported by the Volkswagen Foundation (Hany, 1994; Shi et al., 1995, 1998; Hany & Heller, 1996; Heller & Hany, 1997). The results show that: (1) the mixture of longitudinal and cross-sectional design is very practical and efficient for the study on technical creativity of children from two countries with different cultural backgrounds; (2) two countries as two variables of culture have impact on the development of technical creativity in children; (3) intelligence is one of the factors which plays the most important role in the development of children's creativity; (4) children's performance on technical creative thinking tests increase as they grow up.

Recently, the development of creative thinking in children has received much attention from psychologists and educators due to the need for rapid economic growth and to the educational reform in China. The relationships between creativity and intelligence and personality traits are currently under investigation. In addition, a theoretical model about creativity, called System Model of Creativity, has been proposed (Shi, 1995; Shi & Xu, 1997a, 1997b, 1997c, 1999). It is suggested that, in this model, the intelligence current rather than one's intelligent level itself plays an important role in creativity (Shi & Xu, 1999). The intelligence current is controlled by one's attitude about a task, personality traits, and environmental factors, etc.

Development of Personality Traits

As Chinese psychologists and educators recognized the importance of personality traits in the development of gifted children at the very beginning of the research on giftedness, research on the developmental changes of personality traits of gifted and normal children is among of the most important issues on which the CRGSCC has been working. Some personality questionnaires have been compiled by the CRGSCC. The questionnaire for adolescents named Chinese Adolescents Non-intellectual Personality Inventory (CA-NPI) was widely used in the mainland of China after it was compiled. The researchers of the CRGSCC used CA-NPI to investigate the ambition, independence, emulousness, perseverance, curiosity, and self-awareness (Yuan & Hong, 1990; Hong, 1998). In 1994, some researchers of the CRGSCC started a collaborative cross-cultural study on self-concept of gifted and non-gifted children with researchers from the University of Nijmegen, Netherlands (Peters et al., 1995; Chen et al., 1997; Kong & Ye, 1998). It was found that the gifted children were superior to the normal children not only in many aspects of cognitive abilities, such as memory, reasoning, spatial ability, and so on, but in some personality traits, such as ambition, independence, and curiosity etc.

Education

In China, attention has long been given to talented children in the arts, for example, music, painting and dance. Special schools or classes have been established to nurture these talents. However, special education for intellectually gifted children did not received much attention prior to 1978. The establishment of special classes for gifted adolescents or youth at the University of Science and Technology of China (USTC) in 1978 marked the beginning of experimental educational procedures for gifted children in the mainland of China (Xin & Chen, 1986; Zhu, 1987).

Kinds of Gifted Education

During the past twenty years, four kinds of special education programs have been in existence for gifted children and adolescents, which are summarized in Table 2.

Characteristics of the Gifted Experimental Class

The gifted experimental class differs from normal classes in the following ways (Tao, 1987; Di, 1990; Zha, 1990a; Zha, 1993):

(1) The establishment of the gifted experimental class is based on the children's intelligence or special talent, while the normal class is based on age and cultural knowledge.
(2) The period of schooling has been shortened for the gifted experimental class. In both, primary and high schools, the period is four or five years for the gifted, while in normal schools the period is six years.
(3) In addition to the moral, intellectual, and physical development provided in the normal classes, gifted children are encouraged to develop analytic skills, to solve problems creatively, and to develop good personality traits.
(4) There are alternative courses to meet the special interests and needs of gifted children in the experimental classes that are intended to further develop their potential and abilities.
(5) Teaching materials are modified according to the cognitive levels and traits of the gifted children to promote the development of their creative ability and reasoning skills.
(6) The instructional strategy attempts to make full use of and promote students' ability to study independently. Heuristics, discussion and research methods are adopted instead of cramming.
(7) Attention is focused on the development of students' self-concept and self-evaluation. In

Table 2. Kinds of Gifted Education..

Kind	Description
Enrolled earlier or skip	The gifted children who have passed certain examination are allowed to enter primary/high school or university earlier than the normal, or jump into higher class.
Special class	Gifted experimental classes have been held in more than 50 primary/high schools overall the country; besides, several universities have set up special classes for gifted adolescents.
Special schools	All students of this kind of school are enroled as gifted children. The educational programs of the school are only for the gifted, for example, the Hong Kong G. T. School.
Special activity within/ without the campus	Special courses for computer and the Olympic school of mathematics (physics/chemistry) have been held in certain districts overall the country; children's palace has been set up to organize various science/arts courses; activities concerning scientific research, invention, and arts have been undertaken in school.
Vacational or weekend programs	Many leisure time schools have been setup to devote special courses, such as visual and performing arts, mathematics and sciences, social activities, and so on for the special need of talented children.
Instructed individually	The gifted, who are studying in the normal class, are instructed individually by the teachers/ parents to learn in advance or undertake research work in leisure time.

addition, the students are supported in setting up high ideals and developing abilities of self-regulation, self-education and self-actualization.

(8) A proper balance is maintained in the relationship between collective education and personality development. Students arrange part of their study time at school on their own, in order to develop their own interests and abilities.

(9) The assessment of the results of the educational program depends not only on academic performance (e.g. test results, proportion of students entering a higher grade in school, etc.) but also on appropriate criteria and methods that assess the all-around development of the gifted.

Effects of the Educational Programs

Remarkable progress in gifted education has been achieved in China since 1978. The main results are as follows:

Gifted children and adolescents completed their studies in a shorter period and with excellent results.

Gifted children, who studied in primary or middle school, graduated earlier than the same aged normal children with excellent results through either gifted classes or by skipping grades in normal schools. For example, in Beijing No. 8 Middle School, students of the first gifted class finished the fifth and sixth grade curricula of primary school along with all the of high school curricula within four years, which is four years less than the normal period. They passed the unified university entrance examination with a total score of 35.9 points higher than the normal class of that school. Subsequently, 27 students (average age 14) out of 29 have been enrolled by key universities (Gong, 1990).

The gifted adolescents, averaging less than 15 years of age, have been enrolled in either gifted youth classes or normal undergraduate classes at universities since 1978. Results here have also been excellent. For example, by 1998 the USTC had held twenty one gifted youth classes, with a total registration of more than 800 students. More than 500 students graduated from USTC between 1983 and 1998, and 73.7% had been enrolled in domestic/overseas graduate schools. Among them, more than two hundred students obtained Ph. D.degrees (Ye & Kong, 1998).

Overall, gifted education has been beneficial in developing the potential of gifted children and adolescents. Gifted children and adolescents, who show extraordinary progress in learning, make further gains in intelligence through gifted education. For example, research was done on the students of the first class of the Beijing No. 8 Middle School shortly before graduation using seven tests, including creative thinking and analogical reasoning. The results were compared with both, same aged normal students and older students of the same grade. The comparison showed that the gifted scored notably higher than the same aged normal children on each test and scored higher on five tests than the same grade normal children, who were three to five years older.

A battery of creative thinking tests have been used to examine a sample of gifted students of the third year gifted youth class of USTC and the normal students of the same age (the sample was taken from a population of freshmen and middle school students). The results showed that the mean scores of the students from the gifted youth class are markedly higher than the mean scores of the normal students (Kang, 1985).

Gifted children and adolescents were in good health, physical examinations were carried out for the gifted children and adolescents. In general, the average values of height, weight and chest measurement of the gifted reached or exceeded those of the same-aged normal children in China. For example, the USTC investigated the students from the gifted youth class by physique criteria issued by the State Education Commission. Results showed that most of the students of the gifted youth class exceeded the criteria. This suggests that to enter school earlier or to shorten the period of schooling is not related in a negative way with the health of the gifted (Xin, 1986).

The meaning of the above results can be summarized as follows:

(1) The gifted children possess tremendous potential and the potential could be thoroughly developed through gifted education in accordance with their levels and characteristics.

(2) The gifted education experiments of primary and high school have been established and coordinated with gifted youth classes of universities. Although the gifted education system is still in an embryonic form, it fills in gaps in the regular education system of China.

(3) The gifted experimental classes and youth classes in China provide an experimental base for systematic research on the mental development of gifted children.

Issues

Fruitful results have been obtained in the field of research on and education of supernormal children in China during the last twenty years. However, several essential issues or problems still exist. In summary, the issues or problems are: (a) a severe shortage of financial support and research staff for the study of gifted children; (b) a lack of instruments to study gifted and talented children; (c) a lack of programs for training the teachers of the gifted programs; and (d) a lack of well-designed studies on the development of visual and performing arts and athletics in talented children, especially from the perspectives of psychology and education.

In the future, research efforts in China should be focused on the following topics: (a) implicit learning and creativity; (b) brain function and giftedness; (c) leisure time activities of eminent individuals; (d) personality traits and situational problem solving, etc.

Acknowledgements

The authors would like to express their thanks to Natural Science Foundation of China (Grant No. 3870237 and No. 39700045) and Chinese Academy of Sciences, as well as to Miss Kimblerly from University of Michigan and Prof. Leticia Hernández, University of Munich, who spent much time to correct the English of our manuscript.

References

Chen, G., Peters, W. & Mönks, F. (1997). Comparative study on self-concept of gifted and non-gifted children between China and the Netherlands. *Psychological Sciences*, **20** (1), 19.

Di, G. (1990). Preliminary investigation for the collective education of supernormal children. In: CRGSCC: *The Selected Works on Supernormal Children of the Last Ten Years in China* (pp. 161–170). Beijing: Unity Publishing House.

Freeman, J. (1985). *The psychology of gifted children.* Chichester: Wiley.

Gong, Z. (1990). The educational experiment of the super-normal children in the Beijing No. 8 high school. In: CRGSCC, *The Selected Works on Supernormal Children of the Last Ten Years in China* (pp. 171–178). Beijing: Unity Publishing House.

He, S. (1990). Gifted youth class for ten years. In: CRGSCC, *The Selected Works on Supernormal Children of the Last Ten Years in China* (pp. 179–186). Beijing: Unity Publishing House.

Hany, E. A. (1994). The development of basic cognitive components of technical creativity: a longitudinal comparison of children and youth with high and average intelligence. In: R. F. Subotnik & K. D. Arnold (Eds.), *Beyond Terman: Contemporary Longitudinal Studies of Giftedness and Talent* (pp. 115–154). Norwood, NJ: Ablex.

Hany, E. A. & Heller, K. A. (1996). The development of problem solving capacities in the domain of technics: results from a cross-cultural longitudinal study. *Gifted and Talented International*, **11**, 56–64.

Heller, K. A. & Hany, E. A. (1997). German-Chinese study on technical creativity: cross-cultural perspectives. In: J. Chan, R. Li & J. Spinks (Eds.), *Maximizing Potential: Lengthening and Strengthening our Stride*. Proceedings of the 11th World Conference on Gifted and Talented Children (pp. 237–241). Hong Kong: Social Sciences Research Center, The University of Hong Kong.

Hong, D. (1998). Issues of the application and revision of CA-NPI. In: Z. Zha & J. Shi (Eds.), *The Mystery of the Development of Supernormal Children* (pp. 169–179). Beijing: Chong Qing Publishing House.

Huang, L. (1990). Developing the sub-test of memory for the Cognitive Ability Test of Identifying Supernormal Children (2nd ed.). In: CRGSCC: The selected works on super-normal children of the last ten years in China (pp 84–95). Beijing: Unity Publishing House.

Kang, Z., Zhu, Y. & Liu, Y. (1985). A five-year follow-up study of the third early adolescent class in USTC. *Educational Research*, **11**, 50–57.

Khatena, J. (1982). *Educational psychology of the gifted.* New York: Wiley.

Kong, Y. & Ye, G. (1998). Summary of comparison research on the self-concept of supernormal and normal children from China and the Netherlands. In: Z. Zha & J. Shi (Eds.), *The Mystery of the Development of Supernormal Children* (pp. 111–117). Beijing: Chong Qing Publishing House.

Li, R. & Chan, J. (1996). *Manual of MI (Multiple Intelligences) test.* Hong Kong: Gifted Education Council.

Li, R. & Sze, R.(1997). Teaching the young gifted in an enrichment programme. In: J. Chan, R. Li & J. Spinks (Eds.), *Maximizing Potential: Lengthening and Strengthening our Stride*. Proceedings of the 11th World Conference on Gifted and Talented Children (pp. 290–294). Hong Kong: Social Sciences Research Centre, The University of Hong Kong.

Marland, S. P., Jr. (1971). Education of the gifted and talented - volume 1: Report to the Congress of the United States by the U.S. Commissioner of Education.

Peters, W., Ma, H., Mönks, F. & Ye, G. (1995). Self-concept of Chinese and Dutch gifted and non-gifted children. In: M. Katzko & F. J. Mönks (Eds.), *Nurturing Talent* (pp. 84–95). Assen/Maastricht: Van Gorkum.

Roedell, W. C., Jackson, N. E. & Robinson, H. B. (1980). *Gifted young children.* New York: Teachers College, Columbia University.

Shi, J. (1990a). Memory and organization of memory of gifted and normal children. *Acta Psychologica Sinica*, **22** (2), 127–134.

Shi, J. (1990b). A comparative study of memory and memory monitoring between gifted and normal children. *Acta Psychologica Sinica*, **22** (3), 323–329.

Shi, J. (1995). A system model of creativity. *Journal of Developments in Psychology*, **3** (3), 1–5.

Shi, J. et al. (1998). Cross-cultural study of technical creativity of supernormal and normal children from China and Germany: basic hypothesis and research method. In: Z. Zha & J. Shi (Eds.), *The Mystery of the Development of Supernormal Children* (pp. 25–40). Beijing: Chong Qing Publishing House.

Shi, J. & Xu, F. (1997a). Interest, motivation and creative thinking of supernormal and normal children. *Acta Psychologica Sinica*, **29** (3), 271–277.

Shi, J. & Xu, F. (1997b). On the present situation and trends of studies on gifted children. *Chinese Journal of Special Education*, **1**, 1–4.

Shi, J. & Xu, F. (1997c). The relationship between creativity and intelligence of supernormal children. *Psychological Sciences*, **5**, 468–469.

Shi, J. & Xu, F. (1998). Progress and problems of studies on supernormal children in China in the last 20 years. *Acta Psychologica Sinica*, **30** (3), 298–305.

Shi, J. & Xu, F. (1999). *Recognizing the gifted children.* Beijing: Esperanto Publishing House of China.

Tannenbaum, A. J. (1983). *Gifted children.* New York: Macmillan.

Tao, W. & Gong, B. (1987). Several problems in the education for the supernormal children. In: CRGSCC: *How to Nurture the Supernormal Children* (pp. 170–178). Xi'an: Xi'an Jiaotong University Publishing House.

Tsui, H. F. (1995). Gifted education and the education system of Hong Kong. *Journal of the Gifted and Talented Education Council of the Alberta Teachers Association*, **9** (2), 33–42.

Wang, X. (1990). A comparative study on analogical ability—figural and verbal analogy. In: CRGSCC, *The Selected Works on Supernormal Children of the Last Ten Years in China* (pp. 230–234). Beijing: Unity Publishing House.

Wu, W. T. & Cho, S. (1993). Programs and practices for identifying and nurturing giftedness and talent in Asia (outside the Mainland of China). In: K. A. Heller, F. J. Mönks & A. H. Passow (Eds.), *International Handbook of Research and Development of Giftedness and Talent* (pp. 797–808). Oxford: Pergamon Press.

Wu, Y. (1987). Collective educational experiment of supernormal children. In: CRGSCC, *How to Nurture the Supernormal Children* (pp. 179–184). Xi'an: Xi'an Jiaotong University Publishing House.

Xin, H. & Chen, X. (1986). *An introduction to the education of college gifted youth class.* Hefei: USTC Publishing House.

Yang, X. (1994). *The history of Chinese psychological thoughts.* Beijing: Jiangxi Education Publishing House.

Ye, G. & Kong, Y. (1998). Twenty years gifted education for the special class of gifted adolescents in USTC. In: Z. Zha & J. Shi (Eds.), *The Mystery of the Development of Supernormal Children* (pp. 227–240). Beijing: Chong Qing Publishing House.

Yuan, J. & Hong, D. (1990). A report from the investigation on intellectual gifted adolescents with CA-NPI. In: CRGSCC, *The Selected Works on Supernormal Children of the Last Ten Years in China* (pp. 116–124). Beijing: Unity Publishing House.

Zha, Z. (1983). A three-year longitudinal study of supernormal children. In: CRGSCC, *Monograph of Study on Supernormal Children* (pp. 1–22). Xining: Qinghai Publishing House.

Zha, Z. (1984). A comparison of analogical reasoning between supernormal and normal children of 3 to 6 years old. *Acta Psychologica Sinica,* **4**, 373–382.

Zha, Z. (1985). The psychological development of supernormal children. In: J. Freeman (Ed.), *The Psychology of Gifted Children* (pp. 325–332). Chichester: Wiley.

Zha, Z. (1986). *Manual of Cognitive Ability Test for Identifying the Supernormal Children.* Beijing: Institute of Psychology, Chinese Academy of Sciences.

Zha, Z. (1986a). A five-year study of the mental development of supernormal children. *Acta Psychologica Sinica,* **2**, 123–132.

Zha, Z. (1986b). A study of the mental development of supernormal children in China. In: A. J. Cropley, K. K. Urban, H. Wagner & W. Wieczerkowski (Eds.), *Giftedness: A Continuing Worldwide Challenge* (pp. 31–33). New York: Trillium Press.

Zha, Z. (1987). Gifted children's mental development and education. In: CRGSCC, *How to Nurture the Supernormal Children* (pp. 1–16). Xi'an: Xi'an Jiaotong University Publishing House.

Zha, Z. (1990a). A ten-year study of the mental development of supernormal children. *Acta Psychologica Sinica,* **2**, 114–116.

Zha, Z. (1990b). The concept of gifted children and the methods for distinguishing them. *Educational Research,* **8**, 23–29.

Zha, Z. (1993). Programs and practices for identifying and nurturing giftedness and talent in the People's Republic of China. In: K. A. Heller, F. J. Mönks & A. H. Passow (Eds.), *International Handbook of Research and Development of Giftedness and Talent* (pp. 809–814). Oxford: Pergamon Press.

Zhou, L. & Zha, Z. (1986). Research on selection of supernormal children for a special class at age 10. *Acta Psychologica Sinica,* **4**, 388–394.

Zhu, Y. (1987). A new educational model: gifted youth class of USTC. In CRGSCC, *How to Nurture the Supernormal Children* (pp. 138–152). Xi'an: Xi'an Jiaotong University Publishing House.

Programs and Practices for Identifying and Nurturing Giftedness and Talent in Asia (outside the Mainland of China)

Wu-Tien Wu,[1] Seokhee Cho[2] and Utami Munandar[3]

[1]Department of Special Education, Taiwan Normal University, Taiwan, ROC
[2]Korean Educational Development Institute, Seoul, Korea
[3]Faculty of Psychology, University of Indonesia, Jakarta, Indonesia

Introduction

In terms of human history, the development of *Gifted and Talented Education* (GATE) has been experiencing the following changes in the Asian region: from emphasizing equality to searching for equity and excellence, from educating the elite to developing talent for all, from incidental and fragmental enrichment to systematic and holistic education (Wu, 1998). The current hot topics are: multiple intelligences, cultural diversity, the gifted handicapped, ecological planning, differential programs, and the role of gifted education in educational reform. At the very cross point of the old and new centuries, much attention has been paid to the transition of gifted education. However, each country in Asia differs in the actual practice of providing special education programs for gifted and talented students. A few countries started implementing GATE programs in the 1960s and are now practicing it on a large scale at the national level. Most countries became aware of the need to provide the gifted and talented with special education programs on an experimental basis and/or at a private level only in the 1980s. In the 1990s, a variety of programs were designed according to the worldwide movement of educational reform in many Asian countries.

In this chapter, the current status of GATE in some Asian region countries, namely, India, Indonesia, Japan, Korea, Philippines, Singapore, Taiwan, and Thailand, will be reviewed with respects to policies, identification, programs, and issues for educating the gifted and talented.

India

India's philosophy and policy of education are reflected by the statement of the Ministry of Education that education can be the most effective means for equalizing opportunities and reducing disparities between human beings. In a democratic society, it is considered a fundamental right of citizens. In the ultimate analysis, therefore, the aim must be to enlarge the coverage and improve the quality of education so that a person belonging to any region, caste, creed, sex or economic strata, would have the chance of developing his or her potentials to the full (Maitra, 1997). In India, equity, quality and relevance are the three most important facets in planning the development of the educational system (Maitra, 1997). Since its independence India has made considerable progress in quantity and quality of all types of educational institutions and programs. Education is the second highest sector of budgeted expenditure after defense (a little more than 5% of the country's GNP), gradually becoming balanced in favor of rural areas, which get almost 40%. Three major expert bodies at the national level play crucial roles in educational planning: the National Council of Educational Research and Training, the National Institute of Educational Planning and Administration, and the University Grant Commission. These bodies are responsible for major policy decisions about academic excellence, financing scholarships, higher education abroad, exchange programs, national curriculum, organization of special schools, and selection criteria for teachers, scholars, and eminent persons. Concerning gifted education and development, India believes in the development of giftedness rather than calling a few individuals gifted. The overall educational objectives include all types of GATE. There are no rigid criteria of giftedness; rather, one finds frequent use of the concept 'talent' in official documents. The focus is more on universalization of primary education with an aim of full literacy in India (Maitra, 1997).

Identification

It is estimated that if we restrict the number of gifted and talented children in India to 3%, there will be about 25 million of them. It may vary from 5 to 10% of the population, if we include not only general intellectual and academic abilities but also leadership qualities, talents in visual and performing arts as well as in the emotional domain. To nurture talent particularly among the disadvantaged in society, the government of India, in pursuance of National Policy of Education (1986), launched the *Navodaya Vidyalaya Scheme* (N.V.). Under these schemes, 378 N.V. (residential institutions) have been established throughout the country, with the objective to make quality education accessible to talented children. At least 75% of the seats in a district are for candidates from rural areas. There are provisions for reservations for girls, as well as for disadvantaged students. The screening instruments consist of mental ability tests (60%), arithmetic (20%) and language (20%). The mental ability tests are non-verbal and culture-fair. To identify brilliant students the *National Council of Educational Research and Training* (NCERT) awards 750 scholarships each year including 70 scholarships for socio-economically disadvantaged secondary school students. The selection procedure consists of a two-tier selection through state and national level examination. Also run by the government are the Navyug schools providing quality education to highly able students from low to middle socio-economic strata. Selections are conducted by NCERT for junior section and by SCERT for senior sections. There is however no provision for nursery or pre-school children (Maitra, 1997).

Educational institutions like Jnana Prabodhini (which means 'Awakener of knowledge') started in 1962 with coaching in academics for those gifted in abstract reasoning, using Guilford's SOI model as a stepping stone; now also identify those gifted in creativity and interpersonal behavior for formal educational programs; whereas the non-formal programs identify those who are 'responsible, responsive and cooperative'. These non-formal programs are open to all, especially the under-privileged (Bapat, 1998).

Programs

In India the private sector plays an important role in providing programs for gifted and talented students. The high interest in providing programs for the gifted and talented can be seen from many papers presented by various educational institutions in India at the 5th Asia-Pacific Conference on Giftedness, September 1998.

The Jnana Prabodhine Prashala in Pune is one of the schools for gifted students. It has a program to discover whether a gifted student when motivated and properly guided, can achieve excellence by learning various skills (Bhalerao, 1998). The syllabus is flexible and imparted by the teacher during the regular school hours. This program is implemented in the fifth standard. Gifted secondary school students from Jnana Prabodhini, Yuvati Vibhag, are involved in a program consisting of group tasks to develop attitudes for cooperative working (Patange, 1998). For teachers of the gifted Jnana Prabodhini provides teacher education programs (Mehta, 1998).

Enrichment programs for the gifted are provided by the Mensa (inception 1975 in Pune), an international non-profit organization where the only criterion for membership is a high IQ score. Its aims are: identification and nurturance of intelligence, providing a stimulating and enriched environment for high IQ people, and conducting research in psychology and other social sciences (Damle, 1998).

Problems and Perspectives

As stated by Bapat (1998), ideally all schools should cater programs for the gifted, and various establishments in the community should act as places of exposure and learning, yet it is recognized that this is not yet accepted practice in India and programs for the gifted are few in number. The existing programs are mostly for secondary school students. Some mainstream schools have an important role in catering the needs of the gifted, but most are still in its experimental phase (Bhagwat, 1998). Therefore, to cater to the education of the gifted and talented more teacher educational programs are needed. To date there is no clearly formulated policy for education of the gifted in India. Rather, India believes in "quality education for all," with special attention for the underprivileged and socio-economically disadvantaged people. The perspective of education for the gifted in India has to be seen in this light. However, several institutions and organizations, primarily from the private sector, have established various activities and programs for the benefit of the gifted and talented.

The following intriguing questions posed by Bhagwat (1998) may reflect perspectives of gifted education in India: "It is high time that our system (in India) should think on certain basic questions like 'do the gifted children need a gifted curriculum'?, 'is it possible to have special schools with special curriculum'?, 'does the economy of the nation have the provision for it'?, 'what can be the compromise for developing the programs for gifted children'?, 'can mainstream school provide the enrichment opportunities for the gifted ones'?

Indonesia

In Indonesia's Broad Outline of the State's Policy 1998 (GBHN, 1998) with reference to Education (page 175, paragraph b) it is articulated that "students with extraordinary high intelligence are entitled to special attention and services in order to optimize the development of their achievements and talents/gifts . . ."

This is in line with the 1989 Second Law on the National Education System which states explicitly that "citizens with extraordinary abilities and intelligence are entitled to special attention" (Chapter III, paragraph 8/2). More specifically "each student at levels of education has the right to get educational treatment (opportunities) in accordance with his/her giftedness/ talents, interests and abilities, and to complete an educational program earlier than the regular time," meaning that according to educational policy both enrichment and acceleration are possible.

Identification

With a population of more than 200 million in 1998 and composed of a large number of ethnic groups distributed over about 3000 islands, it is a real challenge for Indonesia to identify its gifted and talented children and youth (Marat, 1992). There is a shortage of experts and testing instruments for the identification of gifted children at a national level (Munandar, 1992, 1996).

When the Ministry of Education and Culture began providing grants to high achieving but economically disadvantaged students of elementary, junior, and senior high schools, the identification was primarily based on achievement tests and when possible on psychological tests (intelligence, aptitude). Since 1982, with the start of the project on education of the gifted by the Ministry of Education and Culture, identification involves intelligence, creativity, and standardized achievement tests, conducted by psychologists and teachers. Simple screening tests were constructed and used by school teachers, items of which include learning behavior (intelligence), creativity and achievement motivation (Munandar, 1996).

In 1990 tests were constructed to identify the underachieving gifted and in 1993 teacher-, peer-, and self-nomination scales (Munandar, 1996). The need for using creativity tests, in addition to intelligence and achievement tests, to identify the gifted has been increasingly recognized and implemented both by state as well as private institutions and practitioners.

Programs

In 1982 a pilot project on educational programs for gifted students was launched by the Ministry of Education and Culture with the establishment of project schools in urban (Jakarta) and rural (Cianjur) areas. This project consisted of enrichment modules for junior and senior high gifted students. A 7-Year Plan of educational provisions for the gifted was formulated with long-term goals for 1982–1989 and an Action Plan for 1982–1983. The project lasted only until 1986, but its main concepts are still used and implemented in the development of a Plus Curriculum since 1994 by the Center for Curriculum Development, Ministry of Education and Culture. This Plus Curriculum has been field-tested in several locations in Java and Sumatra, and is still in the process of development, evaluation, and improvement.

To increase the quality of education throughout the country another policy in the 1990s of the Ministry of Education and Culture has been to promote the establishment of 'High Schools of Excellence' (Sekolah Unggulan) for students with high ability and intelligence in each of the 27 provinces. To date there are 105 schools of this kind, one with an intake of students at a national level (scope), 25 at a provincial level, and 79 at a local level. Some are special schools, others have special classes. The status of these schools are state institutions (64), private (25), collaboration between state and private (14), and collaboration between private institutions, organizations, or foundations (2). One has been existing for more than 15 years, but most of them were established only recently. Therefore, the developmental stage of these High Schools of Excellence varies.

Other existing programs for optimizing high ability and achievement are (Marat, 1992; Munandar, 1998):

- Scholarships for overseas study in science and technology.
- Science contests: schools are urged to form Youth Science groups and contests for innovative-productive performance are held yearly.
- The *University Research for Graduate Education Project* (URGE), competitive grant and fellowship programs: the Graduate Team Research Grant, and the Young Academics Program (for recently achieved PhD and Doctorate).
- Programs for gifted and creative preschool children, established by private organizations/foundations (e.g. the Creativity Development Studio, etc.).

Problems and Perspectives

After nearly two decades of educational programming for the gifted, several inhibiting factors still exist, such as the shortage of expertise and assessment instruments, the lack of trained teachers for the gifted, the scarcity of professionals who are familiar with issues of giftedness, and the want for educational facilities and equipment for implementing enrichment and acceleration programs.

However, there are also contributing factors to mention, e.g. more and more studies are being conducted on giftedness and gifted education, and the participation in and collaboration with regional and international bodies/organizations on G/T (WCGTC, APF-WCGTC, ECHA, etc.) are increasing.

A recent national survey regarding policies in gifted education showed that experts, governmental and school administrators, teachers, and parents are in favor of education for the gifted, and that it should be granted the same priority as education for regular and handicapped students (Munandar, 1998). This indicates a positive public attitude toward GATE.

The monetary and economic crises in Indonesia since mid 1997 will have an impact on the education sector, in terms of the decrease of student enrolment rate, an increase of student dropout rate, and that presumably less funds will be available for educational provisions for the gifted and talented. However, with the backing of state's policy as mentioned above and the support of the society and the private sector, there is still a promising future for GATE in Indonesia.

Japan

After World War II, Japanese education was extensively reformed. Its school system was changed from a 'dual system' into a 'ladder system'. As a result, gifted education has become an almost taboo subject within Japanese society (Chiba, 1980; Hirano, 1992). However, the Japanese government has recently discovered that the Japanese school system fails at developing students' creativity. In an effort to find educational alternatives, Japan hosted an international workshop on 'Education of the gifted in science and technology' in collaboration with UNESCO (NIER, 1993). Afterwards, the Central Council for Education, an advisory body to the Japanese Ministry of Education, introduced proposals aimed at providing differentiated academic programs, which would reflect students' individual differences in abilities. Other exceptional steps would be taken to nurture the special abilities of the gifted.

Programs

After-School Activities

Special opportunities presently exist for public school students who wish to enrich their education through after-school clubs and classes. These extracurricular activities are open to all students and a high percentage choose to participate. While these activities are not offered especially for gifted and talented students, they provide students with a much broader scope of activities than those contained in the regular curriculum.

The Research Institute of Education for Brilliant Children, established as a private organization in 1965, has opened classrooms to intellectually gifted young children. As the scope of intelligence education within Japan has broadened since 1972, important achievements have been continuously made (Chiba, 1980).

High School

High schools are ranked according to their ability to prepare students for the university entrance examination. In contrast, a more egalitarian system is used for ranking elementary and junior high schools. High schools, especially in urban areas, are ranked according to four levels and based upon the number of students who enter the top universities (Stevenson et al., 1992).

Students are admitted to high school, at a given level and school, on the basis of the national entrance examination results. Competition for entrance into the top high schools is keen because they provide better preparation for passing the university examination. It is primarily through entrance examinations, first for high school and later for university, that individual differences in ability among students become acknowledged (Stevenson et al., 1992). However, despite these differences, schools do not provide students with gifted educational programs, in a strict sense, since all students are taught according to the same curriculum even though there are some efforts to cater students' individual differences in regular schools and regular classes.

Early Admission to College

Educational reform for the gifted began with the college level. In accordance with the report made by the *Central Council for Education* (CCE), the Japanese government revised the School Education Acts, as they apply to the college admissions (Japan Ministry of Education, 1997). Henceforth, an exceptional few who display giftedness in maths and physics will be allowed to enter college even before the age of 18. The reasons for restricting the academic areas of giftedness were: (1) it is easier to identify the scientifically and mathematically gifted even among youngsters; (2) giftedness in maths and physics has to be nurtured in a school setting; (3) it has been proven that acceleration is an appropriate approach for nurturing giftedness in physics and maths (Japan Central Council for Education, 1997).

The universities themselves will decide whether or not to accept the accelerated students. However, those colleges that do accept the accelerated students should have doctoral program. They should also provide academic and career guidance, and provide alternatives when these students want to change their academic fields.

In contrast, the CCE report suggested that students talented in dance, music, art and sports do not require special school programs, since their talents will be nurtured enough by extracurricular activities. It also suggested that students below age 17 not be allowed to accelerate, at least for the time being. Acceleration in elementary and junior high is strictly prohibited since grade skipping may provoke severe competition for college entrance.

Admission to College

In 1991, the CCE report discussed modifications to the university entrance requirements that might foster the development of students with special talents and interests. Screening of accelerated students should be based on various data. Some universities, like Cheeba University (1997, 1998), have accepted the proposals and employed such methods as recommendations from teachers, experiments, essay, interview, and performance to identify those who are talented in math and physics.

In an effort to provide various experiences for gifted high school students, a pilot project was launched, which allows them to participate in lectures and seminars hosted by universities or private institutes.

Problems and Perspectives

At last, Japanese officials have come to acknowledge the individual differences in academic achievement and special abilities among older students and have introduced a special policy for these students. However, considering Japanese contemporary philosophy and past educational practice, it may take some time before the Japanese school system provides enrichment programs for gifted students. According to Stevenson (1998) and Stevenson et al. (1992), enrichment programs for gifted youngsters are unlikely to flourish in a culture where elementary school teachers are reluctant to tell parents that their child is gifted or academically advanced and where direct forms of teaching in nursery schools and kindergarten are avoided. This attitude is rooted in a belief that ability is not inherent, but rather the result of practice and hard work, even at the youngest age. That is, "Work hard, then you can achieve better." Japanese people believe that the individual differences, even at the fetus stage, are influenced by the environment and one's efforts rather than by innate, stable, and fixed characteristics. Therefore, they believe that the government should not enhance individual differences by intentionally providing special programs for those who are already doing well. Gifted education will be the responsibility of motivated parents who will provide special programs for their children through private lessons.

Korea

Rapid development of GATE has occurred in Korea. GATE programs in Korea can be characterized by a variety of approaches: special high schools for the gifted and talented, after-school enrichment programs in elementary and junior high schools, acceleration, enrichment programs provided by gifted education centers affiliated with school boards and universities, and the newly established cyber gifted education system.

In Korea GATE started in 1983 with the establishment of the Science High School. Later, the government set up the *Research Center on the Education of the Gifted and Talented* at the *Korean Educational Development Institute* (RCEGT-KEDI) in preparation for formal introduction of GATE programs to regular schools from school year 2001 on.

Programs

Gifted Education in Special High Schools
As of 1999, in Korea there are 16 science high schools, 15 foreign language high schools, 15 sports high schools, 18 performing arts high schools, and a Korean National University of Arts providing differentiated curricular for the gifted. These schools are equipped with advanced educational facilities. Except for the foreign language high schools, the teacher-student ratio is about 1:8, which is much lower than the 1:31 of ordinary high schools.

Junior high school students within the top 1% on relevant subjects or those who won significant competitions are qualified to apply for admission to Special High Schools. The students' GPA, award records, and physical conditions are all taken into account in the admission process. The paper-pencil tests, which had been used for a long time (from 1983 to 1997), have been recently abandoned in this process.

Special High Schools use a unique and customized curriculum. The curriculum is based on a non-graded and individualized instructional system of acceleration and enrichment. It is characterized by more advanced content in a specific field (e.g. more than 45% of the total units are allocated to subjects related to science and math in Science High School), more class hours for activities and performances, and more elective courses and individual studies, as compared to the regular high school curriculum.

After-School Enrichment Programs in Regular School

The 6th revision of the National Curriculum (1995) requires schools to provide gifted and talented students in regular schools with enrichment programs. Enrichment programs have been developed and disseminated to regular schools and gifted education teachers have been trained inside and outside Korea, by the *Ministry of Education of the Republic of Korea* (MOE) in collaboration with the *Korean Educational Development Institute* (KEDI), and by the *United Nations Development Programme* (UNDP) in 1990–1994. About 9.1% of elementary schools, 17.7% of junior high schools and 8.3% of regular senior high schools provide enrichment programs during after-school hours in various subjects such as science, maths, music, dance, foreign languages, and arts (Cho & Kim, 1994; Cho & Oh, 1998).

Acceleration

In 1995, the government revised the education law allowing students to skip grades. This policy has been implemented since 1996, thus gifted students with outstanding academic achievement can enter elementary schools at an earlier age, skip selected grades, be promoted earlier to the next school level. All schools are entitled to identify these students through careful evaluation for acceleration upon parent's agreement. In fact, however, there were only few students who wanted to be accelerated for the reason that it might result in lower academic achievement in the long term. Currently early admission to elementary school is the only option being pursued by parents and pupils.

Gifted Education Centers Affiliated With School Boards And Universities

Sixty three school boards (32.47%) provide enrichment programs for gifted elementary and/or high school students for the time being (Cho & Oh, 1998). In addition, the Ministry of Science and Technology supports 9 universities which provide after-school enrichment programs for gifted junior high school students. It is expected that the number of universities which provide enrichment programs will be increased to 13 in the year 2000.

Cyber Gifted Education System

The cyber gifted education system was established in 1998 to provide enrichment programs on the web for those who live in remote locations. Currently, there are two systems: one for gifted students in elementary school (http://gifted.kedi.re.kr), which is operated by KEDI (Cho & Park, 1998); the other for gifted junior high school students, which is operated by the *Korea Advanced Institute of Science and Technology* (KAIST). These systems will add more courseware in coming years and schools which are not equipped with trained teachers may want to use the systems.

Private Institutions

There are also private institutions that provide enrichment programs for young gifted children. One of the most recognized is the Korea Academy of Gifted Education affiliated with the CBS Cultural Center. It provides enrichment programs to nurture creative problem solving abilities of children from age 3 to the junior high school level. In addition, Korean Minjok Leadership Academy, a private high school, was established in 1996, with the goal of training leadership skills of gifted youths. It provides academically and personally challenging programs.

Problems and Perspectives

There are two main obstacles in nurturing gifted children. One is the university entrance examination, which is mainly a one-shot affair. The other is the insufficient support given to schools with GATE programs, especially in the form of legislation.

In Korea, entering a top university is often viewed by parents and students as a chief criterion of academic achievement (Cho, 1991). Over preparation for this one-shot exam has a negative effect on students' creativity and talent development. In an effort to both boost the creativity of special high school graduates, especially those from science high schools and guarantee the autonomy of universities, the government has established a new university admission policy, focusing on a diversity of entrance requirements rather than the exam. This policy will be implemented in 2001. In the near future, teaching and learning at science high schools will focus more on the development of student's individual aptitudes and talents and less on entrance exam preparations.

Fortunately, the Korean Parliament has just passed the Gifted Education Law (1999) that defines the responsibilities of schools, school boards, and the central government in providing GATE programs from grade 2 to grade 12. When implemented in the near future, it will create a solid foundation for better teacher training and provision of GATE programs as an integrate part of regular school education.

Philippines

The Philippines started its gifted and talented programs earlier than other Asian countries. The earliest seed was planted in 1966 with the opening of the Teacher Training Program for the Gifted in the Department of Special Education, University of Philippines. An official commitment to GATE was written into the 1987 Constitution. Currently, there are 3 high schools devoted to students talented in either arts or science and there are some gifted programs offered by regular schools. Two private organizations, the *Talented and Gifted Philippines* (TAG Philippines) and the *Gifted Philippines, Inc.* (GPI), are committed to promoting and developing education for the gifted and talented.

Identification

The procedure for identifying gifted/talented students relies on a combination of assessments, including standardized tests, classroom grades, teacher recommendations, and interviews with parents and students. For science high schools and arts high schools, the screening criteria are stricter and more relevant to their specific field of talents (Roldan, 1992).

Programs

Since the formal provision of GATE still remains rare in the Philippines, the top challenge in meeting the special needs of gifted and talented children is making use of limited resources. The Manila Science High School and the Philippine Science High School were set up as early as 1963 and 1964 respectively. Both schools provide challenging programs and, each year, select the 'cream of the crop' of young scientific minds from around the country. Scholarships are offered to deserving but underprivileged students and, recently, these schools have branched out to different regions of the country (Roldan, 1992).

Another prestigious special school is the National High School for the Arts. This institution trains promising young artists in music, dance and the visual and performing arts, while at the same time providing them with a complete secondary academic education. Student selection is again very strict and covers all regions of the country (Roldan, 1992).

The private Reading Dynamics Center, founded by the reading specialist Dr. Aurora H. Roldan, has hosted an annual Children's Festival of Words since 1973. The Festival is actually a creative writing workshop for verbally gifted children. It is gradually evolving into a vehicle for identifying children who are not only intellectually and verbally gifted, but also talented in other areas. It also resulted in the birth of TAG Philippines in 1983. This organization provides a support group for gifted young children and their families. Today, TAG not only provides identification and assessment measures for a variety of areas in giftedness, but also offers advice to parents, as well as to the gifted themselves.

The GPI, on the other hand, strives to promote and develop the general welfare of gifted, talented, and creative children, youths and adults. The GPI sponsors teacher training, seminars, workshops, and research projects.

Problems and Perspectives

Being greatly influenced by America, the Philippines' GATE has been in a state of gestation for over three decades. Gifted education, however, has not made great advancements during the last three decades. Due to the unfortunate political situation and economic development, the government's investment in education has been too limited to support GATE in public schools. Consequently, civic groups and business entities are currently the chief advocates for GATE. Nonetheless, it is still written in the constitution that all opportunities should be taken to develop the potentials of children.

TAG Philippines has recently changed its philosophy and now focuses on developing the critical and creative thinking of all students, not just the gifted (TAG Philippines Newsletter, 1997). This change grows from the belief that fostering giftedness depends on making students aware of their hidden power and talents and teaching them how to use these aptitudes to assist humankind.

Singapore

Gifted education in Singapore basically takes one of two forms: the *Gifted Education Program* (GEP) or the Science Research Program that are governed by the Gifted Education Unit, Ministry of Education (Singapore Ministry of Education, 1999). GEP was first implemented in 1984 and its programs cater to the needs of the intellectually gifted. Its programs fall mainly into two categories: Self-contained classes and pull-out programs. GEP does not cover music or art areas, for which there are specific programs such as the Music Elective Programs and the Art Elective Programs. Schools that provide GEP have been increasing every year. It has currently expanded to 9 primary schools and 6 secondary schools, including the notable Raffles Institution and Chinese High School, both of the independent schools that had been given autonomy in staff development and salaries, finance, management

and curriculum, while continuing to enjoy substantial government support (Lim, 1999).

Identification

For self-contained GEP classes, all grade 3 pupils are invited to sit for a Screening Test in English Language and Mathematics. In the end, about 400 students (0.8%) are selected based on their test scores on language ability, numerical ability and general ability. These students are then placed in a GEP program starting with Grade 4. After completing a 3-year primary program, they are then promoted to a 4-year secondary program. Promotion is not automatic. Students are screened on the basis of their primary GEP performance, their attitude towards GEP work, and the results of *Primary School Leaving Examination* (PSLE). A second supplementary entry point into the GEP occurs at Secondary 1 (Grade 7). About 100 students are selected among those who have scored 3 or more A's in the PSLE and have taken the Language Ability, Numerical Ability and General Ability Tests. For pull-out GEP classes, about 25 Secondary students are selected from among 300 Chinese High School students on the basis of their general ability, numerical skills and logic skills (Singapore Ministry of Education, 1999).

Programs

The GPE in Singapore seeks to meet the intellectual needs of the gifted through the provision of an enriched curriculum within a stimulating and interactive environment. The 7th World Congress on Thinking held in Singapore in 1997 attracted the whole country's attention. Many scholars of great renown attended and over 3,000 educators from all around the world participated. This conference was considered very productive and strengthened the country's goal of a 'Thinking School and Learning Nation'. GATE thus became one of the top priorities in national development.

The GATE program in Singapore is essentially one of enrichment rather than acceleration, and of self-contained classes in regular schools, rather than gifted schools (Lim, 1997, 1999). Self-contained classes are kept small with about 25 students. Students have the opportunity to interact with other students through various extra programs. Teachers are specifically selected and trained. Whenever possible, the GE Branch recruits suitable teachers from among the mainstream teachers in the GEP schools. A major part of the GEP teachers' training takes place on the job through supervision and regular meetings with GE Branch officers on matters relating to GEP curriculum and teaching strategies (Singapore Ministry of Education, 1999).

The self-contained GEP classes are essentially enrichment programs, based upon the national curriculum, carried on during regular class hours. In the GEP, topics are dealt with in greater depth and breadth. Greater emphasis is placed on the development of creativity as well as projects. Students also have the opportunity to work with specialists in creative writing, the humanities and the sciences through mentoring programs. Besides developing the intellectual capacities of students, GEP is also concerned with developing students who are active and responsible citizens. This is accomplished through an enriched Civics & Moral Education curriculum, which emphasizes self-awareness, social awareness and community involvement (Singapore Ministry of Education, 1999).

The pull-out program provides a challenging and enriching curriculum in Mathematics, Science and Computer Studies. In addition, individualized projects, which involve an interdisciplinary approach and the participation of university and professional mentors, are also encouraged. Creative computing programs are also provided to develop students' abilities to simulate real-life situations and write programs.

GEP students sit for the PSLE and GCE 'O' Level examination just like any other student. However, for both of these national examinations, they are tested in an additional subject (e.g. Social Studies in the case of the PSLE and one additional elective subject for the 'O' Level Examination).

In addition, the MOE Gifted Education Unit collaborates with the National University of Singapore in organizing special programs such as the Science Research Program, the Creative Arts Program and the Humanities and Social Sciences Research Program. These programs are open to all first-year junior College (grade 11) students and not just former GEP students.

Problems and Perspectives

During the last 15 years, GATE in Singapore has made great advancements in terms of the number of students attending special programs and the diversity of the special programs offered. However, teachers should do more to extend and fully cover the syllabus for fully challenging the gifted and talented students. There is also a need to make non-program teachers more aware of the characteristics and needs of gifted and talented students.

Taiwan

The development of GATE in Taiwan can be divided into four stages: The dawning stage before 1973, the initial experimental stage (1973–1979), the extended experimental stage (1979–1984), and the promoting stage (after 1984) (Wang, 1992; Wu, 2000b).

The framework of GATE in Taiwan is best understood through an analysis of the operational system, which can be broken down into three levels: the implementation level, the supervisory level, and the resource level (Wang, 1992). The implementation level

includes identification and placement of the gifted/talented, curriculum, teaching materials and teaching methods, and the teaching staff. The supervisory systems involve policy and legislation, administrative organizations, and guidance and research. The resource level consists of parental involvement, community resources, and private organizations. The *Special Education Law* (SEL) passed in 1984 (revised in 1997), where GATE was incorporated into all levels of schooling along with education for the disabled, is a milestone and guidepost of GATE development in Taiwan. The SEL sets policy directions for the special education system, curriculum design, teacher development, and resources (Wu, 2000b).

Identification

The identification procedure of gifted/talented students in Taiwan is very strict and systematic, based on multi-assessment and step-by-step screening process (Wu & Cho, 1993; Wu, 2000b). In those classes set up for the intellectually gifted, candidates are first screened by the school itself through group intelligence tests, students' daily performances, and teachers' observations. Then a series of group and individual standardized tests are administered to the upper 10% screened as potential candidates. According to the new regulations, the students finally selected must meet the criteria of high IQ and high grade point average (scores higher than 1.5 standard deviations above the mean are usually required). To be enrolled in the programs for the mathematically/scientifically talented, one must either have a score higher than 1.5 standard deviations above the mean on achievement tests in math and/or science, a grade point average in the top 1% of their school peers at the same grade in maths or science, or demonstrate an outstanding performance in a national or international competition. For the linguistically talented program, the criteria and procedure of identification basically follow that of mathematics and science (Wu, 2000b).

For the special classes for the artistically and musically talented, students are assessed through their performance in fine arts, on musical instruments and through a series of artistic or musical aptitude tests. The eligibility criterion for students talented in dance and drama is mainly focused on performance. Those who won awards for distinguished performance in a national or international contest are also accepted (Wu, 2000b).

It should be noted that the minimum requirement of an IQ test score above the mean for the talented in music, fine arts, dancing, drama, and sports, which had been used for years, has been discarded in the revised SEL of 1997.

Once students have been tentatively identified as gifted or talented, a committee made up of teachers and administrators from the student's school submits a report to the local department of education. After further screening by the department, with the consultation of educational experts, qualified students are placed in appropriate special programs or classes.

Programs

GATE programs implemented in Taiwan are mainly for students with high general ability, students talented in specific academic domains, and students talented in fine arts, music, dancing, drama, and sports. The goals of these programs are: (a) to develop the potential of gifted/talented students, (b) to cultivate good living habits and healthy personality traits, and (c) to teach for high cognitive and/or skill attainment (Ministry of Education, R.O.C., 1979, 1982; Wu, 1992).

Over the past three decades, GATE in Taiwan has expanded through a series of pilot programs. The greatest expansion was during the period of 1981 to 1992 (about 20% increase rate per year), in the last five years, the increase rate has declined to only about 3% per year (Wu, 2000a, 2000b). The 1998 educational statistics (Ministry of Education, R. O. C., 1999) showed that 484 schools, including 188 elementary, 174 junior high, and 122 senior high schools, were conducting programs for gifted and/or talented students. The total number of classes reached 1,422, with 37,225 students. It is estimated that one percent of the total student population were being served in these programs (Wu, 2000a). In addition to special classes and pull-out programs, which emphasize enrichment, there are some acceleration programs for highly gifted students in Taiwan. According to the published measures, they can adopt such means as early entrance, grade-skipping, early graduation, telescoping grades, advanced placement, and exemption from entrance examination, to complete their academic years. According to the new SEL (1997), students who are deemed to be generally gifted and distinguish themselves in all areas of study are allowed to accelerate one year (or more in special cases) in elementary, junior or senior high school.

Additionally, the students identified as being talented in math, science, Chinese, or English, also have the opportunity to take part in special camp programs conducted by universities. Alternatively, they may be qualified to bypass the university entrance examination and be directly admitted to universities majoring in pure sciences, such as physics, chemistry, and maths, or Chinese/English departments.

Program design for gifted students is handled on several levels. Basically, the central government sets goals for the curricula, while the local schools develop specific programs and experimental classes in collaboration with colleges and universities. Recent topics have focused on various enrichment programs, evaluation methods, and follow-up studies on gifted students' development (Wu, 1992, 2000b). Flexible teaching methods, such as peer-tutoring, debate, discussion, brainstorming, experiment, independent study, drama,

contest, and game are employed to stimulate student's creativity and problem-solving ability.

In addition to enrichment of the cognitive domain, affective development is another important component of gifted education. A peer-assisted program entitled 'the caring peer-tutor system' is a good example. In this system, gifted students provide their poorly achieving peers with assistance in academic work. Consequently, gifted children develop not only a gifted mind but, more importantly, a tender and loving heart (Wu, 1992).

Problems and Perspectives

Because the opportunity to be selected in the GATE program is limited, the identification procedure is often viewed as competitive by parents and teachers. To be fair, standardized tests rather than observations and/or performance are emphasized. As a result, very few socially/culturally diverse students are admitted to the GATE program simply because of their limited access to mainstreamed culture, on which the tests are based.

Another identification problem concerns underachieving students with high IQs. Every gifted class has such students, and the teachers complain that it is difficult (if not impossible) to remove them from the class. Rimm (1997) feels that the underachievement of gifted students is a national epidemic (in the USA), and from the research data of Campbell & Wu (1998), it is likely that it is an international epidemic.

In recent years, more educators and administrators are advocating the resource room model as an alternative approach to special class. Among the arguments in favor of mainstreaming the gifted, the focus is on the affective/social domains. A continued expansion of resource rooms for the intellectually gifted children—but not for the talented—has occurred in recent years. Both models, the special class and the resource room (or pull-out program), have their advantages and disadvantages. The decision on the relative efficacy and desirability of each model is still an unsolved problem (Wu, 1992, 2000b).

Another unique condition in Taiwan is the attitude of parents toward gifted/talented education during the junior high years. Many parents are preoccupied with the idea that entering the best senior high school is the most important thing for their children. They feel anxious if the gifted/talented classes have too much curriculum content that is outside the scope of the 'standard curricula' or the high school entrance exam. This perception puts inordinate pressure on the schools, and influences the teaching of gifted/talented classes. Accordingly, many teachers think that teaching the gifted is more of a challenge and more stressful. They also caution against having unrealistic expectations for the gifted (Campbell & Wu, 1998).

In accordance with the nationwide educational reform movement, gifted/talented education in Taiwan is confronted with the following challenges: (a) to design a student-centered, school-based, and pro-fessional-oriented educational program; (b) to identify and nurture the talents of the disabled and the culturally and behaviorally diverse; (c) to bring creative thinking into school reform; (d) to cultivate student's practical competency and vitality through multiple and flexible school entrance systems; (e) to upgrade education quality by developing and sharing educational resources; (f) to create a lifelong learning society by strengthening career planning and follow-up services, and (g) to moderate a conducive ecological environ-ment for the full development of each student's potential (Wu, 1998).

Thailand

Only in the past two decades has research on the gifted and talented in Thailand been carried out in various areas of interest, focusing on teaching strategies, modeling, public attitude, and program efficiency. However, these may not be coordinated or related to the needs of GATE in Thailand (Photisuk, 1999). In the sense of practice, GATE in Thailand is just beginning. A national policy has yet to be established regarding GATE. There have been limited opportunities for gifted/talented students to participate in an enriched or in-depth study, outside of what is already stipulated in the curriculum.

Since 1980, recognition of the educational needs of gifted/talented children has increased and a small number of educators have become interested in provid-ing differentiated educational programs for the gifted and talented. The increasing concern recently resulted in the establishment of the National Center for the Gifted and Talented in 1999, which will focus on developing policy and a national plan regarding GATE and support the set-up of the National Research and Development Institute (Phothisuk, 1999).

Programs

There are three major organizations that work in different areas of GATE in Thailand. They are: the Foundation for the Promotion of Gifted Children, the Department of Special Education of the Srinakhar-inwirot University, and the Institute for the Promotion of Teaching Science and Technology (Sunhachawee, Promboon & Phothisck, 1992).

The Foundation for the Promotion of Gifted Chil-dren, associated with the Department of Special Education, Srinakharinwirot University, provides once-a-year trainings for parents and teachers involved in summer programs in arts and creative writing for young children and in science for gifted high school students. The Foundation also collaborates with 10 schools and universities to prepare reading materials for students and teaching materials for teachers, in the GATE program.

The Department of Special Education, Srinakhar-inwirot University, has offered a M.Ed. program in

GATE since 1991. The Institute for the Promotion of Teaching Science and Technology works on the following projects:

(1) The Long-term Scholarship Project, which started in 1984, grants full government scholarships to outstanding high school and undergraduate stu-dents. This continues throughout their school and college years until they receive Ph. D.degrees and become scientists. Those who graduate are guaran-teed positions in government organizations, mainly in research and development sections or in uni-versities' schools of science, though. Six high schools and 6 Thai universities, constituting 6 pairs of school-university cooperative units, are partici-pating in this project.

(2) The National Science and Mathematics Olympiads project was formally started in 1991. Under the government's full support, this project charters an annual selection and training of high school students to compete in 5 international Science and Math Olympiads, i.e. Maths, Chemistry, Biology, Physics, and Informatics. The Royal Thai Govern-ment sponsored the 6th International Biology Olympiad in 1995 and offered 15 full scholarships to the finalists in National Olympiads for long-term study from 1993.

The proposed *National Research and Development Institute* (NRDI), supported by the National Education Committee, will have the following responsibilities pertaining to GATE (Phothisck, 1999):

• Master plan for research and development in GATE.
• Follow-up research projects.
• Coordination and knowledge and experiences shar-ing with other research
• organizations in GATE, both in domestic and overseas.
• Center for the body of knowledge in GATE.
• Center for resources in GATE.

The NRDI's short-term action plans include the development of identification instruments and the implementation of GATE in accordance with the Education Act, which has been in effect since August 19, 1999. Its long-term plans include expansion of research areas and the accountability evaluation of research projects.

Problems and Perspectives

Despite the fact that there are a number of national projects to enhance giftedness and talents among Thai children and youth, most projects are oriented toward scholarships and competitions or contests only. This results in a very limited number of children who are served in special education programs.

Thailand is in need of more experts in this area to design and develop educational infrastructure aimed at the identification and development of gifted/talented children at early ages. With the newly established National Center for the Gifted and Talented, it is expected that there will be more research, activities and programs for the gifted and talented and, in the near future, a well-defined national policy for GATE in Thailand

Summary and Conclusions

The main factors contributing to the development of GATE in Asia are: the educational philosophy of emphasizing teaching according to individual differences, the societal tendency to value intellectuals and the wise, the principle of governing a nation on the basis of employing the talented, the needs of economic development, the emphasis of children's education by the parents, and the consideration of human power planning by the government (Wu, 1998).

Regarding identification issues, it is hoped that multi-criterion and alternatives other than standardized intelligence tests can be adopted. As the conception of giftedness is broadening and GATE programs are expanding, the identification/assessment procedures will change into a less strict and more flexible system, aimed at developing talents for all.

Programs for gifted and talented children in Asia are new, with the majority having been established during the last one or two decades. The most vigorous efforts are being made in Taiwan, Korea, and Singapore, where the governments have introduced a wide variety of programs for gifted/talented students during the regular school day as well as after school. Elsewhere on the other hand, Japan supports no programs specifically for gifted/talented students prior to the high school years. In India, Indonesia, the Philippines, and Thailand, GATE is mainly operated by private agencies and/or on a small scale.

Political philosophy is obviously not a critical factor in determining whether programs for gifted/talented students will be established (Stevenson et al., 1992; Wu & Cho, 1993). A typical example is Japan. Japan had bitter experience with social elitism before World War II and since then has taken vigorous steps to avoid the emergence of groups that would dominate the political and social life of the country (Hirano, 1992). As a result, Japan makes strong efforts to ensure that all children begin school with equal knowledge and receive equal educational opportunities during their compulsory education years. It was after 1997, that the Japanese government decided to allow limited 'exceptions' in the procedure of entering a university and curriculum flexibility at senior high and college levels (Japan Central Council for Education, 1997).

It appears that neither the level of economic development nor the quality of schools and universities determines whether or not programs for the education of gifted and talented students will be established in any particular country. The critical difference is the culture's philosophy of education (Stevenson, 1998;

Stevenson et al., 1992). In an effort to promote egalitarianism, all the elementary school students in Japan are required to remain with their classmates regardless of their level of intelligence or of academic achievement. In contrast, some countries mentioned in this article, seeking to enhance the contribution of gifted and talented students to their societies, have developed elaborate programs of special education. The natural experiments taking place in these cultures will provide information about gifted and talented students that will be of interest throughout the world (Stevenson et al., 1992).

It is obvious that some countries in the Asian region are not so blessed as to have official state backing for gifted education. In some, the gifted are lumped together under the rubric 'exceptional children' which includes the handicapped. In others, gifted education is a matter of organizational commitment. There is, to be sure, the perennial problematic gap between rhetoric and action, as well as between policy and implementation (Roldan, 1992).

In the overview of GATE worldwide, Passow (1985) gave two reasons for excluding the United States. His reasons were (a) because the diversity of practice is so great and (b) because anything found elsewhere in the world can be found somewhere in the United States. The converse may give a better picture of the reality; practically all programs and curricula for the gifted and talented in Asia have been modeled, if not outrightly transplanted, from somewhere in the West. There is nothing essentially wrong with borrowing from other cultures; however, we should pause to look more closely at what and how we borrow. There are indications in the 1992 Asian survey (Roldan, 1992), that a distinct curriculum for the gifted, different from the regular school curriculum, has made its appearance on the Asian scene.

It seems that, with the acceptance of a differentiated and distinct curriculum for the gifted, rather than merely enrichment of acceleration, the question of the goals of GATE in the Asian area becomes an acute one (Roldan, 1992). Admittedly, Asian countries are at different levels of development and, therefore, are at different levels in their capacity to help gifted/talented children; but it may be at this point where the pooling of expertise and resources becomes important.

In sum, GATE in Asia has made steady progress in the past and has a promising future. Further development should be planned and implemented. To ensure the full development of talents in our society, we must not be content with the limited programs in limited areas on an experimental basis. Multi-flexible GATE programs ought to be designed to meet the divergent needs of the students with multi-capabilities. As Asian countries gain knowledge and experience with GATE, it is hoped that we can continue to improve education for all as well. According to the claim of educational reform in the Asian region, GATE is facing a number of challenges. It is also hoped that GATE will be a leading force in educational reform, fostering the development of modern society and the welfare of all humankind (Wu, 1998).

References

Bapat, G. S. (1998). A unique experiment in gifted education. In: *Abstract Book Fifth Asia-Pacific Conference on Giftedness* (p. 58), New Delhi, September, 1–5, 1998.

Bhagwat, S. (1998). The gifted children in the mainstream school. In: *Abstract Book Fifth Asia-Pacific Conference on Giftedness* (p. 47), New Delhi, 1–5th September 1998.

Bhalerao, S. (1998). Motivating and helping the gifted to achieve excellence in learning skills. In: *Abstract Book Fifth Asia-Pacific Conference on Giftedness* (p. 29), New Delhi, 1–5th September 1998.

Campbell, J. R. & Wu, R. (1998). *Gifted education from a Chinese Perspective.* Symposium paper presented at the 1998 Annual Convention of the American Educational Research Association, San Diego, (USA), April 13–17, 1998.

Cheeba University (1997). *To the way of Scientists for students in second year at the senior high schools and universities,* Cheeba University Advanced Science Program.

Cheeba University (1998). *Admissions rules for the College of Science and Technology, advanced science program in year 1999.* Cheeba University Admissions Office.

Chiba, A. (1980). *Japan's programs for the gifted and talented education.* Tokyo: Japan Head Office, International Society for Intelligence Education.

Cho, S. (1991). Gifted students in Korea. *International Journal of Special Education, 6* (1), 1–5.

Cho, S. & Kim, Y. B. (1994). *Enrichment programs in regular schools in Korea, RR 94–11.* Seoul: Korean Educational Development Institute.

Cho, S. & Oh, Y. J. (1998). *Gifted Education Centers in Korea, CR 98–17.* Seoul: Korean Educational Development Institute.

Damle, S. C. (1998). An enrichment programme for young Mensans. In: *Abstract Book Fifth Asia-Pacific Conference on Giftedness* (p. 32), New Delhi, September 1–5,1998.

Hirano, T. (1992). *The present stage and tasks of gifted education in Japan.* Paper presented at the 2nd Asian Conference on Giftedness, Taipei, (Taiwan), July 24–27, 1992.

Japan Ministry of Education (1997). Regarding the revision of School Education Acts (official order). *Ministry of Education Official Letter No. 320.*

Japan Central Council of Education (1997). *Recommendation on the Direction and methods of the country's education for the 21st century, Second report to the Ministry of Education.* Tokyo: Ministry of Education.

Lim, T. K. (1997). *Maximizing academic potential: The Chinese high school gifted education programme in Singapore.* Singapore: Times Academic Press.

Lim, T. K. (1999). *Gifted education research in Singapore.* Paper presented at a Special Report Session at the 1999 International Symposium on Research of Gifted and Talented Education, Taipei, (Taiwan), December 22–24, 1999.

Maitra, K. (1997). Status of gifted children in India—a country report. *Asia-Pacific Newsletter, 2* (2), November 1997.

Marat, S. (1992). *The gifted and talented in Indonesia.* Paper presented at the 2nd Asia-Pacific Conference on Giftedness, Taipei, (Taiwan), July 24–27, 1992.

Mehta, V. (1998). Special teacher education programs for the teachers of the gifted. In: *Abstract Book Fifth Asia-Pacific Conference on Giftedness* (p. 49). New Delhi, September 1–5, 1998.

Ministry of Education, R. O. C. (1979). *Guidelines for the second-stage experimental educational programs for gifted students in elementary and junior high schools* [in Chinese].

Ministry of Education, R. O. C. (1982). *Guidelines for the third-stage experimental educational programs for gifted students in elementary and junior high schools* [in Chinese].

Ministry of Education, R. O. C. (1982–99). *Education statistics of the Republic of China* [in Chinese].

Munandar, U. (1992). *Model program Pendidikan bagi peserta didik yang memiliki kemampuan dan kecerdasan luar biasa.* Paper presented at the Second National Convention on Education in Indonesia.

Munandar, U. (1996). Education of the Gifted And Talented In Indonesia. In: U. Munandar & C. Semiawan (Eds.), *Optimizing Excellence in Human Resource Development* (pp. 129–141). Jakarta, University of Indonesia Press.

Munandar, U. (1998). *Policy issues on gifted education in the Asia-Pacific region.* Paper presented at the 5th Asia-Pacific Conference on Giftedness. New Delhi, September 1–4, 1998.

NIER (1993). *Nurturing talents in mathematics, science, and technology, the report of APEID workshop.* Tokyo: NIER.

Passow, A. H. (1985). Universal view of G/T programs. In A. H. Roldan (Ed.), *Gifted and talented children, youth and adults: Their social perspective and culture* (pp. 1–15). Manila: Reading Dynamics, Inc.

Patange, V. (1998). Group tasks for developing attitude for cooperative working among secondary school gifted students. In: *Abstract Book Fifth Asia-Pacific Conference on Giftedness* (p. 43). New Delhi, September 1–5, 1998.

Phothisuk, U. (1999). *Gifted researches in Thailand.* Paper presented at the 1999 International Symposium on Research of Gifted and Talented Education. Taipei, (Taiwan), December 22–24, 1999.

Rimm, S. (1997). Underachievement syndrome: A national epidemic. In: N. Colangelo & G. A. Davis (Eds.), *Handbook of Gifted Education* (2nd ed.) (pp. 416–434). Boston, MA: Allyn and Bacon.

Roldan, A. H. (1992). How fares gifted education in Asia? In: W.-T. Wu, C.-C.Kuo & J. Steves (Eds.), *Growing up Gifted and Talented* (pp. 125–133). Taipei, Taiwan: NTNU.

Singapore Ministry of Education (1999). *Gifted education programme handbook:* A pamphlet on gifted education program (2nd ed.).

Stevenson, H. W. (1998). Cultural interpretations of giftedness: The case of East Asia. In R. C. Friedman and K. B. Rogers (Eds.). *Talent in context: Historical and social perspectives on giftedness* (pp. 61–77). Washington, DC: American Psychological Association.

Stevenson, H. W., Lee, S., Chen, C., Kato, S., & Londo, W. (1992). *Education of gifted and talented students in China, Taiwan and Japan.* Unpublished paper.

Sunachawee, A., Promboon, S., & Phothisuk, U. (1992). *Gifted and talented education in Thailand.* Paper presented at the 2nd Asian Conference on Giftedness. Taipei, (Taiwan), July 24–27, 1992.

TAG Philippines Newsletter, 11:2, December, 1997.

Wang, J. D.(1992). A survey on related problems and teaching strategies in gifted education program in Taiwan [in Chinese]. *Bulletin of Special Education*, **8**, 247–264.

Wu, W. T. (1992). Growing up Gifted and Talented in Taiwan, R.O.C. In: W.-T. Wu, C.-C.Kuo & J. Steves (Eds.), *Growing up Gifted and Talented* (pp. 145–154). Taipei, Taiwan: NTNU.

Wu, W. T. (1997). Educational reform and gifted education in Taiwan. In: J. A. Leroux (Ed.), *Connecting the Gifted Community Worldwide* (pp. 299–310). Northridge, CA: World Council for Gifted and Talented Children, Inc.

Wu, W. T. (1998). Thinking globally, acting locally—the development and perspectives of gifted education [in Chinese]. In: Special Education Association, R. O. C. (Ed.), *Proceedings of the Symposium for the 25th Anniversary of Gifted Education in Taiwan*, R.O.C. (pp. 19–39). Taipei, Taiwan. NTNU.

Wu, W. T. (2000a). *Policies and practices in gifted education* [in Chinese]. Taipei, Taiwan: Psychological Publishing Co.

Wu, W. T. (2000b). Talent identification and development in Taiwan. *Roeper Review*, **22** (2), 131–134.

Wu, W. T., & Cho, S. (1993). Programs and practices for identifying and nurturing giftedness and talent in Asia (outside the Mainland of China). In: K. A. Heller, F. J. Mönks & A. H. Passow (Eds.), *International handbook of research and development of giftedness and talent* (pp. 797–807). Oxford: Pergamon.

Programs and Practices for Identifying and Nurturing Giftedness and Talent in Australia and New Zealand

Eddie J. Braggett[1] and Roger I. Moltzen[2]

[1]Charles Sturt University, New South Wales, Australia
[2]The University of Waikato, New Zealand

Introduction

The last quarter of the twentieth century witnessed significant advances in the recognition and education of gifted and talented persons in Australia and New Zealand. These advances stemmed from the increasing realisation of the need to provide for innate giftedness and the necessity of developing high level talent. The eight Australian states and New Zealand (collectively known as *Australasia*) grappled with the concept of giftedness within their egalitarian social systems, seeking to provide for individuality and excellence but striving to avoid the disparaging claims of elitism and privilege. The responses of the two countries varied, as did the reactions of the separate states within Australia, often reflecting the direction of the educational leadership, the strength of lobby groups in society, and the ideologies of prevailing political factions. The following account analyses the ebb and flow of these educational currents under five headings: (1) the influence of egalitarianism, (2) recent influences, (3) state and national policies, (4) educational provisions, (5) research, and (6) future issues.

The Influence of Egalitarianism

In the first half of the twentieth century, Australian and New Zealand education was developed with twin purposes in mind, viz. to provide mass education for students until 14 or 15 years of age and to taper provision for a minority of senior students who aspired to university or college study. Primary education was comprehensive by nature and, with the exception of three Australian states in which a few special classes were provided for selected gifted students (Braggett, 1985), no attempt was made to single out those with ability or potential. In contrast, secondary education in both countries was academically oriented and geared to university entrance requirements while, in New Zealand, streaming (or grouping) was widely implemented based on standardised testing—primarily intelligence testing.

The second half of the century witnessed the rapid expansion of secondary education as student numbers swelled, as retention rates increased, and as an increasing percentage aspired to post-secondary education. This resulted from a changing society in which extended secondary education was deemed to be appropriate for most students and in which the goals of schooling were constantly re-moulded. In a flurry of reform in the 1960s and 1970s, schools were called upon to provide for the full span of intellectual abilities, social (or age) groupings proved popular, and teachers were required to cope with a new breed of students from socioeconomic groups not previously encountered in the senior years of the school system. Teachers were expected to react quickly and positively to the new demands of a rapidly evolving society.

The practice of streaming was increasingly criticised in both countries as being elitist, critics pointing to the disproportionate number of Maori and Aboriginal children who were placed in lower streams. Moreover, the widespread use of intelligence testing was criticised as educators questioned its validity in a modern egalitarian society. Consequently, the school gradually broadened its curriculum, became less selective, and assumed a social function not formerly acknowledged. Comprehensive schools replaced selective schools in some systems, core curricula were developed, elective studies were introduced, teaching was pitched at an average level, and staff were required to provide for so-called disadvantaged groups in a multi-cultural society, an ill-defined role but one aimed at social reconstruction (Braggett, 1985).

779

During the period 1950 to 1980, schools sought to provide more equitably for a wide range of students but unfortunately the needs of the academically and artistically inclined were often downplayed. Resources were required to assist other students with special needs and it was not always believed that gifted students were included in this category. In its starkest form, the issue was seen in terms of alternatives: education could concentrate on those with special needs (the disadvantaged) or on those with special abilities. Society could develop comprehensive schools for all or provide differentially for separate groups. In the spirit of the time, the balance was tilted in favour of those with special needs, often to the neglect of the gifted/talented (Braggett, 1985) or those with special abilities (Moltzen, 1996).

By 1975 a growing reaction was apparent from a variety of educational groups and from concerned parents who believed that more appropriate provision was required for gifted students. At least three New Zealand publications in the 1960s had concentrated on gifted children and these were followed by *Children with special abilities* (NZ Department of Education, 1972), a handbook which brought together much of the earlier thinking. Within Australia, questions were posed in Western Australia, New South Wales, and Victoria, exploring the needs of able students and the type of education required for them. Hence, when a World Conference on Gifted Children was convened in London in 1975, the two countries sent more than 30 delegates, and Professor Parkyn (1976) from New Zealand provided a keynote address on the *Identification and evaluation of gifted children*.

It is now more than 25 years since the gifted movement surfaced, a period in which the two countries have sought to provide for gifted people in their individual ways. There are similarities between the two countries in terms of heritage but no common approach to gifted education has emerged and none is likely because of the diverse nature of the educational systems and the geographical distances involved. The Australian population of almost 20 million is scattered over a large continent equal in size to mainland USA, the majority being found on the coastal strip with a preponderance in the south-east sector. Because education is a state right, Australia has eight distinct educational systems with different organisational structures, system networks, and curriculum development processes, and all are underpinned by political ideologies of varying shades. Twenty-eight percent of Australian students are taught within church and private schools which have an additional degree of independence. New Zealand lies 2000 kms across the Tasman Ocean to the south-east of Australia, a land of geographical contrasts ranging from pastoral plains to rugged alps and glacial rivers. Within this small country of 270,000 km^2, an area smaller than Italy and equal in size to the state of Colorado, the population of 3.4 million has developed a single (national) system of education in which there is considerable devolution of responsibility to the local school.

Recent Influences

During the 1980s and 1990s, there were three major influences that were common to both countries and which influenced educational provision for gifted students. The first was an egalitarian outlook that sought to promote social justice, to remove handicaps, and to develop welfare systems for those in need. In New Zealand, for example, the Ministry of Education sought to remove barriers to achievement, to break down cultural stereotypes that inhibited performance among minority groups, and to develop teacher awareness of the need to cater for a wide range of academic and social behaviours within the school. The NZ Education Act of 1989 decreed that "equity objectives shall underpin all activities within the school," and referred specifically to Maori, Pacific Islands, and other ethnic groups as well as women and girls, students with disabilities, and students with special learning needs (NZ National Education Guidelines, 1990). In Australia, likewise, there was a strong political and educational concern with issues of equity, particularly those that concerned Indigenous students (i.e. Torres Strait Islanders and Aborigines), girls, those with disabilities, students from non-English speaking backgrounds (referred to as NESB students), and those who resided in remote areas.

While it may be argued that gifted education is itself an equity issue, this has not always been accepted by politicians or educators in Australasia. It is often asserted, for example, that students with special abilities do not require assistance beyond that provided by the comprehensive primary or secondary school and that additional provision is tantamount to unwarranted privilege. As a consequence, it is felt to be elitist to identify gifted students and to provide for them in a differential manner: this, it is argued, discriminates even further against those with readily-perceived needs in society. There is little realisation that giftedness is culturally based, that talent is developmental in nature, and that both are intricately related to motivation, self-confidence, interest and sustained effort.

It is difficult to convey the egalitarian sense that permeated Australasian society during the 1980s and 1990s; neither should it be considered a necessarily negative phenomenon. Social justice was—and still is—a very real issue and, despite criticisms that have been levelled against governments in both countries, social attitudes have been modified, less advantaged groups have been assisted, and barriers to achievement have been removed. Those who succeed are now likely to receive genuine approbation, particularly when they overcome obstacles on the way to their success. On the other hand, too much success may engender resentment and lead to the *tall poppy syndrome*: very tall poppies should be cut down (except when sport is involved).

Second, beliefs about giftedness and its definition have been modified over the past two decades. Giftedness was originally seen as an innate quality, relatively fixed, and deserving of provision in special classes or schools. When groups of school students were identified and given the tag of *gifted*, it was usually found that they were drawn from the dominant white society, from the educated middle-class, and from those with positive attitudes to education. Identification techniques were biased against those with different values, against minority groups, and against those who achieved poorly when standardised testing procedures were employed. In one sense, the equity issues referred to above, forced educators to explore more critically the concept of giftedness and its relationship to the culture, leading to a broader concept that was more amenable to education, coaching, or training. More emphasis was placed on developed ability (ie. on performance) and on the ways in which educators could facilitate the development of talent across different domains. The writings of Gardner (1983; 1993) and Lazear (1994) were influential in broadening the approach, including the need to cater for different learning styles.

As a result, increasing emphasis was placed on the comprehensive school and the ability of the teacher to provide for gifted students within the regular classroom. There were moves to downplay the concept of *giftedness* as such and to use different terminology: the *talented*, the *highly able*, or—as favoured in New Zealand—*children with special abilities*. It was increasingly accepted that teachers might influence the development of talent by differentiating the curriculum, varying their teaching strategies, emphasising the teaching of skills and strategies, and modifying their own classroom management practices. While this movement has been generally accepted in both countries and has resulted in very positive gains, there is also a danger that teachers may lose a sense of direction as they develop 'the gifts and talents of all students' and pay less attention to the most advanced students, to those with high potential, and to those with extraordinary abilities. It seems that the greatest success is achieved when a balance between these two approaches is preserved.

Third, there has been a relationship between the political ideology espoused and the degree to which giftedness has been specifically targeted and provided for within government schools. This has been particularly true in Australia where political parties with social democratic traditions have tended to favour policies aimed at equalising social outcomes and overcoming social barriers. While resource teachers have assisted students with learning difficulties, no comparable provision has been made for those with special abilities. The usual classroom setting and the regular teacher, with some inservice or professional development assistance, are believed to afford the most appropriate education for gifted students and it is not accepted that the absence of special provision handicaps their development.

Political parties with a more conservative outlook, those geared to a free-market economy, and those with anti-Labor attitudes, have been more likely to favour wider choice and diversity of school provision. This has been pronounced in Australia where conservative governments have generally been more receptive to the gifted and talented cause and have adopted policies that have led to special schools, special classes, or additional training of staff.

Other political issues, however, have surfaced more recently to complicate the analysis described above. In New Zealand in the late 1980s and early 1990s the New Right ideology was responsible for a raft of public sector reforms. These changes reflected a general view that state intervention to promote egalitarian social goals had caused the economic problems of many western democracies. They embodied what Boston (1991, p. 2) described as "an analytic framework grounded in public choice theory, managerialism and the new economics of organisations, most notably agency theory and transaction cost analysis."

Australian politics in recent years have also reflected an economic rationalist approach in which the outcomes of education have been increasingly intertwined with the goals of the national economy. Funding to government schools has not kept pace with educational needs while concessions have been made to the private education sector. There is a perception in the minds of some that private/independent schools are more desirable and more likely to cater for academically advanced students, a result of their funding and the demands of their fee-paying parents.

At the same time, some labour-oriented political parties have recently modified their approach to educational provision. In New South Wales, for instance, the Labor Party has not only preserved special primary classes and selective secondary schools (both requiring the identification and selection of gifted students and the provision of special schools) but has also campaigned actively for their extension, especially in country regions. In 1989 the New Zealand government introduced the most radical changes in the administration of education seen in more than 100 years. These changes were consistent with the reform of other aspects of the public sector and were characterised by a significant devolution of responsibility and authority from the centre to individual learning institutions. New Zealand has never had a national policy on the education of its gifted students and commentators have variously described the country's attention to its most able as weak, patchy and inconsistent. However, some direction had earlier been provided by the agencies that became disestablished, or whose function excluded such guidance following the introduction of the reforms. This meant the initiative for provisions for gifted students after 1989 resided exclusively at the local school level. In the post-reform era, each school was required to operate within a charter, developed in consultation with its local community. The government required all charters to include clauses relating to such issues as curriculum, equity, and provisions for Maori students. There was no requirement to include content relating to provisions for gifted students. Consequently, what an individual school provides for these students is a direct reflection of the priority it is accorded by the school and its community.

It is within this ethos that gifted and talented programs should be gauged within Australia and New Zealand. There is an undoubted desire on both sides of the Tasman Ocean to widen the benefits of education, to promote high quality schooling within the regular classroom, and for teachers to cater for a wider range of abilities. This is generally conceived within a traditional lockstep method of organisation, however, in which the majority of children cover similar work in groups and do not explore too far from the pre-determined curriculum. As a consequence, some opposition is expressed when withdrawal groups, content or grade acceleration, special classes or differentiated programs are suggested. Some schools, regions and entire systems have accepted an egalitarian thrust and resisted demands for different forms of provision but others have forged ahead and introduced innovative and exciting programs that cater for individual needs.

In line with these advances, it is evident that major advances have been made within Australia and New Zealand over the past 20 years. There is decidedly less opposition to students with special abilities and educational consultants who visit schools report a deeper appreciation of the need to cater for a wider range of abilities/talents. There is some indication also that, when government (state) schools are involved, an increased level of teacher awareness is related to the existence of a publicised policy by the Minister or the State Department on the education of gifted/talented students.

State and National Policies

Australia

The eight Australian Departments or Ministries of Education have all developed State Policies that draw attention to the needs of gifted students and to the types of provisions that might be made. Each provides a short rationale, a general definition of giftedness/talent, approaches to identification, ways of differentiating provision, programs available at state level, lists of resources, contact persons, and—sometimes—sources of funding. It is informative to peruse these policy statements, beginning in 1979, as they reflect changing attitudes to giftedness and pinpoint considerable differences in the extent of each state's commitment to gifted education.

In the 1980s, Western Australia adopted the most radical of all policies based on a pyramid-type structure. Programs for the lower primary years (ages 5–8) were school based and designed to cater for approximately 5% of the age group; at the middle primary level (ages 8–10), 3% of children were selected for part-time withdrawal programs in strategically chosen schools with *special interest centres*; and, at the upper primary level (ages 10–12), classes were introduced for 2% of the children who were totally withdrawn for fast-paced scholastic courses but integrated with the rest of the school for expressive arts, physical education, and other informal activities. At the secondary level, approximately 1.5% were offered places in designated secondary schools where high calibre programs met their advanced intellectual needs while others attended secondary schools with specialities in such areas as music, dance/drama and languages (WA Policy, 1981).

It was maintained that this was a total approach to gifted education as it provided enrichment, extension and accelerated progression within the range of normal school options. An Academic Extension Branch was established at the state level, resources were committed, *talent searches* were conducted across the state each year, and professional development was provided for teachers. The purpose was to legitimatise and embed provision for gifted students within the mainstream of educational practice.

Most other states moved more cautiously and developed less radical policies, most being influenced by the Marland Report (1972) in which giftedness was conceived in a broadened form and by Renzulli's (1977) *Enrichment Triad Model* which was often used (but frequently misinterpreted) as the basis for in-class enrichment. An analysis of the policies developed by New South Wales, South Australia, Northern Territory, Queensland, Tasmania and the Australian Capital Territory (ACT) reveals a spectrum of provisions ranging from special schools/classes, regional consultants and centralised mentor programs at one end of the continuum to enrichment for able students in the regular class at the other end.

In the state of Victoria, enrichment and extension programs were provided on a cluster group basis (often involving both state and private schools), a mentor register was developed for the state, and one high school in Melbourne introduced a radically differentiated acceleration program in which students could complete six years of secondary education in four or five years. Victoria proved to be an early leader in gifted education (GCTF, 1983).

Present State Policies

At the start of a new millenium, some Australian states are revising their policies once again in order to reflect changing views about giftedness and its development, and the desire to embrace more inclusive approaches. As explained in an earlier section, there is a strong thrust for the regular classroom teacher to be involved in program provision and for special classes to be de-emphasised. Moreover, the 1990s witnessed cut-backs in government expenditure resulting in financial pruning of educational services. Driven by educational and financial considerations, authorities questioned the need for separate programs and required the comprehensive school and the regular classroom teacher to assume increased responsibility for differentiated programs, often without any increase in resources.

At the commencement of 2000, all Australian states had policies relating to gifted and talented students: some were relatively general in nature while others reflected a system concern that led to quality program implementation. The main policy provisions, currently in effect, are outlined below.

- The strong thrust that earlier characterised Western Australia changed in some ways when responsibility for gifted education was transferred from the state's central office to the regional and district level. Nevertheless, the specialised secondary school programs continue and are genuinely entrenched within mainstream provision; the part-time PEAC withdrawal programs for primary children continue based on an annual state-wide *talent search*; and a range of school-based programs operate throughout the state. Staff professional development is stressed (Pears, 1999).

- Queensland stresses the need for extension, enrichment and acceleration at the school level and provides support through a state coordinator of gifted and talented education who has developed networks, provides inservice training, develops and distributes resources, and implements school programs and policies. Enrichment and extension concentrate on high-level skills development, creative and critical thinking and metacognition (Queensland Department of Education, 1993; Hewett, 1999).

- While stressing the need for school-based programs, South Australia also seeks to develop *Focus Schools* at the primary school level to act as models for other schools to emulate, to render support, and to provide professional development for teachers. Special Interest Secondary Schools are provided and supported in the areas of music, languages, agriculture, sports and SHIP (*S*tudents with *H*igh *I*ntellectual *P*otential). Three full-time Coordinators work across the state, developing resources and providing support (SA State Policy, 1995; Minchin, 1999).

- Northern Territory, in addition to a system-wide identification program, provides special primary school classes, permits accelerated progression, inservices teachers in enrichment strategies, and provides state-sponsored camps. Advanced senior secondary students may study a university subject in the final year of school, while the Aboriginal and Islander Tertiary Aspirations Program seeks to increase the number of Indigenous students who successfully complete secondary education and proceed to tertiary studies (Day, 1999).

- Tasmania reworked its policy in 1996 and committed funds for gifted education by assigning part-time coordinators in each of the state's districts and appointing a state-wide coordinator. Four special schools were designated in the areas of information technology, performing arts and off-site programs, while guidelines for early school entry and for acceleration were developed and trialled in 1998. In response to teacher needs, the new policy emphasises 'user friendly' identification and assessment procedures and outlines the development of a mentor program (Tasmania, 1996; Fagg, 1999).

- The Australian Capital Territory (ACT) is responsible for the smallest Australian system and the most compact geographically. Its 1998 draft policy placed emphasis on school-based programs and the development of students' skills. Strategies to provide for gifted and talented students included school and classroom grouping patterns, acceleration, workshops, and mentor programs (ACT Draft Policy, 1998).

- New South Wales is different from other states in that it provides Secondary Selective and Agricultural Schools and selective classes (termed OC Classes) in primary schools, entry to which is highly competitive. The number of such classes has increased over the last 10 years. Early entry to school is permitted and accelerated progression may take the form of year or content promotion. A Mentor Links Program has been developed as well as a Talent Development Project for students with outstanding talents in the field of popular entertainment. While school-based programs are emphasised, district network initiatives are promoted and have steadily increased over the past three years (NSW Government Strategy, 1991; Bradburn, 1999).

- The 1995 policy in Victoria places considerable stress on, and has led to the development of, statewide networks of schools and clusters of primary and secondary schools in particular curriculum areas; local gifted education networks; special programs to connect country schools; international programs; a diversity of programs to provide for Individual Learning Pathways; enrichment, extension, acceleration and mentor programs; a sustained and well coordinated central program aimed at resource development, school assistance, and teacher professional development; and a range of specific programs in concert with institutions, community organisations and parent organisations. The approach has targeted teacher and public awareness and has included state and international conferences since 1995 (*Bright Futures*, 1995; Morris, 1999; Reynen, 1999; Stewart, 1999).

Private (independent) and Catholic schools are not part of wider systems and it is therefore difficult to refer to their policies as such. Each school may develop its own policy relating to gifted students and, as indicated in a later section, these range from general statements to those which are highly specific and which result in high quality, innovative programs.

Even though education is a state concern, the Australian Government has also been pressed to develop a *national* policy on gifted and talented education. A Senate Select Committee (1988) urged the Government to "make a clear statement that special educational strategies should be provided for gifted children throughout Australia" but this has not yet materialised, although there are current moves to influence and renew government interest (Geake, 1999).

New Zealand

New Zealand's history of providing for gifted students has been characterised by ebbs and flows of interest and attention, where positive developments have frequently resulted from the efforts of concerned individuals, and where gains have often been short-lived (Moltzen, 1996). During the 1980s there was a strong call from those committed to the gifted cause for a national policy, which would require schools to demonstrate the provision made for this group of students. It was argued that this would ensure consistency of provision and end a pattern whereby real progress was negated in the next era. This lobby group reminded educators that, among the countries represented in Sydney at the 8th World Conference on the Gifted and Talented in 1989, New Zealand was the only country without a policy on the education of the gifted (McAlpine, 1991).

At the same time there began a process of educational reform in New Zealand, characterised by decentralisation, devolution of responsibility, and increased parental choice. While the direction of reform reflected changes in other countries, New Zealand was committed to carrying the process much further than other educational jurisdictions. Lawton (1992), for example, reported in an international educational survey that New Zealand had taken decentralisation to a level beyond that of any other system studied.

According to the Ministry of Education, the post-reform environment in New Zealand has made the development of a national policy less appropriate than it has ever been. The principles of decentralisation and devolution mean that the chief educational authority

[the Centre] limits to a bare minimum the policies it imposes on local schools. While schools are required to develop policies in some areas, the gifted do not need such special consideration, the Ministry of Education defending its position by pointing to the country's recently-developed National Curriculum which is specifically designed to challenge "all students to fulfil their potential" (NZ Ministry of Education, 1991). This Curriculum advocates higher order thinking skills, open-ended activities, and problem solving approaches; contains achievement objectives across a range of levels covering 13 years of schooling; and encourages teachers to place students at levels commensurate with their ability, and not according to their age or grade level. To many, however, this provides an inadequate guarantee that the needs of the gifted will be met in an appropriate fashion. For example, the provision exists to accelerate the learning of the gifted but many teachers and principals remain reluctant to advance students beyond what is perceived as the level for the average child at a particular age and stage (Townsend, 1996). Where some acceleration is acceptable, any movement of a child in advance of his or her peers is likely to be very conservative indeed.

The arguments of the Ministry of Education when defending the lack of a national policy have failed to lessen the pressure for some national direction. In what could be interpreted as a response to increasing lobbying, the Ministry of Education in 1998 established an 'Advisory Group on Gifted Education' to advise the Ministry on issues associated with the education of the gifted. While the Ministry has held its position that a national policy is inappropriate, it has agreed with the Advisory Group's recommendation that national Guidelines be developed and distributed to every school in the country. The contract for this project has been let and these Guidelines are expected to be in all schools early in 2000. The Ministry has also agreed to fund a modest professional development program to accompany the distribution of the Guidelines and appears committed to exploring and supporting future developments for the gifted.

The Guidelines seek to provide schools with a platform on which to build their own policies and practices. The current educational climate in New Zealand emphasises the need for schools to work with their communities and to develop philosophies and approaches that reflect the needs of each individual community. Because the Guidelines will be required to reflect this principle, considerable variation is expected among schools as they define giftedness and seek to provide for their gifted students.

It is difficult to ascertain with accuracy the full nature of the influences that have resulted in this dramatic change of direction. It is 27 years since a similar initiative resulted in the publication of a booklet containing suggestions for teaching children with special abilities (NZ Department of Education, 1972).

There appears to be a greater appreciation of diversity and a weakening of the *one-size-fits-all* attitude, both inside and outside education. This is exemplified particularly in a variety of developments to improve the levels of Maori achievement. There is also an increased national awareness that New Zealand's collective attitude towards high achievement (except in sport) has been unjustifiably negative. It might be part of a developing maturity in a nation when the success of one group is not automatically interpreted as a threat to others. Perhaps it not inconsequential that New Zealand's preference for the term *children with special abilities* seems to have disappeared, allowing the national Guidelines to refer to these children as *gifted*.

Educational Provisions

There is a wide diversity of provisions made for gifted and talented students at school, district and system levels throughout Australia and New Zealand. Moreover, terms such as *enrichment* and *extension* are often used interchangeably or with particular connotations that are specific to schools or to developed programs. Hence, the present analysis which includes some thousands of Australasian programs necessitates a conceptualisation that, while accurate, must be open to the charge of generality. The two countries are reported separately.

Australia

Seven types of provision may be discerned across Australia, involving individual schools, small clusters of schools, wider district initiatives, and overall system strategies.

Special Schools/Classes

During the first half of the twentieth century when high school education was a privilege for an intellectual elite, selective high schools became an important segment of secondary education in most Australian states. Designed for students with university aspirations, they were often single-sex schools and were located mainly in metropolitan areas. When secondary education was extended and reformed in the 1960s and 1970s, many of these academic schools were converted to comprehensive establishments and made co-educational in the process. A few, however, missed the reformers' zeal and were preserved as selective schools with competitive academic entrance requirements. During the 1990s, in a changing political scene, New South Wales once again increased the number of selective schools, so that 23 specifically cater for 'academically gifted and talented students' (Bradburn, 1999). These schools are renowned for their high academic results at the end of Year 12 when students sit for an external examination on which university selection is based. Except for a few selective establishments in Victoria, however, virtually all similar high

schools in Australia have been abolished. A Conservatorium High School exists in Sydney for talented musical students and is operated in conjunction with the NSW Conservatorium of Music.

With the growth of comprehensive secondary schools in the 1970s, it was found that gifted students were not always extended, and this resulted in two important modifications. First, extension courses were introduced into the senior years of the high school curriculum so that subjects might be studied at different levels of difficulty, a decision which assisted the academically capable. Second, the organisation of the high school itself came under scrutiny as alternatives within a comprehensive framework were canvassed.

Western Australia was one of the first states to react, introducing a Talent Search for students with high intellectual potential in the final year of the primary school, a scheme which continues to find favour with the community. On the basis of this quest, approximately 300 students are offered places in 10 comprehensive high schools, each having a special academic class which provides advanced courses and permits accelerated learners to work at their own pace. While each of the schools has developed its own approach, most place the students in a separate class for academic subjects for the first two or three years of their studies but require them to join regular classes for elective and non-elective studies.

One of the aims of these classes (and of the selective schools in New South Wales) has been to stem the drift of students to private schools because of the perception that independent schools might offer more academically rigorous programs. There is no doubt that selective schools/classes attract high quality students and enhance the academic reputation of the state systems.

Other states have introduced schemes to increase the academic orientation of the secondary school. Three South Australian secondary schools are designated SHIP schools (providing for *S*tudents with *H*igh *I*ntellectual *P*otential) and have acquired a reputation for high quality output (Minchin, 1999). As part of state school provision, Tasmania and the Australian Capital Territory provide separate Senior Colleges for students in the last two years of the high school, a form of organisation which may enhance enrichment and specialisation because of the larger number of students enrolled and the expertise of the staff. University High School, Melbourne, accepts an intake of 25 students in Year 7 each year and permits them to extend and accelerate their learning through the grades.

Special classes have also been created at the *primary* school level, mainly for students in Years 5, 6 or 7. New South Wales introduced special classes for gifted students in the final years of the primary school in 1932, a concept which still exists in 1999/2000 despite the vagaries of different political policies. There are currently 104 such classes, known as Opportunity or OC classes, in 65 primary schools (Bradburn, 1999). Special primary classes are likewise provided in the Northern Territory at Darwin and Alice Springs (Day, 1999).

Full-time special classes for gifted students at the primary level are not immune from controversy, however, as the Western Australian experience has indicated. After the WA Department of Education commenced Full-time Extension Classes for able students in Years 6 and 7 in 1982, there was opposition on the grounds that early specialisation was undesirable, leading to the discontinuation of the units after 1986 and to a concentration on part-time programs and on cluster group provision.

While the above examples may indicate a range of special school/class provisions, the majority of Australian schools do not have special, standardised identification procedures for gifted students and do not provide special classes for them. Most primary schools retain whole-class instruction in comprehensive settings and promote children on a lock-step basis. Many high schools grade students in mathematics and languages, placing the highest performers in selected classes in each grade and leaving the rest of the students ungraded. The debate on the merits of *graded* vs. *ungraded* classes is ongoing.

Cluster Groups/Networks

Cluster groups are seen as a specialised and economical way of providing for gifted students at primary and secondary level, allowing a number of schools which are in close geographic proximity to plan and implement joint educational programs for teachers or students. When students are involved, they permit small numbers from two or more schools to combine for enrichment or extension activities on a part-time basis, the schools sharing the costs involved and having access to expertise that each could not provide individually.

During the 1980s they were particularly popular in Victoria and Western Australia although they existed in all Australian states in some form. Since that time their popularity has declined because of the time and organisation involved, the problems of transporting students between schools, and the consequent absence of pupils from regular classes on a continuing basis. Other forms of joint activities and networking have now been developed in their place.

One exception to this decline is found in Western Australia where cluster groups have been perfected and embedded in mainstream provision. Developed from the original pyramid-approach to gifted education, the Primary Extension and Challenge (PEAC) program is a statewide initiative that offers challenging experiences to gifted students in Years 5–7 (ages 10–12) as part of their normal school program. Most children are tested in Year 4 and, if they meet the relevant criteria, are

Table 1. Examples of Programs offered at PEAC Centres in Western Australia.

Statistics	What if . . . ?	Solar energy
Electronics	Aborigines	Man in flight
Japanese culture	Italian	French
Meteorology	Zoology	Theatre
Anthropology	Computers	Propaganda
Magnetism	Astronomy	Chemistry
Extension math	Forestry	Paleontology
Left to write	Polyominoes	Algebra
Aviation	Esperanto	Microscopes
Nordic myths	Poetry	Natural disasters

placed in a pool of students who may attend courses in PEAC centres throughout the state over the next few years. These courses are provided on a wide range of themes which vary from year to year depending on the self-expressed interests of local students. Examples of courses are outlined in Table 1.

PEAC Centres are located throughout Western Australia in both metropolitan areas and country towns. They operate for the entire school year providing withdrawal programs for children who are drawn from surrounding schools and who attend for half a day each week for 6–10 weeks or longer. Programs are designed to provide challenging content and to train research and independent study skills, as well as affording a chance for gifted and talented students to meet and support each other in their interests. Entry to these extension courses has been broadened over time so that children who are not in the selected pool are also permitted to attend individual courses if they demonstrate high ability and interest in a specified area.

PEAC courses have proved popular with students and teachers because of the interest they provide, the motivation they generate, the enrichment and extension they impart, and the positive attitudes to learning which they foster. They have not only won the approbation of parents but have also been accepted by all major political parties in the state. This form of gifted education has now been accepted as normal mainstream provision, Western Australia being the only state to achieve this commendation.

In the north of Australia, three sectors—the NT Department of Education, community groups, and the Northern Territory University—provide and coordinate regular vacation schools for senior secondary students in order to encourage study at post-secondary level and to introduce all ethnic groups to advanced study. At the same time, the *Aboriginal and Islander Tertiary*

Aspirations Program (AITAP) is designed to increase the number of Indigenous students who successfully complete the Northern Territory Certificate of Education and proceed to college/university studies (Day, 1999). Both programs assist motivation and broaden the horizons of students.

As part of its *Bright Futures* program, Victoria has emphasised local teacher networks to "assist teachers and parents in Government, Catholic and independent schools to meet gifted students' needs" and has developed clusters of primary and secondary schools "to offer a world class standard in particular curriculum areas such as science, sport, LOTE [languages other than English], visual and performing arts, and information technology" (*Bright Futures*, 1995). It is apparent that the original concept of school clusters has now been broadened, aided by interactive information technology.

Networking assumes a new dimension when schools develop particular expertise and become models for others to emulate. There are eight Focus Schools in Queensland which act as centres for training and research and invite others to visit and observe their approach (Education Queensland, 1999). Networking also forms the basis of the South Australian *Focus School Program* where teams assist local schools and groups of teachers (Minchin, 1999).

Special Interest Centres

Special Interest Centres are secondary schools, usually comprehensive in nature and serving all students in the neighbourhood. Additionally, they have a specialised discipline area that attracts highly talented students from a wide geographic area because of the high quality instruction that is available. In South Australia there are currently four Special Interest Secondary Schools which specialise in music, one in languages, one in agriculture, and two in sports (Minchin, 1999).

In the music centres, students follow a normal high school course as well as specialising in the theoretical and performance strands of music. In one school, tuition is available in flute, piccolo, oboe, clarinet, saxophone, bassoon, trumpet, french horn, trombone, tuba, violin, viola, cello, classical guitar, untuned percussion (xylophone, etc.), piano, pipe organ and voice. It is not unusual for students to integrate their studies in the performance arts, and to excel in many aspects of academic and social life. The staff are highly qualified and develop excellence that spreads to other teaching departments.

Influenced to a degree by this South Australian concept, New South Wales created the Newtown High School of the Performing Arts in Sydney, a comprehensive school with specialities in the visual arts, dance, drama, and music. Students who concentrate on dance, for example, must study composition, appreciation and performance, and may select from the following styles: traditional, modern, classical, jazz,

African-derived modern, Aboriginal, ballroom, and Latin and American dance. Other students who do not specialise in the performing arts are still included in a wide array of related activities (set production, audio backup, organisational activities, publicity, design, technology, etc) and benefit from the excellence engendered within the school.

The special interest high schools with the longest history are found in Western Australia where the Department of Education has grafted specialist disciplines onto 11 existing comprehensive schools in the Perth metropolitan area. These schools, some with special programs dating from 1968, provide high level instruction in the areas of art, languages, music, dance and/or theatre arts, and select students on the basis of interview, performance, folio presentation, and standardised testing if appropriate. In general the students who enter the 11 classes each year are expected to work at a sustained pace and to aspire to excellence. The programs are widely acclaimed throughout the state because of their high quality and the outstanding levels of student performance.

More recently, Tasmania has developed four schools with special programs in performing arts, information technology, and off-site studies (Fagg, 1999) while New South Wales has a widely acclaimed Talent Development Project in the arts area which identifies and provides for students with outstanding talents in the field of popular entertainment (Bradburn, 1999).

Acceleration

Attitudes to acceleration have softened in Australia over the past decade and there is now less suspicion and a wider acceptance of the practice. In the Northern Territory, for example, the Policy for the Education of Gifted and Talented Students (NT Policy 1992) indicates unequivocally that acceleration can assist some gifted students. In other states such as the Australian Capital Territory (ACT Draft Policy, 1998), it is spelt out in considerable detail and safeguards are outlined. Nonetheless, all states and territories specifically detail it as one strategy, often in concert with others, to provide more adequately for the education of the gifted.

Western Australia was the first to espouse acceleration at system level when it encouraged the ten high schools with special classes for intellectually talented students to accelerate the progress of those whose learning was advanced. The Ministry of Education in New South Wales formally accepted and publicised the benefits of accelerated progression in 1991, issuing a publication entitled *Guidelines for accelerated progression* (Board of Studies, NSW, 1991) to all schools. School principals have the final responsibility for deciding cases of early entry to school and of accelerated progression through the grades.

Subject acceleration is more widespread than total grade skipping, and occurs naturally in vertically organised classes, in classrooms where teachers encourage children to work at their own pace, or where individualised programs are devised. Despite these changing attitudes, there is still considerable opposition to acceleration in individual schools on the alleged grounds of negative social-emotional outcomes or because of the restrictions imposed by the ubiquitous high school timetable.

In its widest sense, acceleration is multi-faceted as indicated in the Northern Territory Policy. Schools are informed that acceleration may assume many forms but essentially means that a student will complete some or all of his/her formal schooling requirements in a faster time than average peers. Some of the ways in which this can be achieved include:

- early admission to preschool, primary school, junior high school, senior high school;
- curriculum presented above year level;
- students accelerated into an older age group to work in one or more subjects;
- full-time classes of identified gifted students;
- family (vertical) grouping in the secondary school;
- curriculum presented at a faster rate in the mainstream classroom;
- students given credit for successful completion of courses at other institutions (NT Policy, 1992).

Victoria, having already established an acceleration program at University High School, Melbourne, in 1981 decided to create additional *select entry accelerated learning programs* in the mid–1990s, allowing students to complete their six years of secondary schooling in five years. As an extension of this type of acceleration, Victoria allows selected secondary students to study first-year university subjects as part of their Year 12 school program (*Bright Futures*, 1995). A similar scheme operates in other states including New South Wales and the Northern Territory.

Overall, therefore, the practice of acceleration is more widely accepted than in previous years although it is still likely to produce negative emotive responses from those who are not convinced by the overwhelming amount of research findings on the topic or who cling to age groupings that supposedly create homogeneous ability classrooms.

Enrichment

Enrichment is nominated to be the most widely used strategy across Australia in providing for gifted and talented students. Significantly, it is often referred to by the term *enrichment activities* rather than *enrichment programs,* an indication of the fragmented nature of the approach frequently adopted. In defence of enrichment as a strategy, it is claimed that it may be integrated with regular classroom instruction and that it causes less disruption to the normal school organisation than some other approaches. It is obvious, however, that much

confused thinking exists about the purposes of enrichment and the target group for whom it is intended. Some teachers confine enrichment activities to a small, select group of children who are considered to be gifted in some way, but the majority believe that enrichment is appropriate to the needs of all children and should not be restricted to predetermined groups. It takes time for some teachers to realise that enrichment is a complex concept that may be implemented at different levels and for different purposes.

Queensland has developed a model of curriculum provision "for gifted education and talent identification" that operates at four interrelated levels and incorporates enrichment within a wider framework. While it is applicable to all students in primary or secondary schools, it is "specifically intended for schools to identify and meet the needs of potentially gifted students" (Education Queensland, 1999).

Strand 1 activities are designed to expand interests and to identify the talents of all children. Such activities include concerts, debating clubs, competitions, sports days, chess clubs, camps, choirs, musicals and art/drama festivals which, while providing cultural enrichment, help to identify students who may benefit from similar activities at a higher level. The teacher observes those who meet the criteria of advanced studies, discusses extension/enrichment possibilities with parents (if children are young or if money is involved), and encourages students to participate in higher level activities. This may include extra-curricular activities such as mini courses (in a sport for example), drama and dance classes, music lessons, a Double Helix Science Club, Aboriginal art classes, a Vietnamese Saturday School, or a writers' circle.

Strand 2 introduces or extends higher level thinking activities, thereby allowing students to participate in school and regional events or competitions. Its purpose is to identify students, including those who underachieve, to participate in teams and withdrawal programs and develop self confidence and self understanding. Identification opportunities are provided through Maths Challenge Days, art festivals, leadership courses, mini Thinkfests and mini-*Tournament of Minds.* The criteria to enter various programs are specified and students are tutored in the skills required. A Maths Challenge, for example, is based on problem solving skills, motivation and analytical processes and, hence, these are developed so that particular students may enjoy and excel in the Challenge. *Tournament of Minds* requires creativity, leadership, problem solving ability, communication and interpersonal skills and these are taught and stressed for those who desire to participate in the Tournament. Other school and community-based activities are similarly analysed in order to extrapolate the requisite skills and strategies which are then developed over time. As a result of the teacher's observations, students may be offered places in pull-out programs such as leadership courses, writers' camps, philosophy forums, industry place-ments, Thinkfest programs, *Tournament of Minds,* or Excellence Expos.

Strand 3, termed *implementing gifted education,* seeks to identify students who need differentiation, provide an appropriate curriculum for them, and empower them to be autonomous learners. Based partly on Maker's four basic modifications (content, process, product, environment) and on Braggett's seven cate-gories of differentiation (speed, cognitive processes, enrichment/extension, personal experience/autonomy, multiple intelligences, deductive thinking, social change), the Queensland model encourages students to be involved in a differentiated curriculum that permits and develops independent learning, research and reporting skills, problem finding and solving ability, high level critical and creative thinking skills (eg. analysis, synthesis and evaluation), communication skills, and task commitment. Teachers are required to identify their learning objectives, pretest students for prior mastery, and eliminate unnecessary teaching. The end product allows students to be involved in nego-tiated activities, extension programs or independent study.

Strand 4 is designed to "identify students who need negotiated, differentiated curriculum (an individualised work program) and to facilitate independent learning." Influenced by a number of researchers including Renzulli, the negotiated curriculum may entail accel-eration/compaction, mentor programs, contracts, dual enrolments and extension programs. Individualised Education Plans are integral to this level of the program. The model makes it clear, however, that students do not pass through these four strands in a linear fashion but that they are simply guides for identification and curriculum provision. Students who perform at an advanced level in Strand 1, for example, may proceed directly to Strand 4 if they possess the requisite skills and strategies.

While there are many other equally useful models available to teachers, the Queensland model illustrates a trend in many Australian schools whereby increasing numbers of teachers are seeking to base their enrich-ment programs—indeed their entire teaching—on a sound theoretical basis. Bloom's *Taxonomy* was one of the first models to achieve widespread appeal, partic-ularly at the primary school level. Hence, while there is legitimate criticism that some enrichment activities are low level and lack educational rigour, it is encouraging to see a widening awareness of the concept of enrichment and a willingness to combine it with a differentiated and negotiated curriculum. In addition to the Queensland model, this move has been assisted by the Western Australian *TAGS* Kits for primary (Educa-tion Department of WA, 1995) and secondary schools (Education Department of WA, 1996); a range of publications by the South Australian, ACT, and Victo-rian Departments/Ministries of Education; and recent Australian educational publications that emphasise the need for differentiation.

Supplementary Programs

In addition to class-based programs, there are other initiatives which influence gifted education and fre-quently involve wider community input. First, there are numerous mentor programs for individual students who exhibit outstanding performance or potential. These exist in most Australian states and territories, sometimes coordinated by the State Department of Education, sometimes by district or school authorities, and occasionally by a parent association. In New South Wales, for example, the mentor program is designed for students 10 years of age and over, and operates in 26 districts across the state.

Second, the rapidly increasing use of information technology is having a decided impact on the delivery of services for gifted and talented education. Not only is this opening opportunities for students who live in more remote areas of the country but it is also providing an unprecedented array of programs for city and rural areas alike. In Victoria the Department of Education and the University of Melbourne combine to provide mentor programs for secondary school stu-dents via e-mail and other interactive technology between face-to-face sessions, while programs such as *As the Crow Flies* and *Horizons Programs* permit students to use the Internet and other technology in high quality enrichment and extension programs. Interactive television also permits teachers to partici-pate in professional development courses despite the separation of distance.

Third, there is enthusiastic support for camps that provide enrichment/extension in such talent areas as creative writing, drama, art, music, maths, science, languages, computers and gymnastics. In most states the camps are organised by individual schools or on a district basis but the Northern Territory Department of Education arranges vacation schools and provides funds for students to attend from all over the Territory.

Fourth, there are numerous national challenges and competitions that are open to students and which promote excellence. The *Tournament of Minds* has achieved a high degree of popularity since 1987. An extension of the American *Odyssey of Minds,* the Tournament is conducted in divisions that allow primary and secondary schools to participate, each school presenting a team that competes against others in problem solving situations. It is well known in every Australian state and territory and involves students from state, Catholic and independent schools. Another venture, the *Future Problem Solving Program*, is a year-long program that promotes critical, creative and futuristic thinking among students at all levels of schooling and challenges them to apply advanced thinking strategies to significant issues. Literacy, mathematics, science, and other reputable competitions are conducted by associations, banks, universities, and major firms.

Fifth, the education of gifted and talented students often incorporates other bodies, associations, and institutions as well as schools. Business houses are involved in some programs, while museums, art schools, zoological gardens, botanical gardens, Aboriginal Centres, industrial complexes, and other specialist groups contribute across Australia. Some universities and colleges have always contributed, both to individual programs and to the professional development of teachers.

Other Organisations

There are two other groups which have a major input into gifted education and provide important services to the community. The first group comprises the State Associations which were established during the late 1970s when the gifted movement was in its infancy. At that time the assistance of parents and community members was crucial because it broadened the base of the agitation for change and pressured governments to respond. Parents and professional educators banded together and established state associations, all of which have continued to have a significant input into the gifted cause. In general the associations operate in a professional manner and supply a valuable service for parents and teachers alike. This is done through advisory services when parents/teachers write or telephone for assistance, through publications that explain giftedness and gifted education, through programs for children (usually at weekends or in vacation time), and through conferences and regular meetings that involve local, national and international speakers. Most publish a journal that is distributed to members on a regular basis, while in some states there is a close working relationship between the Association, the Department or Ministry of Education, schools, universities and/or teacher organisations.

The Australian Association for the Education of the Gifted and Talented (AAEGT) was formed in 1985 and has assisted in developing awareness of giftedness across the country. It organises conferences and workshops, publishes the *Australasian Journal of Gifted Education,* conducts national competitions for students, acts as a lobby group, and liaises with all state associations. It contributes to National Conferences which are hosted in the various states every two years and, in 1989, organised the *8th World Conference on the Gifted and Talented* in Sydney.

The second major group includes academics who work in universities and colleges across Australia. They have been, and continue to be, at the forefront of the movement in many states and at the national level, providing strong support in teaching, writing, and researching about giftedness. In contrast to the early 1980s, it is now possible to specialise in gifted education at undergraduate and graduate levels in a number of universities. Academics also play an important role at the inservice level where they provide professional development programs. The publication, *TALENT-ED*, edited by Bailey at the University of New England, provides very useful material for teachers.

Overall, therefore, one may discern seven major types of provision for gifted and talented students in Australia, ranging from state-wide programs with Departmental imprimatur to in-school enrichment programs that reflect local-school initiatives. While the range of these programs is considerable, it must be stressed that gifted initiatives are not uniform across the states and territories, that state political priorities are usually reflected in the educational policies espoused, and that egalitarian philosophies are strong among some teachers and community groups. Nevertheless, the advances over the past decade have been numerous and reflect an ever-increasing awareness of the needs of the gifted.

New Zealand

The last decade has seen a dramatic shift in the perception of giftedness and in provisions for the gifted in New Zealand. The educational reform process, begun in 1989, has contributed to these changes, and has been more positive than negative. In an earlier national survey into the restructuring process, there was evidence of a growth in programs for the gifted (Keown, McGee & Oliver, 1992), while the growth of 'special' programs across the country was greatest for Maori children and for the gifted.

Studies by Moltzen (1992) and Moltzen and Mitchell (1992) sought to understand how the process of change impacted upon the gifted. The reforms had their origins in the report of the Picot Taskforce (Taskforce to Review Education Administration, 1988), later interpreted in a government white paper, *Tomorrow's Schools* (Lange, 1988), and finally expressed in the Education Act 1989 and its amendment. While none of these documents made reference to the gifted, there were aspects of the reforms that were to affect such students. Devolution of responsibility to local schools carried with it the possibility of change which was translated into positive educational initiatives. For example, while little direction had been previously provided by central or regional bodies, many principals in Moltzen's (1992) study felt an increased responsibility to provide for their gifted students. In this new era, schools are encouraged to design/develop their own programs in consultation with their communities, and they have the financial autonomy and flexibility to appoint staff and allocate resources to this end. It quickly became evident that schools used this new-found freedom to develop programs for their gifted (Moltzen, 1992). Moreover, the enhanced role of parents in school governance resulted in a higher priority for gifted programs than in previous years (Moltzen, 1992; Moltzen & Mitchell, 1992) as it was found that many parent trustees raised concerns about the gifted and frequently expressed dissatisfaction with their school's provisions for this group.

An aim of the reforms was to create an educational environment which encouraged parents to select schools that best suited the needs of their children: it is believed that competition improves the quality of school education, that 'good' schools experience growth, and that 'poor' schools suffer a loss of enrolments, forcing them to address their inadequacies. In this environment, school image is of primary concern, and the gifted become a 'marketable commodity' (Moltzen, 1992). In Moltzen's study (1992), programs for the gifted were seen as a positive 'shop window' for the school, while some principals unabashedly admitted that promoting programs for the gifted was sound 'marketplace practice'.

Ten years after the introduction of the reforms, these trends have continued and many gifted students have gained from the increased attention. Nevertheless, the increased provision has not been universal. Without specific 'national' direction, any initiatives are dependent upon local interest: if a school does not identify the gifted as a priority, little is likely to occur. While some schools are doing well, others are achieving very poorly. Moreover, it is apparent that schools in higher socioeconomic areas have had a monopoly on developments for the gifted because the parents in these communities are more likely to press the cause with the school and its trustees.

There also appears to have been some change in the type of provision for these students. The diversity of programs is definitely greater than in previous years, the result in part of schools seeking to offer something in advance of their 'competitors'. New Zealand educators retain an affinity for more inclusive approaches to giftedness but seem less self conscious about implementing strategies that may draw attention to these students.

The Regular Classroom

Provisions for the gifted beyond the regular classroom have traditionally been very limited in New Zealand, egalitarian attitudes constraining any initiatives to place the gifted child in a setting other than with his/her peers of the same age and grade. Within the regular classroom the gifted are usually offered a program of enrichment, which is frequently criticised for being little more than 'busy work' and offering more of the same (Townsend, 1996). The extent to which their special abilities are identified and nurtured is almost entirely dependent on the knowledge and skill of the regular classroom teacher. However, what could previously be viewed as a 'default' provision, is increasingly being selected as a preferred approach. Many schools, in reviewing their programs, have examined a range of possible approaches and have decided that the regular classroom is the most appro-priate context in which to place their efforts (Moltzen, 1998), a viable option within the New Zealand Curriculum Framework. Frequently this approach is supplemented with other programs but the major provision is based in the regular classroom and delivered by the regular class teacher. Most schools which choose this preferred approach recognise the importance of providing a comprehensive professional development program to assist teachers with the knowledge and skill to undertake the role.

Pullout Programs

Pullout programs continue to be the most popular 'supplementary' provision for the gifted in primary schools, a more conservative approach which finds favour in New Zealand because it is less likely to attract charges of elitism while still offering the gifted something in the way of a dedicated and special program (Moltzen, 1998). It usually sees gifted students withdrawn from their regular classes for a morning or afternoon (sometimes an entire day) for a period of about six weeks, to work together on a specialised area of study. They are usually drawn from classes at different levels, and thus the age range of the group may cover three or four years. As the program focus varies greatly, it is sometimes related directly to curriculum areas, but more often it seeks to allow students of like mind to work on topics outside the regular classroom program. In the country's egalitarian tradition, a broad range of topics is usually provided so that as many children as possible are included in such enrichment programs.

Acceleration

Reid (1991) referred to acceleration as the 'Cinderella' provision for gifted students in New Zealand. When 152 primary school teachers and 140 trainee teachers in their final year of training were surveyed, it was found that both groups held relatively positive views about acceleration (i.e. grade-skipping) but that approximately 50% had reservations about the social and emotional effects associated with the practice. In an earlier study, McDonald (1988) reported that "virtually no children are accelerated in New Zealand schools" (p. 2), despite legislative provision for flexible promotion, and revealed that Maori children (particularly boys) were less likely to be promoted out of the junior classes. Girls, on the other hand, were more likely to be promoted at an earlier age than boys, regardless of their demonstrated level of academic achievement. Although there is some anecdotal evidence that schools are now somewhat more likely to accept acceleration, there is still a belief that it will do more harm than good. Moltzen (1995) suggested that the positive findings from numerous research studies on acceleration were largely unknown.

Curriculum acceleration is more widely practised. The National Curriculum is designed to allow vertical movement, and teachers are encouraged to place children at levels commensurate with their ability. This may occur in the regular primary classroom, if a teacher allows children to work at a range of levels, or by accelerating children to a higher level in specific subjects, notably in reading and language. Some primary schools make provision for gifted children to study a subject at a neighbouring intermediate- or high school. While still uncommon, a few secondary schools make provision for their most able students to study university courses. Curriculum acceleration at the secondary level is most likely to occur in mathematics but the practice also occurs in science and music.

Separate Schools/Classes

The only New Zealand school specifically established to cater for gifted students is the Thomas Kennedy Academy at Raumati South, just north of Wellington. It currently enrols 62 children, ranging in age from four to 13 years, and caters for children with special abilities in a spectrum of areas, not confining itself to exceptional intellectual and academic ability.

In the 10 years since the latest educational reforms, there has been a growth in the number of separate full time classes for gifted students, most evident in intermediate (middle) schools and high schools. This organisational option is easier to implement in an intermediate school, where students spend more time with a 'home class' teacher. In high schools it is more difficult, requiring some to limit the subject choices available to gifted classes to maximise the time that students spend together as a group.

Nawton Primary School in Hamilton is a rare example of a primary school that provides for gifted students in two separate classes—one for five to seven year olds and the other for children eight to 11. Situated in a low socioeconomic area, the school reports that, because teachers were required to meet the diverse range of special needs in their classrooms, the most able students frequently missed out as their needs were perceived as less urgent and less demanding (Bendikson, 1997). The school community debated the issue and agreed to educate the gifted in separate classes. Significantly, the principal believed she would not have considered this option in a higher socio-economic area, where—with fewer students with special needs—the regular classroom teacher is more capable of providing for the gifted.

Cluster Grouping

Bendikson (1997) found that the most common method of assigning students to particular teachers is the pepper pot approach, in which children with common characteristics are spread across a number of classes to ensure that no teacher is assigned a disproportionate number of children of a particular character. In this way, the children who manifest challenging behaviour, have special needs, exhibit learning disabilities or display giftedness are divided on an 'equitable' basis among the classes. While there are occasional attempts to place children with teachers who can meet their particular needs, there is an overriding concern that no one teacher is overburdened or overblessed. Some schools have concluded that this is not the best use of resources and 'cluster' gifted children in a class with an empathetic teacher. Ilam Primary School in Christchurch adopted this approach some years ago and believes it is a most effective way to cater for these students.

New Zealand Correspondence School

The Correspondence School, established in 1922, provides for students who cannot attend school or pre-school, because of remoteness or sickness or because they live overseas. Nevertheless, this School is increasingly providing for gifted students who receive the majority of their education at their local school, while the Correspondence School provides tuition in subjects not locally available. In 1999 the Correspondence School enrolled 239 gifted students in its courses; 198 primary and 41 secondary, with eligibility being limited to the top 5% of the age group in general ability. The verification process was not particularly rigorous, however, and there are a number of present students who do not meet this requirement. Enrolments are highest in mathematics and foreign languages.

Other Groups

The country's first education centre devoted specifically to gifted education was opened in 1995. Named after a distinguished New Zealand scholar, the George Parkyn Centre for Gifted Education was established to meet a significant gap in official education services. By 1999 the centre had developed a wide range of activities, including the delivery of professional development workshops throughout New Zealand for parents of gifted children and for schools. It also supports research projects, produces resources, and lobbies for improved provisions for gifted children.

The New Zealand Association for Gifted Children (NZAGC), formed in 1975, continues to play a very important role in supporting parents, children and professionals. With 400 members and six branches, the NZAGC supports parents and teachers through meetings, seminars and publications, and provides children with camps, courses, holiday programs and opportunities to mix socially. The National Council of NZAGC organises conferences, provides resource material/library services, raises sponsorship, and advocates and lobbies on behalf of gifted children. NZAGC publishes *Tall Poppies*, a magazine aimed primarily at parents and teachers, and *APEX: The New Zealand Journal of Gifted Education,* a peer-reviewed academic journal designed to provide a forum for the dissemination of research.

The institutions involved in teacher education in New Zealand generally devote a minimal amount of time to the needs of the gifted (Taylor, 1995). Taylor's study found that, where giftedness was included, it was frequently an optional course or a small module within a compulsory course on special education. It would not appear that the time has increased since 1995 given the fact that there has been a significant 'reduction' in the period of time now required to complete a teaching degree. On the other hand, Christchurch College of Education will offer a Masters level course in the education of gifted children from 2000, while Massey University and the University of Waikato continue to be the tertiary sector leaders in this field. Both universities offer undergraduate and graduate courses in the education of the gifted. The Flinders University of South Australia's *Certificate in Gifted Education* is offered in association with the University of Waikato, is co-taught by staff from both institutions and is the only tertiary qualification in gifted education available in New Zealand. Riley, the coordinator of gifted courses at Massey University, and Moltzen at the University of Waikato both report a recent growth in course enrolments, particularly among practising teachers at graduate level.

The Education Review Office (ERO) is the government department that reports on the quality of education in all New Zealand schools and early childhood centres. In fulfilling this function, its officers inspect and evaluate the quality of teaching and student learning and they consistently highlight issues associated with the education of gifted students (Moltzen, 1999). In 1998 the office produced a handbook entitled *Working with students with special abilities* (Education Review Office, 1998) and, while some of the perspectives attracted criticism, the publication reflected the agency's commitment to improving the quality of education for these students (Moltzen, 1999). The contribution ERO has made in raising the awareness of teachers and principals to the needs of the gifted has been significant.

Research

Australia

Research into giftedness in Australia falls into three distinct periods. Up to 1984, much of the research writing was descriptive in character, often reflecting a curriculum concern or reiterating equally descriptive overseas publications (Braggett, 1986). Giftedness was seen as a relatively static concept and identification was a major issue for academic discussion. In the second period from 1985 to the beginning of the 1990s, research explored the multidimensional quality of giftedness and began to highlight the need to develop talent through well delineated programs. Attitudes to giftedness were canvassed, surveys were conducted (Braggett, 1985), 'disadvantaged' groups were tar-

geted, and research funds were related to *Projects of National Significance*. Graduate programs in gifted education became increasingly available at some Australian universities and graduate research began to develop. The third stage, embracing the 1990s and spilling into the new millenium, has witnessed the growth of qualitative and quantitative research, characterised by academic rigour and often involving ongoing longitudinal projects. While some of this has been university-based, much has been in concert with Ministries of Education, school districts, and educational institutions. Graduate Schools of Education have seen a marked increase in the number of graduate students who wish to research the area of giftedness and talent.

A number of themes have assumed increasing importance. Aspects of school organisation have included student acceleration in mixed ability classes and the effects of acceleration on vocational and social outcomes; special class provision and special schools (O'Brien & Vialle, 1998; Geake, 1999; Gross, 1999; Hoekman, 1999; Wood, 1999); the effectiveness of school mentoring programs; vertical timetabling in schools; ability grouping (Geake, 1999); and the ability of the middle school to provide for the needs of gifted students (Braggett, 1997; Braggett, Day & Morris, 1999). Creativity in its various manifestations has been researched by McCann (1999) and Botticchio (Vialle, 1999) while thinking skills, metacognition and multiple intelligences have attracted continuing attention (McGrath, 1998; Chan, 1999; Jewell, 1999a; Vialle, 1999). Geake & O'Boyle (1999) have extended these studies into the brain functioning and neural organisation of highly gifted mathematicians while musical ability has also been researched at different centres (Geake, 1999; Hoekman, 1999). Gender-related issues have been explored in depth (Kerr & Kupius, 1998; Landvogt, Leder & Forgasz, 1998; Lysaght & Vialle, 1998; Flood, 1999) while the attitudes and influence of parents on gifted children continue to attract attention (Knight & Bailey, 1997; Taplin & White, 1998). The socialisation of gifted young children has been studied by Geake (1999) and Porter (1999) while their thinking strategies have been explored by Braggett, Kay & Lowrie (1998). Related research themes include teacher attitudes to giftedness (Pohl, 1998; Smith & Chan, 1998), the education of Indigenous students (Harslett, 1998), gifted disabled students, intervention programs, curriculum innovations, and underachieving students.

While cognitive aspects of development continue to attract the attention of researchers, affective outcomes form an increasing focus where the effects of school organisation, curriculum provision, and teacher approach are viewed in relation to self-confidence and self esteem (Gross, 1999; Marsh & Craven, 1998; Smee, 1999), to motivation (Chan, 1999; Flood, 1999; Gross, 1999; Hoekman, 1999; Street, 1999), and to learning styles (Hall, 1999). Leadership forms another emerging theme (Jewell, 1999b; Webster, 1999). Much of this research is within the broader parameters of socio-affective development of gifted students, a theme increasingly pursued by Gross (1999) at the Gerric Centre at the University of New South Wales. Other universities actively involved in ongoing research include Wollongong University, Charles Sturt University, the Gifted Development and Education Unit at the University of Melbourne, Flinders University, and the University of New England. Additional research is pursued in other universities, in State Departments/Ministries and in individual schools.

New Zealand

There has been a steady increase in New Zealand-based research in the area of giftedness in recent years, the majority undertaken by the growing number of graduate students, but led by a small group of academics. The publication of *Gifted and Talented: New Zealand Perspectives* (McAlpine & Moltzen, 1996), the first New Zealand text in the field, brought together the work of most of these researchers. One of the more significant investigations reported in this text was that of Bevan-Brown (1996) who focused on special abilities from a Maori perspective, the first comprehensive study to do so. Other researchers include Holton (talented mathematical students); McAlpine (identification of gifted students, and creativity); Moltzen (the life stories of gifted adults); Rawlinson (self concept, self efficacy and enrichment); Reid (program evaluation for gifted students); Riley (computers with gifted students); and Townsend (teachers' perceptions of acceleration and enrichment).

In 1987 Freeman established the journal *APEX* for the purpose of publishing articles about gifted children and their education. In 1993 the New Zealand Associations of Gifted Children purchased the journal and in 1997 it became the peer-reviewed *APEX: The New Zealand Journal of Gifted Education*, providing a forum for the dissemination of articles dealing with practice, policies and research in gifted education.

Since its first publication, the *Scale for Rating Behavioral Characteristics of Superior Students* (SRBCSS) (Renzulli & Hartman, 1971) has been employed by many New Zealand teachers despite shortcomings in the New Zealand context. Accordingly, a modified instrument, the *Teacher Observation Scales for Identifying Children with Special Abilities*, was developed, a New Zealand equivalent to the original scale (McAlpine & Reid, 1996). These scales are the outcome of a comprehensive program of research and trialling, and have been well received by teachers.

At the same time, there has been a steady increase in the number of 'gifted' conferences and seminars, often involving high profile speakers from overseas, but simultaneously providing a forum for local researchers to share their findings.

Future Issues

It is now 25 years since the so-called gifted movement developed in Australia and New Zealand, leading to an increased awareness of the needs of gifted students and a demand for schools to respond with more appropriate provisions. During that time, there have been marked advances as curriculum developers have sought to introduce more flexible approaches and to depart from grade-related content. It is now more widely accepted that children should move at a pace commensurate with their abilities, be enriched in their daily education, be extended when required, and—in less usual circumstances—be accelerated by year or content. While these trends are obvious in both countries, they are not uniformly observed and there are many conservative elements which continue to advocate egalitarian policies.

There are three pressing issues that need to be addressed if sustained progress is to be made. First, a prolonged public education campaign is required to convince teachers, parents and legislators that the manifestation of giftedness is usually dependent on the home, the school and the community, and that parents and teachers have a significant role to play in the development of talent over time. There is still an acceptance by many that giftedness/talent is fixed by inheritance and that it will materialise in spite of the environment: such people do not see the necessity for high quality programs and appropriate provision. They do not realise the importance of motivation, of self-esteem, of a sustaining mentor, and of sympathetic teachers who nurture giftedness, differentiate the curriculum, and develop children's skills and strategies to the highest level. If this message could be accepted by the community, it would provoke a revolution in education.

Second, when gifted education is envisaged as an appendage to mainstream provision, it is placed in a precarious position when governments change, when budgets are constricted, or when rationalisation is implemented. The education of gifted children must be seen within a *total school approach* in which all children's abilities are catered for and where individual differences are respected. The education of gifted and talented students is a mainstream concern, a part of everyday school life. Moreover, there is no one panacea for all gifted students, just as there is no one approach to students with learning difficulties. The education of the gifted requires the entire staff to be involved, the curriculum to be scrutinised and differentiated when required, and the welfare of all students to be paramount. There has been so much debate on organisational matters such as streaming, acceleration and extension that educators have sometimes forgotten the central concern of the school—appropriate education for all students.

Third, the situation in Australia and New Zealand demands that considerable attention be focused on regular classroom teachers and their ability to cope with an extended range of abilities in the classroom. While it might be desirable to create special schools and classes, to involve students in pullout programs, and have access to specialist teachers and resources, the reality is different. Most schools will continue to rely on the efforts of dedicated classroom teachers who will do the best they can in the limited hours that are available and with the limited resources that exist. It is encouraging that so much has been achieved over the past 25 years and that teachers are increasingly aware of the need to change. They need to be further supported and encouraged through professional development programs that cater for their needs.

In summary, therefore, Australia and New Zealand have witnessed positive changes over the last quarter of the century and the cause of gifted students has been significantly advanced. As the two countries enter the 21st century, they can look forward with a degree of optimism to an educational future that is challenging, yet most promising.

References

ACT Draft Policy (1998). *School policy: Gifted and talented students.* Canberra: ACT Department of Education and Training and Children's, Youth and Family Services Bureau.

Bendikson, L (1997). *The placement rationale: How large schools organise classes.* Master of Education thesis, University of Waikato, New Zealand.

Bevan-Brown, J. (1996). Special abilities: a Maori perspective. In: D. McAlpine & R. Moltzen (Eds.), *Gifted and talented: New Zealand perspectives* (pp. 91–109). Palmerston North: Educational Research and Development Centre; Massey University, New Zealand.

Board of Studies, NSW (1991). *Guidelines of accelerated progression.* Sydney: Board of Studies, NSW.

Boston, J. (1991). The theoretical underpinnings of public sector restructuring in New Zealand. In: J. Boston, J. Martin, J. Pallot & P. Walsh (Eds.), *Reshaping the state: New Zealand's bureaucratic revolution.* Auckland: Oxford University Press.

Bright Futures (1995). *A policy statement to support gifted students* [Victoria]. Melbourne: Directorate of School Education.

Bradburn, K. (1999). *Selective Schools Unit*, NSW Department of Education and Training. Personal communication, March 1999.

Braggett, E. J. (1997). *The middle years of schooling: An Australian perspective.* Melbourne: Hawker Brownlow Education.

Braggett, E. J. (1986). *Talented, gifted, creative: Australian writings.* Canberra: Commonwealth Schools Commission.

Braggett, E. J. (1985). *Education of gifted and talented children: Australian provision.* Canberra: Commonwealth Schools Commission.

Braggett, E. J., Day, A. & Morris, G. (1999). *Reforming the middle years of schooling.* Melbourne: Hawker Brownlow Education.

Braggett, E. J., Kay, R. & Lowrie, T. (1998). *Thinking skills and their development in young children.* Report to the Australian Research Council (ARC), 1998.

Chan, L. K. S. (1999). Metacognition and motivational orientations of intellectually gifted students: Metacognition and motivation. *Australasian Journal of Gifted Education,* **8** (1), 15–22.

Day, A. (1999). NT Board of Studies, Exceptional Children, NT Department of Education. Personal communication, August 1999.

Education Department of WA (1996). *Secondary teaching TAGS.* Belmont, WA: Supply West.

Education Department of WA (1995). *Teaching TAGS (Primary).* Belmont WA: Supply West.

Education Queensland (1999). *A model of curriculum provision for gifted education and talent identification.* Brisbane: Education Queensland.

Education Review Office (1998). *Working with students with special abilities.* Education Evaluation Reports, New Zealand.

Fagg, S. (1999). Gifted Education, Tasmanian Education Department. Personal communication, March 1999.

Flood, A. (1999). The evidence for gender differences in academic giftedness: A study of top 1000 TER achievers in the NSW Higher School Certificate. *Australasian Journal of Gifted Education,* **8** (1), 44–56.

Gardner, H. (1983). *Frames of mind.* London: Fontana Press.

Gardner, H. (1993). *Multiple intelligences.* New York: Basic Books.

GCTF (1983). *Gifted and talented children: A teacher's guide.* Melbourne: Gifted Children Task Force, Education Department, Victoria.

Geake, J. (1999). Gifted Education Unit, University of Melbourne, Victoria. Personal communication, August 1999.

Geake, J. & O'Boyle, M. (1999). University of Melbourne. Personal communication, August 1999.

Gross, M. U. M. (1999). Gerric Centre, University of New South Wales. Personal communication, August 1999.

Gross, M. U. M. (1998). Fishing for the facts: A response to Marsh and Craven (1998). *Australasian Journal of Gifted Education,* **7** (1), 6–15.

Hall, M. (1999). *Research into the learning styles of gifted adolescents,* Adelaide. Personal communication, August 1999.

Harslett, M. (1998). Education Department of Western Australia. Personal communication, July 1997.

Hewett, J. (1999). Gifted and Talented Education, Education Queensland. Personal communication, June, 1999.

Hoekman, K. (1999). Gerric Centre, University of New South Wales. Personal communication, August 1999.

Jewell, P. (1999a). Flinders University. Personal communication, August 1999.

Jewell, P (1999b). Leaders and followers: A response to Webster. *Australasian Journal of Gifted Education,* **8** (1), 33–38.

Kerr, B. & Kupius, S. R. (1998). Brynhilds fire: Talent, courage and betrayal in the lives of at-risk girls. *Australasian Journal of Gifted Education,* **7** (2), 5–8.

Keown, P., McGee, C. & Oliver, D. (1992). National survey of secondary schools 1. *Report No. 5. Monitoring today's schools research project.* Hamilton: University of Waikato.

Knight, B. A. & Bailey, S. (Eds.). (1997). *Parents as lifelong partners.* Melbourne: Hawker Brownlow Education.

Landvogt, J. E., Leder, G. C. & Forgasz, H. J. (1998). Sugar, spice and puppy dog tails: gendered perceptions of talent and high achievement. *Australasian Journal of Gifted Education, 7* (2), 9–20.

Lange, D. (1988). *Tomorrow's schools: The reform of education administration in New Zealand.* Wellington: New Zealand Government Printer.

Lawton, S. B. (1992). Why restructure? An international survey of the roots of reform. *Journal of Education Policy, 7* (2), 139–154.

Lazear, D. (1994). *Seven ways of knowing.* Melbourne: Hawker Brownlow Education.

Lysaght, P. & Vialle, W. (1998). Reflections on giftedness: A preliminary survey of gifted girls. *Australasian Journal of Gifted Education, 7* (2), 21–27.

Marland. S. P. (1972). *Education of the gifted and talented.* Vol. 1. *Report of the Congress of the United States by the US Commissioner of Education.* Washington DC.: Government Printing Office.

Marsh, H. W. & Craven, R. G. (1998). The big fish little pond effect, optical illusions, and misinterpretations: a response to Gross. *Australasian Journal of Gifted Education, 7* (1), 16–28.

McAlpine, D. (1991). Issues in the education of the gifted and talented. In: *Education for the gifted and talented child.* Proceedings of the 1991 NZAGC teachers' conference (pp. 112–119). Palmerston North, NZ.

McAlpine, D. & Moltzen, R. (Eds.). (1996). *Gifted and talented: New Zealand perspectives.* Palmerston North: Educational Research and Development Centre: Massey University, New Zealand.

McAlpine, D. & Reid, N. (1996). *Teacher observation scales for children with special abilities.* Wellington: New Zealand Council for Educational Research.

McCann, M. (1999). Flinders University. Personal communication, August 1999.

McDonald, G. (1988). Promotion, retention and acceleration: How a school produces inequality in the face of good intentions. *Ser, 2* Item 1.

McGrath, C. (1998). *An investigation of a new approach to teaching and learning designed to focus teachers and students on their thinking.* Ph.D. Thesis, University of South Australia.

Minchin, M. (1999). Curriculum Division, Gifted and Talented, SA Department of Education. Personal communication, March 1999.

Moltzen, R. (1992). *The impact of reforms in education of provisions for gifted children.* Master of Education Thesis, University of Waikato, New Zealand.

Moltzen, R. (1995). Students with special abilities. In: D. Fraser, R. Moltzen & K. Ryba (Eds.), *Learners with special needs in Aotearoa New Zealand* (pp. 267–306). Palmerston North: The Dunmore Press.

Moltzen, R. (1996). Historical perspectives. In: D. McAlpine & R. Moltzen (Eds.), *Gifted and talented: New Zealand perspectives* (pp. 1–21). Palmerston North: Educational Research and Development Centre: Massey University, New Zealand.

Moltzen, R. (1998). Maximising the potential of the gifted child in the regular classroom: A professional development issue. *Gifted Education International, 13* (1), 36–45.

Moltzen, R. (1999). Young, gifted and living in New Zealand. In: *Inside out: Understanding the needs of the gifted:* Proceedings from the Gifted Conference. Christchurch, New Zealand, April 16, 17.

Moltzen, R. & Mitchell, D. (1992). *Children with special needs. Report No. 6. Monitoring today's schools research project.* Hamilton: University of Waikato.

Morris, G. (1999). Bright Futures, Education Victoria. Personal communication. June, 1999.

NT Policy (1992). *Revised policy for the education of gifted and talented students in Northern Territory schools.* Darwin: The Northern Territory Board of Studies.

NZ Department of Education (1972). *Children with special abilities: Suggestions for teaching gifted children in primary schools.* Wellington: New Zealand Government Printer.

NZ Ministry of Education (1991). *The national curriculum of New Zealand: A discussion document.* Wellington: New Zealand Ministry of Education.

NZ National Educational Guidelines (1990). *Supplement to the Education Gazette (New Zealand).* Feb. 1.

NSW Government Strategy (1991). *NSW government strategy for the education of gifted and talented students.* Sydney: New South Wales Government.

O'Brien, P. & Vialle, W. (1998). Students' and teachers' perceptions of selective schooling. *Australasian Journal of Gifted Education, 7* (1), 50–55.

Parkyn, G. W. (1976). The identification and evaluation of gifted children. In: J. Gibson & P. Chennells (Eds.), *Gifted children: Looking to their future* (pp. 35–36). London: Latimer.

Pears, G. (1999). Gifted Education, Education Department of Western Australia. Personal communication, March 1999.

Pohl, M. L. (1998). *Teachers' attitudes towards the education of the gifted.* Master of Gifted Education Thesis, Flinders University.

Porter, L. (1999). *Young gifted children.* Sydney: Allyn & Unwin.

Queensland Department of Education (1993). *The education of gifted students in Queensland schools* (State Policy Statement). Brisbane: Studies Directorate, Education Queensland.

Reid, N. (1991). The Cinderella provision: Research on accelerated learning. *Gifted Children, 16,* 96–103.

Renzulli, J. S. (1977). *The enrichment triad model: A guide for developing defensible programs for the gifted and talented.* Mansfield Center, CN: Creative Learning Press.

Renzulli, J. S. & Hartman, R. K. (1971). Scale for rating behavioral characteristics of superior students. *Exceptional Children, 38* (3), 243–248.

Reynen, K. (1999). Bright Futures, Education Victoria. Personal communication, March 1999.

SA State Policy (1995). *State policy for the education of gifted children and students.* Adelaide: SA Department of Education.

Senate Select Committee (1988). *The report of the Senate Select Committee on the education of gifted and talented children* (The Parliament of the Commonwealth of Australia). Canberra: Australian Government Publishing Service.

Smee, R. (1999). Big fish need to occasionally swim with other big fish. *Australasian Journal of Gifted Education*, **8** (1), 39–43.

Smith, S. R. & Chan, L. K. S. (1998). The attitudes of catholic primary school teachers towards educational provisions for gifted and talented students. *Australasian Journal of Gifted Education*, **7** (1), 29–41.

Stewart, J. (1999). Bright Futures, Education Victoria. Personal communication, March 1999.

Street, P. (1999). *High achievements of students in the middle school (years 5–9): The relationship to curriculum, teaching strategies and school provision for affective needs.* Ph.D. Thesis, Charles Sturt University, NSW.

Taplin, M. & White, M. (1998). Parents' and teachers' perceptions of selective schooling. *Australasian Journal of Gifted Education,* **7**(1), 42–49.

Taskforce to Review Education Administration (1988). *Administering for excellence.* Wellington: Government Printer.

Tasmania (1996). *Education for students who are gifted* (State Policy). Hobart: Tasmanian Education Department.

Taylor, S. (1995). *Preservice education in teaching children with special abilities at the primary school level.* Master of Education Thesis, Massey University, New Zealand.

Townsend, M. A. R. (1996). Enrichment and acceleration: lateral and vertical perspectives in provisions for gifted and talented. In: D. McAlpine & R. Moltzen (Eds.), *Gifted and Talented: New Zealand perspectives* (pp. 361–375). Educational Research and Development Centre: Massey University, New Zealand.

Townsend, M. A. R. & Patrick, H. (1993). Academic and psychosocial apprehensions of teachers and teacher trainees toward the educational acceleration of gifted children. *New Zealand Journal of Educational Studies*, **28**, 29–41.

Vialle, W. (1999). University of Wollongong. Personal communication, August 1999.

WA Policy (1981). *Policy No.31. The education of gifted and talented students. Policy from the Director-General's Office.* Perth: Education Department of Western Australia.

Webster, P. (1999). Developing leadership talent for our global civilization. *Australasian Journal of Gifted Education*, **8** (1), 23–32.

Were, E. (1997). The placement rationale: Ena Were talks to Linda Bendikson. *Tall Poppies*, **22** (2), 16–17.

Wood, D. (1999). *Factors involved in the establishment and development of a special primary school class for academically gifted students: A case study.* M.Ed (Hons) Thesis, Charles Sturt University, NSW.

The Status of Gifted Child Education in Africa

Cedric A. Taylor[1] and Shirley J. Kokot[2]

[1]*University of Port Elizabeth, South Africa*
[2]*University of South Africa in Pretoria, South Africa*

Introduction

Educational developments in Africa cannot be understood without a knowledge of traditional African culture and of political developments in sub-Saharan Africa during and after colonial rule. Therefore a brief historical background is given of political developments in that region. A number of issues which determine educational planning and priorities and also have implications for decisions regarding gifted education emanate from that complex set of historical, political and cultural factors. Those issues concern the historical background of unequal and segregated education, African culture, different and elitist conceptions of gifted education, different interpretations of equal educational rights, the goal of universal primary education, the priority of majority needs, economic conditions, and the marginalization of education. A brief historical overview is given of gifted education in sub-Saharan Africa that illustrates the inequalities inherited from a combination of First World and Third World education systems on the same continent. The same pattern is discernible in the search for an identification procedure that would apply within diverse cultural, ethnic and national groups. Future development of gifted education in African countries is seen as dependent on a restructuring of gifted education in the context of national developmental needs. Some aspects that need to be researched in this respect are outlined.

A Historical Perspective

Brief Historical Background of Political Developments in Africa

The colonial past of Africa and events subsequent to the attainment of independence by sub-Saharan African countries need to be taken into account to understand political, social and economic issues that may directly influence policy decisions regarding formal provision for gifted children in the education system. A brief overview is given of the situation immediately preceding and after the granting of independence to African countries by colonial powers.

During the pre-independence period most colonial powers unscrupulously exploited the human and natural resources of sub-Saharan African countries for their own purposes. The political, economic, social and educational development of these countries and their peoples were considered of lesser or no concern. In some cases a minority of African elites were educated in Western education systems and allowed limited participation in government. Missionary schools provided basic training in reading and writing to a small percentage of the masses.

In the 1960s the winds of change began to sweep over the African continent, heralding the end of colonial rule and the dawn of uhuru ('freedom'). In a relatively short period of time, however, independence led to authoritarian regimes of one kind or another. In most cases, the demise of constitutional democracy began with a movement to one-party and ultimately one-man rule. This was due in some countries to the electoral supremacy of the ruling party and the high degree of elite cohesiveness before independence. In others, one-party regimes were established with extensive coercion and personalization of power (Diamond, 1988). A period of prolonged instability followed, characterized by successive power struggles, coups and dictatorships which in many cases led to civil war, and the destruction of the economy and poverty. An important contributing factor to this state of affairs may have been the fact that at independence most new African states were left in conditions of more or less acute economic dependence and not prepared politically and administratively for independence by the colonial powers. This may have led to a heightened sense of vulnerability felt by African leaders for their young countries which served to justify a concentration of power as a means of asserting control (Diamond, 1988).

In recent times some African countries have started to rebuild their economies and a move has become apparent towards a more democratic form of government. This observation is supported by the following events:

- In 1981 the African Charter on Human and Peoples' Rights was adopted in Nairobi, Kenya by the Organization of African Unity (Shiman, 1988).
- Two sub-Saharan African states, Senegal and Ivory Coast, participated in the Second Strasbourg Conference on Parliamentary democracy in 1987 (Council of Europe, 1987).
- Botswana continues to be one of the best examples of multi-party democracy in Africa. Moreover, in a decade and half, Botswana moved from being one of the poorest countries in Africa to one of the richest, with per capita GNP increasing from $100 to over $900 (Holm, 1988, p. 197). Heavy and well-distributed investments were made, amongst others, in education (Diamond, 1988).
- Namibia has established a democracy and multi-party elections have taken place in Zambia and more recently in Nigeria; a democracy persisted for a period of time in Zimbabwe.
- A Pan-African Conference on Democracy, organized by the Minister of State of Senegal in Dakar in 1992, was attended by 47 states.
- South Africa held its first democratic election in 1994.

Countries in Africa are entering a new phase of development, learning what democracy means in practice, for government and society. Democracy, however, means different things to different people. The form of democracy that will develop in the African context and its implications for education remains to be seen.

Events in South Africa followed a different course. Colonies formerly under British rule and granted self-government in 1905, formed the Union of South Africa in 1910 as an independent country. A multi-party democratic form of government was established with qualified franchise for coloureds, Indians and blacks that in effect limited representation in parliament to whites. The Nationalist party which came into power in 1948 progressively consolidated social, residential, cultural, economic and political apartheid constitutionally over the next four decades. While separate Houses of Parliament were created for coloureds and Indians in 1984, the blacks who form the majority of the population had neither vote nor representation in Parliament. The speech by President F. W. de Klerk on February 2, 1990, however, heralded the beginning of the end of apartheid. On June 17, 1991, the legal foundation of the apartheid system was eliminated when Parliament scrapped the law classifying South Africans by race from birth. A new constitution has been drawn up that is based on human rights and democratic principles.

Issues Impacting on the Provision of Education for the Gifted

Certain issues that emanate from the historical and cultural context of a country may directly influence policy decisions regarding gifted education. Issues that are relevant in the African context are discussed below.

Pre- and Post-Apartheid Educational History in Southern Africa

Little is known about traditional education in pre-colonial southern Africa. Ceremonial forms may still be seen in initiation (amakweta) ceremonies, but the social meaning has often changed. For example, such ceremonies had increasingly sought to make social distinctions between the 'red' (traditional) and 'school' (Christian modernizing) people during the nineteenth century. While traditionalists looked to the practices of the rural past for the methods of shaping educational meaning in a 'tribal' context, there was a gradual increase in the number of 'school' people attending a network of Christian mission schools throughout the region. These schools were seen as the gateway to 'Western civilization' and the formal labor market (Middelton, 1997, p. 5). Apart from 'flagship' schools that were run by missionary institutions in certain towns and cities, a vast network of small rural schools was established by the mid-twentieth century. Among these were a range of educational initiatives by African Independent Churches, controlled by black Africans. Even before the advent of an apartheid regime under the National party in 1948, a colour bar existed that protected white workers from black competition. Yet for the small number of blacks—an emergent elite—who managed to survive to high school in the missionary run 'flagship' schools, the quality of the education received was on a par with the education of the Europeans. It was from this group that the African nationalist leadership was drawn (Middelton, 1997).

In 1948 the Nationalist Party came into power with fundamental implications for the sphere of education: time-honoured segregationist policies were honed into the racist dogma of apartheid (Middelton, 1997). The notorious Eiselen Report on Native Education (1951) set the tone by arguing that each cultural group should have its 'own education' suitable to its 'own needs' and focused on the development of its 'own people in their own areas'. Subsequently, all education other than that intended for white children was removed from the control of education departments in the various provinces and placed in the hands of state departments concerned with the affairs of the various racial groups as defined by apartheid. The missionaries were forced to hand their schools over to the state.

Gradually, education was increasingly fragmented, first into the Bantu (African), Coloured and Indian categories; then, the control of African education was divided between no less than ten 'homeland' administrations and the Department of Bantu Education which served the African population outside of the homelands.

While these developments were taking place in South Africa, the neighbouring anglophone states of southern and central Africa were moving toward independence an establishing themselves as part of the African family of nations in the era of Uhuru (English: freedom). In the first rush of independence, there was great emphasis on education for development, and many new schools and universities were opened in all areas (Middelton, 1997). The major difference between African education in these areas and in South Africa is that in the former there was an unbroken tradition of church-state cooperation, which enabled the quality and the quantity of education to develop apace despite declining resources (Middelton, 1997). The only exception was Rhodesia (now Zimbabwe), where white privilege played a significant role in the shaping of the politics of education.

The 1980s are considered as the era of reformism in South African education and in 1981 the report of the (De Lange) Committee of Investigation into Education, recommended "equal opportunities for education, including equal standards in education, for every inhabitant, irrespective of race, colour, creed or sex." Yet the committee stopped short of recommending a non-racial system. Many of the reforms recommended by this report were implemented during the 1980s and they also formed the core of the Department of National Education's Educational Renewal Strategy, published in 1992, which was to be the blueprint for the National party's educational policy for the post-apartheid era (Middelton, 1997).

With the advent of the new, black, government in 1994, education has been high on the list of priority matters to be rapidly addressed in South Africa's emerging democracy. The issues surrounding the drive towards educational reform has been a dominant and intense subject of debate even before the current political transition. The debate, while focusing on the needs of the historically disadvantaged population groups, strives for a solution that should, according to Hartshorn (1992), provide all children with relevant and equal education of an acceptable standard. The merging of segregated Third World and First World schools into a unitary system of education has not been without many problems and accompanying tension. A major problem has been a lack of finance to redress past inequalities without lowering the standard of education in previously advantaged schools. Government introduced 'outcomes-based education' (OBE) in an attempt to transform the system, as well as the policy of inclusion in order to answer to the human rights issues of equality for all learners. Their answer to the lack of finances has been to increase the learner-teacher ratio in all classrooms to 35–1. Teachers in

schools with previously low learner-teacher ratios have been forced to either relocate to other schools or have lost their posts. In many cases, teachers are unwilling to move to rural areas where school buildings are inadequate in terms of facilities and resources and the staffing of schools remains a problem. Many classes in rural areas may number upward of 60 learners to a single teacher, while the previously white schools are struggling to accommodate as many as 40 children in classrooms designed for 25. Many schools in poorer provinces, such as the Northwest Province lack textbooks and even leadership. Poor matriculation results at the end of 1998 have been blamed on the fact that hundreds of schools in this province lack a principal and over 1000 schools lack a deputy principal (SABC-TV news broadcast, April 10, 1999).

In the light of this, making special provision for a relatively small group of gifted pupils is seen as a waste of resources and those built up over years in this respect have and are being abandoned in order to make provision for needs considered as more pressing. Thus, gifted education is rejected by many because it is considered to be a part of the education system of an oppressive regime. Others consider it to be an expensive luxury. However, it is also important to understand the culture of black Africans in order to fully understand issues regarding gifted education.

The Culture of Black Africans

In the aftermath of independence when African countries were struggling to escape from their colonial past and re-establish a traditional African way of life, leading thinkers such as Kwame Nkrumah, Julius Nyerere, Leopold Senghor, Koli Busia and Kenneth Kaunda responded with a new philosophy: African socialism. African socialism, according to du Plessis (1992, p. 9), professes to make sense of the traditional (African) way of life in a modern world. Its perception of society is said to be rooted in the idea of ujamaa (English: familyhood, togetherness) and both its foundation and objective is the extended family. Within this context the state is considered to be but an extended family requiring an involved personal loyalty from its citizens. A multi-party system is seen as inherently divisive. Moreover, ujamaa represents a call for communal co-responsibility towards the upliftment of those in society who, in some or other respect, have remained behind. African society's values are directed towards the maintenance of cohesiveness and solidarity, and one of the strongest social control agencies is the extended family, imbued with the principle of collective responsibility. In this context children who have fallen behind or have been disadvantaged will receive priority educational treatment before those who are managing well, which in many cases may be perceived to be the gifted.

African culture values and nurtures the attitude and behavior of identifying with others, understanding and responding to another person's needs and sharing emotions. Archbishop Desmond Tutu (1991) has referred to ". . . our sense of ubuntu—our humaneness, caring, hospitality, our sense of connectedness, our sense that my humanity is bound up in your humanity." Traditionally, the African's concept of who he/she is can be summed up in the words: "I am, because we are, and because we are, therefore I am" (Mbiti, 1969, pp. 108–109; Ray, 1976, p. 32).

This value is expressed in African music. Traditional African musical performances are occasions not for passive listening but for participating and doing. Each person contributes only one note, a small part of the whole sound. For a white person from a Western culture, this may appear very inefficient because one person could for instance produce the whole sound with one hand on a keyboard synthesizer. That, however, is irrelevant in this case. The music is a social thing, aimed at expressing cooperation (Tracey, 1990, pp. 36–37).

From the above, it may be hypothesized that traditional African culture nurtures the affective development of children. Gifted programs that under-emphasize or exclude the affective and social dimensions of child development may be seen as contrary to traditional culture and be rejected.

Different Conceptions of Giftedness

All cultures include individuals who excel and who have special abilities (O'Tuel, Swanson & Elam, 1997). Forbes-Harper (1997, p. 483) states that "recent research has revealed that any concept of giftedness is a product of a society at a particular time." Thus, giftedness would appear to have meaning relative to a given cultural context and each culture should define giftedness in its own image, in terms of the abilities that the members of that culture value at that time. Because of this, throughout history the meaning of giftedness has shifted according to the interests and preconceptions of people using the term. However, most of the definitions that are commonly accepted around the world today have arisen from the interests of Westerners and may not reflect the culture of a certain people. Some definitions refer to certain areas in which high performance needs to be demonstrated. If areas that are considered to be of major importance in a specific culture are excluded such conceptions of giftedness may not be acceptable. Modern technological societies greatly value logical mathematical intelligence and certain forms of linguistic competence. On the other hand, African cultural tradition ascribes greater weight to social than technological facts of intelligence, views child-rearing goals primarily in terms of social skills and regards interactions with people as inherently more important than objects, thus fostering a more socially orientated set of cognitive skills. Defining and identifying giftedness in other cultures is therefore a "cultural and academic

minefield" (Forbes-Harper, 1997, p. 486). It is also feasible that in the modern information age, causing so much interaction with other cultures, the inhabitants of our 'global village' are sharing more common interests than in the past. Thus many African cultures are composed of individuals clinging to traditional values as well as those who value so-called 'Western' ideals and share many 'Western' interests. An African definition of giftedness would thus have to accommodate both groups.

Benedict (in Khatena, 1992, p. 6) reports that "culture shapes man although more slowly man shapes culture as well." In Africa, there is a dearth of research concerning gifted black youths and in the little there is, it is noticeable that the authors attempt to 'fit' black gifted learners to views of giftedness foreign to African culture (for example, Mwamwenda, 1990). It is possible that Africans are shaping their culture towards Western patterns but it would be tragic if they lose knowledge of their original cultural identity in the process. For this reason, it is important to understand how giftedness may have been viewed in traditional African cultures and whether this view is changing.

African Views of Giftedness

Considering views of giftedness in African countries, one can see the influence and impact of cultural and ethnic motives (Yossufu, 1986; Lumadi, 1998). Many believe strongly in maintaining their traditional past and as such encourage the fundamental and traditional arts of their various cultures such as wood carving, basket weaving, pottery, music, dance and many others that are held in high esteem.

Anim (1992) provides valuable insight into traditional African conceptions and manifestations of giftedness. He describes the custom whereby a young child addresses a visiting chief in drum language while another sings his praises in terms of traditional poems and then, to the rhythm of his companion's drumming, executes a beautiful and very intricate dance. This is repeated for other chiefs attending a festival. Each praise is sung spontaneously with no rehearsal and no prior knowledge except the name of a chief and where he came from. Anim points out that such a performance requires creativity and quick thinking. Another manifestation of giftedness is found in the role of the linguist who is the traditional mouthpiece of the Akan chief (Anim, 1992). As the traditional Akan chief is not allowed to talk directly with his people, the linguist becomes the intermediary. A linguist should have a great sense of humour, be a master of court language, be able to think fast and take quick rational decisions. In short, he should be an accomplished diplomat. A chief's drummer would be required to advise the chief during talks with rhythmic codes on the drum and would likewise have to be a very talented person (Anim, 1991, p. 24). In traditional African culture the concept of giftedness acquires meaning in terms of performances such as those of the linguist and the drummer.

According to Lumadi (1998), giftedness in individuals is recognized and valued in African culture so long as the ability is used for the greater good of the family and/or the community rather than promoting only the wellbeing of the individual. Thus the cohesiveness of social groups is emphasized again. In the traditional Vhavenda culture, exceptional abilities were encouraged in various fields including sport, art, music, courage and prowess in battle, and leadership. In modern Vhavenda families, the emphasis has broadened to include academic abilities. Child rearing patterns followed by the Vhavenda tend to support and develop high ability in children. These include (Lumadi, 1998):

- Family pride in individual achievement.
- Encouragement to do one's best and strive for excellence.
- Competition.
- Reward for a job well done.
- Valuing persistence and hard work.
- Choosing role models.
- Cooperation and helping one another.
- Building self-esteem and a determination to succeed.

In a study to investigate the effect of gender stereotyping on urbanised black gifted adolescents, Kokot & Kokot (1998) find that the adolescents as well as their families reject traditional roles and support high individual achievement in all spheres.

Elitist Conceptions of Gifted Education

For some, gifted education is associated with elitist education. For historical and cultural reasons this may be a view commonly held in present day Africa. In colonial times and even thereafter educational opportunities in some instances were provided for the few at the expense of the many. African elites, i.e. those with social status and belonging to ruling families, were mostly assured of an education in Western-oriented systems. Members of such elites, according to Giri (1990, p. 66), owed much of their personal success to their passage through such systems. It is therefore understandable that conceptions of giftedness that result in singling out for special treatment a selected group of children, say with high IQs, may be associated with earlier forms of elite education and seen as reinforcing still existing inequalities and providing for a minority who are already perceived as privileged by virtue of their unique gifts. Tembela (1987, p. 65), in rejecting special schools for the gifted, given an indication of how deep-seated that feeling is by associating such an educational measure with 'intellectual aristocracy' and "a perpetuation of class distinction."

However, perhaps due to the present rapid cultural transition and adoption of 'modern' values, many African families are increasingly keen to support children to become achievers in their particular fields. There is an emphasis on good education, which is seen by many Africans as being the key to a future that allows freedom from the shackles of poverty and other problems of being disadvantaged and those children who have the opportunity of gaining a better education tend to seize it rather than refuse on the grounds of elitism. The support of rapid advancement of black women through affirmative action in South Africa (Kokot & Kokot, 1998) also signals changing social norms and a movement away from communalism—at least in the academic and financial arenas. Therefore, the concept of 'elitism' that is still association with the identification of and provision for gifted children in South Africa at least appears to be a political rather than a social issue.

Different Interpretations of Equal Educational Rights

The most basic and widely accepted proposal about human rights is the Universal Declaration of Human Rights adopted by the United Nations in 1948. Article 26 of the declaration states that "Everyone has the right to education" (Human rights, 1983, p. 3). The document makes no mention of special provision for the gifted. Principle 7 of the Declaration of the Rights of the Child (1959) states inter alia that "The child . . . shall be given an education . . . on a basis of equal opportunity, to develop his abilities . . ." (Tarrow, 1987, p. 238). Although this could be interpreted to include the gifted, educational rights for the gifted and talented are not directly mentioned in human rights documents. A society that does not provide for the gifted can therefore not be accused of not honoring the idea of equal education rights.

Even if the idea of equal educational rights for the gifted is accepted, people may disagree about what is meant by equal educational rights (Thomas, 1987). For some, equal educational rights means equality of opportunity, i.e. the right to be treated differently according to one's particular abilities and one's particular needs. Equality of opportunity is interpreted to mean not equal, but different offerings and treatment (Bishop, 1989). It may also be expressed in the words: "Help each child to become all that he or she is capable of being." All children are not alike and should therefore not be treated the same. This would imply special provision for the gifted. For others, equal implies equal access to educational opportunities and that everyone deserves a place in the regular educational system. This means that every child, of whatever ability, should have a chance to enter a typical classroom. All learners are therefore admitted to school and all are treated equally, meaning that everyone is treated the same. Those who fail to progress under regular instruction will usually drop out of school or be forced to repeat their present grade level.

African countries that are struggling to provide greater educational access to their people will probably adhere to the latter interpretation of equal educational rights, i.e. give as many children as possible the opportunity to enter the regular educational system. South African introduced the concept of 'inclusion' to its new post–1994 education system. This policy ensures that all children may receive tuition in mainstream schools, regardless of any barriers to learning that they may experience, such as visual, auditory, physical or other handicaps. It expects teachers to be able to provide support for all kinds of differing dis/abilities in the classrooms, and serves to illustrate the government's interpretation of equality in education. It is thus likely that programs for gifted children would be considered as elitist.

The Goal of Universal Primary Education

Article 4 of the Convention Against Discrimination in Education (1960) called for free and compulsory primary education. African countries that were signatories to the UNESCO Addis Ababa Conference of 1961 established universal primary education as a regional goal set to be accomplished within a decade (Ahmed & Coombs, 1975). This has not been accomplished in spite of very good achievement in educational access and equity during recent decades. The problem is compounded by the fact that Africa, with the world's highest birth rate, will have doubled its population by the year 2000 (Poats, 1984). The population of Africa at present is about 550 million people of whom the majority are of low socioeconomic status.

In countries that are still some distance from achieving universal primary schooling, equalizing educational opportunity will in these instances probably mean that everyone deserves the same chance to try the standard course of study offered in the schools.

The Priority of Majority Needs

It is to be expected that educational authorities will give first priority to providing education to the great mass of average learners. Only after facilities have been provided for the 'average majority' can attention be given to special provisions, first the handicapped and then the gifted. In countries that are struggling at present to provide at least 6 years of primary education for all, special provision for the exceptional minority may be postponed indefinitely.

Other reasons for serving the non-exceptional majority before the exceptional also exist. First, the average majority of the population forms a more powerful political body than do the exceptional. The non-exceptional are far larger in number and can exert more effective political pressure to have its educational needs fulfilled than can the exceptional minority. Second, the non-handicapped majority composes the

Table 1. Enrolment Rations in Sub-Saharan Africa, 1995.

Pre-primary	Primary	Secondary	Tertiary
9.2%	73.9%	24.3%	3.5%

Source: World Education Report: Teachers and Teaching in a Changing World. UNESCO: Paris, 1998.

labor force needed for developing a country's economic growth, so that an investment in educating the majority is expected to yield benefits in increased production. Third, as a developing nation desperately tries to enroll all of its growing population of children in school, its educators are hardly able to train enough teachers and print enough textbooks to serve the average majority, much less to finance the more expensive services needed by the exceptional (Thomas, 1987). Enrolment figures for sub-Saharan Africa are given in Table 1 and illiteracy rates in Table 2.

Economic Conditions

The more affluent a community the more likely it is that a wide variety of special educational services will

Table 2. Estimated Adult Illiterate Population (%) in Some Sub-Saharan African Countries, 1995.

Medium human development countries	Adult literacy rate (%)
South Africa	81.8
Botswana	69.8
Namibia	76.0
Congo	74.9
Zimbabwe	85.1
Swaziland	76.7

Low human development countries	Adult literacy rate (%)
Lesotho	71.3
Kenya	78.1
Nigeria	57.1
Dem. Rep. of the Congo	77.3
Zambia	78.2
Cote D'Ivoire	40.1
Tanzania	67.8
Central African Rep.	60.1
Angola	42.0
Uganda	61.8
Malati	56.4
Mozambique	40.1
Ethiopia	35.5
Burundi	35.3
Niger	13.6

Source: Human Development Report 1998. United Nations Development Program (UNDP). New York: Oxford University Press.

be provided. When resources for education are seriously limited, it becomes a difficult question to decide who should get how much. If resources are equally divided among everyone, an equal share may be too small to be of much practical significance. Training teachers in gifted education will place a further burden on scarce resources because of a longer training period and the need for additional trainers. This will be difficult to justify in the light of a World Bank report that states that in more than half of the countries in sub-Saharan Africa, 50% or more of the teaching staff lack formal training and do not meet the standards the countries themselves require (Rideout, 1987).

Marginalization of Education

Education systems in some sub-Saharan African states have been criticized for turning out too many graduates with doubtful qualifications of even more doubtful use and that they do so at a high cost that is beyond the means of the national economies (Giri, 1990). Scientists, technicians, economists and others are in many instances trained for a Western-style economy geared to sustained development and high productivity. It appeared reasonable to think that the very existence of more and more professionals trained to cater for the needs of a modern society would help sustain economic growth.

The expected growth however seems not to have taken place. In the seventies, growth slowed in most countries and in the eighties, the superficially modern societies of sub-Saharan Africa declined and in some cases collapsed altogether, according to Giri (1990). On the other hand, informal activity flourished in every sector—in trade, transport and crafts and even in small industries and banking. There was a burgeoning of initiative outside the formal framework and of low-productivity activities in general. A stage has been reached where it is the informal sector that largely dominates employment in the townships of Africa. In addition, the outbreak of wars, political unrest and disruption during the nineties has hardly contributed to economic stability or growth.

Education is being perceived by some as having failed to lead African societies to economic growth and turning out young people whose only prospects are jobs in the informal sector that bear little relation to the training they have received. The result is that the aims of the education system have been questioned, that it has been seen as too expensive and unsuitable and in the process marginalized to some extent. Under these circumstances allocation of scarce resources to gifted education may be seen as a bad investment.

Historical Overview of Gifted Education in Sub-Saharan Africa

South Africa is the only sub-Saharan African country in which notable developments in the field of gifted education have taken place. After 1910 a sophisticated

education system for whites was developed in South Africa. In spite of the well-developed education system for the whites, little was done to meet the needs of gifted children in that system. Prominent educationists pointed out from time to time that the country could not afford to neglect its gifted youth and that special provision should be made for their needs. In 1918 Dr W. T. Viljoen, Superintendent General of Education in the Cape Province, remarked on the rigid uniformity of teaching in the schools and in his annual report called for the introduction of differentiated courses which would provide for the slow and the gifted learner (Cape of Good Hope Department of Public Education, 1919). In 1931, an article was written by an educator who advised grouping pupils according to their cognitive abilities, as determined by intelligence testing (Kimmins, 1931). Much later, two Presidents of the influential Suid-Afrikaanse Onderwysersunie (English: South African Teachers' Union), G. J. Smit in 1954 and F. S. Robertson in 1963, devoted their presidential addresses to the theme of gifted education and expressed concern that gifted pupils were underachieving and that their full potential was not being developed in the schools.

No significant research on the gifted child was undertaken before the 1940s. The first important work was done by Biesheuwel on African intelligence with special reference to the extent that growth and measurement of intelligence can be determined by factors other than heredity such as cultural milieu, home environment, school environment, nutrition and temperament (Biesheuwel, 1943). Further studies by Biesheuwel on African ability focused on the intellectual potentialities of Africans and the identification and description of research problems in this field. These included the following: mental characteristics of African languages and the influence that they have on the process of thought and structure of the mind, musical ability (e.g. the ability to excel in the manipulation of auditory relations), a psychological study of the manual and perceptual skills involved in arts and crafts and their transferability outside their cultural context, and the high order perceptual and imaginal thinking processes required by traditional African games (Biesheuwel, 1952).

In 1946 the point was made that the education system should provide for the "right of every pupil to undergo school training that enables him to experience a daily task or career that matches his aptitude" (Archer in Coetzer & Van Zyl, 1989, p.147, translated). In the 1950s more academic works appeared. One concerned a study of the intellectually superior school child, with special reference to social adjustment. Venter (1955) experimentally investigated different procedures whereby special provision could be made for gifted pupils and Duminy, who defended his doctoral thesis on psychological and pedagogical aspects of giftedness in December 1959 at the Free University, Amsterdam, in the Netherlands (Duminy, 1960). Articles concerned with the plight of the gifted child and descriptions of attempts to bring this plight to the attention of teachers and education authorities appeared. To accommodate differences in learners, differentiated education within schools in the white education departments became an aim of the South African education system in the 1950s. This approach was to provide for learner's disparate intellectual abilities, aptitudes and interests and also to provide gifted pupils with more challenging learning matter.

During the 1960s, interest in gifted learners grew considerably. In 1964 the findings of a committee were that (Jacobs & White, 1994):

- gifted children should be homogenously grouped in primary schools so that teaching methods could be adapted to meet their needs;
- curriculum content should be adjusted for gifted primary school children;
- acceleration and enrichment should be practised as methods of accommodating the needs of able learners in schools;
- secondary schools offering specialized study in the technical, commercial, agricultural, scientific and arts fields be established.

In 1965, the Institute for Manpower Research of the National Bureau for Educational and Social Research launched project Talent Search, described by Lategan (1986) as "probably the largest educational research project yet undertaken in South Africa" (translated from the Afrikaans). This long-term project investigated the academic progress of about 70 000 high ability white Standard 6 (Grade 9) pupils to create a basis for effective special educational provision for gifted children.

From around 1969 Jock L. Omond, a retired headmaster and inspector of schools, accelerated the propagation of the idea of gifted education. Over the next few years he put the case of the gifted to education authorities and the public at meetings all over the country, delivered papers at conferences, and gave interviews over the radio and TV. The educational authorities reacted negatively at first to Omond's pleas so he decided to proceed on his own. On June 14, 1976, he established the Office for the Gifted and Talented in Port Elizabeth with the aim of providing for the gifted on an extra-curricular basis and in an out-of-school setting.

In 1970 the Human Sciences Research Council (Haasbroek, 1988) reported that differentiated education was being practised in different ways at different levels in the various provinces. Following this, various task committees to investigate gifted education were established and further reports were published in 1981, 1984, 1987 and 1988. It is noticeable that the first real attempts to investigate the needs of gifted black children were made during the 1980s and a report was published in 1988 that motivated the establishment of a special school for black gifted learners.

In 1979, the first National Conference on Gifted Education was organized by the University of Stellenbosch. Gradually a more positive attitude was developing towards gifted education on the part of the education authorities and official recognition was gained with the appointment of the first education planner for the gifted, Dr J. S. Neethling on October 1, 1980 by the Education Department of the Cape Province. At the end of 1980 the Transvaal Education Department followed suit and established extra-curricular centers to provide for the needs of gifted children. Shortly afterwards the province of Natal also established a system to provide for the gifted and similarly the Orange Free State in 1986.

During 1982 and 1983 various developments took place in the Cape Province. Twenty-five schools were selected and virtually given carte blanche to introduce and develop gifted education. One of the major tasks of these schools was to provide guidance and support to other schools starting out on gifted education. An editorial board was formed for the publication of Creata, the first bilingual journal on gifted education in the world and the first Problem-Solving Bowl, based on the Torrance model, was held. In-service courses were held for principals, teachers and school psychologists (Neethling, 1985).

It was also realized that apart from limited in-service courses for teachers formal training programs needed to be established at tertiary institutions. The first extensive training program for teachers of the gifted was established at the University of Port Elizabeth in 1983. The University of South Africa followed and these universities offer basic modules on gifted education in pre-service education courses as well as specialized training at post-graduate level.

Further impetus was given to the idea of gifted education by the First International Conference on Giftedness (Ingenium 1000) that was held in Stellenbosch in 1984. Major inputs at the conference were made by speakers from the United States of America and their influence has been clearly visible in programs that were subsequently established in various parts of South Africa. This was followed by a Second International Conference (Children of Gold) in Johannesburg in 1987. Unfortunately, the unstable political climate of this time restricted the number of overseas attendants and impacted as well on the black schools. Even though financial support had been obtained to enable black teachers to attend, boycotts and disruption of many of these schools made attendance impossible.

By the end of the 1980s, it was clear that the provincial authorities responsible for diverse population groups were developing different approaches to gifted child education. These approaches included two high schools for Art, Ballet and Music, extracurricular centers, parent-driven enrichment programs and enrichment programs for black pupils that were run as outreach programs. Other familiar activities, such as subject Olympiads, Problem-Solving Bowls and Speech and Drama contests were also held in various parts of the country (Kokot, 1994). Leadership courses were regularly offered to senior primary and high school pupils. Furthermore, high school pupils were no longer limited in the number of subjects studied for the matriculation examination. Instead of the usual six subjects, most highly able students were now studying seven subjects, with many sitting for up to ten subjects at the end of their matriculation year.

In view of these diverse efforts, it is not surprising that in their investigation of the 'state of the art' of education for the gifted in member and non-member countries of UNESCO, Mitchell & Williams (1987) found that the "two developed nations that lead the world in level of commitment to gifted/talented education are Israel and South Africa" (p. 532). However, there is no doubt that the same commitment was not in evidence in education departments responsible for black education in the less developed areas of South Africa. It is, therefore, understandable that gifted education was regarded as part of the elitist, white regime.

Other African Countries

Outside of South Africa hardly any development of note has taken place in the field of gifted education. In Nigeria the National Policy on Education (1981) states that Ministries of Education will, in consultation with appropriate bodies, provide special programs for gifted children (Gwany, 1989). It is not clear whether any further development took place before 1986 when a National Planning Committee of ten members from tertiary institutions was constituted by the Federal Minister of Education. A First Workshop on the Identification and Nurturing of the Gifted was held in 1986 at Kaduna (Adesokan, 1986). A blueprint was outlined and policy formulated on the identification and education of the gifted in Nigeria. According to Oladokun (1987) and Gwany (1989), however, the existing system was not significantly adapted to accommodate the gifted child and nothing of real note has been done to generally encourage gifted education in Nigeria. Adesokan (1987) states that the Nigerian teacher is unlikely to assume the function of identifying and nurturing giftedness unless specific attention is given to gifted education in teacher training.

In some African countries with limited secondary school places pupils attending those schools are a highly select group. Secondary education may in those circumstances be regarded as a form of special education provision for a group of pupils which may resemble the highly able in some respects. In Tanzania a quota system exists for selection to secondary school.

Such a scheme was necessary to prevent most of the places going to educationally wealthy areas in the country. The poorer areas can now send pupils for secondary education even though their academic achievement may be well below those of some pupils in the richer areas who are not selected. Furthermore, better-equipped primary schools tended to send a disproportionate number of pupils to the secondary schools. To achieve more equitable distribution of places to the secondary school, the top pupil from each primary school is selected to go on for further education. In this way children in every school in Tanzania have at least some chance of making it to secondary school (Bishop, 1989).

Yoder (1986) states that secondary education and certainly post-secondary education was, by definition, education of the gifted during the pre-independence days of Botswana. Those few individuals who rose to the top and who were selected for further advancement of their education were typically those who displayed exceptional potential. Often, it was because of this potential that they received the educational opportunities that they did. It is true that social status and membership in the ruling family also affected educational opportunity, particularly in the very early days. In time, as the concept of education became more broadly accepted, however, access to schooling became more dependent on factors such as academic ability. Access to advanced schooling, particularly, was influenced by academic potential. Advanced education, therefore, was available primarily for academic achievers who could be said to be academically gifted.

According to Yoder (1986) Botswana has no programs that are identified as being specifically for the benefit of the gifted. The one possible exception to this is a private secondary school in the Gaborone area that offers a moderately accelerated program for pupils who demonstrate the required aptitude. Those pupils selected for this program may compress a five-year secondary school program into four years. Additional Mathematics was offered in some schools at one stage but this has been dropped. The training program of teachers' colleges in Botswana does not include gifted education.

Gifted education in Kenya seems to be in the embryonic stage. Interest has been generated amongst teachers, parents and the public by means of conferences. A first conference was held in 1991 and the Second Eastern African Conference on Gifted and Talented persons was held in August 1992 in Nairobi on the theme of "Caring, educating and harnessing gifted and talented persons for national development." Objectives of the conference were the following:

- To develop and increase public awareness on the plight of gifted and talented persons.
- To encourage individual and/or collaborative research work in the area of giftedness and talent.

- To encourage efforts to establish and implement intervention programs.
- To identify in general terms the handicaps which gifted and talented people experience, and to suggest possible solutions.
- To encourage the utilization of the gifted and talented in society for national development.

The Search for an Identification Procedure

Giftedness is culture-specific. What is recognized as gifted behaviour in one culture or environment may be beside the point in another. An identification model or procedure for giftedness that does not attend to a specific sociocultural context would therefore fail to identify the gifted in that context. This is especially relevant in traditional African society.

Identification of the Gifted in Traditional African Culture

Certain characteristics are highly valued in traditional African society. These include a quick wit, wisdom, humour, an active, dynamic disposition, leadership, linguistic excellence, one who knows everything, and one who is good with his hands around the house (Anim, 1992). Children who are seen to reflect these characteristics may be given names accordingly. For example, parents may give their boy the name Okabae (English: he has returned) because their child showed exceptional intelligence that led them to believe that a wise and long dead member of the family had returned. Names can therefore be an indicator of intelligence (Anim, 1991).

In traditional African society gifted children were selected for very special roles and could be found at a very early age serving in the chief's court, learning the intricate life styles of a courtier. Certain roles, for example, that of the linguist and drummer, cannot be inherited. It is something that a person becomes because of the qualities that s/he possesses. The linguist of the village who is the spokesman and adviser of the chief will be selected on the grounds of his wisdom, diplomacy and quick wit. Likewise the drummer who transmits messages in drum language to the chief during discussions will be selected on the grounds of possessing certain special qualities (Anim, 1991).

Pre–1994 Identification Procedures

A general intelligence test based on the South African Individual Scale has been developed and standardized for nine African languages by the Institute for Psychological and Edumetric Research of the Human Sciences Research Council (HSRC), e.g. the Individual Scale for Xhosa-speaking pupils (1988). These tests could be described as culture-fair but are generally not accepted to be culture-free for various reasons. For example, these tests may be regarded as favoring an inner locus-of-control orientation which is typical of Western

culture. Other tests developed by the HSRC that may be applied to assess Black secondary school learners' abilities are the Guidance Test Battery for Secondary Pupils (GBS) in Grade 10, the Scholastic Aptitude Test Battery (SATB) for learners in Grades 4/5, 6/7 and 8/9 and the Academic Aptitude Test (AAT) for Grade 12 learners. The SATB 4/5 has been standardized for seven language groups, namely Northern Sotho, Southern Sotho, Tswana, Tsonga, Venda, Xhosa and Zulu. These tests are used for guidance purposes and not specifically to identify gifted pupils. Tlale (1990) is of the opinion that the above-mentioned tests are based on Western culture and therefore cannot reveal the full ability of black children.

A more flexible approach to the identification of gifted pupils was followed by the Cape Province Education Department (now the Western Cape Education Department) in South Africa. Instruments and procedures that were used include IQ tests, Torrance Creativity Tests, assessment of reading and spelling age, assessment of mathematical ability and further teacher or parent assessment. Formal application of these, however, only continues if it is required to clear up doubts or to assess specific abilities. Where identification is obvious testing will not be completed.

A more formal approach was followed by the Transvaal Education Department in South Africa (now the Gauteng Department of Education). The first phase of the identification procedure required the collection of data about academic achievement in school, characteristics of a child, and by means of teacher and peer evaluation, using checklists. Secondly, a panel of evaluators at a school would identify those nominated as gifted on the basis of the data available. In the third phase all particulars of the pupils identified in phase two were sent to the regional office of the Educational Support Services for a final selection of pupils. This department implemented this identity procedure to all Grade 3 pupils for selection for admission to gifted programs run at extra-curricular centers from Grade 4 onwards.

In most African countries the task of identifying the gifted presents a mammoth problem (Anim, 1992). An acute shortage of teachers and a near total absence of school psychologists or guidance counselors mean that identification procedures used in developed countries are largely non-existent. The only means remaining for schools are the teacher's cumulative assessment of a child's achievement and, in most cases, the teacher's intuition. No specialized way is possible of identifying the gifted in the large classes in which over-extended teachers must function.

Recent Research on Identification

Many studies concerned with issues and aspects of gifted education have been conducted in South Africa amongst the white population group. There has, however, been a dearth of research concerning black gifted children and even more rare are studies completed by black researchers. One major area of concern over the years has been the lack of a definition and identification procedure that is valid for African culture.

The Development of Principles for the Design of an Instrument to Identify Gifted Black Children

Tlale (1990) undertook an investigation in South Africa to determine principles for the design of a culturally relevant instrument to identify gifted black secondary school children. He identified six principles, namely that the instrument should

- measure cognitive and metacognitive functions;
- be divided into subtests, each measuring a specific ability;
- be culturally appropriate, i.e. based on the socio-cultural environment of black children;
- use appropriate language, i.e. be written in the first language of the child;
- effectively discriminate between children of different ages while taking into account language development in particular;
- avoid biasing factors found in rural and urban cultures (Tlale 1990; pp. 115–119).

These principles are applied to design an instrument to identify gifted Tswana secondary school learners (ages 13–17 years). The instrument comprises six tests. The first five tests are verbal tests and similar to the first five tests of the Senior South African Individual Scale-R (SSAIS Revised); the sixth test is similar to the eighth test (Absurdities) of the SSAIS-R. The above-mentioned six tests of the SSAIS-R were used as a basis for the design of the instrument because they are primarily verbal or composed of pictures which can easily be adapted to African culture (Tlale, 1990). The tests are designed to be administered orally and individually.

After empirical application and testing, the researcher concludes that it has been proved possible to design an instrument, written in Tswana and based on black African culture, to identify gifted Tswana secondary school learners. Nor reference, however, is made to the validity of the instrument as an indicator of giftedness. The researcher also concludes that, as black people in South Africa share a common culture with only a few variations, the instrument can be translated and adapted to other African languages.

Moving Away from IQ Testing

More recently, a study has been completed that attempts to identifying giftedness without resorting to tests. Lumadi (1998) studied the Venda culture to ascertain what cultural and social factors contribute to the development and nurturance of giftedness. He studied identification models described in the literature and concluded that Dabrowski's Overexcitabilities and Gardner's Multiple Intelligence Theory (MIT) are valid

to the culture of the Vhavenda. As a result, he was able to compile a checklist of attributes that would enable teachers to recognize signs of high ability. A qualitative study was conducted with six high school learners. He also concluded that the views of Tannenbaum (1983) and Kokot (1992, 1994) were appropriate to the Venda culture and recommended that either be adopted by African cultures as being suitable definitions of giftedness.

Predictors of Performance of Disadvantaged Adolescents

Skuy and his associates (Skuy et al., 1990) conducted a study at the University of the Witwatersrand in Johannesburg, to determine which of Feuerstein's Learning Potential Assessment Device (LPAD), standardized ability tests and ratings of temperament, creativity and self-concept were significant predictors of performance. It was hoped that the study would provide the basis for developing an appropriate assessment battery for the identification of suitable candidates for a gifted program.

Of the 300 children participating in the Soweto Gifted Child Program, 100 were randomly selected for inclusion in the sample. Subjects were 13–18 years of age and of low socioeconomic status. Performance in the Soweto Gifted Child Program (SGCP) was the criterion against which the predictive value of the independent measures was determined. The findings of this study corroborated those of Skuy, Kaniel and Tzuriel (1988) in Israel by demonstrating the value of the LPAD and, in particular, the Organiser, for identifying giftedness among disadvantaged children.

These studies are limited and represent an initial stage in the much-needed research on gifted black African children. More research needs to be encouraged, especially by black academics who understand their culture, to validate these early findings and broaden knowledge relating this neglected group.

Nurturing the Gifted

From the discussion of historical and current issues that impact on the provision of education in sub-Saharan African countries one may conclude that very little or no formal provision for the gifted will be made in most of these countries. As already indicated South Africa is the exception in this respect that the gifted were relatively well served by formal and non-formal programs in the old regime. Outside of the well-developed and, for many years, well-funded provincial Education Departments serving mostly the white sector of the population, universities, parent/community associations and private sector groups also provided for the needs of the gifted in various ways.

Although many of the programs have been abandoned due to withdrawal of government funding, it is worth describing certain of the long-term programs that were successful. Programs and opportunities for gifted learners which are still in existence, but which are of limited scope or shorter duration are not described. These include the following: olympiads (e.g. mathematics, accountancy), competitions (e.g. history, music, choir) art exhibitions, science expo's, problem-solving bowls, leadership seminars, writers' workshops, parent-driven enrichment programs and publication opportunities (e.g. Wakening Word; Voices from young Africa (Mda & Van Wyk, no date), youth orchestras and business/stock market games.

Formal In-School Programs
Four-area Curriculum Enrichment and Extension Model

This model was implemented by the Cape Education Department and was based on a wide, flexible interpretation of giftedness. It made provision for the gifted at four levels referred to as areas (Meintjies, 1988; Mentz, 1991). Area 1 provided for all pupils to receive training the thinking skills, problem-solving, research skills, creativity and life-skills (communication, interpersonal relationships). This area formed the basis of the gifted education program. Area 2 was aimed at the top 10–12% of pupils and represented a subject-directed approach. Enrichment and acceleration were provided in the regular classroom situation in each subject and every grade. Area 3 was more child-directed and allowed for a variety of withdrawal and grouping arrangements in-and out-of-class and school. A changing group of pupils was withdrawn for special and inter-school activities, taking into account specific giftedness. Area 4 attempted to provide for the exceptionally brilliant pupils by means of individualization and mentors. These pupils qualified for acceleration. Gifted underachievers received specific attention in the Area 4 program.

Support for teachers was provided by coordinators appointed and paid by the Education Department. They were based at regional Teachers' Centers. Additional support was offered by the Psychological, Educational Guidance and Curriculum Services of the Education Department. The main task of the coordinators was to equip teachers with the skills, strategies and techniques that enabled them to integrate activities for the gifted with the normal teaching program in the school. Workshop, lectures, talks, consultations, personal interviews, advice and information relating to any aspect of gifted education were some of the services provided, not only to teachers but also to parents, pupils, private and tertiary institutions or any other interested organization.

Special Schools
In some African countries special schools were established with the purpose of providing a model for other schools to follow. These schools were given various names such as Apex institutions, Special or International Schools. Schools in these categories include

King's College at Yaba in Nigeria, Suleja Academy at Abuja in Nigeria, Prince of Wales College at Achimoto in Ghana, Makerere College in Kampala, Uganda, and Waterford and St. Mark's in Swaziland. Although the establishment of these schools was to the advantage of gifted children, many of them very soon became preparation grounds for university entrance examinations. Cognitive abilities were highlighted and in the process those gifted in other areas lost interest and became underachievers (Anim, 1992). Whether these special schools get their fair share of gifted pupils is unknown. Special schools that are privatized are very expensive and only the financially well-off can afford to send their children to them.

In Ghana available places in secondary schools are so few that clusters of primary schools developed called Preparatory, International or Experimental Schools. The primary purpose of these schools was to prepare pupils for the common entrance examination to the secondary school. These schools do not particularly provide for the gifted and talented.

In 1993 in Johannesburg, South Africa, the Rand Afrikaans University initiated a special secondary school for academically talented black adolescents, known as Raucoll. Funding was obtained from the private sector that considers the school to be an ideal opportunity for training future black business leaders. Subjects offered are English, Afrikaans, Mathematics, Science, Accounting and Business Economics. Top achieving Grade 7 pupils (mainly from schools in Soweto) form the pool from which successful pupils are selected. Part of the admission criteria includes a financial means test as pupils must be drawn from families of low socioeconomic status. Success at matriculation is expected so if a pupil fails to thrive at the school, he or she may be referred to nearby state schools after Grade 9.

In 1995, Dr Shirley Kokot established Radford House, a primary school for gifted children ages 4–13, in Johannesburg. This was in response to parent requests following the rapid increase in problems manifested by gifted children in classrooms subjected to increasing teacher-pupil ratios and the rapidly increasing influx of previously disadvantaged black children. Teachers faced with the problem of a high percentage of children with poor English and very limited academic skills in the same class as gifted and 'average' children proclaimed that the situation made it impossible to adequately accommodate the gifted. This led to many behavioral and emotional problems amongst bright children.

Radford House serves children of high potential by keeping class sizes small (the teacher-pupil ratio is a maximum of 1–16 but averages at 1–12); focuses on skills rather than content (including thinking skills and research skills) and promotes discovery learning and exploration. The unique teaching approach integrates Howard Gardner's Multiple Intelligence Theory into a thematic approach where the children are guided to be active rather than passive participants in the teaching process. Extracurricular activities, aimed at providing the children with an holistic education, include sports (ball skills, cricket, soccer, hockey, tennis, swimming and netball) as well as chess, choir, public speaking, debating, art, drama, a wildlife club, and a French language club. Ballet and Karate are offered at the school by private teachers. The school receives no funding and operates purely on school fees.

Special Schools for the Arts and Commercial Subjects

In the province of Gauteng in South Africa provision for specific talents in fine and performing arts, ballet, music and commercial subjects is made by means of two special schools (in Pretoria and Johannesburg) which cater specifically for these areas of giftedness. Originally, the Arts and Ballet school in Pretoria was separate from the Commercial High schools but owing to lack of funds, these combined to share a single school building after 1994.

Formal Out-of-School Programs

Extra-Curricular Centers

The Transvaal Education Department in South Africa made provision for the gifted in out-of-school settings. These aimed to provide enrichment in various fields not normally encountered by pupils in school (e.g. Philosophical Studies, Astronomy, Electronics, Petrochemical and Geological Studies, Money and Banking, Drama etc.). These centers were situated in the larger cities in the province. Only pupils who were identified as gifted according to a three phase selection procedure could attend the centers. Classes were offered after school hours, once or twice weekly for an hour at a time. Curricula were designed jointly by curriculum experts, universities, staff attached to the centers and the private sector.

Certain of the centers ran courses were during school vacations to enable children from outlying areas to have the enrichment opportunity and interact socially.

The center in Pretoria, serving 2000 pupils annually, has been closed down. The remaining centers are unsure of how long they will be able to function, owing to lack of state funding.

The Orange Free State had one enrichment center situated in Bloemfontein. This center included a boarding establishment so that groups of gifted pupils from all over the province could attend a week-long course twice a year. This center has been closed down.

In 1984, Dr Cedric Taylor established an Academic Vacation School at the University of Port Elizabeth. This was a two week residential program that was attended by Grade 9–12 gifted pupils every year from all over South Africa. The school was funded by the University Council and by sponsors from the private sector. The objectives of the school were to provide the pupils with intellectually challenging experiences

within the academic framework of the university; to promote good relationships between black and white pupils in South Africa and to create the opportunity for pupils from disadvantaged communities to learn and live together with their intellectual peers from more privileged communities and thus to facilitate their transition from school to university. After 1994, the Vacation School changed to a facility for only black, previously disadvantaged pupils.

The Office for the Gifted and Talented

Voluntary parent or community associations played a pioneering role in the 1970s in providing for the gifted in South Africa. During this decade the educational authorities were opposed to the idea of special provision for the gifted in schools. The parents and community responded by establishing parent/community associations in various big centers that provided extra-curricular activities for the gifted. The pioneer in this respect was Jock Omond, who established the Office for the Gifted and Talented in Port Elizabeth, South Africa, in 1976. The Office offered courses and lecturers on a variety of topics and arranged visits to centers of interest. Periodicals, books and newspapers from all over the world were scrutinized and a newsletter was published which summarized articles from these sources that were of possible interest to parents and teachers. A collection, possibly unique in the world, of 28 volumes of approximately 12 000 press cuttings on gifted education from all countries was regularly brought up to date. The collection is available for research and study by appointment. The death in 1990 of Omond who was the driving force behind the Office, signaled its discontinuation.

THe National Association for Gifted and Talented Children in South Africa

In 1992, Shirley Kokot, a senior lecturer responsible for teacher training in gifted child education at the University of South Africa, Pretoria, identified the need for networking advocates of gifted education throughout Southern Africa and launched the newsletter Excedo (English: We go beyond). The mailing list of this newsletter grew to over 2000 addresses. In 1997, Dr Kokot organized a National Conference at the University of South Africa in Pretoria to address the plight of the gifted in the light of the new dispensation. A result of the conference was the formation of the National Association of Gifted and Talented Children in South Africa (NAGTCSA). Dr Kokot was elected President and the Excedo newsletter became the mouthpiece of the Association. Consequently, NAGTCSA representatives were able to represent gifted children and their families in discussions regarding policy decisions in education. Gifted learners continue to fall under the structures established to provide for education for learners with special educational needs (ELSEN) in South Africa but the focus in education discussions and policy documents is on 'disabled' and 'disadvantaged' learners. Because of this emphasis, mention of the highly able has been almost non-existent in the various new policy proposals. The final policies regarding special needs education are currently being drawn up and the success of the lobbying by the NAGTCSA is awaited.

Growth of Children's Potential (GCP)

In 1982 Stan Edkins, a retired headmaster, in liaison with the Department of Education and Training (the department responsible for black education) provided the impetus for a Saturday enrichment program in the sprawling black township of Soweto. It became known as the Soweto Saturday School. In 1983 a second program was started in Alexandra, an overcrowded black ghetto, a third in 1988 in Northern Soweto and a similar program was started in the Johannesburg suburb of Bedfordview for pupils from Daveyton, yet another black township. These projects developed into what was called the Gifted child program. In 1992 the name was changed to Growth of Children's Potential.

The focus of the program is the previously disadvantaged gifted pupil from black township schools who, because of the inadequate schooling system and deprived sociopolitical background, would not reach potential.

The selection process consists of an initial screening by the school whereby the top 2–3 academic pupils from each school are invited for further assessment using a general intelligence test normed in South Africa and the Torrance Test of Creative Thinking. The top 25 pupils per area and per grade are selected.

The main components of the program are Saturday morning enrichment of academic areas. An integrated studies themes approach is used which dovetails with the syllabi of the state schools. Afternoon special interest groups follow the morning program and after a light lunch, the pupils take part in relaxing and creative activities. Workshops are run by tutors, volunteer community people and experts and include current affairs seminars, drama, chess, dance, art, swimming, other sports and nature awareness. Excursions, camps and cross-cultural activities are also organized during the year.

All Grade 7 and 8 pupils on the program are tested annually using a battery of aptitude tests. Based on the test results and in consultation with GCP center directors, pupils are selected to write the private school entrance examinations. In 1991 thirty of these pupils were accepted into private schools and scholarships secured for twenty-one.

The GCP achieved measurable success and stability in its first 10 years with over 600 pupils being accommodated in their programs per year and another 400 in programs run in other regions using the same model. The future of the GCP is uncertain.

Non-Formal In-School Programs

Thinking Actively in a Social Context (TASC)

A Curriculum Development Unit (CDU) under the co-directorship of Belle Wallace and Harvey B. Adams was established at the University of Natal, Pietermaritzburg, South Africa in 1985 with the overall aim of undertaking research, teaching and community-service activities to help teachers maximise the extent to which all pupils develop their potential. Under the broad aim of the CDU and in the light of the perceived needs of high school pupils an initial pilot project was launched in 1986 to develop a course to teach thinking skills to pupils in Grade 10. The focus was on developing higher levels of thinking skills and problem-solving strategies amongst black pupils in Kwazulu Natal schools (Adams & Wallace, 1991). The TASC program has since been revised and its aims have been extended to develop in the pupils certain attitudes towards learning (in all contexts, not only the school); basic thinking skills necessary for making sense of experience; tools for effective thinking and problem-solving and metacognition.

The extended TASC program also aimed to improve the effectiveness of teachers as facilitators of children's 'learning to learn'. Short-term adaptation and long-term reconstruction of the curriculum is seen as part of the TASC program (Adams & Wallace, 1991). According to the authors the program is based of Vygotsky's work on the development of higher levels of thinking and its connection to social transaction, Feuerstein's theory of cognitive modifiability and the concept of mediated learning experiences, and Sternberg's theory of intelligence (Adams & Wallace 1988, p. 132).

Basic underlying principles of TASC are as follows:

- Adopt a model of the problem-solving process and explicitly teach it.
- Identify a set of specific skills and strategies and give training in these.
- Develop a vocabulary.
- Give ample practice in both the skills and the strategies using situations that are significant and relevant to the learners.
- Give attention to the motivational aspects of problem-solving.
- Progress in the teaching from modeling by the teacher, to guided activity by the learner and eventually autonomous action by the learner.
- Assist the learner to transfer skills and strategies to new contexts.
- Emphasize cooperative learning in small groups.
- Encourage self-monitoring and self-education.
- Require learners to develop their metacognitive knowledge (Adams & Wallace, 1991, p. 107).

Several courses based on underlying principles of TASC have been developed and tested. These courses, each spread over a 5 day (25 hours) period, were taught to high achieving white and black Grade 10 pupils. Adams & Wallace (1991) state that the outcomes were similar in each case, namely rapid learning, high motivation, improvements in self-image and lasting improvements in performance on specified cognitive tasks. No statistics are provided to substantiate these claims. It is, however, mentioned that an evaluation by members of the Schools' Psychological Service teachers, the pupils and the researchers revealed certain difficulties. Firstly, it was felt that pupils not already achieving highly within the school system for whatever reason (e.g. inadequate mastery of English) would need a foundation course in basic thinking, and assistance in achieving oral fluency in English. It was also felt that gains made during the course would be rapidly dissipated unless constant call was made upon the newly acquired skills and metacognitive knowledge during the pupils' subject lessons.

A major pilot course was subsequently run for a mixed ability Grade 10 class of 40 black pupils. This extended over a 6 week period consisting of two 2-hourly sessions after school each week. The researchers state that an evaluation of the course again revealed that the approach was highly successful for those pupils already achieving at a relatively high level and with a reasonable command of the English language. The remainder progressed at a much slower rate. No statistics are given.

Following this, the work of the program was expanded in two directions: the first four years of the 5 year secondary school curriculum will be included in the program of instruction; and secondly, the syllabi of all major school subjects will be examined to identify and develop opportunities for building the use of the newly acquired skills into regular subject lessons (Adams & Wallace, 1991).

The TASC program represents a systematic, multi-phase model of problem-solving, incorporating basic thinking skills and tools for effective thinking. The researchers claim that there are good grounds for believing that the TASC approach has the possibility of achieving significant changes in the capacity of pupils to benefit from their schooling, and the ability to meet problems in their day to day existence. This type of research is important especially to the South African context, where the majority has not been adequately schooled in either content areas or higher level thinking skills. This research is continuing.

Future Development

A number of issues have been described that emanate from the political, historical and cultural context of Africa and that have a direct bearing on the provision of education for the gifted and talented. In general, those issues seem to imply that gifted education will probably not be a priority item on the education agenda of most African countries in the near future. A restructuring of gifted education on a broader base and

contextualized for the needs and priorities of a developing country may be needed to establish legitimacy in future. Some aspects that need to be researched in this respect are briefly outlined below:

• Linking gifted education programs to national development needs and traditional culture

National Service Schemes that aim to relate education to practical service to the nation and to promote national unity have been established in Ghana, Nigeria and Sierra Leone (Anim, 1992). The restructuring of programs for the gifted within the wider context of national developmental needs may ensure the legitimacy of such provision in the education system. Likewise, gifted education may be linked to the traditional social structure of ujamaa and the improvement of the quality of life of the whole community.

• Building on the strengths of African culture

Competencies and attitudes that are highly valued in African culture and that can be utilized in the development of gifted programs are social-affective competence, interpersonal intelligence and orality (e.g. the Mukama—the tradition of oral history and poetry) (Bhola, 1990). Building on the strengths of African culture may increase the relevancy of gifted programs. Traditional orality, for example, could be developed in the context of a modern democratic state in the form of public and political oratory. At the same time programs should also augment those kinds of intelligence that are tradtionally not favored in the African culture, e.g. technological competence.

• The integration of gifted programs in regular classroom teaching

Gifted education should be seen to be affording all pupils the opportunity to participate in and gain from enrichment and extension and to discover and develop their potential. Therefore special programs should not be provided separately for a select few but be open to all who are interested in and able to benefit from such opportunities. Models need to be researched that integrate gifted programs in regular classroom teaching.

References

Adams, H. B. & Wallace, B. (1991). A model for curriculum development. Gifted Education International1, **7**, 104–113.

Adesokan, E. (1987). Emerging concepts of giftedness: the implementation of gifted education in Nigeria. *Gifted International*, **4**, 106–113.

Adesokan, E. (1986). Education of the gifted in Nigeria. *World Gifted Newsletter*, **7**, 8. Tampa, Florida: World Council for Gifted and Talented Children, Inc.

Ahmed, M. 7 Coombs, P. H. (1975). *Education for rural development: case studies for planners*. New York: Praeger.

Anim, N. O. (1992). *In pursuit of relevance in education in Africa*. Conference on Current Trends in Comparative Education. Pretoria: University of South Africa.

Anim, N. O. (1992). The gifted and talented in the third world: a case of gross under-development. In: F. J. Mönks & W. A. M. Peters (Eds.), *Talent for the Future. Social and Personality Development of Gifted Children* (pp. 1–9). Assen: Van Gorcum.

Anim, N. O. (1991). Let's push out the schoolwalls of the third world. *World gifted Newsletter*, **12**, 24. Beaumont, Texas: World Council for Gifted and Talented Children, Inc.

Bhola, H. S. (1990). An overview of literacy in sub-Sahara Africa—Images in the making. *African Studies Review*, **33**, 5–20.

Biesheuvel, S. (1943). *African intelligence*. Johannesburg: South African Institute of Race Relations.

Biesheuvel, S. (1952). The study of African ability. *African Studies*, **11**, 45–58, 105–117.

Bishop, G. (1989). Alternative strategies for education. London: Macmillan Publishers.

Cape of Good Hope Department of Public Education (1919). *Report of the Superintendent General of Education*. Cape Town.

Coetzer, I. A. & Van Zyl, A. E. (1989). *Die historiese opvoedkunde: enkele eietydse opvoedingsvraagstukke* [English: History of Education: certain issues]. Pretoria: University of South Africa.

Council of Europe (1987). *Second Strasbourg Conference on Parliamentary Democracy*. Compendium of documents, 29–30 September. Strasbourg.

Diamond, L. (1988). Introduction: roots of failure, seeds of hope. In: L. Diamond, J. J. Linz & S. M. Lipset (Eds.), *Democracy in Developing Countries. Africa,* Vol. 2 (pp. 1–32). Boulder, CO: Lynne Rienner Publishers.

Duminy, P. A. (1960). *Begaafdheid: enkele psigologiese en pedagogiese aspekte* [English: Giftedness: Psychological and pedagogical aspects]. Pretoria: Van Schaik.

Du Plessis, L. M. (1992). The relevance of a Christian approach to politics (with particular reference to Higher Learning in the African context). *Journal of Theology for Southern Africa*, **78**, 3–14.

Forbes-Harper, M. (1997). Providing for gifted students in an Independent Multi-Cultural school in Australia. In: J. Chan, R. Li & J. Spinks (Eds.), *Maximising Potential: Lengthening and Strengthening Our Stride* (pp. 476–487). Hong Kong: Hong Kong University.

Gifted Child Program. (1991). *Annual report*. Doornfontein: GCP Trust.

Giri, J. (1990). Crisis in growth or structural crisis? *The Courier, 123*, 65–67. Brussels: Dueter Frish.

Gwany, D. M. (1989). The gifted child in the Nigerian 6–3–3–4 system of education. *Gifted Education International*, **6**, 117–122.

Haasbroek, J. B. (1988). *Report on the working committee: education for highly gifted pupils*. Pretoria: Human Sciences Research Council.

Hartshorne, K. (1992). Foreword. In: R. McGregor & A. McGregor (Eds.), *McGregor's education alternatives*. Kenwyn, Cape Town: Juta.

Holm, J. D.(1988). Botswana: a paternalistic democracy. In: J. Diamond, J. J. Linz, & S. M. Lipset (Eds.), *Democracy in Developing Countries, Africa,* Vol. 2 (pp. 179–215). Boulder, CO: Lynne Rienner Publishers.

Human Rights (1983). *A compilation of international instruments*. New York: United Nations.

Human Sciences Research Council (1986). *Education for gifted pupils*. Pretoria: Human Sciences Research Council.

Jacobs, L. L. & White, L. (1994). *A draft model for gifted child education*. Transvaalse Onderwysdepartement Onderwysnavorsingsburo. Werkstuk 515, Augustus.

Khatena, J. Gifted (1992). *Challenge and response for education*. Itasca: Peacock Publishers, Inc.

Kimmins, C. W. (1931). *Modern movements in education*. The Transvaal Education News, VII(1).

Kokot, S. J. (1992). *Understanding giftedness: a South African perspective*. Durban: Butterworths.

Kokot, S. J. (1994). *Help, our child is gifted*. Pretoria: Promedia.

Kokot, S. J. & Kokot, P. L. (1998). The effect of gender stereotyping on gifted black adolescents. *Gifted and Talented International*, **13** (1), 19–27.

Lategan, M. M. (1986). *Onderwys vir die begaafde kind—'n Histories-pedagogiese deurskouing* [English: Education of the gifted child—a Historical/pedagogical view]. Unpublished thesis. Pretoria: University of South Africa.

Lumadi, T. E. (1998). *Sociocultural factors in the family significant for the development of giftedness in Vhavenda children*. Unpublished M.Ed. dissertation: Pretoria: University of South Africa.

Mbiti, J. S. (1969). *African religions and philosophy*. London: Heineman.

Mda, L. & Van Wyk, C. (Eds.). (no date). *Voices from young Africa*. Johannesburg: The South African Committee for Higher Education/Macmillan Boleswa.

Meintjies, C. (1988). Gifted child education in the Cape. *Creata*, **6**, 1–4.

Mentz, H. J. (1991). *An investigation of the four-area curriculum extension and enrichment model for gifted education as viewed through the Cartesian, Socialist and Deep Ecology epistemologies*. Unpublished M.Phil. Cape Town: University of Cape Town.

Middelton, J. (Ed.). (1997). *Encyclopedia of Africa South of the Sahara,* Vol. 2. New York: Macmillan.

Mitchell, B. M. & Williams, W. G. (1987). Education of the gifted and talented in the world community. *Phi Delta Kappan*, **68**, 531–534.

Mwamwenda, T. S. (1990). *Educational psychology: an African perspective*. Durban: Butterworths.

Neethling, J. S. (1985). Historical overview of gifted education in South Africa from about 1918. *Gifted International*, **111**, 51–64.

Oladokun, T. O. (1987). Factors militating against gifted education in Nigeria. *Gifted International*, **4**, 114–117.

O'Teul, F. S., Swanson, J. D.& Elam, A. (1997). Early identification of potentially gifted students using non-traditional measurements. In: J. Chan, R. Li & J. Spinks (Eds.), *Maximising Potential: Lengthening and Strengthening Our Stride* (pp. 532–536). Hong Kong: Hong Kong University.

Poats, R. (1984). Crisis and response in Africa. *OECD Observer*, **13**, 26–29.

Ray, B. C. (1976). *Systems and models for developing programs for gifted and talented*. Englewood Cliffs, N.J.: Prentice Hall.

Rideout, W. M. J. Jr. (1987). Rights of access and equal opportunity: focus on sub-Saharan Africa. In: N. B. Tarrow

(Ed.), *Human Rights and Education* (pp. 17–36). New York:

Robertson, F. S. (1963). Opvoeding tot leierskap [English: Education for leadership]. *Die Unie, 60,* 79–87.

Shiman, D. (1988). *Teaching about human rights. Issues of justice in a global age.* Denver: Center for Teaching International Relations, University of Denver.

Sithole, M. (1988). Zimbabwe: in search of a stable democracy. In: L. Diamond, J. J. Linz & S. M. Lipset (Eds.), *Democracy in Developing Countries. Africa,* Vol. 2. (pp. 217–257). Boulder, CO: Lynne Rienner Publishers.

Skuy, M., Gaydon, V., Hoffenber, S. & Fridjhon. (1990). Predictors of performance of disadvantaged adolescents in a gifted program. *Gifted Child Quarterly,* **34,** 92–101.

Skuy, M., Kaniel, S. & Tzuriel, D. (1988). Dynamic assessment of intellectually superior Istraeli children in a low socioeconomic status community. *Gifted Education International,* **5,** 90–96.

Smit, G. J. (1954). Die begaafde kind [English: The gifted child]. *Die Unie,* **49,** 268–278.

Tannenbaum, A. J. (1983). *Gifted children: Psychological and educational perspectives.* New York: Macmillan.

Tarrow, N. B. (Ed.) (1987). *Human rights and education.* New York: Pergamon Press.

Taylor, C. A. (1985). The university and the gifted child: a generic link? *Gifted Child Today, 39,* 14.

Tembela, A. J. (1987). Training teachers for the gifted. *Gifted International,* **4,** (2), 64–67.

Thomas, R. M. (1987). Exceptional abilities and educational rights: concern for the handicapped and gifted in Britain, China and Indonesia. In: N. B. Tarrow (Ed.), *Human Rights and Education* (pp. 57–79). New York: Pergamon Press.

Tlale, C. D.(1990). *Principles for the design of a culturally relevant instrument to identify gifted black secondary school children.* Unpublished Ph. D.Thesis. Pretoria: University of Pretoria.

Tracey, A. (1990). *Keywords in African music.* Stellenbosch: Music Educator's Conference.

Tutu, D. (1991). *Sunday Times. March 31.*

Union of South Africa. (1953). *Debates of Parliament (Hansard).* Elsiesriver: Nasionale handelsdrukkery Beperk.

Venter, E. H. (1955). *Die verskynsel van begaafdheid en 'n eksperimentele onsoek van verskillende prosedures waardeur spesiale onderwys vir begaafde leerlinge voorsien kan word* [English: The phenomenon of giftedness and an experimental study of different procedures whereby special education can be provided for gifted pupils]. Unpublished D.Ed. thesis. Bloemfontein: University of the Orange Free State.

UNESCO (1998). *World Education Report: teachers and teaching in a changing world.* Paris: UNESCO.

United Nations Development Program (UNDP) (1998). *Human development report 1998.* New York: Oxford University Press.

Yoder, J. H. (1986). Gifted education: a view from the third world. *Gifted Education International,* **4,** 74–79.

Yossufu, A. (1983). Giftedness in context. In: B. M. Shore, F. Gagné, S. Larivee, R. H. Tali & R. E. Tremblay (Eds.), *Face to face with giftedness.* Montreal, Canada: McGill University Printing Service.

Programs and Practices for Identifying and Nurturing Giftedness and Talent in Latin American Countries

Eunice M. L. Soriano de Alencar,[1] Sheyla Blumen-Pardo[2] and Doris Castellanos-Simons[3]

[1]Catholic University of Brasilia, Brasilia, Brazil
[2]Catholic University of Peru, Lima, Peru
[3]Pedagogical University Enrique J. Varona, Havana, Cuba

Introduction

We are beginning the third millennium and gifted education in Latin American countries is still very heterogeneous and complex in its development. While Brazil, the largest and only Portuguese speaking country, is consolidating its special services in different levels of education, and other countries such as Peru, Cuba, Mexico, and Argentina, have shown a significant progress, others have little or no provision at all for their gifted and talented population.

The purpose of this chapter is to provide an overview of gifted education in Latin American countries. It will focus first on Peru and South American Spanish spoken countries. Following, gifted education in Brazil will be described as the country which offers the greatest diversity of programs for gifted students. Next, attention for the gifted and the talented in Cuba, Central, and North American countries will be presented. The chapter finalizes with issues and perspectives on gifted education in Latin America.

Gifted and Talented Education in South American Spanish Spoken Countries

Do the gifted make the country, or does the country make the gifted? This question becomes dramatic when we consider the intellectual functioning levels of the majority of South American children, who, beginning the third millennium, live under poor conditions (Pereyra, 1987; Thorne & Blumen, 1996; Casassus, Froemel, Palafox & Cusato, 1998).

The South American Spanish spoken countries are mainly multicultural and multilingual. Peru, Chile, and Venezuela, among other Andean countries, are passing through an Educational Reform sponsored by many international agencies, in which constructivism plays a very important role (Cardó, 1990; Peruvian Ministry of Education, 1995). Dramatic reduction in the negative indicators of schooling, such as absenteeism and school failure, has been exhibited in these countries, and the goal of universal education is close to being achieved (Blumen, 1998a).

Several attempts to nurture the gifted and talented can be seen in Peru and other South American Spanish spoken countries. Some of them based on scientific research coming from university research centers (Zubiria & Gonzales, 1982; Samper, 1987; Mönks, Ypenburg & Blumen, 1997), or coming from technical institutes (CONCYTEC, 1989, 1998). Others came from the government and are politically influenced (Gonzales, 1991; Ruiz, 1991), and very few come from enterprises or private institutes (i.e. *MENTE FUTURA*, Fundación para la Creatividad y el Talento, among others) and have a hands-on, practical approach (Blumen, 1999b). However, all of them are significant attempts to meet the needs of the gifted and talented of the region (Alencar & Blumen, 1993).

The State-of-Art of Gifted and Talented Education

Provisions for nurturing the gifted and talented in South American Spanish spoken countries began in the late 70s under the influence of Renzulli's theory (Renzulli, 1978). However, due to the multicultural diversity of most of the Andean countries, the need to consider the context as an important factor to assess high ability focused the attention on models which considered the context as an important factor to explain high ability, such as Mönks Interdependence Triadic Model (Mönks, 1992) among others.

The development of educational policies and programs for the gifted and talented in South American Spanish spoken countries varies greatly. While policies are not essential to the existence of programs for gifted learners in the classroom, countries such as Peru,

Colombia and Venezuela, which have legislation-based policies appear to offer better programs according to the educational needs of the gifted and talented.

Peru is leading the South American Spanish spoken countries in the education of the gifted, with a broader provision of programs, both in the public and private school system. Other countries such as Venezuela and Colombia, that first began with special programs for the gifted and talented, have deactivated most of their programs due to financial difficulties; and others, such as Chile and Argentina, have isolated efforts in the private school system. However, there are still countries in the region, such as Ecuador, Bolivia, and Paraguay, which do not provide their public schools with special programs for the gifted and talented learners.

Argentina

Towards the beginning of the year 2000, three private institutions were created to attend the needs of gifted children in Argentina: two in the capital city of Buenos Aires and the third in the province of Mendoza (Kloosterman, 1999). They are all private institutes whose main goal was to identify and encourage the abilities of the gifted children coming from the middle and middle-upper class. The identification and attention programs were based on Renzulli's (1978) conception of giftedness and the methodology involved parents and teachers counseling services. In 1994, the First Iberoamerican Conference on Talented Children was held in Buenos Aires. Later, the First International Conference on High Intelligence and Education was organized in Mendoza (Kloosterman, 1999). However, the public sector does not yet provide a comprehensive program for the gifted, and the great majority of gifted and talented children in Argentina, most of them coming from poor environments, are still waiting to be attended by the public sector.

Chile

Since 1964, Chile has attempted to fulfill the gifted and talented needs, led by Dr. Gambra, who founded The Chilean Institute for the Gifted. In 1979, the Andes-Chile National Association for the Development of the Gifted Education, as well as the Latin American Association for the Integral Development of the Gifted was founded; the following year, Supraxia Universal, an Institute for gifted youngsters and adults from all countries was also founded. However, most of these institutes were deactivated in the following years. In 1985, a new method for developing gifted behavior from the first days of life was put in practice by Dr. Gambra (1991) who is promoting his method in the other Spanish spoken countries of the region.

Colombia

In 1986, the Alberto Merani Foundation for the Development of Intelligence was established with the goal of being an enrichment center for 12 year olds and older gifted children. The foundation was developed based on the results obtained in a study about the cognitive abilities of 14- to 15- year old high school students, which indicated a delay in the cognitive development due to the adverse living and schooling conditions. In 1987, the First International Conference on Intelligence was organized. This conference was the starting point for the creation of the Institute for the Gifted Children in Bogota, which had started its activities in the previous year. The activities of the foundation are continuing, and focused on the validity of their pedagogical proposals.

Peru

Peru has quickly developed a concern about gifted and talented children (Blumen, 1995, 1997, 1998a, c, 1999b). In the past seven years, changes of misconceptions and efforts to understand and nurture the gifted and talented have been exhibited, both in public and private education, as well as in the mass media. Although there is a tremendous gap between public and private education (Blumen, 1996, 1999b; Thorne & Blumen, 1996), it is important to recognize that the Educational Reform which began in 1993 nationwide has stated the attention towards the individual needs of the learner (Peruvian Ministry of Education, 1995).

Research on creativity expressed through artistic tasks began during the Educational Reform of 1972 in an attempt to achieve the integral education of the student. In the first half of the 1970s, theoretical and methodological proposals were submitted and the Ministry of Education with the former Federal Republic of Germany, carried out a project on the Education for the Arts. Since 1978, the research carried out in Peru was experimental and comparative. The relationship between variables such as the demographic and socioeconomic level and creativity were examined (Stahr, 1979). In the 1980s, various mediating and conditioning processes were incorporated in the research (Blumen, 2000; Neuhaus, 1982).

In the mid 80s, the first research in the field of gifted education was carried out on a national basis to identify the gifted and talented, involving 3,000 children. Theoretical and methodological proposals aimed at achieving a complete use of human resources to improve the development of the country (CON-CYTEC, 1989; Pereyra, 1987).

The most important result of this study took place in 1983, when a Law of Education for the highly able was established (Ministry of Education, 1983). Then, enrichment educational practices began in both public and private school systems. Although limited in number, these programs represented the first attempts to detect and attend the needs of the gifted and talented children in Peru (CONCYTEC, 1989; Gonzales, 1991; Ruiz, 1991). In the early 90s, research focused on the development of creative abilities and on creative behavior, and a more practical approach to research has emerged.

More recently, the Catholic University of Peru in cooperation with the Catholic University of Nijmegen, has supported most of the research on gifted education in Peru (Blumen, 1996, 1998b, 1999a). As a starting point, doctoral research in the field began in 1994, under the supervision of Prof. Dr. Franz Mönks. Two years later, the First Symposium *Creativity, Intelligence, and Talent* was organized, sponsored by the Graduate Program of Psychology, at the Catholic University of Peru. In addition, from then on, the symposium is organized on a yearly basis.

In May 1997, an experimental teacher training workshop, which benefited 3,000 children and 100 teachers was developed as the first effort to train regular public school teachers to meet the needs of the disadvantaged gifted and talented students. This experimental workshop was sponsored by the *Teacher Training National Plan* (PLANCAD), the *German Cooperation Agency for Education* (GTZ) and the *Catholic University of Peru* (PUCP), coordinated by Dr. Eva Gefferth and Prof. Sheyla Blumen. The follow-up and the evaluation process results were positive and strongly recommended application on a national basis (Blumen, 2000), and were introduced as a relevant topic in the regular national teacher training programs.

Later, in December 1997, the book *Nuestros niños son talentosos* (Mönks, Ypenburg & Blumen, 1997) was published by the Catholic University of Peru. This was the first book in the country to call attention to the characteristics of the gifted and talented to promote appropriate educational programs. During 1998, two workshops on gifted and talented education showed that the need to train teachers was increasing dramatically. In 1999 *Mente Futura* started its functioning with a dynamic program of activities involving identification, differentiation and training workshops on the needs of the poor gifted children attending public schools of both, Lima City and the Peruvian Provinces.

In January 1999, the *European Advanced Diploma in Educating the Gifted*, sponsored by the *European Council for High Ability* (ECHA) and the University of Nijmegen, and coordinated by *Mente Futura* was started in Lima City. The *Leon Pinelo School* of Lima provided the infrastructure and the well-equipped Auditorium for the ECHA meetings to take place, in order to train teachers from the region in gifted and talented education. The school, very well-known for its integral philosophy on child development, was also open for the candidates to visit as a relevant setting or for practicing purposes (Robotics, Special Advanced Science or Maths programs, Visual arts enrichment programs, among others).

Peruvian ECHA Diploma candidates come mostly from the public sector, although there are some from the private sector; they belong to all the different levels of education, from preschool to superior education levels. Some of them are staff members of the Ministry of Education, others are university professors, school directors, pedagogical coordinators, special education and homeroom teachers, as well as psychologists. Although most of them come from Lima, around 12% come from the provinces.

Following the characteristic of the psycho/pedagogical research on this part of the planet, most of them focus their attention on practical outcomes of their research, such as identification and attention alternatives inside the regular classroom. However, on a macro level, the focus is related to the legal determinants for establishing an acceleration program as an official alternative for those who deserve it.

The impact of these changes in policies and practices towards the education for the gifted, must be monitored to establish new research lineaments on the psychology and education of the gifted in this part of the world.

Venezuela

In Venezuela there are two programs supervised by governmental organizations that serve gifted and talented children. The first is a branch of the Ministry of Education and is responsible for the whole area of special education. The second is the Galileo Program of the Gran Mariscal of Ayacucho Foundation. The Galileo Program goal is to select and prepare secondary students with outstanding academic performance for continuing advanced studies in foreign universities. The program is based on four stages (preselection, selection course, reinforcement and preparation program, results) which provide a complete psycho/pedagogical assessment through the program.

Issues and Trends

In South American Spanish spoken countries, where each school establishes its own criteria for identification, ecological validity of the assessment process needs to be taking into account on the selection of an identification process. One of the most important considerations of this process is the establishment of Norms for the general population, which in multicultural and multilingual countries such as the Andean countries is very difficult to achieve. Therefore, in most cases, norms for specific subgroups need to be established.

Each country and school looks for a way to serve the gifted and talented needs. Acceleration, which was an exception in most South America Spanish spoken countries a decade ago, is slowly being considered as a learning alternative for gifted children (Blumen, 2000). Enrichment activities such as, drama, knowledge bowl, chess club, Model UN, debate, drama, music classes, and science-related clubs are available in some of the schools. The students also participate in the various talent searches programs sponsored by universities in their own countries and in countries of the region, such as science fairs, inventors fairs, maths competitions, among others, and can also compete or get together on international events.

Another common procedure, especially for grades 1–5, is clustering. When students have been identified, they are grouped in the same classroom. The teacher for this class receives special support on the characteristics of the gifted and talented, problems that are often found in a gifted population and an introduction to methods that have been successful with highly capable students. Clustering provides opportunities for the students to be grouped together on some occasions as well as having opportunities to work with non-gifted peers.

Education of the gifted in South America Spanish spoken countries has developed over the last decade. However, this seemed to happen due to isolated efforts. There is a danger that any such major thrust might become a panacea, in which case there is a risk that the needs of the individual would not be met.

Special resources such as universities, research institutions, museums, and other professional organizations are still neglected in educating the gifted and talented children. These institutions have the knowledge, the personnel and the equipment that can cater for gifted and talented students, and give them insight into attractive and challenging areas and methods. These places can also supply mentors for gifted individuals. However, there appear to be only sporadic efforts to use these resources.

The promising sectors are, on the one hand, the schools that belong to foreign communities, such as the German, British, Jewish, and American schools, among others, which have European, Israeli or American influence. And, on the other hand, the science-based industries with research and development departments, and the National Council of Science and Technology who is presenting laws for these industries to adopt youngsters into their research and development departments, and enable them to work with their professionals (CONCYTEC, 1998).

To monitor the impact of these changes in policies and practices on the education for the gifted, ongoing research will be needed as well as a sense of advocacy on behalf of educators and parents.

Gifted and Talented Education in Brazil

Educational concern for the gifted began in Brazil under the influence of a Russian teacher, Helena Antipoff, who arrived in this country in 1929. Before coming to Brazil, Helena Antipoff studied in France and Switzerland, where she conducted studies on intelligence and testing. After arriving in the country, Antipoff continued her research on gifted children, which resulted in several publications in the 1930s and 1940s, calling attention to the need of early identification and educational services for the gifted.

In the beginning of the 1970s, two important facts called attention to the special needs of gifted children. The first was a national general law for education established by the federal government in 1971. This law included an article about special education, stating that "all students, with mental and physical deficiencies, those who are late in their schooling as well as the gifted should receive special treatment, according to the policy at the state level." The second was the First National Conference on Gifted Children, also in 1971, sponsored by the Ministry of Education. For the first time in Brazil, different aspects of gifted education were broadly discussed among psychologists and educators.

Since then, policies in support of gifted and talented education were reported in several documents from the Federal Government. One of the most important reports was published by the Federal Education Council in 1987. This report was entitled The Hour of the Gifted. A Federal Education Council Proposal (Conselho Federal de Educação, 1987) encouraged actions that would be of immediate help in meeting the needs of gifted students. This document outlined the basic principles of special education, criteria, and methods for identifying the gifted, different kinds of programs for the gifted, presented the definition of giftedness adopted in the country, and included several recommendations related to gifted education.

More recently, in 1995, the Special Education Office, from the Ministry of Education, published a report outlining the federal education policies and guidelines for educating the gifted and talented students (Secretaria de Educação Especial, 1995). To reinforce the need for implementing the federal policies at the state level, the Office organized a two-day seminar in 1996 for the staff of the State Special Education Offices from the 26 Brazilian states. During this seminar, guidelines for implementing programs for gifted students were provided, and different models of programs for educating gifted students and provisions for special talents in specific areas of giftedness were discussed.

A new stimulus to the field of gifted education was the III Ibero-American Conference in Brasilia, in 1998. This conference was organized by the Special Education Office, with the support of UNESCO, the Federal District Government, and the Catholic University of Brasilia. Several well-known scholars from the field were invited as keynote speakers, promoting discussions on the importance of nurturing special talents in different areas of giftedness. The State Special Education secretaries attended the conference, at the request of the Ministry of Education. The Brazilian federal government once again called attention to the state educational government to the need of implementing programs for the gifted.

However, as described by Alencar (1986, 1991, 1998), misconceptions about gifted and talented education are still present among educators and in the community at large. One misconception is the idea that gifted students should always show outstanding performance in all fields; another common belief is that giftedness is a very rare phenomenon. It is also believed that gifted students demonstrate extremely high level of performance and achievement from very early in their lives and that expressions of high ability continue throughout life independent of environmental conditions. Educators also ignore the reality that to be superior in one area does not necessarily imply a superior performance in others. Ambivalence about gifted students prevails in Brazilian society; sometimes the children are perceived with admiration and sometimes with indifference or even hostility.

Current Programs

Before presenting the major Brazilian programs for gifted students, it is important to note that some programs described previously by Alencar and Blumen (1993) were discontinued. This is the case of the program for the gifted and talented sponsored by the National Service of Industry and the program for disadvantaged gifted student sponsored by AVIBRAS Foundation. Other programs, which included different projects and support for talents in specific areas, are facing many difficulties, due to the lack of adequate direction and leadership. In addition to the programs described in this chapter, a few others are being implemented in some private and military schools in Rio de Janeiro, Soã Paulo, and other Brazilian cities. However specific details were not available.

The Gifted College Student: Special Program of Training

The Special Training Program for gifted college students was initiated in 1979 by the Department of Improvement of Graduate Personnel of the Ministry of Education. This programs aims:

(1) To provide an excellent academic preparation to those college students who demonstrate an outstanding performance in their academic activities.
(2) To supply those students with opportunities to further develop higher level thinking abilities and communication abilities.
(3) To stimulate new pedagogical experiences to improve college education (Dessen, 1994).

Students are selected for this program during their second or third semester at the university. The main criteria for the selection are: high academic achievement, nomination by university professors, and high interest and motivation in carrying out their studies. The selected students receive scholarships and remain in the program throughout their undergraduate program.

The program started with 15 students from two universities. This number increased during this last decade when universities from all parts of the country requested authorization to implement the program in some of their departments. In 1997, 3,556 university students from 317 departments at 59 private and public Brazilian universities participated in the program (CAPES, 1997). In each department, a professor is chosen as the mentor and is responsible for organizing a program of activities and supervising the students. Mentors are selected from the university professors who demonstrate real interest in the program, high academic productivity, and a good relationship with colleagues and students. Every mentor is responsible for 12 students and has to evaluate each of them at the end of each semester.

The program was evaluated in 1997 by a team of scholars (CAPES, 1997). According to the evaluation, 92% of the students across the 317 university departments presented a good performance. Recently, two studies were conducted to analyze the effects of the programs, how the students were perceived by their university teachers and colleagues, and how the program was perceived by non-participating students (Balbachevsky, 1997; Bottura, 1997). A positive impact of the program on the students as well as on their University departments was observed. In addition, teachers and students shared a highly positive image of the participating students.

Project to Orient and Identify Talents: A Program in the Private School System

Among the programs for the gifted in the private school system, the most well-known is in Objetivo Education Center in So Paulo. The Center is an educational complex ranging from kindergarten to college, with several schools in different states.

This project was initiated in 1972 and included separate classes for gifted students, followed by the organization of an advanced study program. In 1986, a series of extracurricular courses for the gifted and talented students began with the general purpose of challenging the students' potential and encouraging them to use their own resources in a creative manner and respecting their own pace. The identification procedures are based on the results of intelligence tests and teachers' nominations. Children with exceptional talent in literature and visual arts are also accepted, when indicated by the school psychologist (Cuppertino, 1998).

The courses comprise two areas: Technology and humanities. The former aims to help the gifted students become more familiar with technical advances and to find answers for technological problems. The purpose of the humanities course is the exploration of different experiences which in turn would lead to the development of creative and critical thinking, leadership abilities and communication skills. A description of these courses is provided by Di Genio, Ancona-Lopez & Brandão (1990) and Cuppertino (1998).

Besides the enrichment programs for gifted and talented students, the Project to Orient and Identify Talents (POIT) organizes regular courses on gifted education for educators and psychologists in São Paulo. It also has a counseling service for gifted students and their families. Conferences on giftedness and talent are organized periodically with the most well-known scholars in the field.

A Center for Talent Development

In 1993, a Center for the Development of Potential and Talent was founded in Lavras, a city in the state of Minas Gerais. Its main purpose is to provide an enrichment program for the gifted children. Other goals of the Center are:

(1) To identify the special interests and educational needs of talented children and adolescents and to provide assistance toward meeting these needs.
(2) To offer support to gifted children in their personal and emotional developmental needs.
(3) To ensure proper stimulation of youth so as to develop specific abilities and talents (Guenther, 1995, p. 27).

The identification procedure occurs in three stages. At first, elementary school teachers nominate students on the basis of a list of characteristics related to several abilities; nominated students are then examined by the school technical personnel who reevaluate and complete the observations. The students who are selected, as well as their parents, are then interviewed by the facilitator. The final stage occurs during the first year of the child's participation in the enrichment program; during this period, selected students are observed by the facilitator who analyzes the program's benefits for the children.

In 1996, 644 children from different socio-economic classes were enrolled in the enrichment program; these children participate in activities organized in different areas, such as communication and humanities and science and technology. Interest groups are formed with children with defined common interests. Projects are also developed under the supervision of a mentor. Regular encounters, with about 100 children, occur once a month (Guenther, 1997).

Public School Programs for the Gifted and Talented

Programs for the gifted and talented have been implemented in the public school system in several states. However, according to Sabatella (in press), the number of students participating in the program is very small. She contacted all the state special education office requesting information about programs for the gifted and concluded that the only public educational

system with a large number of identified students was in the Federal District, where 210 students were participating in special programs in 1997.

The program from the public school system in the Federal District offers gifted students opportunities to optimally develop their potential and talents; to promote their personal social and school adjustment; to expose the students to experiences, materials and information outside the bounds of the regular curriculum; and to expose students to more difficult or more in-depth material (Fonseca, Caixeta, Souza & Cavalcante, 1990).

As described elsewhere (Alencar, 1991), the nomination of the students for this program is made by the teachers who refer students who have demonstrated high intellectual ability, leadership, creativity, academic achievement or talents in the performing and visual arts. The teacher then observes the nominated students for one month, using a checklist to guide these observations. The nominated students fill out a questionnaire about their own interests, hobbies, favorite sports, preference for working individually or in groups, among other topics. Psychological tests, such as Raven's Progressive Matrice Test—General Scale, are also administered.

Educational support for the gifted students occurs in Resource Centers at their own schools and at the Park School. At the Resource Centers, gifted and talented students are exposed to in-depth material on the typical curriculum subjects. At the Park School, students study music, visual arts, ceramics and performing arts once a week; according to their interests, students also participate in one of several clubs (science, flute, photography, foreign language, folklore and others). The Park School also has some learning centers where different enrichment programs are offered.

Provisions for Special Talents

A large number of schools for talented students in music, ballet, sports and visual arts are available in many cities of all states. Brazilian middle class children usually have other classes besides those in their regular school. These classes allow the identification of talents and it is the starting point for a professional specialization. There are also several competitions at the local, state and national level in mathematics, chess and science. The oldest and most famous is a project known as Scientists for the Future, described by Alencar (1986), which is a nationwide competition that aims to discover new talents in the field of science and to help those students to continue their studies until the university level.

Issues and Trends

Despite the efforts from the Special Education Office, at the Ministry of Education, the majority of the Brazilian states are resistant to the implementation of special programs for the gifted and talented students. This is mostly explained by the educational problems of the country, as the high rate of illiteracy, limited number of educational institutions, and reduced financial resources for the educational field. Misconceptions about gifted also mask the real needs of this group of students.

Research on giftedness and talent is scarce due to the shortage of experts in the field in Brazil. Most of the research studies have been conducted on creativity and ways to foster creative abilities among the students (Alencar, 1994, 1995a, 1995b; Alencar & Virgolim, 1995; Wechsler, 1995).

There is a lack of programs at the university level to prepare teachers to work with the gifted and talented students; this explains the lack of certification requirements for teachers of the gifted. Courses on giftedness and gifted education have been offered only in a very limited number of Brazilian universities. In general, teachers' preparation for dealing with gifted students is accomplished by special in-service programs; experts from the Brazilian Association for the Gifted have contributed to this training.

We hope that the III Ibero-American Conference on Giftedness in Brasilia, in 1998, was a significant stimulus for discussions among parents, teachers, state government, university staff, and the population in general, about the needs of gifted and talented students, and the importance of generating new programs and implementing different services for these students, whose talents and abilities have been neglected.

Gifted and Talented Education in Cuba, North and Central America Spanish Speaking Countries

Research on giftedness and talent has had a relatively recent development in Cuba, as well as in most of the countries of the region. However, it is necessary to point up that this development has been preceded and stimulated by practical innovative intervention, since education has been a priority and one of the most relevant milestones of the Cuban social project.

Concerns about the education of the gifted and talented were already present in the classics of Cuba's social, pedagogical and scientific thinking. Nevertheless, very few studies on identification and nurturing of giftedness were conducted until the 40s and 50s, where some of them are reported, especially in the University of Havana (Lorenzo, 1996).

Basically, research on outstanding and competent individuals has been approached since 1970 from studies on creativity. González (1985) analyzed the role of moral development and motivational instances such as aspirations, ideals, self-concept, and career motivations, on the emergency of creative performances among high school and college students. Likewise, González (1990), Labarrere (1994), Mitjans (1995), among others, developed related topics concerning the personality of technically creative individuals, the

relations between high abilities and self-regulation, as well as integrative approaches to creativity and its education. The latter could be considered an early expression of Cuban scholar's concerns for giftedness and talent research whereas those notions were not explicitly assumed at the moment.

A very sensitive period for development and reset on giftedness in Cuba began in the eighties. That was the time of the first official projects of research and educational intervention for identifying and fostering intellectual abilities and giftedness in children and adolescents. Examples of very well known projects are ARGOS—Development of Intelligence, Creativity and Talent, PRYCREA—Project for Reflexive Thinking and Creativity, TEDI—Intellectual Development Techniques, and Learning to Learn, inspired on the Venezuelan project Learning to Think and also conducted with children from rural zones of the country.

A meaningful moment for the recognition of this field within Cuban educational and scientific milieus was also the celebration of the I Ibero-American Symposium Pensar y Crear: Desarrollo de la Inteligencia, in Havana, 1991. Supported by the Ministry of Education and the Pedagogical University of Havana, the conference allowed for the first time the explicit discussion of the topic and motivated a cooperative search for contextual solutions to the educational issues of giftedness and talent. From 1990, the most important psycho-pedagogical meetings, such as the well known Pedagogía and Hacia la Educación del Siglo XXI, are systematically including the exchange of experiences about giftedness, thus giving a new impulse to the social commitments with its investigation and education.

Misconceptions about Giftedness

Social stereotypes and misconceptions about the gifted still remain a gap in the educational progress of this field. A strong prejudice is firmly rooted in the popular and teachers thinking that any differentiated practice with the gifted threaten equity and democratic principles of education. In the scientific domain, concepts like talent, creativity and high abilities have substituted notions like giftedness, intelligence and exceptionally, in order to avoid the elitist and genetic connotation associated to those terms. In general, Cuban society, especially educators, have been more sensitive to the ideal of an education which promotes giftedness and talent within the regular classes, for all the students, according to their potential and without segregation, than to the acceptance of an especial education for the gifted and talented.

Some of the most common misconceptions in this field are the prevalence of cognitive dimensions and academic success when defining giftedness, the belief that gifted individuals do not need special provisions because they "succeed anyway without external support," the idea that their superiority will be shown in all the contents or activity domains and psychological areas (i.e. advanced emotional development) or, on the contrary, the feeling that gifted and talented always experience emotional troubles and social difficulties (Castellanos, 1997).

An Overview of the Research on Giftedness and Talent in Cuba: Its Impact on Education

As indicated before, the explicit research on giftedness and talent in Cuba dates back to the late eighties; with very few exceptions, the hallmark of these first works was its commitment to education.

In the Faculty of Educational Sciences of the Pedagogical University of Havana, a research team was established in 1986 to study questions related to giftedness education and provide teachers training on that domain. Some of their tasks concerned the search of identification procedures and techniques suitable to the specific context and mass conditions schools, and the experimentation of instructional strategies aiming at developing higher intellectual skills and student self-management within the regular curriculum of high school and pedagogical careers (Martinez, 1994; Córdova, 1996).

ARGOS project was created in 1986, supported by the Ministry of Education, and with the participation of collaborators from the Pedagogical University of Havana, and educators and researchers from several institutions. The project undertook the task of sensitizing some strategic milieus with the educational needs of the gifted and talented. Its general goals encompassed working with school children (mainly at elementary and secondary level), parents, teachers and directive instances to promote an ambiance of transformation and excellence at school. Definition of giftedness adopted was, to a large extent, inspired by Renzulli's conception of giftedness. Research developed by the project between 1986–1996 focused on topics such as the psycho-pedagogical characterization of Cuban gifted children, the study of their families and its functional dynamic and the diagnostic of teachers' preparation for identifying and nurturing giftedness and talent. Likewise, special programs and strategies for fostering giftedness and talent in the regular classroom were experimentally implemented, with attention to special populations such as disabled and handicapped students, and to their families. As part of the project, Scientific Community PAIDOS was intending to develop scientific abilities and attitudes as well as creative talents among children and their teachers. Unfortunately, ARGOS was discontinued in 1997 whereas a part of its programs is still in progress.

One of the most relevant consequences of this incipient progress in gifted research has been the concern for qualifying teachers and promoting awareness about giftedness and its education. Just to give some examples, the Pedagogical University included two optional courses devoted to the identification of

potential talents, and to the enrichment programs available within the regular curriculum as a part of its Masters in Education program. The higher level career of Primary Education added an academic program, "Attention to individual differences in the regular classroom," which mainly focus on differentiated treatments to stimulate the more able and creative students, and to promote intellectual development. A course about the special needs of the gifted and talented was offered for the first time in 1996 to the teachers and directors of the Vocational High Schools, special centers where a large majority of high able and talented adolescents are attending to.

New research and intervention projects are emerging. That is the case of the Group for Talent Orientation, at the Pedagogical University, and the recent project for Leadership in Talent Youth, of the Center of Psychological and Sociological Research. Educational investigation and experimental practices conducted from schools and universities have proliferated in the last years. As far as can be observed in the proceedings of the psycho-pedagogical congresses and workshops realized, the latter are mostly centered on the development of creative thinking, general and specific domain skills and strategies and metacognitive abilities as well as it moral, affective and social issues. Basic and applied research on the gifted and talented, its identification and education has still a long way to go in Cuba.

State Concerns and Policies Related to Gifted Education

Since the early years of the sixties, considerable efforts were deployed to provide special attention to talents education whereas this intention was not explicitly stated on official documents and legislation. It remained rather subsumed in a general aspiration of nurturing 'a many-sided personality' with a particular emphasis on integrality (encompassing moral, affective and social dimensions, in addition to the development of intellectual abilities and talents).

At the moment, only a few documents deal with explicit indications for differentiated treatment of the gifted and talented. An official definition of giftedness and talent is still absent. Educational response to the special needs of the gifted and talented is commonly conceived as a part of general strategies of attention to individual differences. However, a suggestive exception is the normative, existing since 1991 in the higher education level which rules a special organization of the instructional processes for individuals categorized as high performance students. They are described as those individuals who:

(1) Show more rapid pace of assimilation and more advanced learning aptitudes in one or more of the disciplines or content areas, or in scientific research and technical activities.

(2) Could be identified by their superior performances, creativity and independence in the solution of their academic, technical or research tasks, and have shown to be able to assimilate complementary tasks in their studies project (Reglamento de Trabajo Docente-Metodologico para la Educación Superior. Resolución 269/1991, p. 10).

A differentiated curriculum is recommended for these youth according to their potentialities and individual interests. Several kinds of curricular adaptation, such as compacting courses, the addition, elimination or substitution of academic subjects or topics, should give them more time for scientific and research activities. Mentorships, provided by teachers and outstanding professionals and researchers, is stipulated as a part of the special provisions regulated in the law.

Unfortunately, the existence of these sort of documents is not yet generalized for the rest of the levels and types of instruction, so that most of the efforts done to adapt school process to the gifted and talented educational characteristics are originated by the teachers own initiative and school administration with more or less success.

Provisions for the Gifted and Talented in Cuba

Special provisions for the gifted and talented in Cuba are carried out in different ways. It is important to point out that Cuban education is totally public. In the framework of the formal school (National System of Education), attention to special talents has been a historical concern.

Vocational High Schools for Sciences and for Pedagogical Sciences, Schools for Sports Initiation, Vocational Schools for Arts, among others, constitute special pre-university level centers; the students are mainly selected on the basis of specific aptitudes and performances. In addition to a general curriculum, they can benefit from a flexible cycle of specialization and complementary (enriched) programs aiming at developing talents, vocation and careers orientation within specific domains. Focus on investigation work, and the search of concrete and applicable solutions to the regional problems are important features of the pedagogical conception of those schools, particularly in High Schools for Sciences. There, intervention for the giftedness can adopt the way of instructional variants of enrichment and subject matter acceleration, advanced thinking skills training in the classroom and mentorship.

Likewise, organizations such as Children Innovators's Movement, Interests Centers like regional and international Competitions and school Olympics are conceived as stimulus for the gifted and talented development.

On the other hand, attention to special talents is provided by specific institutions in each community. That is the case of the Culture Community Centers, the

Young Computational Clubs, the Centers for Creative Youth (Visual Arts), the Centers for the Young Musicians, the museums and sports-centers, among others. Courses, activities and programs are organized to promote apprenticeships as well as development of interests and creative productivity in children, adolescents and youth, who may freely attend them.

In 1997, a specialized Chair for the Development of Intelligence, Creativity and Talent was initiated, sponsored by the Pedagogical University of Havana, attending to promote necessary research and intervention in the area, social awareness and support, and to create the basis for scientific understandings and exchanges between Cuban investigators and practitioners. Also, the need for a greater communication with the international scientific community is recognized.

Programs and Practices for the Education of the Gifted and Talented in Central America

The precarious situations of the countries from the Central region of America, in the economic, social and educational aspects, determines to a large extent the fact that financial resources and efforts have to necessarily be spent on the projects devoted to more elementary goals such as, for example, to increase schooling attendance.

In **Puerto Rico**, we know about the existence of the Organización para el Fomento del Desarrollo del Pensamiento, directed by A. Villarini (Zilberstein, 1996), which develops a pedagogy to fostering intellectual abilities and giftedness within the curricular contents.

In the Institute of Psychological Research of the University of Costa Rica, research on giftedness is focused on intellectual competence (intelligence) and creativity, with special emphasis in developing identification and diagnosis procedures for students selection, as well as conceptual frames to understand those processes (Tapia & Molina, 1998).

In **Guatemala**, although experimental research on highly capable children has not been carried out, supporting programs for highly capable students have been established, as the Asociación Pro Alumno Talentoso y Superdotado, which aims to identify and to promote the talents of the gifted and talented. The Universidad del Valle, through its Programa de Orientación y Becas para Estudios Superiores assesses giftedness through batteries of Aptitude Tests, and scholarships for university studies are available for the high capable students identified. In addition to this, in 1992, a program to identify highly capable students was initiated at the Universidad del Valle. in order to provide them scholarships and other economic support for continuing university studies (Alencar & Blumen, 1993).

Mexico, a Spanish speaking country located in North America has developed several proposals that attempt to meet the needs of the gifted children in regular classrooms, based on the Renzulli (1978) model, in an effort to cope with the conditions of the gifted children attending regular public elementary schools, that followed the educational philosophy that the General Direction of Special Education stated.

The Mexican proposal considers five fundamental aspects: (a) a continuous sensitivity program on the needs of the gifted children applied to the whole school community, (b) activities to identify gifted children in the classroom, (c) general and specific thinking skills activities to the school population, (d) research and creative productive activities to all the students of special populations, and (e) permanent identification programs from a broad conception of the human being, which considers multiple identification criteria as well as direct observation in every student activities. The main goal is to identify and to develop the creative and productive potential of all children as well as to promote their academic achievement.

In 1982, the first public school for Mexican gifted children was established in Puebla, a city located 100 km South of Mexico City. The school began with 143 children having an IQ higher than 120, coming from 23 public schools, 10 federal schools, and 13 private schools.

Later, the *Centro de Desarrollo del Intelecto* (Center for the Development of the Intellect), a private organisation that served children of middle-high socio-economic level was also established in Puebla, to promote favourable conditions for the development of their gifts and talents, and to provide psychological and pedagogical support for skills that were not attended to in the traditional school system (Arroyo, 1989).

Also in Mexico City, there has been a proposal that attempted to meet the conditions of the public primary schools as well as the educational philosophy followed by the Head Office of Special Education. The main objective of the proposal was to identify and promote the creative and productive potential of children and to encourage their academic performance.

During the 1987–88 school year, a program for gifted and talented children was begun in 38 primary schools in Mexico City. A variety of identification and enrichment programs was developed. One of the initial results was that 5430 children in regular schools and 993 children in special education schools benefited from this program.

In June 1988, the works of 45 children was exhibited to the public; and later, on July 30 and 31, the First International Seminar 'Meeting the Needs of Gifted Children' was held in Guadalajara, Jalisco, Mexico. The event was organised by the Psychology Department of Guadalajara University and the Special Education Department of the Mexican State Education Office, and provided an opportunity to share and to exchange experiences related to gifted children and their educational needs and problems. Some of the problems faced by Mexican researchers (Cortes &

Schwanke, 1988), such as administrative difficulties and a lack of physical conditions, are very common in Latin American countries.

Issues and Perspectives

This chapter addressed gifted and talented education in Latin American countries. It pointed out the huge differences in services available for nurturing the gifted students among the countries in this part of the world. While in some of them, as in Brazil, educational policies related to gifted education were proposed more than 25 years ago, there are countries where the first programs are being initiated as experimental proposals, and others with no educational provisions for attending the gifted and talented students.

An analysis of the current situation of gifted education in Latin America also indicates that several programs which were implemented in different countries were discontinued. This was due to the lack of financial support as well as to stereotypes, prejudices and misconceptions about the gifted students. On the other hand, much progress was observed in Peru and Cuba in this last decade, where several initiatives in favor of the gifted and the talented have occurred.

In order to enable the gifted students to develop their abilities to the full, several initiatives are urgently required. One of them is the need for disseminating information about giftedness among school staff, teachers and parents, in order to make them more aware of the cognitive, social and emotional needs of these students.

It is specially important to prepare teachers to become more effective in working with the gifted. It is also necessary to make them aware that by ignoring the gifted, society loses many talents and leaders who could make a significant contribution to the solution of the problems of the country and to the progress that the society desires.

More research needs to be carried out in this area, to gain a better knowledge about the gifted and the talented children that belong to different socioeconomic levels in Latin American countries. The socioeconomic level should be taken into account in future studies, because it is very probable that more similarities would be found between children of similar socioeconomic status among the Latin American countries, than between the different socioeconomic levels in the same country.

It is also important that college and universities include gifted and talented education in their curriculum, in order to prepare teachers to identify and nurture the gifted and talented children.

Finally it is imperative that the educational authorities in Latin American countries acknowledge several issues identified previously in the chapter and that they respond by contributing to the implementation of educational conditions favorable to the gifted and talented development.

References

Alencar, E. M. L. S. (1986). *Psicologia e educação do superdotado* [Psychology and education of the gifted]. São Paulo: Pioneira.

Alencar, E. M. L. S. (1991). Developing the potential of disadvantaged pupils in Brazil. In: B. Wallace (Ed.), *Worldwide Perspectives on the Gifted Disadvantaged* (pp. 330–342). Bicester, England: A B Academic Publishers.

Alencar, E. M. L. S. (1994). Creativity in the Brazilian educational context: two decades of research. *Gifted and Talented International*, **9** (1), 4–7.

Alencar, E. M. L. S. (1995a). *Criatividade* [Creativity]. Brasilia: Editora da Universidade de Brasilia.

Alencar, E. M. L. S. (1995b). Challenges to the development of creative talent. *Gifted and Talented International*, **10**, 5–9.

Alencar, E. M. L. S. (1998). *Programas para estudantes que se destacam por um potencial superior* [Programs for students with a superior potential]. Educação Brasileira, **20**, 173–187.

Alencar, E. M. L. S. & Blumen, S. (1993). Programs and practices for identifying and nurturing giftedness and talent in Central and South America. In: K. A. Heller, F. J. Mönks & A. H. Passow (Eds.), *International Handbook of Research and Development of Giftedness and Talent* (pp. 849–864). Oxford: Pergamon Press.

Alencar, E. M. L. S. & Virgolim, A. M. R. (Eds.). (1995). *Criatividade: expressão e desenvolvimento* [Creativity: Expression and development]. Petrópolis: Vozes.

Arroyo, I. (1989). *Experiencias educativas en las escuelas públicas de Puebla* [Educational experiences in the public schools of Puebla]. Barcelona; Paper presented at the first conference of Eurotalent.

Balbachevsky, E. (1997). *O impacto do Programa Especial de Treinamento na graduação* [The impact of the Special Program of Training at the undergraduate courses]. Technical Report. Brasilia: Coordenação de Aperfeiçoamento de Pessoal de Nível Superior.

Blumen, S. (1995). Contribuciones para el desarrollo de programas para talentosos dentro del centro educativo [Contributions to the development of programs for the gifted within the educational environment]. *Revista de Psicología de la Pontificia Universidad Católica del Perú*, **1**, 37–49.

Blumen, S. (1996). *Nurturing/promotion of giftedness and creativity in early childhood*. Paper presented at the V European Council of High Ability Conference in Vienna, Austria.

Blumen, S. (1997). El desarrollo de las habilidades cognoscitivas según los avances en las teoras psicológicas [The development of cognitive abilities following the new outcomes of psychological theories]. *Revista de Psicología de la Pontificia Universidad Católica del Perú, 1*, 54–95.

Blumen, S. (1998a). *Identificación del niño talentoso en Lima*. Unpublished Master's Thesis in Psychology. Lima: Pontificia Universidad Católica del Perú.

Blumen, S. (1998b). *Talent detection inside organizations*. Paper presented at the Seminar on New Dimmensions on Organizational Psychology. University of Lima. Lima, Perú.

Blumen, S. (1998c). *New dimensions on the identification and attention of the gifted*. Paper presented at the National Forum on Young Inventors. University Ricardo Palma. Lima, Perú.

Blumen, S. (1999a). *Brain Functioning*. Paper presented at the International Scientific Meeting of the Peruvian Society of Science & Technology. Lima, Perú.

Blumen, S. (1999b). *Detection of the disadvantaged highly able in Lima*. Paper presented at the II Conference of the Iberoamerican Association of Psychological Assessment, Caracas, Venezuela.

Blumen, S. (2000). *Identification of and Attention for the Highly Able in Lima*. Nijmegen: KUN.

Bottura, M. C. S. (1997). *O que é o Programa Especial de Treinamento?* [What is the Special Program of Training?]. Technical report. Braslia: Coordenação de Aperfeiçoamento de Pessoal de Nível Superior.

CAPES (1997). *Programa Especial de Treinamento* [Special Program of Training]. Technical report. Brasília: Coordenação de Aperfeiçoamento de Pessoal de Nível Superior.

Cardó, F. A (1990). *Tendencias de la educación em América Latina* [Tendencies of education in Latin America]. Paper presented at the III Conference about Analysis and Perspectives of the Education in Peru, Lima.

Casassus, J., Froemel, J. E., Palafox, J. C. & Cusato, S. (1998). *Primer Estudio Internacional Comparativo* [First International Comparative Study]. Laboratorio Latinoamericano de Evaluación de la Calidad de la Educación [Latin American Laboratory on the Assessment of the Quality of Education]. Santiago: UNESCO-OREALC.

Castellanos, D. (1997). *Modelo heurístico para la identificación del talento en el contexto escolar: una alternativa para el profesor* [Heuristic model for talent identification in the school context]. Unpublished Master's Thesis, Universidad Pedagógica Enrique José Varona, Havana.

CONCYTEC (1989). *Programa de detección y apoyo a niños superdotados* [Detection program and support for gifted children]. Lima: CONCYTEC.

CONCYTEC (1998). *VIII Feria de ciencia y tecnología* [VIII Science and Technology Fair]. Lima: CONCYTEC.

Conselho Federal de Educação (1987). *A hora do superdotado* [The hour of the gifted]. Braslia: Conselho Federal de Educação.

Córdova, M. D. (1996). *La estimulación intelectual en situaciones de aprendizaje* [Intellectual stimulation in learning environments]. Unpublished doctoral dissertation, Universidad de La Habana, Havana.

Cortes, C. & Schwanke, P. E. (1988). *Atención a niños con capacidades y aptitudes sobresalientes en la Dirección General de Educación Especial en México* (Attention programs for gifted children in the General Education Superintendency of Mexico). Mexico: Dirección General de Educación Especial/Secretaría de Educación Pública.

Cuppertino. C. M. (1998). *Educación de los 'diferentes' en Brasil: el caso de la superdotación* [Education of the different students in Brazil: the gifted]. In: Proceedings of the First International Conference on High Intelligence Education in Mendonza, Argentina (pp. 98–107).

Dessen, M. A. (1994). O Programa Especial de Treinamento: evolução e perspectivas futuras [The Special Program of Training: Evolution and future perspectives]. *Revista Didáctica, 30*, 27–49.

Di Genio, J. C., Ancona-Lopez, M. & Brandão, A. (1990). Project to orient and identify talents—extra-curricular courses for talented children and their effects: a parents' point of view. In: S. Bailey, E. Braggett & M. Robinson

(Eds.), *The Challenge of Excellence: A Vision Splendid* (pp. 270–281). Melbourne: Barker.

Fonseca, F. G., Caixeta, G. S., Souza, L. M. & Cavalcante, M. A. M. (1990). *Atendimento educacional ao aluno superdotado* [Educational attendance for the gifted]. Brasília: Fundação Educacional do Distrito Federal.

Gambra, M. J. (1991). *Los métodos cientficos para superdotar al bebé* [Scientific methods to make the child gifted]. Santiago de Chile: Instituto de Superdotados de Chile.

González, A (1990). *Cómo propiciar la creatividad* [How to foster creativity]. La Habana: Editorial de Ciencias Sociales.

Gonzáles, A. (1991). *Detección de talentos y desarrollo para la regionalización* [Talent detection and development for regionalization]. Lima: CONCYTEC.

González, F. (1985). *Psicologia de la personalidad* [Psychology of personality]. Havana: Pueblo y Educación.

Guenther, Z. C. (1995). A center for talent development in Brazil. *Gifted and Talented International, 10,* 26–30.

Guenther, Z. C. (1997). *CEDET—Quarto ano de atendimento aos escolares bem-dotados* [The Center for Potential and Talent Development—four years of attending the gifted children]. Paper presented at the II National Seminar on Gifted Education in Lavras, Brazil.

Kloosterman, V. I. (1999). Treasures of the South: Gifted and talented children in Argentina. *Gifted and Talented International,* **14** (2), 112–117.

Labarrere, A. (1994). *Pensamiento. Análisis y autorregulación en la actividad cognitiva de los alumnos* [Thinking: analysis and self-regulation in students' cognitive activity]. México: Angeles.

Lorenzo, R. (1996). *El talento em la escuela primaria* [Giftedness in elementary school]. Doctoral dissertation. La Habana: Universidad Pedagogica E. J. Verona.

Martinez, M. (1994). *Enseñanza problemática y pensamiento creador* [Problematic teaching and creative thinking]. La Habana: Ediciones IPLAC.

Ministerio de Educatión (1991). *Reglamento de Trabajo Docente Metodológico para la Educación Superior. Resolución 269/1991* [Regulations for teaching and methodological work in higher education]. Havana: Ministerio de Educación.

Ministry of Education. (1983). *Ley general de educación* [General law of education], Lima: Ministry of Education.

Mitjans, A. (1995). *Creatividad, personalidad y educación* [Creativity, personality and education]. Havana: Pueblo y Educación.

Mönks, F. J. (1992). Development of gifted children: the issue of identification and programming. In: F. J. Mönks & W. Peters (Eds.), *Talent for the Future* (pp. 191–202). Assen/Maastricht: Van Gorcum.

Mönks, F., Ypenburg, I. & Blumen, S. (1997). *Nuestros niños son talentosos* [Our children are gifted]. Lima: Fondo Editorial de la Pontificia Universidad Católica del Perú.

Neuhaus, G. M. (1982). *Estudio comparativo de la capacidad creativa en artes plásticas en niños de diferentes edades y sexo* [Comparative study on the creative ability in visual arts on children of different ages and sex]. Unpublished Bachellor thesis in Psychology. Lima: Catholic University of Peru.

Pereyra, C. (1987). *Nivel de inteligencia y rendimiento académico en la Universidad Nacional de Ingeniería* [Intelligence level and academic achievement at UNI], Vol. 2. Lima : UNI.

Peruvian Ministry of Education (1995). *Integración de niños con necesidades educativas especiales a la escuela común* [Integration of children with special educational needs to the regular classroom]. Lima: UNESCO/OREALC.

Renzulli, J. S. (1978). What makes giftedness? Reexamining a definition. *Phi Delta Kappa, 60,* 180–184.

Ruiz, C. (1991). *Diferencias en las características de personalidad entre niños de ambos sexos bien dotados intelectualmente y aquellos de inteligencia normal* [Personality differences by gender between normal and gifted children]. Lima: Universidad Nacional Mayor de San Marcos.

Sabatella, M. L. P. Gifted education in Brazil. In: J. F. Smutny (Ed.), *Serving Under-Represented Population.* Creskill, NJ: Hampton Press. (In press).

Samper, M. Z. (1987). *Las inteligencias superiores* [The superior inteligences]. Bogota: Fundación Alberto Merani para el Desarrollo de la Inteligencia.

Secretaria de Educação Especial (1995). *Diretrizes gerais para o atendimento educacional aos alunos portadores de altas habilidades/superdotação e talentos* [General guides to the educational attention to the high ability students, giftedness and talent]. Brasília: Secretaria de Educação Especial.

Stahr, M. (1979). *Estudio comparativo de la imaginación creativa en niños de diferente nivel socio-económico* [Comparative study on creative imagination of children of different socioeconomic levels]. Unpublished Bachelor thesis in Psychology, Lima: Catholic University of Peru.

Tapia, N. & Molina, M. (1998). Procesos cognoscitivos, aptitud y competencias académicas en la Universidad de Costa Rica [Cognitive processes, aptitude and academic competencies at the University of Costa Rica]. *Actualidades en Psicologia,* **14,** 97.

Thorne, C. & Blumen, S. (1996). *Componente textos y materiales educativos* [Texts and educational materials]. Lima: Ministerio de Educación/Banco Mundial.

Thorne, C., López, E. & Moreno, M. (1996). *El niño eje del cambio social para una educación de calidad* [The child as axis of the social change for an education of quality]. Cuadernos de la Facultad de Letras y Ciencias Humanas. Lima: Pontificia Universidad Católica del Perú.

Wechsler, S. M. (1995). *Criatividade. Descobrindo e encorajando* [Discovering and encouraging creativity]. Campinas: PSY.

Zilberstein, J, (1996). *Sabe Ud. estimular el desarrollo intelectual de sus alumnos en la clase de Ciencias Naturales?* [Do you know how to stimulate intellectual development in your students at Science class?]. Havana: MINED.

Zubiria, M. & Gonzalez, M. A. (1982). *El Instituto Alberto Morani: Una institución para la educación de superdotados* [The Alberto Merani Institute: An Institute for the education of the gifted]. Bogotá: Secretaría del Convenio Andrés Bello.

Part VII

Present and Future of Research and Education of the Gifted and Talented

A Multidimensional Framework for Synthesizing Disparate Issues in Identifying, Selecting, and Serving Gifted Children

Robert J. Sternberg[1] and Rena F. Subotnik[2]

[1]Yale University, USA
[2]Hunter College, City Univerity of New York, USA

The Case of Justine Handley

Justine Handley, 8 years old, is being considered for selection into the gifted program at Cotswold Primary School. She has been recommended by her classroom teacher, but so have 17 other students, and there are only 10 open slots in the program. Right now the selection committee is deciding whether to admit Justine. They have available the following information:

(1) Full-scale IQ: 99th percentile
(2) Full-scale creativity score: 85th percentile
(3) Achievement tests: Verbal—98th percentile; Maths—85th percentile
(4) Teacher evaluation of motivation: 90th percentile (the committee's evaluation of her current teacher's recommendation)
(5) Peer nomination: 3 of her current classmates out of 25 identified her as the most able student in the class.

Should the committee admit Justine into the gifted program?

A discussion ensues among the five committee members, yet the deliberations are not achieving consensus. Consider their views.

Andrea Erickson, the principal, enthusiastically supports Justine's admission based on her scoring in the 99th percentile on an individually-administered IQ test. Andrea would not consider someone acceptable with an IQ score below the 95th percentile, and Justine is well above this level. Andrea points out that IQ has been shown to be a reliable measure and a valid predictor of success in rigorous academic programs like the one at Cotswold School.

Francesca Priestly's reasoning is somewhat different. As a gifted education consultant, Francesca believes that there are many different ways to demonstrate giftedness besides IQ, and that children selected for the Cotswold program can be identified as gifted by meeting any one of the criteria. The Cotswold program offers challenging individual and group activities in reading, writing, mathematics, science, foreign language, arts, music, and physical education. There are thus many ways to succeed in the program. Francesca believes that Justine qualifies for the program on the basis of her being in the 98th percentile or above with respect to either her IQ score *or* her verbal achievement score.

Jerry Baumgartner, a psychologist, is reluctant to admit Justine simply on the basis of IQ. He has seen that many students are able to remember and analyze other people's ideas without being able to come up with any good ideas of their own. According to Jerry, creativity is just as important as IQ. Therefore, to be identified as gifted, a student should attain scores in the 95th percentile or above on *both* IQ and measured creativity. It is not clear to Jerry that Justine could meet the demands of the Cotswold gifted program, which require students to produce creative work on a regular basis. He views Justine as sufficiently intelligent but as insufficiently creative for admission to the gifted program.

Curtis Hill, a teacher, believes that strengths in certain areas can compensate for weaknesses in other areas. In fact, the Cotswold faculty has been trained to assist students in using their special aptitudes to offset their academic or social weaknesses. Therefore he believes that the best policy is to average scores across criterion measures and to select those students with the highest average score. In this way, Justine's higher scores in IQ and verbal achievement can compensate for her relatively lower scores in creativity, maths achievement, and the estimation of her peers.

Another teacher, Ronnie Shabad, believes that what should matter in making selection decisions is how far you have come rather than where you are at a given point in time. She points out that although Justine's test scores are generally quite high, Justine's parents are well educated, economically successful, and have been actively involved in Justine's education. For Ronnie, a teacher's recommendation is key, and Justine's teacher-rated motivation score is not consistent with a picture of someone who is prepared to commit herself to the effort expected of students in the Cotswold gifted program. She points out that other candidates with similar test scores have made better use of the opportunities provided them. In fact, some of them have achieved at a very high level coming from homes with less well-educated or economically successful parents.

The five committee members are all committed to an excellent gifted program and to ensuring that the children selected for the program can optimally benefit from the experience. But the committee members differ in their preferred approaches to combining the criterion information available. The difference in approaches leads them to different decisions regarding Justine and other candidates.

In this chapter, we provide a unified framework for understanding disparate issues elucidated in this handbook that are often viewed as unrelated or only weakly related to each other. The chapter is divided into three major parts. The first part presents a multidimensional model and describes four approaches to the identification and selection of candidates for gifted programs. The second part deals with the application of the multidimensional model to challenges confronting gifted education, as described in this handbook. The third part draws some conclusions.

Four Approaches to Identification and Selection of Candidates for Gifted Programs

Static Models

Static models of identification and selection assess performance at a given point in time. Conventional intelligence tests, creativity tests, achievement tests, and peer nominations are all examples of static assessments.

The five approaches promoted by the various members of the Cotswold committee represent an array of mathematical combination rules for a given set of selection criteria. Approaches are not 'right' or 'wrong', but rather, appropriate to given goals set for identification, instruction, and assessment of performance. These goals, in turn, may vary, depending on the values they reflect. Because of limited resources, identification tied to theory can be unwittingly transformed into selection based on available space in programs (Subotnik & Coleman, 1996; Louis, Subotnik, Breland & Lewis, 2000). Thus decisions on who will be served take into consideration cultural and community resources, which vary from place to place.

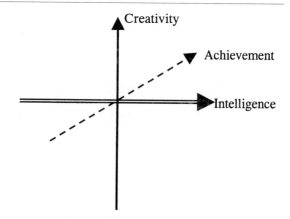

Figure 1. Example of a Static Model

Each of the approaches personified by Cotswold committee members sets a different combination rule for dimensions of a multidimensional space of giftedness and talents. In this space, certain people are identified as being in 'regions' that entitle them to be labeled as gifted and to consequently receive services; other people are not. For example, IQ might be conceived of as one dimension of the space; creativity test scores as another; achievement test scores as one or more others; and motivation and peer nominations as still another (see Fig. 1). The regions of the multidimensional space that represent 'giftedness' differ for each different approach.

Single Cutoff: Targeted Criterion

Andrea Erickson supports a single-cutoff, targeted criterion approach (see Fig. 2). In this approach, one considers only a pre-specified single piece of information, such as an IQ score, and makes a decision based on whether an individual's score is above a certain predetermined threshold (or cutoff). The rest of the data collected for each applicant would be used only for curriculum planning if the child is admitted to the program.

Andrea happened to use IQ in her decision making, but the model refers to any single targeted decision criterion applied to a pool of potentially eligible candidates. The cut-off might refer to IQ, maths SAT, a creativity test score, grade-point average, or any other single piece of data collected for each individual. Note that the single criterion can be more nearly domain general, such as a measure of IQ, or more nearly domain specific, such as maths SAT.

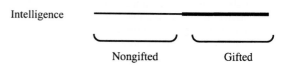

Figure 2. Example of a Single Cutoff: Targeted Criterion

The assumption underlying this model is that, although various criteria may be informative, only one is definitive and hence should be decisive in making selection decisions. The decision to use one targeted criterion over others may be because performance on this criterion has been shown to be highly predictive of performance in a particular gifted program or similar ones, or it may be a philosophical decision based on a unidimensional conception of giftedness (e.g. giftedness as determined by IQ). For this model, the bottom line is that a score above a certain cutoff on the targeted criterion is necessary and sufficient for admission to a program.

There are several potential advantages to the single-cutoff, targeted-criterion approach. For one thing, it is uncomplicated, especially for parents and the public. A criterion is announced in advance, and children must either make the designated cut-off or they do not get in. Also, adding selection criteria can produce diminishing returns. In other words, the incremental predictive value of additional criteria may not justify the addition of these criteria. Finally, using a single criterion tends to be quicker and cheaper, and involves less deliberation than is the case for multiple criteria.

There are also potential disadvantages to this approach. The single-cutoff, targeted criterion approach may not do justice to the full richness of the giftedness construct. Whether additional criteria contribute to prediction of success in a gifted program is an empirical question, and unless one starts off with these additional criteria, one may never find out whether they would have been useful. Given the investment that must go into the construction of a gifted program, the approach may be too simplistic for making defensible high stakes decisions about candidate selection.

Single Cutoff: Flexible Criterion

Francesca Priestly supports a single-cutoff, flexible-criterion approach (see Fig. 3). In this approach, like the previous one, the decision-makers consider only a single piece of information, but they are flexible as to which piece that information might be. For one individual, it may be an IQ score, for another, it may be a motivational rating. The key is to find the attribute that represents the individuals' greatest decision-relevant strength, and to use that attribute in making a

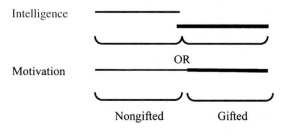

Figure 3. Example of a Single Cutoff: Flexible Criterion

decision. The decision is based on whether an individual's score is above a certain threshold (or cutoff) for the criterion relevant to that individual.

This approach may be viewed as a disjunctive generalization of the first approach. In the single-cutoff, targeted-criterion approach, one index is chosen in advance as decisive. In the single-cutoff, flexible-criterion approach, surpassing the cutoff on any one of a set of criteria is sufficient for entry into the gifted program.

Sometimes cutoffs are used negatively; students are rejected if any one of their scores falls *below* a certain point. Positive and negative cutoffs may be used together, whereby selection entails a candidate's being above a high threshold on at least one criterion but not below a low threshold on any other criteria.

The single-cutoff, flexible-criterion approach is attractive for several reasons. For one thing, this approach recognizes the multiplicity of gifts and talents (see, e.g. Gardner, 1983; Sternberg, 1985, 1997). Although people may prefer different models or theories of giftedness, virtually all people recognize that gifts and talents are, in fact, multiple. This approach therefore promotes greater diversity among those selected for admission to a gifted program, and adding a negative cutoff can ensure that there is a basic level of competence that exists among all students. The single-cutoff, flexible-criterion approach may also encourage a certain kind of synergism that arises when people's strengths are complementary rather than identical. For example, a group project to design a new form of transportation might require the talents of people who excel in creativity, writing, social skills, and problem solving (each reflected in various admission criteria for the Cotswold program).

The single-cutoff, flexible-criterion approach also has its drawbacks. First, it may be difficult to construct a curriculum that does justice to the broad range of gifts and talents that can be identified with this approach. The diversity of skills in the classroom may require more individualization of instruction than the teacher is able to provide. In addition, the number of potential talent domains and hence selection criteria a program might use is extremely large. It can become difficult—both philosophically and politically – to decide which talents or gifts are potentially relevant for decision making. Third, this approach is potentially costly and time-consuming if too many criteria are taken into account.

Multiple Cutoff

Jerry Baumgartner, in the case study above, supports a multiple-cutoff approach (see Fig. 4). In this approach, one considers a set of pre-specified pieces of information, such as an IQ score, a creativity-test score, and an achievement-test score, and makes a decision based on whether an individual's scores are above certain predetermined thresholds (or cutoffs) on all of the

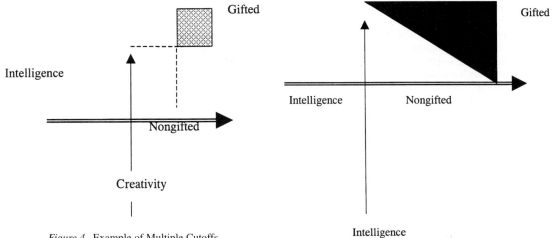

Figure 4. Example of Multiple Cutoffs

Figure 5. Example of Averaging

measures. Jerry, for example, believes that both IQ and creativity-test score should be incorporated into the selection procedure for admission into the Cotswold gifted program (see also Sternberg & Lubart, 1995).

This approach assumes that giftedness is best described conjunctively—as someone's scoring above a pre-specified threshold on each of a set of measures, all of which in combination are believed to predict success. In this approach, therefore, each above-cutoff score is necessary but individually not sufficient for the student to be selected for the program.

By implication, only a relatively limited number of criteria can be used, and cutoffs have to be set at a reasonable level so that a sufficient number of people can be identified as gifted. Consider three advantages of this approach. First, this approach takes into account the interactive nature of gifts and talents by having multiple cutoffs, for example, on tests of IQ, creativity, and achievement. Second, this approach ensures that selected students are at a relatively high level on *all* of the skills deemed to be important for success in the program. Consequently, teachers can prepare instruction without worrying that individual students' weaknesses will undermine the effectiveness of that instruction. Third, this approach is relatively cost- and time-efficient if one limits the number of criteria that are used in decision-making.

As with all the other approaches discussed thus far, there are also disadvantages. Individuals whose gifts or talents are exceedingly high in one area but non-exceptional in one or more other areas may be excluded. For example, in a system that requires above-threshold scores on IQ and achievement tests, someone with an exceptionally high IQ or an exceptionally high achievement score may be rejected because his or her other score is merely high, but not exceptional. Because of the need to set reasonable cutoff levels it would be possible to identify as gifted an individual

who shows a high level of skill in several areas, but perhaps an extraordinary level of skill in none of them. Finally, use of this approach may require a relatively substantial investment of time and other resources in the identification procedure with little room to maneuver in the process except in determining cutoffs.

Averaging

Curtis Hill supports an averaging approach (see Fig. 5). In this approach, scores on each of multiple criteria are converted to a common unit (such as a standard score), and then averaged. Because the various criteria are not necessarily viewed as being of equal predictive validity, they may be weighted to reflect their perceived importance. For example, Justine's percentile scores might all be converted to standard (z) scores, weighted, and then assigned an average value as a single index of her suitability for selection into the gifted program.

This approach assumes that giftedness is multidimensional and that higher scores in some dimensions of giftedness can compensate for lower scores in other dimensions. As typically used, it also assumes linear weighting of the variables with no interactions. Linearity implies that a score difference of a certain number of points is consistent at any two points along a continuum (e.g. the difference between IQs of 120 and 130 is identical to the difference between IQs of 150 and 160). *No interactions* means that, for example, the relation between IQ and creativity would be the same at all points along the continua of both.

A main positive feature of this approach is the fact that it uses all of the available (linear) information, whereas in other models, information is essentially wasted for the purposes of identification. The approach guarantees that no candidate who is selected is fairly weak in several dimensions or extremely weak in any of them. In other words, several fairly low scores or one extremely low score is likely to take the candidate out of consideration. This fact ensures that teachers will have to do little or no remediation with their gifted students. Also, employment of this approach is likely to lead to diversity among selected students, because the criteria along which people score well are likely to differ.

This approach also has weaknesses. First, some people believe that giftedness is a construct that should deal with true exceptionalities, not averages. Second, the sheer diversity in number and kinds of talent profiles may challenge teachers in ways for which they are not prepared. Third, just one extremely low score may knock someone out of the running for admission to a gifted program, even if the low level of functioning represented by this score would not necessarily be problematical for successful performance in the program, e.g. not being nominated by peers from a non-selective environment. Finally, it may be difficult to find criteria for which there are no interactions (cf. literature on correlation between IQ and creativity test scores in Sternberg & O'Hara, 1999).

Dynamic Models

Dynamic models involve assessment of estimated change over time (see Fig. 6) (Grigorenko & Sternberg, 1998; Kanevsky, this handbook), taking into account the context in which the assessment takes place. Before comparing the children to each other, the children are compared to themselves at two or more hypothesized points in time. The idea is to determine how far a child has come and thereby predict how far the child can go. Children who have come further, it is assumed, are those who take better advantage of the opportunities they are given.

For example, Ronnie Shabad has pointed out that, although Justine's profile is a good one, it does not indicate that she took maximal advantage of opportunities. Other students with comparable profiles may have been reared in families without the Handley's eco-

nomic wherewithal to be actively involved in their child's schooling. Or they may have grown up in households with poorly educated parents.

Each of the approaches described above can be operationalized in a dynamic way. For the single-cutoff, target-criterion approach, one would look at growth in the single criterion, considering, for example, not only current knowledge base, but also, early opportunities for acquiring this knowledge base. For the single-cutoff, flexible-criteria approach, one would look at maximal growth in any one of the criteria. For the multiple-cutoff approach, one would look at a minimal required level of growth in each of the criteria; and for the averaging approach, one would average growth across the multiple criteria.

The dynamic model has one overarching advantage. Children start at different metaphorical points of origin and so may have relatively longer or shorter routes to traverse to meet preset identification or selection criteria. Consequently, this approach promotes diversity with respect to the origins and family backgrounds of the children likely to be selected for a given gifted program.

The dynamic model also has potential disadvantages. It is difficult to operationalize concepts such as 'point of origin', 'environmental advantage', or 'family background'. What measures does one use to operationalize 'environmental advantage'? For example, two children may come from environments that are equally disadvantaged financially, but in one environment, the children were strongly encouraged to engage themselves in their schoolwork, whereas in the other environment, they were not (Olszewski, Kulieke & Buescher, 1987). Most important for the discussion at hand, one can come a long way but still not excel. For a particular child from a particularly difficult environment, reaching an average level of performance on several measures may be impressive, but does that level of performance entitle the child to be labeled as gifted (Noble, Subotnik & Arnold, 1999)?

Up to this point, we have been describing various models and approaches to the identification and selection of the gifted. How do these models help us synthesize some of the disparate issues in selecting, identifying, and serving gifted children?

Application of the Multidimensional Model

Many pressing issues confront gifted education today. These issues not only affect the research agenda of the field, but also the day-to-day operations of gifted programs, like the one at Cotswold School.

The Role of Gatekeepers

Gatekeepers operate at two different levels. At one level, they identify and select gifted students. In terms of the multidimensional model, they: (a) select which dimensions in the multidimensional space they view as relevant to identification and selection, and (b) form a

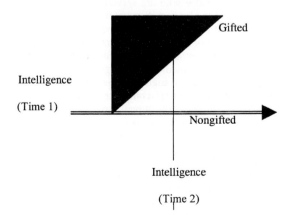

Figure 6. Example of a Dynamic Model

combination rule (what we have called an *approach*) for combining the information contained in multiple dimensions. For example, they might select IQ and creativity score as two dimensions, and then use a multiple-cutoff rule as their approach for combining information from those two dimensions. At a second level, they determine the criteria by which people advance in their education or in their field of endeavor (Feldman, Csikszentmihalyi & Gardner, 1994). For example, they decide which areas of research will be funded and which ones will not be, or which kinds of art works will be displayed and which kinds will not be. In terms of the multidimensional model, they judge the creations that emanate from the hypothetical constructs underlying the dimensions (e.g. creativity is the hypothetical construct underlying one or more scores on a test of creativity).

The Cultural Context of Giftedness

The cultural context in which giftedness is judged affects the dimensions and combination rule that are selected. Thus, people who excel on a particular dimension, such as hunting prowess, may be viewed as gifted in one culture but as undistinguished in another (Bourdieu, 1977; DiMaggio, 1982; Gardner, 1983; Sternberg, 1985; Bronfenbrenner, 1993; Meyer, 1994) because hunting is peripheral to the central enterprises of the culture. A highly precocious and competent reader might be valued in one culture, but hardly recognized in non-literate cultures.

When people move from one culture to another, they may find themselves either newly labeled or no longer labeled as gifted. The difference may be due to the dimensions that are valued or of the qualifying level of performance on those dimensions. For example, some Asian students whose mathematics performance might be above average but undistinguished in their own countries might look gifted in the United States, where the levels of mathematics achievement are, on average, lower.

In extreme cases, excellence in the dimensions that are valued in one culture or one time may lead to one's execution in another culture or time (Simonton, 1994). For example, in some countries in some periods of time, people perceived to be intellectuals have been viewed as highly dangerous. A charismatic leader who is gifted during an epoch of dictatorship may find him or herself in line to be executed when the culture or mores of the country change.

People whose cultures or subcultures are distant from the mainstream may find themselves having developed skills that are valued among their own group of people but not among the people in the cultural mainstream (Scott, Peron, Urbano, Hogan & Gold, 1992; Ford, 1996; Subotnik & LeBlanc, 2001). It may be quite a bit more difficult for people from distinct cultures to be labeled as gifted by the mainstream simply because they have so far, metaphorically, to

travel to acquire the skills that the mainstream values (Olszewski-Kubilius, Grant & Seibert, 1993). In such cases, the dynamic model may be useful in showing just how far they have come (Feuerstein, 1973; Wright & Borland, 1993; Borland & Wright, 1994).

Domain Generality versus Domain Specificity of Giftedness

Dimensions in the multidimensional space differ in terms of the degree to which they represent general vs. domain-specific characteristics. For example, many psychologists view IQ as general (although not completely) intelligence because the aspects of intelligence it measures apply across many domains of endeavor. Musical-composition skills, in contrast, would be viewed as more domain specific, because these skills apply in fewer domains of endeavor. Because humans tend to specialize over time, identification of the gifted often focuses on more general abilities when applied to children and young adolescents, and more domain-specific abilities and skills when applied to older adolescents and adults (Feldman, 1986; Subotnik & Olszewski-Kubilius, 1997). Indeed, with few exceptions, it is harder to measure domain-specific expertise in younger than in older individuals.

Different domains have different trajectories. A highly successful career in violin performance or ballet is dependent on early investment in instruction and practice (Feldman, 1986). In contrast, most psychologists, do not decide on their domain of specialization until they reach the high school or university level.

Who Gets Served?

Who gets served in gifted programs depends on the dimensions of the multidimensional space that are valued and on how these dimensions are combined. It also depends on whether one uses a static or a dynamic model of assessment. In the former model, those who are served will be those who have the highest value(s) on the relevant dimension(s) at a given point. In the latter model, those who are served will be those who have traveled the longest distance from some perceived starting point to where they are now.

Another factor that might be taken into account is the level or kind or service that a child will receive if he or she is not accepted into a program for the gifted. Some families will arrange for their children to receive services that are almost comparable, whereas others may be thrown into educational environments that are stultifying and even alienating.

How Do the Gifted Get Served?

Ideally, a gifted program like the one at the Cotswold School should have parallel dimensions for identification, selection, curriculum design, and assessment of performance. For example, if the program selects students on the basis of IQ and creativity-test scores, then the underlying abilities relevant to performance on each should apply to performance in the gifted program.

Many domains in which giftedness is assessed make a distinction between performance-related aspects and creative- productivity related aspects. The way students are identified, taught, and assessed may differ depending on which aspect is to be emphasized. For example, both musical performers and composers will study music theory, but the emphasis will be different. Performers will employ theory to interpret what they play, while composers need theory to help them structure and improvise effectively.

Will Those Who Get Served become Gifted Adults?

Many children who are identified as gifted children will not be viewed so when they become adults, just as many adults who are viewed as gifted will not have been identified as gifted when they were young. There are a number of reasons for this discrepancy. First, the dimensions used to assess giftedness during childhood and adulthood may differ (Subotnik & Olszewski-Kubilius, 1997). For example, scoring brilliantly on reading and mathematics achievement tests may be essential and sufficient for success in school but not for success in many jobs. Second, as noted earlier, domain-specific dimensions typically become more important with age. For example, advanced interpretational skills in music may not be easy to assess until an individual first has acquired a considerable level of technique. Third, assessment of giftedness among children tends to stress potentialities, whereas assessment of giftedness among adults tends to be based on assessed accomplishments (Subotnik & Arnold, 1999).

There are at least two points of view regarding discrepancies in childhood vs. adult giftedness. One is that we are mistaken in whom we identify as gifted in childhood, and that we need to pay more attention to the dimensions that will be relevant to career performance later on. In science, for example, the ability to learn the basic material may be important earlier on, but the ability to generate interesting questions will become more important later on. Perhaps we need to expend more effort promoting question-generating ability among young people. From another perspective, giftedness is a different construct for children than for adults, and children should be served on the basis of the dimensions that are relevant for childhood giftedness, regardless of whether these dimensions will be relevant to occupational success later on.

Conclusion

In this chapter, we have presented a multidimensional model for understanding the identification and selection of the gifted. We have described two different ways of using the model through static and dynamic assessment. We have also described four different approaches that fall under the model: the single-cutoff, targeted-criterion approach; the single-cutoff, flexible-

criterion approach; the multiple-cutoff approach; and the averaging approach. We have also discussed several issues that can be informed by our model.

We believe that a unified model provides an umbrella under which a large number of issues can be covered. More specifically, it helps prevent different activities from operating at cross-purposes to one another, as when one set of dimensions matters for selection into a program but a different set of dimensions matters for success in the same program. A unified model also clarifies how the dimensions that are valued in childhood giftedness can be either the same as or different from those dimensions that contribute to giftedness in adults.

It is certainly possible that we have tried to be too all-encompassing, missing the fine grain thinking taken into account by gifted-education specialists. However, we believe the advantages outweigh the disadvantages. This handbook is so rich with information and theory that readers may find it helpful to view the field through such a lens. Alternatively, we look forward to the handbook serving as a catalyst to our readers in their own model development.

References

Borland, J. H., & Wright, L. (1994). Identifying young, potentially gifted, economically disadvantaged students. *Gifted Child Quarterly*, **38** (4), 164–171.

Bourdieu, P. (1977). *Reproduction in education, society, culture*. Beverly Hills, CA: Sage.

Bronfenbrenner, U. (1993). The ecology of cognitive development: Research models and fugitive findings. In: R. H. Wozniak & K. Fischer (Eds.), *Scientific environments* (pp. 3–44). Hillsdale, NJ: Erlbaum.

DiMaggio, P. (1982). Cultural capital and school success: the impact of status culture participation on the grades of U.S. high school students. *American Sociological Review*, **47**, 189–201.

Feldman, D. H. (1986). *Nature's gambit: child prodigies and the development of human potential*. New York: Basic Books.

Feldman, D. H., Csikszentmihalyi, M., & Gardner H. (Eds.) (1994). *Changing the world. A framework for the study of creativity*. Westport, CT: Praeger.

Ford, D. Y. (1996). *Reversing underachievement among gifted black students: Promising practices and programs*. New York: Teachers College Press.

Feuerstein, R. (1973). *Instrumental Enrichment*. Baltimore: University Park Press.

Gardner, H. (1983). *Frames of mind: the theory of multiple intelligences*. New York: Basic Books.

Grigorenko, E. L., & Sternberg, R. J. (1998). Dynamic testing. *Psychological Bulletin*, **124**, 75–111.

Louis, B., Subotnik, R. F., Breland, P., & Lewis, M. (2000). Identification vs. admissions practices: implications for policies and practices in gifted education. *Educational Psychology Review* **12** (3), 295–314.

Meyer, J. W. (1994). The evolution of modern stratification systems. In: D. B. Grusky (Ed.), *Social Stratification in Sociological Perspective*, (pp. 730–737). Boulder, CO: Westview.

Noble, K. D., Subotnik, R. F., & Arnold, K. D.(1999). To thine own self be true: a new model of female talent development. *Gifted Child Quarterly*, **43**, 140–149.

Olszewski-Kubilius, P., Grant, B., & Seibert, C. (1993). Social support systems and the disadvantaged gifted: a framework for developing programs and services. *Roeper Review*, **17** (1), 20–25.

Olszewski, P., Kulieke, M. J., & Buescher, T. (1987). The influence of the family environment on the development of talent: a literature review. *Journal of the Education of the Gifted*, **11** (1), 6–28.

Scott, M. S., Perou, R., Urbano, R., Hogan A., & Gold, S. (1992). The Identification of Giftedness: a Comparison of White, Hispanic, and Black Families. *Gifted Child Quarterly*, **36** (3), 131–139.

Simonton, D. K. (1994). *Greatness: who makes history and why?* New York: Guilford.

Sternberg, R. J. (1985). *Beyond IQ: a triarchic theory of human intelligence.* New York: Cambridge University press.

Sternberg, R. J. (1997). *Successful intelligence.* New York: Plume.

Sternberg, R. J., & O'Hara, L. (1999). Creativity and intelligence. In R. J. Sternberg (Ed.), *Handbook of Creativity* (pp. 251–272.) New York: Cambridge University Press.

Subotnik, R. F., & Arnold, K. D.(1999). Longitudinal studies of creativity. In: M. A. Runco & S. Pritzker (Eds.), *Encyclopedia of Creativity*, Vol 2. (pp. 163–168). San Diego, CA: Academic Press.

Subotnik, R. F., & Coleman, L. J. (1996). Establishing the foundations for a talent development school: applying principles to creating an ideal. *Journal for the Education of the Gifted*, **20**, 175–189.

Subotnik, R. F., & LeBlanc, G. (2001). Teaching gifted children in a multicultural world. In: J. A. Banks & C. McGee Banks (Eds.), *Multicultural Education: Issues and Perspectives* (4th ed.) (pp. 353–376) Boston: Allyn & Bacon.

Subotnik, R. F., & Olszewski-Kubilius, P. (1997). Distinctions between children's and adults' experiences of giftedness. *The Peabody Journal of Education*, **72** (3 & 4), 101–116.

Subotnik, R. F., Olszewski-Kubilius, P., & Arnold, K. Beyond Bloom: revisiting environmental factors that enhance or impeded talent development. In: J. Borland (Ed.) *Rethinking Gifted Education*. New York: Teachers College Press. (In press).

Wright, L., & Borland, J. H. (1993). Using early childhood developmental portfolios in the identification and education of young, economically disadvantaged, potentially gifted students. *Roeper Review*, **15** (4), 205–210.

The Study of Giftedness: Reflections on Where We Are and Where We Are Going

Franz J. Mönks,[1] Kurt A. Heller[2] and A. Harry Passow[†]

[1]*University of Nijmegen, The Netherlands*
[2]*University of Munich, Germany*

Introduction

At the entrance to the third millenium, people and groups concerned with the nature and nurture of giftedness and talent—educators, policy-makers, researchers, the public—find that, despite a large and growing knowledge base, issues concerning the education and development of the gifted continue to be discussed and debated. It might even be said that, as in other fields, the more that is known, the more issues are raised and controversies are fueled. Issues concerning the gifted field have never been confined to a small group of children and youth identified as 'gifted or talented' but have an impact on the whole of education. For example, the issues surrounding questions of *excellence and equity* affect all educational decisions, not just provisions made for the gifted. Despite a century of programming for the gifted, such efforts are still debated as to whether or not they are elitist, undemocratic and even necessary (cf. Henry, 1994; Herrnstein & Murray, 1994; Jacoby & Glauberman, 1995; Mönks, 1996). Towards the end of the 20th century 'cluster grouping', one kind of ability grouping, had once again become the focus of policy debates with research cited to support both sides of the controversy (Gentry et al., 1999). These are just a few examples of the perennial issues which are unresolved despite the accumulation of research, theory and experience over the past century. In fact, it is likely that they will never be fully resolved; supporters of gifted education will only find a more solid basis for their positions with the growing base of research and theory.

In the first report on his longitudinal study, Terman (1925) suggested that, as more is learned about giftedness and how gifted children should be educated, we will learn more about increasing the talent reservoir:

> When the sources of our intellectual talent have been determined, it is conceivable that means may be found which would increase our supply. When the physical, mental and character traits of gifted children are better understood it will be possible to set about their education with better hope of success . . . In the gifted child, Nature has moved far back the usual limits of educability, but the realms thus thrown open to the educator are still *terra incognita*. It is time to move forward, explore and consolidate (pp. 16–17).

The German psychologist Stern emphasized in 1916:

> It is strange that until now there exist thorough diagnostic processes only for the children for whom we have concern because of some handicap but not for the children of hope (p. 114). For 2% of the highly gifted and another 10% of the gifted elementary school children we need provisions for appropriate nurturing (p. 109).

To reflect on research and education of the gifted at the beginning of the new century requires a look at the issues and problems in the field—many of which are perennial—which will shape the future of talent development.

The Beginnings of Study of the Gifted

Modern giftedness research has a long past but a short history. Confucius in China and Plato in Greece (in politeia, VI) discussed 'heavenly' (gifted) children. They attempted not only to explain giftedness or high ability theoretically, but also made practical suggestions for the identification and selection of the gifted and for nurturing them in society. In this way giftedness or talent was considered as a national resource, to be encouraged and multiplied for the good of the community. It is interesting to note that both East

839

Asian and Classical European traditions adopted largely identical interpretations of giftedness and talent, which were considered to be gifts from nature, in the form of exceptional cognitive abilities (perception, thinking, learning and memory).

The close relationship of giftedness to the concept of intelligence is shown etymologically not only in the Chinese attributes 'Tsung' and 'Ming' (exceptional sight and hearing) but also both in the Latin meaning of 'intellect' in the philosophy of Aristotle and in the writings of the later English Sensualists (e.g. John Locke, 1632–1704). This European attitude or hypothesis was expressed in the assumption: Nihil est in intellectu, quod non prius fuerit in sensu (the intellect contains nothing that did not come to it through the senses). This intellectual conception of giftedness or talent was probably first broadened to include motivational and environmental components by Terman (1954). In the New Testament parable (Matthew 25, 28) Jesus spoke of the talents entrusted to mankind. The term 'talent' (*talanton* in Greek, *talentum* in Latin) was derived originally from an ancient unit of weight or token. In Vulgate Latin (fourth century) *talentum* adopted, possibly for the first time, the meaning 'mental aptitude'. In the Middle Ages the term 'talent' took on the meaning of giftedness in the sense of inborn ability; this meaning persisted into the first half of this century (e.g. Révész as late as 1952). The concept of genius, long native to psychiatry (cf. Anastasi, 1958), can also be traced back to its classical roots (Heller, 1993b).

In a more narrow sense, research on the nature and nurture of the gifted began at the turn of the last century but has intensified and become increasingly more sophisticated, focused and informative in the last few decades. Americans tend to mark the beginning of serious research on the gifted with the 1922 initiation of Terman's so-called *Genetic Studies of Genius* when a life-span longitudinal study "was designed to discover what physical, mental and personality traits are characteristic of gifted children as a class and what sort of adult the typical gifted child becomes" (Terman & Oden, 1951, p. 21). Europeans sometimes cite William Stern's 1916 publication *Psychologische Begabungsforschung und Begabungsdiagnose* [Psychological research and detection of the gifted] as having preceded the Terman study and a better benchmark.

There were, of course, earlier studies about the nature of 'genius', the training and exploits of '*Wunderkinder*' and other prodigies and the provisions made for rapid learners and academic achievers (see Chapters I, 7 and II, 8). The editor of a 1924 yearbook of the National Society for the Study of Education (NSSE) observed that:

Lombroso's *Man of genius* (1891), Galton's English *Men of science* (1874), Galton's *Hereditary genius* (1869), Constable's *Poverty and hereditary* genius

(1905), Cattell's *A statistical study of American men of science* (1906–1910) are characteristic studies that have helped define the problem of the origin of superior achievement, especially to raise the issue as to the relative contribution of inherited constitution and educational training in the production of greatness (Whipple, 1924, p. 2).

The 1924 NSSE yearbook entitled *The Education of Gifted Children* contains an annotated bibliography of 453 entries—mostly American although several German citations are included. The sheer volume provides clear evidence that there was considerable interest in the nature and education of the gifted in the early part of the last century. The content of the articles as reflected in the titles and annotations suggests that many of the topics discussed or reported were not unlike those one finds in more recent literature. There were articles on intelligence testing as a means of identification, descriptions of 'superior groups', comparisons of 'bright and dull pupils', honors plans, studies of precocious and 'super-normal' children, outcomes of ability grouping, the nature of genius and even a 1906 article by Terman titled 'Genius and stupidity'. (This was a report on his doctoral dissertation which he finished in 1905. In June 1905 he received his doctoral diploma from the hands of President Theodore Roosevelt.)

In his Editor's Preface to the 1924 NSSE yearbook, Whipple noted that the "Committee has not found itself in agreement upon some fundamental principles involved in the education of gifted children" (p. iv) including the various means "for the selection of gifted pupils or the administration of their training" (p. 24). These same two classes of issues persist.

Themes and Issues from Earlier Research

In 1960, in connection with legislation being considered by the State of Illinois, Gallagher prepared a report whose purpose was "to review and summarize all of the information now available relating to the education of gifted children" (p. 3). Gallagher summarized his findings under the following headings: identification, cultural background, intellectual patterns, academic achievement, social popularity, emotional adjustment, elementary programs and program evaluation. He concluded that a clear generalization that can be drawn from the review of research was that "special programming for gifted children requires additional personnel and services" (p. 131).

In 1963, Mönks published a review article entitled *Contributions to the study of giftedness in childhood and adolescence*. In this article a survey was made of the then existing trends in the study of gifted children and adolescents. Six theoretical approaches were identified and summarized as follows: (1) clinical approach or the theory of disharmony, (2) socio-

840

cultural/psychosocial approach, (3) psychoanalytical approach, (4) hereditary theory, (5) theory of differentiation and (6) theory of harmony (after Terman's correlation of giftedness with psychological and physical health). The same article proposed a longitudinal study to develop an empirical basis for the improvement of psychological educational as well as instructional guidance of gifted students (see Mönks, 1992).

About 40 years before the 1963 Mönks' article there already existed in the Netherlands scientific interest in the gifted child. The contribution of the Dutch psychologist Révész (Hungarian by origin, residing in Amsterdam after 1921) about a musical prodigy in 1925 is well known. Other psychologists like Waterink and De Groot contributed to the study of giftedness theoretically and empirically. But at that time (1938, 1956) policy makers were more interested in "equal opportunities for all" and this meant for the children with handicaps (see Mönks, 1992). Concern for the appropriate education of the gifted and interest in theoretical conceptualizations of giftedness have a long history in Europe but a minimal impact on research and practice. During the last decade of the 20th century, however, there is not only a growing awareness of the needs of gifted learners in almost all European countries (see Chapter VI, 4), but a substantial improvement of gifted education in schools and also expanding research activities in universities.

While many perennial research themes are still being studied, other topics are now the focus of investigation, often using more insightful or more sophisticated means to probe more meaningful questions. For example, Heller (1992, pp. 75–76) proposed the following research topics which seemed important to him in understanding talent and its nurture:

- Development of instructional concepts and pedagogy for the gifted.
- Curricular development for special academic courses, special classes or even special high schools for certain acceleration groups, for enrichment groups and for extracurricular support of the gifted—including evaluation of such courses and programs.
- The construction of identification instruments for process diagnosis or dynamic assessment (as a complement to the 'status diagnosis'), the testing of successive decision strategies and multidimensional classification models.
- Construction of area-specific counseling tests for talented adolescents.
- Longitudinal studies of the gifted including analyses of the living environment over the whole life span.
- Study of leisure-time activities of talented adolescents and their influence on personality development.
- Career problems of talented girls and women especially in the fields of mathematics, natural sciences and technology.

- Analyses of metacognition, causal attribution, achievement motivation, self control, heuristic skills, the self concept (including sex differences) and self-evaluation of abilities.
- Quasi-experimental intervention studies for counseling and supporting gifted children and adolescents.

Definitions and Conceptions of Giftedness

A basic problem in building a theory about giftedness is that it is a multifaceted phenomenon, the nature of which is still at issue. Can a single theory account for the appearance of precocity as in 4-year olds who play chess or who write publishable poems or 10-year olds who are concert-class performers or children who perform exceptionally well on academic tasks or school-age children who develop patentable inventions? Put another way, can a single theory explain the rare Einsteins, Shakespeares, Nijinskys and similar talented individuals as well as the child whose 'giftedness' appears to be achieving unusually well academically as measured by standardized achievement tests?

Research and experience over the past decades have underscored the range and variety of individuals whom school personnel and different communities (e.g. cultural, artistic, business and industry) have identified and labeled 'gifted' or 'talented'. Depending on the criteria being applied, there are some children who are only slightly above average while others are so far above the average as to be extremely rare. In the U.S.A., the latter are sometimes called, only partly in jest, "severely and profoundly gifted." Some individuals seem to have talent potential in a single area while others appear to have potential in a variety of areas. Some individuals who have manifested talent potential seem to have little or no interest or motivation to develop or use that capacity while others are highly interested, motivated, committed and involved. Some youngsters are especially precocious, manifesting unusual talent potential at very early ages, while others are 'late bloomers' who do not show unusual potential or performance until much later in their development. There are youngsters who educators believe are academically gifted—i.e. high achievers, good test-takers, good designers and implementers of school projects—but who are not necessarily outstanding performers and producers outside the classroom. Some talent areas seem to be manifested earlier than others. Some 'academic absorbers' deal with their learnings in straightforward ways, while others seem to take delight in 'playing around' with ideas and challenges in creative and innovative ways.

Thus, the gifted and the talented are clearly a very heterogeneous set of persons and it is this multidimensional heterogeneity which may preclude a comprehensive theory. The absence of such a theory, however, does not prevent us from deepening our insights and understandings of the phenomena nor intensifying efforts to identify talent potential and nurture talented performance.

Giftedness and *talent* are terms which have been variously defined over the years and a variety of conceptions have emerged related to these diverse definitions. Feldhusen & Jarwan (1993, pp. 234–235) suggested that definitions of giftedness can be classified into six categories: psychometric, trait, social needs orientated, educationally oriented, special talent and multidimensional (also see Chapter III, 1 in this handbook). Eysenck & Barrett (1993) viewed giftedness as a 'fuzzy concept' that can be defined in three major ways: "(1) as synonymous with *general intelligence*; (2) as synonymous with *creativity*; (3) as synonymous with *special (artistic or scientific) ability*."

Renzulli (1982) has asserted that despite efforts throughout the century, "the precise definition of giftedness remains a question with no universally accepted answer" (p. 723). He suggests that the many definitions of gifted range along a continuum from a 'conservative' end represented by Terman's definition of the top 1% in general intellectual ability to the more 'liberal' definition of Witty who recommended that the definition of giftedness be expanded to include any child "whose performance, in a potentially valuable line of human activity, is consistently remarkable." Also see Chapter IV, 3 in this handbook.

Heller (1989) notes that "giftedness belongs to the class of so-called hypothetical 'construct' terms whose definition is dependent on the chosen theoretical frame of reference," a term which "is strongly convoluted with relatively complex behavioral phenomena" (pp. 140–141). Gallagher & Courtright (1986) have argued that "one term, *gifted*, has been used to describe two different constructs . . . [which] "although overlapping, emerge from different traditions and have a number of subtle differences that create confusion and contradiction" (p. 93). One construct derives from the studies of psychological scientists on individual differences while the other "stems from educational practice and the need for schools to design special educational programs for students who possess abilities and perform far in excess of their age mates" (p. 93). Gallagher (see Chapter VI, 2) asserts that the educational definition of giftedness has significant policy implications with identification and program goals following from the constructs accepted.

In Sternberg & Davidson's (1986) *Conceptions of giftedness*, some 17 different conceptions of the construct are presented and discussed by the persons who proposed and advanced them. These constructs, as Sternberg and Davidson put it, "although distinct, are interrelated in certain ways" (p. 3). They divide these different conceptions into those which are *implicit-theoretical*—each presenting "a somewhat different implicit theory of giftedness that seeks to define this elusive concept" (p. 4)—and those which are *explicit-*

theoretical—each emphasizing explicit theories of giftedness in terms of cognitive or developmental psychology. The different conceptions of giftedness are also divided between those which are school-centered and those which focus on adult performance and productive behavior.

An example of an implicit-theoretical conception is that of Tannenbaum (1983) who views the interaction of five factors resulting in gifted/talented performance. These include: (1) *general ability* or tested general intelligence with different threshold IQs being required for various kinds of accomplishment; (2) *special ability* or special capacities or affinities for various kinds of work; (3) *non-intellective factors*, a confluence of affective elements such as ego strength, persistence, delayed gratification, (4) *environmental factors* including "stimulating home, school and community settings [which] are indispensable not only for maximizing potentialities but also for helping to determine the directions they take" and (5) *chance factors*, "unpredictable events in a person's life that are critical both to the realization of promise and to the demonstration of talents" (pp. 87–88).

Another example of clustering the different orientations and conceptions is the following: (1) trait oriented definitions, (2) cognitive component models, (3) achievement-oriented models and (4) socio-cultural/psychosocial oriented models (see Chapter II, 1). These models have to be seen as complementary since each of them emphasizes an important aspect.

Sternberg's (1986) triarchic theory of intellectual giftedness is an example of an explicit-theoretical conception based on cognitive theory. This theory consists of three subtheories: The first "relates intelligence to the internal world of the individual, specifying the mental mechanisms that lead to more or less intelligent behavior"; the second "specifies those points along the continuum of one's experience with tasks or situations that most critically involve the use of intelligence"; and the third relates intelligence to the individual's external world, "specifying three classes of acts—environmental adaptation, selection and shaping—that characterize intelligent behavior in the everyday world" (p. 223).

Sternberg & Davidson (1986) see definitions of giftedness as having particular significance in identification and development:

> Giftedness is something we invent, not something we discover. It is what one society or another wants it to be, and hence its conceptualization can change over time and place. If the definition of giftedness is a useful one, then it can lead to favorable consequences of many kinds, both for society and for individuals. If the definition of giftedness is not useful, valuable talents may be wasted, and less valuable ones fostered and encouraged. It is thus important for all of us to understand just what it is

we, and others, mean by the concept of *giftedness* (pp. 3–4).

Many different decisions regarding identification, education and counseling, for example, depend on the often only implicit conception and definition of giftedness. Therefore clarification of underlying constructs is essential for both program and research design.

Definitions, concepts and constructs which guide research and educational planning today are much more diverse, much more research and theory based and much more influential on the planning and program decisions being made for the identification and development of talent. At the beginning of 21st century, it would appear that efforts to develop better theories and conceptions of giftedness and talent in order to improve program and practice will continue but the focus will no longer be on devising a single, comprehensive conception or construct of giftedness and talent (Feldhusen, 1998; Benito & Moro, 1999). There is increasing recognition that theory building and conceptualization of the phenomena of giftedness have considerable significance in determining what should be done to bring giftedness potential to talent realization (see Chapters I, 3–4) or to develop high expertise and excellence in a specific domain (see Chapters II, 3–5).

Developmental Issues

Studying Giftedness from a Life-Span Perspective

Charlotte Bühler, the pioneer of life-span psychology published in 1933 the groundbreaking book 'Der menschliche Lebenslauf als psychologisches Problem' [The human course of life as a psychological problem]. The life-span view in developmental psychology has its roots in Europe (Mönks & Spiel, 1994; see also Chapter II, 1 in this handbook). Only in the latter half of the 20th century human development was not longer seen as being synonymous with child and adolescent development. The traditional approach to human development emphasized extreme change from birth to adolescence, stability in adulthood, and decline in old age; e.g. the decrease of cognitive functioning has been discussed extensively in the literature under the heading 'deficit model'. According to the deficit view there is indeed a decrease of cognitive functioning from adulthood on. The age of onset lies somewhere between 20 and 40. If, however, a distinction is made between *fluid* and *cristallized* intelligence (cf. Cattell & Horn, 1978), the outcome is different. From longitudinal data one can draw the conclusion that there is no decline of *cristallized* intelligence with age, while the *fluid* intelligence decreases, indeed, beginning roughly at the age of 30 years. Furthermore, it is not age as such which has influence on cognitive functioning, more important is rather the amount and quality of academic training and health conditions. Age must be regarded as

an index of experiences and not as an independent variable which influences human behavior.

The life-span perspective has seven explicit characteristics (Baltes 1987; cf. Mönks & Spiel, 1994, pp. 137–138).

(1) *Life-long development:* Development as a process of change takes place throughout the whole life.
(2) *Multidimensionality:* Human development consists of different dimensions and a variety of components within these dimensions.
(3) *Multidirectionality:* Some dimensions or components may increase, while others decrease.
(4) *Plasticity:* Human development may take different paths, depending on the individual's life conditions.
(5) *Historical embeddedness:* Development is influenced by historical as well as economical and cultural conditions.
(6) *Contextualism:* The individual is responding to and acting on contexts; heredity is not a fate but is always heredity in a specific environment.
(7) *Multidisciplinarity:* Human development needs to be studied in an interdisciplinary context.

The most famous life-span study is Terman's *Genetic Study of Genius* which started in the 20s and is still ongoing (Terman, 1925; Terman & Oden, 1951; Walberg et al., 1994). His 1528 subjects (672 girls and 856 boys) were selected on the basis of an IQ score of 135 or higher. His selection was based on IQ as the only crucial factor of giftedness. Actually, his selection was very careful and he did try to apply the high scientific standards of that time. In spite of the many deficits of such pioneering approach, his data provided us with rich material and new perspectives on the development of gifted subjects. Terman, convinced by his own empirical data, came to the conclusion that intelligence is important, a necessary condition, but that a supportive home and school environment as well as high achievement motivation contribute in an essential way to the realization of high potential.

It is evident that many researchers avoid longitudinal studies since it takes years to get data. At the time the data become available for interpretation, they may no longer be relevant for the new situation due to societal and cultural changes. But it is also evident that we need longitudinal studies to get insight into the development, i.e. changes over time, of gifted individuals (cf. Subotnik & Arnold, 1994). For recent longitudinal studies see e.g. Heller (1991, 1996, 2000), Rost (1993), Perleth & Heller (1994), Benbow & Lubinski (1996), Achter et al. (1999), Lubinski & Benow (1994, 2000), and Chapter VI, 4 in this handbook. An effective approach seems to be the so called mixed longitudinal study according to Schaie's (1970, 1983) most efficient design. Studies of this kind could provide us with information on (Mönks & Spiel, 1994, p. 139):

- which conditions facilitate or hinder the development of gifted potential,
- whether there are 'typical' developmental processes characteristic for the gifted in comparison to the non-gifted,
- whether there are domain specific patterns of development in gifted individuals,
- whether there exists a relationship between creativity and giftedness or not, or to what extent,
- what the *g*-factor contributes to the cognitive development of gifted individuals and whether the *g*-factor shows stability and/or variability over the life-span or parts of the life-span.

These kinds of questions can only be solved when disciplinarity (e.g. behavior genetics) forms the guideline for research projects.

According to Subotnik & Arnold (1994; see also Chapter II, 9 in this handbook), future longitudinal studies should attend to the interactions between talented individuals and their field, by examining domains and fields over time, and by carefully specifying the definitions of eminence, genius, giftedness, or talent. A systems approach to longitudinal research offers three distinct advantages. First, this approach offers an empirical base on which to judge significant innovation in a domain. Second, it accounts for the social context of accomplishment. Third and finally, the person-domain-field conception focuses research on the products of greatest significance to our lives. Subotnik and Arnold argue that longitudinal studies of both everyday creative giftedness and creative eminence are valuable, complementary endeavors—one improves daily life in our homes and schools, the other can attune us to recognize, value, and develop talent with the potential to reach beyond the individual to the transformation of society.

Expectations from Cross-Cultural Socialization Research

Important advances in our knowledge about developmental conditions of gifted children and adolescents can also be expected from cross-cultural investigations in the field. This has thus far been somewhat neglected in the research of giftedness.

The reason for relatively few cross-cultural studies which can be referred to as more than international cooperations but also meet scientific methodology requirements, is not only the enormous cost but also specific methodological problems which frequently confound work and financial loads. One expects *cross-cultural* research approaches within giftedness to bring about an increase in knowledge with regard to various cultural influences on individual developmental and educational processes. This goal should be met by a specific research strategy. This means that cross-cultural psychology should be defined by research methods rather than by the object of research. A good

example here is the comparative study of Peters (1998) concerning the self-concept of gifted adolescents in China and the Netherlands.

Three types of comparison are relevant: (a) cross-national, (b) cross-cultural, (c) cross-societal. In this context the second, cross-cultural studies, is of interest. With regard to the cross-national view, e.g. see Wilgosh (1994).

Culturally caused behavioral differences in the individual development should be identified through the systematic comparison of psychological patterns obtained in different cultural conditions; equivalent measurement instruments must be employed. This is a major problem of cross-cultural research; on the basis of such research designs, universal assumptions can be examined in relevant developmental, educational, learning or instructional areas. This is a function which was already emphasized by Wilhelm Wundt in his psychology of different cultures over one hundred years ago. Thus, the so-called *etic* (from phonetic) approach starts with a universal hypothesis of human behavior and personality, e.g. intelligence, creativity or achievement motivation. In contrast, the so-called *emic* (from phonemic) approach looks at cultural socialization influences within specific cultures (cultural-relativity hypothesis). Newer ecopsychological models attempt to integrate concepts of 'emic' and 'etic'.

Cross-cultural studies can provide new recognitions about social-cultural developmental and nurturance conditions of the gifted solely from their change of the perspective. This could lead to greater variety in the support of developing giftedness and program ideas. Not only this but also tolerance toward foreign cultures is increased. The meeting of different cultures can also be supported by international conferences (for greater detail see Chapter IV, 15 in this handbook).

Identification of Talent Potential

The procedures and processes by which talent potential is measured have changed dramatically since Terman (1925) selected the 1528 subjects (see p. 837 above) for his life-long longitudinal study: "The standard set for inclusion in the group was 140 IQ for Binet-tested subjects and 135 for high school subjects selected on the basis of the Terman Group Test" (Terman & Oden, 1951, p. 22). High intelligence, as measured by an individual or group test, became the basis for both defining giftedness and identifying gifted individuals. For an overview see Chapters III, 1-4 in this handbook.

Sternberg (1993) has reviewed procedures for identifying alternative approaches to assessing intellectual potential, arguing that "'giftedness' can be viewed as quite broader than a high score on a conventional intelligence test' and that 'there can be different sorts of tests within each metaphor, depending upon the particular theory within the metaphor that generates the test'." Concerning methodological problems cf. Hany (1993).

Feldhusen & Jarwan (1993) submitted that a sound identification system must deal with a number of issues: "(1) the rationale and goals, (2) defining the target population, (3) use of single or multiple criteria, (4) types of test performance, (5) criteria for test selection and (6) selection strategies" (for further information see Chapters III, 1 and VII, 1 in this handbook; also Mönks & Heller, 1994).

Operational definitions and conceptions of giftedness guide identification and program planning. As Renzulli (1982) has pointed out: "there are very few educators who cling to a 'straight IQ' definition or purely academic criteria for identifying giftedness. 'Multiple talent' and 'multiple criteria' are almost the bywords of the present day interest in the gifted" (p. 723). Also see Chapter IV, 3 in this handbook.

Depending on the definition of giftedness or talent, multiple sources of information about individual differences may include some or all of the following (Passow, 1985a, p. 2049):

- Evidence of general ability and/or multiple intelligences including group and individual intelligence tests.
- Evidence of scholastic achievement, including standardized tests of achievement and teacher grades.
- Evidence from 'creativity' measures, including standardized tests of creativity, divergent thinking and productive thinking.
- Nomination by teachers on various kinds of rating scales and checklists.
- Nomination by peers on various kinds of rating scales, inventories, check lists.
- Nomination by parents on various kinds of rating scales, inventories, check lists.
- Evidence of productivity through products of individuals such as writings, compositions, sculpture, science projects, reports and so on.
- Evidence of noncognitive behaviors—for example, work habits, task commitment, self-directedness, pride in accomplishment, etc.—on inventories, check lists and rating scales.
- Autobiography and self-nominations.
- Evidence from judgment by experts in various talent areas, such judgments based on student products and/ or performances, especially in areas such as dramatics, graphic arts, and music.

In addition to relying more on student performance and products in the identification process, another significant development involves the design of environments or settings which provide opportunities for a larger number of students to engage in a self-identification process by participating in enrichment activities which enable them to demonstrate their capabilities and manifest their talent potential. Milgram (2000) demonstrated in a recent special issue of the *Roeper Review* that the strategies and procedures of *talent identification* and *talent search* vary worldwide. Hence an international sharing of knowledge and experiences in this field could enlarge the research and practice of identifying and nurturing the gifted and talented.

Identification procedures have been seriously criticized for their failure to identify gifted in such populations as racial and ethnic minorities, the disadvantaged and poor and those with limited language in their land of residence. There are increasing numbers of such students not only from a given country itself but also those displaced by political and/ or economic hardship. Increasing attention is being paid to procedures and techniques which will enlarge the talent pool from these seriously underrepresented populations. For dynamic assessment see Chapter III, 2; for early identification Chapter III, 3 in this handbook.

Three examples of such effort are *The National Research Center on the Gifted and Talented* at the University of Connecticut and the University of Georgia (USA), which is developing methods for identifying diverse populations and training teachers to recognize such giftedness; *The Center for the Study of Giftedness* at the University of Nijmegen (The Netherlands), where work is ongoing in identifying and providing enrichment for both minority students (primarily Turkish and Moroccan) and disadvantaged Dutch students; and the *Center for the Study of Excellence (CSE)* at the University of Munich (Germany), where the Munich High Ability Test System (MHBT)—consisting of two dozen scales—has been developed (Heller & Perleth, 2000).

In the year 2000, it would appear that the multi-dimensions of giftedness and the concept of multiple talents will prompt the design and employment of much more authentic and complex identification procedures; less reliance on single tests, particularly IQ tests; more design and dependence on self-identification wherein individuals can demonstrate their talent potential by their performances and products; much more use of enrichment curricular opportunities to provide the basis for manifestation of talent potential and increased efforts to identify talent potential among the many seriously underrepresented populations.

Gifted Education

Perhaps the fundamental question educators of the gifted must deal with has always been and continues to be: What kinds of education and socialization opportunities and experiences are needed to transform talent potential into talented performance? See Chapters IV, 4 in this handbook.

More than four decades ago, pointing to the tendency to believe that if only children with talent potential could be identified then they could readily be provided with appropriate experiences to nurture that talent, McClelland (1958) observed:

> Suppose we could locate that sleepy boy in the back row, the potential poet; what would we do for him? Would we offer him a liberal scholarship to one of our better private schools? Would we 'enrich' his curriculum with special readings in poetry, or in the Greek classics? Or would we perhaps excuse him from school altogether on the ground that he would do better as a self-educated man? Or would we supply him with a vocational counselor who would help him find his real niche in life? . . . The plain fact is that we do not know what we would do; we do not know enough about what goes into the making of a poet . . . we still know far too little to be confident about how to develop talented performance out of talent potential (pp. 23–24).

While what goes into the making of a poet, a scientist, a painter, a musician, an orator or any other talent domain may not be known with the certainty that specific actions will result in nurturing particular giftedness, we do know that the absence of certain kinds of experiences will impede or thwart the realization of talent. For example, a strong case can be made that the 'potential poet' whose language is not cultivated and enriched, whose understanding of the beauty and esthetics of language is not nurtured, who has not experienced various genres of poetry, who has not acquired the connoisseurship that enables him/her to distinguish between 'good and bad' poetry, who has not had opportunities to produce poetry, who has not been encouraged to play around with words and ideas and who has not had opportunities to 'do poetry'—is not likely to transform his/her potential into superior performance. We do not know that the 'potential poet' will emerge but we are pretty certain that without these kinds of experiences and learning opportunities, he/she is very unlikely to become a gifted poet. The same arguments could be made for other areas of giftedness or talent.

Every area of specialized talent has a content and a substance, its very special methodologies and processes, its modes of problem definition and problem solving, its ways of exercising creativity, innovation and originality. A specialized curriculum for the gifted should activate and motivate the commitment and the development of the competencies and affective behaviors needed for nurturing one's special talent potential.

To be able to meet the learning and developmental needs of gifted students, appropriate teacher training is an imperative. So far, the education and instruction of gifted students have not been included in teacher training. Therefore post graduate training for teachers and/or inservice-training should have priority in order to increase the number of teachers as gifted education specialists. The ECHA diploma may serve as an example for that, which has been established as *European Advanced Diploma in Educating the Gifted* in connection with the University of Nijmegen in 1994 (cf. Katzko, 1996, pp. 2–5).

Curricular Programs and Provisions for the Gifted

Educators planning for the gifted are concerned with designing educational settings and learning engagements that make available opportunities for students to acquire the knowledge, insights, skills, understandings, motivation, interest, values and other learning that will enable them to perform at levels of excellence that might be described as 'gifted' or 'talented'. Not every potential poet will emerge as a poet but it is unlikely that potential will be realized without appropriate experiences. It is the nature of 'appropriate experiences' that is at issue.

For more than a century schools have provided programs of various kinds aimed at nurturing the potential of gifted and talented children and youth. Practically every aspect of the educational process— the goals and objectives, curriculum content, instructional strategies, teaching/learning resources, personnel resources and evaluation and assessment programs—have been modified and adapted "to meet the needs of the gifted."

As the Marland Report (1971) put it, the gifted "are children who require differentiated educational programs and/or services beyond those normally provided by the regular school program in order to realize their contribution to self and society" (p. 2). The phrase "beyond those normally provided by the regular school program" implies that there is a curriculum which may be accelerated (experienced at an earlier age, in less time than is usual or at a more rapid pace), enriched (experienced in greater depth and/or breadth), or amplified (experienced beyond what is provided for other students, differing in nature or kind).

Programming for the gifted, i.e. the provision of differentiated curricula, raises a number of issues such as: Are there bodies of content and educational experiences that are essential for talent development? Is there a common body of curriculum content for all talent development? What kinds of specialized curricula are needed to nurture diverse talents? A curriculum and the instruction form the heart of any school system, thus also for gifted education. Because the "curriculum is *what* is taught to students, i.e. intended and unintended information, skills, and attitudes that are communicated to students in schools" (Sowell, 1996, p. 5), whereas the instruction is *how* the curriculum is delivered to students.

Are there education imperatives which are applicable to all gifted—i.e. are there learnings which are essential for all gifted and talented, regardless of their specific talent domain? Are there essential learnings that all gifted must experience if they are to achieve maximum self-realization and fulfill their potential? Positions taken on these issues vary widely. Most curricular and instructional programs are based on a particular conception of giftedness albeit in most instances this is only implicit (see Chapters in Part IV, 1–15 and VI, 1–11).

There is a general consensus on the need for specialized curricula aimed at nurturing the diverse special areas of talent, providing learning engagements and opportunities that enable the individual to identify and develop the skills, knowledge, insights, understandings and values needed to realize one's area of specialized talent potential. The specialized curriculum starts the individual toward the development of his/her talent potential by activating and motivating the acquisition of and commitment to knowledge, skills and affective behaviors that contribute to talented performance (see Heller, 1999).

Not only are there issues concerning the nature of such specialized curricula but there are questions about the appropriate balance between the differentiated basic or general curriculum and the specialized curricula. Which subjects, which disciplines, which learning opportunities are appropriate at the early stages of talent development and how do these change as the talent matures and comes closer to the behaviors of a gifted adult performer? To what extent should the individual be permitted or encouraged to focus his/her learnings on a specific talent domain or to what extent should he/she be required to engage in basic/general or common learnings? Should the potential poet and the exceptionally able mathematician have opportunities to pursue more intensive study of creative writing or of advanced mathematics 'at the expense' of the general or basic education? These issues are essentially questions as to what constitutes a sound and appropriate general education which can serve as a foundation or base for the development of specialized talents and what comprises the specialized curricula.

A closely related issue of curricular balance is that of acceleration vis-a-vis enrichment—when and how to accelerate learning and when and how to enrich learning. For many years, literature on gifted education posed acceleration and enrichment as opposing concepts and the controversy still rages among some advocates of each process. Passow (1985b) has argued that acceleration "enables the student to deal with more advanced concepts at higher cognitive levels and thus represents an enriching experience" while providing opportunities for more advanced study in the area being accelerated or in another area or areas (p. 37). On the other hand, by providing "learning experiences that enable the student to probe more broadly or more intensively" using advanced resources "enabling gifted individuals to attain higher levels of insight, understanding, performance, or product development," enrichment also involves acceleration (p. 37). For

further information see Chapters IV, 1–4 in this handbook.

Both acceleration and enrichment have qualitative as well as quantitative dimensions which make it possible for gifted individuals to pursue differential experiences through a greater variety of opportunities and engagements. Thus, the issue is now beginning to be reformulated, not in terms of acceleration vs. enrichment, but rather as the question: *When* is it more appropriate to alter the tempo or pace of instruction and learning and *when* is it more appropriate to alter the breadth or depth of experience and *how* shall this be accomplished?

During the past decades, mainly in the USA, there has been a proliferation of systems and models for designing programs for the gifted and talented (Fox, 1979; Maker, 1982; Renzulli, 1986; Renzulli & Reis, 1997). These models may focus on organizing for instruction (i.e. administrative models) or "consist of principles that guide the instructional process and give direction to the content, thinking processes and outcomes of learning experiences" (Renzulli, 1986). Maker (1982) observed that these models differ in terms of the theoretical assumptions made, "both regarding the nature of the learner (for example, learning, motivation, intellectual and emotional characteristics) and the nature or effectiveness of certain teaching methods" (p. 2). See also Heller & Hany (1996).

Some ideas of the diverse foci, nature and comprehensiveness of the models and systems that are currently being implemented in the USA can be gathered from the following listing (for greater detail see Chapters VI, 1 and 2 in this handbook):

- SMPY's model for teaching mathematically precocious students.
- The Autonomous Learner Model for the gifted and talented.
- The Integrative Education Model.
- The Learning Enrichment Service (LES): A participatory model for gifted adolescents.
- The Purdue Three-Stage Enrichment Model for Gifted Education at the Elementary Level.
- The Purdue Secondary Model for Gifted and Talented Youth.
- The Grid: A model to construct differentiated curricula for the gifted.
- The SOI System for Gifted Education.
- The Enrichment Triad/Revolving Door Model: A schoolwide plan for the development of creative productivity (see Chapter IV, 3).
- The Secondary Triad Model.
- Cultivating simultaneous student growth in both multiple creative talents and knowledge.
- Talents unlimited: Applying the multiple talent approach in mainstream and gifted programs.
- The Enrichment Matrix Model.

- Fostering effective independent learning through individualized programming.
- The Cognitive-Affective Interaction Model for Enriching Gifted Programs.
- The cognitive and affective taxonomies.
- The basic structure of a discipline.
- Discussions of moral dilemmas.
- Creative problem solving.
- Teaching Strategies Programs (Maker, 1982; Renzulli, 1986; Gallagher & Gallagher, 1994; Heller & Hany, 1996; Gallagher, 1997; Renzulli & Reis, 1997; Heller, 1999).

A criticism made of many of these models is that, with very few exceptions, they fail to deal with the total curricular experience and usually consider only one aspect of instruction and learning—whether to select and implement a particular system or model depends on the congruence between the conception and assumptions underlying the model and the particular goals of the school's program.

In the early 1920s the reform movement had a great impact on reshaping instructional and educational methods in schools. According to this movement education should be child centered. One of the most prominent reformers was Maria Montessori. Her educational system has been and continues to be a great help in optimizing individual development. Montessori education, like other individualized programs (Jenaplan, Daltonplan), has never explicitly formulated a gifted program. But in reality Montessori education realizes the core principles of gifted education: The level and pace of individual ability determines the content and speed of the individual student. These 'hidden' gifted programs should be made explicit and be made better known to parents and teachers.

Another issue regarding a curriculum for the gifted is that of the balance between cognitive and affective development. Most of the focus of curriculum design for the gifted is on cognitive development: the stimulation of problem-solving and thinking skills and academic and intellectual growth. Far less attention is given to the affective development of the gifted (the feelings, values, motivation, attitudes, morality, self-concepts) although some of the models mentioned above do attend to this domain (Dixon, Meyer & Hardy, 1986). Only a few models—e.g. Williams' (1986) Cognitive-Affective Interaction and Betts' (1986) Autonomous Learner Model for the Gifted and Talented—have the affective domain as a major focus. See Chapters II, 5–6 in this handbook. Passow (1992, p. 224) has observed that:

> Regardless of their specific interests or degree of talent, a [curriculum] should foster self-direction and independence, intellectual and emotional self-reliance, self-set goals and a love of learning. It should stimulate a desire to create and experiment with ideas and things. It should nurture an understanding

and appreciation of one's cultural heritage. It should cultivate what Brandwein (1955) describes as persistence—a willingness "to labor beyond a prescribed time . . . to withstand discomfort . . . to face failure" (p. 10) and questing—"a dissatisfaction with present explanations of aspects of reality" (p. 11).

The processes of nurturing the affective development of the gifted has several dimensions: instructional, counseling and environmental. From a curricular and instructional perspective, every discipline or subject has the potential for enhancing affective growth through self-awareness, sensitivity to others, understanding, empathy, esthetic appreciation, interpersonal understandings and moral values (see Chapters IV, 9–10). From the counseling perspective, gifted and talented students face particular affective problems of a personal and interpersonal nature for which guidance and support are needed. From the environmental perspective, classroom, school and community climates are powerful influences on student behavior and learning, especially on affective development: self-concepts, attitudes, motivations, task commitment. As educators of the gifted have become more concerned with the affective dimensions nurturing talent, more attention is being given to curriculum, guidance and climate for learning, as these have an impact on affective development.

Still another dimension of curricular significance for the gifted focuses on interdisciplinary study. Curriculum content, Passow (1982) has suggested, should "include more elaborate, complex and in-depth study of major ideas, problems and themes that integrate knowledge with and across systems of thought" (p. 7). Curricula which are organized across themes or problem areas, using interdisciplinary approaches of a high order, drawing on knowledge and multidisciplinary resources appropriate to deriving understandings and gaining insights into those problems and themes are increasingly being perceived as germane to the education of the gifted (see Chapters IV, 1–2 and 12).

Another curricular issue focuses on the suitable balance between individual and group activity for the gifted. Independent study and individualized instruction are widely advocated for gifted students: opportunities to pursue their own interests, concerns, problems and preoccupations on their own and by themselves. On the other hand, in addition to the learning which come from interaction with students with a wide range of abilities, there is a good deal of research regarding the stimulation and exhilaration that come from interaction with other equally able gifted students. A differentiated curriculum for the gifted must provide opportunities for independent study as well as group learning activities depending on the particular goals and objectives being pursued. The request for individualized and differentiated curricula for the gifted is a realistic claim in accordance with leading textbooks on curriculum. Sowell (1996) made a valuable distinction between: (a) curriculum conception, (b) purpose of education, and (c) primary source of content. He came to the following overview (cf. Table 1).

Dishart (1980) is critical of curricula which must be either enriched or accelerated in order to be used with the gifted and argues:

> Educational programs for the gifted should be based upon the needs of the individual learners rather than upon making up for the program deficits in a curriculum for the non-gifted. There is a resultant difference between enriching or accelerating an inadequate and inappropriate curriculum and designing an adequate and appropriate curriculum for use in the first place (p. 26).

Educators of the gifted are taking heed of the concept of differentiated curricula which are "adequate and appropriate . . . in the first place." Educational planners are giving more thoughtful attention to the creation of a community of learners, to problems of sequence and articulation over the school years, to devising opportunities for individualized/independent study, to meaningful implementation of the concepts of acceleration and enrichment and to integrating curricular elements for the gifted within the total curriculum.

Moreover, increasingly planners are beginning to think in terms of curricula and learning experiences which extend beyond the classroom and into the community, using a broad array of relevant resources, both school and non-school. Mentorships and apprenticeships, for example, relate students with talent potential to talented adults who provide learning opportunities and serve as role models (Maoz, 1993; Zorman, 1993).

There is, as yet, no certainty regarding appropriate and adequate curricula for the gifted but gradually the 'busy work' and 'fun-and-games' approaches to educating the gifted are being eliminated and there is increasing understanding and congruence between operating concepts of giftedness, goals and objectives and the design of learning opportunities and learning environments (Van Tassel-Baska, 1998; Heller, 1999). For an international overview by country see Part VI of this handbook.

Extracurricular Programs and Experiences

Learning experiences outside school are often necessary and in any case very useful for the development of giftedness and talent, especially creative productivity. Because such individual activities are self-regulated learning processes, special interests are supported in an optimal way. Community facilities and opportunities for individualized leisure time activities are very important not only for the development of domain-specific competencies but also for the enhancement of self-concept and task commitment. Furthermore, leisure time activities offer chances for many relationships between gifted peers, which are important for the development of giftedness and talent. Therefore extracurricular programs like after school work groups, Saturday and summer programs or academies, academic olympiads, competitions, etc. provide gifted adolescents with a great variety of challenging experiencies (see Chapter IV, 13 in this handbook).

Such learning opportunities are especially supportive for the development of gifted or talented girls and women (see Chapters V, 7–8). Inasmuch as the risk of limited sozialization experiences, e.g. in the field of 'hard' sciences and technology, is quite higher for gifted/talented girls than boys, balancing leisure time activities are necessary for girls in such fields. An affiliated problem is the lower participation quota of girls in competitions in comparison to boys. Hence group competitions offer useful supplementary learning experiences for girls. Much research with respect to gender specific differences between gifted girls and boys and instructional approaches to cope with that problem has been carried out in recent years, in Germany e.g. Beerman, Heller & Menacher (1992), Heller & Ziegler (1996), Ziegler, Heller & Broome (1996), Ziegler & Heller (1998, 1999).

Table 1. Curriculum Conceptions, Purposes of Education and Primary Sources of Content (according to Sowell, 1996, p. 41).

Curriculum Conception	Purpose of Education	Primary Source of Content
Cumulative tradition of organized knowledge	To cultivate cognitive achievement and the intellect	Academic disciplines, subject matter
Social relevance-reconstruction	To prepare people for life in an unstable, changing world; to reform society	Needs of society and culture
Self-actualization	To develop individuals to their fullest potential	Needs and interests of learners

Community Agencies and Institutions

As schools come to understand more about the nature of giftedness and its nurture, community agencies and institutions are being recognized as another essential element in talent development. Kough (1958) has argued that there are many specialized areas that schools can expose students to, but often they cannot provide the expertise needed for developing potential to a high level as well as a nonschool group can, and that "many of the educational functions which are directed by the schools can be enhanced by community activities" (p. 378).

Research and experience support the idea that education, socialization and enculturation take place in many different settings and that many agencies and institutions, besides the school, teach. A second important idea is that there are personnel and material resources in non-school agencies which can enrich the learning opportunities and thus challenge gifted and talented students far beyond that which the school can do (for greater detail see Maoz, 1993).

Community agencies and institutions often have far more appropriate, up-to-date and state-of-the-art equipment than that which the school can provide. Such agencies and institutions are not only sources for much needed materials and equipment but, equally if not more importantly, they are the places where practicing specialists—scientists, artists, musicians, researchers, artisans, technicians, media personnel, writers, government leaders, other professionals and other creative and productive individuals—are available who can serve as mentors, teachers and role models for young persons with talent potential.

Increasingly, the human and material resources of non-school individuals and groups are being used to extend educational opportunities and challenges for the gifted and talented. These resources are now recognized as not being simply enriching but, in many cases, they are absolutely essential and critical in talent nurturing efforts. A sound mentoring experience, for example, can have a significant impact on both the cognitive and affective growth of the child.

Administrative and Organizational Arrangements

Curricula may be implemented and learning opportunities for the gifted may be provided in a variety of settings. These settings can be in or out of school, within regular classes, special classes or special schools, part-time or full time, beginning at and available in every grade level.

Special groups may be organized on the basis of ability, achievement, aptitude, interests or motivation and may involve students or the entire school population. Groups may meet for a few minutes a day or for the entire school day. The groups may be organized for a variety of purposes such as practice for debate or academic bowls, for drama or chess. Groups may include special classes or sections, special schools or school-within-schools (e.g. the German Gymnasium with an eight year accelerated program in the regular nine year Gymnasium; cf. Heller, Osterrieder & Wystrychowski, 1995; Heller & Rindermann, 1999).

Despite the various kinds of grouping used in providing for the gifted, the general practice—usually called ability grouping or tracking—has a long and controversial history on philosophical, psychological, sociological and educational grounds. Because ability grouping has been an issue and been studied for almost a century, there is a considerable body of research available but the controversy is hardly resolved. In the United States, ability grouping/tracking has been linked to provisions for the gifted and, from time to time, has been condemned as 'elitist' and 'undemocratic', hindering both equity and excellence. Currently the U.S. pendulum is swinging away from ability grouping to cluster grouping (homogeneous achievement classes). For an overview of ability grouping vs. cooperative learning see Slavin (1992), Kulik & Kulik (1997), Robinson (1997, 1998), Van Tassel-Baska (1998), Gentry & Owen (1999); also cf. Chapters IV, 1 to 4, 12 and 13 in this handbook.

Some gifted programs do separate the gifted from other students but, except for full-time special classes or special schools, complete isolation is rare. Research has indicated that, depending on the circumstances, there are positive outcomes from the stimulation of gifted students interacting with each other and the competition as well as the cooperation that occurs in those settings.

Grouping and tracking are organization procedures intended to facilitate teaching and learning. What appears to be emerging is a consensus that the issue is not one of grouping vs. no grouping but rather one of *what kinds of grouping*—together with other elements of curriculum and instruction—are needed to foster optimum learning for all children, including those believed to have talent potential. A balance needs to be attained between learning experiences optimally engaged in with intellectual and creative peers and those that are best experienced with a broad mix of learners (Tannenbaum, 1998).

A variety of special schools for the gifted and talented, schools which usually have selected admissions and which provide distinctive domain specific learning opportunities, are still rare. Examples of such schools are the *Bronx High School of Science* (USA), *The Israel Academy of Arts and Science* (Israel) and the *Yehudi Menuhin Music School* (UK). In Europe there are many secondary schools for Dance, Music and the Fine Arts, or the *selective German Gymnasium*, eight year (instead of the regular nine year) accelerated program in Baden-Württemberg and Rhineland-Palatinate or several *private Gymnasia* in Germany, Austria and Switzerland. In the United States there has been a growth of residential Governer's schools which select students from entire states who are gifted in specific areas: *The North Carolina High School for Mathematics and Science, The North Carolina School of Fine Arts, The Louisiana School for Arts, Science and the Performing Arts* and *The Illinois Math and Science Academy* exemplify such state supported selective special-purpose schools.

Despite the attainments of such schools as with other forms of grouping, they continue to be controversial. The basic argument advanced for their support is that they provide the kind of stimulating environment and appropriate personnel and material resources which are not possible in any other setting. The argument against such special schools is that they are elitist, undemocratic and use scarce resources needed by other less able students. Although the issue of special schools has never been resolved to the satisfaction of all due to deep philosophical and political differences regarding the extent that the student body is inclusive of minorities and disadvantaged gifted—i.e. the equity question is dealt with, special schools and special programs appear to be more acceptable.

At the beginning of the 21st century, it seems likely that the many controversies surrounding various kinds of administrative and organizational provisions will not be resolved, essentially because they are part of the larger issue of equity and excellence. Planners of programs for the gifted will need to draw on research for support of special provisions but use these insights in the context of planning rich opportunities for learning for all. See also Chapters V, 3 and 9.

Socio-Emotional Development, Counseling and Guidance

Superior performance is determined by the interaction of many factors, cognitive, affective and social. The social and emotional issues, including self-concept can release or inhibit the full use of an individual's abilities (VanTassel-Baska, 1989; Freeman, 1991, 1997; Tannenbaum, 1998). How an individual functions cognitively is affected by and affects the individual's affective functioning—cognitive and affective systems are congruent and interactive. Tannenbaum (1983) argues that:

> Ability alone cannot facilitate great accomplishment. It also requires a confluence of various non-intellective factors such as ego strength, dedication to a chosen field of productivity or performance, willingness to sacrifice short-term satisfactions for the sake of long-term accomplishment and many others. These traits are integral to the achieving personality regardless of the areas in which the talent manifests itself (p. 88).

Regardless of specific interests or degree of talent, opportunities are needed to foster such qualities as self-direction and independence, intellectual and emotional self-reliance, self-set goals and a love of learning, a desire to create and experiment with ideas and things—

all affective behaviors. Opportunities are needed to cultivate what Brandwein (1955) called *persistence* a willingness "to labor beyond a prescribed time . . . to withstand discomfort . . . to face failure" (p. 10)—and questing "a dissatisfaction with present explanations of aspects of reality" (p. 11).

As a group, gifted children tend to be more highly motivated, often have a strong desire for self-advancement and unusual emotional depth and intensity; they tend to have higher self-concepts and stronger ego strengths; are inclined to be greater risk-takers; tend to be more sensitive to the expectations and feelings of others; often express idealism and a sense of justice earlier and tend to be more independent, more forceful and more competitive.

By virtue of their being 'different', the gifted often encounter socio-emotional problems which can become serious. For example, sometimes, the gifted child's cognitive development far outstrips his/her affective development and adults expect equally 'mature behavior', creating problems by such expectations. Adult uncertainty about the nature of giftedness can result in their pressuring a child to conform or behave in particular ways or in their avoiding or ignoring recognition of unusual ability. Excesses in either direction can contribute to socio-emotional problems which require guidance and counseling.

Classroom curriculum and instruction can be boring and unchallenging or the classroom climate and school environment can influence student behavior and learning, positively or negatively.

Alan & Fox (1979) have categorized the affective problems of gifted children as environmental, interpersonal and intrapersonal. *Environmental* problems arise in a school setting where lack of a sufficiently interesting or challenging curriculum leaves the child feeling bored, resentful, hostile or disengaged. School problems arise when mediocrity is accepted, excellence is not recognized or rewarded and superior performance is denigrated or ignored. *Interpersonal* problems stem from the gifted child being perceived as 'different' by peers, teachers and adults whose consequent behavior may cause the gifted student to reject or deny his/her potential in order to become 'more acceptable'. Interpersonal problems may also arise when parents, teachers, counselors and other adults have unrealistic expectations regarding the gifted child's performance and behavior. The gifted child's *intrapersonal* problems are those of self-concept, self-esteem and self-acceptance which can lead either to the development of appropriate coping strategies or dysfunctional behavioral responses.

In addition to these three classes of problems, the gifted child also faces problems of educational and career choice-decisions regarding higher education and professional pursuits stemming from their greater potential and higher achievements. All of these problems or potential problems call for guidance and counseling which meets the particular needs of gifted children (see Chapters V, 3–6).

The still new history of the counseling of gifted students includes few publications (St Clair, 1989). Some of them are aimed at teachers, others at the students' parents. Some publications also focus on the personality of the individual looking for counseling. Need for counseling arises directly from giftedness or talent when, for example, there is an inappropriate interaction between the gifted child and the environment. Often age-related distributions of counseling needs specific to the gifted/talented can be found: These age-related problems are frequently confounded with gender-related socialization effects (Silverman, 1993, 1997; Colangelo, 1997; Kerr, 1997). Also see Chapters V, 7–8 in this handbook.

The task of counseling the gifted must be oriented toward individual needs and thus toward concrete counseling problems and at the same time toward the goal of optimal development of the student. In this sense, the counseling of adolescents is very important in supporting their identity formation. The essential importance of counseling in a sufficient program for gifted is emphasized by Silverman (1993). She reminds us that the development of gifted children is frequently asynchronous. Such uneven development leads to greater vulnerability for the gifted, especially for the highly gifted. Such children need counseling to assist them in dealing with their intense emotional lives, their heightened awareness and their difficulties in fitting in with age peers and rigid educational systems. Silverman postulates that the aim of counseling is not just the remediation of problems: Its main goal should be guidance toward self-actualization.

Those being served by counseling services for the gifted include also the gifted's parents, teachers and other important socialization agents including siblings and peers. Parents and teachers of the gifted often need

support because of the specific/unique needs of the gifted. Although scholastic counseling and individual psychological counseling are sometimes indistinguishable because of the inevitable overlapping of these two areas, they can be differentiated as follows (cf. Heller 1993a, 1996, 1999; Elbing & Heller, 1996):

(1) *Scholastic counseling* includes problems of identification, nurturance or cognitive learning and achievement, appropriate classes as well as acceleration measures such as special schools, early admittance to school and skipping grades, extracurricular enrichment activities and guidance toward appropriate post-secondary education.

(2) In *individual counseling*, issues such as those listed in Table 2 are prominent.

One must always take the gifted individual's learning and thinking characteristics, interests and social-emotional needs into account (see Parts II, 4–8 and V, 1–6).

One should take the gifted's natural superiority in information processing into consideration when developing programs for the gifted in order to avoid boredom and loss of motivation. An extended period of non-challenging education frequently leads to later difficulties, usually when the task difficulty increases rapidly during secondary education and the gifted elementary school child has not learned how to learn, study or experience academic failure or frustration. For counseling and nurturing talented girls in particular see Chapter V, 8 in this handbook.

Counseling services also need to be appropriate and adequate for gifted students with learning disabilities and for those with physical handicaps. Counseling agents should also be trained to deal with populations too often underrepresented in gifted programming such as racial and ethnic minorities, the disadvantaged and those with limited language ability in their current land

Table 2. Percentual Frequencies[a] of Counseling Needs Specific to the Gifted from a German Gifted Counseling Center at the University of Munich (according to Heller, 1993a, p. 54).

Boys:		%	Girls:		%
(1)	Search for nurturance possibilities	43.7	(1)	Search for nurturance possibilities	54.5
(2)	Academic achievement problems	31.3	(2)	Identification of giftedness	45.5
(3)	Identification of giftedness	31.0	(3)	Educational counseling	24.2
(4)	Boredom at school	22.3	(4)	Skipping a class	21.2
(5)	Doctor's recommendation	12.6	(5)	Academic achievement problems	15.2
(6)	Skipping a class	11.7	(6)	Boredom at school	12.1
(7)	Behaviour problems	11.7	(7)	Doctor's recommendation	6.1
(8)	Discrepancy between intellectual and social development	10.7	(8)	Discrepancy between intellectual and social development	6.1
(9)	Educational counseling	8.7	(9)	Psychological problems	6.1
(10)	Concentration problems	4.9	(10)	Discrepancy between intellectual and motivational development	3.1

[a]Multiple listings possible

of residence. Increasingly, all over the world, perhaps especially in the United States and in Western Europe, there are students with the added psychological and/or economic handicaps that come from being uprooted from their original homeland. Additional counseling concerns are dealt with in Chapters V, 2–6 and 9.

An integrative model of counseling the gifted has been presented by Perleth & Heller (1992). The model explicates the necessity for cooperation between various counseling agents (school psychologists, school and vocational counselors, social workers, teachers of the gifted) and institutions (school, counseling agencies, research institutes) in order to meet the challenge of counseling the gifted and talented.

For this purpose, it is very important to strengthen the training of those involved in counseling students by including the area of giftedness in developmental, educational and clinical psychology. Counseling personnel should be able to identify and counsel gifted students. There is also a need for inservice counselor training programs (Milgram, 1991).

In the year 2000, it seems likely that increased attention to the mental health and affective development of the gifted will result in making available group and individual guidance and counseling appropriate to the particular needs of the gifted and talented. As educators become more sensitive to the affective characteristics and needs of the gifted, they will design and adopt educational, counseling and socializing experiences to meet those needs.

Creativity

For some researchers, creativity is a basic component of giftedness, a characteristic or trait to be assessed in the process of identifying and selecting gifted and talented students. Some writers use the term as synonymous with giftedness. For others, creativity is a trait to be nurtured if talent potential is to become talented performance. Some researchers write of creative scientists, creative mathematicians or creative artists, for example. Others use the term creativity as synonymous with productive thinking, divergent thinking, critical thinking and even problem solving and view it as a quality to be stimulated and nurtured. For them creativity is more than intelligence and results from the synthesis of many brain functions.

A number of theories of the nature of creativity have been advanced—e.g. psychoanalytic, humanistic, personal attribute, developmental stage and right and left brain, to cite a few (cf. Tannenbaum, 1983; Gardner, 1993; Weisberg, 1993; Feldman, Csikszentmihalyi & Gardner, 1994; Hany, 1994; Milgram & Hong, 1994; Runco & Pritzler, 1999; Sternberg, 1999a). These theories attempt to explain the nature of creativity—some in terms of creative processes or abilities, others in terms of creative potential (see Chapters I, 5–7).

Research on creativity has focused on understanding its nature and functioning, on procedures for assessing its nature and on ways of stimulating or nurturing it. Each focus has raised a number of issues. One perennial issue is the relation between intelligence and creativity—are they distinct and different or are they related and, if so, how? See Simonton (1988, 1999).

Guilford's work became, as Stein (1986) observed, "not only the starting point for those who study the intellect and those who wish to develop creativity tests, but it has also become a model for curriculum development." A social-psychological approach to education of creativity stems from Hennessey (1997); for providing creative school environments see Daniels (1997) and Chapters I, 5 and IV, 11 in this handbook.

A number of test batteries have been developed to identify creativity and these have been replete with controversy (Davis, 1997). One kind of problem has to deal with the validity of such tests. Tannenbaum (1983), for example, asserts that: "For a test to have good face validity, its content must resemble in some way the essential phenomenon it is measuring. This would be especially difficult to demonstrate in tests of creativity, considering the multidimensionality of the concept, how it develops in the human psyche and the mental processes involved in activating it" (p. 270). There have been a number of batteries of tests of creativity developed, and these have their supporters and their critics. While numerous studies have been carried out on many such batteries, as Tannenbaum notes, "from the research produced thus far, it is impossible to draw a clear picture about the relationships among tested creativity, IQ and achievement" (p. 293). Also see Heller (1989, 1991, 1992), Hany (1994).

Efforts to nurture creativity fall into two main categories: One is the development of a number of 'programs' for in-school or extracurricular use, and the second is the adaptation of the regular curriculum in order to stimulate the creative processes. Among the former, for example, are programs aimed at direct instruction to nurture creativity—such as the Meyers-Torrance Workbooks, the Purdue Creativity Training Program, Parne's Creative Problem Solving and Williams' Classroom Ideas for Encouraging Thinking and Feeling, to cite a few. Extracurricular programs are exemplified by the Future Problem-Solving Program and the Odyssey of the Mind, both national competitions designed to stimulate creativity. The latter involve a variety of instructional strategies—e.g. differentiated assignments, independent projects, real-life problems—which require students to deal with the regular curriculum in novel and innovative ways resulting in the stimulation of the creative processes. A basic issue posed is the extent to which these various school-centered curricula and activities actually stimulate creativity—however conceptualized and defined—and whether there is a carry-over to fulfillment of potential beyond the classroom. That is, are children who experience these programs and engage in these activities 'more creative' in their fields of endeavor as adults? Chapter IV, 11 in this handbook provides programs and strategies for nurturing creativity.

Clearly, issues concerning the assessment, identification and nurturing of creativity continue to involve both researchers and practitioners. In the coming years, it is likely that the theories and studies of creativity—its nature, assessment and nurture—will lead to a better understanding of the creative process and its relation to gifted and talented behaviors.

Underachievement

A report by the *Fund for the Advancement of Education* (1957) framed the problem of underachievement as follows:

> Despite the great strides made by American education over the last 50 years, we are still far short of the goal of enabling and encouraging every young person to develop his full potential. The resulting waste of rich human resources is enormous and is deeply rooted in our educational system, right down to the earliest grades. We must therefore attack the long-run problems of talent supply primarily through our school and colleges (p. i).

The phenomenon of underachievement is both a puzzling and a challenging one—puzzling in its complexities and challenging in the difficulty in reversing or overcoming it. Underachievement is essentially a school-centered concept—i.e. most definitions refer to a serious gap between predicted and actual school achievement. As Raph, Goldberg & Passow (1966) have noted: "The broadest definition of underachievement among the more able would refer to all those who, for whatever reasons, fail to develop their potentialities maximally. Only if it were possible to assess potential with sufficient accuracy to enable prediction of performance for all individuals would such a definition become operationally meaningful" (p. 2). Clearly, the accuracy of assessment and predictions has not reached that stage. Thus, Raph et al. (1966) suggested a much narrower definition of underachievement to include:

> intellectual or academic ability on intelligence and aptitude tests but fail to develop their abilities . . . all those who rank in the upper third of the population in ability, but who do not graduate from high school, do not go on to college, or drop out of college before completing their studies, thus failing to acquire the academic preparation needed for the high level jobs they are potentially able to fill (p. 3).

Researchers and practitioners have used variations of this definition but almost all have focused on some variant of the discrepancy between actual attainment and expected attainment. Tannenbaum (1983) observes that "studies of underachievement show variations not only in symptoms but in etiology as well" (p. 224).

Explanations of the nature and causes of underachievement vary considerably. They include what Raph et al. (1966) called "phenomenological factors related to the underachiever's self-concept, self-ideal, motivation and adult models" (p. 181) as well as a variety of home and family factors such as parental pressures, expectations and attitudes as well as home climate and support (Butler-Por, 1987, 1993). Other researchers focus on school programs and classroom conditions as well as personality characteristics (Whitmore, 1980; Rimm, 1997; Supplee, 1990).

At the beginning of the third millennium, the seriousness of the phenomenon of achievement and its effects on individuals and society are being recognized and better understood. Because the probable causes of underachievement are so diverse, the identification strategies proposed for reversing it are diverse as well (Butler-Por, 1993; Ziegler, Dresel & Schober, 2000). Suggested intervention strategies include: changing the classroom climate to affect "the teacher's values, expectations, educational aims and her ability to establish accepting and supportive relationships between her and the children among the class members" (Butler-Por, 1987, p. 103); "systematic curriculum work in basic subjects" together with "stimulating curricula experiences" and curriculum enrichment (Butler-Por, 1987, pp. 108–109); focused counseling and guidance; and mentors and role models from the community and school. For further information see Chapter V, 5 in this handbook.

Underrepresented Populations: Gifted Minority and Disadvantaged

Over the years, the under-representation of minority groups in programs for the gifted and in various fields of specialized talents has been a real concern for educators and society at large all over the world. The minority groups which have been of particular concern in the United States, include African Americans, Hispanic, Native Americans, Asian Americans and the disadvantaged—i.e. children who live in poverty. Research has not contradicted the belief that talent potential is actually equally distributed across lines of race, class and socioeconomic status (see Chapters V, 3 and 9 in this handbook).

As studies have shown, it is not simply a question of becoming "interested and acquiring a good education" but rather one of removing a variety of barriers to identifying and nurturing disadvantaged and minority gifted. Passow (1986, pp. 152–155) identified these barriers as including, but not limited to the following:

- Attitudes and expectations of educators who often do not believe there is giftedness in culturally different populations.
- Over-reliance on intelligence tests as the prime criterion for identification.

- A rigid learning environment and an inflexible curriculum which fail to take into account the individual needs and learning styles of these populations.
- Failure to provide the necessary general education, basic skills foundation and learning-how-to-learn skills which are required for the further development of specialized talents.
- Failure of the schools to understand the significance of a mother tongue other than English, denigrating language habits and speech patterns and failing to provide bilingual education where needed.
- Failure to create a learning environment and a climate for learning in which attention is given to both the affective and cognitive elements or talent development.
- Failure to select, assign and provide appropriate inservice education to teachers, counselors, administrators and other educators who must create the conditions for learning and who, by serving as the gatekeepers for programs and services are critical in talent development.
- Failure to help culturally different students enhance their self-esteem and recognize that systematic and longterm discrimination contributes to lower self-perceptions.

In countries around the world, there have been numerous programs aimed at increasing the participation of minority and disadvantaged populations in talent identification and talent development programs. These are generally focused on the perceived barriers and are aimed at using more appropriate multiple techniques and procedures in the identification processes, designing curricula and instructional strategies accelerating and enriching educational opportunities for underrepresented groups, providing appropriate counseling and other affective supports, rendering guidance to families and building support, involving community personnel as a way of extending resources and enlarging learning opportunities, developing culturally pluralistic, multicultural programs, creating a 'climate for excellence' in the school and community. Several countries have extended the school day and the school year in order to provide enrichment experiences.

In the United States, the *Jacob K. Javits Gifted and Talented Students Education Grants Program* provides financial support to help build a nationwide capability in meeting the special education needs of gifted and talented students in elementary and secondary schools. Since its passage in 1988, at least half of the appropriations have gone to proposals designed to serve gifted and talented students who are economically disadvantaged.

An outstanding example of serving such populations is the *Inanç High School* in Istanbul. This school—for academically gifted students from all parts of Turkey—provides a free quality education for children between the ages of 11 and 18, who are economically disadvantaged.

Currently, there is a clear and widespread recognition that minorities and disadvantaged populations around the world represent the largest reservoir of undeveloped potential available and the identification and development of this talent potential has become especially apparent. The driving force behind the efforts to increase the representation of minorities and disadvantaged populations in the programs for the gifted is essentially one of achieving the twin goals of equity and excellence.

Parents and Families

The family and parents constitute a child's first school. Research has shown that parents and families play a particularly important role in the development of the gifted child—especially in the affective domain, in the nurturing of self-concepts, values, attitudes, motivation, interests and commitment. For example, Bloom's (1985) study of 120 "'immensely talented' musicians, artists, athletes, mathematicians and scientists" found "strong evidence that no matter what the initial characteristics (or gifts) of the individuals, unless there is a long and intensive process of encouragement, nurturance, education and training, the individuals will not attain extreme levels of capability in these particular fields" (p. 3). Bloom found certain family values in all four talent groups studied: The value of achievement and the importance of doing one's best whatever the task was very important in the subject's homes. The parents' commitment to the productive use of time, the introduction of the child to the talent field, parental encouragement, the provision of resources and materials, and the arrangement of learning opportunities were very significant in the child's ultimate achievement. As Bloom and his colleagues concluded:

> The parents' interest and participation in the child's learning contributed significantly to his or her achievement in the field. We find it difficult to imagine how these children could have gotten good teachers, learned to practice regularly and thoroughly and developed a value of and a commitment to achievement in the talent field without a great deal of parental guidance and support. The role of the home in supporting the long process of talent development is only one piece of the picture, but it is a crucial one (p. 476).

Parenting of gifted children involves many of the same issues, problems and challenges which arise in the parenting of any child—but much more. Fine (1977) has observed:

855

There is a need for parents to be very self-aware regarding their personal investments in the child and also to maintain an accurate and balanced perception of the child as a growing person. Gifted and creative children need parents for emotional support and encouragement, for value and behavioral guidance and to set realistic goals; it is appropriate and important that parents of gifted and creative children in fact do fulfill a parenting 'contract' with their children (p. 500).

Research has found that having a gifted child in the family affects relations among family members. Coleman (1985) has described the effects as follows:

The presence of a gifted child in a family can affect relationships among family members and their thoughts about their relationships. Changes are a product of the family rearranging itself to deal with a member who presents a behavioral pattern that departs from typical expectations . . . Once a child is suspected of being different, parental concerns begin to surface. These concerns become enhanced and even exaggerated as the differences between the gifted and other children become clearer and the parents feel the need to respond in some special way . . . The intrusion of official recognition by the school can create concerns for the family that were previously dormant or non-existent (p. 126).

Mentally and physically handicapped children have had strong advocacy for many years from their parents as well as from other concerned citizens. However, the gifted have a more recent and less effective advocacy. Parents and others who perceive the needs of gifted children have sometimes been hesitant to ask support for those who 'have it all'. Fortunately, parents have been aided by organizations such as the *National Association for Gifted Children* (NAGC) in the United States, the *European Council for High Ability* (ECHA), the *World Council for Gifted and Talented Children* (WCGT), parent organizations in several European countries and groups on the more local level—organizations who have developed programs of advocacy (Maier, 1993). NAGC, having a 50 year history, has developed a strong legislative branch and has obtained the attention and support of legislators. This support led to the *Jacob Javits Grant* which currently funds the *National Research Center* at four state university sites (see Renzulli & Gubbins, 1998, and Chapter I, 2). Parents are encouraged to participate in these local, regional, national and international organizations. Thus, parental concerns can be addressed, their understanding increased and their voices strengthened.

At the beginning of the year 2000, there is increased recognition that the identification of talent and its nurture is not a task which can be accomplished by the school alone. Research and experience have made clear that parents and families are essential in the identification and fostering of giftedness but, just as the school cannot fully develop potential without the nurturance that takes place in the home, parents cannot play out their roles fully without the nurturance that occurs in the school. The role of parents and families in talent development is being acknowledged and studied. Increasingly, meaningful two-way communication channels are being established to facilitate mutual support between home and school. Counseling and advising services are being provided—not just the schools providing services to the parents and family but mutual interaction as parents provide information about the child from which the school can benefit as well (cf. Freeman, 1996, 1998, and Chapter V, 2 of this handbook).

Needed Research and Related Topics

Finally, some state of the art consequences are formulated (for a general overview see Waldmann & Weinert, 1990). The following topics seem to be of the utmost importance for research on giftedness and talent (for greater detail see Heller, 1993b and c; in this handbook the Chapters I, 1 and 8):

- Increase in *basic research*: Cognitive science studies focusing on explanation of the nature of giftedness and talent are needed as a supplement to psychometric studies, which are indispensable to the prediction of excellence (see Chapters III, 2 and 4). Also longitudinal studies of giftedness are indispensable in uncovering causal explanations of intra- vs. interindividual differences in changes over the time and of the interactions of developmental variables (see Chapters II, 1, 7–10). Interdisciplinary research projects including neuro-psychological and biological approaches or genetic studies (see Chapter II, 2) as well as cross-national/cultural studies (see Chapter IV, 15) should continue to be intensified, especially to examine the generalizability or universal validity of many theories in the field. Quasi-experimental and qualitative studies are also increasing our understanding of the nature of giftedness and of developmental changes. Without such basic scientific findings, applied research will wither and the quality of gifted education will be affected in the near future. Additionally, ontological and meta-theoretical difficulties with conceptions of giftedness and talent must be considered (see Chapter I, 1).
- Deficiencies in *applied research*: Elaboration of multidimensional and multiple theory based identification strategies as well as dynamic assessment approaches to the diagnosis of giftedness (see Chapter III, 2) are needed for the practical tasks of gifted counseling, guidance and education. Further desired ends are the development of intervention programs—and prevention measures—for balancing gender-specific differences in cognitive abilities and

performances, especially in the fields of mathematics, 'hard' sciences and technology (see Chapters V, 7–8). Finally, new conceptions and methods of evaluating school and extracurricular programs are needed (see Chapter IV, 14).

There is a continuing evolution in the creativity programs from an emphasis primarily on divergent thinking in the 1950s and 1960s to models including a wide range of dynamic and expanding conceptions including critical thinking and varied abilities. Most creativity programs are still based on the older, limited models. Hence existing programs and curricular materials should be rethought in light of new concepts, such as Simonton's Chance Configuration Theory (1988a/b), or Sternberg's Investment Theory (Sternberg & Lubart, 1991) and social-environmental approaches (see Chapters I, 5–7). It seems especially important to revise one-sided training programs based on promotion of divergent thought processes which however neglect the mediation of knowledge (Weisberg, 1993). Investigations of the expertise-novice paradigm could provide useful information to domain-specific concepts of creativity and giftedness (see Chapters I, 3 and II, 3). Additionally the life-span approach to exceptionality and the study on late-life potential should be included in the study of creativity; see Simonton (1992, 1994, 1999a/b) and Chapter II, 10 of this handbook).

Last but not least, more interest needs to be dedicated to the evaluation of new gifted education programs and counseling or support measures. In connection with evaluation, problems arise concerning the qualification of teachers, counselors and other gifted education related personnel.

Real progress in knowledge, which provides a theoretical basis to practice, can be expected only in the long run. Thus, applied research can often serve only to optimize pragmatic procedures. More important is the demand for careful evaluation of concrete identification and effective gifted methods and curriculum. These measures, of course, always depend on value decisions and aims. These values should be explicitly taken into account in corresponding evaluation models (cf. Heller et al., 1995; Heller & Viek, 2000). Well planned evaluation can have the positive side-effect of bridging the often criticized gap between scientific research and educational practice (see Chapter IV, 14). Progress in knowledge from giftedness research is closely connected with material and personnel resources.

Internationally these are quite differently distributed. In the USA and a few other countries there are basic training programs for future expert personnel in the field of gifted education (see Chapter V, 1). In Europe (Chapters VI, 1, 4–5) and in many other countries around the world (see Chapters VI, 6–11), inservice training programs dominate, e.g. for teachers and/or counselors. As far as we know, special gifted qualification programs for scientific research personnel are very rare. Hence post-graduate (master or doctorate) programs are necessary for recruiting the ablest junior scientists into the field of giftedness research. Examples for that are the new international MA study program 'Psychology of Excellence' at the University of Munich (Germany), directed by K. A. Heller (*e-mail address*: heller@edupsy.uni-muenchen.de; *internet page*: http://www.paed.uni-muenchen.de/excellence/) or the postgraduate training program provided by the University of Nijmegen in cooperation with ECHA, directed by F. J. Mönks (cf. Katzko, 1996). Other examples are the MA study programs in Educational Psychology with a focus on Giftedness at the University of Virginia in Charlottesville (USA), directed by C. M. Callahan (*e-mail address*: cmc@virginia.edu) and the University of Calgary (Canada), directed by J. L. Lupart. Unquestionably, the scientific and practical outcome of giftedness research is highly dependent on the level of qualification of the scholars working in this area. In Table 3, the modules of the MA study program 'Psychology of Excellence' mentioned above are listed. This curriculum could serve as an example to the demands for qualifying practitioners (e.g. gifted educators and counselors) and researchers in the field.

On the other hand, "efforts to increase connections between studies of giftedness and mainstream psychological and educational research" (Jackson, 1993, p. 46) are necessary, because most mainstream researchers ignore or pay little attention to gifted journals (see Chapter I, 8 in this handbook). "However, studies of giftedness have contributed to mainstream theory and may play some special roles in theory development. Strategies for overcoming barriers to further integration with mainstream research are proposed" (Jackson, 1993, pp. 46–50).

Conclusion

As we entered the third millennium, there are important advances to anticipate challenging tasks in gifted education and giftedness research. Most significant are the increasing tendencies toward interdisciplinary communication in research and practice, cross-cultural research and sharing of conceptions and practices and the continued tendency to perceive giftedness from a developmental perspective. There is evidence of evolving interdependence of research and practice, and we continue to press for greater understanding and awareness of giftedness by highly trained researchers.

The emergence of interdisciplinary approaches to the study of giftedness and related fields is a strong and promising trend. In reflection of a new world order there is increasing cross-cultural research and shared understanding. Internationally there is an increasing awareness of the special needs of gifted students and broader understanding of identification methods. Thus, this handbook may enhance the exchange of information and experience of researchers and practitioners both in the gifted field and in the overall educational field. With encouraged and enlightened teachers, administrators, psychological advisors and counselors as well as parents, gifted young people will more probably be enabled to develop fully their potential and their own contributions to the world.

Table 3. Curriculum (Module Structure) of the International Two Year MA Study Program "Psychology of Excellence" at the LMU in Munich, Germany.

Module 1: Excellence: Models, Research, and Development

1a	Conceptions of Excellence (obligatory) (3 hrs)
1b	Cognitive Aspects of Excellence (2 hrs)
1c	Motivational Aspects of Excellence (2 hrs)

Module 2: Identification and Programming

2a	Models of Gifted Education (obligatory) (3 hrs)
2b	Identification and Talent Search (2 hrs)
2c	Promoting Excellence in School: Nurturing Strategies and Programs (2 hrs)
2d	Promoting Excellence in the Corporate World (Business and Industry) (2 hrs)

Module 3: Educational Psychology

3a	Introduction to Learning and Instruction (obligatory) (3 hrs)
3b	Instructional Design (3 hrs)
3c	Learning Environments and Educational Technology (3 hrs)
3d	Self-regulated Learning, Metacognition, and Discovery (3 hrs)
3e	Communication and Cooperation (3 hrs)

Module 4: Differential Psychology

4a	Personality Psychology (obligatory) (2 hrs)
4b	Diagnosis of Giftedness and Counseling Psychology (2 hrs)
4c	Gender and Cross-Cultural Studies (2 hrs)

Module 5: Research and Evaluation

5a	Research Design and Program Evaluation (obligatory) (3 hrs)
5b	Advanced Statistics (obligatory) (3 hrs)
5c	Research Practice I (obligatory) (3 hrs)
5d	Research Practice II (3 hrs)

Module 6: Social and Organizational Psychology (three obligatory)

6a	Center of Excellence (2 hrs)
6b	Quality Management (2 hrs)
6c	Career Development in Higher Education and in the Corporate World (2 hrs)
6d	Career Counseling (2 hrs)
6e	Leadership (2 hrs)

Students focusing on "Psychology of Excellence" with the **major in Educational & Differential Psychology** and the **first minor in Social & Organizational Psychology** (Modules 1 through 6) must choose **one of the following three modules** (7–1, 7–2, 7–3) to accomplish the requirements **for the second Minor**. In the chosen module three classes are obligatory. The program is taught entirely in English and includes **two internships** (consisting of six weeks each).

Module 7–1: Science Education (all obligatory)

7–1a	Introduction to Science Education (2 hrs)
7–1b	Physics Education (2 hrs)
7–1c	Didactics in another subject (2 hrs)

Module 7–2: Philosophy (all obligatory)

7–2a	Philosophy of Science (2 hrs)
7–2b	Philosophy of Mind (2 hrs)
7–2c	Corporate Ethics (2 hrs)

Module 7–3: Sociology (all obligatory)

7–3a	Introduction to Sociology (2 hrs)
7–3b	Family and Kinship Systems (2 hrs)
7–3c	Comparative Religions (2 hrs)

References

Achter, J. A., Lubinski, D., Benbow, C. B., & Eftekhari-Sanjani, H. (1999). Assessing vocational preferences among gifted adolescents adds incremental validity to abilities: A discriminant analysis of educational outcomes over a 10-year interval. *Journal of Educational Psychology*, **91** (4), 777–786.

Alan, S. D., & Fox, D. K. (1979). Group counseling of the gifted. In J. H. Orlloff (Ed.), *Beyond awareness: Providing for the gifted*. Falls Church, VA: Northern Virginian Council for Gifted/Talented Education.

Anastasi, A. (1958). *Differential psychology* (3rd ed.). New York: MacMillan.

Baltes, P. B. (1987). Theoretical positions of life-span developmental psychology: on the dynamics between growth and decline. *Developmental Psychology*, **23**, 611–626.

Beerman, L., Heller, K. A. & Menacher, P. (1992). *Mathe: nichts für Mädchen? Begabung und Geschlecht am Beispiel von Mathematik, Naturwissenschaft und Technik* [Mathematics: nothing for girls? Gender-specific talents in Math, Natural Sciences and Technology]. Bern: Huber.

Benbow, C. P., & Lubinski, D. (Eds.). (1996). *Intellectual Talent*. Baltimore: Johns Hopkins University Press.

Benito, Y. & Moro, J. (1999). An empirically-based proposal for screening in the early identification of intellectually gifted students. *Gifted and Talented International*, **14**, 80–91.

Betts, G. T. (1986). The autonomous learner model for the gifted child. In: J. S. Renzulli (Ed.), *Systems and Models for Developing Programs for the Gifted and Talented* (pp. 27–56). Mansfield Center, CT: Creative Learning Press, Inc.

Bloom, B. S. (Ed.). (1985). *Developing talent in young people*. New York: Ballantine Books.

Brandwein, P. F. (1955). *The gifted child as future scientist*. New York: Harcourt.

Bray, D. W. (1954). *Issues in the study of talent*. New York: John Wiley.

Butler-Por, N. (1987). *Underachievers in school*. New York: John Wiley.

Butler-Por, N. (1993). Underachieving gifted students. In: K. A. Heller, F. J. Mönks & A. H. Passow (Eds.), *International Handbook of Research and Development of Giftedness and Talent* (pp. 649–668). Oxford: Pergamon.

Cattell, R. B. & Horn, J. L. (1978). A check on the theory of fluid and crystallized intelligence with description of new subtest designs. *Journal of Educational Measurement*, **15**, 139–164.

Colangelo, N. (1997). Counseling gifted students: issues and practices. In: N. Colangelo & G. A. Davis (Eds.), *Handbook of Gifted Education* (pp. 353–365). Boston: Allyn and Bacon.

Coleman, L. J. (1985). *Schooling the gifted*. Menlo Park, CA: Addison-Wesley Publ.

Daniels, S. (1997). Creativity in the classroom: characteristics, climate, and curriculum. In: N. Colangelo & G. A. Davis (Eds.), *Handbook of Gifted Education* (pp. 292–307). Boston: Allyn and Bacon.

Davis, G. A. (1997). Identifying creative students and measuring creativity. In: N. Colangelo & G. A. Davis (Eds.), *Handbook of Gifted Education* (pp. 269–281). Boston: Allyn and Bacon.

Dishart, M. (1980). The gifted and talented: their education and development. *Educational Researcher*, **9**, 26–27.

Dixon, B., Meyer, J. & Hardy, A. (1986). *Reaching the gifted: a resource book for affective development*. Toronto, Canada: Ontario Institute for Studies in Education.

Elbing, E. & Heller, K. A. (1996.). Beratungsanlässe in der Hochbegabtenberatung [Counseling Needs and Issues in Gifted Students]. *Psychologie in Erziehung und Unterricht*, **43**, 57–69.

Eysenck, H. J. & Barrett, P. T. (1993). Brain research related to giftedness. In: K. A. Heller, F. J. Mönks & A. H. Passow (Eds.), *International Handbook of Research and Development of Giftedness and Talent* (pp. 115–131). Oxford: Pergamon.

Feldhusen, J. F. (1998). Talent, creativity, and expertise. In: J. A. Leroux (Ed.), *Connecting the Gifted Community Worldwide* (pp. 177–187). Seattle: WCGT.

Feldhusen, J. F. & Jarwan, F. A. (1993). Identification of gifted and talented youth for educational programs. In: K. A. Heller, F. J. Mönks & A. H. Passow (Eds.), *International Handbook of Research and Development of Giftedness and Talent* (pp. 233–251). Oxford: Pergamon.

Feldman, D. H., Csikszentmihalyi, M. & Gardner, H. (1994). *Changing the World: A Framework for the Study of Creativity*. Westport, CT: Praeger.

Fine, M. J. (1977). Facilitating parent-child relationships for creativity. *Gifted Child Quarterly*, **4**, 487–500.

Fox, L. H. (1979). Programs for the gifted and talented: an overview. In: A. H. Passow (Ed.), *The Gifted and the Talented: Their Education and Development* (pp. 104–126). 78th Yearbook, Part 1, National Society for the Study of Education. Chicago: University of Chicago Press.

Freeman, J. (1991). *Gifted children growing up*. London: Cassell.

Freeman, J. (1996). *Highly able girls and boys*. London: Department of Education and Employment.

Freeman, J. (1997). The emotional development of the highly able. *European Journal of Psychology in Education*, **12**, 479–493.

Freeman, J. (1998). *Educating the very able: current international research*. London. The Stationery Office.

Fund for the Advancement of Education (1957). *They went to college early*. New York: Fund for the Advancement of Education.

Gallagher, J. J. (1960). *Analysis of research on the education of gifted children*. Springfield, IL: Office of the Superintendent of Public Instruction.

Gallagher, J. J. (1997). Issues in the education of gifted students. In: N. Colangelo & G. A. Davis (Eds.), *Handbook of Gifted Education* (pp. 10–23). Boston: Allyn and Bacon.

Gallagher, J. J. & Courtright, R. D. (1986). The educational definition of giftedness and its policy implications. In: R. J. Sternberg & J. E. Davidson (Eds.), *Conceptions of Giftedness* (pp. 93–111). New York: Cambridge University Press.

Gallagher, J. J. & Gallagher, S. (1994). *Teaching the gifted child* (4th ed.). Boston: Allyn and Bacon.

Gardner, H. (1993). *Creating Minds: An anatomy of creativity seen through the lives of Freud, Einstein, Picasso, Stravinski, Eliot, Graham, and Gandhi*. New York: Basic Books.

Gentry, M. & Owen, S. V. (1999). An investigation of the effects of total school flexible cluster grouping on identification, achievement, and classroom practices. *Gifted Child Quarterly, 43*, 224–243.

Guilford, J. P. (1968). *Intelligence, creativity and their educational implications.* San Diego, CA: Knapp.

Hany, E. A. (1993). Methodology problems and issues concerning identification. In: K. A. Heller, F. J. Mönks & A. H. Passow (Eds.), *International Handbook of Research and Development of Giftedness and Talent* (pp. 209–232). Oxford: Pergamon Press.

Hany, E. A. (1994). The development of basic cognitive components of technical creativity: a longitudinal comparison of children and youth with high and average intelligence. In: R. F. Subotnik & K. D. Arnold (Eds.), *Beyond Terman. Contemporary Longitudinal Studies of Giftedness and Talent* (pp. 115–154). Norwood, NJ: Ablex.

Heller, K. A. (1989). Perspectives on the diagnosis of giftedness. *The German Journal of Psychology, 13*, 140–159.

Heller, K. A. (1991). The nature and development of giftedness: a longitudinal study. *European Journal for High Ability, 2*, 174–188.

Heller, K. A. (1992). Giftedness research and education of the gifted and talented in Germany. In F. J. Mönks, M. W. Katzko & H. W. van Boxtel (Eds.), *Education of the Gifted in Europe: Theoretical and Research Issues* (pp. 71–85). Amsterdam/Lisse: Swets & Zeitlinger.

Heller, K. A. (1993a). Identifying and counselling gifted students. In: E. G. Demetropoulos et al. (Eds.), *Europe 2000—Tendencies and Perspectives in Counselling and Guidance* (pp. 48–62). Athens: Hellenic Society of Counselling and Guidance (HE.S.CO.G.).

Heller, K. A. (1993b). International trends and issues of research on giftedness. In: W. T. Wu, C. C. Kuo & J. Steeves (Eds.), *Proceedings of the Second Asian Conference on Giftedness: Growing up Gifted and Talented* (pp. 93–110). Taipei, Taiwan: NTNU.

Heller, K. A. (1993c). Structural tendencies and issues of research on giftedness and talent. In: K. A. Heller, F. J. Mönks & A. H. Passow (Eds.), *International Handbook of Research and Development of Giftedness and Talent* (pp. 49–67). Oxford: Pergamon.

Heller, K. A. (1994). Responsibility in research on high ability. In: K. A. Heller & E. A. Hany (Eds.), *Competence and Responsibility,* Vol. 2 (pp. 7–12). Seattle: Hogrefe & Huber Publ.

Heller, K. A. (1996). The nature and development of giftedness: a longitudinal study. In: A. J. Cropley & D. Dehn (Eds.), *Fostering the Growth of High Ability: European Perspectives* (pp. 41–56). Norwood, NJ: Ablex.

Heller, K. A. (1999). Individual (Learning and Motivational) Needs vs. Instructional Conditions of Gifted Education. *High Ability Studies, 9*, 9–21.

Heller, K. A. (Ed.) (2000). *Hochbegabung im Kindes-und Jugendalter* [High Ability in Children and Adolescents] (2nd ed.). Göttingen: Hogrefe.

Heller, K. A. & Hany, E. A. (1996). Psychologische Modelle der Hochbegabtenförderung. [Psychological Models of Gifted Education]. In: F. E. Weinert (Ed.), *Psychologie des Lernens und der Instruktion, Bd. 2 der Pädagogischen*

Psychologie (Enzyklopädie der Psychologie) (pp. 477–513). Göttingen: Hogrefe.

Heller, K. A. & Perleth, Ch. (2000). *Münchner Hochbegabungs-Testsystem* [Munich High Ability Test System]. Göttingen: Hogrefe.

Heller, K. A., & Rindermann, H. (1999). Hochbegabung, Motivation und Leistungs-exzellenz: Aktuelle Forschungsbefunde zum achtjährigen Gymnasium in Baden-Württemberg [High Ability, Motivation, and Performance Escellence]. In: Th. Fitzner, W. Stark, H. P. Kagelmacher & Th. Müller (Eds.), *Erkennen, Anerkennen und Fördern von Hochbegabten* (pp. 81–107). Stuttgart: Klett.

Heller, K. A., & Viek, P. (2000). Support for gifted university students: Individual and social factors. In: C. F. M. van Lieshout & P. G. Heymans (Eds.), *Talent, resilience, and wisdom across the life span* (pp. 299–321). Hove: Psychology Press.

Heller, K. A. & Ziegler, A. (1996). Gender differences in mathematics and the natural sciences: Can attributional retraining improve the performance of gifted females? *Gifted Child Quarterly, 40*, 200–210.

Heller, K. A., Osterrieder, K. & Wystrychowski, W. (1995). A longitudinal follow-up evaluation study of a statewide acceleration program for highly gifted students at the German gymnasium. In: M. Katzko & F. J. Mönks (Eds.), *Nurturing Talent: Individual Needs and Social Ability* (pp. 269–274). Assen/Maastricht: Van Gorcum.

Hennessey, B. A. (1997). Teaching for creative development: a social psychological approach. In: N. Colangelo & G. A. Davis (Eds.), *Handbook of Gifted Education* (pp. 282–291). Boston: Allyn and Bacon.

Henry, W. A. 3rd (1994). *In Defense of Elitism.* New York: Doubleday.

Herrnstein, R. J. & Murray, C. (1994). *The Bell Curve: Intelligence and class structure in American life.* New York: The Free Press.

Jackson, N. E. (1993). Moving into the mainstream? Reflections on the study of giftedness. *Gifted Child Quarterly, 37*, 46–50.

Jacoby, R. & Glauberman, N. (1995). *The bell curve debate.* New York: Times Books.

Katzko, M. (1996). ECHA Diploma. *ECHA News, 10* (1), 2–4.

Kerr, B. (1997). Developing talents in girls and young women. In: N. Colangelo & G. A. Davis (Eds.), *Handbook of Gifted Education* (pp. 483–497) Boston: Allyn and Bacon.

Kough, J. (1958). Community agencies and the gifted. In N. B. Henry (Ed.), *Education of the Gifted.* 57th Yearbook, Part 11, National Society for the Study of Education. Chicago: University of Chicago Press.

Kulik, J. A. & Kulik, C.-L. C. (1997). Ability grouping. In: N. Colangelo & G. A. Davis (Eds.), *Handbook of Gifted Education* (pp. 230–242). Boston: Allyn and Bacon.

Lubinski, D., & Benbow, C. P. (1994). The Study of Mathematically Precocious Youth: The First Three Decades of a Planned 50-year Study of Intellectual Talent. In: R. F. Subotnik and K. D. Arnold (Eds.), *Beyond Terman: Contemporary Longitudinal Studies of Giftedness and Talent* (pp. 255–281). Norwood, NJ: Ablex.

Lubinski, D. & Benbow, C. P. (2000). States of Excellence. *American Psychologist, 55* (1), 137–150.

Maier, N. (1993). Advocacy as a force in the education of the gifted and talented. In: K. A. Heller, F. J. Mönks & A. H. Passow (Eds.), *International Handbook of Research and Development of Giftedness and Talent* (pp. 865–879). Oxford: Pergamon.

Maker, C. (1982). *Teaching models in education of the gifted.* Rockville, MD: Aspen Systems Corporation.

Maoz, N. (1993). Nurturing giftedness in non-school educative settings—using the personnal and material resources of the community. In: K. A. Heller, F. J. Mönks & A. H. Passow (Eds.), *International Handbook of Research and Development of Giftedness and Talent* (pp. 743–752). Oxford: Pergamon.

Marland, S. P. Jr. (1971). *Education of the gifted and talented.* Washington, DC: U.S. Government Printing Office.

McClelland, D. C., Baldwin, A. L., Bronfenbrenner, U. & Strodtbeck, F. L. (1958). *Talent and society: New perspectives on identification of talent.* Princeton, NJ: Van Nostrand.

Milgram, R. M. (Ed.) (1991). *Counseling gifted and talented children.* Norwood, NJ: Ablex.

Milgram, R. M. (Ed.). (2000). Talent identification and development: an international perspective. Special issue. *Roeper Review, 22* (2), 76–134.

Milgram, R. M. & Hong, E, E. (1994). Creative thinking and creative performance in adolescents as predictors of creative attainments in adults: a follow-up study after 18 Years. In: R. F. Subotnik & K. D. Arnold (Eds.), *Beyond Terman: Contemporary Longitudinal Studies of Giftedness and Talent* (pp. 212–228). Norwood, NJ: Ablex.

Mönks, F. J. (1963). Beiträge zur Begabtenforschung im Kindes- und Jugendalter [Contributions to giftedness research]. *Archiv für die gesamte Psychologie, 115,* 362–382.

Mönks, F. J. (1992). From conception to realization. In: F. J. Mönks, M. W. Katzko & H. W. van Boxtel (Eds.), *Education of the Gifted in Europe: Theoretical and Research Issues* (pp. 13–21). Amsterdam/Lisse: Swets & Zeitlinger.

Mönks, F. J. (1996). Elite-Debatte im Scheinwerfer [The Elitism Debate]. *Psychologie in Erziehung und Unterricht, 43,* 219–224.

Mönks, F. J., & Heller, K. A. (1994). Identification and programming of the gifted and talented. In T. Husén & T. N. Postlethwaite (Eds.), *The International Encyclopedia of Education, Vol. 5* (2nd ed., pp. 2725–2733). Oxford: Pergamon.

Mönks, F. J. & Spiel, Ch. (1994). Development of giftedness in a life-span perspective. In: K. A. Heller & E. A. Hany (Eds.), *Competence and Responsibility,* Vol. 2 (pp. 136–139). Seattle: Hogrefe & Huber Publ.

Passow, A. H. (1982). Differentiated curriculum for the gifted/talented: a point of view. In: S. N. Kaplan et al. (Eds.), *Curricula for the Gifted* (pp. 4–20). Ventura, CA: Ventura County Superintendent of Schools Office.

Passow, A. H. (1985a). Gifted and talented, education of. In: T. Husén & T. N. Postlethwaite (Eds.), *The International Encyclopedia of Education* (pp. 2045–2056). Oxford, U.K.: Pergamon.

Passow, A. H. (1985b). Intellectual development of the gifted. In: F. R. Link (Ed.), *Essays on the Intellect* (pp. 23–43). Alexandria, VA: Association for Supervision and Curriculum Development.

Passow, A. H. (1986). Educational programs for minority/disadvantaged gifted students. In: L. Kanevsky (Ed.), *Issues in Gifted Education: A Collection of Readings* (pp. 148–172). San Diego, CA: San Diego City Schools.

Passow, A. H. (1992). Nurturing the affective aspects of giftedness: a neglected component of talent development. In: F. J. Mönks & W. Peters (Eds.), *Talent for the Future* (pp. 222–226). Assen/Maastricht: Van Gorcum.

Perleth, Ch. & Heller, K. A. (1992). Results and implications of the Munich study of giftedness. In: J. Kotásková (Ed.), *Psychological Development and personality Formative Processes* (pp. 366–376). Proceedings of the 6th Prague International Conference. Prague: Institute of Psychology, Czechoslovak Academy of Sciences.

Perleth, Ch. & Heller, K. A. (1994). The Munich Longitudinal Study of Giftedness. In: R. F. Subotnik & K. D.Arnold (Eds.), *Beyond Terman: Contemporary Longitudinal Studies of Giftedness and Talent* (pp. 77–114). Norwood, NJ: Ablex.

Peters, W. A. M. (1998). *The Self-Concept of Able Young Adolescents in China and the Netherlands.* Ph.D. Dissertation, University of Nijmegen (KUN). Nijmegen, NL: KUN.

Raph, J. B., Goldberg, M. L. & Passow, A. H. (1966). *Bright underachievers.* New York: Teachers College Press.

Renzulli, J. S. (1982). Gifted persons. In: H. E. Mitzel (Ed.), *Encyclopedia of educational research* (5th ed., pp. 723–730). New York: The Free Press.

Renzulii, J. S. (Ed.). (1986). *Strategies and models for developing programs for the gifted and talented.* Mansfield Center, CT: Creative Learning Press, Inc.

Renzulli, J. S. & Gubbins, E. J. (1998). The national research center on the gifted and talented: lessons learned and promises to keep. In: J. A. Leroux (Ed.), *Connecting the Gifted Community Worldwide* (pp. 51–70). Seattle:WCGT.

Renzulli, J. S. & Reis, S. M. (1997). The schoolwide enrichment model: new directions for developing high-end learning. In: N. Colangelo & G. A. Davis (Eds.), *Handbook of Gifted Education* (pp. 136–154). Boston: Allyn and Bacon.

Renzulli, J. S., Reid, B. D. & Gubbins, E. J. (1992). *Setting an agenda: research priorities for the gifted and talented through the year 2000.* Storrs, CT: NRCG/T.

Révécz, G. (1952). *Talent und Genie* [Talent and genius]. Bern: A. Francke.

Rimm, S. B. (1997). Underachievement syndrome: a national epidemic. In: N. Colangelo & G. A. Davis (Eds.), *Handbook of Gifted Education* (pp. 416–434). Boston: Allyn and Bacon.

Robinson, A. (1997). Cooperative learning for talented students: emergent issues and implications. In: N. Colangelo & G. A. Davis (Eds.), *Handbook of Gifted Education* (pp. 243–252). Boston: Allyn and Bacon.

Robinson, N. M. (1998). The interface between secondary and post-secondary schools: U.S. alternatives before and during college for academically gifted students. In: J. A. Leroux (Ed.), *Connecting the Gifted Community Worldwide* (pp. 287–298). Seattle: WCGT.

Rost, D. H. (Ed.) (1993). *Lebensumweltanalyse hochbegabbter Grundschulkinder* [Learning Environments of Gifted Children in Primary Schools]. Göttingen: Hogrefe.

Runco, M. A. & Pritzker, S. (Eds.). (1999). *Encyclopedia of Creativity.* San Diego, CA: Academic Press.

Schaie, K. W. (1970). A reinterpretation of age-related changes in cognitive structure and functioning. In: L. R. Goulet & P. B. Baltes (Eds.), *Life-span developmental psychology* (pp. 485–507). London: Academic Press.

Schaie, K. W. (Ed.). (1983). *Longitudinal studies of adult psychological development.* London: Guilford Press.

Shore, B. M. & Kanevsky, L. S. (1993). Thinking processes: being and becoming gifted. In: K. A. Heller, F. J. Mönks & A. H. Passow (Eds.), *International Handbook of Research and Development of Giftedness and Talent* (pp. 133–147). Oxford: Pergamon.

Silverman, L. K. (1993). Counseling needs and programs for the gifted. In: K. A. Heller, F. J. Mönks & A. H. Passow (Eds.), *International Handbook of Research and Development of Giftedness and Talent* (pp. 631–647). Oxford: Pergamon.

Siverman, L. K. (1997). Family counseling with the gifted. In: N. Colangela & G. A. Davis (Eds.), *Handbook of Gifted Education* (pp. 382–397). Boston: Allyn and Bacon.

Simonton, D. K. (1988a). Creativity, leadership and chance. In R. J. Sternberg (Ed.), *The Nature of Creativity: Contemporary Psychological Perspectives* (pp. 386–426). Cambridge: Cambridge University Press.

Simonton, D. K. (1988b). *Scientific Genius.* Cambridge: Cambridge University Press.

Simonton, D. K. (1992). The social context of career success and course for 2,026 scientists and inventors. *Personality and Social Psychology Bulletin,* **18,** 452–463.

Simonton, D. K. (1994). *Greatness: who makes history and why.* New York: Guilford Press.

Simonton, D. K. (1999a). Creativity from a historiometric perspective. In: R. J. Sternberg (Ed.), *Handbook of Creativity* (pp. 116–133). New York: Cambridge University Press.

Simonton, D. K. (1999b). *Origins of genius. Darwinian perspectives on creativity.* New York: Oxford University Press.

Slavin, R. E. (1992). When and why does cooperative learning increase achievement? Theoretical and empirical perspectives. In: R. Hertz-Lazarowitz & N. Miller (Eds.), *Interaction in Cooperative groups: The Theoretical Anatomy of Group Learning* (pp. 145–173). New York: Cambridge University Press.

Sowell, E. J. (1996). *Curriculum—An Integrative Instruction.* Englewood Cliffs, NJ: Prentice Hall.

St. Clair, K. L. (1989). Counseling gifted students: a historical review. *Roeper Review* 12, 98–102.

Stein, M. I. (1986). *Gifted, talented and creative young people: a guide to theory, teaching and research.* New York: Garland Publishing Inc.

Stern, W. (1916). *Psychologische Begabungsforschung und Begabungsdiagnose* [Psychological giftedness research and identification of the gifted]. Leipzig, Germany: Teubner.

Sternberg, R. J. (1986). A triarchic theory of intellectual giftedness. In: R. J. Sternberg & J. E. Davidson (Eds.), *Conceptions of Giftedness* (pp. 223–243). New York: Cambridge University Press.

Sternberg, R. J. (1993). Procedures for identifying intellectual potential in the gifted: a perspective on alternative 'metaphors of mind'. In: K. A. Heller, F. J. Mönks & A. H. Passow (Eds.), *International Handbook of Research and Development of Giftedness and Talent* (pp. 185–207). Oxford: Pergamon.

Sternberg, R. J. (1997). Successful intelligence: a broader view of who is smart in school and life. *International Schools Journal,* **17,** 19–31.

Sternberg, R. J. (Ed.). (1999a). *Handbook of Creativity.* New York: Cambridge University Press.

Sternberg, R. J. (1999b). The theory of successful intelligence. *Review of General Psychology,* **3** (4), 1–25.

Sternberg, R. J. & Davidson, J. E. (Eds.). (1986). *Conceptions of giftedness.* New York: Cambridge University Press.

Sternberg, R. J. & Lubart, T. (1991). An investment theory of creativity and its development. *Human Development,* **34,** 1–31.

Subotnik, R. F., & Arnold, K. D. (1994). Beyond Terman: Contemporary Longitudinal Studies of Giftedness and Talent. Norwood, NJ: Ablex.

Supplee, P. L. (1990). *Reaching the gifted underachiever: program strategy and design.* New York: Teachers College Press.

Tannenbaum, A. J. (1983). *Gifted children: psychological and educational perspectives.* New York: Macmillan.

Tannenbaum, A. J. (1993). History of giftedness and 'gifted education' in world perspective. In K. A. Heller, F. J. Mönks & A. H. Passow (Eds.). International Handbook of Research and Development of Giftedness and Talent (pp 3–27). Oxford: Pergamon.

Tannenbaum, A. J. (1997). The meaning and making of giftedness. In: N. Colangelo & G. A. Davis (Eds.), *Handbook of Gifted Education* (pp. 27–42). Boston: Allyn and Bacon.

Tannenbaum, A. J. (1998). Programs for the gifted: to be or not to be. In: J. A. Leroux (Ed.), *Connecting the Gifted Community Worldwide* (pp. 5–36). Seattle: WCGT.

Terman, L. M. (1906). Genius and stupidity: a study of some of the intellectual processes of seven 'bright' and seven 'stupid' boys. *Pedagogical Seminary,* **13,** 307–373.

Terman, L. M. (1925). *Genetic studies of genius.* Volume 1: Mental and physical characteristics of a thousand gifted children. Stanford, CA: Stanford University Press.

Terman, L. M. (1954). Scientists and nonscientists in a group of 800 gifted men. *Psychological Monographs: General and Applied, 68* (Whole No. 378), 1–44.

Terman, L. M. & Oden, M. H. (1951). The Stanford studies of the gifted. In: P. Witty (Ed.), *The Gifted Child.* Boston, MA: D. C. Heath.

VanTassel-Baska, J. (1989). The role of the family in the success of disadvantaged gifted learners. *Journal for the Education of the Gifted,* **13,** 22–36.

VanTassel-Baska, J. (1998). Can appropriate curriculum become a reality in schools. In: J. A. Leroux (Ed.), *Connecting the Gifted Community Worldwide* (pp. 71–80). Seattle: WCGT.

Walberg, H. J., Zhang, G., Haller, E. P., Sares, Z. A., Stariha, W. E., Wallace, T. & Zeiser, S. F. (1994). Early educative influences on later outcomes: the terman data revisited. In: K. A. Heller & E. A. Hany (Eds.), *Competence and Responsibility,* Vol. 2 (pp. 164–177). Seattle: Hogrefe & Huber Publ.

Waldmann, M. & Weinert, F. E. (1990). *Intelligenz und Denken. Perspektiven der Hochbegabungsforschung* [Intelligence and Thinking Processes. Perspectives on the Research of Giftedness]. Göttingen: Hogrefe.

Weisberg, R. E. (1993). *Creativity. Beyond the Myth of Genius.* New York: Freeman.

Whipple, G. M. (Ed.). (1924). The education of gifted children. 23rd Yearbook, Part 1, National Society for the Study of Education. Bloomington, IL: Public School Publishing Company.

Whitmore, J. R. (1980). *Giftedness, conflict and underachievement.* Boston, MA: Allyn and Bacon.

Wilgosh, L. (1994). High achievement and underachievement in a cross-national context. In: K. A. Heller & E. A. Hany (Eds.), *Competence and Responsibility,* Vol. 2 (pp. 407–411). Seattle: Hogrefe & Huber Publ.

Williams, F. E. (1972). *A total creativity program kit.* Englewood Cliffs, NJ: Educational Technology Publications.

Williams, F. E. (1986). The cognitive-affective interaction model for enriching gifted programs. In: J. S. Renzulli (Ed.), *Systems and Models for Developing Programs for the Gifted and Talented* (pp. 306–350). Mansfield Center, CT: Creative Learning Press.

Williams, W. M. (1999). Peering into the nature-nurture debate. *Contemporary Psychology,* **44,** 267–269.

Ziegler, A. & Heller, K. A. (1998). Attribution retraining for self-related cognitions among women. *Gifted and Talented International,* **12,** 36–41.

Ziegler, A. & Heller, K. A. (1999). Conditions for self-confidence among boys and girls achieving highly in chemistry. *Journal of Secondary Education of the Gifted,* **10,** 192–199.

Ziegler, A., Heller, K. A. & Broome, P. (1996). Motivational preconditions for girls gifted and highly gifted in physics. *High Ability Studies,* **7,** 129–143.

Ziegler, A., Dresel, M. & Schober, B. (2000). Underachievementdiagnose: Ein Modell zur Diagnose partieller Lernbeeinträchtigung [Identifying Underachievers: A Diagnostic Model]. In: K. A. Heller (Ed.), *Begabungsdiagnostik in der Schul- und Erziehungsberatung* (2nd. ed.), pp. 259–278. Bern: Huber.

Zorman, R. (1993). Mentoring and role modeling programs for the gifted. In: K. A. Heller, F. J. Mönks & A. H. Passow (Eds.), *International Handbook of Research and Development of Giftedness and Talent* (pp. 727–741). Oxford: Pergamon.

List of Contributors

Contributors are listed in alphabetical order together with their affiliations. Titles of articles which they have written follow in alphabetical order, along with the respective page numbers. Co-authorship is indicated by *.

Clarke, C. (Newcastle University, UK)
Global Professionalism and Perceptions of Teachers of the Gifted: 565

Cohen, L. M. (Oregon State University, Corvallis, Oregon, USA)
Conceptual Foundations and Theoretical Lenses for the Diversity of Giftedness and Talent: 331

Colangelo, N. (The Connie Belin & Jacqueline N. Blank International Center for Gifted Education and Talent Development, University of Iowa, Iowa City, USA)
Counseling Gifted Students: 595

Coleman, L. J. (College of Education, University of Tennessee, USA)
Social-Emotional Development and the Personal Experience of Giftedness: 203

Cropley, A. J. (University of Hamburg, Germany)
Nurturing Talents/Gifts in Mathematics: 413; *Programs and Strategies for Nurturing Creativity*: 485

Cross, T. L. (Teachers College, Ball State University, USA)
Social-Emotional Development and the Personal Experience of Giftedness: 203

Csikszentmihalyi, M. (Claremont Graduate University and The University of Chicago, USA)
New Conceptions and Research Approaches to Creativity: Implications of a Systems Perspective for Creativity in Education: 81

Feldhusen, J. F. (Purdue University, USA)
Identification of Gifted and Talented Youth for Educational Programs: 271

Feldman, D. H. (Tufts University, Medford, Massachusetts, USA)
Prodigies, Savants and Williams Syndrome: Windows Into Talent and Cognition: 227

Freeman, J. (School of Lifelong Learning and Education, Middlesex University, London, UK)
Families the Essential Context for Gifts and Talents: 573

Gagné, F. (Université du Québec à Montréal, Montreal, Canada)
Understanding the Complex Choreography of Talent Development Through DMGT-Based Analysis: 67

Gallagher, J. J. (The University of North Carolina at Chapel Hill, The Frank Porter Graham Child Development Center, USA)
Changing Paradigms for Gifted Education in the United States: 681

Grager-Loidl, H. (Center for the Study of Giftedness, University of Nijmegen, Netherlands)
Underachievement in Gifted Children and Adolescents: Theory and Practice: 609

Grigorenko, E. L. (Department of Psychology, Yale University, New Haven, Connecticut, USA)
Russian Gifted Education in Technical Disciplines: Tradition and Transformation: 735

Gross, M. U. M. (The University of New South Wales, Sydney, Australia)
Issues in the Cognitive Development of Exceptionally and Profoundly Gifted Individuals: 179

Gruber, H. (University of Regensburg, Germany)
Instructional Psychology and the Gifted: 383

Heller, K. A. (University of Munich, Germany)
Conceptions of Giftedness from a Meta-Theoretical Perspective: 3; *International Trends and Topics of Research on Giftedness and Talent*: 123; *The Study of Giftedness: Reflections on Where We Are and Where We Are Going*: 839

Hernández de Hahn, E. L. (University of Munich, Germany and Iboamerican and National University, San Diego, California, USA)
Cross-Cultural Studies in Gifted Education: 549

Jarwan, F. A. (Noor-Hussein Foundation, Jordan)
Identification of Gifted and Talented Youth for Educational Programs: 271

Joswig, H. (Rostock University, Rostock, Germany)
Gifted Education in Europe: Programs, Practices, and Current Research: 703

Kanevsky, L. (Faculty of Education, Simon Fraser University, Burnaby, British Columbia, Canada)
Dynamic Assessment of Gifted Students: 283

Kaufmann, F. A. (6520 Lone Oak Court, Bethesda, Maryland, USA)
Attention-Deficit/Hyperactivity Disorder in Gifted Students: 621

Kerr, B. (Arizona State University, USA)
Guiding Gifted Girls and Young Women: 649

Kokot, S. J. (University of South Africa in Pretoria, South Africa)
The Status of Gifted Child Education in Africa: 799

Lens, W. (University of Leuven, Belgium)
Motivation and Cognition: Their Role in the Development of Giftedness: 193

Leroux, J. A. (University of Ottawa, Canada)
A Study of Education for High Ability Students in Canada: Policy, Programs and Student Needs: 695

Lubinski, D. (Vanderbilt University, USA)
Gender Differences in Engineering and the Physical Sciences Among the Gifted: An Inorganic-Organic Distinction: 633

Lupart, J. (University of Calgary, Canada)
Inclusive Education for Gifted Students with Disabilities: 659

Mandl, H. (University of Munich, Germany)
Instructional Psychology and the Gifted: 383

Manstetten, R. (University of Osnabrück, Germany)
Promotion of the Gifted in Vocational Training: 439

Maoz, N. (Weizmann Institute of Science in Rehovot, Israel)
Middle East Region: Efforts, Policies, Programs and Issues: 743

Martino, G. (John B. Pierce Laboratory and Yale University School of Medicine, USA)
Giftedness in Non-Academic Domains: The Case of the Visual Arts and Music: 95

Mason, E. J. (Northeastern University, Boston, Massachusetts, USA)
Developmental Psychology and Giftedness: Theories and Research: 141

Moltzen, R. I. (The University of Waikato, New Zealand)
Programs and Practices for Identifying and Nurturing Giftedness and Talent in Australia and New Zealand: 779

Mönks, F. J. (University of Nijmegen, The Netherlands)
Early Identification of High Ability: 297; *Developmental Psychology and Giftedness: Theories and Research*: 141; *The Study of Giftedness: Reflections on Where We Are and Where We Are Going*: 839

Moon, S. M. (Purdue University, West Lafayette, Indiana, USA)
Developing Gifted Programs: 499

Morelock, M. J. (Elmira College, Elmira, NY, USA)
Gender Differences in Engineering and the Physical Sciences Among the Gifted: An Inorganic-Organic Distinction: 633; *Prodigies, Savants and Williams Syndrome: Windows Into Talent and Cognition*: 227

Munandar, U. (Faculty of Psychology, University of Indonesia, Jakarta, Indonesia)
Programs and Practices for Identifying and Nurturing Giftedness and Talent in Asia (outside the Mainland of China): 765

Olszewski-Kubilius, P. (Center for Talent Development, Northwestern University, Evanston, IL, USA)
The Education and Development of Verbally Talented Students: 397

Pagnin, A. (Istituto di Psicologia, Universita di Pavia, Italy)
New Trends in Research on Moral Development in the Gifted: 467

Passow, A. H.
The Study of Giftedness: Reflections on Where We Are and Where We Are Going: 839

Pasupathi, M. (Center for Lifespan Psychology, Max Planck Institute for Human Development, Berlin, Germany)
A 'Talent' for Knowledge and Judgment about Life: The Lifespan Development of Wisdom: 253

Perleth, C. (University of Rostock, Germany)
Early Identification of High Ability: 297

Persson, R. S. (Jönköping University, Jönköping, Sweden)
Gifted Education in Europe: Programs, Practices, and Current Research: 703

Peters, W. A. M. (Center for the Study of Giftedness, University of Nijmegen, Netherlands)
Underachievement in Gifted Children and Adolescents: Theory and Practice: 609

Plomin, R. (Institute of Psychiatry, London, UK)
Genetic Tools for Exploring Individual Differences in Intelligence: 157

Powell, W. N. (Oregon State University, Corvallis, Oregon, USA)
Conceptual Foundations and Theoretical Lenses for the Diversity of Giftedness and Talent: 331

Prado, T. M. (University of Hamburg, Germany)
Nurturing Talents/Gifts in Mathematics: 413

Pyryt, M. C. (University of Calgary, Centre for Gifted Education, Calgary, Alberta, Canada)
Talent Development in Science and Technology: 427

Rand, P. (University of Oslo, Norway)
Motivation and Cognition: Their Role in the Development of Giftedness: 193

Reis, S. M. (University of Connecticut, Storrs, Connecticut, USA)
The Schoolwide Enrichment Model: 367

Renzulli, J. S. (University of Connecticut, Storrs, Connecticut, USA)
The Schoolwide Enrichment Model: 367

Rosselli, H. C. (University of South Florida, Tampa, Florida, USA)
Developing Gifted Programs: 499

Rudnitski, R. A. (State University of New York at New Paltz, USA)
National/Provincial Gifted Education Policies: Present State, Future Possibilities: 673

Schatz, T. (University of Rostock, Germany)
Early Identification of High Ability: 297

Schneider, W. (University of Würzburg, Germany)
Giftedness, Expertise, and (Exceptional) Performance: A Developmental Perspective: 165

Schofield, N. J. (University of Newcastle, Australia)
International Trends and Topics of Research on Giftedness and Talent: 123

Schoon, I. (Department of Psychology, City University, London, UK)
A Life Span Approach to Talent Development: 213

Shi, J. (Institute of Psychology, Chinese Academy of Sciences, Beijing, China)
Psychological Research on and Education of Gifted and Talented Children in China: 757

Simonton. D. K. (Department of Psychology, University of California, Davis, USA)
Genius and Giftedness Same or Different?: 111

Soriano de Alencar, E. M. L. (Catholic University of Brasilia, Brasilia, Brazil)
Programs and Practices for Identifying and Nurturing Giftedness and Talent in Latin American Countries: 817

Staudinger, U. M. (Center for Lifespan Psychology, Max Planck Institute for Human Development, Berlin, Germany)
A 'Talent' for Knowledge and Judgment about Life: The Lifespan Development of Wisdom: 253

Sternberg, R. J. (Yale University, New Haven, Connecticut, USA)
A Multidimensional Framework for Synthesizing Disparate Issues in Identifying, Selecting, and Serving Gifted Children: 831; *Giftedness as Developing Expertise*: 55

Subhi, T. (Al al-Bayt University in Amman, Jordan)
Middle East Region: Efforts, Policies, Programs and Issues: 743

Subotnik, R. F. (Hunter College, City University of New York, USA)
A Multidimensional Framework for Synthesizing Disparate Issues in Identifying, Selecting, and Serving Gifted Children: 831; *Addressing the Most Challenging Questions in Gifted Education and Psychology: A Role Best Suited to Longitudinal Research*: 243

Supplee, P. (Center for the Study of Giftedness, University of Nijmegen, Netherlands)
Underachievement in Gifted Children and Adolescents: Theory and Practice: 609

Tannenbaum, A. J. (Teachers College, Columbia University, New York, USA)
A History of Giftedness in School and Society: 23; *Giftedness: The Ultimate Instrument for Good and Evil*: 447

Taylor, C. A. (University of Port Elizabeth, South Africa)
The Status of Gifted Child Education in Africa: 799

Thompson, L. A. (Case Western Reserve University, USA)
Genetic Tools for Exploring Individual Differences in Intelligence: 157

Trost, G. (Institute for Test Development and Talent Research Ltd., Bonn, Germany)
Prediction of Excellence in School, Higher Education, and Work: 317

Urban, K. K. (University of Hanover, Germany)
Programs and Strategies for Nurturing Creativity: 485

VanTassel-Baska, J. (College of William and Mary, Williamsburg, Virginia, USA)
Theory and Research on Curriculum Development for the Gifted: 345

Vialle, W. (University of Wollongong, Australia)
Global Professionalism and Perceptions of Teachers of the Gifted: 565

Wagner, H. (Institute Bildung und Begabung, Bonn, Germany)
Academic Competitions and Programs Designed to Challenge the Exceptionally Talented: 523

Walberg, H. J. (University of Illinois at Chicago, USA)
Academic Competitions and Programs Designed to Challenge the Exceptionally Talented: 523

Whalen, S. P. (Chapin Hall Center for Children at the University of Chicago, Chicago, IL, USA)
The Education and Development of Verbally Talented Students: 397

Wieczerkowski, W. (University of Hamburg, Germany)
Nurturing Talents/Gifts in Mathematics: 413

Winner, E. (Boston College and Harvard Project Zero, USA)
Giftedness in Non-Academic Domains: The Case of the Visual Arts and Music: 95

Wolfe, R. (Claremont Graduate University and The University of Chicago, USA)
New Conceptions and Research Approaches to Creativity: Implications of a Systems Perspective for Creativity in Education: 81

Wright, L. (Teachers College, Columbia University, USA)
Identifying and Educating Poor and Under-Represented Gifted Students: 587

Wu, W.-T. (Department of Special Education, Taiwan Normal University, Taiwan, ROC)
Programs and Practices for Identifying and Nurturing Giftedness and Talent in Asia (outside the Mainland of China): 765

Yewchuk, C. (University of Alberta, Canada)
Inclusive Education for Gifted Students with Disabilities: 659

Zha, Z. (Institute of Psychology, Chinese Academy of Sciences, Beijing, China)
Psychological Research on and Education of Gifted and Talented Children in China: 757

Ziegler, A. (University of Munich, Germany)
Conceptions of Giftedness from a Meta-Theoretical Perspective: 3

Author Index

Page numbers not in brackets refer to the reference lists; those in brackets refer to the citations in the text. Only authors named in the reference lists appear in this index.

Haroutounian, J., 109 (103), 281 (278)
Harradine, C., 692 (686)
Harrington, D. M., 92 (82), 119 (112)
Harris J. J. III, 594
Harris, C. R., 223 (218), 755 (750)
Harris, J. J., 312 (308), 342 (331, 334), 361 (358), 517 (506), 618 (613)
Harris, J. R., 52 (49)
Harris, P. L., 728 (723)
Harris, R., 325
Harrison, C., 190 (183)
Harsányi, L., 728 (706)
Harslett, M., 795 (793)
Hart, D., 482 (474, 476)
Hart, E. L., 628 (622), 630
Hart, L. A., 163
Harter, S., 201 (198, 200), 607 (598)
Hartley, D., 667 (664)
Hartman, R. K., 281, 796 (794)
Hartmann, Ch., 728 (713)
Hartmann, T., 630 (626)
Hartshorne, H., 464 (452, 460)
Hartshorne, K., 814
Hartsough, C. S., 630 (628)
Harvey, J. A., 630
Hasselbring, T. S., 293 (285)
Hasselhorn, M., 312 (305)
Hassenstein, M., 497 (485)
Hastings, T. H., 223 (221)
Hastings, T. J., 175 (166)
Hastorf, A. H., 175 (165, 166)
Hatch, T., 281 (273), 362 (352)
Hattie, J. A., 325 (318)
Hausdorf, P. A., 496 (487)
Havighurst, R. J., 19 (6), 52 (24, 41), 189 (180), 265 (253, 260), 280, 464 (448)
Hawkins, W. L., 482 (471)
Hawkridge, D., 756 (749)
Hayes, F. B., 312 (301)
Hayes, J. R., 119 (114), 497 (487)
Hayes-Jacobs, H., 435 (433)
Haywood, H. C., 294 (283, 285, 287)
He, S., 763
Heal, M. M., 362 (351)
Hébert, T. P., 360, 362 (351), 381, 618, 619 (611, 614, 615, 616)
Hechtman, L., 630
Heckhausen, J., 223 (220), 265
Hedges, L. V., 646 (640)
Heggestad. E. D., 645 (643)
Heid, H., 445 (440)
Heid, M. K., 424 (414)
Heilmann, K., 325 (321)
Heinbokel, A., 312 (305), 619 (612), 728
Heincke, S. G., 266 (255)
Heine, C., 92 (88)
Hektner, J., 92 (88)

Heller, K. A., 20 (3, 5, 6, 7, 9, 17), 52 (44, 49), 53, 137 (123, 124, 129, 134, 136), 152 (149, 150), 155, 175 (166), 202 (199), 223, 224 (220, 221), 250 (244), 266 (263), 312, 314 (297, 299, 300, 307), 325, 326 (317, 318, 323), 342 (331, 336), 394 (383, 384, 385, 389), 435, 445 (441, 442, 444), 482 (478), 535 (526), 559 (549, 555), 585 (574, 581), 619 (609, 614, 615, 617), 656 (655), 667 (659), 728, 729, 731, 734 (703, 710, 713, 714), 763 (760), 859 (839, 840, 841, 842, 843, 845, 847, 848, 849, 850, 852, 853, 856), 860 (857), 861, 863
Helmke, A., 325 (318), 619 (615)
Helmreich, R. L., 119 (116)
Helson, R., 119, 435 (427), 497 (487)
Helwig, C., 484 (471)
Hempel, C. G., 20 (16)
Henderson, B. B., 153 (147)
Hendricks, M., 362 (350), 435 (430, 431)
Hendricks, S., 313
Hendrickson, L., 190 (184)
Hengen, T., 362 (353)
Henle, M., 497 (487)
Henmon, V. A. C., 294 (284)
Hennessey, B. A., 52 (27), 860 (853)
Henson, R., 109 (103)
Her Majesty's Inspectorate, 572
Herbert, E., 360 (346)
Herbert, T., 691
Herma, J. L., 223 (216, 220, 221)
Herman, E., 109 (106)
Herman, G. N., 667 (664)
Hermans, H. J. M., 559 (551)
Hermelin, B., 153 (147), 239, 240 (229, 233, 238)
Hernandez, S., 362 (348)
Herrnstein, R. J., 52 (49), 64 (56), 342 (336), 394 (383), 410 (398, 399), 860 (839)
Herrold, W. G., 667 (666)
Hersh, R., 424 (413)
Hershberger, S. L., 311 (302)
Herskovits, M., 250 (247), 728 (707), 729
Hertel, E., 535 (527)
Hertzog, N. B., 517 (509)
Hess, R. D., 585 (575)
Hesselink, J., 239 (238)
Hetherington, E. M., 585 (580)
Hewett, J., 795 (783)
Hey, V., 559 (553)
Heyman, G. D., 201 (200), 585 (578)
Hiatt, E. L., 517 (503), 687 (677)
Hickey, J., 464
Hickok, G., 239 (238)
Hickson, J., 294 (287)
Hiddemann, W., 483 (477)
Higgins, S., 668 (660)
Hill, A. L., 239, 240 (228, 229), 668 (666)
Hill, L., 163 (162)
Hills, J. R., 281 (277)
Hilton, T. L., 325 (319)

Subject Index

909